PROFESSIONAL CAREERS SOURCEBOOK

ISSN 1045-9863

PROFESSIONAL CAREERS SOURCEBOOK

Where to find help planning careers that require college or technical degrees

FOURTH EDITION

Sara T. Bernstein and Kathleen M. Savage, Editors

Compiled in cooperation with InfoPLACE, the Job, Career, and Education Service of the Cuyahoga County Public Library, Cleveland, Ohio

Gale Research Inc.

An International Thomson Publishing Company

Changing the Way the World Learns

NEW YORK • LONDON • BONN • BOSTON • DETROIT • MADRID
MELBOURNE • MEXICO CITY • PARIS • SINGAPORE • TOKYO
TORONTO • WASHINGTON • ALBANY NY • BELMONT CA • CINCINNATI OH

Editors: Sara T. Bernstein and Kathleen M. Savage
Associate Editors: Ian Goodhall and Theresa J. MacFarlane
Assistant Editor: Tara Sheets

Research Manager: Victoria B. Cariappa
Research Specialist: Gary J. Oudersluys
Research Associates: Tamara C. Nott and Amy Terese Steel

Production Director: Mary Beth Trimper
Assistant Production Manager: Evi Seoud
Production Assistant: Deborah Milliken
Product Design Manager: Cynthia Baldwin
Graphic Designer: Michelle DiMercurio
Graphic Services Supervisor: Barbara J. Yarrow

Manager, Data Entry Services: Benita L. Spight
Data Entry Supervisor: Gwendolyn S. Tucker
Data Entry Associate: Johnny Carson

Manager, Technical Support Services: Theresa Rocklin
Programmer/Analyst: Charles Beaumont
Programmer: Parveen Parikh

⊗™ The paper used in this publication meets the minimum requirements of American National Standard for Information Sciences--Permanence Paper for Printed Library Materials, ANSI Z39.48-1984.

♲ This book is printed on recycled paper that meets Environmental Protection Agency standards.

ISBN 0-8103-8915-0
ISSN 1045-9863

Printed in the United States of America

I(T)P™   Gale Research Inc., an International Thomson Publishing Company.
ITP logo is a trademark under license.

Contents

Executive, Administrative, and Managerial Occupations

Professional Specialty Occupations

Engineers

Architects and Surveyors

Computer, Mathematical, and Operations Research Occupations

Life Scientists

Physical Scientists

Lawyers and Judges

Social Scientists and Urban Planners

Social and Recreation Workers

Highlights

Students, parents, career changers, and professionals involved with career guidance can turn first to *Professional Careers Sourcebook* to locate essential career planning sources.

PCS identifies and pulls together a broad spectrum of resources used to explore professional career opportunities. It profiles 121 professional and technical occupations, ranging from accountant and aircraft pilot to visual artist and writer. Each profile lists up to 11 categories of career information:

- Job descriptions
- Career guides
- Professional associations
- Standards/certification agencies
- Test guides and certification examinations
- Educational directories and programs
- Awards, scholarships, grants, and fellowships
- Basic reference guides and handbooks
- Professional and trade periodicals
- Professional meetings and conventions
- Other sources of interest to professionals

Each entry includes, as appropriate and available:

- Organization, association, or publication name
- Contact information, including address, phone, toll-free, and facsimile numbers
- Author/editor, dates, and frequency
- Brief description of purpose, services, or content

The fourth edition is a complete revision incorporating thousands of organization, title, address, and text changes.

Also included in the fourth edition:

- A Master List of Profiled Careers referencing covered occupations and professions by job titles, alternate names, popular names, and synonymous and related names
- State Occupational and Professional Licensing Agencies listings
- Employment Growth Rankings and Statistics of profiled careers as projected by the U.S. Department of Labor's Bureau of Labor Statistics
- Index to Information Sources listed in *PCS*.

New Features include:

- Fully updated contact/order information--including addresses and phone, fax, and toll-free numbers
- Over 750 new career guides, test guides, directories, and basic reference guides and handbooks produced by over 25 major publishers of career resources
- Overall entry count has increased by nearly 20 percent, while the new, three-column format makes a more compact book

Compiled in Cooperation
With Career Information Center

Many of the sources listed in *PCS* were identified in the career collection of InfoPlace, the job, career, and education service of the Cuyahoga County Public Library, and are used daily to develop career planning strategies and provide answers to career-related questions.

Career Research Resources—
Step by Step

Step 1: Beginning Your Career Search	Step 2: Planning Your Career	Step 3: Finding the Job You Want

Occupational Outlook Handbook (OOH)

Vocational Careers Sourcebook (VCS) and Professional Careers Sourcebook (PCS)

Job Hunter's Sourcebook (JHS)

Describes careers in detail:
    nature of work
    working conditions
    employment statistics ·
    job outlook
    earnings
    job training, qualifications,
      and advancement
Provides additional information
sources:
    associations, organizations,
      unions, and governmental
      agencies
    publications

Provide concise job descriptions
noting:
    employment outlook
    salaries
Offer descriptive listings:
    directories and catalogs of
      educational programs
    special training programs
    standards/certification agencies
Expand *OOH*'s additional
information sources:
    complete information on
      professional associations
      and related organizations
    comprehensive entries for
      professional reference works
      and trade periodicals
Provide extensive listings for
other categories of resources:
    career guides
    test guides
    awards, scholarships, grants,
      and fellowships
    meetings and conventions

Features profiles of job-hunting
information for specific careers:
    sources of help-wanted ads
    placement and job referral
      services
    employer directories and
      networking lists
    handbooks and manuals
    employment agencies and
      executive search firms
    other leads
Identifies sources of general job-
hunting information:
    reference works
    newspapers, magazines, and
      journals
    audio/visual resources
    online services
    software
    other sources
Includes an essay offering tips
on using the public library as a
career information center.

Preface

Each of us is different, with talents, traits, and values that may be highly unique, so the ideal job complements the individual, bringing out the best of a person's character and qualities. Whatever the talents or interests, chances are that a career exists that values those traits. The trick is identifying the careers that meet an individual's needs, an often bewildering task given the complexity of the modern world. Madeleine Swain, president of an outplacement firm in New York, explained in a *Savvy* article that "you've got to find a blending of what you've got and what's out there.... The best thing to do is to see where there's growth and opportunity, and then mesh that with what you can bring to the party. Then you create something marketable."

Career Choices

Early career planning increases the chance of identifying the career choices most suited to an individual's talents, abilities, interests, and goals. This is the key to finding an enjoyable and fulfilling job, which is crucial since the average adult spends more than 2,000 hours per year at work. According to William F. Shanahan, author of *College--Yes or No?,* career planning should begin in high school with careful course selection, some work experience, and career research. Shanahan suggests students take more difficult math, science, language, and English courses in preparation for future goals, encouraging students to look for summer and part-time jobs in occupational areas that interest them. Most important, though, is his advice to read books about various careers, to talk with professionals in fields of interest, to visit offices, and to investigate the different colleges and schools offering educational programs for particular careers.

The major benefit of this research is that it results in an understanding of which careers appeal to an individual, who typically will gain valuable self-knowledge in the process. Looking at the array of occupations available in today's society encourages introspection and allows an individual to determine likes and dislikes, goals, interests, and abilities. Such an approach helps an individual--no matter what age--to form career goals. As Martha C. Douglas advised in *Go for It! How to Get Your First Good Job: A Career Planning Guide for Young Adults,* "It's important you find out what's right for you. You are unique. You have developed certain strengths and weaknesses from the time you were little. If you can find a way to tap this knowledge about yourself, you will find clues to your future."

Career Changes

As people grow and mature, though, their career goals may change, often precipitating second and third careers. Phyllis Macklin, a partner in the outplacement firm of Minsuk, Macklin, Stein & Associates, claims that the average worker changes jobs five times for such reasons as dismissal, boredom, dissatisfaction, changed values, or--for some--greater independence.

Teachers are a case in point. Despite the common belief that many are fleeing from careers in education, more and more disillusioned professionals are leaving business and industry for teaching jobs, sometimes accepting lower wages and completing lengthy and expensive certification programs to do so. "They are coming into education in droves," noted John Kean, chairman of the University of Wisconsin--Madison's Department of Curriculum and Instruction. In her *Time* article titled "The Lure of the Classroom," Susan Tifft quotes one midcareer student teacher as saying: "Today you can put everything into a company and still get pink-slipped. No machine can ever take the place of a teacher." Apparently, this midcareer teacher had to learn the painful truth that "company" and "career" are not the same. "Very often," Macklin explained in the *Detroit News,* "when people start their jobs, they think of the company. They don't think of their careers as something apart."

Careful career planning and continued career research are very possibly the best ways to avoid such pitfalls and ensure fulfilling employment. *Professional Careers Sourcebook* is dedicated to furthering such planning. *PCS* will prove to be a valuable map for those journeying to a rich and happy work life. Both the student and those with careers in transition can consult *PCS* first in their career research. Career and guidance counselors, too, will find it an important tool, as will information professionals expanding their career collections: Because no one should make decisions about careers with just a little information.

Introduction

Statistics show that current and future employment markets are following economic conditions and trends in the 1990s. The official word from the U.S. Department of Labor for students seeking jobs and professionals changing careers is that "the emphasis on education will continue. Three out of the four fastest growing occupational groups will be the executive, administrative, and managerial; professional specialty; and technicians and related support occupations. These occupations generally require the highest levels of education and skill. Office and factory automation, changes in consumer demand, and substitution of imports for domestic products are expected to cause employment to stagnate or decline in many occupations that require little formal education---apparel workers and textile machinery operators, for example. Opportunities for high school dropouts will be increasingly limited, and workers who cannot read and follow directions may not even be considered for most jobs" (*Occupational Outlook Handbook, 1994-1995*). Clearly, then, college graduates and those completing specialized education programs have the advantage in today's economy.

Professional Careers Sourcebook (*PCS*), now in its fourth edition, provides expanded and updated coverage of career planning resources for 121 careers requiring college degrees or specialized education. *PCS* provides a comprehensive overview of the literature and professional organizations that aid career planning and related research. It completes the time-consuming task of locating and organizing needed information, enabling its users to move more efficiently from career planning to career fulfillment. It appeals to the full spectrum of individuals involved in career planning. Students, parents, job changers, career librarians, employment and guidance counselors, and others in need of career information will find that the convenience and thoroughness of *PCS* facilitates their planning and strategy objectives.

Comprehensive Content and Convenient Arrangement

While other titles primarily describe occupations, *PCS* supplies the most in-depth coverage of information sources related to 121 specific professions. *PCS* is arranged by profession; each career profile can be used to:

- Research occupations. Brief career descriptions summarize the duties and responsibilities that each profession entails, complete with salary levels and growth potentials for each.

- Explore professional careers. Specific professions are described in listed career guides, including books, articles, kits, pamphlets, brochures, and other materials that are often difficult to identify or locate quickly.

- Find professional or certification test guides. Students and professionals can locate information on test guides and handbooks designed to assist with preparing for professional or certification examinations.

- Identify career-enhancing resources. *PCS* identifies newsletters, magazines, newspapers, trade journals, and other serials that offer information to, and are used by professionals in the profiled careers. Valuable resources such as manuals, textbooks, directories, dictionaries, encyclopedias, films, videocassettes, and other significant reference materials used by professionals are also identified.

- Target professional associations and organizations. *PCS* lists organizations that will assist individuals seeking advice on career planning, professional development, and networking, including:
    Professional and trade associations.
    Standards and certification agencies.
    State professional and occupational licensing agencies.
    Meetings, conventions, trade shows, and conferences within given fields.
    Award and financial support programs that encourage students and professionals
        to further pursue a given career.

Easy access to information on specific occupations is facilitated by the Master List of Profiled Careers. This definitive guide to *PCS* contents refers to covered professions by occupation names, job titles, popular names, and by synonymous or related terms. The Index to Information Sources alphabetically lists specific publication titles and organization names. Please consult the User's Guide for more information about the arrangement, content, and indexing of the information sources cited in *PCS*.

PCS Complements the *Occupational Outlook Handbook*

Owing to the importance of career information to students, parents, counselors, and librarians, *PCS* is designed as a companion to today's foremost career resource–the Department of Labor's *Occupational Outlook Handbook* (*OOH*). The *OOH* provides detailed descriptions of some 250 occupations, covering areas such as the nature of the work, working conditions, job outlook, earnings, job training, qualifications, and advancement. It also offers selected sources of additional information for each of the occupations covered, listing the names and addresses of associations, organizations, unions, government agencies, and publications.

PCS has been designed to complement–not replace–*OOH* by augmenting the information about the 121 professional careers included in *OOH*. *PCS* greatly expands the Additional Sources of Information sections in each *OOH* chapter, by providing complete information about professional associations and related organizations and comprehensive entries for professional reference works and trade periodicals. In addition, *PCS* provides extensive listings of career guides, test guides, awards, scholarships, grants, fellowships, professional meetings and conventions, and more. The 121 careers profiled in *PCS* correspond to the jobs defined as "professional" by the 1994-1995 edition of *OOH*. *PCS* profiles are arranged in the same order as *OOH* chapters on the covered professions, allowing the books to be used in tandem to create a complete career research program. Gale's *Vocational Careers Sourcebook* provides the same types of information on the balance of the occupations covered by *OOH*, those that do not require more than a high school diploma for entry-level positions. See the chart on page viii for an outline of how *PCS, OOH,* and other job-related Gale titles can be used together in selecting and developing a career.

PCS Compiled in Cooperation With
Career Information Center

Many of the information sources included in this edition of *PCS* were identified in the more than 3,000 books, pamphlets, newspapers, and periodicals that comprise the career collection of InfoPLACE, the highly regarded job, career, and education service of the Cuyahoga County Public Library in Cleveland, Ohio. Kathleen M. Savage, the InfoPLACE information librarian, selected career resources that have been successfully used by patrons and counselors at InfoPLACE. InfoPLACE also conducts individual consultations and sponsors workshops such as "Career Decisions" for career planning and "Career Realities" for job hunters seeking professional positions.

Additional information contained in *PCS* was compiled through direct contact with selected associations, agencies, and organizations; from career collections of other major public libraries; and from selected material from other Gale databases. This fourth edition represents a complete revision and updating from the third edition of *PCS*.

Comments and Suggestions Are Welcome

Libraries, associations, career counseling firms, agencies, publishers, and other organizations active in career planning and research are encouraged to submit material about their programs, activities, publications, or other resources for use in future editions of *PCS*. Other comments and suggestions from users of this directory also are appreciated. Please contact:

Professional Careers Sourcebook
Gale Research Inc.
835 Penobscot Bldg.
Detroit, MI 48226-4094
Toll-free: 800-347-GALE
Facsimile: (313)961-6815
Telex: 810 221 7087

User's Guide

Professional Careers Sourcebook (*PCS*) consists of:

- Master List of Profiled Careers
- 121 Career Profiles
- State Occupational and Professional Licensing Agencies
- Job Rankings and Statistics
- Employment Growth Rankings and Statistics
- Index to Information Sources

Master List of Profiled Careers

The Master List of Profiled Careers, following this guide, lists in a single alphabetic sequence the job titles used to identify the 121 careers profiled in *PCS*, as well as alternate, popular, synonymous, and related job titles and names, and occupation names contained within job titles. "See" references lead from alternate names to the appropriate career profiles and their beginning page numbers.

Career Profile Content and Arrangement

The order of the 121 career profiles contained in *PCS* reflects the arrangement used in the *Occupational Outlook Handbook*, as listed on the Contents pages. Profiles are organized into ten major sections by general profession type (which are further subdivided into more specific occupation types in some cases) and are then listed alphabetically.

Each profile contains up to 11 categories of information sources, as described below. Within each category, individual entries are organized alphabetically by name or title. (Entries are numbered and arranged sequentially, beginning with the first entry in the first profile.) The organizations, publications, and other sources listed are fully cited in all relevant chapters and categories, providing the user with a complete selection of information resources for each career in a single, convenient location.

Categories of Information in Career Profiles

- **Job Descriptions.** Each profile contains a summary explaining the duties and responsibilities that a particular occupation or profession entails, including educational and training require-ments, if available. The description abstracts the 1994-1995 *Occupational Outlook Handbook's* coverage of the profession. Salaries and growth potential for an occupation also will be noted.

- **Career Guides.** This section lists books, articles, kits, pamphlets, brochures, and other materials that describe a given profession. Often these works will be part of a career/vocational series. Entries in this section will include the source's title; name, address, and phone number of its publisher or distributor; name of the editor or author; publication date or frequency; description of contents; arrangement; indexes; toll-free or additional phone numbers; and facsimile numbers, when applicable. Publication, videocassette, and film titles appear in italics.

- **Professional Associations.** This category of information covers trade and professional associations that offer career-related information and services. Entries note the association's name, address, and phone number; its membership; purpose and objectives; publications; toll-free or additional phone numbers; and facsimile numbers, when known. Publication titles are rendered in italics. In some cases, the publications mentioned in these entries are described in greater detail as separate entries cited in the Career Guides, Basic Reference Guides and Handbooks, and Professional and Trade Periodicals categories.

- **Standards/Certification Agencies.** This section offers information about accrediting agencies, certification examinations, national or professional standards programs, or association-sponsored certification and testing programs. Entries in this section provide the certifying agency or program's name, address, and phone number; a description; publication titles; toll-free or additional phone numbers; and facsimile numbers, when available.

- **Test Guides.** This section lists guides and handbooks designed to assist in preparing for professional or certification examinations; for instance, medical school entrance examinations, bar exams, the CPA exam, real estate licensing exams, or nursing boards. These entries include the guide's title; its publisher's or distributor's name, address, and phone number; editor's or author's name; publication date or frequency; description of contents; arrangement; indexes; toll-free or additional phone numbers; and facsimile numbers, when available. Publication titles appear in italics.

- **Educational Directories and Programs.** This category notes directories, catalogs, and other publications that list career-related course offerings of colleges, universities, schools, associations, and other organizations. Association and special school programs exclusively for the profiled career may be listed here as well. Entries for directories and other publications will offer the title; name, address, and phone number of the publisher or distributor; name of the editor or author; publication date or frequency; description of contents; arrangement; indexes; toll-free or additional phone numbers; and facsimile numbers, when known. Entries for programs will offer the name, address, and phone number of the institution; a description of course offerings; toll-free or additional phone numbers; and facsimile numbers, when available. Publication titles appear in italics.

- **Awards, Scholarships, Grants, and Fellowships.** This section lists awards given in recognition of professional achievement and financial support programs that aid students and professionals in fulfilling or continuing their education in a given career. Entries in this section include the name of the award or program; the name, address, and phone number of the sponsoring organization; a description; toll-free or additional phone numbers; and facsimile number, when applicable.

- **Basic Reference Guides and Handbooks.** This category provides information about manuals, textbooks, directories, dictionaries, encyclopedias, films and videocassettes, and other published reference material used by professionals working in the profiled career. Entries offer the resource's title; the name, address, and phone number of its publisher or distributor; the editor's or author's name; publication date or frequency; description of contents; arrangement; indexes; toll-free and additional phone numbers; and facsimile numbers, when applicable. Publication and film title are rendered in italics.

- **Professional and Trade Periodicals.** This section lists newsletters, magazines, newspapers, trade journals, and other serials that offer information to professionals in the profiled career. Entries note the resource's title; the name, address, and phone number of the publisher; the editor's name; frequency; description of contents; toll-free and additional phone numbers; and facsimile numbers, when available. Publication titles appear in italics.

- **Professional Meetings and Conventions.** This section includes trade shows, conferences, conventions, and meetings that provide opportunities for networking and professional development. Entries feature the event's name; the name, address, and phone number of the event's organizer or sponsor; the frequency of the event and forthcoming dates and locations; toll-free and additional phone numbers; and facsimile numbers, when known.

- **Other Sources of Information.** This category lists online databases, compilations of performance standards, statistical sources, sources of supply, special reference works, films and videocassettes, annual reviews, or other miscellaneous material that might be of interest to individuals working in the given profession. (Material routinely used by professionals in a profiled career will be found in the Basic Reference Guides and Handbooks category.) Entries for sources of information feature the title; the name, address, and phone number of the publisher or distributor; editor's or author's name; publication date or frequency; description of contents; arrangement; indexes; toll-free and additional phone numbers; and facsimile numbers, when known. Publication and film titles appear in italics.

Special Sections Enhance the Usefulness of Career Profiles

Appendix I: State Occupational and Professional Licensing Agencies, following the main section, covers state government agencies responsible for granting professional and occupational licenses. Entries are arranged alphabetically by state and include the state agency's or department's name, address, and phone number.

Appendix II: Employment Growth Rankings and Statistics reprints Bureau of Labor Statistics figures indicating the employment growth for occupations covered in this edition of *PCS*.

Index to Information Sources

PCS includes a comprehensive Index to Information Sources that lists all associations, organizations, agencies, publications, database services, and information sources cited in the career profiles and state agencies section. Entries are arranged alphabetically and are referenced by their entry numbers. Publication and film titles are rendered in italics.

Master List of Profiled Careers

This lists outlines references to covered occupations and professions by job titles, alternate names, occupation names contained within job titles, popular names, and synonymous and related names. Beginning page numbers for each occupation's profile are provided. Title of profiles appear in **boldface**.

Master List of Profiled Careers

Accountants and Auditors

Accountants and auditors prepare, analyze, and verify financial reports needed by managers in business, industrial, and government organizations. **Public accountants** have their own businesses or work for accounting firms. They are employed primarily in auditing, but may also concentrate on tax matters, such as preparing income tax returns and advising clients of the tax advantages and disadvantages of certain business decisions. **Management accountants** provide the financial information executives need to make sound business decisions. They prepare financial reports to meet the public disclosure requirements of various stock exchanges, the Securities and Exchange Commission, and other regulatory bodies. They may work in other areas such as taxation, budgeting, costs, or investments. **Internal auditors** examine and evaluate their firms' financial and information systems, management procedures, and internal controls to insure that records are accurate and controls are adequate to protect against fraud and waste. They also review company operations, evaluating their efficiency, effectiveness, and compliance with corporate policies and procedures, laws, and government regulations. **Government accountants and auditors** see that revenues are received and expenditures are made in accordance with laws and regulations.

Salaries

Average earnings for accountants with bachelor's degree is $28,000/year; with master's degrees $30,000/year.

Beginning public accountants	$28,000/year
Experienced public accountants	$42,400/year
Certified public accountants	$61,900/year
Certified management accountants	$58,700/year
Beginning junior government accountants and auditors	$18,300-$22,700/year
Federal government accountants and auditors	$46,300-$48,200/year

Employment Outlook

Growth rate until the year 2005: Faster than the average.

Accountants and Auditors

CAREER GUIDES

★1★ Accountant
Careers, Inc.
PO Box 135
Largo, FL 34649-0135
Ph: (813)584-7333

1994. Four page brief offering the definition, history, duties, working conditions, personal qualifications, educational requirements, earnings, hours, employment outlook, advancement, and careers related to this position.

★2★ "Accountant" in 100 Best Careers for the Year 2000 (pp. 167-169)
Arco Pub.
201 W. 103rd St.
Indianapolis, IN 46290
Ph: 800-428-5331   Fax: 800-835-3202

Shelly Field. 1992. Describes 100 job opportunities expected to grow fast throughout the next decade. Provides information on job duties and responsibilities, training requirements, education, advancement opportunities, experience and qualifications, and typical salaries.

★3★ "Accountant" and "Accountant Student Trainee" in Guide to Federal Jobs (pp. 124, 127)
Resource Directories
3361 Executive Pkwy., Ste. 302
Toledo, OH 43606
Ph: (419)536-5353   Fax: (419)536-7056
Fr: 800-274-8515

Rod W. Durgin, editor. Third edition, 1992. Contains information on finding and applying for federal jobs. Describes more than 200 professional and technical jobs for college graduates. Covers the nature of the work, salary, and geographic location. Lists college majors preferred for that occupation. Section one describes the function and work of government agencies that hire the most significant number of college graduates.

★4★ "Accountant/Auditor" in BLR Encyclopedia of Prewritten Job Descriptions
Business and Legal Reports, Inc.
39 Academy St.
Madison, CT 06443-1513
Ph: (203)245-7448

Stephen D. Bruce, editor-in-chief. 1994. This book contains hundreds of sample job descriptions arranged by functional job category. The 1-3 page job descriptions cover what the worker normally does in the position, who they report to, and how that position fits in the organizational structure.

★5★ "Accountant" in College Board Guide to Jobs and Career Planning (pp. 127-128)
The College Board
45 Columbus Ave.
New York, NY 10023-6992
Ph: (212)713-8165   Fax: (212)713-8143
Fr: 800-323-7155

Second edition, 1994. Describes the job, salaries, related careers, education needed, and where to write for more information.

★6★ Accountant, Cost
Careers, Inc.
PO Box 135
Largo, FL 34649-0135
Ph: (813)584-7333

1992. Two-page summary describing duties, working conditions, personal qualifications, training, earnings and hours, employment outlook, places of employment, related careers, and where to write for more information.

★7★ "Accountant" in Jobs Rated Almanac
World Almanac
1 International Blvd., Ste. 444
Mahwah, NJ 07495
Ph: (201)529-6900   Fax: (201)529-6901

Les Krantz. Second edition, 1992. Ranks 250 jobs by environment, salary, outlooks, physical demands, stress, security, travel opportunities, and extra perks. Includes jobs the editor feels are the most common, most interesting, and the most rapidly growing.

★8★ "Accountant" in Opportunities in Office Occupations (pp. 131-145)
National Textbook Co. (NTC)
VGM Career Books
4255 W. Touhy Ave.
Lincolnwood, IL 60646-1975
Ph: (708)679-5500   Fax: (708)679-2494
Fr: 800-323-4900

Blanche Ettinger. 1989. This book reflects current changes in office work and discusses trends for the next decade. Describes the job market, opportunities, job duties, educational preparation, the work environment, and earnings.

★9★ "Accountant" in VGM's Careers Encyclopedia (pp. 1-4)
National Textbook Co. (NTC)
VGM Career Books
4255 W. Touhy Ave.
Lincolnwood, IL 60646-1975
Ph: (708)679-5500   Fax: (708)679-2494
Fr: 800-323-4900

Graig T. Norback, editor. Third edition, 1991. Describes job duties, places of employment, working conditions, qualifications, education and training, advancement potential, and salary for each occupation.

★10★ "Accountant" in VGM's Handbook of Business and Management Careers
National Textbook Co.
4255 W. Touhy Ave.
Lincolnwood, IL 60646-1975
Ph: (708)679-5500   Fax: (708)679-2494
Fr: 800-323-4900

Annette Selden. Second edition, 1993. Contains 42 two-page occupational profiles describing job duties, places of employment, working conditions, qualifications, education, employment outlook, and income.

★11★ Accountants
Chronicle Guidance Publications, Inc.
66 Aurora St.
PO Box 1190
Moravia, NY 13118-1190
Ph: (315)497-0330   Fax: (315)497-3359
Fr: 800-622-7284

1991. Career brief describing the nature of the job, working conditions, hours and earnings, education and training, licensure, certification, unions, personal qualifications, social and psychological factors, location, employment outlook, entry methods, advancement, and related occupations.

★12★ "Accountants" in *American Almanac of Jobs and Salaries* (pp. 262-272)
Avon Books
1350 Avenue of the Americas
New York, NY 10019
Ph: (212)261-6800   Fr: 800-238-0658
John Wright, editor. Revised and updated, 1994-95. This is a comprehensive guide to the wages of hundreds of occupations in a wide variety of industries and organizations.

★13★ "Accountants and Auditors" in *101 Careers: A Guide to the Fastest-Growing Opportunities* (pp. 1-3)
John Wiley & Sons, Inc.
605 3rd Ave.
New York, NY 10158-0012
Ph: (212)850-6645   Fax: (212)850-6088
Michael Harkavy. 1990. Describes the nature of the job, working conditions, employment growth, qualifications, personal skills, projected salaries, and where to write for more information.

★14★ "Accountants and Auditors" in *America's 50 Fastest Growing Jobs* (pp. 12)
JIST Works, Inc.
720 N. Park Ave.
Indianapolis, IN 46202-3431
Ph: (317)264-3720   Fax: (317)264-3709
Fr: 800-648-5478
Michael J. Farr, compiler. 1994. Describes the 50 fastest growing jobs within major career clusters such as technicians, and marketing and sales. Each job profile explains the nature of the work, skills and abilities required, employment outlook, average earnings, related occupations, education and training requirements, and employment opportunities. Also contains career planning information and job search tips.

★15★ "Accountants and Auditors" in *Encyclopedia of Careers and Vocational Guidance* (Vol.2, pp. 1-4)
J.G. Ferguson Publishing Co.
200 W. Madison St., Ste. 300
Chicago, IL 60606
Ph: (312)580-5480   Fax: (312)580-4948
William E. Hopke, editor-in-chief. Ninth edition, 1993. Four-volume set that profiles 900 occupations and describes job trends in 74 industries. Includes career description, educational requirements, history of the job, methods of entry, advancement, employment outlook, earnings, conditions of work, social and psychological factors, and sources of further information.

★16★ "Accountants and Auditors" in *Jobs! What They Are—Where They Are—What They Pay* (p. 156)
Simon & Schuster, Inc.
Simon & Schuster Bldg.
1230 Avenue of the Americas
New York, NY 10020
Ph: (212)698-7000   Fr: 800-223-2348
Robert O. Snelling and Anne M. Snelling. 3rd edition, 1992. Describes duties and responsibilities, earnings, employment opportunities, training, and qualifications.

★17★ "Accountants and Auditors" in *Occupational Outlook Handbook*
U.S. Government Printing Office
Superintendent of Documents
Washington, DC 20402
Ph: (202)512-1800   Fax: (202)512-2250
Biennial; latest edition, 1994-95. Encyclopedia of careers describing about 250 occupations and comprising about 85 percent of all jobs in the economy. Occupations that require lengthy education or training are given the most attention. Each occupation's profile describes what the worker does on the job, working conditions, education and training requirements, advancement possibilities, job outlook, earnings, and sources of additional information.

★18★ "Accountants" in *Career Discovery Encyclopedia* (Vol.1, pp. 7-9)
J.G. Ferguson Publishing Co.
200 W. Madison St., Ste. 300
Chicago, IL 60606
Ph: (312)580-5480   Fax: (312)580-4948
Russell E. Primm, editor-in chief. 1993. This six volume set contains two-page articles for 504 occupations. Each article describes job duties, earnings, and educational and training requirements. The whole set is arranged alphabetically by job title. Designed for junior high and older students.

★19★ "Accountants" in *Opportunities in Insurance Careers* (pp. 129-132)
National Textbook Co. (NTC)
VGM Career Books
4255 W. Touhy Ave.
Lincolnwood, IL 60646-1975
Ph: (708)679-5500   Fax: (708)679-2494
Fr: 800-323-4900
Robert M. Schrayer. 1993. Provides an introduction to the world of insurance careers through an exploration of the industry's history, academic requirements, certification, licensing and education requirements, positions available, as well as some careers associated with the insurance industry, such as data processing, human resources and public relations.

★20★ "Accountants", "Public Accountants", and "Auditor" in *Career Information Center* (Vol.1)
Simon and Schuster
200 Old Tappan Rd.
Old Tappan, NJ 07675
Fax: 800-445-6991   Fr: 800-223-2348
Richard Lidz and Linda Perrin, editorial directors. Fifth edition, 1993. A multi-volume set that profiles over 600 occupations. Each occupational profile describes job duties, educational requirements, advancement possibilities, employment outlook, working conditions, earnings and benefits, and where to write for more information.

★21★ "Accounting" in *Black Woman's Career Guide* (pp. 244-248)
Bantam Doubleday Dell
1540 Broadway
New York, NY 10036
Fax: 800-233-3294   Fr: 800-223-5780
Beatryce Nivens. Revised edition, 1987. Part 1 describes career planning, resume writing, job hunting, and interviewing. Part 2 profiles

60 black women pioneers in 20 different career areas.

★22★ "Accounting" in *Career Choices for the 90's for Students of Business* (pp. 1-23)
Walker and Co.
435 Hudson St.
New York, NY 10014
Ph: (212)727-8300   Fax: (212)727-0984
Fr: 800-289-2553
Compiled by Career Associates Staff. 1990. This book offers alternatives for students of business. Gives information about the outlook and competition for entry-level candidates. Provides job hunting tips.

★23★ "Accounting" in *Career Choices for the 90's for Students of Economics* (pp. 1-23)
Walker and Co.
435 Hudson St.
New York, NY 10014
Ph: (212)727-8300   Fax: (212)727-0984
Fr: 800-289-2553
Compiled by Career Associates Staff. 1990. This book offers alternatives for students of economics. Gives information about the outlook and competition for entry-level candidates. Provides job hunting tips.

★24★ "Accounting" in *Career Choices for the 90's for Students of MBA* (pp. 1-22)
Walker and Co.
435 Hudson St.
New York, NY 10014
Ph: (212)727-8300   Fax: (212)727-0984
Fr: 800-289-2553
Compiled by Career Associates Staff. 1990. This book offers alternatives for students interested in business. Gives information about the outlook and competition for entry-level candidates. Provides job hunting tips.

★25★ "Accounting" in *College Majors and Careers: A Resource Guide to Effective Life Planning* (pp. 7-8)
Garrett Park Press
PO Box 1907
Garrett Park, MD 20896
Ph: (301)946-2553
Paul Phifer. 1993. Lists 60 college majors, with definitions; related occupations and leisure activities; skills, values, and personal needed attributes; suggested readings; and a list of associations.

★26★ "Accounting" in *Encyclopedia of Career Choices for the 1990s: A Guide to Entry Level Jobs* (pp. 1-23)
Walker and Co.
435 Hudson St.
New York, NY 10014
Ph: (212)727-8300   Fax: (212)727-0984
Fr: 800-289-2553
1990. Describes entry-level careers in a variety of industries. Presents qualifications required, working conditions, salary, internships, and professional associations.

★27★ "Accounting" in *Encyclopedia of Careers and Vocational Guidance* **(Vol.1, pp. 1-6)**
J.G. Ferguson Publishing Co.
200 W. Madison St., Ste. 300
Chicago, IL 60606
Ph: (312)580-5480   Fax: (312)580-4948
William E. Hopke, editor-in-chief. Ninth edition, 1993. Four-volume set that profiles 900 occupations and describes job trends in 74 industries. Includes career description, educational requirements, history of the job, methods of entry, advancement, employment outlook, earnings, conditions of work, social and psychological factors, and sources of further information.

★28★ *Accounting and Finance Salary Survey*
Source Finance, Accounting and Financial
   Recruiting Specialists
1375 E. 9th St., Ste. 1960
Cleveland, OH 44114
Ph: (216)765-8808
Annual. This booklet describing career plan development in accounting, future opportunities, the organizational structure of staff in public accounting and private accounting firms, and compensation by job title and years of experience, and geographical area.

★29★ "Accounting" in *Internships 1995*
Petersons Guides, Inc.
PO Box 2123
Princeton, NJ 08543-2123
Ph: (609)243-9111   Fr: 800-338-3282
Fifteenth edition, 1995. Lists internship opportunities under six broad categories: communications, creative, performing, and fine arts, human services, international relations, business and technology, and public affairs. For each internship program, gives the names, phone number, contact person, description, eligibility requirements, and benefits.

★30★ "Accounting" in *Liberal Arts Jobs*
Petersons Guides, Inc.
PO Box 2123
Princeton, NJ 08543-2123
Ph: (609)243-9111   Fax: (609)243-9150
Fr: 800-338-3282
Burton Jay Nadler. Revised edition, 1989. Strives to help the liberal arts graduate identify skills for entry-level positions. Gives goal setting and job search advice.

★31★ "Accounting" in *Opportunities in Financial Careers* **(pp. 77-94)**
National Textbook Co. (NTC)
VGM Career Books
4255 W. Touhy Ave.
Lincolnwood, IL 60646-1975
Ph: (708)679-5500   Fax: (708)679-2494
Fr: 800-323-4900
Michael J. Sumichrast and Dean Crist. 1991. Describes jobs in banking, security sales, and accounting occupations. Explains trends in the field, training requirements, advancement possibilities, licensing, and earnings.

★32★ "Accounting" in *Opportunities in Hotel and Motel Careers* **(pp. 37-86)**
National Textbook Co. (NTC)
VGM Career Books
4255 W. Touhy Ave.
Lincolnwood, IL 60646-1975
Ph: (708)679-5500   Fax: (708)679-2494
Fr: 800-323-4900
Shepard Henkin. 1992. Describes jobs in the hospitality industry, employment outlook, personal requirements, educational preparation, apprenticeship and training, salary, and job hunting techniques.

★33★ "Accounting" in *Where the Jobs Are: The Hottest Careers for the 90s* **(pp. 43-51)**
Career Press
180 5th Ave.
Hawthorne, NJ 07507
Ph: (201)427-0229   Fax: (201)427-2037
Fr: 800-CAREER-1
Joyce Hadley. 1995. Offers a job-hunting strategy for the 1990s as well as descriptions of growing careers of the decade. Each profile includes general information, forecasts, growth, education and training, licensing requirements, and salary information.

★34★ *Auditor*
Careers, Inc.
PO Box 135
Largo, FL 34649-0135
Ph: (813)584-7333
1992. Two-page summary describing duties, working conditions, personal qualifications, training, earnings and hours, employment outlook, places of employment, related careers, and where to write for more information.

★35★ *Auditors*
Chronicle Guidance Publications, Inc.
66 Aurora St.
PO Box 1190
Moravia, NY 13118-1190
Ph: (315)497-0330   Fax: (315)497-3359
Fr: 800-622-7284
1991. Career brief describing the nature of the job, working conditions, hours and earnings, education and training, licensure, certification, unions, personal qualifications, social and psychological factors, location, employment outlook, entry methods, advancement, and related occupations.

★36★ *The Bottom Line: Inside Accounting Today*
New American Library (Nal/Dutton)
375 Hudson St.
New York, NY 10014-3657
Ph: (212)366-2000
Grace W. Weinstein. 1987. This book gives an overview of trends and changes in the accounting profession.

★37★ *Careers in Accounting*
National Textbook Co. (NTC)
VGM Career Books
4255 W. Touhy Ave.
Lincolnwood, IL 60646-1975
Ph: (708)679-5500   Fax: (708)679-2494
Fr: 800-323-4900
Gloria Gaylord, editor. 1991. Career guide covering the field of accounting.

★38★ "Careers in Accounting" in *Careers in Business* **(pp. 16-31)**
National Textbook Co. (NTC)
VGM Career Books
4255 W. Touhy Ave.
Lincolnwood, IL 60646-1975
Ph: (708)679-5500   Fax: (708)679-2494
Fr: 800-323-4900
Lila B. Stair and Dorothy Domkowski. 1992. Provides facts about business areas such as marketing, accounting, production, human resources, management, and finance. Focuses on job duties, salaries, career paths, employment outlook, trends, educational preparation and skills needed.

★39★ *Careers in Finance*
National Textbook Co. (NTC)
VGM Career Books
4255 W. Touhy Ave.
Lincolnwood, IL 60646-1975
Ph: (708)679-5500   Fax: (708)679-2494
Fr: 800-323-4900
Trudy Ring, editor. 1993. Covers financial careers in such areas as higher education, corporate and public finance, and commercial and investment banking.

★40★ *Careers in Public Accounting: A Comprehensive Comparison of the Top Tier Firms*
Emerson Co.
12356 Northrup Way, No. 103
Bellevue, WA 98005
Ph: (206)869-0655
James C. Emerson. Fourth edition, 1993. This book gives statistics on the big eight accounting firms, and, history, operating strategy, key personnel, operating statistics, major officers, major clients, and primary practice emphasis. Also includes analyses of eleven industries.

★41★ *Exploring Careers in Accounting*
Rosen Publishing Group
29 E. 21st St.
New York, NY 10010
Ph: (212)777-3017   Fax: (212)777-0277
Fr: 800-237-9932
Lawrence Rosenthal. 1993. Describes job duties, personal qualities needed, advantages, job opportunities, educational preparation, future trends, and job hunting.

★42★ "Harvey A. Goldstein" in *Straight Talk on Careers: Eighty Pros Take You Into Their Professions* **(pp. 20-21)**
Garrett Park Press
PO Box 1907
Garrett Park, MD 20896
Ph: (301)946-2553
Mary Barbera-Hogan. 1987. Contains candid interviews from people who give an inside view of their work in 80 different careers. These professionals describe a day's work and the stresses and rewards accompanying their work.

★43★ *The Insider's Guide to the Top 20 Careers in Business and Management*
McGraw-Hill
1221 Avenue of the Americas
New York, NY 10020
Ph: (212)512-3493   Fax: (212)512-3050
Tom Fischgrund. 1994. Contains information on different business careers including ac-

counting, banking, finance, and retail sales. Includes tips on choosing a careers, preparing a resume, interviewing, and succeeding on the job.

★44★ "International Accounting" in *Opportunities in International Business Careers* (pp. 60-69)

National Textbook Co. (NTC)
VGM Career Books
4255 W. Touhy Ave.
Lincolnwood, IL 60646-1975
Ph: (708)679-5500   Fax: (708)679-2494
Fr: 800-323-4900

Jeffry S. Arpan. 1989. Describes what types of jobs exist in international business, where they are located, what challenges and rewards they bring, and how to prepare for and obtain jobs in international business.

★45★ *Opportunities in Accounting Careers*

National Textbook Co. (NTC)
VGM Career Books
4255 W. Touhy Ave.
Lincolnwood, IL 60646-1975
Ph: (708)679-5500   Fax: (708)679-2494
Fr: 800-323-4900

Martin Rosenberg. 1991. Offers information about career opportunities in the field and how to prepare for them. Describes job opportunities, how to make a career decision, job hunting techniques, and future trends.

★46★ *Successfully Managing Your Accounting Career*

John Wiley and Sons, Inc.
605 3rd Ave.
New York, NY 10158-0012
Ph: (212)850-6000   Fax: (212)850-6088
Fr: 800-526-5368

Henry Lubus. 1988. Gives advice on career planning, job hunting and changing, and how to succeed on the job. Describes trends, continuing education, membership in professional associations, and careers in public and private accounting and in teaching.

★47★ *Take the CPA Challenge*

American Institute of Certified Public
    Accountants
1211 Avenue of the Americas
New York, NY 10036-8775
Ph: (212)596-6200   Fr: 800-862-4272

1987. This 12-page pamphlet describes what a CPA does, and certification and education requirements. Covers career opportunities in public accounting, business and industry, government, nonprofit organizations, and accounting education.

★48★ *Why Graduate School for Careers in Professional Accounting?*

American Institute of Certified Public
    Accountants
1211 Avenue of the Americas
New York, NY 10036-8775
Ph: (212)596-6200   Fr: 800-862-4272

1987. This six-panel brochure describes the career benefits for accountants who pursue advanced studies.

PROFESSIONAL ASSOCIATIONS

★49★ American Assembly of Collegiate Schools of Business (AACSB)

600 Emerson Rd., Ste. 300
St. Louis, MO 63141
Ph: (314)872-8481   Fax: (314)872-8495

Members: Institutions offering accredited programs of instruction in business administration and accounting at the college level; nonaccredited schools; business firms; governmental and professional organizations; educational institutions and organizations outside the U.S. **Purpose:** Provides accreditation for bachelor's and master's degree programs in business administration and accounting. Compiles statistics and conducts research. **Publications:** *Achieving Quality and Continuous Improvement Through Self-Evaluation and Peer Review (Standards for Accreditation)*, annual. • *American Assembly of Collegiate Schools of Business— Membership Directory*, annual. • *Business and Management Education Funding Alert*, monthly. • *Guide to Doctoral Programs in Business and Management*, periodic. • *Newsline*, quarterly. • *Salary Survey*, annual.

★50★ American Institute of Certified Public Accountants (AICPA)

1211 Avenue of the Americas
New York, NY 10036-8775
Ph: (212)596-6200   Fax: (212)596-6213
Fr: 800-862-4272

Members: Professional society of accountants certified by the states and territories. **Purpose:** Responsibilities include establishing auditing and reporting standards; influencing the development of financial accounting standards underlying the presentation of U.S. corporate financial statements; preparing and grading the national Uniform CPA Examination for the state licensing bodies. Conducts research and continuing education programs and surveillance of practice. Maintains over 100 committees including Accounting Standards, Accounting and Review Services, AICPA Effective Legislation Political Action, Auditing Standards, Federal Taxation, Management Consulting Services, Professional Ethics, Quality Review, Women and Family Issues, and Information Technology. Maintains speakers' bureau. **Publications:** *Accounting Trends and Techniques*, annual. • *American Institute of Certified Public Accountants—Catalog of Publications and CPE Materials*, periodic. • *CPA Client Bulletin*, monthly. • *CPA Examinations*, semiannual. • *CPA Letter*, semimonthly. • *Digest of Washington Issues*. • *Journal of Accountancy*, monthly. • *Practicing CPA*, monthly. • *Tax Adviser: A Magazine of Tax Planning, Trends and Techniques*, monthly.

★51★ Information Systems Audit and Control Association (ISACA)

3701 Algonquin Rd., Ste. 1010
Rolling Meadows, IL 60008
Ph: (708)253-1545   Fax: (708)253-1443

Members: Dedicated to the establishment of standards and systems of control designed to effectively organize and utilize data processing resources. **Purpose:** Aids auditors, man-

agers, and systems specialists in addressing problems related to controls in data processing systems. Offers Certified Information Systems Auditor Professional Designation Program. Administers the Information Systems Audit & Control Foundation, which sponsors research in the field. **Publications:** *Control Objectives*, periodic. • *Global Communique*. • *I.S. Audit and Control Journal*, bimonthly.

★52★ Institute of Internal Auditors (IIA)

249 Maitland Ave.
Altamonte Springs, FL 32701-4201
Ph: (407)830-7600   Fax: (407)831-5171

Members: International professional organization of internal auditors, comptrollers, accountants, educators, and computer specialists in functions of internal auditing in corporations, government agencies, and institutions. **Purpose:** Grants professional certification. Offers benchmarking subscription service and quality reviews. **Publications:** *IIA Educator*, semiannual. • *IIA Today*, bimonthly. • *Institute of Internal Auditors— Membership/Certified Internal Auditor Directory*, biennial. • *Internal Auditor*, bimonthly. • *Pistas de Auditoria*, bimonthly.

★53★ Institute of Management Accountants (IMA)

10 Paragon Dr.
Montvale, NJ 07645
Ph: (201)573-9000   Fax: (201)573-8185
Fr: 800-638-4427

Members: Management accountants in industry, public accounting, government, and academia; other persons interested in internal and management uses of accounting. **Purpose:** Conducts research on accounting methods and procedures and the management purposes served. Established Institute of Certified Management Accountants to implement and administer examination for the Cerified Management Accountant (CMA) program. Annually presents chapter medals for competition, manuscripts and for the highest scores on the CMA Examination. Offers continuing education programs comprising courses, conferences, and a self-study program in management accounting areas. Offers ethics counseling services for members by telephone. Sponsors the Stuart Cameron McLeod Society, the Continuous Improvement Center, and the Foundation for Applied Research. **Publications:** *The Focus*, bimonthly. • *Management Accounting*, monthly.

★54★ National Association of State Boards of Accountancy (NASBA)

380 Lexington Ave., Ste. 200
New York, NY 10168
Ph: (212)490-3868   Fax: (212)490-5841

State and territorial boards of public accountancy. Serves as a forum for communication among state boards of accountancy. Assists member boards in obtaining services needed for the administration of public accountancy laws and the protection of the public interest. Sponsors Uniform CPA Examination Corporation (CPAES), a division of NASBA that provides exam services including processing exam applications, administering the CPA exam, and issuing grades. Compiles annual statistics on CPA candidate performance on the Uniform CPA Examination. **Publications:** *CPA Candidate Performance on the*

Uniform CPA Examination, annual. • *Digest of State Accountancy Laws and State Board Regulations.* • *Handbook and Checklist for CPA Examination Administration.* • *Model Positive Enforcement Program.* • *Report of the CPA Examination Review Board*, annual. • *Standards and Checklist for State Regulation of Public Accountancy.* • *State Board Report*, monthly. • *State Boards of Accountancy of the United States*, periodic. • *Uniform Accountancy Act.*

★55★ National Society of Public Accountants (NSPA)

1010 N. Fairfax St.
Alexandria, VA 22314-1574
Ph: (703)549-6400   Fax: (703)549-2984
Fr: 800-966-6679

Members: Professional society of practicing accountants and tax practitioners. **Purpose:** Represents the independent practitioner. Conducts correspondence courses and seminars; operates speakers' bureau. Maintains 21 committees. **Publications:** *Income and Fees of Accountants in Public Practice*, triennial. • *National Public Accountant*, monthly. • *National Society of Public Accountants—Annual Report.* • *National Society of Public Accountants—Yearbook.* • *NSPA Washington Reporter.*

STANDARDS/CERTIFICATION AGENCIES

★56★ Accreditation Council for Accountancy and Taxation

1010 N. Fairfax St.
Alexandria, VA 22314-1574
Ph: (703)549-6400   Fax: (703)549-2984
Conducts semiannual certification examination in accountancy and annual certification examination in taxation.

★57★ American Institute of Certified Public Accountants (AICPA)

1211 Avenue of the Americas
New York, NY 10036-8775
Ph: (212)596-6200   Fax: (212)596-6213
Fr: 800-862-4272

Professional society of accountants certified by the states and territories. Responsibilities include establishing auditing and reporting standards; influencing the development of financial accounting standards underlying the presentation of U.S. corporate financial statements; preparing and grading the national Uniform CPA Examination for the state licensing bodies.

★58★ Community Associations Institute (CAI)

1630 Duke St.
Alexandria, VA 22314
Ph: (703)548-8600   Fax: (703)684-1581
Purpose is to develop and provide the most advanced and effective guidance for the creation, financing, operation, and maintenance of the common facilities and services in condominiums, townhouse projects, planned unit developments, and open-space communities.

★59★ EDP Auditors Association (EDPAA)

455 E. Kehoe Blvd., No. 106
PO Box 88180
Carol Stream, IL 60188
Ph: (708)682-1200   Fax: (708)682-4010
Establishes standards and systems of control designed to effectively organize and utilize data processing resources. Offers Certified Information Systems Auditor Program.

★60★ Financial Accounting Standards Board
Financial Accounting Foundation

401 Merritt 7
PO Box 5116
Norwalk, CT 06856
Ph: (203)847-0700

Defines, issues, and promotes financial accounting standards.

★61★ Information Systems Audit and Control Association (ISACA)

3701 Algonquin Rd., Ste. 1010
Rolling Meadows, IL 60008
Ph: (708)253-1545   Fax: (708)253-1443
Dedicated to the establishment of standards and systems of control designed to effectively organize and utilize data processing resources. Aids auditors, managers, and systems specialists in addressing problems related to controls in data processing systems. Offers Certified Information Systems Auditor Professional Designation Program.

★62★ Institute of Certified Management Accountants

10 Paragon Dr.
Montvale, NJ 07645
Ph: (201)573-6300   Fax: (201)573-8185
Fr: 800-638-4427

Evaluates the credentials of Certified Management Accountant (CMA) candidates; conducts CMA examinations and grants certificates to those who qualify. Ensures that CMAs continue to meet the professional development requirements necessary to retain their certificates.

★63★ Institute of Internal Auditors (IIA)

249 Maitland Ave.
Altamonte Springs, FL 32701-4201
Ph: (407)830-7600   Fax: (407)831-5171
Grants professional certification. Offers benchmarking subscription service and quality reviews.

★64★ Institute of Management Accountants (IMA)

10 Paragon Dr.
Montvale, NJ 07645
Ph: (201)573-9000   Fax: (201)573-8185
Fr: 800-638-4427

Established Institute of Certified Management Accountants to implement and administer examination for the Cerified Management Accountant (CMA) program. Offers continuing education programs comprising courses, conferences, and a self-study program in management accounting areas.

★65★ National Society of Public Accountants (NSPA)

1010 N. Fairfax St.
Alexandria, VA 22314-1574
Ph: (703)549-6400   Fax: (703)549-2984
Fr: 800-966-6679

Conducts correspondence courses and seminars; operates speakers' bureau.

TEST GUIDES

★66★ *Accounting*

National Learning Corp.
212 Michael Dr.
Syosset, NY 11791
Ph: (516)921-8888   Fax: (516)921-8743
Fr: 800-645-6337

Jack Rudman. Part of the Regents College Proficiency Examination series. A sample test for college credit-by-examination programs in the field of accounting. Multiple-choice style with answers included.

★67★ *ACT Proficiency Examination Program: Auditing*

National Learning Corp.
212 Michael Dr.
Syosset, NY 11791
Ph: (516)921-8888   Fax: (516)921-8743
Fr: 800-645-6337

Jack Rudman. A series of practice test guides containing multiple-choice examinations designed to demonstrate proficiency in the subject of accounting. Titles in the series include *Introductory Accounting; Intermediate Accounting; Cost Accounting and Analysis; Advanced Accounting.*

★68★ *The AICPA's Uniform CPA Exam*

Arco Publishing Co.
Macmillan General Reference
15 Columbus Cir.
New York, NY 10023
Fax: 800-835-3202   Fr: 800-858-7674
Compiled by American Institute of Certified Public Accountants (AICPA). 1995. Contains a complete exam.

★69★ *Barron's How to Prepare for the Certified Public Accountant Examination (CPA)*

Barron's Educational Series, Inc.
250 Wireless Blvd.
Hauppauge, NY 11788
Ph: (516)434-3311   Fax: 800-645-3476
Fr: 800-645-3476

Samuel Person. Third edition, 1992. (paper). Includes guidelines and strategies for taking the CPA Examination as well as practice tests.

★70★ *Career Examination Series: Accountant*

National Learning Corp.
212 Michael Dr.
Syosset, NY 11791
Ph: (516)921-8888   Fax: (516)921-8743
Fr: 800-645-6337

Jack Rudman. A series of study guides with multiple-choice examination questions and solutions for trainees and professional accountants and auditors. Titles in the series include *Accountant II; Accountant III; Accountant IV; Accountant-Auditor; Accounting and Auditing Careers; Accounting Executive; Accounting Systems Specialist; Administrative Accountant; Administrative Auditor of Accounts; Assessor; Assessment and Tax Accounting Supervisor; Assistant State Accounts Auditor/Examiner of Municipal Affairs; Associate Management Auditor; Associate Tax Auditor; Auditor; Chief Accountant; Chief Auditor; Chief Excise Tax Investigator; Chief Field Accountant; County Director of Accounting; Deputy Assessor; Field Accountant; Field Auditor; Internal Auditor; Internal Revenue Agent; Internal Revenue Officer; Principal Accountant; Principal Auditor; Senior Accountant; Senior Assessor; Senior Auditor; Senior Field Accountant; Senior Internal Auditor; Supervising Accountant; Supervising Assessor; Supervising Auditor; Tax Auditor.*

★71★ *Career Examination Series:*
   Accountant/Auditor
National Learning Corp.
212 Michael Dr.
Syosset, NY 11791
Ph: (516)921-8888   Fax: (516)921-8743
Fr: 800-645-6337

Jack Rudman. Test guide including questions and answers for students or professionals in the field who seek advancement through examination.

★72★ *Career Examination Series:*
   Accounting Assistant
National Learning Corp.
212 Michael Dr.
Syosset, NY 11791
Ph: (516)921-8888   Fax: (516)921-8743
Fr: 800-645-6337

Jack Rudman. 1993. Test guide including questions and answers for students or professionals in the field who seek advancement through examination.

★73★ *Career Examination Series:*
   Administrative Claim Examiner
National Learning Corp.
212 Michael Dr.
Syosset, NY 11791
Ph: (516)921-8888   Fax: (516)921-8743
Fr: 800-645-6337

Jack Rudman. 1993. Test guide including questions and answers for students or professionals in the field who seek advancement through examination.

★74★ *Career Examination Series:*
   Administrative Management Auditor
National Learning Corp.
212 Michael Dr.
Syosset, NY 11791
Ph: (516)921-8888   Fax: (516)921-8743
Fr: 800-645-6337

Jack Rudman. 1993. Test guide including questions and answers for students or professionals in the field who seek advancement through examination.

★75★ *Career Examination Series:*
   Assistant Accountant
National Learning Corp.
212 Michael Dr.
Syosset, NY 11791
Ph: (516)921-8888   Fax: (516)921-8743
Fr: 800-645-6337

Jack Rudman. 1993. Test guide including questions and answers for students or professionals in the field who seek advancement through examination.

★76★ *Career Examination Series:*
   Compensation Claims Auditor
National Learning Corp.
212 Michael Dr.
Syosset, NY 11791
Ph: (516)921-8888   Fax: (516)921-8743
Fr: 800-645-6337

Jack Rudman. 1993. Test guide including questions and answers for students or professionals in the field who seek advancement through examination.

★77★ *Career Examination Series: Field*
   Accountant/Auditor
National Learning Corp.
212 Michael Dr.
Syosset, NY 11791
Ph: (516)921-8888   Fax: (516)921-8743
Fr: 800-645-6337

Jack Rudman. Test guide including questions and answers for students or professionals in the field who seek advancement through examination.

★78★ *Career Examination Series: Junior*
   Accountant
National Learning Corp.
212 Michael Dr.
Syosset, NY 11791
Ph: (516)921-8888   Fax: (516)921-8743
Fr: 800-645-6337

Jack Rudman. Test guide including questions and answers for students or professionals in the field who seek advancement through examination.

★79★ *Career Examination Series:*
   Management Auditor
National Learning Corp.
212 Michael Dr.
Syosset, NY 11791
Ph: (516)921-8888   Fax: (516)921-8743
Fr: 800-645-6337

Jack Rudman. 1993. Test guide including questions and answers for students or professionals in the field who seek advancement through examination.

★80★ *Career Examination Series:*
   Payroll Auditor
National Learning Corp.
212 Michael Dr.
Syosset, NY 11791
Ph: (516)921-8888   Fax: (516)921-8743
Fr: 800-645-6337

Jack Rudman. 1993. Test guide including questions and answers for students or professionals in the field who seek advancement through examination.

★81★ *Career Examination Series:*
   Principal Accountant/Auditor
National Learning Corp.
212 Michael Dr.
Syosset, NY 11791
Ph: (516)921-8888   Fax: (516)921-8743
Fr: 800-645-6337

Jack Rudman. Test guide including questions and answers for students or professionals in the field who seek advancement through examination.

★82★ *Career Examination Series:*
   Senior Accountant/Auditor
National Learning Corp.
212 Michael Dr.
Syosset, NY 11791
Ph: (516)921-8888   Fax: (516)921-8743
Fr: 800-645-6337

Jack Rudman. Test guide including questions and answers for students or professionals in the field who seek advancement through examination.

★83★ *Career Examination Series: State*
   Accounts Auditor/Examiner of
   Municipal Affairs
National Learning Corp.
212 Michael Dr.
Syosset, NY 11791
Ph: (516)921-8888   Fax: (516)921-8743
Fr: 800-645-6337

Jack Rudman. 1993. Test guide including questions and answers for students or professionals in the field who seek advancement through examination.

★84★ *Career Examination Series:*
   Supervising Accountant/Auditor
National Learning Corp.
212 Michael Dr.
Syosset, NY 11791
Ph: (516)921-8888   Fax: (516)921-8743
Fr: 800-645-6337

Jack Rudman. Test guide including questions and answers for students or professionals in the field who seek advancement through examination.

★85★ *Certified Public Accountant*
   Examination (CPA)
National Learning Corp.
212 Michael Dr.
Syosset, NY 11791
Ph: (516)921-8888   Fax: (516)921-8743
Fr: 800-645-6337

Jack Rudman. Part of the Admission Test series. A sample test for those seeking admission to graduate and professional schools or seeking entrance or advancement in institutional and public career service in the field of certified public accounting.

★86★ *CPA Examination Review:*
   Auditing
John Wiley and Sons, Inc.
605 3rd Ave.
New York, NY 10158-0012
Ph: (212)850-6000   Fax: (212)850-6088
Fr: 800-526-5368

Patrick R. Delaney, 1994. Includes illustrations.

★87★ EZ 101 Study Keys: Accounting
Barron's Educational Series, Inc.
250 Wireless Blvd.
Hauppauge, NY 11788
Ph: (516)434-3311   Fax: (516)434-3723
Fr: 800-645-3476
1992. Provides themes, formulas, and a glossary of accounting terms.

★88★ Financial Accounting
National Learning Corp.
212 Michael Dr.
Syosset, NY 11791
Ph: (516)921-8888   Fax: (516)921-8743
Fr: 800-645-6337
Jack Rudman. Part of the Dantes Subject Standardized Test series. A standardized graduate and college-level examination given by graduate schools, colleges, and the U.S. Armed Forces as a final examination for course evaluation in the field of accounting. Multiple-choice format with correct answers.

★89★ Regents External Degree Series: Accounting
National Learning Corp.
212 Michael Dr.
Syosset, NY 11791
Ph: (516)921-8888   Fax: (516)921-8743
Fr: 800-645-6337
Jack Rudman. A multiple-choice examination for accounting professionals preparing to enter the Regents External Degree Program, an alternate route to a college degree. Test contains multiple-choice questions with answers provided. Titles in the series include *Accounting I; Accounting II; Accounting III.*

EDUCATIONAL DIRECTORIES AND PROGRAMS

★90★ American Assembly of Collegiate Schools of Business—Membership Directory
American Assembly of Collegiate Schools of Business
600 Emerson Rd., Ste. 300
St. Louis, MO 63141-6762
Ph: (314)872-8481   Fax: (314)872-8495
Sharon Barber, Director of Communications
Annual, September. Covers over 800 member institutions offering instructional programs in business administration at the college level; member businesses, governmental agencies, and professional organizations. Entries include: Institution or company name, address, phone, fax, e-mail, name and title of member representative. Arrangement: Alphabetical by organization.

★91★ Business and Finance Career Directory
Gale Research Inc.
835 Penobscot Bldg.
Detroit, MI 48226-4094
Ph: (313)961-2242   Fax: (313)961-6083
Fr: 800-877-GALE
Bradley J. Morgan and Joseph M. Palmisano. Second edition, 1992. A directory in the Career Advisor Series that provides essays written by industry professionals; job search in-

formation on resume and cover letter preparation, networking, and the interviewing process; approximately 300 companies and organizations offering job opportunities and internships, and additional job-hunting resources.

AWARDS, SCHOLARSHIPS, GRANTS, AND FELLOWSHIPS

★92★ AAHCPA Scholarship
American Association of Hispanic CPA'S (AAHCPA)
2424 Pennsylvania Ave., NW, No. 402
Washington, DC 20037
Ph: (202)337-4069
Qualifications: Candidates must be hispanic students majoring in accounting. Selection criteria: Grade point averages and financial need. Funds available: Two awards of $750 and $1,000 each.

★93★ AICPA Doctoral Fellowships
American Institute of Certified Public Accountants (AICPA)
Academic and Career Development Division
1211 Avenue of the Americas
New York, NY 10036-8775
Ph: (212)575-5504
Purpose: To encourage qualified students to enter and complete doctoral programs in accounting and become accounting teachers. Qualifications: Applicant may be of any nationality. Candidate must hold a CPA certificate and plan to enter an academic career in accounting in the United States. Grants are tenable in doctoral programs accredited by the American Assembly of Collegiate Schools of Business. Funds available: $5,000. Application details: Write to AICPA for application materials. Submit form with copies of relevant standardized test scores, a statement of career objectives, transcripts, and three letters of recommendation. Non-U.S. citizens also must supply scores from the Test of Spoken English. Deadline: 1 April. All applicants will be notified by 1 May.

★94★ American Accounting Association Fellowship Program in Accounting
American Accounting Association
5717 Bessie Dr.
Sarasota, FL 34233-2399
Ph: (813)921-7747   Fax: (813)923-4093
Purpose: To encourage and increase the supply of qualified teachers of accounting at the University level in the United States and Canada. Qualifications: Candidate must have been accepted into a doctoral program. Awards will only go to those students in their first year. Foreign students are eligble if a resident of the U.S. or Canada at the time of application and are enrooled in or have a degree from a U.S. or Canadian accredited graduate progarm and plan to teach in the U.S. or Canada. Funds available: $5,000. Application details: Contact the office manager for application guidelines, available in September. Deadline: 1 February. Notification by 31 March.

★95★ Michael J. Barrett Doctoral Dissertation Grant
Institute of Internal Auditors Research Foundation (IIA)
249 Maitland Ave.
Altamonte Springs, FL 32701-4201
Ph: (407)830-7600   Fax: (407)831-5171
Purpose: To encourage internal audit research by doctoral candidates. Qualifications: Applicants must be pursuing a doctoral degree in business with a concentration in auditing or accounting from an accredited institution. They must intend to teach in the field of auditing for at least two years and have completed or be within one year of completing the necessary course requirements and pre-dissertation examinations required by the degree-granting institution, and be at the dissertation stage at the time of the award. If all requirements have not been completed, a schedule of completion of the remaining requirements should be included in the cover letter. They should also devote full-time to the dissertation during the term of the award; however, if less than full-time work is expected, and the reason is justified on the cover letter, the candidate will not be disqualified. Selection criteria: Selection of candidates is the responsibility of the Doctoral Dissertations Committee of the IIA Research Foundation Board of Research Advisors, which includes professionals actively involved in internal auditing. Funds available: Grants vary from $1,000 to $10,000 each, based on the amount required to complete the dissertation within one year. The grant is paid over a period generally not exceeding one year and usually divided into three installments corresponding with dissertation progress reports. Application details: Applicants must submit two letters of recommendation, a dissertation proposal that includes their name, dissertation title, and name of the degree-granting institution; the objective of the research; the need for the research; the research plan; the candidate's qualifications; and a schedule that lists individual tasks and estimated completion time, in months, from the starting date. Proposals should not exceed six pages. Cover letter must be submitted dicussing the degree the candidate will receive; the major and minor fields covered in the doctoral program; the full name of the degree granting institution where they will complete their dissertation and its business school accreditations; the names and positions of the two professors who will send letters of recommendation to the IIA and who are directly involved in the supervision of the applicant's dissertation; the schedule for completion of course work, qualifying examinations, and beginning of the dissertation research; the future professional and careeer plans after completing the doctoral program; and a one-half page summary (abstract) of the dissertation. Deadline: May 15 and October 31. The Foundation reviews proposals in June and December.

★96★ Bradford Cadmus Memorial Award
Institute of Internal Auditors
249 Maitland Ave.
Altamonte Springs, FL 32701-4201
Ph: (407)830-7600   Fax: (407)851-5171
For recognition of outstanding contributions in the field of internal auditing to research, education, or literature. This is the highest honor or tribute bestowed by the Institute. A calligraphic scroll and all expenses to the Institute's International Conferences for the winner and spouse are awarded annually. Established in 1966 in honor of the first managing director of the Institute, Bradford Cadmus.

★97★ Arthur H. Carter Scholarship
American Accounting Association
5717 Bessie Dr.
Sarasota, FL 34233-2399
Ph: (813)921-7747   Fax: (813)923-4093
Purpose: To defray the costs of the accounting student's undergraduate or graduate education for one year. Qualifications: Undergraduate or master's degree students who are United States citizens and have completed two years of study at an accredited college or university and have a minimum of one more year of study at the time the award is made may apply. Recipient must be enrolled a minimum of 12 semester hours (or equivalent), of which two courses should be accounting related, during the scholarship period. The school must be an Assembly member of the AACSB. Applicants are screened by a committee composed of members of the American Accounting Association. Their recommendations are submitted to the Carter Estate Trustees for final approval. Funds available: $2,500 will be sent to the school for disbursement to the student. Application details: Student must obtain application from the accounting department at their school and submit letters of recommendation and transcripts with the application to the department chairman. Deadline: Application and supporting material due April 1.

★98★ Thomas H. Fitzgerald Award
EDP Auditors Association and the EDP Auditors Foundation
3701 W Algonquin Rd., Ste. 1010
Rolling Meadows, IL 60008-3192
Ph: (708)253-1545   Fax: (708)253-1443
For recognition of the five highest scores on the Certified Information Systems Auditor (CISA) examinations. Plaques are awarded to each of the five individuals. The persons achieving the highest scores receive admission to the annual conference. Awarded annually at the conference in June. Established in 1981.

★99★ Frank Greathouse Distinguished Leadership Award
Association of Government Accountants
2200 Mount Vernon Ave.
Alexandria, VA 22301-1314
Ph: (703)684-6931   Fax: (703)548-9367
To recognize individuals in government service (federal, state, and local) who have provided sustained outstanding leadership in financial management over a period of years, resulting in a notable contribution to financial management. The awardees need not be members of the Association. A plaque and formal citations are awarded annually.

★100★ Robert Kaufman Memorial Scholarships
Independent Accountants International Educational Foundation
9200 S. Dadeland Blvd., Ste. 510
Miami, FL 33156
Ph: (305)670-0580   Fax: (305)670-3818
Purpose: To assist young people in furthering their education in the field of accounting. Qualifications: Students who are pursuing, or planning to pursue, an education in accounting at recognized academic institutions anywhere in the world are eligible to apply. Selection criteria: Applications are evaluated on the basis of past academic achievement, standardized test scores, extracurricular activities, and courses taken. Applicants compete on an academic basis only, without reference to financial need. Financial need is considered only after the winning applicants are selected and the amount of the award is to be set. Funds available: An honorary award of up to $250 to assist in the purchase of textbooks may be given to any full-time student without demonstration of financial need. A scholarship of up to $5,000 may be awarded to a full-time student demonstrating financial need. The size of this award is based on the student's financial need as determined by an analysis of the student's finanical circumstances. Application details: Applications may be obtained from a college financial aid office, an IA member, or IA International headquarters. To be considered, the application must bear the signature of an endorsing IA member firm. If applicant is not familiar with an IA member, the IA headquarters will provide the name and address of the nearest member firm. Deadline: February 28.

★101★ Laurels Fund Scholarships
American Society of Women Accountants (ASWA)
1755 Lynnfield Road, Ste. 222
Memphis, TN 38119
Ph: (901)680-0470   Fax: (901)680-0505
Purpose: To assist women seeking advanced accounting degrees. Qualifications: Applicant may be of any nationality. Applicant must be working toward a master's or doctoral degree in the field of accounting. Applicant does not have to be a member of either ASWA or AWSCPA. Funds available: $1,000-5,000. Application details: Write to ASWA or AWSCPA for application form and guidelines, available in September. Submit application materials to the scholarship chair, whose address is included in the guidelines. Deadline: 15 February.

★102★ NSPA Scholarship Awards
National Society of Public Accountants Scholarship Foundation (NSPA)
1010 N. Fairfax St.
Alexandria, VA 22314-1574
Ph: (703)549-6400   Fax: (703)549-2984
Purpose: To emphasize and perpetuate the prestige and status of the public accounting profession. Qualifications: Candidates should be students majoring in accounting with a B or better grade point average, and should be enrolled full-time in a degree program at an accredited two-year or four-year college or university. Evening program students will be considered full-time if they are pursuing an accounting degree. Only undergraduate students are eligible. Students in an accredited two-year college may apply during their first year or during their second year if transferring to a four-year institution, provided they have committed themselves to major in accounting throughout the remainder of their college career. Students in an accredited four-year college may apply for a scholarship for their second, third, or fourth year of studies, provided they have committed themselves to a major in accounting throughout the remainder of their college career. Selection criteria: Scholarships are awarded primarily for academic attainment, demonstrated leadership ability, and financial need. Funds available: Approximately $1,000 each for students entering their third or fourth year of studies and approximately $500 each for students entering their second year of studies. In addition, the outstanding student in the competition, designated the Charles H. Earp Memorial Scholar, receives an additional stipend. Application details: Applications and appraisal forms may be obtained from the candidate's school or by writing the NSPA Scholarship Foundation. Completed applications must be accompanied by official transcripts bearing the official seal or registrar signature from the issuing institution from each college attended. They should also be accompanied by a completed appraisal form that can be submitted by the student or the issuing professor. Deadline: March 10.

★103★ Elijah Watt Sells Awards
American Institute of Certified Public Accountants
1211 Avenue of the Americas
New York, NY 10036-8775
Ph: (212)575-6417
To recognize individuals who achieve the highest scores on the nationwide CPA examination. CPA candidates who sit for all four parts of the exam during the same examination are eligible. Gold, Silver and Bronze medals are awarded biannually for three highest scores. Established in 1933.

★104★ Stanley H. Stearman Scholarships
National Society of Public Accountants Scholarship Foundation (NSPA)
1010 N. Fairfax St.
Alexandria, VA 22314-1574
Ph: (703)549-6400   Fax: (703)549-2984
Purpose: To emphasize and perpetuate the prestige and status of the public accounting profession. Qualifications: Candidates must be enrolled in a full-time graduate or undergraduate accounting program and have a B or better grade point average in all courses. Evening program students will be considered full-time if they are pursuing an accounting degree. Undergraduate students at two-year colleges may apply during their first or second years if they will be transferring to a four-year institution for a major in accounting. Four-year undergraduate college students may apply for this scholarship for their second, third, or fourth year of study towards a major in accounting. Recipients must be sons, daughters, grandchildren, nieces, nephews, or sons- or daughters-in-law of active or deceased NSPA members. Funds available: One scholarship of $2,000 per year

not to exceed three years. Application details: Applications and appraisal forms may be obtained by writing the NSPA Scholarship Foundation. Along with official transcripts and a completed appraisal form, applicants must include a letter of intent outlining their reasons for seeking the award, their intended career objective, and how this scholarship award would be used to accomplish that objective. Deadline: March 10.

BASIC REFERENCE GUIDES AND HANDBOOKS

★105★ The Accountant's Business Manual
American Institute of Certified Public Accountants (AICPA)
1211 Avenue of the Americas
New York, NY 10036-8775
Ph: (212)596-6200
William H. Behrenfeld and Andrew R. Biebl. Semiannual. Covers regulations and new legislation for 20 industries. Includes information on insurance, corporations, and investments.

★106★ Accountant's Desk Handbook
Prentice-Hall, Inc.
Rte. 9W
Englewood Cliffs, NJ 07632
Ph: (201)592-2000
Albert P. Ameiss, and Nicholas A. Kargas. Third edition, 1988. Sourcebook for managerial and tax acccounting, tax planning, and auditing standards.

★107★ Accounting and Auditing in a New Environment
AMACOM
135 W. 50th St.
New York, NY 10020-1201
Ph: (212)903-8089   Fr: 800-262-9696
Albert J. Harnois. 1994. Describes the nontechnical skills that accountants and auditors need.

★108★ Accounting Desk Book: The Accountant's Everyday Instant Answerbook
Prentice-Hall, Inc.
Rte. 9W
Englewood Cliffs, NJ 07632
Ph: (201)592-2000
Tom M. Plank and Douglas Blensley. Ninth edition, 1989. Reference manual for business managers, accountants, investors, and attorneys.

★109★ Accounting: Systems and Procedures
McGraw-Hill, Inc.
1221 Avenue of the Americas
New York, NY 10020
Ph: (212)512-2000   Fr: 800-722-4726
D.I. Weaver and E. B. Bower, et al. Fifth edition, 1988. Introductory text covering basic accounting, the accounting cycle, and accounting subsystems and special procedures.

★110★ Auditing Concepts and Methods: A Guide to Current Auditing Theory and Practice
McGraw-Hill, Inc.
1221 Avenue of the Americas
New York, NY 10020
Ph: (212)512-2000   Fr: 800-722-4726
D. R. Carmichael and John J. Willingham. Fifth edition, 1989. Introductory text describing the auditing profession, the audit process, audit examinations, and the auditor's report.

★111★ Auditing: Integrated Concepts and Procedures
John Wiley and Sons, Inc.
605 3rd Ave.
New York, NY 10158-0012
Ph: (212)850-6000   Fax: (212)850-6088
Fr: 800-526-5368
Donald H. Taylor and Patrick B. Delaney. Sifth edition, 1993. Includes theoretical and practical approaches to auditing. Covers auditing ethics and responsibility.

★112★ Compensation in the Accounting/Financial Field
Abbott, Langer and Associates
548 1st St.
Crete, IL 60417
Ph: (708)672-4200
Dr. Stewart Langer. Annual.

★113★ The Desktop Encyclopedia of Corporate Finance and Accounting
Probus Publishing Co., Inc.
1925 N. Clybourne
Chicago, IL 60614
Ph: (312)868-1100
Charles J. Woelfel. Second edition, 1987. Contains short articles on 270 major accounting and financial concepts. Includes references for further investigation.

★114★ Handbook of Health Care Accounting and Finance
Aspen Publishers, Inc.
200 Orchard Ridge Dr., Ste. 200
Gaithersburg, MD 20878
Ph: (301)417-7500
William O. Cleverly, editor. 1989. Includes bibliographies and indexes.

★115★ Handbook of Management Accounting
Gower Publishing Co.
Old Post Rd.
Brookfield, VT 05036
Ph: (802)276-3162
Roger Cowe. Second edition, 1988.

★116★ Hospitality Management Accounting
Van Nostrand Reinhold
115 5th Ave.
New York, NY 10013
Michael M. Coltman. Fifth edition, 1993.

★117★ Management of an Accounting Practice Handbook
American Institute of Certified Public Accountants (AICPA)
1211 Avenue of the Americas
New York, NY 10036-8775
Ph: (212)575-6200
1993.

★118★ Miller Comprehensive GAAS Guide
Arco Publishing Co.
Macmillan General Reference
15 Columbus Cir.
New York, NY 10023
Fax: 800-835-3202   Fr: 800-858-7674
Martin A. Miller and Larry P. Bailey. Annual. States generally accepted auditing standards and practices.

★119★ Miller Comprehensive Governmental GAAP Guide
Arco Publishing Co.
Macmillan General Reference
15 Columbus Cir.
New York, NY 10023
Fax: 800-835-3202   Fr: 800-858-7674
Larry P. Bailey. Annual. States generally accepted accounting principles.

★120★ The Portable MBA in Finance and Accounting
John Wiley and Sons, Inc.
605 3rd Ave.
New York, NY 10158-0012
Ph: (212)850-6000   Fax: (212)850-6088
Fr: 800-526-5368
John Leslie Livingstone. 1992. Offers advices to businesses. Includes preparing budgets, implementing business plans, and evaluating acquisition targets.

PROFESSIONAL AND TRADE PERIODICALS

★121★ The Accountant
Lafferty Publications
1422 W. Peachtree St., No. 800
Atlanta, GA 30309
Ph: (404)874-5120   Fax: (404)874-5123
D. Daly, Contact
Monthly. Contains articles on the international accounting industry as viewed from a British perspective. Recurring features include news of research and book reviews.

★122★ Accounting Review
American Accounting Assn.
5717 Bessie Drive
Sarasota, FL 34233
Ph: (813)921-7747   Fax: (813)923-4093
William R. Kinney
Quarterly. Accounting education, research, financial reporting, and book reviews.

★123★ The CPA Journal
New York State Society of CPAs
530 5th Ave.
New York, NY 10036-5701
Ph: (212)719-8300   Fax: (212)719-3364
James Craig
Monthly. Refereed accounting journal.

★124★ Government Accountants Journal
Assn. of Government Accountants
2200 Mount Vernon Ave.
Alexandria, VA 22301-1314
Ph: (703)684-6931   Fax: (703)548-9367
Mimi Stewart

Quarterly. Accounting and financial management magazine.

★125★ IIA Today
Institute of Internal Auditors (IIA)
249 Maitland Ave.
Altamonte Springs, FL 32701-4201
Ph: (407)830-7600   Fax: (407)831-5171
Lisa M. Krist

Consists of articles designed to keep auditors up to date. Includes current information on Institute and chapter activities and reports of IIA seminars and conferences. Recurring features include editorials, news of research, news of members, book reviews, educational products, member services, and columns titled Odyssey, Chapter News, Quizmaster, Headquarters News, Profile, Visitors, and In Memorium.

★126★ Internal Auditor
Institute of Internal Auditors, Inc.
249 Maitland Ave.
Altamonte Springs, FL 32701-4201
Ph: (407)830-7600   Fax: (407)831-5171

Bimonthly. Internal auditing.

★127★ Journal of Accountancy
The American Institute of Certified Public Accountants
1211 Avenue of the Americas
New York, NY 10036
Ph: (212)596-6200   Fax: (212)596-6213
Colleen Katz

Monthly. Accounting journal.

★128★ Management Accounting
Institute of Management Accountants
10 Paragon Drive
Montvale, NJ 07645-1760
Ph: (201)573-9000   Fax: (201)573-0639
Fr: 800-638-4427
Robert F. Randall

Monthly. Journal reporting on corporate finance, accounting, cash management, and budgeting.

★129★ National Public Accountant
National Society of Public Accountants
1010 N. Fairfax St.
Alexandria, VA 22314
Ph: (703)549-6400   Fax: (703)549-2984

Monthly. Public accounting magazine,

★130★ The Practical Accountant
Faulkner and Gray
110 Penn Plaza
New York, NY 10001
Ph: (212)967-7000   Fax: (212)967-7155
Jeannie MandelkerVice President

Monthly. "How-to" magazine for accountants covering every aspect of accounting and taxation.

★131★ The Practical Accountant Alert
Warren, Gorham & Lamont, Inc.
1 Penn Plaza, 40th Fl.
New York, NY 10119
Ph: (212)971-5041   Fax: (212)971-5025
Fr: 800-922-0066
Robert W. McGee

Semimonthly. Monitors developments in areas such as taxes, financial planning and reporting, accounting and auditing, Security and Exchange Commission (SEC) regulations, computers, practice management, and MAS as they affect accounting practices. Recurring features include columns titled Professional Societies, Accounting Firms, and ERISA.

PROFESSIONAL MEETINGS AND CONVENTIONS

★132★ American Institute of Certified Public Accountants Microcomputer Conference and Exhibition
American Institute of Certified Public Accountants
Harborside Financial Center
201 Plaza III
Jersey City, NJ 07311-3881
Ph: (201)332-2300
Annual.

★133★ Midwest Accounting and Business Management Show
Illinois Certified Public Accounting Society
222 S. Riverside Plaza, 16th Fl.
Chicago, IL 60606
Ph: (312)933-0393   Fax: (312)993-9432
Annual. Always held during August at the O'Hare Expocenter, in Rosemont, Illinois. **Dates and Locations:** 1995; Chicago, IL.

★134★ National Association of Tax Practitioners Convention
National Association of Tax Practitioners
720 Association Dr.
Appleton, WI 54914-1483
Ph: (414)749-1040   Fax: (414)749-1062
Annual. Always held during August.

OTHER SOURCES OF INFORMATION

★135★ "Accountant/Auditor" in 100 Best Jobs for the 1990s & Beyond
Dearborn Financial Publishing, Inc.
520 N. Dearborn St.
Chicago, IL 60610-4354
Ph: (312)836-4400   Fax: (312)836-1021
Fr: 800-621-9621

Carol Kleiman. 1992. Describes 100 jobs ranging from accountants to veterinarians.. Each job profile includes such information as education, experience, and certification needed, salaries, and job search suggestions.

★136★ "Accountant" in Career Selector 2001
Barron's Educational Series, Inc.
250 Wireless Blvd.
Hauppauge, NY 11788
James C. Gonyea. 1993.

★137★ The NSPA Annual Scholarship Awards
National Society of Public Accountants (NSPA)
1010 N. Fairfax St.
Alexandria, VA 22314-1574
Ph: (703)549-6400   Fax: (703)549-2984
This six-panel brochure describes scholarship eligibility requirements and application procedures for accountanting students.

Administrative Services Managers

Administrative services managers, who work throughout private industry and government, coordinate and direct supportive services such as secretarial and correspondence; conference planning and travel; information processing; personnel and financial records processing; communication; mail; materials scheduling and distribution; printing and reproduction; personal property procurement, supply and disposal; data processing; library; food; and transportation. They are often involved in the hiring and dismissal of employees. **Supervisory level managers** directly oversee supervisors or staffs involved in supportive services. **Mid-level administrative services managers** develop overall plans, set goals and deadlines, develop procedures to direct and improve supportive services, define supervisory level managers' responsibilities, and delegate authority.

Salaries

Earnings for administrative services managers vary substantially depending upon the managerial level, size of firm, and type of industry. Salaries of administrative services managers are as follows:

Administrative services managers	$28,000-$58,000/year or more

Employment Outlook

Growth rate until the year 2005: More slowly than the average.

Administrative Services Managers

TEST GUIDES

★144★ Career Examination Series: Administrative Associate
National Learning Corp.
212 Michael Dr.
Syosset, NY 11791
Ph: (516)921-8888   Fax: (516)921-8743
Fr: 800-645-6337

Jack Rudman. 1993. Test guide including questions and answers for students or professionals in the field who seek advancement through examination.

★145★ Career Examination Series: Administrative Careers with America
National Learning Corp.
212 Michael Dr.
Syosset, NY 11791
Ph: (516)921-8888   Fax: (516)921-8743
Fr: 800-645-6337

Jack Rudman. 1993. Test guide including questions and answers for students or professionals in the field who seek advancement through examination.

★146★ Career Examination Series: Administrative Careers Examination
National Learning Corp.
212 Michael Dr.
Syosset, NY 11791
Ph: (516)921-8888   Fax: (516)921-8743
Fr: 800-645-6337

Jack Rudman. 1993. Test guide including questions and answers for students or professionals in the field who seek advancement through examination.

★147★ Career Examination Series: Administrative Manager
National Learning Corp.
212 Michael Dr.
Syosset, NY 11791
Ph: (516)921-8888   Fax: (516)921-8743
Fr: 800-645-6337

Jack Rudman. 1993. Test guide including questions and answers for students or professionals in the field who seek advancement through examination.

★148★ Career Examination Series: Administrative Service Officer
National Learning Corp.
212 Michael Dr.
Syosset, NY 11791
Ph: (516)921-8888   Fax: (516)921-8743
Fr: 800-645-6337

Jack Rudman. 1993. Test guide including questions and answers for students or professionals in the field who seek advancement through examination.

★149★ Career Examination Series: Administrative Services Manager
National Learning Corp.
212 Michael Dr.
Syosset, NY 11791
Ph: (516)921-8888   Fax: (516)921-8743
Fr: 800-645-6337

Jack Rudman. A study guide for professionals and trainees in the field of administrative services management. Includes a multi-

ple-choice examination section; provides answers.

★150★ Career Examination Series: Personnel, Administration and Computer Occupations
National Learning Corp.
212 Michael Dr.
Syosset, NY 11791
Ph: (516)921-8888   Fax: (516)921-8743
Fr: 800-645-6337

Jack Rudman. 1993. Test guide including questions and answers for students or professionals in the field who seek advancement through examination.

★151★ Career Examination Series: Professional Careers in Administrative and Technical Services
National Learning Corp.
212 Michael Dr.
Syosset, NY 11791
Ph: (516)921-8888   Fax: (516)921-8743
Fr: 800-645-6337

Jack Rudman. 1993. Test guide including questions and answers for students or professionals in the field who seek advancement through examination.

★152★ Career Examination Series: Senior Office Manager
National Learning Corp.
212 Michael Dr.
Syosset, NY 11791
Ph: (516)921-8888   Fax: (516)921-8743
Fr: 800-645-6337

Jack Rudman. 1993. Test guide including questions and answers for students or professionals in the field who seek advancement through examination.

EDUCATIONAL DIRECTORIES AND PROGRAMS

★153★ Public Administration Career Directory
Gale Research Inc.
835 Penobscot Bldg.
Detroit, MI 48226
Ph: (313)961-2242   Fr: 800-877-GALE
1994. For job seekers contemplating careers in public service.

PROFESSIONAL AND TRADE PERIODICALS

★154★ Administrative Science Quarterly
Cornell University
425 Caldwell Hall
Ithaca, NY 14853-2602
Ph: (607)255-5581   Fax: (607)255-7524
Stephen R. Barley
Quarterly. Journal publishes empirical and theoretical articles on business, government, military, health, and other organizations.

★155★ Dynamic Supervision—Office and Staff Edition
Bureau of Business Practice
24 Rope Ferry Rd.
Waterford, CT 06386
Ph: (203)442-4365   Fax: (203)434-3078
Fr: 800-243-0876
Shelley Wolf
Semimonthly. Provides methods and techniques for supervision in an office setting.

★156★ The Office Professional
Professional Training Associates, Inc.
210 Commerce Blvd.
Round Rock, TX 78664-2189
Ph: (512)255-6006   Fax: (512)255-7532
Fr: 800-424-2112
Marilyn Johnson
Monthly. Provides information on new developments and ideas in office systems and procedures. Covers topics such as successful communication techniques, professional human relation skills, career development, secretarial methods, management thinking, and office technology. Recurring features include columns titled Top Pro; Never, Never; This Way To Success; and Feedback, and Top Notes.

★157★ Office World News
1905 Swarthmore Ave.
Lakewood, NJ 08701
Ph: (908)363-0708   Fax: (908)367-2426
Kim Chandlee McCabe
Monthly. Tabloid focusing on office products industry.

★158★ Supervision
National Research Bureau, Inc.
200 N. 4th
PO Box 1
Burlington, IA 52601-0001
Ph: (319)752-5415   Fax: (319)752-3421
Barbara Boeding
Monthly. Magazine for first-line foremen, supervisors, and office managers.

★159★ Supervisor's Bulletin for Administration and Office Support Groups
Bureau of Business Practice
24 Rope Ferry Rd.
Waterford, CT 06386
Ph: (203)442-4365   Fax: (203)434-3078
Fr: 800-243-0876
Patricia Thunberg
Semimonthly. Presents tips for increased effectiveness in solving daily problems such as achieving better teamwork, motivation, delegation, training, cost control, planning and scheduling, and discipline. Also discusses methods for dealing with compliance-related topics and legal situations.

★160★ Today's Supervisor
National Safety Council
1121 Spring Lake Drive
Itasca, IL 60143-3201
Ph: (708)285-1121   Fax: (708)775-2285
Fr: 800-621-7619
Kathy Henderson
Monthly. Magazine for the front-line supervisor containing articles related to safety and health.

PROFESSIONAL MEETINGS AND CONVENTIONS

★161★ Association of Legal Administrators Meeting
Association of Legal Administrators
175 E. Hawthorne Pkwy., Ste. 325
Vernon Hills, IL 60061
Ph: (708)816-1212   Fax: (708)816-1213
Annual. Always held during April or May.

Budget Analysts

Budget analysts provide advice and technical assistance in the preparation of annual budgets for firms or organizations. They seek to find the most efficient distribution of funds and resources among various departments and programs. Budget analysts in private industry also seek to increase profits. Through the process of examining past and current budgets, researching economic developments, and reviewing company objectives, analysts assess an organization's financial position, address policy issues, and establish company goals for the coming year. Budget analysts also keep program managers and others within their organization informed on the status and availability of funds in different budget accounts and methods to control their distribution.

Salaries

Salaries of business analysts vary widely by experience, education, and employer. Salaries of business analysts are as follows:

Beginning business analysts	$23,500-$28,000/year
Analysts, 1-3 years experience	$27,000-$35,000/year
Senior analysts	$34,500-$41,200/year
Budget analysts, federal government (average)	$42,033/year

Employment Outlook

Growth rate until the year 2005: Average.

Budget Analysis

ership News, semiannual. • *Society Programs*, quarterly.

TEST GUIDES

★170★ Career Examination Series: Budget Analyst
National Learning Corp.
212 Michael Dr.
Syosset, NY 11791
Ph: (516)921-8888   Fax: (516)921-8743
Fr: 800-645-6337
Jack Rudman. Test guide including questions and answers for students or professionals in the field who seek advancement through examination. Also included in the series: Senior Budget Analyst, Principal Budget Analyst, Associate Budget Analyst, and Assistant Budget Analyst.

★171★ Career Examination Series: Chief Compensation Investigator
National Learning Corp.
212 Michael Dr.
Syosset, NY 11791
Ph: (516)921-8888   Fax: (516)921-8743
Fr: 800-645-6337
Jack Rudman. 1993. Test guide including questions and answers for students or professionals in the field who seek advancement through examination.

★172★ Career Examination Series: Cost and Statistical Analyst
National Learning Corp.
212 Michael Dr.
Syosset, NY 11791
Ph: (516)921-8888   Fax: (516)921-8743
Fr: 800-645-6337
Jack Rudman. 1993. Test guide including questions and answers for students or professionals in the field who seek advancement through examination.

EDUCATIONAL DIRECTORIES AND PROGRAMS

★173★ Business and Finance Career Directory
Gale Research Inc.
835 Penobscot Bldg.
Detroit, MI 48226-4094
Ph: (313)961-2242   Fax: (313)961-6083
Fr: 800-877-GALE
Bradley J. Morgan and Joseph M. Palmisano. Second edition, 1992. A directory in the Career Advisor Series that provides essays written by industry professionals; job search information on resume and cover letter preparation, networking, and the interviewing process; approximately 300 companies and organizations offering job opportunities and internships, and additional job-hunting resources.

AWARDS, SCHOLARSHIPS, GRANTS, AND FELLOWSHIPS

★174★ Graham and Dodd Award
Association for Investment Management and Research
5 Boar's Head Ln.
PO Box 3668
Charlottesville, VA 22903
Ph: (804)977-6600   Fax: (804)977-1103
For recognition of excellence in financial writing as demonstrated in an article in the *Financial Analysts Journal* during the previous year. A plaque is awarded annually. Established in 1960 to honor Benjamin Graham and David L. Dodd for their enduring contributions to the field of financial analysis.

★175★ Nicholas Molodovsky Award
Association for Investment Management and Research
5 Boar's Head Ln.
PO Box 3668
Charlottesville, VA 22903
Ph: (804)977-6600   Fax: (804)977-1103
This, the highest honor bestowed by the Federation, is given to recognize those individuals who have made contributions of such significance as to change the direction of the profession and to raise it to higher standards of accomplishment. A plaque and a financial contribution in the laureate's name to an important research project are awarded periodically. First presented in 1968 to Nicholas Molodovsky, one of the profession's outstanding scholars.

BASIC REFERENCE GUIDES AND HANDBOOKS

★176★ The Basics of Budgeting
AMACOM
135 W. 50th St.
New York, NY 10020-1201
Ph: (212)903-8089   Fr: 800-262-9696
Robert G. Finney. 1993.

★177★ Handbook of Budgeting
John Wiley and Sons, Inc.
605 3rd Ave.
New York, NY 10158-0012
Ph: (212)850-6000   Fax: (212)850-6088
Fr: 800-526-5368
Robert Rachlin, editor. Third edition, 1993. Discusses budgeting preparation, presentation, and analysis. Contains examples of forms, techniques, and reports.

★178★ The Portable MBA in Finance and Accounting
John Wiley and Sons, Inc.
605 3rd Ave.
New York, NY 10158-0012
Ph: (212)850-6000   Fax: (212)850-6088
Fr: 800-526-5368
John Leslie Livingstone. 1992. Offers advices to businesses. Includes preparing budgets,

implementing business plans, and evaluating acquisition targets.

PROFESSIONAL AND TRADE PERIODICALS

★179★ Barron's National Business and Financial Weekly
Dow Jones & Co., Inc.
World Financial Center
200 Liberty
New York, NY 10281
Ph: (212)416-2700   Fax: (212)416-2829
James P. Meagher
Weekly. Business and finance magazine.

★180★ Controller
Peed Corp.
120 W. Harvest Drive
PO Box 85518
Lincoln, NE 68521-5380
Ph: (402)477-8900   Fax: (402)477-9252
Roger D. MinerPublisher
Biweekly. Aviation sales tabloid.

★181★ Credit Union Management
Credit Union Executives Society
6410 Enterprise Ln., Ste. 300
Madison, WI 53719-1143
Ph: (608)271-2664   Fax: (608)271-2303
Mary Auestad Arnold
Monthly. Magazine on the development of technical and management skills for credit union executives.

★182★ The Federal Employee
National Federation of Federal Employees
1016 16th St. NW
Washington, DC 20036
Ph: (202)862-4400   Fax: (202)862-4432
Lisa Harris Kelly
Monthly. Provides news and information on issues (legislative and regulatory) affecting federal employees.

★183★ The Fednews
National Association of Government Employees
2011 Crystal Dr., Ste. 206
Arlington, VA 22202
Ph: (703)979-0290
Monthly. Reviews issues and developments affecting federal government employees. Covers areas such as contract negotiations, employee benefits, lobbying and representation, and legal assistance. Recurring features include legislative updates, Association reports, news of members, and a calendar of events.

★184★ Finance and Commerce
Finance & Commerce, Inc.
615 S. 7th St.
Minneapolis, MN 55415
Ph: (612)333-4244   Fax: (612)333-3243
Patrick Boulay
Business newspaper.

★185★ *Finance & Development*
International Monetary Fund & The World
  Bank
IMF Building
700 19th St. NW
Washington, DC 20431
Ph: (202)623-8300   Fax: (202)623-4738
Claire Liuksila

Quarterly. Magazine explaining work and policies of the Bretton Woods institutions. Carries articles on financial and developmental issues. Published in seven languages (English, French, Spanish, German, Arabic, Portuguese, and Chinese).

★186★ *Financial Analysts Journal*
AIMR
PO Box 3668
Charlottesville, VA 22903
Ph: (804)980-9775
Charles D'Ambrosio

Bimonthly. Journal for investment professionals including portfolio managers, securities analysts, and investment strategists.

★187★ *Financial Management*
Financial Management Assn.
Florida State University
College of Business
Dept. of Finance
Tallahassee, FL 32306-1042
Ph: (904)644-6512   Fax: (904)644-7671
James S. Ang

Quarterly. Magazine covering business, economics, and management.

★188★ *Financial Planning*
SDC Publishing
40 W. 57th St., 8th Fl.
New York, NY 10019
Ph: (212)765-5311   Fax: (212)765-6123
E van Simonoff

Monthly.

★189★ *Global Finance*
Global Finance Joint Venture
11 W. 19th St, 2nd Fl.
New York, NY 10011
Ph: (212)337-5900   Fax: (212)337-5055
Carl G. Burger

Monthly. International finance magazine for professionals.

★190★ *The Government Manager*
Bureau of National Affairs, Inc. (BNA)
1231 25th St. NW
Washington, DC 20037
Ph: (202)452-4200   Fax: (202)822-8092
Fr: 800-372-1033
Anthony A. Harris

Biweekly. Covers developments in public sector human resource management. Recurring features include columns titled A Three Page Rundown, Working With People, Ground Rules, and Special Report.

★191★ *Professional Managers
  Association—Update*
Professional Managers Association
Box 895, Ben Franklin Sta.
Washington, DC 20044
Ph: (202)343-0883
Helene Benson

Bimonthly. Provides information of interest to federal civil service employees in mid-level management positions. Discusses issues such as fairness of pay and appraisal systems and innovative management practices.

★192★ *Small Business Controller*
Warren, Gorham and Lamont, Inc.
1 Penn Plaza
New York, NY 10119
Ph: (212)971-5000   Fax: (212)971-5025
Stephan Collins

Quarterly. Source for technical information in accounting and financial management. For

financial managers in growing and emerging businesses.

PROFESSIONAL MEETINGS AND CONVENTIONS

★193★ **FIM-New York - Financial Investment Management Exposition and Conference**
Flagg Management, Inc.
PO Box 4440
New York, NY 10017
Ph: (212)286-0333   Fax: (212)286-0086

Annual. Always held during September at the Hilton Hotel in New York, New York.

OTHER SOURCES OF INFORMATION

★194★ "Budget Analyst" in *Career Selector 2001*
Barron's Educational Series, Inc.
250 Wireless Blvd.
Hauppauge, NY 11788
Ph: (516)434-3311   Fax: (516)434-3723
Fr: 800-645-3476

James C. Gonyea. 1993.

Construction and Building Inspectors

Construction and building inspectors examine the construction, alteration, or repair of highways, streets, sewer and water systems, dams, bridges, buildings, and other structures to ensure compliance with building codes and ordinances, zoning regulations, and contract specifications. **Building inspectors** check the structural quality of buildings. **Electrical inspectors** review the installation of electrical systems and equipment to verify that they function properly and comply with electrical codes and standards. **Elevator inspectors** examine lifting and conveying devices such as elevators, escalators, moving sidewalks, lifts and hoists, inclined railways, ski lifts, and various amusement rides. **Mechanical inspectors** review the installation of the mechanical components of kitchen appliances, heating and air-conditioning equipment, gasoline and butane tanks, gas and oil piping, gas-fired and oil-fired appliances, and boilers. **Plumbing inspectors** examine plumbing systems, including private disposal systems, water supply and distribution systems, plumbing fixtures and traps, and drain, waste, and vent lines. **Public works inspectors** ensure that federal, state, and local government construction of water and sewer systems, highways, streets, bridges, and dams conforms to detailed contract specifications. **Home inspectors** examine newly built homes to insure adherence to regulations.

Salaries

Building inspectors typically command the highest salaries. Generally, earnings for all inspectors are substantially higher in large metropolitan areas.

Median salary of construction and building inspectors	$31,200/year

Employment Outlook

Growth rate until the year 2005: Faster than the average.

Construction and Building Inspectors

★195★ *Building Inspection as a Career*
International Conference of Building
 Officials
5360 S. Workman Mill Rd.
Whittier, CA 90601
Ph: (213)699-0541   Fr: 800-423-6587
This eight-page pamphlet defines different
types of inspectors, such as specification,
government, public works, and special inspectors. Explains personal qualities needed
by inspectors and growth possibilities of the
profession.

★196★ *Building Inspector*
Careers, Inc.
PO Box 135
Largo, FL 34649-0135
Ph: (813)584-7333
1994. Two-page summary describing duties,
working conditions, personal qualifications,
training, earnings and hours, employment
outlook, places of employment, related careers, and where to write for more information.

**★197★ "Building Inspector" in *Career
Information Center* (Vol.4)**
Simon and Schuster
200 Old Tappan Rd.
Old Tappan, NJ 07675
Fax: 800-445-6991   Fr: 800-223-2348
Richard Lidz and Linda Perrin, editorial directors. Fifth edition, 1993. A multi-volume set
that profiles more than 600 occupations. Volume 4 includes the chapter "Building Inspector" (p. 117). Each occupational profile describes job duties, educational requirements,
getting a job, advancement possibilities, employment outlook, working conditions, earnings and benefits, and sources of additional
information.

**★198★ "Construction and Building
Inspectors" in *Occupational Outlook
Handbook***
U.S. Government Printing Office
Superintendent of Documents
Washington, DC 20402
Ph: (202)512-1800   Fax: (202)512-2250
Biennial; latest edition, 1994-95. Encyclopedia of careers describing about 250 occupations and comprising about 85 percent of all
jobs in the economy. Occupations that require lengthy education or training are given
the most attention. Each occupation's profile
describes what the worker does on the job,
working conditions, education and training requirements, advancement possibilities, job
outlook, earnings, and sources of additional
information.

**★199★ "Construction Inspector" in
*Jobs! What They Are—Where They
Are—What They Pay* (p. 134)**
Simon & Schuster, Inc.
Simon & Schuster Bldg.
1230 Avenue of the Americas
New York, NY 10020
Ph: (212)698-7000   Fr: 800-223-2348
Robert O. Snelling and Anne M. Snelling. 3rd
edition, 1992. Describes duties and responsi-
bilities, earnings, employment opportunities,
training, and qualifications. ·

★200★ *Construction Inspectors*
Chronicle Guidance Publications, Inc.
66 Aurora St.
PO Box 1190
Moravia, NY 13118-1190
Ph: (315)497-0330   Fax: (315)497-3359
Fr: 800-622-7284
1991. Career brief describing the nature of
the job, working conditions, hours and earnings, education and training, licensure, certification, unions, personal qualifications, social
and psychological factors, location, employment outlook, entry methods, advancement,
and related occupations.

**★201★ "Construction Inspectors" in
Career Discovery Encyclopedia (Vol.2,
pp. 52-53)**
J.G. Ferguson Publishing Co.
200 W. Madison St., Ste. 300
Chicago, IL 60606
Ph: (312)580-5480   Fax: (312)580-4948
Russell E. Primm, editor-in chief. 1993. This
six volume set contains two-page articles for
504 occupations. Each article describes job
duties, earnings, and educational and training
requirements. The whole set is arranged alphabetically by job title. Designed for junior
high and older students.

**★202★ "Construction Inspectors,
Government" in *Encyclopedia of
Careers and Vocational Guidance*
(Vol.2, pp. 377-380)**
J.G. Ferguson Publishing Co.
200 W. Madison St., Ste. 300
Chicago, IL 60606
Ph: (312)580-5480   Fax: (312)580-4948
William E. Hopke, editor-in-chief. Ninth edition, 1993. Four-volume set that profiles 900
occupations and describes job trends in 74
industries. Includes career description, educational requirements, history of the job,
methods of entry, advancement, employment
outlook, earnings, conditions of work, social
and psychological factors, and sources of further information.

**★203★ *Exploring Careers in the
Construction Industry***
Rosen Publishing Group
29 E. 21st St.
New York, NY 10010
Ph: (212)777-3017   Fax: (212)777-0277
Fr: 800-237-9932
Elizabeth Stewart Lytle. 1994. Includes information on specific trades. Also overviews the
economic considerations, unions, opportunities for minorities and women, necessary education and training, and necessary tools and
equipment.

★204★ Opportunities in Building Construction Trades
National Textbook Co. (NTC)
VGM Career Books
4255 W. Touhy Ave.
Lincolnwood, IL 60646-1975
Ph: (708)679-5500   Fax: (708)679-2494
Fr: 800-323-4900

Michael Sumichrast. 1989. Contains illustrations. Includes a bibliography. Explains job duties, educational requirements, salary, working conditions, employment outlook, and advancement opportunities.

PROFESSIONAL ASSOCIATIONS

★205★ American Society of Home Inspectors (ASHI)
85 W. Algonquin Rd.
Arlington Heights, IL 60005
Ph: (708)290-1919   Fax: (708)290-1920
Members: Professional home inspectors. **Purpose:** To establish home inspector qualifications; set practice standards for home inspections; adhere to a code of ethics; keep the concept of "objective third party" intact; inform members of the most advanced methods and techniques. Conducts seminars through local chapters. **Publications:** The Reporter, monthly.

★206★ Building Officials and Code Administrators International (BOCA)
4051 W. Flossmoor Rd.
Country Club Hills, IL 60478-5795
Ph: (708)799-2300   Fax: (708)799-4981
Members: Governmental officials and agencies responsible for administering or formulating building, zoning, or housing regulations. **Purpose:** Promotes establishment of minimum, unbiased building codes and provides services for keeping them up-to-date. Supplies information on quality and acceptability of building materials and systems and on new construction techniques and materials. Maintains services for local governments in connection with building codes and their administration; provides consulting, training and education, plan review, and other advisory services; conducts correspondence courses; prepares in-service training programs and assists local organizations in such activities. Maintains placement services. **Publications:** Annual Supplements to National Codes. • BOCA Bulletin, bimonthly. • Building Code Manual and Property Maintenance Manual. • Building Official and Code Administrator Magazine, bimonthly. • National Building Code, triennial. • National Energy Conservation Code, triennial. • National Fire Prevention Code, triennial. • National Mechanical Code, triennial. • National Plumbing Code, triennial. • National Property Maintenance Code, periodic. • One- and Two-Family Dwelling Code. • Plumbing Manual. • Proposed Code Changes, annual. • Research Report, quarterly.

★207★ International Association of Plumbing and Mechanical Officials (IAPMO)
20001 Walnut Dr. S
Walnut, CA 91789-2825
Ph: (909)595-8449   Fax: (909)594-1537
Members: Government agencies, administrative officials, sales representatives, manufacturers, associations, and members of associations related to the plumbing field. **Purpose:** Sponsors and writes Uniform Plumbing Codes; also sponsors Uniform Mechanical Code. Sponsors speakers' bureau. National Air Conditioning, Heating, Ventilating and Refrigeration Officials became a mechanical division of IAPMO in 1977. **Publications:** Directory of Listed Plumbing Products, monthly. • Directory of Listed Plumbing Products for Mobile Homes and Recreational Vehicles, bimonthly. • Interpretation Manual. • Official, bimonthly. • Uniform Mechanical Code. • Uniform Plumbing Code Illustrated Training Manual. • Uniform Plumbing Code Study Guide. • Uniform Solar Energy Code. • Uniform Swimming Pool Code.

★208★ International Conference of Building Officials (ICBO)
5360 Workman Mill Rd.
Whittier, CA 90601
Ph: (310)699-0541   Fax: (310)692-3853
Fr: 800-336-1963
Members: Representatives of local, regional, and state governments. **Purpose:** Seeks to publish, maintain, and promote the Uniform Building Code and related documents; investigate and research principles underlying safety to life and property in the construction, use, and location of buildings and related structures; develop and promulgate uniformity in regulations pertaining to building construction; educate the building official; formulate guidelines for the administration of building inspection departments. Conducts training programs, courses, and certification programs for code enforcement inspectors. Maintains speakers' bureau. **Publications:** Building Standards Magazine, monthly. • Building Standards Newsletter, monthly. • ICBO Certification Roster, annual. • ICBO Membership Roster, annual. • The Uniform Building Code, triennial.

★209★ Southern Building Code Congress, International (SBCCI)
900 Montclair Rd.
Birmingham, AL 35213
Ph: (205)591-1853   Fax: (205)592-7001
Members: Active members are state, county, municipal, or other government subdivisions (2200); associate members are trade associations, architects, engineers, contractors, and related groups or persons (5100). **Purpose:** Seeks to develop, maintain, and promote the adoption of the Standard Building, Gas, Plumbing, Mechanical, Fire Prevention, and Housing Codes. Encourages uniformity in building regulations through the Standard Codes and their application and enforcement. Provides technical and educational services to members and others; participates in the development of nationally recognized consensus standards. Provides research on new materials and methods of construction; conducts seminars on code enforcement, inspection, and special topics. **Publications:**

Southern Building Magazine, bimonthly. • Standard Building Code, triennial. • Standard Fire Prevention Code, triennial. • Standard Gas Code, triennial. • Standard Mechanical Code, triennial. • Standard Plumbing Code, triennial.

STANDARDS/CERTIFICATION AGENCIES

★210★ Building Officials and Code Administrators International (BOCA)
4051 W. Flossmoor Rd.
Country Club Hills, IL 60478-5795
Ph: (708)799-2300   Fax: (708)799-4981
Promotes establishment of minimum, unbiased building codes and provides services for keeping them up-to-date. Provides consulting, training and education, plan review, and other advisory services.

★211★ International Association of Plumbing and Mechanical Officials (IAPMO)
2001 Walnut Dr., S.
Walnut, CA 91789
Ph: (714)595-8449   Fax: (714)594-3690
Sponsors and writes codes.

★212★ International Conference of Building Officials (ICBO)
5360 Workman Mill Rd.
Whittier, CA 90601
Ph: (310)699-0541   Fax: (310)692-3853
Fr: 800-336-1963
Conducts training programs, courses, and certification programs for code enforcement inspectors.

★213★ Southern Building Code Congress, International (SBCCI)
900 Montclair Rd.
Birmingham, AL 35213
Ph: (205)591-1853   Fax: (205)592-7001
Seeks to develop, maintain, and promote the adoption of the Standard Building, Gas, Plumbing, Mechanical, Fire Prevention, and Housing Codes. Encourages uniformity in building regulations through the Standard Codes and their application and enforcement.

TEST GUIDES

★214★ Career Examination Series: Building Construction Inspector
National Learning Corp.
212 Michael Dr.
Syosset, NY 11791
Ph: (516)921-8888   Fax: (516)921-8743
Fr: 800-645-6337

Jack Rudman. 1993. Test guide including questions and answers for students or professionals in the field who seek advancement through examination.

★215★ Career Examination Series: Construction Inspector
National Learning Corp.
212 Michael Dr.
Syosset, NY 11791
Ph: (516)921-8888   Fax: (516)921-8743
Fr: 800-645-6337

Jack Rudman. 1993. Test guide including questions and answers for students or professionals in the field who seek advancement through examination.

★216★ Career Examination Series: Principal Engineering Inspector
National Learning Corp.
212 Michael Dr.
Syosset, NY 11791
Ph: (516)921-8888   Fax: (516)921-8743
Fr: 800-645-6337

Jack Rudman. 1993. Test guide including questions and answers for students or professionals in the field who seek advancement through examination.

★217★ Career Examination Series: Sanitary Construction Inspector
National Learning Corp.
212 Michael Dr.
Syosset, NY 11791
Ph: (516)921-8888   Fax: (516)921-8743
Fr: 800-645-6337

Jack Rudman. 1993. Test guide including questions and answers for students or professionals in the field who seek advancement through examination.

AWARDS, SCHOLARSHIPS, GRANTS, AND FELLOWSHIPS

★218★ John Fies Award
International Conference of Building Officials
5360 S. Workman Mill Rd.
Whittier, CA 90601
Ph: (310)699-0541   Fax: (310)692-3853

To honor members of the building industry whose contributions exemplify the ideals and purposes of the ICBO. Nominations may be submitted. A plaque is awarded annually at the meeting in September. Established in 1977 in honor of John Fies, recognized throughout the building industry for his continued diligent efforts and dedication both in building code work and as a conscientious construction industry representative.

★219★ Phil Roberts Award
International Conference of Building Officials
5360 S. Workman Mill Rd.
Whittier, CA 90601
Ph: (310)699-0541   Fax: (310)692-3853

To recognize outstanding building officials and to honor contributions by building officials to the code enforcement field. Nominations may be submitted. A plaque is presented annually at the meeting in September. Established in 1974 in memory of Phil Roberts, former president of ICBO and building official of Boise, Idaho.

BASIC REFERENCE GUIDES AND HANDBOOKS

★220★ Complete Construction Handbook
McGraw-Hill Inc.
11 W. 19 St.
New York, NY 10011
Ph: 800-722-4726

Joseph J. Waddell and Joseph A. Dobrowlski. 1993.

★221★ Construction Inspection Handbook: Quality Assurance and Quality Control
Van Nostrand Reinhold Co., Inc.
115 5th Ave.
New York, NY 10003
Ph: (212)254-3232

James J. O'Brien. Third edition, 1989.

★222★ Encyclopedia of Building Technology
Prentice-Hall, Inc.
Rte. 9W
Englewood Cliffs, NJ 07632
Ph: (201)592-2000

Henry J. Cowan, editor. 1988. Includes bibliographies and indexes.

★223★ Field Inspection Manual
International Conference of Building Officials (ICBO)
5360 S. Workman Mill Rd.
Whittier, CA 90601
Ph: (310)699-0541   Fax: (213)692-3853
Fr: 800-423-6587

Describes inspection techniques and includes checklists and sample forms.

★224★ Glossary of Construction Industry Terms: With Particular Emphasis on Use in AIA Documents: Glossary, Glossary References, Bibliography
American Institute of Architects (AIA)
1735 New York Ave., NW
Washington, DC 20006
Ph: (202)626-7300

1991. Includes a bibliography.

★225★ Handbook to the Uniform Building Code: An Illustrated Commentary
International Conference of Building Officials (ICBO)
5360 S. Workman Mill Rd.
Whittier, CA 90601
Ph: (310)699-0541

Vincent R. Bush. 1991. Handbook providing a commentary to the Uniform Building Codes describing practical application.

★226★ Inspecting and Advising: A Handbook for Inspectors and Advisors and Advisory Teachers
Routledge, Chapman & Hall, Inc.
29 W. 35th St.
New York, NY 10001-2291
Ph: (212)244-3336   Fax: (212)563-2269

Joan Dean, editor. 1992.

★227★ McGraw-Hill's Handbook of Electrical Construction Calculations
McGraw-Hill Inc.
11 W. 19th St.
New York, NY 10011
Ph: 800-722-4726

Joseph F. McPartland, Brian J. McPartland, Steven P. McPartland, and Jack Pullizzi. 1993.

★228★ Means Illustrated Construction Dictionary
R. S. Means Co., Inc.
100 Construction Plaza
Kingston, MA 02364
Ph: (617)585-7880

Kornelis Smit, editor. Second edition, 1991. Illustrated.

★229★ National Building Code
Building Officials and Code Administrators International (BOCA)
4051 W. Flossmoor Rd.
Country Club Hills, IL 60478
Ph: (708)799-2300   Fax: (708)799-4981
Fr: 800-343-1103

Twelfth edition, 1993.

★230★ National Electrical Code
Prentice-Hall, Inc.
Rte. 9W
Englewood Cliffs, NJ 07632
Ph: (201)592-2000   Fr: 800-634-2863

1994. Handbook that explains and illustrates the National Electrical Code.

★231★ Public Works Inspectors' Manual
McGraw-Hill, Inc.
1221 Avenue of the Americas
New York, NY 10020
Ph: (212)512-2000   Fr: 800-722-4726

S. B. Birch and S. Jaffe. 1993. Written for professionals responsible for the inspection of public works. Covers construction material, as well as methods and construction procedures.

★232★ Safety and Management in Construction and Industry
McGraw-Hill, Inc.
1221 Avenue of the Americas
New York, NY 10020
Ph: (212)512-2000   Fr: 800-722-4726

David Goldsmith. 1987. Illustrated. Includes a bibliography and an index.

★233★ Uniform Building Code Standards
International Conference of Building Officials (ICBO)
5360 S. Workman Mill Rd.
Whittier, CA 90601
Ph: (310)699-0541

1994. Contains all the standard specifications referred to in the Uniform Building Code.

PROFESSIONAL AND TRADE PERIODICALS

★234★ ABC Today
Associated Builders and Contractors, Inc.
   (ABC)
N. 17th St.
Rosslyn, VA 22209
Ph: (202)637-8800   Fax: (703)812-8203
Pamela E. Hunter

Semimonthly. Designed to keep readers alerted to important changes within ABC and the construction industry. Reports on legislative issues, construction trends, conferences and meetings, and ABC services. Recurring features include news of members and columns titled Industry Briefs, Safety Notebook, Computer Corner, Bottom Line, and Chapter News.

★235★ Construction Newsletter
National Safety Council
1121 Spring Lake Dr.
Itasca, IL 60143-3201
Ph: (708)775-2282   Fax: (708)775-2285
Diane A. Ghazarian

Bimonthly. Focuses on industrial and occupational safety in the construction industry. Carries items on such topics as safe work practices and products; accident prevention; and successful industrial safety programs and policies.

PROFESSIONAL MEETINGS AND CONVENTIONS

★236★ A/E/C SYSTEMS - International Computer and Management Show for the Design and Construction Industries
A/E/C Systems, Inc.
1 Farron Dr.
Chadds Ford, PA 19317
Ph: (215)444-9690   Fax: (215)444-9583

OTHER SOURCES OF INFORMATION

★237★ "Building Inspector" in Career Selector 2001
Barron's Educational Series, Inc.
250 Wireless Blvd.
Hauppauge, NY 11788
Ph: (516)434-3311   Fax: (516)434-3723
Fr: 800-645-3476

James C. Gonyea. 1993.

★238★ "Construction-Maintenance Inspector" in Career Selector 2001
Barron's Educational Series, Inc.
250 Wireless Blvd.
Hauppauge, NY 11788
Ph: (516)434-3311   Fax: (516)434-3723
Fr: 800-645-3476

James C. Gonyea. 1993.

Construction Contractors and Managers

Construction contractors and managers determine appropriate construction methods and schedule all required construction activities for the completion of particular construction projects. They determine labor requirements, obtain necessary permits and licenses, meet with cost estimators to monitor construction costs and avoid overruns, monitor the progress of construction activities, and direct construction supervisors. They often use computers to evaluate different construction methods and to determine the most cost-effective plan.

Salaries

Salaries of construction managers vary depending upon the size and nature of the construction project, its geographic location, and economic conditions.

Beginning construction managers	$32,000/year
Experienced construction managers	$35,000-$110,000/year

Employment Outlook

Growth rate until the year 2005: Much faster than the average.

Construction Contractors and Managers

**★248★ "Contractors and Builders" in
Opportunities in Building Construction
Trades (pp. 77-90)**
National Textbook Co. (NTC)
VGM Career Books
4255 W. Touhy Ave.
Lincolnwood, IL 60646-1975
Ph: (708)679-5500   Fax: (708)679-2494
Fr: 800-323-4900
Michael Sumichrast. 1989. Gives an overview of the construction industry and describes the jobs of various craftwokers. Covers different kinds of builders: home, custom; and describes management skills needed and industry trends affecting opportunities.

**★249★ Exploring Careers in the
Construction Industry**
Rosen Publishing Group
29 E. 21st St.
New York, NY 10010
Ph: (212)777-3017   Fax: (212)777-0277
Fr: 800-237-9932
Elizabeth Stewart Lytle. 1994. Includes information on specific trades. Also overviews the economic considerations, unions, opportunities for minorities and women, necessary education and training, and necessary tools and equipment.

**★250★ "General Contractor" in
Moonlighting: 148 Great Ways to Make
Money on the Side (pp. 134-136)**
Avon Books
1350 Avenue of the Americas
New York, NY 10019
Ph: (212)261-6800   Fr: 800-238-0658
Carl Hausman, author. 1989. Explains why people moonlight and its benefits: extra money, low overhead, develop new skills, own boss. Guides the reader in analyzing personal potential for succeeding in a moonlighting business, analyzing possible business opportunities, and setting up a home office. Lists 148 possible moonlighting jobs and describes start-up cost, estimated hours per week, the work involved, marketing ideas, and resources to read and contact.

**★251★ "Heavy Construction Contractor"
in Career Information Center (Vol.4)**
Simon and Schuster
200 Old Tappan Rd.
Old Tappan, NJ 07675
Fax: 800-445-6991   Fr: 800-223-2348
Richard Lidz and Dale Anderson, editorial directors. Fifth edition, 1993. For 600 occupations, tis 13 volume set describes job duties, entry-level requirements, education and training needed, advancement possibilities, employment outlook, earnings, and benefits. Each of the first 12 volumes includes jobs related under a broad career field; volume 4 covers construction. Volume 13 is the index.

**★252★ "Highway Contractor" in Career
Information Center (Vol.4)**
Simon and Schuster
200 Old Tappan Rd.
Old Tappan, NJ 07675
Fax: 800-445-6991   Fr: 800-223-2348
Richard Lidz and Dale Anderson, editorial directors. Fifth edition, 1993. For 600 occupations, this 13 volume set describes job duties, entry-level requirements, education and

training needed, advancement possibilities, employment outlook, earnings, and benefits. Each of the first 12 volumes includes jobs related under a broad career field; volume 4 covers construction. Volume 13 is the index.

**★253★ "Rural Builder" in Hard-Hatted
Women: Stories of Struggle and
Sucess in the Trades (pp. 202-211)**
Seal Press
Western Ave., Ste. 410
Seattle, WA 98121
Ph: (206)283-7844   Fax: (206)285-9410
Molly Martin, editor. 1988. Twenty-six women describe their experiences working in blue collar occupations. They tell how they got in, the work they do on the job, their relationships in predominantly male occupations, and the training they have received.

**★254★ What is CM?: An Introduction to
Professional Construction Management**
Construction Management Association of America
12355 Sunrise Valley Dr., Ste. 640
Reston, VA 22091
Ph: (703)391-1200
1990. This six panel brochure defines construction management as a service performed and explains its importance in the scheduling and cost of building projects.

PROFESSIONAL ASSOCIATIONS

**★255★ American Council for
Construction Education (ACCE)**
901 Hudson Ln.
Monroe, LA 71201
Ph: (318)323-2413   Fax: (318)323-2413
Members: Construction-oriented associations, corporations, and individuals united to: promote and improve construction education at the postsecondary level; engage in accrediting construction education programs offered by colleges and universities nationwide; maintain procedures consistent with the accrediting policies of the Commission on Recognition of Postsecondary Accreditation and report the results of its activities and list the colleges and universities with accredited programs of study in construction; review at regular intervals the criteria, standards, and procedures that the council has adopted to evaluate programs in construction education. Provides visiting teams for campus program evaluations; compiles statistics.

**★256★ American Institute of
Constructors (AIC)**
466 94th Ave.
St. Petersburg, FL 33702
Ph: (813)578-0317   Fax: (813)578-9982
Members: Professionals engaged in construction practice, education, and research. Serves as the certifying body for the professional constructor. **Purpose:** Objectives are to promote the study and to advance the practice of construction. Facilitates the exchange of information and ideas relating to construction. Conducts educational programs. **Publications:** AIC Newsletter, bimonthly. • American Professional Con-

structor, quarterly. • Ethics Manual. • Roster of Members, annual.

**★257★ Associated Builders and
Contractors (ABC)**
1300 N. 17th St.
Rosslyn, VA 22204
Ph: (703)812-2000
Members: Construction contractors, subcontractors, suppliers, and associates. **Purpose:** Aim is to foster and perpetuate the principles of rewarding construction workers and management on the basis of merit. Sponsors management education programs and craft training; also sponsors apprenticeship and skill training programs. Disseminates technological and labor relations information. Maintains placement service. Compiles statistics. **Publications:** ABC Today, semimonthly. • National Membership Directory and Users Guide, annual.

**★258★ Associated General Contractors
of America (AGC)**
1957 E St. NW
Washington, DC 20006
Ph: (202)393-2040   Fax: (202)347-4004
Members: General construction contractors; subcontractors; industry suppliers; service firms. **Purpose:** Provides market services through its divisions. Conducts special conferences and seminars designed specifically for construction firms. Compiles statistics on job accidents reported by member firms. ors. Maintains 65 committees, including joint cooperative committees with other associations and liaison committees with federal agencies. **Publications:** AGC Membership Directory and Buyers' Guide, annual. • AGC Mobile Directory. • Associated General Contractors of America—National Newsletter, biweekly. • Constructor, monthly.

**★259★ Associated Schools of
Construction (ASC)**
PO Box 834
Peoria, IL 61652
Members: Colleges and universities offering a program leading to an undergraduate or advanced degree with major emphasis on construction. **Purpose:** Aims to establish objectives for the development of construction education and to assist institutions of higher education in establishing construction education and management programs. Has undertaken an intensive study of the curricula of member institutions, with resulting recommendations. Compiles statistics. **Publications:** Construction Education Chronicle, semiannual. • Proceedings of the Annual Meeting, annual.

**★260★ Construction Management
Association of America (CMAA)**
7918 Jones Branch Dr., Ste. 540
Mc Lean, VA 22102
Ph: (703)356-2622   Fax: (703)356-6388
Members: Corporations and individuals who furnish construction management as a professional service. **Purpose:** Promotes the growth and development of construction management as a professional service; encourages high professional standards. Conducts forum on construction management. **Publications:** CM Advisor, bimonthly. • CM Member Services Directory, annual. • CMAA

Manual: Standard CM Services and Practice, annual.

★261★ Professional Construction Estimators Association of America (PCEA)
PO Box 11626
Charlotte, NC 28220-1626
Ph: (704)522-6376   Fax: (704)522-7013
Professional construction estimators. Objectives are to further recognition of construction estimating; to collect and disseminate information; to research and solve problems relating to the construction industry; to establish educational programs for youth and promote construction estimating as a career; to maintain ethical standards. **Publications:** *National Estimator*, quarterly. • *National PCEA Directory*, annual.

STANDARDS/CERTIFICATION AGENCIES

★262★ Mechanical Contractors Association of America (MCAA)
1385 Piccard Dr.
Rockville, MD 20850-4329
Ph: (301)869-5800   Fax: (301)990-9690
Works to standardize materials and methods used in the industry. Conducts business overhead, labor wage, and statistical surveys. Promotes apprenticeship training programs. Conducts seminars on contracts, labor estimating, job cost control, project management, marketing, collective bargaining, contractor insurance, and other management topics. Promotes methods to conserve energy in new and existing buildings.

TEST GUIDES

★263★ Career Examination Series: Building Construction Program Manager
National Learning Corp.
212 Michael Dr.
Syosset, NY 11791
Ph: (516)921-8888   Fax: (516)921-8743
Fr: 800-645-6337
Jack Rudman. 1993. Test guide including questions and answers for students or professionals in the field who seek advancement through examination.

★264★ Career Examination Series: Construction Analyst
National Learning Corp.
212 Michael Dr.
Syosset, NY 11791
Ph: (516)921-8888   Fax: (516)921-8743
Fr: 800-645-6337
Jack Rudman. A series of study guides with multiple-choice examination questions and solutions for trainees and professionals in construction and building inspection. Titles in the series include *Construction Cost Specialist; Construction Manager*.

★265★ Career Examination Series: Director of Engineering, Building and Housing
National Learning Corp.
212 Michael Dr.
Syosset, NY 11791
Ph: (516)921-8888   Fax: (516)921-8743
Fr: 800-645-6337
Jack Rudman. 1993. Test guide including questions and answers for students or professionals in the field who seek advancement through examination.

★266★ Career Examination Series: Highway Construction Coordinator
National Learning Corp.
212 Michael Dr.
Syosset, NY 11791
Ph: (516)921-8888   Fax: (516)921-8743
Fr: 800-645-6337
Jack Rudman. 1993. Test guide including questions and answers for students or professionals in the field who seek advancement through examination.

★267★ Career Examination Series: Park Construction Coordinator
National Learning Corp.
212 Michael Dr.
Syosset, NY 11791
Ph: (516)921-8888   Fax: (516)921-8743
Fr: 800-645-6337
Jack Rudman. 1993. Test guide including questions and answers for students or professionals in the field who seek advancement through examination.

EDUCATIONAL DIRECTORIES AND PROGRAMS

★268★ Collegiate Construction Education Directory
AGC Information, Inc.
1957 E St. NW
Washington, DC 20006
Ph: (202)393-2040   Fax: (202)347-4004
E. W. Jones, Contact
Irregular, previous edition June 1987; latest edition June 1992. Covers construction and construction-related programs at colleges and universities. Entries include: Institution name, fees, program name, address, phone, names of key personnel, program enrollment, accreditation. Arrangement: Geographical.

BASIC REFERENCE GUIDES AND HANDBOOKS

★269★ Complete Construction Handbook
McGraw-Hill Inc.
11 W. 19 St.
New York, NY 10011
Ph: 800-722-4726
Joseph J. Waddell and Joseph A. Dobrowlski. 1993.

★270★ The Complete Standard Handbook of Construction Personnel Management
Prentice Hall
Rte. 9W
Englewood Cliffs, NJ 07632
Ph: (201)592-2000
Carleton Coulter, III. 1989. Includes illustrations.

★271★ The Construction Manager - 1991
Prentice Hall
Rte. 9W
Englewood Cliffs, NJ 07632
Ph: (201)592-2000
Andrew M. Civitello, Jr. 1991.

★272★ Contractor's Management Handbook
McGraw-Hill Publishing Co.
11 W. 19th St.
New York, NY 10011
Ph: (212)337-6010   Fr: 800-722-4726
James J. O'Brien. Second edition, 1991.

★273★ From Plan to Profit: A Management Handbook for Home Builders
National Association of Home Builders
15th and M St., NW
Washington, DC 20005
Ph: (202)822-0463   Fax: (202)822-0391
J. Frank Newton. 1990.

★274★ McGraw-Hill's Handbook of Electrical Construction Calculations
McGraw-Hill Inc.
11 W. 19th St.
New York, NY 10011
Ph: 800-722-4726
Joseph F. McPartland, Brian J. McPartland, Steven P. McPartland, and Jack Pullizzi. 1993.

★275★ Strategic Management in Construction
Gower Publishing Co.
Old Post Rd.
Brookfield, VT 05036
Ph: (802)276-3162
David Langford. 1991. First edition.

★276★ The Surveying Handbook
Van Nostrand Reinhold
115 5th Ave.
New York, NY 10013
Russell C. Brinker and Roy Minnick. Second edition, 1994.

PROFESSIONAL AND TRADE PERIODICALS

★277★ *Building Design & Construction*
Cahners Publishing Co.
1350 E. Touhy Ave.
PO Box 5080
Des Plaines, IL 60017-5080
Ph: (708)635-8800   Fax: (708)390-2618
Jack HollfelderPublisher
Monthly. Magazine on business and technology for commercial, institutional, and industrial buildings.

★278★ *CIM Construction Journal*
Construction Industries of Massachusetts
1500 Providence Hwy.
PO Box 667
Norwood, MA 02062
Ph: (617)551-0182   Fax: (617)551-0916
Patricia A. Mikes
Weekly. Magazine on heavy and highway construction.

★279★ *Construction Bulletin Magazine*
Chapin Publishing Co.
8401 N. 73rd Ave., No. 82
Brooklyn Park, MN 55428
Ph: (612)537-7730   Fax: (612)537-1363
Fr: 800-328-4827
George R. Rekela
Weekly. Magazine covering Minnesota, North Dakota, and South Dakota construction activities.

★280★ *The Construction Contractor*
Federal Publications, Inc.
1120 20th St. NW
Washington, DC 20036
Ph: (202)337-7000   Fax: (202)659-2233
Richard L. Shea
Biweekly. Contains news, insight, and analysis of construction industry developments and cases.

★281★ *Construction Digest*
Construction Magazine Group, Inc.
PO Box 6132
Indianapolis, IN 46206-6132
Ph: (317)329-3100   Fax: (317)329-3110
William A. Orth
Semiweekly. Magazine for the public works and construction engineering industries.

★282★ *Construction Equipment*
Cahners Publishing Co.
1350 E. Touhy Ave.
PO Box 5080
Des Plaines, IL 60017-5080
Ph: (708)635-8800   Fax: (708)390-2618
Kirk Landers
Monthly. Magazine with information and ideas for managers of equipment and trucks.

★283★ *Construction Market Data*
Construction News Service
7623-B Ora Glen Dr.
Greenbelt, MD 20770
Ph: (301)441-3063
Jim Meehan
Weekly. Covers residential, commercial, and engineering construction in the Washington metropolitan area.

★284★ *Construction News*
10835 Financial Centre Pkwy., Ste. 133
Little Rock, AR 72211-3555
Ph: (501)376-1931   Fax: (501)375-5831
Robert Alvey
Weekly. Construction industry magazine.

★285★ *Construction Newsletter*
National Safety Council
1121 Spring Lake Dr.
Itasca, IL 60143-3201
Ph: (708)775-2282   Fax: (708)775-2285
Diane A. Ghazarian
Bimonthly. Focuses on industrial and occupational safety in the construction industry. Carries items on such topics as safe work practices and products; accident prevention; and successful industrial safety programs and policies.

★286★ *Construction Review*
U.S. Government Printing Office
Superintendent of Documents
Washington, DC 20402-9322
Ph: (202)783-3238   Fax: (202)512-2250
U.S. Department of CommercePublisher
Bimonthly. Magazine listing government statistics on construction.

★287★ *Construction Supervision & Safety Letter*
Bureau of Business Practice
24 Rope Ferry Rd.
Waterford, CT 06386
Ph: (203)442-4365   Fax: (201)592-3179
Fr: 800-243-0876
Barry Richardson
Semimonthly. Serves supervisors of blue-collar workers with discussion and advice on organizing, planning, and operating. Covers construction safety, the use of communication and motivation as productive management tools, ways to simplify discipline, and building teamwork. Recurring features include interviews with safety professionals, case histories, and cartoons.

★288★ *Construction Times*
PO Box 268
Stillwater, MN 55082-0268
W.E. Baker
Monthly. Building trade magazine (tabloid).

★289★ *CONSTRUCTOR*
Associated General Contractors Information
1957 E St. NW
Washington, DC 20006-5199
Ph: (202)393-2040   Fax: (202)628-1369
William F. Heavey
Monthly.

★290★ *Contracting Business*
Penton Publishing
1100 Superior Ave.
Cleveland, OH 44114
Ph: (216)696-7000   Fax: (216)696-7932
Dominick Guarino
Monthly.

★291★ *Contractors Guide*
Century Publishing Co.
990 Grove St.
Evanston, IL 60201-4370
Ph: (708)491-6440   Fax: (708)491-0867
Greg Ettling
Monthly. Trade magazine on roofing and insulation.

★292★ *Daily Construction Reporter*
7670 Opprtunity Rd.
San Diego, CA 92111-1112
Ph: (619)492-1402   Fax: (619)565-4182
Bernado RomanowskyPublisher
Daily. Construction newspaper covering jobs that are out for bid, bid results, building permits, and other information.

★293★ *ENR: Engineering News-Record*
McGraw-Hill, Inc.
1221 Avenue of the Americas
New York, NY 10020
Ph: (212)512-4686   Fax: (212)512-4256
Arthur J. Fox
Weekly. Magazine focusing on engineering and construction.

★294★ *The Journal of Light Construction*
RR 2, Box 146
Richmond, VT 05477-9607
Ph: (802)434-4747   Fax: (802)434-4467
Steve Bliss
Monthly. Magazine (tabloid) for residential and light professionals involved in new and rehabilitative construction. Each issue covers a single aspect of construction.

★295★ *Plastics in Building Construction*
Technomic Publishing Co., Inc.
851 New Holland Ave.
PO Box 3535
Lancaster, PA 17604
Ph: (717)291-5609   Fax: (717)295-4538
Fr: 800-233-9936
Monthly. Publication reporting exclusively on new developments in plastics in building construction.

PROFESSIONAL MEETINGS AND CONVENTIONS

★296★ *A/E/C Systems and CMC Fall*
A/E/C Systems, Inc.
1 Farron Dr.
Chadds Ford, PA 19317
Ph: (215)444-9690   Fax: (215)444-9583
Annual.

★297★ *Associated General Contractors National Convention and Constructor Exposition*
Associated General Contractors
1957 E St., NW
Washington, DC 20006
Ph: (202)393-2040   Fax: (202)347-4004
Annual. **Dates and Locations:** 1996 Feb 29-05; San Diego, CA.

★298★ **CONBUILD - Construction and Building Machinery, Equipment, and Materials**
Glahe International, Inc.
1700 K St., NW, Ste. 403
Washington, DC 20006-3824
Ph: (202)659-4557   Fax: (202)457-0776

★299★ **CONEXPO - International Construction Equipment Expostion**
Construction Industry Manufacturers Association
111 E. Wisconsin Ave., Ste. 940
Milwaukee, WI 53202
Ph: (414)272-0943   Fax: (414)272-2672
Every three years. **Dates and Locations:** 1996 Mar 20-24; Las Vegas, NV.

OTHER SOURCES OF INFORMATION

★300★ **"Construction Worker" in Encyclopedia of Danger: Dangerous Professions (pp. 34-37)**
Chelsea House Publishers
1974 Sproul Rd., Ste. 400
Broomall, PA 19008
Ph: (215)353-5166   Fax: (215)359-1439
Missy Allen and Michel Peissel. 1993. Provides descriptions of 24 dangerous occupations, their risky characteristics, and safety precautions.

★301★ **Management Development in the Construction Industry**
American Society of Civil Engineers
345 E. 47th St.
New York, NY 10017-2398
Ph: (212)705-7288   Fax: (212)980-4681
1992.

Cost Estimators

Cost estimators predict the cost of projects for owners or managers to use in making bids for contracts, in determining if a new product will be profitable, or in determining if the firms products are making a profit. Estimators compile and analyze data on all factors that might influence costs: materials, labor, location, and special machinery, among others. The estimator compares the cost of purchasing parts to the firm's cost of manufacturing them to determine which is more cost effective.

Salaries

Salaries for cost estimators vary widely by experience, education, size of firm, and industry.

Beginning cost estimators in construction	$17, 000-$21,000/year
Beginning cost estimators in engineering or construction management	$30,000/year or more
Highly experienced cost estimators	$75,000/year or more

Employment Outlook

Growth rate until the year 2005: Faster than the average.

Cost Estimators

CAREER GUIDES

★302★ Careers in Cost Engineering and Related Industry Specialties
American Association of Cost Engineers
PO Box 1557
Morgantown, WV 26507-1557
Ph: (304)296-8444
This one-page guide describes how to become a cost engineer, what cost engineers do, and which industries employ cost engineers.

★303★ Careers in Finance
National Textbook Co. (NTC)
VGM Career Books
4255 W. Touhy Ave.
Lincolnwood, IL 60646-1975
Ph: (708)679-5500   Fax: (708)679-2494
Fr: 800-323-4900
Trudy Ring, editor. 1993. Covers financial careers in such areas as higher education, corporate and public finance, and commercial and investment banking.

★304★ "Cost Estimators" in Career Discovery Encyclopedia (Vol.2, pp. 66-67)
J.G. Ferguson Publishing Co.
200 W. Madison St., Ste. 300
Chicago, IL 60606
Ph: (312)580-5480   Fax: (312)580-4948
Russell E. Primm, editor-in chief. 1993. This six volume set contains two-page articles for 504 occupations. Each article describes job duties, earnings, and educational and training requirements. The whole set is arranged alphabetically by job title. Designed for junior high and older students.

★305★ "Cost Estimators" in Encyclopedia of Careers and Vocational Guidance (Vol.2, pp.399-401)
J.G. Ferguson Publishing Co.
200 W. Madison St., Ste. 300
Chicago, IL 60606
Ph: (312)580-5480   Fax: (312)580-4948
William E. Hopke, editor-in-chief. Ninth edition, 1993. Four-volume set that profiles 900 occupations and describes job trends in 74 industries. Includes career description, educational requirements, history of the job, methods of entry, advancement, employment outlook, earnings, conditions of work, social and psychological factors, and sources of further information.

★306★ "Cost Estimators" in Occupational Outlook Handbook
U.S. Government Printing Office
Superintendent of Documents
Washington, DC 20402
Ph: (202)512-1800   Fax: (202)512-2250
Biennial; latest edition, 1994-95. Encyclopedia of careers describing about 250 occupations and comprising about 85 percent of all jobs in the economy. Occupations that require lengthy education or training are given the most attention. Each occupation's profile describes what the worker does on the job, working conditions, education and training requirements, advancement possibilities, job outlook, earnings, and sources of additional information.

PROFESSIONAL ASSOCIATIONS

★307★ AACE International (AACE)
209 Prairie Ave.
Morgantown, WV 26505
Ph: (304)296-8444   Fax: (304)291-5728
Fr: 800-858-2678
Members: Professional society of cost managers, cost engineers, estimators, schedulers and planners, economic evaluators, educators, representatives of all branches of engineering, engineering students, and others. **Purpose:** Conducts technical and educational programs. Offers placement service. Compiles statistics. **Publications:** AACE International—Directory of Members, annual. • AACE Transactions, annual. • Cost Engineering: The Journal of Total Cost Management, monthly. • Cost Engineer's Notebook, 3/year.

★308★ American Society of Professional Estimators (ASPE)
11141 Georgia Ave., Ste. 412
Wheaton, MD 20902
Ph: (301)929-8848   Fax: (301)929-0231
Members: Construction cost estimators; firms allied to the construction industry; construction educators. **Purpose:** Fosters and upholds high professional and ethical standards in construction estimating. Sponsors efforts to enhance the education of young people entering the estimating profession; offers continuing education to established professionals; provides certification for estimators. Encourages the use of estimators throughout the construction industry. Conducts charitable program. Library is under development. **Publications:** The Estimator, bimonthly. • National Roster, annual. • Standard Estimating Practice Manual.

★309★ Coalition for State Prompt Pay (CSPP)
3150 Spring St.
Fairfax, VA 22031-2399
Ph: (703)273-7200   Fax: (703)278-8082
Members: National, state, regional, and local trade associations whose members sell products and services to state agencies. **Purpose:** Purpose is to lobby for the enactment of prompt payment legislation in all states. Maintains a national clearinghouse of information on state payment practices such as statutes, rules, and regulations. **Publications:** Coalition for State Prompt Pay—Newsletter, periodic. • Guide to Getting Paid Promptly by State and Local Agencies, periodic. • Model State Prompt Pay Law. • State-by-State Report on Prompt Pay Legislation, periodic.

★310★ Society of Cost Estimating and Analysis (SCEA)
101 S. Whiting St., Ste. 201
Alexandria, VA 22304
Ph: (703)751-8069   Fax: (703)461-7328
Members: Individuals in cost estimating and analysis and price analysis-oriented professions. **Purpose:** Facilitates the professional association of the cost estimating and analysis disciplines; enhances the efficiency and effectiveness of cost estimating and analysis activities in proprietary industry, nonprofit organizations, and government. Activities include: identification of technical and ethical

standards; establishment and maintenance of standards; assistance in the identification of qualified members for industry and government. Maintains code of ethics to promote cooperation and good relations among members of the profession and to enhance the stature of the profession. Provides certification program that supports technical and ethical standards through participation in oral workshops, involvement in professional programs, completion of accredited university courses, and successful completion of certification examination. **Publications:** *Journal of Cost Analysis*, annual. • *National Estimator*, semiannual. • *SCEA Newsletter*, quarterly.

STANDARDS/CERTIFICATION AGENCIES

★311★ American Society of Professional Estimators (ASPE)
11141 Georgia Ave., Ste. 412
Wheaton, MD 20902
Ph: (301)929-8848   Fax: (301)929-0231
Fosters and upholds high professional and ethical standards in construction estimating. Sponsors efforts to enhance the education of young people entering the estimating profession; offers continuing education to established professionals; provides certification for estimators.

★312★ Society of Cost Estimating and Analysis (SCEA)
101 S. Whiting St., Ste. 201
Alexandria, VA 22304
Ph: (703)751-8069   Fax: (703)461-7328
Activities include: identification of technical and ethical standards; establishment and maintenance of standards; assistance in the identification of qualified members for industry and government. Maintains code of ethics to promote cooperation and good relations among members of the profession and to enhance the stature of the profession. Provides certification program that supports technical and ethical standards through participation in oral workshops, involvement in professional programs, completion of accredited university courses, and successful completion of certification examination.

TEST GUIDES

★313★ Career Examination Series: Construction Cost Specialist
National Learning Corp.
212 Michael Dr.
Syosset, NY 11791
Ph: (516)921-8888   Fax: (516)921-8743
Fr: 800-645-6337
Jack Rudman. A study guide for professionals and trainees in the field of construc-

tion cost estimating. Includes a multiple-choice examination section; provides answers.

★314★ Career Examination Series: Cost and Statistical Analyst
National Learning Corp.
212 Michael Dr.
Syosset, NY 11791
Ph: (516)921-8888   Fax: (516)921-8743
Fr: 800-645-6337
Jack Rudman. 1993. Test guide including questions and answers for students or professionals in the field who seek advancement through examination.

★315★ Career Examination Series: Estimator
National Learning Corp.
212 Michael Dr.
Syosset, NY 11791
Ph: (516)921-8888   Fax: (516)921-8743
Fr: 800-645-6337
Jack Rudman. 1993. Test guide including questions and answers for students or professionals in the field who seek advancement through examination.

EDUCATIONAL DIRECTORIES AND PROGRAMS

★316★ Seminars in Compensation and Benefits Management
American Compensation Association (ACA)
14040 N. Northsight Blvd.
Scottsdale, AZ 85260-3601
Ph: (602)951-9191   Fax: (602)483-8352
1993. This catalog describes courses offered for compensation and benefits professionals, human resource executives, and training and development professionals. Gives dates, locations, and prices.

AWARDS, SCHOLARSHIPS, GRANTS, AND FELLOWSHIPS

★317★ Award of Merit
American Association of Cost Engineers
PO Box 1557
Morgantown, WV 26507-1557
Ph: (304)296-8444   Fax: (304)291-5728
This, the organization's highest award, is presented to an individual for contributions to cost engineering. Membership is not necessary for consideration. Awarded annually. Established in 1957.

★318★ Fellow
American Association of Cost Engineers
PO Box 1557
Morgantown, WV 26507-1557
Ph: (304)296-8444   Fax: (304)291-5728
To recognize those members who have advanced cost engineering by service within the organization and to organizations outside of AACE. Awarded annually upon recommendation. Established in 1976.

PROFESSIONAL AND TRADE PERIODICALS

★319★ Cost Control News
Siefer Consultants, Inc.
525 Cayuga St.
Storm Lake, IA 50588
Ph: (712)732-7340
Steve Stepanek

Semimonthly. Discusses cost cutting measures and opportunities. Considers such topics as eliminating miscellaneous expenses, charitable contributions, using budgets, self insuring prescription coverage, and mail sorting.

★320★ The Journal of Cost Analysis
Institute of Cost Analysis
201 S. Whiting St.
Alexandria, VA 22306
Ph: (703)751-8069

Dr. Kankey, editor. Semiannual.

PROFESSIONAL MEETINGS AND CONVENTIONS

★321★ American Association of Cost Engineers Annual Meeting
American Association of Cost Engineers
PO Box 1557
Morgantown, WV 26507-1557
Ph: (304)296-8444   Fax: (304)291-5728
Annual. **Dates and Locations:** 1996 Jun 23-26; Vancouver, BC.

Education Administrators

Education administrators provide direction, leadership, and day-to-day management of educational activities in preschools; elementary, secondary, religious, vocational, and technical schools; colleges and universities; businesses; correctional institutions; museums; and job training and community service organizations. Their main responsibility is to insure high quality instruction. **Principals** manage elementary and secondary schools. **Assistant principals** usually handle scheduling of classes, coordinating transportation, custodial and cafeteria services, discipline, social and recreational programs, health and safety, building and grounds maintenance, and student counseling. Public school administrators, such as **education supervisors**, plan, evaluate, and improve curriculum and teaching techniques. Similarly, **academic deans** assist college and university presidents and develop budgets and academic policies and programs. **College or university department heads or chairpersons** coordinate schedules of classes and teaching assignments, propose budgets, recruit and interview applicants for teaching positions, perform other administrative duties, and teach. **Directors of student services** direct and coordinate admissions, foreign student services, health and counseling services, and social, recreational, and other programs. **Registrars** maintain students' education records, including transcripts. **Directors of admissions** manage the process of admitting students, oversee the preparation of college catalogs, recruit students, and work closely with **financial aid directors**, who oversee scholarship, fellowship, and loan programs. **Directors of student activities** plan and arrange social, cultural, recreational, and orientation activities. **Athletic directors** plan and direct intramural and intercollegiate athletic activities.

Salaries

Salaries vary according to position, level of responsibility, experience, and size and location of institution.

Senior high school principal	$63,000/year
Junior high/middle school principal	$58,600/year
Elementary school principal	$54,900/year
Senior high school assistant principal	$52,300/year
Junior high/middle school assistant principal	$49,900/year
Elementary school assistant principal	$45,400/year
Academic deans	$53,400-$182,600/year
Student services directors	$30,900-$47,500/year

Employment Outlook

Growth rate until the year 2005: Average.

Education Administrators

CAREER GUIDES

★322★ *Academic Deans*
Chronicle Guidance Publications, Inc.
66 Aurora St.
PO Box 1190
Moravia, NY 13118-1190
Ph: (315)497-0330   Fax: (315)497-3359
Fr: 800-622-7284
1993. Career brief describing the nature of the job, working conditions, hours and earnings, education and training, licensure, certification, unions, personal qualifications, social and psychological factors, location, employment outlook, entry methods, advancement, and related occupations.

★323★ *Admissions Directors (College and University)*
Chronicle Guidance Publications, Inc.
66 Aurora St.
PO Box 1190
Moravia, NY 13118-1190
Ph: (315)497-0330   Fax: (315)497-3359
Fr: 800-622-7284
1993. Career brief describing the nature of the job, working conditions, hours and earnings, education and training, licensure, certification, unions, personal qualifications, social and psychological factors, location, employment outlook, entry methods, advancement, and related occupations.

★324★ *Careers in Teaching*
TAB/McGraw-Hill, Inc.
PO Box 182607
Columbus, OH 43218-2607
Fax: (614)759-3644   Fr: 800-822-8158
Glen W. Cutlip, Ph.D. and Robert J. Schockley, Ph.D. 1994.

★325★ "College Administration" in *Liberal Arts Jobs*
Petersons Guides, Inc.
PO Box 2123
Princeton, NJ 08543-2123
Ph: (609)243-9111   Fax: (609)243-9150
Fr: 800-338-3282
Burton Jay Nadler. Second edition, 1989. Strives to help the liberal arts graduate identify skills for entry-level positions. Gives goal setting and job search advice.

★326★ "College Administrators" in *Career Discovery Encyclopedia* (Vol.2, pp. 28-29)
J.G. Ferguson Publishing Co.
200 W. Madison St., Ste. 300
Chicago, IL 60606
Ph: (312)580-5480   Fax: (312)580-4948
Russell E. Primm, editor-in chief. 1993. This six volume set contains two-page articles for 504 occupations. Each article describes job duties, earnings, and educational and training requirements. The whole set is arranged alphabetically by job title. Designed for junior high and older students.

★327★ *Dean of Students*
Careers, Inc.
PO Box 135
Largo, FL 34649-0135
Ph: (813)584-7333
1994. Two-page occupational summary card describing duties, working conditions, personal qualifications, training, earnings and hours, employment outlook, places of employment, related careers, and where to write for more information.

★328★ "Director of Graduate Studies" in *Opportunities in Marketing Careers* (pp. 77-79)
National Textbook Co. (NTC)
VGM Career Books
4255 W. Touhy Ave.
Lincolnwood, IL 60646-1975
Ph: (708)679-5500   Fax: (708)679-2494
Fr: 800-323-4900
Margery S. Steinberg. 1988. Defines marketing and surveys marketing fields, such as research and retailing. Gives the employment outlook and describes the rewards of a career in marketing. Includes information on the education needed, and how to find a job. Lists colleges with majors in marketing.

★329★ "Education Administrators" in *Occupational Outlook Handbook*
U.S. Government Printing Office
Superintendent of Documents
Washington, DC 20402
Ph: (202)512-1800   Fax: (202)512-2250
Biennial; latest edition, 1994-95. Encyclopedia of careers describing about 250 occupations and comprising about 85 percent of all jobs in the economy. Occupations that require lengthy education or training are given the most attention. Each occupation's profile describes what the worker does on the job, working conditions, education and training requirements, advancement possibilities, job outlook, earnings, and sources of additional information.

★330★ "Education Directors" in *Encyclopedia of Careers and Vocational Guidance* (Vol.2, pp. 527-530)
J.G. Ferguson Publishing Co.
200 W. Madison St., Ste. 300
Chicago, IL 60606
Ph: (312)580-5480   Fax: (312)580-4948
William E. Hopke, editor-in-chief. Ninth edition, 1993. Four-volume set that profiles 900 occupations and describes job trends in 74 industries. Includes career description, educational requirements, history of the job, methods of entry, advancement, employment outlook, earnings, conditions of work, social and psychological factors, and sources of further information.

★331★ *Elementary School Principal*
Vocational Biographies, Inc.
PO Box 31
Sauk Centre, MN 56378-0031
Ph: (612)352-6516   Fax: (612)352-5546
Fr: 800-255-0752
1991. Four-page pamphlet containing a personal narrative about a worker's job, work likes and dislikes, career path from high school to the present. Education and training, the rewards and frustrations, and the effects of the job on the rest of the worker's life. The data file portion of this pamphlet gives a concise occupational summary, including work descriptions, working conditions, places of employment, personal characteristics, education and training, job outlook, and salary range.

★332★ *Financial Aid Administrators (Education)*
Chronicle Guidance Publications, Inc.
66 Aurora St.
PO Box 1190
Moravia, NY 13118-1190
Ph: (315)497-0330   Fax: (315)497-3359
Fr: 800-622-7284
1993. Career brief describing the nature of the job, working conditions, hours and earnings, education and training, licensure, certifi-

cation, unions, personal qualifications, social and psychological factors, location, employment outlook, entry methods, advancement, and related occupations.

★333★ Jobs! What They Are—Where They Are—What They Pay! (p. 108-110)
Simon & Schuster, Inc.
Simon & Schuster Bldg.
1230 Avenue of the Americas
New York, NY 10020
Ph: (212)698-7000   Fr: 800-223-2348
Robert O. Snelling and Anne M. Snelling. Third revised edition, 1992. Describes duties and responsibilities, earnings, employment opportunities, training, and qualifications.

★334★ Proficiencies for Principals: Elementary and Middle Schools
National Association of Elementary School Principles (NAESP)
1615 Duke St.
Alexandria, VA 22314
Ph: (703)684-3345
1991.

★335★ Registrars (College and University)
Chronicle Guidance Publications, Inc.
66 Aurora St.
PO Box 1190
Moravia, NY 13118-1190
Ph: (315)497-0330   Fax: (315)497-3359
Fr: 800-622-7284
1993. Career brief describing the nature of the job, working conditions, hours and earnings, education and training, licensure, certification, unions, personal qualifications, social and psychological factors, location, employment outlook, entry methods, advancement, and related occupations.

★336★ "School Administrator" in College Board Guide to Jobs and Career Planning (pp. 191)
The College Board
415 Columbus Ave.
New York, NY 10023-6992
Ph: (212)713-8165   Fax: (212)713-8143
Fr: 800-323-7155
Joyce S. Mitchell. Second edition, 1994. Describes the job, salaries, related careers, education needed, and where to write for more information.

★337★ "School Administrator" in VGM's Handbook of Business and Management Careers
National Textbook Co.
4255 W. Touhy Ave.
Lincolnwood, IL 60646-1975
Ph: (708)679-5500   Fax: (708)679-2494
Fr: 800-323-4900
Annette Selden. Second edition, 1993. Contains 42 two-page occupational profiles describing job duties, places of employment, working conditions, qualifications, education, employment outlook, and income.

★338★ School Administrators
Careers, Inc.
PO Box 135
Largo, FL 34649-0135
Ph: (813)584-7333
1994. Four-page brief offering the definition, history, duties, working conditions, personal qualifications, educational requirements,

earnings, hours, employment outlook, advancement, and careers related to this position.

★339★ "School Administrators" in Career Discovery Encyclopedia (Vol.5, pp. 170-171)
J.G. Ferguson Publishing Co.
200 W. Madison St., Ste. 300
Chicago, IL 60606
Ph: (312)580-5480   Fax: (312)580-4948
Russell E. Primm, editor-in chief. 1993. This six volume set contains two-page articles for 504 occupations. Each article describes job duties, earnings, and educational and training requirements. The whole set is arranged alphabetically by job title. Designed for junior high and older students.

★340★ "School Administrators" in Career Information Center (Vol.11)
Simon and Schuster
200 Old Tappan Rd.
Old Tappan, NJ 07675
Fax: 800-445-6991   Fr: 800-223-2348
Richard Lidz and Linda Perrin, editorial directors. Fifth edition, 1993. This 13-volume set profiles over 600 occupations. Each occupational profile describes job duties, educational requirements, how to get the job, advancement possibilities, employment outlook, working conditions, earnings and benefits, and where to write for more information.

★341★ "School Administrators" in Encyclopedia of Careers and Vocational Guidance (Vol.4, pp. 325-328)
J.G. Ferguson Publishing Co.
200 W. Madison St., Ste. 300
Chicago, IL 60606
Ph: (312)580-5480   Fax: (312)580-4948
William E. Hopke, editor-in-chief. Ninth edition, 1993. Four-volume set that profiles 900 occupations and describes job trends in 74 industries. Includes career description, educational requirements, history of the job, methods of entry, advancement, employment outlook, earnings, conditions of work, social and psychological factors, and sources of further information.

★342★ "School Principal" in Jobs Rated Almanac
World Almanac
1 International Blvd., Ste. 444
Mahwah, NJ 07495
Ph: (201)529-6900   Fax: (201)529-6901
Les Krantz. Second edition, 1992. Ranks 250 jobs by environment, salary, outlooks, physical demands, stress, security, travel opportunities, and extra perks. Includes jobs the editor feels are the most common, most interesting, and the most rapidly growing.

★343★ School Principals
Chronicle Guidance Publications, Inc.
66 Aurora St.
PO Box 1190
Moravia, NY 13118-1190
Ph: (315)497-0330   Fax: (315)497-3359
Fr: 800-622-7284
1991. Career brief describing the nature of the job, working conditions, hours and earnings, education and training, licensure, certification, unions, personal qualifications, social and psychological factors, location, employ-

ment outlook, entry methods, advancement, and related occupations.

★344★ "University and College Administrators" in American Almanac of Jobs and Salaries (p. 117)
Avon Books
1350 Avenue of the Americas
New York, NY 10019
Ph: (212)261-6800   Fr: 800-238-0658
John Wright, editor. Revised and updated, 1994-95. This is comprehensive guide to the wages of hundreds of occupations in a wide variety of industries and organizations.

PROFESSIONAL ASSOCIATIONS

★345★ American Association of Collegiate Registrars and Admissions Officers (AACRAO)
1 Dupont Cir. NW, Ste. 330
Washington, DC 20036
Ph: (202)293-9161   Fax: (202)872-8857
Members: Degree-granting postsecondary institutions, government agencies, and higher education coordinating boards, private educational organizations, and education-oriented businesses. **Purpose:** Promotes higher education and furthers the professional development of members working in admissions, enrollment management, institutional research, records, and registration. **Publications:** AACRAD Employment Referral Bulletin. • AACRAO Data Dispenser, monthly. • AACRAO Member Guide, annual. • College and University, quarterly. • Transfer Credit Practices of Designated Educational Institutions, biennial. • World Education Series.

★346★ American Association of School Administrators (AASA)
1801 N. Moore St.
Arlington, VA 22209
Ph: (703)528-0700   Fax: (703)841-1543
Members: Professional association of administrators and executives of school systems and educational service agencies; school district superintendents; central, building, and service unit administrators; presidents of colleges, deans, and professors of educational administration; placement officers; executive directors and administrators of education associations; heads of private schools. **Purpose:** Sponsors numerous professional development seminars annually through its National Academy for School Executives, "dedicated to excellence in educational system leadership." Founded Educational Research Service Maintains numerous standing and ad hoc committees. **Publications:** Leadership News, semimonthly. • The School Administrator.

★347★ American Association of University Administrators (AAUA)
PO Box 2183
Tuscaloosa, AL 35403
Ph: (205)758-0636   Fax: (205)345-9778
Members: Promotes excellence in the administration of higher education and assists career administrators in continuing their pro-

fessional growth. **Purpose:** Conducts periodic professional development program. **Publications:** *AAUA Communique*, quarterly. • *Journal for Higher Education Management: A Journal of the AAUA*, 3/year.

★348★ American Federation of School Administrators (AFSA)
1729 21st St. NW
Washington, DC 20009
Ph: (202)986-4209   Fax: (202)986-4211
Principals, vice-principals, directors, supervisors, and administrators involved in pedagogical education. Purposes are to: achieve the highest goals in education; maintain and improve standards, benefits, and conditions for personnel without regard to color, race, sex, background, or national origin; obtain job security; protect seniority and merit; cooperate with all responsible organizations in education; promote understanding, participation, and support of the public, communities, and agencies; be alert to resist attacks and campaigns that would create or entrench a spoils system; promote democratic society by supporting full educational opportunities for every child and student in the nation. **Publications:** *AFSA News*, monthly.

★349★ American Federation of Teachers (AFT)
555 New Jersey Ave. NW
Washington, DC 20001
Ph: (202)879-4400   Fr: 800-238-1133
Members: AFL-CIO. Works with teachers and other educational employees at the state and local level in organizing, collective bargaining, research, educational issues, and public relations. **Purpose:** Conducts research in areas such as educational reform, bilingual education, teacher certification, and evaluation and national assessments and standards. Represents members' concerns through legislative action; offers technical assistance. Seeks to serve professionals with concerns similar to those of teachers, including state employees, healthcare workers, and paraprofessionals. **Publications:** *AFT Action: A Newsletter for AFT Leaders*, weekly. • *American Educator*, quarterly. • *American Teacher*, 8/year. • *Healthwire*, 10/year. • *On Campus*, 9/year. • *Public Sevice Reporter*, 9/year.

★350★ Association of International Education Administrators (AIEA)
PO Box 13288
Denton, TX 76203-3288
Ph: (817)565-2483
Publications: *Bridges to the Future: Strategies for Internationalizing Higher Education.* • *International Education Forum*, semiannual.

★351★ Association for the Study of Higher Education (ASHE)
Texas A&M University
Department of Educational Admin.
College Station, TX 77843-4226
Ph: (409)845-0393   Fax: (409)862-4347
Members: Professors, researchers, administrators, policy analysts, graduate students, and others concerned with the study of higher education. **Purpose:** Purposes are to advance the study of higher education and facilitate and encourage discussion of priority issues for research in the study of higher

education. **Publications:** *ASHE Newsletter*, periodic. • *Directory of ASHE Membership and Higher Education Program Faculty*, annual. • *Review of Higher Education*, quarterly.

★352★ National Association of Elementary School Principals (NAESP)
1615 Duke St.
Alexandria, VA 22314
Ph: (703)684-3345   Fax: (703)548-6021
Members: Professional association of principals, assistant or vice principals, and aspiring principals; persons engaged in educational research and in the professional education of elementary and middle school administrators. **Purpose:** Sponsors National Distinguished Principals Program, President's Award for Educational Excellence, American Student Council Association, National Fellows Program, and Institute for Reflective Practice. Offers professional development workshops throughout the year. **Publications:** *Communicator*, 10/year. • *Focus on Finance*, 3/year. • *Here's How*, bimonthly. • *The K-8 Principal.* • *Middle Matters*, 3/year. • *Principal*, 5/year. • *Principals' Opinion Polls.* • *Report to Parents*, bimonthly. • *Research Roundup*, 3/year. • *Streamlined Seminar*, bimonthly.

★353★ National Association of Secondary School Principals (NASSP)
1904 Association Dr.
Reston, VA 22091
Ph: (703)860-0200   Fax: (703)476-5432
Members: Secondary school principals and assistant principals; other persons engaged in secondary school administration and/or supervision; college professors teaching courses in secondary education. **Purpose:** Sponsors National Association of Student Councils, National Honor Society, and National Junior Honor Society. Conducts competitions. **Publications:** *Administrative Information Report*, annual. • *AP Special*, bimonthly. • *Leadership for Student Activities*, monthly. • *NASSP Bulletin: The Journal for Middle Level and High School Administrators.* • *NASSP—Curriculum Report*, 5/year. • *NASSP—Legal Memorandum*, quarterly. • *NASSP—NewsLeader*, monthly. • *The Practitioner*, quarterly. • *Schools in the Middle*, quarterly. • *Tips for Principals*, monthly.

★354★ National Association of Student Personnel Administrators (NASPA)
1875 Connecticut Ave. NW, Ste. 418
Washington, DC 20009
Ph: (202)265-7500
Members: Representatives of degree-granting institutions of higher education which have been fully accredited. **Purpose:** Works to enrich the educational experience of all students. Serves colleges and universities by providing leadership and professional growth opportunities for the chief student affairs officer and other professionals who consider higher education and student affairs issues from an institutional perspective. Provides professional development; improves information and research; acts as an advocate for students in higher education. Promotes diversity in NASPA and the profession. Maintains career service and conducts the Richard F. Stevens Institute. Supports minority undergraduate fellows program. **Publications:** *Career Services Bulletin*, annual. • *Member-*

ship Handbook, annual. • *NASPA Forum*, monthly. • *NASPA Journal*, periodic.

★355★ National Council for Accreditation of Teacher Education (NCATE)
2010 Massachusetts Ave. NW, Ste. 500
Washington, DC 20036-1023
Ph: (202)466-7496   Fax: (202)296-6620
Members: Representatives from constituent colleges and universities, state departments of education, school boards, teacher and other professional groups. **Purpose:** Voluntary accrediting body devoted exclusively to: evaluation and accreditation of institutions for preparation of elementary and secondary school teachers; preparation of school service personnel, including school principals, supervisors, superintendents, guidance counselors, school psychologists, instructional technologists, and other specialists for school-oriented positions. **Publications:** *Handbook for Institutional Visits.* • *NCATE-Approved Curriculum Guidelines.* • *Quality Teaching*, 3/year. • *Standards, Procedures, and Policies for the Accreditation of Professional Education Units.* • *Teacher Preparation: A Guide to Colleges and Universities.*

STANDARDS/CERTIFICATION AGENCIES

★356★ American Federation of Teachers (AFT)
555 New Jersey Ave. NW
Washington, DC 20001
Ph: (202)879-4400   Fr: 800-238-1133
Conducts research in areas such as educational reform, bilingual education, teacher certification, and evaluation and national assessments and standards.

★357★ National Council for Accreditation of Teacher Education (NCATE)
2010 Massachusetts Ave. NW, Ste. 500
Washington, DC 20036-1023
Ph: (202)466-7496   Fax: (202)296-6620
Voluntary accrediting body devoted exclusively to: evaluation and accreditation of institutions for preparation of elementary and secondary school teachers; preparation of school service personnel, including school principals, supervisors, superintendents, guidance counselors, school psychologists, instructional technologists, and other specialists for school-oriented positions.

TEST GUIDES

★358★ Career Examination Series: Coordinator of Drug Abuse Educational Programs
National Learning Corp.
212 Michael Dr.
Syosset, NY 11791
Ph: (516)921-8888   Fax: (516)921-8743
Fr: 800-645-6337
Jack Rudman. 1993. Test guide including questions and answers for students or professionals in the field who seek advancement through examination.

★359★ Career Examination Series: Education Director
National Learning Corp.
212 Michael Dr.
Syosset, NY 11791
Ph: (516)921-8888   Fax: (516)921-8743
Fr: 800-645-6337
Jack Rudman. A series of study guides with multiple-choice examination questions and solutions for trainees and professional educational administrators. Titles in the series include *Administrative Education Officer; Coordinator of Educational Affairs; College Administrative Associate; Director of School Facilities and Operations; Education Officer; Education Supervisor; Education Supervisor (Developmental Disabilities); Education Supervisor (Special Subjects); Education Supervisor (Vocational); School Finance Manager.*

★360★ National Teacher Examination Series
National Learning Corp.
212 Michael Dr.
Syosset, NY 11791
Ph: (516)921-8888   Fax: (516)921-8743
Fr: 800-645-6337
Jack Rudman. Practice multiple-choice examinations for education certification. Includes solutions. Titles in the series include *National Teacher Examination (Core Battery)* (one-volume combined edition); *Educational Leadership: Administration and Supervision;* as well as a number of specific education subjects.

★361★ Teachers License Examination Series: Principal
National Learning Corp.
212 Michael Dr.
Syosset, NY 11791
Ph: (516)921-8888   Fax: (516)921-8743
Fr: 800-645-6337
Jack Rudman. A series of preparatory study guides for professionals studying for licensing examinations. Includes a multiple-choice test section; provides answers. Titles in the series include *Assistant Principal, Elementary School; Assistant Principal, Junior High School; Principal, Elementary School; Principal, Junior High School; Principal, Academic High School; Principal, Vocational High School; Supervision Test; Supervisor's Handbook of Mnemonic Devices; Principal, Comprehensive High School; Assistant Administrative Director;* and titles for a number of departmental chairperson positions.

EDUCATIONAL DIRECTORIES AND PROGRAMS

★362★ Educational Career Directory
Gale Research Inc.
835 Penobscot Bldg.
Detroit, MI 48226
Ph: (313)961-2242   Fr: 800-877-GALE
1994.

AWARDS, SCHOLARSHIPS, GRANTS, AND FELLOWSHIPS

★363★ AASA and Convention Exhibitors Scholarships
American Association of School Administrators (AASA)
1801 North Moore St.
Arlington, VA 22209
Ph: (703)528-0700
Purpose: To encourage and support outstanding graduate students who intend to pursue careers in public school administration. Qualifications: Applicant must be a graduate student in the field of school administration enrolled at a U.S. or Canadian institution. Candidate must intend to pursue the public school superintendency as a career. Candidate must be nominated by the dean of the department. Funds available: $2,000. Application details: Write for nomination guidelines. Deadline: 1 May.

★364★ AASL Distinguished School Administrators Award
American Library Association
American Association of School Librarians
50 E. Huron St.
Chicago, IL 60611
Ph: (312)944-6780   Fax: (312)440-9374
To recognize school administrators for developing an exemplary school library media program and for having made an outstanding and sustained contribution to advancing the role of the school library media center as an agency for the improvement of education. State, county, or district school superintendents and building principals currently in administrative office and directly responsible for a school or group of schools at any level are eligible. District administrators responsible for broad instructional leadership such as assistant superintendents, directors of curriculum and instruction, and directors of elementary and/or secondary education are also eligible. The deadline is December 1. A monetary award of $2,000 and a plaque are awarded annually at the ALA conference. Established in 1968. Sponsored by Social Issues Resources Series.

★365★ ACE Fellows Program
American Council on Education (ACE)
1 Dupont Circle
Washington, DC 20036-1193
Ph: (202)939-9420
Purpose: To enable college and university administrators to acquire more sophisticated knowledge of funding, planning, budgeting, personnel management, and legal strategies. Qualifications: Nominees must have a minimum of five years of college-level experience as faculty members or as administrators and must have a record of leadership accomplishments. Selection criteria: Candidates are nominated by their institution's chief executive or chief academic officer. After an initial screening of candidates' credentials by a committee of higher education leaders, finalists are interviewed and approximately 30 fellows are selected by a panel of presidents and senior officers in higher education. Funds available: The nominating institution continues to pay the fellow's full salary and benefits during the fellowship year. The institution hosting a fellow is responsible for providing funds to cover the fellow's travel and meeting attendance costs, which amount to approximately $10,000. The institution providing the internship experience is also responsible for a $2,500 placement fee payable to ACE. Several grants are available on a competitive basis to nominating institutions that are ACE members and release their fellows for an off-campus fellowship. The grants range between $9,000 and $12,000 and are intended to help offset the institution's expense in replacing the fellow. Institutions that are not ACE members may nominate a candidate, but must pay an additional fee if the candidate is selected as a fellow. Application details: Nominations and candidates' application materials are sent to presidents and chief academic officers of all accredited institutions during the summer. Deadline: November 1. Finalists are selected and notified by January 15. Finalists are interviewed in Washington, DC, in late January and early February. Approximately 30 ACE Fellows are selected and notified of their appointment by March 1.

★366★ American Education Award
American Association of School Administrators
1801 N. Moore St.
Arlington, VA 22209
Ph: (703)528-0700
To recognize an American citizen who has achieved a distinguished career in his or her profession by serving as a role model to others. Awarded at the annual convention. Established in 1928 by the National School Supply and Equipment Association. Additional information is available from Rena Barnes.

★367★ Jack A. Culbertson Award
University Council for Educational Administration
212 Rackley Bldg.
University Park, PA 16802-3200
Ph: (602)965-6690   Fax: (814)863-7532
To recognize individuals for accomplishments in the early years of their professional careers in educational administration. The contribution can be in the form of an innovation in training, a published book, instructional materials produced, a new course or program developed, a completed research project, and/or other related products. Individuals are judged for innovativeness, originality, ability to generalize, potential impact, relation to UCEA goals, significance with respect to the training mission at the individual's institution, degree of effort required to produce the con-

tribution, and extent of support for the effort provided by the candidate's employing institution. Young or beginning professors from member universities may be nominated by April 1. A monetary award and a plaque are presented annually at the Plenary Session Representatives meeting in October. Established in 1983 in honor of Jack A. Culbertson, UCEA's first full-time Executive Director.

★368★ Exemplary Preparation Award
American Association of School
    Administrators
1801 N. Moore St.
Arlington, VA 22209
Ph: (703)528-0700

To recognize institutions of higher education for exemplary programs for the preparation of school administrators. Awarded when merited at the annual convention awards banquet. Sponsored by the Higher Education Committee. Additional information is available from Linda Klopfenstein, (703) 875-0707.

★369★ James R. Kirkpatrick Memorial Award
American Association of School
    Administrators
1801 N. Moore St.
Arlington, VA 22209
Ph: (703)528-0700

To recognize an educator who has demonstrated outstanding lobbying efforts on behalf of quality education. Candidates are nominated by their state executives, and the winner is chosen by the Federal Policy and Legislation Committee. A plaque is awarded annually at the "I Care" legislative conference.

★370★ Leadership Award
National Council of Administrative Women
    in Education
c/o Dr. Jill Berman
476 12th St., No. 11215
Brooklyn, NY 11215
Ph: (718)499-1593   Fax: (718)919-0781

For recognition of outstanding research pertaining to women in educational administration or to the development of leadership skills. Application must be submitted by December 30. A monetary award and transportation to the national conference are awarded biennially. Established in 1984.

★371★ Leadership for Learning Award
American Association of School
    Administrators
1801 N. Moore St.
Arlington, VA 22209
Ph: (703)528-0700

To recognize outstanding administrative leadership leading to improved learning by students. Superintendents who have served in their present districts or institutions for at least five years are eligible. A Steuben glass creation is presented to the honoree; and a monetary award of $2,000 is presented to his school district. Awarded annually. Established in 1984. Additional information is available from Linda Klopfenstein, (703) 875-0707.

★372★ Harold W. McGraw, Jr. Prize in Education
McGraw-Hill
1221 Avenue of the Americas
New York, NY 10020
Ph: (212)512-3493   Fax: (212)512-3050

To recognize individuals who have made significant contributions to the advancement of knowledge through education. The prize honors individuals whose accomplishments are making a difference today, and whose programs and ideas can serve as effective models for the education of future generations of Americans. Only individuals who are presently committed to the cause of education are eligible. Institutions, boards, organizations and other groups are not. Nominees need not be professional educators, nor is eligibility limited to traditional educational achievement. Individuals may be nominated in the areas of teaching, administration, policy planning, business, government, publishing and adult education. Each year, a Nominating Committee, consisting of leaders in the educational community across the country, submit nominations to the Board of Judges. In addition, the Board of Judges considers nominations received directly, if they meet eligibility requirements, and include references from the educational community. The deadline is July 1. The following criteria are used for consideration: (1) Prize winners must have made a significant impact in their fields relating to the advancement of knowledge through education; (2) Prize winners must have displayed a sense of innovation in attempting to creatively change, improve, enhance or further a specific area of education; (3) Individuals may be nominated for lifetime achievement; (4) Winners from teaching, administration or policy planning must have instituted or enhanced curriculums, developed exceptional programs, changed or improved policy; and (5) Winners from the business sector must display a sense of commitment beyond financial contributions, and must have taken a significant leadership role in furthering a specific aspect of education. Up to three monetary prizes of $25,000 each are awarded annually. Established in 1988 in honor of the Centennial celebration of McGraw-Hill and Harold W. McGraw, Jr., chairman emeritus, McGraw Hill, Inc.

★373★ National Academy for School Executives Internships
American Association of School
    Administrators (AASA)
1801 North Moore St.
Arlington, VA 22209
Ph: (703)528-0700

Purpose: To provide professional development opportunities to school administrators. Qualifications: Applicant must be a U.S. or Canadian resident. Candidate must be a practicing school administrator, or have equivalent administrative credentials. Interns work as executive assistants for the National Academy for School Executives in Washington, D.C. Interns learn through on-the-job responsibilities and extensive travel throughout the United States. Participation in the annual convention is also required. Funds available: $25,000 stipend, plus $1,500 relocation allowance. Application details: Write to AASA

for application guidelines, specifying interest in the internship program. Deadline: 15 April.

★374★ Salmon Memorial Lecture
American Association of School
    Administrators
1801 N. Moore St.
Arlington, VA 22209
Ph: (703)528-0700

To recognize an outstanding lecturer in the field of educational administration. Nominations may be submitted by June 15. The recipient of this honor speaks at the annual convention and also receives an honorarium, travel expenses, and one night's lodging at the convention. Additional information is available from M. Don Thomas, Wasatch Education Systems, 1214 Wilmington Ave., Salt Lake City, UT 84106, (801) 532-5340.

★375★ Signature of Excellence Award
National University Continuing Education
    Association
1 Dupont Circle, NW, Ste. 615
Washington, DC 20036
Ph: (202)659-3130   Fax: (202)785-0374

To recognize a chief executive officer of a higher education institution who has demonstrated exemplary service to the field of continuing higher education. Service may include leadership concerning federal legislation, a major research project, or policies in higher education. Awarded when merited. Established in 1985.

★376★ The Washington Post Distinguished Educational Leadership Awards
The Washington Post Company
    Educational Foundation
1150 15th St. NW
Washington, DC 20071
Ph: (202)334-6834   Fax: (202)334-5609

To recognize a vital member of the educational system - the school principal. The program honors 18 principals in the metropolitan Washington area who go beyond the day-to-day demands of the position to create an exceptional educational environment. Awarded annually. Established in 1986.

BASIC REFERENCE GUIDES AND HANDBOOKS

★377★ *The Business-Education Partnership*
International Information Associates, Inc.
PO Box 773
Morrisville, PA 19067-0773
Ph: (215)493-9214   Fax: (215)493-9421
Arthur G. Sharp, editor. 1992.

★378★ *The Elementary Principal's Handbook: A Guide to Effective Action*
Prentice-Hall, Inc.
Rte. 9W
Englewood Cliffs, NJ 07632
Ph: (201)592-2000   Fr: 800-223-1360
L. Hughes and G. Ubben. Fourth edition, 1994. Presents the principal's role in the development of an effective school program.

Covers pupil relations, facilities management, and financial management.

★379★ Encyclopedia of School Administration and Supervision
Oryx Press
2214 N. Central Ave.
Phoenix, AZ 85004-1483
Ph: (602)254-6156   Fr: 800-457-6799
Richard A. Gorton, Gail T. Schneider, and James C. Fisher, editors. 1988. Contains articles about current issues of concern to today's school administrators. Defines educational terminology. Reports research on a wide variety of topics.

★380★ The International Encyclopedia of Higher Education
Jossey-Bass, Inc., Publishers
350 Samsone
San Francisco, CA 94104
Ph: (415)433-1767
Asa S. Knowles, editor in chief. 1977. Ten-volume set covering national systems of higher education; includes reports on higher education.

PROFESSIONAL AND TRADE PERIODICALS

★381★ AAHE Bulletin
American Association for Higher Education (AAHE)
1 Dupont Circle, Ste. 360
Washington, DC 20036
Ph: (202)293-6440   Fax: (202)462-7326
Bry Pollack
Monthly. Discusses effectiveness in higher education. Focuses on academic affairs, employment, public policy, teaching methods, technology, and assessment. Recurring features include interviews, news of research, and practical articles.

★382★ Academic Leader
Magna Publications, Inc.
2718 Dryden Dr.
Madison, WI 53704
Ph: (608)249-2455
Doris Green
Monthly. Presents news and information of concern to academic deans and chairpersons. Covers aspects of educational administration such as budgeting and personnel. Carries information on using leadership skills to improve the performance of the individual faculty and staff members, as well as the department as a whole. Recurring features include reports on conferences and trends in education.

★383★ AFSA News
American Federation of School Administrators (AFSA)
1729 21st St. NW
Washington, DC 20009
Ph: (202)986-4209   Fax: (202)986-4211
Kelly A. Griffin
Monthly. Covers issues of concern to school administrators and supervisors.

★384★ American Association of School Administrators—Leadership News
American Association of School Administrators
Communications Department
1801 N. Moore St.
Arlington, VA 22209
Ph: (703)528-0700   Fax: (703)528-2146
Natalie Carter Holmes
Semiannual. Publishes news, information, and opinion relating to education and school administration. Recurring features include letters to the editor, interviews, news of research, reports of meetings, job listings, notices of publications available.

★385★ American Educator
American Federation of Teachers
555 New Jersey Ave. NW
Washington, DC 20001
Ph: (202)879-4430
Liz McPike
Quarterly. Magazine on education.

★386★ American School & University
North American Publishing Co.
401 N. Broad St.
Philadelphia, PA 19108
Ph: (215)238-5300   Fax: (215)238-5457
Joseph Agron
Monthly. Trade magazine.

★387★ The Department Chair
Anker Publishing Company
PO Box 249
Bolton, MA 01740
James D. Anker
Quarterly. Provides information on faculty recruiting and status, salaries and tenure, enrollment, politics, economic aspects, training and development, and sexual harassment.

★388★ The Developer
National Staff Development Council
PO Box 240
Oxford, OH 45056
Ph: (513)523-6029   Fax: (513)523-0638
Concerned with staff development programs for teachers and other educational personnel. Discusses effective staff development programs, news models of staff development, theories of adult learning, and planning and funding district-based staff development programs. Recurring features include news of research and reports of Council activities.

★389★ Educational Leadership
Assn. for Supervision and Curriculum Development
1250 N. Pitt St.
Alexandria, VA 22314-1453
Ph: (703)549-9110   Fax: (703)549-3891
Ronald S. Brandt
Magazine on curriculum, instruction, supervision, and leadership in schools.

★390★ Holmes Group—Forum
Holmes Group
501 Erickson Hall
Michigan State University
East Lansing, MI 48824-1034
Ph: (517)353-3874
Kathleen Devaney
Quarterly. Provides information on the national, regional, and local activities of the Holmes Group—a nonprofit corporation of research universities committed to the improvement of the preparation of educators.

★391★ International Journal of Educational Reform
Technomic Publishing Co., Inc.
851 New Holland Ave.
PO Box 3535
Lancaster, PA 17604
Ph: (717)291-5609   Fax: (717)295-4538
Fr: 800-233-9936
Fenwick W. English
Quarterly. Journal acting as the roundtable of educational reform worldwide.

★392★ Journal of Higher Education
Ohio State University Press
1070 Carmack Rd.
Columbus, OH 43210
Ph: (614)292-6930   Fax: (614)292-2065
Robert J. Silverman
Bimonthly. Scholarly journal on the institution of higher education. Articles combine disciplinary methods with critical insight to investigate issues important to faculty, administrators, and program managers.

★393★ NASPA Forum
National Association of Student Personnel Administrators, Inc. (NASPA)
1875 Connecticut Ave. NW
Washington, DC 20009
Ph: (202)265-7500
Sybil Walker
Reports on Association activities and discusses topics related to student affairs. Covers subjects such as commuting students, college costs, minority students, the fraternity systems, and graduate and professional programs. Recurring features include conference reports and a calendar of events.

★394★ The Practitioner
National Association of Secondary School Principals (NASSP)
1904 Association Dr.
Reston, VA 22091
Ph: (703)860-0200   Fax: (703)476-5432
Patricia George
Quarterly. Focuses on topics of special concern to middle and high school principals. Called "a newsletter for the on-line administrator," emphasizing such management concerns as program-types, scheduling, curriculum, and innovations.

★395★ Principal
National Assn. of Elementary School Principals
1615 Duke St.
Alexandria, VA 22314-3483
Ph: (703)684-3345   Fax: (703)548-6021
Leon E. Greene
Magazines for NACSP members.

★396★ The School Administrator
American Assn. of School Administrators
1801 N. Moore St.
Arlington, VA 22209
Ph: (703)528-0700   Fax: (703)528-2146
Jay P. Goldman
Monthly. Magazine for superintendents and school leaders.

★397★ Schools in the Middle
National Association of Secondary School
Principals (NASSP)
1904 Association Dr.
Reston, VA 22091
Ph: (703)860-0200   Fax: (703)476-5432
Patricia George

Quarterly. Addresses issues of concern to teachers and administrators in middle level education (grades 7-9).

★398★ SMSG Newsletter
School Management Study Group (SMSG)
860 18th Ave.
Salt Lake City, UT 84103
Ph: (801)532-5340   Fax: (801)484-2089
Donald Thomas

Concerned with how education is affected by such issues as educational leadership, conflict management, personnel and program evaluation, school finance, federal legislation, and school law. Covers trends in educational governance, reform, and the improvement of school practices. Recurring features include book reviews and a column of resources and practical ideas.

★399★ Updating School Board Policies
National School Boards Association
1680 Duke St.
Alexandria, VA 22314
Ph: (703)838-6722   Fax: (703)683-7590
Karen Powe

Offers educational policy advice for school board members and administrators in various areas of school governance, including budgeting, financial management, teacher evaluation, negotiation, and curriculum development. Identifies trends, court decisions and changing legal requirements that affect a school system's policies and regulations. Recurring features include columns titled Court View, Trends, Tips 'n Techniques, and Policy Adviser (a question and answer column).

★400★ The Washington Update
Office of Government Relations
1801 N. Moore St.
Arlington, VA 22209
Ph: (703)528-0700
Nicholas Penning

Bimonthly. Reports and analyzes legislative, executive, and judicial activity in the areas of education and school management issues. Covers U.S. Department of Education, Supreme Court, congressional legislation, and proposed legislation that affects the school districts and superintendents.

PROFESSIONAL MEETINGS AND CONVENTIONS

★401★ American Adult and Continuing Education Conference
American Association for Adult and
Continuing Education
2101 Wilson Blvd., No. 925
Arlington, VA 22201-3062
Ph: (703)522-2234   Fax: (703)522-2250
Annual. Always held during November.
Dates and Locations: 1995 Nov; Kansas City, MO. • 1996 Nov; Charlotte, NC.

★402★ American Association of Bible Colleges Annual Meeting
American Association of Bible Colleges
Box 1523
Fayetteville, AR 72701
Ph: (501)521-8164   Fax: (501)521-9202
Annual.

★403★ American Association of Community and Junior Colleges Annual Convention
American Association of Community and
Junior Colleges
1 Dupont Circle, NW, Ste. 410
Washington, DC 20036-1176
Ph: (202)728-0200   Fax: (202)833-2467
Annual.

★404★ American Association of School Administrators Convention
American Association of School
Administrators (AASA)
1801 N. Moore St.
Arlington, VA 22209
Ph: (703)875-0748   Fax: (703)841-1543
Annual. **Dates and Locations:** 1999 Mar 08-11; San Diego, CA.

★405★ Association of Teacher Educators Annual Conference
Glencoe
15319 Chatsworth St.
Mission Hills, CA 91345
Ph: (818)898-1391
Annual. Always held during February. **Dates and Locations:** 1996 Feb.

★406★ NAFSA - Association of International Educators Annual Conference
NAFSA - Association of International
Educator
1875 Connecticut Ave. NW, Ste. 1000
Washington, DC 20009-5728
Ph: (202)462-4811   Fax: (202)667-3419
Annual.

★407★ National Association for the Education of Young Children Annual Conference
National Association for the Education of
Young Children
1509 16th St., NW
Washington, DC 20036
Ph: (202)232-8777   Fax: (202)328-1846
Annual. Usually held during November.

★408★ National Association of Elementary School Principals Convention and Exhibition
National Association of Elementary School
Principals
1615 Duke St.
Alexandria, VA 22314
Ph: (703)684-3345   Fax: (703)549-5298
Annual. Always held during March or April.
Dates and Locations: 1996 Mar 23-27; Washington, DC. • 1997 Apr 12-16; San Antonio, TX. • 1998 Mar 14-18; Orlando, FL. • 1999 Mar 24-01; San Francisco, CA.

★409★ National Association of Secondary School Principals Annual Convention
National Association of Secondary School
Principals
1904 Association Dr.
Reston, VA 22091
Ph: (703)860-0200   Fax: (703)476-5432
Fr: 800-253-7746
Biennial. **Dates and Locations:** 1996 Feb 23-27; San Francisco, CA. • 1997 Mar 07-11; Orlando, FL. • 1998 Feb 06-10; San Diego, CA.

★410★ Southwestern Federation of Administrative Disciplines Convention
Southwestern Federation of Administrative
Disciplines
2700 Bay Area Blvd.
Houston, TX 77058
Ph: (713)283-3122   Fax: (713)283-3951
Annual. Always held during March. **Dates and Locations:** 1996 Mar 05-09; Houston, TX. • 1997 Mar 11-15; New Orleans, LA. • 1998 Mar 03-07; Dallas, TX.

OTHER SOURCES OF INFORMATION

★411★ "Educational Administration" in Accounting to Zoology: Graduate Fields Defined (pp. 75-77)
Petersons Guides, Inc.
PO Box 2123
Princeton, NJ 08543-2123
Ph: (609)243-9111   Fax: (609)243-9150
Fr: 800-338-3282
Amy J. Goldstein, editor. Revised and updated, 1987. Discusses types of graduate programs and degrees, graduate research, applied work, employment prospects and trends.

★412★ "Educational Administrator" in 100 Best Jobs for the 1990s & Beyond
Dearborn Financial Publishing, Inc.
520 N. Dearborn St.
Chicago, IL 60610-4354
Ph: (312)836-4400   Fax: (312)836-1021
Fr: 800-621-9621
Carol Kleiman. 1992. Describes 100 jobs ranging from accountants to veterinarians. Each job profile includes such information as education, experience, and certification needed, salaries, and job search suggestions.

Employment Interviewers

Employment interviewers help jobs seekers find employment and help employers find qualified staff by acting as brokers who match jobs and applicants. Employment interviewers work largely in private personnel consultant firms or in state employment security offices.

Salaries

Private sector earnings vary, in part because the basis for compensation varies. For instance, workers in personnel consulting firms generally are paid on a commission basis while those in temporary help service companies receive a salary.

Employment interviewers in personnel consulting and temporary help services firms	$17,000-$25,000/year
Employment interviewers at state job centers	$13,000-$24,000/year

Employment Outlook

Growth rate until the year 2005: Average.

Employment Interviewers

CAREER GUIDES

★413★ Employment Firm Workers
Chronicle Guidance Publications, Inc.
66 Aurora St.
PO Box 1190
Moravia, NY 13118-1190
Ph: (315)497-0330   Fax: (315)497-3359
Fr: 800-622-7284
1993. Career brief describing the nature of the job, working conditions, hours and earnings, education and training, licensure, certification, unions, personal qualifications, social and psychological factors, location, employment outlook, entry methods, advancement, and related occupations.

★414★ Employment Interviewer
Careers, Inc.
PO Box 135
Largo, FL 34649-0135
Ph: (813)584-7333
1994. Two-page occupational summary card describing duties, working conditions, personal qualifications, training, earnings and hours, employment outlook, places of employment, related careers, and where to write for more information.

★415★ "Employment Interviewer" in Opportunities in Airline Careers (pp. 108-109)
National Textbook Co. (NTC)
VGM Career Books
4255 W. Touhy Ave.
Lincolnwood, IL 60646-1975
Ph: (708)679-5500   Fax: (708)679-2494
Fr: 800-323-4900
Adrian A. Paradis. 1987. Gives an overview of the airline industry including job opportunities and salaries. Describes careers in management, finance, sales, customer service and safety.

★416★ "Employment Interviewers" in Occupational Outlook Handbook
U.S. Government Printing Office
Superintendent of Documents
Washington, DC 20402
Ph: (202)512-1800   Fax: (202)512-2250
Biennial; latest edition, 1994-95. Encyclopedia of careers describing about 250 occupa-

tions and comprising about 85 percent of all jobs in the economy. Occupations that require lengthy education or training are given the most attention. Each occupation's profile describes what the worker does on the job, working conditions, education and training requirements, advancement possibilities, job outlook, earnings, and sources of additional information.

PROFESSIONAL ASSOCIATIONS

★417★ International Association of Personnel in Employment Security (IAPES)
1801 Louisville Rd.
Frankfort, KY 40601
Ph: (502)223-4459   Fax: (502)223-4127
Members: Officials and others engaged in job placement, unemployment compensation, and labor market information administration through municipal, state, provincial, and federal government employment agencies and unemployment compensation agencies. **Purpose:** Conducts workshops and research. Offers professional development program of study guides and tests. **Publications:** IAPES News, bimonthly. • International Association of Personnel in Employment Security—Proceedings, annual. • Workforce, quarterly.

★418★ National Association of Personnel Services (NAPS)
3133 Mt. Vernon Ave.
Alexandria, VA 22305
Ph: (703)684-0180   Fax: (703)684-0071
Members: Private employment and temporary service firms. **Purpose:** Compiles statistics on professional agency growth and development; conducts certification program and educational programs. Association is distinct from former name of National Personnel Consultants ** **Publications:** Inside NAPS, 10/year.

★419★ National Association of Temporary Services (NATS)
119 S. St. Asaph St.
Alexandria, VA 22314
Ph: (703)549-6287   Fax: (703)549-4808
Members: Companies supplying workers to other firms on a temporary basis. **Purpose:** Sponsors ten to 12 regional workshops and in-depth industry studies. **Publications:** Contemporary Times, quarterly. • National Association of Temporary Services—Membership Directory, annual. • NATS Managers Guide to Employment Law.

STANDARDS/CERTIFICATION AGENCIES

★420★ National Association of Personnel Consultants (NAPC)
3133 Mt. Vernon Ave.
Alexandria, VA 22305
Ph: (703)684-0180   Fax: (703)684-0071
Conducts certification program.

★421★ National Association of Personnel Services (NAPS)
3133 Mt. Vernon Ave.
Alexandria, VA 22305
Ph: (703)684-0180   Fax: (703)684-0071
Compiles statistics on professional agency growth and development; conducts certification program and educational programs.

TEST GUIDES

★422★ Career Examination Series: Employment Consultant (Testing)
National Learning Corp.
212 Michael Dr.
Syosset, NY 11791
Ph: (516)921-8888   Fax: (516)921-8743
Fr: 800-645-6337
Jack Rudman. A study guide for professionals and trainees in the field of employ-

ment interviewing. Includes a multiple-choice examination section; provides answers.

★423★ Career Examination Series: Employment Interviewer
National Learning Corp.
212 Michael Dr.
Syosset, NY 11791
Ph: (516)921-8888　　Fax: (516)921-8743
Fr: 800-645-6337

Jack Rudman. A study guide for professionals and trainees in the field of employment interviewing. Includes a multiple-choice examination section; provides answers.

★424★ Career Examination Series: Senior Employment Interviewer
National Learning Corp.
212 Michael Dr.
Syosset, NY 11791
Ph: (516)921-8888　　Fax: (516)921-8743
Fr: 800-645-6337

Jack Rudman. A study guide for professionals and trainees in the field of employment interviewing. Includes a multiple-choice examination section; provides answers.

★425★ Career Examination Series: Supervising Employment Consultant (Testing)
National Learning Corp.
212 Michael Dr.
Syosset, NY 11791
Ph: (516)921-8888　　Fax: (516)921-8743
Fr: 800-645-6337

Jack Rudman. A study guide for professionals and trainees in the field of employment interviewing. Includes a multiple-choice examination section; provides answers.

AWARDS, SCHOLARSHIPS, GRANTS, AND FELLOWSHIPS

★426★ Award of Merit
International Association of Personnel in Employment Security
1801 Louisville Rd.
Frankfort, KY 40601
Ph: (502)223-4459　　Fax: (502)223-4127

To recognize an individual and a group for outstanding service to the employment security profession, the Association, and the community. A chapter's nominee must be a current and have been a member during the year of activity. The deadline for nominations is March. A monetary award, a plaque, a desk plate, and travel expenses to the Convention are awarded to first place winners annually. Established in 1944.

★427★ Robert B. Irwin Award
National Industries for the Blind
524 Hamburg Tpke., CN 969
Wayne, NJ 07474
Ph: (201)595-9200　　Fax: (201)595-9122

To recognize an individual for significant contributions to an area related to sheltered workshop employment for blind persons. A plaque is awarded annually at the National Sales Meeting of The General Council of Workshops for the Blind. Established in 1953 in memory of Dr. Robert B. Irwin, who pioneered and led the way for creating employment opportunities for the blind.

★428★ Outstanding Local Veterans' Employment Representative
Disabled American Veterans
Natl. Service & Legislative Headquarters
807 Maine Ave. SW
Washington, DC 20024
Ph: (202)554-3501　　Fax: (202)554-3581

To recognize significant contributions made by local veterans' employment representatives to enhance employment and training opportunities for disabled veterans. Nominations are accepted. A large wood and bronze plaque and an all-expense paid trip to the DAV national convention are awarded annually. Established in 1973.

PROFESSIONAL AND TRADE PERIODICALS

★429★ College Placement Council— Spotlight
College Placement Council
62 Highland Ave.
Bethlehem, PA 18017
Ph: (215)868-1421　　Fax: (215)868-0208
Fr: 800-544-5272
Mimi Collins

Devoted to career planning and employment of college graduates. Recurring features include news of regulations and legislation, technological developments statistics, research, trends, publications, and events related to career development and employment.

★430★ Executive Recruiter News
Kennedy Publications
Templeton Rd.
Fitzwilliam, NH 03447
Ph: (603)585-3101　　Fax: (603)585-6401
Fr: 800-531-0007
David A. Lord

Monthly. Concerned with executive search. Contains news, commentary, and advice on how to manage a search practice. Recurring features include interviews, book reviews, reports of meetings, and columns titled Recruiters on the Move and Feedback.

★431★ Issues & Observations
Center for Creative Leadership
PO Box 26300
Greensboro, NC 27438-6300
Ph: (910)288-7210　　Fax: (910)288-3999
Martin Wilcox

Quarterly. Presents information on applied creativity, organizational psychology, executive development, leadership, and psychometrics. Recurring features include interviews, news of research, news of educational opportunities, and a column titled Inklings.

★432★ Personnel Manager's Letter
Bureau of Business Practice
24 Rope Ferry Rd.
Waterford, CT 06386
Ph: (203)442-4365
Jill Whitney, Contact

Semimonthly. Provides the Human Resources manager with how-to information. Topics include benefits, training, recruiting, termination, and compensation policies. Recurring features include interviews, news of research and columns titled You Be the Judge, Workplace News, and Our Readers Ask.

★433★ Recruiting Trends
Remy Publishing Company
350 W. Hubbard St., Ste. 440
Chicago, IL 60610
Ph: (312)464-0300　　Fax: (312)464-0166
Fr: 800-542-6670
Elizabeth M. Hintch

Monthly. Covers trends and practices in recruiting people for jobs in science, engineering, management, and hard-to-fill technical positions, including hourly and part-time work. Reports on successful techniques, new developments in interviewing and testing, and regulatory agencies and government requirements affecting employment.

OTHER SOURCES OF INFORMATION

★434★ "Employment Interviewer" in 100 Best Jobs for the 1990s & Beyond
Dearborn Financial Publishing, Inc.
520 N. Dearborn St.
Chicago, IL 60610-4354
Ph: (312)836-4400　　Fax: (312)836-1021
Fr: 800-621-9621

Carol Kleiman. 1992. Describes 100 jobs ranging from accountants to veterinarians. Each job profile includes such information as education, experience, and certification needed, salaries, and job search suggestions.

Engineering, Science, and Data Processing Managers

Engineering, science, and data processing managers plan, coordinate, and direct technical and scientific activities. They determine scientific and technical goals within broad outlines provided by top management and then supervise a staff of engineers, scientists, or data processing workers who perform the necessary technical tasks. For example, engineering managers supervise engineering activities in testing, production, operations, or maintenance, or plan and coordinate the design and development of machinery, products, systems, and processes. Natural science managers oversee activities in agricultural science, chemistry, biology, geology, or physics. They coordinate testing, quality control, and production activities in industrial plants. Electronic data processing managers review the work of systems analysts, computer programmers, and computer operators, or coordinate computer operations and software development.

Salaries

Salaries for engineering, science, and data processing managers vary by specialty and level of management. Salaries are as follows:

Engineering and science managers	$50,000-$100,000/year
Data processing managers	$35,000-$80,000/year

Employment Outlook

Growth rate until the year 2005: Faster than the average.

Engineering, Science, and Data Processing Managers

CAREER GUIDES

★435★ Career Management for Engineers: Forty Essays on the Relationship Between You, Your Employer, and Your Profession
Vantage Press, Inc.
516 W. 34 St.
New York, NY 10001
Ph: (212)736-1767
Robert B. Herden, author. 1988. This "how-to-succeed" guide for engineers explores entry-level career opportunities for new graduates, and offers advice on succeeding and advancing on the job. Includes suggestions on mentoring, dress, writing skills, supervision, finance, team work, career mistakes, communicating, and how to chair a meeting.

★436★ "Career Profile: Interview With a Systems Manager" in Exploring Careers in the Computer Field
Rosen Publishing Group
29 E. 21st St.
New York, NY 10010
Ph: (212)777-3017   Fax: (212)777-0277
Fr: 800-237-9932
Joseph Weintraub, author. 1993. Surveys the newest growth areas in the computer industry including artificial intelligence, desktop publishing, and personal computers. Discusses entry into the field, salaries, future trends, and offers job search advice. Contains interviews with five people who describe their real-life experiences working in computer related jobs. Lists organizations and colleges.

★437★ Careers for Computer Buffs and Other Technological Types
National Textbook Co. (NTC)
VGM Career Books
4255 W. Touhy Ave.
Lincolnwood, IL 60646-1975
Ph: (708)679-5500   Fax: (708)679-2494
Fr: 800-323-4900
Marjorie Eberts and Margaret Gisler, editors. 1993. Career manual for those interested in computers and other technological fields.

★438★ Careers in Science
National Textbook Co. (NTC)
VGM Career Books
4255 W. Touhy Ave.
Lincolnwood, IL 60646-1975
Ph: (708)679-5500   Fax: (708)679-2494
Fr: 800-323-4900

Thomas A. Easton, editor. Explores careers in life science, physical science, social science, earth science, engineering, mathematics, and computer science.

★439★ "Computer Database Manager" in Career Information Center (Vol.1)
Simon and Schuster
200 Old Tappan Rd.
Old Tappan, NJ 07675
Fax: 800-445-6991   Fr: 800-223-2348

Richard Lidz and Dale Anderson, editorial directors. Fifth edition, 1993. For 600 occupations, this 13 volume set describes job duties, entry-level requirements, education and training needed, advancement possibilities, employment outlook, and earnings and benfits. Each of the first 12 volumes includes jobs related under a broad career field; volume 1 covers administration, business, and office. Volume 13 is the index.

★440★ "Computer and Information Services" in Where the Jobs Are: The Hottest Careers for the 90s (pp. 77-96)
Career Press
180 5th Ave.
Hawthorne, NJ 07507
Ph: (201)427-0229   Fax: (201)427-2037
Fr: 800-CAREER-1

Joyce Hadley. 1995. Offers a job-hunting strategy for the 1990s as well as descriptions of growing careers of the decade. Each profile includes general information, forecasts, growth, education and training, licensing requirements, and salary information.

★441★ "Computing or Information Center Operations" in Opportunities in Computer Science Careers (pp. 32-33)
National Textbook Co. (NTC)
VGM Career Books
4255 W. Touhy Ave.
Lincolnwood, IL 60646-1975
Ph: (708)679-5500   Fax: (708)679-2494
Fr: 800-323-4900

Julie Lepick Kling, author. 1991. Surveys careers in the computer field (programming, software development, hardware, research, and technical writing). Profiles five people working in the field. Separate chapters discuss educational preparation and employment outlook. An appendix contains salary information.

★442★ Data Base Managers
Chronicle Guidance Publications, Inc.
66 Aurora St.
PO Box 1190
Moravia, NY 13118-1190
Ph: (315)497-0330   Fax: (315)497-3359
Fr: 800-622-7284

1991. Pamphlet describes the nature of the job, working conditions, hours and earnings, education and training, licensure, certification, unions, personal qualifications, social and psychological factors, location, employment outlook, entry methods, advancement, and related occupations.

★443★ "Data Base Managers" in Career Discovery Encyclopedia (Vol.2, pp. 80-81)
J.G. Ferguson Publishing Co.
200 W. Madison St., Ste. 300
Chicago, IL 60606
Ph: (312)580-5480   Fax: (312)580-4948
Russell E. Primm, editor-in-chief. This six volume set contains two-page articles for 504 occupations. Each article describes job duties, earnings, and educational and training requirements. The whole set is arranged alphabetically by job title. Written for junior high and older students.

★444★ "Data Base Managers" in
Encyclopedia of Careers and
Vocational Guidance (Vol.2, pp. 427-430)
J.G. Ferguson Publishing Co.
200 W. Madison St., Ste. 300
Chicago, IL 60606
Ph: (312)580-5480   Fax: (312)580-4948
William E. Hopke, editor-in-chief. Ninth edition, 1993. This four-volume set describes 74 industries and 900 occupations. The occupational profiles cover the nature of the work, educational requirements, history, methods of entry, advancement, employment outlook, earnings, working conditions, social and psychological factors, and sources of further information.

★445★ *Data Processing Manager*
Careers, Inc.
PO Box 135
Largo, FL 34649-0135
Ph: (813)584-7333
1995. Two-page occupational summary card describing duties, working conditions, personal qualifications, training, earnings and hours, employment outlook, places of employment, related careers, and where to write for more information.

★446★ "Data Processing Manager" in
Career Information Center (Vol.1)
Simon and Schuster
200 Old Tappan Rd.
Old Tappan, NJ 07675
Fax: 800-445-6991   Fr: 800-223-2348
Richard Lidz and Dale Anderson, editorial directors. Fifth edition, 1993. For 600 occupations, this 13 volume set describes job duties, entry-level requirements, education and training needed, advancement possiblities, employment outlook, earnings, and benefits. Each of the first 12 volumes includes job related under a broad career field; volume 1 covers business, administration, and office. Volume 13 is an index.

★447★ "Data Processing Manager" in
Occu-Facts: Information on 580
Careers in Outline Form
Careers, Inc.
PO Box 135
Largo, FL 34649-0135
Ph: (813)584-7333
Biennial, 1995-96 edition. Each one-page occupational profile describes duties, working conditions, physical surroundings and demands, aptitudes, temperament, educational requirement, employment outlook, earnings, and places of employment.

★448★ "Database Administrator" in
Careers in High Tech: Exciting Jobs in
Today's Fastest-Growing Fields (pp. 50-51)
Prentice Hall, Inc.
200 Old Tappan Rd.
Old Tappan, NJ 07675
Ph: (201)767-5000
Connie Winkler, author. 1987. Surveys career opportunities in data processing, technology, personal computers, telecommunications, manufacturing technology, artificial intelligence, computer graphics, biotechnology, lasers, technical writing, and publishing. There is a chapter on educational prepartion.

Appendies include associations, periodicals, and a bibliography.

★449★ "Database Administrator" in
Complete Computer Career Guide (pp. 32-34)
Tab/McGraw-Hill
Blue Ridge Summit, PA 17294-0850
Ph: (717)794-2191
Judith Norback, author. 1987. This guide offers career planning tips and describes the educational preparation needed, employment outlook, industry certification. Offers job search advice. There is a separate section on opportunities for women and minorities.

★450★ "Database Administrator" in
Opportunities in High Tech Careers (pp. 104-105)
National Textbook Co. (NTC)
VGM Career Books
4255 W. Touhy Ave.
Lincolnwood, IL 60646-1975
Ph: (708)679-5500   Fax: (708)679-2494
Fr: 800-323-4900
Gary D. Golter, author. 1987. Explores high technology careers and describes opportunities, qualifications, educational preparation, and suggests job search strategies.

★451★ "Engineering Management" in
Accounting to Zoology: Graduate
Fields Defined (pp. 369-370)
Petersons Guides, Inc.
PO Box 2123
Princeton, NJ 08543-2123
Ph: (609)243-9111   Fax: (609)243-9150
Fr: 800-338-3282
Amy J. Goldstein, editor. 1987. Comprehensive volume defines graduate and professional fields in health sciences; physical sciences and mathematics; and engineering and applied sciencs.

★452★ "Engineering Management" in
Opportunities in Civil Engineering (pp. 87-89)
National Textbook Co. (NTC)
VGM Career Books
4255 W. Touhy Ave.
Lincolnwood, IL 60646-1975
Ph: (708)679-5500   Fax: (708)679-2494
Fr: 800-323-4900
Joseph D. Hagerty, author. 1987. Describes the scope of, educational preparation, specialities, job duties, salaries, working conditions, and employment and advancement possibilities for civil engineers. Lists professional organizations.

★453★ "Engineering and Operations
Manager" in *Careers in High Tech* (pp. 104-105)
Arco Publishing Co.
Macmillan General Reference
15 Columbus Cir.
New York, NY 10023
Fax: 800-835-3202   Fr: 800-858-7674
Connine Winkler, author. 1987. Surveys career opportunities in data processing, technology, personal computers, telecommunications, manufacturing technology, artificial intelligence, computer graphics, biotechnology, lasers, technical writing, and publishing. There is a chapter on educational preparation. Appendices include associations, periodicals, and a biliography.

★454★ "Engineering and Plant
Maintenance Superintendent" in *BLR*
Encyclopedia of Prewritten Job
Descriptions
Business and Legal Reports, Inc.
39 Academy St.
Madison, CT 06443-1513
Ph: (203)245-7448
Stephen D. Bruce, Editor-in-Chief. 1994. This book contains hundreds of sample job descriptions arranged by functional job category. The 1-3 page job descriptions cover what the worker normally does in that position, who they report to, and how that position fits in the organizational struture.

★455★ "Engineering, Science and Data
Processing Manager" in *Occupational*
Outlook Handbook
U.S. Government Printing Office
Superintendent of Documents
Washington, DC 20402
Ph: (202)512-1800   Fax: (202)512-2250
Biennial. 1994-95. This encyclopedia of careers describes in detail 250 occupations—comprising about 85 percent of all jobs in the economy. Occupations that require lengthy education or training are given the most attention. For each occupation, the handbook covers job duties, working conditions, training, educational preparation, personal qualities, advancement possibilities, job outlook, earnings, and sources of additional information.

★456★ "Engineering, Science, and Data
Processing Managers" in *America's 50*
Fastest Growing Jobs (pp. 15)
JIST Works, Inc.
720 N. Park Ave.
Indianapolis, IN 46202-3431
Ph: (317)264-3720   Fax: (317)264-3709
Fr: 800-648-5478
Michael J. Farr, compiler. 1994. Describes the 50 fastest growing jobs within major career clusters such as technicians, and marketing and sales. Each job profile explains the nature of the work, skills and abilities required, employment outlook, average earnings, related occupations, education and training requirements, and employment opportunities. Also contains career planning information and job search tips.

★457★ *Get the Best Jobs in DP: The*
Computer Professional's Technical
Interview Guide
Mind Management
24304 100 Ave. W.
PO Box 998
Edmonds, WA 98020
David Krause, author. 1989. Supplies written interview checklist, model letters and resumes, applications, professional references, and forms to organize applicant and company information. Includes sample screening, management, and four technical interviews.

★458★ "Industrial/Management Engineering" in *Accounting to Zoology: Graduate Fields Defined* **(pp. 349-350)**
Petersons Guides, Inc.
PO Box 2123
Princeton, NJ 08543-2123
Ph: (609)243-9111   Fax: (609)243-9150
Fr: 800-338-3282
Amy J. Goldstein. 1987. Comprehensive volume defines graduate and professional fields in health sciences; physical sciences and mathematics; and engineering and applied sciences. Includes an alphabetical index.

★459★ *Making It Big in Data Processing: A Total Program for Success Based on Over 35 Years of Experience With Data Processing Professionals*
Crown Publishers, Inc.
201 E. 50th St.
New York, NY 10002
Ph: (212)254-1600   Fr: 800-726-0600
Robert Half. 1987. Written for the person planning to use a data processing job as a springboard to a career. Includes advice on educational preparation, job hunting, succeeding on the job, and moving into a supervisory position.

★460★ *Opportunities in Data Processing Careers*
National Textbook Co. (NTC)
VGM Career Books
4255 W. Toughy Ave.
Lincolnwood, IL 60646-1975
Ph: (708)679-5500   Fax: (708)679-2494
Fr: 800-323-4900
Norman N. Noerper.

★461★ "Positions in Management" in *Opportunities in Computer Science Careers* **(pp. 49-53)**
National Textbook Co. (NTC)
VGM Career Books
4255 W. Touhy Ave.
Lincolnwood, IL 60646-1975
Ph: (708)679-5500   Fax: (708)679-2494
Fr: 800-323-4900
Julie Lepick Kling, author. 1991. Provides an overview of the history and development of data processing careers. For each job included, describes responsibilities, salary, and job outlook. Contains separate chapters on educational preparation and job hunting. Lists professional organizations, publications, and schools.

PROFESSIONAL ASSOCIATIONS

★462★ American Society for Engineering Management (ASEM)
PO Box 867
Annapolis, MD 21401
Ph: (410)263-7065   Fr: 800-728-7065
Members: Persons with management experience in engineering, production, technical marketing, or related activities, or who hold a degree in engineering management. **Purpose:** Seeks to advance engineering computer science in theory and practice; to pro-

mote development of the profession; and to maintain high professional standards. Provides forum for professional contact and discussion; operates speakers' bureau; conducts educational and research programs. **Publications:** *Engineering Management Journal*, quarterly.

★463★ Data Processing Management Association (DPMA)
505 Busse Hwy.
Park Ridge, IL 60068
Ph: (708)825-8124   Fax: (708)825-1693
Members: Managerial personnel, staff, educators, and individuals interested in the management of information resources. **Purpose:** Founder of the Certificate in Data Processing examination program, now administered by an intersociety organization. Maintains Legislative Communications Network. Professional education programs include EDP-oriented business and management principles self-study courses and a series of videotaped management development seminars. Sponsors student organizations around the country interested in data processing and encourages members to serve as counselors for the Scout computer merit badge. Conducts research projects, including a business information systems curriculum for two- and four-year colleges. **Publications:** *Industry Structure Model, A Framework for Career Development for IS Professionals.* • *Information Systems, The DPMA Model Corriculum for a Four-Year Undergraduate Degree for the 1990's.* • *Inside DPMA*, monthly.

★464★ IEEE Engineering Management Society (EMS)
c/o Institute of Electrical and Electronics Engineers
345 E. 47th St.
New York, NY 10017
Ph: (212)705-7900   Fax: (212)705-4929
Members: A society of the Institute of Electrical and Electronics Engineers. **Purpose:** Gathers and disseminates information concerning management science as applied to all aspects of the production and operation of electronic components and systems. Studies socioeconomic implications of emerging electronic technologies. Sponsors book series for IEEE; operates speakers' bureau; compiles statistics; bestows Engineering Manager of the Year Award and IEEE Engineering Recognition Award. **Publications:** *Engineering Management Review*, quarterly. • *Transactions on Engineering Management*, quarterly.

★465★ Information Systems Audit and Control Association (ISACA)
3701 Algonquin Rd., Ste. 1010
Rolling Meadows, IL 60008
Ph: (708)253-1545   Fax: (708)253-1443
Members: Dedicated to the establishment of standards and systems of control designed to effectively organize and utilize data processing resources. **Purpose:** Aids auditors, managers, and systems specialists in addressing problems related to controls in data processing systems. Offers Certified Information Systems Auditor Professional Designation Program. Administers the Information Systems Audit & Control Foundation, which sponsors research in the field. **Publications:** *Control*

Objectives, periodic. • *Global Communique.* • *I.S. Audit and Control Journal*, bimonthly.

★466★ Reliability Engineering and Management Institute (REMI)
7340 N. La Oesta Ave.
Tucson, AZ 85704
Ph: (602)297-2679   Fax: (602)621-8191
Members: Purpose: Publicizes all aspects, particularly implementation and management, of reliability, availability, maintainability, testing, and mechanical reliability engineering. Holds seminars for professional training. **Publications:** *Proceedings of the Reliability Engineering and Management Institute*, annual. • *REMI Proceedings*, annual.

STANDARDS/CERTIFICATION AGENCIES

★467★ Data Processing Management Association (DPMA)
505 Busse Hwy.
Park Ridge, IL 60068
Ph: (708)825-8124   Fax: (708)825-1693
Founder of the Certificate in Data Processing examination program, now administered by an intersociety organization. Maintains Legislative Communications Network. Professional education programs include EDP-oriented business and management principles self-study courses and a series of videotaped management development seminars.

TEST GUIDES

★468★ *Career Examination Series: Data Processing Operations Supervisor*
National Learning Corp.
212 Michael Dr.
Syosset, NY 11791
Ph: (516)921-8888   Fax: (516)921-8743
Fr: 800-645-6337
Jack Rudman. A series of study guides with multiple-choice examination questions and solutions for trainees and professionals in data processing. A titles in the series includes *Data Processing Operations Coordinator*.

★469★ *Career Examination Series: Director of Data Processing*
National Learning Corp.
212 Michael Dr.
Syosset, NY 11791
Ph: (516)921-8888   Fax: (516)921-8743
Fr: 800-645-6337
Jack Rudman. 1993. Test guide including questions and answers for students or professionals in the field who seek advancement through examination.

★470★ Career Examination Series: Director of Engineering, Building and Housing
National Learning Corp.
212 Michael Dr.
Syosset, NY 11791
Ph: (516)921-8888   Fax: (516)921-8743
Fr: 800-645-6337
Jack Rudman. 1993. Test guide including questions and answers for students or professionals in the field who seek advancement through examination.

★471★ Career Examination Series: Engineering Inspector
National Learning Corp.
212 Michael Dr.
Syosset, NY 11791
Ph: (516)921-8888   Fax: (516)921-8743
Fr: 800-645-6337
Jack Rudman. A study guide for professionals and trainees in the field of engineering inspection. Includes a multiple-choice examination section; provides answers.

EDUCATIONAL DIRECTORIES AND PROGRAMS

★472★ Computing and Software Design Career Directory
Gale Research Inc.
835 Penobscot Bldg.
Detroit, MI 48226-4094
Ph: (313)961-2242   Fax: (313)961-6083
Fr: 800-877-GALE
Bradley J. Morgan and Joseph M. Palmisano. 1993. A directory in the Career Advisor Series that provides essays written by industry professionals; job search information on resume and cover letter preparation, networking, and the interviewing process; approximately 300 companies and organizations offering job opportunities and internships, and additional job-hunting resources.

AWARDS, SCHOLARSHIPS, GRANTS, AND FELLOWSHIPS

★473★ Glenn Seaborg Award
International Platform Association
PO Box 250
Winnetka, IL 60093
Ph: (312)446-4321
To recognize an individual who has done the most to increase the public's interest in science. An engraved silver bowl is awarded annually. Established in 1979 to honor Glenn Seaborg, the American chemist.

BASIC REFERENCE GUIDES AND HANDBOOKS

★474★ Computer Security Test Manual
Van Nostrand Reinhold
115 5th Ave.
New York, NY 10013
Philip Fites and Martin P. J. Kratz. 1993.

★475★ Electrical Power Engineering
McGraw-Hill Inc.
11 W. 19 St.
New York, NY 10011
Ph: 800-722-4726
Henslay William Kabisama. 1993.

★476★ Engineering Project Management
Marcel Dekker, Inc.
270 Madison Ave.
New York, NY 10016
Ph: (212)696-9000
Blanchard. 1990.

★477★ Management of Innovation & Change
John Wiley and Sons, Inc.
605 3rd Ave.
New York, NY 10158-0012
Ph: (212)850-6000   Fax: (212)850-6088
Fr: 800-526-5368
Sankar. 1991.

★478★ Standard Handbook for Electrical Engineers
McGraw-Hill, Inc.
1221 Avenue of the Americas
New York, NY 10020
Ph: (212)512-2000   Fr: 800-722-4726
Donald G. Fink and H. Wayne Beaty, editors. Thirteenth edition, 1993. Covers new developments, and the generation, transmission, distribution, control, conservation, and application of electrical power. Lists current standards governing the electrical engineering field.

PROFESSIONAL AND TRADE PERIODICALS

★479★ The Bridge
National Academy of Engineering
2101 Constitution Ave. NW
Washington, DC 20418
Ph: (202)334-1562   Fax: (202)334-1595
Douglas L. Wolford
Quarterly. Publishes authored articles and information on programs and general activities of the Academy.

★480★ COM-AND: Computer Audit News and Developments
Management Advisory Publications
PO Box 81151
Wellesley Hills, MA 02181-0001
Ph: (617)235-2895
Javier F. Kuong
Focuses on trends and developments in the electronic data processing (EDP) and data communications fields, as well as providing practical guidelines, standards, and ideas on data processing technology as they affect audit and control matters. Presents tutorials on a topic of current interest in the field of EDP audit and internal controls. Suggests "key steps" to be taken by readers in order to "harness new technology and train personnel to cope with new developments." Recurring features include interviews, news of research, a calendar of events, reports of meetings, news of educational opportunities, book reviews, and notices of publications available.

★481★ Computer Economics Report
Computer Economics, Inc.
5841 Edison Pl.
Carlsbad, CA 92008
Ph: (619)438-8100   Fax: (619)431-1126
Fr: 800-326-8100
Monthly. Provides analyses of new IBM technologies and acquisition and financial management strategies from an end-user perspective. Recurring features include cost comparisons, price/performance analyses, new product forecasts, and evaluations of acquisition techniques for medium and large computer systems.

★482★ EDI World
EDI World, Inc.
2021 Coolidge St.
Hollywood, FL 33020
Ph: (305)925-5900   Fax: (305)925-7533
Raymond G. Feldman
Monthly. Magazine emphasizing electronic data interchange.

★483★ Engineering Journal
American Institute of Steel Construction
1 E. Wacker Dr., Ste. 3100
Chicago, IL 60601-2001
Ph: (312)670-2400   Fax: (312)670-5403
Jacqueline Joseffer
Quarterly. Magazine devoted exclusively to the design of steel structures featuring papers of practical design value. Provides the latest information on steel design, research, and constuction to structural engineers, architects, and educators.

★484★ Engineering Outlook
University of Illinois at Urbana-Champaign
College of Engineering
112 Engineering Hall
1308 W. Green St.
Urbana, IL 61801
Ph: (217)333-1510   Fax: (217)244-7705
Maureen L. Tan
Quarterly. Covers, in non-technical language, research at the University of Illinois in the areas of aeronautical, astronautical, ceramic, agricultural, chemical, civil, computer, electrical, general, nuclear, mechanical, industrial, and materials science engineering; as well as computer science, physics, theoretical and applied mechanics, and bioengineering. Recurring features include columns titled Engineering Perspective, From the Dean, and Focus on Engineering.

★485★ Engineering & Science
The California Institute of Technology
 Alumni Assn.
Caltech 1-71
Pasadena, CA 91125
Ph: (818)356-6811   Fax: (818)577-0636
Jane Dietrich

Quarterly. Journal on research at California
Institute of Technology.

★486★ Engineering Times
National Society of Professional Engineers
1420 King St.
Alexandria, VA 22314
Ph: (703)684-2875   Fax: (703)836-4875
Stefan Jaeger

Monthly. Magazine (tabloid) covering professional, legislative, and techology issues for
an engineering audience.

★487★ ERC Update
Engineering Research Center (ERC)
College of Engineering
Wind Tunnel Bldg.
Room 2104
College Park, MD 20742
Ph: (301)405-3906   Fax: (301)405-6707
Judith Mays

Features news concerning the Center's programs supporting research and assistance to
businesses and industry.

**★488★ International Journal of Human
 Computer Interaction**
Ablex Publishing Corp.
355 Chestnut St.
Norwood, NJ 07648
Ph: (201)767-8450   Fax: (201)767-6717
Michael Smith

Quarterly. Computer journal.

★489★ Journal of Managerial Issues
Pittsburg State University
Dept. of Economics, Finance & Banking
Pittsburg, KS 66762
Ph: (316)235-4547   Fax: (316)232-7515
Charles C. Fischer

Quarterly. Scholarly refereed journal for business managers and business educators.

**★490★ Journal of Product Innovation
 Management**
Elsevier Science Publishing Co., Inc.
655 Avenue of the Americas
New York, NY 10010
Ph: (212)633-3977   Fax: (212)633-3820
Thomas P. Hustad

Research journal on strategies for new product development and marketing.

★491★ Managers Magazine
Life Insurance Marketing & Research Assn.
PO Box 208
Hartford, CT 06141-0208
Ph: (203)677-0033   Fax: (203)678-0187
Daniel J. Nahorney

Monthly. Magazine on life insurance agency
management.

**★492★ Medical Group Management
 Update**
Medical Group Management Assn.
104 Inverness Terrace E.
Englewood, CO 80112-5306
Ph: (303)799-1111   Fax: (303)643-4427
Eileen Barker

Monthly. Newspaper (tabloid) covering current legislative events, practical management
issues, trends in the health care community,
and Association activities, services, and
news.

★493★ Midwest Engineer
Western Society of Engineers
176 W. Adams, Ste. 1734
Chicago, IL 60603
Ph: (312)372-3760   Fax: (312)372-3761

★494★ National Engineer
National Assn. of Power Engineers
5-7 Springfield St.
Chicopee, MA 01013-2624
Ph: (413)592-6273   Fax: (413)592-1998
William F. Judd
Monthly.

**★495★ NTIS Foreign Technology
 Newsletter**
National Technical Information Service
 (NTIS)
5285 Port Royal Rd.
Springfield, VA 22161
Ph: (703)487-4630

Biweekly. Carries abstracts of reports on the
field of foreign technology. Covers biomedical
technology; civil, construction, structural, and
building engineering; communications; computer, electro, and optical technology; energy, manufacturing, and industrial engineering; and physical and materials sciences.
Recurring features include notices of publications available and a form for ordering reports
from NTIS.

★496★ Organization Science
The Institute of Management Sciences
290 Westminster St.
Providence, RI 02903
Ph: (401)274-2525   Fax: (401)274-3189
Arie Y. Lewin

Quarterly. Innovative research on organizations drawing upon multiple disciplines.

★497★ The Professional Engineer
Professional Engineers of North Carolina
4000 Wake Forest Rd., Ste. 108
Raleigh, NC 27609
Ph: (919)872-0683   Fax: (919)876-9748
Marilyn R. Banks

Bimonthly. Magazine for Professional Engineers in North Carolina

★498★ Project Management
Practice Management Associates, Ltd.
10 Midland Ave.
Newton, MA 02158
Ph: (617)965-0055   Fax: (617)965-5152
Frank A. Stasiowski

Monthly. Offers tactics and techniques for
hands-on project management.

★499★ RAC Journal
Reliability Analysis Center (RAC)
PO Box 4700
Rome, NY 13440-8200
Ph: (315)337-0900   Fax: (315)337-9932
Fr: 800-526-4802
Anthony Coppola

Quarterly. Discusses current reliability-re-
lated research. Covers RAC publications,
programs and workshops, and calls for papers. Recurring features include a calendar of
events and technical briefs.

**★500★ Science, Technology & Human
 Values**
Sage Periodicals Press
2455 Teller Rd.
Thousand Oaks, CA 91320
Ph: (805)499-0721   Fax: (805)499-0871
Susan E. Cozzens

Quarterly. Journal evaluating the ethics of
science and technology.

**★501★ TEST Engineering &
 Management**
The Mattingley Publishing Co., Inc.
3756 Grand Ave., Ste. 205
Oakland, CA 94610
Ph: (510)839-0909   Fax: (510)839-2950
Eve Mattingley-Hannigan

Bimonthly. Reliability/qualifications test engineering magazine.

PROFESSIONAL MEETINGS AND CONVENTIONS

★502★ A/E/C Systems and CMC Fall
A/E/C Systems, Inc.
1 Farron Dr.
Chadds Ford, PA 19317
Ph: (215)444-9690   Fax: (215)444-9583
Annual.

**★503★ American Association for the
 Advancement of Science and
 Technology Exhibition**
American Association for the Advancement
 of Science (AAAS)
Meetings Office
1333 H St., NW
Washington, DC 20005
Ph: (202)326-6459   Fax: (202)289-4021
Annual.

**★504★ Data Processing Management
 Association Convention**
Data Processing Management Association
505 Busse Hwy.
Park Ridge, IL 60068
Ph: (708)825-8124   Fax: (708)825-1693
Annual.

Financial Managers

Financial managers prepare reports required by firms to conduct operations and to satisfy tax and regulatory requirements. Financial managers also oversee the flow of cash and financial instruments and develop information to assess the present and future financial status of firm. **Chief financial officers,** for example, may oversee all financial management functions of small firms or departments of a large firm. **Controllers** direct the preparation of all financial reports such as income statements, balance sheets, and special reports such as depreciation schedules. **Cash managers** monitor and control the flow of cash receipts and disbursements and other financial instruments. **Risk and insurance managers** are responsible for programs to minimize risks and losses that may arise from financial transactions and business operations undertaken by an institution. **Credit card operations managers** establish credit card rating criteria, determine credit ceilings, and monitor their institution's extension of credit. **Reserve officers** review financial statements and direct the purchase and sale of bonds and other securities to maintain the asset-liability ratio required by law. **User representatives** in international accounting develop integrated international financial and accounting systems for the banking transactions of multinational organizations. Managers in financial institutions make decisions in accordance with federal and state laws, and policies established by the institution's board of directors. These include **bank branch managers, saving and loan association managers, consumer credit managers**, and **credit union managers**.

Salaries

Salary levels for financial managers depend on the size and location of the firm. Salaries are likely to be higher in large institutions and cities.

Lowest 10 percent	Less than $20,200 year
Median	$39,700/year
Top 10 percent	More than $77,800/year

Employment Outlook

Growth rate until the year 2005: Average.

Financial Managers

CAREER GUIDES

★505★ "Bank Administrators and Managers" in *101 Careers: A Guide to the Fastest-Growing Opportunities* **(pp. 8-9)**
John Wiley & Sons, Inc.
605 3rd Ave.
New York, NY 10158-0012
Ph: (212)850-6645   Fax: (212)850-6088
Michael Harkavy. 1990. Describes the nature of the job, working conditions, employment growth, qualifications, personal skills, projected salaries, and where to write for more information.

★506★ *Bank Careers*
Careers, Inc.
PO Box 135
Largo, FL 34649-0135
Ph: (813)584-7333
1994. Two-page occupational summary card describing duties, working conditions, personal qualifications, training, earnings and hours, employment outlook, places of employment, related careers, and where to write for more information.

★507★ *Bank Loan Officer*
Vocational Biographies, Inc.
PO Box 31
Sauk Centre, MN 56378-0031
Ph: (612)352-6516   Fax: (612)352-5546
Fr: 800-255-0752
1995. Four-page pamphlet containing a personal narrative about a worker's job, work likes and dislikes, career path from high school to the present, education and training, the rewards and frustrations, and the effects of the job on the rest of the worker's life. The data file portion of this pamphlet gives a concise occupational summary, including work description, working conditions, places of employment, personal characteristics, education and training, job outlook, and salary range.

★508★ "Bank Manager" in *College Board Guide to Jobs and Career Planning* **(pp. 131)**
The College Board
415 Columbus Ave.
New York, NY 10023-6992
Ph: (212)713-8165   Fax: (212)713-8143
Fr: 800-323-7155
Joyce S. Mitchell. Second edition, 1994. Describes the job, salaries, related careers, education needed, and where to write for more information.

★509★ "Bank Officer" in *Jobs Rated Almanac*
World Almanac
1 International Blvd., Ste. 444
Mahwah, NJ 07495
Ph: (201)529-6900   Fax: (201)529-6901
Les Krantz. Second edition, 1992. Ranks 250 jobs by environment, salary, outlooks, physical demands, stress, security, travel opportunities, and extra perks. Includes jobs the editor feels are the most common, most interesting, and the most rapidly growing.

★510★ "Bank Officer" in *VGM's Careers Encyclopedia* **(pp. 57-59)**
National Textbook Co. (NTC)
VGM Career Books
4255 W. Touhy Ave.
Lincolnwood, IL 60646-1975
Ph: (708)679-5500   Fax: (708)679-2494
Fr: 800-323-4900
Third edition, 1991. Describes job duties, places of employment, working conditions, qualifications, education, and training, advancement potential, and salary for each occupation.

★511★ "Bank Officers" in *American Almanac of Jobs and Salaries* **(p. 397)**
Avon Books
1350 Avenue of the Americas
New York, NY 10019
Ph: (212)261-6800   Fr: 800-238-0658
John Wright, editor. Revised and updated, 1994-95. This is comprehensive guide to the wages of hundreds of occupations in a wide variety of industries and organizations.

★512★ "Banking and Finance" in *College Majors and Careers: A Resource Guide to Effective Life Planning* **(pp.25-26)**
Garrett Park Press
PO Box 1907
Garrett Park, MD 20896
Ph: (301)946-2553
Paul Phifer. 1993. Lists 60 college majors, with definitions; related occupations and leisure activities; skills, values, and personal needed attributes; suggested readings; and a list of associations.

★513★ "Banking and Financial Services" in *Where the Jobs Are: The Hottest Careers for the 90s* **(pp. 52-76)**
Career Press
180 5th Ave.
Hawthorne, NJ 07507
Ph: (201)427-0229   Fax: (201)427-2037
Fr: 800-CAREER-1
Joyce Hadley. 1995. Offers a job-hunting strategy for the 1990s as well as descriptions of growing careers of the decade. Each profile includes general information, forecasts, growth, education and training, licensing requirements, and salary information.

★514★ "Banking" in *Internships 1995*
Petersons Guides, Inc.
PO Box 2123
Princeton, NJ 08543-2123
Ph: (609)243-9111   Fr: 800-338-3282
Fifteenth edition, 1995. Lists internship opportunities under six broad categories: communications, creative, performing, and fine arts, human services, international relations, business and technology, and public affairs. For each internship program, gives the names, phone number, contact person, description, eligibility requirements, and benefits.

★515★ "Barbara Bemister—Bank Branch" in *Straight Talk on Careers: Eighty Pros Take You Into Their Professions* **(pp. 18-19)**
Garrett Park Press
PO Box 1907
Garrett Park, MD 20896
Ph: (301)946-2553
Mary Barbera-Hogan. 1987. Contains candid interviews from people who give an inside view of their work in 80 different careers.

These professionals describe a day's work and the stresses and rewards accompanying their work.

★516★ Careers in Banking and Finance
Rosen Publishing Group
29 E. 21st St.
New York, NY 10010
Ph: (212)777-3017   Fax: (212)777-0277
Fr: 800-237-9932

Patricia Haddock. 1990. Includes information on job availability, and describes specialized areas of banking and finance.

★517★ Careers in Finance
National Textbook Co. (NTC)
VGM Career Books
4255 W. Touhy Ave.
Lincolnwood, IL 60646-1975
Ph: (708)679-5500   Fax: (708)679-2494
Fr: 800-323-4900

Trudy Ring, editor. 1993. Covers financial careers in such areas as higher education, corporate and public finance, and commercial and investment banking.

★518★ Careers in the Investment World
Chelsea House Publishers
Div. of Main Line Book Co.
95 Madison Ave.
New York, NY 10016
Ph: (212)683-4400   Fax: (212)683-4412

Rachel S. Epstein. 1988.

★519★ "Controller" in VGM's Careers Encyclopedia (pp. 118-120)
National Textbook Co. (NTC)
VGM Career Books
4255 W. Touhy Ave.
Lincolnwood, IL 60646-1975
Ph: (708)679-5500   Fax: (708)679-2494
Fr: 800-323-4900

Third edition, 1991. Describes job duties, places of employment, working conditions, qualifications, education, and training, advancement potential, and salary for each occupation.

★520★ "Corporate Finance" in American Almanac of Jobs and Salaries (p. 409)
Avon Books
1350 Avenue of the Americas
New York, NY 10019
Ph: (212)261-6800   Fr: 800-238-0658

John Wright, editor. Revised and updated, 1994-95. This is comprehensive guide to the wages of hundreds of occupations in a wide variety of industries and organizations.

★521★ Credit Manager
Careers, Inc.
PO Box 135
Largo, FL 34649-0135
Ph: (813)584-7333

1994. Four-page brief offering the definition, history, duties, working conditions, personal qualifications, educational requirements, earnings, hours, employment outlook, advancement, and careers related to this position.

★522★ "Credit Manager" in VGM's Careers Encyclopedia (pp. 125-126)
National Textbook Co. (NTC)
VGM Career Books
4255 W. Touhy Ave.
Lincolnwood, IL 60646-1975
Ph: (708)679-5500   Fax: (708)679-2494
Fr: 800-323-4900

Third edition, 1991. Describes job duties, places of employment, working conditions, qualifications, education, and training, advancement potential, and salary for each occupation.

★523★ Credit Managers
Chronicle Guidance Publications, Inc.
66 Aurora St.
PO Box 1190
Moravia, NY 13118-1190
Ph: (315)497-0330   Fax: (315)497-3359
Fr: 800-622-7284

1991. Career brief describing the nature of the job, working conditions, hours and earnings, education and training, licensure, certification, unions, personal qualifications, social and psychological factors, location, employment outlook, entry methods, advancement, and related occupations.

★524★ "Credit Managers" in Jobs! What They Are—Where They Are—What They Pay! (pp. 160)
Simon & Schuster, Inc.
Simon & Schuster Bldg.
1230 Avenue of the Americas
New York, NY 10020
Ph: (212)698-7000   Fr: 800-223-2348

Robert O. Snelling and Anne M. Snelling. Third revised edition, 1992. Also includes a chapter titled "Bank Officers" (p. 147). Describes duties and responsibilities, earnings, employment opportunities, training, and qualifications.

★525★ "Director of Finance" in Career Opportunities in Art (pp. 69-70)
Facts on File
460 Park Ave. S.
New York, NY 10016-7382
Ph: (212)683-2244   Fax: 800-678-3633
Fr: 800-322-8755

Susan H. Haubenstock. 1988. This book profiles seventy-five art-related jobs. Each profile includes a career description, career ladder, employment and advancement prospects, education, experience and skills required, salary range, and tips for entry into the field.

★526★ "Finance" in Internships 1995
Petersons Guides, Inc.
PO Box 2123
Princeton, NJ 08543-2123
Ph: (609)243-9111   Fr: 800-338-3282

Fifteenth edition, 1995. Lists internship opportunities under six broad categories: communications, creative, performing, and fine arts, human services, international relations, business and technology, and public affairs. For each internship program, gives the names, phone number, contact person, description, eligibility requirements, and benefits.

★527★ "Financial Analysts" in Jobs! What They Are—Where They Are— What They Pay (pp. 142)
Fireside
Simon & Schuster Bldg.
1230 Avenue of the Americas
New York, NY 10020
Ph: (212)698-7000   Fr: 800-223-2348

Robert O. Snelling and Anne M. Snelling. Revised and updated, 1992. Describes duties and responsibilities, earnings, employment opportunities, training, and qualifications.

★528★ "Financial Institution Officers and Managers" in Encyclopedia of Careers and Vocational Guidance (Vol.2, pp. 657-661)
J.G. Ferguson Publishing Co.
200 W. Madison St., Ste. 300
Chicago, IL 60606
Ph: (312)580-5480   Fax: (312)580-4948

William E. Hopke, editor-in-chief. Ninth edition, 1993. Four-volume set that profiles 900 occupations and describes job trends in 74 industries. Includes career description, educational requirements, history of the job, methods of entry, advancement, employment outlook, earnings, conditions of work, social and psychological factors, and sources of further information.

★529★ "Financial Manager" in College Board Guide to Jobs and Career Planning (pp. 134)
The College Board
415 Columbus Ave.
New York, NY 10023-6992
Ph: (212)713-8165   Fax: (212)713-8143
Fr: 800-323-7155

Joyce S. Mitchell. Second edition, 1994. Describes the job, salaries, related careers, education needed, and where to write for more information.

★530★ "Financial Managers" in Occupational Outlook Handbook
U.S. Government Printing Office
Superintendent of Documents
Washington, DC 20402
Ph: (202)512-1800   Fax: (202)512-2250

Biennial; latest edition, 1994-95. Encyclopedia of careers describing 250 occupations and comprising about 85 percent of all jobs in the economy. Occupations that require lengthy education or training are given the most attention. Each occupation's profile describes what the worker does on the job, working conditions, education and training requirements, advancement possibilities, job outlook, earnings, and sources of additional information.

★531★ "Financial Planners and Business Managers" in Jobs! What They Are—Where They Are—What They Pay (pp. 161)
Fireside
Simon & Schuster Bldg.
1230 Avenue of the Americas
New York, NY 10020
Ph: (212)698-7000   Fr: 800-223-2348

Robert O. Snelling and Anne M. Snelling. Revised and updated, 1992. Describes duties and responsibilities, earnings, employment opportunities, training, and qualifications.

★532★ "Financial Planners and Managers" in *101 Careers: A Guide to the Fastest-Growing Opportunities* **(pp. 14-16)**
John Wiley & Sons, Inc.
605 3rd Ave.
New York, NY 10158-0012
Ph: (212)850-6645   Fax: (212)850-6088
Michael Harkavy. 1990. Describes the nature of the job, working conditions, employment growth, qualifications, personal skills, projected salaries, and where to write for more information.

★533★ "Hospital Controller" in *Opportunities in Hospital Administration Careers* **(pp. 31-32)**
National Textbook Co. (NTC)
VGM Career Books
4255 W. Touhy Ave.
Lincolnwood, IL 60646-1975
Ph: (708)679-5500   Fax: (708)679-2494
Fr: 800-323-4900
Donald I. Snook. 1989. Describes hospital administration in varied work settings. Covers educational preparation, skills, compensation, getting started in the profession, and job hunting.

★534★ "Hospital Credit Manager" in *Opportunities in Hospital Administration Careers* **(pp. 33-34)**
National Textbook Co. (NTC)
VGM Career Books
4255 W. Touhy Ave.
Lincolnwood, IL 60646-1975
Ph: (708)679-5500   Fax: (708)679-2494
Fr: 800-323-4900
Donald I. Snook. 1989. Describes hospital administration in varied work settings. Covers educational preparation, skills, compensation, getting started in the profession, and job hunting.

★535★ *The Insider's Guide to the Top 20 Careers in Business and Management*
McGraw-Hill
1221 Avenue of the Americas
New York, NY 10020
Ph: (212)512-3493   Fax: (212)512-3050
Tom Fischgrund. 1994. Contains information on different business careers including accounting, banking, finance, and retail sales. Includes tips on choosing a careers, preparing a resume, interviewing, and succeeding on the job.

★536★ "Investment Bankers", "Controllers", and "Bank Officer" in *Career Information Center* **(Vol.1)**
Simon and Schuster
200 Old Tappan Rd.
Old Tappan, NJ 07675
Fax: 800-445-6991   Fr: 800-223-2348
Richard Lidz and Linda Perrin, editorial directors. Fifth edition, 1993. A multi-volume set that profiles over 600 occupations. Each occupational profile describes job duties, educational requirements, advancement possibilities, employment outlook, working conditions, earnings and benefits, and where to write for more information.

★537★ *Loan Officers (Banking)*
Chronicle Guidance Publications, Inc.
66 Aurora St.
PO Box 1190
Moravia, NY 13118-1190
Ph: (315)497-0330   Fax: (315)497-3359
Fr: 800-622-7284
1992. Career brief describing the nature of the job, working conditions, hours and earnings, education and training, licensure, certification, unions, personal qualifications, social and psychological factors, location, employment outlook, entry methods, advancement, and related occupations.

★538★ *Opportunities in Banking*
National Textbook Co. (NTC)
VGM Career Books
4255 W. Touhy Ave.
Lincolnwood, IL 60646-1975
Ph: (708)679-5500   Fax: (708)679-2494
Fr: 800-323-4900
Philip Perry. Details positions and career paths, offers advice on preparing for the field, and projects the future market for jobs. Also overviews the evolution of the Federal Reserve Band and other federal institutions such as the Export-Import Bank and the Farm Credit Administration.

★539★ *Opportunities in Financial Careers*
National Textbook Co. (NTC)
VGM Career Books
4255 W. Touhy Ave.
Lincolnwood, IL 60646-1975
Ph: (708)679-5500   Fax: (708)679-2494
Fr: 800-323-4900
Michael J. Sumichrast and Dean Crist. 1991. Describes jobs in banking, security sales, and accounting occupations. Explains trends in the field, training requirements, advancement possibilities, licensing, and earnings.

PROFESSIONAL ASSOCIATIONS

★540★ American Bankers Association (ABA)
1120 Connecticut Ave. NW
Washington, DC 20036
Ph: (202)663-5000   Fax: (202)663-7533
Members: Members are principally commercial banks and trust companies; combined assets of members represent approximately 90% of the U.S. banking industry; approximately 94% of members are community banks with less than $500 million in assets. **Purpose:** Seeks to enhance the role of commerical bankers as preeminent providers of financial services through communications, research, legal action, lobbying of federal legislative and regulatory bodies, and education and training programs. Serves as spokesperson for the banking industry; facilitates exchange of information among members. Maintains the American Institute of Banking, an industry-sponsored adult education program. Conducts educational and training programs for bank employees and officers through a wide range of banking schools and national conferences. Maintains liaison with federal bank regulators; submits draft legislation and lobbies Congress on issues affecting commercial banks; testifies before congressional committees; represents members in U.S. postal rate proceedings. Serves as secretariat of the International Monetary Conference and the Financial Institutions Committee for the American National Standards Institute. Compiles briefs and lawsuits in major court cases affecting the industry. Conducts teleconferences with state banking associations on such issues as regulatory compliance; works to build consensus and coordinate activities of leading bank and financial service trade groups. Provides services to members including: public advocacy; news media contact; insurance program providing directors and officers with liability coverage, financial institution bond, and trust errors and omissions coverage; research service operated through ABA Center for Banking Information; fingerprint set processing in conjunction with the Federal Bureau of Investigation; discounts on operational and income-producing projects through the Corporation for American Banking. Conducts conferences, forums, and workshops covering subjects such as small business, consumer credit, agricultural and community banking, trust management, bank operations, and automation. Sponsors the Personal Economics Program, which educates schoolchildren and the community on banking, economics, and personal finance. **Publications:** *ABA Banking Journal*, monthly. • *ABA Management Update of Personal Trust and Private Banking*, bimonthly. • *AIB Leader Letter*, quarterly. • *Bank Compliance Magazine*, quarterly. • *Bank Insurance and Protection Bulletin*, monthly. • *Bank Operations Bulletin*, monthly. • *Bank Personnel News*, monthly. • *Bank Security News*, monthly. • *Bankers News*, biweekly. • *Commercial Lending Review*, quarterly. • *Consumer Credit Delinquency Bulletin*, quarterly. • *Employee Benefits Quarterly*, quarterly. • *Journal of Agricultural Lending*, quarterly. • *Network News*, 3/year. • *Retail Banking Digest*, bimonthly. • *Retail Delivery Systems Quarterly*, quarterly. • *Securities Processing Digest*, quarterly. • *Stonier Forum*, semiannual. • *Trends*, bimonthly. • *Trust and Financial Advisor*, quarterly. • *Trust Letter*, monthly.

★541★ American Financial Services Association (AFSA)
919 18th St. NW
Washington, DC 20006
Ph: (202)296-5544   Fax: (202)223-0321
Fr: 800-843-3280
Members: Companies whose business is primarily direct credit lending to consumers and/or the purchase of sales finance paper on consumer goods. Some members have insurance and retail subsidiaries; some are themselves subsidiaries of highly diversified parent corporations. **Purpose:** Encourages the business of financing individuals and families for necessary and useful purposes, at reasonable charges, including interest; promotes consumer understanding of basic money management principles as well as constructive uses of consumer credit. Educational services include films, textbooks, and study units for the classroom and budgeting guides for individuals and families. Compiles statistical reports; offers seminars. **Publications:** *Consumer Finance Law Bulle-*

tin, monthly. • *CREDIT magazine*, bimonthly. • *Executive Letter*, monthly. • *Independent Operations: A Quarterly Report for Financial Services Independents.*

★542★ Bank Administration Institute (BAI)
1 N. Franklin St.
Chicago, IL 60606
Ph: (312)553-4600   Fax: (312)683-2373
Fr: 800-323-8552
Members: Purpose: Works to provides research, technical studies, publications, professional development programs, and advisory services to bank executives seeking to improve bank performance. Offers educational programs through conferences and research and technical studies in retail, payment systems, human resources, operations, lending, finance, executive education, audit, security, and compliance. Maintains the BAI School. **Publications:** *Bank Fraud*, monthly. • *Bank Management Magazine*, bimonthly. • *Compliance Alert*, biweekly.

★543★ Credit Union Executives Society (CUES)
6410 Enterprise Ln., Ste. 300
Madison, WI 53719-1143
Ph: (608)271-2664   Fax: (608)271-2303
Fr: 800-252-2664
Members: Serves the professional development and competency enhancement needs of credit union chief executives and their vice presidents. **Purpose:** Supports related credit union board development and its contribution to executvie effectiveness. Encourages senior management development. **Publications:** *Compensation Survey Manual*, annual. • *Credit Union Director Magazine*, quarterly. • *Credit Union Executives Society—Membership Directory*, annual. • *Credit Union Management Magazine*, monthly. • *Disaster Recovery Planning Manual*. • *FYI Management Memo*, monthly.

★544★ Environmental Bankers Association (EBA)
1020 N. Fairfax St., Ste. 201
Alexandria, VA 22314
Ph: (703)549-0977   Fax: (703)548-5945
Banks interested in environmental risk management and liability issues. Aims to help members preserve net income and assets from environmental liability issues resulting from lending and trust activities. Updates members on environmental risk management programs, auditing procedures, legislation and government regulation, environmental banking case law, and pollution insurance/risk management procedures.

★545★ Financial Executives Institute (FEI)
10 Madison Ave.
PO Box 1938
Morristown, NJ 07962-1938
Ph: (201)898-4600   Fax: (201)898-4649
Members: Professional organization of corporate financial executives performing duties of chief financial officer, controller, treasurer, or vice-president-finance. **Purpose:** Sponsors research activities through its affiliated Financial Executives Research Foundation. Maintains offices in Toronto, Canada, and Washington, DC. **Publications:** *FEI Briefing*, monthly. • *Financial Executive*, bimonthly. •

Financial Executives Institute Directory, semiannual.

★546★ Financial Management Association (FMA)
School of Bus.
University of South Florida
Tampa, FL 33620-5500
Ph: (813)974-2084   Fax: (813)974-3318
Members: Professors of financial management; corporate financial officers. **Purpose:** Facilitates exchange of ideas among persons involved in financial management or the study thereof. Conducts workshops for comparison of current research projects and development of cooperative ventures in writing and research. Sponsors honorary society for superior students at 300 colleges and universities. Offers placement services. **Publications:** *Careers in Finance*, periodic. • *Financial Management*, quarterly. • *Financial Management Collection*, triennial. • *Financial Practice and Education*, semiannual. • *Membership/Professional Directory*, periodic.

★547★ Financial Managers Society (FMS)
8 S. Michigan Ave., Ste. 500
Chicago, IL 60603-3307
Ph: (312)578-1300   Fax: (312)578-1308
Members: Technical information exchange for financial managers of financial institutions. **Purpose:** Sponsors Fundamentals of Investments Portfolio Management Program and Asset and Liability Management for the 90's, Implementing FAS 107. **Publications:** *Cost Accounting Manual*. • *Financial Managers Society—Membership Directory*, annual. • *Internal Audit Manual*. • *Internal Audit Manual Update*. • *Records Retention Manual*. • *Update*, biweekly.

★548★ Forex U.S.A.
Tradition North America
61 Broadway
New York, NY 10006
Ph: (212)797-5580   Fax: (212)797-7463
Members: Individuals engaged by banks in foreign exchange trading and deposit dealing; brokers in these markets. **Purpose:** Encourages public and professional education in foreign exchange and furthers awareness of the effect of foreign exchange on economics and finance. Fosters better relations among members and strives to improve professional responsibility and the market environment. Works with other organizations and government officials and agencies. Conducts annual seminar for junior traders, semiannual seminar for senior traders, educational meetings, and presentations. **Publications:** *Forex Newsletter*, quarterly.

★549★ Healthcare Financial Management Association (HFMA)
2 Westbrook Corporate Center, Ste. 700
Westchester, IL 60154
Ph: (708)531-9600   Fax: (708)531-0032
Members: Financial management professionals employed by hospitals and long-term care facilities, public accounting and consulting firms, insurance companies, medical groups, managed care organizations, government agencies, and other organizations. **Purpose:** Conducts educational seminars and two annual examinations, awarding rating of Fellow or Certified Manager of Pa-

tient Accounts to successful candidates. **Publications:** *Healthcare Financial Management*, monthly. • *Notes from National*, monthly. • *Patient Accounts*, monthly.

★550★ Institute of Financial Education (IFE)
111 E. Wacker Dr., 9th Fl.
Chicago, IL 60601-4680
Ph: (312)946-8801   Fax: (312)946-8802
Members: Nationwide educational organization conducting courses for personnel of savings institutions, commercial banks, and credit unions. **Purpose:** Conducts educational programs. **Publications:** *Bringing in Business*. • *Chapter Briefing*, monthly. • *Consumer Lending: From Application to Servicing*. • *Deposit Account Operations*. • *Deposit Accounts and Services*. • *Glossary of Financial Services Terminology*. • *HUD/FHA Quality Control Manual*. • *Insurance of Accounts: A Practical Guide to the FDIC Regulations*. • *IRA Basics*. • *1994 FHA/VA Loan Processing Information Service*. • *1994 FHA/VA Loan Servicing Manual*. • *Person to Person: Helping Customers Make Financial Decisions*. • *Residential Mortgage Lending Documentation*. • *Residential Mortgage Lending: From Application to Servicing*. • *Residential Mortgage Lending Origination*. • *Retail Banking: Serving the Financial Needs of Customers*. • *Sales Skills for Financial Professionals*. • *Service Excellence: New Techniques for Banking Professionals*. • *Supervisory Personnel Management: Building Work Relationships*. • *Supervisory Personnel Management: Maximizing Your Effectiveness*. • *Talking and Listening: Keys to Success with Customers and Co-Workers*. • *Teller Operations*. • *Truth in Savings Handbook for Front-Line Staff*. • *Write with Confidence: Tools for Financial Business Writing*. • *Your New Job: Tips for Career Success*.

★551★ National Association of Credit Management (NACM)
8815 Centre Park Dr.
Columbia, MD 21045
Ph: (410)740-5560   Fax: (410)740-5574
Members: Credit and financial executives representing manufacturers, wholesalers, financial institutions, insurance companies, utilities, and other businesses interested in business credit. **Purpose:** Promotes sound credit practices and legislation. Conducts Graduate School of Credit and Financial Management at Dartmouth College, Hanover, NH. **Publications:** *Business Credit*. • *Credit Executives Handbook*. • *Credit Manual of Commercial Laws*, annual. • *Digest of Commercial Laws*.

★552★ National Association of State Credit Union Supervisors (NASCUS)
1901 N. Fort Myer Dr., Ste. 201
Arlington, VA 22209
Ph: (703)528-8351   Fax: (703)528-3248
Fr: 800-819-0660
Members: State credit union supervisors (48) and state chartered credit unions (500); state credit union leagues, and law and accounting firms are supporters. **Purpose:** Seeks improvement of state regulatory system and educational programs for supervisors and examiners. Conducts continuing education   program   for   examiners.

Publications: *NASCUS Stateline*, monthly. • *President's Report.*

★553★ Treasury Management Association (TMA)
7315 Wisconsin Ave., Ste. 1250W
Bethesda, MD 20814
Ph: (301)907-2862   Fax: (301)907-2864
Members: Seeks to establish a National Forum for the exchange of concepts and techniques related to improving the management of treasury through education, communication, and recognition of the treasury management profession. **Purpose:** Conducts educational programs. Offers placement service. **Publications:** *Account Analysis Standards.* • *Banking Relations Compendium.* • *Corporate Treasury Guide to UCC4A.* • *EDI Payment Primer.* • *Essentials of Cash Management.* • *Financial EDI Compendium.* • *International Treasury Management Compendium.* • *TMA Journal*, bimonthly. • *TMA Newsletter*, monthly. • *Treasury Management Association*, annual. • *Treasury Management Guide.* • *Wholesale Lockbox Questionnaire.*

STANDARDS/CERTIFICATION AGENCIES

★554★ Healthcare Financial Management Association (HFMA)
2 Westbrook Corporate Center, Ste. 700
Westchester, IL 60154
Ph: (708)531-9600   Fax: (708)531-0032
Conducts educational seminars and two annual examinations, awarding rating of Fellow or Certified Manager of Patient Accounts to successful candidates.

TEST GUIDES

★555★ ACT Proficiency Examination Program: Corporate Finance
National Learning Corp.
212 Michael Dr.
Syosset, NY 11791
Ph: (516)921-8888   Fax: (516)921-8743
Fr: 800-645-6337
Jack Rudman. A series of practice test guides containing multiple-choice examinations.

★556★ Career Examination Series: Financial Analyst
National Learning Corp.
212 Michael Dr.
Syosset, NY 11791
Ph: (516)921-8888   Fax: (516)921-8743
Fr: 800-645-6337
Jack Rudman. A series of study guides with multiple-choice examination questions and solutions for trainees and professional financial managers. Titles in the series include *Assistant Budget Analyst; Assistant Budget Director; Assistant Budget Examiner; Associate Budget Analyst; Budget Analyst; Budget Assistant (USPS); Budget Director; Budget Examiner; Budget Examining Trainee; Bud-*

get Officer; Budget Supervisor; Budget Technician; Chief Budget Examiner; Fiscal Administrator; Fiscal Analyst; Fiscal Director; Fiscal Manager; Fiscal Officer; Principal Budget Analyst; Principal Budget Examiner; Principal Budget Officer; Principal Financial Analyst; Senior Budget Analyst; Senior Budget Examiner; Senior Budget Officer; Senior Financial Analyst.

★557★ Career Examination Series: Investment Analyst
National Learning Corp.
212 Michael Dr.
Syosset, NY 11791
Ph: (516)921-8888   Fax: (516)921-8743
Fr: 800-645-6337
Jack Rudman. 1993. Test guide including questions and answers for students or professionals in the field who seek advancement through examination.

★558★ Money and Banking
National Learning Corp.
212 Michael Dr.
Syosset, NY 11791
Ph: (516)921-8888   Fax: (516)921-8743
Fr: 800-645-6337
Jack Rudman. Part of the Dantes Subject Standardized Test series. A standardized graduate and college-level examination given by graduate schools, colleges, and the U.S. Armed Forces as a final examination for course evaluation in the field of finance. Multiple-choice format with correct answers.

★559★ Principles of Finance
National Learning Corp.
212 Michael Dr.
Syosset, NY 11791
Ph: (516)921-8888   Fax: (516)921-8743
Fr: 800-645-6337
Jack Rudman. Part of Dantes Subject Standardized Tests.

★560★ Regents External Degree Series: Finance
National Learning Corp.
212 Michael Dr.
Syosset, NY 11791
Ph: (516)921-8888   Fax: (516)921-8743
Fr: 800-645-6337
Jack Rudman. A multiple-choice examination for financial professionals preparing to enter the Regents External Degree Program, an alternate route to a college degree. Test contains multiple-choice questions with answers provided. Titles in the series include *Finance I; Finance II; Finance III.*

EDUCATIONAL DIRECTORIES AND PROGRAMS

★561★ American Banker—Top Finance Companies Issue
American Banker—Bond Buyer
1 State St. Plaza
New York, NY 10004
Ph: (212)943-5288   Fax: (212)480-0165
Fr: 800-367-3989
Dave Branch
Publication includes: List of top finance companies with $10 million or more in capital funds. Entries include: Finance company name, headquarters, city; rankings of net receivables by type, business, consumer, and other; total capital funds for two preceding years; capital and surplus, total assets, net receivables, net income, deferred income, receivables acquired, and amount of bank credit at end of the preceding year.

★562★ Business and Finance Career Directory
Gale Research Inc.
835 Penobscot Bldg.
Detroit, MI 48226-4094
Ph: (313)961-2242   Fax: (313)961-6083
Fr: 800-877-GALE
Bradley J. Morgan and Joseph M. Palmisano. Second edition, 1992. A directory in the Career Advisor Series that provides essays written by industry professionals; job search information on resume and cover letter preparation, networking, and the interviewing process; approximately 300 companies and organizations offering job opportunities and internships, and additional job-hunting resources.

★563★ Finance Companies Directory
American Business Directories, Inc.
5711 S. 86th Circle
Omaha, NE 68127
Ph: (402)593-4600   Fax: (402)331-1505
Number of listings: 16,552 (U.S. edition); 1,139 (Canadian edition). Entries include: Name, address, phone (including area code). Compiled from telephone company "Yellow Pages," nationwide.

★564★ Finance, Insurance & Real Estate USA: Industry Analyses, Statistics, and Leading Organizations
Gale Research Inc.
835 Penobscot Bldg.
Detroit, MI 48226-4094
Ph: (313)961-2242   Fax: (313)961-6083
Fr: 800-877-GALE
Kristin Hart, Contact
Latest edition November; new edition expected 1996. Publication includes: Lists of up to 75 leading companies in banking, finance, insurance, real estate, and related sectors, selected on the basis of annual revenue. Entries include: Co. name, address, phone, chief executive, type of company, annual sales, number of employees. Principal content of publication is statistical profiles of the finance, insurance, and real estate industries. Each industry division includes tables, graphs, and maps that provide general statistics on number of firms and employees, compensation,

and revenues; changes in these statistics between 1985 and 1991 (1992 where available); inputs and outputs; occupations employed; and industry data by state. Arrangement: Classified by industry, then ranked by annual sales.

★565★ Legal and Financial Directory
The Daily Journal
2000 S. Colorado Blvd., Ste. 2000
Denver, CO 80222
Ph: (303)756-9995   Fax: (303)756-4465
Fr: 800-323-2362
Arla Haley, Contact
Annual, summer. Covers over 15,000 firms and individuals serving the law, real estate, insurance, and financial industries in Colorado. Entries include: Name, address, phone, fax, telex, geographical area served, description of product/service. Arrangement: Alphabetical.

★566★ Marketing and Sales Career Directory
Gale Research Inc.
835 Penobscot Bldg.
Detroit, MI 48226-4094
Ph: (313)961-2242   Fax: (313)961-6083
Fr: 800-877-GALE
Bradley J. Morgan and Joseph M. Palmisano. Fourth edition, 1992. A directory in the Career Advisor Series that provides essays written by industry professionals; job search information on resume and cover letter preparation, networking, and the interviewing process; approximately 300 companies and organizations offering job opportunities and internships, and additional job-hunting resources.

★567★ Newspapers Career Directory
Gale Research Inc.
835 Penobscot Bldg.
Detroit, MI 48226-4094
Ph: (313)961-2242   Fax: (313)961-6083
Fr: 800-877-GALE
Bradley J. Morgan and Joseph M. Palmisano. 1993. A directory in the Career Advisor Series that provides essays written by industry professionals; job search information on resume and cover letter preparation, networking, and the interviewing process; approximately 300 companies and organizations offering job opportunities and internships, and additional job-hunting resources.

AWARDS, SCHOLARSHIPS, GRANTS, AND FELLOWSHIPS

★568★ Award for Achievement in Business Growth
Commercial Finance Association
225 W. 34th St., Ste. 1815
New York, NY 10122
Ph: (212)594-3490   Fax: (212)564-6053
To demonstrate to the general public the positive aspects of the asset-based financial services industry in helping companies with potential to grow and prosper and to recognize projects financed by an NCFA member. A

plaque is awarded annually. Established in 1955.

★569★ Nicholas Molodovsky Award
Association for Investment Management and Research
5 Boar's Head Ln.
PO Box 3668
Charlottesville, VA 22903
Ph: (804)977-6600   Fax: (804)977-1103
This, the highest honor bestowed by the Federation, is given to recognize those individuals who have made contributions of such significance as to change the direction of the profession and to raise it to higher standards of accomplishment. A plaque and a financial contribution in the laureate's name to an important research project are awarded periodically. First presented in 1968 to Nicholas Molodovsky, one of the profession's outstanding scholars.

★570★ Roger F. Murray Prize Competition
Institute for Quantitative Research in Finance
c/o Legal Offices: Walsh & Valdespino
William Fouse, Prize Chm.
230 Park Ave., Ste. 1550
New York, NY 10169
Ph: (212)869-1190
To recognize scientific achievement in quantitative research in finance. Research presented at an Institute seminar is considered. Monetary awards of $5,000 for first prize, $3,000 for second prize, $2,000 for third prize, and framed certificates are awarded annually. Established to honor Roger F. Murray, S. Sloan Colt Professor Emeritus of Banking and International Finance, Columbia University.

★571★ Donald L. Scantlebury Memorial Award
Joint Financial Management Improvement Program
666 11th St. NW, Ste. 320
Washington, DC 20001
Ph: (202)376-5415   Fax: (202)376-5396
To recognize senior financial management executives who, through outstanding and continuous leadership in financial management, have been principally responsible for significant economies, efficiencies, and improvements in federal, state, or local government. Federal, state, or local government employees who are senior executives are eligible. Nominations must be submitted by January 8. A plaque is awarded annually in March. Established in 1970 and renamed in memory of Donald L. Scantlebury, who was the Chief Accountant of the General Accounting Office and chairman of the JFMIP Steering Committee.

BASIC REFERENCE GUIDES AND HANDBOOKS

★572★ Bank Administration Manual: A Comprehensive Reference Guide
Dow Jones-Irwin
1818 Ridge Rd.
Homewood, IL 60430
Ph: (708)206-2349   Fr: 800-634-3963
Jeffry L. Seglin. Third revised edition, 1988. Defines key banking and investment terms. Lists financial-related associations, organizations, and groups. Summarizes important banking laws and regulations.

★573★ Bankers Desk Reference
Warren, Gorham and Lamont, Inc.
1 Penn Plaza
New York, NY 10119
Ph: (212)971-5000   Fr: 800-922-0066
Annual. Provides sections on different areas of banking such as commercial lending and bank regulation.

★574★ The Banker's Handbook
Dow Jones-Irwin, Inc.
1818 Ridge Rd.
Homewood, IL 60430
Ph: (708)206-2349   Fr: 800-634-3963
William Hubert Baughn, et al., editors. Third edition, 1988. Covers a broad range of banking topics including investments and personnel.

★575★ Branch Management: What You Need to Know to Succeed
Institute of Financial Education (IFE)
111 E. Wacker Dr., 9th Fl.
Chicago, IL 60601
Ph: (312)946-8800
1987. Covers topics such as marketing, financial management, and recruiting and training employees.

★576★ Commercial Banking
Prentice-Hall, Inc.
Rte. 9W
Englewood Cliffs, NJ 07632
Ph: (201)592-2000   Fr: 800-922-0579
Edward W. Reed and E. Gill. Fourth edition, 1989. Addresses the day-to-day concerns of bank management. Covers rate swaps, bank transactions, and interstate banking.

★577★ Dictionary of Finance
Macmillan Publishing Co., Inc.
866 3rd Ave.
New York, NY 10022
Ph: (212)702-2000   Fr: 800-257-5755
Eitan A. Avneyon. 1988. Defines 6200 terms in economics, accounting, banking, investment, and public and private financing. Also includes slang and industry jargon.

★578★ Encyclopedia of Banking and Finance
Bank Administration Institute (BAI)
2550 Golf Rd.
Rolling Meadows, IL 60008
Ph: (708)228-6200   Fr: 800-323-8552
Glenn Gaywaine Munn and Ferdinand L. Garcia. 1993. Includes definitions of banking

terms and articles on a wide variety of banking topics.

★579★ Financial Decision Making: Concepts, Problems and Cases
Prentice-Hall, Inc.
Rte. 9W
Englewood Cliffs, NJ 07632
Ph: (201)592-2000   Fr: 800-634-2863
James Hampton. Fourth edition, 1989. Presents a step-by-step approach to the process of making financial decisions with practical applications and case studies.

★580★ Fundamentals of Financial Management
Prentice Hall
113 Sylvan Ave., Rte. 9W
Englewood Cliffs, NJ 07632
Ph: (201)592-2000   Fr: 800-922-0579
James Van Horne. Ninth edition, 1995. Provides an introduction to business finance; covers financial decision making and allocation of and raising of funds.

★581★ Glossary of Financial Services Terminology
Institute of Financial Education (IFE)
111 E. Wacker Dr., 9th Fl.
Chicago, IL 60601
Ph: (312)946-8800
Fourth edition. 1990. Gives definitions of more than 650 key terms used in savings, lending, appraising, real estate, investing, and accounting operations.

★582★ Handbook of Financial Markets and Institutions
John Wiley and Sons, Inc.
605 3rd Ave.
New York, NY 10158-0012
Ph: (212)850-6000   Fax: (212)850-6088
Fr: 800-526-5368
Edward I. Altman and Mary Jane McKinney, editors. Sixth edition, 1987. Contains current information on a broad range of financial topics including commercial banking, real estate, and investments.

★583★ Introduction to Financial Management
McGraw-Hill, Inc.
1221 Avenue of the Americas
New York, NY 10020
Ph: (212)512-2000   Fr: 800-722-4726
Lawrence D. Schall and Charles W. Haley. Sixth edition, 1991. Introductory text providing an overview of financial management including the American financial system, taxes, and capital.

★584★ The Portable MBA in Finance and Accounting
John Wiley and Sons, Inc.
605 3rd Ave.
New York, NY 10158-0012
Ph: (212)850-6000   Fax: (212)850-6088
Fr: 800-526-5368
John Leslie Livingstone. 1992. Offers advices to businesses. Includes preparing budgets, implementing business plans, and evaluating acquisition targets.

PROFESSIONAL AND TRADE PERIODICALS

★585★ ABA Banking Journal
Simmons-Boardman Publishing
345 Hudson St.
New York, NY 10014
Ph: (212)620-7200   Fax: (212)633-1165
William Streeter
Monthly. Official magazine of the American Bankers Association.

★586★ American Banker
American Banker, Inc.
1 State St. Plaza
New York, NY 10004
Ph: (212)943-6700   Fax: (212)943-2984
William Zimmerman
Daily. Newspaper for senior executives in banking and other financial services industries. Coverage includes news on the financial service industry, news analysis, statistical data ranking financial institutions, investigative pieces, and financial industry trend stories for decision-makers.

★587★ Bank News
912 Baltimore
Kansas City, MO 64105
Ph: (816)421-7941   Fax: (816)472-0397
R.W. Poquette
Monthly. Magazine for the banking industry.

★588★ The Bankers Magazine
Warren, Gorham and Lamont, Inc.
1 Penn Plaza
New York, NY 10119
Ph: (212)971-5000   Fax: (212)971-5025
Paul Blocklyn
Bimonthly. Magazine on banking.

★589★ Bankers Monthly
Hanover Publishers
200 W. 57th St.
New York, NY 10019
Ph: (212)399-1084   Fax: (212)245-1973
Robert Bruce Slater
Monthly. Magazine covering current banking topics of interest to senior bank executives.

★590★ Banks in Insurance Report
John Wiley and Sons, Inc.
Subscription Dept.
605 3rd Ave.
New York, NY 10158
Ph: (212)850-6000   Fax: (212)850-6799
Edward J. Stone
Monthly. Journal containing current information of interest to bankers involved in insurance.

★591★ CFP Today
Institute of Certified Financial Planners
7600 E. Eastman Ave., No. 301
Denver, CO 80231-4370
Ph: (303)751-7600   Fax: (303)751-1037
Jill Ladouceur
Bimonthly. Provides coverage of industry events and developments as well as happenings within the association. Carries articles on regulatory, ethical, and public relations aspects of the industry. Recurring features include letters to the editor, news of

members, a calendar of events, feature articles, and news of educational opportunities.

★592★ Consumer Finance Newsletter
Financial Publishing Company
82 Brookline Ave.
Boston, MA 02215
Ph: (617)262-4040
James C. Senay
Provides information on effective and pending credit insurance and installment loan regulations on the state and federal levels. Supplies news of potential state changes in regulations.

★593★ Financial Executive
Financial Executives Institute
10 Madison Ave.
PO Box 1938
Morristown, NJ 07962-1938
Ph: (201)898-4600   Fax: (201)898-4649
Robin Couch Cardillo
Bimonthly. Magazine covering corporate financial management for senior executives of major corporations.

★594★ Financial Marketing
Charles E. Bartling, Contact
Provides marketing professionals from banks, savings institutions, and credit unions with pertinent information on current trends and developments in the marketing of financial services. Recurring features include letters to the editor, news of research, book reviews, job listing, and a calendar of events.

★595★ Financial Planning News
2 Concourse Pkwy., Ste. 800
Atlanta, GA 30328
Ph: (404)395-1605   Fax: (404)668-7758
Lindsay Wyatt
Carries general news for the financial services industry. Covers such topics as financial planning, banking, insurance, mergers and acquisitions, industry personnel, and new products. Also reports on legislation and regulatory developments and chapter news. Recurring features include letters to the editor, interviews, news of research, meeting reports, and a calendar of events, as well as job listings and notices of publications available.

★596★ FMS Update
Financial Managers Society, Inc. (FMS)
8 S. Michigan Ave., Ste. 500
Chicago, IL 60603-3307
Ph: (312)578-1300
Beatrice J. McLean
Semimonthly. Provides financial managers of savings and loan institutions with the latest industry news. Features legislative and regulatory updates and thrift industry accounting issues reports regularly. Recurring features include notices of publications available, reports of meetings, a calendar of events, and a regulatory checklist.

★597★ Independent Consultant's Briefing
Christopher Juillet
PO Box 1725
Ann Arbor, MI 48106
Ph: (313)449-0310   Fax: (313)449-0351
Christopher Juillet, Contact
Quarterly. Provides articles on a wide variety of consulting-related topics, as well as news of tax and other legislation of importance to

consultants. Features articles by actual practicing independent consultants which gives advice on establishing and running an independent consulting business. Also covers retirement, investments, and insurance. Recurring features include letters to the editor, book reviews, and notices of publications available.

★598★ Institutional Investor
488 Madison Ave.
New York, NY 10022
Ph: (212)303-3300   Fax: (212)303-3171
Monthly. Magazine for the investment or financial industry.

★599★ Investment Dealer's Digest
Investment Dealer's Digest
2 World Trade Center, 18th Fl.
New York, NY 10048
Ph: (212)227-1200   Fax: (212)321-3805
Philip Maher
Weekly. Magazine focusing on securities and finance.

★600★ Journal of Finance
American Finance Assn.
Ohio State University
College of Business
1775 College Rd.
Columbus, OH 43210
Ph: (614)292-8449   Fax: (614)292-2359
Rene Stultz
Academic research journal.

★601★ The Leahy Newsletter
Leahy Newsletter, Inc.
17782 E. 17th St., No. 108
PO Box 467
Tustin, CA 92681
Ph: (714)832-7811   Fax: (714)835-3396
Robert Leahy
Monthly. Provides information on treasury management.

★602★ Letters of Credit Report
John Wiley and Sons, Inc.
Subscription Dept.
605 3rd Ave.
New York, NY 10158
Ph: (212)850-6000   Fax: (212)850-6799
Thomas Whitehill
Bimonthly. Journal publishing information on law and commercial practice for bankers and lawyers.

★603★ Money Management Letter
Institutional Investor, Inc.
488 Madison Ave., 12th Fl.
New York, NY 10022
Ph: (212)303-3300   Fax: (212)303-3353
Fr: 800-543-4444
Tom Lamont
Biweekly. Serves as an information source for professionals involved in U.S. pension fund management. Reports on new strategies and investment products, pension fund searches and hires for consultants, managers and custodians, performance measurement, developing markets, and important personnel changes.

★604★ Retail Banker International
Lafferty Publications
1422 W. Peachtree St., No. 800
Atlanta, GA 30309
Ph: (404)874-5120   Fax: (404)874-5123
Damian Daly, Contact
Biweekly. Covers the international consumer financial services industry. Includes news and articles on banking in the U.S. and foreign countries.

★605★ Retail Banking Digest
American Bankers Association (ABA)
1120 Connecticut Ave. NW
Washington, DC 20036
Ph: (202)663-5071   Fax: (202)828-4544
Fr: 800-338-0626
Craig Sablosky
Provides in -depth treatment of key consumer banking issues, including industry trends, innovative programs, organizational issues, changing market conditions, and other subjects of interest to the competitive banker.

★606★ Review for CFOs & Investment Bankers
Brumberg Publications
124 Harvard St.
Brookline, MA 02146
Ph: (617)734-1979
Bruce Brumberg
Monthly. Strategies and trends in capital raising and financial restructuring.

★607★ Savings & Community Banker
Savings & Community Bank of America
111 E. Wacker Dr., Ste. 2600
Chicago, IL 60601
Ph: (312)644-3100   Fax: (312)644-9358
Mary Nowesnick
Monthly. Magazine for managers and supervisors of savings institutions.

★608★ Tax Management Financial Planning Journal
Tax Management, Inc.
1250 23rd St. NW
Washington, DC 20037
Ph: (202)833-7240   Fax: (202)833-7297
Fr: 800-372-1033
Glenn Davis
Monthly. Covers topics in financial planning, including memoranda on current financial and tax planning strategies.

★609★ Wall Street Journal
Dow Jones & Co., Inc.
420 Lexington Ave.
New York, NY 10170
Ph: (212)808-6600   Fax: (212)808-6898
Robert Bartley
Daily. Newspaper reporting on national business and finance.

PROFESSIONAL MEETINGS AND CONVENTIONS

★610★ American Bankers Association Annual Convention
American Bankers Association
1120 Connecticut Ave., NW
Washington, DC 20036-3905
Ph: (202)663-5191
Annual.

★611★ American Bankers Association National Operations and Automation Conference
American Bankers Association
1120 Connecticut Ave., NW
Washington, DC 20036-5191
Ph: (202)663-5191
Annual.

★612★ American Bankers Association National Trust and Financial Services Conference
American Bankers Association
1120 Connecticut Ave. NW
Washington, DC 20036
Ph: (202)663-5191
Annual.

★613★ Bank Marketing Association Annual Convention and Exhibit
Bank Marketing Association
1120 Connecticut Ave., NW, No. 300
Washington, DC 20036-3902
Ph: (312)782-1442
Annual.

★614★ Bank Marketing Association Trust and Personal Financial Services Marketing Conference
Bank Marketing Association
1120 Connecticut Ave., NW, No. 300
Washington, DC 20036-3902
Ph: (312)782-1442
Annual.

★615★ FIM-New York - Financial Investment Management Exposition and Conference
Flagg Management, Inc.
PO Box 4440
New York, NY 10017
Ph: (212)286-0333   Fax: (212)286-0086
Annual. Always held during September at the Hilton Hotel in New York, New York.

★616★ GEWINN - International Banking & Investments Trade Fair
Glahe International, Inc.
1700 K St., NW, Ste. 403
Washington, DC 20006-4557
Ph: (202)659-4557   Fax: (202)457-0776
Annual. **Dates and Locations:** 1995; Vienna

★617★ Independent Bankers Association of America National Convention and Exposition
Independent Bankers Association of America (IBAA)
1168 S. Main St.
Sauk Centre, MN 56378
Ph: (612)352-6546
Annual.

OTHER SOURCES OF INFORMATION

★618★ "Corporate Financial Analyst" in
100 Best Jobs for the 1990s & Beyond
Dearborn Financial Publishing, Inc.
520 N. Dearborn St.
Chicago, IL 60610-4354
Ph: (312)836-4400   Fax: (312)836-1021
Fr: 800-621-9621
Carol Kleiman. 1992. Describes 100 jobs
ranging from accountants to veterinarians.

Each job profile includes such information as
education, experience, and certification
needed, salaries, and job search suggestions.

Funeral Directors

Funeral Directors, also called **morticians or undertakers** interview the family to learn what they desire with regard to the nature of the funeral, the clergy members or other persons who will officiate, and the final disposition of the remains. Directors establish with the family the location, dates, and times of wakes, memorial services, and burials. They also send a hearse to carry the body to the funeral home or mortuary. Directors also arrange the details and logistics of funerals. They prepare obituary notices and have them placed in newspapers. Arrange for pallbearers and clergy, schedule with the cemetery the opening and closing of a grave, decorate and prepare the sides of all services, and provide for the transportation of the remains, mourners, and flowers between sites. Although this career does not appeal to everyone, the men and women who work as funeral directors take great pride in the fact that they provide efficient and appropriate services that give comfort to their customers.

Salaries

Earnings for funeral directors are as follows:

Funeral directors (owners/managers)	$59,754/year
Mid-level managers	$41,393/year
Embalmers	$27,421/year
Apprentices	$17,489/year

Employment Outlook

Growth rate until the year 2005: Average.

Funeral Directors

CAREER GUIDES

★619★ *Are You Interested in: Helping Others? . . . Have You Considered . . . Funeral Service?*
National Funeral Directors Association
PO Box 27641
Milwaukee, WI 53227-0641
1993. Describes the funeral service professional's job duties, career opportunities, and educational requirements. Lists schools offering mortuary science programs.

★620★ *Crematory Owner/Funeral Director*
Vocational Biographies, Inc.
PO Box 31
Sauk Centre, MN 56378-0031
Ph: (612)352-6516   Fax: (612)352-5546
Fr: 800-255-0752
1992. Four-page pamphlet containing a personal narrative about a worker's job, work likes and dislikes, career path from high school to the present. Education and training, the rewards and frustrations, and the effects of the job on the rest of the worker's life. The data file portion of this pamphlet gives a concise occupational summary, including work descriptions, working conditions, places of employment, personal characteristics, education and training, job outlook, and salary range.

★621★ *Embalmer/Funeral Director*
Vocational Biographies, Inc.
PO Box 31
Sauk Centre, MN 56378-0031
Ph: (612)352-6516   Fax: (612)352-5546
Fr: 800-255-0752
1991. Four-page pamphlet containing a personal narrative about a worker's job, work likes and dislikes, career path from high school to the present. Education and training, the rewards and frustrations, and the effects of the job on the rest of the worker's life. The data file portion of this pamphlet gives a concise occupational summary, including work descriptions, working conditions, places of employment, personal characteristics, education and training, job outlook, and salary range.

★622★ "Funeral Director" in *Career Information Center* (Vol.5)
Simon and Schuster
200 Old Tappan Rd.
Old Tappan, NJ 07675
Fax: 800-445-6991   Fr: 800-223-2348
Richard Lidz and Linda Perrin, editorial directors. Fifth edition, 1993. This 13-volume set profiles over 600 occupations. Each occupational profile describes job duties, entry-level requirements, educational requirements, advancement possibilities, employment outlook, working conditions, earnings and benefits, and where to write for more information.

★623★ *Funeral Directors*
Chronicle Guidance Publications, Inc.
66 Aurora St.
PO Box 1190
Moravia, NY 13118-1190
Ph: (315)497-0330   Fax: (315)497-3359
Fr: 800-622-7284
1991. Career brief describing the nature of the job, working conditions, hours and earnings, education and training, licensure, certification, unions, personal qualifications, social and psychological factors, location, employment outlook, entry methods, advancement, and related occupations.

★624★ "Funeral Directors" in *Career Discovery Encyclopedia* (Vol.3, pp. 46-47)
J.G. Ferguson Publishing Co.
200 W. Madison St., Ste. 300
Chicago, IL 60606
Ph: (312)580-5480   Fax: (312)580-4948
Russell E. Primm, editor-in chief. 1993. This six volume set contains two-page articles for 504 occupations. Each article describes job duties, earnings, and educational and training requirements. The whole set is arranged alphabetically by job title. Designed for junior high and older students.

★625★ "Funeral Directors and Embalmers" in *Encyclopedia of Careers and Vocational Guidance* (Vol.3, pp. 51-52)
J.G. Ferguson Publishing Co.
200 W. Madison St., Ste. 300
Chicago, IL 60606
Ph: (312)580-5480   Fax: (312)580-4948
William E. Hopke, editor-in-chief. Ninth edition, 1993. Four-volume set that profiles 900 occupations and describes job trends in 74 industries. Includes career description, educational requirements, history of the job, methods of entry, advancement, employment outlook, earnings, conditions of work, social and psychological factors, and sources of further information.

★626★ "Funeral Directors and Embalmers" in *Jobs! What They Are—Where They Are—What They Pay* (pp. 349)
Fireside
Simon & Schuster Bldg.
1230 Avenue of the Americas
New York, NY 10020
Ph: (212)698-7000   Fr: 800-223-2348
Robert O. Snelling and Anne M. Snelling. Revised and updated, 1992. Describes duties and responsibilities, earnings, employment opportunities, training, and qualifications.

★627★ "Funeral Directors" in *Occupational Outlook Handbook* (pp. 40-41)
U.S. Government Printing Office
Superintendent of Documents
Washington, DC 20402
Ph: (202)512-1800   Fax: (212)512-2250
Biennial; latest edition, 1994-95. Encyclopedia of careers. Describes about 250 occupations that comprise about 85 percent of all jobs in the economy. Occupations that require lengthy education or training are given the most attention.

★628★ *Funeral Service: A Tradition of Caring. A Future of Promise*
National Funeral Directors Association
PO Box 27641
Milwaukee, WI 53201
1992. Describes the services funeral directors provide, duties and responsibilities, employment outlook, and salaries. Lists accred-

ited colleges and schools of mortuary science.

★629★ In Service of Others: The Professional Funeral Director
National Funeral Directors Association
PO Box 27641
Milwaukee, WI 53227-8641
Describes the role of the funeral director and career opportunities for men and women.

★630★ "Mortuary Science Technicians" in Encyclopedia of Careers and Vocational Guidance (Vol.3, pp. 470-475)
J.G. Ferguson Publishing Co.
200 W. Madison St., Ste. 300
Chicago, IL 60606
Ph: (312)580-5480   Fax: (312)580-4948
William E. Hopke, editor-in-chief. Ninth edition, 1993. Four-volume set that profiles 900 occupations and describes job trends in 74 industries. Includes career description, educational requirements, history of the job, methods of entry, advancement, employment outlook, earnings, conditions of work, social and psychological factors, and sources of further information.

PROFESSIONAL ASSOCIATIONS

★631★ American Board of Funeral Service Education (ABFSE)
PO Box 1305
Brunswick, ME 04011
Ph: (207)798-5801   Fax: (207)798-5988
Representatives from National Funeral Directors Association and Conference of Funeral Service Examining Boards of the United States; university and college program representatives and public members. Seeks to: formulate and enforce rules and regulations setting up standards concerning the schools and colleges teaching mortuary science; accredit schools and colleges of mortuary science. Sponsors the National Scholarship for Funeral Service program to provide capable young men and women studying in the field with financial assistance. Compiles statistics. **Publications:** Accredited Colleges of Mortuary Science, periodic. • Directory of Accredited College Programs in Mortuary Science and Committees of the American Board of Funeral Service Education, annual. • National Scholarships for Funeral Service, periodic.

★632★ Associated Funeral Directors International (AFDSI)
PO Box 1382
Largo, FL 34649
Ph: (813)593-0709   Fax: (813)593-9937
Fr: 800-346-7151
Funeral homes and mortuaries; franchise-membership granted to one establishment in a community. Services other funeral directors in the shipping of human remains. Provides members with business and professional aids, including public relations and advertising programs, booklets and leaflets, and co-operative buying of products. **Publications:** AFDS Today, bimonthly. • Associated Fu-

neral Directors Service International—Shipping Directory, annual.

★633★ Flying Funeral Directors of America (FFDA)
256 Spring Cove Dr.
Elgin, IL 60123
Ph: (708)931-4232
Members: Funeral directors who own planes, have a pilot's license, or are interested in flying; persons associated with allied funeral industries who are licensed pilots. **Purpose:** to create and further a common interest in flying and funeral service; to join together in case of mass disaster; to improve flying safety. **Publications:** Crosswinds, quarterly. • Membership Roster, biennial.

★634★ Funeral and Memorial Societies of America (CAFMS)
6900 Lost Lake Rd.
Egg Harbor, WI 54209-9231
Ph: (414)868-3136   Fax: (414)868-3136
Fr: 800-458-5563
Works to: promote the affordability, dignity, and simplicity of funeral rites and memorial services; reduce unjustifiable costs of burial and other funeral services; provide every person with the opportunity to predetermine the type of funeral or memorial service he or she desires; make available information on body or organ donation. Promotes reciprocity of benefits among member societies; informs public on funeral costs and methods of reducing costs; lobbies for reform of funeral regulations at the state and federal levels. Maintains speakers' bureau. **Publications:** FAMSA—Directory of Member Societies, periodic. • The Leader, periodic.

★635★ Jewish Funeral Directors of America (JFDA)
399 E. 72nd St., Ste. 3F
New York, NY 10021
Ph: (212)628-3465   Fax: (212)517-4647
Professional society of Jewish funeral directors. **Publications:** Funeral Etiquette. • How to Explain Death to Children, 3/year. • If You Will Lift the Load. • Jewish Funeral Director, annual. • Jewish Funeral in Contemporary Life. • Suicide in the Young.

★636★ National Foundation of Funeral Service (NFFS)
2250 E. Devon Ave., Ste. 250
Des Plaines, IL 60018
Ph: (708)827-6337   Fax: (708)827-6342
Operates school of funeral service management, extension courses, library, and research, charitable, and educational program. **Publications:** NFFS News, quarterly.

★637★ National Funeral Directors Association (NFDA)
11121 W. Oklahoma Ave.
Milwaukee, WI 53227-4096
Ph: (414)541-2500   Fax: (414)541-1909
Members: Federation of state funeral directors' associations. Founded by and associated with the Academy of Professional Funeral Service Practice (voluntary certification program). Maintains speakers' bureau and conducts professional education seminars and home study courses. Compiles statistics. **Publications:** The Director, monthly. • National Funeral Directors Association—Membership/Resource Guide, annual.

★638★ National Funeral Directors and Morticians Association (NFDMA)
1800 E. Linwood Blvd.
Kansas City, MO 64109-2097
Ph: (816)921-1800   Fax: (816)924-2113
State, district, and local funeral directing and embalming associations and their members. Promotes ethical practices; encourages just and uniform laws pertaining to funeral directing and embalming.

★639★ National Selected Morticians (NSM)
5 Revere Dr., Ste. 340
Northbrook, IL 60062
Ph: (708)559-9569
Members: Funeral directors. **Publications:** The Bulletin, monthly. • Membership Roster, annual. • Personal Roster, biennial.

STANDARDS/CERTIFICATION AGENCIES

★640★ American Board of Funeral Service Education (ABFSE)
PO Box 1305
Brunswick, ME 04011
Ph: (207)798-5801   Fax: (207)798-5988
Representatives from National Funeral Directors Association and Conference of Funeral Service Examining Boards of the United States; university and college program representatives and public members. Seeks to: formulate and enforce rules and regulations setting up standards concerning the schools and colleges teaching mortuary science; accredit schools and colleges of mortuary science. Sponsors the National Scholarship for Funeral Service program to provide capable young men and women studying in the field with financial assistance.

★641★ National Funeral Directors Association (NFDA)
11121 W. Oklahoma Ave.
Milwaukee, WI 53227-4096
Ph: (414)541-2500   Fax: (414)541-1909
Founded by and associated with the Academy of Professional Funeral Service Practice (voluntary certification program). Maintains speakers' bureau and conducts professional education seminars and home study courses.

TEST GUIDES

★642★ Career Examination Series: Funeral Directing Investigator
National Learning Corp.
212 Michael Dr.
Syosset, NY 11791
Ph: (516)921-8888   Fax: (516)921-9743
Fr: 800-645-6337
Jack Rudman. Test guide including questions and answers for students or professionals in the field who seek advancement through examination.

EDUCATIONAL DIRECTORIES AND PROGRAMS

★643★ American Blue Book of Funeral Directors
Kates-Boylston Publication, Inc.
1501 Broadway
New York, NY 10036
Ph: (212)398-9266   Fax: (212)768-9140
Adrian F. BoylstonPublisher

Covers: about 22,000 funeral homes primarily in the United States and Canada. Manufacturers and suppliers of supplies and equipment for funeral homes are also listed. Entries include: For funeral homes—Name, address, phone. For manufacturers and suppliers—Name, address, toll-free phone, fax, products.

★644★ Associated Funeral Directors International—Membership Directory
Associated Resources, Inc.
11691 Oval Dr. W.
PO Box 1382
Largo, FL 34644
Ph: (813)593-0709   Fax: (813)593-9937
Fr: 800-346-7151
Richard A. Santore, Contact

Annual, fall. Covers Approximately 18,000 funeral service providers in the U.S. Entries include: Co. name, address, phone, telex, name and title of contact.

★645★ Embalmers Directory
American Business Directories, Inc.
5711 S. 86th Circle
Omaha, NE 68127
Ph: (402)593-4600   Fax: (402)331-1505
Entries include: Name, address, phone, size of advertisement, name of owner or manager, number of employees, year first in "Yellow Pages." Compiled from telephone company "Yellow Pages," nationwide.

★646★ Funeral Directors Directory
American Business Directories, Inc.
5711 S. 86th Circle
Omaha, NE 68127
Ph: (402)593-4600   Fax: (402)331-1505
Number of listings: 30,176 (U.S. edition); 3,133 (Canadian edition). Entries include: Name, address, phone (including area code), size of advertisement, year first in "Yellow Pages," name of owner or manager, number of employees. Regional editions available: Eastern, $760.00; Western, $395.00. Compiled from telephone company "Yellow Pages," nationwide.

★647★ Funeral and Memorial Societies of America
Funeral and Memorial Societies of America
6900 Lost Lake Rd.
Egg Harbor, WI 54209-9231
Ph: (414)868-3136   Fax: (414)868-3136
Fr: 800-458-5563
John L. Blake, Contact

Covers: over 150 nonprofit memorial societies which assist members in obtaining simple funeral arrangements at reasonable cost. Includes members of the Memorial Society Association of Canada. Entries include: Name, address, phone.

★648★ Funeral Plans—Pre-Arranged Directory
American Business Directroies, Inc.
5711 S. 86th Circle
Omaha, NE 68127
Ph: (402)593-4600   Fax: (402)331-1505
Number of listings: 1,937. Entries include: Name, address, phone, size of advertisement, name of owner or manager, number of employees, year first in "Yellow Pages." Compiled from telephone company "Yellow Pages," nationwide.

★649★ National Funeral Directors Association—Membership Listing and Resources
NFDA Publications, Inc.
11121 W. Oklahoma Ave.
Milwaukee, WI 53227
Ph: (414)541-2500   Fax: (414)541-1909
Kellie Schilling

Covers: 20,000 members of state funeral director associations affiliated with the National Funeral Directors Association. Entries include: Company name, address, phone, and principal executive.

★650★ The National Yellow Book of Funeral Directors
Nomis Publications, Inc.
PO Box 5122
Youngstown, OH 44514
Ph: 800-321-7479   Fax: (216)788-1112
Twentieth edition, 1994. A directory of funeral homes across the country. Includes the name, address, and phone, of all its listees.

★651★ Purple Directory: National Listing of Minority Funeral Firms
Shugar's
15873 Hartwell St.
Detroit, MI 48227
Ph: (313)836-8300   Fax: (313)836-8600
Miriam E. Pipes

Covers: Approximately 2,500 minority funeral firms in the U.S. Entries include: Firm name, address, phone; some listings include fax and name and title of contact.

★652★ Texas Funeral Services Directory
TSD Press
1800 Nueces
Austin, TX 78701
Ph: (512)477-5698   Fax: (512)473-2447
Julie Sayers

Annual, August.

★653★ Yellow Book of Funeral Directors
Nomis Publications, Inc.
PO Box 5122
Youngstown, OH 44514
Ph: (216)788-9608   Fax: (216)788-1112
Fr: 800-321-7479
Margaret Rouzzo, Secretary/Treasurer

Covers: 23,000 United States and Canadian funeral homes; Veteran's Administration hospitals and regional offices; major hospitals; foreign consulates and branch offices; daily papers; mortuary colleges. Entries include: Name of home, address, phone, code for shipping points, city code for daily papers available for obituaries.

AWARDS, SCHOLARSHIPS, GRANTS, AND FELLOWSHIPS

★654★ Award of Recognition
Conference of Funeral Service Examining Boards
15 NE 3rd. St.
PO Box 497
Washington, IN 47501
Ph: (812)254-7887   Fax: (812)254-6966

To recognize those individuals who have contributed to the continued efforts of funeral service education. Institution directors, state board representatives, funeral service organizations, and funeral service educators are eligible. A plaque is awarded annually during the convention. Established in 1952.

★655★ Hilgenfeld Research and Publications Grants; Hilgenfeld Scholarship Grants
Hilgenfeld Foundation for Mortuary Education
PO Box 4311
Fullerton, CA 92634

Purpose: To expand the knowledge and understanding of funeral service through education, research, and thanatology books publication. Qualifications: Applicant must be a high school graduate or actively involved in the mortuary science industry. Scholarship applicant must be student pursuing career in funeral service, or in the funeral service industry seeking a graduate degree. Funds available: $250-10,000. Application details: Write to the Foundation for guidelines. Deadline: None.

★656★ National Scholarships for Funeral Service
American Board of Funeral Service Education
14 Crestwood Rd.
Cumberland, ME 04021

Qualifications: Applicants must be citizens of the United States and have completed at least one term of study in a program in Funeral Service or Mortuary Science Education that is accredited by the American Board of Funeral Service Education. Selection criteria: Recipients are chosen on the basis of financial need, academic performance, extracurricular and/or community activities, recommendations, and the articulateness of the scholarship application. Funds available: Either $250 or $500 and are remitted directly to the college upon satisfactory proof of enrollment. Application details: Applicants are required to file an application (including one essay), one letter of recommendation, transcripts of all previous college work attempted, and their federal 1040 tax form. Deadline: March 15 and September 15.

BASIC REFERENCE GUIDES AND HANDBOOKS

★657★ The Funeral Director's Practice Management Handbook
Prentice Hall
Rte. 9W
Englewood Cliffs, NJ 07632
Ph: (201)592-2000

Howard C. Raether, editor. 1989. Contains different responsibilities of the funeral director. Includes personalizing funerals, grief counseling, self-help support groups, and prearranged funerals.

PROFESSIONAL AND TRADE PERIODICALS

★658★ American Funeral Director
Kates-Bolyston Publications, Inc.
1501 Broadway
New York, NY 10036
Ph: (212)398-9266   Fax: (212)768-9140
Nick Verrastro

Monthly. Magazine featuring articles on home management, including construction, finance, laws, developments, and association news.

★659★ Continental Association of Funeral and Memorial Societies— Leader
Continental Association of Funeral and Memorial Societies
6900 Lost Lake Rd.
Egg Harbor, WI 54209-9231
Ph: (301)913-0030
John Blake

Quarterly. Concerned with the funeral industry, activities of memorial societies, and legislation related to consumer rights in making funeral arrangements. Includes articles and bibliographies pertaining to funerals, death, and dying.

★660★ The Director
National Funeral Directors Assn.
11121 W. Oklahoma Ave.
Milwaukee, WI 53227-4096
Ph: (414)541-2500   Fax: (414)541-1909
Susan Daniels

Monthly. Magazine for the funeral service profession. Includes medical updates, business trends, funeral regulations, and bereavement issues.

★661★ Florida Funeral Director
Florida Funeral Directors Service, Inc.
502 E. Jefferson St.
Tallahassee, FL 32314
Ph: (904)224-1969   Fax: (904)224-7965
Jan Scheff
Bimonthly.

★662★ Funeral Service Business & Legal Guide
CB Legal Publishing Corporation
555 Skokie Blvd., Ste.500
Northbrook, IL 60062
Ph: (708)480-1020   Fax: (708)480-7859
Cheryl A. Lapin

Discusses business and legal problems pertinent to the funeral service industry. Covers such topics as antitrust issues, tax matters, consumer trade practice, government regulations, and environmental concerns.

★663★ Funeral Service "Insider"
United Communications Group
11300 Rockville Pike, No. 1100
Rockville, MD 20852
Ph: (301)816-8945
Lance Helgerson

Covers the latest trends in funeral service education, legislation, franchising, marketing, and consumer purchasing. Recurring features include editorials, news of research, letters to the editor, and a calendar of events.

★664★ Morticians of the Southwest
Farring, Inc.
2514 National Dr.
Garland, TX 75041-2329
Ph: (214)840-1060
Sharon M. Farrell

Monthly. Funeral service industry magazine.

★665★ Mortuary Management
315 Silver Lake Blvd.
Los Angeles, CA 90026
Ph: (213)665-0101   Fax: (213)665-3068
Ronald Hast

Monthly. Magazine for those involved in the funeral industry.

★666★ Southern Funeral Director
PO Box 1147
Beaufort, SC 29902
Ph: (803)521-0239   Fax: (803)521-1398
Fr: 800-849-9677
Mary Vopp Cronley

Monthly. Magazine for funeral directors.

★667★ Texas Director
Texas Funeral Directors Assn.
PO Box 14667
Austin, TX 78761
Ph: (512)454-5262   Fax: (512)451-9556
Jeannette Brown, Contact

Monthly. Business and professional magazine for funeral directors.

PROFESSIONAL MEETINGS AND CONVENTIONS

★668★ Kansas Funeral Directors and Embalmers Association Convention
National Funeral Directors Association
11121 W. Oklahoma Ave.
Milwaukee, WI 53227
Ph: (414)541-2500   Fax: (414)541-1909
Annual. **Dates and Locations:** 1995, Oct. 28-02, Fl.

★669★ Michigan Funeral Directors Association Convention
Michigan Funeral Directors Association
PO Box 27158
Lansing, MI 48909
Ph: (517)482-3928   Fax: (517)482-8212
Annual.

★670★ Missouri Funeral Directors Association Annual Convention
Missouri Funeral Directors Association
600 Ellis Blvd.
Jefferson City, MO 65101
Ph: (314)635-1661   Fax: (314)635-9494
Annual.

★671★ National Funeral Directors and Morticians Association Convention
National Funeral Directors and Morticians Association
1800 E. Linwood
Kansas City, MO 64109
Ph: (816)921-1800
Annual.

★672★ New Jersey State Funeral Directors Assocaition Convention
New Jersey State Funeral Directors Association
Manasquan, NJ 08736
Ph: (908)974-9444
Annual.

★673★ Ohio Funeral Directors Annual Convention
Ohio Funeral Directors Assocaition
2501 N. Star Rd.
Columbus, OH 43221
Ph: (614)486-5339   Fax: (614)486-5358
Annual. Always held during April or May at the Hyatt Regency Convention Center in Columbus Ohio. **Dates and Locations:** 1996, May 01-03 • 1997, Apr 22-25.

★674★ South Dakota Funeral Directors Association Annual Convention
South Dakota Funeral Directors Association
PO Box 1037
Pierre, SD 57501
Ph: (605)224-1591   Fax: (605)224-7426
Annual. Always held during January at the Downtown Convention Center in San Antonio, Texas.

★675★ Texas Funeral Directors Association Convention
Texas Funeral Directors Association
1513 S. Interstate 35
Austin, TX 78741
Ph: (512)442-2304   Fax: (512)443-3559
Annual. **Dates and Locations:** 1996, Jun 03-07, Austin, TX • 1997, Jun 10-14, Arlington, TX • 1998, Jun 01-05, Corpus Christi, TX.

★676★ Virginia Funeral Directors Assocaiton Convention
Virginia Funeral Directors Association
5803 Staple Mill Rd.
Richmond, VA 23228-5427
Ph: (804)264-0505   Fax: (804)264-3260
Annual. Always held during June.

OTHER SOURCES OF INFORMATION

★677★ "Funeral Director" in *Career Selector 2001*
Barron's Educational Series, Inc.
250 Wireless Blvd.
Hauppauge, NY 11788
Ph: (516)434-3311   Fax: (516)434-3723
Fr: 800-645-3476
James C. Gonyea. 1993.

General Managers and Top Executives

General managers and top executives are at the top of the management hierarchy. They formulate the policies and direct the operations of both private firms and government agencies. **Chief executive officers**, for example, establish an organization's general goals and policies in collaboration with executive vice-presidents and the board of directors.

Salaries

Salaries vary substantially depending upon the level of managerial responsibility, length of service, and type, size, and location of firm. Chief executive officers are the most highly paid top-level managers, many receiving base salaries of $3.2 million or more, plus additional compensation in the way of fringe benefits and company stock, equivalent, on the average, to nearly half of their base salary.

Employment Outlook

Growth rate until the year 2005: More slowly than the average.

General Managers and Top Executives

CAREER GUIDES

CAREER GUIDES

★678★ "Business Administration and Management" in *College Majors and Careers: A Resource Guide to Effective Life Planning* (pp. 31-32)
Garrett Park Press
PO Box 1907
Garrett Park, MD 20896
Ph: (301)946-2553
Paul Phifer. Revised, 1993. Lists 61 college majors, with definitions; related occupations and leisure activities; skills, values, and personal needed attributes; suggested readings; and a list of associations.

★679★ "Business Executive" in *College Board Guide to Jobs and Career Planning* (pp. 90)
The College Board
415 Columbus Ave.
New York, NY 10023-6992
Ph: (212)713-8165   Fax: (212)713-8143
Fr: 800-323-7155
Joyce S. Mitchell. Second edition, 1994. Describes the job, salaries, related careers, education needed, and where to write for more information.

★680★ *Business and Management Jobs*
Petersons Guides, Inc.
PO Box 2123
Princeton, NJ 08543-2123
Ph: (609)243-9111   Fax: (609)243-9150
Fr: 800-338-3282
Billy Christopher, editor. Annual. This guide gives job hunting advice and profiles companies across the United States that hire business degree program graduates at the bachelor and masters level. Company profiles give name, address, describes what the company does, describe entry level hires, gives the starting location and contact information. Companies are indexed by degree level, major of new hires, industry, and starting location.

★681★ *Career Choices for the 90's for Students of Business*
Walker and Co.
435 Hudson St.
New York, NY 10014
Ph: (212)727-8300   Fax: (212)727-0984
Fr: 800-289-2553
Compiled by Career Associates Staff. 1990. This book offers alternatives for students of business, including the career of underwriter. Gives information about the outlook and competition for entry-level candidates. Provides job hunting tips.

★682★ *Career Choices for the 90's for Students of MBA*
Walker and Co.
435 Hudson St.
New York, NY 10014
Ph: (212)727-8300   Fax: (212)727-0984
Fr: 800-289-2553
Compiled by Career Associates Staff. 1990. This book offers alternatives for students interested in business. Gives information about the outlook and competition for entry-level candidates. Provides job hunting tips.

★683★ *Careers in Business*
National Textbook Co. (NTC)
VGM Career Books
4255 W. Touhy Ave.
Lincolnwood, IL 60646-1975
Ph: (708)679-5500   Fax: (708)679-2494
Fr: 800-323-4900
Lila B. Stair and Dorothy Domkowski. 1992. Provides facts about business areas such as marketing, accounting, production, human resources, management and finance. Focuses on job duties, salaries, career paths, employment outlook, trends, educational preparation and skills needed.

★684★ *Careers and the MBA: Targeting Your Search*
Bob Adams, Inc.
260 Center St.
Holbrook, MA 02343-1074
Ph: (617)767-8100   Fr: 800-872-5627
Gigi Ranno, editor. 1994. Features articles by leaders in business and addresses trends in business, industry reports. Includes the ad-dresses of 700 companies currently recruiting M.B.A.'s.

★685★ "City Manager" in *VGM's Handbook of Business and Management Careers*
National Textbook Co.
4255 W. Touhy Ave.
Lincolnwood, IL 60646-1975
Ph: (708)679-5500   Fax: (708)679-2494
Fr: 800-323-4900
Annette Selden. Second edition, 1993. Contains 42 two-page occupational profiles describing job duties, places of employment, working conditions, qualifications, education, employment outlook, and income.

★686★ "Executive Director" in *Profitable Careers in Non-Profit* (pp. 27-46)
John Wiley and Sons, Inc.
605 3rd Ave.
New York, NY 10158-0012
Ph: (212)850-6000   Fax: (212)850-6088
Fr: 800-526-5368
William Lewis and Carol Milano. 1987. Examines nonprofit organizations and the career opportunities they offer. Offers tips on how to target and explore occupational opportunities in the nonprofit sector.

★687★ *Executive Resume Handbook*
Prentice-Hall, Inc.
200 Old Tappan Rd.
Old Tappan, NJ 07675
Ph: (201)767-5000   Fr: 800-634-2863
Harold W. Dickhut. 1987. Describes how to write resumes and cover letters. Gives advice on job hunting and interviewing. Includes samples of skill-oriented resumes.

★688★ "General Business" in *Internships: 1995* (pp. 24-31)
Petersons Guides, Inc.
PO Box 2123
Princeton, NJ 08543-2123
Ph: (609)243-9111   Fax: (609)243-9150
Fr: 800-338-3282
Fifteenth edition, 1995. Lists internship opportunities under six broad categories: communications, creative, performing, and fine, performing, and fine, performing, and fine

arts, human services, international relations, business and technology, and public relations. Includes a special section on internships in Washington, DC. For each internship program, gives the name, phone number, contact person, description, eligibility requirements, and benefits.

★689★ "General Managers" in *Career Information Center* (Vol.1)
Simon and Schuster
200 Old Tappan Rd.
Old Tappan, NJ 07675
Fax: 800-445-6991   Fr: 800-223-2348
Richard Lidz and Linda Perrin, editorial directors. Fifth edition, 1993. A multi-volume set that profiles over 600 occupations. Each occupational profile describes job duties, educational requirements, advancement possibilities, employment outlook, working conditions, earnings and benefits, and where to write for more information.

★690★ "General Managers and Top Executives" in *Occupational Outlook Handbook*
U.S. Government Printing Office
Superintendent of Documents
Washington, DC 20402
Ph: (202)512-1800   Fax: (202)512-2250
Biennial; latest edition, 1994-95. Encyclopedia of careers describing about 250 occupations and comprising about 85 percent of all jobs in the economy. Occupations that require lengthy education or training are given the most attention. Each occupation's profile describes what the worker does on the job, working conditions, education and training requirements, advancement possibilities, job outlook, earnings, and sources of additional information.

★691★ *How to Get the Hot Jobs in Business & Finance*
Perennial Library
10 E. 53rd St.
New York, NY 10022
Ph: (212)207-7000
Mary E. Calhoun. 1988.

★692★ *Make Them Choose You: The Executive Selection Process, Replacing Mystery With Strategy*
Prentice-Hall, Inc.
200 Old Tappan Rd.
Old Tappan, NJ 07675
Ph: (201)767-5000   Fr: 800-634-2863
James D. Kohlmann. 1988. Written for executives, managers, and professionals at all levels. Focuses on the psychology of the interview. The author suggests responses to interview questions that will generate positive feedback. Gives advice on salary negotiation.

★693★ *Managers (Business and Manufacturing)*
Careers, Inc.
PO Box 135
Largo, FL 34649-0135
Ph: (813)584-7333
1994. Four-page brief offering the definition, history, duties, working conditions, personal qualifications, educational requirements, earnings, hours, employment outlook, advancement, and careers related to this position.

★694★ *Opportunities in Business Management Careers*
National Textbook Co. (NTC)
VGM Career Books
4255 W. Touhy Ave.
Lincolnwood, IL 60646-1975
Ph: (708)679-5500   Fax: (708)679-2494
Fr: 800-323-4900
Irene Magdaline Place. 1991. Describes the management field and the employment outlook for managers. Explains management education, advancement opportunities, and benefits. Gives job hunting strategies.

★695★ *Pack Your Own Parachute: How to Survive Mergers, Takeovers and Other Corporate Disasters*
Addison-Wesley Publishing Co.
1 Jacob Way
Reading, MA 01867
Ph: (617)944-3700   Fr: 800-447-2226
Paul Morris Hirsch. 1987. Explains company takeovers; describes the human cost of restructuring. Includes a discussion of the free agent concept for managers.

★696★ *Rate Your Executive Potential*
John Wiley and Sons, Inc.
605 3rd Ave.
New York, NY 10158-0012
Ph: (212)850-6000   Fax: (212)850-6088
Fr: 800-526-5368
Roger Fritz. 1988. Provides guidelines to become a successful manager and a better candidate for promotion to the executive level. Outlines key elements of good management. Describes self-evaluation and gives suggestions for improvement.

★697★ "Richard Huback—Chairman of the Board" in *Straight Talk on Careers: Eighty Pros Take You Into Their Professions* (pp. 46-48)
Garrett Park Press
PO Box 1907
Garrett Park, MD 20896
Ph: (301)946-2553
Mary Barbera-Hogan. 1987. Contains candid interviews from people who give an inside view of their work in 80 different careers. These professionals describe a day's work and the stresses and rewards accompanying their work.

★698★ *Rites of Passage at $100,000 Plus: The Insider's Lifetime Guide to Executive Job-Changing and Faster Career Progress*
Henry Holt & Co.
115 W. 18th St., 6th Fl.
New York, NY 10011
Ph: (212)886-9200
John Lucht. Revised edition, 1993. This book describes how to change jobs and includes information on networking, job search strategies, interviewing, and negotiating the employment contract. Gives advice on working with executive recruiters.

★699★ *VGM's Handbook of Business & Management Careers*
National Textbook Co. (NTC)
VGM Career Books
4255 W. Touhy Ave.
Lincolnwood, IL 60646-1975
Ph: (708)679-5500   Fax: (708)679-2494
Fr: 800-323-4900
DES Annette Selden, editor. Second edition, 1993. Contains 42 occupational profiles. Each profile contains information on job duties, places of employment, working conditions, qualifications, educational requirements, employment outlook, and income.

PROFESSIONAL ASSOCIATIONS

★700★ **American Management Association (AMA)**
135 W. 50th St.
New York, NY 10020-1201
Ph: (212)586-8100   Fax: (212)903-8168
Members: Provides educational forums worldwide to teach members and their colleagues about superior, practical business skills and explore best practices of world-class organizations through interaction with each other and expert faculty practitioners. **Purpose:** Publishing program provides tools individuals use to extend learning beyond the classroom in a process of life-long professional growth and development through education. **Publications:** *Compensation and Benefits Review*, bimonthly. • *CompFlash*, monthly. • *HR Focus*, monthly. • *Management Review*, monthly. • *Organizational Dynamics: A Quarterly Review of Organizational Behavior for Professional Managers*. • *The President*, monthly. • *Supervisory Management*, monthly.

★701★ **Chief Executives Organization (CEO)**
5430 Grosvenor Ln., Ste. 210
Bethesda, MD 20814
Ph: (301)564-9614   Fax: (301)564-0060
Members: Members of the Young Presidents' Organization who have reached the age of 49, the mandatory "retirement" age for YPO. (Young Presidents' Organization comprises presidents of corporations with gross annual revenue of at least one million dollars and a minimum of 50 employees, of nonindustrial corporations with revenue of two million dollars and 25 employees, or of banking corporations with average deposits of 15 million dollars and 25 employees. Each member must have been elected president of a corporation before reaching the age of 35.) **Purpose:** Sponsors educational programs. **Publications:** *News*, quarterly.

★702★ **National Certification Agency for Medical Lab Personnel (NCA)**
7910 Woodmont Ave., Ste. 1301
Bethesda, MD 20814
Ph: (301)654-1622   Fax: (301)657-2909
Members: Persons who direct, educate, supervise, or practice in clinical laboratory science. **Purpose:** To assure the public and employers of the competence of clinical laboratory personnel; to provide a mecha-

nism for individuals demonstrating competency in the field to achieve career mobility. Develops and administers competency-based examinations for certification of clinical laboratory personnel; provides for periodic recertification by examination or through documentation of continuing education. Compiles statistics.

★703★ National Management Association (NMA)
2210 Arbor Blvd.
Dayton, OH 45439
Ph: (513)294-0421   Fax: (513)294-2374
Members: Business and industrial management personnel; membership comes from supervisory level, with the remainder from middle management and above. **Purpose:** Seeks to develop and recognize management as a profession and to promote the free enterprise system. Prepares chapter programs on basic management, management policy and practice, communications, human behavior, industrial relations, economics, political education, and liberal education. Maintains speakers' bureau and hall of fame. Maintains educational, charitable, and research programs. Sponsors charitable programs. **Publications:** *Board of Directors Directory*, annual. • *Manage*, quarterly. • *National Speakers' Directory*, periodic.

★704★ Society for Advancement of Management (SAM)
PO Box 889
Vinton, VA 24179
Ph: (703)342-5563   Fax: (703)342-6413
Members: Professional organization of management executives in industry commerce, government, and education. **Purpose:** Fields of interest include management education, international management, administration, budgeting, collective bargaining, distribution, incentives, materials handling, quality control, and training. Sponsors numerous conferences, study groups, and seminars; conducts special programs on economics, material handling, distribution, industrial relations, and operation of small businesses. Sponsors National Management Case Competition. **Publications:** *Advanced Management Journal*, quarterly. • *SAM Focus on Management*, quarterly. • *The SAM Manager*, quarterly. • *Society for Advancement of Management— Annual Directory of Officers*.

STANDARDS/CERTIFICATION AGENCIES

★705★ American Society of International Executives (ASIE)
18 Sentry Pkwy., Ste. 1
Blue Bell, PA 19422
Ph: (215)540-2295   Fax: (215)540-2290
Awards certification as Certified Documentary Specialist (CDS), Certified International Executive (CIE), or Experienced International Executive (EIE-EM).

TEST GUIDES

★706★ Barrons' How to Prepare for the Graduate Management Admission Test (GMAT)
Barron's Educational Series, Inc.
250 Wireless Blvd.
Hauppauge, NY 11788
Ph: (516)434-3311   Fax: 800-645-3476
Fr: 800-645-3476

Eugene D. Jaffe and Stephen Hilbert. Tenth edition, 1994. This guide includes five practice tests and one full-length diagnostic test. All answers are explained.

★707★ Career Examination Series: Administrator
National Learning Corp.
212 Michael Dr.
Syosset, NY 11791
Ph: (516)921-8888   Fax: (516)921-8743
Fr: 800-645-6337

Jack Rudman. A series of study guides with multiple-choice examination questions and solutions for trainees and professional general managers. Titles in the series include *Administrative Officer; Administrative Officer I; Administrative Officer II; Administrator I; Administrator II; Administrator III; Administrator IV; Board Member; Chief Executive Officer; Director of Administration; Director of Administrative Services; Executive Director; Senior Business Manager*.

★708★ GMAT: Graduate Management Admission Test
Arco Publishing Co.
Macmillan General Reference
15 Columbus Cir.
New York, NY 10023
Fax: 800-835-3202   Fr: 800-858-7674

Thomas Martinson. et al. Sixth edition, 1994. Includes six sample tests with an explanation of the answers. Also provides inside advice on business school admissions and financing graduate education.

★709★ SuperCourse for the GMAT
Arco Publishing Co.
Macmillan General Reference
15 Columbus Cir.
New York, NY 10023
Fax: 800-835-3202   Fr: 800-858-7674

Thomas Martinson. Fourth edition, 1993. Includes study plans, test-taking strategies, model exams, and drills.

EDUCATIONAL DIRECTORIES AND PROGRAMS

★710★ American Assembly of Collegiate Schools of Business— Membership Directory
American Assembly of Collegiate Schools of Business
600 Emerson Rd., Ste. 300
St. Louis, MO 63141-6762
Ph: (314)872-8481   Fax: (314)872-8495
Sharon Barber, Director of Communications

Annual, September. Covers over 800 member institutions offering instructional programs in business administration at the college level; member businesses, governmental agencies, and professional organizations. Entries include: Institution or company name, address, phone, fax, e-mail, name and title of member representative. Arrangement: Alphabetical by organization.

★711★ Bricker's International Directory: Long-Term University—Based Executive Programs
Peterson's Guides, Inc.
202 Carnegie Center
PO Box 2123
Princeton, NJ 08543-2123
Ph: (609)243-9111   Fax: (609)243-9150
Fr: 800-338-3282
Dorothy Q. Power, Contact

Annual, October. Covers several hundred residential management development programs at academic institutions in the United States and abroad. Criteria for listing include that program must be residential, at least one week in length, in English, not introductory in content, and with emphasis on "strategic" issues and functions covering a wide range of organizations. Entries include: Name of program; sponsoring institution; location, dates, and duration of program; tuition fees; curriculum content; modes of instruction; size of classes; information on participants; living accommodations; faculty; special features; official contact. Arrangement: Classified by subject, then alphabetical by institution.

AWARDS, SCHOLARSHIPS, GRANTS, AND FELLOWSHIPS

★712★ AMS Award for Achievements in and Contributions to Management
Administrative Management Society
1101 14th St. NW, Ste. 1100
Washington, DC 20005-5601
Ph: (202)371-8299

To recognize distinguished achievements in and significant contributions to the profession of management. Nominations and selection are based on the following criteria: (1) outstanding achievements in and contributions to management and business; (2) contributions to the advancement of education and/or training in the field of management; (3) contributions to the enhancement of management as a profession or recognition as a management professional through outstanding contributions to society in general through professional, community and civic activities; and (4) demonstrated professional competence in management. The deadline for nominations is February 1. A gold medal is presented annually. Established in 1982.

★713★ Arts Management Award for Arts Administrator of the Year
Arts Management
408 W. 57th St.
New York, NY 10019
Ph: (212)245-3850

To honor an outstanding arts administrator for specific accomplishments of note and to focus national attention on the entire profession. An individual professionally employed as administrator of a cultural program during the year by an organization whose primary activity is in the field of the performing or visual arts is eligible. A wood plaque is awarded annually. Established in 1969.

★714★ Arts Management Award for Career Service
Arts Management
408 W. 57th St.
New York, NY 10019
Ph: (212)245-3850

To honor an outstanding arts administrator for contributions to cultural development over the past decade. An individual professionally employed as an administrator of a cultural program for the previous ten years by an organization whose primary activity is in the field of the performing or visual arts is eligible. A wood plaque is awarded annually. Established in 1969.

★715★ Phil Carroll Advancement of Management Awards
Society for Advancement of Management
PO Box 889
Vinton, VA 24179
Ph: (703)342-5563   Fax: (703)342-6413

To recognize a specific contribution as represented by a published article, and a case history of implementation of the new idea or technique. Awards are given in the following categories: (1) Operations Management; (2) Marketing Management; (3) Management of Product or Service Development; (4) Financial Management; (5) Personnel Management; and (6) General Management. Any key management person, whether a member or not, is eligible. A writeup of the contribution must have been published at least one year prior to the selection. Individuals of any nationality may be nominated. Awarded as merited.

★716★ Henry Laurence Gantt Medal
American Management Association
135 W. 50th St.
New York, NY 10020-1201
Ph: (212)903-7915

To recognize distinguished achievement in management as a service to the community. A medal is awarded annually. Established in 1929 to memorialize the acomplishments and service to the community by Henry Laurence Gantt, a distinguished management engineer, industrial leader, and humanitarian. Co-sponsored by the American Society of Mechanical Engineers.

★717★ Taylor Key Award
Society for Advancement of Management
PO Box 889
Vinton, VA 24179
Ph: (703)342-5563   Fax: (703)342-6413

This, one of the highest awards of the Society, is given for recognition of outstanding contributions to the art and science of management as conceived by Frederick W. Taylor. Individuals of any nationality are eligible. A gold key is awarded annually. Established in 1937.

BASIC REFERENCE GUIDES AND HANDBOOKS

★718★ Dictionary of Business and Management
John Wiley and Sons, Inc.
605 3rd Ave.
New York, NY 10158-0012
Ph: (212)850-6000   Fax: (212)850-6088
Fr: 800-526-5368

Jerry Martin Rosenberg. Third edition, 1992. Defines about 10,000 business-related terms.

★719★ Essentials of Management
McGraw-Hill, Inc.
1221 Avenue of the Americas
New York, NY 10020
Ph: (212)512-2000   Fr: 800-722-4726

Harold D. Koontz, Cyril O'Donnell, et al. Fifth edition, 1990. Basic text covering management theory, planning, organizing, staffing, leading, and controlling.

★720★ Handbook of International Business
John Wiley and Sons, Inc.
605 3rd Ave.
New York, NY 10158-0012
Ph: (212)850-6000   Fax: (212)850-6088
Fr: 800-526-5368

Ingo Walter and Tracy Murray, editors. Second edition, 1988. Contains sections on all areas of international business. Includes bibliographies.

★721★ Handbook of International Management
John Wiley and Sons, Inc.
605 3rd Ave.
New York, NY 10158-0012
Ph: (212)850-6000   Fax: (212)850-6088
Fr: 800-526-5368

Ingo Walter and Tracy Murray, editors. 1988. Covers forecasting, market research, international financial accounting, and international labor relations.

★722★ Handbook of Management and Development
Gower Publishing Co.
Old Post Rd.
Brookfield, VT 05036
Ph: (802)276-3162

Alan Mumford. Third edition, 1991.

★723★ Leadership in Organizations
Prentice-Hall, Inc.
Rte. 9W
Englewood Cliffs, NJ 07632
Ph: (201)592-2000   Fr: 800-634-2863

Gary Yukl. Second edition, 1989. Details major theories of leadership and provides practical guidelines for application. Covers power, activity patterns in managerial work, leadership behavior, and managerial traits.

★724★ Management
Prentice Hall
113 Sylvan Ave., Rte. 9W
Englewood Cliffs, NJ 07632
Ph: (201)592-2000   Fr: 800-922-0579

James A. Stoner and R. Freeman. Sixth edition, 1995. Provides an introduction to management; covers ethics, strategic planning, and entrepreneurship.

★725★ Management
McGraw-Hill, Inc.
1221 Avenue of the Americas
New York, NY 10020
Ph: (212)512-2000   Fr: 800-722-4726

Harold D. Koontz and Heinz Weihrich. Ninth edition, 1988. Basic text that covers management theory, planning, organizing, staffing, and controlling.

★726★ Managing People
Facts on File
460 Park Ave. S.
New York, NY 10016-7382
Ph: (212)683-2244   Fax: 800-678-3633
Fr: 800-322-8755

Dale A. Timpe, editor. 1988. Includes a bibliography and an index.

★727★ The Minority Executives Handbook
Warner Books, Inc.
666 5th Ave.
New York, NY 10103
Ph: (212)522-7200   Fr: 800-343-9204

Randolph W. Cameron. 1993.

★728★ The NMA Handbook for Managers
Prentice-Hall, Inc.
Rte. 9W
Englewood Cliffs, NJ 07632
Ph: (201)592-2000

Patricia H. Virga, editor. 1987. Includes bibliographical references and an index.

★729★ Principles of Modern Management: Functions and Systems
Allyn & Bacon, Inc.
160 Gould St.
Needham Heights, MA 02194-2310
Ph: (617)455-1200   Fr: 800-278-3525

S. Certo. Fourth edition, 1989. A basic introduction to management theory and practice.

★730★ Supervision, Techniques and New Dimensions
Prentice-Hall, Inc.
Rte. 9W
Englewood Cliffs, NJ 07632
Ph: (201)592-2000

Alfred W. Travers. Second edition, 1992. Includes bibliographies and an index.

★731★ Value at the Top: Solutions to the Executive Compensation Crisis
HarperBusiness
10 E. 53rd St.
New York, NY 10022
Ph: (212)207-7000   Fax: (212)207-7145
Ira T. Kay, editor. 1992.

PROFESSIONAL AND TRADE PERIODICALS

★732★ Advance Business Reports
Advance Business Reports, Inc.
250 W. 57th St., Ste. 307
New York, NY 10107-0001
Ph: (212)956-4460
Murray Ansell
Weekly. Provides information on occupancy and expansion of new business facilities. Published in multiple editions by geographic area.

★733★ Business Week
McGraw-Hill, Inc.
1221 Avenue of the Americas
New York, NY 10020
Ph: (212)512-4686   Fax: (212)512-4256
Stephen B. Shepard
Weekly. Magazine providing business news and interpretation.

★734★ Forbes
Forbes Inc.
60 5th Ave.
New York, NY 10011
Ph: (212)620-2200   Fr: 800-888-9896
Malcolm S. Forbes
Biweekly. Magazine reporting on industry, business and finance management.

★735★ Fortune
Time-Warner, Inc.
Time-Life Bldg.
Rockefeller Center
New York, NY 10019
Ph: (212)522-4158   Fax: (212)522-0074
Marshall Loeb
Business and industry magazine printed in regional and demographic editions.

★736★ Harvard Business Review
Harvard Graduate School of Business Administration
1554 South Sepolveda, No. 209
Los Angeles, CA 90025
Ph: (310)575-5610   Fax: (310)575-5615
Laurence AllenPublisher
Bimonthly. Magazine for business executives.

★737★ Industry Week
Penton Publishing
1100 Superior Ave.
Cleveland, OH 44114
Ph: (216)696-7000   Fax: (216)696-7932
Charles R. Day
Semiweekly. Magazine containing articles to help industry executives sharpen their managerial skills and increase their effectiveness.

★738★ Management Report
Executive Enterprises Publications Company, Inc.
22 W. 21st St.
New York, NY 10010-6904
Ph: (212)645-7880   Fax: (212)675-4883
Fr: 800-332-8804
Jane A. Bensahel
Monthly. Deals with preventing and combating union organization drives. Recurring features include advice and tips on topics such as feasible schedulings and the role it plays in stopping unions in their tracks, how to respond to union attempts to organize white-collar workers, handling union threats against voters, explaining the delay of a scheduled wage increase, and training supervisors.

★739★ Management Review
American Management Assn.
135 W. 50th St., 15th Fl.
New York, NY 10020-1201
Ph: (212)903-8393   Fax: (212)903-8083
Martha Peak
Monthly. Magazine covering general business and management issues for top and middle managers.

★740★ The President Newsletter
Periodicals Division
135 W. 50th St.
New York, NY 10020
Ph: (212)903-8075   Fax: (212)903-8168
Barbara J. Parker
Monthly. Consists of features, columns, and advisory articles on topics of interest to the CEOs and presidents of small to mid-size organizations. Recurring features include management practice, economic watch, legal update, technology trends, money matters, family business, and president profiles.

OTHER SOURCES OF INFORMATION

★741★ "Business Administration and Management" in Accounting to Zoology: Graduate Fields Defined (pp. 31-33)
Petersons Guides, Inc.
PO Box 2123
Princeton, NJ 08543-2123
Ph: (609)243-9111   Fax: (609)243-9150
Fr: 800-338-3282
Amy J. Goldstein, editor. Revised and updated, 1987. Discusses types of graduate programs and degrees, graduate research, applied work, employment prospects and trends.

★742★ The Career Makers: America's Top One Hundred Fifty Executive Recruiters
HarperBusiness
10 E. 53rd St.
New York, NY 10022
Ph: (212)207-7000   Fax: (212)207-7145
John Sibbald, editor. 1993.

★743★ Top Executive Compensation Report No. 1016: 1992 Edition
Conference Board, Inc.
845 3rd Ave.
New York, NY 10022
Ph: (212)759-0900   Fax: (212)980-7014
Fr: 800-US-BOARD
Elizabeth R. Arreglado, editor. 1992.

Government Chief Executives and Legislators

Government executives are officials who run governmental units that help formulate, carry out and enforce laws. Government chief executives have overall responsibility for the performance of their organization. In coordination with legislators, they establish goals and objectives, then organize programs and formulate policies to attain these goals. They appoint people to head departments, such as highways, health, police, and finance; prepare budgets; solicit bids from and select contractors to do work for the government; and insure that resources are being used properly and that programs are carried out as planned. **Legislators** are the elected officials who make laws or amend existing ones in order to remedy problems or to promote certain activities. Legislators introduce bills in the legislative body and examine and vote on bills introduced by other legislators. They also approve budgets and the appointments of department heads and commission members submitted by the chief executive.

Salaries

Salaries of public administrators vary widely depending on the size of the government unit and on whether the job is part time, full time year round, or full time for only a few months a year. Salaries are as follows:

City managers	$33,000-$125,000/year
Mayors	$9,900-$78,000/year
Legislators, state, (average)	$23,000/year
Governors	$35,000-$130,000/year
Lieutenant governors (average)	$57,000/year

Employment Outlook

Growth rate until the year 2005: Little change.

Government Chief Executives
and Legislators.

CAREER GUIDES

★744★ *Careers in Government*
National Textbook Co. (NTC)
VGM Career Books
4255 W. Toughy Ave.
Lincolnwood, IL 60646-1975
Ph: (708)679-5500   Fax: (708)679-2494
Fr: 800-323-4900

Mary Elizabeth Pitz. Explores many different aspects to careers in the government.

★745★ **"City County Managers and Assistants" in** *Jobs! What They Are—Where They Are—What They Pay* **(p.133)**
Fireside/Simon & Schuster, Inc.
Simon & Schuster Bldg.
1230 Avenue of the Americas
New York, NY 10020
Ph: (212)698-7000

Robert O. Snelling, author. Revised edition. 1992. This book profiles 241 occupations, describing duties and responsibilities, educational preparation, earnings, opportunities, qualifications, and where to write for more information. Occupations are arranged under 29 broad career fields.

★746★ **"City Manager" in** *College Board Guide to Jobs and Career Planning* **(pp. 211)**
The College Board
415 Columbus Ave.
New York, NY 10023-6992
Ph: (212)713-8165   Fax: (212)713-8143
Fr: 800-323-7155

Joyce Slayton Mitchell, author. Second edition, 1994. Written for high school and college students, this guide includes career planning tips and information about the 90's labor market.

★747★ **"City Manager" in** *Encyclopedia of Careers and Vocational Guidance* **(Vol.2, pp. 300-302)**
J.G. Ferguson Publishing Co.
200 W. Madison St., Ste. 300
Chicago, IL 60606
Ph: (312)580-5480   Fax: (312)580-4948

William E. Hopke, editor-in-chief. Ninth edition, 1993. This four volume set describes 74 industries and 900 occupations. The occupational profiles cover the nature of the work, educational requirements, history, methods of entry, advancement, employment outlook, earnings, working conditions, social and psychological factors, and sources of further information.

★748★ **"City Manager" in** *Occu-facts: Information on 580 Careers in Outline Form*
Careers, Inc.
PO Box 135
Largo, FL 34649-0135
Ph: (813)584-7333

Biennial, 1995-96 edition. Each one-page occupational profile describes duties, working conditions, physical surroundings and demands, aptitudes, temperament, educational requirements, employment outlook, earning, and places of employment.

★749★ **"City Manager" in** *VGM's Careers Encyclopedia* **(pp. 98-100)**
National Textbook Co. (NTC)
VGM Career Books
4255 W. Touhy Ave.
Lincolnwood, IL 60646-1975
Ph: (708)679-5500   Fax: (708)679-2494
Fr: 800-323-4900

Third edition. 1991. Arranged alphabetically A-Z, this book contains descriptions of 200 managerial, professional, technical, trade and service occupations. Each profile describes job duties, places of employment, qualifications, educational preparation, training, employment potential, advancement, income, and additional sources of information.

★750★ *City Managers*
Chronicle Guidance Publications, Inc.
66 Aurora St.
PO Box 1190
Moravia, NY 13118-1190
Ph: (315)497-0330   Fax: (315)497-3359
Fr: 800-622-7284

1994. This career brief describes the nature of the job, working conditions, hours and earnings, education and training, licensure, certification, unions, personal qualifications, social and psychological factors, location, employment outlook, entry methods, advancement, and related occupations.

★751★ **"City Managers" in** *Career Discovery Encyclopedia* **(Vol.1, pp. 176-178)**
J.G. Ferguson Publishing Co.
200 W. Madison St., Ste. 300
Chicago, IL 60606
Ph: (312)580-5480   Fax: (312)580-4948

Russell E. Primm, editor-in-chief. Second edition, 1993. This six volume set contains two-page articles for 504 occupations. Each article describes job duties, earnings, and educational and training requirements. The set is arranged alphabetically by job title.

★752★ *The Complete Guide to Public Employment*
Impact Publications
PO Box 1896
Evanston, IL 60204
Ph: (312)475-5748

Ronald L. Krannich and Caryl Rae Krannich, authors. Third edition, 1995. Describes jobs and career opportunites with local, state, and federal government including elected office and government administration. Lists many resources and offers career planning and job search advice.

★753★ **"Congressperson/Senator" and "President (U.S.)" in** *Jobs Rated Almanac*
World Almanac
1 International Blvd., Ste. 444
Mahwah, NJ 07495
Ph: (201)529-6900   Fax: (201)529-6901

Les Krantz. Second edition, 1992. Ranks 250 jobs by environment, salary, outlooks, physical demands, stress, security, travel opportunities, and extra perks. Includes jobs the editor feels are the most common, most interesting, and the most rapidly growing.

★754★ "Elected Government Official" in
College Board Guide to Jobs and
Career Planning (pp. 217-219)
The College Board
45 Columbus Ave.
New York, NY 10023-6992
Ph: (212)713-8165   Fax: (212)713-8143
Fr: 800-323-7155
Second edition, 1994. Describes the job, salaries, related careers, education needed, and where to write for more information.

★755★ FEW's News & Views
Federally Employed Women, Inc.
1400 Eye St. NW, Ste. 425
Washington, DC 20005
Ph: (202)898-0994
Joanne Dumene, editor. Six per year. Tabloid outlining job opportunities for women in government.

★756★ "Government Chief Executives
and Legislators" in Occupational
Outlook Handbook
U.S. Government Printing Office
Superintendent of Documents
Washington, DC 20402
Ph: (202)512-1800   Fax: (202)512-2250
1992-1993. This encyclopedia of careers describes in detail 250 occupations—comprising about 85 percent of all jobs in the economy. Occupations that require lengthy education or training are given the most attention. For each occupation, the handbook covers job duties, working conditions, training, educational preparation, personal qualities, advancement possibilities, job outlook, earnings, and sources of additional information.

★757★ "Government/Political Science"
in Accounting to Zoology: Graduate
Fields Defined (pp. 174-175)
Petersons Guides, Inc.
PO Box 2123
Princeton, NJ 08543-2123
Ph: (609)243-9111   Fax: (609)243-9150
Fr: 800-338-3282
Amy J. Goldstein, editor. 1987. A comprehensive volume of definitions of graduate and professional science; physical sciences and mathematics; and engineering and applied sciences. Includes an alphabetical index.

★758★ "Mayor" in Profiles in
Achievement (pp. 21-38)
The College Board
45 Columbus Ave.
New York, NY 10023-6992
Ph: (212)713-8165   Fax: (212)713-8143
Fr: 800-323-7155
Charles M. Hollway, author. 1987. This book contains interviews with eight successful men and women who have used hard work, determination, and their educations to reach their goals. These men and women overcame barriers of race, gender, tradition, and lack of money.

★759★ "On the Public Payroll" in
American Almanac of Jobs and
Salaries (pp. 1-120)
Avon Books
1350 Avenue of the Americas
New York, NY 10019
Ph: (212)261-6800   Fr: 800-238-0658
John Wright and Edward J. Dwyer, authors. 1994-95. Contains salary surveys of high-level government executives and administrative officials at the local, state, and federal levels, including legislators, governors, and the president.

★760★ Opportunities in Federal
Government Careers
National Textbook Co. (NTC)
VGM Career Books
4255 W. Touhy Ave.
Lincolnwood, IL 60646-1975
Ph: (708)679-5500   Fax: (708)679-2494
Fr: 800-323-4900
Neale Baxter. Explores the intricacies of the federal government, the federal hiring practices and the personnel classification system. Also overviews the opportunities available, including professional, clerical, technical, and blue collar jobs. Cross-indexes college majors and federal jobs.

★761★ Opportunities in State and Local
Government Careers
National Textbook Co. (NTC)
VGM Career Books
4255 W. Touhy Ave.
Lincolnwood, IL 60646-1975
Ph: (708)679-5500   Fax: (708)679-2494
Fr: 800-323-4900
Neale A. Baxter. Reviews opportunities in state and local government, including administration and legislation, correction, education, fire and police protection, health, transportation, housing and community development, natural resources, sanitation, and welfare and human services.

★762★ "Politics and Public Service" in
Encyclopedia of Careers and
Vocational Guidance (Vol.1, pp. 374-380)
J.G. Ferguson Publishing Co.
200 W. Madison St., Ste. 300
Chicago, IL 60606
Ph: (312)580-5480   Fax: (312)580-4948
William E. Hopke, editor-in-chief. Ninth edition, 1993. This four volume set describes 74 industries and 900 occupations. The occupational profiles cover the nature of the work, educational requirements, history, methods of entry, advancement, employment outlook, earnings, working conditions, social and psychological factors, and sources of further information.

★763★ "Public Administrator" in Top
Professions: The 100 Most Popular,
Dynamic, and Profitable Careers in
America Today (pp. 17-19)
Petersons Guides, Inc.
PO Box 2123
Princeton, NJ 08543-2123
Ph: (609)243-9111   Fax: (609)243-9150
Fr: 800-338-3282
1989. Includes occupations requiring a college or advanced degree. Describes job duties, earnings, typical job titles, career op-

portunities at different degree levels, and lists associations to write to for more information.

★764★ "State Legislator" in Profiles in
Achievement (pp. 145-165)
The College Board
45 Columbus Ave.
New York, NY 10023-6992
Ph: (212)713-8165   Fax: (212)713-8143
Fr: 800-323-7155
Charles M. Holloway, author. 1987. This book contains interviews with eight successful men and women who have used hard work, determination, and their educations to reach their goals.

★765★ "Urban Administration Careers"
in Occu-Facts: Information on 580
Careers in Outline Form
Careers, Inc.
PO Box 135
Largo, FL 34649-0135
Ph: (813)584-7333
Biennial, 1995-96 edition. Each four-page occupational profile describes duties, working conditions, physcial surroundings and demands, aptitudes, temperament, educational requirements, employment outlook, earnings, and places of employment outlook, earnings, and places of employment.

★766★ VGM's Handbook for
Government and Public Service
Careers
National Textbook Co. (NTC)
VGM Career Books
4255 W. Touhy Ave.
Lincolnwood, IL 60646-1975
Ph: (708)679-5500   Fax: (708)679-2494
Fr: 800-323-4900
Annette Selden, editor. 1993. Describes jobs in federal, state, and local governments.

PROFESSIONAL ASSOCIATIONS

★767★ Council of State Governments
(CSG)
3560 Iron Works Pike
PO Box 11910
Lexington, KY 40578-1910
Ph: (606)244-8000   Fax: (606)244-8001
Fr: 800-800-1910
Joint agency of all state governments and six commonwealths and territories. Governing board consists of the 50 governors and two legislators per state. Works to strengthen state government by: improving administrative and managerial capability and performance; promoting intergovernmental cooperation; collecting, processing, generating, and disseminating information needed by states; assisting states in solving specific problems of policy formulation and operations; serving as a catalyst and representative on issues and opportunities affecting the states. Provides staff services to other organizations of state officals in various fields of activity. Arranges and implements conferences attended by legislators and state officials. Offers constituent services of research, surveys, and data search to the private sector. Maintains collection of state govern-

ment department and agency reports. Operates speakers' bureau; conducts research and educational programs; compiles statistics. **Publications:** *Book of the States*, biennial. • *Spectrum: The Journal of State Government*, quarterly. • *State Administrative Officials Classified by Functions*, annual. • *State Elective Officials and the Legislatures*, annual. • *State Government News*, monthly. • *State Government Research Checklist*, bimonthly. • *State Legislative Leadership Committees and Staff*, annual.

★768★ ICMA - International City/County MGT Association (ICMA)
777 N. Capitol St. NE, Ste. 500
Washington, DC 20002-4201
Ph: (202)289-4262   Fax: (202)962-3500
Members: International professional and educational organization for appointed administrators and assistant administrators serving cities, counties, districts, and regions. **Purpose:** Conducts Management Information Service and Urban Data Service. Operates ICMA Training Institute, which conducts correspondence courses and training seminars for municipal employees in various fields of municipal administration. Collects data on local governments. **Publications:** *Guide to Management Improvement Projects in Local Government*, quarterly. • *Hispanic Network and Job Opportunities Bulletin*, periodic. • *Management Information Service Report*, monthly. • *Municipal Management*. • *Municipal Year Book*. • *Practical Management*. • *Public Management*, monthly. • *Who's Who in Local Government Management*, annual.

★769★ National Association of Counties (NACo)
440 1st St. NW, 8th Fl.
Washington, DC 20001
Ph: (202)393-6226   Fax: (202)393-2630
Members: Elected and appointed county governing officials at management or policy level. **Purpose:** Provides research for county officials and represents them at the national level. Compiles statistics. **Publications:** *County News*, bimonthly.

STANDARDS/CERTIFICATION AGENCIES

★770★ Community Associations Institute (CAI)
1630 Duke St.
Alexandria, VA 22314
Ph: (703)548-8600   Fax: (703)684-1581
Purpose is to develop and provide the most advanced and effective guidance for the creation, financing, operation, and maintenance of the common facilities and services in condominiums, townhouse projects, planned unit developments, and open-space communities.

AWARDS, SCHOLARSHIPS, GRANTS, AND FELLOWSHIPS

★771★ Award of Merit/Distinguished Service Award
National Council of Senior Citizens
1331 F St. NW
Washington, DC 20004
Ph: (202)624-9532   Fax: (202)624-9595
To recognize lawmakers (usually one U.S. Representative and one U.S. Senator) who have consistently demonstrated dedication and commitment to America's elderly by outstanding work on their behalf in the U.S. Congress or State Legislatures. Also, used on occasion to honor NCSC members, club leaders and other supporters for outstanding work to achieve NCSC's goal of "a better life for older people. . .and for people of all ages." A certificate and framed citation are awarded when meritted. Established in 1963.

★772★ Barbed Wire Award
American Ex-Prisoners of War
3201 E. Pioneer Pkwy., Ste. 40
Arlington, TX 76010-5396
Ph: (817)649-2979
To recognize the member of Congress who has supported and helped former POWs with legislative actions. Current members of Congress are considered. A trophy is awarded annually at a reception in Washington, DC. Established in 1988. Additional information is available from Charles M. Williams, Executive Director, Room 9109, 941 North Capitol Street, Washington, DC 20421.

★773★ Lindy Boggs Award
American Occupational Therapy Association
c/o Strahan
1383 Piccard Dr., Ste. 301
PO Box 1725
Rockville, MD 20849-1725
Ph: (301)948-9626   Fax: (301)948-5512
To recognize significant contributions by a registered occupational therapist or a certified occupational therapy assistant in promoting occupational therapy in the political arena by increasing recognition of the field in federal or state legislations, regulations, and/or policies, or by increasing appreciation and understanding of occupational therapy by elected or appointed officials and to provide an incentive for others to take an active role in the legislation process, advocacy, and/or policy making that affects occupational therapy. Nominees must be members of the Association in good standing and must have demonstrated outstanding participation in one or more of the following categories: training and organizing therapists to take part in federal or state legislation, regulations, and/or policies; the education of legislators or other key government officials in the purpose and function of occupational therapy; response to requests for action from the Government and Legal Affairs Division of the Association; advocacy for consumers of health care and educational services; and state activities related to AOTA/PAC and/or state PACs. A certificate is awarded annually at the the AOTA Conference. Established in 1983 in honor of

Coreen C. (Lindy) Boggs, U.S. Congresswoman of Louisiana.

★774★ Congressional Award
Small Business Council of America
4800 Hampton Ln., 7th Fl.
Bethesda, MD 20814
Ph: (301)951-9325
To recognize a U.S. Congressman or Senator for efforts on behalf of small business in connection with federal tax matters. A plaque is awarded annually. Established in 1981.

★775★ Congressman of the Year
National Multiple Sclerosis Society
733 3rd Ave.
New York, NY 10017-3288
Ph: (212)986-3240   Fax: (212)986-7981
To recognize members of Congress with distinguished records of support for medical research, rehabilitation services, and legislation affecting people with multiple sclerosis. Incumbent U.S. Represntatives or U.S. Senators may be nominated by March 1 by any chapter of the Society or other source. The awardee is chosen by the Society's Government Relations Committee and the Board of Directors. A society grant for current research investigation is often named for the recipient. Awarded annually. Established in 1984.

★776★ Global Statesman Award
Campaign for United Nations Reform
713 D St. SE
Washington, DC 20003
Ph: (202)546-3956   Fax: (202)543-4878
To honor those members of the House and Senate who have a 100 percent voting record on issues concerning world order chosen by the Campaign for each Congress. A plaque and press coverage are awarded biennially after the end of each Congress. Established in 1978.

★777★ Golden Carrot Award
Public Voice for Food and Health Policy
1001 Connecticut Ave. NW, Ste. 522
Washington, DC 20036
Ph: (202)659-5930   Fax: (202)659-3683
For recognition of progressive food safety, nutrition, and agriculture policy leadership. Members of Congress are eligible. A plaque is awarded annually in September. Established in 1983.

★778★ Governmental Affairs and Public Service Award
National Rehabilitation Association
633 S. Washington St.
Alexandria, VA 22314
Ph: (703)715-9090
To recognize a public official who has demonstrated leadership in improving rehabilitation services for persons with disabilities through legislative action at the national level. Members of Congress and their staff or members of the executive and judicial branches of government who have made outstanding contributions to rehabilitation through their formation, integration, or administration of significant legislation are eligible. The deadline for nominations is August 1. Awarded when merited. Established in 1981.

★779★ Governor of the Year
National Multiple Sclerosis Society
733 3rd Ave.
New York, NY 10017-3288
Ph: (212)986-3240   Fax: (212)986-7981

To recognize Governors with distinguished records of leadership in support of medical research, rehabilitation services and legislation affecting people with multiple sclerosis. Incumbent Governors must be nominated by September 1. A Society grant for current research investigation will be named for the recipient. Awarded annually. Established in 1985.

★780★ I Care Awards
American Association of School
   Administrators
1801 N. Moore St.
Arlington, VA 22209
Ph: (703)528-0700

To recognize legislators for outstanding efforts in promoting quality education. Awarded annually at the "I Care" legislative conference. The Office of Governmental Relations staff is responsible for the selection of winners.

★781★ Leadership in Human Services Award
American Public Welfare Association
810 1st St. NE, Ste. 500
Washington, DC 20002-4267
Ph: (202)682-0100   Fax: (202)289-6555

To recognize outstanding efforts by national and state policy-makers to assist poor Americans. Awarded annually.

★782★ Legislative Award
Association of Federal Investigators
3299 K St. NW, 7th Fl.
Washington, DC 20007
Ph: (202)337-5234   Fax: (202)333-5365

To recognize a member of Congress who through his efforts has contributed significantly towards enhancing Federal law enforcement and investigations. A plaque is awarded annually. Established in 1966.

★783★ Legislator of the Year
Vietnam Veterans of America
1224 M St. NW
Washington, DC 20005-5783
Ph: (202)628-2700   Fax: (202)628-5881

To recognize a legislator for outstanding advocacy of positive veteran legislation. A plaque is awarded annually. Established in 1984.

★784★ National Congressional Award
National Recreation and Park Association
2775 S. Quincy St., Ste. 300
Arlington, VA 22206
Ph: (703)820-4940   Fax: (703)671-6772

To recognize a member of the U.S. Senate or House of Representatives who has demonstrated continuing national leadership in efforts to improve and/or protect the quality and quantity of leisure opportunities through park, recreation, and conservation programs and projects. Usually one award is presented.

★785★ NWRA Distinguished Service Award
National Water Resources Association
3800 N. Fairfax Dr., Ste. 4
Arlington, VA 22203-1703
Ph: (703)524-1544   Fax: (703)524-1548

To recognize individuals in federal and state government for significant contributions to the development and conservation of our nation's water resources. A plaque is awarded annually when merited. Established in 1987.

★786★ Outstanding Elected Democratic Woman Holding Public Office
National Federation of Democratic Women
3311 NW Roosevelt
Corvallis, OR 97330
Ph: (503)752-5708

To recognize a current statewide, regional, or national woman office holder who has demonstrated support of the Federation, the Democratic Party, and its principles and commitment to the success of other Democratic women. Established in 1987. In addition, special awards are presented at the Convention.

★787★ Presidents Award
National Rehabilitation Association
633 S. Washington St.
Alexandria, VA 22314
Ph: (703)715-9090

To recognize outstanding achievement in behalf of persons with disabilities. Individuals or organizations whose activities in the preceding years have made a major contribution to the rehabilitation of persons with disabilities on a nationwide basis, in an area not generally considered technical, are eligible. Eligible for this award are members of Congress who have demonstrated a leadership role in the development and/or passage of legislation which increases rehabilitation opportunities for persons with disabilities, employers who have made intelligent and persistent efforts to provide employment opportunities for persons with disabilities and have inspired others to do likewise, members of a profession or other group whose zeal for rehabilitation have heightened the interest and enlarged the contribution of that profession or group, or people with disabilities whose examples or whose concern for persons with disabilities has so inspired others as to effect a nationwide impact upon rehabilitation. The deadline for nominations is August 1.

★788★ Edgar Wayburn Award
Sierra Club
Exec. Office Mgr.
730 Polk St.
San Francisco, CA 94109
Ph: (415)776-2211   Fax: (415)776-0350

To recognize outstanding service to the cause of conservation and the environment by a government official, either executive or legislative. Selection is made by the Executive Committee of the Board of Directors. Awarded annually. Established in 1979.

PROFESSIONAL AND TRADE PERIODICALS

★789★ Congress in Print
Congressional Quarterly Inc.
1414 22nd St. NW
Washington, DC 20037
Ph: (202)887-8500   Fax: (202)728-1862
Laura Michaelis

Weekly. News on Congressional documents.

★790★ Congressional Digest
3231 P St. NW
Washington, DC 20007
Ph: (202)333-7332   Fax: (202)625-6670
Griff Thomas President

Magazine covering major controversies in the Congress, pro and con.

★791★ Congressional Quarterly Weekly Report
Congressional Quarterly Inc.
1414 22nd St. NW
Washington, DC 20037
Ph: (202)887-8500   Fax: (202)728-1862
Robert Merry

Weekly. Congressional news research service.

★792★ Governing, The States and Localities
Congressional Quarterly Inc.
1414 22nd St. NW
Washington, DC 20037
Ph: (202)887-8500   Fax: (202)728-1862
Peter A. Harkness

Monthly. Magazine for decision makers and others with an interest in state and local government.

★793★ Government Executive
National Journal, Inc.
1730 M St. NW, Ste. 1100
Washington, DC 20036
Ph: (202)862-0600   Fax: (202)833-8069
Tim Clark

Magazine for government executives.

★794★ Government Finance Review
Government Finance Officers Assn.
180 N. Michigan Ave., Ste. 800
Chicago, IL 60601
Ph: (312)977-9700   Fax: (312)977-4806
Barbara Weiss

Bimonthly. Membership magazine covering finance and financial management for state and local governments.

★795★ Government Information Quarterly
JAI Press, Inc.
55 Old Post Rd., No. 2
PO Box 1678
Greenwich, CT 06836-7678
Ph: (203)661-7602   Fax: (203)661-0792
Peter Hunon

Quarterly.

★796★ *Independent Consultant's Briefing*
Christopher Juillet
PO Box 1725
Ann Arbor, MI 48106
Ph: (313)449-0310   Fax: (313)449-0351
Christopher Juillet, Contact
Quarterly. Provides articles on a wide variety of consulting-related topics, as well as news of tax and other legislation of importance to consultants. Features articles by actual practicing independent consultants which gives advice on establishing and running an independent consulting business. Also covers retirement, investments, and insurance. Recurring features include letters to the editor, book reviews, and notices of publications available.

★797★ *State Government News*
The Council of State Governments
Iron Works Pike
PO Box 11910
Lexington, KY 40578-1910
Ph: (606)231-1939   Fax: (606)231-1858
Fr: 800-800-1910
Dag Ryan
Monthly. State government magazine.

★798★ *State Legislatures*
National Conference of State Legislatures
1560 Broadway, Ste. 700
Denver, CO 80202
Ph: (303)830-2200   Fax: (303)863-8003
Karen Hansen

Monthly. Magazine bringing a national perspective to state politics and government by tracking legislation and issues, examining innovations and ideas, monitoring trends and developments, and exploring operations and procedures in the 50 state legislatures.

Health Services Managers

Health services managers are responsible for health care facilities, services, programs, staff, budgets, and relations with other organizations. These professionals plan, organize, coordinate, and supervise the delivery of health care at hospitals, medical group practices, outpatient clinics, health maintenance organizations (HMOs), nursing homes, hospices, home health agencies, rehabilitation centers, community mental health centers, urgent care centers, diagnostic imaging centers, and the offices of health practitioners, such as doctors and dentists. **Health care CEO's** must assess the need for services, personnel, facilities, and equipment and recommend such changes as opening a home health service or closing a burn center. They are also concerned with community outreach, response to government agencies and regulations, and negotiating. **Assistant administrators** to the CEO handle day-to-day management decisions. **Health specialists** provide the day-to-day management of specialized departments like surgery, rehabilitation therapy, nursing, medical records, and so on. These managers have more narrowly defined responsibilities than the managers to whom they report.

Salaries

Salaries vary depending on personal performance type and size of health care institution, and geographic location.

Median for all health service managers	$46,600-$166,700/year
Hospital CEO's	$77,000-$223,600/year

Employment Outlook

Growth rate until the year 2005: Much faster than the average.

Health Services Managers

CAREER GUIDES

★799★ *A Career in Long-Term Health Care Administration: Your Key to Success*
American College of Health Care Administrators
325 S. Patrick St.
Alexandria, VA 22314
Ph: (703)549-5822
Annual. This eight-panel brochure describes licensure requirements, salary, and entering the field of nursing home administration.

★800★ *Careers in Health and Fitness*
Rosen Publishing Group
29 E. 21st St.
New York, NY 10010
Ph: (212)777-3017   Fax: (212)777-0277
Fr: 800-237-9932
Jackie Heron, R.N. 1990. Explores the opportunities and responsibilities of a career in health or fitness.

★801★ *Careers in Social and Rehabilitation Services*
National Textbook Co. (NTC)
VGM Career Books
4255 W. Touhy Ave.
Lincolnwood, IL 60646-1975
Ph: (708)679-5500   Fax: (708)679-2494
Fr: 800-323-4900
Geraldine O. Garner, Ph.D., editor. 1993. Describes dozens of careers in the field of social and rehabilitation services.

★802★ *"Health Administration, Management, & Related Services" in College Majors and Careers: Resource Guide to Effective Life Planning* (pp. 67-68)
Garrett Park Press
PO Box 1907
Garrett Park, MD 20896
Ph: (301)946-2553
Paul Phifer. Revised, 1993. Lists 60 college majors, with definitions; related occupations and leisure activities; skills, values, and personal attributes needed; suggested readings; and a list of associations.

★803★ *"Health Care" in Where the Jobs Are: The Hottest Careers for the 90s* (pp. 143-166)
Career Press
180 5th Ave.
Hawthorne, NJ 07507
Ph: (201)427-0229   Fax: (201)427-2037
Fr: 800-CAREER-1
Joyce Hadley. 1995. Offers a job-hunting strategy for the 1990s as well as descriptions of growing careers of the decade. Each profile includes general information, forecasts, growth, education and training, licensing requirements, and salary information.

★804★ *"Health Service Manager" in College Board Guide to Jobs and Career Planning* (pp. 234)
The College Board
415 Columbus Ave.
New York, NY 10023-6992
Ph: (212)713-8165   Fax: (212)713-8143
Fr: 800-323-7155
Joyce S. Mitchell. Second edition, 1994. Describes the job, salaries, related careers, education needed, and where to write for more information.

★805★ *"Health Services Administration" in 150 Careers in the Health Care Field*
Reed Reference Publishing
121 Chanlon Rd.
PO Box 31
New Providence, NJ 07974
Fax: (908)665-6688   Fr: 800-521-8110
Stanley Alperin. Third edition, 1993. Profiles health care occupations requiring a bachelor's degree or less. Describes the nature of the work, educational preparation, licensing requirements, and salary. Lists accredited educational programs.

★806★ *Health Services Administrator*
Careers, Inc.
PO Box 135
Largo, FL 34649-0135
Ph: (813)584-7333
1992. Four-page brief offering the definition, history, duties, working conditions, personal qualifications, educational requirements, earnings, hours, employment outlook, advancement, and careers related to this position.

★807★ *"Health Services Administrator" in 100 Best Careers for the Year 2000* (pp. 56-58)
Arco Pub.
201 W. 103rd St.
Indianapolis, IN 46290
Ph: 800-428-5331   Fax: 800-835-3202
Shelly Field. 1992. Describes 100 job opportunities expected to grow fast throughout the next decade. Provides information on job duties and responsibilities, training requirements, education, advancement opportunities, experience and qualifications, and typical salaries.

★808★ *"Health Services Administrators" in Encyclopedia of Careers and Vocational Guidance* (Vol.3, pp. 126-129)
J.G. Ferguson Publishing Co.
200 W. Madison St., Ste. 300
Chicago, IL 60606
Ph: (312)580-5480   Fax: (312)580-4948
William E. Hopke, editor-in-chief. Ninth edition, 1993. Four-volume set that profiles 900 occupations and describes job trends in 74 industries. Includes career description, educational requirements, history of the job, methods of entry, advancement, employment outlook, earnings, conditions of work, social and psychological factors, and sources of further information.

★809★ *"Health Services" in Internships 1995*
Petersons Guides, Inc.
PO Box 2123
Princeton, NJ 08543-2123
Ph: (609)243-9111   Fr: 800-338-3282
Fifteenth edition, 1995. Lists internship opportunities under six broad categories: communications, creative, performing, and fine arts, human services, international relations, business and technology, and public affairs. For each internship program, gives the names, phone number, contact person, description, eligibility requirements, and benefits.

★810★ "Health Services Managers" in *America's 50 Fastest Growing Jobs* **(pp. 16)**
JIST Works, Inc.
720 N. Park Ave.
Indianapolis, IN 46202-3431
Ph: (317)264-3720   Fax: (317)264-3709
Fr: 800-648-5478
Michael J. Farr, compiler. 1994. Describes the 50 fastest growing jobs within major career clusters such as technicians, and marketing and sales. Each job profile explains the nature of the work, skills and abilities required, employment outlook, average earnings, related occupations, education and training requirements, and employment opportunities. Also contains career planning information and job search tips.

★811★ "Health Services Managers" in *Occupational Outlook Handbook*
U.S. Government Printing Office
Superintendent of Documents
Washington, DC 20402
Ph: (202)512-1800   Fax: (202)512-2250
Biennial; latest edition, 1994-95. Encyclopedia of careers describing about 250 occupations and comprising about 85 percent of all jobs in the economy. Occupations that require lengthy education or training are given the most attention. Each occupation's profile describes what the worker does on the job, working conditions, education and training requirements, advancement possibilities, job outlook, earnings, and sources of additional information.

★812★ "Health Services Managers" in *VGM's Handbook of Health Care Careers*
National Textbook Co.
4255 W. Touhy Ave.
Lincolnwood, IL 60646-1975
Ph: (708)679-5500   Fax: (708)679-2494
Fr: 800-323-4900
Annette Selden. 1993. Contains 42 two-page occupational profiles describing job duties, places of employment, working conditions, qualifications, education, employment outlook, and income.

★813★ "Hospital Administration" in *Liberal Arts Jobs*
Petersons Guides, Inc.
PO Box 2123
Princeton, NJ 08543-2123
Ph: (609)243-9111   Fax: (609)243-9150
Fr: 800-338-3282
Burton Jay Nadler. Second edition, 1989. Strives to help the liberal arts graduate identify skills for entry-level positions. Gives goal setting and job search advice.

★814★ "Hospital Administrator" in *VGM's Handbook of Business and Management Careers*
National Textbook Co.
4255 W. Touhy Ave.
Lincolnwood, IL 60646-1975
Ph: (708)679-5500   Fax: (708)679-2494
Fr: 800-323-4900
Annette Selden. Second edition, 1993. Contains 42 two-page occupational profiles describing job duties, places of employment, working conditions, qualifications, education, employment outlook, and income.

★815★ "Hospital Administrators" in *American Almanac of Jobs and Salaries* **(p. 452)**
Avon Books
1350 Avenue of the Americas
New York, NY 10019
Ph: (212)261-6800   Fr: 800-238-0658
John Wright, editor. Revised and updated, 1994-95. This is comprehensive guide to the wages of hundreds of occupations in a wide variety of industries and organizations.

★816★ "Hospital and Health Service Adminstrators" in *Jobs! What They Are—Where They Are—What They Pay* **(p. 166)**
Simon & Schuster, Inc.
Simon & Schuster Bldg.
1230 Avenue of the Americas
New York, NY 10020
Ph: (212)698-7000   Fr: 800-223-2348
Robert O. Snelling and Anne M. Snelling. 3rd edition, 1992. Describes duties and responsibilities, earnings, employment opportunities, training, and qualifications.

★817★ *Hospital and Health Services Administrators*
Chronicle Guidance Publications, Inc.
66 Aurora St.
PO Box 1190
Moravia, NY 13118-1190
Ph: (315)497-0330   Fax: (315)497-3359
Fr: 800-622-7284
1993. Career brief describing the nature of the job, working conditions, hours and earnings, education and training, licensure, certification, unions, personal qualifications, social and psychological factors, location, employment outlook, entry methods, advancement, and related occupations.

★818★ *Hospital Salary Survey Report*
Hospital Compensation Service
John R. Zabka Associates, Inc.
69 Minnehaha Blvd.
PO Box 376
Oakland, NJ 07436
Ph: (201)405-0075   Fax: (201)405-1258
Annual. 1994-95. Reports salaries for management employees, registered nurses, and licensed practical nurses by hospital bed size, by profit and nonprofit status for governmental hospitals, and by geographic area.

★819★ *New Careers in Hospitals*
Rosen Publishing Group
29 E. 21st St.
New York, NY 10010
Ph: (212)777-3017   Fax: (212)777-0277
Fr: 800-237-9932
Lois S. Sigel. 1990. Describes a variety of hospital positions, including careers in public relations. Covers background, professional preparation, functions, salary, and job outlook.

★820★ "Nursing Home Administrators" in *Career Paths in the Field of Aging: Professional Gerontology* **(pp. 35-36)**
Simon and Schuster
200 Old Tappan Rd.
Old Tappan, NJ 07675
Fax: 800-445-6991   Fr: 800-223-2348
David A. Peterson. 1987. Provides a history of the gerontology profession, and describes

jobs, education and skills required, employment outlook and trends in the field.

★821★ *Opportunities in Hospital Administration Careers*
National Textbook Co. (NTC)
VGM Career Books
4255 W. Touhy Ave.
Lincolnwood, IL 60646-1975
Ph: (708)679-5500   Fax: (708)679-2494
Fr: 800-323-4900
I. Donald Snook. 1989. Describes hospital administration in varied work settings. Covers educational preparation, skills, compensation, getting started in the profession, and job hunting.

PROFESSIONAL ASSOCIATIONS

★822★ Accrediting Commission on Education for Health Services Administration (ACEHSA)
1911 N. Fort Myer Dr., Ste. 503
Arlington, VA 22209
Ph: (703)524-0511   Fax: (703)525-4791
Accredits graduate degree programs in health services administration, health planning, and health policy. Goal is the improvement of professional education. **Publications:** *Official List of Accredited Programs*, semiannual.

★823★ American Association of Homes and Services for the Aging (AAHSA)
901 E St. NW, Ste. 500
Washington, DC 20004-2037
Ph: (202)783-2242   Fax: (202)783-2255
Members: Voluntary not-for-profit nursing homes, housing, retirement communities, and health-related facilities and services for the elderly; state associations; interested individuals. **Purpose:** Provides a unified means of identifying and solving problems in order to protect and advance the interests of the residents served. Believes that long-term care should be geared toward individual needs and provided in a spectrum ranging from nursing care to independent living and community-based care. Is committed to community involvement in the home to ensure the highest quality of care for residents. Maintains liaison with Congress and federal agencies. Provides educational programs, publications, group purchasing program, capital financing, and in surance programs. **Publications:** *AAHA Provider News*, monthly. • *American Association of Homes for the Aging Publications Catalog.* • *Washington Report*, biweekly.

★824★ American College of Health Care Administrators (ACHCA)
325 S. Patrick St.
Alexandria, VA 22314
Ph: (703)549-5822   Fax: (703)739-7901
Members: Persons actively engaged in the administration of long-term care facilities, assisted-living facilities in medical administration, or activities designed to improve the quality of long-term administration. **Purpose:** Certifies members' ability to meet and maintain a standard of competence in nursing

home and long-term care administration. Works to elevate the standards in the field and to develop and promote a code of ethics and standards of education and training. Seeks to inform allied professions and the public that good administration of long-term care facilities calls for special formal academic training and experience. Encourages research in all aspects of geriatrics, the chronically ill, and administration. Maintains placement service. Conducts research and special education programs. **Publications:** *Journal of Long-Term Care Administration*, quarterly. • *Long-Term Care Administrator*, bimonthly.

★825★ **American College of Healthcare Executives (ACHE)**
1 N. Franklin, Ste. 1700
Chicago, IL 60606-3491
Ph: (312)424-2800   Fax: (312)424-0023
Members: Professional society for hospital and health service executives. **Purpose:** Works to: keep members abreast of current and future trends, issues, and developments; shape productive and effective organizational strategies and professional performance; increase the visibility and recognition of the health care management profession; act as advocate for health care management in legislative activities and with government agencies; develop cooperation among professional societies and other health care associations in dealing with current issues; strengthen and encourage the profession's code of ethics; maintain professional standards. Maintains database of personal and career data on its membership. Holds educational seminars and training programs on health care management. Offers student loans and personal loan program. Operates Healthcare Executives Career Resource Center. Maintains numerous committees and task forces; conducts research programs; compiles statistics. **Publications:** *Frontiers of Health Services Management*, quarterly. • *Health Services Research*, bimonthly. • *Healthcare Executive*, bimonthly. • *Hospital and Health Services Administration*, quarterly.

★826★ **American Society for Healthcare Education and Training - of the American Hospital Association (ASHET)**
840 N. Lake Shore Dr.
Chicago, IL 60611
Ph: (312)280-3556   Fr: 800-621-6712
Educators and trainers from hospitals and other healthcare institutions involved in staff development, and patient and community education. Purposes are: to foster professional development of members; to demonstrate the value of comprehensive education as a management strategy; to promote continuing education among all healthcare personnel; to develop coordination among organizations involved in the education of healthcare personnel; to formulate information and evaluation programs; to recommend action on national issues relating to healthcare education. Conducts educational programs. Sponsors competitions. **Publications:** *Healthcare Education Dateline*. • *Hospitals*, biweekly. • *Journal of Healthcare Education and Training*, periodic.

★827★ **Association of University Programs in Health Administration (AUPHA)**
1911 N. Fort Myer Dr., Ste. 503
Arlington, VA 22209
Ph: (703)524-5500
Members: Universities offering graduate and undergraduate study in health services and hospital administration. **Purpose:** To improve the quality of education in health services administration. Undertakes research and educational programs, such as studies of the criteria used for selection of students and curriculum patterns adopted by various universities. Conducts faculty institutes on topics relating to health administration. Compiles statistics. **Publications:** *AUPHA Exchange*, bimonthly. • *Health Services Administration Education*, biennial. • *Journal of Health Administration Education*, quarterly.

★828★ **Family and Health Section of the National Council on Family Relations (FHS)**
3989 Central Ave. NE, Ste. 550
Minneapolis, MN 55421
Ph: (612)781-9331   Fax: (612)781-9348
Members: A section of the National Council on Family Relations. Health and education professionals. **Purpose:** Serves as a forum for all professionals involved in interdisciplinary work in the family and health fields. Presents clinical research and educational programs at NCFR conferences. **Publications:** *Family Health News*, periodic.

★829★ **Medical Group Management Association (MGMA)**
104 Inverness Ter. E.
Englewood, CO 80112
Ph: (303)799-1111   Fax: (303)643-4427
Members: Persons actively engaged in the business management of medical groups consisting of three or more physicians in medical practice with centralized business functions. Sponsors educational training programs. Provides placement and information services. Compiles statistics. **Publications:** *Administrators' Bookshelf*, annual. • *Cost Survey Report*, annual. • *Health Exchange*, quarterly. • *Medical Group Management Journal*, bimonthly. • *Medical Group Management—Management Update*, monthly. • *Medical Group Management Washington Report*, monthly. • *MGMA Directory*, annual. • *MGMA Membership Compensation Survey Report*, annual.

★830★ **National Health Council (NHC)**
1730 M St. NW, Ste. 500
Washington, DC 20036
Ph: (202)785-3910   Fax: (202)785-5923
Members: National membership association of voluntary and professional societies in the health field; national organizations and business groups with strong health interests. **Purpose:** Seeks to improve the health of the nation. Holds annual National Health Forum. Distributes printed material on health careers and related subjects. Promotes standardization of financial reporting for voluntary health groups. **Publications:** *Congress and Health*. • *Council Currents*, bimonthly. • *Directory of Health Groups in Washington*. • *Guide to America's Voluntary Health Agencies*. • *Long-Term Care*. • *Standards of Accounting*

and Reporting for Voluntary Health and Welfare Organizations (The Black Book)*. • *200 Ways to Put Your Talent to Work in the Health Field*.

STANDARDS/CERTIFICATION AGENCIES

★831★ **American College of Health Care Administrators (ACHCA)**
325 S. Patrick St.
Alexandria, VA 22314
Ph: (703)549-5822   Fax: (703)739-7901
Certifies members' ability to meet and maintain a standard of competence in nursing home and long-term care administration. Works to elevate the standards in the field and to develop and promote a code of ethics and standards of education and training.

★832★ **American College of Healthcare Executives (ACHE)**
1 N. Franklin, Ste. 1700
Chicago, IL 60606-3491
Ph: (312)424-2800   Fax: (312)424-0023
Develops cooperation among professional societies and other health care associations in dealing with current issues; strengthen and encourage the profession's code of ethics; maintain professional standards.

★833★ **National Health Council (NHC)**
1730 M St. NW, Ste. 500
Washington, DC 20036
Ph: (202)785-3910   Fax: (202)785-5923
Promotes standardization of financial reporting for voluntary health groups.

★834★ **Professional Association of Health Care Office Managers (PAHCOM)**
461 E. 10 Mile Rd.
Pensacola, FL 32534
Ph: (904)474-9460   Fax: (904)474-6352
Fr: 800-451-9311
Operates certification program for health care office managers.

TEST GUIDES

★835★ *Career Examination Series: Health Services Manager*
National Learning Corp.
212 Michael Dr.
Syosset, NY 11791
Ph: (516)921-8888   Fax: (516)921-8743
Fr: 800-645-6337
Jack Rudman. Test guide including questions and answers for students or professionals in the field who seek advancement through examination.

★836★ Career Examination Series: Hospital Administrator
National Learning Corp.
212 Michael Dr.
Syosset, NY 11791
Ph: (516)921-8888   Fax: (516)921-8743
Fr: 800-645-6337
Jack Rudman. A series of study guides with multiple-choice examination questions and solutions for trainees and professional hospital administration. Titles in the series include *Assistant Director of Nursing Care; Assistant Hospital Administrator; Clinic Administrator; Coordinator of Community Mental Health Services; Director of Nursing Care; Director of Patient Services; Hospice Coordinator; Hospital Administration Intern; Junior Hospital Administrator; Nursing Home Administrator; Senior Medical Services Specialist.*

★837★ The Licensing Exam Review Guide in Nursing Home Administration
Springer Publishing Co.
536 Broadway
New York, NY 10012
Ph: (212)431-4370
James E. Allen. Second edition, 1992. Contains 560 test questions and 1100 key terms and concepts essential to the federally recommended core of knowledge relevant to nursing home administration.

EDUCATIONAL DIRECTORIES AND PROGRAMS

★838★ Health & Medical Industry Directory
American Business Directories, Inc.
5711 S. 86th Circle
Omaha, NE 68127
Ph: (402)593-4600   Fax: (402)331-1505
Released 1993. Lists over 1.1 million physicians and surgeons, dentists, clinics, health clubs, and other health-related businesses in the U.S. and Canada. Entries include: Name, address, phone.

★839★ Health Services Administration Education
Association of University Programs in Health Administration
1911 N. Fort Myer Dr., Ste. 503
Arlington, VA 22209
Ph: (703)524-5500   Fax: (703)525-4791
Donna Royston
Biennial, May of odd years. Covers undergraduate, graduate, and nontraditional member programs in health services administration; coverage includes Canada. Entries include: Program name, address, department name, name of director, phone; program history and description; curriculum description; admission procedures and requirements; financial assistance available; placement services; enrollment and student characteristics; fees. Arrangement: Separate alphabetical sections for graduate and undergraduate programs.

AWARDS, SCHOLARSHIPS, GRANTS, AND FELLOWSHIPS

★840★ Richard P. Covert Scholarships
Healthcare Information and Management Systems Society (HIMSS)
840 North Lake Shore Dr.
Chicago, IL 60611
Ph: (312)280-6148
Purpose: To encourage scholarship by students in the fields of health care information and management systems. Qualifications: Candidate may be of any nationality. Applicant must be enrolled in an accredited undergraduate or graduate program related to health care information or management systems, such as management engineering, operations research, computer science and information systems, mathematics, business administration, or hospital administration. Candidate must be a student member of HIMSS or apply for membership. Normally, one scholarship is reserved for a graduate student and one for an undergraduate. Funds available: $1,000; plus all-expense-paid trip to the HIMSS annual conference. Application details: Write to HIMSS for application form and guidelines. Submit form with transcripts, technical paper and/or essay, completed federal student financial aid form, and a faculty recommendation. Application for membership, including dues, may accompany the scholarship application. Deadline: 15 October. Notification by mid-January.

★841★ F. Stanton Deland Fellowships in Health Care and Society
Brigham and Women's Hospital
75 Francis St.
Boston, MA 02115
Ph: (617)732-5559
Purpose: To provide the opportunity to participate in the management of an eminent health care institution. Qualifications: Applicant must hold an advanced degree. There are no other specific background requirements. Fellows will be located primarily at Brigham and Women's Hospital in Boston, Massachusetts. Fellows are expected to give occasional seminars or tutorials, and to complete a project. Funds available: Stipend varies, according to professional and educational experience as well as need. Application details: Write for application forms. Submit completed forms with curriculum vitae, personal and professional goals statement, and a project proposal. Deadline: 1 February.

★842★ Albert W. Dent Scholarship
American College of Healthcare Executives Foundation
1 N. Franklin St., Ste. 1700
Chicago, IL 60606-3491
Ph: (312)943-0544   Fax: (312)943-3791
Purpose: To provide financial aid and increase the enrollment of minority and physically disabled students in healthcare management graduate programs and to encourage them to obtain middle- and upper-level positions in health care management. Qualifications: Applicants must be United States or Canadian citizens who are either Student Associates in good standing in the

American College of Healthcare Executives, minority or physically disabled undergraduate students who either have been accepted for full-time study for the fall term in a health care management graduate program accredited by the Accrediting Commission on Education for Health Services Administration, or students enrolled full-time and in good academic standing in an accredited graduate program in health care management. Previous recipients are not eligible. Financial need must be demonstrated. Funds available: Each scholarship is $3,000. The number of awards varies from year to year. Deadline: Completed applications must be filed between January 1 and March 31.

★843★ Distinguished Service Award
American Hospital Association
840 N. Lake Shore Dr.
Chicago, IL 60611
Ph: (312)280-6000
This, the Association's highest award, is given for recognition of noteworthy service, contributions or achievements in hospital administration activities. Individuals who have made a career in the hospital or health field are eligible. In selecting the recipient, primary consideration is given to the following factors: welfare of hospital patients; improvements in administrative methods and practices; service in local, state or provincial, or national organizations in the health care field; furtherance of good public relations; assistance to and collaboration with other hospitals; promotion of social and other legislation relating to better patient care; and advancement of the art and science of health care administration. A medallion is awarded annually. Established in 1934.

★844★ Harry J. Harwick Award
American College of Medical Practice Executives
104 Inverness Terr. E.
Englewood, CO 80112-5306
Ph: (303)799-1111   Fax: (303)643-4427
For recognition of an individual who has displayed a lifetime of achievement and made outstanding contributions to the field of health care delivery, administration, and education, with particular attention to medical group practice. A bronze casting and a $2,000 scholarship in the recipient's name to a student currently enrolled in a University Health Administration program interested in ambulatory care/group practice administration are awarded annually when merited. Established in 1976 to honor Harry J. Harwick, Mayo Clinic business manager and first group practice administrator.

★845★ Honorary Fellowship Award
American College of Health Care Administrators
325 S. Patrick St.
Alexandria, VA 22314-3571
Ph: (703)549-5822   Fax: (703)739-7901
To recognize a professional individual who has demonstrated distinguished service in long-term health care or related fields, (e.g., government, education, community service, or professional health care). The nominee need not be a College member. He/she must be ineligible for active membership in the College as defined in Article II, Section 1 of the ACHCA Bylaws. The deadline for submis-

sions is November 15. A plaque is awarded annually during the ACHCA Convocation. Established in 1964.

★846★ Honorary Fellowships
American Academy of Medical
  Administrators
Congress Bldg.
30555 Southfield Rd., Ste. 150
Southfield, MI 48076
Ph: (313)540-4310   Fax: (313)645-0590
To recognize distinguished service in the field of health care administration. All health care executives in the United States and Canada are eligible. The deadline is June 1. A plaque is awarded yearly at the annual conference and convocation. Established in 1959.

★847★ Robert S. Hudgens Memorial Award - Young Healthcare Executive of the Year
American College of Healthcare Executives
840 N. Lake Shore Dr., Ste. 1103W
Chicago, IL 60611
Ph: (312)943-0544   Fax: (312)943-3791
To recognize an exceptional health care executive under 40 years of age serving as a CEO or COO of a health care organization. Candidates must be nominated by an ACHE Committee. A plaque is awarded annually. Established in 1969 by the Alumni Association of the Department of Hospital and Health Administration of Medical College of Virginia, Virginia Commonwealth University in memory Robert S. Hudgens, the College's first elected vice president.

★848★ Marriott Corporation Health Care Services Charles U. Letourneau Student Research Paper of the Year Award
American Academy of Medical
  Administrators
Congress Bldg.
30555 Southfield Rd., Ste. 150
Southfield, MI 48076
Ph: (313)540-4310   Fax: (313)645-0590
To recognize a student of health care administration for excellence, quality, and originality in health care administration research and writing. A monetary award of $500, a plaque, publication in the Academy publication, and travel expenses to the annual conference and convocation are awarded annually. Established in 1973 in honor of Charles U. Letourneau, M.D. Sponsored by the Marriott Corporation.

★849★ Foster G. McGaw Student Loans
American College of Healthcare Executives
  Foundation
1 N. Franklin St., Ste. 1700
Chicago, IL 60606-3491
Ph: (312)943-0544   Fax: (312)943-3791
Purpose: To assist financially needy persons to better prepare for health care management careers, thereby contributing to improvements in the field. Qualifications: Applicants must be enrolled full-time and in good academic standing in graduate programs in healthcare management that are accredited by the Accrediting Commission on Education for Health Services Administration; student associates in good standing in the ACHE may also apply. Candidates must also be United States or Canadian citizens. Previous recipients are not eligible. Applicants must provide

evidence of financial need. Selection criteria: The Director of each graduate program must recommend students with the greatest financial need. Funds available: Loan amounts are dependent on applicants' needs, but are limited to $4,000 each, interest free, for the first three years. After that time, the loan is repayable over the next five years at a pre-established interest rate. Application details: Applications may be obtained from the Program Director. Deadline: Applications are accepted each year between January 1 and March 31.

★850★ Presidential Award for Mental Health Administration
National Association of Psychiatric Health
  Systems
1319 F St. NW, Ste. 1000
Washington, DC 20004
Ph: (202)393-6700   Fax: (202)783-6041
To honor individuals for their personal and professional efforts on behalf of psychiatric hospitals and the patients they serve, and their contributions to their community in health related matters. Non-physician professional administrators who have demonstrated outstanding contributions to the advancement of patient care and the delivery of mental illness care through creative and efficient management or resources are eligible. A plaque and the opportunity to present a lecture at the NAPHS Annual Meeting the following year are awarded. Established in 1980.

BASIC REFERENCE GUIDES AND HANDBOOKS

★851★ The Facts on File Dictionary of Health Care Management
Facts on File
460 Park Ave. S.
New York, NY 10016-7382
Ph: (212)683-2244   Fax: 800-678-3633
Fr: 800-322-8755
Joseph C. Rhea, J. Steven Ott, and Jay M. Shafritz. 1988. Incudes a bibliography and more than 40 charts and diagrams.

★852★ Health Services Administration Handbook
Warren H. Green, Inc.
8356 Olive Blvd.
St. Louis, MO 63132
Ph: (314)991-1335
Karen M. Lorentzen and Linda Roemer. 1988.

★853★ Healthcare Quality and Productivity: Practical Management Tools
Aspen Publishers, Inc.
200 Orchard Ridge Dr., Ste. 200
Gaithersburg, MD 20878
Ph: (301)417-7500   Fr: 800-638-8437
Kirk Roey. 1988. Includes bibliographical references.

★854★ Manual of Clinical Evaluation: Strategies for Cost-Effective Care
Little, Brown and Co., Inc.
34 Beacon St.
Boston, MA 02108
Ph: (617)227-0730
Mark D. Aronson and Thomas L. Delbanco, editors. First edition, 1988. Includes bibliographies and an index.

★855★ Nursing Home Administrator's Deskbook
Prentice-Hall, Inc.
Rte. 9W
Englewood, NJ 07632
Ph: (201)592-2000   Fr: 800-634-2863
Monroe Title. 1989. Shows how to operate a nursing home in full compliance with state and federal regulations.

★856★ Professional Writing Skills for Health Care Managers
Mosby-Year Book, Inc.
11830 Westline Industrial Dr.
St. Louis, MO 63146
Ph: (314)872-8370   Fax: (314)432-1380
Fr: 800-325-4177
1987.

★857★ U.S. Hospitals: The Future of Health Care
Deloitte & Touche
125 Summer St.
Boston, MA 02110
Ph: (617)261-8000
1990. Survey of 25 per cent of all acute care hospitals in the United States. The report describes financial losses, low occupancy rates, and nursing shortages.

PROFESSIONAL AND TRADE PERIODICALS

★858★ American Hospital Association— Outreach
American Hospital Association (AHA)
840 N. Lake Shore Dr.
Chicago, IL 60611
Ph: (312)280-5921   Fax: (312)280-6012
Fr: 800-621-6902
David C. King
Bimonthly. Analyzes the factors influencing market supply, demand, and competition. Recurring features include statistics, details on the latest accreditation standards, reviews of current literature, education and technical assistance updates, news of research, and resources.

★859★ The Health Care M & A Report
Irving Levin Associates, Inc.
72 Park St.
New Canaan, CT 06840
Ph: (203)966-4343   Fax: (203)966-8510
Fr: 800-248-1668
Stephen M. Monroe
Quarterly. Journal detailing merger activities in subsectors of the health care industry.

★860★ Health Care Management Review
Aspen Publishers, Inc.
200 Orchard Ridge Dr., Ste. 200
Gaithersburg, MD 20878
Ph: (301)417-7500   Fax: (301)417-7550
Jack Bruggeman, Contact

Quarterly. Journal devoted to management issues in health care and administration.

★861★ Healthcare Executive
American College of Healthcare Executives
840 N. Lake Shore Dr.
Chicago, IL 60611
Ph: (312)943-0544   Fax: (312)943-3791
Walter Wachel

Bimonthly. Health care management magazine examining trends, issues, and innovations.

★862★ Healthcare Information Management
Healthcare Information and Management
  Systems Society (HIMSS)
230 E. Ohio St., Ste. 600
Chicago, IL 60611
Ph: (312)664-4467   Fax: (312)664-6143
Andrew Pasternak

Quarterly. Reports on health care information management systems, including the latest management trends in information systems, management engineering, and telecommunications.

★863★ Healthcare Management Team Letter
Health Resources Publishing
Brinley Professional Plaza
3100 Hwy. 38
PO Box 1442
Wall, NJ 07719-1442
Ph: (908)681-1133
Robert K. Jenkins

Monthly. Alerts management teams or department heads to information that may help them in their roles as decision makers.

★864★ Hospital & Health Services Administration
Health Administration Press
1021 E. Huron St.
Ann Arbor, MI 48104
Ph: (313)764-1380   Fax: (313)763-1105
Richard S. Kurz

Quarterly. Professional journal focusing on hospital and health services administration.

★865★ Hospital Practice
HP Publishing Co.
55 Fifth Ave.
New York, NY 10003
Ph: (212)989-2100   Fax: (212)727-7316
Robert W. Schrier

Monthly. Magazine providing information on developments and problem areas in medicine and clinical research. Emphasizes application of medical knowledge to the direct care of patients.

★866★ Managed Care Quarterly
Aspen Publishers, Inc.
7201 McKinney Circle
Frederick, MD 21701
Lenda P. Hill

Quarterly. Journal providing current information to health care executives who require in-depth material on specific managed care issues.

★867★ Modern Healthcare
Crain Communications, Inc.
740 N. Rush St.
Chicago, IL 60611-2590
Ph: (312)649-5286   Fax: (312)280-3174
Clark Bell

Weekly.

★868★ Physician Services Report
Society for Healthcare Planning and
  Marketing
840 N. Lakeshore Dr.
Chicago, IL 60611
Ph: (312)280-6086
Ruth Ann Grant

Quarterly. Covers physician recruitment, services, and medical staff marketing. Recurring features include news of research and notices of publications available.

PROFESSIONAL MEETINGS AND CONVENTIONS

★869★ American Academy of Medical Administrators Convention
American Academy of Medical
  Administrators
30555 Southfield Rd., Ste. 150
Southfield, MI 48076
Ph: (313)540-4310   Fax: (313)645-0590

Annual. **Dates and Locations:** 1995 Nov 02-04; Anaheim, CA.

★870★ American Association for Continuity of Care Annual Conference
American Association for Continuity of Care
1730 N. Lynn St., Ste. 502
Arlington, VA 22209-2004
Ph: (305)386-3855   Fax: (703)276-8196

Annual. Always held during September. **Dates and Locations:** 1996; New York, NY.

★871★ American Health Care Association Annual Convention and Exposition
American Health Care Association
1201 L St., NW
Washington, DC 20005
Ph: (202)842-4444   Fax: (202)842-3860

Annual. Always held during October.

★872★ Federation of American Health Systems Annual Convention & Business Exposition
Federation of American Health Systems
PO Box 8708
Little Rock, AR 72217-8708
Ph: (501)661-9555   Fax: (501)663-4903
Fr: 800-880-FAHS

Annual.

★873★ Health Care Information and Management Systems Society Show
American Hospital Association
Convention and Meetings Division
230 E. Ohio St., Ste. 600
Chicago, IL 60611
Ph: (312)664-4467   Fax: (313)664-6143

Annual.

★874★ Healthcare Forum Annual Meeting
The Healthcare Forum
830 Market St., 8th Fl.
San Francisco, CA 94102
Ph: (415)421-8810   Fax: (415)421-8837

Annual.

★875★ Middle Atlantic Health Congress
Middle Atlantic Health Congress
760 Alexander Rd., CN 1
Princeton, NJ 08543-0001
Ph: (609)924-0049   Fax: (609)275-4100

Annual. Always held at the Trump Taj Mahal in Atlantic City, New Jersey. **Dates and Locations:** 1996 May 22-23; Atlantic City, NJ.

OTHER SOURCES OF INFORMATION

★876★ "Health Services Administrator" in 100 Best Jobs for the 1990s & Beyond
Dearborn Financial Publishing, Inc.
520 N. Dearborn St.
Chicago, IL 60610-4354
Ph: (312)836-4400   Fax: (312)836-1021
Fr: 800-621-9621

Carol Kleiman. 1992. Describes 100 jobs ranging from accountants to veterinarians. Each job profile includes such information as education, experience, and certification needed, salaries, and job search suggestions.

★877★ "Health Services Management and Hospital Administration" in Accounting to Zoology: Graduate Fields Defined (pp. 117-119)
Petersons Guides, Inc.
PO Box 2123
Princeton, NJ 08543-2123
Ph: (609)243-9111   Fax: (609)243-9150
Fr: 800-338-3282

Amy J. Goldstein, editor. Revised and updated, 1987. Discusses types of graduate programs and degrees, graduate research, applied work, employment prospects, and trends.

Hotel Managers and Assistants

Hotel managers are responsible for the efficient and profitable operation of their establishments. The **general manager** has overall responsibility for the operation of the hotel and sets room rates, allocates funds to departments, approves expenditures, and establishes standards for service to guests, decor, housekeeping, food quality, and banquet operations. **Assistant managers** must insure that the day-to-day operations of their departments meet the general manager's standards. **Resident managers** who live in the hotel, oversee the day-to-day operations of the hotel, and are on call 24 hours a day to resolve any problems or emergencies. **Executive housekeepers** are responsible for insuring that guest rooms, meeting and banquet rooms, and public areas are clean, orderly, and well maintained. **Front office managers** coordinate reservations and room assignments, and train and direct the hotel's front desk staff that deals with the public. **Food and beverage managers** oversee the operation of the hotel's restaurants, cocktail lounges, and banquet facilities. **Convention services managers** coordinate the activities of large hotels' various departments for meetings, conventions, and other special events. Other assistant managers may be specialists responsible for activities such as personnel, accounting and office administration, marketing and sales, security, maintenance and recreational facilities.

Salaries

Salaries vary greatly according to responsibilities, experience, and hotel size.

Assistant managers of small hotels	$26,000/year
Assistant managers of large hotels	$38,400/year
General managers of small hotels	$44,900/year
General managers of large hotels	$86,700/year
Food and beverage managers	$41,200/year
Front office managers	$26,500/year

Employment Outlook

Growth rate until the year 2005: Average.

Hotel Managers and Assistants

CAREER GUIDES

★878★ **Hospitality Industry Compensation Survey**
American Hotel and Motel Assn.
1201 New York Ave., NW, Ste. 600
Washington, DC 20005-3931
Ph: (202)289-3100
1987. Reports the salaries of 17 managerial positions by region, property size, and revenue.

★879★ **"Hospitality Manager" in** *College Board Guide to Jobs and Career Planning* (pp. 93)
The College Board
415 Columbus Ave.
New York, NY 10023-6992
Ph: (212)713-8165   Fax: (212)713-8143
Fr: 800-323-7155
Joyce S. Mitchell. Second edition, 1994. Describes the job, salaries, related careers, education needed, and where to write for more information.

★880★ **Hospitality and Recreation**
Franklin Watts, Inc.
387 Park Ave., S.
New York, NY 10016
Ph: (212)686-7070
Marjorie R. Schulz. 1990. Part of the Careers for Today series.

★881★ **Hotel Guest Services Director**
Vocational Biographies, Inc.
PO Box 31
Sauk Centre, MN 56378-0031
Ph: (612)352-6516   Fax: (612)352-5546
Fr: 800-255-0752
1994. Four-page pamphlet containing a personal narrative about a worker's job, work likes and dislikes, career path from high school to the present. Education and training, the rewards and frustrations, and the effects of the job on the rest of the worker's life. The data file portion of this pamphlet gives a concise occupational summary, including work descriptions, working conditions, places of employment, personal characteristics, education and training, job outlook, and salary range.

★882★ **"Hotel Management" in** *Career Choices for the 90's for Students of Business* (pp. 89-108)
Walker and Co.
435 Hudson St.
New York, NY 10014
Ph: (212)727-8300   Fax: (212)727-0984
Fr: 800-289-2553
Compiled by Career Associates Staff. 1990. This book offers alternatives for students of business. Gives information about the outlook and competition for entry-level candidates. Provides job hunting tips.

★883★ **"Hotel Management" in** *Career Connection for Technical Education* (pp. 90-91)
JIST Works, Inc.
720 N. Park Ave.
Indianapolis, IN 46202-3431
Ph: (317)264-3720   Fax: (317)264-3709
Fred A. Rowe. 1994, second edition. Describes in detail technical occupations. Includes information on recommended high school courses, course requirements, related careers, and a self-assessment guide.

★884★ **"Hotel Management" in** *Encyclopedia of Career Choices for the 1990s: A Guide to Entry Level Jobs* (pp. 397-416)
Berkley Pub.
PO Box 506
East Rutherford, NJ 07073
Fax: (201)933-2316   Fr: 800-788-6262
1992. Describes entry-level careers in a variety of industries. Presents qualifications required, working conditions, salary, internships, and professional associations.

★885★ **Hotel Manager**
Vocational Biographies, Inc.
PO Box 31
Sauk Centre, MN 56378-0031
Ph: (612)352-6516   Fax: (612)352-5546
Fr: 800-255-0752
1995. Four-page pamphlet containing a personal narrative about a worker's job, work likes and dislikes, career path from high school to the present. Education and training, the rewards and frustrations, and the effects of the job on the rest of the worker's life. The data file portion of this pamphlet gives a concise occupational summary, including work descriptions, working conditions, places of employment, personal characteristics, education and training, job outlook, and salary range.

★886★ **"Hotel Manager" in** *Career Information Center* (Vol.8)
Simon and Schuster
200 Old Tappan Rd.
Old Tappan, NJ 07675
Fax: 800-445-6991   Fr: 800-223-2348
Richard Lidz and Linda Perrin, editorial directors. Fifth edition, 1993. This 13-volume set profiles over 600 occupations. Each occupational profile describes job duties, entry-level requirements, educational requirements, advancement possibilities, employment outlook, working conditions, earnings and benefits, and where to write for more information.

★887★ **"Hotel Manager" in** *Jobs Rated Almanac*
World Almanac
1 International Blvd., Ste. 444
Mahwah, NJ 07495
Ph: (201)529-6900   Fax: (201)529-6901
Les Krantz. Second edition, 1992. Ranks 250 jobs by environment, salary, outlooks, physical demands, stress, security, travel opportunities, and extra perks. Includes jobs the editor feels are the most common, most interesting, and the most rapidly growing.

★888★ **"Hotel Managers and Assistants" in** *America's 50 Fastest Growing Jobs* (pp. 19)
JIST Works, Inc.
720 N. Park Ave.
Indianapolis, IN 46202-3431
Ph: (317)264-3720   Fax: (317)264-3709
Fr: 800-648-5478
Michael J. Farr, compiler. 1994. Describes the 50 fastest growing jobs within major career clusters such as technicians, and marketing and sales. Each job profile explains the nature of the work, skills and abilities required, employment outlook, average earnings, related occupations, education and training requirements, and employment opportunities. Also contains career planning information and job search tips.

★889★ "Hotel Managers and Assistants" in *Occupational Outlook Handbook*
U.S. Government Printing Office
Superintendent of Documents
Washington, DC 20402
Ph: (202)512-1800   Fax: (202)512-2250
Biennial; latest edition, 1994-95. Encyclopedia of careers describing about 250 occupations and comprising about 85 percent of all jobs in the economy. Occupations that require lengthy education or training are given the most attention. Each occupation's profile describes what the worker does on the job, working conditions, education and training requirements, advancement possibilities, job outlook, earnings, and sources of additional information.

★890★ *Hotel/Motel Careers: Check It Out!*
Educational Institute of the American Hotel and Motel Association
PO Box 1240
East Lansing, MI 48826
Ph: (517)353-5500   Fr: 800-752-4567
This pamphlet describes career opportunities in the hotel/motel industry, as well as education, training, and scholarships.

★891★ "Hotel and Motel Management" in *Career Discovery Encyclopedia* **(Vol.3, pp. 104-105)**
J.G. Ferguson Publishing Co.
200 W. Madison St., Ste. 300
Chicago, IL 60606
Ph: (312)580-5480   Fax: (312)580-4948
Russell E. Primm, editor-in chief. 1993. This six volume set contains two-page articles for 504 occupations. Each article describes job duties, earnings, and educational and training requirements. The whole set is arranged alphabetically by job title. Designed for junior high and older students.

★892★ "Hotel and Motel Management" in *College Majors and Careers: A Resource Guide to Effective Life Planning* **(pp. 75-76)**
Garrett Park Press
PO Box 1907
Garrett Park, MD 20896
Ph: (301)946-2553
Paul Phifer. Revised, 1993. Lists 60 college majors, with definitions; related occupations and leisure activities; skills, values, and personal attributesneeded; suggested readings; and a list of associations.

★893★ "Hotel/Motel Management" in *Liberal Arts Jobs*
Petersons Guides, Inc.
PO Box 2123
Princeton, NJ 08543-2123
Ph: (609)243-9111   Fax: (609)243-9150
Fr: 800-338-3282
Burton Jay Nadler. Second edition, 1989. Strives to help the liberal arts graduate identify skills for entry-level positions. Gives goal setting and job search advice.

★894★ *Hotel-Motel Manager*
Careers, Inc.
PO Box 135
Largo, FL 34649-0135
Ph: (813)584-7333
1994. Four-page brief offering the definition, history, duties, working conditions, personal qualifications, educational requirements, earnings, hours, employment outlook, advancement, and careers related to this position.

★895★ "Hotel/Motel Manager" in *100 Best Careers for the Year 2000* **(pp. 230-232)**
Arco Pub.
201 W. 103rd St.
Indianapolis, IN 46290
Ph: 800-428-5331   Fax: 800-835-3202
Shelly Field. 1992. Describes 100 job opportunities expected to grow fast throughout the next decade. Provides information on job duties and responsibilities, training requirements, education, advancement opportunities, experience and qualifications, and typical salaries.

★896★ "Hotel/Motel Manager" in *VGM's Careers Encyclopedia* **(pp. 215-217)**
National Textbook Co. (NTC)
VGM Career Books
4255 W. Touhy Ave.
Lincolnwood, IL 60646-1975
Ph: (708)679-5500   Fax: (708)679-2494
Fr: 800-323-4900
Third edition, 1991. Describes job duties, places of employment, working conditions, qualifications, education, and training, advancement potential, and salary for each occupation.

★897★ "Hotel/Motel Manager" in *VGM's Handbook of Business and Management Careers*
National Textbook Co.
4255 W. Touhy Ave.
Lincolnwood, IL 60646-1975
Ph: (708)679-5500   Fax: (708)679-2494
Fr: 800-323-4900
Annette Selden. Second edition, 1993. Contains 42 two-page occupational profiles describing job duties, places of employment, working conditions, qualifications, education, employment outlook, and income.

★898★ *Hotel or Motel Managers*
Chronicle Guidance Publications, Inc.
66 Aurora St.
PO Box 1190
Moravia, NY 13118-1190
Ph: (315)497-0330   Fax: (315)497-3359
Fr: 800-622-7284
1992. Career brief describing the nature of the job, working conditions, hours and earnings, education and training, licensure, certification, unions, personal qualifications, social and psychological factors, location, employment outlook, entry methods, advancement, and related occupations.

★899★ "Hotel and Motel Managers and Assistants" in *Jobs! What They Are—Where They Are—What They Pay* **(p. 204)**
Simon & Schuster, Inc.
Simon & Schuster Bldg.
1230 Avenue of the Americas
New York, NY 10020
Ph: (212)698-7000   Fr: 800-223-2348
Robert O. Snelling and Anne M. Snelling. 3rd edition, 1992. Describes duties and responsibilities, earnings, employment opportunities, training, and qualifications.

★900★ "Hotel and Motel Managers" in *Encyclopedia of Careers and Vocational Guidance* **(Vol.3, pp. 149-151)**
J.G. Ferguson Publishing Co.
200 W. Madison St., Ste. 300
Chicago, IL 60606
Ph: (312)580-5480   Fax: (312)580-4948
William E. Hopke, editor-in-chief. Ninth edition, 1993. Four-volume set that profiles 900 occupations and describes job trends in 74 industries. Includes career description, educational requirements, history of the job, methods of entry, advancement, employment outlook, earnings, conditions of work, social and psychological factors, and sources of further information.

★901★ "Jobs in Hotel and Motel Management" in *American Almanac of Jobs and Salaries* **(p. 416)**
Avon Books
1350 Avenue of the Americas
New York, NY 10019
Ph: (212)261-6800   Fr: 800-238-0658
John Wright, editor. Revised and updated, 1994-95. This is a comprehensive guide to the wages of hundreds of occupations in a wide variety of industries and organizations.

★902★ *Opportunities in Hotel and Motel Management*
National Textbook Co. (NTC)
VGM Career Books
4255 W. Touhy Ave.
Lincolnwood, IL 60646-1975
Ph: (708)679-5500   Fax: (708)679-2494
Fr: 800-323-4900
Shepard Henkin. Revised edition, 1992. Describes jobs in the hospitality industry, employment outlook, personal requirements, educational preparation, apprenticeship and training, salary, and job hunting techniques.

★903★ "Robert Marsili—Hotel Manager" in *Straight Talk on Careers: Eighty Pros Take You Into Their Professions* **(pp. 27-30)**
Garrett Park Press
PO Box 1907
Garrett Park, MD 20896
Ph: (301)946-2553
Mary Barbera-Hogan. 1987. Contains candid interviews from people who give an inside view of their work in 80 different careers. These professionals describe a day's work and the stresses and rewards accompanying their work.

★904★ So . . . You Want to Be an Innkeeper: The Complete Guide to Operating a Successful Bed and Breakfast Inn
Chronicle Books
275 5th St.
San Francisco, CA 94103
Ph: (415)777-7240   Fax: (415)777-8887
Mary E. Davies. 1990.

★905★ "Travel and Hospitality" in Where the Jobs Are: The Hottest Careers for the 90s (pp. 279)
Career Press
180 5th Ave.
Hawthorne, NJ 07507
Ph: (201)427-0229   Fax: (201)427-2037
Fr: 800-CAREER-1
Joyce Hadley. 1995. Offers a job-hunting strategy for the 1990s as well as descriptions of growing careers of the decade. Each profile includes general information, forecasts, growth, education and training, licensing requirements, and salary information.

PROFESSIONAL ASSOCIATIONS

★906★ American Hotel & Motel Association (AH&MA)
1201 New York Ave. NW, Ste. 600
Washington, DC 20005-3931
Ph: (202)289-3100   Fax: (202)289-3199
Members: Federation of 50 state and regional hotel associations, representing over 1.4 million hotel and motel rooms. **Purpose:** Promotes business of hotels and motels through publicity and promotion programs. Works to improve operating methods through dissemination of information on industry methods. Conducts educational institute for training at all levels, through home study, adult education, and colleges. Provides guidance on member and labor relations. Reviews proposed legislation affecting hotels. Sponsors study group programs. Maintains speakers' bureau and library; conducts research; compiles statistics; sponsors competitions. Operates the American Hotel Foundation, which absorbed the Hospitality Lodging and Travel Research Foundation in 1993. **Publications:** AH&MA Reports. • Directory of Hotel and Motel Systems, annual. • Innside Government. • Lodging, monthly. • Who's Who Directory, annual.

★907★ Career College Association (CCA)
750 1st St. NE, Ste. 900
Washington, DC 20002
Ph: (202)336-6700   Fax: (202)336-6828
Members: Private postsecondary schools providing career education. **Purpose:** Seeks to inform members of the accreditation process and regulations affecting vocational education. Conducts workshops and institutes for staffs of member schools; provides legislative, administrative, and public relations assistance. Has established Career Training Foundation to support research into private vocational education. Sponsors research programs. Maintains hall of fame; compiles statistics. **Publications:** Career College

Times, monthly. • Career Education. • Career News Digest. • Classroom Companion, quarterly. • Directory of Private Accredited Career Colleges and Schools, annual.

★908★ Council on Hotel, Restaurant, and Institutional Education (CHRIE)
1200 17th St. NW
Washington, DC 20036-3097
Ph: (202)331-5990   Fax: (202)785-2511
Members: Schools and colleges offering specialized education and training in cooking, baking, tourism and hotel, restaurant, and institutional administration; individuals, executives, and students. **Purpose:** Sponsors competitions. **Publications:** CHRIE Communique, biweekly. • Guide to Hospitality Education, semiannual. • Hospitality and Tourism Educator, quarterly. • Hospitality Education and Research Journal. • Hosteur Magazine, annual. • Membership Directory and Research Guide, annual.

★909★ National Executive Housekeepers Association (NEHA)
1001 Eastwind Dr., Ste. 301
Westerville, OH 43081-3361
Ph: (614)895-7166   Fax: (614)895-1248
Fr: 800-200-NEHA
Members: Persons engaged in institutional housekeeping management in hospitals, hotels and motels, schools, and industrial establishments. Has established educational standards. Sponsors certificate and collegiate degree programs. Holds annual National Housekeepers Week celebration during the second week in September. Created the N.E.H.A. Educational Foundation to allocate financial awards to recognized schools to assist students in institutional housekeeping. Maintains referral service. **Publications:** Executive Housekeeping Today, monthly. • Shop Talk, quarterly.

STANDARDS/CERTIFICATION AGENCIES

★910★ Bed & Breakfast Reservation Services World-Wide (B&BRSWW)
PO Box 14841
Baton Rouge, LA 70898-4841
Ph: (504)336-4035   Fax: (504)343-0672
Fr: 800-364-7242
Certifies bed and breakfast operators through Gold Medallion Host Certification program. Assists members in compliance with zoning and government regulations; offers assistance in development of local regulations where none exist.

★911★ National Executive Housekeepers Association (NEHA)
1001 Eastwind Dr., Ste. 301
Westerville, OH 43081-3361
Ph: (614)895-7166   Fax: (614)895-1248
Fr: 800-200-NEHA
Has established educational standards. Sponsors certificate and collegiate degree programs.

EDUCATIONAL DIRECTORIES AND PROGRAMS

★912★ A Guide to College Programs in Hospitality and Tourism
Council on Hotel, Restaurant and Institutional Education (CHRIE)
1200 17th St. NW
Washington, DC 20036-3097
Ph: (202)331-5990   Fax: (202)785-2511
Douglas E. Adair, Contact
Biennial, March of odd years. Covers about 400 secondary and technical institutes, colleges, and universities; international coverage. Entries include: School name, address, areas of study, degrees offered, name and title of contact, program description, financial aid information, tuition and fees, admission and graduation requirements. Arrangement: Alphabetical, geographical, specialization.

★913★ Travel and Hospitality Career Directory
Gale Research Inc.
835 Penobscot Bldg.
Detroit, MI 48226-4094
Ph: (313)961-2242   Fax: (313)961-6083
Fr: 800-877-GALE
Bradley J. Morgan and Joseph M. Palmisano. Second edition, 1992. A directory in the Career Advisor Series that provides essays written by industry professionals; job search information on resume and cover letter preparation, networking, and the interviewing process; approximately 300 companies and organizations offering job opportunities and internships, and additional job-hunting resources.

AWARDS, SCHOLARSHIPS, GRANTS, AND FELLOWSHIPS

★914★ Convention Service Manager of the Year
Successful Meetings Magazine
355 Park Ave. S.
New York, NY 10010
Ph: (212)592-6400   Fax: (212)592-6409
To recognize hotel and resort convention service managers who excel in helping meeting planners. Individuals who have worked as a convention service manager for a hotel or resort for a minimum of one year are eligible. A winner is chosen from each of the following categories: hotels, convention and visitor bureaus, and convention centers. A plaque is awarded annually.

★915★ Environmental Quality Achievement Awards
American Hotel & Motel Association
1201 New York Ave. NW
Washington, DC 20005-3931
Ph: (202)289-3133
To honor a lodging property that has improved the environmental quality of the area where it is located, or has otherwise maintained an outstanding natural-resource con-

servation/enhancement program to do so. The award is given for contribution to the general welfare of the environment and the community in areas of property/community beautification, natural resources, conservation (including the natural elements and wildlife), active participation in civic planning to provide for any of the aforementioned, or active participation in a recycling program. Entries may be submitted only by AH&MA member properties by January 24. A plaque is awarded annually at the association's convention. Sponsored by Visa U.S.A.

★916★ NAMP Scholarships
National Association of Meat Purveyors (NAMP)
1920 Association Dr., Ste. 400
Reston, VA 22091-1547
Ph: (703)758-1900   Fax: (703)758-8001
Purpose: To promote and sponsor outstanding and deserving students who are training for careers in the foodservice industry. Qualifications: Applicants must be enrolled at an accredited undergraduate institution and seeking a degree in foodservice management, meat science, hotel/restaurant management, or culinary arts. Selection criteria: A member of NAMP's Scholarship Committee selects the school at which the scholarship will be offered. This committee member, with the help of school representatives, selects the candidate on the basis of need and ability. Funds available: $10,000 is distibuted each year, generally in increments of $1500.00 to 2500.00 to Universities and Culinary Arts Institutions. Application details: NAMP attempts to achieve a geographical balance that corresponds to its membership make-up. Students can inquire as to the availability of a scholarship at their school by contacting the school's department.

★917★ Statler Foundation Scholarship
Statler Foundation
107 Delaware Ave., Ste. 508
Buffalo, NY 14202
Ph: (716)852-1104
Purpose: To further education in the field of hospitality. Qualifications: Applicants must be enrolled in food service, culinary arts, or hotel/motel management programs on a fulltime basis in the U.S. Selection criteria: Scholarships are awarded through State Hotel-Motel Associations. Funds available: Amounts differ for each state. Application details: Students must be co-sponsored by the hotel/motel association in their state of residence. Deadline: Decided by each individual State Association.

BASIC REFERENCE GUIDES AND HANDBOOKS

★918★ The Hotel and Restaurant Business
Van Nostrand Reinhold
115 5th Ave.
New York, NY 10013
Donald Lundberg. Sixth edition, 1994.

★919★ INNovation: Creativity Techniques for Hospitality Managers
John Wiley and Sons, Inc.
605 3rd Ave.
New York, NY 10158-0012
Ph: (212)850-6000   Fax: (212)850-6088
Fr: 800-526-5368
Florence Berger and Dennis H. Ferguson. 1990.

★920★ The Lodging and Food Service Industry
Educational Institute of the American Hotel & Motel Association
1201 New York Ave. NW, Ste. 600
Washington, DC 20005-3931
Ph: (202)289-3100
Gerald W. Lattin. Second edition, 1993. Describes the lodging industry; covers growth and development, organization, and structure, as well as such areas as operations, maintenance, marketing, and personnel. Describes career opportunities.

★921★ Managing Front Office Operations
Educational Institute of the American Hotel & Motel Association
1201 New York Ave., NW, Ste. 600
Washington, DC 20005
Ph: (202)289-3100
Charles E. Steadman and Michael L. Kasavana; edited by Matthew O. Rowe. 1991. Explains guest registration, accounting, and how to evaluate and manage the operations and staff of the front office.

★922★ Managing Quality Services
American Hotel & Motel Association (AH&MA)
1201 New York Ave., NW, Ste. 600
Washington, DC 20005
Ph: (202)289-3100
Stephen J. Shriver; edited by George Glazer. 1988. Shows managers how to increase profitability and productivity by solving problems and standards of performance. Includes case studies, sample flip charts and agendas, and a perfo rmance standard model.

★923★ Resort Development and Management
Educational Institute of the AH & MA
1407 S. Harrison Rd.
PO Box 1240
East Lansing, MI 48826
Ph: (517)353-5500   Fr: 800-752-4567
Chuck Y. Gee; edited by Marjorie Harless. Second edition, 1988. Offers extensive details on the process of planning and development, managing the health club/spa facility, computer systems, security, safety, and risk management.

★924★ Training for the Hospitality Industry
Educational Institute of the American Hotel & Motel Association
1201 New York Ave., NW
Washington, DC 20005
Ph: (202)289-3100
Lewis C. Forrest, Jr. Second edition, 1990.

PROFESSIONAL AND TRADE PERIODICALS

★925★ The Art and Science of Hospitality Management
Educational Institute of the American Hotel & Motel Association (AH&MA)
1407 S. Harrsion Rd.
PO Box 1240
East Lansing, MI 48826
Ph: (517)353-5500   Fr: 800-752-4567
James R. Abbey and Jerome J. Vallen. 1987. Offers a clear understanding of the skills specific to managing a hotel, motel, or restaurant, including management responsibilities, operational responsibilities, and the personal and professional demands of managing and maintaining the management image.

★926★ The Cornell Hotel and Restaurant Administration Quarterly
Cornell University School of Hotel Administration
Statler Hall
Ithaca, NY 14853-6902
Ph: (607)255-3025   Fax: (607)255-4179
Glenn Withiam
Bimonthly. Magazine of applied research and ideas for hotel and restaurant managers.

★927★ Entree
Entree Travel
1470 E. Valley Rd.
Santa Barbara, CA 93108
Ph: (805)969-5848   Fax: (805)966-7095
William Tomicki
Monthly. Features "an insider's look at hotels, restaurants, and travel around the world." Contains advice and tips on travel, bargains, and services. Recurring features include book reviews and notices of publications available.

★928★ Foodservice East
The Newbury Street Group, Inc.
76 Summer St.
Boston, MA 02110
Ph: (617)695-9080   Fr: 800-852-5212
Susan Holaday
Tabloid covering restaurant, hotel, school, college, and hospital food service in the Northeast.

★929★ Hotel & Motel Management
Advanstar Communications Inc.
7500 Old Oak Blvd.
Cleveland, OH 44130
Ph: (216)896-2839   Fax: (216)891-2726
Robert Nozar
Magazine (tabloid) covering the global lodging industry.

★930★ Hotel and Resort Industry
Coastal Communications Corp.
488 Madison Ave.
New York, NY 10022
Ph: (212)888-1500   Fax: (212)888-8008
Stefani O'Connor
Monthly. Magazine for headquarters executives, owners, operations management, specifiers, and purchasing directors in hotels, resorts, motels, and motor inns.

★931★ Innkeeping World
Charles Nolte
PO Box 84108
Seattle, WA 98124
Ph: (206)362-7125   Fax: (206)362-7847
Dedicated to providing information "to enhance the hotel executive's skillful management of all aspects of hotel operation through concisely written articles incorporating ideas and case-histories which communicate useful knowledge for lasting benefit." Features regular columns covering market and industry developments, marketing advice, personnel concerns, and other topics of interest to management level staff. Recurring features include columns titled Reports and Trends, Managing, Marketing, Guest Relations, Staff Relations, and Ideas.

★932★ Inside Preferred of America
Preferred Hotels Worldwide
1901 S. Meyers Rd., Ste. 220
Oakbrook Terrace, IL 60181-5206
Ph: (312)953-0404
Patti Temple

Monthly. Provides information for executives and general managers of the independently-owned Preferred Hotels. Reports personnel changes, statistics, and meeting and convention dates and locations. Also includes news of awards and items relating to the hotel business which might not appear in trade journals.

★933★ Lodging Hospitality
Penton Publishing
1100 Superior Ave.
Cleveland, OH 44114
Ph: (216)696-7000   Fax: (216)696-7932
Ed Watkins

Monthly. Magazine serving managers of independent, franchise, chain-owned, and referral groups in the hospitality industry.

★934★ Restaurants & Institutions
Cahners Publishing Co.
1350 E. Touhy Ave.
PO Box 5080
Des Plaines, IL 60017-5080
Ph: (708)635-8800   Fax: (708)390-2618
Mike Bartlett

Semiweekly. Magazine focusing on foodservice and lodging management.

PROFESSIONAL MEETINGS AND CONVENTIONS

★935★ American Hotel and Motel Association Fall Conference
American Hotel and Motel Association
1201 New York Ave., NW, Ste. 600
Washington, DC 20005-3931
Ph: (202)289-3115   Fax: (202)289-3199
Annual. **Dates and Locations:** 1995 Nov 06-10; New York, NY.

★936★ CHRIE - Council on Hotel, Restaurant, and Institutional Education International Conference
Council on Hotel, Restaurant, and Institutional Education
1200 17th St., NW
Washington, DC 20036-3097
Ph: (202)331-5990   Fax: (202)785-2511
Annual. **Dates and Locations:** 1995

★937★ EUROEXPO HOREGA - International Trade Fair for Hotel, Restaurant, and Catering Equipment
Glahe International, Inc.
1700 K St., NW, Ste. 403
Washington, DC 20006-4557
Ph: (202)659-4557   Fax: (202)457-0776
Biennial. **Dates and Locations:** 1995; St. Petersburg.

★938★ Hotel, Motel, and Restaurant Supply Show of the Southeast
Leisure Time Unlimited, Inc.
708 Main St.
PO Box 332
Myrtle Beach, SC 29578
Ph: (803)448-9483   Fax: (803)626-1513
Annual. Always held during January at the Convention Center in Myrtle Beach, South Carolina. **Dates and Locations:** 1996 Jan 30-01; Myrtle Beach, SC. • 1997 Jan 28-30; Myrtle Beach, SC. • 1998 Jan 27-20; Myrtle Beach, SC.

★939★ Hotelympia - International Hotel and Catering Exhibition
Reed Exhibition Companies (World Headquarters)
255 Washington St.
Newton, MA 02158-1630
Ph: (617)630-2200   Fax: (617)630-2222
Biennial. **Dates and Locations:** 1996 Feb; London.

★940★ International Hotel/Motel and Restaurant Show
George Little Management, Inc.
10 Bank St., Ste. 1200
White Plains, NY 10606-1933
Ph: (914)421-3200   Fax: (914)948-6180
Annual. Always held during November at the Jacob K. Javits Convention Center in New York City. **Dates and Locations:** 1995 Nov 10-14; New York, NY. • 1996 Nov 09-12; New York, NY. • 1997 Nov 08-11; New York, NY. • 1998 Nov 07-10; New York, NY.

★941★ KUK Prage - International Trade Fair for Hotel & Catering, Food & Beverages
Glahe International, Inc.
1700 K St., NW, Ste. 403
Washington, DC 20006-4557
Ph: (202)659-4557   Fax: (202)457-0776
Dates and Locations: 1996; Prague.

★942★ National Restaurant Association Restaurant, Hotel-Motel Show
National Restaurant Association
150 N. Michigan Ave., Ste. 2000
Chicago, IL 60601
Ph: (312)853-2525   Fax: (312)853-2548
Annual. Always held during May at the McCormick Place Complex in Chicago, Illinois. **Dates and Locations:** 1996 May 20-18; Chicago, IL.

★943★ Northeast Food Service and Lodging Exposition and Conference
Reed Exhibition Companies (World Headquarters)
255 Washington St.
Newton, MA 02158-1630
Ph: (617)630-2200   Fax: (617)630-2222
Annual. Always held during April at the Bayside Exposition Center in Boston, Massachusetts. **Dates and Locations:** 1996 Apr; Boston, MA.

★944★ Southeastern Restaurant, Hospitality Foodservice Show
Reed Exhibition Companies (World Headquarters)
255 Washington St.
Newton, MA 02158-1630
Ph: (617)630-2200   Fax: (617)630-2222
Annual. Always held during October at the Georgia World Congress Center in Atlanta, Georgia.

★945★ Upper Midwest Hospitality, Restaurant, and Lodging Show
Upper Midwest Hospitality Inc.
871 Jefferson Ave.
St. Paul, MN 55102
Ph: (612)222-7401   Fax: (612)222-7347
Annual. **Dates and Locations:** 1996 Feb; Minneapolis, MN.

OTHER SOURCES OF INFORMATION

★946★ "Hospitality Administration" in Accounting to Zoology: Graduate Fields Defined (pp. 37-38)
Petersons Guides, Inc.
PO Box 2123
Princeton, NJ 08543-2123
Ph: (609)243-9111   Fax: (609)243-9150
Fr: 800-338-3282
Amy J. Goldstein, editor. Revised and updated, 1987. Discusses types of graduate programs and degrees, graduate research, applied work, employment prospects and trends.

★947★ "Hotel Manager/Assistant" in 100 Best Jobs for the 1990s & Beyond
Dearborn Financial Publishing, Inc.
520 N. Dearborn St.
Chicago, IL 60610-4354
Ph: (312)836-4400   Fax: (312)836-1021
Fr: 800-621-9621
Carol Kleiman. 1992. Describes 100 jobs ranging from accountants to veterinarians.. Each job profile includes such information as education, experience, and certification needed, salaries, and job search suggestions.

★948★ "Hotel/Motel Manager" in Career Selector 2001
Barron's Educational Series, Inc.
250 Wireless Blvd.
Hauppauge, NY 11788
Ph: (516)434-3311   Fax: (516)434-3723
Fr: 800-645-3476
James C. Gonyea. 1993.

Industrial Production Managers

Industrial production managers direct the work of first-line supervisors and coordinate all other activities related to production within factories, including production scheduling, staffing, selection and installation of equipment, quality control, inventory control, and coordination of activities between departments. Computers are used by production managers to provide current data on such things as inventory and product standards.

Salaries

Salaries of industrial production managers vary significantly by industry and plant size. Median salaries are as follows:

Industrial production managers $60,000/year

Employment Outlook

Growth rate until the year 2005: Slower than the average.

Industrial Production Managers

★949★ "Industrial Production Managers" in *Occupational Outlook Handbook*
U.S. Government Printing Office
Superintendent of Documents
Washington, DC 20402
Ph: (202)512-1800   Fax: (202)512-2250
Biennial. 1994-95. This encyclopedia of careers describes in detail 250 occupations—comprising about 85 percent of all jobs in the economy. Occupations that require lengthy education or training are given the most attention. For each occupation, the handbook covers job duties, working conditions, training, educational preparation, personal qualities, advancement possibilities, job outlook, earnings, and sources of additional information.

★950★ "Inventory Management Officer" in *Guide to Federal Jobs* (pp. 257)
Resource Directories
3361 Executive Pkwy., Ste. 302
Toledo, OH 43606
Ph: (419)536-5353   Fax: (419)536-7056
Fr: 800-274-8515
Rod W. Durgin, editor. Third edition. 1992. Covers locating and ap plying for federal jobs. For 200 professional and technical jobs requiring a college degree, this guide describes the nature of the work and lists college majors preferred for that occupation. Section 1 surveys the functions and work of the government agencies that hire the most significant number of college graduates.

★951★ "Production Management" in *Career Choices for the 90's for Students of M.B.A.* (pp. 77-78)
Walker and Co.
435 Hudson St.
New York, NY 10014
Ph: (212)727-8300   Fax: (212)727-0984
Fr: 800-289-2553
1990. Describes jobs in various industries and cntains interviews with people working in related occupations. Presents employment outlook, best geographic location, entry-level opportunities, career paths, job responsibilities, advancement possibilities, personal and professional qualifications, salaries, working conditions, material for further reading, and associations.

★952★ "Production Management" in *Encyclopedia of Career Choices for the 1990's: A Guide to Entry Level Jobs* (pp. 307-308)
Berkley Pub.
PO Box 506
East Rutherford, NJ 07073
Fax: (201)933-2316   Fr: 800-788-6262
1992. Written for college and professional associations. Related interviews with people working in the field. There is a cross index of college majors to career fields.

★953★ "Production Manager" in *Career Information Center* (Vol.9)
Simon and Schuster
200 Old Tappan Rd.
Old Tappan, NJ 07675
Fax: 800-445-6991   Fr: 800-223-2348
Richard Lidz and Dale Anderson, editorial directors. Fifth edition, 1993. For 600 occupations, this 13 volume set describes job duties, entry-level requirements, education and training needed, advancement possibilities, employment outlook, earnings and benefits. Each of the first 12 volumes includes jobs related under a broad career field; volume 9 covers manufacturing. Volume 13 is the index.

★954★ "Production Manager, Industrial" in *VGM's Careers Encyclopedia* (pp. 373-374)
National Textbook Co. (NTC)
VGM Career Books
4255 W. Touhy Ave.
Lincolnwood, IL 60646-1975
Ph: (708)679-5500   Fax: (708)679-2494
Fr: 800-323-4900
Third edition. 1991. Arranged alphabetically A-Z, this book contains 2 to 5 page descriptions of 200 managerial, professional, technical, trade and service occupations. Each profile describes job duties, places of employment, qualifications, educational preparation, training, employment potential, advancement possibilities, income, and additional sources of information.

★955★ "Production Manager, Industrial" in *VGM's Handbook of Business and Management Careers* (pp. 71-72)
National Textbook Co. (NTC)
VGM Career Books
4255 W. Touhy Ave.
Lincolnwood, IL 60646-1975
Ph: (708)679-5500   Fax: (708)679-2494
Fr: 800-323-4900
Annette Selden, editor. Second ed., 1993. Arranged alphabetically, this guide contains 42 occupational profiles describing job duties, places of employment, working conditions, qualifications, education, employment outlook, and income.

★956★ *Production Planners*
Chronicle Guidance Publications, Inc.
66 Aurora St.
PO Box 1190
Moravia, NY 13118-1190
Ph: (315)497-0330   Fax: (315)497-3359
Fr: 800-622-7284
1993. This career brief describes the nature of the job, working conditions, hours and earnings, education and training, licensure, certification, unions, personal qualifications, social and psychological factors, location, employment outlook, entry methods, advancement, and related occupations.

★957★ "Production Supervisor" in *Career Information Center* (Vol.9)
Simon and Schuster
200 Old Tappan Rd.
Old Tappan, NJ 07675
Fax: 800-445-6991   Fr: 800-223-2348
Richard Lidz and Dale Anderson, editorial directors. Fifth edition. 1993. For 600 occupations, this 13 volume set describes entry-level requirements, education and training needed, advancement possibilities, employment outlook, earnings and benefits. Each of the first 12 volumes include jobs related under a broad career field; volume 9 covers manufacturing. Volume 13 is the Index.

PROFESSIONAL ASSOCIATIONS

★958★ American Association of Industrial Management (AAIM)
Stearns Bldg., Ste. 324
293 Bridge St.
Springfield, MA 01103
Ph: (413)737-8766   Fax: (413)737-9724
Members: Companies in manufacturing, automotive, textile, chemical, paper, and insurance fields; banks; colleges and universities; town and city governments; hospitals. **Purpose:** Conducts activities in the industrial relations and industrial management fields; gives advice and/or assistance in all aspects of labor relations, training, industrial relations research, management and supervisory education, job evaluation, wage and salary administration, and communications. **Publications:** Consumer Price Index. • Executive Manager, periodic. • Job Evaluation Manuals. • Signs of the Times, periodic. • U.S. News Washington Business Report, monthly.

★959★ APICS — The Educational Society for Resource Management (APICS)
500 W. Annandale Rd.
Falls Church, VA 22046
Ph: (703)237-8344   Fax: (703)237-4316
Fr: 800-444-2742
Purpose: Offers programs and materials on resource management concepts and techniques. Develops and provides education on materials for all areas of manufacturing and service industries. Recognizes persons certified in production and inventory management (CPIM) and integrated resource management (CIRM). Maintians speakers' bureau; compiles statistics; produces monthly Business Outlook Index. Maintains special interest groups. **Publications:** APICS, The Performance Advantage, monthly. • Production and Inventory Management Journal, quarterly.

★960★ Industrial Relations Research Association (IRRA)
7226 Social Science Bldg.
1180 Observatory Dr.
Madison, WI 53706
Ph: (608)262-2762   Fax: (608)265-4591
Businesspersons, union leaders, government officials, lawyers, arbitrators, academics, and others interested in research and exchange of ideas on social, political, economic, legal, and psychological aspects of labor, including employer and employee organization, labor relations, personnel administration, social security, and labor legislation. Disseminates research results. Maintains placement service. **Publications:** Dialogues, semiannual. • Industrial Relations Research Association— Annual Research Volume, annual. • Industrial Relations Research Association— Annual Spring Proceedings, annual. • Industrial Relations Research Association— Annual Winter Proceedings, annual. • Industrial Relations Research Association— Membership Directory, quadrennial. • Industrial Relations Research Association— Series Newsletter, quarterly.

★961★ International Management Council (IMC)
430 S. 20th St., Ste. 3
Omaha, NE 68102-2506
Ph: (402)345-1904   Fax: (402)345-4480
Members: Supervisors and managers in all fields. **Purpose:** Seeks to help supervisory managers develop as leaders in their industries and communities. Maintains speakers' bureau; offers specialized education program. **Publications:** In Focus, bimonthly. • International Management Council— "Management Forum", quarterly.

TEST GUIDES

★962★ ACT Proficiency Examination Program: Production/Operations Management
National Learning Corp.
212 Michael Dr.
Syosset, NY 11791
Ph: (516)921-8888   Fax: (516)921-8743
Fr: 800-645-6337
Jack Rudman. A series of practice test guides containing multiple-choice examinations designed to demonstrate proficiency in the subject of production/operations management.

★963★ Career Examination Series: Director of Industrial Development
National Learning Corp.
212 Michael Dr.
Syosset, NY 11791
Ph: (516)921-8888   Fax: (516)921-8743
Fr: 800-645-6337
Jack Rudman. 1993. Test guide including questions and answers for students or professionals in the field who seek advancement through examination.

PROFESSIONAL AND TRADE PERIODICALS

★964★ Business & Industry
Business Magazines, Inc.
1720 28th St., Ste. B
West Des Moines, IA 50265-1436
Ph: (515)225-2545   Fax: (515)225-2318
James V. Snyder
Monthly. Magazine for top level and purchasing management, manufacturing and design engineers, and quality control personnel.

★965★ Industrial Distribution
Cahners Publishing Co.
275 Washington St.
Newton, MA 02158-1630
Ph: (617)964-3030   Fax: (617)558-4456
George Berkwitt
Monthly. Magazine covering industrial supplies, marketing, management, sales, telecommunications, computers, inventory, and warehouse management.

★966★ Industrial Maintenance and Plant Operation
Capital Cities/ABC/Chilton Co.
Chilton Way
Radnor, PA 19087
Ph: (215)964-4000   Fax: (215)964-4647
Jerry Steinbrink
Monthly. Product news magazine (tabloid) serving the plant engineering, maintenance, replacement, and operations markets.

★967★ The Industrial News
Welch Daily News, Inc.
100 RR Ave.
PO Box 180
Iaeger, WV 24844
Ph: (304)938-2142   Fax: (304)436-3146
William A. Johnson
Weekly. Newspaper with demographic orientation.

★968★ Journal of Operations Management
Elessseier Science
500 W. Annandale Rd.
Falls Church, VA 22046-4274
Ph: (703)237-8344   Fax: (703)237-4316
Christina Khojasteh
Quarterly. Journal covering manufacturing operations management topics.

★969★ Journal of Productivity Analysis
Kluwer Academic Publishers
101 Philip Drive
Norwell, MA 02061
Ph: (617)871-6600   Fax: (617)871-6528
Ali Dogramari
Quarterly. Scholoarly journal on measuring, explaining, and improving productivity in the production and distribution of goods and services.

★970★ Occupational Health & Safety Letter
Business Publishers, Inc.
951 Pershing Dr.
Silver Spring, MD 20910
Ph: (301)587-6300   Fax: (301)587-1081
Fr: 800-274-0122
Hiram Reisner
Biweekly. Covers federal and state legislation, standards, regulations, research activities, and enforcement cases concerning safety and health in the workplace environment. Concerned particularly with the Occupational Safety and Health Act (OSHA) of 1970. Recurring features include information on the medical, economic, and technological aspects of occupational health, and a calendar of events.

★971★ Occupational Safety & Health Reporter
Bureau of National Affairs, Inc. (BNA)
1231 25th St. NW
Washington, DC 20037
Ph: (202)452-4200   Fax: (202)822-8092
Fr: 800-372-1033
Stanley S. Pond
Weekly. Provides a notification and reference service covering federal and state regulation of occupational safety and health, standards, legislation, enforcement activities, research, and legal decisions. Recurring features include a calendar of meetings and seminars and the full text of selected administrative

rulings, proposed standards, criteria documents, variance notices, and compliance manuals.

★972★ **Production and Inventory Management Journal**
American Production and Inventory Control Society, Inc.
500 W. Annandale Rd.
Falls Church, VA 22046
Ph: (303)279-7658   Fax: (303)273-3278
R.E.D. Woolsey

Quarterly. Trade refereed journal covering production and inventory management.

★973★ **Production Management Bulletin**
Bureau of Business Practice
24 Rope Ferry Rd.
Waterford, CT 06386
Ph: (203)442-4365   Fax: (203)434-3078
Fr: 800-876-9105
Mary-Lou Brockett Devine

Semimonthly. Covers production department topics such as employee motivation, creation and maintenance of a safe workplace, solving common job problems, and ensuring a quality product.

★974★ **Safety Management**
Bureau of Business Practice
24 Rope Ferry Rd.
Waterford, CT 06386
Ph: (203)442-4365   Fax: (203)434-3078
Fr: 800-243-0876
Heather Vaughn

Monthly. Discusses successful safety programs and legal issues pertinent to safety management.

★975★ **Utility Supervision**
Bureau of Business Practice
24 Rope Ferry Rd.
Waterford, CT 06386
Ph: (203)442-4365   Fax: (203)434-3078
Fr: 800-243-0876
Winifred Bonney

Semimonthly. Covers techniques of supervising nonclerical employees of electric, gas, telephone, municipal power, water, and sanitation organizations. Considers such topics as organizing and planning, effective deployment of workers, ensuring a safe work environment, effective cost management, and utilizing teamwork, communication, and motivation as productive management tools. Also discusses the high cost of poor quality and disciplinary policies involving attendance, production, and safety. Recurring features include interviews with supervisors and managers, practical tips, and columns titled Supervisory Clinic and Utility Safety.

Inspectors and Compliance Officers, except Construction

Inspectors and compliance officers enforce adherence to a wide range of laws, regulations, policies, and procedures that protect the public on matters such as health, safety, food, immigration, licensing, interstate commerce, and international trade. Depending upon their employer, inspectors vary widely in titles and responsibilities. **Health inspectors** work with engineers, chemists, microbiologists, health workers, and lawyers to insure compliance with public health and safety regulations governing food, drugs, cosmetics, and other consumer products. **Consumer safety inspectors** specialize in food, feeds and pesticides, weights and measures, cosmetics, or drugs and medical equipment. **Food inspectors** inspect meat, poultry, and their byproducts to insure that they are wholesome and safe for public consumption. They also check for proper product labeling and sanitation. **Environmental health inspectors, or sanitarians**, who work primarily for state and local governments, insure that food, water, and air meet government standards. **Agricultural commodity graders** apply quality standards to aid the buying and selling of commodities and to insure that retailers and consumers receive wholesome and reliable products. **Immigration inspectors** interview and examine people seeking to enter the United States and its territories. They inspect passports to determine whether people are legally eligible to enter and verify their citizenship status and identity. **Aviation safety inspectors** insure that Federal Aviation Administration (FAA) regulations, which govern the quality and safety of aircraft equipment and personnel, are maintained. **Motor vehicle inspectors** verify the compliance of automobiles and trucks with state requirements for safe operation and emissions. **Traffic inspectors** oversee the scheduled service of streetcar, bus, or railway systems and determine the need for additional vehicles, revised schedules, or other changes to improve service. **Park rangers** register vehicles and visitors, collect fees, and provide information regarding state and national parks. **Occupational safety and health inspectors** visit places of employment to detect unsafe machinery and equipment or unhealthy working conditions. **Equal opportunity representatives** ascertain and correct unfair employment practices through consultation with and mediation between employers and minority groups. **Alcohol, tobacco, and firearms inspectors** inspect distilleries, wineries, and breweries; cigar and cigarette manufacturing plants; wholesale liquor dealers and importers; firearms and explosives manufacturers, dealers, and users; and other regulated facilities.

Salaries

Salaries of inspectors and compliance officers in state and local governments and in private industry are generally lower than those in federal government jobs.

Lowest 10 percent	less than $19,500/year
Median	$32,760/year
Highest 10 percent	More than $52,000/year
Federal government inspector (average)	$24,800-$59,300/year

Employment Outlook

Growth rate until the year 2005: Faster than the average.

Inspectors and Compliance Officers, Except Construction

CAREER GUIDES

★976★ "Alcohol, Tobacco and Firearms Inspector" in *Guide to Federal Jobs* (pp. 252)
Resource Directories
3361 Executive Pkwy., Ste. 302
Toledo, OH 43606
Ph: (419)536-5353   Fax: (419)536-7056
Fr: 800-274-8515

Rod W. Durgin, editor. Third edition, 1992. Contains information on finding and applying for federal jobs. Describes more than 200 professional and technical jobs for college graduates. Also includes chapters titled "Customs Inspector" (p. 254), "Immigration Inspector" (p. 250), "Consumer Safety Inspector" (p. 149), "Wage and Hour Compliance Specialists" (p. 255), and "Quality Assurance Specialist" (p. 255). Covers the nature of the work, salary, and geographic location. Lists college majors preferred for that occupation. Section one describes the function and work of government agencies that hire the most significant number of college graduates.

★977★ *Consumer Safety Officers*
Chronicle Guidance Publications, Inc.
66 Aurora St.
PO Box 1190
Moravia, NY 13118-1190
Ph: (315)497-0330   Fax: (315)497-3359
Fr: 800-622-7284

1993. Career brief describing the nature of the job, working conditions, hours and earnings, education and training, licensure, certification, unions, personal qualifications, social and psychological factors, location, employment outlook, entry methods, advancement, and related occupations.

★978★ "Government Inspectors and Examiners" in *Career Information Center* (Vol.11)
Simon and Schuster
200 Old Tappan Rd.
Old Tappan, NJ 07675
Fax: 800-445-6991   Fr: 800-223-2348
Richard Lidz and Linda Perrin, editorial directors. Fifth edition, 1993. This 13-volume set profiles over 600 occupations. Each occupational profile describes job duties, educational requirements, how to get the job, advancement possibilities, employment outlook, working conditions, earnings and benefits, and where to write for more information.

★979★ "Health Inspectors" in *Jobs! What They Are—Where They Are—What They Pay!* (pp. 136)
Simon & Schuster, Inc.
Simon & Schuster Bldg.
1230 Avenue of the Americas
New York, NY 10020
Ph: (212)698-7000   Fr: 800-223-2348
Robert O. Snelling and Anne M. Snelling. Third revised edition, 1992. Also includes a chapter titled "Regulatory Inspectors" (p. 139). Describes duties and responsibilities, earnings, employment opportunities, training, and qualifications.

★980★ "Health and Regulatory Inspectors" in *Encyclopedia of Careers and Vocational Guidance* (Vol.3, pp. 122-125)
J.G. Ferguson Publishing Co.
200 W. Madison St., Ste. 300
Chicago, IL 60606
Ph: (312)580-5480   Fax: (312)580-4948
William E. Hopke, editor in chief. Ninth edition, 1993. Four-volume set that profiles 900 occupations and describes job trends in 74 industries. Volume 2—*Professional Careers*—contains a chapter on "Health and Regulatory Inspectors" (p. 286). Includes career description, educational requirements, history of the job, methods of entry, advancement, employment outlook, earnings, conditions of work, social and psychological factors, and sources of further information.

★981★ "Inspectors and Compliance Officers" in *Best Jobs for the 1990s and Into the 21st Century*
Impact Publications
9104-N Manassas Dr.
Manassas Park, VA 22111
Ph: (703)361-7300   Fax: (703)335-9486

Ronald L. Krannich and Caryl Rae Krannich. 1993.

★982★ "Inspectors and Compliance Officers, except Construction" in *Occupational Outlook Handbook*
U.S. Government Printing Office
Superintendent of Documents
Washington, DC 20402
Ph: (202)512-1800   Fax: (202)512-2250

Biennial; latest edition, 1994-95. Encyclopedia of careers describing about 250 occupations and comprising about 85 percent of all jobs in the economy. Occupations that require lengthy education or training are given the most attention. Each occupation's profile describes what the worker does on the job, working conditions, education and training requirements, advancement possibilities, job outlook, earnings, and sources of additional information.

★983★ "Quality Control Inspectors" in *Career Information Center* (Vol.9)
Simon and Schuster
200 Old Tappan Rd.
Old Tappan, NJ 07675
Fax: 800-445-6991   Fr: 800-223-2348

Richard Lidz and Linda Perrin, editorial directors. Fifth edition, 1993. This 13-volume set profiles over 600 occupations. Each occupational profile describe job duties, educational requirements, how to get the job, advancement possibilities, employment outlook, working conditions, earnings and benefits, and where to write for more information.

PROFESSIONAL ASSOCIATIONS

★984★ National Association of Government Inspectors and Quality Assurance Personnel (NAGI & QAP)
c/o William C. Stanley
PO Box 484
Beaufort, NC 28516
Ph: (919)466-8031
Publications: *News Letter*, monthly.

★985★ National Association of Governmental Labor Officials (NAGLO)
4 W. Edenton St.
Raleigh, NC 27601
Ph: (919)733-7166   Fax: (919)733-6197
Members: Elected and appointed heads of state labor departments. **Purpose:** Seeks to assist labor officials in performing their duties and to improve employment conditions for American workers. **Publications:** *NAGLO Membership Directory*, annual. • *NAGLO News*, periodic.

★986★ National Association of Property Inspectors
303 W. Cypress St.
PO Box 12528
San Antonio, TX 78212-0528
Fax: (210)225-8450   Fr: 800-486-3676
Members: Property inspectors throughout North America wishing to be certified. **Purpose:** Provides certification and recognition for real estate professionals who have completed specialized educational courses, demonstrated competence, and agreed to abide by a code of ethics. Works with Lincoln Graduate Center to offer educational courses and programs. Plans to offer seminars throughout the country. **Publications:** *Property Inspector News*, quarterly.

STANDARDS/CERTIFICATION AGENCIES

★987★ American Association of Automatic Door Manufacturers (AAADM)
1300 Sumner Ave.
Cleveland, OH 44115-2851
Ph: (216)241-7333   Fax: (216)241-0105
Works to promote the industry and provide a forum for members to communicate. Currently working on certification program for inspectors.

★988★ American Institute of Inspectors
1117 47th St.
Sacramento, CA 95819
Ph: (916)451-0304   Fax: (916)455-7106
Certified home inspectors. Works to set standards for impartial evaluations of residential properties. Certifies members in four areas: residential homes, mobile homes, mechanics, and earthquake hazard reduction.

★989★ National Association of Property Inspectors
303 W. Cypress St.
PO Box 12528
San Antonio, TX 78212-0528
Fax: (210)225-8450   Fr: 800-486-3676
Property inspectors throughout North America wishing to be certified. Provides certification and recognition for real estate professionals who have completed specialized educational courses, demonstrated competence, and agreed to abide by a code of ethics.

★990★ National Board of Boiler and Pressure Vessel Inspectors (NBBI)
1055 Crupper Ave.
Columbus, OH 43229
Ph: (614)888-8320   Fax: (614)888-0750
Represents agencies empowered to assure adherence to the ASME Boiler and Pressure Vessel Construction Code and the National Board Inspection Code.

TEST GUIDES

★991★ *Career Examination Series: Associate Water Use Inspector*
National Learning Corp.
212 Michael Dr.
Syosset, NY 11791
Ph: (516)921-8888   Fax: (516)921-8743
Fr: 800-645-6337
Jack Rudman. 1993. Test guide including questions and answers for students or professionals in the field who seek advancement through examination.

★992★ *Career Examination Series: Auto Equipment Inspector*
National Learning Corp.
212 Michael Dr.
Syosset, NY 11791
Ph: (516)921-8888   Fax: (516)921-8743
Fr: 800-645-6337
Jack Rudman. 1993. Test guide including questions and answers for students or professionals in the field who seek advancement through examination.

★993★ *Career Examination Series: Automotive Facilities Inspector*
National Learning Corp.
212 Michael Dr.
Syosset, NY 11791
Ph: (516)921-8888   Fax: (516)921-8743
Fr: 800-645-6337
Jack Rudman. 1993. Test guide including questions and answers for students or professionals in the field who seek advancement through examination.

★994★ *Career Examination Series: Beverage Control Inspector*
National Learning Corp.
212 Michael Dr.
Syosset, NY 11791
Ph: (516)921-8888   Fax: (516)921-8743
Fr: 800-645-6337
Jack Rudman. 1993. Test guide including questions and answers for students or pro-

fessionals in the field who seek advancement through examination.

★995★ *Career Examination Series: Beverage Control Investigator*
National Learning Corp.
212 Michael Dr.
Syosset, NY 11791
Ph: (516)921-8888   Fax: (516)921-8743
Fr: 800-645-6337
Jack Rudman. 1993. Test guide including questions and answers for students or professionals in the field who seek advancement through examination.

★996★ *Career Examination Series: Chief Beverage Control Investigator*
National Learning Corp.
212 Michael Dr.
Syosset, NY 11791
Ph: (516)921-8888   Fax: (516)921-8743
Fr: 800-645-6337
Jack Rudman. 1993. Test guide including questions and answers for students or professionals in the field who seek advancement through examination.

★997★ *Career Examination Series: Chief Compliance Investigator*
National Learning Corp.
212 Michael Dr.
Syosset, NY 11791
Ph: (516)921-8888   Fax: (516)921-8743
Fr: 800-645-6337
Jack Rudman. 1993. Test guide including questions and answers for students or professionals in the field who seek advancement through examination.

★998★ *Career Examination Series: Chief Consumer Affairs Investigator*
National Learning Corp.
212 Michael Dr.
Syosset, NY 11791
Ph: (516)921-8888   Fax: (516)921-8743
Fr: 800-645-6337
Jack Rudman. 1993. Test guide including questions and answers for students or professionals in the field who seek advancement through examination.

★999★ *Career Examination Series: Chief Meat Inspector*
National Learning Corp.
212 Michael Dr.
Syosset, NY 11791
Ph: (516)921-8888   Fax: (516)921-8743
Fr: 800-645-6337
Jack Rudman. 1993. Test guide including questions and answers for students or professionals in the field who seek advancement through examination.

★1000★ *Career Examination Series: Chief Multiple Residence Inspector*
National Learning Corp.
212 Michael Dr.
Syosset, NY 11791
Ph: (516)921-8888   Fax: (516)921-8743
Fr: 800-645-6337
Jack Rudman. 1993. Test guide including questions and answers for students or professionals in the field who seek advancement through examination.

★1001★ Career Examination Series: Chief Water Pollution Control Inspector
National Learning Corp.
212 Michael Dr.
Syosset, NY 11791
Ph: (516)921-8888   Fax: (516)921-8743
Fr: 800-645-6337

Jack Rudman. 1993. Test guide including questions and answers for students or professionals in the field who seek advancement through examination.

★1002★ Career Examination Series: Farm Products Grading Inspector
National Learning Corp.
212 Michael Dr.
Syosset, NY 11791
Ph: (516)921-8888   Fax: (516)921-8743
Fr: 800-645-6337

Jack Rudman. 1993. Test guide including questions and answers for students or professionals in the field who seek advancement through examination.

★1003★ Career Examination Series: Inspector
National Learning Corp.
212 Michael Dr.
Syosset, NY 11791
Ph: (516)921-8888   Fax: (516)921-8743
Fr: 800-645-6337

Jack Rudman. A series of study guides with multiple-choice examination questions and solutions for trainees and professional inspectors and compliance officers. Titles in the series include Compliance Investigator; Food Inspector; Food Inspector Trainee; Inspector of Low Pressure Boilers; Inspector of Markets, Weights, and Measures; Institutional Inspector; Investigator—Inspector; License Inspector; Lighting Inspector; Lottery Inspector; Meat Inspector; Meat Inspector Trainee; Meat Inspector-Poultry Inspector; Medical Inspector; Motor Vehicle Inspector; Ordinance Inspector; Painting Inspector; Pharmaceutical Examiner; Pharmacy Inspector; Postal Inspector (U.S.P.S.); Principal Consumer Affairs Inspector; Principal Purchase Inspector; Principal Zoning Inspector; Public Health Inspector; Railroad Equipment Inspector; Railroad Inspector; Railroad Track and Structure Inspector; Rehabilitation Inspector; Rent Inspector; Road Car Inspector; Safety and Health Inspector; Sanitation Inspector; Sanitation Inspector Trainee; Senior Air Pollution Inspector; Senior Automotive Facilities Inspector; Senior Boiler Inspector; Senior Consumer Affairs Inspector; Senior Fire Prevention Inspector; Senior Food Inspector; Senior Inspector of Low Pressure Boilers; Senior Inspector of Markets, Weights, and Measures; Senior Inspector, Meat and Poultry; Senior Meat Inspector; Senior Pesticide Control Inspector; Senior Pharmacy Inspector; Senior Purchase Inspector; Senior Rent Inspector; Senior Taxi and Limousine Inspector; Senior Telephone Inspector; Senior Transportation Inspector; Senior Zoning Inspector; Sewer Inspector; Shelter Inspector (Civil Defense); Supervising Air Pollution Inspector; Supervising Automotive Facilities Inspector; Supervising Consumer Affairs Inspector; Supervising Food Inspector; Supervising Inspector of Markets, Weights, and Measures; Supervising Meat Inspector; Supervising Plumbing Inspector; Supervising Sanitation Inspector; Supervising Taxi and Limousine Inspector; Supervising Water Use Inspector; Tax Compliance Agent; Tax Compliance Agent (Spanish Speaking); Tax Compliance Representative; Tax i and Limousine Inspector; Water Use Inspector; Zoning Inspector; Zoning Inspector II.

★1004★ Career Examination Series: Senior Electrical Inspector
National Learning Corp.
212 Michael Dr.
Syosset, NY 11791
Ph: (516)921-8888   Fax: (516)921-8743
Fr: 800-645-6337

Jack Rudman. 1993. Test guide including questions and answers for students or professionals in the field who seek advancement through examiation.

PROFESSIONAL AND TRADE PERIODICALS

★1005★ The Food & Drug Letter
Washington Business Information, Inc.
1117 N. 19th St.
Arlington, VA 22209-1978
Ph: (703)247-3424   Fax: (703)247-3421
Michael Dolan

Biweekly. Seeks to provide a detailed analysis of federal regulatory activity relating to food, drugs, and cosmetics. Interprets policy and regulatory changes, focusing on the impact of specific actions on industry in both the long and short term.

★1006★ Food Protection Report
Charles Felix Associates
PO Box 1581
Leesburg, VA 22075
Ph: (703)777-7448
Charles W. Felix

Monthly. Addresses developments in food protection that will have an impact on safety programs. Incorporates a four-page insert titled Inside Report that provides features, editorials, and analysis, and discusses innovations in the industry. Recurring features include columns titled Bulletin, Commentary, and Profile.

★1007★ Job Safety Consultant
BRP Publications Inc.
1333 H St. NW, Ste. 1100 W.
Washington, DC 20005
Ph: (202)842-3022
Marsha Wagshol

Monthly. Covers industrial safety and health, Occupational Safety and Health Administration (OSHA) and company safety strategies. Recurring features include columns titled Editor's Corner, Updates & Alerts, Safety in Action, Technical Tips, and Safety Talks.

★1008★ U.S. Regulatory Reporter
Parexel International Corporation
195 West St.
Waltham, MA 02154-1116
Ph: (617)487-9900   Fax: (617)487-0525
Fr: 800-937-7795
Mark Mathieu

Monthly. Reports regulatory news from the FDA and other government agencies for companies in the drug, medical device, diagnostic, and biotechnology industries. Recurring features include analyses of FDA product approval standards and review processes and sections titled Regulatory Review and the Biologies and Biotech Regulatory Report.

PROFESSIONAL MEETINGS AND CONVENTIONS

★1009★ National Safety Council Congress and Exposition
National Safety Council
1121 Spring Lake Dr.
Itasca, IL 60143
Ph: (708)285-1121   Fax: (708)285-0798
Annual. **Dates and Locations:** 1995 Nov 05-10; Dallas, TX. • 1996 Oct 27-01; Orlando, FL.

Loan Officers and Counselors

Loan officers prepare, analyze, and verify loan applications, make decisions regarding the extension of credit, and help borrowers fill out loan applications. Loan officers usually specialize in commercial, consumer, or mortgage loans. Commercial or business loans help companies pay for new equipment or to expand operations. **Loan counselors** help consumers with low income or a poor credit history qualify for credit, usually a home mortgage. Loan counselors meet with consumers who are attempting to purchase a home or refinance debt, but who do not qualify for loans with banks.

Salaries

Earnings for loan officers and counselors are as follows:

Real estate mortgage loan officers	$25,000-$45,000/year
Consumer loan officers	$27,000-$47,000/year
Loan counselors	$15,000-$35,000/year

Employment Outlook

Growth rate until the year 2005: Faster than the average.

Loan Officers and Counselors

CAREER GUIDES

★1010★ **Bank Loan Officer**
Vocational Biographies, Inc.
PO Box 31
Sauk Centre, MN 56378-0031
Ph: (612)352-6516   Fax: (612)352-5546
Fr: 800-255-0752

1995. Four-page pamphlet containing a personal narrative about a worker's job, work likes and dislikes, career path from high school to the present, education and training, the rewards and frustrations, and the effects of the job on the rest of the worker's life. The data file portion of this pamphlet gives a concise occupational summary, including work description, working conditions, places of employment, personal characteristics, education and training, job outlook, and salary range.

★1011★ **"Banking and Financial Services"** in *Where the Jobs Are: The Hottest Careers for the 90s* (pp. 52-76)
Career Press
180 5th Ave.
Hawthorne, NJ 07507
Ph: (201)427-0229   Fax: (201)427-2037
Fr: 800-CAREER-1

Joyce Hadley. 1995. Offers a job-hunting strategy for the 1990s as well as descriptions of growing careers of the decade. Each profile includes general information, forecasts, growth, education and training, licensing requirements, and salary information.

★1012★ **"Loan Officer"** in *BLR Encyclopedia of Prewritten Job Descriptions*
Business and Legal Reports, Inc.
39 Academy St.
Madison, CT 06443-1513
Ph: (203)245-7448

Stephen D. Bruce, editor-in-chief. 1994. This book contains hundreds of sample job descriptions arranged by functional job category. The 1-3 page job descriptions cover what the worker normally does in the position, who they report to, and how that position fits in the organizational structure.

★1013★ **"Loan Officers"** in *101 Careers: A Guide to the Fastest-Growing Opportunities* (pp. 23-25)
John Wiley & Sons, Inc.
605 3rd Ave.
New York, NY 10158-0012
Ph: (212)850-6645   Fax: (212)850-6088

Michael Harkavy. 1990. Describes the nature of the job, working conditions, employment growth, qualifications, personal skills, projected salaries, and where to write for more information.

★1014★ **Loan Officers (Banking)**
Chronicle Guidance Publications, Inc.
66 Aurora St.
PO Box 1190
Moravia, NY 13118-1190
Ph: (315)497-0330   Fax: (315)497-3359
Fr: 800-622-7284

1992. Career brief describing the nature of the job, working conditions, hours and earnings, education and training, licensure, certification, unions, personal qualifications, social and psychological factors, location, employment outlook, entry methods, advancement, and related occupations.

★1015★ **"Loan Officers and Counselors"** in *Occupational Outlook Handbook* (pp. 53-54)
U.S. Government Printing Office
Superintendent of Documents
Washington, DC 20402
Ph: (202)512-1800   Fax: (202)512-2250

Biennial; latest edition, 1994-95. Encyclopedia of careers. Describes about 250 occupations that comprise about 85 percent of all jobs in the economy. Occupations that require lengthy education or training are given the most attention.

★1016★ **Loan Officers (Financial Institutions)**
Chronicle Guidance Publications, Inc.
66 Aurora St.
PO Box 1190
Moravia, NY 13118-1190
Ph: (315)497-0330   Fax: (315)497-3359
Fr: 800-622-7284

1992. Career brief describing the nature of the job, working conditions, hours and earnings, education and training, licensure, certification, unions, personal qualifications, social and psychological factors, location, employ-

ment outlook, entry methods, advancement, and related occupations.

★1017★ **Loan Processing Clerk**
Vocational Biographies, Inc.
PO Box 31
Sauk Centre, MN 56378-0031
Ph: (612)352-6516   Fax: (612)352-5546
Fr: 800-255-0752

1995. Four-page pamphlet containing a personal narrative about a worker's job, work likes and dislikes, career path from high school to the present. Education and training, the rewards and frustrations, and the effects of the job on the rest of the worker's life. The data file portion of this pamphlet gives a concise occupational summary, including work descriptions, working conditions, places of employment, personal characteristics, education and training, job outlook, and salary range.

★1018★ **So You Want to be in Financial Services: It's Time to Consider a Career in the Savings Institution Business**
Institute of Financial Education
111 E. Wacker Dr.
Chicago, IL 60601
Ph: (312)644-3100

Describes savings institutions, and lists jobs in each department, including loan processors and officers.

PROFESSIONAL ASSOCIATIONS

★1019★ **Collateral Loan Brokers Association of New York (CLBANY)**
486 8th Ave.
New York, NY 10001
Ph: (212)736-0755

Owners of pawnbroking stores in New York City. Seeks to: promote and protect business interests of its members in relation to each other, the public, and public authorities; create favorable public relations by dispelling misconceptions; disseminate information with respect to modern practices and the desirability of "pledge loans."

★1020★ National Association of Affordable Housing Lenders
1726 18th St. NW
Washington, DC 20009
Ph: (202)328-9171   Fax: (202)265-4435
Members: Lenders specializing in affordable housing finance, including banks and loan consortia. **Purpose:** Sponsors forums on banking and housing finance. Represents members' interests before congress and government agencies. **Publications:** *Compendium of Loan Consortia.* • *Directions in Affordable Housing Finance*, quarterly.

★1021★ National Association of Professional Mortgage Women (NAPMW)
PO Box 2016
Edmonds, WA 98020-0999
Ph: (206)778-6162   Fax: (206)771-9588
Sponsors educational and professional development programs for women in mortgage banking professions. Aims to maintain high standards of professional conduct and to encourage women to pursue careers in mortgage banking. Works for equal recognition and professsional opportunities for women. Offers professional certification through its Institute of Mortgage Lending. **Publications:** *Notes & Deeds*, quarterly.

★1022★ Robert Morris Associates - Association of Bank Loan and Credit Officers (RMA)
1 Liberty Pl.
1650 Market St., Ste. 2300
Philadelphia, PA 19103
Ph: (215)851-9100   Fax: (215)851-9206
Commercial and savings banks and savings and loan institutions represented by more than 15,000 commercial loan and credit officers. Conducts research and professional development activities in areas of loan administration, asset management, and commercial lending and credit to increase professionalism. Named in honor of Robert Morris (1734-1806), a financier and politician. Provides Mentor training curriculum for commercial lending professionals. From more than 90,000 financial statements supplied by member institutions, annually compiles the Statement Studies containing average composite balance sheets for more than 360 different lines of business in manufacturing, wholesaling, retailing, and contracting. **Publications:** *Commercial Lending Newsletter*, monthly. • *Journal of Commercial Lending*, monthly. • *Member Roster*, annual. • *RMA Annual Statement Studies*, annual.

STANDARDS/CERTIFICATION AGENCIES

★1023★ National Association of Professional Mortgage Women (NAPMW)
PO Box 2016
Edmonds, WA 98020-0999
Ph: (206)778-6162   Fax: (206)771-9588
Sponsors educational and professional development programs for women in mortgage

banking professions. Aims to maintain high standards of professional conduct and to encourage women to pursue careers in mortgage banking. Works for equal recognition and professsional opportunities for women. Offers professional certification through its Institute of Mortgage Lending.

EDUCATIONAL DIRECTORIES AND PROGRAMS

★1024★ Loan Broker—Annual Directory
Ben Campbell, Publisher
917 S. Park St.
Owosso, MI 48867-4422
Ben Campbell
Covers: Approximately 800 loan brokers, private funding sources, and business financing services operation in the continental U.S. Entries include: Co. name, address, phone, names and titles of key personnel, number of employees, financial data, subsidiary and branch names and locations, requirements for membership, admission, or eligibility, product/service.

★1025★ Loans Directory
American Business Directories, Inc.
5711 S. 86th Circle
Omaha, NE 68127
Ph: (402)593-4600   Fax: (402)331-1505
Number of listings: 53,516 (U.S. edition); 2,205 (Canadian edition). Entries include: Name, address, phone (including area code), size of advertisement, year first in "Yellow Pages," name of owner or manager, number of employees. Regional editions available: North East (Connecticut, Maine, Massachusetts, New Hampshire, New Jersey, New York, Pennsylvania, Rhode Island, Vermont), $310.00; East North Central (Illinois, Indiana, Michigan, Ohio, Wisconsin), $360.00; West North Central (Iowa, Kansas, Minnesota, Missouri, Nebraska, North Dakota, South Dakota), $240.00; South Atlantic (Washington D.C., Delaware, Florida, Georgia, Maryland, North Carolina, South Carolina, Virginia, West Virginia), $460.00; South Central (Alabama, Arkansas, Kentucky, Louisiana, Mississippi, Oklahoma, Tennessee, Texas), $460.00; Mountain (Arizona, Colorado, Idaho, Montana, Nevada, New Mexico, Utah, Wyoming) $150.00; Pacific (Alaska, California, Hawaii, Oregon, Washington), $360.00. Compiled from telephone company "Yellow Pages," nationwide.

★1026★ New Mexico Financial Institutions Division—Annual Report
Financial Institutions Division
PO Box 25101
Santa Fe, NM 87504
Ph: (505)827-7100   Fax: (505)827-7107
Janis Rutschman, Contact
Covers: state and federally chartered financial institutions in New Mexico, including commercial banks, savings and loan associations, credit unions, mortgage loan companies, escrow companies, collection agencies, consumer credit bureaus, agencies licensed to isseeee money orders, and motor vehicle

sales finance companies. Entries include: For banks, savings and loans, and credit unions—Name, location, balance sheet data. For others—Name, address.

BASIC REFERENCE GUIDES AND HANDBOOKS

★1027★ Commercial Lending
American Bankers Association
1120 Connecticut Ave., NW
Washington, DC 20036
George E. Ruth. 3rd edition, 1995. Offers information for those interested in financial analysis, loan structuring, documentation, and credit investigation.

★1028★ Commercial Loan Practices and Operations
Bankers Publishing Co.
210 South St.
Boston, MA 02111
Ph: (617)426-4495
Vincent J. Signoriello. 1990.

★1029★ Job Descriptions for Financial Institutions: A Comprehensive Reference Guide
Bank Administration Institute
1 N. Franklin St.
Chicago, IL 60606-3401
Ph: 800-323-8552
W. Frank Kelly. 1987. Describes different jobs in the banking world.

★1030★ The Loan Officer's Handbook
Dow Jones-Irwin
PO Box 300
Princeton, NJ 08543-0300
Ph: (609)452-2820
William J. Korsvik and Charles O. Meiburg, editors. 1986. Describes different aspects of loaning money. Includes business conditions, the federal reserve systems, strategic planning, marketing loan services, and other valuable information.

PROFESSIONAL AND TRADE PERIODICALS

★1031★ CREDIT Magazine
American Financial Services Association
919 18th St., NW
Washington, DC 20006
Ph: (202)296-5544
Bimonthly.

★1032★ Journal of Commerical Lending
Robert Morris Associates-Association of Bank Loan and Credit Officers
1 Liberty Pl.
1650 Market St., Ste. 2300
Philadelphia, PA 19103
Ph: (215)851-9100
Monthly. Covers commercial lending and credit issues. Includes book reviews, technol-

ogy update, and legislative and regulatory issues.

★1033★ *Loan Officer's Legal Alert*
Executive Enterprises Publications
  Company, Inc.
22 W. 21st St., 10th Fl.
New York, NY 10010-6904
Ph: (212)645-7880   Fax: (212)675-4883
Fr: 800-332-8804
Isabelle Cohen

Monthly. Informs on the legal aspects of commercial lending. Covers secured transactions under Article 9 of the Uniform Credit Code (UCC) and other legal ramifications of commercial lending. Recurring features include a column titled Lender Liability.

★1034★ *Mortgage Bank Weekly*
SNL Securities
410 E. Main St.
PO Box 2124
Charlottesville, VA 22902
Ph: (804)977-1600   Fax: (804)977-4466
Tom Ward

Weekly. Reports by fax the latest industry news, earnings, trends, and up-to-date market information on mortgage banking. Recurring features include news of research.

★1035★ *Mortgage Securities Newsletter*
Public Securities Association
40 Broad St.
New York, NY 10004
Ph: (212)809-7000   Fax: (212)742-1549
William Levy

Monthly. Reports current developments regarding mortgage securities, including regulation, legislation, and market practices and operations. Recurring features include a calendar of events and reports of meetings.

★1036★ *National Mortgage News*
212 W. 35th St., 13th Fl.
New York, NY 10001
Ph: (212)563-4008

Contains articles on developments in mortgage securities.

OTHER SOURCES OF INFORMATION

★1037★ **"Bank Loan Counselor" in**
Career Selector 2001
Barron's Educational Series, Inc.
250 Wireless Blvd.
Hauppauge, NY 11788
Ph: (516)434-3311   Fax: (516)434-3723
Fr: 800-645-3476
James C. Gonyea. 1993.

★1038★ **"Bank Loan Officer" in** *100*
Best Jobs for the 1990s & Beyond
Dearborn Financial Publishing, Inc.
520 N. Dearborn St.
Chicago, IL 60610-4354
Ph: (312)836-4400   Fax: (312)836-1021
Fr: 800-621-9621

Carol Kleiman. 1992. Describes 100 jobs ranging from accountants to veterinarians. Each job profile includes such information as education, experience, and certification needed, salaries, and job search suggestions.

★1039★ *Credit Executive*
New York Credit and Financial
  Management Association
520 8th Ave., Ste. 2201
New York, NY 10018
Ph: (212)268-8711

Magazine on business and commerical credit and finance.

Management Analysts and Consultants

The work of **management analysts and consultants** varies from employer to employer and from project to project. In general, analysts and consultants collect, review, and analyze information; make recommendations; and assist in the implementation of their proposals. Firms providing consulting services range in size from solo practitioners to large international organizations employing thousands of consultants. These services usually are provided on a contract basis–a company chooses a consulting firm specializing in the area in which it needs assistance and then the two firms determine the conditions of the contract. Management analysts in government agencies use the same skills as their private-sector colleagues to advise managers in government on many types of issues–most of which are similar to the problems faced by private firms.

Salaries

Salaries for management analysts and consultants vary widely by experience, education, and employer.

Median earnings of wage-and-salary analysts
and consultants $40,300/year

Employment Outlook

Growth rate until the year 2005: Much faster than the average.

Management Analysts and Consultants

★1040★ *Management Analysts and Consultants*
Chronicle Guidance Publications, Inc.
66 Aurora St.
PO Box 1190
Moravia, NY 13118-1190
Ph: (315)497-0330   Fax: (315)497-3359
Fr: 800-622-7284
1992. Career brief describing the nature of the job, working conditions, hours and earnings, education and training, licensure, certification, unions, personal qualifications, social and psychological factors, location, employment outlook, entry methods, advancement, and related occupations.

★1041★ "Management Analysts and Consultants" in *America's 50 Fastest Growing Jobs* (pp. 20)
JIST Works, Inc.
720 N. Park Ave.
Indianapolis, IN 46202-3431
Ph: (317)264-3720   Fax: (317)264-3709
Fr: 800-648-5478
Michael J. Farr, compiler. 1994. Describes the 50 fastest growing jobs within major career clusters such as technicians, and marketing and sales. Each job profile explains the nature of the work, skills and abilities required, employment outlook, average earnings, related occupations, education and training requirements, and employment opportunities. Also contains career planning information and job search tips.

★1042★ "Management Analysts and Consultants" in *Career Discovery Encyclopedia* (Vol.4, pp. 42-43)
J.G. Ferguson Publishing Co.
200 W. Madison St., Ste. 300
Chicago, IL 60606
Ph: (312)580-5480   Fax: (312)580-4948
Russell E. Primm, editor-in chief. 1993. This six volume set contains two-page articles for 504 occupations. Each article describes job duties, earnings, and educational and training requirements. The whole set is arranged al-phabetically by job title. Designed for junior high and older students.

★1043★ "Management Analysts and Consultants" in *Encyclopedia of Careers and Vocational Guidance* (Vol.3, pp. 357-360)
J.G. Ferguson Publishing Co.
200 W. Madison St., Ste. 300
Chicago, IL 60606
Ph: (312)580-5480   Fax: (312)580-4948
William E. Hopke, editor-in-chief. Ninth edition, 1993. Four-volume set that profiles 900 occupations and describes job trends in 74 industries. Includes career description, educational requirements, history of the job, methods of entry, advancement, employment outlook, earnings, conditions of work, social and psychological factors, and sources of further information.

★1044★ "Management Analysts and Consultants" in *Occupational Outlook Handbook*
U.S. Government Printing Office
Superintendent of Documents
Washington, DC 20402
Ph: (202)512-1800   Fax: (202)512-2250
Biennial; latest edition, 1994-95. Encyclopedia of careers describing about 250 occupations and comprising about 85 percent of all jobs in the economy. Occupations that require lengthy education or training are given the most attention. Each occupation's profile describes what the worker does on the job, working conditions, education and training requirements, advancement possibilities, job outlook, earnings, and sources of additional information.

★1045★ "Management Analysts" in *Guide to Federal Jobs* (p. 97)
Resource Directories
3361 Executive Pkwy., Ste. 302
Toledo, OH 43606
Ph: (419)536-5353   Fax: (419)536-7056
Fr: 800-274-8515
Rod W. Durgin, editor. Third edition, 1992. Contains information on finding and applying for federal jobs. Describes more than 200 professional and technical jobs for college graduates. Covers the nature of the work, salary, and geographic location. Lists college majors preferred for that occupation. Section one describes the function and work of government agencies that hire the most significant number of college graduates.

★1046★ "Management Consultant" in *College Board Guide to Jobs and Career Planning* (pp. 96)
The College Board
415 Columbus Ave.
New York, NY 10023-6992
Ph: (212)713-8165   Fax: (212)713-8143
Fr: 800-323-7155
Joyce S. Mitchell. Second edition, 1994. Describes the job, salaries, related careers, education needed, and where to write for more information.

★1047★ "Management Consultant" in *VGM's Careers Encyclopedia* (pp. 256-257)
National Textbook Co. (NTC)
VGM Career Books
4255 W. Touhy Ave.
Lincolnwood, IL 60646-1975
Ph: (708)679-5500   Fax: (708)679-2494
Fr: 800-323-4900
Third edition, 1991. Describes job duties, places of employment, working conditions, qualifications, education, and training, advancement potential, and salary for each occupation.

★1048★ "Management Consultant" in *VGM's Handbook of Business and Management Careers*
National Textbook Co.
4255 W. Touhy Ave.
Lincolnwood, IL 60646-1975
Ph: (708)679-5500   Fax: (708)679-2494
Fr: 800-323-4900
Annette Selden. Second edition, 1993. Contains 42 two-page occupational profiles describing job duties, places of employment, working conditions, qualifications, education, employment outlook, and income.

★1049★ "Management Consultants" in
101 Careers: A Guide to the Fastest-
Growing Opportunities (pp. 26-28)
John Wiley & Sons, Inc.
605 3rd Ave.
New York, NY 10158-0012
Ph: (212)850-6645   Fax: (212)850-6088
Michael Harkavy. 1990. Describes the nature of the job, working conditions, employment growth, qualifications, personal skills, projected salaries, and where to write for more information.

★1050★ "Management Consultants" in
American Almanac of Jobs and
Salaries (p. 344)
Avon Books
1350 Avenue of the Americas
New York, NY 10019
Ph: (212)261-6800   Fr: 800-238-0658
John Wright, editor. Revised and updated, 1994-95. This is a comprehensive guide to the wages of hundreds of occupations in a wide variety of industries and organizations.

★1051★ "Management Consultants" in
Jobs! What They Are—Where They
Are—What They Pay (p. 239)
Simon & Schuster, Inc.
Simon & Schuster Bldg.
1230 Avenue of the Americas
New York, NY 10020
Ph: (212)698-7000   Fr: 800-223-2348
Robert O. Snelling and Anne M. Snelling. 3rd edition, 1992. Describes duties and responsibilities, earnings, employment opportunities, training, and qualifications.

★1052★ Management Consulting 1991-
1992
Harvard Business School Press
Harvard Business School
Gallatin E-115
Boston, MA 02163
Ph: (617)495-6700
Kathleen Johnson, editor. Third edition, 1990. This book profiles management consulting firms that hire MBA graduates. Describes companies, giving the name, address, contact person, and office locations. Explains what the company does and the recruiting process.

★1053★ "Management Consulting" in
Career Choices for the 90s for
Students of MBA (pp. 122-138)
Walker and Co.
435 Hudson St.
New York, NY 10014
Ph: (212)727-8300   Fax: (212)727-0984
Fr: 800-289-2553
Compiled by Career Associates Staff. 1990. This book offers alternatives for students interested in business. Gives information about the outlook and competition for entry-level candidates. Provides job hunting tips.

★1054★ "Management Consulting" in
Encyclopedia of Career Choices for the
1990s: A Guide to Entry Level Jobs
(pp. 521-537)
Berkley Pub.
PO Box 506
East Rutherford, NJ 07073
Fax: (201)933-2316   Fr: 800-788-6262
1992. Describes entry-level careers in a variety of industries. Presents qualifications required, working conditions, salary, internships, and professional associations.

★1055★ MBA's Guide to Self-
Assessment and Career Development
Prentice-Hall, Inc.
200 Old Tappan Rd.
Old Tappan, NJ 07675
Ph: (201)767-5000   Fr: 800-922-0579
James G. Clawson. Third edition, 1991. Contains self-assessment exercises to help the entry-level job seeker avoid the wrong career choice. Provides information on consulting as a career. Occupational profiles describe a typical work day, skills and credentials needed, career paths, and typical employers.

★1056★ Professional Profile of
Management Consultants: A Body of
Expertise, Skills, and Attributes
Association of Management Consulting
    Firms (ACME)
521 5th Ave., 35th Fl.
New York, NY 10175-3599
Ph: (212)697-9693
1992. Brochure that defines management consulting and describes the attributes of a successful management consultant.

★1057★ Your Career in Management
Consulting
Institute of Mangement Consultants (IMC)
230 Park Ave., Ste. 544
New York, NY 10169
Ph: (212)697-8262
1990. This four-page fact sheet describes why consultants are used, educational requirements, skills and attributes, and certification.

PROFESSIONAL ASSOCIATIONS

★1058★ ACME - The Association of
Management Consulting Firms
521 5th Ave.
New York, NY 10175
Ph: (212)697-9693   Fax: (212)949-6571
Division of Council of Consulting Organizations. Management consulting organizations that provide a broad range of managerial services to commercial, industrial, governmental, and other organizations and individuals. Seeks to unite management consulting firms in order to develop and improve professional standards and practice in the field. Offers information and referral services on management consultants; administers public relations program. Conducts research. **Publications:** ACME—Directory of Members, annual. • ACME Newsletter, quarterly. • ACME Survey of Key Management Information, annual. • Career Kit. • How to Select and

Use Management Consultants. • Management Consulting: Annotated Bibliography of Selected Resource Materials, semi-annual. • Professional Profile of Management Consultants: A Body of Expertise, Skills, and Attributes.

★1059★ National Society of
Environmental Consultants (NSEC)
PO Box 12528
San Antonio, TX 78212-0528
Fax: (210)225-8450   Fr: 800-486-3676
Members: Environmental consulting professionals and others interested in the environmentally responsible use of real estate. **Purpose:** Encourages an awareness of environmental risks and regulations regarding their impact on real property value; promotes the development of ethics and standards of professional practice for environmental consultants. Conducts educational programs. Bestows the Environmental Assessment Consultant (EAC) designation. **Publications:** Environmental Consultant, quarterly. • Membership Directory, annual.

TEST GUIDES

★1060★ Career Examination Series:
Administrative Consultant
National Learning Corp.
212 Michael Dr.
Syosset, NY 11791
Ph: (516)921-8888   Fax: (516)921-8743
Fr: 800-645-6337
Jack Rudman. 1993. Test guide including questions and answers for students or professionals in the field who seek advancement through examination.

★1061★ Career Examination Series:
Administrative Education Analyst
National Learning Corp.
212 Michael Dr.
Syosset, NY 11791
Ph: (516)921-8888   Fax: (516)921-8743
Fr: 800-645-6337
Jack Rudman. 1993. Test guide including questions and answers for students or professionals in the field who seek advancement through examination.

★1062★ Career Examination Series:
Associate Transit Management Analyst
National Learning Corp.
212 Michael Dr.
Syosset, NY 11791
Ph: (516)921-8888   Fax: (516)921-8743
Fr: 800-645-6337
Jack Rudman. 1993. Test guide including questions and answers for students or professionals in the field who seek advancement through examination.

★1063★ Career Examination Series: Consultant
National Learning Corp.
212 Michael Dr.
Syosset, NY 11791
Ph: (516)921-8888   Fax: (516)921-8743
Fr: 800-645-6337

Jack Rudman. 1993. Test guide including questions and answers for students or professionals in the field who seek advancement through examination.

★1064★ Career Examination Series: Hospital Administration Consultant
National Learning Corp.
212 Michael Dr.
Syosset, NY 11791
Ph: (516)921-8888   Fax: (516)921-8743
Fr: 800-645-6337

Jack Rudman. 1993. Test guide including questions and answers for students or professionals in the field who seek advancement through examination.

★1065★ Career Examination Series: Management Analyst
National Learning Corp.
212 Michael Dr.
Syosset, NY 11791
Ph: (516)921-8888   Fax: (516)921-8743
Fr: 800-645-6337

Jack Rudman. A series of study guides with multiple-choice examination questions and solutions for trainees and professionals in the field of management analysis and consulting. Titles in the series include *Assistant Management Analyst; Associate Management Analyst; Chief Management Analyst; Management Analysis Trainee; Principal Management Analyst; Senior Management Analyst.*

★1066★ Career Examination Series: Senior Personnel Analyst
National Learning Corp.
212 Michael Dr.
Syosset, NY 11791
Ph: (516)921-8888   Fax: (516)921-8743
Fr: 800-645-6337

Jack Rudman. 1993. Test guide including questions and answers for students or professionals in the field who seek advancement through examination.

★1067★ Career Examination Series: Social Services Management Specialist
National Learning Corp.
212 Michael Dr.
Syosset, NY 11791
Ph: (516)921-8888   Fax: (516)921-8743
Fr: 800-645-6337

Jack Rudman. 1993. Test guide including questions and answers for students or professionals in the field who seek advancement through examination.

EDUCATIONAL DIRECTORIES AND PROGRAMS

★1068★ Acme—Directory of Members, 1994-95
Association of Management Consulting Firms (ACME)
521 5th Ave., 35th Fl.
New York, NY 10175
Ph: (212)697-9693

1994. Lists 35 companies with name, address, contact person, and a description of services to aid users in identifying appropriate firms for specific assignments.

★1069★ Business and Finance Career Directory
Gale Research Inc.
835 Penobscot Bldg.
Detroit, MI 48226-4094
Ph: (313)961-2242   Fax: (313)961-6083
Fr: 800-877-GALE

Bradley J. Morgan and Joseph M. Palmisano. Second edition, 1992. A directory in the Career Advisor Series that provides essays written by industry professionals; job search information on resume and cover letter preparation, networking, and the interviewing process; approximately 300 companies and organizations offering job opportunities and internships, and additional job-hunting resources.

★1070★ Institute of Management Sciences/Operations Research Society of America—Combined Membership Directory
Institute of Management Sciences
290 Westminster St.
Providence, RI 02903
Ph: (401)274-2525   Fax: (401)274-3189
Diane Folanaris, Contact

Biennial, odd years. Covers over 14,000 managers, educators, and practicing management scientists; international coverage. Entries include: Name, address, phone, electronic mail address, affiliations within organization. Arrangement: Alphabetical.

AWARDS, SCHOLARSHIPS, GRANTS, AND FELLOWSHIPS

★1071★ Taylor Key Award
Society for Advancement of Management
PO Box 889
Vinton, VA 24179
Ph: (703)342-5563   Fax: (703)342-6413

This, one of the highest awards of the Society, is given for recognition of outstanding contributions to the art and science of management as conceived by Frederick W. Taylor. Individuals of any nationality are eligible. A gold key is awarded annually. Established in 1937.

BASIC REFERENCE GUIDES AND HANDBOOKS

★1072★ Profitable Consulting: Guiding America's Managers Into the Next Century
Addison-Wesley Publishing Co., Inc.
1 Jacob Way
Reading, MA 01867
Ph: (617)944-3700   Fr: 800-447-2226
Robert O. Metzger. 1988.

PROFESSIONAL AND TRADE PERIODICALS

★1073★ Consultants News
Kennedy Publications
Templeton Rd.
Fitzwilliam, NH 03447
Ph: (603)585-3101   Fax: (603)585-6401
Fr: 800-531-0007
David A. Lord

Monthly. Offers independent coverage of management consulting, including news, commentary, and advice on how to manage a consulting practice.

★1074★ Consultant's Newsletter
Society of Medical-Dental Management Consultants
6215 Larson
Kansas City, MO 64133
Ph: (816)353-8488   Fr: 800-826-2264
William H. Kidd

Monthly. Discusses news of the Society, including notices and reports of meetings, group activities, and information regarding members. Also covers management consulting for the health professional in such areas as taxes, medical design, retirement, medical economics, estate planning, and trends in medical and dental practices.

★1075★ Executive Excellence
Executive Excellence
One E. Center, Ste. 303
Provo, UT 84606
Ph: (801)375-4014
Kenneth M. Shelton

Monthly. Provides articles by CEOs, educators, consultants, and trainers for individuals interested in developing management leadership and skills and find excellence in the workplace.

★1076★ The Professional Consultant
National Training Center
123 NW 2nd Ave., No. 403
Portland, OR 97209
Ph: (503)224-8834   Fax: (503)224-2104
Paul L. Franklin

Monthly. Addresses marketing and management of consulting services, seminars, training, and information products. Recurring features include letters to the editor, interviews, news of research, a calendar of events, reports of meetings, news of educational opportunities, book reviews, and an annual report on research regarding fees, incomes, and operating ratios of consultants and advisors.

★1077★ *The Spokesman*
Association of Productivity Specialists
Pan Am Bldg.
200 Park Ave., Ste. 303E
New York, NY 10017
Ph: (212)286-0943
Robert A. Jacobson

Quarterly. Covers information and published materials relevant to the productivity specialist segment of the management consultant profession.

OTHER SOURCES OF INFORMATION

★1078★ "Consulting" in *Wanted: Liberal Arts Graduates* (pp. 37-39)
Doubleday and Co., Inc.
724 5th Ave.
New York, NY 10109
Ph: (212)397-0550   Fr: 800-223-5780
Marian L. Salzman. 1987. This book recommends that liberal arts graduates analyze their skills and research the job market. Describes companies that hire liberal arts graduates. Gives tips on how to get in and move up.

★1079★ *How to Make it Big as a Consultant*
AMACOM
135 W. 50th St.
New York, NY 10020-1201
Ph: (212)903-8089   Fr: 800-262-9696
William A. Cohen. 2nd edition, 1990.

★1080★ "Management Consultant" in *100 Best Jobs for the 1990s & Beyond*
Dearborn Financial Publishing, Inc.
520 N. Dearborn St.
Chicago, IL 60610-4354
Ph: (312)836-4400   Fax: (312)836-1021
Fr: 800-621-9621
Carol Kleiman. 1992. Describes 100 jobs ranging from accountants to veterinarians. Each job profile includes such information as education, experience, and certification needed, salaries, and job search suggestions.

★1081★ *Marketing Your Consulting and Professional Services*
John Wiley and Sons, Inc.
605 3rd Ave.
New York, NY 10158-0012
Ph: (212)850-6000   Fax: (212)850-6088
Fr: 800-526-5368
Richard A. Connor and Jeffrey P. Davidson. 1990. Step-by-step guide to entering the consulting field including developing a marketing plan.

Marketing, Advertising, and Public Relations Managers

The fundamental objective of any firm is to market its products or services profitably. **Marketing managers** develop the firm's detailed marketing strategy. **Sales managers** direct the firm's sales program. **Advertising managers** oversee the account services, creative services, and media services departments. The account services department is managed by **account executives**, who assess the need for advertising and, in advertising agencies, maintain the accounts of clients. The creative services department, which develops the subject matter and presentation of advertising, is supervised by a **creative director**, who oversees the copy chief and art director and their staffs. The media services department is supervised by the **media director** who oversees planning groups which select the communication media–for example, radio, television, newspapers, magazines, or outdoor signs–to disseminate the advertising. **Sales promotion managers** supervise staffs of sales promotion specialists, and direct sales promotion programs that combine advertising with financial incentives to increase sales of products and services. **Public relations managers** supervise staffs of public relations specialists; direct publicity programs designed to promote the image of the firm to various groups such as consumers, stockholders, or the general public, using any necessary communication media; and may assist company executives in drafting speeches, scheduling interviews, and other forms of public contact.

Salaries

Salaries vary substantially depending on the level of managerial responsibility, length of service, and size and location of the firm; size of sales territory is also a factor for sales managers.

Lowest 10 percent	Less than $22,000/year
Median	$41,000/year
Top 10 percent	More than $79,000/year

Employment Outlook

Growth rate until the year 2005: Faster than the average.

Marketing, Advertising, and Public Relations Managers

CAREER GUIDES

★1082★ "Advertising Account Executive" in Career Opportunities in the Music Industry (pp. 33-34)
Facts on File
460 Park Ave. S.
New York, NY 10016-7382
Ph: (212)683-2244   Fax: 800-678-3633
Fr: 800-322-8755
Shelly Field. 1990. Discusses approximately 80 jobs in music including the performing arts, business, and education. Each job description provides basic career information, salary, employment prospects, advancement opportunities, education, training, and experience required.

★1083★ "Advertising Account Executive" in VGM's Careers Encyclopedia (pp. 11-13)
National Textbook Co. (NTC)
VGM Career Books
4255 W. Touhy Ave.
Lincolnwood, IL 60646-1975
Ph: (708)679-5500   Fax: (708)679-2494
Fr: 800-323-4900
Third edition, 1991. Describes job duties, places of employment, working conditions, qualifications, education, and training, advancement potential, and salary for each occupation.

★1084★ "Advertising Account Executives" in Jobs! What They Are— Where They Are—What They Pay! (pp. 34)
Simon & Schuster, Inc.
Simon & Schuster Bldg.
1230 Avenue of the Americas
New York, NY 10020
Ph: (212)698-7000   Fr: 800-223-2348
Robert O. Snelling and Anne M. Snelling. Third revised edition, 1992. Includes chapters titled "Market Research Analysts" (p. 39), "Product Managers" (p. 260), "Sales Administrators" (p. 334), and "Sales Managers" (p. 335). Describes duties and responsibili-

ties, earnings, employment opportunities, training, and qualifications.

★1085★ "The Advertising Agency" in American Almanac of Jobs and Salaries (pp. 389-399)
Avon Books
1350 Avenue of the Americas
New York, NY 10019
Ph: (212)261-6800   Fr: 800-238-0658
John Wright, editor. Revised and updated, 1994-95. A comprehensive guide to the wages of hundreds of occupations in a wide variety of industries and organizations.

★1086★ Advertising Agency Workers
Chronicle Guidance Publications, Inc.
66 Aurora St.
PO Box 1190
Moravia, NY 13118-1190
Ph: (315)497-0330   Fax: (315)497-3359
Fr: 800-622-7284
1991. Career brief describing the nature of the job, working conditions, hours and earnings, education and training, licensure, certification, unions, personal qualifications, social and psychological factors, location, employment outlook, entry methods, advancement, and related occupations.

★1087★ "Advertising" in Black Woman's Career Guide (pp. 208-214)
Bantam Doubleday Dell
1540 Broadway
New York, NY 10036
Fax: 800-233-3294   Fr: 800-223-5780
Beatryce Nivens. Revised edition, 1987. Part 1 describes career planning, resume writing, job hunting, and interviewing. Part 2 profiles 60 black women pioneers in 20 different career areas.

★1088★ "Advertising" in Careers in Communications (pp. 101-114)
National Textbook Co. (NTC)
VGM Career Books
4255 W. Touhy Ave.
Lincolnwood, IL 60646-1975
Ph: (708)679-5500   Fax: (708)679-2494
Fr: 800-323-4900
Shonan Noronha. 1987. This book examines the fields of journalism, photography, radio,

television, film, public relations, and advertising. Gives concrete advice on where the jobs are and how to get them. Suggests many resources for job hunting.

★1089★ "Advertising" in College Board Guide to Jobs and Career Planning (pp. 110)
The College Board
415 Columbus Ave.
New York, NY 10023-6992
Ph: (212)713-8165   Fax: (212)713-8143
Fr: 800-323-7155
Joyce S. Mitchell. Second edition, 1994. Describes the job, salaries, related careers, education needed, and where to write for more information.

★1090★ "Advertising" in Desk Guide to Training and Work Advertisement (pp. 137-139)
Charles C. Thomas, Publisher
2600 S. 1st St.
Springfield, IL 62794-9265
Ph: (217)789-8980   Fax: (217)789-9130
Fr: 800-258-8980
Gail Baugher Keunstler. 1988. Describes alternative methods of gaining entry into an occupation through different types of educational programs, internships, and apprenticeships.

★1091★ "Advertising Directors" in Career Discovery Encyclopedia (Vol.1, pp. 22-23)
J.G. Ferguson Publishing Co.
200 W. Madison St., Ste. 300
Chicago, IL 60606
Ph: (312)580-5480   Fax: (312)580-4948
Russell E. Primm, editor-in-chief. 1993. This six volume set contains two-page articles for 504 occupations. Each article describes job duties, earnings, and educational and training requirements. The whole set is arranged alphabetically by job title. Designed for junior high and older students.

★1092★ "Advertising" in *Encyclopedia of Careers and Vocational Guidance*
J.G. Ferguson Publishing Co.
200 W. Madison St., Ste. 300
Chicago, IL 60606
Ph: (312)580-5480   Fax: (312)580-4948
William E. Hopke, editor-in chief. Ninth edition, 1993. Four-volume set that profiles 900 occupations and describes job trends in 74 industries. Volume 1—*Industry Profiles*—includes a chapter titled "Advertising" (p. 7). Includes career description, educational requirements, history of the job, methods of entry, advancement, employment outlook, earnings, conditions of work, social and psychological factors, and sources of further information.

★1093★ "Advertising" in *Fast Track Careers: A Guide to the Highest Paying Jobs* (pp. 41-64)
John Wiley and Sons, Inc.
605 3rd Ave.
New York, NY 10158-0012
Ph: (212)850-6000   Fax: (212)850-6088
Fr: 800-526-5368
William Lewis and Nancy Schuman. 1987. Describes eight fast-track careers, the industry, entry-level opportunities, leading companies, expected earnings; includes a glossary of the industry jargon.

★1094★ "Advertising Manager" in *VGM's Careers Encyclopedia* (pp. 13-15)
National Textbook Co. (NTC)
VGM Career Books
4255 W. Touhy Ave.
Lincolnwood, IL 60646-1975
Ph: (708)679-5500   Fax: (708)679-2494
Fr: 800-323-4900
Third edition, 1991. Describes job duties, places of employment, working conditions, qualifications, education, and training, advancement potential, and salary for each occupation.

★1095★ "Advertising Manager" in *VGM's Handbook of Business and Management Careers*
National Textbook Co.
4255 W. Touhy Ave.
Lincolnwood, IL 60646-1975
Ph: (708)679-5500   Fax: (708)679-2494
Fr: 800-323-4900
Annette Selden. Second edition, 1993. Contains 42 two-page occupational profiles describing job duties, places of employment, working conditions, qualifications, education, employment outlook, and income.

★1096★ "Advertising Managers and Account Executives" in *101 Careers: A Guide to the Fastest-Growing Opportunities* (pp. 36-38)
John Wiley & Sons, Inc.
605 3rd Ave.
New York, NY 10158-0012
Ph: (212)850-6645   Fax: (212)850-6088
Michael Harkavy. 1990. Describes the nature of the job, working conditions, employment growth, qualifications, personal skills, projected salaries, and where to write for more information.

★1097★ "Advertising" in *Opportunities in Airline Careers* (pp. 26-28)
National Textbook Co. (NTC)
VGM Career Books
4255 W. Touhy Ave.
Lincolnwood, IL 60646-1975
Ph: (708)679-5500   Fax: (708)679-2494
Fr: 800-323-4900
Adrian A. Paradis. 1987. Gives an overview of the airline industry including job opportunities and salaries. Describes careers in management, finance, sales, customer service and safety.

★1098★ "Advertising Sales" in *Opportunities in Magazine Publishing Careers* (pp. 91-100)
National Textbook Co. (NTC)
VGM Career Books
4255 W. Touhy Ave.
Lincolnwood, IL 60646-1975
Ph: (708)679-5500   Fax: (708)679-2494
Fr: 800-323-4900
S. William Pattis. 1992. Describes history, organizations, and types of magazine publishing (such as consumer, business, technical, and trade magazines). Covers career opportunities in different departments in a publishing company, future trends, and job hunting techniques.

★1099★ *Advertising Workers*
Careers, Inc.
PO Box 135
Largo, FL 34649-0135
Ph: (813)584-7333
1994. Four-page brief offering the definition, history, duties, working conditions, personal qualifications, educational requirements, earnings, hours, employment outlook, advancement, and careers related to this position.

★1100★ *Career Choices for the 90's for Students of Communications and Journalism*
Walker and Co.
435 Hudson St.
New York, NY 10014
Ph: (212)727-8300   Fax: (212)727-0984
Fr: 800-289-2553
1990. Offers alternatives for students of communications and journalism. Gives information about the job outlook and competition for entry-level candidates. Provides job-hunting tips.

★1101★ *Career Choices for the 90's for Students of English*
Walker and Co.
435 Hudson St.
New York, NY 10014
Ph: (212)727-8300   Fax: (212)727-0984
Fr: 800-289-2553
Compiled by Career Associates Staff. Revised edition, 1990. The goal of this book is to offer career alternatives for students of English. It includes information on advertising careers. Gives the outlook and competition for entry-level candidates. Provides job hunting tips.

★1102★ *Career Choices for the 90's for Students of Psychology*
Walker and Co.
435 Hudson St.
New York, NY 10014
Ph: (212)727-8300   Fax: (212)727-0984
Fr: 800-289-2553
Compiled by Career Associates Staff. 1990. This book offers alternatives for students of psychology, including careers within the advertising field. Gives information about the outlook and competition for entry-level candidates. Provides job hunting tips.

★1103★ *Career Information Center*
Simon and Schuster
200 Old Tappan Rd.
Old Tappan, NJ 07675
Fax: 800-445-6991   Fr: 800-223-2348
Richard Lidz and Linda Perrin, editorial directors. Fifth edition, 1993. This multi-volume set profiles hundreds of occupations, including those of advertising account executive, sales manager, and marketing director. Each occupational profile describes job duties, educational requirements, how to get the job, advancement possibilities, employment outlook, working conditions, earnings and benefits, and where to write for more information.

★1104★ *Career Opportunities in Advertising and Public Relations*
Facts on File
460 Park Ave. S.
New York, NY 10016-7382
Ph: (212)683-2244   Fax: 800-678-3633
Fr: 800-322-8755
Shelly Field. 1993. Guidebook offering complete career information for those entering advertising or public relations. Describes 85 jobs and includes salary information, employment prospects, and education and skills needed for the jobs.

★1105★ *Career Opportunities in the Sports Industry*
Facts on File
460 Park Ave. S.
New York, NY 10016-7382
Ph: (212)683-2244   Fax: 800-678-3633
Fr: 800-322-8755
Shelly Field. 1993. Sourcebook combining a variety of information including sports-related academic programs, league lists, professional associations, and more of interest to those considering employment in organized amateur or professional sports.

★1106★ *Career Opportunities in Television, Cable and Video*
Facts on File
460 Park Ave. S.
New York, NY 10016-7382
Ph: (212)683-2244   Fax: 800-678-3633
Fr: 800-322-8755
Maxine K. Reed and Robert M. Reed. Third edition, 1993. Includes information on employment and advancement prospects, education, experience and skills requiresn salary range, and tips for entry into the field.

★1107★ Careers in Advertising
National Textbook Co. (NTC)
VGM Career Books
4255 W. Touhy Ave.
Lincolnwood, IL 60646-1975
Ph: (708)679-5500   Fax: (708)679-2494
Fr: 800-323-4900
S. William Pattis. 1990. Describes employment in creative and media services, research, account management, production and traffic, agency management, and sales.

★1108★ Careers in Marketing
National Textbook Co. (NTC)
VGM Career Books
4255 W. Touhy Ave.
Lincolnwood, IL 60646-1975
Ph: (708)679-5500   Fax: (708)679-2494
Fr: 800-323-4900
Lila B. Stair, editor. 1991. Examines careers in the field of marketing. Careers include: Marketing Research, Product Development, Direct Marketing, and International Marketing.

★1109★ "Director of Public Relations"
in Career Opportunities in the Music
Industry (pp. 165-166)
Facts on File
460 Park Ave. S.
New York, NY 10016-7382
Ph: (212)683-2244   Fax: 800-678-3633
Fr: 800-322-8755
Shelly Field. 1990. Discusses approximately 80 jobs in music including the performing arts, business, and education. Each job description provides basic career information, salary, employment prospects, advancement opportunities, education, training, and experience required.

★1110★ "International Marketing" in
Opportunities in International Business
Careers (pp. 77-85)
National Textbook Co. (NTC)
VGM Career Books
4255 W. Touhy Ave.
Lincolnwood, IL 60646-1975
Ph: (708)679-5500   Fax: (708)679-2494
Fr: 800-323-4900
Jeffry S. Arpan. 1989. Describes what types of jobs exist in international business, where they are located, what challenges and rewards they bring, and how to prepare for and obtain jobs in international business.

★1111★ Making It in Public Relations:
An Insider's Guide to Career
Opportunities
Macmillan Publishing Co.
866 3rd Ave.
New York, NY 10022
Ph: (212)702-2000
Leonard Mogel. 1993.

★1112★ "Marketing" in Advertising: A
VGM Career Planner (pp. 58-61)
National Textbook Co. (NTC)
VGM Career Books
4255 W. Touhy Ave.
Lincolnwood, IL 60646-1975
Ph: (708)679-5500   Fax: (708)679-2494
Fr: 800-323-4900
William S. Pattis. 1989. Describes the development of advertising. Explains the role of the media in advertising, personal characteristics

needed to succeed in this field, educational requirements, and related jobs. Gives job hunting tips.

★1113★ "Marketing, Advertising, and
Public Relations Managers" in
America's 50 Fastest Growing Jobs
(pp. 23)
JIST Works, Inc.
720 N. Park Ave.
Indianapolis, IN 46202-3431
Ph: (317)264-3720   Fax: (317)264-3709
Fr: 800-648-5478
Michael J. Farr, compiler. 1994. Describes the 50 fastest growing jobs within major career clusters such as technicians, and marketing and sales. Each job profile explains the nature of the work, skills and abilities required, employment outlook, average earnings, related occupations, education and training requirements, and employment opportunities. Also contains career planning information and job search tips.

★1114★ "Marketing, Advertising, and
Public Relations Managers" in Career
Opportunities for Writers
Facts on File
460 Park Ave. S.
New York, NY 10016-7382
Ph: (212)683-2244   Fax: 800-678-3633
Fr: 800-322-8755
Rosemary Guiley. 1992. Offers details on careers such as duties, salaries, prerequisites, employment and advancement oportunities, organizations to join, and opportunities for women and minorities.

★1115★ "Marketing, Advertising, and
Public Relations Managers" in
Occupational Outlook Handbook
U.S. Government Printing Office
Superintendent of Documents
Washington, DC 20402
Ph: (202)512-1800   Fax: (202)512-2250
Biennial; latest edition, 1994-95. Encyclopedia of careers describing some 250 occupations and comprising about 85 percent of all jobs in the economy. Occupations that require lengthy education or training are given the most attention. Each occupation's profile describes what the worker does on the job, working conditions, education and training requirements, advancement possibilities, job outlook, earnings, and sources of additional information.

★1116★ "Marketing and Advertising" in
Where the Jobs Are: The Hottest
Careers for the 90s (pp. 195-210)
Career Press
180 5th Ave.
Hawthorne, NJ 07507
Ph: (201)427-0229   Fax: (201)427-2037
Fr: 800-CAREER-1
Joyce Hadley. 1995. Offers a job-hunting strategy for the 1990s as well as descriptions of growing careers of the decade. Each profile includes general information, forecasts, growth, education and training, licensing requirements, and salary information.

★1117★ "Marketing Analyst" in College
Board Guide to Jobs and Career
Planning (pp. 113-114)
The College Board
45 Columbus Ave.
New York, NY 10023-6992
Ph: (212)713-8165   Fax: (212)713-8143
Fr: 800-323-7155
Second edition, 1994. Describes the job, salaries, related careers, education needed, and where to write for more information.

★1118★ "Marketing and Distribution" in
College Majors and Careers: A
Resource Guide to Effective Life
Planning (pp. 87-88)
Garrett Park Press
PO Box 1907
Garrett Park, MD 20896
Ph: (301)946-2553
Paul Phifer. 1993. Lists 60 college majors, with definitions; related occupations and leisure activities; skills, values, and personal needed attributes; suggested readings; and a list of associations.

★1119★ "Marketing" in Encyclopedia of
Careers and Vocational Guidance
(Vol.1, pp. 279)
J.G. Ferguson Publishing Co.
200 W. Madison St., Ste. 300
Chicago, IL 60606
Ph: (312)580-5480   Fax: (312)580-4948
William E. Hopke, editor-in-chief. Ninth edition, 1993. Four-volume set that profiles 900 occupations and describes job trends in 74 industries. Includes career description, educational requirements, history of the job, methods of entry, advancement, employment outlook, earnings, conditions of work, social and psychological factors, and sources of further information.

★1120★ "Marketing Manager" in 100
Best Careers for the Year 2000 (pp.
162-165)
Arco Pub.
201 W. 103rd St.
Indianapolis, IN 46290
Ph: 800-428-5331   Fax: 800-835-3202
Shelly Field. 1992. Describes 100 job opportunities expected to grow fast throughout the next decade. Provides information on job duties and responsibilities, training requirements, education, advancement opportunities, experience and qualifications, and typical salaries.

★1121★ Marketing Managers
Chronicle Guidance Publications, Inc.
66 Aurora St.
PO Box 1190
Moravia, NY 13118-1190
Ph: (315)497-0330   Fax: (315)497-3359
Fr: 800-622-7284
1992. Occupational brief describing the nature of the job, working conditions, hours and earnings, education and training, licensure, certification, unions, personal qualifications, social and psychological factors, location, employment outlook, entry methods, advancement, and related occupations.

★1122★ Opportunities in Advertising
National Textbook Co. (NTC)
VGM Career Books
4255 W. Touhy Ave.
Lincolnwood, IL 60646-1975
Ph: (708)679-5500   Fax: (708)679-2494
Fr: 800-323-4900

S. William Pattis. 1988. Illustrated. Includes a bibliography. Explains job duties, educational requirements, salary, working conditions, employment outlook, and advancement opportunities.

★1123★ Opportunities in Business Communications
National Textbook Co. (NTC)
VGM Career Books
4255 W. Touhy Ave.
Lincolnwood, IL 60646-1975
Ph: (708)679-5500   Fax: (708)679-2494
Fr: 800-323-4900

Overviews opportunities in marketing, public relations, promotions, and community relations, and describes the ways businesses deal with employee relations, investor relations, and instructional technology.

★1124★ Opportunities in Magazine Publishing Careers
National Textbook Co. (NTC)
VGM Career Books
4255 W. Touhy Ave.
Lincolnwood, IL 60646-1975
Ph: (708)679-5500   Fax: (708)679-2494
Fr: 800-323-4900

S. William Pattis. 1992. Describes history, organizations, and types of magazine publishing (such as consumer, business, technical, and trade magazines). Covers career opportunities in different departments in a publishing company, including public relations, as well as future trends, and job hunting techniques.

★1125★ Opportunities in Marketing Careers
National Textbook Co. (NTC)
VGM Career Books
4255 W. Touhy Ave.
Lincolnwood, IL 60646-1975
Ph: (708)679-5500   Fax: (708)679-2494
Fr: 800-323-4900

Margery S. Steinberg. 1988. Defines marketing and surveys marketing fields, such as research and retailing. Gives the employment outlook and describes the rewards of a career in marketing. Includes information on the education needed, and how to find a job. Lists colleges with majors in marketing.

★1126★ Opportunities in Public Relations Careers
National Textbook Co. (NTC)
VGM Career Books
4255 W. Touhy Ave.
Lincolnwood, IL 60646-1975
Ph: (708)679-5500   Fax: (708)679-2494
Fr: 800-323-4900

Morris B. Rotman. 1988. Describes the history and future of public relations; what public relations people do; and the market for public relations. Lists colleges offering public relations courses and the largest public relations firms. Charts public relations salaries.

★1127★ Public Relations Director, School
Careers, Inc.
PO Box 135
Largo, FL 34649-0135
Ph: (813)584-7333

1991. Two-page summary describing duties, working conditions, personal qualifications, training, earnings and hours, employment outlook, places of employment, related careers, and where to write for more information.

★1128★ "Public Relations Executive" in Jobs Rated Almanac
World Almanac
1 International Blvd., Ste. 444
Mahwah, NJ 07495
Ph: (201)529-6900   Fax: (201)529-6901

Les Krantz. Second edition, 1992. Ranks 250 jobs by environment, salary, outlooks, physical demands, stress, security, travel opportunities, and extra perks. Includes jobs the editor feels are the most common, most interesting, and the most rapidly growing.

★1129★ "Public Relations Manager" in Career Information Center (Vol.3)
Simon and Schuster
200 Old Tappan Rd.
Old Tappan, NJ 07675
Fax: 800-445-6991   Fr: 800-223-2348

Richard Lidz and Linda Perrin, editorial directors. Fifth edition, 1993. This 13-volume set profiles over 600 occupations. Each occupational profile describes job duties, entry-level requirements, educational requirements, advancement possibilities, employment outlook, working conditions, earnings and benefits, and where to write for more information.

★1130★ "Public Relations" in New Careers in Hospitals
Rosen Publishing Group
29 E. 21st St.
New York, NY 10010
Ph: (212)777-3017   Fax: (212)777-0277
Fr: 800-237-9932

Lois S. Siegel. Revised edition, 1990. Describes a variety of hospital careers and covers background, professional preparation, functions, salary, and job outlook.

★1131★ "Public Relations Officer" in Career Opportunities in Art (pp. 31-32)
Facts on File
460 Park Ave. S.
New York, NY 10016-7382
Ph: (212)683-2244   Fax: 800-678-3633
Fr: 800-322-8755

Susan H. Haubenstock. 1988. This book profiles seventy-five art-related jobs. Each profile includes a career description, career ladder, employment and advancement prospects, education, experience and skills required, salary range, and tips for entry into the field.

★1132★ "Public Relations and Publicity" in Advertising: A VGM Career Planner (pp. 93-98)
National Textbook Co. (NTC)
VGM Career Books
4255 W. Touhy Ave.
Lincolnwood, IL 60646-1975
Ph: (708)679-5500   Fax: (708)679-2494
Fr: 800-323-4900

Pattis, S. William. 1989. Describes the development of advertising. Explains the role of the media in advertising, personal characteristics needed to succeed in this field, educational requirements, and related jobs. Gives job hunting tips.

★1133★ "Public Relations Specialists" in Career Discovery Encyclopedia (Vol.5, pp. 108-109)
J.G. Ferguson Publishing Co.
200 W. Madison St., Ste. 300
Chicago, IL 60606
Ph: (312)580-5480   Fax: (312)580-4948

Russell E. Primm, editor-in chief. 1993. This six volume set contains two-page articles for 504 occupations. Each article describes job duties, earnings, and educational and training requirements. The whole set is arranged alphabetically by job title. Designed for junior high and older students.

★1134★ "Public Relations" in Where the Jobs Are: The Hottest Careers for the 90s (pp. 211-220)
Career Press
180 5th Ave.
Hawthorne, NJ 07507
Ph: (201)427-0229   Fax: (201)427-2037
Fr: 800-CAREER-1

Joyce Hadley. 1995. Offers a job-hunting strategy for the 1990s as well as descriptions of growing careers of the decade. Each profile includes general information, forecasts, growth, education and training, licensing requirements, and salary information.

★1135★ Sales Manager
Careers, Inc.
PO Box 135
Largo, FL 34649-0135
Ph: (813)584-7333

1993. Two-page occupational summary card describing duties, working conditions, personal qualifications, training, earnings and hours, employment outlook, places of employment, related careers, and where to write for more information.

★1136★ "Sales Manager" in VGM's Careers Encyclopedia (pp. 418-421)
National Textbook Co. (NTC)
VGM Career Books
4255 W. Touhy Ave.
Lincolnwood, IL 60646-1975
Ph: (708)679-5500   Fax: (708)679-2494
Fr: 800-323-4900

Third edition, 1991. Describes job duties, places of employment, working conditions, qualifications, education, and training, advancement potential, and salary for each occupation.

★1137★ Sales Managers
Chronicle Guidance Publications, Inc.
66 Aurora St.
PO Box 1190
Moravia, NY 13118-1190
Ph: (315)497-0330   Fax: (315)497-3359
Fr: 800-622-7284

1991. Career brief describing the nature of the job, working conditions, hours and earnings, education and training, licensure, certification, unions, personal qualifications, social and psychological factors, location, employment outlook, entry methods, advancement, and related occupations.

★1138★ Sales Promotion/Marketing Manager (Retail)
Careers, Inc.
PO Box 135
Largo, FL 34649-0135
Ph: (813)584-7333

1993. Two-page occupational summary card describing duties, working conditions, personal qualifications, training, earnings and hours, employment outlook, places of employment, related careers, and where to write for more information.

PROFESSIONAL ASSOCIATIONS

★1139★ American Advertising Federation (AAF)
1101 Vermont Ave. NW, Ste. 500
Washington, DC 20005
Ph: (202)898-0089   Fax: (202)898-0159

Purpose: Works to advance the business of advertising as a vital and essential part of the American economy and culture through government and public relations; professional development and recognition; community service, social responsibility and high standards; and benefits and services to members. Operates Advertising Hall of Fame, Hall of Achievement, and speakers' bureau. **Publications:** American Advertising Federation—Annual Report to the Members. • American Advertising Federation—Government Report, monthly. • American Advertising Magazine, quarterly. • Communicator, monthly. • Newsline, monthly.

★1140★ American Association of Advertising Agencies (AAAA)
666 3rd Ave., 13th Fl.
New York, NY 10017
Ph: (212)682-2500   Fax: (212)682-8136

Members: Fosters development of the advertising industry; assists member agencies to operate more efficiently and profitably. **Purpose:** Sponsors member information and international services. Maintains 44 committees. Compiles statistics. **Publications:** Agency Magazine, quarterly. • 401(K) News, monthly. • Roster, annual.

★1141★ American Society for Health Care Marketing and Public Relations (ASHCMPR)
c/o American Hospital Association
840 N. Lake Shore Dr.
Chicago, IL 60611
Ph: (312)422-3737   Fax: (312)422-4579

Persons in hospitals, hospital councils or associations, hospital-related schools, and health care organizations responsible for marketing and public relations. **Publications:** Directory of Health Care Strategic Management and Communications Consultants, annual. • Membership Directory of the American Society for Health Care Marketing and Public Relations, annual. • MPR Exchange, bimonthly.

★1142★ Council of Sales Promotion Agencies (CSPA)
750 Summer St.
Stamford, CT 06901
Ph: (203)325-3911   Fax: (203)969-1499

Members: Agencies with a primary interest in sales promotion. **Purpose:** Seeks to increase understanding, by management, of sales promotion as a special component of the total marketing management and corporate communication function; will stimulate methods of scientific research and evaluation of sales promotion. Sponsors intern program; conducts research; maintains speakers' bureau and hall of fame. Plans to establish library.

★1143★ Food Marketing Institute (FMI)
800 Connecticut Ave. NW, Ste. 500
Washington, DC 20006-2701
Ph: (202)452-8444   Fax: (202)429-4519

Members: Grocery retailers and wholesalers. **Purpose:** Maintains liaison with government and consumers. Conducts 75 educational conferences and seminars per year. Conducts research programs; compiles statistics. **Publications:** Cumulative Index, annual. • Facts About Supermarket Development, annual. • Food Marketing Industry Speaks, annual. • Issues Bulletin, monthly. • Supermarket Industry Financial Review, annual. • Trends: Consumer Attitudes and the Supermarket. • Washington Report, weekly.

★1144★ Promotion Marketing Association of America (PMAA)
257 Park Ave. S., 11th Fl.
New York, NY 10001
Ph: (212)420-1100   Fax: (212)533-7622

Members: Promotion service companies, sales incentive organizations, and companies using promotion programs; supplier members are manufacturers of premium merchandise, consultants, and advertising agencies. **Purpose:** Conducts surveys and studies of industry groups and premium usage. **Publications:** Outlook. • PMAA Membership Directory, annual. • Promotion Marketing Abstract Quotes, semiannual.

★1145★ Public Relations Society of America (PRSA)
33 Irving Pl., 3rd Fl.
New York, NY 10003
Ph: (212)995-2230   Fax: (212)995-0757

Members: Professional society of public relations practitioners in business and industry, counseling firms, government, associations,

hospitals, schools, and nonprofit organizations. **Purpose:** Conducts professional development programs. Maintains job referral service, speakers' bureau, and research information center. Offers accreditation program. **Publications:** Public Relations Journal, semiannual. • Public Relations Tactics, monthly.

★1146★ Sales and Marketing Executives International (SMEI)
Statler Office Tower, No. 977
Cleveland, OH 44115
Ph: (216)771-6650   Fax: (216)771-6652

Members: Executives concerned with sales and marketing management, research, training, and other managerial aspects of distribution. **Purpose:** Members control activities of 3,000,000 salespersons. Undertakes studies in the field of selling and sales management; sponsors sales workshops, rallies, clinics, and seminars. Conducts career education programs, working with teachers, establishing sales clubs and fraternities, and cooperating with Junior Achievement and Distributive Education Clubs of America to interest young people in sales careers. Offers Graduate School of Sales Management and Marketing at Syracuse University, NY. Seeks to make overseas markets more accessible by interchange of selling information and marketing techniques with executives in other countries; affiliated associations are located in 49 countries. Maintains hall of fame and speakers' bureau; sponsors competitions. **Publications:** Marketing Times, quarterly. • SMEI Leadership Directory, annual.

TEST GUIDES

★1147★ Basic Marketing
National Learning Corp.
212 Michael Dr.
Syosset, NY 11791
Ph: (516)921-8888   Fax: (516)921-8743
Fr: 800-645-6337

Jack Rudman. Part of the Dantes Subject Standardized Test series. A standardized graduate and college-level examination given by graduate schools, colleges, and the U.S. Armed Forces as a final examination for course evaluation in the field of marketing. Multiple-choice format with correct answers.

★1148★ Career Examination Series: Chief Marketing Representative
National Learning Corp.
212 Michael Dr.
Syosset, NY 11791
Ph: (516)921-8888   Fax: (516)921-8743
Fr: 800-645-6337

Jack Rudman. A study guide for professionals and trainees in the field of marketing, advertising, and public relations management. Includes a multiple-choice examination section; provides answers.

★1149★ Career Examination Series: Director of Advertising
National Learning Corp.
212 Michael Dr.
Syosset, NY 11791
Ph: (516)921-8888   Fax: (516)921-8743
Fr: 800-645-6337

Jack Rudman. A study guide for professionals and trainees in the field of marketing, advertising, and public relations management. Includes a multiple-choice examination section; provides answers.

★1150★ Career Examination Series: Director of Public Information
National Learning Corp.
212 Michael Dr.
Syosset, NY 11791
Ph: (516)921-8888   Fax: (516)921-8743
Fr: 800-645-6337

Jack Rudman. 1993. Test guide including questions and answers for students or professionals in the field who seek advancement through examination.

★1151★ Career Examination Series: Public Relations Director
National Learning Corp.
212 Michael Dr.
Syosset, NY 11791
Ph: (516)921-8888   Fax: (516)921-8743
Fr: 800-645-6337

Jack Rudman. A study guide for professionals and trainees in the field of marketing, advertising, and public relations management. Includes a multiple-choice examination section; provides answers.

★1152★ Marketing
National Learning Corp.
212 Michael Dr.
Syosset, NY 11791
Ph: (516)921-8888   Fax: (516)921-8743
Fr: 800-645-6337

Jack Rudman. Part of the Test Your Knowledge Series. Contains multiple choice questions with answers.

★1153★ "Principles om Marketing" in ACT Proficiency Examination Program
National Learning Corp.
212 Michael Dr.
Syosset, NY 11791
Ph: (516)921-8888   Fax: (516)921-8743
Fr: 800-645-6337

Jack Rudman. A series of practice test guides. Part of a series which contains multiple-choice examinations designed to demonstrate proficiency in the subject of marketing.

★1154★ Regents External Degree Series: Marketing
National Learning Corp.
212 Michael Dr.
Syosset, NY 11791
Ph: (516)921-8888   Fax: (516)921-8743
Fr: 800-645-6337

Jack Rudman. A multiple-choice examination for marketing professionals preparing to enter the Regents External Degree Program, an alternate route to a college degree. Test contains multiple-choice questions with answers provided. Titles in the series include Marketing I; Marketing II; Marketing III.

EDUCATIONAL DIRECTORIES AND PROGRAMS

★1155★ Advertising Career Directory
Gale Research Inc.
835 Penobscot Bldg.
Detroit, MI 48226-4094
Ph: (313)961-2242   Fax: (313)961-6083
Fr: 800-877-GALE

Bradley J. Morgan and Joseph M. Palmisano. Fifth edition, 1992. A directory in the Career Advisor Series that provides essays written by industry professionals; job search information on resume and cover letter preparation, networking, and the interviewing process; approximately 300 companies and organizations offering job opportunities and internships, and additional job-hunting resources.

★1156★ Journalism and Mass Communication Directory
Association for Education in Journalism and Mass Communication
University of South Carolina
1621 College St.
Columbia, SC 29208
Ph: (803)777-2005   Fax: (803)777-4728
Jennifer McGill, Executive Director

Annual, October. Covers more than 3,000 professionals, academics, and graduate students; more than 400 journalism and mass communications schools and departments in four-year colleges and universities (including many with broadcasting, public relations, and advertising curriculums), including 200 members of the Association of Schools of Journalism and Mass Communication; journalism education associations at the college and university level; national funds, fellowships, and foundations in journalism; college and scholastic journalistic services; media and professional associations; information centers and special interest groups; and professional and student societies; coverage includes Arrangement: Individuals are alphabetical; schools are geographical; others are alphabetical within organization type.

★1157★ Magazine Career Directory
Gale Research Inc.
835 Penobscot Bldg.
Detroit, MI 48226-4094
Ph: (313)961-2242   Fax: (313)961-6083
Fr: 800-877-GALE

Bradley J. Morgan and Joseph M. Palmisano. Fifth edition, 1993. A directory in the Career Advisor Series that provides essays written by industry professionals; job search information on resume and cover letter preparation, networking, and the interviewing process; approximately 300 companies and organizations offering job opportunities and internships, and additional job-hunting resources.

★1158★ Marketing and Sales Career Directory
Gale Research Inc.
835 Penobscot Bldg.
Detroit, MI 48226-4094
Ph: (313)961-2242   Fax: (313)961-6083
Fr: 800-877-GALE

Bradley J. Morgan and Joseph M. Palmisano. Fourth edition, 1992. A directory in the Career Advisor Series that provides essays written by industry professionals; job search information on resume and cover letter preparation, networking, and the interviewing process; approximately 300 companies and organizations offering job opportunities and internships, and additional job-hunting resources.

★1159★ Newspapers Career Directory
Gale Research Inc.
835 Penobscot Bldg.
Detroit, MI 48226-4094
Ph: (313)961-2242   Fax: (313)961-6083
Fr: 800-877-GALE

Bradley J. Morgan and Joseph M. Palmisano. 1993. A directory in the Career Advisor Series that provides essays written by industry professionals; job search information on resume and cover letter preparation, networking, and the interviewing process; approximately 300 companies and organizations offering job opportunities and internships, and additional job-hunting resources.

★1160★ Public Administration Career Directory
Gale Research Inc.
835 Penobscot Bldg.
Detroit, MI 48226
Ph: (313)961-2242   Fr: 800-877-GALE

1994. For job seekers contemplating careers in public service.

★1161★ Public Relations Career Directory
Gale Research Inc.
835 Penobscot Bldg.
Detroit, MI 48226-4094
Ph: (313)961-2242   Fax: (313)961-6083
Fr: 800-877-GALE
Bradley J. Morgan, Contact

Latest edition 1993. Covers Approximately 125 companies offering job opportunities, internships, and training possibilities for those seeking a career in public relations; sources of help-wanted ads, professional associations, videos, databases, career guides, and professional guides and handbooks. Entries include: For companies—Name, address, phone, fax, business description, names and titles of key personnel, number of employees, average number of entry-level positions available, human resources contact, description of internships including contact, type and number available, application procedures, qualifications, and duties. For others—Name or title, address, phone, description. Paperback edition is available from Visible Ink Press. Arrangement: Companies are alphabetical; others are classified by type of resource.

★1162★ Where Shall I Go to Study Advertising and Public Relations?
Advertising Education Publications
PO Box 4164
Lubbock, TX 79424
Ph: (806)798-0610   Fax: (806)798-0616
Billy I. Ross, Contact
Annual, January. Covers more than 175 colleges and universities in 42 states with advertising and public relations curricula. Entries include: Institution name and location; program identification and content, degrees offered, accreditation; number of advertising and public relations students, graduates, and full-time faculty; scholarship assistance available; admission requirements; fees; contact name. Arrangement: Geographical.

AWARDS, SCHOLARSHIPS, GRANTS, AND FELLOWSHIPS

★1163★ Advertising Age Awards
Advertising Age
Crain Communications
740 N. Rush St.
Chicago, IL 60611
Ph: (312)649-5205   Fax: (312)649-5331
To recognize the best in advertising. The following awards are presented: Advertising Executive of the Year - to recognize excellence in the advertising industry, established in 1971; Agency of the Year - established in 1973; Best TV Commercials - for recognition of achievement in television commercials. Awards are presented in 12 categories. One category winner is designated best of show. Established in 1982; Magazine of the Year and Magazine Editor of the Year - to recognize an editor for quality of writing and graphics, as well as circulation and advertising gains; International Ad Agency of the Year - established in 1984; Star Presenter of the Year - to recognize a celebrity/star for outstanding performance in advertisements, established in 1986; Best TV Commercial of the Year - to recognize creative excellence and production values, sales results are considered; Best Original Commercial Music; Best Adaptation of Music for Commercial Use; Best Magazine Ad of the Year - sales results are considered; Best Newspaper Ad of the Year - sales results are considered; Best Radio Commercial of Year - sales results are considered; and Best Outdoor Ad of the Year.

★1164★ Advertising Leader of the Year Award
Western States Advertising Agencies
  Association
6404 Wilshire Blvd., No. 111
Los Angeles, CA 90048
Ph: (213)655-1951   Fax: (213)655-8627
For outstanding contributions to the advertising industry in the West and to public and community service. A plaque, silver bowl, or other appropriate piece is awarded annually. Established in 1957.

★1165★ AWNY Advertising Woman of the Year
Advertising Women of New York
153 E. 57th St.
New York, NY 10022
Ph: (212)593-1950   Fax: (212)759-2865
To recognize a woman who has made outstanding contributions to advertising throughout her professional career. Awarded annually when merited. Established in 1965.

★1166★ Alden G. Clayton Doctoral Dissertation Proposal Award
Marketing Science Institute
1000 Massachusetts Ave.
Cambridge, MA 02138
Ph: (617)491-2060   Fax: (617)491-2065
To stimulate and support research by doctoral students on subjects of importance and relevance to marketing practitioners. Marketing doctoral students must submit proposals dealing with specified topics by August 1. A monetary award of $2,500 and a certificate are awarded annually at the American Marketing Association Educators Conference. Established in 1984 to honor Alden G. Clayton, former MSI president who retired in 1986 after more than a decade of leadership at the Institute.

★1167★ Effie Awards
American Marketing Association/New York
310 Madison Ave., Ste. 1211
New York, NY 10017
Ph: (212)687-3280   Fax: (212)986-8329
For recognition of effective advertising campaigns. The Effie is a unique award because it recognizes the team effort of client and agency. Campaigns must currently be running to be considered. Entries must be submitted by December 1. Awards are given in more than 40 categories. Gold, silver and bronze E statuettes are awarded annually. The Grand Effie is given for the most effective campaign in all categories. Established in 1969.

★1168★ International Advertising Association Award
International Advertising Association
342 Madison Ave., 20th Fl., Ste. 2000
New York, NY 10173-0073
Ph: (212)557-1133   Fax: (212)983-0455
To recognize an individual for significant contributions to the advancement of international advertising and marketing. A Tiffany crystal globe and pedestal with an inscribed sterling silver plaque is awarded biennially. Established in 1951.

★1169★ International Broadcasting Awards
Hollywood Radio and Television Society
13701 Riverside Dr., Ste. 205
Sherman Oaks, CA 91423-2467
Ph: (818)789-1182
To promote and improve broadcast advertising, honor men and women who create and produce it, and increase international cooperation in this field. Finalists are selected in 17 television and 12 radio categories. In May, an international board of final judges chooses one trophy winner in each category, and in June, chooses overall sweepstakes winners for both television and radio. The competition is open on an equal basis to television and

radio commercials transmitted anywhere in the world during the year. The deadline for entries is in January. "Ollie" trophies are awarded for the best commercial in each category, certificates are awarded to all finalists, and plaques are awarded to sweepstakes winners. Awarded annually at the IBA Presentation Show. Established in 1960.

★1170★ Marketing Executive of the Year
National Account Management Association
38 E. 23rd St.
New York, NY 10010
Ph: (212)260-6262   Fax: (212)674-6997
For recognition of outstanding executive ability. Top management executives with a proven record in organizational development who support the National Accounts principle, and are known in the sales and marketing function may be nominated by any NAM member. Awarded each year at NAMA's annual conference. Established in 1965.

★1171★ Mobius Advertising Awards
United States Festivals Association
841 N. Addison Ave.
Elmhurst, IL 60126-1291
Ph: (708)834-7773   Fax: (708)834-5565
For recognition of outstanding creativity in television and radio commercials, print advertising, and package design. Advertising produced or aired nationally, regionally, or locally anywhere in the world within the year preceding the annual October 1st entry deadline is eligible. Within the North American and international divisions, production may be entered in any of 79 subject categories and may also be entered in any of 15 production technique categories (not all apply for each medium). Entries are eligible for recognition in each category entered. The Mobius statuette is presented annually to winners of first place recognition in the various categories. A Best of Festival award is also presented to the television and radio commercial and print advertisement that best exemplifies the production talents of the industry. Certificates are presented to the runners-up. Established in 1971.

★1172★ MPA Kelly Award
Magazine Publishers of America
Special Events
919 Third Ave.
New York, NY 10022
Ph: (212)872-3700   Fax: (212)888-4217
To recognize and encourage excellence in magazine advertising creativity. Any advertising campaign is eligible if it appears during the current year in consumer magazines published in the United States, regardless of product or service advertised, size or coloration. Advertising campaigns for magazines are not eligible. A monetary prize of $100,000 is awarded annually. The winning campaign is announced at an award dinner during which the campaigns of all 25 finalists are presented. In addition to the cash prize, which is to be allocated to members of the winning agency's creative department by its director, a trophy is awarded. The remaining Kelly Award finalists also receive trophies. Established in 1981 in memory of Stephen E. Kelly, a former MPA president.

★1173★ New Clio Awards
New Clio Awards Inc.
720 N. Wabash Ave.
Chicago, IL 60611
Ph: (312)337-5900   Fax: (312)664-8425
Fr: 800-WIN-CLIO

To recognize creative excellence in advertising worldwide. Open to television, print, radio, poster and outdoor advertising introduced during the previous year. The entry deadline is April 30. U.S. entries and international entries are judged separately, but finalists are judged to ascertain winners in approximately 150 categories, including technique and Classic Television Hall of Fame. Entries are judged against a scale of criteria, which includes concept, execution, music, illustration, direction, etc. Clio statuettes are awarded to top winners in each category at the annual awards show at the New York State Theatre at Lincoln Center. Finalists in each category receive certificates. Established in 1959 by Wallace Ross as the American TV Commercials Festival. Re-structured in 1991 by New Clio Awards, Inc.

★1174★ Parlin Award
American Marketing Association
250 S. Wacker Dr., Ste. 200
Chicago, IL 60606
Ph: (312)648-0536   Fax: (312)648-9713

To recognize significant contributions to the field of marketing. Business persons from the United States or Canada are eligible. A plaque is awarded annually. Established and administered by the Philadelphia chapter of the association. Established in 1945 in honor of Charles Coolidge Parlin.

★1175★ RAC Hall of Fame
Retail Advertising Conference
500 N. Michigan Ave., Ste. 600
Chicago, IL 60611
Ph: (312)245-9011   Fax: (312)245-9015

To recognize individuals who have contributed the most each year to the advancement of the retail advertising profession. Established in 1955.

★1176★ Reggie Awards
Promotion Marketing Association of
    America, Inc.
257 Park Ave. S.
New York, NY 10010
Ph: (212)206-1100   Fax: (212)533-7622

For recognition of the 10 best promotion marketing programs of the year on the basis of the success of the promotion including effective solution to promotion objectives, originality of concept, and execution and results of elements that communicated an entry to the marketplace. Open to all promotion marketers, advertising/promotion agencies, manufacturers, and suppliers. Both member and non-member entries are accepted. Ten trophies representing an old-fashioned cash register are awarded annually at PMAA's Update Conference. The super REGGIE award is an actual functioning cash register. Entry fees are $245 for each PMAA member and $295 for each nonmember company. Established in 1984.

★1177★ Silver Medal Award Program
American Advertising Federation
1101 Vermont Ave. NW, Ste. 500
Washington, DC 20005
Ph: (202)898-0089   Fax: (202)898-0159
Fr: 800-999-AAF1

To recognize men and women who have made outstanding contributions to advertising and have been active in furthering the industry's standards, creative excellence, and responsibility in areas of social concern. Nominations are accepted. The honoree is voted upon by local advertising clubs. A silver medal plaque or silver medal medallion are awarded when merited.

★1178★ Myles Standish Award
Outdoor Advertising Association of America
1850 M. St. NW, Ste. 1040
Washington, DC 20036
Ph: (202)833-5566   Fax: (202)833-1522

To recognize an individual who has made an outstanding contribution to outdoor advertising. The honoree must be active in the outdoor advertising industry. A framed medal is awarded biennially. Established in 1954 in honor of Myles Standish, an early pioneer in the standardized outdoor industry.

★1179★ Touchstone Awards
American Society for Health Care
    Marketing and Public Relations
c/o American Hospital Association
840 N. Lake Shore Dr.
Chicago, IL 60611
Ph: (312)280-6359   Fax: (312)280-5923

To recognize excellence in the practice of hospital public relations, marketing and advertising. Awards are given in the following categories: (1) Advertising - Outdoor; Print Media; Radio; Television; and Total Campaign; (2) Annual Reports; (3) Audiovisuals; (4) Marketing, Total Effort; (5) Photography; (6) Public Service; (7) Research Project; (8) Solution to a Public Relations Problem; and (9) Writing. Members and nonmembers may be nominated by May 1. Gold and silver trophies are awarded annually in each category at the conference in the fall. Established in 1983. Sponsored by American Hospital Association.

BASIC REFERENCE GUIDES AND HANDBOOKS

★1180★ Advertising: What It Is and How to Do It
McGraw-Hill, Inc.
1221 Avenue of the Americas
New York, NY 10020
Ph: (212)512-2000   Fr: 800-722-4726

Roderick White. Third edition, 1993. Introductory text that discusses media ad agencies, ad design, economics, and legal issues.

★1181★ The Dictionary of Marketing
Fairchild Books and Visuals
7 W. 34th St.
New York, NY 10001
Ph: (212)630-3880   Fr: 800-247-6622

Rona Ostrow and Sweetman R. Smith. 1987. Illustrated.

★1182★ Dictionary of Marketing and Advertising
Nichols Publishing
11 Harts Ln., Ste. I
East Brunswick, NJ 08816
Ph: (908)238-4880

Michael J. Baker. Second edition, 1990. Illustrated.

★1183★ Environmental Marketing
McGraw-Hill Inc.
11 W. 19 St.
New York, NY 10011
Ph: 800-722-4726

Walter Coddington. 1993.

★1184★ Fundamentals of Marketing
McGraw-Hill, Inc.
1221 Avenue of the Americas
New York, NY 10020
Ph: (212)512-2000   Fr: 800-722-4726

William J. Stanton and C. M. Futrell. 1993. Basic text that covers marketing principles and practices including pricing, distribution, and promotion.

★1185★ Great Print Advertising: Creative Approaches, Strategies, and Tactics
John Wiley and Sons, Inc.
605 3rd Ave.
New York, NY 10158-0012
Ph: (212)850-6000   Fax: (212)850-6088
Fr: 800-526-5368

Tony Antin. 1993. Gives detailed instructions for developing print ads. Provides examples of ads that work and those that don't, plus explains the differences between them.

★1186★ The Manager's Desk Reference
AMACOM
135 W. 50th St.
New York, NY 10020-1201
Ph: (212)903-8089   Fr: 800-262-9699

Cynthia Berryman-Fink. 1991. Designed for marketing management.

★1187★ The Manager's Guide to Competitive Marketing Strategies
AMACOM
135 W. 50th St.
New York, NY 10020-1201
Ph: (212)903-8089   Fr: 800-262-9699

Norton Paley. 1992.

★1188★ The Marketer's Guide to Public Relations: How Today's Top Companies Are Using the New PR to Gain a Competitive Edge
John Wiley and Sons, Inc.
605 3rd Ave.
New York, NY 10158-0012
Ph: (212)850-6000   Fax: (212)850-6088
Fr: 800-526-5368

Thomas L. Harris. 1991. Simplifies public relations into a tool that can be used by marketing departments of companies for increased business success.

★1189★ Marketing
Macmillan Publishing Co., Inc.
866 3rd Ave.
New York, NY 10022
Ph: (202)702-2000   Fr: 800-257-5755

Joel R. Evans and Barry Berman. Third edition, 1993.

★1190★ Marketing Management: Strategies and Programs
McGraw-Hill, Inc.
1221 Avenue of the Americas
New York, NY 10020
Ph: (212)512-2000   Fr: 800-722-4726

Joseph P. Guiltinan and Paul Gordon. Fifth edition, 1993. Covers managerial perspectives on marketing, planning, strategy, promotion, and distribution.

★1191★ Principles of Marketing
Prentice-Hall, Inc.
Rte. 9W
Englewood Cliffs, NJ 07632
Ph: (201)592-2000   Fr: 800-634-2863

Philip Kotler. Fifth edition, 1991. Introduces the fundamentals of marketing. Covers marketing goals and planning, the marketing environment, and consumer behavior.

★1192★ Public Relations Handbook
Dartnell Corp.
4660 Ravenswood Ave.
Chicago, IL 60640
Ph: (312)561-4000   Fr: 800-621-5463

Robert L. Dilenschneider and Dan J. Forrestal. Third revised edition, 1987. Covers planning, policy making, budgeting, staffing, and creative writing.

★1193★ Public Relations Management by Objectives
Longman, Inc.
Longman Bldg.
95 Church St.
White Plains, NY 10601
Ph: (914)993-5000

Norman R. Nager and T. Harrell Allen. 1984. Part of the Longman Series in Public Communication. Illustrated. Includes bibliographical references and an index.

★1194★ Retail Marketing for Employees, Managers, and Entrepreneurs
McGraw-Hill, Inc.
1221 Avenue of the Americas
New York, NY 10020
Ph: (212)512-2000   Fr: 800-722-4726

Warren G. Meyer and E. E. Harris, et al. Eighth edition, 1988. Covers the basics of retail marketing. Includes information on career planning for the marketing professional.

PROFESSIONAL AND TRADE PERIODICALS

★1195★ Advertising Age
Crain Communications, Inc.
740 N. Rush St.
Chicago, IL 60611
Ph: (312)649-5215   Fax: (312)649-5228
Fred Danzig

Weekly. Advertising trade publication covering agency, media, and advertiser news and trends.

★1196★ Adweek
Billboard Magazine
33 Commercial St.
Gloucester, MA 01930
Ph: (508)281-3110   Fax: (508)281-0136
Andrew Jaffe

Weekly. Advertising news magazine.

★1197★ Business Ideas Newsletter
Dan Newman Company
1051 Bloomfield Ave.
Clifton, NJ 07012
Ph: (201)778-6677
Dan Newman

Publishes information for advertising and marketing executives to "increase results, returns, and profits." Reports on and interprets developments affecting the business community, including issues such as legislative and regulatory activities and tax reform. Covers new product developments, employment strategies, advertising techniques, and direct marketing potential. Recurring features include news of research, reports of meetings, news of educational opportunities, and book reviews.

★1198★ Communication Briefings
Encoders, Inc.
700 Black Horse Pike, Ste. 110
Blackwood, NJ 08012
Ph: (609)232-6380   Fax: (609)232-8229
Frank Grazian

Monthly. Provides communication ideas and techniques for a wide variety of areas, including public relations, advertising, fund raising, speeches, media relations, human resources, and employee/manager relations. Carries interviews with top communicators, business leaders, university experts, and research specialists. Recurring features include news of research, book reviews, and abstracts of articles from national publications.

★1199★ Financial Marketing
Charles E. Bartling, Contact
Provides marketing professionals from banks, savings institutions, and credit unions with pertinent information on current trends and developments in the marketing of financial services. Recurring features include letters to the editor, news of research, book reviews, job listing, and a calendar of events.

★1200★ Graphic Design: USA
Kaye Publishing
1556 3rd Ave., Ste. 405
New York, NY 10128
Ph: (212)534-5500   Fax: (212)534-4415
Susan Benson

Monthly. Magazine reporting on creating and producing advertising art.

★1201★ Grayson Report
Grayson Associates, Inc.
108 Loma Media Rd.
Santa Barbara, CA 93103
Ph: (805)564-1313   Fax: (805)564-8800
I. Robert Parket

Quarterly. Academic journal written for consumer marketing practitioners.

★1202★ Industrial Marketing Management
Elsevier Science Publishing Co., Inc.
655 Avenue of the Americas
New York, NY 10010
Ph: (212)989-5800   Fax: (212)633-3913
James D. Hlavacek

Quarterly. Research journal exploring marketing techniques and solutions.

★1203★ Interactive Age
CMP Publications, Inc.
600 Community Drive
Manhasset, NY 11030
Ph: (516)562-5000   Fax: (516)562-5101
Chuck MartinPublisher

Newspaper containing articles on interactive marketing and the information highway.

★1204★ Journal of Advertising Research
Advertising Research Foundation, Inc.
641 Lexington Ave.
New York, NY 10022
Ph: (212)751-5656   Fax: (212)319-5265
Kathryn Kucharski Grubb

Bimonthly. Journal of advertising and marketing research.

★1205★ Journal of Direct Marketing
John Wiley and Sons, Inc.
605 3rd Ave.
New York, NY 10158
Ph: (212)850-6000   Fax: (212)850-6799
Don E. Schultz

Quarterly. Journal containing articles, as well as software and book reviews, on the field of direct marketing.

★1206★ Journal of Strategic Marketing
Chapman & Hall
29 W. 35th St.
New York, NY 10001-2291
Ph: (212)244-3336

Quarterly. Journal containing articles on the relationship between marketing and management.

★1207★ Marketing and Media Decisions
ACT III Publishing, Media Group
401 Park Ave. S.
New York, NY 10036
Ph: (212)695-4215
Sandra Rifkin

Monthly. Advertising magazine.

★1208★ Marketing News
American Marketing Assn.
250 S. Wacker Dr., Ste. 200
Chicago, IL 60606-5819
Ph: (312)648-0536   Fax: (312)993-7540
Thomas E. Caruso

Biweekly. Trade magazine.

★1209★ The Media Messenger
Western Press Clipping Services
8401 73rd Ave. N., Ste. 82
Brooklyn Park, MN 55428
Ph: (612)537-7730   Fr: 800-328-4827
Mary Sis

Monthly. Reports news summaries within the publishing, advertising, public relations, radio, and television industries.

★1210★ The National Business Wire Newsletter
Business Wire
44 Montgomery St., No. 3900
San Francisco, CA 94104
Ph: (415)986-4422   Fax: (415)788-5335
Lorry I. Lokey

Monthly. Published for those who use the Business Wire service to transmit news releases nationally and internationally via high speed (9600 baud) satellite. Carries updates on personnel changes in the media and public relations world as well as news items concerning print and electronic journalism and all aspects of public relations. Recurring features include job listings and obituaries.

★1211★ O'Dwyer's PR Services Report
J.R. O'Dwyer Co., Inc.
271 Madison Ave.
New York, NY 10016
Ph: (212)679-2471   Fax: (212)683-2750

Monthly. Professional magazine covering the public relations industry.

★1212★ The Perceptive Report
Perceptive Marketers Agency, Ltd.
1100 E. Hector St., Ste. 301
Conshohocken, PA 19428
Ph: (215)825-8710   Fax: (215)825-9186
Allen P. Solovitz

Monthly. Carries industry news, tips for managers, and profiles of those in the industry.

★1213★ PR News
Phillips Business Information, Inc.
7811 Montrose Rd.
Potomac, MD 20854
Ph: (212)879-7090
Tom Moore

Weekly. Carries public relations news and information of interest to high-level executives. Offers a two-page case study in each issue on an aspect of public relations within business, industry, government, education, or nonprofit organizations. Recurring features include mention of awards and honors in the field, personnel and account changes, excerpts from major speeches, interviews with prominent speakers, and recommendations of public relations material.

★1214★ PR Reporter
PR Publishing Company, Inc.
Dudley House
PO Box 600
Exeter, NH 03833-0600
Ph: (603)778-0514   Fax: (603)778-1741
Patrick Jackson

Weekly. Gives news of developments, trends, and research in the field of public relations. Provides alternating biweekly supplements: Tips and Tactics, Managing the Human Climate, and Purview (summarizing pertinent articles and books relating to social science). Recurring features include and columns titled Who's Who in Public Relations and Annual Survey of the Profession.

★1215★ The Professional Consultant
Howard L. Shenson
123 NW 2nd Ave., No. 403
Portland, OR 97209-3927
Ph: (818)703-1415   Fax: (818)703-6295
Paul L. Franklin, Contact

Monthly. Covers topics of importance to consultants of all disciplines. Contains how-to articles and trends in the profession. Recurring features include marketing tips and the column Briefly.

★1216★ Pub Relations Quarterly
44 W. Market St.
Rhinebeck, NY 12572
Ph: (914)876-2081   Fax: (914)876-2561
Howard Penn Hudson

Quarterly. Public relations magazine.

★1217★ Public Relations Journal
Public Relations Society of America
33 Irving Pl.
New York, NY 10003-2376
Ph: (212)460-1413   Fax: (212)995-0757
Anne Fetsch

Monthly. Public relations magazine containing articles on theory and practice for practitioners and those in related fields.

★1218★ Sales and Marketing Executive Report
Dartnell Corporation
4660 Ravenswood Ave.
Chicago, IL 60640
Ph: (312)561-4000   Fax: (312)561-3801
Fr: 800-621-5463
Christen P. Heide

Biweekly. Discusses topics of interest to managers, including motivating and training sales personnel, executive self-improvement, and advertising and public relations strategies. Recurring features include news of research, letters to the editor, book reviews, a calendar of events, and columns titled Sales/Marketing Briefs and Special Report.

★1219★ Sales & Marketing Management
Bill Communications, Inc.
355 Park Ave. S.
New York, NY 10010-1789
Ph: (212)592-6200   Fax: (212)592-6359
Charles Butler

Business magazine.

PROFESSIONAL MEETINGS AND CONVENTIONS

★1220★ Bank Marketing Association Annual Convention and Exhibit
Bank Marketing Association
1120 Connecticut Ave., NW, No. 300
Washington, DC 20036-3902
Ph: (312)782-1442

Annual.

★1221★ Direct Marketing Association Convention
Direct Marketing Association
11 W. 42nd St.
New York, NY 10036-8096
Ph: (212)768-7277   Fax: (212)768-4546
Fr: 800-255-0006

Annual. **Dates and Locations:** 1995 Oct; Dallas, TX. ● 1996 Oct; New Orleans, LA.

★1222★ Direct Selling Association Annual Meeting
Direct Selling Association
1776 K St., NW, Ste. 600
Washington, DC 20006
Ph: (202)293-5760   Fax: (202)463-4569

Annual.

★1223★ Professional Photographers of America Marketing and Management Conference
Professional Photographers of America
1090 Executive Way
Des Plaines, IL 60018
Ph: (708)299-8161   Fax: (708)299-1975

Annual. Always held during January.

★1224★ Public Relations Society of America Annual Conference
Public Relations Society of America
33 Irving Pl.
New York, NY 10003
Ph: (212)995-2230   Fax: (212)995-0757

Annual. **Dates and Locations:** 1995 Nov 05-08; Seattle, WA.

★1225★ Retail Advertising Conference Expo
Retail Advertising and Marketing Association International
500 N. Michigan Ave., Ste. 600
Chicago, IL 60611
Ph: (312)245-9011   Fax: (312)245-9015

Annual. **Dates and Locations:** 1995

★1226★ XL Exposition and Conference
Advanstar Expositions
1800 Augusta, Ste. 300
Houston, TX 77057
Ph: (713)974-6637   Fax: (713)974-6272

Annual.

OTHER SOURCES OF INFORMATION

★1227★ "Advertising and Marketing Account Supervisor" in *100 Best Jobs for the 1990s & Beyond*
Dearborn Financial Publishing, Inc.
520 N. Dearborn St.
Chicago, IL 60610-4354
Ph: (312)836-4400   Fax: (312)836-1021
Fr: 800-621-9621
Carol Kleiman. 1992. Describes 100 jobs ranging from accountants to veterinarians. Each job profile includes such information as education, experience, and certification needed, salaries, and job search suggestions.

★1228★ "Advertising and Public Relations" in *Accounting to Zoology: Graduate Fields Defined* **(pp. 33-36)**
Petersons Guides, Inc.
PO Box 2123
Princeton, NJ 08543-2123
Ph: (609)243-9111   Fax: (609)243-9150
Fr: 800-338-3282
Amy J. Goldstein, editor. Revised and updated, 1987. Discusses types of graduate programs and degrees, graduate research, applied work, employment prospects and trends.

★1229★ *Careers in Marketing*
Macmillian Publishing Co., Inc.
866 3rd Ave.
New York, NY 10022
Ph: (202)702-2000   Fr: 800-257-5755
1993.

★1230★ "Marketing" in *Accounting to Zoology: Graduate Fields Defined* **(p. 45)**
Petersons Guides, Inc.
PO Box 2123
Princeton, NJ 08543-2123
Ph: (609)243-9111   Fax: (609)243-9150
Fr: 800-338-3282
Amy J. Goldstein, editor. Revised and updated, 1987. Discusses types of graduate programs and degrees, graduate research, applied work, employment prospects and trends.

★1231★ *The Marketing Glossary*
AMACOM
135 W. 50th St.
New York, NY 10020-1201
Ph: (212)903-8089   Fr: 800-262-9696
Mark N. Clemente. 1992. Provides key terms, concepts, and applications.

Personnel, Training, and Labor Relations Specialists and Managers

Personnel, training, and labor relations specialists and managers, also commonly known as **human resources specialists and managers**, help management make effective use of employees' skills, and help employees find satisfaction in their jobs and working conditions. Dealing with people is an essential part of the job. The **director of human resources**, oversees several departments—each headed by an experienced manager concerned with basic personnel activities. **Employment and placement managers** oversee the hiring and separation of employees. **Recruiters** maintain contacts within the community and may travel extensively—often to college campuses—to search for promising job applicants. **Equal employment opportunity (EEO) representatives** or **affirmative action coordinators** investigate and resolve EEO grievances, examine corporate practices for possible violations, and compile and submit EEO statistical reports. **Job analysts**, sometimes called **position classifiers**, collect and examine detailed information about job duties to prepare job descriptions. **Occupational analysts** conduct research, generally in large firms. They are concerned with occupational classification systems and study the effects of industry and occupational trends upon worker relationships. **Employee benefits managers** handle the company's employee benefits program, notably its health insurance and pension plans. Training or, more broadly, human resource development is supervised by **training and development managers**. **Training specialists** are responsible for planning, organizing, and directing a wide range of training activities. **Employee welfare managers** are responsible for a wide array of programs covering occupational safety and health standards and practices; health promotion and physical fitness, medical examinations, and minor health treatment, such as first aid; plant security; publications; food service and recreation activities; van-pooling; employee suggestion systems; child care; and counseling services—an area of rapidly growing importance. The **director of industrial relations** formulates labor policy, oversees industrial labor relations, negotiates collective bargaining agreements, and coordinates grievance procedures to handle complaints resulting from disputes under the contract for firms with unionized employees. Industrial labor relations programs are implemented by labor relations managers and their staff.

Salaries

Salaries vary widely and depend on the size and location of the firm and the nature of the business.

Lowest 10 percent	Less than $17,000/year
Median	$32,000/year
Top 10 percent	More than $64,000/year
Federal government labor relations Specialists	$50,400/year
Federal government personnel managers	$48,200/year

Employment Outlook

Growth rate until the year 2005: Faster than the average.

Personnel, Training, and Labor Relations Specialists and Managers

CAREER GUIDES

★1232★ *Career Choices for the 90's for Students of Psychology*
Walker and Co.
435 Hudson St.
New York, NY 10014
Ph: (212)727-8300   Fax: (212)727-0984
Fr: 800-289-2553
Compiled by Career Associates Staff. 1990. This book offers alternatives for students of psychology, including careers within the advertising field. Gives information about the outlook and competition for entry-level candidates. Provides job hunting tips.

★1233★ *Career Opportunities in the Music Industry*
Facts on File
460 Park Ave. S.
New York, NY 10016-7382
Ph: (212)683-2244   Fax: 800-678-3633
Fr: 800-322-8755
Shelly Field. 1990. Discusses approximately 80 jobs in music, including the performing arts, business, and education. Each job description provides basic career information, salary, employment prospects, advancement opportunities, education, training, and experience required.

★1234★ "Compensation Specialists", "Personnel Recruiters", and "Training Specialists" in *Career Information Center* (Vol.1)
Simon and Schuster
200 Old Tappan Rd.
Old Tappan, NJ 07675
Fax: 800-445-6991   Fr: 800-223-2348
Richard Lidz, and Linda Perrin, editorial directors. Fifth edition, 1993. A multi-volume set that profiles over 600 occupations. Volume 1 chapters include personnel, training, and labor relations specialists and managers. Each occupational profile describes job duties, educational requirements, advance-

ment possibilities, employment outlook, working conditions, earnings and benefits, and where to write for more information.

★1235★ "Corporate Benefits Manager" in *Jobs! What They Are—Where They Are—What They Pay!* (pp. 236)
Simon & Schuster, Inc.
Simon & Schuster Bldg.
1230 Avenue of the Americas
New York, NY 10020
Ph: (201)767-5937   Fr: 800-223-2348
Robert O. Snelling and Anne M. Snelling. Third revised edition, 1992. Includes chapter titled "Personnel and Labor Relations Specialist" (p. 241) and "Training-and-Development Specialist" (p. 245). Describes duties and responsibilities, earnings, employment opportunities, training, and qualifications.

★1236★ "Employee Benefits" in *Profitable Careers in Non-Profit* (pp. 100-102)
John Wiley and Sons, Inc.
605 3rd Ave.
New York, NY 10158-0012
Ph: (212)850-6000   Fax: (212)850-6088
Fr: 800-526-5368
William Lewis and Carol Milano. 1987. Examines nonprofit organizations and the career opportunities they offer. Offers tips on how to target and explore occupational opportunities in the nonprofit sector.

★1237★ "Employee/Labor Relations (Personnel)" in *Encyclopedia of Career Choices for the 1990s: Guide to Entry Level Jobs* (pp. 639-657)
Berkley Pub.
PO Box 506
East Rutherford, NJ 07073
Fax: (201)933-2316   Fr: 800-788-6262
1992. Describes entry-level careers in a variety of industries. Presents qualifications required, working conditions, salary, internships, and professional associations.

★1238★ "Human Resources Department" in *Opportunities in Hotel and Motel Management* (pp. 37-86)
National Textbook Co. (NTC)
VGM Careers
4255 W. Touhy Ave.
Lincolnwood, IL 60646-1975
Ph: (708)679-5500   Fax: (708)679-2494
Fr: 800-323-4900
Shepard Hankin. 1992. Describes jobs in the hospitality industry, employment outlook, personal requirements, educational preparation, apprenticeship and training, salary, and job hunting techniques.

★1239★ "Human Resources Development" in *Careers in Business*
National Textbook Co. (NTC)
VGM Career Books
4255 W. Touhy Ave.
Lincolnwood, IL 60646-1975
Ph: (708)679-5500   Fax: (708)679-2494
Fr: 800-323-4900
Lila B. Stair and Dorothy Domkowski, editors. 1992. Provides facts about business areas such as marketing, accounting, production, human resources development, management and finance. Focuses on job duties, salaries, career paths, employment outlook, trends, educational preparation and skills needed.

★1240★ "Human Resources and Employee Services" in *Where the Jobs Are: The Hottest Careers for the 90s* (pp. 167-182)
Career Press
180 5th Ave.
Hawthorne, NJ 07507
Ph: (201)427-0229   Fax: (201)427-2037
Fr: 800-CAREER-1
Joyce Hadley. 1995. Offers a job-hunting strategy for the 1990s as well as descriptions of growing careers of the decade. Each profile includes general information, forecasts, growth, education and training, licensing requirements, and salary information.

★1241★ Human Resources Managers
Chronicle Guidance Publications, Inc.
66 Aurora St.
PO Box 1190
Moravia, NY 13118-1190
Ph: (315)497-0330   Fax: (315)497-3359
Fr: 800-622-7284
1992. Occupational brief describing the nature of the job, working conditions, hours and earnings, education and training, licensure, certification, unions, personal qualifications, social and psychological factors, location, employment outlook, entry methods, advancement, and related occupations.

★1242★ "Human Resources Personnel" in Opportunities in Insurance Careers (pp. 129-132)
National Textbook Co. (NTC)
VGM Career Books
4255 W. Touhy Ave.
Lincolnwood, IL 60646-1975
Ph: (708)679-5500   Fax: (708)679-2494
Fr: 800-323-4900
Robert M. Schrayer. 1993. Provides an introduction to the world of insurance careers through an exploration of the industry's history academic requirements, certification, licensing and education requirements, positions available, as well as some careers associated with the insurance industry, such as data processing, human resources and public relations.

★1243★ Industrial, Human Resource, and Labor Relations Director
Careers, Inc.
PO Box 135
Largo, FL 34649-0135
Ph: (813)584-7333
1995. Two-page occupational summary card describing duties, working conditions, personal qualifications, training, earnings and hours, employment outlook, places of employment, related careers, and where to write for more information.

★1244★ "International Personnel" in Opportunities in International Business Careers (pp. 91-93)
National Textbook Co. (NTC)
VGM Career Books
4255 W. Touhy Ave.
Lincolnwood, IL 60646-1975
Ph: (708)679-5500   Fax: (708)679-2494
Fr: 800-323-4900
Jeffry S. Arpan. 1989. Describes what types of jobs exist in international business, where they are located, what challenges and rewards they bring, and how to prepare for and obtain jobs in international business.

★1245★ Introduction to Human Resource Development Careers
American Society for Training and Development
1640 King St.
Box 1443
Alexandria, VA 22313
Ph: (703)683-8100
Richard Y. Chang. Third Edition, 1990. This 21-page booklet describes the training and development profession; discusses roles, functions performed, how to get into training and development, and current trends.

★1246★ Job Analyst
Careers, Inc.
PO Box 135
Largo, FL 34649-0135
Ph: (813)584-7333
1993. Two-page occupational summary card describing duties, working conditions, personal qualifications, training, earnings and hours, employment outlook, places of employment, related careers, and where to write for more information.

★1247★ Job Analysts
Chronicle Guidance Publications, Inc.
66 Aurora St.
PO Box 1190
Moravia, NY 13118-1190
Ph: (315)497-0330   Fax: (315)497-3359
Fr: 800-622-7284
1991. Career brief describing the nature of the job, working conditions, hours and earnings, education and training, licensure, certification, unions, personal qualifications, social and psychological factors, location, employment outlook, entry methods, advancement, and related occupations.

★1248★ "Labor Relations Specialist" in VGM's Careers Encyclopedia (pp. 237-239)
National Textbook Co. (NTC)
VGM Career Books
4255 W. Touhy Ave.
Lincolnwood, IL 60646-1975
Ph: (708)679-5500   Fax: (708)679-2494
Fr: 800-323-4900
Third edition, 1991. Describes job duties, places of employment, working conditions, qualifications, education, and training, advancement potential, and salary for each occupation.

★1249★ "Labor Relations Specialist" in VGM's Handbook of Business and Management Careers
National Textbook Co.
4255 W. Touhy Ave.
Lincolnwood, IL 60646-1975
Ph: (708)679-5500   Fax: (708)679-2494
Fr: 800-323-4900
Annette Selden. Second edition, 1993. Contains 42 two-page occupational profiles describing job duties, places of employment, working conditions, qualifications, education, employment outlook, and income.

★1250★ "Labor Relations Specialists" in Career Information Center (Vol.9)
Simon and Schuster
200 Old Tappan Rd.
Old Tappan, NJ 07675
Fax: 800-445-6991   Fr: 800-223-2348
Richard Lidz and Linda Perrin, editorial directors. Fifth edition, 1993. This 13-volume set profiles over 600 occupations. Each occupational profile describe job duties, educational requirements, how to get the job, advancement possibilities, employment outlook, working conditions, earnings and benefits, and where to write for more information.

★1251★ "Manpower Development Specialist" in Guide to Federal Jobs (pp. 71)
Resource Directories
3361 Executive Pkwy., Ste. 302
Toledo, OH 43606
Ph: (419)536-5353   Fax: (419)536-7056
Fr: 800-274-8515
Rod W. Durgin, editor. Third edition, 1992. Contains information on finding and applying for federal jobs. Describes more than 200 professional and technical jobs for college graduates. Also includes chapters titled "Equal Employment Specialist" (p. 94), "Labor Management Relations Examiner" (p. 91), "Labor Relations Specialist" (p. 89), and "Personnel Staffing Specialist" (p. 84), "Salary and Wage Administration Specialist", "Position Classification Specialist" (p. 85), "Employee Development Specialist" (p. 90), "Employee Relations Specialist" (p. 88), and "Occupational Analyst" (p. 86). Covers the nature of the work, salary, and geographic location. Lists college majors preferred for that occupation. Section one describes the function and work of government agencies that hire the most significant number of college graduates.

★1252★ Personnel Administrator Careers
Careers, Inc.
PO Box 135
Largo, FL 34649-0135
Ph: (813)584-7333
1995. Four-page brief offering the definition, history, duties, working conditions, personal qualifications, educational requirements, earnings, hours, employment outlook, advancement, and careers related to this position.

★1253★ Personnel Administrators
Chronicle Guidance Publications, Inc.
66 Aurora St.
PO Box 1190
Moravia, NY 13118-1190
Ph: (315)497-0330   Fax: (315)497-3359
Fr: 800-622-7284
1991. Career brief describing the nature of the job, working conditions, hours and earnings, education and training, licensure, certification, unions, personal qualifications, social and psychological factors, location, employment outlook, entry methods, advancement, and related occupations.

★1254★ "Personnel" in Black Woman's Career Guide (pp. 309-313)
Bantam Doubleday Dell
1540 Broadway
New York, NY 10036
Fax: 800-233-3294   Fr: 800-223-5780
Beatryce Nivens. Revised edition, 1987. Part 1 describes career planning, resume writing, job hunting, and interviewing. Part 2 profiles 60 black women pioneers in 20 different career areas.

★1255★ "Personnel Director" in *BLR Encyclopedia of Prewritten Job Descriptions*
Business and Legal Reports (BLR)
Bureau of Law and Business, Inc.
Hazardous Waste Bulletin
39 Academy St.
Madison, CT 06443-1513
Ph: (203)245-7448

Stephen D. Bruce, editor in chief. 1994. Part I describes how to write job descriptions. Part II contains hundreds of sample job descriptions which explain the position function and authority, major duties, and minimum qualifications.

★1256★ "Personnel Director/Director of Human Resources" in *Opportunities in Hospital Administration Careers* **(pp. 36-37)**
National Textbook Co. (NTC)
VGM Career Books
4255 W. Touhy Ave.
Lincolnwood, IL 60646-1975
Ph: (708)679-5500   Fax: (708)679-2494
Fr: 800-323-4900

I. Donald Snook. 1989. Describes hospital administration in varied work settings. Covers educational preparation, skills, compensation, getting started in the profession, and job hunting.

★1257★ "Personnel" and "Human Resources" in *Liberal Arts Jobs*
Petersons Guides, Inc.
PO Box 2123
Princeton, NJ 08543-2123
Ph: (609)243-9111   Fax: (609)243-9150
Fr: 800-338-3282

Burton Jay Nadler. 1989. Strives to help the liberal arts graduate identify skills for entry-level positions. Gives goal setting and job search advice.

★1258★ "Personnel and Labor Relations Specialists" in *Encyclopedia of Careers and Vocational Guidance* **(Vol.4, pp. 20-24)**
J.G. Ferguson Publishing Co.
200 W. Madison St., Ste. 300
Chicago, IL 60606
Ph: (312)580-5480   Fax: (312)580-4948

William E. Hopke, editor in chief. Ninth edition, 1993. Four-volume set that profiles 900 occupations and describes job trends in 74 industries. Includes career description, educational require ments, history of the job, methods of entry, advancement, employment outlook, earnings, conditons of work, social and psychological factors, and sources of further information.

★1259★ "Personnel or Labor Relations Workers" in *College Board Guide to Jobs and Career Planning* **(pp. 100)**
The College Board
415 Columbus Ave.
New York, NY 10023-6992
Ph: (212)713-8165   Fax: (212)713-8143
Fr: 800-323-7155

Joyce S. Mitchell. Second edition, 1994. Describes the job, salaries, related careers, education needed, and where to write for more information.

★1260★ *Personnel Manager*
Vocational Biographies, Inc.
PO Box 31
Sauk Centre, MN 56378-0031
Ph: (612)352-6516   Fax: (612)352-5546
Fr: 800-255-0752

1992. Four-page pamphlet containing a personal narrative about a worker's job, work likes and dislikes, career path from high school to the present. Education and training, the rewards and frustrations, and the effects of the job on the rest of the worker's life. The data file portion of this pamphlet gives a concise occupational summary, including work descriptions, working conditions, places of employment, personal characteristics, education and training, job outlook, and salary range.

★1261★ "Personnel Manager" in *VGM's Careers Encyclopedia* **(pp. 336-339)**
National Textbook Co. (NTC)
VGM Career Books
4255 W. Touhy Ave.
Lincolnwood, IL 60646-1975
Ph: (708)679-5500   Fax: (708)679-2494
Fr: 800-323-4900

Third edition, 1991. Describes job duties, places of employment, working conditions, qualifications, education, and training, advancement potential, and salary for each occupation.

★1262★ "Personnel Manager" in *VGM's Handbook of Business and Management Careers*
National Textbook Co.
4255 W. Touhy Ave.
Lincolnwood, IL 60646-1975
Ph: (708)679-5500   Fax: (708)679-2494
Fr: 800-323-4900

Annette Selden. Second edition, 1993. Contains 42 two-page occupational profiles describing job duties, places of employment, working conditions, qualifications, education, employment outlook, and income.

★1263★ "Personnel" in *Opportunities in Airline Careers* **(pp. 107-115)**
National Textbook Co. (NTC)
VGM Career Books
4255 W. Touhy Ave.
Lincolnwood, IL 60646-1975
Ph: (708)679-5500   Fax: (708)679-2494
Fr: 800-323-4900

Adrian A. Paradis. 1987. Gives an overview of the airline industry including job opportunities and salaries. Describes careers in management, finance, sales, customer service and safety.

★1264★ *Personnel Recruiters*
Chronicle Guidance Publications, Inc.
66 Aurora St.
PO Box 1190
Moravia, NY 13118-1190
Ph: (315)497-0330   Fax: (315)497-3359
Fr: 800-622-7284

1991. Career brief describing the nature of the job, working conditions, hours and earnings, education and training, licensure, certification, unions, personal qualifications, social and psychological factors, location, employment outlook, entry methods, advancement, and related occupations.

★1265★ "Personnel Specialists" in *Career Discovery Encyclopedia* **(Vol.5, pp. 10-11)**
J.G. Ferguson Publishing Co.
200 W. Madison St., Ste. 300
Chicago, IL 60606
Ph: (312)580-5480   Fax: (312)580-4948

Russell E. Primm, editor-in chief. 1993. This six volume set contains two-page articles for 504 occupations. Each article describes job duties, earnings, and educational and training requirements. The whole set is arranged alphabetically by job title. Designed for junior high and older students.

★1266★ "Personnel, Training, and Labor Relations Specialists and Managers" in *Occupational Outlook Handbook*
U.S. Government Printing Office
Superintendent of Documents
Washington, DC 20402
Ph: (202)512-1800   Fax: (202)512-2250

Biennial; latest edition, 1994-95. Encyclopedia of careers describing more than 250 occupations and comprising about 85 percent of all jobs in the economy. Occupations that require lengthy education or training are given the most attention. Each occupation's profile describes what the worker does on the job, working conditions, education and training requirements, advancement possibilities, job outlook, earnings, and sources of additional information.

★1267★ "Training Coordinator/Director" in *Opportunities in Public Health Careers* **(pp. 78-79)**
National Textbook Co. (NTC)
VGM Career Books
4255 W. Touhy Ave.
Lincolnwood, IL 60646-1975
Ph: (708)679-5500   Fax: (708)679-2494
Fr: 800-323-4900

George E. Pickett. 1988. Defines the public health field and describes career opportunities as well as educational preparation and the future of the public health field. The appendixes list public health organizations, state and federal public health agencies, and graduate schools offering public health programs.

★1268★ *Training Director*
Careers, Inc.
PO Box 135
Largo, FL 34649-0135
Ph: (813)584-7333

1995. Four-page brief offering the definition, history, duties, working conditions, personal qualifications, educational requirements, earnings, hours, employment outlook, advancement, and careers related to this position.

★1269★ *You Want to Be a Labor Arbitrator?*
American Arbitration Association
140 W. 51st St.
New York, NY 10020
Ph: (212)484-4000   Fax: (212)765-4874

1989. This 12-page booklet describes the education and experience needed by labor arbitrators, as well as how to become a member of the American Arbitration Association. Includes a bibliography for the new arbitrator.

★1270★ *Your Career in Human Resource Development: A Guide to Information and Decision Making*
American Society For Training and Development
1640 Duke St.
Box 1443
Alexandria, VA 22313
Ph: (703)683-8100
Robert W. Stump and the HRD Careers Committee. Revised second edition, 1990. This guide helps prospective practitioners identify the skills they already have that suit them to the field; also explains where to go for help and how to keep up with the profession.

PROFESSIONAL ASSOCIATIONS

★1271★ **American Arbitration Association (AAA)**
140 W. 51st St.
New York, NY 10020
Ph: (212)484-4000   Fax: (212)765-4874
Members: Businesses, unions, trade and educational associations, law firms, arbitrators, and interested individuals. **Purpose:** Dedicated to the resolution of disputes of all kinds through the use of arbitration, mediation, democratic elections, and other voluntary methods. Provides administrative services for arbitrating, mediating, or negotiating disputes and impartial administration of elections. Maintains Panel of Arbitrators and Mediators for referrals to parties involved in disputes. Conducts skill-building sessions to promote a more complete understanding of conflict resolution processes. **Publications:** *Arbitration and the Law*, annual. • *Arbitration Times*, quarterly. • *Dispute Resolution Journal*, quarterly. • *Labor Arbitration in Government*, monthly. • *Lawyers' Arbitration Letter*, quarterly. • *New York No-Fault Arbitration Reports*, monthly. • *Study Time*, quarterly. • *Summary of Labor Arbitration Awards*, monthly.

★1272★ **American Compensation Association (ACA)**
14040 N. Northsight Blvd.
Scottsdale, AZ 85260
Ph: (602)951-9191   Fax: (602)483-8352
Members: Managerial, professional, and executive level administrative personnel in business, industry, and government who are responsible for the design, establishment, execution, administration, or application of total compensation practices (including benefits) and policies in their organizations. **Purpose:** Conducts surveys, research, and certification program; confers Certified Compensation Professional (CCP) designation and Certified Benefits Professional (CBP) designation. Furthers the exchange of information on current practice and research in all phases of employee compensation including wages, salaries, pensions, group insurance, and other related forms of employee remuneration. Organizes more than 400 seminars annually. Compiles statistics. Maintains speakers' bureau. **Publications:** *ACA Journal*, quarterly. • *ACA News*, 10/year. • *American Compensation Association—*

Membership Directory, annual. • *Annual Seminar Catalog*, annual. • *Building Blocks in Total Compensation*. • *Publications Catalog*, annual. • *Salary Budget Survey*, annual.

★1273★ **American Society for Healthcare Human Resources Administration (ASHHRA)**
1 N. Franklin
Chicago, IL 60606
Ph: (312)280-6722   Fax: (312)280-4152
Members: Purpose: Purposes are: to provide effective and continuous leadership in the field of health care human resources administration; to promote cooperation with hospitals and allied associations in matters pertaining to hospital human resources administration; to further the professional and educational development of members; to encourage and promote research; to encourage and assist local groups in chapter formation through regular programs and institutes on health care human resources issues. Offers placement service. **Publications:** *Directory of Health Care Human Resources Consultants*, annual. • *Hospitals*, bimonthly. • *Human Resources Administrator*, bimonthly. • *Roster of Membership*, annual.

★1274★ **American Society for Training and Development (ASTD)**
Box 1443
1640 King St.
Alexandria, VA 22313
Ph: (703)683-8100   Fax: (703)683-8103
Members: Professional association for persons engaged in the training and development of business, industry, education, and government employees. **Purpose:** Undertakes special research projects and acts as clearinghouse. Operates 3000 volume information center on human resource development. Maintains 18 committees, 15 networks, and 30 industry groups. **Publications:** *ASTD Buyer's Guide and Consultant Directory*, annual. • *HRD quarterly*. • *Info-Line: Practical Guidelines for Human Resource Development Professionals*, monthly. • *Models for HRD Practice*. • *National Report on Human Resources*, monthly. • *Technical and Skills Training*, 8/year. • *Trainer's Toolkits*. • *Training and Development Literature Index*, bimonthly. • *Training & Development*, monthly. • *Who's Who in Training and Development*, annual.

★1275★ **Industrial Relations Research Association (IRRA)**
7226 Social Science Bldg.
1180 Observatory Dr.
Madison, WI 53706
Ph: (608)262-2762   Fax: (608)265-4591
Businesspersons, union leaders, government officials, lawyers, arbitrators, academics, and others interested in research and exchange of ideas on social, political, economic, legal, and psychological aspects of labor, including employer and employee organization, labor relations, personnel administration, social security, and labor legislation. Disseminates research results. Maintains placement service. **Publications:** *Dialogues*, semiannual. • *Industrial Relations Research Association— Annual Research Volume*, annual. • *Industrial Relations Research Association— Annual Spring Proceedings*, annual. • *Industrial Relations Research Association—*

Annual Winter Proceedings, annual. • *Industrial Relations Research Association— Membership Directory*, quadrennial. • *Industrial Relations Research Association— Series Newsletter*, quarterly.

★1276★ **International Association of Personnel in Employment Security (IAPES)**
1801 Louisville Rd.
Frankfort, KY 40601
Ph: (502)223-4459   Fax: (502)223-4127
Members: Officials and others engaged in job placement, unemployment compensation, and labor market information administration through municipal, state, provincial, and federal government employment agencies and unemployment compensation agencies. **Purpose:** Conducts workshops and research. Offers professional development program of study guides and tests. **Publications:** *IAPES News*, bimonthly. • *International Association of Personnel in Employment Security—Proceedings*, annual. • *Workforce*, quarterly.

★1277★ **International Foundation of Employee Benefit Plans**
18700 W. Bluemound Rd.
PO Box 69
Brookfield, WI 53008
Ph: (414)786-6700   Fax: (414)786-2990
Members: Jointly trusteed, public, Canadian, and company-sponsored employee benefit plans; administrators, labor organizations, employer associations, benefit consultants, investment counselors, insurance consultants, banks, attorneys, accountants, actuaries, and others who service or are interested in the field of employee benefit plans. **Purpose:** Cosponsors the Certified Employee Benefit Specialist Program (CEBS) in the United States and Canada, a ten-course college-level study program leading to a professional designation in the employee benefits field. Conducts research on all aspects of employee benefit plan management; funds graduate and postgraduate studies. Sponsors Academy of Authors, recognizing authors of books published by the foundation. Conducts more than 50 educational programs. **Publications:** *Employee Benefit Issues: The Multiemployee Perspective*, annual. • *Employee Benefit Plans: A Glossary of Terms*. • *Employee Benefits Basics*, quarterly. • *Employee Benefits Journal*, quarterly. • *Employee Benefits Practices*, quarterly. • *Flexible Benefits: A How-To Guide*. • *International Foundation of Employee Benefit Plans Digest*, monthly. • *Legal-Legislative Reporter News Bulletin*, monthly. • *Self-Funding of Health Care Benefits*. • *Trustees Handbook*.

★1278★ **International Personnel Management Association (IPMA)**
1617 Duke St.
Alexandria, VA 22314
Ph: (703)549-7100   Fax: (703)684-0948
Members: Public personnel agencies (1400); individuals, including personnel workers, consultants, and professors (4400). **Purpose:** Seeks to improve personnel practices in government through provision of testing services, advisory service, conferences, professional development programs, research, and publications. Sponsors seminars

and workshops on various phases of public personnel administration. Compiles statistics. **Publications:** *Agency Issues,* biweekly. • *International Personnel Management Association—Membership Directory,* annual. • *IPMA News,* monthly. • *Public Employee Relations Library,* periodic. • *Public Personnel Management,* quarterly.

★1279★ Interstate Conference of Employment Security Agencies (ICESA)
444 N. Capitol St. NW, Ste. 142
Washington, DC 20001
Ph: (202)628-5588   Fax: (202)783-5023
State agencies responsible for administering unemployment insurance, employment and training programs, and labor market information. Strives to improve the public employment service, unemployment insurance programs, and employment and training programs; to encourage effective state action in training and placing unemployed workers, paying unemployment benefits, stabilizing the labor market and developing labor market information; to engage in public policy research and education in order to secure enactment of sound legislation; to identify the positions of member agencies and act as their collective voice in communicating those positions to federal officials, to national groups and to the public. **Publications:** *Labor Notes/Labor Market Inform-The Nation.* • *Workforce,* quarterly. • *Workforce Trends - An Assessment of the Future by Employment Security Agencies.*

★1280★ Society for Human Resource Management (SHRM)
606 N. Washington St.
Alexandria, VA 22314
Ph: (703)548-3440   Fax: (703)836-0367
Fr: 800-283-7476
Members: Professional organization of human resource, personnel, and industrial relations professionals and executives. **Purpose:** Promotes the advancement of human resource management. Sponsors SHRM Foundation. Offers certification through the Human Resource Certification Institute. **Publications:** *HR Magazine,* monthly. • *HR News,* monthly. • *Issues in HR,* bimonthly. • *Speakers Directory,* periodic.

STANDARDS/CERTIFICATION AGENCIES

★1281★ American Compensation Association (ACA)
14040 N. Northsight Blvd.
Scottsdale, AZ 85260
Ph: (602)951-9191   Fax: (602)483-8352
Conducts surveys, research, and certification program; confers Certified Compensation Professional (CCP) designation and Certified Benefits Professional (CBP) designation. Furthers the exchange of information on current practice and research in all phases of employee compensation including wages, salaries, pensions, group insurance, and

other related forms of employee remuneration.

★1282★ International Foundation of Employee Benefit Plans
18700 W. Bluemound Rd.
PO Box 69
Brookfield, WI 53008
Ph: (414)786-6700   Fax: (414)786-2990
Cosponsors the Certified Employee Benefit Specialist Program (CEBS) in the United States and Canada, a ten-course college-level study program leading to a professional designation in the employee benefits field. Conducts more than 50 educational programs.

★1283★ Society for Human Resource Management (SHRM)
606 N. Washington St.
Alexandria, VA 22314
Ph: (703)548-3440   Fax: (703)836-0367
Fr: 800-283-7476
Promotes the advancement of human resource management. Sponsors SHRM Foundation. Offers certification through the Human Resource Certification Institute.

TEST GUIDES

★1284★ *Career Examination Series: Director of Human Development*
National Learning Corp.
212 Michael Dr.
Syosset, NY 11791
Ph: (516)921-8888   Fax: (516)921-8743
Fr: 800-645-6337
Jack Rudman. 1993. Test guide including questions and answers for students or professionals in the field who seek advancement through examination.

★1285★ *Career Examination Series: Director of Personnel*
National Learning Corp.
212 Michael Dr.
Syosset, NY 11791
Ph: (516)921-8888   Fax: (516)921-8743
Fr: 800-645-6337
Jack Rudman. A series of study guides with multiple-choice examination questions and solutions for trainees and professionals in personnel, training, and labor relations. Titles in the series include *Administrative Labor Relations Specialist; Administrative Personnel Examiner; Assistant Employment and Training Program Administrator; Assistant Labor Relations Specialist; Assistant Personnel Examiner; Assistant Retirement Benefits Examiner; Associate Personnel Administrator; Chief Personnel Administrator; Director of Training; Employee Benefits Supervisor; Employment and Training Coordinator; Employment and Training Fiscal Auditor; Employment and Training Programs Administrator; Labor-Management Practices Adjuster; Labor Mediator; Labor Mediation Trainee; Labor Relations Analyst; Labor Relations Assistant; Labor Relations Representative; Mediator (Labor Relations); Personnel Administrator; Personnel Analyst; Personnel Associate; Personnel Manager; Personnel*

Officer; Personnel Specialist; Personnel Systems Analyst; Personnel Transactions Supervisor; Principal Human Resources Specialist; Principal Labor Relations Analyst; Principal Labor Specialist; Principal Personnel Administrator; Senior Labor Specialist; Senior Personnel Administrator; Staff Development Coordinator; Staff Development Specialist; Supervising Human Resources Specialist; Training Specialist; Training Specialist I; Training Specialist II.

★1286★ *Career Examination Series: Employee Relations Director*
National Learning Corp.
212 Michael Dr.
Syosset, NY 11791
Ph: (516)921-8888   Fax: (516)921-8743
Fr: 800-645-6337
Jack Rudman. 1993. Test guide including questions and answers for students or professionals in the field who seek advancement through examination.

★1287★ *Career Examination Series: General Industrial Training Supervisor*
National Learning Corp.
212 Michael Dr.
Syosset, NY 11791
Ph: (516)921-8888   Fax: (516)921-8743
Fr: 800-645-6337
Jack Rudman. 1993. Test guide including questions and answers for students or professionals in the field who seek advancement through examination.

★1288★ *Career Examination Series: Human Relations Specialist*
National Learning Corp.
212 Michael Dr.
Syosset, NY 11791
Ph: (516)921-8888   Fax: (516)921-8743
Fr: 800-645-6337
Jack Rudman. 1993. Test guide including questions and answers for students or professionals in the field who seek advancement through examination.

★1289★ *Career Examination Series: Human Resources Specialist*
National Learning Corp.
212 Michael Dr.
Syosset, NY 11791
Ph: (516)921-8888   Fax: (516)921-8743
Fr: 800-645-6337
Jack Rudman. 1993. Test guide including questions and answers for students or professionals in the field who seek advancement through examination.

★1290★ *Career Examination Series: Labor Specialist*
National Learning Corp.
212 Michael Dr.
Syosset, NY 11791
Ph: (516)921-8888   Fax: (516)921-8743
Fr: 800-645-6337
Jack Rudman. 1993. Test guide including questions and answers for students or professionals in the field who seek advancement through examination.

★1291★ *Career Examination Series: Personnel, Administration and Computer Occupations*
National Learning Corp.
212 Michael Dr.
Syosset, NY 11791
Ph: (516)921-8888   Fax: (516)921-8743
Fr: 800-645-6337

Jack Rudman. 1993. Test guide including questions and answers for students or professionals in the field who seek advancement through examination.

★1292★ *Career Examination Series: Personnel Manager*
National Learning Corp.
212 Michael Dr.
Syosset, NY 11791
Ph: (516)921-8888   Fax: (516)921-8743
Fr: 800-645-6337

Jack Rudman. Test guide including questions and answers for students or professionals in the field who seek advancement through examination.

★1293★ *Career Examination Series: Principal Personnel Analyst*
National Learning Corp.
212 Michael Dr.
Syosset, NY 11791
Ph: (516)921-8888   Fax: (516)921-8743
Fr: 800-645-6337

Jack Rudman. 1993. Test guide including questions and answers for students or professionals in the field who seek advancement through examination.

★1294★ *Career Examination Series: Social Services Human Resources Development Specialist*
National Learning Corp.
212 Michael Dr.
Syosset, NY 11791
Ph: (516)921-8888   Fax: (516)921-8743
Fr: 800-645-6337

Jack Rudman. 1993. Test guide including questions and answers for students or professionals in the field who seek advancement through examination.

★1295★ *Career Examination Series: Training Development Specialist*
National Learning Corp.
212 Michael Dr.
Syosset, NY 11791
Ph: (516)921-8888   Fax: (516)921-8743
Fr: 800-645-6337

Jack Rudman. 1993. Test guide including questions and answers for students or professionals in the field who seek advancement through examination.

★1296★ *Personnel/Human Resource Management*
National Learning Corp.
212 Michael Dr.
Syosset, NY 11791
Ph: (516)921-8888   Fax: (516)921-8743
Fr: 800-645-6337

Jack Rudman. Part of Dantes Subject Standardized Tests.

★1297★ *Principles of Management: Organizational Behavior; Labor Relations; Personnel Management*
National Learning Corp.
212 Michael Dr.
Syosset, NY 11791
Ph: (516)921-8888   Fax: (516)921-8743
Fr: 800-645-6337

Jack Rudman. A series of practice test guides containing multiple-choice examinations designed to demonstrate proficiency in the subject of personnel management. Part of the series titled *ACT Proficiency Examination Program.*

★1298★ *Regents External Degree Series: Human Resources*
National Learning Corp.
212 Michael Dr.
Syosset, NY 11791
Ph: (516)921-8888   Fax: (516)921-8743
Fr: 800-645-6337

Jack Rudman. A multiple-choice examination for personnel professionals preparing to enter the Regents External Degree Program, an alternate route to a college degree. Test contains multiple-choice questions with answers provided. Titles in the series include *Management of Human Resources I; Management of Human Resources II; Management of Human Resources III.*

EDUCATIONAL DIRECTORIES AND PROGRAMS

★1299★ *University and College Labor Education Association—Membership and Resource Directory of Institutions and Professional Staff*
University and College Labor Education Association
Mary Ruth Gross, Secretary
Center For Labor Research and Education
Univeristy of California-Berkeley
Berkeley, CA 94720
Ph: (510)642-0323
Susan Schurman, President

Annual, fall. Covers universities with full-time labor education programs. Entries include: University or college name, address, phone, names and titles of professional staff. Arrangement: Geographical.

AWARDS, SCHOLARSHIPS, GRANTS, AND FELLOWSHIPS

★1300★ **Distinguished Performance Award**
National Alliance of Business
1201 New York Ave. NW, Ste. 700
Washington, DC 20005
Ph: (202)289-2888   Fax: (202)289-1303

To recognize excellence in job training and education programs aimed at helping structurally unemployed and other jobless people become productive citizens. Awards are given in the following categories: Outstanding Job Training Professional; Distinguished Business Volunteer of the Year; Company of the Year; Outstanding Service Delivery Area; State Leadership in Job Training Partnership, Employment, and Economic Development; and other categories that vary each year. Nominations are open to representatives of any state or local job training or educational organization, business, state or local government, trade union, and other enterprises engaged in training or retraining America's workforce. Selection is made on the basis of performance, achievement of goals, and innovative use of public and private resources. Individuals must demonstrate active and significant business participation as well as cooperation between the public and private sectors in the community. A plaque is awarded annually at the convention. Established in 1982.

★1301★ **Pericles Awards**
Employment Management Association
4101 Lake Boone Trail, Ste. 201
Raleigh, NC 27607
Ph: (919)787-6010   Fax: (919)787-5302

To recognize outstanding achievements in the area of human resources, promote professionalism in the employment field, and focus national attention on the value of effective human resources programs. Awards of Excellence are given in three categories. The EMA Achievement Awardacknowledges an outstanding contribution by an employment executive in a manager-level position or above whose contributions to the employment field have influence and impact within and outside the employing organization, and whose ideas, programs, techniques, or knowledge can be recognized as applicable, useful, and effective outside the employing organization. The EMA Special Award is given for outstanding contributions to the human resources field by an individual outside the field. The recipient may be a business executive, academician, writer, or any other individual of outstanding leadership or vision whose work and ideas influence the course of human resource management. The EMA National Service Awardis presented to a company, organization, or institution in recognition of its development of one or more innovative and worthwhile human resources programs, or for its outstanding awareness of and leadership in addressing social and economic problems that impact the human resources field. Individuals may submit nominees for any or all categories, or may submit their own candidacy by January 31. Established in 1975.

★1302★ **Warner W. Stockberger Achievement Award**
International Personnel Management Association
1617 Duke St.
Alexandria, VA 22314
Ph: (703)549-7100   Fax: (703)684-0948

To recognize and honor a person in public or private life who has made an outstanding contribution to public personnel management in terms of any of the following: encouraging acceptance of personnel administration principles as an aid to better management; skillful application of personnel administration principles to any group of employees; leadership in favor of sound personnel principles by developing, sponsoring, or promoting progressive legislation strengthening personnel management in the public service; leadership in developing creative responses to new and unusual challenges in personnel management; and distinguished teaching, authorship, or research. A plaque is awarded annually. Established in 1947 to honor Dr. Warner W. Stockberger, a pioneer and leader in federal personnel administration and the first Director of Personnel of the U.S. Department of Agriculture.

BASIC REFERENCE GUIDES AND HANDBOOKS

★1303★ *Achieving Results From Training: How to Evaluate Human Resource Development to Strengthen Programs and Increase Impact*
Jossey-Bass, Inc., Publishers
350 Samsone
San Francisco, CA 94104
Ph: (415)433-1767   Fax: (415)433-0499
Robert O. Brinkeroff. 1987. Explains how to find out whether human resource development programs are meeting the needs they were designed to address. Provides guidelines and checklists for carrying out each step of an evaluation, as well as several evaluation techniques.

★1304★ *Arbitration and the Law, 1992-93*
American Arbitration Association (AAA)
140 W. 51st St.
New York, NY 10020
Ph: (212)484-4000   Fr: 800-333-3303
Linda Miller and Margaret Doyle, editors. Annual. 1993. Explores recent legal and judicial developments in arbitration. Digests of significant court decisions are presented, as well as expert commentary examining the current trends in alternative dispute resolution. Arbitration statutes and relevant legislation, both domestic and foreign, are reprinted.

★1305★ *The Career Training Sourcebook*
McGraw-Hill Inc.
11 W. 19 St.
New York, NY 10011
Ph: 800-722-4726
Sara Gilbert. 1993.

★1306★ *A Checklist for Technical Skills and Other Training*
American Society for Training and
   Development (ASTD)
1640 King
PO Box 1443
Alexandria, VA 22313
Ph: (703)683-8100
William Garry and Rosemary Springborn, editors. Contains 700 items covering every facet of training organized in a logical, easy-to-use sequence under precisely defined headings.

★1307★ *Choosing Effective Development Programs: An Appraisal Guide for Human Resources and Training Managers*
Greenwood Press, Inc.
88 Post Rd., W.
PO Box 5007
Westport, CT 06881
Ph: (203)226-3571
James E. Gardner, 1987. Provides a checklist of questions under the headings of components common to programs (motivation, goal setting and feedback, job "performability," leadership, rank-and-file training, and supervisory training) to elicit the basic information for preappraisal.

★1308★ *Critical Skills: The Guide to Top Performance for Human Resources Managers*
American Management Association (AMA)
135 W. 50th St.
New York, NY 10020
Ph: (212)586-8100
William R. Tracey. 1988. Includes bibliographies and an index.

★1309★ *Employee Benefit Plans: A Glossary of Terms*
International Foundation of Employee
   Benefits Plans (IFEBP)
18700 Bluemound Rd.
PO Box 69
Brookfield, WI 53008-0069
Ph: (414)786-6700
June Lehman, editor. 1993. Includes more than 2200 definitions derived from all apsects of the employee benefit field. Also included is a dictionary of some 650 employee benefit-related acronyms and abbreviations.

★1310★ *Employee Discipline and Discharge Policies*
Matthew Bender and Co., Inc.
11 Penn Plaza
New York, NY 10001
Ph: (212)967-7707
Bruce S. Harrison and J. Michael McGuire. 1991 (loose-leaf).

★1311★ *Handbook of Human Resource Development*
Nichols Publishing Co.
11 Harts Ln., Ste. I
East Brunswick, NY 08816
Ph: (908)238-4880
Michael Armstrong. 1988.

★1312★ *A Handbook of Human Resource Management*
Nichols Publishing
11 Harts Ln., Ste. I
East Brunswick, NJ 08816
Ph: (908)238-4880
Michael Armstrong. 1988. Includes indexes.

★1313★ *A Handbook of Personnel Management Practice*
Nichols Pub.
Englewood Cliffs, NJ 07632
Ph: (201)592-2000
Michael Armstrong and John F. Lorentzen. 1988. A Spectrum book. Includes bibliographical references and an index.

★1314★ *How to Be an Effective Trainer: Skills for Managers and New Trainers*
John Wiley and Sons, Inc.
605 3rd Ave.
New York, NY 10158-0012
Ph: (212)850-6000   Fax: (212)850-6088
Fr: 800-526-5368
Barry J. Smith and Brian L. DeLahaye. Second edition, 1987. Provides an overview of training, planning, learning, training techniques, and training aides. Shows how to use basic skills in practice.

★1315★ *Human Resource Problem Solving*
Prentice-Hall, Inc.
Rte. 9W
Englewood Cliffs, NJ 07632
Ph: (201)592-2000   Fr: 800-634-2863
Robert B. Bowin. 1987. Presents human resource issues such as recruiting, job evaluation, performance appraisal, and "real-life" problems. Includes solutions from research data and professional journal articles.

★1316★ *Human Resources Management and Development Handbook*
AMACOM
135 W. 50th St.
New York, NY 10020-1201
Ph: (212)903-8089   Fr: 800-262-9699
William R. Tracy, editor. 1992. Practical handbook that identifies and illustrates workable concepts, principles, strategies, methods, and procedures to help the human resource development professional improve productivity, reduce costs, and integrate human resources within the organization.

★1317★ *Human Resources and Personnel Management*
McGraw-Hill, Inc.
1221 Avenue of the Americas
New York, NY 10020
Ph: (212)512-2000   Fr: 800-722-4726
William B. Werther and Keith Davis. Fourth edition, 1992. This basic text gives an overview of the human resource field including employee selection, job analysis and design, employee appraisal, and labor relations.

★1318★ *The IFM Guide to the Preparation of a Company Policy Manual*
Institute for Management (IFM)
c/o Panel Publishers
14 Plaza Rd.
Greenvale, NY 11548-4728
Second edition, 1987. Includes an index.

★1319★ *Managing Human Resources*
South-Western Publishing Co.
5101 Madison Rd.
Cincinnati, OH 45227
Ph: (513)271-8811
Arthur W. Sherman, Jr., George W. Bohlander, and Herbert J. Chruden. Ninth edition, 1991. Illustrated. Includes bibliographies and indexes.

★1320★ Managing Human Resources: Productivity, Quality of Work Life, Profits
McGraw-Hill, Inc.
1221 Avenue of the Americas
New York, NY 10020
Ph: (212)512-2000   Fr: 800-722-4726
Wayne F. Cascio. Second edition, 1989. Shows the practical application of human resource theory and research.

★1321★ Managing Human Resources in Small and Mid-Sized Companies
American Management Association (AMA)
135 W. 50th St.
New York, NY 10020
Ph: (212)586-8100
Diane Arthur. 1987. Contains forms and tables. Includes a bibliography and an index.

★1322★ Manual of Personnel Policies, Procedures, and Operations
Prentice-Hall, Inc.
Rte. 9W
Englewood Cliffs, NJ 07632
Ph: (201)592-2000
Joseph D. Levesque. Second edition, 1993. Includes bibliographies and an index.

★1323★ The Mediation Process: Practical Strategies for Resolving Conflict
Jossey-Bass, Inc., Publishers
350 Samsone
San Francisco, CA 94104
Ph: (415)433-1767
Christopher W. Moore. 1987. Comprehensive guide to the principles and practices of mediation; offers strategies and techniques for every stage of the process. Presents an in-depth step-by-step account of how mediation is actually applied in resolving conflicts of all kinds, including family, divorce, labor-management, home-school, and landlord-tenant.

★1324★ Modern Personnel Checklists, With Commentary
Warren, Gorham and Lamont, Inc.
1 Penn Plaza
New York, NY 10119
Ph: (212)971-5000
Richard J. Melucci. Second edition, 1991 (loose-leaf). Includes an index.

★1325★ Personnel/Human Resource Management
Prentice-Hall, Inc.
Rte. 9W
Englewood Cliffs, NJ 07632
Ph: (201)592-2000
David A. DeCenzo and Stephen P. Robbins. Fifth edition, 1991. Illustrated. Includes bibliographies and indexes.

★1326★ Personnel Planning Guide: Successful Management of Your Most Important Asset
Upstart Publishing Co.
12 Portland St.
Dover, NH 03820
Ph: (603)749-5071
David H. Bangs, Jr. 1989. Includes forms and a bibliograph y.

★1327★ Recruiting, Training and Retaining New Employees: Managing the Transition From College to Work
Jossey-Bass, Inc., Publishers
350 Samsone
San Francisco, CA 94104
Ph: (415)433-1767
Jack J. Philips. 1987. Gives advice on developing a recruiting program that will draw the best-suited new grads into an organization and then retain them. Explains how to design and implement effective recruitment and entry-level training and development programs.

★1328★ Supervisor's Standard Reference Handbook
Prentice-Hall, Inc.
Rte. 9W
Englewood Cliffs, NJ 07632
Ph: (201)592-2000
W. H. Weiss. Second edition, 1988. Includes an index.

★1329★ The Trainer's Handbook: The AMA Guide to Effective Training
AMACOM
135 W. 50th St.
New York, NY 10020-1201
Ph: (212)903-8089   Fr: 800-262-9699
Gray Mitchell. 1992. Covers training, planning for training, and the management of training facilities, personnel, and operations. Presents workable solutions to many training problems.

★1330★ The Trainer's Professional Development Handbook
Jossey-Bass, Inc., Publishers
350 Sansome St.
San Francisco, CA 94104
Ph: (415)433-1740
Ray Bard et al. 1987. Part One gives step-by-step tips for planning professional growth and discusses career options and learning styles. Part Two is an extensive catalog of learning resources, complete with costs, ordering information, and suppliers addresses. Part Three, a concise encyclopedia of HRD and OD, summarizes the key concepts, theories, and contributions in the field.

PROFESSIONAL AND TRADE PERIODICALS

★1331★ The Arbitration Journal
American Arbitration Assn.
140 W. 51st St.
New York, NY 10020-1203
Ph: (212)484-4000   Fax: (212)765-4874
Jack A. Smith
Quarterly. Professional journal.

★1332★ The Better-Work Supervisor
Clement Communications, Inc.
Concord Industrial Park
PO Box 500
Concordville, PA 19331
Ph: (610)459-4200   Fax: (610)459-0936
Fr: 800-345-8101
Semimonthly. Provides advice and suggestions for supervisors on how to handle their employees and potential problems in the workplace. Features proven case histories, examples of typical management problems and solutions, ways to promote teamwork, and methods of inspiring confidence in workers. A minimum of five copies must be ordered.

★1333★ Bulletin to Management
Bureau of National Affairs, Inc. (BNA)
9435 Keywest
Rockville, MD 20850
Ph: (202)452-4358   Fax: (202)452-4603
Fr: 800-372-1033
Bill L. Manville
Weekly. Features summaries of current developments in human resource/personnel management and labor relations, including key court decisions, legislation, and collective bargaining. Provides information on "real-life job situations" and ready-to-use policy guides. Recurring features include statistics.

★1334★ Dynamic Supervision—Office and Staff Edition
Bureau of Business Practice
24 Rope Ferry Rd.
Waterford, CT 06386
Ph: (203)442-4365   Fax: (203)434-3078
Fr: 800-243-0876
Shelley Wolf
Semimonthly. Provides methods and techniques for supervision in an office setting.

★1335★ The EEO Review
John Wiley and Sons, Inc.
Subscription Dept.
605 3rd Ave.
New York, NY 10158
Ph: (212)850-6000   Fax: (212)850-6799
Sarah Magee
Monthly. Journal focussing on legal issues and policies that concern personnel managers and supervisors.

★1336★ Employee Benefits Alert
Research Institute of America
90 5th Ave., 10th Fl.
New York, NY 10011
Ph: (212)645-4800
Biweekly. Reports on up-to-date federal compliance rules and regulations and related information.

★1337★ Employee Benefits Journal
International Foundation of Employee Benefit Plans
PO Box 69
Brookfield, WI 53008-0069
Ph: (414)786-6700   Fax: (414)786-2990
Fr: 800-466-2366
Mary E. Brennan
Quarterly. Journal covering topics on employee benefits.

★1338★ Employee Benefits Report
Warren, Gorham and Lamont, Inc.
1 Penn Plaza
New York, NY 10119
Ph: (212)971-5000   Fax: (212)971-5025
David Beck
Monthly. Newsletter presenting articles on benefits and pensions for benefits and personnel specialists.

★1339★ Employee Relations and Human Resources Bulletin
Bureau of Business Practice
24 Rope Ferry Rd.
Waterford, CT 06386
Ph: (203)442-4365   Fax: (203)434-3078
Fr: 800-243-0876
Barbara Kelsey
Semimonthly. Explores the personnel and human relations field. Examines such topics as career planning, affirmative action, compensation practices, pensions, union disputes, and salary and benefit policies. Recurring features include a four-page supplement titled Management People are Talking About . . . , occasional interviews with top personnel directors, and a column that analyzes specific personnel legal cases. Also includes 3 special reports a year and a 24-page in-depth look at a single topic of interest in the human resources field.

★1340★ The Government Manager
Bureau of National Affairs, Inc. (BNA)
1231 25th St. NW
Washington, DC 20037
Ph: (202)452-4200   Fax: (202)822-8092
Fr: 800-372-1033
Anthony A. Harris
Biweekly. Covers developments in public sector human resource management. Recurring features include columns titled A Three Page Rundown, Working With People, Ground Rules, and Special Report.

★1341★ HR Focus
American Management Assn.
135 W. 50th St., 15th Fl.
New York, NY 10020
Ph: (212)903-8160   Fax: (212)903-8168
Bob Smith
Monthly. Newsletter focusing on personnel management.

★1342★ HRMagazine
Society for Human Resource Management
606 N. Washington St.
Alexandria, VA 22314
Ph: (703)548-3440   Fax: (703)836-0367
Ceel Pasternak
Monthly. Magazine for human resource management professionals.

★1343★ Human Resource Management News
Remy Publishing Company
350 W. Hubbard St., Ste. 440
Chicago, IL 60610
Ph: (312)464-0300   Fax: (312)464-0166
Fr: 800-542-6670
John V. Hickey
Weekly. Reports on employee relations, personnel administration, and industrial relations. Offers a telephone query service.

★1344★ IAPES News
International Assn. of Personnel in Employment Security
1801 Louisville Rd.
Frankfort, KY 40601
Ph: (502)223-4459   Fax: (502)223-4127
Michael R. Stone
Bimonthly. Magazine on employment security.

★1345★ Personnel Consultant
National Assn. of Personnel Consultants
3133 Mount Vernon Ave.
Alexandria, VA 22305-2540
Ph: (703)684-0180   Fax: (703)684-0071
J.P. Moery
Bimonthly. Private placement industry magazine.

★1346★ Personnel Journal
ACC Communications Inc.
245 Fischer Ave., B-2
Costa Mesa, CA 92626
Ph: (714)751-1883   Fax: (714)751-4106
Allan Halcrow
Monthly.

★1347★ Personnel Management
Bureau of National Affairs, Inc. (BNA)
1231 25th St. NW
Washington, DC 20037
Ph: (202)452-4238   Fax: (202)452-4603
Fr: 800-372-1033
Bill L. Manville
Biweekly. Provides legal clarification and practical advice on employers' pay and benefit policies, including detailed discussions of pertinent federal and state laws. Discusses such topics as health care compensation laws, pension law (ERISA), job evaluation, benefit plans, compensation administration, incentive systems, and independent contractors. Part of the BNA Policy and Practice Series; can be purchased alone or in any combination with other binder sets titled Compensation, Fair Employment Practices, Wages and Hours, and Labor Relations.

★1348★ Personnel Manager's Letter
Bureau of Business Practice
24 Rope Ferry Rd.
Waterford, CT 06386
Ph: (203)442-4365
Jill Whitney, Contact
Semimonthly. Provides the Human Resources manager with how-to information. Topics include benefits, training, recruiting, termination, and compensation policies. Recurring features include interviews, news of research and columns titled You Be the Judge, Workplace News, and Our Readers Ask.

★1349★ Supervisor's Guide to Employment Practices
Clement Communications, Inc.
Concord Industrial Park
Concordville, PA 19331
Ph: (215)459-4200   Fax: (610)459-0936
Fr: 800-345-8101
Biweekly. Provides information to managers and supervisors regarding sensitive human resource issues.

★1350★ Training & Development
American Society for Training and Development
1640 King St.
PO Box 1443
Alexandria, VA 22313
Ph: (703)683-8100   Fax: (703)683-8103
Patricia Galagan
Monthly. Magazine on training and development.

PROFESSIONAL MEETINGS AND CONVENTIONS

★1351★ American Management Association Human Resources Conference and Exhibition
Flagg Management, Inc.
PO Box 4440
New York, NY 10163
Ph: (212)286-0333   Fax: (212)286-0086
Annual. Always held during April.

★1352★ Best of America Human Resources Conference and Exposition
Lakewood Conferences
50 S. 9th St.
Minneapolis, MN 55402
Ph: (612)333-0471   Fax: (612)340-4759
Annual.

★1353★ International Registry of Organization Development Professionals Convention
International Registry of Organization Development Professionals
781 Beta Dr., Ste. K
Cleveland, OH 44143
Ph: (216)461-4333   Fax: (216)729-9319
Semiannual. Always held during May & July at George Williams College in Williams Bay, Wisconsin, and once a year internationally.

★1354★ Society for Human Resource Management's - Annual Conference and Exposition-The Leadership Challenge
Society for Human Resource Management
606 N. Washington St.
Alexandria, VA 22314
Ph: (703)548-3440   Fax: (703)836-0367
Annual. **Dates and Locations:** 1996 Jun 25-26; Chicago, IL. • 1997 Jun 22-25; San Diego, CA.

OTHER SOURCES OF INFORMATION

★1355★ *HR Words You Gotta Know!*
AMACOM
135 W. 50th St.
New York, NY 10020-1201
Ph: (212)903-8089   Fr: 800-262-9696

William R. Tracey. 1994. A glossary of human resource terms, laws, accronyms, and abbreviations.

★1356★ "Human Resources Management" in *Accounting to Zoology: Graduate Fields Defined* (pp. 39-40)
Petersons Guides, Inc.
PO Box 2123
Princeton, NJ 08543-2123
Ph: (609)243-9111   Fax: (609)243-9150
Fr: 800-338-3282

Amy J. Goldstein, editor. Revised and updated, 1987. Discusses types of graduate programs and degrees, graduate research, applied work, employment prospects and trends.

★1357★ "Human Resources Manager/ Executive" in *100 Best Jobs for the 1990s & Beyond*
Dearborn Financial Publishing, Inc.
520 N. Dearborn St.
Chicago, IL 60610-4354
Ph: (312)836-4400   Fax: (312)836-1021
Fr: 800-621-9621

Carol Kleiman. 1992. Describes 100 jobs ranging from accountants to veterinarians.

Each job profile includes such information as education, experience, and certification needed, salaries, and job search suggestions.

★1358★ "Industrial and Labor Relations" in *Accounting to Zoology: Graduate Fields Defined* (pp. 129-130)
Petersons Guides, Inc.
PO Box 2123
Princeton, NJ 08543-2123
Ph: (609)243-9111   Fax: (609)243-9150
Fr: 800-338-3282

Amy J. Goldstein, editor. Revised and updated, 1987. Discusses types of graduate programs and degrees, graduate research, applied work, employment prospects and trends.

Property and Real Estate Managers

Property and real estate managers control income-producing commercial and residential properties, and manage the communal property and services of condominium and community associations. They also plan and direct the purchase, development, and disposal of real estate for businesses. When owners of apartments, office buildings, retail and industrial properties, or condominiums lack the time or expertise to assume the day-to-day management of their real estate investments, they often hire a property manager, or contract for one's services with a real estate management company. Property managers act as the owners' agent and advisor for the property. Businesses employ real estate managers to locate, acquire, and develop real estate needed for their operations and to dispose of property no longer suited to their uses. Real estate managers employed by corporations that operate chains of restaurants, apparel and grocery stores, and gasoline service stations locate sites well suited for these types of establishments, and arrange to purchase or lease the property from the owners. Real estate managers who work for land development companies acquire land and plan the construction of shopping centers, houses and apartments, office buildings, or industrial parks. Real estate managers also work as land and permit agents for companies engaged in mining and quarrying, oil exploration, and constructing pipe and utility lines.

Salaries

Earnings vary greatly according to levels of responsibility. Median salaries include:

On-site apartment managers	$33,000/year
Property managers	$67,200/year
Property managers, shopping centers	$72,700/year
Property managers, office buildings	$75,200/year
Corporate real estate managers, restaurants	$62,300/year
Corporate real estate managers, apparel chains	$64,700/year

Employment Outlook

Growth rate until the year 2005: Faster than the average.

Property and Real Estate Managers

CAREER GUIDES

★1359★ Building Managers
Chronicle Guidance Publications, Inc.
66 Aurora St.
PO Box 1190
Moravia, NY 13118-1190
Ph: (315)497-0330   Fax: (315)497-3359
Fr: 800-622-7284

1994. Career brief describing the nature of the job, working conditions, hours and earnings, education and training, licensure, certification, unions, personal qualifications, social and psychological factors, location, employment outlook, entry methods, advancement, and related occupations.

**★1360★ "Building or Property Manager"
in VGM's Careers Encyclopedia (pp. 69-71)**
National Textbook Co. (NTC)
VGM Career Books
4255 W. Touhy Ave.
Lincolnwood, IL 60646-1975
Ph: (708)679-5500   Fax: (708)679-2494
Fr: 800-323-4900

Third edition, 1991. Describes job duties, places of employment, working conditions, qualifications, education, and training, advancement potential, and salary for each occupation.

**★1361★ "Building or Property Manager"
in VGM's Handbook of Business and Management Careers**
National Textbook Co.
4255 W. Touhy Ave.
Lincolnwood, IL 60646-1975
Ph: (708)679-5500   Fax: (708)679-2494
Fr: 800-323-4900

Annette Selden. Second edition, 1993. Contains 42 two-page occupational profiles describing job duties, places of employment, working conditions, qualifications, education, employment outlook, and income.

★1362★ Career Choices for the 90's for Students of Business
Walker and Co.
435 Hudson St.
New York, NY 10014
Ph: (212)727-8300   Fax: (212)727-0984
Fr: 800-289-2553

Compiled by Career Associates Staff. 1990. This book offers alternatives for students of business, including the career of underwriter. Gives information about the outlook and competition for entry-level candidates. Provides job hunting tips.

★1363★ Career Choices for the 90's for Students of Psychology
Walker and Co.
435 Hudson St.
New York, NY 10014
Ph: (212)727-8300   Fax: (212)727-0984
Fr: 800-289-2553

Compiled by Career Associates Staff. 1990. This book offers alternatives for students of psychology, including careers within the advertising field. Gives information about the outlook and competition for entry-level candidates. Provides job hunting tips.

★1364★ Compensation and Benefit Salary for Corporate Real Estate Executives
NACORE International
471 Spencer Dr. S., Ste. 8
West Palm Beach, FL 33409-6685
Ph: (407)683-8111

Annua1. Results of a survey of 900 corporate real estate executives representing 29 positions. Gives the type of company, annual sales, geographic area, education, age, and salary (overall average, overall medium, medium lower third, medium upper third) for 29 different job titles.

★1365★ Facilities Management Administrator
Building Owners and Managers Institute International (BOMII)
1521 Ritchie Hwy., Ste. 2A
Arnold, MD 21012
Ph: (301)974-1410

This booklet describes the course of study and procedure to become a designated Facilities Management Administrator.

**★1366★ "Industrial Property Manager"
in Guide to Federal Jobs (pp. 196)**
Resource Directories
3361 Executive Pkwy., Ste. 302
Toledo, OH 43606
Ph: (419)536-5353   Fax: (419)536-7056
Fr: 800-274-8515

Rod W. Durgin, editor. Third edition, 1992. Contains information on finding and applying for federal jobs. Describes more than 200 professional and technical jobs for college graduates. Covers the nature of the work, salary, and geographic location. Lists college majors preferred for that occupation. Section one describes the function and work of government agencies that hire the most significant number of college graduates.

★1367★ Opportunities in Property Management
National Textbook Co. (NTC)
VGM Career Books
4255 W. Touhy Ave.
Lincolnwood, IL 60646-1975
Ph: (708)679-5500   Fax: (708)679-2494
Fr: 800-323-4900

Mariwyn Evans. Explores opportunities in property management, including mall management and land acquisition and development. Includes information on training and typical career paths.

★1368★ "Property Management and Leasing" in *Opportunities in Real Estate Careers* **(pp. 86-89)**
National Textbook Co. (NTC)
VGM Career Books
4255 W. Touhy Ave.
Lincolnwood, IL 60646-1975
Ph: (708)679-5500   Fax: (708)679-2494
Fr: 800-323-4900

Mariwyn Evans. 1988. Gives an overview of the real estate industry. Describes jobs and specialties in the estate field. Lists schools and addresses to write to for more information.

★1369★ "Property Management" in *Your Successful Real Estate Career: Building a Future in Real Estate Sales*
AMACOM
135 W. 50th St.
New York, NY 10020-1201
Ph: (212)903-8089   Fr: 800-262-9699

Kenneth W. Edwards. 1992. Provides an overview of career opportunities in real estate. Gives tips on beginning and succeeding in real estate.

★1370★ *Property Manager*
Careers, Inc.
PO Box 135
Largo, FL 34649-0135
Ph: (813)584-7333

1991. Four-page brief offering the definition, history, duties, working conditions, personal qualifications, educational requirements, earnings, hours, employment outlook, advancement, and careers related to this position.

★1371★ "Property Manager" in *College Board Guide to Jobs and Career Planning* **(pp. 102-103)**
The College Board
45 Columbus Ave.
New York, NY 10023-6992
Ph: (212)713-8165   Fax: (212)713-8143
Fr: 800-323-7155

Second edition, 1994. Describes the job, salaries, related careers, education needed, and where to write for more information.

★1372★ "Property and Real Estate Managers" in *America's 50 Fastest Growing Jobs* **(p. 25)**
JIST Works, Inc.
720 N. Park Ave.
Indianapolis, IN 46202-3431
Ph: (317)264-3720   Fax: (317)264-3709
Fr: 800-648-5478

Michael J. Farr, compiler. 1994. Describes the 50 fastest growing jobs within major career clusters such as technicians, and marketing and sales. Each job profile explains the nature of the work, skills and abilities required, employment outlook, average earnings, related occupations, education and training requirements, and employment opportunities. Also contains career planning information and job search tips.

★1373★ "Property and Real Estate Managers" in *Best Jobs for the 1990s and Into the 21st Century*
Impact Publications
9104-N Manassas Dr.
Manassas Park, VA 22111
Ph: (703)361-7300   Fax: (703)335-9486

Ronald L. Krannich and Caryl Rae Krannich. 1993.

★1374★ "Property and Real Estate Managers" in *Career Discovery Encyclopedia* **(Vol.5, pp. 92-93)**
J.G. Ferguson Publishing Co.
200 W. Madison St., Ste. 300
Chicago, IL 60606
Ph: (312)580-5480   Fax: (312)580-4948

Russell E. Primm, editor-in chief. 1993. This six volume set contains two-page articles for 504 occupations. Each article describes job duties, earnings, and educational and training requirements. The whole set is arranged alphabetically by job title. Designed for junior high and older students.

★1375★ "Property and Real Estate Managers" in *Occupational Outlook Handbook*
U.S. Government Printing Office
Superintendent of Documents
Washington, DC 20402
Ph: (202)512-1800   Fax: (202)512-2250

Biennial; latest edition, 1994-95. Encyclopedia of careers describing more than 250 occupations and comprising about 85 percent of all jobs in the economy. Occupations that require lengthy education or training are given the most attention. Each occupation's profile describes what the worker does on the job, working conditions, education and training requirements, advancement possibilities, job outlook, earnings, and sources of additional information.

★1376★ *Real Estate: A VGM Career Planner*
National Textbook Co. (NTC)
VGM Career Books
4255 W. Touhy Ave.
Lincolnwood, IL 60646-1975
Ph: (708)679-5500   Fax: (708)679-2494
Fr: 800-323-4900

Mariwyn Evans. 1989. Part of the VGM Career Planner series. Provides information on different aspects of real estate, including: overview of the field, employment outlook, tips for career advancement, educational requirements, salary figures, and where to find more information.

★1377★ "Real Estate" in *Encyclopedia of Career Choices for the 1990s: A Guide to Entry Level Jobs* **(pp. 742-765)**
Berkley Pub.
PO Box 506
East Rutherford, NJ 07073
Fax: (201)933-2316   Fr: 800-788-6262

1992. Describes entry-level careers in a variety of industries. Presents qualifications required, working conditions, salary, internships, and professional associations.

★1378★ "Real Estate" in *Encyclopedia of Careers and Vocational Guidance*
J.G. Ferguson Publishing Co.
200 W. Madison St., Ste. 300
Chicago, IL 60606
Ph: (312)580-5480   Fax: (312)580-4948

William E. Hopke, editor-in-chief. Ninth edition, 1993. Four-volume set that profiles 900 occupations and describes job trends in 74 industries. Volume 1—*Industry Profiles*—contains the chapter "Real Estate" (p. 401). Includes career description, educational requirements, history of the job, methods of entry, advancement, employment outlook, earnings, conditions of work, social and psychological factors, and sources of further information.

★1379★ *Real Property Administrator*
Building Owners and Managers Institute
  International (BOMII)
1521 Ritchie Hwy., Ste. 3A
Arnold, MD 21012
Ph: (301)974-1410

Booklet that accompanies the course of study needed to become a designated Real Property Administrator (RPA).

★1380★ *Systems Maintenance Administrator*
Building Owners and Managers Institute
  International (BOMII)
1521 Ritchie Hwy., Ste. 3A
Arnold, MD 21012
Ph: (301)974-1410

Booklet that accompanies the courses of study and procedures to become a designated Systems Maintenance Technician or a Systems Maintenance Administrator.

★1381★ *Your Successful Real Estate Career*
American Management Association
135 W. 50th St.
New York, NY 10020
Ph: (212)903-8089

Kenneth W. Edwards. 1993.

PROFESSIONAL ASSOCIATIONS

★1382★ Apartment Owners and Managers Association of America (AOMA)
65 Cherry Plz.
Watertown, CT 06795-0238
Ph: (203)274-2589   Fax: (203)274-2580
Members: Builders who also manage the multifamily housing they construct; most members operate garden-type and mid-rise buildings constructed within the past two decades. **Publications:** *AOMA Newsletter*, monthly. • *Apartment Management Report*, monthly.

★1383★ Building Owners and Managers Association International (BOMA)
1201 New York Ave. NW, Ste. 300
Washington, DC 20005
Ph: (202)408-2662   Fax: (202)371-0181
Members: Owners, managers, investors, and developers of commercial office buildings. **Purpose:** Purpose is to promote the

office building industry as a business enterprise through mutual discussion and cooperation, education, dissemination of information, and establishment of standards of practice and performance. The Building Owners and Managers Institute, BOMA's educational arm, provides courses leading to RPA (Real Property Administrator), SMA (Systems Maintenance Administrator), and FMA (Facilities Maintenance Administrator) certifications. Conducts research programs. Operates placement service; maintains speakers' bureau; compiles statistics. Also maintains 20 sections including: Accounting Systems and Procedures; Corporate and Financial Buildings; Legislative and Urban Affairs; Office Building Leasing. **Publications:** *Buyer's Guide*, annual. • *Cleaning Study.* • *EOMA Office Market Review*, annual. • *Experience Exchange Report for Downtown and Suburban Office Buildings*, annual. • *Functional Accounting Guide and Chart of Accounts.* • *Office Tenant Moves and Changes.* • *Skylines*, monthly.

★1384★ **Community Associations Institute (CAI)**
1630 Duke St.
Alexandria, VA 22314
Ph: (703)548-8600   Fax: (703)684-1581
Members: Builders, developers, lawyers, accountants, condominium associations, homeowners associations, property managers, insurance and real estate agents, and government officials or agencies. **Purpose:** Purpose is to develop and provide the most advanced and effective guidance for the creation, financing, operation, and maintenance of the common facilities and services in condominiums, townhouse projects, planned unit developments, and open-space communities. Seeks to educate new owners about their responsibilities in order to attract more people to leadership positions within housing developments. Compiles statistics. **Publications:** *Board Briefs*, bimonthly. • *Common Ground*, bimonthly. • *Community Association Law Reporter*, monthly. • *Creating a Community Association.* • *Financial Management of Associations.* • *Ledger Quarterly.*

★1385★ **Institute of Real Estate Management (IREM)**
430 N. Michigan Ave.
Chicago, IL 60611-4090
Ph: (312)329-6000   Fax: (312)661-0217
Members: Professional organization of real property and asset managers. **Purpose:** Awards professional designation CERTIFIED PROPERTY MANAGER (CPM) to qualifying individuals and ACCREDITED MANAGEMENT ORGANIZATION (AMO) to qualifying management firms. Also awards ACCREDITED RESIDENTIAL MANAGER which recognizes outstanding residential site managers. Monitors legislation affecting real estate management. Maintains software vendor self-certification program. Offers management courses and seminars; conducts research and educational programs; supports formal code of ethics; compiles statistics; maintains speakers' bureau and job referral service. **Publications:** *AMO Presepective.* • *Annual Apartment Building, Office Building, Condominium/Cooperative, Shopping Center, and Federally-Assisted Apartment Income/Expense Analyses*, annual. • *ARM*

News, 7/year. • *The Bulletin*, 10/year. • *Catalog of Courses and Publications*, annual. • *CPM, AMO, and ARM Profiles/Compensation Studies*, triennial. • *CPM Aspects*, bimonthly. • *Hot Topics*, 3/year. • *Journal of Property Management*, bimonthly.

★1386★ **Nacore International (NACORE)**
440 Columbia Dr., Ste. 100
West Palm Beach, FL 33409
Ph: (407)683-8111   Fax: (407)697-4853
Members: Executives, attorneys, real estate department heads, architects, engineers, analysts, researchers, and anyone responsible for the management, administration, and operation of national and regional real estate departments of national and international corporations. **Purpose:** Provides a meeting ground for the exchange of ideas, experience, and problems among members; encourages professionalism within corporate real estate through education and communication; protects the interests of corporate realty in dealing with adversaries, public or private; maintains contact with other real estate organizations; publicizes the availability of fully qualified members to the job market. Maintains Institute for Corporate Real Estate as educational arm. Conducts seminars, including concentrated workshops on the corporate real estate field. Compiles statistics; sponsors competitions; maintains biographical archives and placement service. **Publications:** *Corporate Real Estate Executive*, 9/year. • *Placement Northwestern*, monthly. • *Welcome! Program*, annual. • *Who's Who in Corporate Real Estate*, annual.

★1387★ **National Apartment Association (NAA)**
1111 14th St. NW, Ste. 900
Washington, DC 20005
Ph: (202)842-4050   Fax: (202)842-4056
Members: Federation of 150 state and local associations of industry professionals engaged in all aspects of the multifamily housing industry, including owners, builders, investors, developers, managers, and allied service representatives. **Purpose:** Provides education and certification for property management executives, on-site property managers, maintenance personnel, property supervisors, and leasing agents. Offers a nationwide legislative network concerned with governmental decisions at the federal, state, and local levels. **Publications:** *NAA Organizational Manual*, annual. • *Survey of Income and Operation Expenses in Rental Apartment Communities*, annual. • *UNITS*, 9/year.

★1388★ **National Association of Home Builders of the U.S. (NAHB)**
1201 15th St. NW
Washington, DC 20005
Ph: (202)822-0200   Fax: (202)822-0559
Members: Single and multifamily home builders, commercial builders, and others associated with the building industry. **Purpose:** Lobbies on behalf of the housing industry and conducts public affairs activities to increase public understanding of housing and the economy. Collects and disseminates data on current developments in home building and home builders' plans through its Economics Department and nationwide Metropolitan Housing Forecast. Maintains NAHB Re-

search Center, which functions as the research arm of the home building industry. Sponsors seminars and workshops on construction, mortgage credit, labor relations, cost reduction, land use, remodeling, and business management. Compiles statistics; offers charitable program, spokesman training, and placement service; maintains speakers' bureau, and hall of fame. Subsidiaries include Home Builders Institute and National Council of the Housing Industry. Maintains over 50 committees in many areas of construction; operates National Commercial Builders Council, National Council of the Multifamily Housing Industry, National Remodelers Council and National Sales and Marketing Council. **Publications:** *Builder Magazine*, monthly. • *Forecast of Housing Activity*, monthly. • *Housing Economics*, monthly. • *Housing Market Statistics*, monthly. • *Nation's Building News*, semi-monthly. • *Reference Guide to Homebuilding Articles*, quarterly.

STANDARDS/CERTIFICATION AGENCIES

★1389★ **Building Owners and Managers Association International (BOMA)**
1201 New York Ave. NW, Ste. 300
Washington, DC 20005
Ph: (202)408-2662   Fax: (202)371-0181
Purpose is to promote the office building industry as a business enterprise through mutual discussion and cooperation, education, dissemination of information, and establishment of standards of practice and performance. The Building Owners and Managers Institute, BOMA's educational arm, provides courses leading to RPA (Real Property Administrator), SMA (Systems Maintenance Administrator), and FMA (Facilities Maintenance Administrator) certifications.

★1390★ **Community Associations Institute (CAI)**
1630 Duke St.
Alexandria, VA 22314
Ph: (703)548-8600   Fax: (703)684-1581
Purpose is to develop and provide the most advanced and effective guidance for the creation, financing, operation, and maintenance of the common facilities and services in condominiums, townhouse projects, planned unit developments, and open-space communities.

★1391★ **Institute of Real Estate Management (IREM)**
430 N. Michigan Ave.
Chicago, IL 60611-4090
Ph: (312)329-6000   Fax: (312)661-0217
Monitors legislation affecting real estate management. Maintains software vendor self-certification program. Offers management courses and seminars; conducts research and educational programs; supports formal code of ethics; compiles statistics; maintains speakers' bureau and job referral service.

★1392★ National Apartment Association (NAA)
1111 14th St. NW, Ste. 900
Washington, DC 20005
Ph: (202)842-4050   Fax: (202)842-4056
Provides education and certification for property management executives, on-site property managers, maintenance personnel, property supervisors, and leasing agents.

Test Guides

★1393★ Barron's How to Prepare for Real Estate Licensing Examinations: Salesperson and Broker
Barron's Educational Series, Inc.
250 Wireless Blvd.
Hauppauge, NY 11788
Ph: (516)434-3311   Fax: (516)434-3723
Fr: 800-645-3476
Bruce J. Lindeman. Fourth edition, 1990. Study guide containing five practice tests; includes forms and maps.

★1394★ Career Examination Series: Principal Real Estate Manager
National Learning Corp.
212 Michael Dr.
Syosset, NY 11791
Ph: (516)921-8888   Fax: (516)921-8743
Fr: 800-645-6337
Jack Rudman. 1993. Test guide including questions and answers for students or professionals in the field who seek advancement through examination.

★1395★ Career Examination Series: Real Estate Management Trainee
National Learning Corp.
212 Michael Dr.
Syosset, NY 11791
Ph: (516)921-8888   Fax: (516)921-8743
Fr: 800-645-6337
Jack Rudman. 1993. Test guide including questions and answers for students or professionals in the field who seek advancement through examination.

★1396★ Career Examination Series: Real Property Manager
National Learning Corp.
212 Michael Dr.
Syosset, NY 11791
Ph: (516)921-8888   Fax: (516)921-8743
Fr: 800-645-6337
Jack Rudman. A series of study guides with multiple-choice examination questions and solutions for trainees and professional property and real estate managers. Titles in the series include *Assistant Housing Manager; Assistant Real Estate Agent; Associate Real Property Manager; Building Manager; Housing Management Assistant; Housing Management Representative; Housing Manager; Land Management Specialist; Principal Buildings Manager; Principal Land Management Specialist; Public Buildings Manager; Real Estate Manager; Senior Housing Management Assistant; Senior Housing Management Representative; Senior Land Management Specialist; Senior Real Estate Manager; Supervising Real Estate Manager.*

★1397★ Career Examination Series: Senior Real Estate Agent
National Learning Corp.
212 Michael Dr.
Syosset, NY 11791
Ph: (516)921-8888   Fax: (516)921-8743
Fr: 800-645-6337
Jack Rudman. 1991. Part of the Career Examination Series. A study guide for professionals and trainees in the field of real estate. Includes a multiple-choice examination section; provides answers.

Awards, Scholarships, Grants, and Fellowships

★1398★ BOMA International Awards Program
Building Owners and Managers Association International
1201 New York Ave. NW, Ste. 300
Washington, DC 20005
Ph: (202)408-2662   Fax: (202)371-0181
To salute excellence in the office building industry. Each year, three awards are presented. The Office Building of the Year Award (TOBY Awards) are given to honor an outstanding example of a commercial office building in each of four size categories (under 100,000 square feet, 100,000 to 249,999 square feet, 250,000 to 500,000 square feet, and over 500,000 square feet); rehabilitated/modernized buildings; corporate headquarters facilities; historical buildings; medical office buildings; government buildings; and suburban office parks. The building must be at least three years old from the date of occupancy of the first tenant by June of the current competition year and must not have won at the international level during the past 10 years. The building must be a member, or be managed by an entity, that is a member in good standing of both the local BOMA association and BOMA International. Buildings entering the historical category must be at least 50 years old. Each local BOMA association may submit one building in each category to the Regional panel of judges. Each Regional Conference submits winners to the International panel of judges. Three major factors are considered in judging: building management, efficiency of operation, and impact on the community. Judging occurs at the regional and international levels. Trophies are presented annually at the International Convention in June. The Outstanding Local Member of the Year Award is given to honor members of a local BOMA association who have demonstrated leadership skills, participated in local association activities as officers or committee members, contributed time and talent to their field, written articles on their field, and shown an interest in keeping up-to-date by participating in educational programs. The award, given to all regional winners, recognizes activity during the previous year rather than service rendered over many years. Judging occurs at the local and regional levels. The Association of the Year Award is also given to honor a local BOMA association that has done an outstanding job

of keeping its members informed through programs, educational opportunities, and social activities at the regional or national levels; participated in government affairs at any level; and has shown evidence of responsible financial planning. Awarded annually at the International Convention in June. Established in 1985.

★1399★ Presidents Award
Building Owners and Managers Association International
1201 New York Ave. NW, Ste. 300
Washington, DC 20005
Ph: (202)408-2662   Fax: (202)371-0181
To recognize outstanding achievement in the field of commercial real estate development and management. Members and nonmembers are eligible. A parchment certificate is awarded annually. The award is presented at the President's discretion. Established in 1975.

Basic Reference Guides and Handbooks

★1400★ Corporate Real Estate Handbook: Strategies for Improving Bottom-Line Performance
McGraw-Hill, Inc.
1221 Avenue of the Americas
New York, NY 10020
Ph: (212)512-2000   Fr: 800-722-4726
Robert A. Silverman, editor. 1987. Basic guide that describes how proper management of a corporation's real estate assets can contribute to the organization's profits.

★1401★ Dictionary of Real Estate Terms
Barrons' Educational Series, Inc.
250 Wireless Blvd.
Hauppauge, NY 11788
Ph: (516)434-3311   Fax: (516)434-3723
Fr: 800-645-3476
Jack P. Friedman, Jack C. Harris, and J. Bruce Lindeman. 1993. Second revised edition, 1987. Defines 1200 words and phrases.

★1402★ Facilities Maintenance Management
R. S. Means Co., Inc.
100 Construction Plaza
Kingston, MA 02364
Ph: (617)585-7880
Gregory H. Magee, edited by William Mahoney. 1988. How-to guide to planning and executing a comprehensive maintenance management program. Discusses the interior building components and operating systems and also the exterior structure and facilities, such as parking lots.

★1403★ Facilities Planning
AMACOM
135 W. 50th St.
New York, NY 10020-1201
Ph: (212)903-8089   Fr: 800-262-9699
Roger L. Brauer. 1992. Describes how to identify and define user requirements, how to compile user requirement data, and how to employ the user requirements method in fea-

sibility studies, design review, building evaluation, and facilities and space management. Helps to translate user's needs into concrete space and equipment specifications.

★1404★ **The Guide to Real Estate Exchanging**
John Wiley and Sons, Inc.
605 3rd Ave.
New York, NY 10158-0012
Ph: (212)850-6000   Fax: (212)850-6088
Fr: 800-526-5368
Jack Cummings. 1991. Discusses many different angles of real estate investing.

★1405★ **Handbook of Real Estate (Encyclopedia of Terms)**
National Learning Corp.
212 Michael Dr.
Syosset, NY 11791
Ph: (516)921-8888   Fax: (516)921-8743
Fr: 800-645-6337
Jack Rudman. Part of the Admission Test series. A sample test for those who are seeking admission to graduate and professional schools or seeking entrance or advancement in institutional and public career service in the field of real estate.

★1406★ **Landlording: A Handy Manual for Scrupulous Landlords and Landladies Who Do It Themselves**
Express
PO Box 1639
El Cerrito, CA 94530-4639
Ph: (510)236-5496
Leigh Robinson. 1994. Includes a bibliography and an index. Illustrated.

★1407★ **The Landlord's Handbook: A Complete Guide to Managing Small Residential Properties**
Dearborn Financial Publishing, Inc.
520 Dearborn St.
Chicago, IL 60610
Ph: (312)836-0490
Daniel Goodwin and Richard Rusdorf. 1989. Includes a bibliography and an index.

★1408★ **Planned Maintenance for Productivity and Energy Conservation**
Fairmont Press, Inc.
700 Indian Trail
Lilburn, GA 30247
Ph: (404)925-9388
John Criswell. Third edition, 1989. This handbook provides a comprehensive set of guidelines that will aid efficiency of all aspects of a building maintenance program. Explains how to obtain maximum benefits from preventative and emergency maintenance; reduce utility costs through improving maintenance performance; and implement measures for effective energy conservation.

★1409★ **Rental Management Made Easy**
Tower Publishing Co.
34 Diamond St.
PO Box 7220
Portland, ME 04101
Ph: (207)774-9813   Fax: (207)775-1740
W.G. Roberts, editor. 1992.

PROFESSIONAL AND TRADE PERIODICALS

★1410★ **Buildings**
Stamats Communications, Inc.
427 6th Ave. SE
PO Box 1888
Cedar Rapids, IA 52406
Ph: (319)364-6167   Fax: (319)364-4278
Linda Monroe
Monthly. Publication featuring management techniques, development, and ownership of facilities.

★1411★ **CPM Aspects**
Institute of Real Estate Management
PO Box 109025
Chicago, IL 60610-9025
Ph: (312)329-6055   Fax: (312)661-0217
Pam Chwedyk
Bimonthly. Discusses new trends in real estate management and asset fair housing, including management techniques, rent control, government-subsidized housing, environmental and ethnic issues. Covers federal, state, and local legislation affecting real estate management. Informs members of Institute activities and programs. Recurring features include a column entitled Jobs Bulletin.

★1412★ **Journal of Property Management**
Institute of Real Estate Management
430 N. Michigan Ave.
Chicago, IL 60611
Ph: (312)661-1930   Fax: (312)661-0217
Mariwyn Evans
Bimonthly. Magazine serving real estate managers.

★1413★ **Mr. Landlord**
Home Rental Publishing
PO Box 1366
Norfolk, VA 23501
Ph: (804)467-1427
Jeffrey E. Taylor
Monthly. Covers all aspects of management of small rental properties.

★1414★ **The Property Professional**
National Property Management Association
380 Main St., Ste. 290
Dunedin, FL 34698
Ph: (813)736-3788
James Lerch
Bimonthly. Provides information on government/contractor property asset management. Carries news of courses, seminars, personalities in the field, and the activities of the Association and its chapters. Recurring features include editorials, news of members, and calendar of events.

★1415★ **Units**
National Apartment Assn.
1111 14th St. NW, Ste. 900
Washington, DC 20005
Ph: (202)842-4050   Fax: (202)842-4056
Stephanie Oetjen
Bimonthly. Magazine for the rental housing industry. Aimed at owners, management firms, and management personnel of multifamily housing. Includes but is not limited to the NAA.

PROFESSIONAL MEETINGS AND CONVENTIONS

★1416★ **Building Owners and Managers Association International Annual Convention and the Office Building Show**
Production Group International
2200 Wilson Blvd., Ste. 200
Arlington, VA 22201-3324
Ph: (703)528-8484   Fax: (703)528-1724
Annual. Usually held during the third week of June. **Dates and Locations:** 1996 Jun 23-26; Boston, MA.

★1417★ **Nacore International Symposium and Exposition**
NACORE International (West Palm Beach)
440 Columbia Dr., Ste. 100
West Palm Beach, FL 33409-1968
Ph: (407)683-8111
Annual. **Dates and Locations:** 1995; Los Angeles, CA. • 1996; Chicago, IL.

★1418★ **PMEXPO - Property Management Exposition**
Bachner Communications
8811 Colesville Rd.
Silver Spring, MD 20910
Ph: (301)587-6543   Fax: (301)589-2017
Annual. Always held during late September at the Capital Centre, in Landover, Maryland.

OTHER SOURCES OF INFORMATION

★1419★ **"Real Estate"** in *Accounting to Zoology: Graduate Fields Defined* (pp. 46-47)
Petersons Guides, Inc.
PO Box 2123
Princeton, NJ 08543-2123
Ph: (609)243-9111   Fax: (609)243-9150
Fr: 800-338-3282
Amy J. Goldstein, editor. Revised and updated, 1987. Discusses types of graduate programs and degrees, graduate research, applied work, employment prospects and trends.

Purchasers and Buyers

Purchasers and buyers, sometimes called **industrial buyers**, purchase the goods, materials, supplies, and services that are required by their organization. They insure that products are of suitable quality and sufficient quantity, secured at the right price, and available when needed. Purchasing agents and managers use computers to obtain current product and price listings, to track inventory, and to process orders.

Salaries

Median annual salaries vary between private sector and federal jobs, with government workers earning less.

Lowest 10 percent	Less than $13,959/year
Median	$33,067/year
Top 10 percent	More than $56,581/year
Federal government	$24,400/year
Contract specialists, federal government	$43,800/year

Employment Outlook

Growth rate until the year 2005: More slowly than the average.

Purchasers and Buyers

CAREER GUIDES

★1420★ "International Purchasing" in Opportunities in International Business Careers (pp. 85-87)
National Textbook Co. (NTC)
VGM Career Books
4255 W. Touhy Ave.
Lincolnwood, IL 60646-1975
Ph: (708)679-5500   Fax: (708)679-2494
Fr: 800-323-4900
Jeffry S. Arpan. 1989. Describes what types of jobs exist in international business, where they are located, what challenges and rewards they bring, and how to prepare for and obtain jobs in international business.

★1421★ Opportunities in Purchasing Careers
National Textbook Co. (NTC)
VGM Career Books
4255 W. Touhy Ave.
Lincolnwood, IL 60646-1975
Ph: (708)679-5500   Fax: (708)679-2494
Fr: 800-323-4900
Kent B. Banning. 1990. Part of the VGM Opportunities series.

★1422★ Procurement Career Development Handbook
U.S. Department of the Treasury
Washington, DC 20219
1988.

★1423★ "Purchasers and Buyers" in Occupational Outlook Handbook
U.S. Government Printing Office
Superintendent of Documents
Washington, DC 20402
Ph: (202)512-1800   Fax: (202)512-2250
Biennial; latest edition, 1994-95. Encyclopedia of careers describing more than 225 occupations and comprising about 80 percent of all jobs in the economy. Occupations that require lengthy education or training are given the most attention. Each occupation's profile describes what the worker does on the job, working conditions, education and training requirements, advancement possibilities, job

outlook, earnings, and sources of additional information.

★1424★ Purchasing Agent
Vocational Biographies, Inc.
PO Box 31
Sauk Centre, MN 56378-0031
Ph: (612)352-6516   Fax: (612)352-5546
Fr: 800-255-0752
1993. Four-page pamphlet containing a personal narrative about a worker's job, work likes and dislikes, career path from high school to the present. Education and training, the rewards and frustrations, and the effects of the job on the rest of the worker's life. The data file portion of this pamphlet gives a concise occupational summary, including work descriptions, working conditions, places of employment, personal characteristics, education and training, job outlook, and salary range.

★1425★ "Purchasing Agent" in Guide to Federal Technical, Trades and Labor Jobs (p. 197)
Resource Directories
3361 Executive Pkwy., Ste. 302
Toledo, OH 43606
Ph: (419)536-5353   Fax: (419)536-7056
Fr: 800-274-8515
Rod W. Durgin, editor-in-chief. 1992. Describes where and how to apply for a federal job as a purchasing agent. For each job included, gives a description, salary, locations, and the agencies that hire the most employees for that job.

★1426★ "Purchasing Agent" in Jobs Rated Almanac
World Almanac
1 International Blvd., Ste. 444
Mahwah, NJ 07495
Ph: (201)529-6900   Fax: (201)529-6901
Les Krantz. Second edition, 1992. Ranks 250 jobs by environment, salary, outlooks, physical demands, stress, security, travel opportunities, and extra perks. Includes jobs the editor feels are the most common, most interesting, and the most rapidly growing.

★1427★ "Purchasing Agent" in VGM's Careers Encyclopedia (pp. 384-386)
National Textbook Co. (NTC)
VGM Career Books
4255 W. Touhy Ave.
Lincolnwood, IL 60646-1975
Ph: (708)679-5500   Fax: (708)679-2494
Fr: 800-323-4900
Third edition, 1991. Describes job duties, places of employment, working conditions, qualifications, education, and training, advancement potential, and salary for each occupation.

★1428★ "Purchasing Agent" in VGM's Handbook of Business and Management Careers
National Textbook Co.
4255 W. Touhy Ave.
Lincolnwood, IL 60646-1975
Ph: (708)679-5500   Fax: (708)679-2494
Fr: 800-323-4900
Annette Selden. Second edition, 1993. Contains 42 two-page occupational profiles describing job duties, places of employment, working conditions, qualifications, education, employment outlook, and income.

★1429★ "Purchasing Agents" in American Almanac of Jobs and Salaries (p. 358)
Avon Books
1350 Avenue of the Americas
New York, NY 10019
Ph: (212)261-6800   Fr: 800-238-0658
John Wright, editor. Revised and updated, 1994-95. This is a comprehensive guide to the wages of hundreds of occupations in a wide variety of industries and organizations.

★1430★ "Purchasing Agents" in Career Discovery Encyclopedia (Vol.5, pp. 114-115)
J.G. Ferguson Publishing Co.
200 W. Madison St., Ste. 300
Chicago, IL 60606
Ph: (312)580-5480   Fax: (312)580-4948
Russell E. Primm, editor-in chief. 1993. This six volume set contains two-page articles for 504 occupations. Each article describes job duties, earnings, and educational and training requirements. The whole set is arranged al-

phabetically by job title. Designed for junior high and older students.

★1431★ "Purchasing Agents" in *Career Information Center* (Vol.10)
Simon and Schuster
200 Old Tappan Rd.
Old Tappan, NJ 07675
Fax: 800-445-6991   Fr: 800-223-2348
Richard Lidz and Linda Perrin, editorial directors. Fifth edition, 1993. This 13-volume set profiles over 600 occupations. Each occupational profile describes job duties, educational requirements, how to get the job, advancement possibilities, employment outlook, working conditions, earnings and benefits, and where to write for more information.

★1432★ "Purchasing Agents" in *Encyclopedia of Careers and Vocational Guidance* (Vol.4, pp. 208-211)
J. G. Ferguson Publishing Co.
200 W. Monroe, Ste. 250
Chicago, IL 60606
Ph: (312)580-5480
William Hopke, editor-in-chief. Eighth edition, 1990. Four-volume set that profiles 900 occupations and describes job trends in 76 industries. Includes career description, educational requirements, history of the job, methods of entry, advancement, employment outlook, earnings, conditions of work, social and psychological factors, and sources of further information.

★1433★ "Purchasing Agents" in *Jobs! What They Are—Where They Are— What They Pay* (p. 242)
Simon & Schuster, Inc.
Simon & Schuster Bldg.
1230 Avenue of the Americas
New York, NY 10020
Ph: (212)698-7000   Fr: 800-223-2348
Robert O. Snelling and Anne M. Snelling. 3rd edition, 1992. Describes duties and responsibilities, earnings, employment opportunities, training, and qualifications.

★1434★ "Purchasing Agents and Managers" in *101 Careers: A Guide to the Fastest-Growing Opportunities* (pp. 45-47)
John Wiley & Sons, Inc.
605 3rd Ave.
New York, NY 10158-0012
Ph: (212)850-6645   Fax: (212)850-6088
Michael Harkavy. 1990. Describes the nature of the job, working conditions, employment growth, qualifications, personal skills, projected salaries, and where to write for more information.

★1435★ "Purchasing Director/Materials Manager" in *Opportunities in Hospital Administration Careers* (pp. 37-38)
National Textbook Co. (NTC)
VGM Career Books
4255 W. Touhy Ave.
Lincolnwood, IL 60646-1975
Ph: (708)679-5500   Fax: (708)679-2494
Fr: 800-323-4900
I. Donald Snook. 1989. Describes hospital administration in varied work settings. Covers educational preparation, skills, compensation, getting started in the profession, and job hunting.

★1436★ "Purchasing Manager" in *BLR Encyclopedia of Prewritten Job Descriptions*
Business and Legal Reports, Inc.
39 Academy St.
Madison, CT 06443-1513
Ph: (203)245-7448
Stephen D. Bruce, editor-in-chief. 1994. This book contains hundreds of sample job descriptions arranged by functional job category. The 1-3 page job descriptions cover what the worker normally does in the position, who they report to, and how that position fits in the organizational structure.

★1437★ "Purchasing Manager" in *College Board Guide to Jobs and Career Planning* (pp. 104-105)
The College Board
45 Columbus Ave.
New York, NY 10023-6992
Ph: (212)713-8165   Fax: (212)713-8143
Fr: 800-323-7155
Second edition, 1994. Describes the job, salaries, related careers, education needed, and where to write for more information.

★1438★ *Purchasing Managers (Agents)*
Chronicle Guidance Publications, Inc.
66 Aurora St.
PO Box 1190
Moravia, NY 13118-1190
Ph: (315)497-0330   Fax: (315)497-3359
Fr: 800-622-7284
1994. Career brief describing the nature of the job, working conditions, hours and earnings, education and training, licensure, certification, unions, personal qualifications, social and psychological factors, location, employment outlook, entry methods, advancement, and related occupations.

★1439★ "Purchasing" in *Opportunities in Airline Careers* (pp. 23-25)
National Textbook Co. (NTC)
VGM Career Books
4255 W. Touhy Ave.
Lincolnwood, IL 60646-1975
Ph: (708)679-5500   Fax: (708)679-2494
Fr: 800-323-4900
Adrian A. Paradis. 1987. Gives an overview of the airline industry including job opportunities and salaries. Describes careers in management, finance, sales, customer service and safety.

Professional Associations

★1440★ American Purchasing Society (APS)
11910 Oak Trail Way
Port Richey, FL 34668
Ph: (813)862-7998   Fax: (813)862-8199
Purpose: Seeks to certify qualified purchasing personnel. Maintains speakers' bureau and placement service. Conducts research programs; compiles statistics including salary surveys. Provides consulting service for purchasing, materials management, and marketing. **Publications:** *Cost Cutter*, quarterly. • *Directory of Buyers and Purchasing Executives*, biennial. • *50 Tips for Outstanding Pur-*

chasing. • *How to Become a Smart MRO Buyer.* • *Professional Purchasing*, monthly. • *The Search of How to Get a Higher Salary.* • *10 Checklists for Buyers and Purchasing Managers.* • *25 Cost Saving Tips for Businesses.* • *What a Salesperson Should Know about the Law.*

★1441★ National Association of Purchasing Management (NAPM)
2055 E. Centennial Cir.
PO Box 22160
Tempe, AZ 85285-2160
Ph: (602)752-6276   Fax: (602)752-7890
Fr: 800-888-6276
Members: Purchasing and materials managers for industrial, commercial, and utility firms; educational institutions and government agencies. **Purpose:** Disseminates information on procurement. Works to develop more efficient purchasing methods. Conducts program for certification as a purchasing manager. Cosponsors executive purchasing management institutes at Michigan State University, Cornell University, University of North Carolina, Arizona State University, and the University of California at Los Angeles. Provides in-company training. Maintains speakers' bureau and reference service. **Publications:** *International Journal of Purchasing and Materials Management*, quarterly. • *NAPM Insights*, monthly. • *Report on Business*, monthly.

★1442★ National Contract Management Association (NCMA)
1912 Woodford Rd.
Vienna, VA 22182
Ph: (703)448-9231   Fax: (703)448-0939
Members: Individuals concerned with administration, procurement, acquisition, negotiation, and management of government contracts and subcontracts. **Purpose:** Works for the education, improvement, and professional development of members and nonmembers through national and chapter programs, symposia, and workshops. Develops training materials to serve the procurement field. Offers certification in Contract Management (CPCM and CACM) designations. Conducts annual education seminar in 80 locations throughout the U.S. Operates speakers' bureau; maintains job listing service. **Publications:** *Contract Management*, monthly. • *National Contract Management Journal*, semiannual.

★1443★ National Institute of Governmental Purchasing (NIGP)
11800 Sunrise Valley Dr., Ste. 1050
Reston, VA 22091
Ph: (703)715-9400   Fax: (703)715-9897
Fr: 800-FOR-NIGP
Members: Federal, state, provincial, county, and local government buying agencies; hospital, school, prison, and public utility purchasing agencies in the U.S. and Canada. **Purpose:** Develops simplified standards and specifications for governmental buying; promotes uniform purchasing laws and procedures; conducts specialized education and research programs. Conducts certification program for Certified Professional Public Buyer (CPPB) and Certified Public Purchasing Officer (CPPO); offers consulting services and cost-saving programs and tools for governmental agencies, including purchasing

software for desktop computers. Maintains specifications library for public purchasing. Maintains speakers' bureau; compiles statistics. **Publications:** *Chapter Networker.* • *Government Procurement*, quarterly. • *Technical Bulletin*, bimonthly.

STANDARDS/CERTIFICATION AGENCIES

★1444★ National Association of Purchasing Management (NAPM)
2055 E. Centennial Cir.
PO Box 22160
Tempe, AZ 85285-2160
Ph: (602)752-6276   Fax: (602)752-7890
Fr: 800-888-6276

Conducts program for certification as a purchasing manager.

★1445★ National Contract Management Association (NCMA)
1912 Woodford Rd.
Vienna, VA 22182
Ph: (703)448-9231   Fax: (703)448-0939

Develops training materials to serve the procurement field. Offers certification in Contract Management (CPCM and CACM) designations. Conducts annual education seminar in 80 locations throughout the U.S. Operates speakers' bureau; maintains job listing service.

★1446★ National Institute of Governmental Purchasing (NIGP)
11800 Sunrise Valley Dr., Ste. 1050
Reston, VA 22091
Ph: (703)715-9400   Fax: (703)715-9897
Fr: 800-FOR-NIGP

Develops simplified standards and specifications for governmental buying; promotes uniform purchasing laws and procedures; conducts specialized education and research programs. Conducts certification program for Certified Professional Public Buyer (CPPB) and Certified Public Purchasing Officer (CPPO); offers consulting services and cost-saving programs and tools for governmental agencies.

TEST GUIDES

★1447★ *Career Examination Series: Purchasing Agent*
National Learning Corp.
212 Michael Dr.
Syosset, NY 11791
Ph: (516)921-8888   Fax: (516)921-8743
Fr: 800-645-6337

Jack Rudman. A series of study guides with multiple-choice examination questions and solutions for trainees and professional pur-

chasing agents and managers. Titles in the series include *Assistant Purchasing Agent; Chief Purchasing Agent; Director of Purchasing; Medical Purchasing Specialist; Principal Purchasing Agent; Purchasing Agent (Food); Purchasing Agent (Lumber); Purchasing Agent (Medical); Purchasing Agent (Printing); Purchasing Supervisor; School Purchasing Agent.*

BASIC REFERENCE GUIDES AND HANDBOOKS

★1448★ *The Purchasing Handbook*
McGraw-Hill Inc.
11 W. 19 St.
New York, NY 10011
Ph: 800-722-4726

Harold Fearon. 1993.

PROFESSIONAL AND TRADE PERIODICALS

★1449★ *American Logistics Association—Executive Briefing*
American Logistics Association
1133 15th St. NW, Ste. 640
Washington, DC 20005
Ph: (202)466-2520   Fax: (202)296-4419
Patricia M. Bartosch

Monthly. Carries articles intended to promote cooperation between the Defense Department and the industries with which it does business. Recurring features include statistics.

★1450★ *Buying Strategy Forecast*
Purchasing Magazine
275 Washington St.
Newton, MA 02158
Ph: (617)558-4650   Fax: (617)558-4327
Tom Stundza

Biweekly. Provides purchasing managers with price and supply forecasts, industrial commodity market analyses, manufacturing outlooks, and buying strategies to cut costs and increase company profits. Alerts readers to spot shortages, favorably priced items, and product changes.

★1451★ *Purchasing Executive's Bulletin*
Bureau of Business Practice
24 Rope Ferry Rd.
Waterford, CT 06386
Ph: (203)442-4365   Fax: (203)434-3078
Fr: 800-243-0876
Wayne Muller

Semimonthly. Profiles the practices of successful purchasing operations in manufacturing and service companies and organizations. Features advice from purchasing

executives and managers on controlling costs, improving quality and assuring optimum supplier performance.

★1452★ *Update: The Executive's Purchasing Advisor*
Buyers Laboratory, Inc. (BLI)
20 Railroad Ave.
Hackensack, NJ 07601
Ph: (201)488-0404
Daria Hoffman

Monthly. Focusses on office equipment and supplies, offering purchasing advice and exploring methods of increasing office productivity through appropriate management of the equipment and its operators. Offers readers a chance to share their experiences, evaluate products and equipment, and gives results of Buyers Laboratory's testing.

PROFESSIONAL MEETINGS AND CONVENTIONS

★1453★ Great Lakes Industrial Show
North American Exposition Co.
33 Rutherford Ave.
Boston, MA 02129
Ph: (617)242-6092   Fax: (617)242-1817
Fr: 800-225-1577

Annual. Always held during November at the Convention Center in Cleveland, Ohio. **Dates and Locations:** 1995 Nov 07-09; Cleveland, OH. • 1996 Nov 12-14; Cleveland, OH.

★1454★ International Die Casting Congress and Exposition
North American Die Casting Association
9701 W. Higgins Rd., Ste. 880
Rosemont, IL 60018-4721
Ph: (708)292-3600   Fax: (708)292-3620

Biennial. **Dates and Locations:** 1997 Nov 03-06; Minneapolis, MN. • 1999 Oct 18-21; Milwaukee, WI.

OTHER SOURCES OF INFORMATION

★1455★ "Purchasing Agent" in *Career Selector 2001*
Barron's Educational Series, Inc.
250 Wireless Blvd.
Hauppauge, NY 11788
Ph: (516)434-3311   Fax: (516)434-3723
Fr: 800-645-3476

James C. Gonyea. 1993.

Restaurant and Food Service Managers

Efficient and profitable operation of restaurants and institutional food service facilities requires that **restaurant/food service managers and assistant managers** select and appropriately price interesting menu items, efficiently use food and other supplies, achieve consistent quality in food preparation and service, recruit and train adequate numbers of workers and supervise their work, and attend to the various administrative aspects of the business. In most restaurants and institutional food service facilities, the manager is assisted by one or more assistant managers, depending on the size and business hours of the establishment. Restaurant and food service managers supervise the kitchen and dining room, oversee food preparation and cooking, and check the quality of the food.

Salaries

Earnings vary greatly according to the type and size of establishment.

Restaurant/food service managers, fast food	$24,900/year
Restaurant/food service managers, full menu, table service	$30,400/year
Commercial/institutional food service managers	$29,300/year
Executive Chefs	$33,600-$49,000/year
Assistant managers	$31,700/year
Manager trainees	$20,200-$27,900/year

Employment Outlook

Growth rate until the year 2005: Much faster than the average.

Restaurant and Food Service Managers

★1456★ *Cafeteria Manager Industrial*
Careers, Inc.
PO Box 135
Largo, FL 34649-0135
Ph: (813)584-7333
1993. Two-page occupational summary card describing duties, working conditions, personal qualifications, training, earnings and hours, employment outlook, places of employment, related careers, and where to write for more information.

★1457★ *Careers in Foods and Nutrition*
Glencoe Publishing Co.
866 3rd Ave.
New York, NY 10022-6299
Ph: (212)702-3276
Videotape that explores foods and nutrition career fields that require special training or an advanced degree.

★1458★ *Careers in the Restaurant Industry*
Rosen Publishing Group
29 E. 21st St.
New York, NY 10010
Ph: (212)777-3017   Fax: (212)777-0277
Fr: 800-237-9932
Mary Price Lee and Richard S. Lee. 1990. Discusses opportunities and training for jobs in the restaurant industry including fast food franchises, and bartending. Covers opening a restaurant, culinary education and financial aid.

★1459★ *College Majors and Careers: A Resource Guide to Effective Life Planning*
Garrett Park Press
PO Box 1907
Garrett Park, MD 20896
Ph: (301)946-2553
Paul Phifer. Revised, 1993. Lists college majors, with definitions; related occupations and leisure activities; skills, values, and personal needed attributes; suggested readings; and a

list of associations. Includes information on food service.

★1460★ "Food and Beverage Services" in *Career Choices for the 90's for Students of Business* (pp. 96-99)
Walker and Co.
435 Hudson St.
New York, NY 10014
Ph: (212)727-8300   Fax: (212)727-0984
Fr: 800-289-2553
Compiled by Career Associates Staff. 1990. This book offers alternatives for students of business. Gives information about the outlook and competition for entry-level candidates. Provides job hunting tips.

★1461★ *Food Service Director*
Vocational Biographies, Inc.
PO Box 31
Sauk Centre, MN 56378-0031
Ph: (612)352-6516   Fax: (612)352-5546
Fr: 800-255-0752
1994. Four-page pamphlet containing a personal narrative about a worker's job, work likes and dislikes, career path from high school to the present, education and training, the rewards and frustrations, and the effects of the job on the rest of the worker's life. The data file portion of this pamphlet gives a concise occupational summary, including work description, working conditions, places of employment, personal characteristics, education and training, job outlook, and salary range.

★1462★ *Food Service Supervisor*
Careers, Inc.
PO Box 135
Largo, FL 34649-0135
Ph: (813)584-7333
1992. Two-page occupational summary card describing duties, working conditions, personal qualifications, training, earnings and hours, employment outlook, places of employment, related careers, and where to write for more information.

★1463★ *Food Service Supervisors*
Chronicle Guidance Publications, Inc.
66 Aurora St.
PO Box 1190
Moravia, NY 13118-1190
Ph: (315)497-0330   Fax: (315)497-3359
Fr: 800-622-7284
1993. Career brief describing the nature of the job, working conditions, hours and earnings, education and training, licensure, certification, unions, personal qualifications, social and psychological factors, location, employment outlook, entry methods, advancement, and related occupations.

★1464★ "Food Service Supervisors" in *Jobs! What They Are—Where They Are—What They Pay* (p.166)
Simon & Schuster, Inc.
Simon & Schuster Bldg.
1230 Avenue of the Americas
New York, NY 10020
Ph: (212)698-7000   Fr: 800-223-2348
Robert O. Snelling and Anne M. Snelling. 3rd edition, 1992. Describes duties and responsibilities, earnings, employment opportunities, training, and qualifications.

★1465★ "Food Services Administration" in *Opportunities in Hospital Administration Careers* (pp. 38-39)
National Textbook Co. (NTC)
VGM Career Books
4255 W. Touhy Ave.
Lincolnwood, IL 60646-1975
Ph: (708)679-5500   Fax: (708)679-2494
Fr: 800-323-4900
Donald I. Snook. 1989. Describes hospital administration in varied work settings. Covers educational preparation, skills, compensation, getting started in the profession, and job hunting.

★1466★ The Lodging and Food Service Industry
Educational Institute of the American Hotel & Motel Association (AH&MA)
1407 S. Harrsion Rd.
PO Box 1240
East Lansing, MI 48826
Ph: (517)353-5500
Gerald W. Lattin; edited by Timothy Eaton. Third edition, 1993. Describes the food service industry: growth and development, organization and structure, and management and operations. Covers career opportunities.

★1467★ "Personnel and Labor Relations Specialists" in Encyclopedia of Careers and Vocational Guidance (Vol.4, pp. 20-24)
J.G. Ferguson Publishing Co.
200 W. Madison St., Ste. 300
Chicago, IL 60606
Ph: (312)580-5480   Fax: (312)580-4948
William E. Hopke, editor in chief. Ninth edition, 1993. Four-volume set that profiles 900 occupations and describes job trends in 74 industries. Includes career description, educational require ments, history of the job, methods of entry, advancement, employment outlook, earnings, conditons of work, social and psychological factors, and sources of further information.

★1468★ "Restaurant and Food Service Managers" in Encyclopedia of Careers and Vocational Guidance (Vol.4, pp. 288-290)
J.G. Ferguson Publishing Co.
200 W. Madison St., Ste. 300
Chicago, IL 60606
Ph: (312)580-5480   Fax: (312)580-4948
William E. Hopke, editor-in-chief. Ninth edition, 1993. Four-volume set that profiles 900 occupations and describes job trends in 74 industries. Includes career description, educational requirements, history of the job, methods of entry, advancement, employment outlook, earnings, conditions of work, social and psychological factors, and sources of further information.

★1469★ "Restaurant and Food Service Managers" in Occupational Opportunities Handbook (pp. 58-60)
Superintendent of Documents
U.S. Government Printing Office
Washington, DC 20402-9325
Ph: (202)783-3238
Biennial, 1992-93. Encyclopedia of careers describing more than 225 occupations and comprising about 80 percent of all jobs in the economy. Occupations that require lengthy education or training are given the most attention. Each occupation's profile describes what the worker does on the job, working conditions, education and training requirements, advancement possibilities, job outlook, earnings, and sources of additional information.

★1470★ Restaurant Manager
Careers, Inc.
PO Box 135
Largo, FL 34649-0135
Ph: (813)584-7333
1992. Two-page occupational summary card describing duties, working conditions, personal qualifications, training, earnings and hours, employment outlook, places of employment, related careers, and where to write for more information.

★1471★ "Restaurant Manager" in 100 Best Careers for the Year 2000 (pp. 233-235)
Arco Pub.
201 W. 103rd St.
Indianapolis, IN 46290
Ph: 800-428-5331   Fax: 800-835-3202
Shelly Field. 1992. Describes 100 job opportunities expected to grow fast throughout the next decade. Provides information on job duties and responsibilities, training requirements, education, advancement opportunities, experience and qualifications, and typical salaries.

★1472★ "Restaurant Manager" in Career Information Center (Vol.8)
Simon and Schuster
200 Old Tappan Rd.
Old Tappan, NJ 07675
Fax: 800-445-6991   Fr: 800-223-2348
Richard Lidz and Linda Perrin, editorial directors. Fifth edition, 1993. This 13-volume set profiles over 600 occupations. Each occupational profile describes job duties, entry-level requirements, educational requirements, advancement possibilities, employment outlook, working conditions, earnings and benefits, and where to write for more information.

★1473★ Restaurant Managers
Chronicle Guidance Publications, Inc.
66 Aurora St.
PO Box 1190
Moravia, NY 13118-1190
Ph: (315)497-0330   Fax: (315)497-3359
Fr: 800-622-7284
1992. Career brief describing the nature of the job, working conditions, hours and earnings, education and training, licensure, certification, unions, personal qualifications, social and psychological factors, location, employment outlook, entry methods, advancement, and related occupations.

★1474★ "Restaurant Managers" in Career Discovery Encyclopedia (Vol.5, pp. 150-151)
J.G. Ferguson Publishing Co.
200 W. Madison St., Ste. 300
Chicago, IL 60606
Ph: (312)580-5480   Fax: (312)580-4948
Russell E. Primm, editor-in-chief. 1993. This six volume set contains two-page articles for 504 occupations. Each article describes job duties, earnings, and educational and training requirements. The whole set is arranged alphabetically by job title. Designed for junior high and older students.

★1475★ "Tom Kaplan—Restaurant Manager" in Straight Talk on Careers: Eighty Pros Take You Into Their Professions (pp. 36-37)
Garrett Park Press
PO Box 1907
Garrett Park, MD 20896
Ph: (301)946-2553
Mary Barbera-Hogan. 1987. Contains candid interviews from people who give a n inside view of their work in 80 different careers.

These professionals describe a day's work and the stresses and rewards accompanying their work.

PROFESSIONAL ASSOCIATIONS

★1476★ Career College Association (CCA)
750 1st St. NE, Ste. 900
Washington, DC 20002
Ph: (202)336-6700   Fax: (202)336-6828
Members: Private postsecondary schools providing career education. **Purpose:** Seeks to inform members of the accreditation process and regulations affecting vocational education. Conducts workshops and institutes for staffs of member schools; provides legislative, administrative, and public relations assistance. Has established Career Training Foundation to support research into private vocational education. Sponsors research programs. Maintains hall of fame; compiles statistics. **Publications:** Career College Times, monthly. • Career Education. • Career News Digest. • Classroom Companion, quarterly. • Directory of Private Accredited Career Colleges and Schools, annual.

★1477★ Council on Hotel, Restaurant, and Institutional Education (CHRIE)
1200 17th St. NW
Washington, DC 20036-3097
Ph: (202)331-5990   Fax: (202)785-2511
Members: Schools and colleges offering specialized education and training in cooking, baking, tourism and hotel, restaurant, and institutional administration; individuals, executives, and students. **Purpose:** Sponsors competitions. **Publications:** CHRIE Communique, biweekly. • Guide to Hospitality Education, semiannual. • Hospitality and Tourism Educator, quarterly. • Hospitality Education and Research Journal. • Hosteur Magazine, annual. • Membership Directory and Research Guide, annual.

★1478★ Educational Foundation of the National Restaurant Association (EFNRA)
250 S. Wacker Dr., No. 1400
Chicago, IL 60606
Ph: (312)715-1010   Fax: (312)715-0807
Fr: 800-765-2122
Members: Educational foundation supported by the National Restaurant Association and all segments of the foodservice industry including restaurateurs, foodservice companies, food and equipment manufacturers, distributors, and trade associations. **Purpose:** Dedicated to the advancement of professional standards in the industry through education and research. Offers video training programs, management courses, and careers information. Conducts research. Maintains hall of fame. **Publications:** Careers in Foodservice, A Guide for Two-and Four-Year Hospitality Programs. • The Instructor, semiannual.

★1479★ National Association of Convenience Stores (NACS)
1605 King St.
Alexandria, VA 22314-2792
Ph: (703)684-3600   Fax: (703)836-4564
Retail stores that sell gasoline, fast foods, soft drinks, dairy products, beer, cigarettes, publications, grocery items, snacks, and nonfood items and are usually open seven days per week for longer hours than conventional supermarkets. (Convenience stores generally stock 1500 to 3000 items, compared to 7000 or more in most supermarkets. NACS estimates there are some 70,000 convenience stores, most are chain owned, with 1000 more established each year in the suburbs and concentrated city areas.) Conducts educational and legislative activities; sponsors management seminars. Also maintains task forces; compiles statistics. **Publications:** *Compensation Survey*, annual. • *FACT Book*, annual. • *NACS News Summary*, biweekly. • *NACS SCAN*, monthly. • *National Association of Convenience Stores—Membership and Services Directory*, annual. • *National Association of Convenience Stores—State of the Industry Report*, annual. • *Washington Report*, biweekly.

TEST GUIDES

★1480★ Career Examination Series: Food Service Manager
National Learning Corp.
212 Michael Dr.
Syosset, NY 11791
Ph: (516)921-8888   Fax: (516)921-8743
Fr: 800-645-6337
Jack Rudman. 1993. Test guide including questions and answers for students or professionals in the field who seek advancement through examination.

★1481★ Career Examination Series: Food Service Supervisor
National Learning Corp.
212 Michael Dr.
Syosset, NY 11791
Ph: (516)921-8888   Fax: (516)921-8743
Fr: 800-645-6337
Jack Rudman. A study guide for professionals and trainees in the field of restaurant and food service management. Includes a multiple-choice examination section; provides answers.

EDUCATIONAL DIRECTORIES AND PROGRAMS

★1482★ Directory of Foodservice Distribution
Lebhar-Friedman Books
425 Park Ave.
New York, NY 10022
Ph: (212)319-9400
Gael Murhpy, editor. 1992.

★1483★ Foodservice/Hospitality College Directory
Educational Foundation of the National Restaurant Association
250 S. Wacker Dr., Ste. 1400
Chicago, IL 60606-5834
Ph: (312)715-1010   Fax: (312)715-0807
Fr: 800-765-2122
Julie Bayles, Contact
Irregular, latest edition December 1990. Covers Approximately 150 senior college and 300 junior college or vocational-technical school programs in the foodservice/hospitality industry. Entries include: Institution name, name of department or program, address, phone. Arrangement: Geographical.

★1484★ Travel and Hospitality Career Directory
Gale Research Inc.
835 Penobscot Bldg.
Detroit, MI 48226-4094
Ph: (313)961-2242   Fax: (313)961-6083
Fr: 800-877-GALE
Bradley J. Morgan and Joseph M. Palmisano. Second edition, 1992. A directory in the Career Advisor Series that provides essays written by industry professionals; job search information on resume and cover letter preparation, networking, and the interviewing process; approximately 300 companies and organizations offering job opportunities and internships, and additional job-hunting resources.

AWARDS, SCHOLARSHIPS, GRANTS, AND FELLOWSHIPS

★1485★ Foodservice Operator of the Year
International Foodservice Manufacturers Association
180 N. Stetson, Ste. 4400
Chicago, IL 60601
Ph: (312)540-4400   Fax: (312)540-4401
To recognize lasting and outstanding contributions to the advancement of the food service industry. Awards are given in the following categories: independent restaurant operator, chain full service, chain fast service, health care, elementary and secondary schools, colleges and universities, business and industry/contract food management, specialty food services, and hotels and lodging. Any person, worldwide, engaged in the active ownership, management, supervision, or employment of an establishment in one of the nine classes of the food service industry is eligible to receive a Silver Plate Award. The Gold Plate Award recipient, who is designated Food service Operator of the Year, is selected from among the nine Silver Plate winners. The deadline for nominations is in December. Awarded annually in May. Established in 1955.

★1486★ Great Menu Award
National Restaurant Association
1200 17th St. NW
Washington, DC 20036
Ph: (202)331-5900   Fr: 800-424-5156
To recognize an owner or manager of a foodservice operation for outstanding restaurant menus based on imagination, design, and merchandising power. Awards are given in the following categories: restaurant average per person check less than $8; between $8 and $15; over $15; specialty; banquet/catering; institutional foodservice; most imaginative; best design; and greatest merchandising power. The menus are judged by a panel of designers, food writers, and editors. The judges select first, second, and third place winners who receive plaques and menu stickers. Awarded annually. Established in 1963. Additional information is available from Jennifer Batty, telephone: (202) 331-5942.

★1487★ NAMP Scholarships
National Association of Meat Purveyors (NAMP)
1920 Association Dr., Ste. 400
Reston, VA 22091-1547
Ph: (703)758-1900   Fax: (703)758-8001
Purpose: To promote and sponsor outstanding and deserving students who are training for careers in the foodservice industry. Qualifications: Applicants must be enrolled at an accredited undergraduate institution and seeking a degree in foodservice management, meat science, hotel/restaurant management, or culinary arts. Selection criteria: A member of NAMP's Scholarship Committee selects the school at which the scholarship will be offered. This committee member, with the help of school representatives, selects the candidate on the basis of need and ability. Funds available: $10,000 is distibuted each year, generally in increments of $1500.00 to 2500.00 to Universities and Culinary Arts Institutions. Application details: NAMP attempts to achieve a geographical balance that corresponds to its membership make-up. Students can inquire as to the availability of a scholarship at their school by contacting the school's department.

BASIC REFERENCE GUIDES AND HANDBOOKS

★1488★ The Art and Science of Hospitality Management
Educational Institute of the American Hotel & Motel Association (AH&MA)
1407 S. Harrsion Rd.
PO Box 1240
East Lansing, MI 48826
Ph: (517)353-5500   Fr: 800-752-4567
James R. Abbey and Jerome J. Vallen. 1987. Offers a clear understanding of the skills specific to managing a hotel, motel, or restaurant, including management responsibilities, operational responsibilities, and the personal and professional demands of managing and maintaining the management image.

★1489★ Fundamentals of Meal Management
Plycon Press
PO Box 220
Redondo Beach, CA 90277
Ph: (310)379-9725
Margaret McWilliams, editor. 1993.

★1490★ The Hotel and Restaurant Business
Van Nostrand Reinhold
115 5th Ave.
New York, NY 10013
Donald Lundberg. 1993.

★1491★ Inventory Control Systems in Foodservice Organizations: Programmed Study Guide
Iowa State University Press
Iowa State University
2121 S. State Ave.
Ames, IA 50010
Ph: (515)292-0140   Fax: (515)292-3348
Iowa Dietetic Association Staff, editors. 1992.

★1492★ Knight's Foodservice Dictionary
Van Nostrand Reinhold Co., Inc.
115 5th Ave.
New York, NY 10003
Ph: (212)254-3232
John B. Knight; edited by Charles A. Salter. 1987. A CBI book.

★1493★ Nutrition for the Foodservice Professional
Van Nostrand Reinhold
115 5th Ave.
New York, NY 10013
Karen Eich Drummond. 1993.

★1494★ Planning and Control for Food and Beverage Operations
Educational Institute of the American Hotel & Motel Association (AH&MA)
1407 S. Harrison Rd.
PO Box 1240
East Lansing, MI 48826
Ph: (517)353-5500   Fr: 800-752-4567
Jack D. Ninemeir, et al.; edited by Marjorie Harless and John Glazer. Third edition, 1991. Includes sections on computer operations, menu planning, and cost analysis. Written for small and large operations.

★1495★ Professional Dining Room Management
Van Nostrand Reinhold Co., Inc.
115 5th Ave.
New York, NY 10003
Ph: (212)254-3232
Carol A. King. Second edition, 1988. Illustrated. Includes a bibliography and an index.

★1496★ Purchasing For Hospitality Operations
Educational Institute of the American Hotel & Motel Association (AH&MA)
1407 S. Harrison Rd.
PO Box 1240
East Lansing, MI 48826
Ph: (517)353-5500
William B. Virts; edited by Kent F. Premo. 1987. Gives advice on distributors and suppliers, quality control, and purchasing. Explains specific food purchasing—meat, poultry,

dairy products, fruits, vegetables, and alcoholic beverages.

★1497★ The Restaurant Managers Handbook: How to Set Up, Operate, and Manage a Financially Successful Restaurant
Atlantic Publishing, Inc.
1210 SW 23rd Pl.
Ocala, FL 34474
Douglas R. Brown. Second edition, 1989.

★1498★ Successful Buffet Management
Van Nostrand Reinhold, Inc.
115 5th Ave.
New York, NY 10003
Ph: (212)254-3232
Ronald Yudd. 1990.

★1499★ Successful Kitchen Operation and Staff Management Handbook
Prentice-Hall, Inc.
Rte. 9W
Englewood Cliffs, NJ 07632
Ph: (201)592-2000
J. A. Van Duyn. 1979. Illustrated. Includes a bibliography and an index.

PROFESSIONAL AND TRADE PERIODICALS

★1500★ Entree
Entree Travel
1470 E. Valley Rd.
Santa Barbara, CA 93108
Ph: (805)969-5848   Fax: (805)966-7095
William Tomicki
Monthly. Features "an insider's look at hotels, restaurants, and travel around the world." Contains advice and tips on travel, bargains, and services. Recurring features include book reviews and notices of publications available.

★1501★ Food Management
Penton Publishing
1100 Superior Ave.
Cleveland, OH 44114
Ph: (216)696-7000   Fax: (216)696-7932
Donna Boss
Monthly. Professional magazine for foodservice directors.

★1502★ Food Talk
Charles Felix Associates
PO Box 1581
Leesburg, VA 22075
Ph: (703)777-7448
Charles W. Felix
Quarterly. Meant to be distributed by health departments to restaurant managers and retail food store operators in their jurisdictions. Offers articles dealing with the sanitary handling of foods, including news reports on foodborne outbreaks, contaminations, court cases, U.S. Food and Drug Administration (FDA) regulatory decisions, and epidemiological notes from the Centers for Disease Control (CDC).

★1503★ Restaurant Briefing
Walter Mathews Associates, Inc.
28 W. 38th St.
New York, NY 10018
Ph: (212)533-9445   Fax: (212)933-9295
Scott Wagandorf
Carries news briefs of interest to restaurant owners and managers in the areas of customer trends, management, foods, equipment, decor, entertainment, labor costs, government regulations, advertising and promotion, research, employee relations, and security. Recurring features include news of research and book reviews.

★1504★ Restaurant Business
Bill Communications, Inc.
355 Park Ave. S.
New York, NY 10010-1789
Ph: (212)592-6200   Fax: (212)592-6359
Scott Allmendinger
Trade magazine for restaurants and commercial food service.

★1505★ Restaurant Hospitality
Penton Publishing
1100 Superior Ave.
Cleveland, OH 44114
Ph: (216)696-7000   Fax: (216)696-7932
Mike DeLuca
Monthly. Magazine for managers and other executives of independent restaurants, restaurant chains, and hotels.

★1506★ Restaurants & Institutions
Cahners Publishing Co.
1350 E. Touhy Ave.
PO Box 5080
Des Plaines, IL 60017-5080
Ph: (708)635-8800   Fax: (708)390-2618
Mike Bartlett
Semiweekly. Magazine focusing on foodservice and lodging management.

PROFESSIONAL MEETINGS AND CONVENTIONS

★1507★ American School Food Service Association Conference
American School Food Service Association
1600 Duke St., 7th Fl.
Alexandria, VA 22314
Ph: (703)739-3900   Fax: (703)739-3915
Fr: 800-877-8822
Annual.

★1508★ CHRIE - Council on Hotel, Restaurant, and Institutional Education International Conference
Council on Hotel, Restaurant, and Institutional Education
1200 17th St., NW
Washington, DC 20036-3097
Ph: (202)331-5990   Fax: (202)785-2511
Annual.

★1509★ EUROEXPO HOREGA - International Trade Fair for Hotel, Restaurant, and Catering Equipment
Glahe International, Inc.
1700 K St., NW, Ste. 403
Washington, DC 20006-4557
Ph: (202)659-4557   Fax: (202)457-0776

Biennial. **Dates and Locations:** 1995; St. Petersburg.

★1510★ Foodservice Expo
Kentucky Restaurant Association
422 Executive Pk.
Louisville, KY 40207-4204
Ph: (502)896-0464   Fax: (502)896-0465

Annual. Always held during September at the Expo Center in Louisville, Kentucky. **Dates and Locations:** 1996 Sep; Louisville, KY.

★1511★ Hotel, Motel, and Restaurant Supply Show of the Southeast
Leisure Time Unlimited, Inc.
708 Main St.
PO Box 332
Myrtle Beach, SC 29578
Ph: (803)448-9483   Fax: (803)626-1513

Annual. Always held during January at the Convention Center in Myrtle Beach, South Carolina. **Dates and Locations:** 1996 Jan 30-01; Myrtle Beach, SC. • 1997 Jan 28-30; Myrtle Beach, SC. • 1998 Jan 27-20; Myrtle Beach, SC.

★1512★ Hotelympia - International Hotel and Catering Exhibition
Reed Exhibition Companies (World Headquarters)
255 Washington St.
Newton, MA 02158-1630
Ph: (617)630-2200   Fax: (617)630-2222

Biennial. **Dates and Locations:** 1996 Feb; London.

★1513★ KUK Prage - International Trade Fair for Hotel & Catering, Food & Beverages
Glahe International, Inc.
1700 K St., NW, Ste. 403
Washington, DC 20006-4557
Ph: (202)659-4557   Fax: (202)457-0776

Dates and Locations: 1996; Prague.

★1514★ Mid-Southwest Foodservice Convention and Exposition
Oklahoma Restaurant Association
3800 N. Portland
Oklahoma City, OK 73112
Ph: (405)942-8181   Fax: (405)942-0541

Annual. Always held during April at the Myriad Convention Center in Oklahoma City, Oklahoma. **Dates and Locations:** 1996 Apr 15-18; Oklahoma City, OK. • 1997 Apr 22-24; Oklahoma City, OK.

★1515★ Midwestern Foodservice and Equipment Exposition
Missouri Restaurant Association
PO Box 10277
4049 Pennsylvania
Kansas City, MO 64111
Ph: (816)753-5222   Fax: (816)753-6993

Annual. Always held during October alternating between St. Louis and Kansas City, Missouri.

★1516★ National Association of Food Equipment Manufacturers Convention
National Association of Food Equipment Manufacturers
401 N. Michigan Ave.
Chicago, IL 60611
Ph: (312)644-6610

Biennial. **Dates and Locations:** 1997 Sep; New Orleans, LA.

★1517★ National Restaurant Association Restaurant, Hotel-Motel Show
National Restaurant Association
150 N. Michigan Ave., Ste. 2000
Chicago, IL 60601
Ph: (312)853-2525   Fax: (312)853-2548

Annual. Always held during May at the McCormick Place Complex in Chicago, Illinois. **Dates and Locations:** 1996 May 20-18; Chicago, IL.

★1518★ New York Restaurant & Food Service Show
Reed Exhibition Companies (World Headquarters)
255 Washington St.
Newton, MA 02158-1630
Ph: (617)630-2200   Fax: (617)630-2222

Annual. Always held during February in New York, New York. **Dates and Locations:** 1996 Feb; New York, NY.

★1519★ Northeast Food Service and Lodging Exposition and Conference
Reed Exhibition Companies (World Headquarters)
255 Washington St.
Newton, MA 02158-1630
Ph: (617)630-2200   Fax: (617)630-2222

Annual. Always held during April at the Bayside Exposition Center in Boston, Massachusetts. **Dates and Locations:** 1996 Apr; Boston, MA.

★1520★ Pacific Northwest Regional Restaurant Exposition
Oregon Restaurant Association
8565 SW Salish Ln. No. 120
Wilsonville, OR 97070
Ph: (503)628-4422   Fax: (503)682-4455
Fr: 800-462-0619

Biennial. Always held at the Convention Center in Portland, Oregon. **Dates and Locations:** 1997 Apr 12-14; Portland, OR.

★1521★ Southeastern Restaurant, Hospitality Foodservice Show
Reed Exhibition Companies (World Headquarters)
255 Washington St.
Newton, MA 02158-1630
Ph: (617)630-2200   Fax: (617)630-2222

Annual. Always held during October at the Georgia World Congress Center in Atlanta, Georgia.

★1522★ Upper Midwest Hospitality, Restaurant, and Lodging Show
Upper Midwest Hospitality Inc.
871 Jefferson Ave.
St. Paul, MN 55102
Ph: (612)222-7401   Fax: (612)222-7347

Annual. **Dates and Locations:** 1996 Feb; Minneapolis, MN.

★1523★ Western Restaurant Show
California Restaurant Association
3435 Wilshire Blvd., Ste. 2606
Los Angeles, CA 90010
Ph: (213)384-1200   Fax: (213)384-1623
Fr: 800-744-4272

Annual. Alternates between Los Angeles and San Francisco, California. **Dates and Locations:** 1996 Aug 17-20; San Francisco, CA. • 1997 Aug 16-19; Los Angeles, CA.

OTHER SOURCES OF INFORMATION

★1524★ *Careers in the Restaurant Industry*
Rosen Publishing Group
29 E. 21st St.
New York, NY 10010
Ph: 800-237-9932   Fax: (212)777-0277

Mary Price Lee and Richard Lee. Revised edition, 1990.

★1525★ "Restaurant/Food Service Manager" in *100 Best Jobs for the 1990s & Beyond*
Dearborn Financial Publishing, Inc.
520 N. Dearborn St.
Chicago, IL 60610-4354
Ph: (312)836-4400   Fax: (312)836-1021
Fr: 800-621-9621

Carol Kleiman. 1992. Describes 100 jobs ranging from accountants to veterinarians. Each job profile includes such information as education, experience, and certification needed, salaries, and job search suggestions.

Retail Managers

Retail managers have many responsibilities, depending on the size and type of establishment. Managers coordinate and direct all aspects o retail trade, including ordering, inspection, pricing, and inventory o goods; monitoring sales activity; developing merchandising plans; maintaining good customer relations; monitoring profits and losses; and coordinating displays, advertisements, and sales announcements.

Salaries

Earnings for retail managers are as follows:

Assistant store managers	$13,100-$14,300/year
Store managers	$18,400-$23,700/year
District managers	$29,800-$62,700/year
Regional managers	$47,000-$128,000/year

Employment Outlook

Growth rate until the year 2005: Average.

Retail Managers

CAREER GUIDES

★1526★ Careers in Farm, Industrial and Outdoor Power Equipment Retailing
North American Equipment Dealers Association
10877 Watson Rd.
St. Louis, MO 63127-1081
1994. Describes job opportunities (sales, services, inventory control, accounting, and retail computer technology), departments, job duties, and methods of entry.

★1527★ The Insider's Guide to the Top 20 Careers in Business and Management
McGraw-Hill
1221 Avenue of the Americas
New York, NY 10020
Ph: (212)512-3493   Fax: (212)512-3050
Tom Fischgrund. 1994. Contains information on different business careers including accounting, banking, finance, and retail sales. Includes tips on choosing a careers, preparing a resume, interviewing, and succeeding on the job.

★1528★ "Manager, Retail Store" in Museum Jobs form A-Z: What They Are, How to Prepare, and Where to Find Them
Batax Museum Publishing
301 Racquet Club Rd., Ste. 202
Fort Lauderdale, FL 33326
G.W. Bates. 1994.

★1529★ "Regional Retail Sales Manager" in BLR Encyclopedia of Prewritten Job Descriptions
Business and Legal Reports, Inc.
39 Academy St.
Madison, CT 06443-1513
Ph: (203)245-7448
Stephen D. Bruce, editor-in-chief. 1994. This book contains hundreds of sample job descriptions arranged by functional job category. The 1-3 page job descriptions cover what the worker normally does in the position, who they report to, and how that position fits in the organizational structure.

★1530★ "Retail" in Internships 1995
Petersons Guides, Inc.
PO Box 2123
Princeton, NJ 08543-2123
Ph: (609)243-9111   Fr: 800-338-3282
Fifteenth edition, 1995. Lists internship opportunities under six broad categories: communications, creative, performing, and fine arts, human services, international relations, business and technology, and public affairs. For each internship program, gives the names, phone number, contact person, description, eligibility requirements, and benefits.

★1531★ "Retail Managers" in Encyclopedia of Careers and Vocational Guidance (Vol.4, pp. 294-296)
J.G. Ferguson Publishing Co.
200 W. Madison St., Ste. 300
Chicago, IL 60606
Ph: (312)580-5480   Fax: (312)580-4948
William E. Hopke, editor-in-chief. Ninth edition, 1993. Four-volume set that profiles 900 occupations and describes job trends in 74 industries. Includes career description, educational requirements, history of the job, methods of entry, advancement, employment outlook, earnings, conditions of work, social and psychological factors, and sources of further information.

★1532★ "Retail Managers" in Occupational Outlook Handbook (pp. 70-73)
U.S. Government Printing Office
Superintendent of Documents
Washington, DC 20402
Ph: (202)512-1800   Fax: (202)512-2250

★1533★ "Retail Store Manager" in VGM's Handbook of Business and Management Careers
National Textbook Co.
4255 W. Touhy Ave.
Lincolnwood, IL 60646-1975
Ph: (708)679-5500   Fax: (708)679-2494
Fr: 800-323-4900
Annette Selden. Second edition, 1993. Contains 42 two-page occupational profiles describing job duties, places of employment, working conditions, qualifications, education, employment outlook, and income.

★1534★ "Retail Store Managers" in Career Discovery Encyclopedia (Vol.5, pp. 154-155)
J.G. Ferguson Publishing Co.
200 W. Madison St., Ste. 300
Chicago, IL 60606
Ph: (312)580-5480   Fax: (312)580-4948
Russell E. Primm, editor-in chief. 1993. This six volume set contains two-page articles for 504 occupations. Each article describes job duties, earnings, and educational and training requirements. The whole set is arranged alphabetically by job title. Designed for junior high and older students.

★1535★ "Retailing and Marketing" in Career Connection for Technical Education (pp. 134-135)
JIST Works, Inc.
720 N. Park Ave.
Indianapolis, IN 46202-3431
Ph: (317)264-3720   Fax: (317)264-3709
Fred A. Rowe. 1994, second edition. Describes in detail technical occupations. Includes information on recommended high school courses, course requirements, related careers, and a self-assessment guide.

★1536★ Sales Promotion/Marketing Manager (Retail)
Careers, Inc.
PO Box 135
Largo, FL 34649-0135
Ph: (813)584-7333
1993. Two-page occupational summary card describing duties, working conditions, personal qualifications, training, earnings and hours, employment outlook, places of employment, related careers, and where to write for more information.

PROFESSIONAL ASSOCIATIONS

★1537★ Institute of Store Planners
25 N. Broadway
Tarrytown, NY 10591
Ph: (914)332-1806
Purpose: Dedicated to the professional growth of members while providing service to the public through improvement of the retail

environment. Provides forum for debate and discussion by store design experts, retailers, and public figures.

★1538★ International Mass Retail Association
1901 Pennsylvania Ave., NW, 10th Fl.
Washington, DC 20006
Ph: (202)861-0774
Purpose: To conduct research and educational programs on every phase of self-service general merchandising retailing. Conducts studies on industry practices and procedures and generates informaiton on all areas of the business.

★1539★ National Association of Retail Dealers of America
10 E. 22nd St.
Lombard, IL 60148
Ph: (708)953-8950
Retailers of appliances, home electronics, computers, furniture, and audio components.

BASIC REFERENCE GUIDES AND HANDBOOKS

★1540★ Modern Retailing: Theory and Practice
BPI
9605 Scranton Rd., Ste. 503
San Diego, CA 92121-1774
Ph: (619)457-7577   Fax: (619)453-1091
J. Barry Mason, Morris L. Mayer, and J.B. Wilkinson. Sixth edition, 1993.

PROFESSIONAL AND TRADE PERIODICALS

★1541★ Chain Merchandiser Magazine
Rte. 1, Box 956
Baker City, OR 97814
Ph: (503)523-3642
Magazine on improved merchandising methods at every level of the distribution process.

Covers customer values, lower costs, and greater profists.

★1542★ Chain Store Age Executive
Lebhar-Friedman, Inc.
425 Park Ave.
New York, NY 10022
Ph: (212)756-5000   Fax: (212)756-5125
Murray Forester
Monthly. Magazine for management of retail chain headquarters. Reports on marketing, merchandising, strategic planning, physical supports, and shopping center developments.

★1543★ General Merchandise News
712 Fair Oaks Ave.
South Pasadena, CA 91030
Magazine covering the sale, distribution, marketing, and retailing of non-food products in the U.S. and Canada.

★1544★ Inside Retailing
Lebhar-Friedman, Inc.
425 Park Ave.
New York, NY 10022
Ph: (212)756-5017   Fax: (516)935-4958
David Mahler
Biweekly. Provides up-to-date information on what is happening in the retail industry and how current economic conditions affect retailing. Summarizes actions, acquisitions, and policies of major retail chains across the U.S. Discusses problems facing retail operations, i.e., shoplifting and retaining customer loyalty.

★1545★ Journal of Retailing
New York University
44 W. 4th St.
New York, NY 10012-1126
Ph: (212)998-0550
Journal focuses on retailing, marketing, and general business.

★1546★ The Retail Challenge
International Council of Shopping Centers
665 5th Ave.
New York, NY 10022
Ph: (212)421-8181
Quarterly. Covers "the nuts and bolts of retailing and provides the industry know-how to boost your merchant's productivity." Features how-to information on selling tech-

niques, customer service, motivation, operations, advertising, promotion, and marketing.

★1547★ Retail Control
National Retail Federation
100 W. 31st St.
New York, NY 10001
Ph: (212)244-8780
Journal providing retail management and financial information.

★1548★ Retailing Today
Robert Kahn and Associates
PO Box 249
Lafayette, CA 94549
Ph: (510)254-4434   Fax: (510)284-5612
Robert Kahn
Monthly. Focuses on general merchandise, apparel, furniture, hardware, automotive, and food retailing. Offers "original research, comments on current trends and conditions, recommendations for company policy, and emphasis on ethical conduct in business."

★1549★ Stores
NRF Enterprises, Inc.
Liberty Pl.
Washington, DC 20004-2802
Ph: (202)783-7971   Fax: (202)737-2849
Monthly.

PROFESSIONAL MEETINGS AND CONVENTIONS

★1550★ International Mass Retail Association Convention
International Mass Retail Association
1901 Pennsylvania Ave., NW, 10th Fl.
Washington, DC 20006
Ph: (202)861-0774
Annual in May. Features exhibits.

Underwriters

Underwriters appraise and select the risks their company will insure. The underwriter must analyze information in insurance applications, reports from loss control consultants, medical reports, and actuarial studies (reports that describe the probability of insured loss) and then decide whether to issue a policy. An insurance company may lose business to competitors if the underwriter appraises risks too conservatively, or it may have to pay more claims if the underwriting actions are too liberal.

Salaries

Salaries vary according to type of insurance.

Personal line entry-level underwriters	$25,000/year
Commercial line underwriters	$28,000/year
Personal line senior underwriters	$40,400/year
Commercial line senior underwriters	$40,600/year
Commercial line underwriting supervisor	$45,500/year
Personal line underwriting supervisors	$45,300/year
Personal line underwriting managers	$61,000/year
Commercial line underwriting managers	$61,000/year

Employment Outlook

Growth rate until the year 2005: Average.

Underwriters

CAREER GUIDES

★1551★ *Career Choices for the 90's for Students of Business*
Walker and Co.
435 Hudson St.
New York, NY 10014
Ph: (212)727-8300   Fax: (212)727-0984
Fr: 800-289-2553
Compiled by Career Associates Staff. 1990. This book offers alternatives for students of business, including the career of underwriter. Gives information about the outlook and competition for entry-level candidates. Provides job hunting tips.

★1552★ *Career Choices for the 90's for Students of Mathematics*
Walker and Co.
435 Hudson St.
New York, NY 10014
Ph: (212)727-8300   Fax: (212)727-0984
Fr: 800-289-2553
Revised edition, 1990. Offers alternatives for students of mathematics. Gives information about the outlook and competition for entry-level candidates. Provides job-hunting tips.

★1553★ *"Chartered Life Underwriters"* in *Opportunities in Insurance Careers* (p. 71-84)
National Textbook Co. (NTC)
VGM Career Books
4255 W. Touhy Ave.
Lincolnwood, IL 60646-1975
Ph: (708)679-5500   Fax: (708)679-2494
Fr: 800-323-4900
Robert M. Schrayer. 1993. Provides an introduction to the world of insurance careers through an exploration of the industry's history, academic requirements, certification, licensing and education requirements, positions available, as well as some careers associated with the insurance industry, such as data processing, human resources and public relations.

★1554★ *"Chartered Property and Casualty Underwriter"* in *Opportunities in Insurance Careers* (pp. 71-75)
National Textbook Co. (NTC)
VGM Career Books
4255 W. Touhy Ave.
Lincolnwood, IL 60646-1975
Ph: (708)679-5500   Fax: (708)679-2494
Fr: 800-323-4900
Robert M. Schrayer. 1993. Provides an introduction to the world of insurance careers through an exploration of the industry's history, academic requirements, certification, licensing and education requirements, positions available, as well as some careers associated with the insurance industry, such as data processing, human resources and public relations.

★1555★ *"Insurance"* in *Encyclopedia of Career Choices for the 1990s: A Guide to Entry Level Jobs* (pp. 437-456)
Berkley Pub.
PO Box 506
East Rutherford, NJ 07073
Fax: (201)933-2316   Fr: 800-788-6262
1992. Describes entry-level careers in a variety of industries. Presents qualifications required, working conditions, salary, internships, and professional associations.

★1556★ *"Insurance Underwriter"* in *Jobs Rated Almanac*
World Almanac
1 International Blvd., Ste. 444
Mahwah, NJ 07495
Ph: (201)529-6900   Fax: (201)529-6901
Les Krantz. Second edition, 1992. Ranks 250 jobs by environment, salary, outlooks, physical demands, stress, security, travel opportunities, and extra perks. Includes jobs the editor feels are the most common, most interesting, and the most rapidly growing.

★1557★ *Insurance Underwriters*
Chronicle Guidance Publications, Inc.
66 Aurora St.
PO Box 1190
Moravia, NY 13118-1190
Ph: (315)497-0330   Fax: (315)497-3359
Fr: 800-622-7284
1994. Career brief describing the nature of the job, working conditions, hours and earnings, education and training, licensure, certification, unions, personal qualifications, social and psychological factors, location, employment outlook, entry methods, advancement, and related occupations.

★1558★ *"Underwriter"* in *College Board Guide to Jobs and Career Planning* (pp. 106)
The College Board
415 Columbus Ave.
New York, NY 10023-6992
Ph: (212)713-8165   Fax: (212)713-8143
Fr: 800-323-7155
Joyce S. Mitchell. Second edition, 1994. Describes the job, salaries, related careers, education needed, and where to write for more information.

★1559★ *"Underwriter"* in *VGM's Careers Encyclopedia* (pp. 475-477)
National Textbook Co. (NTC)
VGM Career Books
4255 W. Touhy Ave.
Lincolnwood, IL 60646-1975
Ph: (708)679-5500   Fax: (708)679-2494
Fr: 800-323-4900
Third edition, 1991. Describes job duties, places of employment, working conditions, qualifications, education, and training, advancement potential, and salary for each occupation.

★1560★ *"Underwriter"* in *VGM's Handbook of Business and Management Careers*
National Textbook Co.
4255 W. Touhy Ave.
Lincolnwood, IL 60646-1975
Ph: (708)679-5500   Fax: (708)679-2494
Fr: 800-323-4900
Annette Selden. Second edition, 1993. Contains 42 two-page occupational profiles describing job duties, places of employment, working conditions, qualifications, education, employment outlook, and income.

★1561★ *"Underwriters"* in *American Almanac of Jobs and Salaries* (p. 422)
Avon Books
1350 Avenue of the Americas
New York, NY 10019
Ph: (212)261-6800   Fr: 800-238-0658
John Wright, editor. Revised and updated, 1994-95. This is a comprehensive guide to the wages of hundreds of occupations in a wide variety of industries and organizations.

★1562★ "Underwriters" in *Best Jobs for the 1990s and Into the 21st Century*
Impact Publications
9104-N Manassas Dr.
Manassas Park, VA 22111
Ph: (703)361-7300   Fax: (703)335-9486
Ronald L. Krannich and Caryl Rae Krannich. 1993.

★1563★ "Underwriters" in *Career Discovery Encyclopedia* (Vol.6, pp. 134-135)
J.G. Ferguson Publishing Co.
200 W. Madison St., Ste. 300
Chicago, IL 60606
Ph: (312)580-5480   Fax: (312)580-4948
Russell E. Primm, editor-in chief. 1993. This six volume set contains two-page articles for 504 occupations. Each article describes job duties, earnings, and educational and training requirements. The whole set is arranged alphabetically by job title. Designed for junior high and older students.

★1564★ "Underwriters" in *Career Information Center* (Vol.1)
Simon and Schuster
200 Old Tappan Rd.
Old Tappan, NJ 07675
Fax: 800-445-6991   Fr: 800-223-2348
Richard Lidz and Linda Perrin, editorial directors. Fifth edition, 1993. A multi-volume set that profiles over 600 occupations. Each occupational profile describes job duties, educational requirements, advancement possibilities, employment outlook, working conditions, earnings and benefits, and where to write for more information.

★1565★ "Underwriters" in *Encyclopedia of Careers and VocationalGuidance* (Vol.4, pp. 578-580)
J.G. Ferguson Publishing Co.
200 W. Madison St., Ste. 300
Chicago, IL 60606
Ph: (312)580-5480   Fax: (312)580-4948
William E. Hopke, editor in chief. Ninth edition, 1993. Four-volume set that profiles 900 occupations and describes job trends in 74 industries. Includes career description, educational requirements, history of the job, methods of entry, advancement, employment outlook, earnings, conditions of work, social and psychological factors, and sources of further information.

★1566★ "Underwriters" in *Jobs! What They Are—Where They Are—What They Pay* (p. 155)
Simon & Schuster, Inc.
Simon & Schuster Bldg.
1230 Avenue of the Americas
New York, NY 10020
Ph: (201)767-5937   Fr: 800-223-2348
Robert O. and Anne M. Snelling. 3rd edition, 1992. Describes duties and responsibilities, earnings, employment opportunities, training, and qualifications.

★1567★ "Underwriters" in *Occupational Outlook Handbook*
U.S. Government Printing Office
Superintendent of Documents
Washington, DC 20402
Ph: (202)512-1800   Fax: (202)512-2250
Biennial; latest edition, 1994-95. Encyclopedia of careers describing more than 250 occupations and comprising about 85 percent of all jobs in the economy. Occupations that require lengthy education or training are given the most attention. Each occupation's profile describes what the worker does on the job, working conditions, education and training requirements, advancement possibilities, job outlook, earnings, and sources of additional information.

★1568★ "Underwriters" in *Opportunities in Insurance Careers* (p. 43)
National Textbook Co. (NTC)
VGM Career Books
4255 W. Touhy Ave.
Lincolnwood, IL 60646-1975
Ph: (708)679-5500   Fax: (708)679-2494
Fr: 800-323-4900
Robert M. Schrayer. 1987. Provides an introduction to the world of insurance careers through an exploration of the industry's history academic requirements, certification, licensing and education requirements, positions available, as well as some careers associated with the insurance industry, such as data processing, human resources and public relations.

★1569★ "Underwriting" in *Career Choices for the 90's for Students of Economics* (pp. 77-78)
Walker and Co.
435 Hudson St.
New York, NY 10014
Ph: (212)727-8300   Fax: (212)727-0984
Fr: 800-289-2553
Compiled by Career Associates Staff. 1990. This book offers alternatives for students of economics, including the career of underwriter. Gives information about the outlook and competition for entry-level candidates. Provides job hunting tips.

PROFESSIONAL ASSOCIATIONS

★1570★ **Alliance of American Insurers (ALLIANCE)**
1501 Woodfield Rd., Ste. 400 W
Schaumburg, IL 60173-4980
Ph: (708)330-8500   Fax: (708)330-8602
Members: Property and casualty insurance companies.

★1571★ **American Association of Crop Insurers (AACI)**
1 Massachusetts Ave. NW, Ste. 800
Washington, DC 20001-1431
Ph: (202)789-4100   Fax: (202)408-7763
Members: Private sector companies or agencies that sell multiple-peril crop insurance. **Purpose:** Purposes are to educate Congress on crop insurance issues, to monitor crop insurance legislation, and to inform members about these activities. Compiles statistics. Works with academics to develop software that will aid agents in selling crop insurance. **Publications:** *Agent Newsletter*, quarterly. • *American Association of Crop Insurers—Affiliate Member Newsletter*, quarterly.

★1572★ **American Council of Life Insurance (ACLI)**
1001 Pennsylvania Ave. NW
Washington, DC 20004-2599
Ph: (202)624-2000   Fax: (202)624-2319
Fr: 800-942-4242
Members: Legal reserve life insurance companies authorized to do business in the U.S. **Purpose:** Works to advance the interests of the life insurance industry and to provide effective government relations. Conducts investment and social research programs; compiles statistics. Maintains Insurance Industry's Citizen Action Network and Center for Corporate Public Involvement and Medical Research Fund. **Publications:** *ACLI Digest*, biweekly. • *Forum 500 Forecast*, quarterly. • *Life Insurance Fact Book*, annual.

★1573★ **American Institute for Chartered Property Casualty Underwriters (AICPCU)**
720 Providence Rd.
PO Box 3016
Malvern, PA 19355-0716
Ph: (610)644-2100   Fax: (610)251-9995
Members: Determines qualifications for professional certification of insurance personnel; cooperates with colleges and universities in establishing educational standards; conducts examinations and awards designation of Chartered Property Casualty Underwriter (CPCU). **Publications:** *CPCU Course Guides*, annual. • *CPCU/IIA Catalogue*, annual. • *Institute Insights*, semiannual. • *Key Information*, annual. • *Malvern Examiner*, semiannual. • *Solutions - An Idea Exchange for CPCU/ITA Course headers*, semiannual.

★1574★ **CPCU Society**
720 Providence Rd.
PO Box 3009
Malvern, PA 19355
Ph: (610)251-CPCU   Fax: (215)251-2761
Members: Professional society of individuals who have passed ten national examinations of the American Institute for Chartered Property Casualty Underwriters, have 3 years of work experience, have agreed to be bound by a code of ethics, and have been awarded CPCU designation. **Purpose:** Promotes education, research, social responsibility, and professionalism in the field. Holds seminars, symposia, videoconferences, and workshops; conducts research projects. Operates speakers' bureau. **Publications:** *CPCU Journal*, quarterly. • *CPCU News*, 10/year. • *CPCU Society—Society Shop*, biennial. • *Electronic Underwriter: Artificial Intelligence and Insurance*. • *The Impact of Consumer Activism on the Insurance Industry*. • *The Risk Retention Act: Bane or Blessing*. • *Team Up with Your Insurance Adjuster*. • *There is a Career for You in Insurance*. • *You Deserve the Best Insurance Advice*.

★1575★ Home Office Life Underwriters Association (HOLUA)
5770 Powers Ferry Rd., Ste. 300
Atlanta, GA 30317-4308
Ph: (404)984-9840   Fax: (404)984-0441
Members: Underwriters of legal reserve life insurance companies. **Purpose:** Offers educational program, through the Academy Life Underwriting, designed specifically for professional home office life underwriters.

★1576★ Insurance Information Institute (III)
110 William St.
New York, NY 10038
Ph: (212)669-9200   Fax: (212)732-1916
Members: Property and liability insurance companies. **Purpose:** Provides information and educational services to mass media, educational institutions, trade associations, businesses, government agencies, and the public. Conducts public opinion surveys. Sponsors seminars and briefings on insurance, safety, research, public policy, and economic topics. **Publications:** *Executive Media Alert*, biweekly. • *I.I.I. Insurance Daily*. • *Insurance Facts*, annual. • *Insurance Issues Update*, monthly. • *Insurance Pulse*, quarterly.

★1577★ Insurance Services Office (ISO)
7 World Trade Center
New York, NY 10048
Ph: (212)898-6000
Members: Property and liability insurance companies. **Purpose:** Seeks to: make available to any insurer, on a voluntary basis, statistical, actuarial, policy forms, and other related services; function as an insurance advisory organization and statistical agent.

★1578★ Life Underwriter Training Council (LUTC)
7625 Wisconsin Ave.
Bethesda, MD 20814
Ph: (301)913-5882   Fax: (301)913-0123
Members: Established by the Life Insurance Marketing and Research Association, the National Association of Life Underwriters, and the American Council of Life Insurance. Members are students who are life underwriters taking part in sales training courses sponsored by local life underwriters associations. **Purpose:** Promotes improved quality of life insurance marketing by providing training, a clearinghouse for information on life underwriter education and training, and assistance to anyone interested in the life insurance sales and service training. The LUTC programs comprise: two 26-week sales training courses in personal insurance and business insurance; one 13-week course in disability income sales; a 13-week fundamentals of financial services course; a 13-week multiline skills course; a 13-week professional growth course; two 13-week courses in advanced sales; a series of seminars based on various aspects of insurance. (Successful completion of three courses and membership in a local association of NALU lead to the designation of LUTC Fellow.) Prepares textbooks, examinations, and recognition certificates. **Publications:** *Focus*, quarterly. • *LUTC to CMOs*, quarterly. • *LUTC to Editors*, quarterly. • *LUTC Today*, 8/year. • *LUTCF*

Review, annual. • *This Month in LUTC*, 8/year. • *This Year in LUTC*, annual.

★1579★ National Association of Review Appraisers and Mortgage Underwriters (NARA/MU)
8383 E. Evans Rd.
Scottsdale, AZ 85260
Ph: (602)998-3000   Fax: (602)998-8022
Members: Real estate professionals and mortgage underwriters who aid in determining value of property. **Purpose:** Acts as umbrella group for real estate appraisers. Conducts educational seminars; maintains speakers' bureau; operates placement service. **Publications:** *Appraisal Review Journal*, quarterly. • *National Association of Review Appraisers and Mortgage Underwriters—Directory*, annual. • *National Association of Review Appraisers and Mortgage Underwriters—Reviews*, quarterly.

STANDARDS/CERTIFICATION AGENCIES

★1580★ American Institute for Chartered Property Casualty Underwriters (AICPCU)
720 Providence Rd.
PO Box 3016
Malvern, PA 19355-0716
Ph: (610)644-2100   Fax: (610)251-9995
Determines qualifications for professional certification of insurance personnel; cooperates with colleges and universities in establishing educational standards; conducts examinations and awards designation of Chartered Property Casualty Underwriter (CPCU).

★1581★ American Institute for Property and Liability Underwriters (AIPLU)
720 Providence Rd.
Malvern, PA 19355-0770
Ph: (215)644-2100
Determines qualifications for professional certification of insurance personnel; cooperates with colleges and universities in establishing educational standards; conducts examinations and awards designation of Chartered Property Casualty Underwriter (CPCU).

★1582★ Health Insurance Association of America (HIAA)
1025 Connecticut Ave. NW, Ste. 1200
Washington, DC 20036
Ph: (202)223-7780
Issues data on benefits and products, tracks legislation and regulations, and offers insurance education.

★1583★ Insurance Institute of America (IIA)
720 Providence Rd.
Malvern, PA 19355-0716
Ph: (215)644-2100   Fax: (215)251-9995
Sponsors 18 educational programs for property and liability insurance personnel. Conducts exams and awards certificates and diplomas.

★1584★ Life Office Management Association (LOMA)
5770 Powers Ferry Rd. NW
Atlanta, GA 30327
Ph: (404)951-1770   Fax: (404)984-0441
Administers FLMI Insurance Education Program, which awards FLMI (Fellow, Life Management Institute) designation to life and health insurance company employees and others who complete the ten-examination program.

★1585★ National Association of Health Underwriters (NAHU)
1000 Connecticut Ave. NW, Ste. 810
Washington, DC 20036
Ph: (202)223-5533   Fax: (202)785-2274
Testifies before federal and state committees on pending health insurance legislation. Grants RHU certification to qualified Registered Disability Income and Health Insurance Underwriters.

TEST GUIDES

★1586★ *Career Examination Series: Underwriter*
National Learning Corp.
212 Michael Dr.
Syosset, NY 11791
Ph: (516)921-8888   Fax: (516)921-8743
Fr: 800-645-6337
Jack Rudman. A series of study guides with multiple-choice examination questions and solutions for trainees and professional underwriters. Titles in the series include *Insurance Contract Analysts; Insurance Examiner; Principal Insurance Examiner; Senior Insurance Examiner; Senior Underwriting Clerk; Workers' Compensation Review Analyst*.

EDUCATIONAL DIRECTORIES AND PROGRAMS

★1587★ *Business and Finance Career Directory*
Gale Research Inc.
835 Penobscot Bldg.
Detroit, MI 48226-4094
Ph: (313)961-2242   Fax: (313)961-6083
Fr: 800-877-GALE
Bradley J. Morgan and Joseph M. Palmisano. Second edition, 1992. A directory in the Career Advisor Series that provides essays written by industry professionals; job search information on resume and cover letter preparation, networking, and the interviewing process; approximately 300 companies and organizations offering job opportunities and internships, and additional job-hunting resources.

Awards, Scholarships, Grants, and Fellowships

★1588★ Distinguished Graduate Award in Premium Auditing
National Society of Insurance Premium
  Auditors
PO Box 323
Boys Town, NE 68010
For recognition of achievement of the highest grade average in the national examinations leading to the Associate in Premium Auditing Program of the Insurance Institute of America. A monetary award of $500 and a plaque are presented annually. Established in 1982 by the Insurance Institute of America.

★1589★ Harold R. Gordon Memorial Award - Health Insurance Industry Man of the Year
National Association of Health Underwriters
1000 Connecticut Ave. NW, Ste. 1111
Washington, DC 20036
Ph: (202)223-5533   Fax: (202)785-2274
To recognize an individual for significant contributions to the development and progress of the health insurance business either during the year or over a sustained period of time. A plaque and certificate are awarded annually. Established in 1948.

Basic Reference Guides and Handbooks

★1590★ Corporations: Estate, Business, and Compensation Planning
National Underwriter Co.
505 Gest St.
Cincinnati, OH 45203-1716
Ph: (513)721-2140
Dennis C. Reardon, editor. 1992.

★1591★ Dictionary of Insurance Terms
Barron's Educational Series, Inc.
250 Wireless Blvd.
Hauppauge, NY 11788
Ph: (516)434-3311   Fax: (516)434-3723
Fr: 800-645-3476
Harvey W. Rubin. Second edition. 1991.

★1592★ Field Guide to Estate Planning, Business Planning, and Employee Benefits
National Underwriter Co.
505 Gest St.
Cincinnati, OH 45203-1716
Ph: (513)721-2140
Donald F. Cady, editor. 1992.

★1593★ Financial Planning for the Older Client
National Underwriter Co.
505 Gest St.
Cincinnati, OH 45203-1716
Ph: (513)721-2140
Dana Shilling, editor. 1992.

★1594★ Who Writes What
National Underwriter Co.
505 Gest St.
Cincinnati, OH 45203-1716
Ph: (513)721-2140
Jaclyn M. Ruzsa, editor. 1992.

Professional and Trade Periodicals

★1595★ American Institute for Chartered Property Casualty Underwriters—Institute Insights
American Institute for Chartered Property
  Casualty Underwriters
PO Box 3016
Malvern, PA 19355-0716
Ph: (215)644-2100   Fax: (215)644-7629
Anne Swigart
Semiannual. Covers programs, activities, and news at the Institutes. Designed to inform those interested in the Institutes of "the ongoing commitment to high standards in continuing education, professionalism, and the promotion of ethical behavior in the property-liability insurance industry."

★1596★ American Society of Chartered Life Underwriters and Chartered Financial Consultants—Query
American Society of Chartered Life
  Underwriters and Chartered Financial
  Consultants
270 Bryn Mawr Ave.
Bryn Mawr, PA 19010
Ph: (215)526-2500
Chuck Hall
Monthly. Contains news of interest to clients of chartered life underwriters. Covers such topics as life insurance, trusts, taxation, and financial planning.

★1597★ American Society of Chartered Life Underwriters and Chartered Financial Consultants—Society Page
American Society of Chartered Life
  Underwriters and Chartered Financial
  Consultants
270 Bryn Mawr Ave.
Bryn Mawr, PA 19010
Ph: (215)526-2500
Deanne Sherman
Bimonthly. Reports Society and member news, notices of the Society's upcoming conferences and seminars, and continuing education information. Features signed insurance, finance, and management articles.

★1598★ CPCU News
Society of Chartered Property & Casualty
  Underwriters (CPCU)
PO Box 3009
720 Providence Rd.
Malvern, PA 19355
Ph: (215)251-2743   Fax: (215)251-2761
Lisa Fittipaldi
Publishes news of the Society, its members, and its services.

★1599★ Inland Marine Underwriters Association—Impact
Inland Marine Underwriters Association
111 Broadway, 15th Fl.
New York, NY 10006
Ph: (212)233-7958
Karen Sherbine
Quarterly. Disseminates news and views of interest to insurance companies transacting inland marine insurance in the U.S. Provides a forum for the discussion of problems which are of common concern. Reports on legislative and regulatory activities affecting the industry and advocates an insurance contract language which is clear, simple, and adequate for the protection of the public. Recurring features include news of members, news of research, and a calendar of events.

★1600★ NAMS News
National Association of Marine Surveyors,
  Inc. (NAMS)
PO Box 9306
Chesapeake, VA 23321-9306
Ph: (609)722-5515   Fax: 800-822-6267
Fr: 800-822-6267
Kim I. MacCartney
Quarterly. Provides news of interest to marine surveyors, underwriters, and adjusters. Covers developments at the International Maritime Bureau, government regulations affecting the field, the national marine conference, and regional meetings. Recurring features include news of research, news of members, information on publications available, and columns titled Cargo and Yachts.

★1601★ National Underwriter Life and Health/Financial Services
Thomas Slattery
Weekly. Life and health/financial services newsweekly.

★1602★ Risk Analysis
Plenum Publishing Corp.
233 Spring St.
New York, NY 10013
Ph: (212)620-8000   Fax: (212)463-0742
Curtis Travis
Quarterly. Official journal of the Society for Risk Analysis.

Professional Meetings and Conventions

★1603★ National Association of Review Appraisers and Mortgage Underwriters Convention
National Association of Review Appraisers
  and Mortgage Underwriters
8383 E. Evans Rd.
Scottsdale, AZ 85260
Ph: (602)998-3000   Fax: (602)998-8022
Annual.

OTHER SOURCES OF INFORMATION

★1604★ "Insurance Underwriter" in
Career Selector 2001
Barron's Educational Series, Inc.
250 Wireless Blvd.
Hauppauge, NY 11788
Ph: (516)434-3311   Fax: (516)434-3723
Fr: 800-645-3476
James C. Gonyea. 1993.

★1605★ "Underwriter" in *100 Best Jobs*
for the 1990s & Beyond
Dearborn Financial Publishing, Inc.
520 N. Dearborn St.
Chicago, IL 60610-4354
Ph: (312)836-4400   Fax: (312)836-1021
Fr: 800-621-9621

Carol Kleiman. 1992. Describes 100 jobs
ranging from accountants to veterinarians.
Each job profile includes such information as
education, experience, and certification
needed, salaries, and job search suggestions.

Wholesale and Retail Buyers and Merchandise Managers

Wholesale and retail buyers purchase merchandise for resale. Regardless of what they are buying–from clothing to machinery they seek the best available merchandise at the lowest possible price. Working with sales and marketing managers, they also determine how the merchandise will be distributed and marketed. Wholesale and retail buyers are an integral part of a complex system of production, distribution, and merchandising that caters to the vast variety of consumer needs and desires. Buyers working for large and medium-sized firms usually specialize in acquiring one or two lines of merchandise. However, buyers working for small stores may purchase their complete stock of merchandise. Wholesale buyers purchase goods directly from manufacturers or from other wholesale firms for resale to retail firms or to commercial establishments and other institutions. Retail buyers purchase goods from wholesale firms or directly from manufacturers for resale to the public.

Salaries

A buyer's income depends on the amount and type of product purchased, the employer's sales volume and, to some extent, the buyer's seniority.

Lowest 10 percent	Less than $13,500/year
Median	$25,100/year
Top 10 percent	More than $46,700/year

Employment Outlook

Growth rate until the year 2005: Slower than the average.

Wholesale and Retail Buyers and Merchandise Managers

★1606★ "Assistant Buyers and Buyers" and "Resident Buying Offices and Central Buying Offices" in *Opportunities in Retailing Careers* (chaps. 4 and 6)
National Textbook Co. (NTC)
VGM Career Books
4255 W. Touhy Ave.
Lincolnwood, IL 60646-1975
Ph: (708)679-5500   Fax: (708)679-2494
Fr: 800-323-4900

Roslyn Dolber. 1988. Gives the history of modern retailing, and describes retailing organization. Includes the required educational preparation and gives job hunting advice on writing the resume and preparing for the interview.

★1607★ *Buyers*
Chronicle Guidance Publications, Inc.
66 Aurora St.
PO Box 1190
Moravia, NY 13118-1190
Ph: (315)497-0330   Fax: (315)497-3359
Fr: 800-622-7284

1992. Career brief describing the nature of the job, working conditions, hours and earnings, education and training, licensure, certification, unions, personal qualifications, social and psychological factors, location, employment outlook, entry methods, advancement, and related occupations.

★1608★ "Buyers" in *Jobs! What They Are—Where They Are—What They Pay* (p. 316)
Simon & Schuster, Inc.
Simon & Schuster Bldg.
1230 Avenue of the Americas
New York, NY 10020
Ph: (212)698-7000   Fr: 800-223-2348

Robert O. Snelling and Anne M. Snelling. 3rd edition, 1992. Describes duties and responsibilities, earnings, employment opportunities, training, and qualifications.

★1609★ "Buyers" in *Liberal Arts Jobs*
Petersons Guides, Inc.
PO Box 2123
Princeton, NJ 08543-2123
Ph: (609)243-9111   Fax: (609)243-9150
Fr: 800-338-3282

Burton Jay Nadler. Second edition 1989. Strives to help the liberal arts graduate identify skills for entry-level positions. Gives goal setting and job search advice.

★1610★ "Buyers, Wholesale and Retail" in *Encyclopedia of Careers and Vocational Guidance* (Vol.2, pp. 229-232)
J.G. Ferguson Publishing Co.
200 W. Madison St., Ste. 300
Chicago, IL 60606
Ph: (312)580-5480   Fax: (312)580-4948

William E. Hopke, editor-in-chief. Ninth edition, 1993. Four-volume set that profiles 900 occupations and describes job trends in 74 industries. Includes career description, educational requirements, history of the job, methods of entry, advancement, employment outlook, earnings, conditions of work, social and psychological factors, and sources of further information.

★1611★ "Buying" in *Career Choices for the 90's for Students of Art* (pp. 52-54)
Walker and Co.
435 Hudson St.
New York, NY 10014
Ph: (212)727-8300   Fax: (212)727-0984
Fr: 800-289-2553

Compiled by Career Associates Staff. 1990. This book offers alternatives for students of art. Gives information about the outlook and competition for entry-level candidates. Provides job hunting tips.

★1612★ "Buying" in *Career Choices for the 90's for Students of Business* (pp. 75-77)
Walker and Co.
435 Hudson St.
New York, NY 10014
Ph: (212)727-8300   Fax: (212)727-0984
Fr: 800-289-2553

Compiled by Career Associates Staff. 1990. This book offers alternatives for students of business. Gives information about the outlook and competition for entry-level candidates. Provides job hunting tips.

★1613★ "Buying" in *Career Choices for the 90's for Students of English*
Walker and Co.
435 Hudson St.
New York, NY 10014
Ph: (212)727-8300   Fax: (212)727-0984
Fr: 800-289-2553

Compiled by Career Associates Staff. 1990. The goal of this book is to offer career alternatives for students of English. Gives the outlook and competition for entry-level candidates. Provides job hunting tips.

★1614★ "Buying" in *Career Choices for the 90's for Students of Political Science and Government*
Walker and Co.
435 Hudson St.
New York, NY 10014
Ph: (212)727-8300   Fax: (212)727-0984
Fr: 800-289-2553

Compiled by Career Associates Staff. 1990. This book offers alternatives for students of political science. Gives information about job outlook and competition for entry-level candidates. Provides job hunting tips.

★1615★ "Buying" in *Career Choices for the 90's for Students of Psychology* (pp. 30-32)
Walker and Co.
435 Hudson St.
New York, NY 10014
Ph: (212)727-8300   Fax: (212)727-0984
Fr: 800-289-2553

Compiled by Career Associates Staff. 1990. This book offers alternatives for students of psychology. Gives information about the outlook and competition for entry-level candidates. Provides job hunting tips.

★1616★ *Careers in Clothing and Textiles*
Glencoe Publishing Co.
866 3rd Ave.
New York, NY 10022-6299
Ph: (212)702-3276

Videotape that explores career possibilities in the manufacturing, designing, merchandising, and selling of clothes.

★1617★ *Department Store Buyer*
Vocational Biographies, Inc.
PO Box 31
Sauk Centre, MN 56378-0031
Ph: (612)352-6516   Fax: (612)352-5546
Fr: 800-255-0752

1994. Four-page pamphlet containing a personal narrative about a worker's job, work likes and dislikes, career path from high school to the present. Education and training, the rewards and frustrations, and the effects of the job on the rest of the worker's life. The data file portion of this pamphlet gives a concise occupational summary, including work descriptions, working conditions, places of employment, personal characteristics, education and training, job outlook, and salary range.

★1618★ "Department Store Retailing" in *Encyclopedia of Career Choices for the 1990s: A Guide to Entry Level Jobs* (pp. 252-272)
Berkley Pub.
PO Box 506
East Rutherford, NJ 07073
Fax: (201)933-2316   Fr: 800-788-6262

1992. Describes entry-level careers in a variety of industries. Presents qualifications required, working conditions, salary, internships, and professional associations.

★1619★ "Fashion Merchandising" in *Opportunities in Fashion* (pp. 49-76)
National Textbook Co. (NTC)
VGM Career Books
4255 W. Touhy Ave.
Lincolnwood, IL 60646-1975
Ph: (708)679-5500   Fax: (708)679-2494
Fr: 800-323-4900

Roslyn Dolber. 1993. Describes career opportunities in apparel design and production textile, and fashion merchandising. Gives job hunting advice. Lists schools that offer fashion-related majors.

★1620★ "Merchandisers" in *Jobs! What They Are—Where They Are—What They Pay* (pp. 321)
Fireside
Simon & Schuster Bldg.
1230 Avenue of the Americas
New York, NY 10020
Ph: (212)698-7000   Fr: 800-223-2348

Robert O. Snelling and Anne M. Snelling. Revised and updated, 1992. Describes duties and responsibilities, earnings, employment opportunities, training, and qualifications.

★1621★ *Opportunities in Retailing Careers*
National Textbook Co. (NTC)
VGM Career Books
4255 W. Touhy Ave.
Lincolnwood, IL 60646-1975
Ph: (708)679-5500   Fax: (708)679-2494
Fr: 800-323-4900
Roslyn Dolber. 1989.

★1622★ "Purchasers and Buyers" in *Occupational Outlook Handbook*
U.S. Government Printing Office
Superintendent of Documents
Washington, DC 20402
Ph: (202)512-1800   Fax: (202)512-2250

Biennial; latest edition, 1994-95. Encyclopedia of careers describing more than 225 occupations and comprising about 80 percent of all jobs in the economy. Occupations that require lengthy education or training are given the most attention. Each occupation's profile describes what the worker does on the job, working conditions, education and training requirements, advancement possibilities, job outlook, earnings, and sources of additional information.

★1623★ "Retail Buyer" in *Guide to Careers Without College* (pp. 21-22)
Franklin Watts, Inc.
387 Park Ave., S.
New York, NY 10016
Ph: (212)686-7070   Fax: (212)213-6435

Kathleen S. Abrams. 1988. Discusses rewarding careers that do not require a college degree.

★1624★ "Retail Buyer" in *VGM's Careers Encyclopedia* (pp. 407-409)
National Textbook Co. (NTC)
VGM Career Books
4255 W. Touhy Ave.
Lincolnwood, IL 60646-1975
Ph: (708)679-5500   Fax: (708)679-2494
Fr: 800-323-4900

Third edition, 1991. Describes job duties, places of employment, working conditions, qualifications, education, and training, advancement potential, and salary for each occupation.

★1625★ "Retail Buyers" in *Career Information Center* (Vol.10)
Simon and Schuster
200 Old Tappan Rd.
Old Tappan, NJ 07675
Fax: 800-445-6991   Fr: 800-223-2348

Richard Lidz and Linda Perrin, editorial directors. Fifth edition, 1993. This 13-volume set profiles over 600 occupations. Each occupational profile describes job duties, educational requirements, how to get the job, advancement possibilities, employment outlook, working conditions, earnings and benefits, and where to write for more information.

★1626★ "Retail" in *Internships 1995*
Petersons Guides, Inc.
PO Box 2123
Princeton, NJ 08543-2123
Ph: (609)243-9111   Fr: 800-338-3282

Fifteenth edition, 1995. Lists internship opportunities under six broad categories: communications, creative, performing, and fine arts, human services, international relations, business and technology, and public affairs. For each internship program, gives the names, phone number, contact person, description, eligibility requirements, and benefits.

★1627★ "Retail and Wholesale Buyer" in *College Board Guide to Jobs and Career Planning* (pp. 146)
The College Board
415 Columbus Ave.
New York, NY 10023-6992
Ph: (212)713-8165   Fax: (212)713-8143
Fr: 800-323-7155

Joyce S. Mitchell. Second edition, 1994. Describes the job, salaries, related careers, education needed, and where to write for more information.

★1628★ *Retailing*
Prentice-Hall, Inc.
200 Old Tappan Rd.
Old Tappan, NJ 07675
Ph: (201)767-5000   Fr: 800-722-4726

Gerald Pintel and Jay Diamond. Fifth edition, 1991. Includes an index.

★1629★ "Wholesale and Retail Buyers" in *101 Careers: A Guide to the Fastest-Growing Opportunities* (pp. 54-57)
John Wiley & Sons, Inc.
605 3rd Ave.
New York, NY 10158-0012
Ph: (212)850-6645   Fax: (212)850-6088

Michael Harkavy. 1990. Describes the nature of the job, working conditions, employment growth, qualifications, personal skills, projected salaries, and where to write for more information.

★1630★ "Wholesale and Retail Trade" in *Career Choices for the 90's for Students of Mathematics* (pp. 82-84)
Walker and Co.
435 Hudson St.
New York, NY 10014
Ph: (212)727-8300   Fax: (212)727-0984
Fr: 800-289-2553

Compiled by Career Associates Staff. 1990. This book offers alternatives for students of mathematics. Gives information about the outlook and competition for entry-level candidates. Provides job hunting tips.

★1631★ "Wholesaler" in *VGM's Handbook of Business and Management Careers*
National Textbook Co.
4255 W. Touhy Ave.
Lincolnwood, IL 60646-1975
Ph: (708)679-5500   Fax: (708)679-2494
Fr: 800-323-4900

Annette Selden. Second edition, 1993. Contains 42 two-page occupational profiles describing job duties, places of employment, working conditions, qualifications, education, employment outlook, and income.

PROFESSIONAL ASSOCIATIONS

★1632★ National Association of Men's Sportswear Buyers (NAMSB)
500 5th Ave., Ste. 1425
New York, NY 10110
Ph: (212)391-8580
Members: Sponsors trade shows for buyers of clothes for men's wear stores. Conducts media interviews to discuss men's wear and educational programs.

★1633★ National Retail Federation (NRF)
325 7th St. NW, Ste. 1000
Washington, DC 20004-2802
Ph: (202)783-7971   Fax: (202)737-2849
Members: Purpose: Represents 50 state retail association, several dozen national retail associations as well as large and small corporate members representing the breadth and diversity of the retail industry's establishment and employees. Conducts informational and educational conferences related to all phases of retailing including financial planning and cash management, taxation, economic forecasting, expense planning, shortage control, credit, electronic data processing, telecommunications, merchandise management, buying, traffic, security, supply, materials handling, store planning and construction, personnel administration, recruitment and training, and advertising and display. **Publications:** *STORES Magazine*, monthly. • *Washington Retail Report*, weekly.

★1634★ United Buying Services (NABS)
39 S. Milwaukee Ave.
Wheeling, IL 60090
Ph: (708)215-7000
Members: Buying service organizations. **Purpose:** Serves as a clearinghouse for the exchange of information and ideas relating to buying services. Acts as a centralized distribution source for promotion of national products.

TEST GUIDES

★1635★ Career Examination Series: Buyer
National Learning Corp.
212 Michael Dr.
Syosset, NY 11791
Ph: (516)921-8888   Fax: (516)921-8743
Fr: 800-645-6337
Jack Rudman. A series of study guides with multiple-choice examination questions and solutions for trainees and professional buy-ers. Titles in the series include *Assistant Buyer; Buyer I; Buyer II; Principal Buyer; Senior Buyer.*

BASIC REFERENCE GUIDES AND HANDBOOKS

★1636★ Modern Retailing: Theory and Practice
BPI
9605 Scranton Rd., Ste. 503
San Diego, CA 92121-1774
Ph: (619)457-7577   Fax: (619)453-1091
J. Barry Mason, Morris L. Mayer, and J.B. Wilkinson. Sixth edition, 1993.

★1637★ Retail Buying
Prentice-Hall, Inc.
Rte. 9W
Englewood Cliffs, NJ 07632
Ph: (201)592-2000   Fr: 800-634-2863
Jay Diamond and Gerald Pintel. Fourth edition, 1992. Practical guide describing procedures and practices used by professional retail buyers. Covers purchasing goods off price.

PROFESSIONAL AND TRADE PERIODICALS

★1638★ Barnard's Retail Marketing Report
Barnard Enterprises, Inc.
25 Sutton Pl. S.
New York, NY 10022
Ph: (212)752-9810
Kurt Barnard
Monthly. Reports, forecasts, analyzes, explains, and identifies trends and events affecting retail operations. Recurring features include market statistics and news of research.

★1639★ The Distributor's & Wholesaler's Advisor
Alexander Research & Communications, Inc.
215 Park Ave. S., Ste. 1301
New York, NY 10003-1603
Ph: (212)228-0246   Fax: (212)228-0376
Anita Rosepka
Semiannual. Provides case studies, how-to-do-it reports, and industry news of interest to wholesalers and distributors. Covers management strategies, working with manufacturers, logistics and warehousing, finance, personnel issues, sales management, tech-nology, customer service, and law and regulation.

★1640★ Retailing Today
Robert Kahn and Associates
PO Box 249
Lafayette, CA 94549
Ph: (510)254-4434   Fax: (510)284-5612
Robert Kahn
Monthly. Focuses on general merchandise, apparel, furniture, hardware, automotive, and food retailing. Offers "original research, comments on current trends and conditions, recommendations for company policy, and emphasis on ethical conduct in business."

PROFESSIONAL MEETINGS AND CONVENTIONS

★1641★ National Association of Men's Sportswear Buyers (NAMSB) Show
Schimel Co., Inc.
535 5th Ave.
New York, NY 10017
Ph: (212)986-1811   Fax: (212)697-8493
Always held during January, March, June, and October at the Jacob K. Javits Convention Center in New York City.

★1642★ Supermarket Industry Convention and Educational Exposition
Food Marketing Institute
800 Connecticut Ave., NW Ste. 500
Washington, DC 20006-2701
Ph: (202)452-8444   Fax: (202)429-4519
Annual. Always held during May at McCormick Place Complex in Chicago, Illinois. **Dates and Locations:** 1996 May 05-08; Chicago, IL. • 1997 May 04-07; Chicago, IL.

OTHER SOURCES OF INFORMATION

★1643★ "Wholesale Sales Representative" in *100 Best Jobs for the 1990s & Beyond*
Dearborn Financial Publishing, Inc.
520 N. Dearborn St.
Chicago, IL 60610-4354
Ph: (312)836-4400   Fax: (312)836-1021
Fr: 800-621-9621
Carol Kleiman. 1992. Describes 100 jobs ranging from accountants to veterinarians. Each job profile includes such information as education, experience, and certification needed, salaries, and job search suggestions.

Aerospace Engineers

Aerospace engineers design, develop, test, and help manufacture commercial and military aircraft, missiles, and spacecraft. They develop new technologies in commercial aviation, defense systems, and space exploration, often specializing in areas like structural design, guidance, navigation and control, instrumentation and communication, or production methods. They also may specialize in one type of aerospace product, such as commercial transportation, helicopters, spacecraft, or rockets.

Salaries

Starting salaries for engineers with bachelor's degrees are significantly higher than starting salaries of college graduates in other fields.

Beginning aerospace engineers	$31,826/year
Mid-level engineers	$52,500/year
Senior managerial engineers	$102,544/year

Employment Outlook

Growth rate until the year 2005: More slowly than the average.

Aerospace Engineers

CAREER GUIDES

★1644★ *Aerospace Careers*
Franklin Watts, Inc.
387 Park Ave., S.
New York, NY 10016
Ph: (212)686-7070
James L. Schefter. 1987.

★1645★ *Aerospace Engineer*
Careers, Inc.
PO Box 135
Largo, FL 34649-0135
Ph: (813)584-7333
1991. Four-page brief offering the definition, history, duties, working conditions, personal qualifications, educational requirements, earnings, hours, employment outlook, advancement, and careers related to this position.

★1646★ "Aerospace Engineer" in *Career Information Center* (Vol.6)
Simon and Schuster
200 Old Tappan Rd.
Old Tappan, NJ 07675
Fax: 800-445-6991   Fr: 800-223-2348
Richard Lidz and Linda Perrin, editorial directors. Fifth edition, 1993. This 13-volume set profiles over 600 occupations. Each occupational profile describes job duties, entry-level requirements, educational requirements, advancement possibilities, employment outlook, working conditions, earnings and benefits, and where to write for more information.

★1647★ "Aerospace Engineer" in *Guide to Federal Jobs* (p. 163)
Resource Directories
3361 Executive Pkwy., Ste. 302
Toledo, OH 43606
Ph: (419)536-5353   Fax: (419)536-7056
Fr: 800-274-8515
O'Rod W. Durgin, editor. Third edition, 1992. Contains information on finding and applying for federal jobs. Describes more than 200 professional and technical jobs for college graduates. Covers the nature of the work, salary, and geographic location. Lists college majors preferred for that occupation. Section one describes the function and work of gov-

ernment agencies that hire the most significant number of college graduates.

★1648★ "Aerospace Engineer" in *Jobs Rated Almanac*
World Almanac
1 International Blvd., Ste. 444
Mahwah, NJ 07495
Ph: (201)529-6900   Fax: (201)529-6901
Les Krantz. Second edition, 1992. Ranks 250 jobs by environment, salary, outlooks, physical demands, stress, security, travel opportunities, and extra perks. Includes jobs the editor feels are the most common, most interesting, and the most rapidly growing.

★1649★ "Aerospace Engineer" in *VGM's Careers Encyclopedia* (pp. 22-25)
National Textbook Co. (NTC)
VGM Career Books
4255 W. Touhy Ave.
Lincolnwood, IL 60646-1975
Ph: (708)679-5500   Fax: (708)679-2494
Fr: 800-323-4900
Third edition, 1991. Profiles 200 occupations. Describes job duties, places of employment, working conditions, qualifications, education and training, advancement potential, and salary for each occupation.

★1650★ *Aerospace Engineers*
Chronicle Guidance Publications, Inc.
66 Aurora St.
PO Box 1190
Moravia, NY 13118-1190
Ph: (315)497-0330   Fax: (315)497-3359
Fr: 800-622-7284
1993. Occupational brief describing the nature of the job, working conditions, hours and earnings, education and training, licensure, certification, unions, personal qualifications, social and psychological factors, location, employment outlook, entry methods, advancement, and related occupations.

★1651★ "Aerospace Engineers" in *101 Careers: A Guide to the Fastest-Growing Opportunities* (pp. 58-60)
John Wiley & Sons, Inc.
605 3rd Ave.
New York, NY 10158-0012
Ph: (212)850-6645   Fax: (212)850-6088
Michael Harkavy. 1990. Describes the nature of the job, working conditions, employment

growth, qualifications, personal skills, projected salaries, and where to write for more information.

★1652★ "Aerospace Engineers" in *Best Jobs for the 1990s and Into the 21st Century*
Impact Publications
9104-N Manassas Dr.
Manassas Park, VA 22111
Ph: (703)361-7300   Fax: (703)335-9486
Ronald L. Krannich and Caryl Rae Krannich. 1993.

★1653★ "Aerospace Engineers" in *Career Discovery Encyclopedia* (Vol.1, pp. 30-31)
J.G. Ferguson Publishing Co.
200 W. Madison St., Ste. 300
Chicago, IL 60606
Ph: (312)580-5480   Fax: (312)580-4948
Russell E. Primm, editor-in-chief. 1993. This six volume set contains two-page articles for 504 occupations. Each article describes job duties, earnings, and educational and training requirements. The whole set is arranged alphabetically by job title. Designed for junior high and older students.

★1654★ "Aerospace Engineers" in *College Majors and Careers: A Resource Guide to Effective Life Planning* (pp. 9-10)
Garrett Park Press
PO Box 1907
Garrett Park, MD 20896
Ph: (301)946-2553
Paul Phifer. 1993. Lists 60 college majors, with definitions; related occupations and leisure activities; skills, values, and personal attributes needed; suggested readings; and a list of associations.

★1655★ "Aerospace Engineers" in *Encyclopedia of Careers and Vocational Guidance* (Vol.2, pp. 35-38)
J.G. Ferguson Publishing Co.
200 W. Madison St., Ste. 300
Chicago, IL 60606
Ph: (312)580-5480   Fax: (312)580-4948
William E. Hopke, editor-in-chief. Ninth edition, 1993. Four-volume set that profiles 900 occupations and describes job trends in 74 industries. Includes career description, educational requirements, history of the job,

methods of entry, advancement, employment outlook, earnings, conditions of work, social and psychological factors, and sources of further information.

★1656★ "Aerospace Engineers" in Jobs! What They Are—Where They Are—What They Pay (p. 117)
Simon & Schuster, Inc.
Simon & Schuster Bldg.
1230 Avenue of the Americas
New York, NY 10020
Ph: (212)698-7000   Fr: 800-223-2348
Robert O. Snelling and Anne M. Snelling. 3rd edition, 1992. Describes duties and responsibilities, earnings, employment opportunities, training, and qualifications.

★1657★ "Aerospace Engineers" in Occupational Outlook Handbook
U.S. Government Printing Office
Superintendent of Documents
Washington, DC 20402
Ph: (202)512-1800   Fax: (202)512-2250
Biennial; latest edition, 1994-95. Encyclopedia of careers describing about 250 occupations and comprising about 85 percent of all jobs in the economy. Occupations that require lengthy education or training are given the most attention. Each occupation's profile describes what the worker does on the job, working conditions, education and training requirements, advancement possibilities, job outlook, earnings, and sources of additional information.

★1658★ Career Development for Engineers and Scientists: Organizational Programs and Individual Choices
Van Nostrand Reinhold Co., Inc.
115 5th Ave.
New York, NY 10003
Ph: (212)254-3232   Fr: 800-842-3636
Robert F. Morrison and Richard M. Vosburgh. 1987. Includes bibliographies and an index. Illustrated.

★1659★ Careers and the Engineer
Bob Adams, Inc.
260 Center St.
Holbrook, MA 02343
Ph: (617)268-9570
Gigi Ranno, editor. Annual.

★1660★ Careers in Engineering
National Textbook Co. (NTC)
VGM Career Books
4255 W. Touhy Ave.
Lincolnwood, IL 60646-1975
Ph: (708)679-5500   Fax: (708)679-2494
Fr: 800-323-4900
Geraldine O. Garner, Ph.D., editor. 1993. Career guide covering 14 different engineering specialties.

★1661★ The Civilized Engineer
St. Martin's Press, Inc.
175 5th Ave.
New York, NY 10010
Ph: (212)674-5151   Fax: 800-258-2769
Fr: 800-221-7945
Samuel C. Florman. 1989. Published by Thomas Dunne Books. Discusses engineering education, the relationship between engineers and nontechnical executives, and the role of women in engineering.

★1662★ "Engineering" in American Almanac of Jobs and Salaries (pp. 261)
Avon Books
1350 Avenue of the Americas
New York, NY 10019
Ph: (212)261-6800   Fr: 800-238-0658
John Wright, editor. Revised and updated, 1994-95. A comprehensive guide to the wages of hundreds of occupations in a wide variety of industries and organizations.

★1663★ "Engineering" in Encyclopedia of Careers and Vocational Guidance (Vol.1, pp. 165-171)
J.G. Ferguson Publishing Co.
200 W. Madison St., Ste. 300
Chicago, IL 60606
Ph: (312)580-5480   Fax: (312)580-4948
William E. Hopke, editor-in-chief. Ninth edition, 1993. Four-volume set that profiles 900 occupations and describes job trends in 74 industries. Includes career description, educational requirements, history of the job, methods of entry, advancement, employment outlook, earnings, conditions of work, social and psychological factors, and sources of further information.

★1664★ Engineering Salary Survey
Source Engineering
1290 Oakmead, Ste. 318
Sunnyvale, CA 94086
Ph: (408)738-8440
Annual. Discusses the structure of the engineering profession, trends, and compensation. Salaries are listed by job function, industry, and years of experience.

★1665★ "Engineering" in Where the Jobs Are: The Hottest Careers for the 90s (pp. 111-124)
Career Press
180 5th Ave.
Hawthorne, NJ 07507
Ph: (201)427-0229   Fax: (201)427-2037
Fr: 800-CAREER-1
Joyce Hadley. 1995. Offers a job-hunting strategy for the 1990s as well as descriptions of growing careers of the decade. Each profile includes general information, forecasts, growth, education and training, licensing requirements, and salary information.

★1666★ Engineering for You: A Career Guide
Iowa State University Press
2121 S. State Ave.
Ames, IA 50010
Ph: (515)292-0140   Fax: (515)292-3348
John T. Jones. 1991.

★1667★ Flight Engineer
Careers, Inc.
PO Box 135
Largo, FL 34649-0135
Ph: (813)584-7333
1992. Four-page brief describing duties, working conditions, personal qualifications, training, earnings and hours, employment outlook, places of employment, related careers, and where to write for more information.

★1668★ How to Become a Professional Engineer: The Road to Registration
McGraw-Hill, Inc.
1221 Avenue of the Americas
New York, NY 10020
Ph: (212)512-2000   Fr: 800-722-4726
John D. Constance. Fourth edition, 1988. Includes a bibliography and an index.

★1669★ Opportunities in Aerospace Careers
National Textbook Co. (NTC)
VGM Career Books
4255 W. Touhy Ave.
Lincolnwood, IL 60646-1975
Ph: (708)679-5500   Fax: (708)679-2494
Fr: 800-323-4900
Wallace R. Maples, author. 1991. Surveys jobs with the airlines, airports, the government, the military, in manufacturing, and in research and development. Describes educational requirements, working conditions, salaries, employment outlook, and certification.

★1670★ Opportunities in Engineering
National Textbook Co. (NTC)
VGM Career Books
4255 W. Touhy Ave.
Lincolnwood, IL 60646-1975
Ph: (708)679-5500   Fax: (708)679-2494
Fr: 800-323-4900
Nicholas Basta. 1990. Profiles specialties in the engineering field including civil, chemical, mechanical, biomedical, and aerospace. Offers information on salaries, career paths and educational requirements.

★1671★ Opportunities in Engineering Technology Careers
National Textbook Co. (NTC)
VGM Career Books
4255 W. Touhy Ave.
Lincolnwood, IL 60646-1975
Ph: (708)679-5500   Fax: (708)679-2494
Fr: 800-323-4900
John E. Heer and D. Joseph Hagerty. 1987. Describes the many opportunities available for engineering technicians. Explains job duties, educational requirements, salary, working conditions, employment outlook, and advancement opportunities. Lists accredited engineering technology programs.

★1672★ Peterson's Job Opportunities for Engineering and Technology
Petersons Guides, Inc.
PO Box 2123
Princeton, NJ 08543-2123
Ph: (609)243-9111   Fax: (609)243-9150
Fr: 800-338-3282
1994. Gives job hunting advice including information on resume writing, interviewing, and handling salary negotiations. Lists companies that hire college graduates in science and engineering at the bachelor and master's level. Companies are indexed by industry, starting location, and major. Company profiles include contact information and types of hires.

★1673★ Successful Engineering: A Guide to Achieving Your Career Goals
McGraw-Hill, Inc.
1221 Avenue of the Americas
New York, NY 10020
Ph: (212)512-2000   Fr: 800-722-4726
Lawrence J. Kamm. 1989. Written for the practicing and graduating engineer. Gives advice about working with accountants, the politics of design, and engineering ethics.

★1674★ VGM'S Handbook of Scientific and Technical Careers
National Textbook Co. (NTC)
VGM Career Books
4255 W. Touhy Ave.
Lincolnwood, IL 60646-1975
Ph: (708)679-5500   Fax: (708)679-2494
Fr: 800-323-4900
Annette Selden, editor. Second ed. Overview of nearly 60 science-related careers, with emphasis on educational preparation. Includes information on job responsibilities, working conditions, salaries, and growth opportunities.

PROFESSIONAL ASSOCIATIONS

★1675★ American Institute of Aeronautics and Astronautics (AIAA)
370 L'Enfant Promenade SW
Washington, DC 20024
Ph: (202)646-7400   Fax: (202)646-7508
Members: Scientists and engineers in the field of aeronautics and astronautics. Facilitates interchange of technological information through publications and technical meetings in order to foster overall technical progress in the field and increase the professional competence of members. **Purpose:** Operates Public Policy program to provide federal decision-makers with the technical information and policy guidance needed to make effective policy on aerospace issues. Public Policy program activities include congressional testimony, position papers, section public policy activities, and workshops. Offers placement assistance; compiles statistics; offers educational programs. Provides abstracting services through its Acroplus Access. **Publications:** AAIA Bulletin, monthly. • Aerospace America, monthly. • AIAA Education Series. • AIAA Journal, monthly. • AIAA Student Journal, quarterly. • International Aerospace Abstracts, monthly. • Journal of Aircraft, bimonthly. • Journal of Guidance, Control, and Dynamics, bimonthly. • Journal of Propulsion and Power, bimonthly. • Journal of Spacecraft and Rockets, bimonthly. • Journal of Thermophysics and Heat Transfer, quarterly. • Progress in Astronautics and Astronautics Series. • Roster, biennial.

★1676★ American Institute of Aeronautics and Astronautics Aeroplus Access (AIAAAA)
85 John St.
New York, NY 10038
Ph: (212)349-1120   Fax: (212)349-1283
Fr: 800-348-7737
Members: A division of the American Institute of Aeronautics and Astronautics devoted to the acquisition, processing, and dissemination of technical and engineering information. **Publications:** Aerospace Access, periodic. • International Aerospace Abstracts, monthly.

★1677★ American Institute of Engineers (AIE)
4666 San Pablo Dam Rd., No. 8
El Sobrante, CA 94803-3142
Ph: (510)223-8911   Fax: (510)223-3400
Members: Professional engineers and engineering students. **Purpose:** Seeks to advance the professional interests of engineers and scientists. Fosters the interchange of ideas and information among members. Compiles statistics; maintains speakers' bureau. **Publications:** AIE Newsmagazine, monthly.

★1678★ Sigma Gamma Tau
c/o Dr. John E. LaGraff
Syracuse University
Department of Mechanical and Aerospace Engineering
151 Link Hall
Syracuse, NY 13244-1240
Ph: (315)443-4366   Fax: (315)443-9099
Members: National honor society - aerospace engineering.

TEST GUIDES

★1679★ Career Examination Series: Aerospace Engineer
National Learning Corp.
212 Michael Dr.
Syosset, NY 11791
Ph: (516)921-8888   Fax: (516)921-8743
Fr: 800-645-6337
Jack Rudman. Test guide including questions and answers for students or professionals in the field who seek advancement through examination.

★1680★ Career Examination Series: Engineer
National Learning Corp.
212 Michael Dr.
Syosset, NY 11791
Ph: (516)921-8888   Fax: (516)921-8743
Fr: 800-645-6337
Jack Rudman. A series of study guides with multiple-choice examination questions and solutions for trainees and professional petroleum engineers. Titles in the series include Administrative Engineer; Chief Engineer; Engineering Aide and Science Assistant; Engineering Aide; Engineering Assistant; Engineering Trainee; Senior Engineer; Senior Engineering Aide.

★1681★ Engineer-in-Training Exam File
Engineering Press, Inc.
PO Box 1
San Jose, CA 95103-0001
Ph: (408)258-4503   Fax: 800-700-1651
Fr: 800-800-1651
Donald G. Newnan and Dean Newnan. Eleventh edition. 1990. Contains 505 problems with step-by-step solutions. Covers: mathematics; statics; fluid mechanics. Includes an index.

★1682★ Engineer-In-Training Sample Examinations
Professional Publications, Inc.
1250 5th Ave.
Belmont, CA 94002-3863
Ph: 800-426-1178
Michael R. Lindeburg. 1991. Contains two complete practice exams, including detailed solutions.

★1683★ Engineering Economic Analysis Exam File
Engineering Press, Inc.
PO Box 1
San Jose, CA 95103-0001
Ph: (408)258-4503   Fax: 800-700-1651
Fr: 800-800-1651
Contains 386 exam problems with step-by-step solutions.

★1684★ Graduate Record Examination: Engineering
National Learning Corp.
212 Michael Dr.
Syosset, NY 11791
Ph: (516)921-8888   Fax: (516)921-8743
Fr: 800-645-6337
Jack Rudman. Multiple-choice test for those seeking admission to graduate school for study in the field of engineering. Includes solutions to examination questions.

★1685★ Graduate Record Examination in Engineering
Arco Publishing Co.
Macmillan General Reference
15 Columbus Cir.
New York, NY 10023
Fax: 800-835-3202   Fr: 800-858-7674
C.W. Tan, et al. First edition. 1988. Contains two sample tests with an explanation to answers.

★1686★ Practicing to Take the GRE Engineering Test: An Official Publication of the GRE Board
Educational Testing Service
Rosedale Rd.
Princeton, NJ 08541
Ph: (609)921-9000
Second edition, 1989. Summarizes the purpose and scope of the Graduate Record Examination Subject Test for engineering. Contains sample questions.

★1687★ Professional Engineer
National Learning Corp.
212 Michael Dr.
Syosset, NY 11791
Ph: (516)921-8888   Fax: (516)921-8743
Fr: 800-645-6337
Jack Rudman. A sample test for engineers who are seeking admission to graduate and professional schools or seeking entrance or

advancement in institutional and public career service.

★1688★ *Undergraduate Program Field Test: Engineering*
National Learning Corp.
212 Michael Dr.
Syosset, NY 11791
Ph: (516)921-8888   Fax: (516)921-8743
Fr: 800-645-6337

Jack Rudman. A practice examination fashioned after tests given in the Regents External Degree Program. Designed to measure knowledge received outside the college classroom in the subject of engineering. Contains multiple-choice questions; provides solutions.

EDUCATIONAL DIRECTORIES AND PROGRAMS

★1689★ *ABET Accreditation Yearbook*
Accreditation Board for Engineering and Technology
345 E. 47th St., 14th Fl.
New York, NY 10017-2397
Ph: (212)705-7685   Fax: (212)838-8062
Simona C. Mardale, Contact

Annual, September. Covers about 300 U.S. colleges and universities with engineering programs, 242 institutions with programs in engineering technology, and 11 institutions with engineering-related programs accredited by the Board; also lists accredited Canadian programs. Entries include: For United States institutions—Name, year of next full accreditation review, location, program names, year of initial accreditation for each program, coding to indicate degrees offered, format of program (day, night, cooperative, etc.). For Canadian programs—Name, location, names of programs, year of initial accredition for each program. Arrangement: Classified by program area.

AWARDS, SCHOLARSHIPS, GRANTS, AND FELLOWSHIPS

★1690★ *AIAA Aerodynamic Decelerator Systems Award*
American Institute of Aeronautics and Astronautics
370 L'Enfant Promenade SW
Washington, DC 20024-2518
Ph: (202)646-7537   Fax: (202)646-7508

To recognize significant contributions to the effectiveness and/or safety of aeronautical or aerospace systems through development or application of the art and science of aerodynamic decelerator technology. A medal, certificate of citation, and a rosette pin are awarded at the Aerodynamic Deceleration Conference. Established in 1976.

★1691★ *AIAA Aerospace Contribution to Society Award*
American Institute of Aeronautics and Astronautics
370 L'Enfant Promenade SW
Washington, DC 20024-2518
Ph: (202)646-7537   Fax: (202)646-7508

To recognize a notable contribution to society through the application of aerospace technology to societal needs. A medal, certificate of citation, and a rosette pin are presented annually at the Aerospace Sciences Meeting and Exhibit. Established in 1977.

★1692★ *AIAA Aerospace Power Systems Award*
American Institute of Aeronautics and Astronautics
370 L'Enfant Promenade SW
Washington, DC 20024-2518
Ph: (202)646-7537   Fax: (202)646-7508

For recognition of a significant contribution in the broad field of aerospace power systems, specifically as related to the application of engineering sciences and systems engineering to the production, storage, distribution, and processing of aerospace power. The award consists of a medal, certificate of citation, and rosette pin and is generally presented annually at the Intersociety Energy Conversion Engineering Conference. Established in 1981.

★1693★ *AIAA Lawrence Sperry Award*
American Institute of Aeronautics and Astronautics
370 L'Enfant Promenade SW
Washington, DC 20024-2518
Ph: (202)646-7537   Fax: (202)646-7508

To recognize a notable contribution made by a young person to the advancement of aeronautics or astronautics. Individuals under the age of 35 are eligible. A medal, certificate, and a rosette pin are awarded annually at the Aerospace Sciences Conference. Established in 1936 to honor Lawrence B. Sperry, pioneer aviator and inventor, who died in 1923 in a forced landing while attempting a flight across the English Channel.

★1694★ *AIAA Mechanics and Control of Flight Award*
American Institute of Aeronautics and Astronautics
370 L'Enfant Promenade SW
Washington, DC 20024-2518
Ph: (202)646-7537   Fax: (202)646-7508

To recognize an outstanding recent technical or scientific contribution by an individual to the mechanics, guidance, or control of flight in space or the atmosphere. A medal, certificate, and a rosette pin are awarded annually at the Guidance, Navigation, and Control Conference. Established in 1967.

★1695★ *AIAA Support Systems Award*
American Institute of Aeronautics and Astronautics
370 L'Enfant Promenade SW
Washington, DC 20024-2518
Ph: (202)646-7537   Fax: (202)646-7508

To recognize significant contribution to the overall effectiveness of aeronautical or aerospace systems through the development of improved support systems technology. A medal, certificate, and a rosette pin are presented annually at the Space Logistics Symposium. Established in 1975.

★1696★ *AIAA Von Karman Lectureship in Astronautics*
American Institute of Aeronautics and Astronautics
370 L'Enfant Promenade SW
Washington, DC 20024-2518
Ph: (202)646-7537   Fax: (202)646-7508

To honor an individual who has performed notably and distinguished him or herself technically in the field of astronautics. A medal and citation are awarded annually. The awardee is expected to present a lecture at the Aerospace Sciences meeting. Established in 1962 in honor of Theodore von Karman, a fundamentalist in the aerospace sciences.

★1697★ *Dirk Brouwer Award*
American Astronautical Society
6352 Rolling Mill Pl., Ste. 102
Springfield, VA 22152
Ph: (703)866-0020   Fax: (703)866-3526

To recognize significant technical contributions to space flight mechanics and astrodynamics. Awarded annually. Established in 1972.

★1698★ *Engineering Rotation Program*
Hughes Aircraft Company
Technical Education Center
PO Box 80028
Los Angeles, CA 90080-0028
Ph: (310)568-6711

Purpose: To enable engineering and science graduates to find and develop the special field of work and the career position best suited to their interests and education. Qualifications: Applicant must be a U.S. citizen and have a bachelor's degree in electrical, mechanical, systems, computer or aerospace engineering; computer science; physics; or mathematics. Candidate must have a grade point average of at least 3.0/4.0, with emphasis on technical classes and related disciplines. Participants in the Rotation Program gain practical experience through up to four different work assignments at Hughes facilities, usually in southern California. Upon completion of the program, participants may be placed in permanent positions with the Company, based on their interests and assignments available. Funds available: Salary and company benefits. Application details: Write to the educational coordinator for application form and guidelines. Include pertinent information regarding academic status (university, field of interest for both undergraduate and graduate work, year of graduation, and grade point average) in initial letter of interest. Deadline: 1 March.

★1699★ *Engineer Degree Fellowships; Howard Hughes Doctoral Fellowships*
Hughes Aircraft Company
Technical Education Center
PO Box 80028
Los Angeles, CA 90080-0028
Ph: (310)568-6711

Purpose: To support doctoral studies in engineering and related sciences and to provide students with practical work experience. Qualifications: Applicant for either type of fellowship must be a U.S. citizen and have a bachelor's and master's degree or equivalent graduate experience in electrical, mechanical, systems, computer or aerospace engineering; computer science; physics; or mathematics. Engineer Degree Fellowships are reserved for candidates who have first degrees in engineering. For both awards, priority is given to individuals with experience in electronics and related disciplines. Candidate must have a minimum grade point average of 3.0/4.0, and be qualified for admission to an approved graduate program in the United States. Fellows are considered employees of the Hughes Aircraft Company and, in addition to their graduate studies, gain work experience in one of two programs: work-study or full-study. Fellows in the work-study program attend a university near a Hughes facility (usually in southern California) and complete coursework while working at the facility for 20 to 36 hours per week. Work-study fellows may switch to full-study status to complete their dissertations. Full-study fellows attend a university distant from Hughes and are on leave of absence from the company while studying full-time. Full-study fellows are required to spend the summer term working for the Company, and may work eight hours a week during the school year if attending a university within commuting distance. Funds available: Company salary and benefits, plus tuition, book and living allowances. Application details: Write to the educational coordinator for application form and guidelines. Include pertinent information regarding academic status (university, field of interest for both undergraduate and graduate work, year of graduation, and grade point average) in initial letter of interest. Deadline: 10 January. Fellows are announced in April.

★1700★ W. Randolph Lovelace II Award
American Astronautical Society
6352 Rolling Mill Pl., Ste. 102
Springfield, VA 22152
Ph: (703)866-0020   Fax: (703)866-3526

To recognize an individual for significant contributions to space science and technology. Awarded when merited. Established in 1965.

★1701★ Victor A. Prather Award
American Astronautical Society
6352 Rolling Mill Pl., Ste. 102
Springfield, VA 22152
Ph: (703)866-0020   Fax: (703)866-3526

To recognize researchers, engineers, and flight crew members in the field of extra-vehicular protection in space. Awarded annually. Established in 1962.

★1702★ Theodore von Karman Award
Air Force Association
1501 Lee Hwy.
Arlington, VA 22209-1198
Ph: (703)247-5810   Fax: (703)247-5853

For distinguished service in the field of aerospace science. A metal plaque on a walnut base is awarded. The majority of the Association's awards are presented at the national conference in September. Established in 1948.

BASIC REFERENCE GUIDES AND HANDBOOKS

★1703★ Eshbach's Handbook of Engineering Fundamentals
Professional Publications, Inc.
1250 5th Ave.
Belmont, CA 94002-3863
Ph: 800-426-1178

Byron Tapley. 4th edition, 1990.

★1704★ Jane's Aerospace Dictionary
Jane's Information Group
1340 Braddock Pl., Ste. 300
PO Box 1436
Alexandria, VA 22314-1651
Ph: (703)683-3700

Bill Gunston. Third edition, 1989.

PROFESSIONAL AND TRADE PERIODICALS

★1705★ A & D Digest
American Production and Inventory Control Society (APICS)
500 W. Annandale Rd.
Falls Church, VA 22046
Ph: (703)237-8344   Fax: (703)534-4767
Fr: 800-444-2742

Quarterly. Covers production, consulting, and manufacturing in the aerospace and defense (A & D) fields.

★1706★ Aeronautical Engineering
National Technical Information Service (NTIS)
5285 Port Royal Rd.
Springfield, VA 22161
Ph: (703)487-4630

Monthly. Covers documents on the engineering and theoretical aspects of design, construction, evaluation, testing, operation, and performance of aircraft and associated components, equipment, and systems.

★1707★ Aerospace America
AIAA/American Institute of Aeronautics and Astronautics
370 L'Enfant Promenade SW
Washington, DC 20024
Ph: (202)646-7400   Fax: (202)646-7508
Michael J. Lewis

Monthly. Aerospace engineering and technology magazine.

★1708★ Aerospace Daily
McGraw-Hill, Inc.
1156 15th St. NW, Ste. 600
Washington, DC 20005
Ph: (202)822-4600

Daily. Reports on developments in the aerospace industry in the U.S. and overseas. Covers related political decisions.

★1709★ Aerospace Engineering
Society of Automotive Engineers, Inc.
400 Commonwealth Drive
Warrendale, PA 15096
Ph: (412)776-4841   Fax: (412)776-4026
Dan Holt

Monthly. Magazine for aerospace manufacturing engineers providing technical and design information.

★1710★ AIAA Journal
AIAA/American Institute of Aeronautics and Astronautics
370 L'Enfant Promenade SW
Washington, DC 20024
Ph: (202)646-7400   Fax: (202)646-7508
George W. Sutton

Monthly. Technical journal providing original archival research papers on new theoretical developments and/or experimental results in the fields of aeronautics and astronautics. For research-oriented readers.

★1711★ Aviation Week & Space Technology
McGraw-Hill, Inc.
1221 Avenue of the Americas
New York, NY 10020
Ph: (212)512-4686   Fax: (212)512-4256
Donald E. Fink

Weekly. Magazine focusing on aviation space engineering.

★1712★ Graduating Engineer
Peterson's/COG Publishing Group
16030 Ventura Blvd., No. 560
Encino, CA 91436
Ph: (818)789-5293
Charlotte Chandler-Thomas

Magazine focusing on employment, education, and career development for entry-level engineers.

★1713★ Optimal Control Applications and Methods
John Wiley and Sons, Inc.
Subscription Dept.
605 3rd Ave.
New York, NY 10158
Ph: (212)850-6000   Fax: (212)850-6799
B.L. Pierson

Quarterly. Journal containing information on optimal control applications. Topics include aerospace, robots and manufacturing systems, and electrical and electronic systems.

PROFESSIONAL MEETINGS AND CONVENTIONS

★1714★ Advanced Aerospace Materials and Processes Conference and Expo
ASM International
9639 Kinsman Rd.
Materials Park, OH 44073-0002
Ph: (216)338-5151   Fax: (216)338-4634

Annual. Always held in Long Beach, California. **Dates and Locations:** 1995; Long Beach, CA.

★1715★ **Aerospace Medical Association Annual Scientific Meeting**
The Herlitz Co., Inc.
404 Park Ave., S.
New York, NY 10016
Ph: (212)532-9400   Fax: (212)696-4104
Annual.

★1716★ **AIAA International Aerospace Conference and Show**
American Institute of Aeronautics and Astronautics (AIAA)
370 L'Enfant Promenade, SW
Washington, DC 20024
Ph: (202)646-7400   Fax: (202)646-7508
Annual.

★1717★ **Society of Automotive Engineers Aerospace Technology Congress and Exposition**
Society of Automotive Engineers
400 Commonwealth Dr.
Warrendale, PA 15096-0001
Ph: (412)776-4841   Fax: (412)776-5760
Annual. Always held during October at the Convention Center in Long Beach, California. **Dates and Locations:** 1995 Oct; Long Beach, CA. • 1996 Oct; Long Beach, CA.

OTHER SOURCES OF INFORMATION

★1718★ **"Aerospace/Aeronautical Engineering" in** *Accounting to Zoology: Graduate Fields Defined* **(pp. 361-362)**
Petersons Guides, Inc.
PO Box 2123
Princeton, NJ 08543-2123
Ph: (609)243-9111   Fax: (609)243-9150
Fr: 800-338-3282
Amy J. Goldstein, editor. Revised and updated, 1987. Defines 298 graduate and professional fields. Discusses types of graduate programs and degrees, graduate research, applied work, employment prospects, and trends.

★1719★ *Aerospace Facts and Figures 1993-94*
McGraw-Hill, Inc.
1221 Avenue of the Americas
New York, NY 10020
Ph: (212)512-2000   Fr: 800-722-4726
1993. Provides a financial summary of the aerospace industry.

★1720★ *Financial Aid for Minorities in Engineering & Science*
Garrett Park Press
PO Box 190
Garrett Park, MD 20896
Ph: (301)946-2553
1993.

★1721★ *GEM: National Consortium for Graduate Degrees for Minorities in Engineering*
National Consortium for Graduate Degrees for Minorities in Engineering
PO Box 537
Notre Dame, IN 46556
Ph: (219)287-1097
1988. Describes the graduate fellowship program for minorities in engineering including financial support, application, and internship. Lists universities offering this program.

★1722★ *How to Become a Professional Engineer*
McGraw-Hill, Inc.
1221 Avenue of the Americas
New York, NY 10020
Ph: (212)512-2000   Fr: 800-722-4726
J.D. Constance. Fourth edition, 1987. Describes how to register for the professional engineer's license in all fifty states. Gives a state-by-state list of licensing regulations. Gives advice on how to take the written examination.

Chemical Engineers

Chemical engineers work in many phases of the production of chemicals and chemical products. They design equipment and plants, determine and test methods of manufacturing the products, and supervise production. Chemical engineers also work in industries other than chemical manufacturing such as electronics or aircraft manufacturing. Because the duties of chemical engineers cut across many fields, they apply principles of chemistry, physics, mathematics, and mechanical and electrical engineering. They frequently specialize in a particular operation such as oxidation or polymerization. Others specialize in a particular area such as pollution control or the production of a specific product like plastics or rubber.

Salaries

Starting salaries for engineers with bachelor's degrees are significantly higher than starting salaries of college graduates in other fields.

Beginning chemical engineers	$39,203/year
Experienced mid-level engineers	$52,500/year
Senior managerial engineers	$102,544/year

Employment Outlook

Growth rate until the year 2005: Average.

Chemical Engineers

CAREER GUIDES

★1723★ *Career Development for Engineers and Scientists: Organizational Programs and Individual Choices*
Van Nostrand Reinhold Co., Inc.
115 5th Ave.
New York, NY 10003
Ph: (212)254-3232   Fr: 800-842-3636
Robert F. Morrison and Richard M. Vosburgh. 1987. Includes bibliographies and an index. Illustrated.

★1724★ *Careers in Chemical Engineering*
American Institute of Chemical Engineers (AIChE)
345 E. 47th St.
New York, NY 10017
Ph: (212)705-7657
1989. Describes chemical engineers' job functions and educational preparation. Lists the industries and jobs in which chemical engineers work.

★1725★ *Careers and the Engineer*
Bob Adams, Inc.
260 Center St.
Holbrook, MA 02343
Ph: (617)268-9570
Gigi Ranno, editor. Annual.

★1726★ *Careers in Engineering*
National Textbook Co. (NTC)
VGM Career Books
4255 W. Touhy Ave.
Lincolnwood, IL 60646-1975
Ph: (708)679-5500   Fax: (708)679-2494
Fr: 800-323-4900
Geraldine O. Garner, Ph.D., editor. 1993. Career guide covering 14 different engineering specialties.

★1727★ *Chemical Engineer*
Careers, Inc.
PO Box 135
Largo, FL 34649-0135
Ph: (813)584-7333
1992. Two-page occupational summary card describing duties, working conditions, personal qualifications, training, earnings and hours, employment outlook, places of employment, related careers, and where to write for more information.

★1728★ *Chemical Engineer*
Vocational Biographies, Inc.
PO Box 31
Sauk Centre, MN 56378-0031
Ph: (612)352-6516   Fax: (612)352-5546
Fr: 800-255-0752
1994. Four-page pamphlet containing a personal narrative about a worker's job, work likes and dislikes, career path from high school to the present, education and training, the rewards and frustrations, and the effects of the job on the rest of the worker's life. The data file portion of this pamphlet gives a concise occupational summary, including work description, working conditions, places of employment, personal characteristics, education and training, job outlook, and salary range.

★1729★ "Chemical Engineer" in *Career Information Center* (Vol.6)
Simon and Schuster
200 Old Tappan Rd.
Old Tappan, NJ 07675
Fax: 800-445-6991   Fr: 800-223-2348
Richard Lidz and Linda Perrin, editorial directors. Fifth edition, 1993. This 13-volume set profiles over 600 occupations. Each occupational profile describes job duties, entry-level requirements, educational requirements, advancement possibilities, employment outlook, working conditions, earnings and benefits, and where to write for more information.

★1730★ "Chemical Engineer" in *Guide to Federal Jobs* (p. 169)
Resource Directories
3361 Executive Pkwy., Ste. 302
Toledo, OH 43606
Ph: (419)536-5353   Fax: (419)536-7056
Fr: 800-274-8515
Rod W. Durgin, editor. Third edition, 1992. Contains information on finding and applying for federal jobs. Describes more than 200 professional and technical jobs for college graduates. Covers the nature of the work, salary, and geographic location. Lists college majors preferred for that occupation. Section one describes the function and work of government agencies that hire the most significant number of college graduates.

★1731★ "Chemical Engineer" in *Opportunities in High-Tech Careers* (pp. 49-50, 127-128)
National Textbook Co. (NTC)
VGM Career Books
4255 W. Touhy Ave.
Lincolnwood, IL 60646-1975
Ph: (708)679-5500   Fax: (708)679-2494
Fr: 800-323-4900
Gary D. Golter and Deborah Yanuck. 1987. Explores high technology careers. Written for the student and displaced worker. Describes job opportunities, how to make a career decision, how to prepare for high-technology jobs, job hunting techniques, and future trends.

★1732★ "Chemical Engineer" in *VGM's Careers Encyclopedia* (pp. 86-88)
National Textbook Co. (NTC)
VGM Career Books
4255 W. Touhy Ave.
Lincolnwood, IL 60646-1975
Ph: (708)679-5500   Fax: (708)679-2494
Fr: 800-323-4900
Third edition, 1991. Profiles 200 occupations. Describes job duties, places of employment, working conditions, qualifications, education and training, advancement potential, and salary for each occupation.

★1733★ "Chemical Engineering" in *College Majors and Careers: A Resource Guide to Effective Life Planning* (pp. 33-34)
Garrett Park Press
PO Box 1907
Garrett Park, MD 20896
Ph: (301)946-2553
Paul Phifer. Revised, 1993. Lists 60 college majors, with definitions; related occupations and leisure activities; skills, values, and personal attributesneeded; suggested readings; and a list of associations.

★1734★ Chemical Engineers
Chronicle Guidance Publications, Inc.
66 Aurora St.
PO Box 1190
Moravia, NY 13118-1190
Ph: (315)497-0330   Fax: (315)497-3359
Fr: 800-622-7284

1994. Career brief describing the nature of the job, working conditions, hours and earnings, education and training, licensure, certification, unions, personal qualifications, social and psychological factors, location, employment outlook, entry methods, advancement, and related occupations.

★1735★ "Chemical Engineers" in 101 Careers: A Guide to the Fastest-Growing Opportunities (pp. 64-66)
John Wiley & Sons, Inc.
605 3rd Ave.
New York, NY 10158-0012
Ph: (212)850-6645   Fax: (212)850-6088

Michael Harkavy. 1990. Describes the nature of the job, working conditions, employment growth, qualifications, personal skills, projected salaries, and where to write for more information.

★1736★ "Chemical Engineers" in Best Jobs for the 1990s and Into the 21st Century
Impact Publications
9104-N Manassas Dr.
Manassas Park, VA 22111
Ph: (703)361-7300   Fax: (703)335-9486

Ronald L. Krannich and Caryl Rae Krannich. 1993.

★1737★ "Chemical Engineers" in Career Discovery Encyclopedia (Vol.1, pp. 160-161)
J.G. Ferguson Publishing Co.
200 W. Madison St., Ste. 300
Chicago, IL 60606
Ph: (312)580-5480   Fax: (312)580-4948

Russell E. Primm, editor-in chief. 1993. This six volume set contains two-page articles for 504 occupations. Each article describes job duties, earnings, and educational and training requirements. The whole set is arranged alphabetically by job title. Designed for junior high and older students.

★1738★ "Chemical Engineers" in Encyclopedia of Careers and Vocational Guidance (Vol.2, p. 275)
J.G. Ferguson Publishing Co.
200 W. Madison St., Ste. 300
Chicago, IL 60606
Ph: (312)580-5480   Fax: (312)580-4948

William E. Hopke, editor-in-chief. Ninth edition, 1993. Four-volume set that profiles 900 occupations and describes job trends in 74 industries. Includes career description, educational requirements, history of the job, methods of entry, advancement, employment outlook, earnings, conditions of work, social and psychological factors, and sources of further information.

★1739★ "Chemical Engineers" in Jobs! What They Are—Where They Are—What They Pay (p. 120)
Simon & Schuster, Inc.
Simon & Schuster Bldg.
1230 Avenue of the Americas
New York, NY 10020
Ph: (212)698-7000   Fr: 800-223-2348

Robert O. Snelling and Anne M. Snelling. 3rd edition, 1992. Describes duties and responsibilities, earnings, employment opportunities, training, and qualifications.

★1740★ "Chemical Engineers" in Occupational Outlook Handbook
U.S. Government Printing Office
Superintendent of Documents
Washington, DC 20402
Ph: (202)512-1800   Fax: (202)512-2250

Biennial; latest edition, 1994-95. Encyclopedia of careers describing about 250 occupations and comprising about 85 percent of all jobs in the economy. Occupations that require lengthy education or training are given the most attention. Each occupation's profile describes what the worker does on the job, working conditions, education and training requirements, advancement possibilities, job outlook, earnings, and sources of additional information.

★1741★ "Chemists" in Encyclopedia of Careers and Vocational Guidance (Vol.2, pp. 285-287)
J.G. Ferguson Publishing Co.
200 W. Madison St., Ste. 300
Chicago, IL 60606
Ph: (312)580-5480   Fax: (312)580-4948

William E. Hopke, editor-in-chief. Ninth edition, 1993. Four-volume set that profiles 900 occupations and describes job trends in 74 industries. Includes career description, educational requirements, history of the job, methods of entry, advancement, employment outlook, earnings, conditions of work, social and psychological factors, and sources of further information.

★1742★ The Civilized Engineer
St. Martin's Press, Inc.
175 5th Ave.
New York, NY 10010
Ph: (212)674-5151   Fax: 800-258-2769
Fr: 800-221-7945

Samuel C. Florman. 1989. Published by Thomas Dunne Books. Discusses engineering education, the relationship between engineers and nontechnical executives, and the role of women in engineering.

★1743★ "Engineering" in American Almanac of Jobs and Salaries (pp. 261)
Avon Books
1350 Avenue of the Americas
New York, NY 10019
Ph: (212)261-6800   Fr: 800-238-0658

John Wright, editor. Revised and updated, 1994-95. A comprehensive guide to the wages of hundreds of occupations in a wide variety of industries and organizations.

★1744★ "Engineering" in Encyclopedia of Careers and Vocational Guidance (Vol.1, pp. 165-171)
J.G. Ferguson Publishing Co.
200 W. Madison St., Ste. 300
Chicago, IL 60606
Ph: (312)580-5480   Fax: (312)580-4948

William E. Hopke, editor-in-chief. Ninth edition, 1993. Four-volume set that profiles 900 occupations and describes job trends in 74 industries. Includes career description, educational requirements, history of the job, methods of entry, advancement, employment outlook, earnings, conditions of work, social and psychological factors, and sources of further information.

★1745★ Engineering Salary Survey
Source Engineering
1290 Oakmead, Ste. 318
Sunnyvale, CA 94086
Ph: (408)738-8440

Annual. Discusses the structure of the engineering profession, trends, and compensation. Salaries are listed by job function, industry, and years of experience.

★1746★ Engineering for You: A Career Guide
Iowa State University Press
2121 S. State Ave.
Ames, IA 50010
Ph: (515)292-0140   Fax: (515)292-3348

John T. Jones. 1991.

★1747★ How to Become a Professional Engineer: The Road to Registration
McGraw-Hill, Inc.
1221 Avenue of the Americas
New York, NY 10020
Ph: (212)512-2000   Fr: 800-722-4726

John D. Constance. Fourth edition, 1988. Includes a bibliography and an index.

★1748★ Opportunities in Chemical Engineering
National Textbook Co. (NTC)
VGM Career Books
4255 W. Touhy Ave.
Lincolnwood, IL 60646-1975
Ph: (708)679-5500   Fax: (708)679-2494
Fr: 800-323-4900

D. Joseph Hagerty

★1749★ Opportunities in Engineering
National Textbook Co. (NTC)
VGM Career Books
4255 W. Touhy Ave.
Lincolnwood, IL 60646-1975
Ph: (708)679-5500   Fax: (708)679-2494
Fr: 800-323-4900

Nicholas Basta. 1990. Profiles specialties in the engineering field including civil, chemical, mechanical, biomedical, and aerospace. Offers information on salaries, career paths and educational requirements.

★1750★ Opportunities in Engineering Technology Careers
National Textbook Co. (NTC)
VGM Career Books
4255 W. Touhy Ave.
Lincolnwood, IL 60646-1975
Ph: (708)679-5500   Fax: (708)679-2494
Fr: 800-323-4900
John E. Heer and D. Joseph Hagerty. 1987. Describes the many opportunities available for engineering technicians. Explains job duties, educational requirements, salary, working conditions, employment outlook, and advancement opportunities. Lists accredited engineering technology programs.

★1751★ Peterson's Job Opportunities for Engineering and Technology
Petersons Guides, Inc.
PO Box 2123
Princeton, NJ 08543-2123
Ph: (609)243-9111   Fax: (609)243-9150
Fr: 800-338-3282
1994. Gives job hunting advice including information on resume writing, interviewing, and handling salary negotiations. Lists companies that hire college graduates in science and engineering at the bachelor and master's level. Companies are indexed by industry, starting location, and major. Company profiles include contact information and types of hires.

★1752★ Successful Engineering: A Guide to Achieving Your Career Goals
McGraw-Hill, Inc.
1221 Avenue of the Americas
New York, NY 10020
Ph: (212)512-2000   Fr: 800-722-4726
Lawrence J. Kamm. 1989. Written for the practicing and graduating engineer. Gives advice about working with accountants, the politics of design, and engineering ethics.

PROFESSIONAL ASSOCIATIONS

★1753★ Accreditation Board for Engineering and Technology (ABET)
111 Market Pl., Ste. 1050
Baltimore, MD 21202
Ph: (410)347-7700   Fax: (410)625-2238
Members: Professional societies representing over one million engineers are participating bodies (21); affiliate bodies (5); board of directors has 29 representatives. Is responsible for the quality control of engineering education. Accredits college curricula in engineering, engineering technology, and engineering-related areas. **Publications:** Accreditation Yearbook, annual. • Criteria for Accrediting Programs in Engineering in the United States, annual. • Criteria for Accrediting Programs in Engineering Technology, annual.

★1754★ American Association of Engineering Societies (AAES)
1111 19th St. NW, Ste. 608
Washington, DC 20036
Ph: (202)296-2237   Fax: (202)296-1151
Members: Societies representing over 500,000 engineers. **Purpose:** Works to: advance the knowledge and practice of engineering in the public interest; act as an advisory, communication, and information exchange agency for member activities, especially regarding public policy issues. Conducts studies sponsored by Engineering Manpower Commission. Compiles statistics. **Publications:** AAES Update, quarterly. • Directory of Engineering Societies, biennial. • Engineering and Technology Degrees, annual. • Engineering and Technology Enrollments, annual. • Engineers Salary Survey, annual. • The Role of Engineering in Sustainable Development. • Who's Who in Engineering, biennial.

★1755★ American Chemical Society (ACS)
1155 16th St. NW
Washington, DC 20036
Ph: (202)872-4600   Fr: 800-227-5558
Members: Scientific and educational society of chemists and chemical engineers. Conducts: studies and surveys; special programs for disadvantaged persons; legislation monitoring, analysis, and reporting; courses for graduate chemists and chemical engineers; radio and television programming. Offers career guidance counseling; administers the Petroleum Research Fund and other grants and fellowship programs. Operates Employment Clearing Houses. Compiles statistics. Maintains speakers' bureau. Maintains 33 divisions. **Publications:** Accounts of Chemical Research, monthly. • Analytical Chemistry, semimonthly. • Biochemistry, weekly. • Bioconjugate Chemistry, bimonthly. • Biotechnology Progress, bimonthly. • Chemical Abstracts, weekly. • Chemical and Engineering News, weekly. • Chemical Health & Safety, bimonthly. • Chemical Research in Toxicology, bimonthly. • Chemical Reviews, 8/year. • Chemical Titles. • Chemistry of Materials, monthly. • Chemtech, monthly. • Energy and Fuels, bimonthly. • Environmental Science and Technology, monthly. • Industrial and Engineering Chemistry Research, monthly. • Inorganic Chemistry, biweekly. • Journal of Agricultural and Food Chemistry, monthly. • Journal of Chemical and Engineering Data, quarterly. • Journal of Chemical Information and Computer Sciences, bimonthly. • Journal of Medicinal Chemistry, biweekly. • Journal of Organic Chemistry, biweekly. • Journal of Pharmaceutical Sciences, monthly. • Journal of Physical and Chemical Reference Data, bimonthly. • Journal of Physical Chemistry, weekly. • Journal of the American Chemical Society, biweekly. • Langmuir, monthly. • Macromolecules, biweekly. • Organometallics, monthly.

★1756★ American Institute of Chemical Engineers (AICHE)
345 E. 47th St.
New York, NY 10017
Ph: (212)705-7338   Fax: (212)752-3294
Members: Professional society of chemical engineers. **Purpose:** Establishes standards for chemical engineering curricula; offers employment services. Sponsors petrochemical and refining, exposition, and continuing education programs. Sponsors competitions. Offers speakers' bureau; compiles statistics. Maintains numerous committees including: Career Guidance; Chemical Engineering Education Projects; International Activities; Research. **Publications:** AIChE Journal, monthly. • AIChE Symposium Series, bimonthly. • AIChEMI Modular Instruction Series, periodic. • AIChExtra, monthly. • American Institute of Chemical Engineers—Directory, periodic. • Ammonia Plant Safety, annual. • Biotechnology Progress, bimonthly. • Chapter One, quarterly. • Chemical Engineering Faculties, annual. • Chemical Engineering Progress, monthly. • Environmental Progress, quarterly. • International Chemical Engineering, quarterly. • Plant/Operations Progress, quarterly.

★1757★ American Institute of Chemists (AIC)
7315 Wisconsin Ave.
Bethesda, MD 20814
Ph: (301)652-2447   Fax: (301)657-3549
Members: Chemists and chemical engineers. **Purpose:** Promotes advancement of chemical professions in the U.S.; protects public welfare by establishing and enforcing high practice standards; represents professional interests of chemists and chemical engineers. Sponsors American Board of Clinical Chemistry; National Registry in Clinical Chemistry; National Certification Commission in Chemistry and Chemical Engineering; AIC Foundation; National Inventors Hall of Fame; Public Education Fund. Offers placement services. **Publications:** American Institute of Chemists—Professional Directory, annual. • The Chemist.

★1758★ American Institute of Engineers (AIE)
4666 San Pablo Dam Rd., No. 8
El Sobrante, CA 94803-3142
Ph: (510)223-8911   Fax: (510)223-3400
Members: Professional engineers and engineering students. **Purpose:** Seeks to advance the professional interests of engineers and scientists. Fosters the interchange of ideas and information among members. Compiles statistics; maintains speakers' bureau. **Publications:** AIE Newsmagazine, monthly.

★1759★ Association of Consulting Chemists and Chemical Engineers (ACC&CE)
295 Madison Ave., 27th Fl.
New York, NY 10017
Ph: (212)983-3160   Fax: (212)983-3161
Members: Chemists and chemical engineers engaged in consulting practice as individuals, partners, or executives of organizations. Operates Clearing House for Consultants, through which industry is introduced to qualified and experienced members in any given field. **Publications:** Consulting Services, biennial.

★1760★ National Organization for the Professional Advancement of Black Chemists and Chemical Engineers (NOBCCHE)
525 College St. NW
Washington, DC 20059
Ph: (202)667-1699   Fax: (202)667-1705
Fr: 800-776-1419
Members: Black professionals in science and chemistry. **Purpose:** Seeks to aid black scientists and chemists in reaching their full professional potential; encourages black students to pursue scientific studies and employ-

ment; promotes participation of blacks in scientific research. Provides volunteers to teach science courses in selected elementary schools; sponsors scientific field trips for students; maintains speakers' bureau for schools; provides summer school for students of the U.S. Naval Academy. Conducts technical seminars in Africa; operates exchange program of scientific and chemical professionals with the People's Republic of China. Sponsors competitions; presents awards for significant achievements to individuals in the field. Maintains library of materials pertaining to chemistry, science, and black history; keeps archive of organization's books and records. Maintains placement service; compiles statistics. **Publications:** *Newsmagazine*, quarterly. • *Proceedings of Annual Meeting.*

★1761★ **National Society of Professional Engineers (NSPE)**
1420 King St.
Alexandria, VA 22314
Ph: (703)684-2800   Fax: (703)836-4875
Members: Professional engineers and engineers-in-training in all fields registered in accordance with the laws of states or territories of the U.S. or provinces of Canada; qualified graduate engineers, student members, and registered land surveyors. Is concerned with social, professional, ethical, and economic considerations of engineering as a profession; encompasses programs in public relations, employment practices, ethical considerations, education, and career guidance. Monitors legislative and regulatory actions of interest to the engineering profession. **Publications:** *Directory of Professional Engineers in Private Practice*, biennial. • *Engineering Times*, monthly. • *PEG Times*, quarterly.

★1762★ **Society of Women Engineers (SWE)**
120 Wall St., 11th Fl.
New York, NY 10005
Ph: (212)509-9577   Fax: (212)509-0224
Members: Educational service society of women engineers; membership is also open to men. **Purpose:** Supplies information on the achievements of women engineers and the opportunities available to them; assists women engineers in preparing for return to active work following temporary retirement. Serves as an informational center on women in engineering. Administers several certificate and scholarship programs. Offers tours and career guidance; conducts surveys. Compiles statistics. **Publications:** *National Survey of Women and Men Engineers.*

STANDARDS/CERTIFICATION AGENCIES

★1763★ **Accreditation Board for Engineering and Technology (ABET)**
111 Market Pl., Ste. 1050
Baltimore, MD 21202
Ph: (410)347-7700   Fax: (410)625-2238
Is responsible for the quality control of engineering education. Accredits college curricula in engineering, engineering technology, and engineering-related areas.

★1764★ **American Institute of Chemical Engineers (AICHE)**
345 E. 47th St.
New York, NY 10017
Ph: (212)705-7338   Fax: (212)752-3294
Establishes standards for chemical engineering curricula; offers employment services. Sponsors petrochemical and refining, exposition, and continuing education programs.

★1765★ **American Institute of Chemists (AIC)**
7315 Wisconsin Ave.
Bethesda, MD 20814
Ph: (301)652-2447   Fax: (301)657-3549
Promotes advancement of chemical professions in the U.S.; protects public welfare by establishing and enforcing high practice standards; represents professional interests of chemists and chemical engineers. Sponsors American Board of Clinical Chemistry; National Registry in Clinical Chemistry; National Certification Commission in Chemistry and Chemical Engineering; AIC Foundation; National Inventors Hall of Fame; Public Education Fund.

★1766★ **Society of Women Engineers (SWE)**
120 Wall St., 11th Fl.
New York, NY 10005
Ph: (212)509-9577   Fax: (212)509-0224
Administers several certificate and scholarship programs. Compiles statistics.

TEST GUIDES

★1767★ *Career Examination Series: Assistant Chemical Engineer*
National Learning Corp.
212 Michael Dr.
Syosset, NY 11791
Ph: (516)921-8888   Fax: (516)921-8743
Fr: 800-645-6337
Jack Rudman. Test guide including questions and answers for students or professionals in the field who seek advancement through examination.

★1768★ *Career Examination Series: Chemical Engineer*
National Learning Corp.
212 Michael Dr.
Syosset, NY 11791
Ph: (516)921-8888   Fax: (516)921-8743
Fr: 800-645-6337
Jack Rudman. Test guide including questions and answers for students or professionals in the field who seek advancement through examination.

★1769★ *Career Examination Series: Engineer*
National Learning Corp.
212 Michael Dr.
Syosset, NY 11791
Ph: (516)921-8888   Fax: (516)921-8743
Fr: 800-645-6337
Jack Rudman. A series of study guides with multiple-choice examination questions and solutions for trainees and professional petroleum engineers. Titles in the series include *Administrative Engineer; Chief Engineer; Engineering Aide and Science Assistant; Engineering Aide; Engineering Assistant; Engineering Trainee; Senior Engineer; Senior Engineering Aide.*

★1770★ *Career Examination Series: Junior Chemical Engineer*
National Learning Corp.
212 Michael Dr.
Syosset, NY 11791
Ph: (516)921-8888   Fax: (516)921-8743
Fr: 800-645-6337
Jack Rudman. 1993. Test guide including questions and answers for students or professionals in the field who seek advancement through examination.

★1771★ *Engineer-in-Training Exam File*
Engineering Press, Inc.
PO Box 1
San Jose, CA 95103-0001
Ph: (408)258-4503   Fax: 800-700-1651
Fr: 800-800-1651
Donald G. Newnan and Dean Newnan. Eleventh edition. 1990. Contains 505 problems with step-by-step solutions. Covers: mathematics; statics; fluid mechanics. Includes an index.

★1772★ *Engineering Economic Analysis Exam File*
Engineering Press, Inc.
PO Box 1
San Jose, CA 95103-0001
Ph: (408)258-4503   Fax: 800-700-1651
Fr: 800-800-1651
Contains 386 exam problems with step-by-step solutions.

★1773★ *Graduate Record Examination: Engineering*
National Learning Corp.
212 Michael Dr.
Syosset, NY 11791
Ph: (516)921-8888   Fax: (516)921-8743
Fr: 800-645-6337
Jack Rudman. Multiple-choice test for those seeking admission to graduate school for study in the field of engineering. Includes solutions to examination questions.

★1774★ *Graduate Record Examination in Engineering*
Arco Publishing Co.
Macmillan General Reference
15 Columbus Cir.
New York, NY 10023
Fax: 800-835-3202   Fr: 800-858-7674
C.W. Tan, et al. First edition. 1988. Contains two sample tests with an explanation to answers.

★1775★ Practing to Take the GRE Engineering Test: An Offical Publication of the GRE Board
Educational Testing Service
Rosedale Rd.
Princeton, NJ 08541
Ph: (609)921-9000

Second edition, 1989. Summarizes the purpose and scope of the Graduate Record Examination Subject Test for engineering. Contains sample questions.

★1776★ Professional Engineer
National Learning Corp.
212 Michael Dr.
Syosset, NY 11791
Ph: (516)921-8888   Fax: (516)921-8743
Fr: 800-645-6337

Jack Rudman. A sample test for engineers who are seeking admission to graduate and professional schools or seeking entrance or advancement in institutional and public career service.

★1777★ Undergraduate Program Field Test: Engineering
National Learning Corp.
212 Michael Dr.
Syosset, NY 11791
Ph: (516)921-8888   Fax: (516)921-8743
Fr: 800-645-6337

Jack Rudman. A practice examination fashioned after tests given in the Regents External Degree Program. Designed to measure knowledge received outside the college classroom in the subject of engineering. Contains multiple-choice questions; provides solutions.

EDUCATIONAL DIRECTORIES AND PROGRAMS

★1778★ ABET Accreditation Yearbook
Accreditation Board for Engineering and Technology
345 E. 47th St., 14th Fl.
New York, NY 10017-2397
Ph: (212)705-7685   Fax: (212)838-8062
Simona C. Mardale, Contact

Annual, September. Covers about 300 U.S. colleges and universities with engineering programs, 242 institutions with programs in engineering technology, and 11 institutions with engineering-related programs accredited by the Board; also lists accredited Canadian programs. Entries include: For United States institutions—Name, year of next full accreditation review, location, program names, year of initial accreditation for each program, coding to indicate degrees offered, format of program (day, night, cooperative, etc.). For Canadian programs—Name, location, names of programs, year of initial accredition for each program. Arrangement: Classified by program area.

★1779★ ACS Directory of Graduate Research
American Chemical Society (ACS)
1155 16th St. NW
Washington, DC 20036
Ph: (202)872-4589   Fax: (202)872-6067
Fr: 800-227-5558
Cathy A. Nelson, Contact

Biennial, November of odd years. Covers about 738 departments offering masters' and/or doctoral degrees in chemistry, chemical engineering, biochemistry, medicinal/pharmaceutical chemistry, clinical chemistry, polymer science, food science, forensic science, marine science, and toxicology located in the United States and Canada. Entries include: Institution name, address, phone, fax, department name, name of chairperson, degrees offered, fields of specialization; names and birth dates of faculty members, their educational backgrounds, special research interests, personal phone number, computer addresses, and recent publications; names and thesis titles of recent Masters' and Ph.D. graduates. Arrangement: Classified by discipline, then alphabetical by keyword in institution name.

★1780★ American Chemical Society— List of Approved Schools
Office of Professional Training
American Chemical Society (ACS)
1155 16th St. NW
Washington, DC 20036
Ph: (202)872-4589   Fax: (202)872-6066
Dolphine S. Hite, Contact

Annual, April. Covers about 600 institutions offering undergraduate programs in chemistry that are approved by the American Chemical Society. Entries include: Institution name, address; asterisk indicates whether also accredited by the American Institute of Chemical Engineers and the Accreditation Board for Engineering and Technology. Arrangement: Geographical.

★1781★ Chemical Engineering Progress Software Directory
American Institute of Chemical Engineers
345 E. 47th St.
New York, NY 10017
Ph: (212)705-7576   Fax: (212)752-3294

Published 1993.. Covers Over 1,500 chemical engineering progress software programs and approximately 450 vendors. Engineering programs categories include biochemical engineering, data conversion, equipment design, expert systems, flowsheet simulations, petroleum production, reactor design, software utilities, and thermodynamics. Entries include: Name, address, phone; description of product/service.

★1782★ Chemical Research Faculties: An International Directory
American Chemical Society (ACS)
1155 16th St. NW
Washington, DC 20036
Ph: (202)872-4600   Fax: (202)452-8913
Fr: 800-227-5558
M. Joan Comstock, Books Department

Irregular, latest edition 1988. Covers about 600 educational institutions with departments granting advanced degrees in chemical research fields of study, including pharmaceutical chemistry, chemical engineering, and bio-

chemistry; 65 chemical associations. Omits institutions in the United States and Canada that are covered in the American Chemical Society's "ACS Directory of Graduate Research" (described separately). Entries include: For educational institutions—Name, name of department, address, phone, degrees offered, fields of specialization; names of faculty members, their educational backgrounds, special research interests, personal phone numbers, recent publications. For associations—Name, address, Arrangement: Classified by four major disciplines (chemistry, chemical engineering, biochemistry, and pharmaceutical), then geographical.

★1783★ College Chemistry Faculties
American Chemical Society (ACS)
1155 16th St. NW
Washington, DC 20036
Ph: (202)872-4364   Fax: (202)872-6067
Fr: 800-227-5558
M. Joan Constock, Head, Books Department

Triennial, latest edition August 1993. Covers 2,200 departments in two-, three-, and four-year colleges and universities in the United States and Canada offering instruction in chemistry, biochemistry, chemical engineering, and related disciplines. Entries include: Institution name, address, department name and phone, degrees offered, and names of faculty, with major teaching field, highest earned degree, and academic rank. Arrangement: Geographical.

★1784★ The Directory of Chemical Engineering Consultants
American Institute of Chemical Engineers
345 E. 47th St.
New York, NY 10017
Ph: (212)705-7338

June Sewer, editor. Ninth edition, 1992.

★1785★ Environmental Career Directory
Gale Research Inc.
835 Penobscot Bldg.
Detroit, MI 48226-4094
Ph: (313)961-2242   Fax: (313)961-6083
Fr: 800-877-GALE

Bradley J. Morgan and Joseph M. Palmisano. 1993. A directory in the Career Advisor Series that provides essays written by industry professionals; job search information on resume and cover letter preparation, networking, and the interviewing process; approximately 300 companies and organizations offering job opportunities and internships, and additional job-hunting resources.

★1786★ Physical Science Career Directory
Gale Research Inc.
835 Penobscot Bldg.
Detroit, MI 48226-4094
Ph: (313)961-2242   Fax: (313)961-6083
Fr: 800-877-GALE
Bradley J. Morgan, Contact

First edition March 1994. Covers over 210 chemical companies, testing and research laboratories, and consulting firms in the U.S. offering entry-level positions and internships; sources of help-wanted ads, professional associations, producers of videos, databases, career guides, and professional guides and handbooks. Entries include: For companies—Name, address, phone, fax, business description, research activities, names and titles of key personnel, number of employees, average number of entry-level positions available, human resources contact, description of internship opportunities including contact, type and number available, application procedures, qualifications, and duties. For others—Name or title, address, phone, description. Paperback edition Arrangement: Companies are alphabetical; others are classified by type of resource.

AWARDS, SCHOLARSHIPS, GRANTS, AND FELLOWSHIPS

★1787★ ACS Award for Creative Invention
American Chemical Society
Research, Grants, and Awards
1155 16th St. NW
Washington, DC 20036
Ph: (202)872-4408

To recognize individual inventors for successful applications of research in chemistry and/or chemical engineering that contribute to the material prosperity and happiness of people. The nominee must be a resident of the United States or Canada. A patent must have been granted for the work to be recognized and it must have been developed during the preceding 17 years. The deadline for nominations is February 1. A monetary award of $5,000, a gold medal, and an allowance of up to $1,000 for travel to the award ceremony are awarded annually. Established in 1966. Sponsored by the ASC Committee on Corporation Associates.

★1788★ Award in Chemical Engineering Practice
American Institute of Chemical Engineers
345 E. 47th St.
New York, NY 10017
Ph: (212)705-7329

To recognize outstanding contributions by a chemical engineer in the industrial practice of the profession. Institute members are eligible. A monetary award of $4,000, a $500 travel allowance, and a plaque are awarded annually when merited. Established in 1972. Sponsored by Bechtel National, Inc.

★1789★ Lawrence K. Cecil Award
American Institute of Chemical Engineers
345 E. 47th St.
New York, NY 10017
Ph: (212)705-7329

For recognition of of outstanding chemical engineering contributions and achievements toward the preservation or improvement of man's natural environmental (air, water, or land). A monetary award of $2,500 and a plaque are awarded annually if merited at the annual meeting, where the winner presents an address. Established in 1972 in honor of Lawrence K. Cecil. Sponsored by BP America, Inc.

★1790★ Allan P. Colburn Award for Excellence in Publications by a Young Member of the Institute
American Institute of Chemical Engineers
345 E. 47th St.
New York, NY 10017
Ph: (212)705-7329

To recognize a notable contribution to the publications of the Institute by a younger member. Individuals who have made significant contributions to chemical engineering through publications are eligible. The recipient must be under the age of 36 at the end of the calendar year. A monetary award of $5,000 and a $500 travel allowance are awarded annually when merited at the annual meeting. Established in 1945. Sponsored by E. I. du Pont de Nemours and Company.

★1791★ Food, Pharmaceutical and Bioengineering Division Award in Chemical Engineering
American Institute of Chemical Engineers
345 E. 47th St.
New York, NY 10017
Ph: (212)705-7329

To recognize an individual for outstanding chemical engineering contributions and achievements industries involved in food, pharmaceutical, and bioengineering activities. Contributions may have been made in industrial, governmental, academic, or other organizations. The recipient need not be a member of the Institute. The deadline for nominations is March 31 each year. A monetary award of $3,000 and a plaque are awarded annually. Established in 1970. Sponsored by Merck.

★1792★ Donald Q. Kern Award
American Institute of Chemical Engineers
345 E. 47th St.
New York, NY 10017
Ph: (212)705-7329

To recognize individuals who have demonstrated outstanding expertise in some field of heat transfer or energy conversion. Nominations may be submitted by June 1. Membership in AIChE is not required. The award consists of a monetary award of $1,000 and a plaque, and the honoree is invited to present a lecture at the National Heat Transfer Conference. Additionally, a written review is printed and distributed to division members. Awarded annually when merited at a meeting sponsored by the Institute. Established in 1973 in honor of Donald Q. Kern. Supported by Heat Transfer Research, Inc.

★1793★ Kirkpatrick Chemical Engineering Achievement Award
Chemical Engineering
McGraw-Hill, Inc.
1221 Avenue of the Americas
New York, NY 10020
Ph: (212)512-2197   Fax: (212)512-4762

To recognize and honor outstanding accomplishments by a group of chemical engineers during the two-year period preceding the award year. Companies, divisions of a company, or groups of companies are eligible. A cast bronze plaque mounted on walnut and a write up in *Chemical Engineering* are awarded biennially. Established in 1933 and named to honor the former editorial director of *Chemical Engineering*.

★1794★ E. V. Murphree Award in Industrial and Engineering Chemistry
American Chemical Society
Research, Grants, and Awards
1155 16th St. NW
Washington, DC 20036
Ph: (202)872-4408

To stimulate fundamental research in industrial and engineering chemistry, the development of chemical engineering principles, and their application to industrial processes. A nominee must have accomplished outstanding research of a theoretical or experimental nature in the fields of industrial chemistry or chemical engineering. The award is granted without regard to age, sex, or nationality. The deadline for nominations is February 1. A monetary award of $5,000, a certificate, and an allowance of not more than $1,000 for travel expenses to attend the meeting where the award is presented are awarded annually. Established in 1955. Sponsored by Exxon Research and Engineering Companyand Exxon Chemical Company.

★1795★ Personal Achievement in Chemical Engineering Awards
Chemical Engineering
McGraw-Hill, Inc.
1221 Avenue of the Americas
New York, NY 10020
Ph: (212)512-2197   Fax: (212)512-4762

To give the recipient due professional recognition to act as a stimulant to other engineers in industry, and to help bolster the stature of chemical engineering in the eyes of the general public. Selection is based on outstanding personal achievement in chemical engineering in one of the following four fields: research and development, design, production, and unusual achievements that do not readily fall into the previous categories. An inscribed plaque and recognition in *Chemical Engineering* are awarded to as many as four individuals annually. Established in 1968.

★1796★ Professional Progress Award for Outstanding Progress in Chemical Engineering
American Institute of Chemical Engineers
345 E. 47th St.
New York, NY 10017
Ph: (212)705-7329

To recognize outstanding progress in the field of chemical engineering. Individuals under 45 years of age at the time of receipt of the award are eligible. A monetary award of $4,000 plus $500 travel allowance and a plaque are presented, and the recipient is invited to deliver an address. Awarded not more than once every calendar year. Established in 1948 by Air Products and Chemicals, Inc.

★1797★ R. H. Wilhelm Award in Chemical Reaction Engineering
American Institute of Chemical Engineers
345 E. 47th St.
New York, NY 10017
Ph: (212)705-7329

To recognize significant and new contributions in chemical reaction engineering. Individuals who have advanced the frontiers of chemical reaction engineering with emphasis on originality, creativity, and novelty of concept and application are eligible. A monetary award of $3,000, a $500 travel allowance, and a plaque are awarded once a year. Established in 1972. Sponsored by Mobil Research and Development Corporation.

BASIC REFERENCE GUIDES AND HANDBOOKS

★1798★ *Chemical Technology: An Encyclopedic Treatment*
Barnes and Noble Books (Imports and Reprints)
Rte. 47-23
Wayne, NJ 07470
Ph: (201)256-6465

T.J.W. Thoor, editor. 1975. Describes the application of natural and synthetic materials to manufacturing processes.

★1799★ *Encyclopedia of Chemical Processing and Design*
Marcel Dekker, Inc.
270 Madison Ave., 4th Fl.
New York, NY 10016
Ph: (212)696-9000

John J. McKetta, editor. 1994. Includes bibliographical references.

★1800★ *Engineer-In-Training Reference Manual*
Professional Publications, Inc.
1250 5th Ave.
Belmont, CA 94002-3863
Fax: (415)592-4519   Fr: 800-426-1178

Michael R. Lindeburg. Eighth edition. Comprehensive guide to preparing for the F.E. exam that covers mathematics, engineering economic analysis, systems of units, fluid statics and dynamics, open channel flow, thermodynamics, and more. Intended to be a broad review of engineering fundamentals.

★1801★ *Formulas, Facts, and Constants for Students and Professionals in Engineering, Chemistry, and Physics*
Springer-Verlag New York, Inc.
175 5th Ave.
New York, NY 10010
Ph: (212)460-1500   Fr: 800-777-4643

Helmut J. Fischbeck and K. H. Fischbeck. Second edition, 1987. Includes an index. Illustrated.

★1802★ *Kirk-Othmer Encyclopedia of Chemical Technology*
John Wiley and Sons, Inc.
605 3rd Ave.
New York, NY 10158-0012
Ph: (212)850-6000   Fax: (212)850-6088
Fr: 800-526-5368

Herman F. Mark, Donald F. Othmer, Charles G. Overberger, and Glen T. Seaborg, editors. Fourth edition. Covers basic chemistry and industrial processes.

★1803★ *Riegel's Handbook of Industrial Chemistry*
Van Nostrand Reinhold Co., Inc.
115 5th Ave.
New York, NY 10003
Ph: (212)254-3232

Emil Raymond Riegel. Ninth edition, 1992. Reviews current developements in the chemical process industry.

PROFESSIONAL AND TRADE PERIODICALS

★1804★ *ACS Washington Alert*
American Chemical Society (ACS)
1155 16th St. NW
Washington, DC 20036
Ph: (202)872-8724   Fax: (202)872-6206
Keith Belton

Biweekly. Focuses on such chemical issues as hazardous waste, air and water quality, biotechnology, and toxic substances, and how they are affected by government regulatory and legislative activities.

★1805★ *AICHE Journal*
American Institute of Chemical Engineers
345 E. 47th St.
New York, NY 10017
Ph: (212)705-7576   Fax: (212)752-3294
Matthew V. Tirrell

Monthly. Journal with articles on chemical engineering research and development, stressing the immediate and potential values in engineering.

★1806★ *Biotechnology & Bioengineering*
John Wiley and Sons, Inc.
605 3rd Ave.
New York, NY 10158
Ph: (212)850-6000   Fax: (212)850-6799
Daniel I.C. Wang

Monthly. Journal providing an international forum for original research on all aspects of biochemical and microbial technology, including products, process development and design, and equipment.

★1807★ *Chemical Design Automation News*
Charlotte Romanicle, Contact
Monthly. Focuses on matters of technical interest relating to the use of computer automation techniques in chemical and engineered materials research. Recurring features include news of research and a calendar of events.

★1808★ *Chemical Engineering*
McGraw-Hill, Inc.
1221 Avenue of the Americas
New York, NY 10020
Ph: (212)512-4686   Fax: (212)512-4256
Nicholas P. Chopey

Biweekly. Chemical process industries magazine.

★1809★ *Chemical and Engineering News*
American Chemical Society
1155 16th St. NW
Washington, DC 20036
Ph: (202)872-4570   Fax: (202)872-4574
Michael Heylin

Weekly. Chemical process industries trade journal.

★1810★ *Chemical Engineering Progress*
American Institute of Chemical Engineers
345 E. 47th St.
New York, NY 10017
Ph: (212)705-7576   Fax: (212)752-3294
Mark Rosenzweig

Monthly. Chemical process industries magazine.

★1811★ *Chemical Heritage*
Chemical Heritage Foundation
3401 Walnut St., Ste. 460B
Philadelphia, PA 19104-6228
Ph: (215)898-4896   Fax: (215)898-3327
Theodor Benfrey

Concerned with the history of chemistry, chemical engineering, and the chemical process industries. Contains brief historical articles; news of history projects, societies, and sources; and news of the Beckman Center and the Othmer Library of Chemical History. Recurring features include news of research, news of members, book reviews, news of recent publications, and a calendar of events.

★1812★ *Environment Engineer*
Professional Engineers in Government (PEG)
1420 King St.
Alexandria, VA 22314-2715
Ph: (703)684-2882
Marji Bayers

Bimonthly. Covers legislation and judicial activities in federal, state, and local government; regulations of the Office of Personnel Management; and labor, management, and personnel relations affecting professional engineers in government. Recurring features include editorials, news of members, book reviews, a calendar of events, and notices of workshops and awards.

★1813★ *Journal of the American Chemical Society*
American Chemical Society
1155 16th St. NW
Washington, DC 20036
Ph: (202)872-4570   Fax: (202)872-4574
Allen J. Bard

Biweekly. Chemistry research journal.

PROFESSIONAL MEETINGS AND CONVENTIONS

★1814★ AOCS Annual Meeting & Expo
American Oil Chemists' Society
PO Box 3489
Champaign, IL 61826-3489
Ph: (217)359-2344   Fax: (217)351-8091

Annual. Usually held during spring. **Dates and Locations:** 1996 Apr 28-01; Indianapolis, IN.

★1815★ Chemical Processing Table Top Show
Chemical Processing Table Top Show
Putman Publishing Co.
310 E. Erie St.
Chicago, IL 60611
Ph: (312)644-2020   Fax: (312)644-1131

Ten per year.

OTHER SOURCES OF INFORMATION

★1816★ "Chemical Engineering" in *Accounting to Zoology: Graduate Fields Defined* (pp. 323-324)
Petersons Guides, Inc.
PO Box 2123
Princeton, NJ 08543-2123
Ph: (609)243-9111   Fax: (609)243-9150
Fr: 800-338-3282

Amy J. Goldstein, editor. Revised and updated, 1987. Defines 298 graduate and professional fields. Discusses types of graduate programs and degrees, graduate research, applied work, employment prospects, and trends.

★1817★ *Financial Aid for Minorities in Engineering & Science*
Garrett Park Press
PO Box 190
Garrett Park, MD 20896
Ph: (301)946-2553
1993.

★1818★ *GEM: National Consortium for Graduate Degrees for Minorities in Engineering*
National Consortium for Graduate Degrees for Minorities in Engineering
PO Box 537
Notre Dame, IN 46556
Ph: (219)287-1097

1988. Describes the graduate fellowship program for minorities in engineering including financial support, application, and internship. Lists universities offering this program.

★1819★ *How to Become a Professional Engineer*
McGraw-Hill, Inc.
1221 Avenue of the Americas
New York, NY 10020
Ph: (212)512-2000   Fr: 800-722-4726

J.D. Constance. Fourth edition, 1987. Describes how to register for the professional engineer's license in all fifty states. Gives a state-by-state list of licensing regulations. Gives advice on how to take the written examination.

Civil Engineers

Civil engineers, who work in the oldest branch of engineering, design and supervise the construction of roads, airports, tunnels, bridges, water supply and sewage systems, and buildings. Major specialties within civil engineering are structural, water resources, environmental, construction, transportation, highway, and geotechnical engineering.

Salaries

Starting salaries in private industry for engineers with bachelor degrees are significantly higher than starting salaries of college graduates in other fields.

Beginning civil engineers	$29,376/year
Experienced engineers	$52,500/year
Senior managerial engineers	$102,544/year

Employment Outlook

Growth rate until the year 2005: Average.

Civil Engineers

CAREER GUIDES

★1820★ *ASCE Guide to Employment Conditions for Civil Engineers*
American Society of Civil Engineers
345 E. 47th St.
New York, NY 10017
Ph: (212)705-7288   Fax: (212)980-4681
Third edition, 1988.

★1821★ *ASCE Salary Survey*
American Society of Civil Engineers
345 E. 47th St.
New York, NY 10017
Ph: (212)705-7288   Fax: (212)980-4681
1991.

★1822★ *Career Development for Engineers and Scientists: Organizational Programs and Individual Choices*
Van Nostrand Reinhold Co., Inc.
115 5th Ave.
New York, NY 10003
Ph: (212)254-3232   Fr: 800-842-3636
Robert F. Morrison and Richard M. Vosburgh. 1987. Includes bibliographies and an index. Illustrated.

★1823★ *Careers and the Engineer*
Bob Adams, Inc.
260 Center St.
Holbrook, MA 02343
Ph: (617)268-9570
Gigi Ranno, editor. Annual.

★1824★ *Careers in Engineering*
National Textbook Co. (NTC)
VGM Career Books
4255 W. Touhy Ave.
Lincolnwood, IL 60646-1975
Ph: (708)679-5500   Fax: (708)679-2494
Fr: 800-323-4900
Geraldine O. Garner, Ph.D., editor. 1993. Career guide covering 14 different engineering specialties.

★1825★ *Civil Engineer*
Careers, Inc.
PO Box 135
Largo, FL 34649-0135
Ph: (813)584-7333
1994. Four-page brief offering the definition, history, duties, working conditions, personal qualifications, educational requirements, earnings, hours, employment outlook, advancement, and careers related to this position.

★1826★ *Civil Engineer*
Vocational Biographies, Inc.
PO Box 31
Sauk Centre, MN 56378-0031
Ph: (612)352-6516   Fax: (612)352-5546
Fr: 800-255-0752
1991. Four-page pamphlet containing a personal narrative about a worker's job, work likes and dislikes, career path from high school to the present. Education and training, the rewards and frustrations, and the effects of the job on the rest of the worker's life. The data file portion of this pamphlet gives a concise occupational summary, including work descriptions, working conditions, places of employment, personal characteristics, education and training, job outlook, and salary range.

★1827★ "Civil Engineer" in *100 Best Careers for the Year 2000* (pp. 252-254)
Arco Pub.
201 W. 103rd St.
Indianapolis, IN 46290
Ph: 800-428-5331   Fax: 800-835-3202
Shelly Field. 1992. Describes 100 job opportunities expected to grow fast throughout the next decade. Provides information on job duties and responsibilities, training requirements, education, advancement opportunities, experience and qualifications, and typical salaries.

★1828★ "Civil Engineer" in *Guide to Federal Jobs* (p. 156)
Resource Directories
3361 Executive Pkwy., Ste. 302
Toledo, OH 43606
Ph: (419)536-5353   Fax: (419)536-7056
Fr: 800-274-8515
Rod W. Durgin, editor. Third edition, 1992. Contains information on finding and applying for federal jobs. Describes more than 200 professional and technical jobs for college graduates. Covers the nature of the work, salary, and geographic location. Lists college majors preferred for that occupation. Section one describes the function and work of government agencies that hire the most significant number of college graduates.

★1829★ "Civil Engineer" in *Jobs Rated Almanac*
World Almanac
1 International Blvd., Ste. 444
Mahwah, NJ 07495
Ph: (201)529-6900   Fax: (201)529-6901
Les Krantz. Second edition, 1992. Ranks 250 jobs by environment, salary, outlooks, physical demands, stress, security, travel opportunities, and extra perks. Includes jobs the editor feels are the most common, most interesting, and the most rapidly growing.

★1830★ "Civil Engineer" in *Opportunities in High-Tech Careers* (p. 123)
National Textbook Co. (NTC)
VGM Career Books
4255 W. Touhy Ave.
Lincolnwood, IL 60646-1975
Ph: (708)679-5500   Fax: (708)679-2494
Fr: 800-323-4900
Gary D. Golter and Deborah Yanuck. 1987. Explores high technology careers. Written for the student and displaced worker. Describes job opportunities, how to make a career decision, how to prepare for high-technology jobs, job hunting techniques, and future trends.

★1831★ "Civil Engineer" in *VGM's Careers Encyclopedia* (pp. 100-102)
National Textbook Co. (NTC)
VGM Career Books
4255 W. Touhy Ave.
Lincolnwood, IL 60646-1975
Ph: (708)679-5500   Fax: (708)679-2494
Fr: 800-323-4900
Third edition, 1991. Profiles 200 occupations. Describes job duties, places of employment, working conditions, qualifications, education and training, advancement potential, and salary for each occupation.

★1832★ "Civil Engineering" in *College Majors and Careers: A Resource Guide to Effective Life Planning* **(pp. 37-38)**
Garrett Park Press
PO Box 1907
Garrett Park, MD 20896
Ph: (301)946-2553
Paul Phifer. Revised, 1993. Lists 60 college majors, with definitions; related occupations and leisure activities; skills, values, and personal attributes needed; suggested readings; and a list of associations.

★1833★ *Civil Engineers*
Chronicle Guidance Publications, Inc.
66 Aurora St.
PO Box 1190
Moravia, NY 13118-1190
Ph: (315)497-0330   Fax: (315)497-3359
Fr: 800-622-7284
1993. Occupational brief describing the nature of the job, working conditions, hours and earnings, education and training, licensure, certification, unions, personal qualifications, social and psychological factors, location, employment outlook, entry methods, advancement, and related occupations.

★1834★ "Civil Engineers" in *101 Careers: A Guide to the Fastest-Growing Opportunities* **(pp. 70-72)**
John Wiley & Sons, Inc.
605 3rd Ave.
New York, NY 10158-0012
Ph: (212)850-6645   Fax: (212)850-6088
Michael Harkavy. 1990. Describes the nature of the job, working conditions, employment growth, qualifications, personal skills, projected salaries, and where to write for more information.

★1835★ "Civil Engineers" in *Career Discovery Encyclopedia* **(Vol.2, pp. 12-13)**
J.G. Ferguson Publishing Co.
200 W. Madison St., Ste. 300
Chicago, IL 60606
Ph: (312)580-5480   Fax: (312)580-4948
Russell E. Primm, editor-in chief. 1993. This six volume set contains two-page articles for 504 occupations. Each article describes job duties, earnings, and educational and training requirements. The whole set is arranged alphabetically by job title. Designed for junior high and older students.

★1836★ "Civil Engineers" in *Career Information Center* **(Vol.4)**
Simon and Schuster
200 Old Tappan Rd.
Old Tappan, NJ 07675
Fax: 800-445-6991   Fr: 800-223-2348
Richard Lidz and Linda Perrin, editorial directors. Fifth edition, 1993. A multi-volume set that profiles more than 600 occupations. Each occupational profile describes job duties, educational requirements, getting a job, advancement possibilities, employment outlook, working conditions, earnings and benefits, and sources of additional information.

★1837★ "Civil Engineers" in *Encyclopedia of Careers and Vocational Guidance* **(Vol.2, pp.307-311)**
J.G. Ferguson Publishing Co.
200 W. Madison St., Ste. 300
Chicago, IL 60606
Ph: (312)580-5480   Fax: (312)580-4948
William E. Hopke, editor-in-chief. Ninth edition, 1993. Four-volume set that profiles 900 occupations and describes job trends in 74 industries. Includes career description, educational requirements, history of the job, methods of entry, advancement, employment outlook, earnings, conditions of work, social and psychological factors, and sources of further information.

★1838★ "Civil Engineers" in *Jobs! What They Are—Where They Are—What They Pay* **(p. 58)**
Simon & Schuster, Inc.
Simon & Schuster Bldg.
1230 Avenue of the Americas
New York, NY 10020
Ph: (212)698-7000   Fr: 800-223-2348
Robert O. Snelling and Anne M. Snelling. 3rd edition, 1992. Describes duties and responsibilities, earnings, employment opportunities, training, and qualifications.

★1839★ "Civil Engineers" in *Occupational Outlook Handbook*
U.S. Government Printing Office
Superintendent of Documents
Washington, DC 20402
Ph: (202)512-1800   Fax: (202)512-2250
Biennial; latest edition, 1994-95. Encyclopedia of careers describing about 250 occupations and comprising about 85 percent of all jobs in the economy. Occupations that require lengthy education or training are given the most attention. Each occupation's profile describes what the worker does on the job, working conditions, education and training requirements, advancement possibilities, job outlook, earnings, and sources of additional information.

★1840★ *The Civilized Engineer*
St. Martin's Press, Inc.
175 5th Ave.
New York, NY 10010
Ph: (212)674-5151   Fax: 800-258-2769
Fr: 800-221-7945
Samuel C. Florman. 1989. Published by Thomas Dunne Books. Discusses engineering education, the relationship between engineers and nontechnical executives, and the role of women in engineering.

★1841★ "Engineering" in *American Almanac of Jobs and Salaries* **(pp. 261)**
Avon Books
1350 Avenue of the Americas
New York, NY 10019
Ph: (212)261-6800   Fr: 800-238-0658
John Wright, editor. Revised and updated, 1994-95. A comprehensive guide to the wages of hundreds of occupations in a wide variety of industries and organizations.

★1842★ "Engineering" in *Encyclopedia of Careers and Vocational Guidance* **(Vol.1, pp. 165-171)**
J.G. Ferguson Publishing Co.
200 W. Madison St., Ste. 300
Chicago, IL 60606
Ph: (312)580-5480   Fax: (312)580-4948
William E. Hopke, editor-in-chief. Ninth edition, 1993. Four-volume set that profiles 900 occupations and describes job trends in 74 industries. Includes career description, educational requirements, history of the job, methods of entry, advancement, employment outlook, earnings, conditions of work, social and psychological factors, and sources of further information.

★1843★ *Engineering Salary Survey*
Source Engineering
1290 Oakmead, Ste. 318
Sunnyvale, CA 94086
Ph: (408)738-8440
Annual. Discusses the structure of the engineering profession, trends, and compensation. Salaries are listed by job function, industry, and years of experience.

★1844★ "Engineering" in *Where the Jobs Are: The Hottest Careers for the 90s* **(pp. 111-124)**
Career Press
180 5th Ave.
Hawthorne, NJ 07507
Ph: (201)427-0229   Fax: (201)427-2037
Fr: 800-CAREER-1
Joyce Hadley. 1995. Offers a job-hunting strategy for the 1990s as well as descriptions of growing careers of the decade. Each profile includes general information, forecasts, growth, education and training, licensing requirements, and salary information.

★1845★ *Engineering for You: A Career Guide*
Iowa State University Press
2121 S. State Ave.
Ames, IA 50010
Ph: (515)292-0140   Fax: (515)292-3348
John T. Jones. 1991.

★1846★ "Howard Simons—Structural Engineer" in *Straight Talk on Careers: Eighty Pros Take You Into Their Professions* **(pp. 51-53)**
Garrett Park Press
PO Box 1907
Garrett Park, MD 20896
Ph: (301)946-2553
Mary Barbera-Hogan. 1987. Contains candid interviews from people who give an inside view of their work in 80 different careers. These professionals describe a day's work and the stresses and rewards accompanying their work.

★1847★ *Opportunities in Civil Engineering Careers*
National Textbook Co. (NTC)
VGM Career Books
4255 W. Touhy Ave.
Lincolnwood, IL 60646-1975
Ph: (708)679-5500   Fax: (708)679-2494
Fr: 800-323-4900
Joseph D. Hagerty and Louis F. Cohn. 1987. Includes a bibliography. Explains job duties, educational requirements, salary, working

conditions, employment outlook, and advancement opportunities.

★1848★ Opportunities in Engineering
National Textbook Co. (NTC)
VGM Career Books
4255 W. Touhy Ave.
Lincolnwood, IL 60646-1975
Ph: (708)679-5500   Fax: (708)679-2494
Fr: 800-323-4900

Nicholas Basta. 1990. Profiles specialties in the engineering field including civil, chemical, mechanical, biomedical, and aerospace. Offers information on salaries, career paths and educational requirements.

★1849★ Opportunities in Engineering Technology Careers
National Textbook Co. (NTC)
VGM Career Books
4255 W. Touhy Ave.
Lincolnwood, IL 60646-1975
Ph: (708)679-5500   Fax: (708)679-2494
Fr: 800-323-4900

John E. Heer and D. Joseph Hagerty. 1987. Describes the many opportunities available for engineering technicians. Explains job duties, educational requirements, salary, working conditions, employment outlook, and advancement opportunities. Lists accredited engineering technology programs.

★1850★ Peterson's Job Opportunities for Engineering and Technology
Petersons Guides, Inc.
PO Box 2123
Princeton, NJ 08543-2123
Ph: (609)243-9111   Fax: (609)243-9150
Fr: 800-338-3282

1994. Gives job hunting advice including information on resume writing, interviewing, and handling salary negotiations. Lists companies that hire college graduates in science and engineering at the bachelor and master's level. Companies are indexed by industry, starting location, and major. Company profiles include contact information and types of hires.

★1851★ Successful Engineering: A Guide to Achieving Your Career Goals
McGraw-Hill, Inc.
1221 Avenue of the Americas
New York, NY 10020
Ph: (212)512-2000   Fr: 800-722-4726

Lawrence J. Kamm. 1989. Written for the practicing and graduating engineer. Gives advice about working with accountants, the politics of design, and engineering ethics.

PROFESSIONAL ASSOCIATIONS

★1852★ Accreditation Board for Engineering and Technology (ABET)
111 Market Pl., Ste. 1050
Baltimore, MD 21202
Ph: (410)347-7700   Fax: (410)625-2238
Members: Professional societies representing over one million engineers are participating bodies (21); affiliate bodies (5); board of directors has 29 representatives. Is responsible for the quality control of engineer-

ing education. Accredits college curricula in engineering, engineering technology, and engineering-related areas. **Publications:** Accreditation Yearbook, annual. • Criteria for Accrediting Programs in Engineering in the United States, annual. • Criteria for Accrediting Programs in Engineering Technology, annual.

★1853★ American Association of Engineering Societies (AAES)
1111 19th St. NW, Ste. 608
Washington, DC 20036
Ph: (202)296-2237   Fax: (202)296-1151
Members: Societies representing over 500,000 engineers. **Purpose:** Works to: advance the knowledge and practice of engineering in the public interest; act as an advisory, communication, and information exchange agency for member activities, especially regarding public policy issues. Conducts studies sponsored by Engineering Manpower Commission. Compiles statistics. **Publications:** AAES Update, quarterly. • Directory of Engineering Societies, biennial. • Engineering and Technology Degrees, annual. • Engineering and Technology Enrollments, annual. • Engineers Salary Survey, annual. • The Role of Engineering in Sustainable Development. • Who's Who in Engineering, biennial.

★1854★ American Institute of Engineers (AIE)
4666 San Pablo Dam Rd., No. 8
El Sobrante, CA 94803-3142
Ph: (510)223-8911   Fax: (510)223-3400
Members: Professional engineers and engineering students. **Purpose:** Seeks to advance the professional interests of engineers and scientists. Fosters the interchange of ideas and information among members. Compiles statistics; maintains speakers' bureau. **Publications:** AIE Newsmagazine, monthly.

★1855★ American Society of Civil Engineers (ASCE)
c/o Kelly Cunningham
1015 15th St. NW, Ste. 600
Washington, DC 20005
Ph: (202)789-2200
Members: Professional society of civil engineers. **Purpose:** Supports research and engineering societies library. Offers continuing education courses and technical specialty conferences. Maintains numerous committees. **Publications:** ASCE News, monthly. • Civil Engineering, monthly. • Manuals and Reports on Engineering Practice, periodic. • Official Register, annual. • Publications Abstracts, bimonthly. • Transactions, annual.

★1856★ National Action Council for Minorities in Engineering (NACME)
3 W. 35th St.
New York, NY 10001
Ph: (212)279-2626   Fax: (212)629-5178
Members: Seeks to increase the number of African American, Hispanic, and Native American students enrolled in and graduating from engineering schools. **Purpose:** Offers incentive grants to engineering schools to recruit and provide financial assistance to increasing numbers of minority students. Works with local, regional, and national support organizations to motivate and encourage

precollege students to engage in engineering careers. Conducts educational and research programs; operates project to assist engineering schools in improving the retention and graduation rates of minority students. Maintains speakers' bureau; compiles statistics. **Publications:** Directory of Pre-College and University Minority Engineering Programs, periodic. • Financial Aid Unscrambled: A Guide for Minority Engineering Students, biennial. • Gearing Up: How to Start a Pre-College Minority Engineering Program. • NACME News, semiannual. • NACME Statistical Report, biennial.

★1857★ National Society of Professional Engineers (NSPE)
1420 King St.
Alexandria, VA 22314
Ph: (703)684-2800   Fax: (703)836-4875
Members: Professional engineers and engineers-in-training in all fields registered in accordance with the laws of states or territories of the U.S. or provinces of Canada; qualified graduate engineers, student members, and registered land surveyors. Is concerned with social, professional, ethical, and economic considerations of engineering as a profession; encompasses programs in public relations, employment practices, ethical considerations, education, and career guidance. Monitors legislative and regulatory actions of interest to the engineering profession. **Publications:** Directory of Professional Engineers in Private Practice, biennial. • Engineering Times, monthly. • PEG Times, quarterly.

★1858★ Society of Women Engineers (SWE)
120 Wall St., 11th Fl.
New York, NY 10005
Ph: (212)509-9577   Fax: (212)509-0224
Members: Educational service society of women engineers; membership is also open to men. **Purpose:** Supplies information on the achievements of women engineers and the opportunities available to them; assists women engineers in preparing for return to active work following temporary retirement. Serves as an informational center on women in engineering. Administers several certificate and scholarship programs. Offers tours and career guidance; conducts surveys. Compiles statistics. **Publications:** National Survey of Women and Men Engineers.

STANDARDS/CERTIFICATION AGENCIES

★1859★ Accreditation Board for Engineering and Technology (ABET)
111 Market Pl., Ste. 1050
Baltimore, MD 21202
Ph: (410)347-7700   Fax: (410)625-2238
Is responsible for the quality control of engineering education. Accredits college curricula in engineering, engineering technology, and engineering-related areas.

★1860★ **Society of Women Engineers (SWE)**
120 Wall St., 11th Fl.
New York, NY 10005
Ph: (212)509-9577   Fax: (212)509-0224
Administers several certificate and scholarship programs. Compiles statistics.

TEST GUIDES

★1861★ *Career Examination Series: Building Structural Engineer*
National Learning Corp.
212 Michael Dr.
Syosset, NY 11791
Ph: (516)921-8888   Fax: (516)921-8743
Fr: 800-645-6337
Jack Rudman. 1993. Test guide including questions and answers for students or professionals in the field who seek advancement through examination.

★1862★ *Career Examination Series: Civil Engineer*
National Learning Corp.
212 Michael Dr.
Syosset, NY 11791
Ph: (516)921-8888   Fax: (516)921-8743
Fr: 800-645-6337
Jack Rudman. Test guide including questions and answers for students or professionals in the field who seek advancement through examination. Also included in the series: Senior Civil Engineer, Principal Civil Engineer, Junior Civil Engineer, and Assistant Civil Engineer.

★1863★ *Career Examination Series: Engineer*
National Learning Corp.
212 Michael Dr.
Syosset, NY 11791
Ph: (516)921-8888   Fax: (516)921-8743
Fr: 800-645-6337
Jack Rudman. A series of study guides with multiple-choice examination questions and solutions for trainees and professional petroleum engineers. Titles in the series include *Administrative Engineer; Chief Engineer; Engineering Aide and Science Assistant; Engineering Aide; Engineering Assistant; Engineering Trainee; Senior Engineer; Senior Engineering Aide.*

★1864★ *Career Examination Series: Highway Engineer*
National Learning Corp.
212 Michael Dr.
Syosset, NY 11791
Ph: (516)921-8888   Fax: (516)921-8743
Fr: 800-645-6337
Jack Rudman. 1993. Test guide including questions and answers for students or professionals in the field who seek advancement through examination.

★1865★ *Career Examination Series: Senior Building Structural Engineer*
National Learning Corp.
212 Michael Dr.
Syosset, NY 11791
Ph: (516)921-8888   Fax: (516)921-8743
Fr: 800-645-6337
Jack Rudman. 1993. Test guide including questions and answers for students or professionals in the field who seek advancement through examination.

★1866★ *Career Examination Series: Senior Civil Engineer (Structures)*
National Learning Corp.
212 Michael Dr.
Syosset, NY 11791
Ph: (516)921-8888   Fax: (516)921-8743
Fr: 800-645-6337
Jack Rudman. 1993. Test guide including questions and answers for students or professionals in the field who seek advancement through examination.

★1867★ *Civil Engineering License Exam File*
Engineering Press, Inc.
PO Box 1
San Jose, CA 95103-0001
Ph: (408)258-4503   Fax: 800-700-1651
Fr: 800-800-1651
Donald G. Newnan and Robert E. Lindskog. Eleventh edition, 1991. 93 problems and solutions for the Civil Engineering Principles and Practice Exam.

★1868★ *Civil Engineering Reference Manual*
Professional Publications, Inc.
1250 5th Ave.
Belmont, CA 94002-3863
Ph: 800-426-1178
Michael R. Lindeburg. 6th edition, 1992. Covers 22 different exam topics.

★1869★ *Civil Engineering Sample Examination*
Professional Publications, Inc.
1250 5th Ave.
Belmont, CA 94002-3863
Ph: 800-426-1178
Michael R. Lindeburg. 3rd edition, 1992. Offers 25 typical exam problems with complete answers.

★1870★ *Engineer-in-Training Exam File*
Engineering Press, Inc.
PO Box 1
San Jose, CA 95103-0001
Ph: (408)258-4503   Fax: 800-700-1651
Fr: 800-800-1651
Donald G. Newnan and Dean Newnan. Eleventh edition. 1990. Contains 505 problems with step-by-step solutions. Covers: mathematics; statics; fluid mechanics. Includes an index.

★1871★ *Engineering Economic Analysis Exam File*
Engineering Press, Inc.
PO Box 1
San Jose, CA 95103-0001
Ph: (408)258-4503   Fax: 800-700-1651
Fr: 800-800-1651
Contains 386 exam problems with step-by-step solutions.

★1872★ *Graduate Record Examination: Engineering*
National Learning Corp.
212 Michael Dr.
Syosset, NY 11791
Ph: (516)921-8888   Fax: (516)921-8743
Fr: 800-645-6337
Jack Rudman. Multiple-choice test for those seeking admission to graduate school for study in the field of engineering. Includes solutions to examination questions.

★1873★ *Graduate Record Examination in Engineering*
Arco Publishing Co.
Macmillan General Reference
15 Columbus Cir.
New York, NY 10023
Fax: 800-835-3202   Fr: 800-858-7674
C.W. Tan, et al. First edition. 1988. Contains two sample tests with an explanation to answers.

★1874★ *Practicing to Take the GRE Engineering Test: An Official Publication of the GRE Board*
Educational Testing Service
Rosedale Rd.
Princeton, NJ 08541
Ph: (609)921-9000
Second edition, 1989. Summarizes the purpose and scope of the Graduate Record Examination Subject Test for engineering. Contains sample questions.

★1875★ *Professional Engineer*
National Learning Corp.
212 Michael Dr.
Syosset, NY 11791
Ph: (516)921-8888   Fax: (516)921-8743
Fr: 800-645-6337
Jack Rudman. A sample test for engineers who are seeking admission to graduate and professional schools or seeking entrance or advancement in institutional and public career service.

★1876★ *Timber Design for the Civil Professional Engineering Examination*
Professional Publications, Inc.
1250 5th Ave.
Belmont, CA 94002-3863
Fax: (415)592-4519   Fr: 800-426-1178
Robert L. Brungraber. Third edition, 1990. Includes a bibliography and an index. Contains codes, standard references, and practice problems.

★1877★ *Undergraduate Program Field Test: Engineering*
National Learning Corp.
212 Michael Dr.
Syosset, NY 11791
Ph: (516)921-8888   Fax: (516)921-8743
Fr: 800-645-6337
Jack Rudman. A practice examination fashioned after tests given in the Regents External Degree Program. Designed to measure knowledge received outside the college classroom in the subject of engineering. Contains multiple-choice questions; provides solutions.

EDUCATIONAL DIRECTORIES AND PROGRAMS

★1878★ ABET Accreditation Yearbook
Accreditation Board for Engineering and Technology
345 E. 47th St., 14th Fl.
New York, NY 10017-2397
Ph: (212)705-7685   Fax: (212)838-8062
Simona C. Mardale, Contact
Annual, September. Covers about 300 U.S. colleges and universities with engineering programs, 242 institutions with programs in engineering technology, and 11 institutions with engineering-related programs accredited by the Board; also lists accredited Canadian programs. Entries include: For United States institutions—Name, year of next full accreditation review, location, program names, year of initial accreditation for each program, coding to indicate degrees offered, format of program (day, night, cooperative, etc.). For Canadian programs—Name, location, names of programs, year of initial accredition for each program. Arrangement: Classified by program area.

★1879★ Environmental Career Directory
Gale Research Inc.
835 Penobscot Bldg.
Detroit, MI 48226-4094
Ph: (313)961-2242   Fax: (313)961-6083
Fr: 800-877-GALE
Bradley J. Morgan and Joseph M. Palmisano. 1993. A directory in the Career Advisor Series that provides essays written by industry professionals; job search information on resume and cover letter preparation, networking, and the interviewing process; approximately 300 companies and organizations offering job opportunities and internships, and additional job-hunting resources.

AWARDS, SCHOLARSHIPS, GRANTS, AND FELLOWSHIPS

★1880★ ASCE President's Medal
American Society of Civil Engineers
1015 15th N.W, Ste. 600
Washington, DC 20005
Ph: (202)789-2200   Fax: (202)289-6797
To recognize the accomplishments and contributions of eminent engineers to the profession, the Society or the public. A bronze medal is awarded annually. Established in 1986.

★1881★ Award for Service To People
American Society of Civil Engineers
1015 15th N.W, Ste. 600
Washington, DC 20005
Ph: (202)789-2200   Fax: (202)289-6797
To recognize individuals who have performed outstanding service to people in their communities, and to further public understanding and recognition of the identification, "Civil Engineering: A People-Serving Profession." A certificate is awarded annually. Established in 1980.

★1882★ Arthur J. Boase Award of the Reinforced Concrete Research Council
American Society of Civil Engineers
1015 15th N.W, Ste. 600
Washington, DC 20005
Ph: (202)789-2200   Fax: (202)289-6797
To recognize a person, persons, or organizations for outstanding activities and achievements in the reinforced concrete field. Nominations must be submitted by November 1. A certificate is awarded annually. Established in honor of Arthur J. Boase (1892-1949).

★1883★ Can-AM Civil Engineering Amity Award
American Society of Civil Engineers
1015 15th N.W, Ste. 600
Washington, DC 20005
Ph: (202)789-2200   Fax: (202)289-6797
To recognize civil engineers who have made outstanding and unusual contributions toward the advancement of professional relationships between the civil engineers of the United States and Canada. Nominations must be submitted by November 1. A plaque and a certificate are awarded annually. Established in 1972.

★1884★ Freeman Fellowship
American Society of Civil Engineers
1015 15th N.W, Ste. 600
Washington, DC 20005
Ph: (202)789-2200   Fax: (202)289-6797
To aid and encourage young engineers, especially in research work. Grants are awarded biennially in odd-numbered years. In addition, traveling scholarships are available to members younger than 45 years of age. Established in 1924 by John R. Freeman, past President and Honorary Member, ASCE.

★1885★ Simon W. Freese Environmental Engineering Award and Lecture
American Society of Civil Engineers
1015 15th N.W, Ste. 600
Washington, DC 20005
Ph: (202)789-2200   Fax: (202)289-6797
To invite a distinguished person to prepare for publication and deliver the Simon W. Freese Environmental Engineering Lecture. A certificate and an honorarium are awarded annually. Established in 1975 by the Environmental Engineering Division and endowed by the firm of Freese and Nichols in honor of their partner, Simon W. Freese.

★1886★ Alfred M. Freudenthal Medal
American Society of Civil Engineers
1015 15th N.W, Ste. 600
Washington, DC 20005
Ph: (202)789-2200   Fax: (202)289-6797
To recognize an individual for distinguished achievement in safety and reliability studies applicable to any branch of civil engineering. Nominations must be submitted by November 1. A bronze medal is awarded every two years. Established in 1975 by the Engineering Mechanics Division.

★1887★ Edmund Friedman Young Engineer Award for Professional Achievement
American Society of Civil Engineers
1015 15th N.W, Ste. 600
Washington, DC 20005
Ph: (202)789-2200   Fax: (202)289-6797
To recognize members who are 32 years of age or less and who have attained significant professional achievement. Nominations must be submitted by Februrary 1. A certificate is presented at the National Convention. Established in 1972.

★1888★ John Fritz Medal
United Engineering Trustees
345 E. 47th St.
New York, NY 10017
Ph: (212)705-7828   Fax: (212)705-7441
For recognition of outstanding scientific or industrial achievement in any field of pure or applied science. A gold medal and/or certificate are awarded annually. Established in 1902 by the United Engineering Society in honor of John Fritz, a noted developer of the iron and steel industry, an exceptional engineer, and an influential founder of U.S. industry. Sponsored by the American Institute of Chemical Engineers; American Society of Mechanical Engineering; American Institute of Mining, Metallurgical and Petroleum Engineers; American Society of Civil Engineers; and the Institute of Electrical and Electronics Engineers, Inc.

★1889★ Government Civil Engineer of the Year Award
American Society of Civil Engineers
1015 15th N.W, Ste. 600
Washington, DC 20005
Ph: (202)789-2200   Fax: (202)289-6797
To recognize distinguished civil engineers employed in public service for significant contributions to Public Service Engineering. Engineers of recognized standing, preferably registered and citizens of the United States are eligible. Award nominees are judged on the following: sustained outstanding civil engineering performance in the public sector; evidence of high character and professional integrity; minimum of 15 years of public service as a civil engineer; and five of the fifteen years at the senior administrative level. Nominations must be submitted by October 1. Up to four recipients may be designated in any year, no more than one from each Zone. The award consists of a suitably inscribed certificate. Established by the Committee on Civil Engineers in Government.

★1890★ Shortridge Hardesty Award
American Society of Civil Engineers
1015 15th N.W, Ste. 600
Washington, DC 20005
Ph: (202)789-2200   Fax: (202)289-6797
To recognize an individual(s) who has contributed substantially in applying fundamental results of research to solution of practical engineering problems in the field of structural stability. Members must be nominated by November 1. An honorarium and a certificate are awarded annually. Established in 1987 by the firm of Hardesty & Hanover to honor the contributions of Shortridge Hardesty as first chairman of the Column Research Council.

★1891★ International Coastal Engineering Award
American Society of Civil Engineers
1015 15th N.W, Ste. 600
Washington, DC 20005
Ph: (202)789-2200   Fax: (202)289-6797

To provide international recognition for outstanding leadership and development in the field of coastal engineering. There is no restriction to nationality or Society membership. Selection is based on contribution to the advancement of coastal engineering in the manner of engineering design, teaching, professional leadership, construction, research, planning, or a combination thereof. Nominations must be submitted by November 1. A specially designed plaque, a certificate, and an honorarium are awarded annually. In even-numbered years the award will, if possible, be presented at the International Coastal Engineering Conference. In odd-numbered years the award will be presented at an ASCE national or specialty conference as desired by the recipient. Established in 1977 in honor of Mauricio Porraz.

★1892★ John G. Moffat - Frank E. Nichol Harbor and Coastal Engineering Award
American Society of Civil Engineers
1015 15th N.W, Ste. 600
Washington, DC 20005
Ph: (202)789-2200   Fax: (202)289-6797

To recognize new ideas and concepts that can be efficiently implemented to expand the engineering or construction techniques available for harbor and coastal projects. Nominations must be submitted by November 1. An honorarium, a plaque, and a certificate are awarded annually. Established in 1977 by the firm of Moffat & Nichol to honor John G. Moffat and Frank E. Nichol.

★1893★ Outstanding Civil Engineering Achievement
American Society of Civil Engineers
1015 15th N.W, Ste. 600
Washington, DC 20005
Ph: (202)789-2200   Fax: (202)289-6797

To recognize an engineering project that demonstrates the greatest engineering skills and represents the greatest contribution to engineering progress and mankind. A plaque is presented to the owner of the project. In addition, Awards of Merit winners may be selected. Awarded annually. Established in 1960.

★1894★ Roebling Award
American Society of Civil Engineers
1015 15th N.W, Ste. 600
Washington, DC 20005
Ph: (202)789-2200   Fax: (202)289-6797

To recognize and honor an individual who has made an outstanding contribution toward the advancement of construction engineering. Nominations may be submitted by November 1. The recipient of the Award will deliver a Roebling Lecture at an appropriate meeting of the Society. An honorarium and a plaque are awarded annually when merited. Awarded without restrictions as to Society membership or nationality. Established in 1987 by the Construction Division of the Society in memory of three outstanding construc-

tors, John A. Roebling, Washington Roebling and Emily Roebling.

★1895★ J. Waldo Smith Hydraulic Fellowship
American Society of Civil Engineers
1015 15th N.W, Ste. 600
Washington, DC 20005
Ph: (202)789-2200   Fax: (202)289-6797

To assist that graduate student, preferably an Associate Member of the Society, who gives promise of best fulfilling the ideals of the fellowship. The fellowship is offered every third year. It runs for one full academic year and provides $4,000, plus up to $1,000 as may be required for physical equipment connected with the research. Such equipment becomes the property of the institution upon completion of the work. Established in 1938 and made possible by J. Waldo Smith, past Vice President and Hon. M. ASCE, who bequeathed funds to the Society.

★1896★ Theodore von Karman Medal
American Society of Civil Engineers
1015 15th N.W, Ste. 600
Washington, DC 20005
Ph: (202)789-2200   Fax: (202)289-6797

To recognize an individual for distinguished achievement in engineering mechanics applicable to any branch of civil engineering. Individuals regardless of age, nationality, and Society membership are eligible. A bronze medal is awarded annually. Established in 1960 by the Engineering Mechanics Division of the Society in honor of Theodore von Karman.

BASIC REFERENCE GUIDES AND HANDBOOKS

★1897★ Civil Engineer's Reference Book
Butterworth-Heinemann Publishers
80 Montvale Ave.
Stoneham, MA 02180
Ph: (617)438-8464   Fr: 800-548-4001

Leslie Spencer Blake, editor. 1994. Contains articles on all aspects of civil engineering and site management.

★1898★ Encyclopedia of Building Technology
Prentice-Hall, Inc.
Rte. 9W
Englewood Cliffs, NJ 07632
Ph: (201)592-2000

Henry J. Cowan, editor. 1988. Includes bibliographies and indexes.

★1899★ Engineer-In-Training Reference Manual
Professional Publications, Inc.
1250 5th Ave.
Belmont, CA 94002-3863
Fax: (415)592-4519   Fr: 800-426-1178

Michael R. Lindeburg. Eighth edition. Comprehensive guide to preparing for the F.E. exam that covers mathematics, engineering economic analysis, systems of units, fluid statics and dynamics, open channel flow,

thermodynamics, and more. Intended to be a broad review of engineering fundamentals.

★1900★ Engineering Materials: Properties and Selection
Prentice-Hall, Inc.
Rte. 9W
Englewood Cliffs, NJ 07632
Ph: (201)592-2000   Fr: 800-634-2863

Kenneth Budinski. Third edition, 1989. A guide to the material specifications of methods, plastics, ceramics, and cements. Provides recommendations for construction with these materials and tips for proper specification on engineering drawings.

★1901★ The VNR Dictionary of Civil Engineering
Van Nostrand Reinhold
115 5th Ave.
New York, NY 10013

John S. Scott. 1993.

PROFESSIONAL AND TRADE PERIODICALS

★1902★ The CERCular
U.S. Army Engineer Waterways Experiment Station
c/o CEWES-CV-I
3909 Halls Ferry Rd.
Vicksburg, MS 39180-6199
Ph: (601)634-2012   Fax: (601)634-3433
Fred E. Camfield

Quarterly. Covers CERC, the U.S. Army Coastal Engineering Research Center and its work on shore and beach erosion; coastal flood and storm protection; navigation improvements; and the design, construction, operation, and maintenance of coastal structures. Reports on meetings of the Coastal engineering Research Board and a calendar of coastal related events of interest. Recurring features include listings of CERC reports published, notices of upcoming conferences, and notices of new publications.

★1903★ Civil Engineering: An Abstract Newsletter
National Technical Information Service (NTIS)
5285 Port Royal Rd.
Springfield, VA 22161
Ph: (703)487-4630

Biweekly. Publishes abstracts with full bibliographic citations in the areas of highway engineering, civil engineering, soil and rock mechanics, flood control, and construction equipment, materials and supplies. Alerts readers to related published materials available from NTIS and other sources.

★1904★ Civil Engineering-ASCE
American Society of Civil Engineers
345 E. 47th St.
New York, NY 10017-2398
Ph: (212)705-7463   Fax: (212)705-7712
Virginia Fairweather

Monthly. Professional magazine.

★1905★ Journal of Urban Planning and Development
American Society of Civil Engineers
345 E. 47th St.
New York, NY 10017-2398
Ph: 800-548-2723   Fax: (212)705-7300
R. Ian Kingham

Quarterly. Journal on the application of civil engineering to urban planning.

★1906★ Public Works Digest
U.S. Army Center for Public Works
7701 Telegraph Rd.
Alexandria, VA 22310-3862
Ph: (703)355-3404   Fax: (703)355-2805
Mark Ray

Bimonthly. Provides Army engineering and housing managers worldwide with news, technical information, and headquarter updates pertaining to their jobs. Covers automated management systems, engineering and technical developments, energy management, commercial activities, and housing. Recurring features include news of research and success stories.

OTHER SOURCES OF INFORMATION

★1907★ "Civil Engineer" in Career Selector 2001
Barron's Educational Series, Inc.
250 Wireless Blvd.
Hauppauge, NY 11788
Ph: (516)434-3311   Fax: (516)434-3723
Fr: 800-645-3476

James C. Gonyea. 1993.

★1908★ "Civil Engineering" in Accounting to Zoology: Graduate Fields Defined (pp. 325-327)
Petersons Guides, Inc.
PO Box 2123
Princeton, NJ 08543-2123
Ph: (609)243-9111   Fax: (609)243-9150
Fr: 800-338-3282

Amy J. Goldstein, editor. Revised and updated, 1987. Defines 298 graduate and professional fields. Discusses types of graduate programs and degrees, graduate research, applied work, employment prospects, and trends.

★1909★ Financial Aid for Minorities in Engineering & Science
Garrett Park Press
PO Box 190
Garrett Park, MD 20896
Ph: (301)946-2553
1993.

★1910★ GEM: National Consortium for Graduate Degrees for Minorities in Engineering
National Consortium for Graduate Degrees for Minorities in Engineering
PO Box 537
Notre Dame, IN 46556
Ph: (219)287-1097

1988. Describes the graduate fellowship program for minorities in engineering including financial support, application, and internship. Lists universities offering this program.

★1911★ How to Become a Professional Engineer
McGraw-Hill, Inc.
1221 Avenue of the Americas
New York, NY 10020
Ph: (212)512-2000   Fr: 800-722-4726
J.D. Constance. Fourth edition, 1987. Describes how to register for the professional engineer's license in all fifty states. Gives a state-by-state list of licensing regulations. Gives advice on how to take the written examination.

Electrical and Electronics Engineers

Electrical and electronics engineers design, develop, test, and supervise the manufacture of electrical and electronic equipment. Electrical equipment includes power generating and transmission equipment used by electric utilities, and electric motors, machinery controls, and lighting and wiring in buildings, automobiles, and aircraft. Electronic equipment includes radar, computers, communications equipment, and TV sets. The specialties of electrical and electronics engineers include several major areas such as power distributing equipment, integrated circuits, computers, electrical equipment manufacturing, communications industrial robot control systems, and aviation electronics.

Salaries

Starting salaries for engineers with bachelor's degrees are significantly higher than starting salaries of college graduates in other fields.

Beginning electrical and electronics engineers	$33,754/year
Experienced mid-level engineers	$52,500/year
Senior managerial engineers	$102,544/year

Employment Outlook

Growth rate until the year 2005: Average.

Electrical and Electronics Engineers

★1912★ **Career Development for Engineers and Scientists: Organizational Programs and Individual Choices**
Van Nostrand Reinhold Co., Inc.
115 5th Ave.
New York, NY 10003
Ph: (212)254-3232   Fr: 800-842-3636
Robert F. Morrison and Richard M. Vosburgh. 1987. Includes bibliographies and an index. Illustrated.

★1913★ **Careers and the Engineer**
Bob Adams, Inc.
260 Center St.
Holbrook, MA 02343
Ph: (617)268-9570
Gigi Ranno, editor. Annual.

★1914★ **Careers in Engineering**
National Textbook Co. (NTC)
VGM Career Books
4255 W. Touhy Ave.
Lincolnwood, IL 60646-1975
Ph: (708)679-5500   Fax: (708)679-2494
Fr: 800-323-4900
Geraldine O. Garner, Ph.D., editor. 1993. Career guide covering 14 different engineering specialties.

★1915★ **The Civilized Engineer**
St. Martin's Press, Inc.
175 5th Ave.
New York, NY 10010
Ph: (212)674-5151   Fax: 800-258-2769
Fr: 800-221-7945
Samuel C. Florman. 1989. Published by Thomas Dunne Books. Discusses engineering education, the relationship between engineers and nontechnical executives, and the role of women in engineering.

★1916★ **"Electrical/Electronic Engineering" in College Majors and Careers: A Resource Guide to Effective Life Planning (pp. 51-52)**
Garrett Park Press
PO Box 1907
Garrett Park, MD 20896
Ph: (301)946-2553

Paul Phifer. Revised, 1993. Lists 60 college majors, with definitions; related occupations and leisure activities; skills, values, and personal attributes needed; suggested readings; and a list of associations.

★1917★ **"Electrical/Electronics Engineer" in VGM's Careers Encyclopedia (pp. 152-155)**
National Textbook Co. (NTC)
VGM Career Books
4255 W. Touhy Ave.
Lincolnwood, IL 60646-1975
Ph: (708)679-5500   Fax: (708)679-2494
Fr: 800-323-4900

Third edition, 1991. Profiles 200 occupations. Describes job duties, places of employment, working conditions, qualifications, education and training, advancement potential, and salary for each occupation.

★1918★ **"Electrical and Electronics Engineers" in 101 Careers: A Guide to the Fastest-Growing Opportunities (pp. 81-83)**
John Wiley & Sons, Inc.
605 3rd Ave.
New York, NY 10158-0012
Ph: (212)850-6645   Fax: (212)850-6088

Michael Harkavy. 1990. Describes the nature of the job, working conditions, employment growth, qualifications, personal skills, projected salaries, and where to write for more information.

★1919★ **"Electrical and Electronics Engineers" in America's 50 Fastest Growing Jobs (pp. 40)**
JIST Works, Inc.
720 N. Park Ave.
Indianapolis, IN 46202-3431
Ph: (317)264-3720   Fax: (317)264-3709
Fr: 800-648-5478

Michael J. Farr, compiler. 1994. Describes the 50 fastest growing jobs within major career clusters such as technicians, and marketing and sales. Each job profile explains the nature of the work, skills and abilities required, employment outlook, average earnings, related occupations, education and training requirements, and employment opportunities. Also contains career planning information and job search tips.

★1920★ **"Electrical and Electronics Engineers" in Career Discovery Encyclopedia (Vol.2, pp. 138-139)**
J.G. Ferguson Publishing Co.
200 W. Madison St., Ste. 300
Chicago, IL 60606
Ph: (312)580-5480   Fax: (312)580-4948

Russell E. Primm, editor-in-chief. 1993. This six volume set contains two-page articles for 504 occupations. Each article describes job duties, earnings, and educational and training requirements. The whole set is arranged alphabetically by job title. Designed for junior high and older students.

★1921★ **"Electrical/Electronics Engineers" in Career Information Center (Vol.6)**
Simon and Schuster
200 Old Tappan Rd.
Old Tappan, NJ 07675
Fax: 800-445-6991   Fr: 800-223-2348
Richard Lidz and Linda Perrin, editorial directors. Fifth edition, 1993. This 13-volume set profiles over 600 occupations. Each occupational profile describes job duties, entry-level requirements, educational requirements, advancement possibilities, employment outlook, working conditions, earnings and benefits, and where to write for more information.

★1922★ "Electrical and Electronics Engineers" in *Encyclopedia of Careers and Vocational Guidance* (Vol.2, pp. 534-537)
J.G. Ferguson Publishing Co.
200 W. Madison St., Ste. 300
Chicago, IL 60606
Ph: (312)580-5480   Fax: (312)580-4948
William E. Hopke, editor-in-chief. Ninth edition, 1993. Four-volume set that profiles 900 occupations and describes job trends in 74 industries. Includes career description, educational requirements, history of the job, methods of entry, advancement, employment outlook, earnings, conditions of work, social and psychological factors, and sources of further information.

★1923★ "Electrical and Electronics Engineers" in *Jobs! What They Are— Where They Are—What They Pay* (p. 121)
Simon & Schuster, Inc.
Simon & Schuster Bldg.
1230 Avenue of the Americas
New York, NY 10020
Ph: (212)698-7000   Fr: 800-223-2348
Robert O. Snelling and Anne M. Snelling. 3rd edition, 1992. Describes duties and responsibilities, earnings, employment opportunities, training, and qualifications.

★1924★ "Electrical and Electronics Engineers" in *Occupational Outlook Handbook*
U.S. Government Printing Office
Superintendent of Documents
Washington, DC 20402
Ph: (202)512-1800   Fax: (202)512-2250
Biennial; latest edition, 1994-95. Encyclopedia of careers describing about 250 occupations and comprising about 85 percent of all jobs in the economy. Occupations that require lengthy education or training are given the most attention. Each occupation's profile describes what the worker does on the job, working conditions, education and training requirements, advancement possibilities, job outlook, earnings, and sources of additional information.

★1925★ *Electrical Engineer*
Careers, Inc.
PO Box 135
Largo, FL 34649-0135
Ph: (813)584-7333
1991. Two-page occupational summary card describing duties, working conditions, personal qualifications, training, earnings and hours, employment outlook, places of employment, related careers, and where to write for more information.

★1926★ *Electrical Engineer*
Vocational Biographies, Inc.
PO Box 31
Sauk Centre, MN 56378-0031
Ph: (612)352-6516   Fax: (612)352-5546
Fr: 800-255-0752
1993. Four-page pamphlet containing a personal narrative about a worker's job, work likes and dislikes, career path from high school to the present. Education and training, the rewards and frustrations, and the effects of the job on the rest of the worker's life. The data file portion of this pamphlet gives a concise occupational summary, including work descriptions, working conditions, places of employment, personal characteristics, education and training, job outlook, and salary range.

★1927★ "Electrical Engineer" in *Jobs Rated Almanac*
World Almanac
1 International Blvd., Ste. 444
Mahwah, NJ 07495
Ph: (201)529-6900   Fax: (201)529-6901
Les Krantz. Second edition, 1992. Ranks 250 jobs by environment, salary, outlooks, physical demands, stress, security, travel opportunities, and extra perks. Includes jobs the editor feels are the most common, most interesting, and the most rapidly growing.

★1928★ "Electrical Engineer" in *Opportunities in High-Tech Careers* (pp. 54-56, 122-123)
National Textbook Co. (NTC)
VGM Career Books
4255 W. Touhy Ave.
Lincolnwood, IL 60646-1975
Ph: (708)679-5500   Fax: (708)679-2494
Fr: 800-323-4900
Gary D. Golter and Deborah Yanuck. 1987. Explores high technology careers. Written for the student and displaced worker. Describes job opportunities, how to make a career decision, how to prepare for high-technology jobs, job hunting techniques, and future trends.

★1929★ "Electrical Engineers" in *Profiles in Achievement* (pp. 85-100)
The College Board
45 Columbus Ave.
New York, NY 10023-6992
Ph: (212)713-8165   Fax: (212)713-8143
Fr: 800-323-7155
Charles M. Holloway. 1987. Profiles eight men and women who have overcome the the barriers of race, gender, tradition, and economic circumstances in their quest to become successful professionals.

★1930★ "Electronics Engineer" in *Guide to Federal Jobs* (pp. 161)
Resource Directories
3361 Executive Pkwy., Ste. 302
Toledo, OH 43606
Ph: (419)536-5353   Fax: (419)536-7056
Fr: 800-274-8515
Rod W. Durgin, editor. Third edition, 1992. Contains information on finding and applying for federal jobs. Describes more than 200 professional and technical jobs for college graduates. Also includes a chapter titled "Electrical Engineer" (p. 160). Covers the nature of the work, salary, and geographic location. Lists college majors preferred for that occupation. Section one describes the function and work of government agencies that hire the most significant number of college graduates.

★1931★ *Electronics Engineers and Technicians*
Chronicle Guidance Publications, Inc.
66 Aurora St.
PO Box 1190
Moravia, NY 13118-1190
Ph: (315)497-0330   Fax: (315)497-3359
Fr: 800-622-7284
1992. Career brief describing the nature of the job, working conditions, hours and earnings, education and training, licensure, certification, unions, personal qualifications, social and psychological factors, location, employment outlook, entry methods, advancement, and related occupations.

★1932★ "Engineering" in *American Almanac of Jobs and Salaries* (pp. 261)
Avon Books
1350 Avenue of the Americas
New York, NY 10019
Ph: (212)261-6800   Fr: 800-238-0658
John Wright, editor. Revised and updated, 1994-95. A comprehensive guide to the wages of hundreds of occupations in a wide variety of industries and organizations.

★1933★ "Engineering" in *Encyclopedia of Careers and Vocational Guidance* (Vol.1, pp. 165-171)
J.G. Ferguson Publishing Co.
200 W. Madison St., Ste. 300
Chicago, IL 60606
Ph: (312)580-5480   Fax: (312)580-4948
William E. Hopke, editor-in-chief. Ninth edition, 1993. Four-volume set that profiles 900 occupations and describes job trends in 74 industries. Includes career description, educational requirements, history of the job, methods of entry, advancement, employment outlook, earnings, conditions of work, social and psychological factors, and sources of further information.

★1934★ *Engineering Salary Survey*
Source Engineering
1290 Oakmead, Ste. 318
Sunnyvale, CA 94086
Ph: (408)738-8440
Annual. Discusses the structure of the engineering profession, trends, and compensation. Salaries are listed by job function, industry, and years of experience.

★1935★ "Engineering" in *Where the Jobs Are: The Hottest Careers for the 90s* (pp. 111-124)
Career Press
180 5th Ave.
Hawthorne, NJ 07507
Ph: (201)427-0229   Fax: (201)427-2037
Fr: 800-CAREER-1
Joyce Hadley. 1995. Offers a job-hunting strategy for the 1990s as well as descriptions of growing careers of the decade. Each profile includes general information, forecasts, growth, education and training, licensing requirements, and salary information.

★1936★ *Engineering for You: A Career Guide*
Iowa State University Press
2121 S. State Ave.
Ames, IA 50010
Ph: (515)292-0140   Fax: (515)292-3348
John T. Jones. 1991.

★1937★ Opportunities in Electronics Careers
National Textbook Co. (NTC)
VGM Career Books
4255 W. Touhy Ave.
Lincolnwood, IL 60646-1975
Ph: (708)679-5500   Fax: (708)679-2494
Fr: 800-323-4900

Mark Rowh. 1992. Overviews opportunities in commercial and industrial electronics equipment repair, electronics home entertainment repair, electronics engineering, and engineering technology. Lists schools offering electronics programs.

★1938★ Opportunities in Engineering Technology Careers
National Textbook Co. (NTC)
VGM Career Books
4255 W. Touhy Ave.
Lincolnwood, IL 60646-1975
Ph: (708)679-5500   Fax: (708)679-2494
Fr: 800-323-4900

John E. Heer and D. Joseph Hagerty. 1987. Describes the many opportunities available for engineering technicians. Explains job duties, educational requirements, salary, working conditions, employment outlook, and advancement opportunities. Lists accredited engineering technology programs.

★1939★ Peterson's Job Opportunities for Engineering and Technology
Petersons Guides, Inc.
PO Box 2123
Princeton, NJ 08543-2123
Ph: (609)243-9111   Fax: (609)243-9150
Fr: 800-338-3282

1994. Gives job hunting advice including information on resume writing, interviewing, and handling salary negotiations. Lists companies that hire college graduates in science and engineering at the bachelor and master's level. Companies are indexed by industry, starting location, and major. Company profiles include contact information and types of hires.

★1940★ Successful Engineering: A Guide to Achieving Your Career Goals
McGraw-Hill, Inc.
1221 Avenue of the Americas
New York, NY 10020
Ph: (212)512-2000   Fr: 800-722-4726

Lawrence J. Kamm. 1989. Written for the practicing and graduating engineer. Gives advice about working with accountants, the politics of design, and engineering ethics.

PROFESSIONAL ASSOCIATIONS

★1941★ Accreditation Board for Engineering and Technology (ABET)
111 Market Pl., Ste. 1050
Baltimore, MD 21202
Ph: (410)347-7700   Fax: (410)625-2238
Members: Professional societies representing over one million engineers are participating bodies (21); affiliate bodies (5); board of directors has 29 representatives. Is responsible for the quality control of engineering education. Accredits college curricula in engineering, engineering technology, and engineering-related areas. **Publications:** Accreditation Yearbook, annual. • Criteria for Accrediting Programs in Engineering in the United States, annual. • Criteria for Accrediting Programs in Engineering Technology, annual.

★1942★ Airlines Electronic Engineering Committee (AEEC)
2551 Riva Rd.
Annapolis, MD 21401
Ph: (410)266-4114   Fax: (410)266-2047
Members: Airline and other transport aircraft electronics and electrical engineers. **Purpose:** Develops voluntary standards for air transport avionics equipment and systems. Monitors legislation concerning regulatory matters; acts as a representative for the airline engineering community. Provides technical support. Operates subcommittees; maintains library. **Publications:** Aeroline, monthly.

★1943★ American Association of Engineering Societies (AAES)
1111 19th St. NW, Ste. 608
Washington, DC 20036
Ph: (202)296-2237   Fax: (202)296-1151
Members: Societies representing over 500,000 engineers. **Purpose:** Works to: advance the knowledge and practice of engineering in the public interest; act as an advisory, communication, and information exchange agency for member activities, especially regarding public policy issues. Conducts studies sponsored by Engineering Manpower Commission. Compiles statistics. **Publications:** AAES Update, quarterly. • Directory of Engineering Societies, biennial. • Engineering and Technology Degrees, annual. • Engineering and Technology Enrollments, annual. • Engineers Salary Survey, annual. • The Role of Engineering in Sustainable Development. • Who's Who in Engineering, biennial.

★1944★ American Institute of Engineers (AIE)
4666 San Pablo Dam Rd., No. 8
El Sobrante, CA 94803-3142
Ph: (510)223-8911   Fax: (510)223-3400
Members: Professional engineers and engineering students. **Purpose:** Seeks to advance the professional interests of engineers and scientists. Fosters the interchange of ideas and information among members. Compiles statistics; maintains speakers' bureau. **Publications:** AIE Newsmagazine, monthly.

★1945★ IEEE Electron Devices Society (EDS)
c/o Institute of Electrical and Electronics Engineers
345 E. 47th St.
New York, NY 10017
Ph: (212)705-7900   Fax: (212)705-4929
Members: A society of the Institute of Electrical and Electronics Engineers. **Purpose:** Concerned with the theory, design, and performance of electron devices, including electron tubes, solid-state devices, integrated electron devices, energy sources, power devices, displays, and device reliability. **Publications:** Electron Device Letters, monthly. • Journal Electronic Materials, bimonthly. • Transactions on Electron Devices, monthly. • Transactions on Semiconductor Manufacturing, quarterly.

★1946★ Institute of Electrical and Electronics Engineers (IEEE)
345 E. 47th St.
New York, NY 10017
Ph: (212)705-7900   Fax: (212)705-4929
Members: Engineers and scientists in electrical engineering, electronics, and allied fields; membership includes 47,000 students. **Purpose:** Conducts lecture courses at the local level on topics of current engineering and scientific interest. Assists student groups. Supports Engineering Societies Library in New York City in conjunction with other groups. **Publications:** Spectrum, monthly. • Standards, periodic.

★1947★ National Action Council for Minorities in Engineering (NACME)
3 W. 35th St.
New York, NY 10001
Ph: (212)279-2626   Fax: (212)629-5178
Members: Seeks to increase the number of African American, Hispanic, and Native American students enrolled in and graduating from engineering schools. **Purpose:** Offers incentive grants to engineering schools to recruit and provide financial assistance to increasing numbers of minority students. Works with local, regional, and national support organizations to motivate and encourage precollege students to engage in engineering careers. Conducts educational and research programs; operates project to assist engineering schools in improving the retention and graduation rates of minority students. Maintains speakers' bureau; compiles statistics. **Publications:** Directory of Pre-College and University Minority Engineering Programs, periodic. • Financial Aid Unscrambled: A Guide for Minority Engineering Students, biennial. • Gearing Up: How to Start a Pre-College Minority Engineering Program. • NACME News, semiannual. • NACME Statistical Report, biennial.

★1948★ National Society of Professional Engineers (NSPE)
1420 King St.
Alexandria, VA 22314
Ph: (703)684-2800   Fax: (703)836-4875
Members: Professional engineers and engineers-in-training in all fields registered in accordance with the laws of states or territories of the U.S. or provinces of Canada; qualified graduate engineers, student members, and registered land surveyors. Is concerned with social, professional, ethical, and economic considerations of engineering as a profession; encompasses programs in public relations, employment practices, ethical considerations, education, and career guidance. Monitors legislative and regulatory actions of interest to the engineering profession. **Publications:** Directory of Professional Engineers in Private Practice, biennial. • Engineering Times, monthly. • PEG Times, quarterly.

★1949★ **Society of Women Engineers (SWE)**
120 Wall St., 11th Fl.
New York, NY 10005
Ph: (212)509-9577   Fax: (212)509-0224
Members: Educational service society of women engineers; membership is also open to men. **Purpose:** Supplies information on the achievements of women engineers and the opportunities available to them; assists women engineers in preparing for return to active work following temporary retirement. Serves as an informational center on women in engineering. Administers several certificate and scholarship programs. Offers tours and career guidance; conducts surveys. Compiles statistics. **Publications:** *National Survey of Women and Men Engineers.*

STANDARDS/CERTIFICATION AGENCIES

★1950★ **Accreditation Board for Engineering and Technology (ABET)**
111 Market Pl., Ste. 1050
Baltimore, MD 21202
Ph: (410)347-7700   Fax: (410)625-2238
Is responsible for the quality control of engineering education. Accredits college curricula in engineering, engineering technology, and engineering-related areas.

★1951★ **Society of Women Engineers (SWE)**
120 Wall St., 11th Fl.
New York, NY 10005
Ph: (212)509-9577   Fax: (212)509-0224
Administers several certificate and scholarship programs. Compiles statistics.

TEST GUIDES

★1952★ *Career Examination Series: Electrical Engineer*
National Learning Corp.
212 Michael Dr.
Syosset, NY 11791
Ph: (516)921-8888   Fax: (516)921-8743
Fr: 800-645-6337
Jack Rudman. Test guide including questions and answers for students or professionals in the field who seek advancement through examination. Also included in the series: Senior Electrical Engineer, Junior Electrical Engineer, and Assistant Electrical Engineer.

★1953★ *Career Examination Series: Electronic Engineer*
National Learning Corp.
212 Michael Dr.
Syosset, NY 11791
Ph: (516)921-8888   Fax: (516)921-8743
Fr: 800-645-6337
Jack Rudman. Test guide including questions and answers for students or professionals in the field who seek advancement through examination.

★1954★ *Career Examination Series: Engineer*
National Learning Corp.
212 Michael Dr.
Syosset, NY 11791
Ph: (516)921-8888   Fax: (516)921-8743
Fr: 800-645-6337
Jack Rudman. A series of study guides with multiple-choice examination questions and solutions for trainees and professional petroleum engineers. Titles in the series include *Administrative Engineer; Chief Engineer; Engineering Aide and Science Assistant; Engineering Aide; Engineering Assistant; Engineering Trainee; Senior Engineer; Senior Engineering Aide.*

★1955★ *Circuit Analysis Exam File*
Engineering Press, Inc.
PO Box 1
San Jose, CA 95103-0001
Ph: (408)258-4503   Fax: 800-700-1651
Fr: 800-800-1651
Contains 291 exam problems with step-by-step solutions. Covers: restrictive circuits; network theorems; transient analysis, complex frequency, and 2-part networks.

★1956★ *Electrical Engineering*
National Learning Corp.
212 Michael Dr.
Syosset, NY 11791
Ph: (516)921-8888   Fax: (516)921-8743
Fr: 800-645-6337
Jack Rudman. Part of the Test Your Knowledge Series. Contains multiple choice questions with answers.

★1957★ *Electrical Engineering Reference Manual*
Professional Publications, Inc.
1250 5th Ave.
Belmont, CA 94002-3863
Fax: (415)592-4519   Fr: 800-426-1178
Raymond B. Yarbrough. Fifth edition, 1990. Includes an index. Subjects covered include: digital logic, power systems, rotating machines, mathematics, and engineering economic analysis.

★1958★ *Engineer-in-Training Exam File*
Engineering Press, Inc.
PO Box 1
San Jose, CA 95103-0001
Ph: (408)258-4503   Fax: 800-700-1651
Fr: 800-800-1651
Donald G. Newnan and Dean Newnan. Eleventh edition. 1990. Contains 505 problems with step-by-step solutions. Covers: mathematics; statics; fluid mechanics. Includes an index.

★1959★ *Engineering Economic Analysis Exam File*
Engineering Press, Inc.
PO Box 1
San Jose, CA 95103-0001
Ph: (408)258-4503   Fax: 800-700-1651
Fr: 800-800-1651
Contains 386 exam problems with step-by-step solutions.

★1960★ *Graduate Record Examination: Engineering*
National Learning Corp.
212 Michael Dr.
Syosset, NY 11791
Ph: (516)921-8888   Fax: (516)921-8743
Fr: 800-645-6337
Jack Rudman. Multiple-choice test for those seeking admission to graduate school for study in the field of engineering. Includes solutions to examination questions.

★1961★ *Graduate Record Examination in Engineering*
Arco Publishing Co.
Macmillan General Reference
15 Columbus Cir.
New York, NY 10023
Fax: 800-835-3202   Fr: 800-858-7674
C.W. Tan, et al. First edition. 1988. Contains two sample tests with an explanation to answers.

★1962★ *Practicing to Take the GRE Engineering Test: An Official Publication of the GRE Board*
Educational Testing Service
Rosedale Rd.
Princeton, NJ 08541
Ph: (609)921-9000
Second edition, 1989. Summarizes the purpose and scope of the Graduate Record Examination Subject Test for engineering. Contains sample questions.

★1963★ *Professional Engineer*
National Learning Corp.
212 Michael Dr.
Syosset, NY 11791
Ph: (516)921-8888   Fax: (516)921-8743
Fr: 800-645-6337
Jack Rudman. A sample test for engineers who are seeking admission to graduate and professional schools or seeking entrance or advancement in institutional and public career service.

EDUCATIONAL DIRECTORIES AND PROGRAMS

★1964★ *ABET Accreditation Yearbook*
Accreditation Board for Engineering and Technology
345 E. 47th St., 14th Fl.
New York, NY 10017-2397
Ph: (212)705-7685   Fax: (212)838-8062
Simona C. Mardale, Contact
Annual, September. Covers about 300 U.S. colleges and universities with engineering programs, 242 institutions with programs in engineering technology, and 11 institutions with engineering-related programs accredited by the Board; also lists accredited Canadian programs. Entries include: For United States institutions—Name, year of next full accreditation review, location, program names, year of initial accreditation for each program, coding to indicate degrees offered, format of program (day, night, cooperative, etc.). For Canadian programs—Name, location, names of programs, year of initial ac-

credition for each program. Arrangement: Classified by program area.

AWARDS, SCHOLARSHIPS, GRANTS, AND FELLOWSHIPS

★1965★ Control Systems Award
Institute of Electrical and Electronics
  Engineers
345 E. 47th St.
New York, NY 10017-2394
Ph: (212)705-7882   Fax: (212)223-2911

To recognize an individual for meritorious achievement in contributions to theory, design, or techniques, as evidenced by publications or patents in the area of control systems engineering, science, and technology. A monetary award of $3,000, a bronze medal, and a certificate are awarded annually. The deadline for nominations is January 31. Established in 1980. Sponsored by IEEE Control Systems Society.

★1966★ Engineering Rotation Program
Hughes Aircraft Company
Technical Education Center
PO Box 80028
Los Angeles, CA 90080-0028
Ph: (310)568-6711

Purpose: To enable engineering and science graduates to find and develop the special field of work and the career position best suited to their interests and education. Qualifications: Applicant must be a U.S. citizen and have a bachelor's degree in electrical, mechanical, systems, computer or aerospace engineering; computer science; physics; or mathematics. Candidate must have a grade point average of at least 3.0/4.0, with emphasis on technical classes and related disciplines. Participants in the Rotation Program gain practical experience through up to four different work assignments at Hughes facilities, usually in southern California. Upon completion of the program, participants may be placed in permanent positions with the Company, based on their interests and assignments available. Funds available: Salary and company benefits. Application details: Write to the educational coordinator for application form and guidelines. Include pertinent information regarding academic status (university, field of interest for both undergraduate and graduate work, year of graduation, and grade point average) in initial letter of interest. Deadline: 1 March.

★1967★ Founders Medal
Institute of Electrical and Electronics
  Engineers
345 E. 47th St.
New York, NY 10017-2394
Ph: (212)705-7882   Fax: (212)223-2911

To recognize major contributions in the leadership, planning, or administration of affairs of great value to the electrical and electronics engineering profession. Members of IEEE may be nominated. Nominations and two supporting letters must be received by July 1. The award consists of a monetary award of $10,000, a gold medal, a bronze replica, and

a certificate. Awarded annually. Established in 1952.

★1968★ Engineer Degree Fellowships; Howard Hughes Doctoral Fellowships
Hughes Aircraft Company
Technical Education Center
PO Box 80028
Los Angeles, CA 90080-0028
Ph: (310)568-6711

Purpose: To support doctoral studies in engineering and related sciences and to provide students with practical work experience. Qualifications: Applicant for either type of fellowship must be a U.S. citizen and have a bachelor's and master's degree or equivalent graduate experience in electrical, mechanical, systems, computer or aerospace engineering; computer science; physics; or mathematics. Engineer Degree Fellowships are reserved for candidates who have first degrees in engineering. For both awards, priority is given to individuals with experience in electronics and related disciplines. Candidate must have a minimum grade point average of 3.0/4.0, and be qualified for admission to an approved graduate program in the United States. Fellows are considered employees of the Hughes Aircraft Company and, in addition to their graduate studies, gain work experience in one of two programs: work-study or full-study. Fellows in the work-study program attend a university near a Hughes facility (usually in southern California) and complete coursework while working at the facility for 20 to 36 hours per week. Work-study fellows may switch to full-study status to complete their dissertations. Full-study fellows attend a university distant from Hughes and are on leave of absence from the company while studying full-time. Full-study fellows are required to spend the summer term working for the Company, and may work eight hours a week during the school year if attending a university within commuting distance. Funds available: Company salary and benefits, plus tuition, book and living allowances. Application details: Write to the educational coordinator for application form and guidelines. Include pertinent information regarding academic status (university, field of interest for both undergraduate and graduate work, year of graduation, and grade point average) in initial letter of interest. Deadline: 10 January. Fellows are announced in April.

★1969★ IEEE Medal for Engineering Excellence
Institute of Electrical and Electronics
  Engineers
345 E. 47th St.
New York, NY 10017-2394
Ph: (212)705-7882   Fax: (212)223-2911

To recognize an achievement of exceptional application engineering in the technical disciplines of the IEEE, for the benefit of the public and the engineering profession. An individual or a team of not more than three may be nominated by July 1. A monetary award of $10,000, a gold medal, a bronze replica, and a certificate are awarded annually. Established in 1986.

★1970★ IEEE Medal of Honor
Institute of Electrical and Electronics
  Engineers
345 E. 47th St.
New York, NY 10017-2394
Ph: (212)705-7882   Fax: (212)223-2911

This, the highest award offered by the Institute, is awarded for a particular contribution which forms a clearly exceptional addition to the science and technology of concern to the Institute. The award is normally made within a few years after recognition of the exceptional nature of such a contribution. The recipient need not be a member of the IEEE. The nomination deadline is July 1. The award consists of a monetary prize of $20,000, an inscribed gold Medal of Honor, a bronze replica, and a certificate. Established in 1917.

★1971★ Morris E. Leeds Award
Institute of Electrical and Electronics
  Engineers
345 E. 47th St.
New York, NY 10017-2394
Ph: (212)705-7882   Fax: (212)223-2911

To recognize an individual, or group of individuals not larger than three, making an outstanding contribution to the field of electrical measurement. Special consideration is given to the value of contributions made before the candidate's 36th birthday. The deadline for nominations is January 31. The award consists of $1,000 and an illuminated certificate. Established in 1958. Sponsored by the Leeds and Northrup Foundation.

★1972★ Outstanding Young Electrical Engineer Award
Eta Kappa Nu
Box HKN
Univ. of Missouri-Rolla
Rolla, MO 65401
Ph: (314)341-6400

For recognition of distinguished achievement in the field of electrical engineering and community work by a young electrical engineer in the United States. Engineers under 35 years of age who have graduated not more than ten years are eligible. An honorarium and certificate are awarded annually. Established in 1935 by R.I. Wilkinson.

★1973★ General Emmett Paige Scholarship
Armed Forces Communications &
  Electronics Association (AFCEA)
Educational Foundation
4400 Fair Lakes Ct.
Fairfax, VA 22033-3899
Ph: (703)631-6149   Fax: (703)631-4693

Purpose: To promote excellence in scientific and engineering education. Qualifications: Applicants must be United States citizens enrolled in an accredited four-year college or university and working toward a bachelor degree in electrical engineering, electronics, communications engineering, mathematics, computer technology, physics, or information management. Selection criteria: The scholarship is awarded on the basis of demonstrated academic achievement, high "moral character," leadership ability, and potential to contribute to the defense of the United States. Financial need is also a consideration. Funds available: Scholarships of $1,000 are awarded each year. Except under unusual circumstances, students may receive only one award from AFCEA per year. Application details: Application forms are available from school ROTC units or by contacting Mrs. Phyllis R. Lau, Administrator of Scholarships and Awards, at the above address. Toll-free telephone: 800-336-4583, ext. 6149. Students competing for other AFCEA scholarships are automatically considered for the General Emmett Paige Scholarship. Deadline: May 1.

★1974★ **Judith A. Resnik Award**
Institute of Electrical and Electronics
  Engineers
345 E. 47th St.
New York, NY 10017-2394
Ph: (212)705-7882   Fax: (212)223-2911

To recognize an electrical engineer for contributions to space engineering. Preference is given to an individual who has made the contribution prior to the 37th birthday and who holds membership in IEEE. Nominations may be submitted by January 31. A monetary award of $2,000, a bronze medal, a certificate, and up to $1,000 for travel expenses for the recipient and a companion to attend the award ceremony are awarded annually. Established in 1987 in memory of the Challenger astronaut, Judith A. Resnik. Sponsored by IEEE Aerospace and Electronic Systems Society.

★1975★ **Charles Proteus Steinmetz Award**
Institute of Electrical and Electronics
  Engineers
345 E. 47th St.
New York, NY 10017-2394
Ph: (212)705-7882   Fax: (212)223-2911

To recognize an individual for major contributions to the development of standards in the field of electrical and electronics engineering. The deadline for nominations is January 31. A monetary award of $5,000, a bronze medal, and a certificate are awarded annually. Established in 1979. Sponsored by the IEEE Standards Board.

★1976★ **Alton B. Zerby Outstanding Student (Electrical Engineering) Award**
Eta Kappa Nu
Box HKN
Univ. of Missouri-Rolla
Rolla, MO 65401
Ph: (314)341-6400

To recognize an outstanding electrical engineering student for classwork and extra-curricular activities. Students must be a U.S. citizen and nominated by one of the chapters of Eta Kappa Nu. A monetary prize and a certificate are awarded annually. Established in 1965 in memory of Alton Zerby and Carl T. Koerner.

Basic Reference Guides and Handbooks

★1977★ *Electric Motor Handbook*
Butterworth-Heinemann Publishers
80 Montvale Ave.
Stoneham, MA 02180
Ph: (617)438-8464   Fr: 800-548-4001
B.J. Chalmers, editor. 1988. Contains articles on electric motors above ten kilowatts and covers selection, components, testing, maintenance, and installation.

★1978★ *Electrical Power Engineering*
McGraw-Hill Inc.
11 W. 19 St.
New York, NY 10011
Ph: 800-722-4726
Henslay William Kabisama. 1993.

★1979★ *Electrical Technology*
John Wiley and Sons, Inc.
605 3rd Ave.
New York, NY 10158-0012
Ph: (212)850-6000   Fax: (212)850-6088
Fr: 800-526-5368
E. Hughes. Sixth edition, 1987. Covers the basics of electrical and electronics engineering including theories and their applications.

★1980★ *Electronic Engineers' Handbook*
McGraw-Hill, Inc.
1221 Avenue of the Americas
New York, NY 10020
Ph: (212)512-2000   Fr: 800-722-4726
Donald G. Fink and Donald Christiansen, editors. Third edition, 1989. A practical reference guide for the working electronic engineer.

★1981★ *Electronics Engineer's Reference Book*
Butterworth-Heinemann Publishers
80 Montvale Ave.
Stoneham, MA 02180
Ph: (617)438-8464   Fr: 800-548-4001
F.F. Mazda, editor. Sixth edition, 1989. Contains information on a broad range of new technologies including fiber optics and microprocessors.

★1982★ *Encyclopedia of Electronics*
Tab Books, Inc.
PO Box 40
Blue Ridge Summit, PA 17294-0850
Ph: (717)794-2191   Fr: 800-223-1128
Neil J. Sclater, editor. Second edition, 1990. Contains practical information on current developments in electronics.

★1983★ *Engineer-In-Training Reference Manual*
Professional Publications, Inc.
1250 5th Ave.
Belmont, CA 94002-3863
Fax: (415)592-4519   Fr: 800-426-1178
Michael R. Lindeburg. Eighth edition. Comprehensive guide to preparing for the F.E. exam that covers mathematics, engineering economic analysis, systems of units, fluid statics and dynamics, open channel flow, thermodynamics, and more. Intended to be a broad review of engineering fundamentals.

★1984★ *Illustrated Encyclopedic Dictionary of Electronics*
Prentice-Hall, Inc.
Rte. 9W
Englewood Cliffs, NJ 07632
Ph: (201)592-2000   Fr: 800-634-2863
John Douglas-Young. Second edition, 1987. Briefly defines thousands of electronic terms.

★1985★ *Standard Handbook for Electrical Engineers*
McGraw-Hill, Inc.
1221 Avenue of the Americas
New York, NY 10020
Ph: (212)512-2000   Fr: 800-722-4726
Donald G. Fink and H. Wayne Beaty, editors. Thirteenth edition, 1993. Covers new developments, and the generation, transmission, distribution, control, conservation, and application of electrical power. Lists current standards governing the electrical engineering field.

Professional and Trade Periodicals

★1986★ *Electronic Industries Association—Executive Report*
Electronic Industries Association
2001 Pennsylvania Ave. NW
Washington, DC 20006
Ph: (202)457-4980   Fax: (202)457-4985
Mack V. Rosenker

Bimonthly. Provides news of electronics and the electronics industry. Focuses on legislative proposals and hearings, engineering standards, sales trends in the industry and general Association news. Recurring features include news of Association business and meetings, seminars, and notices of publications available.

★1987★ *Electronic Materials Technology News*
Business Communications Company, Inc.
25 Van Zant St.
Norwalk, CT 06855-1781
Ph: (203)853-4266   Fax: (203)853-0348
Kurt Miska

Monthly. Contains "analyses of new products, patents, and industry trends" in the electronics market for the chemical and materials industries. Covers specialty chemicals, fiber optics, commercialization of existing technology, patents, processes, and business opportunities.

★1988★ *IEEE Spectrum*
Institute of Electrical and Electronics
  Engineers, Inc.
345 E. 47th St.
New York, NY 10017
Ph: (212)705-7555   Fax: (212)705-7453
Fr: 800-678-4333
Donald Christiansen

Monthly. Magazine for the scientific and engineering professional. Provides information on developments and trends in engineering, physics, mathematics, chemistry, medicine/biology, and the nuclear sciences.

★1989★ *International Journal of Numerical Modelling*
John Wiley and Sons, Inc.
Subscription Dept.
605 3rd Ave.
New York, NY 10158
Ph: (212)850-6000   Fax: (212)850-6799
W.J.R. Hoefer

Bimonthly. Journal containing information on electrical and eletronic engineering, with a focus on numerical modelling.

★1990★ *Multimedia Magazine*
Institute of Electrical and Electronics
   Engineers, Inc.
345 E. 47th St.
New York, NY 10017
Ph: (212)705-7555   Fax: (212)705-7453
Fr: 800-678-4333

Quarterly. Journal focusing on multimedia computing and communications systems.

★1991★ *Optimal Control Applications and Methods*
John Wiley and Sons, Inc.
Subscription Dept.
605 3rd Ave.
New York, NY 10158
Ph: (212)850-6000   Fax: (212)850-6799
B.L. Pierson

Quarterly. Journal containing information on optimal control applications. Topics include aerospace, robots and manufacturing systems, and electrical and electronic systems.

★1992★ *Personal Communications Magazine*
Institute of Electrical and Electronics
   Engineers, Inc.
345 E. 47th St.
New York, NY 10017
Ph: (212)705-7555   Fax: (212)705-7453
Fr: 800-678-4333

Quarterly. Journal concerning technical and policy issues related to personalized communications.

★1993★ *Power*
McGraw-Hill, Inc.
1221 Avenue of the Americas
New York, NY 10020
Ph: (212)512-4686   Fax: (212)512-4256
R. Schwieger

Monthly. Magazine for engineers in electric utilities, process and manufacturing plants, commercial and service establishments, and consulting, design, and construction engineering firms working in the power technology field.

★1994★ *Quality and Reliability Engineering International*
John Wiley and Sons, Inc.
Subscription Dept.
605 3rd Ave.
New York, NY 10158
Ph: (212)850-6000   Fax: (212)850-6799
Finn Jensen

Bimonthly. Journal centered on scientific theories versus industrial realities in the areas of electronic, electrical, and mechanical engineering.

★1995★ *Robotics & Automation Magazine*
Institute of Electrical and Electronics
   Engineers, Inc.
345 E. 47th St.
New York, NY 10017
Ph: (212)705-7555   Fax: (212)705-7453
Fr: 800-678-4333

Quarterly. Journal concerning prototyping, demonstration and evaluation, and commercialization of robotic and automation technology.

PROFESSIONAL MEETINGS AND CONVENTIONS

★1996★ Electronic Imaging International
World Access Corp.
15 Bemis Rd.
PO Box 171
Wellesley Hills, MA 02181
Ph: (617)235-8095

Annual. Always held during September at the Hynes Convention Center in Boston, Massachusetts.

★1997★ Ideas in Science and Electronics - Electronics Exposition and Symposium
Ideas in Science and Electronics, Inc.
8100 Mountain Rd., NE, Ste. 109
Albuquerque, NM 87110-7827
Ph: (505)262-1023   Fax: (505)265-1143

Annual. Always held during May at the Convention Center in Albuquerque, New Mexico.
Dates and Locations: 1996 May 14-16; Albuquerque, NM.

★1998★ O-E/LASE - Optoelectronics and Laser Applications in Science and Engineering Exhibit
SPIE - International Society for Optical
   Engineering
PO Box 10
Bellingham, WA 98227
Ph: (206)676-3290   Fax: (206)647-1445
Annual. Four symposia per year.

OTHER SOURCES OF INFORMATION

★1999★ "Electrical and Power Engineering" in *Accounting to Zoology: Graduate Fields Defined* (pp. 339-342)
Petersons Guides, Inc.
PO Box 2123
Princeton, NJ 08543-2123
Ph: (609)243-9111   Fax: (609)243-9150
Fr: 800-338-3282

Amy J. Goldstein, editor. Revised and updated, 1987. Defines 298 graduate and professional fields. Discusses types of graduate programs and degrees, graduate research, applied work, employment prospects, and trends.

★2000★ *Financial Aid for Minorities in Engineering & Science*
Garrett Park Press
PO Box 190
Garrett Park, MD 20896
Ph: (301)946-2553

1993.

★2001★ *GEM: National Consortium for Graduate Degrees for Minorities in Engineering*
National Consortium for Graduate Degrees
   for Minorities in Engineering
PO Box 537
Notre Dame, IN 46556
Ph: (219)287-1097

1988. Describes the graduate fellowship program for minorities in engineering including financial support, application, and internship. Lists universities offering this program.

★2002★ *How to Become a Professional Engineer*
McGraw-Hill, Inc.
1221 Avenue of the Americas
New York, NY 10020
Ph: (212)512-2000   Fr: 800-722-4726

J.D. Constance. Fourth edition, 1987. Describes how to register for the professional engineer's license in all fifty states. Gives a state-by-state list of licensing regulations. Gives advice on how to take the written examination.

Industrial Engineers

Industrial engineers determine the most effective ways for an organization to use the basic factors of production–people, machines, materials, information, and energy. They bridge the gap between management and operations, and are more concerned with people and methods of business organization than are engineers in other specialties, who generally work more with products or processes. To solve organizational, production, and related problems most efficiently, industrial engineers design data processing systems and apply mathematical analyses such as operations research. They also develop management control systems to aid in financial planning and cost analysis, design production planning and control systems to coordinate activities and control product quality, and design or improve systems for the physical distribution of goods and services.

Salaries

Starting salaries for engineers with bachelor's degrees are significantly higher than starting salaries of college graduates in other fields.

Beginning industrial engineers	$32,348/year
Experienced mid-level engineers	$52,500/year
Senior managerial engineers	$102,544/year

Employment Outlook

Growth rate until the year 2005: Average.

Industrial Engineers

CAREER GUIDES

★2003★ *Career Development for Engineers and Scientists: Organizational Programs and Individual Choices*
Van Nostrand Reinhold Co., Inc.
115 5th Ave.
New York, NY 10003
Ph: (212)254-3232   Fr: 800-842-3636
Robert F. Morrison and Richard M. Vosburgh. 1987. Includes bibliographies and an index. Illustrated.

★2004★ *Careers and the Engineer*
Bob Adams, Inc.
260 Center St.
Holbrook, MA 02343
Ph: (617)268-9570
Gigi Ranno, editor. Annual.

★2005★ *Careers in Engineering*
National Textbook Co. (NTC)
VGM Career Books
4255 W. Touhy Ave.
Lincolnwood, IL 60646-1975
Ph: (708)679-5500   Fax: (708)679-2494
Fr: 800-323-4900
Geraldine O. Garner, Ph.D., editor. 1993. Career guide covering 14 different engineering specialties.

★2006★ *The Civilized Engineer*
St. Martin's Press, Inc.
175 5th Ave.
New York, NY 10010
Ph: (212)674-5151   Fax: 800-258-2769
Fr: 800-221-7945
Samuel C. Florman. 1989. Published by Thomas Dunne Books. Discusses engineering education, the relationship between engineers and nontechnical executives, and the role of women in engineering.

★2007★ *"Engineering" in American Almanac of Jobs and Salaries* (pp. 261)
Avon Books
1350 Avenue of the Americas
New York, NY 10019
Ph: (212)261-6800   Fr: 800-238-0658
John Wright, editor. Revised and updated, 1994-95. A comprehensive guide to the wages of hundreds of occupations in a wide variety of industries and organizations.

★2008★ *"Engineering" in BLR Encyclopedia of Prewritten Job Descriptions*
Business and Legal Reports, Inc.
64 Wall St.
Madison, CT 06443
Ph: (203)245-7448
Stephen D. Bruce, editor in chief. 1994. Describes how to write job descriptions. Contains hundreds of sample job descriptions which explain major duties and minimum qualifications.

★2009★ *"Engineering" in Encyclopedia of Careers and Vocational Guidance* (Vol.1, pp. 165-171)
J.G. Ferguson Publishing Co.
200 W. Madison St., Ste. 300
Chicago, IL 60606
Ph: (312)580-5480   Fax: (312)580-4948
William E. Hopke, editor-in-chief. Ninth edition, 1993. Four-volume set that profiles 900 occupations and describes job trends in 74 industries. Includes career description, educational requirements, history of the job, methods of entry, advancement, employment outlook, earnings, conditions of work, social and psychological factors, and sources of further information.

★2010★ *Engineering Salary Survey*
Source Engineering
1290 Oakmead, Ste. 318
Sunnyvale, CA 94086
Ph: (408)738-8440
Annual. Discusses the structure of the engineering profession, trends, and compensation. Salaries are listed by job function, industry, and years of experience.

★2011★ *"Engineering" in Where the Jobs Are: The Hottest Careers for the 90s* (pp. 111-124)
Career Press
180 5th Ave.
Hawthorne, NJ 07507
Ph: (201)427-0229   Fax: (201)427-2037
Fr: 800-CAREER-1
Joyce Hadley. 1995. Offers a job-hunting strategy for the 1990s as well as descriptions of growing careers of the decade. Each profile includes general information, forecasts, growth, education and training, licensing requirements, and salary information.

★2012★ *Engineering for You: A Career Guide*
Iowa State University Press
2121 S. State Ave.
Ames, IA 50010
Ph: (515)292-0140   Fax: (515)292-3348
John T. Jones. 1991.

★2013★ *Industrial Engineer*
Careers, Inc.
PO Box 135
Largo, FL 34649-0135
Ph: (813)584-7333
1993. Four-page brief offering the definition, history, duties, working conditions, personal qualifications, educational requirements, earnings, hours, employment outlook, advancement, and careers related to this position.

★2014★ *"Industrial Engineer" in Career Information Center* (Vol.9)
Simon and Schuster
200 Old Tappan Rd.
Old Tappan, NJ 07675
Fax: 800-445-6991   Fr: 800-223-2348
Richard Lidz and Linda Perrin, editorial directors. Fifth edition, 1993. This 13-volume set profiles over 600 occupations. Each occupational profile describes job duties, educational requirements, advancement possibilities, employment outlook, working conditions, earnings and benefits, and where to write for more information.

★2015★ *"Industrial Engineer" in Guide to Federal Jobs* (p. 171)
Resource Directories
3361 Executive Pkwy., Ste. 302
Toledo, OH 43606
Ph: (419)536-5353   Fax: (419)536-7056
Fr: 800-274-8515
Rod W. Durgin, editor. Third edition, 1992. Contains information on finding and applying for federal jobs. Describes more than 200 professional and technical jobs for college graduates. Covers the nature of the work, salary, and geographic location. Lists college majors preferred for that occupation. Section one describes the function and work of government agencies that hire the most significant number of college graduates.

★2016★ "Industrial Engineer" in *Jobs Rated Almanac*
World Almanac
1 International Blvd., Ste. 444
Mahwah, NJ 07495
Ph: (201)529-6900   Fax: (201)529-6901
Les Krantz. Second edition, 1992. Ranks 250 jobs by environment, salary, outlooks, physical demands, stress, security, travel opportunities, and extra perks. Includes jobs the editor feels are the most common, most interesting, and the most rapidly growing.

★2017★ "Industrial Engineer" in *VGM's Careers Encyclopedia* (pp. 219-221)
National Textbook Co. (NTC)
VGM Career Books
4255 W. Touhy Ave.
Lincolnwood, IL 60646-1975
Ph: (708)679-5500   Fax: (708)679-2494
Fr: 800-323-4900
Third edition, 1991. Profiles 200 occupations. Describes job duties, places of employment, working conditions, qualifications, education and training, advancement potential, and salary for each occupation.

★2018★ "Industrial Engineering" in *College Majors and Careers: A Resource Guide to Effective Life Planning* (pp. 77-78)
Garrett Park Press
PO Box 1907
Garrett Park, MD 20896
Ph: (301)946-2553
Paul Phifer. Revised, 1993. Lists 60 college majors, with definitions; related occupations and leisure activities; skills, values, and personal attributes needed; suggested readings; and a list of associations.

★2019★ *Industrial Engineers*
Chronicle Guidance Publications, Inc.
66 Aurora St.
PO Box 1190
Moravia, NY 13118-1190
Ph: (315)497-0330   Fax: (315)497-3359
Fr: 800-622-7284
1993. Career brief describing the nature of the job, working conditions, hours and earnings, education and training, licensure, certification, unions, personal qualifications, social and psychological factors, location, employment outlook, entry methods, advancement, and related occupations.

★2020★ "Industrial Engineers" in *101 Careers: A Guide to the Fastest-Growing Opportunities* (pp. 84-86)
John Wiley & Sons, Inc.
605 3rd Ave.
New York, NY 10158-0012
Ph: (212)850-6645   Fax: (212)850-6088
Michael Harkavy. 1990. Describes the nature of the job, working conditions, employment growth, qualifications, personal skills, projected salaries, and where to write for more information.

★2021★ "Industrial Engineers" in *Career Discovery Encyclopedia* (Vol.3, pp. 114-115)
J.G. Ferguson Publishing Co.
200 W. Madison St., Ste. 300
Chicago, IL 60606
Ph: (312)580-5480   Fax: (312)580-4948
Russell E. Primm, editor-in chief. 1993. This six volume set contains two-page articles for 504 occupations. Each article describes job duties, earnings, and educational and training requirements. The whole set is arranged alphabetically by job title. Designed for junior high and older students.

★2022★ "Industrial Engineers" in *Encyclopedia of Careers and Vocational Guidance* (Vol.3, pp. 177-181)
J.G. Ferguson Publishing Co.
200 W. Madison St., Ste. 300
Chicago, IL 60606
Ph: (312)580-5480   Fax: (312)580-4948
William E. Hopke, editor-in-chief. Ninth edition, 1993. Four-volume set that profiles 900 occupations and describes job trends in 74 industries. Includes career description, educational requirements, history of the job, methods of entry, advancement, employment outlook, earnings, conditions of work, social and psychological factors, and sources of further information.

★2023★ "Industrial Engineers" in *Jobs! What They Are—Where They Are—What They Pay* (p. 123)
Simon & Schuster, Inc.
Simon & Schuster Bldg.
1230 Avenue of the Americas
New York, NY 10020
Ph: (212)698-7000   Fr: 800-223-2348
Robert O. Snelling and Anne M. Snelling. 3rd edition, 1992. Describes duties and responsibilities, earnings, employment opportunities, training, and qualifications.

★2024★ "Industrial Engineers" in *Occupational Outlook Handbook*
U.S. Government Printing Office
Superintendent of Documents
Washington, DC 20402
Ph: (202)512-1800   Fax: (202)512-2250
Biennial; latest edition, 1994-95. Encyclopedia of careers describing about 250 occupations and comprising about 85 percent of all jobs in the economy. Occupations that require lengthy education or training are given the most attention. Each occupation's profile describes what the worker does on the job, working conditions, education and training requirements, advancement possibilities, job outlook, earnings, and sources of additional information.

★2025★ "Industrial Engineers" in *Opportunities in High-Tech Careers* (pp. 59-61, 129-130)
National Textbook Co. (NTC)
VGM Career Books
4255 W. Touhy Ave.
Lincolnwood, IL 60646-1975
Ph: (708)679-5500   Fax: (708)679-2494
Fr: 800-323-4900
Gary D. Colter and Deborah Yanuck. 1987. Explores high technology careers. Written for the student and displaced worker. Describes

job opportunities, how to make a career decision, how to prepare for high-technology jobs, job hunting techniques, and future trends.

★2026★ *Opportunities in Engineering Technology Careers*
National Textbook Co. (NTC)
VGM Career Books
4255 W. Touhy Ave.
Lincolnwood, IL 60646-1975
Ph: (708)679-5500   Fax: (708)679-2494
Fr: 800-323-4900
John E. Heer and D. Joseph Hagerty. 1987. Describes the many opportunities available for engineering technicians. Explains job duties, educational requirements, salary, working conditions, employment outlook, and advancement opportunities. Lists accredited engineering technology programs.

★2027★ *Peterson's Job Opportunities for Engineering and Technology*
Petersons Guides, Inc.
PO Box 2123
Princeton, NJ 08543-2123
Ph: (609)243-9111   Fax: (609)243-9150
Fr: 800-338-3282
1994. Gives job hunting advice including information on resume writing, interviewing, and handling salary negotiations. Lists companies that hire college graduates in science and engineering at the bachelor and master's level. Companies are indexed by industry, starting location, and major. Company profiles include contact information and types of hires.

★2028★ *Planning Your Career as an IE: The People-Oriented Engineering Profession*
Institute of Industrial Engineers (IIE)
25 Technology Park/Atlanta
Norcross, GA 30092
Ph: (404)449-0460
Annual. Explains the industrial engineering profession and describes the issues to consider when making a career choice.

★2029★ *Successful Engineering: A Guide to Achieving Your Career Goals*
McGraw-Hill, Inc.
1221 Avenue of the Americas
New York, NY 10020
Ph: (212)512-2000   Fr: 800-722-4726
Lawrence J. Kamm. 1989. Written for the practicing and graduating engineer. Gives advice about working with accountants, the politics of design, and engineering ethics.

PROFESSIONAL ASSOCIATIONS

★2030★ Accreditation Board for Engineering and Technology (ABET)
111 Market Pl., Ste. 1050
Baltimore, MD 21202
Ph: (410)347-7700   Fax: (410)625-2238
Members: Professional societies representing over one million engineers are participating bodies (21); affiliate bodies (5); board of directors has 29 representatives. Is responsible for the quality control of engineering education. Accredits college curricula in

engineering, engineering technology, and engineering-related areas. **Publications:** *Accreditation Yearbook*, annual. • *Criteria for Accrediting Programs in Engineering in the United States*, annual. • *Criteria for Accrediting Programs in Engineering Technology*, annual.

★2031★ American Association of Engineering Societies (AAES)
1111 19th St. NW, Ste. 608
Washington, DC 20036
Ph: (202)296-2237   Fax: (202)296-1151
Members: Societies representing over 500,000 engineers. **Purpose:** Works to: advance the knowledge and practice of engineering in the public interest; act as an advisory, communication, and information exchange agency for member activities, especially regarding public policy issues. Conducts studies sponsored by Engineering Manpower Commission. Compiles statistics. **Publications:** *AAES Update*, quarterly. • *Directory of Engineering Societies*, biennial. • *Engineering and Technology Degrees*, annual. • *Engineering and Technology Enrollments*, annual. • *Engineers Salary Survey*, annual. • *The Role of Engineering in Sustainable Development*. • *Who's Who in Engineering*, biennial.

★2032★ American Institute of Engineers (AIE)
4666 San Pablo Dam Rd., No. 8
El Sobrante, CA 94803-3142
Ph: (510)223-8911   Fax: (510)223-3400
Members: Professional engineers and engineering students. **Purpose:** Seeks to advance the professional interests of engineers and scientists. Fosters the interchange of ideas and information among members. Compiles statistics; maintains speakers' bureau. **Publications:** *AIE Newsmagazine*, monthly.

★2033★ Institute of Industrial Engineers (IIE)
25 Technology Park/Atlanta
Norcross, GA 30092
Ph: (404)449-0460   Fax: (404)263-8532
Members: Professional society of industrial engineers and student members. **Purpose:** Concerned with the design, improvement, and installation of integrated systems of people, materials, equipment, and energy. Draws upon specialized knowledge and skill in the mathematical, physical, and social sciences together with the principles and methods of engineering analysis and design, to specify, predict, and evaluate the results obtained from such systems. Maintains technical societies and divisions. **Publications:** *The Engineering Economist*, quarterly. • *Industrial Engineering*, monthly. • *Industrial Management*. • *Transactions*, bimonthly.

★2034★ National Action Council for Minorities in Engineering (NACME)
3 W. 35th St.
New York, NY 10001
Ph: (212)279-2626   Fax: (212)629-5178
Members: Seeks to increase the number of African American, Hispanic, and Native American students enrolled in and graduating from engineering schools. **Purpose:** Offers incentive grants to engineering schools to recruit and provide financial assistance to in-

creasing numbers of minority students. Works with local, regional, and national support organizations to motivate and encourage precollege students to engage in engineering careers. Conducts educational and research programs; operates project to assist engineering schools in improving the retention and graduation rates of minority students. Maintains speakers' bureau; compiles statistics. **Publications:** *Directory of Pre-College and University Minority Engineering Programs*, periodic. • *Financial Aid Unscrambled: A Guide for Minority Engineering Students*, biennial. • *Gearing Up: How to Start a Pre-College Minority Engineering Program*. • *NACME News*, semiannual. • *NACME Statistical Report*, biennial.

★2035★ National Society of Professional Engineers (NSPE)
1420 King St.
Alexandria, VA 22314
Ph: (703)684-2800   Fax: (703)836-4875
Members: Professional engineers and engineers-in-training in all fields registered in accordance with the laws of states or territories of the U.S. or provinces of Canada; qualified graduate engineers, student members, and registered land surveyors. Is concerned with social, professional, ethical, and economic considerations of engineering as a profession; encompasses programs in public relations, employment practices, ethical considerations, education, and career guidance. Monitors legislative and regulatory actions of interest to the engineering profession. **Publications:** *Directory of Professional Engineers in Private Practice*, biennial. • *Engineering Times*, monthly. • *PEG Times*, quarterly.

★2036★ Society of Women Engineers (SWE)
120 Wall St., 11th Fl.
New York, NY 10005
Ph: (212)509-9577   Fax: (212)509-0224
Members: Educational service society of women engineers; membership is also open to men. **Purpose:** Supplies information on the achievements of women engineers and the opportunities available to them; assists women engineers in preparing for return to active work following temporary retirement. Serves as an informational center on women in engineering. Administers several certificate and scholarship programs. Offers tours and career guidance; conducts surveys. Compiles statistics. **Publications:** *National Survey of Women and Men Engineers*.

STANDARDS/CERTIFICATION AGENCIES

★2037★ Accreditation Board for Engineering and Technology (ABET)
111 Market Pl., Ste. 1050
Baltimore, MD 21202
Ph: (410)347-7700   Fax: (410)625-2238
Is responsible for the quality control of engineering education. Accredits college curricula in engineering, engineering technology, and engineering-related areas.

★2038★ Society of Women Engineers (SWE)
120 Wall St., 11th Fl.
New York, NY 10005
Ph: (212)509-9577   Fax: (212)509-0224
Administers several certificate and scholarship programs. Compiles statistics.

TEST GUIDES

★2039★ *Career Examination Series: Assistant Heating & Ventilating Engineer*
National Learning Corp.
212 Michael Dr.
Syosset, NY 11791
Ph: (516)921-8888   Fax: (516)921-8743
Fr: 800-645-6337
Jack Rudman. 1993. Test guide including questions and answers for students or professionals in the field who seek advancement through examination.

★2040★ *Career Examination Series: Engineer*
National Learning Corp.
212 Michael Dr.
Syosset, NY 11791
Ph: (516)921-8888   Fax: (516)921-8743
Fr: 800-645-6337
Jack Rudman. A series of study guides with multiple-choice examination questions and solutions for trainees and professional petroleum engineers. Titles in the series include *Administrative Engineer; Chief Engineer; Engineering Aide and Science Assistant; Engineering Aide; Engineering Assistant; Engineering Trainee; Senior Engineer; Senior Engineering Aide*.

★2041★ *Career Examination Series: Industrial Engineer*
National Learning Corp.
212 Michael Dr.
Syosset, NY 11791
Ph: (516)921-8888   Fax: (516)921-8743
Fr: 800-645-6337
Jack Rudman. 1993. Test guide including questions and answers for students or professionals in the field who seek advancement through examination.

★2042★ *Engineer-in-Training Exam File*
Engineering Press, Inc.
PO Box 1
San Jose, CA 95103-0001
Ph: (408)258-4503   Fax: 800-700-1651
Fr: 800-800-1651
Donald G. Newnan and Dean Newnan. Eleventh edition. 1990. Contains 505 problems with step-by-step solutions. Covers: mathematics; statics; fluid mechanics. Includes an index.

★2043★ Engineering Economic Analysis Exam File
Engineering Press, Inc.
PO Box 1
San Jose, CA 95103-0001
Ph: (408)258-4503   Fax: 800-700-1651
Fr: 800-800-1651

Contains 386 exam problems with step-by-step solutions.

★2044★ Graduate Record Examination: Engineering
National Learning Corp.
212 Michael Dr.
Syosset, NY 11791
Ph: (516)921-8888   Fax: (516)921-8743
Fr: 800-645-6337

Jack Rudman. Multiple-choice test for those seeking admission to graduate school for study in the field of engineering. Includes solutions to examination questions.

★2045★ Graduate Record Examination in Engineering
Arco Publishing Co.
Macmillan General Reference
15 Columbus Cir.
New York, NY 10023
Fax: 800-835-3202   Fr: 800-858-7674

C.W. Tan, et al. First edition. 1988. Contains two sample tests with an explanation to answers.

★2046★ Practicing to Take the GRE Engineering Test: An Official Publication of the GRE Board
Educational Testing Service
Rosedale Rd.
Princeton, NJ 08541
Ph: (609)921-9000

Second edition, 1989. Summarizes the purpose and scope of the Graduate Record Examination Subject Test for engineering. Contains sample questions.

★2047★ Professional Engineer
National Learning Corp.
212 Michael Dr.
Syosset, NY 11791
Ph: (516)921-8888   Fax: (516)921-8743
Fr: 800-645-6337

Jack Rudman. A sample test for engineers who are seeking admission to graduate and professional schools or seeking entrance or advancement in institutional and public career service.

★2048★ Undergraduate Program Field Test: Engineering
National Learning Corp.
212 Michael Dr.
Syosset, NY 11791
Ph: (516)921-8888   Fax: (516)921-8743
Fr: 800-645-6337

Jack Rudman. A practice examination fashioned after tests given in the Regents External Degree Program. Designed to measure knowledge received outside the college classroom in the subject of engineering. Contains multiple-choice questions; provides solutions.

EDUCATIONAL DIRECTORIES AND PROGRAMS

★2049★ ABET Accreditation Yearbook
Accreditation Board for Engineering and Technology
345 E. 47th St., 14th Fl.
New York, NY 10017-2397
Ph: (212)705-7685   Fax: (212)838-8062
Simona C. Mardale, Contact

Annual, September. Covers about 300 U.S. colleges and universities with engineering programs, 242 institutions with programs in engineering technology, and 11 institutions with engineering-related programs accredited by the Board; also lists accredited Canadian programs. Entries include: For United States institutions—Name, year of next full accreditation review, location, program names, year of initial accreditation for each program, coding to indicate degrees offered, format of program (day, night, cooperative, etc.). For Canadian programs—Name, location, names of programs, year of initial accredition for each program. Arrangement: Classified by program area.

AWARDS, SCHOLARSHIPS, GRANTS, AND FELLOWSHIPS

★2050★ Award for Technical Innovation in Industrial Engineering
Institute of Industrial Engineers
Member & Chapter Services
25 Technology Park/Atlanta
Norcross, GA 30092
Ph: (404)449-0460   Fax: (404)263-8532

To recognize significant innovative technical contributions to the industrial engineering profession as evidenced by: significantly expanding the body of knowledge in an Industrial Engineering function; meaningfully establishing yet another functional area of the profession; or providing exceptional technical leadership in a major interdisciplinary project. Members and non-members are eligible. Awarded annually. Established in 1984.

★2051★ Dwight D. Gardner Memorial Scholarship
Institute of Industrial Engineers
25 Technology Park/Atlanta
Norcross, GA 30092
Ph: (404)449-0460   Fax: (404)263-8532

Purpose: To encourage and assist industrial engineering education and aid men and women in becoming qualified to practice as professional industrial engineers. Qualifications: Candidates must be undergraduate industrial engineering students enrolled full-time in any school in the United States and its territories, Canada, or Mexico that is accredited by an agency recognized by IIE. They must be active Institute members and have a grade point average of 3.40 out of 4.00. They must also have at least five full quarters or three full semesters remaining from the date of nomination to be eligible. Funds available:

Number of awards presented and amounts vary. In the 1989-90 academic year, 12 scholarships of $1,500 each were awarded. Application details: Nominations are solicited each fall from the academic department heads of all accredited programs. Interested students are urged to contact their respective department head and indicate their interest. Application packets are sent directly to all nominated students for completion. Deadline: Nominations must be completed by November 15.

★2052★ Frank and Lillian Gilbreth Industrial Engineering Award
Institute of Industrial Engineers
Member & Chapter Services
25 Technology Park/Atlanta
Norcross, GA 30092
Ph: (404)449-0460   Fax: (404)263-8532

This, the most esteemed honor presented by the Institute, is given for recognition of distinguished accomplishments and outstanding contributions to the welfare of mankind in the field of industrial engineering. A plaque is awarded annually when merited. Established in 1962 in honor of Frank and Lillian Gilbreth, who were pioneers in the field of industrial engineering.

★2053★ Frank and Lillian Gilbreth Memorial Fellowships
Institute of Industrial Engineers
25 Technology Park/Atlanta
Norcross, GA 30092
Ph: (404)449-0460   Fax: (404)263-8532

Purpose: To encourage and assist industrial engineering education and aid men and women in becoming qualified to practice as professional industrial engineers. Qualifications: Candidates must be graduate industrial engineering students enrolled full-time in any school in the United States and its territories, Canada, or Mexico. They must be active Institute members and have a grade point average of at least 3.40 out of 4.00. They must also have at least five full quarters or three full semesters remaining from the date of nomination to be eligible for consideration. Funds available: The number of awards presented and amount of award varies. In the 1989-90 academic year, four fellowships of $2,500 each were awarded. Application details: Nominations are solicited each fall from the academic department heads of all accredited programs. Interested students are urged to contact their respective department head and indicate their interest. Application packets are sent directly to all nominated students for completion. Deadline: Nominations must be completed by November 15.

★2054★ IIE Doctoral Dissertation Award
Institute of Industrial Engineers
Member & Chapter Services
25 Technology Park/Atlanta
Norcross, GA 30092
Ph: (404)449-0460   Fax: (404)263-8532

To recognize outstanding graduate research in the field of industrial engineering, thus promoting better industrial engineering research. Members and nonmembers are eligible. Awarded annually when merited. Established in 1986.

★2055★ Richard Harold Kaufmann Award
Institute of Electrical and Electronics Engineers
345 E. 47th St.
New York, NY 10017-2394
Ph: (212)705-7882   Fax: (212)223-2911

To recognize an outstanding achievement in the field of industrial systems engineering. Preference is given to an individual, but may be conferred on a team of not more than three. Nominations may be submitted by January 31. A monetary award of $2,000, a bronze medal, and an certificate are awarded annually. Established in 1987. Sponsored by the IEEE Industry Applications Society.

★2056★ MTM Fellowships
Institute of Industrial Engineers
25 Technology Park/Atlanta
Norcross, GA 30092
Ph: (404)449-0460   Fax: (404)263-8532

Purpose: To encourage and assist industrial engineering education and aid men and women in becoming qualified to practice as professional industrial engineers. Qualifications: Candidates must be full-time undergraduate students who have demonstrated specific interest in the field of work measurement. They must be active Institute members, have a grade point average of 3.4 out of 4.0 and have at least five full quarters or three full semesters remaining from the date of nomination to be eligible. Funds available: Two fellowships of $1,500. Application details: Nominations are solicited each fall from the academic department heads of all accredited programs. Interested students are urged to contact their respective department heads and indicate their interest. Application packets are sent directly to all nominated students for completion. Deadline: Nominations must be completed by November 15.

★2057★ MTM Scholarships
Institute of Industrial Engineers
25 Technology Park/Atlanta
Norcross, GA 30092
Ph: (404)449-0460   Fax: (404)263-8532

Purpose: To encourage and assist industrial engineering education and aid men and women in becoming qualified to practice as professional industrial engineers. Qualifications: Candidates must be full-time graduate students who have demonstrated specific interest in the field of work measurement. They must be active Institute members, have a grade point average of 3.4 out of 4.0, and have at least five full quarters or three full semesters remaining from the date of nomination to be eligible. Funds available: One $2,000 scholarship. Application details: Nominations are solicited each fall from the academic department heads of all accredited programs. Interested students are urged to contact their respective department heads and indicate their interest. Application packets are sent directly to all nominated students for completion. Deadline: Nominations must be completed by November 15.

★2058★ Outstanding Young Industrial Engineer Award
Institute of Industrial Engineers
Member & Chapter Services
25 Technology Park/Atlanta
Norcross, GA 30092
Ph: (404)449-0460   Fax: (404)263-8532

To recognize individuals in academia and business who have demonstrated outstanding characteristics of leadership, professionalism, and potential in the field of industrial engineering. Open to individuals not over 35 years of age who have been members of a senior chapter for a minimum of five years. Awarded annually when merited. Established in 1983.

BASIC REFERENCE GUIDES AND HANDBOOKS

★2059★ Electrical Power Engineering
McGraw-Hill Inc.
11 W. 19 St.
New York, NY 10011
Ph: 800-722-4726

Henslay William Kabisama. 1993.

★2060★ Engineer-In-Training Reference Manual
Professional Publications, Inc.
1250 5th Ave.
Belmont, CA 94002-3863
Fax: (415)592-4519   Fr: 800-426-1178

Michael R. Lindeburg. Eighth edition. Comprehensive guide to preparing for the F.E. exam that covers mathematics, engineering economic analysis, systems of units, fluid statics and dynamics, open channel flow, thermodynamics, and more. Intended to be a broad review of engineering fundamentals.

★2061★ Handbook of Industrial Engineering
John Wiley and Sons, Inc.
605 3rd Ave.
New York, NY 10158-0012
Ph: (212)850-6000   Fax: (212)850-6088
Fr: 800-526-5368

Gavriel Salvendy, editor. Second edition, 1991. Contain articles on industrial engineering theory and practice.

★2062★ Production Handbook
John Wiley and Sons, Inc.
605 3rd Ave.
New York, NY 10158-0012
Ph: (212)850-6000   Fax: (212)850-6088
Fr: 800-526-5368

John A. White. Fourth edition, 1987. Covers definition, design, and management of production requirements and systems. Includes information on manufacturing, employees, forecasting, and robotics.

PROFESSIONAL AND TRADE PERIODICALS

★2063★ AIPE Newsline
American Institute of Plant Engineers (AIPE)
8180 Corporate Park Dr., Ste. 305
Cincinnati, OH 45242
Ph: (513)561-6000
Linda A. Niesz

Discusses "engineering practice and management as applied to facilities in the public and private sectors." Carries news of local, regional, and national AIPE activities, and announcements of contests, awards, conferences, and employment opportunities. Recurring features include chapter news and news of members.

★2064★ Design Perspectives
Industrial Designers Society of America (IDSA)
1142 Walker Rd., Ste. E
Great Falls, VA 22066-1836
Ph: (703)759-0100   Fax: (703)759-7679
Karen Berube

Discusses issues relevant to the profession. Recurring features include reports of chapter and national activities of IDSA, a section on employment opportunities in the field, resource section, and a calendar of events.

★2065★ IE News: Energy, Environment & Plant Engineering
Institute of Industrial Engineers
25 Technology Park
Norcross, GA 30092
Ph: (404)449-0460
L. Jackson Turvaville

Considers environmental and energy issues in the design and operation of industrial plants.

★2066★ Industrial Engineering
Institute of Industrial Engineers
25 Technology Park/Atlanta
Norcross, GA 30092
Ph: (404)449-0461   Fax: (404)263-8532
Eric Torrey

Monthly. Magazine covering industrial engineering, facilities design, systems integration, production control, and material handling management.

PROFESSIONAL MEETINGS AND CONVENTIONS

★2067★ Society for the Advancement of Material and Process Engineering Symposium and Exhibition
Society for the Advancement of Material and Process Engineering
PO Box 2459
Covina, CA 91722
Ph: (818)331-0616   Fax: (818)332-8751

Annual. Always held during May at the Convention Center in Anaheim, California. **Dates and Locations:** 1996 May; Anaheim, CA.

OTHER SOURCES OF INFORMATION

★2068★ Financial Aid for Minorities in Engineering & Science
Garrett Park Press
PO Box 190
Garrett Park, MD 20896
Ph: (301)946-2553
1993.

★2069★ GEM: National Consortium for Graduate Degrees for Minorities in Engineering
National Consortium for Graduate Degrees
for Minorities in Engineering
PO Box 537
Notre Dame, IN 46556
Ph: (219)287-1097

1988. Describes the graduate fellowship program for minorities in engineering including financial support, application, and internship. Lists universities offering this program.

★2070★ How to Become a Professional Engineer
McGraw-Hill, Inc.
1221 Avenue of the Americas
New York, NY 10020
Ph: (212)512-2000   Fr: 800-722-4726

J.D. Constance. Fourth edition, 1987. Describes how to register for the professional engineer's license in all fifty states. Gives a state-by-state list of licensing regulations. Gives advice on how to take the written examination.

Mechanical Engineers

Mechanical engineers are concerned with the production, transmission, and use of mechanical power and heat. They design and develop power-producing machines such as internal combustion engines, steam and gas turbines, and jet rocket engines. They also design and develop power-using machines such as refrigeration and air-conditioning equipment, robots, machine tools, materials handling systems, and industrial production equipment.

Salaries

Starting salaries for engineers with bachelor's degrees are significantly higher than starting salaries of college graduates in other fields.

Beginning mechanical engineers	$34,462/year
Experienced mid-level engineers	$52,500/year
Senior managerial engineers	$102,544/year

Employment Outlook

Growth rate until the year 2005: Average.

Mechanical Engineers

CAREER GUIDES

★2071★ *Career Development for Engineers and Scientists: Organizational Programs and Individual Choices*
Van Nostrand Reinhold Co., Inc.
115 5th Ave.
New York, NY 10003
Ph: (212)254-3232   Fr: 800-842-3636
Robert F. Morrison and Richard M. Vosburgh. 1987. Includes bibliographies and an index. Illustrated.

★2072★ *Careers and the Engineer*
Bob Adams, Inc.
260 Center St.
Holbrook, MA 02343
Ph: (617)268-9570
Gigi Ranno, editor. Annual.

★2073★ *Careers in Engineering*
National Textbook Co. (NTC)
VGM Career Books
4255 W. Touhy Ave.
Lincolnwood, IL 60646-1975
Ph: (708)679-5500   Fax: (708)679-2494
Fr: 800-323-4900
Geraldine O. Garner, Ph.D., editor. 1993. Career guide covering 14 different engineering specialties.

★2074★ *The Civilized Engineer*
St. Martin's Press, Inc.
175 5th Ave.
New York, NY 10010
Ph: (212)674-5151   Fax: 800-258-2769
Fr: 800-221-7945
Samuel C. Florman. 1989. Published by Thomas Dunne Books. Discusses engineering education, the relationship between engineers and nontechnical executives, and the role of women in engineering.

★2075★ *"Engineering" in American Almanac of Jobs and Salaries* (pp. 261)
Avon Books
1350 Avenue of the Americas
New York, NY 10019
Ph: (212)261-6800   Fr: 800-238-0658
John Wright, editor. Revised and updated, 1994-95. A comprehensive guide to the wages of hundreds of occupations in a wide variety of industries and organizations.

★2076★ *Engineering Salary Survey*
Source Engineering
1290 Oakmead, Ste. 318
Sunnyvale, CA 94086
Ph: (408)738-8440
Annual. Discusses the structure of the engineering profession, trends, and compensation. Salaries are listed by job function, industry, and years of experience.

★2077★ *"Engineering" in Where the Jobs Are: The Hottest Careers for the 90s* (pp. 111-124)
Career Press
180 5th Ave.
Hawthorne, NJ 07507
Ph: (201)427-0229   Fax: (201)427-2037
Fr: 800-CAREER-1
Joyce Hadley. 1995. Offers a job-hunting strategy for the 1990s as well as descriptions of growing careers of the decade. Each profile includes general information, forecasts, growth, education and training, licensing requirements, and salary information.

★2078★ *Engineering for You: A Career Guide*
Iowa State University Press
2121 S. State Ave.
Ames, IA 50010
Ph: (515)292-0140   Fax: (515)292-3348
John T. Jones. 1991.

★2079★ *Mechanical Engineer*
Careers, Inc.
PO Box 135
Largo, FL 34649-0135
Ph: (813)584-7333
1992. Two-page occupational summary card describing duties, working conditions, personal qualifications, training, earnings and hours, employment outlook, places of employment, related careers, and where to write for more information.

★2080★ *Mechanical Engineer*
Vocational Biographies, Inc.
PO Box 31
Sauk Centre, MN 56378-0031
Ph: (612)352-6516   Fax: (612)352-5546
Fr: 800-255-0752
1990. Four-page pamphlet containing a personal narrative about a worker's job, work likes and dislikes, career path from high school to the present. Education and training, the rewards and frustrations, and the effects of the job on the rest of the worker's life. The data file portion of this pamphlet gives a concise occupational summary, including work descriptions, working conditions, places of employment, personal characteristics, education and training, job outlook, and salary range.

★2081★ *"Mechanical Engineer" in 100 Best Careers for the Year 2000* (pp. 255-258)
Arco Pub.
201 W. 103rd St.
Indianapolis, IN 46290
Ph: 800-428-5331   Fax: 800-835-3202
Shelly Field. 1992. Describes 100 job opportunities expected to grow fast throughout the next decade. Provides information on job duties and responsibilities, training requirements, education, advancement opportunities, experience and qualifications, and typical salaries.

★2082★ *"Mechanical Engineer" in Career Information Center* (Vol.6)
Simon and Schuster
200 Old Tappan Rd.
Old Tappan, NJ 07675
Fax: 800-445-6991   Fr: 800-223-2348
Richard Lidz and Linda Perrin, editorial directors. Fifth edition, 1993. This 13-volume set profiles over 600 occupations. Each occupational profile describes job duties, entry-level requirements, educational requirements, advancement possibilities, employment outlook, working conditions, earnings and benefits, and where to write for more information.

★2083★ "Mechanical Engineer" in Guide to Federal Jobs (p. 158)
Resource Directories
3361 Executive Pkwy., Ste. 302
Toledo, OH 43606
Ph: (419)536-5353   Fax: (419)536-7056
Fr: 800-274-8515

Rod W. Durgin, editor. Third edition, 1992. Contains information on finding and applying for federal jobs. Describes more than 200 professional and technical jobs for college graduates. Covers the nature of the work, salary, and geographic location. Lists college majors preferred for that occupation. Section one describes the function and work of government agencies that hire the most significant number of college graduates.

★2084★ "Mechanical Engineer" in Jobs Rated Almanac
World Almanac
1 International Blvd., Ste. 444
Mahwah, NJ 07495
Ph: (201)529-6900   Fax: (201)529-6901

Les Krantz. Second edition, 1992. Ranks 250 jobs by environment, salary, outlooks, physical demands, stress, security, travel opportunities, and extra perks. Includes jobs the editor feels are the most common, most interesting, and the most rapidly growing.

★2085★ "Mechanical Engineer" in Opportunities in High-Tech Careers (pp. 58-59)
National Textbook Co. (NTC)
VGM Career Books
4255 W. Touhy Ave.
Lincolnwood, IL 60646-1975
Ph: (708)679-5500   Fax: (708)679-2494
Fr: 800-323-4900

Gary D. Colter and Deborah Yanuck. 1987. Explores high technology careers. Written for the student and displaced worker. Describes job opportunities, how to make a career decision, how to prepare for high-technology jobs, job hunting techniques, and future trends.

★2086★ "Mechanical Engineer" in VGM's Careers Encyclopedia (pp. 269-271)
National Textbook Co. (NTC)
VGM Career Books
4255 W. Touhy Ave.
Lincolnwood, IL 60646-1975
Ph: (708)679-5500   Fax: (708)679-2494
Fr: 800-323-4900

Third edition, 1991. Profiles 200 occupations. Describes job duties, places of employment, working conditions, qualifications, education and training, advancement potential, and salary for each occupation.

★2087★ "Mechanical Engineering" in College Majors and Careers: A Resource Guide to Effective Life Planning (pp. 91-92)
Garrett Park Press
PO Box 1907
Garrett Park, MD 20896
Ph: (301)946-2553

Paul Phifer. 1993. Lists 60 college majors, with definitions; related occupations and leisure activities; skills, values, and personal needed attributes; suggested readings; and a list of associations.

★2088★ Mechanical Engineers
Chronicle Guidance Publications, Inc.
66 Aurora St.
PO Box 1190
Moravia, NY 13118-1190
Ph: (315)497-0330   Fax: (315)497-3359
Fr: 800-622-7284

1993. Career brief describing the nature of the job, working conditions, hours and earnings, education and training, licensure, certification, unions, personal qualifications, social and psychological factors, location, employment outlook, entry methods, advancement, and related occupations.

★2089★ "Mechanical Engineers" in 101 Careers: A Guide to the Fastest-Growing Opportunities (pp. 87-88)
John Wiley & Sons, Inc.
605 3rd Ave.
New York, NY 10158-0012
Ph: (212)850-6645   Fax: (212)850-6088

Michael Harkavy. 1990. Describes the nature of the job, working conditions, employment growth, qualifications, personal skills, projected salaries, and where to write for more information.

★2090★ "Mechanical Engineers" in Career Discovery Encyclopedia (Vol.4, pp. 66-67)
J.G. Ferguson Publishing Co.
200 W. Madison St., Ste. 300
Chicago, IL 60606
Ph: (312)580-5480   Fax: (312)580-4948

Russell E. Primm, editor-in chief. 1993. This six volume set contains two-page articles for 504 occupations. Each article describes job duties, earnings, and educational and training requirements. The whole set is arranged alphabetically by job title. Designed for junior high and older students.

★2091★ "Mechanical Engineers" in Encyclopedia of Careers and Vocational Guidance (Vol.3, pp. 388-391)
J.G. Ferguson Publishing Co.
200 W. Madison St., Ste. 300
Chicago, IL 60606
Ph: (312)580-5480   Fax: (312)580-4948

William E. Hopke, editor-in-chief. Ninth edition, 1993. Four-volume set that profiles 900 occupations and describes job trends in 74 industries. Includes career description, educational requirements, history of the job, methods of entry, advancement, employment outlook, earnings, conditions of work, social and psychological factors, and sources of further information.

★2092★ "Mechanical Engineers" in Jobs! What They Are—Where They Are—What They Pay (p. 125)
Simon & Schuster, Inc.
Simon & Schuster Bldg.
1230 Avenue of the Americas
New York, NY 10020
Ph: (212)698-7000   Fr: 800-223-2348

Robert O. Snelling and Anne M. Snelling. 3rd edition, 1992. Describes duties and responsibilities, earnings, employment opportunities, training, and qualifications.

★2093★ "Mechanical Engineers" in Occupational Outlook Handbook
U.S. Government Printing Office
Superintendent of Documents
Washington, DC 20402
Ph: (202)512-1800   Fax: (202)512-2250

Biennial; latest edition, 1994-95. Encyclopedia of careers describing about 250 occupations and comprising about 85 percent of all jobs in the economy. Occupations that require lengthy education or training are given the most attention. Each occupation's profile describes what the worker does on the job, working conditions, education and training requirements, advancement possibilities, job outlook, earnings, and sources of additional information.

★2094★ "Mechanical Engineers" in Profiles in Achievement (pp. 61-83)
The College Board
45 Columbus Ave.
New York, NY 10023-6992
Ph: (212)713-8165   Fax: (212)713-8143
Fr: 800-323-7155

Charles M. Holloway. 1987. Profiles eight men and women who have overcome the the the barriers of race, gender, tradition, and economic circumstances in their quest to become successful professionals.

★2095★ Opportunities in Engineering
National Textbook Co. (NTC)
VGM Career Books
4255 W. Touhy Ave.
Lincolnwood, IL 60646-1975
Ph: (708)679-5500   Fax: (708)679-2494
Fr: 800-323-4900

Nicholas Basta. 1990. Profiles specialties in the engineering field including civil, chemical, mechanical, biomedical, and aerospace. Offers information on salaries, career paths and educational requirements.

★2096★ Opportunities in Engineering Technology Careers
National Textbook Co. (NTC)
VGM Career Books
4255 W. Touhy Ave.
Lincolnwood, IL 60646-1975
Ph: (708)679-5500   Fax: (708)679-2494
Fr: 800-323-4900

John E. Heer and D. Joseph Hagerty. 1987. Describes the many opportunities available for engineering technicians. Explains job duties, educational requirements, salary, working conditions, employment outlook, and advancement opportunities. Lists accredited engineering technology programs.

★2097★ Opportunities in Mechanical Engineering Careers
National Textbook Co. (NTC)
VGM Career Books
4255 W. Toughy Ave.
Lincolnwood, IL 60646-1975
Ph: (708)679-5500   Fax: (708)679-2494
Fr: 800-323-4900

Seichi Karni.

★2098★ Peterson's Job Opportunities for Engineering and Technology
Petersons Guides, Inc.
PO Box 2123
Princeton, NJ 08543-2123
Ph: (609)243-9111   Fax: (609)243-9150
Fr: 800-338-3282
1994. Gives job hunting advice including information on resume writing, interviewing, and handling salary negotiations. Lists companies that hire college graduates in science and engineering at the bachelor and master's level. Companies are indexed by industry, starting location, and major. Company profiles include contact information and types of hires.

★2099★ Successful Engineering: A Guide to Achieving Your Career Goals
McGraw-Hill, Inc.
1221 Avenue of the Americas
New York, NY 10020
Ph: (212)512-2000   Fr: 800-722-4726
Lawrence J. Kamm. 1989. Written for the practicing and graduating engineer. Gives advice about working with accountants, the politics of design, and engineering ethics.

★2100★ What Is a Mechanical Engineer?
American Society of Mechanical Engineers (ASME)
345 E. 47th St.
New York, NY 10017
Ph: (212)705-7722
1988. Examines the profession of mechanical engineering. Includes information on job location and educational requirements.

PROFESSIONAL ASSOCIATIONS

★2101★ Accreditation Board for Engineering and Technology (ABET)
111 Market Pl., Ste. 1050
Baltimore, MD 21202
Ph: (410)347-7700   Fax: (410)625-2238
Members: Professional societies representing over one million engineers are participating bodies (21); affiliate bodies (5); board of directors has 29 representatives. Is responsible for the quality control of engineering education. Accredits college curricula in engineering, engineering technology, and engineering-related areas. **Publications:** Accreditation Yearbook, annual. • Criteria for Accrediting Programs in Engineering in the United States, annual. • Criteria for Accrediting Programs in Engineering Technology, annual.

★2102★ American Association of Engineering Societies (AAES)
1111 19th St. NW, Ste. 608
Washington, DC 20036
Ph: (202)296-2237   Fax: (202)296-1151
Members: Societies representing over 500,000 engineers. **Purpose:** Works to: advance the knowledge and practice of engineering in the public interest; act as an advisory, communication, and information exchange agency for member activities, especially regarding public policy issues. Conducts studies sponsored by Engineering Manpower Commission. Compiles statistics. **Publications:** AAES Update, quarterly. • Directory of Engineering Societies, biennial. • Engineering and Technology Degrees, annual. • Engineering and Technology Enrollments, annual. • Engineers Salary Survey, annual. • The Role of Engineering in Sustainable Development. • Who's Who in Engineering, biennial.

★2103★ American Institute of Engineers (AIE)
4666 San Pablo Dam Rd., No. 8
El Sobrante, CA 94803-3142
Ph: (510)223-8911   Fax: (510)223-3400
Members: Professional engineers and engineering students. **Purpose:** Seeks to advance the professional interests of engineers and scientists. Fosters the interchange of ideas and information among members. Compiles statistics; maintains speakers' bureau. **Publications:** AIE Newsmagazine, monthly.

★2104★ American Society of Mechanical Engineers (ASME)
345 E. 47th St.
New York, NY 10017
Ph: (212)705-7722   Fax: (212)705-7739
Fr: 800-THE-ASME
Members: Technical society of mechanical engineers and students. **Purpose:** Conducts research; develops boiler, pressure vessel, and power test codes. Develops safety codes and standards for equipment. Conducts short course programs, and Identifying Research Needs Program. Maintains 19 research committees and 38 divisions. **Publications:** Applied Mechanics Review, monthly. • Applied Mechanics Transactions, quarterly. • ASME News, monthly. • Biomechanical Engineering Transactions, quarterly. • Dynamic Systems, Measurement and Control Transactions, quarterly. • Electronic Packaging Transactions, quarterly. • Energy Resources Technology Transactions, quarterly. • Engineering for Gas Turbines and Power Transactions, quarterly. • Engineering for Industry Transactions, quarterly. • Engineering Materials and Technology Transactions, quarterly. • Fluids Engineering Transactions, quarterly. • Heat Transfer Transactions, quarterly. • Mechanical Design Transactions Journal, quarterly. • Mechanical Engineering, monthly. • Offshore Mechanics and Arctic Engineering Transactions, quarterly. • Pressure Vessel Technology Transactions, quarterly. • Solar Energy Engineering Transactions, quarterly. • Tribology Transactions, quarterly. • Turbomachinery Transactions, quarterly. • Vibration and Acoustics Transactions Journal, quarterly.

★2105★ National Action Council for Minorities in Engineering (NACME)
3 W. 35th St.
New York, NY 10001
Ph: (212)279-2626   Fax: (212)629-5178
Members: Seeks to increase the number of African American, Hispanic, and Native American students enrolled in and graduating from engineering schools. **Purpose:** Offers incentive grants to engineering schools to recruit and provide financial assistance to increasing numbers of minority students. Works with local, regional, and national support organizations to motivate and encourage precollege students to engage in engineering careers. Conducts educational and research programs; operates project to assist engineering schools in improving the retention and graduation rates of minority students. Maintains speakers' bureau; compiles statistics. **Publications:** Directory of Pre-College and University Minority Engineering Programs, periodic. • Financial Aid Unscrambled: A Guide for Minority Engineering Students, biennial. • Gearing Up: How to Start a Pre-College Minority Engineering Program. • NACME News, semiannual. • NACME Statistical Report, biennial.

★2106★ National Society of Professional Engineers (NSPE)
1420 King St.
Alexandria, VA 22314
Ph: (703)684-2800   Fax: (703)836-4875
Members: Professional engineers and engineers-in-training in all fields registered in accordance with the laws of states or territories of the U.S. or provinces of Canada; qualified graduate engineers, student members, and registered land surveyors. Is concerned with social, professional, ethical, and economic considerations of engineering as a profession; encompasses programs in public relations, employment practices, ethical considerations, education, and career guidance. Monitors legislative and regulatory actions of interest to the engineering profession. **Publications:** Directory of Professional Engineers in Private Practice, biennial. • Engineering Times, monthly. • PEG Times, quarterly.

★2107★ Society of Women Engineers (SWE)
120 Wall St., 11th Fl.
New York, NY 10005
Ph: (212)509-9577   Fax: (212)509-0224
Members: Educational service society of women engineers; membership is also open to men. **Purpose:** Supplies information on the achievements of women engineers and the opportunities available to them; assists women engineers in preparing for return to active work following temporary retirement. Serves as an informational center on women in engineering. Administers several certificate and scholarship programs. Offers tours and career guidance; conducts surveys. Compiles statistics. **Publications:** National Survey of Women and Men Engineers.

STANDARDS/CERTIFICATION AGENCIES

★2108★ Accreditation Board for Engineering and Technology (ABET)
111 Market Pl., Ste. 1050
Baltimore, MD 21202
Ph: (410)347-7700   Fax: (410)625-2238
Is responsible for the quality control of engineering education. Accredits college curricula in engineering, engineering technology, and engineering-related areas.

★2109★ American Society of Mechanical Engineers (ASME)
345 E. 47th St.
New York, NY 10017
Ph: (212)705-7722   Fax: (212)705-7739
Fr: 800-THE-ASME
Conducts research; develops boiler, pressure vessel, and power test codes. Develops safety codes and standards for equipment.

★2110★ Society of Women Engineers (SWE)
120 Wall St., 11th Fl.
New York, NY 10005
Ph: (212)509-9577   Fax: (212)509-0224
Administers several certificate and scholarship programs. Compiles statistics.

TEST GUIDES

★2111★ Career Examination Series: Building Mechanical Engineer
National Learning Corp.
212 Michael Dr.
Syosset, NY 11791
Ph: (516)921-8888   Fax: (516)921-8743
Fr: 800-645-6337
Jack Rudman. 1993. Test guide including questions and answers for students or professionals in the field who seek advancement through examination.

★2112★ Career Examination Series: Engineer
National Learning Corp.
212 Michael Dr.
Syosset, NY 11791
Ph: (516)921-8888   Fax: (516)921-8743
Fr: 800-645-6337
Jack Rudman. A series of study guides with multiple-choice examination questions and solutions for trainees and professional petroleum engineers. Titles in the series include *Administrative Engineer; Chief Engineer; Engineering Aide and Science Assistant; Engineering Aide; Engineering Assistant; Engineering Trainee; Senior Engineer; Senior Engineering Aide.*

★2113★ Career Examination Series: Hydraulic Engineer
National Learning Corp.
212 Michael Dr.
Syosset, NY 11791
Ph: (516)921-8888   Fax: (516)921-8743
Fr: 800-645-6337
Jack Rudman. 1993. Test guide including questions and answers for students or professionals in the field who seek advancement through examination.

★2114★ Career Examination Series: Mechanical Engineer
National Learning Corp.
212 Michael Dr.
Syosset, NY 11791
Ph: (516)921-8888   Fax: (516)921-8743
Fr: 800-645-6337
Jack Rudman. Test guide including questions and answers for students or professionals in the field who seek advancement through examination. Also included in the series: Senior Mechanical Engineer, Junior Mechanical Engineer, and Assistant Mechanical Engineer.

★2115★ Engineer-in-Training Exam File
Engineering Press, Inc.
PO Box 1
San Jose, CA 95103-0001
Ph: (408)258-4503   Fax: 800-700-1651
Fr: 800-800-1651
Donald G. Newnan and Dean Newnan. Eleventh edition. 1990. Contains 505 problems with step-by-step solutions. Covers: mathematics; statics; fluid mechanics. Includes an index.

★2116★ Engineer-In-Training Reference Manual
Professional Publications, Inc.
1250 5th Ave.
Belmont, CA 94002-3863
Fax: (415)592-4519   Fr: 800-426-1178
Michael R. Lindeburg. Eighth edition. Comprehensive guide to preparing for the F.E. exam that covers mathematics, engineering economic analysis, systems of units, fluid statics and dynamics, open channel flow, thermodynamics, and more. Intended to be a broad review of engineering fundamentals.

★2117★ Fluid Mechanics Exam File
Engineering Press, Inc.
PO Box 1
San Jose, CA 95103-0001
Ph: (408)258-4503   Fax: 800-700-1651
Fr: 800-800-1651
Contains 203 exam problems with step-by-step solutions. Covers: fluid properties; dimensional analysis; viscosity; momemtum and energy; and conduits.

★2118★ Graduate Record Examination in Engineering
Arco Publishing Co.
Macmillan General Reference
15 Columbus Cir.
New York, NY 10023
Fax: 800-835-3202   Fr: 800-858-7674
C.W. Tan, et al. First edition. 1988. Contains two sample tests with an explanation to answers.

★2119★ Graduate Record Examination: Engineering
National Learning Corp.
212 Michael Dr.
Syosset, NY 11791
Ph: (516)921-8888   Fax: (516)921-8743
Fr: 800-645-6337
Jack Rudman. Multiple-choice test for those seeking admission to graduate school for study in the field of engineering. Includes solutions to examination questions.

★2120★ Journeyman, General Mechanical Examination: An Illustrated Review
Engineer's Press
PO Box 141651
Coral Gables, FL 33114-1651
Ph: (305)856-0031
John Gladstone. Second edition, 1988.

★2121★ Mechanical Engineering
National Learning Corp.
212 Michael Dr.
Syosset, NY 11791
Ph: (516)921-8888   Fax: (516)921-8743
Fr: 800-645-6337
Jack Rudman. Part of the Test Your Knowledge Series. Contains multiple choice questions with answers.

★2122★ Mechanical Engineering Reference Manual
Professional Publications, Inc.
1250 5th Ave.
Belmont, CA 94002-3863
Ph: 800-426-1178
Michael R. Lindeburg. 9th edition, 1994. Includes charts and diagrams.

★2123★ Mechanical Engineering Sample Examination
Professional Publications, Inc.
1250 5th Ave.
Belmont, CA 94002-3863
Fax: (415)592-4519   Fr: 800-426-1178
Michael R. Lindeburg. 1989. Second edition. Features 20 exam-type problems, including five in the multiple-choice format.

★2124★ Mechanical Work Examinations; A Study Guide for Civil Service, Labor Organization, and Industrial Examinations
Ken-Books
56 Midcrest Way
San Francisco, CA 94131
Ph: (415)584-0799
Harry Walter Koch. Revised edition, 1987.

★2125★ Practicing to Take the GRE Engineering Test: An Official Publication of the GRE Board
Educational Testing Service
Rosedale Rd.
Princeton, NJ 08541
Ph: (609)921-9000
Second edition, 1989. Summarizes the purpose and scope of the Graduate Record Examination Subject Test for engineering. Contains sample questions.

★2126★ Professional Engineer
National Learning Corp.
212 Michael Dr.
Syosset, NY 11791
Ph: (516)921-8888   Fax: (516)921-8743
Fr: 800-645-6337
Jack Rudman. A sample test for engineers who are seeking admission to graduate and professional schools or seeking entrance or advancement in institutional and public career service.

★2127★ Undergraduate Program Field Test: Engineering
National Learning Corp.
212 Michael Dr.
Syosset, NY 11791
Ph: (516)921-8888   Fax: (516)921-8743
Fr: 800-645-6337
Jack Rudman. A practice examination fashioned after tests given in the Regents External Degree Program. Designed to measure knowledge received outside the college classroom in the subject of engineering. Con-

tains multiple-choice questions; provides solutions.

EDUCATIONAL DIRECTORIES AND PROGRAMS

★2128★ *ABET Accreditation Yearbook*
Accreditation Board for Engineering and Technology
345 E. 47th St., 14th Fl.
New York, NY 10017-2397
Ph: (212)705-7685   Fax: (212)838-8062
Simona C. Mardale, Contact
Annual, September. Covers about 300 U.S. colleges and universities with engineering programs, 242 institutions with programs in engineering technology, and 11 institutions with engineering-related programs accredited by the Board; also lists accredited Canadian programs. Entries include: For United States institutions—Name, year of next full accreditation review, location, program names, year of initial accreditation for each program, coding to indicate degrees offered, format of program (day, night, cooperative, etc.). For Canadian programs—Name, location, names of programs, year of initial accredition for each program. Arrangement: Classified by program area.

AWARDS, SCHOLARSHIPS, GRANTS, AND FELLOWSHIPS

★2129★ ASME Medal
American Society of Mechanical Engineers
345 E. 47th St.
New York, NY 10017
Ph: (212)705-7722   Fax: (212)705-7674
For recognition of eminently distinguished engineering achievement. The nominations deadline is March 1. One ASME Medal may be awarded annually. A monetary award of $10,000, a gold medal, and a certificate are presented. Established in 1920.

★2130★ Per Bruel Noise Control and Acoustics Medal
American Society of Mechanical Engineers
345 E. 47th St.
New York, NY 10017
Ph: (212)705-7722   Fax: (212)705-7674
For recognition of eminent achievement and extraordinary merit in the field of noise control and acoustics. The achievement must include useful applications of the principles of Noise Control and Acoustics to the art and science of mechanical engineering. An honorarium of $1,000, a vermeil medal, a certificate, and travel expenses are awarded. Established in 1987.

★2131★ Engineering Rotation Program
Hughes Aircraft Company
Technical Education Center
PO Box 80028
Los Angeles, CA 90080-0028
Ph: (310)568-6711
Purpose: To enable engineering and science graduates to find and develop the special field of work and the career position best suited to their interests and education. Qualifications: Applicant must be a U.S. citizen and have a bachelor's degree in electrical, mechanical, systems, computer or aerospace engineering; computer science; physics; or mathematics. Candidate must have a grade point average of at least 3.0/4.0, with emphasis on technical classes and related disciplines. Participants in the Rotation Program gain practical experience through up to four different work assignments at Hughes facilities, usually in southern California. Upon completion of the program, participants may be placed in permanent positions with the Company, based on their interests and assignments available. Funds available: Salary and company benefits. Application details: Write to the educational coordinator for application form and guidelines. Include pertinent information regarding academic status (university, field of interest for both undergraduate and graduate work, year of graduation, and grade point average) in initial letter of interest. Deadline: 1 March.

★2132★ Fluids Engineering Award
American Society of Mechanical Engineers
345 E. 47th St.
New York, NY 10017
Ph: (212)705-7722   Fax: (212)705-7674
To recognize outstanding contributions over a period of years to the engineering profession, and especially to the field of fluids engineering through research, practice, and/or teaching. Nominations must be submitted by September 30. A bronze medal and a certificate are awarded. Established in 1968 by the Fluids Engineering Division.

★2133★ Freeman Scholar Award
American Society of Mechanical Engineers
345 E. 47th St.
New York, NY 10017
Ph: (212)705-7722   Fax: (212)705-7674
To recognize a person of wide experience in fluids engineering who will review a topic in his or her specialty (including a comprehensive statement of the state of the art) and suggest key future research needs. The recipient may be from industry, government, education, or private professional practice. The nominations deadline is February 1, in odd-numbered years. An honorarium of $7,500, a certificate, and a travel allowance are awarded biennially in even-numbered years. Established in 1926.

★2134★ Engineer Degree Fellowships; Howard Hughes Doctoral Fellowships
Hughes Aircraft Company
Technical Education Center
PO Box 80028
Los Angeles, CA 90080-0028
Ph: (310)568-6711
Purpose: To support doctoral studies in engineering and related sciences and to provide students with practical work experience.

Qualifications: Applicant for either type of fellowship must be a U.S. citizen and have a bachelor's and master's degree or equivalent graduate experience in electrical, mechanical, systems, computer or aerospace engineering; computer science; physics; or mathematics. Engineer Degree Fellowships are reserved for candidates who have first degrees in engineering. For both awards, priority is given to individuals with experience in electronics and related disciplines. Candidate must have a minimum grade point average of 3.0/4.0, and be qualified for admission to an approved graduate program in the United States. Fellows are considered employees of the Hughes Aircraft Company and, in addition to their graduate studies, gain work experience in one of two programs: work-study or full-study. Fellows in the work-study program attend a university near a Hughes facility (usually in southern California) and complete coursework while working at the facility for 20 to 36 hours per week. Work-study fellows may switch to full-study status to complete their dissertations. Full-study fellows attend a university distant from Hughes and are on leave of absence from the company while studying full-time. Full-study fellows are required to spend the summer term working for the Company, and may work eight hours a week during the school year if attending a university within commuting distance. Funds available: Company salary and benefits, plus tuition, book and living allowances. Application details: Write to the educational coordinator for application form and guidelines. Include pertinent information regarding academic status (university, field of interest for both undergraduate and graduate work, year of graduation, and grade point average) in initial letter of interest. Deadline: 10 January. Fellows are announced in April.

★2135★ Internal Combustion Engine Award
American Society of Mechanical Engineers
345 E. 47th St.
New York, NY 10017
Ph: (212)705-7722   Fax: (212)705-7674
To recognize eminent achievement or distinguished contributions in any phase of research or engineering of internal combustion engines. Citizens of the United States are eligible. The nomination deadline is February 1. An honorarium award of $1,000 (to be divided equally if there is more than one recipient) and a bronze plaque are awarded annually. Established in 1966 by the Diesel and Gas Engine Power Division.

★2136★ Max Jakob Memorial Award
American Society of Mechanical Engineers
345 E. 47th St.
New York, NY 10017
Ph: (212)705-7722   Fax: (212)705-7674
To recognize eminent achievement or distinguished service in the area of heat transfer. A bronze plaque, certificate, and cash honorarium are presented. Established in 1961. In 1962 the award became a joint activity of the Society and the American Institute of Chemical Engineers.

★2137★ Machine Design Award
American Society of Mechanical Engineers
345 E. 47th St.
New York, NY 10017
Ph: (212)705-7722   Fax: (212)705-7674
To recognize distinguished service or eminent achievement in the field of machine design. The deadline for nominations is February 1. An honorarium of $1,000, a bronze plaque, and a certificate are awarded annually. Established in 1958.

★2138★ M. Eugene Merchant Manufacturing Medal
American Society of Mechanical Engineers
345 E. 47th St.
New York, NY 10017
Ph: (212)705-7722   Fax: (212)705-7674
To recognize significant efforts in improving the productivity and efficiency of manufacturing operation(s). Established in 1986.

★2139★ Percy W. Nicholls Award
Society for Mining, Metallurgy, and
    Exploration
PO Box 625002
Littleton, CO 80162-5002
Ph: (303)973-9550   Fax: (303)973-3845
To recognize notable scientific or industrial achievement in the field of solid fuels. Established in 1942 by the Coal Division of the American Institute of Mining, Metallurgical and Petroleum Engineers, and the Fuels Division of the American Society of Mechanical Engineers.

★2140★ Rufus Oldenburger Medal
American Society of Mechanical Engineers
345 E. 47th St.
New York, NY 10017
Ph: (212)705-7722   Fax: (212)705-7674
In recognition of an individual for significant contributions and outstanding achievements in the field of automatic control. The nominations deadline is February 1. A monetary award of $1,000, a bronze medal, and certificate are awarded annually. Established in 1968.

★2141★ Pi Tau Sigma Gold Medal
American Society of Mechanical Engineers
345 E. 47th St.
New York, NY 10017
Ph: (212)705-7722   Fax: (212)705-7674
To recognize outstanding achievement in mechanical engineering in up to ten years following graduation. Nominations are accepted by February 1. A monetary award of $1,000, a gold medal, a certificate, and travel expenses are awarded annually. Established in 1938 by Pi Tau Sigma, Honorary Mechanical Engineering Fraternity.

★2142★ James Harry Potter Gold Medal
American Society of Mechanical Engineers
345 E. 47th St.
New York, NY 10017
Ph: (212)705-7722   Fax: (212)705-7674
To recognize eminent achievement or distinguished service in the appreciation of the science of thermodynamics in mechanical engineering. The basis of the award includes contributions involving the teaching, appreciation, or utilization of thermodynamic principles in research, development, and design in mechanical engineering. The nomination

deadline is February 1. A monetary award of $1,500, a vermeil medal, and a certificate are awarded annually. Established in 1980.

★2143★ Pressure Vessel and Piping Award
American Society of Mechanical Engineers
345 E. 47th St.
New York, NY 10017
Ph: (212)705-7722   Fax: (212)705-7674
To recognize outstanding contributions in the field of pressure vessel and piping technology including, but not limited to, research, development, teaching, and significant advancements of the state of the art. The nomination deadline is June 1. A monetary award of $1,000, a bronze medal, and certificate are awarded annually. Established in 1980 by the Pressure Vessel and Piping Division.

★2144★ Charles Russ Richards Memorial Award
American Society of Mechanical Engineers
345 E. 47th St.
New York, NY 10017
Ph: (212)705-7722   Fax: (212)705-7674
To recognize an individual for outstanding achievement in mechanical engineering twenty years or more following graduation. The nomination deadline is February 1. A monetary award of $1,000, a certificate, and travel expenses, are awarded annually. Established in 1944 by Pi Tau Sigmain memory of Charles Russ Richards, the founder of Pi Tau Sigma at the University of Illinois, former head of mechanical engineering, and Dean of Engineering at the University of Illinois.

★2145★ R. Tom Sawyer Award
American Society of Mechanical Engineers
International Gas Turbine Institute
5801 Peachtree Dunwoody Rd., Ste. 1
Atlanta, GA 30342
Ph: (404)847-0072   Fax: (404)847-0151
To recognize important contributions to the gas turbine industry and to the International Gas Turbine Institute over a substantial period of time. The nominations deadline is September 1. A plaque and a certificate are awarded annually. Established in 1972 to honor R. Tom Sawyer, who worked zealously for four decades to advance gas turbine technology in all of its aspects.

★2146★ Soichiro Honda Medal
American Society of Mechanical Engineers
345 E. 47th St.
New York, NY 10017
Ph: (212)705-7722   Fax: (212)705-7674
To recognize outstanding achievement or significant contributions in the field of personal transportation. The nomination deadline is February 1. A monetary award of $2,500, a gold medal, travel expenses, a certificate are awarded. Established in 1980 in honor of Honda's contribution to personal transporation. Sponsored by the Honda Motor Company.

★2147★ Timoshenko Medal
American Society of Mechanical Engineers
345 E. 47th St.
New York, NY 10017
Ph: (212)705-7722   Fax: (212)705-7674
To recognize distinguished contributions to applied mechanics. The nomination deadline is November 1. An honorarium of $1,000, a

bronze medal, and a certificate are awarded annually. Established in 1957 to honor Stephen Timoshenko, an author and teacher of applied mechanics.

★2148★ Henry R. Worthington Medal
American Society of Mechanical Engineers
345 E. 47th St.
New York, NY 10017
Ph: (212)705-7722   Fax: (212)705-7674
To recognize an individual for eminent achievement in the field of pumping machinery in the areas of research, development, design, innovation, management, education, or literature. The nomination deadline is February 1. A monetary award of $2,500, a bronze medal, and a certificate are awarded annually. Established in 1980 by Worthington Pump, Inc.

BASIC REFERENCE GUIDES AND HANDBOOKS

★2149★ Engineer-In-Training Reference Manual
Professional Publications, Inc.
1250 5th Ave.
Belmont, CA 94002-3863
Fax: (415)592-4519   Fr: 800-426-1178
Michael R. Lindeburg. Eighth edition. Comprehensive guide to preparing for the F.E. exam that covers mathematics, engineering economic analysis, systems of units, fluid statics and dynamics, open channel flow, thermodynamics, and more. Intended to be a broad review of engineering fundamentals.

★2150★ Handbook of Engineering Fundamentals
John Wiley and Sons, Inc.
605 3rd Ave.
New York, NY 10158-0012
Ph: (212)850-6000   Fax: (212)850-6088
Fr: 800-526-5368
Byron D. Tapley. Fourth edition, 1990. Covers mathematics, rigid body and fluid mechanics, and properties of materials.

★2151★ Machinery's Handbook: A Reference Book for the Mechanical Engineer, Designer, Manufacturing Engineer, Draftsman, Toolmaker, and Machinist
Industrial Press, Inc.
200 Madison Ave.
New York, NY 10016
Ph: (212)889-6330
Erik Oberg, Franklin D. Jones, and Holbrook L. Horton, editors. Twenty-fourth edition, 1992. Covers all aspects of machine shop practice.

★2152★ Marks' Standard Handbook for Mechanical Engineers
McGraw-Hill, Inc.
1221 Avenue of the Americas
New York, NY 10020
Ph: (212)512-2000   Fr: 800-722-4726
Eugene A. Avallone and Theodore Baumeister, editors. Ninth edition, 1987.

Covers mechnical engineering principles, standards, and practices.

PROFESSIONAL AND TRADE PERIODICALS

★2153★ *Applied Mechanics Reviews*
American Society of Mechanical Engineers
345 E. 47th St.
New York, NY 10017
Ph: (212)705-7722   Fax: (212)705-7841
A.W. Kenneth Metzner

Monthly. Mechanical engineering journal. Includes annual index and two supplements.

★2154★ *CTI News*
Cooling Tower Institute (CTI)
PO Box 73383
Houston, TX 77273
Ph: (713)583-4087   Fax: (713)537-1721
Dennis Shea

Quarterly. Discusses news and events of concern to the Institute.

★2155★ *Materials Sciences: An Abstract Newsletter*
National Technical Information Service (NTIS)
5285 Port Royal Rd.
Springfield, VA 22161
Ph: (703)487-4630

Biweekly. Reports on all types of materials and composites. Provides information on adhesives and sealants, coatings and finishes, colorants, solvents, and cleaners and abrasives. Discusses ablation, corrosion, and materials degradation and fouling. Recurring features include bibliographies.

★2156★ *Mechanical Engineering*
American Society of Mechanical Engineers
345 E. 47th St.
New York, NY 10017
Ph: (212)705-7722   Fax: (212)705-7841
Jay O'Leary

Monthly. Mechanical engineering.

★2157★ *Quality and Reliability Engineering International*
John Wiley and Sons, Inc.
Subscription Dept.
605 3rd Ave.
New York, NY 10158
Ph: (212)850-6000   Fax: (212)850-6799
Finn Jensen

Bimonthly. Journal centered on scientific theories versus industrial realities in the areas of electronic, electrical, and mechanical engineering.

★2158★ *Society of Automotive Engineers—UPdate*
Society of Automotive Engineers (SAE)
400 Commonwealth Dr.
Warrendale, PA 15096-0001
Ph: (412)776-4841   Fax: (412)776-5760
Martha B. Swiss

Monthly. Reports on meetings and expositions, activities of engineering professionals, awards, education, professional development opportunities, publications, and regional section projects. Includes a calendar of events.

OTHER SOURCES OF INFORMATION

★2159★ *Financial Aid for Minorities in Engineering & Science*
Garrett Park Press
PO Box 190
Garrett Park, MD 20896
Ph: (301)946-2553
1993.

★2160★ *GEM: National Consortium for Graduate Degrees for Minorities in Engineering*
National Consortium for Graduate Degrees for Minorities in Engineering
PO Box 537
Notre Dame, IN 46556
Ph: (219)287-1097

1988. Describes the graduate fellowship program for minorities in engineering including financial support, application, and internship. Lists universities offering this program.

★2161★ *How to Become a Professional Engineer*
McGraw-Hill, Inc.
1221 Avenue of the Americas
New York, NY 10020
Ph: (212)512-2000   Fr: 800-722-4726

J.D. Constance. Fourth edition, 1987. Describes how to register for the professional engineer's license in all fifty states. Gives a state-by-state list of licensing regulations. Gives advice on how to take the written examination.

★2162★ *"Mechanical Engineering" in Accounting to Zoology: Graduate Fields Defined* (pp. 362-363)
Petersons Guides, Inc.
PO Box 2123
Princeton, NJ 08543-2123
Ph: (609)243-9111   Fax: (609)243-9150
Fr: 800-338-3282

Amy J. Goldstein, editor. Revised and updated, 1987. Defines 298 graduate and professional fields. Discusses types of graduate programs and degrees, graduate research, applied work, employment prospects, and trends.

Metallurgical, Ceramic, and Materials Engineers

Metallurgical, ceramic, and materials engineers develop new types of metals, ceramics, composites, and other materials which meet special requirements. Most metallurgical engineers work in one of the three main branches of metallurgy: extractive or chemical, physical, and mechanical or process. **Extractive metallurgists** are concerned with removing metals from ores, and refining and alloying them to obtain useful metal. **Physical metallurgists** study the nature, structure, and physical properties of metals and their alloys, and methods of converting refined metals into final products. **Mechanical metallurgists** develop and improve metalworking processes such as casting, forging, rolling, and drawing. Ceramic engineers develop methods for creating new materials and determine ways to mold new ceramic materials into useful products. Materials engineers evaluate technical and economic factors to determine which of the many metals, plastics, ceramics, or other materials available is best for each application.

Salaries

Starting salaries for engineers with bachelor's degrees are significantly higher than starting salaries of college graduates in other fields.

Beginning metallurgical engineers	$33,502/year
Experienced mid-level engineers	$52,500/year
Senior managerial engineers	$102,544/year

Employment Outlook

Growth rate until the year 2005: Faster than the average.

Metallurgical, Ceramic, and Materials Engineers

★2163★ Career Development for Engineers and Scientists: Organizational Programs and Individual Choices
Van Nostrand Reinhold Co., Inc.
115 5th Ave.
New York, NY 10003
Ph: (212)254-3232   Fr: 800-842-3636
Robert F. Morrison and Richard M. Vosburgh. 1987. Includes bibliographies and an index. Illustrated.

★2164★ Careers in Ceramics
National Institute of Ceramic Engineers (NICE)
757 Brooksedge Plaza Dr.
Westerville, OH 43081
Ph: (614)890-4700
Describes the use of ceramics in a variety of industries, examines career opportunities in research and development, production, business, and management. Gives advice on entering the profession and lists colleges and universities with ceramic engineering programs accredited by the Accreditation Board for Engineering and Technology.

★2165★ Careers and the Engineer
Bob Adams, Inc.
260 Center St.
Holbrook, MA 02343
Ph: (617)268-9570
Gigi Ranno, editor. Annual.

★2166★ Careers in Engineering
National Textbook Co. (NTC)
VGM Career Books
4255 W. Touhy Ave.
Lincolnwood, IL 60646-1975
Ph: (708)679-5500   Fax: (708)679-2494
Fr: 800-323-4900
Geraldine O. Garner, Ph.D., editor. 1993. Career guide covering 14 different engineering specialties.

★2167★ Ceramic Engineer
Careers, Inc.
PO Box 135
Largo, FL 34649-0135
Ph: (813)584-7333
1994. Two-page occupational summary card describing duties, working conditions, personal qualifications, training, earnings and hours, employment outlook, places of employment, related careers, and where to write for more information.

★2168★ Ceramic Engineer
Vocational Biographies, Inc.
PO Box 31
Sauk Centre, MN 56378-0031
Ph: (612)352-6516   Fax: (612)352-5546
Fr: 800-255-0752
1990. Four-page pamphlet containing a personal narrative about a worker's job, work likes and dislikes, career path from high school to the present. Education and training, the rewards and frustrations, and the effects of the job on the rest of the worker's life. The data file portion of this pamphlet gives a concise occupational summary, including work descriptions, working conditions, places of employment, personal characteristics, education and training, job outlook, and salary range.

★2169★ "Ceramic Engineer" in Career Information Center (Vol.6)
Simon and Schuster
200 Old Tappan Rd.
Old Tappan, NJ 07675
Fax: 800-445-6991   Fr: 800-223-2348
Richard Lidz and Linda Perrin, editorial directors. Fifth edition, 1993. This 13-volume set profiles over 600 occupations. Each occupational profile describes job duties, entry-level requirements, educational requirements, advancement possibilities, employment outlook, working conditions, earnings and benefits, and where to write for more information.

★2170★ "Ceramic Engineer" in Opportunities in Craft Careers (pp. 33-54)
National Textbook Co. (NTC)
VGM Career Books
4255 W. Touhy Ave.
Lincolnwood, IL 60646-1975
Ph: (708)679-5500   Fax: (708)679-2494
Fr: 800-323-4900
Marianne Munday. 1994. Provides a general overview of crafts and some traditional and non-traditional jobs related to crafts. Gives information on how to start a crafts business.

★2171★ "Ceramic Engineer" in VGM's Careers Encyclopedia (pp. 81-83)
National Textbook Co. (NTC)
VGM Career Books
4255 W. Touhy Ave.
Lincolnwood, IL 60646-1975
Ph: (708)679-5500   Fax: (708)679-2494
Fr: 800-323-4900
Third edition, 1991. Profiles 200 occupations. Describes job duties, places of employment, working conditions, qualifications, education and training, advancement potential, and salary for each occupation.

★2172★ Ceramic Engineers
Chronicle Guidance Publications, Inc.
66 Aurora St.
PO Box 1190
Moravia, NY 13118-1190
Ph: (315)497-0330   Fax: (315)497-3359
Fr: 800-622-7284
1994. Career brief describing the nature of the job, working conditions, hours and earnings, education and training, licensure, certification, unions, personal qualifications, social and psychological factors, location, employment outlook, entry methods, advancement, and related occupations.

★2173★ "Ceramic Engineers" in Career Discovery Encyclopedia (Vol.1, pp. 156-157)
J.G. Ferguson Publishing Co.
200 W. Madison St., Ste. 300
Chicago, IL 60606
Ph: (312)580-5480   Fax: (312)580-4948
Russell E. Primm, editor-in chief. 1993. This six volume set contains two-page articles for

504 occupations. Each article describes job duties, earnings, and educational and training requirements. The whole set is arranged alphabetically by job title. Designed for junior high and older students.

★2174★ "Ceramic Engineers" in *Jobs! What They Are—Where They Are—What They Pay!* (p. 119)
Simon & Schuster, Inc.
Simon & Schuster Bldg.
1230 Avenue of the Americas
New York, NY 10020
Ph: (212)698-7000   Fr: 800-223-2348
Robert O. Snelling and Anne M. Snelling. Third revised edition, 1992. Includes a chapter titled "Metallurgical Engineers." (pp. 126) Describes duties and responsibilities, earnings, employment opportunities, training, and qualifications.

★2175★ "Chemical Technicians" in *Career Discovery Encyclopedia* (Vol.1, pp. 162-163)
J.G. Ferguson Publishing Co.
200 W. Madison St., Ste. 300
Chicago, IL 60606
Ph: (312)580-5480   Fax: (312)580-4948
Russell E. Primm, editor-in chief. 1993. This six volume set contains two-page articles for 504 occupations. Each article describes job duties, earnings, and educational and training requirements. The whole set is arranged alphabetically by job title. Designed for junior high and older students.

★2176★ *The Civilized Engineer*
St. Martin's Press, Inc.
175 5th Ave.
New York, NY 10010
Ph: (212)674-5151   Fax: 800-258-2769
Fr: 800-221-7945
Samuel C. Florman. 1989. Published by Thomas Dunne Books. Discusses engineering education, the relationship between engineers and nontechnical executives, and the role of women in engineering.

★2177★ *The Encyclopedia of Careers and Vocational Guidance*
J.G. Ferguson Publishing Co.
200 W. Madison St., Ste. 300
Chicago, IL 60606
Ph: (312)580-5480   Fax: (312)580-4948
William E. Hopke, editor-in-chief. Ninth edition, 1993. Four-volume set that profiles 900 occupations and describes job trends in 74 industries. Volume 1—*Industry Profiles*—includes chapters on "Ceramics" (p. 95) and "Physical Sciences" (p. 356). Includes career description, educational requirements, history of the job, methods of entry, advancement, employment outlook, earnings, conditions of work, social and psychological factors, and sources of further information.

★2178★ "Engineering" in *American Almanac of Jobs and Salaries* (pp. 261)
Avon Books
1350 Avenue of the Americas
New York, NY 10019
Ph: (212)261-6800   Fr: 800-238-0658
John Wright, editor. Revised and updated, 1994-95. A comprehensive guide to the wages of hundreds of occupations in a wide variety of industries and organizations.

★2179★ *Engineering Salary Survey*
Source Engineering
1290 Oakmead, Ste. 318
Sunnyvale, CA 94086
Ph: (408)738-8440
Annual. Discusses the structure of the engineering profession, trends, and compensation. Salaries are listed by job function, industry, and years of experience.

★2180★ "Engineering" in *Where the Jobs Are: The Hottest Careers for the 90s* (pp. 111-124)
Career Press
180 5th Ave.
Hawthorne, NJ 07507
Ph: (201)427-0229   Fax: (201)427-2037
Fr: 800-CAREER-1
Joyce Hadley. 1995. Offers a job-hunting strategy for the 1990s as well as descriptions of growing careers of the decade. Each profile includes general information, forecasts, growth, education and training, licensing requirements, and salary information.

★2181★ *Engineering for You: A Career Guide*
Iowa State University Press
2121 S. State Ave.
Ames, IA 50010
Ph: (515)292-0140   Fax: (515)292-3348
John T. Jones. 1991.

★2182★ "Materials Engineer" in *Guide to Federal Jobs* (pp. 153)
Resource Directories
3361 Executive Pkwy., Ste. 302
Toledo, OH 43606
Ph: (419)536-5353   Fax: (419)536-7056
Fr: 800-274-8515
Rod W. Durgin, editor. Third edition, 1992. Contains information on finding and applying for federal jobs. Describes more than 200 professional and technical jobs for college graduates. Also includes a chapter titled "Ceramic Engineer" (p. 168). Covers the nature of the work, salary, and geographic location. Lists college majors preferred for that occupation. Section one describes the function and work of government agencies that hire the most significant number of college graduates.

★2183★ "Materials Engineer" in *Opportunities in High-Tech Careers* (pp. 50-52)
National Textbook Co. (NTC)
VGM Career Books
4255 W. Touhy Ave.
Lincolnwood, IL 60646-1975
Ph: (708)679-5500   Fax: (708)679-2494
Fr: 800-323-4900
Gary D. Colter and Deborah Yanuck. 1987. Explores high technology careers. Written for the student and displaced worker. Describes job opportunities, how to make a career decision, how to prepare for high-technology jobs, job hunting techniques, and future trends.

★2184★ *Materials: Engineering a Bright Future for Yourself*
ASM International
9639 Kinsman Rd.
Materials Park, OH 44073
Ph: (216)338-5151
Explores the many career opportunities in the field of materials engineering; describes educational preparation required. Lists colleges and universities which offer programs in materials/metallurgy, ceramics, and polymers.

★2185★ *Materials Engineers*
Chronicle Guidance Publications, Inc.
66 Aurora St.
PO Box 1190
Moravia, NY 13118-1190
Ph: (315)497-0330   Fax: (315)497-3359
Fr: 800-622-7284
1992. Career brief describing the nature of the job, working conditions, hours and earnings, education and training, licensure, certification, unions, personal qualifications, social and psychological factors, location, employment outlook, entry methods, advancement, and related occupations.

★2186★ "Metallurgical, Ceramic, and Materials Engineers" in *101 Careers: A Guide to the Fastest-Growing Opportunities* (pp. 89-91)
John Wiley & Sons, Inc.
605 3rd Ave.
New York, NY 10158-0012
Ph: (212)850-6645   Fax: (212)850-6088
Michael Harkavy. 1990. Describes the nature of the job, working conditions, employment growth, qualifications, personal skills, projected salaries, and where to write for more information.

★2187★ "Metallurgical, Ceramic, and Materials Engineers" in *Occupational Outlook Handbook*
U.S. Government Printing Office
Superintendent of Documents
Washington, DC 20402
Ph: (202)512-1800   Fax: (202)512-2250
Biennial; latest edition, 1994-95. Encyclopedia of careers describing about 250 occupations and comprising about 85 percent of all jobs in the economy. Occupations that require lengthy education or training are given the most attention. Each occupation's profile describes what the worker does on the job, working conditions, education and training requirements, advancement possibilities, job outlook, earnings, and sources of additional information.

★2188★ *Metallurgical Engineer*
Careers, Inc.
PO Box 135
Largo, FL 34649-0135
Ph: (813)584-7333
1992. Two-page occupational summary card describing duties, working conditions, personal qualifications, training, earnings and hours, employment outlook, places of employment, related careers, and where to write for more information.

★2189★ "Metallurgical Engineer" in
Career Information Center **(Vol.6)**
Simon and Schuster
200 Old Tappan Rd.
Old Tappan, NJ 07675
Fax: 800-445-6991   Fr: 800-223-2348
Richard Lidz and Linda Perrin, editorial directors. Fifth edition, 1993. This 13-volume set profiles over 600 occupations. Each occupational profile describes job duties, entry-level requirements, educational requirements, advancement possibilities, employment outlook, working conditions, earnings and benefits, and where to write for more information.

★2190★ "Metallurgical Engineer" in
VGM's Careers Encyclopedia **(pp. 281-283)**
National Textbook Co. (NTC)
VGM Career Books
4255 W. Touhy Ave.
Lincolnwood, IL 60646-1975
Ph: (708)679-5500   Fax: (708)679-2494
Fr: 800-323-4900

Third edition, 1991. Profiles 200 occupations. Describes job duties, places of employment, working conditions, qualifications, education and training, advancement potential, and salary for each occupation.

★2191★ "Metallurgical Engineers" in
Encyclopedia of Careers and
Vocational Guidance **(Vol.3, pp. 429-432)**
J.G. Ferguson Publishing Co.
200 W. Madison St., Ste. 300
Chicago, IL 60606
Ph: (312)580-5480   Fax: (312)580-4948
William E. Hopke, editor-in-chief. Ninth edition, 1993. Four-volume set that profiles 900 occupations and describes job trends in 74 industries. Includes career description, educational requirements, history of the job, methods of entry, advancement, employment outlook, earnings, conditions of work, social and psychological factors, and sources of further information.

★2192★ "Metallurgical and Mining
Engineering" in *College Majors and*
Careers: A Resource Guide to Effective
Life Planning **(pp. 97-98)**
Garrett Park Press
PO Box 1907
Garrett Park, MD 20896
Ph: (301)946-2553

Paul Phifer. Revised, 1993. Lists 60 college majors, with definitions; related occupations and leisure activities; skills, values, and personal attributesneeded; suggested readings; and a list of associations.

★2193★ Metallurgists
Chronicle Guidance Publications, Inc.
66 Aurora St.
PO Box 1190
Moravia, NY 13118-1190
Ph: (315)497-0330   Fax: (315)497-3359
Fr: 800-622-7284

1991. Occupational brief describing the nature of the job, working conditions, hours and earnings, education and training, licensure, certification, unions, personal qualifications, social and psychological factors, location,

employment outlook, entry methods, advancement, and related occupations.

★2194★ Opportunities in Materials
Science
National Textbook Co. (NTC)
VGM Career Books
4255 W. Touhy Ave.
Lincolnwood, IL 60646-1975
Ph: (708)679-5500   Fax: (708)679-2494
Fr: 800-323-4900

Charles A. Wert. Describes careers available in metallurgy, plastics, engineering, solid state physics, jet turbine engineering, highway and bridge engineering and other fields.

★2195★ Peterson's Job Opportunities
for Engineering and Technology
Petersons Guides, Inc.
PO Box 2123
Princeton, NJ 08543-2123
Ph: (609)243-9111   Fax: (609)243-9150
Fr: 800-338-3282

1994. Gives job hunting advice including information on resume writing, interviewing, and handling salary negotiations. Lists companies that hire college graduates in science and engineering at the bachelor and master's level. Companies are indexed by industry, starting location, and major. Company profiles include contact information and types of hires.

★2196★ Successful Engineering: A
Guide to Achieving Your Career Goals
McGraw-Hill, Inc.
1221 Avenue of the Americas
New York, NY 10020
Ph: (212)512-2000   Fr: 800-722-4726
Lawrence J. Kamm. 1989. Written for the practicing and graduating engineer. Gives advice about working with accountants, the politics of design, and engineering ethics.

PROFESSIONAL ASSOCIATIONS

★2197★ Accreditation Board for
Engineering and Technology (ABET)
111 Market Pl., Ste. 1050
Baltimore, MD 21202
Ph: (410)347-7700   Fax: (410)625-2238
Members: Professional societies representing over one million engineers are participating bodies (21); affiliate bodies (5); board of directors has 29 representatives. Is responsible for the quality control of engineering education. Accredits college curricula in engineering, engineering technology, and engineering-related areas. **Publications:** *Accreditation Yearbook*, annual. • *Criteria for Accrediting Programs in Engineering in the United States*, annual. • *Criteria for Accrediting Programs in Engineering Technology*, annual.

★2198★ American Association of
Engineering Societies (AAES)
1111 19th St. NW, Ste. 608
Washington, DC 20036
Ph: (202)296-2237   Fax: (202)296-1151
Members: Societies representing over 500,000 engineers. **Purpose:** Works to: ad-

vance the knowledge and practice of engineering in the public interest; act as an advisory, communication, and information exchange agency for member activities, especially regarding public policy issues. Conducts studies sponsored by Engineering Manpower Commission. Compiles statistics. **Publications:** *AAES Update*, quarterly. • *Directory of Engineering Societies*, biennial. • *Engineering and Technology Degrees*, annual. • *Engineering and Technology Enrollments*, annual. • *Engineers Salary Survey*, annual. • *The Role of Engineering in Sustainable Development*. • *Who's Who in Engineering*, biennial.

★2199★ American Ceramic Society
(ACerS)
735 Ceramic Pl.
PO Box 6136
Westerville, OH 43086-6136
Ph: (614)890-4700   Fax: (614)899-6109
Members: Professional society of scientists, engineers, educators, plant operators, and others interested in the glass, cements, refractories, nuclear ceramics, whitewares, electronics, engineering, and structural clay products industries. **Purpose:** Disseminates scientific and technical information through its publications and technical meetings. Conducts continuing education courses and training such as the Precollege Education Program. Sponsors over 10 meetings yearly; encourages high school and college students' interest in ceramics. Maintains Ross C. Purdy Museum of Ceramics; offers placement service and speakers' bureau. **Publications:** *American Ceramic Society Bulletin*, monthly. • *Ceramic Engineering and Science Proceedings*, bimonthly. • *Ceramic Source*, annual. • *Ceramics Abstracts*, bimonthly. • *Journal of the American Ceramic Society*, monthly.

★2200★ American Institute of Engineers
(AIE)
4666 San Pablo Dam Rd., No. 8
El Sobrante, CA 94803-3142
Ph: (510)223-8911   Fax: (510)223-3400
Members: Professional engineers and engineering students. **Purpose:** Seeks to advance the professional interests of engineers and scientists. Fosters the interchange of ideas and information among members. Compiles statistics; maintains speakers' bureau. **Publications:** *AIE Newsmagazine*, monthly.

★2201★ ASM International (ASM)
9639 Kinsman
Materials Park, OH 44073-0002
Ph: (216)338-5151   Fax: (216)338-4634
Fr: 800-336-5152

Metallurgists, materials engineers, executives in materials producing and consuming industries; teachers and students. Disseminates technical information about the manufacture, use, and treatment of engineered materials. Offers in-plant, home study, and intensive courses through Materials Engineering Institute. Conducts career development program. Established ASM Foundation for Education and Research. Maintains library of 10,000 volumes on metals and other materials. **Publications:** *Advanced Materials and Processes*, monthly. • *Alloys Index*, monthly. • *ASM Handbook*. • *ASM News*, monthly. •

Casting Digest Digest, monthly. • *Cleaning/Finishing/Coating Digest*, monthly. • *Corrosion Prevention/Inhibition Digest*, monthly. • *Cutting Tool/Machining Digest*, monthly. • *Engineered Materials Abstracts*, monthly. • *Guide to Engineered Materials*, annual. • *Heat Processing Digest*, monthly. • *International Materials Reviews*, bimonthly. • *Journal of Materials Engineering and Performance*, bimonthly. • *Journal of Phase Equilibria*, bimonthly. • *Metalforming Digest*, monthly. • *Metallurgical Transactions A*, monthly. • *Metallurgical Transactions B*, bimonthly. • *Metals Abstracts*, monthly. • *Metals Abstracts Index*, monthly. • *Nonferrous Alert*, monthly. • *Polymers/Ceramics/Composites Alert*, monthly. • *Stainless Steels Digest*, monthly. • *Steels Alert*, monthly. • *Testing and Control Digest*, monthly. • *Titanium Digest*, monthly. • *UPDATE Newsletter*, quarterly. • *Welding/Brazing/Soldering Digest*, monthly. • *World Calendar*, quarterly.

★2202★ Association of Iron and Steel Engineers (AISE)
3 Gateway Center, Ste. 2350
Pittsburgh, PA 15222
Ph: (412)281-6323   Fax: (412)281-4657
Members: Engineers and operators in the basic steel industry; suppliers to the industry. **Purpose:** To advance the technical and engineering phases of the production and processing of iron and steel. Develops technical reports for the industry; conducts studies. District sections sponsor various social events. **Publications:** *AISE Yearbook.* • *Directory Iron and Steel Plants*, annual. • *Directory of Iron and Steel Works of the United States and Canada*, annual. • *Iron and Steel Engineer*, monthly. • *The Making, Shaping and Treating of Steel.*

★2203★ Minerals, Metals, and Materials Society
420 Commonwealth Dr.
Warrendale, PA 15086
Ph: (412)776-9000   Fax: (412)776-3770
Members: A member society of American Institute of Mining, Metallurgical and Petroleum Engineers. Professional society of metallurgists, metallurgical engineers, and materials scientists. Maintains 35 committees. **Publications:** *JOM*, monthly. • *Journal of Electronic Materials*, bimonthly. • *Metallurgical Transactions A*, monthly. • *Metallurgical Transactions B*, quarterly.

★2204★ National Action Council for Minorities in Engineering (NACME)
3 W. 35th St.
New York, NY 10001
Ph: (212)279-2626   Fax: (212)629-5178
Members: Seeks to increase the number of African American, Hispanic, and Native American students enrolled in and graduating from engineering schools. **Purpose:** Offers incentive grants to engineering schools to recruit and provide financial assistance to increasing numbers of minority students. Works with local, regional, and national support organizations to motivate and encourage precollege students to engage in engineering careers. Conducts educational and research programs; operates project to assist engineering schools in improving the retention and graduation rates of minority students. Maintains speakers' bureau; compiles statis-

tics. **Publications:** *Directory of Pre-College and University Minority Engineering Programs*, periodic. • *Financial Aid Unscrambled: A Guide for Minority Engineering Students*, biennial. • *Gearing Up: How to Start a Pre-College Minority Engineering Program.* • *NACME News*, semiannual. • *NACME Statistical Report*, biennial.

★2205★ National Institute of Ceramic Engineers (NICE)
735 Ceramic Pl.
Westerville, OH 43081
Ph: (614)890-4700   Fax: (614)899-6109
Members: Promotes the professional status of ceramic engineering, accreditation of educational programs in ceramic engineering and science, and high ethical engineering standards and practices. Sponsors continuing education courses. Offers employment service and promotes professional engineer registration.

★2206★ National Society of Professional Engineers (NSPE)
1420 King St.
Alexandria, VA 22314
Ph: (703)684-2800   Fax: (703)836-4875
Members: Professional engineers and engineers-in-training in all fields registered in accordance with the laws of states or territories of the U.S. or provinces of Canada; qualified graduate engineers, student members, and registered land surveyors. Is concerned with social, professional, ethical, and economic considerations of engineering as a profession; encompasses programs in public relations, employment practices, ethical considerations, education, and career guidance. Monitors legislative and regulatory actions of interest to the engineering profession. **Publications:** *Directory of Professional Engineers in Private Practice*, biennial. • *Engineering Times*, monthly. • *PEG Times*, quarterly.

★2207★ Society for Mining, Metallurgy, and Exploration (SME)
PO Box 625002
Littleton, CO 80162-5002
Ph: (303)973-9550   Fax: (303)973-3845
Members: A member society of the American Institute of Mining, Metallurgical and Petroleum Engineers. Persons engaged in the finding, exploitation, treatment, and marketing of all classes of minerals (metal ores, industrial minerals, and solid fuels) except petroleum. **Purpose:** Promotes the arts and sciences connected with the production of useful minerals and metals. Offers specialized education programs; compiles enrollment and graduation statistics from schools offering engineering degrees in mining, mineral, mineral processing/metallurgical, geological, geophysical, and mining technology. Provides placement service and sponsors charitable programs. **Publications:** *Minerals and Metallurgical Processing*, quarterly. • *Mining Engineering*, monthly. • *Transactions*, annual. • *Who's Who in Mineral Engineering*, annual.

★2208★ Society of Women Engineers (SWE)
120 Wall St., 11th Fl.
New York, NY 10005
Ph: (212)509-9577   Fax: (212)509-0224
Members: Educational service society of women engineers; membership is also open to men. **Purpose:** Supplies information on the achievements of women engineers and the opportunities available to them; assists women engineers in preparing for return to active work following temporary retirement. Serves as an informational center on women in engineering. Administers several certificate and scholarship programs. Offers tours and career guidance; conducts surveys. Compiles statistics. **Publications:** *National Survey of Women and Men Engineers.*

STANDARDS/CERTIFICATION AGENCIES

★2209★ Accreditation Board for Engineering and Technology (ABET)
111 Market Pl., Ste. 1050
Baltimore, MD 21202
Ph: (410)347-7700   Fax: (410)625-2238
Is responsible for the quality control of engineering education. Accredits college curricula in engineering, engineering technology, and engineering-related areas.

★2210★ National Institute of Ceramic Engineers (NICE)
735 Ceramic Pl.
Westerville, OH 43081
Ph: (614)890-4700   Fax: (614)899-6109
Promotes the professional status of ceramic engineering, accreditation of educational programs in ceramic engineering and science, and high ethical engineering standards and practices. Offers employment service and promotes professional engineer registration.

★2211★ Society of Women Engineers (SWE)
120 Wall St., 11th Fl.
New York, NY 10005
Ph: (212)509-9577   Fax: (212)509-0224
Administers several certificate and scholarship programs. Compiles statistics.

TEST GUIDES

★2212★ *Career Examination Series: Engineer*
National Learning Corp.
212 Michael Dr.
Syosset, NY 11791
Ph: (516)921-8888   Fax: (516)921-8743
Fr: 800-645-6337
Jack Rudman. A series of study guides with multiple-choice examination questions and solutions for trainees and professional petroleum engineers. Titles in the series include *Administrative Engineer; Chief Engineer; Engineering Aide and Science Assistant; Engi-*

neering Aide; Engineering Assistant; Engineering Trainee; Senior Engineer; Senior Engineering Aide.

★2213★ Career Examination Series: Materials Engineer
National Learning Corp.
212 Michael Dr.
Syosset, NY 11791
Ph: (516)921-8888   Fax: (516)921-8743
Fr: 800-645-6337

Jack Rudman. Test guide including questions and answers for students or professionals in the field who seek advancement through examination.

★2214★ Career Examination Series: Metallurgist
National Learning Corp.
212 Michael Dr.
Syosset, NY 11791
Ph: (516)921-8888   Fax: (516)921-8743
Fr: 800-645-6337

Jack Rudman. Test guide including questions and answers for students or professionals in the field who seek advancement through examination.

★2215★ Engineer-in-Training Exam File
Engineering Press, Inc.
PO Box 1
San Jose, CA 95103-0001
Ph: (408)258-4503   Fax: 800-700-1651
Fr: 800-800-1651

Donald G. Newnan and Dean Newnan. Eleventh edition. 1990. Contains 505 problems with step-by-step solutions. Covers: mathematics; statics; fluid mechanics. Includes an index.

★2216★ Engineering Economic Analysis Exam File
Engineering Press, Inc.
PO Box 1
San Jose, CA 95103-0001
Ph: (408)258-4503   Fax: 800-700-1651
Fr: 800-800-1651

Contains 386 exam problems with step-by-step solutions.

★2217★ Graduate Record Examination: Engineering
National Learning Corp.
212 Michael Dr.
Syosset, NY 11791
Ph: (516)921-8888   Fax: (516)921-8743
Fr: 800-645-6337

Jack Rudman. Multiple-choice test for those seeking admission to graduate school for study in the field of engineering. Includes solutions to examination questions.

★2218★ Graduate Record Examination in Engineering
Arco Publishing Co.
Macmillan General Reference
15 Columbus Cir.
New York, NY 10023
Fax: 800-835-3202   Fr: 800-858-7674

C.W. Tan, et al. First edition. 1988. Contains two sample tests with an explanation to answers.

★2219★ Practicing to Take the GRE Engineering Test: An Official Publication of the GRE Board
Educational Testing Service
Rosedale Rd.
Princeton, NJ 08541
Ph: (609)921-9000

Second edition, 1989. Summarizes the purpose and scope of the Graduate Record Examination Subject Test for engineering. Contains sample questions.

★2220★ Professional Engineer
National Learning Corp.
212 Michael Dr.
Syosset, NY 11791
Ph: (516)921-8888   Fax: (516)921-8743
Fr: 800-645-6337

Jack Rudman. A sample test for engineers who are seeking admission to graduate and professional schools or seeking entrance or advancement in institutional and public career service.

★2221★ Undergraduate Program Field Test: Engineering
National Learning Corp.
212 Michael Dr.
Syosset, NY 11791
Ph: (516)921-8888   Fax: (516)921-8743
Fr: 800-645-6337

Jack Rudman. A practice examination fashioned after tests given in the Regents External Degree Program. Designed to measure knowledge received outside the college classroom in the subject of engineering. Contains multiple-choice questions; provides solutions.

EDUCATIONAL DIRECTORIES AND PROGRAMS

★2222★ ABET Accreditation Yearbook
Accreditation Board for Engineering and Technology
345 E. 47th St., 14th Fl.
New York, NY 10017-2397
Ph: (212)705-7685   Fax: (212)838-8062
Simona C. Mardale, Contact

Annual, September. Covers about 300 U.S. colleges and universities with engineering programs, 242 institutions with programs in engineering technology, and 11 institutions with engineering-related programs accredited by the Board; also lists accredited Canadian programs. Entries include: For United States institutions—Name, year of next full accreditation review, location, program names, year of initial accreditation for each program, coding to indicate degrees offered, format of program (day, night, cooperative, etc.). For Canadian programs—Name, location, names of programs, year of initial accredition for each program. Arrangement: Classified by program area.

★2223★ Metallurgy/Materials Education Yearbook
ASM International
9639 Kinsman Rd.
Materials Park, OH 44073-0002
Ph: (216)338-5151   Fax: (216)338-4634
Fr: 800-336-5152
Mary Allen, Administrative Secretary

Annual, July. Covers 1,050 professors of metallurgy, materials science, and polymer and ceramics, primarily in the United States, Canada, and Europe. Entries include: For North American schools—Name of school, address, name of department head, degrees offered, list of faculty members with specialties and phone numbers; number of seniors and graduate students. Listings for foreign schools have less detail. Arrangement: Alphabetical by school name.

★2224★ SME Guide to Minerals Schools
Society for Mining, Metallurgy, and Exploration Inc. (SME)
PO Box 625002
Littleton, CO 80162-5002
Ph: (303)973-9550   Fax: (303)973-3845

Annual, January. Covers over 50 educational institutions offering programs in geological, geophysical, metallurgical, mineral processing, and mining engineering along with mining engineering technology. Entries include: Institution name; program title; department name, address, phone, fax, electronic mail code; references for admissions information; names and titles of program administrators; name, title, highest degree earned, and teaching specialty for faculty members; enrollment statistics by level and year; degrees offered and special requirements; number of degrees conferred by level and year; contact, address, and phone for job placement assistance. Arrangement: Classified by program area.

AWARDS, SCHOLARSHIPS, GRANTS, AND FELLOWSHIPS

★2225★ Henry J. Albert Award
International Precious Metals Institute
4905 Tilghman St., Ste. 160
Allentown, PA 18104
Ph: (215)395-9700   Fax: (215)395-5855

To recognize and encourage outstanding theoretical or experimental contributions to the metallurgy of precious metals. A palladium medal and a certificate are awarded. Established in 1979. Sponsored by Engelhard Corporation.

★2226★ Application to Practice Award
Minerals, Metals, and Materials Society
420 Commonwealth Dr.
Warrendale, PA 15086
Ph: (412)776-9035   Fax: (412)776-3770

To recognize an individual who has demonstrated outstanding achievement in transferring research results or findings in some aspect of the field of metallurgy and materials into commercial production and practical use as a representative of an industrial, academic, governmental, or technical organization. Nominations must be submitted by October 31. A certificate and an engraved crystal piece are awarded annually. Established in 1985.

★2227★ ASM International and The Minerals, Metals and Materials Society Distinguished Lectureship in Materials and Society
ASM International
Materials Park, OH 44073
Ph: (216)338-5151   Fax: (216)338-4634
To clarify the role of materials science and engineering in technology and in society in its broadest sense, to present an evaluation of progress made in developing new technology for the ever changing needs of technology and society, and to define new frontiers for materials science and engineering. Awarded annually. Established in 1971.

★2228★ Edward DeMille Campbell Memorial Lecture
ASM International
Materials Park, OH 44073
Ph: (216)338-5151   Fax: (216)338-4634
To recognize outstanding demonstrated ability in materials science and engineering. A monetary award of $3,000 and a certificate are presented. Established in 1926 in memory of Professor Campbell who was blind for all but two years of his professional life.

★2229★ Francis J. Clamer Medal
Franklin Institute
Benjamin Franklin National Memorial
20th & The Parkway
Philadelphia, PA 19103-1194
Ph: (215)448-1329   Fax: (215)448-1364
To recognize meritorious inventions, discoveries, or research in the field of metallurgy. A gold medal is awarded. Established in 1943.

★2230★ Distinguished Life Member
ASM International
Materials Park, OH 44073
Ph: (216)338-5151   Fax: (216)338-4634
To recognize those leaders who have devoted their time, knowledge, and abilities to the advancement of the materials industries. Established in 1954.

★2231★ James Douglas Gold Medal
American Institute of Mining, Metallurgical and Petroleum Engineers
345 E. 47th St., 14th Fl.
New York, NY 10017
Ph: (212)705-7695
To recognize an individual for distinguished achievement in nonferrous metallurgy, including both the benefication of ores and the alloying and utilization of nonferrous metals. A gold medal is awarded annually. Established in 1922.

★2232★ Extraction & Processing Science Award
Minerals, Metals, and Materials Society
420 Commonwealth Dr.
Warrendale, PA 15086
Ph: (412)776-9035   Fax: (412)776-3770
To recognize an individual for notable contributions to the scientific understanding of extractive metallurgy. An engraved plaque is awarded annually. Established in 1955.

★2233★ Extraction & Processing Technology Award
Minerals, Metals, and Materials Society
420 Commonwealth Dr.
Warrendale, PA 15086
Ph: (412)776-9035   Fax: (412)776-3770
To recognize an individual for notable contributions to the advancement of the technology of extractive metallurgy. An engraved plaque is awarded annually. Established in 1955.

★2234★ Benjamin F. Fairless Award
American Institute of Mining, Metallurgical and Petroleum Engineers
345 E. 47th St., 14th Fl.
New York, NY 10017
Ph: (212)705-7695
To recognize an individual for distinguished achievement in iron and steel production and ferrous metallurgy. A silver plaque is awarded annually. Established in 1954 by the US Steel Corporation in memory of its longtime Chairman of the Board.

★2235★ Antoine M. Gaudin Award
Society for Mining, Metallurgy, and Exploration
PO Box 625002
Littleton, CO 80162-5002
Ph: (303)973-9550   Fax: (303)973-3845
For recognition of specific engineering or scientific achievements that have furthered understanding of the technology of mineral processing. Eligible areas for contributions are agglomeration, classification, comminution, electrical and magnetic separation, flocculation and sedimentation, froth flotation, hydrometallurgy, particulate behavior, and other related mineral processing operations. The deadline for nomination is July 15. A plaque is awarded when merited. Established in 1975.

★2236★ Gold Medal
ASM International
Materials Park, OH 44073
Ph: (216)338-5151   Fax: (216)338-4634
To recognize outstanding knowledge and great versatility in the application of science to the field of materials science and engineering, as well as exceptional ability in the diagnosis and solution of diversified materials problems. A gold medal designed by Walter Sinz is generally presented annually. Established in 1943.

★2237★ Hal Williams Hardinge Award
Society for Mining, Metallurgy, and Exploration
PO Box 625002
Littleton, CO 80162-5002
Ph: (303)973-9550   Fax: (303)973-3845
To recognize outstanding achievement in the field of industrial minerals. A plaque and citation are awarded annually. Established in 1958.

★2238★ Honorary Member
International Magnesium Association
1303 Vincent Pl., No. 1
Mc Lean, VA 22102
Ph: (703)442-8888   Fax: (703)821-1824
To recognize, on an international level, an individual who has made consistent and significant contributions to the industry. This

award is an echelon higher than the Special Award. Established in 1954.

★2239★ Howe Memorial Lecturer
Iron and Steel Society
410 Commonwealth Dr.
Warrendale, PA 15086
Ph: (412)776-1534   Fax: (412)776-0430
To recognize outstanding contributions to the science and practice of iron and steel metallurgy or metallography. The awardee presents a lecture and receives a certificate. Established in 1923 in honor of Henry Marion Howe, Past President of the Institute.

★2240★ William Hume-Rothery Award
Minerals, Metals, and Materials Society
420 Commonwealth Dr.
Warrendale, PA 15086
Ph: (412)776-9035   Fax: (412)776-3770
To recognize an outstanding scientific leader for scholarly contributions to the science of alloys. Nominations must be submitted by October 31. A plaque is awarded annually. Established in 1972 by the Institute of Metals Division of The Metallurgical Society of AIME.

★2241★ Institute of Metals Lecture and Robert Franklin Mehl Award
Minerals, Metals, and Materials Society
420 Commonwealth Dr.
Warrendale, PA 15086
Ph: (412)776-9035   Fax: (412)776-3770
To recognize an outstanding scientific leader who is selected to present the lecture in his or her field of accomplishment. A medal and a plaque in walnut book are awarded annually. Established in 1921. The Robert Franklin Mehl Award was added in 1972.

★2242★ IPMI Distinguished Achievement Award
International Precious Metals Institute
4905 Tilghman St., Ste. 160
Allentown, PA 18104
Ph: (215)395-9700   Fax: (215)395-5855
To recognize important career contributions to the advancement of precious metals, either technological, economic, or business. A plaque bearing a precious metal medallion is awarded and the recipient is invited to present the award lecture at the IPMI Annual Meeting. Established in 1977.

★2243★ IPMI Student Award
International Precious Metals Institute
4905 Tilghman St., Ste. 160
Allentown, PA 18104
Ph: (215)395-9700   Fax: (215)395-5855
To recognize and encourage outstanding work by graduate or undergraduate students who have started or plan to do research or development projects in the field of precious metals. Nominations from faculty members must be received by December 6. Three monetary prizes of $2,000 each, an invitation to the IPMI Annual Conference in Vancouver, and $500 toward travel expenses are awarded to the students. In addition, an IPMI Graduate Student Award of $3,000 is presented to the university to support the work of graduate students. The IPMI Graduate Student Award is sponsored by Gemini Industries, Inc. Established in 1980.

★2244★ IMS and AMS Jacquet-Lucas Award for Excellence in Metallography
ASM International
Materials Park, OH 44073
Ph: (216)338-5151   Fax: (216)338-4634

To recognize the best entry in the annual ASM metallographic competition. Awarded annually. Established in 1946 and co-sponsored by the International Metallographic Societysince 1972. Endowed by Buehler Limited.

★2245★ J. E. Johnson, Jr., Award
Iron and Steel Society
410 Commonwealth Dr.
Warrendale, PA 15086
Ph: (412)776-1534   Fax: (412)776-0430

To recognize creative work in the metallurgy or manufacture of pig iron. Individuals under the age of 40 are eligible. A monetary award and a certificate are awarded annually. Established in 1921 in memory of J.E. Johnson, Jr., a prominent engineer and author of two valuable volumes on iron blast furnace construction and practice.

★2246★ Leadership Award
Minerals, Metals, and Materials Society
420 Commonwealth Dr.
Warrendale, PA 15086
Ph: (412)776-9035   Fax: (412)776-3770

To recognize an individual who has demonstrated outstanding leadership in some aspect of the fields of metallurgy and materials as a representative of an industrial, academic, governmental, or technical organization. Nominations must be submitted by October 31. A certificate and crystal piece are awarded annually. Established in 1985.

★2247★ Charles F. Rand Memorial Gold Medal
American Institute of Mining, Metallurgical and Petroleum Engineers
345 E. 47th St., 14th Fl.
New York, NY 10017
Ph: (212)705-7695

To recognize an individual for distinguished achievement in mining administration including metallurgy and petroleum. A gold medal is awarded annually. Established in 1939.

★2248★ Robert H. Richards Award
Society for Mining, Metallurgy, and Exploration
PO Box 625002
Littleton, CO 80162-5002
Ph: (303)973-9550   Fax: (303)973-3845

To recognize achievement in any form that unmistakably furthers the art of mineral beneficiation in any of its branches. A citation and sterling silver Vanning Dish are awarded annually.

★2249★ Rock Mechanics Award
Society for Mining, Metallurgy, and Exploration
PO Box 625002
Littleton, CO 80162-5002
Ph: (303)973-9550   Fax: (303)973-3845

For recognition of distinguished contributions to the advancement of the field of rock mechanics. A plaque and citation are awarded annually. Established in 1967.

★2250★ Rocky Mountain Coal Mining Institute Scholarships
Rocky Mountain Coal Mining Institute (RMCMI)
3000 Youngfield, No. 324
Lakewood, CO 80215
Ph: (303)238-9099   Fax: (303)238-0509

Purpose: To assist students who have chosen a career in the mining industry. Qualifications: Candidates must be sophomores in good academic standing, U.S. citizens and residents of one of the member states (Arizona, Colorado, Montana, North Dakota, New Mexico, Texas, Utah, and Wyoming), pursuing a degree in a mining-related field or in engineering disciplines such as geology or mineral processing and metallurgy, and have expressed an interest in western coal as a possible career. Selection criteria: Completed application and personal interview. Funds available: Sixteen students from the Institute's eight member states receive $750 annually. Application details: The RMCMI Scholarship Chairman contacts the various colleges and universities in the member states and request nominations from students and each dean of the mining department. The chairman and the RMCMI state vice president interview the various nominees. The scholarship is presented at the end of the recipient's sophomore year and renewed, upon recommendation from the dean of the college or university involved, at the close of the recipient's junior year. Deadline: February 1.

★2251★ Albert Sauveur Achievement Award
ASM International
Materials Park, OH 44073
Ph: (216)338-5151   Fax: (216)338-4634

To recognize pioneering materials science and engineering achievements that have stimulated organized work leading to a basic advance in materials knowledge. A plaque is awarded. Established in 1934 in honor of Albert Sauveur, a distinguished teacher, metallographer and metallurgist.

★2252★ TMS/ASM Joint Distinguished Lectureship in Materials and Society
Minerals, Metals, and Materials Society
420 Commonwealth Dr.
Warrendale, PA 15086
Ph: (412)776-9035   Fax: (412)776-3770

To clarify the role of materials engineering in technology and in society in its broadest sense, to present an evaluation of progress made in developing new technology for the ever changing needs of technology and society, and to define new frontiers for materials engineering. Suggestions may be submitted prior to April 1 each year for consideration for an award to be given two years hence. A certificate with citation are awarded at the joint fall meeting of the societies. Established in 1970 by The Minerals, Metals, and Materials Society. (Formerly the Metallurgical Society) and the American Society for Metals.

★2253★ WAAIME Scholarship Loans
American Institute of Mining, Metallurgical and Petroleum Engineers, Inc. (WAAIME)
Woman's Auxiliary
345 E. 47th St., 14th Fl.
New York, NY 10017

Qualifications: Applicants must be undergraduate students studying for a degree at an accredited United States engineering school in engineering science as applied to industries within the mineral field. These include mining, geology, metallurgy, petroleum, mineral science, materials science, mining economics and other related fields that further the interests of the mineral industry. Scholarship loans also are available for graduate students on the same terms as for undergraduates. These cannot be given to students who have also had an undergraduate grant from WAAIME unless that loan has been repaid. Graduate scholarship loans are limited to two years. Selection criteria: Each applicant is considered on an individual basis by a local Section Scholarship Loan Fund Chairman through personal interviews and research of academic standing, character, need, and personality, and then by the National Scholarship Loan Fund Committee. Preference is given to college juniors and seniors. Funds available: The amount of the scholarship loans is individually determined. Each recipient is expected to repay 50 percent of the monies loaned without interest. Repayment starts after graduation and is to be completed within six years. Application details: Applications should not be sent before the interview. Applications must be accompanied by recent grade transcripts, supporting letters including the personal evaluation by the Section Scholarship Loan Fund Chairman. Deadline: All application material must be in the hands of the Chairman of the National Scholarship Loan Fund Committee by March 15.

BASIC REFERENCE GUIDES AND HANDBOOKS

★2254★ *1994 Annual Book of ASTM Standards*
ASTM
1916 Race St.
Philadelphia, PA 19103
Ph: (215)299-5400

1994. Includes approved ASTM standard and tentative test methods, definitions, recommended, practices, classifications, specifications, and other related material.

★2255★ *Dictionary of Ceramic Science and Engineering*
Plenum Publishing Co.
233 Spring St.
New York, NY 10013
Ph: (212)620-8000   Fr: 800-221-9369

I.J. McColm. Second edition, 1994. Defines terms related to ceramic science and industry.

★2256★ Engineer-In-Training Reference Manual
Professional Publications, Inc.
1250 5th Ave.
Belmont, CA 94002-3863
Fax: (415)592-4519   Fr: 800-426-1178
Michael R. Lindeburg. Eighth edition. Comprehensive guide to preparing for the F.E. exam that covers mathematics, engineering economic analysis, systems of units, fluid statics and dynamics, open channel flow, thermodynamics, and more. Intended to be a broad review of engineering fundamentals.

★2257★ Engineered Materials Handbook: Volume 1 Composites
ASM International
9639 Kinsman Rd.
Materials Park, OH 44073
Ph: (216)338-5151
Cyril A. Dostal, editor. 1987. Contains information on the newest developments in composite materials. Covers properties of components, design, testing, and applications.

★2258★ Materials Handbook: An Encyclopedia for Managers, Technical Professionals, Purchasing and Production Managers, Technicians, and Supervisors . . .
McGraw-Hill, Inc.
1221 Avenue of the Americas
New York, NY 10020
Ph: (212)512-2000   Fr: 800-722-4726
George Stuart Brady and Henry R. Clauser. Thirteenth editon, 1991. Contains descriptions of all materials and substances related to engineering technologies. Arranged alphabetically.

★2259★ Metals Handbook
ASM International (ASMI)
9639 Kinsman Rd.
Materials Park, OH 44073
Ph: (216)338-5151
Eighteen volumes. Describes the properties of ferrous and non-ferrous metals and processes and testing.

PROFESSIONAL AND TRADE PERIODICALS

★2260★ Advanced Materials
Advanced Publications, Inc.
PO Box 6249
Hilton Head, SC 29938
Ph: (803)842-4940   Fax: (803)842-4940
Philip West
Reviews recent developments in composites, ceramics, high-performance plastics, adhesives, metals, and coatings. Concentrates on materials specifically designed for demanding conditions. Recurring features include news of research and product development and technology, reports of meetings, book reviews, notices of publications available, and patent reviews.

★2261★ Electronic Materials Technology News
Business Communications Company, Inc.
25 Van Zant St.
Norwalk, CT 06855-1781
Ph: (203)853-4266   Fax: (203)853-0348
Kurt Miska
Monthly. Contains "analyses of new products, patents, and industry trends" in the electronics market for the chemical and materials industries. Covers specialty chemicals, fiber optics, commercialization of existing technology, patents, processes, and business opportunities.

★2262★ International Journal of Purchasing & Materials Management
National Assn. of Purchasing Management
PO Box 22160
Tempe, AZ 85285-2160
Ph: (602)752-6276   Fax: (602)752-7890
Donald W. Dobler C.P.M.
Quarterly. Academic journal covering purchasing and materials management.

★2263★ Journal of the American Ceramic Society
The American Ceramic Society
735 Ceramic Pl.
Westerville, OH 43081-8720
Ph: (614)890-4700   Fax: (614)899-6109
John B. Wachtman
Monthly. Ceramic research journal.

★2264★ Journal of Materials Technology and Performance
ASM International
9639 Kinsman Rd.
Materials Pk, OH 44073
Ph: (216)338-5151   Fax: (216)338-4634
John R. Ogren
Quarterly. Metal/materials engineering trade journal.

★2265★ Material Handling Outlook
Materials Handling and Management Society
8720 Red Oak Blvd., Ste. 224
Charlotte, NC 28217
Ph: (704)525-4667   Fax: (704)558-4753
Pete Youngs
Quarterly. Reflects the aims of the Society, which are to advance the theory and practice of material management and material handling systems in manufacturing, distribution, warehousing, transportation, and health care operations. Recurring features include news of members and Society activities, a calendar of events, and columns by the president and the executive director.

★2266★ Mining and Metallurgical Society of America—Newsletter
Mining and Metallurgical Society of America
9 Escalle Ln.
Larkspur, CA 94939
Ph: (415)924-7441
Robert Crum
Quarterly. Reports Society activities in the areas of conservation of mineral resources, industrial advancement, protection of investors and workers, increasing scientific knowledge of the mineral industries, and encouragement of professional ideals and ethics. Recurring features include news of members and prospective members, news of research, statistics, and obituaries.

★2267★ Technimet Topics
Technimet Corporation
2345 S. 170th St.
New Berlin, WI 53151
Ph: (414)782-6344
Barbara J. Suess
Presents technical articles detailing the use of metallurgical science to solve problems of manufacture or failure of components. Covers subjects such as machinability, weldability, and various failure mechanisms such as fatigue, corrosion, and brittle fracture.

PROFESSIONAL MEETINGS AND CONVENTIONS

★2268★ American Ceramic Society Annual Meeting and Exposition
American Ceramic Society
735 Ceramic Place
Westerville, OH 43081
Ph: (614)794-5877   Fax: (614)899-6109
Annual. **Dates and Locations:** 1995; Indianapolis, IN.

★2269★ Minerals, Metals, and Materials Society Annual Meeting and Exhibition
Minerals, Metals, and Materials Society
420 Commonwealth Dr.
Warrendale, PA 15086
Ph: (412)776-9040   Fax: (412)776-3770
Fr: 800-966-4867
Annual.

OTHER SOURCES OF INFORMATION

★2270★ Financial Aid for Minorities in Engineering & Science
Garrett Park Press
PO Box 190
Garrett Park, MD 20896
Ph: (301)946-2553
1993.

★2271★ GEM: National Consortium for Graduate Degrees for Minorities in Engineering
National Consortium for Graduate Degrees for Minorities in Engineering
PO Box 537
Notre Dame, IN 46556
Ph: (219)287-1097
1988. Describes the graduate fellowship program for minorities in engineering including financial support, application, and internship. Lists universities offering this program.

★2272★ *How to Become a Professional Engineer*
McGraw-Hill, Inc.
1221 Avenue of the Americas
New York, NY 10020
Ph: (212)512-2000   Fr: 800-722-4726
J.D. Constance. Fourth edition, 1987. Describes how to register for the professional engineer's license in all fifty states. Gives a state-by-state list of licensing regulations. Gives advice on how to take the written examination.

★2273★ "Materials Sciences and Engineering" in *Accounting to Zoology: Graduate Fields Defined*
Petersons Guides, Inc.
PO Box 2123
Princeton, NJ 08543-2123
Ph: (609)243-9111   Fax: (609)243-9150
Fr: 800-338-3282
Amy J. Goldstein, editor. Revised and updated, 1987. Defines 298 graduate and professional fields. Discusses types of graduate programs and degrees, graduate research, applied work, employment prospects, and trends.

Mining Engineers

Mining engineers find, extract, and prepare minerals for manufacturing industries to use. They design open pit and underground mines, supervise the construction of mine shafts and tunnels in underground operations, and devise methods for transporting minerals to processing plants. Mining engineers are responsible for the safe and economical operation of mines, including ventilation, water supply, power, communications, and equipment maintenance. With increased emphasis on protecting the environment, many mining engineers have been working to solve problems related to land reclamation and water and air pollution.

Salaries

Starting salaries for engineers with bachelor degrees are significantly higher than starting salaries of college graduates in other fields.

Beginning mining engineers	$31,177/year
Experienced mid-level engineers	$52,500/year
Senior managerial engineers	$102,544/year

Employment Outlook

Growth rate until the year 2005: Little change.

Mining Engineers

★2274★ *Career Development for Engineers and Scientists: Organizational Programs and Individual Choices*
Van Nostrand Reinhold Co., Inc.
115 5th Ave.
New York, NY 10003
Ph: (212)254-3232   Fr: 800-842-3636
Robert F. Morrison and Richard M. Vosburgh. 1987. Includes bibliographies and an index. Illustrated.

★2275★ *Careers and the Engineer*
Bob Adams, Inc.
260 Center St.
Holbrook, MA 02343
Ph: (617)268-9570
Gigi Ranno, editor. Annual.

★2276★ *Careers in Engineering*
National Textbook Co. (NTC)
VGM Career Books
4255 W. Touhy Ave.
Lincolnwood, IL 60646-1975
Ph: (708)679-5500   Fax: (708)679-2494
Fr: 800-323-4900
Geraldine O. Garner, Ph.D., editor. 1993. Career guide covering 14 different engineering specialties.

★2277★ *Careers for Engineers in the Minerals Industry*
Society of Mining Engineers (SME)
PO Box 625002
Littleton, CO 80162
Ph: (303)973-9550
1990. Identifies career options in the minerals industry; describes specific professions and basic educational background required; lists colleges and universities with accredited engineering and engineering technology programs in mineral fields.

★2278★ *The Civilized Engineer*
St. Martin's Press, Inc.
175 5th Ave.
New York, NY 10010
Ph: (212)674-5151   Fax: 800-258-2769
Fr: 800-221-7945
Samuel C. Florman. 1989. Published by Thomas Dunne Books. Discusses engineering education, the relationship between engineers and nontechnical executives, and the role of women in engineering.

★2279★ *"Engineering" in American Almanac of Jobs and Salaries* (pp. 261)
Avon Books
1350 Avenue of the Americas
New York, NY 10019
Ph: (212)261-6800   Fr: 800-238-0658
John Wright, editor. Revised and updated, 1994-95. A comprehensive guide to the wages of hundreds of occupations in a wide variety of industries and organizations.

★2280★ *Engineering Salary Survey*
Source Engineering
1290 Oakmead, Ste. 318
Sunnyvale, CA 94086
Ph: (408)738-8440
Annual. Discusses the structure of the engineering profession, trends, and compensation. Salaries are listed by job function, industry, and years of experience.

★2281★ *Engineering for You: A Career Guide*
Iowa State University Press
2121 S. State Ave.
Ames, IA 50010
Ph: (515)292-0140   Fax: (515)292-3348
John T. Jones. 1991.

★2282★ *Engineering Your Career: Which Way to Turn*
Society of Mining Engineers (SME)
PO Box 625002
Littleton, CO 80162
Ph: (303)973-9550
1987. Contains papers prepared by presenters at the Career Planning Workshop. Topics covered include labor market for mining engineers, job interviewing techniques, and continuing education.

★2283★ *"Mining" in Encyclopedia of Careers and Vocational Guidance* (Vol. 1, pp. 307-314)
J.G. Ferguson Publishing Co.
200 W. Madison St., Ste. 300
Chicago, IL 60606
Ph: (312)580-5480   Fax: (312)580-4948
William E. Hopke, editor-in-chief. Ninth edition, 1993. Four-volume set that profiles 900 occupations and describes job trends in 74 industries. Includes career description, educational requirements, history of the job, methods of entry, advancement, employment outlook, earnings, conditions of work, social and psychological factors, and sources of further information.

★2284★ *Mining Engineer*
Careers, Inc.
PO Box 135
Largo, FL 34649-0135
Ph: (813)584-7333
1995. Two-page occupational summary card describing duties, working conditions, personal qualifications, training, earnings and hours, employment outlook, places of employment, related careers, and where to write for more information.

★2285★ *"Mining Engineer" in VGM's Careers Encyclopedia* (pp. 286-288)
National Textbook Co. (NTC)
VGM Career Books
4255 W. Touhy Ave.
Lincolnwood, IL 60646-1975
Ph: (708)679-5500   Fax: (708)679-2494
Fr: 800-323-4900
Third edition, 1991. Profiles 200 occupations. Describes job duties, places of employment, working conditions, qualifications, education and training, advancement potential, and salary for each occupation.

★2286★ *Mining Engineers*
Chronicle Guidance Publications, Inc.
66 Aurora St.
PO Box 1190
Moravia, NY 13118-1190
Ph: (315)497-0330   Fax: (315)497-3359
Fr: 800-622-7284
1994. Occupational brief describing the nature of the job, working conditions, hours and earnings, education and training, licensure, certification, unions, personal qualifications, social and psychological factors, location,

employment outlook, entry methods, advancement, and related occupations.

★2287★ "Mining Engineers" in *Career Information Center* **(Vol.2)**
Simon and Schuster
200 Old Tappan Rd.
Old Tappan, NJ 07675
Fax: 800-445-6991   Fr: 800-223-2348
Richard Lidz and Linda Perrin, editorial directors. Fifth edition, 1993. A multi-volume set that profiles over 600 occupations. Each occupational profile describes job duties, educational requirements, advancement possibilities, employment outlook, working conditions, earnings and benefits, and where to write for more information.

★2288★ "Mining Engineers" in *Encyclopedia of Careers and Vocational Guidance* **(Vol.3, pp. 450-454)**
J.G. Ferguson Publishing Co.
200 W. Madison St., Ste. 300
Chicago, IL 60606
Ph: (312)580-5480   Fax: (312)580-4948
William E. Hopke, editor-in-chief. Ninth edition, 1993. Four-volume set that profiles 900 occupations and describes job trends in 74 industries. Includes career description, educational requirements, history of the job, methods of entry, advancement, employment outlook, earnings, conditions of work, social and psychological factors, and sources of further information.

★2289★ "Mining Engineers" in *Guide to Federal Jobs* **(p. 165)**
Resource Directories
3361 Executive Pkwy., Ste. 302
Toledo, OH 43606
Ph: (419)536-5353   Fax: (419)536-7056
Fr: 800-274-8515
Rod W. Durgin, editor. Third edition, 1992. Contains information on finding and applying for federal jobs. Describes more than 200 professional and technical jobs for college graduates. Covers the nature of the work, salary, and geographic location. Lists college majors preferred for that occupation. Section one describes the function and work of government agencies that hire the most significant number of college graduates.

★2290★ "Mining Engineers" in *Jobs! What They Are—Where They Are—What They Pay* **(p. 127)**
Simon & Schuster, Inc.
Simon & Schuster Bldg.
1230 Avenue of the Americas
New York, NY 10020
Ph: (212)698-7000   Fr: 800-223-2348
Robert O. Snelling and Anne M. Snelling. 3rd edition, 1992. Describes duties and responsibilities, earnings, employment opportunities, training, and qualifications.

★2291★ "Mining Engineers" in *Occupational Outlook Handbook*
U.S. Government Printing Office
Superintendent of Documents
Washington, DC 20402
Ph: (202)512-1800   Fax: (202)512-2250
Biennial; latest edition, 1994-95. Encyclopedia of careers describing about 250 occupations and comprising about 85 percent of all jobs in the economy. Occupations that re-

quire lengthy education or training are given the most attention. Each occupation's profile describes what the worker does on the job, working conditions, education and training requirements, advancement possibilities, job outlook, earnings, and sources of additional information.

★2292★ *Opportunities in Engineering Technology Careers*
National Textbook Co. (NTC)
VGM Career Books
4255 W. Touhy Ave.
Lincolnwood, IL 60646-1975
Ph: (708)679-5500   Fax: (708)679-2494
Fr: 800-323-4900
John E. Heer and D. Joseph Hagerty. 1987. Describes the many opportunities available for engineering technicians. Explains job duties, educational requirements, salary, working conditions, employment outlook, and advancement opportunities. Lists accredited engineering technology programs.

★2293★ *Peterson's Job Opportunities for Engineering and Technology*
Petersons Guides, Inc.
PO Box 2123
Princeton, NJ 08543-2123
Ph: (609)243-9111   Fax: (609)243-9150
Fr: 800-338-3282
1994. Gives job hunting advice including information on resume writing, interviewing, and handling salary negotiations. Lists companies that hire college graduates in science and engineering at the bachelor and master's level. Companies are indexed by industry, starting location, and major. Company profiles include contact information and types of hires.

★2294★ *Successful Engineering: A Guide to Achieving Your Career Goals*
McGraw-Hill, Inc.
1221 Avenue of the Americas
New York, NY 10020
Ph: (212)512-2000   Fr: 800-722-4726
Lawrence J. Kamm. 1989. Written for the practicing and graduating engineer. Gives advice about working with accountants, the politics of design, and engineering ethics.

PROFESSIONAL ASSOCIATIONS

★2295★ Accreditation Board for Engineering and Technology (ABET)
111 Market Pl., Ste. 1050
Baltimore, MD 21202
Ph: (410)347-7700   Fax: (410)625-2238
Members: Professional societies representing over one million engineers are participating bodies (21); affiliate bodies (5); board of directors has 29 representatives. **Responsible for the quality control of engineering education. Accredits college curricula in engineering, engineering technology, and engineering-related areas. **Publications:** *Accreditation Yearbook*, annual. • *Criteria for Accrediting Programs in Engineering in the United States*, annual. • *Criteria for Accrediting Programs in Engineering Technology*, annual.

★2296★ American Association of Engineering Societies (AAES)
1111 19th St. NW, Ste. 608
Washington, DC 20036
Ph: (202)296-2237   Fax: (202)296-1151
Members: Societies representing over 500,000 engineers. **Purpose:** Works to: advance the knowledge and practice of engineering in the public interest; act as an advisory, communication, and information exchange agency for member activities, especially regarding public policy issues. Conducts studies sponsored by Engineering Manpower Commission. Compiles statistics. **Publications:** *AAES Update*, quarterly. • *Directory of Engineering Societies*, biennial. • *Engineering and Technology Degrees*, annual. • *Engineering and Technology Enrollments*, annual. • *Engineers Salary Survey*, annual. • *The Role of Engineering in Sustainable Development*. • *Who's Who in Engineering*, biennial.

★2297★ American Institute of Engineers (AIE)
4666 San Pablo Dam Rd., No. 8
El Sobrante, CA 94803-3142
Ph: (510)223-8911   Fax: (510)223-3400
Members: Professional engineers and engineering students. **Purpose:** Seeks to advance the professional interests of engineers and scientists. Fosters the interchange of ideas and information among members. Compiles statistics; maintains speakers' bureau. **Publications:** *AIE Newsmagazine*, monthly.

★2298★ National Action Council for Minorities in Engineering (NACME)
3 W. 35th St.
New York, NY 10001
Ph: (212)279-2626   Fax: (212)629-5178
Members: Seeks to increase the number of African American, Hispanic, and Native American students enrolled in and graduating from engineering schools. **Purpose:** Offers incentive grants to engineering schools to recruit and provide financial assistance to increasing numbers of minority students. Works with local, regional, and national support organizations to motivate and encourage precollege students to engage in engineering careers. Conducts educational and research programs; operates project to assist engineering schools in improving the retention and graduation rates of minority students. Maintains speakers' bureau; compiles statistics. **Publications:** *Directory of Pre-College and University Minority Engineering Programs*, periodic. • *Financial Aid Unscrambled: A Guide for Minority Engineering Students*, biennial. • *Gearing Up: How to Start a Pre-College Minority Engineering Program*. • *NACME News*, semiannual. • *NACME Statistical Report*, biennial.

★2299★ National Society of Professional Engineers (NSPE)
1420 King St.
Alexandria, VA 22314
Ph: (703)684-2800   Fax: (703)836-4875
Members: Professional engineers and engineers-in-training in all fields registered in accordance with the laws of states or territories of the U.S. or provinces of Canada; qualified graduate engineers, student members, and

registered land surveyors. Is concerned with social, professional, ethical, and economic considerations of engineering as a profession; encompasses programs in public relations, employment practices, ethical considerations, education, and career guidance. Monitors legislative and regulatory actions of interest to the engineering profession. **Publications:** *Directory of Professional Engineers in Private Practice,* biennial. • *Engineering Times,* monthly. • *PEG Times,* quarterly.

★2300★ Society for Mining, Metallurgy, and Exploration (SME)
PO Box 625002
Littleton, CO 80162-5002
Ph: (303)973-9550   Fax: (303)973-3845
Members: A member society of the American Institute of Mining, Metallurgical and Petroleum Engineers. Persons engaged in the finding, exploitation, treatment, and marketing of all classes of minerals (metal ores, industrial minerals, and solid fuels) except petroleum. **Purpose:** Promotes the arts and sciences connected with the production of useful minerals and metals. Offers specialized education programs; compiles enrollment and graduation statistics from schools offering engineering degrees in mining, mineral, mineral processing/metallurgical, geological, geophysical, and mining technology. Provides placement service and sponsors charitable programs. **Publications:** *Minerals and Metallurgical Processing,* quarterly. • *Mining Engineering,* monthly. • *Transactions,* annual. • *Who's Who in Mineral Engineering,* annual.

★2301★ Society of Women Engineers (SWE)
120 Wall St., 11th Fl.
New York, NY 10005
Ph: (212)509-9577   Fax: (212)509-0224
Members: Educational service society of women engineers; membership is also open to men. **Purpose:** Supplies information on the achievements of women engineers and the opportunities available to them; assists women engineers in preparing for return to active work following temporary retirement. Serves as an informational center on women in engineering. Administers several certificate and scholarship programs. Offers tours and career guidance; conducts surveys. Compiles statistics. **Publications:** *National Survey of Women and Men Engineers.*

STANDARDS/CERTIFICATION AGENCIES

★2302★ Accreditation Board for Engineering and Technology (ABET)
111 Market Pl., Ste. 1050
Baltimore, MD 21202
Ph: (410)347-7700   Fax: (410)625-2238
Is responsible for the quality control of engineering education. Accredits college curricula in engineering, engineering technology, and engineering-related areas.

★2303★ Society of Women Engineers (SWE)
120 Wall St., 11th Fl.
New York, NY 10005
Ph: (212)509-9577   Fax: (212)509-0224
Administers several certificate and scholarship programs. Compiles statistics.

TEST GUIDES

★2304★ Career Examination Series: Engineer
National Learning Corp.
212 Michael Dr.
Syosset, NY 11791
Ph: (516)921-8888   Fax: (516)921-8743
Fr: 800-645-6337
Jack Rudman. A series of study guides with multiple-choice examination questions and solutions for trainees and professional petroleum engineers. Titles in the series include *Administrative Engineer; Chief Engineer; Engineering Aide and Science Assistant; Engineering Aide; Engineering Assistant; Engineering Trainee; Senior Engineer; Senior Engineering Aide.*

★2305★ Engineer-in-Training Exam File
Engineering Press, Inc.
PO Box 1
San Jose, CA 95103-0001
Ph: (408)258-4503   Fax: 800-700-1651
Fr: 800-800-1651
Donald G. Newnan and Dean Newnan. Eleventh edition. 1990. Contains 505 problems with step-by-step solutions. Covers: mathematics; statics; fluid mechanics. Includes an index.

★2306★ Engineering Economic Analysis Exam File
Engineering Press, Inc.
PO Box 1
San Jose, CA 95103-0001
Ph: (408)258-4503   Fax: 800-700-1651
Fr: 800-800-1651
Contains 386 exam problems with step-by-step solutions.

★2307★ Graduate Record Examination: Engineering
National Learning Corp.
212 Michael Dr.
Syosset, NY 11791
Ph: (516)921-8888   Fax: (516)921-8743
Fr: 800-645-6337
Jack Rudman. Multiple-choice test for those seeking admission to graduate school for study in the field of engineering. Includes solutions to examination questions.

★2308★ Graduate Record Examination in Engineering
Arco Publishing Co.
Macmillan General Reference
15 Columbus Cir.
New York, NY 10023
Fax: 800-835-3202   Fr: 800-858-7674
C.W. Tan, et al. First edition. 1988. Contains two sample tests with an explanation to answers.

★2309★ Practicing to Take the GRE Engineering Test: An Official Publication of the GRE Board
Educational Testing Service
Rosedale Rd.
Princeton, NJ 08541
Ph: (609)921-9000
Second edition, 1989. Summarizes the purpose and scope of the Graduate Record Examination Subject Test for engineering. Contains sample questions.

★2310★ Professional Engineer
National Learning Corp.
212 Michael Dr.
Syosset, NY 11791
Ph: (516)921-8888   Fax: (516)921-8743
Fr: 800-645-6337
Jack Rudman. A sample test for engineers who are seeking admission to graduate and professional schools or seeking entrance or advancement in institutional and public career service.

★2311★ Undergraduate Program Field Test: Engineering
National Learning Corp.
212 Michael Dr.
Syosset, NY 11791
Ph: (516)921-8888   Fax: (516)921-8743
Fr: 800-645-6337
Jack Rudman. A practice examination fashioned after tests given in the Regents External Degree Program. Designed to measure knowledge received outside the college classroom in the subject of engineering. Contains multiple-choice questions; provides solutions.

EDUCATIONAL DIRECTORIES AND PROGRAMS

★2312★ ABET Accreditation Yearbook
Accreditation Board for Engineering and Technology
345 E. 47th St., 14th Fl.
New York, NY 10017-2397
Ph: (212)705-7685   Fax: (212)838-8062
Simona C. Mardale, Contact
Annual, September. Covers about 300 U.S. colleges and universities with engineering programs, 242 institutions with programs in engineering technology, and 11 institutions with engineering-related programs accredited by the Board; also lists accredited Canadian programs. Entries include: For United States institutions—Name, year of next full accreditation review, location, program names, year of initial accreditation for each program, coding to indicate degrees offered, format of program (day, night, cooperative, etc.). For Canadian programs—Name, location, names of programs, year of initial accredition for each program. Arrangement: Classified by program area.

★2313★ Environmental Career Directory
Gale Research Inc.
835 Penobscot Bldg.
Detroit, MI 48226-4094
Ph: (313)961-2242   Fax: (313)961-6083
Fr: 800-877-GALE
Bradley J. Morgan and Joseph M. Palmisano. 1993. A directory in the Career Advisor Series that provides essays written by industry professionals; job search information on resume and cover letter preparation, networking, and the interviewing process; approximately 300 companies and organizations offering job opportunities and internships, and additional job-hunting resources.

★2314★ SME Guide to Minerals Schools
Society for Mining, Metallurgy, and
   Exploration Inc. (SME)
PO Box 625002
Littleton, CO 80162-5002
Ph: (303)973-9550   Fax: (303)973-3845
Annual, January. Covers over 50 educational institutions offering programs in geological, geophysical, metallurgical, mineral processing, and mining engineering along with mining engineering technology. Entries include: Institution name; program title; department name, address, phone, fax, electronic mail code; references for admissions information; names and titles of program administrators; name, title, highest degree earned, and teaching specialty for faculty members; enrollment statistics by level and year; degrees offered and special requirements; number of degrees conferred by level and year; contact, address, and phone for job placement assistance. Arrangement: Classified by program area.

Awards, Scholarships, Grants, and Fellowships

★2315★ AIME Distinguished Service Award
American Institute of Mining, Metallurgical
   and Petroleum Engineers
345 E. 47th St., 14th Fl.
New York, NY 10017
Ph: (212)705-7695
For recognition of extraordinary and dedicated service in furtherance of the goals, purposes and traditions of AIME. An engraved plaque is awarded annually at the Annual Meeting of the Institute. Established in 1988.

★2316★ Distinguished Member Award
International Facility Management
   Association
1 E. Greenway Plaza, 11th Fl.
Houston, TX 77046-0194
Ph: (713)623-4362   Fax: (713)623-6124
Fr: 800-359-4362
This, the highest recognition that IFMA gives its members, is given to recognize facility management executives for outstanding contributions to IFMA and the professionalism of facility management. Respected leaders, men and women who ably contribute to IFMA and its affiliated chapters, are considered.

Full-time facility management executives employed in their present position for at least one year, and who are professional or associate members of IFMA for at least the past three years are eligible. Nominations may be submitted. Awards are presented at the annual conference in October. Winners are also profiled in *FMA News*. Established in 1983.

★2317★ Antoine M. Gaudin Award
Society for Mining, Metallurgy, and
   Exploration
PO Box 625002
Littleton, CO 80162-5002
Ph: (303)973-9550   Fax: (303)973-3845
For recognition of specific engineering or scientific achievements that have furthered understanding of the technology of mineral processing. Eligible areas for contributions are agglomeration, classification, comminution, electrical and magnetic separation, flocculation and sedimentation, froth flotation, hydrometallurgy, particulate behavior, and other related mineral processing operations. The deadline for nomination is July 15. A plaque is awarded when merited. Established in 1975.

★2318★ Gold Medal Award
Mining and Metallurgical Society of America
9 Escalle Lane
Larkspur, CA 94939-1217
Ph: (415)924-7441
For recognition of conspicuous professional or public service in the advancement of the science of mining and metallurgy or of economic geology, for the betterment of the conditions under which these industries are carried on, and for the protection of the health and safety of workmen in the mines and in metallurgical establishments. The recipient need not necessarily be a member of the society. Awarded when merited. Established in 1914.

★2319★ Erskine Ramsay Medal
American Institute of Mining, Metallurgical
   and Petroleum Engineers
345 E. 47th St., 14th Fl.
New York, NY 10017
Ph: (212)705-7695
To recognize an individual for distinguished achievement in coal mining including both bituminous coal and anthracite. Awarded annually. Established in 1948.

★2320★ Rocky Mountain Coal Mining Institute Scholarships
Rocky Mountain Coal Mining Institute
   (RMCMI)
3000 Youngfield, No. 324
Lakewood, CO 80215
Ph: (303)238-9099   Fax: (303)238-0509
Purpose: To assist students who have chosen a career in the mining industry. Qualifications: Candidates must be sophomores in good academic standing, U.S. citizens and residents of one of the member states (Arizona, Colorado, Montana, North Dakota, New Mexico, Texas, Utah, and Wyoming), pursuing a degree in a mining-related field or in engineering disciplines such as geology or mineral processing and metallurgy, and have expressed an interest in western coal as a possible career. Selection criteria: Completed application and personal interview. Funds available: Sixteen students from the

Institute's eight member states receive $750 annually. Application details: The RMCMI Scholarship Chairman contacts the various colleges and universities in the member states and request nominations from students and each dean of the mining department. The chairman and the RMCMI state vice president interview the various nominees. The scholarship is presented at the end of the recipient's sophomore year and renewed, upon recommendation from the dean of the college or university involved, at the close of the recipient's junior year. Deadline: February 1.

★2321★ William Lawrence Saunders Gold Medal
Society for Mining, Metallurgy, and
   Exploration
PO Box 625002
Littleton, CO 80162-5002
Ph: (303)973-9550   Fax: (303)973-3845
To recognize distinguished achievement in mining substances other than coal. The term "mining" includes the production of metals as well as nonmetallic minerals. A gold medal and certificate are awarded annually. Established in 1927.

★2322★ WAAIME Scholarship Loans
American Institute of Mining, Metallurgical
   and Petroleum Engineers, Inc. (WAAIME)
Woman's Auxiliary
345 E. 47th St., 14th Fl.
New York, NY 10017
Qualifications: Applicants must be undergraduate students studying for a degree at an accredited United States engineering school in engineering science as applied to industries within the mineral field. These include mining, geology, metallurgy, petroleum, mineral science, materials science, mining economics and other related fields that further the interests of the mineral industry. Scholarship loans also are available for graduate students on the same terms as for undergraduates. These cannot be given to students who have also had an undergraduate grant from WAAIME unless that loan has been repaid. Graduate scholarship loans are limited to two years. Selection criteria: Each applicant is considered on an individual basis by a local Section Scholarship Loan Fund Chairman through personal interviews and research of academic standing, character, need, and personality, and then by the National Scholarship Loan Fund Committee. Preference is given to college juniors and seniors. Funds available: The amount of the scholarship loans is individually determined. Each recipient is expected to repay 50 percent of the monies loaned without interest. Repayment starts after graduation and is to be completed within six years. Application details: Applications should not be sent before the interview. Applications must be accompanied by recent grade transcripts, supporting letters including the personal evaluation by the Section Scholarship Loan Fund Chairman. Deadline: All application material must be in the hands of the Chairman of the National Scholarship Loan Fund Committee by March 15.

★2323★ Young Engineer Award
Society for Mining, Metallurgy, and
  Exploration
PO Box 625002
Littleton, CO 80162-5002
Ph: (303)973-9550   Fax: (303)973-3845
For recognition of engineering professionalism of young people working in the coal industry. SME members under the age of 35 who have prepared a technical report for presentation at any coal industry meeting or publication in any coal industry journal are eligible. The deadline for nominations is July 1. Awarded annually. Established in 1976.

BASIC REFERENCE GUIDES AND HANDBOOKS

★2324★ Introductory Mining Engineering
John Wiley and Sons, Inc.
605 3rd Ave.
New York, NY 10158-0012
Ph: (212)850-6000   Fax: (212)850-6088
Fr: 800-526-5368
Howard L. Hartman. 1987. Covers the fundamentals of mining, mining operations, and surface and underground mining.

PROFESSIONAL AND TRADE PERIODICALS

★2325★ Coal
Maclean Hunter Publishing Co.
29 N. Wacker Drive
Chicago, IL 60606
Ph: (312)726-2802   Fax: (312)726-2574
Art Sandy
Monthly. Coal production magazine.

★2326★ Colorado School of Mines Quarterly
CSM Press
1500 Illinois
Golden, CO 80401
Ph: (303)273-3300   Fax: (303)273-3310
Quarterly. Mineral engineering and earth science magazine.

★2327★ Concentrates
Mining Foundation of the Southwest
PO Box 42317
Tucson, AZ 85733
Ph: (602)622-6257
Monthly. Monitors developments in the mining industry. Provides information on the Club's educational and social events for professionals in the industry. Recurring features include historical items, news of research, notes on members, and a calendar of events.

★2328★ Engineering and Mining Journal
Maclean Hunter Publishing Co.
29 N. Wacker Drive
Chicago, IL 60606
Ph: (312)726-2802   Fax: (312)726-2574
Robert Wyllie
Monthly. Magazine focusing on metal and non-metallic mining.

★2329★ Mine Regulation Reporter
Pasha Publications, Inc.
1616 N. Ft. Myer Dr., Ste. 1000
Arlington, VA 22209
Ph: (703)528-1244   Fax: (703)528-1253
Fr: 800-424-2908
Ellen E. Smith
Biweekly. Presents news of events and court decisions affecting the mining industry. Includes notices of new rules, proposed changes, and fines assessed by state and federal agencies. Carries case summaries listing state agency, issue involved, synopsis of decision, and name and address of counsel. Carries full text of all court decisions affecting mining companies and contracts. Recurring features include an index listing cases by subject.

★2330★ Mining Activity Digest
E&MJ International Directory of Mining
29 N. Wacker Dr.
Chicago, IL 60606
Ph: (312)726-2802   Fax: (312)726-4103
Catherine Henchek
Monthly. Provides updates on mine/plant activity for copper, zinc, gold, and other metals. Supplements the E&MJ International Directory of Mining.

★2331★ Mining and Metallurgical Society of America—Newsletter
Mining and Metallurgical Society of America
9 Escalle Ln.
Larkspur, CA 94939
Ph: (415)924-7441
Robert Crum
Quarterly. Reports Society activities in the areas of conservation of mineral resources, industrial advancement, protection of investors and workers, increasing scientific knowledge of the mineral industries, and encouragement of professional ideals and ethics. Recurring features include news of members and prospective members, news of research, statistics, and obituaries.

★2332★ Productivity Report
Pasha Publications, Inc.
1616 N. Ft. Myer Dr., Ste. 1000
Arlington, VA 22209
Ph: (703)528-1244   Fax: (703)528-1253
Quarterly. Reports mining productivity giving data for individual mines, as well as past performance data.

PROFESSIONAL MEETINGS AND CONVENTIONS

★2333★ MINExpo International
American Mining Congress
1920 N St., NW, Ste. 300
Washington, DC 20036
Ph: (202)861-2800   Fax: (202)861-2821
Fr: 800-296-8890
Every four years. Dates and Locations: 1996 Sep 09-12; Las Vegas, NV. • 2000

★2334★ Northwest Mining Association Convention and Trade Show
ShoWorks, Inc.
702 S. Washington
Spokane, WA 99204-2524
Ph: (509)838-8755   Fax: (509)838-2838
Annual. Always held at the AG Trade Center in Spokane, Washington. Dates and Locations: 1995 Dec 06-08; Spokane, WA. • 1996 Dec 02-06; Spokane, WA.

OTHER SOURCES OF INFORMATION

★2335★ Financial Aid for Minorities in Engineering & Science
Garrett Park Press
PO Box 190
Garrett Park, MD 20896
Ph: (301)946-2553
1993.

★2336★ GEM: National Consortium for Graduate Degrees for Minorities in Engineering
National Consortium for Graduate Degrees for Minorities in Engineering
PO Box 537
Notre Dame, IN 46556
Ph: (219)287-1097
1988. Describes the graduate fellowship program for minorities in engineering including financial support, application, and internship. Lists universities offering this program.

★2337★ How to Become a Professional Engineer
McGraw-Hill, Inc.
1221 Avenue of the Americas
New York, NY 10020
Ph: (212)512-2000   Fr: 800-722-4726
J.D. Constance. Fourth edition, 1987. Describes how to register for the professional engineer's license in all fifty states. Gives a state-by-state list of licensing regulations. Gives advice on how to take the written examination.

★2338★ "Mineral/Mining Engineering"
in *Accounting to Zoology: Graduate*
Fields Defined (pp. 347-348)
Petersons Guides, Inc.
PO Box 2123
Princeton, NJ 08543-2123
Ph: (609)243-9111   Fax: (609)243-9150
Fr: 800-338-3282
Amy J. Goldstein, editor. Revised and updated, 1987. Defines 298 graduate and professional fields. Discusses types of graduate programs and degrees, graduate research, applied work, employment prospects, and trends.

Nuclear Engineers

Nuclear engineers design, develop, monitor, and operate nuclear power plants used to generate electricity and power Navy ships. They also conduct research on nuclear energy and radiation. Some specialize in the development of nuclear weapons; others develop industrial and medical uses for radioactive materials.

Salaries

Starting salaries for engineers with bachelor degrees are significantly higher than starting salaries of college graduates in other fields.

Beginning nuclear engineers	$34,447/year
Experienced mid-level engineers	$52,500/year
Senior managerial engineers	$102,544/year

Employment Outlook

Growth rate until the year 2005: Slower than the average.

Nuclear Engineers

CAREER GUIDES

★2339★ Career Development for Engineers and Scientists: Organizational Programs and Individual Choices
Van Nostrand Reinhold Co., Inc.
115 5th Ave.
New York, NY 10003
Ph: (212)254-3232   Fr: 800-842-3636
Robert F. Morrison and Richard M. Vosburgh. 1987. Includes bibliographies and an index. Illustrated.

★2340★ Careers and the Engineer
Bob Adams, Inc.
260 Center St.
Holbrook, MA 02343
Ph: (617)268-9570
Gigi Ranno, editor. Annual.

★2341★ Careers in Engineering
National Textbook Co. (NTC)
VGM Career Books
4255 W. Touhy Ave.
Lincolnwood, IL 60646-1975
Ph: (708)679-5500   Fax: (708)679-2494
Fr: 800-323-4900
Geraldine O. Garner, Ph.D., editor. 1993. Career guide covering 14 different engineering specialties.

★2342★ The Civilized Engineer
St. Martin's Press, Inc.
175 5th Ave.
New York, NY 10010
Ph: (212)674-5151   Fax: 800-258-2769
Fr: 800-221-7945
Samuel C. Florman. 1989. Published by Thomas Dunne Books. Discusses engineering education, the relationship between engineers and nontechnical executives, and the role of women in engineering.

★2343★ "Engineering" in American Almanac of Jobs and Salaries (pp. 261)
Avon Books
1350 Avenue of the Americas
New York, NY 10019
Ph: (212)261-6800   Fr: 800-238-0658
John Wright, editor. Revised and updated, 1994-95. A comprehensive guide to the wages of hundreds of occupations in a wide variety of industries and organizations.

★2344★ Engineering Salary Survey
Source Engineering
1290 Oakmead, Ste. 318
Sunnyvale, CA 94086
Ph: (408)738-8440
Annual. Discusses the structure of the engineering profession, trends, and compensation. Salaries are listed by job function, industry, and years of experience.

★2345★ Engineering for You: A Career Guide
Iowa State University Press
2121 S. State Ave.
Ames, IA 50010
Ph: (515)292-0140   Fax: (515)292-3348
John T. Jones. 1991.

★2346★ How to Become a Professional Engineer: The Road to Registration
McGraw-Hill, Inc.
1221 Avenue of the Americas
New York, NY 10020
Ph: (212)512-2000   Fr: 800-722-4726
John D. Constance. Fourth edition, 1988. Includes a bibliography and an index.

★2347★ "Nuclear Engineer" in Guide to Federal Jobs (p. 159)
Resource Directories
3361 Executive Pkwy., Ste. 302
Toledo, OH 43606
Ph: (419)536-5353   Fax: (419)536-7056
Fr: 800-274-8515
Rod W. Durgin, editor. Third edition, 1992. Contains information on finding and applying for federal jobs. Describes more than 200 professional and technical jobs for college graduates. Covers the nature of the work, salary, and geographic location. Lists college majors preferred for that occupation. Section one describes the function and work of government agencies that hire the most significant number of college graduates.

★2348★ "Nuclear Engineer" in Jobs Rated Almanac
World Almanac
1 International Blvd., Ste. 444
Mahwah, NJ 07495
Ph: (201)529-6900   Fax: (201)529-6901
Les Krantz. Second edition, 1992. Ranks 250 jobs by environment, salary, outlooks, physical demands, stress, security, travel opportunities, and extra perks. Includes jobs the editor feels are the most common, most interesting, and the most rapidly growing.

★2349★ "Nuclear Engineer" in Opportunities in High-Tech Careers (pp. 120-122)
National Textbook Co. (NTC)
VGM Career Books
4255 W. Touhy Ave.
Lincolnwood, IL 60646-1975
Ph: (708)679-5500   Fax: (708)679-2494
Fr: 800-323-4900
Gary D. Colter and Deborah Yanuck. 1987. Explores high technology careers. Written for the student and displaced worker. Describes job opportunities, how to make a career decision, how to prepare for high-technology jobs, job hunting techniques, and future trends.

★2350★ "Nuclear Engineers" in 101 Careers: A Guide to the Fastest-Growing Opportunities (pp. 92-94)
John Wiley & Sons, Inc.
605 3rd Ave.
New York, NY 10158-0012
Ph: (212)850-6645   Fax: (212)850-6088
Michael Harkavy. 1990. Describes the nature of the job, working conditions, employment growth, qualifications, personal skills, projected salaries, and where to write for more information.

★2351★ "Nuclear Engineers" in Career Discovery Encyclopedia (Vol.4, pp. 124-124)
J.G. Ferguson Publishing Co.
200 W. Madison St., Ste. 300
Chicago, IL 60606
Ph: (312)580-5480   Fax: (312)580-4948
Russell E. Primm, editor-in-chief. 1993. This six volume set contains two-page articles for 504 occupations. Each article describes job duties, earnings, and educational and training requirements. The whole set is arranged al-

phabetically by job title. Designed for junior high and older students.

★2352★ "Nuclear Engineers" in *Encyclopedia of Careers and Vocational Guidance* **(Vol.3, pp. 553-557)**
J.G. Ferguson Publishing Co.
200 W. Madison St., Ste. 300
Chicago, IL 60606
Ph: (312)580-5480   Fax: (312)580-4948
William E. Hopke, editor-in-chief. Ninth edition, 1993. Four-volume set that profiles 900 occupations and describes job trends in 74 industries. Includes career description, educational requirements, history of the job, methods of entry, advancement, employment outlook, earnings, conditions of work, social and psychological factors, and sources of further information.

★2353★ "Nuclear Engineers" in *Jobs! What They Are—Where They Are—What They Pay* **(pp. 128)**
Fireside
Simon & Schuster Bldg.
1230 Avenue of the Americas
New York, NY 10020
Ph: (212)698-7000   Fr: 800-223-2348
Robert O. Snelling and Anne M. Snelling. Revised and updated, 1992. Describes duties and responsibilities, earnings, employment opportunities, training, and qualifications.

★2354★ "Nuclear Engineers" in *Occupational Outlook Handbook*
U.S. Government Printing Office
Superintendent of Documents
Washington, DC 20402
Ph: (202)512-1800   Fax: (202)512-2250
Biennial; latest edition, 1994-95. Encyclopedia of careers describing about 250 occupations and comprising about 85 percent of all jobs in the economy. Occupations that require lengthy education or training are given the most attention. Each occupation's profile describes what the worker does on the job, working conditions, education and training requirements, advancement possibilities, job outlook, earnings, and sources of additional information.

★2355★ *Nuclear Engineers and Scientists*
Careers, Inc.
PO Box 135
Largo, FL 34649-0135
Ph: (813)584-7333
1992. Four-page brief describing duties, working conditions, personal qualifications, training, earnings and hours, employment outlook, places of employment, related careers, and where to write for more information.

★2356★ *Nuclear Power Plant Engineers & Technicians*
Chronicle Guidance Publications, Inc.
66 Aurora St.
PO Box 1190
Moravia, NY 13118-1190
Ph: (315)497-0330   Fax: (315)497-3359
Fr: 800-622-7284
1993. Career brief describing the nature of the job, working conditions, hours and earnings, education and training, licensure, certification, unions, personal qualifications, social

and psychological factors, location, employment outlook, entry methods, advancement, and related occupations.

★2357★ *Opportunities in Engineering Technology Careers*
National Textbook Co. (NTC)
VGM Career Books
4255 W. Touhy Ave.
Lincolnwood, IL 60646-1975
Ph: (708)679-5500   Fax: (708)679-2494
Fr: 800-323-4900
John E. Heer and D. Joseph Hagerty. 1987. Describes the many opportunities available for engineering technicians. Explains job duties, educational requirements, salary, working conditions, employment outlook, and advancement opportunities. Lists accredited engineering technology programs.

★2358★ *Peterson's Job Opportunities for Engineering and Technology*
Petersons Guides, Inc.
PO Box 2123
Princeton, NJ 08543-2123
Ph: (609)243-9111   Fax: (609)243-9150
Fr: 800-338-3282
1994. Gives job hunting advice including information on resume writing, interviewing, and handling salary negotiations. Lists companies that hire college graduates in science and engineering at the bachelor and master's level. Companies are indexed by industry, starting location, and major. Company profiles include contact information and types of hires.

★2359★ *Successful Engineering: A Guide to Achieving Your Career Goals*
McGraw-Hill, Inc.
1221 Avenue of the Americas
New York, NY 10020
Ph: (212)512-2000   Fr: 800-722-4726
Lawrence J. Kamm. 1989. Written for the practicing and graduating engineer. Gives advice about working with accountants, the politics of design, and engineering ethics.

PROFESSIONAL ASSOCIATIONS

★2360★ Accreditation Board for Engineering and Technology (ABET)
111 Market Pl., Ste. 1050
Baltimore, MD 21202
Ph: (410)347-7700   Fax: (410)625-2238
Members: Professional societies representing over one million engineers are participating bodies (21); affiliate bodies (5); board of directors has 29 representatives. Is responsible for the quality control of engineering education. Accredits college curricula in engineering, engineering technology, and engineering-related areas. **Publications:** *Accreditation Yearbook*, annual. • *Criteria for Accrediting Programs in Engineering in the United States*, annual. • *Criteria for Accrediting Programs in Engineering Technology*, annual.

★2361★ American Association of Engineering Societies (AAES)
1111 19th St. NW, Ste. 608
Washington, DC 20036
Ph: (202)296-2237   Fax: (202)296-1151
Members: Societies representing over 500,000 engineers. **Purpose:** Works to: advance the knowledge and practice of engineering in the public interest; act as an advisory, communication, and information exchange agency for member activities, especially regarding public policy issues. Conducts studies sponsored by Engineering Manpower Commission. Compiles statistics. **Publications:** *AAES Update*, quarterly. • *Directory of Engineering Societies*, biennial. • *Engineering and Technology Degrees*, annual. • *Engineering and Technology Enrollments*, annual. • *Engineers Salary Survey*, annual. • *The Role of Engineering in Sustainable Development.* • *Who's Who in Engineering*, biennial.

★2362★ American Institute of Engineers (AIE)
4666 San Pablo Dam Rd., No. 8
El Sobrante, CA 94803-3142
Ph: (510)223-8911   Fax: (510)223-3400
Members: Professional engineers and engineering students. **Purpose:** Seeks to advance the professional interests of engineers and scientists. Fosters the interchange of ideas and information among members. Compiles statistics; maintains speakers' bureau. **Publications:** *AIE Newsmagazine*, monthly.

★2363★ American Nuclear Society (ANS)
555 N. Kensington Ave.
La Grange Park, IL 60525
Ph: (708)352-6611   Fax: (708)352-0499
Members: Physicists, chemists, educators, mathematicians, life scientists, engineers, metallurgists, managers, and administrators with professional experience in nuclear science or nuclear engineering. Works to advance science and engineering in the nuclear industry. **Purpose:** Disseminates information; promotes research; conducts meetings devoted to scientific and technical papers; works with government agencies, educational institutions, and other organizations dealing with nuclear issues. **Publications:** *ANS/DOE Series.* • *ANS News*, monthly. • *ANS Topical Meeting Proceedings*, quarterly. • *Fusion Technology.* • *Nuclear News*, monthly. • *Nuclear Science and Engineering*, monthly. • *Nuclear Standards News*, monthly. • *Nuclear Technology*, monthly. • *Re-actions*, 3/year. • *Transactions*, semiannual.

★2364★ National Action Council for Minorities in Engineering (NACME)
3 W. 35th St.
New York, NY 10001
Ph: (212)279-2626   Fax: (212)629-5178
Members: Seeks to increase the number of African American, Hispanic, and Native American students enrolled in and graduating from engineering schools. **Purpose:** Offers incentive grants to engineering schools to recruit and provide financial assistance to increasing numbers of minority students. Works with local, regional, and national support organizations to motivate and encourage

precollege students to engage in engineering careers. Conducts educational and research programs; operates project to assist engineering schools in improving the retention and graduation rates of minority students. Maintains speakers' bureau; compiles statistics. **Publications:** *Directory of Pre-College and University Minority Engineering Programs*, periodic. • *Financial Aid Unscrambled: A Guide for Minority Engineering Students*, biennial. • *Gearing Up: How to Start a Pre-College Minority Engineering Program.* • *NACME News*, semiannual. • *NACME Statistical Report*, biennial.

★2365★ National Society of Professional Engineers (NSPE)
1420 King St.
Alexandria, VA 22314
Ph: (703)684-2800   Fax: (703)836-4875
Members: Professional engineers and engineers-in-training in all fields registered in accordance with the laws of states or territories of the U.S. or provinces of Canada; qualified graduate engineers, student members, and registered land surveyors. Is concerned with social, professional, ethical, and economic considerations of engineering as a profession; encompasses programs in public relations, employment practices, ethical considerations, education, and career guidance. Monitors legislative and regulatory actions of interest to the engineering profession. **Publications:** *Directory of Professional Engineers in Private Practice*, biennial. • *Engineering Times*, monthly. • *PEG Times*, quarterly.

★2366★ Society of Women Engineers (SWE)
120 Wall St., 11th Fl.
New York, NY 10005
Ph: (212)509-9577   Fax: (212)509-0224
Members: Educational service society of women engineers; membership is also open to men. **Purpose:** Supplies information on the achievements of women engineers and the opportunities available to them; assists women engineers in preparing for return to active work following temporary retirement. Serves as an informational center on women in engineering. Administers several certificate and scholarship programs. Offers tours and career guidance; conducts surveys. Compiles statistics. **Publications:** *National Survey of Women and Men Engineers.*

STANDARDS/CERTIFICATION AGENCIES

★2367★ Accreditation Board for Engineering and Technology (ABET)
111 Market Pl., Ste. 1050
Baltimore, MD 21202
Ph: (410)347-7700   Fax: (410)625-2238
Is responsible for the quality control of engineering education. Accredits college curricula in engineering, engineering technology, and engineering-related areas.

★2368★ Society of Women Engineers (SWE)
120 Wall St., 11th Fl.
New York, NY 10005
Ph: (212)509-9577   Fax: (212)509-0224
Administers several certificate and scholarship programs. Compiles statistics.

TEST GUIDES

★2369★ *Career Examination Series: Engineer*
National Learning Corp.
212 Michael Dr.
Syosset, NY 11791
Ph: (516)921-8888   Fax: (516)921-8743
Fr: 800-645-6337
Jack Rudman. A series of study guides with multiple-choice examination questions and solutions for trainees and professional petroleum engineers. Titles in the series include *Administrative Engineer; Chief Engineer; Engineering Aide and Science Assistant; Engineering Aide; Engineering Assistant; Engineering Trainee; Senior Engineer; Senior Engineering Aide.*

★2370★ *Engineer-in-Training Exam File*
Engineering Press, Inc.
PO Box 1
San Jose, CA 95103-0001
Ph: (408)258-4503   Fax: 800-700-1651
Fr: 800-800-1651
Donald G. Newnan and Dean Newnan. Eleventh edition. 1990. Contains 505 problems with step-by-step solutions. Covers: mathematics; statics; fluid mechanics. Includes an index.

★2371★ *Engineering Economic Analysis Exam File*
Engineering Press, Inc.
PO Box 1
San Jose, CA 95103-0001
Ph: (408)258-4503   Fax: 800-700-1651
Fr: 800-800-1651
Contains 386 exam problems with step-by-step solutions.

★2372★ *Graduate Record Examination: Engineering*
National Learning Corp.
212 Michael Dr.
Syosset, NY 11791
Ph: (516)921-8888   Fax: (516)921-8743
Fr: 800-645-6337
Jack Rudman. Multiple-choice test for those seeking admission to graduate school for study in the field of engineering. Includes solutions to examination questions.

★2373★ *Graduate Record Examination in Engineering*
Arco Publishing Co.
Macmillan General Reference
15 Columbus Cir.
New York, NY 10023
Fax: 800-835-3202   Fr: 800-858-7674
C.W. Tan, et al. First edition. 1988. Contains two sample tests with an explanation to answers.

★2374★ *Practicing to Take the GRE Engineering Test: An Official Publication of the GRE Board*
Educational Testing Service
Rosedale Rd.
Princeton, NJ 08541
Ph: (609)921-9000
Second edition, 1989. Summarizes the purpose and scope of the Graduate Record Examination Subject Test for engineering. Contains sample questions.

★2375★ *Professional Engineer*
National Learning Corp.
212 Michael Dr.
Syosset, NY 11791
Ph: (516)921-8888   Fax: (516)921-8743
Fr: 800-645-6337
Jack Rudman. A sample test for engineers who are seeking admission to graduate and professional schools or seeking entrance or advancement in institutional and public career service.

★2376★ *Undergraduate Program Field Test: Engineering*
National Learning Corp.
212 Michael Dr.
Syosset, NY 11791
Ph: (516)921-8888   Fax: (516)921-8743
Fr: 800-645-6337
Jack Rudman. A practice examination fashioned after tests given in the Regents External Degree Program. Designed to measure knowledge received outside the college classroom in the subject of engineering. Contains multiple-choice questions; provides solutions.

EDUCATIONAL DIRECTORIES AND PROGRAMS

★2377★ *ABET Accreditation Yearbook*
Accreditation Board for Engineering and Technology
345 E. 47th St., 14th Fl.
New York, NY 10017-2397
Ph: (212)705-7685   Fax: (212)838-8062
Simona C. Mardale, Contact
Annual, September. Covers about 300 U.S. colleges and universities with engineering programs, 242 institutions with programs in engineering technology, and 11 institutions with engineering-related programs accredited by the Board; also lists accredited Canadian programs. Entries include: For United States institutions—Name, year of next full accreditation review, location, program names, year of initial accreditation for each program, coding to indicate degrees offered, format of program (day, night, cooperative, etc.). For Canadian programs—Name, location, names of programs, year of initial accredition for each program. Arrangement: Classified by program area.

★2378★ *Environmental Career Directory*
Gale Research Inc.
835 Penobscot Bldg.
Detroit, MI 48226-4094
Ph: (313)961-2242   Fax: (313)961-6083
Fr: 800-877-GALE

Bradley J. Morgan and Joseph M. Palmisano. 1993. A directory in the Career Advisor Series that provides essays written by industry professionals; job search information on resume and cover letter preparation, networking, and the interviewing process; approximately 300 companies and organizations offering job opportunities and internships, and additional job-hunting resources.

AWARDS, SCHOLARSHIPS, GRANTS, AND FELLOWSHIPS

★2379★ ANS Environmental Sciences Division Scholarship
American Nuclear Society
555 North Kensington Ave.
La Grange Park, IL 60525
Ph: (708)352-6611   Fax: (708)352-0499

Qualifications: Applicants must be undergraduate students at an accredited institution in the United States who have completed two or more years in a course of study leading to a degree in nuclear science or nuclear engineering. They must be U.S. citizens or possess permanent resident visas. Funds available: $2,500 scholarship. Application details: Transcript and application form must be submitted. Deadline: March 1.

★2380★ ANS Fuel Cycle and Waste Management Scholarship
American Nuclear Society
555 North Kensington Ave.
La Grange Park, IL 60525
Ph: (708)352-6611   Fax: (708)352-0499

Qualifications: Applicants must be undergraduate students at an accredited institution in the United States who have completed two or more years in a course of study leading to a degree in nuclear science or nuclear engineering. They must be U.S. citizens or possess permanent resident visas. Funds available: $1,000 scholarship. Application details: Transcript and application form must be submitted. Deadline: March 1.

★2381★ ANS Graduate Scholarships
American Nuclear Society
555 North Kensington Ave.
La Grange Park, IL 60525
Ph: (708)352-6611   Fax: (708)352-0499

Qualifications: Candidates must be graduate students at an accredited institution in the United States who are enrolled full-time in a program leading to an advanced degree in nuclear science or nuclear engineering, and must be sponsored by an ANS Local Section, Division, Student Branch, Committee, Member, or Organization Member. More than one They must be U.S. citizens or possess permanent resident visas. Funds available: Seven $3,000 scholarships. Application de-

tails: Transcript and application form must be submitted. Deadline: March 1.

★2382★ ANS Power Division Scholarship
American Nuclear Society
555 North Kensington Ave.
La Grange Park, IL 60525
Ph: (708)352-6611   Fax: (708)352-0499

Qualifications: Applicants must be undergraduate students at an accredited institution in the United States who have completed two or more years in a course of study leading to a degree in nuclear science or nuclear engineering. They must be a U.S. citizen or possess permanent resident visas. Funds available: $2,500 scholarship. Application details: Transcript and application form must be submitted. Deadline: March 1.

★2383★ ANS Reactor Operations Division Scholarship
American Nuclear Society
555 North Kensington Ave.
La Grange Park, IL 60525
Ph: (708)352-6611   Fax: (708)352-0499

Qualifications: Applicants must be undergraduate students at an accredited institution in the United States who have completed two or more years in a course of study leading to a degree in nuclear science or nuclear engineering. They must be U.S. citizens or possess permanent resident visas. Funds available: $1,000 scholarship. Application details: Transcript and application form must be submitted. Deadline: March 1.

★2384★ ANS Undergraduate Scholarships
American Nuclear Society
555 North Kensington Ave.
La Grange Park, IL 60525
Ph: (708)352-6611   Fax: (708)352-0499

Qualifications: Candidates must be undergraduate students at an accredited institution in the United States who have completed one year in a course of study leading to a degree in nuclear science, nuclear engineering, or a nuclear related field. They must be U.S. citizens or possess permanent resident visas. Funds available: Four $1,000 scholarships for sophomores and eleven $2,000 scholarships for students who have completed two or more years and will be entering as juniors or seniors. Application details: Transcript and application form must be submitted. Deadline: March 1.

★2385★ Robert A. Dannels Scholarships
American Nuclear Society
555 North Kensington Ave.
La Grange Park, IL 60525
Ph: (708)352-6611   Fax: (708)352-0499

Qualifications: Applicants must be a graduate students in an accredited institution in the United States who are enrolled full-time in a program leading to an advanced degree in nuclear science or nuclear engineering. They must be U.S. citizens or possess permanent resident visas. Selection criteria: Nominations of handicapped persons is encouraged. Funds available: Seven $4,000 scholarships. Application details: Transcript and application form must be submitted. Deadline: March 1.

★2386★ Verne R. Dapp Scholarship
American Nuclear Society
555 North Kensington Ave.
La Grange Park, IL 60525
Ph: (708)352-6611   Fax: (708)352-0499

Qualifications: Applicants must be graduate students in an accredited institution in the United States who are enrolled full-time in a program leading to an advanced degree in nuclear science or nuclear engineering. They must be U.S. citizens or possess permanent resident visas. Funds available: $2,000 scholarship. Application details: Transcript and application form must be submitted. Deadline: March 1.

★2387★ Joseph R. Dietrich Scholarships
American Nuclear Society
555 North Kensington Ave.
La Grange Park, IL 60525
Ph: (708)352-6611   Fax: (708)352-0499

Qualifications: Applicants must be undergraduate students in an accredited institution in the United States who have completed two or more years in a course of study leading to a degree in nuclear science or nuclear engineering. They must be U.S. citizens or possess permanent resident visas. Funds available: $3,000 scholarship. Application details: Transcript and application form must be submitted. Deadline: March 1.

★2388★ Paul A. Greebler Scholarship
American Nuclear Society
555 North Kensington Ave.
La Grange Park, IL 60525
Ph: (708)352-6611   Fax: (708)352-0499

Qualifications: Applicatns must be undergraduate students at an accredited institution in the United States who have completed two or more years in a course of study leading to a degree in nuclear science or nuclear engineering. They must be U.S. citizens or possess permanent resident visas. Funds available: $3,000 scholarship. Application details: Transcript and application form must be submitted. Deadline: March 1.

★2389★ John R. Lamarsh Scholarship
American Nuclear Society
555 North Kensington Ave.
La Grange Park, IL 60525
Ph: (708)352-6611   Fax: (708)352-0499

Qualifications: Applicants must be undergraduate students at an accredited institution in the United States who have completed two or more years in a course of study leading to a degree in nuclear science or nuclear engineering. They must be U.S. citizens or possess permanent resident visas. Funds available: $3,000 scholarship. Application details: Transcript and application form must be submitted. Deadline: March 1.

★2390★ John and Muriel Landis Scholarships
American Nuclear Society
555 North Kensington Ave.
La Grange Park, IL 60525
Ph: (708)352-6611   Fax: (708)352-0499

Qualifications: Applicants must be United States citizens or permanent residents and undergraduate or graduate students in any U.S. college or university who are planning to pursue a career in nuclear engineering, nuclear science, or a nuclear-related field. They must be sponsored by an ANS local section, division, student branch, committee, member, or organization member. Applicants must have a greater than average financial need or exhibit conditions or experiences that render them disadvantaged, such as poor high school or undergraduate preparation due to family poverty. Qualified high school seniors are also eligible to apply. Selection criteria: Based on financial need. Minorities and women are especially encouraged to apply, although selections are made without regard to race, creed, or gender. Funds available: A maximum of eight $3,000 scholarships. Application details: Application requests should include name of univeristy that will be attended, letter of commitment from that school, status (sophomore, junior) for the next fall semester, and major course of study. Completed applications should include a transcript of grades and a sponsoring organization form. Deadline: March 1.

★2391★ James R. Vogt Scholarship
American Nuclear Society
555 North Kensington Ave.
La Grange Park, IL 60525
Ph: (708)352-6611   Fax: (708)352-0499

Qualifications: Applicants must be undergraduate students at an accredited institution in the United States who are enrolled in or proposing to undertake research in radio-analytical chemistry or analytical applications of nuclear science. They must be U.S. citizens or possess permanent resident visas. Funds available: $3,000 scholarship. Application details: Transcript and application form must be submitted. Deadline: March 1.

BASIC REFERENCE GUIDES AND HANDBOOKS

★2392★ Nuclear Reactor Engineering, Vol. 1: Reactor Design Basics
Van Nostrand Reinhold
115 5th Ave.
New York, NY 10013

Samuel Glasstone and Alexander Sesonske. 1993.

★2393★ Nuclear Reactor Engineering, Vol. 2: Reactor System Engineering
Van Nostrand Reinhold
115 5th Ave.
New York, NY 10013

Samuel Glasstone and Alexander Sesonske. 1993.

PROFESSIONAL AND TRADE PERIODICALS

★2394★ ANS News
American Nuclear Society (ANS)
555 N. Kensington Ave.
La Grange Park, IL 60525
Ph: (708)579-8257   Fax: (708)352-0499
Tara L. Brady

Monthly. Reports on activities of the Society and its professional members, who are dedicated to the advancement of engineering, science, and management relating to the nuclear power industry. Recurring features include a calendar of events and columns titled Reader Views, News About Members, New ANS Members, Public Information/Education, Speakers Corner, Professional Divisions Report, President's Column, and ANS Journal Contents.

★2395★ Fusion Power Report
Business Publishers, Inc.
951 Pershing Dr.
Silver Spring, MD 20910
Ph: (301)587-6300   Fax: (301)587-1081
Fr: 800-274-0122
Thecla R. Fabian

Monthly. Focuses on scientific, engineering, economic, and political developments in the field of fusion energy. Provides concise coverage of significant fusion energy activities and achievement in the U.S. and internationally. Recurring features include a calendar of events, calls for papers, news of research, and the column Contracts & Negotiations.

★2396★ NRMA Newsletter
Nuclear Records Management Association (NRMA)
210 5th Ave.
New York, NY 10010
Ph: (212)683-9221
Rodd S. Excelbert

Quarterly. Covers computer services, nuclear utilities, Nuclear Regulatory Commission and other agency regulations, and other subjects related to records management. Recurring features include Association news, publication notices, news of research, and information on symposia and conferences.

★2397★ Nuclear Reactor Safety
National Technical Information Service (NTIS)
5285 Port Royal Rd.
Springfield, VA 22161
Ph: (703)487-4630

Monthly. Abstracts worldwide technical information on safety-related aspects of reactors.

★2398★ NuclearFuel
Energy and Business Newsletters
1200 G. St. NW, Ste. 1100
Washington, DC 20005
Ph: (202)383-2170   Fax: (202)383-2125
Fr: 800-223-6180
Michael Knapik

Biweekly. Functions as an information service on the nuclear fuel cycle. Discusses regulatory agencies; summarizes reports and studies; and contains analyses and critiques by experts in the field. Covers worldwide uranium exploration, production, and demand; enrichment and fuel fabrication; fuel management; spent fuel storage, reprocessing plutonium, and waste handling.

★2399★ Nucleonics Week
Energy and Business Newsletters
1200 G St. NW, Ste. 1100
Washington, DC 20005
Ph: (202)383-2190   Fax: (202)383-2125
Margaret Ryan

Weekly. Provides an overview of all international developments relating to commercial nuclear power. Offers coverage of plant construction, low-level waste issues, government policies, plant performance, services, and decommissioning, as well as "comprehensive statistical coverage of plant production and the economics of nuclear power." Recurring features include a monthly listing of nuclear power electric generation worldwide.

★2400★ Professional Reactor Operator Society—Communicator
Professional Reactor Operator Society
PO Box 181
Mishicot, WI 54228-0181
Ph: (414)755-2725
Gregory Veith

Quarterly. Acts as a forum for the exchange of information between nuclear reactor operators and government agencies, Congress, and industry in order to promote safety and efficiency in nuclear facilities. Evaluates the educational requirements of operators and the consequences of job stress. Reports on news in the nuclear energy field.

★2401★ Utility Quarterly
American Nuclear Society (ANS)
555 N. Kensington Ave.
La Grange Park, IL 60525
Ph: (708)579-8257   Fax: (708)352-0499
Tara L. Brady

Quarterly. Reports on activities and issues at nuclear power plants.

PROFESSIONAL MEETINGS AND CONVENTIONS

★2402★ Nuclear Science Symposium and Power Systems Exposition
Trade Associates, Inc.
6001 Montrose Rd., Ste. 900
Rockville, MD 20852-1608
Ph: (301)468-3210   Fax: (301)468-3662
Annual.

OTHER SOURCES OF INFORMATION

★2403★ *Financial Aid for Minorities in Engineering & Science*
Garrett Park Press
PO Box 190
Garrett Park, MD 20896
Ph: (301)946-2553
1993.

★2404★ *GEM: National Consortium for Graduate Degrees for Minorities in Engineering*
National Consortium for Graduate Degrees for Minorities in Engineering
PO Box 537
Notre Dame, IN 46556
Ph: (219)287-1097
1988. Describes the graduate fellowship program for minorities in engineering including financial support, application, and internship. Lists universities offering this program.

★2405★ *How to Become a Professional Engineer*
McGraw-Hill, Inc.
1221 Avenue of the Americas
New York, NY 10020
Ph: (212)512-2000   Fr: 800-722-4726
J.D. Constance. Fourth edition, 1987. Describes how to register for the professional engineer's license in all fifty states. Gives a state-by-state list of licensing regulations. Gives advice on how to take the written examination.

★2406★ "Nuclear Engineer" in *Career Selector 2001*
Barron's Educational Series, Inc.
250 Wireless Blvd.
Hauppauge, NY 11788
Ph: (516)434-3311   Fax: (516)434-3723
Fr: 800-645-3476
James C. Gonyea. 1993.

★2407★ "Nuclear Engineering" in *Accounting to Zoology: Graduate Fields Defined* (pp. 364-365)
Petersons Guides, Inc.
PO Box 2123
Princeton, NJ 08543-2123
Ph: (609)243-9111   Fax: (609)243-9150
Fr: 800-338-3282

Amy J. Goldstein, editor. Revised and updated, 1987. Defines 298 graduate and professional fields. Discusses types of graduate programs and degrees, graduate research, applied work, employment prospects, and trends.

Petroleum Engineers

Petroleum engineers explore for and produce oil and gas. Many petroleum engineers plan and supervise drilling operations. If the drilling is successful, petroleum engineers work to achieve the maximum profitable recovery of oil and gas from a petroleum reservoir by determining and developing the most efficient production methods.

Salaries

Starting salaries in private industry for engineers with bachelor degrees are significantly higher than starting salaries of college graduates in other fields.

Beginning petroleum engineers	$40,679/year
Experienced mid-level engineers	$52,500/year
Senior managerial engineers	$102,544/year

Employment Outlook

Growth rate until the year 2005: Decline.

Petroleum Engineers

CAREER GUIDES

★2408★ Career Development for Engineers and Scientists: Organizational Programs and Individual Choices
Van Nostrand Reinhold Co., Inc.
115 5th Ave.
New York, NY 10003
Ph: (212)254-3232   Fr: 800-842-3636
Robert F. Morrison and Richard M. Vosburgh. 1987. Includes bibliographies and an index. Illustrated.

★2409★ Careers and the Engineer
Bob Adams, Inc.
260 Center St.
Holbrook, MA 02343
Ph: (617)268-9570
Gigi Ranno, editor. Annual.

★2410★ Careers in Engineering
National Textbook Co. (NTC)
VGM Career Books
4255 W. Touhy Ave.
Lincolnwood, IL 60646-1975
Ph: (708)679-5500   Fax: (708)679-2494
Fr: 800-323-4900
Geraldine O. Garner, Ph.D., editor. 1993. Career guide covering 14 different engineering specialties.

★2411★ The Civilized Engineer
St. Martin's Press, Inc.
175 5th Ave.
New York, NY 10010
Ph: (212)674-5151   Fax: 800-258-2769
Fr: 800-221-7945
Samuel C. Florman. 1989. Published by Thomas Dunne Books. Discusses engineering education, the relationship between engineers and nontechnical executives, and the role of women in engineering.

★2412★ "Engineering" in American Almanac of Jobs and Salaries (pp. 261)
Avon Books
1350 Avenue of the Americas
New York, NY 10019
Ph: (212)261-6800   Fr: 800-238-0658
John Wright, editor. Revised and updated, 1994-95. A comprehensive guide to the wages of hundreds of occupations in a wide variety of industries and organizations.

★2413★ The Engineering/High-Tech Student's Handbook: Preparing for Careers of the Future
Petersons Guides, Inc.
PO Box 2123
Princeton, NJ 08543-2123
Ph: (609)243-9111   Fax: (609)243-9150
Fr: 800-338-3282
David R. Reyes-Guerra and Alan M. Fischer. 1988. Pamphlet that provides an overview of the engineering profession. Contains information on engineering study opportunities; profiles colleges and universities offering engineering programs.

★2414★ Engineering Salary Survey
Source Engineering
1290 Oakmead, Ste. 318
Sunnyvale, CA 94086
Ph: (408)738-8440
Annual. Discusses the structure of the engineering profession, trends, and compensation. Salaries are listed by job function, industry, and years of experience.

★2415★ Engineering for You: A Career Guide
Iowa State University Press
2121 S. State Ave.
Ames, IA 50010
Ph: (515)292-0140   Fax: (515)292-3348
John T. Jones. 1991.

★2416★ How to Become a Professional Engineer: The Road to Registration
McGraw-Hill, Inc.
1221 Avenue of the Americas
New York, NY 10020
Ph: (212)512-2000   Fr: 800-722-4726
John D. Constance. Fourth edition, 1988. Includes a bibliography and an index.

★2417★ Opportunities in Engineering Technology Careers
National Textbook Co. (NTC)
VGM Career Books
4255 W. Touhy Ave.
Lincolnwood, IL 60646-1975
Ph: (708)679-5500   Fax: (708)679-2494
Fr: 800-323-4900
John E. Heer and D. Joseph Hagerty. 1987. Describes the many opportunities available for engineering technicians. Explains job duties, educational requirements, salary, working conditions, employment outlook, and advancement opportunities. Lists accredited engineering technology programs.

★2418★ Opportunities in Petroleum
National Textbook Co. (NTC)
VGM Career Books
4255 W. Touhy Ave.
Lincolnwood, IL 60646-1975
Ph: (708)679-5500   Fax: (708)679-2494
Fr: 800-323-4900
Gretchen Krueger. Overviews the careers available in finding oil, including geopolitics, drilling and producing oil, and transporting, refining and marketing. Also lists information on salaries, opportunities for advancement, and the employment outlook.

★2419★ Peterson's Job Opportunities for Engineering and Technology
Petersons Guides, Inc.
PO Box 2123
Princeton, NJ 08543-2123
Ph: (609)243-9111   Fax: (609)243-9150
Fr: 800-338-3282
1994. Gives job hunting advice including information on resume writing, interviewing, and handling salary negotiations. Lists companies that hire college graduates in science and engineering at the bachelor and master's level. Companies are indexed by industry, starting location, and major. Company profiles include contact information and types of hires.

★2420★ Petroleum Engineer
Vocational Biographies, Inc.
PO Box 31
Sauk Centre, MN 56378-0031
Ph: (612)352-6516   Fax: (612)352-5546
Fr: 800-255-0752
1994. Four-page pamphlet containing a personal narrative about a worker's job, work likes and dislikes, career path from high school to the present. Education and training, the rewards and frustrations, and the effects of the job on the rest of the worker's life. The data file portion of this pamphlet gives a concise occupational summary, including work descriptions, working conditions, places of employment, personal characteristics, education and training, job outlook, and salary range.

★2421★ "Petroleum Engineer" in *Guide to Federal Jobs* **(p. 166)**
Resource Directories
3361 Executive Pkwy., Ste. 302
Toledo, OH 43606
Ph: (419)536-5353   Fax: (419)536-7056
Fr: 800-274-8515
Rod W. Durgin, editor-in-chief. Third edition, 1992. Contains information on finding and applying for federal jobs. Describes more than 200 professional and technical jobs for college graduates. Covers the nature of the work, salary, and geographic location. Lists college majors preferred for that occupation. Section one describes the function and work of government agencies that hire the most significant number of college graduates.

★2422★ "Petroleum Engineer" in *Jobs Rated Almanac*
World Almanac
1 International Blvd., Ste. 444
Mahwah, NJ 07495
Ph: (201)529-6900   Fax: (201)529-6901
Les Krantz. Second edition, 1992. Ranks 250 jobs by environment, salary, outlooks, physical demands, stress, security, travel opportunities, and extra perks. Includes jobs the editor feels are the most common, most interesting, and the most rapidly growing.

★2423★ "Petroleum Engineer" in *VGM's Careers Encyclopedia* **(pp. 339-341)**
National Textbook Co. (NTC)
VGM Career Books
4255 W. Touhy Ave.
Lincolnwood, IL 60646-1975
Ph: (708)679-5500   Fax: (708)679-2494
Fr: 800-323-4900
Third edition, 1991. Profiles 200 occupations. Describes job duties, places of employment, working conditions, qualifications, education and training, advancement potential, and salary for each occupation.

★2424★ *Petroleum Engineers*
Careers, Inc.
PO Box 135
Largo, FL 34649-0135
Ph: (813)584-7333
1993. Two-page occupational summary card describing duties, working conditions, personal qualifications, training, earnings and hours, employment outlook, places of employment, related careers, and where to write for more information.

★2425★ *Petroleum Engineers*
Chronicle Guidance Publications, Inc.
66 Aurora St.
PO Box 1190
Moravia, NY 13118-1190
Ph: (315)497-0330   Fax: (315)497-3359
Fr: 800-622-7284
1994. Occupational brief describing the nature of the job, working conditions, hours and earnings, education and training, licensure, certification, unions, personal qualifications, social and psychological factors, location, employment outlook, entry methods, advancement, and related occupations.

★2426★ "Petroleum Engineers" in *Career Discovery Encyclopedia* **(Vol.5, pp. 16-17)**
J.G. Ferguson Publishing Co.
200 W. Madison St., Ste. 300
Chicago, IL 60606
Ph: (312)580-5480   Fax: (312)580-4948
Russell E. Primm, editor-in chief. 1993. This six volume set contains two-page articles for 504 occupations. Each article describes job duties, earnings, and educational and training requirements. The whole set is arranged alphabetically by job title. Designed for junior high and older students.

★2427★ "Petroleum Engineers" in *Career Information Center* **(Vol.2)**
Simon and Schuster
200 Old Tappan Rd.
Old Tappan, NJ 07675
Fax: 800-445-6991   Fr: 800-223-2348
Richard Lidz and Linda Perrin, editorial directors. Fifth edition, 1993. A multi-volume set that profiles over 600 occupations. Each occupational profile describes job duties, educational requirements, advancement possibilities, employment outlook, working conditions, earnings and benefits, and where to write for more information.

★2428★ "Petroleum Engineers" in *Encyclopedia of Careers and Vocational Guidance* **(Vol.4, pp. 31-34)**
J.G. Ferguson Publishing Co.
200 W. Madison St., Ste. 300
Chicago, IL 60606
Ph: (312)580-5480   Fax: (312)580-4948
William E. Hopke, editor-in-chief. Ninth edition, 1993. Four-volume set that profiles 900 occupations and describes job trends in 74 industries. Includes career description, educational requirements, history of the job, methods of entry, advancement, employment outlook, earnings, conditions of work, social and psychological factors, and sources of further information.

★2429★ "Petroleum Engineers" in *Jobs! What They Are—Where They Are—What They Pay* **(p. 129)**
Simon & Schuster, Inc.
Simon & Schuster Bldg.
1230 Avenue of the Americas
New York, NY 10020
Ph: (212)698-7000   Fr: 800-223-2348
Robert O. Snelling and Anne M. Snelling. 3rd edition, 1992. Describes duties and responsibilities, earnings, employment opportunities, training, and qualifications.

★2430★ "Petroleum Engineers" in *Occupational Outlook Handbook*
U.S. Government Printing Office
Superintendent of Documents
Washington, DC 20402
Ph: (202)512-1800   Fax: (202)512-2250
Biennial; latest edition, 1994-95. Encyclopedia of careers describing about 250 occupations and comprising about 85 percent of all jobs in the economy. Occupations that require lengthy education or training are given the most attention. Each occupation's profile describes what the worker does on the job, working conditions, education and training requirements, advancement possibilities, job

outlook, earnings, and sources of additional information.

★2431★ *Petroleum Exploration/ Production Occupations*
Careers, Inc.
PO Box 135
Largo, FL 34649-0135
Ph: (813)584-7333
1992. Four-page brief offering the definition, history, duties, working conditions, personal qualifications, educational requirements, earnings, hours, employment outlook, advancement, and careers related to this position.

★2432★ "Petroleum Refining Workers" in *Encyclopedia of Careers and Vocational Guidance* **(Vol.4, pp. 35-39)**
J.G. Ferguson Publishing Co.
200 W. Madison St., Ste. 300
Chicago, IL 60606
Ph: (312)580-5480   Fax: (312)580-4948
William E. Hopke, editor-in-chief. Ninth edition, 1993. Four-volume set that profiles 900 occupations and describes job trends in 74 industries. Includes career description, educational requirements, history of the job, methods of entry, advancement, employment outlook, earnings, conditions of work, social and psychological factors, and sources of further information.

★2433★ *Successful Engineering: A Guide to Achieving Your Career Goals*
McGraw-Hill, Inc.
1221 Avenue of the Americas
New York, NY 10020
Ph: (212)512-2000   Fr: 800-722-4726
Lawrence J. Kamm. 1989. Written for the practicing and graduating engineer. Gives advice about working with accountants, the politics of design, and engineering ethics.

PROFESSIONAL ASSOCIATIONS

★2434★ Accreditation Board for Engineering and Technology (ABET)
111 Market Pl., Ste. 1050
Baltimore, MD 21202
Ph: (410)347-7700   Fax: (410)625-2238
Members: Professional societies representing over one million engineers are participating bodies (21); affiliate bodies (5); board of directors has 29 representatives. Is responsible for the quality control of engineering education. Accredits college curricula in engineering, engineering technology, and engineering-related areas. **Publications:** *Accreditation Yearbook*, annual. • *Criteria for Accrediting Programs in Engineering in the United States*, annual. • *Criteria for Accrediting Programs in Engineering Technology*, annual.

★2435★ Alliance to Save Energy (ASE)
1725 K St. NW, Ste. 509
Washington, DC 20006-1401
Ph: (202)857-0666   Fax: (202)331-9588
Members: Coalition of business, government, environmental, and consumer leaders who seek to increase the efficiency of energy

use. **Purpose:** Conducts research, pilot projects, and educational programs. **Publications:** *Alliance Update*, quarterly.

★2436★ **American Association of Engineering Societies (AAES)**
1111 19th St. NW, Ste. 608
Washington, DC 20036
Ph: (202)296-2237   Fax: (202)296-1151
Members: Societies representing over 500,000 engineers. **Purpose:** Works to: advance the knowledge and practice of engineering in the public interest; act as an advisory, communication, and information exchange agency for member activities, especially regarding public policy issues. Conducts studies sponsored by Engineering Manpower Commission. Compiles statistics. **Publications:** *AAES Update*, quarterly. • *Directory of Engineering Societies*, biennial. • *Engineering and Technology Degrees*, annual. • *Engineering and Technology Enrollments*, annual. • *Engineers Salary Survey*, annual. • *The Role of Engineering in Sustainable Development.* • *Who's Who in Engineering*, biennial.

★2437★ **American Institute of Engineers (AIE)**
4666 San Pablo Dam Rd., No. 8
El Sobrante, CA 94803-3142
Ph: (510)223-8911   Fax: (510)223-3400
Members: Professional engineers and engineering students. **Purpose:** Seeks to advance the professional interests of engineers and scientists. Fosters the interchange of ideas and information among members. Compiles statistics; maintains speakers' bureau. **Publications:** *AIE Newsmagazine*, monthly.

★2438★ **National Action Council for Minorities in Engineering (NACME)**
3 W. 35th St.
New York, NY 10001
Ph: (212)279-2626   Fax: (212)629-5178
Members: Seeks to increase the number of African American, Hispanic, and Native American students enrolled in and graduating from engineering schools. **Purpose:** Offers incentive grants to engineering schools to recruit and provide financial assistance to increasing numbers of minority students. Works with local, regional, and national support organizations to motivate and encourage precollege students to engage in engineering careers. Conducts educational and research programs; operates project to assist engineering schools in improving the retention and graduation rates of minority students. Maintains speakers' bureau; compiles statistics. **Publications:** *Directory of Pre-College and University Minority Engineering Programs*, periodic. • *Financial Aid Unscrambled: A Guide for Minority Engineering Students*, biennial. • *Gearing Up: How to Start a Pre-College Minority Engineering Program.* • *NACME News*, semiannual. • *NACME Statistical Report*, biennial.

★2439★ **National Society of Professional Engineers (NSPE)**
1420 King St.
Alexandria, VA 22314
Ph: (703)684-2800   Fax: (703)836-4875
Members: Professional engineers and engineers-in-training in all fields registered in accordance with the laws of states or territories of the U.S. or provinces of Canada; qualified graduate engineers, student members, and registered land surveyors. Is concerned with social, professional, ethical, and economic considerations of engineering as a profession; encompasses programs in public relations, employment practices, ethical considerations, education, and career guidance. Monitors legislative and regulatory actions of interest to the engineering profession. **Publications:** *Directory of Professional Engineers in Private Practice*, biennial. • *Engineering Times*, monthly. • *PEG Times*, quarterly.

★2440★ **Society for Mining, Metallurgy, and Exploration (SME)**
PO Box 625002
Littleton, CO 80162-5002
Ph: (303)973-9550   Fax: (303)973-3845
Members: A member society of the American Institute of Mining, Metallurgical and Petroleum Engineers. Persons engaged in the finding, exploitation, treatment, and marketing of all classes of minerals (metal ores, industrial minerals, and solid fuels) except petroleum. **Purpose:** Promotes the arts and sciences connected with the production of useful minerals and metals. Offers specialized education programs; compiles enrollment and graduation statistics from schools offering engineering degrees in mining, mineral, mineral processing/metallurgical, geological, geophysical, and mining technology. Provides placement service and sponsors charitable programs. **Publications:** *Minerals and Metallurgical Processing*, quarterly. • *Mining Engineering*, monthly. • *Transactions*, annual. • *Who's Who in Mineral Engineering*, annual.

★2441★ **Society of Petroleum Engineers (SPE)**
PO Box 833836
Richardson, TX 75083-3836
Ph: (214)952-9393   Fax: (214)952-9435
Members: Worldwide professional society of engineers in the field of petroleum engineering. **Purpose:** Conducts videotape courses, continuing education short courses, and distinguished lecturer program; sponsors contests; offers placement service; compiles statistics; maintains speakers' bureau. Conducts charitable programs and offers children's services. **Publications:** *Journal of Petroleum Technology*, monthly. • *SPE Computer Applications*, bimonthly. • *SPE Drilling Engineering*, quarterly. • *SPE Formation Evaluation*, quarterly. • *SPE Production Engineering*, quarterly. • *SPE Reservoir Engineering*, quarterly. • *Transactions*, annual.

★2442★ **Society of Women Engineers (SWE)**
120 Wall St., 11th Fl.
New York, NY 10005
Ph: (212)509-9577   Fax: (212)509-0224
Members: Educational service society of women engineers; membership is also open to men. **Purpose:** Supplies information on the achievements of women engineers and the opportunities available to them; assists women engineers in preparing for return to active work following temporary retirement. Serves as an informational center on women in engineering. Administers several certificate and scholarship programs. Offers tours and career guidance; conducts surveys. Compiles statistics. **Publications:** *National Survey of Women and Men Engineers*.

STANDARDS/CERTIFICATION AGENCIES

★2443★ **Accreditation Board for Engineering and Technology (ABET)**
111 Market Pl., Ste. 1050
Baltimore, MD 21202
Ph: (410)347-7700   Fax: (410)625-2238
Is responsible for the quality control of engineering education. Accredits college curricula in engineering, engineering technology, and engineering-related areas.

★2444★ **Society of Women Engineers (SWE)**
120 Wall St., 11th Fl.
New York, NY 10005
Ph: (212)509-9577   Fax: (212)509-0224
Administers several certificate and scholarship programs. Compiles statistics.

TEST GUIDES

★2445★ *Career Examination Series: Engineer*
National Learning Corp.
212 Michael Dr.
Syosset, NY 11791
Ph: (516)921-8888   Fax: (516)921-8743
Fr: 800-645-6337
Jack Rudman. A series of study guides with multiple-choice examination questions and solutions for trainees and professional petroleum engineers. Titles in the series include *Administrative Engineer; Chief Engineer; Engineering Aide and Science Assistant; Engineering Aide; Engineering Assistant; Engineering Trainee; Senior Engineer; Senior Engineering Aide*.

★2446★ *Engineer-in-Training Exam File*
Engineering Press, Inc.
PO Box 1
San Jose, CA 95103-0001
Ph: (408)258-4503   Fax: 800-700-1651
Fr: 800-800-1651
Donald G. Newnan and Dean Newnan. Eleventh edition. 1990. Contains 505 problems with step-by-step solutions. Covers: mathematics; statics; fluid mechanics. Includes an index.

★2447★ *Engineering Economic Analysis Exam File*
Engineering Press, Inc.
PO Box 1
San Jose, CA 95103-0001
Ph: (408)258-4503   Fax: 800-700-1651
Fr: 800-800-1651
Contains 386 exam problems with step-by-step solutions.

★2448★ Graduate Record Examination: Engineering
National Learning Corp.
212 Michael Dr.
Syosset, NY 11791
Ph: (516)921-8888   Fax: (516)921-8743
Fr: 800-645-6337

Jack Rudman. Multiple-choice test for those seeking admission to graduate school for study in the field of engineering. Includes solutions to examination questions.

★2449★ Graduate Record Examination in Engineering
Arco Publishing Co.
Macmillan General Reference
15 Columbus Cir.
New York, NY 10023
Fax: 800-835-3202   Fr: 800-858-7674

C.W. Tan, et al. First edition. 1988. Contains two sample tests with an explanation to answers.

★2450★ Practicing to Take the GRE Engineering Test: An Official Publication of the GRE Board
Educational Testing Service
Rosedale Rd.
Princeton, NJ 08541
Ph: (609)921-9000

Second edition, 1989. Summarizes the purpose and scope of the Graduate Record Examination Subject Test for engineering. Contains sample questions.

★2451★ Professional Engineer
National Learning Corp.
212 Michael Dr.
Syosset, NY 11791
Ph: (516)921-8888   Fax: (516)921-8743
Fr: 800-645-6337

Jack Rudman. A sample test for engineers who are seeking admission to graduate and professional schools or seeking entrance or advancement in institutional and public career service.

★2452★ Undergraduate Program Field Test: Engineering
National Learning Corp.
212 Michael Dr.
Syosset, NY 11791
Ph: (516)921-8888   Fax: (516)921-8743
Fr: 800-645-6337

Jack Rudman. A practice examination fashioned after tests given in the Regents External Degree Program. Designed to measure knowledge received outside the college classroom in the subject of engineering. Contains multiple-choice questions; provides solutions.

EDUCATIONAL DIRECTORIES AND PROGRAMS

★2453★ ABET Accreditation Yearbook
Accreditation Board for Engineering and Technology
345 E. 47th St., 14th Fl.
New York, NY 10017-2397
Ph: (212)705-7685   Fax: (212)838-8062
Simona C. Mardale, Contact

Annual, September. Covers about 300 U.S. colleges and universities with engineering programs, 242 institutions with programs in engineering technology, and 11 institutions with engineering-related programs accredited by the Board; also lists accredited Canadian programs. Entries include: For United States institutions—Name, year of next full accreditation review, location, program names, year of initial accreditation for each program, coding to indicate degrees offered, format of program (day, night, cooperative, etc.). For Canadian programs—Name, location, names of programs, year of initial accredition for each program. Arrangement: Classified by program area.

★2454★ Environmental Career Directory
Gale Research Inc.
835 Penobscot Bldg.
Detroit, MI 48226-4094
Ph: (313)961-2242   Fax: (313)961-6083
Fr: 800-877-GALE

Bradley J. Morgan and Joseph M. Palmisano. 1993. A directory in the Career Advisor Series that provides essays written by industry professionals; job search information on resume and cover letter preparation, networking, and the interviewing process; approximately 300 companies and organizations offering job opportunities and internships, and additional job-hunting resources.

★2455★ Petroleum Engineering and Technology Schools
Society of Petroleum Engineers
PO Box 833836
Richardson, TX 75083
Ph: (214)952-9393   Fax: (214)952-9435
Fr: 800-456-6863
Kate Aberle, Contact

Annual, December. Covers 97 petroleum engineering schools and petroleum technology schools in the United States and abroad. Entries include: Institution name, address, undergraduate and graduate enrollment, faculty members and their specialties, degrees offered, curriculum description, number of degrees granted, entrance requirements. Arrangement: Geographical within degree levels.

AWARDS, SCHOLARSHIPS, GRANTS, AND FELLOWSHIPS

★2456★ John Franklin Carll Award
Society of Petroleum Engineers
PO Box 833836
Richardson, TX 75083-3836
Ph: (214)952-9393   Fax: (214)952-9435

To honor distinguished achievements that advance petroleum engineering technology or professionalism. Nominations must be submitted by March 15. A bronze plaque, inscribed and mounted on walnut is awarded annually when merited. Established in 1956.

★2457★ DeGolyer Distinguished Service Medal
Society of Petroleum Engineers
PO Box 833836
Richardson, TX 75083-3836
Ph: (214)952-9393   Fax: (214)952-9435

To recognize distinguished service to SPE, the professions of engineering and geology, and the petroleum industry. Individuals who are members of SPE and have at least 15 years of professional experience in the petroleum industry may be nominated by March 15. A silver medal is awarded when merited. Established in 1965.

★2458★ Distinguished Service Award
Society of Petroleum Engineers
PO Box 833836
Richardson, TX 75083-3836
Ph: (214)952-9393   Fax: (214)952-9435

This, the Society's oldest honor, recognizes Society-wide contributions that exhibit such exceptional devotion of time, effort, thought, and action as to set them apart from other contributions to SPE. Members must be nominated by March 15. A walnut and silver-plated plaque is awarded when merited. Established in 1947.

★2459★ Drilling Engineering Award
Society of Petroleum Engineers
PO Box 833836
Richardson, TX 75083-3836
Ph: (214)952-9393   Fax: (214)952-9435

To recognize an individual for outstanding technical achievements in or contributions to the advancement of drilling. Identifiable technical achievements and advances are the primary criteria for selection of recipients. Awarded annually. Established in 1983.

★2460★ Honorary Member
Society of Petroleum Engineers
PO Box 833836
Richardson, TX 75083-3836
Ph: (214)952-9393   Fax: (214)952-9435

This, the highest honor conferred by the Society of Petroleum Engineers, recognizes distinguished scientific or engineering achievement. Members must be nominated by March 15. Awarded when merited. Established in 1960.

★2461★ Anthony F. Lucas Gold Medal
Society of Petroleum Engineers
PO Box 833836
Richardson, TX 75083-3836
Ph: (214)952-9393   Fax: (214)952-9435
This, the Society's major technical award, is given to recognize an individual for distinguished achievement in improving the technique and practice of finding and producing petroleum. Nominations of members and non-members must be submitted by March 15. A gold medal is awarded annually when merited. Established in 1936 by the American Institute of Mining, Metallurgical and Petroleum Engineers.

★2462★ Production Engineering Award
Society of Petroleum Engineers
PO Box 833836
Richardson, TX 75083-3836
Ph: (214)952-9393   Fax: (214)952-9435
To recognize an individual for outstanding technical achievements in or contributions to the advancement of petroleum production. Identifiable technical achievements and advances are the primary criteria for the selection of recipients. Awarded annually. Established in 1983.

★2463★ Reservoir Engineering Award
Society of Petroleum Engineers
PO Box 833836
Richardson, TX 75083-3836
Ph: (214)952-9393   Fax: (214)952-9435
To recognize an individual for outstanding technical achievements in or contributions to the advancement of reservoir engineering. Identifiable technical achievements and advances are the primary criteria for the selection of recipients. Awarded annually. Established in 1983.

★2464★ SPE Distinguished Lecturers
Society of Petroleum Engineers
PO Box 833836
Richardson, TX 75083-3836
Ph: (214)952-9393   Fax: (214)952-9435
To recognize outstanding achievements in petroleum engineering technology. Lecturers are selected annually to present lectures to the Society's sections. Established in 1961.

★2465★ WAAIME Scholarship Loans
American Institute of Mining, Metallurgical and Petroleum Engineers, Inc. (WAAIME) Woman's Auxiliary
345 E. 47th St., 14th Fl.
New York, NY 10017
Qualifications: Applicants must be undergraduate students studying for a degree at an accredited United States engineering school in engineering science as applied to industries within the mineral field. These include mining, geology, metallurgy, petroleum, mineral science, materials science, mining economics and other related fields that further the interests of the mineral industry. Scholarship loans also are available for graduate students on the same terms as for undergraduates. These cannot be given to students who have also had an undergraduate grant from WAAIME unless that loan has been repaid. Graduate scholarship loans are limited to two years. Selection criteria: Each applicant is considered on an individual basis by a local Section Scholarship Loan Fund Chairman through personal interviews and research of academic standing, character, need, and personality, and then by the National Scholarship Loan Fund Committee. Preference is given to college juniors and seniors. Funds available: The amount of the scholarship loans is individually determined. Each recipient is expected to repay 50 percent of the monies loaned without interest. Repayment starts after graduation and is to be completed within six years. Application details: Applications should not be sent before the interview. Applications must be accompanied by recent grade transcripts, supporting letters including the personal evaluation by the Section Scholarship Loan Fund Chairman. Deadline: All application material must be in the hands of the Chairman of the National Scholarship Loan Fund Committee by March 15.

PROFESSIONAL AND TRADE PERIODICALS

★2466★ Improved Recovery Week
Pasha Publications, Inc.
1616 N. Ft. Myer Dr., Ste. 1000
Arlington, VA 22209
Ph: (703)528-1244
Jay Schempt
Weekly. Provides news and information on oil recovery methods and economics.

★2467★ International Oil News— Management Edition
William F. Bland Company
PO Box 16666
Chapel Hill, NC 27516-6666
Ph: (919)490-0700   Fax: (919)490-3002
William F. Bland
Weekly. Covers "timely and significant developments in the international oil business, including exploration, production, transportation, refining, and marketing."

★2468★ International Petroleum Finance
Petroleum Analysis, Ltd.
PO Box 130, FDR Sta.
New York, NY 10150-0130
Ph: (212)755-7484   Fax: (212)750-0189
Dillard P. Spriggs
Semimonthly. Analyzes the profits, finances, and management strategies of publicly and nationally owned companies in the oil industry. Includes OPEC financial developments, loans, borrowing, spending by oil companies, and statistics on stocks, drilling operations, and production.

★2469★ National Petroleum News
Hunter Publishing Ltd. Partnership
950 Lee St.
Des Plaines, IL 60016
Ph: (708)296-0770   Fax: (708)803-3328
Frank M. Victoria
Monthly. Magazine for the oil marketing industry.

★2470★ Petroleum Newsletter
National Safety Council
1121 Spring Lake Dr.
Itasca, IL 60143-3201
Ph: (708)775-2282   Fax: (708)775-2285
Diane A. Ghazarian
Bimonthly. Serves as a medium for the exchange of accident prevention information and techniques for personnel in occupations involving petroleum. Promotes safety awareness, safe practices, and safe products at home, on the road, and on the job.

★2471★ Petroleum Outlook
John S. Herold, Inc.
5 Edgewood Ave.
Greenwich, CT 06830
Ph: (203)869-2585
Randy S. Rose
Monthly. Reports on and analyzes the latest petroleum industry developments for energy investors. Supplies statistics on finding costs, reserves, and prices for a "universe of 50 small oil companies," alternating monthly with similar information on 50 larger companies. Coverage includes petroleum, exploration drilling, and oil industry service companies.

★2472★ PRRC Newsletter
New Mexico Petroleum Recovery Research Center
Campus Sta.
Socorro, NM 87801
Ph: (505)835-5406   Fax: (505)835-6031
F.K. Stanley
Semiannual. Provides news and information on research work conducted at the Center and in New Mexico.

PROFESSIONAL MEETINGS AND CONVENTIONS

★2473★ Society of Petroleum Engineers Department of Energy Improved Oil Recovery Symposium
Society of Petroleum Engineers
PO Box 833836
Richardson, TX 75083-3836
Ph: (214)952-9494   Fax: (214)952-9435
Biennial.

★2474★ Society of Petroleum Engineers Production Operations Symposium
Society of Petroleum Engineers
PO Box 833836
Richardson, TX 75803-3836
Ph: (214)952-9494   Fax: (214)952-9435
Biennial.

OTHER SOURCES OF INFORMATION

★2475★ *Financial Aid for Minorities in Engineering & Science*
Garrett Park Press
PO Box 190
Garrett Park, MD 20896
Ph: (301)946-2553
1993.

★2476★ *GEM: National Consortium for Graduate Degrees for Minorities in Engineering*
National Consortium for Graduate Degrees for Minorities in Engineering
PO Box 537
Notre Dame, IN 46556
Ph: (219)287-1097
1988. Describes the graduate fellowship program for minorities in engineering including financial support, application, and internship. Lists universities offering this program.

★2477★ *How to Become a Professional Engineer*
McGraw-Hill, Inc.
1221 Avenue of the Americas
New York, NY 10020
Ph: (212)512-2000   Fr: 800-722-4726
J.D. Constance. Fourth edition, 1987. Describes how to register for the professional engineer's license in all fifty states. Gives a state-by-state list of licensing regulations. Gives advice on how to take the written examination.

★2478★ *International Petroleum Encyclopedia, 1994*
PennWell Books
PO Box 1260
Tulsa, OK 74101
Ph: (918)835-3161
John C. McCaslin, editor. Annual. Contains articles on petroleum and natural gas production around the world. Includes maps on oil deposits. Describes drilling techniques and use of equipment.

★2479★ *"Petroleum Engineering" in Accounting to Zoology: Graduate Fields Defined* (pp. 348-349)
Petersons Guides, Inc.
PO Box 2123
Princeton, NJ 08543-2123
Ph: (609)243-9111   Fax: (609)243-9150
Fr: 800-338-3282

Amy J. Goldstein, editor. Revised and updated, 1987. Defines 298 graduate and professional fields. Discusses types of graduate programs and degrees, graduate research, applied work, employment prospects, and trends.

Architects

Architects provide a wide variety of professional services to individuals and organizations planning a building project. They may be involved in all phases of development, from the initial discussion of general ideas with the client through construction. Their duties require a variety of skills: design, engineering, managerial, and supervisory. Architects design a wide variety of buildings, such as office and apartment buildings, schools, churches, factories, hospitals, houses, and airport terminals. They also design multi building complexes such as urban centers, college campuses, industrial parks, and entire communities. In addition to designing buildings, architects may advise on the selection of building sites, prepare cost analysis and land-use studies, and do long range planning for land development.

Salaries

Architects who are partners in well established architectural firms or solo practitioners generally earn much more than their salaried employees, but their incomes may fluctuate due to changing business conditions. Earnings for salaried architects are as follows:

Median $36,700/year

Employment Outlook

Growth rate until the year 2005: Average.

Architects

CAREER GUIDES

★2480★ Architect
Careers, Inc.
PO Box 135
Largo, FL 34649-0135
Ph: (813)584-7333

1994. Four-page brief offering the definition, history, duties, working conditions, personal qualifications, educational requirements, earnings, hours, employment outlook, advancement, and careers related to this position.

★2481★ Architect
Vocational Biographies, Inc.
PO Box 31
Sauk Centre, MN 56378-0031
Ph: (612)352-6516   Fax: (612)352-5546
Fr: 800-255-0752

1991. Four-page pamphlet containing a personal narrative about a worker's job, work likes and dislikes, career path from high school to the present. Education and training, the rewards and frustrations, and the effects of the job on the rest of the worker's life. The data file portion of this pamphlet gives a concise occupational summary, including work descriptions, working conditions, places of employment, personal characteristics, education and training, job outlook, and salary range.

★2482★ "Architect" in College Board Guide to Jobs and Career Planning (pp. 200)
The College Board
415 Columbus Ave.
New York, NY 10023-6992
Ph: (212)713-8165   Fax: (212)713-8143
Fr: 800-323-7155

Joyce S. Mitchell. Second edition, 1994. Profiles a variety of careers. Each profile contains information on salaries, related careers, education needed, and sources of additional information.

★2483★ "Architect" in Guide to Federal Jobs (p. 155)
Resource Directories
3361 Executive Pkwy., Ste. 302
Toledo, OH 43606
Ph: (419)536-5353   Fax: (419)536-7056
Fr: 800-274-8515

Rod W. Durgin, editor. Third edition, 1992. Contains information on finding and applying for federal jobs. Describes more than 200 professional and technical jobs for college graduates. Covers the nature of the work, salary, and geographic location. Lists college majors preferred for that occupation. Section one describes the function and work of government agencies that hire the most significant number of college graduates.

★2484★ "Architect" in Jobs Rated Almanac
World Almanac
1 International Blvd., Ste. 444
Mahwah, NJ 07495
Ph: (201)529-6900   Fax: (201)529-6901

Les Krantz. Second edition, 1992. Ranks 250 jobs by environment, salary, outlooks, physical demands, stress, security, travel opportunities, and extra perks. Includes jobs the editor feels are the most common, most interesting, and the most rapidly growing.

★2485★ "Architect" in VGM's Careers Encyclopedia (pp. 46-49)
National Textbook Co. (NTC)
VGM Career Books
4255 W. Touhy Ave.
Lincolnwood, IL 60646-1975
Ph: (708)679-5500   Fax: (708)679-2494
Fr: 800-323-4900

Third edition, 1991. Profiles 200 occupations. Describes job duties, places of employment, working conditions, qualifications, education and training, advancement potential, and salary for each occupation.

★2486★ "Architect" in VGM's Handbook of Business and Management Careers
National Textbook Co.
4255 W. Touhy Ave.
Lincolnwood, IL 60646-1975
Ph: (708)679-5500   Fax: (708)679-2494
Fr: 800-323-4900

Annette Selden. Second edition, 1993. Contains 42 two-page occupational profiles describing job duties, places of employment, working conditions, qualifications, education, employment outlook, and income.

★2487★ Architects
Chronicle Guidance Publications, Inc.
66 Aurora St.
PO Box 1190
Moravia, NY 13118-1190
Ph: (315)497-0330   Fax: (315)497-3359
Fr: 800-622-7284

1994. Career brief describing the nature of the job, working conditions, hours and earnings, education and training, licensure, certification, unions, personal qualifications, social and psychological factors, location, employment outlook, entry methods, advancement, and related occupations.

★2488★ "Architects" in 101 Careers: A Guide to the Fastest-Growing Opportunities (pp. 61-63)
John Wiley & Sons, Inc.
605 3rd Ave.
New York, NY 10158-0012
Ph: (212)850-6645   Fax: (212)850-6088

Michael Harkavy. 1990. Describes the nature of the job, working conditions, employment growth, qualifications, personal skills, projected salaries, and where to write for more information.

★2489★ "Architects" in American Almanac of Jobs and Salaries (pp. 220)
Avon Books
1350 Avenue of the Americas
New York, NY 10019
Ph: (212)261-6800   Fr: 800-238-0658

John Wright, editor. Revised and updated, 1994-95. A comprehensive guide to the wages of hundreds of occupations in a wide variety of industries and organizations.

★2490★ "Architects and Builders" in Opportunities in Real Estate Careers (pp. 112-115)
National Textbook Co. (NTC)
VGM Career Books
4255 W. Touhy Ave.
Lincolnwood, IL 60646-1975
Ph: (708)679-5500   Fax: (708)679-2494
Fr: 800-323-4900

M. Evans. 1988. Gives an overview of the real estate industry. Describes jobs and specialties in the estate field. Lists schools and addresses to write to for more information.

★2491★ "Architects" in *Career Discovery Encyclopedia* (Vol.1, pp. 56-57)
J.G. Ferguson Publishing Co.
200 W. Madison St., Ste. 300
Chicago, IL 60606
Ph: (312)580-5480   Fax: (312)580-4948
Russell E. Primm, editor-in chief. 1993. This six volume set contains two-page articles for 504 occupations. Each article describes job duties, earnings, and educational and training requirements. The whole set is arranged alphabetically by job title. Designed for junior high and older students.

★2492★ "Architects" in *Career Information Center* (Vol.4)
Simon and Schuster
200 Old Tappan Rd.
Old Tappan, NJ 07675
Fax: 800-445-6991   Fr: 800-223-2348
Richard Lidz and Linda Perrin, editorial directors. Fifth edition, 1993. A multi-volume set that profiles more than 600 occupations. Each occupational profile describes job duties, educational requirements, getting a job, advancement possibilities, employment outlook, working conditions, earnings and benefits, and sources of additional information.

★2493★ "Architects" in *Encyclopedia of Careers and Vocational Guidance* (Vol. 2, pp. 94-96)
J.G. Ferguson Publishing Co.
200 W. Madison St., Ste. 300
Chicago, IL 60606
Ph: (312)580-5480   Fax: (312)580-4948
William E. Hopke, editor-in-chief. Ninth edition, 1993. Four-volume set that profiles 900 occupations and describes job trends in 74 industries. Includes career description, educational requirements, history of the job, methods of entry, advancement, employment outlook, earnings, conditions of work, social and psychological factors, and sources of further information.

★2494★ "Architects" in *Jobs! What They Are—Where They Are—What They Pay* (p. 56)
Simon & Schuster, Inc.
Simon & Schuster Bldg.
1230 Avenue of the Americas
New York, NY 10020
Ph: (212)698-7000   Fr: 800-223-2348
Robert O. Snelling and Anne M. Snelling. 3rd edition, 1992. Describes duties and responsibilities, earnings, employment opportunities, training, and qualifications.

★2495★ "Architects" in *Occupational Outlook Handbook*
U.S. Government Printing Office
Superintendent of Documents
Washington, DC 20402
Ph: (202)512-1800   Fax: (202)512-2250
Biennial; latest edition, 1994-95. Encyclopedia of careers describing about 250 occupations and comprising about 85 percent of all jobs in the economy. Occupations that require lengthy education or training are given the most attention. Each occupation's profile describes what the worker does on the job, working conditions, education and training requirements, advancement possibilities, job outlook, earnings, and sources of additional information.

★2496★ "Architecture" in *College Majors and Careers: A Resource Guide to Effective Life Planning* (pp. 19-20)
Garrett Park Press
PO Box 1907
Garrett Park, MD 20896
Ph: (301)946-2553
Paul Phifer. Revised, 1993. Lists 60 college majors, with definitions; related occupations and leisure activities; skills, values, and personal attributesneeded; suggested readings; and a list of associations.

★2497★ "Architecture" in *Exploring Careers in Computer Graphics* (pp. 62-66)
Rosen Publishing Group
29 E. 21st St.
New York, NY 10010
Ph: (212)777-3017   Fax: (212)777-0277
Fr: 800-237-9932
Richard Masterson. 1987. Explores careers in computer graphics, describing educational preparation and job-hunting strategies. Includes information on applications such as CAD/CAM and business. Appendices include a glossary, trade journals, associations, colleges, and a bibliography.

★2498★ "Architecture" in *Liberal Arts Jobs*
Petersons Guides, Inc.
PO Box 2123
Princeton, NJ 08543-2123
Ph: (609)243-9111   Fax: (609)243-9150
Fr: 800-338-3282
Burton Jay Nadler. Second edition, 1989. Strives to help the liberal arts graduate identify skills for entry-level positions. Gives goal setting and job search advice.

★2499★ "Architecture" in *Opportunities in Environmental Careers*
National Textbook Co. (NTC)
VGM Career Books
4255 W. Touhy Ave.
Lincolnwood, IL 60646-1975
Ph: (708)679-5500   Fax: (708)679-2494
Fr: 800-323-4900
Odom Fanning. 1991. Describes a broad range of opportunities in fields such as environmental health, recreation, physics, and hygiene.

★2500★ *Career Opportunities in Art*
Facts on File
460 Park Ave. S.
New York, NY 10016-7382
Ph: (212)683-2244   Fax: 800-678-3633
Fr: 800-322-8755
Susan H. Haubenstock and David Joselit. 1993. Guidebook containing valuable information on obtaining practical employment in 83 art-related fields. Includes contact information for degree programs as well as professional associations. Includes information on jobs in advertising, graphic desing, printmaking, photography, architecture, interior design, textile design, and others.

★2501★ *Career Profile: Architect*
American Institute of Architects (AIA)
1735 New York Ave., NW
Washington, DC 20006
Ph: (202)626-7300
1990. Describes personal qualifications, high school preparation, educational preparation, income, and employment outlook.

★2502★ *Careers in Architecture: A Salary Survey of Architects Working in Settings Other Than Private Practice*
American Institute of Architects (AIA)
Office of International Relations
1735 New York Ave., NW
Washington, DC 20006
Ph: (202)626-7345
1993.

★2503★ *IDP Training Guidelines*
National Council of Architectural Registration Boards (NCARB)
1735 New York Ave., NW, Ste. 700
Washington, DC 20006
Ph: (202)783-6500
Annual. Describes the training standards for the Intern-Architect Development program. Provides information on acquring exposure to architectural practice, areas where exposure should be gained, and how much experience is required to satisfy the IDP training standard for NCARB certification.

★2504★ *Opportunities in Architecture*
National Textbook Co. (NTC)
VGM Career Books
4255 W. Touhy Ave.
Lincolnwood, IL 60646-1975
Ph: (708)679-5500   Fax: (708)679-2494
Fr: 800-323-4900
Robert J. Piper. Revised edition, 1993. Gives an overview of the field of architecture, employment outlook, advancement opportunities, educational requirements, salary, and sources of more information.

★2505★ *Restoration Architect*
Vocational Biographies, Inc.
PO Box 31
Sauk Centre, MN 56378-0031
Ph: (612)352-6516   Fax: (612)352-5546
Fr: 800-255-0752
1994. Four-page pamphlet containing a personal narrative about a worker's job, work likes and dislikes, career path from high school to the present. Education and training, the rewards and frustrations, and the effects of the job on the rest of the worker's life. The data file portion of this pamphlet gives a concise occupational summary, including work descriptions, working conditions, places of employment, personal characteristics, education and training, job outlook, and salary range.

★2506★ *Rules of Conduct*
National Council of Architectural Registration Boards (NCARB)
1735 New York Ave., NW
Washington, DC 20006
Ph: (202)783-6500
Revised, 1993. Describes the rules of conduct enforced by state boards of architectural registration. This edition supersedes all previous editions.

PROFESSIONAL ASSOCIATIONS

★2507★ American Institute of Architects (AIA)
1735 New York Ave. NW
Washington, DC 20006
Ph: (202)626-7300   Fax: (202)626-7421
Members: Professional society of architects: regular members are professional, licensed architects; associate members are graduate architects, not yet licensed; emeritus members are retired architects. **Purpose:** Fosters professionalism and accountability among members through continuing education and training; promotes design excellence by influencing change in the industry. Sponsors educational programs with schools of architecture, graduate students, and elementary and secondary schools; conducts professional development programs. Advises on professional competitions; supplies construction documents. Established the American Architectural Foundation and sponsors Octagon Museum; operates bookstore; stages exhibitions; compiles statistics. Provides monthly news service on design and construction. Operates speakers' bureau, placement services, conducts research programs, charitable activities, and children's services. **Publications:** *American Institute of Architects—Memo*, monthly. • *ARCHITECTURE*, monthly. • *Profile*, annual.

★2508★ Asian American Architects and Engineers
1670 Pine St.
San Francisco, CA 94109
Ph: (415)928-5910   Fax: (415)921-0182
Members: Minorities. **Purpose:** Provides contracts and job opportunities for minorities in the architectural and eningeering fields. Serves as a network for the promotion in professional fields.

★2509★ Association of Collegiate Schools of Architecture (ACSA)
1735 New York Ave. NW
Washington, DC 20006
Ph: (202)785-2324   Fax: (202)628-0448
Members: Full members are architectural schools; affiliate members are foreign schools or schools without professional architectural programs; participating members are individuals. **Publications:** *ACSA News*, 9/year. • *Architecture Schools: Special Programs*, annual. • *Guide to Architecture Schools*, quinquennial. • *Journal of Architectural Education*, quarterly. • *Proceedings of the ACSA Annual Meeting*.

★2510★ Center for Architectural and Design Research
632 Arch St.
Spring City, PA 19475
Ph: (610)948-5787
Purpose: Promotes research and documentation of art and architecture, especially that designed or inspired by Rudolf Steiner and Anthroposophy. Offers consulting services; maintains speakers' bureau.

★2511★ National Organization of Minority Architects (NOMA)
Howard University
School of Architecture and Planning
2366 6th St.
Washington, DC 20059
Members: Purpose: Seeks to increase the number and influence of minority architects by encouraging minority youth and taking an active role in the education of new architects. Works in cooperation with other associations, professionals, and architectural firms to promote the professional advancement of members. Sponsors competitions; offers children's services, educational programs, and charitable programs; maintains speakers' bureau; compiles statistics. **Publications:** *NOMA News*, quarterly. • *Roster of Minority Firms*, periodic.

★2512★ Society of American Registered Architects (SARA)
1245 S. Highland Ave.
Lombard, IL 60148
Ph: (708)932-4622
Members: Architects registered or licensed under the laws of states and territories of the U.S. **Purpose:** Sponsors seminars and professional and student design competitions. Offers placement service. **Publications:** *SARA Membership Directory*, annual. • *SARAScope Newsletter*, bimonthly.

STANDARDS/CERTIFICATION AGENCIES

★2513★ National Council of Architectural Registration Boards (NCARB)
1735 New York Ave. NW, Ste. 700
Washington, DC 20006
Ph: (202)783-6500   Fax: (202)783-0290
Federation of state boards for the registration of architects in the United States, District of Columbia, Puerto Rico, Virgin Islands, Guam, and the Northern Mariana Islands.

TEST GUIDES

★2514★ *Career Examination Series: Architect*
National Learning Corp.
212 Michael Dr.
Syosset, NY 11791
Ph: (516)921-8888   Fax: (516)921-8743
Fr: 800-645-6337
Jack Rudman. A series of study guides with multiple-choice examination questions and solutions for trainees and professional architects. Titles in the series include *Architectural Draftsman; Architectural Specifications Writer; Assistant Architect; Assistant Architectural Draftsman; Senior Architect*.

★2515★ *Licensed Architect: Building Design Examination Primer*
Arcade Publishing
141 5th Ave.
New York, NY 10010
Ph: (212)353-8148
Ken Zinns. Third edition, 1991.

★2516★ *NCARB Architecture Registration Examination Handbook*
National Council of Architectural Registration Boards (NCARB)
1735 New York Ave., NW, Ste. 700
Washington, DC 20006
Ph: (202)783-6500
1990. Published in conjuction with Architectural Record Books.

EDUCATIONAL DIRECTORIES AND PROGRAMS

★2517★ *Architecture Schools: Special Programs*
Association of Collegiate Schools of Architecture, Inc. (ACSA)
1735 New York Ave. NW
Washington, DC 20006
Ph: (202)785-2324   Fax: (202)628-0448
Christine Hess, Project Manager
Annual, March. Covers member academic institutions that offer architectural off-campus study programs, on-campus summer programs, and introductory programs; international coverage. Entries include: School name, address, name and title of contact, geographical area covered, restrictions for admission, programs offered, tuition and fees. Arrangement: Geographical.

★2518★ *Directory of Consultants*
Society of American Archivists
600 S. Federal, Ste. 504
Chicago, IL 60605
Ph: (312)922-0140   Fax: (312)347-1452
Teresa Brinati, Contact
Biennial, odd years. Covers Approximately 48 archivists, 17 conservators and preservation administrators, and 23 manuscript appraisers in the U.S. Entries include: Name, address, phone, fax, e-mail, description of services or areas of specialty. Arrangement: Classified by line of business, then alphabetical.

★2519★ *Guide to Architecture Schools*
Association of Collegiate Schools of Architecture (ACSA)
1735 New York Ave. NW
Washington, DC 20006
Ph: (202)785-2324   Fax: (202)628-0448
Richard McCommons, Executive Director
Irregular, previous edition January 1989; latest edition spring 1994. Covers 120 ACSA member schools and related organizations. Entries include: For schools—Name, address; statistics on the student body; percent of applications accepted; tuition rates; scholarship information; names and specialties of faculty; descriptions of graduate, undergraduate, and special programs; entrance requirements; application deadlines. For orga-

nizations—Contact name, address, phone. Arrangement: Alphabetical.

AWARDS, SCHOLARSHIPS, GRANTS, AND FELLOWSHIPS

★2520★ AHA/American Institute of Architects Fellowships in Health Facilities Design
American Hospital Association (AHA)
One North Franklin
Chicago, IL 60606
Ph: (312)422-3807   Fax: (312)422-4571
Purpose: To encourage research and study related to the architectural design of health care facilities. Qualifications: Candidate must be a U.S. citizen. Applicant must be a graduate-level student in architecture with an interest in the design of health care facilities. Fellowships, which are co-sponsored by the American Institute of Architecture, may be used for graduate study at an accredited school of architecture associated with a school of hospital administration or near hospital resources adequate to supplement prescribed graduate architecture courses in health facilities design. Awards may also be used for independent graduate-level study, research, or design in the health facilities field; or for travel with in-residence research at selected hospitals in a predetermined area. Funds available: $20,000. Application details: Write to AHA for application materials. Deadline: January 15. Awards are announced in March.

★2521★ AIA/American Architectural Foundation Scholarships for Advanced Study or Research
American Institute of Architects (AIA)
Scholarship Program
1735 New York Ave., N.W.
Washington, DC 20006
Ph: (202)626-7511   Fax: (202)626-7364
Purpose: To assist architects with professional degrees who wish to continue their education. Qualifications: Applicant must either be a student currently in the final year of a professional degree program resulting in a B.Arch., M.Arch., or the equivalent; or be a practitioner, intern, educator, or other who has received a professional degree in architecture. Scholarships may be used to pursue a second professional degree in architecture or a closely related field of study. Funds available: $1,000-2,500. Application details: Write to the AIA Scholarship Program for application form and guidelines. Deadline: 15 February. Scholarship winners will be announced in late April.

★2522★ AIA/American Architectural Foundation Scholarships for First Professional Degree Candidates
American Institute of Architects (AIA)
Scholarship Program
1735 New York Ave., N.W.
Washington, DC 20006
Ph: (202)626-7511   Fax: (202)626-7364
Purpose: To assist students who are in professional degree programs in architecture.

Qualifications: Candidate may be of any nationality. Applicant must be enrolled in one of the last two years of a professional degree program in architecture at a school accredited by the National Architectural Accrediting Board or recognized by the Royal Architectural Institute of Canada. Candidate must not have previously received a professional architecture degree. Candidate's application must be screened and endorsed by his/her school. Funds available: $500-2,500. Application details: Application forms are only available from the office of the head of an accredited school of architecture, or through its scholarship committee. The number of application forms is limited; schools screen candidates before selecting those who will receive forms. Submit application to the AIA with letters of recommendation and financial aid form. Deadline: 1 February. Scholarship winners will be announced in late April.

★2523★ American Architectural Foundation Minority/Disadvantaged Scholarship
American Architectural Foundation (AAF)
1735 New York Ave., NW
Washington, DC 20006-5292
Ph: (202)626-7500   Fax: (202)626-7420
Purpose: To financially assist minority and disadvantaged students in their pursual of a professional degree in architecture at schools of architecture accredited by The National Architectural Accrediting Board (NAAB). Qualifications: Qualified applicants are high school seniors, technical school/junior college students transferring to an NAAB school, or college freshmen beginning a program that will lead to either a bachelor's or master's degree. Applicants must be residents of the United States. Students who have completed heir first year of a standard four-year curriculum are not eligible. Funds available: The award amount is determined by the financial need of the student and in cooperation with the scholarship program director and the directors of financial aid at the school. The scholarship is not intended to cover the full cost of education. Twenty scholarships are awarded each year and may be renewed for an additional two years, provided the student remains in good standing at an accredited school of architecture, has continued financial need, and adheres to all program requirements. Application details: Candidates must first submit a nomination in order to receive an application. Suitable nominations may be made by an architect or architectural firm, a local chapter of The American Institute of Architects, a community design center, a guidance counselor or teacher, a dean, department head, or professor from an accredited school of architecture, or a director of a community, civic, or religious organization. Deadline: 1993 nominations were received no later than December 4, 1992, and completed applications were received by January 15, 1993. Finalists are announced in April.

★2524★ Architectural Awards of Excellence
American Institute of Steel Construction
One E. Wacker Dr., Ste. 3100
Chicago, IL 60601-2001
Ph: (312)670-2400   Fax: (312)670-5403
To recognize and applaud designers of steel framed buildings that are outstanding in their

appearance and show imaginative creation. Buildings must be located in the United States and framed with steel produced and fabricated in the United States. A mounted bronze bas relief is presented to the architect, and a certificate is awarded to the structural engineer, fabricator, general contractor, steel erector and owner. Awarded biennially in alternate years with the Prize Bridge Award. Established in 1960.

★2525★ Artists' Fellowship Program
New York Foundation for the Arts
155 6th Ave., No. 14FL
New York, NY 10013-1507
Ph: (212)233-3900   Fax: (212)791-1813
To encourage professional development and to provide fellowships to individual New York State creative artists in the following categories: Architecture, Choreography, Crafts, Fiction, Film, Music Composition, Nonfiction Literature, Painting, Performance Art/Emergent Forms, Photography, Playwriting/Screenwriting, Poetry, Printmaking/Drawing/Artists' Books, Sculpture, and Video. The Program assists eligible New York State artists in their work through direct grants awarded solely on the basis of creative excellence. These awards are not to be considered project support. All applicants to the Artists' Fellowship Program are required to submit a representative body of work to demonstrate professional accomplishment and commitment to a professional career. They must be at least 18 years of age, and must have resided in New York State for the two years immediately prior to application. Graduate or undergraduate matriculated students enrolled in a degree program at the time of application may not apply. No faxed applications are accepted. Fellowships of $7,000 are awarded in some of the categories annually. In 1992, an average of 11 Fellowships were awarded in each of the following categories: Crafts, Film, Nonfiction, Literature, Performance Art/Emergent Forms, Poetry, Printmaking/Drawing/Artists' Books and Sculpture. Established in 1984. The New York Foundation for the Arts also administers four other major statewide programs: (1) The Artists-in-Residence Program, a re-grant program to create artists-in-residence opportunities in educational, cultural, and community organizations; (2) The Artists' New Works Program, a sponsorship program that provides advisory and fiscal services to professional artists who are developing individual projects; and (3) The Revolving Loan Program, a short-term, loan service for nonprofit cultural organizations.

★2526★ Ashworth Fellowship
Municipal Art Society of New York
457 Madison Ave.
New York, NY 10022
Ph: (212)935-3960   Fax: (212)753-1816
To provide an annual opportunity for a college student, recent graduate, or graduate student to complete a project relating to architecture, landscape architecture, urban planning and design, historic preservation, zoning, urban environmental controls, public art, or the history of architecture. Support of the Society's staff and resources, office space in the Urban Center, and a stipend of $2,500 are awarded.

★2527★ Henry Bacon Medal for Memorial Architecture
American Institute of Architects
1735 New York Ave. NW
Washington, DC 20006-5292
Ph: (202)626-7300   Fax: (202)626-7364

To recognize excellence in memorial architecture having no purpose other than to portray, promote, or symbolize an idea of high spiritual concern. Selection is made by the Jury on Institute Honors. The deadline is November 4. Awarded biennially on behalf of the American Architectal Foundation. Established in 1966 in honor of Henry Bacon, the architect who designed the Lincoln Memorial in Washington, D.C.

★2528★ Best in American Living Awards
Professional Builder
1350 E. Touhy Ave.
PO Box 5080
Des Plaines, IL 60018
Ph: (312)635-8800   Fax: (708)635-9950

To recognize the nation's most successful new housing designs for quality design and construction, energy efficiency, and successful market acceptance. Entries may be submitted by June 1 in the following categories: best attached house, best detached house, best one-of-a-kind custom house, and best overall rental project. Awards are presented in January at the National Association of Home BuildersConvention. Winning projects are featured in *Better Homes and Gardens*and *Professional Builder*. Co-sponsored by the National Association of Home Builders and *Better Homes and Gardens*.

★2529★ Arnold W. Brunner Memorial Prize in Architecture
American Academy of Arts and Letters
633 W. 155 St.
New York, NY 10032
Ph: (212)368-5900   Fax: (212)491-4615

For recognition of an architect from any country who contributes to architecture as an art. Applications are not accepted. Nominations are made by members of the Academy. A monetary award of $5,000 is presented annually. Established in 1955 by Mrs. Emma Beatrice Brunner in memory of her husband, Arnold W. Brunner.

★2530★ College of Fellows Grants
American Institute of Architects Foundation
1735 New York Ave. NW
Washington, DC 20006
Ph: (202)626-7563   Fax: (202)626-7364

To advance the understanding and awareness of architecture, both to the general public and the profession; and to provide for significant scholarly research that results in publications, exhibitions, symposia, lectures and conferences. The preservation of architectural records is also considered a high priority. All applications are accepted for review. The deadline for submission of applications is March. A monetary prize is awarded annually in May at the annual convention of AIA. Established in 1963.

★2531★ Gold Medal
American Institute of Architects
1735 New York Ave. NW
Washington, DC 20006-5292
Ph: (202)626-7300   Fax: (202)626-7364

This, the highest honor the Institute can bestow upon an individual, is given in recognition of most distinguished service to the profession or the Institute. Individuals must be nominated by a Board member. Any person, living or dead and not necessarily an architect or an American, that the Board believes is qualified may receive the award. Nominations must be postmarked by May 10. A gold medal is awarded annually. Established in 1907.

★2532★ Graham Foundation Grants
Graham Foundation for Advanced Studies in the Fine Arts
4 West Burton Place
Chicago, IL 60610
Ph: (312)787-4071

Purpose: To support research, independent study, exhibitions, and publications in educational areas directly concerned with architecture and other arts that are immediately contributive to architecture. Qualifications: Candidate may be of any nationality. Grants are not awarded for construction, or for direct scholarship aid. No aid is granted for projects done in pursuit of a degree. Fellowship grants to individuals for independent study normally must have some end objective such as a book or a monograph. Funds available: $10,000 maximum. Application details: There are no application forms. Submit project proposal with resume; budget; work plan and schedule; and specific amount requested. Three letters of reference, evaluating the applicant and the proposed project, should be sent directly from the referees to the Foundation. Deadline: January 15 and July 15. Awards are usually made approximately 120 days after the deadline.

★2533★ Thomas Jefferson Memorial Foundation Medal in Architecture
Thomas Jefferson Memorial Foundation
Monticello Box 316
Charlottesville, VA 22901
Ph: (804)293-2158

To recognize excellence in architecture in the world. Architects, regardless of their nationality, are eligible. An honorarium of $5,000, a medal, and travel expenses to attend the awards ceremony and present a lecture are awarded annually at the University of Virginia. The award is presented on April 13 at an official University ceremony celebrating Thomas Jefferson's birthday. Established in 1966 through the School of Architecture of the University of Virginia.

★2534★ Landscape Architecture Student Competition
National Stone Association
1415 Elliot Pl., NW
Washington, DC 20007-2599
Ph: (202)342-1100   Fax: (202)342-0702

Purpose: To encourage architecture students to become familiar with the unique needs and special circumstances involved in the beautification and reclamation of stone quarries. Qualifications: Applicants must be undergraduate seniors or graduate students enrolled in landscape architecture degree programs at schools located in the United States or Canada. Entries must be based on active or proposed commercial crushed stone operations and can be submitted by individuals or groups of up to three students. Sites that are abandoned or where mining operations have been completed are not eligible for consideration. Selection criteria: Prizes are awarded for projects that make mining sites more usable and visually attractive. Entries are judged on overall excellence in design, creativity, and sensitivity to community needs. Each of the three components are given equal consideration by the judges, who are members of the American Society of Landscape Architects. Funds available: Prizes are split between students and their respective departments of landscape architecture. First prize is $1,000 for the student and $700 for the school. Second prize is $500 for the student and $300 for the school; and third prize is $300 for the student and $200 for the school. Application details: Students must first develop problem statements and then design solutions. Their plans should identify factors important in the siting and design of a mining processing site and describe how the design would mitigate the various impacts. Entries must show a solution containing three distinct components, each presented on a separate foam board that measures 30x40 inches. The three components are: site and operational analysis, which documents existing conditions and the potential assets and liabilities of the site; site improvement and beautification, which includes a plan to reduce the adverse impact of the operating site on the environment and community; and a final use or reclamation plan, to take effect as the site begins to cease operations. Applications should also include a narrative description of the project and an extensive cost analysis. Students should be aware of state and local reclamation, zoning, and safety regulations that may impact upon their project. Candidates are encouraged to research laws that relate to their project and incorporate them into the final proposal. Deadline: In 1993, the preliminary application deadline was April 9; the final entry deadline was May 14.

★2535★ Emily Munson Memorial Student Award
Society of American Registered Architects (SARA)
1245 S. Highland Ave.
Lombard, IL 60148
Ph: (312)932-4622   Fax: (708)495-3054

Purpose: To recognize creative and unusually imaginative architectural designs. Qualifications: Applicants must be attending an NAAB-accredited architectural school and be in their third or fourth year of a Bachelor of Arts or Bachelor of Science architectural program, or be in the third, fourth, or fifth year of a Bachelor of Architecture program. Students must also secure faculty sponsorship. Selection criteria: The jury seeks those submissions that clearly demonstrate a response to typical architectural concepts such as human activity needs, climatic considerations, structural integrity, cultural influences, site planning, creative insight, and coherence of architectural vocabulary. Applicants must show the ability to recognize and resolve situational problems of mechanical and electrical systems, envrionmental context, and external support systems, and to integrate functional aspects of the problem in an appropriate manner. Funds available: Cash prizes vary. In 1992, they were $2,000 (first place), $1,000 (second place), and $500 (third place), plus two special merit awards of $100 each. Deadline: Varies each year, depending on the date of the Society's national convention, where winners are announced.

★2536★ National Endowment for the Arts - Design Arts Program USA Fellowships
National Endowment for the Arts
Visual Arts Program/Fellowships, Rm. 729
Nancy Hanks Center
1100 Pennsylvania Ave., NW
Washington, DC 20506-0001
Ph: (202)682-5422   Fax: (202)682-5699
Purpose: To enable designers and those in design-related professions who have made significant contributions to the design field to travel and study independently within the United States. The grants provide desingers the time and flexibility to explore new concepts, generate fresh ideas, or compile information for a book or study. Qualifications: Fellowships are awarded to professional designers and other qualified individuals working on innovative design projects. They are intended for those for whom a more extensive first-hand knowledge of the American design environment is critical to their work. Eligible fields include architecture, landscape architecture, urban design and planning, historic preservation, interior design, industrial and product design, and graphic design. Applicants must be United States citizens or permanent residents. Selection criteria: The Endowment places a strong emphasis on quality as the first criterion in evaluating applications. Funds available: Fellowships include awards of up to $20,000.

★2537★ Augustus St. Gaudens Medal
Cooper Union for the Advancement of
   Science and Art
30 Cooper Sq.
New York, NY 10003-7120
Ph: (212)353-4164
To recognize professional achievement in art and architecture. A committee evaluates past achievements of the candidates for the award. A medal is presented annually. Established in 1955 and named after one of America's leading sculptors, Augustus St. Gaudens.

★2538★ Society of American Registered Architects Student Design Competition
Society of American Registered Architects
   (SARA)
1245 S. Highland Ave.
Lombard, IL 60148
Ph: (312)932-4622   Fax: (708)495-3054
Qualifications: Competition is open to students who are attending NAAB-accredited architectural schools and are in their third or fourth year of a Bachelor of Arts or Bachelor of Science architectural program. Submissions may be the product of work for a design studio, a technical course, or an independent effort completed since January 1, 1991. Students must also secure the sponsorship of a faculty member. Selection criteria: The jury seeks submissions that clearly demonstrate

a response to typical architectural concepts such as human activity needs, climatic considerations, structural integrity, cultural influences, site planning, creative insight, and coherence of architectural vocabulary. They must also be able to recognize and resolve situational problems of mechanical and electrical systems, environmental context, and external support systems, and to integrate functional aspects of the problem in an appropriate manner. Funds available: First prize is $2,000, second prize is $1,000, and third prize is $500. Winning entries are displayed at the Society of American Registered Architects National Convention. Application details: Applicants must complete and return a registration form, which is available from the Dean's offices or from the Society of American Registered Architects. Submissions may be any medium-sized architectural project other than a single-family home or vacation residence. Faculty and students are encouraged to select design problems pertaining to buildings that are representative of a significant functional type, such as schools, libraries, and museums. Projects must be of sufficient scale and complexity to present an appropriate challenge to design and technical skills. Site information and the original program statement must be clearly communicated as part of the presentation, in detail sufficient to be understood by persons completely unfamiliar with the project. Faculty sponsors must provide a copy of the problem statement. Students must include a concise description of the design problem on the Project Summary Form. Partipants must address the climate conditions consistent with their chosen site. Sites need not be local, but entrants are encouraged to work with site specific conditions. Climatic conditions must be clearly communicated in all cases. Local regulations should be applied to the design problem. Submissions should reflect reasonable regard for the health and safety of occupants. Design drawings are limited to four display boards with sufficient graphics to explain the solution completely. Deadline: September 25. Recipients are announced November 6.

★2539★ Synergy Award
Society of American Registered Architects
1245 S. Highland Ave.
Lombard, IL 60148
Ph: (708)932-4622
To recognize an individual who has performed outstanding service to the architectural profession. A certificate is awarded annually when merited. Established in 1970.

★2540★ Tucker Architectural Awards Competition
Building Stone Institute
PO Box 507
Purdys, NY 10578
Ph: (914)232-5725   Fax: (914)232-5259
To recognize and honor those architectural firms whose excellence in concept and design have contributed significantly to architecture worldwide. Awards are given in the following categories: Category I - a non-residential structure completed within the last 5 years; Category II - a stone structure completed at least 40 years ago and still in use today; Category III - a residential structure completed within the last five years; Category

IV - landscape project in a residential or non-residential site development completed within the last five years; and Category V - a renovation or restoration project completed within the last five years. The program is open to all architects, designers, contractors and others who feel that their projects, or other projects with which they are familiar, have achieved the ideal of excellence and incorporate the use of natural stone. The entry deadline is December 1. Trophies are awarded annually at a special luncheon usually in April. Established in 1977 in memory of Beverley R. Tucker, Jr., a past president of the Institute.

★2541★ William Van Alen International Student Design Competition Prizes
National Institute for Architectural Education
30 West 22nd St.
New York, NY 10010
Ph: (212)924-7000   Fax: (212)366-5836
Purpose: To encourage students to study architecture and undertake international travel. Qualifications: Competitor may be of any nationality. Applicant must be working toward a professional degree in an architectural or engineering school anywhere in the world. Competitor may be a full- or part-time student. Recipients may use the award for study toward the degree, to conduct research of an architectural nature, or to travel to a country other than their own for study or research. Recipients who wish to use the award for travel must begin trip within 18 months of winning competition. Funds available: First prize: $5,000; second prize: $3,000; third prize: $1,500. Application details: Write to NIAE for competition guidelines and registration application form. Or contact dean of home institution for registration materials. Completed forms may be submitted to NIAE anytime before the final entry deadline. After submitting registration form, candidate has eight weeks during which he/she must complete and submit project. Deadline: Mid-May.

★2542★ Lloyd Warren Fellowships/Paris Prize Architectural Design Competition
National Institute for Architectural Education
30 West 22nd St.
New York, NY 10010
Ph: (212)924-7000   Fax: (212)366-5836
Purpose: To encourage creative architectural designs, and to support study and travel by architectural students and recent graduates. Qualifications: Recipients are selected from participants in an annual architectural design competition. Each year NIAE selects a project for which competitors must submit designs. Competitor must be a U.S. permanent resident. Competitor must either have received his/her first professional degree in architecture during the two academic years prior to the competition, or complete the degree by December in the year in which the fellowship is awarded. Competitor's degree must be from a U.S. school of architecture. Recipients must use the award to travel outside of the United States for study or research. Travel must begin within one year of winning competition. Funds available: First prize: $6,000; second prize: $4,000. Application details: Write to NIAE for competition guidelines and registration application form, available between September and March. Or contact dean of home institution for registra-

tion materials. Completed forms may be submitted to NIAE anytime before the final registration deadline. Candidate has two weeks during which he/she must complete and submit project. Deadline: 1 March.

BASIC REFERENCE GUIDES AND HANDBOOKS

★2543★ Architect's Handbook of Professional Practice
American Institute of Architects (AIA)
1735 New York Ave., NW
Washington, DC 20006
Ph: (202)626-7300
David Haviland, editor. 1994. Contains information on the architectural profession and architectural office management. Includes sample business forms.

★2544★ Architectural Programming
Van Nostrand Reinhold
115 5th Ave.
New York, NY 10013
Donna Duerk. 1993.

★2545★ Dictionary of Architecture and Construction
McGraw-Hill, Inc.
1221 Avenue of the Americas
New York, NY 10020
Ph: (212)512-2000   Fr: 800-722-4726
C.M. Harris. Second edition, 1992. Defines terms in architecture and the building trades used from medieval times to the present. Lists materials, structures, and equipment used in construction.

★2546★ Encyclopedia of Architecture: Design, Engineering, and Construction
John Wiley and Sons, Inc.
605 3rd Ave.
New York, NY 10158-0012
Ph: (212)850-6000   Fax: (212)850-6088
Fr: 800-526-5368
Joseph A. Wilkes, editor in chief. 1990. Covers architectural processes, technology, history, aesthetics, and biographical information.

★2547★ Encyclopedia of Building Technology
Prentice-Hall, Inc.
Rte. 9W
Englewood Cliffs, NJ 07632
Ph: (201)592-2000
Henry J. Cowan, editor. 1988. Includes bibliographies and indexes.

★2548★ Uniform Building Code Standards
International Conference of Building Officials (ICBO)
5360 S. Workman Mill Rd.
Whittier, CA 90601
Ph: (310)699-0541
1994. Contains all the standard specifications referred to in the Uniform Building Code.

PROFESSIONAL AND TRADE PERIODICALS

★2549★ American Institute of Architects—Memo
American Institute of Architects (AIA)
1735 New York Ave. NW
Washington, DC 20006
Ph: (202)626-7439   Fax: (202)626-7365
Stephanie Stubbs
Monthly. Concerned with the architectural profession. Discusses business and legislative trends, practice and design information, and AIA activities. Recurring features include news of members and a calendar of events.

★2550★ Architectural Digest
Knapp Communications Corp.
6300 Wilshire Blvd.
Los Angeles, CA 90048
Ph: (213)965-3700   Fax: (213)937-1458
Thomas P. LoseePublisher
Monthly. Magazine on interior design, art, and antiques.

★2551★ Architectural Record
McGraw-Hill, Inc.
1221 Avenue of the Americas
New York, NY 10020
Ph: (212)512-4686   Fax: (212)512-4256
Magazine focusing on architecture.

★2552★ Architecture
Billboard Magazine
33 Commercial St.
Gloucester, MA 01930
Ph: (508)281-3110   Fax: (508)281-0136
Monthly. Official publication of the American Institute of Architects. For architects, interior designers, engineers, and architectural students.

★2553★ Building Industry Technology: An Abstract Newsletter
National Technical Information Service (NTIS)
5285 Port Royal Rd.
Springfield, VA 22161
Ph: (703)487-4630
Biweekly. Consists of abstracts of reports on architectural and environmental design, building standards, construction materials and equipment, and structural analyses. Recurring features include a form for ordering reports from NTIS.

★2554★ Design Quarterly
MIT Press Journals
55 Hayward St.
Cambridge, MA 02142
Ph: (617)253-2889   Fax: (617)258-6779
Martin Filler
Quarterly. Journal covering architecture, design, and contemporary graphics.

★2555★ Progressive Architecture
P/A 600 Summer St.
Stamford, CT 06904
Ph: (203)348-7531   Fax: (203)348-4023
Monthly. National magazine on architecture, interior designs, and planning.

PROFESSIONAL MEETINGS AND CONVENTIONS

★2556★ American Institute of Architects Convention and Upper Midwest Regional Building and Design Exhibition
American Institute of Architects-Minnesota
275 Market St., Ste. 54
Minneapolis, MN 55405
Ph: (612)338-6763   Fax: (612)338-7981
Annual. Always held during October at the Convention Center in Minneapolis, Minnesota. **Dates and Locations:** 1995; Minneapolis, MN.

★2557★ American Institute of Architects National Convention and Exposition of New Products, Technology, and Design
American Institute of Architects
1735 New York Ave., NW
Washington, DC 20006
Ph: (202)626-7395   Fax: (202)626-7518
Annual. **Dates and Locations:** 1996 May 10-12; Minneapolis, MN.

★2558★ Architectural Woodwork Institute Annual Trade Show and Convention
Architectural Woodwork Institute
13924 Braddock Rd.
Centreville, VA 22020
Ph: (703)222-1100   Fax: (703)222-2499
Annual. **Dates and Locations:** 1995 Oct 12-14; New Orleans, LA.

★2559★ Design Professionals Annual Convention and Products Show/Louisiana Architects Association/American Society of Interior Design
Louisiana Architects Association
521 America St.
Baton Rouge, LA 70802
Ph: (504)387-5579   Fax: (504)387-2743
Annual. **Dates and Locations:** 1995 Oct 19-21; Kenner, LA.

OTHER SOURCES OF INFORMATION

★2560★ American Institute of Architects Scholarship Programs 1989
American Institute of Architects (AIA)
1735 New York Ave., NW
Washington, DC 20006
Ph: (202)626-7345
1989. Describes eligibility requirements, application procedures, deadlines, and duration of the scholarship for undergraduates, graduates and professionals.

★2561★ "Architect" in *100 Best Jobs for the 1990s & Beyond*
Dearborn Financial Publishing, Inc.
520 N. Dearborn St.
Chicago, IL 60610-4354
Ph: (312)836-4400   Fax: (312)836-1021
Fr: 800-621-9621

Carol Kleiman. 1992. Describes 100 jobs ranging from accountants to veterinarians.. Each job profile includes such information as education, experience, and certification needed, salaries, and job search suggestions.

★2562★ "Architect" in *Career Selector 2001*
Barron's Educational Series, Inc.
250 Wireless Blvd.
Hauppauge, NY 11788
Ph: (516)434-3311   Fax: (516)434-3723
Fr: 800-645-3476

James C. Gonyea. 1993.

★2563★ "Architecture" in *Accounting to Zoology: Graduate Fields Defined* (pp. 12-13)
Petersons Guides, Inc.
PO Box 2123
Princeton, NJ 08543-2123
Ph: (609)243-9111   Fax: (609)243-9150
Fr: 800-338-3282

Amy J. Goldstein, editor. Revised and updated, 1987. Defines 298 graduate and professional fields. Discusses types of graduate programs and degrees, graduate research, applied work, employment prospects, and trends.

★2564★ *The Complete Illustration Guide For Architects, Designers, Artists, and Students*
Van Nostrand Reinhold
115 5th Ave.
New York, NY 10013

Larry Evans. 1993.

★2565★ *The Practice of Architecture as It Differs From the Practice of Engineering*
National Council of Architectural Registration Boards (NCARB)
1735 New York Ave., NW
Washington, DC 20006
Ph: (202)783-6500

1987. Compares the education, training, and professional examination of architects with civil, mechanical, and electrical engineers.

★2566★ *Success Strategies for Design Professionals: Superpositioning for Architecture and Engineering Firms*
McGraw-Hill, Inc.
1221 Avenue of the Americas
New York, NY 10020
Ph: (212)512-2000

W. Coxe and D.H. Maister. 1987. Suggests methods to achieve financial success in the field of design.

Landscape Architects

Landscape architects design areas so that they are not only functional, but beautiful and environmentally appropriate as well. They may plan the location of buildings, roads, and walkways and the arrangement of flowers, shrubs, and trees. They also may redesign streets to limit automobile traffic and to improve pedestrian access and safety. Natural resource conservation and historic preservation are other important objectives to which landscape architects may apply their knowledge of the environment as well as their design and artistic talents.

Salaries

Salaries for landscape architects vary by location, experience, and size of firm.

Beginning landscape architects with bachelor's degrees	$20,400/year
Beginning landscape architects with master's degrees	$30,600/year
Experienced landscape architects	$41,900/year
Landscape architects, federal government	$46,855/year

Employment Outlook

Growth rate until the year 2005: Average.

Landscape Architects

CAREER GUIDES

★2567★ Architect, Landscape
Careers, Inc.
PO Box 135
Largo, FL 34649-0135
Ph: (813)584-7333
1994. Two-page occupational summary card describing duties, working conditions, personal qualifications, training, earnings and hours, employment outlook, places of employment, related careers, and where to write for more information.

★2568★ Between People and Nature: The Profession of Landscape Architecture
American Society of Landscape Architects (ASLA)
4401 Connecticut Ave., NW, 5th Fl.
Washington, DC 20008
Ph: (202)686-2752
1991. Describes the field of landscape architecture, educational preparation, and employment and earnings.

★2569★ "Landscape Architect" in College Board Guide to Jobs and Career Planning (pp. 208-209)
The College Board
45 Columbus Ave.
New York, NY 10023-6992
Ph: (212)713-8165   Fax: (212)713-8143
Fr: 800-323-7155
Second edition, 1994. Describes the job, salaries, related careers, education needed, and where to write for more information.

★2570★ "Landscape Architect" in Desk Guide to Training and Work Advisement (p. 57)
Charles C. Thomas, Publisher
2600 S. 1st St.
Springfield, IL 62794-9265
Ph: (217)789-8980   Fax: (217)789-9130
Fr: 800-258-8980
Gail Baugher Keunstler. 1988. Describes alternative methods of gaining entry into an occupation through different types of educational programs, internships, and apprenticeships.

★2571★ "Landscape Architect" in Guide to Federal Jobs (p. 154)
Resource Directories
3361 Executive Pkwy., Ste. 302
Toledo, OH 43606
Ph: (419)536-5353   Fax: (419)536-7056
Fr: 800-274-8515
Rod W. Durgin, editor. Third edition, 1992. Contains information on finding and applying for federal jobs. Describes more than 200 professional and technical jobs for college graduates. Covers the nature of the work, salary, and geographic location. Lists college majors preferred for that occupation. Section one describes the function and work of government agencies that hire the most significant number of college graduates.

★2572★ "Landscape Architect" in Museum Jobs form A-Z: What They Are, How to Prepare, and Where to Find Them
Batax Museum Publishing
301 Racquet Club Rd., Ste. 202
Fort Lauderdale, FL 33326
G.W. Bates. 1994.

★2573★ "Landscape Architect" in Opportunities in Environmental Careers
National Textbook Co. (NTC)
VGM Career Books
4255 W. Touhy Ave.
Lincolnwood, IL 60646-1975
Ph: (708)679-5500   Fax: (708)679-2494
Fr: 800-323-4900
Odom Fanning. 1991. Describes a broad range of opportunities in fields such as environmental health, recreation, physics, and hygiene.

★2574★ "Landscape Architect" in Opportunities in Real Estate Careers (pp. 110-111)
National Textbook Co. (NTC)
VGM Career Books
4255 W. Touhy Ave.
Lincolnwood, IL 60646-1975
Ph: (708)679-5500   Fax: (708)679-2494
Fr: 800-323-4900
Evans, Mariwyn. 1988. Gives an overview of the real estate industry. Describes jobs and specialties in the estate field. Lists schools and addresses to write to for more information.

★2575★ "Landscape Architect" in VGM's Careers Encyclopedia (pp. 240-241)
National Textbook Co. (NTC)
VGM Career Books
4255 W. Touhy Ave.
Lincolnwood, IL 60646-1975
Ph: (708)679-5500   Fax: (708)679-2494
Fr: 800-323-4900
Third edition, 1991. Profiles 200 occupations. Describes job duties, places of employment, working conditions, qualifications, education and training, advancement potential, and salary for each occupation.

★2576★ Landscape Architects
Chronicle Guidance Publications, Inc.
66 Aurora St.
PO Box 1190
Moravia, NY 13118-1190
Ph: (315)497-0330   Fax: (315)497-3359
Fr: 800-622-7284
1993. Career brief describing the nature of the job, working conditions, hours and earnings, education and training, licensure, certification, unions, personal qualifications, social and psychological factors, location, employment outlook, entry methods, advancement, and related occupations.

★2577★ "Landscape Architects" in Career Discovery Encyclopedia (Vol.3, pp. 158-159)
J.G. Ferguson Publishing Co.
200 W. Madison St., Ste. 300
Chicago, IL 60606
Ph: (312)580-5480   Fax: (312)580-4948
Russell E. Primm, editor-in chief. 1993. This six volume set contains two-page articles for 504 occupations. Each article describes job duties, earnings, and educational and training requirements. The whole set is arranged alphabetically by job title. Designed for junior high and older students.

★2578★ "Landscape Architects" in Career Information Center (Vol.4)
Simon and Schuster
200 Old Tappan Rd.
Old Tappan, NJ 07675
Fax: (800)445-6991   Fr: 800-223-2348
Richard Lidz and Linda Perrin, editorial directors. Fifth edition, 1993. A multi-volume set that profiles more than 600 occupations. Each occupational profile describes job

duties, educational requirements, getting a job, advancement possibilities, employment outlook, working conditions, earnings and benefits, and sources of additional information.

★2579★ "Landscape Architects" in Encyclopedia of Careers and Vocational Guidance (Vol.3, pp. 263-266)

J.G. Ferguson Publishing Co.
200 W. Madison St., Ste. 300
Chicago, IL 60606
Ph: (312)580-5480   Fax: (312)580-4948

William E. Hopke, editor-in-chief. Ninth edition, 1993. Four-volume set that profiles 900 occupations and describes job trends in 74 industries. Includes career description, educational requirements, history of the job, methods of entry, advancement, employment outlook, earnings, conditions of work, social and psychological factors, and sources of further information.

★2580★ "Landscape Architects" in Jobs! What They Are—Where They Are—What They Pay (p. 63)

Simon & Schuster, Inc.
Simon & Schuster Bldg.
1230 Avenue of the Americas
New York, NY 10020
Ph: (212)698-7000   Fr: 800-223-2348

Robert O. Snelling and Anne M. Snelling. 3rd edition, 1992. Describes duties and responsibilities, earnings, employment opportunities, training, and qualifications.

★2581★ "Landscape Architects" in Occupational Outlook Handbook

U.S. Government Printing Office
Superintendent of Documents
Washington, DC 20402
Ph: (202)512-1800   Fax: (202)512-2250

Biennial; latest edition, 1994-95. Encyclopedia of careers describing about 250 occupations and comprising about 85 percent of all jobs in the economy. Occupations that require lengthy education or training are given the most attention. Each occupation's profile describes what the worker does on the job, working conditions, education and training requirements, advancement possibilities, job outlook, earnings, and sources of additional information.

★2582★ Landscape Designer

Vocational Biographies, Inc.
PO Box 31
Sauk Centre, MN 56378-0031
Ph: (612)352-6516   Fax: (612)352-5546
Fr: 800-255-0752

1992. Four-page pamphlet containing a personal narrative about a worker's job, work likes and dislikes, career path from high school to the present. Education and training, the rewards and frustrations, and the effects of the job on the rest of the worker's life. The data file portion of this pamphlet gives a concise occupational summary, including work descriptions, working conditions, places of employment, personal characteristics, education and training, job outlook, and salary range.

★2583★ Opportunities in Landscape Architecture

National Textbook Co. (NTC)
VGM Career Books
4255 W. Touhy Ave.
Lincolnwood, IL 60646-1975
Ph: (708)679-5500   Fax: (708)679-2494
Fr: 800-323-4900

Ralph E. Griswold and William G. Swain. 1987. Includes a bibliography. Offers information about career opportunities in the field and how to prepare for them.

PROFESSIONAL ASSOCIATIONS

★2584★ American Society of Landscape Architects (ASLA)

4401 Connecticut Ave. NW, 5th Fl.
Washington, DC 20008
Ph: (202)686-2752   Fax: (202)686-1001

Members: Professional society of landscape architects. **Purpose:** Purpose is to promote the advancement of education and skill in the art of landscape architecture as an instrument in service to the public welfare. As the official accrediting agency, seeks to strengthen existing and proposed university programs in landscape architecture. Offers counsel to new and emerging programs; encourages state registration of landscape architects. Sponsors annual educational exhibit. Offers placement service; conducts specialized education and research. **Publications:** *ASLA Members Handbook*, annual. • *Landscape Architecture*, monthly. • *Landscape Architecture News Digest*, monthly. • *National Directory of Landscape Architecture Firms*, periodic.

★2585★ Council of Landscape Architectural Registration Boards (CLARB)

12700 Fair Lakes Cir., Ste. 110
Fairfax, VA 22033
Ph: (703)818-1300   Fax: (703)818-1309

Members: State and provincial registration boards for landscape architects. **Purpose:** Works for coordination of state and provincial registration; seeks to facilitate reciprocal registration between states and provinces. Prepares Annual Landscape Architect Registration. **Publications:** *C.L.A.R.B. News*, quarterly. • *Understanding the L.A.R.E.*, annual.

★2586★ Landscape Architecture Foundation (LAF)

4401 Connecticut Ave. NW, 5th Fl.
Washington, DC 20008
Ph: (202)686-0068   Fax: (202)686-1001

Members: Education and research vehicle for the landscape architecture profession in the U.S. **Purpose:** Combines the capabilities of landscape architects, interests of environmentalists, and needs of agencies and resource foundations. To encourage development of environmental research; to support and disseminate information on landscape architecture. Provides for the preparation and dissemination of educational and scientific information through publications, exhibits, lectures, and seminars. Solicits and expends

gifts, legacies, and grants; has established an endowment fund; finances new programs. Sponsors California Landscape Architectural Student Scholarship Fund; endows and establishes professorships at colleges and universities. Develops programmed teaching materials in landscape architectural planning and construction; encourages submittal of proposals for unique and/or interdisciplinary educational research projects. Prepares slide, film, and tape presentations; operates charitable program. Has conducted a study of the profession to establish goals in terms of education, research needs, practice, and formulation of public policy. **Publications:** *Grade Easy.* • *Handbook of Landscape Architectural Construction.* • *Street Graphics.*

★2587★ National Landscape Association (NLA)

1250 Eye St. NW, Ste. 500
Washington, DC 20005
Ph: (202)789-2900   Fax: (202)789-1893

Members: Landscape firms. **Purpose:** Works to: enhance the professionalism of its member firms in designing, building, and maintaining quality landscapes in a profitable and environmentally responsible manner; represent the landscape perspective within the industry. Sponsors annual landscape tour in conjunction with American Association of Nurserymen. **Publications:** *NLA Landscape News*, bimonthly.

TEST GUIDES

★2588★ Career Examination Series: Landscape Architect

National Learning Corp.
212 Michael Dr.
Syosset, NY 11791
Ph: (516)921-8888   Fax: (516)921-8743
Fr: 800-645-6337

Jack Rudman. A series of study guides with multiple-choice examination questions and solutions for trainees and professional landscape architects. Titles in the series include *Assistant Landscape Architect; Assistant Landscape Engineer; Junior Landscape Architect; Senior Landscape Architect.*

EDUCATIONAL DIRECTORIES AND PROGRAMS

★2589★ Landscape Architecture Accredited Programs

American Society of Landscape Architects
4401 Connecticut Ave. NW, Ste. 500
Washington, DC 20008-2302
Ph: (202)686-2752   Fax: (202)686-1001
Ron Leighton, Contact

Annual, September. Covers 71 programs in landscape architecture that are accredited by the society. Entries include: Institution name, address, and phone; name of director, department chairman, or contact; degrees offered; years of latest and next accreditation review, and accreditation status. Arrangement: Alphabetical.

AWARDS, SCHOLARSHIPS, GRANTS, AND FELLOWSHIPS

★2590★ AILA Yamagami Hope Fellowship
Landscape Architecture Foundation (LAF)
4401 Connecticut Ave., NW, Ste. 500
Washington, DC 20008
Ph: (202)686-0068

Qualifications: Candidates must be landscape architects who have been in practice for a minimum of three years and wish to use the funds for continuing education. They must have a bachelor's degree or a master's degree in landscape architecture. Selection criteria: Submissions will be evaluated on the innovative nature of the proposed endeavor, the benefits that may accrue to other members of the profession and the profession in general, the personal goals to be achieved, and the qualifications of the applicant. Funds available: The fellowship grant may be used to support credit or non-credit courses, seminars or workshops, development of a history of the American Institute of Landscape Architects from 1954 to 1982, travel or related expenses in support of an independent research project, or development of post-secondary educational materials or curriculum plans. Application details: Applications consist of: a summary addressing several questions supplied by the Foundation; a statement of intent detailing how the funds would be used; two letters of recommendation from licensed landscape architects; and a completed application form. Deadline: August 17.

★2591★ Ashworth Fellowship
Municipal Art Society of New York
457 Madison Ave.
New York, NY 10022
Ph: (212)935-3960   Fax: (212)753-1816

To provide an annual opportunity for a college student, recent graduate, or graduate student to complete a project relating to architecture, landscape architecture, urban planning and design, historic preservation, zoning, urban environmental controls, public art, or the history of architecture. Support of the Society's staff and resources, office space in the Urban Center, and a stipend of $2,500 are awarded.

★2592★ ASLA Medal
American Society of Landscape Architects
4401 Connecticut Ave. NW, 5th Fl.
Washington, DC 20008-2302
Ph: (202)686-2752   Fax: (202)686-1001
Fr: 800-787-2752

This, the Society's highest award, is given to recognize an individual who has made extraordinary contributions to the profession of landscape architecture. Nominations must be submitted by March 1. A medal is awarded annually. Established in 1971.

★2593★ Grace and Robert Fraser Landscape Heritage Award
Landscape Architecture Foundation (LAF)
4401 Connecticut Ave., NW, Ste. 500
Washington, DC 20008
Ph: (202)686-0068

Purpose: To recognize innovative horticultural design as it relates to the profession of landscape architecture. Qualifications: Candidate must be an undergraduate or graduate student currently pursuing research on new approaches to landscape architecture through horticulture. Funds available: $500. Application details: Write to the Foundation for application form and guidelines. Submit form with essay (500-word maximum) outlining the research or design project. Deadline: 4 May.

★2594★ Grace and Robert Fraser Landscape Heritage Fund Award
Landscape Architecture Foundation
4401 Connecticut Ave. NW, Ste. 500
Washington, DC 20008
Ph: (202)686-0068   Fax: (202)686-1001

To recognize innovative horticultural research or design as it relates to the profession of landscape architecture. A landscape architectural student currently pursuing research on new approaches to landscape architecture through horticulture or a landscape architect who has made a significant contribution to the profession through unique horticultural research or design is eligible. The deadline for applications is May 4. A monetary prize of $500 is awarded.

★2595★ Ralph Hudson Environmental Fellowship
Landscape Architecture Foundation (LAF)
4401 Connecticut Ave., NW, Ste. 500
Washington, DC 20008
Ph: (202)686-0068

Purpose: To advance the profession of landscape architecture through research activities with emphasis on concern for open space, parks, and recreation. Qualifications: Applicants must hold a degree in landscape architecture, have at least five years experience in professional practice (private, public, academic, or any combination thereof), be residents of the U.S., Canada, Mexico, islands of the Caribbean, or citizens of the U.S. residing or working abroad. Application details: Applications may be obtained from the Foundation. Deadline: August 17.

★2596★ LaGasse Medal
Landscape Architecture Foundation
4401 Connecticut Ave. NW, Ste. 500
Washington, DC 20008
Ph: (202)686-0068   Fax: (202)686-1001

To honor both a landscape architect and a layperson who, through their professional achievements, encourage resource and land management. Nominations may be submitted to the Board of Directors. A medal and a certificate are awarded annually. Established in 1981 to commemorate the professional life of Alfred B. LaGasse.

★2597★ LANDCADD, Inc. Scholarship
Landscape Architecture Foundation (LAF)
4401 Connecticut Ave., NW, Ste. 500
Washington, DC 20008
Ph: (202)686-0068

Purpose: To encourage the use of emerging technologies in the study and practice of landscape architecture. Qualifications: Candidate must be an undergraduate or graduate landscape architecture student who wishes to utilize such technological advancements as computer-aided design, video imaging or telecommunications in his/her career. Funds available: $500, plus $500 in LANDCADD software to the recipient's department. Application details: Write to the Foundation for application form and guidelines. Submit form with two recommendation letters and essay (500-word maximum) addressing one of the following: how these technologies could affect the future of landscape architecture; research plans and how research will be implemented; how the knowledge and use of emerging technologies have contributed to your studies in landscape architecture. Deadline: 4 May.

★2598★ Landscape Architecture Student Competition
National Stone Association
1415 Elliot Pl., NW
Washington, DC 20007-2599
Ph: (202)342-1100   Fax: (202)342-0702

Purpose: To encourage architecture students to become familiar with the unique needs and special circumstances involved in the beautification and reclamation of stone quarries. Qualifications: Applicants must be undergraduate seniors or graduate students enrolled in landscape architecture degree programs at schools located in the United States or Canada. Entries must be based on active or proposed commercial crushed stone operations and can be submitted by individuals or groups of up to three students. Sites that are abandoned or where mining operations have been completed are not eligible for consideration. Selection criteria: Prizes are awarded for projects that make mining sites more usable and visually attractive. Entries are judged on overall excellence in design, creativity, and sensitivity to community needs. Each of the three components are given equal consideration by the judges, who are members of the American Society of Landscape Architects. Funds available: Prizes are split between students and their respective departments of landscape architecture. First prize is $1,000 for the student and $700 for the school. Second prize is $500 for the student and $300 for the school; and third prize is $300 for the student and $200 for the school. Application details: Students must first develop problem statements and then design solutions. Their plans should identify factors important in the siting and design of a mining processing site and describe how the design would mitigate the various impacts. Entries must show a solution containing three distinct components, each presented on a separate foam board that measures 30x40 inches. The three components are: site and operational analysis, which documents existing conditions and the potential assets and liabilities of the site; site improvement and beautification, which includes a plan to reduce the adverse impact of the operating site on the environment and community; and a final use or reclamation plan, to take effect as the site begins to cease operations. Applications should also include a narrative description of the project and an extensive cost analysis. Students should be aware of state and local reclamation, zoning, and safety regulations that may impact upon their project. Candidates are encouraged to research laws that relate to their project and incorporate them into the final proposal. Deadline: In 1993, the preliminary application deadline was April 9; the final entry deadline was May 14.

★2599★ Landscape Design Award
American Horticultural Society
7931 E. Boulevard Dr.
Alexandria, VA 22308
Ph: (703)768-5700   Fax: (703)765-6032
Fr: 800-777-7931

To recognize an individual whose work in landscape architecture or design contributes to a better awareness of the field of horticulture. A plaque is presented each year at the annual meeting. Established in 1974.

★2600★ National Endowment for the Arts - Design Arts Program USA Fellowships
National Endowment for the Arts
Visual Arts Program/Fellowships, Rm. 729
Nancy Hanks Center
1100 Pennsylvania Ave., NW
Washington, DC 20506-0001
Ph: (202)682-5422   Fax: (202)682-5699

Purpose: To enable designers and those in design-related professions who have made significant contributions to the design field to travel and study independently within the United States. The grants provide desingers the time and flexibility to explore new concepts, generate fresh ideas, or compile information for a book or study. Qualifications: Fellowships are awarded to professional designers and other qualified individuals working on innovative design projects. They are intended for those for whom a more extensive first-hand knowledge of the American design environment is critical to their work. Eligible fields include architecture, landscape architecture, urban design and planning, historic preservation, interior design, industrial and product design, and graphic design. Applicants must be United States citizens or permanent residents. Selection criteria: The Endowment places a strong emphasis on quality as the first criterion in evaluating applications. Funds available: Fellowships include awards of up to $20,000.

★2601★ National Landscape Award
American Association of Nurserymen
1250 I St. NW, Ste. 500
Washington, DC 20005
Ph: (202)789-2900   Fax: (202)789-1893
This, the nation's oldest and most honored environmental and community improvement program, is designed to single out businesses, institutions, and governmental organizations that have made a significant contribution to the quality of life in their communities through landscape beautification, and to bring those valued contributions to the attention of the American public. A framed parchment certificate is awarded annually. Established in 1952.

★2602★ National Landscape Design Awards
National Landscape Association
1250 I St. NW, Ste. 500
Washington, DC 20005
Ph: (202)789-2900   Fax: (202)789-1893
To recognize professionals who have created outstanding residential and commercial landscape designs and those responsible for executing such designs. Awards are presented in the following categories: single-family residence; entrance; active use area; pools, patios, and active recreation areas; public use area; schools, parks, restaurants; and passive use area. A framed certificate is awarded annually. Established in 1970.

★2603★ NCSGC National Scholarships
National Council of State Garden Clubs, Inc. (NCSGC)
4402 Magnolia Ave.
St. Louis, MO 63110-3492
Qualifications: Applicants must be United States citizens who are studying horticulture, floriculture, landscape design, city planning, or an allied subject. They must also be endorsed by their State Garden Club. Selection criteria: Selection is based on academic record and financial need. Funds available: Thirty awards of $4,000 each are given annually. Application details: Candidates should write to obtain the name of their state scholarship chairperson. Deadline: National deadline is December 1. State deadlines vary.

★2604★ Rain Bird Company Scholarship
Landscape Architecture Foundation (LAF)
4401 Connecticut Ave., NW, Ste. 500
Washington, DC 20008
Ph: (202)686-0068
Purpose: To recognize an outstanding landscape architecture student. Qualifications: Applicants must be students in their final two years of undergraduate study (third, fourth, fifth years) in need of financial assistance. Eligible applicants include those who have demonstrated commitment to the profession through participation in extracurricular activities and exemplary scholastic achievements. Funds available: $1,000. Application details: Applicants must submit an application form, Financial Aid Form, and a 300-word essay. Deadline: May 4.

★2605★ James K. Rathmell, Jr., Memorial Scholarship to Work/Study Abroad
Bedding Plants Foundation
PO Box 27241
Lansing, MI 48909
Ph: (517)694-8537
Purpose: To encourage overseas work and study in the fields of horticulture, floriculture, and landscape architecture by U.S. students. Qualifications: Applicant must be an undergraduate or graduate student in the United States who wishes to pursue work or study abroad. Candidate is responsible for making all arrangements for his/her overseas program. Preference will be given to applicants with well-defined objectives that will benefit the bedding and container plant industry. Funds available: $2,000 maximum. Application details: Write for application materials. Submit application form with undergraduate and graduate transcripts, a letter of invitation

from host firm/institution abroad, an academic letter of recommendation, and a personal letter of recommendation. Deadline: 1 April.

★2606★ Edward D. Stone Jr. and Associates Minority Scholarship
Landscape Architecture Foundation (LAF)
4401 Connecticut Ave., NW, Ste. 500
Washington, DC 20008
Ph: (202)686-0068
Purpose: To help continue the education of students entering their final years of undergraduate study in landscape architecture. Qualifications: Applicants must be minority students in their final years of study. Funds available: Two $1,000 scholarships are awarded. Application details: Applications consist of the following: a typed, double-spaced 500-word essay; between four and eight 35mm color slides neatly arranged in a plastic folder or three to five 8x10 black and white or color photographs that demonstrate the student's best work; two letters of recommendation; a completed application form; and a completed Financial Aid Form. Deadline: May 4.

BASIC REFERENCE GUIDES AND HANDBOOKS

★2607★ *A Dictionary of Landscape Architecture*
University of New Mexico Press
1720 Lomas Blvd., NE
Albuquerque, NM 87131-1591
Ph: (505)277-2346
Baker H. Morrow. First edition, 1987. Includes a bibliography. Illustrated.

★2608★ *From Concept to Form in Landscape Architecture*
Van Nostrand Reinhold
115 5th Ave.
New York, NY 10013
Grant Reid. 1993.

★2609★ *Landscape Construction, Procedures, Techniques, and Design*
Stipes Publishing Co.
10-12 Chester St.
PO Box 526
Champaign, IL 61820
Ph: (217)356-8391
Floyd A. Giles. 1991. Illustrated.

★2610★ *The Oxford Companion to Gardens*
Oxford University Press, Inc.
200 Madison Ave.
New York, NY 10016
Ph: (212)679-7300
Patrick Goode and Michael Lancaster, editors. 1991. Includes a bibliography. Illustrated.

★2611★ Site Engineering for Landscape Architects
Van Nostrand Reinhold
115 5th Ave.
New York, NY 10013

Steven Strom and Kurt Nathan. 1993.

★2612★ Time-Saver Standards for Landscape Architecture: Design and Construction Data
McGraw-Hill, Inc.
1221 Avenue of the Americas
New York, NY 10020
Ph: (212)512-2000   Fr: 800-722-4726

Charles W. Harris and Nicholas T. Dines, editors. 1988. Includes bibliographies and an index.

PROFESSIONAL AND TRADE PERIODICALS

★2613★ City Trees
Society of Municipal Arborists
PO Box 364
Wellesley Hills, MA 02181
Ph: (617)235-7600   Fax: (627)237-1936
Leonard E. Phillips

Bimonthly. Addresses all aspects of municipal (urban) forestry. Contains technical articles on species of trees, pest control, conservation, planning, design, and equipment. Recurring features include lists of new publications, statistics, news of research, letters to the editor, announcements of meetings, and columns titled President's Column, Professor's Column, City of the Month, Park of the Month, Tree of the Month, and Editor's Corner.

★2614★ LAND: Landscape Architectural News Digest
American Society of Landscape Architecture
4401 Connecticut Ave. NW, 5th Fl.
Washington, DC 20008
Ph: (202)686-8335   Fax: (202)686-1001
Lee V. Fleming

Carries news and monitors developments in landscape architecture, environmental design, and related fields. Focuses on public policy, education, and other areas affecting landscape architecture.

★2615★ Landscape Architecture
American Society of Landscape Architects
4401 Connecticut Ave. NW, 5th Fl.
Washington, DC 20008
Ph: (202)686-2752   Fax: (202)686-1001
Lee Fleming

Monthly. Professional magazine covering land planning and design.

PROFESSIONAL MEETINGS AND CONVENTIONS

★2616★ American Society of Landscape Architects Annual Meeting and Educational Exhibit
American Society of Landscape Architects
4401 Connecticut Ave., NW, Ste. 500
Washington, DC 20008
Ph: (202)686-2752   Fax: (202)686-1001
Annual. **Dates and Locations:** 1996 Oct 04-07; Los Angeles, CA. • 1997 Nov 08-11; Atlanta, GA.

★2617★ Southwest Horticultural Trade Show
Arizona Nursery Association
1430 W. Broadway Rd., A125
Tempe, AZ 85282-1127
Ph: (602)966-1610   Fax: (602)966-0923
Annual. Always held during September at the Civic Plaza in Phoenix, Arizona.

OTHER SOURCES OF INFORMATION

★2618★ The Complete Illustration Guide For Architects, Designers, Artists, and Students
Van Nostrand Reinhold
115 5th Ave.
New York, NY 10013

Larry Evans. 1993.

★2619★ "Landscape Architect" in 100 Best Jobs for the 1990s & Beyond
Dearborn Financial Publishing, Inc.
520 N. Dearborn St.
Chicago, IL 60610-4354
Ph: (312)836-4400   Fax: (312)836-1021
Fr: 800-621-9621

Carol Kleiman. 1992. Describes 100 jobs ranging from accountants to veterinarians.. Each job profile includes such information as education, experience, and certification needed, salaries, and job search suggestions.

★2620★ "Landscape Architecture" in Accounting to Zoology: Graduate Fields Defined (pp. 13-14)
Petersons Guides, Inc.
PO Box 2123
Princeton, NJ 08543-2123
Ph: (609)243-9111   Fax: (609)243-9150
Fr: 800-338-3282

Amy J. Goldstein, editor. Revised and updated, 1987. Defines 298 graduate and professional fields. Discusses types of graduate programs and degrees, graduate research, applied work, employment prospects, and trends.

Surveyors

Surveyors measure and map the earth's surface. **Land surveyors** establish official land, air space, and water boundaries, write descriptions of land for deeds, leases, and other legal documents, and measure construction and mineral sites. They are assisted by **survey technicians**, who operate surveying instruments and collect information. **Mapping scientists** and other surveyors collect information for and prepare maps and charts. Mapping scientists include workers in several occupations. **Cartographers** prepare maps using information provided by geodetic surveys, aerial photographs, and satellite data. **Photogrammetrists** prepare maps and drawings by measuring and interpreting aerial photographs, using analytical processes and mathematical formulas. Photogrammetrists make detailed maps of areas that are inaccessible or difficult to survey by other methods. **Map editors** develop and verify map contents from aerial photographs and other reference sources. Some surveyors perform specialized functions. **Geodetic surveyors** use special high-accuracy techniques, including satellite observations, to measure large areas of the earth's surface. **Geophysical prospecting surveyors** mark sites for subsurface exploration, usually petroleum related. **Marine surveyors** survey harbors, rivers, and other bodies of water to determine shorelines, topography of the bottom, water depth, and other features. New technology is changing the nature of the work of surveyors. The **geographic information specialist** combines the functions of mapping science and surveying into a broader field concerned with the collection and analysis of geographic spatial information.

Salaries

Earnings, especially starting salaries, depend on candidates' qualifications.

Survey technicians	$23,700/year
Survey technicians, federal government	$24,000/year
Land surveyors, federal government	$41,000/year
Cartographers, federal government	$44,000/year
Geodesists, federal government	$47,600/year

Employment Outlook

Growth rate until the year 2005: More slowly than the average.

Surveyors

CAREER GUIDES

★2621★ *Cartographer*
Careers, Inc.
PO Box 135
Largo, FL 34649-0135
Ph: (813)584-7333

1994. Two-page occupational summary card describing duties, working conditions, personal qualifications, training, earnings and hours, employment outlook, places of employment, related careers, and where to write for more information.

★2622★ "Land Surveyor" in *Desk Guide to Training and Work Advisement* (p. 167)
Charles C. Thomas, Publisher
2600 S. 1st St.
Springfield, IL 62794-9265
Ph: (217)789-8980   Fax: (217)789-9130
Fr: 800-258-8980

Gail Baugher Keunstler. 1988. Describes alternative methods of gaining entry into an occupation through different types of educational programs, internships, and apprenticeships.

★2623★ "Land Surveyor" in *Guide to Federal Jobs* (pp. 225)
Resource Directories
3361 Executive Pkwy., Ste. 302
Toledo, OH 43606
Ph: (419)536-5353   Fax: (419)536-7056
Fr: 800-274-8515

Rod W. Durgin, editor. Third edition, 1992. Contains information on finding and applying for federal jobs. Describes more than 200 professional and technical jobs for college graduates. Includes chapters titled "Geodesist" (p. 224), and "Cartographers" (p. 223). Covers the nature of the work, salary, and geographic location. Lists college majors preferred for that occupation. Section one describes the function and work of government agencies that hire the most significant number of college graduates.

★2624★ "Surveying and Mapping Technicians" in *Encyclopedia of Careers and Vocational Guidance* (Vol.4, pp. 460-465)
J.G. Ferguson Publishing Co.
200 W. Madison St., Ste. 300
Chicago, IL 60606
Ph: (312)580-5480   Fax: (312)580-4948

William E. Hopke, editor-in-chief. Ninth edition, 1993. Four-volume set that profiles 900 occupations and describes job trends in 74 industries. Includes career description, educational requirements, history of the job, methods of entry, advancement, employment outlook, earnings, conditions of work, social and psychological factors, and sources of further information.

★2625★ "Surveying" in *Opportunities in Civil Engineering* (pp. 64-67)
National Textbook Co. (NTC)
VGM Career Books
4255 W. Touhy Ave.
Lincolnwood, IL 60646-1975
Ph: (708)679-5500   Fax: (708)679-2494
Fr: 800-323-4900

D. Joseph Hagerty and Louis F. Cohn. 1987. Defines surveying and describes educational requirements, specialties, duties, salaries, working conditions, advancement opportunities, and employment trends. List professional organizations.

★2626★ *Surveying Sisters: The Positions and Perceptions of Women in an Erstwhile Male Profession*
Routledge, Chapman & Hall, Inc.
29 W. 35th St.
New York, NY 10001-2291
Ph: (212)244-3336   Fax: (212)563-2269

Clara Greed. 1990.

★2627★ *Surveyor*
Careers, Inc.
PO Box 135
Largo, FL 34649-0135
Ph: (813)584-7333

1993. Two-page occupational summary card describing duties, working conditions, personal qualifications, training, earnings and hours, employment outlook, places of employment, related careers, and where to write for more information.

★2628★ *Surveyor*
Vocational Biographies, Inc.
PO Box 31
Sauk Centre, MN 56378-0031
Ph: (612)352-6516   Fax: (612)352-5546
Fr: 800-255-0752

1992. Four-page pamphlet containing a personal narrative about a worker's job, work likes and dislikes, career path from high school to the present. Education and training, the rewards and frustrations, and the effects of the job on the rest of the worker's life. The data file portion of this pamphlet gives a concise occupational summary, including work descriptions, working conditions, places of employment, personal characteristics, education and training, job outlook, and salary range.

★2629★ "Surveyor" in *BLR Encyclopedia of Prewritten Job Descriptions*
Business and Legal Reports, Inc.
39 Academy St.
Madison, CT 06443-1513
Ph: (203)245-7448

Stephen D. Bruce, editor-in-chief. 1994. This book contains hundreds of sample job descriptions arranged by functional job category. The 1-3 page job descriptions cover what the worker normally does in the position, who they report to, and how that position fits in the organizational structure.

★2630★ "Surveyor" in *Jobs Rated Almanac*
World Almanac
1 International Blvd., Ste. 444
Mahwah, NJ 07495
Ph: (201)529-6900   Fax: (201)529-6901

Les Krantz. Second edition, 1992. Ranks 250 jobs by environment, salary, outlooks, physical demands, stress, security, travel opportunities, and extra perks. Includes jobs the editor feels are the most common, most interesting, and the most rapidly growing.

★2631★ "Surveyor" in *VGM's Careers Encyclopedia* (pp. 444-447)
National Textbook Co. (NTC)
VGM Career Books
4255 W. Touhy Ave.
Lincolnwood, IL 60646-1975
Ph: (708)679-5500   Fax: (708)679-2494
Fr: 800-323-4900
Third edition, 1991. Profiles 200 occupations. Describes job duties, places of employment, working conditions, qualifications, education and training, advancement potential, and salary for each occupation.

★2632★ *Surveyors*
Chronicle Guidance Publications, Inc.
66 Aurora St.
PO Box 1190
Moravia, NY 13118-1190
Ph: (315)497-0330   Fax: (315)497-3359
Fr: 800-622-7284
1992. Career brief describing the nature of the job, working conditions, hours and earnings, education and training, licensure, certification, unions, personal qualifications, social and psychological factors, location, employment outlook, entry methods, advancement, and related occupations.

★2633★ "Surveyors" in *101 Careers: A Guide to the Fastest-Growing Opportunities* (pp. 95-98)
John Wiley & Sons, Inc.
605 3rd Ave.
New York, NY 10158-0012
Ph: (212)850-6645   Fax: (212)850-6088
Michael Harkavy. 1990. Describes the nature of the job, working conditions, employment growth, qualifications, personal skills, projected salaries, and where to write for more information.

★2634★ "Surveyors" in *Career Information Center* (Vol.4)
Simon and Schuster
200 Old Tappan Rd.
Old Tappan, NJ 07675
Fax: 800-445-6991   Fr: 800-223-2348
Richard Lidz and Linda Perrin, editorial directors. Fifth edition, 1993. A multi-volume set that profiles more than 600 occupations. Each occupational profile describes job duties, educational requirements, getting a job, advancement possibilities, employment outlook, working conditions, earnings and benefits, and sources of additional information.

★2635★ "Surveyors" in *Encyclopedia of Careers and Vocational Guidance* (Vol.4, pp. 466-469)
J.G. Ferguson Publishing Co.
200 W. Madison St., Ste. 300
Chicago, IL 60606
Ph: (312)580-5480   Fax: (312)580-4948
William E. Hopke, editor-in-chief. Ninth edition, 1993. Four-volume set that profiles 900 occupations and describes job trends in 74 industries. Includes career description, educational requirements, history of the job, methods of entry, advancement, employment outlook, earnings, conditions of work, social and psychological factors, and sources of further information.

★2636★ "Surveyors" in *Guide to Careers Without College* (pp. 80-82)
Franklin Watts, Inc.
387 Park Ave., S.
New York, NY 10016
Ph: (212)686-7070   Fr: 800-843-3749
Kathleen S. Abrams. 1988. Discusses rewarding careers that do not require a college degree.

★2637★ "Surveyors" in *Occupational Outlook Handbook*
U.S. Government Printing Office
Superintendent of Documents
Washington, DC 20402
Ph: (202)512-1800   Fax: (202)512-2250
Biennial; latest edition, 1994-95. Encyclopedia of careers describing about 250 occupations and comprising about 85 percent of all jobs in the economy. Occupations that require lengthy education or training are given the most attention. Each occupation's profile describes what the worker does on the job, working conditions, education and training requirements, advancement possibilities, job outlook, earnings, and sources of additional information.

★2638★ "Surveyors" in *Opportunities inReal Estate Careers* (pp. 108-110)
National Textbook Co. (NTC)
VGM Career Books
4255 W. Touhy Ave.
Lincolnwood, IL 60646-1975
Ph: (708)679-5500   Fax: (708)679-2494
Fr: 800-323-4900
Evans, Mariwyn. 1988. Gives an overview of the real estate industry. Describes jobs and specialties in the estate field. Lists schools and addresses to write to for more information.

★2639★ "Surveyors and Surveying Technicians" in *Jobs! What They Are—Where They Are—What They Pay* (p. 65)
Simon & Schuster, Inc.
Simon & Schuster Bldg.
1230 Avenue of the Americas
New York, NY 10020
Ph: (212)698-7000   Fr: 800-223-2348
Robert O. Snelling and Anne M. Snelling. 3rd edition, 1992. Describes duties and responsibilities, earnings, employment opportunities, training, and qualifications.

Professional Associations

★2640★ American Congress on Surveying and Mapping (ACSM)
5410 Grosvenor Ln.
Bethesda, MD 20814-2122
Ph: (301)493-0200   Fax: (301)493-8245
Members: Professionals, technicians, and students in the field of surveying and mapping including surveying of all disciplines, land and geographic information systems, cartography, geodesy, photogrammetry, engineering, geophysics, geography, and computer graphics; American Association for Geodetic Surveying, American Cartographic Association, and National Society of Professional Surveyors. **Purpose:** Objectives are to: advance the sciences of surveying and mapping; promote public understanding and use of surveying and mapping; speak on the national level as the collective voice of the profession; provide publications to serve the surveying and mapping community. Member organizations encourage improvement of university and college curricula for surveying and mapping. **Publications:** *ACSM Bulletin*, bimonthly. • *Cartography and Geographic Information Systems*, quarterly. • *Membership Roster*, periodic. • *Surveying and Land Information Systems*, quarterly. • *Technical Papers*, semiannual.

★2641★ American Society for Photogrammetry and Remote Sensing (ASPRS)
5410 Grosvenor Ln., Ste. 210
Bethesda, MD 20814-2160
Ph: (301)493-0290   Fax: (301)493-0208
Members: Firms, individuals, government employees, and academicians engaged in photogrammetry, photointerpretation, remote sensing, and geographic information systems and their application to such fields as archaeology, geographic information systems, military reconnaissance, urban planning, engineering, traffic surveys, meteorological observations, medicine, geology, forestry, agriculture, construction, and topographic mapping. Offers voluntary certification program open to persons associated with one or more functional area of photogrammetry, remote sensing, and GIS. Surveys the profession of private firms in photogrammetry and remote sensing in the areas of products and services. **Publications:** *Photogrammetric Engineering and Remote Sensing*, monthly.

★2642★ Council of American Survey Research Organizations (CASRO)
3 Upper Devon Belle Terre
Port Jefferson, NY 11777
Ph: (516)928-6954   Fax: (516)928-6041
Members: Survey research companies in the U.S. **Purpose:** Seeks to: provide a vehicle whereby survey research companies can interact with one another, sharing relevant information and addressing common problems; promote the establishment, maintenance, and improvement of professional standards in survey research. **Publications:** *CASRO Journal*, annual.

★2643★ National Society of Professional Surveyors (NSPS)
5410 Grosvenor Ln., Ste. 100
Bethesda, MD 20814-2122
Ph: (301)493-0200   Fax: (301)493-8245
Members: A member organization of the American Congress on Surveying and Mapping. Professional surveyors, preprofessionals, technicians, and students. **Purpose:** Encourages members to adopt and adhere to standards of ethical and professional behavior and to provide a professional service to the public. Maintains liaison with other professional societies; promotes public confidence in services rendered by members; monitors laws and regulations affecting the profession; helps to develop curricula for teaching surveying. **Publications:** *Surveying and Land Information Systems*, quarterly.

STANDARDS/CERTIFICATION AGENCIES

★2644★ American Society for Photogrammetry and Remote Sensing (ASPRS)
5410 Grosvenor Ln., Ste. 210
Bethesda, MD 20814-2160
Ph: (301)493-0290   Fax: (301)493-0208
Offers voluntary certification program open to persons associated with one or more functional area of photogrammetry, remote sensing, and GIS.

TEST GUIDES

★2645★ *Career Examination Series: Coordinator of Surveying Services*
National Learning Corp.
212 Michael Dr.
Syosset, NY 11791
Ph: (516)921-8888   Fax: (516)921-8743
Fr: 800-645-6337
Jack Rudman. 1993. Test guide including questions and answers for students or professionals in the field who seek advancement through examination.

★2646★ *Career Examination Series: Land Surveyor*
National Learning Corp.
212 Michael Dr.
Syosset, NY 11791
Ph: (516)921-8888   Fax: (516)921-8743
Fr: 800-645-6337
Jack Rudman. A series of study guides with multiple-choice examination questions and solutions for trainees and professional surveyors. Titles in the series include *Assistant Land Surveyor; Assistant Surveyor; City Surveyor; Health Care Surveyor; Land Surveyor Trainee.*

★2647★ *Career Examination Series: Surveyor*
National Learning Corp.
212 Michael Dr.
Syosset, NY 11791
Ph: (516)921-8888   Fax: (516)921-8743
Fr: 800-645-6337
Jack Rudman. Test guide including questions and answers for students or professionals in the field who seek advancement through examination. Also included in the series: Land Surveyor, City Surveyor, and Assistant Land Surveyor.

★2648★ *Land Surveyor-in-Training Sample Examination*
Professional Publications, Inc.
1250 5th Ave.
Belmont, CA 94002-3863
Ph: 800-426-1178
George M. Cole. 1994. Offers over 160 multiple choice questions to simulate the actual FLS/LSIT exam. Provides detailed solutions and answer keys.

AWARDS, SCHOLARSHIPS, GRANTS, AND FELLOWSHIPS

★2649★ ACA Outstanding Achievement Award
American Cartographic Association
5410 Grosvenor Ln.
Bethesda, MD 20814
Ph: (301)493-0200   Fax: (301)493-8245
To recognize outstanding achievement in the field of cartography. Members of ACA are eligible. A framed certificate is awarded. Established in 1982.

★2650★ ACSM Map Design Competition Awards
American Congress on Surveying and
  Mapping
5410 Grosvenor Ln.
Bethesda, MD 20814
Ph: (301)493-0200   Fax: (301)493-8245
The following awards are presented: (1) Awards for Outstanding Achievement in Cartographic Design - to promote concern for map design and to recognize significant advances in cartography. Certificates and Exhibition at ACSM Annual Convention and conventions of other professional organizations are awarded. Maps become part of the U.S. Library of Congress permanent collection; (2) R.R. Donnelley & Sons Co. Awards- to recognize the best student entries in the ACSM Map Design Competition on the basis of overall design, impression, use of color, and achievement of stated design objectives. One award is given to a student from an academic program and one to a student from a technical program. Entries may be submitted by February 15. A monetary award of $100 and a certificate are awarded in each category; and (3) Rand McNally Awards- to recognize the best student entries. Sponsored by Rand McNally Company and R. R. Donnelley and Sons Company.

★2651★ American Association for Geodetic Surveying Graduate Fellowship Award
American Association for Geodetic
  Surveying
5410 Grosvenor Ln.
Bethesda, MD 20814
Ph: (301)493-0200   Fax: (301)493-8245
To recognize outstanding graduate students committed to the pursuit of knowledge in geodetic surveying and by so doing to enhance the ability of the profession to better serve the needs of society. Nominations may be made by any member of ACSM or ASPRS. The criteria upon which the nominee is evaluated include: (1) enrollment in or acceptance by a graduate program with a significant focus upon geodetic surveying and/or geodesy; (2) academic record including scope of course work and level of achievement as indicated by grade point average; (3) letter(s) of recommendation with respect to academic qualification from not more than two faculty members familiar with the nominee's performance; (4) a letter of recommendation with respect to the ethical standards of the nominee; and (5) a personal statement of course of study and its relationship to career

goals prepared by the nominee. A monetary award of $2,000 and an appropriate citation are presented annually at the annual meeting. Established in 1983.

★2652★ American Cartographic Association Scholarship Award
American Cartographic Association
5410 Grosvenor Ln.
Bethesda, MD 20814
Ph: (301)493-0200   Fax: (301)493-8245
To recognize outstanding cartography and mapping sciences students and to encourage the completion of an undergraduate program and/or the pursuit of graduate education in cartography or other mapping sciences. Any person who is a full-time student of junior or senior standing enrolled in a cartography or other mapping sciences curriculum, in a 4-year degree granting institution, is eligible. Previous candidates can be renominated in succeeding years. Any ACSM member may nominate a qualified student with appropriate documentation. Students may nominate themselves by completing the standard ACSM-ASPRS Fellowship or Scholarship Awards Application. The ACA Awards Committee selects the Scholarship recipient from among those nominated. A monetary prize of $1,000 and an appropriate certificate are presented at the annual meeting. Established in 1986.

★2653★ Berntsen Scholarship in Surveying
American Congress on Surveying and
  Mapping
5410 Grosvenor Ln.
Bethesda, MD 20814
Ph: (301)493-0200   Fax: (301)493-8245
To provide financial assistance to a full-time undergraduate student pursuing a four-year degree in surveying. Any person who is enrolled in a four-year degree program in surveying may apply for this scholarship by January 1. Selection is based on appraisal of the applicant's (1) justification of award; (2) educational plan; (3) academic performance and standing; (4) potential for development; and (5) financial need. A scholarship of $1,500 is awarded. Sponsored by Berntsen International, Inc. of Madison, Wisconsin.

★2654★ Walter S. Dix Award
American Congress on Surveying and
  Mapping
5410 Grosvenor Ln.
Bethesda, MD 20814
Ph: (301)493-0200   Fax: (301)493-8245
To recognize an individual who represents and embodies outstanding contributions to ACSM and the surveying and mapping profession.

★2655★ Joseph F. Dracup Scholarship Award
American Association for Geodetic
  Surveying
5410 Grosvenor Ln.
Bethesda, MD 20814
Ph: (301)493-0200   Fax: (301)493-8245
To encourage outstanding undergraduates committed to a career in geodetic surveying. A monetary award of $2,000 and a citation are presented at the annual meeting. Established in 1988.

★2656★ Honorary Member
American Congress on Surveying and
Mapping
5410 Grosvenor Ln.
Bethesda, MD 20814
Ph: (301)493-0200   Fax: (301)493-8245
To honor the leaders in surveying and
mapping science. Any person who has attained outstanding national or international
recognition by contributions to the surveying
and mapping profession may be elected by
the Board of Direction. A plaque is awarded.

★2657★ Leica Surveying Scholarships
American Congress on Surveying and
Mapping
5410 Grosvenor Ln.
Bethesda, MD 20814
Ph: (301)493-0200   Fax: (301)493-8245
To provide financial assistance to undergraduate students studying surveying at schools
with two-or four-year degree programs in surveying or a related field. Applications may be
submitted by January 1. Two monetary
awards of $1,000 each are presented.

★2658★ O. M. Miller Cartographic Medal
American Geographical Society
156 5th Ave.
New York, NY 10010
Ph: (212)242-0214   Fax: (212)989-1583
To recognize outstanding contributions in the
field of cartography or geodesy. A gold medal
is awarded when merited. Established in
1968.

**★2659★ Most Interesting Surveying
Project of the Year Award**
National Society of Professional Surveyors
5410 Grosvenor Ln.
Bethesda, MD 20814-2122
Ph: (301)493-0200   Fax: (301)493-8245
To recognize individuals, companies, governmental units, or state associations having
knowledge of interesting projects and the
ability to provide documentation of the
project, including technical information, releases, photographs, and a record of the personnel and equipment involved. Members of
NSPS or affiliates are eligible. The project
need not have occurred within the last year.
Projects must be submitted by December 31.
A Pentax camera, plaque, and 1,000 reprints
of the resulting published article are awarded.
Sponsored by Pentax Corporation, Englewood, Colorado. Contact Pat Canfield at
ACSM/NSPS for more information.

**★2660★ Schonstedt Scholarship in
Surveying**
American Congress on Surveying and
Mapping
5410 Grosvenor Ln.
Bethesda, MD 20814
Ph: (301)493-0200   Fax: (301)493-8245
To provide for undergraduate study in sur-
veying. Students who have completed at
least two years of a four-year curriculum lead-
ing to a degree in surveying may apply by
January 1. A scholarship of $1,500 is
awarded. Sponsored by Schonstedt Instru-
ment Companyof Reston, Virginia.

**★2661★ Student Project of the Year
Award**
National Society of Professional Surveyors
5410 Grosvenor Ln.
Bethesda, MD 20814-2122
Ph: (301)493-0200   Fax: (301)493-8245
To encourage and recognize students who
participate, research, and write about surveying projects. Any undergraduate student
enrolled in a surveying or surveying related
program is eligible for this award. Papers may
be submitted by December 31. A plaque,
$150 honorarium, and travel expenses to at-
tend the ACSM-ASPRS Spring Convention
are awarded. Sponsored by C&G Software
Systems, Inc.Contact Pat Canfield at ACSM/
NSPS for more information.

★2662★ Surveying Excellence Award
National Society of Professional Surveyors
5410 Grosvenor Ln.
Bethesda, MD 20814-2122
Ph: (301)493-0200   Fax: (301)493-8245
To recognize and honor a person who has
performed outstanding service to the development and advancement of the surveying
profession. Candidates, who don't necessarily have to be surveyors or members of NSPS
or ACSM, must be nominated by an ACSM
affiliate section or two NSPS members by
December 31. A plaque and $500 hon-
orarium are awarded. Sponsored by P.O.B.
Publishing Company, Canton, Michigan.
Contact Pat Canfield at ACSM/NSPS for
more information.

★2663★ Surveying and Mapping Award
American Society of Civil Engineers
1015 15th N.W, Ste. 600
Washington, DC 20005
Ph: (202)789-2200   Fax: (202)289-6797
To recognize a member who has made a
contribution during the year to the advancement of surveying and mapping in either
teaching, writing, research, planning, design,
construction, or management. Nominations
must be submitted by November 1. A plaque
and certificate are awarded annually. Established in 1969.

**★2664★ Wild Heerbrugg Geodetic
Fellowship**
American Congress on Surveying and
Mapping
5410 Grosvenor Ln.
Bethesda, MD 20814
Ph: (301)493-0200   Fax: (301)493-8245
To encourage qualified candidates to pursue
graduate education in geodesy and to pro-
mote the development of geodetic science.
Competition is open to any member of the
Congress on Surveying and Mapping or the
American Society for Photogrammetry and
Remote Sensing or any regular student of an
accredited school who is sponsored by a
member of the American Congress on Surveying and Mapping or the American Society
for Photogrammetry and Remote Sensing.
Every applicant must have completed at least
one undergraduate course in surveying or
photogrammetry prior to the receipt of the
fellowship. The applications are judged on
the following criteria: (1) previous academic
record; (2) applicant's statement of his or her
study objectives; (3) applicability of previous
courses to graduate work in geodesy; (4) rec-

ommendation of faculty member; and (5) financial need. The deadline for application is
January 15. A $4,000 fellowship is awarded
annually for graduate study at an accredited
school of his or her choice. Sponsored by
Wild Heerbrugg Instruments, Inc.

BASIC REFERENCE GUIDES
AND HANDBOOKS

★2665★ *The Surveying Handbook*
Van Nostrand Reinhold
115 5th Ave.
New York, NY 10013
Russell C. Brinker and Roy Minnick. Second
edition, 1994.

**★2666★ *Surveying: Principles and
Applications***
Prentice-Hall, Inc.
Rte. 9W
Englewood Cliffs, NJ 07632
Ph: (201)592-2000   Fr: 800-634-2863
Barry F. Kavangh and S.J. Glenn Bird. Third
edition, 1992. This introductory text ad-
dresses both theory and applications. Covers
highway curves, construction surveying, pho-
togrammetry, and hydrographic surveying.
Includes exercises with answers.

**★2667★ *Surveying Ready-Reference
Manual***
McGraw-Hill, Inc.
1221 Avenue of the Americas
New York, NY 10020
Ph: (212)512-2000   Fr: 800-722-4726
G.O. Stenstrom. 1987.

PROFESSIONAL AND TRADE
PERIODICALS

★2668★ *The ASPRS Newsletter*
American Society for Photogrammetry and
Remote Sensing (ASPRS)
5410 Grosvenor Lane, Ste. 210
Bethesda, MD 20814-2160
Ph: (301)493-0290   Fax: (301)493-0208
Joann Treadwell
Monthly. Reports on the activities of the Society, which is involved in analysis of images for
measuring topographical features and objects. Recurring features include news of
members and announcements of awards received.

★2669★ *Backsights*
Surveyors Historical Society
c/o Myron A. Lewis
31457 Hugh Way
Hayward, CA 94544-7741
Ph: (510)471-3905
Semiannual. Reflects the Society's commitment to the preservation of surveying instruments, records, and memorabilia. Features
articles on the history of surveying. Recurring

features include news of the activities of the Society and its members.

★2670★ Land Degradation & Rehabilitation
John Wiley and Sons, Inc.
Subscription Dept.
605 3rd Ave.
New York, NY 10158
Ph: (212)850-6000   Fax: (212)850-6799
C.J. Wiley

Quarterly. Journal publishing information on rehabilitation and degradation in terrestrial environments.

★2671★ Professional Surveyor
American Surveyors Publishing Co.
2300 South Ninth Street, Suite 501
Arlington, VA 22204
Ph: (703)892-0733   Fax: (703)920-3652
Nick Harrison

Bimonthly. Magazine for land surveyors, mappers, and civil engineers.

★2672★ Progress & Perspectives: Affirmative Action in Surveying and Mapping
Wendy J.W. Straight
12 E. 5th St.
Dunkirk, NY 14048
Ph: (716)366-1990
Wendy J.W. Straight

Bimonthly. Addresses equal opportunity issues in surveying and mapping. Recurring features include letters to the editor, interviews, news of research, reports of meetings, news of educational opportunities, and notices of publications available.

★2673★ Surveying and Land Information Systems
American Congress on Surveying and Mapping
5410 Grosvenor Ln.
Bethesda, MD 20814
Ph: (301)493-0200   Fax: (301)493-8245
Charles R. Schwarz

Quarterly. Scholarly journal for surveying and land information systems professsionals.

PROFESSIONAL MEETINGS AND CONVENTIONS

★2674★ California Land Surveyors Association Conference
California Land Surveyors Association
795 Farmers Ln., No. 11
PO Box 9098
Santa Rosa, CA 95405
Ph: (707)578-6016   Fax: (707)578-4406
Annual. Usually held during the spring in either California or Nevada.

★2675★ Michigan Society of Professional Land Surveyors Annual Meeting
Michigan Society of Professional Surveyors
220 S. Museum Dr.
Lansing, MI 48933
Ph: (517)484-2413   Fax: (517)484-3711
Annual. Always held during February, in Michigan. **Dates and Locations:** 1996 Feb 20-23; Lansing, MI. • 1997 Feb 18-21; Traverse City, MI. • 1998 Feb 17-20; Lansing, MI. • 1999 Feb 15-18; Grand Rapids, MI. • 2000 Feb 15-18; Traverse City, MI.

Actuaries

Actuaries design insurance and pension plans and keep informed on their operation to make sure that they are maintained on a sound financial basis. Actuaries assemble and analyze statistics to calculate probabilities of death, sickness, injury, disability, unemployment, retirement, and property loss from accident, theft, fire, and other hazards. They use this information to determine the expected insured loss. They must make sure that the price charged for the insurance will enable the company to pay all claims and expenses as they occur. Finally, this price must be profitable and yet be competitive with other insurance companies. In a similar manner, the actuary calculates premium rates and determines policy contract provisions for each type of insurance offered. Most actuaries specialize in either life and health insurance or property and liability (casualty) insurance; others specialize in pension plans, financial planning, or investment.

Salaries

Earnings depend on experience and passage of actuarial examinations.

Recent college graduates	$31,800/year
Associate status	$46,000/year
Fellow status	$65,500/year

Employment Outlook

Growth rate until the year 2005: Faster than the average.

Actuaries

describes what the worker does on the job, working conditions, education and training requirements, advancement possibilities, job outlook, earnings, and sources of additional information.

★2688★ Actuary
Careers, Inc.
PO Box 135
Largo, FL 34649-0135
Ph: (813)584-7333
1993. Two-page occupational summary card describing duties, working conditions, personal qualifications, training, earnings and hours, employment outlook, places of employment, related careers, and where to write for more information.

★2689★ "Actuary" in 100 Best Careers for the Year 2000 (pp. 170-173)
Arco Pub.
201 W. 103rd St.
Indianapolis, IN 46290
Ph: 800-428-5331   Fax: 800-835-3202
Shelly Field. 1992. Describes 100 job opportunities expected to grow fast throughout the next decade. Provides information on job duties and responsibilities, training requirements, education, advancement opportunities, experience and qualifications, and typical salaries.

★2690★ "Actuary" in College Board Guide to Jobs and Career Planning (pp. 129)
The College Board
415 Columbus Ave.
New York, NY 10023-6992
Ph: (212)713-8165   Fax: (212)713-8143
Fr: 800-323-7155
Joyce S. Mitchell. Second edition, 1994. Profiles a variety of careers. Each profile contains information on salaries, related careers, education needed, and sorces of additional information.

★2691★ "Actuary" in Desk Guide to Training and Work Advisement (p. 169)
Charles C. Thomas, Publisher
2600 S. 1st St.
Springfield, IL 62794-9265
Ph: (217)789-8980   Fax: (217)789-9130
Fr: 800-258-8980
Gail Baugher Keunstler. 1988. Describes alternative methods of gaining entry into an occupation through different types of educational programs, internships, and apprenticeships.

★2692★ "Actuary" in Guide to Federal Jobs (p. 235)
Resource Directories
3361 Executive Pkwy., Ste. 302
Toledo, OH 43606
Ph: (419)536-5353   Fax: (419)536-7056
Fr: 800-274-8515
Rod W. Durgin, editor. Third edition, 1992. Contains information on finding and applying for federal jobs. Describes more than 200 professional and technical jobs for college graduates. Covers the nature of the work, salary, and geographic location. Lists college majors preferred for that occupation. Section one describes the function and work of government agencies that hire the most significant number of college graduates.

★2693★ "Actuary" in Jobs Rated Almanac
World Almanac
1 International Blvd., Ste. 444
Mahwah, NJ 07495
Ph: (201)529-6900   Fax: (201)529-6901
Les Krantz. Second edition, 1992. Ranks 250 jobs by environment, salary, outlooks, physical demands, stress, security, travel opportunities, and extra perks. Includes jobs the editor feels are the most common, most interesting, and the most rapidly growing.

★2694★ "Actuary" in Opportunities in Insurance Careers (pp. 40-41)
National Textbook Co. (NTC)
VGM Career Books
4255 W. Touhy Ave.
Lincolnwood, IL 60646-1975
Ph: (708)679-5500   Fax: (708)679-2494
Fr: 800-323-4900
Robert M. Schrayer. 1987. Provides an introduction to the world of insurance careers through an exploration of the industry's history; academic requirements; certification, licensing, and education requirements; positions available; as well as some careers associated with the insurance industry, such as data processing, human resources, and public relations.

★2695★ "Actuary" in VGM's Careers Encyclopedia (pp. 7-11)
National Textbook Co. (NTC)
VGM Career Books
4255 W. Touhy Ave.
Lincolnwood, IL 60646-1975
Ph: (708)679-5500   Fax: (708)679-2494
Fr: 800-323-4900
Third edition, 1991. Profiles 200 occupations. Describes job duties, places of employment, working conditions, qualifications, education and training, advancement potential, and salary for each occupation.

★2696★ "Actuary" in VGM's Handbook of Business and Management Careers
National Textbook Co.
4255 W. Touhy Ave.
Lincolnwood, IL 60646-1975
Ph: (708)679-5500   Fax: (708)679-2494
Fr: 800-323-4900
Annette Selden. Second edition, 1993. Contains 42 two-page occupational profiles describing job duties, places of employment, working conditions, qualifications, education, employment outlook, and income.

PROFESSIONAL ASSOCIATIONS

★2697★ American Academy of Actuaries
1100 17th N.W., 7th Fl.
Washington, DC 20036
Ph: (202)223-8196   Fax: (202)872-1948
Members: Qualified actuaries (professionals trained in the application of mathematical probability and statistics to the design of insurance and pension programs). **Purpose:** Seeks to: facilitate relations between actuaries and government bodies; conduct public relations activities; promulgate standards of

practice for the actuarial profession. The academy was founded by 4 specialty actuarial associations in the U.S. to represent the entire profession: Casualty Actuarial Society; Conference of Actuaries in Public Practice (now Conference of Consulting Actuaries); Society of Actuaries; Fraternal Actuarial Association (now defunct). Maintains speakers' bureau. **Publications:** Actuarial Update, monthly. • American Academy of Actuaries Yearbook. • Contingencies, bimonthly. • Directory of Actuarial Memberships, annual. • Enrolled Actuaries Report, quarterly.

★2698★ American Society of Pension Actuaries (ASPA)
4350 N. Fairfax Dr., Ste. 820
Arlington, VA 22203
Ph: (703)516-9300   Fax: (703)516-9308
Members: Individuals involved in the consulting, administrative, and design aspects of the employee benefit business. **Purpose:** Promotes high standards in the profession; provides nine-part educational program. **Publications:** American Society of Pension Actuaries—Yearbook, annual. • Pension Actuary, monthly.

★2699★ Casualty Actuarial Society (CAS)
1100 N. Glebe Rd., Ste. 600
Arlington, VA 22201
Ph: (703)276-3100   Fax: (703)276-3108
Members: Professional society of insurance actuaries promoting actuarial and statistical science as applied to insurance problems (such as casualty, fire, and social) other than life insurance. Examination required for membership. **Publications:** Actuarial Review, quarterly. • Syllabus of Examinations, annual. • Year Book.

★2700★ Conference of Consulting Actuaries (CCA)
475 N. Martingale, No. 800
Schaumburg, IL 60173-2226
Ph: (708)706-3535   Fax: (708)706-3599
Members: Full-time consulting actuaries or governmental actuaries. **Publications:** Consulting Actuary, 3/year. • Proceedings of the Conference of Consulting Actuaries, annual. • Yearbook.

★2701★ Society of Actuaries (SOA)
475 N. Martingale Rd., Ste. 800
Schaumburg, IL 60173-2226
Ph: (708)706-3500   Fax: (708)706-3599
Members: Professional organization of individuals trained in the application of mathematical probabilities to the design of insurance, pension, and employee benefit programs. **Purpose:** Sponsors series of examinations leading to designation of fellow or associate in the society. Maintains speakers' bureau; conducts educational and research programs. **Publications:** The Actuary. • Directory of Actuarial Memberships, periodic. • Index to Publications, annual. • Society of Actuaries—Record. • Society of Actuaries—Transactions, annual. • Society of Actuaries Yearbook. • Statistics for Pension Actuaries, annual.

STANDARDS/CERTIFICATION AGENCIES

★2702★ American Academy of Actuaries
1100 17th N.W., 7th Fl.
Washington, DC 20036
Ph: (202)223-8196   Fax: (202)872-1948
Seeks to: facilitate relations between actuaries and government bodies; conduct public relations activities; promulgate standards of practice for the actuarial profession.

★2703★ American Society of Pension Actuaries (ASPA)
4350 N. Fairfax Dr., Ste. 820
Arlington, VA 22203
Ph: (703)516-9300   Fax: (703)516-9308
Promotes high standards in the profession; provides nine-part educational program.

★2704★ Society of Actuaries (SOA)
475 N. Martingale Rd., Ste. 800
Schaumburg, IL 60173-2226
Ph: (708)706-3500   Fax: (708)706-3599
Professional organization of individuals trained in the application of mathematical probabilities to the design of insurance, pension, and employee benefit programs. Sponsors series of examinations leading to designation of fellow or associate in the society.

TEST GUIDES

★2705★ Career Examination Series: Actuary
National Learning Corp.
212 Michael Dr.
Syosset, NY 11791
Ph: (516)921-8888   Fax: (516)921-8743
Fr: 800-645-6337
Jack Rudman. A series of study guides with multiple-choice examination questions and solutions for trainees and professional actuaries. Titles in the series include *Assistant Actuary; Principal Actuary; Senior Actuarial Clerk; Senior Actuary.*

AWARDS, SCHOLARSHIPS, GRANTS, AND FELLOWSHIPS

★2706★ AERF Practitioners Award
Actuarial Education and Research Fund
475 N. Martingale Rd., Ste. 800
Schaumburg, IL 60173-2226
Ph: (708)706-3570   Fax: (708)706-3599
To acknowledge the considerable research done by actuaries in a nonacademic setting and to encourage the publication of research performed in the working environment. The research must be practical and innovative. The work must be done by an individual who is not substantially employed by an academic

institution and who is a member of one of the sponsoring organizations. The research must be actuarial in nature and not already published in a journal or a newsletter. A monetary award and publication in *ARCH (Actuarial Research Learning House)* are awarded annually. Established in 1988.

★2707★ Annual Prize
Society of Actuaries
475 N. Martingale, Rd. Ste. 800
Schaumburg, IL 60173-2226
Ph: (708)706-3500   Fax: (708)706-3599
For recognition of the best eligible *Transactions* paper released to members of the Society in preprint page-proof form during each year. Papers eligible must be those released between July 1 and June 30 of the year of the award. A monetary prize of $500 and a plaque are awarded annually when merited. Established in 1982.

★2708★ Dorweiler Prize
Casualty Actuarial Society
1100 N. Glebe Rd., Ste. 600
Arlington, VA 22201
Ph: (301)547-3205   Fax: (703)276-3100
To stimulate original thinking and research in the solution of advanced insurance problems by recognizing outstanding papers by an Associate or Fellow of the Society who has attained his designation more than five years ago. A monetary prize of $1,000 is awarded annually if merited. Established in 1970 in honor of Paul Dorweiler.

★2709★ Halmstad Prize
Actuarial Education and Research Fund
475 N. Martingale Rd., Ste. 800
Schaumburg, IL 60173-2226
Ph: (708)706-3570   Fax: (708)706-3599
For recognition of the best paper on actuarial research published each year. Papers may be nominated. A monetary prize is awarded annually. Established in 1978 in memory of David Garrick Halmstad, an associate of the Society of Actuaries, for his significant contributions to actuarial science and research.

★2710★ Michelbacher Prize
Casualty Actuarial Society
1100 N. Glebe Rd., Ste. 600
Arlington, VA 22201
Ph: (301)547-3205   Fax: (703)276-3100
To recognize the author of the best paper submitted in response to a call for discussion papers whenever the program is conducted by the Casualty Actuarial Society. Selection is based on originality, research, readability, and completeness of papers. Recipients need not be members of the CAS. A monetary prize of $1,000 is awarded annually. Established in 1979 in memory of Gustav F. Michelbacher.

★2711★ Harold W. Schloss Memorial Scholarship Fund
Casualty Actuarial Society
1100 N. Glebe Rd., Ste. 600
Arlington, VA 22201
Ph: (301)547-3205   Fax: (703)276-3100
To benefit deserving and academically outstanding students in the actuarial program of the Department of Statistics and Actuarial Science at the University of Iowa. The student recipient is selected each spring by the Trustees of the CAS Trust based on the rec-

ommendation of the department chairman at the University of Iowa. A scholarship of $500 is awarded annually. Established in 1984 in memory of Harold W. Schloss, a past president of the Society.

★2712★ Triennial Prize
Society of Actuaries
475 N. Martingale, Rd. Ste. 800
Schaumburg, IL 60173-2226
Ph: (708)706-3500   Fax: (708)706-3599
For recognition of the best eligible *Transactions* paper released to members of the Society in preprint page-proof form during each successive three-year period. The paper must have been submitted to the Executive Director of the Society before the end of the fifth year succeeding the calendar year in which the author first qualified as an Associate of a recognized actuarial society. Members may submit papers written during the three years preceding the award. A monetary prize of $500 and a plaque are awarded triennially, when merited. Established in 1912.

★2713★ Woodward - Fondiller Prize
Casualty Actuarial Society
1100 N. Glebe Rd., Ste. 600
Arlington, VA 22201
Ph: (301)547-3205   Fax: (703)276-3100
To stimulate original thinking and research in the solution of advanced insurance problems by recognizing outstanding papers by an Associate or Fellow of the Society who has attained his designation within the last five years. A monetary award of $1,000 is awarded annually if merited. Established in 1963 in memory of Joseph H. Woodward and Richard Fondiller.

BASIC REFERENCE GUIDES AND HANDBOOKS

★2714★ Actuarial Mathematics
American Mathematical Society (AMS)
PO Box 6248
Providence, RI 02940
Ph: 800-321-4267
Harry H. Panjer, editor. Thirty-fifth edition, 1990. Includes bibliographies.

★2715★ Insurance Risk Models
Society of Actuaries
475 N. Martingale Rd., Ste. 800
Schaumburg, IL 60173-3226
Ph: (708)706-3500   Fax: (708)706-3599
H.H. Panjer, editor. 1992.

★2716★ Options and the Management of Financial Risk
Society of Actuaries
475 N. Martingale Rd., Ste. 800
Schaumburg, IL 60173-3226
Phelim Boyle, editor. 1992.

PROFESSIONAL AND TRADE PERIODICALS

★2717★ AAIS Viewpoint
American Association of Insurance Services (AAIS)
1035 S. York Rd.
Bensenville, IL 60106
Ph: (708)595-3225   Fax: (708)595-4647
Carol Poynter
Quarterly. Contains news of current insurance issues, AAIS activities, insurance legislation, and other subjects of interest.

★2718★ Actuarial Digest
PO Box 1167
Ponte Vedra, FL 32004
Ph: (904)273-1245
Gene Hubbard
Bimonthly. Covers issues of concern to working actuaries. Recurring features include letters to the editor, interviews, news of research, a calendar of events, news of educational opportunities, job listings, book reviews, notices of publications available, and a column titled What's New.

★2719★ Actuarial Futures
Society of Actuaries
475 N. Martingale, Ste. 800
Schaumburg, IL 60173-2226
Ph: (708)706-3500   Fax: (708)706-3599
Susan Martz, Contact
Irregular. Facilitates the professional development of Society members in the field of futurism. Recurring features include letters to the editor and a column titled Chairperson's Corner.

★2720★ Actuarial Update
American Academy of Actuaries
1720 I St. NW, 7th Fl.
Washington, DC 20006
Ph: (202)223-8196   Fax: (202)872-1948
Adam Reese
Monthly. Supports the Academy's efforts to provide standards or criteria for actuaries, to promote education in actuarial science, and to educate the public on the actuarial profession. Facilitates the exchange of information among actuarial organizations. Recurring features include reports on developments affecting the actuarial profession, news of members, news of research, and a calendar of Academy events and activities of interest.

★2721★ Actuary of the Future
Society of Actuaries
475 N. Martingale, Ste. 800
Schaumburg, IL 60173-2226
Ph: (708)706-3500   Fax: (708)706-3599
Susan Martz, Contact
Encourages and facilitates communication and professional development of members of the Society who have nontraditional experience or have an interest in exploring nontraditional roles and opportunities for actuaries. Recurring features include a column titled Editor's Note.

★2722★ Digital Doings
Society of Actuaries
475 N. Martingale, Ste. 800
Schaumburg, IL 60173-2226
Ph: (708)706-3500   Fax: (708)706-3599
Susan Martz, Contact
Disseminates information concerning developments in computer science as it relates to the work of actuaries. Recurring features include a column titled Sound Bytes.

★2723★ Expanding Horizons
Society of Actuaries
475 N. Martingale, Ste. 800
Schaumburg, IL 60173-2226
Ph: (708)706-3500   Fax: (708)706-3599
Susan Martz, Contact
Facilitates the professional development of Society members in the areas of actuarial education and research. Recurring features include letters to the editor, news of educational opportunities, news of research, and a calendar of events.

★2724★ Financial Reporter
Society of Actuaries
475 N. Martingale, Ste. 800
Schaumburg, IL 60173-2226
Ph: (708)706-3500   Fax: (708)706-3599
Susan Martz
Encourages the professional development of Society members in the field of life insurance company financial reporting. Recurring features include letters to the editor, news of research, news of educational opportunities, and a calendar of events.

★2725★ The Future Actuary
Society of Actuaries
475 N. Martingale, Ste. 800
Schaumburg, IL 60173-2226
Ph: (708)706-3500   Fax: (708)706-3599
Judy Bluder-Wohlt
Quarterly. Provides actuarial students with the latest information on jobs, internships, study techniques, career development, professional conduct, and ethics. Recurring features include a calendar of events, news of educational opportunities, and job listings.

★2726★ Insurance Industry Newsletter
Smith & Associates
PO Box 3006
Savannah, GA 31402-3006
Ph: (912)355-4117   Fax: (912)355-4117
George V.R. Smith
Weekly. Provides news and comment on the insurance industry in the U.S. Contains information on legislation and regulation, trends, promotions, and new products. Recurring features include book reviews, news of research, statistics, obituaries, and meetings in the fields of liability, property, life, and health insurance.

PROFESSIONAL MEETINGS AND CONVENTIONS

★2727★ Society of Actuaries Convention
Society of Actuaries
475 N. Martingale Rd., Ste. 800
Schaumburg, IL 60173-2226
Ph: (708)706-3500   Fax: (708)706-3599
Annual. **Dates and Locations:** 1995 Oct 15-18; Boston, MA.

OTHER SOURCES OF INFORMATION

★2728★ "Actuary" in Career Selector 2001
Barron's Educational Series, Inc.
250 Wireless Blvd.
Hauppauge, NY 11788
Ph: (516)434-3311   Fax: (516)434-3723
Fr: 800-645-3476
James C. Gonyea. 1993.

★2729★ "Insurance and Actuarial Science" in Accounting to Zoology: Graduate Fields Defined (p. 42)
Petersons Guides, Inc.
PO Box 2123
Princeton, NJ 08543-2123
Ph: (609)243-9111   Fax: (609)243-9150
Fr: 800-338-3282
Amy J. Goldstein, editor. Revised and updated, 1987. Defines 298 graduate and professional fields. Discusses types of graduate programs and degrees, graduate research, applied work, employment prospects, and trends.

★2730★ Principles of Professional Conduct
American Society of Pension Actuaries (ASPA)
2029 K St. NW, 4th Fl.
Washington, DC 20006
Ph: (202)659-3620
Describes actuarial professional conduct, responsibility to clients, relations with other professionals, competition, advertising, and solicitation.

★2731★ Rules of Conduct and Practice Procedures Concerning Enrolled Actuaries and Their Interrelationships With Pension Practitioners
American Society of Pension Actuaries (ASPA)
2029 K St. NW, 4th Fl.
Washington, DC 20006
Ph: (202)659-3620
1987.

Computer Scientists and Systems Analysis

Computer scientists conduct research, design computers, and discover and use principles of applying computers. They have a high level of theoretical expertise that apply to the complex problems and innovative ideas for the application or creation of new technology. **Systems analysts** define business, scientific, or engineering problems and design solutions using computers. They may design entirely new systems, including hardware and software, or add a single new software application.

Salaries

Systems analysts salaries vary by region of the country and by industry.

Lowest 10 percent	Less than $25,200/year
Median	$42,100/year
Top 10 percent	More than $65,500/year
Federal government entry level	$18,300/year

Employment Outlook

Growth rate until the year 2005: Much faster than the average.

Computer Scientists and Systems Analysts

CAREER GUIDES

★2732★ *Career Choices for the 90's for Students of Computer Science*
Walker and Co.
435 Hudson St.
New York, NY 10014
Ph: (212)727-8300   Fax: (212)727-0984
Fr: 800-289-2553
1990. Offers alternatives for students of computer science. Gives information about the job outlook and competition for entry-level candidates. Provides job-hunting tips.

★2733★ *Careers for Computer Buffs and Other Technological Types*
National Textbook Co. (NTC)
VGM Career Books
4255 W. Touhy Ave.
Lincolnwood, IL 60646-1975
Ph: (708)679-5500   Fax: (708)679-2494
Fr: 800-323-4900
Marjorie Eberts and Margaret Gisler, editors. 1993. Career manual for those interested in computers and other technological fields.

★2734★ "Computer Careers" in *Best Jobs for the 1990s and Into the 21st Century*
Impact Publications
9104-N Manassas Dr.
Manassas Park, VA 22111
Ph: (703)361-7300   Fax: (703)335-9486
Ronald L. Krannich and Caryl Rae Krannich. 1993. Includes information on computer programmers, systems analysts, and operations research analysts.

★2735★ "The Computer Industry" in *Encyclopedia of Career Choices for the 1990s: A Guide to Entry Level Jobs (pp. 152-173)*
Berkley Pub.
PO Box 506
East Rutherford, NJ 07073
Fax: (201)933-2316   Fr: 800-788-6262
1992. Describes entry-level careers in a variety of industries. Presents qualifications re-

quired, working conditions, salary, internships, and professional associations.

★2736★ "Computer and Information Services" in *Where the Jobs Are: The Hottest Careers for the 90s (pp. 77-96)*
Career Press
180 5th Ave.
Hawthorne, NJ 07507
Ph: (201)427-0229   Fax: (201)427-2037
Fr: 800-CAREER-1
Joyce Hadley. 1995. Offers a job-hunting strategy for the 1990s as well as descriptions of growing careers of the decade. Each profile includes general information, forecasts, growth, education and training, licensing requirements, and salary information.

★2737★ *Computer, Salary Survey and Career Planning Guide*
Source EDP
120 Broadway, Ste. 1010
New York, NY 10271
Ph: (212)557-8611
Annual. Describes career paths in the computer field and trends in the computer field. Lists job titles. Charts salaries by job titles, years of experience, and industry.

★2738★ "Computer Scientists and Systems Analysts" in *Occupational Outlook Handbook*
U.S. Government Printing Office
Superintendent of Documents
Washington, DC 20402
Ph: (202)512-1800   Fax: (202)512-2250
Biennial; latest edition, 1994-95. Encyclopedia of careers describing about 250 occupations and comprising about 85 percent of all jobs in the economy. Occupations that require lengthy education or training are given the most attention. Each occupation's profile describes what the worker does on the job, working conditions, education and training requirements, advancement possibilities, job outlook, earnings, and sources of additional information.

★2739★ "Computer Technologists and Professionals" in *American Almanac of Jobs and Salaries (pp. 284-295)*
Avon Books
1350 Avenue of the Americas
New York, NY 10019
Ph: (212)261-6800   Fr: 800-238-0658
John Wright, editor. Revised and updated, 1994-95. A comprehensive guide to the wages of hundreds of occupations in a wide variety of industries and organizations.

★2740★ "Computers" in *College Majors and Careers: A Resource Guide to Effective Life Planning (pp. 41-42)*
Garrett Park Press
PO Box 1907
Garrett Park, MD 20896
Ph: (301)946-2553
Paul Phifer. 1993. Lists 60 college majors, with definitions; related occupations and leisure activities; skills, values, and personal needed attributes; suggested readings; and a list of associations.

★2741★ "Computers" in *Internships 1995*
Petersons Guides, Inc.
PO Box 2123
Princeton, NJ 08543-2123
Ph: (609)243-9111   Fr: 800-338-3282
Fifteenth edition, 1995. Lists internship opportunities under six broad categories: communications, creative, performing, and fine arts, human services, international relations, business and technology, and public affairs. For each internship program, gives the names, phone number, contact person, description, eligibility requirements, and benefits.

★2742★ *Exploring Careers in the Computer Field*
Rosen Publishing Group
29 E. 21st St.
New York, NY 10010
Ph: (212)777-3017   Fax: (212)777-0277
Fr: 800-237-9932
Joseph Weintraub. Revised edition, 1993. Describes future trends in computers including opportunities in hardware and software. Includes interviews with people in different

computer careers including programming, consulting, and systems management. Provides state-by-state listing of universities and colleges offering two- and four-year degree programs in data processing and computer science.

★2743★ Exploring High-Tech Careers
Rosen Publishing Group
29 E. 21st St.
New York, NY 10010
Ph: (212)777-3017   Fax: (212)777-0277
Fr: 800-237-9932

Scott Southworth. Revised edition, 1993. Gives an orientation to the field of high technology and high-tech jobs. Describes educational preparation and job hunting. Includes a glossary and a bibliography.

★2744★ Making It Big in Data Processing: A Total Program for Success Based on Over 35 Years of Experience With Data Processing Professionals
Crown Publishers, Inc.
201 E. 50th St.
New York, NY 10002
Ph: (212)254-1600   Fr: 800-726-0600

Robert Half. 1987. Written for the person planning to use a data processing job as a springboard to a career. Includes advice on educational preparation, job hunting, succeeding on the job, and moving into a supervisory position.

★2745★ "Michael Ati—Systems Analyst" in Straight Talk on Careers: Eighty Pros Take You Into Their Professions (pp. 3-5)
Garrett Park Press
PO Box 1907
Garrett Park, MD 20896
Ph: (301)946-2553

Mary Barbera-Hogan. 1987. Contains candid interviews from people who give an inside view of their work in 80 different careers. These professionals describe a day's work and the stresses and rewards accompanying their work.

★2746★ Opportunities in Computer Science Careers
National Textbook Co. (NTC)
VGM Career Books
4255 W. Touhy Ave.
Lincolnwood, IL 60646-1975
Ph: (708)679-5500   Fax: (708)679-2494
Fr: 800-323-4900

Julie L. Kling. 1991. Includes a bibliography. Describes job duties, educaitonal requirements, salary, working conditions, employment outlook, and advancement opportunities.

★2747★ Opportunities in Word Processing Careers
National Textbook Co. (NTC)
VGM Career Books
4255 W. Touhy Ave.
Lincolnwood, IL 60646-1975
Ph: (708)679-5500   Fax: (708)679-2494
Fr: 800-323-4900

Marianne Forrester Munday. 1991. Explains the development of word processing and how it works. Discusses the training needed, major employers of word processing person-

nel, and related careers, including systems analyst.

★2748★ Peterson's Job Opportunities for Engineering and Technology
Petersons Guides, Inc.
PO Box 2123
Princeton, NJ 08543-2123
Ph: (609)243-9111   Fax: (609)243-9150
Fr: 800-338-3282

1994. Gives job hunting advice including information on resume writing, interviewing, and handling salary negotiations. Lists companies that hire college graduates in science and engineering at the bachelor and master's level. Companies are indexed by industry, starting location, and major. Company profiles include contact information and types of hires.

★2749★ "Systems Analysis" in Choices for the 90's for Students of Mathematics (pp. 52-55)
Walker and Co.
435 Hudson St.
New York, NY 10014
Ph: (212)727-8300   Fax: (212)727-0984
Fr: 800-289-2553

1990. Offers alternatives for students of mathematics. Gives information about the outlook and competition for entry-level candidates. Provides job-hunting tips.

★2750★ Systems Analyst
Careers, Inc.
PO Box 135
Largo, FL 34649-0135
Ph: (813)584-7333

1991. Two-page occupational summary card describing duties, working conditions, personal qualifications, training, earnings and hours, employment outlook, places of employment, related careers, and where to write for more information.

★2751★ "Systems Analyst" in 100 Best Careers for the Year 2000 (pp. 110-112)
Arco Pub.
201 W. 103rd St.
Indianapolis, IN 46290
Ph: 800-428-5331   Fax: 800-835-3202

Shelly Field. 1992. Describes 100 job opportunities expected to grow fast throughout the next decade. Provides information on job duties and responsibilities, training requirements, education, advancement opportunities, experience and qualifications, and typical salaries.

★2752★ "Systems Analyst" in BLR Encyclopedia of Prewritten Job Descriptions
Business and Legal Reports, Inc.
39 Academy St.
Madison, CT 06443-1513
Ph: (203)245-7448

Stephen D. Bruce, editor-in-chief. 1994. This book contains hundreds of sample job descriptions arranged by functional job category. The 1-3 page job descriptions cover what the worker normally does in the position, who they report to, and how that position fits in the organizational structure.

★2753★ "Systems Analyst" in Career Information Center (Vol.1)
Simon and Schuster
200 Old Tappan Rd.
Old Tappan, NJ 07675
Fax: 800-445-6991   Fr: 800-223-2348

Richard Lidz and Linda Perrin, editorial directors. Fifth edition, 1993. A multi-volume set that profiles over 600 occupations. Each occupational profile describes job duties, educational requirements, advancement possibilities, employment outlook, working conditions, earnings and benefits, and where to write for more information.

★2754★ "Systems Analyst" in Careers in Business (pp. 32-60)
National Textbook Co. (NTC)
VGM Career Books
4255 W. Touhy Ave.
Lincolnwood, IL 60646-1975
Ph: (708)679-5500   Fax: (708)679-2494
Fr: 800-323-4900

Lila B. Stair and Dorothy Domkowski, editors. 1992. Provides facts about business areas such as marketing, accounting, production, human resources, management, and finance. Focuses on job duties, salaries, career paths, employment outlook, trends, educational preparation, and skills needed.

★2755★ "Systems Analyst" in Careers in High-Tech
Arco Publishing Co.
Macmillan General Reference
15 Columbus Cir.
New York, NY 10023
Fax: 800-835-3202   Fr: 800-858-7674

Connie Winkler. 1987. Surveys occupations in data processing, personal computers, telecommunications, manufacturing technology, artificial intelligence, computer graphics, medicine, biotechnology, lasers, technical writing, and publishing. Separate chapters cover education and training.

★2756★ "Systems Analyst" in College Board Guide to Jobs and Career Planning (pp. 123)
The College Board
415 Columbus Ave.
New York, NY 10023-6992
Ph: (212)713-8165   Fax: (212)713-8143
Fr: 800-323-7155

Joyce S. Mitchell. Second edition, 1994. Covers a variety of careers. Each career profile contains information on salaries, related careers, education needed, and sources of additional information.

★2757★ "Systems Analyst" in Opportunities in High-Tech Careers (pp. 100-101)
National Textbook Co. (NTC)
VGM Career Books
4255 W. Touhy Ave.
Lincolnwood, IL 60646-1975
Ph: (708)679-5500   Fax: (708)679-2494
Fr: 800-323-4900

Gary D. Colter and Deborah Yanuck. 1987. Explores high technology careers. Written for the student and displaced worker. Describes job opportunities, how to make a career decision, how to prepare for high-technology jobs, job hunting techniques, and future trends.

★2758★ "Systems Analyst" in VGM's Careers Encyclopedia (pp. 447-449)
National Textbook Co. (NTC)
VGM Career Books
4255 W. Touhy Ave.
Lincolnwood, IL 60646-1975
Ph: (708)679-5500   Fax: (708)679-2494
Fr: 800-323-4900
Third edition, 1991. Profiles 200 occupations. Describes job duties, places of employment, working conditions, qualifications, education and training, advancement potential, and salary for each occupation.

★2759★ "Systems Analyst" in VGM's Handbook of Business and Management Careers
National Textbook Co.
4255 W. Touhy Ave.
Lincolnwood, IL 60646-1975
Ph: (708)679-5500   Fax: (708)679-2494
Fr: 800-323-4900
Annette Selden. Second edition, 1993. Contains 42 two-page occupational profiles describing job duties, places of employment, working conditions, qualifications, education, employment outlook, and income.

★2760★ Systems Analysts
Chronicle Guidance Publications, Inc.
66 Aurora St.
PO Box 1190
Moravia, NY 13118-1190
Ph: (315)497-0330   Fax: (315)497-3359
Fr: 800-622-7284
1993. Career brief describing the nature of the job, working conditions, hours and earnings, education and training, licensure, certification, unions, personal qualifications, social and psychological factors, location, employment outlook, entry methods, advancement, and related occupations.

★2761★ "Systems and Analysts" in Encyclopedia of Careers and Vocational Guidance (Vol.4, pp. 476-477)
J.G. Ferguson Publishing Co.
200 W. Madison St., Ste. 300
Chicago, IL 60606
Ph: (312)580-5480   Fax: (312)580-4948
William E. Hopke, editor-in-chief. Ninth edition, 1993. Four-volume set that profiles 900 occupations and describes job trends in 74 industries. Includes career description, educational requirements, history of the job, methods of entry, advancement, employment outlook, earnings, conditions of work, social and psychological factors, and sources of further information.

★2762★ "Systems Analysts" in Jobs! What They Are—Where They Are—What They Pay (p. 82)
Simon & Schuster, Inc.
Simon & Schuster Bldg.
1230 Avenue of the Americas
New York, NY 10020
Ph: (212)698-7000   Fr: 800-223-2348
Robert O. Snelling and Anne M. Snelling. 3rd edition, 1992. Describes duties and responsibilities, earnings, employment opportunities, training, and qualifications.

PROFESSIONAL ASSOCIATIONS

★2763★ Association for Computing Machinery (ACM)
1515 Broadway
New York, NY 10036-5701
Ph: (212)869-7440   Fax: (212)944-1318
Computer scientists, engineers, physical scientists, business system specialists, analysts, and social scientists interested in computing and data processing. Works to advance information processing including the study, design, development, construction, and application of modern technology and computing techniques. Encourages appropriate language for general information processing, storage, retrieval, and transmission/communication. Promotes the automatic control and simulation of processes. Maintains over 30 special interest groups that focus on specific computer issues. Holds 60 special interest group meetings per year. **Publications:** Association for Computing Machinery—Conference Proceedings, annual. • Communications of the ACM, monthly. • Computing Reviews, monthly. • Computing Surveys, quarterly. • Guide to Computing Literature, annual. • Journal of the Association for Computing Machinery, quarterly. • Quote Quad, quarterly. • Transactions on Computer Systems, quarterly. • Transactions on Database Systems, quarterly. • Transactions on Graphics, quarterly. • Transactions on Mathematical Software, quarterly. • Transactions on Office Information Systems, quarterly. • Transactions on Programming Languages and Systems, quarterly.

★2764★ Association for Systems Management (ASM)
1433 W. Bagley Rd.
PO Box 38370
Cleveland, OH 44138-0370
Ph: (216)243-6900   Fax: (216)234-2930
Members: International professional organization of executives and specialists in management information systems serving business, commerce, education, government, and the military. **Purpose:** Expresses concern with communications, electronics, equipment, forms control, human relations, organization, procedure writing, and systems applications. Offers seminars, conferences, and courses in all phases of information systems and management. **Publications:** Journal of Systems Management, monthly.

STANDARDS/CERTIFICATION AGENCIES

★2765★ Institute for Certification of Computer Professionals (ICCP)
2200 E. Devon Ave., Ste. 268
Des Plaines, IL 60018
Ph: (708)299-4227   Fax: (708)299-4280
Individuals passing the exams automatically become members of the Association of the Institute for Certification of Computer Professionals. Has developed code of ethics and good practice to which those taking the exams promise to adhere.

TEST GUIDES

★2766★ Advanced Placement Examination in Computer Science
Arco Publishing Co.
Macmillan General Reference
15 Columbus Cir.
New York, NY 10023
Fax: 800-835-3202   Fr: 800-858-7674
Elayne Schulman. Second edition, 1988. Includes two full-length model examinations in computer science, plus review and drill.

★2767★ Career Examination Series: Computer Systems Analyst
National Learning Corp.
212 Michael Dr.
Syosset, NY 11791
Ph: (516)921-8888   Fax: (516)921-8743
Fr: 800-645-6337
Jack Rudman. A series of study guides with multiple-choice examination questions and solutions for trainees and professional computer systems analysts. Titles in the series include Associate Computer Programmer/Analyst; Associate Computer Systems Analysts; Computer Associate (Systems Programming); Computer Specialist; Computer Specialist (Data Base Administration); Computer Systems Analyst Trainee; Computer Systems Manager; Principal Systems Analyst; Senior Computer Systems Analyst; Senior Systems Analyst; Supervising Systems Analyst.

★2768★ Career Examination Series: Database Programmer Analyst
National Learning Corp.
212 Michael Dr.
Syosset, NY 11791
Ph: (516)921-8888   Fax: (516)921-8743
Fr: 800-645-6337
Jack Rudman. 1993. Test guide including questions and answers for students or professionals in the field who seek advancement through examination.

★2769★ Career Examination Series: Digital Computer Specialist
National Learning Corp.
212 Michael Dr.
Syosset, NY 11791
Ph: (516)921-8888   Fax: (516)921-8743
Fr: 800-645-6337
Jack Rudman. 1993. Test guide including questions and answers for students or professionals in the field who seek advancement through examination.

★2770★ Career Examination Series: Digital Computer Systems Analyst
National Learning Corp.
212 Michael Dr.
Syosset, NY 11791
Ph: (516)921-8888 Fax: (516)921-8743
Fr: 800-645-6337
Jack Rudman. 1993. Test guide including questions and answers for students or professionals in the field who seek advancement through examination.

★2771★ Career Examination Series: Digital Computer Systems Specialist
National Learning Corp.
212 Michael Dr.
Syosset, NY 11791
Ph: (516)921-8888 Fax: (516)921-8743
Fr: 800-645-6337
Jack Rudman. 1993. Test guide including questions and answers for students or professionals in the field who seek advancement through examination.

★2772★ Career Examination Series: Management Information Systems Specialist
National Learning Corp.
212 Michael Dr.
Syosset, NY 11791
Ph: (516)921-8888 Fax: (516)921-8743
Fr: 800-645-6337
Jack Rudman. 1993. Test guide including questions and answers for students or professionals in the field who seek advancement through examination.

★2773★ Career Examination Series: Personnel, Administration and Computer Occupations
National Learning Corp.
212 Michael Dr.
Syosset, NY 11791
Ph: (516)921-8888 Fax: (516)921-8743
Fr: 800-645-6337
Jack Rudman. 1993. Test guide including questions and answers for students or professionals in the field who seek advancement through examination.

★2774★ Career Examination Series: Senior Systems Analyst
National Learning Corp.
212 Michael Dr.
Syosset, NY 11791
Ph: (516)921-8888 Fax: (516)921-8743
Fr: 800-645-6337
Jack Rudman. Test guide including questions and answers for students or professionals in the field who seek advancement through examination.

★2775★ Career Examination Series: Systems Analyst
National Learning Corp.
212 Michael Dr.
Syosset, NY 11791
Ph: (516)921-8888 Fax: (516)921-8743
Fr: 800-645-6337
Jack Rudman. 1993. Test guide including questions and answers for students or professionals in the field who seek advancement through examination.

★2776★ Computer Science
National Learning Corp.
212 Michael Dr.
Syosset, NY 11791
Ph: (516)921-8888 Fax: (516)921-8743
Fr: 800-645-6337
Jack Rudman. A test from the Graduate Record Examination series. Multiple-choice test for those seeking admission to graduate school for study in the field of computer science. Includes solutions to examination questions.

★2777★ EZ 101 Study Keys: Computer Science
Barron's Educational Series, Inc.
250 Wireless Blvd.
Hauppauge, NY 11788
Ph: (516)434-3311 Fax: (516)434-3723
Fr: 800-645-3476
1991. Provides themes and a glossary of terms.

★2778★ Graduate Record Examination in Computer Science
Arco Pub.
201 W. 103rd St.
Indianapolis, IN 46290
Ph: 800-428-5331 Fax: 800-835-3202
Yusuf Efe and Stephen Ben-Avi. 1988. Provides two complete sample exams with detailed answers. Areas covered include: software systems, computer organization, theory, and mathematics.

★2779★ Graduate Record Examination: Computers
Arco Publishing Co.
Macmillan General Reference
15 Columbus Cir.
New York, NY 10023
Fax: 800-835-3202 Fr: 800-858-7674
Thomas H. Martinson. Fifth edition, 1994. Includes six practice exams.

EDUCATIONAL DIRECTORIES AND PROGRAMS

★2780★ Computing and Software Design Career Directory
Gale Research Inc.
835 Penobscot Bldg.
Detroit, MI 48226-4094
Ph: (313)961-2242 Fax: (313)961-6083
Fr: 800-877-GALE
Bradley J. Morgan and Joseph M. Palmisano. 1993. A directory in the Career Advisor Series that provides essays written by industry professionals; job search information on resume and cover letter preparation, networking, and the interviewing process; approximately 300 companies and organizations offering job opportunities and internships, and additional job-hunting resources.

AWARDS, SCHOLARSHIPS, GRANTS, AND FELLOWSHIPS

★2781★ Engineering Rotation Program
Hughes Aircraft Company
Technical Education Center
PO Box 80028
Los Angeles, CA 90080-0028
Ph: (310)568-6711
Purpose: To enable engineering and science graduates to find and develop the special field of work and the career position best suited to their interests and education. Qualifications: Applicant must be a U.S. citizen and have a bachelor's degree in electrical, mechanical, systems, computer or aerospace engineering; computer science; physics; or mathematics. Candidate must have a grade point average of at least 3.0/4.0, with emphasis on technical classes and related disciplines. Participants in the Rotation Program gain practical experience through up to four different work assignments at Hughes facilities, usually in southern California. Upon completion of the program, participants may be placed in permanent positions with the Company, based on their interests and assignments available. Funds available: Salary and company benefits. Application details: Write to the educational coordinator for application form and guidelines. Include pertinent information regarding academic status (university, field of interest for both undergraduate and graduate work, year of graduation, and grade point average) in initial letter of interest. Deadline: 1 March.

★2782★ Engineer Degree Fellowships; Howard Hughes Doctoral Fellowships
Hughes Aircraft Company
Technical Education Center
PO Box 80028
Los Angeles, CA 90080-0028
Ph: (310)568-6711
Purpose: To support doctoral studies in engineering and related sciences and to provide students with practical work experience. Qualifications: Applicant for either type of fellowship must be a U.S. citizen and have a bachelor's and master's degree or equivalent graduate experience in electrical, mechanical, systems, computer or aerospace engineering; computer science; physics; or mathematics. Engineer Degree Fellowships are reserved for candidates who have first degrees in engineering. For both awards, priority is given to individuals with experience in electronics and related disciplines. Candidate must have a minimum grade point average of 3.0/4.0, and be qualified for admission to an approved graduate program in the United States. Fellows are considered employees of the Hughes Aircraft Company and, in addition to their graduate studies, gain work experience in one of two programs: work-study or full-study. Fellows in the work-study program attend a university near a Hughes facility (usually in southern California) and complete coursework while working at the facility for 20 to 36 hours per week. Work-study fellows may switch to full-study status to complete their dissertations. Full-study fellows attend a university distant from Hughes and are on

leave of absence from the company while studying full-time. Full-study fellows are required to spend the summer term working for the Company, and may work eight hours a week during the school year if attending a university within commuting distance. Funds available: Company salary and benefits, plus tuition, book and living allowances. Application details: Write to the educational coordinator for application form and guidelines. Include pertinent information regarding academic status (university, field of interest for both undergraduate and graduate work, year of graduation, and grade point average) in initial letter of interest. Deadline: 10 January. Fellows are announced in April.

★2783★ NAACP Willems Scholarship
National Association for the Advancement
  of Colored People (NAACP)
4805 Mt. Hope Dr.
Baltimore, MD 21215-3297
Ph: (410)358-8900

Qualifications: Applicants must be majoring in engineering, chemistry, physics, or computer and mathematical sciences and possess a cumulative grade point average of at least 3.0 or B average. They must be members of the NAACP. Funds available: Undergraduates will receive a maximum award of $8,000 to be paid in annual installments of $2,000. Graduates will be awarded a $3,000 renewable scholarship. Application details: Updated application forms are available in January. Deadline: April 30.

★2784★ General Emmett Paige
  Scholarship
Armed Forces Communications &
  Electronics Association (AFCEA)
Educational Foundation
4400 Fair Lakes Ct.
Fairfax, VA 22033-3899
Ph: (703)631-6149   Fax: (703)631-4693

Purpose: To promote excellence in scientific and engineering education. Qualifications: Applicants must be United States citizens enrolled in an accredited four-year college or university and working toward a bachelor degree in electrical engineering, electronics, communications engineering, mathematics, computer technology, physics, or information management. Selection criteria: The scholarship is awarded on the basis of demonstrated academic achievement, high "moral character," leadership ability, and potential to contribute to the defense of the United States. Financial need is also a consideration. Funds available: Scholarships of $1,000 are awarded each year. Except under unusual circumstances, students may receive only one award from AFCEA per year. Application details: Application forms are available from school ROTC units or by contacting Mrs. Phyllis R. Lau, Administrator of Scholarships and Awards, at the above address. Toll-free telephone: 800-336-4583, ext. 6149. Students competing for other AFCEA scholarships are automatically considered for the General Emmett Paige Scholarship. Deadline: May 1.

★2785★ U.S. Department of Energy
  Internship
Oak Ridge Institute for Science and
  Education
Science/Engineering Education Division
University Programs Division
PO Box 117
Oak Ridge, TN 37831-0117
Ph: (615)576-3427   Fax: (615)576-0202

Qualifications: Applicants must be United States citizens or permanent resident aliens who are currently at the junior or senior level at a college or university, are majoring in computer sciences, engineering, environmental/life sciences, or physical sciences, and have a minimum grade point average of 3.0 or higher on a 4.0 scale. Selection criteria: Participants are selected on the basis of academic merit, future research interests, and an availability of the position at the National Laboratory. Funds available: A stipend of $225 per week, plus complimentary housing (or housing allowance) and round trip transportation to the laboratory. Approximately 400 Recipients are given internships as student research participants at one of the following locations: Argonne National Laboratory, Illinois; Brookhaven National Laboratory, New York; Lawrence Berkeley Laboratory, California; Lawrence Livermore Laboratory, California; Los Alamos National Laboratory, New Mexico; Oak Ridge National Laboratory, Tennessee; or Pacific Northwest Laboratory, Washington. Students will participate with National Laboratory scientists in ongoing research and will have access to state-of-the-art equipment and facilities. Seminars, workshops, and coursework are also conducted in the student's chosen field of study. Student appointments are normally for one academic term; however, extension of appointments through the summer are encouraged. Tuition and fees for the academic credit to be received for the semester experience are the responsibility of the participants. Application details: Applications are mailed to the Department of Energy (DOE) for processing and review. Completed, eligible files are sent to the students laboratories of choice, and are forwarded to the laboratory scientists for review and selection. Laboratory decisions are forwarded back to DOA, which, in turn, sends decision letters to the students. Students may receive offers from both their first- and second-choice laboratories. Subsequent placement of students is attempted as student responses are received. Deadline: The 1993 deadlines were March 15 for the Fall Semster and October 20 for the Spring Semester.

BASIC REFERENCE GUIDES
AND HANDBOOKS

★2786★ Analysis and Design of
  Information Systems
McGraw-Hill, Inc.
1221 Avenue of the Americas
New York, NY 10020
Ph: (212)512-2000   Fr: 800-722-4726
J.A. Senn. Second edition, 1989. Covers the fundamentals of systems analysis and sys-

tems design. Also describes designing and implementing information systems.

★2787★ The Computer Glossary: The
  Complete Illustrated Desk Reference
AMACOM
135 W. 50th St.
New York, NY 10020-1201
Ph: (212)903-8089   Fr: 800-262-9699
Alan Freedman. 1994.

★2788★ Computer Science Source Book
McGraw-Hill, Inc.
1221 Avenue of the Americas
New York, NY 10020
Ph: (212)512-2000   Fr: 800-722-4726
1989. Sixty articles cover topics such as computer science, data processing, artificial intelligence, operating systems, programming languages, electronic mail, and super computers.

★2789★ Computer Security Test Manual
Van Nostrand Reinhold
115 5th Ave.
New York, NY 10013
Philip Fites and Martin P. J. Kratz. 1993.

★2790★ Computers Today with BASIC
McGraw-Hill, Inc.
1221 Avenue of the Americas
New York, NY 10020
Ph: (212)512-2000   Fr: 800-722-4726
D.H. Sanders. Third edition, 1989. Covers computer capabilities and limitations, software applications, information systems, and the computer's impact on society.

★2791★ Dictionary of Computer Terms
Barron's Educational Series, Inc.
250 Wireless Blvd.
Hauppauge, NY 11788
Ph: (516)434-3311   Fax: (516)434-3723
Fr: 800-645-3476
Douglas Downing and Michael Covington. Third edition, 1992.

★2792★ McGraw-Hill Encyclopedia of
  Electronics and Computers
McGraw-Hill, Inc.
1221 Avenue of the Americas
New York, NY 10020
Ph: (212)512-2000   Fr: 800-722-4726
Sybil P. Parker, editor. Second edition, 1988. Contains articles on electronics and computers.

★2793★ McGraw-Hill Microcomputing
McGraw-Hill, Inc.
1221 Avenue of the Americas
New York, NY 10020
Ph: (212)512-2000   Fr: 800-722-4726
Timothy J. O'Leary and Bryan K. Williams. Annual, third edition 1991-92. Describes computer concepts in general and specific software such as Wordperfect, dBase, and Lotus.

★2794★ McGraw-Hill Personal Computer
  Programming Encyclopedia:
  Languages and Operating Systems
McGraw-Hill, Inc.
1221 Avenue of the Americas
New York, NY 10020
Ph: (212)512-2000   Fr: 800-722-4726
William J. Birnes, editor. Second edition, 1989. Provides functional and operating defi-

nitions for all statement commands, and source codes in all high-level programming languages. Includes articles on CAD/CAM, desktop publishing, and artificial intelligence.

★2795★ Professional Industries Software Directory for IBM & Compatible DOS Computers
International Computer Programs, Inc.
823 E. Westfield Blvd.
Indianapolis, IN 46220
Ph: (317)251-7727
Edited by ICP Staff. 1990.

★2796★ A Professional's Guide to Systems Analysis
McGraw-Hill, Inc.
1221 Avenue of the Americas
New York, NY 10020
Ph: (212)512-2000   Fr: 800-722-4726
Martin E. Modell. 1988. Defines systems analysis and provides a step-by-step guide to analyzing systems. Covers applications and security.

PROFESSIONAL AND TRADE PERIODICALS

★2797★ Chemical Design Automation News
Charlotte Romanicle, Contact
Monthly. Focuses on matters of technical interest relating to the use of computer automation techniques in chemical and engineered materials research. Recurring features include news of research and a calendar of events.

★2798★ Computer Wave
PO Box 19491
Seattle, WA 98109
Ph: (206)284-5476   Fax: (206)283-1020
Robert L. Crowther

★2799★ Computerworld
MacWorld
7 E. 12th St.
New York, NY 10003
Ph: (212)909-5900   Fax: (212)755-2751
Bill Laberis
Weekly. Newspaper for information systems executives.

★2800★ Concurrency
John Wiley and Sons, Inc.
Subscription Dept.
605 3rd Ave.
New York, NY 10158
Ph: (212)850-6000   Fax: (212)850-6799
G.C. Fox
Scientific journal focussing on concurrent computers and solutions to problems specific to concurrent computer designers.

★2801★ Datamation
Cahners Publishing Co.
275 Washington St.
Newton, MA 02158-1630
Ph: (617)964-3030   Fax: (617)558-4656
David R. Bronsell
Semiweekly. Magazine on computers and information processing.

★2802★ Journal of Intelligent & Fuzzy Systems
John Wiley and Sons, Inc.
605 3rd Ave.
New York, NY 10158
Ph: (212)850-6000   Fax: (212)850-6799
Mohammad Jamshidi
Quarterly. Journal providing information on fuzzy logic and intelligent systems in the fields of computer science, engineering and manufacturing.

★2803★ SIGDOC Newsletter
Special Interest Group for Systems Documentation (SIGDOC)
1515 Broadway, 17th Fl.
New York, NY 10036
Ph: (212)869-7440   Fr: 800-932-0878
Russel Boiland
Quarterly. Contains announcements and reports about international conferences on systems documentation. Examines documents produced by systems analysts, programmers, and project managers in their work to investigate, design, and develop new systems. Reviews techniques applied by technical writers and others in preparing user documents and reference material. Reports on hardware and software used to aid the documentation process.

OTHER SOURCES OF INFORMATION

★2804★ The Computer Industry Almanac, 1989: The Insider's Guide to People, companies, Products, & Trends in the Fascinating Fast-Paced Computer . . .
Simon & Schuster, Inc.
Simon & Schuster Bldg.
1230 Avenue of the Americas
New York, NY 10020
Ph: (212)698-7000   Fr: 800-223-2348
Juliussen, Egil, and Kawren Juliussen, editors. 1989. A compendium of a variety of information on the computer industry compiled from newsletters, reports and magazines.

★2805★ "Computer Systems Analyst" in 100 Best Jobs for the 1990s & Beyond
Dearborn Financial Publishing, Inc.
520 N. Dearborn St.
Chicago, IL 60610-4354
Ph: (312)836-4400   Fax: (312)836-1021
Fr: 800-621-9621
Carol Kleiman. 1992. Describes 100 jobs ranging from accountants to veterinarians.. Each job profile includes such information as education, experience, and certification needed, salaries, and job search suggestions.

★2806★ Introduction to Information Processing
McGraw-Hill, Inc.
1221 Avenue of the Americas
New York, NY 10020
Ph: (212)512-2000   Fr: 800-722-4726
Beryl Robichaud and Eugene J. Muscat. Fourth edition, 1989. Covers networks, telecommunications, computer conferencing, and artificial intelligence. Describes job opportunities in information processing in the public and private sectors.

Mathematicians

Mathematicians are engaged in solving a wide variety of activities, ranging from the creation of new theories and techniques to the translation of economic, scientific, engineering, and business problems into mathematical terms. Mathematical work falls into two broad classes: theoretical (pure) mathematics and applied mathematics. **Theoretical mathematicians** advance mathematical science by developing new principles and new relationships between existing principles of mathematics. **Applied mathematicians** use theories and techniques, such as mathematical modeling, and to solve practical problems in business, government, engineering, and the natural and social sciences. Mathematicians use computers extensively to analyze and process data, develop models, and solve complex problems.

Salaries

Salaries are generally higher in industry than in government or educational institutions. Average starting salaries for mathematicians are as follows:

Mathematicians, bachelor's degree	$28,400/year
Mathematicians, master's degree	$33,600/year
Mathematicians, Ph.D.	$41,000/year
Mathematicians, federal government	$53,232/year

Employment Outlook

Growth rate until the year 2005: Slower than the average.

Mathematicians

★2807★ *Career Choices for the 90's for Students of Mathematics*
Walker and Co.
435 Hudson St.
New York, NY 10014
Ph: (212)727-8300   Fax: (212)727-0984
Fr: 800-289-2553
Revised edition, 1990. Offers alternatives for students of mathematics. Gives information about the outlook and competition for entry-level candidates. Provides job-hunting tips.

★2808★ *Careers in Mathematical Sciences*
Mathematical Association of America (MAA)
1529 18th St., NW
Washington, DC 20036
Ph: (202)387-5200
1990.

★2809★ *Careers in Mathematics*
American Mathematical Society
PO Box 6248
Providence, RI 02940-6248
Ph: (401)272-9500
1991. Describes career opportunities for persons with a bachelor degree, discusses how to choose a university, and lists scholarships and fellowships.

★2810★ *Careers in Mathematics*
Association for Women in Mathematics (AWM)
Wellesley College
106 Central St.
Wellesley, MA 02181-8201
Ph: (617)235-0320
Margaret Menzin and Robert Goldman. 1987. Explores career opportunities for mathematicians in statistics, actuarial science, mathematical modeling, and cryptography.

★2811★ *Mathematician*
Careers, Inc.
PO Box 135
Largo, FL 34649-0135
Ph: (813)584-7333
1994. Four-page brief describing duties, working conditions, personal qualifications, training, earnings and hours, employment outlook, places of employment, related careers, and where to write for more information.

★2812★ "Mathematician" in *Career Information Center* (Vol.6)
Simon and Schuster
200 Old Tappan Rd.
Old Tappan, NJ 07675
Fax: 800-445-6991   Fr: 800-223-2348
Richard Lidz and Linda Perrin, editorial directors. Fifth edition, 1993. This 13-volume set profiles over 600 occupations. Each occupational profile describes job duties, entry-level requirements, educational requirements, advancement possibilities, employment outlook, working conditions, earnings and benefits, and where to write for more information.

★2813★ "Mathematician" in *College Board Guide to Jobs and Career Planning* (pp. 119)
The College Board
415 Columbus Ave.
New York, NY 10023-6992
Ph: (212)713-8165   Fax: (212)713-8143
Fr: 800-323-7155
Joyce S. Mitchell. Second edition, 1994. Describes a variety of careers. Each profile includes information on salaries, related careers, education needed, and sources of additional information.

★2814★ "Mathematician" in *Guide to Federal Jobs* (pp. 237)
Resource Directories
3361 Executive Pkwy., Ste. 302
Toledo, OH 43606
Ph: (419)536-5353   Fax: (419)536-7056
Fr: 800-274-8515
Rod W. Durgin, editor. Third edition, 1992. Contains information on finding and applying for federal jobs. Describes more than 200 professional and technical jobs for college graduates. Covers the nature of the work, salary, and geographic location. Lists college majors preferred for that occupation. Section one describes the function and work of government agencies that hire the most significant number of college graduates.

★2815★ "Mathematician" in *Jobs Rated Almanac*
World Almanac
1 International Blvd., Ste. 444
Mahwah, NJ 07495
Ph: (201)529-6900   Fax: (201)529-6901
Les Krantz. Second edition, 1992. Ranks 250 jobs by environment, salary, outlooks, physical demands, stress, security, travel opportunities, and extra perks. Includes jobs the editor feels are the most common, most interesting, and the most rapidly growing.

★2816★ "Mathematician" in *VGM's Careers Encyclopedia* (pp. 267-269)
National Textbook Co. (NTC)
VGM Career Books
4255 W. Touhy Ave.
Lincolnwood, IL 60646-1975
Ph: (708)679-5500   Fax: (708)679-2494
Fr: 800-323-4900
Third edition, 1991. Profiles 200 occupations. Describes job duties, places of employment, working conditions, qualifications, education and training, advancement potential, and salary for each occupation.

★2817★ "Mathematicians" in *101 Careers: A Guide to the Fastest-Growing Opportunities* (pp. 111-113)
John Wiley & Sons, Inc.
605 3rd Ave.
New York, NY 10158-0012
Ph: (212)850-6645   Fax: (212)850-6088
Michael Harkavy. 1990. Describes the nature of the job, working conditions, employment growth, qualifications, personal skills, projected salaries, and where to write for more information.

★2818★ "Mathematicians" in *Career Discovery Encyclopedia* (Vol.4, pp. 60-61)
J.G. Ferguson Publishing Co.
200 W. Madison St., Ste. 300
Chicago, IL 60606
Ph: (312)580-5480   Fax: (312)580-4948
Russell E. Primm, editor-in chief. 1993. This six volume set contains two-page articles for 504 occupations. Each article describes job duties, earnings, and educational and training requirements. The whole set is arranged alphabetically by job title. Designed for junior high and older students.

★2819★ "Mathematicians" in
Encyclopedia of Careers and
Vocational Guidance **(Vol.3, pp. 378-**
380)
J.G. Ferguson Publishing Co.
200 W. Madison St., Ste. 300
Chicago, IL 60606
Ph: (312)580-5480   Fax: (312)580-4948
William E. Hopke, editor-in-chief. Ninth edition, 1993. Four-volume set that profiles 900 occupations and describes job trends in 74 industries. Includes career description, educational requirements, history of the job, methods of entry, advancement, employment outlook, earnings, conditions of work, social and psychological factors, and sources of further information.

★2820★ "Mathematicians" in *Jobs!*
What They Are—Where They Are—
What They Pay **(p. 79)**
Simon & Schuster, Inc.
Simon & Schuster Bldg.
1230 Avenue of the Americas
New York, NY 10020
Ph: (212)698-7000   Fr: 800-223-2348
Robert O. Snelling and Anne M. Snelling. 3rd edition, 1992. Describes duties and responsibilities, earnings, employment opportunities, training, and qualifications.

★2821★ "Mathematicians" in
Occupational Outlook Handbook
U.S. Government Printing Office
Superintendent of Documents
Washington, DC 20402
Ph: (202)512-1800   Fax: (202)512-2250
Biennial; latest edition, 1994-95. Encyclopedia of careers describing about 250 occupations and comprising about 85 percent of all jobs in the economy. Occupations that require lengthy education or training are given the most attention. Each occupation's profile describes what the worker does on the job, working conditions, education and training requirements, advancement possibilities, job outlook, earnings, and sources of additional information.

★2822★ *Mathematicians and*
Technicians
Chronicle Guidance Publications, Inc.
66 Aurora St.
PO Box 1190
Moravia, NY 13118-1190
Ph: (315)497-0330   Fax: (315)497-3359
Fr: 800-622-7284
1994. Career brief describing the nature of the job, working conditions, hours and earnings, education and training, licensure, certification, unions, personal qualifications, social and psychological factors, location, employment outlook, entry methods, advancement, and related occupations.

★2823★ "Mathematics" in *College*
Majors and Careers: A Resource Guide
to Effective Life Planning **(pp. 89-90)**
Garrett Park Press
PO Box 1907
Garrett Park, MD 20896
Ph: (301)946-2553
Paul Phifer. Revised, 1993. Lists 60 college majors, with definitions; related occupations and leisure activities; skills, values, and per-

sonal attributes needed; suggested readings; and a list of associations.

★2824★ "Mathematics" in *Encyclopedia*
of Careers and Vocational Guidance
(Vol.1, pp. 284-289)
J.G. Ferguson Publishing Co.
200 W. Madison St., Ste. 300
Chicago, IL 60606
Ph: (312)580-5480   Fax: (312)580-4948
William E. Hopke, editor-in-chief. Ninth edition, 1993. Four-volume set that profiles 900 occupations and describes job trends in 74 industries. Includes career description, educational requirements, history of the job, methods of entry, advancement, employment outlook, earnings, conditions of work, social and psychological factors, and sources of further information.

PROFESSIONAL ASSOCIATIONS

★2825★ American Mathematical Society
(AMS)
PO Box 6248
Providence, RI 02940
Ph: (401)455-4000   Fax: (401)331-3842
Fr: 800-321-4AMS
Members: Professional society of mathematicians and educators. **Purpose:** Promotes the interests of mathematical scholarship and research. Holds institutes, seminars, short courses, and symposia to further mathematical research; awards prizes. Offers placement services; compiles statistics. **Publications:** *Abstracts of Papers Presented to the AMS*, bimonthly. • *Assistantships and Graduate Fellowships in the Mathematical Sciences*, annual. • *Bulletin of the AMS*, quarterly. • *Combined Membership List*, annual. • *Current Mathematical Publications*. • *Employment Information in the Mathematical Sciences*, bimonthly. • *Journal of the American Mathematical Society*, quarterly. • *Mathematical Reviews*, monthly. • *Mathematics of Computation*, quarterly. • *Memoirs of the AMS*, bimonthly. • *Notices of the AMS*, 10/year. • *Proceedings of the AMS*, monthly. • *St. Petersburg Mathematical Journal*, bimonthly. • *Sugaku Expositions*, semiannual. • *Theory of Probability and Mathematical Statistics*, semiannual. • *Transactions of the American Mathematical Society*, monthly. • *Transactions of the Moscow Mathematical Society*, annual.

★2826★ Institute of Mathematical
Statistics (IMS)
3401 Investment Blvd., Ste. 7
Hayward, CA 94545-3819
Ph: (510)783-8141   Fax: (510)783-4131
Members: Professional society of mathematicians and others interested in mathematical statistics and probability theory. **Purpose:** Seeks to further research in mathematical statistics and probability. **Publications:** *Annals of Applied Probability*, quarterly. • *Annals of Probability*, quarterly. • *Annals of Statistics*, bimonthly. • *Current Index to Statistics*. • *IMS Lecture Notes*. • *Institute of Mathematical Statistics Bulletin*, bimonthly. • *Statistical Science*, quarterly.

★2827★ Mathematical Association of
America (MAA)
1529 18th St. NW
Washington, DC 20036
Ph: (202)387-5200   Fax: (202)265-2384
Members: College mathematics teachers; individuals using mathematics as a tool in a business or profession. **Purpose:** Sponsors annual high school mathematics contests and W.L. Putnam Competition for college students. Conducts faculty enhancement workshops and promotes the use of computers through classroom training. Offers college placement test program; operates speakers' bureau. **Publications:** *American Mathematical Monthly*. • *College Mathematics Journal*. • *Mathematical Association of America—Focus*, bimonthly. • *Mathematics Magazine*. • *Membership List*, annual.

★2828★ National Council of Teachers of
Mathematics (NCTM)
1906 Association Dr.
Reston, VA 22091
Ph: (703)620-9840   Fax: (703)476-2970
Members: Teachers of mathematics in grades K-12, two-year colleges, and teacher education personnel on college campuses. **Publications:** *Journal for Research in Mathematics Education*, 5/year. • *Mathematics Teacher*, monthly. • *Mathematics Teaching in the Middle School*, quarterly. • *National Council of Teachers of Mathematics—Yearbook*. • *NCTM News Bulletin*, 10/year. • *Teaching Children Mathematics*, monthly.

★2829★ Society for Industrial and
Applied Mathematics (SIAM)
3600 University City Science Center
Philadelphia, PA 19104-2688
Ph: (215)382-9800   Fax: (215)386-7999
Members: Mathematicians, engineers, computer scientists, physical scientists, bioscientists, educators, social scientists, and others utilizing mathematics for the solution of problems. **Purpose:** Purposes are to: promote research in applied mathematics and computational science; further the application of mathematics to new methods and techniques useful in industry and science; provide for the exchange of information between the mathematical, industrial, and scientific communities. Founded the SIAM Institute for the Advancement of Scientific Computing in 1984. Conducts workshops; offers courses; supports sections and university chapters. **Publications:** *CBMS-NSF Regional Conference Series in Applied Mathematics*. • *Classics in Applied Mathematics and Proceedings*, periodic. • *Frontiers in Applied Mathematics*, periodic. • *Membership List*, annual. • *Review*, quarterly. • *SIAM Journal on Applied Mathematics*, bimonthly. • *SIAM Journal on Computing*, bimonthly. • *SIAM Journal on Control and Optimization*, bimonthly. • *SIAM Journal on Discrete Mathematics*, quarterly. • *SIAM Journal on Mathematical Analysis*, bimonthly. • *SIAM Journal on Matrix Analysis and Applications*, quarterly. • *SIAM Journal on Numerical Analysis*, bimonthly. • *SIAM Journal on Optimization*, quarterly. • *SIAM Journal on Scientific Computing*, bimonthly. • *SIAM News*. • *SIAM Review*, quarterly. • *Studies in Applied Mathematics*, periodic. • *Theory of Probability and Its Applications*, quarterly.

TEST GUIDES

★2830★ Advanced Placement Examinations in Mathematics Calculus AB and Calculus BC
Arco Publishing Co.
Macmillan General Reference
15 Columbus Cir.
New York, NY 10023
Fax: 800-835-3202   Fr: 800-858-7674
Sanderson M. Smith and Frank W. Griffin. Second edition, 1990. Two full-length model examinations, course outline, and formulas.

★2831★ Career Examination Series: Mathematician
National Learning Corp.
212 Michael Dr.
Syosset, NY 11791
Ph: (516)921-8888   Fax: (516)921-8743
Fr: 800-645-6337
Jack Rudman. A series of study guides with multiple-choice examination questions and solutions for trainees and professional mathematicians. A title in the series includes Senior Mathematician.

★2832★ Career Examination Series: Senior Mathematician
National Learning Corp.
212 Michael Dr.
Syosset, NY 11791
Ph: (516)921-8888   Fax: (516)921-8743
Fr: 800-645-6337
Jack Rudman. Test guide including questions and answers for students or professionals in the field who seek advancement through examination.

★2833★ College Board Achievement Test in Mathematics Level 1
Arco Publishing Co.
Macmillan General Reference
15 Columbus Cir.
New York, NY 10023
Fax: 800-835-3202   Fr: 800-858-7674
Morris Bramson, editor. Sixth edition, 1991. Math review plus six full-length sample examinations.

★2834★ College-Level Examination Series: Mathematics
National Learning Corp.
212 Michael Dr.
Syosset, NY 11791
Ph: (516)921-8888   Fax: (516)921-8743
Fr: 800-645-6337
Jack Rudman. Multiple-choice preparatory examinations for professional mathematicians considering the College-Level Examination Program (CLEP) as an alternative to college course matriculation. Includes solutions to sample test questions. Titles in the series include Mathematics; Calculus with Analytical Geometry.

★2835★ Dantes Subject Standardized Tests: Calculsus
National Learning Corp.
212 Michael Dr.
Syosset, NY 11791
Ph: (516)921-8888   Fax: (516)921-8743
Fr: 800-645-6337
Jack Rudman. Multiple-choice graduate- and college-level examination given by graduate schools, colleges and the Armed Forces as a final examination for course evaluation. Includes answers. Titles in the series include Differential Equations; Linear Algebra; Plane Trigonometry.

★2836★ Graduate Record Examination: Mathematics
National Learning Corp.
212 Michael Dr.
Syosset, NY 11791
Ph: (516)921-8888   Fax: (516)921-8743
Fr: 800-645-6337
Jack Rudman. Multiple-choice test for those seeking admission to graduate school for study in the field of mathematics. Includes solutions to examination questions.

★2837★ Practicing to Take the GRE Mathematics Test
Educational Testing Service
Rosedale Rd.
Princeton, NJ 08541
Ph: (609)921-9000
1987. Includes test preparation information, answer sheets, and test instructions. Contains an actual test.

★2838★ Undergraduate Program Field Test: Mathematics
National Learning Corp.
212 Michael Dr.
Syosset, NY 11791
Ph: (516)921-8888   Fax: (516)921-8743
Fr: 800-645-6337
Jack Rudman. A practice examination fashioned after tests given in the Regents External Degree Program. Designed to measure knowledge received outside the college classroom in the subject of mathematics. Contains multiple-choice questions; provides solutions.

EDUCATIONAL DIRECTORIES AND PROGRAMS

★2839★ Peterson's Guide to Graduate Programs in the Physical Sciences and Mathematics
Peterson's Guides, Inc.
202 Carnegie Center
PO Box 2123
Princeton, NJ 08543-2123
Ph: (609)243-9111   Fax: (609)243-9150
Fr: 800-338-3282
Dorothy Q. Power, Contact
Annual, December. Covers colleges and universities in the United States and Canada that offer more than 2,300 accredited graduate and professional programs in physical sciences and mathematics fields. Entries include: School name, address, phone, name and title of contact, admission requirements, description of school and programs. Publication is fourth in a series called "Grad Guides." Arrangement: Classified by academic fields.

AWARDS, SCHOLARSHIPS, GRANTS, AND FELLOWSHIPS

★2840★ Certificate of Merit
Mathematical Association of America
1529 18th St. NW
Washington, DC 20036
Ph: (202)387-5200   Fax: (202)265-2384
To recognize an individual for some special work or service associated with mathematics or the wider mathematical community. Awarded at irregular intervals.

★2841★ George B. Dantzig Prize
Society for Industrial and Applied Mathematics
3600 Univ. City Science Center
Philadelphia, PA 19104-2688
Ph: (215)382-9800   Fax: (215)386-7999
To recognize original work which, by its breadth and scope, constitutes an outstanding contribution to the field of mathematical programming. The contributions must be publicly available and may belong to any aspect of mathematical programming in its broadest sense. Strong preference is given to candidates under the age of 50. A monetary prize and a certificate are presented every three years at the International Symposium of MPS or the SIAM annual meeting. Established in 1979. Co-sponsored by the Mathematical Programming Society.

★2842★ Engineering Rotation Program
Hughes Aircraft Company
Technical Education Center
PO Box 80028
Los Angeles, CA 90080-0028
Ph: (310)568-6711
Purpose: To enable engineering and science graduates to find and develop the special field of work and the career position best suited to their interests and education. Qualifications: Applicant must be a U.S. citizen and have a bachelor's degree in electrical, mechanical, systems, computer or aerospace engineering; computer science; physics; or mathematics. Candidate must have a grade point average of at least 3.0/4.0, with emphasis on technical classes and related disciplines. Participants in the Rotation Program gain practical experience through up to four different work assignments at Hughes facilities, usually in southern California. Upon completion of the program, participants may be placed in permanent positions with the Company, based on their interests and assignments available. Funds available: Salary and company benefits. Application details: Write to the educational coordinator for application form and guidelines. Include pertinent information regarding academic status (university, field of interest for both undergraduate and graduate work, year of graduation, and grade point average) in initial letter of interest. Deadline: 1 March.

★2843★ Delbert Ray Fulkerson Fund
American Mathematical Society
PO Box 6248
Providence, RI 02940
Ph: (401)455-4000
To recognize outstanding work in discrete mathematics. The fund's proceeds are used jointly by the American Mathematical Society and the Mathematical Programming Society. Awarded as merited. Established in 1979.

★2844★ Yueh-Gin Gung and Dr. Charles Y. Hu Award for Distinguished Service to Mathematics
Mathematical Association of America
1529 18th St. NW
Washington, DC 20036
Ph: (202)387-5200   Fax: (202)265-2384
To recognize distinguished service to mathematics other than the creation of new mathematics. A monetary prize of $4,000, a certificate, and a silver cup are awarded annually at the January meeting. Established in 1960, and revised in 1988.

★2845★ Hedrick Lectureship
Mathematical Association of America
1529 18th St. NW
Washington, DC 20036
Ph: (202)387-5200   Fax: (202)265-2384
To recognize an individual for a significant contribution to the field of mathematics. A certificate and appropriate publicity are awarded annually in August. The recipient presents a lecture at the annual Board of Governors' meeting the following August.

★2846★ Engineer Degree Fellowships; Howard Hughes Doctoral Fellowships
Hughes Aircraft Company
Technical Education Center
PO Box 80028
Los Angeles, CA 90080-0028
Ph: (310)568-6711
Purpose: To support doctoral studies in engineering and related sciences and to provide students with practical work experience. Qualifications: Applicant for either type of fellowship must be a U.S. citizen and have a bachelor's and master's degree or equivalent graduate experience in electrical, mechanical, systems, computer or aerospace engineering; computer science; physics; or mathematics. Engineer Degree Fellowships are reserved for candidates who have first degrees in engineering. For both awards, priority is given to individuals with experience in electronics and related disciplines. Candidate must have a minimum grade point average of 3.0/4.0, and be qualified for admission to an approved graduate program in the United States. Fellows are considered employees of the Hughes Aircraft Company and, in addition to their graduate studies, gain work experience in one of two programs: work-study or full-study. Fellows in the work-study program attend a university near a Hughes facility (usually in southern California) and complete coursework while working at the facility for 20 to 36 hours per week. Work-study fellows may switch to full-study status to complete their dissertations. Full-study fellows attend a university distant from Hughes and are on leave of absence from the company while studying full-time. Full-study fellows are required to spend the summer term working for the Company, and may work eight hours a week during the school year if attending a university within commuting distance. Funds available: Company salary and benefits, plus tuition, book and living allowances. Application details: Write to the educational coordinator for application form and guidelines. Include pertinent information regarding academic status (university, field of interest for both undergraduate and graduate work, year of graduation, and grade point average) in initial letter of interest. Deadline: 10 January. Fellows are announced in April.

★2847★ NAACP Willems Scholarship
National Association for the Advancement of Colored People (NAACP)
4805 Mt. Hope Dr.
Baltimore, MD 21215-3297
Ph: (410)358-8900
Qualifications: Applicants must be majoring in engineering, chemistry, physics, or computer and mathematical sciences and possess a cumulative grade point average of at least 3.0 or B average. They must be members of the NAACP. Funds available: Undergraduates will receive a maximum award of $8,000 to be paid in annual installments of $2,000. Graduates will be awarded a $3,000 renewable scholarship. Application details: Updated application forms are available in January. Deadline: April 30.

★2848★ National Academy of Sciences Award in Applied Mathematics and Numerical Analysis
National Academy of Sciences
2101 Constitution Ave. NW
Washington, DC 20418
Ph: (202)334-2444
To recognize outstanding work in applied mathematics and numerical analysis. Individuals engaged in a program of research carried out in institutions located in North America are eligible. A monetary prize of $10,000 is awarded approximately every three years. Established in 1967. Sponsored by IBM.

★2849★ National Academy of Sciences Award in Mathematics
National Academy of Sciences
2101 Constitution Ave. NW
Washington, DC 20418
Ph: (202)334-2444
To recognize an individual for excellence of research in the mathematical sciences published within the preceding ten years. A monetary award of $5,000 is presented once every four years. Established in 1988 by the American Mathematical Society in commemoration of its centennial.

★2850★ Newcomen Award for Notable Proficiency in Mathematics, Physics and Chemistry
Newcomen Society of the United States
412 Newcomen Rd.
Exton, PA 19341
Ph: (215)363-6600   Fax: (215)363-0612
For recognition of notable proficiency in mathematics, physics, and chemistry. A monetary prize of $250 and a scroll are awarded annually. Established in 1960. Administered by Drexel University.

★2851★ President's National Medal of Science
National Science Foundation
4201 Wilson Blvd., Rm. 1225
Arlington, VA 22203
Ph: (202)357-7512   Fax: (202)357-7346
To recognize individuals who are deserving of special recognition by reason of their outstanding contributions to knowledge in the physical, biological, mathematical, engineering, behavioral, or social sciences. The President's Committee on the National Medal of Science receives recommendations of various nationally representative scientific or engineering organizations as well as the recommendations of the National Academy of Sciences. The guidelines for selection are as follows: the total impact of an individual's work on the present state of physical, biological, mathematical, engineering, behavioral, or social sciences and any achievements of an unusually significant nature judged in relation to their potential effects on the development of scientific thought. Unusually distinguished service in the general advancement of science and engineering, when accompanied by substantial contributions to the content of science, may also be recognized. Established in 1959 by the Congress of the United States and first awarded in 1962. Additional information is available from Susan Fannoney, telephone: (202) 357-7512.

★2852★ John von Neumann Lecture
Society for Industrial and Applied Mathematics
3600 Univ. City Science Center
Philadelphia, PA 19104-2688
Ph: (215)382-9800   Fax: (215)386-7999
To recognize an individual for distinguished contributions to pure and/or applied mathematics. The recipient may be a mathematician or a scientist in another field. An honorarium of $2,500, travel expenses to the award ceremony, and a framed certificate are awarded. The recipient presents the John von Neumann Lecture that surveys and evaluates a significant contribution to mathematics and its applications. A manuscript representing the lecture is required for publication in *SIAM Review*. Awarded annually at the SIAM annual meeting. Established in 1959.

★2853★ James H. Wilkinson Prize in Numerical Analysis and Scientific Computing
Society for Industrial and Applied Mathematics
3600 Univ. City Science Center
Philadelphia, PA 19104-2688
Ph: (215)382-9800   Fax: (215)386-7999
To stimulate younger contributors and to help them in their research. Selection is based on research in, or other contributions to, numerical analysis and scientific computing during the six years preceding the award. There are no eligibility restrictions. A monetary award of $1,000 and an engraved plaque are awarded every fourth year, normally at the SIAM annual meeting. Established in 1979.

BASIC REFERENCE GUIDES AND HANDBOOKS

★2854★ CRC Handbook of Mathematical Sciences
CRC Press, Inc.
2000 Corporate Blvd., NW
Boca Raton, FL 33431
Ph: (407)994-0555   Fr: 800-272-7737
William H. Beyer, editor. Sixth edition, 1987. Includes tables, formulas, and some explanatory text for elementary mathematics, higher mathematics, probability, and statistics.

★2855★ Dictionary of Mathematics Terms
Barron's Educational Series, Inc.
250 Wireless Blvd.
Hauppauge, NY 11788
Ph: (516)434-3311   Fax: (516)434-3723
Fr: 800-645-3476
Douglas Downing. 1992.

★2856★ Dynamic Programming
Van Nostrand Reinhold
115 5th Ave.
New York, NY 10013
Salah E. Elmaghraby. 1993.

★2857★ Encyclopedic Dictionary of Mathematics
MIT Press
55 Hayward St.
Cambridge, MA 02142
Ph: (617)625-8569
Kiyosi Ito, editor. Second edition, 1993. Contains articles on a broad range of mathematical topics.

★2858★ The Facts on File Dictionary of Mathematics
Facts on File
460 Park Ave. S.
New York, NY 10016-7382
Ph: (212)683-2244   Fax: 800-678-3633
Fr: 800-322-8755
Carol Gibson, editor. Revised, expanded edition, 1990. Defines commonly used mathematical terms, including terms in fields such as computer graphics, artificial intelligence, and robotics.

★2859★ Handbook of Applied Mathematics: Selected Results and Methods
Van Nostrand Reinhold Co., Inc.
115 5th Ave.
New York, NY 10003
Ph: (212)254-3232
Carl E. Pearson, editor. Second edition, 1990. Contains formulas and techniques for the application of mathematics to practical problems.

★2860★ Introduction to Mathematics
Prentice-Hall, Inc.
Rte. 9W
Englewood Cliffs, NJ 07632
Ph: (201)592-2000   Fr: 800-634-2863
Bruce E. Meserve, Max Sobel, and J. Dossey. Sixth edition, 1989. Covers basic mathematical principles for geometry, algebra, probability, and statistics. Describes the use of calculators and computers to aid in determining solutions.

★2861★ The VNR Concise Encyclopedia of Mathematics
Van Nostrand Reinhold Co., Inc.
115 5th Ave.
New York, NY 10003
Ph: (212)254-3232
W. Gellert, editor. 1977. Includes an index. Illustrated.

★2862★ Webster's New World Dictionary of Mathematics
Prentice-Hall, Inc.
Rte. 9W
Englewood Cliffs, NJ 07632
Ph: (201)592-2000   Fr: 800-634-2863
William Karush. 1989. Published by Webster's New World. Provides an alphabetical listing of 1400 key mathematical terms.

PROFESSIONAL AND TRADE PERIODICALS

★2863★ Employment Information in the Mathematical Sciences/Journal
American Mathematical Society
PO Box 6248
Providence, RI 02940
Ph: (401)272-9500   Fax: (401)331-3842
Fr: 800-556-7774
Provides concise listings of open positions (1,400-1,500/yr.) "suitable for mathematicians with education and experience at every level beyond the Bachelor's degree." Lists positions by state.

★2864★ Mathematical Association of America—Focus
Mathematical Association of America (MAA)
1529 18th St. NW
Washington, DC 20036
Ph: (202)387-5200   Fax: (202)265-2384
Fr: 800-331-1622
Peter L. Renz
Presents articles of interest to those using mathematics as a tool in a business or profession and reports on Association news. Recurring features include a calendar of events, editorials, and member news.

★2865★ Mathematics Magazine
Mathematical Assn. of America
1529 18th St. NW
Washington, DC 20036
Ph: (202)387-5200   Fax: (202)265-2384
G.L. Alexanderson
Bimonthly. Magazine featuring informal mathematical articles and notes designed to appeal to faculty and students at the undergraduate level. Also contains a problems section, a reviews section, a news and letters section featuring early publication of problems and solutions from Olympiads and Putnam Competitions.

★2866★ Numerical Linear Algebra with Applications
John Wiley and Sons, Inc.
Subscription Dept.
605 3rd Ave.
New York, NY 10158
Ph: (212)850-6000   Fax: (212)850-6799
O. Axelsson
Bimonthly. Journal emphasizing new methods in numerical linear algebra, including their analysis and applications.

★2867★ Random Structures & Algorithms
John Wiley and Sons, Inc.
Subscription Dept.
605 3rd Ave.
New York, NY 10158
Ph: (212)850-6000   Fax: (212)850-6799
Michal Karonski
Journal describing research on random structures and applications of probabilistic techniques to problem solving in mathematics, computer science and operations research.

★2868★ Russian Journal of Mathematical Physics
John Wiley and Sons, Inc.
Subscription Dept.
605 3rd Ave.
New York, NY 10158
Ph: (212)850-6000   Fax: (212)850-6799
Victor P. Maslov
Journal publishing articles on recent achievements and reviews of modern mathematical physics.

★2869★ SIAM Journal on Applied Mathematics
Society for Industrial and Applied Mathematics
3600 University City Science Center
Philadelphia, PA 19104-2688
Ph: (215)382-9800   Fax: (215)386-7999
J.P. Keener
Bimonthly. Journal containing research articles in the applied mathematics of physical, engineering, biological, medical, and social sciences.

★2870★ SIAM News
Society for Industrial and Applied Mathematics
3600 University City Science Center
Philadelphia, PA 19104-2688
Ph: (215)382-9800   Fax: (215)386-7999
Gail R. Corbett
Bimonthly. Applied mathematics news journal (tabloid).

OTHER SOURCES OF INFORMATION

★2871★ "Applied Mathematics" in *Accounting to Zoology: Graduate Fields Defined* (pp. 304-305)
Petersons Guides, Inc.
PO Box 2123
Princeton, NJ 08543-2123
Ph: (609)243-9111   Fax: (609)243-9150
Fr: 800-338-3282
Amy J. Goldstein, editor. Revised and updated, 1987. Defines 298 graduate and professional fields. Discusses types of graduate programs and degrees, graduate research, applied work, employment prospects, and trends.

★2872★ "Mathematician" in *Career Selector 2001*
Barron's Educational Series, Inc.
250 Wireless Blvd.
Hauppauge, NY 11788
Ph: (516)434-3311   Fax: (516)434-3723
Fr: 800-645-3476
James C. Gonyea. 1993.

★2873★ "Mathematician/Statistician" in *100 Best Jobs for the 1990s & Beyond*
Dearborn Financial Publishing, Inc.
520 N. Dearborn St.
Chicago, IL 60610-4354
Ph: (312)836-4400   Fax: (312)836-1021
Fr: 800-621-9621
Carol Kleiman. 1992. Describes 100 jobs ranging from accountants to veterinarians.. Each job profile includes such information as education, experience, and certification needed, salaries, and job search suggestions.

★2874★ "Mathematics" in *Accounting to Zoology: Graduate Fields Defined* (pp. 307-308)
Petersons Guides, Inc.
PO Box 2123
Princeton, NJ 08543-2123
Ph: (609)243-9111   Fax: (609)243-9150
Fr: 800-338-3282
Amy J. Goldstein, editor. Revised and updated, 1987. Defines 298 graduate and professional fields. Discusses types of graduate programs and degrees, graduate research, applied work, employment prospects, and trends.

Operations Research Analysts

Operations research analysts also called **management science analysts** help organizations plan and operate in the most efficient and effective manner. They accomplish this by applying the scientific method and mathematical principles to organizational problems so that managers can evaluate alternatives and choose the course of action that best suits the organization. Operations research analysts are problem solvers. The problems they tackle are for the most part those encountered in large business organizations: business strategy, forecasting, resource allocation, facilities layout, inventory control, personnel schedules, and distribution systems. Operations research analysts use computers extensively and are typically proficient in database management and programming.

Salaries

Median annual earnings for operations research analysts are as follows:

Beginning analyst, master's degree	$30,000-$35,000/year
Experienced analyst	$50,000-$90,000/year or more
Federal government analyst	$57,419/year

Employment Outlook

Growth rate until the year 2005: Much faster than the average.

Operations Research Analysts

CAREER GUIDES

★2875★ *Careers in Operations Research*
Operations Research Society of America (ORSA)
1314 Guilford Ave.
Baltimore, MD 21202
Ph: (301)528-4146

1991. Provides an introduction to the field of operations research and describes typical careers in operations research. Gives a sampling of colleges and universities across the United States which offer degree programs in operations research.

★2876★ "Computer Careers" in *Best Jobs for the 1990s and Into the 21st Century*
Impact Publications
9104-N Manassas Dr.
Manassas Park, VA 22111
Ph: (703)361-7300   Fax: (703)335-9486

Ronald L. Krannich and Caryl Rae Krannich. 1993. Includes information on computer programmers, systems analysts, and operations research analysts.

★2877★ "Operations Research Analyst" in *Guide to Federal Jobs* (p. 236)
Resource Directories
3361 Executive Pkwy., Ste. 302
Toledo, OH 43606
Ph: (419)536-5353   Fax: (419)536-7056
Fr: 800-274-8515

Rod W. Durgin, editor. Third edition, 1992. Contains information on finding and applying for federal jobs. Describes more than 200 professional and technical jobs for college graduates. Covers the nature of the work, salary, and geographic location. Lists college majors preferred for that occupation. Section one describes the function and work of government agencies that hire the most significant number of college graduates.

★2878★ "Operations Research Analyst" in *VGM's Careers Encyclopedia*
National Textbook Co. (NTC)
VGM Career Books
4255 W. Touhy Ave.
Lincolnwood, IL 60646-1975
Ph: (708)679-5500   Fax: (708)679-2494
Fr: 800-323-4900

Third edition, 1991. Profiles 200 occupations. Describes job duties, places of employment, working conditions, qualifications, education and training, advancement potential, and salary for each occupation.

★2879★ "Operations Research Analyst" in *VGM's Handbook of Business and Management Careers*
National Textbook Co.
4255 W. Touhy Ave.
Lincolnwood, IL 60646-1975
Ph: (708)679-5500   Fax: (708)679-2494
Fr: 800-323-4900

Annette Selden. Second edition, 1993. Contains 42 two-page occupational profiles describing job duties, places of employment, working conditions, qualifications, education, employment outlook, and income.

★2880★ *Operations Research Analysts*
Chronicle Guidance Publications, Inc.
66 Aurora St.
PO Box 1190
Moravia, NY 13118-1190
Ph: (315)497-0330   Fax: (315)497-3359
Fr: 800-622-7284

1993. Career brief describing the nature of the job, working conditions, hours and earnings, education and training, licensure, certification, unions, personal qualifications, social and psychological factors, location, employment outlook, entry methods, advancement, and related occupations.

★2881★ "Operations Research Analysts" in *America's 50 Fastest Growing Jobs* (pp. 50)
JIST Works, Inc.
720 N. Park Ave.
Indianapolis, IN 46202-3431
Ph: (317)264-3720   Fax: (317)264-3709
Fr: 800-648-5478

Michael J. Farr, compiler. 1994. Describes the 50 fastest growing jobs within major career clusters such as technicians, and marketing and sales. Each job profile explains the nature of the work, skills and abilities required, employment outlook, average earnings, related occupations, education and training requirements, and employment opportunities. Also contains career planning information and job search tips.

★2882★ "Operations Research Analysts" in *Career Information Center* (Vol.1)
Simon and Schuster
200 Old Tappan Rd.
Old Tappan, NJ 07675
Fax: 800-445-6991   Fr: 800-223-2348

Richard Lidz and Linda Perrin, editorial directors. Fifth edition, 1993. A multi-volume set that profiles over 600 occupations. Each occupational profile describes job duties, educational requirements, advancement possibilities, employment outlook, working conditions, earnings and benefits, and where to write for more information.

★2883★ "Operations-Research Analysts" in *Encyclopedia of Careers and Vocational Guidance* (Vol.3, pp. 618-620)
J.G. Ferguson Publishing Co.
200 W. Madison St., Ste. 300
Chicago, IL 60606
Ph: (312)580-5480   Fax: (312)580-4948

William E. Hopke, editor-in-chief. Ninth edition, 1993. Four-volume set that profiles 900 occupations and describes job trends in 74 industries. Includes career description, educational requirements, history of the job, methods of entry, advancement, employment outlook, earnings, conditions of work, social and psychological factors, and sources of further information.

★2884★ "Operations Research Analysts" in *Occupational Outlook Handbook*
U.S. Government Printing Office
Superintendent of Documents
Washington, DC 20402
Ph: (202)512-1800   Fax: (202)512-2250

Biennial; latest edition, 1994-95. Encyclopedia of careers describing about 250 occupations and comprising about 85 percent of all jobs in the economy. Occupations that require lengthy education or training are given the most attention. Each occupation's profile describes what the worker does on the job, working conditions, education and training requirements, advancement possibilities, job outlook, earnings, and sources of additional information.

PROFESSIONAL ASSOCIATIONS

★2885★ The Institute of Management Sciences (TIMS)
290 Westminster St.
Providence, RI 02903
Ph: (401)274-2525   Fax: (401)274-3189
Members: Professional society for scientists and management in business, labor, government, teaching, and research. **Purpose:** Aim is to advance scientific knowledge and improve management practices; members contribute to or learn about important findings in management technology, applied mathematics, psychology, economics, and other sciences. Compiles statistics; conducts research programs; maintains speakers' bureau. Maintains 20 colleges, including Artificial Intelligence, Innovation Management and Entrepreneurship, and Simulation and Gaming. **Publications:** *Annual Comprehensive Index.* • *Information Systems Research,* quarterly. • *Interfaces,* bimonthly. • *Management Science,* monthly. • *Marketing Science,* quarterly. • *Mathematics of Operations Research,* quarterly. • *OR/MS Today,* bimonthly. • *Organization Science,* quarterly.

★2886★ Military Operations Research Society (MORS)
Landmark Towers
101 S. Whiting St., Ste. 202
Alexandria, VA 22304
Ph: (703)751-7290   Fax: (703)751-8171
Members: Purpose: Works to improve the quality and effectiveness of military operations research. Sponsors colloquia; facilitates exchange of information and peer criticism among students, theoreticians, practitioners, and users of military operations research. Does not make or advocate official policy nor does it attempt to influence policy formulation. **Publications:** *Careers in Military Operations Research.* • *Military Operations Research,* quarterly. • *PHALANX,* quarterly. • *Proceedings of the Military Operations Research Symposium,* annual. • *World of MORS.*

★2887★ Operations Research Society of America (ORSA)
1314 Guilford Ave.
Baltimore, MD 21202
Ph: (410)528-4146   Fax: (410)528-8556
Members: Scientists, educators, and practitioners engaged or interested in methodological subjects such as optimization, probabilistic models, decision analysis, and game theory. Also involved in areas of public concern such as health, energy, urban issues, and defense systems through industrial applications including marketing, operations management, finance, and decision support sys-

tems. Operates a visiting lecturers program. Offers placement service; compiles statistics. **Publications:** *Interfaces,* bimonthly. • *Marketing Science,* quarterly. • *Mathematics of Operations Research,* quarterly. • *Operations Research,* bimonthly. • *Operations Research Letters,* bimonthly. • *OR/MS Today,* bimonthly. • *ORSA Journal on Computing,* quarterly. • *ORSA/TIMS Bulletin,* semiannual. • *ORSA/TIMS Membership Directory,* biennial. • *Stochastic Models.* • *Transportation Science,* quarterly.

TEST GUIDES

★2888★ Career Examination Series: Office Systems Analyst
National Learning Corp.
212 Michael Dr.
Syosset, NY 11791
Ph: (516)921-8888   Fax: (516)921-8743
Fr: 800-645-6337
Jack Rudman. 1993. Test guide including questions and answers for students or professionals in the field who seek advancement through examination.

★2889★ Career Examination Series: Operations Research Analyst
National Learning Corp.
212 Michael Dr.
Syosset, NY 11791
Ph: (516)921-8888   Fax: (516)921-8743
Fr: 800-645-6337
Jack Rudman. Test guide including questions and answers for students or professionals in the field who seek advancement through examination.

★2890★ Career Examination Series: Program Research Analyst
National Learning Corp.
212 Michael Dr.
Syosset, NY 11791
Ph: (516)921-8888   Fax: (516)921-8743
Fr: 800-645-6337
Jack Rudman. A series of study guides with multiple-choice examination questions and solutions for trainees and professional operations research analysts. Titles in the series include *Administrative Staff Analyst; Computer Associate (Operations); Operations Research Analyst; Principal Research Analyst.*

AWARDS, SCHOLARSHIPS, GRANTS, AND FELLOWSHIPS

★2891★ ORSA/TIMS von Neumann Prize
Operations Research Society of America
Mt. Royal & Guilford Aves.
Baltimore, MD 21202
Ph: (410)528-4146
To recognize the scholar who has made fundamental theoretical contributions to opera-

tions research and management science. A monetary award of $3,000, an engraved medal, and a certificate are awarded annually. Established in 1974 by the Councils of the Operations Research Society of America and The Institute of Management Sciences(TIMS).

BASIC REFERENCE GUIDES AND HANDBOOKS

★2892★ Introduction to Operations Research
McGraw-Hill Publishing Co.
11 W. 19th St.
New York, NY 10011
Ph: (212)337-6010   Fr: 800-722-4726
Frederick S. Hiller. 1995.

★2893★ Operations Research Problem Solver
Research & Education Association
61 Ethel Rd., W.
Piscataway, NJ 08854
Ph: (908)819-8880
Revised edition, 1994.

PROFESSIONAL AND TRADE PERIODICALS

★2894★ Operations Research
Operations Research Society of America
1314 Guilford Ave.
Baltimore, MD 21202
Ph: (410)528-4146   Fax: (410)361-8044
Donald Ratliff
Bimonthly. Journal publishing new operations research for practitioners and Operations Research Society of America members.

★2895★ Organizations and Change
International Registry of Organization Development Professionals
11234 Walnut Ridge Rd.
Chesterland, OH 44026
Ph: (216)461-4333   Fax: (216)729-9319
Donald W. Cole
Monthly. Serves organization development professionals, teachers of organizational behavior, management consultants, personnel directors and executives by carrying news items, interest surveys, economic information, and committee reports. Recurring features include announcements of conferences, meetings, publications, consulting opportunities, and employment openings.

OTHER SOURCES OF INFORMATION

★2896★ "Operations Research" in
***Accounting to Zoology: Graduate
Fields Defined*** (pp. 350-351)
Petersons Guides, Inc.
PO Box 2123
Princeton, NJ 08543-2123
Ph: (609)243-9111   Fax: (609)243-9150
Fr: 800-338-3282

Amy J. Goldstein, editor. Revised and updated, 1987. Defines 298 graduate and professional fields. Discusses types of graduate programs and degrees, graduate research, applied work, employment prospects, and trends.

Statisticians

Statisticians design, implement, compile, and interpret the numerical results of surveys and experiments. In doing so, they apply their knowledge of statistical methods to a particular subject area, such as biology, economics, engineering, medicine, or psychology. They may use statistical techniques to predict population growth or economic conditions, develop quality control tests for manufactured products, assess the nature of environmental problems, analyze legal and social problems, or help business managers and government officials make decisions and evaluate the results of new programs.

Salaries

Assistant statistics professor	$40,000/year
Associate statistics professor	$43,500/year
Statistics professor	$54,500/year
Statistician, federal government	$51,893/year

Employment Outlook

Growth rate until the year 2005: Slower than the average.

Statisticians

CAREER GUIDES

★2897★ Career Opportunities in the Sports Industry
Facts on File
460 Park Ave. S.
New York, NY 10016-7382
Ph: (212)683-2244   Fax: 800-678-3633
Fr: 800-322-8755

Shelly Field. 1993. Sourcebook combining a variety of information including sports-related academic programs, league lists, professional associations, and more of interest to those considering employment in organized amateur or professional sports.

★2898★ Careers in Statistics
American Statistical Association (ASA)
1429 Duke St.
Alexandria, VA 22314-3402
Ph: (703)684-1221

1990. Describes what statisticians do, opportunities for future employment, education required, and sources of additional information. Lists U.S. and Canadian schools offering degrees in statistics.

★2899★ "Mathematical Statistician" in Guide to Federal Jobs (p. 238)
Resource Directories
3361 Executive Pkwy., Ste. 302
Toledo, OH 43606
Ph: (419)536-5353   Fax: (419)536-7056
Fr: 800-274-8515

Rod W. Durgin, editor. Third edition, 1992. Contains information on finding and applying for federal jobs. Describes more than 200 professional and technical jobs for college graduates. Covers the nature of the work, salary, and geographic location. Lists college majors preferred for that occupation. Section one describes the function and work of government agencies that hire the most significant number of college graduates.

★2900★ Minorities! . . . Looking for a Challenging Career? What About Statistics?
American Statistical Association (ASA)
1429 Duke St.
Alexandria, VA 22314-3402
Ph: (703)684-1221

Briefly describes the field of statistics, programs of study, salaries, and sources of additional information.

★2901★ Opportunities in Social Science Careers
National Textbook Co. (NTC)
VGM Career Books
4255 W. Touhy Ave.
Lincolnwood, IL 60646-1975
Ph: (708)679-5500   Fax: (708)679-2494
Fr: 800-323-4900

Rosanne J. Marek. Overviews a wide range of career opportunities in social science including anthropology, economics, political science, statistics, history, psychology, sociology, urban and regional planning, and geography. Includes information on salary levels and the employment outlook.

★2902★ "Sports Statistician" in Careers in Health and Fitness
Rosen Publishing Group
29 E. 21st St.
New York, NY 10010
Ph: (212)777-3017   Fax: (212)777-0277
Fr: 800-237-9932

Jackie Heron. 1990. Occupational profiles contain information on job duties, skills, advantages, basic equipment used, employment possibilities, certification, and salary.

★2903★ Statistician
Chronicle Guidance Publications, Inc.
66 Aurora St.
PO Box 1190
Moravia, NY 13118-1190
Ph: (315)497-0330   Fax: (315)497-3359
Fr: 800-622-7284

1992. Career brief describing the nature of the job, working conditions, hours and earnings, education and training, licensure, certification, unions, personal qualifications, social and psychological factors, location, employment outlook, entry methods, advancement, and related occupations.

★2904★ Statistician
Careers, Inc.
PO Box 135
Largo, FL 34649-0135
Ph: (813)584-7333

1994. This two-page occupational summary card describes duties, working conditions, personal qualifications, training, earnings and hours, employment outlook, places of employment, related careers, and where to write for more information.

★2905★ "Statistician" in Career Information Center (Vol.1)
Simon and Schuster
200 Old Tappan Rd.
Old Tappan, NJ 07675
Fax: 800-445-6991   Fr: 800-223-2348

Richard Lidz and Linda Perrin, editorial directors. Fifth edition, 1993. This 13-volume set profiles over 600 occupations. Each occupational profile describes job duties, entry-level requirements, educational requirements, advancement possibilities, employment outlook, working conditions, earnings and benefits, and where to write for more information.

★2906★ "Statistician" in Careers in Health and Fitness
Rosen Publishing Group
29 E. 21st St.
New York, NY 10010
Ph: (212)777-3017   Fax: (212)777-0277
Fr: 800-237-9932

Jackie Heron. 1990. Explains primary functions, fundamental skills, pros and cons, and employment possibilities of statisticians. Covers education needed and salary range of statisticians.

★2907★ "Statistician" in College Board Guide to Jobs and Career Planning (pp. 121-122)
The College Board
45 Columbus Ave.
New York, NY 10023-6992
Ph: (212)713-8165   Fax: (212)713-8143
Fr: 800-323-7155

Second edition, 1994. Describes the job, salaries, related careers, education needed, and where to write for more information.

★2908★ "Statistician" in *Guide to Federal Jobs* (p. 239)
Resource Directories
3361 Executive Pkwy., Ste. 302
Toledo, OH 43606
Ph: (419)536-5353   Fax: (419)536-7056
Fr: 800-274-8515

Rod W. Durgin, editor. Third edition, 1992. Contains information on finding and applying for federal jobs. Describes more than 200 professional and technical jobs for college graduates. Covers the nature of the work, salary, and geographic location. Lists college majors preferred for that occupation. Section one describes the function and work of government agencies that hire the most significant number of college graduates.

★2909★ "Statistician" in *Jobs Rated Almanac*
World Almanac
1 International Blvd., Ste. 444
Mahwah, NJ 07495
Ph: (201)529-6900   Fax: (201)529-6901
Les Krantz. Second edition, 1992. Ranks 250 jobs by environment, salary, outlooks, physical demands, stress, security, travel opportunities, and extra perks. Includes jobs the editor feels are the most common, most interesting, and the most rapidly growing.

★2910★ "Statistician" in *VGM's Career Encyclopedia* (pp. 440-442)
National Textbook Co. (NTC)
VGM Career Books
4255 W. Touhy Ave.
Lincolnwood, IL 60646-1975
Ph: (708)679-5500   Fax: (708)679-2494
Fr: 800-323-4900

Third edition, 1991. Describes 200 jobs. Explains places of employment, working conditions, qualifications, education and training needed, advancement possibilities and income for each occupation.

★2911★ "Statisticians" in *Encyclopedia of Careers and Vocational Guidance* (Vol.4, pp. 433-435)
J.G. Ferguson Publishing Co.
200 W. Madison St., Ste. 300
Chicago, IL 60606
Ph: (312)580-5480   Fax: (312)580-4948
William E. Hopke, editor-in-chief. Ninth edition, 1993. Four-volume set that profiles 900 occupations and describes job trends in 74 industries. Includes career description, educational requirements, history of the job, methods of entry, advancement, employment outlook, earnings, conditions of work, social and psychological factors, and sources of further information.

★2912★ "Statisticians" in *Occupational Outlook Handbook*
U.S. Government Printing Office
Superintendent of Documents
Washington, DC 20402
Ph: (202)512-1800   Fax: (202)512-2250
Biennial; latest edition, 1994-95. Encyclopedia of careers describing about 250 occupations and comprising about 85 percent of all jobs in the economy. Occupations that require lengthy education or training are given the most attention. Each occupation's profile describes what the worker does on the job, working conditions, education and training requirements, advancement possibilities, job outlook, earnings, and sources of additional information.

★2913★ *Statistics as a Career: Women at Work*
American Statistical Association (ASA)
1429 Duke St.
Alexandria, VA 22314-3402
Ph: (703)684-1221

Briefly describes women as statisticians. Explains the field of statistics, earnings, how to become a statistician, and where to write for more information.

PROFESSIONAL ASSOCIATIONS

★2914★ **American Statistical Association (ASA)**
1429 Duke St.
Alexandria, VA 22314-3402
Ph: (703)684-1221   Fax: (703)684-2037
Members: Professional society of persons interested in the theory, methodology, and application of statistics to all fields of human endeavor. **Publications:** *American Statistician*, quarterly. • *AMSTAT News*, 11/year. • *Chance*, quarterly. • *Current Index to Statistics*, annual. • *Directory of Statisticians*, periodic. • *Journal of ASA*, quarterly. • *Journal of Business and Economic Statistics*, quarterly. • *Journal of Computational and Graphical Statistics*, quarterly. • *Journal of Educational Statistics*, quarterly. • *STATS*, biennial. • *Technometrics*, quarterly.

★2915★ **Institute of Mathematical Statistics (IMS)**
3401 Investment Blvd., Ste. 7
Hayward, CA 94545-3819
Ph: (510)783-8141   Fax: (510)783-4131
Members: Professional society of mathematicians and others interested in mathematical statistics and probability theory. **Purpose:** Seeks to further research in mathematical statistics and probability. **Publications:** *Annals of Applied Probability*, quarterly. • *Annals of Probability*, quarterly. • *Annals of Statistics*, bimonthly. • *Current Index to Statistics*. • *IMS Lecture Notes*. • *Institute of Mathematical Statistics Bulletin*, bimonthly. • *Statistical Science*, quarterly.

TEST GUIDES

★2916★ *ACT Proficiency Examination Program: Statistics*
National Learning Corp.
212 Michael Dr.
Syosset, NY 11791
Ph: (516)921-8888   Fax: (516)921-8743
Fr: 800-645-6337
Jack Rudman. A practice test that demonstrates proficiency in the area of statistics. Multiple-choice format with solutions included.

★2917★ *Basic Statistics*
National Learning Corp.
212 Michael Dr.
Syosset, NY 11791
Ph: (516)921-8888   Fax: (516)921-8743
Fr: 800-645-6337
Jack Rudman. Dantes Subject Standardized Test series. A standardized graduate and college level examination given by graduate schools, colleges, and the Armed Forces as a final examination for course evaluation in the field of statistics. Multiple-choice format with correct answers.

★2918★ *Career Examination Series: Cost and Statistical Analyst*
National Learning Corp.
212 Michael Dr.
Syosset, NY 11791
Ph: (516)921-8888   Fax: (516)921-8743
Fr: 800-645-6337
Jack Rudman. 1993. Test guide including questions and answers for students or professionals in the field who seek advancement through examination.

★2919★ *Career Examination Series: Statistician*
National Learning Corp.
212 Michael Dr.
Syosset, NY 11791
Ph: (516)921-8888   Fax: (516)921-8743
Fr: 800-645-6337
Jack Rudman. A series of study guides with multiple-choice examination questions and solutions for trainees and professional statisticians. Titles in the series include *Assistant Statistician; Associate Statistician; Chief Biostatistician; Principal Statistician; Senior Statistician.*

★2920★ *College-Level Examination: Statistics*
National Learning Corp.
212 Michael Dr.
Syosset, NY 11791
Ph: (516)921-8888   Fax: (516)921-8743
Fr: 800-645-6337
Jack Rudman. A sample test that parallels those administered in the College-Level Examination Program which grants college credit for knowledge acquired outside the college classroom. Multiple-choice format; contains answers.

★2921★ *Probability and Statistics Exam File*
Engineering Press, Inc.
PO Box 1
San Jose, CA 95103-0001
Ph: (408)258-4503   Fax: 800-700-1651
Fr: 800-800-1651
Contains 371 exam problems with step-by-step solutions. Covers: descriptive statistics; probability; discrete random variables; variances; regression.

★2922★ *Regents College Proficiency Examination Series: Statistics*
National Learning Corp.
212 Michael Dr.
Syosset, NY 11791
Ph: (516)921-8888   Fax: (516)921-8743
Fr: 800-645-6337
Jack Rudman. A sample test for college credit-by-examination programs in the field of

statistics. Multiple-choice style with answers included.

AWARDS, SCHOLARSHIPS, GRANTS, AND FELLOWSHIPS

★2923★ Fellow of the American Statistical Association
American Statistical Association
1429 Duke St.
Alexandria, VA 22314
Ph: (703)684-1221   Fax: (703)684-2037
For recognition of individuals in the field of statistics. Individuals with activities in the following areas are eligible: consulting on statistical problems, statistical applications and data collection, administration of statistical activities, teaching and dissemination of statistical knowledge, list of major publications having statistical content, activities in the Association, and activities in related professional organizations. Awarded annually.

★2924★ Fisher Memorial Lecture
Institute of Mathematical Statistics
3401 Investment Blvd., Ste. 7
Hayward, CA 94545
Ph: (510)783-8141   Fax: (510)783-4131
To honor a statistician and to stimulate contribution to the field. The honoree presents a lecture annually. Established in 1964.

★2925★ Samuel S. Wilks Memorial Medal Award
American Statistical Association
1429 Duke St.
Alexandria, VA 22314
Ph: (703)684-1221   Fax: (703)684-2037
To recognize a statistician for contributions to statistical theory or practice, through publications or participation in programs of instruction on practical application that directly or indirectly have benefited the United States Government or the country generally. A medal, citation, and an honorarium are awarded annually. Established in 1964.

BASIC REFERENCE GUIDES AND HANDBOOKS

★2926★ Advances in Statistical Analysis and Statistical Computing
JAI Press, Inc.
PO Box 1678
Greenwich, CT 06836
Ph: (203)661-7602
Roberto S. Mariano. 1991.

★2927★ Computational Handbook of Statistics
Scott, Foresman and Co.
1900 E. Lake Ave.
Glenview, IL 60025
Ph: (708)729-3000   Fr: 800-782-2665
James L. Bruning and B. L. Kintz. Third edition, 1990. Includes a bibliogra phy and an index.

★2928★ Encyclopedia of Statistical Sciences
John Wiley and Sons, Inc.
605 3rd Ave.
New York, NY 10158-0012
Ph: (212)850-6000   Fax: (212)850-6088
Fr: 800-526-5368
Samuel Kotz and Norman L. Johnston, editors. 1988. Contains information on statistical theory and applications.

PROFESSIONAL AND TRADE PERIODICALS

★2929★ The American Statistician
American Statistical Assn.
1429 Duke St.
Alexandria, VA 22314-2304
Ph: (703)684-1221   Fax: (703)684-2037
Kinley Larntz
Quarterly. Statistical journal.

★2930★ AMSTAT News
American Statistical Association (AMSTAT)
1429 Duke St.
Alexandria, VA 22314-3402
Ph: (703)684-1221   Fax: (703)684-2036
Alison Stern-Dunyak
Publishes news of the Association, its activities, and members. Recurring features include a calendar of events and employment opportunities.

★2931★ The Annals of Statistics
Institute of Mathematical Statistics
3401 Investment Blvd., Ste. 7
Hayward, CA 94545
Ph: (510)783-8141   Fax: (510)783-4131
Michael Woodroofe
Quarterly. Journal publishing contributions to the theory of statistics and to its applications.

★2932★ Biometric Bulletin
Biometric Society
808 17th St., Ste. 200
Washington, DC 20006
Ph: (703)836-8311
R. Tomassone
Quarterly. Describes member and Society activities in the field of biometry. Recurring features include letters to the editor, news of research, and a calendar of events.

★2933★ Journal of the American Statistical Association
American Statistical Assn.
1429 Duke St.
Alexandria, VA 22314-3402
Ph: (703)684-1221   Fax: (703)684-2037
Roderick Little
Quarterly. Statistical journal.

★2934★ Journal of Forecasting
John Wiley and Sons, Inc.
605 3rd Ave.
New York, NY 10158
Ph: (212)850-6000   Fax: (212)850-6799
Derek W. Bunn
Journal containing articles on recent developments in forecasting. Aimed at business forecasters and statisticians.

★2935★ News From COPAFS
Council of Professional Associations on Federal Statistics (COPAFS)
1429 Duke St., Ste. 402
Alexandria, VA 22314
Ph: (703)836-0404   Fax: (703)684-2037
Edward J. Spar
Covers developments in Federal statistics policy and programs, including data collection efforts, quality of data, and access to information. Describes major statistical activities within the Federal government.

★2936★ Statistical Indicator Report
Statistical Indicator Associates
North Egremont, MA 01252
Ph: (413)528-3280
Leonard H. Lempert
Weekly. Deals with economics and business cycles. Reports on the Bureau of Economic Analysis leading, coincident, and lagging indicators. Recurring features include monthly articles on summary indexes (percentage expanding, average duration of run, and composite).

★2937★ Texas Economic Indicators
Bureau of Business Research
PO Box 7549
Austin, TX 78713
Ph: (512)471-1616   Fax: (512)471-1063
Rita J. Wright
Monthly. Provides statistical data from 1983-1993 for major metropolitan areas.

PROFESSIONAL MEETINGS AND CONVENTIONS

★2938★ Joint Statistical Meetings
American Statistical Association
1429 Duke St.
Alexandria, VA 22314
Ph: (703)684-1221   Fax: (703)684-2037
Annual. **Dates and Locations:** 1996 Aug 04-08; Chicago, IL.

OTHER SOURCES OF INFORMATION

★2939★ "Mathematician/Statistician" in
    100 Best Jobs for the 1990s & Beyond
Dearborn Financial Publishing, Inc.
520 N. Dearborn St.
Chicago, IL 60610-4354
Ph: (312)836-4400   Fax: (312)836-1021
Fr: 800-621-9621
Carol Kleiman. 1992. Describes 100 jobs
ranging from accountants to veterinarians..

Each job profile includes such information as
education, experience, and certification
needed, salaries, and job search suggestions.

★2940★ "Statistician" in *Career
    Selector 2001*
Barron's Educational Series, Inc.
250 Wireless Blvd.
Hauppauge, NY 11788
Ph: (516)434-3311   Fax: (516)434-3723
Fr: 800-645-3476

James C. Gonyea. 1993.

Agricultural Scientists

Agricultural scientists study farm crops and animals and develop ways of improving their quantity and quality. They look for ways to improve crop yield and quality with less labor, control pests and weeds more safely and effectively, and conserve soil and water. Agricultural science is closely related to biological science, and agricultural scientists use the principles of biology and other sciences to solve problems in agriculture. They often work with biological scientists on basic biological research and in applying to agriculture the advances in knowledge brought about by biotechnology. Agricultural scientists usually specialize. **Agronomists** study ways to improve the nutritional value of crops and the quality of seed. **Animal scientists** develop more efficient ways of producing and processing meat, poultry, eggs, and milk. **Dairy scientists** and **poultry scientists** study the genetics, nutrition, reproduction, growth and development of domestic farm animals. **Food technologists** study the chemical, physical, and biological nature of food to learn how to safely process, preserve, package, distribute, and store it. **Soil scientists** study soil characteristics, map soil types, and determine the best types of crops for each soil.

Salaries

Median annual earnings for beginning agricultural scientists are as follows:

Bachelor's degree, animal science	$20,189/year
Federal government, animal science	$55,631/year
Agronomists	$45,911/year

Employment Outlook

Growth rate until the year 2005: Average.

Agricultural Scientists

CAREER GUIDES

★2941★ *Agricultural and Biological Engineer*
Careers, Inc.
PO Box 135
Largo, FL 34649-0135
Ph: (813)584-7333
1995. Two-page summary describing duties, working conditions, personal qualifications, training, earnings and hours, employment outlook, places of employment, related careers, and where to write for more information.

★2942★ "Agricultural and Biological Scientists" in *Jobs! What They Are— Where They Are—What They Pay* (pp. 44)
Simon & Schuster, Inc.
Simon & Schuster Bldg.
1230 Avenue of the Americas
New York, NY 10020
Ph: (212)698-7000   Fr: 800-223-2348
Robert O. Snelling and Anne M. Snelling. 3rd edition, 1992. Describes duties and responsibilities, earnings, employment opportunities, training, and qualifications.

★2943★ "Agricultural Engineer" and "Soil Scientists" in *Career Information Center* (Vol.2)
Simon and Schuster
200 Old Tappan Rd.
Old Tappan, NJ 07675
Fax: 800-445-6991   Fr: 800-223-2348
Richard Lidz and Linda Perrin, editorial directors. Fifth edition, 1993. A multi-volume set that profiles over 600 occupations. Each oocupational profile describes job duties, educational requirements, advancement possibilities, employment outlook, working conditions, earnings and benefits, and where to write for more information.

★2944★ *Agricultural Researchers*
Careers, Inc.
PO Box 135
Largo, FL 34649-0135
Ph: (813)584-7333
1992. Four-page brief describing duties, working conditions, personal qualifications, training, earnings and hours, employment outlook, places of employment, related careers, and where to write for more information.

★2945★ "Agricultural Scientist" in *College Board Guide to Jobs and Career Planning* (pp. 276)
The College Board
415 Columbus Ave.
New York, NY 10023-6992
Ph: (212)713-8165   Fax: (212)713-8143
Fr: 800-323-7155
Joyce S. Mitchell. Second edition, 1994. Profiles a variety of careers. Each profile contains information on salaries, related careers, education needed, and sources of additional information.

★2946★ "Agricultural Scientist" in *Jobs Rated Almanac*
World Almanac
1 International Blvd., Ste. 444
Mahwah, NJ 07495
Ph: (201)529-6900   Fax: (201)529-6901
Les Krantz. Second edition, 1992. Ranks 250 jobs by environment, salary, outlooks, physical demands, stress, security, travel opportunities, and extra perks. Includes jobs the editor feels are the most common, most interesting, and the most rapidly growing.

★2947★ "Agricultural Scientist" in *Opportunities in Environmental Careers*
National Textbook Co. (NTC)
VGM Career Books
4255 W. Touhy Ave.
Lincolnwood, IL 60646-1975
Ph: (708)679-5500   Fax: (708)679-2494
Fr: 800-323-4900
Odom Fanning. 1991. Describes a broad range of opportunities in fields such as environmental health, recreation, physics, and hygiene.

★2948★ "Agricultural Scientists" in *American Almanac of Jobs and Salaries* (p. 259)
Avon Books
1350 Avenue of the Americas
New York, NY 10019
Ph: (212)261-6800   Fr: 800-238-0658
John Wright, editor. Revised and updated, 1994-95. A comprehensive guide to the wages of hundreds of occupations in a wide variety of industries and organizations.

★2949★ "Agricultural Scientists" in *Encyclopedia of Careers and Vocational Guidance* (Vol.2, pp. 53-56)
J.G. Ferguson Publishing Co.
200 W. Madison St., Ste. 300
Chicago, IL 60606
Ph: (312)580-5480   Fax: (312)580-4948
William E. Hopke, editor-in-chief. Ninth edition, 1993. Four-volume set that profiles 900 occupations and describes job trends in 74 industries. Includes career description, educational requirements, history of the job, methods of entry, advancement, employment outlook, earnings, conditions of work, social and psychological factors, and sources of further information.

★2950★ "Agricultural Scientists" in *Occupational Outlook Handbook*
U.S. Government Printing Office
Superintendent of Documents
Washington, DC 20402
Ph: (202)512-1800   Fax: (202)512-2250
Biennial; latest edition, 1994-95. Encyclopedia of careers describing about 250 occupations and comprising about 85 percent of all jobs in the economy. Occupations that require lengthy education or training are given the most attention. Each occupation's profile describes what the worker does on the job, working conditions, education and training requirements, advancement possibilities, job outlook, earnings, and sources of additional information.

★2951★ "Agriculture" in *College Majors and Careers: A Resource Guide to Effective Life Planning* (pp.11-12)
Garrett Park Press
PO Box 1907
Garrett Park, MD 20896
Ph: (301)946-2553
Paul Phifer. 1993. Lists 60 college majors, with definitions; related occupations and leisure activities; skills, values, and personal needed attributes; suggested readings; and a list of associations.

★2952★ "Agriculture" in *Encyclopedia of Careers and Vocational Guidance* (Vol.1, pp. 14-21)
J.G. Ferguson Publishing Co.
200 W. Madison St., Ste. 300
Chicago, IL 60606
Ph: (312)580-5480   Fax: (312)580-4948
William E. Hopke, editor-in-chief. Ninth edition, 1993. Four-volume set that profiles 900 occupations and describes job trends in 74 industries. Includes career description, educational requirements, history of the job, methods of entry, advancement, employment outlook, earnings, conditions of work, social and psychological factors, and sources of further information.

★2953★ Agronomist
Careers, Inc.
PO Box 135
Largo, FL 34649-0135
Ph: (813)584-7333

1995. Two-page occupational summary card describing duties, working conditions, personal qualifications, training, earnings and hours, employment outlook, places of employment, related careers, and where to write for more information.

★2954★ "Agronomist" in *Guide to Federal Jobs* (p. 117)
Resource Directories
3361 Executive Pkwy., Ste. 302
Toledo, OH 43606
Ph: (419)536-5353   Fax: (419)536-7056
Fr: 800-274-8515
Rod W. Durgin, editor. Third edition, 1992. Contains information on finding and applying for federal jobs. Describes more than 200 professional and technical jobs for college graduates. Also includes chapters titled "Horticulturist" (p. 111), "Soil Scientist" (p. 116), and "Entomologist" (p. 107). Covers the nature of the work, salary, and geographic location. Lists college majors preferred for that occupation. Section one describes the function and work of government agencies that hire the most significant number of college graduates.

★2955★ Agronomists
Chronicle Guidance Publications, Inc.
66 Aurora St.
PO Box 1190
Moravia, NY 13118-1190
Ph: (315)497-0330   Fax: (315)497-3359
Fr: 800-622-7284
1991. Occupational brief describing the nature of the job, working conditions, hours and earnings, education and training, licensure, certification, unions, personal qualifications, social and psychological factors, location, employment outlook, entry methods, advancement, and related occupations.

★2956★ Careers in Agribusiness and Industry
Interstate Printers & Publishers, Inc.
510 N. Vermillion St.
PO Box 50
Danville, IL 61834-0050
Ph: (217)446-0500
Marcella Smith, Jean M. Underwood, and Mark Bultmann. Fourth revised edition, 1991.

★2957★ Careers in Floriculture
Society of American Florists (SAF)
1601 Duke St.
Alexandria, VA 22314
Ph: (703)836-8700

1988. Briefly describes career opportunities as a retail florist, a wholesale florist, and a greenhouse producer. Covers educational preparation.

★2958★ Careers in Foods and Nutrition
Glencoe Publishing Co.
866 3rd Ave.
New York, NY 10022-6299
Ph: (212)702-3276

Videotape that explores foods and nutrition career fields that require special training or an advanced degree.

★2959★ Careers in Science
National Textbook Co. (NTC)
VGM Career Books
4255 W. Touhy Ave.
Lincolnwood, IL 60646-1975
Ph: (708)679-5500   Fax: (708)679-2494
Fr: 800-323-4900

Thomas A. Easton, editor. Explores careers in life science, physical science, social science, earth science, engineering, mathematics, and computer science.

★2960★ Entomologist
Careers, Inc.
PO Box 135
Largo, FL 34649-0135
Ph: (813)584-7333

1995. Two-page occupational summary card describing duties, working conditions, personal qualifications, training, earnings and hours, employment outlook, places of employment, related careers, and where to write for more information.

★2961★ Exploring Careers in Agronomy, Crops, and Soils
American Society of Agronomy (ASA)
677 S. Segoe Rd.
Madison, WI 53711
Ph: (608)273-8080

1991. Describes agronomic sciences and the various roles which agronomists, crop scientists, and soil scientists fulfill. Includes description of various job opportunities as well as salaries in the agronomic sciences. Includes a list of colleges and universities offering degrees in agronomic science. Published in cooperation with the Crop Science Society of America and the Soil Science Society of America.

★2962★ "Food Technologist" in *150 Careers in the Health Care Field*
Reed Reference Publishing
121 Chanlon Rd.
PO Box 31
New Providence, NJ 07974
Fax: (908)665-6688   Fr: 800-521-8110
Stanley Alperin. Third edition, 1993. Profiles 150 health care occupations requiring a bachelor's degree or less. Describes the nature of the work, educational preparation, licensing requirements, and salary. Lists accredited educational programs.

★2963★ "Food Technologist" in *Careers in Health Care* (pp. 84-87)
National Textbook Co. (NTC)
VGM Career Books
4255 W. Touhy Ave.
Lincolnwood, IL 60646-1975
Ph: (708)679-5500   Fax: (708)679-2494
Fr: 800-323-4900

Barbara M. Swanson. Third edition, 1995. Profiles 58 health careers. Describes job duties, work settings, salaries, licensing and certification requirements, educational preparation, and future outlook.

★2964★ "Food Technologist" in *Encyclopedia of Careers and Vocational Guidance*
J.G. Ferguson Publishing Co.
200 W. Madison St., Ste. 300
Chicago, IL 60606
Ph: (312)580-5480   Fax: (312)580-4948
William E. Hopke, editor-in-chief. Ninth edition, 1993. Four-volume set that profiles 900 occupations and describes job trends in 74 industries. Includes career description, educational requirements, history of the job, methods of entry, advancement, employment outlook, earnings, conditions of work, social and psychological factors, and sources of further information.

★2965★ "Horticulture" in *College Majors and Careers: A Resource Guide to Effective Life Planning* (pp. 73-74)
Garrett Park Press
PO Box 1907
Garrett Park, MD 20896
Ph: (301)946-2553

Paul Phifer. Revised, 1993. Lists 60 college majors, with definitions; related occupations and leisure activities; skills, values, and personal attributes needed; suggested readings; and a list of associations.

★2966★ "Horticulture" in *Desk Guide to Training and Work Advisement* (pp. 55-58)
Charles C. Thomas, Publisher
2600 S. 1st St.
Springfield, IL 62794-9265
Ph: (217)789-8980   Fax: (217)789-9130
Fr: 800-258-8980

Gail Baugher Keunstler. 1988. Describes alternative methods of gaining entry into an occupation through different types of educational programs, internships, and apprenticeships.

★2967★ Horticulturist
Careers, Inc.
PO Box 135
Largo, FL 34649-0135
Ph: (813)584-7333

1992. Two-page occupational summary card describing duties, working conditions, personal qualifications, training, earnings and hours, employment outlook, places of employment, related careers, and where to write for more information.

★2968★ *Making a World of Difference*
Higher Education Programs
Office of Grants and Program Systems
U.S. Department of Agriculture
14th & Dependence Aves.
Washington, DC 20250
Ph: (202)447-5626

1991. Describes employment opportunities.

★2969★ *Opportunities in Agriculture Careers*
National Textbook Co. (NTC)
VGM Career Books
4255 W. Touhy Ave.
Lincolnwood, IL 60646-1975
Ph: (708)679-5500   Fax: (708)679-2494
Fr: 800-323-4900

Sampling of more than 200 careers available in agriculture-related fields as a result of the application of technology to agriculture. Describes careers in agriculture production industries, food processing, marketing, environmental protection and communications. Chapters include "Forestry", and "Soil Conservation".

★2970★ *Peterson's Job Opportunities for Engineering and Technology*
Petersons Guides, Inc.
PO Box 2123
Princeton, NJ 08543-2123
Ph: (609)243-9111   Fax: (609)243-9150
Fr: 800-338-3282

1994. Gives job hunting advice including information on resume writing, interviewing, and handling salary negotiations. Lists companies that hire college graduates in science and engineering at the bachelor and master's level. Companies are indexed by industry, starting location, and major. Company profiles include contact information and types of hires.

★2971★ *"Science" in Where the Jobs Are: The Hottest Careers for the 90s (pp. 245-260)*
Career Press
180 5th Ave.
Hawthorne, NJ 07507
Ph: (201)427-0229   Fax: (201)427-2037
Fr: 800-CAREER-1

Joyce Hadley. 1995. Offers a job-hunting strategy for the 1990s as well as descriptions of growing careers of the decade. Each profile includes general information, forecasts, growth, education and training, licensing requirements, and salary information.

★2972★ *A Scientific Career With the Agricultural Research Service*
United States Department of Agriculture
Agricultural Research Service
Personnel Division-Personnel Operations
 Branch
6303 Ivy Lane
Greenbelt, MD 20770
Ph: (301)344-2152

1990. Brochure describing the work of the agricultural research service and jobs with the service.

★2973★ *"Soil Scientist" in VGM's Careers Encyclopedia (pp. 437-438)*
National Textbook Co. (NTC)
VGM Career Books
4255 W. Touhy Ave.
Lincolnwood, IL 60646-1975
Ph: (708)679-5500   Fax: (708)679-2494
Fr: 800-323-4900

Third edition, 1991. Profiles 200 occupations. Describes job duties, places of employment, working conditions, qualifications, education and training, advancement potential, and salary for each occupation.

★2974★ *Soil Scientists*
Chronicle Guidance Publications, Inc.
66 Aurora St.
PO Box 1190
Moravia, NY 13118-1190
Ph: (315)497-0330   Fax: (315)497-3359
Fr: 800-622-7284

1991. Career brief describing the nature of the job, working conditions, hours and earnings, education and training, licensure, certification, unions, personal qualifications, social and psychological factors, location, employment outlook, entry methods, advancement, and related occupations.

★2975★ *Think About It*
National FFA Center
5632 Mount Vernon Memorial Hwy.
PO Box 15160
Alexandria, VA 22309-0160
Ph: (703)360-3600

Outlines career opportunities in agricultural production, processing, research, agribusiness, and resource management.

★2976★ *VGM'S Handbook of Scientific and Technical Careers*
National Textbook Co. (NTC)
VGM Career Books
4255 W. Touhy Ave.
Lincolnwood, IL 60646-1975
Ph: (708)679-5500   Fax: (708)679-2494
Fr: 800-323-4900

Annette Selden, editor. Second ed. Overview of nearly 60 science-related careers, with emphasis on educational preparation. Includes information on job responsibilities, working conditions, salaries, and growth opportunities.

PROFESSIONAL ASSOCIATIONS

★2977★ *American Society of Agronomy (ASA)*
677 S. Segoe Rd.
Madison, WI 53711
Ph: (608)273-8080   Fax: (608)273-2021
Members: Professional society of agronomists, plant breeders, physiologists, soil scientists, chemists, educators, technicians, and others concerned with crop production and soil management, and conditions affecting them. **Purpose:** Sponsors fellowship program and student essay and speech contests. Provides placement service. **Publications:** *Agronomy Abstracts*, annual. • *Agronomy Journal*, bimonthly. • *Agronomy News*, monthly. • *ARCPACS Consultant Di-*

rectory, periodic. • *International Directory*, periodic. • *Journal of Environmental Quality*, quarterly. • *Journal of Natural Resources and Life Sciences Education*, semiannual. • *Journal of Production Agriculture*, quarterly.

★2978★ *American Society for Horticultural Science (ASHS)*
113 S. West St., Ste. 400
Alexandria, VA 22314-2824
Ph: (703)836-4606   Fax: (703)836-2024
Members: Educators and government workers engaged in research, teaching, or extension work in horticultural science; firms, associations, and others interested in horticulture. **Purpose:** Promotes and encourages interest in scientific research and education in horticulture. Maintains hall of fame. Offers placement service. Operates 42 committees and 46 working groups. **Publications:** *ASHS Newsletter*, monthly. • *HortScience*, monthly. • *HortTecnology*, quarterly. • *Journal of the American Society for Horticultural Science*, bimonthly.

★2979★ *Council for Agricultural Science and Technology (CAST)*
4420 Lincoln Way
Ames, IA 50010-3447
Ph: (515)292-2125   Fax: (515)292-4512
Members: Scientific societies, associate societies, individuals, corporations, foundations, and trade associations. **Purpose:** Purpose is to disseminate information to the public, news media, and the government on the science and technology of food and agricultural matters of broad public concern. Sponsors educational programs. **Publications:** *Comments*, periodic. • *Issue Papers*, periodic. • *NewsCAST*, quarterly. • *Papers*, periodic. • *Science of Food and Agriculture*, semiannual. • *Special Publications*, periodic. • *Task Force Reports*, periodic.

★2980★ *Institute of Food Technologists (IFT)*
221 N. LaSalle St., Ste. 300
Chicago, IL 60601
Ph: (312)782-8424   Fax: (312)782-8348
Members: Scientific educational society of technical personnel in food industries, production, product development, research, and product quality. **Purpose:** Promotes application of science and engineering to the evaluation, production, processing, packaging, distribution, preparation, and utilization of foods. Aids educational institutions in developing curricula for training in this area. **Publications:** *Food Technology*, monthly. • *IFT Membership Directory*, annual. • *Journal of Food Science*, bimonthly.

★2981★ *IRI Research Institute (IRI)*
PO Box 1276
169 Greenwich Ave.
Stamford, CT 06904-1276
Ph: (203)327-5985   Fax: (203)359-1595
Members: International technical specialists working in agricultural and agribusiness development. Projects have included: development and management of pasture seed industry in Venezuela; livestock improvement in Belize; nontraditional crop improvement program in the Dominican Republic; roadside vegetation and rice production in Brazil; food crops extension program in Indonesia; rice production and management in Guyana; a

crop diversification program in Peru, including the Amazon region; coffee production, El Salvador feasibility and evaluation studies, most recently in Costa Rica, Ecuador, Egypt, Honduras, Kenya, Paraguay, Guyana, Saudi Arabia, and the Yemen Arab Republic. Most projects incorporate a training program for academic credit or practical on-the-job training.

★2982★ Soil Science Society of America (SSSA)
677 S. Segoe Rd.
Madison, WI 53711
Ph: (608)273-8080   Fax: (608)273-2021
Members: Professional soil scientists, including soil physicists, soil classifiers, land use and management specialists, chemists, microbiologists, soil fertility specialists, soil cartographers, conservationists, mineralogists, engineers, and others interested in fundamental and applied soil science.
Publications: *Journal of Environmental Quality*, quarterly. • *Journal of Production Agriculture*, quarterly. • *110-Year Indices*, periodic. • *Soil Science Society of America—Journal*, bimonthly. • *Soil Survey Horizons*, quarterly.

Test Guides

★2983★ *Career Examination Series: Dairy Products Specialist*
National Learning Corp.
212 Michael Dr.
Syosset, NY 11791
Ph: (516)921-8888   Fax: (516)921-8743
Fr: 800-645-6337
Jack Rudman. 1993. Test guide including questions and answers for students or professionals in the field who seek advancement through examination.

★2984★ *Career Examination Series: Horticultural Inspector*
National Learning Corp.
212 Michael Dr.
Syosset, NY 11791
Ph: (516)921-8888   Fax: (516)921-8743
Fr: 800-645-6337
Jack Rudman. 1993. Test guide including questions and answers for students or professionals in the field who seek advancement through examination.

★2985★ *Career Examination Series: Horticulturist*
National Learning Corp.
212 Michael Dr.
Syosset, NY 11791
Ph: (516)921-8888   Fax: (516)921-8743
Fr: 800-645-6337
Jack Rudman. A study guide for professionals and prospective science technicians. Includes a multiple-choice examination section; provides answers.

Educational Directories and Programs

★2986★ *Directory of American Agriculture*
Agricultural Resources & Communications, Inc.
4210 Wam-Teau Dr.
Wamego, KS 66547-9377
Ph: (913)456-9705   Fax: (913)456-9705
Fr: 800-404-7940
Chris Wilson, Contact
Annual, Previous edition September 1993; latest edition September 1994. Covers national and state agricultural organizations; federal and state agricultural departments, agencies, and programs; colleges of agriculture at land grant universities, state 4-H leaders, farm broadcastors and publications, farm credit councils, agricultural information services and other agricultural organizations, agencies and institutions. Entries include: Organization name, address, phone, fax, name and title of contact. National organization entries include additional information. Arrangement: Classified by type of organizations.

★2987★ *Environmental Career Directory*
Gale Research Inc.
835 Penobscot Bldg.
Detroit, MI 48226-4094
Ph: (313)961-2242   Fax: (313)961-6083
Fr: 800-877-GALE
Bradley J. Morgan and Joseph M. Palmisano. 1993. A directory in the Career Advisor Series that provides essays written by industry professionals; job search information on resume and cover letter preparation, networking, and the interviewing process; approximately 300 companies and organizations offering job opportunities and internships, and additional job-hunting resources.

Awards, Scholarships, Grants, and Fellowships

★2988★ John Deere Medal
American Society of Agricultural Engineers
2950 Niles Rd.
St. Joseph, MI 49085-9659
Ph: (616)429-0300   Fax: (616)429-3852
For recognition of distinguished achievement in the application of science and art to the soil. An inscribed gold medal is awarded annually. Established in 1937 in memory of John Deere, who forged a piece of saw blade into a plow form to create the world's first all-steel moldboard.

★2989★ Henry Giese Structures and Environment Award
American Society of Agricultural Engineers
2950 Niles Rd.
St. Joseph, MI 49085-9659
Ph: (616)429-0300   Fax: (616)429-3852
For recognition of excellence in the structures and environment area of agricultural engineering. ASAE members are eligible. A plaque is awarded annually. Established in 1958. Renamed in 1988 to honor Henry Giese for his lifelong accomplishments in farm building design, research and teaching.

★2990★ Massey - Ferguson Medal
American Society of Agricultural Engineers
2950 Niles Rd.
St. Joseph, MI 49085-9659
Ph: (616)429-0300   Fax: (616)429-3852
To honor dedication to the spirit of learning and teaching in the field of agricultural engineering by which agricultural knowledge and practice has been advanced. A gold medal is awarded annually. Established in 1965 to honor Daniel Massey, a pioneer innovator and agricultural machinery manufacturer, and Harry Ferguson, inventor and ardent exponent of agricultural mechanization.

★2991★ Cyrus Hall McCormick - Jerome Increase Case Medal
American Society of Agricultural Engineers
2950 Niles Rd.
St. Joseph, MI 49085-9659
Ph: (616)429-0300   Fax: (616)429-3852
For recognition of exceptional and meritorious engineering achievements in agriculture. An inscribed gold medal is awarded annually. Established in 1931 by Mrs. Emmons Blaine, Cyrus H. McCormick, and Mrs. Harold F. McCormick in memory of their father, Cyrus H. McCormick, the inventor of the self-rake reaper. In 1986, the award name was changed to honor Jerome Increase Case, the developer of the reliable threshing machine. Co-sponsored by Case IH.

★2992★ National Food and Energy Council Electrification Award
American Society of Agricultural Engineers
2950 Niles Rd.
St. Joseph, MI 49085-9659
Ph: (616)429-0300   Fax: (616)429-3852
To honor individual agricultural engineers for their personal and professional contributions to the progress made in the utilization of electrical energy in the production and processing of agriculatural products. A plaque is awarded annually. Established in 1969.

Basic Reference Guides and Handbooks

★2993★ *Agriculture in Dry Lands: Principles and Practice*
Elsevier Science Publishing Co., Inc.
655 Avenue of the Americas
New York, NY 10010
Ph: (212)989-5800
I Arnon, editor. 1992.

★2994★ *Microclimate and Spray Dispersion*
Routledge, Chapman & Hall, Inc.
29 W. 35th St.
New York, NY 10001-2291
Ph: (212)244-3336
David H. Bache, editor. 1992.

★2995★ Systems Approaches to Agricultural Development
Elsevier Science Publishing Co., Inc.
655 Avenue of the Americas
New York, NY 10010
Ph: (212)989-5800
Paul S. Teng, editor. 1992.

PROFESSIONAL AND TRADE PERIODICALS

★2996★ Agricultural & Food: An Abstract Newsletter
National Technical Information Service (NTIS)
5285 Port Royal Rd.
Springfield, VA 22161
Ph: (703)487-4630
Biweekly. Publishes abstracts of reports on agricultural chemistry, agricultural equipment, facilities, and operations. Also covers agronomy, horticulture, and plant pathology; fisheries and aquaculture; animal husbandry and veterinary medicine; and food technology.

★2997★ Agricultural Outlook
U.S. Government Printing Office
Superintendent of Documents
Washington, DC 20402
Ph: (202)783-3238   Fax: (202)275-0019
Monthly. Magazine updating and analyzing developments affecting the outlook of the food and fiber economy of the U.S.

★2998★ Agronomy Journal
American Society of Agronomy
677 S. Segoe Rd.
Madison, WI 53711
Ph: (608)273-8080   Fax: (608)273-2021
J.L. Hatfield
Bimonthly. Agriculture science trade journal.

★2999★ ARI Newsletter
Agricultural Research Institute (ARI)
9650 Rockville Pike
Bethesda, MD 20814
Ph: (301)530-7122   Fax: (301)530-7007
Stan Cath
Bimonthly. Designed to keep members up-to-date on current work study panels, committees, and special task forces of the Institute. Provides a vehicle for exchange of professional information on agricultural research and related national policies and issues.

★3000★ NewsCAST
Council for Agricultural Science and Technology (CAST)
4420 Lincoln Way
Ames, IA 50010
Ph: (515)292-2125   Fax: (515)292-4512
Robert J. Ver Straeten
Quarterly. Serves a consortium of 30 food and agricultural science societies, which promotes understanding by providing a factual background in agricultural science and technology. Carries features of interest to food and agricultural scientists and news of the organization's activities and programs. Recurring features include announcements of available publications and honors awarded; and a progress report on the work of specific, authorized task forces.

★3001★ Science of Food, Agriculture, and Environment: Supplement for Teaching
Council of Agricultural Science and Technology
4420 Lincoln Way
Ames, IA 50014-3447
Ph: (515)292-2125   Fax: (515)292-4512
Robert J. Ver Straeten
Tracks developments in the agricultural and environmental sectors.

PROFESSIONAL MEETINGS AND CONVENTIONS

★3002★ National Western Stock Show and Rodeo
National Western Stock Show Association
4655 Humboldt St.
Denver, CO 80216
Ph: (303)297-1166   Fax: (303)292-1708
Annual. Always held during January at the National Western Complex in Denver, Colorado. **Dates and Locations:** 1996 Jan 09-21; Denver, CO. • 1997 Jan 07-19; Denver, CO. • 1998 Jan 13-25; Denver, CO. • 1999 Jan 12-24; Denver, CO.

★3003★ Northwest Agricultural Show
Northwest Agricultural Congress
4672 Drift Creek Rd., SE
Sublimity, OR 97385
Ph: (503)769-7120   Fax: (503)769-3549
Annual. Always held during January at the Expo Center in Portland, Oregon.

OTHER SOURCES OF INFORMATION

★3004★ "Agricultural Scientist" in 100 Best Jobs for the 1990s & Beyond
Dearborn Financial Publishing, Inc.
520 N. Dearborn St.
Chicago, IL 60610-4354
Ph: (312)836-4400   Fax: (312)836-1021
Fr: 800-621-9621
Carol Kleiman. 1992. Describes 100 jobs ranging from accountants to veterinarians.. Each job profile includes such information as education, experience, and certification needed, salaries, and job search suggestions.

★3005★ "Horticulture" in Accounting to Zoology: Graduate Fields Defined
Petersons Guides, Inc.
PO Box 2123
Princeton, NJ 08543-2123
Ph: (609)243-9111   Fax: (609)243-9150
Fr: 800-338-3282
Goldstein, Amy J., editor. Revised and updated, 1987. Defines 298 graduate and professional fields. Discusses types of graduate programs and degrees, graduate research, applied work, employment prospects, and trends. Contains chapters titled "Agricultural Sciences" (pp. 235-236), "Agronomy and Soil Sciences" (pp. 236-237), "Animal Sciences" (p. 237), "Entomology" (pp. 214, 215), and "Food Science and Technology" (pp. 237-238).

★3006★ Salaries of Scientists, Engineers, and Technicians: A Summary of Salary Surveys
Commission on Professionals in Science and Technology (CPST)
1500 Massachusetts Ave., NW, Ste. 831
Washington, DC 20005
Ph: (202)223-6995
1993.

★3007★ Yearbook of Agriculture
Superintendent of Documents
U.S. Government Printing Office
Washington, DC 20402
Ph: (202)783-3238
Annual. Published by the U.S. Department of Agriculture. Each yearbook provides in-depth coverage of a single topic.

Biological Scientists

Biological scientists study living organisms and their relationship to their environment. Most specialize in some area such as ornithology (the study of birds) or microbiology (the study of microscopic organisms). Biological scientists work in management or administration. They may plan and administer programs for testing foods and drugs for example, or direct activities at zoos or botanical gardens. Some work as consultants to business firms or to government, while others test and inspect foods, drugs, and other products or write for technical publications. Some work in sales and service jobs for companies manufacturing chemicals or other technical products. **Aquatic biologists** study plants and animals living in water. **Marine biologists** study salt water organisms and **limnologists** study fresh water organisms. **Biochemists** study the chemical composition of living things. **Botanists** deal with plants and their environment. **Microbiologists** investigate the growth and characteristics of microscopic organisms such as bacteria, viruses and fungi. **Medical microbiologists** study the relationship between bacteria and disease or the effect of antibiotics on microorganisms. **Physiologists** study life functions of plants and animals both at the whole organism and at the cellular or molecular level, under normal and abnormal conditions. **Zoologists** study animals, their origin, behavior, diseases and life processes. **Ecologists** study the relationship between organisms and their environments and the effects of influences such as pollutants, rainfall, temperature, and altitude on organisms.

Salaries

Salaries for biological scientists differ depending on the type of study:

Biological scientists, bachelor's degree (private industry)	$21,850/year
Biological scientists, (federal government)	$45,155/year
Medical scientists	$32,400/year
Microbiologists	$49,440/year
Ecologists	$44,657/year
Physiologists	$55,326/year

Employment Outlook

Growth rate until the year 2005: Faster than the average.

Biological Scientists

CAREER GUIDES

★3008★ Biochemist
Careers, Inc.
PO Box 135
Largo, FL 34649-0135
Ph: (813)584-7333
1991. Four-page brief offering the definition, history, duties, working conditions, personal qualifications, educational requirements, earnings, hours, employment outlook, advancement, and careers related to this position.

★3009★ "Biochemist" in *VGM's Careers Encyclopedia* (pp. 62-63)
National Textbook Co. (NTC)
VGM Career Books
4255 W. Touhy Ave.
Lincolnwood, IL 60646-1975
Ph: (708)679-5500   Fax: (708)679-2494
Fr: 800-323-4900
Third edition, 1991. Profiles 200 occupations. Describes job duties, places of employment, working conditions, qualifications, education and training, advancement potential, and salary for each occupation.

★3010★ Biochemists
Chronicle Guidance Publications, Inc.
66 Aurora St.
PO Box 1190
Moravia, NY 13118-1190
Ph: (315)497-0330   Fax: (315)497-3359
Fr: 800-622-7284
1992. Career brief describing the nature of the job, working conditions, hours and earnings, education and training, licensure, certification, unions, personal qualifications, social and psychological factors, location, employment outlook, entry methods, advancement, and related occupations.

★3011★ "Biological Sciences" in *Encyclopedia of Careers and Vocational Guidance* (Vol.1, pp. 61-68)
J.G. Ferguson Publishing Co.
200 W. Madison St., Ste. 300
Chicago, IL 60606
Ph: (312)580-5480   Fax: (312)580-4948
William E. Hopke, editor-in-chief. Ninth edition, 1993. Four-volume set that profiles 900 occupations and describes job trends in 74 industries. Includes career description, educational requirements, history of the job, methods of entry, advancement, employment outlook, earnings, conditions of work, social and psychological factors, and sources of further information.

★3012★ "Biological Scientists" in *American Almanac of Jobs and Salaries* (p. 257)
Avon Books
1350 Avenue of the Americas
New York, NY 10019
Ph: (212)261-6800   Fr: 800-238-0658
John Wright, editor. Revised and updated, 1994-95. A comprehensive guide to the wages of hundreds of occupations in a wide variety of industries and organizations.

★3013★ "Biological Scientists" in *America's 50 Fastest Growing Jobs* (pp. 32)
JIST Works, Inc.
720 N. Park Ave.
Indianapolis, IN 46202-3431
Ph: (317)264-3720   Fax: (317)264-3709
Fr: 800-648-5478
Michael J. Farr, compiler. 1994. Describes the 50 fastest growing jobs within major career clusters such as technicians, and marketing and sales. Each job profile explains the nature of the work, skills and abilities required, employment outlook, average earnings, related occupations, education and training requirements, and employment opportunities. Also contains career planning information and job search tips.

★3014★ "Biological Scientists" in *Best Jobs for the 1990s and Into the 21st Century*
Impact Publications
9104-N Manassas Dr.
Manassas Park, VA 22111
Ph: (703)361-7300   Fax: (703)335-9486
Ronald L. Krannich and Caryl Rae Krannich. 1993.

★3015★ "Biological Scientists" in *Encyclopedia of Careers and Vocational Guidance* (Vol.2, pp. 182-185)
J.G. Ferguson Publishing Co.
200 W. Madison St., Ste. 300
Chicago, IL 60606
Ph: (312)580-5480   Fax: (312)580-4948
William E. Hopke, editor-in-chief. Ninth edition, 1993. Four-volume set that profiles 900 occupations and describes job trends in 74 industries. Includes career description, educational requirements, history of the job, methods of entry, advancement, employment outlook, earnings, conditions of work, social and psychological factors, and sources of further information.

★3016★ "Biological Scientists" in *Occupational Outlook Handbook*
U.S. Government Printing Office
Superintendent of Documents
Washington, DC 20402
Ph: (202)512-1800   Fax: (202)512-2250
Biennial; latest edition, 1994-95. Encyclopedia of careers describing about 250 occupations and comprising about 85 percent of all jobs in the economy. Occupations that require lengthy education or training are given the most attention. Each occupation's profile describes what the worker does on the job, working conditions, education and training requirements, advancement possibilities, job outlook, earnings, and sources of additional information.

★3017★ Biologist
Careers, Inc.
PO Box 135
Largo, FL 34649-0135
Ph: (813)584-7333
1994. Four-page brief offering the definition, history, duties, working conditions, personal qualifications, educational requirements, earnings, hours, employment outlook, advancement, and careers related to this position.

★3018★ "Biologist" in *College Board Guide to Jobs and Career Planning* (pp. 278)
The College Board
415 Columbus Ave.
New York, NY 10023-6992
Ph: (212)713-8165   Fax: (212)713-8143
Fr: 800-323-7155

Joyce S. Mitchell. Second edition, 1994. Covers a variety of job opportunities. Each career profile contains information on salaries, related careers, education needed, and sources of additional information.

★3019★ "Biologist" in *Guide to Federal Jobs* (pp. 107)
Resource Directories
3361 Executive Pkwy., Ste. 302
Toledo, OH 43606
Ph: (419)536-5353   Fax: (419)536-7056
Fr: 800-274-8515

Rod W. Durgin, editor. Third edition, 1992. Contains information on finding and applying for federal jobs. Describes more than 200 professional and technical jobs for college graduates. Also includes chapters titled "Biological Scientist Student Trainee" (p. 125), "Zoologist" (p. 105), "Wildlife Biologist" (p. 38), "Microbiologist" (p. 102), "Botanist" (p. 108), and "Plant Physiologist" (p. 110). Covers the nature of the work, salary, and geographic location. Lists college majors preferred for that occupation. Section one describes the function and work of government agencies that hire the most significant number of college graduates.

★3020★ "Biologist" in *Opportunities in High-Tech Careers* (p. 136)
National Textbook Co. (NTC)
VGM Career Books
4255 W. Touhy Ave.
Lincolnwood, IL 60646-1975
Ph: (708)679-5500   Fax: (708)679-2494
Fr: 800-323-4900

Golter, Gary D., and Deborah Yanuck. 1987. Explores high-technology careers. Written for the student and displaced worker. Describes job opportunities, how to make a career decision, how to prepare for high-technology jobs, job hunting techniques, and future trends.

★3021★ "Biologists" in *Encyclopedia of Careers and Vocational Guidance*
J.G. Ferguson Publishing Co.
200 W. Madison St., Ste. 300
Chicago, IL 60606
Ph: (312)580-5480   Fax: (312)580-4948

William E. Hopke, editor-in-chief. Eighth edition, 19903. Four-volume set that profiles 900 occupations and describes job trends in 74 industries. Includes career description, educational requirements, history of the job, methods of entry, advancement, employment outlook, earnings, conditions of work, social and psychological factors, and sources of further information.

★3022★ "Biology", "Botony", and "Physiology" in *College Majors and Careers: A Resource Guide to Effective Life Planning*
Garrett Park Press
PO Box 1907
Garrett Park, MD 20896
Ph: (301)946-2553

Paul Phifer. Revised, 1993. Lists 60 college majors, with definitions; related occupations and leisure activities; skills, values, and personal attributesneeded; suggested readings; and a list of associations.

★3023★ "Biology" in *Opportunities in Environmental Careers*
National Textbook Co. (NTC)
VGM Career Books
4255 W. Touhy Ave.
Lincolnwood, IL 60646-1975
Ph: (708)679-5500   Fax: (708)679-2494
Fr: 800-323-4900

Odom Fanning. 1991. Describes a broad range of opportunities in fields such as environmental health, recreation, physics, and hygiene.

★3024★ *Botanist*
Careers, Inc.
PO Box 135
Largo, FL 34649-0135
Ph: (813)584-7333

1992. Four-page brief offering the definition, history, duties, working conditions, personal qualifications, educational requirements, earnings, hours, employment outlook, advancement, and careers related to this position.

★3025★ *Career Opportunities in Genetics*
Genetics Society of America
Administrative Office
9650 Rockville Pike
Bethesda, MD 20814
Ph: (301)571-1825

1987. Defines genetics and outlines career opportunities in genetics. Covers where geneticists work, training needed, and the future of genetics.

★3026★ *Careers in Botany*
Botanical Society of America, Business Office
1735 Neil Ave.
Columbus, OH 43210-1293
Ph: (614)292-3519

1988. Describes botany, the connection between botany and society, specializations in the field of botany, current issues, salary, and educational preparation.

★3027★ *Careers in Physiology*
American Physiological Society
9650 Rockville Pike
Bethesda, MD 20814-3991
Ph: (301)530-7164

1990. Briefly describes physiology careers and the education required.

★3028★ *Careers in Public Garden*
American Association of Botanical Gardens and Arboreta
786 Church Rd.
Wayne, PA 19087
Ph: (215)688-1120

Brochure that describes the function of public gardens, the types of jobs available in public gardens, and the training required for positions in botanical gardens.

★3029★ *Careers in Science*
National Textbook Co. (NTC)
VGM Career Books
4255 W. Touhy Ave.
Lincolnwood, IL 60646-1975
Ph: (708)679-5500   Fax: (708)679-2494
Fr: 800-323-4900

Thomas A. Easton, editor. Explores careers in life science, physical science, social science, earth science, engineering, mathematics, and computer science.

★3030★ "Ecology" in *Opportunities in Environmental Careers*
National Textbook Co. (NTC)
VGM Career Books
4255 W. Touhy Ave.
Lincolnwood, IL 60646-1975
Ph: (708)679-5500   Fax: (708)679-2494
Fr: 800-323-4900

Odom Fanning. 1991. Describes a broad range of opportunities in fields such as environmental health, recreation, physics, and hygiene.

★3031★ *Internship Directory 1994: Internships and Summer Jobs at Public Gardens*
American Association of Botanical Gardens and Arboreta (AABGA)
786 Church Rd.
Wayne, PA 19087
Ph: (215)688-1120   Fax: (610)293-0149

Wood Frey. Annual. Lists more than 500 summer jobs and internships at 122 botanical gardens, arboreta, and other horticultural institutions.

★3032★ *Microbiologist*
Careers, Inc.
PO Box 135
Largo, FL 34649-0135
Ph: (813)584-7333

1992. Two-page occupational summary card describing duties, working conditions, personal qualifications, training, earnings and hours, employment outlook, places of employment, related careers, and where to write for more information.

★3033★ *Microbiologists*
Chronicle Guidance Publications, Inc.
66 Aurora St.
PO Box 1190
Moravia, NY 13118-1190
Ph: (315)497-0330   Fax: (315)497-3359
Fr: 800-622-7284

1993. Career brief describing the nature of the job, working conditions, hours and earnings, education and training, licensure, certification, unions, personal qualifications, social and psychological factors, location, employment outlook, entry methods, advancement, and related occupations.

★3034★ *Opportunities in Biological Science*
National Textbook Co. (NTC)
VGM Career Books
4255 W. Touhy Ave.
Lincolnwood, IL 60646-1975
Ph: (708)679-5500   Fax: (708)679-2494
Fr: 800-323-4900

Charles S. Winter. 1990. Includes a bibliography. Explains job duties, educaitonal requirements, salary, working conditions, employment outlook, and advancement opportunities.

★3035★ *Opportunities for Women in Science Careers*
National Textbook Co. (NTC)
VGM Career Books
4255 W. Touhy Ave.
Lincolnwood, IL 60646-1975
Ph: (708)679-5500   Fax: (708)679-2494
Fr: 800-323-4900

Alice Fins. 1979. Profiles women professionals in science careers such as biology, chemistry, geology, astronomy, physics, math, and others.

★3036★ *Peterson's Job Opportunities for Engineering and Technology*
Petersons Guides, Inc.
PO Box 2123
Princeton, NJ 08543-2123
Ph: (609)243-9111   Fax: (609)243-9150
Fr: 800-338-3282

1994. Gives job hunting advice including information on resume writing, interviewing, and handling salary negotiations. Lists companies that hire college graduates in science and engineering at the bachelor and master's level. Companies are indexed by industry, starting location, and major. Company profiles include contact information and types of hires.

★3037★ *Physiologist, Animal*
Careers, Inc.
PO Box 135
Largo, FL 34649-0135
Ph: (813)584-7333

1995. Two-page occupational summary card describing duties, working conditions, personal qualifications, training, earnings and hours, employment outlook, places of employment, related careers, and where to write for more information.

★3038★ *"Physiologist"* in *Guide to Federal Jobs* (p. 106)
Resource Directories
3361 Executive Pkwy., Ste. 302
Toledo, OH 43606
Ph: (419)536-5353   Fax: (419)536-7056
Fr: 800-274-8515

Rod W. Durgin, editor. Third edition, 1992. Contains information on finding and applying for federal jobs. Describes more than 200 professional and technical jobs for college graduates. Covers the nature of the work, salary, and geographic location. Lists college majors preferred for that occupation. Section one describes the function and work of government agencies that hire the most significant number of college graduates.

★3039★ *"Science"* in *Where the Jobs Are: The Hottest Careers for the 90s* (pp. 245-260)
Career Press
180 5th Ave.
Hawthorne, NJ 07507
Ph: (201)427-0229   Fax: (201)427-2037
Fr: 800-CAREER-1

Joyce Hadley. 1995. Offers a job-hunting strategy for the 1990s as well as descriptions of growing careers of the decade. Each profile includes general information, forecasts, growth, education and training, licensing requirements, and salary information.

★3040★ *VGM'S Handbook of Scientific and Technical Careers*
National Textbook Co. (NTC)
VGM Career Books
4255 W. Touhy Ave.
Lincolnwood, IL 60646-1975
Ph: (708)679-5500   Fax: (708)679-2494
Fr: 800-323-4900

Annette Selden, editor. Second ed. Overview of nearly 60 science-related careers, with emphasis on educational preparation. Includes information on job responsibilities, working conditions, salaries, and growth opportunities.

★3041★ *Wildlife/Fishery Biologists*
Careers, Inc.
PO Box 135
Largo, FL 34649-0135
Ph: (813)584-7333

1991. Four-page brief offering the definition, history, duties, working conditions, personal qualifications, educational requirements, earnings, hours, employment outlook, advancement, and careers related to this position.

★3042★ *Working for Life: Careers in Biology*
Plexus Publishing, Inc.
143 Old Marlton Pike
Medford, NJ 08055
Ph: (609)654-6500

Thomas A. Easton. Second edition, 1988. Includes a bibliography.

★3043★ *Zoologist*
Careers, Inc.
PO Box 135
Largo, FL 34649-0135
Ph: (813)584-7333

1994. Four-page brief offering the definition, history, duties, working conditions, personal qualifications, educational requirements, earnings, hours, employment outlook, advancement, and careers related to this position.

★3044★ *Zoologists*
Chronicle Guidance Publications, Inc.
66 Aurora St.
PO Box 1190
Moravia, NY 13118-1190
Ph: (315)497-0330   Fax: (315)497-3359
Fr: 800-622-7284

1994. Career brief describing the nature of the job, working conditions, hours and earnings, education and training, licensure, certification, unions, personal qualifications, social and psychological factors, location, employ-

ment outlook, entry methods, advancement, and related occupations.

PROFESSIONAL ASSOCIATIONS

★3045★ **American Institute of Biological Sciences (AIBS)**
730 11th St. NW
Washington, DC 20001-4521
Ph: (202)628-1500   Fax: (202)628-1509
Fr: 800-992-AIBS

Members: Professional biological associations and laboratories whose members have an interest in the life sciences. **Purpose:** Promotes unity and effectiveness of effort among persons engaged in biological research, education, and application of biological sciences, including agriculture, environment, and medicine. Seeks to further the relationships of biological sciences to other sciences, the arts, and industries. Conducts symposium series; provides names of prominent biologists who are willing to serve as speakers and curriculum consultants; provides advisory committees and other services to the Department of Energy, Environmental Protection Agency, National Science Foundation, Department of Defense, and National Aeronautics and Space Administration. Maintains educational consultant panel. **Publications:** *American Institute of Biological Sciences—Forum: Public Issues, the Life Sciences, and You*, bimonthly. • *Annual Meeting Program*, annual. • *BioScience*, 11/year.

★3046★ **American Physiological Society (APS)**
9650 Rockville Pike
Bethesda, MD 20814-3991
Ph: (301)530-7164   Fax: (301)571-8305
Members: Professional society of physiologists. **Publications:** *Advances in Physiology Education*, semiannual. • *American Journal of Physiology*, monthly. • *American Journal of Physiology: Cell Physiology*, monthly. • *American Journal of Physiology: Endocrinology and Metabolism*, monthly. • *American Journal of Physiology: Gastrointestinal and Liver Physiology*, monthly. • *American Journal of Physiology: Heart and Circulatory Physiolog*, monthly. • *American Journal of Physiology: Lung Cellular and Molecular Physiology*, monthly. • *American Journal of Physiology: Regulatory, Integrative, and Comparative Physiology*, monthly. • *American Journal of Physiology: Renal, Fluid and Electrolyte Physiology*, monthly. • *FASEB Directory*, annual. • *Journal of Applied Physiology*, monthly. • *Journal of Neurophysiology*, monthly. • *News in Physiological Sciences*, bimonthly. • *Physiological Reviews*, quarterly. • *The Physiologist*, bimonthly.

★3047★ **American Society for Biochemistry and Molecular Biology (ASBMB)**
9650 Rockville Pike
Bethesda, MD 20814-3996
Ph: (301)530-7145   Fax: (301)571-1824
Members: Biochemists and molecular biologists who have conducted and published

original investigations in biological chemistry and/or molecular biology. Operates placement service. **Publications:** *Journal of Biological Chemistry*, weekly. • *Minireview Compendium*, annual.

★3048★ American Society for Microbiology (ASM)
1325 Massachusetts Ave. NW
Washington, DC 20005
Ph: (202)737-3600
Members: Scientific society of microbiologists. **Purpose:** Promotes the advancement of scientific knowledge in order to improve education in microbiology. Encourages the highest professional and ethical standards, and the adoption of sound legislative and regulatory policies affecting the discipline of microbiology at all levels. Communicates microbiological scientific achievements to the public. Maintains numerous committees and 23 divisions, and placement services; compiles statistics. **Publications:** *Abstracts of Annual Meeting.* • *Antimicrobial Agents and Chemotherapy*, monthly. • *Applied and Environmental Microbiology*, monthly. • *ASM Directory of Members.* • *ASM News*, monthly. • *Clinical Microbiology Reviews*, quarterly. • *Infection and Immunity*, monthly. • *International Journal of Systematic Bacteriology*, quarterly. • *Journal of Bacteriology*, semimonthly. • *Journal of Clinical Microbiology*, monthly. • *Journal of Virology*, monthly. • *Microbiological Reviews*, quarterly. • *Molecular and Cellular Biology*, monthly.

★3049★ American Society of Zoologists (ASZ)
401 N. Michigan Ave.
Chicago, IL 60611-4267
Ph: (312)527-6697   Fax: (312)527-6640
Members: Professional society of zoologists. **Purpose:** Maintains placement service; conducts educational programs. **Publications:** *American Zoologist*, bimonthly. • *Careers in Animal Biology.*

★3050★ Botanical Society of America (BSA)
c/o Kimberly E. Hiser
Business Manager Botanical Society of America
1735 Neil Ave.
Columbus, OH 43210-1293
Ph: (614)292-3519
Professional society of botanists and others interested in plant science. Conducts special research programs. **Publications:** *American Journal of Botany*, monthly. • *Botanical Society of America—Membership Directory*, biennial. • *Career Bulletin*, periodic. • *Guide to Graduate Study in Botany for the U.S. and Canada.* • *Plant Science Bulletin*, bimonthly.

★3051★ Soil and Water Conservation Society (SWCS)
7515 NE Ankeny Rd.
Ankeny, IA 50021
Ph: (515)289-2331   Fax: (515)289-1227
Fr: 800-843-7645
Soil and water conservationists and others in fields related to the use, conservation, and management of natural resources. Objective is to advance the science and art of good land and water use. Offers internships to qualified students. Operates educational programs for children. **Publications:** *Conservogram*,

bimonthly. • *Journal of Soil and Water Conservation*, bimonthly. • *Technical Monographs*, periodic.

TEST GUIDES

★3052★ Advanced Placement Examination in Biology
Arco Publishing Co.
Macmillan General Reference
15 Columbus Cir.
New York, NY 10023
Fax: 800-835-3202   Fr: 800-858-7674
Richard F. Heller and Rachael F. Heller. Second Edition, 1990. Contains a subject review and two full-length practice tests.

★3053★ Career Examination Series: Bacteriologist
National Learning Corp.
212 Michael Dr.
Syosset, NY 11791
Ph: (516)921-8888   Fax: (516)921-8743
Fr: 800-645-6337
Jack Rudman. A series of study guides with multiple-choice examination questions and solutions for trainees and professional biologists. Titles in the series include *Assistant Bacteriologist; Assistant Microbiologist; Entomologist; Senior Microbiologist.*

★3054★ Career Examination Series: Biologist
National Learning Corp.
212 Michael Dr.
Syosset, NY 11791
Ph: (516)921-8888   Fax: (516)921-8743
Fr: 800-645-6337
Jack Rudman. 1993. Test guide including questions and answers for students or professionals in the field who seek advancement through examination.

★3055★ Career Examination Series: Conservation Biologist
National Learning Corp.
212 Michael Dr.
Syosset, NY 11791
Ph: (516)921-8888   Fax: (516)921-8743
Fr: 800-645-6337
Jack Rudman. 1993. Test guide including questions and answers for students or professionals in the field who seek advancement through examination.

★3056★ Career Examination Series: Forensic Scientist (Toxicology)
National Learning Corp.
212 Michael Dr.
Syosset, NY 11791
Ph: (516)921-8888   Fax: (516)921-8743
Fr: 800-645-6337
Jack Rudman. 1993. Test guide including questions and answers for students or professionals in the field who seek advancement through examination.

★3057★ Career Examination Series: Junior Bacteriologist
National Learning Corp.
212 Michael Dr.
Syosset, NY 11791
Ph: (516)921-8888   Fax: (516)921-8743
Fr: 800-645-6337
Jack Rudman. 1993. Test guide including questions and answers for students or professionals in the field who seek advancement through examination.

★3058★ Career Examination Series: Microbiologist
National Learning Corp.
212 Michael Dr.
Syosset, NY 11791
Ph: (516)921-8888   Fax: (516)921-8743
Fr: 800-645-6337
Jack Rudman. 1993. Test guide including questions and answers for students or professionals in the field who seek advancement through examination.

★3059★ EZ 101 Study Keys: Biology
Barron's Educational Series, Inc.
250 Wireless Blvd.
Hauppauge, NY 11788
Ph: (516)434-3311   Fax: (516)434-3723
Fr: 800-645-3476
1991. Provides themes and a glossary of terms.

★3060★ General Biology
National Learning Corp.
212 Michael Dr.
Syosset, NY 11791
Ph: (516)921-8888   Fax: (516)921-8743
Fr: 800-645-6337
Jack Rudman. College-Level Examination series. A sample test that parallels those administered in the College-Level Examination Program which grants college credit for knowledge acquired outside the college classroom. Multiple-choice format; contains answers.

★3061★ Graduate Record Examination: Biology
National Learning Corp.
212 Michael Dr.
Syosset, NY 11791
Ph: (516)921-8888   Fax: (516)921-8743
Fr: 800-645-6337
Jack Rudman. Multiple-choice test for those seeking admission to graduate school for study in the field of biology. Includes solutions to examination questions.

★3062★ Graduate Record Examination (GRE) in Biology
Barron's Educational Series, Inc.
250 Wireless Blvd.
Hauppauge, NY 11788
Ph: (516)434-3311   Fax: (516)434-3723
Fr: 800-645-3476
John A. Snyder, Ph.D. and C. Leland Rodgers, Ph.D. Third edition, 1989. Contains four model GRE Biology Tests with answers, plus an up-to-date review of college-level biology.

★3063★ Microbiology
National Learning Corp.
212 Michael Dr.
Syosset, NY 11791
Ph: (516)921-8888   Fax: (516)921-8743
Fr: 800-645-6337
Jack Rudman. ACT Proficiency Examination Program series. A practice test that demonstrates proficiency in the area of biology. Multiple-choice format with solutions included.

★3064★ Practicing to Take the GRE Biology Test
Educational Testing Service
Rosedale Rd.
Princeton, NJ 08541
Ph: (609)921-9000
Second edition, 1990. Summarizes the purpose and scope of the Graduate Record Examination Subject Test for biology. Contains sample questions.

★3065★ Regents College Prociciency Examination Series: Biology
National Learning Corp.
212 Michael Dr.
Syosset, NY 11791
Ph: (516)921-8888   Fax: (516)921-8743
Fr: 800-645-6337
Jack Rudman. A sample test for college credit-by-examination programs in the field of biology. Multiple-choice style with answers included.

★3066★ Undergraduate Program Field Test: Biology
National Learning Corp.
212 Michael Dr.
Syosset, NY 11791
Ph: (516)921-8888   Fax: (516)921-8743
Fr: 800-645-6337
Jack Rudman. A practice examination fashioned after tests given in the Regents External Degree Program. Designed to measure knowledge received outside the college classroom in the subject of biology. Contains multiple-choice questions; provides solutions.

EDUCATIONAL DIRECTORIES AND PROGRAMS

★3067★ Environmental Career Directory
Gale Research Inc.
835 Penobscot Bldg.
Detroit, MI 48226-4094
Ph: (313)961-2242   Fax: (313)961-6083
Fr: 800-877-GALE
Bradley J. Morgan and Joseph M. Palmisano. 1993. A directory in the Career Advisor Series that provides essays written by industry professionals; job search information on resume and cover letter preparation, networking, and the interviewing process; approximately 300 companies and organizations offering job opportunities and internships, and additional job-hunting resources.

★3068★ Internship Directory: Internships and Summer Jobs at Public Gardens
American Association of Botanical Gardens and Arboreta (AABGA)
786 Church Rd.
Wayne, PA 19087
Ph: (610)688-1120   Fax: (610)293-0149
Annual, October. Covers over 130 gardens, arboreta, and other horticultural organizations that offer student internships and summer jobs. Entries include: Name of institution, address, name of contact, deadline for application, number of students hired, whether internships are available, employment period, hours, rate of pay, whether housing is available, other comments. Arrangement: Alphabetical.

★3069★ Physical Science Career Directory
Gale Research Inc.
835 Penobscot Bldg.
Detroit, MI 48226-4094
Ph: (313)961-2242   Fax: (313)961-6083
Fr: 800-877-GALE
Bradley J. Morgan, Contact
First edition March 1994. Covers over 210 chemical companies, testing and research laboratories, and consulting firms in the U.S. offering entry-level positions and internships; sources of help-wanted ads, professional associations, producers of videos, databases, career guides, and professional guides and handbooks. Entries include: For companies—Name, address, phone, fax, business description, research activities, names and titles of key personnel, number of employees, average number of entry-level positions available, human resources contact, description of internship opportunities including contact, type and number available, application procedures, qualifications, and duties. For others—Name or title, address, phone, description. Paperback edition Arrangement: Companies are alphabetical; others are classified by type of resource.

AWARDS, SCHOLARSHIPS, GRANTS, AND FELLOWSHIPS

★3070★ AIBS Distinguished Service Award
American Institute of Biological Sciences
730 11th St. NW
Washington, DC 20001-4521
Ph: (202)628-1500   Fax: (202)628-1509
To recognize contributions in the service of biology, especially in the advancement and integration of biological disciplines, the application of biological knowledge to the solution of mankind's problems, and the improvement of public policy and planning by the introduction of pertinent biological considerations. Nominations must be submitted by October 1 and include a statement of the individual's service to biological science as a profession. A plaque is bestowed at the annual meeting and the winner's acceptance address is published in *BioScience*. Established in 1972.

★3071★ Eppley Foundation Support for Advanced Scientific Research
Eppley Foundation for Research, Inc.
575 Lexington Ave.
New York, NY 10022
Purpose: To support and encourage postdoctoral work in the physical and biological sciences. Qualifications: Applicants must be qualified investigators conducting post-doctoral, original research in the physical and biological sciences. Candidates must have a Ph.D. or M.D., and be affiliated with a recognized educational or research institution. Persons who have recently received their doctorates are unlikely to receive funding. Grant proposals from foreign countries are considered without prejudice, but such applicants must explain in a covering letter why they are unable to obtain research funds in their own countries. Funds available: Up to 12 grants ranging from several thousand dollars to $25,000. The average grant is $15,000. Most awards are for one year. Funds are issued to the institution for the individual. Institutions must acknowledge in writing their willingness to administer the grant. Up to 15 percent of the grant will go for institutional administration costs. Recipients must submit a final report one year after the grant period, which includes an itemized accounting of funds disbursed. Application details: Five reprints of any publication arising from work sponsored by the Foundation must be sent to the Foundation office. A formal application, a proposal that is concise and states clearly the methods and goals of the researcher, a vita (proposals involving more than one investigator should include vitae for all researchers), itemized budget and a sponsoring letter from the institution must be submitted. Deadline: All application materials must be filed by the first of February, May, August or November.

★3072★ Guest Lectureship Award on Basic Cell Research in Cytology
American Society of Cytology
409 W. 9th St.
Wilmington, DE 19808
Ph: (215)922-3880   Fax: (215)922-7347
To honor a cytologist with the presentation of the Basic Cytology Lecture at the Meeting. An honorarium of $2,000, a certificate, and travel expenses to attend the annual meeting are awarded each year. Established in 1967. Made possible by a contribution from SmithKline Beecham Clinical Laboratories.

★3073★ Louisa Gross Horwitz Prize
Columbia University
Office of the Pres.
202 Low Memorial Library
New York, NY 10027
Ph: (212)854-5017
To recognize an individual for outstanding basic research in biology or biochemistry. A monetary prize of $25,000 is awarded annually. Established in 1967 to honor Louisa Gross Horwitz, the daughter of Dr. Samuel David Gross (1805-1889), a prominent surgeon of Philadelphia, author of "Systems of Surgery" and a president of the American Medical Association.

★3074★ Life Sciences Research Foundation Fellowships

Life Sciences Research Foundation
Lewis Thomas Laboratories
Princeton University
Princeton, NJ 08544
Ph: (609)258-3551

Purpose: To support postdoctoral research in the biological sciences. Qualifications: Applicant may be of any nationality, but must hold an M.D. or Ph.D. in any of the biological sciences. Fellowship is competitive and is based primarily on the quality of the applicant's past achievements. U.S. fellows are not restricted in their choice of laboratory. Foreign citizens must conduct their fellowship research in a U.S. laboratory. Funds available: $35,000/year. Application details: Send self-addressed return envelope to the Fellowship Coordinator for application form and guidelines. Deadline: October 1.

★3075★ National Academy of Sciences Award in Molecular Biology

National Academy of Sciences
2101 Constitution Ave. NW
Washington, DC 20418
Ph: (202)334-2444

To recognize a recent notable discovery in the field of molecular biology by a young scientist. A monetary prize of $20,000 is awarded annually. Established in 1961 with funds provided by the United States Steel Foundation. Sponsored by Monsanto Company.

★3076★ National Physical Science Consortium Graduate Fellowships For Minorities and Women

National Physical Sciences Consortium for Minorities and Women
c/o New Mexico State University
O'Loughlin House
University Ave.
Box 30001, Dept. 3 NPS
Las Cruces, NM 88003-8001
Ph: (505)646-6037   Fax: (505)646-6097
Fr: 800-952-4118

Purpose: To expand the pool of women and minorities in graduate physical science studies. Qualifications: Applicants must be United States citizens who are African American, Hispanic, Native American, and/or female. They must also have undergraduate standing as seniors with a GPA of at least 3.0 on a 4.0 scale, be eligible to pursue graduate study at a participating member university, and be an entering or returning student. Study must be in the fields of astronomy, chemistry, computer science, geology, materials science, mathematics, sciences, physics, or subdisciplines. Selection criteria: Selection is based on grade point average, GRE scores, transcripts, letters of recommendation, and prior research and/or employment experience. Photocopies of each candidate's application are sent to major research laboratories, national corporations, and leading Ph.D. granting universities. Two review committees, consisting of scientists, academic deans, and sponsoring employers, review the applications. Funds available: Fellowships from $150,000 to $180,000 depending on the cost of graduate school for a period of six years, to cover tuition, fees, and a stipend. Stipends are $12,500 per year, for years 1

through 4, plus summer employment for the first and second year; and $15,000 per year for the fifth and sixth years. Application details: Application is a Macintosh formatted computer diskette. Applications must be submitted with official transcripts for each post-secondary school attended, GRE test scores, and a one-page statement describing research experience, educational objectives, and professional goals within the application. Deadline: November 15. Recipients will be announced the following January.

★3077★ Papanicolaou Award of the American Society of Cytology

American Society of Cytology
409 W. 9th St.
Wilmington, DE 19808
Ph: (215)922-3880   Fax: (215)922-7347

To recognize an individual for meritorious contributions in the field of cytology. The deadline for nominations is February 18. A monetary award of $1,500, a certificate, a bronze medal, and travel expenses to attend the annual meeting are awarded each year. Established in 1958. Sponsored by the late Harry and Helen C. Roth. Mr. Roth was Chairman of the Board, Clay-Adams Company, Division of Becton Dickenson Company, Parsippany, New Jersey.

★3078★ Predoctoral Fellowships in Biological Sciences

Howard Hughes Medical Institute
Office of Grants and Special Programs
4000 Jones Bridge Road
Chevy Chase, MD 20815-6789
Ph: (301)215-8889

Purpose: To encourage graduate students who are beginning doctoral studies in the biological sciences. Qualifications: Candidate may be of any nationality. Applicant must be entering or enrolled in a full-time Ph.D. or Sc.D. program in the biological sciences. Fellowships are intended to assist doctoral candidates at the beginning of their studies; students who will have completed the first year of graduate study by the application deadline are not eligible. U.S. citizens may study at educational institutions in the United States or abroad; citizens of other countries must enroll at institutions in the United States. Funds available: $14,000/year, plus $12,000/year cost-of-education allowance. Application details: General fellowship information and the application may be obtained from the Fellowship Office at the NRC for application forms. Submit to the NRC the form with proposed plan of study, transcripts, four letters of reference, and Graduate Record Examination general and subject test scores. Some foreign applicants must also submit scores from the Test of English as a Foreign Language. Deadline: Early November. Notification in early April.

★3079★ President's National Medal of Science

National Science Foundation
4201 Wilson Blvd., Rm. 1225
Arlington, VA 22203
Ph: (202)357-7512   Fax: (202)357-7346

To recognize individuals who are deserving of special recognition by reason of their outstanding contributions to knowledge in the physical, biological, mathematical, engineering, behavioral, or social sciences. The Presi-

dent's Committee on the National Medal of Science receives recommendations of various nationally representative scientific or engineering organizations as well as the recommendations of the National Academy of Sciences. The guidelines for selection are as follows: the total impact of an individual's work on the present state of physical, biological, mathematical, engineering, behavioral, or social sciences and any achievements of an unusually significant nature judged in relation to their potential effects on the development of scientific thought. Unusually distinguished service in the general advancement of science and engineering, when accompanied by substantial contributions to the content of science, may also be recognized. Established in 1959 by the Congress of the United States and first awarded in 1962. Additional information is available from Susan Fannoney, telephone: (202) 357-7512.

★3080★ William C. Rose Award in Biochemisty

American Society for Biochemistry and Molecular Biology
9650 Rockville Pike
Bethesda, MD 20814
Ph: (301)530-7145   Fax: (301)571-1824

For recognition of outstanding research in biochemistry and molecular biology and to promote an interest in training young scientists. A monetary prize of $3,000 and a plaque are awarded annually at the scientific meeting. Established in 1976 by a group of students of the late William C. Rose, a professor of Biochemistry at the University of Illinois, Urban, on his 90th birthday.

★3081★ Smithsonian Research Fellowships

Smithsonian Institution
Office of Public Affairs
900 Jefferson Dr. SW, Rm. 2410
Washington, DC 20560
Ph: (202)357-2470   Fax: (202)786-2515

To support independent research in residence at the Smithsonian in association with the research staff and using the Institution's resources. Fellowships are awarded in the fields of history of science and technology, social and cultural history, history of art, anthropology, biological sciences, earth sciences, and materials analysis. Open to all qualified individuals without reference to race, color, religion, sex, national origin, age, or condition of handicap of any applicant. Predoctoral and postdoctoral fellowship appointments for six to twelve months, senior postdoctoral appointments for three to twelve months and graduate student appointments for ten weeks are awarded. Additional information is available from Smithsonian Institution, Office of Fellowships and Grants, 7300 l'Enfant Plaza, Washington, DC 20560.

★3082★ Herbert Sober Memorial Lectureship

American Society for Biochemistry and Molecular Biology
9650 Rockville Pike
Bethesda, MD 20814
Ph: (301)530-7145   Fax: (301)571-1824

For recognition of outstanding research in biochemistry and molecular biology with an emphasis on techniques and methods. A monetary prize of $1,000 and a plaque are awarded biennially in even-numbered years at the scientific meeting. Established in 1978 by friends of Dr. Sober.

★3083★ **U.S. Department of Energy Internship**
Oak Ridge Institute for Science and
    Education
Science/Engineering Education Division
University Programs Division
PO Box 117
Oak Ridge, TN 37831-0117
Ph: (615)576-3427   Fax: (615)576-0202

Qualifications: Applicants must be United States citizens or permanent resident aliens who are currently at the junior or senior level at a college or university, are majoring in computer sciences, engineering, environmental/life sciences, or physical sciences, and have a minimum grade point average of 3.0 or higher on a 4.0 scale. Selection criteria: Participants are selected on the basis of academic merit, future research interests, and an availability of the position at the National Laboratory. Funds available: A stipend of $225 per week, plus complimentary housing (or housing allowance) and round trip transportation to the laboratory. Approximately 400 Recipients are given internships as student research participants at one of the following locations: Argonne National Laboratory, Illinois; Brookhaven National Laboratory, New York; Lawrence Berkeley Laboratory, California; Lawrence Livermore Laboratory, California; Los Alamos National Laboratory, New Mexico; Oak Ridge National Laboratory, Tennessee; or Pacific Northwest Laboratory, Washington. Students will participate with National Laboratory scientists in ongoing research and will have access to state-of-the-art equipment and facilities. Seminars, workshops, and coursework are also conducted in the student's chosen field of study. Student appointments are normally for one academic term; however, extension of appointments through the summer are encouraged. Tuition and fees for the academic credit to be received for the semester experience are the responsibility of the participants. Application details: Applications are mailed to the Department of Energy (DOE) for processing and review. Completed, eligible files are sent to the students laboratories of choice, and are forwarded to the laboratory scientists for review and selection. Laboratory decisions are forwarded back to DOA, which, in turn, sends decision letters to the students. Students may receive offers from both their first- and second-choice laboratories. Subsequent placement of students is attempted as student responses are received. Deadline: The 1993 deadlines were March 15 for the Fall Semster and October 20 for the Spring Semester.

BASIC REFERENCE GUIDES AND HANDBOOKS

★3084★ *Biological Science*
W.W. Norton & Co., Inc.
500 5th Ave.
New York, NY 10110
Ph: (212)354-5500   Fax: (212)869-0856
Fr: 800-223-4830
William T. Keeton, editor. 1992.

★3085★ *The Facts on File Dictionary of Biology*
Facts on File
460 Park Ave. S.
New York, NY 10016-7382
Ph: (212)683-2244   Fax: 800-678-3633
Fr: 800-322-8755
Elizabeth Toothill, editor. Revised edition, 1990. Defines terms for all areas of the biological sciences, including genetics and molecular biology.

★3086★ *Manual of Clinical Microbiology*
American Society for Microbiology (ASM)
1325 Massachusetts Ave. NW
Washington, DC 20005
Ph: (202)737-3600
Edwin H. Lennette, editor in chief. Fifth edition, 1991. Covers standard procedures materials, common pathogens, and diseases. Has a section on computer applications.

PROFESSIONAL AND TRADE PERIODICALS

★3087★ *American Journal of Botany*
Botanical Society of America
Ohio State University
1735 Neil Ave.
Columbus, OH 43210-1293
Ph: (614)292-3519   Fax: (614)292-3519
Nels Lersten
Magazine containing botanical research papers.

★3088★ *American Zoologist*
American Society of Zoologists
401 N. Michigan Ave.
Chicago, IL 60611-4267
Ph: (312)527-6697   Fax: (312)245-1085
Milton Fingerman
Bimonthly. Journal of zoological research.

★3089★ *BioScience*
American Institute of Biological Sciences
730 11th St. NW
Washington, DC 20001-4521
Ph: (202)628-1500   Fax: (202)628-1509
Julie Ann Miller
Monthly. Review journal for biologists, containing articles, book reviews, new product reviews, features, and announcements.

★3090★ *BIOSIS Evolution*
BioSciences Information Service (BIOSIS)
2100 Arch St.
Philadelphia, PA 19103-1399
Ph: (215)587-4800   Fax: (215)587-2016
Fr: 800-523-4806
Denise Civa
Bimonthly. Serves subscribers to BIOSIS, "the world's largest English language abstracting and indexing service for biological and biomedical research." Reports on new BIOSIS product developments, pricing and distribution of current products and services, and educational programs. Provides descriptions on training courses for BIOSIS online services, vendor news affecting BIOSIS databases, information on the availability of the databases, and tips on searching the databases. Recurring features include news of employees, a BIOSIS training schedule, news of research, columns titled title CD-ROM Corner, Vendor News, International Notes, and In Search of . . . (sample searches on various life science topics).

★3091★ *Microbiological Reviews*
American Society for Microbiology
1325 Massachusetts Ave. NW
Washington, DC 20005
Ph: (202)737-3600
W.K. Joklik
Quarterly. Review journal on microbiology.

★3092★ *The Research Reporter*
Worcester Foundation for Experimental
    Biology
222 Maple Ave.
Shrewsbury, MA 01545
Ph: (508)842-9632   Fax: (508)842-7187
Patricia Kelleher Martin
Monitors current activities at the Foundation and relates ongoing research in the areas of neurobiology, cancer and cell biology, and endocrine-reproductive biology. Recurring features include items on grants and awards, personal profiles, meeting and conference reports, and a column titled Distillations.

PROFESSIONAL MEETINGS AND CONVENTIONS

★3093★ **American Institute of Biological Sciences Annual Meeting**
American Institute of Biological Sciences
730 11th St., NW
Washington, DC 20001
Ph: (202)628-1500   Fax: (202)628-1509
Fr: 800-992-2427
Annual. Usually held during August.

★3094★ **American Society for Cell Biology Annual Meeting**
American Society for Cell Biology (ASCB)
9650 Rockville Pike
Bethesda, MD 20814
Ph: (301)530-7153   Fax: (301)530-7139
Annual. **Dates and Locations:** 1995 Dec 07-12; Washington, DC. • 1996 Dec 07-12; San Francisco, CA. • 1997 Dec 13-18; Washington, DC.

★3095★ Biophysical Society Annual Meeting
Biophysical Society
9650 Rockville Pke.
Bethesda, MD 20814
Ph: (301)530-7010   Fax: (301)530-7014
Annual. **Dates and Locations:** 1996 Feb 18-22; Baltimore, MD. • 1997 Mar 02-06; New Orleans, LA. • 1998 Feb 22-26; Kansas City, MO. • 1999 Feb 13-18; Baltimore, MD.

OTHER SOURCES OF INFORMATION

★3096★ *American Men and Women of Science: A Biographical Directory of Today's Leaders in Physical, Biological, and Related Sciences*
R.R. Bowker Co.
121 Chanlon Rd.
New Providence, NJ 07974
Ph: (908)464-6800   Fax: (908)464-3553
1994.

★3097★ "Biologic Scientist" in *100 Best Jobs for the 1990s & Beyond*
Dearborn Financial Publishing, Inc.
520 N. Dearborn St.
Chicago, IL 60610-4354
Ph: (312)836-4400   Fax: (312)836-1021
Fr: 800-621-9621

Carol Kleiman. 1992. Describes 100 jobs ranging from accountants to veterinarians.. Each job profile includes such information as education, experience, and certification needed, salaries, and job search suggestions.

★3098★ "Biologist" in *Career Selector 2001*
Barron's Educational Series, Inc.
250 Wireless Blvd.
Hauppauge, NY 11788
Ph: (516)434-3311   Fax: (516)434-3723
Fr: 800-645-3476

James C. Gonyea. 1993.

★3099★ "Biology" in *Accounting to Zoology: Graduate Fields Defined* (pp. 199-200)
Petersons Guides, Inc.
PO Box 2123
Princeton, NJ 08543-2123
Ph: (609)243-9111   Fax: (609)243-9150
Fr: 800-338-3282

Amy J. Goldstein, editor. Revised and updated, 1987. Defines 298 graduate and professional fields. Discusses types of graduate programs and degrees, graduate research, applied work, employment prospects, and trends.

★3100★ *Salaries of Scientists, Engineers, and Technicians: A Summary of Salary Surveys*
Commission on Professionals in Science and Technology (CPST)
1500 Massachusetts Ave., NW, Ste. 831
Washington, DC 20005
Ph: (202)223-6995
1993.

Foresters and Conservations Scientists

Foresters and conservation scientists manage, develop, use, and help protect forests, rangelands, and other natural resources. Foresters plan and supervise the growth, protection, and harvesting of trees. They map forest areas, estimate the amount of standing timber and future growth, and manage timber sales. Foresters also protect the trees from fire, harmful insects, and disease. **Range managers**, also called **range conservationists**, and **range ecologists** or **range scientists**, manage, improve, and protect rangelands to maximize their use without damaging the environment. **Soil conservationists** provide technical assistance to farmers, ranchers, and others concerned with the conservation of soil, water, and related natural resources. They develop programs that are designed to get the most productive use of land without damaging it. Foresters and conservation scientists often specialize in one area of work, such as forest resource management, urban forestry, wood technology, or forest economics.

Salaries

Salaries in state and local government and in private industry are generally lower than in the federal government. Average federal salaries are as follows:

Forester, range managers, soil conservationists with a bachelor's degree	$18,340-$22,717/year
Foresters, range managers, soil conservationists with a master's degree	$22,717-$27,789/year
Forester	$42,440/year
Soil conservationists	$39,448/year
Forest products technologists	$56,559/year

Employment Outlook

Growth rate until the year 2005: Slower than the average.

Foresters and Conservation Scientists

CAREER GUIDES

★3101★ *Career Information Question and Answer Sheet*
Society of American Foresters (SAF)
5400 Grosvenor Ln.
Bethesda, MD 20814-2198
Ph: (301)897-8720

P. Gregory Smith, editor. 1992. Describes the differences between foresters and forestry technicians, including job duties, educational preparation, and employment opportunities.

★3102★ *Career Profiles: Forestry Conservation, Ecology, and Environmental Management*
U.S. Department of Agriculture
Forest Service
PO Box 96090
Washington, DC 20090-6090
Ph: (202)205-0957

Slightly revised 1987. Describes the job of forester; lists places of employment, educational requirements, and other characteristics needed to be successful in the field of forestry.

★3103★ *Careers in Science*
National Textbook Co. (NTC)
VGM Career Books
4255 W. Touhy Ave.
Lincolnwood, IL 60646-1975
Ph: (708)679-5500   Fax: (708)679-2494
Fr: 800-323-4900

Thomas A. Easton, editor. Explores careers in life science, physical science, social science, earth science, engineering, mathematics, and computer science.

★3104★ *Conservation Officer*
Chronicle Guidance Publications, Inc.
66 Aurora St.
PO Box 1190
Moravia, NY 13118-1190
Ph: (315)497-0330   Fax: (315)497-3359
Fr: 800-622-7284

1994. Career brief describing the nature of the job, working conditions, hours and earnings, education and training, licensure, certifi-

cation, unions, personal qualifications, social and psychological factors, location, employment outlook, entry methods, advancement, and related occupations.

★3105★ "Conservationist" in *College Board Guide to Jobs and Career Planning* (pp. 281)
The College Board
415 Columbus Ave.
New York, NY 10023-6992
Ph: (212)713-8165   Fax: (212)713-8143
Fr: 800-323-7155

Joyce S. Mitchell. Second edition, 1994. Describes a variety of careers. Career profiles include information on salaries, related careers, education needed, and sources of additional information.

★3106★ "Ecologist" in *Guide to Federal Jobs* (p. 104)
Resource Directories
3361 Executive Pkwy., Ste. 302
Toledo, OH 43606
Ph: (419)536-5353   Fax: (419)536-7056
Fr: 800-274-8515

Rod W. Durgin, editor. Third edition, 1992. Contains information on finding and applying for federal jobs. Describes more than 200 professional and technical jobs for college graduates. Covers the nature of the work, salary, and geographic location. Lists college majors preferred for that occupation. Section one describes the function and work of government agencies that hire the most significant number of college graduates.

★3107★ *Exploring Careers in the National Parks*
Rosen Publishing Group
29 E. 21st St.
New York, NY 10010
Ph: (212)777-3017   Fax: (212)777-0277
Fr: 800-237-9932

Bob Gartner. 1993. Offers advice on how to land that hard-to-get summer job with the park service. Profiles the position which includes being surrounded by some of the most beautiful scenery in the world.

★3108★ "Forest and Conservation Workers" in *Jobs! What They Are—Where They Are—What They Pay* (pp. 100)
Fireside
Simon & Schuster Bldg.
1230 Avenue of the Americas
New York, NY 10020
Ph: (212)698-7000   Fr: 800-223-2348

Robert O. Snelling and Anne M. Snelling. Revised and updated, 1992. Describes duties and responsibilities, earnings, employment opportunities, training, and qualifications.

★3109★ *Forester*
Vocational Biographies, Inc.
PO Box 31
Sauk Centre, MN 56378-0031
Ph: (612)352-6516   Fax: (612)352-5546
Fr: 800-255-0752

1991. Four-page pamphlet containing a personal narrative about a worker's job, work likes and dislikes, career path from high school to the present, education and training, the rewards and frustrations, and the effects of the job on the rest of the worker's life. The data file portion of this pamphlet gives a concise occupational summary, including work description, working conditions, places of employment, personal characteristics, education and training, job outlook, and salary range.

★3110★ *Forester*
Careers, Inc.
PO Box 135
Largo, FL 34649-0135
Ph: (813)584-7333

1994. Four-page brief offering the definition, history, duties, working conditions, personal qualifications, educational requirements, earnings, hours, employment outlook, advancement, and careers related to this position.

★3111★ "Forester" in *Guide to Federal Jobs* (pp. 115)
Resource Directories
3361 Executive Pkwy., Ste. 302
Toledo, OH 43606
Ph: (419)536-5353   Fax: (419)536-7056
Fr: 800-274-8515
Rod W. Durgin, editor. Third edition, 1992. Contains information on finding and applying for federal jobs. Describes more than 200 professional and technical jobs for college graduates. Also includes chapters titled "Soil Conservationist" (p. 114) and "Range Conservationist" (p. 113). Covers the nature of the work, salary, and geographic location. Lists college majors preferred for that occupation. Section one describes the function and work of government agencies that hire the most significant number of college graduates.

★3112★ "Forester" in *Jobs! What They Are—Where They Are—What They Pay!* (p. 99)
Simon & Schuster, Inc.
Simon & Schuster Bldg.
1230 Avenue of the Americas
New York, NY 10020
Ph: (212)698-7000   Fr: 800-223-2348
Robert O. Snelling and Anne M. Snelling. Third revised edition, 1992. Includes a chapter titled "Soil Conservationist" (p. 101). Describes duties and responsibilities, earnings, employment opportunities, training, and qualifications.

★3113★ "Forester" in *Opportunities in Crafts Careers* (pp. 31-32)
National Textbook Co. (NTC)
VGM Career Books
4255 W. Touhy Ave.
Lincolnwood, IL 60646-1975
Ph: (708)679-5500   Fax: (708)679-2494
Fr: 800-323-4900
Marianne Munday. 1994. Provides a general overview of crafts and some traditional and non-traditional jobs related to crafts. Gives information on how to start a crafts business.

★3114★ "Forester", "Range Manager", and "Soil Conservationist" in *VGM's Careers Encylopedia*
National Textbook Co. (NTC)
VGM Career Books
4255 W. Touhy Ave.
Lincolnwood, IL 60646-1975
Ph: (708)679-5500   Fax: (708)679-2494
Fr: 800-323-4900
Third edition, 1991. Profiles 200 occupations. Describes job duties, places of employment, working conditions, qualifications, education and training, advancement potential, and salary for each occupation.

★3115★ *Foresters*
Chronicle Guidance Publications, Inc.
66 Aurora St.
PO Box 1190
Moravia, NY 13118-1190
Ph: (315)497-0330   Fax: (315)497-3359
Fr: 800-622-7284
1994. Career brief describing the nature of the job, working conditions, hours and earnings, education and training, licensure, certification, unions, personal qualifications, social and psychological factors, location, employ-ment outlook, entry methods, advancement, and related occupations.

★3116★ "Foresters and Conservation Scientists" in *Occupational Outlook Handbook*
U.S. Government Printing Office
Superintendent of Documents
Washington, DC 20402
Ph: (202)512-1800   Fax: (202)512-2250
Biennial; latest edition, 1994-95. Encyclopedia of careers describing about 250 occupations and comprising about 85 percent of all jobs in the economy. Occupations that require lengthy education or training are given the most attention. Each occupation's profile describes what the worker does on the job, working conditions, education and training requirements, advancement possibilities, job outlook, earnings, and sources of additional information.

★3117★ "Foresters" in *Encyclopedia of Careers and Vocational Guidance* (Vol.3, pp. 32-36)
J.G. Ferguson Publishing Co.
200 W. Madison St., Ste. 300
Chicago, IL 60606
Ph: (312)580-5480   Fax: (312)580-4948
William E. Hopke, editor-in-chief. Ninth edition, 1993. Four-volume set that profiles 900 occupations and describes job trends in 74 industries. Includes career description, educational requirements, history of the job, methods of entry, advancement, employment outlook, earnings, conditions of work, social and psychological factors, and sources of further information.

★3118★ "Forestry" in *College Majors and Careers: A Resource Guide to Effective Life Planning* (pp. 61-62)
Garrett Park Press
PO Box 1907
Garrett Park, MD 20896
Ph: (301)946-2553
Paul Phifer. Revised, 1993. Lists 60 college majors, with definitions; related occupations and leisure activities; skills, values, and personal attributes needed; suggested readings; and a list of associations.

★3119★ "Forestry" in *Liberal Arts Jobs*
Petersons Guides, Inc.
PO Box 2123
Princeton, NJ 08543-2123
Ph: (609)243-9111   Fax: (609)243-9150
Fr: 800-338-3282
Jay Burton Nadler. Second edition, 1989. Strives to help the liberal arts graduate identify skills for entry-level positions. Gives goal setting and job search advice.

★3120★ "Forestry Technicians" in *Encyclopedia of Careers and Vocational Guidance* (Vol.3, pp. 37-42)
J.G. Ferguson Publishing Co.
200 W. Madison St., Ste. 300
Chicago, IL 60606
Ph: (312)580-5480   Fax: (312)580-4948
William E. Hopke, editor-in-chief. Ninth edition, 1993. Four-volume set that profiles 900 occupations and describes job trends in 74 industries. Includes career description, educational requirements, history of the job, methods of entry, advancement, employment outlook, earnings, conditions of work, social and psychological factors, and sources of further information.

★3121★ *Make a Difference: Challenge Yourself With a Career in Forest Service*
U.S. Department of Agriculture
Forest Service
PO Box 96090
Washington, DC 20090-6090
Ph: (202)205-0957
1991. Covers careers managing timber, land, wildlife, and water.

★3122★ *Opportunities in Agriculture Careers*
National Textbook Co. (NTC)
VGM Career Books
4255 W. Touhy Ave.
Lincolnwood, IL 60646-1975
Ph: (708)679-5500   Fax: (708)679-2494
Fr: 800-323-4900
Sampling of more than 200 careers available in agriculture-related fields as a result of the application of technology to agriculture. Describes careers in agriculture production industries, food processing, marketing, environmental protection and communications. Chapters include "Forestry", and "Soil Conservation".

★3123★ *Opportunities in Environmental Careers*
National Textbook Co. (NTC)
VGM Career Books
4255 W. Touhy Ave.
Lincolnwood, IL 60646-1975
Ph: (708)679-5500   Fax: (708)679-2494
Fr: 800-323-4900
Odom Fanning. 1991. Describes a broad range of opportunities in fields such as environmental health, recreation, physics, and hygiene. Chapters include "Forestry", "Range Manager", "Soil Conservation", and "Wildlife Conservation". Lists federal government agencies, colleges and universities, and citizen organizations that provide opportunities in environment-related careers. Entries include organization name and address.

★3124★ *Opportunities in Forestry*
National Textbook Co. (NTC)
VGM Career Books
4255 W. Touhy Ave.
Lincolnwood, IL 60646-1975
Ph: (708)679-5500   Fax: (708)679-2494
Fr: 800-323-4900
Christopher M. Wille. Discusses jobs in forestry including opportunities in government, the private sector, and self-employment. Also offers information on education and training.

★3125★ "Range Manager" and "Foresters" in *Career Information Center* (Vol.2)
Simon and Schuster
200 Old Tappan Rd.
Old Tappan, NJ 07675
Fax: 800-445-6991   Fr: 800-223-2348
Richard Lidz and Linda Perrin, editorial directors. Fifth edition, 1993. A multi-volume set that profiles over 600 occupations. Each occupational profile describes job duties, educational requirements, advancement possibilities, employment outlook, working conditions, earnings and benefits, and where to write for more information.

★3126★ *So You Want to Be in Forestry*
American Forestry Association (AFA)
1516 P St., NW
Washington, DC 20005
Ph: (202)667-3300

Brochure describing forestry, how to become a forester, and employment opportunities and related fields.

★3127★ *Soil Conservationist*
Careers, Inc.
PO Box 135
Largo, FL 34649-0135
Ph: (813)584-7333

1992. Two-page occupational summary card describing duties, working conditions, personal qualifications, training, earnings and hours, employment outlook, places of employment, related careers, and where to write for more information.

★3128★ *Soil Conservationists*
Chronicle Guidance Publications, Inc.
66 Aurora St.
PO Box 1190
Moravia, NY 13118-1190
Ph: (315)497-0330   Fax: (315)497-3359
Fr: 800-622-7284

1994. Career brief describing the nature of the job, working conditions, hours and earnings, education and training, licensure, certification, unions, personal qualifications, social and psychological factors, location, employment outlook, entry methods, advancement, and related occupations.

★3129★ *VGM'S Handbook of Scientific and Technical Careers*
National Textbook Co. (NTC)
VGM Career Books
4255 W. Touhy Ave.
Lincolnwood, IL 60646-1975
Ph: (708)679-5500   Fax: (708)679-2494
Fr: 800-323-4900

Annette Selden, editor. Second ed. Overview of nearly 60 science-related careers, with emphasis on educational preparation. Includes information on job responsibilities, working conditions, salaries, and growth opportunities.

PROFESSIONAL ASSOCIATIONS

★3130★ American Forests
1516 P St. NW
PO Box 2000
Washington, DC 20005
Ph: (202)667-3300   Fax: (202)667-7751
Fr: 800-368-5748

Members: A citizens' conservation organization working to advance the intelligent management and use of forests, soil, water, wildlife, and all other natural resources. **Purpose:** Promotes public appreciation of natural resources and the part they play in the social, recreational, and economic life of the U.S. **Publications:** *American Forests*, bimonthly. • *National Registry of Champion Big Trees and Famous Historical Trees.* • *Resource Hotline*, biweekly. • *Urban Forests*, bimonthly.

★3131★ National Association of Conservation Districts (NACD)
509 Capitol Ct. NE
Washington, DC 20002
Ph: (202)547-6223   Fax: (202)547-6450

Members: Soil and water conservation districts organized by the citizens of watersheds, counties, or communities under provisions of state laws. **Purpose:** Directs and coordinates, through local self-government efforts, the conservation and development of soil, water, and related natural resources. Districts include over 90% of the nation's privately owned land. Conducts educational programs and children's services. **Publications:** *District Leader*, monthly. • *NACD Directory*, annual. • *Proceedings of Annual Convention.* • *Tuesday Letter*, quarterly.

★3132★ Society of American Foresters (SAF)
5400 Grosvenor Ln.
Bethesda, MD 20814
Ph: (301)897-8720   Fax: (301)897-3690

Members: Professional society of foresters and scientists working in related fields. **Purpose:** Serves as accrediting agency for professional forestry education. Provides professional training. Supports 28 subject-oriented working groups. **Publications:** *Forest Science*, quarterly. • *Journal of Forestry*, monthly. • *Northern Journal of Applied Forestry*, quarterly. • *Southern Journal of Applied Forestry*, quarterly. • *Western Journal of Applied Forestry*, quarterly.

★3133★ Society for Range Management (SRM)
1839 York St.
Denver, CO 80206
Ph: (303)355-7070   Fax: (303)355-5059

Members: Professional international society of scientists, technicians, ranchers, administrators, teachers, and students interested in the study, use, and management of rangeland resources for livestock, wildlife, watershed, and recreation. Sponsors placement service. **Publications:** *Journal of Range Management*, bimonthly. • *Rangelands*, bimonthly. • *Society for Range Management—Mini-Directory*, periodic. • *Trail Boss News*, periodic.

★3134★ The Wilderness Society (TWS)
900 17th St. NW
Washington, DC 20006-2596
Ph: (202)833-2300   Fax: (202)429-3958

Members: Purposes include the establishment of the land ethic as a basic element of American culture and philosophy, and the education of a broader and more committed wilderness preservation and land protection constituency. Focuses on federal, legislative, and administrative actions affecting public lands, including national forests, parks, and wildlife refuges, and Bureau of Land Management lands. Encourages Congress to designate appropriate public lands as wilderness areas. Programs include grass roots organizing, economic analysis, lobbying, research, and public education. Compiles statistics. **Publications:** *Wilderness*, quarterly.

STANDARDS/CERTIFICATION AGENCIES

★3135★ Society of American Foresters (SAF)
5400 Grosvenor Ln.
Bethesda, MD 20814
Ph: (301)897-8720   Fax: (301)897-3690

Serves as accrediting agency for professional forestry education.

TEST GUIDES

★3136★ *Career Examination Series: Forest Ranger*
National Learning Corp.
212 Michael Dr.
Syosset, NY 11791
Ph: (516)921-8888   Fax: (516)921-8743
Fr: 800-645-6337

Jack Rudman. A series of study guides with multiple-choice examination questions and solutions for trainees and professional foresters and conservation scientists. Titles in the series include *Air Pollution Control Chemist; Air Pollution Control Engineer; Air Pollution Control Engineering Trainee; Air Pollution Control Technician; Air Pollution Inspector; Associate Urban Park Ranger; Director of Environmental Health Services; Environmental Analyst; Environmental Assistant; Environmental Conservation Investigator; Environmental Conservation Officer; Environmental Conservation Officer Trainee; Environmental Control Specialist; Environmental Control Specialist Trainee; Environmentalist; Forester; Forester Trainee; Forestry Technician; Principal Forestry Technician; Range Conservationist; Senior Forestry Technician; Soil Conservationist; Soil Scientist; Supervising Environmentalist; Supervisor of Conservation Areas; Urban Forester.*

★3137★ *Introduction to Forestry*
National Learning Corp.
212 Michael Dr.
Syosset, NY 11791
Ph: (516)921-8888   Fax: (516)921-8743
Fr: 800-645-6337

Jack Rudman. Dantes Subject Standardized Test series. A standardized graduate and college level examination given by graduate schools, colleges, and the Armed Forces as a final examination for course evaluation in the field of forestry. Multiple-choice format with correct answers.

EDUCATIONAL DIRECTORIES AND PROGRAMS

★3138★ *Conservation Directory, 1994*
National Wildlife Federation
1400 16th St., NW
Washington, DC 20036
Ph: (202)797-6800   Fr: 800-432-6564
Annual. Thirty-ninth edition, 1994. Lists organizations, agencies, and officials concerned with natural resource use and management.

★3139★ *Environmental Career Directory*
Gale Research Inc.
835 Penobscot Bldg.
Detroit, MI 48226-4094
Ph: (313)961-2242   Fax: (313)961-6083
Fr: 800-877-GALE
Bradley J. Morgan and Joseph M. Palmisano. 1993. A directory in the Career Advisor Series that provides essays written by industry professionals; job search information on resume, resume and cover letter preparation, networking, and the interviewing process; approximately 300 companies and organizations offering job opportunities and internships, and additional job-hunting resources.

★3140★ *Society of American Foresters Accredited Professional and Recognized Technical Forestry Degree Programs*
Society of American Foresters
5400 Grosvenor Ln.
Bethesda, MD 20814
Ph: (301)897-8720   Fax: (301)897-3690
P. Gregory Smith, Contact
Annual, January. Covers nearly 50 forestry schools and institutions offering programs in professional forestry; about 20 institutions offering forestry technician programs are also listed. Entries include: Institution name, address; date of first accreditation, date of last on-site accreditation, date accreditation expires. Arrangement: Geographical.

AWARDS, SCHOLARSHIPS, GRANTS, AND FELLOWSHIPS

★3141★ **Audubon Medal**
National Audubon Society
700 Broadway
New York, NY 10003
Ph: (212)979-3000   Fax: (212)353-0377
To honor distinguished, individual service to conservation. Achievements of national or international significance are considered. Audubon directors and staff are not eligible. A gold medal is awarded when merited. Established in 1947.

★3142★ **Eugene Baker Memorial Award**
Association of Conservation Engineers
Alabama Dept. of Conservation
64 N. Union St.
Montgomery, AL 36130
Ph: (205)242-3476   Fax: (205)242-0289
To recognize an engineer for outstanding contributions to conservation engineering. A bronze plaque is awarded as merited. Established in 1964.

★3143★ **Paul Bartsch Award**
Audubon Naturalist Society of the Central
    Atlantic States
8940 Jones Mill Rd.
Chevy Chase, MD 20815
Ph: (301)652-9188
To recognize individuals for outstanding contributions to the field of natural history and conservation. Preference is given to nominees who have had some connection with the Society. Nominations may be made at any time. A bronze medal and a certificate are awarded as merited. Established in 1962 in honor of Paul Bartsch, an outstanding naturalist who was active in the Society during the first half of this century and worked at the Smithsonian in the field of malacology (study of mollusks).

★3144★ **Chandler - Misener Award**
International Association for Great Lakes
    Research
2200 Bonisteel Blvd.
Ann Arbor, MI 48109-2099
Ph: (313)747-1673   Fax: (313)747-2748
To acknowledge excellence in the fields of natural or social science or environmental engineering directly related to a Great Lake or other large lakes of the world based on an article published in the *Journal of Great Lakes Research*. A certificate is awarded annually. Established in 1970.

★3145★ **Edward J. Cleary Award**
American Academy of Environmental
    Engineers
130 Holiday Court, Ste. 100
Annapolis, MD 21401
Ph: (410)266-3311   Fax: (410)266-7653
To honor an outstanding performer in the management of environmental protection enterprises conducted either under public (local, state, regional, federal, international) or private auspices. A walnut plaque is awarded biennially. Established in 1972.

★3146★ **Climatics Award**
Institute of Environmental Sciences
940 E. Northwest Hwy.
Mount Prospect, IL 60056
Ph: (708)255-1561   Fax: (708)255-1699
For recognition in the field of environmental sciences. Established in 1986.

★3147★ **Conservationist of the Year**
Adirondack Council
PO Box D-2
Elizabethtown, NY 12932
Ph: (518)873-2240   Fax: (518)873-6675
Fr: 800-842-PARK
To recognize individuals for support and initiatives in working for lasting protection and preservation of the Adirondack Park. Selection is by nomination. A hand carved loon with a plaque is awarded annually at the awards banquet. Established in 1984.

★3148★ **Distinguished Service/ Achievement Awards**
Sierra Club
Exec. Office Mgr.
730 Polk St.
San Francisco, CA 94109
Ph: (415)776-2211   Fax: (415)776-0350
To recognize persons who are or have been in public service. Distinguished Service recognition is for strong and consistent commitment to conservation over a considerable period of time; whereas Distinguished Achievement recognition is for some particular action of singular importance to conservation. Selection is made by the Executive Committee of the Board of Directors upon recommendation of the Honors and Awards Committee. Awarded annually to one, but no more than three, individuals. Established in 1971.

★3149★ **Distinguished Service Award**
American Forestry Association
PO Box 2000
Washington, DC 20013
Ph: (202)667-3300   Fax: (202)667-7751
To recognize individuals who have rendered distinguished service of national significance to forestry and other aspects of resource conservation. Both members and non-members of the association who have distinguished themselves in their professional activities as legislators, foresters, or other resource professionals are eligible. A plaque is awarded annually. Established in 1948.

★3150★ **Federal Environmental Engineer of the Year**
Conference of Federal Environmental
    Engineers
17 Nicholson Court
Sterling, VA 22170
To recognize exemplary work and accomplishments by environmental engineers in the Federal service. An environmental engineer is one who possesses: (1) a Baccalaureate or higher degree in engineering; or (2) a Professional Engineering license; or (3) an engineer classification awarded by OPM, and (4) prepared himself or herself through additional study, training, and experience in the sciences to complement engineering skills, and applied them in the protection of the environment and the public health. A plaque is awarded annually. Established in 1974.

★3151★ **Bernhard Eduard Fernow Award**
American Forestry Association
PO Box 2000
Washington, DC 20013
Ph: (202)667-3300   Fax: (202)667-7751
To recognize an individual for notable scientific achievements and contributions to forestry. Nominees may be nationals of any country. A medallion is awarded biennially in odd-numbered years by the American Forestry Association and in even-numbered years by the German Forestry Association. Established in 1965.

★3152★ William B. Greeley Award
American Forestry Association
PO Box 2000
Washington, DC 20013
Ph: (202)667-3300 Fax: (202)667-7751

To recognize distinguished service to forestry and other aspects of resource conservation of regional significance. Both members and non-members of the association who have distinguished themselves in their professional activities as legislators, foresters, and other resource professionals are eligible. Awarded annually. Established in 1983.

★3153★ Stephen Tyng Mather Award
National Parks and Conservation
    Association
1776 Massachusetts Ave. NW, Ste. 200
Washington, DC 20036
Ph: (202)223-6722 Fax: (202)659-0650

To recognize individuals who put principle before personal gain in the preservation of natural and/or archaeological resources. Any federal employee who has been employed for two years or more in the preservation or management of natural and archaeological resources may be nominated. A monetary award of $1,000, a certificate, and travel allowance to the ceremony are presented annually at the March Board Meeting. Established in 1983 in honor of Stephen T. Mather, the first director of the National Park Service and co-founder of NPCA.

**★3154★ Outstanding Achievement
 Award**
Society for Range Management
1839 York St.
Denver, CO 80206
Ph: (303)355-7070

To recognize individuals or organizations whose contributions or careers have become eminently noteworthy in the advancement of the science and art of range-related resource management. A certificate is awarded annually. Established in 1956.

★3155★ Gifford Pinchot Medal
Society of American Foresters
5400 Grosvenor Ln.
Bethesda, MD 20814-2198
Ph: (301)897-8720 Fax: (301)897-3690

To recognize outstanding contributions by forestry professionals to administration, practice, and professional development in North American forestry. The deadline is June 15 of even-numbered years. An engraved medallion is awarded biennially in odd-numbered years at the national convention. Established in 1950.

★3156★ Frederick G. Renner Award
Society for Range Management
1839 York St.
Denver, CO 80206
Ph: (303)355-7070

For special recognition to individuals or small groups for exceptional accomplishments in, or contributions to, range management and range science. Accomplishments of the previous five years are considered for the award. A monetary award of $750, a plaque, and a citation are awarded annually. Established in 1972 by Frederic G. Renner from funds donated to the Society.

★3157★ Urban Forestry Awards
American Forestry Association
PO Box 2000
Washington, DC 20013
Ph: (202)667-3300 Fax: (202)667-7751

To recognize outstanding leadership and service resulting in the advancement of urban forestry concepts. Two awards are given each year, one to a citizen activist and one to a professional urban forester. Established in 1982.

**★3158★ Western Forestry Award for
 Current Achievement**
Western Forestry and Conservation
    Association
4033 SW Canyon Rd.
Portland, OR 97221
Ph: (503)226-4562 Fax: (503)226-2515

To recognize individuals for significant service to western North American forestry and to inspire others to greater performance. A plaque is awarded annually when merited. Established in 1961.

**★3159★ Western Forestry Award for
 Lifetime Service**
Western Forestry and Conservation
    Association
4033 SW Canyon Rd.
Portland, OR 97221
Ph: (503)226-4562 Fax: (503)226-2515

To recognize individuals for significant service to western North American forestry through a lifetime of service and to inspire others to greater performance. A plaque is awarded annually when merited. Established in 1951.

BASIC REFERENCE GUIDES
AND HANDBOOKS

★3160★ *Essentials of Forestry Practice*
John Wiley and Sons, Inc.
605 3rd Ave.
New York, NY 10158-0012
Ph: (212)850-6000 Fax: (212)850-6088
Fr: 800-526-5368

Charles H. Stoddard and Glenn M. Stoddard. Fourth edition, 1987. Includes history and future trends in forestry. Covers managing forests and administration of forestry programs.

**★3161★ *Forest Resource Management
in the Twenty-First Century: Will
Forestry Education Meet the Challenge***
Society of American Foresters
5400 Grosvenor Ln.
Bethesda, MD 20814
Ph: (301)897-8720 Fax: (301)897-3690
1992.

PROFESSIONAL AND TRADE
PERIODICALS

★3162★ *American Forests*
PO Box 2000
Washington, DC 20013-2000
Ph: (202)667-3300 Fax: (202)667-7751
Bill Rooney

Bimonthly. Forest conservation magazine.

★3163★ *American Rivers*
American Rivers
801 Pennsylvania Ave. SE, Ste. 400
Washington, DC 20003
Ph: (202)547-6900 Fax: (202)543-6142
Deborah Conn

Quarterly. Concerned with the protection and restoration of America's rivers. Covers local, state, and federal on river issues.

★3164★ *The Amicus Journal*
Natural Resources Defense Council
40 W. 20 St.
New York, NY 10011
Ph: (212)727-2700 Fax: (212)727-1773
Kathrin Day Lassila

Quarterly. Journal covering national and international environmental affairs.

★3165★ *City Trees*
Society of Municipal Arborists
PO Box 364
Wellesley Hills, MA 02181
Ph: (617)235-7600 Fax: (627)237-1936
Leonard E. Phillips

Bimonthly. Addresses all aspects of municipal (urban) forestry. Contains technical articles on species of trees, pest control, conservation, planning, design, and equipment. Recurring features include lists of new publications, statistics, news of research, letters to the editor, announcements of meetings, and columns titled President's Column, Professor's Column, City of the Month, Park of the Month, Tree of the Month, and Editor's Corner.

★3166★ *The Conservationist*
New York State Dept. of Environmental
    Conservation
50 Wolf Rd., Rm. 516
Albany, NY 12233-4502
Ph: (518)457-5547 Fax: (518)457-1088
Robert deVilleneuve

Bimonthly. Magazine covering conservation issues.

★3167★ *Journal of Forestry*
Society of American Foresters
5400 Grosvenor Ln.
Bethesda, MD 20814-2198
Ph: (301)897-8720 Fax: (301)897-3690
Rebecca Staebler

Monthly. Journal covering measurement, protection, management, and use of forests for wildlife, recreation, water, wilderness, and graying, as well as the growing and harvesting for timber and energy.

★3168★ *Natural Resources Newsletter*
Forestry Department
University of Kentucky
Lexington, KY 40546-0073
Allan J. Worms

Quarterly. Dedicated to "improved management and enjoyment of Kentucky's natural resources."

★3169★ *Soil Science Society of America Journal*
Soil Science Society of America
677 S. Segoe Rd.
Madison, WI 53711-1086
Ph: (608)273-8080   Fax: (608)273-2021
Robert Luxmoore

Bimonthly. Soil research journal.

★3170★ *Timber Bulletin*
United Nations Publications
PO Box 361
Birmingham, AL 35201-0361
Fax: (205)995-1588   Fr: 800-633-4931

Journal providing information on forest products, including a survey of monthly prices, a market review and trade flow data.

★3171★ *The Timberline*
New England Forestry Foundation, Inc.
238 Main St.
Cambridge, MA 02142
Ph: (617)864-4229   Fax: (617)868-7329
L.J.G. Kopp

Quarterly. Contains forestry-related articles.

PROFESSIONAL MEETINGS AND CONVENTIONS

★3172★ **Society of American Foresters National Convention**
Society of American Foresters
5400 Grosvenor Ln.
Bethesda, MD 20814
Ph: (301)897-8720   Fax: (301)897-3690

Annual. **Dates and Locations:** 1995 Oct 28-01; Portland, ME. • 1996 Oct 17-20; Atlanta, GA.

★3173★ **Society for Range Management Annual Conference**
Society for Range Management
1839 York St.
Denver, CO 80206
Ph: (303)355-7070   Fax: (303)355-5059

Annual. **Dates and Locations:** 1996 Feb 10-15; Wichita, KS. • 1997 Feb 16-21; Rapid City, SD.

★3174★ **Western Forestry Conference**
Western Forestry and Conservation Association
4033 SW Canyon Rd.
Portland, OR 97221
Ph: (503)226-4562   Fax: (503)228-4562

Annual. Always held during the first week of December. **Dates and Locations:** 1995 Dec 03-05; Coeur D'Alene

OTHER SOURCES OF INFORMATION

★3175★ **"Forester"** in *Career Selector 2001*
Barron's Educational Series, Inc.
250 Wireless Blvd.
Hauppauge, NY 11788
Ph: (516)434-3311   Fax: (516)434-3723
Fr: 800-645-3476
James C. Gonyea. 1993.

★3176★ **"Forestry"** in *Accounting to Zoology: Graduate Fields Defined* (pp. 241-242)
Petersons Guides, Inc.
PO Box 2123
Princeton, NJ 08543-2123
Ph: (609)243-9111   Fax: (609)243-9150
Fr: 800-338-3282

Amy J. Goldstein, editor. Revised and updated, 1987. Defines 298 graduate and professional fields. Discusses types of graduate programs and degrees, graduate research, applied work, employment prospects, and trends.

★3177★ *Salaries of Scientists, Engineers, and Technicians: A Summary of Salary Surveys*
Commission on Professionals in Science and Technology (CPST)
1500 Massachusetts Ave., NW, Ste. 831
Washington, DC 20005
Ph: (202)223-6995
1993.

Chemists

Chemists search for and put to practical use new knowledge about chemicals. Chemists have developed a tremendous variety of new and improved synthetic fibers, paints, adhesives, drugs, electronic components, lubricants, and other products. They also develop processes which save energy and reduce pollution, such as improved oil refining methods. Research on the chemistry of living things provides the basis for advances in medicine, agriculture, and other areas. Many chemists work in research and development. Chemists also work in production and inspection in chemical manufacturing plants. Chemists often specialize in a subfield. **Analytical chemists** determine the structure, composition, and nature of substances and develop analytical techniques. **Organic chemists** study the chemistry of the vast number of carbon compounds. **Inorganic chemists** study compounds mainly of elements other than carbon, such as those in electronic components. **Physical chemists** study the physical characteristics of atoms and molecules and investigate how chemical reactions work.

Salaries

Salaries for chemists depend on education and experience.

Chemists, bachelor's degree	$24,000/year
Chemists, master's degree	$32,000/year
Chemists, doctorate	$48,000/year
Chemists, federal government (average)	$51,537/year

Employment Outlook

Growth rate until the year 2005: Average.

Chemists

CAREER GUIDES

★3178★ "Biochemist" in *100 Best Careers for the Year 2000* (pp. 250-251)
Arco Pub.
201 W. 103rd St.
Indianapolis, IN 46290
Ph: 800-428-5331   Fax: 800-835-3202
Shelly Field. 1992. Describes 100 job opportunities expected to grow fast throughout the next decade. Provides information on job duties and responsibilities, training requirements, education, advancement opportunities, experience and qualifications, and typical salaries.

★3179★ *Careers in Science*
National Textbook Co. (NTC)
VGM Career Books
4255 W. Touhy Ave.
Lincolnwood, IL 60646-1975
Ph: (708)679-5500   Fax: (708)679-2494
Fr: 800-323-4900
Thomas A. Easton, editor. Explores careers in life science, physical science, social science, earth science, engineering, mathematics, and computer science.

★3180★ *Chemist*
Careers, Inc.
PO Box 135
Largo, FL 34649-0135
Ph: (813)584-7333
1994. Four-page brief offering the definition, history, duties, working conditions, personal qualifications, educational requirements, earnings, hours, employment outlook, advancement, and careers related to this position.

★3181★ "Chemist" in *Career Information Center* (Vol.6)
Simon and Schuster
200 Old Tappan Rd.
Old Tappan, NJ 07675
Fax: 800-445-6991   Fr: 800-223-2348
Richard Lidz and Linda Perrin, editorial directors. Fifth edition, 1993. This 13-volume set profiles over 600 occupations. Each occupational profile describes job duties, entry-level requirements, educational requirements, advancement possibilities, employment

outlook, working conditions, earnings and benefits, and where to write for more information.

★3182★ "Chemist" in *College Board Guide to Jobs and Career Planning* (pp. 280)
The College Board
415 Columbus Ave.
New York, NY 10023-6992
Ph: (212)713-8165   Fax: (212)713-8143
Fr: 800-323-7155
Joyce S. Mitchell. Second edition, 1994. Covers a variety of careers. Each career profile contains information on salaries, related careers, education needed, and sources of additional information.

★3183★ "Chemist" in *Guide to Federal Jobs* (p. 217)
Resource Directories
3361 Executive Pkwy., Ste. 302
Toledo, OH 43606
Ph: (419)536-5353   Fax: (419)536-7056
Fr: 800-274-8515
Rod W. Durgin, editor. Third edition, 1992. Contains information on finding and applying for federal jobs. Describes more than 200 professional and technical jobs for college graduates. Covers the nature of the work, salary, and geographic location. Lists college majors preferred for that occupation. Section one describes the function and work of government agencies that hire the most significant number of college graduates.

★3184★ "Chemist" in *Jobs Rated Almanac*
World Almanac
1 International Blvd., Ste. 444
Mahwah, NJ 07495
Ph: (201)529-6900   Fax: (201)529-6901
Les Krantz. Second edition, 1992. Ranks 250 jobs by environment, salary, outlooks, physical demands, stress, security, travel opportunities, and extra perks. Includes jobs the editor feels are the most common, most interesting, and the most rapidly growing.

★3185★ "Chemist" in *Opportunities in High-Tech Careers* (pp. 49-50)
National Textbook Co. (NTC)
VGM Career Books
4255 W. Touhy Ave.
Lincolnwood, IL 60646-1975
Ph: (708)679-5500   Fax: (708)679-2494
Fr: 800-323-4900
Gary D. Golter, and Deborah Yanuck. 1987. Explores high technology careers. Written for the student and displaced worker. Describes job opportunities, how to make a career decision, how to prepare for high-technology jobs, job hunting techniques, and future trends.

★3186★ "Chemist" in *VGM's Careers Encyclopedia* (pp. 88-91)
National Textbook Co. (NTC)
VGM Career Books
4255 W. Touhy Ave.
Lincolnwood, IL 60646-1975
Ph: (708)679-5500   Fax: (708)679-2494
Fr: 800-323-4900
Third edition, 1991. Profiles 200 occupations. Describes job duties, places of employment, working conditions, qualifications, education and training, advancement potential, and salary for each occupation.

★3187★ "Chemistry" in *College Majors and Careers: A Resource Guide to Effective Life Planning* (pp. 35-36)
Garrett Park Press
PO Box 1907
Garrett Park, MD 20896
Ph: (301)946-2553
Paul Phifer. Revised, 1993. Lists 60 college majors, with definitions; related occupations and leisure activities; skills, values, and personal attributesneeded; suggested readings; and a list of associations.

★3188★ "Chemistry" in *Encyclopedia of Careers and Vocational Guidance* (Vol.1, pp. 105-109)
J.G. Ferguson Publishing Co.
200 W. Madison St., Ste. 300
Chicago, IL 60606
Ph: (312)580-5480   Fax: (312)580-4948
William E. Hopke, editor-in-chief. Ninth edition, 1993. Four-volume set that profiles 900 occupations and describes job trends in 74 industries. Includes career description, educational requirements, history of the job, methods of entry, advancement, employment

outlook, earnings, conditions of work, social and psychological factors, and sources of further information.

★3189★ "Chemistry" in Liberal Arts Jobs
Petersons Guides, Inc.
PO Box 2123
Princeton, NJ 08543-2123
Ph: (609)243-9111   Fax: (609)243-9150
Fr: 800-338-3282

Burton Jay Nadler. Second edition, 1989. Strives to help the liberal arts graduate identify skills for entry-level positions. Gives goal setting and job search advice.

★3190★ "Chemistry" in Opportunities in Environmental Careers
National Textbook Co. (NTC)
VGM Career Books
4255 W. Touhy Ave.
Lincolnwood, IL 60646-1975
Ph: (708)679-5500   Fax: (708)679-2494
Fr: 800-323-4900

Odom Fanning. 1991. Describes a broad range of opportunities in fields such as environmental health, recreation, physics, and hygiene.

★3191★ Chemistry and Your Career: Questions and Answers
American Chemical Society (ACS)
1155 16th St., NW
Washington, DC 20036
Ph: (202)872-4600

1993. Describes what chemists do, where chemists work, what they earn, educational preparation, how to choose a school, and financial aid. Covers career options in special areas of chemistry.

★3192★ Chemists
Chronicle Guidance Publications, Inc.
66 Aurora St.
PO Box 1190
Moravia, NY 13118-1190
Ph: (315)497-0330   Fax: (315)497-3359
Fr: 800-622-7284

1992. Career brief describing the nature of the job, working conditions, hours and earnings, education and training, licensure, certification, unions, personal qualifications, social and psychological factors, location, employment outlook, entry methods, advancement, and related occupations.

★3193★ "Chemists" in 101 Careers: A Guide to the Fastest-Growing Opportunities (pp. 105-106)
John Wiley & Sons, Inc.
605 3rd Ave.
New York, NY 10158-0012
Ph: (212)850-6645   Fax: (212)850-6088

Michael Harkavy. 1990. Describes the nature of the job, working conditions, employment growth, qualifications, personal skills, projected salaries, and where to write for more information.

★3194★ "Chemists" in American Almanac of Jobs and Salaries (pp. 252)
Avon Books
1350 Avenue of the Americas
New York, NY 10019
Ph: (212)261-6800   Fr: 800-238-0658

John Wright, editor. Revised and updated, 1994-95. A comprehensive guide to the

wages of hundreds of occupations in a wide variety of industries and organizations.

★3195★ "Chemists" in Best Jobs for the 1990s and Into the 21st Century
Impact Publications
9104-N Manassas Dr.
Manassas Park, VA 22111
Ph: (703)361-7300   Fax: (703)335-9486

Ronald L. Krannich and Caryl Rae Krannich. 1993.

★3196★ "Chemists" in Jobs! What They Are—Where They Are—What They Pay (p. 309)
Simon & Schuster, Inc.
Simon & Schuster Bldg.
1230 Avenue of the Americas
New York, NY 10020
Ph: (212)698-7000   Fr: 800-223-2348

Robert O. Snelling and Anne M. Snelling. 3rd edition, 1992. Describes duties and responsibilities, earnings, employment opportunities, training, and qualifications.

★3197★ "Chemists" in Occupational Outlook Handbook
U.S. Government Printing Office
Superintendent of Documents
Washington, DC 20402
Ph: (202)512-1800   Fax: (202)512-2250

Biennial; latest edition, 1994-95. Encyclopedia of careers describing about 250 occupations and comprising about 85 percent of all jobs in the economy. Occupations that require lengthy education or training are given the most attention. Each occupation's profile describes what the worker does on the job, working conditions, education and training requirements, advancement possibilities, job outlook, earnings, and sources of additional information.

★3198★ "Chief Chemist" in BLR Encyclopedia of Prewritten Job Descriptions
Business and Legal Reports, Inc.
39 Academy St.
Madison, CT 06443-1513
Ph: (203)245-7448

Stephen D. Bruce, editor-in-chief. 1994. This book contains hundreds of sample job descriptions arranged by functional job category. The 1-3 page job descriptions cover what the worker normally does in the position, who they report to, and how that position fits in the organizational structure.

★3199★ Employment Outlook
American Chemical Society (ACS)
1155 16th St., NW
Washington, DC 20036
Ph: (202)872-4600

Annual. Describes career opportunities for chemists, demands, salaries, and trends in education. Charts the supply and demand for chemists. Gives career planning and job hunting advice.

★3200★ Opportunities in Chemistry Careers
National Textbook Co. (NTC)
VGM Career Books
4255 W. Touhy Ave.
Lincolnwood, IL 60646-1975
Ph: (708)679-5500   Fax: (708)679-2494
Fr: 800-323-4900

John H. Woodburn. 1987. Defines chemistry and describes history, entry-level jobs, future trends, personal qualities needed, educational requirements, earnings, and career specializations. Includes a list of professional associations and a bibliograpy of further readings.

★3201★ Opportunities for Women in Science Careers
National Textbook Co. (NTC)
VGM Career Books
4255 W. Touhy Ave.
Lincolnwood, IL 60646-1975
Ph: (708)679-5500   Fax: (708)679-2494
Fr: 800-323-4900

Alice Fins. 1979. Profiles women professionals in science careers such as biology, chemistry, geology, astronomy, physics, math, and others.

★3202★ Peterson's Job Opportunities for Engineering and Technology
Petersons Guides, Inc.
PO Box 2123
Princeton, NJ 08543-2123
Ph: (609)243-9111   Fax: (609)243-9150
Fr: 800-338-3282

1994. Gives job hunting advice including information on resume writing, interviewing, and handling salary negotiations. Lists companies that hire college graduates in science and engineering at the bachelor and master's level. Companies are indexed by industry, starting location, and major. Company profiles include contact information and types of hires.

★3203★ Salary 1993: Analysis of the American Chemical Society's 1993 Survey of Salaries and Employment
American Chemical Society (ACS)
1155 16th St., NW
Washington, DC 20036
Ph: (202)872-4600

Joan Burrelli. Annual. Gives salaries for chemists and notes how they vary by degree level, years of experience, industry, and job function.

★3204★ "Science" in Where the Jobs Are: The Hottest Careers for the 90s (pp. 245-260)
Career Press
180 5th Ave.
Hawthorne, NJ 07507
Ph: (201)427-0229   Fax: (201)427-2037
Fr: 800-CAREER-1

Joyce Hadley. 1995. Offers a job-hunting strategy for the 1990s as well as descriptions of growing careers of the decade. Each profile includes general information, forecasts, growth, education and training, licensing requirements, and salary information.

★3205★ Scientists, Physical

Careers, Inc.
PO Box 135
Largo, FL 34649-0135
Ph: (813)584-7333
1994. Four-page brief describing duties, working conditions, personal qualifications, training, earnings and hours, employment outlook, places of employment, related careers, and where to write for more information.

PROFESSIONAL ASSOCIATIONS

★3206★ American Association for Clinical Chemistry (AACC)

2101 L St. NW, Ste. 202
Washington, DC 20037-1526
Ph: (202)857-0717   Fax: (202)887-5093
Fr: 800-892-1400
Members: Clinical laboratory scientists and others engaged in the practice of clinical chemistry in independent laboratories, hospitals, and allied institutions. **Purpose:** Maintains Endowment Fund for Research in Clinical Chemistry. Maintains employment service. Sponsors: therapeutic drug monitoring and endocrinology programs; continuing education programs; quality control programs. Compiles statistics; sponsors speakers' bureau. **Publications:** Clinical Chemistry Journal, monthly. • Clinical Chemistry News, monthly. • Clinical Chemistry Reference Edition, monthly.

★3207★ American Chemical Society (ACS)

1155 16th St. NW
Washington, DC 20036
Ph: (202)872-4600   Fr: 800-227-5558
Members: Scientific and educational society of chemists and chemical engineers. Conducts: studies and surveys; special programs for disadvantaged persons; legislation monitoring, analysis, and reporting; courses for graduate chemists and chemical engineers; radio and television programming. Offers career guidance counseling; administers the Petroleum Research Fund and other grants and fellowship programs. Operates Employment Clearing Houses. Compiles statistics. Maintains speakers' bureau. Maintains 33 divisions. **Publications:** Accounts of Chemical Research, monthly. • Analytical Chemistry, semimonthly. • Biochemistry, weekly. • Bioconjugate Chemistry, bimonthly. • Biotechnology Progress, bimonthly. • Chemical Abstracts, weekly. • Chemical and Engineering News, weekly. • Chemical Health & Safety, bimonthly. • Chemical Research in Toxicology, bimonthly. • Chemical Reviews, 8/year. • Chemical Titles. • Chemistry of Materials, monthly. • Chemtech, monthly. • Energy and Fuels, bimonthly. • Environmental Science and Technology, monthly. • Industrial and Engineering Chemistry Research, monthly. • Inorganic Chemistry, biweekly. • Journal of Agricultural and Food Chemistry, monthly. • Journal of Chemical and Engineering Data, quarterly. • Journal of Chemical Information and Computer Sciences, bimonthly. • Journal of Medicinal Chemistry,

biweekly. • Journal of Organic Chemistry, biweekly. • Journal of Pharmaceutical Sciences, monthly. • Journal of Physical and Chemical Reference Data, bimonthly. • Journal of Physical Chemistry, weekly. • Journal of the American Chemical Society, biweekly. • Langmuir, monthly. • Macromolecules, biweekly. • Organometallics, monthly.

★3208★ American Institute of Chemists (AIC)

7315 Wisconsin Ave.
Bethesda, MD 20814
Ph: (301)652-2447   Fax: (301)657-3549
Members: Chemists and chemical engineers. **Purpose:** Promotes advancement of chemical professions in the U.S.; protects public welfare by establishing and enforcing high practice standards; represents professional interests of chemists and chemical engineers. Sponsors American Board of Clinical Chemistry; National Registry in Clinical Chemistry; National Certification Commission in Chemistry and Chemical Engineering; AIC Foundation; National Inventors Hall of Fame; Public Education Fund. Offers placement services. **Publications:** American Institute of Chemists—Professional Directory, annual. • The Chemist.

★3209★ American Society for Biochemistry and Molecular Biology (ASBMB)

9650 Rockville Pike
Bethesda, MD 20814-3996
Ph: (301)530-7145   Fax: (301)571-1824
Members: Biochemists and molecular biologists who have conducted and published original investigations in biological chemistry and/or molecular biology. Operates placement service. **Publications:** Journal of Biological Chemistry, weekly. • Minireview Compendium, annual.

★3210★ Association of Analytical Chemists (ANACHEM)

2017 Hyde Park Rd.
Detroit, MI 48207
Ph: (313)393-3685
Members: Analytical chemists. **Purpose:** Promotes the welfare of analytical chemists and their profession. Offers technical presentations and social affairs.

★3211★ Association of Consulting Chemists and Chemical Engineers (ACC&CE)

295 Madison Ave., 27th Fl.
New York, NY 10017
Ph: (212)983-3160   Fax: (212)983-3161
Members: Chemists and chemical engineers engaged in consulting practice as individuals, partners, or executives of organizations. Operates Clearing House for Consultants, through which industry is introduced to qualified and experienced members in any given field. **Publications:** Consulting Services, biennial.

★3212★ Center for Process Analytical Chemistry

Mail Stop BG-10
Seattle, WA 98195
Ph: (206)685-2326   Fax: (206)543-6506
Members: Companies involved in analytical chemistry. Conducts research in analytical

chemistry. **Publications:** Monitor, semiannual.

★3213★ Chemical Manufacturers Association (CMA)

2501 M St. NW
Washington, DC 20037
Ph: (202)887-1100   Fax: (202)887-1237
Members: Manufacturers of chemicals. **Purpose:** Conducts advocacy and administers research in areas of broad import to chemical manufacturing, such as pollution prevention and other special research programs. Conducts committee studies. Operates Chemical Emergency Center (CHEMTREC) for guidance to emergency services on handling emergencies involving chemicals; also operates Chemical Referral Center which offers health and safety information about chemicals to the public. Maintains 62 biomedical and special program panels. **Publications:** ChemEcology, 10/year. • CMA Directory and User's Guide, annual. • CMA News. • Emergency Response Guidebook: A Tool for Safety.

★3214★ International Organization for Chemical Sciences in Development (U.S.A. Office) (IOCD)

PO Box 8156
Falls Church, VA 22041
Ph: (703)845-9078   Fax: (703)845-9078
Members: Scientists from around the world concerned about the barriers that hinder research efforts of chemists in developing countries. **Purpose:** Links chemists in developing countries with investigators in industrial countries in collaborative research in the areas of health, agriculture, and industry. Organizes laboratory workshops in developing countries to provide chemists hands-on instruction in research techniques. **Publications:** IOCD Update, semiannual.

★3215★ National Mole Day Foundation

1220 S. 5th St.
Prairie du Chien, WI 53821
Ph: (608)326-6036   Fax: (608)326-2333
Members: Individuals interested in the mole concept, chemistry, and Avogadro's number (the number 6.023×10 to the 23rd power, indicating the number of atoms or molecules in a mole of any substance.) **Purpose:** Promotes the importance and awareness of chemistry in everyday life. Originates activities for school chemistry clubs; celebrates Mole Day (October 23).

★3216★ Society of Nuclear Medicine (SNM)

1850 Samuel Morse Dr.
Reston, VA 22090
Ph: (703)708-9000   Fax: (703)708-9015
Members: Professional society of physicians, physicists, chemists, radiopharmacists, nuclear medicine technologists, and others interested in nuclear medicine, nuclear magnetic resonance, and the use of radioactive isotopes in clinical practice, research, and teaching. **Purpose:** Disseminates information concerning the utilization of nuclear phenomena in the diagnosis and treatment of disease. Oversees the Technologist Section of the Society of Nuclear Medicine. **Publications:** The Journal of Nuclear Medicine, monthly. • Journal of Nuclear Medicine

Technology, quarterly. • *Society of Nuclear Medicine Membership Directory.*

★3217★ U.S. National Committee for the International Union of Pure and Applied Chemistry
c/o Tamae Maeda Wong
National Research Council
2101 Constitution Ave. NW, Rm. 273
Washington, DC 20418
Ph: (202)334-2156   Fax: (202)334-2154
Members: Chemists from academia, government, and industry. **Purpose:** Investigates and makes recommendations for action on chemical matters of international importance that need regulation, standardization, or codification. Cooperates with other organizations on topics concerning chemicals; promotes cooperation among chemists. Maintains the Chemical Research Applied to World Needs Committee (CHEMRAWN). Holds symposia. **Publications:** *Pure and Applied Chemistry*, monthly.

STANDARDS/CERTIFICATION AGENCIES

★3218★ American Institute of Chemists (AIC)
7315 Wisconsin Ave.
Bethesda, MD 20814
Ph: (301)652-2447   Fax: (301)657-3549
Promotes advancement of chemical professions in the U.S.; protects public welfare by establishing and enforcing high practice standards; represents professional interests of chemists and chemical engineers. Sponsors American Board of Clinical Chemistry; National Registry in Clinical Chemistry; National Certification Commission in Chemistry and Chemical Engineering; AIC Foundation; National Inventors Hall of Fame; Public Education Fund.

★3219★ American Oil Chemists' Society (AOCS)
PO Box 3489
Champaign, IL 61826-3489
Ph: (217)359-2344   Fax: (217)351-8091
Sponsors short courses; certifies referee chemists; distributes cooperative check samples; sells official reagents. Maintains 100 committees.

TEST GUIDES

★3220★ AP Chemistry
Arco Pub.
201 W. 103rd St.
Indianapolis, IN 46290
Ph: 800-428-5331   Fax: 800-835-3202
Frederick J. Rowe. 1993, Second edition. Provides samples of multiple-choice and free response questions. Includes a topic review.

★3221★ Career Examination Series: Assistant Chemist
National Learning Corp.
212 Michael Dr.
Syosset, NY 11791
Ph: (516)921-8888   Fax: (516)921-8743
Fr: 800-645-6337

Jack Rudman. Test guide including questions and answers for students or professionals in the field who seek advancement through examination.

★3222★ Career Examination Series: Associate Chemist
National Learning Corp.
212 Michael Dr.
Syosset, NY 11791
Ph: (516)921-8888   Fax: (516)921-8743
Fr: 800-645-6337

Jack Rudman. Test guide including questions and answers for students or professionals in the field who seek advancement through examination.

★3223★ Career Examination Series: Chemist
National Learning Corp.
212 Michael Dr.
Syosset, NY 11791
Ph: (516)921-8888   Fax: (516)921-8743
Fr: 800-645-6337

Jack Rudman. A series of study guides with multiple-choice examination questions and solutions for trainees and professional chemists. Titles in the series include *Assistant Chemist; Associate Analytical Chemist; Associate Chemist; Biochemist; Biochemist Trainee; Chemist I (Environmental Control); Chemist II (Environmental Control); Chemist Trainee; Environmental Chemist; Junior Chemist; Laboratory Assistant (Chemistry); Principal Chemist; Sanitary Chemist; Senior Chemist; Senior Analytical Chemist.*

★3224★ Career Examination Series: Junior Chemist
National Learning Corp.
212 Michael Dr.
Syosset, NY 11791
Ph: (516)921-8888   Fax: (516)921-8743
Fr: 800-645-6337

Jack Rudman. Test guide including questions and answers for students or professionals in the field who seek advancement through examination.

★3225★ Career Examination Series: Principal Chemist
National Learning Corp.
212 Michael Dr.
Syosset, NY 11791
Ph: (516)921-8888   Fax: (516)921-8743
Fr: 800-645-6337

Jack Rudman. Test guide including questions and answers for students or professionals in the field who seek advancement through examination.

★3226★ Career Examination Series: Senior Chemist
National Learning Corp.
212 Michael Dr.
Syosset, NY 11791
Ph: (516)921-8888   Fax: (516)921-8743
Fr: 800-645-6337

Jack Rudman. Test guide including questions and answers for students or professionals in the field who seek advancement through examination.

★3227★ College-Level Examination Series: Chemistry
National Learning Corp.
212 Michael Dr.
Syosset, NY 11791
Ph: (516)921-8888   Fax: (516)921-8743
Fr: 800-645-6337

Jack Rudman. Multiple-choice preparatory examinations for students considering the College-Level Examination Program (CLEP) as an alternative to college course matriculation. Includes solutions to sample test questions. Titles in the series include *General Chemistry; Clinical Chemistry.*

★3228★ Dantes Subject Standardized Tests: College Chemistry
National Learning Corp.
212 Michael Dr.
Syosset, NY 11791
Ph: (516)921-8888   Fax: (516)921-8743
Fr: 800-645-6337

Jack Rudman. Multiple-choice graduate- and college-level examination given by graduate schools, colleges and the Armed Forces as a final examination for course evaluation. Includes answers.

★3229★ EZ 101 Study Keys: Chemistry
Barron's Educational Series, Inc.
250 Wireless Blvd.
Hauppauge, NY 11788
Ph: (516)434-3311   Fax: (516)434-3723
Fr: 800-645-3476

1992. Provides themes, formulas, and a glossary of terms.

★3230★ Graduate Record Examination: Chemistry
National Learning Corp.
212 Michael Dr.
Syosset, NY 11791
Ph: (516)921-8888   Fax: (516)921-8743
Fr: 800-645-6337

Jack Rudman. Multiple-choice test for those seeking admission to graduate school for study in the field of chemistry. Includes solutions to examination questions.

★3231★ Regents College Proficiency Examination Series: Chemistry
National Learning Corp.
212 Michael Dr.
Syosset, NY 11791
Ph: (516)921-8888   Fax: (516)921-8743
Fr: 800-645-6337

Jack Rudman. A sample test for college credit-by-examination programs in the field of chemistry. Multiple-choice style with answers included.

★3232★ Undergraduate Program Field Test: Chemistry
National Learning Corp.
212 Michael Dr.
Syosset, NY 11791
Ph: (516)921-8888   Fax: (516)921-8743
Fr: 800-645-6337

Jack Rudman. A practice examination fashioned after tests given in the Regents External Degree Program. Designed to measure knowledge received outside the college classroom in the subject of chemistry. Contains multiple-choice questions; provides solutions.

EDUCATIONAL DIRECTORIES AND PROGRAMS

★3233★ ACS Directory of Graduate Research
American Chemical Society (ACS)
1155 16th St. NW
Washington, DC 20036
Ph: (202)872-4589   Fax: (202)872-6067
Fr: 800-227-5558
Cathy A. Nelson, Contact

Biennial, November of odd years. Covers about 738 departments offering masters' and/or doctoral degrees in chemistry, chemical engineering, biochemistry, medicinal/pharmaceutical chemistry, clinical chemistry, polymer science, food science, forensic science, marine science, and toxicology located in the United States and Canada. Entries include: Institution name, address, phone, fax, department name, name of chairperson, degrees offered, fields of specialization; names and birth dates of faculty members, their educational backgrounds, special research interests, personal phone number, computer addresses, and recent publications; names and thesis titles of recent Masters' and Ph.D. graduates. Arrangement: Classified by discipline, then alphabetical by keyword in institution name.

★3234★ American Chemical Society—List of Approved Schools
Office of Professional Training
American Chemical Society (ACS)
1155 16th St. NW
Washington, DC 20036
Ph: (202)872-4589   Fax: (202)872-6066
Dolphine S. Hite, Contact

Annual, April. Covers about 600 institutions offering undergraduate programs in chemistry that are approved by the American Chemical Society. Entries include: Institution name, address; asterisk indicates whether also accredited by the American Institute of Chemical Engineers and the Accreditation Board for Engineering and Technology. Arrangement: Geographical.

★3235★ Chemical Research Faculties: An International Directory
American Chemical Society (ACS)
1155 16th St. NW
Washington, DC 20036
Ph: (202)872-4600   Fax: (202)452-8913
Fr: 800-227-5558
M. Joan Comstock, Books Department

Irregular, latest edition 1988. Covers about 600 educational institutions with departments granting advanced degrees in chemical research fields of study, including pharmaceutical chemistry, chemical engineering, and biochemistry; 65 chemical associations. Omits institutions in the United States and Canada that are covered in the American Chemical Society's "ACS Directory of Graduate Research" (described separately). Entries include: For educational institutions—Name, name of department, address, phone, degrees offered, fields of specialization; names of faculty members, their educational backgrounds, special research interests, personal phone numbers, recent publications. For associations—Name, address, Arrangement: Classified by four major disciplines (chemistry, chemical engineering, biochemistry, and pharmaceutical), then geographical.

★3236★ Physical Science Career Directory
Gale Research Inc.
835 Penobscot Bldg.
Detroit, MI 48226-4094
Ph: (313)961-2242   Fax: (313)961-6083
Fr: 800-877-GALE
Bradley J. Morgan, Contact

First edition March 1994. Covers over 210 chemical companies, testing and research laboratories, and consulting firms in the U.S. offering entry-level positions and internships; sources of help-wanted ads, professional associations, producers of videos, databases, career guides, and professional guides and handbooks. Entries include: For companies—Name, address, phone, fax, business description, research activities, names and titles of key personnel, number of employees, average number of entry-level positions available, human resources contact, description of internship opportunities including contact, type and number available, application procedures, qualifications, and duties. For others—Name or title, address, phone, description. Paperback edition Arrangement: Companies are alphabetical; others are classified by type of resource.

★3237★ Research in Chemistry at Primarily Undergraduate Institutions
Council on Undergraduate Research
University of North Carolina at Asheville
1 University Hts.
Asheville, NC 28804-3299
Ph: (704)251-6006   Fax: (704)251-6002
Laurel Ferejohn, Contact

Irregular, latest edition June 1993; new edition expected Feb. 1995. Covers 550 primarily undergraduate chemistry departments with about 1,800 faculty members; 212 departments are featured in more detail. Institutions contacted were selected based on primarily undergraduate enrollment. Entries include: College name, address; department chairman, phone, fax; enrollment, number of faculty, number of staff, facilities, size of library, equipment available, research funding, student research activity. For faculty members—Name, phone, research interests, current publications, and grants received. Arrangement: Alphabetical.

AWARDS, SCHOLARSHIPS, GRANTS, AND FELLOWSHIPS

★3238★ ACS Award in Analytical Chemistry
American Chemical Society
Research, Grants, and Awards
1155 16th St. NW
Washington, DC 20036
Ph: (202)872-4408

To recognize and encourage outstanding contributions to the science of analytical chemistry, pure or applied, carried out in the United States or Canada. The nominee must be a resident of the United States or Canada and must have made an outstanding contribution to analytical chemistry. Special consideration is given to the independence of thought and the originality shown, or to the importance of the work when applied to public welfare, economics, or the needs and desires of humanity. The deadline for nominations is February 1. A monetary prize of $5,000, an etching, and travel expenses incidental to the conferring of the award are awarded annually. Established in 1947. Sponsored by Fisher Scientific Company, Ltd.

★3239★ ACS Award in the Chemistry of Materials
American Chemical Society
Research, Grants, and Awards
1155 16th St. NW
Washington, DC 20036
Ph: (202)872-4408

To recognize and encourage creative work in the chemistry of materials. The nominee must have made outstanding contributions to the chemistry of materials, with particular emphasis on research relating to materials of actual or potential technological importance, where fundamental understanding of chemistry associated with materials preparation, processing, or use is critical. The deadline for nominations is February 1. A monetary award of $5,000, an inscribed certificate, and reimbursed travel expenses to attend the presentation ceremony are awarded annually, beginning in 1990. Established in 1988 by E. I. duPont de Nemours and Company to commemorate the fiftieth anniversary of the commercialization of nylon and of the discovery of Teflon. Sponsored by E. I. du Pont de Nemours and Company.

★3240★ ACS Award for Creative Invention
American Chemical Society
Research, Grants, and Awards
1155 16th St. NW
Washington, DC 20036
Ph: (202)872-4408

To recognize individual inventors for successful applications of research in chemistry and/or chemical engineering that contribute to the material prosperity and happiness of people. The nominee must be a resident of the United States or Canada. A patent must have been granted for the work to be recognized and it must have been developed during the preceding 17 years. The deadline for nominations is February 1. A monetary award of $5,000, a gold medal, and an allowance of up to $1,000 for travel to the award ceremony are awarded annually. Established in 1966. Sponsored by the ASC Committee on Corporation Associates.

★3241★ ACS Award in Inorganic Chemistry
American Chemical Society
Research, Grants, and Awards
1155 16th St. NW
Washington, DC 20036
Ph: (202)872-4408

To recognize and encourage fundamental research in the field of inorganic chemistry. The nominee must have accomplished outstanding research in the preparation, properties, reactions, or structure of inorganic substances. Special consideration is given to the independence of thought and originality shown. The award is granted without regard to age, nationality, or sex. The deadline for nominations is February 1. A monetary award of $5,000, a certificate, and a travel allowance of not more than $1,000 to attend the meeting where the award is presented are awarded annually. Established in 1960 by Texas Instruments Incorporated. Sponsored by Monsanto Company.

★3242★ ACS Award in Pure Chemistry
American Chemical Society
Research, Grants, and Awards
1155 16th St. NW
Washington, DC 20036
Ph: (202)872-4408

To recognize and encourage fundamental research in pure chemistry carried out in North America by young men and women. The nominee must be under the age of 36 on April 30, and must have accomplished research of unusual merit for an individual on the threshold of his or her career. Special consideration is given to independence of thought and the originality shown in the research, which must have been carried out in North America. The nomination deadline is February 1. A monetary prize of $4,000, a certificate setting forth the reasons for the award, and a travel allowance of up to $1,000 to attend the meeting where the award is presented are awarded annually. Established in 1931 by A. C. Langmuir. Sponsored by Alpha Chi Sigma Fraternity.

★3243★ Roger Adams Award in Organic Chemistry
American Chemical Society
Research, Grants, and Awards
1155 16th St. NW
Washington, DC 20036
Ph: (202)872-4408

To recognize and encourage outstanding contributions to research in organic chemistry defined in its broadest sense. The award is granted to an individual without regard to nationality. The deadline for nominations is February 1. A monetary prize of $25,000, a gold medal, and a sterling silver replica of the medal are awarded biennially in odd-num-

bered years. Additionally, the recipient delivers a lecture at the Biennial National Organic Chemistry Symposium of the American Chemical Society where the award is presented. The travel expenses to the Symposium are paid. Established in 1959. Sponsored by Organic Reactions, Inc., and Organic Syntheses, Inc.

★3244★ Award for Professional Excellence
Iota Sigma Pi
c/o Jeanne Buccigross
Mt. St. Joseph College
Dept. of Chemistry
Mt. St. Joseph, OH 45051

To recognize outstanding contributions to chemistry and allied fields. Nominees are judged on the significance of their accomplishments in academic, governmental, or industrial chemistry; in education; in administration; or in a combination of these areas. Achievements may include innovative design, development, application, or promotion of a principle or practice that has widespread significance to the scientific community or society on a national level. The nominee must be a member of Iota Sigma Pi. The deadline is December 15. A monetary prize of $500 and a certificate are presented at the National Convention in June. Established in 1984.

★3245★ Alfred Bader Award in Bioinorganic or Bioorganic Chemistry
American Chemical Society
Research, Grants, and Awards
1155 16th St. NW
Washington, DC 20036
Ph: (202)872-4408

To recognize significant accomplishments that are at the interface between biology and organic or inorganic chemistry. Special consideration is given to applications of the fundamental principles and experimental methodology of chemistry to areas of biological significance. The deadline for nominations is February 1. A monetary award of $3,000, an inscribed certificate, and travel expenses incidental to conferment of the award are granted annually. The recipient's award address is reprinted in *Aldrichimica Acta*. Established in 1986 and financed by a gift to the ACS by Alfred R. Bader.

★3246★ Charles Frederick Chandler Medal
Columbia University
Office of the Pres.
202 Low Memorial Library
New York, NY 10027
Ph: (212)854-5017

For recognition of achievement in pure or applied chemistry. A gold medal is awarded biennially. Established in 1910 and funded through a foundation receiving gifts from students of Professor Chandler.

★3247★ Arthur C. Cope Award
American Chemical Society
Research, Grants, and Awards
1155 16th St. NW
Washington, DC 20036
Ph: (202)872-4408

To recognize outstanding achievement in the field of organic chemistry that has had apparent significance within the preceding five years. The award is granted to an individual

without regard to age, sex, or nationality. The deadline for nominations is February 1. A monetary prize of $25,000, a gold medal, and a bronze replica of the medal are awarded annually. In addition, an unrestricted grant-in-aid of $50,000 for research in organic chemistry under the direction of the recipient, designated as an Arthur C. Cope Fund Grant, is made to any university or nonprofit institution selected by the recipient. A recipient may choose to assign the Arthur C. Cope Fund Grant to an institution for use by others than the recipient for research or education in organic chemistry. Established in 1972 under the terms of the will of Arthur C. Cope.

★3248★ Arthur C. Cope Scholar Award
American Chemical Society
Research, Grants, and Awards
1155 16th St. NW
Washington, DC 20036
Ph: (202)872-4408

To recognize and encourage excellence in organic chemistry. Up to ten Scholars are named annually, with a balanced distribution among the following age groups: under age 36, between ages 26-49 (inclusive), and over age 50. The deadline for nominations is February 1. No individual may receive a second Arthur C. Cope Scholar Award; Arthur C. Cope Medalists are ineligible to be named Cope Scholars. A certificate and a $25,000 unrestricted research grant, to be assigned by the recipient to any university or nonprofit institution, are awarded. The recipient is required to deliver a lecture at the annual Arthur C. Cope Symposium. Established in 1984 under the terms of the will of Arthur C. Cope.

★3249★ Francis P. Garvan - John M. Olin Medal
American Chemical Society
Research, Grants, and Awards
1155 16th St. NW
Washington, DC 20036
Ph: (202)872-4408

To recognize distinguished service to chemistry by women chemists who are citizens of the United States. The deadline for nominations is February 1. A monetary prize of $5,000, an inscribed gold medal, a bronze replica of the medal, and an allowance of $1,000 for travel expenses to attend the meeting where the award is presented are awarded annually. Established in 1936 through a donation from Francis P. Garvan. Sponsored and funded by Olin Corporation.

★3250★ Gold Medal
American Institute of Chemists
7315 Wisconsin Ave., Ste. 518E
Bethesda, MD 20814
Ph: (301)652-2447   Fax: (301)657-3549

This, the institute's highest honor, is presented to recognize a person who has stimulated activities of service to the science of chemistry, or the chemistry or chemical engineering professions in the United States. Life fellowship in the institute is awarded annually. Established in 1926.

★3251★ E. B. Hershberg Award for Important Discoveries in Medicinally Active Substances
American Chemical Society
Research, Grants, and Awards
1155 16th St. NW
Washington, DC 20036
Ph: (202)872-4408

To recognize and encourage outstanding discoveries in the chemistry of medicinally active substances made during the previous two decades. The deadline for nominations is February 1 of even-numbered years. A monetary award of $3,000, a certificate, and a travel allowance of $1,000 to attend the presentation ceremony are awarded biennially in odd-numbered years. Established in 1988 by Schering-Plough Corporation in honor of the contributions of Emanuel B. Hershberg to the pharmaceutical industry, especially the application of organic chemistry, for the discovery and development of novel drugs. Sponsored by Schering-Plough Corporation.

★3252★ Joel Henry Hildebrand Award in the Theoretical and Experimental Chemistry of Liquids
American Chemical Society
Research, Grants, and Awards
1155 16th St. NW
Washington, DC 20036
Ph: (202)872-4408

To recognize distinguished contributions to the understanding of the chemistry and physics of liquids. The award is granted without regard to age, sex, or nationality. The deadline for nominations is February 1. A monetary prize of $5,000, a certificate, and an allowance of up to $1,000 for travel expenses incidental to conferral of the award are presented annually. Established in 1980 in recognition of the scientific contributions of ACS past president, Joel H. Hildebrand. The first award was presented to Dr. Hildebrand as part of the observances of his hundredth birthday in November, 1981. Sponsored by Exxon Research and Engineering Company and Exxon Chemical Company.

★3253★ Honorary Member
Phi Lambda Upsilon, National Honorary Chemical Society
Dept. of Chemistry
Virginia Polytechnic Institution & State Univ.
Blacksburg, VA 24061
Ph: (703)231-5997   Fax: (703)231-3255
To recognize individuals for outstanding contributions to the science of chemistry.

★3254★ Ipatieff Prize
American Chemical Society
Research, Grants, and Awards
1155 16th St. NW
Washington, DC 20036
Ph: (202)872-4408

To recognize outstanding chemical experimental work in the field of catalysis or high pressure, carried out by men or women under 40 years of age of any nationality forty years of age. The award may be made for investigations carried out in any country, but reference is given to American chemists. The deadline for nominations is February 1. The award consists of the income from a trust fund and a diploma setting forth the reasons for the award. The financial value of the prize may

vary, but it is expected to be approximately $5,000. Awarded every three years. An allowance is provided to cover travel expenses incidental to conferment of the award. Established in 1943 by the Ipatieff Trust Fund and Northwestern University.

★3255★ Irving Langmuir Award in Chemical Physics
American Chemical Society
Research, Grants, and Awards
1155 16th St. NW
Washington, DC 20036
Ph: (202)872-4408

To recognize and encourage outstanding interdisciplinary research in chemistry and physics. Nominees must have made an outstanding contribution to chemical physics or physical chemistry within the ten preceding years. The nominee must be a resident of the United States. The deadline for nominations is February 1 in any odd-numbered year. A monetary award of $10,000 and a scroll are awarded biennially in even-numbered years. Selection of the recipient in odd-numbered years is conducted by the Division of Chemical Physics of the American Physical Society. Established in 1964. Sponsored by General Electric Foundation.

★3256★ NAACP Willems Scholarship
National Association for the Advancement of Colored People (NAACP)
4805 Mt. Hope Dr.
Baltimore, MD 21215-3297
Ph: (410)358-8900

Qualifications: Applicants must be majoring in engineering, chemistry, physics, or computer and mathematical sciences and possess a cumulative grade point average of at least 3.0 or B average. They must be members of the NAACP. Funds available: Undergraduates will receive a maximum award of $8,000 to be paid in annual installments of $2,000. Graduates will be awarded a $3,000 renewable scholarship. Application details: Updated application forms are available in January. Deadline: April 30.

★3257★ National Academy of Sciences Award in Chemical Sciences
National Academy of Sciences
2101 Constitution Ave. NW
Washington, DC 20418
Ph: (202)334-2444

To recognize innovative research in the chemical sciences that contributes, in the broadest sense, to the better understanding of the natural sciences and to the benefit of humanity. Researchers with broad fundamental impact are eligible. A monetary prize of $10,000 and a medal are awarded annually. Established in 1978 in honor of Armand Hammer. Sponsored by Occidental Petroleum Corporation.

★3258★ National Fresenius Award
Phi Lambda Upsilon, National Honorary Chemical Society
Dept. of Chemistry
Virginia Polytechnic Institution & State Univ.
Blacksburg, VA 24061
Ph: (703)231-5997   Fax: (703)231-3255
For recognition of an outstanding contribution in chemical research, education, and/or administration by a chemist under 35 years of age. A monetary award, travel expenses, and

a plaque are awarded annually. Established in 1965.

★3259★ Newcomen Award for Notable Proficiency in Mathematics, Physics and Chemistry
Newcomen Society of the United States
412 Newcomen Rd.
Exton, PA 19341
Ph: (215)363-6600   Fax: (215)363-0612
For recognition of notable proficiency in mathematics, physics, and chemistry. A monetary prize of $250 and a scroll are awarded annually. Established in 1960. Administered by Drexel University.

★3260★ Nobel Laureate Signature Award for Graduate Education in Chemistry
American Chemical Society
Research, Grants, and Awards
1155 16th St. NW
Washington, DC 20036
Ph: (202)872-4408

To recognize an outstanding graduate student and his or her preceptor(s) in the field of chemistry, as broadly defined. The graduate student nominee must have completed a Ph.D. dissertation in chemistry within the 12-month period before the deadline for receipt of nominations. The award recognizes only work done while the nominee was a graduate student. This award is granted without regard to age, sex, or nationality. The deadline for nominations is February 1. The graduate student receives a monetary prize of $3,000 and a plaque containing the signatures of Nobel Laureates. The student's preceptor(s) receives $3,000 and a plaque for permanent display in the institution's Chemistry Department. Travel expenses of recipients incidental to the conferring of the award are paid. Awarded annually. Established in 1978. Sponsored by J. T. Baker, Inc.

★3261★ James Flack Norris Award in Physical Organic Chemistry
American Chemical Society
Research, Grants, and Awards
1155 16th St. NW
Washington, DC 20036
Ph: (202)872-4408

To encourage and reward outstanding contributions to physical organic chemistry. The deadline for nominations is February 1. A monetary prize of $3,000, an engraved certificate, and an allowance of not more than $1,000 for travel expenses to the meeting where the award is presented are awarded annually. Established in 1963 in commemoration of James Flack Norris. Sponsored by the Northeastern Section, ACS.

★3262★ Henry H. Storch Award in Fuel Chemistry
American Chemical Society
Research, Grants, and Awards
1155 16th St. NW
Washington, DC 20036
Ph: (202)872-4408

To recognize distinguished contributions within the preceding five years to fundamental or engineering research on the chemistry and utilization of coal or related materials. The deadline for nominations is February 1. A monetary award of $5,000, a plaque, and an expense allowance of up to $1,500 for travel to the presentation ceremony are presented annually. Established in 1964 by the Division of Fuel Chemistry, ACS and administered by the Division until 1985. Sponsored by Exxon Research and Engineering Company.

★3263★ Robert A. Welch Award in Chemistry
Robert A. Welch Foundation
4605 Post Oak Pl., Ste. 200
Houston, TX 77027
Ph: (713)961-9884   Fax: (713)961-5168

To encourage basic chemical research and to recognize the value of chemical research contributions for the benefit of mankind. Nominations are solicited from appropriate scientific organizations, and nominations received from appropriate organizations and individuals are considered (no self nominations). A monetary prize of $225,000, a gold medal, and a certificate are awarded annually at a dinner in honor of the recipient. Established in 1972 under the terms of the will of Robert Alonzo Welch.

BASIC REFERENCE GUIDES AND HANDBOOKS

★3264★ Chemistry
Allyn and Bacon, Inc.
PO Box 11071
Des Moines, IA 50336
Fr: 800-278-3525

Ronald J. Gillespie. Second edition, 1989. Covers chemical principles and reaction chemistry.

★3265★ CRC Handbook of Chemistry and Physics
CRC Press, Inc.
2000 Corporate Blvd., NW
Boca Raton, FL 33431
Ph: (305)994-0555   Fr: 800-272-7737

Robert C. Weast, editor in chief. Sixty-ninth edition, 1988. Contains mathematical tables and a section on physical constants.

★3266★ The Facts on File Dictionary of Chemistry
Facts on File
460 Park Ave. S.
New York, NY 10016-7382
Ph: (212)683-2244   Fax: 800-678-3633
Fr: 800-322-8755

Dr. John Daintith, editor. Revised edition, 1990. This is a nontechnical dictionary defining basic chemical terms and reactions.

★3267★ Formulas, Facts, and Constants for Students and Professionals in Engineering, Chemistry, and Physics
Springer-Verlag New York, Inc.
175 5th Ave.
New York, NY 10010
Ph: (212)460-1500   Fr: 800-777-4643

Helmut J. Fischbeck and K. H. Fischbeck. Second edition, 1987. Includes an index. Illustrated.

★3268★ Fundamentals of Chemistry with Qualitative Analysis
John Wiley and Sons, Inc.
605 3rd Ave.
New York, NY 10158-0012
Ph: (212)850-6000   Fax: (212)850-6088
Fr: 800-526-5368

James E. Brady and J. R. Holum. Third edition, 1988. This introductry text covers chemical principals, theory, reactions, and properties.

★3269★ Grant & Hackh's Chemical Dictionary
McGraw-Hill, Inc.
1221 Avenue of the Americas
New York, NY 10020
Ph: (212)512-2000   Fr: 800-722-4726

Ingo W. D. Hackh, Roger Grant, and Claire Grant. Fifth edition, 1987. Includes an index. Illustrated.

★3270★ Handbook of Chemistry and Physics: A Ready-Reference Book of Chemical and Physical Data
CRC Press, Inc.
2000 Corporate Blvd., NW
Boca Raton, FL 33431
Ph: (407)994-0555

Robert C. Weast, editor. Sixty-eighth edition, 1987. Includes bibliographical references and an index.

★3271★ Hawley's Condensed Chemical Dictionary
Van Nostrand Reinhold Co., Inc.
115 5th Ave.
New York, NY 10003
Ph: (212)254-3232

N. Irving Sax and Richard J. Lewis, editors. Twelfth edition, 1992. Includes an index. Illustrated.

★3272★ Lange's Handbook of Chemistry
McGraw-Hill, Inc.
1221 Avenue of the Americas
New York, NY 10020
Ph: (212)512-2000   Fr: 800-722-4726

John A. Dean, editor. Fourteenth edition, 1992. Includes tables on atomic and molecular structure, inorganic chemistry, analytical chemistry, electrochemistry, organic chemistry, spetroscopy, thermodynamic properties, and physical properties.

★3273★ Materials Handbook: An Encyclopedia for Managers, Technical Professionals, Purchasing and Production Managers, Technicians, and Supervisors . . .
McGraw-Hill, Inc.
1221 Avenue of the Americas
New York, NY 10020
Ph: (212)512-2000   Fr: 800-722-4726

George Stuart Brady and Henry R. Clauser. Thirteenth editon, 1991. Contains descriptions of all materials and substances related to engineering technologies. Arranged alphabetically.

★3274★ Merck Index: An Encyclopedia of Chemicals, Drugs, and Biologicals
Merck and Co., Inc.
PO Box 2000
Rahway, NJ 07065
Ph: (908)750-7470

Martha Windholz, editor. Eleventh edition. 1990. A source of data on chemicals including name, alternate names, molecular formula, molecular weight, composition, literature references, structural diagram, physical data, derivatives, and use. Toll free: 800-594-4600.

PROFESSIONAL AND TRADE PERIODICALS

★3275★ ACS Washington Alert
American Chemical Society (ACS)
1155 16th St. NW
Washington, DC 20036
Ph: (202)872-8724   Fax: (202)872-6206
Keith Belton

Biweekly. Focuses on such chemical issues as hazardous waste, air and water quality, biotechnology, and toxic substances, and how they are affected by government regulatory and legislative activities.

★3276★ The Chemical Bulletin
American Chemical Society, Chicago Section
7173 N. Austin
Niles, IL 60714
Ph: (708)647-8405   Fax: (708)647-8364

Monthly. Contains information of interest to members of the Chicago branch of the American Chemical Society.

★3277★ Chemical Design Automation News
Charlotte Romanicle, Contact
Monthly. Focuses on matters of technical interest relating to the use of computer automation techniques in chemical and engineered materials research. Recurring features include news of research and a calendar of events.

★3278★ Chemical Heritage
Chemical Heritage Foundation
3401 Walnut St., Ste. 460B
Philadelphia, PA 19104-6228
Ph: (215)898-4896   Fax: (215)898-3327
Theodor Benfrey

Concerned with the history of chemistry, chemical engineering, and the chemical process industries. Contains brief historical articles; news of history projects, societies, and sources; and news of the Beckman Center and the Othmer Library of Chemical History. Recurring features include news of research, news of members, book reviews, news of recent publications, and a calendar of events.

★3279★ Chemical Week
Chemical Week Associates
888 7th Ave. 26th Fl.
New York, NY 10106
Ph: (212)621-4900   Fax: (212)621-4949
David Hunter

Weekly. Chemical process industries magazine.

★3280★ The Chemist
American Institute of Chemists, Inc.
7315 Wisconsin Ave.
Bethesda, MD 20814
Ph: (301)652-2447
Robert S. Melville

Covers news items relating to the chemical profession and membership in the Institute. Reports on legislation, licensure, earnings, awards, and professional education. Recurring features include news of employment opportunities and news of members.

★3281★ Magnetic Resonance in Chemistry
John Wiley and Sons, Inc.
Subscription Dept.
605 3rd Ave.
New York, NY 10158
Ph: (212)850-6000   Fax: (212)850-6799
H. Gunther

Monthly. Scholastic journal publishing papers on spectrometry in chemistry.

★3282★ Soap/Cosmetics/Chemical Specialties
PTN Publishing Co.
445 Broad Hollow Rd., Ste. 21
Melville, NY 11747-3601
Ph: (516)845-2700   Fax: (516)845-2797
Anita Hipius Shaw

Monthly. Soap, cosmetics, and chemical specialties trade magazine.

PROFESSIONAL MEETINGS AND CONVENTIONS

★3283★ American Association for Clinical Chemistry National Meeting
Scherago International, Inc.
11 Penn Plaza, Ste. 1003
New York, NY 10001
Ph: (212)643-1750   Fax: (212)643-1758
Annual. Always held during July.

★3284★ AOAC International Meeting and Exposition
AOAC International
2200 Wilson Blvd., Ste. 400
Arlington, VA 22201-3301
Ph: (703)522-3032   Fax: (703)522-5468
Annual.

★3285★ Federation of Analytical Chemistry and Spectroscopy Societies Convention
Federation of Analytical Chemistry and Spectroscopy Societies
13 N. Cliffe Dr.
Wilmington, DE 19809
Ph: (302)798-5161   Fax: (302)944-8837
Annual. **Dates and Locations:** 1995; Philadelphia, PA.

OTHER SOURCES OF INFORMATION

★3286★ "Chemist" in 100 Best Jobs for the 1990s & Beyond
Dearborn Financial Publishing, Inc.
520 N. Dearborn St.
Chicago, IL 60610-4354
Ph: (312)836-4400   Fax: (312)836-1021
Fr: 800-621-9621
Carol Kleiman. 1992. Describes 100 jobs ranging from accountants to veterinarians.

Each job profile includes such information as education, experience, and certification needed, salaries, and job search suggestions.

★3287★ "Chemist" in Career Selector 2001
Barron's Educational Series, Inc.
250 Wireless Blvd.
Hauppauge, NY 11788
Ph: (516)434-3311   Fax: (516)434-3723
Fr: 800-645-3476
James C. Gonyea. 1993.

★3288★ "Chemistry" in Accounting to Zoology: Graduate Fields Defined (p. 295)
Petersons Guides, Inc.
PO Box 2123
Princeton, NJ 08543-2123
Ph: (609)243-9111   Fax: (609)243-9150
Fr: 800-338-3282
Amy J. Goldstein, editor. Revised and updated, 1987. Defines 298 graduate and professional fields. Discusses types of graduate programs and degrees, graduate research, applied work, employment prospects, and trends.

★3289★ Salaries of Scientists, Engineers, and Technicians: A Summary of Salary Surveys
Commission on Professionals in Science and Technology (CPST)
1500 Massachusetts Ave., NW, Ste. 831
Washington, DC 20005
Ph: (202)223-6995
1993.

★3290★ The Skeptical Chemist
Kessinger Publishing Co.
PO Box 160
Kila, MT 59920-0160
Ph: (406)756-0167
Robert Boyle, editor. 1992.

Geologists and Geophysicists

Geologists and geophysicists study the physical aspects and history of the earth. They identify and examine rocks, conduct geological surveys, construct maps, and use instruments to measure the earth's gravity and magnetic field. They also analyze information collected through seismic prospecting, which involves bouncing sound waves off buried rock layers. Geoscientists play an increasingly important part in studying, preserving, and cleaning up the environment. Many monitor and design waste disposal sites, preserve water supplies, and locate safe sites for hazardous waste facilities, nuclear powerplants, and landfills. Many geologists search for oil, natural gas, minerals, and underground water. Geologists and geophysicists usually specialize. **Geological oceanographers** study and map the ocean floor. They collect information using remote sensing devices aboard surface ships or underwater research craft. **Physical oceanographers** study the physical aspects of oceans such as currents and the interaction of the sea's surface with the atmosphere. **Chemical oceanographers** study the chemical composition, dissolved elements, and nutrients of oceans. **Hydrologists** study the distribution, circulation, and physical properties of underground and surface waters. **Petroleum Geologists** explore for oil and gas by studying and mapping the subsurface of the ocean or land. **Mineralogists** analyze and classify minerals and precious stones according to composition and structure. **Paleontologists** study fossils found in geological formations to trace the evolution of plant and animal life and the geologic history of the earth. **Seismologists** interpret data from seismographs and other instruments to locate earthquakes and earthquake-related faults. **Stratigraphers** study the distribution and arrangement of sedimentary rock layers by examining their fossil and mineral content.

Salaries

Average salaries for geologists and geophysicists are as follows:

Geologists and geophysicists with a bachelor's degree	$25,704,/year
Geologists and geophysicists with a master's degree	$28,100/year
Geologists and geophysicists with a doctorate	$33,600/year
Geologists, federal government	$51,800/year
Geophysicists, federal government	$57,929/year
Hydrologists	$47,793/year
Oceanographers	$54,552/year

Employment Outlook

Growth rate until the year 2005: Average.

Geologists and Geophysicists

CAREER GUIDES

★3291★ Careers in Exploration Geophysics

Society of Exploration Geophysicists (SEG)
PO Box 702740
Tulsa, OK 74170-2740
Ph: (918)493-3516

Explores careers in geophysics, briefly describing the fields and education preparation.

★3292★ Careers in Geophysics. Solid Earth, Hydrologic, Oceanic, Atmospheric, and Space Sciences

American Geophysical Union (AGU)
2000 Florida Ave., NW
Washington, DC 20009
Ph: (202)462-6900

1993. Describes the geophysical disciplines, personal qualification needed for a career in geophysics, educational preparation, and employment oppportunities and outlook.

★3293★ Careers in Science

National Textbook Co. (NTC)
VGM Career Books
4255 W. Touhy Ave.
Lincolnwood, IL 60646-1975
Ph: (708)679-5500   Fax: (708)679-2494
Fr: 800-323-4900

Thomas A. Easton, editor. Explores careers in life science, physical science, social science, earth science, engineering, mathematics, and computer science.

★3294★ Future Employment Opportunities in the Geological Sciences

Geological Society of America (GSA)
3300 Penrose Pl.
PO Box 9140
Boulder, CO 80301
Ph: (303)447-2020   Fr: 800-472-1988

1991. Examines employment opportunities in the petroleum, mining, and consulting industries; in academia; and in federal, state, and local governments. Gives some tips on resume writing and interviewing.

★3295★ Geologist

Careers, Inc.
PO Box 135
Largo, FL 34649-0135
Ph: (813)584-7333

1993. Two-page occupational summary card describing duties, working conditions, personal qualifications, training, earnings and hours, employment outlook, places of employment, related careers, and where to write for more information.

★3296★ "Geologist", "Geophysicist", and "Oceanographer" in VGM's Careers Encyclopedia

National Textbook Co. (NTC)
VGM Career Books
4255 W. Touhy Ave.
Lincolnwood, IL 60646-1975
Ph: (708)679-5500   Fax: (708)679-2494
Fr: 800-323-4900

Norback, Craig T., editor. Third edition, 1991. Profiles 200 occupations. Describes job duties, places of employment, working conditions, qualifications, education and training, advancement potential, and salary for each occupation.

★3297★ "Geologist" in Guide to Federal Jobs (pp. 221)

Resource Directories
3361 Executive Pkwy., Ste. 302
Toledo, OH 43606
Ph: (419)536-5353   Fax: (419)536-7056
Fr: 800-274-8515

Rod W. Durgin, editor. Third edition, 1992. Contains information on finding and applying for federal jobs. Describes more than 200 professional and technical jobs for college graduates. Also includes chapters titled: "Geophysicist" (p. 215) and "Hydrologist" (p. 211). Covers the nature of the work, salary, and geographic location. Lists college majors preferred for that occupation. Section one describes the function and work of government agencies that hire the most significant number of college graduates.

★3298★ "Geologist" in Jobs Rated Almanac

World Almanac
1 International Blvd., Ste. 444
Mahwah, NJ 07495
Ph: (201)529-6900   Fax: (201)529-6901

Les Krantz. Second edition, 1992. Ranks 250 jobs by environment, salary, outlooks, physical demands, stress, security, travel opportunities, and extra perks. Includes jobs the editor feels are the most common, most interesting, and the most rapidly growing.

★3299★ "Geologist" in Jobs! What They Are—Where They Are—What They Pay!

Simon & Schuster, Inc.
Simon & Schuster Bldg.
1230 Avenue of the Americas
New York, NY 10020
Ph: (212)698-7000   Fr: 800-223-2348

Robert O. Snelling and Anne M. Snelling. Third revised edition, 1992. Includes chapters titled "Geophysicists" and "Oceanographers". Describes duties and responsibilities, earnings, employment opportunities, training, and qualifications.

★3300★ Geologists

Chronicle Guidance Publications, Inc.
66 Aurora St.
PO Box 1190
Moravia, NY 13118-1190
Ph: (315)497-0330   Fax: (315)497-3359
Fr: 800-622-7284

1993. Occupational brief describing the nature of the job, working conditions, hours and earnings, education and training, licensure, certification, unions, personal qualifications, social and psychological factors, location, employment outlook, entry methods, advancement, and related occupations.

★3301★ "Geologists" in American Almanac of Jobs and Salaries (p. 254)

Avon Books
1350 Avenue of the Americas
New York, NY 10019
Ph: (212)261-6800   Fr: 800-238-0658

John Wright, editor. Revised and updated, 1994-95. A comprehensive guide to the wages of hundreds of occupations in a wide variety of industries and organizations.

★3302★ "Geologists" in *Career Discovery Encyclopedia* **(Vol.3, pp. 60-61)**
J.G. Ferguson Publishing Co.
200 W. Madison St., Ste. 300
Chicago, IL 60606
Ph: (312)580-5480   Fax: (312)580-4948
Russell E. Primm, editor-in chief. 1993. This six volume set contains two-page articles for 504 occupations. Each article describes job duties, earnings, and educational and training requirements. The whole set is arranged alphabetically by job title. Designed for junior high and older students.

★3303★ "Geologists" in *Encyclopedia of Careers and Vocational Guidance* **(Vol.3, pp. 83-85)**
J.G. Ferguson Publishing Co.
200 W. Madison St., Ste. 300
Chicago, IL 60606
Ph: (312)580-5480   Fax: (312)580-4948
William E. Hopke, editor-in-chief. Ninth edition, 1993. Four-volume set that profiles 900 occupations and describes job trends in 74 industries. Includes career description, educational requirements, history of the job, methods of entry, advancement, employment outlook, earnings, conditions of work, social and psychological factors, and sources of further information.

★3304★ "Geologists and Geophysicists" in *Occupational Outlook Handbook*
U.S. Government Printing Office
Superintendent of Documents
Washington, DC 20402
Ph: (202)512-1800   Fax: (202)512-2250
Biennial; latest edition, 1994-95. Encyclopedia of careers describing about 250 occupations and comprising about 85 percent of all jobs in the economy. Occupations that require lengthy education or training are given the most attention. Each occupation's profile describes what the worker does on the job, working conditions, education and training requirements, advancement possibilities, job outlook, earnings, and sources of additional information.

★3305★ "Geology" in *College Majors and Careers: A Resource Guide to Effective Life Planning* **(pp. 65-66)**
Garrett Park Press
PO Box 1907
Garrett Park, MD 20896
Ph: (301)946-2553
Paul Phifer. Revised, 1993. Lists 60 college majors, with definitions; related occupations and leisure activities; skills, values, and personal attributesneeded; suggested readings; and a list of associations.

★3306★ *Geophysicist*
Careers, Inc.
PO Box 135
Largo, FL 34649-0135
Ph: (813)584-7333
1991. Four-page brief offering the definition, history, duties, working conditions, personal qualifications, educational requirements, earnings, hours, employment outlook, advancement, and careers related to this position.

★3307★ *Geophysicist*
Vocational Biographies, Inc.
PO Box 31
Sauk Centre, MN 56378-0031
Ph: (612)352-6516   Fax: (612)352-5546
Fr: 800-255-0752
1994. Four-page pamphlet containing a personal narrative about a worker's job, work likes and dislikes, career path from high school to the present. Education and training, the rewards and frustrations, and the effects of the job on the rest of the worker's life. The data file portion of this pamphlet gives a concise occupational summary, including work descriptions, working conditions, places of employment, personal characteristics, education and training, job outlook, and salary range.

★3308★ *Geophysicists*
Chronicle Guidance Publications, Inc.
66 Aurora St.
PO Box 1190
Moravia, NY 13118-1190
Ph: (315)497-0330   Fax: (315)497-3359
Fr: 800-622-7284
1993. Career brief describing the nature of the job, working conditions, hours and earnings, education and training, licensure, certification, unions, personal qualifications, social and psychological factors, location, employment outlook, entry methods, advancement, and related occupations.

★3309★ "Geophysicists" in *American Almanac of Jobs and Salaries* **(p. 257)**
Avon Books
1350 Avenue of the Americas
New York, NY 10019
Ph: (212)261-6800   Fr: 800-238-0658
John Wright, editor. Revised and updated, 1994-95. A comprehensive guide to the wages of hundreds of occupations in a wide variety of industries and organizations.

★3310★ "Geophysicists" in *Career Discovery Encyclopedia* **(Vol.3, pp. 62-63)**
J.G. Ferguson Publishing Co.
200 W. Madison St., Ste. 300
Chicago, IL 60606
Ph: (312)580-5480   Fax: (312)580-4948
Russell E. Primm, editor-in chief. 1993. This six volume set contains two-page articles for 504 occupations. Each article describes job duties, earnings, and educational and training requirements. The whole set is arranged alphabetically by job title. Designed for junior high and older students.

★3311★ "Geophysicists" in *Encyclopedia of Careers and Vocational Guidance* **(Vol.3, pp. 86-89)**
J.G. Ferguson Publishing Co.
200 W. Madison St., Ste. 300
Chicago, IL 60606
Ph: (312)580-5480   Fax: (312)580-4948
William E. Hopke, editor-in-chief. Ninth edition, 1993. Four-volume set that profiles 900 occupations and describes job trends in 74 industries. Includes career description, educational requirements, history of the job, methods of entry, advancement, employment outlook, earnings, conditions of work, social and psychological factors, and sources of further information.

★3312★ "Geophysicists" and "Geologists" in *Encyclopedia of Careers and Vocational Guidance*
J.G. Ferguson Publishing Co.
200 W. Madison St., Ste. 300
Chicago, IL 60606
Ph: (312)580-5480   Fax: (312)580-4948
William E. Hopke, editor-in-chief. Ninth edition, 1993. Four-volume set that profiles 900 occupations and describes job trends in 74 industries. Includes career description, educational requirements, history of the job, methods of entry, advancement, employment outlook, earnings, conditions of work, social and psychological factors, and sources of further information.

★3313★ *Geoscience Employment and Hiring Survey*
American Geological Institute (AGI)
c/o AGI Publications Center
PO Box 205
Annapolis Junction, MO 20701
Ph: (301)953-1744
Annual. Gives current and projected employment statistics and approximate starting salaries for graduates by degree level.

★3314★ *Hydrologists*
Chronicle Guidance Publications, Inc.
66 Aurora St.
PO Box 1190
Moravia, NY 13118-1190
Ph: (315)497-0330   Fax: (315)497-3359
Fr: 800-622-7284
1993. Career brief describing the nature of the job, working conditions, hours and earnings, education and training, licensure, certification, unions, personal qualifications, social and psychological factors, location, employment outlook, entry methods, advancement, and related occupations.

★3315★ *North American Survey of Geoscientists, U.S. Section: Summary: Survey Results and Forecast of Employment Trends*
American Geological Institute (AGI)
4220 King St.
Alexandria, VA 22302
Ph: (703)379-2480
Nick Claudy, editor. 1988. Profiles geoscientists in the United States and Canada. Each Profile includes information on employment, years of experience, annual income, occupational levels and objectives, educational background, and training.

★3316★ *Oceanographer*
Careers, Inc.
PO Box 135
Largo, FL 34649-0135
Ph: (813)584-7333
1992. Four-page brief offering the definition, history, duties, working conditions, personal qualifications, educational requirements, earnings, hours, employment outlook, advancement, and careers related to this position.

★3317★ *Oceanographer*
Chronicle Guidance Publications, Inc.
66 Aurora St.
PO Box 1190
Moravia, NY 13118-1190
Ph: (315)497-0330   Fax: (315)497-3359
Fr: 800-622-7284
1992. Career brief describing the nature of the job, working conditions, hours and earnings, education and training, licensure, certification, unions, personal qualifications, social and psychological factors, location, employment outlook, entry methods, advancement, and related occupations.

★3318★ "Oceanographer" in *Guide to Federal Jobs* (p. 222)
Resource Directories
3361 Executive Pkwy., Ste. 302
Toledo, OH 43606
Ph: (419)536-5353   Fax: (419)536-7056
Fr: 800-274-8515
Rod W. Durgin, editor. Third edition, 1992. Contains information on findin g and applying for federal jobs. Describes more than 200 professional and technical jobs for college graduates. Covers the nature of the work, salary, and geographic location. Lists college majors preferred for that occupation. Section one describes the function fand work of government agencies that hire the most significant number of college graduates.

★3319★ "Oceanographers" in *American Almanac of Jobs and Salaries* (pp.258)
Avon Books
1350 Avenue of the Americas
New York, NY 10019
Ph: (212)261-6800   Fr: 800-238-0658
John Wright, editor. Revised and updated, 1994-95. A comprehensive guide to the wages of hundreds of occupations in a wide variety of industries and organizations.

★3320★ "Oceanographers", "Geologists", and "Geophysicists" in *Career Information Center* (Vol.2)
Simon and Schuster
200 Old Tappan Rd.
Old Tappan, NJ 07675
Fax: 800-445-6991   Fr: 800-223-2348
Richard Lidz and Linda Perrin, editorial directors. Fifth edition, 1993. A multi-volume set that profiles over 600 occupations. Each occupational profile describes job duties, educational requirements, advancement possibilities, employment outlook, working conditions, earnings and benefits, and where to write for more information.

★3321★ "Oceanography" in *Opportunities in Marine and Maritime Careers* (pp. 19-27)
National Textbook Co. (NTC)
VGM Career Books
4255 W. Touhy Ave.
Lincolnwood, IL 60646-1975
Ph: (708)679-5500   Fax: (708)679-2494
Fr: 800-323-4900
Heitzmann, William Ray. 1988. Includes careers in cruise ships, oceanography, marine sciences, fishing, commercial diving, maritime transportation, shipbuilding, the Navy, and the Coast Guard. Describes job duties, training requirements, and how to get started. Lists schools.

★3322★ *Opportunities for Women in Science Careers*
National Textbook Co. (NTC)
VGM Career Books
4255 W. Touhy Ave.
Lincolnwood, IL 60646-1975
Ph: (708)679-5500   Fax: (708)679-2494
Fr: 800-323-4900
Alice Fins. 1979. Profiles women professionals in science careers such as biology, chemistry, geology, astronomy, physics, math, and others.

★3323★ *Paleontologist*
Careers, Inc.
PO Box 135
Largo, FL 34649-0135
Ph: (813)584-7333
1993. Two-page occupational summary card describing duties, working conditions, personal qualifications, training, earnings and hours, employment outlook, places of employment, related careers, and where to write for more information.

★3324★ *Peterson's Job Opportunities for Engineering and Technology*
Petersons Guides, Inc.
PO Box 2123
Princeton, NJ 08543-2123
Ph: (609)243-9111   Fax: (609)243-9150
Fr: 800-338-3282
1994. Gives job hunting advice including information on resume writing, interviewing, and handling salary negotiations. Lists companies that hire college graduates in science and engineering at the bachelor and master's level. Companies are indexed by industry, starting location, and major. Company profiles include contact information and types of hires.

★3325★ *Scientists, Earth*
Careers, Inc.
PO Box 135
Largo, FL 34649-0135
Ph: (813)584-7333
1991. Four-page brief describing duties, working conditions, personal qualifications, training, earnings and hours, employment outlook, places of employment, related careers, and where to write for more information.

★3326★ *Scientists, Physical*
Careers, Inc.
PO Box 135
Largo, FL 34649-0135
Ph: (813)584-7333
1994. Four-page brief describing duties, working conditions, personal qualifications, training, earnings and hours, employment outlook, places of employment, related careers, and where to write for more information.

★3327★ *Women Exploring the Earth*
Society of Exploration Geophysicists (SEG)
PO Box 702740
Tulsa, OK 74170-2740
Ph: (918)493-3516
1987. Profiles five women who have productive careers in geophysics.

PROFESSIONAL ASSOCIATIONS

★3328★ **American Geological Institute (AGI)**
4220 King St.
Alexandria, VA 22302
Ph: (703)379-2480   Fax: (703)379-7563
Members: Federation of national scientific and technical societies in the earth sciences. **Purpose:** Seeks to: stimulate public understanding of geological sciences; improve teaching of the geological sciences in schools, colleges, and universities; maintain high standards of professional training and conduct; work for the general welfare of members. Provides career guidance program. **Publications:** *Directory of GeoScience Departments*, annual. • *Geotimes*, monthly.

★3329★ **American Geophysical Union (AGU)**
2000 Florida Ave. NW
Washington, DC 20009
Ph: (202)462-6900   Fax: (202)328-0566
Fr: 800-966-AGU1
Members: Individuals professionally associated with the field of geophysics; associate membership is open to all others; supporting members are companies and other organizations whose work involves geophysics. **Purpose:** Promotes the study of problems concerned with the figure and physics of the earth; initiates and coordinates research that depends upon national and international cooperation and provides for scientific discussion of research results. Offers science and policy lecture series. Sponsors placement service at semiannual meeting. **Publications:** *Antarctic Research Series*. • *Coastal and Estuarine Sciences*, periodic. • *Directory of U.S. Ocean Scientists and Engineers*, periodic. • *Earth in Space*. • *EOS*, weekly. • *Geophysical Monograph Series*, periodic. • *Geophysical Research Letters*, monthly. • *Geotectonics*, bimonthly. • *Global Biogeochemical Cycles*, quarterly. • *Izvestiya, Atmospheric and Oceanic Physics*, monthly. • *Izvestiya, Physics of the Solid Earth*, monthly. • *Journal of Geophysical Research*. • *Maurice Ewing Volumes*, periodic. • *Oceanology*, bimonthly. • *Paleoceanography*, bimonthly. • *Planetology Papers*, monthly. • *Radio Science*, bimonthly. • *Reviews of Geophysics*, quarterly. • *Tectonics*, bimonthly. • *Water Resources Monograph Series*, periodic. • *Water Resources Research*, monthly.

★3330★ **Association of American State Geologists (AASG)**
Bureau of Topographic and Geologic Survey
PO Box 9453
Harrisburg, PA 17105-8453
Ph: (717)787-2169   Fax: (717)783-7267
Members: State geologists, or equivalent officials from each state, who direct and conduct research in geology and mineral resources (including ground water). **Purpose:** Stimulates exchange of scientific and administrative information; seeks to improve coordination of work with federal agencies and other state agencies. **Publications:** *The*

State Geological Surveys - A History. • *State Geologists Journal,* annual.

★3331★ Association of Engineering Geologists (AEG)
323 Boston Post Rd., Ste. 2D
Sudbury, MA 01776
Ph: (508)443-4639
Members: Graduate geologists and geological engineers; full members must have five years experience in the field of engineering geology. **Purpose:** Seeks to: provide a forum for the discussion and dissemination of technical and scientific information; encourage the advancement of professional recognition, scientific research, and high ethical and professional standards. Has compiled information on engineering geology curricula of colleges and universities. Promotes public understanding, health, safety and welfare, and acceptance of the engineering geology profession. Conducts technical sessions, symposia, abstracts, and short courses; cosponsors seminars and conferences with other professional and technical societies and organizations. **Publications:** *AEG Directory,* annual. • *AEG Newsletter,* quarterly.

★3332★ Geological Society of America (GSA)
3300 Penrose Pl.
PO Box 9140
Boulder, CO 80301-9140
Ph: (303)447-2020   Fax: (303)447-1133
Fr: 800-472-1988
Members: Professional society of geologists. Promotes the science of geology. **Purpose:** Maintains placement service. **Publications:** *Decade of North American Geology Series.* • *Engineering Geology Series.* • *Geological Society of America—Abstracts with Programs,* periodic. • *Geological Society of America—Bulletin,* monthly. • *Geology,* monthly. • *GSA Today,* monthly.

★3333★ Gungywamp Society (GS)
334 Brook St.
Noank, CT 06340
Ph: (203)536-2887
Members: Avocational archaeologists, anthropologists, historians, geologists, astronomers, and interested individuals. **Purpose:** Seeks to protect and preserve sites throughout the northeastern United States that show evidence of ancient and pre-Columbian cultures. Investigates and studies lithic features, architecture, artifacts, ancient inscriptions, and historic records. Has discovered an archaeological site in Connecticut that shows evidence of serial occupancy since 3000 B.C. Conducts tours through the Gungywamp Complex, an archaeological area preserved by the group. Sponsors educational and charitable programs. Maintains speakers' bureau. **Publications:** *The Greater Gungywamp: A Guide.* • *Stonewatch,* quarterly.

★3334★ Marine Technology Society (MTS)
1828 L St. NW, No. 906
Washington, DC 20036
Ph: (202)775-5966   Fax: (202)429-9417
Members: Scientists, engineers, educators, and others with professional interests in the marine sciences or related fields; includes institutional and corporate members. **Purpose:** Disseminates marine scientific and technical information, including institutional, environmental, physical, and biological aspects; fosters a deeper understanding of the world's seas and attendant technologies. Maintains 14 sections and 28 professional committees. Conducts tutorials. **Publications:** *Marine Technology Society Journal,* quarterly.

★3335★ National Association of Black Geologists and Geophysicists (NABGG)
PO Box 720157
Houston, TX 77272
Members: Black geologists and geophysicists. **Purpose:** Assists minority geologists and geophysicists in establishing professional and business relationships. Informs minority students of career opportunities in geology and geophysics. Seeks to motivate minority students to utilize existing programs, grants, and loans. Provides annual scholarships and oversees the educational careers of scholarship recipients. Assists minority students in their pursuit for summer employment and members interested in obtaining employees for summer positions. **Publications:** *Platform Network,* quarterly.

★3336★ Society of Exploration Geophysicists (SEG)
PO Box 702740
Tulsa, OK 74170
Ph: (918)493-3516   Fax: (918)493-2074
Members: Individuals having eight years of education and experience in exploration geophysics or geology. **Purpose:** Promotes the science of geophysics, especially as it applies to the exploration for petroleum and other minerals. Encourages high professional standards among members; supports the common interests of members. Maintains SEG Foundation, which receives contributions from companies and individuals and distributes them in the form of scholarships to students of geophysics and related subjects. Offers short continuing education courses to geophysicists and geologists. Maintains 37 committees including: Development and Production; Engineering and Groundwater Geophysics; Mining and Geothermal; Offshore Exploration and Oceanography. **Publications:** *Geophysics,* monthly. • *Geophysics: The Leading Edge of Exploration,* monthly. • *Roster,* annual.

STANDARDS/CERTIFICATION AGENCIES

★3337★ American Institute of Professional Geologists (AIPG)
7828 Vance Dr., Ste. 103
Arvada, CO 80003-2125
Ph: (303)431-0831   Fax: (303)431-1332
Provides certification to geologists attesting to their competence and integrity.

TEST GUIDES

★3338★ ACT Proficiency Examination Program: Physical Geology
National Learning Corp.
212 Michael Dr.
Syosset, NY 11791
Ph: (516)921-8888   Fax: (516)921-8743
Fr: 800-645-6337
Jack Rudman. A series of practice test guides containing multiple-choice examinations designed to demonstrate proficiency in the subject of geology.

★3339★ Career Examination Series: Geologist
National Learning Corp.
212 Michael Dr.
Syosset, NY 11791
Ph: (516)921-8888   Fax: (516)921-8743
Fr: 800-645-6337
Jack Rudman. A series of study guides with multiple-choice examination questions and solutions for trainees and professional geologists. Titles in the series include *Geophysicist; Hydrogeologist; Junior Geologist; Oceanographer; Senior Geologist.*

★3340★ Career Examination Series: Geologist/Geophysicist
National Learning Corp.
212 Michael Dr.
Syosset, NY 11791
Ph: (516)921-8888   Fax: (516)921-8743
Fr: 800-645-6337
Jack Rudman. Test guide including questions and answers for students or professionals in the field who seek advancement through examination.

★3341★ Career Examination Series: Junior Geologist
National Learning Corp.
212 Michael Dr.
Syosset, NY 11791
Ph: (516)921-8888   Fax: (516)921-8743
Fr: 800-645-6337
Jack Rudman. Test guide including questions and answers for students or professionals in the field who seek advancement through examination.

★3342★ Career Examination Series: Senior Geologist
National Learning Corp.
212 Michael Dr.
Syosset, NY 11791
Ph: (516)921-8888   Fax: (516)921-8743
Fr: 800-645-6337
Jack Rudman. Test guide including questions and answers for students or professionals in the field who seek advancement through examination.

★3343★ College-Level Examination Series: Geology
National Learning Corp.
212 Michael Dr.
Syosset, NY 11791
Ph: (516)921-8888   Fax: (516)921-8743
Fr: 800-645-6337
Jack Rudman. A sample test that parallels those administered in the College-Level Ex-

amination Program which grants college credit for knowledge acquired outside the college classroom. Multiple-choice format; contains answers.

★3344★ *Dantes Subject Standardized Tests: Geology*
National Learning Corp.
212 Michael Dr.
Syosset, NY 11791
Ph: (516)921-8888   Fax: (516)921-8743
Fr: 800-645-6337

Jack Rudman. Multiple-choice graduate- and college-level examination given by graduate schools, colleges and the Armed Forces as a final examination for course evaluation. Includes answers. Titles in the series include *General Geophysics; Physical Science.*

★3345★ *Geology*
National Learning Corp.
212 Michael Dr.
Syosset, NY 11791
Ph: (516)921-8888   Fax: (516)921-8743
Fr: 800-645-6337

Jack Rudman. Part of the Test Your Knowledge Series. Contains multiple choice questions with answers.

★3346★ *Graduate Record Examination: Geology*
National Learning Corp.
212 Michael Dr.
Syosset, NY 11791
Ph: (516)921-8888   Fax: (516)921-8743
Fr: 800-645-6337

Jack Rudman. Multiple-choice test for those seeking admission to graduate school for study in the field of geology. Includes solutions to examination questions.

★3347★ *Regents College Proficiency Examination Series: Geology*
National Learning Corp.
212 Michael Dr.
Syosset, NY 11791
Ph: (516)921-8888   Fax: (516)921-8743
Fr: 800-645-6337

Jack Rudman. Multiple-choice preparatory examinations for professional geologists and geophysicists considering college credit-by-examination programs as an alternative to college course matriculation. Includes solutions to sample test questions. Titles in the series include *Earth Science; Geology.*

★3348★ *Undergraduate Program Field Test: Geology*
National Learning Corp.
212 Michael Dr.
Syosset, NY 11791
Ph: (516)921-8888   Fax: (516)921-8743
Fr: 800-645-6337

Jack Rudman. A practice examination fashioned after tests given in the Regents External Degree Program. Designed to measure knowledge received outside the college classroom in the subject of geology. Contains multiple-choice questions; provides solutions.

EDUCATIONAL DIRECTORIES AND PROGRAMS

★3349★ *Environmental Career Directory*
Gale Research Inc.
835 Penobscot Bldg.
Detroit, MI 48226-4094
Ph: (313)961-2242   Fax: (313)961-6083
Fr: 800-877-GALE

Bradley J. Morgan and Joseph M. Palmisano. 1993. A directory in the Career Advisor Series that provides essays written by industry professionals; job search information on resume and cover letter preparation, networking, and the interviewing process; approximately 300 companies and organizations offering job opportunities and internships, and additional job-hunting resources.

★3350★ *Physical Science Career Directory*
Gale Research Inc.
835 Penobscot Bldg.
Detroit, MI 48226-4094
Ph: (313)961-2242   Fax: (313)961-6083
Fr: 800-877-GALE
Bradley J. Morgan, Contact

First edition March 1994. Covers over 210 chemical companies, testing and research laboratories, and consulting firms in the U.S. offering entry-level positions and internships; sources of help-wanted ads, professional associations, producers of videos, databases, career guides, and professional guides and handbooks. Entries include: For companies—Name, address, phone, fax, business description, research activities, names and titles of key personnel, number of employees, average number of entry-level positions available, human resources contact, description of internship opportunities including contact, type and number available, application procedures, qualifications, and duties. For others—Name or title, address, phone, description. Paperback edition Arrangement: Companies are alphabetical; others are classified by type of resource.

★3351★ *SME Guide to Minerals Schools*
Society for Mining, Metallurgy, and Exploration Inc. (SME)
PO Box 625002
Littleton, CO 80162-5002
Ph: (303)973-9550   Fax: (303)973-3845
Annual, January. Covers over 50 educational institutions offering programs in geological, geophysical, metallurgical, mineral processing, and mining engineering along with mining engineering technology. Entries include: Institution name; program title; department name, address, phone, fax, electronic mail code; references for admissions information; names and titles of program administrators; name, title, highest degree earned, and teaching specialty for faculty members; enrollment statistics by level and year; degrees offered and special requirements; number of degrees conferred by level and year; contact, address, and phone for job placement assistance. Arrangement: Classified by program area.

AWARDS, SCHOLARSHIPS, GRANTS, AND FELLOWSHIPS

★3352★ **William Bowie Medal**
American Geophysical Union
2000 Florida Ave. NW
Washington, DC 20009
Ph: (202)462-6900   Fax: (202)328-0566

For recognition of outstanding contributions to fundamental geophysics and for unselfish cooperation in research. A medal is awarded annually. Established in 1939.

★3353★ **Walter H. Bucher Medal**
American Geophysical Union
2000 Florida Ave. NW
Washington, DC 20009
Ph: (202)462-6900   Fax: (202)328-0566

For recognition of original contributions to the basic knowledge of the earth's crust. A medal is awarded biennially in odd-numbered years. Established in 1968.

★3354★ **Gilbert H. Cady Award**
Geological Society of America
3300 Penrose Pl.
PO Box 9140
Boulder, CO 80301
Ph: (303)447-2020   Fax: (303)447-1133

To honor contribution that advance the field of coal geology in North America. Contributions by workers outside North America deemed to advance coal geology in North America may also be considered. The deadline for receipt of nominations is February 1. A silver tray and a certificate are awarded annually when merited. Established in 1971. Sponsored by the Coal Geology Division.

★3355★ **Arthur L. Day Medal**
Geological Society of America
3300 Penrose Pl.
PO Box 9140
Boulder, CO 80301
Ph: (303)447-2020   Fax: (303)447-1133

To recognize outstanding distinction in contributions to geologic knowledge through the application of physics and chemistry and to inspire further efforts in the field. The deadline for receipt of nominations is February 1. A gold medal, a bronze replica, and the remission of society dues for life are awarded annually when merited. Established in 1948.

★3356★ **Maurice Ewing Medal**
American Geophysical Union
2000 Florida Ave. NW
Washington, DC 20009
Ph: (202)462-6900   Fax: (202)328-0566

For recognition of significant original contributions to understanding physical, geophysical, and geological processes in the ocean; significant original contributions to scientific ocean engineering, technology, and instrumentation; and/or outstanding service to marine sciences. A medal is awarded annually. Established in 1976. Co-sponsored by the United States Navy.

★3357★ Arnold Guyot Memorial Award
National Geographic Society
1600 M St. NW
Washington, DC 20036
Ph: (202)857-7000   Fax: (202)775-6141

To recognize outstanding scientific investigations in geology or paleontology. Awarded irregularly. Established in 1968.

**★3358★ Michel T. Halbouty Human
Needs Award**
American Association of Petroleum
   Geologists
PO Box 979
Tulsa, OK 74101
Ph: (918)584-2555   Fax: (918)584-0469

To recognize an individual(s) for the most outstanding application of geology to the benefit of human needs and to recognize scientific excellence. Two silver medals mounted on a plaque are awarded annually. Established in 1972. Renamed in 1988.

★3359★ Honorary Member
Society of Exploration Geophysicists
Box 702740
Tulsa, OK 74170-2740
Ph: (918)493-3516   Fax: (918)493-2074

To recognize a distinguished contribution to exploration geophysics or a related field, or to the advancement of the profession of exploration geophysics through service to the Society. Awarded when merited.

★3360★ Virgil Kauffman Gold Medal
Society of Exploration Geophysicists
Box 702740
Tulsa, OK 74170-2740
Ph: (918)493-3516   Fax: (918)493-2074

To recognize outstanding contributions of a technical or professional nature to the advancement of the science of geophysical exploration, as manifested during the previous five years. Awarded annually.

★3361★ James Furman Kemp Award
Columbia University
Office of the Pres.
202 Low Memorial Library
New York, NY 10027
Ph: (212)854-5017

To recognize distinguished public service in geology. A gold medal is awarded at infrequent intervals by the Department of Geology of the University. Established in 1948.

★3362★ Ben H. Parker Memorial Medal
American Institute of Professional
   Geologists
7828 Vance Dr., Ste. 103
Arvada, CO 80003
Ph: (303)431-0831   Fax: (303)431-1332

This, the Institute's most distinguished award, is given to recognize outstanding service to the profession of geology. Consideration of an individual for this medal should emphasize a continual record of contribution to the profession of geology. A wide variety of contributions can be considered, such as the education and training of geologists; professional development of geologists; service to the institute; leadership in the surveillance of laws, rules, and regulations affecting geology, geologists, and the public; and activity in local and regional affairs of geologists. Publication and scientific achievement are not a requisite for

consideration. A bronze medal mounted on a marble base is awarded annually at the annual meeting. Established in 1969.

★3363★ Penrose Medal Award
Geological Society of America
3300 Penrose Pl.
PO Box 9140
Boulder, CO 80301
Ph: (303)447-2020   Fax: (303)447-1133

To recognize eminent research in pure geology and outstanding original contributions or achievements which mark a decided advance in the science of geology. The deadline for receipt of nominations is February 1. A gold medal, a bronze replica, and the remission of Society dues for life are awarded annually when merited. Established in 1927.

**★3364★ Rip Rapp Archaeological
Geology Award**
Geological Society of America
3300 Penrose Pl.
PO Box 9140
Boulder, CO 80301
Ph: (303)447-2020   Fax: (303)447-1133

To recognize an individual who has contributed in an outstanding manner to the interdisciplinary field of archaeological geology. The recipient of the award need not be a member of the Geological Society of America nor a citizen of the United States. The deadline for receipt of nominations is February 15. An engrossed certificate and a small pewter Revere bowl are awarded annually when merited. Renamed in 1993. Established in 1982. Sponsored by the Archaeological Geology Division.

**★3365★ Rocky Mountain Coal Mining
Institute Scholarships**
Rocky Mountain Coal Mining Institute
   (RMCMI)
3000 Youngfield, No. 324
Lakewood, CO 80215
Ph: (303)238-9099   Fax: (303)238-0509

Purpose: To assist students who have chosen a career in the mining industry. Qualifications: Candidates must be sophomores in good academic standing, U.S. citizens and residents of one of the member states (Arizona, Colorado, Montana, North Dakota, New Mexico, Texas, Utah, and Wyoming), pursuing a degree in a mining-related field or in engineering disciplines such as geology or mineral processing and metallurgy, and have expressed an interest in western coal as a possible career. Selection criteria: Completed application and personal interview. Funds available: Sixteen students from the Institute's eight member states receive $750 annually. Application details: The RMCMI Scholarship Chairman contacts the various colleges and universities in the member states and request nominations from students and each dean of the mining department. The chairman and the RMCMI state vice president interview the various nominees. The scholarship is presented at the end of the recipient's sophomore year and renewed, upon recommendation from the dean of the college or university involved, at the close of the recipient's junior year. Deadline: February 1.

★3366★ Frank H. Spedding Award
Rare Earth Research Conference
c/o F.S. Richardson
Chemistry Department
University of Virginia
Charlottesville, VA 22901
Ph: (804)924-3905

To recognize excellence in contributions to the science and technology of rare earth materials. Nominations of those engaged in rare earth research are accepted. A plaque and travel expenses to the conference are awarded biennially. Established in 1979.

★3367★ Mary Clark Thompson Medal
National Academy of Sciences
2101 Constitution Ave. NW
Washington, DC 20418
Ph: (202)334-2444

To recognize outstanding services to geology and paleontology. Preference is given to American scholars. A monetary prize of $7,500 and a medal are presented every three to five years. Established in 1919.

★3368★ WAAIME Scholarship Loans
American Institute of Mining, Metallurgical
   and Petroleum Engineers, Inc. (WAAIME)
Woman's Auxiliary
345 E. 47th St., 14th Fl.
New York, NY 10017

Qualifications: Applicants must be undergraduate students studying for a degree at an accredited United States engineering school in engineering science as applied to industries within the mineral field. These include mining, geology, metallurgy, petroleum, mineral science, materials science, mining economics and other related fields that further the interests of the mineral industry. Scholarship loans also are available for graduate students on the same terms as for undergraduates. These cannot be given to students who have also had an undergraduate grant from WAAIME unless that loan has been repaid. Graduate scholarship loans are limited to two years. Selection criteria: Each applicant is considered on an individual basis by a local Section Scholarship Loan Fund Chairman through personal interviews and research of academic standing, character, need, and personality, and then by the National Scholarship Loan Fund Committee. Preference is given to college juniors and seniors. Funds available: The amount of the scholarship loans is individually determined. Each recipient is expected to repay 50 percent of the monies loaned without interest. Repayment starts after graduation and is to be completed within six years. Application details: Applications should not be sent before the interview. Applications must be accompanied by recent grade transcripts, supporting letters including the personal evaluation by the Section Scholarship Loan Fund Chairman. Deadline: All application material must be in the hands of the Chairman of the National Scholarship Loan Fund Committee by March 15.

★3369★ G. K. Warren Prize
National Academy of Sciences
2101 Constitution Ave. NW
Washington, DC 20418
Ph: (202)334-2444

To recognize noteworthy and distinguished accomplishment in any field of science coming within the scope of the Academy, preferably for fluviatile geology. Individuals of noteworthy and distinguished accomplishment are eligible. A monetary prize of $6,000 is awarded approximately every four years. Established in 1961 by Emily B. Warren in memory of her father.

BASIC REFERENCE GUIDES AND HANDBOOKS

★3370★ The Encyclopedia of Field and General Geology
Van Nostrand Reinhold Co., Inc.
115 5th Ave.
New York, NY 10003
Ph: (212)254-3232   Fr: 800-842-3636

Charles W. Finkl, editor. 1988. Contains information for practicing field geologists.

★3371★ The Facts on File Dictionary of Geology and Geophysics
Facts on File
460 Park Ave. S.
New York, NY 10016-7382
Ph: (212)683-2244   Fax: 800-678-3633
Fr: 800-322-8755

Dorothy F. Lapidus. 1988. Illustrated.

★3372★ The Field Guide to Geology
Facts on File
460 Park Ave. S.
New York, NY 10016-7382
Ph: (212)683-2244   Fax: 800-678-3633
Fr: 800-322-8755

David Lambert and Diagram Group staff. 1989. Contains articles on all aspects of geology. Includes diagrams, charts, maps, and photographs.

★3373★ Glossary of Geology
American Geological Institute (AGI)
4220 King St.
Alexandria, VA 22302
Ph: (703)379-2480

Robert L. Bates and Julia A. Jackson, editors. Third edition, 1988. Defines 36,000 geoscience terms including more than 4,000 mineral names.

★3374★ Hydrothermal Mineral Deposits: Principles and Fundamental Concepts for the Exploration Geologist
Springer-Verlag New York, Inc.
175 5th Ave., 19th Fl.
New York, NY 10010
Ph: (212)460-1500

F. Pirajno, editor. 1992.

★3375★ McGraw-Hill Encyclopedia of the Geological Sciences
McGraw-Hill, Inc.
1221 Avenue of the Americas
New York, NY 10020
Ph: (212)512-2000   Fr: 800-722-4726

Sybil P. Parker, editor in chief. Second edition, 1988. Contains 520 articles covering the geological sciences, and essential materials, processes, compositions, and physical characteristics of the solid part of the earth.

★3376★ The Practical Geologist
Simon & Schuster, Inc.
Simon & Schuster Bldg.
1230 Avenue of the Americas
New York, NY 10020
Ph: (212)698-7000

Dougal Dixon, editor. 1992.

PROFESSIONAL AND TRADE PERIODICALS

★3377★ Archaeological Prospection
John Wiley and Sons, Inc.
Subscription Dept.
605 3rd Ave.
New York, NY 10158
Ph: (212)850-6000   Fax: (212)850-6799
A.M. Pollard

Quarterly. Journal with articles relating to archaeological prospection techniques, including geophysical and geochemical methods, and underlying geology.

★3378★ Consortium for Continental Reflection Profiling—Newsletter
Consortium for Continental Reflection Profiling (COCORP)
c/o L. Brown
Ithaca, NY 14853
Ph: (607)255-3474   Fax: (607)254-4780
L. Brown

Periodic. Carries technical information concerning the Consortium's seismic reflection surveys. Contains abstracts of papers based on COCORP profiling as well as maps of the areas being studied and COCORP lines in these areas. Also mentions symposia of interest and provides notices of display prints and tapes available.

★3379★ Geological Journal
John Wiley and Sons, Inc.
Subscription Dept.
605 3rd Ave.
New York, NY 10158
Ph: (212)850-6000   Fax: (212)850-6799
A.E. Adams

Quarterly. Journal of interdisciplinary earth science containing research papers and articles on current topics.

★3380★ The Geological Newsletter
Geological Society of the Oregon Country
PO Box 907
Portland, OR 97207-0709
Ph: (503)284-4320
Donald Barr

Monthly. Disseminates news concerning geology and the earth sciences. Recurring features include reports on lectures, field trips, and activities of the Society, news of members, news of research, and a calendar of events.

★3381★ Geological Society of America Bulletin
Geological Society of America
PO Box 9140
Boulder, CO 80301
Ph: (303)447-2020   Fax: (303)447-1133
Jean Thyfault

Monthly. Geology journal.

★3382★ Geology
Geological Society of America
PO Box 9140
Boulder, CO 80301
Ph: (303)447-2020   Fax: (303)447-1133
Ann H. Crawford

Monthly. Geology journal.

★3383★ Geotimes
American Geological Institute
4220 King St.
Alexandria, VA 22302-1507
Ph: (703)379-2480   Fax: (703)379-7563
Julia A. Jackson

Monthly. Magazine for geology and geophysics professionals.

★3384★ IAMG News Letter
International Association for Mathematical Geology (IAMG)
c/o James R. Carr
Geological Sciences, MS172
University of Nevada
Reno, NV 89557
Ph: (702)784-4244   Fax: (702)784-1766
James R. Carr

Semiannual. Focuses on the applications of mathematics and statistics to the earth and planetary sciences. Provides information on computer applications, listings of job opportunities in geoscience, news of research, and news of coming events.

★3385★ International Journal for Numerical and Analytical Methods in Geomechanics
John Wiley and Sons, Inc.
Subscription Dept.
605 3rd Ave.
New York, NY 10158
Ph: (212)850-6000   Fax: (212)850-6799
C.S. Desai

Monthly. Journal covering on geomechanics. Topics include soil and rock mechanics, structure and foundation mechanics, earth structure interaction, geothermal energy, and ice mechanics.

★3386★ The Journal of Geology
University of Chicago Press
5720 S. Woodlawn Ave.
Chicago, IL 60637
Ph: (312)702-7600   Fax: (312)702-0172
Alfred T. Anderson

Bimonthly. Journal presenting original contributions on all aspects of earth sciences from geochemistry and geophysics to paleontology and related space sciences.

★3387★ Ocean Technology & Engineering: An Abstract Newsletter
National Technical Information Service (NTIS)
5285 Port Royal Rd.
Springfield, MO 22161
Ph: (703)487-4630

Biweekly. Carries abstracts from publications concerned with marine engineering, dynamic oceanography, physical and chemical oceanography, biological oceanography, marine geophysics and geology, hydrography, and underwater construction and habitats.

★3388★ Oil & Gas Journal
PennWell Publishing Co.
3050 Post Oak Blvd., Ste. 200
Houston, TX 77056
Ph: (713)621-9720   Fax: (713)963-6285
John L. Kennedy

Weekly. Trade magazine serving engineers and managers in international petroleum operations.

PROFESSIONAL MEETINGS AND CONVENTIONS

★3389★ Geological Society of America Annual Meeting and GeoScience Expo
Geological Society of America
3300 Penrose Pl.
PO Box 9140
Boulder, CO 80301
Ph: (303)447-2020   Fax: (303)447-0648
Fr: 800-472-1988

Annual. **Dates and Locations:** 1995 Nov 06-; New Orleans, LA. ● 1996 Oct 28-31; Denver, CO. ● 1997 Oct 27-30; Salt Lake City, UT.

★3390★ Society of Exploration Geophysicists Annual International Meeting and Exposition
Society of Exploration Geophysicists
PO Box 702740
Tulsa, OK 74170
Ph: (918)493-3516   Fax: (918)493-2074

Annual. **Dates and Locations:** 1996 Nov 05-09; Denver, CO.

OTHER SOURCES OF INFORMATION

★3391★ "Geologist" in Career Selector 2001
Barron's Educational Series, Inc.
250 Wireless Blvd.
Hauppauge, NY 11788
Ph: (516)434-3311   Fax: (516)434-3723
Fr: 800-645-3476
James C. Gonyea. 1993.

★3392★ "Geology" in Accounting to Zoology: Graduate Fields Defined
Petersons Guides, Inc.
PO Box 2123
Princeton, NJ 08543-2123
Ph: (609)243-9111   Fax: (609)243-9150
Fr: 800-338-3282

Amy J. Goldstein, editor. Revised and updated, 1987. Defines 298 graduate and professional fields. Discusses types of graduate programs and degrees, graduate research, applied work, employment prospects, and trends. Chapters include "Geophysics" (pp. 300-301), and "Marine Sciences/Oceanography" (pp. 303-304).

★3393★ Salaries of Scientists, Engineers, and Technicians: A Summary of Salary Surveys
Commission on Professionals in Science and Technology (CPST)
1500 Massachusetts Ave., NW, Ste. 831
Washington, DC 20005
Ph: (202)223-6995
1993.

Meteorologists

Meteorology is the study of the atmosphere, the air that surrounds the earth. **Meteorologists** study the atmosphere's physical characteristics, motions, and processes, and the way the atmosphere affects the rest of our environment. The best-known application of this knowledge is in forecasting the weather. However, weather information and meteorological research are also applied in air-pollution control, agriculture, air and sea transportation, defense, and the study of trends in the earth's climate such as global warming or ozone depletion. Meteorologists who forecast the weather, known professionally as **operational meteorologists**, are the largest group of specialists. They study information on air pressure, temperature, humidity, and wind velocity, and apply physical and mathematical relationships to make short- and long-range forecasts. **Physical meteorologists** study the atmosphere's chemical and physical properties, the transmission of light, sound, and radio waves, and the transfer of energy in the atmosphere. They also study factors affecting formation of clouds, rain, snow, and other weather phenomena. **Climatologists** analyze past records of wind, rainfall, sunshine, and temperature in specific areas or regions. Their studies are used to plan heating and cooling systems, design buildings, and aid in effective land utilization.

Salaries

Average starting salaries for meteorologists employed by the federal government vary according to educational background.

Meteorologist, bachelor's degree	$18,340-$22,717/year
Meteorologist, master's degree	$22,717-$27,790/year
Meteorologist, doctorate	$33,623-$40-299/year

Employment Outlook

Growth rate until the year 2005: Average.

Meteorologists

CAREER GUIDES

★3394★ *Broadcast Meteorologist*
Vocational Biographies, Inc.
PO Box 31
Sauk Centre, MN 56378-0031
Ph: (612)352-6516   Fax: (612)352-5546
Fr: 800-255-0752

1992. Four-page pamphlet containing a personal narrative about a worker's job, work likes and dislikes, career path from high school to the present. Education and training, the rewards and frustrations, and the effects of the job on the rest of the worker's life. The data file portion of this pamphlet gives a concise occupational summary, including work descriptions, working conditions, places of employment, personal characteristics, education and training, job outlook, and salary range.

★3395★ *Careers in Science*
National Textbook Co. (NTC)
VGM Career Books
4255 W. Touhy Ave.
Lincolnwood, IL 60646-1975
Ph: (708)679-5500   Fax: (708)679-2494
Fr: 800-323-4900

Thomas A. Easton, editor. Explores careers in life science, physical science, social science, earth science, engineering, mathematics, and computer science.

★3396★ *Meteorologist*
Careers, Inc.
PO Box 135
Largo, FL 34649-0135
Ph: (813)584-7333

1995. Two-page occupational summary card describing duties, working conditions, personal qualifications, training, earnings and hours, employment outlook, places of employment, related careers, and where to write for more information.

★3397★ "Meteorologist" in *100 Best Careers for the Year 2000* (pp. 247-249)
Arco Pub.
201 W. 103rd St.
Indianapolis, IN 46290
Ph: 800-428-5331   Fax: 800-835-3202

Shelly Field. 1992. Describes 100 job opportunities expected to grow fast throughout the next decade. Provides information on job duties and responsibilities, training requirements, education, advancement opportunities, experience and qualifications, and typical salaries.

★3398★ "Meteorologist" in *Guide to Federal Jobs* (p. 220)
Resource Directories
3361 Executive Pkwy., Ste. 302
Toledo, OH 43606
Ph: (419)536-5353   Fax: (419)536-7056
Fr: 800-274-8515

Rod W. Durgin, editor. Third edition, 1992. Contains information on finding and applying for federal jobs. Describes more than 200 professional and technical jobs for college graduates. Covers the nature of the work, salary, and geographic location. Lists college majors preferred for that occupation. Section one describes the function and work of government agencies that hire the most significant number of college graduates.

★3399★ "Meteorologist" in *Jobs Rated Almanac*
World Almanac
1 International Blvd., Ste. 444
Mahwah, NJ 07495
Ph: (201)529-6900   Fax: (201)529-6901

Les Krantz. Second edition, 1992. Ranks 250 jobs by environment, salary, outlooks, physical demands, stress, security, travel opportunities, and extra perks. Includes jobs the editor feels are the most common, most interesting, and the most rapidly growing.

★3400★ "Meteorologist" in *VGM's Careers Encyclopedia* (pp. 284-285)
National Textbook Co. (NTC)
VGM Career Books
4255 W. Touhy Ave.
Lincolnwood, IL 60646-1975
Ph: (708)679-5500   Fax: (708)679-2494
Fr: 800-323-4900

Third edition, 1991. Profiles 200 occupations. Describes job duties, places of employment,

working conditions, qualifications, education and training, advancement potential, and salary for each occupation.

★3401★ *Meteorologists*
Chronicle Guidance Publications, Inc.
66 Aurora St.
PO Box 1190
Moravia, NY 13118-1190
Ph: (315)497-0330   Fax: (315)497-3359
Fr: 800-622-7284

1992. Career brief describing the nature of the job, working conditions, hours and earnings, education and training, licensure, certification, unions, personal qualifications, social and psychological factors, location, employment outlook, entry methods, advancement, and related occupations.

★3402★ "Meteorologists" in *101 Careers: A Guide to the Fastest-Growing Opportunities* (pp. 114-116)
John Wiley & Sons, Inc.
605 3rd Ave.
New York, NY 10158-0012
Ph: (212)850-6645   Fax: (212)850-6088

Michael Harkavy. 1990. Describes the nature of the job, working conditions, employment growth, qualifications, personal skills, projected salaries, and where to write for more information.

★3403★ "Meteorologists" in *American Almanac of Jobs and Salaries* (pp. 258)
Avon Books
1350 Avenue of the Americas
New York, NY 10019
Ph: (212)261-6800   Fr: 800-238-0658

John Wright, editor. Revised and updated, 1994-95. A comprehensive guide to the wages of hundreds of occupations in a wide variety of industries and organizations.

★3404★ "Meteorologists" in *Career Discovery Encyclopedia* (Vol.4, pp. 86-87)
J.G. Ferguson Publishing Co.
200 W. Madison St., Ste. 300
Chicago, IL 60606
Ph: (312)580-5480   Fax: (312)580-4948

Russell E. Primm, editor-in chief. 1993. This six volume set contains two-page articles for 504 occupations. Each article describes job duties, earnings, and educational and training requirements. The whole set is arranged al-

phabetically by job title. Designed for junior high and older students.

★3405★ "Meteorologists" in *Career Information Center* (Vol.2)
Simon and Schuster
200 Old Tappan Rd.
Old Tappan, NJ 07675
Fax: 800-445-6991   Fr: 800-223-2348
Richard Lidz and Linda Perrin, editorial directors. Fifth edition, 1993. A multi-volume set that profiles over 600 occupations. Each occupational profile describes job duties, educational requirements, advancement possibilities, employment outlook, working conditions, earnings and benefits, and where to write for more information.

★3406★ "Meteorologists" in *Encyclopedia of Careers and Vocational Guidance* (Vol.3, pp. 439-441)
J.G. Ferguson Publishing Co.
200 W. Madison St., Ste. 300
Chicago, IL 60606
Ph: (312)580-5480   Fax: (312)580-4948
William E. Hopke, editor-in-chief. Ninth edition, 1993. Four-volume set that profiles 900 occupations and describes job trends in 74 industries. Includes career description, educational requirements, history of the job, methods of entry, advancement, employment outlook, earnings, conditions of work, social and psychological factors, and sources of further information.

★3407★ "Meteorologists" in *Jobs! What They Are—Where They Are—What They Pay* (p. 312)
Simon & Schuster, Inc.
Simon & Schuster Bldg.
1230 Avenue of the Americas
New York, NY 10020
Ph: (212)698-7000   Fr: 800-223-2348
Robert O. Snelling and Anne M. Snelling. 3rd edition, 1992. Describes duties and responsibilities, earnings, employment opportunities, training, and qualifications.

★3408★ "Meteorologists" in *Occupational Outlook Handbook*
U.S. Government Printing Office
Superintendent of Documents
Washington, DC 20402
Ph: (202)512-1800   Fax: (202)512-2250
Biennial; latest edition, 1994-95. Encyclopedia of careers describing about 250 occupations and comprising about 85 percent of all jobs in the ecomony. Occupations that require lengthy education or training are given the most attention.Each occupation's profile describes what the worker does on the job, working conditions, education and training requirements, advancement possibilities, job outlook, earnings, and sources of additional information.

★3409★ *Peterson's Job Opportunities for Engineering and Technology*
Petersons Guides, Inc.
PO Box 2123
Princeton, NJ 08543-2123
Ph: (609)243-9111   Fax: (609)243-9150
Fr: 800-338-3282
1994. Gives job hunting advice including information on resume writing, interviewing, and handling salary negotiations. Lists companies that hire college graduates in science and engineering at the bachelor and master's level. Companies are indexed by industry, starting location, and major. Company profiles include contact information and types of hires.

★3410★ *Scientists, Physical*
Careers, Inc.
PO Box 135
Largo, FL 34649-0135
Ph: (813)584-7333
1994. Four-page brief describing duties, working conditions, personal qualifications, training, earnings and hours, employment outlook, places of employment, related careers, and where to write for more information.

PROFESSIONAL ASSOCIATIONS

★3411★ **American Meteorological Society (AMS)**
45 Beacon St.
Boston, MA 02108
Ph: (617)227-2425   Fax: (617)742-8718
Members: Professional meteorologists, oceanographers, and hydrologists; interested students and nonprofessionals. **Purpose:** Develops and disseminates information on the atmospheric and related oceanic and hydrospheric sciences; seeks to advance professional applications. Activities include guidance service, scholarship programs, career information, certification of consulting meteorologists, and a seal of approval program to recognize competence in radio and television weathercasting. Issues statements of policy to assist public understanding on subjects such as weather modification, forecasting, tornadoes, hurricanes, flash floods, and meteorological satellites. Provides abstracting services. Has prepared educational films, filmstrips, and slides for a new curriculum in meteorology at the ninth grade level. Issues monthly announcements of job openings for meteorologists. **Publications:** *AMS Newsletter*, periodic. • *Bulletin of the American Meteorological Society*, monthly. • *Journal of Applied Meteorology*, monthly. • *Journal of Atmospheric and Oceanic Technology*, bimonthly. • *Journal of Climate*, monthly. • *Journal of Physical Oceanography*, monthly. • *Journal of the Atmospheric Sciences*, semimonthly. • *Meteorological and Geoastrophysical Abstracts*, monthly. • *Monthly Weather Review*. • *Weather and Forecasting*, quarterly.

STANDARDS/CERTIFICATION AGENCIES

★3412★ **American Meteorological Society (AMS)**
45 Beacon St.
Boston, MA 02108
Ph: (617)227-2425   Fax: (617)742-8718
Activities include guidance service, scholarship programs, career information, certification of consulting meteorologists, and a seal of approval program to recognize competence in radio and television weathercasting.

TEST GUIDES

★3413★ *Career Examination Series: Meteorologist*
National Learning Corp.
212 Michael Dr.
Syosset, NY 11791
Ph: (516)921-8888   Fax: (516)921-8743
Fr: 800-645-6337
Jack Rudman. 1993. Test guide including questions and answers for students or professionals in the field who seek advancement through examination.

★3414★ *Career Examination Series: Senior Meteorologist*
National Learning Corp.
212 Michael Dr.
Syosset, NY 11791
Ph: (516)921-8888   Fax: (516)921-8743
Fr: 800-645-6337
Jack Rudman. 1993. Test guide including questions and answers for students or professionals in the field who seek advancement through examination.

★3415★ *Dantes Subject Standardized Tests: Climatology/Meteorology*
National Learning Corp.
212 Michael Dr.
Syosset, NY 11791
Ph: (516)921-8888   Fax: (516)921-8743
Fr: 800-645-6337
Jack Rudman. Multiple-choice graduate- and college-level examination given by graduate schools, colleges and the Armed Forces as a final examination for course evaluation. Includes answers.

EDUCATIONAL DIRECTORIES AND PROGRAMS

★3416★ *Curricula in the Atmospheric, Oceanic, Hydrologic and Related Sciences—Colleges and Universities*
American Meteorological Society
45 Beacon St.
Boston, MA 02108
Ph: (617)227-2425   Fax: (617)742-8718
Linda S. Esche, Contact

Biennial, September of even years. Actual title is "Curricula in the Atmospheric, Oceanic, Hydrologic, and related Sciences" and describes over 108 schools. Entries include: School name, address, phone; names and specialties of staff, degrees offered, courses, special facilities. Arrangement: Alphabetical.

★3417★ *Environmental Career Directory*
Gale Research Inc.
835 Penobscot Bldg.
Detroit, MI 48226-4094
Ph: (313)961-2242   Fax: (313)961-6083
Fr: 800-877-GALE

Bradley J. Morgan and Joseph M. Palmisano. 1993. A directory in the Career Advisor Series that provides essays written by industry professionals; job search information on resume and cover letter preparation, networking, and the interviewing process; approximately 300 companies and organizations offering job opportunities and internships, and additional job-hunting resources.

★3418★ *Physical Science Career Directory*
Gale Research Inc.
835 Penobscot Bldg.
Detroit, MI 48226-4094
Ph: (313)961-2242   Fax: (313)961-6083
Fr: 800-877-GALE
Bradley J. Morgan, Contact

First edition March 1994. Covers over 210 chemical companies, testing and research laboratories, and consulting firms in the U.S. offering entry-level positions and internships; sources of help-wanted ads, professional associations, producers of videos, databases, career guides, and professional guides and handbooks. Entries include: For companies—Name, address, phone, fax, business description, research activities, names and titles of key personnel, number of employees, average number of entry-level positions available, human resources contact, description of internship opportunities including contact, type and number available, application procedures, qualifications, and duties. For others—Name or title, address, phone, description. Paperback edition Arrangement: Companies are alphabetical; others are classified by type of resource.

AWARDS, SCHOLARSHIPS, GRANTS, AND FELLOWSHIPS

★3419★ **Cleveland Abbe Award for Distinguished Service to Atmospheric Sciences by an Individual**
American Meteorological Society
45 Beacon St.
Boston, MA 02108-3693
Ph: (617)227-2425   Fax: (617)742-8718

For recognition of notable contributions to the progress of the atmospheric sciences or to the application of atmospheric sciences to general social, economic or humanitarian welfare. A certificate is awarded irregularly. Established in 1963.

★3420★ **AIAA Losey Atmospheric Science Award**
American Institute of Aeronautics and Astronautics
370 L'Enfant Promenade SW
Washington, DC 20024-2518
Ph: (202)646-7537   Fax: (202)646-7508

To recognize outstanding contributions to the atmospheric sciences as applied to the advancement of aeronautics and astronautics. A medal and certificate are usually presented at the Aerospace Sciences Meeting and Exhibit. Established in 1940 in memory of Captain Robert M. Losey, a meteorological officer who was killed while serving as an observer for the U.S. Army, the first officer in the service of the United States to die in World War II.

★3421★ **Award for Outstanding Achievement in Biometeorology**
American Meteorological Society
45 Beacon St.
Boston, MA 02108-3693
Ph: (617)227-2425   Fax: (617)742-8718

For recognition of distinguished contributions made by an individual in the field of biometerology. The nominations are made by the Awards Committee from a list submitted by the Committee of Biometeorology and Aerobiology. A certificate is awarded irregularly. Established in 1960.

★3422★ **Award for Outstanding Contribution to the Advance of Applied Meteorology**
American Meteorological Society
45 Beacon St.
Boston, MA 02108-3693
Ph: (617)227-2425   Fax: (617)742-8718

For outstanding contributions by an individual to the advancement of applied meterology, either in the direct application of meterological or climatological knowledge to the fulfillment of industrial or agricultural needs, or to research and development of scientific knowledge that can meet such needs. A certificate is awarded annually. Established in 1956.

★3423★ **Award for Outstanding Service by a Broadcast Meteorologist**
American Meteorological Society
45 Beacon St.
Boston, MA 02108-3693
Ph: (617)227-2425   Fax: (617)742-8718

To recognize outstanding service to the community by a weathercaster. Nominations may be made by an individual or a group. A certificate is awarded annually. Established in 1975.

★3424★ **Award for Outstanding Service by a Weather Forecaster**
American Meteorological Society
45 Beacon St.
Boston, MA 02108-3693
Ph: (617)227-2425   Fax: (617)742-8718

To recognize an individual for distinguished performance in forecasting which promotes the public safety and well-being. Three awards are given: Francis W. Reichelderfer Award for distinguished public service contributions by weather service personnel; Charles L. Mitchell Award for an exceptional long-term service by individuals engaged in weather forecasting activities; and an award for exceptional specific prediction. Certificates are awarded annually. Established in 1967.

★3425★ **Jule G. Charney Award**
American Meteorological Society
45 Beacon St.
Boston, MA 02108-3693
Ph: (617)227-2425   Fax: (617)742-8718

To recognize an individual for highly significant research or development achievement in the atmospheric or hydrospheric sciences. Not more than three awardees are selected annually. Each receives a medallion and a stipend. Established in 1969 on the 50th Anniversary of the Society. The award is now named in memory of Professor Jule G. Charney of the Massachusetts Institute of Technology.

★3426★ **Max A. Eaton Prize**
American Meteorological Society
45 Beacon St.
Boston, MA 02108-3693
Ph: (617)227-2425   Fax: (617)742-8718

For recognition of the best student paper presented at each technical conference on hurricanes and tropical meteorology. Entrants must be currently enrolled in high school, college, or graduate school. Students who have just completed a degree but not begun regular employment at the time of the conference are also eligible. A certificate is awarded. Established in 1977 by Captain Eaton's colleagues, to recognize Max A. Eaton's lifelong contributions to tropical meteorology and the encouragement he gave to so many young researchers.

★3427★ **Howard H. Hanks, Jr., Scholarship in Meteorology**
American Meteorological Society
45 Beacon St.
Boston, MA 02108-3693
Ph: (617)227-2425   Fax: (617)742-8718

In recognition of academic excellence and achievement in meteorology by a college or university student entering his final undergraduate year. He must be a major in a meteorology department or some aspect of the atmospheric sciences, intend to make atmospheric science his career. A cash prize of $700 is awarded annually. The scholarship honors the late Howard H. Hanks, Jr., Vice President of Weather Corporation of America, who was engaged in applied and industrial meteorology at the time of his death in 1969. William J. Hartnett, Board Chairman of Weather Corporation of America, provided funds for the scholarship. Established in 1973.

★3428★ **Bernhard Haurwitz Memorial Lecturer**
American Meteorological Society
45 Beacon St.
Boston, MA 02108-3693
Ph: (617)227-2425   Fax: (617)742-8718

To recognize an individual for significant contributions to the understanding of waves in the atmosphere, the circulation of the middle atmosphere, or the dynamics of climate. The lecture is presented at the AMS annual meeting or at an appropriate topical meeting and is published in the *Bulletin*. The lecture is presented occasionally. Established in 1989.

★3429★ **Honorary Life Membership**
American Association of State
 Climatologists
Minnesota State Climatologist
S-325 Borlaug Hall
University of Minnesota
St. Paul, MN 55108
Ph: (612)296-4214   Fax: (612)625-2208

For recognition of significant contributions in the science of climatology. The executive committee makes the nominations. A certificate is awarded when merited at the annual meeting. Established in 1978.

★3430★ **Helmut Landberg Award for Excellence in Applied Climatology**
American Association of State
 Climatologists
Minnesota State Climatologist
S-325 Borlaug Hall
University of Minnesota
St. Paul, MN 55108
Ph: (612)296-4214   Fax: (612)625-2208

For recognition of outstanding public service in the field of applied climatology. Members of the Association are eligible. A monetary prize of $200 and a plaque are awarded when merited at the convention. Established in 1987 in honor of Helmut Landberg, the founder of the State Climatology Programs.

★3431★ **Robert Leviton Award**
American Meteorological Society
45 Beacon St.
Boston, MA 02108-3693
Ph: (617)227-2425   Fax: (617)742-8718

For recognition of the best student paper on development or evaluation of atmospheric instrumentation or unique measurement techniques. The paper selected for the award may be chosen either from those given at a designated national meeting or technical conference of the Society, or papers appearing in one of its journals. Nominations are made by the Committee on Measurements. To be considered for the award an entrant should either be enrolled as a full-time student or be a student who has just completed a degree but has not begun employment at the time the

paper is given or submitted for publication. A monetary award of $300 is awarded. This award honors Robert Leviton, who devoted nearly his entire professional career to endeavors related to the measurement of wind, temperature, pressure and humidity in the atmosphere.

★3432★ **Father James B. Macelwane Annual Awards in Meteorology**
American Meteorological Society
45 Beacon St.
Boston, MA 02108-3693
Ph: (617)227-2425   Fax: (617)742-8718

To stimulate interest in the atmospheric sciences among college and university students. The papers must be original and must be concerned with some phase of the atmospheric sciences. All registered undergraduate students of a college or university in the Americas are eligible for participation, but no more than two students from any one institution may enter papers in any one contest. The following prizes are awarded: first prize - $300; second prize - $200; and third prize - $100. Established in 1960.

★3433★ **Banner I. Miller Award**
American Meteorological Society
45 Beacon St.
Boston, MA 02108-3693
Ph: (617)227-2425   Fax: (617)742-8718

To recognize an individual for the best contribution to the science of hurricane and tropical weather forecasting published during the preceding 24 months prior to the presentation of the award in a journal with international circulation. The nomination for the award will be submitted to the Awards Committee by the Committee on Tropical Meteorology and Tropical Cyclones. A monetary award of $300 is presented annually. Established by colleagues and peers of Dr. Miller in 1977.

★3434★ **Howard T. Orville Scholarship in Meteorology**
American Meteorological Society
45 Beacon St.
Boston, MA 02108-3693
Ph: (617)227-2425   Fax: (617)742-8718

In recognition of academic excellence and achievement in meteorology by a college or university student entering his final undergraduate year. He must be a major in a meteorology department or some aspect of the atmospheric sciences and intend to make atmospheric science his career. A cash prize of $1,000 is awarded annually. The Orville Scholarship honors the late Howard T. Orville, Head of the Naval Aerological Service, 1940-1950, when he retired as Captain, USN. Captain Orville was President of the American Meteorological Society 1948-1949. Established in 1965.

★3435★ **Carl-Gustaf Rossby Research Medal**
American Meteorological Society
45 Beacon St.
Boston, MA 02108-3693
Ph: (617)227-2425   Fax: (617)742-8718

This, the highest honor the Society can bestow, is given in recognition of outstanding and distinguished contributions to man's understanding of the structure or behavior of the atmosphere. A gold medal and a certificate

are awarded annually when merited. Established in 1951.

★3436★ **Sverdrup Gold Medal**
American Meteorological Society
45 Beacon St.
Boston, MA 02108-3693
Ph: (617)227-2425   Fax: (617)742-8718

To recognize researchers for outstanding contributions to the scientific knowledge of interactions between the oceans and the atmosphere. A gold medal and a certificate are awarded irregularly by the President of the Society on the advice of an international committee appointed in consultation with representatives of the Scripps Institution of Oceanography, La Jolla, CA, and the Univeristy of Bergen, Bergen, Norway. Established in 1964 to honor Harald Ulrik Sverdrup.

BASIC REFERENCE GUIDES AND HANDBOOKS

★3437★ *The Atmosphere: An Introduction to Meteorology*
Prentice-Hall, Inc.
Rte. 9W
Englewood Cliffs, NJ 07632
Ph: (201)592-2000   Fr: 800-922-0579

Federick Lutgens and Edward J. Tarbuck. Fifth edition, 1991. This nontechnical introduction focuses on key concepts in meteorology.

★3438★ *Meteorology Source Book: Meteorology*
McGraw-Hill, Inc.
1221 Avenue of the Americas
New York, NY 10020
Ph: (212)512-2000   Fr: 800-722-4726

Sybil P. Parker, editor. 1989. Contains 110 articles covering all types of weather systems and meteorological phenomena, and the technologies for study, forecasting, and prediction.

PROFESSIONAL AND TRADE PERIODICALS

★3439★ *AgMet News*
Department of Agricultural Meteorology
L.W. Chase Hall
Lincoln, NE 68583-0728
Ph: (402)472-3679   Fax: (402)472-6614
Jan Schinstock

Annual. Discusses events, accomplishments, and publications of the Department.

★3440★ Mount Washington Observatory—News Bulletin
Mount Washington Observatory
Main St.
PO Box 2310
North Conway, NH 03860-2310
Ph: (603)356-8345   Fax: (603)356-8345
C. Francis Belcher

Disseminates information of the scientific, observational, and educational programs of the weather Observatory. Publishes news on icing rate studies, radio research, and technology used in the observation field. Recurring features include a calendar of events, news of research, letters to the editor, columns titled Observatory News, Sawdust from the Log, and Interesting Correspondence.

★3441★ Paleoclimate Data Record
NOAA National Geophysical Data Center
325 Broadway, E/GC
Boulder, CO 80303
Ph: (303)497-6227   Fax: (303)497-6513

Irregular. Highlights completed and ongoing research of the Paleoclimate Program, which studies the causes, patterns, and effects of environmental and climate change over time scales of decades to centuries. Covers funding opportunities, data availability and management, and staff activities.

★3442★ Weather
Nautilus Press, Inc.
1054 National Press Bldg.
Washington, DC 20045
Ph: (202)347-6643
John R. Botzum

Monthly. Covers the latest developments in weather and climate research. Reports on federal agency actions in this area and relevant legislation. Recurring features include news of research.

★3443★ Weather and Forecasting
American Meteorological Society
45 Beacon St.
Boston, MA 02108
Ph: (617)227-2425   Fax: (617)742-8718
B. Colman

Quarterly. Journal presenting original research papers related to the atmospheres of the earth and other planets with emphasis on the quantitative and deductive aspects of the physics and dynamics of atmospheric processes and phenomena.

OTHER SOURCES OF INFORMATION

★3444★ "Meteorologist" in Career Selector 2001
Barron's Educational Series, Inc.
250 Wireless Blvd.
Hauppauge, NY 11788
Ph: (516)434-3311   Fax: (516)434-3723
Fr: 800-645-3476

James C. Gonyea. 1993.

★3445★ "Meteorology and Atmospheric Sciences" in Accounting to Zoology: Graduate Fields Defined (pp. 309-310)
Petersons Guides, Inc.
PO Box 2123
Princeton, NJ 08543-2123
Ph: (609)243-9111   Fax: (609)243-9150
Fr: 800-338-3282

Amy J. Goldstein, editor. Revised and updated, 1987. Defines 298 graduate and professional fields. Discusses types of graduate programs and degrees, graduate research, applied work, employment prospects, and trends.

★3446★ Salaries of Scientists, Engineers, and Technicians: A Summary of Salary Surveys
Commission on Professionals in Science and Technology (CPST)
1500 Massachusetts Ave., NW, Ste. 831
Washington, DC 20005
Ph: (202)223-6995

1993.

★3447★ The Weather Almanac
Gale Research Inc.
835 Penobscot Bldg.
Detroit, MI 48226-4094
Ph: (313)961-2242   Fax: (313)961-6083
Fr: 800-347-GALE

Frank E. Bair, editor. Sixth edition, 1992. Describes weather, climate, and air quality in key cities throughout the United States.

Physicists and Astronomers

Physicists attempt to discover basic principles governing the structure and behavior of matter, the generation and transfer of energy, and the interaction of matter and energy. Some physicists use these principles in theoretical areas, such as the nature of time and the origin of the universe, while others work in practical areas such as the development of advanced materials, electronic and optical devices, and medical equipment. Most physicists work in research and development. Some do basic research to increase scientific knowledge and some design research equipment. Astronomy is sometimes considered a subfield of physics. **Astronomers** use the principles of physics and mathematics to learn about the fundamental nature of the universe, and the sun, moon, planets, stars, and galaxies. They may apply their knowledge to problems in navigation and space flight as well. They analyze large quantities of data gathered by observatories and satellites and write scientific papers or reports on their findings.

Salaries

Physicists with master's degrees,	$30,000/year
Physicists with doctorates	$41,000/year
Physicists in the federal government	$61,956/year
Astronomers and space scientists	$65,709/year

Employment Outlook

Growth rate until the year 2005: Decline.

Physicists and Astronomers

CAREER GUIDES

★3448★ Astronomer
Careers, Inc.
PO Box 135
Largo, FL 34649-0135
Ph: (813)584-7333
1991. Two-page occupational summary card describing duties, working conditions, personal qualifications, training, earnings and hours, employment outlook, places of employment, related careers, and where to write for more information.

★3449★ "Astronomer" in Career Information Center (Vol.6)
Simon and Schuster
200 Old Tappan Rd.
Old Tappan, NJ 07675
Fax: 800-445-6991   Fr: 800-223-2348
Richard Lidz and Linda Perrin, editorial directors. Fifth edition, 1993. This 13-volume set profiles over 600 occupations. Each occupational profile describes job duties, entry-level requirements, educational requirements, advancement possibilities, employment outlook, working conditions, earnings and benefits, and where to write for more information.

★3450★ "Astronomer" in Jobs Rated Almanac
World Almanac
1 International Blvd., Ste. 444
Mahwah, NJ 07495
Ph: (201)529-6900   Fax: (201)529-6901
Les Krantz. Second edition, 1992. Ranks 250 jobs by environment, salary, outlooks, physical demands, stress, security, travel opportunities, and extra perks. Includes jobs the editor feels are the most common, most interesting, and the most rapidly growing.

★3451★ Astronomers
Vocational Biographies, Inc.
PO Box 31
Sauk Centre, MN 56378-0031
Ph: (612)352-6516   Fax: (612)352-5546
Fr: 800-255-0752
1995. Four-page pamphlet containing a personal narrative about a worker's job, work likes and dislikes, career path from high school to the present, education and training, the rewards and frustrations, and the effects of the job on the rest of the worker's life. The data file portion of this pamphlet gives a concise occupational summary, including work description, working conditions, places of employment, personal characteristics, education and training, job outlook, and salary range.

★3452★ Astronomers
Chronicle Guidance Publications, Inc.
66 Aurora St.
PO Box 1190
Moravia, NY 13118-1190
Ph: (315)497-0330   Fax: (315)497-3359
Fr: 800-622-7284
1992. Career brief describing the nature of the job, working conditions, hours and earnings, education and training, licensure, certification, unions, personal qualifications, social and psychological factors, location, employment outlook, entry methods, advancement, and related occupations.

★3453★ "Astronomers" in Career Discovery Encyclopedia (Vol.1, pp. 72-73)
J.G. Ferguson Publishing Co.
200 W. Madison St., Ste. 300
Chicago, IL 60606
Ph: (312)580-5480   Fax: (312)580-4948
Russell E. Primm, editor-in chief. 1993. This six volume set contains two-page articles for 504 occupations. Each article describes job duties, earnings, and educational and training requirements. The whole set is arranged alphabetically by job title. Designed for junior high and older students.

★3454★ "Astronomers" in Encyclopedia of Careers and Vocational Guidance (Vol.2, pp. 120-123)
J.G. Ferguson Publishing Co.
200 W. Madison St., Ste. 300
Chicago, IL 60606
Ph: (312)580-5480   Fax: (312)580-4948
William E. Hopke, editor-in-chief. Ninth edition, 1993. Four-volume set that profiles 900 occupations and describes job trends in 74 industries. Includes career description, educational requirements, history of the job, methods of entry, advancement, employment outlook, earnings, conditions of work, social and psychological factors, and sources of further information.

★3455★ "Astronomers" in Jobs! What They Are—Where They Are—What They Pay! (p. 307)
Simon & Schuster, Inc.
Simon & Schuster Bldg.
1230 Avenue of the Americas
New York, NY 10020
Ph: (212)698-7000   Fr: 800-223-2348
Robert O. Snelling and Anne M. Snelling. Third revised edition, 1992. Includes a chapter titled "Physicists". Describes duties and responsibilities, earnings, employment opportunities, training, and qualifications.

★3456★ Biophysicist
Careers, Inc.
PO Box 135
Largo, FL 34649-0135
Ph: (813)584-7333
1994. Two-page summary describing duties, working conditions, personal qualifications, training, earnings and hours, employment outlook, places of employment, related careers, and where to write for more information.

★3457★ Careers in Science
National Textbook Co. (NTC)
VGM Career Books
4255 W. Touhy Ave.
Lincolnwood, IL 60646-1975
Ph: (708)679-5500   Fax: (708)679-2494
Fr: 800-323-4900
Thomas A. Easton, editor. Explores careers in life science, physical science, social science, earth science, engineering, mathematics, and computer science.

★3458★ Health Physicist
Careers, Inc.
PO Box 135
Largo, FL 34649-0135
Ph: (813)584-7333
1994. Four-page brief describing duties, working conditions, personal qualifications, training, earnings and hours, employment outlook, places of employment, related careers, and where to write for more information.

★3459★ "Health Physicist" in
Opportunities in Environmental Careers
National Textbook Co. (NTC)
VGM Career Books
4255 W. Touhy Ave.
Lincolnwood, IL 60646-1975
Ph: (708)679-5500   Fax: (708)679-2494
Fr: 800-323-4900

Odom Fanning. 1991. Describes a broad range of opportunities in fields such as environmental health, recreation, physics, and hygiene.

★3460★ *Opportunities for Women in Science Careers*
National Textbook Co. (NTC)
VGM Career Books
4255 W. Touhy Ave.
Lincolnwood, IL 60646-1975
Ph: (708)679-5500   Fax: (708)679-2494
Fr: 800-323-4900

Alice Fins. 1979. Profiles women professionals in science careers such as biology, chemistry, geology, astronomy, physics, math, and others.

★3461★ *Peterson's Job Opportunities for Engineering and Technology*
Petersons Guides, Inc.
PO Box 2123
Princeton, NJ 08543-2123
Ph: (609)243-9111   Fax: (609)243-9150
Fr: 800-338-3282

1994. Gives job hunting advice including information on resume writing, interviewing, and handling salary negotiations. Lists companies that hire college graduates in science and engineering at the bachelor and master's level. Companies are indexed by industry, starting location, and major. Company profiles include contact information and types of hires.

★3462★ *Physicist*
Careers, Inc.
PO Box 135
Largo, FL 34649-0135
Ph: (813)584-7333

1993. Four-page brief offering the definition, history, duties, working conditions, personal qualifications, educational requirements, earnings, hours, employment outlook, advancement, and careers related to this position.

★3463★ "Physicist" in *Career Information Center* (Vol.6)
Simon and Schuster
200 Old Tappan Rd.
Old Tappan, NJ 07675
Fax: 800-445-6991   Fr: 800-223-2348

Richard Lidz and Linda Perrin, editorial directors. Fifth edition, 1993. This 13-volume set profiles over 600 occupations. Each occupational profile describes job duties, entry-level requirements, educational requirements, advancement possibilities, employment outlook, working conditions, earnings and benefits, and where to write for more information.

★3464★ "Physicist" in *College Board Guide to Jobs and Career Planning* (pp. 287)
The College Board
415 Columbus Ave.
New York, NY 10023-6992
Ph: (212)713-8165   Fax: (212)713-8143
Fr: 800-323-7155

Joyce S. Mitchell. Second edition, 1994. Describes a variety of careers. Includes information on salaries, related careers, education needed, and sources of additional information.

★3465★ "Physicist" in *Guide to Federal Jobs* (pp. 214)
Resource Directories
3361 Executive Pkwy., Ste. 302
Toledo, OH 43606
Ph: (419)536-5353   Fax: (419)536-7056
Fr: 800-274-8515

Rod W. Durgin, editor. Third edition, 1992. Contains information on finding and applying for federal jobs. Describes more than 200 professional and technical jobs for college graduates. Also includes a chapter titled "Astronomy and Space Scientist" (pp. 219). Covers the nature of the work, salary, and geographic location. Lists college majors preferred for that occupation. Section one describes the function and work of government agencies that hire the most significant number of college graduates.

★3466★ "Physicist" in *Jobs Rated Almanac*
World Almanac
1 International Blvd., Ste. 444
Mahwah, NJ 07495
Ph: (201)529-6900   Fax: (201)529-6901

Les Krantz. Second edition, 1992. Ranks 250 jobs by environment, salary, outlooks, physical demands, stress, security, travel opportunities, and extra perks. Includes jobs the editor feels are the most common, most interesting, and the most rapidly growing.

★3467★ "Physicist" in *Opportunities in High-Tech Careers* (pp. 52-53)
National Textbook Co. (NTC)
VGM Career Books
4255 W. Touhy Ave.
Lincolnwood, IL 60646-1975
Ph: (708)679-5500   Fax: (708)679-2494
Fr: 800-323-4900

Gary D. Colter and Deborah Yanuck. 1987. Explores high- technology careers. Written for the student and displaced worker. Describes job opportunities, how to make a career decision, how to prepare for high-technology jobs, job hunting techniques, and future trends.

★3468★ "Physicist" in *VGM's Careers Encyclopedia* (pp. 355-357)
National Textbook Co. (NTC)
VGM Career Books
4255 W. Touhy Ave.
Lincolnwood, IL 60646-1975
Ph: (708)679-5500   Fax: (708)679-2494
Fr: 800-323-4900

Third edition, 1991. Profiles 200 occupations. Describes job duties, places of employment, working conditions, qualifications, education and training, advancement potential, and salary for each occupation.

★3469★ *Physicists*
Chronicle Guidance Publications, Inc.
66 Aurora St.
PO Box 1190
Moravia, NY 13118-1190
Ph: (315)497-0330   Fax: (315)497-3359
Fr: 800-622-7284

1994. Career brief describing the nature of the job, working conditions, hours and earnings, education and training, licensure, certification, unions, personal qualifications, social and psychological factors, location, employment outlook, entry methods, advancement, and related occupations.

★3470★ "Physicists" in *101 Careers: A Guide to the Fastest-Growing Opportunities* (pp. 117-119)
John Wiley & Sons, Inc.
605 3rd Ave.
New York, NY 10158-0012
Ph: (212)850-6645   Fax: (212)850-6088

Michael Harkavy. 1990. Describes the nature of the job, working conditions, employment growth, qualifications, personal skills, projected salaries, and where to write for more information.

★3471★ "Physicists" in *American Almanac of Jobs and Salaries* (p.256)
Avon Books
1350 Avenue of the Americas
New York, NY 10019
Ph: (212)261-6800   Fr: 800-238-0658

John Wright, editor. Revised and updated, 1994-95. A comprehensive guide to the wages of hundreds of occupations in a wide variety of industries and organizations.

★3472★ "Physicists and Astronomers" in *Occupational Outlook Handbook*
U.S. Government Printing Office
Superintendent of Documents
Washington, DC 20402
Ph: (202)512-1800   Fax: (202)512-2250

Biennial; latest edition, 1994-95. Encyclopedia of careers describing about 250 occupations and comprising about 85 percent of all jobs in the economy. Occupations that require lengthy education or training are given the most attention. Each occupation's profile describes what the worker does on the job, working conditions, education and training requirements, advancement possibilities, job outlook, earnings, and sources of additional information.

★3473★ "Physicists" in *Career Discovery Encyclopedia* (Vol.5, pp. 44-45)
J.G. Ferguson Publishing Co.
200 W. Madison St., Ste. 300
Chicago, IL 60606
Ph: (312)580-5480   Fax: (312)580-4948

Russell E. Primm, editor-in chief. 1993. This six volume set contains two-page articles for 504 occupations. Each article describes job duties, earnings, and educational and training requirements. The whole set is arranged alphabetically by job title. Designed for junior high and older students.

★3474★ "Physicists" in *Encyclopedia of Careers and Vocational Guidance* **(Vol.4, pp. 98-102)**
J.G. Ferguson Publishing Co.
200 W. Madison St., Ste. 300
Chicago, IL 60606
Ph: (312)580-5480   Fax: (312)580-4948
William E. Hopke, editor-in-chief. Ninth edition, 1993. Four-volume set that profiles 900 occupations and describes job trends in 74 industries. Includes career description, educational requirements, history of the job, methods of entry, advancement, employment outlook, earnings, conditions of work, social and psychological factors, and sources of further information.

★3475★ "Physics" and "Astronomers" in *College Majors and Careers: A Resource Guide to Effective Life Planning* **(pp. 107-108, 23-24)**
Garrett Park Press
PO Box 1907
Garrett Park, MD 20896
Ph: (301)946-2553
Paul Phifer. Revised, 1993. Lists 60 college majors, with definitions; related occupations and leisure activities; skills, values, and personal attributes needed; suggested readings; and a list of associations.

★3476★ *Scientists, Physical*
Careers, Inc.
PO Box 135
Largo, FL 34649-0135
Ph: (813)584-7333
1994. Four-page brief describing duties, working conditions, personal qualifications, training, earnings and hours, employment outlook, places of employment, related careers, and where to write for more information.

★3477★ *Space Physicist*
Vocational Biographies, Inc.
PO Box 31
Sauk Centre, MN 56378-0031
Ph: (612)352-6516   Fax: (612)352-5546
Fr: 800-255-0752
1995. Four-page pamphlet containing a personal narrative about a worker's job, work likes and dislikes, career path from high school to the present. Education and training, the rewards and frustrations, and the effects of the job on the rest of the worker's life. The data file portion of this pamphlet gives a concise occupational summary, including work descriptions, working conditions, places of employment, personal characteristics, education and training, job outlook, and salary range.

★3478★ *Understanding the Universe: A Career in Astronomy*
American Astronmical Society (AAS)
c/o Dr. Peter B. Boyce
1630 Connecutt Ave., NW, Ste. 200
Washington, DC 20009
Ph: (202)328-2010
Second Edition, 1989. Describes careers in astronomy; places of employment; and educational preparation at the high school, college, and graduate level. Provides a state-by-state list of graduate programs in North America.

PROFESSIONAL ASSOCIATIONS

★3479★ American Association of Physicists in Medicine (AAPM)
1 Physics Ellipse
College Park, MD 20740-3846
Ph: (301)209-3350   Fax: (301)209-0862
Members: Persons professionally engaged in application of physics to medicine and biology in medical research; educational institutions. **Purpose:** Encourages interest and training in medical physics and related fields; promotes high professional standards; disseminates technical information. Maintains placement service. Conducts research programs. Member of American Institute of Physics. **Publications:** *AAPM Report Series*, periodic. ● *American Association of Physicists in Medicine—Membership Directory*, annual. ● *Medical Physics*, monthly.

★3480★ American Astronomical Society (AAS)
2000 Florida Ave. NW, Ste. 400
Washington, DC 20009
Ph: (202)328-2010   Fax: (202)234-2560
Members: Astronomers, physicists, and scientists in related fields. **Purpose:** Conducts Visiting Professor in Astronomy Program. Maintains placement service. **Publications:** *AAS Job Register*, monthly. ● *AAS Newsletter*, 5/year. ● *American Astronomical Society—Membership Directory*, annual. ● *Astronomical Journal*, monthly. ● *Astrophysical Journal.* ● *Bulletin of the American Astronomical Society*, quarterly.

★3481★ American Institute of Physics (AIP)
1 Physics Ellipse
College Park, MD 20740-3843
Ph: (301)209-3100
Members: Corporation of ten national societies in the field of physics with a total of 100,000 members, 17 affiliated societies, 68 corporate associates, and 7500 student members. **Purpose:** Seeks to assist in the advancement and diffusion of the knowledge of physics and its application to human welfare. To this end the institute publishes scientific journals devoted to physics and related sciences; provides secondary information services; conducts research in information systems; serves the public by making available to the press and other channels of public information reliable communications on physics and its progress; carries on extensive career placement activities; maintains projects directed toward providing information about physics education to students, physics teachers, and physics departments; encourages and assists in the documentation and study of the history of recent physics; cooperates with local, national, and international organizations devoted to physics; and fosters the relations of the science of physics to other sciences and to the arts and industry. Provides placement service; compiles statistics; maintains biographical archives and Niels Bohr Library of History of Physics. **Publications:** *Acoustical Physics*, bimonthly. ● *AIP History of Physics Newsletter*, semiannual. ● *Applied Physics Letters*, weekly. ● *Astronomy Letters*,

bimonthly. ● *Astronomy Reports*, bimonthly. ● *Crystallography Report*, bimonthly. ● *Current Physics Index*, quarterly. ● *Directory of Physics and Astronomy Staff*, annual. ● *Graduate Programs in Physics, Astronomy and Related Fields*, annual. ● *JETP Letters*, semimonthly. ● *Journal of Applied Physics.* ● *Journal of Chemical Physics.* ● *Journal of Experimental and Theoretical Physics*, monthly. ● *Journal of Mathematical Physics*, monthly. ● *Journal of Optical Technology*, monthly. ● *Journal of Particles and Nuclei*, bimonthly. ● *Journal of Physical and Chemical Reference Data*, quarterly. ● *Low Temperature Physics*, monthly. ● *Physics Briefs*, semimonthly. ● *Physics—Doklady*, monthly. ● *Physics of Atomic Nuclei*, monthly. ● *Physics of Fluids*, monthly. ● *Physics of Solid State*, monthly. ● *Physics Today*, monthly. ● *Physics—Uspekhi*, monthly. ● *Plasma Physics Report*, monthly. ● *Quantum Electronics*, monthly. ● *Review of Scientific Instruments*, monthly. ● *Semiconductors*, monthly. ● *Technical Physics*, monthly. ● *Technical Physics Letters*, monthly.

★3482★ American Physical Society (APS)
1 Physics Ellipse
College Park, MD 20740-3844
Ph: (301)209-3200   Fax: (301)209-0865
Members: Educators, industrial and government research workers, and students of physics and related fields such as mathematics, astronomy, chemistry, and engineering. **Purpose:** Promotes international cooperation. Sponsors studies of the physics aspect of topics of public concern such as reactor safety, energy use, and plutonium recycling. Maintains education and outreach programs. **Publications:** *APS News*, 11/year. ● *Bulletin of the American Physical Society*, monthly. ● *Physical Review*, monthly. ● *Physical Review Letters*, weekly. ● *Reviews of Modern Physics*, quarterly.

★3483★ American Society for Photogrammetry and Remote Sensing (ASPRS)
5410 Grosvenor Ln., Ste. 210
Bethesda, MD 20814-2160
Ph: (301)493-0290   Fax: (301)493-0208
Members: Firms, individuals, government employees, and academicians engaged in photogrammetry, photointerpretation, remote sensing, and geographic information systems and their application to such fields as archaeology, geographic information systems, military reconnaissance, urban planning, engineering, traffic surveys, meteorological observations, medicine, geology, forestry, agriculture, construction, and topographic mapping. Offers voluntary certification program open to persons associated with one or more functional area of photogrammetry, remote sensing, and GIS. Surveys the profession of private firms in photogrammetry and remote sensing in the areas of products and services. **Publications:** *Photogrammetric Engineering and Remote Sensing*, monthly.

★3484★ Association of Astronomy Educators (AAE)
5103 Burt St.
Omaha, NE 68132
Ph: (402)556-0082   Fax: (402)280-2140
Members: Teachers and educators dedicated to improving astronomy education at all levels, from kindergarten to college. **Purpose:** Promotes astronomy education to enhance the scientific literacy of all students. Brings together resources and knowledge from a number of diverse groups. Works with the National Science Teachers Association. Cosponsors Astronomy Day. **Publications:** *Astronomy Education*, quarterly.

★3485★ Astronomical League (AL)
2112 Kingfisher Ln. E
Rolling Meadows, IL 60008
Ph: (708)398-0562
Members: Members of 196 astronomical societies and other interested individuals. **Purpose:** Promotes the science of astronomy; encourages and coordinates activities of amateur astronomical societies; fosters observational and computational work and craftsmanship in various fields of astronomy; correlates amateur activities with professional research. Operates children's services; sponsors educational programs. **Publications:** *Reflector*, quarterly.

★3486★ Gungywamp Society (GS)
334 Brook St.
Noank, CT 06340
Ph: (203)536-2887
Members: Avocational archaeologists, anthropologists, historians, geologists, astronomers, and interested individuals. **Purpose:** Seeks to protect and preserve sites throughout the northeastern United States that show evidence of ancient and pre-Columbian cultures. Investigates and studies lithic features, architecture, artifacts, ancient inscriptions, and historic records. Has discovered an archaeological site in Connecticut that shows evidence of serial occupancy since 3000 B.C. Conducts tours through the Gungywamp Complex, an archaeological area preserved by the group. Sponsors educational and charitable programs. Maintains speakers' bureau. **Publications:** *The Greater Gungywamp: A Guide.* • *Stonewatch*, quarterly.

★3487★ International Amateur-Professional Photoelectric Photometry (IAPPP)
A. J. Dyer Observatory
Vanderbilt University
Box 1803, Sta. B
Nashville, TN 37235
Ph: (615)373-4897   Fax: (615)343-7263
Members: Amateurs, students, and professionals interested in astronomy. **Purpose:** Facilitates collaborative astronomical research between amateurs, students, and professional astronomers by providing a medium for the exchange of practical information not normally discussed at symposia or published in journals. Provides information on specialized aspects of photoelectric photometry. Solicits manuscripts relevant to astronomical research. Conducts educational and research programs. **Publications:** *I.A.P.P.P. Communications*, quarterly.

★3488★ Society of Nuclear Medicine (SNM)
1850 Samuel Morse Dr.
Reston, VA 22090
Ph: (703)708-9000   Fax: (703)708-9015
Members: Professional society of physicians, physicists, chemists, radiopharmacists, nuclear medicine technologists, and others interested in nuclear medicine, nuclear magnetic resonance, and the use of radioactive isotopes in clinical practice, research, and teaching. **Purpose:** Disseminates information concerning the utilization of nuclear phenomena in the diagnosis and treatment of disease. Oversees the Technologist Section of the Society of Nuclear Medicine . **Publications:** *The Journal of Nuclear Medicine*, monthly. • *Journal of Nuclear Medicine Technology*, quarterly. • *Society of Nuclear Medicine Membership Directory*.

★3489★ Webb Society
1440 S. Marmora Ave.
Tucson, AZ 85713
Ph: (602)628-1077
Members: Amateur and professional astronomers. Conducts research; exchanges astronomical information. **Publications:** *Deep-Sky Magazine*, semiannual. • *Observing Reports*, annual. • *Webb Society Quarterly Journal*, quarterly.

STANDARDS/CERTIFICATION AGENCIES

★3490★ American Society for Photogrammetry and Remote Sensing (ASPRS)
5410 Grosvenor Ln., Ste. 210
Bethesda, MD 20814-2160
Ph: (301)493-0290   Fax: (301)493-0208
Offers voluntary certification program open to persons associated with one or more functional area of photogrammetry, remote sensing, and GIS.

TEST GUIDES

★3491★ *Barron's Regents Exams and Answers: Physics*
Barron's Educational Series, Inc.
250 Wireless Blvd.
Hauppauge, NY 11788
Ph: (516)434-3311   Fax: (516)434-3723
Fr: 800-645-3476
Second edition. 1994. Provides 3 Regents exams and answers and a glossary of important words, people and international organizations.

★3492★ *Career Examination Series: Assistant Physicist*
National Learning Corp.
212 Michael Dr.
Syosset, NY 11791
Ph: (516)921-8888   Fax: (516)921-8743
Fr: 800-645-6337
Jack Rudman. Test guide including questions and answers for students or professionals in the field who seek advancement through examination.

★3493★ *Career Examination Series: Astronomer*
National Learning Corp.
212 Michael Dr.
Syosset, NY 11791
Ph: (516)921-8888   Fax: (516)921-8743
Fr: 800-645-6337
Jack Rudman. A series of study guides with multiple-choice examination questions and solutions for trainees and professional physicists and astronomers. Titles in the series include *Assistant Physicist; Junior Physicist; Physicist.*

★3494★ *Career Examination Series: Physicist/Junior Physicist*
National Learning Corp.
212 Michael Dr.
Syosset, NY 11791
Ph: (516)921-8888   Fax: (516)921-8743
Fr: 800-645-6337
Jack Rudman. Test guide including questions and answers for students or professionals in the field who seek advancement through examination.

★3495★ *Dantes Subject Standardized Tests: Astonomy*
National Learning Corp.
212 Michael Dr.
Syosset, NY 11791
Ph: (516)921-8888   Fax: (516)921-8743
Fr: 800-645-6337
Jack Rudman. Multiple-choice graduate- and college-level examination given by graduate schools, colleges and the Armed Forces as a final examination for course evaluation. Includes answers.

★3496★ *EZ 101 Study Keys: Physics*
Barron's Educational Series, Inc.
250 Wireless Blvd.
Hauppauge, NY 11788
Ph: (516)434-3311   Fax: (516)434-3723
Fr: 800-645-3476
1992. Provides themes, formulas, and a glossary of terms.

★3497★ *Graduate Record Examination: Physics*
National Learning Corp.
212 Michael Dr.
Syosset, NY 11791
Ph: (516)921-8888   Fax: (516)921-8743
Fr: 800-645-6337
Jack Rudman. Multiple-choice test for those seeking admission to graduate school for study in the field of physics. Includes solutions to examination questions.

★3498★ Undergraduate Program Field Test: Physics
National Learning Corp.
212 Michael Dr.
Syosset, NY 11791
Ph: (516)921-8888   Fax: (516)921-8743
Fr: 800-645-6337
Jack Rudman. A practice examination fashioned after tests given in the Regents External Degree Program. Designed to measure knowledge received outside the college classroom in the subject of physics. Contains multiple-choice questions; provides solutions.

EDUCATIONAL DIRECTORIES AND PROGRAMS

★3499★ Graduate Programs in Physics, Astronomy, and Related Fields
American Institute of Physics
500 Sunnyside Blvd.
Woodbury, NY 11797
Ph: (516)576-2203   Fax: (516)349-7669
Fr: 800-809-2247
Jennifer Vancura, Chief Production Editor
Annual, October. Covers more than 300 academic departments in the United States, Canada, and Mexico offering graduate programs in physics, astronomy, and related fields. Entries include: School name, address, department name; admission and graduate degree requirements, including names of contacts for information on admissions, financial aid, and housing; research specialties and areas of concentration of study for each department; stipend awards; list of faculty and their research specialties. Arrangement: Geographical.

★3500★ Physical Science Career Directory
Gale Research Inc.
835 Penobscot Bldg.
Detroit, MI 48226-4094
Ph: (313)961-2242   Fax: (313)961-6083
Fr: 800-877-GALE
Bradley J. Morgan, Contact
First edition March 1994. Covers over 210 chemical companies, testing and research laboratories, and consulting firms in the U.S. offering entry-level positions and internships; sources of help-wanted ads, professional associations, producers of videos, databases, career guides, and professional guides and handbooks. Entries include: For companies—Name, address, phone, fax, business description, research activities, names and titles of key personnel, number of employees, average number of entry-level positions available, human resources contact, description of internship opportunities including contact, type and number available, application procedures, qualifications, and duties. For others—Name or title, address, phone, description. Paperback edition Arrangement: Companies are alphabetical; others are classified by type of resource.

AWARDS, SCHOLARSHIPS, GRANTS, AND FELLOWSHIPS

★3501★ Arctowski Medal
National Academy of Sciences
2101 Constitution Ave. NW
Washington, DC 20418
Ph: (202)334-2444
To recognize studies in solar physics and solar-terrestrial relationships. A monetary prize of $20,000, plus $60,000 to an institution of the recipient's choice, and a medal are presented every three years. Established in 1969.

★3502★ Award for Excellence in Plasma Physics Research
American Physical Society
One Physics Ellipse
College Park, MD 20740
Ph: (301)209-3200   Fax: (301)209-0867
To recognize a particular recent outstanding achievement in plasma physics research. Nominations are open to scientists of all nationalities, regardless of the geographical site at which the work was done. The award consists of a monetary prize of $5,000, to be divided equally in the case of multiple winners, and a certificate to each recipient. Presented at the Annual Meeting Banquet of the Division of Plasma Physics. Awarded annually if merited. Established in 1981.

★3503★ AWIS Educational Foundation Predoctoral Award
Association for Women in Science
1522 K St., NW, Ste. 820
Washington, DC 20005
Ph: (202)408-0742
To recognize women of excellence who are pursuing their doctoral degrees, and to assist them in achieving their career goals. Applicants must be enrolled in a graduate program leading to a Ph.D. degree in any discipline of life, physical, or social science, or engineering. The deadline is January 15. Four monetary awards of $500 each are given annually. The award money may be used for any need associated with the applicant's educational endeavors. In addition, the Luise Meyer-Schutzmeister Memorial Award of $500 is awarded specifically for a graduate student in physics. Other named awards include the Judith G. Pool Memorial Award and the Laura Eisenstein Award.

★3504★ Tom W. Bonner Prize in Nuclear Physics
American Physical Society
One Physics Ellipse
College Park, MD 20740
Ph: (301)209-3200   Fax: (301)209-0867
To recognize and encourage outstanding experimental research in nuclear physics, including the development of a method, technique, or device that significantly contributes in a general way to nuclear physics research. Nominations are open to physicists whose work in nuclear physics is primarily experimental, but a particularly outstanding piece of theoretical work will take precedence over experimental work. There are no time limitations on the work described. A monetary award of $5,000, and a certificate citing the contribution made by the recipient are awarded annually. Established in 1964 as a memorial to Tom W. Bonner by his friends, students, and associates.

★3505★ Herbert P. Broida Prize in Atomic, Molecular, or Chemical Physics
American Physical Society
One Physics Ellipse
College Park, MD 20740
Ph: (301)209-3200   Fax: (301)209-0867
To recognize and enhance outstanding experimental advancements in the fields of atomic, molecular or chemical physics. Emphasis will be given to work done within the five years prior to the award. Preference will be granted to an individual whose contributions have displayed a high degree of breadth, originality, and creativity. The prize consists of a $5,000 stipend and a certificate citing the contributions made by the recipient. Awarded biennially in odd-numbered years. Established in 1979 in memory of Herbert P. Broida, Professor of Physics at the University of California, Santa Barbara, by his friends and the Office of Naval Research.

★3506★ Dirk Brouwer Award
American Astronomical Society
2000 Florida Ave. NW, Ste. 400
Washington, DC 20009
Ph: (202)328-2010   Fax: (202)234-2560
To recognize outstanding contributions in the field of dynamical astronomy, including celestial mechanics, astronomy, geophysics, stellar systems, galactic, and extragalactic dynamics. Candidates of any age, nationality, occupation, or specific field of interest are eligible. An honorarium and a Certificate of Citation are awarded annually. Established in 1978. Awarded by the Division on Dynamical Astronomy.

★3507★ Catherine Wolfe Bruce Medal
Astronomical Society of the Pacific
390 Ashton Ave.
San Francisco, CA 94112
Ph: (415)337-1100   Fax: (415)337-5205
This, one of the most prestigious awards in the field of astronomy, is given in recognition of lifetime research achievement in astronomy and astrophysics. Selection is made by the Board of Directors from nominees proposed by three American and three foreign observatories. A medal with the seal of the Society is awarded annually at the summer meeting. Established in 1897 by Miss Bruce.

★3508★ Oliver E. Buckley Condensed-Matter Physics Prize
American Physical Society
One Physics Ellipse
College Park, MD 20740
Ph: (301)209-3200   Fax: (301)209-0867
To recognize and encourage outstanding theoretical or experimental contributions to condensed-matter physics. The prize consists of $5,000 and a certificate citing the contributions made by the recipient(s). Established in 1952. Sponsored by the AT&T +Bell Laboratoriesas a means of recognizing outstanding scientific work in America.

★3509★ Annie Jump Cannon Award in Astronomy
American Astronomical Society
2000 Florida Ave. NW, Ste. 400
Washington, DC 20009
Ph: (202)328-2010   Fax: (202)234-2560

To recognize a woman for distinguished contributions to astronomy or for similar contributions in related sciences that have immediate application to astronomy. Since 1974, the award has been offered as a research award, by the AAUW with advice from the Society's Annie J. Cannon Award Committee. Awarded annually. Established in 1934.

★3510★ Coblentz Award
Coblentz Society
Perkin - Elmer Corp.
Main Ave.
Norwalk, CT 06859
Ph: (203)762-1000

To recognize an outstanding accomplishment in the field of spectroscopy. Was awarded annually at the Molecular Spectroscopy Meeting at Ohio State University. (Discontinued)

★3511★ Karl Taylor Compton Award
American Institute of Physics
335 E. 45th St.
New York, NY 10017
Ph: (212)661-9404   Fax: (212)949-0473

For outstanding statesmanship in science. Distinguished United States physicists who have made outstanding contributions to physics are eligible. A monetary award of $5,000, a bronze medal and a certificate are awarded at intervals of three to five years. Established in 1957.

★3512★ Comstock Prize
National Academy of Sciences
2101 Constitution Ave. NW
Washington, DC 20418
Ph: (202)334-2444

To recognize an important discovery or investigation in electricity, magnetism, or radiant energy. Bona fide residents of North America are eligible. A monetary prize of $20,000 is presented every five years. Established in 1907 through the Cyrus B. Comstock Fund.

★3513★ Davisson-Germer Prize in Atomic or Surface Physics
American Physical Society
One Physics Ellipse
College Park, MD 20740
Ph: (301)209-3200   Fax: (301)209-0867

To recognize and encourage outstanding work in atomic physics or surface physics. The prize consists of a monetary award of $5,000 and a certificate citing the contributions made by the recipient(s). Awarded in alternate years for outstanding work in atomic physics, and for outstanding work in surface physics. Established in 1965. Sponsored by AT&T +Bell Laboratoriesas a means of recognizing outstanding scientific work in America.

★3514★ John H. Dillon Medal for Research in Polymer Physics
American Physical Society
One Physics Ellipse
College Park, MD 20740
Ph: (301)209-3200   Fax: (301)209-0867

To recognize outstanding research accomplishments by a young polymer physicist. The award consists of the John H. Dillon Medal and a certificate citing the contributions made by the recipient. Awarded annually. Established in 1983 by the American Physical Society Division of High Polymer Physics.

★3515★ Henry Draper Medal
National Academy of Sciences
2101 Constitution Ave. NW
Washington, DC 20418
Ph: (202)334-2444

To recognize outstanding research in astronomical physics. A monetary prize of $10,000 and a medal are presented every four years. Established in 1833 by Mrs. Henry Draper.

★3516★ Maria Goeppert-Mayer Award
American Physical Society
One Physics Ellipse
College Park, MD 20740
Ph: (301)209-3200   Fax: (301)209-0867

To recognize and enhance outstanding achievements by a woman physicist in the early years of her career, and to provide opportunities for her to present these achievements to others through public lectures. Women who are not later than ten years after the granting of the Ph.D. degree or the equivalent career stage are eligible for scientific achievements that demonstrate her potential as an outstanding physicist. The award is open to women of any nationality, and the lectures may be given at institutions in any country within two years after the award is made. The award consists of $2,000 plus a $3,000 travel allowance to provide opportunities for the recipient to give lectures in her field of physics at four institutions of her choice and at the meeting of the Society at which the award is bestowed, and a certificate citing the contributions made by the recipient. Established in 1985 by the General Electric Foundation, to be first awarded in 1986.

★3517★ George Ellery Hale Prize
American Astronomical Society
2000 Florida Ave. NW, Ste. 400
Washington, DC 20009
Ph: (202)328-2010   Fax: (202)234-2560

To recognize a scientist for outstanding contributions over an extended period of time to the field of solar astronomy. Any living scientist without consideration of race, sex, or nationality is eligible. An honorarium, a medal, and a citation are awarded biennially. Awarded by the Solar Physics Division. Established in 1978.

★3518★ Maurice F. Hasler Award
Society for Applied Spectroscopy
198 Thomas Johnsobn Dr. S-2
Frederick, MD 21702-4317
Ph: (301)694-8122   Fax: (301)694-6860

To recognize and encourage notable achievements in spectroscopy that have resulted in significant applications of broad utility. Individuals of any nationality are eligible.

A monetary award of $1,000 and a scroll are awarded biennially. Established in 1969. Sponsored by the Spectroscopy Society of Pittsburgh.

★3519★ Dannie N. Heineman Prize for Astrophysics
American Institute of Physics
335 E. 45th St.
New York, NY 10017
Ph: (212)661-9404   Fax: (212)949-0473

To recognize outstanding work in the field of astrophysics. A monetary prize of $5,000 and a certificate are awarded each year at the Annual Meeting of the American Astronomical Society. Established in 1979 for a ten-year period. Sponsored by the Heineman Foundation for Research, Educational, Charitable, and Scientific Purposes, Inc., and administered jointly by The American Astronomical Society.

★3520★ Engineer Degree Fellowships; Howard Hughes Doctoral Fellowships
Hughes Aircraft Company
Technical Education Center
PO Box 80028
Los Angeles, CA 90080-0028
Ph: (310)568-6711

Purpose: To support doctoral studies in engineering and related sciences and to provide students with practical work experience. Qualifications: Applicant for either type of fellowship must be a U.S. citizen and have a bachelor's and master's degree or equivalent graduate experience in electrical, mechanical, systems, computer or aerospace engineering; computer science; physics; or mathematics. Engineer Degree Fellowships are reserved for candidates who have first degrees in engineering. For both awards, priority is given to individuals with experience in electronics and related disciplines. Candidate must have a minimum grade point average of 3.0/4.0, and be qualified for admission to an approved graduate program in the United States. Fellows are considered employees of the Hughes Aircraft Company and, in addition to their graduate studies, gain work experience in one of two programs: work-study or full-study. Fellows in the work-study program attend a university near a Hughes facility (usually in southern California) and complete coursework while working at the facility for 20 to 36 hours per week. Work-study fellows may switch to full-study status to complete their dissertations. Full-study fellows attend a university distant from Hughes and are on leave of absence from the company while studying full-time. Full-study fellows are required to spend the summer term working for the Company, and may work eight hours a week during the school year if attending a university within commuting distance. Funds available: Company salary and benefits, plus tuition, book and living allowances. Application details: Write to the educational coordinator for application form and guidelines. Include pertinent information regarding academic status (university, field of interest for both undergraduate and graduate work, year of graduation, and grade point average) in initial letter of interest. Deadline: 10 January. Fellows are announced in April.

★3521★ Gerard P. Kuiper Prize
American Astronomical Society
2000 Florida Ave. NW, Ste. 400
Washington, DC 20009
Ph: (202)328-2010   Fax: (202)234-2560

To recognize and honor outstanding contributors to planetary science whose achievements have most advanced our understanding of the universe. Candidates may be of any age or nationality. Awarded annually. Established in 1984. Awarded by the Division for Planetary Sciences.

★3522★ Otto Laporte Award for Research in Fluid Dynamics
American Physical Society
One Physics Ellipse
College Park, MD 20740
Ph: (301)209-3200   Fax: (301)209-0867

To recognize outstanding accomplishments in research in fluid dynamics. The award consists of $1,000, and a certificate citing the contributions made by the recipient. The recipient is invited to present a plenary lecture at the Annual Meeting of the Division of Fluid Dynamics. Established as an APS Award in 1985, but existed as a Division Prize for twelve previous years to honor Otto Laporte. It is supported by the friends of Otto Laporte and the Division of Fluid Dynamics.

★3523★ Fritz London Memorial Award
Duke University
Dept. of Physics
Durham, NC 27706
Ph: (919)684-8234   Fax: (919)684-8101

For recognition of achievement in the field of low temperature physics. Election is by a committee approximately six months before each international meeting of low temperature physics. A monetary prize and a certificate are awarded triennially at the international meeting. Established in 1957 through the generosity of John Bardeen, who gave the money of his second Nobel prize to Duke for the purpose of honoring Fritz London, one of the great theorists of the first half of the twentieth century in condensed matter physics.

★3524★ NAACP Willems Scholarship
National Association for the Advancement of Colored People (NAACP)
4805 Mt. Hope Dr.
Baltimore, MD 21215-3297
Ph: (410)358-8900

Qualifications: Applicants must be majoring in engineering, chemistry, physics, or computer and mathematical sciences and possess a cumulative grade point average of at least 3.0 or B average. They must be members of the NAACP. Funds available: Undergraduates will receive a maximum award of $8,000 to be paid in annual installments of $2,000. Graduates will be awarded a $3,000 renewable scholarship. Application details: Updated application forms are available in January. Deadline: April 30.

★3525★ Newcomen Award for Notable Proficiency in Mathematics, Physics and Chemistry
Newcomen Society of the United States
412 Newcomen Rd.
Exton, PA 19341
Ph: (215)363-6600   Fax: (215)363-0612

For recognition of notable proficiency in mathematics, physics, and chemistry. A monetary prize of $250 and a scroll are awarded annually. Established in 1960. Administered by Drexel University.

★3526★ George E. Pake Prize
American Physical Society
One Physics Ellipse
College Park, MD 20740
Ph: (301)209-3200   Fax: (301)209-0867

To recognize and encourage outstanding work by physicists combining original research accomplishments with leadership in the management of research or development in industry. A monetary award of $5,000, an allowance for travel to the meeting at which the prize is awarded, and a plaque recognizing the contributions of the recipient are awarded annually. Established in 1983 in honor of the outstanding achievements of George E. Pake, a research physicist and a director of industrial research. Sponsored by the Xerox Corporation.

★3527★ W. K. H. Panofsky Prize
American Physical Society
One Physics Ellipse
College Park, MD 20740
Ph: (301)209-3200   Fax: (301)209-0867

To recognize and encourage outstanding achievements in experimental particle physics. Nominations are open to scientists of all nations regardless of the geographical site at which the work was done. The prize is ordinarily awarded to one person but the prize may be shared among recipients when all recipients have contributed to the same accomplishment. The prize is normally awarded for contributions made at an early stage of the recipient's career. The prize consists of $5,000, an allowance for travel to the meeting at which the prize is awarded, and a certificate citing the contributions made by the recipient. Established in 1985 by the friends of W.K.H. Panofsky and the Division of Particles and Fields.

★3528★ Prize for Industrial Applications of Physics
American Institute of Physics
335 E. 45th St.
New York, NY 10017
Ph: (212)661-9404   Fax: (212)949-0473

To recognize outstanding contributions by an individual(s) to the industrial applications of physics. A monetary prize of $7,500 and a certificate are awarded every two years. Established in 1977.

★3529★ Simon Ramo Award
American Physical Society
One Physics Ellipse
College Park, MD 20740
Ph: (301)209-3200   Fax: (301)209-0867

To provide recognition for exceptional young scientists who have performed original doctoral thesis work of outstanding scientific quality and achievements in the area of plasma physics. Nominations are accepted for any doctoral student (present or past) of a college or university in the United States or for U.S. students abroad. The work to be considered must have been performed as part of the requirements for a doctoral degree. Also, the nominee must not have passed his final doctoral examination or started regular employment more than one and a half years before the nomination deadline for the selection cycle in which the nomination is to be considered. The award consists of $1,500, a certificate, and an allowance for travel of up to $500 to attent the annual meeting of the Division of Plasma Physics of the American Physical Society at which the Award will be bestowed. Established in 1985 to honor the many outstanding contributions to the science and application of electromagnetism by Dr. Simon Ramo. Sponsored by TRW, Inc.

★3530★ Bruno Rossi Prize
American Astronomical Society
2000 Florida Ave. NW, Ste. 400
Washington, DC 20009
Ph: (202)328-2010   Fax: (202)234-2560

For a significant contribution to high energy astrophysics, with particular emphasis on recent work. Awarded annually by the High Energy Astrophysics Division. Established in 1984.

★3531★ Rumford Medal
American Academy of Arts and Sciences
Norton's Woods
136 Irving St.
Cambridge, MA 02138
Ph: (617)492-8800

This, the Academy's oldest and most prestigious award, is given to recognize important discoveries concerning heat or light. Nominations are made by committee. A monetary prize and medals are awarded when merited. Established in 1839.

★3532★ Henry Norris Russell Lectureship
American Astronomical Society
2000 Florida Ave. NW, Ste. 400
Washington, DC 20009
Ph: (202)328-2010   Fax: (202)234-2560

To recognize senior astronomers for lifetime eminence in astronomical research. A monetary prize is awarded annually. Established in 1946.

★3533★ Lester W. Strock Award
Society for Applied Spectroscopy
198 Thomas Johnsobn Dr. S-2
Frederick, MD 21702-4317
Ph: (301)694-8122   Fax: (301)694-6860

To recognize a selected publication of substantive research in/or application of analytical atomic spectrochemistry in the fields of earth, life, stellar, and cosmic sciences. A $500 honorarium and a medal are awarded annually at the FACSS Conference. Established in 1979. Sponsored by the New England Section of SAS.

★3534★ Leo Szilard Award for Physics in the Public Interest
American Physical Society
One Physics Ellipse
College Park, MD 20740
Ph: (301)209-3200   Fax: (301)209-0867

To recognize outstanding accomplishments by a physicist in promoting the use of physics for the benefit of society in such areas as the environment, arms control, and science policy. Any living physicist is eligible. The award consists of $250, a certificate citing the contributions of the recipient, and a sculpture to be held one year and passed on to the next winner, and travel expenses to attend the award ceremony. Awarded annually. Established in 1974 by the Forum on Physics and Society as a memorial to Leo Szilard in recognition of his concern for the social consequences of science.

★3535★ John T. Tate International Award
American Institute of Physics
335 E. 45th St.
New York, NY 10017
Ph: (212)661-9404   Fax: (212)949-0473

To recognize foreign nationals for distinguished service to the profession of physics, particularly through efforts that further international understanding and exchange, rather than for research accomplishments. A monetary award of $5,000, a bronze medal and a certificate are awarded at intervals of three to five years. Established in 1964.

★3536★ Beatrice M. Tinsley Prize
American Astronomical Society
2000 Florida Ave. NW, Ste. 400
Washington, DC 20009
Ph: (202)328-2010   Fax: (202)234-2560

To recognize an outstanding research contribution to astronomy or astrophysics of an exceptionally creative or innovative character. No restrictions are placed on a candidate's citizenship or country of residency. Awarded biennially. Established in 1986.

★3537★ Robert J. Trumpler Award
Astronomical Society of the Pacific
390 Ashton Ave.
San Francisco, CA 94112
Ph: (415)337-1100   Fax: (415)337-5205

To recognize a recent recipient of a Ph.D degree whose thesis research is considered unusually important to astronomy, broadly conceived. The thesis must have been written at a North American university and published at the time of the award, and the Ph.D must have been awarded within two years. Nominations may be made by chairpersons of all astronomy and physics departments in North America. The awardee receives $500 and a plaque, and presents a talk about his or her work at the ASP summer meeting. Awarded annually. Reactivated in 1973 in honor of the 20th century astronomer, Robert J. Trumpler, who made major contributions to the study of star clusters and the structure of our galaxy.

★3538★ Harold C. Urey Prize
American Astronomical Society
2000 Florida Ave. NW, Ste. 400
Washington, DC 20009
Ph: (202)328-2010   Fax: (202)234-2560

To recognize outstanding achievement in planetary research by a young scientist. Candidates must be residents of North America and must be either under 36 years of age, or the holder of a recognized doctorate for no more than six years. Awarded annually by the Division for Planetary Sciences. Established in 1984.

★3539★ James Craig Watson Medal
National Academy of Sciences
2101 Constitution Ave. NW
Washington, DC 20418
Ph: (202)334-2444

To recognize contributions to the science of astronomy. A monetary prize of $15,000 and a bronze medal are presented approximately every three years. Established in 1887.

★3540★ Medard W. Welch Award in Vacuum Science
American Vacuum Society
120 Wall St., 32nd Fl.
New York, NY 10005
Ph: (212)248-0200   Fax: (212)248-0245

To recognize outstanding research in fields of interest to the Society. The nominee must have accomplished outstanding theoretical or experimental research within the ten years preceding the year in which the award is made. Special consideration is given to nominees currently engaged in an active career of research. A monetary award of $5,000 and a gold medal are awarded annually. Established in 1969 in memory of M.W. Welch, founder of the Society.

★3541★ Robert R. Wilson Prize for Achievement in the Physics of Particle Accelerators
American Physical Society
One Physics Ellipse
College Park, MD 20740
Ph: (301)209-3200   Fax: (301)209-0867

To recognize and encourage outstanding achievement in the physics of particle accelerators. Nominations are open to scientists of all nations regardless of the geographical site at which the work was done. The prize shall ordinarily be awarded to one person but may be shared among recipients when all recipients have contributed to the same accomplishment. The prize will normally be awarded for contributions made at an early stage of the recipient's career. The prize consists of $5,000, an allowance for travel to the meeting at which the prize is awarded, and a certificate citing the contributions made by the recipient. Established in 1986 by the friends of Robert R. Wilson, the Division of Particles and Fields, and the Topical Group on Particle Beam Physics.

BASIC REFERENCE GUIDES AND HANDBOOKS

★3542★ CRC Handbook of Chemistry and Physics
CRC Press, Inc.
2000 Corporate Blvd., NW
Boca Raton, FL 33431
Ph: (305)994-0555   Fr: 800-272-7737

Robert C. Weast, editor in chief. Sixty-ninth edition, 1988. Contains mathematical tables and a section on physical constants.

★3543★ Encyclopedia of Physics
Hemisphere Publishing Corp.
79 Madison Ave., Ste. 1110
New York, NY 10016
Ph: (212)725-1999   Fr: 800-242-7737

A. M. Prokhorov. 1987.

★3544★ The Encyclopedia of Physics
Van Nostrand Reinhold Co., Inc.
115 5th Ave.
New York, NY 10003
Ph: (212)254-3232

Robert Martin Besancon, editor. Third edition, 1990. Covers the principals and applications of physics. Written for both the professional and non-professional.

★3545★ The Facts on File Dictionary of Physics
Facts on File
460 Park Ave. S.
New York, NY 10016-7382
Ph: (212)683-2244   Fax: 800-678-3633
Fr: 800-322-8755

Dr. John Daintith, editor. Revised expanded edition, 1990. Defines 2000 commonly-used physics terms.

★3546★ Formulas, Facts, and Constants for Students and Professionals in Engineering, Chemistry, and Physics
Springer-Verlag New York, Inc.
175 5th Ave.
New York, NY 10010
Ph: (212)460-1500   Fr: 800-777-4643

Helmut J. Fischbeck and K. H. Fischbeck. Second edition, 1987. Includes an index. Illustrated.

★3547★ Norton's Star Atlas and Reference Handbook
John Wiley and Sons, Inc.
605 3rd Ave.
New York, NY 10158-0012
Ph: (212)850-6000   Fax: (212)850-6088
Fr: 800-526-5368

Arthur P. Norton. Eighteenth edition, 1989. Defines the terminology of observational astronomy.

★3548★ Physics
John Wiley and Sons, Inc.
605 3rd Ave.
New York, NY 10158-0012
Ph: (212)850-6000   Fax: (212)850-6088
Fr: 800-526-5368

Joseph W. Kane and Morton M. Sternheim. Third edition, 1988. Covers the general laws of motion, mechanics, and electricity and magnetism.

★3549★ A Source Book in Astronomy and Astrophysics, 1900-1975
Harvard University Press
79 Garden St.
Cambridge, MA 02138
Ph: (617)495-2600   Fr: 800-448-2242
Kenneth R. Lang and Owen Gingerich, editors. 1979. Follows the programs of the science of astronomy by presenting original papers.

PROFESSIONAL AND TRADE PERIODICALS

★3550★ AIP History of Physics Newsletter
Center for History of Physics
1 Physics Ellipse
College Park, MD 20740
Ph: (212)661-9404
Spencer R. Weart
Semiannual. Summarizes current work of the Center and other institutions in the history of physics. Supplies information on collections of relevant materials located in repositories in the U.S. and abroad.

★3551★ High Power Rocketry Magazine
PO Box 96
Orem, UT 84059
Ph: (801)225-3250
Bruce Kelly
Bimonthly. Carries news of members' research in astronomy, physics, and rockets. Includes news of the Association, which is interested in innovative scientific work and whose members are amateur astronomers.

★3552★ Journal of Mathematical Physics
American Institute of Physics
500 Sunnyside Blvd.
Woodbury, NY 11797
Ph: (516)576-2444   Fax: (516)349-0247
William H. Davis
Monthly. Journal presenting original work of interest to theoretical and mathematical physicists.

★3553★ Physics Today
American Institute of Physics
500 Sunnyside Blvd.
Woodbury, NY 11797-2999
Ph: (516)576-2440   Fax: (516)576-2481
Gloria B. Lubkin
Monthly. Journal covering news of physics research and activities that affect physics.

★3554★ Reviews of Modern Physics
American Institute of Physics
500 Sunnyside Blvd.
Woodbury, NY 11797
Ph: (516)576-2444   Fax: (516)349-0247
D. Pines

★3555★ Russian Journal of Mathematical Physics
John Wiley and Sons, Inc.
Subscription Dept.
605 3rd Ave.
New York, NY 10158
Ph: (212)850-6000   Fax: (212)850-6799
Victor P. Maslov
Journal publishing articles on recent achievements and reviews of modern mathematical physics.

OTHER SOURCES OF INFORMATION

★3556★ "Astronomer" in Career Selector 2001
Barron's Educational Series, Inc.
250 Wireless Blvd.
Hauppauge, NY 11788
Ph: (516)434-3311   Fax: (516)434-3723
Fr: 800-645-3476
James C. Gonyea. 1993.

★3557★ The Astronomers
St. Martin's Press, Inc.
175 5th Ave.
New York, NY 10010
Ph: (212)674-5151
Donald Goldsmith, editor. 1993.

★3558★ Astronomical Almanac
Superintendent of Documents
U.S. Government Printing Office
Washington, DC 20402-3054
Ph: (202)275-2051
Annual. Contains data for astronomy and related sciences.

★3559★ Joy of Insight: Passions of a Physicist
Basic Books, Inc.
10 E. 53rd St.
New York, NY 10022
Ph: (212)207-7057   Fax: (212)207-7203
Victor Weisskopf, editor. 1992.

★3560★ The Light at the Edge of the Universe: Astronomers on the Front Lines of the Cosmological Revolution
Random House, Inc.
201 E. 50th St.
New York, NY 10022
Ph: (212)751-2600
Michael D. Lemonick, editor. 1993.

★3561★ "Physicist/Astronomer" in 100 Best Jobs for the 1990s & Beyond
Dearborn Financial Publishing, Inc.
520 N. Dearborn St.
Chicago, IL 60610-4354
Ph: (312)836-4400   Fax: (312)836-1021
Fr: 800-621-9621
Carol Kleiman. 1992. Describes 100 jobs ranging from accountants to veterinarians. Each job profile includes such information as education, experience, and certification needed, salaries, and job search suggestions.

★3562★ "Physicist" in Career Selector 2001
Barron's Educational Series, Inc.
250 Wireless Blvd.
Hauppauge, NY 11788
Ph: (516)434-3311   Fax: (516)434-3723
Fr: 800-645-3476
James C. Gonyea. 1993.

★3563★ "Physics" in Accounting to Zoology: Graduate Fields Defined (pp. 310-317)
Petersons Guides, Inc.
PO Box 2123
Princeton, NJ 08543-2123
Ph: (609)243-9111   Fax: (609)243-9150
Fr: 800-338-3282
Amy J. Goldstein, editor. Revised and updated, 1987. Defines 298 graduate and professional fields. Discusses types of graduate programs and degrees, graduate research, applied work, employment prospects, and trends.

★3564★ Salaries of Scientists, Engineers, and Technicians: A Summary of Salary Surveys
Commission on Professionals in Science and Technology (CPST)
1500 Massachusetts Ave., NW, Ste. 831
Washington, DC 20005
Ph: (202)223-6995
1993.

Lawyers and Judges

Lawyers or **attorneys**, act as both advocates and advisors. As advocates, they represent one of the opposing parties in criminal and civil trials by presenting arguments that support the client in court. As advisors, lawyers counsel their clients as to their legal rights and obligations and suggest particular courses of action in business and personal matters. The majority of lawyers are in private practice where they may concentrate on criminal or civil law. **Judges** oversee the legal process that in courts of law resolves civil disputes and determines guilt in criminal cases according to Federal and State laws and those of local jurisdictions. They are responsible for ensuring that trials and hearings are conducted fairly and justice is administered in a manner that safeguards the legal rights of all parties involved. Judges preside over trials or hearings and listen as attorneys representing the parties present and argue their cases. They rule on the admissibility of evidence and methods of conducting testimony, and settle disputes between the opposing attorneys. They insure that rules and procedures are followed. **Trial court judges** of the Federal and State court systems have general jurisdiction over any case in their system. Federal and state **appellate court judges** review cases handled by lower courts and administrative agencies. **Administrative law offices judges** formerly called **hearing officers** are employed by government agencies to rule on appeals of agency administrative decisions.

Salaries

Salaries vary by academic background, field of law, and the type, size, and location of employers.

Beginning attorneys, private industry	$36,600/year
Experienced attorneys, private industry	More than $134,000/year
Beginning attorneys, federal government	$27,800-$33,600/year
General attorneys, federal government	$62,200/year
Patent attorneys, federal government	$71.600/year
Federal district court judges	$133,600/year
Circuit court judges	$141,700/year
Federal administrative law judges	$94,800/year

Employment Outlook

Growth rate until the year 2005: Slower than the average for judges; faster than the average for lawyers.

Lawyers and Judges

CAREER GUIDES

★3565★ "Admiralty Law" in
Opportunities in Marine and Maritime
Careers (p. 105)
National Textbook Co. (NTC)
VGM Career Books
4255 W. Touhy Ave.
Lincolnwood, IL 60646-1975
Ph: (708)679-5500   Fax: (708)679-2494
Fr: 800-323-4900
William Ray Heitzman. 1988. Covers careers in cruise ships, oceanography, marine sciences, fishing, commercial diving, maritime transportation, shipbuilding, the Navy, and the Coast Guard. Describes job duties, training requirements, and how to get started. Lists schools.

★3566★ "Attorney" in Guide to Federal
Jobs (p. 173)
Resource Directories
3361 Executive Pkwy., Ste. 302
Toledo, OH 43606
Ph: (419)536-5353   Fax: (419)536-7056
Fr: 800-274-8515
Rod W. Durgin, editor. Third edition, 1992. Contains information on finding and applying for federal jobs. Describes more than 200 professional and technical jobs for college graduates. Covers the nature of the work, salary, and geographic location. Lists college majors preferred for that occupation. Section one describes the function and work of government agencies that hire the most significant number of college graduates.

★3567★ "Attorney" in Jobs Rated
Almanac
World Almanac
1 International Blvd., Ste. 444
Mahwah, NJ 07495
Ph: (201)529-6900   Fax: (201)529-6901
Les Krantz. Second edition, 1992. Ranks 250 jobs by environment, salary, outlooks, physical demands, stress, security, travel opportunities, and extra perks. Includes jobs the editor feels are the most common, most interesting, and the most rapidly growing.

★3568★ "Attorneys" in 101 Careers: A
Guide to the Fastest-Growing
Opportunities (pp. 128-130)
John Wiley & Sons, Inc.
605 3rd Ave.
New York, NY 10158-0012
Ph: (212)850-6645   Fax: (212)850-6088
Michael Harkavy. 1990. Describes the nature of the job, working conditions, employment growth, qualifications, personal skills, projected salaries, and where to write for more information.

★3569★ Career Choices for the 90's for
Students of Law
Walker and Co.
435 Hudson St.
New York, NY 10014
Ph: (212)727-8300   Fax: (212)727-0984
Fr: 800-289-2553
1990. Offers career alternatives for students interested in law. Provides information about the job outlook for entry-level job candidates and competition for jobs; contains tips on how to get the job.

★3570★ Careers in International Law
American Bar Assn.
Section of International Law and Practice
1800 M St., NW, Ste. 450J
Washington, DC 20036
Ph: (202)331-2239
Mark W. Janis, editor. 1993. Includes bibliographies.

★3571★ Careers in Law
National Textbook Co. (NTC)
VGM Career Books
4255 W. Toughy Ave.
Lincolnwood, IL 60646-1975
Ph: (708)679-5500   Fax: (708)679-2494
Fr: 800-323-4900
Gary Munneke. Describes different opportunities for lawyers.

★3572★ Careers in Natural Resources
and Environmental Law
American Bar Association (ABA)
750 N. Lake Shore Dr.
Chicago, IL 60611
Ph: (312)988-6064
Percy R. Luney. 1987. Provides an overview of environmental law, public and private practice, and future trends. Gives job hunting tips.

Profiles law firms, corporations, and governmental and public interest employers.

★3573★ Changing Jobs: A Handbook
for Lawyers for the 1990s
American Bar Association Young Lawyers Division
Section of Law Practice Management
750 N. Lake Shore Dr.
Chicago, IL 60611
Ph: (312)988-5751
Carol Kanarak, editor. 1994.

★3574★ Choosing a Career in the Law
Harvard University Press
79 Garden St.
Cambridge, MA 02138
Ph: (617)495-2600
Dena O. Rakoff. 1991. Gives an overview of professions in law. Describes the law school application process and curriculum, and introduces some law-related fields. Lists additional sources of information.

★3575★ Corporate Attorney
Vocational Biographies, Inc.
PO Box 31
Sauk Centre, MN 56378-0031
Ph: (612)352-6516   Fax: (612)352-5546
Fr: 800-255-0752
1990. Four-page pamphlet containing a personal narrative about a worker's job, work likes and dislikes, career path from high school to the present. Education and training, the rewards and frustrations, and the effects of the job on the rest of the worker's life. The data file portion of this pamphlet gives a concise occupational summary, including work descriptions, working conditions, places of employment, personal characteristics, education and training, job outlook, and salary range.

★3576★ Criminal Defense Attorney
Vocational Biographies, Inc.
PO Box 31
Sauk Centre, MN 56378-0031
Ph: (612)352-6516   Fax: (612)352-5546
Fr: 800-255-0752
1990. Four-page pamphlet containing a personal narrative about a worker's job, work likes and dislikes, career path from high school to the present. Education and training, the rewards and frustrations, and the effects of the job on the rest of the worker's life. The

data file portion of this pamphlet gives a concise occupational summary, including work descriptions, working conditions, places of employment, personal characteristics, education and training, job outlook, and salary range.

★3577★ **District Attorney**
Vocational Biographies, Inc.
PO Box 31
Sauk Centre, MN 56378-0031
Ph: (612)352-6516   Fax: (612)352-5546
Fr: 800-255-0752

1991. Four-page pamphlet containing a personal narrative about a worker's job, work likes and dislikes, career path from high school to the present. Education and training, the rewards and frustrations, and the effects of the job on the rest of the worker's life. The data file portion of this pamphlet gives a concise occupational summary, including work descriptions, working conditions, places of employment, personal characteristics, education and training, job outlook, and salary range.

★3578★ **Environmental Lawyer**
Vocational Biographies, Inc.
PO Box 31
Sauk Centre, MN 56378-0031
Ph: (612)352-6516   Fax: (612)352-5546
Fr: 800-255-0752

1991. Four-page pamphlet containing a personal narrative about a worker's job, work likes and dislikes, career path from high school to the present. Education and training, the rewards and frustrations, and the effects of the job on the rest of the worker's life. The data file portion of this pamphlet gives a concise occupational summary, including work descriptions, working conditions, places of employment, personal characteristics, education and training, job outlook, and salary range.

★3579★ **"International Law"** in *Guide to Careers in World Affairs*
Impact Publications
10655 Big Oak Circle
Manassas Park, VA 22111
Ph: (703)361-7300

Third ed., 1993. Describes jobs in business, government, and nonprofit organizations. Explains the methods and credentials required to secure a job. Contains sections on internships and graduate programs.

★3580★ **"Judge (Federal)"** in *Jobs Rated Almanac*
World Almanac
1 International Blvd., Ste. 444
Mahwah, NJ 07495
Ph: (201)529-6900   Fax: (201)529-6901

Les Krantz. Second edition, 1992. Ranks 250 jobs by environment, salary, outlooks, physical demands, stress, security, travel opportunities, and extra perks. Includes jobs the editor feels are the most common, most interesting, and the most rapidly growing.

★3581★ **Judges**
Chronicle Guidance Publications, Inc.
66 Aurora St.
PO Box 1190
Moravia, NY 13118-1190
Ph: (315)497-0330   Fax: (315)497-3359
Fr: 800-622-7284

1993. Occupational brief describing the nature of the job, working conditions, hours and earnings, education and training, licensure, certification, unions, personal qualifications, social and psychological factors, location, employment outlook, entry methods, advancement, and related occupations.

★3582★ **"Judges"** in *Career Discovery Encyclopedia* **(Vol.3, pp. 152-153)**
J.G. Ferguson Publishing Co.
200 W. Madison St., Ste. 300
Chicago, IL 60606
Ph: (312)580-5480   Fax: (312)580-4948

Russell E. Primm, editor-in chief. 1993. This six volume set contains two-page articles for 504 occupations. Each article describes job duties, earnings, and educational and training requirements. The whole set is arranged alphabetically by job title. Designed for junior high and older students.

★3583★ **"Law"** in *Black Woman's Career Guide* **(pp. 77-91)**
Bantam Doubleday Dell
1540 Broadway
New York, NY 10036
Fax: 800-233-3294   Fr: 800-223-5780

Beatryce Nivens. Revised edition, 1987. Describes career planning, resume writing, job hunting, and interviewing. Profiles 60 black women pioneers in 20 different careers.

★3584★ **Law as a Career**
American Bar Association (ABA)
750 N. Lake Shore Dr.
Chicago, IL 60611
Ph: (312)988-6510

1992. Describes the lawyers role in society, opportunities for women and miniorites, earnings, how to choose and get into law school, and how to secure admission to the bar.

★3585★ **"Law"** in *Career Choices for the 90's for Students of English*
Walker and Co.
435 Hudson St.
New York, NY 10014
Ph: (212)727-8300   Fax: (212)727-0984
Fr: 800-289-2553

1990. Offers career alternatives for students of English. Gives the outlook and competition for entry-level candidates. Provides job-hunting tips.

★3586★ **"Law"** in *Career Choices for the 90's for Students of History*
Walker and Co.
435 Hudson St.
New York, NY 10014
Ph: (212)727-8300   Fax: (212)727-0984
Fr: 800-289-2553

1990. Offers alternatives for students of history. Gives information about the outlook and competition for entry-level candidates. Provides job-hunting tips.

★3587★ **"Law"** in *Career Choices for the 90's for Students of Political Science and Government*
Walker and Co.
435 Hudson St.
New York, NY 10014
Ph: (212)727-8300   Fax: (212)727-0984
Fr: 800-289-2553

1990. Offers alternatives for students of political science. Gives information about job outlook and competition for entry-level candidates. Provides job-hunting tips.

★3588★ **"Law"** in *College Majors and Careers: A Resource Guide to Effective Life Planning* **(pp. 81-82)**
Garrett Park Press
PO Box 1907
Garrett Park, MD 20896
Ph: (301)946-2553

Paul Phifer. Revised, 1993. Lists 60 college majors, with definitions; related occupations and leisure activities; skills, values, and personal attributes needed; suggested readings; and a list of associations.

★3589★ **"Law/Criminal Justice"** in *Internships: 1995* **(pp. 340-346)**
Petersons Guides, Inc.
PO Box 2123
Princeton, NJ 08543-2123
Ph: (609)243-9111   Fax: (609)243-9150
Fr: 800-338-3282

Fifteenth edition, 1995. Lists internship opportunities under six broad categories: communications, creative, performing, and fine arts, human services, international relations, business and technology, and public relations. Includes a special section on internships in Washington, DC. For each internship program, gives the name, phone number, contact person, description, eligibility requirements, and benefits.

★3590★ **"Law"** in *Encyclopedia of Career Choices for the 1990s: A Guide to Entry Level Jobs* **(pp. 477-500)**
Berkley Pub.
PO Box 506
East Rutherford, NJ 07073
Fax: (201)933-2316   Fr: 800-788-6262

1992. Describes entry-level careers in a variety of industries. Presents qualifications required, working conditions, salary, internships, and professional associations.

★3591★ **"Law"** in *Encyclopedia of Careers and Vocational Guidance* **(Vol.1, pp. 248-254)**
J.G. Ferguson Publishing Co.
200 W. Madison St., Ste. 300
Chicago, IL 60606
Ph: (312)580-5480   Fax: (312)580-4948

William E. Hopke, editor-in-chief. Ninth edition, 1993. Four-volume set that profiles 900 occupations and describes job trends in 74 industries. Includes career description, educational requirements, history of the job, methods of entry, advancement, employment outlook, earnings, conditions of work, social and psychological factors, and sources of further information.

★3592★ "Law and Legal Services" in *Where the Jobs Are: The Hottest Careers for the 90s* (pp. 183-194)
Career Press
180 5th Ave.
Hawthorne, NJ 07507
Ph: (201)427-0229   Fax: (201)427-2037
Fr: 800-CAREER-1
Joyce Hadley. 1995. Offers a job-hunting strategy for the 1990s as well as descriptions of growing careers of the decade. Each profile includes general information, forecasts, growth, education and training, licensing requirements, and salary information.

★3593★ "Law" in *Liberal Arts Jobs*
Petersons Guides, Inc.
PO Box 2123
Princeton, NJ 08543-2123
Ph: (609)243-9111   Fax: (609)243-9150
Fr: 800-338-3282
Burton Jay Nadler. Second edition, 1989. Strives to help the liberal arts graduate identify skills for entry-level positions. Gives goal setting and job search advice.

★3594★ "Law" in *Opportunities in Gerontology* (pp. 41-42)
National Textbook Co. (NTC)
VGM Career Books
4255 W. Touhy Ave.
Lincolnwood, IL 60646-1975
Ph: (708)679-5500   Fax: (708)679-2494
Fr: 800-323-4900
Ellen Williams. 1987. Gives a broad overview of career opportunities in gerontology in many fields. Suggest training needed and internships and volunteer opportunities. Lists gerontology-related associations. Gives sources of additional information.

★3595★ "Law" in *Straight Talk on Careers: Eighty Pros Take You Into Their Professions* (pp. 57-73)
Garrett Park Press
PO Box 1907
Garrett Park, MD 20896
Ph: (301)946-2553
Mary Barbera-Hogan. 1987. Contains candid interviews from people who give an inside view of their work in 80 different careers. These professionals describe a day's work and the stresses and rewards accompanying their work.

★3596★ *Lawyer*
Careers, Inc.
PO Box 135
Largo, FL 34649-0135
Ph: (813)584-7333
1992. Four-page brief offering the definition, history, duties, working conditions, personal qualifications, educational requirements, earnings, hours, employment outlook, advancement, and careers related to this position.

★3597★ "Lawyer" in *100 Best Careers for the Year 2000* (pp. 180-181)
Arco Pub.
201 W. 103rd St.
Indianapolis, IN 46290
Ph: 800-428-5331   Fax: 800-835-3202
Shelly Field. 1992. Describes 100 job opportunities expected to grow fast throughout the next decade. Provides information on job

duties and responsibilities, training requirements, education, advancement opportunities, experience and qualifications, and typical salaries.

★3598★ "Lawyer" in *College Board Guide to Jobs and Career Planning* (pp. 222-224)
The College Board
45 Columbus Ave.
New York, NY 10023-6992
Ph: (212)713-8165   Fax: (212)713-8143
Fr: 800-323-7155
Second edition, 1994. Describes the job, salaries, related careers, education needed, and where to write for more information.

★3599★ *Lawyer Professionalism*
Carolina Academic Press
700 Kent St.
Durham, NC 27701
Ph: (919)489-7486
Jack L. Sammons. 1988. Discusses issues concerning professional lawyers.

★3600★ "Lawyer" in *VGM's Careers Encyclopedia* (pp. 242-244)
National Textbook Co. (NTC)
VGM Career Books
4255 W. Touhy Ave.
Lincolnwood, IL 60646-1975
Ph: (708)679-5500   Fax: (708)679-2494
Fr: 800-323-4900
Third edition, 1991. Profiles 200 occupations. Describes job duties, places of employment, working conditions, qualifications, education and training, advancement potential, and salary for each occupation.

★3601★ "Lawyer" in *VGM's Handbook of Business and Management Careers*
National Textbook Co.
4255 W. Touhy Ave.
Lincolnwood, IL 60646-1975
Ph: (708)679-5500   Fax: (708)679-2494
Fr: 800-323-4900
Annette Selden. Second edition, 1993. Contains 42 two-page occupational profiles describing job duties, places of employment, working conditions, qualifications, education, employment outlook, and income.

★3602★ *Lawyers*
Chronicle Guidance Publications, Inc.
66 Aurora St.
PO Box 1190
Moravia, NY 13118-1190
Ph: (315)497-0330   Fax: (315)497-3359
Fr: 800-622-7284
1993. Career brief describing the nature of the job, working conditions, hours and earnings, education and training, licensure, certification, unions, personal qualifications, social and psychological factors, location, employment outlook, entry methods, advancement, and related occupations.

★3603★ "Lawyers" in *American Almanac of Jobs and Salaries* (pp. 236)
Avon Books
1350 Avenue of the Americas
New York, NY 10019
Ph: (212)261-6800   Fr: 800-238-0658
John Wright, editor. Revised and updated, 1994-95. A comprehensive guide to the wages of hundreds of occupations in a wide variety of industries and organizations.

★3604★ "Lawyers" in *Career Discovery Encyclopedia* (Vol.3, pp. 166-167)
J.G. Ferguson Publishing Co.
200 W. Madison St., Ste. 300
Chicago, IL 60606
Ph: (312)580-5480   Fax: (312)580-4948
Russell E. Primm, editor-in-chief. 1993. This six volume set contains two-page articles for 504 occupations. Each article describes job duties, earnings, and educational and training requirements. The whole set is arranged alphabetically by job title. Designed for junior high and older students.

★3605★ "Lawyers" in *Career Information Center* (Vol.11)
Simon and Schuster
200 Old Tappan Rd.
Old Tappan, NJ 07675
Fax: 800-445-6991   Fr: 800-223-2348
Richard Lidz and Linda Perrin, editorial directors. Fifth edition, 1993. This 13-volume set profiles over 600 occupations. Each occupational profile describes job duties, educational requirements, advancement possibilities, employment outlook, working conditions, earnings and benefits, and where to write for more information.

★3606★ "Lawyers" in *Jobs! What They Are—Where They Are—What They Pay* (p. 221)
Simon & Schuster, Inc.
Simon & Schuster Bldg.
1230 Avenue of the Americas
New York, NY 10020
Ph: (212)698-7000   Fr: 800-223-2348
Robert O. Snelling and Anne M. Snelling. 3rd edition, 1992. Describes duties and responsibilities, earnings, employment opportunities, training, and qualifications.

★3607★ "Lawyers and Judges" in *America's 50 Fastest Growing Jobs* (pp. 43)
JIST Works, Inc.
720 N. Park Ave.
Indianapolis, IN 46202-3431
Ph: (317)264-3720   Fax: (317)264-3709
Fr: 800-648-5478
Michael J. Farr, compiler. 1994. Describes the 50 fastest growing jobs within major career clusters such as technicians, and marketing and sales. Each job profile explains the nature of the work, skills and abilities required, employment outlook, average earnings, related occupations, education and training requirements, and employment opportunities. Also contains career planning information and job search tips.

★3608★ "Lawyers and Judges" in *Encyclopedia of Careers and Vocational Guidance* (Vol.3, pp. 281-285)
J.G. Ferguson Publishing Co.
200 W. Madison St., Ste. 300
Chicago, IL 60606
Ph: (312)580-5480   Fax: (312)580-4948
William E. Hopke, editor-in-chief. Ninth edition, 1993. Four-volume set that profiles 900 occupations and describes job trends in 74 industries. Includes career description, educational requirements, history of the job, methods of entry, advancement, employment outlook, earnings, conditions of work, social

and psychological factors, and sources of further information.

★3609★ "Lawyers and Judges" in *Occupational Outlook Handbook*
U.S. Government Printing Office
Superintendent of Documents
Washington, DC 20402
Ph: (202)512-1800   Fax: (202)512-2250
Biennial; latest edition, 1994-95. Encyclopedia of careers describing about 250 occupations and comprising about 85 percent of all jobs in the economy. Occupations that require lengthy education or training are given the most attention. Each occupation's profile describes what the worker does on the job, working conditions, education and training requirements, advancement possibilities, job outlook, earnings, and sources of additional information.

★3610★ "Lawyers" in *Opportunities in Real Estate Careers* **(pp. 115-117)**
National Textbook Co. (NTC)
VGM Career Books
4255 W. Touhy Ave.
Lincolnwood, IL 60646-1975
Ph: (708)679-5500   Fax: (708)679-2494
Fr: 800-323-4900
Mariwyn Evans. 1988. Gives an overview of the real estate industry. Describes jobs and specialties in the estate field. Lists schools and addresses to write to for more information.

★3611★ "Lawyers" in *Profiles in Achievement* **(pp. 103-120)**
The College Board
45 Columbus Ave.
New York, NY 10023-6992
Ph: (212)713-8165   Fax: (212)713-8143
Fr: 800-323-7155
Charles M. Holloway. 1987. Profiles eight men and women who have overcome the the barriers of race, gender, tradition, and economic circumstances in their quest to become successful professionals.

★3612★ *Legal Careers and the Legal System*
Enslow Publishers, Inc.
600 Bloy St. & Ramsey Ave.
PO Box 777
Hillside, NJ 07205
Ph: (908)964-4116   Fr: 800-828-7571
William Fry and Roy Hoopes. 1988. Describes the role of the lawyer in the legal system.

★3613★ *Nonlegal Careers for Lawyers in the Private Sector: Updated Resource Information*
American Bar Association (ABA)
Law Student Division
750 N. Lake Shore Dr.
Chicago, IL 60611
Ph: (312)988-5751
Frances Utley. Second edition, 1994.

★3614★ *Opportunities in Law Careers*
National Textbook Co. (NTC)
VGM Career Books
4255 W. Toughy Ave.
Lincolnwood, IL 60646-1975
Ph: (708)679-5500   Fax: (708)679-2494
Fr: 800-323-4900
Gary A. Munneke.

★3615★ *The Public Interest Handbook: A Guide to Legal Careers in Public Interest Organization*
Locust Hill Press
Main St.
West Cornwall, CT 06796
Ph: (203)672-0060
Geoffrey Kaiser and Barbara Mule. 1987. Profiles public-interest law firms and labor organizations that hire lawyers.

★3616★ *Thinking About Law*
Petersons Guides, Inc.
PO Box 2123
Princeton, NJ 08543-2123
Ph: (609)243-9111   Fax: (609)243-9150
Fr: 800-338-3282
1990. Examines careers in law; discusses how to choose a law school and how to take the LSAT.

PROFESSIONAL ASSOCIATIONS

★3617★ American Bar Association (ABA)
750 N. Lake Shore Dr.
Chicago, IL 60611
Ph: (312)988-5000   Fax: (312)988-6281
Fr: 800-621-6159
Members: Attorneys in good standing of the bar of any state. **Purpose:** Conducts research and educational projects and activities to: encourage professional improvement; provide public services; improve the administration of civil and criminal justice; increase the availability of legal services to the public. Sponsors Law Day USA. Administers numerous standing and special committees such as Committee on Soviet and East European Law, providing seminars and newsletters. Operates 25 sections, including Criminal Justice, Economics of Law Practice, and Family Law. Sponsors essay competitions. Maintains library. **Publications:** *ABA Journal*, monthly. • *Administrative Law Review*, quarterly. • *American Bar Association—Washington Letter*, monthly. • *Antitrust*, 3/year. • *Antitrust Law Journal*, quarterly. • *Barrister*, quarterly. • *The Brief*, quarterly. • *Business Lawyer*, quarterly. • *China Law Reporter*, quarterly. • *Communications Law*, quarterly. • *The Compleat Lawyer*, quarterly. • *Criminal Justice*, quarterly. • *The Entertainment and Sports Lawyer*, quarterly. • *Environmental Law*, quarterly. • *Family Advocate*, quarterly. • *Family Law Quarterly*, quarterly. • *Fidelity and Security News*, quarterly. • *Franchise Law Journal*, quarterly. • *Human Rights*, 3/year. • *Intelligence Report*, monthly. • *International Lawyer*, quarterly. • *The Judges' Journal*, quarterly. • *Jurimetrics: Journal of Law, Science and Technology*, quarterly. • *Juvenile and Child Welfare Law Reporter*, monthly. • *Labor Lawyer*, quarterly. • *Law Practice Management*, 8/year. • *Lawyers' Professional Liability Update*, annual. • *Litigation*, quarterly. • *LRE Project Exchange*, 3/year. • *LRE Report*, 3/year. • *Mental and Physical Disability Law Reporter*, bimonthly. • *Natural Resources and Environment*, quarterly. • *Passport to Legal Understanding: The Newsletter on Public Education*

Programs and Materials, semiannual. • *Preview of U.S. Supreme Court Cases*, biweekly. • *Probate and Property*, bimonthly. • *Public Contract Law Journal*, quarterly. • *Real Property, Probate and Trust Journal*, quarterly. • *Student Lawyer*, monthly. • *Syllabus*, quarterly. • *The Tax Lawyer*, quarterly. • *Tort and Insurance Law Journal*, quarterly. • *The Urban Lawyer*, quarterly.

★3618★ American Judges Association (AJA)
300 Newport Ave.
Williamsburg, VA 23187-8798
Ph: (804)259-1841   Fax: (804)229-7899
Members: Purpose: Seeks to improve the administration of justice at all levels of the courts. **Publications:** *AJA Benchmark*, quarterly. • *Court Review*, quarterly.

★3619★ Association of American Law Schools (AALS)
1201 Connecticut Ave. NW, Ste. 800
Washington, DC 20036-2605
Ph: (202)296-8851   Fax: (202)296-8869
Members: Law schools. **Purpose:** Seeks to improve the legal profession through legal education. Cooperates with state and federal government, other legal education and professional associations, and other national higher education and learned society organizations. Compiles statistics; sponsors teacher placement service. **Publications:** *Association Handbook*, annual. • *Association of American Law Schools—Newsletter*, quarterly. • *Association of American Law Schools—Placement Bulletin*, bimonthly. • *Directory of Law Teachers*, annual. • *Journal of Legal Education*, quarterly.

★3620★ Law School Admission Council/ Law School Admission Services (LSAC/LSAS)
PO Box 40
Newtown, PA 18940
Ph: (215)968-1101
Members: Law schools in the U.S. and Canada. **Purpose:** Develops and administers the law school admission test (LSAT). Provides services to law schools and law school applicants to support the admission process. Holds law school forums. **Publications:** *Law as a Career: A Practical Guide*. • *Official Guide to U.S. Law Schools*. • *Official LSAT PrepKit*. • *Official LSAT TriplePrep: Volume 1*. • *Official LSAT TriplePrep: Volume 2*. • *Prep Tests*. • *Thinking About Law School: A Minority Guide*.

★3621★ National Association for Law Placement (NALP)
1666 Connecticut Ave., Ste. 325
Washington, DC 20009
Ph: (202)667-1666   Fax: (202)265-6735
Members: Law schools, legal employers, and bar associations actively engaged in the recruitment and placement of lawyers. **Purpose:** Purposes are to: provide for the creation and maintenance of standards and ethical procedures to guide law schools and employers in career services and recruitment; promote the exchange of ideas, information, and experiences; develop resource materials and educational programs; enlist employers and law schools in developing well-coordinated placement and recruiting services; provide means for member

organizations to participate in an affirmative policy against discrimination in employment. Conducts annual survey of law school graduates and other research. **Publications:** *Directory of Legal Employers*, annual. • *Federal and State Judicial Clerkship Directory*, annual. • *NALP Bulletin*, monthly. • *National Association for Law Placement—Employment Report and Salary Survey*, annual. • *National Directory of Law Schools*, annual.

★3622★ National Association of Women Judges (NAWJ)
1612 K St. NW, Ste. 1400
Washington, DC 20006-2802
Ph: (202)872-0963   Fax: (202)293-3218
Members: Individuals holding judicial or quasi-judicial positions. **Purpose:** Objectives are to: promote the administration of justice; discuss and formulate solutions to legal, educational, social, and ethical problems encountered by women judges; increase the number of women judges so that the judiciary more appropriately reflects the role of women in a democratic society; address other issues particularly affecting women judges. Conducts research and educational programs and referral services; compiles statistics. **Publications:** *NAWJ Annual Directory*. • *NAWJ Newsletter*.

★3623★ National Judges Association (NJA)
42 Little Horn Rd.
Westcliffe, CO 81252
Ph: (719)783-2562   Fr: 800-654-3099
Members: Incumbent nonlawyer judges and individuals working to publicize the contributions of nonlawyer judges to the court system. Opposes legislation limiting judicial positions to individuals with a law degree. Fosters exchange of ideas, methods, and experiences among members. Seeks to enhance members' judicial performance through further education. Maintains National Judges Education and Research Foundation, which seeks to improve the judicial image and performance through continuing education and training and information exchange. Offers educational courses. **Publications:** *The Gavel*, quarterly.

★3624★ Scandanavian American Lawyers Association
4177 Garrick
Warren, MI 48091
Ph: (313)757-4177   Fax: (313)758-8173
Members: Professional association of Scandanavian-American attorneys. **Purpose:** Provides a forum to discuss and address issues of interest to members. Maintains a placement service.

★3625★ World Association of Judges (WAJ)
1000 Connecticut Ave. NW, Ste. 202
Washington, DC 20036
Ph: (202)466-5428   Fax: (202)452-8540
Members: Members of courts in countries throughout the world. **Purpose:** Promotes the expansion of the rule of law in the world community and the advancement and improvement of the administration of justice for all people.

STANDARDS/CERTIFICATION AGENCIES

★3626★ Community Associations Institute (CAI)
1630 Duke St.
Alexandria, VA 22314
Ph: (703)548-8600   Fax: (703)684-1581
Purpose is to develop and provide the most advanced and effective guidance for the creation, financing, operation, and maintenance of the common facilities and services in condominiums, townhouse projects, planned unit developments, and open-space communities.

★3627★ National Association for Law Placement (NALP)
1666 Connecticut Ave., Ste. 325
Washington, DC 20009
Ph: (202)667-1666   Fax: (202)265-6735
Purposes are to: provide for the creation and maintenance of standards and ethical procedures to guide law schools and employers in career services and recruitment; promote the exchange of ideas, information, and experiences; develop resource materials and educational programs.

TEST GUIDES

★3628★ Admission Test Series: Law School Admission Test
National Learning Corp.
212 Michael Dr.
Syosset, NY 11791
Ph: (516)921-8888   Fax: (516)921-8743
Fr: 800-645-6337
Jack Rudman. A collection of sample examinations designed to prepare prospective lawyers for graduate and professional school entrance tests and for tests administered by private and public institutions for entrance and career advancement. Provides multiple-choice questions; includes correct answers. Titles in the series include *Multistate Bar Examination (MBE); New York State Bar Examination (NYBE)*.

★3629★ Barron's How to Prepare for the Law School Admission Test (LSAT)
Barron's Educational Series, Inc.
250 Wireless Blvd.
Hauppauge, NY 11788
Ph: (516)434-3311   Fax: (516)434-3723
Fr: 800-645-3476
Jerry Bobrow. Seventh edition, 1993. Includes five practice tests with answers.

★3630★ Business Law
National Learning Corp.
212 Michael Dr.
Syosset, NY 11791
Ph: (516)921-8888   Fax: (516)921-8743
Fr: 800-645-6337
Jack Rudman. Dantes Subject Standardized Test series. A standardized graduate and college level examination given by graduate

schools, colleges, and the Armed Forces as a final examination for course evaluation in the field of law. Multiple-choice format with correct answers.

★3631★ Career Examination Series: Attorney
National Learning Corp.
212 Michael Dr.
Syosset, NY 11791
Ph: (516)921-8888   Fax: (516)921-8743
Fr: 800-645-6337
Jack Rudman. Test guide including questions and answers for students or professionals in the field who seek advancement through examination. Also included in the series: Senior Attorney, Principal Attorney, Junior Attorney, Associate Attorney, Assistant Attorney, Administrative Attorney.

★3632★ Career Examination Series: District Attorney
National Learning Corp.
212 Michael Dr.
Syosset, NY 11791
Ph: (516)921-8888   Fax: (516)921-8743
Fr: 800-645-6337
Jack Rudman. Test guide including questions and answers for students or professionals in the field who seek advancement through examination.

★3633★ Career Examination Series: Legal Careers
National Learning Corp.
212 Michael Dr.
Syosset, NY 11791
Ph: (516)921-8888   Fax: (516)921-8743
Fr: 800-645-6337
Jack Rudman. 1993. Test guide including questions and answers for students or professionals in the field who seek advancement through examination.

★3634★ How to Prepare for the Law School Admissions Test (LSAT)
Barron's Educational Series, Inc.
250 Wireless Blvd.
Hauppauge, NY 11788
Ph: (516)434-3311   Fax: (516)434-3723
Fr: 800-645-3476
Jerry Bobrow. Seventh edition, 1993. This book includes a sample LSAT with an explanation of the answers.

★3635★ Law School Admission Test (LSAT)
National Learning Corp.
212 Michael Dr.
Syosset, NY 11791
Ph: (516)921-8888   Fax: (516)921-8743
Fr: 800-645-6337
Jack Rudman. Part of the Admission Test series. A sample test for those seeking admission to graduate and professional schools or seeking entrance or advancement in institutional and public career service.

★3636★ *LSAT Law School Admission Test*
Arco Publishing Co.
Macmillan General Reference
15 Columbus Cir.
New York, NY 10023
Fax: 800-835-3202   Fr: 800-858-7674

Thomas H. Martinson. Fifth edition, 1993. Includes four sample examinations with answers.

★3637★ *Supercourse for the LSAT*
Arco Publishing Co.
Macmillan General Reference
15 Columbus Cir.
New York, NY 10023
Fax: 800-835-3202   Fr: 800-858-7674

Thomas H. Martinson. Fourth edition. 1993. Includes study plans, test-taking strategies, model exams, and drills.

EDUCATIONAL DIRECTORIES AND PROGRAMS

★3638★ *Attorney's Vade Mecum*
Detroit Legal News
2001 W. Lafayette
Detroit, MI 48216
Ph: (313)961-3949   Fax: (313)961-7817
Fr: 800-875-5275
Michelle Scott, Contact

Semiannual, January and July. Covers county, state, and federal courts, agencies, and legal associations in the Michigan counties of Wayne, Oakland, and Macomb. Entries include: For courts—Name, address, phone; judges, clerks, and other personnel, with title and phone. For agencies—name, address, phone, fax, names and titles of key personnel. For associations—Association name, address, phone, names and titles of key personnel. Arrangement: Separate sections for courts, agencies, and associations.

★3639★ *Barron's Guide to Law Schools*
Barron's Educational Series, Inc.
250 Wireless Blvd.
Hauppauge, NY 11788
Ph: (516)434-3311   Fax: (516)434-3723
Fr: 800-645-3476
Patricia M. Wilson, Contact

Biennial, August of even years. Covers 176 American Bar Association (ABA) approved law schools, and law schools not approved by the ABA. Entries include: School name, address, phone, median LSAT percentile, enrollment, accreditation, student demographics, student-faculty ratio, size of library, calendar, degree programs offered, admission and degree requirements, costs, financial aid available, placement services. Arrangement: Alphabetical.

★3640★ *CLE Journal and Register*
Committee on Continuing Professional Education
4025 Chestnut St.
Philadelphia, PA 19104-3099
Ph: (215)243-1600   Fax: (215)243-1664
Fr: 800-253-6397
Harry Kyriakodis, Contact

6 times a year. Covers about 175 sponsors of about 1,000 continuing legal education courses; publishers and producers of continuing legal education books and audio- and videocassettes. Entries include: For sponsors of courses—Course title, location, dates, name and address of sponsor. For publishers—Publication or cassette title, description of contents, author, number of pages, publisher or producer name and address, price. The Committee on Continuing Professional Education is conducted jointly by the American Law Institute and the American Bar Association. Arrangement: Sponsors and publishers are alphabetical by course or publication title; producers of cassettes are by cassette subject.

★3641★ *Directory of Law Teachers*
Association of American Law Schools (AALS)
1201 Connecticut Ave. NW, Ste. 800
Washington, DC 20036-2605
Ph: (202)296-8851   Fax: (202)296-8869
Janet L. Kulick, Contact

Annual, November. Covers law schools approved by the American Bar Association; includes biographical section for about 7,200 deans and full-time faculty members; lists of admissions, alumni affairs, development and placement personnel; list of minority law teachers; Order of the Coif members. Entries include: For schools—Name, address, phone, fax, names of full-time and professional staff, whether school is member of AALS and date of membership. For full-time faculty—Name, institution name, internet/bitnet numbers; professional, education, and career data. Arrangement: Separate alphabetical lists for schools and individuals.

★3642★ *Directory of Legal Employers, 1994*
National Association For Law Placement
1666 Connecticut Ave., Ste. 325
Washington, DC 20009
Ph: (202)667-1666

Annual. Edited by National Association for Law Placement Administrative Offices. Provides general information on law firms, corporations, and government and public interest organizations.

★3643★ *Federal and State Judicial Clerkship Directory*
National Association for Law Placement
1666 Connecticut Ave., Ste. 325
Washington, DC 20009
Ph: (202)667-1666   Fax: (202)265-6735
Janet Smith, Director of Publications

Annual. Covers over 500 federal and state judges offering clerkships. Entries include: Judge name, address, phone, telex, names and titles of key personnel, hiring policies, application procedures. Distribution is primarily to law schools. Arrangement: Geographical.

★3644★ *Gourman Report: A Rating of Graduate and Professional Programs in American and International Universities*
National Education Standards
624 S. Grand Ave., Ste. 1210
Los Angeles, CA 90017
Ph: (213)623-9135
Jack Gourman

Irregular, previous edition 1989; latest edition January, 1993. Covers colleges and universities offering graduate programs in a variety of disciplines; medical schools; law schools; schools of dentistry; optometry; pharmacy. Entries include: Institution name, address, author's description and evaluation. Arrangement: Law, medical, dental, and pharmacy schools are listed by country; others (primarily in United States) are by discipline.

★3645★ *Inside the Law Schools: A Guide by Students for Students*
E. P. Dutton
375 Hudson St.
New York, NY 10014
Ph: (212)366-2000   Fax: (212)366-2888
Fr: 800-526-0275
Hugh Rawson, Contact

Biennial, August of odd years. Covers over 100 law schools. Entries include: School name, address, phone; median entrance scores and grade point averages, acceptance rate, transfer rate; enrollment; percentages of part-time, minority, and women students; student-faculty ratio, expenses, financial aid, library facilities; and descriptions of student life, faculty, curriculum, reputation, and placement success. Arrangement: Alphabetical.

★3646★ *Insider's Guide to Law Firms*
Mobius Press
PO Box 3339
Boulder, CO 80307
Ph: (303)543-9429   Fax: (303)499-5289
Fr: 800-LAW-JOBS
Marie Walsh, Publisher

Annual, August. Covers Over 200 major law firms throughout twelve major U.S. cities: Atlanta, Baltimore, Boston, Chicago, Dallas, Houston, Los Angeles, New York, Philadelphia, Pittsburgh, San Francisco/Palo Alto, and Washington. Entries include: Firm name, address, phone, name and title of contact, names and titles of key personnel, number of partners and associates, salary information, percentage of pro bono work, summer opportunities, area of practice, subsidiary and branch names and locations, description. Arrangement: Geographical.

★3647★ *Law and Legal Information Directory*
Gale Research Inc.
835 Penobscot Bldg.
Detroit, MI 48226-4094
Ph: (313)961-2242   Fax: (313)961-6083
Fr: 800-877-GALE
Holly Selden, Project Coordinator

Biennial, October of even years. Covers more than 33,000 national and international organizations, bar associations, federal and highest state courts, federal regulatory agencies, law schools, firms and organizations offering continuing legal education, paralegal education, sources of scholarships and grants, awards and prizes, special libraries, information systems and services, research centers, publishers of legal periodicals, books, and audiovisual materials, lawyer referral services, legal aid offices, public defender offices, legislature manuals and registers, small claims courts, corporation departments of state, law enforcement agencies, state agencies, including disciplinary agencies, and state bar requirements. Entries include: All Arrangement: Classified by type of organization, activity, service, etc..

★3648★ **Legal and Financial Directory**
The Daily Journal
2000 S. Colorado Blvd., Ste. 2000
Denver, CO 80222
Ph: (303)756-9995   Fax: (303)756-4465
Fr: 800-323-2362
Arla Haley, Contact
Annual, summer. Covers over 15,000 firms and individuals serving the law, real estate, insurance, and financial industries in Colorado. Entries include: Name, address, phone, fax, telex, geographical area served, description of product/service. Arrangement: Alphabetical.

★3649★ **Medical Malpractice Defense Attorney and Health Care Counsel Directory**
PRC Publishing Inc.
4418 Belden Village St. NW
Canton, OH 44718-2516
Ph: (216)492-6063   Fax: (216)492-6063
Fr: 800-336-0083
Molly Romig, Contact
Annual, August. Covers Approximately 70 firms practicing medical malpractice defense law in the U.S. Entries include: Firm name, address, phone, fax, subsidiary and branch names and locations; partner names and biographical data; firm experience and accomplishments; representative clients; name and title of contact; some entries also give hourly rates. Arrangement: Geographical.

★3650★ **North Dakota State Bar Board—Directory of Lawyers & Judges**
State Bar Board
Judicial Wing, 1st Fl.
600 E. Boulevard Ave.
Bismarck, ND 58505-0530
Ph: (701)328-4201   Fax: (701)328-4480
Carla Kolling
Annual, spring. Covers Approximately 1,700 attorneys and judges licensed in the state of North Dakota; U.S. attorneys practicing in the state, state bar association members, state and federal courts, court reporters, and others active in the North Dakota legal system. Entries include: Name, address, phone, fax. Arrangement: Geographical.

★3651★ **Official Guide to U.S. Law Schools**
Law School Admission Council
Box 63
Newtown, PA 18940
Ph: (215)968-1136   Fax: (215)968-1169
Wendy Margolis, Director of Commuications
Annual, spring. 176 listings. Entries include: School name, address, facilities, programs of study and services offered by the school, tuition, and standards for admission. Arrangement: Alphabetical.

★3652★ **Pennsylvania Lawyers Directory**
Pennsylvania Bar Association
PO Box 186
Harrisburg, PA 17108
Ph: (717)238-6715   Fax: (717)238-7182
Fr: 800-932-0311
Marcy Mallory, Contact
Annual, January. Covers all lawyers licensed to practice in Pennsylvania; all federal, state, and local courts and government offices; and all legal organizations. Entries include: Personal, office, or organization name, address, phone, fax; biographical data for individuals. Arrangement: Geographical.

★3653★ **Review of Legal Education in the United States**
Legal Education and Admissions to the Bar
750 N. Lake Shore Dr.
Chicago, IL 60611
Ph: (312)988-5555   Fax: (312)988-6281
Rachel Patrick, Contact
Annual, April. Covers 176 American Bar Association-approved law schools; nonapproved schools; and state bar examination administrators; only a few nonapproved schools responded to survey. Entries include: For law schools—Name, address, phone, year approved, type of school; enrollment for full- and part-time and by level; degrees awarded, tuition and fees, years of college required, weeks and credits required, summer programs offered; teaching staff, and library holdings. For state bar exam administrators—Name, address, phone. Arrangement: Geographical.

★3654★ **So You Want to be a Lawyer: A Practical Guide to Law as a Career**
Law School Admission Council
PO Box 63
Newtown, PA 18940
Ph: (215)968-1001   Fax: (215)968-1169
Wendy Margolis, Director of Communications
Irregular, latest edition 1993; new edition expected 1995. Publication includes: List of law schools approved by the American Bar Association. Entries include: School name, address. Principal content of publication is information on the law school admission process, selecting a law school, and law as a career. Arrangement: Geographical.

★3655★ **Tennessee Attorneys Directory & Buyers Guide**
M. Lee Smith Publishers & Printers
Box 198867
Nashville, TN 37219
Ph: (615)242-7395   Fax: (615)256-6601
Fr: 800-274-6774
Sarah B. Huddleston, Contact
Annual, December. Covers over 12,500 attorneys, paralegals, and legal secretaries in Tennessee. Entries include: Name, address, firm name, phone, fax, Board of Professional Responsibility number. Arrangement: Same information listed geographically, alphabetically, and by law firm.

AWARDS, SCHOLARSHIPS, GRANTS, AND FELLOWSHIPS

★3656★ **Achievement Award**
American Foreign Law Association
Whitman & Ransom
645 Madison Ave.
New York, NY 10022
Ph: (212)759-2400   Fax: (212)755-2025
To recognize a significant contribution to the field of foreign law, comparative law and international law. Awarded annually.

★3657★ **American Bar Association Medal**
American Bar Association
750 N. Lake Shore Dr.
Chicago, IL 60611
Ph: (312)988-6137   Fax: (312)988-6281
To recognize conspicuous service to the cause of American jurisprudence. A medal is awarded at the discretion of the Association. Established in 1929.

★3658★ **Clarence Darrow Award**
International Platform Association
PO Box 250
Winnetka, IL 60093
Ph: (312)446-4321
For recognition of contributions to the American system of justice. An engraved silver bowl is awarded as merited. Established in 1981. The award commemorates Clarence Darrow, the legal crusader of two centuries ago.

★3659★ **Distinguished Service Award**
National Center for State Courts
300 Newport Ave.
PO Box 8798
Williamsburg, VA 23187-8798
Ph: (804)253-2000   Fax: (804)220-0449
To recognize individuals who have made significant contributions to the administration of justice in the United States and to the work of the National Center. Awards are presented in four categories: Present/former state court judge; Present/former non-judge court employee; Lawyer or lay person; and Special Award. An engraved pewter plate and a bound resolution are awarded annually. Established in 1984.

★3660★ **Fifty-Year Award**
Fellows of the American Bar Foundation
750 N. Lake Shore Dr.
Chicago, IL 60611
Ph: (312)988-6606
To recognize a lawyer who has been in the active practice of law for more than fifty years, during which time he manifested adherence to the highest principles and traditions of the legal profession, and service to the community in which he lived. Individuals may be nominated. A plaque is awarded annually. Established in 1957.

★3661★ Clara Shortridge Foltz Award
National Legal Aid and Defender
 Association
1625 K St. NW, 8th Fl.
Washington, DC 20006
Ph: (202)452-0620   Fax: (202)872-1031

To commend a public defender or voluntary defender program for outstanding achievements in the provision of criminal defense services. The deadline for nominations is August 1. The award is named for Clara Shortridge Foltz, the founder of the nation's public defender system. Established in 1985.

★3662★ Hall of Fame
National Association of Black Women
 Attorneys
3711 Macomb St. NW
Washington, DC 20016
Ph: (202)966-9693   Fax: (202)244-6648

For recognition of civic and community leadership. Contributions to the black community are considered. Induction into the Hall of Fame is awarded annually at the Red Dress Ball at the convention. Established in 1987.

★3663★ Judge Learned Hand Award
American Jewish Committee
c/o Judy Rubin
Institute of Human Relations
165 E. 56th St.
New York, NY 10022-2746
Ph: (212)751-4000   Fax: (212)319-6540

To recognize an individual for outstanding achievement in the legal profession and service to the general community to benefit the Society. A plaque is awarded several times a year nationally. Established in 1964 to honor Judge Learned Hand, a distinguished occupant of the Federal bench, and a staunch advocate of the rights of the individual and the importance of democratic values in an orderly society.

★3664★ Learned Hand Medal
Federal Bar Council
145 E. 49th St.
New York, NY 10017
Ph: (212)644-9771   Fax: (212)355-0129

To recognize excellence in Federal jurisprudence. A gold medal, suitably engraved and embossed, is awarded annually at the Law Day Dinner in May. Established in 1961 in memory of Learned Hand, the distinguished jurist.

★3665★ Honoree of the Year Award
National Association of Women Judges
c/o National Center for State Courts
300 Newport Ave.
Williamsburg, VA 23187-8798
Ph: (804)253-2000   Fax: (804)220-0449

To recognize individuals who have assisted women judges to become more proficient in their professions to solve the legal, social and ethical problems associated with the profession; assisted in increasing the number of women judges; and addressed important issues affecting women judges. Individuals, male or female, judges or non-judges, may be nominated. A plaque and other appropriate gifts are awarded at the annual conference in the fall. Established in 1982.

★3666★ Judiciary Award
Association of Federal Investigators
3299 K St. NW, 7th Fl.
Washington, DC 20007
Ph: (202)337-5234   Fax: (202)333-5365

To recognize outstanding members of the bench.

★3667★ Legal Award
Association of Federal Investigators
3299 K St. NW, 7th Fl.
Washington, DC 20007
Ph: (202)337-5234   Fax: (202)333-5365

To recognize Federal prosecutors who have significantly pursued criminal prosecutions at the Federal level. A plaque is awarded annually. Established in 1967.

**★3668★ J. Will Pless International
 Graduate of the Year**
International Legal Fraternity Phi Delta Phi
1750 N St. NW
Washington, DC 20036
Ph: (202)628-0148   Fax: (202)296-7619

To recognize the outstanding law school graduate of the year. Each student Inn selects one candidate by March 15 for the competition. Selection is based on academic achievement, service to the Fraternity, and service to the law school community. An invitation to the biennial convention and a certificate are presented annually to the winner. Each Inn nominee receives a certificate of recognition, and the Inn of the winner receives a plaque.

★3669★ Presidential Commendation
National Association of Criminal Defense
 Lawyers
1627 K St., N.W., 12th Fl.
Washington, DC 20006
Ph: (202)872-8688   Fax: (202)331-8269

To recognize and reward contributions to the improvement of the criminal justice system and the defense of individual liberties. A parchment is awarded at the discretion of the President.

**★3670★ Reporters Committee
 Fellowship**
Reporters Committee for Freedom of the
 Press
1101 Wilson Blvd., Ste.1910
Arlington, VA 22209
Ph: (703)807-2100

Purpose: To provide one year of legal experience working with a non-profit public interest law group in Washington, D.C. Fellows monitor legal issues, provide legal advice and assistance to working journalists, write legal briefs and memoranda, and write for committee publications. Qualifications: Applicants must have earned a law degree by August in the year the fellowship begins. Fellowships run from September to August. Background in journalism, including undergraduate or graduate journalism degree and/or reporting experience is greatly preferred. Preference is given to those who have taken any state bar examination by August. Selection criteria: Based on quality and quantity of journalism/media law background, writing and research ability, and commitment to public interest law. Funds available: Two $20,000 stipends and fully paid health insurance. Application details: No formal application is required. A

cover letter, resume, and legal and non-legal writing samples must be submitted with names, addresses, and phone numbers of three references. Deadline: January 4.

**★3671★ Theodore Roosevelt
 Distinguished Service Medal**
Theodore Roosevelt Association
1864 Muttontown Rd.
PO Box 719
Muttontown, NY 11791
Ph: (516)921-1221   Fax: (516)921-6481

To recognize in contemporary life those who have rendered distinguished service in fields that Theodore Roosevelt worked in his lifetime. The medal is given in the following fields: public and international law, industrial peace, science, American literature, outdoor life, national defense, international affairs, administration of public office, conservation of natural resources, advancement of social justice, expression of pioneer virtues, distinguished public service by a private citizen, and leadership of youth and development of American character. U.S. citizens may be nominated. Selection is made by the executive committee. A medal was awarded annually until 1967; thereafter at the discretion of the executive committee. Established in 1923 to honor Theodore Roosevelt and to encourage the ideals for which he stood.

★3672★ Gertrude E. Rush Award
National Bar Association
1225 11th St. NW
Washington, DC 20001-4217
Ph: (202)842-3900   Fax: (202)289-6170

To recognize individuals who have demonstrated leadership ability in the community within their profession; a pioneer spirit in the pursuit of civil and human rights; and excellence in legal education and perseverance in the law, public policy, or social activism. Nominations are accepted. A trophy is awarded annually during the NBA Mid-Year Conference. Established in 1982 in honor of Gertrude Rush, NBA's only woman co-founder.

★3673★ Scholarship Award
National Association of Black Women
 Attorneys
3711 Macomb St. NW
Washington, DC 20016
Ph: (202)966-9693   Fax: (202)244-6648

To provide a scholarship for black women law students. Several scholarships are presented annually at the Red Dress Ball at the convention. Established in 1978 by Attorney Mabel D. Haden, Washington, DC, with contributions from various businesses, lawyers, and concerned citizens.

**★3674★ Whitney North Seymour, Sr.
 Award**
American Arbitration Association
140 W. 51st St.
New York, NY 10020-1203
Ph: (212)484-4006   Fax: (212)765-4874

To recognize the contribution of a lawyer to the responsible use of arbitration. Lawyers who are active in arbitration are eligible. A bronze medal is awarded annually. Established in 1977 in honor of Whitney North Seymour, Sr., a former president of the American Arbitration Association and the American Bar Association.

★3675★ Student Advocacy Award
International Academy of Trial Lawyers
4 N. 2nd St., Ste. 175
San Jose, CA 95113
Ph: (408)275-6767   Fax: (408)275-6874

To encourage law students to achieve the highest standards possible. Graduating students in law school, who have high standards, moral and ethical, are eligible. Illuminated scrolls are awarded annually to a graduating student at each of the 37 schools participating in the program. Established in 1960.

★3676★ Trial Lawyer of the Year Award
Trial Lawyers for Public Justice
1625 Massachusetts Ave. NW, Ste. 100
Washington, DC 20036
Ph: (202)797-8600   Fax: (202)232-7203

To honor an attorney who has made an outstanding contribution to the public interest by successfully trying or settling a precedent-setting case. To be considered, a case must have broad impact on the public good, involve unique legal issues, and must result in a substantial monetary award to the victims. A plaque is awarded annually at the annual Association of American Trial Attorneys convention. Established in 1983.

★3677★ James "Tick" Vickrey Award
Association of Administrative Law Judges
310 W. Wisconsin Ave., Ste. 880
Milwaukee, WI 53203
Ph: (414)297-3141   Fax: (414)297-3141

To recognize an outstanding contribution to the development of the principles of administrative law during the preceding year. A plaque is awarded annually. Established in 1986 for the honorable James "Tick" Vickrey. Additional information is available from Ronald G. Bernoski, N76 W22260 Cherry Hill Rd., Sussex, WI 53089.

★3678★ Arthur von Briesen Award
National Legal Aid and Defender
   Association
1625 K St. NW, 8th Fl.
Washington, DC 20006
Ph: (202)452-0620   Fax: (202)872-1031

To honor an attorney not employed by a legal services or defender program who has made substantial volunteer contributions to the legal assistance movement. The deadline for nominations is August 1. A plaque is awarded annually. Established in 1961 in honor of the first president of NLADA.

BASIC REFERENCE GUIDES AND HANDBOOKS

★3679★ Black's Law Dictionary; Definitions of the Terms and Phrases of American and English Jurisprodence . . .
West Publishing Co.
50 W. Kellogg Blvd.
PO Box 64526
St. Paul, MN 55164
Ph: (612)228-2778   Fr: 800-328-9424

Nolan Joseph and Michael J. Connolly, editors. Sixth edition, 1993. A standard law dictionary.

★3680★ A Concise Dictionary of Law
Oxford University Press, Inc.
200 Madison Ave.
New York, NY 10016
Ph: (212)679-7300

Second edition, 1990.

★3681★ Encyclopedia of Legal Information Sources
Gale Research Inc.
835 Penobscot Bldg.
Detroit, MI 48226-4094
Ph: (313)961-2242   Fax: (313)961-6083
Fr: 800-347-GALE

Brian L. Baker and Patrick J. Petit, editors. 1992. Lists 23,000 citations in 460 categories. Includes books, periodicals, loose leaf services, statistical sources, research centers, AV, online databases, annual surveys, and associations and professional societies.

★3682★ Law Dictionary
Barron's Educational Series, Inc.
250 Wireless Blvd.
Hauppauge, NY 11788
Ph: (516)434-3311   Fax: (516)434-3723
Fr: 800-645-3476

Steven H. Gifis. Third edition, 1991. Defines 3000 terms. Includes legal citations.

★3683★ Oran's Dictionary of the Law
West Publishing Co.
50 W. Kellogg Blvd.
PO Box 64526
St. Paul, MN 55164
Ph: (612)228-2778

Daniel Oran. Second edition, 1991.

★3684★ Summary of American Law
Lawyer's Co-Operative Publishing Co.
Aqueduct Bldg.
Rochester, NY 14694
Ph: (716)546-5530   Fr: 800-527-0430

Martin Weinstein. Second edition, 1988. A concise treatment of the basic principles of law.

PROFESSIONAL AND TRADE PERIODICALS

★3685★ ABA/BNA Lawyers' Manual on Professional Conduct
Bureau of National Affairs, Inc. (BNA)
1231 25th St. NW
Washington, DC 20037
Ph: (202)452-4200   Fax: (202)822-8092
Fr: 800-372-1033
Robert A. Robbins

Biweekly. Serves as a practical guide to legal ethics and professional responsibility. Covers areas such as conflicts of interest, lawyer-client relationship, malpractice, and other issues of current importance.

★3686★ ABA Journal
American Bar Association
Publications Div.
750 N. Lake Shore Dr.
Chicago, IL 60611-4497
Ph: (312)988-5000   Fax: (312)988-6281
Gary Hengstler

Legal trade journal.

★3687★ American Journal of Family Law
John Wiley and Sons, Inc.
Subscription Dept.
605 3rd Ave.
New York, NY 10158
Ph: (212)850-6000   Fax: (212)850-6799
Laura E. Shapiro

Quarterly. Journal publishing family law resource information.

★3688★ The American Lawyer
The American Lawyer
600 3rd Ave.
New York, NY 10016
Ph: (212)973-2800   Fax: (212)972-6258
Steven Brill

Monthly. Legal magazine.

★3689★ Barrister
American Bar Association
Publications Div.
750 N. Lake Shore Dr.
Chicago, IL 60611-4497
Ph: (312)988-5000   Fax: (312)988-6281
Vicki Quade

Quarterly. Legal and social magazine offering law practice tips.

★3690★ The Cambridge Law Journal
Cambridge University Press
40 W. 20th St.
New York, NY 10011
Ph: (212)924-3900   Fax: (212)691-3239
C.C. Turpin

Journal focusing on all aspects of the law.

★3691★ Conference of Administrative Law Judges Newsletter
National Conference of Administrative Law
   Judges
750 N. Lake Shore Dr.
Chicago, IL 60611
Ph: (312)988-5000

★3692★ Daily Legal News
Legal News Publishing Co.
2935 Prospect Ave.
Cleveland, OH 44115
Ph: (216)696-3322   Fax: (216)696-6329
Lucien B. Karlovec
Legal newspaper featuring general business and local news.

★3693★ EDT
American Bar Association
Publications Div.
750 N. Lake Shore Dr.
Chicago, IL 60611-4497
Ph: (312)988-5000   Fax: (312)988-6281
Sarah Hoban
Legal and social magazine.

★3694★ Fund-Raising Regulation Report
John Wiley and Sons, Inc.
Subscription Dept.
605 3rd Ave.
New York, NY 10158
Ph: (212)850-6000   Fax: (212)850-6799
Bruce R. Hopkins
Bimonthly. Journal publishing information the impact of new laws on fund-raising and charitable giving.

★3695★ Harvard Law Review
Gannett House
Cambridge, MA 02138
Ph: (617)495-4650
Journal publishing legal news.

★3696★ Inside Litigation
Law & Business, Inc.
270 Sylvan
Englewood Cliffs, NJ 07632
Ph: (703)706-8260   Fr: 800-223-0231
J. Stratton Shartel
Monthly. Provides news and information related to law and techniques in litigation practice.

★3697★ Law and Contemporary Problems
Duke University School of Law
PO Box 90364
Durham, NC 27708-0364
Ph: (919)684-5966   Fax: (919)684-3417
Theresa Glover
Quarterly. Law journal.

★3698★ Law & Society Review
Law and Society Assn.
Hampshire House
University of Massachusetts
PO Box 33615
Amherst, MA 01003-3615
Ph: (413)545-4617   Fax: (413)545-1640
William O'Barr
Quarterly. Journal on law and society.

★3699★ Lawyer Hiring & Training Report
Law & Business, Inc.
11 Dupont Circle, Ste. 325
Washington, DC 20036
Ph: (202)328-6662   Fax: (202)332-7122
Fr: 800-223-0231
Larry Smith
Monthly. Carries information on the hiring and training of lawyers. Describes ways a firm can improve on their hiring and training techniques. Features reports on innovative in-house training programs for large and small law firms, legal departments, and government agencies. Recurring features include video and book reviews, listings of educational opportunities, and columns titled Forum on Training, and Forum on Hiring.

★3700★ Lawyer International
Lafferty Publications
1422 W. Peachtree St., No. 800
Atlanta, GA 30309
Ph: (404)874-5120   Fax: (404)874-5123
D. Daly, Contact
Covers international news and features on law firms. Also contains news and analysis affecting lawyers.

★3701★ Legal Briefs
Marshall
600 S. Commonwealth Ave.
Los Angeles, CA 90005-4000
Ph: (213)385-1515
Joan Hendrickson, Contact
Quarterly. Covers appraisal and valuation issues of interest to attorneys.

★3702★ Letters of Credit Report
John Wiley and Sons, Inc.
Subscription Dept.
605 3rd Ave.
New York, NY 10158
Ph: (212)850-6000   Fax: (212)850-6799
Thomas Whitehill
Bimonthly. Journal publishing information on law and commercial practice for bankers and lawyers.

★3703★ The National Law Journal
The National Law Journal
111 8th Ave.
New York, NY 10011
Ph: (212)741-8300   Fax: (212)741-3985
Doreen Weisenhaus
Weekly. Tabloid focusing on the practice of law and trends in law.

★3704★ Prison Legal News
Prison Legal News
PO Box 1684
Lake Worth, FL 33460
Ph: (407)547-9716
Paul Wright
Monthly. Legal and political newsmagazine.

★3705★ SPLC Report
Student Press Law Center
1101 Wilson Blvd., Ste. 1910
Arlington, VA 22209
Tracy Sisser
Report summerizing current cases, legislation and controversies involving student press rights.

★3706★ TRIAL
Assn. of Trial Lawyers of America
1050 31st. St. NW
Washington, DC 20007-4499
Ph: (202)965-3500   Fax: (202)965-0030
Fr: 800-424-2725
Elizabeth Yeary
Monthly. Legal magazine.

★3707★ Trial Diplomacy Journal
John Wiley and Sons, Inc.
Subscription Dept.
605 3rd Ave.
New York, NY 10158
Ph: (212)850-6000   Fax: (212)850-6799
John F. Romano
Bimonthly. Journal focussing on the entire process of trial practice. Covers topics such as forceful methods of cross-examination and key courtroom strategies.

★3708★ Utilities Law Review
John Wiley and Sons, Inc.
Subscription Dept.
605 3rd Ave.
New York, NY 10158
Ph: (212)850-6000   Fax: (212)850-6799
Leigh Hancher
Quarterly. Journal focussing on laws that relate to the utilities sector.

★3709★ Water Law
John Wiley and Sons, Inc.
Subscription Dept.
605 3rd Ave.
New York, NY 10158
Ph: (212)850-6000   Fax: (212)850-6799
Simon Ball
Bimonthly. Journal publishing a legal analysis of environmental, business, and regulatory changes that impact the water industry.

PROFESSIONAL MEETINGS AND CONVENTIONS

★3710★ American Bar Association Annual Meeting/ABA Expo
American Bar Association
750 N. Lake Shore Dr.
Chicago, IL 60611
Ph: (312)988-5880   Fax: (312)988-6281
Annual.

★3711★ Association of American Law Schools Annual Meeting
Association of American Law Schools
1201 Connecticut Ave., NW, Ste. 800
Washington, DC 20036-2605
Ph: (202)296-8851
Annual. Always held during the first week of January. **Dates and Locations:** 1996 Jan.

★3712★ Association of Trial Lawyers of America Convention/Exposition
Association of Trial Lawyers of America
1050 31st St., NW
Washington, DC 20007
Ph: (202)965-3500   Fax: (202)298-6849
Fr: 800-424-2725
Annual.

★3713★ Federal Bar Association Convention
Federal Bar Association
1815 H St., NW, Ste. 408
Washington, DC 20006
Ph: (202)638-0252   Fax: (202)775-0795
Annual. **Dates and Locations:** 1995; Washington, DC.

★3714★ National Bar Association Annual Convention
National Bar Association
1225 11th St., NW
Washington, DC 20001
Ph: (202)842-3900   Fax: (202)289-6170
Annual.

OTHER SOURCES OF INFORMATION

★3715★ *Financing Your Law School Education*
Law School Admission Council/Law School
   Admission Services (LSAC/LSAS)
PO Box 63
Newtown, PA 18940
Ph: (215)968-1001
Debbie Goldberg, and Tom Voss. 1987.

★3716★ *From Here to Attorney*
Professional Publications
1250 5th Ave.
Belmont, CA 94002
Ph: (415)593-9119   Fax: (415)592-4519
Fr: 800-426-1178
1993.

★3717★ *From Law School to Law Practice: The New Associate's Guide*
American Law Institute/American Bar
   Association
Committee on Continuing Professional
   Education
4025 Chestnut St.
Philadelphia, PA 19104
Ph: (215)243-1600
Suzanne B. O'Neill. 1990.

★3718★ "Judge" and "Lawyer" in *Career Selector 2001*
Barron's Educational Series, Inc.
250 Wireless Blvd.
Hauppauge, NY 11788
Ph: (516)434-3311   Fax: (516)434-3723
Fr: 800-645-3476
James C. Gonyea. 1993.

★3719★ "Law" in *Accounting to Zoology: Graduate Fields Defined* (pp. 154-155)
Petersons Guides, Inc.
PO Box 2123
Princeton, NJ 08543-2123
Ph: (609)243-9111   Fax: (609)243-9150
Fr: 800-338-3282
Amy J. Goldstein, editor. Revised and updated, 1987. Defines 298 graduate and professional fields. Discusses types of graduate programs and degrees, graduate research, applied work, employment prospects, and trends.

★3720★ *Law Services Information Book: Law School Admission Test*
Law School Admission Council/Law School
   Admission Services (LSAC/LSAS)
PO Box 63
Newtown, PA 18940
Ph: (215)968-1001
Annual. Covers the Law School Admission Test dates, checklist for the LSAT, information about the LSAT, the law school admission process, the law school data assembly service, and financial aid. Includes a sample law school admission test with answers. Gives a list of law schools with addresses.

★3721★ "Lawyer" in *100 Best Jobs for the 1990s & Beyond*
Dearborn Financial Publishing, Inc.
520 N. Dearborn St.
Chicago, IL 60610-4354
Ph: (312)836-4400   Fax: (312)836-1021
Fr: 800-621-9621
Carol Kleiman. 1992. Describes 100 jobs ranging from accountants to veterinarians. Each job profile includes such information as education, experience, and certification needed, salaries, and job search suggestions.

★3722★ *The Legal Job Interview*
Biennix Corp.
2490 Black Rock Tpke., Ste. 407
Fairfield, CT 06430
Ph: (203)254-1727   Fax: (203)374-2478
1992.

★3723★ *So You Want to Be a Lawyer: A Practical Guide to Law as a Career*
Bantam Doubleday Dell
1540 Broadway
New York, NY 10036
Fax: 800-233-3294   Fr: 800-233-5780
1994.

Anthropologists

Anthropologists study the origin and the physical, social, and cultural development and behavior of humans. They study the way of life, remains, language, and physical characteristics of people in all parts of the world; they compare the customs, values, and social patterns of different cultures. Anthropologists generally concentrate in one of four subfields: cultural anthropology, archeology, linguistics, or biological-physical anthropology. Most anthropologists specialize in cultural, anthropology, studying the customs, cultures, and social lives of groups in a wide range of settings from nonindustrialized societies to modern urban cultures. **Linguistic anthropologists** study the role of language in various cultures. **Biological-physical anthropologists** study the evolution of the human body and look for the earliest evidences of human life.

Salaries

Median annual earnings of social scientists such as anthropologists are as follows:

Lowest 10 percent	Less than $17,800/year
Median	$36,700/year
Top 10 percent	More than $68,700/year
Federal government social scientists	$43,000/year

Employment Outlook

Growth rate until the year 2005: Faster than the average.

Anthropologists

CAREER GUIDES

★3724★ Anthropologist
Careers, Inc.
PO Box 135
Largo, FL 34649-0135
Ph: (813)584-7333
1991. Two-page summary describing duties, working conditions, personal qualifications, training, earnings and hours, employment outlook, places of employment, related careers, and where to write for more information.

★3725★ "Anthropologist" in Career Information Center (Vol.6)
Simon and Schuster
200 Old Tappan Rd.
Old Tappan, NJ 07675
Fax: 800-445-6991   Fr: 800-223-2348
Richard Lidz and Linda Perrin, editorial directors. Fifth edition, 1993. This 13-volume set profiles over 600 occupations. Each occupational profile describes job duties, entry-level requirements, educational requirements, advancement possibilities, employment outlook, working conditions, earnings and benefits, and where to write for more information.

★3726★ "Anthropologist" in College Board Guide to Jobs and Career Planning (pp. 291-292)
The College Board
45 Columbus Ave.
New York, NY 10023-6992
Ph: (212)713-8165   Fax: (212)713-8143
Fr: 800-323-7155
Second edition, 1994. Describes the job, salaries, related careers, education needed, and where to write for more information.

★3727★ Anthropologists
Chronicle Guidance Publications, Inc.
66 Aurora St.
PO Box 1190
Moravia, NY 13118-1190
Ph: (315)497-0330   Fax: (315)497-3359
Fr: 800-622-7284
1993. Career brief describing the nature of the job, working conditions, hours and earnings, education and training, licensure, certifi-

cation, unions, personal qualifications, social and psychological factors, location, employment outlook, entry methods, advancement, and related occupations.

★3728★ "Anthropologists and Archaeologists" in Encyclopedia of Careers and Vocational Guidance (Vol.2, pp. 86-90)
J.G. Ferguson Publishing Co.
200 W. Madison St., Ste. 300
Chicago, IL 60606
Ph: (312)580-5480   Fax: (312)580-4948
William E. Hopke, editor-in-chief. Ninth edition, 1993. Four-volume set that profiles 900 occupations and describes job trends in 74 industries. Includes career description, educational requirements, history of the job, methods of entry, advancement, employment outlook, earnings, conditions of work, social and psychological factors, and sources of further information.

★3729★ "Anthropologists" in Career Discovery Encyclopedia (Vol.1, pp. 48-49)
J.G. Ferguson Publishing Co.
200 W. Madison St., Ste. 300
Chicago, IL 60606
Ph: (312)580-5480   Fax: (312)580-4948
Russell E. Primm, editor-in chief. 1993. This six volume set contains two-page articles for 504 occupations. Each article describes job duties, earnings, and educational and training requirements. The whole set is arranged alphabetically by job title. Designed for junior high and older students.

★3730★ "Anthropologists" in Jobs! What They Are—Where They Are—What They Pay (pp. 354)
Fireside
Simon & Schuster Bldg.
1230 Avenue of the Americas
New York, NY 10020
Ph: (212)698-7000   Fr: 800-223-2348
Robert O. Snelling and Anne M. Snelling. Revised and updated, 1992. Describes duties and responsibilities, earnings, employment opportunities, training, and qualifications.

★3731★ "Anthropology" in College Majors and Careers: A Resource Guide to Effective Life Planning (pp. 17-18)
Garrett Park Press
PO Box 1907
Garrett Park, MD 20896
Ph: (301)946-2553
Paul Phifer. 1993. Lists 60 college majors, with definitions; related occupations and leisure activities; skills, values, and personal needed attributes; suggested readings; and a list of associations.

★3732★ Becoming a Practicing Anthropologist: A Guide to Careers and Training Programs in Applied Anthropology
National Association for the Practice of Anthropology (NAPA)
c/o American Anthropological Association
1703 New Hampshire NW
Washington, DC 20009
Ph: (202)232-8800
John Van Willigen. 1987. Includes a bibliography.

★3733★ Opportunities in Social Science Careers
National Textbook Co. (NTC)
VGM Career Books
4255 W. Touhy Ave.
Lincolnwood, IL 60646-1975
Ph: (708)679-5500   Fax: (708)679-2494
Fr: 800-323-4900
Rosanne J. Marek. Overviews a wide range of career opportunities in social science including anthropology, economics, political science, statistics, history, psychology, sociology, urban and regional planning, and geography. Includes information on salary levels and the employment outlook.

PROFESSIONAL ASSOCIATIONS

★3734★ American Anthropological Association (AAA)
4350 N. Fairfax Dr., Ste. 640
Arlington, VA 22203
Ph: (703)528-1902   Fax: (703)528-3546
Members: Professional society of anthropologists, educators, students, and others interested in the biological and cultural origin and development of humanity. **Purpose:** Sponsors visiting lecturers, congressional fellowship, and departmental services programs. Maintains speakers' bureau, consultants' bureau, and placement service. Sponsors competitions. Conducts research programs and compiles statistics. **Publications:** *American Anthropological Association—Special Publications*, periodic. • *American Anthropologist*, quarterly. • *American Ethnologist*, quarterly. • *Anthropology and Education Quarterly*, quarterly. • *Anthropology and Humanism Quarterly*, quarterly. • *Anthropology Newsletter*, 9/year. • *Central Issues*, biennial. • *Cultural Anthropology*, quarterly. • *Ethos*, quarterly. • *Guide to Departments of Anthropology*, periodic. • *Medical Anthropology*, quarterly.

★3735★ American Association of Physical Anthropologists (AAPA)
Dept. of Anthropology
380 MFAC
SUNY-Buffalo
Buffalo, NY 14261
Ph: (716)645-2942   Fax: (716)645-3808
Members: Professional society of physical anthropologists and scientists in closely related fields interested in the advancement of the science of physical anthropology through research and teaching of human variation, primate paleoanthropology, and primate evolution. **Publications:** *American Journal of Physical Anthropology*, monthly. • *Career Information Bulletin*, periodic. • *Yearbook of Physical Anthropology*.

★3736★ American Ethnological Society (AES)
Oregon State University
Anthropology Department
Corvallis, OR 97331-6403
Ph: (503)737-3852
Members: A division of the American Anthropological Association Anthropologists and others interested in the field of ethnology and social anthropology. Conducts symposia. **Publications:** *American Ethnologist*, quarterly. • *Unit News in Anthropology Newsletter*, monthly.

★3737★ American Society of Primatologists (ASP)
Rush-Presbyterian, St. Lukes Medical Center
Department of OB/GYN
1653 W. Congress Pky.
Chicago, IL 60612
Ph: (312)942-2152   Fax: (312)942-4043
Members: Promotes the discovery and exchange of information regarding nonhuman primates, including all aspects of their anatomy, behavior, development, ecology, evolution, genetics, nutrition, physiology, reproduction, systematics, conservation, husbandry, and use in biomedical research. **Publications:** *American Journal of Primatology*, quarterly. • *ASP Bulletin*, bimonthly.

★3738★ Anthropology Film Center Foundation (AFCF)
PO Box 493
Santa Fe, NM 87501
Ph: (505)983-4127
Members: General anthropologists, visual anthropologists, culture and communication specialists, applied anthropologists, musicologists, linguists, and educators. **Purpose:** Seeks to further scholarship, research, and practice in visual anthropology by using consultation and research services, seminars, publications, teaching, equipment outfitting, and specialized facilities. The Anthropology Film Center develops, reviews, and administers research projects in the following areas: generation and analysis of anthropology film (design, collection, and investigation of naturally occurring human behavior in context through visual technologies and methodologies); film as visual communication; socio-vidistics (investigation of the social organization surrounding the production, use, and display of photographs and film materials in their cultural contexts); culture and human perception; visual/aural arts and media. Other activities include: generation and publication of research films and reports; consultation with universities and institutions; resident fellow program. Offers Ethnographic and Documentary Film Program which provides introductory basics in photography, film making and ethnology, and hands on training with story boarding, camera, sound, editing and lighting exercises.

★3739★ Gungywamp Society (GS)
334 Brook St.
Noank, CT 06340
Ph: (203)536-2887
Members: Avocational archaeologists, anthropologists, historians, geologists, astronomers, and interested individuals. **Purpose:** Seeks to protect and preserve sites throughout the northeastern United States that show evidence of ancient and pre-Columbian cultures. Investigates and studies lithic features, architecture, artifacts, ancient inscriptions, and historic records. Has discovered an archaeological site in Connecticut that shows evidence of serial occupancy since 3000 B.C. Conducts tours through the Gungywamp Complex, an archaeological area preserved by the group. Sponsors educational and charitable programs. Maintains speakers' bureau. **Publications:** *The Greater Gungywamp: A Guide*. • *Stonewatch*, quarterly.

★3740★ Institute for the Study of Man (ISM)
1133 13th St. NW, No. C-2
Washington, DC 20005
Ph: (202)371-2700   Fax: (202)371-1523
Members: Purpose is to publish books and journals in areas related to anthropology and the human sciences. **Publications:** *Journal of Indo-European Studies*, quarterly. • *The Mankind Quarterly*, quarterly.

★3741★ International Women's Anthropology Conference (IWAC)
Anthropology Department
25 Waverly Pl.
New York, NY 10003
Ph: (212)998-8550
Members: Women anthropologists and sociologists who are researching and teaching topics such as women's role in development, feminism, and the international women's movement. **Purpose:** Encourages the exchange of information on research, projects, and funding; addresses policies concerning women from an anthropological perspective. Conducts periodic educational meetings with panel discussions. **Publications:** *IWAC Newsletter*, semiannual.

★3742★ National Association for the Practice of Anthropology (NAPA)
4350 N. Fairfax Dr., Ste. 640
Arlington, VA 22203
Ph: (703)528-1902   Fax: (703)528-3546
Members: A unit of the American Anthropological Association. Professional anthropologists serving social service organizations, government agencies, and business and industrial firms. **Purpose:** Purpose is to help anthropologists develop and market their expertise in areas such as social and political analysis, and program design, evaluation, and management. Compiles statistics. **Publications:** *Bulletin Series*, periodic.

★3743★ Society for Applied Anthropology (SFAA)
PO Box 24083
Oklahoma City, OK 73124
Ph: (405)843-5113   Fax: (405)843-4863
Members: Professional society of anthropologists, sociologists, psychologists, health professionals, industrial researchers, and educators. **Purpose:** Promotes scientific investigation of the principles controlling relations between human beings, and to encourage wide application of these principles to practical problems. **Publications:** *Human Organization*, quarterly. • *Practising Anthropology: A Career-Oriented Publication of the Society for Applied Anthropology*, quarterly. • *SFAA Newsletter*, quarterly.

★3744★ Society for Historical Archaeology (SHA)
PO Box 30446
Tucson, AZ 85751
Ph: (602)886-8006   Fax: (602)886-0182
Members: Archaeologists, historians, anthropologists, and ethnohistorians; other individuals and institutions with an interest in historical archaeology or allied fields. **Purpose:** Aim is to bring together persons interested in studying specific historic sites, manuscripts, and published sources, and to develop generalizations concerning historical periods and cultural dynamics as these emerge through the techniques of archaeological excavation and analysis. Main focus is the era beginning with the exploration of the non-European world by Europeans, and geographical areas in the Western Hemisphere, but also considers Oceanian, African, and Asian archaeology during the relatively late periods. **Publications:** *Guides to the Archaeological Literature of the Immigrant Experience in America*. • *Historical Archaeology*, quarterly.

• *Society for Historical Archaeology Conference: Underwater Proceedings*, annual. • *Society for Historical Archaeology—Newsletter*, quarterly. • *Special Publications Series*, periodic.

★3745★ Wenner-Gren Foundation for Anthropological Research (WGFAR)
220 5th Ave., 16th Fl.
New York, NY 10001
Ph: (212)683-5000
Members: Purpose: Supports research in all branches of anthropology including cultural/social, biological/physical, ethnological, archaeological, and anthropological linguistics, and in closely related disciplines concerned with human origins, development, and variation. **Publications:** *Current Anthropology*, bimonthly.

TEST GUIDES

★3746★ *General Anthropology*
National Learning Corp.
212 Michael Dr.
Syosset, NY 11791
Ph: (516)921-8888   Fax: (516)921-8743
Fr: 800-645-6337
Jack Rudman. Dantes Subject Standardized Test series. A standardized graduate and college level examination given by graduate schools, colleges, and the Armed Forces as a final examination for course evaluation in the field of anthropology. Multiple-choice format with correct answers.

EDUCATIONAL DIRECTORIES AND PROGRAMS

★3747★ *Guide to Departments of Anthropology*
American Anthropological Association
4350 N. Fairfax Dr., Ste. 640
Arlington, VA 22203
Ph: (703)528-1902   Fax: (703)528-3546
Theresa Clifford, Contact
Annual, fall. Covers about 550 departments of anthropology in academic institutions, museums, research associations, and the federal government. Entries include: Institution name, address; degrees offered; names, fields, and areas of interest of faculty and research staff; anthropologists in other departments or programs; graduate student support available; degree requirements; number of degrees granted; and special programs, resources, and facilities. Arrangement: Alphabetical by name of institution.

AWARDS, SCHOLARSHIPS, GRANTS, AND FELLOWSHIPS

★3748★ Juan Comas Award
American Association of Physical Anthropologists
Dept. of Anthropology
SUNY/Buffalo
380 MFAC
Buffalo, NY 14261
Ph: (716)636-2414   Fax: (716)636-3808
To recognize one of the four best student papers presented at the Association's annual meeting. A monetary prize of $200 is awarded annually.

★3749★ Distinguished Service Award
American Anthropological Association
4350 N. Fairfax Dr., Ste. 640
Arlington, VA 22203
Ph: (703)528-1902   Fax: (703)528-3546
To recognize exceptional contributions to anthropology with respect to the increase and dissemination of humanistic and scientific knowledge, and service to the profession. A citation is awarded annually. Established in 1976.

★3750★ Robert F. Heizer Prize
American Society for Ethnohistory
Department of Anthropology
MacGraw Hall
Cornell University
Ithaca, NY 14853
For recognition of the best article in ethnohistory. The awards committee of ASE reviews all books and journals relating to ethnohistory published during the previous year and makes the selection. A monetary prize of $100 and a certificate are awarded annually. Established in 1980 in honor of Dr. Robert F. Heizer, ethnohistorian and archaeologist noted for his research in California and Mesoamerica.

★3751★ Honorary Fellow
Association for Social Anthropology in Oceania
Dept. of Sociology & Anthropology
Univ. of Arkansas
2801 S. University
Little Rock, AR 72204
Ph: (501)569-3173
To acknowledge outstanding professional achievements in the anthropology of Oceania. Candidates are elected by a ballot of ASAO Fellows and voting members. A parchment certificate is presented. The Association can have only 15 Honorary Fellows at one time. Established in 1974.

★3752★ Howard Fellows
George A. and Eliza Gardner Howard Foundation
Brown Univ.
42 Charlesfield St.
PO Box 1956
Providence, RI 02912
Ph: (401)863-2640
To provide individuals in the middle stages of their careers with funds for independent projects in the fields that are selected within the following categories on a rotational basis

each year: Comparative Literature, Language and Literature; History, Anthropology, Political Science and Social Studies; Classical and Archaeological Studies, History of Science, Philosophy, and Religious Studies; Art History and Fine Arts (including painting, sculpture, musicology, music composition, photography and film); and Creative Writing and Literary Criticism. Preference is given to candidates between 25 and 45 years of age who, regardless of their country of citizenship, are professionally based in the United States either by affiliation with an institution or by residence. No fellowships are awarded for work leading to any academic degree or for coursework or training of any other sort. Nominations are accepted between September 1 and October 15. Stipends for the one-year period are $18,000. Established in 1952 by Nicea Howard in memory of her grandparents.

★3753★ Richard Carley Hunt Memorial Postdoctoral Fellowships
Wenner-Gren Foundation for Anthropological Research, Inc.
220 5th Ave., 16th Fl.
New York, NY 10001-7708
Ph: (212)683-5000   Fax: (212)683-9151
Purpose: To aid anthropological research projects. Qualifications: Applicants for both regular grants and Hunt Fellowships may be of any nationality. There are no restrictions regarding the candidate's institutional affiliation for either award, but applicant must have a Ph.D. in anthropology or a related discipline at the time the award is made. Candidates for Hunt Fellowships must have received their Ph.D. within five years of applying for the award, and must use the funds for the write-up of research results for publication. Priority for both awards is given to projects that employ comparative perspectives or integrate more than one subfield of anthropology. Grants are intended for direct research expenses; funds are not available for tuition, salary of awardee, non-project personnel, institutional overhead and support, or travel to meetings. Low priority is given to publication assistance and filmmaking. Funds available: Regular grants: $12,000 maximum; Hunt Fellowships: $7,000 maximum. Application details: Write to the Foundation for application form and guidelines. Deadline: 1 May, 1 November. Applicants are notified six to eight months after the deadline.

★3754★ Margaret Mead Award
American Anthropological Association
4350 N. Fairfax Dr., Ste. 640
Arlington, VA 22203
Ph: (703)528-1902   Fax: (703)528-3546
To recognize a particular accomplishment, such as a film or a service, that interprets anthropological data in ways meaningful to the public. Individuals who are under 40 years of age or who have received a Ph.D. within the past ten years are eligible. A monetary prize of $500 and a plaque are awarded annually. Established in 1979 in memory of Margaret Mead, the noted anthropologist. Co-sponsored by the Society for Applied Anthropology.

★3755★ **Smithsonian Research Fellowships**
Smithsonian Institution
Office of Public Affairs
900 Jefferson Dr. SW, Rm. 2410
Washington, DC 20560
Ph: (202)357-2470   Fax: (202)786-2515
To support independent research in residence at the Smithsonian in association with the research staff and using the Institution's resources. Fellowships are awarded in the fields of history of science and technology, social and cultural history, history of art, anthropology, biological sciences, earth sciences, and materials analysis. Open to all qualified individuals without reference to race, color, religion, sex, national origin, age, or condition of handicap of any applicant. Predoctoral and postdoctoral fellowship appointments for six to twelve months, senior postdoctoral appointments for three to twelve months and graduate student appointments for ten weeks are awarded. Additional information is available from Smithsonian Institution, Office of Fellowships and Grants, 7300 l'Enfant Plaza, Washington, DC 20560.

★3756★ **Sherwood L. Washburn Award**
American Association of Physical
  Anthropologists
Dept. of Anthropology
SUNY/Buffalo
380 MFAC
Buffalo, NY 14261
Ph: (716)636-2414   Fax: (716)636-3808
To recognize one of the four best student papers presented at the Association's annual meeting. A monetary prize of $200 is awarded annually.

★3757★ **Wenner-Gren Foundation Predoctoral Grants**
Wenner-Gren Foundation for
  Anthropological Research, Inc.
220 5th Ave., 16th Fl.
New York, NY 10001-7708
Ph: (212)683-5000   Fax: (212)683-9151
Purpose: Predoctoral Grants are awarded to individuals to aid doctoral dissertation or thesis research in all branches of anthropology. Grants are made to seed innovative approaches and ideas, to cover specific expenses or phases of a project, and/or to encourage aid from other funding agencies. The Foundation particularly invites projects employing comparative perspectives or integrating two or more subfields of anthropology. Qualifications: Applicants must be scholars working on their doctoral dissertation or thesis research. They must be enrolled for a doctoral degree. Those seeking support for postdoctoral research who have not received the degree at the time of application should file a predoctoral application; if an award is approved it will be made after the Ph.D. is in hand. Qualified students of all nationalities are eligible. Funds available: Up to $12,000. Application details: Application forms will be sent upon request. Application must be made jointly with a thesis advisor or other scholar who will undertake responsibility for supervising the project. Awards are contingent upon the applicant's successful completion of all requirements for the degree other than the dissertation/thesis. Applications may be submitted before such requirements have been

met; should an award be approved, the Foundation will at that time request evidence of the applicant's fulfillment of degree requirements. Deadline: There are two deadlines, May 1 and November 1, for applications for funding during the calendar year following. Applicants who will require funds during the first half of the year should meet the May 1 deadline. Projects scheduled to begin in July or later may be submitted by the November 1 deadline. Decisions will be announced six to eight months after the deadline date. Only one application may be submitted during any twelve-month period.

★3758★ **Wenner-Gren Predoctoral Grants**
Wenner-Gren Foundation for
  Anthropological Research, Inc.
220 5th Ave., 16th Fl.
New York, NY 10001-7708
Ph: (212)683-5000   Fax: (212)683-9151
Purpose: To aid thesis or dissertation research projects in anthropology. Qualifications: Applicant may be of any nationality. Candidate must be enrolled in a doctoral program in anthropology or a related discipline, and should have completed all the degree requirements other than the dissertation or thesis before the start of the award tenure. Application must be made jointly with a senior scholar willing to supervise the project. Priority is given to projects employing comparative perspectives or integrating more than one subfield of anthropology. Grants are intended for expenses related directly to the dissertation/thesis research; funds are not available for tuition, salary of awardee, non-project personnel, institutional overhead and support, or travel to meetings. Low priority is given to dissertation write up. Funds available: $12,000 maximum. Application details: Write to the Foundation for application form and guidelines. Deadline: 1 May, 1 November. Applicants are notified six to eight months after the deadline.

★3759★ **Wenner-Gren Regular Grants**
Wenner-Gren Foundation for
  Anthropological Research, Inc.
220 5th Ave., 16th Fl.
New York, NY 10001-7708
Ph: (212)683-5000   Fax: (212)683-9151
Purpose: To encourage anthropological research projects. Qualifications: Applicants for both regular grants and Hunt Fellowships may be of any nationality. There are no restrictions regarding the candidate's institutional affiliation for either award, but applicant must have a Ph.D. in anthropology or a related discipline concerned with human origins, development, and variation. Candidates for Hunt Fellowships must have received their Ph.D. within five years of applying for the award, and must use the funds to aid completion of specific studies or for the write-up of field materials for publication. Priority for both awards is given to projects that employ comparative perspectives or integrate more than one subfield of anthropology. Grants are intended for direct research expenses; funds are not available for tuition, salary of awardee, non-project personnel, institutional overhead and support, or travel to meetings. Low priority is given to dissertation write-up or revision, publication subvention, and filmmaking. Funds available: Regular

grants: $12,000 maximum; Hunt Fellowships: $7,000 maximum. Application details: Write to the Foundation for application form and guidelines. Deadline: 1 May, 1 November. Applicants are notified six to eight months after the deadline.

★3760★ **Erminie Wheeler-Voegelin Prize**
American Society for Ethnohistory
Department of Anthropology
MacGraw Hall
Cornell University
Ithaca, NY 14853
For recognition of the best book-length contribution to ethnohistory. The awards committee of ASE reviews all books relating to ethnohistory from the previous year and makes the selection. A monetary prize of $300 and a certificate are awarded annually. Established in 1981 in honor of Dr. Erminie Wheeler-Voegelin, an early ethnohistorian and founder of the Society.

BASIC REFERENCE GUIDES AND HANDBOOKS

★3761★ *Anthropological Fieldwork: An Annotated Bibliography*
Garland Publishing, Inc.
717 5th Ave.
New York, NY 10022
Ph: (212)751-7447   Fr: 800-627-6273
Pierre B. Gravel. 1988. Part of the Garland Reference Library of Social Science series. Includes indexes.

★3762★ *Finding the Source in Sociology and Anthropology: A Thesaurus-Index to the Reference Collection*
Greenwood Press, Inc.
88 Post Rd. W.
PO Box 5007
Westport, CT 06881
Ph: (203)226-3571
Samuel R. Brown. 1987. Includes indexes.

PROFESSIONAL AND TRADE PERIODICALS

★3763★ *Anthropology of Consciousness*
Dr. Joseph K. Long
155 N. Maine St.
Greenville, KY 42345
Ph: (502)338-7776
Joseph K. Long
Serves as an information exchange for researchers investigating the effect of culture on man's psychological and supernatural behavior patterns. Examines the topics of dreaming, altered states of consciousness, spirit possession, healing, divination, extrasensory perception, mysticism, myth, shamanism, and psychic archeology. Recurring features include book reviews, queries,

notices of publications and symposia, news of members, and obituaries.

★3764★ Anthropology Newsletter
American Anthropological Association
4350 N. Fairfax Dr., Ste. 640
Arlington, VA 22203
Ph: (703)528-1902   Fax: (703)528-3546
Susan N. Skomal
Covers news of the Association and current events of interest to anthropologists, as well as legislation affecting the field. Recurring features include a calendar of events, news of grants, listings of relevant publications, a professional placement service section, and news of members.

★3765★ Association for Social Anthropology in Oceania—Newsletter
Association for Social Anthropology in Oceania
c/o Suzanne Falgout
University of Hawaii-West O'ahu
94-063 Ala Ike
Pearl City, HI 96782
Quarterly. Disseminates information to individuals, university and college libraries, and professional associations with the aim of advancing the study of comparative social anthropology in Oceania through symposia, joint publication, and research coordination. Reports on Association events, activities, and members.

★3766★ Evolutionary Anthropology
John Wiley and Sons, Inc.
Subscription Dept.
605 3rd Ave.
New York, NY 10158
Ph: (212)850-6000   Fax: (212)850-6799
John Fleagle
Bimonthly. Journal covering topics in various areas of biology related to evolution.

★3767★ Institute of Human Origins—Newsletter
Institute of Human Origins
2453 Ridge Rd.
Berkeley, CA 94709
Ph: (510)845-0333   Fax: (510)845-9453
Elisabeth Wilson
Periodic. Covers the fields of paleoanthropology and geochronology, fo-

cusing on research, training, and public outreach activities of the Institute. Recurring features include interviews, a calendar of events, and news of research.

★3768★ ISEM Newsletter
Institute for the Study of Earth and Man (ISEM)
PO Box 274
Dallas, TX 75275
Ph: (214)768-3762   Fax: (214)768-4289
Susan J. Liepins
Semiannual. Reports on research in the anthropological, geological, and statistical sciences. Includes notices of research funds, grants, and contracts awarded. Provides biographical sketches of new faculty members in the anthropological, geological, and statistical sciences departments at Southern Methodist University. Recurring features include news of research and news of members.

★3769★ Museum Anthropology
Council for Museum Anthropology
c/o Natural History Museum of Los Angeles County
Anthropology Section
900 Exposition Blvd.
Los Angeles, CA 90007
Ph: (213)744-3383   Fax: (213)747-4114
Christopher B. Steiner
Covers subject matter including, but not limited to, research on museum collections, theoretical studies of material culture, planning and implementation of exhibitions, public programs, the politics and policies of representation, collections management policy, documentation and conservation of collections, museum training and studies, education in museums, repatriation, and illegal trafficking of antiquities. Recurring features include exhibition reviews, book reviews, conference and symposia announcements, and news and notes.

★3770★ SMRC Newsletter
Southwestern Mission Research Center (SMRC)
University of Arizona
Tucson, AZ 85721
Ph: (602)621-4898   Fax: (602)621-2976
Covers the history and anthropology of northern New Spain (Spanish Colonial South-

west). Features news of tours, meetings, and new publications. Recurring features include an annotated bibliography and news of research members.

OTHER SOURCES OF INFORMATION

★3771★ "Anthropologist" in Career Selector 2001
Barron's Educational Series, Inc.
250 Wireless Blvd.
Hauppauge, NY 11788
Ph: (516)434-3311   Fax: (516)434-3723
Fr: 800-645-3476
James C. Gonyea. 1993.

★3772★ The Innocent Anthropologist: Notes From a Mud Hut
Henry Holt & Co.
115 W. 18th St., 6th Fl.
New York, NY 10011
Ph: (212)886-9200
Nigel Barley, editor. 1992.

★3773★ The Naked Anthropologist: Tales from Around the World
Wadsworth Publishing Co.
10 Davis Dr.
Belmont, CA 94002
Ph: (415)595-2350   Fax: (415)637-9955
Philip R. DeVita, editor. 1992.

★3774★ What the Bones Tell Us: Adventures of an Anthropologist
Henry Holt & Co.
115 W. 18th St., 6th Fl.
New York, NY 10011
Ph: (212)886-9200
Jeffrey H. Schwartz, editor. 1993.

Archaeologists

Archeology is a subfield of anthropology. **Archaeologists** engage the systematic recovery and examination of material evidence, such as graves, buildings, tools, and pottery. This is done to determine the characteristics and history of cultures from the study of artifacts and other buried remains.

Salaries

Median annual earnings of social scientists such as archaeologists are as follows:

Lowest 10 percent	Less than $17,800/year
Median	$36,700/year
Top 10 percent	More than $68,700/year
Federal government social scientists	$43,000

Employment Outlook

Growth rate until the year 2005: Faster than the average.

Archaeologists

CAREER GUIDES

★3775★ "Anthropologists and Archaeologists" in *Encyclopedia of Careers and Vocational Guidance* **(Vol.2, pp. 86-90)**
J.G. Ferguson Publishing Co.
200 W. Madison St., Ste. 300
Chicago, IL 60606
Ph: (312)580-5480   Fax: (312)580-4948
William E. Hopke, editor-in-chief. Ninth edition, 1993. Four-volume set that profiles 900 occupations and describes job trends in 74 industries. Includes career description, educational requirements, history of the job, methods of entry, advancement, employment outlook, earnings, conditions of work, social and psychological factors, and sources of further information.

★3776★ Archaeologist
Vocational Biographies, Inc.
PO Box 31
Sauk Centre, MN 56378-0031
Ph: (612)352-6516   Fax: (612)352-5546
Fr: 800-255-0752
1990. Four-page pamphlet containing a personal narrative about a worker's job, work likes and dislikes, career path from high school to the present. Education and training, the rewards and frustrations, and the effects of the job on the rest of the worker's life. The data file portion of this pamphlet gives a concise occupational summary, including work descriptions, working conditions, places of employment, personal characteristics, education and training, job outlook, and salary range.

★3777★ Archaeologist
Careers, Inc.
PO Box 135
Largo, FL 34649-0135
Ph: (813)584-7333
1994. Two-page summary describing duties, working conditions, personal qualifications, training, earnings and hours, employment outlook, places of employment, related careers, and where to write for more information.

★3778★ "Archaeologist" in *Career Information Center* **(Vol.6)**
Simon and Schuster
200 Old Tappan Rd.
Old Tappan, NJ 07675
Fax: 800-445-6991   Fr: 800-223-2348
Richard Lidz and Linda Perrin, editorial directors. Fifth edition, 1993. This 13-volume set profiles over 600 occupations. Each occupational profile describes job duties, entry-level requirements, educational requirements, advancement possibilities, employment outlook, working conditions, earnings and benefits, and where to write for more information.

★3779★ Archaeologists
Chronicle Guidance Publications, Inc.
66 Aurora St.
PO Box 1190
Moravia, NY 13118-1190
Ph: (315)497-0330   Fax: (315)497-3359
Fr: 800-622-7284
1992. Occupational brief describing the nature of the job, working conditions, hours and earnings, education and training, licensure, certification, unions, personal qualifications, social and psychological factors, location, employment outlook, entry methods, advancement, and related occupations.

★3780★ "Archaeologists" in *Career Discovery Encyclopedia* **(Vol.1, pp. 54-55)**
J.G. Ferguson Publishing Co.
200 W. Madison St., Ste. 300
Chicago, IL 60606
Ph: (312)580-5480   Fax: (312)580-4948
Russell E. Primm, editor-in chief. 1993. This six volume set contains two-page articles for 504 occupations. Each article describes job duties, earnings, and educational and training requirements. The whole set is arranged alphabetically by job title. Designed for junior high and older students.

★3781★ "Archaeologists" in *Jobs! What They Are—Where They Are—What They Pay* **(pp. 355)**
Fireside
Simon & Schuster Bldg.
1230 Avenue of the Americas
New York, NY 10020
Ph: (212)698-7000   Fr: 800-223-2348
Robert O. Snelling and Anne M. Snelling. Revised and updated, 1992. Describes duties and responsibilities, earnings, employment opportunities, training, and qualifications.

PROFESSIONAL ASSOCIATIONS

★3782★ Archaeological Conservancy (AC)
5301 Central Ave. NE, Ste. 1218
Albuquerque, NM 87108
Ph: (505)266-1540
Members: People interested in preserving prehistoric and historic sites for interpretive or research purposes (most members are not professional archaeologists). **Purpose:** Seeks to acquire for permanent preservation, through donation or purchase, the ruins of past American cultures, primarily those of American Indians. Works throughout the U.S. to preserve cultural resources presently on private lands and protect them from the destruction of looters, modern agricultural practices, and urban sprawl. Operates with government agencies, universities, and museums to permanently preserve acquired sites. **Publications:** *The Archaeological Conservancy Newsletter*, quarterly.

★3783★ Archaeological Institute of America (AIA)
656 Beacon St.
Boston, MA 02215
Ph: (617)353-9361   Fax: (617)353-6550
Members: Purpose: Educational and scientific society of archaeologists and others interested in archaeological study and research. Founded five schools of archaeology: American School of Classical Studies (Athens, 1881); School of Classical Studies of the American Academy (Rome, 1895); American Schools of Oriental Research (Jerusalem,

1900 and Baghdad, 1921); School of American Research (1907, with headquarters at Santa Fe, NM). Is allied with three research institutes: American Research Institute in Turkey; American Institute of Iranian Studies (see separate entries); American Research Center in Egypt. Maintains annual lecture program for all branch societies. Operates placement service for archeology educators. Sponsors educational programs for middle school children. **Publications:** *AIA Newsletter*, quarterly. • *American Journal of Archaeology*, quarterly. • *Archaeological Fieldwork Opportunities Bulletin*, annual. • *Archaeology*, bimonthly.

★3784★ Center for American Archeology (CAA)
PO Box 366
Kampsville, IL 62053
Ph: (618)653-4316   Fax: (618)653-4232
Members: Philanthropic organizations, foundations, corporations, professional and amateur archaeologists, students, and others interested in archaeology in the U.S. Conducts archaeological research and disseminates the results. **Purpose:** Excavates, analyzes, and conserves archaeological sites and artifats. Through the Kampsville Archeological Center sponsors tours, lectures, and educational and outreach programs, including university, middle school and junior high, and high school field schools; offers professional training at levels of detail ranging from secondary to postgraduate. Maintains speakers' bureau. Operates Kampsville Archeological Museum. **Publications:** *Center for American Archeology Annual Report.* • *Center for American Archeology Newsletter*, quarterly. • *Kampsville Archeological Center Research Series*, periodic. • *Kampsville Archeological Center Technical Report*, periodic.

★3785★ Epigraphic Society (ES)
2443 Filmore St., Ste. 328
San Francisco, CA 94115
Ph: (619)571-1344   Fax: (619)571-1124
Members: Individuals interested in deciphering ancient inscriptions, including professional and amateur epigraphers (specialists in engraved inscriptions) and linguists. **Purpose:** Members launch expeditions to North America and overseas. Reports discoveries and decipherments and assesses their historical implications. Participates in group lecture and teaching programs with other archaeological societies and university departments of archaeology and history. Conducts specialized education and research programs. Operates museum. Maintains numerous committees. **Publications:** *ESOP Annual.* • *ESOP: Epigraphic Society Occasional Papers.*

★3786★ Foundation for Latin American Anthropological Research (FLAAR)
Brevard Community College
1519 Clearlake Rd.
Cocoa, FL 32922
Ph: (407)632-1111   Fax: (407)633-4565
Members: Purpose: Works to promote a better public understanding of professional archaeology. Sponsors research in the fields of archaeology, pre-Columbian art and architecture, and ethnohistory. Uses the Maya Indians' Fourth - Eighth Century Funerary Vase paintings as a source of reference on the na-

ture of their civilization during the classic period in Mexico, Belize, Guatemala, and Honduras. Photographs in detail all ancient Mayan ceramic art in private collections and museums; analyzes the hieroglyphic inscriptions on this material and prepares scientific publications on the data derived. Sponsors volunteer program in Belize, Guatemala, and Honduras for individuals of all ages and backgrounds. Conducts seminars, lectures, and on-site visits. Sponsors annual two-week study trips to archaeological sites in Mexico, Guatemala, and Peru. Together with WBCC-TV Channel 68 FLAAR produces television documentaries on Maya art, pyramid architecture, and archaeology. Offers a traveling photo exhibit to museums, colleges, and associations. Maintains a speakers' bureau. **Publications:** *Maya Archaeology.* • *Monographs in Art History.*

★3787★ National Association of State Archeologists (NASA)
Oklahoma Archeological Survey
111 E. Chesapeake
Norman, OK 73019-0575
Ph: (405)325-7211   Fax: (405)325-7604
Members: State archaeologists who **Purpose:** oversee the archaeological functions of their state and participate in the management of the state's archaeological resources. Compiles statistics.

★3788★ Society for American Archaeology (SAA)
900 2nd St. NE, No. 12
Washington, DC 20002
Ph: (202)789-8200   Fax: (202)789-0284
Members: Professionals, avocationals, students, and others interested in American archaeology. Stimulates scientific research in the archaeology of the New World by: creating closer professional relations among archaeologists, and between them and others interested in American archaeology; advocating the conservation of archaeological data and furthering the control or elimination of commercialization of archaeological objects; promoting a more rational public appreciation of the aims and limitations of archaeological research. Maintains placement service and educational programs. **Publications:** *American Antiquity*, quarterly. • *Archaeologists of the Americas*, annual. • *Archaeology and Public Education*, quarterly. • *Bulletin of the Society for American Archaeology*, 5/year. • *Latin Amerian Antiquity*, quarterly. • *Special Publications*, periodic.

★3789★ Society for Historical Archaeology (SHA)
PO Box 30446
Tucson, AZ 85751
Ph: (602)886-8006   Fax: (602)886-0182
Members: Archaeologists, historians, anthropologists, and ethnohistorians; other individuals and institutions with an interest in historical archaeology or allied fields. **Purpose:** Aim is to bring together persons interested in studying specific historic sites, manuscripts, and published sources, and to develop generalizations concerning historical periods and cultural dynamics as these emerge through the techniques of archaeological excavation and analysis. Main focus is the era beginning with the exploration of the non-European world by Europeans, and geographical areas

in the Western Hemisphere, but also considers Oceanian, African, and Asian archaeology during the relatively late periods. **Publications:** *Guides to the Archaeological Literature of the Immigrant Experience in America.* • *Historical Archaeology*, quarterly. • *Society for Historical Archaeology Conference: Underwater Proceedings*, annual. • *Society for Historical Archaeology—Newsletter*, quarterly. • *Special Publications Series*, periodic.

★3790★ Society for Industrial Archeology (SIA)
100 Overlook Ctr.
Princeton, NJ 08540
Members: Historians, architects, architectural historians, teachers, museum technical staff, archaeologists, engineers, government staff, and other interested individuals. **Purpose:** To promote the identification, preservation, and use of historic industrial and engineering sites, structures, and equipment; to broaden public awareness of the social significance of America's industrial and technological heritage. Disseminates information; encourages research and field investigations of vanishing works and processes; conducts process tours; offers technical assistance. Members present technical papers. **Publications:** *IA: The Journal of the Society for Industrial Archeology*, semiannual. • *SIA Newsletter*, quarterly.

★3791★ Society of Professional Archeologists (SOPA)
Oklahoma Historical Society
2100 N. Lincoln Blvd.
Oklahoma City, OK 73105
Members: Professional archaeologists satisfying basic requirements in training and experience, including private consultants, individuals working with large firms, and academic personnel. **Purpose:** Objectives are to define professionalism in archaeology; provide a measure against which to evaluate archaeological actions and research; establish certification standards; provide for grievance procedures; demonstrate to other archaeologists and the public the nature of professional archaeology. Monitors related legislative activities; maintains society archives. Is developing educational programs and drafting standards and guidelines for field schools. **Publications:** *Directory of Professional Archeologists*, annual. • *Predicaments, Pragmatics, and Professionalism - Ethical Conduct in Archeology.* • *SOPAnews*, monthly.

STANDARDS/CERTIFICATION AGENCIES

★3792★ Society of Professional Archeologists (SOPA)
Oklahoma Historical Society
2100 N. Lincoln Blvd.
Oklahoma City, OK 73105
Objectives are to define professionalism in archaeology; provide a measure against which to evaluate archaeological actions and research; establish certification standards;

provide for grievance procedures; demonstrate to other archaeologists and the public the nature of professional archaeology. Is developing educational programs and drafting standards and guidelines for field schools.

AWARDS, SCHOLARSHIPS, GRANTS, AND FELLOWSHIPS

★3793★ Award for Distinguished Archaeological Achievement
Archaeological Institute of America
675 Commonwealth Ave.
Boston, MA 02215
Ph: (617)353-9361   Fax: (617)353-6550
To recognize outstanding achievement in the field of archaeology as evidenced by distinguished field work, publication, teaching, or a combination of these achievements. A medal and citation are awarded annually. Established in 1965.

★3794★ George A. Barton Fellowship
American Schools of Oriental Research
3301 N. Charles St.
Baltimore, MD 21218-3207
Ph: (410)516-3498   Fax: (410)516-3499
To provide for one fellowship for seminarians, pre-doctoral or recent post-doctoral students for research in Jerusalem. There is a $2,000 stipend plus free room and half board at the W.F. Albright Institute of Archaeological Researchfor the fellow, but not dependents. Residence at the Albright Institute is required. This award may not be used during the summer. The research period may be up to five months.

★3795★ Lucy Wharton Drexel Medal
The University Museum
Univ. of Pennsylvania
33rd & Spruce St.
Philadelphia, PA 19104
Ph: (215)898-4000   Fax: (215)898-0657
To recognize the most outstanding archaeological work. A gold medal is awarded as merited. Established in 1898 by Lucy Wharton Drexel.

★3796★ Fellowships at the Albright Institute of Archaeological Research in Jerusalem
American Schools of Oriental Research (ASOR)
3301 North Charles St.
Baltimore, MD 21218
Ph: (410)516-3498   Fax: (410)516-3499
Purpose: To enable scholars to undertake research and field projects in the Middle East. Qualifications: There are six different Fellowships available: Annual Professorships; George A. Barton Fellowship; Dorot Research Fellowship; Honorary Appointments; Samuel H. Kress Fellowship; USIA Fellowships. Requirements are as follows: applicant may be of any nationality, but must be a member of ASOR and hold the Ph.D. Special consideration will be given to scholars whose work is affiliated with an ASOR Institute. Fellows are required to take up residence at the Institute and to actively participate in the Insti-

tute's activities. Funds available: Annual Professorship: $10,000, plus room and half board; Barton Fellowship: $2,000, plus $3,000 for room and half board; Dorot Research Fellowship: $30,000 ($22,000 stipend, plus room and half board); Honorary Appointments: no stipend; Samuel H. Kress Fellowship: $4,500, plus $6,500 for room and half board; USIA Fellowships: Stipend up to $7,000 plus room & half board. Application details: Write to the Coordinator of Academic Programs for application form and guidelines Deadline: 15 October (15 September for the Dorot Fellowship). Notification in January.

★3797★ Honorary Member
Missouri Archaeological Society
Univ. of Missouri
103 Swallow Hall
PO Box 958
Columbia, MO 65205
Ph: (314)882-3544   Fax: (314)882-9410
To recognize distinguished members who have made selfless contributions to the Society's programs or objectives. Selection is made by the Board of Directors. For honorary life members, the award consists of free membership and publications for life. For specific year honorary members, the award consists of free memberships and publications for a year and a letter of award. Presented at the annual meeting. Established in 1983.

★3798★ Howard Fellows
George A. and Eliza Gardner Howard Foundation
Brown Univ.
42 Charlesfield St.
PO Box 1956
Providence, RI 02912
Ph: (401)863-2640
To provide individuals in the middle stages of their careers with funds for independent projects in the fields that are selected within the following categories on a rotational basis each year: Comparative Literature, Language and Literature; History, Anthropology, Political Science and Social Studies; Classical and Archaeological Studies, History of Science, Philosophy, and Religious Studies; Art History and Fine Arts (including painting, sculpture, musicology, music composition, photography and film); and Creative Writing and Literary Criticism. Preference is given to candidates between 25 and 45 years of age who, regardless of their country of citizenship, are professionally based in the United States either by affiliation with an institution or by residence. No fellowships are awarded for work leading to any academic degree or for coursework or training of any other sort. Nominations are accepted between September 1 and October 15. Stipends for the one-year period are $18,000. Established in 1952 by Nicea Howard in memory of her grandparents.

★3799★ Alfred Vincent Kidder Award
American Anthropological Association
4350 N. Fairfax Dr., Ste. 640
Arlington, VA 22203
Ph: (703)528-1902   Fax: (703)528-3546
To recognize eminence in the field of American archaeology with emphasis on the American Southwest and Middle America. A medal

and citation are awarded every three years. Established in 1950.

★3800★ Mesopotamian Fellowship
American Schools of Oriental Research
3301 N. Charles St.
Baltimore, MD 21218-3207
Ph: (410)516-3498   Fax: (410)516-3499
To provide for one 3-to 6-month $5,000 fellowship for pre-doctoral students or recent post-doctoral scholars. Applicants should work on a project dealing with ancient Mesopotamian civilization or culture, preferably in Iraq or immediately adjacent sections of bordering countries (ancient Mesopotamia). A fellowship with a stipend of $5,000 is awarded.

★3801★ National Endowment for the Humanities Post Doctoral Fellowships, Nicosia
American Schools of Oriental Research
3301 N. Charles St.
Baltimore, MD 21218-3207
Ph: (410)516-3498   Fax: (410)516-3499
One stipend of up to $30,000 is awarded to a Fellow at the Cyprus American Archaeological Research Institute(CAARI). Humanities scholars holding a Ph.D. degree as of January 1 of the year of the award are eligible. For the following grants, applicants must be or become an individual member of ASOR or be affiliated with an institution that is a corporate member of ASOR.

★3802★ National Endowment for the Humanities Programs
National Endowment for the Humanities
1100 Pennsylvania Ave. NW, Rm. 407
Washington, DC 20506
Ph: (202)606-8438   Fax: (202)606-8243
The National Endowment for the Humanities is an independent federal government grant-making agency to support research, education, and public programs in the humanities. The term *humanities* includes, but is not limited to, the study of the following disciplines: history; philosophy; languages; linguistics; literature; archaeology; jurisprudence; the history, theory, and criticism of the arts; ethics; comparative religion; and those aspects of the social sciences that employ historical or philosophical approaches. Grants are made through six divisions: Education Programs, Fellowships and Seminars, Public Programs, Research Programs, State Programs, and Preservation and Access. The final responsibility for awards rests by law with the Chairman of the Endowment, who is appointed for a four-year term by the President of the United States with the advice and consent of the Senate. The Chairman is advised by the National Council on the Humanities, a board of twenty-six distinguished private citizens. The National Council members, who serve six-year terms, are also nominated by the President and confirmed by the Senate. Established in 1965.

★3803★ Pomerance Award of the Archaeological Institute of America for Scientific Contributions to Archaeology
Archaeological Institute of America
675 Commonwealth Ave.
Boston, MA 02215
Ph: (617)353-9361   Fax: (617)353-6550

To recognize interdisciplinary assistance of scientists to the advancement of archaeological research. A bronze medal and citation are awarded annually. Established in 1980.

★3804★ Rip Rapp Archaeological Geology Award
Geological Society of America
3300 Penrose Pl.
PO Box 9140
Boulder, CO 80301
Ph: (303)447-2020   Fax: (303)447-1133

To recognize an individual who has contributed in an outstanding manner to the interdisciplinary field of archaeological geology. The recipient of the award need not be a member of the Geological Society of America nor a citizen of the United States. The deadline for receipt of nominations is February 15. An engrossed certificate and a small pewter Revere bowl are awarded annually when merited. Renamed in 1993. Established in 1982. Sponsored by the Archaeological Geology Division.

★3805★ Charles Doolittle Walcott Medal
National Academy of Sciences
2101 Constitution Ave. NW
Washington, DC 20418
Ph: (202)334-2444

To recognize outstanding published research, explorations, and discoveries in pre-Cambrian or Cambrian life and history. A monetary prize of $2,000 and a medal are presented once every five years. Established in 1928 by Mary Vaux Walcott.

★3806★ Jesse Wrench Scholarship
Missouri Archaeological Society
Univ. of Missouri
103 Swallow Hall
PO Box 958
Columbia, MO 65205
Ph: (314)882-3544   Fax: (314)882-9410

To recognize an archaeology student who donates time to various society projects. Awarded annually.

BASIC REFERENCE GUIDES AND HANDBOOKS

★3807★ Experimentation and Reconstruction in Environmental Archaeology
David C. Brown
386 Prospect St., No. 192
New Haven, CT 06511
Ph: (203)498-2434

David Robinson, editor. 1992.

★3808★ Interpreting Artifact Scatters
David C. Brown
386 Prospect St., No. 192
New Haven, CT 06511
Ph: (203)498-2434

John Schofield, editor. 1992.

★3809★ Space, Time, and Archeological Landscapes
Plenum Publishing Corp.
233 Spring St.
New York, NY 10013
Ph: (212)620-8000   Fax: (212)463-0742

J. Rossignol, editor. 1992.

★3810★ Understanding Physical Anthropology and Archeology
West Publishing Co.
610 Opperman Dr.
Eagan, MN 55123
Ph: (612)687-7000

William A. Turnbaugh, editor. 1993.

PROFESSIONAL AND TRADE PERIODICALS

★3811★ American Schools of Oriental Research—Newsletter
American Schools of Oriental Research (ASOR)
3301 N. Charles St.
Baltimore, MD 21218
Ph: (410)516-3498   Fax: (410)516-3499
Victor H. Matthews

Quarterly. Reports on ASOR archeological projects in the Middle East. Carries announcements of grant and excavation opportunities and profiles of archeologists and their work. Recurring features include features include listings of teaching jobs available, letters to the editor, and news of members.

★3812★ Amici di Spannocchia
Etruscan Foundation
161 Country Club Dr.
Grosse Pointe Farms, MI 48236
Ph: (313)417-9711   Fax: (313)417-9711
Carol Gove

Annual. Covers activities of the various classical archeology, architectural preservation, and cultural programs conducted at the Foundation's headquarters in Spannocchia, Italy. Recurring features include book reviews and photos.

★3813★ Ancient Mesoamerica
Cambridge University Press
40 W. 20th St.
New York, NY 10011
Ph: (212)924-3900   Fax: (212)691-3239
William R. Fowler

SAY. Journal focusing on Mesoamerican archaeology.

★3814★ Archaeological Conservancy—Newsletter
Archaeological Conservancy
5301 Central Ave. NE, Ste. 1218
Albuquerque, NM 87108-1517
Theresa Oderman

Quarterly. Carries information on the acquisition and preservation of archeological sites in the U.S. Informs readers of research and tour offerings, current efforts, and of the historical significance of sites. Includes news of fundraising activities and contributions to the Conservancy.

★3815★ Archaeological Prospection
John Wiley and Sons, Inc.
Subscription Dept.
605 3rd Ave.
New York, NY 10158
Ph: (212)850-6000   Fax: (212)850-6799
A.M. Pollard

Quarterly. Journal with articles relating to archaeological prospection techniques, including geophysical and geochemical methods, and underlying geology.

★3816★ Backdirt
Institute of Archaeology
A222 Fowler Museum
Los Angeles, CA 90024-7510
Ph: (213)825-7411   Fax: (213)206-4723
Brenda Johnson-Grau

Biennial. Reports on all aspects of archaeological research conducted by the Institute, as well as including some excavation news. Recurring features include columns titled Archaeology Program, Zooarchaeology Laboratory, Archaeological Survey, Bookends, UCLA Friends of Archaeology News, and Public Lectures.

★3817★ Bulletin of the Society for American Archaeology
Society for American Archaeology
900 2nd St. NE, Ste. 12
Washington, DC 20002
Ph: (202)789-8200   Fax: (202)789-0284
Donald Rice

Provides news and information of interest to archaeologists.

★3818★ Cambridge Archaeological Journal
Cambridge University Press
40 W. 20th St.
New York, NY 10011
Ph: (212)924-3900   Fax: (212)691-3239
Chris Scarre

SAY. Journal focusing on archaeological research.

★3819★ Center for Archaeological Investigations—Newsletter
Center for Archaeological Investigations
Southern Illinois University
Carbondale, IL 62901
Ph: (618)453-5031   Fax: (618)453-3253
Donna E. Butler

Annual. Reports on the progress of the Center's projects and research. Contains news of visiting scholars and of the Center's collections. Recurring features include news of members, a calendar of events, listings of recent Center publications, and news of colloquia and conferences.

★3820★ INA Quarterly
Institute of Nautical Archaeology (INA)
PO Drawer HG
College Station, TX 77841-5137
Ph: (409)845-6694
Michael A. Fitzgerald

Quarterly. Features articles about the underwater archeological research being conducted or sponsored by the Institute. Recurring features include news of research and news of members.

★3821★ International Journal of Osteoarchaeology
John Wiley and Sons, Inc.
Subscription Dept.
605 3rd Ave.
New York, NY 10158
Ph: (212)850-6000   Fax: (212)850-6799
Ann Stirland

Quarterly. Journal providing a forum of debate and publication for current research in the study of human and animal bones from an archaeological perspective.

★3822★ Journal of Archaeological Research
Plenum Publishing Corp.
233 Spring St.
New York, NY 10013
Ph: (212)620-8000   Fax: (212)463-0742

Quarterly. Journal targeting archaeological students and professionals covering comparative research, critical articles, and peer-review analyses of studies.

★3823★ Museum Monthly
Denver Museum of Natural History
2001 Colorado Blvd.
Denver, CO 80205
Ph: (303)370-8334   Fax: (303)370-8384
Todd Runestad

Monthly. Focuses on natural history, archeology, and international travel. Carries exhibit information, book reviews, travel and tour information, and educational program news.

Recurring features include notices of awards, news of members, and a calendar of events.

★3824★ Society for Historical Archaeology—Newsletter
Society for Historical Archaeology
College of William and Mary
Department of Anthropology
Williamsburg, VA 23185
Ph: (804)221-1059
Norman F. Barka

Quarterly. Supports the aims of the Society, which "promotes scholarly research and the dissemination of knowledge concerning historical archeology." Presents information on current research, legislative developments, and Society meetings and activities. Recurring features include editorials, letters to the editor, news of members, and a calendar of events.

★3825★ Society for Industrial Archeology—Newsletter
Society for Industrial Archeology
National Museum of American History,
 MRC 629
Smithsonian Institution
Washington, DC 20560
Robert M. Frame

Quarterly. Examines the physical survivals of the technological and industrial past, being concerned with the preservation or loss of historical industrial sites and structures, and interpretation of the sites and artifacts. Covers pertinent laws and legislation, related Museum affairs, and news of the activities of the Society. Recurring features include chapter news, news of members, conferences, grants, exhibits, and publications available, a calendar of events, research queries, and calls for papers.

★3826★ SOPA Newsletter
Society of Professional Archeologists
 (SOPA)
University of South Florida
Department of Anthropology
Tampa, FL 33620
Ph: (813)974-2138
Roger T. Grange

Monthly. Dedicated to archeology and the events, legislation, and people related to the archeological profession. Publishes news of the Society, its members and activities.

★3827★ Stones and Bones Newsletter
Alabama Archaeological Society
c/o McDonald Broom
309 Wallace Hall
Troy State University
Troy, AL 36082
Ph: (205)670-3638   Fax: (205)670-3753
McDonald Broom

Monthly. Reports on the archeology of Alabama, including studies of artifacts, discussions of historic and prehistoric culture, and related topics. Recurring features include Society news, announcements of meetings, book reviews, publication news, calls for papers, news of research, chapter news, and obituaries.

OTHER SOURCES OF INFORMATION

★3828★ "Archaeologist" in Career Selector 2001
Barron's Educational Series, Inc.
250 Wireless Blvd.
Hauppauge, NY 11788
Ph: (516)434-3311   Fax: (516)434-3723
Fr: 800-645-3476
James C. Gonyea. 1993.

Economists and Market Research Analysts

Economists study the production, distribution, and consumption of commodities and services. They analyze the costs and benefits of distributing and consuming these goods and services. Their research might focus on topics such as energy costs, inflation, interest rates, farm prices, or imports. Economists who are primarily theoreticians may use mathematical models to develop theories on the causes of business cycles and inflation or the effects of unemployment and tax policy. Other economists, however, are concerned with practical applications of economic policy in a particular area, such as finance, labor, agriculture, transportation, energy, or health. Economists who work for government agencies assess economic conditions in the United States and abroad and estimate the economic impact of specific changes in legislation or public policy. **Market research analysts** are concerned with the design, promotion, price, and distribution of a product or service. Like economists, market research analysts often design surveys and questionnaires; conduct telephone, personal, or mail interviews; and sometimes offer product samples to assess consumer preferences and indicate current trends. Once the data are compiled, market research analysts code, tabulate, and evaluate the data. They then make recommendations to management based upon their findings and suggest a course of action. They may provide management with information to make decisions on the promotion, distribution, design, and pricing of company products or services; determining the advisability of adding new lines of merchandise, opening new branches, or diversifying the company's operations; or analyzing the effect of changes in the tax laws on future operations.

Salaries

Salaries for economists and market research analysts generally depend on the areas in which they work. For persons with a bachelors degree in economics starting salary averages $25,200/year and for a bachelors degree in marketing $24,000.

Employment Outlook

Growth rate until the year 2005: Average.

Economists and Market Research Analysts

CAREER GUIDES

★3829★ *Career Choices for the 90's for Students of Economics*
Walker and Co.
435 Hudson St.
New York, NY 10014
Ph: (212)727-8300   Fax: (212)727-0984
Fr: 800-289-2553
1990. Offers alternatives for students of economics. Gives information about the outlook and competition for entry-level candidates. Provides job-hunting tips.

★3830★ *Careers in Business Economics*
National Association of Business
    Economists (NABE)
28349 Chagrin Blvd.
Cleveland, OH 44122-4589
Ph: (216)464-7986
1992. Details what business economists do, education required, skills and personality traits needed, salaries, and the future opportunities in business economics. Lists sources of additional information. Explores career opportunities in government, insurance, banking, consulting, investments, industry, and communications.

★3831★ "Consumer Researcher" in *Career Opportunities in the Music Industry* (pp. 31-32)
Facts on File
460 Park Ave. S.
New York, NY 10016-7382
Ph: (212)683-2244   Fax: 800-678-3633
Fr: 800-322-8755
Shelly Field. 1990. Discusses approximately 80 jobs in music including the performing arts, business, and education. Each job description provides basic career information, salary, employment prospects, advancement opportunities, education, training, and experience required.

★3832★ "Economics" in *College Majors and Careers: A Resource Guide to Effective Life Planning* (pp. 47-48)
Garrett Park Press
PO Box 1907
Garrett Park, MD 20896
Ph: (301)946-2553
Paul Phifer. Revised, 1993. Lists 60 college majors, with definitions; related occupations and leisure activities; skills, values, and personal attributesneeded; suggested readings; and a list of associations.

★3833★ *Economist*
Careers, Inc.
PO Box 135
Largo, FL 34649-0135
Ph: (813)584-7333
1992. Four-page brief describing duties, working conditions, personal qualifications, training, earnings and hours, employment outlook, places of employment, related careers, and where to write for more information.

★3834★ "Economist" in *Career Information Center* (Vol.6)
Simon and Schuster
200 Old Tappan Rd.
Old Tappan, NJ 07675
Fax: 800-445-6991   Fr: 800-223-2348
Richard Lidz and Linda Perrin, editorial directors. Fifth edition, 1993. This 13-volume set profiles over 600 occupations. Each occupational profile describes job duties, entry-level requirements, educational requirements, advancement possibilities, employment outlook, working conditions, earnings and benefits, and where to write for more information.

★3835★ "Economist" in *College Board Guide to Jobs and Career Planning* (pp. 293)
The College Board
415 Columbus Ave.
New York, NY 10023-6992
Ph: (212)713-8165   Fax: (212)713-8143
Fr: 800-323-7155
Joyce S. Mitchell. Second edition, 1994. Describes a variety of careers. Career profiles include information on salaries, related careers, education needed, and sources of additional information.

★3836★ "Economist" in *Guide to Federal Jobs* (pp. 53-66)
Resource Directories
3361 Executive Pkwy., Ste. 302
Toledo, OH 43606
Ph: (419)536-5353   Fax: (419)536-7056
Fr: 800-274-8515
Rod W. Durgin, editor. Third edition, 1992. Contains information on finding and applying for federal jobs. Describes more than 200 professional and technical jobs for college graduates. Covers the nature of the work, salary, and geographic location. Lists college majors preferred for that occupation. Section one describes the function and work of government agencies that hire the most significant number of college graduates.

★3837★ "Economist" in *Jobs! What They Are—Where They Are—What They Pay* (p. 152)
Simon & Schuster, Inc.
Simon & Schuster Bldg.
1230 Avenue of the Americas
New York, NY 10020
Ph: (212)698-7000   Fr: 800-223-2348
Robert O. Snelling and Anne M. Snelling. 3rd edition, 1992. Describes duties and responsibilities, earnings, employment opportunities, training, and qualifications.

★3838★ "Economist" and "Market Research Analyst" in *Jobs Rated Almanac*
World Almanac
1 International Blvd., Ste. 444
Mahwah, NJ 07495
Ph: (201)529-6900   Fax: (201)529-6901
Les Krantz. Second edition, 1992. Ranks 250 jobs by environment, salary, outlooks, physical demands, stress, security, travel opportunities, and extra perks. Includes jobs the editor feels are the most common, most interesting, and the most rapidly growing.

★3839★ "Economist" in *VGM's Handbook of Business and Management Careers*
National Textbook Co.
4255 W. Touhy Ave.
Lincolnwood, IL 60646-1975
Ph: (708)679-5500   Fax: (708)679-2494
Fr: 800-323-4900
Annette Selden. Second edition, 1993. Contains 42 two-page occupational profiles describing job duties, places of employment, working conditions, qualifications, education, employment outlook, and income.

★3840★ *Economists*
Chronicle Guidance Publications, Inc.
66 Aurora St.
PO Box 1190
Moravia, NY 13118-1190
Ph: (315)497-0330   Fax: (315)497-3359
Fr: 800-622-7284
1993. Career brief describing the nature of the job, working conditions, hours and earnings, education and training, licensure, certification, unions, personal qualifications, social and psychological factors, location, employment outlook, entry methods, advancement, and related occupations.

★3841★ "Economists" in *101 Careers: A Guide to the Fastest-Growing Opportunities* (pp. 134-135)
John Wiley & Sons, Inc.
605 3rd Ave.
New York, NY 10158-0012
Ph: (212)850-6645   Fax: (212)850-6088
Michael Harkavy. 1990. Describes the nature of the job, working conditions, employment growth, qualifications, personal skills, projected salaries, and where to write for more information.

★3842★ "Economists" in *Encyclopedia of Careers and Vocational Guidance* (Vol.2, pp. 524-526)
J.G. Ferguson Publishing Co.
200 W. Madison St., Ste. 300
Chicago, IL 60606
Ph: (312)580-5480   Fax: (312)580-4948
William E. Hopke, editor-in-chief. Ninth edition, 1993. Four-volume set that profiles 900 occupations and describes job trends in 74 industries. Includes career description, educational requirements, history of the job, methods of entry, advancement, employment outlook, earnings, conditions of work, social and psychological factors, and sources of further information.

★3843★ "Economists and Marketing Research Analysts" in *Occupational Outlook Handbook*
U.S. Government Printing Office
Superintendent of Documents
Washington, DC 20402
Ph: (202)512-1800   Fax: (202)512-2250
Biennial; latest edition, 1994-95. Encyclopedia of careers describing about 250 occupations and comprising about 85 percent of all jobs in the economy. Occupations that require lengthy education or training are given the most attention. Each occupation's profile describes what the worker does on the job, working conditions, education and training requirements, advancement possibilities, job outlook, earnings, and sources of additional information.

★3844★ "Market Analyst" in *VGM's Handbook of Business and Management Careers*
National Textbook Co.
4255 W. Touhy Ave.
Lincolnwood, IL 60646-1975
Ph: (708)679-5500   Fax: (708)679-2494
Fr: 800-323-4900
Annette Selden. Second edition, 1993. Contains 42 two-page occupational profiles describing job duties, places of employment, working conditions, qualifications, education, employment outlook, and income.

★3845★ "Market Research" in *Career Choices for the 90's for Students of Psychology* (pp. 131-145)
Walker and Co.
435 Hudson St.
New York, NY 10014
Ph: (212)727-8300   Fax: (212)727-0984
Fr: 800-289-2553
1990. Offers alternatives for students of psychology. Gives information about the outlook and competition for entry-level candidates. Provides job-hunting tips.

★3846★ *Market Research Consultant*
Vocational Biographies, Inc.
PO Box 31
Sauk Centre, MN 56378-0031
Ph: (612)352-6516   Fax: (612)352-5546
Fr: 800-255-0752
1992. Four-page pamphlet containing a personal narrative about a worker's job, work likes and dislikes, career path from high school to the present. Education and training, the rewards and frustrations, and the effects of the job on the rest of the worker's life. The data file portion of this pamphlet gives a concise occupational summary, including work descriptions, working conditions, places of employment, personal characteristics, education and training, job outlook, and salary range.

★3847★ "Market Research" in *Encyclopedia of Career Choices for the 1990s: A Guide to Entry Level Jobs* (pp. 560-574)
Berkley Pub.
PO Box 506
East Rutherford, NJ 07073
Fax: (201)933-2316   Fr: 800-788-6262
1992. Describes entry-level careers in a variety of industries. Presents qualifications required, working conditions, salary, internships, and professional associations.

★3848★ "Market Research" in *Liberal Arts Jobs*
Petersons Guides, Inc.
PO Box 2123
Princeton, NJ 08543-2123
Ph: (609)243-9111   Fax: (609)243-9150
Fr: 800-338-3282
Burton Jay Nadler. Second edition, 1989. Strives to help the liberal arts graduate identify skills for entry-level positions. Gives goal setting and job search advice.

★3849★ "Market Researchers" in *American Almanac of Jobs and Salaries* (pp. 349)
Avon Books
1350 Avenue of the Americas
New York, NY 10019
Ph: (212)261-6800   Fr: 800-238-0658
John Wright, editor. Revised and updated, 1994-95. A comprehensive guide to the wages of hundreds of occupations in a wide variety of industries and organizations.

★3850★ "Marketing and Market Research" in *Career Choices for the 90's for Students of Business* (pp. 116-119)
Walker and Co.
435 Hudson St.
New York, NY 10014
Ph: (212)727-8300   Fax: (212)727-0984
Fr: 800-289-2553
1990. Offers alternatives for students of business. Gives information about the job outlook and competition for entry-level candidates. Provides job-hunting tips.

★3851★ "Marketing and Market Research" in *Career Choices for the 90's for Students of Mathematics* (pp. 119-122)
Walker and Co.
435 Hudson St.
New York, NY 10014
Ph: (212)727-8300   Fax: (212)727-0984
Fr: 800-289-2553
1990. Offers alternatives for students of mathematics. Gives information about the outlook and competition for entry-level candidates. Provides job-hunting tips.

★3852★ "Marketing Research" in *Opportunities in Marketing Careers* (pp. 13-15)
National Textbook Co. (NTC)
VGM Career Books
4255 W. Touhy Ave.
Lincolnwood, IL 60646-1975
Ph: (708)679-5500   Fax: (708)679-2494
Fr: 800-323-4900
Margery S. Steinberg. 1988. Defines marketing and surveys marketing fields, such as research and retailing. Gives the employment outlook; describes the rewards of a career in marketing. Includes information on the education needed, and how to find a job. Lists colleges with majors in marketing.

★3853★ *Marketing Researcher*
Careers, Inc.
PO Box 135
Largo, FL 34649-0135
Ph: (813)584-7333
1992. Two-page occupational summary card describing duties, working conditions, personal qualifications, training, earnings and hours, employment outlook, places of employment, related careers, and where to write for more information.

★3854★ "Marketing Researcher" in VGM's Careers Encyclopedia (pp. 264-266)
National Textbook Co. (NTC)
VGM Career Books
4255 W. Touhy Ave.
Lincolnwood, IL 60646-1975
Ph: (708)679-5500   Fax: (708)679-2494
Fr: 800-323-4900
Third edition, 1991. Profiles 200 occupations. Describes job duties, places of employment, working conditions, qualifications, education and training, advancement potential, and salary for each occupation.

★3855★ Marketing Researchers
Chronicle Guidance Publications, Inc.
66 Aurora St.
PO Box 1190
Moravia, NY 13118-1190
Ph: (315)497-0330   Fax: (315)497-3359
Fr: 800-622-7284
1992. Career brief describing the nature of the job, working conditions, hours and earnings, education and training, licensure, certification, unions, personal qualifications, social and psychological factors, location, employment outlook, entry methods, advancement, and related occupations.

PROFESSIONAL ASSOCIATIONS

★3856★ American Economic Association (AEA)
2014 Broadway, Ste. 305
Nashville, TN 37203-2418
Ph: (615)322-2595   Fax: (615)343-7590
Members: Educators, business executives, government administrators, journalists, lawyers, and others interested in economics and its application to present-day problems. **Purpose:** Encourages historical and statistical research into actual conditions of industrial life and provides a nonpartisan forum for economic discussion. **Publications:** American Economic Review, quarterly. • Index of Economic Articles. • Job Openings for Economists, bimonthly. • Journal of Economic Literature, quarterly. • Journal of Economic Perspectives, quarterly. • Survey of Members, periodic.

★3857★ American Marketing Association (AMA)
250 S. Wacker Dr., Ste. 200
Chicago, IL 60606
Ph: (312)648-0536   Fax: (312)993-7542
Members: Professional society of marketing and market research executives, sales and promotion managers, advertising specialists, academics, and others interested in marketing. Fosters research; sponsors seminars, conferences, and student marketing clubs; provides educational placement service and doctoral consortium. Offers placement service. **Publications:** American Marketing Association—Proceedings, annual. • International Membership Directory, annual. • Journal of Health Care Marketing, quarterly. • Journal of Marketing, quarterly. • Journal of Marketing Research, quarterly. • Journal of Public Policy and Marketing, semiannual. •

Marketing Management, quarterly. • Marketing News: Reporting on the Marketing Professional and Its Association. • Marketing Research, quarterly.

★3858★ Marketing Research Association (MRA)
2189 Silas Deane Hwy., Ste. 5
Rocky Hill, CT 06067
Ph: (203)257-4008   Fax: (203)257-3990
Members: Companies and individuals involved in any area of marketing research, such as data collection, research, or as an end-user. **Publications:** Alert, monthly. • Blue Books Research Service Directory, annual. • Career Guide. • Communication Responsibilities During Data Collection Process Guidelines. • Facilities Management—Two Perspectives. • Field Auditor Recommended Practices Quality Control Series. • Guidelines and Practices to Promote Respondent Cooperation. • Interviewer Training. • Marketing Research Association—Membership Roster, annual. • Recruiting for Qualitative Research. • Research on Research Report. • We Can Make a Difference.

★3859★ National Association of Business Economists (NABE)
1233 20th St. NW, Ste. 505
Washington, DC 20036
Ph: (202)463-6223   Fax: (202)463-6239
Members: Professional society of institutions, businesses, and students with an active interest in business economics and individuals who are employed by academic, private, or governmental concerns in the area of business-related economic issues. **Purpose:** Maintains placement service for members; conducts several seminars per year. Maintains speakers' bureau. **Publications:** Business Economics, quarterly. • Careers in Business Economics. • Employment Opportunities for Business Economists, quarterly. • NABE News, bimonthly. • NABE Outlook, Industry Survey, and Policy Survey, monthly. • Salary Survey of Business Economists, biennial.

★3860★ National Association of Media Brokers (NAMB)
1650 Tysons Blvd., No. 790
Mc Lean, VA 22102
Ph: (703)827-2727   Fax: (703)827-2728
Members: Media brokerage firms. **Purpose:** Seeks to share information on activities of mutual interest. (Media brokers deal in newspaper, radio, and television properties.) Compiles statistics.

★3861★ National Council on Economic Education (NCEE)
1140 Avenue of the Americas
New York, NY 10036
Ph: (212)730-7007   Fax: (212)730-1793
Fr: 800-336-1192
Members: Economists, educators, and representatives from business, labor, and finance dedicated to improving economic education by improving the quality and increasing the quantity of economics being taught in all levels of schools and colleges. **Purpose:** Initiates curriculum development and research; experiments with new economics courses and ways to prepare teachers and students; provides updated teacher-pupil materials; coordinates national and local programs in eco-

nomics education. Provides consulting services to educators; sponsors workshops; tests new methods in practical school situations. **Publications:** Curriculum Guide. • Economic Education Experiences of Enterprising Teachers, annual. • Economics for Kids, quarterly. • Journal of Economic Education, quarterly. • National Council on Economic Education—Annual Report. • National Council on Economic Education—Directory of Affiliated Councils and Centers, annual. • National Council on Economic Education—Update: For Friends of Economic Education, semiannual. • Senior Economist, quarterly.

TEST GUIDES

★3862★ Career Examination Series: Economist
National Learning Corp.
212 Michael Dr.
Syosset, NY 11791
Ph: (516)921-8888   Fax: (516)921-8743
Fr: 800-645-6337
Jack Rudman. A series of study guides with multiple-choice examination questions and solutions for trainees and professional economists. Titles in the series include Associate Economist; Senior Economist; Supervising Economist.

★3863★ Career Examination Series: Senior Research Analyst
National Learning Corp.
212 Michael Dr.
Syosset, NY 11791
Ph: (516)921-8888   Fax: (516)921-8743
Fr: 800-645-6337
Jack Rudman. 1993. Test guide including questions and answers for students or professionals in the field who seek advancement through examination.

★3864★ Career Examination Series: Supervising Economist
National Learning Corp.
212 Michael Dr.
Syosset, NY 11791
Ph: (516)921-8888   Fax: (516)921-8743
Fr: 800-645-6337
Jack Rudman. Test guide including questions and answers for students or professionals in the field who seek advancement through examination.

★3865★ College-Level Examination Series: Economics
National Learning Corp.
212 Michael Dr.
Syosset, NY 11791
Ph: (516)921-8888   Fax: (516)921-8743
Fr: 800-645-6337
Jack Rudman. Multiple-choice preparatory examinations for professional economists considering the College-Level Examination Program (CLEP) as an alternative to college course matriculation. Includes solutions to sample test questions. Titles in the series include Social Sciences and History; Introductory Microeconomics; Introductory Macroeconomics; Introductory Micro- and Macroeconomics; Introductory Economics.

★3866★ Economics
National Learning Corp.
212 Michael Dr.
Syosset, NY 11791
Ph: (516)921-8888   Fax: (516)921-8743
Fr: 800-645-6337
Jack Rudman. A test from the Graduate Record Examination series. Multiple-choice test for those seeking admission to graduate school for study in the field of economics. Includes solutions to examination questions.

★3867★ Principles of Economics
National Learning Corp.
212 Michael Dr.
Syosset, NY 11791
Ph: (516)921-8888   Fax: (516)921-8743
Fr: 800-645-6337
Jack Rudman. Dantes Subject Standardized Test series. A standardized graduate and college level examination given by graduate schools, colleges, and the Armed Forces as a final examination for course evaluation in the field of economics. Multiple-choice format with correct answers.

Educational Directories and Programs

★3868★ Marketing and Sales Career Directory
Gale Research Inc.
835 Penobscot Bldg.
Detroit, MI 48226-4094
Ph: (313)961-2242   Fax: (313)961-6083
Fr: 800-877-GALE
Bradley J. Morgan and Joseph M. Palmisano. Fourth edition, 1992. A directory in the Career Advisor Series that provides essays written by industry professionals; job search information on resume and cover letter preparation, networking, and the interviewing process; approximately 300 companies and organizations offering job opportunities and internships, and additional job-hunting resources.

Awards, Scholarships, Grants, and Fellowships

★3869★ Thomas F. Divine Award
Association for Social Economics
Louisiana Tech Univ.
College of Admin. & Business
PO Box 10318
Ruston, LA 71272
Ph: (318)257-3701   Fax: (318)257-4253
To recognize the lifetime contributions of an outstanding social economist. A monetary award and a medal are awarded annually at the Association's meeting. Established in 1986 for the Reverend Thomas F. Divine, S.J., founder and first president of the Association.

★3870★ Samuel Z. Westerfield Award
National Economic Association
School of Business
Univ. of Michigan
Ann Arbor, MI 48109-1234
Ph: (313)763-0121   Fax: (313)763-5688
To recognize and encourage scholarly work by African-American economists. Selection is based on outstanding contributions as both a scholar and an economist. A plaque is awarded periodically, usually bienielly.

Basic Reference Guides and Handbooks

★3871★ The Consumer Market Research Handbook
McGraw-Hill, Inc.
1221 Avenue of the Americas
New York, NY 10020
Ph: (212)512-2000   Fr: 800-722-4726
Robert M. Worcester and John Downham. Third revised edition, 1988. Explains how to design, carry out, and apply market research.

★3872★ Dictionary of Marketing Research
St. James Press
c/o Gale Research
835 Penobscot Bldg.
Detroit, MI 48226-4094
Ph: (313)961-2242   Fr: 800-345-0392
Jack R. Van Minden. 1987. This dictionary defines 2000 terms in a classified arranagement.

★3873★ Economics
McGraw-Hill, Inc.
1221 Avenue of the Americas
New York, NY 10020
Ph: (212)512-2000   Fr: 800-722-4726
Paul A. Samuelson and William D. Norhaus. Thirteenth edition, 1989. This introductory text covers basic economic concepts, macroeconomics, microeconomics, and economic growth.

★3874★ Economics of the Firm: Theory and Practice
Prentice Hall
113 Sylvan Ave., Rte. 9W
Englewood Cliffs, NJ 07632
Ph: (201)592-2000   Fr: 800-922-0579
Arthur A. Thompson. Sixth edition, 1993. Covers major aspects of microeconomic theory with an emphasis on practical applications. Focuses on the economics of firms, markets, and competitive behavior.

★3875★ Economics: Principles, Problems, and Policies
McGraw-Hill, Inc.
1221 Avenue of the Americas
New York, NY 10020
Ph: (212)512-2000   Fr: 800-722-4726
Campbell R. McCornell, editor. Tenth edition, 1987. Covers capitalism, fiscal policy, monetary policy, economic growth, and current economic problems.

★3876★ The Economist Atlas of the New Europe
Henry Holt & Co.
115 W. 18th St., 6th Fl.
New York, NY 10011
Ph: (212)886-9200
1992.

★3877★ The Economist Desk Companion: How to Measure, Convert, Calculate, and Define Practically Anything
Henry Holt & Co.
115 W. 18th St., 6th Fl.
New York, NY 10011
Ph: (212)886-9200
1992.

★3878★ The Encyclopedic Dictionary of Economics
Dushkin Publishing Group, Inc.
Sluice Dock
Guilford, CT 06437
Ph: (203)453-4351
Don Cole, editor. Fourth edition, 1991. TO 800-243-6532.

★3879★ The MIT Dictionary of Modern Economics
Massachusetts Institute of Technology
MIT Press
55 Hayward St.
Cambridge, MA 02142
Ph: (617)625-8569
David W. Pearce, editor. Fourth edition, 1992.

★3880★ The New Palgrave: A Dictionary of Economics
Stockton Press
257 Park Ave., S
New York, NY 10010
Ph: (212)673-4400
John Eatwell, Murray Milgate, and Peter Newman, editors. 1987. Includes bibliographies and indexes.

★3881★ The Pocket Economist
Basil Blackwell, Inc.
64 Depot Rd.
Colchester, VT 05446
Ph: (617)225-0430   Fr: 800-445-6638
Rupert Pennant-Rea and Bill Emmott. Second edition, 1988. Defines the most commonly-used economic terms.

★3882★ What Is Economics?
Mayfield Publications
1240 Villa St.
Mountain View, CA 94041
Ph: (415)960-3222   Fax: (415)960-0328
Jim Eggert. Third revised edition, 1993.

PROFESSIONAL AND TRADE PERIODICALS

★3883★ American Economic Review
American Economic Assn.
2014 Broadway, No. 305
Nashville, TN 37203-2418
Ph: (615)322-2595   Fax: (615)343-7590
Orley Ashenfelter
Quarterly. Economics journal.

★3884★ Brandweek
Billboard Magazine
33 Commercial St.
Gloucester, MA 01930
Ph: (508)281-3110   Fax: (508)281-0136
Craig Reiss
Weekly. Advertising and marketing magazine.

★3885★ The Brookings Review
The Brookings Institution
1775 Massachusetts Ave. NW
Washington, DC 20036
Ph: (202)797-6257   Fax: (202)797-6195
Fr: 800-275-1447
Brenda B. Szittya
Quarterly. Journal presenting to a general audience Brookings research and policy proposals on economic, foreign policy, and governmental affairs.

★3886★ Business Economics
National Assn. of Business Economists
28790 Chagrin Blvd., Ste. 300
Cleveland, OH 44122
Ph: (216)241-6223   Fax: (216)241-3830
Edmund A. Mennis
Quarterly. Professional journal of the National Association of Business Economists covering topics such as macro and microeconomics, monetary and fiscal policy, business forecasting, international economics, and deregulation.

★3887★ Business Marketing
Crain Communications, Inc.
740 N. Rush St.
Chicago, IL 60611
Ph: (312)649-5215   Fax: (312)649-5228
Jan Jaben
Monthly. Trade magazine on business-to-business marketing news, strategy, and tactics.

★3888★ Business Trends
Economics Department
PO Box 2900
Honolulu, HI 96846
Ph: (808)537-8307   Fax: (808)536-9433
Bimonthly. Covers foreign investments, capital gains, housing demand and supply, export, and economic growth in Hawaii.

★3889★ Center for Economic Policy Research—Newsletter
Center for Economic Policy Research
100 Encina Commons
Stanford, CA 94305
Ph: (415)725-1874   Fax: (415)723-8611
Carolyn Sherwood
Updates information on conferences, events, and publications.

★3890★ The Economist
The Economist Bldg.
111 W. 57th St.
New York, NY 10019
Ph: (212)541-5730   Fax: (212)541-9378
Bill Emmott
Weekly. International magazine reporting on news, world affairs, business, and finance.

★3891★ The Economist
Marengo Publishing
Box 249
Solon, IA 52333
Ph: (319)644-2233
Brian Fleck
Weekly. Newspaper.

★3892★ Federal Reserve Bank of Cleveland—Economic Commentary
Federal Reserve Bank of Cleveland
PO Box 6387
Cleveland, OH 44101
Ph: (216)579-2000   Fax: (216)579-3050
Robin Ratliff
Biweekly. Features articles on regional, national, and international issues in economics.

★3893★ Journal of Applied Econometrics
John Wiley and Sons, Inc.
Subscription Dept.
605 3rd Ave.
New York, NY 10158
Ph: (212)850-6000   Fax: (212)850-6799
M. Hashem Pesaran
Journal with articles on economics and related subjects.

★3894★ Journal of Economic Literature
American Economic Assn.
2014 Broadway, No. 305
Nashville, TN 37203-2418
Ph: (615)322-2595   Fax: (615)343-7590
Prof. John Pencavel
Quarterly. Economics journal.

★3895★ Journal of International Development
John Wiley and Sons, Inc.
605 3rd Ave.
New York, NY 10158
Ph: (212)850-6000   Fax: (212)850-6799
Paul Mosley
Bimonthly. Journal containing articles on development-related research in economics, political and social areas.

★3896★ Journal of Marketing Research
American Marketing Assn.
250 S. Wacker Dr., Ste. 200
Chicago, IL 60606-5819
Ph: (312)648-0536   Fax: (312)993-7540
Barton A. Weitz
Quarterly. Academic journal publishing scholarly research in the field of marketing.

★3897★ Journal of Strategic Marketing
Chapman & Hall
29 W. 35th St.
New York, NY 10001-2291
Ph: (212)244-3336
Quarterly. Journal containing articles on the relationship between marketing and management.

★3898★ Marketing Research: A Magazine of Management & Applications
American Marketing Assn.
250 S. Wacker Dr., Ste. 200
Chicago, IL 60606-5819
Ph: (312)648-0536   Fax: (312)993-7540
Harry O'Neill
Quarterly. Magazine on the application of marketing research and the management of the marketing research function.

★3899★ Quarterly Journal of Business & Economics
University of Nebraska
CBA Bldg.
PO Box 880407
Lincoln, NE 68588-0407
Ph: (402)472-7931   Fax: (402)472-9777
George M. McCabe
Quarterly. Journal reporting on finance and economics.

★3900★ The Quarterly Journal of Economics
MIT Press Journals
55 Hayward St.
Cambridge, MA 02142
Ph: (617)253-2889   Fax: (617)258-6779
Olivier Blanchard
Quarterly. Journal of analytical articles in economic theory.

★3901★ Trendline Current Market Perspectives
Standard & Poor's
25 Broadway
New York, NY 10004
Ph: (212)208-8392   Fax: (212)208-0040
Kenneth LutzPublisher
Monthly. Price volume charts plotted on a weekly basis; reports on 3 1/2 years of activity on nearly 1,500 NYSE and Amex stocks.

PROFESSIONAL MEETINGS AND CONVENTIONS

★3902★ Western Economic Association International Annual Conference
Western Economic Association International
7400 Center Ave., Ste. 109
Huntington Beach, CA 92647
Ph: (714)898-3222   Fax: (714)891-6715
Annual.

OTHER SOURCES OF INFORMATION

★3903★ "Economics" in *Accounting to Zoology: Graduate Fields Defined* **(pp. 57-60)**
Petersons Guides, Inc.
PO Box 2123
Princeton, NJ 08543-2123
Ph: (609)243-9111   Fax: (609)243-9150
Fr: 800-338-3282

Amy J. Goldstein, editor. Revised and updated, 1987. Defines 298 graduate and professional fields. Discusses types of graduate programs and degrees, graduate research, applied work, employment prospects, and trends.

★3904★ "Economist" in *100 Best Jobs for the 1990s & Beyond*
Dearborn Financial Publishing, Inc.
520 N. Dearborn St.
Chicago, IL 60610-4354
Ph: (312)836-4400   Fax: (312)836-1021
Fr: 800-621-9621

Carol Kleiman. 1992. Describes 100 jobs ranging from accountants to veterinarians. Each job profile includes such information as education, experience, and certification needed, salaries, and job search suggestions.

★3905★ "Economist" in *Career Selector 2001*
Barron's Educational Series, Inc.
250 Wireless Blvd.
Hauppauge, NY 11788
Ph: (516)434-3311   Fax: (516)434-3723
Fr: 800-645-3476

James C. Gonyea. 1993.

Geographers

Geographers study the distribution of both physical and cultural phenomena over an area. Geographers specialize, as a rule. **Economic geographers** deal with the geographic distribution of an area's resources and economic activities. **Political geographers** are concerned with the relationship of geography to political phenomena, local, national and international. **Physical geographers** study the distribution of climates, vegetation, soil, and land forms. **Urban and transportation geographers** study cities and metropolitan areas, while **regional geographers** study the physical, climatic, economic, political, and cultural characteristics of a particular region or area, which may range in size from a river basin to a state, country, or continent. **Medical geographers** study health care delivery systems, epidemiology, and the effect of the environment on health.

Salaries

Median annual earnings for social scientists such as geographers is as follows:

Lowest 10 percent	Less than $17,800/year
Median	$36,700/year
Top 10 percent	More than $68,700/year
Federal government social scientists	$43,000

Employment Outlook

Growth rate until the year 2005: Faster than the average.

Geographers

CAREER GUIDES

★3906★ *Geographer*
Careers, Inc.
PO Box 135
Largo, FL 34649-0135
Ph: (813)584-7333
1992. Two-page occupational summary card describing duties, working conditions, personal qualifications, training, earnings and hours, employment outlook, places of employment, related careers, and where to write for more information.

★3907★ "Geographer" in *Career Information Center* (Vol.2)
Simon and Schuster
200 Old Tappan Rd.
Old Tappan, NJ 07675
Fax: 800-445-6991   Fr: 800-223-2348
Richard Lidz and Linda Perrin, editorial directors. Fifth edition, 1993. This 13-volume set profiles over 600 occupations. Each occupational profile describes job duties, entry-level requirements, educational requirements, advancement possibilities, employment outlook, working conditions, earnings and benefits, and where to write for more information.

★3908★ "Geographer" in *College Board Guide to Jobs and Career Planning* (pp. 295-296)
The College Board
45 Columbus Ave.
New York, NY 10023-6992
Ph: (212)713-8165   Fax: (212)713-8143
Fr: 800-323-7155
Second edition, 1994. Describes the job, salaries, related careers, education needed, and where to write for more information.

★3909★ *Geographers*
Chronicle Guidance Publications, Inc.
66 Aurora St.
PO Box 1190
Moravia, NY 13118-1190
Ph: (315)497-0330   Fax: (315)497-3359
Fr: 800-622-7284
1992. Occupational brief describing the nature of the job, working conditions, hours and earnings, education and training, licensure,

certification, unions, personal qualifications, social and psychological factors, location, employment outlook, entry methods, advancement, and related occupations.

★3910★ "Geographers" in *Career Discovery Encyclopedia* (Vol.3, pp. 58-59)
J.G. Ferguson Publishing Co.
200 W. Madison St., Ste. 300
Chicago, IL 60606
Ph: (312)580-5480   Fax: (312)580-4948
Russell E. Primm, editor-in chief. 1993. This six volume set contains two-page articles for 504 occupations. Each article describes job duties, earnings, and educational and training requirements. The whole set is arranged alphabetically by job title. Designed for junior high and older students.

★3911★ "Geographers" in *Encyclopedia of Careers and Vocational Guidance* (Vol.3, pp.79-81)
J.G. Ferguson Publishing Co.
200 W. Madison St., Ste. 300
Chicago, IL 60606
Ph: (312)580-5480   Fax: (312)580-4948
William E. Hopke, editor-in-chief. Ninth edition, 1993. Four-volume set that profiles 900 occupations and describes job trends in 74 industries. Includes career description, educational requirements, history of the job, methods of entry, advancement, employment outlook, earnings, conditions of work, social and psychological factors, and sources of further information.

★3912★ "Geographers" in *Jobs! What They Are—Where They Are—What They Pay* (pp. 356-257)
Fireside
Simon & Schuster Bldg.
1230 Avenue of the Americas
New York, NY 10020
Ph: (212)698-7000   Fr: 800-223-2348
Robert O. Snelling and Anne M. Snelling. Revised and updated, 1992. Describes duties and responsibilities, earnings, employment opportunities, training, and qualifications.

★3913★ "Geography" in *College Majors and Careers: A Resource Guide to Effective Life Planning* (pp. 63-64)
Garrett Park Press
PO Box 1907
Garrett Park, MD 20896
Ph: (301)946-2553
Paul Phifer. 1993. Lists 60 college majors, with definitions; related occupations and leisure activities; skills, values, and personal needed attributes; suggested readings; and a list of associations.

★3914★ *On Becoming a Professional Geographer*
Merrill Publishing Co.
PO Box 508
Columbus, OH 43216
Ph: (614)890-1111
Martin S. Kenzer, editor. 1989.

PROFESSIONAL ASSOCIATIONS

★3915★ Association of American Geographers (AAG)
1710 16th St. NW
Washington, DC 20009
Ph: (202)234-1450   Fax: (202)234-2744
Members: Professional society of educators and scientists in the field of geography. **Purpose:** Seeks to further professional investigations in geography and to encourage the application of geographic research in education, government, and business. Conducts research; maintains placement service; compiles statistics. **Publications:** *AAG Newsletter*, monthly. • *Annals*, quarterly. • *Geography Department Guide*, annual. • *Professional Geographer*, quarterly.

★3916★ National Geographic Society (NGS)
17th & M Sts. NW
Washington, DC 20036
Ph: (202)857-7000   Fax: (202)775-6141
Members: Persons interested in increasing and diffusing geographic knowledge. **Purpose:** Sponsors expeditions and research in geography, natural history, archaeology, astronomy, ethnology, and oceanography;

sends writers and photographers throughout the world; disseminates information through its magazine, maps, books, television documentaries, films, educational media, and information services for press and radio. Maintains National Geographic Society Geography Education Program to enhance geographic education in grades K-12; also maintains Explorers Hall Museum. **Publications:** *Geography Education Program Update*, quarterly. • *National Geographic*, monthly. • *National Geographic Traveler*, bimonthly. • *National Geographic World*, monthly.

TEST GUIDES

★3917★ *Geography*
National Learning Corp.
212 Michael Dr.
Syosset, NY 11791
Ph: (516)921-8888   Fax: (516)921-8743
Fr: 800-645-6337

Jack Rudman. Part of Dantes Subject Standardized Tests.

★3918★ *Geography*
National Learning Corp.
212 Michael Dr.
Syosset, NY 11791
Ph: (516)921-8888   Fax: (516)921-8743
Fr: 800-645-6337

Jack Rudman. Part of the Test Your Knowledge Series. Contains multiple choice questions with answers.

EDUCATIONAL DIRECTORIES AND PROGRAMS

★3919★ *Guide to Programs in Geography in the United States and Canada/AAG Handbook and Directory of Geographers*
Association of American Geographers
1710 16th St. NW
Washington, DC 20009-3198
Ph: (202)234-1450   Fax: (202)234-2744
Linda Bradshaw, Contact

Annual, September. Covers Approximately 240 institutions and 7,000 individuals. Entries include: For institutions—Department, address, and phone, contact person, requirements, programs, facilities, financial aid, faculty, titles of dissertations and theses completed. For individuals—Name, address, birth date, degrees received, place of employment. Arrangement: Alphabetical.

★3920★ *Schwendeman's Directory of College Geography of the United States*
Geographical Studies and Research Center
Eastern Kentucky University
Roark 201
Richmond, KY 40475
Ph: (606)622-1418   Fax: (606)622-1020
Wilma J. Walker, Contact

Annual, April. Covers 600 college and university geography departments, with their courses, enrollments, and faculties. Entries include: Institution name, department name, address, phone, names and titles of key personnel, enrollment figures. Arrangement: Two directory sections, both geographical—departmental personnel section and a course and enrollment information section.

AWARDS, SCHOLARSHIPS, GRANTS, AND FELLOWSHIPS

★3921★ James R. Anderson Medal of Honor in Applied Geography
Association of American Geographers
1710 16th St. NW
Washington, DC 20009
Ph: (202)234-1450   Fax: (202)234-2744

For recognition of distinguished service to the profession of geography. Any individual (living or dead) or organization engaged in the application of geographic principals may be considered if qualified in one or more of the following areas of achievement: business, industry, or government; literature; education; research; service to the profession; and public service. A plaque is awarded each year at the annual meeting of the Association. Established in 1983 by the Applied Geography Specialty Group of the Association in honor of James R. Anderson's promotion of applied geography.

★3922★ Alexander Graham Bell Medal
National Geographic Society
1600 M St. NW
Washington, DC 20036
Ph: (202)857-7000   Fax: (202)775-6141

To recognize extraordinary achievement in geographic research, broadly construed. A gold medal is awarded irregularly. Established in 1980 in honor of Alexander Graham Bell, the noted inventor, and second president of the Society.

★3923★ Henry Grier Bryant Gold Medal
Geographical Society of Philadelphia
21 S. 12th St.
Philadelphia, PA 19107
Ph: (215)563-0127   Fax: (215)922-2656

To recognize an individual for distinguished service to geography. A gold medal is awarded irregularly. Established in 1933.

★3924★ Franklin L. Burr Award
National Geographic Society
1600 M St. NW
Washington, DC 20036
Ph: (202)857-7000   Fax: (202)775-6141

To recognize especially meritorious work in the field of geographic science. Leaders in

the Society's expeditions and researches are eligible. A monetary award and a certificate are awarded irregularly. Established in 1933 by Mary C. Burr in memory of her father.

★3925★ Cullum Geographical Medal
American Geographical Society
156 5th Ave.
New York, NY 10010
Ph: (212)242-0214   Fax: (212)989-1583

To recognize distinguished contributions to the advancement of geographical science or outstanding geographical discoveries. A gold medal is awarded when merited. Established in 1896 by a bequest from Major General W. Cullum of the U.S. Army, vice president of the society from 1877 to 1892.

★3926★ Helen Culver Gold Medal
Geographic Society of Chicago
30 N. Michigan Ave.
Chicago, IL 60602
Ph: (312)726-5293

To recognize contributions to the science of geography. A gold medal is awarded irregularly. Established in 1907.

★3927★ Charles P. Daly Medal
American Geographical Society
156 5th Ave.
New York, NY 10010
Ph: (212)242-0214   Fax: (212)989-1583

To recognize valuable or distinguished geographical services. A gold medal is awarded when merited. Established in 1902 by a bequest of Judge Daly, president of the society from 1864 to 1899.

★3928★ Honors Award
Association of American Geographers
1710 16th St. NW
Washington, DC 20009
Ph: (202)234-1450   Fax: (202)234-2744

To encourage meritorious achievements in geography by special recognition of outstanding contributions toward the advancement or welfare of the profession. The contributions recognized might be in research, applied research, writing, teaching, committee work, administrative work, collaborative work with nongeographers, or in other aspects of professional geographic work. Honors are given for outstanding achievement and meritorious contributions. Awarded annually at the meeting of the Association. Established in 1951.

★3929★ John Brinckerhoff Jackson Prize
Association of American Geographers
1710 16th St. NW
Washington, DC 20009
Ph: (202)234-1450   Fax: (202)234-2744

For recognition of a popular book of scholarly and literary merit on the human geography of the United States, particularly one that interprets geographical scholarship in language that nonprofessional readers can appreciate and enjoy. Authors of books written by geographers are eligible. Preference is given to U.S. citizens or permanent residents. A monetary prize of $1,000 is awarded at the annual meeting of the Association. Established in 1984 by John Brinckerhoff Jackson, founder and editor of *Landscape* magazine from 1951-1968.

★3930★ Elisha Kent Kane Medal
Geographical Society of Philadelphia
21 S. 12th St.
Philadelphia, PA 19107
Ph: (215)563-0127   Fax: (215)922-2656

To recognize an individual for eminent geographical research. A gold medal is awarded irregularly. Established in 1900.

★3931★ John Oliver La Gorce Medal
National Geographic Society
1600 M St. NW
Washington, DC 20036
Ph: (202)857-7000   Fax: (202)775-6141

To recognize accomplishment in geographic exploration or in the sciences, or for public service to advance international understanding. A gold medal is awarded irregularly. Established in 1967 in honor of John Oliver La Gorce, a former Society President and Editor.

★3932★ Samuel Finley Breese Morse Medal
American Geographical Society
156 5th Ave.
New York, NY 10010
Ph: (212)242-0214   Fax: (212)989-1583

To encourage geographical research. A gold medal is awarded when merited. Established in 1902 with funds bequeathed to the society by Professor Morse, discoverer of the recording telegraph. First awarded in 1928.

★3933★ J. Warren Nystrom Award
Association of American Geographers
1710 16th St. NW
Washington, DC 20009
Ph: (202)234-1450   Fax: (202)234-2744

To recognize outstanding doctoral dissertations in geography. A monetary award is presented at the annual meeting of the Association. Established in 1980 by Warren Nystrom, former executive director of AAG.

★3934★ Outstanding Achievement Award
Society of Woman Geographers
415 E. Capitol St. SE
Washington, DC 20003
Ph: (202)546-9228   Fax: (202)546-5232

To recognize a member of the society for an outstanding contribution or service of lasting benefit to science, the arts, or humanity. Only members of the society are eligible. A certificate is awarded annually when merited. Established in 1978.

BASIC REFERENCE GUIDES AND HANDBOOKS

★3935★ Dictionary of Concepts in Physical Geography
Greenwood Press, Inc.
88 Post Rd., W.
PO Box 5007
Westport, CT 06881
Ph: (203)226-3571
Thomas P. Huber. 1988. Includes bibliographies and an index.

★3936★ Webster's New Geographical Dictionary
Merriam-Webster, Inc.
PO Box 281
Springfield, MA 01102
Ph: (413)734-3134
1988.

PROFESSIONAL AND TRADE PERIODICALS

★3937★ FDG Newsletter
Federal Geographic Data Committee
590 National Center
Reston, VA 22091
Ph: (703)648-4533   Fax: (703)648-5755
Michael Domaratz

Periodic. Provides a forum for the exchange of information on federal digital geographic activities. Tracks the progress of various federal projects and describes federal use of geographic data technology. Contains brief articles on the collection, storage, exchange, and application of digital geographic data.

★3938★ History of Geography Journal
Archives and Association History Committee
c/o Geoffrey J. Martin
Southern Connecticut State University
Department of Geography
New Haven, CT 06515
Ph: (203)397-4355
Geoffrey J. Martin

Periodic. Features essays concerning the history and philosophy of geography, with emphasis on U.S. geographical thought. Carries occasional book reviews.

★3939★ International Journal of Population Geography
John Wiley and Sons, Inc.
Subscription Dept.
605 3rd Ave.
New York, NY 10158
Ph: (212)850-6000   Fax: (212)850-6799
H. Jones

Academic journal publishing international research in population geography. Covers topics such as migration, population and household structure, census analysis, and methods and techniques.

★3940★ National Council for Geographic Education—Perspective
National Council for Geographic Education
Indiana University of Pennsylvania
Indiana, PA 15705
Ph: (412)357-6290
Joseph W. Bencloski

Serves as a forum for the exchange of ideas within the teaching community, offering help to teachers of geography with developing effective geographic education programs and teaching materials for schools, colleges, and continuing education. Recurring features include announcements of awards, obituaries, and a calendar of conventions and meetings.

★3941★ SLA Geography & Map Division—Bulletin
Geography & Map Division
Oregon State University
Kerr Library 121
Corvallis, OR 97331-4501
Ph: (503)737-2971   Fax: (503)737-3453
Joanne M. Perry

Quarterly. Provides a medium of exchange of information, news, and research in the field of geographic and cartographic bibliography, literature, and libraries. Recurring features include a letters to the editor, news of research, a calendar of events, reports of meetings, news of educational opportunities, job listings, book reviews, and notices of publications available.

PROFESSIONAL MEETINGS AND CONVENTIONS

★3942★ Association of American Geographers Annual Meeting
Association of American Geographers
1710 16th St., NW
Washington, DC 20009-3198
Ph: (202)234-1450   Fax: (202)234-2744
Annual. **Dates and Locations:** 1996 Apr; Charlotte, NC.

OTHER SOURCES OF INFORMATION

★3943★ "Geographer" in Career Selector 2001
Barron's Educational Series, Inc.
250 Wireless Blvd.
Hauppauge, NY 11788
Ph: (516)434-3311   Fax: (516)434-3723
Fr: 800-645-3476
James C. Gonyea. 1993.

Historians

Historians research and analyze the past. They usually specialize in a specific country or geographic region; in a particular time period; or in a particular field, such as social, intellectual, political, or diplomatic history. **Biographers** collect detailed information on individuals. **Genealogists** trace family histories. Other historians help study and preserve archives, artifacts, and historic buildings and sites.

Salaries

Median annual earnings of social scientists such as historians are as follows:

Lowest 10 percent	Less than $17,800/year
Median	$36,700/year
Top 10 percent	More than $68,700/year
Federal government social scientists	$43,000/year

Employment Outlook

Growth rate until the year 2005: Faster than the average.

Historians

vancement, and careers related to this position.

CAREER GUIDES

★3944★ Career Choices for the 90's for Students of History
Walker & Co.
720 5th Ave.
New York, NY 10019
Ph: (212)265-3632
Career Associates. 1990. Provides specific information about entry-level opportunities in history and highlights opportunities that might be overlooked. Includes information on where and who the employers are, salaries, entry-level responsibilities, and advancement opportunities.

★3945★ Careers for History Buffs & Others Who Learn from the Past
National Textbook Co. (NTC)
VGM Career Books
4255 W. Toughy Ave.
Lincolnwood, IL 60646-1975
Ph: (708)679-5500   Fax: (708)679-2494
Fr: 800-323-4900
Blythe Camenson. Describes different job opportunities for those interested in history.

★3946★ Careers for Students of History
American Historical Association
400 A St., SE
Washington, DC 20003
Ph: (202)544-2422
Barbara J. Howe. Revised edition, 1989.

★3947★ Great Jobs for History Majors
National Textbook Co. (NTC)
VGM Career Books
4255 W. Toughy Ave.
Lincolnwood, IL 60646-1975
Ph: (708)679-5500   Fax: (708)679-2494
Fr: 800-323-4900
1994.

★3948★ Historian
Careers, Inc.
PO Box 135
Largo, FL 34649-0135
Ph: (813)584-7333
1993. Four-page brief offering the definition, history, duties, working conditions, personal qualifications, educational requirements, earnings, hours, employment outlook, ad-

★3949★ "Historian" in Career Information Center (Vol.6)
Simon and Schuster
200 Old Tappan Rd.
Old Tappan, NJ 07675
Fax: 800-445-6991   Fr: 800-223-2348
Richard Lidz and Linda Perrin, editorial directors. Fifth edition, 1993. This 13-volume set profiles over 600 occupations. Each occupational profile describes job duties, entry-level requirements, educational requirements, advancement possibilities, employment outlook, working conditions, earnings and benefits, and where to write for more information.

★3950★ "Historian" in College Board Guide to Jobs and Career Planning (pp. 297-298)
The College Board
45 Columbus Ave.
New York, NY 10023-6992
Ph: (212)713-8165   Fax: (212)713-8143
Fr: 800-323-7155
Second edition, 1994. Describes the job, salaries, related careers, education needed, and where to write for more information.

★3951★ Historians
Chronicle Guidance Publications, Inc.
66 Aurora St.
PO Box 1190
Moravia, NY 13118-1190
Ph: (315)497-0330   Fax: (315)497-3359
Fr: 800-622-7284
1993. Career brief describing the nature of the job, working conditions, hours and earnings, education and training, licensure, certification, unions, personal qualifications, social and psychological factors, location, employment outlook, entry methods, advancement, and related occupations.

★3952★ "Historians" in Jobs! What They Are—Where They Are—What They Pay (pp. 358)
Fireside
Simon & Schuster Bldg.
1230 Avenue of the Americas
New York, NY 10020
Ph: (212)698-7000   Fr: 800-223-2348
Robert O. Snelling and Anne M. Snelling. Revised and updated, 1992. Describes duties and responsibilities, earnings, employment opportunities, training, and qualifications.

★3953★ "History" in College Majors and Careers: A Resource Guide to Effective Life Planning (pp. 69-70)
Garrett Park Press
PO Box 1907
Garrett Park, MD 20896
Ph: (301)946-2553
Paul Phifer. 1993. Lists 60 college majors, with definitions; related occupations and leisure activities; skills, values, and personal needed attributes; suggested readings; and a list of associations.

PROFESSIONAL ASSOCIATIONS

★3954★ American Association for State and Local History (AASLH)
530 Church St., Ste. 600
Nashville, TN 37219
Ph: (615)255-2971   Fax: (615)255-2979
Members: Organization of educators, historians, writers, and other individuals; state and local historical societies; agencies and institutions interested in improving the study of state and local history in the United States and Canada, and assisting historical organizations in improving their public services. **Publications:** Bicentennial State Histories Series. • Directory of Historical Societies and Agencies in the U.S. and Canada, triennial. • History News, bimonthly. • History News Dispatch, monthly.

★3955★ American Catholic Historical Association (ACHA)
Mullen Library, Rm. 318
Catholic University of America
Washington, DC 20064
Ph: (202)319-5079   Fax: (202)319-4967
Members: Professional society of historians, educators, students, and others interested in the history of the Catholic church in the United States and abroad and in the promotion of historical scholarship among Catholics. Has sponsored the publication of the papers of John Carroll, first Bishop and Archbishop of Baltimore, MD. **Publications:** *Catholic Historical Review*, quarterly.

★3956★ American Historical Association (AHA)
400 A St. SE
Washington, DC 20003
Ph: (202)544-2422   Fax: (202)544-8307
Members: Professional historians, educators, and others interested in promoting historical studies and collecting and preserving historical manuscriptts. **Purpose:** Conducts research and educational programs. Maintains speakers' bureau. **Publications:** *American Historical Association—Perspectives.* • *American Historical Review.* • *Careers for Students of History.* • *Directory of Affiliated Societies.* • *Directory of History Departments and Organizations in the United States and Canada*, annual. • *Doctoral Dissertations in History*, annual. • *Grants, Fellowships, and Prizes of Interest to Historians*, annual.

★3957★ American Society for Eighteenth-Century Studies (ASECS)
Utah State University
USU CC108
Logan, UT 84322-3730
Ph: (801)797-4065   Fax: (801)797-4065
Members: Scholars and others interested in the cultural history of the 18th century. **Purpose:** Encourages and advances study and research in this area; promotes the interchange of information and ideas among scholars from different disciplines (such as librarianship and bibliography) who are interested in the 18th century. Cosponsors seven fellowship programs; sponsors Graduate Student Caucus. **Publications:** *American Society for Eighteenth-Century Studies—Directory*, biennial. • *American Society for Eighteenth-Century Studies—News Circular*, quarterly. • *American Society for Eighteenth-Century Studies—Program for Annual Meeting.* • *Eighteenth-Century Studies*, quarterly. • *Eighteenth-Century Studies: A Cumulative Index, Volumes 1-20.* • *International Directory of Eighteenth-Century Studies/Repertoire International des Dix-Huitiemistes*, periodic. • *Studies in Eighteenth-Century Culture*, annual.

★3958★ Friends of Terra Cotta (FOTC)
771 West End Ave., No. 10E
New York, NY 10025
Ph: (212)932-1750
Members: Architects, engineers, contractors, historians, conservators, and preservationists. **Purpose:** Purpose is to raise awareness of architects, engineers, owners of terra cotta-clad buildings, and the public to the value of and the difficulties associated with the preservation of terra cotta. **Publications:** *American Decorative Tile.* • *Ceramic Ornaments in the New York Subway System.* • *Sites #18: Architectural Terra Cotta.* • *Field Guide to Apartment Building Architecture.* • *Mailing*, quarterly. • *Texture and Design in New York Apartment House Architecture.* • *Tile Roofs of Alfred, New York.*

★3959★ Gungywamp Society (GS)
334 Brook St.
Noank, CT 06340
Ph: (203)536-2887
Members: Avocational archaeologists, anthropologists, historians, geologists, astronomers, and interested individuals. **Purpose:** Seeks to protect and preserve sites throughout the northeastern United States that show evidence of ancient and pre-Columbian cultures. Investigates and studies lithic features, architecture, artifacts, ancient inscriptions, and historic records. Has discovered an archaeological site in Connecticut that shows evidence of serial occupancy since 3000 B.C. Conducts tours through the Gungywamp Complex, an archaeological area preserved by the group. Sponsors educational and charitable programs. Maintains speakers' bureau. **Publications:** *The Greater Gungywamp: A Guide.* • *Stonewatch*, quarterly.

★3960★ National Council on Public History (NCPH)
Indiana University - Purdue University at Indiana
327 Cavanaugh
425 University Blvd.
Indianapolis, IN 46202
Ph: (317)274-2716   Fax: (317)274-2347
Members: Purpose: Objectives are to encourage a broader interest in professional history and to stimulate national interest in public history by promoting its use at all levels of society. (Public history deals with nonacademic history. History is brought to the public rather than the classroom through museum work, public displays, and federal, local, and corporate historians.) Serves as an information clearinghouse; sponsors training programs, local and regional colloquia, projects, and panels. Offers advice to departments of history, historical associations, and others seeking information on public history, professional standards, opportunities, and internships. Conducts surveys and analyses. **Publications:** *Careers for Students of History.* • *The Craft of Public History.* • *Guide to Continuing Education for Public Historians.* • *Guide to Graduate Programs in Public History.* • *The Public Historian*, quarterly. • *Public History News*, quarterly. • *Public History Today.*

★3961★ Newcomen Society of the United States (NSUS)
412 Newcomen Rd.
Exton, PA 19341
Ph: (215)363-6600   Fax: (215)363-0612
Members: Business and professional people in education and industry in the United States and Canada. **Purpose:** Studies material history, as distinguished from political history, in terms of the beginnings, growth, and contributions of industry, transportation, communication, mining, agriculture, banking, insurance, medicine, education, invention, law, and related historical fields. Maintains Thomas Newcomen Memorial Museum in Steam Technology and Industrial History in Chester County, PA. Society named for Thomas Newcomen (1663-1729), British pioneer who invented the first atmospheric steam engine. **Publications:** *Addresses*, periodic.

★3962★ Organization of American Historians (OAH)
112 N. Bryan St.
Bloomington, IN 47408
Ph: (812)855-7311   Fax: (812)855-0696
Members: Professional historians, including college faculty members, secondary school teachers, graduate students, and other individuals in related fields; institutional subscribers are college, university, high school and public libraries, and historical agencies. **Purpose:** Promotes historical research and study. Sponsors 12 prize programs for historical writing; maintains speakers' bureau. Operates a professional job registry at annual meeting. Conducts educational programs. **Publications:** *Journal of American History*, quarterly. • *OAH Magazine of History*, quarterly. • *OAH Newsletter*, quarterly.

★3963★ Society of American Archivists (SAA)
600 S. Federal St., Ste. 504
Chicago, IL 60605
Ph: (312)922-0140   Fax: (312)347-1452
Members: Individuals and institutions concerned with the identification, preservation, and use of records of historical value. **Publications:** *The American Archivist*, quarterly. • *Archival Outlook*, bimonthly. • *SAA Employment Bulletin*, bimonthly. • *SAA Publications Catalog.* • *Society of American Archivists—Directory of Individual Members*, biennial.

★3964★ Society of American Historians (SAH)
Butler Library, Box 2
Columbia University
New York, NY 10027
Ph: (212)854-2221   Fax: (212)932-0602
Members: Authors who have written at least one book of literary and scholarly distinction in the field of American history (membership by invitation only). **Purpose:** Seeks to encourage literary distinction in the writing of history and biography. Promotes the writing of history through prizes for books based on their literary quality.

★3965★ Society for Historians of the Early American Republic (SHEAR)
Lebanon Valley College
History Dept.
101 N. College Ave.
Annville, PA 17003
Ph: (717)867-6355   Fax: (717)867-6124
Members: Individuals interested in the study of U.S. history between 1789-1848. Presents awards. **Publications:** *Journal of the Early Republic*, quarterly.

★3966★ Society for Historical Archaeology (SHA)
PO Box 30446
Tucson, AZ 85751
Ph: (602)886-8006   Fax: (602)886-0182
Members: Archaeologists, historians, anthropologists, and ethnohistorians; other indi-

viduals and institutions with an interest in historical archaeology or allied fields. **Purpose:** Aim is to bring together persons interested in studying specific historic sites, manuscripts, and published sources, and to develop generalizations concerning historical periods and cultural dynamics as these emerge through the techniques of archaeological excavation and analysis. Main focus is the era beginning with the exploration of the non-European world by Europeans, and geographical areas in the Western Hemisphere, but also considers Oceanian, African, and Asian archaeology during the relatively late periods. **Publications:** *Guides to the Archaeological Literature of the Immigrant Experience in America.* • *Historical Archaeology,* quarterly. • *Society for Historical Archaeology Conference: Underwater Proceedings,* annual. • *Society for Historical Archaeology—Newsletter,* quarterly. • *Special Publications Series,* periodic.

★3967★ United States Capitol Historical Society (USCHS)
200 Maryland Ave. NW
Washington, DC 20002
Ph: (202)543-8919   Fax: (202)544-8244
Members: Congressmen, organizations, and others interested in American history in general, and specifically the U.S. Capitol Building in Washington, DC. Encourages understanding of the founding, growth, and significance of the Capitol as a tangible symbol of representative government; conducts research into the history of the Congress and the Capitol. **Purpose:** Sponsored preparation of the color-illustrated book, *We, the People,* describing the construction, art, and architecture of the Capitol building, which was published in cooperation with the National Geographic Society and has gone through 14 editions. Conducts research, pulbications and symposia. **Publications:** *The Capitol Dome,* quarterly. • *Washington DC, Past and Present.*

TEST GUIDES

★3968★ American History
National Learning Corp.
212 Michael Dr.
Syosset, NY 11791
Ph: (516)921-8888   Fax: (516)921-8743
Fr: 800-645-6337
Jack Rudman. Regents College Proficiency Examination series. A sample test for college credit-by-examination programs in the field of history. Multiple-choice style with answers included.

★3969★ Barron's Regents Exams and Answers: U.S. History and Government
Barron's Educational Series, Inc.
250 Wireless Blvd.
Hauppauge, NY 11788
Ph: (516)434-3311   Fax: (516)434-3723
Fr: 800-645-3476
John McGeehan. 1988. Contains sample examination questions and answers for regents examinations in history and government.

★3970★ Career Examination Series: Historian
National Learning Corp.
212 Michael Dr.
Syosset, NY 11791
Ph: (516)921-8888   Fax: (516)921-8743
Fr: 800-645-6337
Jack Rudman. Part of the Career Examination Series. A study guide for professionals and trainees in the field of history. Includes a multiple-choice examination section; provides answers.

★3971★ History
National Learning Corp.
212 Michael Dr.
Syosset, NY 11791
Ph: (516)921-8888   Fax: (516)921-8743
Fr: 800-645-6337
Jack Rudman. Undergraduate Program Field Test series. A practice examination fashioned after tests given in the Regents External Degree Program. Designed to measure knowledge received outside the college classroom in the subject of history. Contains multiple-choice questions; provides solutions.

★3972★ History
National Learning Corp.
212 Michael Dr.
Syosset, NY 11791
Ph: (516)921-8888   Fax: (516)921-8743
Fr: 800-645-6337
Jack Rudman. Part of the Test Your Knowledge Series. Contains multiple choice questions with answers.

EDUCATIONAL DIRECTORIES AND PROGRAMS

★3973★ Directory of History Departments and Organizations in the United States and Canada
American Historical Association
400 A St. SE
Washington, DC 20003-3889
Ph: (202)544-2422   Fax: (202)544-8307
Roxanne Myers Spencer, Contact
Annual, October. Covers over 780 history departments in two- and four-year colleges and universities; historical organizations in the United States and Canada; over 14,000 historians. Entries include: Institution name, address, phone, names of faculty members and their areas of specialization, tuition, application information, enrollment, research facilities and educational programs. Arrangement: Alphabetical.

★3974★ Directory of M.A. and Ph.D. Programs in Art and Art History
College Art Association
275 7th Ave.
New York, NY 10001
Ph: (212)691-1051   Fax: (212)627-2381
Virginia Wageman, Contact
Irregular, latest edition 1992. Covers over 170 institutions offering M.A. and Ph.D. programs in art and art history. Entries include: Institution name, address; names and titles of

faculty; description of program, including admission requirements, degrees offered, degree requirements, tuition, fees; facilities. Arrangement: Alphabetical.

AWARDS, SCHOLARSHIPS, GRANTS, AND FELLOWSHIPS

★3975★ ABC-CLIO America: History and Life Award
Organization of American Historians
112 N. Bryan St.
Bloomington, IN 47408-4199
Ph: (812)855-7311   Fax: (812)855-0696
To encourage and recognize scholarship in American history in the journal literature advancing new perspectives on accepted interpretations or previously unconsidered topics. Individuals as well as editors may submit nominations. The deadline is November 15 of even-numbered years. A monetary award of $750 and a certificate are awarded biennially. First given in 1985.

★3976★ Ashworth Fellowship
Municipal Art Society of New York
457 Madison Ave.
New York, NY 10022
Ph: (212)935-3960   Fax: (212)753-1816
To provide an annual opportunity for a college student, recent graduate, or graduate student to complete a project relating to architecture, landscape architecture, urban planning and design, historic preservation, zoning, urban environmental controls, public art, or the history of architecture. Support of the Society's staff and resources, office space in the Urban Center, and a stipend of $2,500 are awarded.

★3977★ Paul Birdsall Prize in European Military and Strategic History
American Historical Association
400 A St. SE
Washington, DC 20003
Ph: (202)544-2422   Fax: (202)544-8307
To recognize the author of a major work in European military and strategic history since 1870. Preference is given to the international aspects of military history (military/diplomatic) but the impact of technological developments, strategic planning, and military events on society - political, economic, social - also qualify. Purely technical studies divorced from historical context are not eligible. Preference is given to younger academics, but older scholars and nonacademic candidates are not excluded. Authors must be citizens of the United States or Canada. Books published during the preceding two years are eligible to be submitted by May 15. A monetary award of $1,000 is offered biennially. Established in 1986 by an anonymous donor to honor the late Paul Birdsall of Williams College.

★3978★ Herbert Feis Award
American Historical Association
400 A St. SE
Washington, DC 20003
Ph: (202)544-2422   Fax: (202)544-8307
To recognize distinguished research and publication by an independent scholar or public historian in the form of a book, article, or series of articles of seminal importance, or an in-house publication shown to have had a major impact on policy. Individuals outside academe for a minimum of three years prior to the award year are eligible. Works published during the preceding two years must be submitted by May 15. A monetary award of $1,000 is presented annually. Established in 1984 in memory of Herbert Feis, public servant and historian of recent American foreign policy. Sponsored by the Rockefeller Foundation.

★3979★ Fellowship of the Augustan Society
Augustan Society
PO Box P
Torrance, CA 90508
Ph: (213)320-7766   Fax: (213)530-7530
To recognize outstanding contributions to the fields of history, heraldry, genealogy, chivalry, or related fields of study. The award is usually presented to a member of the Society, but occasionally it is given to non-members who have made significant contributions to the field of study of interest to the Society. A certificate is awarded annually. Established in 1965.

★3980★ Louis Gottschalk Prize
American Society for Eighteenth-Century Studies
Computer Center 108
Utah State University
Logan, UT 84322-3730
Ph: (801)750-4065   Fax: (801)750-4065
To recognize an outstanding historical or critical study on a subject of eighteenth-century interest. A book by a member published during the previous year in the field of 18th-century studies, and submitted by a publisher not later than November 15, is eligible. Books that are primarily translations are not eligible. A monetary prize of $1,000 is awarded annually. Established in 1976 in memory of Professor Louis Gottschalk, the second president of the society.

★3981★ Howard Fellows
George A. and Eliza Gardner Howard Foundation
Brown Univ.
42 Charlesfield St.
PO Box 1956
Providence, RI 02912
Ph: (401)863-2640
To provide individuals in the middle stages of their careers with funds for independent projects in the fields that are selected within the following categories on a rotational basis each year: Comparative Literature, Language and Literature; History, Anthropology, Political Science and Social Studies; Classical and Archaeological Studies, History of Science, Philosophy, and Religious Studies; Art History and Fine Arts (including painting, sculpture, musicology, music composition, photography and film); and Creative Writing

and Literary Criticism. Preference is given to candidates between 25 and 45 years of age who, regardless of their country of citizenship, are professionally based in the United States either by affiliation with an institution or by residence. No fellowships are awarded for work leading to any academic degree or for coursework or training of any other sort. Nominations are accepted between September 1 and October 15. Stipends for the one-year period are $18,000. Established in 1952 by Nicea Howard in memory of her grandparents.

★3982★ Jan Ilavsky Memorial Scholarship
Balch Institute for Ethnic Studies
18 S. 7th St.
Philadelphia, PA 19106
Ph: (215)925-8090
To encourage graduate students to select a topic in Slovak history or culture (broadly defined) for their Ph.D. dissertations. Applicants must be enrolled in a doctoral program of an accredited North American university. A scholarship of $2,000 is awarded annually in September. Established in 1985 in memory of Dr. Jan Ilavsky.

★3983★ Individual Award
American Printing History Association
PO Box 4922
Grand Central Sta.
New York, NY 10163
Ph: (212)930-0802   Fax: (212)302-4815
To recognize an individual for distinguished contributions to the study, recording, preservation, and dissemination of printing history. Awarded annually. Established in 1976.

★3984★ G. Wesley Johnson Journal Award
National Council on Public History
327 Cavanaugh Hall - IUPUI
425 Univ. Blvd.
Indianapolis, IN 46202
Ph: (317)274-2716   Fax: (317)274-2347
For recognition of the best article published during the preceding year in *The Public Historian*. All articles published in a single volume (four issues) are eligible and are automatically considered. A monetary prize of $250 and a certificate are awarded annually in April. Established in 1986 by History Associates, Inc. The award was renamed in 1987 to honor G. Wesley Johnson, former editor of *The Public Historian*.

★3985★ National History Day Awards
National History Day
0121 Caroline Hall
University of Maryland
College Park, MD 20742
Ph: (301)314-9739   Fax: (301)314-9767
To recognize academic excellence in the field of history among students in grades 6 through 12. The program seeks to nurture academic achievement and intellectual growth, and to stimulate young people to learn history through the excitement of original research and creative work. Students research and present papers, exhibits, and performances related to a theme. Students between the ages of 12 and 18 may enter. First, second, and third place awards are given both in a Junior and a Senior Division in the following categories: Historical Papers,

Individual Projects, Group Projects, Individual Media, Group Media, Individual Performance, and Group Performances. Special Awards are given in areas such as labor history, naval history, political history, women's history, American Jewish History, and agricultural history. An outstanding entry from each state is also recognized. The application deadline for district contests is mid-March. Monetary prizes, medals, and trophies are awarded annually in June. Established in 1974 by David D. Van Tassel. Sponsored by the Organization of American Historians and the American Historical Association.

★3986★ Paper Prize Award
Phi Alpha Theta
2333 Liberty St.
Allentown, PA 18104
Ph: (610)433-4140   Fax: (610)433-4661
To recognize the author of an essay that combines original historical research on a significant subject based on source material and manuscripts, if possible, with good English composition and superior style. Graduate and undergraduate members of the Society may submit manuscripts by July 1. Six prizes are awarded. The Dr. George P. Hammond Prize of $200 is awarded for the best paper submitted by a graduate student member of the society. The Dr. Lynn W. Turner Prize of $150 is awarded for the best paper submitted by an undergraduate student member of the society. Four prizes, each in the amount of $100, are awarded to papers by other undergraduate student members or graduate student members.

★3987★ Charles E. Peterson Fellowships/Internships
Athenaeum of Philadelphia
E. Washington Sq.
Philadelphia, PA 19106
Ph: (215)925-2688   Fax: (215)925-3755
To provide grants for advanced research in early American history and building technology. Applications are accepted from January 1 to March 1. Grants ranging from $1,000 to $15,000 are awarded annually. Established in 1988 in honor of Charles E. Peterson, one of America's leading restoration architects and founder of the Historic American Buildings Survey.

BASIC REFERENCE GUIDES AND HANDBOOKS

★3988★ *Bibliographies in History: An Index to Bibliographies in History Journals and Dissertations Covering the U.S. and Canada*
ABC-CLIO
PO Box 1911
Santa Barbara, CA 93116-1911
Ph: (805)968-1911
1988. Includes a bibliography and an index.

PROFESSIONAL AND TRADE PERIODICALS

★3989★ American Historical Association—Perspectives
American Historical Association (AHA)
400 A St. SE
Washington, DC 20003
Ph: (202)544-2422   Fax: (202)544-8307
Robert B. Townsend

Publishes news of the Association. Recurring features include editorials, news of research, letters to the editor, news of members, a calendar of events, and columns.

★3990★ American Hospital Association—Outreach
American Hospital Association (AHA)
840 N. Lake Shore Dr.
Chicago, IL 60611
Ph: (312)280-5921   Fax: (312)280-6012
Fr: 800-621-6902
David C. King

Bimonthly. Analyzes the factors influencing market supply, demand, and competition. Recurring features include statistics, details on the latest accreditation standards, reviews of current literature, education and technical assistance updates, news of research, and resources.

★3991★ ASECS News Circular
American Society for Eighteenth-Century Studies (ASECS)
Computer Center 108
Logan, UT 84322-3730
Ph: (801)797-0128   Fax: (801)797-4065
Jeffery R. Smitten

Quarterly. Serves scholars interested in all aspects of the 18th century. Recurring features include announcements of meetings, news of publication projects, news of research, and other related information.

★3992★ Friends of Mamie's Birthplace Newsletter
Mamie Doud Eisenhower Birthplace Foundation, Inc.
PO Box 55
Boone, IA 50036
Larry Adams

Semiannual. Devoted to the preservation of the birthplace and memory of Mamie Doud Eisenhower (1896-1979), former First Lady to President Dwight D. Eishenhower. Includes announcements of activities, programs, deaths; member profiles; and quizzes.

★3993★ IHR Newsletter
Institute for Historical Review (IHR)
1822 1/2 Newport Beach, Ste. 191
Costa Mesa, CA 92627
Ph: (714)631-1490
Theodore J. O'Keefe

Reports on the work of the Institute and revisionist developments around the world.

★3994★ Institute for Historical Study—Newsletter
Institute for Historical Study
2237 Chestnut St.
San Francisco, CA 94123
Ph: (415)441-3759
Elaine Rosenthal

Quarterly. Supports the Institute's desire to "promote the research, the writing, and the public discussion of history." Encourages the discussion of history in a broader public context and the promotion of historical scholarship in both new and traditional areas. Recurring features include profiles of scholars, news of workshops and educational opportunities, book reviews, and news of research, members, and Institute events.

★3995★ Meeting Ground
D'Arcy McNickle Center for the History of the American Indian
Newberry Library
60 W. Walton St.
Chicago, IL 60610
Ph: (312)943-9090
Brenda K. Manuelito

Biennial. Reports past, present, and future activities of the Center which is committed to "improving the quality of teaching and research in the field of Native American history." Recurring features include news of research, news of members, book reviews, reports on Chicago Indian community projects, and columns titled Director's Notes, Center Fellows, Alumni Notes, and New Books.

★3996★ Psychohistory News
International Psychohistorical Association (IPA)
PO Box 314
New York, NY 10024
Ph: (718)857-8075
Jay Sherry

Semiannual. Includes news of Association events, abstracts of papers presented at the Association convention, conference announcements, events in the psychohistorical field, and lists of related publications.

★3997★ The Public Historian
University of California Press
2120 Berkeley Way
Berkeley, CA 94720
Ph: (510)643-7154
Otis L. Graham

Quarterly. Covers public history.

★3998★ Public History News
National Council on Public History (NCPH)
Department of History, 327 Cavanaugh Hall
425 University Blvd.
Indianapolis, IN 46202-5140
Ph: (317)274-2716   Fax: (317)274-2347
Elizabeth B. Monroe

Quarterly. Emphasizes a historical understanding of contemporary issues, policies, problems, and trends. Provides information on the Council's activities, committees, meetings, academic training programs, and public history projects. Announces new publications, job openings, and calls for papers. Recurring features include editorials, a commentary section, and news of research.

PROFESSIONAL MEETINGS AND CONVENTIONS

★3999★ American Association for State and Local History Annual Meeting
American Association for State and Local History
530 Church St., Ste. 600
Nashville, TN 37219
Ph: (615)255-2971   Fax: (615)255-2979
Annual.

★4000★ Organization of American Historians Annual Meeting
Organization of American Historians
112 N. Bryan St.
Bloomington, IN 47408-4199
Ph: (812)855-7311

Annual. **Dates and Locations:** 1996 Mar 28-31; Chicago, IL. • 1997 Apr 17-20; San Francisco, CA.

★4001★ Southern Historical Association Annual Meeting
Southern Historical Association
Dept. of History
University of Georgia
Athens, GA 30602
Ph: (706)542-8848   Fax: (706)542-2455

Annual. **Dates and Locations:** 1995 Nov 08-11; New Orleans, LA. • 1996 Oct 30-02; Little Rock, AR.

OTHER SOURCES OF INFORMATION

★4002★ American Progressive History: An Experiment in Modernization
University of Chicago Press
University of Chicago
5801 Ellis Ave.
Chicago, IL 60637
Ph: (312)702-7700   Fax: (312)702-9756
Ernst A. Breisach, editor. 1993.

★4003★ Grants, Fellowships, and Prizes of Interest to Historians, 1994-95
American Historical Association
400 A St., SE
Washington, DC 20003
Ph: (202)544-2422
Emily Frye, editor. 1994.

★4004★ "Historian" in Career Selector 2001
Barron's Educational Series, Inc.
250 Wireless Blvd.
Hauppauge, NY 11788
Ph: (516)434-3311   Fax: (516)434-3723
Fr: 800-645-3476
James C. Gonyea. 1993.

Political Scientists

Political scientists investigate the ways in which political power is organized, distributed, and used. They study a wide range of subjects such as relations between the U.S. and foreign countries, the beliefs and institutions of foreign nations, the politics of small towns or major metropolises, and the decisions of the U.S. Supreme Court. Studying topics such as public opinion, political decision making, and ideology, they analyze the structure and operation of governments as well as informal political entities. Depending on the topic under study, a political scientist might conduct a public opinion survey, analyze election results, or analyze public documents.

Salaries

Median annual earnings of social scientists such as political scientists are as follows:

Lowest 10 percent	Less than $17,800/year
Median	$36,700/year
Top 10 percent	More than $68,700/year
Federal government social scientists	$43,000/year

Employment Outlook

Growth rate until the year 2005: Faster than the average.

Political Scientists

★4005★ **Career Choices for the 90's for Students of Political Science and Government**
Walker and Co.
435 Hudson St.
New York, NY 10014
Ph: (212)727-8300   Fax: (212)727-0984
Fr: 800-289-2553
Career Associates. 1990. Provides information about entry-level opportunities in political science and government and highlights opportunities that might be overlooked. Includes information on where and who the employers are, salaries, entry-level responsibilities, and advancement opportunities.

★4006★ **Careers and the Study of Political Science: A Guide for Undergraduates**
American Political Science Association (APSA)
1527 New Hampshire Ave., N.W.
Washington, DC 20036
Ph: (202)483-2512
Mary H. Curzan, editor. Fifth edition, 1992.

★4007★ **"Political Science" in College Majors and Careers: A Resource Guide to Effective Life Planning (pp. 111-112)**
Garrett Park Press
PO Box 1907
Garrett Park, MD 20896
Ph: (301)946-2553
Paul Phifer. 1993. Lists 60 college majors, with definitions; related occupations and leisure activities; skills, values, and personal needed attributes; suggested readings; and a list of associations.

★4008★ **Political Scientist**
Careers, Inc.
PO Box 135
Largo, FL 34649-0135
Ph: (813)584-7333
1992. Four-page brief describing duties, working conditions, personal qualifications, training, earnings and hours, employment outlook, places of employment, related careers, and where to write for more information.

★4009★ **"Political Scientist" in Career Information Center (Vol.6)**
Simon and Schuster
200 Old Tappan Rd.
Old Tappan, NJ 07675
Fax: 800-445-6991   Fr: 800-223-2348
Richard Lidz and Linda Perrin, editorial directors. Fifth edition, 1993. This 13-volume set profiles over 600 occupations. Each occupational profile describes job duties, entry-level requirements, educational requirements, advancement possibilities, employment outlook, working conditions, earnings and benefits, and where to write for more information.

★4010★ **"Political Scientist" in College Board Guide to Jobs and Career Planning (pp. 299)**
The College Board
45 Columbus Ave.
New York, NY 10023-6992
Ph: (212)713-8165   Fax: (212)713-8143
Fr: 800-323-7155
Second edition, 1994. Describes the job, salaries, related careers, education needed, and where to write for more information.

★4011★ **Political Scientists**
Chronicle Guidance Publications, Inc.
66 Aurora St.
PO Box 1190
Moravia, NY 13118-1190
Ph: (315)497-0330   Fax: (315)497-3359
Fr: 800-622-7284
1993. Career brief describing the nature of the job, working conditions, hours and earnings, education and training, licensure, certification, unions, personal qualifications, social and psychological factors, location, employment outlook, entry methods, advancement, and related occupations.

★4012★ **"Political Scientists" in Career Discovery Encyclopedia (Vol.5, pp. 66-67)**
J.G. Ferguson Publishing Co.
200 W. Madison St., Ste. 300
Chicago, IL 60606
Ph: (312)580-5480   Fax: (312)580-4948
Russell E. Primm, editor in chief. 1993. This six volume set contains two-page articles for 504 occupations. Each article describes job duties, earnings, and educational and training requirements. The whole set is arranged alphabetically by job title. Designed for junior high and older students.

★4013★ **"Political Scientists" in Encyclopedia of Careers and Vocational Guidance (Vol.4, pp. 145-148)**
J.G. Ferguson Publishing Co.
200 W. Madison St., Ste. 300
Chicago, IL 60606
Ph: (312)580-5480   Fax: (312)580-4948
William E. Hopke, editor-in-chief. Ninth edition, 1993. Four-volume set that profiles 900 occupations and describes job trends in 74 industries. Includes career description, educational requirements, history of the job, methods of entry, advancement, employment outlook, earnings, conditions of work, social and psychological factors, and sources of further information.

★4014★ **"Political Scientists" in Jobs! What They Are—Where They Are—What They Pay (pp. 359)**
Fireside
Simon & Schuster Bldg.
1230 Avenue of the Americas
New York, NY 10020
Ph: (212)698-7000   Fr: 800-223-2348
Robert O. Snelling and Anne M. Snelling. Revised and updated, 1992. Describes duties and responsibilities, earnings, employment opportunities, training, and qualifications.

★4015★ **"Politics" in Encyclopedia of Career Choices for the 1990s: A Guide to Entry Level Jobs (pp. 680-699)**
Berkley Pub.
PO Box 506
East Rutherford, NJ 07073
Fax: (201)933-2316   Fr: 800-788-6262
1992. Written for college and professional associations. Relates interviews with people working in the field. There is a cross index of college majors to career fields.

PROFESSIONAL ASSOCIATIONS

★4016★ Academy of Political Science (APS)
475 Riverside Dr., Ste. 1274
New York, NY 10115-1274
Ph: (212)870-2500   Fax: (212)870-2202
Members: Individual members, libraries and institutions. **Purpose:** Promotes the cultivation of political science and its application to the solution of political, social, and economic problems. **Publications:** *Political Science Quarterly*, quarterly.

★4017★ American Academy of Political and Social Science (AAPSS)
3937 Chestnut St.
Philadelphia, PA 19104
Ph: (215)386-4594   Fax: (215)386-4630
Members: Professionals and laymen concerned with the political and social sciences and related fields. **Purpose:** Promotes the progress of political and social science through publications and meetings. The academy does not take sides in controversial issues, but seeks to gather and present reliable information to assist the public in forming an intelligent and accurate judgment. **Publications:** *The Annals*, bimonthly.

★4018★ American Political Science Association (APSA)
1527 New Hampshire Ave. NW
Washington, DC 20036
Ph: (202)483-2512   Fax: (202)483-2657
Members: College and university teachers of political science, public officials, research workers, and businessmen. "Encourages the impartial study and promotes the development of the art and science of government." **Purpose:** Develops research projects of public interest and educational programs for political scientists and journalists; seeks to improve the knowledge of and increase citizen participation in political and governmental affairs. Serves as clearinghouse for teaching and research positions in colleges, universities, and research bureaus in the U.S. and abroad and for positions open to political scientists in government and private business; conducts Congressional Fellowship Program, which enables political scientists and journalists to spend a year working with members of Congress and congressional committees; conducts the Committee on Professional Ethic, Rights and Freedom which is concerned with the professional ethics, human rights, and academic freedom of political scientists. Gives cash awards and citations for best books and theses of the year in various phases of political science at annual convention. Offers placement service. **Publications:** *American Political Science Association Membership Directory*, triennial. • *American Political Science Review*, quarterly. • *Personnel Service*, monthly. • *PS: Political Science and Politics*, quarterly.

★4019★ Inter-University Consortium for Political and Social Research (ICPSR)
PO Box 1248
Ann Arbor, MI 48106
Ph: (313)764-2570   Fax: (313)764-8041
Members: Cooperative partnership between institutions of higher education represented by departments of political science, history, sociology, and related disciplines concerned with the systematic study of political and social behavior. **Purpose:** Seeks to facilitate research in the social sciences by: developing a major data repository providing access to basic research materials; conducting an advanced training program providing formal course work in methodology, research techniques, and substantive fields for advanced graduate students and faculty; stimulating new research projects; consulting in computer support needs; sponsoring research conferences. Makes available technical facilities to scholars from member institutions. Data repository holdings include survey, election, census, and roll call data, representing nations throughout the world. **Publications:** *Guide to Resources and Services*, annual. • *Summer Program Brochure*, annual.

★4020★ National Association of Schools of Public Affairs and Administration (NASPAA)
1120 G St. NW, Ste. 730
Washington, DC 20005
Ph: (202)628-8965   Fax: (202)626-4978
Members: Universities and government agencies dedicated to the advancement of education, research, and training in public affairs and public administration. **Purpose:** Serves as a national center for information about programs and developments in this field. Fosters goals and standards of educational excellence and represents the concerns and interests of member institutions in the formulation and support of national policies for education in public affairs/public administration. Accredits master's degree program in public affairs and administration. Cooperates with governmental organizations, professional associations, and national public interest groups to improve the quality of public management. **Publications:** *Directory: Graduate Programs in Public Affairs and Administration*, biennial. • *Diversity Guidelines*. • *Doctoral Policy Statement for Programs in Public Affairs/Public Administration*. • *Guidelines and Standards for Baccalaureate*. • *Peer Review/Accreditation Policy*. • *Public Enterprise*, semiannual. • *Roster of Accredited Programs*, annual. • *Standards for Masters*.

★4021★ Women's Caucus for Political Science (WCPS)
Emory University
Department of Political Science
Atlanta, GA 30322
Ph: (404)727-6572   Fax: (404)874-6925
Members: Women professionally trained in political science. **Purpose:** Purposes are to: upgrade the status of women in the profession of political science; promote equal opportunities for women political scientists for graduate admission, financial assistance in such schools, and in employment, promotion, and tenure. Advances candidates for consideration for APSA offices and committees.

Publications: *WCPS Quarterly*. • *Women's Caucus for Political Science Membership Directory*, biennial.

TEST GUIDES

★4022★ *Barron's Regents Exams and Answers: U.S. History and Government*
Barron's Educational Series, Inc.
250 Wireless Blvd.
Hauppauge, NY 11788
Ph: (516)434-3311   Fax: (516)434-3723
Fr: 800-645-3476
John McGeehan. 1988. Contains sample examination questions and answers for regents examinations in history and government.

★4023★ *Political Science*
National Learning Corp.
212 Michael Dr.
Syosset, NY 11791
Ph: (516)921-8888   Fax: (516)921-8743
Fr: 800-645-6337
Jack Rudman. A test from the Graduate Record Examination series. Multiple-choice test for those seeking admission to graduate school for study in the field of political science. Includes solutions to examination questions.

EDUCATIONAL DIRECTORIES AND PROGRAMS

★4024★ *Graduate Faculty and Programs in Political Science*
American Political Science Association (APSA)
1527 New Hampshire Ave. NW
Washington, DC 20036
Ph: (202)483-2512   Fax: (202)483-2657
Patricia B. Spellman
Triennial, latest edition March 1992; new edition expected 1995. Covers more than 300 academic institutions offering master's and Ph.D. programs; 4,500 faculty; coverage includes the U.S. and Canada. Entries include: Name of institution and department, address, phone, fax; admission and degree requirements, costs, financial aid information, description of academic program; departmental faculty members, with titles, degrees, year top degree was awarded, areas of specialization, and E-mail. Arrangement: Separate alphabetical sections for United States and Canadian institutions.

Awards, Scholarships, Grants, and Fellowships

★4025★ Gabriel Almond Award
American Political Science Association
1529 New Hampshire Ave. NW
Washington, DC 20036
Ph: (202)483-2512   Fax: (202)483-2657

For recognition of the best doctoral dissertation in the field of comparative politics. Dissertations completed and accepted during the previous calendar year are eligible. Dissertations must be nominated by a department. A monetary prize of $250 is awarded annually. Established in 1977.

★4026★ William Anderson Award
American Political Science Association
1529 New Hampshire Ave. NW
Washington, DC 20036
Ph: (202)483-2512   Fax: (202)483-2657

For recognition of the best doctoral dissertation in the general field of state and local politics, federalism, or intergovernmental relations in the United States. Dissertations submitted and accepted during the previous calendar year are eligible. Dissertations must be nominated by a department. A monetary prize of $250 is awarded annually. Established in 1977.

★4027★ Best Book Awards
American Political Science Association
Urban Politics and Urban Policy Section
1527 New Hampshire Ave. NW
Washington, DC 20036
Ph: (202)483-2512   Fax: (202)462-7849

To recognize the best book in political science published in the preceding year. Awarded at the annual meeting.

★4028★ Ralph J. Bunche Award
American Political Science Association
1529 New Hampshire Ave. NW
Washington, DC 20036
Ph: (202)483-2512   Fax: (202)483-2657

For recognition of the best scholarly work in political science published within the previous year that explores the phenomenon of ethnic and cultural pluralism. Books must be nominated by the publisher. A monetary prize of $500 is awarded annually. Established in 1978 in memory of Ralph J. Bunche, a prominent black world statesman and diplomat.

★4029★ Franklin L. Burdette Pi Sigma Alpha Award
American Political Science Association
1529 New Hampshire Ave. NW
Washington, DC 20036
Ph: (202)483-2512   Fax: (202)483-2657

For recognition of the author of the best paper presented at the association's annual meeting of the previous year. Papers must be nominated by the program section chairman. A monetary prize of $250 is awarded annually. Established in 1964.

★4030★ Congressional Research Grant Program
Everett McKinley Dirksen Congressional
  Leadership Research Center
Dirksen Congressional Center
301 S. 4th St., Ste. A
Pekin, IL 61554-4219
Ph: (309)347-7113   Fax: (309)347-6432

To provide funds for research on congressional leadership and the U.S. Congress. Anyone with a serious interest in studying Congress is eligible. The center seeks applications specifically from political scientists, historians, biographers, scholars of public administration or American studies, or journalists. Graduate students are encouraged to apply. The deadline is March 31. Grant funds totaling approximately $25,000 are awarded annually for travel to conduct research, duplication of research materials, costs of clerical or research assistance, or other qualified research expenses. Established in 1975. Sponsored by the Catepillar Foundationand the Everett McKinley Dirksen Endowment Fund.

★4031★ CQ Press Award
Congressional Quarterly
1414 22nd St. NW
Washington, DC 20037-1003
Ph: (202)887-8500   Fax: (202)728-1863

To honor the best paper on legislative politics presented at any American Political Science Association meeting during the preceding year. A monetary award of $100 is presented annually at the Labor Day weekend meeting of the APSA. Established in 1985. Sponsored by the American Political Science Association.

★4032★ Eugene V. Debs Award
Eugene V. Debs Foundation
PO Box 843
Terre Haute, IN 47808
Ph: (818)232-2163

To recognize an individual for excellence in the fields of labor, education, or public service. A bronze plaque and citation are awarded annually. Established in 1965.

★4033★ D. B. Hardeman Prize
Lyndon Baines Johnson Foundation
2313 Red River St.
Austin, TX 78705
Ph: (512)478-7829   Fax: (512)478-9104

To encourage scholarship on the U.S. Congress and to recognize the best book published on the Congress or one of its members in the preceding two years. A monetary award of $1,500 is awarded biennially. Established in 1980 by the Lyndon B. Johnson Library in memory of D.B. Hardeman, student of the Congress, and aide and associate of House Speaker Sam Rayburn. Additional information is available from Lyndon B. Johnson Library, c/o Harry Middleton, 2313 Red River Street, Austin, TX 78705; telephone: (512) 482-5137.

★4034★ Howard Fellows
George A. and Eliza Gardner Howard
  Foundation
Brown Univ.
42 Charlesfield St.
PO Box 1956
Providence, RI 02912
Ph: (401)863-2640

To provide individuals in the middle stages of their careers with funds for independent projects in the fields that are selected within the following categories on a rotational basis each year: Comparative Literature, Language and Literature; History, Anthropology, Political Science and Social Studies; Classical and Archaeological Studies, History of Science, Philosophy, and Religious Studies; Art History and Fine Arts (including painting, sculpture, musicology, music composition, photography and film); and Creative Writing and Literary Criticism. Preference is given to candidates between 25 and 45 years of age who, regardless of their country of citizenship, are professionally based in the United States either by affiliation with an institution or by residence. No fellowships are awarded for work leading to any academic degree or for coursework or training of any other sort. Nominations are accepted between September 1 and October 15. Stipends for the one-year period are $18,000. Established in 1952 by Nicea Howard in memory of her grandparents.

★4035★ Harold Lasswell Award
Policy Studies Organization
University of Illinois at Urbana-Champaign
361 Lincoln Hall
702 S. Wright St.
Urbana, IL 61801-3696
Ph: (217)359-8541   Fax: (217)244-5712

To recognize an outstanding scholar contributing to the understanding of the substance or process of public policy. Individuals must be nominated. A plaque is awarded each year at the annual meeting of the Organization (Labor Day weekend). Established in 1983 in honor of Harold Lasswell. For further information, contact Stuart Nagel.

★4036★ James Madison Award
American Political Science Association
1529 New Hampshire Ave. NW
Washington, DC 20036
Ph: (202)483-2512   Fax: (202)483-2657

To recognize an American political scientist who has made a distinguished scholarly contribution to political science. A monetary prize of $2,000 is awarded triennially. Established in 1978 to honor the U.S. President, James Madison.

★4037★ S. C. May Research Award Program
Western Governmental Research
  Association
10900 Los Alamitos Blvd., Ste. 201
Los Alamitos, CA 90720
Ph: (310)795-6694   Fax: (310)795-6697

To recognize outstanding essays that deal with subjects bearing a clear relationship to governmental and public policy research and its application. Authors need not be members of the Association but must reside or be students in one of the 13 western states in the United States. The awards consist of up to four monetary prizes of $350 for papers by university and college graduate students, and one for papers by practitioners. Awarded annually at the annual conference.

★4038★ MOOFW Award
Military Order of the Foreign Wars of the
   United States
45 Robert Circle
Cranston, RI 02905

To recognize outstanding senior cadets at the United States Service Academies. The following awards are presented: United States Military Academy- to recognize excellence in political science. A silver pitcher is awarded annually; United States Air Force Academy- to recognize excellence in physics. A bronze eagle is awarded annually; United States Naval Academy; and United States Coast Guard Academy. Established in 1894.

★4039★ Helen Dwight Reid Award
American Political Science Association
1529 New Hampshire Ave. NW
Washington, DC 20036
Ph: (202)483-2512   Fax: (202)483-2657

For recognition of the best doctoral dissertation in the field of international relations, law, and politics. Dissertations completed and submitted in the previous calendar years are eligible. Dissertations must be nominated by a department. A prize of $250 is awarded annually. Established in 1966.

★4040★ Herbert Roback Scholarship
National Academy of Public Administration
1120 G St. NW, Ste. 850
Washington, DC 20005-3801
Ph: (202)347-3190   Fax: (202)393-0993

To encourage students to pursue careers in public service. A $3,000 scholarship is awarded annually in November for graduate study in public administration, public and international affairs, and/or political science at a metropolitan Washington, DC area college or at New York University. Established in 1979 to honor Herbert Roback.

★4041★ Leo Strauss Award
American Political Science Association
1529 New Hampshire Ave. NW
Washington, DC 20036
Ph: (202)483-2512   Fax: (202)483-2657

For recognition of the best doctoral dissertation in the field of political philosophy. Dissertations submitted and accepted during the previous calendar year are eligible. Dissertations must be nominated by a department. A monetary prize of $250 is awarded annually. Established in 1975.

★4042★ University of Louisville Grawemeyer Award for Ideas Improving World Order
University of Louisville
Department of Political Science
Ford Hall
Univ. of Louisville
Louisville, KY 40292
Ph: (502)588-6831   Fax: (502)588-5682

To recognize the best idea promoting improved relations between nations published or presented in the last five years. The purpose of the award is to stimulate the recognition, dissemination, and critical analysis of outstanding proposals for the improvement of relations between nations. Submissions for the award may address a wide range of international concerns, such as foreign policy and its formation, the conduct of international relations, global economic issues, international trade and investment, resolving regional conflicts, addressing ethnic and racial disputes, halting the proliferation of destructive technologies, international cooperation in environmental protection and other global issues, international law and organization, any combination or particular aspects of these, or any idea that could at least incrementally lead to a more just and peaceful international order. Submissions are judged according to originality, feasibility, and potential impact. The University committee overseeing the award invites nominations from throughout the world by individual political scientists expert in the area, by professional associations of political scientists or related disciplines in international relations, by university presidents, or by publishers and editors of journals and books in political science and international affairs. Self-nominations are not accepted or considered. Entries may be submitted in October. A monetary award of $150,000 is awarded annually. Established in 1988 by H. Charles Grawemeyer, a University graduate and retired industrialist.

★4043★ Urban Politics and Policy Career Achievement Award
American Political Science Association
Urban Politics and Urban Policy Section
1527 New Hampshire Ave. NW
Washington, DC 20036
Ph: (202)483-2512   Fax: (202)462-7849

To recognize individuals for outstanding achievement in urban politics and policy. Awarded at the annual meeting. Established in 1988.

★4044★ Western Political Science Association Awards
Western Political Science Association
c/o Department of Political Science
University of Utah
Salt Lake City, UT 84112
Ph: (916)278-7737   Fax: (916)278-6959

To recognize outstanding unpublished papers in the field of political science. The following awards are presented: Dissertation Award - $250 for the best doctoral dissertation completed at a university within the regional groupings of the WPSA between July 1 and June 30 of the previous academic year; Pi Sigma Alpha Award - $200 for the best paper presented at the last WPSA annual meeting; WPSA Women and Politics Awards - $100 for an outstanding paper on women and politics; WPSA Best Paper Award on Chicano Politics - $100 for an outstanding paper by a Chicano scholar on Chicano politics and its relative aspects; and Award by Committee on the Status of Blacks - $100 for an outstanding paper discussing issues and problems that concern most Black Americans.

BASIC REFERENCE GUIDES AND HANDBOOKS

★4045★ Dictionary of Modern Political Ideologies
St. Martin's Press, Inc.
175 5th Ave., Rm. 1715
New York, NY 10010
Ph: (212)674-5151
M.A. Riff. 1990. Includes bibliographies.

★4046★ Information Sources in Politics and Political Science: A Survey Worldwide
Butterworth Publishers
80 Montvale Ave.
Stoneham, MA 02180
Ph: (617)438-8464   Fr: 800-548-4001
1992. Contains a bibliography of addresses, essays, and lectures in the field of political science. Includes an index.

★4047★ Political Science Research: A Methods Handbook
Iowa State University Press
2121 S. State Ave.
Ames, IA 50010
Ph: (212)292-0140
Madan L. Goel. 1988. Includes a bibliography and an index.

★4048★ World Encyclopedia of Political Systems and Parties
Facts on File
460 Park Ave. S.
New York, NY 10016-7382
Ph: (212)683-2244   Fax: 800-678-3633
Fr: 800-322-8755
George E. Delury, editor. Second edition, 1987. Includes bibliographies, charts, tables, and an index.

PROFESSIONAL AND TRADE PERIODICALS

★4049★ Grass Roots Campaigning
Campaign Consultants, Inc.
PO Box 7281
Little Rock, AR 72217
Ph: (501)225-3996   Fax: (501)225-5167
Jerry L. Russell
Monthly. Offers tips on political campaign techniques. Techniques are non-partisan and non-ideological and are based on actual campaign experiences. Discusses campaign psychology and philosophy.

★4050★ The Howard Phillips Issues and Strategy Bulletin
Policy Analysis, Inc.
9520 Bent Creek Ln.
Vienna, VA 22180
Ph: (703)759-3975
Howard Phillips
Bimonthly. Offers conservative commentary on U.S. and world politics, focusing on congressional actions, Executive Branch and ju-

dicial decisions, federal grants and contracts, geostrategy, and economics.

★4051★ International Report
International Report
PO Box 4882
Irvine, CA 92716
Ph: (714)856-5272   Fax: (714)725-2436
Raul Fernandez

Provides an analysis of world news.

★4052★ Political Finance and Lobby Reporter
Amward Publications, Inc.
2030 Clarendon Blvd., Ste. 305
Arlington, VA 22201
Ph: (703)525-7227   Fax: (703)525-3536
Edward Zuckerman

Reports on federal legislation, regulation, litigation, and enforcement actions relating to the financing of political campaigns and the practice of lobbying. Covers activities of political action committees and foreign and domestic lobby registrations. Recurring features include statistics, book reviews, and announcements of available publications.

★4053★ Political Pulse
Daryl E. Lembke
926 J St., No. 1218
Sacramento, CA 95814
Ph: (916)446-2048   Fax: (916)446-5302
Bud Lembke

Provides information and news regarding California politics and government. Includes columns titled Media Tidbits and Pulse Beats.

★4054★ The Rothenberg Political Report
Stuart Rothenberg
717 2nd St. NE
Washington, DC 20002
Ph: (202)546-2822   Fax: (202)543-8425
Stuart Rothenberg

Biweekly. Covers U.S. House, Senate, gubernatorial, and presidential political campaigns and elections; provides interpretive reports of the actions and announced positions of the candidates. Discusses redistricting and follows local and regional trends. Recurring features include columns titled Report Shorts and The Back Page.

PROFESSIONAL MEETINGS AND CONVENTIONS

★4055★ Annual Meeting of the American Political Science Association
American Political Science Association
1527 New Hampshire Ave., NW
Washington, DC 20036
Ph: (202)483-2512   Fax: (202)483-2657
Annual. Always held the Wednesday through Sunday before Labor Day. **Dates and Locations:** 1996 Aug 05-18; San Francisco, CA. • 1997 Sep 06-18.

★4056★ Western Political Science Association Convention
Western Political Science Association
California State University, Sacramento
6000 J St.
Sacramento, CA 95819
Ph: (916)278-7737
Annual.

Psychologists

Psychologists study human behavior and mental processes to understand, explain, and change people's behavior. They may study the way a person thinks, feels, or behaves. **Research psychologists** investigate the physical, cognitive, emotional, or social aspects of human behavior. Psychologists in applied fields counsel and conduct training programs; do market research; or provide mental health services in hospitals, clinics, or private settings. Like other social scientists, psychologists formulate hypotheses and collect data to test its validity. Psychologists usually specialize. **Clinical psychologists**, who constitute the largest specialty, generally work in hospitals or clinics, or maintain their own practices. They help the mentally or emotionally disturbed adjust to life. **Counseling psychologists** advise people on how to deal with problems of everyday living–personal, social, educational, or vocational. **Educational psychologists** design, develop, and evaluate educational programs. **School psychologists** work with teachers, parents, and administrators to resolve students' learning and behavior problems. **Industrial and organizational psychologists** apply psychological techniques to personnel administration, management, and marketing problems. **Engineering psychologists**, often employed in factories and plants, develop and improve industrial products and human-machine systems. **Community psychologists** apply psychological knowledge to problems of urban and rural life. **Consumer psychologists** study the psychological factors that determine an individual's behavior as a consumer of goods and services. **Health psychologists** counsel the public in health maintenance to help people avoid serious emotional or physical illness and do research on the psychological aspects of medical problems.

Salaries

Psychologists in private practice and in applied specialties generally have higher earnings than other psychologists. Median annual salaries for psychologists with doctoral degrees are listed below.

Psychologists in educational institutions	$41,000/year
Psychologists in business and industry	$67,000/year
Psychologists in federal government	$49,900/year

Employment Outlook

Growth rate until the year 2005: Faster than the average.

Psychologists

CAREER GUIDES

★4057★ Career Choices for the 90's for Students of Psychology
Walker and Co.
435 Hudson St.
New York, NY 10014
Ph: (212)727-8300   Fax: (212)727-0984
Fr: 800-289-2553
Compiled by Career Associates Staff. 1990. This book offers alternatives for students of psychology, including careers within the advertising field. Gives information about the outlook and competition for entry-level candidates. Provides job hunting tips.

★4058★ Careers Helping Children
Glencoe Publishing Co.
866 3rd Ave.
New York, NY 10022-6299
Ph: (212)702-3276
Videotape that explores career possibilities in day care centers, youth programs, community health centers, and government agencies. Educational requirements and personal attributes required for each job are explained.

★4059★ Careers in Psychology
Rosen Publishing Group
29 E. 21st St.
New York, NY 10010
Ph: (212)777-3017   Fax: (212)777-0277
Fr: 800-237-9932
Dr. Lawrence Clayton. 1992. Profiles various mental healthcare professions through high-interest scenarios which demonstrate what work in those professions is like.

★4060★ Children's Clinical Psychologist
Vocational Biographies, Inc.
PO Box 31
Sauk Centre, MN 56378-0031
Ph: (612)352-6516   Fax: (612)352-5546
Fr: 800-255-0752
1994. Four-page pamphlet containing a personal narrative about a worker's job, work likes and dislikes, career path from high school to the present. Education and training, the rewards and frustrations, and the effects of the job on the rest of the worker's life. The data file portion of this pamphlet gives a concise occupational summary, including work descriptions, working conditions, places of employment, personal characteristics, education and training, job outlook, and salary range.

★4061★ Clinical Psychologist
Vocational Biographies, Inc.
PO Box 31
Sauk Centre, MN 56378-0031
Ph: (612)352-6516   Fax: (612)352-5546
Fr: 800-255-0752
1990. Four-page pamphlet containing a personal narrative about a worker's job, work likes and dislikes, career path from high school to the present. Education and training, the rewards and frustrations, and the effects of the job on the rest of the worker's life. The data file portion of this pamphlet gives a concise occupational summary, including work descriptions, working conditions, places of employment, personal characteristics, education and training, job outlook, and salary range.

★4062★ "Consumer Psychology" in Opportunities in Marketing Careers (pp. 29-30)
National Textbook Co. (NTC)
VGM Career Books
4255 W. Touhy Ave.
Lincolnwood, IL 60646-1975
Ph: (708)679-5500   Fax: (708)679-2494
Fr: 800-323-4900
Margery S. Steinberg. 1988. Defines marketing and surveys marketing fields, such as research and retailing. Gives the employment outlook and describes the rewards of a career in marketing. Includes information on the education needed, and how to find a job. Lists colleges with majors in marketing.

★4063★ "Counselors and Psychologists" in Career Paths in the Field of Aging: Professional Gerontology (pp. 30-31)
Simon and Schuster
200 Old Tappan Rd.
Old Tappan, NJ 07675
Fax: 800-445-6991   Fr: 800-223-2348

★4064★ Great Jobs for Psychology Majors
National Textbook Co. (NTC)
VGM Career Books
4255 W. Toughy Ave.
Lincolnwood, IL 60646-1975
Ph: (708)679-5500   Fax: (708)679-2494
Fr: 800-323-4900
1994.

★4065★ Is Psychology the Major for You? Planning For Your Undergraduate Years
American Psychological Association (APA)
750 1st St.
Washington, DC 20002
Ph: (202)336-5500
Paul J. Woods and Charles S. Wilkinson, editors. 1987. Serves as a career planning guide for the undergraduate student. Gives advice on choosing a psychology major, career options, and job hunting.

★4066★ Opportunities in Psychology Careers
National Textbook Co. (NTC)
VGM Career Books
4255 W. Touhy Ave.
Lincolnwood, IL 60646-1975
Ph: (708)679-5500   Fax: (708)679-2494
Fr: 800-323-4900
Dr. Donald Super. Fifth edition, 1988. Defines the field of psychology. Discusses employment outlook, rewards, education required, areas within the field of psychology, and job hunting. Lists scientific and professional organizations, accredited doctoral programs, and internships for clinical and counseling psychology.

★4067★ Opportunities in Social Science Careers
National Textbook Co. (NTC)
VGM Career Books
4255 W. Touhy Ave.
Lincolnwood, IL 60646-1975
Ph: (708)679-5500   Fax: (708)679-2494
Fr: 800-323-4900
Rosanne J. Marek. Overviews a wide range of career opportunities in social science including anthropology, economics, political science, statistics, history, psychology, sociology, urban and regional planning, and geography. Includes information on salary levels and the employment outlook.

★4068★ Psychologist
Careers, Inc.
PO Box 135
Largo, FL 34649-0135
Ph: (813)584-7333
1992. Four-page brief offering the definition, history, duties, working conditions, personal qualifications, educational requirements, earnings, hours, employment outlook, advancement, and careers related to this position.

★4069★ "Psychologist" in Career Information Center (Vol.7)
Simon and Schuster
200 Old Tappan Rd.
Old Tappan, NJ 07675
Fax: 800-445-6991   Fr: 800-223-2348
Richard Lidz and Linda Perrin, editorial directors. Fifth edition, 1993. This 13-volume set profiles over 600 occupations. Each occupational profile describes job duties, entry-level requirements, educational requirements, advancement possibilities, employment outlook, working conditions, earnings and benefits, and where to write for more information.

★4070★ Psychologist, Clinical
Careers, Inc.
PO Box 135
Largo, FL 34649-0135
Ph: (813)584-7333
1992. Two-page occupational summary card describing duties, working conditions, personal qualifications, training, earnings and hours, employment outlook, places of employment, related careers, and where to write for more information.

★4071★ "Psychologist" in College Board Guide to Jobs and Career Planning (pp. 300)
The College Board
415 Columbus Ave.
New York, NY 10023-6992
Ph: (212)713-8165   Fax: (212)713-8143
Fr: 800-323-7155
Joyce S. Mitchell. Second edition, 1994. Describes a variety of careers. Includes information on salaries, related careers, education needed, and sources of additional information.

★4072★ "Psychologist" in Guide to Federal Jobs (p. 75)
Resource Directories
3361 Executive Pkwy., Ste. 302
Toledo, OH 43606
Ph: (419)536-5353   Fax: (419)536-7056
Fr: 800-274-8515
Rod W. Durgin, editor. Third edition, 1992. Contains information on finding and applying for federal jobs. Describes more than 200 professional and technical jobs for college graduates. Covers the nature of the work, salary, and geographic location. Lists college majors preferred for that occupation. Section one describes the function and work of government agencies that hire the most significant number of college graduates.

★4073★ "Psychologist" in Jobs Rated Almanac
World Almanac
1 International Blvd., Ste. 444
Mahwah, NJ 07495
Ph: (201)529-6900   Fax: (201)529-6901
Les Krantz. Second edition, 1992. Ranks 250 jobs by environment, salary, outlooks, physical demands, stress, security, travel opportunities, and extra perks. Includes jobs the editor feels are the most common, most interesting, and the most rapidly growing.

★4074★ "Psychologist" in Opportunities in Child Care (pp. 70-73)
National Textbook Co. (NTC)
VGM Career Books
4255 W. Touhy Ave.
Lincolnwood, IL 60646-1975
Ph: (708)679-5500   Fax: (708)679-2494
Fr: 800-323-4900
Renee Wittenberg. 1987. Offers a detailed survey of the career choices available in child care. Outlines the many job opportunities available in day care, child welfare, child development, and social services. Describes the challenges and rewards as well as the educational and training requirements.

★4075★ "Psychologist" in Opportunities in Social Work Careers (pp. 78-81)
National Textbook Co. (NTC)
VGM Career Books
4255 W. Touhy Ave.
Lincolnwood, IL 60646-1975
Ph: (708)679-5500   Fax: (708)679-2494
Fr: 800-323-4900
Renee Wittenberg. 1988. Describes the skills required for a job in social work, educational preparation, work settings, and related careers. Lists additional resources.

★4076★ Psychologist, School
Careers, Inc.
PO Box 135
Largo, FL 34649-0135
Ph: (813)584-7333
1995. Two-page occupational summary card describing duties, working conditions, personal qualifications, training, earnings and hours, employment outlook, places of employment, related careers, and where to write for more information.

★4077★ "Psychologist" in VGM's Careers Encyclopedia (pp. 378-381)
National Textbook Co. (NTC)
VGM Career Books
4255 W. Touhy Ave.
Lincolnwood, IL 60646-1975
Ph: (708)679-5500   Fax: (708)679-2494
Fr: 800-323-4900
Third edition, 1991. Profiles 200 occupations. Describes job duties, places of employment, working conditions, qualifications, education and training, advancement potential, and salary for each occupation.

★4078★ "Psychologist" in VGM's Handbook of Health Care Careers
National Textbook Co.
4255 W. Touhy Ave.
Lincolnwood, IL 60646-1975
Ph: (708)679-5500   Fax: (708)679-2494
Fr: 800-323-4900
Annette Selden. 1993. Contains 42 two-page occupational profiles describing job duties, places of employment, working conditions, qualifications, education, employment outlook, and income.

★4079★ Psychologists
Chronicle Guidance Publications, Inc.
66 Aurora St.
PO Box 1190
Moravia, NY 13118-1190
Ph: (315)497-0330   Fax: (315)497-3359
Fr: 800-622-7284
1991. Career brief describing the nature of the job, working conditions, hours and earnings, education and training, licensure, certification, unions, personal qualifications, social and psychological factors, location, employment outlook, entry methods, advancement, and related occupations.

★4080★ "Psychologists" in 101 Careers: A Guide to the Fastest-Growing Opportunities (pp. 144-146)
John Wiley & Sons, Inc.
605 3rd Ave.
New York, NY 10158-0012
Ph: (212)850-6645   Fax: (212)850-6088
Michael Harkavy. 1990. Describes the nature of the job, working conditions, employment growth, qualifications, personal skills, projected salaries, and where to write for more information.

★4081★ "Psychologists" in American Almanac of Jobs and Salaries (pp. 481)
Avon Books
1350 Avenue of the Americas
New York, NY 10019
Ph: (212)261-6800   Fr: 800-238-0658
John Wright, editor. Revised and updated, 1994-95. A comprehensive guide to the wages of hundreds of occupations in a wide variety of industries and organizations.

★4082★ "Psychologists" in America's 50 Fastest Growing Jobs (pp. 59)
JIST Works, Inc.
720 N. Park Ave.
Indianapolis, IN 46202-3431
Ph: (317)264-3720   Fax: (317)264-3709
Fr: 800-648-5478
Michael J. Farr, compiler. 1994. Describes the 50 fastest growing jobs within major career clusters such as technicians, and marketing and sales. Each job profile explains the nature of the work, skills and abilities required, employment outlook, average earnings, related occupations, education and training requirements, and employment opportunities. Also contains career planning information and job search tips.

★4083★ "Psychologists" in *Career Discovery Encyclopedia* (Vol.5, pp. 102-103)
J.G. Ferguson Publishing Co.
200 W. Madison St., Ste. 300
Chicago, IL 60606
Ph: (312)580-5480   Fax: (312)580-4948
Russell E. Primm, editor-in chief. 1993. This six volume set contains two-page articles for 504 occupations. Each article describes job duties, earnings, and educational and training requirements. The whole set is arranged alphabetically by job title. Designed for junior high and older students.

★4084★ "Psychologists" in *Encyclopedia of Careers and Vocational Guidance* (Vol.4, pp. 193-197)
J.G. Ferguson Publishing Co.
200 W. Madison St., Ste. 300
Chicago, IL 60606
Ph: (312)580-5480   Fax: (312)580-4948
William E. Hopke, editor-in-chief. Ninth edition, 1993. Four-volume set that profiles 900 occupations and describes job trends in 74 industries. Includes career description, educational requirements, history of the job, methods of entry, advancement, employment outlook, earnings, conditions of work, social and psychological factors, and sources of further information.

★4085★ "Psychologists" in *Jobs! What They Are—Where They Are—What They Pay* (p.91)
Simon & Schuster, Inc.
Simon & Schuster Bldg.
1230 Avenue of the Americas
New York, NY 10020
Ph: (212)698-7000   Fr: 800-223-2348
Robert O. Snelling and Anne M. Snelling. 3rd edition, 1992. Describes duties and responsibilities, earnings, employment opportunities, training, and qualifications.

★4086★ "Psychologists" in *Occupational Outlook Handbook*
U.S. Government Printing Office
Superintendent of Documents
Washington, DC 20402
Ph: (202)512-1800   Fax: (202)512-2250
Biennial; latest edition, 1994-95. Encyclopedia of careers describing about 250 occupations and comprising about 85 percent of all jobs in the economy. Occupations that require lengthy education or training are given the most attention. Each occupation's profile describes what the worker does on the job, working conditions, education and training requirements, advancement possibilities, job outlook, earnings, and sources of additional information.

★4087★ "Psychology" in *Black Woman's Career Guide* (pp. 128-137)
Bantam Doubleday Dell
1540 Broadway
New York, NY 10036
Fax: 800-233-3294   Fr: 800-223-5780
Beatryce Nivens. Revised edition, 1987. Describes career planning, resume writing, job hunting, and interviewing. Profiles 60 black women pioneers in 20 different careers.

★4088★ "Psychology" in *College Majors and Careers: A Resource Guide to Effctive Life Planning* (pp. 113-114)
Garrett Park Press
PO Box 1907
Garrett Park, MD 20896
Ph: (301)946-2553
Paul Phifer. Revised, 1993. Lists 60 college majors, with definitions; related occupations and leisure activities; skills, values, and personal attributesneeded; suggested readings; and a list of associations.

★4089★ *School Psychologists*
Chronicle Guidance Publications, Inc.
66 Aurora St.
PO Box 1190
Moravia, NY 13118-1190
Ph: (315)497-0330   Fax: (315)497-3359
Fr: 800-622-7284
1992. Career brief describing the nature of the job, working conditions, hours and earnings, education and training, licensure, certification, unions, personal qualifications, social and psychological factors, location, employment outlook, entry methods, advancement, and related occupations.

★4090★ "Sports Psychologist" in *Careers in Health and Fitness*
Rosen Publishing Group
29 E. 21st St.
New York, NY 10010
Ph: (212)777-3017   Fax: (212)777-0277
Fr: 800-237-9932
Jackie Heron. 1990. Occupational profiles contain information on job duties, skills, advantages, basic equipment used, employment possibilities, certification, and salary.

PROFESSIONAL ASSOCIATIONS

★4091★ **American Association of Mental Health Professionals in Corrections (AAMHPC)**
c/o John S. Zil, M.D., J.D.
PO Box 163359
Sacramento, CA 95816-9359
Ph: (707)864-0910   Fax: (707)864-0910
Members: Psychiatrists, psychologists, social workers, nurses, and other mental health professionals; individuals working in correctional settings. **Purpose:** Fosters the progress of behavioral sciences related to corrections. Goals are: to improve the treatment, rehabilitation, and care of the mentally ill, mentally retarded, and emotionally disturbed; to promote research and professional education in psychiatry and allied fields in corrections; to advance standards of correctional services and facilities; to foster cooperation between individuals concerned with the medical, psychological, social, and legal aspects of corrections; to share knowledge with other medical practitioners, scientists, and the public. Conducts scientific meetings to contribute to the advancement of the therapeutic community in all its institutional settings, including correctional institutions, hospitals, churches, schools, industry, and the family. **Publications:** *Corrective and Social Psychiatry*, quarterly.

★4092★ **American Psychological Association (APA)**
750 1st St. NE
Washington, DC 20002-4242
Ph: (202)336-5500
Members: Scientific and professional society of psychologists. Students participate as affiliates. **Purpose:** Works to advance psychology as a science, a profession, and as a means of promoting human welfare. **Publications:** *American Psychologist*, monthly. • *APA Membership Register*, annual. • *APA Monitor*, monthly. • *Behavioral Neuroscience*, bimonthly. • *Clinician's Research Digest*, monthly. • *Contemporary Psychology*, monthly. • *Developmental Psychology*, bimonthly. • *Experimental and Clinical Psychopharmacology*, quarterly. • *Health Psychology*, bimonthly. • *Journal of Abnormal Psychology*, quarterly. • *Journal of Applied Psychology*, bimonthly. • *Journal of Comparative Psychology*, quarterly. • *Journal of Consulting and Clinical Psychology*, bimonthly. • *Journal of Counseling Psychology*, quarterly. • *Journal of Educational Psychology*, quarterly. • *Journal of Experimental Psychology: Animal Behavior Processes*, quarterly. • *Journal of Experimental Psychology: Applied*, quarterly. • *Journal of Experimental Psychology: General*, quarterly. • *Journal of Experimental Psychology: Human Perception and Performance*, bimonthly. • *Journal of Experimental Psychology: Learning, Memory, and Cognition*, bimonthly. • *Journal of Family Psychology*, quarterly. • *Journal of Personality and Social Psychology*, monthly. • *Neuropsychology*, quarterly. • *Professional Psychology: Research and Practice*, bimonthly. • *Psychoanalytic Abstracts*, quarterly. • *Psychological Abstracts*, monthly. • *Psychological Assessment: A Journal of Consulting and Clinical Psychology*, quarterly. • *Psychological Bulletin*, bimonthly. • *Psychological Review*, quarterly. • *Psychology and Aging*, quarterly. • *Psychology, Public Policy, and Law*, quarterly. • *PsycSCAN: Applied Experimental and Engineering Psychology*, quarterly. • *PsycSCAN: Applied Psychology*, quarterly. • *PsycSCAN: Behavior Analysis and Therapy*, quarterly. • *PsycSCAN: Clinical Psychology*, quarterly. • *PsycSCAN: Developmental Psychology*, quarterly. • *PsycSCAN: LD/MR*, quarterly. • *PsycSCAN: Neuropsychology*, quarterly.

★4093★ **American Society of Criminology (ASC)**
1314 Kinnear Rd., Ste. 212
Columbus, OH 43212
Ph: (614)292-9207   Fax: (614)292-6767
Members: Professional and academic criminologists; students of criminology in accredited universities; psychiatrists, psychologists, and sociologists. **Purpose:** To develop criminology as a science and academic discipline; to aid in the construction of criminological curricula in accredited universities; to upgrade the practitioner in criminological fields (police, prisons, probation, parole, delinquency workers). Conducts research programs; sponsors three student paper competitions. Provides placement service at annual convention. **Publications:** *American Society of Criminology—Member Directory*, semiannual. • *The Criminologist*, bimonthly. • *Criminology: An*

Interdisciplinary Journal, quarterly. • *Proceedings of Annual Meeting*.

★4094★ Association of Black Psychologists (ABPsi)
PO Box 55999
Washington, DC 20040-5999
Ph: (202)722-0808   Fax: (202)722-5941
Members: Professional psychologists and others in associated disciplines. **Purpose:** Aims to: enhance the psychological well-being of black people in America; define mental health in consonance with newly established psychological concepts and standards; develop policies for local, state, and national decision-making that have impact on the mental health of the black community; support established black sister organizations and aid in the development of new, independent black institutions to enhance the psychological, educational, cultural, and economic situation. Offers training and information on AIDS. Conducts seminars, workshops, and research. **Publications:** *Association of Black Psychologists Publications Manual*. • *Journal of Black Psychology*, semiannual. • *Monographs From the Journal of Black Psychology*, biennial. • *Proceedings of Annual Convention*. • *Psych Discourse*, monthly. • *Resource Manual for Black Psychology Students*. • *Sourcebook on the Teaching of Black Psychology*.

★4095★ Association for Women in Psychology (AWP)
3491 N. Arizona Ave., No. 9
Chandler, AZ 85225
Members: Purpose: Seeks to: end the role that the association feels psychology has had in perpetuating unscientific and unquestioned assumptions about the "natures" of women and men; encourage unbiased psychological research on sex and gender in order to establish facts and expose myths; encourage research and theory directed toward alternative sex-role socialization, child rearing practices, life-styles, and language use; educate and sensitize the science and psychology professions as well as the public to the psychological, social, political, and economic rights of women; combat the oppression of women of color; encourage research on issues of concern to women of color; achieve equality of opportunity for women and men within the profession and science of psychol ogy. Conducts business and professional sessions at meetings of regional psychology associations. Maintains hall of fame and speakers' bureau. Monitors sexism in APA. **Publications:** *AWP Membership Directory*, biennial.

★4096★ International Council of Psychologists (ICP)
Psych Department
San Marcos, TX 78666-4601
Members: Psychologists and individuals professionally active in fields allied to psychology. **Purpose:** Seeks to advance psychology and further the application of its scientific findings. Conducts continuing education workshops and educational programs. **Publications:** *International Psychologist*, quarterly.

★4097★ National Association of School Psychologists (NASP)
8455 Colesville Rd., Ste. 1000
Silver Spring, MD 20910
Ph: (301)608-0500   Fax: (301)608-2514
Members: School psychologists. **Purpose:** Serves the mental health and educational needs of all children and youth. Encourages and provides opportunities for professional growth of individual members. Informs the public on the services and practice of school psychology, and advances the standards of the profession. Operates national school psychologist certification system. Sponsors children's services. **Publications:** *Communique Newspaper*, 8/year. • *School Psychology Review*, quarterly.

STANDARDS/CERTIFICATION AGENCIES

★4098★ American Board of Professional Psychology (ABPP)
2100 E. Broadway, Ste. 313
Columbia, MO 65201
Ph: (314)875-1267   Fax: (314)443-1199
Fr: 800-255-7792
Certification board which conducts oral examinations and awards diplomas to advanced specialists in 9 professional specialties: behavioral psychology, clinical psychology, industrial and organizational psychology, forensic psychology, counseling psychology, clinical neuropsychology, family psychology, health psychology, and school psychology. Candidates must have three years of qualifying experience in psychological practice.

★4099★ National Association of School Psychologists (NASP)
8455 Colesville Rd., Ste. 1000
Silver Spring, MD 20910
Ph: (301)608-0500   Fax: (301)608-2514
Informs the public on the services and practice of school psychology, and advances the standards of the profession. Operates national school psychologist certification system.

TEST GUIDES

★4100★ *ACT Proficiency Examination Program: Educational Psychology*
National Learning Corp.
212 Michael Dr.
Syosset, NY 11791
Ph: (516)921-8888   Fax: (516)921-8743
Fr: 800-645-6337
Jack Rudman. A series of practice test guides containing multiple-choice examinations designed to demonstrate proficiency in the subject of psychology.

★4101★ *Barron's How to Prepare for the Graduate Record Examination-GRE*
Barron's Educational Series, Inc.
250 Wireless Blvd.
Hauppauge, NY 11788
Ph: (516)434-3311   Fax: (516)434-3723
Fr: 800-645-3476
Edward L. Palmer. Third edition, 1989. Includes five practice tests, and complete answers and explanations.

★4102★ *Career Examination Series: Psychologist*
National Learning Corp.
212 Michael Dr.
Syosset, NY 11791
Ph: (516)921-8888   Fax: (516)921-8743
Fr: 800-645-6337
Jack Rudman. Test guide including questions and answers for students or professionals in the field who seek advancement through examination. Also included in the series: Senior Psychologist and Chief Psychologist.

★4103★ *Career Examination Series: Psychology Assistant*
National Learning Corp.
212 Michael Dr.
Syosset, NY 11791
Ph: (516)921-8888   Fax: (516)921-8743
Fr: 800-645-6337
Jack Rudman. A series of study guides with multiple-choice examination questions and solutions for trainees and professional psychologists. Titles in the series include *Chief Psychologist; Clinical Psychologist; Clinical Psychologist Intern; Psychologist; Psychologist Trainee; Psychology Assistant I; Psychology Assistant II; Psychology Assistant III; Senior Psychologist*.

★4104★ *Career Examination Series: Senior Clinical Psychologist*
National Learning Corp.
212 Michael Dr.
Syosset, NY 11791
Ph: (516)921-8888   Fax: (516)921-8743
Fr: 800-645-6337
Jack Rudman. 1993. Test guide including questions and answers for students or professionals in the field who seek advancement through examination.

★4105★ *College-Level Examination Series: Psychology*
National Learning Corp.
212 Michael Dr.
Syosset, NY 11791
Ph: (516)921-8888   Fax: (516)921-8743
Fr: 800-645-6337
Jack Rudman. Multiple-choice preparatory examinations for professional psychologists considering the College-Level Examination Program (CLEP) as an alternative to college course matriculation. Includes solutions to sample test questions. Titles in the series include *Social Sciences and History; Educational Psychology; General Psychology*.

★4106★ Dantes Subject Standardized Tests: Educational Psychology
National Learning Corp.
212 Michael Dr.
Syosset, NY 11791
Ph: (516)921-8888   Fax: (516)921-8743
Fr: 800-645-6337

Jack Rudman. Multiple-choice graduate- and college-level examination given by graduate schools, colleges and the Armed Forces as a final examination for course evaluation. Includes answers.

★4107★ Educational Psychology
National Learning Corp.
212 Michael Dr.
Syosset, NY 11791
Ph: (516)921-8888   Fax: (516)921-8743
Fr: 800-645-6337

Jack Rudman. Regents College Proficiency Examination series. A sample test for college credit-by-examination programs in the field of psychology. Multiple-choice style with answers included.

★4108★ Graduate Record Examination in Psychology
Arco Publishing Co.
Macmillan General Reference
15 Columbus Cir.
New York, NY 10023
Fax: 800-835-3202   Fr: 800-858-7674

Sydney Raphael and Les Halport. 1994. Contains 350 sample questions.

★4109★ Graduate Record Examination: Psychology
Prentice-Hall, Inc.
200 Old Tappan Rd.
Old Tappan, NJ 07675
Ph: (201)767-5000

1992. Includes a bibliography.

★4110★ National Psychology Boards (NPsyB)
National Learning Corp.
212 Michael Dr.
Syosset, NY 11791
Ph: (516)921-8888   Fax: (516)921-8743
Fr: 800-645-6337

Jack Rudman. A sample test for psychologists who are seeking admission to graduate and professional schools or seeking entrance or advancement in institutional and public career service.

★4111★ Practicing to Take the GRE Psychology Test: An Offical Publication of the GRE Board
Educational Testing Service
Rosedale Rd.
Princeton, NJ 08541
Ph: (609)921-9000

Second edition, 1989. Published by Educational Testing Service for the Graduate Record Examinations Board. Summarizes the purpose and scope of the Graduate Record Examination Subject Test for psychology and contain sample questions.

★4112★ Psychology
National Learning Corp.
212 Michael Dr.
Syosset, NY 11791
Ph: (516)921-8888   Fax: (516)921-8743
Fr: 800-645-6337

Jack Rudman. Undergraduate Program Field Test series. A practice examination fashioned after tests given in the Regents External Degree Program. Designed to measure knowledge received outside the college classroom in the subject of psychology. Contains multiple-choice questions; provides solutions.

★4113★ Teachers License Examination Series: School Psychologist
National Learning Corp.
212 Michael Dr.
Syosset, NY 11791
Ph: (516)921-8888   Fax: (516)921-8743
Fr: 800-645-6337

Jack Rudman. A series of preparatory study guides for professionals studying for licensing examinations. Includes a multiple-choice test section; provides answers.

EDUCATIONAL DIRECTORIES AND PROGRAMS

★4114★ Graduate Study in Psychology
American Psychological Association (APA)
750 1st St. NE
Washington, DC 20002-4242
Ph: (202)336-5500
Susan Bedford, Manager

Annual, April. Covers over 600 programs in the United States and Canada offering graduate education in psychology. Entries include: Institution name, address, name of department offering degree, department phone, year program established, chairperson, size of faculty, APA accreditation, academic year system, programs and degrees offered, application procedure, admission requirements, student statistics for the previous year, degree requirements, tuition, financial aid available, and comments on special programs, goals, etc. Arrangement: Geographical.

★4115★ Health & Medical Industry Directory
American Business Directories, Inc.
5711 S. 86th Circle
Omaha, NE 68127
Ph: (402)593-4600   Fax: (402)331-1505

Released 1993. Lists over 1.1 million physicians and surgeons, dentists, clinics, health clubs, and other health-related businesses in the U.S. and Canada. Entries include: Name, address, phone.

★4116★ Internship Programs in Professional Psychology, Including Post-Doctoral Training Programs
Association of Psychology Postdoctoral and Internship Centers
733 15th St. NW, Ste. 719
Washington, DC 20005
Ph: (202)347-0022   Fax: (202)347-8480
Peggy Cantrell

Annual, September. Covers institutions offering PhD internship programs in professional psychology. Entries include: Institution name, name and address of contact, description of program including percentage of time spent in supervision and in seminar attendance, theoretical orientation, number of interns, stipend, admission requirements. Arrangement: Geographical.

★4117★ Mental Health and Social Work Career Directory
Gale Research Inc.
835 Penobscot Bldg.
Detroit, MI 48226-4094
Ph: (313)961-2242   Fax: (313)961-6083
Fr: 800-877-GALE

Bradley J. Morgan and Joseph M. Palmisano. 1993. A directory in the Career Advisor Series that provides essays written by industry professionals; job search information on resume and cover letter preparation, networking, and the interviewing process; approximately 300 companies and organizations offering job opportunities and internships, and additional job-hunting resources.

★4118★ World Sport Psychology Sourcebook
Human Kinetics
1607 N. Market St.
Box 5076
Champaign, IL 61825-5076
Ph: (217)351-5076   Fax: (217)351-2674
Fr: 800-747-4457
Jolene Rupe, Contact

Irregular, previous edition 1981; latest edition 1992. Covers Approximately 1,800 sport psychologists worldwide. Entries include: Name, address, phone, biographical data, academic interests; languages spoken, written, or read. Arrangement: Geographical.

AWARDS, SCHOLARSHIPS, GRANTS, AND FELLOWSHIPS

★4119★ Distinguished Contribution to Psychology in the Public Interest
American Psychological Association
750 1st St. NE
Washington, DC 20002-4242
Ph: (202)336-5700   Fax: (202)336-5708

To recognize two individuals for single extraordinary achievements or lifetime contributions to advance psychology as a science and/or profession. These contributions might include the identification or solution of significant social problems, unusual initiative or dedication to activity in the public interest, or the integration of the science and/or profession of psychology with social action in a manner beneficial to all. One award is reserved to recognize an outstanding psychologist who has not held a Ph.D. for more than 15 years (Early Career). Deadline for nominations is March 1. A monetary prize of $1,000 and a certificate are presented. Additional information is available from the APA Public Interest Directorate.

★4120★ Distinguished Scientific Award for the Applications of Psychology

American Psychological Association
750 1st St. NE
Washington, DC 20002-4242
Ph: (202)336-5700   Fax: (202)336-5708

To recognize an individual who has made distinguished theoretical or empirical advances in psychology leading to the understanding or amelioration of important practical problems. Deadline for nominations is February 1. A citation is presented at the APA convention. The award winner presents an address on some phase of his or her scientific work at the succeeding year's APA convention. Established in 1973. Additional information is available from the APA Science Directorate.

★4121★ Distinguished Scientific Award for an Early Career Contribution to Psychology

American Psychological Association
750 1st St. NE
Washington, DC 20002-4242
Ph: (202)336-5700   Fax: (202)336-5708

To recognize excellent young psychologists. Recipients of this award may not have held a Ph.D for more than nine years. For the purposes of this award, psychology has been divided into eight areas: cognition and human learning, psychopathology, health, developmental, applied research/psychometrics, social/personality, perception/motor performance, and biopsychology/animal behavior. Four areas are considered each year, with areas rotated in two-year cycles. Deadline for nominations is February 1. A citation is awarded at the annual APA convention. Established in 1974. Additional information is available from the APA Science Directorate.

★4122★ Distinguished Scientific Contributions Award

American Psychological Association
Society for Industrial and Organizational Psychology
750 1st St. NE
Washington, DC 20002-4242

To recognize an individual who has made the most distinguished empirical and/or theoretical scientific contributions to the field of industrial and organizational psychology. The setting in which the nominee made the contribution (i.e. industry, academia, government) is not relevant. A monetary award of $500 and a certificate are presented annually.

★4123★ William T. Grant Faculty Scholars

William T. Grant Foundation
515 Madison Ave.
New York, NY 10022-5403
Ph: (212)752-0071

To promote the research development of promising junior scholars who investigate topics relevant to understanding and promoting the well-being and healthy development

of children, adolescents, and youth. Faculty at all universities and nonprofit research institutions, both national and international, are eligible. Nominations may be submitted by July 1. Up to five monetary awards are made to institutions to support a selected faculty member for up to $35,000 per year for five years. Awarded annually. Established in 1982.

★4124★ Ernst Kris Prize

American Society of Psychopathology of Expression
74 Lawton St.
Brookline, MA 02146
Ph: (617)738-9821

For recognition of outstanding scholarly research and for innovative clinical and educational work in the field of psychopathology of expression. A medal is awarded every two to three years. Established in 1973 in honor of Ernst Kris, psychoanalyst and art historian.

★4125★ Kurt Lewin Memorial Award

American Psychological Association
Society for the Psychological Study of Social Issues
PO Box 1248
Ann Arbor, MI 48106-1248
Ph: (313)662-9130   Fax: (313)662-5607

To recognize outstanding contributions to the development and integration of psychological research and social action. A monetary award of $500 and a scroll are awarded annually. The recipient presents a distinguished address at the annual convention. Established in 1948.

★4126★ Masters and Johnson SSTAR Award

Society for Sex Therapy and Research
19910 S. Woodland
Shaker Heights, OH 44122
Ph: (203)324-4894

For recognition of outstanding continuous achievements related to human sexual problems. A trophy and the opportunity to present a lecture are awarded annually at the Society Convention. Established in 1985 in honor of William Masters and Virginia Johnson, sex therapists.

★4127★ President's National Medal of Science

National Science Foundation
4201 Wilson Blvd., Rm. 1225
Arlington, VA 22203
Ph: (202)357-7512   Fax: (202)357-7346

To recognize individuals who are deserving of special recognition by reason of their outstanding contributions to knowledge in the physical, biological, mathematical, engineering, behavioral, or social sciences. The President's Committee on the National Medal of Science receives recommendations of various nationally representative scientific or engineering organizations as well as the recommendations of the National Academy of Sciences. The guidelines for selection are as follows: the total impact of an individual's work on the present state of physical, biological, mathematical, engineering, behavioral, or social sciences and any achievements of an unusually significant nature judged in relation to their potential effects on the development of scientific thought. Unusually distinguished service in the general advancement

of science and engineering, when accompanied by substantial contributions to the content of science, may also be recognized. Established in 1959 by the Congress of the United States and first awarded in 1962. Additional information is available from Susan Fannoney, telephone: (202) 357-7512.

★4128★ Troland Research Award

National Academy of Sciences
2101 Constitution Ave. NW
Washington, DC 20418
Ph: (202)334-2444

To further empirical research in psychology regarding the relationships of consciousness and the physical world. Two monetary prizes of $35,000 each are awarded annually. Established in 1983 with funds bequeathed to the Academy by Leonard T. Troland.

★4129★ Howard Crosby Warren Medal

American Psychological Association
Society of Experimental Psychologists
750 1st St., N.E.
Washington, DC 20002
Ph: (202)336-5500

To recognize a psychologist for outstanding research contributions in experimental psychology. A monetary award of $500 and a bronze medal are awarded each year at the Annual Dinner. Established in 1936.

BASIC REFERENCE GUIDES AND HANDBOOKS

★4130★ American Psychologist Special Issue: The History of American Psychology

American Psychological Association
750 1st St., NE
Washington, DC 20002-4242
Ph: (202)336-5500   Fax: (202)525-5191

Ludy T. Benjamin, Jr., editor. 1992.

★4131★ Concise Encyclopedia of Psychology

John Wiley and Sons, Inc.
605 3rd Ave.
New York, NY 10158-0012
Ph: (212)850-6000   Fax: (212)850-6088
Fr: 800-526-5368

Raymond J. Corsini and George W. Albee, editors. 1987. Includes a bibliogra phy. Illustrated.

★4132★ Dictionary of Concepts in General Psychology

Greenwood Press, Inc.
88 Post Rd., W.
PO Box 5007
Westport, CT 06881
Ph: (203)226-3571   Fax: (203)222-1502

John A. Popplestone and Marion White Mc-Pherson. 1988. Contains short articles on concepts in behavioral psychology and includes references for further reading.

★4133★ **Encyclopedia of Psychology**
John Wiley and Sons, Inc.
605 3rd Ave.
New York, NY 10158-0012
Ph: (212)850-6000   Fax: (212)850-6088
Fr: 800-526-5368

Raymond J. Corsini, editor. Second edition, 1994. Contains articles on different fields of psychology and on psychological topics such as applied, clinical, and theoretical psychology. Includes a bibliography.

★4134★ **The Encyclopedic Dictionary of Psychology**
Dushkin Publishing Group, Inc.
Sluice Dock
Guilford, CT 06437
Ph: (203)453-4351   Fr: 800-243-6532

Terry Pettijohn, editor. Fourth edition, 1991. Illustrated.

★4135★ **Eponyms in Psychology: A Dictionary and Biographical Sourcebook**
Greenwood Press, Inc.
88 Post Rd., W.
PO Box 5007
Westport, CT 06881
Ph: (203)226-3571

Leonard Zusne. 1987. Defines 1800 psychological eponyms- a term or process named after an individual.

★4136★ **Psychology: Principles and Applications**
Prentice-Hall, Inc.
200 Old Tappan Rd.
Old Tappan, NJ 07675
Ph: (201)592-2000

Stephen Worchel and Wayne Shebilske. Fourth edition, 1992. Describes the major subfields of psychology. Covers the application of psychology to fields such as law and health. Explains various psychological theories and their applications.

★4137★ **Stevens' Handbook of Experimental Psychology**
John Wiley and Sons, Inc.
605 3rd Ave.
New York, NY 10158-0012
Ph: (212)850-6000   Fax: (212)850-6088
Fr: 800-526-5368

Richard C. Atkinson, Richard J. Hernstein, and Gardner Lindzey, editors. Second edition, 1988. Covers perception, motivation, learning, and cognition.

★4138★ **Therapeutic Psychology: Fundamentals of Counseling and Psychotherapy**
Prentice-Hall, Inc.
Rte. 9W
Englewood Cliffs, NJ 07632
Ph: (201)592-2000   Fr: 800-634-2963

Lawrence M. Brammer and Everett L. Shostrum. Sixth edition, 1992. Shows how to apply theory to practice. Outlines the therapeutic process from beginning relationships, the middle stages, and terminating the case. Addresses gender and cross-cultural issues.

PROFESSIONAL AND TRADE PERIODICALS

★4139★ **Advance**
Association for Advancement of Psychology
PO Box 38129
Colorado Springs, CO 80937
Ph: (719)520-0688   Fax: (719)520-0375
Fr: 800-869-6595
Stephen Pfeiffer

Quarterly. Concerned with the advancement of psychology. Details the Association's work to represent the interests of professional, social, and scientific psychologists in the public policy arena. Recurring features include news of members, news of research, and a calendar of events.

★4140★ **American Journal of Psychology**
University of Illinois Press
1325 S. Oak St.
Champaign, IL 61820
Ph: (217)333-8935   Fax: (217)244-8082
Donelson Dulany

Quarterly. Journal dealing with experimental psychology and basic principles of psychology.

★4141★ **American Psychologist**
American Psychological Assn.
750 First St. NE
Washington, DC 20002-4242
Ph: (202)336-5500   Fax: (202)336-5568
Raymond D. Fowler

Monthly. Official journal of the Association. Publishes empirical, theoretical, and practical articles.

★4142★ **Applied Cognitive Psychology**
John Wiley and Sons, Inc.
Subscription Dept.
605 3rd Ave.
New York, NY 10158
Ph: (212)850-6000   Fax: (212)850-6799
Michael Pressley

Bimonthly. Journal publishing papers dealing psychological analyses of problems of memory, learning, thinking, language, and consciousness as they are reflected in the real world.

★4143★ **Applied and Preventive Psychology**
Cambridge University Press
40 W. 20th St.
New York, NY 10011
Ph: (212)924-3900   Fax: (212)691-3239
Samuel Osipow

Quarterly. Journal focusing on the treatment of psychological problems.

★4144★ **Applied Psycholinguistics**
Cambridge University Press
40 W. 20th St.
New York, NY 10011
Ph: (212)924-3900   Fax: (212)691-3239
Catherine E. Snow

Quarterly. Journal including research papers on the psychological processes involved in language.

★4145★ **APS Observer**
American Psychological Society
1010 Vermont Ave., NW, Ste. 1100
Washington, DC 20005-4907
Ph: (202)783-2077   Fax: (202)783-2083
Lee Herring

Provides information on issues of interest to members. Offers a monthly employment listing for academic and scientific psychologists.

★4146★ **AWP Newsletter**
Association for Women in Psychology
c/o Mary Kay Biaggio, Pacific Unive
2004 Pacific Ave
Forest Grove, OR 97116
Ph: (503)357-6151   Fax: (503)359-2242
Maryka Biaggio, Contact

Quarterly. Provides information of interest to members of the Association for Women in Psychology. Recurring features include a calendar of events, book reviews, reports of meetings, and job listings.

★4147★ **Behavioral and Brain Sciences**
Cambridge University Press
40 W. 20th St.
New York, NY 10011
Ph: (212)924-3900   Fax: (212)691-3239
Stevan Harnad

Quarterly. Journal focusing on psychology, neuroscience, behavioral biology and cognitive science.

★4148★ **Clinical Psychology & Psychotherapy**
John Wiley and Sons, Inc.
Subscription Dept.
605 3rd Ave.
New York, NY 10158
Ph: (212)850-6000   Fax: (212)850-6799
Paul Emmelkamp

Quarterly. Journal providing an integrative impetus both between theory and practice and between different orientations within clinical psychology and psychotherapy.

★4149★ **Consulting Psychology Journal: Practice and Research**
Educational Publishing Foundation
750 First St. NE
Washington, DC 20002-4242
Ph: (202)336-5600   Fax: (202)336-5568
H. Skipton Leonard

Quarterly. Journal including theoretical/conceptual articles with implications for consulting, original research regarding consultation, reviews in specific areas of practice, and case studies.

★4150★ **Contemporary Psychology**
American Psychological Assn.
750 First St. NE
Washington, DC 20002-4242
Ph: (202)336-5500   Fax: (202)336-5568
John Harvey

Monthly. Journal presenting critical reviews of books, films, tapes, and other media representing a cross section of psychological literature.

★4151★ The Counseling Psychologist
Sage Periodicals Press
2455 Teller Rd.
Thousand Oaks, CA 91320
Ph: (805)499-0721   Fax: (805)499-0871
Gerald Stone

Quarterly. Journal on psychological counseling.

★4152★ Developmental Psychology
American Psychological Assn.
750 First St. NE
Washington, DC 20002-4242
Ph: (202)336-5500   Fax: (202)336-5568
Carolyn Zahn-Waxler

Bimonthly. Journal presenting empirical contributions that advance knowledge and theory about human psychological growth and development from infancy to old age.

★4153★ Diabetic Medicine
John Wiley and Sons, Inc.
Subscription Dept.
605 3rd Ave.
New York, NY 10158
Ph: (212)850-6000   Fax: (212)850-6799
Andrew Boulton

Monthly. Journal informing diabetic patients of research and better health care.

★4154★ European Journal of Personality
John Wiley and Sons, Inc.
Subscription Dept.
605 3rd Ave.
New York, NY 10158
Ph: (212)850-6000   Fax: (212)850-6799
Guus Van Heck

Journal focusing on all areas of current personality psychology with emphasis on human individuality dealing with cognition, emotions, motivation, and interacting with the environment.

★4155★ Industrial and Organizational Psychology
John Wiley and Sons, Inc.
Subscription Dept.
605 3rd Ave.
New York, NY 10158
Ph: (212)850-6000   Fax: (212)850-6799
Cary L. Cooper

Annual. Journal providing reviews in the field of industrial and organizational psychology.

★4156★ International Psychologist
International Council of Psychologists, Inc.
c/o Dr. Carleton Shay
2261 Talmadge St.
Los Angeles, CA 90027
Ph: (213)666-1480
Carleton B. Shay

Quarterly. Publishes news of the professional and scientific activities of the Council while promoting better understanding within the profession. Also contains official announcements and reports of the International Council. Recurring features include book reviews, a list of new members, a message from the president, and sections titled Convention Calendar and News of Members.

★4157★ Journal of Applied Psychology
American Psychological Assn.
750 First St. NE
Washington, DC 20002-4242
Ph: (202)336-5500   Fax: (202)336-5568
Neal Schmitt

Bimonthly. Journal presenting research on applications of psychology in work settings such as industry, correction systems, government, and educational institutions.

★4158★ Journal of Community & Applied Social Psychology
John Wiley and Sons, Inc.
605 3rd Ave.
New York, NY 10158
Ph: (212)850-6000   Fax: (212)850-6799
Geoffrey Stephenson

Quarterly. Journal concerning social psychological analysis and those involved, such as clinical and social psychologists, psychiatrists and health professionals.

★4159★ Journal of Consulting and Clinical Psychology
American Psychological Assn.
750 First St. NE
Washington, DC 20002-4242
Ph: (202)336-5500   Fax: (202)336-5568
Larry Beutler

Bimonthly. Journal presenting research on techniques of diagnosis and treatment in disordered behavior as well as studies of populations of clinical interest.

★4160★ Journal of Counseling Psychology
American Psychological Assn.
750 First St. NE
Washington, DC 20002-4242
Ph: (202)336-5500   Fax: (202)336-5568
Clara E. Hill

Quarterly. Journal presenting empirical studies about counseling processes and interventions, theoretical articles about counseling, and studies dealing with evaluation of counseling applications and programs.

★4161★ Journal of Educational Psychology
American Psychological Assn.
750 First St. NE
Washington, DC 20002-4242
Ph: (202)336-5500   Fax: (202)336-5568
Joel Levin

Quarterly. Journal presenting articles dealing with learning, especially as related to instruction, development, and adjustment.

★4162★ Psychological Bulletin
American Psychological Assn.
750 First St. NE
Washington, DC 20002-4242
Ph: (202)336-5500   Fax: (202)336-5568
Robert Sternberg

Bimonthly. Journal presenting comprehensive and integrative reviews and interpretations of critical substantive and methodological issues and practical problems from all the diverse areas of psychology.

★4163★ Psychology of Addictive Behaviors
Educational Publishing Foundation
750 First St. NE
Washington, DC 20002-4242
Ph: (202)336-5600   Fax: (202)336-5568
H. Miles Cox

Quarterly. Journal including original research related to the psychological aspects of addictive behaviors, such as alcoholism, drug abuse, eating disorders, and other compulsive behaviors.

★4164★ PsycSCAN: Neuropsychology
Educational Publishing Foundation
750 First St. NE
Washington, DC 20002-4242
Ph: (202)336-5600   Fax: (202)336-5568
Jodi Ashcraft

Quarterly. Journal including abstracts from subscriber-selected journals in the area of the relationship between the brain and behavior.

PROFESSIONAL MEETINGS AND CONVENTIONS

★4165★ American Psychological Association Convention
American Psychological Association
750 1st St., NE
Washington, DC 20002-4242
Ph: (202)336-5565   Fax: (202)336-5568

Annual. Always held during August. **Dates and Locations:** 1996 Aug 09-13; Toronto, ON.

★4166★ Association for Advancement of Behavior Therapy Convention
Association for Advancement of Behavior Therapy
c/o Mary Jane Eimer
15 W. 36th St.
New York, NY 10018
Ph: (212)279-7970   Fax: (212)239-8038

Annual. Always held during November. **Dates and Locations:** 1995 Nov

★4167★ Southeastern Psychological Association Convention
Southeastern Psychological Association
University of West Florida
Psychology Dept.
Pensacola, FL 32514
Ph: (904)474-2070   Fax: (904)474-3131
Annual.

OTHER SOURCES OF INFORMATION

★4168★ Careers in Psychology
Rosen Publishing Group
29 E. 21st St.
New York, NY 10010
Ph: 800-237-9932   Fax: (212)777-0277
Dr. Lawrence Clayton. 1992.

★4169★ **"Clinical Psychologist" in** *Career Selector 2001*
Barron's Educational Series, Inc.
250 Wireless Blvd.
Hauppauge, NY 11788
Ph: (516)434-3311   Fax: (516)434-3723
Fr: 800-645-3476

James C. Gonyea. 1993.

★4170★ *Entry Requirements for Professional Practice of Psychology: A Guide for Students and Faculty*
American Assocation of State Psychology
   Boards
PO Box 4389
Montgomery, AL 36103
Ph: (205)832-4580

1993. Explains typical requirements for licensure or certification in the United States and Canada. Describes the Examination for Professional Practice in Psychology.

★4171★ *General Guidelines for Providers of Psychological Services*
American Psychological Association (APA)
1200 17th St., NW
Washington, DC 20036
Ph: (202)336-5500

1987. Lists standards for practice and acceptable levels of quality assurance and performance in psychology.

★4172★ *Is Psychology the Major for You?: Planning for Your Undergraduate Years*
American Psycholocical Association (APA)
1200 17th St., NW
Washington, DC 20036
Ph: (202)336-5500

Paul J. Woods, editor. 1987. Written for academic advisors in psychology. Focuses on career preparation, curricula, and employment options.

★4173★ **"Psychologist" in** *Career Selector 2001*
Barron's Educational Series, Inc.
250 Wireless Blvd.
Hauppauge, NY 11788
Ph: (516)434-3311   Fax: (516)434-3723
Fr: 800-645-3476

James C. Gonyea. 1993.

★4174★ **"Psychologist/Counselor" in** *100 Best Jobs for the 1990s & Beyond*
Dearborn Financial Publishing, Inc.
520 N. Dearborn St.
Chicago, IL 60610-4354
Ph: (312)836-4400   Fax: (312)836-1021
Fr: 800-621-9621

Carol Kleiman. 1992. Describes 100 jobs ranging from accountants to veterinarians. Each job profile includes such information as education, experience, and certification

needed, salaries, and job search suggestions.

★4175★ **"Psychology" in** *Accounting to Zoology: Graduate Fields Defined* (pp. 178-188)
Petersons Guides, Inc.
PO Box 2123
Princeton, NJ 08543-2123
Ph: (609)243-9111   Fax: (609)243-9150
Fr: 800-338-3282

Amy J. Goldstein, editor. Revised and updated, 1987. Defines 298 graduate and professional fields. Discusses types of graduate programs and degrees, graduate research, applied work, employment prospects, and trends.

★4176★ *The Undaunted Psychologist: Adventures in Research*
Temple University Press
Temple University
1601 N. Broad St.
USB 306
Philadelphia, PA 19122
Ph: (215)787-8787   Fax: (215)787-4719
Fr: 800-447-1656

Gary G. Brannigan, editor. 1992.

Sociologists

Sociologists analyze the development, structure, and behavior of groups or social systems such as families, neighborhoods, or clubs. Sociologists may specialize in a particular field such as criminology, rural sociology, or medical sociology. Sociologists are often confused with social workers. While most sociologists conduct research on organizations, groups, and individuals, clinical sociologists, like social workers, may directly help people who are unable to cope with their circumstances.

Salaries

Median annual salaries of sociologists are listed below.

Sociologists in the federal government $53,300/year

Employment Outlook

Growth rate until the year 2005: Most job openings are expected to result from the need to replace sociologists who transfer to other occupations, retire, or leave the labor force. The number of persons who graduate with advanced degrees in sociology through the year 2000 is likely to exceed available job openings.

Sociologists

CAREER GUIDES

★4177★ Career Possibilities for Sociology Graduates
American Sociological Association (ASA)
1722 N St., NW
Washington, DC 20036
Ph: (202)833-3410
1984. Describes the types of jobs held by persons who have bachelor, master's, and doctoral degrees in sociology.

★4178★ "Criminologist" in VGM's Careers Encyclopedia (pp. 127-128)
National Textbook Co. (NTC)
VGM Career Books
4255 W. Touhy Ave.
Lincolnwood, IL 60646-1975
Ph: (708)679-5500   Fax: (708)679-2494
Fr: 800-323-4900
Third edition, 1991. Profiles 200 occupations. Describes job duties, places of employment, working conditions, qualifications, education and training, advancement potential, and salary for each occupation.

★4179★ Criminologists
Chronicle Guidance Publications, Inc.
66 Aurora St.
PO Box 1190
Moravia, NY 13118-1190
Ph: (315)497-0330   Fax: (315)497-3359
Fr: 800-622-7284
1994. Career brief describing the nature of the job, working conditions, hours and earnings, education and training, licensure, certification, unions, personal qualifications, social and psychological factors, location, employment outlook, entry methods, advancement, and related occupations.

★4180★ "Criminologists" in Career information Center (Vol.11)
Simon and Schuster
200 Old Tappan Rd.
Old Tappan, NJ 07675
Fax: 800-445-6991   Fr: 800-223-2348
Richard Lidz and Linda Perrin, editorial directors. Fifth edition, 1993. This 13-volume set profiles over 600 occupations. Each occupational profile describes job duties, educational requirements, advancement possibilities,

employment outlook, working conditions, earnings and benefits, and where to write for more information.

★4181★ Demographers
Chronicle Guidance Publications, Inc.
66 Aurora St.
PO Box 1190
Moravia, NY 13118-1190
Ph: (315)497-0330   Fax: (315)497-3359
Fr: 800-622-7284
1992. Career brief describing the nature of the job, working conditions, hours and earnings, education and training, licensure, certification, unions, personal qualifications, social and psychological factors, location, employment outlook, entry methods, advancement, and related occupations.

★4182★ "Health Sociologist" in Careers in Health Care (pp. 104-107)
National Textbook Co. (NTC)
VGM Career Books
4255 W. Touhy Ave.
Lincolnwood, IL 60646-1975
Ph: (708)679-5500   Fax: (708)679-2494
Fr: 800-323-4900
Swanson, Barbara M. Third edition, 1995. Profiles 58 health careers. Describes job duties, work settings, salaries, licensing and certification requirements, educational preparation, and future outlook.

★4183★ Opportunities in Gerontology Careers
National Textbook Co. (NTC)
VGM Career Books
4255 W. Touhy Ave.
Lincolnwood, IL 60646-1975
Ph: (708)679-5500   Fax: (708)679-2494
Fr: 800-323-4900
Ellen Williams. 1987. Gives a broad overview of career opportunities in gerontology in many fields. Suggest training needed and internships and volunteer opportunities. Lists gerontology-related associations. Gives sources of additional information.

★4184★ Opportunities in Social Science Careers
National Textbook Co. (NTC)
VGM Career Books
4255 W. Touhy Ave.
Lincolnwood, IL 60646-1975
Ph: (708)679-5500   Fax: (708)679-2494
Fr: 800-323-4900
Rosanne J. Marek. Overviews a wide range of career opportunities in social science including anthropology, economics, political science, statistics, history, psychology, sociology, urban and regional planning, and geography. Includes information on salary levels and the employment outlook.

★4185★ Sociologist
Careers, Inc.
PO Box 135
Largo, FL 34649-0135
Ph: (813)584-7333
1995. Four-page brief offering the definition, history, duties, working conditions, personal qualifications, educational requirements, earnings, hours, employment outlook, advancement, and careers related to this position.

★4186★ "Sociologist" in Career Paths in the Field of Aging: Professional Gerontology
Simon and Schuster
200 Old Tappan Rd.
Old Tappan, NJ 07675
Fax: 800-445-6991   Fr: 800-223-2348
David A. Peterson. 1987. Provides a history of the gerontology profession; describes education and skills required, employment outlook, and trends in the field.

★4187★ "Sociologist" in College Board Guide to Jobs and Career Planning (pp. 302)
The College Board
415 Columbus Ave.
New York, NY 10023-6992
Ph: (212)713-8165   Fax: (212)713-8143
Fr: 800-323-7155
Joyce S. Mitchell. Second edition, 1994. Describes a variety of careers. Includes information on salaries, related careers, education needed, and sources of additional information.

★4188★ "Sociologist" in *Guide to Federal Jobs* **(p. 76)**
Resource Directories
3361 Executive Pkwy., Ste. 302
Toledo, OH 43606
Ph: (419)536-5353   Fax: (419)536-7056
Fr: 800-274-8515

Rod W. Durgin, editor. Third edition, 1992. Contains information on finding and applying for federal jobs. Describes more than 200 professional and technical jobs for college graduates. Covers the nature of the work, salary, and geographic location. Lists college majors preferred for that occupation. Section one describes the function and work of government agencies that hire the most significant number of college graduates.

★4189★ "Sociologist" in *VGM's Careers Encyclopedia* **(pp. 434-435)**
National Textbook Co. (NTC)
VGM Career Books
4255 W. Touhy Ave.
Lincolnwood, IL 60646-1975
Ph: (708)679-5500   Fax: (708)679-2494
Fr: 800-323-4900

Third edition, 1991. Profiles 200 occupations. Describes job duties, places of employment, working conditions, qualifications, education and training, advancement potential, and salary for each occupation.

★4190★ *Sociologists*
Chronicle Guidance Publications, Inc.
66 Aurora St.
PO Box 1190
Moravia, NY 13118-1190
Ph: (315)497-0330   Fax: (315)497-3359
Fr: 800-622-7284

1992. Career brief describing the nature of the job, working conditions, hours and earnings, education and training, licensure, certification, unions, personal qualifications, social and psychological factors, location, employment outlook, entry methods, advancement, and related occupations.

★4191★ "Sociologists" in *Career Discovery Encyclopedia* **(Vol.6, pp. 38-39)**
J.G. Ferguson Publishing Co.
200 W. Madison St., Ste. 300
Chicago, IL 60606
Ph: (312)580-5480   Fax: (312)580-4948

Russell E. Primm, editor-in chief. 1993. This six volume set contains two-page articles for 504 occupations. Each article describes job duties, earnings, and educational and training requirements. The whole set is arranged alphabetically by job title. Designed for junior high and older students.

★4192★ "Sociologists" in *Encyclopedia of Careers and Vocational Guidance* **(Vol.4, pp. 377-380)**
J.G. Ferguson Publishing Co.
200 W. Madison St., Ste. 300
Chicago, IL 60606
Ph: (312)580-5480   Fax: (312)580-4948

William E. Hopke, editor-in-chief. Ninth edition, 1993. Four-volume set that profiles 900 occupations and describes job trends in 74 industries. Includes career description, educational requirements, history of the job, methods of entry, advancement, employment outlook, earnings, conditions of work, social

and psychological factors, and sources of further information.

★4193★ "Sociologists" in *Jobs! What They Are—Where They Are—What They Pay* **(p. 360)**
Simon & Schuster, Inc.
Simon & Schuster Bldg.
1230 Avenue of the Americas
New York, NY 10020
Ph: (212)698-7000   Fr: 800-223-2348

Robert O. Snelling and Anne M. Snelling. 3rd edition, 1992. Describes duties and responsibilities, earnings, employment opportunities, training, and qualifications.

★4194★ "Sociologists" in *Occupational Outlook Handbook*
U.S. Government Printing Office
Superintendent of Documents
Washington, DC 20402
Ph: (202)512-1800   Fax: (202)512-2250

Biennial; latest edition, 1994-95. Encyclopedia of careers describing about 250 occupations and comprising about 85 percent of all jobs in the economy. Occupations that require lengthy education or training are given the most attention. Each occupation's profile describes what the worker does on the job, working conditions, education and training requirements, advancement possibilities, job outlook, earnings, and sources of additional information.

★4195★ "Sociology" in *College Majors and Careers: A Resource Guide to Effective Life Planning* **(pp. 123-124)**
Garrett Park Press
PO Box 1907
Garrett Park, MD 20896
Ph: (301)946-2553

Paul Phifer. Revised, 1993. Lists 60 college majors, with definitions; related occupations and leisure activities; skills, values, and personal attributes needed; suggested readings; and a list of associations.

★4196★ *The Sociology Major as Preparation for Careers in Business*
American Sociological Association (ASA)
1722 N St., NW
Washington, DC 20036
Ph: (202)833-3410

Outlines academic and practitioner roles and the job outlook for persons with degrees in sociology.

★4197★ "Sports Sociologist" in *Careers in Health and Fitness*
Rosen Publishing Group
29 E. 21st St.
New York, NY 10010
Ph: (212)777-3017   Fax: (212)777-0277
Fr: 800-237-9932

Jackie Heron. 1990. Occupational profiles contain information on job duties, skills, advantages, basic equipment used, employment possibilities, certification, and salary.

PROFESSIONAL ASSOCIATIONS

★4198★ American Society of Criminology (ASC)
1314 Kinnear Rd., Ste. 212
Columbus, OH 43212
Ph: (614)292-9207   Fax: (614)292-6767

Members: Professional and academic criminologists; students of criminology in accredited universities; psychiatrists, psychologists, and sociologists. **Purpose:** To develop criminology as a science and academic discipline; to aid in the construction of criminological curricula in accredited universities; to upgrade the practitioner in criminological fields (police, prisons, probation, parole, delinquency workers). Conducts research programs; sponsors three student paper competitions. Provides placement service at annual convention. **Publications:** *American Society of Criminology—Member Directory,* semiannual. • *The Criminologist,* bimonthly. • *Criminology: An Interdisciplinary Journal,* quarterly. • *Proceedings of Annual Meeting.*

★4199★ American Sociological Association (ASA)
1722 N St. NW
Washington, DC 20036
Ph: (202)833-3410   Fax: (202)785-0146

Members: Sociologists, social scientists, and others interested in research, teaching, and application of sociology; graduate and undergraduate sociology students who are sponsored by a member of the association. **Purpose:** Compiles statistics. Operates the ASA Teaching Resources Center, which develops a variety of materials useful in teaching sociology. Sponsors Minority Fellowship and Professional Development Programs and Teaching Project. Maintains 23 sections including: Aging; Criminology; Medical; Population. **Publications:** *American Sociological Association—Annual Meeting Proceedings.* • *American Sociological Association—Directory of Departments,* semiannual. • *American Sociological Association—Directory of Members,* biennial. • *American Sociological Association—Employment Bulletin,* monthly. • *American Sociological Association—Footnotes.* • *American Sociological Review,* bimonthly. • *Contemporary Sociology: A Journal of Reviews,* bimonthly. • *Guide to Graduate Departments of Sociology,* annual. • *Journal of Health and Social Behavior,* quarterly. • *Rose Monograph Series,* periodic. • *Social Psychology Quarterly,* quarterly. • *Sociological Methodology,* annual. • *Sociological Theory,* semiannual. • *Sociology of Education,* quarterly. • *Teaching Sociology,* quarterly.

★4200★ Consortium of Social Science Associations (COSSA)
1522 K St. NW, Ste. 836
Washington, DC 20005
Ph: (202)842-3525   Fax: (202)842-2788

Members: National organizations representing professionals in the social and behavioral sciences; affiliates are smaller and/or regional associations; contributors are research universities and scholarly organizations. **Purpose:** Purpose is to inform and educate members of Congress, congressional staff, and officials in the administration and in federal agencies about recent research in the social and behavioral sciences. Stresses the importance of such research and the need for maintaining adequate financial support. Monitors the research budgets and research policy issues of federal agencies; disseminates information on legislative actions and federal policies to social and behavioral scientists. Conducts briefings on current and emerging research, particularly in areas of congressional interest and responsibility. **Publications:** *COSSA Washington Update*, biweekly.

★4201★ International Women's Anthropology Conference (IWAC)
Anthropology Department
25 Waverly Pl.
New York, NY 10003
Ph: (212)998-8550

Members: Women anthropologists and sociologists who are researching and teaching topics such as women's role in development, feminism, and the international women's movement. **Purpose:** Encourages the exchange of information on research, projects, and funding; addresses policies concerning women from an anthropological perspective. Conducts periodic educational meetings with panel discussions. **Publications:** *IWAC Newsletter*, semiannual.

★4202★ PACT Training
Winter Hollow Rd.
PO Box 106
New Kingston, NY 12459-0106
Ph: (914)586-3992   Fax: (914)586-4277

Members: Human service practitioners including police officers, social workers, physicians, nurses, counselors, educators, and theatre professionals. **Purpose:** Purpose is to train people to handle and negotiate sensitive and critical situations such as hostage negotiations, death and dying, child abuse, domestic violence, workforce diversity, and work conflicts, through drama-based instruction. Conducts training programs for those working for airlines, corporations, police and criminal justice agencies, security departments, hospitals, social service agencies, geriatric centers, medical and nursing schools, and educational institutions; these programs include structured improvisations and dramatizations of crisis and conflict situations that require outside inte rvention. Conducts charitable programs.

★4203★ Population Association of America (PAA)
1722 N St. NW
Washington, DC 20036
Ph: (202)429-0891   Fax: (202)785-0146

Members: Professional society of individuals interested in demography and its scientific aspects. **Publications:** *Applied Demography Newsletter*, periodic. • *Demography*, quarterly. • *Directory of Members*, biennial. • *PAA Affairs*, quarterly. • *Population Index*, quarterly.

★4204★ Rural Sociological Society (RSS)
Institute for Environmental Studies
1101 W. Peabody Dr.
Urbana, IL 61801-4723
Ph: (217)333-2916   Fax: (217)333-8046

Members: Educators and others employed in the field of rural sociology. **Purpose:** Promotes the development of rural sociology through research, teahing, and extension work. **Publications:** *Directory of Members*, quadrennial. • *The Rural Sociologist*, quarterly. • *Rural Sociology*, quarterly.

★4205★ Sociological Practice Association (SPA)
Department of Pediatrics/Human Development
Michigan State University
B140 Life Sciences
East Lansing, MI 48824
Ph: (517)353-0709   Fax: (517)353-8464

Members: Purpose: Promtes the application of sociology to individual and social change and advances theory, research, and methods to this end; develops opportunities for the employment and use of clinically trained sociologists; provides a common ground for sociological practitioners, allied professionals, and interested scholars and students. Promotes training and educational opportunities to further sociological practice. Sponsors sessions and programs in clinical and applied sociology at national and regional meetings of other sociological associations. Has conducted a survey on skills, licenses, education, and experience of members. Conducts national certification program. **Publications:** *Clinical Sociology Review*, annual. • *Directory of Members*, periodic. • *Practicing Sociologist*, quarterly. • *Sociological Practice*, annual. • *Using Sociology: An Introduction from the Clinical Perspectives.*

★4206★ Sociological Research Association (SRA)
1722 N St. NW
Washington, DC 20036
Ph: (202)833-3410   Fax: (202)785-0146

Members: Persons, elected from membership of the American Sociological Association, "who have made significant contributions to sociological research, other than a doctoral dissertation, and who maintain an active interest in the advancement of sociological knowledge."

STANDARDS/CERTIFICATION AGENCIES

★4207★ American Society of Criminology (ASC)
1314 Kinnear Rd., Ste. 212
Columbus, OH 43212
Ph: (614)292-9207   Fax: (614)292-6767

Aids in the construction of criminological curricula in accredited universities.

★4208★ Sociological Practice Association (SPA)
Department of Pediatrics/Human Development
Michigan State University
B140 Life Sciences
East Lansing, MI 48824
Ph: (517)353-0709   Fax: (517)353-8464

Has conducted a survey on skills, licenses, education, and experience of members. Conducts national certification program.

TEST GUIDES

★4209★ *College-Level Examination Series: Sociology*
National Learning Corp.
212 Michael Dr.
Syosset, NY 11791
Ph: (516)921-8888   Fax: (516)921-8743
Fr: 800-645-6337

Jack Rudman. Multiple-choice preparatory examinations for professional sociologists considering the College-Level Examination Program (CLEP) as an alternative to college course matriculation. Includes solutions to sample test questions. Titles in the series include *Social Sciences and History; Introductory Sociology.*

★4210★ *Practicing to Take the GRE Sociology Test*
Educational Testing Service
Rosedale Rd.
Princeton, NJ 08541
Ph: (609)921-9000

1987. Published by Educational Testing Service for Graduate Record Examination Board. Includes test preparation information, answer sheets, and test instructions. Contains an actual test.

★4211★ *Sociology*
National Learning Corp.
212 Michael Dr.
Syosset, NY 11791
Ph: (516)921-8888   Fax: (516)921-8743
Fr: 800-645-6337

Jack Rudman. Undergraduate Program Field Test series. A practice examination fashioned after tests given in the Regents External Degree Program. Designed to measure knowledge received outside the college classroom in the subject of sociology. Contains multiple-choice questions; provides solutions.

EDUCATIONAL DIRECTORIES AND PROGRAMS

★4212★ Directory of Departments of Sociology
American Sociological Association
1722 N St. NW
Washington, DC 20036
Ph: (202)833-3410   Fax: (202)785-0146
Fr: 800-877-2693
Karen Gray Edwards, Contact
Biennial, spring of even years. Covers sociology departments in nearly 2,000 institutions; coverage includes Canada. Entries include: Institution name, name and address of department, name and phone of chairperson, number of faculty, number of undergraduate sociology majors, number of graduate sociology students. Arrangement: Alphabetical.

★4213★ Guide to Graduate Departments of Sociology
Boyd Printing
49 Sheridan Ave.
Albany, NY 12210
Nancy Sylvester, Publications Assistant
Annual, spring. Covers over 252 departments of sociology offering master's and/or Ph.D. degrees. Entries include: Institution name, address, phone, fax, e-mail address; department name, chairperson, degrees offered, special programs available, tuition cost; financial aid availability; name and rank of faculty members, highest degree held, institution and date of degree; student enrollment/new admissions figures, number of degrees granted; dissertation titles of recent Ph.D.s, and current positions of recent graduates. Arrangement: Alphabetical.

AWARDS, SCHOLARSHIPS, GRANTS, AND FELLOWSHIPS

★4214★ John Desmond Bernal Prize
Society for Social Studies of Science
Dept. of Sociology
Louisiana State Univ.
Baton Rouge, LA 70803-5411
Ph: (504)388-1647
For recognition of distinguished contributions to social studies of science and technology. A monetary prize of $500 and a commemorative plaque are presented annually. Established in 1981 by the Institute for Scientific Information. The award honors John Desmond Bernal.

★4215★ Jessie Bernard Award
American Sociological Association
1722 N St. NW
Washington, DC 20036
Ph: (202)833-3410
For recognition of a work that has enlarged the horizons of the discipline of sociology to encompass fully the role of women in society. The award may be given for an exceptional single work, or for significant cumulative work done throughout a professional lifetime. A

certificate is awarded biennially in odd-numbered years. Established in 1976.

★4216★ Career of Distinguished Scholarship Award
American Sociological Association
1722 N St. NW
Washington, DC 20036
Ph: (202)833-3410
To honor sociologists who have shown outstanding commitment to the profession of sociology and whose cumulative work has contributed to the advancement of the discipline. A certificate and a lectureship are presented annually. Established in 1980.

★4217★ Distinguished Career in Clinical Sociology
Sociological Practice Association
c/o Mary Cay Sengstock
21502 Wedgewood Ave.
Grosse Pointe Woods, MI 48236
For recognition of a distinguished career in the practice of clinical sociology. Selection is by nomination. A plaque is awarded annually. Established in 1984.

★4218★ DuBois - Johnson - Frazier Award
American Sociological Association
1722 N St. NW
Washington, DC 20036
Ph: (202)833-3410
For recognition of outstanding contributions by sociologists in the tradition of W.E.B. DuBois, Charles S. Johnson, and E. Franklin Frazier, or for work by an institution in assisting the development of scholarly efforts in the same tradition. Certificates are awarded biennially. Established in 1970.

★4219★ President's National Medal of Science
National Science Foundation
4201 Wilson Blvd., Rm. 1225
Arlington, VA 22203
Ph: (202)357-7512   Fax: (202)357-7346
To recognize individuals who are deserving of special recognition by reason of their outstanding contributions to knowledge in the physical, biological, mathematical, engineering, behavioral, or social sciences. The President's Committee on the National Medal of Science receives recommendations of various nationally representative scientific or engineering organizations as well as the recommendations of the National Academy of Sciences. The guidelines for selection are as follows: the total impact of an individual's work on the present state of physical, biological, mathematical, engineering, behavioral, or social sciences and any achievements of an unusually significant nature judged in relation to their potential effects on the development of scientific thought. Unusually distinguished service in the general advancement of science and engineering, when accompanied by substantial contributions to the content of science, may also be recognized. Established in 1959 by the Congress of the United States and first awarded in 1962. Additional information is available from Susan Fannoney, telephone: (202) 357-7512.

BASIC REFERENCE GUIDES AND HANDBOOKS

★4220★ The Encyclopedic Dictionary of Sociology
Dushkin Publishing Group, Inc.
Sluice Dock
Guilford, CT 06437
Ph: (203)453-4351   Fr: 800-243-6532
Richard Lachman, editor. Fourth edition, 1991. Illustrated.

★4221★ The Research Act: A Theoretical Introduction to Sociological Methods
Prentice-Hall, Inc.
Rte. 9W
Englewood Cliffs, NJ 07632
Ph: (201)592-2000   Fr: 800-634-2863
Norman K. Denzin. Third edition, 1989. Examines different methods of sociological research including interviewing, surveys, ethnography, observation, biography, film, and photography.

PROFESSIONAL AND TRADE PERIODICALS

★4222★ American Journal of Economics and Sociology
American Journal of Economics and Sociology, Inc.
41 E. 72 St.
New York, NY 10021
Ph: (212)988-1680
Frank C. Genovese
Quarterly. Journal emphasizing interdisciplinary approach in research of the social sciences.

★4223★ American Journal of Sociology
University of Chicago Press
5720 S. Woodlawn Ave.
Chicago, IL 60637
Ph: (312)702-7600   Fax: (312)702-0172
Marta Tienda
Bimonthly. Journal presenting work on theory, methods, practice, and history of sociology.

★4224★ American Sociological Review
American Sociological Assn.
1722 N St. NW
Washington, DC 20036
Ph: (202)833-3410   Fax: (202)785-0146
Paula England
Bimonthly. Sociology journal. Focus is on issues with the most general bearing on the knowledge of society.

★4225★ *Institute for Public Policy and Social Research—Newsletter*
Institute for Public Policy and Social Research
321 Berkey Hall
East Lansing, MI 48823-1111
Ph: (517)355-6672   Fax: (517)336-1544
Frani Bickart

Provides news of the activities of the Institute, including results of research projects, policy-related outreach activities, and development issues. Includes a list of available reprints of study results in 2 of the 4 issues.

★4226★ *Journal of Sociology and Social Welfare*
Western Michigan University
Kalamazoo, MI 49008-5034
Ph: (616)387-3198   Fax: (616)387-3217
Robert D. Leighninger

Quarterly. Journal presenting a broad range of articles which analyze social welfare institutions, policies, or problems from a social scientific perspective.

★4227★ *Note Us*
Sociological Abstracts, Inc.
PO Box 22206
San Diego, CA 92192-0206
Ph: (619)695-8803   Fax: (619)695-0416
Fr: 800-752-3945
Miriam Chall

Quarterly. Provides information on recent enhancements to Sociological Abstracts, Social Planning/Policy & Development Abstracts, and Linguistics and Language Behavior Abstracts, which are available in print, online, and on CD-ROM. Recurring features include search advice, workshop and exhibit schedules, and book reviews.

★4228★ *Social Forces*
University of North Carolina Press
Dept. of Sociology
Hamilton Hall
Chapel Hill, NC 27599-3210
Ph: (919)962-0513   Fax: (919)962-4777
Richard L. Simpson

Quarterly. Journal covering sociological research and theory.

★4229★ *Society*
Transaction Periodicals Consortium
Rutgers - The State University of New Jersey
New Brunswick, NJ 08903
Ph: (908)932-2280   Fax: (908)932-3138
Irving Louis Horowitz

Bimonthly. Social science and public policy magazine.

PROFESSIONAL MEETINGS AND CONVENTIONS

★4230★ **American Sociological Association Annual Meeting**
American Sociological Association
1722 N St., NW
Washington, DC 20036
Ph: (202)833-3410   Fax: (202)785-0146
Annual. **Dates and Locations:** 1996 Aug 10-14; Chicago, IL.

★4231★ **Eastern Sociological Society Annual Meeting**
Exhibit Promotions Plus
11620 Vixens Path
Ellicott City, MD 21042
Ph: (410)997-0763   Fax: (401)997-0764
Annual.

OTHER SOURCES OF INFORMATION

★4232★ *Annual Review of Sociology*
Annual Reviews, Inc.
4139 El Camino Way
PO Box 10139
Palo Alto, CA 94303-0897
Ph: (415)493-4400   Fr: 800-523-8635

John Hagan, editor. 1995. Reviews recent and contemporary research in sociology and related fields.

★4233★ "Criminology" in *Accounting to Zoology: Graduate Fields Defined*
Petersons Guides, Inc.
PO Box 2123
Princeton, NJ 08543-2123
Ph: (609)243-9111   Fax: (609)243-9150
Fr: 800-338-3282

Amy J. Goldstein, editor. Revised and updated, 1987. Defines 298 graduate and professional fields. Discusses types of graduate programs and degrees, graduate research, applied work, employment prospects, and trends. Chapters include "Gerontology" (pp. 112-113) and "Sociology" (pp. 193-194).

★4234★ "Sociologist" in *Career Selector 2001*
Barron's Educational Series, Inc.
250 Wireless Blvd.
Hauppauge, NY 11788
Ph: (516)434-3311   Fax: (516)434-3723
Fr: 800-645-3476

James C. Gonyea. 1993.

Urban and Regional Planners

Urban and regional planners, often called **community or city planners**, develop programs to provide for growth and revitalization of urban, suburban, and rural communities and their regions. Planners help local officials make decisions on social, economic, and environmental problems. Planners usually devise plans outlining the best use of a community's land–where residential, commercial, recreational, and other human services should take place. Planners are also involved in various other planning activities, including social services, transportation, and resource development. They address such issues as central city redevelopment, traffic congestion, and the impact of growth and change on an area. They formulate capital improvement plans to construct new school, buildings, public housing, and sewage systems. Planners are becoming more involved in social issues, such as sheltering the homeless, securing premises for drug treatment centers, and meeting the needs of an aging population. Planners examine community facilities such as health clinics and schools to be sure these facilities can meet the demands placed upon them. They keep abreast of the economic and legal issues involved in community development or redevelopment and changes in housing and building codes or environmental regulations. Because suburban growth has increased the need for traveling between suburbs and the urban center, the planner's job often includes designing new transportation systems and parking facilities. Urban and regional planners prepare for situations that are likely to develop as a result of population growth or social and economic change.

Salaries

Median annual salaries for urban and regional planners are as follows:

Planners in city government	$40,100/year
Planners in county government	$38,000/year
Planners in city/county government	$36,000/year
Planners in state government	$43,000/year
Planners in private consulting firms	$49,000/year
Planners in business	$58,000/year
Planners in nonprofit organizations	$42,000/year
Planners in federal government	$52,4000/year

Employment Outlook

Growth rate until the year 2005: Average.

Urban and Regional Planners

CAREER GUIDES

★4235★ "Community Planner" in *Guide to Federal Jobs* **(p. 57)**
Resource Directories
3361 Executive Pkwy., Ste. 302
Toledo, OH 43606
Ph: (419)536-5353   Fax: (419)536-7056
Fr: 800-274-8515
Rod W. Durgin, editor. Third edition, 1992. Contains information on finding and applying for federal jobs. Describes more than 200 professional and technical jobs for college graduates. Covers the nature of the work, salary, and geographic location. Lists college majors preferred for that occupation. Section one describes the function and work of government agencies that hire the most significant number of college graduates.

★4236★ "Planner" in *Liberal Arts Jobs*
Petersons Guides, Inc.
PO Box 2123
Princeton, NJ 08543-2123
Ph: (609)243-9111   Fax: (609)243-9150
Fr: 800-338-3282
Burton Jay Nadler. Second edition, 1989. Strives to help the liberal arts graduate identify skills for entry-level positions. Gives goal setting and job search advice.

★4237★ "Planners" in *Opportunities in Environmental Careers*
National Textbook Co. (NTC)
VGM Career Books
4255 W. Touhy Ave.
Lincolnwood, IL 60646-1975
Ph: (708)679-5500   Fax: (708)679-2494
Fr: 800-323-4900
Odom Fanning. 1991. Describes a broad range of opportunities in fields such as environmental health, recreation, physics, and hygiene.

★4238★ *Planners' Salaries and Employment Trends*
American Planning Association (APA)
1313 E. 60th St.
Chicago, IL 60637
Ph: (312)955-9100
1992. Annual. Describes the salaries of planners working in the federal government as consultants and in business. Surveys the average age of planners, percentage of women and minorities in planning, and the differences in salary by geographic area.

★4239★ *Urban Planner*
Careers, Inc.
PO Box 135
Largo, FL 34649-0135
Ph: (813)584-7333
1991. Two-page occupational summary card describing duties, working conditions, personal qualifications, training, earnings and hours, employment outlook, places of employment, related careers, and where to write for more information.

★4240★ "Urban Planner" in *VGM's Careers Encyclopedia* **(pp. 477-479)**
National Textbook Co. (NTC)
VGM Career Books
4255 W. Touhy Ave.
Lincolnwood, IL 60646-1975
Ph: (708)679-5500   Fax: (708)679-2494
Fr: 800-323-4900
Third edition, 1991. Profiles 200 occupations. Describes job duties, places of employment, working conditions, qualifications, education and training, advancement potential, and salary for each occupation.

★4241★ *Urban Planners*
Chronicle Guidance Publications, Inc.
66 Aurora St.
PO Box 1190
Moravia, NY 13118-1190
Ph: (315)497-0330   Fax: (315)497-3359
Fr: 800-622-7284
1992. Career brief describing the nature of the job, working conditions, hours and earnings, education and training, licensure, certification, unions, personal qualifications, social and psychological factors, location, employment outlook, entry methods, advancement, and related occupations.

★4242★ "Urban and Regional Planner" in *Career Information Center* **(Vol.11)**
Simon and Schuster
200 Old Tappan Rd.
Old Tappan, NJ 07675
Fax: 800-445-6991   Fr: 800-223-2348
Richard Lidz and Linda Perrin, editorial directors. Fifth edition, 1993. This 13-volume set profiles over 600 occupations. Each occupational profile describes job duties, entry-level requirements, educational requirements, advancement possibilities, employment outlook, working conditions, earnings and benefits, and where to write for more information.

★4243★ "Urban/Regional Planner" in *Jobs Rated Almanac*
World Almanac
1 International Blvd., Ste. 444
Mahwah, NJ 07495
Ph: (201)529-6900   Fax: (201)529-6901
Les Krantz. Second edition, 1992. Ranks 250 jobs by environment, salary, outlooks, physical demands, stress, security, travel opportunities, and extra perks. Includes jobs the editor feels are the most common, most interesting, and the most rapidly growing.

★4244★ "Urban and Regional Planners" in *101 Careers: A Guide to the Fastest-Growing Opportunities* **(pp. 150-153)**
John Wiley & Sons, Inc.
605 3rd Ave.
New York, NY 10158-0012
Ph: (212)850-6645   Fax: (212)850-6088
Michael Harkavy. 1990. Describes the nature of the job, working conditions, employment growth, qualifications, personal skills, projected salaries, and where to write for more information.

★4245★ "Urban and Regional Planners" in *Encyclopedia of Careers and Vocational Guidance* **(Vol.4, pp. 581-583)**
J.G. Ferguson Publishing Co.
200 W. Madison St., Ste. 300
Chicago, IL 60606
Ph: (312)580-5480   Fax: (312)580-4948
William E. Hopke, editor-in-chief. Ninth edition, 1993. Four-volume set that profiles 900 occupations and describes job trends in 74 industries. Includes career description, educational requirements, history of the job, methods of entry, advancement, employment outlook, earnings, conditions of work, social and psychological factors, and sources of further information.

★4246★ "Urban and Regional Planners" in *Jobs! What They Are—Where They Are—What They Pay* (p. 66)
Simon & Schuster, Inc.
Simon & Schuster Bldg.
1230 Avenue of the Americas
New York, NY 10020
Ph: (212)698-7000   Fr: 800-223-2348
Robert O. Snelling and Anne M. Snelling. 3rd edition, 1992. Describes duties and responsibilities, earnings, employment opportunities, training, and qualifications.

★4247★ "Urban and Regional Planners" in *Occupational Outlook Handbook*
U.S. Government Printing Office
Superintendent of Documents
Washington, DC 20402
Ph: (202)512-1800   Fax: (202)512-2250
Biennial; latest edition, 1994-95. Encyclopedia of careers describing about 250 occupations and comprising about 85 percent of all jobs in the economy. Occupations that require lengthy education or training are given the most attention. Each occupation's profile describes what the worker does on the job, working conditions, education and training requirements, advancement possibilities, job outlook, earnings, and sources of additional information.

PROFESSIONAL ASSOCIATIONS

★4248★ American Planning Association (APA)
1776 Massachusetts Ave. NW, Ste. 400
Washington, DC 20036
Ph: (202)872-0611   Fax: (202)872-0643
Members: Public and private planning agency officials, professional planners, planning educators, elected and appointed officials, and other persons involved in urban and rural development. **Purpose:** Works to foster the best techniques and decisions for the planned development of communities and regions. Provides extensive professional services and publications to professionals and laypeople in planning and related fields; serves as a clearinghouse for information. Through Planning Advisory Service, a research and inquiry-answering service, provides, on an annual subscription basis, advice on specific inquiries and a series of research reports on planning, zoning, and environmental regulations. Supplies information on job openings and makes definitive studies on salaries and recruitment of professional planners. Conducts research; collaborates in joint projects with local, national, and international organizations. **Publications:** *AICP Roster*, biennial. • *Environment and Development*, monthly. • *JobMart*. • *Journal of the American Planning Association*, quarterly. • *Land Use Law and Zoning Digest*, monthly. • *PAS Memo*, monthly. • *Planning Advisory Service Report*. • *Planning Magazine*, monthly. • *Zoning News*, monthly.

★4249★ Association of Collegiate Schools of Planning (ACSP)
Graduate City Planning Program
Atlanta, GA 30332-0155
Ph: (404)894-2351   Fax: (404)894-1628
Members: Schools (117) and faculty (1400) of urban planning at U.S., European, and Canadian colleges and universities. **Purpose:** Conducts research programs; compiles statistics. **Publications:** *Guide to Graduate Education in Urban and Regional Planning*, semiannual. • *Guide to Undegraduate Education in Urban and Regional Planning and Related Fields*, semiannual. • *Journal of Planning Education and Research*, quarterly. • *Update*, quarterly.

STANDARDS/CERTIFICATION AGENCIES

★4250★ American Institute of Certified Planners (AICP)
1776 Massachusetts Ave. NW, Ste. 400
Washington, DC 20036
Ph: (202)872-0611   Fax: (202)872-0643
Maintains code of ethics.

TEST GUIDES

★4251★ *Career Examination Series: Deputy Director of Planning*
National Learning Corp.
212 Michael Dr.
Syosset, NY 11791
Ph: (516)921-8888   Fax: (516)921-8743
Fr: 800-645-6337
Jack Rudman. 1993. Test guide including questions and answers for students or professionals in the field who seek advancement through examination.

★4252★ *Career Examination Series: Economic Development Program Specialist*
National Learning Corp.
212 Michael Dr.
Syosset, NY 11791
Ph: (516)921-8888   Fax: (516)921-8743
Fr: 800-645-6337
Jack Rudman. 1993. Test guide including questions and answers for students or professionals in the field who seek advancement through examination.

★4253★ *Career Examination Series: Urban Designer*
National Learning Corp.
212 Michael Dr.
Syosset, NY 11791
Ph: (516)921-8888   Fax: (516)921-8743
Fr: 800-645-6337
Jack Rudman. A series of study guides with multiple-choice examination questions and solutions for trainees and professional urban and regional planners. Titles in the series include *Assistant Community Development Project Supervisor; Assistant Community Or-*

ganization Specialist (Urban Renewal); Assistant Urban Designer; Building and Zoning Administrator; Regional Planner; Urban Planner.

EDUCATIONAL DIRECTORIES AND PROGRAMS

★4254★ *Accredited University Planning Programs*
Planning Accreditation Board
Iowa State University Research Park
2501 N. Loop Dr., Ste. 800
Ames, IA 50010
Ph: (515)296-7030   Fax: (515)296-9910
Beatrice Clupper, Contact
Annual, December. Covers universities that offer 63 graduate and 11 undergraduate programs in urban and regional planning accredited by the board. Entries include: Institution name, address, phone, name of program, accredited degrees available, name of program administrator, dates first and most recently accredited. Arrangement: Alphabetical.

★4255★ *Guide to Graduate Education in Urban and Regional Planning*
Association of Collegiate Schools of
  Planning Department of Urban Studies
  and Planning
Building 7-338
Massachuetts Institute of Technology
77 Massachuetts Avenue
Cambridge, MA 02139
Ph: (617)253-6164   Fax: (312)955-9100
Cheryl K Contant
Biennial, September of even years. Covers 87 master's degree programs and 29 doctoral programs. Entries include: School name, program name, application address, admission requirements, costs, curriculum, faculty, description of program. Arrangement: Alphabetical.

★4256★ *Public Administration Career Directory*
Gale Research Inc.
835 Penobscot Bldg.
Detroit, MI 48226
Ph: (313)961-2242   Fr: 800-877-GALE
1994. For job seekers contemplating careers in public service.

AWARDS, SCHOLARSHIPS, GRANTS, AND FELLOWSHIPS

★4257★ Annual Award
Parks Council
457 Madison Ave.
New York, NY 10022
Ph: (212)838-9410
To recognize individuals for outstanding contributions to parks, park development, urban beautification, or environmental betterment. Nominations are accepted. An inscribed maple leaf is awarded annually. Established in

1931 by the Park Association of New York City, Inc., which merged with the Council for Parks and Playgrounds in 1970 to offer this award. The award was discontinued but re-established in 1981.

★4258★ **Ashworth Fellowship**
Municipal Art Society of New York
457 Madison Ave.
New York, NY 10022
Ph: (212)935-3960   Fax: (212)753-1816

To provide an annual opportunity for a college student, recent graduate, or graduate student to complete a project relating to architecture, landscape architecture, urban planning and design, historic preservation, zoning, urban environmental controls, public art, or the history of architecture. Support of the Society's staff and resources, office space in the Urban Center, and a stipend of $2,500 are awarded.

★4259★ **ULI Award for Excellence**
Urban Land Institute
625 Indiana Ave. NW, Ste. 400
Washington, DC 20004-2930
Ph: (202)624-7087   Fax: (202)624-7141

To honor innovative land development projects in both the public and private sectors that exemplify superior design, relevance to contemporary issues and needs, and a resourceful use of land while also improving the quality of the living environment. The following requirements must be met: the developer must submit the project; the project must be economically viable; the project must be located in the United States or Canada; and the project must demonstrate relevance to issues and needs of the community. An engraved cube is awarded annually at the institute's fall meeting. Established in 1979.

BASIC REFERENCE GUIDES AND HANDBOOKS

★4260★ *Elsevier's Dictionary of Physical Planning: Defined in English*
French & European Publications Inc.
115 5th Ave.
New York, NY 10003
Ph: (212)673-7400
G. Logie. 1989.

★4261★ *Urban Planning*
McGraw-Hill, Inc.
1221 Avenue of the Americas
New York, NY 10020
Ph: (212)512-2000   Fr: 800-722-4726
Anthony J. Catanese and J. C. Snyder. Second edition, 1988. Covers land use, urban design, and environmental planning.

PROFESSIONAL AND TRADE PERIODICALS

★4262★ *Environment and Development*
American Planning Association
1313 E. 60th St.
Chicago, IL 60637
Ph: (312)955-9100   Fax: (312)955-8312
James Schwab, Contact
Monthly. Covers issues affecting planners, engineers, and others involved in environmental planning. Recurring features include news stories and a column titled Legal Notes.

★4263★ *Journal of the American Planning Association*
American Planning Assn.
1776 Massachusetts Ave. NW, Ste. 704
Washington, DC 20036
Ph: (202)872-0611
Eugenie L. Birch
Quarterly. Journal serving practicing planners and academicians. Reviews developing theory and research, and evaluates trends and methodologies.

★4264★ *Journal of Urban Planning and Development*
American Society of Civil Engineers
345 E. 47th St.
New York, NY 10017-2398
Ph: 800-548-2723   Fax: (212)705-7300
R. Ian Kingham
Quarterly. Journal on the application of civil engineering to urban planning.

★4265★ *Land Use Law Report*
Business Publishers, Inc.
951 Pershing Dr.
Silver Spring, MD 20910
Ph: (301)587-6300   Fax: (301)587-1081
Fr: 800-274-0122
James D. Lawlor
Biweekly. Reports on land use planning and land-use related litigation, especially the activities of federal and state governments. Concerned about the environmental impact of transportation, energy development, water use, and other factors.

★4266★ *Planning*
American Planning Assn.
1313 E. 60th St.
Chicago, IL 60637-2891
Ph: (312)955-9100   Fax: (312)955-8312
Sylvia Lewis
Monthly. Urban planning magazine.

★4267★ *RPA Blueprint*
Regional Plan Association
570 Lexington Ave.
New York, NY 10022
Ph: (212)980-8530   Fax: (212)980-8220
Gabrielle Belson Rattner, Vice Pres.
Focuses on regional planning, forums, and economic development.

★4268★ *Urban Affairs Quarterly*
Sage Periodicals Press
2455 Teller Rd.
Thousand Oaks, CA 91320
Ph: (805)499-0721   Fax: (805)499-0871
Dennis R. Judd
Quarterly. Urban studies journal.

★4269★ *The Urban Age*
World Bank
1818 H St. NW, Rm. S10-107
Washington, DC 20433
Ph: (202)473-3861   Fax: (202)522-3224
Mary McNeil
"Concerned with practical approaches to urban problems in developing countries." Reviews current research, announces publications and studies on urban development, and keeps readers up-to-date on innovative approaches to problems. Recurring features include book reviews and columns titled Letters to the Editor, World View, Newsline, Roundtable, Mayor's Column, Communities Speak, Q & A, From the City Manager's Desk, Book Reviews, and The Urban Calendar.

OTHER SOURCES OF INFORMATION

★4270★ "City & Regional Planning" in *Accounting to Zoology: Graduate Fields Defined* (pp. 172-174)
Petersons Guides, Inc.
PO Box 2123
Princeton, NJ 08543-2123
Ph: (609)243-9111   Fax: (609)243-9150
Fr: 800-338-3282
Amy J. Goldstein, editor. Revised and updated, 1987. Defines 298 graduate and professional fields. Discusses types of graduate programs and degrees, graduate research, applied work, employment prospects, and trends.

★4271★ "Urban Planner" in *Career Selector 2001*
Barron's Educational Series, Inc.
250 Wireless Blvd.
Hauppauge, NY 11788
Ph: (516)434-3311   Fax: (516)434-3723
Fr: 800-645-3476
James C. Gonyea. 1993.

Human Services Workers

Human services worker is a generic term for people who hold professional and paraprofessional jobs in such diverse settings as group homes and halfway houses; correctional, mental retardation, and community mental health centers; family, child, and youth service agencies; and programs concerned with alcoholism, drug abuse, family violence, and aging. Depending on the employment setting and the kinds of clients served there, job titles and duties vary a great deal. Despite differences in what they are called and what they do, human services workers generally perform under the direction of professional staff.

Salaries

Salaries for human services workers are listed below.

Beginning human services workers	$12,000-$20,000/year
Experienced human services workers	Up to $25,000/year

Employment Outlook

Growth rate until the year 2005: Much faster than the average.

Human Services Workers

★4272★ *Becoming a Helper*
Brooks/Cole Publishing Co.
511 Forest Lodge Rd.
Pacific Grove, CA 93950
Ph: (408)373-0728
Marianne S. Corey and Gerald Corey. Second edition, 1993. Includes a bibliography and an index.

★4273★ *Career Explorations in Humans*
Charles C. Thomas, Publisher
2600 S. 1st St.
Springfield, IL 62794-9265
Ph: (217)289-8980   Fax: (217)789-9130
Fr: 800-258-8980
Margaret A. Darrow and William G. Emener, editors. 1991. Describes 15 human service careers/professions.

★4274★ *Careers in Social and Rehabilitation Services*
National Textbook Co. (NTC)
VGM Career Books
4255 W. Touhy Ave.
Lincolnwood, IL 60646-1975
Ph: (708)679-5500   Fax: (708)679-2494
Fr: 800-323-4900
Geraldine O. Garner, Ph.D., editor. 1993. Describes dozens of careers in the field of social and rehabilitation services.

★4275★ "Human Resources" in *BLR Encyclopedia of Prewritten Job Descriptions*
Business and Legal Reports, Inc.
39 Academy St.
Madison, CT 06443-1513
Ph: (203)245-7448
Stephen D. Bruce, editor-in-chief. 1994. This book contains hundreds of sample job descriptions arranged by functional job category. The 1-3 page job descriptions cover what the worker normally does in the position, who they report to, and how that position fits in the organizational structure.

★4276★ "Human Service Worker" in *College Board Guide to Jobs and Career Planning* (pp. 310-311)
The College Board
45 Columbus Ave.
New York, NY 10023-6992
Ph: (212)713-8165   Fax: (212)713-8143
Fr: 800-323-7155
Second edition, 1994. Describes the job, salaries, related careers, education needed, and where to write for more information.

★4277★ "Human Services" in *Career Choices for the 90's for Students of Psychology* (pp. 111-130)
Walker and Co.
435 Hudson St.
New York, NY 10014
Ph: (212)727-8300   Fax: (212)727-0984
Fr: 800-289-2553
1990. Offers alternatives for students of psychology. Gives information about the outlook and competition for entry-level candidates. Provides job-hunting tips.

★4278★ "Human Services" in *Encyclopedia of Career Choices for the 1990s: A Guide to Entry Level Jobs* (pp. 417-436)
Berkley Pub.
PO Box 506
East Rutherford, NJ 07073
Fax: (201)933-2316   Fr: 800-788-6262
1992. Describes entry-level careers in a variety of industries. Presents qualifications required, working conditions, salary, internships, and professional associations.

★4279★ "Human Services" in *Opportunities in Home Economics Careers* (pp. 49-57)
National Textbook Co. (NTC)
VGM Career Books
4255 W. Touhy Ave.
Lincolnwood, IL 60646-1975
Ph: (708)679-5500   Fax: (708)679-2494
Fr: 800-323-4900
Rhea Shields. 1988. Gives the history and trends of home economics. Separate chapters cover home economics-related careers such as art, interior design, and hospitality. Lists colleges and universities offering programs in home economics.

★4280★ "Human Services Workers" in *America's 50 Fastest Growing Jobs* (pp. 42)
JIST Works, Inc.
720 N. Park Ave.
Indianapolis, IN 46202-3431
Ph: (317)264-3720   Fax: (317)264-3709
Fr: 800-648-5478
Michael J. Farr, compiler. 1994. Describes the 50 fastest growing jobs within major career clusters such as technicians, and marketing and sales. Each job profile explains the nature of the work, skills and abilities required, employment outlook, average earnings, related occupations, education and training requirements, and employment opportunities. Also contains career planning information and job search tips.

★4281★ "Human Services Workers" in *Health Care Job Explosion!* (pp. 261-270)
D-Amp Publications
401 Amherst Ave.
Coraopolis, PA 15108
Ph: (412)262-5578
Dennis V. Damp. 1993. Provides information on the nature of work for the major health care occupational groups. Descriptions include working conditions, training, job outlook, qualifications, and related occupations.

★4282★ "Human Services Workers" in *Occupational Outlook Handbook*
U.S. Government Printing Office
Superintendent of Documents
Washington, DC 20402
Ph: (202)512-1800   Fax: (202)512-2250
Biennial; latest edition, 1994-95. Encyclopedia of careers describing about 250 occupations and comprising about 85 percent of all jobs in the economy. Occupations that require lengthy education or training are given the most attention. Each occupation's profile describes what the worker does on the job, working conditions, education and training requirements, advancement possibilities, job outlook, earnings, and sources of additional information.

★4283★ Human Services? . . . That Must Be So Rewarding: A Practical Guide fof Professional Development
Paul H. Brookes Publishing Co.
PO Box 10624
Baltimore, MD 21285-0624
Ph: 800-638-3775
Gail S. Bernstein and Judith A. Halaszyn. 1994. Includes a bibliography and an index.

★4284★ "Mental Health Worker" in Careers in Health Care (pp. 140-142)
National Textbook Co. (NTC)
VGM Career Books
4255 W. Touhy Ave.
Lincolnwood, IL 60646-1975
Ph: (708)679-5500   Fax: (708)679-2494
Fr: 800-323-4900
Barbara M. Swanson. Third edition, 1995. Profiles 58 health careers. Describes job duties, work settings, salaries, licensing and certification requirements, educational preparation, and future outlook.

★4285★ Opportunities in Human Resource Management Careers
National Textbook Co. (NTC)
VGM Career Books
4255 W. Toughy Ave.
Lincolnwood, IL 60646-1975
Ph: (708)679-5500   Fax: (708)679-2494
Fr: 800-323-4900
William J. Traynor.

★4286★ "Social Service" in Internships: 1995 (pp. 289-305)
Petersons Guides, Inc.
PO Box 2123
Princeton, NJ 08543-2123
Ph: (609)243-9111   Fax: (609)243-9150
Fr: 800-338-3282
Fifteen edition, 1995. Lists internship opportunities under six broad categories: communications, creative, performing, and fine arts, human services, international relations, business and technology, and public relations. Includes a special section on internships in Washington, DC. For each internship program, gives the name, phone number, contact person, description, eligibility requirements, and benefits.

PROFESSIONAL ASSOCIATIONS

★4287★ National Organization for Human Service Education (NOHSE)
Box 6257
Fitchburg State College
160 Pearl St.
Fitchburg, MA 01420
Ph: (508)345-2151
Members: Human service professionals, faculty, and students. **Purpose:** To foster excellence in teaching, research and curriculum planning in the human service area; to encourage and support the development of local, state, and national human services organizations; to aid faculty and professional members in their career development. Provides a medium for cooperation and communication among members; maintains registry of qualified consultants in human service ed-

ucation. Conducts professional development workshop; operates speakers' bureau. **Publications:** Journal of Human Service Education, annual. • National Organization for Human Service Education—Link, quarterly.

STANDARDS/CERTIFICATION AGENCIES

★4288★ American Association of Direct Human Service Personnel
1832 Little Rd.
Parma, MI 49269-9506
Ph: (517)531-5820   Fax: (517)531-5820
Conducts two national certification programs; the Certified Human Service Provider (CHSP), and the Certified Service Facilitator (CSF).

TEST GUIDES

★4289★ Career Examination Series: Aging Services Representative
National Learning Corp.
212 Michael Dr.
Syosset, NY 11791
Ph: (516)921-8888   Fax: (516)921-8743
Fr: 800-645-6337
Jack Rudman. 1993. Test guide including questions and answers for students or professionals in the field who seek advancement through examination.

★4290★ Career Examination Series: Alcoholism Counselor
National Learning Corp.
212 Michael Dr.
Syosset, NY 11791
Ph: (516)921-8888   Fax: (516)921-8743
Fr: 800-645-6337
Jack Rudman. 1993. Test guide including questions and answers for students or professionals in the field who seek advancement through examination.

★4291★ Career Examination Series: Alcoholism Educator
National Learning Corp.
212 Michael Dr.
Syosset, NY 11791
Ph: (516)921-8888   Fax: (516)921-8743
Fr: 800-645-6337
Jack Rudman. 1993. Test guide including questions and answers for students or professionals in the field who seek advancement through examination.

★4292★ Career Examination Series: Alcoholism Rehabilitation Consultant
National Learning Corp.
212 Michael Dr.
Syosset, NY 11791
Ph: (516)921-8888   Fax: (516)921-8743
Fr: 800-645-6337
Jack Rudman. 1993. Test guide including questions and answers for students or pro-

fessionals in the field who seek advancement through examination.

★4293★ Career Examination Series: Community Relations Specialist
National Learning Corp.
212 Michael Dr.
Syosset, NY 11791
Ph: (516)921-8888   Fax: (516)921-8743
Fr: 800-645-6337
Jack Rudman. 1993. Test guide including questions and answers for students or professionals in the field who seek advancement through examination.

★4294★ Career Examination Series: Coordinator, Senior Citizen Planning and Research
National Learning Corp.
212 Michael Dr.
Syosset, NY 11791
Ph: (516)921-8888   Fax: (516)921-8743
Fr: 800-645-6337
Jack Rudman. 1993. Test guide including questions and answers for students or professionals in the field who seek advancement through examination.

★4295★ Career Examination Series: Director of Youth Bureau
National Learning Corp.
212 Michael Dr.
Syosset, NY 11791
Ph: (516)921-8888   Fax: (516)921-8743
Fr: 800-645-6337
Jack Rudman. 1993. Test guide including questions and answers for students or professionals in the field who seek advancement through examination.

★4296★ Career Examination Series: Drug Abuse Counselor
National Learning Corp.
212 Michael Dr.
Syosset, NY 11791
Ph: (516)921-8888   Fax: (516)921-8743
Fr: 800-645-6337
Jack Rudman. A series of study guides with multiple-choice examination questions and solutions for trainees and professional human services workers. Titles in the series include Assistant Coordinator of Volunteer Services; Assistant Supervisor of Youth Services; Assistant Youth Corps Project Director; Assistant Youth Guidance Technician; Associate Social Services Management Specialist; Clinic Supervisor (Drug Abuse); Community Development Project Director; Community Improvement Coordinator; Coordinator of Volunteer Services; Director of Child Support Enforcement Bureau; Director of Senior Citizens' Services; Drug Abuse Education Group Leader; Drug Abuse Educator; Drug Abuse Group Worker; Drug Abuse Rehabilitation Counselor; Drug and Alcohol Community Coordinator; Drug and Alcohol Counselor; Drug and Alcohol Program Coordinator; Planner Youth Services; Playground Director; Principal Drug and Alcohol Counselor; Principal Senior Citizens' Program Coordinator; Sanctuary Coordinator; Senior Addiction Specialist; Senior Citizens' Program Coordinator; Senior Citizens' Program Supervisor; Senior Citizens' Services Coordinator; Senior Community Service Worker; Senior Drug Abuse Rehabilitation Counselor; Senior Drug and Alcohol Counselor; Senior

Youth Group Worker; Supervisor of Youth Services; Youth Group Supervisor; Youth Group Worker; Youth Group Worker Aide; Youth Guidance Technician; Youth Services Coordinator; Youth Services Specialist.

★4297★ Career Examination Series: Instructor of the Blind
National Learning Corp.
212 Michael Dr.
Syosset, NY 11791
Ph: (516)921-8888   Fax: (516)921-8743
Fr: 800-645-6337

Jack Rudman. 1993. Test guide including questions and answers for students or professionals in the field who seek advancement through examination.

★4298★ Career Examination Series: Mental Health Geriatric Consultant
National Learning Corp.
212 Michael Dr.
Syosset, NY 11791
Ph: (516)921-8888   Fax: (516)921-8743
Fr: 800-645-6337

Jack Rudman. 1993. Test guide including questions and answers for students or professionals in the field who seek advancement through examination.

EDUCATIONAL DIRECTORIES AND PROGRAMS

★4299★ Mental Health and Social Work Career Directory
Gale Research Inc.
835 Penobscot Bldg.
Detroit, MI 48226-4094
Ph: (313)961-2242   Fax: (313)961-6083
Fr: 800-877-GALE

Bradley J. Morgan and Joseph M. Palmisano. 1993. A directory in the Career Advisor Series that provides essays written by industry professionals; job search information on resume and cover letter preparation, networking, and the interviewing process; approximately 300 companies and organizations offering job opportunities and internships, and additional job-hunting resources.

BASIC REFERENCE GUIDES AND HANDBOOKS

★4300★ Case Management and the Elderly: A Handbook for Planning and Administering Programs
Free Press
866 3rd Ave.
New York, NY 10022
Ph: (212)702-2004   Fr: 800-257-5755
Raymond M. Steinberg and Genevieve W. Carter. 1988. Includes a bibliography and an index.

★4301★ Handbook on Human Service Administration
Marcel Dekker, Inc.
270 Madison Ave.
New York, NY 10016
Ph: (212)696-9000

Jack Rabin and Marcia B. Steinhauer, editors. 1988. Includes bibliographies and an index.

★4302★ Human Services: Concepts & Intervention Strategies
Allyn & Bacon, Inc.
160 Gould St.
Needham Heights, MA 02194
Ph: (617)455-1250   Fax: (617)455-1220
Fr: 800-258-3525

Joseph J. Mehr, editor. 1994.

★4303★ Human Services in Contemporary America
Brooks/Cole Publishing Co.
511 Forest Lodge Rd.
Pacific Grove, CA 93950
Ph: (408)373-0728   Fax: (408)375-6414
Paul Schmolling, Jr., editor. Third edition, 1992.

★4304★ An Introduction to Human Services
Brooks/Cole Publishing Co.
511 Forest Lodge Rd.
Pacific Grove, CA 93950-5098
Ph: (408)373-0728   Fax: (408)375-6414
Marianne Woodside, editor. Second edition, 1994.

★4305★ Managing Aging & Human Service Agencies
Springer Publishing Co., Inc.
536 Broadway
New York, NY 10012
Ph: (212)431-4370   Fax: (212)941-7842
Edward E. Morgan, Jr., editor. 1992.

PROFESSIONAL AND TRADE PERIODICALS

★4306★ AssemblyLine
National Assembly of National Voluntary Health & Social Welfare Organizations, Inc.
1319 F St. NW, Ste. 601
Washington, DC 20004
Ph: (202)347-2080   Fax: (202)393-4517
Kim Pawley Helfgott

Semiannual. Attempts to foster intercommunication and interaction among national voluntary health and social welfare agencies. Discusses topics relating to the impact of voluntarism on human needs, especially in regard to individual health and social welfare agencies. Recurring features include news of research, legislation, resources and funding.

★4307★ Community Mental Health Journal
Human Sciences Press
233 Spring St.
New York, NY 10013
Ph: (212)620-8000   Fax: (212)463-0742
David Cutler

Bimonthly. Mental health journal featuring articles relating to research, theory, and practice.

★4308★ Family Service America— Newswire
Family Service America
11700 W. Lake Park Dr.
Park Place
Milwaukee, WI 53224
Ph: (414)359-1040   Fax: (414)359-1074
Paula J. Purcell

Quarterly. Carries news of programs and services of the Association and member family service agencies. Covers stories on issues related to families, social services, and other non-profit issues.

★4309★ Human Resources Management
John Wiley and Sons, Inc.
605 3rd Ave.
New York, NY 10158
Ph: (212)850-6000   Fax: (212)850-6799
Noel M. Tichy

Quarterly. Journal providing practicing managers and academics with tools and information for problem-solving and decision-making in the human resource field. Explores issues of societal, organizational and individual relevance.

★4310★ Personnel Manager's Letter
Bureau of Business Practice
24 Rope Ferry Rd.
Waterford, CT 06386
Ph: (203)442-4365
Jill Whitney, Contact

Semimonthly. Provides the Human Resources manager with how-to information. Topics include benefits, training, recruiting, termination, and compensation policies. Recurring features include interviews, news of research and columns titled You Be the Judge, Workplace News, and Our Readers Ask.

★4311★ Public Assistance Funding Report
CD Publications
8204 Fenton St.
Silver Spring, MD 20910
Ph: (301)588-6380   Fax: (301)588-6385
Fr: 800-666-6380
Aaron Liebel

Semimonthly. Provides advice on how to create effective job training, housing, and employment programs.

Recreation Workers

Recreation workers plan, organize, and direct activities that help people enjoy and benefit from leisure hours. Recreation programs, whether institutionally or community based, are as diverse as the people they serve and the people who run them. Employment settings range from pristine wilderness areas to health clubs in the city center. At local playgrounds and community centers, for example, recreation personnel organize and conduct a variety of leisure activities, including arts, crafts, fitness, and sports. Recreation workers are also employed by theme parks, tourist attractions, and firms that offer "getaway" vacations or adventure trips. Other employment settings include parks, campgrounds, and recreational areas; schools, churches, and synagogues; retirement communities, senior centers, and adult day care programs; military bases/and correctional institutions; and corporations. Recreation personnel in industry organize and direct leisure activities and athletic programs for employees and their families.

Salaries

Median annual salaries for recreation workers are as follows:

Lowest 10 percent	$7,700/year or less
Median	$14,900/year
Top 10 percent	$27,200/year or more

Employment Outlook

Growth rate until the year 2005: Faster than the average.

Recreation Workers

CAREER GUIDES

★4312★ Career Information: Yours to Discover
American Association for Leisure and Recreation
1900 Association Dr.
Reston, VA 22091
Ph: (703)476-3472   Fax: (703)476-9527
Fr: 800-321-0729

A series of two-page information sheets on 25 separate careers in parks and recreation.

★4313★ Careers in Camping
American Camping Association (ACA)
5000 State Rd., 67 N.
Martinsville, IN 46151-7902
Ph: (317)342-8456

Describes camping careers, job duties, qualifications, salaries, educational preparation, and employment opportunities.

★4314★ Careers Helping Children
Glencoe Publishing Co.
866 3rd Ave.
New York, NY 10022-6299
Ph: (212)702-3276

Videotape that explores career possibilities in day care centers, youth programs, community health centers, and government agencies. Educational requirements and personal attributes required for each job are explained.

★4315★ Careers in Social and Rehabilitation Services
National Textbook Co. (NTC)
VGM Career Books
4255 W. Touhy Ave.
Lincolnwood, IL 60646-1975
Ph: (708)679-5500   Fax: (708)679-2494
Fr: 800-323-4900

Geraldine O. Garner, Ph.D., editor. 1993. Describes dozens of careers in the field of social and rehabilitation services.

★4316★ Opportunities in Recreation and Leisure Careers
National Textbook Co. (NTC)
VGM Career Books
4255 W. Touhy Ave.
Lincolnwood, IL 60646-1975
Ph: (708)679-5500   Fax: (708)679-2494
Fr: 800-323-4900

Clayne R. Jensen and Jay H. Naylor. 1990.

★4317★ "Outdoor Recreation Planner" in Guide to Federal Jobs (pp. 58)
Resource Directories
3361 Executive Pkwy., Ste. 302
Toledo, OH 43606
Ph: (419)536-5353   Fax: (419)536-7056
Fr: 800-274-8515

Rod W. Durgin, editor. Third edition, 1992. Contains information on finding and applying for federal jobs. Describes more than 200 professional and technical jobs for college graduates. Covers the nature of the work, salary, and geographic location. Lists college majors preferred for that occupation.

★4318★ Recreation Leader
Careers, Inc.
PO Box 135
Largo, FL 34649-0135
Ph: (813)584-7333

1992. Two-page occupational summary card describing duties, working conditions, personal qualifications, training, earnings and hours, employment outlook, places of employment, related careers, and where to write for more information.

★4319★ "Recreation and Leisure" in College Majors and Careers: A ResourceGuide to Effective Life Planning (pp. 115-116)
Garrett Park Press
PO Box 1907
Garrett Park, MD 20896
Ph: (301)946-2553

Paul Phifer. Revised, 1993. Lists 60 college majors, with definitions; related occupations and leisure activities; skills, values, and personal attributes needed; suggested readings; and a list of associations.

★4320★ "Recreation/Leisure Services" in Opportunities in Gerontology (pp. 47-49)
National Textbook Co. (NTC)
VGM Career Books
4255 W. Touhy Ave.
Lincolnwood, IL 60646-1975
Ph: (708)679-5500   Fax: (708)679-2494
Fr: 800-323-4900

Ellen Williams. 1987. Gives a broad overview of career opportunities in gerontology in many fields. Suggest training needed and internships and volunteer opportunities. Lists gerontology-related associations. Gives sources of additional information.

★4321★ Recreation Occupations
Chronicle Guidance Publications, Inc.
66 Aurora St.
PO Box 1190
Moravia, NY 13118-1190
Ph: (315)497-0330   Fax: (315)497-3359
Fr: 800-622-7284

1991. Career brief describing the nature of the job, working conditions, hours and earnings, education and training, licensure, certification, unions, personal qualifications, social and psychological factors, location, employment outlook, entry methods, advancement, and related occupations.

★4322★ "Recreation Personnel" in Career Paths in the Field of Aging: Professional Gerontology (pp. 29-30)
Simon and Schuster
200 Old Tappan Rd.
Old Tappan, NJ 07675
Fax: 800-445-6991   Fr: 800-223-2348

David A. Peterson. 1987. Provides a history of the gerontology profession; describes education and skills required, employment outlook, and trends in the field.

★4323★ "Recreation Specialist" in Guide to Federal Jobs (pp. 79)
Resource Directories
3361 Executive Pkwy., Ste. 302
Toledo, OH 43606
Ph: (419)536-5353   Fax: (419)536-7056
Fr: 800-274-8515

Rod W. Durgin, editor. Third edition, 1992. Contains information on finding and applying for federal jobs. Describes more than 200 professional and technical jobs for college graduates. Covers the nature of the work, salary, and geographic location. Lists college majors preferred for that occupation. Section One describes the function and work of government agencies that hire the most significant number of college graduates.

★4324★ Recreation Trends Toward the Year 2000
Management Learning Laboratories
302 W. Hill St.
Champaign, IL 61820
Ph: (217)359-5958
John R. Kelly. 1987. Analyzes future trends in recreation.

★4325★ "Recreation Worker" in Career Information Center (Vol.8)
Simon and Schuster
200 Old Tappan Rd.
Old Tappan, NJ 07675
Fax: 800-445-6991   Fr: 800-223-2348
Richard Lidz and Linda Perrin, editorial directors. Fifth edition, 1993. This 13-volume set profiles over 600 occupations. Each occupational profile describes job duties, entry-level requirements, educational requirements, advancement possibilities, employment outlook, working conditions, earnings and benefits, and where to write for more information.

★4326★ "Recreation Worker" in College Board Guide to Jobs and Career Planning (pp. 312)
The College Board
415 Columbus Ave.
New York, NY 10023-6992
Ph: (212)713-8165   Fax: (212)713-8143
Fr: 800-323-7155
Joyce S. Mitchell. Second edition, 1994. Describes a variety of careers. Includes information on salaries, related careers, education needed, and sources of additional information.

★4327★ Recreation Workers
Chronicle Guidance Publications, Inc.
66 Aurora St.
PO Box 1190
Moravia, NY 13118-1190
Ph: (315)497-0330   Fax: (315)497-3359
Fr: 800-622-7284
1991. Career brief describing the nature of the job, working conditions, hours and earnings, education and training, licensure, certification, unions, personal qualifications, social and psychological factors, location, employment outlook, entry methods, advancement, and related occupations.

★4328★ "Recreation Workers" in Encyclopedia of Careers and Vocational Guidance (Vol.4, pp. 254-257)
J.G. Ferguson Publishing Co.
200 W. Madison St., Ste. 300
Chicago, IL 60606
Ph: (312)580-5480   Fax: (312)580-4948
William E. Hopke, editor-in-chief. Ninth edition, 1993. Four-volume set that profiles 900 occupations and describes job trends in 74 industries. Includes career description, educational requirements, history of the job, methods of entry, advancement, employment outlook, earnings, conditions of work, social and psychological factors, and sources of further information.

★4329★ "Recreation Workers" in Jobs! What They Are—Where They Are—What They Pay (p. 138)
Simon & Schuster, Inc.
Simon & Schuster Bldg.
1230 Avenue of the Americas
New York, NY 10020
Ph: (212)698-7000   Fr: 800-223-2348
Robert O. Snelling and Anne M. Snelling. 3rd edition, 1992. Describes duties and responsibilities, earnings, employment opportunities, training, and qualifications.

★4330★ "Recreation Workers" in Occupational Outlook Handbook
U.S. Government Printing Office
Superintendent of Documents
Washington, DC 20402
Ph: (202)512-1800   Fax: (202)512-2250
Biennial; latest edition, 1994-95. Encyclopedia of careers describing about 250 occupations and comprising about 85 percent of all jobs in the economy. Occupations that require lengthy education or training are given the most attention. Each occupation's profile describes what the worker does on the job, working conditions, education and training requirements, advancement possibilities, job outlook, earnings, and sources of additional information.

★4331★ "Recreation Workers" in Opportunities in Child Care (pp. 68-70)
National Textbook Co. (NTC)
VGM Career Books
4255 W. Touhy Ave.
Lincolnwood, IL 60646-1975
Ph: (708)679-5500   Fax: (708)679-2494
Fr: 800-323-4900
Wittenberg, Renee. 1987. Offers a detailed survey of the career choices available in child care. Outlines the many job opportunities available in day care, child welfare, child development, and social services. Describes the challenges and rewards as well as the educational and training requirements.

PROFESSIONAL ASSOCIATIONS

★4332★ American Camping Association (ACA)
5000 State Rd. 67 N.
Martinsville, IN 46151-7902
Ph: (317)342-8456   Fax: (317)342-2065
Members: Camp owners, directors, program directors, businesses, and students interested in resident and daycamp programming for youth and adults. **Purpose:** Conducts camp standards and camp director certification programs. Offers educational programs in areas of administration, staffing, child development, promotion, and programming. **Publications:** Camping Magazine, bimonthly. • Guide to Accredited Camps, annual.

★4333★ National Council of Young Men's Christian Associations of the United States of America (YMCA-USA)
101 N. Wacker Dr.
Chicago, IL 60606
Ph: (312)977-0031   Fax: (312)977-9063
Members: A volunteer movement characterized by local program control designed to meet the community needs of people of all ages, races, religions, abilities, and incomes. Focus is on nuturing the healthy development of children, promoting positive behavior in teens, and strengthening families. **Purpose:** Provides group activities, facilities for physical and health education and training, youth sports activities, aquatics instruction, camping, parent-child programs, child care, and counseling. Works to address a diversity of social issues through innovative programs in juvenile justice, international exchange and education, job training, relief work, and environmental action. Each YMCA functions independently to meet the needs of the community it serves. Maintains placement service and hall of fame. Compiles statistics. **Publications:** Discovery YMCA, quarterly. • Executive Notes, bimonthly. • Program Notes, quarterly. • Property Management News, quarterly. • Risk Report, quarterly. • Yearbook and Official Roster. • YMCA Directory, annual.

★4334★ National Employee Services and Recreation Association (NESRA)
2211 York Rd., Ste. 207
Oak Brook, IL 60521-2371
Ph: (708)368-1280   Fax: (708)368-1286
Members: Corporations and governmental agencies that sponsor recreation, fitness, and service programs for their employees; associate members are manufacturers and suppliers in the employee recreation market and distributors of consumer products and services. **Purpose:** Helps members contact manufacturers and suppliers who will assist them in meeting their program objectives and employee needs. Provides associate members with advertising services and direct mail and market research assistance. **Publications:** Employee Services Management, 10/ year. • Keynotes, monthly. • National Employee Services and Recreation Association—Membership Directory, annual. • NESRA News, quarterly.

★4335★ National Recreation and Park Association (NRPA)
2775 S. Quincy St., Ste. 300
Arlington, VA 22206-2204
Ph: (703)820-4940   Fax: (703)671-6772
Fr: 800-626-6772
Members: Public interest organization dedicated to improving the human environment through improved park, recreation, and leisure opportunities. Activities include: programs for the development and upgrading of professional and citizen leadership in the park, recreation, and leisure field; dissemination of innovations and research results; technical assistance to affiliated organizations, local communities, and members; providing information on public policy; public education; extensive publications program. Maintains 3000 volume library. **Publications:** Dateline: NRPA, monthly. • EMPLOY, monthly. • Friends of Parks and Recreation News, quar-

terly. • *Guide to Books on Parks and Recreation*, annual. • *Job Opportunities Bulletin*, bimonthly. • *Journal of Leisure Research*, quarterly. • *Legal Issues in Recreation Administration*, quarterly. • *Parks and Recreation Magazine*, monthly. • *Programmers Information Network*, quarterly. • *Recreation. . .Access in the 90's*, bimonthly. • *Recreation and Parks Law Reporter*, quarterly. • *Therapeutic Recreation Journal*, quarterly.

STANDARDS/CERTIFICATION AGENCIES

★4336★ **American Camping Association (ACA)**
5000 State Rd. 67 N.
Martinsville, IN 46151-7902
Ph: (317)342-8456   Fax: (317)342-2065

Conducts camp standards and camp director certification programs. Offers educational programs in areas of administration, staffing, child development, promotion, and programming.

TEST GUIDES

★4337★ *Career Examination Series: Activities Director*
National Learning Corp.
212 Michael Dr.
Syosset, NY 11791
Ph: (516)921-8888   Fax: (516)921-8743
Fr: 800-645-6337

Jack Rudman. A series of study guides with multiple-choice examination questions and solutions for trainees and professional recreation workers. Titles in the series include *Activities Specialist; Administrative Park and Recreation Manager; Assistant Park Supervisor; Assistant Recreation Supervisor; Associate Park Service Worker; Commissioner of Recreation and Community Services; Director of Parks and Recreation; Housing Community Activities Coordinator; Park Manager; ; Park Manager I; Park Manager II; Park Manager III; Park Supervisor; Parks and Recreation Assistant; Principal Park Supervisor; Recreation Aide; Recreation Assistant; Recreation Assistant (Men); Recreation Assistant (Women); Recreation Director; Recreation Director, Handicapped Children's Recreation Program; Recreation Facility Manager; Recreation Instructor; Recreation Leader; Recreation Program Coordinator; Recreation Specialist; Recreation Supervisor; Recreation Worker; Superintendent of Recreation; Supervisor of Park Operations.*

★4338★ *Career Examination Series: Aging Services Representative*
National Learning Corp.
212 Michael Dr.
Syosset, NY 11791
Ph: (516)921-8888   Fax: (516)921-8743
Fr: 800-645-6337

Jack Rudman. 1993. Test guide including questions and answers for students or professionals in the field who seek advancement through examination.

★4339★ *Career Examination Series: Associate Urban Park Ranger*
National Learning Corp.
212 Michael Dr.
Syosset, NY 11791
Ph: (516)921-8888   Fax: (516)921-8743
Fr: 800-645-6337

Jack Rudman. 1993. Test guide including questions and answers for students or professionals in the field who seek advancement through examination.

★4340★ *Career Examination Series: Beach Supervisor*
National Learning Corp.
212 Michael Dr.
Syosset, NY 11791
Ph: (516)921-8888   Fax: (516)921-8743
Fr: 800-645-6337

Jack Rudman. 1993. Test guide including questions and answers for students or professionals in the field who seek advancement through examination.

★4341★ *Career Examination Series: Coordinator, Senior Citizen Planning and Research*
National Learning Corp.
212 Michael Dr.
Syosset, NY 11791
Ph: (516)921-8888   Fax: (516)921-8743
Fr: 800-645-6337

Jack Rudman. 1993. Test guide including questions and answers for students or professionals in the field who seek advancement through examination.

★4342★ *Career Examination Series: Deputy Commissioner of Recreation and Community Services*
National Learning Corp.
212 Michael Dr.
Syosset, NY 11791
Ph: (516)921-8888   Fax: (516)921-8743
Fr: 800-645-6337

Jack Rudman. 1993. Test guide including questions and answers for students or professionals in the field who seek advancement through examination.

★4343★ *Career Examination Series: Director of Youth Bureau*
National Learning Corp.
212 Michael Dr.
Syosset, NY 11791
Ph: (516)921-8888   Fax: (516)921-8743
Fr: 800-645-6337

Jack Rudman. 1993. Test guide including questions and answers for students or professionals in the field who seek advancement through examination.

★4344★ *Career Examination Series: Recreation Worker*
National Learning Corp.
212 Michael Dr.
Syosset, NY 11791
Ph: (516)921-8888   Fax: (516)921-8743
Fr: 800-645-6337

Jack Rudman. Test guide including questions and answers for students or professionals in the field who seek advancement through examination.

★4345★ *Career Examination Series: Senior Recreation Leader*
National Learning Corp.
212 Michael Dr.
Syosset, NY 11791
Ph: (516)921-8888   Fax: (516)921-8743
Fr: 800-645-6337

Jack Rudman. 1993. Test guide including questions and answers for students or professionals in the field who seek advancement through examination.

EDUCATIONAL DIRECTORIES AND PROGRAMS

★4346★ *Mental Health and Social Work Career Directory*
Gale Research Inc.
835 Penobscot Bldg.
Detroit, MI 48226-4094
Ph: (313)961-2242   Fax: (313)961-6083
Fr: 800-877-GALE

Bradley J. Morgan and Joseph M. Palmisano. 1993. A directory in the Career Advisor Series that provides essays written by industry professionals; job search information on resume and cover letter preparation, networking, and the interviewing process; approximately 300 companies and organizations offering job opportunities and internships, and additional job-hunting resources.

★4347★ *Travel and Hospitality Career Directory*
Gale Research Inc.
835 Penobscot Bldg.
Detroit, MI 48226-4094
Ph: (313)961-2242   Fax: (313)961-6083
Fr: 800-877-GALE

Bradley J. Morgan and Joseph M. Palmisano. Second edition, 1992. A directory in the Career Advisor Series that provides essays written by industry professionals; job search information on resume and cover letter preparation, networking, and the interviewing process; approximately 300 companies and organizations offering job opportunities and internships, and additional job-hunting resources.

AWARDS, SCHOLARSHIPS, GRANTS, AND FELLOWSHIPS

★4348★ Delta Psi Kappa Research Award
Delta Psi Kappa
PO Box 90264
Indianapolis, IN 46290
Ph: (317)255-4379

To honor outstanding completed research in the fields of physical education, health, recreation, or dance by a member of Delta Psi Kappa. A monetary prize of $500 is awarded biennially. Established in 1940.

★4349★ Dorothy Mullen National Arts and Humanities Award
National Recreation and Park Association
2775 S. Quincy St., Ste. 300
Arlington, VA 22206
Ph: (703)820-4940   Fax: (703)671-6772

To recognize excellence in arts and humanities programming. Awards are presented in the following categories: Class 1 - programming in areas of populations over 200,000 people; Class 2 - 75,000 to 200,000; Class 3 - 25,000 to 75,000; and Class 4 - less than 25,000. Regional awards are also given.

★4350★ Public Recreation Man and Woman of the Year
Amateur Athletic Union of the United States
Communications Dept.
3400 W. 86th St.
PO Box 68207
Indianapolis, IN 46268
Ph: (317)872-2900   Fax: (317)815-0548

To honor outstanding male and female leaders in the field of public recreation. Awarded annually. Established in 1963.

★4351★ Theodore and Franklin Roosevelt Award for Excellence in Recreation and Park Research
National Recreation and Park Association
2775 S. Quincy St., Ste. 300
Arlington, VA 22206
Ph: (703)820-4940   Fax: (703)671-6772

To recognize an individual whose contributions to recreation and park research have significantly advanced the call of the recreation movement and whose dedication to the field parallels the same dedication and zeal towards parks, recreation, and conservation that was exhibited by the two former presidents, after whom the award is named. A monetary award of $1,500 and a plaque are awarded annually. Established in 1981 by a grant from the Lehman Foundation, New York, NY.

BASIC REFERENCE GUIDES AND HANDBOOKS

★4352★ Leisure Today: Goals for American Recreation
American Alliance for Health, Physical Education, Recreation, and Dance
1900 Association Dr.
Reston, VA 22091
Ph: (703)476-3400   Fr: 800-321-0789
Diana R. Dunn, editor. Semiannual. Focuses on trends in society which will impact on the recreation field such as sunbelt growth, working mothers, and the high-tech society.

★4353★ Recreation and Leisure in Modern Society
Scott, Foresman and Co.
1900 E. Lake Ave.
Glenview, IL 60025
Ph: (708)729-3000

Richard G. Kraus. Fourth edition. 1990. Includes bibliographies and an index.

PROFESSIONAL AND TRADE PERIODICALS

★4354★ Camping Magazine
American Camping Assn.
5000 State Rd. 67 N.
Martinsville, IN 46151-7902
Ph: (317)342-8456   Fax: (317)342-2065
Nancy L. Gordon

Bimonthly. Magazine on organized camping management.

★4355★ Leisure Industry Report
Leisure Industry/Recreation News
PO Box 43563
Washington, DC 20010
Ph: (202)232-7107
Marj Jensen

Reports on trends and the outlook for leisure and discretionary spending in such markets as travel, music, theater, sports, gaming, advertising and publishing, television and movies, and theme parks.

★4356★ National Employee Services and Recreation Association—Keynotes
National Employee Services and Recreation Association
2211 York Rd., Ste. 207
Oak Brook, IL 60521-2371
Ph: (708)562-8130
Karen G. Beagley

Monthly. Provides programming and administration ideas for employee services and recreation managers. Recurring features include new techniques, survey findings, news briefs, management tips, programming ideas, and Association news.

★4357★ Parks and Recreation Magazine
National Recreation and Park Assn.
2775 S. Quincy St., Ste. 300
Arlington, VA 22206-2204
Ph: (703)820-4940   Fax: (703)671-6772
Mike Corwin

Monthly. Magazine focusing on research, technical advances, and professional development for executives, public officials, and community leaders responsible for management of public and private park and recreational facilities.

★4358★ The Recreation Advisor
International Family Recreation Association
PO Drawer 17148
Pensacola, FL 32522
Ph: (904)477-7992
K.W. Stephens

Monthly. Addresses concerns relating to family recreation and recreation safety policies. Monitors the Association's support of recommendations and legislation advantageous to recreation. Recurring features include items on developments in the American Recreation Coalition and the Recreation Vehicle Industry Association and notification of workshops, leadership training, and volunteer instruction programs sponsored by the Association, as well as rallies, caravans, tours, cruises, and tournaments which it conducts.

★4359★ Research Quarterly for Exercise and Sport
American Alliance for Health, Physical Education, Recreation, and Dance
1900 Association Drive
Reston, VA 22091-1599
Ph: (703)476-3400   Fax: (703)476-9527
Maureen R. Weiss

Quarterly. Journal focusing on research in physical education and sports.

★4360★ Strategies
American Alliance for Health, Physical Education, Recreation, and Dance
1900 Association Drive
Reston, VA 22091
Ph: (703)476-3495   Fax: (703)476-9527
Debra LewinDirector

Journal providing practical, hands-on information to physical educators and coaches.

PROFESSIONAL MEETINGS AND CONVENTIONS

★4361★ IDEA Convention
IDEA, The Association for Fitness Professionals
69190 Cornerstone Ct., E., Ste. 204
San Diego, CA 92121
Ph: (619)535-8979   Fax: (619)535-8234
Three times per year at various locations.

Social Workers

Social workers help individuals, families, and groups cope with problems of every description. Mostly, however, they aid people who are having difficulties dealing with circumstances in their lives: the homeless, the unemployed, the seriously ill, the bereaved, and the handicapped. Among the major helping professions, social work is distinguished by a tradition of concern for the poor, the disadvantaged, and the elderly and very young. Through direct counseling and referral to other services, social workers help clients rebuild their lives. Through policy making and advocacy, they help make society more responsive to people's changing needs. Major areas of social work practice include child welfare and family services, mental health, medical social work, school social work community organization, planning and policy development, and social welfare administration.

Salaries

Salaries for social workers at all levels vary greatly by type of agency and geographic region. Generally, though, earnings are highest in large cities and in states with sizable urban populations. Average salaries include:

Medical social workers, private hospitals	$30,000/year
Government social workers	$41,400/year
All settings	$25,600-$38,700/year

Employment Outlook

Growth rate until the year 2005: Faster than the average.

Social Workers

★4362★ Careers in Social and Rehabilitation Services
National Textbook Co. (NTC)
VGM Career Books
4255 W. Touhy Ave.
Lincolnwood, IL 60646-1975
Ph: (708)679-5500   Fax: (708)679-2494
Fr: 800-323-4900
Geraldine O. Garner, Ph.D., editor. 1993. Describes dozens of careers in the field of social and rehabilitation services.

★4363★ Director, Substance Abuse Treatment Center
Careers, Inc.
PO Box 135
Largo, FL 34649-0135
Ph: (813)584-7333
1992. Four-page brief describing duties, working conditions, personal qualifications, training, earnings and hours, employment outlook, places of employment, related careers, and where to write for more information.

★4364★ Educational Career Directory
Gale Research Inc.
835 Penobscot Bldg.
Detroit, MI 48226
Ph: (313)961-2242   Fr: 800-877-GALE
1994.

★4365★ Exploring Careers in Social Work
Rosen Publishing Group
29 E. 21st St.
New York, NY 10010
Ph: (212)777-3017   Fax: (212)777-0277
Fr: 800-237-9932
Carolyn Simpson and Dwain Simpson. 1993. Details the education, training, disadvantages and rewards of social work. Also overviews the special qualities social workers should possess for success such as empathy, patience, and a love for people.

★4366★ "Geriatric Social Worker" in 100 Best Careers for the Year 2000 (pp. 86-88)
Arco Pub.
201 W. 103rd St.
Indianapolis, IN 46290
Ph: 800-428-5331   Fax: 800-835-3202
Shelly Field. 1992. Describes 100 job opportunities expected to grow fast throughout the next decade. Provides information on job duties and responsibilities, training requirements, education, advancement opportunities, experience and qualifications, and typical salaries.

★4367★ Geriatric Social Workers
Chronicle Guidance Publications, Inc.
66 Aurora St.
PO Box 1190
Moravia, NY 13118-1190
Ph: (315)497-0330   Fax: (315)497-3359
Fr: 800-622-7284
1994. Career brief describing the nature of the job, working conditions, hours and earnings, education and training, licensure, certification, unions, personal qualifications, social and psychological factors, location, employment outlook, entry methods, advancement, and related occupations.

★4368★ "Medical Social Worker and Psychiatric Social Worker" in Careers in Health Care (pp. 129-133)
National Textbook Co. (NTC)
VGM Career Books
4255 W. Touhy Ave.
Lincolnwood, IL 60646-1975
Ph: (708)679-5500   Fax: (708)679-2494
Fr: 800-323-4900
Barbara M. Swanson. Third edition, 1995. Profiles 58 health careers. Describes job duties, work settings, salaries, licensing and certification requirements, educational preparation, and future outlook.

★4369★ Opportunities in Social Work Careers
National Textbook Co. (NTC)
VGM Career Books
4255 W. Touhy Ave.
Lincolnwood, IL 60646-1975
Ph: (708)679-5500   Fax: (708)679-2494
Fr: 800-323-4900
Renee Wittenberg. 1988. Describes the skills required for a job in social work, educational preparation, work settings and related careers. Lists additional resources.

★4370★ "Parole Officer" in VGM's Careers Encyclopedia (pp. 334-336)
National Textbook Co. (NTC)
VGM Career Books
4255 W. Touhy Ave.
Lincolnwood, IL 60646-1975
Ph: (708)679-5500   Fax: (708)679-2494
Fr: 800-323-4900
Third edition, 1991. Profiles 200 occupations. Describes job duties, places of employment, working conditions, qualifications, education and training, advancement potential, and salary for each occupation.

★4371★ "Parole Officers" in Career Information Center (Vol.11)
Simon and Schuster
200 Old Tappan Rd.
Old Tappan, NJ 07675
Fax: 800-445-6991   Fr: 800-223-2348
Richard Lidz and Linda Perrin, editorial directors. Fifth edition, 1993. This 13-volume set profiles over 600 occupations. Each occupational profile describes job duties, educational requirements, advancement possibilities, employment outlook, working conditions, earnings and benefits, and where to write for more information.

★4372★ Probation Officer
Careers, Inc.
PO Box 135
Largo, FL 34649-0135
Ph: (813)584-7333
1991. Two-page occupational summary card describing duties, working conditions, personal qualifications, training, earnings and hours, employment outlook, places of employment, related careers, and where to write for more information.

★4373★ Probation Officer
Vocational Biographies, Inc.
PO Box 31
Sauk Centre, MN 56378-0031
Ph: (612)352-6516   Fax: (612)352-5546
Fr: 800-255-0752
1993. Four-page pamphlet containing a personal narrative about a worker's job, work likes and dislikes, career path from high school to the present, education and training, the rewards and frustrations, and the effects

of the job on the rest of the worker's life. The data file portion of this pamphlet gives a concise occupational summary, including work description, working conditions, places of employment, personal characteristics, education and training, job outlook, and salary range.

★4374★ "Probation Officer" in *Career Information Center* (Vol.11)
Simon and Schuster
200 Old Tappan Rd.
Old Tappan, NJ 07675
Fax: 800-445-6991   Fr: 800-223-2348
Richard Lidz and Linda Perrin, editorial directors. Fifth edition, 1993. This 13-volume set profiles over 600 occupations. Each occupational profile describes job duties, educational requirements, advancement possibilities, employment outlook, working conditions, earnings and benefits, and where to write for more information.

★4375★ *Probation and Parole Officers*
Chronicle Guidance Publications, Inc.
66 Aurora St.
PO Box 1190
Moravia, NY 13118-1190
Ph: (315)497-0330   Fax: (315)497-3359
Fr: 800-622-7284
1991. Career brief describing the nature of the job, working conditions, hours and earnings, education and training, licensure, certification, unions, personal qualifications, social and psychological factors, location, employment outlook, entry methods, advancement, and related occupations.

★4376★ "Public Health Social Work" in *Opportunities in Public Health Careers* (pp. 87-89)
National Textbook Co. (NTC)
VGM Career Books
4255 W. Touhy Ave.
Lincolnwood, IL 60646-1975
Ph: (708)679-5500   Fax: (708)679-2494
Fr: 800-323-4900
George E. Pickett. 1988. Defines the public health field and describes career opportunities as well as educational preparation and the future of the public health field. The appendices list public health organizations, state and federal public health agencies, and graduate schools offering public health programs.

★4377★ "Religious Administration and Social Work" in *Opportunities in Religious Service Careers* (pp. 105-114)
National Textbook Co. (NTC)
VGM Career Books
4255 W. Touhy Ave.
Lincolnwood, IL 60646-1975
Ph: (708)679-5500   Fax: (708)679-2494
Fr: 800-323-4900
John Oliver Nelson. 1988. Explains personal qualities needed, educational requirements, and related career opportunities in education, the armed services, missionary work, music, and social work.

★4378★ *School Social Workers*
Chronicle Guidance Publications, Inc.
66 Aurora St.
PO Box 1190
Moravia, NY 13118-1190
Ph: (315)497-0330   Fax: (315)497-3359
Fr: 800-622-7284
1993. Career brief describing the nature of the job, working conditions, hours and earnings, education and training, licensure, certification, unions, personal qualifications, social and psychological factors, location, employment outlook, entry methods, advancement, and related occupations.

★4379★ "Social Service" in *Internships: 1995* (pp. 289-305)
Petersons Guides, Inc.
PO Box 2123
Princeton, NJ 08543-2123
Ph: (609)243-9111   Fax: (609)243-9150
Fr: 800-338-3282
Fifteen edition, 1995. Lists internship opportunities under six broad categories: communications, creative, performing, and fine arts, human services, international relations, business and technology, and public relations. Includes a special section on internships in Washington, DC. For each internship program, gives the name, phone number, contact person, description, eligibility requirements, and benefits.

★4380★ "Social Services" in *Encyclopedia of Careers and Vocational Guidance* (Vol.1, pp. 439-444)
J.G. Ferguson Publishing Co.
200 W. Madison St., Ste. 300
Chicago, IL 60606
Ph: (312)580-5480   Fax: (312)580-4948
William E. Hopke, editor-in-chief. Ninth edition, 1993. Four-volume set that profiles 900 occupations and describes job trends in 74 industries. Includes career description, educational requirements, history of the job, methods of entry, advancement, employment outlook, earnings, conditions of work, social and psychological factors, and sources of further information.

★4381★ "Social Work" in *College Majors and Careers: A Resource Guide to Effective Life Planning* (pp. 121-122)
Garrett Park Press
PO Box 1907
Garrett Park, MD 20896
Ph: (301)946-2553
Paul Phifer. Revised, 1993. Lists 60 college majors, with definitions; related occupations and leisure activities; skills, values, and personal attributes needed; suggested readings; and a list of associations.

★4382★ *Social Worker, Clinical*
Careers, Inc.
PO Box 135
Largo, FL 34649-0135
Ph: (813)584-7333
1991. Two-page occupational summary card describing duties, working conditions, personal qualifications, training, earnings and hours, employment outlook, places of employment, related careers, and where to write for more information.

★4383★ "Social Worker" in *College Board Guide to Jobs and Career Planning* (pp. 315)
The College Board
415 Columbus Ave.
New York, NY 10023-6992
Ph: (212)713-8165   Fax: (212)713-8143
Fr: 800-323-7155
Joyce S. Mitchell. Second edition, 1994. Describes a variety of careers. Career profiles contain information on salaries, related careers, education needed, and sources of additional information.

★4384★ "Social Worker" in *Guide to Federal Jobs* (p. 77)
Resource Directories
3361 Executive Pkwy., Ste. 302
Toledo, OH 43606
Ph: (419)536-5353   Fax: (419)536-7056
Fr: 800-274-8515
Rod W. Durgin, editor. Third edition, 1992. Contains information on finding and applying for federal jobs. Describes more than 200 professional and technical jobs for college graduates. Covers the nature of the work, salary, and geographic location. Lists college majors preferred for that occupation. Section One describes the function and work of government agencies that hire the most significant number of college graduates.

★4385★ *Social Worker, Health Care*
Careers, Inc.
PO Box 135
Largo, FL 34649-0135
Ph: (813)584-7333
1995. Two-page occupational summary card describing duties, working conditions, personal qualifications, training, earnings and hours, employment outlook, places of employment, related careers, and where to write for more information.

★4386★ "Social Worker" in *Jobs Rated Almanac*
World Almanac
1 International Blvd., Ste. 444
Mahwah, NJ 07495
Ph: (201)529-6900   Fax: (201)529-6901
Les Krantz. Second edition, 1992. Ranks 250 jobs by environment, salary, outlooks, physical demands, stress, security, travel opportunities, and extra perks. Includes jobs the editor feels are the most common, most interesting, and the most rapidly growing.

★4387★ "Social Worker" in *Profitable Careers in Non-Profit* (pp. 63-66)
John Wiley and Sons, Inc.
605 3rd Ave.
New York, NY 10158-0012
Ph: (212)850-6000   Fax: (212)850-6088
Fr: 800-526-5368
William Lewis and Carol Milano. 1987. Examines nonprofit organizations and the career opportunities they offer. Offers tips on how to target and explore occupational opportunities in the nonprofit sector.

★4388★ Social Worker, School
Careers, Inc.
PO Box 135
Largo, FL 34649-0135
Ph: (813)584-7333
1993. Two-page occupational summary card describing duties, working conditions, personal qualifications, training, earnings and hours, employment outlook, places of employment, related careers, and where to write for more information.

★4389★ "Social Worker" in VGM's Careers Encyclopedia (pp. 431-433)
National Textbook Co. (NTC)
VGM Career Books
4255 W. Touhy Ave.
Lincolnwood, IL 60646-1975
Ph: (708)679-5500   Fax: (708)679-2494
Fr: 800-323-4900
Third edition, 1991. Profiles 200 occupations. Describes job duties, places of employment, working conditions, qualifications, education, and training, advancement potential, and salary for each occupation.

★4390★ Social Workers
Careers, Inc.
PO Box 135
Largo, FL 34649-0135
Ph: (813)584-7333
1993. Four-page brief offering the definition, history, duties, working conditions, personal qualifications, educational requirements, earnings, hours, employment outlook, advancement, and careers related to this position.

★4391★ Social Workers
Chronicle Guidance Publications, Inc.
66 Aurora St.
PO Box 1190
Moravia, NY 13118-1190
Ph: (315)497-0330   Fax: (315)497-3359
Fr: 800-622-7284
1992. Career brief describing the nature of the job, working conditions, hours and earnings, education and training, licensure, certification, unions, personal qualifications, social and psychological factors, location, employment outlook, entry methods, advancement, and related occupations.

★4392★ "Social Workers" in 101 Careers: A Guide to the Fastest-Growing Opportunities (pp. 147-149)
John Wiley & Sons, Inc.
605 3rd Ave.
New York, NY 10158-0012
Ph: (212)850-6645   Fax: (212)850-6088
Michael Harkavy. 1990. Describes the nature of the job, working conditions, employment growth, qualifications, personal skills, projected salaries, and where to write for more information.

★4393★ "Social Workers" in American Almanac of Jobs and Salaries (pp. 105)
Avon Books
1350 Avenue of the Americas
New York, NY 10019
Ph: (212)261-6800   Fr: 800-238-0658
John Wright, editor. Revised and updated, 1994-95. A comprehensive guide to the wages of hundreds of occupations in a wide variety of industries and organizations.

★4394★ "Social Workers" in America's 50 Fastest Growing Jobs (pp. 69)
JIST Works, Inc.
720 N. Park Ave.
Indianapolis, IN 46202-3431
Ph: (317)264-3720   Fax: (317)264-3709
Fr: 800-648-5478
Michael J. Farr, compiler. 1994. Describes the 50 fastest growing jobs within major career clusters such as technicians, and marketing and sales. Each job profile explains the nature of the work, skills and abilities required, employment outlook, average earnings, related occupations, education and training requirements, and employment opportunities. Also contains career planning information and job search tips.

★4395★ "Social Workers" in Black Woman's Career Guide (pp. 62-65, 92-100)
Bantam Doubleday Dell
1540 Broadway
New York, NY 10036
Fax: 800-233-3294   Fr: 800-223-5780
Beatryce Nivens. Revised edition, 1987. Part 1 describes career planning, resume writing, job hunting, and interviewing. Part Two profiles sixty black women pioneers in twenty different career areas.

★4396★ "Social Workers" in Career Discovery Encyclopedia (Vol.6, pp. 36-37)
J.G. Ferguson Publishing Co.
200 W. Madison St., Ste. 300
Chicago, IL 60606
Ph: (312)580-5480   Fax: (312)580-4948
Russell E. Primm, editor-in chief. 1993. This six volume set contains two-page articles for 504 occupations. Each article describes job duties, earnings, and educational and training requirements. The whole set is arranged alphabetically by job title. Designed for junior high and older students.

★4397★ "Social Workers" in Career Information Center (Vol.11)
Simon and Schuster
200 Old Tappan Rd.
Old Tappan, NJ 07675
Fax: 800-445-6991   Fr: 800-223-2348
Richard Lidz and Linda Perrin, editorial directors. Fifth edition, 1993. This 13-volume set profiles over 600 occupations. Each occupational profile describes job duties, educational requirements, advancement possibilities, employment outlook, working conditions, earnings and benefits, and where to write for more information.

★4398★ "Social Workers" in Career Paths in the Field of Aging: Professional Gerontology (pp. 28-29)
Simon and Schuster
200 Old Tappan Rd.
Old Tappan, NJ 07675
Fax: 800-445-6991   Fr: 800-223-2348
David A. Peterson. 1987. Provides a history of the gerontology profession; describes education and skills required, employment outlook, and trends in the field.

★4399★ "Social Workers" in Encyclopedia of Careers and Vocational Guidance (Vol.4, pp. 373-376)
J.G. Ferguson Publishing Co.
200 W. Madison St., Ste. 300
Chicago, IL 60606
Ph: (312)580-5480   Fax: (312)580-4948
William E. Hopke, editor-in-chief. Ninth edition, 1993. Four-volume set that profiles 900 occupations and describes job trends in 74 industries. Includes career description, educational requirements, history of the job, methods of entry, advancement, employment outlook, earnings, conditions of work, social and psychological factors, and sources of further information.

★4400★ "Social Workers" in Health Care Job Explosion! (pp. 279-290)
D-Amp Publications
401 Amherst Ave.
Coraopolis, PA 15108
Ph: (412)262-5578
Dennis V. Damp. 1993. Provides information on the nature of work for the major health care occupational groups. Descriptions include working conditions, training, job outlook, qualifications, and related occupations.

★4401★ "Social Workers" in Jobs! What They Are—Where They Are—What They Pay (p. 95)
Simon & Schuster, Inc.
Simon & Schuster Bldg.
1230 Avenue of the Americas
New York, NY 10020
Ph: (212)698-7000   Fr: 800-223-2348
Robert O. Snelling and Anne M. Snelling. 3rd edition, 1992. Describes duties and responsibilities, earnings, employment opportunities, training, and qualifications.

★4402★ "Social Workers" in Occupational Outlook Handbook
U.S. Government Printing Office
Superintendent of Documents
Washington, DC 20402
Ph: (202)512-1800   Fax: (202)512-2250
Biennial; latest edition, 1994-95. Encyclopedia of careers describing about 250 occupations and comprising about 85 percent of all jobs in the economy. Occupations that require lengthy education or training are given the most attention. Each occupation's profile describes what the worker does on the job, working conditions, education and training requirements, advancement possibilities, job outlook, earnings, and sources of additional information.

★4403★ "Social Workers" in Opportunities in Child Care (pp. 66-68)
National Textbook Co. (NTC)
VGM Career Books
4255 W. Touhy Ave.
Lincolnwood, IL 60646-1975
Ph: (708)679-5500   Fax: (708)679-2494
Fr: 800-323-4900
Renee Wittenberg. 1987. Offers a detailed survey of the career choices available in child care. Outlines the many job opportunities available in day care, child welfare, child development, and social services. Describes

the challenges and rewards as well as the educational and training requirements.

PROFESSIONAL ASSOCIATIONS

★4404★ American Association of Mental Health Professionals in Corrections (AAMHPC)
c/o John S. Zil, M.D., J.D.
PO Box 163359
Sacramento, CA 95816-9359
Ph: (707)864-0910   Fax: (707)864-0910
Members: Psychiatrists, psychologists, social workers, nurses, and other mental health professionals; individuals working in correctional settings. **Purpose:** Fosters the progress of behavioral sciences related to corrections. Goals are: to improve the treatment, rehabilitation, and care of the mentally ill, mentally retarded, and emotionally disturbed; to promote research and professional education in psychiatry and allied fields in corrections; to advance standards of correctional services and facilities; to foster cooperation between individuals concerned with the medical, psychological, social, and legal aspects of corrections; to share knowledge with other medical practitioners, scientists, and the public. Conducts scientific meetings to contribute to the advancement of the therapeutic community in all its institutional settings, including correctional institutions, hospitals, churches, schools, industry, and the family. **Publications:** *Corrective and Social Psychiatry*, quarterly.

★4405★ Council on Social Work Education (CSWE)
1600 Duke St., Ste. 300
Alexandria, VA 22314
Ph: (703)683-8080   Fax: (703)683-8099
Members: Graduate and undergraduate programs of social work education; national, regional, and local social welfare agencies; libraries and individuals. **Purpose:** Formulates criteria and standards for all levels of social work education; accredits graduate and undergraduate social work programs; provides consulting to social work educators on curriculum, faculty recruitment and development, students and admissions, and teaching methods and materials. Conducts research and compiles data on social work education. **Publications:** *Directory of Colleges and Universities With Accredited Social Work Degree Programs*, annual. • *Journal of Social Work Education*. • *Social Work Education Reporter*. • *Statistics on Social Work Education*, annual. • *Summary Information on Masters of Social Work Programs*, annual.

★4406★ National Association of Social Workers (NASW)
750 First St. NE, Ste. 700
Washington, DC 20002-4241
Ph: (202)408-8600   Fax: (202)336-8312
Fr: 800-638-8799
Members: Regular members are persons who hold a minimum of a baccalaureate degree in social work. Associate members are persons engaged in social work who have a baccalaureate degree in another field. Student members are persons enrolled in accredited (by the Council on Social Work Education) Graduate or undergraduate social work programs. Purposes are to: create professional standards for social work practice; advocate sound public social policies through political and legislative action; provide a wide range of membership services, including continuing education opportunities and an extensive professional program. Operates National Center for Social Policy and Practice. Conducts research; compiles statistics. **Publications:** *Encyclopedia of Social Work.* • *Health and Social Work*, quarterly. • *NASW News.* • *Professional Writing for the Human Services.* • *Social Work*, bimonthly. • *Social Work Abstracts*, quarterly. • *Social Work Almanac.* • *The Social Work Dictionary.* • *Social Work in Education: A Journal for Social Workers in Schools*, quarterly. • *Social Work Research*, quarterly.

★4407★ National Network for Social Work Managers
Administrative Office
6501 N. Federal Hwy., Ste. 5
Boca Raton, FL 33487
Ph: (407)997-7560   Fax: (407)241-6746
Individuals with degrees in social work who are engaged or interested in management within the human services field. Seeks to enhance social work managers' careers in such areas as administration, management, planning, budgeting, economics, and legislative work. Serves as a network to connect social work professionals in human service-related activities. Conducts National Management Institute, regional management development workshops, and other educational programs. Maintains speakers' bureau. **Publications:** *Administration in Social Work*, quarterly. • *Annual Monograph of Papers*, annual. • *Social Work Executive*, quarterly.

STANDARDS/CERTIFICATION AGENCIES

★4408★ Council on Social Work Education (CSWE)
1600 Duke St., Ste. 300
Alexandria, VA 22314
Ph: (703)683-8080   Fax: (703)683-8099
Formulates criteria and standards for all levels of social work education; accredits graduate and undergraduate social work programs.

★4409★ National Association of Social Workers (NASW)
750 First St. NE, Ste. 700
Washington, DC 20002-4241
Ph: (202)408-8600   Fax: (202)336-8312
Fr: 800-638-8799
Regular members are persons who hold a minimum of a baccalaureate. Purposes are to: create professional standards for social work practice; advocate sound public social policies through political and legislative action; provide a wide range of membership services, including continuing education opportunities and an extensive professional program.

TEST GUIDES

★4410★ *Career Examination Series: Addiction Specialist*
National Learning Corp.
212 Michael Dr.
Syosset, NY 11791
Ph: (516)921-8888   Fax: (516)921-8743
Fr: 800-645-6337
Jack Rudman. 1993. Test guide including questions and answers for students or professionals in the field who seek advancement through examination.

★4411★ *Career Examination Series: Alcoholism Rehabilitation Consultant*
National Learning Corp.
212 Michael Dr.
Syosset, NY 11791
Ph: (516)921-8888   Fax: (516)921-8743
Fr: 800-645-6337
Jack Rudman. 1993. Test guide including questions and answers for students or professionals in the field who seek advancement through examination.

★4412★ *Career Examination Series: Certified Social Worker (CSW)*
National Learning Corp.
212 Michael Dr.
Syosset, NY 11791
Ph: (516)921-8888   Fax: (516)921-8743
Fr: 800-645-6337
Jack Rudman. Test guide including questions and answers for students or professionals in the field who seek advancement through examination.

★4413★ *Career Examination Series: Examiner, Social Services*
National Learning Corp.
212 Michael Dr.
Syosset, NY 11791
Ph: (516)921-8888   Fax: (516)921-8743
Fr: 800-645-6337
Jack Rudman. 1993. Test guide including questions and answers for students or professionals in the field who seek advancement through examination.

★4414★ *Career Examination Series: Family and Children Services Specialist*
National Learning Corp.
212 Michael Dr.
Syosset, NY 11791
Ph: (516)921-8888   Fax: (516)921-8743
Fr: 800-645-6337
Jack Rudman. 1993. Test guide including questions and answers for students or professionals in the field who seek advancement through examination.

★4415★ *Career Examination Series: Medical Social Worker*
National Learning Corp.
212 Michael Dr.
Syosset, NY 11791
Ph: (516)921-8888   Fax: (516)921-8743
Fr: 800-645-6337
Jack Rudman. Test guide including questions and answers for students or professionals in

the field who seek advancement through examination.

★4416★ Career Examination Series: Runaway Coordinator
National Learning Corp.
212 Michael Dr.
Syosset, NY 11791
Ph: (516)921-8888   Fax: (516)921-8743
Fr: 800-645-6337

Jack Rudman. 1993. Test guide including questions and answers for students or professionals in the field who seek advancement through examination.

★4417★ Career Examination Series: Social Case Worker
National Learning Corp.
212 Michael Dr.
Syosset, NY 11791
Ph: (516)921-8888   Fax: (516)921-8743
Fr: 800-645-6337

Jack Rudman. Test guide including questions and answers for students or professionals in the field who seek advancement through examination.

★4418★ Career Examination Series: Social Service Collection Representative
National Learning Corp.
212 Michael Dr.
Syosset, NY 11791
Ph: (516)921-8888   Fax: (516)921-8743
Fr: 800-645-6337

Jack Rudman. 1993. Test guide including questions and answers for students or professionals in the field who seek advancement through examination.

★4419★ Career Examination Series: Social Service Representative
National Learning Corp.
212 Michael Dr.
Syosset, NY 11791
Ph: (516)921-8888   Fax: (516)921-8743
Fr: 800-645-6337

Jack Rudman. 1993. Test guide including questions and answers for students or professionals in the field who seek advancement through examination.

★4420★ Career Examination Series: Social Welfare Examiner
National Learning Corp.
212 Michael Dr.
Syosset, NY 11791
Ph: (516)921-8888   Fax: (516)921-8743
Fr: 800-645-6337

Jack Rudman. 1993. Test guide including questions and answers for students or professionals in the field who seek advancement through examination.

★4421★ Career Examination Series: Social Worker
National Learning Corp.
212 Michael Dr.
Syosset, NY 11791
Ph: (516)921-8888   Fax: (516)921-8743
Fr: 800-645-6337

Jack Rudman. A series of study guides with multiple-choice examination questions and solutions for trainees and professional social workers. Titles in the series include *Assistant Director (Child Welfare); Assistant Director of Social Services; Assistant Director (Welfare);*

Assistant Social Worker; Case Aide; Case Manager; Case Supervisor; Casework Supervisor; Case Worker; Caseworker I; Caseworker II; Caseworker Aide; Caseworker Trainee; Certified Social Worker (CSW); Commissioner of Social Services; Director of Social Services; District Director (Social Services); Medical Social Worker; Medical Social Work Assistant; Medical Social Work Coordinator; Principal Social Welfare Examiner; Psychiatric Social Worker; Psychiatric Social Work Assistant; Psychiatric Social Work Supervisor; Psychiatric Social Worker Trainee; Public Health Social Work Assistant; Senior Caseworker; Senior Medical Social Worker; Senior Psychiatric Social Worker; Senior Social Case Worker; Senior Social Services Employment Specialist; Senior Social Services Medical Assistance Specialist; Senior Social Services Program Specialist; Senior Social Welfare Examiner; Senior Social Welfare Examiner (Spanish Speaking); Senior Social Worker; Social Case Worker; Social Work Training Director; Supervising Medical Social Worker; Supervisor III (Social Service); Supervisor (Social Work); Welfare Management System Coordinator; Welfare Representative; Welfare Resources Supervisor; Workers' Compensation Social Worker I; Workers' Compensation Social Worker II.

★4422★ Career Examination Series: Supervisor (Medical and Psychiatric Social Work)
National Learning Corp.
212 Michael Dr.
Syosset, NY 11791
Ph: (516)921-8888   Fax: (516)921-8743
Fr: 800-645-6337

Jack Rudman. 1993. Test guide including questions and answers for students or professionals in the field who seek advancement through examination.

★4423★ Certified Professional Social Worker (CPSW)
National Learning Corp.
212 Michael Dr.
Syosset, NY 11791
Ph: (516)921-8888   Fax: (516)921-8743
Fr: 800-645-6337

Jack Rudman. Part of the Admission Test Series. A sample test for social workers who are seeking admission to graduate and professional schools or seeking entrance or advancement in institutional and public career service.

★4424★ School Social Worker
National Learning Corp.
212 Michael Dr.
Syosset, NY 11791
Ph: (516)921-8888   Fax: (516)921-8743
Fr: 800-645-6337

Jack Rudman. Teachers License Examination series. Study guide to the professional licensing examination for social workers. Includes multiple-choice questions with answers.

★4425★ A Study Guide for ACSW Certification
National Association of Social Workers (NASW)
7981 Eastern Ave.
Silver Spring, MD 20910
Ph: (301)565-0333

Ruth R. Middleman. Third edition, 1994. Includes bibliographical references.

EDUCATIONAL DIRECTORIES AND PROGRAMS

★4426★ Diplomate Directory
American Board of Examiners in Clinical Social Work
3 Mill Rd., Ste. 306
Wilmington, DE 19806
Ph: (302)425-5730   Fax: (302)425-5736
Robert Booth, Contact

Biennial, January of odd years; interedition supplement. Covers Approximately 15,000 board-certified clinical social workers providing advanced mental health care in the U.S. Entries include: Name, address, phone, biographical data, education, healthcare practice information. Arrangement: Geographical.

★4427★ Directory of Colleges and Universities with Accredited Social Work Degree Programs
Council on Social Work Education
1600 Duke St.
Alexandria, VA 22314
Ph: (703)683-8080   Fax: (703)683-8099
Donald W. Beless, Contact

Annual, August. Covers Approximately 550 institutions in North America with undergraduate and graduate programs in social work education accredited by the Council. Entries include: School name, program name and address, name and phone of director or dean, fax number, e-mail address, year first accredited, year of next accreditation review. Arrangement: Geographical within bachelor's and master's degree categories.

★4428★ Mental Health and Social Work Career Directory
Gale Research Inc.
835 Penobscot Bldg.
Detroit, MI 48226-4094
Ph: (313)961-2242   Fax: (313)961-6083
Fr: 800-877-GALE

Bradley J. Morgan and Joseph M. Palmisano. 1993. A directory in the Career Advisor Series that provides essays written by industry professionals; job search information on resume and cover letter preparation, networking, and the interviewing process; approximately 300 companies and organizations offering job opportunities and internships, and additional job-hunting resources.

★4429★ Summary Information on Master of Social Work Programs

Council on Social Work Education
1600 Duke St.
Alexandria, VA 22314
Ph: (703)683-8080
Todd M. Lennon, Information Services Manager

Annual, winter. Covers Over 100 colleges and universities offering Master's degree programs in social work that are accredited by the Council of Social Work Education. Entries include: Name of college or university, address, degrees offered, enrollment dates, academic time unit, fees, usual length of program, concentrations and specializations offered, work/study programs available, whether or not program offers advanced standing, practicum requirements, dual degree programs available. Arrangement: Alphabetical by school.

AWARDS, SCHOLARSHIPS, GRANTS, AND FELLOWSHIPS

★4430★ Ruth P. Brudney Award

National Mental Health Association
1021 Prince St.
Alexandria, VA 22314-2971
Ph: (703)684-7722   Fax: (703)684-5968

To recognize significant contributions made to the care and treatment of people with mental illnesses by practicing professionals in the field of social work. The nominee must hold a master's level (or higher) degree in social work, hold a professional position in an organization that provides/manages social work services to people with mental illnesses. A plaque and all expenses paid to attend the annual meeting are awarded at the Association's Annual Meeting. Established in 1986 through a gift of George Brudney in memory of his wife, Ruth, a psychiatric social worker.

★4431★ National Social Worker of the Year

National Association of Social Workers
Office of News & Media Production
National Office
7981 Eastern Ave.
Silver Spring, MD 20910

To recognize contributions on behalf of people by social workers for enlisting public support for improved social services and contributing to the public's knowledge of social work and social problems. A plaque and an expense paid trip to receive the award at the conference are presented annually. Established in 1968 in memory of Howard F. Gustafson, former President of the Association.

BASIC REFERENCE GUIDES AND HANDBOOKS

★4432★ Continuing Education for Gerontological Careers

Council on Social Work Education
1600 Duke St.
Alexandria, VA 22314
Ph: (703)683-8080

Roberta R. Greene. 1988. Includes bibliographies.

★4433★ Encyclopedia of Social Work

National Association of Social Workers (NASW)
750 1st St., NE, Ste. 700
Washington, DC 20002
Ph: (202)408-8600   Fr: 800-227-3590

Anne Minahon, editor in chief. Eighteenth edition, 1987. Contains articles on social work practice, social issues and problems, and social institutions.

★4434★ Skills for Direct Practice in Social Work

Columbia University Press
562 W. 113th St.
New York, NY 10025
Ph: (212)666-1000   Fr: 800-944-8648

Ruth R. Middleman. 1990.

★4435★ The Social Work Dictionary

National Association of Social Workers (NASW)
750 1st St., NE
Washington, DC 20002
Ph: (202)408-8600   Fr: 800-752-3590

Robert L. Barker. Second edition, 1991. Defines common terms in social work and related fields.

★4436★ Social Work Practice: A Generalist Approach

Allyn & Bacon, Inc.
160 Gould St.
Needham Heights, MA 02194-2310
Ph: (617)455-1200   Fr: 800-278-3525

Louise C. Johnson. Fourth edition, 1992. Introductory text written for the social worker. Presents current and historical literature. Covers human development, human diversity, and social systems theory.

★4437★ Social Work Speaks; NASW Policy Statements

National Association of Social Workers (NASW)
7981 Eastern Ave.
Silver Spring, MD 20910
Ph: (301)565-0333   Fr: 800-752-3590

Third edition, 1994.

★4438★ Supervision in the Helping Professions

Taylor & Francis, Inc.
1990 Frost Rd., Ste. 101
Bristol, PA 19007-1598
Ph: (215)785-5800   Fax: (215)785-5515

Peter Hawkins. 1989.

PROFESSIONAL AND TRADE PERIODICALS

★4439★ AssemblyLine

National Assembly of National Voluntary Health & Social Welfare Organizations, Inc.
1319 F St. NW, Ste. 601
Washington, DC 20004
Ph: (202)347-2080   Fax: (202)393-4517
Kim Pawley Helfgott

Semiannual. Attempts to foster intercommunication and interaction among national voluntary health and social welfare agencies. Discusses topics relating to the impact of voluntarism on human needs, especially in regard to individual health and social welfare agencies. Recurring features include news of research, legislation, resources and funding.

★4440★ Child and Adolescent Social Work Journal

Human Sciences Press
233 Spring St.
New York, NY 10013
Ph: (212)620-8000   Fax: (212)463-0742
Florence Lieberman

Bimonthly. Journal covering social work with children.

★4441★ Families in Society

Families International, Inc.
11700 W. Lake Park Drive
Milwaukee, WI 53224
Ph: (414)359-1040   Fax: (414)359-1074
Ralph J. Burant

Refereed journal for human service professionals.

★4442★ Public Assistance Funding Report

CD Publications
8204 Fenton St.
Silver Spring, MD 20910
Ph: (301)588-6380   Fax: (301)588-6385
Fr: 800-666-6380
Aaron Liebel

Semimonthly. Provides advice on how to create effective job training, housing, and employment programs.

★4443★ Public Welfare

American Public Welfare Assn.
810 1st St. NE, Ste. 500
Washington, DC 20002-4267
Ph: (202)682-0100   Fax: (202)289-6555
Bill Detweiler

Quarterly. Magazine examining public welfare and welfare programs.

★4444★ Social Work

National Association of Social Workers
750 1st St. NE, Ste. 700
Washington, DC 20002-4241
Ph: (202)408-8600   Fax: (202)336-8312
Nancy Winchester

Bimonthly. Magazine for social workers.

PROFESSIONAL MEETINGS AND CONVENTIONS

★4445★ National Association of Black Social Workers Convention
National Association of Black Social Workers
15321 W. McNichols
Detroit, MI 48235
Ph: (313)836-0210
Annual. Always held during April.

★4446★ Showcase for Commitment to Equal Opportunity
National Urban League
500 E. 62nd St.
New York, NY 10021
Ph: (212)310-9000
Annual. Usually held during July.

OTHER SOURCES OF INFORMATION

★4447★ Introduction to Social Work and Social Welfare
Brooks/Cole Publishing Co.
511 Forest Lodge Rd.
Pacific Grove, CA 93950-5098
Ph: (408)373-0728   Fax: (408)375-6414
1993.

★4448★ "Social Work" in Accounting to Zoology: Graduate Fields Defined (pp. 189-190)
Petersons Guides, Inc.
PO Box 2123
Princeton, NJ 08543-2123
Ph: (609)243-9111   Fax: (609)243-9150
Fr: 800-338-3282
Amy J. Goldstein, editor. Revised and updated, 1987. Defines 298 graduate and professional fields. Discusses types of graduate programs and degrees, graduate research, applied work, employment prospects, and trends.

★4449★ "Social Worker" in 100 Best Jobs for the 1990s & Beyond
Dearborn Financial Publishing, Inc.
520 N. Dearborn St.
Chicago, IL 60610-4354
Ph: (312)836-4400   Fax: (312)836-1021
Fr: 800-621-9621

Carol Kleiman. 1992. Describes 100 jobs ranging from accountants to veterinarians. Each job profile includes such information as education, experience, and certification needed, salaries, and job search suggestions.

Protestant Ministers

Protestant ministers lead their congregations in worship services and administer the various rites of the church, such as baptism, confirmation, and Holy Communion. They prepare and deliver sermons and give religious instruction. They also perform marriages; conduct funerals; counsel individuals who seek guidance; visit the sick, aged, and handicapped at home and in the hospital; comfort the bereaved; and serve church members in other ways. Many Protestant ministers write articles for publication, give speeches, and engage in interfaith, community, civic, educational, and recreational activities sponsored by or related to the interests of the church. Some ministers teach in seminaries, colleges and universities, and church-affiliated preparatory or high schools.

Salaries

Salaries of Protestant clergy vary substantially depending on age, experience, denomination, size and wealth of congregation, and geographic location.

Protestant ministers	$27,000/year
Average including fringes such as housing, insurance and transportation	$44,000/year

Employment Outlook

Growth rate until the year 2005: Slower than the average.

Protestant Ministers

CAREER GUIDES

★4450★ *Careers for Women as Clergy*
Rosen Publishing Group
29 E. 21st St.
New York, NY 10010
Ph: (212)777-3017   Fax: (212)777-0277
Fr: 800-237-9932
Rev. Julie Parker. 1993. Overviews the possibilities available to women in the ministry. Discusses hearing one's "calling" and finding a role model.

★4451★ "Clergy" in *College Board Guide to Jobs and Career Planning* (pp. 305)
The College Board
45 Columbus Ave.
New York, NY 10023-6992
Ph: (212)713-8165   Fax: (212)713-8143
Fr: 800-323-7155
Second edition, 1994. Describes the job, salaries, related careers, education needed, and where to write for more information.

★4452★ *Clergy, Protestant*
Careers, Inc.
PO Box 135
Largo, FL 34649-0135
Ph: (813)584-7333
1993. Four-page brief offering the definition, history, duties, working conditions, personal qualifications, educational requirements, earnings, hours, employment outlook, advancement, and careers related to this position.

★4453★ "Minister (Protestant)" in *VGM's Careers Encyclopedia* (pp. 288-289)
National Textbook Co. (NTC)
VGM Career Books
4255 W. Touhy Ave.
Lincolnwood, IL 60646-1975
Ph: (708)679-5500   Fax: (708)679-2494
Fr: 800-323-4900
Third edition, 1991. Profiles 200 occupations. Describes job duties, places of employment, working conditions, qualifications, education and training, advancement potential, and salary for each occupation.

★4454★ "Protestant Minister" in *Jobs! What They Are—Where They Are— What They Pay* (p. 68)
Simon & Schuster, Inc.
Simon & Schuster Bldg.
1230 Avenue of the Americas
New York, NY 10020
Ph: (212)698-7000   Fr: 800-223-2348
Robert O. Snelling and Anne M. Snelling. 3rd edition, 1992. Describes duties and responsibilities, earnings, employment opportunities, training, and qualifications.

★4455★ "Protestant Ministers" in *Career Discovery Encyclopedia* (Vol.5, pp. 96-97)
J.G. Ferguson Publishing Co.
200 W. Madison St., Ste. 300
Chicago, IL 60606
Ph: (312)580-5480   Fax: (312)580-4948
Russell E. Primm, editor-in chief. 1993. This six volume set contains two-page articles for 504 occupations. Each article describes job duties, earnings, and educational and training requirements. The whole set is arranged alphabetically by job title. Designed for junior high and older students.

★4456★ "Protestant Ministers" in *Encyclopedia of Careers and Vocational Guidance* (Vol.4, pp. 181-183)
J.G. Ferguson Publishing Co.
200 W. Madison St., Ste. 300
Chicago, IL 60606
Ph: (312)580-5480   Fax: (312)580-4948
William E. Hopke, editor-in-chief. Ninth edition, 1993. Four-volume set that profiles 900 occupations and describes job trends in 74 industries. Includes career description, educational requirements, history of the job, methods of entry, advancement, employment outlook, earnings, conditions of work, social and psychological factors, and sources of further information.

★4457★ "Protestant Ministers" in *Occupational Outlook Handbook*
U.S. Government Printing Office
Superintendent of Documents
Washington, DC 20402
Ph: (202)512-1800   Fax: (202)512-2250
Biennial; latest edition, 1994-95. Encyclopedia of careers describing about 250 occupations and comprising about 85 percent of all jobs in the economy. Occupations that require lengthy education or training are given the most attention. Each occupation's profile describes what the worker does on the job, working conditions, education and training requirements, advancement possibilities, job outlook, earnings, and sources of additional information.

★4458★ "Religious Ministries" in *Encyclopedia of Careers and Vocational Guidance* (Vol.1, pp.418-425)
J.G. Ferguson Publishing Co.
200 W. Madison St., Ste. 300
Chicago, IL 60606
Ph: (312)580-5480   Fax: (312)580-4948
William E. Hopke, editor-in-chief. Ninth edition, 1993. Four-volume set that profiles 900 occupations and describes job trends in 74 industries. Includes career description, educational requirements, history of the job, methods of entry, advancement, employment outlook, earnings, conditions of work, social and psychological factors, and sources of further information.

PROFESSIONAL ASSOCIATIONS

★4459★ National Council of the Churches of Christ in the U.S.A. (NCC)
475 Riverside Dr.
New York, NY 10115
Ph: (212)870-2227
Members: An agency of 32 Protestant, Anglican, and Orthodox denominations comprising 49,000,000 members, that was formed in 1950 by the action of 29 denominations and by merger of 12 interdenominational agencies. **Purpose:** To serve as a community of its constituent communions in manifesting oneness in Jesus Christ as Divine Lord and Savior and to do together those things which can better be done united than separated. Programs include: publishing materials for religious education; providing disaster relief, refugee assistance, and development aid to people throughout the world in cooperation with overseas churches; coordinating the placement of refugees in U.S. communities;

promoting the use of the New Revised Standard Version of the Bible; strengthening and enriching family life; promoting peace and justice, interfaith activites, and theological dialogue; providing resources in areas such as education for mission and communication, educating and advocating for racial justice, religious liberty, women and childrens's issues and the environment. **Publications:** *Ecu-Link.* • *Yearbook of American and Canadian Churches.*

EDUCATIONAL DIRECTORIES AND PROGRAMS

★4460★ *Accrediting Association of Bible Colleges—Directory*
Accrediting Association of Bible Colleges
Box 1523
Fayetteville, AR 72702
Ph: (501)521-8164   Fax: (501)521-9202
Joniva Mondragon

Annual, spring and summer. Covers over 105 colleges accredited or under consideration by the association. Entries include: Institution name, street and mailing address, phone, fax, toll-free phone; year accredited; years of last and next evaluations; denominational affiliation; degrees, diplomas, and certificates offered; majors; availability of correspondence and extension offerings ; names and titles of administrators; FTE undergraduate enrollment. Arrangement: Classified by type of accreditation.

AWARDS, SCHOLARSHIPS, GRANTS, AND FELLOWSHIPS

★4461★ **Rosa O. Hall Award**
American Baptist Churches in the U.S.A.
National Ministries
c/o American Baptist Historical Society
1106 S. Goodman St.
Rochester, NY 14620
Ph: (716)473-1740

To recognize a minister in a town and country church for outstanding leadership in the church, the community, and the wider Christian fellowship. A rural American Baptist minister is eligible. A monetary award and an engraved plaque are presented at each Biennial Convention of the American Baptist Churches. Established in 1932.

★4462★ **Minister of the Year**
International Evangelism Crusades
14617 Victory Blvd., Ste. 4
Van Nuys, CA 91411
Ph: (818)989-5942   Fax: (818)989-5942
To honor a minister who has distinguished himself with outstanding service to God and mankind. A certificate is awarded annually. Established in 1980.

★4463★ **Outstanding Institutional Chaplain**
American Baptist Churches in the U.S.A.
National Ministries
c/o American Baptist Historical Society
1106 S. Goodman St.
Rochester, NY 14620
Ph: (716)473-1740

To give recognition to an American Baptist-endorsed institutional chaplain currently working on a full-time basis for outstanding contributions at the local, state, and national levels. A monetary award and plaque are presented at each Biennial Convention of the American Baptist Churches. Established in 1963.

★4464★ **Outstanding Military Chaplain**
American Baptist Churches in the U.S.A.
National Ministries
c/o American Baptist Historical Society
1106 S. Goodman St.
Rochester, NY 14620
Ph: (716)473-1740

To give recognition to an American Baptist endorsed military chaplain currently serving on active duty for outstanding contributions at the local, state and national levels. A monetary award and plaque are presented at each Biennial Convention of the American Baptist Churches. Established in 1962.

★4465★ **Outstanding Pastoral Counselor**
American Baptist Churches in the U.S.A.
National Ministries
c/o American Baptist Historical Society
1106 S. Goodman St.
Rochester, NY 14620
Ph: (716)473-1740

To give recognition to an American Baptist endorsed pastoral counselor currently working on a full-time basis for outstanding contributions at the local, state and national levels. A monetary award and plaque are presented at each Biennial Convention of the American Baptist Churches. Established in 1987.

★4466★ **Edward H. Rhoades Award**
American Baptist Churches in the U.S.A.
National Ministries
c/o American Baptist Historical Society
1106 S. Goodman St.
Rochester, NY 14620
Ph: (716)473-1740

To given recognition of a minister in an urban American Baptist church for outstanding leadership in the church, the denomination, the community, and the wider Christian fellowships. A monetary prize and an engraved plaque are awarded biennially. Established in 1962.

BASIC REFERENCE GUIDES AND HANDBOOKS

★4467★ *Eerdman's Handbook to the Bible*
William B. Eerdmans Publishing Co.
255 Jefferson Ave., S.E.
Grand Rapids, MI 49503
Ph: (616)459-4591   Fr: 800-253-7521
David Alexander and Pat Alexander, editors. Sixth edition, 1992.

PROFESSIONAL AND TRADE PERIODICALS

★4468★ *Diakoneo*
North American Association for the Diaconate
PO Box 750156
New Orleans, LA 70175-0156
Ph: (504)895-0058
Ormonde Plater

Promotes the diaconate and diaconal ministry. Aims to enlarge an ecumenical understanding of the ministry of deacons as distinctively oriented toward service. Supplies general news for deacons in the Episcopal Church and Anglican Church of Canada.

★4469★ *Episcopal Peace Fellowship— Newsletter*
Episcopal Peace Fellowship
Box 28156
Washington, DC 20038-8156
Ph: (202)783-3380
Patricia K. Scharf

Quarterly. Promotes the aims of the Fellowship, a "body of Christians, committed to abolishing the causes of war, poverty, hunger, alienation, and economic, social and sexual oppression in their own communities, nation and world." Provides information on peace and justice issues and activities, book reviews, and a calendar of events.

★4470★ *The Noel News*
National Organization of Episcopalians for Life
10523 Main St.
Fairfax, VA 22030
Ph: (703)591-6635
Laurie C. Wieder

Quarterly. Focuses on issues concerning the protection of human life in accordance with the teachings of Scripture. Promotes alternatives to abortion through discussion of religious, ethical, and scientific perspectives. Recurring features include information on the Organization's educational programs and other activities, news of members, and a calendar of events.

★4471★ Views on Education & News of Episcopal Colleges
Association of Episcopal Colleges
815 Second Ave., Ste. 315
New York, NY 10017-4594
Ph: (212)986-0989   Fax: (212)986-5039
Fr: 800-334-7626
John C. Powers

Semiannual. Provides Episcopal church-related colleges and church leaders with news concerning the twelve member colleges. Carries items on educational programs, faculty and student exchanges, scholarships, and conferences. Recurring features include news of members, news of Association-sponsored programs and activities, and a calendar of events.

PROFESSIONAL MEETINGS AND CONVENTIONS

★4472★ American Academy of Religion/ Society of Biblical Literature Annual Meeting
Scholars Press
PO Box 15399
Atlanta, GA 30333-0399
Ph: (404)727-2343   Fax: (404)727-2348

Annual. Always held in November. **Dates and Locations:** 1995 Nov 18-21; Philadelphia, PA.

★4473★ Society for the Scientific Study of Religion Annual Meeting
Society for the Scientific Study of Religion
Pierce Hall, Rm. 193
Purdue University
West Lafayette, IN 47907-1305
Ph: (317)494-6286

Annual.

OTHER SOURCES OF INFORMATION

★4474★ "Pastoral Ministry and Counseling" in Accounting to Zoology: Graduate Fields Defined (pp. 166-167)
Petersons Guides, Inc.
PO Box 2123
Princeton, NJ 08543-2123
Ph: (609)243-9111   Fax: (609)243-9150
Fr: 800-338-3282

Amy J. Goldstein, editor. Revised and updated, 1987. Defines 298 graduate and professional fields. Discusses types of graduate programs and degrees, graduate research, applied work, employment prospects, and trends.

★4475★ Yearbook of American and Canadian Churches
Abingdon Press
201 8th Ave., S.
PO Box 801
Nashville, TN 37203
Ph: (615)749-6290   Fr: 800-251-3320

Kenneth Bedell, editor. Annual.

Rabbis

Rabbis are the spiritual leaders of their congregations, and teachers and interpreters of Jewish law and tradition. They conduct religious services and deliver sermons on the Sabbath and on Jewish holidays. Like other clergy, rabbis conduct weddings and funeral services, visit the sick, help the poor, comfort the bereaved, supervise religious education programs, engage in interfaith activities, and involve themselves in community affairs. Rabbis serve either Orthodox, Conservative, Reform, or Reconstructionist congregations. Rabbis also may write for religious and lay publications and teach in theological seminaries, colleges, and universities.

Salaries

Income varies widely, depending on the size and financial status of the congregation, as well as its denominational branch and geographic location.

Rabbis $38,000-$60,000/year

Employment Outlook

Growth rate until the year 2005: Faster than the average.

Rabbis

CAREER GUIDES

★4476★ "Clergy" in *College Board Guide to Jobs and Career Planning* (pp. 305)
The College Board
45 Columbus Ave.
New York, NY 10023-6992
Ph: (212)713-8165   Fax: (212)713-8143
Fr: 800-323-7155

Second edition, 1994. Describes the job, salaries, related careers, education needed, and where to write for more information.

★4477★ *Rabbi*
Vocational Biographies, Inc.
PO Box 31
Sauk Centre, MN 56378-0031
Ph: (612)352-6516   Fax: (612)352-5546
Fr: 800-255-0752

1993. Four-page pamphlet containing a personal narrative about a worker's job, work likes and dislikes, career path from high school to the present, education and training, the rewards and frustrations, and the effects of the job on the rest of the worker's life. The data file portion of this pamphlet gives a concise occupational summary, including work description, working conditions, places of employment, personal characteristics, education and training, job outlook, and salary range.

★4478★ *Rabbi*
Careers, Inc.
PO Box 135
Largo, FL 34649-0135
Ph: (813)584-7333

1991. Four-page brief offering the definition, history, duties, working conditions, personal qualifications, educational requirements, earnings, hours, employment outlook, advancement, and careers related to this position.

★4479★ "Rabbi" in *VGM's Careers Encyclopedia* (pp. 387-389)
National Textbook Co. (NTC)
VGM Career Books
4255 W. Touhy Ave.
Lincolnwood, IL 60646-1975
Ph: (708)679-5500   Fax: (708)679-2494
Fr: 800-323-4900

Third edition, 1991. Profiles 200 occupations. Describes job duties, places of employment, working conditions, qualifications, education and training, advancement potential, and salary for each occupation.

★4480★ *Rabbinate As Calling & Vocation: Models of Rabbinic Leadership*
Jason Aronson, Inc.
230 Livingston St.
Northvale, NJ 07647
Ph: (201)767-4093   Fax: (201)767-4330

Basil Herring and Robert S. Hirt, Rabbi Isacc Elchanan Theological Seminary. 1991.

★4481★ *Rabbis*
Chronicle Guidance Publications, Inc.
66 Aurora St.
PO Box 1190
Moravia, NY 13118-1190
Ph: (315)497-0330   Fax: (315)497-3359
Fr: 800-622-7284

1994. Career brief describing the nature of the job, working conditions, h ours and earnings, education and training, licensure, certification, unions, personal qualifications, social and psychological factors, location, employment outlook, entry methods, advancement, and related occupations.

★4482★ "Rabbis" in *Career Discovery Encyclopedia* (Vol.5, pp. 118-119)
J.G. Ferguson Publishing Co.
200 W. Madison St., Ste. 300
Chicago, IL 60606
Ph: (312)580-5480   Fax: (312)580-4948
Russell E. Primm, editor-in chief. 1993. This six volume set contains two-page articles for 504 occupations. Each article describes job duties, earnings, and educational and training requirements. The whole set is arranged alphabetically by job title. Designed for junior high and older students.

★4483★ "Rabbis" in *Encyclopedia of Careers and Vocational Guidance* (Vol.4, pp. 216-219)
J.G. Ferguson Publishing Co.
200 W. Madison St., Ste. 300
Chicago, IL 60606
Ph: (312)580-5480   Fax: (312)580-4948

William E. Hopke, editor-in-chief. Ninth edition, 1993. Four-volume set that profiles 900 occupations and describes job trends in 74 industries. Includes career description, educational requirements, history of the job, methods of entry, advancement, employment outlook, earnings, conditions of work, social and psychological factors, and sources of further information.

★4484★ "Rabbis" in *Jobs! What They Are—Where They Are—What They Pay* (p. 70)
Simon & Schuster, Inc.
Simon & Schuster Bldg.
1230 Avenue of the Americas
New York, NY 10020
Ph: (212)698-7000   Fr: 800-223-2348

Robert O. Snelling and Anne M. Snelling. 3rd edition, 1992. Describes duties and responsibilities, earnings, employment opportunities, training, and qualifications.

★4485★ "Rabbis" in *Occupational Outlook Handbook*
U.S. Government Printing Office
Superintendent of Documents
Washington, DC 20402
Ph: (202)512-1800   Fax: (202)512-2250

Biennial; latest edition, 1994-95. Encyclopedia of careers describing about 250 occupations and comprising about 85 percent of all jobs in the economy. Occupations that require lengthy education or training are given the most attention. Each occupation's profile describes what the worker does on the job, working conditions, education and training requirements, advancement possibilities, job outlook, earnings, and sources of additional information.

★4486★ "Religious Ministries" in Encyclopedia of Careers and Vocational Guidance (Vol.1, pp.418-425)
J.G. Ferguson Publishing Co.
200 W. Madison St., Ste. 300
Chicago, IL 60606
Ph: (312)580-5480   Fax: (312)580-4948
William E. Hopke, editor-in-chief. Ninth edition, 1993. Four-volume set that profiles 900 occupations and describes job trends in 74 industries. Includes career description, educational requirements, history of the job, methods of entry, advancement, employment outlook, earnings, conditions of work, social and psychological factors, and sources of further information.

PROFESSIONAL ASSOCIATIONS

★4487★ Central Conference of American Rabbis (CCAR)
192 Lexington Ave.
New York, NY 10016
Ph: (212)684-4990   Fax: (212)689-1649
Members: National organization of Reform rabbis. Offers placement service; compiles statistics. Maintains 38 committees. **Publications:** *CCAR Journal*, quarterly.

★4488★ Federation of Reconstructionist Congregations and Havurot (FRCH)
Church Rd. & Greenwood Ave.
Wyncote, PA 19095
Ph: (215)887-1988   Fax: (215)887-5348
Members: Federation of synagogues and fellowships committed to the philosophy and program of the Jewish Reconstructionist Movement. **Purpose:** Coordinates rabbinical and educational training. Maintains placement service and speakers' bureau. **Publications:** *Reconstructionism Today*, quarterly. • *The Reconstructionist*, semiannual.

★4489★ Rabbinical Alliance of America (RAA)
3 W. 16th St., 4th Fl.
New York, NY 10011
Ph: (212)242-6420   Fax: (212)255-8313
Members: Orthodox rabbis who serve in pulpits and as principals of Jewish day schools and Hebrew schools throughout the world. **Purpose:** Supervises Hebrew Schools Program for Adult Studies. Provides placement service aid for indigent Torah scholars; contributes to Jewish charitable causes. Maintains the Rabbinical Court which handles orthodox Jewish divorces, court of arbitration, Dinei Torahs, and family and marriage counselling. **Publications:** *Perspective*, annual. • *Rabbinic Registry*, biennial. • *Sermon Manual*, biennial. • *Torah Message*, biennial.

★4490★ Rabbinical Assembly (RA)
3080 Broadway
New York, NY 10027
Ph: (212)678-8060   Fax: (212)749-9166
Members: Rabbis serving Conservative Jewish congregations; chaplains in the Armed Forces and in educational or communal organizations. **Purpose:** To promote Conservative Judaism; to cooperate with the Jewish Theological Seminary of America; to advance the cause of Jewish learning; to promote the welfare of the members; and to foster the spirit of fellowship and cooperation among the rabbis and other Jewish scholars. Offers placement service. **Publications:** *Bond of Life*. • *Conservative Judaism*, quarterly. • *Conservative Judaism and Jewish Law*. • *Embracing Judaism*. • *God in the Teachings of Conservative Judaism*. • *Mahzor for Rosh Hashanah and Yom Kippur*. • *Passover Haggadah*. • *RA Newsletter*. • *Rabbinical Assembly Membership List*. • *Selichot Service*. • *Siddur Sim Shalom*. • *Understanding Conservative Judaism*. • *Weekday Prayer Book*.

★4491★ Rabbinical Council of America (RCA)
305 7th Ave.
New York, NY 10001
Ph: (212)807-7888   Fax: (212)727-8452
Members: Ordained Orthodox Jewish rabbis. **Purpose:** Promotes the widespread study of Torah and the fuller observance of traditional Judaism. Sponsors Yeshivath Hadorom in Rehovoth, Israel and Yeshivat Achuzat Yaakov in Gan Yavne, Israel (schools). **Publications:** *Hadorom*, annual. • *Rabbinic Registry*. • *Record*, quarterly. • *Sermon Manual*, annual. • *Tradition*, quarterly.

★4492★ World Union for Progressive Judaism (WUPJ)
838 5th Ave.
New York, NY 10021
Ph: (212)249-0100   Fax: (212)517-3940
Members: Congregations of Reform, Liberal, and Progressive Jews in 29 countries. **Purpose:** Promotes the cause of Progressive Judaism; establishes new congregations and national constituencies; arranges for the training of rabbis and teachers; coordinates activity between constituencies. Represents progressive Jewry at the United Nations and United Nations Educational, Scientific and Cultural Organization (see separate entries). **Publications:** *International Conference Reports*, biennial.

EDUCATIONAL DIRECTORIES AND PROGRAMS

★4493★ Guide to Schools and Departments of Religion and Seminaries in the U.S. and Canada
Macmillan Publishing Co.
100 Front St.
Riverside, NJ 08075
Ph: (609)461-6500   Fax: 800-562-1272
Fr: 800-257-5755
Lists 700 colleges and institutions offering degrees in theology, divinity, and religion.

AWARDS, SCHOLARSHIPS, GRANTS, AND FELLOWSHIPS

★4494★ Hurowitz Award
United Jewish Appeal - Federation of Jewish Philanthropies of New York
130 E. 59th St.
New York, NY 10022
Ph: (212)980-1000

To recognize outstanding cooperative programming involving social work and the religious community. Rabbis and professional social workers who have initiated and implemented major programs involving cooperation and new dimensions of communal relationships are eligible. Citations are awarded annually. Established in 1950.

BASIC REFERENCE GUIDES AND HANDBOOKS

★4495★ Encyclopaedia Judaica
Macmillan Publishing Co., Inc.
866 3rd Ave.
New York, NY 10022
Ph: (212)702-2000   Fr: 800-257-5755

1972. This sixteen-volume set contains 25,000 signed articles on world Jewry. Includes a bibliography and an index.

★4496★ An Encyclopedia of Jewish Concepts
Hebrew Publishing Co.
PO Box 930157
Rockaway Beach, NY 11693
Ph: (718)945-3000

Philip Birnbaum. Revised edition, 1988. Hebrew terms are arranged alphabetically followed by the English term. Definitions range in length from a paragraph to several pages.

★4497★ The New Standard Jewish Encyclopedia
Facts on File
460 Park Ave. S.
New York, NY 10016-7382
Ph: (212)683-2244   Fax: 800-678-3633
Fr: 800-322-8755

Geoffrey Wigoder. Seventh edition, 1992. Covers current Jewish history and recent events in the American Jewish community and in Israel.

PROFESSIONAL AND TRADE PERIODICALS

★4498★ AJC Journal
Institute of Human Relations
165 E. 56th St.
New York, NY 10022
Ph: (212)751-4000
Murray Polner

Quarterly. Covers Jewish events worldwide and news of the American Jewish Committee, whose aim is to protect religious and civil rights, to combat bigotry, and to defend pluralism. Recurring features include editorials and news of research.

★4499★ Association for Jewish Studies—Newsletter
Association for Jewish Studies
University of Maryland
0113 Woods Hall
College Park, MD 20742
Ph: (301)405-4975
Lawrence Fine

Provides information in the field of Jewish Studies and news of the activities of the Association.

★4500★ Nashreeye B'nei Torah
Iranian B'nei Torah Movement
PO Box 351476
Los Angeles, CA 90035
Ph: (310)652-2115   Fax: (310)652-6979
Rabbi Joseph Zargari

Bimonthly. Carries articles on Jewish history, tradition, and culture for Iranian Jews. Tells of the association's work to meet the religious, charitable, and educational needs of Iranian Jews in the U.S. Recurring features include letters to the editor, interviews, notices of publications available, and a calendar of events.

★4501★ Options: The Jewish Resources Newsletter
Options Publishing Company
PO Box 311
Wayne, NJ 07474-0311
Ph: (201)694-2327
Betty J. Singer

Monthly. Describes the variety of resources for American Jewish life, including organizations, cultural activities, political movements, religious variations, publications, and teaching aids. Includes the contact name and address for obtaining information on a particular resource.

Roman Catholic Priests

Roman Catholic priests attend to the spiritual, pastoral, moral, and educational needs of the members of their church. They deliver sermons, administer the sacraments, and preside at liturgical functions such as funeral services. They also comfort the sick, console and counsel those in need of guidance, and assist the poor. In recent years, some priests have paid increasing attention to nonliturgical concerns such as human rights and social welfare. The two main classifications of priests, diocesan (secular) and religious, have the same powers, acquired through ordination by a bishop. The differences lie in their way of life, their type of work, and the church authority to whom they are immediately subject. **Diocesan priests** generally work in parishes assigned by the bishop of their diocese. **Religious priests** generally work as part of a religious order, such as the Jesuits, Dominicans, or Franciscans. They may engage in specialized activities, such as teaching or missionary work, assigned by superiors of their order.

Salaries

Diocesan priests' salaries vary by diocese. Religious priests take a vow of poverty and are supported by their religious order.

Diocesan priests	$9,000/year

Employment Outlook

Growth rate until the year 2005: Much faster than the average.

Roman Catholic Priests

CAREER GUIDES

★4502★ "Clergy" in College Board Guide to Jobs and Career Planning (pp. 305)
The College Board
45 Columbus Ave.
New York, NY 10023-6992
Ph: (212)713-8165   Fax: (212)713-8143
Fr: 800-323-7155
Second edition, 1994. Describes the job, salaries, related careers, education needed, and where to write for more information.

★4503★ A Guide to Religious Ministries for Catholic Men and Women
Catholic News Publishing Co.
210 North Ave.
New Rochelle, NY 10801
Ph: (914)632-1220   Fax: (914)632-3412
Annual. Latest edition 1995. Directory of religious orders.

★4504★ Priest, Roman Catholic
Careers, Inc.
PO Box 135
Largo, FL 34649-0135
Ph: (813)584-7333
1994. Four-page brief offering the definition, history, duties, working conditions, personal qualifications, educational requirements, earnings, hours, employment outlook, advancement, and careers related to this position.

★4505★ "Priest" in VGM's Careers Encyclopedia (pp. 366-368)
National Textbook Co. (NTC)
VGM Career Books
4255 W. Touhy Ave.
Lincolnwood, IL 60646-1975
Ph: (708)679-5500   Fax: (708)679-2494
Fr: 800-323-4900
Third edition, 1991. Profiles 200 occupations. Describes job duties, places of employment, working conditions, qualifications, education and training, advancement potential, and salary for each occupation.

★4506★ "Religious Ministries" in Encyclopedia of Careers and Vocational Guidance (Vol.1, pp.418-425)
J.G. Ferguson Publishing Co.
200 W. Madison St., Ste. 300
Chicago, IL 60606
Ph: (312)580-5480   Fax: (312)580-4948
William E. Hopke, editor-in-chief. Ninth edition, 1993. Four-volume set that profiles 900 occupations and describes job trends in 74 industries. Includes career description, educational requirements, history of the job, methods of entry, advancement, employment outlook, earnings, conditions of work, social and psychological factors, and sources of further information.

★4507★ Roman Catholic Priest
Vocational Biographies, Inc.
PO Box 31
Sauk Centre, MN 56378-0031
Ph: (612)352-6516   Fax: (612)352-5546
Fr: 800-255-0752
1995. Four-page pamphlet containing a personal narrative about a worker's job, work likes and dislikes, career path from high school to the present. Education and training, the rewards and frustrations, and the effects of the job on the rest of the worker's life. The data file portion of this pamphlet gives a concise occupational summary, including work descriptions, working conditions, places of employment, personal characteristics, education and training, job outlook, and salary range.

★4508★ Roman Catholic Priests
Chronicle Guidance Publications, Inc.
66 Aurora St.
PO Box 1190
Moravia, NY 13118-1190
Ph: (315)497-0330   Fax: (315)497-3359
Fr: 800-622-7284
1993. Career brief describing the nature of the job, working conditions, hours and earnings, education and training, licensure, certification, unions, personal qualifications, social and psychological factors, location, employment outlook, entry methods, advancement, and related occupations.

★4509★ "Roman Catholic Priests" in Career Discovery Encyclopedia (Vol.5, pp. 160-161)
J.G. Ferguson Publishing Co.
200 W. Madison St., Ste. 300
Chicago, IL 60606
Ph: (312)580-5480   Fax: (312)580-4948
Russell E. Primm, editor-in chief. 1993. This six volume set contains two-page articles for 504 occupations. Each article describes job duties, earnings, and educational and training requirements. The whole set is arranged alphabetically by job title. Designed for junior high and older students.

★4510★ "Roman Catholic Priests" in Encyclopedia of Careers and Vocational Guidance (Vol.4, pp. 308-311)
J.G. Ferguson Publishing Co.
200 W. Madison St., Ste. 300
Chicago, IL 60606
Ph: (312)580-5480   Fax: (312)580-4948
William E. Hopke, editor-in-chief. Ninth edition, 1993. Four-volume set that profiles 900 occupations and describes job trends in 74 industries. Includes career description, educational requirements, history of the job, methods of entry, advancement, employment outlook, earnings, conditions of work, social and psychological factors, and sources of further information.

★4511★ "Roman Catholic Priests" in Jobs! What They Are—Where They Are—What They Pay (p. 71)
Simon & Schuster, Inc.
Simon & Schuster Bldg.
1230 Avenue of the Americas
New York, NY 10020
Ph: (212)698-7000   Fr: 800-223-2348
Robert O. Snelling and Anne M. Snelling. 3rd edition, 1992. Describes duties and responsibilities, earnings, employment opportunities, training, and qualifications.

★4512★ "Roman Catholic Priests" in Occupational Outlook Handbook
U.S. Government Printing Office
Superintendent of Documents
Washington, DC 20402
Ph: (202)512-1800   Fax: (202)512-2250
Biennial; latest edition, 1994-95. Encyclopedia of careers describing about 250 occupations and comprising about 85 percent of all

jobs in the economy. Occupations that require lengthy education or training are given the most attention. Each occupation's profile describes what the worker does on the job, working conditions, education and training requirements, advancement possibilities, job outlook, earnings, and sources of additional information.

PROFESSIONAL ASSOCIATIONS

★4513★ Bishop's Committee on Vocations (BCV)
3211 4th St. NE
Washington, DC 20017
Ph: (202)541-3033   Fax: (202)541-3222
Members: A committee of the National Conference of Catholic Bishops. **Purpose:** Encourages and promotes religious vocations; develops policies on how to promote vocations. Conducts research and study programs. Works closely with other vocational organizations.

★4514★ Institute on Religious Life (IRL)
PO Box 41007
Chicago, IL 60641
Ph: (312)267-1195
Members: Religious communities or provinces; laity, bishops, priests, and concerned individuals. **Purpose:** Fosters better understanding and implementation of the teachings of the Magisterium of the church on religious life, especially by prayer and sacrifice, study and research, education, consultation, publicity, and communication. Conducts classes and seminars. **Publications:** *Consecrated Life*, semiannual. • *Religious Life*.

★4515★ National Black Catholic Seminarians Association (NBCSA)
780 Porter St.
Beaumont, TX 77701
Members: Black Catholic seminarians united for the growth and development of each member as a person, Christian, and potential priest or religious brother. **Purpose:** "Attempts to reflect both the heritage of the church and black people in terms of the richness of their spirituality." Stresses the importance of individual contribution and total involvement of each black seminarian to the organization. Maintains speakers' bureau and charitable programs; compiles statistics. **Publications:** *National Black Catholic Seminarians Association—Newsletter*, quarterly.

★4516★ National Conference of Diocesan Vocation Directors (NCDVD)
1603 S. Michigan Ave., No. 400
Chicago, IL 60616
Ph: (312)663-5456   Fax: (312)663-5030
Members: Diocesan vocation offices in dioceses affiliated with the National Conference of Catholic Bishops. **Purpose:** Provides communication and continuing education; represents members. **Publications:** *Directory of Diocesan Vocation Office Personnel*, annual. • *NCDVD News*, 5/year. • *Share the Wealth*, triennial.

★4517★ Serra International (SI)
65 E. Wacker Pl., No. 1210
Chicago, IL 60601-7203
Ph: (312)782-2163
Members: Catholic men's and women's clubs in 31 countries. **Purpose:** Seeks to "foster vocations to the Catholic priesthood and religious life, develop appreciation of the ministerial priesthood and of all religious vocations in the Catholic church, and to further Catholicism by encouraging its members to fulfill their Christian vocation to service." Conducts surveys and research projects. Holds seminars and leadership training meetings. Maintains speakers' bureau; sponsors competitions. **Publications:** *Club Information Roster*, annual. • *The Serran*, bimonthly. • *Vocations Activities Guide*.

★4518★ Society of St. Peter Apostle (SSPA)
366 5th Ave.
New York, NY 10001
Ph: (212)563-8700   Fax: (212)563-8725
Fr: 800-431-2222
Members: Purpose: Invites individuals to aid in the training of candidates for the Catholic priesthood in mission lands and to support the formation of men and women candidates for the religious life in the missions.

EDUCATIONAL DIRECTORIES AND PROGRAMS

★4519★ CARA Seminary Directory
Center for Applied Research in the Apostolate (CARA)
Georgetown University
3520 Prospect St. NW
Washington, DC 20057-1033
Ph: (202)687-8080   Fax: (202)687-8083
C. Joseph O'Hara

Biennial, winter. Covers about 350 Catholic seminary programs in the United States and its possessions and American seminaries abroad (Canada, Rome, Belgium). Entries include: Name, address and phone of institution, plus diocesan affiliation, names and titles of superiors, number of staff, degrees held by staff, accreditation, memberships, sponsorship, degree majors offered, cost of tuition and other expenses, certification for governmental student aid programs, and whether scholarships available. Arrangement: Geographical.

AWARDS, SCHOLARSHIPS, GRANTS, AND FELLOWSHIPS

★4520★ Emmanuel d'Alzon Medal
Augustinians of the Assumption
Assumptionist Center
330 Market St.
Brighton, MA 02135
Ph: (617)783-0400   Fax: (617)783-8030
To recognize values, qualitites, and activities that exemplify the ideals of Father Emmanuel d'Alzon, founder of the Assumptionists, in his service to church or country. A bronze medal is awarded as merited. Established in 1954 by the Assumptionists Order, Rome, Italy.

★4521★ Charles Forsyth Award
Catholic Campus Ministry Association
300 College Park
Dayton, OH 45469-2515
Ph: (513)229-4648   Fax: (513)229-4024
For recognition of a contribution to campus ministry on the local, regional, and national level and significant research or experimentation in areas related to campus ministry in such a way as to enlarge the scope and function of ministry. Members who have been campus ministers for at least five years are eligible. A plaque is awarded annually. Established in 1974 in honor of Rev. Charles Forsyth, O.S.B.

★4522★ Good Samaritan Award
American Police Hall of Fame
3801 Biscayne Blvd.
Miami, FL 33137
Ph: (305)573-0070   Fax: (305)573-9819
To recognize both law enforcement and civilians for an act of charity that aids those less fortunate, thus carrying on the biblical act of the Good Samaritan. Nominations of any person, any age, are accepted from another person or him or herself, anytime during the year. Awarded when merited.

★4523★ C. Albert Koob Award
National Catholic Educational Association
1077 30th St. NW, Ste. 100
Washington, DC 20007-3852
Ph: (202)337-6232   Fax: (202)333-6706
To recognize an outstanding contribution to Catholic education in America. Individuals, lay or religious, Catholic or non-Catholic, professional or non-professional, are eligible. The awardee is selected by the NCEA Board of Directors. An engraved plaque is awarded when merited. Established in 1968 and renamed to honor Reverend C. Albert Koob, O. Pream, a former NCEA President (1966-1974).

★4524★ Father McKenna Award
National Association of the Holy Name Society
Office of Communications
PO Box 26038
Baltimore, MD 21224
Ph: (410)276-1166
To recognize a member of the clergy for distinguished service to Holy Name. An inscribed plaque is awarded biennially. Established in 1950 to honor Father McKenna, an

early successful Dominican preacher for Holy Name in the United States.

★4525★ John Francis Meyers Award
National Catholic Educational Association
1077 30th St. NW, Ste. 100
Washington, DC 20007-3852
Ph: (202)337-6232   Fax: (202)333-6706

To recognize outstanding support of Catholic education. Institutions or individuals, lay or religious, professional or non-professional, are eligible. The awardee is selected by the NCEA Board of Directors. An engraved plaque is awarded when merited. Established in 1986 in honor of Msgr. John Francis Meyers, former NCEA President (1976-86).

★4526★ NABE Executive Officer of the Year
National Catholic Educational Association
1077 30th St. NW, Ste. 100
Washington, DC 20007-3852
Ph: (202)337-6232   Fax: (202)333-6706

To honor a currently serving executive officer, pastor or vicar to a Catholic board who demonstrates a high level of skill in and dedication to nurturing the policy process, especially by helping board members to develop the skills for making decisions in the context of a Christian community. Nominations may be made by a non-professional educator who is a member of the nominee's board. An engraved bowl is awarded at the NCEA/NABE Convention when merited. Established in 1984.

BASIC REFERENCE GUIDES AND HANDBOOKS

★4527★ The Catholic Priest as Moral Teacher & Guide
Ignatius Press
2515 Mcallister St.
San Francisco, CA 94118
Ph: (814)835-4216   Fax: (914)835-8406
Fr: 800-322-1531

Joseph C. Ratzinger, editor. 1990.

★4528★ New Catholic Encyclopedia
McGraw-Hill, Inc.
1221 Avenue of the Americas
New York, NY 10020
Ph: (212)512-2000   Fr: 800-722-4726

University of America staff editors. 1967-79. Covers the teachings, history, organization, and activities of the Roman Catholic Church. Includes information on religious, philosophical, scientific, and cultural developments affecting the Roman Catholic Church.

PROFESSIONAL AND TRADE PERIODICALS

★4529★ Eucharistic Minister
Eucharistic Minister
1155 E. Armor Blvd.
Kansas City, MO 64111
Ph: (816)531-0538   Fax: (816)931-5082
Fr: 800-444-8910
Carolyn Hoff
Monthly.

★4530★ Knight of St. John
Knights of St. John
6517 Charles Ave.
Parma, OH 44129
Ph: (216)845-0570
Salvatore La Bianca

Quarterly. Reports on activities and charitable services of the organization, an association of Catholic commanderies in Ghana, Lome, Togo, Nigeria, Trinidad, Tobago, and Panama. Recurring features include listings of members and a calendar of events.

★4531★ NRVC Newsletter
National Religious Vocation Conference (NVRC)
1603 S. Michigan, Ste. 400
Chicago, IL 60616
Ph: (312)663-5454   Fax: (312)663-5030
Patricia Knopp

Quarterly. Contains information pertaining to activities of the Conference, both regionally and nationally. Recurring features include news of meetings and a list of resources for vocation ministry.

★4532★ Religious Life
Institute on Religious Life
PO Box 41007
Chicago, IL 60641
Ph: (312)267-1195
James Downey

Covers religious life, the magisterium or teaching authority of the Catholic Church, talks by the Pope, and reflections on inspirational and religious subjects by noted writers. Serves religious communities primarily, and promotes vocations. Recurring features include profiles of religious communities, announcements of religious formation programs and theology courses, news notes, and book reviews.

★4533★ Xaverian Missions Newsletter
Xaverian Missioners of the United States
101 Summer St.
PO Box 5857
Holliston, MA 01746
Ph: (508)429-2144   Fax: (508)429-4793
Dominic Calarco

Carries reports on Xaverian foreign missions and on related subjects involving the work of this Roman Catholic order of priests. Contains correspondence from missionaries, appeals for vocations and for financial support, and news of activities on the home front.

OTHER SOURCES OF INFORMATION

★4534★ Catholic Almanac
Our Sunday Visitor Publishing
200 Noll Plaza
Huntington, IN 46750
Ph: (219)356-8400   Fr: 800-348-2440

Felician A. Foy and Rose M. Avato. Annual. Contains statistics and information on the Roman Catholic Church in the United States and around the world.

★4535★ Official Catholic Directory
Reed Reference Publishing Co.
PO Box 31
New Providence, NJ 07974
Ph: 800-521-8110   Fr: 800-323-6772

Annual. Contains statistical and institutional information about the churches, schools, and clergy of the Roman Catholic Church in the United States.

Adult and Vocational Education Teachers

Some adult and vocational education programs prepare people who have graduated or left school for occupations that do not require a college degree, such as welder, word processor, dental assistant, and cosmetologist, or help people upgrade current skills. Others offer courses not specifically intended to prepare for an occupation, such as basic education for school dropouts, cooking, dancing, exercise and physical fitness, photography, and the stock market. **Adult and vocational education teachers** may lecture in classrooms, and also give students hands-on experience, much like secondary school shop and home economics teachers. Generally, they demonstrate techniques, have students apply them, and provide criticism so students can learn from mistakes. Some instruct in basic education programs. Teachers may work with students who do not speak English; teach adults reading, writing, and mathematics up to the eighth grade level; or teach adults through a twelfth grade level in preparation for the General Educational Development Examination (GED).

Salaries

Part time adult and vocational education teachers generally earn hourly wages and do not receive benefits or pay for preparation time outside of class. Earnings for full time, salaried adult and vocational education teachers are as follows:

Lowest 10 percent	Less than $13,500/year
Median	$26,900/year
Top 10 percent	More than $49,200/year

Employment Outlook

Growth rate until the year 2005: Faster than the average.

Adult and Vocational Education Teachers

CAREER GUIDES

★4536★ "Adult Education Teacher" in College Board Guide to Jobs and Career Planning (pp. 169-170)
The College Board
45 Columbus Ave.
New York, NY 10023-6992
Ph: (212)713-8165   Fax: (212)713-8143
Fr: 800-323-7155

Second edition, 1994. Describes the job, salaries, related careers, education needed, and where to write for more information.

★4537★ "Adult Education Teachers" in Occupational Outlook Handbook
U.S. Government Printing Office
Superintendent of Documents
Washington, DC 20402
Ph: (202)512-1800   Fax: (202)512-2250

Biennial; latest edition, 1994-95. Encyclopedia of careers describing about 250 occupations and comprising about 85 percent of all jobs in the economy. Occupations that require lengthy education or training are given the most attention. Each occupation's profile describes what the worker does on the job, working conditions, education and training requirements, advancement possibilities, job outlook, earnings, and sources of additional information.

★4538★ "Adult Education Worker" in Career Information Center (Vol.11)
Simon and Schuster
200 Old Tappan Rd.
Old Tappan, NJ 07675
Fax: 800-445-6991   Fr: 800-223-2348

Richard Lidz and Linda Perrin, editorial directors. Fifth edition, 1993. This 13-volume set profiles over 600 occupations. Each occupational profile describes job duties, educational requirements, how to get the job, advancement possibilities, employment outlook, working conditions, earnings and benefits, and where to write for more information.

★4539★ "Adult and Vocational Education Teachers" in 101 Careers: A Guide to the Fastest-Growing Opportunities (pp. 154-156)
John Wiley & Sons, Inc.
605 3rd Ave.
New York, NY 10158-0012
Ph: (212)850-6645   Fax: (212)850-6088

Michael Harkavy. 1990. Describes the nature of the job, working conditions, employment growth, qualifications, personal skills, projected salaries, and where to write for more information.

★4540★ "Adult and Vocational Education Teachers" in Career Discovery Encyclopedia (Vol.1, pp. 20-21)
J.G. Ferguson Publishing Co.
200 W. Madison St., Ste. 300
Chicago, IL 60606
Ph: (312)580-5480   Fax: (312)580-4948

Russell E. Primm, editor-in chief. 1993. This six volume set contains two-page articles for 504 occupations. Each article describes job duties, earnings, and educational and training requirements. The whole set is arranged alphabetically by job title. Designed for junior high and older students.

★4541★ "Adult and Vocational Education Teachers" in Encyclopedia of Careers and Vocational Guidance (Vol.2, pp. 13-16)
J.G. Ferguson Publishing Co.
200 W. Madison St., Ste. 300
Chicago, IL 60606
Ph: (312)580-5480   Fax: (312)580-4948

William E. Hopke, editor-in-chief. Ninth edition, 1993. Four-volume set that profiles 900 occupations and describes job trends in 74 industries. Includes career description, educational requirements, history of the job, methods of entry, advancement, employment outlook, earnings, conditions of work, social and psychological factors, and sources of further information.

★4542★ ASCUS Annual: A Job Search Handbook for Educators
Association for School, College and University Staffing (ASCUS)
1600 Dodge Ave., Ste. 330
Evanston, IL 60201-3451
Ph: (708)864-1999

Annual. Includes articles on the job market, job hunting techniques, locating job vacancies, resume writing, interviewing, job offers, and contracts. Also contains information about overseas employment, and employment in higher education. Includes a list of State Teacher Certification offices.

★4543★ Career in Teaching Technology Education
International Technology Education Association
1914 Association Dr.
Reston, VA 22091
Ph: (703)860-2100   Fax: (703)860-0353

1989. This eight-panel pamphlet describes a career in technology education, educational preparation for the career, and employment opportunities.

★4544★ Careers in Education
National Textbook Co. (NTC)
VGM Career Books
4255 W. Touhy Ave.
Lincolnwood, IL 60646-1975
Ph: (708)679-5500   Fax: (708)679-2494
Fr: 800-323-4900

Roy A. Edelfelt. 1993. Describes career opportunities at all levels of education, from teaching to administration.

★4545★ Careers in Teaching
TAB/McGraw-Hill, Inc.
PO Box 182607
Columbus, OH 43218-2607
Fax: (614)759-3644   Fr: 800-822-8158

Glen W. Cutlip, Ph.D. and Robert J. Schockley, Ph.D. 1994.

★4546★ "Education" in *Career Choices for the 90's for Students of Art* (pp. 170-171)
Walker and Co.
435 Hudson St.
New York, NY 10014
Ph: (212)727-8300   Fax: (212)727-0984
Fr: 800-289-2553
Complied by Career Associates Staff. 1990. This book offers alternatives for students of art. Gives information about the outlook and competition for entry-level candidates. Provides job hunting tips.

★4547★ "Education" in *Career Choices for the 90's for Students of Political Science and Government*
Walker and Co.
435 Hudson St.
New York, NY 10014
Ph: (212)727-8300   Fax: (212)727-0984
Fr: 800-289-2553
Compiled by Career Associates Staff. 1990. This book offers alternatives for students of political science. Gives information about job outlook and competition for entry-level candidates. Provides job hunting tips.

★4548★ "Education" in *College Majors and Careers: A Resource Guide to Effective Life Planning* (pp. 49-50)
Garrett Park Press
PO Box 1907
Garrett Park, MD 20896
Ph: (301)946-2553
Paul Phifer. Revised, 1993. Lists 60 college majors, with definitions; related occupations and leisure activities; skills, values, and personal attributesneeded; suggested readings; and a list of associations.

★4549★ "Education" in *Encyclopedia of Career Choices for the 1990s: A Guide to Entry Level Jobs* (pp. 273-293)
Berkley Pub.
PO Box 506
East Rutherford, NJ 07073
Fax: (201)933-2316   Fr: 800-788-6262
1992. Describes entry-level careers in a variety of industries. Presents qualifications required, working conditions, salary, internships, and professional associations.

★4550★ "Education" in *Liberal Arts Jobs*
Petersons Guides, Inc.
PO Box 2123
Princeton, NJ 08543-2123
Ph: (609)243-9111   Fax: (609)243-9150
Fr: 800-338-3282
Burton Jay Nadler. Second edition, 1989. Strives to help the liberal arts graduate identify skills for entry-level positions. Gives goal setting and job search advice.

★4551★ *Opportunities Abroad for Educators: Fulbright Teacher Exchange Program*
Teacher Exchange Branch
United State Information Agency
301 4 St.
Washington, DC 20547
Ph: (202)619-4700
Annual. This booklet describes the teacher exchange program, and includes applications for teaching positions and seminars abroad; gives a country listing of positions available.

★4552★ *Overseas Employment Opportunities for Educators*
Office of Dependents Schools
U.S. Department of Defense
3461 Eisenhower Ave.
Alexandria, VA 22331-1100
Ph: (703)325-0885
Annual. This booklet describes eligibility requirements, position requirements, application procedures, pay and benefits, housing living, and working conditions. Includes the application form.

★4553★ *The Right Fit: An Educator's Career Handbook and Employment Guide*
Gorsuch Scarisbrick Publishers
8233 Via Paseo del Norte, Ste. F-400
Scottsdale, AZ 85258
Ph: (602)991-7881
Judy A. Strother and Darrel R. Marshall. 1990.

★4554★ "Teacher" in *Jobs Rated Almanac*
World Almanac
1 International Blvd., Ste. 444
Mahwah, NJ 07495
Ph: (201)529-6900   Fax: (201)529-6901
Les Krantz. Second edition, 1992. Ranks 250 jobs by environment, salary, outlooks, physical demands, stress, security, travel opportunities, and extra perks. Includes jobs the editor feels are the most common, most interesting, and the most rapidly growing.

★4555★ *Teaching as a Career*
American Federation of Teachers
555 New Jersey Ave., NW
Washington, DC 20001
Ph: (202)879-4400
1987. This eight-panel brochure describes the rewards of a teaching career, educational preparation, and job locations.

★4556★ "Vocational Education Teachers" in *Career Information Center* (Vol.11)
Simon and Schuster
200 Old Tappan Rd.
Old Tappan, NJ 07675
Fax: 800-445-6991   Fr: 800-223-2348
Richard Lidz and Linda Perrin, editorial directors. Fifth edition, 1993. This 13-volume set profiles over 600 occupations. Each occupational profile describes job duties, educational requirements, how to get the job, advancement possibilities, employment outlook, working conditions, earnings and benefits, and where to write for more information.

PROFESSIONAL ASSOCIATIONS

★4557★ American Association for Adult and Continuing Education (AAACE)
1200 19th St. NW, Ste. 300
Washington, DC 20036
Ph: (202)429-5131   Fax: (202)223-4579
Members: Purpose: Provides leadership in advancing adult education as a lifelong learning process. Serves as a central forum for a wide variety of adult and continuing education special interest groups. Works to stimulate local, state, and regional adult continuing education efforts; encourage mutual cooperation and support; monitor proposed legislation and offer testimony to Congress. **Publications:** *Adult Education Quarterly*, quarterly. • *Adult Learning Practitioner Journal*, bimonthly. • *American Association for Adult and Continuing Education—Newsletter*, bimonthly.

★4558★ American Federation of Teachers (AFT)
555 New Jersey Ave. NW
Washington, DC 20001
Ph: (202)879-4400   Fr: 800-238-1133
Members: AFL-CIO. Works with teachers and other educational employees at the state and local level in organizing, collective bargaining, research, educational issues, and public relations. **Purpose:** Conducts research in areas such as educational reform, bilingual education, teacher certification, and evaluation and national assessments and standards. Represents members' concerns through legislative action; offers technical assistance. Seeks to serve professionals with concerns similar to those of teachers, including state employees, healthcare workers, and paraprofessionals. **Publications:** *AFT Action: A Newsletter for AFT Leaders*, weekly. • *American Educator*, quarterly. • *American Teacher*, 8/year. • *Healthwire*, 10/year. • *On Campus*, 9/year. • *Public Sevice Reporter*, 9/year.

★4559★ American Vocational Association (AVA)
1410 King St.
Alexandria, VA 22314
Ph: (703)683-3111   Fax: (703)683-7424
Fr: 800-892-2274
Members: Teachers, supervisors, administrators, and others interested in the development and improvement of vocational, technical, and practical arts education. **Purpose:** Areas of interest include: secondary, postsecondary, and adult vocational education; education for special population groups; cooperative education. Works with such government agencies as: Bureau of Apprenticeship in Department of Labor; Office of Vocational Rehabilitation in Department of Health and Human Services; Veterans Administration; Office of Vocational and Adult Education of the Department of Education. Maintains hall of fame; bestows awards. **Publications:** *American Vocational Association—Update: The Newspaper for Vocational Educators*, bimonthly. • *Job Market Update*, semiannual. • *Vocational Education Journal*, monthly.

STANDARDS/CERTIFICATION AGENCIES

★4560★ American Federation of Teachers (AFT)
555 New Jersey Ave. NW
Washington, DC 20001
Ph: (202)879-4400   Fr: 800-238-1133
Conducts research in areas such as educational reform, bilingual education, teacher certification, and evaluation and national assessments and standards.

★4561★ Career College Association (CCA)
750 1st St. NE, Ste. 900
Washington, DC 20002
Ph: (202)336-6700   Fax: (202)336-6828
Seeks to inform members of the accreditation process and regulations affecting vocational education. Has established Career Training Foundation to support research into private vocational education.

TEST GUIDES

★4562★ Barron's How to Prepare for the National Teacher Examinations (NTE): Core Battery and Most Specialty Area Tests
Barron's Educational Series, Inc.
250 Wireless Blvd.
Hauppauge, NY 11788
Ph: (516)434-3311   Fax: (516)434-3723
Fr: 800-645-3476
Albertina A. Weinlander. Fifth edition, 1992. Provides review and practice for the Core Battery tests and sample test questions from 19 specialty area tests.

★4563★ Career Examination Series: Alcoholism Educator
National Learning Corp.
212 Michael Dr.
Syosset, NY 11791
Ph: (516)921-8888   Fax: (516)921-8743
Fr: 800-645-6337
Jack Rudman. 1993. Test guide including questions and answers for students or professionals in the field who seek advancement through examination.

★4564★ Career Examination Series: Institutional Trades Instructor
National Learning Corp.
212 Michael Dr.
Syosset, NY 11791
Ph: (516)921-8888   Fax: (516)921-8743
Fr: 800-645-6337
Jack Rudman. A study guide for professionals and trainees in the field of vocational education. Includes a multiple-choice examination section; provides answers.

★4565★ A Guide to the NTE Core Battery Test
Educational Testing Service
Rosedale Rd.
Princeton, NJ 08541
Ph: (609)921-9000
Compiled by the Educational Testing Service staff. Second revised edition, 1992. Contains a form of three previously administered National Teacher Examinations (NTE) Core Battery Test. Also includes a description of each test with sample questions and explanations of the answers as well as test-taking strategies. Also contains answer sheets, answer keys, and scoring instructions.

★4566★ National Teacher Examination Series
National Learning Corp.
212 Michael Dr.
Syosset, NY 11791
Ph: (516)921-8888   Fax: (516)921-8743
Fr: 800-645-6337
Jack Rudman. Practice multiple-choice examinations for education certification. Includes solutions. Titles in the series include *National Teacher Examination (Core Battery)* (one-volume combined edition); *Agriculture; Art Education; Biology and General Science; Business Education; Chemistry and General Science; Chemistry, Physics, and General Science; Earth and Space Science; Education of the Mentally Retarded; English Language and Literature; French; German; Health Education; Home Economics Education; Mathematics; Latin; Marketing and Distributive Education; Men's Physical Education; Music Education; Physics and General Science; Physical Education; Psychological Foundations of Education; Psychology; School Psychology; Science and Mathematics; Social Studies; Social Studies, Literature and Fine Arts; Societal Foundations of Education; Spanish; Special Education; Speech Communication; Teaching Emotionally Disturbed; Teaching Hearing Handicapped; Teaching Learning Disabled; Teaching Orthopedically Handicapped; Teaching Principles and Practices; Teaching Speech Handicapped; Women's Physical Education; Written English Expression.*

★4567★ Occupational Competency Examination Series
National Learning Corp.
212 Michael Dr.
Syosset, NY 11791
Ph: (516)921-8888   Fax: (516)921-8743
Fr: 800-645-6337
Jack Rudman. A series of tests for skilled tradespersons seeking to provide evidence of proficiency in their field in order to become vocational teachers. Multiple choice with solutions.

★4568★ Practicing to Take the GRE Education Test
Educational Testing Service
Rosedale Rd.
Princeton, NJ 08541
Ph: (609)921-9000
Compiled by the Educational Testing Service Staff. Second edition, 1989. This booklet summarizes the purpose and scope of this Graduate Record Examination (GRE) Subject Test. Contains sample questions.

★4569★ Teacher Certification Tests
Arco Publishing Co.
Macmillan General Reference
15 Columbus Cir.
New York, NY 10023
Fax: 800-835-3202   Fr: 800-858-7674
Elna M. Dimock. Third edition, 1993. Covers certification tests administered in 16 states. Tests featured are the California Basic Educational Skills Test, Pre-Professional Skills Test, Connecticut Competency Exam for Prospective Teachers, and Examination for Certification of Educators in Texas. Gives information on testing requirements in all 50 states.

EDUCATIONAL DIRECTORIES AND PROGRAMS

★4570★ Association for Continuing Higher Education—Directory
Association for Continuing Higher Education
PO Box 118067, CE-P
Trident Technical College
Charleston, SC 29423-8067
Ph: (803)722-5546   Fax: (803)722-5520
Irene Barrineau, Administrative Assistant
Annual, March. Covers about 500 individual education professionals and 300 member institutions. Entries include: For institutions—Name, address; names, titles, and phone numbers of institutional representatives. For individuals—Name, title, address, phone. Arrangement: Alphabetical.

★4571★ Educational Career Directory
Gale Research Inc.
835 Penobscot Bldg.
Detroit, MI 48226
Ph: (313)961-2242   Fr: 800-877-GALE
1994.

★4572★ Industrial Teacher Education Directory
National Association of Industrial and Technical Teacher Educators
c/o Dr. Ervin A. Dennis
Department of Industrial Technology
University of Northern Iowa
Cedar Falls, IA 50614-0178
Ph: (319)273-2753   Fax: (319)273-5818
Ervin A. Dennis, Contact
Annual, October. Covers about 2,800 industrial education faculty members at 250 universities and four-year colleges. Entries include: For institutions—Name, address, phone number of industrial education or technology department, degrees granted in previous year, graduate assistantships available, and, for each faculty member, name, academic rank, highest degree held, and areas of specialization. Arrangement: Geographical.

AWARDS, SCHOLARSHIPS, GRANTS, AND FELLOWSHIPS

★4573★ Rutherford B. Lockette Humanitarian Award
International Technology Education Association
1914 Association Dr.
Reston, VA 22091
Ph: (703)860-2100
To recognize an individual who has put forth outstanding efforts to promote humanistic values while serving as a professional in the industrial arts/technology education field. Established in 1984.

★4574★ Outstanding Service Award
American Vocational Association
1410 King St.
Alexandria, VA 22314-2715
Ph: (703)683-3111 Fax: (703)739-9098
To recognize professional educators for meritorious efforts in the improvement, promotion, development, and progress of vocational, technical, and/or practical arts education. Nominations must be submitted by May 1. Not more than five awards are presented annually.

★4575★ Carl Perkins Humanitarian Award
American Vocational Association
1410 King St.
Alexandria, VA 22314-2715
Ph: (703)683-3111 Fax: (703)739-9098
To recognize individuals who have made outstanding meritorious contributions of state or national significance to the improvement, promotion, development, and progress of vocational, technical, or practical arts education. The deadline is May 1. Established in 1985 in memory of Rep. Carl Perkins and designed to recognize individuals who have demonstrated the same humanitarian concerns exemplified by Rep. Perkins.

★4576★ Special Recognition Citation
International Technology Education Association
1914 Association Dr.
Reston, VA 22091
Ph: (703)860-2100
To recognize an individual who has performed outstanding service to or for the Association, or to or for industrial arts/technology education. The citation may be made for persons within or outside the industrial arts/technology profession or a commercial and professional organization.

★4577★ Vocational Teacher of the Year Award
American Vocational Association
1410 King St.
Alexandria, VA 22314-2715
Ph: (703)683-3111 Fax: (703)739-9098
To recognize classroom teachers who are currently providing outstanding vocational education programs for youth and/or adults. Recipients of this award must have made significant contributions toward innovative, unique, and novel programs that serve to improve and promote vocational education.

Awarded annually at the regional and national level.

BASIC REFERENCE GUIDES AND HANDBOOKS

★4578★ The Career Training Sourcebook
McGraw-Hill Inc.
11 W. 19 St.
New York, NY 10011
Ph: 800-722-4726
Sara Gilbert. 1993.

★4579★ Handbook for Adjunct & Part-Time Faculty & Teachers of Adults
Info-Tec, Inc.
20545 Center Ridge Rd., Ste. LL39
Rocky River, OH 44116
Ph: (216)333-3155
Donald Greive. Fifth edtion, 1992.

★4580★ The Handbook of Adult & Continuing Education
Jossey-Bass, Inc., Publishers
350 Sansome St.
San Francisco, CA 94104
Ph: (415)433-1740 Fax: (415)433-0499
Sharan B. Merriam, editor. 1989.

★4581★ An International Dictionary of Adult & Continuing Education
Routledge, Chapman & Hall, Inc.
29 W. 35th St.
New York, NY 10001-2299
Ph: (212)244-3336
Peter Jarvis. 1990.

★4582★ A Practical Guide for Teaching and Training Adults
Krieger Publishing Co., Inc.
PO Box 9542
Melbourne, FL 32902
Ph: (407)724-9542 Fax: (407)951-3671
Franklin W. Spikes, editor. 1994.

PROFESSIONAL AND TRADE PERIODICALS

★4583★ Adult & Continuing Education Today
LERN
1544 Hayes Dr.
Manhattan, KS 66502
Ph: (913)539-5376 Fr: 800-678-5376
William A. Draves
Biweekly. Provides news and information on adult education, including trends, issues, and events such as enrollments, postage rates, funding, legislation, and new growth areas. Features interviews and commentary from prominent national educational leaders.

★4584★ Adult Education Quarterly
American Assn. for Adult & Continuing Education
1200 19th St. NW, Ste. 300
Washington, DC 20036
Ph: (703)522-2234 Fax: (202)331-0509
Ron Cervero
Quarterly. Journal of theory and research in adult and continuing education.

★4585★ American Association for Adult and Continuing Education—Online
American Association for Adult and Continuing Education
1101 Connecticut Ave. NW, Ste. 700
Washington, DC 20036
Ph: (202)429-5131 Fax: (202)223-4579
Features indepth reporting and commentary on developments in national and state legislation and policy, innovative programs, statistics, research, current trends and issues, conferences, and grants. Recurring features include job listings, letters to the editor, and editorials.

★4586★ Continuing Education Alternatives Update
Update Publicare Company
PO Box 570213
Houston, TX 77257-0213
Ph: (713)867-3438
A.C. Doyle
Annual. Furnishes information on various types of continuing education and outlets for the same. Recurring features include news and ideas of continuing education and opportunities in the field.

★4587★ Education: The Changing Scene
Accrediting Council for Continuing Education and Training (ACCET)
600 E. Main St., Ste. 1425
Richmond, VA 23219
Ph: (804)648-6742 Fax: (804)780-0821
Roger J. Williams
Bimonthly. Reports on activities of the Council, which is concerned about improving the quality of continuing education programs. Furnishes discussion of developments and issues in the field, conference reports, and news of members.

★4588★ Industrial Education
Cummins Publishing Co.
6557 Forest Park Drive
Troy, MI 48098-1954
Robin Williams
Magazine on industrial, technical, and vocational education.

★4589★ NAIEC Newsletter
National Association for Industry-Education Cooperation (NAIEC)
235 Hendricks Blvd.
Buffalo, NY 14226-3304
Ph: (716)834-7047 Fax: (716)834-7047
Vito R. Pace
Bimonthly. Concerned with furthering industry-education and joint efforts in school improvement, workplace preparation, and human resource/economic development. Discusses industry-education councils, school improvement, community resources workshops, school-based job placement activities and academic/vocational education.

Also covers educational management, instructional materials, and curriculum and economic development. Recurring features include abstracts of articles, book reviews, statistics, news of research and of members, and a calendar of events.

★4590★ NUCEA Newsletter
National University Continuing Education
   Association (NUCEA)
1 Dupont Circle, Ste. 615
Washington, DC 20036
Ph: (202)659-3130
Susan Goewey

Presents news of legislative and governmental actions pertinent to continuing education, lifelong learning, extension programs, and related educational programs. Includes news from member institutions, coverage of meetings and conferences, and news of Association activities. Recurring features include news of research, news of members, new program ideas, statistical articles, notices of grant opportunities, a professional development calendar, a letter from the President/Executive Director, and a column titled Legislative Backgrounder.

★4591★ TIES Magazine
Trenton State College
Department of Technological Studies
Hillwood Lakes
CN 4700
Trenton, NJ 08650-4700
Ph: (609)771-3335   Fax: (609)771-3330
Ronald Todd

Technology education magazine for teachers.

★4592★ Vocational Education Journal
American Vocational Assn.
1410 King St.
Alexandria, VA 22314-2715
Ph: (703)683-3111   Fax: (703)683-7424
Fr: 800-826-9972
Paul Plawin

Magazine covering trends and issues affecting vocational-technical education.

★4593★ The Written Word
Cega Services
PO Box 81826
Lincoln, NE 68501-1826
Ph: (402)464-0602   Fax: (402)464-5931
Su Perk Davis

Monthly. Encourages "communication and cooperation between individuals, government institutions, schools, libraries and social service agencies working on the problem of illiteracy." Also provides information on programs for Adult Basic Education, General Equivalency Diploma (GED), and English as a Second Language. Recurring features include news of research, publications, and events.

PROFESSIONAL MEETINGS AND CONVENTIONS

★4594★ American Vocational Association Annual Convention and Trade Show
American Vocational Association
1410 King St.
Alexandria, VA 22314
Ph: (703)683-3111   Fax: (703)683-7424
Fr: 800-826-9972

Annual. Held during December. **Dates and Locations:** 1995 Dec 01-05; Denver, CO.

★4595★ Association of School Business Officials Annual Meeting and Exhibits
Association of School Business Officials
   International
11401 N. Shore Dr.
Reston, VA 22090-4232
Ph: (703)478-0405   Fax: (703)478-0205

Annual. Always held during the Fall. **Dates and Locations:** 1996 Nov 08-12; Philadelphia, PA. • 1997 Oct 03-07; Vancouver, BC. • 1998 Oct 16-20; San Antonio, TX. • 1999 Oct 15-19; Orlando, FL.

OTHER SOURCES OF INFORMATION

★4596★ "Adult Education" in Accounting to Zoology: Graduate Fields Defined (pp. 62-63)
Petersons Guides, Inc.
PO Box 2123
Princeton, NJ 08543-2123
Ph: (609)243-9111   Fax: (609)243-9150
Fr: 800-338-3282

Amy J. Goldstein, editor. Revised and updated, 1987. Defines 298 graduate and professional fields. Discusses types of graduate programs and degrees, graduate research, applied work, employment prospects, and trends.

★4597★ Beyond Rhetoric: Fundamental Issues in Adult Literacy Education
Krieger Publishing Co., Inc.
PO Box 9542
Melbourne, FL 32902
Ph: (407)724-9542   Fax: (407)951-3671
Thomas Valentine, editor. 1994. Discusses common concerns of adult education and literacy programs.

★4598★ Designing Instruction for the Adult Learner
Taylor & Francis, Inc.
1900 Frost Rd., Ste. 101
Bristol, PA 19007-1598
Ph: (215)785-5800   Fax: (215)785-5515
Fr: 800-821-8312
Rita Richey, editor. 1992.

★4599★ Designing Instruction for Adult Teachers
Krieger Publishing Co., Inc.
PO Box 9542
Melbourne, FL 32902
Ph: (407)724-9542
Gary J. Dean, editor. 1993.

★4600★ Requirements for Certification of Teachers, Counselors, Librarians, Administrators for Elementary and Secondary Schools, and Junior Colleges
University of Chicago Press
11030 S. Langley Ave.
Chicago, IL 60628
Ph: (312)702-7700   Fr: 800-621-2736
Mary P. Burks, Annual. Fifty-ninth edition, 1994. State-by-state listing of certification requirements for teachers, counselors, librarians, and administrators. Lists addresses of state departments of education.

★4601★ "Teacher (Adult Education)" in Career Selector 2001
Barron's Educational Series, Inc.
250 Wireless Blvd.
Hauppauge, NY 11788
Ph: (516)434-3311   Fax: (516)434-3723
Fr: 800-645-3476
James C. Gonyea. 1993.

★4602★ The Teacher's Almanac
Facts on File
460 Park Ave. S.
New York, NY 10016-7382
Ph: (212)683-2244   Fax: 800-678-3633
Fr: 800-322-8755
Sherwood Harris and Lorna B. Harris, editors. 1988. Contains statistical information such as teachers' salaries, educational finances, and state rankings.

★4603★ "Vocational and Technical Education" in Accounting to Zoology: Graduate Fields Defined (pp. 106-107)
Petersons Guides, Inc.
PO Box 2123
Princeton, NJ 08543-2123
Ph: (609)243-9111   Fax: (609)243-9150
Fr: 800-338-3282
Amy J. Goldstein, editor. Revised and updated, 1987. Defines 298 graduate and professional fields. Discusses types of graduate programs and degrees, graduate research, applied work, employment prospects, and trends.

Archivists and Curators

Archivists, **curators**, **museum technicians**, **conservators**, **and restorers** search for, acquire, analyze, describe, catalog, restore, preserve, exhibit, maintain, and store items of lasting value. Items may include historical documents, audiovisual materials, corporate records, art, coins, stamps, minerals, clothing, maps, live and preserved plants and animals, buildings, or historic sites. Archivists and curators plan and with technicians and restorers, work directly on collection. Archivists and curators may coordinate educational and public service programs such as tour, workshops, lectures, and classes, and may work with the boards of institutions to administer plans and policies. Archivists determine what portion of the vast amount of information produced by government agencies, corporations, educational institutions, and other organizations should be made part of a historical record or put on exhibit. They organize and describe records so they can be located easily, and determine whether records should be stored as original documents, on microfilm, or in computers. Curators manage collections in museums, zoos, aquariums, botanic gardens, and historic sites. They acquire items through purchases, gifts, field exploration, intermuseum loans, or, in the case of plants and animals, breeding. Archivists, curators, and conservators are increasingly using computers to catalog and organize collections and to conduct original research.

Salaries

Earnings of archivists and curators vary considerably by type and size of employer. Average salaries in the federal government are listed below:

Beginning archivists and curators with bachelor's degree	$18,300-$22,700/year
Beginning archivists and curators with master's degree	$27,800/year
Beginning archivists and curators with doctorate	$33,600-$40,300/year

Employment Outlook

Growth rate until the year 2005: Average.

Archivists and Curators

CAREER GUIDES

★4604★ AAMD Salary
Association of Art Museum Directors (AAMD)
1130 Sherbrooke St., W., Ste. 530
Montreal, PQ, Canada H3G 1G1
SAnnual. Survey of art museum salaries from 142 museums.

★4605★ Archivist
Vocational Biographies, Inc.
PO Box 31
Sauk Centre, MN 56378-0031
Ph: (612)352-6516   Fax: (612)352-5546
Fr: 800-255-0752
1991. Four-page pamphlet containing a personal narrative about a worker's job, work likes and dislikes, career path from high school to the present. Education and training, the rewards and frustrations, and the effects of the job on the rest of the worker's life. The data file portion of this pamphlet gives a concise occupational summary, including work descriptions, working conditions, places of employment, personal characteristics, education and training, job outlook, and salary range.

★4606★ Archivist
Careers, Inc.
PO Box 135
Largo, FL 34649-0135
Ph: (813)584-7333
1993. Two-page occupational summary card describing duties, working conditions, personal qualifications, training, earnings and hours, employment outlook, places of employment, related careers, and where to write for more information.

★4607★ "Archivist" in Career Opportunities in Art (pp. 76)
Facts on File
460 Park Ave. S.
New York, NY 10016-7382
Ph: (212)683-2244   Fax: 800-678-3633
Fr: 800-322-8755
Susan H. Haubenstock. 1988. This book profiles seventy-five art-related jobs. Each profile includes a career description, career ladder, employment and advancement prospects, education, experience and skills required, salary range, and tips for entry into the field.

★4608★ "Archivist" and "Curator" in Museum Jobs form A-Z: What They Are, How to Prepare, and Where to Find Them
Batax Museum Publishing
301 Racquet Club Rd., Ste. 202
Fort Lauderdale, FL 33326
G.W. Bates. 1994.

★4609★ "Archivist" in Guide to Federal Jobs (pp. 234)
Resource Directories
3361 Executive Pkwy., Ste. 302
Toledo, OH 43606
Ph: (419)536-5353   Fax: (419)536-7056
Fr: 800-274-8515
Rod W. Durgin, editor. Third edition, 1992. Contains information on finding and applying for federal jobs. Describes more than 200 professional and technical jobs for college graduates. Covers the nature of the work, salary, and geographic location. Lists college majors preferred for that occupation. Section one describes the function and work of government agencies that hire the most significant number of college graduates.

★4610★ Archivists
Chronicle Guidance Publications, Inc.
66 Aurora St.
PO Box 1190
Moravia, NY 13118-1190
Ph: (315)497-0330   Fax: (315)497-3359
Fr: 800-622-7284
1994. Career brief describing the nature of the job, working conditions, hours and earnings, education and training, licensure, certification, unions, personal qualifications, social and psychological factors, location, employment outlook, entry methods, advancement, and related occupations.

★4611★ "Archivists" in Career Discovery Encyclopedia (Vol.1, pp. 60-61)
J.G. Ferguson Publishing Co.
200 W. Madison St., Ste. 300
Chicago, IL 60606
Ph: (312)580-5480   Fax: (312)580-4948
Russell E. Primm, editor-in chief. 1993. This six volume set contains two-page articles for 504 occupations. Each article describes job duties, earnings, and educational and training requirements. The whole set is arranged alphabetically by job title. Designed for junior high and older students.

★4612★ "Archivists and Curators" in 101 Careers: A Guide to the Fastest-Growing Opportunities (pp. 157-160)
John Wiley & Sons, Inc.
605 3rd Ave.
New York, NY 10158-0012
Ph: (212)850-6645   Fax: (212)850-6088
Michael Harkavy. 1990. Describes the nature of the job, working conditions, employment growth, qualifications, personal skills, projected salaries, and where to write for more information.

★4613★ "Archivists and Curators" in Occupational Outlook Handbook
U.S. Government Printing Office
Superintendent of Documents
Washington, DC 20402
Ph: (202)512-1800   Fax: (202)512-2250
Biennial; latest edition, 1994-95. Encyclopedia of careers describing about 250 occupations and comprising about 85 percent of all jobs in the economy. Occupations that require lengthy education or training are given the most attention. Each occupation's profile describes what the worker does on the job, working conditions, education and training requirements, advancement possibilities, job outlook, earnings, and sources of additional information.

★4614★ Careers in Museums: A Variety of Vocations
Technical Information Service
American Association of Museums
1225 Eye St., NW, Ste. 200
Washington, DC 20005
Ph: (202)289-1818   Fax: (202)289-6578
Fourth edition, 1994. Includes a description of museum careers, suggested preparation and education requirements for specific museum jobs, a job placement resource list, and an annotated bibliography for further museum career information.

★4615★ *Code of Ethics for Conservators*
American Association of Museum
1225 I St., NW, Ste. 200
Washington, DC 20005
Ph: (202)289-1818
American Institute for Conservastion of Historic and Artistic Works, Committee on Ethics and Standards. 1992. Describes principles and guidelines for the conservator.

★4616★ *"Curator" in The School of Visual Arts Guide to Careers (pp. 121-122)*
McGraw-Hill, Inc.
1221 Avenue of the Americas
New York, NY 10020
Fr: 800-722-4726
Dee Ito. 1987. Gives a broad overview of each field included, with educational requirements and employment opportunities. Includes ideas on how to get started.

★4617★ *"Curatorial (Art Museums)" in Career Choices for the 90's for Students of Art (pp. 167-169)*
Walker and Co.
435 Hudson St.
New York, NY 10014
Ph: (212)727-8300   Fax: (212)727-0984
Fr: 800-289-2553
Compiled by Career Associates Staff. 1990. This book offers alternatives for students of art. Gives information about the outlook and competition for entry-level candidates. Provides job hunting tips.

★4618★ *"Curators (Art Museums)" in Encyclopedia of Career Choices for 1990s: A Guide to Entry Level Jobs (pp. 46-67)*
Berkley Pub.
PO Box 506
East Rutherford, NJ 07073
Fax: (201)933-2316   Fr: 800-788-6262
1992. Describes entry-level careers in a variety of industries. Presents qualifications required, working conditions, salary, internships, and professional associations.

★4619★ *"Curators" in Career Opportunities in Art*
Facts on File
460 Park Ave. S.
New York, NY 10016-7382
Ph: (212)683-2244   Fax: 800-678-3633
Fr: 800-322-8755
Susan H. Haubenstock. 1988. This book profiles seventy-five art-related jobs. Each profile includes a career description, career ladder, employment and advancement prospects, education, experience and skills required, salary range, and tips for entry into the field.

★4620★ *"Museum Careers: Curator, Archivist" in College Board Guide to Jobs and Career Planning (pp. 184-185)*
The College Board
45 Columbus Ave.
New York, NY 10023-6992
Ph: (212)713-8165   Fax: (212)713-8143
Fr: 800-323-7155
Second edition, 1994. Describes the job, salaries, related careers, education needed, and where to write for more information.

★4621★ *Museum Curator*
Vocational Biographies, Inc.
PO Box 31
Sauk Centre, MN 56378-0031
Ph: (612)352-6516   Fax: (612)352-5546
Fr: 800-255-0752
1993. Four-page pamphlet containing a personal narrative about a worker's job, work likes and dislikes, career path from high school to the present. Education and training, the rewards and frustrations, and the effects of the job on the rest of the worker's life. The data file portion of this pamphlet gives a concise occupational summary, including work descriptions, working conditions, places of employment, personal characteristics, education and training, job outlook, and salary range.

★4622★ *"Museum Curator" in Career Information Center (Vol.8)*
Simon and Schuster
200 Old Tappan Rd.
Old Tappan, NJ 07675
Fax: 800-445-6991   Fr: 800-223-2348
Richard Lidz and Linda Perrin, editorial directors. Fifth edition, 1993. This 13-volume set profiles over 600 occupations. Each occupational profile describes job duties, entry-level requirements, educational requirements, advancement possibilities, employment outlook, working conditions, earnings and benefits, and where to write for more information.

★4623★ *"Museum Curator" in Jobs Rated Almanac*
World Almanac
1 International Blvd., Ste. 444
Mahwah, NJ 07495
Ph: (201)529-6900   Fax: (201)529-6901
Les Krantz. Second edition, 1992. Ranks 250 jobs by environment, salary, outlooks, physical demands, stress, security, travel opportunities, and extra perks. Includes jobs the editor feels are the most common, most interesting, and the most rapidly growing.

★4624★ *"Museum Curator" in Opportunities in Crafts (pp. 55-64)*
National Textbook Co. (NTC)
VGM Career Books
4255 W. Touhy Ave.
Lincolnwood, IL 60646-1975
Ph: (708)679-5500   Fax: (708)679-2494
Fr: 800-323-4900
Marianne Munday. 1994. Provides a general overview of crafts and some traditional and nontraditional jobs related to crafts. Gives information on how to start a crafts business.

★4625★ *"Museum Curator" in VGM's Careers Encyclopedia (pp. 292-294)*
National Textbook Co. (NTC)
VGM Career Books
4255 W. Touhy Ave.
Lincolnwood, IL 60646-1975
Ph: (708)679-5500   Fax: (708)679-2494
Fr: 800-323-4900
Third edition, 1991. Describes job duties, places of employment, working conditions, qualifications, education, and training, advancement potential, and salary for each occupation.

★4626★ *Museum Curators*
Chronicle Guidance Publications, Inc.
66 Aurora St.
PO Box 1190
Moravia, NY 13118-1190
Ph: (315)497-0330   Fax: (315)497-3359
Fr: 800-622-7284
1993. Career brief describing the nature of the job, working conditions, hours and earnings, education and training, licensure, certification, unions, personal qualifications, social and psychological factors, location, employment outlook, entry methods, advancement, and related occupations.

★4627★ *"Museum Curators" in Career Discovery Encyclopedia (Vol.4, pp. 108-109)*
J.G. Ferguson Publishing Co.
200 W. Madison St., Ste. 300
Chicago, IL 60606
Ph: (312)580-5480   Fax: (312)580-4948
Russell E. Primm, editor-in chief. 1993. This six volume set contains two-page articles for 504 occupations. Each article describes job duties, earnings, and educational and training requirements. The whole set is arranged alphabetically by job title. Designed for junior high and older students.

★4628★ *"Museum Curators" in Encyclopedia of Careers and Vocational Guidance (Vol.3, pp. 493-497)*
J.G. Ferguson Publishing Co.
200 W. Madison St., Ste. 300
Chicago, IL 60606
Ph: (312)580-5480   Fax: (312)580-4948
William E. Hopke, editor-in-chief. Ninth edition, 1993. Four-volume set that profiles 900 occupations and describes job trends in 74 industries. Includes career description, educational requirements, history of the job, methods of entry, advancement, employment outlook, earnings, conditions of work, social and psychological factors, and sources of further information.

★4629★ *"Museums/Cultural Organizations" in Internships: 1995 (pp. 122-153)*
Petersons Guides, Inc.
PO Box 2123
Princeton, NJ 08543-2123
Ph: (609)243-9111   Fax: (609)243-9150
Fr: 800-338-3282
Fifteenth edition, 1995. Lists internship opportunities under six broad categories: communications, creative, performing, and fine arts, human services, public relations, and business and technology. Includes a special section on internships in Washington, DC. For each internship program, gives the names, phone number, contact person, description, eligibility requirements, and benefits.

★4630★ *Opportunities for Contract Work in Archaeology and Historic Preservation*
American Anthropological Association
4350 N. Fairfax, Ste. 640
Arlington, VA 22203
Ph: (703)528-1902   Fax: (202)667-5345
This pamphlet describes career opportunities with federal, state, and local agencies which

are required by law to identify and preserve historic properties. Gives a list of agencies employing archivists.

★4631★ Zoo Curator
Vocational Biographies, Inc.
PO Box 31
Sauk Centre, MN 56378-0031
Ph: (612)352-6516   Fax: (612)352-5546
Fr: 800-255-0752
1993. Four-page pamphlet containing a personal narrative about a worker's job, work likes and dislikes, career path from high school to the present. Education and training, the rewards and frustrations, and the effects of the job on the rest of the worker's life. The data file portion of this pamphlet gives a concise occupational summary, including work descriptions, working conditions, places of employment, personal characteristics, education and training, job outlook, and salary range.

PROFESSIONAL ASSOCIATIONS

★4632★ American Association of Botanical Gardens and Arboreta (AABGA)
786 Church Rd.
Wayne, PA 19087
Ph: (610)688-1120   Fax: (610)293-0149
Members: Directors and staffs of botanical gardens, arboreta, institutions maintaining or conducting horticultural courses, and others. **Purpose:** Seeks to serve North American public gardens and horticultural organizations by promoting professional development through its publications and meetings, advocating the interests of public gardens in political, corporate, foundation, and community arenas, and encouraging gardens to adhere to professional standards in their programs and operations. **Publications:** American Association of Botanical Gardens and Arboreta—Newsletter, monthly. • Public Garden, quarterly.

★4633★ American Association of Museums (AAM)
1225 Eye St. NW, Ste. 200
Washington, DC 20005
Ph: (202)289-1818   Fax: (202)289-6578
Members: Art, history, and science museums, art associations and centers, historic houses and societies, preservation projects, planetariums, zoos, aquariums, botanical gardens, college and university museums, libraries, and special museums; trustees and professional employees of museums and others interested in the museum field. Has established an accrediting system for museums. Maintains placement service for museum professionals. **Publications:** The Accessible Museum. • Aviso, monthly. • Caring for Collectibles. • Mermaids, Mummies, and Mastodons. • Museum News, bimonthly. • Museum Registration Methods. • Museums, Adults, and the Humanities. • Museums for a New Century. • Official Museum Directory, annual.

★4634★ American Institute for Conservation of Historic and Artistic Works (AICHAW)
1717 K St. NW, Ste. 301
Washington, DC 20006
Ph: (202)452-9545   Fax: (202)452-9328
Members: Professionals, scientists, administrators, and educators in the field of art conservation; interested individuals. **Purpose:** Advances the practice and promotes the importance of the preservation of cultural property. Coordinates the exchange of knowledge, research, and publications. Establishes and upholds professional standards. Publishes conservation literature. Complies statistics. Represents membership to allied professional associations and advocates on conservation-related issues. Solicits and dispenses money exclusively for charitable, scientific, and educational objectives. **Publications:** AIC Directory, annual. • AIC Newsletter, bimonthly. • Journal of the American Institute for Conservation.

★4635★ Society of American Archivists (SAA)
600 S. Federal St., Ste. 504
Chicago, IL 60605
Ph: (312)922-0140   Fax: (312)347-1452
Members: Individuals and institutions concerned with the identification, preservation, and use of records of historical value. **Publications:** The American Archivist, quarterly. • Archival Outlook, bimonthly. • SAA Employment Bulletin, bimonthly. • SAA Publications Catalog. • Society of American Archivists—Directory of Individual Members, biennial.

STANDARDS/CERTIFICATION AGENCIES

★4636★ American Association of Museums (AAM)
1225 Eye St. NW, Ste. 200
Washington, DC 20005
Ph: (202)289-1818   Fax: (202)289-6578
Has established an accrediting system for museums.

★4637★ American Institute for Conservation of Historic and Artistic Works (AICHAW)
1400 16th St. NW, Ste. 340
Washington, DC 20036
Ph: (202)232-6636   Fax: (202)232-6630
Establishes and maintains a code of ethics and standards of practice.

TEST GUIDES

★4638★ Career Examination Series: Archivist
National Learning Corp.
212 Michael Dr.
Syosset, NY 11791
Ph: (516)921-8888   Fax: (516)921-8743
Fr: 800-645-6337
Jack Rudman. Test guide including questions and answers for students or professionals in the field who seek advancement through examination.

★4639★ Career Examination Series: Museum Curator
National Learning Corp.
212 Michael Dr.
Syosset, NY 11791
Ph: (516)921-8888   Fax: (516)921-8743
Fr: 800-645-6337
Jack Rudman. A series of study guides with multiple-choice examination questions and solutions for trainees and professional archivists and curators. Titles in the series include Museum Director; Museum Supervisor; Principal Museum Curator; Senior Museum Curator.

EDUCATIONAL DIRECTORIES AND PROGRAMS

★4640★ Directory of M.A. and Ph.D. Programs in Art and Art History
College Art Association
275 7th Ave.
New York, NY 10001
Ph: (212)691-1051   Fax: (212)627-2381
Virginia Wageman, Contact
Irregular, latest edition 1992. Covers over 170 institutions offering M.A. and Ph.D. programs in art and art history. Entries include: Institution name, address; names and titles of faculty; description of program, including admission requirements, degrees offered, degree requirements, tuition, fees; facilities. Arrangement: Alphabetical.

★4641★ Environmental Career Directory
Gale Research Inc.
835 Penobscot Bldg.
Detroit, MI 48226-4094
Ph: (313)961-2242   Fax: (313)961-6083
Fr: 800-877-GALE
Bradley J. Morgan and Joseph M. Palmisano. 1993. A directory in the Career Advisor Series that provides essays written by industry professionals; job search information on resume and cover letter preparation, networking, and the interviewing process; approximately 300 companies and organizations offering job opportunities and internships, and additional job-hunting resources.

AWARDS, SCHOLARSHIPS, GRANTS, AND FELLOWSHIPS

★4642★ Louise du Pont Crowninshield Award
National Trust for Historic Preservation
1785 Massachusetts Ave. NW
Washington, DC 20036
Ph: (202)673-4141   Fax: (202)673-4082
This, the oldest and highest award given by the National Trust, is presented to an individual or organization when there is indisputable evidence of superlative leadership achievement in the preservation and interpretation of our national heritage of buildings, structures, districts, sites, cultural landscapes and objects of historical and cultural significance. Nominations must be made by someone other than the nominee and should be directed to the Vice President for Programs, Services and Information. Winners are selected by a special committee of the Board of Trustees. A monetary prize of $2,500 and a citation are awarded annually during National Historic Preservation Week in May. Established in 1959 as a memorial to Louise Evelina du Pont Crowninshield.

★4643★ Fellowships for Art History Research
Metropolitan Museum of Art
Fellowship Program
Office of Academic Programs
1000 5th Ave.
New York, NY 10028-0198
Ph: (212)879-5500
Ten types of fellowships are awarded, including: Classical Fellowship - for an outstanding graduate student who has been admitted to the doctoral program of a university in the United States, and who has submitted an outline of a thesis dealing with Greek and Roman art; Chester Dale Fellowships - for individuals whose fields of study are related to the fine arts of the western world and who are preferably American citizens under the age of forty; Andrew W. Mellon Fellowships - provided by the Andrew W. Mellon Fund for promising young scholars with commendable research projects related to the Museum's collections, as well as for distinguished visiting scholars from this country and abroad who can serve as teachers and advisors and make their expertise available to catalogue and refine the collections; J. Clawson Mills Scholarships - for one year's study or research at the Museum in any branch of the Fine Arts relating to the Metropolitan Museum's collections; Norbert Schimmel Fellowship for Mediterranean Art and Archaeology - to an outstanding graduate student who has been admitted to the doctoral program of a university in the United States and who has submitted an outline of a thesis dealing with ancient Near Eastern art and archaeology or with Greek and Roman art; Jane and Morgan Whitney Fellowships - for study, work or research to students of the fine arts whose fields are related to the Museum's collections, with preference to be given to students in the decorative arts who are under forty years of age; Theodore Rousseau Fellowships - to develop the skills of connoisseurship by sup-

porting first-hand examination of paintings in major European collections, rather than supporting library research. The fellowships are awarded for the training of students whose goal is to enter museums as curators of painting; and Polaire Weissman Fund Fellowships - provides fellowships to qualified graduate students, who preferably have completed graduate studies in the fine arts or studies in costume, and who are interested in pursuing costume history in a museum or teaching career, or other career (including conservation) related to the field of costume. Awarded in alternate years. Applications for all fellowships may be submitted by November 15. The number of fellowships awarded depends upon the funds available; the stipend amount for one year is $25,000 for senior fellows and $15,000 for pre-doctoral fellows, with an additional $2,500 for travel. Awarded annually.

★4644★ Fellowships for Study in Conservation
Metropolitan Museum of Art
Fellowship Program
Office of Academic Programs
1000 5th Ave.
New York, NY 10028-0198
Ph: (212)879-5500
The following fellowships are awarded: Andrew W. Mellon Fellowships in Conservation - for training in one or more of the following departments of the Museum: Paintings Conservation, Objects Conservation (including sculpture, metalwork, glass, ceramics, furniture, and archaeological objects), Musical Instruments, Arms and Armor, Paper Conservation, Textile Conservation, The Costume Institute, and Asian Art Conservation. Sponsored by the Andrew W. Mellon Foundation; L. W. Frohlich Two-Year Fellowship in Conservation - for conservators, art historians or scientists who are at an advanced level in their training and who have demonstrated commitment to the physical examination and treatment of art objects. Sponsored by the Metropolitan Museum of Art; and Starr Fellowship - for training in the conservation and mounting of Asian paintings. Applications may be submitted by January 11.

★4645★ LHAT Award
League of Historic American Theatres
1511 K. St. NW, Ste. 923
Washington, DC 20005
Ph: (202)783-6966   Fax: (202)393-2141
To recognize an individual or an organization that has made a significant contribution to the League and the field of theatre preservation during the past year. Members of the League are eligible. A plaque is awarded annually at the League Conference. Established in 1984.

★4646★ Marquee Award
Theatre Historical Society of America
106 East Ave. E
Robstown, TX 78380
Ph: (512)387-1996
For recognition of theatre preservation or research into the history of theatres. Nominations must be submitted by March 1. Two types of awards are presented: Honorary Member - to recognize an individual who is not a member of the organization and who has contributed to the ideals of organization, and Member of the Year - to recognize an active member who has contributed to the

ideals of the organization. A plaque is awarded annually at the yearly Conclave. Established in 1970 by B. Andrew Corsini and named for *Marquee* , the quarterly theatre publication of the organization.

★4647★ NHPRC/Andrew W. Mellon Foundation Fellowships in Archival Administration
National Historical Publications and
  Records Commission (NHPRC)
National Archives Bldg.
Washington, DC 20408
Ph: (202)501-5610   Fax: (202)501-5601
Purpose: To give archivists actual working experience in administration. The Commission believes that workshops and other types of training, although important aspects of archival education, are not as beneficial as hands-on experience in training future administrators. Qualifications: Fellowship applicants should have between two and five years experience in archival work. While not required, it is desirable that applicants have the equivalent of two semesters of full-time graduate training in a program containing an archives education component. Host institutions are encouraged to provide fellows with a series of supervisory and decision-making experiences. Included in past fellowships have been such diverse areas as appraisal, budget preparation, personnel administration, grants administration, publications, plant operation, long-range planning, disaster planning, collection policy development, committee work, and collection surveys. Funds available: Each of two fellowships runs from nine to twelve months, with the actual length based on the fellow's and host institution's needs. Fellows receive a stipend and benefits package. Applicants should check with Commission staff for the current salary and benefit levels. For 1993-94, the salary is $35,000 plus $7,000 in benefits. Application details: The application process for host institutions and fellows is competitive. The Commission selects the two host institutions from eligible applications received against the September deadline. Institutional staff interested in applying to be hosts should contact Commission staff to discuss their ideas for the program and the technical project. Individual and host application materials may be requested from the Commission. Deadline: Host institutions: September 1. Individual fellowships: March 1.

★4648★ John Wesley Powell Award
Society for History in the Federal
  Government
PO Box 14139, Benjamin Franklin Sta.
Washington, DC 20044
Ph: (301)220-1325
For recognition of achievement in historical preservation and historical display. This includes achievement in the preservation of records, artifacts, buildings, historical sites, or other historical materials. Achievement in a museum exhibit, a historical movie, an audiovisual display, or any other form of visual historical presentation is considered. Awards are given in alternate years for historic preservation and historic display. Entries may be submitted by any branch of the federal government. Non-government organizations and individuals may submit their own or other eligible activities carried out in behalf of the fed-

eral government. A certificate is awarded annually at the April annual meeting. Established in 1983.

★4649★ Preservation Honor Awards
National Trust for Historic Preservation
1785 Massachusetts Ave. NW
Washington, DC 20036
Ph: (202)673-4141   Fax: (202)673-4082

To recognize individuals and organizations for outstanding preservation-related accomplishments. Any aspect of preservation, restoration, rehabilitation or redevelopment of our architectural and maritime heritage that is exemplary is eligible. Candidates and their projects must be in the United States or its territories. Projects must have been completed within the last five years. The nominations deadline is May 1. A plaque is presented to honored individuals or organizations. Awarded at the National Trust's annual conference each October.

★4650★ Renchard Prize for Historic Preservation
Historical Society of Washington, D.C.
1307 New Hampshire Ave. NW
Washington, DC 20036-1507
Ph: (202)785-2068

To recognize an outstanding single or cumulative achievement by an individual, group or organization in the field of historic preservation in Washington, D.C. Aspects of preservation worthy of consideration (but not restricted to) are protection, education, restoration, archaeology (including the protection of early Native American or prehistoric sites), establishment of historic districts and house museums, restoration, photography, research and publication. Activities submitted for consideration may not be part of the requirement of the nominee's salaried position. Nominations may be submitted by February 1. A certificate is awarded annually at a public ceremony and reception in February. Established in 1982 in memory of Ambassador George and Stellita Stapleton Renchard, devotees of historic preservation in the Washington, D.C. area who were killed in an auto accident in Saudi Arabia.

★4651★ Franklin Delano Roosevelt Prize
Society for History in the Federal Government
PO Box 14139, Benjamin Franklin Sta.
Washington, DC 20044
Ph: (301)220-1325

For recognition of an outstanding contribution to the furtherance of history in the federal government. Individuals who have a demonstrated record of outstanding accomplishments in such areas as historical publication, preservation, display, administration, or education are eligible. A citation and a plaque are awarded triennially. Established in 1983 in memory of Franklin Delano Roosevelt, a past President of the United States.

★4652★ Youth Achievement Award
Lewis and Clark Trail Heritage Foundation
Box 3434
Great Falls, MT 59403
Ph: (406)453-7091

For recognition of a person or group of persons under the age of 21 who has increased knowledge of the Lewis and Clark Expedition

through outstanding composition, art, drama, photography, site preservation and enhancement, or other significant contribution. A parchment certificate is presented at the annual meeting in August. Established in 1983.

BASIC REFERENCE GUIDES AND HANDBOOKS

★4653★ Elsevier's Lexicon of Archive Terminology: French, English, German, Spanish, Italian, Dutch
Elsevier Science Publishing Co., Inc.
655 Avenue of the Americas
New York, NY 10010
Ph: (212)989-5800

1964.

★4654★ Keeping Archives
Society of American Archivists (SAA)
600 S. Federal St., Ste. 504
Chicago, IL 60605
Ph: (312)922-0140

Ann Pederson, editor in chief. 1987. Comprehensively covers all the basics of archives administration. This text, with its numerous explanatory tables, sample forms, and helpful illustrations, serves as a guide to establishing and maintaining an effective archives service.

★4655★ A Library, Media & Archival Preservation Glossary
ABC-CLIO
PO Box 1911
Santa Barbara, CA 93116-1911
Ph: (805)688-9685   Fax: (805)968-1911
John N. DePew. 1992.

★4656★ The Management of Local Government Records: A Guide for Local Officials
American Association for State and Local History (AASLH)
172 2nd Ave., N., Ste. 102
Nashville, TN 37201
Ph: (615)255-2971

Bruce W. Dearstyne. 1988. Discusses the nature of public records, the different purposes for keeping them, and the costs of doing so; tells why to save and why to discard certain records, who makes those decisions, and what the benefits are from good records management.

★4657★ Preservation Microfilming: A Guide for Librarians and Archivists
Books on Demand
50 E. Huron St.
Chicago, IL 60611
Ph: (312)944-6780   Fr: 800-545-2433
Nancy E. Gwinn, editor. 1987. Offers a comprehensive step-by-step approach to the planning and implementation of microfilming projects. Gives an overview of the preservation microfilming process.

PROFESSIONAL AND TRADE PERIODICALS

★4658★ The Abbey Newsletter
Abbey Publications, Inc.
7105 Geneva Dr.
Austin, TX 78723
Ph: (512)929-3992   Fax: (512)929-3995
Ellen R. McCrady

Encourages the development of library and archival conservation, particularly technical advances and cross-disciplinary research in the field. Covers bookbinding and the conservation of books, papers, photographs, and non-paper materials. Recurring features include book reviews, news of research, job listings, convention reports, letters to the editor, a calendar of events, and a column about equipment and supplies.

★4659★ The American Archivist
Society of American Archivists
600 S. Federal St., Ste. 504
Chicago, IL 60605
Ph: (312)922-0140   Fax: (312)347-1452
Richard J. Cox

Quarterly. Journal for the North American archival profession disucssing trends in archival theory and practice including book reviews.

★4660★ American Historical Print Collectors Society—News Letter
American Historical Print Collectors Society, Inc.
2368 Old Salem Rd.
Auburn Hills, MI 48326
Ph: (810)332-3902
Donald C. O'Brien

Reports on Society programs, announces museum exhibitions of historical American prints, and lists auction prices of prints. Recurring features include news of members, editorials, and a calendar of events.

★4661★ Archival Outlook
Society of American Archivists
600 S. Fedl., Ste 504
Chicago, IL 60605-1898
Teresa Brinati, Contact

Bimonthly. Publishes news of relevance to the professional archival community. Recurring features include a calendar of events, reports of meetings, news of educational opportunities, and job listings.

★4662★ ConservatioNews
Center for Creative Photography
University of Arizona
Photographers Archives Library
Tucson, AZ 85721
Amy Rule

Quarterly. Concerned with the conservation of paper documents, magnetic media, bound volumes, photographs, and film. Carries articles on the theory and practice of conservation, questions and answers to specific problems, and product news. Recurring features include news of members, book reviews, and a calendar of events.

★4663★ *Manuscript Society—News*
Manuscript Society
350 N. Niagara St.
Burbank, CA 91505
S.L. Carson

Quarterly. Examines news regarding location and collection of handwritten documents, letters, and autographs of historic value. Carries news on preservation, thefts, forgeries, exhibits, and discoveries. Reports current chapter and Society news. Recurring features include news of members, personal profiles, annual meetings, notices of sale and trade opportunities, announcements of auctions, and a column from the president on the collection of historic documents.

★4664★ *Museum News*
American Assn. of Museums
1225 Eye St. NW, Ste. 200
Washington, DC 20005
Ph: (202)289-1818   Fax: (202)289-6578
John Strand

Bimonthly. Magazine for museums, employees, and trustees.

★4665★ *The Primary Source*
Soc. of Mississippi Archivists
PO Box 1151
Jackson, MS 39215-1151
Ph: (601)359-6868
Mattie Sink

Quarterly. Focuses on activities and trends in the archival and library community both regionally and nationally. Includes information on conservation and articles on state repositories and their holdings. Recurring features include news of research, book reviews, and a calendar of events.

OTHER SOURCES OF INFORMATION

★4666★ *A Code of Ethics for Archivists*
Society of American Archivists (SAA)
600 S. Federal St., Ste. 504
Chicago, IL 60605
Ph: (312)347-1452

1992. Provides standards for archivists in the areas of acquisition, access, appraisal, arrangement preservation, and interaction with other archivists.

★4667★ "Historic Preservation and Museum Studies" in *Accounting to Zoology: Graduate Fields Defined* (pp. 119-120)
Petersons Guides, Inc.
PO Box 2123
Princeton, NJ 08543-2123
Ph: (609)243-9111   Fax: (609)243-9150
Fr: 800-338-3282

Amy J. Goldstein, editor. Revised and updated, 1987. Defines 298 graduate and professional fields. Discusses types of graduate programs and degrees, graduate research, applied work, employment prospects, and trends.

★4668★ *Museum Careers and Training: A Professional Guide*
Greenwood Press Inc.
88 Post Rd., W
PO Box 5007
Westport, CT 06881
Ph: (203)226-3571   Fax: (203)222-1502
1994.

★4669★ "Museum Curator" in *Career Selector 2001*
Barron's Educational Series, Inc.
250 Wireless Blvd.
Hauppauge, NY 11788
Ph: (516)434-3311   Fax: (516)434-3723
Fr: 800-645-3476
James C. Gonyea. 1993.

College and University Faculty

College and university faculty teach and advise college students and perform a significant part of our nation's research. They also study and meet with colleagues to keep up with developments in their fields and consult with government, business, nonprofit, and community organizations.

Salaries

Earnings vary according to faculty rank and type of institution, and by field. Average salaries for full-time college and university faculty with nine month contracts are listed below:

Instructors	$27,700/year
Assistant professors	$36,800/year
Associate professors	$44,100/year
Professors	$59,500/year

Employment Outlook

Growth rate until the year 2005: Average.

College and University Faculty

CAREER GUIDES

★4670★ *ASCUS Annual: A Job Search Handbook for Educators*
Association for School, College and University Staffing (ASCUS)
1600 Dodge Ave., Ste. 330
Evanston, IL 60201-3451
Ph: (708)864-1999
Annual. Includes articles on the job market, job hunting techniques, locating job vacancies, resume writing, interviewing, job offers, and contracts. Also contains information about overseas employment, and employment in higher education. Includes a list of State Teacher Certification offices.

★4671★ "Assistant Professor" in *Career Opportunities for Writers* (pp. 164-165)
Facts on File
460 Park Ave. S.
New York, NY 10016-7382
Ph: (212)683-2244   Fax: 800-678-3633
Fr: 800-322-8755
Rosemary Guiley. 1992. Describes approximately 90 careers in eight major fields, offering such details as duties, salaries, prerequisites, employment and advancement oportunities, organizations to join, and opportunities for women and minorities.

★4672★ *Careers in Teaching*
TAB/McGraw-Hill, Inc.
PO Box 182607
Columbus, OH 43218-2607
Fax: (614)759-3644   Fr: 800-822-8158
Glen W. Cutlip, Ph.D. and Robert J. Schockley, Ph.D. 1994.

★4673★ "College Administrators" in *Encyclopedia of Careers and Vocational Guidance* (Vol.2, pp. 335-337)
J.G. Ferguson Publishing Co.
200 W. Madison St., Ste. 300
Chicago, IL 60606
Ph: (312)580-5480   Fax: (312)580-4948
William E. Hopke, editor-in-chief. Ninth edition, 1993. Four-volume set that profiles 900 occupations and describes job trends in 74 industries. Includes career description, educational requirements, history of the job, methods of entry, advancement, employment outlook, earnings, conditions of work, social and psychological factors, and sources of further information.

★4674★ "College Instructor" in *Exploring Careers in the Computer Field*
Rosen Publishing Group
29 E. 21st St.
New York, NY 10010
Ph: (212)777-3017   Fax: (212)777-0277
Fr: 800-237-9932
Joseph Weintraub. Revised edition, 1993. Describes future trends in computers including opportunities in hardware and software. Includes interviews with people in different computer careers including programming, consulting, and systems management. Provides state-by-state listing of universities and colleges offering two- and four-year degree programs in data processing and computer science.

★4675★ "College Professor" in *College Board Guide to Jobs and Career Planning* (pp. 171)
The College Board
415 Columbus Ave.
New York, NY 10023-6992
Ph: (212)713-8165   Fax: (212)713-8143
Fr: 800-323-7155
Joyce S. Mitchell. Second edition, 1994. Describes the job, salaries, related careers, education needed, and where to write for more information.

★4676★ "College Professor" in *Jobs Rated Almanac*
World Almanac
1 International Blvd., Ste. 444
Mahwah, NJ 07495
Ph: (201)529-6900   Fax: (201)529-6901
Les Krantz. Second edition, 1992. Ranks 250 jobs by environment, salary, outlooks, physical demands, stress, security, travel opportunities, and extra perks. Includes jobs the editor feels are the most common, most interesting, and the most rapidly growing.

★4677★ "College Teachers" in *Career Information Center* (Vol.11)
Simon and Schuster
200 Old Tappan Rd.
Old Tappan, NJ 07675
Fax: 800-445-6991   Fr: 800-223-2348
Richard Lidz and Linda Perrin, editorial directors. Fifth edition, 1993. This 13-volume set profiles over 600 occupations. Each occupational profile describes job duties, educational requirements, how to get the job, advancement possibilities, employment outlook, working conditions, earnings and benefits, and where to write for more information.

★4678★ "College and University Faculty" in *101 Careers: A Guide to the Fastest-Growing Opportunities* (pp. 161-163)
John Wiley & Sons, Inc.
605 3rd Ave.
New York, NY 10158-0012
Ph: (212)850-6645   Fax: (212)850-6088
Michael Harkavy. 1990. Describes the nature of the job, working conditions, employment growth, qualifications, personal skills, projected salaries, and where to write for more information.

★4679★ "College and University Faculty" in *Career Discovery Encyclopedia* (Vol.2, pp. 32-33)
J.G. Ferguson Publishing Co.
200 W. Madison St., Ste. 300
Chicago, IL 60606
Ph: (312)580-5480   Fax: (312)580-4948
Russell E. Primm, editor-in chief. 1993. This six volume set contains two-page articles for 504 occupations. Each article describes job duties, earnings, and educational and training requirements. The whole set is arranged alphabetically by job title. Designed for junior high and older students.

★4680★ "College and University Faculty" in *Encyclopedia of Careers and Vocational Guidance* (Vol.2, pp. 338-341)
J.G. Ferguson Publishing Co.
200 W. Madison St., Ste. 300
Chicago, IL 60606
Ph: (312)580-5480   Fax: (312)580-4948
William E. Hopke, editor-in-chief. Ninth edition, 1993. Four-volume set that profiles 900 occupations and describes job trends in 74

industries. Includes career description, educational requirements, history of the job, methods of entry, advancement, employment outlook, earnings, conditions of work, social and psychological factors, and sources of further information.

★4681★ "College and University Faculty" in *Jobs! What They Are—Where They Are—What They Pay* (p. 104)
Simon & Schuster, Inc.
Simon & Schuster Bldg.
1230 Avenue of the Americas
New York, NY 10020
Ph: (212)698-7000   Fr: 800-223-2348
Robert O. Snelling and Anne M. Snelling. 3rd edition, 1992. Describes duties and responsibilities, earnings, employment opportunities, training, and qualifications.

★4682★ "College and University Faculty" in *Occupational Outlook Handbook*
U.S. Government Printing Office
Superintendent of Documents
Washington, DC 20402
Ph: (202)512-1800   Fax: (202)512-2250
Biennial; latest edition, 1994-95. Encyclopedia of careers describing about 250 occupations and comprising about 85 percent of all jobs in the economy. Occupations that require lengthy education or training are given the most attention. Each occupation's profile describes what the worker does on the job, working conditions, education and training requirements, advancement possibilities, job outlook, earnings, and sources of additional information.

★4683★ "College and University Teacher" in *VGM's Careers Encyclopedia* (pp. 451-453)
National Textbook Co. (NTC)
VGM Career Books
4255 W. Touhy Ave.
Lincolnwood, IL 60646-1975
Ph: (708)679-5500   Fax: (708)679-2494
Fr: 800-323-4900
Third edition, 1991. Describes job duties, places of employment, working conditions, qualifications, education, and training, advancement potential, and salary for each occupation.

★4684★ "Education" in *Internships: 1995* (pp. 262-280)
Petersons Guides, Inc.
PO Box 2123
Princeton, NJ 08543-2123
Ph: (609)243-9111   Fax: (609)243-9150
Fr: 800-338-3282
Fifteenth edition, 1995. Lists internship opportunities under six broad categories: communications, creative, performing, and fine arts, human services, public relations, and business and technology. Includes a special section on internships in Washington, DC. For each internship program, gives the names, phone number, contact person, description, eligibility requirements, and benefits.

★4685★ *Faculty Members (College and University)*
Chronicle Guidance Publications, Inc.
66 Aurora St.
PO Box 1190
Moravia, NY 13118-1190
Ph: (315)497-0330   Fax: (315)497-3359
Fr: 800-622-7284
1993. Career brief describing the nature of the job, working conditions, hours and earnings, education and training, licensure, certification, unions, personal qualifications, social and psychological factors, location, employment outlook, entry methods, advancement, and related occupations.

★4686★ *Opportunities Abroad for Educators: Fulbright Teacher Exchange Program*
Teacher Exchange Branch
United State Information Agency
301 4 St.
Washington, DC 20547
Ph: (202)619-4700
Annual. This booklet describes the teacher exchange program, and includes applications for teaching positions and seminars abroad; gives a country listing of positions available.

★4687★ *Overseas Employment Opportunities for Educators*
Office of Dependents Schools
U.S. Department of Defense
3461 Eisenhower Ave.
Alexandria, VA 22331-1100
Ph: (703)325-0885
Annual. This booklet describes eligibility requirements, position requirements, application procedures, pay and benefits, housing living, and working conditions. Includes the application form.

★4688★ "Peter Hammond—University Professor" in *Straight Talk on Careers: Eighty Pros Take You Into Their Professions* (pp. 195-198)
Garrett Park Press
PO Box 1907
Garrett Park, MD 20896
Ph: (301)946-2553
Mary Barbera-Hogan. 1987. Contains candid interviews from people who give an inside view of their work in 80 different careers. These professionals describe a day's work and the stresses and rewards accompanying their work.

★4689★ "Professor" in *Profitable Careers in Non-Profit* (pp. 102-106)
John Wiley and Sons, Inc.
605 3rd Ave.
New York, NY 10158-0012
Ph: (212)850-6000   Fax: (212)850-6088
Fr: 800-526-5368
William Lewis and Carol Milano. 1987. Examines nonprofit organizations and the career opportunities they offer. Offers tips on how to target and explore occupational opportunities in the nonprofit sector.

★4690★ "Teacher" in *100 Best Careers for the Year 2000* (pp. 223-225)
Arco Pub.
201 W. 103rd St.
Indianapolis, IN 46290
Ph: 800-428-5331   Fax: 800-835-3202
Shelly Field. 1992. Describes 100 job opportunities expected to grow fast throughout the next decade. Provides information on job duties and responsibilities, training requirements, education, advancement opportunities, experience and qualifications, and typical salaries.

★4691★ *Teacher, College*
Careers, Inc.
PO Box 135
Largo, FL 34649-0135
Ph: (813)584-7333
1992. Four-page brief offering the definition, history, duties, working conditions, personal qualifications, educational requirements, earnings, hours, employment outlook, advancement, and careers related to this position.

★4692★ *Teaching as a Career*
American Federation of Teachers
555 New Jersey Ave., NW
Washington, DC 20001
Ph: (202)879-4400
1987. This eight-panel brochure describes the rewards of a teaching career, educational preparation, and job locations.

★4693★ "University and College Professors" in *American Almanac of Jobs and Salaries* (pp. 111)
Avon Books
1350 Avenue of the Americas
New York, NY 10019
Ph: (212)261-6800   Fr: 800-238-0658
John Wright, editor. Revised and updated, 1994-95. This is comprehensive guide to the wages of hundreds of occupations in a wide variety of industries and organizations.

PROFESSIONAL ASSOCIATIONS

★4694★ American Association of University Professors (AAUP)
1012 14th St. NW, Ste. 500
Washington, DC 20005
Ph: (202)737-5900   Fax: (202)737-5526
Fr: 800-424-2973
College and university teachers, research scholars, and academic librarians. Purposes are to facilitate cooperation among teachers and research scholars in universities, colleges, and professional schools, for the promotion of higher education and research, and to increase the usefulness and advance the standards, ideals, and welfare of the profession. Bestows awards; compiles statistics.
Publications: *AAUP Redbook.* • *Academe: Bulletin of the AAUP*, bimonthly. • *Collective Bargaining Newsletter.*

★4695★ American Federation of Teachers (AFT)
555 New Jersey Ave. NW
Washington, DC 20001
Ph: (202)879-4400   Fr: 800-238-1133
Members: AFL-CIO. Works with teachers and other educational employees at the state and local level in organizing, collective bargaining, research, educational issues, and public relations. **Purpose:** Conducts research in areas such as educational reform, bilingual education, teacher certification, and evaluation and national assessments and standards. Represents members' concerns through legislative action; offers technical assistance. Seeks to serve professionals with concerns similar to those of teachers, including state employees, healthcare workers, and paraprofessionals. **Publications:** *AFT Action: A Newsletter for AFT Leaders*, weekly. • *American Educator*, quarterly. • *American Teacher*, 8/year. • *Healthwire*, 10/year. • *On Campus*, 9/year. • *Public Sevice Reporter*, 9/year.

★4696★ Association of Astronomy Educators (AAE)
5103 Burt St.
Omaha, NE 68132
Ph: (402)556-0082   Fax: (402)280-2140
Members: Teachers and educators dedicated to improving astronomy education at all levels, from kindergarten to college. **Purpose:** Promotes astronomy education to enhance the scientific literacy of all students. Brings together resources and knowledge from a number of diverse groups. Works with the National Science Teachers Association. Cosponsors Astronomy Day. **Publications:** *Astronomy Education*, quarterly.

★4697★ Association for Business Communication (ABC)
University of North Texas
College of Business
Department of Management
Denton, TX 76203
Ph: (817)565-4423   Fax: (817)565-4930
Members: College teachers of business communication; management consultants in business communications; training directors and correspondence supervisors of business firms, direct mail copywriters, public relations writers, and others interested in communication for business. Sponsors research programs. **Publications:** *Bulletin of the Association for Business Communication*, quarterly. • *Journal of Business Communication*, quarterly.

★4698★ Career College Association (CCA)
750 1st St. NE, Ste. 900
Washington, DC 20002
Ph: (202)336-6700   Fax: (202)336-6828
Members: Private postsecondary schools providing career education. **Purpose:** Seeks to inform members of the accreditation process and regulations affecting vocational education. Conducts workshops and institutes for staffs of member schools; provides legislative, administrative, and public relations assistance. Has established Career Training Foundation to support research into private vocational education. Sponsors research programs. Maintains hall of fame; compiles statistics. **Publications:** *Career College Times*, monthly. • *Career Education*. • *Career News Digest*. • *Classroom Companion*, quarterly. • *Directory of Private Accredited Career Colleges and Schools*, annual.

★4699★ Center for Leadership Development (CLD)
1 Dupont Cir. NW, 8th Fl.
Washington, DC 20036
Ph: (202)939-9418   Fax: (202)785-8056
Members: Organized to provide professional development seminars on administrative decision making and academic leadership for future and current leaders in higher education. **Purpose:** Programs are conducted for presidents, department chairs, and fellows of the American Council on Education. Conducts sessions comprising a program of prominent speakers, seminars, case study analyses, and small group discussions covering concerns, problems, issues, and opportunities in academic administration.

★4700★ College and University Personnel Association (CUPA)
1233 20th St. NW, Ste. 301
Washington, DC 20036
Ph: (202)429-0311   Fax: (202)429-0149
Members: Professional organization made up of colleges and universities interested in the improvement of campus Human Resource administration. **Purpose:** Carries out special research projects and surveys, including annual administrative compensation survey for higher education. Sponsors training seminars to meet members' technical, professional, and developmental needs in human resource management. Disseminates information to members regarding federal legislation and regulations affecting higher education institutions. Compiles statistics. **Publications:** *Administrative Compensation Salary*, annual. • *CEO Survey*. • *Compensation and Benefits Survey of College and University Chief Executive Officers*, biennial. • *CUPA News*, biweekly. • *Faculty Salary Surveys for Public and Private Institutions*, annual. • *Personnel Director's Guide to Employment at Will*.

★4701★ Mathematical Association of America (MAA)
1529 18th St. NW
Washington, DC 20036
Ph: (202)387-5200   Fax: (202)265-2384
Members: College mathematics teachers; individuals using mathematics as a tool in a business or profession. **Purpose:** Sponsors annual high school mathematics contests and W.L. Putnam Competition for college students. Conducts faculty enhancement workshops and promotes the use of computers through classroom training. Offers college placement test program; operates speakers' bureau. **Publications:** *American Mathematical Monthly*. • *College Mathematics Journal*. • *Mathematical Association of America— Focus*, bimonthly. • *Mathematics Magazine*. • *Membership List*, annual.

★4702★ National Association of College and University Business Officers (NACUBO)
1 Dupont Cir. NW, Ste. 500
Washington, DC 20036
Ph: (202)861-2500   Fax: (202)861-2583
Members: Colleges, universities, and companies that are members of a regional association. **Purpose:** Develops and maintains national interest in improving the principles and practices of business and financial administration in higher education. Sponsors workshops in fields such as cash management, grant and contract maintenance, accounting, investment, student loan administration, and costing. Conducts research and information exchange programs between college and university personnel; compiles statistics. **Publications:** *Business Officer*, monthly. • *Financial Accounting and Reporting Manual*, bimonthly. • *NACUBO Membership Directory*, annual. • *National Association of College and University Business Officers— Annual Report*. • *National Association of College and University Business Officers— Special Action and Advisory Reports*.

★4703★ National Education Association (NEA)
1201 16th St. NW
Washington, DC 20036
Ph: (202)833-4000   Fax: (202)822-7974
Members: Professional organization and union of elementary and secondary school teachers, college and university professors, administrators, principals, counselors, and others concerned with education. **Publications:** *Almanac of Higher Education*. • *ESP Annual*. • *ESP Progress*, periodic. • *Handbook*, annual. • *Issues*, annual. • *NEA Higher Education Advocate*. • *NEA Today*, 8/year. • *Thought and Action*.

STANDARDS/CERTIFICATION AGENCIES

★4704★ American Federation of Teachers (AFT)
555 New Jersey Ave. NW
Washington, DC 20001
Ph: (202)879-4400   Fr: 800-238-1133
Conducts research in areas such as educational reform, bilingual education, teacher certification, and evaluation and national assessments and standards.

AWARDS, SCHOLARSHIPS, GRANTS, AND FELLOWSHIPS

★4705★ ACE Fellows Program
American Council on Education (ACE)
1 Dupont Circle
Washington, DC 20036-1193
Ph: (202)939-9420
Purpose: To enable college and university administrators to acquire more sophisticated

knowledge of funding, planning, budgeting, personnel management, and legal strategies. Qualifications: Nominees must have a minimum of five years of college-level experience as faculty members or as administrators and must have a record of leadership accomplishments. Selection criteria: Candidates are nominated by their institution's chief executive or chief academic officer. After an initial screening of candidates' credentials by a committee of higher education leaders, finalists are interviewed and approximately 30 fellows are selected by a panel of presidents and senior officers in higher education. Funds available: The nominating institution continues to pay the fellow's full salary and benefits during the fellowship year. The institution hosting a fellow is responsible for providing funds to cover the fellow's travel and meeting attendance costs, which amount to approximately $10,000. The institution providing the internship experience is also responsible for a $2,500 placement fee payable to ACE. Several grants are available on a competitive basis to nominating institutions that are ACE members and release their fellows for an off-campus fellowship. The grants range between $9,000 and $12,000 and are intended to help offset the institution's expense in replacing the fellow. Institutions that are not ACE members may nominate a candidate, but must pay an additional fee if the candidate is selected as a fellow. Application details: Nominations and candidates' application materials are sent to presidents and chief academic officers of all accredited institutions during the summer. Deadline: November 1. Finalists are selected and notified by January 15. Finalists are interviewed in Washington, DC, in late January and early February. Approximately 30 ACE Fellows are selected and notified of their appointment by March 1.

★4706★ American Accounting Association Fellowship Program in Accounting
American Accounting Association
5717 Bessie Dr.
Sarasota, FL 34233-2399
Ph: (813)921-7747   Fax: (813)923-4093

Purpose: To encourage and increase the supply of qualified teachers of accounting at the University level in the United States and Canada. Qualifications: Candidate must have been accepted into a doctoral program. Awards will only go to those students in their first year. Foreign students are eligble if a resident of the U.S. or Canada at the time of application and are enrooled in or have a degree from a U.S. or Canadian accredited graduate progarm and plan to teach in the U.S. or Canada. Funds available: $5,000. Application details: Contact the office manager for application guidelines, available in September. Deadline: 1 February. Notification by 31 March.

★4707★ Catalyst Awards
Chemical Manufacturers Association
2501 M St. NW
Washington, DC 20037
Ph: (202)887-1205   Fax: (202)887-1237

To publicly recognize exceptional chemistry or chemical engineering teachers within pre-high schools, high schools, and two and four-year colleges throughout the United States and Canada. Individuals with 10 years of ex-

perience are eligible for the national awards. There is no such requirement for the regional award. Only full-time teachers are considered. Nominations may be submitted by January 28. Each year, eight national award winners receive $5,000, a medal and a citation and 16 regional award winners receive $2,500, a medal and a citation. Awarded annually. Established in 1957.

★4708★ Dental Faculty Development Fellowships
ADA Endowment Fund and Assistance Fund Inc.
211 East Chicago Ave., 17th Fl.
Chicago, IL 60611
Ph: (312)440-2567   Fax: (312)440-2822

Purpose: To help dental faculty to improve their research and teaching skills. Qualifications: Applicant must be a U.S. citizen with a D.D.S. or D.M.D. degree. Applicant must be a full-time instructor, or an associate or assistant professor, at an accredited dental school in the United States. Funds available: $20,000. Application details: Write for application form. Submit completed application with curriculum vitae; a detailed outline of proposed course study; a research proposal, including methodology and a supporting statement from a qualified mentor; an outline of personal goals and objectives for the fellowship year; three letters of recommendation; and a letter of acceptance from a post-doctoral program, if applicable. Deadline: September 1. Notification in mid-December.

★4709★ Dental Teacher Training Fellowships
ADA Endowment Fund and Assistance Fund Inc.
211 East Chicago Ave., 17th Fl.
Chicago, IL 60611
Ph: (312)440-2567   Fax: (312)440-2822

Purpose: To support postdoctoral research and teacher training. Qualifications: Applicant must be a U.S. citizen with a D.D.S. or D.M.D. degree. Applicant must be in the final year of a postdoctoral research or teacher training program. Fellowships are tenable in the United States. Funds available: $20,000. Application details: Write for application forms. Submit completed application with curriculum vitae; dental school transcripts, including verification of class standing; verification of enrollment in the final year of a postdoctoral program; and three letters of recommendation, including one from the program director. Deadline: September 1. Notification in mid-December.

★4710★ Distinguished Teaching Award
National Science Teachers Association
1840 Wilson Blvd.
Arlington, VA 22201
Ph: (703)243-7100   Fax: (703)243-7700

To recognize elementary, middle/junior high, high school, and college teachers who have made extraordinary contributions to the field of science teaching. Plaques and complimentary one-year memberships are awarded annually. Sponsored by National Science Teachers Association. Established in 1987.

★4711★ Fulbright Scholar Program
Council for International Exchange of Scholars
3007 Tilden St. NW, Ste. 5M
Washington, DC 20008-3009
Ph: (202)686-7866   Fax: (202)362-3442

To encourage international understanding and the educational exchange of scholars. Applicants must have a doctorate or equivalent professional achievements, and university-level teaching experience. Applications are due August 1. Terms of awards vary from country to country, but generally include round-trip travel, maintenance allowances, and certain supplemental allowances. Approximately 1,000 U.S. academics and professionls are awarded Fulbright grants to lecture or carry out research in over 135 countries each year. Grants range in duration from two months to a full academic year. Except for specified programs, however, summer grants and grants for attendance at international conferences are not available. Awarded annually. Established in 1947 by Senator J. William Fulbright. Sponsored by the United States Information Agency. The CIES is affiliated with the American Council of Learned Societies.

★4712★ Neil A. Miner Award
National Association of Geology Teachers
Dept. of Geology
Western Washington Univ.
Bellingham, WA 98225
Ph: (206)650-3587   Fax: (206)650-7295

For recognition of exceptional contributions to the stimulation of interest in the earth sciences. College level teachers in the United States are eligible for the award. The deadline for nominations is May 1. A plaque is presented annually at the Association's Annual Meeting. Established in 1952 in memory of Neil A. Miner, for his unselfish outlook on life, and for his personal philosophy, which inspired fellow teachers as well as students.

PROFESSIONAL AND TRADE PERIODICALS

★4713★ AAHE Bulletin
American Association for Higher Education (AAHE)
1 Dupont Circle, Ste. 360
Washington, DC 20036
Ph: (202)293-6440   Fax: (202)462-7326
Bry Pollack

Monthly. Discusses effectiveness in higher education. Focuses on academic affairs, employment, public policy, teaching methods, technology, and assessment. Recurring features include interviews, news of research, and practical articles.

★4714★ Academic Leader
Magna Publications, Inc.
2718 Dryden Dr.
Madison, WI 53704
Ph: (608)249-2455
Doris Green

Monthly. Presents news and information of concern to academic deans and chairpersons. Covers aspects of educational administration such as budgeting and personnel. Carries information on using leadership skills to improve the performance of the individual faculty and staff members, as well as the department as a whole. Recurring features include reports on conferences and trends in education.

★4715★ *American Educator*
American Federation of Teachers
555 New Jersey Ave. NW
Washington, DC 20001
Ph: (202)879-4430
Liz McPike

Quarterly. Magazine on education.

★4716★ *Change*
Heldref Publications
Helen Dwight Reid Educational Foundation
1319 18th St. NW
Washington, DC 20036-1802
Ph: (202)296-6267   Fax: (202)296-5149
Fr: 800-365-9753
Nanette Wiese

Bimonthly. Magazine dealing with contemporary issues in higher learning.

★4717★ *Collective Bargaining Newsletter*
American Association of University Professors
1012 14th St., Ste. 500
Washington, DC 20005
Ph: (202)737-5900   Fax: (202)737-5526
Fr: 800-424-2973

Quarterly. Provides news and views relating to salary, contracts, academic positions, advancement of educational standards, and the general welfare of the profession. Recurring features include news of members, news of research, and notices of Association events and activities.

★4718★ *Community College Journal*
American Assn. of Community and Junior Colleges
1 Dupont Circle NW, Ste. 410
Washington, DC 20036-1176
Ph: (202)728-0200   Fax: (202)223-9390
Bonnie Gardner

Bimonthly. Educational magazine.

★4719★ *IHE Newsletter*
Institute of Higher Education (IHE)
Candler Hall
Athens, GA 30602-1772
Ph: (706)542-3464   Fax: (706)542-7588
Cameron Fincher

Periodic. Examines topics of general interest to administrators and faculty members in higher education institutions. Reviews trends and developments in such areas as curriculum reform, administration and governance, institutional assessment and goal-setting and program evaluation. Publishes papers presented at national and regional conferences.

★4720★ *Journal of Higher Education*
Ohio State University Press
1070 Carmack Rd.
Columbus, OH 43210
Ph: (614)292-6930   Fax: (614)292-2065
Robert J. Silverman

Bimonthly. Scholarly journal on the institution of higher education. Articles combine disciplinary methods with critical insight to investi-

gate issues important to faculty, administrators, and program managers.

★4721★ *NASPA Forum*
National Association of Student Personnel Administrators, Inc. (NASPA)
1875 Connecticut Ave. NW
Washington, DC 20009
Ph: (202)265-7500
Sybil Walker

Reports on Association activities and discusses topics related to student affairs. Covers subjects such as commuting students, college costs, minority students, the fraternity systems, and graduate and professional programs. Recurring features include conference reports and a calendar of events.

★4722★ *Phi Delta Kappan*
Phi Delta Kappa, Inc.
408 N. Union
Box 789
Bloomington, IN 47402-0789
Ph: (812)339-1156   Fax: (812)339-0018
Pauline B. Gough

Magazine for professional educators.

★4723★ *Tech Directions*
Prakken Publications, Inc.
275 Metty Dr., Ste. 1
Box 8623
Ann Arbor, MI 48107
Ph: (313)769-1211   Fax: (313)769-8383
Fr: 800-530-9673
Paul J. Bramford

Magazine covering industrial education, technology education, trade and industry, and vocational education. Articles are geared for teacher use and reference from middle school throught postsecondary levels.

PROFESSIONAL MEETINGS AND CONVENTIONS

★4724★ **American Association of Physics Teachers Winter Meeting**
American Association of Physics Teachers (AAPT)
5112 Berwyn Rd.
College Park, MD 20740
Ph: (301)345-4200   Fax: (301)345-1857
Annual. Always held during January.

★4725★ **American Society for Engineering Education Conference and Exhibit**
American Society for Engineering Education
1818 North St., Ste. 600
Washington, DC 20036
Ph: (202)331-3500   Fax: (202)265-8504
Annual. Always held during June. **Dates and Locations:** 1996 Jun 23-26; Washington, DC.

★4726★ **American Technical Education Association National Conference on Technical Education**
American Technical Education Association
800 Sixth St. N.
North Dakota State College of Science
Wahpeton, ND 58076
Ph: (701)671-2240   Fax: (701)671-2260
Always held during March. **Dates and Locations:** 1996 Mar 14-17.

★4727★ **Association for Education in Journalism and Mass Communication Annual Convention**
Association for Education in Journalism and Mass Communication
1621 College St.
University of South Carolina
Columbia, SC 29208-0251
Ph: (803)777-2005   Fax: (803)777-4728
Annual.

★4728★ **Association for Gerontology in Higher Education Annual Meeting**
Association for Gerontology in Higher Education
1001 Connecticut Ave., NW, Ste. 410
Washington, DC 20036-5504
Ph: (202)429-9277
Annual.

★4729★ **Association of Teacher Educators Annual Conference**
Glencoe
15319 Chatsworth St.
Mission Hills, CA 91345
Ph: (818)898-1391
Annual. Always held during February. **Dates and Locations:** 1996 Feb.

★4730★ **NAFSA - Association of International Educators Annual Conference**
NAFSA - Association of International Educator
1875 Connecticut Ave. NW, Ste. 1000
Washington, DC 20009-5728
Ph: (202)462-4811   Fax: (202)667-3419
Annual.

★4731★ **National Association of Biology Teachers National Convention**
National Association of Biology Teachers
11250 Roger Bacon Dr., Ste. 19
Reston, VA 22090
Ph: (703)471-1134
Annual. **Dates and Locations:** 1995 Oct 25-28; Phoenix, AZ. • 1996 Oct 16-19; Charlotte, NC.

★4732★ **National Education Association Annual Meeting and Exposition**
National Educational Association
1201 16th St., NW
Washington, DC 20036
Ph: (202)833-4000   Fax: (202)822-7767
Annual.

★4733★ Southwestern Federation of Administrative Disciplines Convention
Southwestern Federation of Administrative Disciplines
2700 Bay Area Blvd.
Houston, TX 77058
Ph: (713)283-3122   Fax: (713)283-3951
Annual. Always held during March. **Dates and Locations:** 1996 Mar 05-09; Houston, TX. • 1997 Mar 11-15; New Orleans, LA. • 1998 Mar 03-07; Dallas, TX.

OTHER SOURCES OF INFORMATION

★4734★ "Community College Education" in *Accounting to Zoology: Graduate Fields Defined* **(pp. 68-69)**
Petersons Guides, Inc.
PO Box 2123
Princeton, NJ 08543-2123
Ph: (609)243-9111   Fax: (609)243-9150
Fr: 800-338-3282
Amy J. Goldstein, editor. Revised and updated, 1987. Discusses types of graduate programs and degrees, graduate research, applied work, employment prospects and trends.

★4735★ Community College Fact Book
American Council on Education
1 Dupont Circle
Washington, DC 20036
Ph: (212)702-2000   Fr: 800-257-5755
Elaine D. D. El-Khawas, Deborah J. Carter, and Cecilia A. Ottinger, compilers. 1989. Published by American Council on Educa-

tion. Contains statistics on community colleges.

★4736★ "Dean of Students (College)" in *Career Selector 2001*
Barron's Educational Series, Inc.
250 Wireless Blvd.
Hauppauge, NY 11788
Ph: (516)434-3311   Fax: (516)434-3723
Fr: 800-645-3476
James C. Gonyea. 1993.

★4737★ Fostering a Climate for Faculty Scholarship at Community, Technical, and Junior Colleges
American Assn. of Community and Junior Colleges
1 Dupont Circle, NW, Ste. 410
Washington, DC 20036
Ph: (202)728-0200
Jim Palmer, editor. 1992. (202)223-9390.

★4738★ Get Funded!: A Practical Guide for Scholars Seeking Research Support from Business
Sage Publications, Inc.
2455 Teller Rd.
Newbury Park, CA 91320
Ph: (805)499-0721
Dorin Schumacher, editor. 1992. (805)499-0871.

★4739★ "Higher Education" in *Accounting to Zoology: Graduate Fields Defined* **(pp. 88-89)**
Petersons Guides, Inc.
PO Box 2123
Princeton, NJ 08543-2123
Ph: (609)243-9111   Fax: (609)243-9150
Fr: 800-338-3282
Amy J. Goldstein, editor. Revised and updated, 1987. Discusses types of graduate

programs and degrees, graduate research, applied work, employment prospects and trends.

★4740★ The New Faculty Member: Supporting and Fostering Professional Development
Jossey-Bass, Inc., Publishers
350 Sansome St.
San Francisco, CA 94104
Ph: (415)433-1740   Fax: (415)433-0499
Robert Boice, editor. 1992.

★4741★ Requirements for Certification of Teachers, Counselors, Librarians, Administrators for Elementary and Secondary Schools, and Junior Colleges
University of Chicago Press
11030 S. Langley Ave.
Chicago, IL 60628
Ph: (312)702-7700   Fr: 800-621-2736
Mary P. Burks, Annual. Fifty-ninth edition, 1994. State-by-state listing of certification requirements for teachers, counselors, librarians, and administrators. Lists addresses of state departments of education.

★4742★ The Teacher's Almanac
Facts on File
460 Park Ave. S.
New York, NY 10016-7382
Ph: (212)683-2244   Fax: 800-678-3633
Fr: 800-322-8755
Sherwood Harris and Lorna B. Harris, editors. 1988. Contains statistical information such as teachers' salaries, educational finances, and state rankings.

Counselors

Counselors assist people with personal, family, social, educational, and career problems and concerns. Their duties depend on the individuals they serve and the settings in which they work. **School and college counselors** use interviews, counseling sessions, tests, or other tools to help students understand their abilities, interests, talents, and personality characteristics. **College career planning and placement counselors** help students and alumni plan careers and locate jobs. **Rehabilitation counselors** help persons deal with personal, social, and vocational impact of their disabilities. The counselor's goal is to help persons who are disabled become more self-sufficient and productive. **Employment counselors** help individuals make wise career decisions. **Mental health counselors** work with individuals and groups to promote optimum mental health. They help individuals deal with substance abuse, parenting, martial problems, family, suicide, stress management, problems with self-esteem, issues associated with aging, job and career concerns, educational decisions, and issues of mental and emotional health. Other counselors specialize in a particular social issue or population group such as: marriage and family; multi cultural; and gerontological counseling.

Salaries

Self-employed counselors with established practices have the highest earnings. Earnings of rehabilitation, mental health, and employment counselors are usually lower than those of school counselors. The average salary of school counselors is as follows:

School counselors $40,400/year

Employment Outlook

Growth rate until the year 2005: Faster than the average.

Counselors

CAREER GUIDES

★4743★ "AIDS Counselor" in *Career Information Center* (Vol.7)
Simon and Schuster
200 Old Tappan Rd.
Old Tappan, NJ 07675
Fax: 800-445-6991   Fr: 800-223-2348

Richard Lidz and Linda Perrin, editorial directors. Fifth edition, 1993. This 13-volume set profiles over 600 occupations. Each occupational profile describes job duties, entry-level requirements, educational requirements, advancement possibilities, employment outlook, working conditions, earnings and benefits, and where to write for more information.

★4744★ "Alcohol and Drug Abuse Counselor" in *100 Best Careers for the Year 2000* (pp. 32-34)
Arco Pub.
201 W. 103rd St.
Indianapolis, IN 46290
Ph: 800-428-5331   Fax: 800-835-3202

Shelly Field. 1992. Describes 100 job opportunities expected to grow fast throughout the next decade. Provides information on job duties and responsibilities, training requirements, education, advancement opportunities, experience and qualifications, and typical salaries.

★4745★ "Alcohol and Drug Counselors" in *101 Careers: A Guide to the Fastest-Growing Opportunities* (pp. 124-127)
John Wiley & Sons, Inc.
605 3rd Ave.
New York, NY 10158-0012
Ph: (212)850-6645   Fax: (212)850-6088

Michael Harkavy. 1990. Describes the nature of the job, working conditions, employment growth, qualifications, personal skills, projected salaries, and where to write for more information.

★4746★ *Career Counselor*
Vocational Biographies, Inc.
PO Box 31
Sauk Centre, MN 56378-0031
Ph: (612)352-6516   Fax: (612)352-5546
Fr: 800-255-0752

1992. Four-page pamphlet containing a personal narrative about a worker's job, work likes and dislikes, career path from high school to the present, education and training, the rewards and frustrations, and the effects of the job on the rest of the worker's life. The data file portion of this pamphlet gives a concise occupational summary, including work description, working conditions, places of employment, personal characteristics, education and training, job outlook, and salary range.

★4747★ *Career Counselors*
Chronicle Guidance Publications, Inc.
66 Aurora St.
PO Box 1190
Moravia, NY 13118-1190
Ph: (315)497-0330   Fax: (315)497-3359
Fr: 800-622-7284

1993. Career brief describing the nature of the job, working conditions, hours and earnings, education and training, licensure, certification, unions, personal qualifications, social and psychological factors, location, employment outlook, entry methods, advancement, and related occupations.

★4748★ "Career Planning and Placements Staff" in *Liberal Arts Jobs*
Petersons Guides, Inc.
PO Box 2123
Princeton, NJ 08543-2123
Ph: (609)243-9111   Fax: (609)243-9150
Fr: 800-338-3282

Burton Jay Nadler. Second edition, 1989. Strives to help the liberal arts graduate identify skills for entry-level positions. Gives goal setting and job search advice.

★4749★ *Careers in Social and Rehabilitation Services*
National Textbook Co. (NTC)
VGM Career Books
4255 W. Touhy Ave.
Lincolnwood, IL 60646-1975
Ph: (708)679-5500   Fax: (708)679-2494
Fr: 800-323-4900

Geraldine O. Garner, Ph.D., editor. 1993. Describes dozens of careers in the field of social and rehabilitation services.

★4750★ "College Student Personnel Workers" in *Career Information Center* (Vol.11)
Simon and Schuster
200 Old Tappan Rd.
Old Tappan, NJ 07675
Fax: 800-445-6991   Fr: 800-223-2348

Richard Lidz and Linda Perrin, editorial directors. Fifth edition, 1993. This 13-volume set profiles over 600 occupations. Each occupational profile describes job duties, educational requirements, how to get the job, advancement possibilities, employment outlook, working conditions, earnings and benefits, and where to write for more information.

★4751★ "Counseling" in *Career Choices for the 90's for Students of Psychology* (pp. 116-118)
Walker and Co.
435 Hudson St.
New York, NY 10014
Ph: (212)727-8300   Fax: (212)727-0984
Fr: 800-289-2553

Compiled by Career Associates Staff. 1990. This book offers alternatives for students of psychology. Gives information about the outlook and competition for entry-level candidates. Provides job hunting tips.

★4752★ "Counseling" in *Encyclopedia of Career Choices for the 1990s: A Guide to Entry Level Jobs* (pp. 422-424)
Berkley Pub.
PO Box 506
East Rutherford, NJ 07073
Fax: (201)933-2316   Fr: 800-788-6262

1992. Describes entry-level careers in a variety of industries. Presents qualifications required, working conditions, salary, internships, and professional associations.

★4753★ Counselor, School
Careers, Inc.
PO Box 135
Largo, FL 34649-0135
Ph: (813)584-7333
1991. Two-page occupational summary card describing duties, working conditions, personal qualifications, training, earnings and hours, employment outlook, places of employment, related careers, and where to write for more information.

★4754★ Counselor, Vocational Rehabilitation
Careers, Inc.
PO Box 135
Largo, FL 34649-0135
Ph: (813)584-7333
1993. Two-page occupational summary card describing duties, working conditions, personal qualifications, training, earnings and hours, employment outlook, places of employment, related careers, and where to write for more information.

★4755★ "Counselors" in America's 50 Fastest Growing Jobs (pp. 36)
JIST Works, Inc.
720 N. Park Ave.
Indianapolis, IN 46202-3431
Ph: (317)264-3720   Fax: (317)264-3709
Fr: 800-648-5478
Michael J. Farr, compiler. 1994. Describes the 50 fastest growing jobs within major career clusters such as technicians, and marketing and sales. Each job profile explains the nature of the work, skills and abilities required, employment outlook, average earnings, related occupations, education and training requirements, and employment opportunities. Also contains career planning information and job search tips.

★4756★ "Counselors" in Encyclopedia of Careers and Vocational Guidance
J.G. Ferguson Publishing Co.
200 W. Madison St., Ste. 300
Chicago, IL 60606
Ph: (312)580-5480   Fax: (312)580-4948
William E. Hopke, editor-in-chief. Ninth edition, 1993. Four-volume set that profiles 900 occupations and describes job trends in 74 industries. Includes chapters entitled "Career Counselors", "College Student Personnel Workers", "Employment Counselors", "Guidance Counselors", "College Career Planning and Placement Counselors", and "Rehabilitation Counselors". Includes career description, educational requirements, history of the job, methods of entry, advancement, employment outlook, earnings, conditions of work, social and psychological factors, and sources of further information.

★4757★ "Counselors" in Occupational Outlook Handbook
U.S. Government Printing Office
Superintendent of Documents
Washington, DC 20402
Ph: (202)512-1800   Fax: (202)512-2250
Biennial; latest edition, 1994-95. Encyclopedia of careers describing about 250 occupations and comprising about 85 percent of all jobs in the economy. Occupations that require lengthy education or training are given the most attention. Each occupation's profile

describes what the worker does on the job, working conditions, education and training requirements, advancement possibilities, job outlook, earnings, and sources of additional information.

★4758★ "Counselors" in Opportunities in Social Work Careers (pp. 76-78)
National Textbook Co. (NTC)
VGM Career Books
4255 W. Touhy Ave.
Lincolnwood, IL 60646-1975
Ph: (708)679-5500   Fax: (708)679-2494
Fr: 800-323-4900
Renee Wittenberg. 1988. Describes the skills required for a job in social work, educational preparation, work settings and related careers. Lists additional resources.

★4759★ "Counselors and Psychologists" in Career Paths in the Field of Aging: Professional Gerontology (pp. 30-31)
Simon and Schuster
200 Old Tappan Rd.
Old Tappan, NJ 07675
Fax: 800-445-6991   Fr: 800-223-2348
David A. Peterson. 1987. Provides a history of the gerontology profession, and describes jobs, education and skills required, employment outlook and trends in the field.

★4760★ Crisis Counselor
Vocational Biographies, Inc.
PO Box 31
Sauk Centre, MN 56378-0031
Ph: (612)352-6516   Fax: (612)352-5546
Fr: 800-255-0752
1994. Four-page pamphlet containing a personal narrative about a worker's job, work likes and dislikes, career path from high school to the present. Education and training, the rewards and frustrations, and the effects of the job on the rest of the worker's life. The data file portion of this pamphlet gives a concise occupational summary, including work descriptions, working conditions, places of employment, personal characteristics, education and training, job outlook, and salary range.

★4761★ Educational Career Directory
Gale Research Inc.
835 Penobscot Bldg.
Detroit, MI 48226
Ph: (313)961-2242   Fr: 800-877-GALE
1994.

★4762★ Employee Assistance Counselor
Vocational Biographies, Inc.
PO Box 31
Sauk Centre, MN 56378-0031
Ph: (612)352-6516   Fax: (612)352-5546
Fr: 800-255-0752
1992. Four-page pamphlet containing a personal narrative about a worker's job, work likes and dislikes, career path from high school to the present. Education and training, the rewards and frustrations, and the effects of the job on the rest of the worker's life. The data file portion of this pamphlet gives a concise occupational summary, including work descriptions, working conditions, places of employment, personal characteristics, education and training, job outlook, and salary range.

★4763★ "Employment Counselor" in VGM's Careers Encyclopedia (pp. 161-163)
National Textbook Co. (NTC)
VGM Career Books
4255 W. Touhy Ave.
Lincolnwood, IL 60646-1975
Ph: (708)679-5500   Fax: (708)679-2494
Fr: 800-323-4900
Third edition, 1991. Describes job duties, places of employment, working conditions, qualifications, education, and training, advancement potential, and salary for each occupation.

★4764★ "Guidance Counselor" in Profitable Careers in Non-Profit (pp. 77-82)
John Wiley and Sons, Inc.
605 3rd Ave.
New York, NY 10158-0012
Ph: (212)850-6000   Fax: (212)850-6088
Fr: 800-526-5368
William Lewis and Carol Milano. 1987. Examines nonprofit organizations and the career opportunities they offer. Offers tips on how to target and explore occupational opportunities in the nonprofit sector.

★4765★ "Guidance Counselor" in VGM's Careers Encyclopedia (pp. 202-204)
National Textbook Co. (NTC)
VGM Career Books
4255 W. Touhy Ave.
Lincolnwood, IL 60646-1975
Ph: (708)679-5500   Fax: (708)679-2494
Fr: 800-323-4900
Third edition, 1991. Describes job duties, places of employment, working conditions, qualifications, education, and training, advancement potential, and salary for each occupation.

★4766★ "Guidance Counselors" in 101 Careers: A Guide to the Fastest-Growing Opportunities (pp. 170-173)
John Wiley & Sons, Inc.
605 3rd Ave.
New York, NY 10158-0012
Ph: (212)850-6645   Fax: (212)850-6088
Michael Harkavy. 1990. Describes the nature of the job, working conditions, employment growth, qualifications, personal skills, projected salaries, and where to write for more information.

★4767★ "Guidance/Employment Counselor" in Jobs Rated Almanac
World Almanac
1 International Blvd., Ste. 444
Mahwah, NJ 07495
Ph: (201)529-6900   Fax: (201)529-6901
Les Krantz. Second edition, 1992. Ranks 250 jobs by environment, salary, outlooks, physical demands, stress, security, travel opportunities, and extra perks. Includes jobs the editor feels are the most common, most interesting, and the most rapidly growing.

★4768★ Opportunities in Counseling and Development Careers
National Textbook Co. (NTC)
VGM Career Books
4255 W. Touhy Ave.
Lincolnwood, IL 60646-1975
Ph: (708)679-5500   Fax: (708)679-2494
Fr: 800-323-4900
Neale J. Baxter. 1990. This book describes different types of counselors, including rehabilitation and school. For each counseling field, gives a description of the work, employment outlook, salary, benefits, working conditions, entry requirements, and a career ladder. Explores history and current issues in counseling.

★4769★ Pregnancy Counselor
Vocational Biographies, Inc.
PO Box 31
Sauk Centre, MN 56378-0031
Ph: (612)352-6516   Fax: (612)352-5546
Fr: 800-255-0752
1993. Four-page pamphlet containing a personal narrative about a worker's job, work likes and dislikes, career path from high school to the present. Education and training, the rewards and frustrations, and the effects of the job on the rest of the worker's life. The data file portion of this pamphlet gives a concise occupational summary, including work descriptions, working conditions, places of employment, personal characteristics, education and training, job outlook, and salary range.

★4770★ "Professional Employment Counselors" in Jobs! What They Are—Where They Are—What They Pay! (pp. 90)
Simon & Schuster, Inc.
Simon & Schuster Bldg.
1230 Avenue of the Americas
New York, NY 10020
Ph: (212)698-7000   Fr: 800-223-2348
Robert O. Snelling and Anne M. Snelling. Third revised edition, 1992. Includes chapters titled "Rehabilitation Counselor" (p. 92) and "School Guidance Counselors and Career-Planning and Placement Counselors" (p. 93). Describes duties and responsibilities, earnings, employment opportunities, training, and qualifications.

★4771★ Professional Orientation to Counseling
Taylor and Transit Publishing
1900 Frost Rd., Ste. 101
Bristol, PA 19007
Fax: (215)785-5515   Fr: 800-222-1166
Nicholas A. Vacc and Larry C. Loesch. Second edition, 1993. Explains the expectations, activities, and behaviors of professional counselors. Covers counseling theroy and practice, career development, assessment and measurement, consultation, research, and trends in professional counseling.

★4772★ "Rehabilitation Counselor" in Career Information Center (Vol.11)
Simon and Schuster
200 Old Tappan Rd.
Old Tappan, NJ 07675
Fax: 800-445-6991   Fr: 800-223-2348
Richard Lidz and Linda Perrin, editorial directors. Fifth edition, 1993. This 13-volume set

profiles over 600 occupations. Each occupational profile describes job duties, educational requirements, how to get the job, advancement possibilities, employment outlook, working conditions, earnings and benefits, and where to write for more information.

★4773★ "Rehabilitation Counselor" in Careers in Health Care (pp. 245-250)
National Textbook Co. (NTC)
VGM Career Books
4255 W. Touhy Ave.
Lincolnwood, IL 60646-1975
Ph: (708)679-5500   Fax: (708)679-2494
Fr: 800-323-4900
Barbara M. Swanson. Third edition, 1995. Describes job duties, work settings, salaries, licensing and certification requirements, educational preparation, and future outlook.

★4774★ "Rehabilitation Counselor" in College Board Guide to Jobs and Career Planning (pp. 314)
The College Board
415 Columbus Ave.
New York, NY 10023-6992
Ph: (212)713-8165   Fax: (212)713-8143
Fr: 800-323-7155
Joyce S. Mitchell. Second edition, 1994. Describes the job, salaries, related careers, education needed, and where to write for more information.

★4775★ "Rehabilitation Counselor" in VGM's Careers Encyclopedia (pp. 402-404)
National Textbook Co. (NTC)
VGM Career Books
4255 W. Touhy Ave.
Lincolnwood, IL 60646-1975
Ph: (708)679-5500   Fax: (708)679-2494
Fr: 800-323-4900
Third edition, 1991. Describes job duties, places of employment, working conditions, qualifications, education, and training, advancement potential, and salary for each occupation.

★4776★ "Rehabilitation Counselor" in VGM's Handbook of Health Care Careers
National Textbook Co.
4255 W. Touhy Ave.
Lincolnwood, IL 60646-1975
Ph: (708)679-5500   Fax: (708)679-2494
Fr: 800-323-4900
Annette Selden. 1993. Contains 42 two-page occupational profiles describing job duties, places of employment, working conditions, qualifications, education, employment outlook, and income.

★4777★ Rehabilitation Counselors
Chronicle Guidance Publications, Inc.
66 Aurora St.
PO Box 1190
Moravia, NY 13118-1190
Ph: (315)497-0330   Fax: (315)497-3359
Fr: 800-622-7284
1991. Career brief describing the nature of the job, working conditions, hours and earnings, education and training, licensure, certification, unions, personal qualifications, social and psychological factors, location, employment outlook, entry methods, advancement, and related occupations.

★4778★ "School Counselor" in 100 Best Careers for the Year 2000 (pp. 226-228)
Arco Pub.
201 W. 103rd St.
Indianapolis, IN 46290
Ph: 800-428-5331   Fax: 800-835-3202
Shelly Field. 1992. Describes 100 job opportunities expected to grow fast throughout the next decade. Provides information on job duties and responsibilities, training requirements, education, advancement opportunities, experience and qualifications, and typical salaries.

★4779★ "School Counselor" in College Board Guide to Jobs and Career Planning (pp. 193)
The College Board
415 Columbus Ave.
New York, NY 10023-6992
Ph: (212)713-8165   Fax: (212)713-8143
Fr: 800-323-7155
Joyce S. Mitchell. Second edition, 1994. Describes the job, salaries, related careers, education needed, and where to write for more information.

★4780★ School Counselors
Chronicle Guidance Publications, Inc.
66 Aurora St.
PO Box 1190
Moravia, NY 13118-1190
Ph: (315)497-0330   Fax: (315)497-3359
Fr: 800-622-7284
1991. Career brief describing the nature of the job, working conditions, hours and earnings, education and training, licensure, certification, unions, personal qualifications, social and psychological factors, location, employment outlook, entry methods, advancement, and related occupations.

★4781★ "School Counselors" in Career Information Center (Vol.11)
Simon and Schuster
200 Old Tappan Rd.
Old Tappan, NJ 07675
Fax: 800-445-6991   Fr: 800-223-2348
Richard Lidz and Linda Perrin, editorial directors. Fifth edition, 1993. This 13-volume set profiles over 600 occupations. Each occupational profile describes job duties, educational requirements, how to get the job, advancement possibilities, employment outlook, working conditions, earnings and benefits, and where to write for more information.

★4782★ "Vocational Counselors" in Career Information Center (Vol.11)
Simon and Schuster
200 Old Tappan Rd.
Old Tappan, NJ 07675
Fax: 800-445-6991   Fr: 800-223-2348
Richard Lidz and Linda Perrin, editorial directors. Fifth edition, 1993. This 13-volume set profiles over 600 occupations. Each occupational profile describes job duties, educational requirements, how to get the job, advancement possibilities, employment outlook, working conditions, earnings and benefits, and where to write for more information.

★4783★ *Vocational Rehabilitation Counselor*
Vocational Biographies, Inc.
PO Box 31
Sauk Centre, MN 56378-0031
Ph: (612)352-6516   Fax: (612)352-5546
Fr: 800-255-0752

1993. Four-page pamphlet containing a personal narrative about a worker's job, work likes and dislikes, career path from high school to the present. Education and training, the rewards and frustrations, and the effects of the job on the rest of the worker's life. The data file portion of this pamphlet gives a concise occupational summary, including work descriptions, working conditions, places of employment, personal characteristics, education and training, job outlook, and salary range.

★4784★ "Vocational Rehabilitation Specialist" in *Guide to Federal Jobs* (p. 243)
Resource Directories
3361 Executive Pkwy., Ste. 302
Toledo, OH 43606
Ph: (419)536-5353   Fax: (419)536-7056
Fr: 800-274-8515

Rod W. Durgin, editor. Third edition, 1992. Contains information on finding and applying for federal jobs. Describes more than 200 professional and technical jobs for college graduates. Covers the nature of the work, salary, and geographic location. Lists college majors preferred for that occupation. Section one describes the function and work of government agencies that hire the most significant number of college graduates.

★4785★ *What Is Counseling and Human Development*
American Association for Counseling and Development (AACD)
5999 Stevenson Ave.
Alexandria, VA 22304
Ph: (703)823-9800

Eight-panel brochure describing what counselors do, where they work, the training and education required, and certification.

PROFESSIONAL ASSOCIATIONS

★4786★ **American Counseling Association (ACA)**
5999 Stevenson Ave.
Alexandria, VA 22304-3300
Ph: (703)823-9800   Fax: (703)823-0252
Fr: 800-347-6647

Members: Counseling professionals in elementary and secondary schools, higher education, community agencies and organizations, rehabilitation programs, government, industry, business, private practice, career counseling, and mental health counseling. **Purpose:** Provides placement service for members; conducts professional development institutes and provides liability insurance. Maintains Counseling and Human Development Foundation to fund counseling projects. **Publications:** *Career Development Quarterly*. • *Counseling and Values*, 3/year. • *Counseling Today*, monthly. • *Counselor Ed-*

ucation and Supervision, quarterly. • *Elementary School Guidance and Counseling*, quarterly. • *The Journal for Specialists in Group Work*, quarterly. • *Journal of Addictions and Offender Counseling*, semiannual. • *Journal of Counseling and Development*, bimonthly. • *Journal of Employment Counseling*, quarterly. • *The Journal of Humanistic Education and Development*, quarterly. • *Journal of Multicultural Counseling and Development*, quarterly. • *Measurement and Evaluation in Counseling and Development*, quarterly. • *Rehabilitation Counseling Bulletin*, quarterly. • *The School Counselor*.

★4787★ **American Mental Health Counselors Association (AMHCA)**
5999 Stevenson Ave.
Alexandria, VA 22304-3300
Ph: (703)823-9800   Fax: (703)751-1696
Fr: 800-326-2642

Members: A division of the American Counseling Association. Professional counselors employed in mental health services; students. **Purpose:** Aims to: deliver quality mental health services to children, youth, adults, families, and organizations; improve the availability and quality of counseling services through licensure and certification, political and legislative action, training standards, and consumer advocacy. Supports specialty and special interest networks. Fosters communication among members. **Publications:** *Advocate*, 10/year. • *Journal of Mental Health Counseling*, quarterly.

★4788★ **American School Counselor Association (ASCA)**
5999 Stevenson Ave.
Alexandria, VA 22304-3300
Ph: (703)823-9800   Fax: (703)461-3569
Fr: 800-347-6647

Members: School counselors; professionals engaged in school counseling or related activities at least 50% of the time; students; other interested individuals. **Purpose:** Promotes human rights, children's welfare, healthy learning environments, and positive interpersonal relationships; fosters academic, occupational, personal, and social growth among members. Works to improve professional standards in school counseling and in other student personnel services; seeks to further public awareness of such services. Develops and promotes career development programs; sponsors interprofessional activities and leadership development programs. Represents members' interests in governmental and public relations. Serves as liaison among members and counselors in other settings; disseminates educational, professional, and scientific materials. **Publications:** *ASCA Counselor*, 5/year. • *Elementary School Guidance and Counseling*, quarterly. • *The School Counselor*, 5/year.

★4789★ **Council of Rehabilitation Specialists (CRS)**
c/o American Council of the Blind
1155 15th St. NW, Ste. 720
Washington, DC 20005
Ph: (202)467-5081   Fax: (202)467-5085
Fr: 800-424-8666

Members: Rehabilitation and social service professionals, students pursuing careers in these fields, and interested individuals.

Purpose: Promotes the establishment of academic and professional standards; advocates adequate rehabilitation services for all blind and visually impaired persons. **Publications:** *Synergist Newsletter*.

★4790★ **National Board for Certified Counselors (NBCC)**
3-D Terrace Way
Greensboro, NC 27403
Ph: (910)547-0607   Fax: (910)547-0017
Fr: 800-398-5389

Purpose: Establishes and monitors professional credentialing standards for counselors. Identifies individuals who have obtained voluntary certification as a National Certified Counselor, one who assists persons with aging, vocational development, adolescence, family, and marital concerns, or a National Certified Career Counselor, one who aids in developing individualized career plans, or a National Certified School Counselor, one who specializes in counseling within the school setting, or a National Certified Gerontological Counselor, one who specializes in meeting the counseling needs of older people, or a Certified Clinical Mental Health Counselor, one who specializes in working in clinical settings, or a Master Addictions Counselor, one who specializes in addictions counseling. Monitors continuing education activities. Plans to institute online access to a national register. **Publications:** *NBCC News Notes*, quarterly. • *Preparation Guide for the National Clinical Mental Health Counseling Examination*. • *Preparation Guide for the National Counselor Examination for Licensure and Certification*.

★4791★ **National Council on Rehabilitation Education (NCRE)**
c/o Dr. Garth Eldredge
Utah State University
Department of Special Education
Logan, UT 84322-2870
Ph: (801)797-3241   Fax: (801)797-3572

Members: Academic institutions and organizations; professional educators, researchers, and students. **Purpose:** Goals are to: assist in the documentation of the effect of education in improving services to persons with disability; determine the skills and training necessary for effective rehabilitation services; develop role models, standards, and uniform licensure and certification requirements for rehabilitation personnel; interact with consumers and public and private sector policy makers. Disseminates information and provides forum for discussion. Sponsors specialized education and placement service. Compiles statistics. Serves as an advisory body to the National Rehabilitation Association and the Rehabilitation Services Administration; works closely with other agencies and associations in the field. **Publications:** *NCRE Newsletter*, quarterly. • *Rehabilitation Education*, quarterly.

★4792★ **National Rehabilitation Counseling Association (NRCA)**
8807 Sudley Rd., Ste. 102
Manassas, VA 22110-4719
Ph: (703)361-2077   Fax: (703)361-2489

Members: A division of the National Rehabilitation Association. Professional and student rehabilitation counselors. **Purpose:** Works to expand the role of counselors in the rehabilitation process and seeks to advance members' professional development. Supports legislation favoring the profession. **Publications:** *Journal of Applied Rehabilitation Counseling*, quarterly. • *Professional Report of the National Rehabilitation Counseling Association*.

STANDARDS/CERTIFICATION AGENCIES

★4793★ American Mental Health Counselors Association (AMHCA)
5999 Stevenson Ave.
Alexandria, VA 22304-3300
Ph: (703)823-9800   Fax: (703)751-1696
Fr: 800-326-2642

Aims to: deliver quality mental health services to children, youth, adults, families, and organizations; improve the availability and quality of counseling services through licensure and certification, political and legislative action, training standards, and consumer advocacy.

★4794★ Commission on Rehabilitation Counselor Certification (CRCC)
1835 Rohlwing Rd., Ste. E
Rolling Meadows, IL 60008
Ph: (708)394-2104   Fax: (708)394-2108

★4795★ Council of Rehabilitation Specialists (CRS)
c/o American Council of the Blind
1155 15th St. NW, Ste. 720
Washington, DC 20005
Ph: (202)467-5081   Fax: (202)467-5085
Fr: 800-424-8666

Promotes the establishment of academic and professional standards; advocates adequate rehabilitation services for all blind and visually impaired persons.

★4796★ National Board for Certified Counselors (NBCC)
3-D Terrace Way
Greensboro, NC 27403
Ph: (910)547-0607   Fax: (910)547-0017
Fr: 800-398-5389

Establishes and monitors professional credentialing standards for counselors. Identifies individuals who have obtained voluntary certification as a National Certified Counselor, one who assists persons with aging, vocational development, adolescence, family, and marital concerns, or a National Certified Career Counselor, one who aids in developing individualized career plans, or a National Certified School Counselor, one who specializes in counseling within the school setting, or a National Certified Gerontological Counselor, one who specializes in meeting the counseling needs of older people, or a Certified Clinical Mental Health Counselor, one who specializes in working in clinical settings, or a Master Addictions Counselor, one who specializes in addictions counseling.

★4797★ National Council for Accreditation of Teacher Education (NCATE)
2010 Massachusetts Ave. NW, Ste. 500
Washington, DC 20036-1023
Ph: (202)466-7496   Fax: (202)296-6620

Voluntary accrediting body devoted exclusively to: evaluation and accreditation of institutions for preparation of elementary and secondary school teachers; preparation of school service personnel, including school principals, supervisors, superintendents, guidance counselors, school psychologists, instructional technologists, and other specialists for school-oriented positions.

★4798★ National Council on Rehabilitation Education (NCRE)
c/o Dr. Garth Eldredge
Utah State University
Department of Special Education
Logan, UT 84322-2870
Ph: (801)797-3241   Fax: (801)797-3572

Goals are to: develop role models, standards, and uniform licensure and certification requirements for rehabilitation personnel; interact with consumers and public and private sector policy makers.

TEST GUIDES

★4799★ Career Examination Series: Addiction Specialist
National Learning Corp.
212 Michael Dr.
Syosset, NY 11791
Ph: (516)921-8888   Fax: (516)921-8743
Fr: 800-645-6337

Jack Rudman. 1993. Test guide including questions and answers for students or professionals in the field who seek advancement through examination.

★4800★ Career Examination Series: Certified Mental Health Counselor
National Learning Corp.
212 Michael Dr.
Syosset, NY 11791
Ph: (516)921-8888   Fax: (516)921-8743
Fr: 800-645-6337

Jack Rudman. 1993. Test guide including questions and answers for students or professionals in the field who seek advancement through examination.

★4801★ Career Examination Series: Counselor
National Learning Corp.
212 Michael Dr.
Syosset, NY 11791
Ph: (516)921-8888   Fax: (516)921-8743
Fr: 800-645-6337

Jack Rudman. Test guide including questions and answers for students or professionals in the field who seek advancement through examination.

★4802★ Career Examination Series: Mental Health Group Leader
National Learning Corp.
212 Michael Dr.
Syosset, NY 11791
Ph: (516)921-8888   Fax: (516)921-8743
Fr: 800-645-6337

Jack Rudman. 1993. Test guide including questions and answers for students or professionals in the field who seek advancement through examination.

★4803★ Career Examination Series: Supervising Youth Division Counselor
National Learning Corp.
212 Michael Dr.
Syosset, NY 11791
Ph: (516)921-8888   Fax: (516)921-8743
Fr: 800-645-6337

Jack Rudman. 1993. Test guide including questions and answers for students or professionals in the field who seek advancement through examination.

★4804★ Career Examination Series: Veteran Counselor
National Learning Corp.
212 Michael Dr.
Syosset, NY 11791
Ph: (516)921-8888   Fax: (516)921-8743
Fr: 800-645-6337

Jack Rudman. 1993. Test guide including questions and answers for students or professionals in the field who seek advancement through examination.

★4805★ Counselor: National Certification and State Licensing Examinations
Arco Pub.
201 W. 103rd St.
Indianapolis, IN 46290
Ph: 800-428-5331   Fax: 800-835-3202

1990. Covers CRC and NCC exams, state tests, and civil service tests.

★4806★ Fundamentals of Counseling
National Learning Corp.
212 Michael Dr.
Syosset, NY 11791
Ph: (516)921-8888   Fax: (516)921-8743
Fr: 800-645-6337

Jack Rudman. Part of Dantes Subject Standardized Tests.

★4807★ National Teacher Examination Series
National Learning Corp.
212 Michael Dr.
Syosset, NY 11791
Ph: (516)921-8888   Fax: (516)921-8743
Fr: 800-645-6337

Jack Rudman. Practice multiple-choice examinations for education certification. Includes solutions. Titles in the series include *National Teacher Examination (Core Battery)* (one-volume combined edition); *Agriculture; Art Education; Biology and General Science; Business Education; Chemistry and General Science; Chemistry, Physics, and General Science; Earth and Space Science; Education of the Mentally Retarded; English Language and Literature; French; German; Health Education; Home Economics Education; Mathematics; Latin; Marketing and Distributive Education; Men's Physical Educa-*

tion; Music Education; Physics and General Science; Physical Education; Psychological Foundations of Education; Psychology; School Psychology; Science and Mathematics; Social Studies; Social Studies, Literature and Fine Arts; Societal Foundations of Education; Spanish; Special Education; Speech Communication; Teaching Emotionally Disturbed; Teaching Hearing Handicapped; Teaching Learning Disabled; Teaching Orthopedically Handicapped; Teaching Principles and Practices; Teaching Speech Handicapped; Women's Physical Education; Written English Expression.

★4808★ Principles of Guidance
National Learning Corp.
212 Michael Dr.
Syosset, NY 11791
Ph: (516)921-8888   Fax: (516)921-8743
Fr: 800-645-6337

Jack Rudman. Part of the Dantes Subject Standardized Test series. A standardized graduate and college-level examination given by graduate schools, colleges, and the U.S. Armed Forces as a final examination for course evaluation in the field of counseling. Multiple-choice format with correct answers.

★4809★ Rehabilitation Counselor Certification Examination
National Learning Corp.
212 Michael Dr.
Syosset, NY 11791
Ph: (516)921-8888   Fax: (516)921-8743
Fr: 800-645-6337

Jack Rudman. Part of the Admission Test series. A sample test for those seeking admission to graduate and professional schools or seeking entrance or advancement in institutional and public career service in the field of counseling.

★4810★ Teachers License Examination Series: Guidance Counselor
National Learning Corp.
212 Michael Dr.
Syosset, NY 11791
Ph: (516)921-8888   Fax: (516)921-8743
Fr: 800-645-6337

Jack Rudman. A series of preparatory study guides for professionals studying for licensing examinations. Includes a multiple-choice test section; provides answers. Titles in the series related to counseling include Guidance Counselor, Elementary School; Guidance Counselor, Junior High School; Guidance Counselor, Senior High School.

EDUCATIONAL DIRECTORIES AND PROGRAMS

★4811★ Mental Health and Social Work Career Directory
Gale Research Inc.
835 Penobscot Bldg.
Detroit, MI 48226-4094
Ph: (313)961-2242   Fax: (313)961-6083
Fr: 800-877-GALE

Bradley J. Morgan and Joseph M. Palmisano. 1993. A directory in the Career Advisor Se-

ries that provides essays written by industry professionals; job search information on resume and cover letter preparation, networking, and the interviewing process; approximately 300 companies and organizations offering job opportunities and internships, and additional job-hunting resources.

AWARDS, SCHOLARSHIPS, GRANTS, AND FELLOWSHIPS

★4812★ Counselor of the Year Award
National Rehabilitation Counseling Association
8807 Sudley Rd., Ste. 102
Manassas, VA 22110
Ph: (703)620-4404   Fax: (703)361-2489

To recognize a rehabilitation counselor who has made a special contribution to the field of rehabilitation counseling and who has demonstrated excellence in counseling disabled individuals. Awards are presented at the state and regional levels. One award is presented to a rehabilitation counselor at the national level. Special nomination forms must be submitted for the state deadline, April 1; regional deadline, May 15; and national deadline, June 30. Awarded annually.

★4813★ Lullelia W. Harrison Scholarship in Counseling
Zeta Phi Beta Sorority
National Education Foundation
Executive Office
1734 New Hampshire Ave., N.W.
Washington, DC 20009
Ph: (202)387-3103   Fax: (202)232-4593

Qualifications: Applicants must be graduate or undergraduate students enrolled in a degree program in counseling. Funds available: $500 to $1,000 for one academic year. Application details: Completed applications must be returned along with references and an official university transcript. Deadline: February 1. Recipients are notified by August 15.

★4814★ Glen E. Hubele National Graduate Student Award
American Counseling Association
5999 Stevenson Ave.
Alexandria, VA 22304
Ph: (703)823-9800   Fax: (703)823-0252

For recognition of outstanding work in the development of a thesis, dissertation, or an original manuscript prepared and accepted for publication in an AACD or division professional journal. Graduate degree candidates in the field of counseling, guidance, and human development are eligible. The deadline for nominations is December 15. A monetary award of $450 is presented annually. Established by Mrs. Cicely D. Hubele in honor of her son, Glen E. Hubele, a former professor of Educational Psychology and Guidance at Eastern Illinois University, Charleston, IL.

★4815★ National Citations
National Rehabilitation Counseling Association
8807 Sudley Rd., Ste. 102
Manassas, VA 22110
Ph: (703)620-4404   Fax: (703)361-2489

To recognize meritorious service or significant achievements in the field of rehabilitation counseling services of the disabled on a local, state, or regional level. The citations may also be conferred on persons who have made outstanding contributions to the rehabilitation counseling field at the national level. The national deadline for nominations is May 15. Awarded annually.

★4816★ National Distinguished Service Award
National Rehabilitation Counseling Association
8807 Sudley Rd., Ste. 102
Manassas, VA 22110
Ph: (703)620-4404   Fax: (703)361-2489

To recognize unusual or significant professional or technical achievement in the rehabilitation counseling field or in providing services to the disabled on a national basis. The contribution must have had a national impact on the rehabilitation counseling field. Nominations must be submitted by the national deadline, May 15. Awarded annually.

BASIC REFERENCE GUIDES AND HANDBOOKS

★4817★ The Nuts and Bolts of Career Counseling: How to Set up and Succeed in Private Practice
Garrett Park Press
PO Box 190C
Garrett Park, MD 20896-0190
Ph: (301)946-2553

Al Hafer, editor. 1992. Offers advice on how to manage a counseling practice, how to relate to clients, and how to use the latest technology to best advantage.

★4818★ The Professional Counselor: A Process Guide to Helping
Allyn & Bacon, Inc.
160 Gould St.
Needham Heights, MA 02194
Ph: (617)455-1250   Fax: (617)455-1220
Fr: 800-852-8024

Sherilyn Cormier, editor. 1992.

★4819★ Rehabilitation Counseling and Services: Profession and Process
Charles C Thomas, Publisher
2600 S. 1st St.
Springfield, IL 62794-9265
Ph: (217)789-8980

Gerald L. Gandy, et al., editors. 1987.

PROFESSIONAL AND TRADE PERIODICALS

★4820★ AMHCA Advocate
American Mental Health Counselors
  Association (AMHCA)
5999 Stevenson Ave.
Alexandria, VA 22304
Ph: (703)823-9800   Fax: (703)823-0252
Fr: 800-326-2642
Carol Hacker

Publishes news of the programs, members, and activities of AMHCA. Provides updates regarding credentialing of counselors, mental health-related legislation, and insurance coverage of the expenses of mental health counseling. Recurring features include news of meetings and conferences and articles on topics of interest to clinical mental health counselors.

★4821★ Career Development Quarterly
American Assn. for Counseling and
  Development
5999 Stevenson Ave.
Alexandria, VA 22304
Ph: (703)823-9800   Fax: (703)823-0252
Paul R. Salamone

Quarterly. Journal for career counseling and career education professionals in schools, colleges, private practice, government agencies, personnel departments in business and industry, and employment counseling centers.

**★4822★ College Placement Council—
Spotlight**
College Placement Council
62 Highland Ave.
Bethlehem, PA 18017
Ph: (215)868-1421   Fax: (215)868-0208
Fr: 800-544-5272
Mimi Collins

Devoted to career planning and employment of college graduates. Recurring features include news of regulations and legislation, technological developments statistics, research, trends, publications, and events related to career development and employment.

**★4823★ Elementary School Guidance &
Counseling**
American Counseling Assn.
5999 Stevenson Ave.
Alexandria, VA 22304-3300
Ph: (703)823-9800   Fax: (703)823-0252
Stephren Brooks

Quarterly. Journal covering guidance program evaluation, development of new applications for theoretical ideas, and current research in elementary counseling.

★4824★ Guidepost
American Counseling Assn.
5999 Stevenson Ave.
Alexandria, VA 22304-3300
Ph: (703)823-9800   Fax: (703)823-0252
Jennifer L. Sacks

Association newspaper (tabloid) on counseling and human services.

**★4825★ International Academy of
Behavioral Medicine, Counseling, and
Psychotherapy—Newsletter**
International Academy of Behavioral
  Medicine, Counseling, and
  Psychotherapy
6750 Hillcrest Plaza, Ste. 304
Dallas, TX 75230
Ph: (214)458-8334   Fax: (214)490-5228
George R. Mount

Quarterly. Publishes research articles in the field of behavioral medicine, "the systematic application of various principles of behavioral science to health care problems." Contains news of the Academy and its members. Recurring features include book reviews, letters to the editor, and a calendar of events.

**★4826★ Journal of College Student
Development**
American Assn. for Counseling and
  Development
5999 Stevenson Ave.
Alexandria, VA 22304
Ph: (703)823-9800   Fax: (703)823-0252
Stephren Brooks

Bimonthly. Journal covering ideas for improving student services, research and development theory, professional issues, and ethics.

**★4827★ Journal of Counseling &
Development**
American Counseling Assn.
5999 Stevenson Ave.
Alexandria, VA 22304-3300
Ph: (703)823-9800   Fax: (703)823-0252
Ed Herr

Bimonthly. Scholarly journal on counseling and human development.

**★4828★ Journal of Employment
Counseling**
American Assn. for Counseling and
  Development
5999 Stevenson Ave.
Alexandria, VA 22304
Ph: (703)823-9800   Fax: (703)823-0252
Robert Drummond

Quarterly. Journal covering state employee, vocational, college placement, education, business, and industry counseling.

**★4829★ Journal of Mental Health
Counseling**
Sage Periodicals Press
2455 Teller Rd.
Thousand Oaks, CA 91320
Ph: (805)499-0721   Fax: (805)499-0871
Lawrence H. Gerstein

Quarterly. Journal of the American Mental Health Counselors Association containing articles on all aspects of practice, theory, and research relating to mental health counseling.

★4830★ Journal of Rehabilitation
National Rehabilitation Assn.
633 S. Washington St.
Alexandria, VA 22314
Ph: (703)836-0850   Fax: (703)836-0848
Paul Leung

Quarterly. Rehabilitation journal.

**★4831★ The Journal for Specialists in
Group Work**
American Counseling Assn.
5999 Stevenson Ave.
Alexandria, VA 22304-3300
Ph: (703)823-9800   Fax: (703)823-0252
Stephren Brooks

Quarterly. Journal reviewing theory, empirical research related to group medium, legal issues, and related literature.

★4832★ The School Counselor
American Counseling Assn.
5999 Stevenson Ave.
Alexandria, VA 22304-3300
Ph: (703)823-9800   Fax: (703)823-0252
Stephren Brooks

Journal covering current issues affecting teens, and how counselors can deal with them.

PROFESSIONAL MEETINGS AND CONVENTIONS

**★4833★ American Counseling
Association Annual Convention**
American Association for Counseling and
  Development
5999 Stevenson Ave.
Alexandria, VA 22304
Ph: (703)823-9800   Fax: (703)823-0252

Annual. Usually held during March or April. **Dates and Locations:** 1996 Apr 21-24; Pittsburgh, PA. • 1997 Apr 04-07; Orlando, FL. • 1998 Mar 29-01; Indianapolis, IN. • 2000 Mar 22-25; Washington, DC.

OTHER SOURCES OF INFORMATION

**★4834★ Career Planning in Criminal
Justice**
Anderson Publishing Co.
2035 Reading Rd.
Cincinnati, OH 45202
Ph: (513)421-4142

1990. Includes chapters describing careers in corrections, careers in forensic science, and careers in private security.

**★4835★ "Counselor Education" and
"Counseling Psychology" in
Accounting to Psychology: Graduate
Fields Defined (pp. 71-72, 181)**
Petersons Guides, Inc.
PO Box 2123
Princeton, NJ 08543-2123
Ph: (609)243-9111   Fax: (609)243-9150
Fr: 800-338-3282

Amy J. Goldstein, editor. Revised and updated, 1987. Discusses types of graduate programs and degrees, graduate research, applied work, employment prospects and trends.

★4836★ *Counselor Preparation*
Accelerated Development, Inc.
3400 Kilgore Ave.
Muncie, IN 47304-4896
Ph: (317)284-7511   Fax: (317)284-2535
Fr: 800-222-1166

Joseph Hollis, editor. 1994.

★4837★ *"Counselor (Professional)" in*
Career Selector 2001
Barron's Educational Series, Inc.
250 Wireless Blvd.
Hauppauge, NY 11788
Ph: (516)434-3311   Fax: (516)434-3723
Fr: 800-645-3476

James C. Gonyea. 1993.

★4838★ *"Psychologist/Counselor" in*
100 Best Jobs for the 1990s & Beyond
Dearborn Financial Publishing, Inc.
520 N. Dearborn St.
Chicago, IL 60610-4354
Ph: (312)836-4400   Fax: (312)836-1021
Fr: 800-621-9621

Carol Kleiman. 1992. Describes 100 jobs ranging from accountants to veterinarians. Each job profile includes such information as education, experience, and certification needed, salaries, and job search suggestions.

★4839★ *"Rehabilitation Counseling" in*
Accounting to Zoology: Graduate
Fields Defined (pp. 95-96)
Petersons Guides, Inc.
PO Box 2123
Princeton, NJ 08543-2123
Ph: (609)243-9111   Fax: (609)243-9150
Fr: 800-338-3282

Amy J. Goldstein, editor. Revised and updated, 1987. Discusses types of graduate programs and degrees, graduate research, applied work, employment prospects and trends.

★4840★ *Requirements for Certification*
of Teachers, Counselors, Librarians,
Administrators for Elementary and
Secondary Schools, and Junior
Colleges
University of Chicago Press
11030 S. Langley Ave.
Chicago, IL 60628
Ph: (312)702-7700   Fr: 800-621-2736

Mary P. Burks, Annual. Fifty-ninth edition, 1994. State-by-state listing of certification requirements for teachers, counselors, librarians, and administrators. Lists addresses of state departments of education.

★4841★ *Teacher as Counselor:*
Developing the Helping Skills You
Need
Corwin Press
2455 Teller Rd.
Newbury Park, CA 91320
Ph: (805)499-0721   Fax: (805)499-0871

Jeffrey A. Kottler. 1993.

Kindergarten and Elementary School Teachers

Kindergarten and elementary school teachers play a vital role in the development of children. They introduce children to numbers, language, science, and social studies. Teachers lecture and demonstrate to an entire class, and also provide individual attention as much as possible. Kindergarten and elementary school teachers may use games, music, artwork, films, slides, and computers to teach basic skills. They assign lessons, give tests, hear oral presentations, and oversee special projects. They maintain order in the classroom and instill good study habits and an appreciation for learning.

Salaries

Earnings in private schools are generally quite lower than salaries in public elementary schools.

Public elementary school teachers $34,800/year

Employment Outlook

Growth rate until the year 2005: Faster than the average.

Kindergarten and Elementary School Teachers

★4853★ Elementary School Teacher
Vocational Biographies, Inc.
PO Box 31
Sauk Centre, MN 56378-0031
Ph: (612)352-6516   Fax: (612)352-5546
Fr: 800-255-0752

1992. Four-page pamphlet containing a personal narrative about a worker's job, work likes and dislikes, career path from high school to the present, education and training, the rewards and frustrations, and the effects of the job on the rest of the worker's life. The data file portion of this pamphlet gives a concise occupational summary, including work description, working conditions, places of employment, personal characteristics, education and training, job outlook, and salary range.

★4854★ "Elementary School Teacher" in College Board Guide to Jobs and Career Planning (pp. 177)
The College Board
45 Columbus Ave.
New York, NY 10023-6992
Ph: (212)713-8165   Fax: (212)713-8143
Fr: 800-323-7155

Joyce S. Mitchell. Second edition, 1994. Describes the job, salaries, related careers, education needed, and where to write for more information.

★4855★ "Elementary School Teachers" in 101 Careers: A Guide to the Fastest-Growing Opportunities (pp. 167-169)
John Wiley & Sons, Inc.
605 3rd Ave.
New York, NY 10158-0012
Ph: (212)850-6645   Fax: (212)850-6088

Michael Harkavy. 1990. Describes the nature of the job, working conditions, employment growth, qualifications, personal skills, projected salaries, and where to write for more information.

★4856★ "Elementary School Teachers" in Career Discovery Encyclopedia (Vol.2, pp. 154-155)
J.G. Ferguson Publishing Co.
200 W. Madison St., Ste. 300
Chicago, IL 60606
Ph: (312)580-5480   Fax: (312)580-4948

Russell E. Primm, editor-in chief. 1993. This six volume set contains two-page articles for 504 occupations. Each article describes job duties, earnings, and educational and training requirements. The whole set is arranged alphabetically by job title. Designed for junior high and older students.

★4857★ "Elementary School Teachers" in Jobs! What They Are—Where They Are—What They Pay (p. 105)
Simon & Schuster, Inc.
Simon & Schuster Bldg.
1230 Avenue of the Americas
New York, NY 10020
Ph: (212)698-7000   Fr: 800-223-2348

Robert O. Snelling and Anne M. Snelling. 3rd edition, 1992. Describes duties and responsibilities, earnings, employment opportunities, training, and qualifications.

★4858★ How to Get a Job in Education
Bob Adams, Inc.
260 Center St.
Holbrook, MA 02343
Ph: (617)767-8100   Fr: 800-USA-JOBS

Joel Levin. 1995. Provides a comprehensive overview of the entire job search process for teachers, studying for the National Teacher Examination, and applying for the initial teaching certificate. Gives advice on resume writing, contacting school districts, and classroom teaching.

★4859★ "Kindergarten and Elementary School Teacher" in VGM's Careers Encyclopedia (pp. 453-456)
National Textbook Co. (NTC)
VGM Career Books
4255 W. Touhy Ave.
Lincolnwood, IL 60646-1975
Ph: (708)679-5500   Fax: (708)679-2494
Fr: 800-323-4900

Third edition, 1991. Describes job duties, places of employment, working conditions, qualifications, education, and training, advancement potential, and salary for each occupation.

★4860★ "Kindergarten, Elementary and Secondary School Teachers" in Occupational Outlook Handbook
U.S. Government Printing Office
Superintendent of Documents
Washington, DC 20402
Ph: (202)512-1800   Fax: (202)512-2250

Biennial; latest edition, 1994-95. Encyclopedia of careers describing about 250 occupations and comprising about 85 percent of all jobs in the economy. Occupations that require lengthy education or training are given the most attention. Each occupation's profile describes what the worker does on the job, working conditions, education and training requirements, advancement possibilities, job outlook, earnings, and sources of additional information.

★4861★ "Mars Berma—Montessori Elementry School Teacher" in Straight Talk on Careers: Eighty Pros Take You Into Their Professions (pp. 188-190)
Garrett Park Press
PO Box 1907
Garrett Park, MD 20896
Ph: (301)946-2553

Mary Barbera-Hogan. 1987. Contains candid interviews from people who give an inside view of their work in 80 different careers. These professionals describe a day's work and the stresses and rewards accompanying their work.

★4862★ Opportunities Abroad for Educators: Fulbright Teacher Exchange Program
Teacher Exchange Branch
United State Information Agency
301 4 St.
Washington, DC 20547
Ph: (202)619-4700

Annual. This booklet describes the teacher exchange program, and includes applications for teaching positions and seminars abroad; gives a country listing of positions available.

★4863★ Opportunities in Teaching Careers
National Textbook Co. (NTC)
VGM Career Books
4255 W. Touhy Ave.
Lincolnwood, IL 60646-1975
Ph: (708)679-5500   Fax: (708)679-2494
Fr: 800-323-4900

Janet Fine. 1989. Includes a bibliography. Illustrated. Describes the job responsibilities, educational preparation, work settings, and related careers.

★4864★ Overseas Employment Opportunities for Educators
Office of Dependents Schools
U.S. Department of Defense
3461 Eisenhower Ave.
Alexandria, VA 22331-1100
Ph: (703)325-0885

Annual. This booklet describes eligibility requirements, position requirements, application procedures, pay and benefits, housing living, and working conditions. Includes the application form.

★4865★ The Right Fit: An Educator's Career Handbook and Employment Guide
Gorsuch Scarisbrick Publishers
8233 Via Paseo del Norte, Ste. F-400
Scottsdale, AZ 85258
Ph: (602)991-7881

Judy A. Strother and Darrel R. Marshall. 1990.

★4866★ Teacher, Elementary
Careers, Inc.
PO Box 135
Largo, FL 34649-0135
Ph: (813)584-7333

1995. Two-page occupational summary card describing duties, working conditions, personal qualifications, training, earnings and hours, employment outlook, places of employment, related careers, and where to write for more information.

★4867★ "Teacher" in Jobs Rated Almanac
World Almanac
1 International Blvd., Ste. 444
Mahwah, NJ 07495
Ph: (201)529-6900   Fax: (201)529-6901

Les Krantz. Second edition, 1992. Ranks 250 jobs by environment, salary, outlooks, physical demands, stress, security, travel opportunities, and extra perks. Includes jobs the editor feels are the most common, most interesting, and the most rapidly growing.

★4868★ Teachers, Elementary School
Chronicle Guidance Publications, Inc.
66 Aurora St.
PO Box 1190
Moravia, NY 13118-1190
Ph: (315)497-0330   Fax: (315)497-3359
Fr: 800-622-7284

1991. Occupational brief describing the nature of the job, working conditions, hours and earnings, education and training, licensure, certification, unions, personal qualifications, social and psychological factors, location, employment outlook, entry methods, advancement, and related occupations.

★4869★ "Teachers, Kindergarten and Elementary School" in *Encyclopedia of Careers and Vocational Guidance* **(Vol.4, pp. 493-497)**
J.G. Ferguson Publishing Co.
200 W. Madison St., Ste. 300
Chicago, IL 60606
Ph: (312)580-5480   Fax: (312)580-4948
William E. Hopke, editor-in-chief. Ninth edition, 1993. Four-volume set that profiles 900 occupations and describes job trends in 74 industries. Includes career description, educational requirements, history of the job, methods of entry, advancement, employment outlook, earnings, conditions of work, social and psychological factors, and sources of further information.

PROFESSIONAL ASSOCIATIONS

★4870★ American Federation of Teachers (AFT)
555 New Jersey Ave. NW
Washington, DC 20001
Ph: (202)879-4400   Fr: 800-238-1133
Members: AFL-CIO. Works with teachers and other educational employees at the state and local level in organizing, collective bargaining, research, educational issues, and public relations. **Purpose:** Conducts research in areas such as educational reform, bilingual education, teacher certification, and evaluation and national assessments and standards. Represents members' concerns through legislative action; offers technical assistance. Seeks to serve professionals with concerns similar to those of teachers, including state employees, healthcare workers, and paraprofessionals. **Publications:** *AFT Action: A Newsletter for AFT Leaders*, weekly. • *American Educator*, quarterly. • *American Teacher*, 8/year. • *Healthwire*, 10/year. • *On Campus*, 9/year. • *Public Sevice Reporter*, 9/year.

★4871★ Association of Astronomy Educators (AAE)
5103 Burt St.
Omaha, NE 68132
Ph: (402)556-0082   Fax: (402)280-2140
Members: Teachers and educators dedicated to improving astronomy education at all levels, from kindergarten to college. **Purpose:** Promotes astronomy education to enhance the scientific literacy of all students. Brings together resources and knowledge from a number of diverse groups. Works with the National Science Teachers Association. Cosponsors Astronomy Day. **Publications:** *Astronomy Education*, quarterly.

★4872★ National Association for the Education of Young Children (NAEYC)
1509 16th St. NW
Washington, DC 20036
Ph: (202)232-8777   Fax: (202)328-1846
Fr: 800-424-2460
Members: Teachers and directors of preschool and primary schools, kindergartens, child care centers, cooperatives, church schools, and groups having similar programs for young children; early childhood education

and child development professors, trainers, and researchers. Open to all individuals interested in serving and acting on behalf of the needs and rights of young children, with primary focus on the provision of educational services and resources. **Purpose:** Sponsors a public education campaign entitled "Week of the Young Child." Offers voluntary accreditation for early childhood schools and centers through the National Academy of Early Childhood Programs. **Publications:** *Young Children*, bimonthly.

★4873★ National Council for Accreditation of Teacher Education (NCATE)
2010 Massachusetts Ave. NW, Ste. 500
Washington, DC 20036-1023
Ph: (202)466-7496   Fax: (202)296-6620
Members: Representatives from constituent colleges and universities, state departments of education, school boards, teacher and other professional groups. **Purpose:** Voluntary accrediting body devoted exclusively to: evaluation and accreditation of institutions for preparation of elementary and secondary school teachers; preparation of school service personnel, including school principals, supervisors, superintendents, guidance counselors, school psychologists, instructional technologists, and other specialists for school-oriented positions. **Publications:** *Handbook for Institutional Visits.* • *NCATE-Approved Curriculum Guidelines.* • *Quality Teaching*, 3/year. • *Standards, Procedures, and Policies for the Accreditation of Professional Education Units.* • *Teacher Preparation: A Guide to Colleges and Universities.*

★4874★ National Education Association (NEA)
1201 16th St. NW
Washington, DC 20036
Ph: (202)833-4000   Fax: (202)822-7974
Members: Professional organization and union of elementary and secondary school teachers, college and university professors, administrators, principals, counselors, and others concerned with education. **Publications:** *Almanac of Higher Education.* • *ESP Annual.* • *ESP Progress*, periodic. • *Handbook*, annual. • *Issues*, annual. • *NEA Higher Education Advocate.* • *NEA Today*, 8/year. • *Thought and Action.*

★4875★ Waldorf Kindergarten Association of North America
1359 Alderton Ln.
Silver Spring, MD 20906
Ph: (301)460-6287   Fax: (301)779-3272
Members: Kindergarten teachers, parents, professionals, and individuals interested in the Waldorf approach to education. **Purpose:** Follows the educational ideals of Austrian social philosopher Rudolf Steiner (1861-1925), which emphasize a concerted development of the child's physical, spiritual, and emotional abilities. Works with all of the Waldorf Kindergartens in Canada, Mexico, and throughout the United States to create educational programs. **Publications:** *An Overview of the the Waldorf Kindergarten and A Deeper Understanding.* • *Plant Dyeing.* • *Plays for Puppets.* • *Understanding Young Children, Excerpts from Rudolf Steiner.* • *Waldorf Kindergarten Newsletter*, semiannual.

STANDARDS/CERTIFICATION AGENCIES

★4876★ American Federation of Teachers (AFT)
555 New Jersey Ave. NW
Washington, DC 20001
Ph: (202)879-4400   Fr: 800-238-1133
Conducts research in areas such as educational reform, bilingual education, teacher certification, and evaluation and national assessments and standards.

★4877★ National Council for Accreditation of Teacher Education (NCATE)
2010 Massachusetts Ave. NW, Ste. 500
Washington, DC 20036-1023
Ph: (202)466-7496   Fax: (202)296-6620
Voluntary accrediting body devoted exclusively to: evaluation and accreditation of institutions for preparation of elementary and secondary school teachers; preparation of school service personnel, including school principals, supervisors, superintendents, guidance counselors, school psychologists, instructional technologists, and other specialists for school-oriented positions.

TEST GUIDES

★4878★ Barron's How to Prepare for the National Teacher Examinations (NTE): Core Battery and Most Specialty Area Tests
Barron's Educational Series, Inc.
250 Wireless Blvd.
Hauppauge, NY 11788
Ph: (516)434-3311   Fax: (516)434-3723
Fr: 800-645-3476
Albertina A. Weinlander. Fifth edition, 1992. Provides review and practice for the Core Battery tests and sample test questions from 19 specialty area tests.

★4879★ Career Examination Series: Assistant Teacher
National Learning Corp.
212 Michael Dr.
Syosset, NY 11791
Ph: (516)921-8888   Fax: (516)921-8743
Fr: 800-645-6337
Jack Rudman. A study guide for professionals and trainees in the field of education. Includes a multiple-choice examination section; provides answers.

★4880★ Career Examination Series: Indian Education—Elementary Teacher
National Learning Corp.
212 Michael Dr.
Syosset, NY 11791
Ph: (516)921-8888   Fax: (516)921-8743
Fr: 800-645-6337
Jack Rudman. A study guide for professionals and trainees in the field of education. Includes a multiple-choice examination section; provides answers.

★4881★ Career Examination Series: Teacher
National Learning Corp.
212 Michael Dr.
Syosset, NY 11791
Ph: (516)921-8888   Fax: (516)921-8743
Fr: 800-645-6337
Jack Rudman. A study guide for professionals and trainees in the field of education. Includes a multiple-choice examination section; provides answers.

★4882★ Graduate Record Examination: Education
National Learning Corp.
212 Michael Dr.
Syosset, NY 11791
Ph: (516)921-8888   Fax: (516)921-8743
Fr: 800-645-6337
Jack Rudman. A sample multiple-choice test for those seeking admission to graduate school for study in the field of education. Includes solutions to examination questions.

★4883★ A Guide to the NTE Core Battery Test
Educational Testing Service
Rosedale Rd.
Princeton, NJ 08541
Ph: (609)921-9000
Compiled by the Educational Testing Service staff. Second revised edition, 1992. Contains a form of three previously administered National Teacher Examinations (NTE) Core Battery Test. Also includes a description of each test with sample questions and explanations of the answers as well as test-taking strategies. Also contains answer sheets, answer keys, and scoring instructions.

★4884★ Introduction to Education
National Learning Corp.
212 Michael Dr.
Syosset, NY 11791
Ph: (516)921-8888   Fax: (516)921-8743
Fr: 800-645-6337
Jack Rudman. Part of the Dantes Subject Standardized Test series. A standardized graduate and college-level examination given by graduate schools, colleges, and the U.S. Armed Forces as a final examination for course evaluation in the field of education. Multiple-choice format with correct answers.

★4885★ National Teacher Examination Series
National Learning Corp.
212 Michael Dr.
Syosset, NY 11791
Ph: (516)921-8888   Fax: (516)921-8743
Fr: 800-645-6337
Jack Rudman. Practice multiple-choice examinations for education certification. Includes solutions. Titles in the series include *National Teacher Examination (Core Battery)* (one-volume combined edition); *Agriculture; Art Education; Biology and General Science; Business Education; Chemistry and General Science; Chemistry, Physics, and General Science; Earth and Space Science; Education of the Mentally Retarded; English Language and Literature; French; German; Health Education; Home Economics Education; Mathematics; Latin; Marketing and Distributive Education; Men's Physical Education; Music Education; Physics and General Science; Physical Education; Psychological Foundations of Education; Psychology; School Psychology; Science and Mathematics; Social Studies; Social Studies, Literature and Fine Arts; Societal Foundations of Education; Spanish; Special Education; Speech Communication; Teaching Emotionally Disturbed; Teaching Hearing Handicapped; Teaching Learning Disabled; Teaching Orthopedically Handicapped; Teaching Principles and Practices; Teaching Speech Handicapped; Women's Physical Education; Written English Expression.*

★4886★ NTE—National Teacher Examinations
Arco Publishing Co.
Macmillan General Reference
15 Columbus Cir.
New York, NY 10023
Fax: 800-835-3202   Fr: 800-858-7674
Joan O. Levy and Norman Levy. Eleventh edition, 1994. Contains three sample Core Battery tests.

★4887★ Practicing to Take the GRE Education Test
Educational Testing Service
Rosedale Rd.
Princeton, NJ 08541
Ph: (609)921-9000
Compiled by the Educational Testing Service Staff. Second edition, 1989. This booklet summarizes the purpose and scope of this Graduate Record Examination (GRE) Subject Test. Contains sample questions.

★4888★ Reading Instruction in the Elementary School
National Learning Corp.
212 Michael Dr.
Syosset, NY 11791
Ph: (516)921-8888   Fax: (516)921-8743
Fr: 800-645-6337
Jack Rudman. Part of the ACT Proficiency Examination Program series. A practice test that demonstrates proficiency in the area of reading instruction. Multiple-choice format with solutions included.

★4889★ Teacher Certification Tests
Arco Publishing Co.
Macmillan General Reference
15 Columbus Cir.
New York, NY 10023
Fax: 800-835-3202   Fr: 800-858-7674
Elna M. Dimock. Third edition, 1993. Covers certification tests administered in 16 states. Tests featured are the California Basic Educational Skills Test, Pre-Professional Skills Test, Connecticut Competency Exam for Prospective Teachers, and Examination for Certification of Educators in Texas. Gives information on testing requirements in all 50 states.

★4890★ Teachers License Examination Series: Elementary Education
National Learning Corp.
212 Michael Dr.
Syosset, NY 11791
Ph: (516)921-8888   Fax: (516)921-8743
Fr: 800-645-6337
Jack Rudman. A series of preparatory study guides for professionals studying for licensing examinations. Includes a multiple-choice test section; provides answers. Contains numerous titles related to elementary education.

★4891★ Undergraduate Program Field Test: Education
National Learning Corp.
212 Michael Dr.
Syosset, NY 11791
Ph: (516)921-8888   Fax: (516)921-8743
Fr: 800-645-6337
Jack Rudman. A practice examination fashioned after tests given in the Regents External Degree Program. Designed to measure knowledge received outside the college classroom in the subject of education. Contains multiple-choice questions; provides solutions.

EDUCATIONAL DIRECTORIES AND PROGRAMS

★4892★ Educational Career Directory
Gale Research Inc.
835 Penobscot Bldg.
Detroit, MI 48226
Ph: (313)961-2242   Fr: 800-877-GALE
1994.

AWARDS, SCHOLARSHIPS, GRANTS, AND FELLOWSHIPS

★4893★ CIBA-GEIGY Exemplary Elementary Science Teaching Award
National Science Teachers Association
1840 Wilson Blvd.
Arlington, VA 22201
Ph: (703)243-7100   Fax: (703)243-7700
To recognize an elementary teacher who has demonstrated exemplary science teaching performance. A monetary prize of $1,000 and travel to the NSTA National Convention are awarded annually. Established in 1975. Sponsored by the CIBA-GEIGY Corporation and presented by the Council for Elementary Science International.

★4894★ Distinguished Teaching Award
National Science Teachers Association
1840 Wilson Blvd.
Arlington, VA 22201
Ph: (703)243-7100   Fax: (703)243-7700
To recognize elementary, middle/junior high, high school, and college teachers who have made extraordinary contributions to the field of science teaching. Plaques and complimentary one-year memberships are awarded annually. Sponsored by National Science Teachers Association. Established in 1987.

★4895★ **Miriam Joseph Farrell Award for Distinguished Teaching in the Catholic Elementary School**
National Catholic Educational Association
1077 30th St. NW, Ste. 100
Washington, DC 20007-3852
Ph: (202)337-6232   Fax: (202)333-6706
To give public recognition to the excellence of Catholic elementary school teachers. The nominee should be: a teacher within Catholic elementary school(s) for at least ten years; a teacher with a clear, integrated philosophy of Catholic education; a teacher who is highly regarded by peers, students, and parents; and a member, individual or institution of the NCEA Department of Elementary Schools. Entry deadline is November 21. Pen set plaques are awarded annually during the convention to twelve individuals, one from each region. Established in 1982 in memory of the Catholic elementary educator, Sister Miriam Joseph Farrell, P.B.V.M.

★4896★ **Isabel M. Herson Scholarship in Education**
Zeta Phi Beta Sorority
National Education Foundation
Executive Office
1734 New Hampshire Ave., N.W.
Washington, DC 20009
Ph: (202)387-3103   Fax: (202)232-4593
Qualifications: Students must be graduates or undergraduates enrolled in a degree program either in elementary or secondary education. Funds available: $500 to $1,000 for one academic year. Application details: Completed applications must be returned along with references and an official university transcript. Deadline: February 1. Recipients are notified by August 15.

★4897★ **Eleanor M. Johnson Award**
International Reading Association
800 Barksdale Rd.
PO Box 8139
Newark, DE 19714-8139
Ph: (302)731-1600   Fax: (302)731-1057
To recognize a current outstanding elementary classroom teacher of reading and language arts. Candidates must be Association members, have a minimum of five years' teaching experience, and be endorsed by four persons. The deadline is December 1. A monetary award of US $1,000 is presented. Established in 1989 to honor Eleanor M. Johnson, founder and editor-in-chief of *Weekly Reader*. Sponsored by *Weekly Reader* Corporation. Additional information is available from the Executive Office, International Reading Association.

★4898★ **Eleanor Roosevelt Teacher Fellowships**
American Association of University Women (AAUW)
AAUW Educational Foundation
PO Box 4030
Iowa City, IA 52243-4030
Ph: (319)337-1716
Purpose: Eleanor Roosevelt Teacher Fellowships are designed for elementary and secondary school teachers who are seeking to advanced gender equity in the classroom, increase their effectiveness at teaching math and science to girls, and/or tailor their teaching to the needs of minority students and girls

at risk of dropping out. Qualifications: Women teachers who are U.S. citizens or permanent residents, teach full time at U.S. public schools in grades K through 12, have at least five consecutive years full-time teaching experience, plan to continue teaching for the next five years, and able to demonstrate commitment to educational opportunities for women and girls through work in the classroom are eligible. Funds available: Fellowships range from $1,000 to $10,000. Deadline: January 11.

★4899★ **Nila Banton Smith Award**
International Reading Association
800 Barksdale Rd.
PO Box 8139
Newark, DE 19714-8139
Ph: (302)731-1600   Fax: (302)731-1057
To recognize the classroom teacher or reading specialist who has made an outstanding contribution in helping students to become more proficient readers of content instructional materials. Applicants must be actively teaching students in the 7th through 12th grade range or equivalent. The recipient of this award must have demonstrated excellence at the classroom level, in addition to either the building level or district level. The deadline for nominations is December 1. A monetary award of US $1,000 is awarded annually. Established in 1978. The award honors Nila Banton Smith, the ninth president of the Association. Additional information is available from the Executive Office, International Reading Association.

BASIC REFERENCE GUIDES AND HANDBOOKS

★4900★ *Classroom Teaching Skills*
D. C. Heath and Co.
125 Spring St.
Lexington, MA 02173
Ph: (617)862-6650   Fr: 800-334-2284
James M. Cooper, Sandra S. Garrett, et al., editors. Fourth edition, 1990. Includes bibliographies and an index. Illustrated.

★4901★ *Curriculum and Instructional Methods for the Elementary School*
Macmillan Publishing Co.
866 3rd Ave.
New York, NY 10022
Ph: (212)702-2000   Fr: 800-257-5755
Johanna K. Lemlech. Third edition, 1993. Includes a bibliography and indexes.

★4902★ *A Handbook for Substitute Teachers*
Charles C. Thomas, Publisher
2600 S. 1st St.
Springfield, IL 62794-9265
Ph: (217)789-8980   Fax: (217)789-9130
Fr: 800-258-8980
Anne W. Dodd. 1989.

★4903★ *The International Encyclopedia of Teaching and Teacher Education*
Pergamon Press, Inc.
Fairview Park
Elmsford, NY 10523
Ph: (914)592-7700
Michael J. Dunkin, editor. First edition, 1987. Includes bibliographies and indexes. Illustrated.

★4904★ *An Introduction to the Foundations of Education*
Houghton Mifflin Co.
222 Berkeley St.
Boston, MA 02116
Ph: (617)351-5000
Allan C. Ornstein and Daniel Levine. Fifth edition, 1993. Includes bibliographical references and indexes. Illustrated.

★4905★ *Standards for Quality Elementary Schools: Kindergarten Through Eighth Grade*
National Association of Elementary School Principals (NAESP)
1615 Duke St.
Alexandria, VA 22314
Ph: (703)684-3345
Second edition, 1990. Includes forms.

PROFESSIONAL AND TRADE PERIODICALS

★4906★ *American Educator*
American Federation of Teachers
555 New Jersey Ave. NW
Washington, DC 20001
Ph: (202)879-4430
Liz McPike
Quarterly. Magazine on education.

★4907★ *Childhood Education*
Assn. for Childhood Education International
11501 Georgia Ave., Ste. 315
Wheaton, MD 20902-1924
Ph: (301)942-2443   Fax: (301)942-3012
Lucy Prete Martin
Educational journal.

★4908★ *Education Week*
Editorial Projects in Education, Inc.
4301 Connecticut Ave. NW
Washington, DC 20008
Ph: (202)686-0800   Fax: (202)686-0797
Ronald A. Wolk
Weekly. Professional newspaper for elementary and secondary school educators.

★4909★ *The Elementary School Journal*
University of Chicago Press
5720 S. Woodlawn Ave.
Chicago, IL 60637
Ph: (312)702-7600   Fax: (312)702-0172
Thomas L. Good
Bimonthly. Journal relating social science research to elementary education theory and the classroom.

★4910★ Elementary Teacher's Ideas and Materials Workshop
Princeton Educational Publishers
PO Box 280
Plainsboro, NJ 08536
Ph: (609)924-0319   Fax: (609)924-0319
Barry Pavelec

Educational magazine for teachers.

★4911★ ERIC/EECE Bulletin
Educational Resources Information Center
  Clearinghouse on Elementary and Early
  Childhood Education (ERIC/EECE)
ERIC Clearinghouse
University of Illinois
805 W. Pennsylvania Ave.
Urbana, IL 61801-4897
Ph: (217)333-1386   Fax: (217)333-3767
Fr: 800-583-4135
Bernard Cesarone

Focuses on the education, development, and care of children from birth through age 12. Reports on new programs and practices in childhood education, curriculum ideas, and new developments in the ERIC system. Recurring features include references, summaries of documents recently added to the ERIC document collection, announcements of new papers and bibliographies issued by ERIC/EECE, and notes on new publications, training materials, films, and organizations.

★4912★ Erikson
Erikson Institute for Advanced Study in
  Child Development
420 N. Wabash Ave.
Chicago, IL 60611
Ph: (312)280-7302   Fax: (312)280-9270
Jane M. Curry

Semiannual. Provides a perspective on child development and early education, as well as news on the Institute's programs and activities.

★4913★ Extensions
High/Scope Educational Research
  Foundation
600 N. River St.
Ypsilanti, MI 48198-2898
Ph: (313)485-2000   Fax: (313)485-0704
Nancy Altman Brickman

Highlights the latest information on training strategies for early childhood educators, curricula, and specific classroom activity ideas. Includes a column on using computers in the classroom. Incorporates the former Key Notes.

★4914★ The Harvard Education Letter
Gutman 321
6 Appian Way
Cambridge, MA 02138-3704
Ph: (617)496-4841   Fax: (617)496-3584
Fr: 800-422-2681
Edward Miller

Bimonthly. Summarizes current research concerning elementary and secondary education (grades kindergarten-12). Discusses a wide range of school, classroom, and child development issues, addressing the underlying assumptions of current educational debates. Recurring features include case studies, columns titled, and reports on successful and innovative programs.

★4915★ Insights into Open Education
Center for Teaching & Learning
PO Box 8158
Grand Forks, ND 58202
Ph: (701)777-4421   Fax: (701)777-4365
Sara Hanhan

Discusses various aspects of elementary education, including language arts, parent-teacher conferences, special education, reading, writing, science, social studies, and discipline. Focuses on one of the above topics in each issue, including theory and practice, a list of references cited in the article, and a short biography of the author.

★4916★ Report on Education of the Disadvantaged
Business Publishers, Inc.
951 Pershing Dr.
Silver Spring, MD 20910
Ph: (301)587-6300   Fax: (301)587-1081
Fr: 800-274-0122
Rosemary Lally

Biweekly. Covers legislative news affecting the Elementary and Secondary Education Act Chapter I (formerly Title I). Reports on bilingual education, child nutrition and migrant children programs, other program and funding changes, and related topics of interest.

★4917★ TIES Magazine
Trenton State College
Department of Technological Studies
Hillwood Lakes
CN 4700
Trenton, NJ 08650-4700
Ph: (609)771-3335   Fax: (609)771-3330
Ronald ToddPublisher

Technology education magazine for teachers.

PROFESSIONAL MEETINGS AND CONVENTIONS

★4918★ Association for Childhood Education International Annual Study Conference
Association for Childhood Education
  International
11501 Georgia Ave., Ste. 315
Wheaton, MD 20902-1924
Ph: (301)942-2443   Fr: 800-423-3563
Annual.

★4919★ Association of Teacher Educators Annual Conference
Glencoe
15319 Chatsworth St.
Mission Hills, CA 91345
Ph: (818)898-1391

Annual. Always held during February. **Dates and Locations:** 1996 Feb.

★4920★ NAFSA - Association of International Educators Annual Conference
NAFSA - Association of International
  Educator
1875 Connecticut Ave. NW, Ste. 1000
Washington, DC 20009-5728
Ph: (202)462-4811   Fax: (202)667-3419
Annual.

★4921★ National Art Education Association Convention
National Art Education Association
1916 Association Dr.
Reston, VA 22091-1590
Ph: (703)860-8000   Fax: (703)860-2960
Annual.

★4922★ National Association for the Education of Young Children Annual Conference
National Association for the Education of
  Young Children
1509 16th St., NW
Washington, DC 20036
Ph: (202)232-8777   Fax: (202)328-1846
Annual. Usually held during November.

★4923★ National Council for the Social Studies Convention
National Council for the Social Studies
3501 Newark St., NW
Washington, DC 20016
Ph: (202)966-7840   Fax: (202)966-2061

Annual. **Dates and Locations:** 1995 Nov 09-12; Chicago, IL. • 1996 Nov 16-19; Washington, DC. • 1997 Nov 20-23; Cincinnati, OH.

★4924★ National Education Association Annual Meeting and Exposition
National Educational Association
1201 16th St., NW
Washington, DC 20036
Ph: (202)833-4000   Fax: (202)822-7767
Annual.

★4925★ National Middle School Association Annual Conference & Exhibit
National Middle School Association
3600 Corporate Exchange Dr., Ste. 370
Columbus, OH 43231
Ph: (614)848-8211   Fax: (614)848-4301

Annual. **Dates and Locations:** 1995 Nov 01-04; New Orleans, LA. • 1996 Oct 31-03; Baltimore, MD. • 1997; Indianapolis, IN. • 1997 Oct 30-02; Indianapolis, IN. • 1998 Nov 05-08; Denver, CO. • 1999; Orlando, FL.

OTHER SOURCES OF INFORMATION

★4926★ "Elementary Education" in
Accounting to Zoology: Graduate
Fields Defined (p. 84)
Petersons Guides, Inc.
PO Box 2123
Princeton, NJ 08543-2123
Ph: (609)243-9111   Fax: (609)243-9150
Fr: 800-338-3282

Amy J. Goldstein, editor. Revised and updated, 1987. Discusses types of graduate programs and degrees, graduate research, applied work, employment prospects and trends.

★4927★ Elementary Schooling for
Critical Democracy
State University of New York Press
State University Plaza
Albany, NY 12246
Ph: (518)472-5000   Fax: (518)472-5038

Jesse Goodman, editor. 1992. Part of the SUNY Series in Teacher Empowerment and School Reform.

★4928★ An Introduction to Teaching: A
Question of Commitment
Allyn and Bacon, Inc.
160 Gould St.
Needham, MA 02194
Ph: (617)455-1200

Ralph E. Martin, Jr., George H. Wood, and Edward Stevens, Jr. Includes bibliographies and an index. Illustrated.

★4929★ Positively Kindergarten: A
Classroom-Proven, Theme-Based,
Developmental Guide for the
Kindergarten Teacher
Modern Learning Press
PO Box 167
Rosemont, NJ 08556
Ph: (609)397-2214   Fax: (609)397-3467
Fr: 800-627-5867

Beth Lamb, editor. 1991.

★4930★ Requirements for Certification
of Teachers, Counselors, Librarians,
Administrators for Elementary and
Secondary Schools, and Junior
Colleges
University of Chicago Press
11030 S. Langley Ave.
Chicago, IL 60628
Ph: (312)702-7700   Fr: 800-621-2736

Mary P. Burks, Annual. Fifty-ninth edition, 1994. State-by-state listing of certification requirements for teachers, counselors, librarians, and administrators. Lists addresses of state departments of education.

★4931★ "Teacher (Elementary)" in
Career Selector 2001
Barron's Educational Series, Inc.
250 Wireless Blvd.
Hauppauge, NY 11788
Ph: (516)434-3311   Fax: (516)434-3723
Fr: 800-645-3476

James C. Gonyea. 1993.

★4932★ The Teacher's Almanac
Facts on File
460 Park Ave. S.
New York, NY 10016-7382
Ph: (212)683-2244   Fax: 800-678-3633
Fr: 800-322-8755

Sherwood Harris and Lorna B. Harris, editors. 1988. Contains statistical information such as teachers' salaries, educational finances, and state rankings.

Librarians

Librarians make information available to people. They collect, organize, and lend books, periodicals, films, records, videotapes, computer tapes, and cassettes to all types of users. Library work is divided into three basic functions: User services, technical services, and administrative services. Librarians in user services, for example, reference and children's librarians, work directly with users to help them find the information they need. Librarians in technical services such as acquisitions librarians and catalogers acquire and prepare materials for use and generally do not deal with the public. **Acquisitions librarians** select and order books, periodicals, films, and other materials. They read book reviews, publishers' announcements, and catalogs to keep up with current literature. **Catalogers** describe books and other library materials in such a way that users can easily find them. **Bibliographers**, who usually work in research libraries, compile lists of books, periodicals, articles, and audiovisual materials on particular subjects. **Public librarians** serve people of all ages and from all walks of life, including persons who, because of physical handicaps, cannot use conventional print materials. **Children's librarians** find materials children will enjoy and show children how to use the library. **Adult services librarians** handle materials suited for adults and may conduct education programs. **Young adult librarians** help junior and senior high school students select and use books and other materials. **Community outreach librarians and bookmobile librarians** develop library services to meet the needs of underserved groups, such as residents of rural areas, migrant labor camps, inner-city housing projects, and nursing homes. **School librarians**, also called **media specialists**, teach students how to use the school library, or media center. **Academic librarians** serve students, faculty members, and researchers in colleges and universities.

Salaries

Salaries of librarians vary by the individual's qualifications and the type, size, and location of library.

Beginning public librarians	$23,800/year
Beginning school librarians	$27,400/year
Experienced school librarians	$37,900/year
Special librarians, 1-5 years experience	$29,200-$31,800/year
Special library managers	$45,200/year
Beginning university librarians	$25,400/year
Librarians, federal government	$44,500/year

Employment Outlook

Growth rate until the year 2005: More slowly than the average.

Librarians

CAREER GUIDES

★4933★ Academic and Public Librarians: Data by Race, Ethnicity and Sex
Office for Library Personnel Resources
American Library Association
Chicago, IL 60611
Ph: (312)280-2424   Fr: 800-545-2433
1991. This study gives a profile of the library profession for three position groupings: directors and associates, branch department heads, and entry-level librarians in public and academic libraries.

★4934★ Careers for Bookworms & Other Literary Types
National Textbook Co. (NTC)
VGM Career Books
4255 W. Touhy Ave.
Lincolnwood, IL 60646-1975
Ph: (708)679-5500   Fax: (708)679-2494
Fr: 800-323-4900
Marjorie Eberts and Margaret Gisler. 1991. Describes employment opportunities for jobs in education, publishing, libraries, museums, and more.

★4935★ Careers in Research Libraries
Association of Research Libraries
21 Dupont Circle, NW, Ste. 800
Washington, DC 20036
Ph: (202)296-2296
This eight-panel pamphlet describes career opportunities in research libraries, what a research librarian does, rewards of this career, and qualifications and skills needed.

★4936★ Challenging Careers in Information: Join the Information Age
American Society for Information Science
8720 Georgia Ave., Ste. 501
Silver Spring, MD 20910-3602
Ph: (301)495-0900
This booklet describes what information professionals do, job locations, salary, and educational preparation.

★4937★ Educational Career Directory
Gale Research Inc.
835 Penobscot Bldg.
Detroit, MI 48226
Ph: (313)961-2242   Fr: 800-877-GALE
1994.

★4938★ Guide to Careers in Abstracting and Indexing
National Federation of Abstracting and Information Services (NFAIS)
1429 Walnut St.
Philadelphia, PA 19102
Ph: (215)563-2406
Ann Marie Cunningham and Wendey Wicks. 1992.

★4939★ Guide to Library Placement Sources
American Library Association
50 E. Huron St.
Chicago, IL 60611
Ph: (312)280-2424   Fr: 800-545-2433
Margaret Myers. Annual. This pamphlet includes library joblines, specialized library associations and schools offering job postings, state library agencies, state and regional library associations, and information on federal library jobs.

★4940★ "Health Sciences Librarian" in 150 Careers in the Health Care Field
Reed Reference Publishing
121 Chanlon Rd.
PO Box 31
New Providence, NJ 07974
Fax: (908)665-6688   Fr: 800-521-8110
Stanley Alperin. Third edition, 1993. Profiles health care occupations requiring a bachelor's degree or less. Describes the nature of the work, educational preparation, licensing requirements, and salary. Lists accredited educational programs.

★4941★ "Health Sciences Librarian" in Careers in Health Care (pp. 100-103)
National Textbook Co. (NTC)
VGM Career Books
4255 W. Touhy Ave.
Lincolnwood, IL 60646-1975
Ph: (708)679-5500   Fax: (708)679-2494
Fr: 800-323-4900
Barbara M. Swanson. Third edition, 1995. Describes job duties, work settings, salaries,

licensing and certification requirements, educational preparation, and future outlook.

★4942★ Health Sciences Librarians
Chronicle Guidance Publications, Inc.
66 Aurora St.
PO Box 1190
Moravia, NY 13118-1190
Ph: (315)497-0330   Fax: (315)497-3359
Fr: 800-622-7284
1994. Career brief describing the nature of the job, working conditions, hours and earnings, education and training, licensure, certification, unions, personal qualifications, social and psychological factors, location, employment outlook, entry methods, advancement, and related occupations.

★4943★ "Indexer" in Offbeat Careers: Directory of Unusual Work
Ten Speed Press
PO Box 7123
Berkeley, CA 94707
Fax: (510)559-1629   Fr: 800-841-2665
Al Sacharov. 1991. Each occupational profile describes places of employment, how to get the job, employment outlook, advantages and disadvantages of the work, and personal characteristics needed.

★4944★ "Information Management" in New Emerging Careers: Today, Tomorrow, and in the 21st Century (pp. 57-64)
Garrett Park Press
PO Box 1907
Garrett Park, MD 20896
Ph: (301)946-2553
Norman S. Feingold and Maxine N. Atwater. 1988. This book focuses on ten of the most promising new technologies giving an overview and descibing employment opportunities. Includes information on specific jobs with education and training requirements.

★4945★ Is It for You? Music Librarianship
Music Library Association
PO Box 487
Canton, MA 02021
Ph: (617)828-8450
This four-panel brochure describes what music librarians do, where they work, and necessary educational preparation.

★4946★ Law Librarian
Vocational Biographies, Inc.
PO Box 31
Sauk Centre, MN 56378-0031
Ph: (612)352-6516   Fax: (612)352-5546
Fr: 800-255-0752
1993. Four-page pamphlet containing a personal narrative about a worker's job, work likes and dislikes, career path from high school to the present. Education and training, the rewards and frustrations, and the effects of the job on the rest of the worker's life. The data file portion of this pamphlet gives a concise occupational summary, including work descriptions, working conditions, places of employment, personal characteristics, education and training, job outlook, and salary range.

★4947★ Librarian
Careers, Inc.
PO Box 135
Largo, FL 34649-0135
Ph: (813)584-7333
1993. Four-page brief offering the definition, history, duties, working conditions, personal qualifications, educational requirements, earnings, hours, employment outlook, advancement, and careers related to this position.

★4948★ "Librarian" in BLR Encyclopedia of Prewritten Job Descriptions
Business and Legal Reports, Inc.
39 Academy St.
Madison, CT 06443-1513
Ph: (203)245-7448
Stephen D. Bruce, editor-in-chief. 1994. This book contains hundreds of sample job descriptions arranged by functional job category. The 1-3 page job descriptions cover what the worker normally does in the position, who they report to, and how that position fits in the organizational structure.

★4949★ "Librarian" in Career Opportunities in Art
Facts on File
460 Park Ave. S.
New York, NY 10016-7382
Ph: (212)683-2244   Fax: 800-678-3633
Fr: 800-322-8755
Susan H. Haubenstock. 1988. This book profiles seventy-five art-related jobs. Each profile includes a career description, career ladder, employment and advancement prospects, education, experience and skills required, salary range, and tips for entry into the field.

★4950★ "Librarian" in Career Opportunities for Writers (pp. 168-169)
Facts on File
460 Park Ave. S.
New York, NY 10016-7382
Ph: (212)683-2244   Fax: 800-678-3633
Fr: 800-322-8755
Rosemary Guiley. 1992. Describes approximately 90 careers in eight major fields, offering such details as duties, salaries, prerequisites, employment and advancement oportunities, organizations to join, and opportunities for women and minorities.

★4951★ Librarian Career Resource Network Directory
American Library Association
50 E. Huron St.
Chicago, IL 60611
Ph: (312)280-2424   Fr: 800-545-2433
1987. This booklet lists persons who are willing to answer career-related questions about librarianship. Contacts are listed alphabetically and indexed by state and subject area and type of library.

★4952★ Librarian, Children's
Careers, Inc.
PO Box 135
Largo, FL 34649-0135
Ph: (813)584-7333
1995. Two-page occupational summary card describing duties, working conditions, personal qualifications, training, earnings and hours, employment outlook, places of employment, related careers, and where to write for more information.

★4953★ "Librarian" in College Board Guide to Jobs and Career Planning (pp. 182)
The College Board
415 Columbus Ave.
New York, NY 10023-6992
Ph: (212)713-8165   Fax: (212)713-8143
Fr: 800-323-7155
Joyce S. Mitchell. Second edition, 1994. Describes the job, salaries, related careers, education needed, and where to write for more information.

★4954★ Librarian, Health Sciences
Careers, Inc.
PO Box 135
Largo, FL 34649-0135
Ph: (813)584-7333
1994. Two-page occupational summary card describing duties, working conditions, personal qualifications, training, earnings and hours, employment outlook, places of employment, related careers, and where to write for more information.

★4955★ "Librarian" in Jobs Rated Almanac
World Almanac
1 International Blvd., Ste. 444
Mahwah, NJ 07495
Ph: (201)529-6900   Fax: (201)529-6901
Les Krantz. Second edition, 1992. Ranks 250 jobs by environment, salary, outlooks, physical demands, stress, security, travel opportunities, and extra perks. Includes jobs the editor feels are the most common, most interesting, and the most rapidly growing.

★4956★ Librarian, Music
Careers, Inc.
PO Box 135
Largo, FL 34649-0135
Ph: (813)584-7333
1994. Two-page occupational summary card describing duties, working conditions, personal qualifications, training, earnings and hours, employment outlook, places of employment, related careers, and where to write for more information.

★4957★ "Librarian" in Profitable Careers in Non-Profit (pp. 66—71)
John Wiley and Sons, Inc.
605 3rd Ave.
New York, NY 10158-0012
Ph: (212)850-6000   Fax: (212)850-6088
Fr: 800-526-5368
William Lewis and Carol Milano. 1987. Examines nonprofit organizations and the career opportunities they offer. Offers tips on how to target and explore occupational opportunities in the nonprofit sector.

★4958★ Librarian, Special
Careers, Inc.
PO Box 135
Largo, FL 34649-0135
Ph: (813)584-7333
1991. Four-page brief offering the definition, history, duties, working conditions, personal qualifications, educational requirements, earnings, hours, employment outlook, advancement, and careers related to this position.

★4959★ "Librarian, Special Library" in Museum Jobs form A-Z: What They Are, How to Prepare, and Where to Find Them
Batax Museum Publishing
301 Racquet Club Rd., Ste. 202
Fort Lauderdale, FL 33326
G.W. Bates. 1994.

★4960★ "Librarian" in VGM's Careers Encyclopedia (pp. 245-248)
National Textbook Co. (NTC)
VGM Career Books
4255 W. Touhy Ave.
Lincolnwood, IL 60646-1975
Ph: (708)679-5500   Fax: (708)679-2494
Fr: 800-323-4900
Third edition, 1991. Describes job duties, places of employment, working conditions, qualifications, education, and training, advancement potential, and salary for each occupation.

★4961★ Librarians
Chronicle Guidance Publications, Inc.
66 Aurora St.
PO Box 1190
Moravia, NY 13118-1190
Ph: (315)497-0330   Fax: (315)497-3359
Fr: 800-622-7284
1993. Career brief describing the nature of the job, working conditions, hours and earnings, education and training, licensure, certification, unions, personal qualifications, social and psychological factors, location, employment outlook, entry methods, advancement, and related occupations.

★4962★ "Librarians" in 101 Careers: A Guide to the Fastest-Growing Opportunities (pp. 174-177)
John Wiley & Sons, Inc.
605 3rd Ave.
New York, NY 10158-0012
Ph: (212)850-6645   Fax: (212)850-6088
Michael Harkavy. 1990. Describes the nature of the job, working conditions, employment growth, qualifications, personal skills, projected salaries, and where to write for more information.

★4963★ "Librarians" in *American Almanac of Jobs and Salaries* (p. 99)
Avon Books
1350 Avenue of the Americas
New York, NY 10019
Ph: (212)261-6800   Fr: 800-238-0658
John Wright, editor. Revised and updated, 1994-95. This is a comprehensive guide to the wages of hundreds of occupations in a wide variety of industries and organizations.

★4964★ "Librarians" in *Career Discovery Encyclopedia* (Vol.3, pp. 176-177)
J.G. Ferguson Publishing Co.
200 W. Madison St., Ste. 300
Chicago, IL 60606
Ph: (312)580-5480   Fax: (312)580-4948
Russell E. Primm, editor-in chief. 1993. This six volume set contains two-page articles for 504 occupations. Each article describes job duties, earnings, and educational and training requirements. The whole set is arranged alphabetically by job title. Designed for junior high and older students.

★4965★ "Librarians" in *Encyclopedia of Careers and Vocational Guidance* (Vol.3, pp. 292-296)
J.G. Ferguson Publishing Co.
200 W. Madison St., Ste. 300
Chicago, IL 60606
Ph: (312)580-5480   Fax: (312)580-4948
William E. Hopke, editor-in-chief. Ninth edition, 1993. Four-volume set that profiles 900 occupations and describes job trends in 74 industries. Includes career description, educational requirements, history of the job, methods of entry, advancement, employment outlook, earnings, conditions of work, social and psychological factors, and sources of further information.

★4966★ "Librarians" in *Guide to Federal Jobs* (p. 232)
Resource Directories
3361 Executive Pkwy., Ste. 302
Toledo, OH 43606
Ph: (419)536-5353   Fax: (419)536-7056
Fr: 800-274-8515
Rod W. Durgin, editor. Third edition, 1992. Contains information on finding and applying for federal jobs. Describes more than 200 professional and technical jobs for college graduates. Covers the nature of the work, salary, and geographic location. Lists college majors preferred for that occupation. Section one describes the function and work of government agencies that hire the most significant number of college graduates.

★4967★ "Librarians" in *Jobs! What They Are—Where They Are—What They Pay* (p. 112)
Simon & Schuster, Inc.
Simon & Schuster Bldg.
1230 Avenue of the Americas
New York, NY 10020
Ph: (212)698-7000   Fr: 800-223-2348
Robert O. Snelling and Anne M. Snelling. 3rd edition, 1992. Describes duties and responsibilities, earnings, employment opportunities, training, and qualifications.

★4968★ "Librarians" in *Occupational Outlook Handbook*
U.S. Government Printing Office
Superintendent of Documents
Washington, DC 20402
Ph: (202)512-1800   Fax: (202)512-2250
Biennial; latest edition, 1994-95. Encyclopedia of careers describing about 250 occupations and comprising about 85 percent of all jobs in the economy. Occupations that require lengthy education or training are given the most attention. Each occupation's profile describes what the worker does on the job, working conditions, education and training requirements, advancement possibilities, job outlook, earnings, and sources of additional information.

★4969★ "Library and Information Science" in *Encyclopedia of Careers and Vocational Guidance* (Vol.1, pp.261-267)
J.G. Ferguson Publishing Co.
200 W. Madison St., Ste. 300
Chicago, IL 60606
Ph: (312)580-5480   Fax: (312)580-4948
William E. Hopke, editor-in-chief. Ninth edition, 1993. Four-volume set that profiles 900 occupations and describes job trends in 74 industries. Includes career description, educational requirements, history of the job, methods of entry, advancement, employment outlook, earnings, conditions of work, social and psychological factors, and sources of further information.

★4970★ "Library and Information Sciences" in *College Majors and Careers: A Resource Guide to Effective Life Planning*
Garrett Park Press
PO Box 1907
Garrett Park, MD 20896
Ph: (301)946-2553
Paul Phifer. Revised, 1993. Lists 60 college majors, with definitions; related occupations and leisure activities; skills, values, and personal attributesneeded; suggested readings; and a list of associations.

★4971★ *Library Jobs: How to Fill Them, How to Find Them*
Oryx Press
4041 N. Central, Ste. 700
Phoenix, AZ 85012-3330
Ph: (602)265-2651   Fr: 800-279-6799
Barbara I. Dewey. 1987. This is a guide for librarians seeking professional positions, and library administrators responsible for hiring at all levels. The book's emphasis is on the careful examination of knowledge, skills, and abilities needed for different positions in libraries. Includes information on resume writing, cover letters, and references.

★4972★ "Library" in *Opportunities in Airline Careers* (pp. 25-26)
National Textbook Co. (NTC)
VGM Career Books
4255 W. Touhy Ave.
Lincolnwood, IL 60646-1975
Ph: (708)679-5500   Fax: (708)679-2494
Fr: 800-323-4900
Adrian A. Paradis. 1987. Gives an overview of the airline industry including job opportunities and salaries. Describes careers in management, finance, sales, customer service and safety.

★4973★ *Media Specialists (Education)*
Chronicle Guidance Publications, Inc.
66 Aurora St.
PO Box 1190
Moravia, NY 13118-1190
Ph: (315)497-0330   Fax: (315)497-3359
Fr: 800-622-7284
1992. Career brief describing the nature of the job, working conditions, hours and earnings, education and training, licensure, certification, unions, personal qualifications, social and psychological factors, location, employment outlook, entry methods, advancement, and related occupations.

★4974★ *MLA Salary Survey*
Medical Library Association
6 N. Michigan Ave., Ste. 300
Chicago, IL 60602
Ph: (312)419-4094
1992. Edited by the Health Science Library, Status and Economic Interests Committee.

★4975★ "Music Librarian" in *Career Opportunities in the Music Industry* (pp. 201-204)
Facts on File
460 Park Ave. S
New York, NY 10016-7382
Ph: (212)683-2244   Fax: 800-678-3633
Fr: 800-322-8755
Shelly Field. 1990. Discusses approximately 80 jobs in music including the performing arts, business, and education. Each job description provides basic career information, salary, employment prospects, advancement opportunities, education, training, and experience required.

★4976★ *Newspaper Librarian*
Vocational Biographies, Inc.
PO Box 31
Sauk Centre, MN 56378-0031
Ph: (612)352-6516   Fax: (612)352-5546
Fr: 800-255-0752
1995. Four-page pamphlet containing a personal narrative about a worker's job, work likes and dislikes, career path from high school to the present. Education and training, the rewards and frustrations, and the effects of the job on the rest of the worker's life. The data file portion of this pamphlet gives a concise occupational summary, including work descriptions, working conditions, places of employment, personal characteristics, education and training, job outlook, and salary range.

★4977★ *Opportunities in Library and Information Science*
National Textbook Co. (NTC)
VGM Career Books
4255 W. Touhy Ave.
Lincolnwood, IL 60646-1975
Ph: (708)679-5500   Fax: (708)679-2494
Fr: 800-323-4900
Kathleen M. Heim and Margaret Myers. 1992. Presents a description of the work library professionals perform. Covers specialization by library type and job function. Includes information about educational preparation and job hunting. Includes a bibliography.

★4978★ "Public Librarians" in *Career Information Center* **(Vol.11)**
Simon and Schuster
200 Old Tappan Rd.
Old Tappan, NJ 07675
Fax: 800-445-6991   Fr: 800-223-2348
Richard Lidz and Linda Perrin, editorial directors. Fifth edition, 1993. This 13-volume set profiles over 600 occupations. Each occupational profile describes job duties, educational requirements, how to get the job, advancement possibilities, employment outlook, working conditions, earnings and benefits, and where to write for more information.

★4979★ *School Librarian*
Vocational Biographies, Inc.
PO Box 31
Sauk Centre, MN 56378-0031
Ph: (612)352-6516   Fax: (612)352-5546
Fr: 800-255-0752
1992. Four-page pamphlet containing a personal narrative about a worker's job, work likes and dislikes, career path from high school to the present. Education and training, the rewards and frustrations, and the effects of the job on the rest of the worker's life. The data file portion of this pamphlet gives a concise occupational summary, including work descriptions, working conditions, places of employment, personal characteristics, education and training, job outlook, and salary range.

★4980★ "School Librarians" in *Career Information Center* **(Vol.11)**
Simon and Schuster
200 Old Tappan Rd.
Old Tappan, NJ 07675
Fax: 800-445-6991   Fr: 800-223-2348
Richard Lidz and Linda Perrin, editorial directors. Fifth edition, 1993. This 13-volume set profiles over 600 occupations. Each occupational profile describes job duties, educational requirements, how to get the job, advancement possibilities, employment outlook, working conditions, earnings and benefits, and where to write for more information.

★4981★ "School Media Specialists" in *Career Information Center* **(Vol.11)**
Simon and Schuster
200 Old Tappan Rd.
Old Tappan, NJ 07675
Fax: 800-445-6991   Fr: 800-223-2348
Richard Lidz and Linda Perrin, editorial directors. Fifth edition, 1993. This 13-volume set profiles over 600 occupations. Each occupational profile describes job duties, educational requirements, how to get the job, advancement possibilities, employment outlook, working conditions, earnings and benefits, and where to write for more information.

★4982★ "Special Librarians" in *Career Information Center* **(Vol.11)**
Simon and Schuster
200 Old Tappan Rd.
Old Tappan, NJ 07675
Fax: 800-445-6991   Fr: 800-223-2348
Richard Lidz and Linda Perrin, editorial directors. Fifth edition, 1993. This 13-volume set profiles over 600 occupations. Each occupational profile describes job duties, educational requirements, how to get the job, advancement possibilities, employment outlook,

working conditions, earnings and benefits, and where to write for more information.

★4983★ What Is a Special Librarian?
Special Libraries Association
1700 18th St., NW
Washington, DC 20009-2508
Ph: (202)234-4700
1991. The eight-page booklet describes special librarianship, the need for special librarians, skills needed, employment opportunities, salary, and educational preparation.

★4984★ Whatever You Like to Do . . . A Librarian Probably Is Already Doing It
American Library Association
50 E. Huron St.
Chicago, IL 60611
Ph: (312)280-2424   Fr: 800-545-2433
This 13-page booklet explores career opportunities for librarians, profiling librarians in different work settings. Describes educational requirements and salary.

PROFESSIONAL ASSOCIATIONS

★4985★ American Association of Law Libraries (AALL)
53 W. Jackson Blvd., Ste. 940
Chicago, IL 60604
Ph: (312)939-4764   Fax: (312)431-1097
Librarians who serve the legal profession in the courts, bar associations, law societies, law schools, private law firms, federal, state, and county governments, and business; associate members are legal publishers and other interested persons. Sponsors institutes which are generally held in mid-winter and in the summer during the week preceding the annual meeting; directs procedure for exchange of duplicate materials among law libraries. Maintains placement service. **Publications:** *American Association of Law Libraries Newsletter*, monthly. • *Biographical Directory.* • *Directory of Law Libraries*, annual. • *Index to Foreign Legal Periodicals*, quarterly. • *Law Library Journal*, quarterly. • *Salary Survey.*

★4986★ American Library Association (ALA)
50 E. Huron St.
Chicago, IL 60611
Ph: (312)944-6780   Fax: (312)280-3255
Fr: 800-545-2433
Members: Librarians, libraries, trustees, friends of libraries, and others interested in the responsibilities of libraries in the educational, social, and cultural needs of society. **Purpose:** Promotes and improves library service and librarianship. Establishes standards of service, support, education, and welfare for libraries and library personnel; promotes the adoption of such standards in libraries of all kinds; safeguards the professional status of librarians; encourages the recruiting of competent personnel for professional careers in librarianship; promotes popular understanding and public acceptance of the value of library service and librarianship. Works in liaison with federal agencies to initiate the enactment and administration of legislation that will

extend library services. Offers placement services. **Publications:** *ALA Handbook of Organization and Membership Directory*, annual. • *ALA Washington Newsletter*, periodic. • *American Libraries*, 11/year. • *Book Links*, bimonthly. • *Booklist*, biweekly. • *Library Systems Newsletter*, monthly. • *Library Technology Reports*, bimonthly.

★4987★ American Society for Information Science (ASIS)
8720 Georgia Ave., Ste. 501
Silver Spring, MD 20910-3602
Ph: (301)495-0900   Fax: (301)495-0810
Members: Information specialists, scientists, librarians, administrators, social scientists, and others interested in the use, organization, storage, retrieval, evaluation, and dissemination of recorded specialized information. **Purpose:** Seeks to improve the information transfer process through research, development, application, and education. Provides a forum for the discussion, publication, and critical analysis of work dealing with the theory, practice, research, and development of elements involved in communication of information. Members are engaged in a variety of activities and specialties including classification and coding systems, automatic and associative indexing, machine translation of languages, special librarianship and library systems analysis, and copyright issues. Sponsors National Auxiliary Publications Service, which provides reproduction services and a central depository for all types of information (operated for ASIS by Microfiche Publications). Maintains placement service. Sponsors numerous special interest groups. Conducts continuing education programs and professional development workshops. **Publications:** *Annual Review of Information Science and Technology.* • *Handbook and Directory*, annual. • *Jobline*, monthly. • *Journal of the American Society for Information Science.*

★4988★ Association for Library and Information Science Education (ALISE)
4101 Lake Boone Trl., Ste. 201
Raleigh, NC 27607
Ph: (919)787-5181   Fax: (919)787-4916
Members: Graduate schools offering degree programs in library science and their faculties. **Purpose:** Seeks to: promote excellence in education for library and information science as a means of increasing the effectiveness of library and information services; provide a forum for the active interchange of ideas and information among library educators; promote research related to teaching and to library and information science; formulate and promulgate positions on matters related to library education. Offers employment program. **Publications:** *Journal of Education for Library and Information Science.* • *Library and Information Science Education Statistical Report*, annual.

★4989★ Special Libraries Association (SLA)
1700 18th St. NW
Washington, DC 20009-2508
Ph: (202)234-4700   Fax: (202)265-9317
Members: International association of information professionals who work in special libraries serving business, research, government, universities, newspapers, museums,

and institutions that use or produce specialized information. **Purpose:** Seeks to advance the leadership role of special librarians. Offers consulting services to organizations that wish to establish or expand a library or information services. Conducts continuing education courses, public relations, and government relations programs. Provides employment services. Operates Information Resources Center on topics pertaining to the development and management of special libraries. Maintains Hall of Fame. **Publications:** *Special Libraries*, quarterly. • *SpeciaList*, monthly. • *Who's Who in Special Libraries*, annual.

STANDARDS/CERTIFICATION AGENCIES

★4990★ American Library Association (ALA)
50 E. Huron St.
Chicago, IL 60611
Ph: (312)944-6780   Fax: (312)280-3255
Fr: 800-545-2433
Establishes standards of service, support, education, and welfare for libraries and library personnel; promotes the adoption of such standards in libraries of all kinds.

TEST GUIDES

★4991★ *Career Examination Series: Junior Librarian*
National Learning Corp.
212 Michael Dr.
Syosset, NY 11791
Ph: (516)921-8888   Fax: (516)921-8743
Fr: 800-645-6337
Jack Rudman. 1993. Test guide including questions and answers for students or professionals in the field who seek advancement through examination.

★4992★ *Career Examination Series: Librarian*
National Learning Corp.
212 Michael Dr.
Syosset, NY 11791
Ph: (516)921-8888   Fax: (516)921-8743
Fr: 800-645-6337
Jack Rudman. A series of study guides with multiple-choice examination questions and solutions for trainees and professional librarians. Titles in the series include *Assistant Library Director; Assistant Library Director I; Assistant Library Director II; Assistant Library Director III; Assistant Library Director IV; Assistant Library Director V; Department Librarian; Department Senior Librarian; Director of Library; Librarian I; Librarian II; Librarian III; Librarian IV; Librarian V; Librarian Trainee; Library Director; Library Director I; Library Director II; Library Director III; Library Dire ctor IV; Library Director V; Medical Record Librarian; Principal Librarian; Professional Library*

Examination; Public Librarian; Senior Librarian; Senior Librarian I.

★4993★ *Career Examination Series: Magnetic Tape Librarian*
National Learning Corp.
212 Michael Dr.
Syosset, NY 11791
Ph: (516)921-8888   Fax: (516)921-8743
Fr: 800-645-6337
Jack Rudman. 1993. Test guide including questions and answers for students or professionals in the field who seek advancement through examination.

★4994★ *Career Examination Series: Senior Medical Records Librarian*
National Learning Corp.
212 Michael Dr.
Syosset, NY 11791
Ph: (516)921-8888   Fax: (516)921-8743
Fr: 800-645-6337
Jack Rudman. 1993. Test guide including questions and answers for students or professionals in the field who seek advancement through examination.

★4995★ *Library Science*
National Learning Corp.
212 Michael Dr.
Syosset, NY 11791
Ph: (516)921-8888   Fax: (516)921-8743
Fr: 800-645-6337
Jack Rudman. Part of the Test Your Knowledge Series. Contains multiple choice questions with answers.

★4996★ *National Teacher Examination Series*
National Learning Corp.
212 Michael Dr.
Syosset, NY 11791
Ph: (516)921-8888   Fax: (516)921-8743
Fr: 800-645-6337
Jack Rudman. Practice multiple-choice examinations for education certification. Includes solutions. Titles in the series include *National Teacher Examination (Core Battery)* (one-volume combined edition); *Agriculture; Art Education; Biology and General Science; Business Education; Chemistry and General Science; Chemistry, Physics, and General Science; Earth and Space Science; Education of the Mentally Retarded; English Language and Literature; French; German; Health Education; Home Economics Education; Mathematics; Latin; Marketing and Distributive Education; Men's Physical Education; Music Education; Physics and General Science; Physical Education; Psychological Foundations of Education; Psychology; School Psychology; Science and Mathematics; Social Studies; Social Studies, Literature and Fine Arts; Societal Foundations of Education; Spanish; Special Education; Speech Communication; Teaching Emotionally Disturbed; Teaching Hearing Handicapped; Teaching Learning Disabled; Teaching Orthopedically Handicapped; Teaching Principles and Practices; Teaching Speech Handicapped; Women's Physical Education; Written English Expression.*

★4997★ *Teachers License Examination Series: Elementary Education*
National Learning Corp.
212 Michael Dr.
Syosset, NY 11791
Ph: (516)921-8888   Fax: (516)921-8743
Fr: 800-645-6337
Jack Rudman. A series of preparatory study guides for professionals studying for licensing examinations. Includes a multiple-choice test section; provides answers. Contains numerous titles related to elementary education.

EDUCATIONAL DIRECTORIES AND PROGRAMS

★4998★ *American Library Directory*
R. R. Bowker Co.
121 Chanlon Rd.
New Providence, NJ 07974
Ph: (908)464-6800   Fax: (908)771-7704
Nan Hudes, Marketing Director
Annual, June. Covers over 35,000 U.S. and Canadian academic, public, county, provincial, and regional libraries; library systems; medical, law, and other special libraries; and libraries for the blind and physically handicapped. Separate section lists over 350 library networks and consortia and 220 accredited and unaccredited library school programs. Entries include: For libraries—Name, supporting or affiliated institution or firm name, address, phone, fax, electronic mail address, Standard Address Number (SANs), names of librarian and department heads, income, collection size, special collections, computer hardware, automated functions, and type of catalog. For library systems—Name, location. For library Arrangement: Geographical.

★4999★ *Association for Library and Information Science Education— Annual Directory*
Association for Library and Information Science Education
4101 Lake Boone Trail, Ste. 201
Raleigh, NC 27607
Ph: (919)787-5181   Fax: (919)787-4916
Penney DePas, Contact
Annual, fall. Publication includes: List of 82 member graduate-level library schools and 1,800 faculty members; international coverage. Entries include: School name, address, phone, electronic mail address, date established, dean, list of faculty. Arrangement: Alphabetical by school name.

★5000★ *Bowker Annual: Library and Book Trade Almanac*
R. R. Bowker Co.
121 Chanlon Rd.
New Providence, NJ 07974
Ph: (908)464-6800   Fax: (908)665-6688
Katherine Barr, Contact
Annual, May. Publication includes: Lists of accredited library schools; scholarships for education in library science; library organizations; library statistics; publishing and bookselling organizations. Entries include: Directory listings give name of institution, address,

phone, fax, name of officer or contact, publications; scholarship listings include requirements, value of grant, contact name. Principal content is articles and special reports on topics of interest to those in library/information science and publishers; international reports; annual reports from federal agencies and libraries and from national associations; information on legislation, funding, etc. Arrangement: Topical.

★5001★ Directory of Library School Offerings in Music Librarianship
Music Library Association
c/o Richard Griscom, Executive Secretary
University of Louisville Music Library
2301 S. 3rd St.
Louisville, KY 40292
Ph: (502)588-5659   Fax: (502)588-7701
Richard Griscom, Executive Secretary

Irregular, latest edition July 1994. Covers about 50 library schools that offer programs in music librarianship. Entries include: School name, address, contact name, phone, internships offered, courses offered, and number of music credits possible. Arrangement: Geographical.

★5002★ Educational Media and Technology Yearbook
Libraries Unlimited
PO Box 6633
Englewood, CO 80155-6633
Ph: (303)770-1220   Fax: (303)220-8843
Fr: 800-237-6124
Debbie Taylor, Contact

Annual, November. Publication includes: Lists of media-related organizations and associations; institutions offering graduate degrees in media and instructional technology; foundation and federal funding sources; and producers, distributors, and publishers of audiovisual materials; international coverage. Entries include: Institution or organization name, address, phone, name of contact; most listings also contain brief additional detail pertinent to subject of listing. Principal content is articles reviewing current state of the field. Arrangement: Separate sections for associations, institutions, funding sources, and suppliers.

★5003★ Financial Assistance for Library and Information Studies
Standing Committee on Library Education
50 E. Huron St.
Chicago, IL 60611
Ph: (312)280-4277   Fax: (312)280-3256
Fr: 800-545-2433
Margaret Myers, Contact

Annual, November. Covers colleges, universities, and other organizations offering scholarships and other assistance in library education. Entries include: Organization or institution name, award name, program level, type of assistance, requirements, application deadline; contact name, address for application. Each annual edition lists financial sources for the next academic year. Arrangement: State awards are geographical; regional and national are alphabetical.

★5004★ Library Education, Human Resource, & Development Program— Abstracts of Funded Projects
U.S. Office of Educational Research and Improvement
555 New Jersey Ave. NW
Washington, DC 20208-5571
Ph: (202)219-1315   Fax: (202)219-1725
Janice Owens, Contact

Irregular, latest edition 1992. Covers colleges and universities which have received library education grants from the Department of Education to train persons in librarianship through fellowships, institutes, and traineeships. Grants are authorized under Title II-B of the Higher Education Act (HEA) to institutions of higher education and library organizations and agencies. Entries include: Institution name, address, name of project director, total funding for the year, number of available grants, dates of availability, study level, program priorities and objectives. Arrangement: Geographical.

★5005★ Master's Programs in Library & Information Studies Accredited by the American Library Association
Office for Accreditation
50 E. Huron St.
Chicago, IL 60611
Ph: (312)280-2432   Fax: (312)280-2433
Fr: 800-545-2433
Prudence Dalrymple, Director

Semiannual, March and October. Covers about 60 institutions in the United States and Canada that offer graduate programs in library and information studies. Entries include: Institution name, address; name and phone of dean, director, or contact; degrees offered. Arrangement: Geographical.

★5006★ Newspapers Career Directory
Gale Research Inc.
835 Penobscot Bldg.
Detroit, MI 48226-4094
Ph: (313)961-2242   Fax: (313)961-6083
Fr: 800-877-GALE

Bradley J. Morgan and Joseph M. Palmisano. 1993. A directory in the Career Advisor Series that provides essays written by industry professionals; job search information on resume and cover letter preparation, networking, and the interviewing process; approximately 300 companies and organizations offering job opportunities and internships, and additional job-hunting resources.

AWARDS, SCHOLARSHIPS, GRANTS, AND FELLOWSHIPS

★5007★ ACRL Doctoral Dissertation Fellowship
American Library Association
Association of College and Research Libraries
50 E. Huron St.
Chicago, IL 60611
Ph: (312)280-3248   Fax: (312)280-2520
Fr: 800-545-2433

To foster research in academic librarianship by encouraging and assisting doctoral students with their dissertation research. Candidates who have completed their coursework and have had a dissertation proposal accepted in the area of academic librarianship are considered. The nomination deadline is December 1. A monetary award of $1,000 and a plaque are presented annually at the conference. Established in 1983. Sponsored by the Institute for Scientific Information.

★5008★ Bound to Stay Bound Books Scholarships
American Library Association (ALA)
Association for Library Service to Children
50 East Huron St.
Chicago, IL 60611
Ph: (312)280-2163

Purpose: To encourage advanced degree study in the field of library service to children. Qualifications: Applicant must be a U.S. citizen. Applicant must be planning to work in the field of library service to children. The scholarships may be used for study toward the M.L.S. degree or other graduate work at an ALA-accredited library school. Funds available: $5,000. Application details: Write for the ALA handbook, which lists all awards available, application form and guidelines. Deadline: 1 March.

★5009★ Reverend Andrew L. Bouwhuis Memorial Scholarships
Catholic Library Association
St. Joseph Central High School
22 Maplewood Ave.
Pittsfield, MA 01201
Ph: (413)447-9121

Purpose: To encourage college students to enter the library profession. Qualifications: Applicant must be a college senior or graduate who has been accepted by a master's of library science program. Candidates are evaluated on the basis of academic scholarship and financial need. Funds available: $1,500. Application details: Write to the Scholarship Committee for application materials. Submit application form with statement of interest in librarianship, statement of financial need, transcripts, and Graduate Record Examination, Miller, or other applicable test scores. Letters of reference and supporting financial documents are also welcome. Deadline: February 1. The scholarship winner is announced during the week following Easter.

★5010★ Bowker/Ulrich's Serials Librarianship Award
American Library Association
Association for Library Collections and
  Technical Services
50 E. Huron St.
Chicago, IL 60611
Ph: (312)280-5034   Fax: (312)280-3257
Fr: 800-545-2433

In recognition of distinguished contributions to serials librarianship within the previous three years as demonstrated through such activities as leadership in serials-related activities through participation in professional associations and/or library education programs, contributions to the body of serials literature, conduct of research in the area of serials, development of tools or methods to enhance access to or management of serials, or other advances leading to a better understanding of the field of serials. Nominations must be submitted by December 1. The award may be divided among two or more individuals who have participated in the achievement for which it is granted. A monetary award of $1,500 and a citation are presented annually at the American Library Association Conference. Established in 1985. The award is donated by R. R. Bowker.

★5011★ David H. Clift Scholarship
American Library Association
Office for Library Personnel Resources
50 E. Huron St.
Chicago, IL 60611
Ph: (312)944-6780   Fax: (312)280-3256

To provide funds for a U.S. or Canadian citizen to begin an MLS degree in an ALA-accredited program. A monetary award of $3,000 is presented. Established in 1969.

★5012★ Facts On File Current Affairs Grant
American Library Association
Reference and Adult Services Division
50 E. Huron St.
Chicago, IL 60611
Ph: (312)280-4398   Fax: (312)944-8085
Fr: 800-545-2433

To recognize a library for imaginative programming that makes current affairs more meaningful to an adult audience. The grant is awarded for projects conducted in an informal setting whether in a public, academic, or school library and emphasizes quality rather than the magnitude of the project. Programs, bibliographies, pamphlets, and innovative approaches of all types and in all media are considered. A monetary grant of up to $2,000 is awarded annually. Established in 1979. Sponsored by Facts On File, Inc.

★5013★ Louise Giles Minority Scholarship
American Library Association
Office for Library Personnel Resources
50 E. Huron St.
Chicago, IL 60611
Ph: (312)944-6780   Fax: (312)280-3256

To provide funds for a U.S. or Canadian minority student to begin an MLS degree in ALA-accredited program. A monetary award of $3,000 is presented. Established in 1977.

★5014★ Hubbard Scholarship
Georgia Library Association
c/o Donna Mancini
215 Sycamore St.
Decatur, GA 30030
Ph: (404)370-3070

Purpose: To encourage the study of librarianship, and to recruit excellent librarians for the state of Georgia. Qualifications: Applicant must be a U.S. citizen accepted for admission to a master's program at a library school accredited by the American Library Association (ALA). Candidate must indicate an intention to complete the degree requirements within two years. An accepted scholar must work in a Georgia library for one year following completion of degree. Funds available: $3,000. Application details: Write for application form. Submit with three letters of reference, transcripts, and proof of acceptance by an ALA-accredited library school. Deadline: May 1. Applicants will be notified by June 1.

★5015★ Harold Lancour Scholarship for Foreign Study
Beta Phi Mu International Library Science
  Honor Society
School of Library and Information Science
University of Pittsburgh
Pittsburgh, PA 15260
Ph: (412)624-9435

Purpose: To allow U.S. library scholars to study abroad. Qualifications: Applicant may be of any nationality, but must be a librarian or graduate student in library sciences. Awards are tenable outside of the United States; foreign study must relate to graduate or professional goals. Funds available: $1,000. Application details: Write to the executive secretary for application form and guidelines. Submit form and resume with statement indicating the relevance of proposed foreign study to work or studies. Deadline: March 1.

★5016★ Law Degree Scholarships for Library School Graduates
American Association of Law Libraries
401 N. Michigan Ave.
Chicago, IL 60611-4212
Ph: (312)939-4764   Fax: (312)431-1097

Purpose: To support students who plan to pursue careers in law librarianship. Qualifications: Candidate should preferably be a U.S. or Canadian citizen. Applicant must be a graduate of an accredited library school who is working toward a law degree in an accredited law school, with no more than 36 semester (or 54 quarter) credit hours of study remaining before qualifying for the degree. Candidate must have meaningful law library experience. Scholarships are tenable at a law school accredited by the American Bar Association. Funds available: $2,500 maximum. Application details: Write for application form and guidelines. Deadline: 1 April.

★5017★ LDA Award for Excellence in Library Achievement
LDA Publishers
42-36 209th St.
Bayside, NY 11361
Ph: (718)224-9484   Fax: (718)224-9487

To call attention to the importance of libraries, librarians, and their work. The following criteria are considered: outstanding achievement

in developing and publishing library materials; long and distinguished service in the advancement of librarianship; an original contribution for promoting the library; progressive legislative activity; promoting of intellectual freedom; and creative, innovative utilization of technologies. Librarians, trustees, support staff, friends of the library, vendors, and publishers may be nominated by April 15. A plaque is awarded annually at the Long Island Libraries Conference. Established in 1978.

★5018★ Library Degree Scholarships for Law Graduates
American Association of Law Libraries
401 N. Michigan Ave.
Chicago, IL 60611-4212
Ph: (312)939-4764   Fax: (312)431-1097

Purpose: To support students who plan to pursue careers in law librarianship. Qualifications: Candidate should preferably be a U.S. or Canadian citizen. Applicant must be a graduate of an accredited law school who is a degree candidate in an accredited library school. Funds available: $3,000 maximum. Application details: Write for application form and guidelines. Deadline: 1 April. Notification by 31 May.

★5019★ Library Degree Scholarships for Non-Law School Graduates
American Association of Law Libraries
401 N. Michigan Ave.
Chicago, IL 60611-4212
Ph: (312)939-4764   Fax: (312)431-1097

Purpose: To support students who plan to pursue careers in law librarianship. Qualifications: Candidate should preferably be a U.S. or Canadian citizen. Applicant must be a graduate of an accredited college; a degree candidate in an accredited library school; and have some law library experience. Funds available: $2,500 maximum. Application details: Write for application form and guidelines. Deadline: 1 April. Notification by 31 May.

★5020★ LITA/GEAC Scholarships in Library and Information Technology.
American Library Association (ALA)
Library and Information Technology
  Association
50 E. Huron St.
Chicago, IL 60611
Ph: (312)280-4270   Fax: (312)280-3257

Purpose: To encourage students committed to a career in library automation and information technology. Qualifications: Applicant must be a student entering a ALA-accredited master's program of library education, with an emphasis on library automation. Funds available: $2,500. Application details: Write to the ALA at the above address for application form and guidelines. Deadline: April 1.

★5021★ LITA/OCLC Minority Scholarship
American Library Association (ALA)
Library and Information Technology
  Association
50 E. Huron St.
Chicago, IL 60611
Ph: (312)280-4270   Fax: (312)280-3257

Purpose: To encourage minority students committed to a career in library automation and information technology. Qualifications:

Applicant must be a U.S. or Canadian citizen, a member of a principle minority group, and a student entering a ALA-accredited master's program of library education, with an emphasis on library automation. Funds available: $2,500. Application details: Write to the ALA at the above address for application form and guidelines. Deadline: 1 April.

★5022★ Allie Beth Martin Award
American Library Association
Public Library Association
50 E. Huron St.
Chicago, IL 60611
Ph: (312)280-5752   Fax: (312)280-5029
Fr: 800-545-2433

To recognize a librarian who, in a public library setting, has demonstrated an extraordinary range and depth of knowledge about books or other library materials and has exhibited a distinguished ability to share that knowledge. Application deadline is December 1. A $3,000 honorarium and a citation are presented annually at the ALA Annual Conference. Established in 1977 in honor of Allie Beth Martin. Sponsored by the Baker and Taylor.

★5023★ Medal of Merit
American Numismatic Association
818 N. Cascade Ave.
Colorado Springs, CO 80903-3279
Ph: (719)632-2646   Fax: (719)634-4085

This, ANA's second highest award, is given to recognize individuals for outstanding contributions to the science of numismatics. A silver medal is awarded annually. Established in 1947.

★5024★ Frederic G. Melcher Book Award
Unitarian Universalist Association
25 Beacon St.
Boston, MA 02108
Ph: (617)742-2100   Fax: (617)367-3237

To recognize the author of an outstanding literary work that contributes to religious liberalism. A monetary award of $1,000 and a citation are awarded annually. Established in 1964 to honor Frederic G. Melcher, dean of American publishers.

★5025★ Frederic G. Melcher Scholarships
American Library Association (ALA)
Association for Library Service to Children
50 East Huron St.
Chicago, IL 60611
Ph: (312)280-2163

Purpose: To encourage advanced degree study in the field of library service to children. Qualifications: Applicant must reside in the U.S. or Canada. Applicant must be planning to work in the field of library service to children for at least two years upon graduation. The scholarships may be used for study toward the M.L.S. degree or other graduate work at an ALA-accredited library school. Funds available: $5,000; Melcher: $5,000. Application details: Write for the ALA handbook, which lists all awards available, application form and guidelines. Deadline: 1 March.

★5026★ MLA Doctoral Fellowship
Medical Library Association (MLA)
6 North Michigan Ave., Ste. 300
Chicago, IL 60602-4805
Ph: (312)419-9094

Purpose: To encourage superior students to conduct doctoral work in medical librarianship or information science. Qualifications: Applicants must be citizens or permanent residents of the United States or Canada and graduates of ALA-accredited schools of library science pursuing a doctoral degree. Programs must emphasize biomedical and health-related information science. Candidates should already be accepted in a doctoral program to assure acceptance of the project toward Ph.D requirements. Previous winners of Doctoral Fellowships are not eligible. Selection criteria: Preference is given to applicants who have at least 80 percent of their course work completed and an approved dissertation prospectus. Funds available: One fellowship of $1,000 is awarded annually. Funds may be used for project and travel expenses, as well as augmenting larger, separately funded projects relevant to doctoral degree requirements. Funds may not be used to pay for tuition, equipment, clinical support except preparation of the final report for MLA, and living expenses. Application details: Applicants must submit formal application form, two letters of reference including one from the applicant's doctoral advisor and one from a person recognized for expertise in the proposed field, official graduate transcripts, a summary and detailed budget for the doctoral project, and a signed statement of terms and conditions. Deadline: February 1.

★5027★ Margaret E. Monroe Library Adult Services Award
American Library Association
Reference and Adult Services Division
50 E. Huron St.
Chicago, IL 60611
Ph: (312)280-4398   Fax: (312)944-8085
Fr: 800-545-2433

To recognize and honor a librarian who has made significant contributions to library adult services and who has had an impact on the profession. Practicing librarians, library and information science researchers or educators, or retired librarians who have brought distinction to the profession's understanding and practice of services for adults are eligible. "Adult" is defined to exclude young adults. A citation is awarded annually at the ALA Annual Conference. Established in 1985 in honor of Margaret E. Monroe, scholar, mentor, administrator, and author in the field of library services to adults.

★5028★ Shirley Olofson Memorial Award
American Library Association
New Members Round Table
c/o Staff Liaison
50 E. Huron St.
Chicago, IL 60611
Ph: (312)944-6780   Fax: (312)280-3257

To provide funds for individuals to attend their second ALA Annual Conference. The deadline is December 11. A monetary award is presented.

★5029★ Esther J. Piercy Award
American Library Association
Association for Library Collections and Technical Services
50 E. Huron St.
Chicago, IL 60611
Ph: (312)280-5034   Fax: (312)280-3257
Fr: 800-545-2433

To recognize the contribution to librarianship in the field of technical services by a librarian, with not more than 10 years of professional experience, who has shown outstanding promise for continuing contributions and leadership. Criteria for the award are: leadership in professional associations at the local, state, regional, or national level; contributions to the development, application, or utilization of new or improved methods, techniques, and routines; significant contributions to professional literature; or conduct of studies or research in the technical services. Nominations must be submitted by December 1. A citation is presented each year at the ALA Annual Conference. Established in 1969 in honor of Esther J. Piercy.

★5030★ Herbert W. Putnam Honor Award
American Library Association
ALA Awards Committee
50 E. Huron St.
Chicago, IL 60611
Ph: (312)944-6780   Fax: (312)280-3257
Fr: 800-545-2433

To provide a grant-in-aid to an American librarian of outstanding ability for travel, writing, or any other use that might improve his or her service to the library profession or to society. The $500 grant awarded quadrennially is made possible by the income received from the Herbert W. Putnam Honor Fund.

★5031★ Sarah Rebecca Reed Scholarships
Beta Phi Mu International Library Science Honor Society
School of Library and Information Science
University of Pittsburgh
Pittsburgh, PA 15260
Ph: (412)624-9435

Purpose: To assist graduate students in the library sciences. Qualifications: Applicant may be of any nationality, but must be accepted into a program of study accredited by the American Library Association. Funds available: $1,500. Application details: Write to the executive secretary for application form and guidelines. Submit form with five letters of reference. Deadline: March 1.

★5032★ Frank B. Sessa Scholarship for Continuing Education
Beta Phi Mu International Library Science Honor Society
School of Library and Information Science
University of Pittsburgh
Pittsburgh, PA 15260
Ph: (412)624-9435

Purpose: To encourage librarians to pursue further education. Qualifications: Applicant may be of any nationality, but must be a member of Beta Phi Mu. Scholarship is tenable worldwide. Funds available: $750. Application details: Write to the executive secretary for application form and guidelines. Submit form with resume and an explanation of proposed study or research. Deadline: March 1.

★5033★ Fannie Simon Award
Special Libraries Association
Museums, Arts and Humanities Division
1700 18th St. NW
Washington, DC 20009-2508
Ph: (202)234-4700   Fax: (202)265-9317
To recognize a member of the Division for distinguished service to publishing librarianship or the field of publishing. The award consists of a cash stipend of $100 and a plaque. Established in 1980 in honor of Fannie Simon, founder of the SLA Publishing Division, and a 1962 SLA Hall of Fame Award winner.

BASIC REFERENCE GUIDES AND HANDBOOKS

★5034★ ALA Survey of Librarian Salaries
American Library Association (ALA)
Publishing Services
50 E. Huron St.
Chicago, IL 60611
Ph: (312)944-6780   Fax: (312)944-2641
Fr: 800-545-2433
Mary J. Lynch, Margaret Myers, and Jeneice Guy, editors. 1992.

★5035★ CD-ROM Librarian Index: 1986-1990
Meckler Publishing
11 Ferry Ln., W.
Westport, CT 06880
Ph: (203)226-6967   Fax: (203)454-5840
Ann Babits, editor. 1991.

★5036★ Handbook for Small, Rural, and Emerging Public Libraries
Oryx Press
2214 N. Central at Encanto, Ste. 103
Phoenix, AZ 85004
Ph: (602)265-2651
Anne Gervasi and Betty K. Seibt. 1988. Includes bibliographies and an index.

★5037★ Introduction to Reference Work: Reference Services and Reference Practices
McGraw-Hill, Inc.
1221 Avenue of the Americas
New York, NY 10020
Ph: (212)512-2000   Fr: 800-722-4726
William A. Katz. Sixth edition, 1992. Two-volume work that covers basic reference sources, and principles and practices of reference work.

★5038★ Knowing Where to Look: The Ultimate Guide to Research
Writer's Digest Books
1507 Dana Ave.
Cincinnati, OH 45207
Ph: (513)531-2222
Lois Horowitz, editor. 1988. Includes an index.

★5039★ Manual of Online Search Strategies
Macmillan Publishing Co., Inc.
866 3rd Ave.
New York, NY 10022
Ph: (212)702-2000
Chris Armstrong and Andy Large, editors. 1992. Part of the Professional Librarian Series.

★5040★ The Prentice-Hall Encyclopedia of Information Technology
Prentice-Hall, Inc.
Rte. 9W
Englewood Cliffs, NJ 07632
Ph: (201)592-2000   Fr: 800-634-2863
Robert A. Edmunds. 1987. Contains articles, written in a basic, nontechnical style, on information technology.

★5041★ Reference Readiness: A Manual for Librarians and Students
Shoe String Press, Inc.
PO Box 4327
Hamden, CT 06514
Ph: (203)248-6307
Agnes Ann Hede. Fourth edition, 1990. Lists basic reference sources and points out notable features.

★5042★ Special Libraries: A Guide for Management
Special Libraries Association (SLA)
1700 18th St., NW
Washington, DC 20009
Ph: (202)234-4700
Janet L. Ahrensfeld, Elin B. Christianson, and David E. King. Third edition, 1991. Includes a bibliography and an index. Illustrated.

★5043★ The Video Librarian's Guide to Collection Development and Management
Macmillan Publishing Co., Inc.
866 3rd Ave.
New York, NY 10022
Ph: (212)702-2000
Randy Pitman, editor. 1992. Part of the Professional Librarian Series.

PROFESSIONAL AND TRADE PERIODICALS

★5044★ ALCTS Newsletter
Association for Library Collections and Technical Services (ALCTS)
50 E. Huron St.
Chicago, IL 60611
Ph: (708)892-7465   Fax: (708)892-7466
Ann Swartzell
Concerned with collection development, cataloging, acquisitions, microform management, serials management, and preservation of materials in libraries. Contains news of activities of the Division and news items contributed by press releases from agencies and publishers. Recurring features include a calendar of events, notices of new publications, and a column titled Council of Regional Groups Update.

★5045★ American Libraries
American Library Assn.
50 E. Huron St.
Chicago, IL 60611
Ph: (312)944-6780   Fax: (312)944-8085
Thomas Gaughan
Magazine including news and features of interest to library service professionals.

★5046★ American Theological Library Association—Newsletter
American Theological Library Association
820 Church St., 3rd Fl.
Evanston, IL 60201
Ph: (708)869-7788
Janice P. Anderson, Contact
Quarterly. Presents news of interest to library professionals at theological schools. Recurring features include notices of publications available and job listings.

★5047★ B/ITE
Information Technology Division
c/o Karol Feltes Battelle
505 King Ave.
Columbus, OH 43201
Ph: (614)424-6307   Fax: (614)424-4738
Karol Feltes
Quarterly. Presents information technology and its applications to libraries. Provides a forum and means of communication for Division members. Recurring features include a calendar of events, reports of meetings, news of educational opportunities, and notices of publications available.

★5048★ Collection Management
The Haworth Press, Inc.
10 Alice St.
Binghamton, NY 13904-1580
Ph: (607)722-5857   Fax: (607)722-1424
Fr: 800-342-9678
Peter Gellatly
Quarterly. Journal examining developments in the field of collection management and their implications for college, university, and research libraries of all types.

★5049★ Friends of Libraries U.S.A. News Update
American Library Association, Reference and Adult Services Division
E Huron St.
Chicago, IL 60611-2795
Ph: (312)944-6780   Fax: (312)440-9374
Sandy Dolnick, Contact
Quarterly. Informs members on activities of benefit to them, including organizing, fundraising, literacy programs, and book and author events. Recurring features include book reviews. columns titled Friends in Action and New Books: Eclectic Selections for Reading Groups, Programs and Reading Enjoyment.

★5050★ Journal of the American Society for Information Science
John Wiley and Sons, Inc.
605 3rd Ave.
New York, NY 10158
Ph: (212)850-6000   Fax: (212)850-6799
Donald H. Kraft
Bimonthly. International journal serves as a forum for discussion and experimentation concerning the theory and practice of communicating information. Covers computer

technology, operations research, librarianship, communications, management, information storage and retrieval, reprography, and systems design.

★5051★ Journal of Library Administration
The Haworth Press, Inc.
10 Alice St.
Binghamton, NY 13904-1580
Ph: (607)722-5857   Fax: (607)722-1424
Fr: 800-342-9678
Sul H. Lee

Quarterly. Journal representing the viewpoints and concerns of top administration and middle-management in libraries.

★5052★ Library Administration & Management
American Library Assn.
50 E. Huron St.
Chicago, IL 60611
Ph: (312)944-6780   Fax: (312)944-8085
Diane Graves

Quarterly. Journal reporting on current administrative issues of concern to library managers and executives.

★5053★ Library Journal
Cahners Publishing Co.
249 W. 17th St.
New York, NY 10011
Ph: (212)463-6759   Fax: (212)463-6734
John N. Berry

Library management and book selection journal.

★5054★ The Library Quarterly
University of Chicago Press
5720 S. Woodlawn Ave.
Chicago, IL 60637
Ph: (312)702-7600   Fax: (312)702-0172
Stephen P. Harter

Quarterly. Journal serving library researchers.

★5055★ Library Trends
University of Illinois Graduate School of Library & Information Science Publications
501 E. Daniel St.
Champaign, IL 61820-6211
Ph: (217)333-1359   Fax: (217)244-7329
F.W. Lancaster

Quarterly. Library and information science Journal.

★5056★ The National Librarian: The NLA Newsletter
National Librarians Association (NLA)
PO Box 486
Alma, MI 48801
Ph: (517)463-7227   Fax: (517)463-8694
Peter Dollard

Quarterly. Reports on news of concern to professional librarians. Reports on certification, education, relevant legal cases, and news of the Association and related library and educational organizations. Recurring features include book reviews and a section titled Bibliography on Professionalism.

★5057★ The Primary Source
Soc. of Mississippi Archivists
PO Box 1151
Jackson, MS 39215-1151
Ph: (601)359-6868
Mattie Sink

Quarterly. Focuses on activities and trends in the archival and library community both regionally and nationally. Includes information on conservation and articles on state repositories and their holdings. Recurring features include news of research, book reviews, and a calendar of events.

★5058★ Public Library Quarterly
The Haworth Press, Inc.
10 Alice St.
Binghamton, NY 13904-1580
Ph: (607)722-5857   Fax: (607)722-1424
Fr: 800-342-9678
Richard L. Waters

Quarterly. Journal addressing the major administrative challenges facing public libraries.

★5059★ School Library Journal
Cahners Publishing Co.
249 W. 17th St.
New York, NY 10011
Ph: (212)463-6759   Fax: (212)463-6734
Lillian N. Gerhardt

★5060★ SLA Geography & Map Division—Bulletin
Geography & Map Division
Oregon State University
Kerr Library 121
Corvallis, OR 97331-4501
Ph: (503)737-2971   Fax: (503)737-3453
Joanne M. Perry

Quarterly. Provides a medium of exchange of information, news, and research in the field of geographic and cartographic bibliography, literature, and libraries. Recurring features include a letters to the editor, news of research, a calendar of events, reports of meetings, news of educational opportunities, job listings, book reviews, and notices of publications available.

★5061★ Special Libraries
Special Libraries Assn.
1700 Eighteenth St. NW
Washington, DC 20009
Ph: (202)234-4700   Fax: (202)265-9317
Gail L. Repsher

Quarterly. Official journal of the Special Libraries Association. Includes papers on the administration, organization, and operation of special libraries and information centers; scholarly research reports in librarianship, documentation, education, information science and technology; and articles on such concerns as professional standards, salary information, education, and public relations.

★5062★ Wilson Library Bulletin
The H.W. Wilson Co.
950 University Ave.
Bronx, NY 10452
Ph: (718)588-8400   Fax: (718)590-1617
Fr: 800-367-6770
Grace Anne DeCandido

Monthly. Magazine for library professionals.

PROFESSIONAL MEETINGS AND CONVENTIONS

★5063★ American Association of School Librarians Conference and Exhibition
American Association of School Librarians
50 E. Huron St.
Chicago, IL 60611
Ph: (312)280-4387   Fax: (312)280-3224
Annual.

★5064★ American Library Association Annual Conference
American Library Association
50 E. Huron St.
Chicago, IL 60611
Ph: (312)944-6780   Fax: (312)280-3224
Annual. **Dates and Locations:** 1996 Jun 20-27; Orlando, FL. • 1997 Jun 26-03; San Francisco, CA.

★5065★ American Library Association Mid-Winter Meeting
American Library Association
50 E. Huron St.
Chicago, IL 60611
Ph: (312)944-6780   Fax: (312)280-3224
Annual. **Dates and Locations:** 1996 Jan 19-25, TX.

★5066★ Annual Meeting of the American Association of Law Libraries
American Association of Law Libraries
53 W. Jackson Blvd., Ste. 940
Chicago, IL 60604
Ph: (312)939-4764   Fax: (312)431-1097
Annual.

★5067★ Art Libraries Society of North America Annual Conference
Art Libraries Society of North America
3900 E. Timrod St.
Tucson, AZ 85711
Ph: (602)881-8479   Fax: (602)322-6778
Annual. **Dates and Locations:** 1996; Miami Beach, FL.

★5068★ Association of College and Research Libraries National Conference
Association of College and Research Libraries
50 E. Huron St.
Chicago, IL 60611
Ph: (312)944-6780   Fax: (312)440-9374
Every three years.

★5069★ Church and Synagogue Library Association Conference
Church and Synagogue Library Association
PO Box 19357
Portland, OR 97280-0357
Ph: (503)244-6919
Annual.

★5070★ **Midwest Federation of Library Associations Quadrennial Convention**
Ohio Library Association
67 Jefferson Ave.
Columbus, OH 43215
Ph: (614)221-9057   Fax: (614)221-6234
Every four years. **Dates and Locations:** 1995 Nov 08-11; Chicago, IL.

★5071★ **Public Library Association National Conference**
Public Library Association
50 E. Huron St.
Chicago, IL 60611
Ph: (312)944-6780   Fax: (312)440-9374
Biennial.

★5072★ **Special Libraries Association Annual Conference**
Special Libraries Association
1700 18th St., NW
Washington, DC 20009
Ph: (202)234-4700   Fax: (202)265-9317
Annual. **Dates and Locations:** 1996 Jun 09-12; Boston, MA. • 1997 Jun 08-11; Seattle, WA. • 1998 Jun 07-10; Indianapolis, IN. • 1999 Jun 05-10; Minneapolis, MN. • 2000 Jun 10-15; Philadelphia, PA. •

OTHER SOURCES OF INFORMATION

★5073★ **"Children's Librarian"** in *Career Selector 2001*
Barron's Educational Series, Inc.
250 Wireless Blvd.
Hauppauge, NY 11788
Ph: (516)434-3311   Fax: (516)434-3723
Fr: 800-645-3476
James C. Gonyea. 1993.

★5074★ *Education for Professional Librarians*
Macmillan Publishing Co.
100 Front St.
Box 500
Riverside, NJ 08075
Ph: 800-257-5755
Herbert S. White, editor. 1990. Includes a bibliography and an index.

★5075★ *Guide to the Use of Libraries and Information Sources*
McGraw-Hill, Inc.
1221 Avenue of the Americas
New York, NY 10020
Ph: (212)512-2000
Jean Key Gates, editor. 1989. Includes an index. Illustrated.

★5076★ **"Information Science"** in *Accounting to Zoology: Graduate Fields Defined* (pp. 336-338)
Petersons Guides, Inc.
PO Box 2123
Princeton, NJ 08543-2123
Ph: (609)243-9111   Fax: (609)243-9150
Fr: 800-338-3282
Amy J. Goldstein, editor. Revised and updated, 1987. Discusses types of graduate programs and degrees, graduate research, applied work, employment prospects and trends.

★5077★ **"Librarian"** in *100 Best Jobs for the 1990s & Beyond*
Dearborn Financial Publishing, Inc.
520 N. Dearborn St.
Chicago, IL 60610-4354
Ph: (312)836-4400   Fax: (312)836-1021
Fr: 800-621-9621
Carol Kleiman. 1992. Describes 100 jobs ranging from accountants to veterinarians. Each job profile includes such information as education, experience, and certification needed, salaries, and job search suggestions.

★5078★ **"Librarian"** in *Career Selector 2001*
Barron's Educational Series, Inc.
250 Wireless Blvd.
Hauppauge, NY 11788
Ph: (516)434-3311   Fax: (516)434-3723
Fr: 800-645-3476
James C. Gonyea. 1993.

★5079★ *Library and Information Science Annual*
Libraries Unlimited
6931 S. Yosemite St.
Englewood, CO 80112
Ph: (303)770-1220   Fr: 800-237-6124
Bohdan S. Wynar, Ann E. Prentice, and Anna Grace Patterson, editors. Annual. Contains essays, book reviews, reviews of periodicals, and abstracts of library science dissertations.

★5080★ *Library Programs: Library Career Training Programs—Abstracts of Funded Projects*
U.S. Department of Education
Office of Educational Research and Improvement
Washington, DC 20208
Ph: (202)245-3192
Annual. This booklet describes colleges offering fellowships and grants under Title II-B of the Higher Education Act of 1965 for the master's, post-master's, and doctoral degrees in library science.

★5081★ **"Library Science"** in *Accounting to Zoology: Graduate Fields Defined* (pp. 156-157)
Petersons Guides, Inc.
PO Box 2123
Princeton, NJ 08543-2123
Ph: (609)243-9111   Fax: (609)243-9150
Fr: 800-338-3282
Amy J. Goldstein, , editor. Revised and updated, 1987. Discusses types of graduate programs and degrees, graduate research, applied work, employment prospects and trends.

★5082★ *Requirements for Certification of Teachers, Counselors, Librarians, Administrators for Elementary and Secondary Schools, and Junior Colleges*
University of Chicago Press
11030 S. Langley Ave.
Chicago, IL 60628
Ph: (312)702-7700   Fr: 800-621-2736
Mary P. Burks, Annual. Fifty-ninth edition, 1994. State-by-state listing of certification requirements for teachers, counselors, librarians, and administrators. Lists addresses of state departments of education.

Secondary School Teachers

Secondary school teachers help students move from childhood to adulthood. They help them delve more deeply into subjects introduced in elementary school and learn more about the world and about themselves. Secondary school teachers specialize in specific subjects, such as English, Spanish, mathematics, history, or biology, in junior high or high school. They may teach a variety of related courses, for example, American history, contemporary American problems, and world geography. Special education teachers work with students who are mentally retarded, emotionally disturbed, learning disabled, or speech and hearing impaired. Others work with very bright or "gifted" students.

Salaries

Earnings in private schools are generally quite lower than salaries of teachers in public secondary schools.

Public secondary school teachers $36,000/year

Employment Outlook

Growth rate until the year 2005: Faster than the average.

Secondary School Teachers

CAREER GUIDES

★5083★ ASCUS Annual: A Job Search Handbook for Educators
Association for School, College and
    University Staffing (ASCUS)
1600 Dodge Ave., Ste. 330
Evanston, IL 60201-3451
Ph: (708)864-1999

Annual. Includes articles on the job market, job hunting techniques, locating job vacancies, resume writing, interviewing, job offers, and contracts. Also contains information about overseas employment, and employment in higher education. Includes a list of State Teacher Certification offices.

★5084★ Becoming a Teacher: Accepting the Challenge of a Profession
Allyn & Bacon, Inc.
160 Gould St.
Needham Heights, MA 02194
Ph: (617)455-1250   Fax: (617)455-1220
Fr: 800-278-3525

Forrest W. Parkay, editor. 1992.

★5085★ Careers in Education
National Textbook Co. (NTC)
VGM Career Books
4255 W. Touhy Ave.
Lincolnwood, IL 60646-1975
Ph: (708)679-5500   Fax: (708)679-2494
Fr: 800-323-4900

Roy A. Edelfelt. 1993. Describes career opportunities at all levels of education, from teaching to administration.

★5086★ Careers in Teaching
TAB/McGraw-Hill, Inc.
PO Box 182607
Columbus, OH 43218-2607
Fax: (614)759-3644   Fr: 800-822-8158

Glen W. Cutlip, Ph.D. and Robert J. Schockley, Ph.D. 1994.

★5087★ "Education" in Career Choices for the 90's for Students of Art (pp. 170-171)
Walker and Co.
435 Hudson St.
New York, NY 10014
Ph: (212)727-8300   Fax: (212)727-0984
Fr: 800-289-2553

Complied by Career Associates Staff. 1990. This book offers alternatives for students of art. Gives information about the outlook and competition for entry-level candidates. Provides job hunting tips.

★5088★ "Education" in Career Choices for the 90's for Students of Political Science and Government
Walker and Co.
435 Hudson St.
New York, NY 10014
Ph: (212)727-8300   Fax: (212)727-0984
Fr: 800-289-2553

Compiled by Career Associates Staff. 1990. This book offers alternatives for students of political science. Gives information about job outlook and competition for entry-level candidates. Provides job hunting tips.

★5089★ "Education" in College Majors and Careers: A Resource Guide to Effective Life Planning (pp. 49-50)
Garrett Park Press
PO Box 1907
Garrett Park, MD 20896
Ph: (301)946-2553

Paul Phifer. Revised, 1993. Lists 60 college majors, with definitions; related occupations and leisure activities; skills, values, and personal attributesneeded; suggested readings; and a list of associations.

★5090★ "Education" in Internships: 1995 (pp. 262-280)
Petersons Guides, Inc.
PO Box 2123
Princeton, NJ 08543-2123
Ph: (609)243-9111   Fax: (609)243-9150
Fr: 800-338-3282

Fifteenth edition, 1995. Lists internship opportunities under six broad categories: communications, creative, performing, and fine arts, human services, public relations, and business and technology. Includes a special section on internships in Washington, DC. For each internship program, gives the names, phone number, contact person, description, eligibility requirements, and benefits.

★5091★ "Education" in Liberal Arts Jobs
Petersons Guides, Inc.
PO Box 2123
Princeton, NJ 08543-2123
Ph: (609)243-9111   Fax: (609)243-9150
Fr: 800-338-3282

Burton Jay Nadler. Second edition, 1989. Strives to help the liberal arts graduate identify skills for entry-level positions. Gives goal setting and job search advice.

★5092★ High School Agriculture Teacher
Vocational Biographies, Inc.
PO Box 31
Sauk Centre, MN 56378-0031
Ph: (612)352-6516   Fax: (612)352-5546
Fr: 800-255-0752

1995. Four-page pamphlet containing a personal narrative about a worker's job, work likes and dislikes, career path from high school to the present. Education and training, the rewards and frustrations, and the effects of the job on the rest of the worker's life. The data file portion of this pamphlet gives a concise occupational summary, including work descriptions, working conditions, places of employment, personal characteristics, education and training, job outlook, and salary range.

★5093★ "High School Teacher" in College Board Guide to Jobs and Career Planning (pp. 180)
The College Board
415 Columbus Ave.
New York, NY 10023-6992
Ph: (212)713-8165   Fax: (212)713-8143
Fr: 800-323-7155

Joyce S. Mitchell. Second edition, 1994. Describes the job, salaries, related careers, education needed, and where to write for more information.

★5094★ "Joan Moylett—High School Teacher" in *Straight Talk on Careers: Eighty Pros Take You Into Their Professions* **(pp. 191-194)**
Garrett Park Press
PO Box 1907
Garrett Park, MD 20896
Ph: (301)946-2553
Mary Barbera-Hogan. 1987. Contains candid interviews from people who give an inside view of their work in 80 different careers. These professionals describe a day's work and the stresses and rewards accompanying their work.

★5095★ *Leadership for the 21st Century: Teaching in Hawaii*
Communications Branch
Office of the Superintendent
State Department of Education
PO Box 2360
Honolulu, HI 96804
Ph: (808)586-3230
1990. This eight-panel pamphlet describes employment opportunities, excellence in education issues, performance expectations, qualifications and requirements, salaries and benefits, equal employment opportunities, the application procedure, and other sources of information.

★5096★ *Opportunities Abroad for Educators: Fulbright Teacher Exchange Program*
Teacher Exchange Branch
United State Information Agency
301 4 St.
Washington, DC 20547
Ph: (202)619-4700
Annual. This booklet describes the teacher exchange program, and includes applications for teaching positions and seminars abroad; gives a country listing of positions available.

★5097★ *Opportunities in Teaching Careers*
National Textbook Co. (NTC)
VGM Career Books
4255 W. Touhy Ave.
Lincolnwood, IL 60646-1975
Ph: (708)679-5500   Fax: (708)679-2494
Fr: 800-323-4900
Janet Fine. 1989. Includes a bibliography. Illustrated. Describes the job responsibilities, educational preparation, work settings, and related careers.

★5098★ *Overseas Employment Opportunities for Educators*
Office of Dependents Schools
U.S. Department of Defense
3461 Eisenhower Ave.
Alexandria, VA 22331-1100
Ph: (703)325-0885
Annual. This booklet describes eligibility requirements, position requirements, application procedures, pay and benefits, housing living, and working conditions. Includes the application form.

★5099★ *The Right Fit: An Educator's Career Handbook and Employment Guide*
Gorsuch Scarisbrick Publishers
8233 Via Paseo del Norte, Ste. F-400
Scottsdale, AZ 85258
Ph: (602)991-7881
Judy A. Strother and Darrel R. Marshall. 1990.

★5100★ *Secondary School Teacher*
Careers, Inc.
PO Box 135
Largo, FL 34649-0135
Ph: (813)584-7333
1995. Two-page occupational summary card describing duties, working conditions, personal qualifications, training, earnings and hours, employment outlook, places of employment, related careers, and where to write for more information.

★5101★ "Secondary School Teacher" in *VGM's Careers Encyclopedia* **(pp. 456-458)**
National Textbook Co. (NTC)
VGM Career Books
4255 W. Touhy Ave.
Lincolnwood, IL 60646-1975
Ph: (708)679-5500   Fax: (708)679-2494
Fr: 800-323-4900
Third edition, 1991. Describes job duties, places of employment, working conditions, qualifications, education and training, advancement potential, and salary for each occupation.

★5102★ "Secondary School Teachers" in *101 Careers: A Guide to the Fastest-Growing Opportunities* **(pp. 181-184)**
John Wiley & Sons, Inc.
605 3rd Ave.
New York, NY 10158-0012
Ph: (212)850-6645   Fax: (212)850-6088
Michael Harkavy. 1990. Describes the nature of the job, working conditions, employment growth, qualifications, personal skills, projected salaries, and where to write for more information.

★5103★ "Secondary School Teachers" in *America's 50 Fastest Growing Jobs* **(pp. 67)**
JIST Works, Inc.
720 N. Park Ave.
Indianapolis, IN 46202-3431
Ph: (317)264-3720   Fax: (317)264-3709
Fr: 800-648-5478
Michael J. Farr, compiler. 1994. Describes the 50 fastest growing jobs within major career clusters such as technicians, and marketing and sales. Each job profile explains the nature of the work, skills and abilities required, employment outlook, average earnings, related occupations, education and training requirements, and employment opportunities. Also contains career planning information and job search tips.

★5104★ "Secondary School Teachers" in *Career Discovery Encyclopedia* **(Vol.6, pp. 10-11)**
J.G. Ferguson Publishing Co.
200 W. Madison St., Ste. 300
Chicago, IL 60606
Ph: (312)580-5480   Fax: (312)580-4948
Russell E. Primm, editor-in-chief. 1993. This six volume set contains two-page articles for 504 occupations. Each article describes job duties, earnings, and educational and training requirements. The whole set is arranged alphabetically by job title. Designed for junior high and older students.

★5105★ "Secondary School Teachers" in *Career Information Center* **(Vol.11)**
Simon and Schuster
200 Old Tappan Rd.
Old Tappan, NJ 07675
Fax: 800-445-6991   Fr: 800-223-2348
Richard Lidz and Linda Perrin, editorial directors. Fifth edition, 1993. This 13-volume set profiles over 600 occupations. Each occupational profile describes job duties, educational requirements, how to get the job, advancement possibilities, employment outlook, working conditions, earnings and benefits, and where to write for more information.

★5106★ "Secondary School Teachers" in *Jobs! What They Are—Where They Aree—What They Pay* **(p. 106)**
Simon & Schuster, Inc.
Simon & Schuster Bldg.
1230 Avenue of the Americas
New York, NY 10020
Ph: (212)698-7000   Fr: 800-223-2348
Robert O. Snelling and Anne M. Snelling. Revised and updated, 1989. Each profile gives duties and responsibilities, earnings and opportunities, training and qualifications. Arranged by job title within broad industry categories.

★5107★ "Secondary School Teachers" in *Occupational Outlook Handbook*
U.S. Government Printing Office
Superintendent of Documents
Washington, DC 20402
Ph: (202)512-1800   Fax: (202)512-2250
Biennial; latest edition, 1994-95. Encyclopedia of careers describing about 250 occupations and comprising about 85 percent of all jobs in the economy. Occupations that require lengthy education or training are given the most attention. Each occupation's profile describes what the worker does on the job, working conditions, education and training requirements, advancement possibilities, job outlook, earnings, and sources of additional information.

★5108★ "Teacher" in *Jobs Rated Almanac*
World Almanac
1 International Blvd., Ste. 444
Mahwah, NJ 07495
Ph: (201)529-6900   Fax: (201)529-6901
Les Krantz. Second edition, 1992. Ranks 250 jobs by environment, salary, outlooks, physical demands, stress, security, travel opportunities, and extra perks. Includes jobs the editor feels are the most common, most interesting, and the most rapidly growing.

★5109★ Teachers, Secondary School
Chronicle Guidance Publications, Inc.
66 Aurora St.
PO Box 1190
Moravia, NY 13118-1190
Ph: (315)497-0330   Fax: (315)497-3359
Fr: 800-622-7284

1993. Career brief describing the nature of the job, working conditions, hours and earnings, education and training, licensure, certification, unions, personal qualifications, social and psychological factors, location, employment outlook, entry methods, advancement, and related occupations.

★5110★ "Teachers, Secondary School" in Encyclopedia of Careers and Vocational Guidance (Vol.4, pp. 501-504)
J.G. Ferguson Publishing Co.
200 W. Madison St., Ste. 300
Chicago, IL 60606
Ph: (312)580-5480   Fax: (312)580-4948
William E. Hopke, editor-in-chief. Ninth edition, 1993. Four-volume set that profiles 900 occupations and describes job trends in 74 industries. Includes career description, educational requirements, history of the job, methods of entry, advancement, employment outlook, earnings, conditions of work, social and psychological factors, and sources of further information.

★5111★ Teaching as a Career
American Federation of Teachers
555 New Jersey Ave., NW
Washington, DC 20001
Ph: (202)879-4400
1987. This eight-panel brochure describes the rewards of a teaching career, educational preparation, and job locations.

PROFESSIONAL ASSOCIATIONS

★5112★ American Federation of Teachers (AFT)
555 New Jersey Ave. NW
Washington, DC 20001
Ph: (202)879-4400   Fr: 800-238-1133
Members: AFL-CIO. Works with teachers and other educational employees at the state and local level in organizing, collective bargaining, research, educational issues, and public relations. **Purpose:** Conducts research in areas such as educational reform, bilingual education, teacher certification, and evaluation and national assessments and standards. Represents members' concerns through legislative action; offers technical assistance. Seeks to serve professionals with concerns similar to those of teachers, including state employees, healthcare workers, and paraprofessionals. **Publications:** AFT Action: A Newsletter for AFT Leaders, weekly. • American Educator, quarterly. • American Teacher, 8/year. • Healthwire, 10/year. • On Campus, 9/year. • Public Sevice Reporter, 9/year.

★5113★ Association of Astronomy Educators (AAE)
5103 Burt St.
Omaha, NE 68132
Ph: (402)556-0082   Fax: (402)280-2140
Members: Teachers and educators dedicated to improving astronomy education at all levels, from kindergarten to college. **Purpose:** Promotes astronomy education to enhance the scientific literacy of all students. Brings together resources and knowledge from a number of diverse groups. Works with the National Science Teachers Association. Cosponsors Astronomy Day. **Publications:** Astronomy Education, quarterly.

★5114★ National Council for Accreditation of Teacher Education (NCATE)
2010 Massachusetts Ave. NW, Ste. 500
Washington, DC 20036-1023
Ph: (202)466-7496   Fax: (202)296-6620
Members: Representatives from constituent colleges and universities, state departments of education, school boards, teacher and other professional groups. **Purpose:** Voluntary accrediting body devoted exclusively to: evaluation and accreditation of institutions for preparation of elementary and secondary school teachers; preparation of school service personnel, including school principals, supervisors, superintendents, guidance counselors, school psychologists, instructional technologists, and other specialists for school-oriented positions. **Publications:** Handbook for Institutional Visits. • NCATE-Approved Curriculum Guidelines. • Quality Teaching, 3/year. • Standards, Procedures, and Policies for the Accreditation of Professional Education Units. • Teacher Preparation: A Guide to Colleges and Universities.

★5115★ National Education Association (NEA)
1201 16th St. NW
Washington, DC 20036
Ph: (202)833-4000   Fax: (202)822-7974
Members: Professional organization and union of elementary and secondary school teachers, college and university professors, administrators, principals, counselors, and others concerned with education. **Publications:** Almanac of Higher Education. • ESP Annual. • ESP Progress, periodic. • Handbook, annual. • Issues, annual. • NEA Higher Education Advocate. • NEA Today, 8/year. • Thought and Action.

STANDARDS/CERTIFICATION AGENCIES

★5116★ American Federation of Teachers (AFT)
555 New Jersey Ave. NW
Washington, DC 20001
Ph: (202)879-4400   Fr: 800-238-1133
Conducts research in areas such as educational reform, bilingual education, teacher certification, and evaluation and national assessments and standards.

★5117★ National Council for Accreditation of Teacher Education (NCATE)
2010 Massachusetts Ave. NW, Ste. 500
Washington, DC 20036-1023
Ph: (202)466-7496   Fax: (202)296-6620
Voluntary accrediting body devoted exclusively to: evaluation and accreditation of institutions for preparation of elementary and secondary school teachers; preparation of school service personnel, including school principals, supervisors, superintendents, guidance counselors, school psychologists, instructional technologists, and other specialists for school-oriented positions.

TEST GUIDES

★5118★ Barron's How to Prepare for the National Teacher Examinations (NTE): Core Battery and Most Specialty Area Tests
Barron's Educational Series, Inc.
250 Wireless Blvd.
Hauppauge, NY 11788
Ph: (516)434-3311   Fax: (516)434-3723
Fr: 800-645-3476
Albertina A. Weinlander. Fifth edition, 1992. Provides review and practice for the Core Battery tests and sample test questions from 19 specialty area tests.

★5119★ Career Examination Series: Assistant Teacher
National Learning Corp.
212 Michael Dr.
Syosset, NY 11791
Ph: (516)921-8888   Fax: (516)921-8743
Fr: 800-645-6337
Jack Rudman. A study guide for professionals and trainees in the field of education. Includes a multiple-choice examination section; provides answers.

★5120★ Career Examination Series: Indian Education—Secondary Teacher
National Learning Corp.
212 Michael Dr.
Syosset, NY 11791
Ph: (516)921-8888   Fax: (516)921-8743
Fr: 800-645-6337
Jack Rudman. A study guide for professionals and trainees in the field of education. Includes a multiple-choice examination section; provides answers.

★5121★ Career Examination Series: Teacher
National Learning Corp.
212 Michael Dr.
Syosset, NY 11791
Ph: (516)921-8888   Fax: (516)921-8743
Fr: 800-645-6337
Jack Rudman. A study guide for professionals and trainees in the field of education. Includes a multiple-choice examination section; provides answers.

★5122★ Graduate Record Examination: Education
National Learning Corp.
212 Michael Dr.
Syosset, NY 11791
Ph: (516)921-8888   Fax: (516)921-8743
Fr: 800-645-6337

Jack Rudman. A sample multiple-choice test for those seeking admission to graduate school for study in the field of education. Includes solutions to examination questions.

★5123★ A Guide to the NTE Core Battery Test
Educational Testing Service
Rosedale Rd.
Princeton, NJ 08541
Ph: (609)921-9000

Compiled by the Educational Testing Service staff. Second revised edition, 1992. Contains a form of three previously administered National Teacher Examinations (NTE) Core Battery Test. Also includes a description of each test with sample questions and explanations of the answers as well as test-taking strategies. Also contains answer sheets, answer keys, and scoring instructions.

★5124★ Introduction to Education
National Learning Corp.
212 Michael Dr.
Syosset, NY 11791
Ph: (516)921-8888   Fax: (516)921-8743
Fr: 800-645-6337

Jack Rudman. Part of the Dantes Subject Standardized Test series. A standardized graduate and college-level examination given by graduate schools, colleges, and the U.S. Armed Forces as a final examination for course evaluation in the field of education. Multiple-choice format with correct answers.

★5125★ National Teacher Examination Series
National Learning Corp.
212 Michael Dr.
Syosset, NY 11791
Ph: (516)921-8888   Fax: (516)921-8743
Fr: 800-645-6337

Jack Rudman. Practice multiple-choice examinations for education certification. Includes solutions. Titles in the series include National Teacher Examination (Core Battery) (one-volume combined edition); Agriculture; Art Education; Biology and General Science; Business Education; Chemistry and General Science; Chemistry, Physics, and General Science; Earth and Space Science; Education of the Mentally Retarded; English Language and Literature; French; German; Health Education; Home Economics Education; Mathematics; Latin; Marketing and Distributive Education; Men's Physical Education; Music Education; Physics and General Science; Physical Education; Psychological Foundations of Education; Psychology; School Psychology; Science and Mathematics; Social Studies; Social Studies, Literature and Fine Arts; Societal Foundations of Education; Spanish; Special Education; Speech Communication; Teaching Emotionally Disturbed; Teaching Hearing Handicapped; Teaching Learning Disabled; Teaching Orthopedically Handicapped; Teaching Principles and Practices; Teaching Speech Handi-

capped; Women's Physical Education; Written English Expression.

★5126★ NTE—National Teacher Examinations
Arco Publishing Co.
Macmillan General Reference
15 Columbus Cir.
New York, NY 10023
Fax: 800-835-3202   Fr: 800-858-7674

Joan O. Levy and Norman Levy. Eleventh edition, 1994. Contains three sample Core Battery tests.

★5127★ Practicing to Take the GRE Education Test
Educational Testing Service
Rosedale Rd.
Princeton, NJ 08541
Ph: (609)921-9000

Compiled by the Educational Testing Service Staff. Second edition, 1989. This booklet summarizes the purpose and scope of this Graduate Record Examination (GRE) Subject Test. Contains sample questions.

★5128★ Teacher Certification Tests
Arco Publishing Co.
Macmillan General Reference
15 Columbus Cir.
New York, NY 10023
Fax: 800-835-3202   Fr: 800-858-7674

Elna M. Dimock. Third edition, 1993. Covers certification tests administered in 16 states. Tests featured are the California Basic Educational Skills Test, Pre-Professional Skills Test, Connecticut Competency Exam for Prospective Teachers, and Examination for Certification of Educators in Texas. Gives information on testing requirements in all 50 states.

★5129★ Teachers License Examination Series: Elementary Education
National Learning Corp.
212 Michael Dr.
Syosset, NY 11791
Ph: (516)921-8888   Fax: (516)921-8743
Fr: 800-645-6337

Jack Rudman. A series of preparatory study guides for professionals studying for licensing examinations. Includes a multiple-choice test section; provides answers. Contains numerous titles related to elementary education.

★5130★ Undergraduate Program Field Test: Education
National Learning Corp.
212 Michael Dr.
Syosset, NY 11791
Ph: (516)921-8888   Fax: (516)921-8743
Fr: 800-645-6337

Jack Rudman. A practice examination fashioned after tests given in the Regents External Degree Program. Designed to measure knowledge received outside the college classroom in the subject of education. Contains multiple-choice questions; provides solutions.

EDUCATIONAL DIRECTORIES AND PROGRAMS

★5131★ Educational Career Directory
Gale Research Inc.
835 Penobscot Bldg.
Detroit, MI 48226
Ph: (313)961-2242   Fr: 800-877-GALE
1994.

AWARDS, SCHOLARSHIPS, GRANTS, AND FELLOWSHIPS

★5132★ Catalyst Awards
Chemical Manufacturers Association
2501 M St. NW
Washington, DC 20037
Ph: (202)887-1205   Fax: (202)887-1237

To publicly recognize exceptional chemistry or chemical engineering teachers within pre-high schools, high schools, and two and four-year colleges throughout the United States and Canada. Individuals with 10 years of experience are eligible for the national awards. There is no such requirement for the regional award. Only full-time teachers are considered. Nominations may be submitted by January 28. Each year, eight national award winners receive $5,000, a medal and a citation and 16 regional award winners receive $2,500, a medal and a citation. Awarded annually. Established in 1957.

★5133★ CIBA-GEIGY Exemplary High School Science Teaching Award
National Science Teachers Association
1840 Wilson Blvd.
Arlington, VA 22201
Ph: (703)243-7100   Fax: (703)243-7700

To recognize a high school teacher who has demonstrated exemplary science teaching performance. A monetary prize of $1,000 and travel to the NSTA National Convention are awarded annually. Established in 1979. Sponsored by CIBA-GEIGY Corporation.

★5134★ CIBA-GEIGY Exemplary Middle Level Science Teaching Award
National Science Teachers Association
1840 Wilson Blvd.
Arlington, VA 22201
Ph: (703)243-7100   Fax: (703)243-7700

To recognize a middle level school teacher who has demonstrated exemplary science teaching performance. A monetary prize of $1,000 and travel to the NSTA National Convention are awarded annually. Established in 1982. Sponsored by CIBA-GEIGY Corporation.

★5135★ James Bryant Conant Award in High School Chemistry Teaching
American Chemical Society
Research, Grants, and Awards
1155 16th St. NW
Washington, DC 20036
Ph: (202)872-4408

To recognize, encourage, and stimulate outstanding teachers of high school chemistry in the United States, its possessions or territories, at both the regional and national levels. Nominations for the regional awards are submitted only by ACS local sections. The deadline for submissions is December 1. Each winner of an ACS Regional Award in High School Chemistry Teaching automatically becomes a candidate for the James Bryant Conant Award in the following year and remains a candidate for three successive years unless: he or she is selected as a recipient of the Conant Award, or his or her nomination is withdrawn by the nominating local section. One of the regional winners or candidates is selected by the national award committee as the recipient of the James Bryant Conant Award in High School Chemistry Teaching. The national award consists of a monetary prize of $5,000, a certificate, and travel expenses to attend the meeting where the award is presented. Established in 1965 by E. I. du Pont de Nemours and Company Incorporated. Sponsored by Ethyl Corporation.

★5136★ Distinguished Teaching Award
National Science Teachers Association
1840 Wilson Blvd.
Arlington, VA 22201
Ph: (703)243-7100   Fax: (703)243-7700

To recognize elementary, middle/junior high, high school, and college teachers who have made extraordinary contributions to the field of science teaching. Plaques and complimentary one-year memberships are awarded annually. Sponsored by National Science Teachers Association. Established in 1987.

★5137★ Jack Fishleder Photography Award
National Science Teachers Association
1840 Wilson Blvd.
Arlington, VA 22201
Ph: (703)243-7100   Fax: (703)243-7700

To provide science teachers with the incentive to photograph. Award categories are: a photo documentation that illustrates exemplary science instruction and learning and scientific or natural phenomena that can be utilized for instruction in the classroom. Teachers, supervisors, and educators in all science disciplines from elementary to college level are eligible. Monetary awards of $750 are presented in each category. Established in 1989. Sponsored by Creative Dimensions.

★5138★ Isabel M. Herson Scholarship in Education
Zeta Phi Beta Sorority
National Education Foundation
Executive Office
1734 New Hampshire Ave., N.W.
Washington, DC 20009
Ph: (202)387-3103   Fax: (202)232-4593

Qualifications: Students must be graduates or undergraduates enrolled in a degree program either in elementary or secondary education. Funds available: $500 to $1,000 for one academic year. Application details: Completed applications must be returned along with references and an official university transcript. Deadline: February 1. Recipients are notified by August 15.

★5139★ Innovative Teaching of Secondary School Physics Award
American Association of Physics Teachers
1 Physics Ellipse
College Park, MD 20740
Ph: (301)209-3300   Fax: (301)209-0845

To encourage change in instructional practices used in teaching high school physics courses. Up to five awards may be presented, each consisting of $500, a citation, and a certificate. Awarded annually at the Association's Winter Meeting. Established in 1970.

★5140★ NCEA Secondary Department Award
National Catholic Educational Association
1077 30th St. NW, Ste. 100
Washington, DC 20007-3852
Ph: (202)337-6232   Fax: (202)333-6706

To recognize extraordinary contributions to Catholic secondary education in the United States. Outstanding school personnel associated with Catholic secondary education with demonstrable achievements in Catholic secondary education at the local, diocesan, state or national level, may be nominated by NCEA members. A plaque is presented annually at the convention. Established in 1983.

★5141★ Outstanding Biology Teacher Award
National Association of Biology Teachers
11250 Roger Bacon Dr., Ste. 19
Reston, VA 22090
Ph: (703)471-1134   Fax: (703)435-5582

To recognize outstanding performance in the classroom and to bring this type of performance to the attention of the general public. Secondary school teachers of biology in each state of the United States and selected territories are eligible to be nominated by March 15. Membership in NABT is not required. Certificates and a world class pair of binoculars are awarded annually. Established in 1960. Sponsored by Prentice-Hall.

★5142★ Outstanding Earth Science Teacher Award
National Association of Geology Teachers
Dept. of Geology
Western Washington Univ.
Bellingham, WA 98225
Ph: (206)650-3587   Fax: (206)650-7295

For recognition of earth science teachers who are considered exemplary and deserving of recognition for their accomplishments. One secondary school teacher from each state and one from each of 11 NAGT sections are eligible. Nomination deadline is approximately January 1. Established in 1971.

★5143★ Outstanding High School Teacher Awards
Inland Steel - Ryerson Foundation
30 W. Monroe St.
Chicago, IL 60603
Ph: (312)899-3420   Fax: (312)899-3323

To encourage and recognize excellence in teaching, particularly in high schools where Inland Steel Company draws its employees. Peers may submit nominations in April. A monetary award of $300 and a plaque for the recipient and school are presented annually. Established in 1981.

★5144★ Program to Recognize Excellence in Student Literary Magazines
National Council of Teachers of English
1111 Kenyon Rd.
Urbana, IL 61801
Ph: (217)328-3870   Fax: (217)328-0977

To recognize students, teachers, and schools producing excellent literary magazines; to improve the quality of such magazines; and to encourage all schools to develop literary magazines, seeking excellence in writing and schoolwide participation in production. All senior high, junior high, and middle schools throughout the United States, Canada, and American schools abroad are eligible. Entries must be submitted by July 1. Entries are placed in the following award categories and listed in a ranked booklet: superior, excellent, above average, unranked, and Highest Award - selected from the superior-ranked journals and given to several magazines in a particular year, or to none. Awarded annually. Established in 1984.

★5145★ Eleanor Roosevelt Teacher Fellowships
American Association of University Women (AAUW)
AAUW Educational Foundation
PO Box 4030
Iowa City, IA 52243-4030
Ph: (319)337-1716

Purpose: Eleanor Roosevelt Teacher Fellowships are designed for elementary and secondary school teachers who are seeking to advanced gender equity in the classroom, increase their effectiveness at teaching math and science to girls, and/or tailor their teaching to the needs of minority students and girls at risk of dropping out. Qualifications: Women teachers who are U.S. citizens or permanent residents, teach full time at U.S. public schools in grades K through 12, have at least five consecutive years full-time teaching experience, plan to continue teaching for the next five years, and able to demonstrate commitment to educational opportunities for women and girls through work in the classroom are eligible. Funds available: Fellowships range from $1,000 to $10,000. Deadline: January 11.

★5146★ Nila Banton Smith Award
International Reading Association
800 Barksdale Rd.
PO Box 8139
Newark, DE 19714-8139
Ph: (302)731-1600   Fax: (302)731-1057

To recognize the classroom teacher or reading specialist who has made an outstanding contribution in helping students to become more proficient readers of content instructional materials. Applicants must be actively teaching students in the 7th through 12th grade range or equivalent. The recipient of this award must have demonstrated excellence at the classroom level, in addition to either the building level or district level. The deadline for nominations is December 1. A monetary award of US $1,000 is awarded annually. Established in 1978. The award honors Nila Banton Smith, the ninth president of the Association. Additional information is available from the Executive Office, International Reading Association.

BASIC REFERENCE GUIDES AND HANDBOOKS

★5147★ Classroom Teaching Skills
D. C. Heath and Co.
125 Spring St.
Lexington, MA 02173
Ph: (617)862-6650   Fr: 800-334-2284
James M. Cooper, Sandra S. Garrett, et al., editors. Fourth edition, 1990. Includes bibliographies and an index. Illustrated.

★5148★ A Handbook for Substitute Teachers
Charles C. Thomas, Publisher
2600 S. 1st St.
Springfield, IL 62794-9265
Ph: (217)789-8980   Fax: (217)789-9130
Fr: 800-258-8980
Anne W. Dodd. 1989.

★5149★ The International Encyclopedia of Teaching and Teacher Education
Pergamon Press, Inc.
Fairview Park
Elmsford, NY 10523
Ph: (914)592-7700
Michael J. Dunkin, editor. First edition, 1987. Includes bibliographies and indexes. Illustrated.

★5150★ An Introduction to the Foundations of Education
Houghton Mifflin Co.
222 Berkeley St.
Boston, MA 02116
Ph: (617)351-5000
Allan C. Ornstein and Daniel Levine. Fifth edition, 1993. Includes bibliographical references and indexes. Illustrated.

★5151★ Secondary Instruction: A Manual for Classroom Teaching
Allyn & Bacon, Inc.
PO Box 11071
Des Moines, IA 50336
Fr: 800-278-3525
Joel M. Levine. 1989.

PROFESSIONAL AND TRADE PERIODICALS

★5152★ American Educator
American Federation of Teachers
555 New Jersey Ave. NW
Washington, DC 20001
Ph: (202)879-4430
Liz McPike
Quarterly. Magazine on education.

★5153★ The Harvard Education Letter
Gutman 321
6 Appian Way
Cambridge, MA 02138-3704
Ph: (617)496-4841   Fax: (617)496-3584
Fr: 800-422-2681
Edward Miller

Bimonthly. Summarizes current research concerning elementary and secondary education (grades kindergarten-12). Discusses a wide range of school, classroom, and child development issues, addressing the underlying assumptions of current educational debates. Recurring features include case studies, columns titled, and reports on successful and innovative programs.

★5154★ Report on Education of the Disadvantaged
Business Publishers, Inc.
951 Pershing Dr.
Silver Spring, MD 20910
Ph: (301)587-6300   Fax: (301)587-1081
Fr: 800-274-0122
Rosemary Lally

Biweekly. Covers legislative news affecting the Elementary and Secondary Education Act Chapter I (formerly Title I). Reports on bilingual education, child nutrition and migrant children programs, other program and funding changes, and related topics of interest.

★5155★ Schools in the Middle
National Association of Secondary School Principals (NASSP)
1904 Association Dr.
Reston, VA 22091
Ph: (703)860-0200   Fax: (703)476-5432
Patricia George

Quarterly. Addresses issues of concern to teachers and administrators in middle level education (grades 7-9).

★5156★ Tech Directions
Prakken Publications, Inc.
275 Metty Dr., Ste. 1
Box 8623
Ann Arbor, MI 48107
Ph: (313)769-1211   Fax: (313)769-8383
Fr: 800-530-9673
Paul J. Bramford

Magazine covering industrial education, technology education, trade and industry, and vocational education. Articles are geared for teacher use and reference from middle school throught postsecondary levels.

★5157★ TIES Magazine
Trenton State College
Department of Technological Studies
Hillwood Lakes
CN 4700
Trenton, NJ 08650-4700
Ph: (609)771-3335   Fax: (609)771-3330
Ronald ToddPublisher

Technology education magazine for teachers.

PROFESSIONAL MEETINGS AND CONVENTIONS

★5158★ American Association of Physics Teachers Winter Meeting
American Association of Physics Teachers (AAPT)
5112 Berwyn Rd.
College Park, MD 20740
Ph: (301)345-4200   Fax: (301)345-1857
Annual. Always held during January.

★5159★ American Council on the Teaching of Foreign Languages Convention
American Council on the Teaching of Foreign Languages
6 Executive Plaza
Yonkers, NY 10701
Ph: (914)963-8830   Fax: (914)963-1275
Annual. Always held during November. **Dates and Locations:** 1995 Nov 18-20; Anaheim, CA. • 1996 Nov 22-24; Philadelphia, PA.

★5160★ American Technical Education Association National Conference on Technical Education
American Technical Education Association
800 Sixth St. N.
North Dakota State College of Science
Wahpeton, ND 58076
Ph: (701)671-2240   Fax: (701)671-2260
Always held during March. **Dates and Locations:** 1996 Mar 14-17.

★5161★ Association of Teacher Educators Annual Conference
Glencoe
15319 Chatsworth St.
Mission Hills, CA 91345
Ph: (818)898-1391
Annual. Always held during February. **Dates and Locations:** 1996 Feb.

★5162★ NAFSA - Association of International Educators Annual Conference
NAFSA - Association of International Educator
1875 Connecticut Ave. NW, Ste. 1000
Washington, DC 20009-5728
Ph: (202)462-4811   Fax: (202)667-3419
Annual.

★5163★ National Art Education Association Convention
National Art Education Association
1916 Association Dr.
Reston, VA 22091-1590
Ph: (703)860-8000   Fax: (703)860-2960
Annual.

★5164★ National Association of Biology Teachers National Convention
National Association of Biology Teachers
11250 Roger Bacon Dr., Ste. 19
Reston, VA 22090
Ph: (703)471-1134
Annual. **Dates and Locations:** 1995 Oct 25-28; Phoenix, AZ. • 1996 Oct 16-19; Charlotte, NC.

★5165★ **National Council for the Social Studies Convention**
National Council for the Social Studies
3501 Newark St., NW
Washington, DC 20016
Ph: (202)966-7840   Fax: (202)966-2061

Annual. **Dates and Locations:** 1995 Nov 09-12; Chicago, IL. • 1996 Nov 16-19; Washington, DC. • 1997 Nov 20-23; Cincinnati, OH.

★5166★ **National Education Association Annual Meeting and Exposition**
National Educational Association
1201 16th St., NW
Washington, DC 20036
Ph: (202)833-4000   Fax: (202)822-7767

Annual.

★5167★ **Vocational Home Economics Teachers Association of Texas**
Vocational Home Economics Teachers Association of Texas
3737 Executive Center Dr., Ste. 210
Austin, TX 78731
Ph: (512)794-8370   Fr: 800-880-8438

Annual. Usually held during August in Dallas, Texas.

OTHER SOURCES OF INFORMATION

★5168★ *An Introduction to Teaching: A Question of Commitment*
Allyn and Bacon, Inc.
160 Gould St.
Needham, MA 02194
Ph: (617)455-1200

Ralph E. Martin, Jr., George H. Wood, and Edward Stevens, Jr. Includes bibliographies and an index. Illustrated.

★5169★ *Requirements for Certification of Teachers, Counselors, Librarians, Administrators for Elementary and Secondary Schools, and Junior Colleges*
University of Chicago Press
11030 S. Langley Ave.
Chicago, IL 60628
Ph: (312)702-7700   Fr: 800-621-2736

Mary P. Burks, Annual. Fifty-ninth edition, 1994. State-by-state listing of certification requirements for teachers, counselors, librarians, and administrators. Lists addresses of state departments of education.

★5170★ *"Secondary Education" in Accounting to Zoology: Graduate Fields Defined* (pp. 99-101)
Petersons Guides, Inc.
PO Box 2123
Princeton, NJ 08543-2123
Ph: (609)243-9111   Fax: (609)243-9150
Fr: 800-338-3282

Amy J. Goldstein, editor. Revised and updated, 1987. Discusses types of graduate programs and degrees, graduate research, applied work, employment prospects and trends.

★5171★ *"Teacher (Secondary)" in Career Selector 2001*
Barron's Educational Series, Inc.
250 Wireless Blvd.
Hauppauge, NY 11788
Ph: (516)434-3311   Fax: (516)434-3723
Fr: 800-645-3476

James C. Gonyea. 1993.

★5172★ *The Teacher's Almanac*
Facts on File
460 Park Ave. S.
New York, NY 10016-7382
Ph: (212)683-2244   Fax: 800-678-3633
Fr: 800-322-8755

Sherwood Harris and Lorna B. Harris, editors. 1988. Contains statistical information such as teachers' salaries, educational finances, and state rankings.

Chiropractors

Chiropractors are health practitioners who primarily treat patients whose health problems are associated with the body's muscular, nervous, and skeletal systems, especially the spine. Interference with these systems is believed to impair normal functions and lower resistance to disease. Chiropractors hold that misalignment or compression of the spinal nerves, for example, can alter many important body functions by affecting the neurological system. The chiropractic approach to health care reflects a holistic view, which stresses the patient's overall well-being. It recognizes that many factors affect health, including exercise, diet, rest, environment, and heredity. In keeping with the holistic tradition, chiropractors encourage the use of natural, nondrug, nonsurgical health treatment in cases where chiropractic care is inappropriate, chiropractors refer patients to other health practitioners. They also recommend lifestyle changes in eating and sleeping habits to their patients. Some chiropractors specialize in areas related to athletic injuries, diseases and disorders of children, or mental and nervous disorders. Others specialize in taking and interpreting X-rays and other diagnostic images.

Salaries

Earnings are influenced by the characteristics and qualifications of the practitioner, the number of years in practice, and geographic location.

Lowest 10 percent	$21,000/year
Median	$70,000/year
Top 10 percent	$190,000/year

Employment Outlook

Growth rate until the year 2005: Faster than the average.

Chiropractors

★5173★ Career for the Future: Chiropractic Health Care
International Chiropractors Association
1110 N. Glebe Rd., Ste. 1000
Arlington, VA 22201
Ph: (703)528-5000
1991. This six-panel pamphlet describes personal qualifications, nature of the job, educational preparation, professional practice, licensure, income, and financial aid.

★5174★ Careers in Medicine
National Textbook Co. (NTC)
VGM Career Books
4255 W. Touhy Ave.
Lincolnwood, IL 60646-1975
Ph: (708)679-5500   Fax: (708)679-2494
Fr: 800-323-4900
Terry Sacks, editor. 1993. Guide to the various careers in the field of medicine.

★5175★ Careers in Medicine
Rosen Publishing Group
29 E. 21st St.
New York, NY 10010
Ph: (212)777-3017   Fax: (212)777-0277
Fr: 800-237-9932
Carolyn Simpson and Penelope Hall, M.D. 1993. Discusses the qualities a good doctor must possess and how a young person can combine a desire to help others with the practical aspects of getting into and through medical school.

★5176★ Chiropractic State of the Art, 1994-95
American Chiropractic Association (ACA)
1701 Clarendon Blvd.
Arlington, VA 22209
Ph: (703)276-8800   Fr: 800-368-3083
Annual. 1994. This 47-page booklet gives history, occupational information, educational information, licensure, and employment outlook. Lists accredited chiropractic colleges.

★5177★ Chiropractor
Careers, Inc.
PO Box 135
Largo, FL 34649-0135
Ph: (813)584-7333
1994. Two-page occupational summary card describing duties, working conditions, personal qualifications, training, earnings and hours, employment outlook, places of employment, related careers, and where to write for more information.

★5178★ Chiropractor
Vocational Biographies, Inc.
PO Box 31
Sauk Centre, MN 56378-0031
Ph: (612)352-6516   Fax: (612)352-5546
Fr: 800-255-0752
1990. Four-page pamphlet containing a personal narrative about a worker's job, work likes and dislikes, career path from high school to the present. Education and training, the rewards and frustrations, and the effects of the job on the rest of the worker's life. The data file portion of this pamphlet gives a concise occupational summary, including work descriptions, working conditions, places of employment, personal characteristics, education and training, job outlook, and salary range.

★5179★ "Chiropractor" in 100 Best Careers for the Year 2000 (pp.9-11)
Arco Pub.
201 W. 103rd St.
Indianapolis, IN 46290
Ph: 800-428-5331   Fax: 800-835-3202
Shelly Field. 1992. Describes 100 job opportunities expected to grow fast throughout the next decade. Provides information on job duties and responsibilities, training requirements, education, advancement opportunities, experience and qualifications, and typical salaries.

★5180★ "Chiropractor" in Career Information Center (Vol.7)
Simon and Schuster
200 Old Tappan Rd.
Old Tappan, NJ 07675
Fax: 800-445-6991   Fr: 800-223-2348
Richard Lidz and Linda Perrin, editorial directors. Fifth edition, 1993. This 13-volume set profiles over 600 occupations. Each occupational profile describes job duties, entry-level requirements, educational requirements, advancement possibilities, employment outlook, working conditions, earnings and benefits, and where to write for more information.

★5181★ "Chiropractor" in College Board Guide to Jobs and Career Planning (pp. 239)
The College Board
415 Columbus Ave.
New York, NY 10023-6992
Ph: (212)713-8165   Fax: (212)713-8143
Fr: 800-323-7155
Joyce S. Mitchell. Second edition, 1994. Describes the job, salaries, related careers, education needed, and where to write for more information.

★5182★ "Chiropractor" in Jobs Rated Almanac
World Almanac
1 International Blvd., Ste. 444
Mahwah, NJ 07495
Ph: (201)529-6900   Fax: (201)529-6901
Les Krantz. Second edition, 1992. Ranks 250 jobs by environment, salary, outlooks, physical demands, stress, security, travel opportunities, and extra perks. Includes jobs the editor feels are the most common, most interesting, and the most rapidly growing.

★5183★ "Chiropractor" in VGM's Careers Encyclopedia (pp. 93-95)
National Textbook Co. (NTC)
VGM Career Books
4255 W. Touhy Ave.
Lincolnwood, IL 60646-1975
Ph: (708)679-5500   Fax: (708)679-2494
Fr: 800-323-4900
Third edition, 1991. Describes job duties, places of employment, working conditions, qualifications, education, and training, advancement potential, and salary for each occupation.

★5184★ "Chiropractor" in VGM's Handbook of Health Care Careers
National Textbook Co.
4255 W. Touhy Ave.
Lincolnwood, IL 60646-1975
Ph: (708)679-5500   Fax: (708)679-2494
Fr: 800-323-4900
Annette Selden. 1993. Contains 42 two-page occupational profiles describing job duties,

places of employment, working conditions, qualifications, education, employment outlook, and income.

★5185★ Chiropractors
Chronicle Guidance Publications, Inc.
66 Aurora St.
PO Box 1190
Moravia, NY 13118-1190
Ph: (315)497-0330   Fax: (315)497-3359
Fr: 800-622-7284

1991. Career brief describing the nature of the job, working conditions, hours and earnings, education and training, licensure, certification, unions, personal qualifications, social and psychological factors, location, employment outlook, entry methods, advancement, and related occupations.

★5186★ "Chiropractors" in 101 Careers: A Guide to the Fastest-Growing Opportunities (pp. 185-187)
John Wiley & Sons, Inc.
605 3rd Ave.
New York, NY 10158-0012
Ph: (212)850-6645   Fax: (212)850-6088

Michael Harkavy. 1990. Describes the nature of the job, working conditions, employment growth, qualifications, personal skills, projected salaries, and where to write for more information.

★5187★ "Chiropractors" in American Almanac of Jobs and Salaries (p. 477)
Avon Books
1350 Avenue of the Americas
New York, NY 10019
Ph: (212)261-6800   Fr: 800-238-0658

John Wright, editor. Revised and updated, 1994-95. This is comprehensive guide to the wages of hundreds of occupations in a wide variety of industries and organizations.

★5188★ "Chiropractors" in Best Jobs for the 1990s and Into the 21st Century (pp. 102)
Impact Publications
9104-N Manassas Dr.
Manassas Park, VA 22111
Ph: (703)361-7300   Fax: (703)335-9486

Ronald L. Krannich and Caryl Rae Krannich. 1993.

★5189★ "Chiropractors" in Career Discovery Encyclopedia (Vol.1, pp. 170-171)
J.G. Ferguson Publishing Co.
200 W. Madison St., Ste. 300
Chicago, IL 60606
Ph: (312)580-5480   Fax: (312)580-4948

Russell E. Primm, editor-in chief. 1993. This six volume set contains two-page articles for 504 occupations. Each article describes job duties, earnings, and educational and training requirements. The whole set is arranged alphabetically by job title. Designed for junior high and older students.

★5190★ "Chiropractors" in Encyclopedia of Careers and Vocational Guidance (Vol.2, pp. 295-296)
J.G. Ferguson Publishing Co.
200 W. Madison St., Ste. 300
Chicago, IL 60606
Ph: (312)580-5480   Fax: (312)580-4948

William E. Hopke, editor-in-chief. Eight edition, 1990. Four-volume set that profiles 900 occupations and describes job trends in 74 industries. Includes career description, educational requirements, history of the job, methods of entry, advancement, employment outlook, earnings, conditions of work, social and psychological factors, and sources of further information.

★5191★ "Chiropractors" in Health Care Job Explosion! (pp. 293-300)
D-Amp Publications
401 Amherst Ave.
Coraopolis, PA 15108
Ph: (412)262-5578

Dennis V. Damp. 1993. Provides information on the nature of work for the major health care occupational groups. Descriptions include working conditions, training, job outlook, qualifications, and related occupations.

★5192★ "Chiropractors" in Jobs! What They Are—Where They Are—What They Pay (p. 284)
Simon & Schuster, Inc.
Simon & Schuster Bldg.
1230 Avenue of the Americas
New York, NY 10020
Ph: (212)698-7000   Fr: 800-223-2348

Robert O. Snelling and Anne M. Snelling. 3rd edition, 1992. Describes duties and responsibilities, earnings, employment opportunities, training, and qualifications.

★5193★ "Chiropractors" in Occupational Outlook Handbook
U.S. Government Printing Office
Superintendent of Documents
Washington, DC 20402
Ph: (202)512-1800   Fax: (202)512-2250

Biennial; latest edition, 1994-95. Encyclopedia of careers describing about 250 occupations and comprising about 85 percent of all jobs in the economy. Occupations that require lengthy education or training are given the most attention. Each occupation's profile describes what the worker does on the job, working conditions, education and training requirements, advancement possibilities, job outlook, earnings, and sources of additional information.

★5194★ The Confusion About Chiropractors; What They Are, What They Do, & What They Can Do for You
Impulse Publishing
PO Box 3321
Danbury, CT 06813-3321
Ph: (203)790-8430

Richard E. DeRoeck. 1989.

★5195★ Fact Sheet on Chiropractic
American Chiropractic Association
1701 Clarendon Blvd.
Arlington, VA 22209
Ph: (703)276-8800   Fax: (703)243-2593
Fr: 800-368-3083

1990. Describes the position of chiropractors in the health care system.

★5196★ Facts About Chiropractic Education: Patient Information
American Chiropractic Association
1701 Clarendon Blvd.
Arlington, VA 22209
Ph: (703)276-8800   Fax: (703)243-2593
Fr: 800-368-3083

1990. This pamphlet describes the educational preparation and licensure of chiropractors and gives a profile of a typical chiropractic student.

★5197★ Health Careers
Careers, Inc.
PO Box 135
Largo, FL 34649-0135
Ph: (813)584-7333

1994. Four-page brief describing duties, working conditions, personal qualifications, training, earnings and hours, employment outlook, places of employment, related careers, and where to write for more information.

★5198★ Opportunities in Chiropractic Health Careers
National Textbook Co. (NTC)
VGM Career Books
4255 W. Touhy Ave.
Lincolnwood, IL 60646-1975
Ph: (708)679-5500   Fax: (708)679-2494
Fr: 800-323-4900

R.C. Schafer, Louis Spartelli. 1987. Presents an overview of the profession, its history and development, the science and philosophy of chiropractic therapy. Describes the basic role of the chiropractic physician, career opportunities educational requirements, licensure, and the future of the profession.

★5199★ Planning a Career in Chiropractic
American Chiropractic Association
1701 Clarendon Blvd.
Arlington, VA 22209
Ph: (703)276-8800   Fr: 800-368-3083

1992. This 15-page booklet provides general information on the history, growth, and goals of chiropractic as well as the educational requirements necessary for a doctor's degree, licensure information, and scholarship opportunities.

PROFESSIONAL ASSOCIATIONS

★5200★ American Chiropractic Association (ACA)
1701 Clarendon Blvd.
Arlington, VA 22209
Ph: (703)276-8800   Fax: (703)243-2593
Fr: 800-986-4636

Members: Enhances the philosophy, science, and art of chiropractic, and the professional welfare of individuals in the field. **Purpose:** Promotes legislation defining chiropractic health care and improves the public's awareness and utilization of chiropractic. Conducts chiropractic survey and statistical study; maintains library. Sponsors Correct Posture Week in May and Spinal Health Month in October. Chiropractic colleges have student ACA groups. **Publications:** *ACA/Today*, monthly. • *American Chiropractic Association Membership Directory*, annual. • *Journal of Chiropractic*, monthly.

★5201★ Council on Chiropractic Education (CCE)
7975 N. Hayden Rd., No. A-210
Scottsdale, AZ 85258-3246
Ph: (602)443-8877   Fax: (602)483-7333
Members: Representatives of member colleges. **Purpose:** Advocates high standards in chiropractic education; establishes criteria of institutional excellence for educating chiropractic physicians; acts as national accrediting agency for chiropractic colleges. Conducts workshops for college teams, consultants, and chiropractic college staffs. **Publications:** *CCE Board of Directors*, annual. • *Educational Standards for Chiropractic Colleges*, semiannual.

★5202★ International Chiropractors Association (ICA)
1110 N. Glebe Rd., Ste. 1000
Arlington, VA 22201
Ph: (703)528-5000   Fax: (703)528-5023
Members: Professional society of chiropractors, chiropractic educators, students, and laypersons. Sponsors professional development programs and practice management seminars. **Publications:** *Congressional Directory*, annual. • *ICA Today*, bimonthly. • *International Chiropractors Association Membership Directory*, annual. • *International Review of Chiropractic*, bimonthly.

STANDARDS/CERTIFICATION AGENCIES

★5203★ Council on Chiropractic Education (CCE)
7975 N. Hayden Rd., No. A-210
Scottsdale, AZ 85258-3246
Ph: (602)443-8877   Fax: (602)483-7333
Advocates high standards in chiropractic education; establishes criteria of institutional excellence for educating chiropractic physicians; acts as national accrediting agency for chiropractic colleges.

★5204★ International Chiropractors Association (ICA)
1110 N. Glebe Rd., Ste. 1000
Arlington, VA 22201
Ph: (703)528-5000   Fax: (703)528-5023
Sponsors professional development programs and practice management seminars.

EDUCATIONAL DIRECTORIES AND PROGRAMS

★5205★ *The Chiropractic College Directory*
K M Enterprises
PO Box 25978
Los Angeles, CA 90025
Ph: (818)710-6868   Fax: (818)710-6855
Kevin McNamee, Contact
Biennial, January of even years. Covers over 17 chiropractic colleges, state and national licensing boards, national associations. international coverage. Entries include: College name, address, phone, names and titles of key personnel, history, financial data, admissions requirements, curriculum, typical questions, clinical opportunities, postgraduate and residency programs. Arrangement: Alphabetical.

★5206★ *Encyclopedia of Medical Organizations and Agencies*
Gale Research Inc.
835 Penobscot Bldg.
Detroit, MI 48226-4094
Ph: (313)961-2242   Fax: (313)961-6741
Fr: 800-877-GALE
Karen Boyden, Contact
Biennial, November of odd years. Covers over 13,400 state, national, and international medical associations, foundations, research institutes, federal and state agencies, and medical and allied health schools. Entries include: Organization name, address, phone; many listings include names and titles of key personnel, descriptive annotations. Arrangement: Classified by subject, then by type of organization.

★5207★ *Health & Medical Industry Directory*
American Business Directories, Inc.
5711 S. 86th Circle
Omaha, NE 68127
Ph: (402)593-4600   Fax: (402)331-1505
Released 1993. Lists over 1.1 million physicians and surgeons, dentists, clinics, health clubs, and other health-related businesses in the U.S. and Canada. Entries include: Name, address, phone.

★5208★ *Therapists and Allied Health Professionals Career Directory*
Gale Research Inc.
835 Penobscot Bldg.
Detroit, MI 48226-4094
Ph: (313)961-2242   Fax: (313)961-6083
Fr: 800-877-GALE
Bradley J. Morgan and Joseph M. Palmisano. 1993. A directory in the Career Advisor Series that provides essays written by industry professionals; job search information on resume and cover letter preparation, networking, and the interviewing process; approximately 300 companies and organizations offering job opportunities and internships, and additional job-hunting resources.

AWARDS, SCHOLARSHIPS, GRANTS, AND FELLOWSHIPS

★5209★ Chiropractor of the Year
International Chiropractors Association
1110 N. Glebe Rd., Ste. 1000
Arlington, VA 22201
Ph: (703)528-5000   Fax: (703)528-5023
To recognize outstanding achievement within the chiropractic profession. Members of the Association are eligible. A plaque is awarded annually. Established in 1926.

★5210★ Lee - Homewood Honorary Award
Association for the History of Chiropractic
1000 Brady St.
Davenport, IA 52803
Ph: (319)326-9656   Fax: (319)326-8414
For recognition of lifetime achievements benefitting the social and scientific advancement of the chiropractic profession. A certificate is awarded annually at the conference. Established in 1981 and renamed in 1983 for its first two recipients.

BASIC REFERENCE GUIDES AND HANDBOOKS

★5211★ *Advances in Chiropractic*
Mosby-Year Book, Inc..
11830 Westline Industrial Dr.
St. Louis, MO 63146
Ph: (314)872-8370   Fax: (314)432-1380
Fr: 800-325-4177
1994.

★5212★ *Chiropractic: An Illustrated History*
Mosby-Year Book, Inc..
11830 Westline Industrial Dr.
St. Louis, MO 63146
Ph: (314)872-8370   Fax: (314)432-1380
Fr: 800-325-4177
Dennis Peterson and Glenda Wiese. 1994.

★5213★ *Fact Sheet: Health Education Assistance Loan Program (HEAL)*
U.S. Department of Health and Human Services
Public Health Service
Health Resources and Services Administration
Bureau of Health Professions, Division of Student Assistance
Rockville, MD 20857
Ph: (301)443-2086
Fact sheet describing the HEAL Program; covers eligible schools, borrowers, and lenders, as well as loan limitations, interest, and repayment.

PROFESSIONAL AND TRADE PERIODICALS

★5214★ Advance
Foundation for Chiropractic Education and
  Research
1701 Clarendon Blvd.
Arlington, VA 22209-2712
Ph: (703)276-7445
Mary E. Johnson
Bimonthly. Provides information on programs
and projects related to the Foundation, in-
cluding research sponsored by the Founda-
tion.

**★5215★ Association for the History of
Chiropractic—Bulletin**
Association for the History of Chiropractic,
  Inc.
1000 Brady St.
Davenport, IA 52803
Fax: (319)326-8414   Fr: 800-722-2586
Willaim S. Rehm
Periodic. Relates information on events and
developments in the field of chiropractic his-
tory. Reviews Association activities. Recur-
ring features include listings of educational
opportunities and news of members.

★5216★ Journal of Chiropractic
American Chiropractic Assn.
8229 Maryland Ave.
Saint Louis, MO 63105
Ph: (314)862-7800   Fax: (314)721-5171
Greg Lammert
Monthly. Chiropractic journal providing edito-
rials, reports, association news, and informa-
tion about legislation affecting the profession.

★5217★ Staying Well Newsletter
Foundation for Chiropractic Education and
  Research
66 Washington Ave.
Des Moines, IA 50314
Ph: (515)282-7118   Fax: (515)282-3347
Fr: 800-622-6309
Robin Merrifield
Bimonthly. Promotes chiropractic health and
fitness. Carries a feature article and news
briefs on such topics as living a better life
after age 65, the effect of fitness on life insur-
ance premiums and other health-related is-
sues. Recurring features include news of chi-
ropractic research and a column titled Ask
Your Doctor.

PROFESSIONAL MEETINGS AND CONVENTIONS

**★5218★ American Chiropractic
Association Annual Convention and
Exhibition**
American Chiropractic Association
1701 Clarendon Blvd.
Arlington, VA 22209
Ph: (703)276-8800   Fax: (703)243-2593
Annual. Always held during June.

OTHER SOURCES OF INFORMATION

**★5219★ "Chiropractic" in Accounting to
Zoology: Graduate Fields Defined (pp.
251-253)**
Petersons Guides, Inc.
PO Box 2123
Princeton, NJ 08543-2123
Ph: (609)243-9111   Fax: (609)243-9150
Fr: 800-338-3282
Amy J. Goldstein, editor. Revised and up-
dated, 1987. Discusses types of graduate
programs and degrees, graduate research,
applied work, employment prospects, and
trends.

**★5220★ "Chiropractor" in Allied Health
Professions (pp. 7-8; 134)**
Arco Publishing Co.
Simon & Schuster, Inc.
201 W. 103rd St.
Indianapolis, IN 46290
Ph: 800-428-5331   Fax: 800-835-3202
1993. Contains information on 28 representative careers in health care. Provides a sample
of the Allied Health Professions Admission
Test, lists professional societies and associations, and offers a directory of schools and
programs for the careers listed.

**★5221★ "Chiropractor" in Career
Selector 2001**
Barron's Educational Series, Inc.
250 Wireless Blvd.
Hauppauge, NY 11788
Ph: (516)434-3311   Fax: (516)434-3723
Fr: 800-645-3476
James C. Gonyea. 1993.

**★5222★ Scholarships From the
International Chiropractors Association**
International Chiropractors Association
  (ICA)
1110 N. Glebe Rd., Ste. 1000
Arlington, VA 22201
Ph: (703)528-5000
This one-page information sheet describes
the King Koil Scholarship and lists the chi-
ropractic colleges that offer it.

Dentists

Dentists diagnose and treat problems of the teeth and tissues of the mouth. They examine X-rays, place protective plastic sealants on childrens' teeth, fill cavities, straighten teeth, repair fractured teeth, and treat gum disease. Dentists remove teeth only when necessary and may provide dentures to replace missing teeth. They also perform corrective surgery of the gums and supporting bones. Increasingly, dentists are concerned with preventing dental problems. In addition to cleaning teeth, dentists may provide instruction in diet, flossing, the use of fluorides, and other aspects of dental care. Dentists may devote some time to laboratory work such as making dentures and crowns. Despite the trend toward specialization, most dentists are general practitioners who handle a wide variety of dental needs. The largest group of specialists is **orthodontists**, who straighten teeth. The next largest group, **oral and maxillofacial surgeons**, operate on the mouth and jaws. The remainder specialize in pediatric dentistry (dentistry for children); periodontics (treating the gums); prosthodontics (making artificial teeth or dentures); endodontics (root canal therapy); public health dentistry (community dental health); and oral pathology (diseases of the mouth).

Salaries

Specialists generally earn considerably more than general practitioners.

Net median for general practitioners	$90,000/year
Net median for specialists	$130,000/year

Employment Outlook

Growth rate until the year 2005: More slowly than the average.

Dentists

CAREER GUIDES

★5223★ Career Planning: Consider All the Angles: Orthodontics
American Associaton of Orthodontists (AAO)
460 N. Lindbergh Blvd.
St. Louis, MO 63141
Ph: (314)993-1700
1988. This six-panel brochure describes the rewards of a career in orthodontics.

★5224★ Dentist
Careers, Inc.
PO Box 135
Largo, FL 34649-0135
Ph: (813)584-7333
1994. Four-page brief offering the definition, history, duties, working conditions, personal qualifications, educational requirements, earnings, hours, employment outlook, advancement, and careers related to this position.

★5225★ Dentist
Vocational Biographies, Inc.
PO Box 31
Sauk Centre, MN 56378-0031
Ph: (612)352-6516   Fax: (612)352-5546
Fr: 800-255-0752
1994. Four-page pamphlet containing a personal narrative about a worker's job, work likes and dislikes, career path from high school to the present, education and training, the rewards and frustrations, and the effects of the job on the rest of the worker's life. The data file portion of this pamphlet gives a concise occupational summary, including work description, working conditions, places of employment, personal characteristics, education and training, job outlook, and salary range.

★5226★ "Dentist" in 100 Best Careers for the Year 2000 (pp. 23-25)
Arco Pub.
201 W. 103rd St.
Indianapolis, IN 46290
Ph: 800-428-5331   Fax: 800-835-3202
Shelly Field. 1992. Describes 100 job opportunities expected to grow fast throughout the next decade. Provides information on job duties and responsibilities, training requirements, education, advancement opportunities, experience and qualifications, and typical salaries.

★5227★ "Dentist" in Career Information Center (Vol.7)
Simon and Schuster
200 Old Tappan Rd.
Old Tappan, NJ 07675
Fax: 800-445-6991   Fr: 800-223-2348
Richard Lidz and Linda Perrin, editorial directors. Fifth edition, 1993. This 13-volume set profiles over 600 occupations. Each occupational profile describes job duties, entry-level requirements, educational requirements, advancement possibilities, employment outlook, working conditions, earnings and benefits, and where to write for more information.

★5228★ "Dentist" in College Board Guide to Jobs and Career Planning (pp. 242)
The College Board
415 Columbus Ave.
New York, NY 10023-6992
Ph: (212)713-8165   Fax: (212)713-8143
Fr: 800-323-7155
Joyce S. Mitchell. Second edition, 1994. Describes the job, salaries, related careers, education needed, and where to write for more information.

★5229★ "Dentist" in Jobs Rated Almanac
World Almanac
1 International Blvd., Ste. 444
Mahwah, NJ 07495
Ph: (201)529-6900   Fax: (201)529-6901
Les Krantz. Second edition, 1992. Ranks 250 jobs by environment, salary, outlooks, physical demands, stress, security, travel opportunities, and extra perks. Includes jobs the editor feels are the most common, most interesting, and the most rapidly growing.

★5230★ "Dentist" in VGM's Careers Encyclopedia (pp. 136-139)
National Textbook Co. (NTC)
VGM Career Books
4255 W. Touhy Ave.
Lincolnwood, IL 60646-1975
Ph: (708)679-5500   Fax: (708)679-2494
Fr: 800-323-4900
Third edition, 1991. Describes job duties, places of employment, working conditions, qualifications, education, and training, advancement potential, and salary for each occupation.

★5231★ "Dentist" in VGM's Handbook of Health Care Careers
National Textbook Co.
4255 W. Touhy Ave.
Lincolnwood, IL 60646-1975
Ph: (708)679-5500   Fax: (708)679-2494
Fr: 800-323-4900
Annette Selden. 1993. Contains 42 two-page occupational profiles describing job duties, places of employment, working conditions, qualifications, education, employment outlook, and income.

★5232★ "Dentistry" in Black Woman's Career Guide (pp. 105-106)
Bantam Doubleday Dell
1540 Broadway
New York, NY 10036
Fax: 800-233-3294   Fr: 800-223-5780
Beatryce Nivens. Revised edition, 1987. Part 1 describes career planning, resume writing, job hunting, and interviewing. Part 2 profiles 60 black women pioneers in 20 different career areas.

★5233★ Dentistry Today
American Dental Association (ADA)
211 E. Chicago Ave.
Chicago, IL 60611
Ph: (312)440-2639
Latest revision, 1992. A two-page statistical fact sheet on the number of dentists, earnings of dentists, dental practice, and future opportunities in dentistry.

★5234★ "Dentists" in *101 Careers: A Guide to the Fastest-Growing Opportunities* (pp. 195-197)
John Wiley & Sons, Inc.
605 3rd Ave.
New York, NY 10158-0012
Ph: (212)850-6645   Fax: (212)850-6088
Michael Harkavy. 1990. Describes the nature of the job, working conditions, employment growth, qualifications, personal skills, projected salaries, and where to write for more information.

★5235★ "Dentists" in *American Almanac of Jobs and Salaries* (pp. 227)
Avon Books
1350 Avenue of the Americas
New York, NY 10019
Ph: (212)261-6800   Fr: 800-238-0658
John Wright, editor. Revised and updated, 1994-95. This is comprehensive guide to the wages of hundreds of occupations in a wide variety of industries and organizations.

★5236★ "Dentists" in *Best Jobs for the 1990s and Into the 21st Century*
Impact Publications
9104-N Manassas Dr.
Manassas Park, VA 22111
Ph: (703)361-7300   Fax: (703)335-9486
Ronald L. Krannich and Caryl Rae Krannich. 1993.

★5237★ "Dentists" in *Career Discovery Encyclopedia* (Vol.2, pp. 90-91)
J.G. Ferguson Publishing Co.
200 W. Madison St., Ste. 300
Chicago, IL 60606
Ph: (312)580-5480   Fax: (312)580-4948
Russell E. Primm, editor-in chief. 1993. This six volume set contains two-page articles for 504 occupations. Each article describes job duties, earnings, and educational and training requirements. The whole set is arranged alphabetically by job title. Designed for junior high and older students.

★5238★ *Dentists and Dental Specialists*
Chronicle Guidance Publications, Inc.
66 Aurora St.
PO Box 1190
Moravia, NY 13118-1190
Ph: (315)497-0330   Fax: (315)497-3359
Fr: 800-622-7284
1994. Career brief describing the nature of the job, working conditions, hours and earnings, education and training, licensure, certification, unions, personal qualifications, social and psychological factors, location, employment outlook, entry methods, advancement, and related occupations.

★5239★ "Dentists" in *Encyclopedia of Careers and Vocational Guidance* (Vol.2, pp. 455-457)
J.G. Ferguson Publishing Co.
200 W. Madison St., Ste. 300
Chicago, IL 60606
Ph: (312)580-5480   Fax: (312)580-4948
William E. Hopke, editor-in-chief. Ninth edition, 1993. Four-volume set that profiles 900 occupations and describes job trends in 74 industries. Includes career description, educational requirements, history of the job, methods of entry, advancement, employment outlook, earnings, conditions of work, social

and psychological factors, and sources of further information.

★5240★ "Dentists" in *Health Care Job Explosion!* (pp. 301-308)
D-Amp Publications
401 Amherst Ave.
Coraopolis, PA 15108
Ph: (412)262-5578
Dennis V. Damp. 1993. Provides information on the nature of work for the major health care occupational groups. Descriptions include working conditions, training, job outlook, qualifications, and related occupations.

★5241★ "Dentists" in *Jobs! What They Are—Where They Are—What They Pay* (p. 285)
Simon & Schuster, Inc.
Simon & Schuster Bldg.
1230 Avenue of the Americas
New York, NY 10020
Ph: (212)698-7000   Fr: 800-223-2348
Robert O. Snelling and Anne M. Snelling. 3rd edition, 1992. Describes duties and responsibilities, earnings, employment opportunities, training, and qualifications.

★5242★ "Dentists" in *Occupational Outlook Handbook*
U.S. Government Printing Office
Superintendent of Documents
Washington, DC 20402
Ph: (202)512-1800   Fax: (202)512-2250
Biennial; latest edition, 1994-95. Encyclopedia of careers describing about 250 occupations and comprising about 85 percent of all jobs in the economy. Occupations that require lengthy education or training are given the most attention. Each occupation's profile describes what the worker does on the job, working conditions, education and training requirements, advancement possibilities, job outlook, earnings, and sources of additional information.

★5243★ *Exploring Careers in Dentistry*
Rosen Publishing Group
29 E. 21st St.
New York, NY 10010
Ph: (212)777-3017   Fax: (212)777-0277
Fr: 800-237-9932
Jessica A. Rickert. Revised edition, 1991. Describes the nature of the work, educational requirements, salary and future trends in dentistry. Includes a glossary, a list of dental schools, the American Dental Association's Principle of Ethics, and Code of Professional Conduct.

★5244★ *Have You Considered Dentistry?*
American Dental Association (ADA)
211 E. Chicago Ave.
Chicago, IL 60611
Ph: (312)440-2639
Describes the benefits of choosing a career in dentistry, including security, advancements, flexibility, variety, creativity, and prestige.

★5245★ *Health Careers*
Careers, Inc.
PO Box 135
Largo, FL 34649-0135
Ph: (813)584-7333
1994. Four-page brief describing duties, working conditions, personal qualifications, training, earnings and hours, employment outlook, places of employment, related careers, and where to write for more information.

★5246★ *Opportunities in Dental Care*
National Textbook Co. (NTC)
VGM Career Books
4255 W. Touhy Ave.
Lincolnwood, IL 60646-1975
Ph: (708)679-5500   Fax: (708)679-2494
Fr: 800-323-4900
Norman N. Noerper. Describes job responsibilities, working conditions, salary, and educational requirements.

★5247★ *Orthodontist*
Careers, Inc.
PO Box 135
Largo, FL 34649-0135
Ph: (813)584-7333
1992. Two-page summary describing duties, working conditions, personal qualifications, training, earnings and hours, employment outlook, places of employment, related careers, and where to write for more information.

★5248★ *Orthontics: Career Planning: Consider All The Angles: Orthodontics*
American Association of Orthodontists (AAO)
401 N. Lindbergh Blvd.
St. Louis, MO 63141
Ph: (314)993-1700   Fax: (314)997-1745
1991. This six-panel pamphlet describes orthodontics, educational requirements, and employment outlook.

★5249★ *Pediatric Dentist*
Vocational Biographies, Inc.
PO Box 31
Sauk Centre, MN 56378-0031
Ph: (612)352-6516   Fax: (612)352-5546
Fr: 800-255-0752
1993. Four-page pamphlet containing a personal narrative about a worker's job, work likes and dislikes, career path from high school to the present, education and training, the rewards and frustrations, and the effects of the job on the rest of the worker's life. The data file portion of this pamphlet gives a concise occupational summary, including work description, working conditions, places of employment, personal characteristics, education and training, job outlook, and salary range.

★5250★ "Public Health Dentist" in *Opportunities in Public Health Careers* (pp. 64-65)
National Textbook Co. (NTC)
VGM Career Books
4255 W. Touhy Ave.
Lincolnwood, IL 60646-1975
Ph: (708)679-5500   Fax: (708)679-2494
Fr: 800-323-4900
George E. Pickett, 1988. Defines the public health field and describes career opportuni-

ties as well as educational preparation and the future of the public health field. The appendixes list public health organizations, state and federal public health agencies, and graduate schools offering public health programs.

★5251★ "Select—A National Program to Attract Qualified Individuals to a Career in Dentistry" in Journal of Dental Education (Vol. 51, No. 2, 1987)
American Dental Association (ADA)
211 E. Chicago Ave.
Chicago, IL 60611
Ph: (312)440-2639
This four-page article describes the decline in the number of dental school applicants and the select national recruitment program designed to encourage practicing dentists, dental professionals, educators, and counselors to recruiting students to dental careers.

PROFESSIONAL ASSOCIATIONS

★5252★ Academy of Laser Dentistry
401 N. Michigan Ave.
Chicago, IL 60611
Ph: (312)644-6610   Fax: (312)321-6869
Members: Dentists, hygienists, dental teachers, and corporate laser dental vendors. **Purpose:** Promotes clinical education, research, and development of standards and guidelines for the safe and ethical use of dental laser technology. Conducts educational programs. Provides certification. **Publications:** *Journal of Clinical, Laser, Medical, and Surgery*, bimonthly. • *Wavelengths*, quarterly.

★5253★ American Association of Dental Schools (AADS)
1625 Massachusetts Ave. NW
Washington, DC 20036
Ph: (202)667-9433   Fax: (202)667-0642
Members: Individuals interested in dental education; schools of dentistry, graduate dentistry, and dental auxiliary education in the U.S., Canada, and Puerto Rico; affiliated institutions of the federal government. **Purpose:** To promote better teaching and education in dentistry and dental research and to facilitate exchange of ideas among dental educators. Sponsors meetings, conferences, and workshops; conducts surveys, studies, and special projects and publishes their results. Maintains 37 sections representing teaching and administrative areas of dentistry. **Publications:** *Admission Requirements of United States and Canadian Dental Schools*, annual. • *Bulletin of Dental Education*, monthly. • *Directory of Dental Educators*, periodic. • *Directory of Institutional Members*, annual. • *Journal of Dental Education*, monthly.

★5254★ American Central European Dental Institute (ACEDI)
60 Federal St.
Boston, MA 02110-2510
Ph: (617)423-6165   Fax: (617)426-0006
Members: Dentists and others serving in capacities related to the dental profession. **Purpose:** Seeks to advance standards in the profession of dentistry. Conducts educational programs; maintains speakers' bureau. **Publications:** *ACEDI*, annual.

★5255★ American Dental Association (ADA)
211 E. Chicago Ave.
Chicago, IL 60611
Ph: (312)440-2500   Fax: (312)440-7494
Members: Professional society of dentists. Encourages the improvement of the health of the public and promotes the art and science of dentistry in matters of legislation and regulations. **Purpose:** Inspects and accredits dental schools and schools for dental hygienists, assistants, and laboratory technicians. Conducts research programs at ADA Health Foundation Research Institute. Produces most of the dental health education material used in the U.S. Sponsors National Children's Dental Health Month. Compiles statistics on personnel, practice, and dental care needs and attitudes of patients with regard to dental health. Sponsors 12 councils. **Publications:** *American Dental Directory*, annual. • *Dental Teamwork*, bimonthly. • *Index to Dental Literature*, quarterly. • *Journal of the American Dental Association*, monthly. • *News*, biweekly.

★5256★ Federation of Special Care Organizations and Dentistry
211 E. Chicago Ave., 17th Fl.
Chicago, IL 60611-9361
Ph: (312)440-2660   Fax: (312)440-7494
Members: Dentists and dental care providers. **Purpose:** Seeks to improve the effectiveness of health care providers in providing quality patient care, especially for patients who for reasons of medical diagnosis, disabilities, or frailties prevalent in advanced age require special care and/or special settings for dental care. Conducts educational programs. **Publications:** *Special Care in Dentistry*, bimonthly.

★5257★ International Academy of Oral Medicine and Toxicology (IAOMT)
PO Box 608531
Orlando, FL 32860-8531
Ph: (407)298-2450   Fax: (407)298-2450
Members: Dentists, physicians, and medical scientists. **Purpose:** Encourages, sponsors, and disseminates scientific research on the biocompatibility of materials used in dentistry. Offers educational programs; maintains speakers' bureau. **Publications:** *Bio-Probe Newsletter*, bimonthly. • *IN VIVO*, quarterly.

STANDARDS/CERTIFICATION AGENCIES

★5258★ Academy of Laser Dentistry
401 N. Michigan Ave.
Chicago, IL 60611
Ph: (312)644-6610   Fax: (312)321-6869
Promotes clinical education, research, and development of standards and guidelines for the safe and ethical use of dental laser technology. Provides certification.

★5259★ American Dental Association (ADA)
211 E. Chicago Ave.
Chicago, IL 60611
Ph: (312)440-2500   Fax: (312)440-7494
Inspects and accredits dental schools and schools for dental hygienists, assistants, and laboratory technicians.

TEST GUIDES

★5260★ Admission Test Series: National Dental Boards
National Learning Corp.
212 Michael Dr.
Syosset, NY 11791
Ph: (516)921-8888   Fax: (516)921-8743
Fr: 800-645-6337
Jack Rudman. A collection of sample tests for those seeking admission to graduate and professional schools or seeking entrance or advancement in institutional and public career service in the field of dentistry. Titles in the series include *National Dental Boards (NDB)/Part I; National Dental Boards (NDB)/Part II*.

★5261★ Career Examination Series: Dentist
National Learning Corp.
212 Michael Dr.
Syosset, NY 11791
Ph: (516)921-8888   Fax: (516)921-8743
Fr: 800-645-6337
Jack Rudman. A study guide for professionals and trainees in the field of dentistry. Includes a multiple-choice examination section; provides answers.

★5262★ Career Examination Series: Senior Dentist
National Learning Corp.
212 Michael Dr.
Syosset, NY 11791
Ph: (516)921-8888   Fax: (516)921-8743
Fr: 800-645-6337
Jack Rudman. A study guide for professionals and trainees in the field of dentistry. Includes a multiple-choice examination section; provides answers.

★5263★ Dental Admission Test (DAT)
National Learning Corp.
212 Michael Dr.
Syosset, NY 11791
Ph: (516)921-8888   Fax: (516)921-8743
Fr: 800-645-6337
Jack Rudman. Part of the Admission Test series. A sample test for those seeking admission to graduate and professional schools or seeking entrance or advancement in institutional and public career service in the field of dentistry.

★5264★ *Dental Admission Test Preparation Materials*
American Dental Association (ADA)
211 E. Chicago Ave.
Chicago, IL 60611
Ph: (312)440-2500

1990. Contains copies of four examinations used in the Dental Admission Testing Program.

EDUCATIONAL DIRECTORIES AND PROGRAMS

★5265★ *Accredited Advanced Dental Educational Programs*
Commission on Dental Accreditation
211 E. Chicago Ave.
Chicago, IL 60611
Ph: (312)440-2686   Fax: (312)440-2915
Fr: 800-621-8099
Tom Berger, Manager

Semiannual, February and August. Covers about 700 dental education programs accredited for postdoctoral work, dentistry specialties, general practice residency, and advanced general dentistry; coverage includes Canada. Entries include: Institution name, address, years of past and next accreditation reviews. Arrangement: Geographical.

★5266★ *Admission Requirements of U.S. and Canadian Dental Schools*
American Association of Dental Schools (AADS)
1625 Massachusetts Ave. NW
Washington, DC 20036
Ph: (202)667-9433   Fax: (202)667-0642
Amy Siegel, Contact

Annual, July. Covers Approximately 65 schools. Entries include: School name, dean, address, program, admission requirements, calendar, expenses, characteristics of entering class, financial aid, name and title of contact. Arrangement: Geographical.

★5267★ *American Association of Dental Schools—Directory of Institutional Members & Association Officers*
American Association of Dental Schools (AADS)
1625 Massachusetts Ave. NW
Washington, DC 20036
Ph: (202)667-9433   Fax: (202)667-0642
Amy Siegel, Contact

Annual, November. Covers over 170 member dental schools, dental education programs, and dental service programs offered by hospitals and other institutions not affiliated with dental schools. Entries include: School or program name, address, phone, names and titles of chief administrators and department chairs. Now includes Department Chairs. Arrangement: Alphabetical.

★5268★ *American Dental Directory*
American Dental Association
211 E. Chicago Ave.
Chicago, IL 60611
Ph: (312)440-2500   Fax: (312)440-3542
Fr: 800-947-4746
B. Ranallo, Contact

Annual, January. Covers over 170,000 dentists. Also includes list of active and historic dental schools, dental organizations, and state dental examining boards. Entries include: Name, address, year of birth, educational data, specialty, membership status. Arrangement: Geographical.

★5269★ *Barron's Guide to Medical and Dental Schools*
Barron's Educational Series, Inc.
250 Wireless Blvd.
Hauppauge, NY 11788
Ph: 800-645-3476   Fax: (516)434-3723
Fr: 800-645-3476
Max Reed, Contact

Biennial, fall of odd years. Covers about 220 medical, osteopathic, and dental schools. Entries include: School name, address, admission requirements, housing, grading and promotion policies, facilities, description of curriculum. Arrangement: Classified by type of school, then geographical.

★5270★ *Encyclopedia of Medical Organizations and Agencies*
Gale Research Inc.
835 Penobscot Bldg.
Detroit, MI 48226-4094
Ph: (313)961-2242   Fax: (313)961-6741
Fr: 800-877-GALE
Karen Boyden, Contact

Biennial, November of odd years. Covers over 13,400 state, national, and international medical associations, foundations, research institutes, federal and state agencies, and medical and allied health schools. Entries include: Organization name, address, phone; many listings include names and titles of key personnel, descriptive annotations. Arrangement: Classified by subject, then by type of organization.

★5271★ *Gourman Report: A Rating of Graduate and Professional Programs in American and International Universities*
National Education Standards
624 S. Grand Ave., Ste. 1210
Los Angeles, CA 90017
Ph: (213)623-9135
Jack Gourman

Irregular, previous edition 1989; latest edition January, 1993. Covers colleges and universities offering graduate programs in a variety of disciplines; medical schools; law schools; schools of dentistry; optometry; pharmacy. Entries include: Institution name, address, author's description and evaluation. Arrangement: Law, medical, dental, and pharmacy schools are listed by country; others (primarily in United States) are by discipline.

★5272★ *Health & Medical Industry Directory*
American Business Directories, Inc.
5711 S. 86th Circle
Omaha, NE 68127
Ph: (402)593-4600   Fax: (402)331-1505

Released 1993. Lists over 1.1 million physicians and surgeons, dentists, clinics, health clubs, and other health-related businesses in the U.S. and Canada. Entries include: Name, address, phone.

★5273★ *Healthcare Career Directory— Nurses and Physicians*
Gale Research Inc.
835 Penobscot Bldg.
Detroit, MI 48226-4094
Ph: (313)961-2242   Fax: (313)961-6083
Fr: 800-877-GALE

Bradley J. Morgan and Joseph M. Palmisano. Second edition, 1993. A directory in the Career Advisor Series that provides essays written by industry professionals; job search information on resume and cover letter preparation, networking, and the interviewing process; approximately 300 companies and organizations offering job opportunities and internships, and additional job-hunting resources.

★5274★ *Medical and Health Information Directory*
Gale Research Inc.
835 Penobscot Bldg.
Detroit, MI 48226-4094
Ph: (313)961-2242   Fax: (313)961-6741
Fr: 800-877-GALE
Karen Boyden, Contact

Approximately biennial; latest edition 1994. Covers in Volume 1, almost 18,600 medical and health oriented associations, organizations, institutions, and government agencies, including health maintenance organizations (HMOs), preferred provider organizations (PPOs), insurance companies, pharmaceutical companies, research centers, and medical and allied health schools. In Volume 2, nearly 11,800 medical book publishers; medical periodicals, directories, audiovisual producers and services, medical libraries and information centers, and electronic resources. In Volume 3, nearly 26,000 clinics, treatment centers, care programs, and counseling/diagnostic services for 30 subject areas. Entries include: Institution, service, or firm name, address, phone; many include names of key personnel Arrangement: Classified by organization activity, service, etc..

★5275★ *Physicians and Dentists Database*
FIRSTMARK, Inc.
34 Juniper Ln.
Newton Center, MA 02159-2861
Ph: (617)965-7989   Fax: (617)965-8510
Fr: 800-729-2600

Awards, Scholarships, Grants, and Fellowships

★5276★ American Academy of Periodontology Student Award
American Academy of Periodontology
737 N. Michigan Ave., Ste. 800
Chicago, IL 60611
Ph: (312)787-5518   Fax: (312)787-3670
To honor senior dental students who have done outstanding work in the field of periodontics. A certificate and a year's subscription to the *Journal of Periodontology* are awarded annually. Established in 1964.

★5277★ American Association for Dental Research-Student Research Fellowships
American Association for Dental Research (AADR)
1111 14th St., NW, Ste. 1000
Washington, DC 20005
Ph: (202)898-1050   Fax: (202)789-1033
Purpose: To encourage dental students living in the United States to consider careers in oral health research. Qualifications: Students must be enrolled in an accredited DDS/DMD or hygiene program in a dental (health associated) institution within the United States and must be sponsored by a faculty member at that institution. Students should not have received their degree, nor should they be due to receive their degree in the year of the award. Applicants may have an advanced degree in a basic science subject. Selection criteria: Selection is based on scientific merit, creativity, feasibility, and potential significance to oral health research. Funds available: Each fellowship includes a stipend of $1,600. In addition, each preceptor receives $300 for supplies and funds for travel when research is presented. Application details: Ten sets of the following material must be submitted: a proposal no longer than eight pages, cover letter from the applicant's sponsor, curriculum vitae no longer than two pages, and a copy of the sponsor's biographical sketch. Deadline: All materials must be received by January 6.

★5278★ American Society of Dentistry for Children Prize
American Society of Dentistry for Children
John Hancock Center
875 N. Michigan Ave., Ste. 4040
Chicago, IL 60611-1901
Ph: (312)943-1244   Fax: (312)943-5341
To recognize the graduating student who is judged to be the most outstanding in the field of dentistry for children. A Certificate of Merit, together with a one year's subscription to the *Journal of Dentistry for Children* is awarded.

★5279★ Award of Merit
American College of Dentists
839 Quince Orchard Blvd., Ste. J
Gaithersburg, MD 20878
Ph: (301)977-3223   Fax: (301)977-3330
For recognition of unusual contributions made toward the advancement of the profession of dentistry and its service to humanity by persons other than Fellows of the College. An engraved certificate is awarded when merited at the Convocation. In addition, in

1970 and 1983 Awards of Excellence were presented. Established in 1959.

★5280★ Award for Special Service to Hospital Dentistry
American Association of Hospital Dentists
211 E. Chicago Ave., 17th Fl.
Chicago, IL 60611
Ph: (312)440-2661
For recognition of special and unusual service to hospital dentistry. A plaque is presented when merited. Established in 1977.

★5281★ Clinical Dental Fellowships
Eastman Dental Center
625 Elmwood Ave.
Rochester, NY 14620-2989
Ph: (716)275-8315   Fax: (716)256-3153
Purpose: To support postdoctoral dental training and research. Qualifications: Applicant must have D.D.S., D.M.D. or equivalent. Fellowships are tenable at the Center, and are intended for advanced clinical training and/or research in general or pediatric dentistry. Funds available: $11,000. Application details: Write for application form and guidelines. Deadline: November 1st.

★5282★ Colgate-Palmolive Award
American Association of Women Dentists (AAWD)
401 N. Michigan Ave.
Chicago, IL 60611
Ph: (312)644-6610   Fax: (312)321-6869
Purpose: To recognize excellence in the field of dentistry. Qualifications: Must be a senior student in good standing at dental school. Selection criteria: Ten dental schools are selected annually be AAWD Awards Committee and are notified of their selection. Deans of the 10 schools then select candidates to receive the scholarships. Funds available: Ten $500 scholarships annually. Application details: Students cannot apply directly, but must be nominated through the dental college.

★5283★ Community Preventive Dentistry Award
American Dental Association
Council on Community Health, Hospital, Institutional & Medic
Institutional & Medical Affairs
211 E. Chicago Ave., 17th Fl.
Chicago, IL 60611-2678
Ph: (312)440-2868   Fax: (312)440-7494
To recognize achievements in community preventive dentistry. The award is open to any individual or organization responsible for creating and implementing a community preventive dentistry program. The first prize includes a monetary award of $2,000 and a plaque, and meritorious awards include $300 and a plaque. The entry deadline is June 1. Awarded annually at the ADA annual session. Established in 1972 with assistance from the JOHNSON & JOHNSON Consumer Products, Inc., Professional Division.

★5284★ Dental Faculty Development Fellowships
ADA Endowment Fund and Assistance Fund Inc.
211 East Chicago Ave., 17th Fl.
Chicago, IL 60611
Ph: (312)440-2567   Fax: (312)440-2822
Purpose: To help dental faculty to improve their research and teaching skills. Qualifica-

tions: Applicant must be a U.S. citizen with a D.D.S. or D.M.D. degree. Applicant must be a full-time instructor, or an associate or assistant professor, at an accredited dental school in the United States. Funds available: $20,000. Application details: Write for application form. Submit completed application with curriculum vitae; a detailed outline of proposed course study; a research proposal, including methodology and a supporting statement from a qualified mentor; an outline of personal goals and objectives for the fellowship year; three letters of recommendation; and a letter of acceptance from a postdoctoral program, if applicable. Deadline: September 1. Notification in mid-December.

★5285★ Dental Student Scholarship Program
ADA Endowment Fund and Assistance Fund Inc
211 East Chicago Ave., 17th Fl.
Chicago, IL 60611
Ph: (312)440-2567   Fax: (312)440-2822
Purpose: To assist students in need of financial assistance in the field of dentistry. Qualifications: Applicants must be a U.S. citizen in their first or second year of dental school. Selection criteria: Applicants need a 3.0 GPA; demonstrate financial need; 2 letters of reference; typed summary of personal/professional goals. Funds available: $2,500. Application details: Contact the Fund for guidelines and application forms. Deadline: June 15.

★5286★ Dental Teacher Training Fellowships
ADA Endowment Fund and Assistance Fund Inc.
211 East Chicago Ave., 17th Fl.
Chicago, IL 60611
Ph: (312)440-2567   Fax: (312)440-2822
Purpose: To support postdoctoral research and teacher training. Qualifications: Applicant must be a U.S. citizen with a D.D.S. or D.M.D. degree. Applicant must be in the final year of a postdoctoral research or teacher training program. Fellowships are tenable in the United States. Funds available: $20,000. Application details: Write for application forms. Submit completed application with curriculum vitae; dental school transcripts, including verification of class standing; verification of enrollment in the final year of a postdoctoral program; and three letters of recommendation, including one from the program director. Deadline: September 1. Notification in mid-December.

★5287★ William John Gies Award
American College of Dentists
839 Quince Orchard Blvd., Ste. J
Gaithersburg, MD 20878
Ph: (301)977-3223   Fax: (301)977-3330
To recognize and encourage unusual services in dentistry and in the allied fields of education, research, literature, etc. Fellows of the College are eligible for the award. An engraved certificate is awarded annually during the Convocation. Established in 1939 in honor of William John Gies who contributed much to the advancement of dentistry.

★5288★ Hillenbrand Fellowship in Dental Administration
ADA Endowment Fund and Assistance Fund Inc.
211 East Chicago Ave., 17th Fl.
Chicago, IL 60611
Ph: (312)440-2567   Fax: (312)440-2822
Purpose: To provide an individual with a year of study and practical experience in the field of dental administration. Qualifications: Applicant must be a U.S. citizen with a graduate degree from an accredited dental school. Fellowship is tenable in Chicago. Funds available: $40,000. Application details: Write for application form. Submit completed application with dental school transcripts, three letters of recommendation, and a one-page statement describing area of interest and goals and objectives for career development. Applicant may be interviewed. Deadline: Varies; December 1 in odd years. The fellowship is awarded biennially.

★5289★ HRSA-BHP Health Professions Student Loans
U.S. Public Health Service
Health Resources and Services Administration
Parklawn Bldg., Rm. 8-38
5600 Fishers Ln.
Rockville, MD 20857
Purpose: To assist students with need for financial assistance to undertake the course of study required to become physicians, dentists, osteopathic physicians, optometrists, pharmacists, podiatrists, or veterinarians. Qualifications: Applicants must be enrolled or accepted for enrollment as full-time students in a program leading to a doctoral degree in medicine, dental surgery or equivalent degree, pharmacy, osteopathic medicine, optometry or equivalent degree, podiatric medicine or equivalent degree, or veterinary medicine or equivalent degree; or a bachelor of science in pharmacy or equivalent degree. Applicants must also be citizens, nationals, or permanent residents of the United States or the District of Columbia, the Commonwealths of Puerto Rico or the Marianna Islands, the Virgin Islands, Guam, The American Samoa, the Trust Territory of the Pacific Islands, the Republic of Palau, the Republic of the Marshall Islands, and the Federated State of Micronesia. Applicants must also demonstrate financial need. Professional students, interns, residents, and students seeking advanced training are not eligible. Funds available: Up to the cost of tuition plus $2,500 or the amount of financial need, whichever is less. The interest rate is five percent and accrues during the repayment period. Loans are repayable over a ten year period and beginning one year after the student graduates or ceases to enroll full-time in a health program.

★5290★ HRSA-BHP Loans for Disadvantaged Students
U.S. Public Health Service
Health Resources and Services Administration
Parklawn Bldg., Rm. 8-38
5600 Fishers Ln.
Rockville, MD 20857
Purpose: To assist students who need financial assistance to pursue careers in medicine, osteopathic medicine, dentistry, optometry, podiatric medicine, pharmacy, or veterinary medicine. Qualifications: Applicants must be citizens, nationals, or lawful permanent residents of the United States or the District of Columbia, the Commonwealths of Puerto Rico or the Marianna Islands, the Virgin Islands, Guam, American Samoa, the Trust Territory of the Pacific Islands, the Republic of Palau, the Republic of the Marshall Islands, or the Federated State of Micronesia. They must also be enrolled or accepted for enrollment at a participating health professionals school full-time. Students must be determined by their school's financial aid director to meet financial need and "disadvantaged background" criteria. Those enrolled in schools of medicine or osteopathic medicine must demonstrate exceptional financial need. Preprofessional students, interns, residents, and students seeking advanced training are not eligible. Selection criteria: Schools are responsible for selecting recipients and for determining the amount of assistance. Funds available: The maximum loan amount allowed for each school year is the cost of tuition plus $2,500, or the amount of financial need, whichever is lesser. The repayment interest rate is five percent over a ten-year period, which begins one year after completion of cessation of full-time study. Interest begins accruing at the time the loan becomes rapayable. Repayment may be deferred under special circumstances, and interest does not accrue during periods of deferment.

★5291★ Minority Dental Student Scholarship Program
ADA Endowment Fund and Assistance Fund Inc.
211 East Chicago Ave., 17th Fl.
Chicago, IL 60611
Ph: (312)440-2567   Fax: (312)440-2822
Purpose: To assist students from minority groups that are traditionally under-represented in the fields of medicine and dentistry. Qualifications: Applicant must be a U.S. citizen entering the first or second year of a U.S. dental school. Applicant must be African-American Native American, or Hispanic. Selection criteria: 2.5 GPA; demonstrate financial need; 2 letters of reference; typed summary of personal/professional goals. Funds available: $2,000. Application details: Write to the Fund for guidelines and application. Deadline: July 1. Notification in mid-August.

★5292★ Senior Dental and Dental Hygiene Student Awards
Academy of Dentistry for the Handicapped
211 E. Chicago, 17th Fl.
Chicago, IL 60611
Ph: (312)440-2660
To encourage the sensitivity and sensibility of the dental profession and allied health professionals toward the needs of the handicapped and special patient populations. Graduating senior dental and dental hygiene students may qualify for the award by demonstrating a sincere interest and concern for the dental needs of the handicapped and special patients while an undergraduate dental or dental hygiene student. Certificates are awarded annually.

★5293★ Henry Spenadel Award
First District Dental Society
295 Madison Ave.
New York, NY 10017
Ph: (212)889-8940   Fax: (212)949-4745
To recognize contributions to the welfare of humanity in the field of dentistry. A gold medal and plaque are awarded annually. Established in 1950.

★5294★ Student Merit Award for Outstanding Achievement in Community Dentistry
American Association of Public Health Dentistry
National Office
10619 Jousting Ln.
Richmond, VA 23235
Ph: (804)272-8344   Fax: (804)272-0802
To recognize outstanding achievement by dental students and dental hygiene students in the field of community dentistry. Full-time dental hygiene students or predoctoral dental students in an accredited dental or dental hygiene school in the United States are eligible. First prize includes a monetary award, a one-year subscription to the *Journal of Public Health Dentistry*, and partial expenses to the association's annual meeting; second and third prizes consist of plaques and *Journal* subscriptions. Awarded annually. Established in 1970.

BASIC REFERENCE GUIDES AND HANDBOOKS

★5295★ *Boucher's Clinical Dental Terminology: Glossary of Accepted Terms in All Disciplines of Dentistry*
Mosby-Year Book, Inc.
11830 Westline Industrial Dr.
St. Louis, MO 63146
Ph: (314)872-8370   Fax: (314)432-1380
Fr: 800-325-4177
Thomas J. Zwemer, editor. Fourth edition, 1993. Includes a bibliography.

★5296★ *Fact Sheet: Health Education Assistance Loan Program (HEAL)*
U.S. Department of Health and Human Services
Public Health Service
Health Resources and Services Administration
Bureau of Health Professions, Division of Student Assistance
Rockville, MD 20857
Ph: (301)443-2086
Fact sheet describing the HEAL Program; covers eligible schools, borrowers, and lenders, as well as loan limitations, interest, and repayment.

★5297★ Health Professions Student Loan Program
Bureau of Health Professions
Division of Student Assistance
5600 Fishers Ln., Rm. 834
Rockville, MD 20857
Ph: (301)443-2086

This information sheet explains who is qualifed to apply for the Health Professions Student Loan, where to apply, the amount of money that can borrowed, and repayment.

PROFESSIONAL AND TRADE PERIODICALS

★5298★ AAOMS Surgical Update
American Association of Oral and
    Maxillofacial Surgeons (AAOMS)
9700 W. Bryn Mawr Ave.
Rosemont, IL 60018
Ph: (708)678-6200   Fax: (708)678-6286
Fr: 800-822-6637

Provides "the dental profession and others with current information on the speciality of oral and maxillofacial surgery and patient care."

★5299★ AGD Impact
Academy of General Dentistry (AGD)
211 E. Chicago Ave., Ste. 1200
Chicago, IL 60611
Ph: (312)440-4300   Fax: (312)440-0559
William W. Howard

Seeks to keep Academy members abreast of issues, legislation, and trends that affect their practice, relationships in the profession, and their position in the healthcare community.

★5300★ American Academy of Implant Dentistry—Newsletter
American Academy of Implant Dentistry
6900 Grove Rd.
Thorofare, NJ 08086
Ph: (609)848-7027   Fax: (312)335-9090
Mark V. Davis

Quarterly. Covers current activities in the field of implant dentistry, particularly the educational programs of the Academy.

★5301★ American Association of Hospital Dentists—InterFace
American Association of Hospital Dentists
211 E. Chicago Ave.
Chicago, IL 60611
Ph: (312)440-2661
Joseph D'Ambrosio

Quarterly. Carries information about trends, legislation, policy changes, and issues that affect the practices of hospital dentists. Recurring features include Association news, news of research, a calendar of events, and columns titled Fellowships, Funding, Sources, In Brief, and What to Write For.

★5302★ American College of Dentists— News & Views
American College of Dentists
839-J Quince Orchard Blvd.
Gaithersburg, MD 20878
Ph: (301)986-0555   Fax: (301)977-3330
Sherry Reramidas

Quarterly. Presents accounts of College meetings, as well as remarks from the College's president. Publishes notices of scheduled events, spotlights individuals recognized or given awards by the College, and profiles convocation speakers, and other dental organizations. Recurring features include reports of meetings.

★5303★ American Society for Dental Aesthetics—Newsletter
American Society for Dental Aesthetics
   (ASDA)
635 Madison Ave., 12th Floor
New York, NY 10022
Ph: (212)751-3263   Fax: (212)308-5184
Michael M. Friedman

Biennial. Focuses on upcoming meetings and lectures of interest to ASDA members. Includes contributed items of a technical nature from members, discussing current projects, techniques, and products. Recurring features include interviews, news of research, a calendar of events, and columns titled But Paul You Can't Do That, Implants, Photography, The President Speaks, and Office Management.

★5304★ American Society for Geriatric Dentistry—Newsletter
American Society for Geriatric Dentistry
211 East Chicago Ave.
Chicago, IL 60611
Ph: (212)343-2100
Saul Kamen

Quarterly. Publishes news of geriatric dentistry as well as the Society, its members and activities. Recurring features include legislative updates, a calendar of events, news of members, book reviews, editorials, a message from the president, bibliographies, and biographies.

★5305★ ASGD-InterFace
John S. Rutkauskas, Contact
Quarterly. Informs members of the American Society for Geriatric Dentistry of news and activities. Recurring features include letters to the editor, news of research, a calendar of events, and notices of publications available.

★5306★ The Cranial Letter
The Cranial Academy
3500 Depauw Blvd. No. 1080
Indianapolis, IN 46268-1136
Ph: (317)879-0713
Dalla Hessler

Quarterly. Provides information about osteopathy in the cranio-sacral field for doctors of osteopathy, dentistry, and medicine. Carries news of reports, papers, seminars, courses offered by the Academy, and research projects. Recurring features include obituaries, a calendar of events, and columns titled President's Message, The Dental Corner, and Scientific Section.

★5307★ Current Opinion in Dentistry
Current Science
20 N. 3rd St.
Philadelphia, PA 19106-2113
Ph: (215)574-2266   Fax: (215)574-2270
Fr: 800-552-5866
S.T. Sonis

Quarterly. Journal for dental professionals.

★5308★ Holistic Dental Association— Communicator
Richard Shepard
Presents news and information supporting holistic dentistry. Recurring features include news of upcoming meetings and courses.

★5309★ Implantologist
Academy for Implants and Transplants
PO Box 223
Springfield, VA 22150
Ph: (703)451-0001

Annual. Discusses developments in the field of implant and transplant dentistry, with the purpose of assisting dentists in general practice. Carries articles on techniques and procedures in implant and transplant dentistry.

★5310★ JADA
ADA Publishers Inc.
211 E. Chicago Ave.
Chicago, IL 60611
Ph: (312)440-2740   Fax: (312)440-2550
James Berry

Monthly. Dental magazine.

★5311★ Journal of Dental Research
American Assn. for Dental Research
1111 14th St. NW, Ste. 1000
Washington, DC 20005
Ph: (202)898-1050   Fax: (202)789-1033
Linda T. Hemphill

Monthly. Dental science journal.

★5312★ Journal of the Michigan Dental Association
Michigan Dental Assn.
230 N. Washington Ave., Ste. 208
Lansing, MI 48933
Ph: (517)372-9070   Fax: (517)372-0008
David Foe

Journal focusing on the Michigan Dental Association and dentistry.

★5313★ NIDR Research Digest
National Institute of Dental Research
   (NIDR)
National Institute of Health
Bldg. 31, Rm. 2C35
Bethesda, MD 20892
Ph: (301)496-4261
Jody Dove

Irregular. Highlights recent dental research advances.

★5314★ Pediatric Dentistry Today
American Academy of Pediatric Dentistry
211 E. Chicago Ave., Ste. 1036
Chicago, IL 60611
Ph: (312)351-8387   Fax: (312)337-6329
Amy Fox

Reports on the activities of the Academy, which seeks to advance the specialty of pediatric dentistry through practice, education, and research. Recurring features include news of research, profiles of members, and legislative updates.

★5315★ *Westviews*
Western Dental Society (WDS)
6242 Westchester Pkwy., Ste. 220
Los Angeles, CA 90045
Ph: (213)641-5561   Fax: (213)641-3258
James Mead
Carries items relating to organized dentistry
and the clinical aspects of dentistry. Covers
local community events involving the organization or the profession; provides updates of
states agency actions affecting dentistry.

PROFESSIONAL MEETINGS AND CONVENTIONS

★5316★ Academy of General Dentistry
Annual Meeting
Anthony J. Jannetti, Inc.
N. Woodbury Rd., Box 56
Pitman, NJ 08071
Ph: (609)589-2319   Fax: (609)589-7463
Annual.

★5317★ American Academy of Pediatric
Dentistry Annual Meeting
American Academy of Pediatric Dentistry
211 E. Chicago Ave., Ste. 1036
Chicago, IL 60611
Ph: (312)337-2169
Annual. **Dates and Locations:** 1996 May;
Chicago, IL. • 1997 May; Philadelphia, PA.

★5318★ American Association of Dental
Schools Annual Session and
Exposition
American Association of Dental Schools
1625 Massachusetts Ave., NW
Washington, DC 20036
Ph: (202)667-9433   Fax: (202)667-0642
Annual.

★5319★ American Association of
Orthodontists Annual Session
American Association of Orthodontists
401 N. Lindbergh Blvd.
St. Louis, MO 63141-7816
Ph: (314)993-1700   Fax: (314)997-1745
Annual.

★5320★ American Dental Association
Annual Session
American Dental Association
211 E. Chicago Ave., Ste. 200
Chicago, IL 60611-2678
Ph: (312)440-2657   Fax: (312)440-2707
Annual. **Dates and Locations:** 1996 Sep 28-
02; Orlando, FL. • 1997 Oct 18-22; Washington, DC. • 1998 Oct 10-15; San Antonio, TX. •
1999 Oct 16-21; Las Vegas, NV. • 2000 Oct
28-02; Chicago, IL. •

★5321★ American Dental Society of
Anesthesiology Convention
American Dental Society of Anesthesiology
211 E. Chicago Ave., Ste. 948
Chicago, IL 60611
Ph: (312)664-8270   Fax: (312)642-9713
Annual.

★5322★ International Education
Congress of Dental Technology
Dental Laboratory Association of New York
State
42-01 215th Pl.
Bayside, NY 11361
Ph: (718)229-1001
Annual. **Dates and Locations:** 1995; Tarry-
town, NY.

★5323★ Liberty Dental Conference
Philadelphia County Dental Society
225 Washington E.
Philadelphia, PA 19106
Ph: (215)925-6050   Fax: (215)925-6998
Annual. **Dates and Locations:** 1996 Mar 08-
10; Philadelphia, PA.

★5324★ Mid-Continent Dental Congress
Convention
Greater St. Louis Dental Society
13667 Manchester Rd.
St. Louis, MO 63131
Ph: (314)965-5960   Fax: (314)965-4746
Annual.

★5325★ National Dental Association
Annual Convention
National Dental Association, Inc.
5506 Connecticut Ave., NW, Ste. 24-25
Washington, DC 20015
Ph: (202)244-7555   Fax: (202)244-5992
Annual. **Dates and Locations:** 1995; Phila-
delphia, PA.

★5326★ Star of the North Dental
Meeting
Minnesota Dental Association
2236 Marshall Ave.
St. Paul, MN 55104
Ph: (612)646-7454   Fax: (612)646-8246
Annual. Always held at the Convention Cen-
ter in Minneapolis, Minnesota.

★5327★ Thomas P. Hinman Dental
Meeting
Thomas P. Hinman Dental Society
60 Lenox Pte.
Atlanta, GA 30324
Ph: (404)231-1476   Fax: (404)231-9638
Annual. Always held during March at the At-
lanta Market Center in Atlanta, Georgia.
Dates and Locations: 1996 Mar 21-24; At-
lanta, GA. • 1997 Mar 20-23; Atlanta, GA.

★5328★ Yankee Dental Congress
Massachusetts Dental Society
83 Speen St.
Natick, MA 01760-4125
Ph: (508)651-7511   Fax: (508)653-7115

OTHER SOURCES OF INFORMATION

★5329★ *ASDA Handbook*
American Student Dental Association
(ASDA)
211 E. Chicago Ave., Ste. 840
Chicago, IL 60611
Ph: (312)440-2795
Annual. Contains extensive information on
succeeding in dental school. Includes information about scholarships, loans, research
opportunities, essay contests, and much
more.

★5330★ "Dentist" in *100 Best Jobs for
the 1990s & Beyond*
Dearborn Financial Publishing, Inc.
520 N. Dearborn St.
Chicago, IL 60610-4354
Ph: (312)836-4400   Fax: (312)836-1021
Fr: 800-621-9621
Carol Kleiman. 1992. Describes 100 jobs
ranging from accountants to veterinarians.
Each job profile includes such information as
education, experience, and certification
needed, salaries, and job search suggestions.

★5331★ "Dentist" in *Career Selector
2001*
Barron's Educational Series, Inc.
250 Wireless Blvd.
Hauppauge, NY 11788
Ph: (516)434-3311   Fax: (516)434-3723
Fr: 800-645-3476
James C. Gonyea. 1993.

★5332★ "Dentistry and Oral Sciences"
in *Accounting to Zoology: Graduate
Fields Defined* (pp. 253-255)
Petersons Guides, Inc.
PO Box 2123
Princeton, NJ 08543-2123
Ph: (609)243-9111   Fax: (609)243-9150
Fr: 800-338-3282
Amy J. Goldstein, editor. Revised and up-
dated, 1987. Discusses types of graduate
programs and degrees, graduate research,
applied work, employment prospects, and
trends.

★5333★ *Esthetic Restorations:
Improved Dentist-Laboratory
Communication*
Quintessence Publishing Co., Inc.
551 Kimberly Dr.
Carol Stream, IL 60188
Ph: (708)682-3223
Paul J. Muia, editor. 1993.

★5334★ *The Preveterinary Planning
Guide*
Betz Publishing Co.
PO Box 1745
Rockville, MD 20849
Ph: (301)340-0030   Fr: 800-634-4365
Jane D. Crawford. 1992. This book is a guide
to the veterinary school admission process.
Includes information on career opportunities
and standardized exams, interviewing, and
veterinary college enrollments.

Optometrists

Optometrists are primary eye care providers who examine people's eyes to diagnose and treat vision problems and, eye disease. They also test to insure that the patient has proper depth and color perception and the ability to focus and coordinate the eyes. Optometrists prescribe eyeglasses, contact lenses, vision therapy, and low-vision aids. When optometrists diagnose conditions requiring treatment beyond the optometric scope of practice, they arrange for consultation with the appropriate health care practitioners. Although most optometrists are in general practice, some specialize in work with the elderly or with children. Others work with partially sighted persons, who use microscopic or telescopic lenses. Still others concentrate on contact lenses, sports vision, or vision therapy. Optometrists also teach, do research, consult, and serve on health advisory committees of various kinds.

Salaries

Salaries vary greatly depending on location, specialization, and other factors.

Net earnings, beginning optometrists	$45,000/year
Experienced optometrists	$75,000/year

Employment Outlook

Growth rate until the year 2005: Average.

Optometrists

CAREER GUIDES

★5335★ Careers in Medicine
National Textbook Co. (NTC)
VGM Career Books
4255 W. Touhy Ave.
Lincolnwood, IL 60646-1975
Ph: (708)679-5500   Fax: (708)679-2494
Fr: 800-323-4900

Terry Sacks, editor. 1993. Guide to the various careers in the field of medicine.

★5336★ Careers in Medicine: Traditional and Alternative Opportunities
Garrett Park Press
PO Box 1907
Garrett Park, MD 20896-0190
Ph: (301)946-2553

T. Donald Rucker and Martin D. Keller. Revised edition, 1990. Written for college students who are considering applying to medical school, medical students attempting to select a specialty, and physicians who want to explore nonclinical work. Provides descriptions and employment outlook for 900 medical-oriented occupations.

★5337★ Health Careers
Careers, Inc.
PO Box 135
Largo, FL 34649-0135
Ph: (813)584-7333

1994. Four-page brief describing duties, working conditions, personal qualifications, training, earnings and hours, employment outlook, places of employment, related careers, and where to write for more information.

★5338★ Is Your Future in Sight
American Optometric Association (AOA)
243 N. Lindbergh Blvd.
St. Louis, MO 63141-9982
Ph: (314)991-4100

This eight-panel brochure briefly describes the advantages and variety of a career in optometry. Lists schools and colleges of optometry.

★5339★ Opportunities in Eye Care Careers
National Textbook Co. (NTC)
VGM Career Books
4255 W. Touhy Ave.
Lincolnwood, IL 60646-1975
Ph: (708)679-5500   Fax: (708)679-2494
Fr: 800-323-4900

Kathleen M. Ahrens. 1991. Describes job responsibilities, working conditions, salaries, and educational requirements.

★5340★ Opportunities in Optometry
National Textbook Co. (NTC)
VGM Career Books
4255 W. Touhy Ave.
Lincolnwood, IL 60646-1975
Ph: (708)679-5500   Fax: (708)679-2494
Fr: 800-323-4900

Frank M. Kitchell. Overviews the latest trends in treatment and technology, including the use of soft contact lenses.

★5341★ Optometrist
Vocational Biographies, Inc.
PO Box 31
Sauk Centre, MN 56378-0031
Ph: (612)352-6516   Fax: (612)352-5546
Fr: 800-255-0752

1994. Four-page pamphlet containing a personal narrative about a worker's job, work likes and dislikes, career path from high school to the present, education and training, the rewards and frustrations, and the effects of the job on the rest of the worker's life. The data file portion of this pamphlet gives a concise occupational summary, including work description, working conditions, places of employment, personal characteristics, education and training, job outlook, and salary range.

★5342★ Optometrist
Careers, Inc.
PO Box 135
Largo, FL 34649-0135
Ph: (813)584-7333

1994. Two-page occupational summary card describing duties, working conditions, personal qualifications, training, earnings and hours, employment outlook, places of employment, related careers, and where to write for more information.

★5343★ "Optometrist" in Career Information Center (Vol.7)
Simon and Schuster
200 Old Tappan Rd.
Old Tappan, NJ 07675
Fax: 800-445-6991   Fr: 800-223-2348

Richard Lidz and Linda Perrin, editorial directors. Fifth edition, 1993. This 13-volume set profiles over 600 occupations. Each occupational profile describes job duties, entry-level requirements, educational requirements, advancement possibilities, employment outlook, working conditions, earnings and benefits, and where to write for more information.

★5344★ "Optometrist" in College Board Guide to Jobs and Career Planning (pp. 250)
The College Board
415 Columbus Ave.
New York, NY 10023-6992
Ph: (212)713-8165   Fax: (212)713-8143
Fr: 800-323-7155

Joyce S. Mitchell. Second edition, 1994. Describes the job, salaries, related careers, education needed, and where to write for more information.

★5345★ "Optometrist" in Guide to Federal Jobs (p. 140)
Resource Directories
3361 Executive Pkwy., Ste. 302
Toledo, OH 43606
Ph: (419)536-5353   Fax: (419)536-7056
Fr: 800-274-8515

Rod W. Durgin, editor. Third edition, 1992. Contains information on finding and applying for federal jobs. Describes more than 200 professional and technical jobs for college graduates. Covers the nature of the work, salary, and geographic location. Lists college majors preferred for that occupation. Section one describes the function and work of government agencies that hire the most significant number of college graduates.

★5346★ "Optometrist" in Jobs Rated Almanac
World Almanac
1 International Blvd., Ste. 444
Mahwah, NJ 07495
Ph: (201)529-6900   Fax: (201)529-6901

Les Krantz. Second edition, 1992. Ranks 250 jobs by environment, salary, outlooks, physical demands, stress, security, travel opportunities, and extra perks. Includes jobs the editor feels are the most common, most interesting, and the most rapidly growing.

★5347★ "Optometrist" in *VGM's Careers Encyclopedia*
National Textbook Co. (NTC)
VGM Career Books
4255 W. Touhy Ave.
Lincolnwood, IL 60646-1975
Ph: (708)679-5500   Fax: (708)679-2494
Fr: 800-323-4900

Third edition, 1991. Describes job duties, places of employment, working conditions, qualifications, education, and training, advancement potential, and salary for each occupation.

★5348★ "Optometrist" in *VGM's Handbook of Health Care Careers*
National Textbook Co.
4255 W. Touhy Ave.
Lincolnwood, IL 60646-1975
Ph: (708)679-5500   Fax: (708)679-2494
Fr: 800-323-4900

Annette Selden. 1993. Contains 42 two-page occupational profiles describing job duties, places of employment, working conditions, qualifications, education, employment outlook, and income.

★5349★ *Optometrists*
Chronicle Guidance Publications, Inc.
66 Aurora St.
PO Box 1190
Moravia, NY 13118-1190
Ph: (315)497-0330   Fax: (315)497-3359
Fr: 800-622-7284

1993. Career brief describing the nature of the job, working conditions, hours and earnings, education and training, licensure, certification, unions, personal qualifications, social and psychological factors, location, employment outlook, entry methods, advancement, and related occupations.

★5350★ "Optometrists" in *101 Careers: A Guide to the Fastest-Growing Opportunities* (pp. 235-237)
John Wiley & Sons, Inc.
605 3rd Ave.
New York, NY 10158-0012
Ph: (212)850-6645   Fax: (212)850-6088

Michael Harkavy. 1990. Describes the nature of the job, working conditions, employment growth, qualifications, personal skills, projected salaries, and where to write for more information.

★5351★ "Optometrists" in *American Almanac of Jobs and Salaries* (p. 478)
Avon Books
1350 Avenue of the Americas
New York, NY 10019
Ph: (212)261-6800   Fr: 800-238-0658

John Wright, editor. Revised and updated, 1994-95. This is comprehensive guide to the wages of hundreds of occupations in a wide variety of industries and organizations.

★5352★ "Optometrists" in *Best Jobs for the 1990s and Into the 21st Century*
Impact Publications
9104-N Manassas Dr.
Manassas Park, VA 22111
Ph: (703)361-7300   Fax: (703)335-9486

Ronald L. Krannich and Caryl Rae Krannich. 1993.

★5353★ "Optometrists" in *Career Discovery Encyclopedia* (Vol.4, pp. 148-149)
J.G. Ferguson Publishing Co.
200 W. Madison St., Ste. 300
Chicago, IL 60606
Ph: (312)580-5480   Fax: (312)580-4948

Russell E. Primm, editor-in-chief. 1993. This six volume set contains two-page articles for 504 occupations. Each article describes job duties, earnings, and educational and training requirements. The whole set is arranged alphabetically by job title. Designed for junior high and older students.

★5354★ "Optometrists" in *Encyclopedia of Careers and Vocational Guidance* (Vol.3, pp. 637-639)
J.G. Ferguson Publishing Co.
200 W. Madison St., Ste. 300
Chicago, IL 60606
Ph: (312)580-5480   Fax: (312)580-4948

William E. Hopke, editor-in-chief. Ninth edition, 1993. Four-volume set that profiles 900 occupations and describes job trends in 74 industries. Includes career description, educational requirements, history of the job, methods of entry, advancement, employment outlook, earnings, conditions of work, social and psychological factors, and sources of further information.

★5355★ "Optometrists" in *Health Care Job Explosion!* (pp. 309-316)
D-Amp Publications
401 Amherst Ave.
Coraopolis, PA 15108
Ph: (412)262-5578

Dennis V. Damp. 1993. Provides information on the nature of work for the major health care occupational groups. Descriptions include working conditions, training, job outlook, qualifications, and related occupations.

★5356★ "Optometrists" in *Jobs! What They Are—Where They Are—What They Pay* (p. 256)
Simon & Schuster, Inc.
Simon & Schuster Bldg.
1230 Avenue of the Americas
New York, NY 10020
Ph: (212)698-7000   Fr: 800-223-2348

Robert O. Snelling and Anne M. Snelling. 3rd edition, 1992. Describes duties and responsibilities, earnings, employment opportunities, training, and qualifications.

★5357★ "Optometrists" in *Occupational Outlook Handbook*
U.S. Government Printing Office
Superintendent of Documents
Washington, DC 20402
Ph: (202)512-1800   Fax: (202)512-2250

Biennial, latest edition, 1994-95. Encyclopedia of careers describing about 250 occupations and comprising about 85 percent of all

jobs in the economy. Occupations that require lengthy education or training are given the most attention. Each occupation's profile describes what the worker does on the job, working conditions, education and training requirements, advancement possibilities, job outlook, earnings, and sources of additional information.

★5358★ "Optometry" in *Black Woman's Career Guide* (pp. 108-109)
Bantam Doubleday Dell
1540 Broadway
New York, NY 10036
Fax: 800-233-3294   Fr: 800-223-5780

Beatryce Nivens. Revised edition, 1987. Part 1 describes career planning, resume writing, job hunting, and interviewing. Part 2 profiles 60 black women pioneers in 20 different career areas.

PROFESSIONAL ASSOCIATIONS

★5359★ American Optometric Association (AOA)
243 N. Lindbergh Blvd.
St. Louis, MO 63141
Ph: (314)991-4100   Fax: (314)991-4101

Members: Professional society of optometrists, students of optometry, and paraoptometric assistants and technicians. **Purpose:** To improve the quality, availability, and accessibility of eye and vision care; to represent the optometric profession; to help members conduct their practices; to promote the highest standards of patient care. Monitors and promotes legislation concerning the scope of optometric practice, alternate health care delivery systems, health care cost containment, Medicare, and other issues relevant to eye/vision care. Supports the International Library, Archives and Museum of Optometry which includes references on ophthalmic and related sciences with emphasis on the history and socieconomic aspects of optometry. Operates Vision U.S.A. program, which provides free eye care to the working poor. Conducts specialized education program and charitable programs; operates placement service; compiles statistics. Maintains museum. Conducts Seal of Certification and Acceptance Program. **Publications:** *American Optometric Association—News*, semimonthly. • *Journal of the American Optometric Association*, monthly. • *Optometric Economics*, monthly.

★5360★ Association of Schools and Colleges of Optometry (ASCO)
6110 Executive Blvd., Ste. 690
Rockville, MD 20852
Ph: (301)231-5944   Fax: (301)770-1828

Members: Institutional members of 17 schools and colleges of optometry in the U.S. and two in Canada. **Purpose:** Promotes academic optometry. **Publications:** *Admissions to Schools and Colleges of Optometry*, annual. • *Annual Survey of Optometric Education*, annual. • *Eye on Education*, quarterly. • *Faculty Directory*, semiannual. • *Journal of Optometric Education*, quarterly. •

Optometric Education, quarterly. • *Residency and Graduate Program Directory*, annual.

STANDARDS/CERTIFICATION AGENCIES

★5361★ American Optometric Association (AOA)
243 N. Lindbergh Blvd.
St. Louis, MO 63141
Ph: (314)991-4100   Fax: (314)991-4101
Promotes the highest standards of patient care. Monitors and promotes legislation concerning the scope of optometric practice, alternate health care delivery systems, health care cost containment, Medicare, and other issues relevant to eye/vision care. Conducts Seal of Certification and Acceptance Program.

TEST GUIDES

★5362★ *Career Examination Series: Optometrist*
National Learning Corp.
212 Michael Dr.
Syosset, NY 11791
Ph: (516)921-8888   Fax: (516)921-8743
Fr: 800-645-6337
Jack Rudman. A study guide for professionals and trainees in the field of optometry. Includes a multiple-choice examination section; provides answers.

★5363★ *Optometry Admission Test (OAT)*
National Learning Corp.
212 Michael Dr.
Syosset, NY 11791
Ph: (516)921-8888   Fax: (516)921-8743
Fr: 800-645-6337
Jack Rudman. Part of the Admission Test series. A sample test for potential optometrists who are seeking admission to graduate and professional schools or seeking entrance or advancement in institutional and public career service.

EDUCATIONAL DIRECTORIES AND PROGRAMS

★5364★ *Blue Book of Optometrists*
Butterworth-Heinemann
313 Washington St.
Newton, MA 02158
Ph: (617)928-2646   Fax: (617)279-4851
Fr: 800-366-2665
Christine Swanson, Contact
Annual, November. Covers nearly 30,000 optometrists, optical supply houses, manufacturers and import firms, associations, national and state examining board members, colleges and programs concerned with optometry and para-optometry; coverage includes Canada. Entries include: For optometrists—Name, office address, phone; personal, education, and career data; specialty. Arrangement: Geographical.

★5365★ *Encyclopedia of Medical Organizations and Agencies*
Gale Research Inc.
835 Penobscot Bldg.
Detroit, MI 48226-4094
Ph: (313)961-2242   Fax: (313)961-6741
Fr: 800-877-GALE
Karen Boyden, Contact
Biennial, November of odd years. Covers over 13,400 state, national, and international medical associations, foundations, research institutes, federal and state agencies, and medical and allied health schools. Entries include: Organization name, address, phone; many listings include names and titles of key personnel, descriptive annotations. Arrangement: Classified by subject, then by type of organization.

★5366★ *Gourman Report: A Rating of Graduate and Professional Programs in American and International Universities*
National Education Standards
624 S. Grand Ave., Ste. 1210
Los Angeles, CA 90017
Ph: (213)623-9135
Jack Gourman
Irregular, previous edition 1989; latest edition January, 1993. Covers colleges and universities offering graduate programs in a variety of disciplines; medical schools; law schools; schools of dentistry; optometry; pharmacy. Entries include: Institution name, address, author's description and evaluation. Arrangement: Law, medical, dental, and pharmacy schools are listed by country; others (primarily in United States) are by discipline.

★5367★ *Health & Medical Industry Directory*
American Business Directories, Inc.
5711 S. 86th Circle
Omaha, NE 68127
Ph: (402)593-4600   Fax: (402)331-1505
Released 1993. Lists over 1.1 million physicians and surgeons, dentists, clinics, health clubs, and other health-related businesses in the U.S. and Canada. Entries include: Name, address, phone.

★5368★ *Healthcare Career Directory— Nurses and Physicians*
Gale Research Inc.
835 Penobscot Bldg.
Detroit, MI 48226-4094
Ph: (313)961-2242   Fax: (313)961-6083
Fr: 800-877-GALE
Bradley J. Morgan and Joseph M. Palmisano. Second edition, 1993. A directory in the Career Advisor Series that provides essays written by industry professionals; job search information on resume and cover letter preparation, networking, and the interviewing process; approximately 300 companies and organizations offering job opportunities and internships, and additional job-hunting resources.

★5369★ *Optometry: A Career with Vision*
American Optometric Association
243 N. Lindbergh Blvd.
St. Louis, MO 63141
Ph: (314)991-4100   Fax: (314)991-4100
L. Baumstark, Contact
Annual, January; latest edition fall 1994. Covers about 20 optometry schools. Entries include: School name, address, phone; name of contact; admission requirements; statistical profile of students in program. Arrangement: Alphabetical.

AWARDS, SCHOLARSHIPS, GRANTS, AND FELLOWSHIPS

★5370★ Apollo Award
American Optometric Association
234 N. Lindbergh Blvd.
St. Louis, MO 63141
Ph: (314)991-4100   Fax: (314)991-4101
This, optometry's highest honor, is given to recognize individuals or groups who have made, or are making significant contributions to the visual welfare of the public. The nomination deadline is December 1. A bronze trophy of Phoebus Apollo is awarded annually at the national meeting in June. Established in 1961.

★5371★ Garland W. Clay Award
American Academy of Optometry
4330 East West Hwy., Ste. 1117
Bethesda, MD 20814
Ph: (301)718-6500   Fax: (301)656-0989
For recognition of the author of a significant paper on clinical optometry published in *Optometry and Vision Science* and selected by the editorial council. A plaque and expenses to attend the annual meeting are awarded annually. Established in 1978 by the Clay family in memory of Garland W. Clay, academy president 1975-76.

★5372★ Distinguished Service Award
American Optometric Association
234 N. Lindbergh Blvd.
St. Louis, MO 63141
Ph: (314)991-4100   Fax: (314)991-4101
For recognition of doctors of optometry for unusually significant contributions to the advancement of the profession. The award is designed to recognize long term dedication rather than any single contribution. A plaque is awarded annually. Established in 1980.

★5373★ Eminent Service Award
American Academy of Optometry
4330 East West Hwy., Ste. 1117
Bethesda, MD 20814
Ph: (301)718-6500   Fax: (301)656-0989
For recognition of a fellow who has made distinguished, exemplary, or unique contributions to the academy. Nominations may be made to the awards committee by any member of the academy. Established in 1960.

★5374★ William Feinbloom Award
American Academy of Optometry
4330 East West Hwy., Ste. 1117
Bethesda, MD 20814
Ph: (301)718-6500   Fax: (301)656-0989

To recognize an individual who has made a distinguished and significant contribution to clinical excellence and the direct clinical advancement of visual and optometric service, and thus the visual enhancement of the public. Individuals who have made a distinguished and significant contribution to the total spectrum of clinical achievements are considered. Nominations must be received by the Academy Awards Chairman by June 1. A metallic wall shield and expenses to attend the annual meeting are awarded when merited. Established in 1983 in memory of William Feinbloom, a pioneer in low vision.

★5375★ G. N. Getman Award
College of Optometrists in Vision
    Development
PO Box 285
Chula Vista, CA 91912-0285
Ph: (619)425-6191   Fax: (619)425-0733

For recognition of outstanding contributions in the field of vision development by an optometrist. A plaque is awarded annually. Established in 1970.

★5376★ Honorary and Life Fellowships
American Academy of Optometry
4330 East West Hwy., Ste. 1117
Bethesda, MD 20814
Ph: (301)718-6500   Fax: (301)656-0989

Honorary Fellowships recognize individuals who are not academy fellows for distinguished contributions in the academy and/or the science and art of optometry. Life Fellowships recognize those fellows who through long-time memberships in the academy have rendered distinguished service to the science and art of optometry. Established about 1964.

★5377★ HRSA-BHP Health Professions Student Loans
U.S. Public Health Service
Health Resources and Services
    Administration
Parklawn Bldg., Rm. 8-38
5600 Fishers Ln.
Rockville, MD 20857

Purpose: To assist students with need for financial assistance to undertake the course of study required to become physicians, dentists, osteopathic physicians, optometrists, pharmacists, podiatrists, or veterinarians. Qualifications: Applicants must be enrolled or accepted for enrollment as full-time students in a program leading to a doctoral degree in medicine, dental surgery or equivalent degree, pharmacy, osteopathic medicine, optometry or equivalent degree, podiatric medicine or equivalent degree, or veterinary medicine or equivalent degree; or a bachelor of science in pharmacy or equivalent degree. Applicants must also be citizens, nationals, or permanent residents of the United States or the District of Columbia, the Commonwealths of Puerto Rico or the Marianna Islands, the Virgin Islands, Guam, The American Samoa, the Trust Territory of the Pacific Islands, the Republic of Palau, the Republic of the Marshall Islands, and the Federated State of Micronesia. Applicants must also demonstrate

financial need. Professional students, interns, residents, and students seeking advanced training are not eligible. Funds available: Up to the cost of tuition plus $2,500 or the amount of financial need, whichever is less. The interest rate is five percent and accrues during the repayment period. Loans are repayable over a ten year period and beginning one year after the student graduates or ceases to enroll full-time in a health program.

★5378★ HRSA-BHP Loans for Disadvantaged Students
U.S. Public Health Service
Health Resources and Services
    Administration
Parklawn Bldg., Rm. 8-38
5600 Fishers Ln.
Rockville, MD 20857

Purpose: To assist students who need financial assistance to pursue careers in medicine, osteopathic medicine, dentistry, optometry, podiatric medicine, pharmacy, or veterinary medicine. Qualifications: Applicants must be citizens, nationals, or lawful permanent residents of the United States or the District of Columbia, the Commonwealths of Puerto Rico or the Marianna Islands, the Virgin Islands, Guam, American Samoa, the Trust Territory of the Pacific Islands, the Republic of Palau, the Republic of the Marshall Islands, or the Federated State of Micronesia. They must also be enrolled or accepted for enrollment at a participating health professionals school full-time. Students must be determined by their school's financial aid director to meet financial need and "disadvantaged background" criteria. Those enrolled in schools of medicine or osteopathic medicine must demonstrate exceptional financial need. Preprofessional students, interns, residents, and students seeking advanced training are not eligible. Selection criteria: Schools are responsible for selecting recipients and for determining the amount of assistance. Funds available: The maximum loan amount allowed for each school year is the cost of tuition plus $2,500, or the amount of financial need, whichever is lesser. The repayment interest rate is five percent over a ten-year period, which begins one year after completion of cessation of full-time study. Interest begins accruing at the time the loan becomes rapayable. Repayment may be deferred under special circumstances, and interest does not accrue during periods of deferment.

★5379★ Julius F. Neumueller Award in Optics
American Academy of Optometry
4330 East West Hwy., Ste. 1117
Bethesda, MD 20814
Ph: (301)718-6500   Fax: (301)656-0989

For recognition of an outstanding paper of not more than 3,000 words on one of the following topics: geometrical optics, physical optics, opthalmic optics, or optics of the eye. Students enrolled in accredited schools of optometry may submit papers by May 1. A monetary prize of about $500 and a plaque are awarded annually when merited. Established in 1969 through a trust fund set up by Dr. Julius F. Neumueller.

★5380★ Optometrist of the Year Award
American Optometric Association
234 N. Lindbergh Blvd.
St. Louis, MO 63141
Ph: (314)991-4100   Fax: (314)991-4101

For recognition of outstanding service by a doctor of optometry to the profession of optometry, service on behalf of the visual welfare of the public, and service to the community at large. Members of the Association are eligible for nomination by May 1. A plaque is awarded annually at the national meeting in June. Established in 1967.

★5381★ A. M. Skeffington Award
College of Optometrists in Vision
    Development
PO Box 285
Chula Vista, CA 91912-0285
Ph: (619)425-6191   Fax: (619)425-0733

For recognition of outstanding contributions by a Fellow to optometric literature. A plaque is awarded annually. Established in 1970.

BASIC REFERENCE GUIDES AND HANDBOOKS

★5382★ Contact Lenses: Procedures and Techniques
Butterworth-Heinemann Publishers
80 Montvale Ave.
Stoneham, MA 02180
Ph: (617)775-4438   Fr: 800-548-4001

Gerald E. Lowther. 1992. Includes bibliographical references and an index.

★5383★ Fact Sheet: Health Education Assistance Loan Program (HEAL)
U.S. Department of Health and Human
    Services
Public Health Service
Health Resources and Services
    Administration
Bureau of Health Professions, Division of
    Student Assistance
Rockville, MD 20857
Ph: (301)443-2086

Fact sheet describing the HEAL Program; covers eligible schools, borrowers, and lenders, as well as loan limitations, interest, and repayment.

★5384★ Optometrists Desk Reference
Butterworth-Heinemann Publishers
80 Montvale Ave.
Stoneham, MA 02180
Ph: (617)438-8464   Fr: 800-548-4001

Leroy Rubin, editor. 1987. Includes an index.

PROFESSIONAL AND TRADE PERIODICALS

★5385★ Eyewitness
Contact Lens Society of America
11735 Bowman Green Dr.
Reston, VA 22090
Ph: (703)437-5100   Fax: (703)437-0727
Thomas V. Appler

Quarterly. Informs members of developments in the contact lens industry. Also reports on related educational information and technical papers. Recurring features include news of research, calendar of events, reports of meetings, and associate member listing.

★5386★ Journal of the American Optometric Association
American Optometric Assn.
243 N. Lindbergh Blvd.
Saint Louis, MO 63141
Ph: (314)991-4100   Fax: (314)991-4101
John Potter

Monthly. Optometry journal.

PROFESSIONAL MEETINGS AND CONVENTIONS

★5387★ Contact Lens Association of Ophthalmologists National Meeting
Contact Lens Association of Ophthalmologists
523 Decatur, Ste. 1
New Orleans, LA 70130
Ph: (504)581-4000   Fax: (504)581-5884
Annual.

★5388★ International Vision Expo and Conference East
Association Expositions & Services
1100 Summer St.
Stamford, CT 06905
Ph: (203)325-5099   Fax: (203)325-5001

Annual. Always held during March at the Jacob Javits Convention Center in New York, New York. **Dates and Locations:** 1996 Mar 29-31; New York, NY. • 1997 Mar 21-23; New York, NY.

★5389★ Southern Educational Congress of Optometry
Southern Council of Optometrists
4661 N. Shallowford Rd.
Atlanta, GA 30338
Ph: (404)451-8206   Fax: (404)451-3156
Annual. Always held during February at the Inforum in Atlanta, Georgia. **Dates and Locations:** 1996 Feb 21-25; Atlanta, GA. • 1997 Feb 27-03; Atlanta, GA.

OTHER SOURCES OF INFORMATION

★5390★ "Optometry and Vision Sciences" in Accounting to Zoology: Graduate Fields Defined (pp. 279-280)
Petersons Guides, Inc.
PO Box 2123
Princeton, NJ 08543-2123
Ph: (609)243-9111   Fax: (609)243-9150
Fr: 800-338-3282

Amy J. Goldstein, editor. Revised and updated, 1987. Discusses types of graduate programs and degrees, graduate research, applied work, employment prospects and trends.

Physicians

Physicians perform medical examinations, diagnose illnesses, and treat people who are suffering from injury or disease. They also advise patients on good health practices. There are two types of physicians: the M.D., Doctor of Medicine, and the D.O., Doctor of Osteopathic Medicine. While M.D.'s and D.O.'s may use all accepted methods of treatment, including drugs and surgery, D.O.'s place special emphasis on the body's muscoskeletal system. They believe that good health requires proper alignment of the bones, muscles, ligaments, and nerves. Physicians may be general practitioners or they may specialize in a particular field of medicine. High-technology medicine requires much skill and training. Its dominant role in American medical care underlies the system of specialty medicine. In fact, most M.D.'s are specialists. Medical specialties for which there is training include internal medicine, general surgery, obstetrics and gynecology, psychiatry, pediatrics, radiology, anesthesiology, ophthalmology, pathology, and orthopedic surgery. While most M.D.'s specialize, D.O.'s tend to be primary care providers such as family practitioners.

Salaries

Physicians have among the highest average annual earnings of any occupation, although earnings vary according to specialty, years in practice, geographic region, hours worked, and the physician's skill, personality, and professional reputation.

Residents	$28,618-$36,258/year
Physicians	$155,000/year

Employment Outlook

Growth rate until the year 2005: Faster than the average.

Physicians

CAREER GUIDES

★5391★ Careers in Medicine
National Textbook Co. (NTC)
VGM Career Books
4255 W. Touhy Ave.
Lincolnwood, IL 60646-1975
Ph: (708)679-5500   Fax: (708)679-2494
Fr: 800-323-4900
Terry Sacks, editor. 1993. Guide to the various careers in the field of medicine.

★5392★ Careers in Medicine
Rosen Publishing Group
29 E. 21st St.
New York, NY 10010
Ph: (212)777-3017   Fax: (212)777-0277
Fr: 800-237-9932
Carolyn Simpson and Penelope Hall, M.D. 1993. Discusses the qualities a good doctor must possess and how a young person can combine a desire to help others with the practical aspects of getting into and through medical school.

★5393★ Careers in Medicine: Traditional and Alternative Opportunities
Garrett Park Press
PO Box 1907
Garrett Park, MD 20896-0190
Ph: (301)946-2553
T. Donald Rucker and Martin D. Keller. Revised edition, 1990. Written for college students who are considering applying to medical school, medical students attempting to select a specialty, and physicians who want to explore nonclinical work. Provides descriptions and employment outlook for 900 medical-oriented occupations.

★5394★ "Doctor" in College Board Guide to Jobs and Career Planning (pp. 245)
The College Board
415 Columbus Ave.
New York, NY 10023-6992
Ph: (212)713-8165   Fax: (212)713-8143
Fr: 800-323-7155
Joyce S. Mitchell. Second edition, 1994. Describes the job, salaries, related careers, education needed, and where to write for more information.

★5395★ "Doctors" in American Almanac of Jobs and Salaries (pp. 230)
Avon Books
1350 Avenue of the Americas
New York, NY 10019
Ph: (212)261-6800   Fr: 800-238-0658
John Wright, editor. Revised and updated, 1994-95. This is a comprehensive guide to the wages of hundreds of occupations in a wide variety of industries and organizations.

★5396★ "Environmental Physician" in Opportunities in Environmental Careers
National Textbook Co. (NTC)
VGM Career Books
4255 W. Touhy Ave.
Lincolnwood, IL 60646-1975
Ph: (708)679-5500   Fax: (708)679-2494
Fr: 800-323-4900
Odom Fanning. 1991. Describes a broad range of opportunities in fields such as environmental health, recreation, physics, and hygiene.

★5397★ Family Practice Physician
Vocational Biographies, Inc.
PO Box 31
Sauk Centre, MN 56378-0031
Ph: (612)352-6516   Fax: (612)352-5546
Fr: 800-255-0752
1993. Four-page pamphlet containing a personal narrative about a worker's job, work likes and dislikes, career path from high school to the present, education and training, the rewards and frustrations, and the effects of the job on the rest of the worker's life. The data file portion of this pamphlet gives a concise occupational summary, including work description, working conditions, places of employment, personal characteristics, education and training, job outlook, and salary range.

★5398★ "Health Care" in Where the Jobs Are: The Hottest Careers for the 90s (pp. 143-166)
Career Press
180 5th Ave.
Hawthorne, NJ 07507
Ph: (201)427-0229   Fax: (201)427-2037
Fr: 800-CAREER-1
Joyce Hadley. 1995. Offers a job-hunting strategy for the 1990s as well as descriptions of growing careers of the decade. Each pro-

file includes general information, forecasts, growth, education and training, licensing requirements, and salary information.

★5399★ Health Careers
Careers, Inc.
PO Box 135
Largo, FL 34649-0135
Ph: (813)584-7333
1994. Four-page brief describing duties, working conditions, personal qualifications, training, earnings and hours, employment outlook, places of employment, related careers, and where to write for more information.

★5400★ "Medical Officer (Physician)" in Guide to Federal Jobs (p. 128)
Resource Directories
3361 Executive Pkwy., Ste. 302
Toledo, OH 43606
Ph: (419)536-5353   Fax: (419)536-7056
Fr: 800-274-8515
Rod W. Durgin, editor. Third edition, 1992. Contains information on finding and applying for federal jobs. Describes more than 200 professional and technical jobs for college graduates. Covers the nature of the work, salary, and geographic location. Lists college majors preferred for that occupation. Section one describes the function and work of government agencies that hire the most significant number of college graduates.

★5401★ "Medicine" in Black Woman's Career Guide (pp. 100-105)
Bantam Doubleday Dell
1540 Broadway
New York, NY 10036
Fax: 800-233-3294   Fr: 800-223-5780
Beatryce Nivens. Revised edition, 1987. Part 1 discusses career planning, resume writing, job hunting, and interviewing. Part 2 profiles 60 black women pioneers in 20 different career areas.

★5402★ "Medicine" in College Majors and Careers: A Resource Guide to Effective Life Planning (p. 95)
Garrett Park Press
PO Box 1907
Garrett Park, MD 20896
Ph: (301)946-2553
Paul Phifer. Revised, 1993. Lists 60 college majors, with definitions; related occupations

and leisure activities; skills, values, and personal attributes needed; suggested readings; and a list of associations.

★5403★ "Medicine" in *Straight Talk on Careers: Eighty Pros Take You Into Their Professions* (pp. 160-174)
Garrett Park Press
PO Box 1907
Garrett Park, MD 20896
Ph: (301)946-2553

Mary Barbera-Hogan. 1987. Contains candid interviews from people who give an inside view of their work in 80 different careers. These professionals describe a day's work and the stresses and rewards accompanying their work.

★5404★ *Ophthalmologist*
Careers, Inc.
PO Box 135
Largo, FL 34649-0135
Ph: (813)584-7333

1994. Two-page summary describing duties, working conditions, personal qualifications, training, earnings and hours, employment outlook, places of employment, related careers, and where to write for more information.

★5405★ "Ophthalmologist" in *VGM's Handbook of Health Care Careers*
National Textbook Co.
4255 W. Touhy Ave.
Lincolnwood, IL 60646-1975
Ph: (708)679-5500   Fax: (708)679-2494
Fr: 800-323-4900

Annette Selden. 1993. Contains 42 two-page occupational profiles describing job duties, places of employment, working conditions, qualifications, education, employment outlook, and income.

★5406★ *Opportunities in Fitness Careers*
National Textbook Co. (NTC)
VGM Career Books
4255 W. Touhy Ave.
Lincolnwood, IL 60646-1975
Ph: (708)679-5500   Fax: (708)679-2494
Fr: 800-323-4900

Jean Rosenbaum and Mary Prine. 1991. Surveys fitness related careers, including the physical therapy profession. Describes career opportunities, education and experience needed, how to get into entry-level jobs and what income to expect. Schools are listed in the appendix.

★5407★ *Opportunities in Health and Medical Careers*
National Textbook Co. (NTC)
VGM Career Books
4255 W. Touhy Ave.
Lincolnwood, IL 60646-1975
Ph: (708)679-5500   Fax: (708)679-2494
Fr: 800-323-4900

I. Donald Snook Jr., Leo D'Orazio. Describes the working conditions of physicians, physician assistants, therapists, nurses, technicians, administrators, and hospital staff. Also includes information on educational requirements and salaries.

★5408★ *Opportunities in Physician Careers*
National Textbook Co. (NTC)
VGM Career Books
4255 W. Touhy Ave.
Lincolnwood, IL 60646-1175
Ph: (708)679-5500   Fax: (708)679-2494
Fr: 800-323-4900

Jan Sugar-Webb. Overviews specialities in medicine, including pediatrics, neurology, dermatology, and internal medicine. Also offers information on preparing for medical school, working conditions, salary ranges, and employment prospects.

★5409★ *Osteopathic Physician*
Careers, Inc.
PO Box 135
Largo, FL 34649-0135
Ph: (813)584-7333

1994. Four-page brief offering the definition, history, duties, working conditions, personal qualifications, educational requirements, earnings, hours, employment outlook, advancement, and careers related to this position.

★5410★ "Osteopathic Physician" in *College Board Guide to Jobs and Career Planning* (pp. 252)
The College Board
415 Columbus Ave.
New York, NY 10023-6992
Ph: (212)713-8165   Fax: (212)713-8143
Fr: 800-323-7155

Joyce S. Mitchell. Second edition, 1994. Describes the job, salaries, related careers, education needed, and where to write for more information.

★5411★ "Osteopathic Physician" in *VGM's Careers Encyclopedia*
National Textbook Co. (NTC)
VGM Career Books
4255 W. Touhy Ave.
Lincolnwood, IL 60646-1975
Ph: (708)679-5500   Fax: (708)679-2494
Fr: 800-323-4900

Third edition, 1991. Describes job duties, places of employment, working conditions, qualifications, education, training, advancement potential, and salary for each occupation.

★5412★ "Osteopathic Physician" in *VGM's Handbook of Health Care Careers*
National Textbook Co.
4255 W. Touhy Ave.
Lincolnwood, IL 60646-1975
Ph: (708)679-5500   Fax: (708)679-2494
Fr: 800-323-4900

Annette Selden. 1993. Contains 42 two-page occupational profiles describing job duties, places of employment, working conditions, qualifications, education, employment outlook, and income.

★5413★ "Osteopathic Physicians" in *Career Discovery Encyclopedia* (Vol.4, pp. 154-155)
J.G. Ferguson Publishing Co.
200 W. Madison St., Ste. 300
Chicago, IL 60606
Ph: (312)580-5480   Fax: (312)580-4948

Russell E. Primm, editor-in chief. 1993. This six volume set contains two-page articles for 504 occupations. Each article describes job duties, earnings, and educational and training requirements. The whole set is arranged alphabetically by job title. Designed for junior high and older students.

★5414★ *Pediatrician*
Vocational Biographies, Inc.
PO Box 31
Sauk Centre, MN 56378-0031
Ph: (612)352-6516   Fax: (612)352-5546
Fr: 800-255-0752

1994. Four-page pamphlet containing a personal narrative about a worker's job, work likes and dislikes, career path from high school to the present, education and training, the rewards and frustrations, and the effects of the job on the rest of the worker's life. The data file portion of this pamphlet gives a concise occupational summary, including work description, working conditions, places of employment, personal characteristics, education and training, job outlook, and salary range.

★5415★ *Physician*
Careers, Inc.
PO Box 135
Largo, FL 34649-0135
Ph: (813)584-7333

1994. Four-page brief describing duties, working conditions, personal qualifications, training, earnings and hours, employment outlook, places of employment, related careers, and where to write for more information.

★5416★ "Physician" in *100 Best Careers for the Year 2000* (pp. 1-2)
Arco Pub.
201 W. 103rd St.
Indianapolis, IN 46290
Ph: 800-428-5331   Fax: 800-835-3202

Shelly Field. 1992. Describes 100 job opportunities expected to grow fast throughout the next decade. Provides information on job duties and responsibilities, training requirements, education, advancement opportunities, experience and qualifications, and typical salaries.

★5417★ "Physician (General Practice)" in *Jobs Rated Almanac*
World Almanac
1 International Blvd., Ste. 444
Mahwah, NJ 07495
Ph: (201)529-6900   Fax: (201)529-6901

Les Krantz. Second edition, 1992. Ranks 250 jobs by environment, salary, outlooks, physical demands, stress, security, travel opportunities, and extra perks. Includes jobs the editor feels are the most common, most interesting, and the most rapidly growing.

★5418★ **"Physician" and "Osteopathic Physician" in** *Career Information Center* **(Vol.7)**
Simon and Schuster
200 Old Tappan Rd.
Old Tappan, NJ 07675
Fax: 800-445-6991   Fr: 800-223-2348
Richard Lidz and Linda Perrin, editorial directors. Fifth edition, 1993. This 13-volume set profiles over 600 occupations. Each occupational profile describes job duties, entry-level requirements, educational requirements, advancement possibilities, employment outlook, working conditions, earnings and benefits, and where to write for more information.

★5419★ *Physician Salary Survey Report, Hospital-Based and Group Practice*
Hospital & Healthcare Compensation
  Service
John R. Zabka Associates, Inc.
69 Minnehaha Blvd.
PO Box 376
Oakland, NJ 07436
Ph: (201)405-0075
Annual Describes compensation and benefits for the chief of staff or medical director, staff physicians, and heads of departments. Includes information on bonuses, base salary, number of hours worked annually by each physician, housing and meal allowances, hospital bed size, group practice organization size, and governmental and nongovernmental facilities. Compensation report on hospital-based and group practice physicians.

★5420★ **"Physician" in** *VGM's Careers Encyclopedia* **(pp. 350-353)**
National Textbook Co. (NTC)
VGM Career Books
4255 W. Touhy Ave.
Lincolnwood, IL 60646-1975
Ph: (708)679-5500   Fax: (708)679-2494
Fr: 800-323-4900
Third edition, 1991. Describes job duties, places of employment, working conditions, qualifications, education, training, advancement potential, and salary for each occupation.

★5421★ **"Physician" in** *VGM's Handbook of Health Care Careers*
National Textbook Co.
4255 W. Touhy Ave.
Lincolnwood, IL 60646-1975
Ph: (708)679-5500   Fax: (708)679-2494
Fr: 800-323-4900
Annette Selden. 1993. Contains 42 two-page occupational profiles describing job duties, places of employment, working conditions, qualifications, education, employment outlook, and income.

★5422★ **"Physicians" in** *101 Careers: A Guide to the Fastest-Growing Opportunities* **(pp. 250-252)**
John Wiley & Sons, Inc.
605 3rd Ave.
New York, NY 10158-0012
Ph: (212)850-6645   Fax: (212)850-6088
Michael Harkavy. 1990. Describes the nature of the job, working conditions, employment growth, qualifications, personal skills, pro-

jected salaries, and where to write for more information.

★5423★ **"Physicians" in** *America's 50 Fastest Growing Jobs* **(pp. 55)**
JIST Works, Inc.
720 N. Park Ave.
Indianapolis, IN 46202-3431
Ph: (317)264-3720   Fax: (317)264-3709
Fr: 800-648-5478
Michael J. Farr, compiler. 1994. Describes the 50 fastest growing jobs within major career clusters such as technicians, and marketing and sales. Each job profile explains the nature of the work, skills and abilities required, employment outlook, average earnings, related occupations, education and training requirements, and employment opportunities. Also contains career planning information and job search tips.

★5424★ **"Physicians" in** *Best Jobs for the 1990s and Into the 21st Century*
Impact Publications
9104-N Manassas Dr.
Manassas Park, VA 22111
Ph: (703)361-7300   Fax: (703)335-9486
Ronald L. Krannich and Caryl Rae Krannich. 1993.

★5425★ **"Physicians" in** *Career Discovery Encyclopedia* **(Vol.5, pp. 42-43)**
J.G. Ferguson Publishing Co.
200 W. Madison St., Ste. 300
Chicago, IL 60606
Ph: (312)580-5480   Fax: (312)580-4948
Russell E. Primm, editor-in chief. 1993. This six volume set contains two-page articles for 504 occupations. Each article describes job duties, earnings, and educational and training requirements. The whole set is arranged alphabetically by job title. Designed for junior high and older students.

★5426★ **"Physicians" in** *Career Paths in the Field of Aging: Professional Gerontology* **(pp. 27-28)**
Simon and Schuster
200 Old Tappan Rd.
Old Tappan, NJ 07675
Fax: 800-445-6991   Fr: 800-223-2348
David A. Peterson. 1987. Provides a history of the gerontology profession, and describes jobs, education and skills required, employment outlook and trends in the field.

★5427★ **"Physicians" in** *Careers in Health and Fitness*
Rosen Publishing Group
29 E. 21st St.
New York, NY 10010
Ph: (212)777-3017   Fax: (212)777-0277
Fr: 800-237-9932
Jackie Heron. 1990. Occupational profiles contain information on job duties, skills, advantages, basic equipment used, employment possibilities, certification, and salary.

★5428★ **"Physicians" in** *Encyclopedia of Careers and Vocational Guidance* **(Vol.4, pp. 92-97)**
J.G. Ferguson Publishing Co.
200 W. Madison St., Ste. 300
Chicago, IL 60606
Ph: (312)580-5480   Fax: (312)580-4948
William E. Hopke, editor-in-chief. Ninth edition, 1993. Four-volume set that profiles 900 occupations and describes job trends in 74 industries. Includes career description, educational requirements, history of the job, methods of entry, advancement, employment outlook, earnings, conditions of work, social and psychological factors, and sources of further information.

★5429★ **"Physicians" in** *Health Care Job Explosion!* **(pp. 324-339)**
D-Amp Publications
401 Amherst Ave.
Coraopolis, PA 15108
Ph: (412)262-5578
Dennis V. Damp. 1993. Provides information on the nature of work for the major health care occupational groups. Descriptions include working conditions, training, job outlook, qualifications, and related occupations.

★5430★ **"Physicians" in** *Jobs! What They Are—Where They Are—What They Pay!* **(p. 290)**
Simon & Schuster, Inc.
Simon & Schuster Bldg.
1230 Avenue of the Americas
New York, NY 10020
Ph: (212)698-7000   Fr: 800-223-2348
Robert O. Snelling and Anne M. Snelling. Third revised edition, 1992. Includes chapters titled "Osteopathic Physicians" (p. 242) and "Physicians" (p. 244). Describes duties and responsibilities, earnings, employment opportunities, training, and qualifications.

★5431★ *Physicians (Medical and Osteopathic)*
Chronicle Guidance Publications, Inc.
66 Aurora St.
PO Box 1190
Moravia, NY 13118-1190
Ph: (315)497-0330   Fax: (315)497-3359
Fr: 800-622-7284
1991. Career brief describing the nature of the job, working conditions, hours and earnings, education and training, licensure, certification, unions, personal qualifications, social and psychological factors, location, employment outlook, entry methods, advancement, and related occupations.

★5432★ **"Physicians" in** *Occupational Outlook Handbook*
U.S. Government Printing Office
Superintendent of Documents
Washington, DC 20402
Ph: (202)512-1800   Fax: (202)512-2250
Biennial; latest edition, 1994-95. Encyclopedia of careers describing about 250 occupations and comprising about 85 percent of all jobs in the economy. Occupations that require lengthy education or training are given the most attention. Each occupation's profile describes what the worker does on the job, working conditions, education and training requirements, advancement possibilities, job

★5433★ Psychiatrist
Careers, Inc.
PO Box 135
Largo, FL 34649-0135
Ph: (813)584-7333
1994. Two-page summary describing duties, working conditions, personal qualifications, training, earnings and hours, employment outlook, places of employment, related careers, and where to write for more information.

★5434★ "Psychiatrist" in VGM's Handbook of Health Care Careers
National Textbook Co.
4255 W. Touhy Ave.
Lincolnwood, IL 60646-1975
Ph: (708)679-5500   Fax: (708)679-2494
Fr: 800-323-4900
Annette Selden. 1993. Contains 42 two-page occupational profiles describing job duties, places of employment, working conditions, qualifications, education, employment outlook, and income.

★5435★ "Public Health Physician" in Opportunities in Public Health Careers (pp. 84-86)
National Textbook Co. (NTC)
VGM Career Books
4255 W. Touhy Ave.
Lincolnwood, IL 60646-1975
Ph: (708)679-5500   Fax: (708)679-2494
Fr: 800-323-4900
George E. Pickett. 1988. Defines the public health field and describes career opportunities as well as educational preparation and the future of the public health field. The appendixes list public health organizations, state and federal public health agencies, and graduate schools offering public health programs.

★5436★ What Everyone Should Know About Osteopathic Physicians
Channing L. Bete Co., Inc.
200 State Rd.
South Deerfield, MA 01373
Ph: (413)665-7611
1987. Booklet describing osteopathic physicians, their views about health care, where they work, and their education and training.

★5437★ What Is a D.O.? What Is an M.D.?
American Osteopathic Assocation
142 E. Ontario St.
Chicago, IL 60611
Ph: (312)280-5800
1991. This six-panel brochure compares and contrasts medical doctors and osteopathic physicians.

★5438★ You . . . The Doctor: A Basic Guide to a Rewarding Career
American Medical Association
515 N. State St.
Chicago, IL 60610
Ph: (312)464-5000   Fr: 800-621-8335
1987. This pamphlet describes high school and college educational preparation, medical school qualification, and what it takes to succeed as a medical doctor.

PROFESSIONAL ASSOCIATIONS

★5439★ American Association of Colleges of Osteopathic Medicine (AACOM)
6110 Executive Blvd., No. 405
Rockville, MD 20852
Ph: (301)468-0990   Fax: (301)770-5738
Members: Osteopathic medical colleges. **Purpose:** Operates centralized application service; monitors and works with Congress and other government agencies in the planning of health care programs. Gathers statistics on osteopathic medical students, faculty, and diplomates. **Publications:** AACOM Organizational Guide, annual. ● American Association of Colleges of Osteopathic Medicine—Annual Statistical Report. ● Debts and Career Plans of Osteopathic Medical Students, annual. ● Education of the Osteopathic Physician. ● Osteopathic Medical Education. ● Osteopathic Medical Education: A Handbook for Minority Applicants.

★5440★ American College of Cardiology (ACC)
9111 Old Georgetown Rd.
Bethesda, MD 20814-1699
Ph: (301)897-5400   Fax: (301)897-9745
Fr: 800-253-4636
Professional society of physicians, surgeons, and scientists specializing in cardiology (heart) and cardiovascular (circulatory) diseases. Operates Heart House Learning Center. Maintains numerous committees. **Publications:** ACC Current Journal Review, bimonthly. ● ACCEL, monthly. ● Affiliates in Training, bimonthly. ● Cardiology, monthly. ● Journal of the American College of Cardiology, monthly.

★5441★ American Medical Association (AMA)
515 N. State St.
Chicago, IL 60610
Ph: (312)464-5000   Fax: (312)464-4184
Members: County medical societies and physicians. **Purpose:** Disseminates scientific information to members and the public. Informs members on significant medical and health legislation on state and national levels and represents the profession before Congress and governmental agencies. Cooperates in setting standards for medical schools, hospitals, residency programs, and continuing medical education courses. Offers physician placement service and counseling on practice management problems. Operates library which lends material and provides specific medical information to physicians. Ad-hoc committees are formed for such topics as health care planning and principles of medical ethics. **Publications:** American Medical News, weekly. ● Archives of Dermatology, monthly. ● Archives of Family Medicine, monthly. ● Archives of General Psychiatry, monthly. ● Archives of Internal Medicine, semimonthly. ● Archives of Neurology, monthly. ● Archives of Ophthalmology, monthly. ● Archives of Otolaryngology—Head and Neck Surgery, monthly. ● Archives of Pediatrics & Adolescent Medicine, monthly. ● Archives of Surgery, monthly. ●

Journal of the American Medical Association, weekly.

★5442★ American Osteopathic Association (AOA)
142 E. Ontario St.
Chicago, IL 60611
Ph: (312)280-5800   Fax: (312)280-3860
Fr: 800-621-1773
Members: Osteopathic physicians, surgeons, and graduates of approved colleges of osteopathic medicine. Associate members include teaching, research, administrative, and executive employees of approved colleges, hospitals, divisional societies, and affiliated organizations. Forms (with its affiliates) an officially recognized structure of the osteopathic profession. Promotes the public health, to encourage scientific research, and to maintain and improve high standards of medical education in osteopathic colleges. Inspects and accredits colleges and hospitals; conducts a specialty certification program; sponsors a national examining board satisfactory to state licensing agencies; maintains mandatory program of continuing medical education for members. Compiles statistics on location and type of practice of osteopathic physicians. Sponsors research activities through Bureau of Research in osteopathic colleges and hospitals. Maintains Physician Placement Service. Produces public service radio and television programs; maintains 2000 item library and biographical archives on osteopathic medicine and history. Offers speakers' bureau. **Publications:** American Osteopathic Association Yearbook and Directory. ● The D.O., monthly. ● Journal of AOA, monthly.

★5443★ Association of American Medical Colleges (AAMC)
2450 N St. NW
Washington, DC 20037
Ph: (202)828-0400   Fax: (202)828-1125
Members: Medical schools, graduate affiliate medical colleges, academic societies, teaching hospitals, and individuals interested in the advancement of medical education, biomedical research, and healthcare. **Purpose:** Provides centralized application service. Offers management education program for medical school deans, teaching hospital directors, department chairmen, and service chiefs of affiliated hospitals. Develops and administers the Medical College Admissions Test (MCAT). Operates student loan program. Maintains information management system and institutional profile system. Compiles statistics. **Publications:** Academic Medicine, monthly. ● Curriculum Directory, annual. ● Directory of American Medical Education, annual. ● Medical School Admission Requirements, annual. ● Weekly Report.

★5444★ Council on Medical Education - of the American Medical Association (CME-AMA)
515 N. State St.
Chicago, IL 60610
Ph: (312)464-4804   Fax: (312)464-5830
Members: A council of the American Medical Association. **Purpose:** Participates in the accreditation of and provides consultation to medical school programs, graduate medical educational programs, and educational programs for several allied health occupations.

Provides information on medical and allied health education at all levels. **Publications:** *Allied Health Education Directory*, annual. • *Annual Report of Medical Education in the Journal of the AMA.* • *Continuing Education Courses for Physicians Supplement to the Journal of the AMA*, semiannual. • *Directory of Graduate Medical Education Programs*, annual.

★5445★ International Academy of Oral Medicine and Toxicology (IAOMT)
PO Box 608531
Orlando, FL 32860-8531
Ph: (407)298-2450   Fax: (407)298-2450
Members: Dentists, physicians, and medical scientists. **Purpose:** Encourages, sponsors, and disseminates scientific research on the biocompatibility of materials used in dentistry. Offers educational programs; maintains speakers' bureau. **Publications:** *Bio-Probe Newsletter*, bimonthly. • *IN VIVO*, quarterly.

STANDARDS/CERTIFICATION AGENCIES

★5446★ American Association of Osteopathic Examiners (AAOE)
300 5th St. NE
Washington, DC 20002
Ph: (202)544-5060   Fax: (202)544-3525
Works for adequate osteopathic representation on all physician licensing boards. Conducts examinations and offers certification of osteopathic physicians.

★5447★ American Association of Osteopathic Specialists (AAOS)
804 Main St., Ste. D
Forest Park, GA 30050
Ph: (404)363-8263   Fax: (404)361-2285
Fr: 800-447-9397
Allopathic physicians. Provides certification programs in 26 different areas of specialization.

★5448★ American Board of Sleep Medicine
1610 14th St. NW, Ste. 302
Rochester, MN 55901-0246
Ph: (507)287-9819   Fax: (507)287-6008
Offers certification in sleep medicine to licensed physicians and individuals with Ph.D.s in health related fields.

★5449★ American College of Pain Medicine (ACPM)
5700 Old Orchard Rd.
Skokie, IL 60077-1057
Ph: (708)966-0459   Fax: (708)966-9418
Awards certification to physicians successfully completing the examination and credentialing process.

★5450★ American Medical Association (AMA)
515 N. State St.
Chicago, IL 60610
Ph: (312)464-5000   Fax: (312)464-4184
Cooperates in setting standards for medical schools, hospitals, residency programs, and continuing medical education courses.

★5451★ American Osteopathic Association (AOA)
142 E. Ontario St.
Chicago, IL 60611
Ph: (312)280-5800   Fax: (312)280-3860
Fr: 800-621-1773
Inspects and accredits colleges and hospitals; conducts a specialty certification program; sponsors a national examining board satisfactory to state licensing agencies; maintains mandatory program of continuing medical education for members.

★5452★ American Sports Medicine Association Board of Certification (ASMA)
660 W. Duarte Rd.
Arcadia, CA 91007
Ph: (818)445-1978
Verifies and qualifies the educational competency of active athletic trainers and sports medicine trainers for certification. Establishes minimum competency standards of education required for the prevention and care of athletic injuries and sports medicine.

★5453★ Educational Commission for Foreign Medical Graduates (ECFMG)
3624 Market St.
Philadelphia, PA 19104
Ph: (215)386-5900
Aims to provide information to foreign medical graduates regarding entry into graduate medical education and the U.S. health care system; evaluate their qualifications; identify foreign medical graduates' cultural and professional needs; assist in the establishment of educational policies and programs.

TEST GUIDES

★5454★ *Admission Test Series: Medical College Admission Test*
National Learning Corp.
212 Michael Dr.
Syosset, NY 11791
Ph: (516)921-8888   Fax: (516)921-8743
Fr: 800-645-6337
Jack Rudman. A collection of sample examinations designed to prepare potential doctors for graduate and professional school entrance tests and for tests administered by private and public institutions for entrance and career advancement. Provides multiple-choice questions; includes correct answers. Titles in the series include *National Medical Boards (NMB)/Combined Volumes; National Medical Boards (NMB)/Part I; National Medical Boards (NMB)/Part II; Educational Commission for Foreign Medical Graduates Examination; Foreign Medical Graduates Examination in Medical Science/Combined Volumes; Foreign Medical Graduates Examination in Medical Science/Part I—Basic Medical Science; Foreign Medical Graduates Examination in Medical Science/Part II—Clinical Sciences.*

★5455★ *Barron's How to Prepare for the Medical College Admission Test (MCAT)*
Barron's Educational Series, Inc.
250 Wireless Blvd.
Hauppauge, NY 11788
Ph: (516)434-3311   Fax: (516)434-3723
Fr: 800-645-3476
Hugo R. Seibel and Kenneth E. Guyer. Seventh edition, 1991. Contains four practice tests; includes answers.

★5456★ *Career Examination Series: Physician*
National Learning Corp.
212 Michael Dr.
Syosset, NY 11791
Ph: (516)921-8888   Fax: (516)921-8743
Fr: 800-645-6337
Jack Rudman. A series of study guides with multiple-choice examination questions and solutions for trainees and professional physicians. Titles in the series include *Psychiatrist; Staff Physician; Supervising Physician and Surgeon; Surgeon.*

★5457★ *A Complete Preparation for the MCAT*
TAB/McGraw-Hill, Inc.
PO Box 182607
Columbus, OH 43218-2607
Fax: (614)759-3644   Fr: 800-822-8158
James L. Flowers. et al. Sixth edition, 1992. This two-volume set presents review materials for biology, general chemistry, organic chemistry, and physics. Gives samples of each section of the test with answers.

★5458★ *Comprehensive Review for FMGEMS*
Harwal Publishing Co.
605 W. State St.
Media, PA 19063
Ph: (215)565-0746
John Bullock and Abdool Sattar Moosa. 1989. Part of the National Medical Series for Independent Study. Covers questions for the Foreign Medical Graduate Examination in the Medical Sciences.

★5459★ FLEX, Federation Licensing Examination
Federation of State Medical Boards of the United States (FSMB)
6000 Western Place, Ste. 707
Fort Worth, TX 12489
Ph: (817)735-8445
Annual.

★5460★ *How to Prepare for the Medical College Admission Test*
Arco Publishing Co.
Macmillan General Reference
15 Columbus Cir.
New York, NY 10023
Fax: 800-835-3202   Fr: 800-858-7674
William R. Bishai, et al. Revised edition, 1987. Describes the Medical College Admission Test and includes three practice tests. An appendix lists colleges of medicine in the United States and Canada.

★5461★ How to Prepare for the Medical College Admission Test (MCAT)
Barron's Educational Series, Inc.
250 Wireless Blvd.
Hauppauge, NY 11788
Ph: (516)434-3311   Fax: (516)434-3723
Fr: 800-645-3476
Hugo R. Seibel and Kenneth E. Guyer. Seventh edition. 1991. Contains four sample test with answers explained.

★5462★ MCAT SuperCoures
Arco Pub.
201 W. 103rd St.
Indianapolis, IN 46290
Ph: 800-428-5331   Fax: 800-835-3202
Stefan Bosworth and Marion Brisk. 1994, second edition. Provides lesson by lesson instruction.

★5463★ Medical College Admission Test (MCAT)
National Learning Corp.
212 Michael Dr.
Syosset, NY 11791
Ph: (516)921-8888   Fax: (516)921-8743
Fr: 800-645-6337
Jack Rudman. Part of the Admission Test series. A sample test for those seeking admission to graduate and professional schools or seeking entrance or advancement in institutional and public career service.

★5464★ Medical College Admission Test (MCAT)
Arco Publishing Co.
Macmillan General Reference
15 Columbus Cir.
New York, NY 10023
Fax: 800-835-3202   Fr: 800-858-7674
Lawrence Solomon and Morris Bramson. Third edition, 1988. Includes four sample test and a general review.

EDUCATIONAL DIRECTORIES AND PROGRAMS

★5465★ Association of American Medical Colleges—Curriculum Directory
Association of American Medical Colleges (AAMC)
2450 N St. NW
Washington, DC 20037-1126
Ph: (202)828-0400   Fax: (202)828-1123
Cynthia T. Bennett, Contact
Annual, October. Covers accredited medical schools in the U.S., Puerto Rico, and Canada. Entries include: School name, address, contact person, academic programs offered, curriculum characteristics, required and elective courses, length of program, type of instruction, conditions for learning, grading evaluation, instructional innovations, and trends of interest to applicants, faculties, and deans. Arrangement: Geographical.

★5466★ Association of American Medical Colleges—Directory of American Medical Education
Association of American Medical Colleges (AAMC)
2450 N St. NW
Washington, DC 20037-1126
Ph: (202)828-0400   Fax: (202)828-1123
Cynthia T. Bennett, Contact
Annual, September. Covers accredited medical schools; coverage includes U.S., Puerto Rico, and Canada. Entries include: Name of school, address, phone, fax, history, whether public or private, enrollment, names of clinical facilities; names and titles of university officials, medical school administrative staff, and department, division, or section chairpersons and a brief historical statement. Officers and members of various AAMC organizations are listed, including member medical academic societies, teaching hospitals, and steering committees. Arrangement: Geographical.

★5467★ Barron's Guide to Medical and Dental Schools
Barron's Educational Series, Inc.
250 Wireless Blvd.
Hauppauge, NY 11788
Ph: 800-645-3476   Fax: (516)434-3723
Fr: 800-645-3476
Max Reed, Contact
Biennial, fall of odd years. Covers about 220 medical, osteopathic, and dental schools. Entries include: School name, address, admission requirements, housing, grading and promotion policies, facilities, description of curriculum. Arrangement: Classified by type of school, then geographical.

★5468★ Best Doctors in America
Woodward/White, Inc.
129 1st Ave. SW
Aiken, SC 29801
Ph: (803)648-0300   Fax: (803)641-1709
Steven Neifel, Vice President
Biennial, January of even years.. Covers Approximately 3,800 doctors selected as "the best" in their specialties by a survey of about 5,500 doctors. Entries include: Name, address, phone, academic/hospital affiliations.

★5469★ Directory of Training Programs in Internal Medicine: Residency and Subspecialty Fellowships
National Study of Internal Medicine Manpower
969 E. 60th St.
Chicago, IL 60637
Ph: (312)702-7105   Fax: (312)702-7222
Christopher Lyttle, Contact
Annual, March. Covers about 440 training programs accredited by the Accreditation Council for Graduate Medical Education and about 1,700 fellowships in internal medicine and 15 subspecialties. Entries include: Name of institution, center, or medical department, address, contact name, category or subspecialty in which residency or fellowship is offered, number of residents and fellows trained annually, size of institution, type of ownership, number of filled positions. Arrangement: Residency programs are geographical; fellowships are by subspecialty, then geographical.

★5470★ Encyclopedia of Medical Organizations and Agencies
Gale Research Inc.
835 Penobscot Bldg.
Detroit, MI 48226-4094
Ph: (313)961-2242   Fax: (313)961-6741
Fr: 800-877-GALE
Karen Boyden, Contact
Biennial, November of odd years. Covers over 13,400 state, national, and international medical associations, foundations, research institutes, federal and state agencies, and medical and allied health schools. Entries include: Organization name, address, phone; many listings include names and titles of key personnel, descriptive annotations. Arrangement: Classified by subject, then by type of organization.

★5471★ Health & Medical Industry Directory
American Business Directories, Inc.
5711 S. 86th Circle
Omaha, NE 68127
Ph: (402)593-4600   Fax: (402)331-1505
Released 1993. Lists over 1.1 million physicians and surgeons, dentists, clinics, health clubs, and other health-related businesses in the U.S. and Canada. Entries include: Name, address, phone.

★5472★ Healthcare Career Directory— Nurses and Physicians
Gale Research Inc.
835 Penobscot Bldg.
Detroit, MI 48226-4094
Ph: (313)961-2242   Fax: (313)961-6083
Fr: 800-877-GALE
Bradley J. Morgan and Joseph M. Palmisano. Second edition, 1993. A directory in the Career Advisor Series that provides essays written by industry professionals; job search information on resume and cover letter preparation, networking, and the interviewing process; approximately 300 companies and organizations offering job opportunities and internships, and additional job-hunting resources.

★5473★ Infact Medical School Information System
Dataflow Systems Inc.
7758 Wisconsin Ave.
Bethesda, MD 20814
Ph: (301)654-9133
J. B. Malcom, Contact
Updated 3 times per year. Not a directory, but a compilation of the complete catalogs of over 140 North American medical schools; coverage includes Canada.

★5474★ International Health Electives for Medical Students
American Medical Student Association
1890 Preston White Dr.
Reston, VA 22091
Ph: (703)620-6600   Fax: (703)620-5873
Nancy Busse, Contact
Irregular, previous edition 1990; latest edition 1993. Covers in four volumes, more than 200 clinical sites worldwide that offer learning experiences outside the United States to American medical students. Volume 1 covers Africa and the Middle East; volume 2, the Americas; volume 3, Asia and western Pacific; and volume 4, Europe. Entries include: Name and

address of clinic, hospital or organization; contact person; duration of program, number of students permitted in program, time of year program is offered, fees, financial aid available, nature of duties and other details, name and address of contact. Arrangement: Geographical.

★5475★ Medical Directory of the Dakotas
Jola Publications
2933 N. 2nd St.
Minneapolis, MN 55411
Ph: (612)529-5001   Fax: (612)521-2289
Dennis Schapiro, Contact

Annual. Covers Approximately 5,000 doctors, hospitals, clinics, nursing homes, and other selected health care providers in North Dakota and South Dakota. Entries include: Doctor or facility name, address, phone. Arrangement: Classified by type of facility or care provided.

★5476★ Medical and Health Information Directory
Gale Research Inc.
835 Penobscot Bldg.
Detroit, MI 48226-4094
Ph: (313)961-2242   Fax: (313)961-6741
Fr: 800-877-GALE
Karen Boyden, Contact

Approximately biennial; latest edition 1994. Covers in Volume 1, almost 18,600 medical and health oriented associations, organizations, institutions, and government agencies, including health maintenance organizations (HMOs), preferred provider organizations (PPOs), insurance companies, pharmaceutical companies, research centers, and medical and allied health schools. In Volume 2, nearly 11,800 medical book publishers; medical periodicals, directories, audiovisual producers and services, medical libraries and information centers, and electronic resources. In Volume 3, nearly 26,000 clinics, treatment centers, care programs, and counseling/diagnostic services for 30 subject areas. Entries include: Institution, service, or firm name, address, phone; many include names of key personnel Arrangement: Classified by organization activity, service, etc..

★5477★ Medical School Admission Requirements—United States and Canada
Association of American Medical Colleges (AAMC)
2450 N St. NW
Washington, DC 20037-1126
Ph: (202)828-0400   Fax: (202)828-1123
Cynthia T. Bennett, Contact

Annual, April. Covers accredited medical schools; in the U.S., Canada, and Puerto Rico. Entries include: School name, address, name and title of contact, admission requirements, application procedures, premedical planning, financial aid programs, fees, selection factors, curriculum features, first year current expenses, premedical planning, MCAT and AMCAS information, applicant statistics. Arrangement: Geographical.

★5478★ Mental Health and Social Work Career Directory
Gale Research Inc.
835 Penobscot Bldg.
Detroit, MI 48226-4094
Ph: (313)961-2242   Fax: (313)961-6083
Fr: 800-877-GALE

Bradley J. Morgan and Joseph M. Palmisano. 1993. A directory in the Career Advisor Series that provides essays written by industry professionals; job search information on resume and cover letter preparation, networking, and the interviewing process; approximately 300 companies and organizations offering job opportunities and internships, and additional job-hunting resources.

★5479★ Minority Student Opportunities in United States Medical Schools
Association of American Medical Colleges (AAMC)
2450 N St. NW
Washington, DC 20037-1126
Ph: (202)828-0573   Fax: (202)828-1125
Lily May Johnson, Contact

Biennial. Covers Programs for minority group students at 126 medical schools. Entries include: Name of school, name of parent institution, if applicable, address, phone, name of contact; descriptions of recruitment, admissions, financial aid, and academic assistance programs for underrepresented minority students; statistical table on minority admissions, enrollment, and graduation. Arrangement: Geographical.

★5480★ The Official ABMS Directory of Board Certified Medical Specialists
Marquis Who's Who
121 Chanlon Rd.
New Providence, NJ 07974
Ph: (908)771-7730   Fax: (908)665-6688
Fr: 800-521-8110
Leigh Carol Yuster-Freeman, VP, Bibliographies

Annual, November. Covers more than 447,000 board-certified specialists in 25 areas of medical practice from allergy to urology. Entries include: Name, certifications, office address, phone, date and place of birth, education, career data, date certified, type of practice, professional memberships. Arrangement: Classified by specialty, then geographical.

★5481★ Physicians and Dentists Database
FIRSTMARK, Inc.
34 Juniper Ln.
Newton Center, MA 02159-2861
Ph: (617)965-7989   Fax: (617)965-8510
Fr: 800-729-2600

AWARDS, SCHOLARSHIPS, GRANTS, AND FELLOWSHIPS

★5482★ AAFP President's Award
American Academy of Family Physicians
8880 Ward Pkwy.
Kansas City, MO 64114
Ph: (816)333-9700

To recognize exceptional service in furthering the purpose of the Academy. Awarded annually if merited.

★5483★ AMA Distinguished Service Award
American Medical Association
515 N. State
Chicago, IL 60610
Ph: (312)464-4344   Fax: (312)464-5896

To recognize a physician for scientific achievements. Selection is made by the House of Delegates at the interim meeting preceding the annual convention where the presentation is made. A medallion is presented to the winner before the House of Delegates. Awarded annually. Established in 1938.

★5484★ Elizabeth Blackwell Medal
American Medical Women's Association
801 N. Fairfax St., Ste. 400
Alexandria, VA 22314
Ph: (703)838-0500   Fax: (703)549-3864

To recognize the physician who has made the most outstanding contribution to the cause of women in the field of medicine. A medal is awarded annually. Established in 1949.

★5485★ William and Charlotte Cadbury Award
National Medical Fellowships
254 W. 31st St., 7th Fl.
New York, NY 10001-2813
Ph: (212)714-0933

To recognize the outstanding achievement of a fourth year minority medical student. Academic achievement, leadership, and social consciousness are criteria for the award. A monetary prize of $2,000 and a certificate of merit are awarded annually at the annual meeting of American Medical Colleges. Established in 1977 by Dr. Irving Graef in honor of the organization's former Executive Director and Staff Associate.

★5486★ General Practitioner of the Year
American College of General Practitioners in Osteopathic Medicine and Surgery
330 E. Algonquin
Arlington Heights, IL 60005
Ph: (708)228-6090   Fr: 800-323-0790

To recognize an outstanding general practitioner in osteopathic medicine and surgery. A plaque is awarded annually. Established in 1955.

★5487★ Janet M. Glasgow Certificate Award
American Medical Women's Association
801 N. Fairfax St., Ste. 400
Alexandria, VA 22314
Ph: (703)838-0500   Fax: (703)549-3864

To recognize women medical students graduating first or in the top ten percent of their classes. Established in 1941. In addition, a Janet M. Glasgow Essay Award of $1,500 is awarded to a medical student who has written the best essay identifying a woman physician who has been a significant role model. Established in 1958.

★5488★ Henry G. Halladay Awards
National Medical Fellowships
254 W. 31st St., 7th Fl.
New York, NY 10001-2813
Ph: (212)714-0933

To recognize the achievement of black males in the first year of medical school who have overcome significant obstacles to obtain a medical education. Five supplemental scholarships of $760 each are awarded annually. Established in 1970 by an endowment from Mrs. Henry G. Halladay in memory of her husband.

★5489★ Honorary Member
American Academy of Family Physicians
8880 Ward Pkwy.
Kansas City, MO 64114
Ph: (816)333-9700

This, the highest honor the Academy can bestow, is given to recognize individuals of distinction who have rendered outstanding service to the AAFP or to the medical profession. Awarded as merited.

★5490★ HRSA-BHP Health Professions Student Loans
U.S. Public Health Service
Health Resources and Services
   Administration
Parklawn Bldg., Rm. 8-38
5600 Fishers Ln.
Rockville, MD 20857

Purpose: To assist students with need for financial assistance to undertake the course of study required to become physicians, dentists, osteopathic physicians, optometrists, pharmacists, podiatrists, or veterinarians. Qualifications: Applicants must be enrolled or accepted for enrollment as full-time students in a program leading to a doctoral degree in medicine, dental surgery or equivalent degree, pharmacy, osteopathic medicine, optometry or equivalent degree, podiatric medicine or equivalent degree, or veterinary medicine or equivalent degree; or a bachelor of science in pharmacy or equivalent degree. Applicants must also be citizens, nationals, or permanent residents of the United States or the District of Columbia, the Commonwealths of Puerto Rico or the Marianna Islands, the Virgin Islands, Guam, The American Samoa, the Trust Territory of the Pacific Islands, the Republic of Palau, the Republic of the Marshall Islands, and the Federated State of Micronesia. Applicants must also demonstrate financial need. Professional students, interns, residents, and students seeking advanced training are not eligible. Funds available: Up to the cost of tuition plus $2,500 or the amount of financial need, whichever is

less. The interest rate is five percent and accrues during the repayment period. Loans are repayable over a ten year period and beginning one year after the student graduates or ceases to enroll full-time in a health program.

★5491★ HRSA-BHP Loans for Disadvantaged Students
U.S. Public Health Service
Health Resources and Services
   Administration
Parklawn Bldg., Rm. 8-38
5600 Fishers Ln.
Rockville, MD 20857

Purpose: To assist students who need financial assistance to pursue careers in medicine, osteopathic medicine, dentistry, optometry, podiatric medicine, pharmacy, or veterinary medicine. Qualifications: Applicants must be citizens, nationals, or lawful permanent residents of the United States or the District of Columbia, the Commonwealths of Puerto Rico or the Marianna Islands, the Virgin Islands, Guam, American Samoa, the Trust Territory of the Pacific Islands, the Republic of Palau, the Republic of the Marshall Islands, or the Federated State of Micronesia. They must also be enrolled or accepted for enrollment at a participating health professionals school full-time. Students must be determined by their school's financial aid director to meet financial need and "disadvantaged background" criteria. Those enrolled in schools of medicine or osteopathic medicine must demonstrate exceptional financial need. Preprofessional students, interns, residents, and students seeking advanced training are not eligible. Selection criteria: Schools are responsible for selecting recipients and for determining the amount of assistance. Funds available: The maximum loan amount allowed for each school year is the cost of tuition plus $2,500, or the amount of financial need, whichever is lesser. The repayment interest rate is five percent over a ten-year period, which begins one year after completion of cessation of full-time study. Interest begins accruing at the time the loan becomes rapayable. Repayment may be deferred under special circumstances, and interest does not accrue during periods of deferment.

★5492★ Robert A. Kehoe Award of Merit
American College of Occupational and
   Environmental Medicine
55 West Seegers Rd.
Arlington Heights, IL 60005
Ph: (708)228-6850   Fax: (708)228-1856

To recognize distinguished contributions to the development of the specialty of occupational medicine. A bronze plaque mounted on walnut is awarded annually in the fall. Established in 1956 and named for Robert A. Kehoe, M.D., a pioneer in the field of environmental medicine and a past president of the College from 1949-1950.

★5493★ Franklin C. McLean Award
National Medical Fellowships
254 W. 31st St., 7th Fl.
New York, NY 10001-2813
Ph: (212)714-0933

This, the oldest and most prestigious honor of NMF, is given to recognize a senior minority medical student for distinguished academic

achievement, leadership ability, and community service. A monetary prize of $3,000 and a certificate of merit are awarded annually at the annual meeting of the Association of Medical Colleges. Established in 1968 in memory of NMF's founder, Franklin C. McLean.

★5494★ Benjamin Rush Award for Citizenship and Community Service
American Medical Association
515 N. State
Chicago, IL 60610
Ph: (312)464-4344   Fax: (312)464-5896

To recognize outstanding contributions to the community for citizenship and public service above and beyond the call of duty as a practicing physician. A plaque is presented at the interim meeting. Established in 1973.

★5495★ Special Recognition Award
American College of Preventive Medicine
1015 15th St. NW, Ste. 403
Washington, DC 20005
Ph: (202)789-0003   Fax: (202)289-8274

To recognize and honor outstanding achievement in and contributions to the field of preventive medicine. Awardee must be a physician or other scientist who has made contributions to humanity in research, teaching, or service. A plaque and travel expenses are awarded annually at the PREVENTION meeting. Established in 1970.

★5496★ John G. Walsh Award
American Academy of Family Physicians
8880 Ward Pkwy.
Kansas City, MO 64114
Ph: (816)333-9700

To recognize long-term dedication and effective leadership in furthering the development of family practice. Awarded as merited.

BASIC REFERENCE GUIDES AND HANDBOOKS

★5497★ Clinician's Pocket Reference: A Scutmonkey's Handbook
Appleton and Lange
PO Box 56303
Norwalk, CT 06856
Ph: (203)838-4400   Fr: 800-423-1359

Leonard G. Gomella, G. Richard Braen, and Michael Olding, editors. Seventh edition, 1993. Covers procedures, techniques, and patient care information; features many charts and tables for quick and easy reference. Gives common lab values, medication actions, and dosages. Explains intravenous therapy, emergency care, operating room procedures, and suturing techniques.

★5498★ Conn's Current Therapy: Latest Approved Methods of Treatment for the Practicing Physician
W. B. Saunders Co.
Curtis Center
Independence Ave.
Philadelphia, PA 19106
Ph: (215)238-7800
Howard F. Conn; edited by Robert E. Rakel. Annual 1992. Presents current recommended therapy.

★5499★ Dorland's Illustrated Medical Dictionary
W. B. Saunders Co.
Curtis Center
Independence Sq.,W.
Philadelphia, PA 19106
Ph: (215)238-7800
Irregular. Twenty-seventh edition, 1988.

★5500★ Fact Sheet: Health Education Assistance Loan Program (HEAL)
U.S. Department of Health and Human Services
Public Health Service
Health Resources and Services Administration
Bureau of Health Professions, Division of Student Assistance
Rockville, MD 20857
Ph: (301)443-2086
Fact sheet describing the HEAL Program; covers eligible schools, borrowers, and lenders, as well as loan limitations, interest, and repayment.

★5501★ Health Professions Student Loan Program
Bureau of Health Professions
Division of Student Assistance
5600 Fishers Ln., Rm. 834
Rockville, MD 20857
Ph: (301)443-2086
This information sheet explains who is qualifed to apply for the Health Professions Student Loan, where to apply, the amount of money that can borrowed, and repayment.

★5502★ The Merck Manual of Diagnosis and Therapy
Merck and Co., Inc.
PO Box 2000
Rahway, NJ 07065
Ph: (908)750-7470   Fr: 800-594-4600
Sixteenth edition, 1992. Describes symptoms to facilitate diagnosis; explains recommended treatment.

★5503★ Mosby's Medical Dictionary
Mosby-Year Book, Inc.
11830 Westline Industrial Dr.
St. Louis, MO 63146
Ph: (314)872-8370   Fax: (314)432-1380
Fr: 800-325-4177
Walter D. Glanze, Kenneth N. Anderson, and Lois E. Anderson, editors. 1993. Illustrated.

★5504★ The New American Medical Dictionary and Health Manual
New American Library
1633 Broadway
New York, NY 10019
Ph: (212)366-2000   Fr: 800-526-0275
Robert E. Rothenberg. Sixth revised edition, 1992. Illustrated.

★5505★ Osteopathic Medicine: An American Reformation
American Osteopathic Association (AOA)
142 E. Ontario St.
Chicago, IL 60611-2864
Ph: (312)280-5800
George W. Northup, editor in chief. Third edition, 1987. Provides an overview of osteopathic medicine, its history and theory, and a picture of the past and present of the profession.

★5506★ Osteopathic Research: Growth and Development
American Osteopathic Association (AOA)
142 E. Ontario St.
Chicago, IL 60611-2864
Ph: (312)280-5800
George W. Northup, editor. 1987. Traces the development of osteopathic research.

★5507★ PDR: Physicians' Desk Reference
Medical Economics Books
680 Kinderkamack Rd.
Oradell, NJ 07649
Ph: (201)358-7200   Fr: 800-223-0581
Barbara B. Huff, et al., editors. Annual. 1995. Contains descriptions of drugs including medical indications, pharmacological actions, and adverse reactions.

★5508★ The Principles and Practice of Medicine
Appleton and Lange
PO Box 56303
Norwalk, CT 06856
Ph: (203)838-4400   Fr: 800-423-1359
Harvey A. McGehee, et al., editors. Twenty-second edition, 1988. Practical guide to diagnosis and treatment.

★5509★ Professional Guide to Diseases
Springhouse Corp.
1111 Bethlehem Pike
Spring House, PA 19477
Ph: (215)646-8700
Fourth edition, 1991. An encyclopedia of illnesses, disorders, injuries, and their treatments. Includes bibliographies and an index.

★5510★ Radiology
McGraw-Hill Inc.
11 W. 19 St.
New York, NY 10011
Ph: 800-722-4726
David Hovsepian, M.D. 1993.

★5511★ Taber's Cyclopedic Medical Dictionary
F. A. Davis Co.
1915 Arch St.
Philadelphia, PA 19103
Ph: (215)568-2270
Clarence W. Taber. Edited by Clayton L. Thomas. Seventeenth edition, 1993. Includes an index.

PROFESSIONAL AND TRADE PERIODICALS

★5512★ ACEP News
American College of Emergency Physicians (ACEP)
PO Box 619911
Dallas, TX 75261-9911
Ph: (214)550-0911   Fax: (214)580-2816
Fr: 800-798-1822
Earl Schwartz
Monthly. Informs emergency physicians of socioeconomic issues affecting the specialty of emergency medicine. Contains information on medical practice management, pertinent federal and state legislation, and college activities and services.

★5513★ Advanced Technology in Surgical Care
American Health Consultants, Inc.
3525 Piedmont Rd., Bldg. 6, Ste. 400
Atlanta, GA 30305
Ph: (404)262-7436   Fax: (404)262-7837
Fr: 800-688-2421
Fran Rothbard
Monthly. Concerned with topics related to lasers in surgery and medicine in general. Considers safety, legal issues, reimbursement, cost containment, and new products and procedures. Recurring features include news of research and conferences, a calendar of events, guest columns, and laser practice reports.

★5514★ American Association of Senior Physicians—Newsletter
American Association of Senior Physicians (AASP)
515 N. State St., 14th Fl.
Chicago, IL 60610
Ph: (312)464-2460   Fax: (312)464-5845
Gerald L. Farley
Bimonthly. Focuses on successful retirement for physicians. Supplies information on finances, social security, taxes, residence relocation, closing a medical practice, travel opportunities, estate considerations, and related subjects.

★5515★ American College of Medical Quality—Focus
American College of Utilization Review Physicians
9005 Congressional Ct.
Potomac, MD 20854-4608
Ph: (813)497-3340   Fax: (813)497-5573
Russell E. Barker, Contact
Bimonthly. Highlights news on the quality assurance of the utilization review field. Recurring features include letters to the editor, news of research, a calendar of events, job listings, and book reviews.

★5516★ American Family Physician
American Academy of Family Physicians
8880 Ward Pkwy.
Kansas City, MO 64114
Ph: (816)333-9700   Fax: (816)333-0303
Sharon Scott Morey
Medical journal.

★5517★ Annals of Internal Medicine
American College of Physicians
Independence Mall W.
6th St. at Race
Philadelphia, PA 19106-1572
Ph: (215)351-2651   Fax: (215)351-2644
Suzanne W. Fletcher
Semiweekly. Medical journal.

**★5518★ Clinical and Diagnostic
Virology**
Elsevier Science Publishing Co., Inc.
655 Avenue of the Americas
New York, NY 10010
Ph: (212)633-3977   Fax: (212)633-3820
Max Chernesky
Journal in the field of virology.

★5519★ Cope
Media America, Inc.
2019 N. Carothers
Franklin, TN 37064
Ph: (615)790-2400   Fax: (615)791-4719
Michael D. HoltPublisher
Bimonthly. Journal covering the field of oncology.

★5520★ The Cranial Letter
The Cranial Academy
3500 Depauw Blvd. No. 1080
Indianapolis, IN 46268-1136
Ph: (317)879-0713
Dalla Hessler
Quarterly. Provides information about osteopathy in the cranio-sacral field for doctors of osteopathy, dentistry, and medicine. Carries news of reports, papers, seminars, courses offered by the Academy, and research projects. Recurring features include obituaries, a calendar of events, and columns titled President's Message, The Dental Corner, and Scientific Section.

★5521★ Family Practice Management
American Academy of Family Physicians
8880 Ward Pkwy.
Kansas City, MO 64114
Ph: (816)333-9700   Fax: (816)333-0303
Magazine covering socio-economic and management topics concerning family physicians.

**★5522★ JAMA: Journal of the American
Medical Association**
American Medical Assn.
515 N. State St.
Chicago, IL 60610
Ph: (312)464-5000   Fax: (312)464-4184
George D. Lundberg
Weekly. Scientific general medical journal.

**★5523★ Journal of the American
Osteopathic Association**
American Osteopathic Assn.
142 E. Ontario St.
Chicago, IL 60611-2864
Ph: (312)280-5870   Fax: (312)280-5893
Thomas Wesley Allen
Monthly. Osteopathic clinical journal.

★5524★ The Journal of Family Practice
Appleton & Lange
25 Van Zant St.
PO Box 5630
Norwalk, CT 06856
Ph: (203)838-4400   Fax: (203)854-9486
Paul Fischer
Monthly. Journal covering clinical, family practice, and osteopathic medicine.

**★5525★ The Journal of Perinatal
Education**
American Society for Psychoprophylaxis in
   Obstetrics, Inc. (APSO)
1200 19th St. NW, Ste. 300
Washington, DC 20036-4579
Ph: (202)857-1128   Fax: (202)857-1130
Fr: 800-368-4404
Francine Nichols
Quarterly. Journal containing original research data and teaching aids for physicians, health care educators, and family members who promote and support the APSO/Lamaza method of prepared childbirth.

**★5526★ The Lancet (North American
Edition)**
Williams & Wilkins
428 E. Preston St.
Baltimore, MD 21202
Ph: (410)528-8553   Fax: (410)528-4452
Robin Fox
Weekly. Medical journal. Contents identical to British edition.

★5527★ Medical Staff Leader
American Hospital Publishing, Inc.
737 N. Michigan Ave., Ste. 700
Chicago, IL 60611
Ph: (312)440-6800   Fr: 800-621-6902
Jim Montague
Monthly. Devoted to specific and common concerns of medical staff and hospital administration. Recurring features include articles on joint ventures, ethics, legislation, malpractice, and medical by-laws.

★5528★ MM News
Medical Soc. of the County of NY
40 W. 57th St.
New York, NY 10019-4001
Loretta Lewis, Contact
Bimonthly. Provides Society news and information for member doctors. Recurring features include letters to the editor, a calendar of events, and reports of meetings.

**★5529★ The New England Journal of
Medicine**
Massachusetts Medical Society
1440 Main St.
Waltham, MA 02154-1649
Ph: (617)893-3800   Fax: (617)893-0413
Jerome P. Kassirer
Weekly. Journal for the medical profession.

**★5530★ Operative Techniques in Sports
Medicine**
W.B. Saunders Co.
The Curtis Center
Independence Sq. W.
Philadelphia, PA 19106-3399
Ph: (215)238-7800   Fax: (215)238-6445
David Drez
Quarterly. Journal covering the field of orthopedics in sports medicine.

★5531★ Physicians' Newsletter
Blue Shield of California
2 N. Point
San Francisco, CA 94133
Ph: (415)445-5090   Fax: (415)445-5070
Ken Duchscherer
Bimonthly. Provides information pertaining to Blue Shield of California's private healthcare plans in the areas of new coverage, expenditures, policy guidelines, and items of general healthcare financing affecting physicians in California.

★5532★ Political Stethoscope
American Medical Political Action
   Committee (AMPAC)
1101 Vermont Ave. NW
Washington, DC 20005
Ph: (202)789-7400   Fax: (202)789-7469
James H. Jackson
Quarterly. Focuses on physicians and spouses who are actively involved in the political process of running for office or working on election campaigns. Promotes AMPAC educational programs and activities.

★5533★ The Practice Builder
Alan Bernstein
2755 Bristol, No. 100
Costa Mesa, CA 92626
Ph: (714)545-8900   Fax: (714)662-1002
Alan Bernstein
Offers marketing strategies to small health care practices.

**★5534★ Primary Care Update for OB/
GYNS**
Elsevier Science Publishing Co., Inc.
655 Avenue of the Americas
New York, NY 10010
Ph: (212)633-3977   Fax: (212)633-3820
Magazine for members of the American College of Obstetricians and Gynecologists.

★5535★ Seizure
W.B. Saunders Co.
The Curtis Center
Independence Sq. W.
Philadelphia, PA 19106-3399
Ph: (215)238-7800   Fax: (215)238-6445
Tim Betts
Quarterly. Journal including topics related to epilepsy and seizure disorders.

**★5536★ Voice of the Pharmacist—
Newsletter**
American College of Apothecaries
205 Daingerfield Rd.
Alexandria, VA 22314
Ph: (703)684-8603   Fax: (703)683-3619
D.C. Huffman
Quarterly. Examines current issues and opportunities affecting the retail, hospital, and consultant practices of pharmacy. Discusses controversial issues, often with commentary by pharmacists. Recurring features include editorials, news of research, and letters to the editor.

PROFESSIONAL MEETINGS AND CONVENTIONS

★5537★ American Academy of Family Physicians Annual Scientific Assembly
American Academy of Family Physicians
8880 Ward Pkwy.
Kansas City, MO 64114
Ph: (816)333-9700   Fax: (816)333-0303
Fr: 800-274-2237

Annual. **Dates and Locations:** 1996 Oct 03-05; New Orleans, LA. • 1997 Sep 25-27; Kansas City, MO. • 1998 Sep 17-19; San Francisco, CA. • 1999 Sep 16-19; Orlando, FL. • 2000 Sep 21-24; Dallas, TX.

★5538★ American Academy of Ophthalmology Annual Meeting
American Academy of Ophthalmology
PO Box 7424
San Francisco, CA 94120-7424
Ph: (415)561-8500   Fax: (415)561-8576

Annual. **Dates and Locations:** 1995 Oct 27-31; Chicago, IL. • 1995 Oct 29-02; Atlanta, GA. • 1996 Oct 26-30; San Francisco, CA. • 1997 Nov 08-12; New Orleans, LA. • 1998 Oct 24-28; Orlando, FL. • 1998 Nov 08-12; New Orleans, LA. • 1999 Oct 24-28; Orlando, FL. • 2000 Oct 29-02; San Francisco, CA.

★5539★ American Academy of Pediatrics Annual Meeting
American Academy of Pediatrics
141 Northwest Point Blvd.
PO Box 927
Elk Grove Village, IL 60009
Ph: (708)981-7885   Fax: (708)228-5097
Fr: 800-433-9016

Annual. **Dates and Locations:** 1995 Oct 14-18; San Francisco, CA. • 1996 Oct 26-30; Boston, MA.

★5540★ American Academy of Physical Medicine and Rehabilitation Annual Meetings
American Academy of Physical Medicine and Rehabilitation
122 S. Michigan Ave., Ste. 1300
Chicago, IL 60603
Ph: (312)922-9366   Fax: (312)922-6754

Annual. **Dates and Locations:** 1995 Nov 17-22; Orlando, FL. • 1996 Oct 08-12; Chicago, IL.

★5541★ American College of Osteopathic Obstetricians and Gynecologists Annual Convention and Exhibition
American College of Osteopathic Obstetricians and Gynecologists
900 Auburn Rd.
Pontiac, MI 48342
Ph: (313)332-6360   Fax: (313)332-4607
Annual.

★5542★ American College of Sports Medicine Annual Meeting
American College of Sports Medicine
401 W. Michigan St.
Indianapolis, IN 46202
Ph: (317)637-9200   Fax: (317)634-7817
Annual. Usually held during the end of May.
Dates and Locations: 1996 May 29-01; Cincinnati, OH.

★5543★ American College of Surgeons Annual Clinical Congress
American College of Surgeons
55 E. Erie St.
Chicago, IL 60611
Ph: (312)664-4050   Fax: (312)440-7014
Annual. **Dates and Locations:** 1995 Oct 22-27; New Orleans, LA. • 1996 Oct 06-11; San Francisco, CA. • 1997 Oct 12-17; Chicago, IL. • 1998 Oct 25-30; Orlando, FL. • 1999 Oct 10-15; San Francisco, CA. • 2000 Oct 22-27; Chicago, IL. •

★5544★ American Geriatrics Society Annual Meeting
Thomas S. Clark and Associates
4970 Cleveland St., Ste. 107
Virginia Beach, VA 23462
Ph: (804)490-1389   Fax: (804)497-4209

Annual. **Dates and Locations:** 1996 May 02-05; Chicago, IL. • 1997 May 08-11; Atlanta, GA.

★5545★ American Heart Association Scientific Sessions
American Heart Association
7272 Greenville Ave.
Dallas, TX 75231
Ph: (214)706-1230   Fax: (214)373-3406
Annual. **Dates and Locations:** 1995 Nov 13-16; Anaheim, CA. • 1996 Nov 11-14; New Orleans, LA. • 1997 Nov 10-13; Orlando, FL. • 1998 Nov 09-12; Dallas, TX.

★5546★ American Medical Women's Association Annual Meeting
American Medical Women's Association
801 N. Fairfax St., Ste. 400
Alexandria, VA 22314
Ph: (703)838-0500   Fax: (703)549-3864
Annual. Always held during November.
Dates and Locations: 1995 Nov 01-05; Seattle, WA. • 1996 Nov 06-10; Boston, MA. • 1997 Nov 05-09; Chicago, IL.

★5547★ American Pain Society Scientific Meeting
American Pain Society
5700 Old Orchard Rd., 1st Fl.
Skokie, IL 60077-1024
Ph: (708)966-5595   Fax: (708)966-9418
Annual. **Dates and Locations:** 1995 Nov 08-12; Beverly Hills, CA.

★5548★ American Psychiatric Association Annual Meeting
American Psychiatric Association
1400 K St. NW
Washington, DC 20005
Ph: (202)682-6100   Fax: (202)682-6114
Annual. **Dates and Locations:** 1996 May 04-09; New York, NY. • 1997 May 17-22; San Diego, CA. • 1998 May 30-04; Toronto, ON.

★5549★ American Psychiatric Association Institute on Hospital and Community Psychiatry
American Psychiatric Association
1400 K St., NW
Washington, DC 20005
Ph: (202)682-6000   Fax: (202)682-6132
Annual. Always held during October. **Dates and Locations:** 1996 Oct 18-22; Chicago, IL.

★5550★ Eastern Regional Osteopathic Convention
New Jersey Association of Osteopathic Physicians and Surgeons
1212 Stuyvesant Ave.
Trenton, NJ 08618
Ph: (609)393-8114

Annual. Always held at Bally's Park Place Hotel in Atlantic City, New Jersey. **Dates and Locations:** 1995; Atlantic City, NJ.

★5551★ International College of Surgeons, U.S. Section Annual Meeting
International College of Surgeons, U.S. Section
1516 N. Lake Shore Dr.
Chicago, IL 60610-1694
Ph: (312)787-6274   Fax: (312)787-1624
Annual. Usually held in the spring/summer. **Dates and Locations:** 1995; San Diego, CA. • 1996; Washington, DC.

★5552★ Western States Osteopathic Convention
Stanley Schultz, Inc.
6730 E. McDowell Rd., Ste. 114
Scottsdale, AZ 85257-3142
Ph: (602)941-8981   Fr: 800-528-9906
Annual. Always held in Las Vegas, Nevada. **Dates and Locations:** 1995; Las Vegas, NV.

OTHER SOURCES OF INFORMATION

★5553★ *Annual Statistical Report*
American Association of Colleges of Osteopathic Medicine (AACOM)
6110 Executive Blvd., Ste. 405
Rockville, MD 20852
Ph: (301)468-0990

Annual. A compilation of information gathered from the colleges of osteopathic medicine. The statistical data, which are presented in tables and charts with accompanying text, relate to the characteristics of applicants and matriculants, faculty, curriculum, sources of grants and loans, and distribution of revenues and expenditures.

★5554★ *Current Medical Diagnosis and Treatment*
Appleton and Lange
25 Van Zant St.
East Norwalk, CT 06855
Ph: (203)838-4400   Fr: 800-423-1359
1994. Describes diagnosis and treatment for more than a thousand diseases.

★5555★ From Residency to Reality: Health Professions
McGraw-Hill, Inc.
1221 Avenue of the Americas
New York, NY 10020
Ph: (212)512-2000
Patricia A. Hoffmeir and Jean A. Bohner. 1988. Written for senior medical students and residents. Gives advice on choosing a residency, job hunting, interviewing, and setting up and managing a practice.

★5556★ Information Regarding AMCAS
Association of American Medical Colleges (AAMC)
2450 N St., NW
Washington, DC 20037
Ph: (202)828-0400
Annual. Describes the American Medical Colleges Application Service as a centralized application processing service for medical school applicants.

★5557★ Internal Medicine: Diagnosis and Therapy
Appleton and Lange
25 Van Zant St.
East Norwalk, CT 06855
Ph: (203)838-4400   Fr: 800-423-1359
Jay H. Stein, editor. 1993. This pocket-sized manual is a guide to diagnosis, treatment, and drug therapy.

★5558★ Medical School: Getting in, Staying in, Staying Human
Williams and Wilkins
428 E. Preston St.
Baltimore, MD 21202
Ph: (410)528-4000   Fr: 800-638-0672
Keith R. Ablow. 1992.

★5559★ "Medicine" in Accounting to Zoology: Graduate Fields Defined (pp. 255-260)
Petersons Guides, Inc.
PO Box 2123
Princeton, NJ 08543-2123
Ph: (609)243-9111   Fax: (609)243-9150
Fr: 800-338-3282
Amy J. Goldstein, editor. Revised and updated, 1987. Discusses types of graduate programs and degrees, graduate research, applied work, employment prospects and trends.

★5560★ "Physician" in 100 Best Jobs for the 1990s & Beyond
Dearborn Financial Publishing, Inc.
520 N. Dearborn St.
Chicago, IL 60610-4354
Ph: (312)836-4400   Fax: (312)836-1021
Fr: 800-621-9621
Carol Kleiman. 1992. Describes 100 jobs ranging from accountants to veterinarians.. Each job profile includes such information as education, experience, and certification needed, salaries, and job search suggestions.

★5561★ "Physician (General Practitioner)" in Career Selector 2001
Barron's Educational Series, Inc.
250 Wireless Blvd.
Hauppauge, NY 11788
Ph: (516)434-3311   Fax: (516)434-3723
Fr: 800-645-3476
James C. Gonyea. 1993.

★5562★ The Premedical Planning Guide to Allopathic (M.D.), Osteopathic (D.O.), and Podiatric Medical Schools
Betz Publishing Co., Inc.
PO Box 1745
Rockville, MD 20849
Ph: (301)340-0030   Fr: 800-634-4365
Jane D. Crawford. 1993. Guide to the podiatric college admission process, including preparation, application, and admission procedures. Includes advice on how to choose a podiatrics medical college.

★5563★ Thinking About Medicine
Petersons Guides, Inc.
PO Box 2123
Princeton, NJ 08543-2123
Ph: (609)243-9111   Fax: (609)243-9150
Fr: 800-338-3282
Charles J. Shields. This pamphlet describes the educational preparation needed to get into medical school, the MCAT, and how to improve the chances of being selected.

★5564★ Yearbook and Directory of Osteopathic Physicians
American Osteopathic Association (AOA)
142 E. Ontario St.
Chicago, IL 60611-2864
Ph: (312)280-5800
Annual. Contains alphabetic and geographic listings of osteopathic physicians in the United States and foreign countries. Also lists colleges, hospitals, and affiliated groups. Includes a compendium of educational, regulatory, and organizational information.

Podiatrists

Podiatrists, also known as doctors of podiatric medicine (DPM's), diagnose and treat disorders and diseases of the foot and lower leg. Podiatrists treat corns, calluses, ingrown toenails, bunions, and other deformities. Other conditions treated by podiatrists include ankle and foot injuries, and foot complaints associated with diseases such as diabetes. Some practitioners specialize in surgery, orthopedics, and public health. Besides these three recognized specialties, podiatrists may choose subspecialty areas such as sports medicine, pediatrics, dermatology, geriatrics, and diabetic foot care.

Salaries

Income of podiatrists generally rises significantly as their practices grow.

Median net for podiatrists with 1-2 years experience	$100,287/year
Median net for podiatrists with 10-15 years experience	$119,674/year

Employment Outlook

Growth rate until the year 2005: Faster than the average.

Podiatrists

CAREER GUIDES

★5565★ Careers in Medicine
National Textbook Co. (NTC)
VGM Career Books
4255 W. Touhy Ave.
Lincolnwood, IL 60646-1975
Ph: (708)679-5500   Fax: (708)679-2494
Fr: 800-323-4900

Terry Sacks, editor. 1993. Guide to the various careers in the field of medicine.

★5566★ Careers in Medicine
Rosen Publishing Group
29 E. 21st St.
New York, NY 10010
Ph: (212)777-3017   Fax: (212)777-0277
Fr: 800-237-9932

Carolyn Simpson and Penelope Hall, M.D. 1993. Discusses the qualities a good doctor must possess and how a young person can combine a desire to help others with the practical aspects of getting into and through medical school.

★5567★ Careers in Medicine: Traditional and Alternative Opportunities
Garrett Park Press
PO Box 1907
Garrett Park, MD 20896-0190
Ph: (301)946-2553

T. Donald Rucker and Martin D. Keller. Revised edition, 1990. Written for college students who are considering applying to medical school, medical students attempting to select a specialty, and physicians who want to explore nonclinical work. Provides descriptions and employment outlook for 900 medical-oriented occupations.

★5568★ Doctor of Podiatric Medicine: Partner for Health
American Podiatric Medical Association
9312 Old Georgetown Rd.
Bethesda, MD 20814-1621
Ph: (301)571-9200

1986. Pamphlet describing the profession, practice, educational background, and responsibilities of podiatrists.

★5569★ Health Careers
Careers, Inc.
PO Box 135
Largo, FL 34649-0135
Ph: (813)584-7333

1994. Four-page brief describing duties, working conditions, personal qualifications, training, earnings and hours, employment outlook, places of employment, related careers, and where to write for more information.

★5570★ Podiatric Medicine: The Profession, the Practice
American Podiatric Medical Association
9312 Old Georgetown Rd.
Bethesda, MD 20814-1621
Ph: (301)571-9200

1990. This eight-page booklet outlines preprofessional, professional, postdoctoral and continuing education for podiatrists; describes the profession, and discusses practice in hospitals, public health, and federal service. Lists colleges of podiatric medicine and organizations for the profession.

★5571★ The Podiatric Physician: Meeting the Challenge
American Association of Colleges of Podiatric Medicine
1350 Piccard Dr., Ste. 322
Rockville, MD 20850
Ph: (301)990-7400   Fax: (301)990-2807
Fr: 800-922-9266

This 19-page booklet describes careers in podiatric medicine, specialties in the field, and how to get into a college of podiatric medicine. Contains a two-page profile on eight colleges of podiatric medicine.

★5572★ Podiatrist
Vocational Biographies, Inc.
PO Box 31
Sauk Centre, MN 56378-0031
Ph: (612)352-6516   Fax: (612)352-5546
Fr: 800-255-0752

1991. Four-page pamphlet containing a personal narrative about a worker's job, work likes and dislikes, career path from high school to the present. Education and training, the rewards and frustrations, and the effects of the job on the rest of the worker's life. The data file portion of this pamphlet gives a concise occupational summary, including work descriptions, working conditions, places

of employment, personal characteristics, education and training, job outlook, and salary range.

★5573★ Podiatrist
Careers, Inc.
PO Box 135
Largo, FL 34649-0135
Ph: (813)584-7333

1993. Two-page occupational summary card describing duties, working conditions, personal qualifications, training, earnings and hours, employment outlook, places of employment, related careers, and where to write for more information.

★5574★ "Podiatrist" in 100 Best Careers for the Year 2000 (pp. 6-8)
Arco Pub.
201 W. 103rd St.
Indianapolis, IN 46290
Ph: 800-428-5331   Fax: 800-835-3202

Shelly Field. 1992. Describes 100 job opportunities expected to grow fast throughout the next decade. Provides information on job duties and responsibilities, training requirements, education, advancement opportunities, experience and qualifications, and typical salaries.

★5575★ "Podiatrist" in Career Information Center (Vol.7)
Simon and Schuster
200 Old Tappan Rd.
Old Tappan, NJ 07675
Fax: 800-445-6991   Fr: 800-223-2348

Richard Lidz and Linda Perrin, editorial directors. Fifth edition, 1993. This 13-volume set profiles over 600 occupations. Each occupational profile describes job duties, entry-level requirements, educational requirements, advancement possibilities, employment outlook, working conditions, earnings and benefits, and where to write for more information.

★5576★ "Podiatrist" in *College Board Guide to Jobs and Career Planning* (pp. 257)
The College Board
415 Columbus Ave.
New York, NY 10023-6992
Ph: (212)713-8165   Fax: (212)713-8143
Fr: 800-323-7155

Joyce S. Mitchell. Second edition, 1994. Describes the job, salaries, related careers, education needed, and where to write for more information.

★5577★ "Podiatrist" in *Guide to Federal Jobs* (p. 142)
Resource Directories
3361 Executive Pkwy., Ste. 302
Toledo, OH 43606
Ph: (419)536-5353   Fax: (419)536-7056
Fr: 800-274-8515

Rod W. Durgin, editor. Third edition, 1992. Contains information on finding and applying for federal jobs. Describes more than 200 professional and technical jobs for college graduates. Covers the nature of the work, salary, and geographic location. Lists college majors preferred for that occupation. Section one describes the function and work of government agencies that hire the most significant number of college graduates.

★5578★ "Podiatrist" in *Jobs Rated Almanac*
World Almanac
1 International Blvd., Ste. 444
Mahwah, NJ 07495
Ph: (201)529-6900   Fax: (201)529-6901

Les Krantz. Second edition, 1992. Ranks 250 jobs by environment, salary, outlooks, physical demands, stress, security, travel opportunities, and extra perks. Includes jobs the editor feels are the most common, most interesting, and the most rapidly growing.

★5579★ "Podiatrist" in *VGM's Careers Encyclopedia* (pp. 359-361)
National Textbook Co. (NTC)
VGM Career Books
4255 W. Touhy Ave.
Lincolnwood, IL 60646-1975
Ph: (708)679-5500   Fax: (708)679-2494
Fr: 800-323-4900

Third edition, 1991. Describes job duties, places of employment, working conditions, qualifications, education, and training, advancement potential, and salary for each occupation.

★5580★ "Podiatrist" in *VGM's Handbook of Health Care Careers*
National Textbook Co.
4255 W. Touhy Ave.
Lincolnwood, IL 60646-1975
Ph: (708)679-5500   Fax: (708)679-2494
Fr: 800-323-4900

Annette Selden. 1993. Contains 42 two-page occupational profiles describing job duties, places of employment, working conditions, qualifications, education, employment outlook, and income.

★5581★ *Podiatrists*
Chronicle Guidance Publications, Inc.
66 Aurora St.
PO Box 1190
Moravia, NY 13118-1190
Ph: (315)497-0330   Fax: (315)497-3359
Fr: 800-622-7284

1993. Career brief describing the nature of the job, working conditions, hours and earnings, education and training, licensure, certification, unions, personal qualifications, social and psychological factors, location, employment outlook, entry methods, advancement, and related occupations.

★5582★ "Podiatrists" in *101 Careers: A Guide to the Fastest-Growing Opportunities* (pp. 253-255)
John Wiley & Sons, Inc.
605 3rd Ave.
New York, NY 10158-0012
Ph: (212)850-6645   Fax: (212)850-6088

Michael Harkavy. 1990. Describes the nature of the job, working conditions, employment growth, qualifications, personal skills, projected salaries, and where to write for more information.

★5583★ "Podiatrists" in *American Almanac of Jobs and Salaries* (p. 479)
Avon Books
1350 Avenue of the Americas
New York, NY 10019
Ph: (212)261-6800   Fr: 800-238-0658

John Wright, editor. Revised and updated, 1994-95. This is a comprehensive guide to the wages of hundreds of occupations in a wide variety of industries and organizations.

★5584★ "Podiatrists" in *America's 50 Fastest Growing Jobs* (pp. 57)
JIST Works, Inc.
720 N. Park Ave.
Indianapolis, IN 46202-3431
Ph: (317)264-3720   Fax: (317)264-3709
Fr: 800-648-5478

Michael J. Farr, compiler. 1994. Describes the 50 fastest growing jobs within major career clusters such as technicians, and marketing and sales. Each job profile explains the nature of the work, skills and abilities required, employment outlook, average earnings, related occupations, education and training requirements, and employment opportunities. Also contains career planning information and job search tips.

★5585★ "Podiatrists" in *Best Jobs for the 1990s and Into the 21st Century*
Impact Publications
9104-N Manassas Dr.
Manassas Park, VA 22111
Ph: (703)361-7300   Fax: (703)335-9486

Ronald L. Krannich and Caryl Rae Krannich. 1993.

★5586★ "Podiatrists" in *Career Discovery Encyclopedia* (Vol.5, pp. 62-63)
J.G. Ferguson Publishing Co.
200 W. Madison St., Ste. 300
Chicago, IL 60606
Ph: (312)580-5480   Fax: (312)580-4948

Russell E. Primm, editor-in chief. 1993. This six volume set contains two-page articles for 504 occupations. Each article describes job duties, earnings, and educational and training requirements. The whole set is arranged alphabetically by job title. Designed for junior high and older students.

★5587★ "Podiatrists" in *Encyclopedia of Careers and Vocational Guidance* (Vol.4, pp. 137-139)
J.G. Ferguson Publishing Co.
200 W. Madison St., Ste. 300
Chicago, IL 60606
Ph: (312)580-5480   Fax: (312)580-4948

William E. Hopke, editor-in-chief. Ninth edition, 1993. Four-volume set that profiles 900 occupations and describes job trends in 74 industries. Includes career description, educational requirements, history of the job, methods of entry, advancement, employment outlook, earnings, conditions of work, social and psychological factors, and sources of further information.

★5588★ "Podiatrists" in *Jobs! What They Are—Where They Are—What They Pay* (p. 291)
Simon & Schuster, Inc.
Simon & Schuster Bldg.
1230 Avenue of the Americas
New York, NY 10020
Ph: (212)698-7000   Fr: 800-223-2348

Robert O. Snelling and Anne M. Snelling. 3rd edition, 1992. Describes duties and responsibilities, earnings, employment opportunities, training, and qualifications.

★5589★ "Podiatrists" in *Occupational Outlook Handbook*
U.S. Government Printing Office
Superintendent of Documents
Washington, DC 20402
Ph: (202)512-1800   Fax: (202)512-2250

Biennial; latest edition, 1994-95. Encyclopedia of careers describing about 250 occupations and comprising about 85 percent of all jobs in the economy. Occupations that require lengthy education or training are given the most attention. Each occupation's profile describes what the worker does on the job, working conditions, education and training requirements, advancement possibilities, job outlook, earnings, and sources of additional information.

★5590★ "Podiatry" in *Black Woman's Career Guide* (pp. 106-108)
Bantam Doubleday Dell
1540 Broadway
New York, NY 10036
Fax: 800-233-3294   Fr: 800-223-5780

Beatryce Nivens. Revised edition, 1987. Part 1 describes career planning, resume writing, job hunting, and interviewing. Part 2 profiles 60 black women pioneers in 20 different career areas.

★5591★ "Sports Podiatrist" in *Careers in Health and Fitness*
Rosen Publishing Group
29 E. 21st St.
New York, NY 10010
Ph: (212)777-3017   Fax: (212)777-0277
Fr: 800-237-9932

Jackie Heron. 1990. Occupational profiles contain information on job duties, skills, advantages, basic equipment used, employment possibilities, certification, and salary.

★5592★ Your Podiatrist Talks About Podiatric Medicine
American Podiatric Medical Association (APMA)
9312 Old Georgetown Rd.
Bethesda, MD 20814-1621
Ph: (301)571-9200
1991. This pamphlet describes career opportunities, educational preparation, and financial aid for potential podiatrists. Lists accredited colleges of podiatric medicine.

PROFESSIONAL ASSOCIATIONS

★5593★ American Association of Colleges of Podiatric Medicine (AACPM)
1350 Piccard Dr., Ste. 322
Rockville, MD 20850
Ph: (301)990-7400   Fax: (301)990-2807
Fr: 800-922-9266
Members: Professional organization of administrators, faculty, practitioners, students, and other individuals associated with podiatric medical education. **Purpose:** Provides vocational guidance material for secondary schools and colleges. Conducts public affairs activities and legislative advocacy. Compiles statistics.

★5594★ American Podiatric Medical Association (APMA)
9312 Old Georgetown Rd.
Bethesda, MD 20814
Ph: (301)571-9200   Fax: (301)530-2752
Members: Professional society of podiatrists. **Publications:** *APMA News*, monthly. • *Catalogue of Audiovisual, Informational and Educational Materials*, periodic. • *Desk Reference of the APMA*, annual. • *Journal of the American Podiatric Medical Association*, monthly.

STANDARDS/CERTIFICATION AGENCIES

★5595★ American Board of Podiatric Orthopedics and Primary Medicine (ABPOPPM)
401 N. Michigan Ave.
Chicago, IL 60611-4267
Ph: (312)321-5139   Fax: (312)644-1815
Offers certifying examinations in foot orthopedics for podiatrists; aims at improving public health by encouraging and elevating standards for practicing podiatric orthopedists.

★5596★ American Board of Podiatric Surgery (ABPS)
1601 Dolores St.
San Francisco, CA 94110-4906
Ph: (415)826-3200   Fax: (415)826-4640
Objectives are: to protect and improve public health by advancing the science of foot surgery and by encouraging the study and evaluation of standards of foot surgery; to act upon application for certification of legally licensed podiatrists to ascertain their competency in foot surgery; to grant certificates to candidates who have met all qualifications.

TEST GUIDES

★5597★ Colleges of Podiatry Admission Test (CPAT)
National Learning Corp.
212 Michael Dr.
Syosset, NY 11791
Ph: (516)921-8888   Fax: (516)921-8743
Fr: 800-645-6337
Jack Rudman. Part of the Admission Test series. A sample test for potential podiatrists who are seeking admission to graduate and professional schools or seeking entrance or advancement in institutional and public career service.

EDUCATIONAL DIRECTORIES AND PROGRAMS

★5598★ Encyclopedia of Medical Organizations and Agencies
Gale Research Inc.
835 Penobscot Bldg.
Detroit, MI 48226-4094
Ph: (313)961-2242   Fax: (313)961-6741
Fr: 800-877-GALE
Karen Boyden, Contact
Biennial, November of odd years. Covers over 13,400 state, national, and international medical associations, foundations, research institutes, federal and state agencies, and medical and allied health schools. Entries include: Organization name, address, phone; many listings include names and titles of key personnel, descriptive annotations. Arrangement: Classified by subject, then by type of organization.

★5599★ Health & Medical Industry Directory
American Business Directories, Inc.
5711 S. 86th Circle
Omaha, NE 68127
Ph: (402)593-4600   Fax: (402)331-1505
Released 1993. Lists over 1.1 million physicians and surgeons, dentists, clinics, health clubs, and other health-related businesses in the U.S. and Canada. Entries include: Name, address, phone.

★5600★ Healthcare Career Directory— Nurses and Physicians
Gale Research Inc.
835 Penobscot Bldg.
Detroit, MI 48226-4094
Ph: (313)961-2242   Fax: (313)961-6083
Fr: 800-877-GALE
Bradley J. Morgan and Joseph M. Palmisano. Second edition, 1993. A directory in the Career Advisor Series that provides essays written by industry professionals; job search information on resume and cover letter preparation, networking, and the interviewing process; approximately 300 companies and organizations offering job opportunities and internships, and additional job-hunting resources.

★5601★ Medical and Health Information Directory
Gale Research Inc.
835 Penobscot Bldg.
Detroit, MI 48226-4094
Ph: (313)961-2242   Fax: (313)961-6741
Fr: 800-877-GALE
Karen Boyden, Contact
Approximately biennial; latest edition 1994. Covers in Volume 1, almost 18,600 medical and health oriented associations, organizations, institutions, and government agencies, including health maintenance organizations (HMOs), preferred provider organizations (PPOs), insurance companies, pharmaceutical companies, research centers, and medical and allied health schools. In Volume 2, nearly 11,800 medical book publishers; medical periodicals, directories, audiovisual producers and services, medical libraries and information centers, and electronic resources. In Volume 3, nearly 26,000 clinics, treatment centers, care programs, and counseling/diagnostic services for 30 subject areas. Entries include: Institution, service, or firm name, address, phone; many include names of key personnel Arrangement: Classified by organization activity, service, etc..

AWARDS, SCHOLARSHIPS, GRANTS, AND FELLOWSHIPS

★5602★ HRSA-BHP Health Professions Student Loans
U.S. Public Health Service
Health Resources and Services Administration
Parklawn Bldg., Rm. 8-38
5600 Fishers Ln.
Rockville, MD 20857
Purpose: To assist students with need for financial assistance to undertake the course of study required to become physicians, dentists, osteopathic physicians, optometrists, pharmacists, podiatrists, or veterinarians. Qualifications: Applicants must be enrolled or accepted for enrollment as full-time students in a program leading to a doctoral degree in medicine, dental surgery or equivalent degree, pharmacy, osteopathic medicine, optometry or equivalent degree, podiatric medicine or equivalent degree, or veterinary medicine or equivalent degree; or a bachelor of science in pharmacy or equivalent degree. Applicants must also be citizens, nationals, or permanent residents of the United States or the District of Columbia, the Commonwealths of Puerto Rico or the Marianna Islands, the Virgin Islands, Guam, The American Samoa, the Trust Territory of the Pacific Islands, the Republic of Palau, the Republic of the Marshall Islands, and the Federated State of Micronesia. Applicants must also demonstrate financial need. Professional students, interns, residents, and students seeking ad-

vanced training are not eligible. Funds available: Up to the cost of tuition plus $2,500 or the amount of financial need, whichever is less. The interest rate is five percent and accrues during the repayment period. Loans are repayable over a ten year period and beginning one year after the student graduates or ceases to enroll full-time in a health program.

★**5603**★ **HRSA-BHP Loans for Disadvantaged Students**
U.S. Public Health Service
Health Resources and Services
  Administration
Parklawn Bldg., Rm. 8-38
5600 Fishers Ln.
Rockville, MD 20857

Purpose: To assist students who need financial assistance to pursue careers in medicine, osteopathic medicine, dentistry, optometry, podiatric medicine, pharmacy, or veterinary medicine. Qualifications: Applicants must be citizens, nationals, or lawful permanent residents of the United States or the District of Columbia, the Commonwealths of Puerto Rico or the Marianna Islands, the Virgin Islands, Guam, American Samoa, the Trust Territory of the Pacific Islands, the Republic of Palau, the Republic of the Marshall Islands, or the Federated State of Micronesia. They must also be enrolled or accepted for enrollment at a participating health professionals school full-time. Students must be determined by their school's financial aid director to meet financial need and "disadvantaged background" criteria. Those enrolled in schools of medicine or osteopathic medicine must demonstrate exceptional financial need. Preprofessional students, interns, residents, and students seeking advanced training are not eligible. Selection criteria: Schools are responsible for selecting recipients and for determining the amount of assistance. Funds available: The maximum loan amount allowed for each school year is the cost of tuition plus $2,500, or the amount of financial need, whichever is lesser. The repayment interest rate is five percent over a ten-year period, which begins one year after completion of cessation of full-time study. Interest begins accruing at the time the loan becomes rapayable. Repayment may be deferred under special circumstances, and interest does not accrue during periods of deferment.

★**5604**★ **Lifetime Achievement Award**
Podiatry Management
7000 Terminal Sq., Ste. 210
Upper Darby, PA 19082
Ph: (610)734-2420   Fax: (610)734-2423

To recognize individuals who promote and advance the podiatry profession. Podiatrists vote for the winning candidate. A plaque and publicity are awarded annually. Established in 1984. The Award has been recognized by the White House with letters from Presidents Bush and Clinton.

★**5605**★ **Practitioner of the Year Award**
American Society of Podiatric Medicine
7331 Collins Ave.
Miami Beach, FL 33141
Ph: (305)866-9608

To recognize individuals for contributions to podiatric medicine through the ASPM. Recipi-

ents are selected by the Executive Board of the Society prior to the annual meeting. A framed certificate is awarded annually. Established in 1980.

BASIC REFERENCE GUIDES AND HANDBOOKS

★**5606**★ *Desk Reference*
American Podiatric Medical Association
  (APMA)
9312 Old Georgetown Rd.
Bethesda, MD 20814
Ph: (301)571-9200
Periodic. 1993.

★**5607**★ *Fact Sheet: Health Education Assistance Loan Program (HEAL)*
U.S. Department of Health and Human
  Services
Public Health Service
Health Resources and Services
  Administration
Bureau of Health Professions, Division of
  Student Assistance
Rockville, MD 20857
Ph: (301)443-2086

Fact sheet describing the HEAL Program; covers eligible schools, borrowers, and lenders, as well as loan limitations, interest, and repayment.

★**5608**★ *Handbook of Common Foot Problems*
Churchill Livingstone, Inc.
650 6th Ave.
New York, NY 10011
Ph: (212)206-5000   Fr: 800-553-5426
Lawrence B. Harkless, editor. 1990.

★**5609**★ *Podiatric Medicine*
Williams and Wilkins
428 E. Preston St.
Baltimore, MD 21202
Ph: (410)528-4000

Irving Yale. Third edition, 1987. Includes a bibliography and an index.

PROFESSIONAL AND TRADE PERIODICALS

★**5610**★ *AAPSM Newsletter*
American Academy of Podiatric Sports
  Medicine (AAPSM)
1729 Glastonberry Rd.
Potomac, MD 20854
Ph: (301)424-7440
Larry I. Shane

Quarterly. Features articles discussing injuries and treatments in the field of podiatry. Reports on Academy activities and meetings. Recurring features include news of research, editorials, and a calendar of events.

★**5611**★ *American Academy of Podiatry Administration—Newsletter*
American Academy of Podiatry
  Administration
2737 E. Oakland Park Blvd.
Ft. Lauderdale, FL 33306
Ph: (305)561-3338
Gary S. Wallach

Quarterly. Supplies management information for Academy members. Covers such subjects as investments, advertising and marketing, and tax planning. Recurring features include book reviews, news of the Academy and its members, news of research, a calendar of events, and columns titled President's Corner, Practice Management Points, and Money Management.

★**5612**★ *APMA News*
American Podiatric Medical Association
  (APMA)
9312 Old Georgetown Rd.
Bethesda, MD 20814-1621
Ph: (301)571-9200   Fax: (301)530-2752
David Zych

Monthly. Covers news of the Association as well as reporting on bylaws and on regulations that affect the profession. Recurring features include a calendar of events, statistics, news of research, and news of workshops.

★**5613**★ *The Podiatrist's Patient Newsletter*
Doctor's Press, Inc.
Pitney Rd.
PO Box 11177
Lancaster, PA 17605
Ph: (717)393-1010   Fr: 800-233-0196
Lee J. Dmitzak

Quarterly. Intended for distribution to podiatrists' patients. Carries articles and items on topics related to foot health. Recurring features include quizzes and cartoons.

PROFESSIONAL MEETINGS AND CONVENTIONS

★**5614**★ **American College of Foot and Ankle Surgeons Annual Meeting and Seminar**
American College of Foot and Ankle
  Surgeons
444 NW Hwy. 150
Park Ridge, IL 60068
Ph: (708)292-2237   Fax: (708)292-2022

Annual. **Dates and Locations:** 1996 Mar 20-23; New Orleans, LA.

★**5615**★ **American Podiatric Medical Association Annual Meeting**
American Podiatric Medical Association
9312 Old Georgetown Rd.
Bethesda, MD 20814
Ph: (301)571-9200   Fax: (301)530-2752

Annual. Always held in August.

★5616★ Western Podiatric Congress
California Podiatric Medical Association
2430 K St., Ste. 200
Sacramento, CA 95816
Ph: (916)448-0248   Fax: (916)448-0258
Annual.

OTHER SOURCES OF INFORMATION

★5617★ A Guide to Financing Your Podiatric Medical Education
American Association of Colleges of
Podiatric Medicine (AACPM)
6110 Executive Blvd., Ste. 204
Rockville, MD 20852
Ph: (301)984-9350   Fr: 800-922-9266

Pamphlet describing how to determine financial need and lists sources of financial aid for podiatry students.

★5618★ "Podiatric Medicine" in Accounting to Zoology: Graduate Fields Defined (pp. 284-285)
Petersons Guides, Inc.
PO Box 2123
Princeton, NJ 08543-2123
Ph: (609)243-9111   Fax: (609)243-9150
Fr: 800-338-3282

Amy J. Goldstein, editor. Revised and updated, 1987. Discusses types of graduate programs and degrees, graduate research, applied work, employment prospects and trends.

★5619★ "Podiatrist" in 100 Best Jobs for the 1990s & Beyond
Dearborn Financial Publishing, Inc.
520 N. Dearborn St.
Chicago, IL 60610-4354
Ph: (312)836-4400   Fax: (312)836-1021
Fr: 800-621-9621

Carol Kleiman. 1992. Describes 100 jobs ranging from accountants to veterinarians. Each job profile includes such information as education, experience, and certification needed, salaries, and job search suggestions.

★5620★ "Podiatrist" in Allied Health Professions (pp. 5-6; 134)
Arco Publishing Co.
Simon & Schuster, Inc.
201 W. 103rd St.
Indianapolis, IN 46290
Ph: 800-428-5331   Fax: 800-835-3202

1993. Contains information on 28 representative careers in health care. Provides a sample of the Allied Health Professions Admission Test, lists professional societies and associations, and offers a directory of schools and programs for the careers listed.

★5621★ The Premedical Planning Guide to Allopathic (M.D.), Osteopathic (D.O.), and Podiatric Medical Schools
Betz Publishing Co., Inc.
PO Box 1745
Rockville, MD 20849
Ph: (301)340-0030   Fr: 800-634-4365

Jane D. Crawford. 1993. Guide to the podiatric college admission process, including preparation, application, and admission procedures. Includes advice on how to choose a podiatrics medical college.

Veterinarians

Veterinarians care for pets, livestock, sporting and laboratory animals, and protect the public from exposure to animal diseases. Typically, veterinarians diagnose medical problems, dress wounds, set broken bones, perform surgery, and prescribe and administer medicines and vaccines. Most veterinarians engage in private practice. The majority treat small animals such as dogs, cats, and birds. Others concentrate on larger animals or have a mixed practice of both large and small animals. Some veterinarians teach in veterinary colleges, work in zoos or animal laboratories, or engage in a combination of clinical and research activities.

Salaries

Earnings of veterinarians rise significantly as they gain experience.

Beginning veterinarians, private practice	$27,858/year
Veterinarians, private practice	$63,069/year
Veterinarians, federal government	$50,482/year

Employment Outlook

Growth rate until the year 2005: Faster than the average.

Veterinarians

CAREER GUIDES

★5622★ Animal Scientists
Chronicle Guidance Publications, Inc.
66 Aurora St.
PO Box 1190
Moravia, NY 13118-1190
Ph: (315)497-0330   Fax: (315)497-3359
Fr: 800-622-7284

1994. Career brief describing the nature of the job, working conditions, hours and earnings, education and training, licensure, certification, unions, personal qualifications, social and psychological factors, location, employment outlook, entry methods, advancement, and related occupations.

★5623★ Careers for Animal Lovers and Other Zoological Types
National Textbook Co. (NTC)
VGM Career Books
4255 W. Touhy Ave.
Lincolnwood, IL 60646-1975
Ph: (708)679-5500   Fax: (708)679-2494
Fr: 800-323-4900

Louise Miller, editor. 1991. Explores careers working with animals.

★5624★ Careers in Medicine
National Textbook Co. (NTC)
VGM Career Books
4255 W. Touhy Ave.
Lincolnwood, IL 60646-1975
Ph: (708)679-5500   Fax: (708)679-2494
Fr: 800-323-4900

Terry Sacks, editor. 1993. Guide to the various careers in the field of medicine.

★5625★ Careers in Veterinary Medicine
Rosen Publishing Group
29 E. 21st St.
New York, NY 10010
Ph: (212)777-3017   Fax: (212)777-0277
Fr: 800-237-9932

Jane Caryl Duncan. 1994. Describes working in veterinary medicine and gives an overview of future career possibilities.

★5626★ Health Careers
Careers, Inc.
PO Box 135
Largo, FL 34649-0135
Ph: (813)584-7333

1994. Four-page brief describing duties, working conditions, personal qualifications, training, earnings and hours, employment outlook, places of employment, related careers, and where to write for more information.

★5627★ Large Animal Veterinarian
Vocational Biographies, Inc.
PO Box 31
Sauk Centre, MN 56378-0031
Ph: (612)352-6516   Fax: (612)352-5546
Fr: 800-255-0752

1994. Four-page pamphlet containing a personal narrative about a worker's job, work likes and dislikes, career path from high school to the present. Education and training, the rewards and frustrations, and the effects of the job on the rest of the worker's life. The data file portion of this pamphlet gives a concise occupational summary, including work descriptions, working conditions, places of employment, personal characteristics, education and training, job outlook, and salary range.

★5628★ Opportunities in Animal and Pet Care
National Textbook Co. (NTC)
VGM Career Books
4255 W. Touhy Ave.
Lincolnwood, IL 60646-1975
Ph: (708)679-5500   Fax: (708)679-2494
Fr: 800-323-4900

Mary Price Lee, Richard S. Lee. Overviews careers in animal and pet care including veterinary positions, zoo work, wild animal training, animal shelters, pet shops and pet therapy. Describes necessary educational background and lists programs in animal technology.

★5629★ Opportunities in Veterinary Medicine Careers
National Textbook Co. (NTC)
VGM Career Books
4255 W. Touhy Ave.
Lincolnwood, IL 60646-1975
Ph: (708)679-5500   Fax: (708)679-2494
Fr: 800-323-4900

Sara Mikesell. Discusses history and educational requirements, and, employment opportunities for veterinarians in industry, government, academia, and the military.

★5630★ "Public Health Veterinarian" in Opportunities in Environmental Careers
National Textbook Co. (NTC)
VGM Career Books
4255 W. Touhy Ave.
Lincolnwood, IL 60646-1975
Ph: (708)679-5500   Fax: (708)679-2494
Fr: 800-323-4900

Odom Fanning. 1991. Describes a broad range of opportunities in fields such as environmental health, recreation, physics, and hygiene.

★5631★ Today's Veterinarian
American Veterinary Medical Association
1931 N. Meacham Rd., Ste. 100
Schaumburg, IL 60173-4360
Ph: (708)925-8070

1987. This 20-page booklet describes what veterinarians do, specialties of veterinary medicine, personal abilities and education required, getting into veterinary school, rewards and drawbacks of the profession, earnings, outlook, and related occupations. Lists accredited veterinary medical colleges.

★5632★ Veterinarian
Careers, Inc.
PO Box 135
Largo, FL 34649-0135
Ph: (813)584-7333

1994. Four-page brief offering the definition, history, duties, working conditions, personal qualifications, educational requirements, earnings, hours, employment outlook, advancement, and careers related to this position.

★5633★ *Veterinarian*
Vocational Biographies, Inc.
PO Box 31
Sauk Centre, MN 56378-0031
Ph: (612)352-6516   Fax: (612)352-5546
Fr: 800-255-0752
1992. Four-page pamphlet containing a personal narrative about a worker's job, work likes and dislikes, career path from high school to the present. Education and training, the rewards and frustrations, and the effects of the job on the rest of the worker's life. The data file portion of this pamphlet gives a concise occupational summary, including work descriptions, working conditions, places of employment, personal characteristics, education and training, job outlook, and salary range.

★5634★ "Veterinarian" in *100 Best Careers for the Year 2000* (pp. 79-81)
Arco Pub.
201 W. 103rd St.
Indianapolis, IN 46290
Ph: 800-428-5331   Fax: 800-835-3202
Shelly Field. 1992. Describes 100 job opportunities expected to grow fast throughout the next decade. Provides information on job duties and responsibilities, training requirements, education, advancement opportunities, experience and qualifications, and typical salaries.

★5635★ "Veterinarian" in *Black Woman's Career Guide* (pp. 109-110)
Bantam Doubleday Dell
1540 Broadway
New York, NY 10036
Fax: 800-233-3294   Fr: 800-223-5780
Beatryce Nivens. Revised edition, 1987. Part 1 describes career planning, resume writing, job hunting, and interviewing. Part 2 profiles 60 black women pioneers in 20 different career areas.

★5636★ "Veterinarian" in *College Board Guide to Jobs and Career Planning* (pp. 258)
The College Board
415 Columbus Ave.
New York, NY 10023-6992
Ph: (212)713-8165   Fax: (212)713-8143
Fr: 800-323-7155
Joyce S. Mitchell. Second edition, 1994. Describes the job, salaries, related careers, education needed, and where to write for more information.

★5637★ "Veterinarian" in *Jobs Rated Almanac*
World Almanac
1 International Blvd., Ste. 444
Mahwah, NJ 07495
Ph: (201)529-6900   Fax: (201)529-6901
Les Krantz. Second edition, 1992. Ranks 250 jobs by environment, salary, outlooks, physical demands, stress, security, travel opportunities, and extra perks. Includes jobs the editor feels are the most common, most interesting, and the most rapidly growing.

★5638★ "Veterinarian" in *VGM's Careers Encyclopedia* (pp. 481-483)
National Textbook Co. (NTC)
VGM Career Books
4255 W. Touhy Ave.
Lincolnwood, IL 60646-1975
Ph: (708)679-5500   Fax: (708)679-2494
Fr: 800-323-4900
Third edition, 1991. Describes job duties, places of employment, working conditions, qualifications, education, and training, advancement potential, and salary for each occupation.

★5639★ "Veterinarian" in *VGM's Handbook of Health Care Careers*
National Textbook Co.
4255 W. Touhy Ave.
Lincolnwood, IL 60646-1975
Ph: (708)679-5500   Fax: (708)679-2494
Fr: 800-323-4900
Annette Selden. 1993. Contains 42 two-page occupational profiles describing job duties, places of employment, working conditions, qualifications, education, employment outlook, and income.

★5640★ *Veterinarians*
Chronicle Guidance Publications, Inc.
66 Aurora St.
PO Box 1190
Moravia, NY 13118-1190
Ph: (315)497-0330   Fax: (315)497-3359
Fr: 800-622-7284
1993. Career brief describing the nature of the job, working conditions, hours and earnings, education and training, licensure, certification, unions, personal qualifications, social and psychological factors, location, employment outlook, entry methods, advancement, and related occupations.

★5641★ "Veterinarians" in *101 Careers: A Guide to the Fastest-Growing Opportunities* (pp. 269-272)
John Wiley & Sons, Inc.
605 3rd Ave.
New York, NY 10158-0012
Ph: (212)850-6645   Fax: (212)850-6088
Michael Harkavy. 1990. Describes the nature of the job, working conditions, employment growth, qualifications, personal skills, projected salaries, and where to write for more information.

★5642★ "Veterinarians" in *Best Jobs for the 1990s and Into the 21st Century*
Impact Publications
9104-N Manassas Dr.
Manassas Park, VA 22111
Ph: (703)361-7300   Fax: (703)335-9486
Ronald L. Krannich and Caryl Rae Krannich. 1993.

★5643★ "Veterinarians" in *Career Discovery Encyclopedia* (Vol.6, pp. 138-139)
J.G. Ferguson Publishing Co.
200 W. Madison St., Ste. 300
Chicago, IL 60606
Ph: (312)580-5480   Fax: (312)580-4948
Russell E. Primm, editor in chief. 1993. This six volume set contains two-page articles for 504 occupations. Each article describes job duties, earnings, and educational and training requirements. The whole set is arranged alphabetically by job title. Designed for junior high and older students.

★5644★ "Veterinarians" in *Career Information Center* (Vol.2)
Simon and Schuster
200 Old Tappan Rd.
Old Tappan, NJ 07675
Fax: 800-445-6991   Fr: 800-223-2348
Richard Lidz and Linda Perrin, editorial directors. Fifth edition, 1993. A multi-volume set that profiles over 600 occupations. Each occupational profile describes job duties, educational requirements, advancement possibilities, employment outlook, working conditions, earnings and benefits, and where to write for more information.

★5645★ "Veterinarians" in *Encyclopedia of Careers and Vocational Guidance* (Vol.4, pp. 584-586)
J.G. Ferguson Publishing Co.
200 W. Madison St., Ste. 300
Chicago, IL 60606
Ph: (312)580-5480   Fax: (312)580-4948
William E. Hopke, editor-in-chief. Ninth edition, 1993. Four-volume set that profiles 900 occupations and describes job trends in 74 industries. Includes career description, educational requirements, history of the job, methods of entry, advancement, employment outlook, earnings, conditions of work, social and psychological factors, and sources of further information.

★5646★ "Veterinarians" in *Health Care Job Explosion!* (pp. 340-346)
D-Amp Publications
401 Amherst Ave.
Coraopolis, PA 15108
Ph: (412)262-5578
Dennis V. Damp. 1993. Provides information on the nature of work for the major health care occupational groups. Descriptions include working conditions, training, job outlook, qualifications, and related occupations.

★5647★ "Veterinarians" in *Jobs! What They Are—Where They Are—What They Pay* (p. 53)
Simon & Schuster, Inc.
Simon & Schuster Bldg.
1230 Avenue of the Americas
New York, NY 10020
Ph: (212)698-7000   Fr: 800-223-2348
Robert O. Snelling and Anne M. Snelling. 3rd edition, 1992. Describes duties and responsibilities, earnings, employment opportunities, training, and qualifications.

★5648★ "Veterinarians" in *Occupational Outlook Handbook*
U.S. Government Printing Office
Superintendent of Documents
Washington, DC 20402
Ph: (202)512-1800   Fax: (202)512-2250
Biennial; latest edition, 1994-95. Encyclopedia of careers describing about 250 occupations and comprising about 85 percent of all jobs in the economy. Occupations that require lengthy education or training are given the most attention. Each occupation's profile describes what the worker does on the job, working conditions, education and training requirements, advancement possibilities, job

outlook, earnings, and sources of additional information.

★5649★ "Zoo Veterinarian" in *Museum Jobs form A-Z: What They Are, How to Prepare, and Where to Find Them*
Batax Museum Publishing
301 Racquet Club Rd., Ste. 202
Fort Lauderdale, FL 33326
G.W. Bates. 1994.

PROFESSIONAL ASSOCIATIONS

★5650★ American Association of Industrial Veterinarians (AAIV)
c/o Caroline & Co.
1015 E. Broadway
Columbia, MO 65201
Ph: (314)449-3109   Fax: (314)874-2451
Members: Veterinarians, many of whom are members of the American Veterinary Medical Association and are employed in a professional capacity in industrial activities, for example, with drug and chemical firms, in livestock and poultry enterprises, or in independent research. Holds workshops. **Publications:** *AAIV Highlights*, semiannual.

★5651★ American Association of Wildlife Veterinarians (AAWV)
Colorado Division of Wildlife
317 W. Prospect
Fort Collins, CO 80526-2097
Ph: (303)484-2836
Members: Veterinarians in state and federal wildlife resource agencies, universities, private practice, public health service agencies, agricultural agencies, and diagnostic laboratories; veterinary students; and interested individuals. **Purpose:** To deal with problems confronting veterinarians who work with free-ranging wildlife. Encourages colleges of veterinary medicine to increase emphasis on management of and preventive medicine for free-ranging species; educates governmental agencies and wildlife resource interest groups; promotes utilization of veterinarians in the field of wildlife resource management and research; encourages cooperation among resource management professionals and wildlife veterinarians; promotes continuing education programs for wildlife veterinarians; emphasizes interrelationships of man, domestic animals, and wildlife with disease; encourages recognition of disease syndromes as potentially influenced by habitat succession, alteration, and pollution.

★5652★ American Association of Zoo Veterinarians (AAZV)
3400 W. Girard Ave.
Philadelphia, PA 19104-1196
Ph: (215)387-9094   Fax: (215)387-2165
Members: Veterinarians actively engaged in the practice of zoo and wildlife medicine for at least four years; veterinarians who do not qualify for active membership; persons interested in diseases of wildlife; students of veterinary medicine in any accredited veterinary school. **Purpose:** Purposes are to: advance programs for preventive medicine, husbandry, and scientific research dealing with

captive and free-ranging wild animals; provide a forum for the presentation and discussion of problems related to the field; enhance and uphold the professional ethics of veterinary medicine. **Publications:** *Conference Proceedings*, annual. • *Journal of Zoo and Wildlife Medicine*, quarterly.

★5653★ American Society of Animal Science (ASAS)
309 W. Clark St.
Champaign, IL 61820-4690
Ph: (217)356-3182   Fax: (217)398-4119
Members: Professional society of persons engaged in investigation, instruction, or extension in animal science or in the production, processing, and dissemination of livestock and livestock products. **Publications:** *ASAS Handbook and Membership Directory*, biennial. • *Combined Abstracts*, annual. • *Journal of Animal Science*, annual.

★5654★ American Veterinary Medical Association (AVMA)
1931 N. Meacham Rd., Ste. 100
Schaumburg, IL 60173-4360
Ph: (708)925-8070   Fax: (708)925-1329
Fr: 800-248-2862
Members: Professional society of veterinarians. **Purpose:** Conducts educational and research programs. Provides placement service. Maintains the American Society of Laboratory Animal Practitioners. Sponsors American Veterinary Medical Association Foundation (also known as AVMA Foundation) and Educational Commission for Foreign Veterinary Graduates. Compiles statistics. **Publications:** *American Journal of Veterinary Research*, monthly. • *Journal of the AVMA*, semimonthly.

★5655★ Association of American Veterinary Medical Colleges (AAVMC)
1101 Vermont Ave., Ste. 710
Washington, DC 20005
Ph: (202)371-9195   Fax: (202)842-0773
Members: Purpose: Represents colleges of veterinary medicine in the United States and Canada; departments of veterinary science and departments of comparative medicine. **Publications:** *Journal of Veterinary Medical Education*, semiannual.

★5656★ Association for Women Veterinarians (AWV)
c/o Chris Stone Payne, D.V.M.
32205 Allison Dr.
Union City, CA 94587
Ph: (510)471-8379   Fax: (510)471-8379
Members: Women veterinarians; students of veterinary medicine. **Publications:** *AWV Bulletin*, quarterly. • *Roster of Women Veterinarians*, periodic.

★5657★ National Association of Federal Veterinarians (NAFV)
1101 Vermont Ave. NW, Ste. 710
Washington, DC 20005-3521
Ph: (202)289-6334
Members: Professional society of veterinarians employed by the U.S. Government. Maintains speakers' bureau. **Publications:** *Federal Veterinarian*, monthly. • *National Association of Federal Veterinarians—Directory*, annual. • *National Association of Federal Veterinarians—Proceedings of Symposia*, annual.

TEST GUIDES

★5658★ *Admission Test Series: Veterinary College Admission Test*
National Learning Corp.
212 Michael Dr.
Syosset, NY 11791
Ph: (516)921-8888   Fax: (516)921-8743
Fr: 800-645-6337

Jack Rudman. A collection of sample examinations designed to prepare potential veterinarians for graduate and professional school entrance tests and for tests administered by private and public institutions for entrance and career advancement. Provides multiple-choice questions; includes correct answers. Titles in the series include *Educational Commission for Foreign Veterinary Graduates Examination/Combined Volumes; Educational Commission for Foreign Veterinary Graduates Examination/Part I—Anatomy, Physiology, Pathology; Educational Commission for Foreign Veterinary Graduates Examination/Part II—Pharmacology, Therapeutics, Parasitology, Hygiene; Educational Commission for Foreign Veterinary Graduates Examination/Part III—Physical Diagnosis, Medicine, Surgery; National Veterinary Boards/Combined Volumes; National Veterinary Boards/Part I—Anatomy, Physiology, Pathology; National Veterinary Boards/Part II—Pharmacology, Therapeutics, Parasitology, Hygiene; National Veterinary Boards/Part III—Physical Diagnosis, Medicine, Surgery.*

★5659★ *Career Examination Series: Veterinarian*
National Learning Corp.
212 Michael Dr.
Syosset, NY 11791
Ph: (516)921-8888   Fax: (516)921-8743
Fr: 800-645-6337

Jack Rudman. A study guide for professionals and trainees in the field of veterinary medicine. Includes a multiple-choice examination section; provides answers.

★5660★ *Career Examination Series: Veterinarian Trainee*
National Learning Corp.
212 Michael Dr.
Syosset, NY 11791
Ph: (516)921-8888   Fax: (516)921-8743
Fr: 800-645-6337

Jack Rudman. A study guide for professionals and trainees in the field of veterinary medicine. Includes a multiple-choice examination section; provides answers.

★5661★ *National Veterinary Boards (NVB)*
National Learning Corp.
212 Michael Dr.
Syosset, NY 11791
Ph: (516)921-8888   Fax: (516)921-8743
Fr: 800-645-6337

Jack Rudman. Part of the Admission Test series. A sample test for those seeking admission to graduate and professional schools or seeking entrance or advancement in institutional and public career service.

★5662★ Veterinary Aptitude Test: Practice Examination
Datar Publishing Co.
PO Box 16464
St. Louis, MO 63125
Ph: (314)843-5343   Fr: 800-633-8378
David M. Tarlow. 1993. Part of the Practice Examination Series.

EDUCATIONAL DIRECTORIES AND PROGRAMS

★5663★ Colleges of Veterinary Medicine Accredited or Approved by American Veterinary Medical Association
American Veterinary Medical Association (AVMA)
1931 N. Meacham Rd., Ste. 100
Schaumburg, IL 60173-4360
Ph: (708)925-8070   Fax: (708)925-1329
Fr: 800-248-2862
Edward R. Ames, Contact

Semiannual, April and November. Covers veterinary colleges in the United States, Canada and Europe. Entries include: Institution name, address; name of dean, accreditation status, year of latest review. Arrangement: Geographical.

★5664★ Encyclopedia of Medical Organizations and Agencies
Gale Research Inc.
835 Penobscot Bldg.
Detroit, MI 48226-4094
Ph: (313)961-2242   Fax: (313)961-6741
Fr: 800-877-GALE
Karen Boyden, Contact

Biennial, November of odd years. Covers over 13,400 state, national, and international medical associations, foundations, research institutes, federal and state agencies, and medical and allied health schools. Entries include: Organization name, address, phone; many listings include names and titles of key personnel, descriptive annotations. Arrangement: Classified by subject, then by type of organization.

★5665★ Healthcare Career Directory— Nurses and Physicians
Gale Research Inc.
835 Penobscot Bldg.
Detroit, MI 48226-4094
Ph: (313)961-2242   Fax: (313)961-6083
Fr: 800-877-GALE

Bradley J. Morgan and Joseph M. Palmisano. Second edition, 1993. A directory in the Career Advisor Series that provides essays written by industry professionals; job search information on resume and cover letter preparation, networking, and the interviewing process; approximately 300 companies and organizations offering job opportunities and internships, and additional job-hunting resources.

★5666★ Horse Industry Directory
American Horse Council
1700 K St. NW, Ste. 300
Washington, DC 20006
Ph: (202)296-4031   Fax: (202)296-1970
K. A. Luedeke, Director of Administration

Annual, previous edition January 1994, new edition expected January 1995. Covers organizations concerned with all aspects of the horse industry, including breed registries, racing and showing organizations, transportation and sales companies, and rodeo/trail organizations. Entries include: Organization name, address, phone, names and titles of key personnel. Arrangement: Classified by service.

★5667★ Medical and Health Information Directory
Gale Research Inc.
835 Penobscot Bldg.
Detroit, MI 48226-4094
Ph: (313)961-2242   Fax: (313)961-6741
Fr: 800-877-GALE
Karen Boyden, Contact

Approximately biennial; latest edition 1994. Covers in Volume 1, almost 18,600 medical and health oriented associations, organizations, institutions, and government agencies, including health maintenance organizations (HMOs), preferred provider organizations (PPOs), insurance companies, pharmaceutical companies, research centers, and medical and allied health schools. In Volume 2, nearly 11,800 medical book publishers; medical periodicals, directories, audiovisual producers and services, medical libraries and information centers, and electronic resources. In Volume 3, nearly 26,000 clinics, treatment centers, care programs, and counseling/diagnostic services for 30 subject areas. Entries include: Institution, service, or firm name, address, phone; many include names of key personnel Arrangement: Classified by organization activity, service, etc..

AWARDS, SCHOLARSHIPS, GRANTS, AND FELLOWSHIPS

★5668★ AABP Amstutz - Williams Award
American Association of Bovine Practitioners
c/o James A. Jarrett
PO Box 1755
Rome, GA 30162-1755
Ph: (706)232-2220   Fax: (706)232-2232
Fr: 800-269-2227

To honor an individual for outstanding service to the veterinary profession. A hand carved wooden bull is awarded when merited. Established in 1986 and named for Harold E. Amstutz and Eric L. Williams.

★5669★ AAHA Award
American Animal Hospital Association
Denver West Office Park
PO Box 150899
Denver, CO 80215-0899
Ph: (303)986-2800   Fax: (303)986-1700

To recognize either a veterinarian or nonveterinarian who has made outstanding contributions, directly or indirectly, toward the betterment AAHA and the veterinary profession. Established in 1958.

★5670★ AFIA Award
American Veterinary Medical Association
1931 N. Meacham Rd., Ste. 100
Schaumburg, IL 60173-4360
Ph: (708)925-8070   Fax: (708)925-1329

To recognize outstanding research by a veterinarian on nutrition or disease affecting livestock or poultry production. Original work published during the five calendar years immediately preceding the year the award is to be given is eligible for consideration. Private practitioners as well as institutional workers and others residing in the United States and Canada are eligible. Selection is made by the AVMA Council on Research. A monetary award of $1,500 and a plaque are awarded annually. Established in 1948 by the American Feed Industry Association. AVMA was invited to participate in 1969.

★5671★ AVES Honorary Diploma
American Veterinary Epidemiology Society
Univ. of Texas Health Science Center
PO Box 20186
Houston, TX 77225
Ph: (713)792-4451

To recognize veterinarians and public health scientists who have made contributions to public health. Individuals with at least 20 years experience in public health and related fields are eligible. A diploma is awarded several times a year. Established in 1968.

★5672★ Charles E. Bild Practitioner of the Year Award
American Animal Hospital Association
Denver West Office Park
PO Box 150899
Denver, CO 80215-0899
Ph: (303)986-2800   Fax: (303)986-1700

To recognize on the national level the year's most outstanding practicing veterinarian. The recipient is drawn from a slate of the two previous year's winners of the Regional Outstanding Practitioner Award. A plaque is awarded annually at the convention. Established in 1975 in memory of Dr. Charles E. Bild.

★5673★ Distinguished Service Award
Association for Women Veterinarians
PO Box 1051
Littleton, CO 80160-1051
Ph: (303)795-0130

To recognize an individual for contributing toward advancing the status of women veterinarians. Awarded annually when merited. Established in 1976.

★5674★ Friskies PetCare Award
American Animal Hospital Association
Denver West Office Park
PO Box 150899
Denver, CO 80215-0899
Ph: (303)986-2800   Fax: (303)986-1700
In recognition of outstanding contributions to feline medicine and/or nutrition. The recipient may or may not be a veterinarian. A monetary award of $750 and an engraved plaque are awarded annually. Established in 1982.

★5675★ Charles A. Griffin Award
American Association for Laboratory Animal Science
70 Timber Creek Dr., Ste. 5
Cordova, TN 38018
Ph: (901)754-8620   Fax: (901)753-0046
This, AALAS's most prestigious professional recognition, is given to an individual for outstanding accomplishments in the improvement of the care and quality of animals used in biologic and medical research. A monetary award of $500 and a bronze plaque are awarded annually. Established in 1957 in memory of Charles A. Griffin, D.V.M. of the Division of Laboratories and Research, New York State Department of Health, who was one of the active leaders of the Animal Care Panel in its early years.

★5676★ HRSA-BHP Health Professions Student Loans
U.S. Public Health Service
Health Resources and Services
   Administration
Parklawn Bldg., Rm. 8-38
5600 Fishers Ln.
Rockville, MD 20857
Purpose: To assist students with need for financial assistance to undertake the course of study required to become physicians, dentists, osteopathic physicians, optometrists, pharmacists, podiatrists, or veterinarians. Qualifications: Applicants must be enrolled or accepted for enrollment as full-time students in a program leading to a doctoral degree in medicine, dental surgery or equivalent degree, pharmacy, osteopathic medicine, optometry or equivalent degree, podiatric medicine or equivalent degree, or veterinary medicine or equivalent degree; or a bachelor of science in pharmacy or equivalent degree. Applicants must also be citizens, nationals, or permanent residents of the United States or the District of Columbia, the Commonwealths of Puerto Rico or the Marianna Islands, the Virgin Islands, Guam, The American Samoa, the Trust Territory of the Pacific Islands, the Republic of Palau, the Republic of the Marshall Islands, and the Federated State of Micronesia. Applicants must also demonstrate financial need. Professional students, interns, residents, and students seeking advanced training are not eligible. Funds available: Up to the cost of tuition plus $2,500 or the amount of financial need, whichever is less. The interest rate is five percent and accrues during the repayment period. Loans are repayable over a ten year period and beginning one year after the student graduates or ceases to enroll full-time in a health program.

★5677★ HRSA-BHP Loans for Disadvantaged Students
U.S. Public Health Service
Health Resources and Services
   Administration
Parklawn Bldg., Rm. 8-38
5600 Fishers Ln.
Rockville, MD 20857
Purpose: To assist students who need financial assistance to pursue careers in medicine, osteopathic medicine, dentistry, optometry, podiatric medicine, pharmacy, or veterinary medicine. Qualifications: Applicants must be citizens, nationals, or lawful permanent residents of the United States or the District of Columbia, the Commonwealths of Puerto Rico or the Marianna Islands, the Virgin Islands, Guam, American Samoa, the Trust Territory of the Pacific Islands, the Republic of Palau, the Republic of the Marshall Islands, or the Federated State of Micronesia. They must also be enrolled or accepted for enrollment at a participating health professionals school full-time. Students must be determined by their school's financial aid director to meet financial need and "disadvantaged background" criteria. Those enrolled in schools of medicine or osteopathic medicine must demonstrate exceptional financial need. Preprofessional students, interns, residents, and students seeking advanced training are not eligible. Selection criteria: Schools are responsible for selecting recipients and for determining the amount of assistance. Funds available: The maximum loan amount allowed for each school year is the cost of tuition plus $2,500, or the amount of financial need, whichever is lesser. The repayment interest rate is five percent over a ten-year period, which begins one year after completion of cessation of full-time study. Interest begins accruing at the time the loan becomes rapayable. Repayment may be deferred under special circumstances, and interest does not accrue during periods of deferment.

★5678★ James A. McCallam Award
Association of Military Surgeons of the
   United States
9320 Old Georgetown Rd.
Bethesda, MD 20814
Ph: (301)897-8800   Fax: (301)530-5446
To recognize a Doctor of Veterinary Medicine for outstanding accomplishments in the field of medicine and health. Nominations are encouraged. An honorarium and a plaque are presented. This award honors the late Brigadier General James A. McCallam, a former Chief, United States Army Veterinary Corps and the first Washington Representative of the American Veterinary Medical Association.

★5679★ MSD AGVET AABP Award for Excellence in Preventive Veterinary Medicine - Beef Cattle
American Association of Bovine
   Practitioners
c/o James A. Jarrett
PO Box 1755
Rome, GA 30162-1755
Ph: (706)232-2220   Fax: (706)232-2232
Fr: 800-269-2227
To promote bovine practice with an emphasis on preventive medicine. Veterinarians in bo-

vine practice are eligible. A scholarship of $1,500 in the name of the recipient to the veterinary college of his choice, and a bronze plaque are awarded annually. Established in 1982 by MSD AGVET. Sponsored by MSD AGVET Division of Merck and Company.

★5680★ Outstanding Veterinary Public Health Student
Conference of Public Health Veterinarians
1919 N. Wayne St.
Arlington, VA 22201
For recognition of an outstanding performance in the area of veterinary public health. Students in good academic standing at a college of veterinary medicine in the United States, accredited by the American Veterinary Medical Association, are eligible for nomination by deans of colleges of veterinary medicine by March 1. Selection criteria include the following: (1) consistent demonstration of interest and aptitude in subjects pertinent to veterinary public health; (2) demonstrated superior scholarship in subjects specifically related to veterinary public health; (3) demonstrated potential for leadership in the veterinary medical profession, in general, and in veterinary public health specifically; and (4) good academic standing. A stipend of $300 and a plaque are awarded annually. Established in 1980.

★5681★ Outstanding Woman Veterinarian Award
Association for Women Veterinarians
PO Box 1051
Littleton, CO 80160-1051
Ph: (303)795-0130
For recognition of a woman veterinarian who has made a significant contribution to the field of veterinary medicine. Nominations are accepted. A plaque is presented annually. Established in 1951 and awarded annually between 1951 and 1958. The award was reinstituted in 1972.

★5682★ James H. Steele Award
American Veterinary Epidemiology Society
Univ. of Texas Health Science Center
PO Box 20186
Houston, TX 77225
Ph: (713)792-4451
To recognize an outstanding young veterinary public health epidemiologist, and to encourage epidemiological studies of animal diseases that affect the public welfare and peace. A scroll and an art object are awarded at the World Veterinary Congress. Established in 1971.

★5683★ Syntex Animal Health - Bovine Practitioner of the Year Award
American Association of Bovine
   Practitioners
c/o James A. Jarrett
PO Box 1755
Rome, GA 30162-1755
Ph: (706)232-2220   Fax: (706)232-2232
Fr: 800-269-2227
To recognize a veterinarian in bovine practice for outstanding accomplishments. A diamond ring and a commemorative plaque are awarded annually. Established in 1978 by Syntex Animal Health.

★5684★ Veterinarian of the Year
Gaines Dog Care Center
Quaker Oats Co.-23-1
PO Box 9001
Chicago, IL 60604
Ph: (312)222-7894

To recognize an outstanding accomplishment in the veterinary field. A monetary award and a Cycle Fido Statuette are awarded annually to two veterinarians. Cosponsored by the American Animal Hospital Associationand the American Veterinary Medical Association.

BASIC REFERENCE GUIDES AND HANDBOOKS

★5685★ Black's Veterinary Dictionary
Barnes and Noble Imports
81 Adams Dr.
Totowa, NJ 07512
Ph: (201)256-6465

Geoffry P. West, editor. 1994. Published by Adam and Charles Black, London.

★5686★ Current Veterinary Therapy
W. B. Saunders Co.
Curtis Center
Independence Sq. W.
Philadelphia, PA 19106
Ph: (215)238-7800

R.W. Kirk, editor. 1989.

★5687★ Fact Sheet: Health Education Assistance Loan Program (HEAL)
U.S. Department of Health and Human
Services
Public Health Service
Health Resources and Services
Administration
Bureau of Health Professions, Division of
Student Assistance
Rockville, MD 20857
Ph: (301)443-2086

Fact sheet describing the HEAL Program; covers eligible schools, borrowers, and lenders, as well as loan limitations, interest, and repayment.

★5688★ Handbook of Veterinary Procedures and Emergency Treatment
W. B. Saunders Co.
Curtis Center
Independence Sq., W.
Philadelphia, PA 19106
Ph: (215)238-7800

Robert W. Kirk and Stephen I. Bistner. Fifth edition, 1990.

★5689★ The Merck Veterinary Manual
Merck and Co., Inc.
PO Box 2000
Rahway, NJ 07065
Ph: (908)750-7470   Fr: 800-999-3633

Clarence M. Fraser, editor. Seventh edition, 1991.

★5690★ Veterinary Pharmaceuticals and Biologicals
Veterinary Medicine Publishing Co.
9073 Lenexa Dr.
Lenexa, KS 66215
Ph: (913)492-4300

Seventh edition, 1990. Includes indexes.

PROFESSIONAL AND TRADE PERIODICALS

★5691★ AHI Quarterly
Animal Health Institute
PO Box 1417-D50
Alexandria, VA 22313-1480
Ph: (703)684-0011   Fax: (703)684-0125
Patrick McCabe

Discusses developments of significance to animal health, livestock, and veterinary industries. Includes legislative and regulatory updates and news of research.

★5692★ AVEA Newsletter
American Veterinary Exhibitors Association
(AVEA)
106 W. 11th St., Ste. 1600
Kansas City, MO 64105-1806
Ph: (816)474-0876   Fax: (816)842-2603
James Fries

Quarterly. Reports on the Association's involvement in the area of veterinary exhibitions. Provides a forum to give firms exhibiting at veterinary conventions a voice in planning the time, place, programs, and facilities of such meetings. Also offers suggestions for more effective exhibits. Recurring features include letters to the editor, interviews, news of research, reports of meetings, notice of educational opportunities, job listings, book reviews, notices of publications available, and a calendar of events. Includes columns titled Budget Statement and President's Page.

★5693★ DVM Newsmagazine
Advanstar Communications Inc.
280 Madison Ave.
New York, NY 10016
Ph: (216)243-8100   Fax: (216)891-2675
Maureen Hrehocik

Monthly. Recipients are veterinarians in private practices in the U.S.

★5694★ Federal Veterinarian
National Association of Federal
Veterinarians
1101 Vermont Ave. NW, Ste. 710
Washington, DC 20005
Ph: (202)289-6334
Edward Menning

Monthly. Reports developments in federal veterinary medicine and in personnel policy affecting veterinarians.

★5695★ Journal of the American Veterinary Medical Association
American Veterinary Medical Association
1931 N. Meacham Rd., Ste. 100
Schaumburg, IL 60173-4360
Ph: (708)925-8070   Fax: (708)925-1329

Semimonthly. Trade journal for veterinary medical professionals.

★5696★ New Methods
Ronald S. Lippert, A.H.T.
PO Box 22605
San Francisco, CA 94122-0605
Ph: (415)664-3469   Fr: 800-435-3218
Ronald S. Lippert

Monthly. Examines common problems and concerns in the field of animal health technology. "Provides professionals with the best in network sources" as well as items on animal care and protection and medical breakthroughs. Recurring features include letters to the editor, interviews, notices of publications available, job listings, news of educational opportunities, and news of research.

★5697★ Vet Industry Newsletter
Good Communications, Inc.
PO Box 31292
Charleston, SC 29417
Ph: (803)795-9555   Fax: (803)795-2930
Fr: 800-968-1738

Monthly. Provides information for executives at veterinary pharmaceutical and pet product companies. Covers new products, strategies, and promotions to the veterinary market.

★5698★ Veterinary Medicine
Veterinary Medicine Publishing Co.
9073 Lenexa Drive
Lenexa, KS 66215
Ph: (913)492-4300   Fax: (913)492-4157
Tracy L. Revoir

Monthly. Clinical veterinary medicine magazine.

PROFESSIONAL MEETINGS AND CONVENTIONS

★5699★ American Animal Hospital Association Annual Meeting
American Animal Hospital Association
PO Box 150899
Denver, CO 80215-0899
Ph: (303)986-2800   Fax: (303)986-1700
Fr: 800-252-2242

Annual. Always held during March or April.

★5700★ American Association of Bovine Practitioners Annual Conference
American Association of Bovine
Practitioners
PO Box 218
South Barre, VT 05670
Ph: (802)476-5711

Annual. **Dates and Locations:** 1996 Sep 12-15; San Antonio, TX. • 1997 Sep 18-21 • 1998 Sep 24-27

★5701★ American Humane Association Annual Meeting and Training Conference/Animal Protection
American Humane Association
63 Inverness Dr., E.
Englewood, CO 80112-5117
Ph: (303)792-9900   Fax: (303)792-5333
Annual. Usually held during October.

★5702★ American Veterinary Medical Association Annual Convention
American Veterinary Medical Association
1931 N. Meacham Rd., Ste. 100
Schaumburg, IL 60173-4360
Ph: (708)925-8070   Fax: (708)925-1329
Annual. **Dates and Locations:** 1995; Pittsburgh, PA.

★5703★ Western Veterinary Conference
Western Veterinary Conference
2425 E. Oquendo Rd.
Las Vegas, NV 89120
Ph: (702)739-6698
Annual. Always held during February at the Hilton Riviera in Las Vegas, Nevada. **Dates and Locations:** 1996 Feb 18-22; Las Vegas, NV. • 1997 Feb 16-20; Las Vegas, NV. • 1998 Feb 15-19; Las Vegas, NV.

OTHER SOURCES OF INFORMATION

★5704★ Developing Communication & Counseling Skills in Medicine
Routledge, Chapman & Hall, Inc.
29 W. 35th St.
New York, NY 10001-2291
Ph: (212)244-3336
Roslyn Corney, editor. 1992.

★5705★ The Preveterinary Planning Guide
Betz Publishing Co.
PO Box 1745
Rockville, MD 20849
Ph: (301)340-0030   Fr: 800-634-4365
Jane D. Crawford. 1992. This book is a guide to the veterinary school admission process. Includes information on career opportunities and standardized exams, interviewing, and veterinary college enrollments.

★5706★ Say Woof! The Day of a Country Veterinarian
Macmillian Publishing Co., Inc.
866 3rd Ave.
New York, NY 10022
Ph: (202)702-2000   Fr: 800-257-5755
1992.

★5707★ Standard Emergency Procedures for the Small Animal Veterinarian
W.B. Saunders Co.
Curtis Center
Independence Sq., W
Philadelphia, PA 19106
Ph: (215)238-7800
Signe J. Plunkett. 1993.

★5708★ "Veterinarian" in 100 Best Jobs for the 1990s & Beyond
Dearborn Financial Publishing, Inc.
520 N. Dearborn St.
Chicago, IL 60610-4354
Ph: (312)836-4400   Fax: (312)836-1021
Fr: 800-621-9621
Carol Kleiman. 1992. Describes 100 jobs ranging from accountants to veterinarians. Each job profile includes such information as education, experience, and certification needed, salaries, and job search suggestions.

★5709★ "Veterinarian" in Career Selector 2001
Barron's Educational Series, Inc.
250 Wireless Blvd.
Hauppauge, NY 11788
Ph: (516)434-3311   Fax: (516)434-3723
Fr: 800-645-3476
James C. Gonyea. 1993.

★5710★ "Veterinary Medicine and Sciences" in Accounting to Zoology: Graduate Fields Defined (pp. 290-292)
Petersons Guides, Inc.
PO Box 2123
Princeton, NJ 08543-2123
Ph: (609)243-9111   Fax: (609)243-9150
Fr: 800-338-3282
Amy J. Goldstein, editor. Revised and updated, 1987. Discusses types of graduate programs and degrees, graduate research, applied work, employment prospects and trends.

★5711★ "Veterinary Technician" in Allied Health Professions (pp. 52-53; 174)
Arco Publishing Co.
Simon & Schuster, Inc.
201 W. 103rd St.
Indianapolis, IN 46290
Ph: 800-428-5331   Fax: 800-835-3202
1993. Contains information on 28 representative careers in health care. Provides a sample of the Allied Health Professions Admission Test, lists professional societies and associations, and offers a directory of schools and programs for the careers listed.

Dietitians and Nutrionists

Dietitians and nutritionists use their knowledge of the principles of nutrition to help people develop healthy eating habits. Professionals trained in the science of nutrition can scientifically evaluate an individual's diet. They may suggest modifications such as instructing a client with high blood pressure to avoid salty foods, for example, or help an overweight person identify sources of fats and sugars. **Clinical dietitians** provide nutritional services for patients in hospitals, nursing homes, clinics, or doctors' offices. **Community dietitians** counsel individuals and groups on nutritional practices to prevent disease and to promote good health. **Administrative dietitians** are responsible for large-scale meal planning and preparation in such places as hospitals, nursing homes, company cafeterias, prisons, elementary and secondary schools, and colleges and universities. **Research dieticians** are usually employed in academic medical centers or educational institutions, although some work in community health programs.

Salaries

Salaries for dietitians are as follows:

Beginning dietitians, hospital	$23,320/year
Dietitians, hospital	$34,833/year or less
Beginning dietitians, federal government	$16,973/year
Dietitians, federal government	$36,247/year

Employment Outlook

Growth rate until the year 2005: Average.

Dietitians and Nutritionists

CAREER GUIDES

★5712★ **Allied Health Professions**
Simon & Schuster, Inc.
200 Old Tappan Rd.
Old Tappan, NJ 07675

1993. Includes information on available jobs, required training, a directory of training programs, and a full-sample Allied Health Professions Admission Test (AHPAT).

★5713★ **Careers in Foods and Nutrition**
Glencoe Publishing Co.
866 3rd Ave.
New York, NY 10022-6299
Ph: (212)702-3276

Videotape that explores foods and nutrition career fields that require special training or an advanced degree.

★5714★ **Careers in Health and Fitness**
Rosen Publishing Group
29 E. 21st St.
New York, NY 10010
Ph: (212)777-3017   Fax: (212)777-0277
Fr: 800-237-9932

Jackie Heron, R.N. 1990. Explores the opportunities and responsibilities of a career in health or fitness.

★5715★ **Careers in Medicine: Traditional and Alternative Opportunities**
Garrett Park Press
PO Box 1907
Garrett Park, MD 20896-0190
Ph: (301)946-2553

T. Donald Rucker and Martin D. Keller. Revised edition, 1990. Written for college students who are considering applying to medical school, medical students attempting to select a specialty, and physicians who want to explore nonclinical work. Provides descriptions and employment outlook for 900 medical-oriented occupations.

★5716★ **"Dietetic Technicians" in Encyclopedia of Careers and Vocational Guidance (Vol.2, pp.476-481)**
J.G. Ferguson Publishing Co.
200 W. Madison St., Ste. 300
Chicago, IL 60606
Ph: (312)580-5480   Fax: (312)580-4948

William E. Hopke, editor-in-chief. Ninth edition, 1993. Four-volume set that profiles 900 occupations and describes job trends in 74 industries. Includes career description, educational requirements, history of the job, methods of entry, advancement, employment outlook, earnings, conditions of work, social and psychological factors, and sources of further information.

★5717★ **"Dietetics and Nutritional Care" in 150 Careers in the Health Care Field**
Reed Reference Publishing
121 Chanlon Rd.
PO Box 31
New Providence, NJ 07974
Fax: (908)665-6688   Fr: 800-521-8110

Stanley Alperin. Third edition, 1993. Profiles health care occupations requiring a bachelor's degree or less. Describes the nature of the work, educational preparation, licensing requirements, and salary. Lists accredited educational programs.

★5718★ **"Dietetics Professions" in Careers in Health Care (pp. 67-73)**
National Textbook Co. (NTC)
VGM Career Books
4255 W. Touhy Ave.
Lincolnwood, IL 60646-1975
Ph: (708)679-5500   Fax: (708)679-2494
Fr: 800-323-4900

Barbara M. Swanson. Third edition, 1995. Describes job duties, work settings, salaries, licensing and certification requirements, educational preparation, and future outlook.

★5719★ **"Dietician" in 100 Best Careers for the Year 2000 (pp. 35-37)**
Arco Pub.
201 W. 103rd St.
Indianapolis, IN 46290
Ph: 800-428-5331   Fax: 800-835-3202

Shelly Field. 1992. Describes 100 job opportunities expected to grow fast throughout the next decade. Provides information on job duties and responsibilities, training requirements, education, advancement opportunities, experience and qualifications, and typical salaries.

★5720★ **"Dietician" in Jobs Rated Almanac**
World Almanac
1 International Blvd., Ste. 444
Mahwah, NJ 07495
Ph: (201)529-6900   Fax: (201)529-6901

Les Krantz. Second edition, 1992. Ranks 250 jobs by environment, salary, outlooks, physical demands, stress, security, travel opportunities, and extra perks. Includes jobs the editor feels are the most common, most interesting, and the most rapidly growing.

★5721★ **"Dietician and Nutritionist" in Career Information Center (Vol.5)**
Simon and Schuster
200 Old Tappan Rd.
Old Tappan, NJ 07675
Fax: 800-445-6991   Fr: 800-223-2348

Richard Lidz and Linda Perrin, editorial directors. Fifth edition, 1993. This 13-volume set profiles over 600 occupations. Each occupational profile describes job duties, entry-level requirements, educational requirements, advancement possibilities, employment outlook, working conditions, earnings and benefits, and where to write for more information.

★5722★ **"Dietician" in Profitable Careers in Non-Profit (pp. 96-98)**
John Wiley and Sons, Inc.
605 3rd Ave.
New York, NY 10158-0012
Ph: (212)850-6000   Fax: (212)850-6088
Fr: 800-526-5368

William Lewis and Carol Milano. 1987. Examines nonprofit organizations and the career opportunities they offer. Offers tips on how to target and explore occupational opportunities in the nonprofit sector.

★5723★ "Dietician" in *VGM's Careers Encyclopedia* (pp. 139-141)
National Textbook Co. (NTC)
VGM Career Books
4255 W. Touhy Ave.
Lincolnwood, IL 60646-1975
Ph: (708)679-5500   Fax: (708)679-2494
Fr: 800-323-4900

Third edition, 1991. Describes job duties, places of employment, working conditions, qualifications, education, and training, advancement potential, and salary for each occupation.

★5724★ "Dietician" in *VGM's Handbook of Health Care Careers*
National Textbook Co.
4255 W. Touhy Ave.
Lincolnwood, IL 60646-1975
Ph: (708)679-5500   Fax: (708)679-2494
Fr: 800-323-4900

Annette Selden. 1993. Contains 42 two-page occupational profiles describing job duties, places of employment, working conditions, qualifications, education, employment outlook, and income.

★5725★ "Dieticians and Nutritionists" in *Guide to Federal Jobs* (p. 131)
Resource Directories
3361 Executive Pkwy., Ste. 302
Toledo, OH 43606
Ph: (419)536-5353   Fax: (419)536-7056
Fr: 800-274-8515

Rod W. Durgin, editor. Third edition, 1992. Contains information on finding and applying for federal jobs. Describes more than 200 professional and technical jobs for college graduates. Covers the nature of the work, salary, and geographic location. Lists college majors preferred for that occupation. Section one describes the function and work of government agencies that hire the most significant number of college graduates.

★5726★ "Dieticians and Nutritionists" in *Health Care Job Explosion!* (pp. 152-158)
D-Amp Publications
401 Amherst Ave.
Coraopolis, PA 15108
Ph: (412)262-5578

Dennis V. Damp. 1993. Provides information on the nature of work for the major health care occupational groups. Descriptions include working conditions, training, job outlook, qualifications, and related occupations.

★5727★ *Dietitian*
Careers, Inc.
PO Box 135
Largo, FL 34649-0135
Ph: (813)584-7333

1994. Four-page brief offering the definition, history, duties, working conditions, personal qualifications, educational requirements, earnings, hours, employment outlook, advancement, and careers related to this position.

★5728★ "Dietitian" in *BLR Encyclopedia of Prewritten Job Descriptions*
Business and Legal Reports, Inc.
39 Academy St.
Madison, CT 06443-1513
Ph: (203)245-7448

Stephen D. Bruce, editor-in-chief. 1994. This book contains hundreds of sample job descriptions arranged by functional job category. The 1-3 page job descriptions cover what the worker normally does in the position, who they report to, and how that position fits in the organizational structure.

★5729★ "Dietitian" in *College Board Guide to Jobs and Career Planning* (pp. 244)
The College Board
415 Columbus Ave.
New York, NY 10023-6992
Ph: (212)713-8165   Fax: (212)713-8143
Fr: 800-323-7155

Joyce S. Mitchell. Second edition, 1994. Describes the job, salaries, related careers, education needed, and where to write for more information.

★5730★ "Dietitian/Nutritionist" in *150 Careers in the Health Care Field*
Reed Reference Publishing
121 Chanlon Rd.
PO Box 31
New Providence, NJ 07974
Fax: (908)665-6688   Fr: 800-521-8110

Stanley Alperin. Third edition, 1993. Profiles health care occupations requiring a bachelor's degree or less. Describes the nature of the work, educational preparation, licensing requirements, and salary. Lists accredited educational programs.

★5731★ *Dietitians*
Chronicle Guidance Publications, Inc.
66 Aurora St.
PO Box 1190
Moravia, NY 13118-1190
Ph: (315)497-0330   Fax: (315)497-3359
Fr: 800-622-7284

1992. Career brief describing the nature of the job, working conditions, hours and earnings, education and training, licensure, certification, unions, personal qualifications, social and psychological factors, location, employment outlook, entry methods, advancement, and related occupations.

★5732★ "Dietitians" in *Career Discovery Encyclopedia* (Vol.2, pp. 104-105)
J.G. Ferguson Publishing Co.
200 W. Madison St., Ste. 300
Chicago, IL 60606
Ph: (312)580-5480   Fax: (312)580-4948

Russell E. Primm, editor-in chief. 1993. This six volume set contains two-page articles for 504 occupations. Each article describes job duties, earnings, and educational and training requirements. The whole set is arranged alphabetically by job title. Designed for junior high and older students.

★5733★ "Dietitians" in *Encyclopedia of Careers and Vocational Guidance* (Vol.2, pp. 482-484)
J.G. Ferguson Publishing Co.
200 W. Madison St., Ste. 300
Chicago, IL 60606
Ph: (312)580-5480   Fax: (312)580-4948

William E. Hopke, editor-in-chief. Ninth edition, 1993. Four-volume set that profiles 900 occupations and describes job trends in 74 industries. Includes career description, educational requirements, history of the job, methods of entry, advancement, employment outlook, earnings, conditions of work, social and psychological factors, and sources of further information.

★5734★ "Dietitians" in *Jobs! What They Are—Where They Are—What They Pay* (p. 164)
Simon & Schuster, Inc.
Simon & Schuster Bldg.
1230 Avenue of the Americas
New York, NY 10020
Ph: (212)698-7000   Fr: 800-223-2348

Robert O. Snelling and Anne M. Snelling. 3rd edition, 1992. Describes duties and responsibilities, earnings, employment opportunities, training, and qualifications.

★5735★ "Dietitians and Nutritionists" in *101 Careers: A Guide to the Fastest-Growing Opportunities* (pp. 198-200)
John Wiley & Sons, Inc.
605 3rd Ave.
New York, NY 10158-0012
Ph: (212)850-6645   Fax: (212)850-6088

Michael Harkavy. 1990. Describes the nature of the job, working conditions, employment growth, qualifications, personal skills, projected salaries, and where to write for more information.

★5736★ "Dietitians and Nutritionists" in *Best Jobs for the 1990s and Into the 21st Century*
Impact Publications
9104-N Manassas Dr.
Manassas Park, VA 22111
Ph: (703)361-7300   Fax: (703)335-9486

Ronald L. Krannich and Caryl Rae Krannich. 1993.

★5737★ "Dietitians and Nutritionists" in *Occupational Outlook Handbook*
U.S. Government Printing Office
Superintendent of Documents
Washington, DC 20402
Ph: (202)512-1800   Fax: (202)512-2250

Biennial; latest edition, 1994-95. Encyclopedia of careers describing about 250 occupations and comprising about 85 percent of all jobs in the economy. Occupations that require lengthy education or training are given the most attention. Each occupation's profile describes what the worker does on the job, working conditions, education and training requirements, advancement possibilities, job outlook, earnings, and sources of additional information.

★5738★ "Dietitians" in *Opportunities in Home Economics Careers* **(pp. 59-65)**
National Textbook Co. (NTC)
VGM Career Books
4255 W. Touhy Ave.
Lincolnwood, IL 60646-1975
Ph: (708)679-5500   Fax: (708)679-2494
Fr: 800-323-4900

Rhea Shields. 1988. Gives the history and trends of home economics. Separate chapters cover home economics related careers such as art, interior design, and hospitality. Lists colleges and universities offering programs in home economics.

★5739★ *Food Scientists*
Chronicle Guidance Publications, Inc.
66 Aurora St.
PO Box 1190
Moravia, NY 13118-1190
Ph: (315)497-0330   Fax: (315)497-3359
Fr: 800-622-7284

1987. Career brief describing the nature of the job, working conditions, hours and earnings, education and training, licensure, certification, unions, personal qualifications, social and psychological factors, location, employment outlook, entry methods, advancement, and related occupations.

★5740★ "Food Technologist" in *Guide to Federal Jobs* **(p. 227)**
Resource Directories
3361 Executive Pkwy., Ste. 302
Toledo, OH 43606
Ph: (419)536-5353   Fax: (419)536-7056
Fr: 800-274-8515

Rod W. Durgin, editor. Third edition, 1992. Contains information on finding and applying for federal jobs. Describes more than 200 professional and technical jobs for college graduates. Covers the nature of the work, salary, and geographic location. Lists college majors preferred for that occupation. Section one describes the function and work of government agencies that hire the most significant number of college graduates.

★5741★ "Food Technologists" in *Jobs! What They Are—Where They Are—What They Pay* **(p. 51)**
Simon & Schuster, Inc.
Simon & Schuster Bldg.
1230 Avenue of the Americas
New York, NY 10020
Ph: (212)698-7000   Fr: 800-223-2348
Robert O. Snelling and Anne M. Snelling. 3rd edition, 1992. Describes duties and responsibilities, earnings, employment opportunities, training, and qualifications.

★5742★ *The Health Care Worker: An Introduction to Health Occupations*
Prentice-Hall, Inc.
200 Old Tappan Rd.
Old Tappan, NJ 07675
Ph: (201)767-5000

Shirley A. Badasch, and Doreen S. Chesebro. Second edition, 1988. Includes a bibliography and an index.

★5743★ *Health Careers*
Careers, Inc.
PO Box 135
Largo, FL 34649-0135
Ph: (813)584-7333

1994. Four-page brief describing duties, working conditions, personal qualifications, training, earnings and hours, employment outlook, places of employment, related careers, and where to write for more information.

★5744★ *Opportunities in Nutrition*
National Textbook Co. (NTC)
VGM Career Books
4255 W. Touhy Ave.
Lincolnwood, IL 60646-1975
Ph: (708)679-5500   Fax: (708)679-2494
Fr: 800-323-4900

Carol Coles Caldwell. Overviews careers in nutrition and subspecialties suchas research, pediatric, renal, and sports and cardiovascular dietetics. Includesinterviews with nutritionists, and information on training.

★5745★ *Opportunities in Nutrition Careers*
National Textbook Co. (NTC)
VGM Career Books
4255 W. Touhy Ave.
Lincolnwood, IL 60646-1975
Ph: (708)679-5500   Fax: (708)679-2494
Fr: 800-323-4900

Carol C. Caldwell. 1992. Describes how to become a registered dietitian and discusses different educational programs. Suggests many different work environments and overviews new career opportunities.

★5746★ "Public Health Nutritionist" in *Opportunities in Public Health Careers* **(pp. 82-84)**
National Textbook Co. (NTC)
VGM Career Books
4255 W. Touhy Ave.
Lincolnwood, IL 60646-1975
Ph: (708)679-5500   Fax: (708)679-2494
Fr: 800-323-4900

George E. Pickett. 1988. Defines the public health field and describes career opportunities as well as educational preparation and the future of the public health field. The appendixes list public health organizations, state and federal public health agencies, and graduate schools offering public health programs.

★5747★ *Set Your Sights: Your Future in Dietetics—Educational Pathways*
American Dietetic Association (ADA)
216 W. Jackson Blvd., Ste. 800
Chicago, IL 60606-6995
Ph: (312)899-0040   Fr: 800-877-1600
Three-page pamphlet describing different types of dietitians in different work settings, education, salary, financial aid, and job outlook.

★5748★ "Sports Nutritionist" in *Careers in Health and Fitness*
Rosen Publishing Group
29 E. 21st St.
New York, NY 10010
Ph: (212)777-3017   Fax: (212)777-0277
Fr: 800-237-9932

Jackie Heron. 1990. Occupational profiles contain information on job duties, skills, advantages, basic equipment used, employment possibilities, certification, and salary.

PROFESSIONAL ASSOCIATIONS

★5749★ American Association of Nutritional Consultants (AANC)
880 Canarios Court, Ste. 210
Chula Vista, CA 91910
Ph: (619)482-8533

Members: Professional nutritional consultants. **Purpose:** Seeks to: develop a certification board; create a forum for exchange of nutritional information; establish state chapters. Offers benefits such as car rental and laboratory discounts. **Publications:** *Nutrition and Dietary Consultant*, monthly.

★5750★ American Dietetic Association (ADA)
216 W. Jackson Blvd., Ste. 800
Chicago, IL 60606
Ph: (312)899-0040   Fax: (312)899-1979

Members: Dietetic professionals, registered dietitians and dietetic technicians serving the public through promotion of optimal nutrition, health and well being. **Purpose:** Seeks to shape the food choices and impact the nutritional status of the public in hospitals, colleges, universities, schools, day care centers, research, business and industry. Sets and approves standards of education and practice. Provides career guidance. **Publications:** *Journal of the American Dietetic Association*, monthly.

★5751★ Consultant Dietitians in Health Care Facilities (CDHCF)
216 W. Jackson Blvd., Ste. 800
Chicago, IL 60606
Ph: (312)899-0040   Fax: (312)899-1758
Fr: 800-877-1600

Members: A special interest group of the American Dietetic Association. Dietitians employed in extended care facilities, nursing homes, and a variety of food service operations. Disseminates information; assists in solving their problems in the field. Conducts workshops; offers networking opportunities for professionals. **Publications:** *The Consultant Dietitian*, quarterly. • *Dining Skills.* • *How to Consult Manual.* • *Video Tapes on Dysphagia and Chemical Hazards.*

STANDARDS/CERTIFICATION AGENCIES

★5752★ American Association of Nutritional Consultants (AANC)
880 Canarios Court, Ste. 210
Chula Vista, CA 91910
Ph: (619)482-8533
Develops a certification board; create a forum for exchange of nutritional information; establish state chapters.

★5753★ American Dietetic Association (ADA)
216 W. Jackson Blvd., Ste. 800
Chicago, IL 60606
Ph: (312)899-0040   Fax: (312)899-1979
Sets and approves standards of education and practice.

TEST GUIDES

★5754★ Career Examination Series: Dietitian
National Learning Corp.
212 Michael Dr.
Syosset, NY 11791
Ph: (516)921-8888   Fax: (516)921-8743
Fr: 800-645-6337
Jack Rudman. Test guide including questions and answers for students or professionals in the field who seek advancement through examination.

★5755★ Career Examination Series: Head Dietician
National Learning Corp.
212 Michael Dr.
Syosset, NY 11791
Ph: (516)921-8888   Fax: (516)921-8743
Fr: 800-645-6337
Jack Rudman. 1993. Test guide including questions and answers for students or professionals in the field who seek advancement through examination.

★5756★ Career Examination Series: Nutritionist
National Learning Corp.
212 Michael Dr.
Syosset, NY 11791
Ph: (516)921-8888   Fax: (516)921-8743
Fr: 800-645-6337
Jack Rudman. Test guide including questions and answers for students or professionals in the field who seek advancement through examination.

★5757★ Registration Examination for Dietitians (RED)
National Learning Corp.
212 Michael Dr.
Syosset, NY 11791
Ph: (516)921-8888   Fax: (516)921-8743
Fr: 800-645-6337
Jack Rudman. Part of the Admission Test series. A sample test for prospective dietitians who are seeking admission to graduate and professional schools or seeking entrance or advancement in institutional and public career service.

★5758★ Study Guide for the Registration Examination for Dietetic Technicians
American Dietetic Association (ADA)
Commisaion on Dietetic Registration
216 W. Jackson Blvd., Ste. 800
Chicago, IL 60606
Ph: (312)899-0040
Second edition, 1991. Includes a bibliography.

EDUCATIONAL DIRECTORIES AND PROGRAMS

★5759★ Directory of Dietetic Programs
American Dietetic Association (ADA)
216 W. Jackson Blvd., Ste. 800
Chicago, IL 60606-6995
Ph: (312)899-4814   Fax: (312)899-1758
Beverly E. Mitchell, Admin., Dept. of Ed.
Annual, August. Covers about 600 ADA-approved or accredited dietetic education programs; advanced degree programs in dietetics and related areas. Entries include: Institution name, department name, address, phone, name and title of contact, program concentration. Arrangement: Classified by type of program, then geographical.

★5760★ Health Information Resources in the Federal Government
ODPHP National Health Information Center
330 C St. SW, Rm. 2132
Washington, DC 20201
Ph: (301)565-4167   Fax: (301)984-4256
Erin Henderson
Irregular, previous edition 1990; latest edition 1993. Covers over 120 federal and federally sponsored offices and programs providing health information and assistance. Entries include: Organization name, address, phone, name of administrator, description of services, intended users, restrictions on use, fees, publications, online databases (if any). Arrangement: Classified by subject.

★5761★ Health & Medical Industry Directory
American Business Directories, Inc.
5711 S. 86th Circle
Omaha, NE 68127
Ph: (402)593-4600   Fax: (402)331-1505
Released 1993. Lists over 1.1 million physicians and surgeons, dentists, clinics, health clubs, and other health-related businesses in the U.S. and Canada. Entries include: Name, address, phone.

★5762★ Life Sciences Organizations and Agencies Directory
Gale Research Inc.
835 Penobscot Bldg.
Detroit, MI 48226-4094
Ph: (313)961-2242   Fax: (313)961-6083
Fr: 800-877-GALE
Brigitte Darnay, Contact
Published 1988. Covers about 7,500 associations, government agencies, research centers, educational institutions, libraries and information centers, museums, consultants, electronic information services, and other organizations and agencies active in agriculture, biology, ecology, forestry, marine science, nutrition, wildlife and animal sciences, and other natural and life sciences. Entries include: Organization or agency name, address, phone, name and title of contact, description. Arrangement: Classified by type of organization.

★5763★ Medical and Health Information Directory
Gale Research Inc.
835 Penobscot Bldg.
Detroit, MI 48226-4094
Ph: (313)961-2242   Fax: (313)961-6741
Fr: 800-877-GALE
Karen Boyden, Contact
Approximately biennial; latest edition 1994. Covers in Volume 1, almost 18,600 medical and health oriented associations, organizations, institutions, and government agencies, including health maintenance organizations (HMOs), preferred provider organizations (PPOs), insurance companies, pharmaceutical companies, research centers, and medical and allied health schools. In Volume 2, nearly 11,800 medical book publishers; medical periodicals, directories, audiovisual producers and services, medical libraries and information centers, and electronic resources. In Volume 3, nearly 26,000 clinics, treatment centers, care programs, and counseling/diagnostic services for 30 subject areas. Entries include: Institution, service, or firm name, address, phone; many include names of key personnel Arrangement: Classified by organization activity, service, etc..

★5764★ Therapists and Allied Health Professionals Career Directory
Gale Research Inc.
835 Penobscot Bldg.
Detroit, MI 48226-4094
Ph: (313)961-2242   Fax: (313)961-6083
Fr: 800-877-GALE
Bradley J. Morgan and Joseph M. Palmisano. 1993. A directory in the Career Advisor Series that provides essays written by industry professionals; job search information on resume and cover letter preparation, networking, and the interviewing process; approximately 300 companies and organizations offering job opportunities and internships, and additional job-hunting resources.

AWARDS, SCHOLARSHIPS, GRANTS, AND FELLOWSHIPS

★5765★ ADA Foundation Awards for Excellence
American Dietetic Association Foundation
216 W. Jackson Blvd., Ste. 800
Chicago, IL 60606-6995
Ph: (312)899-4821   Fax: (312)899-1758
Fr: 800-877-1600

To recognize excellence in the practice of six areas of dietetics. The deadline for nominations is April 15. A monetary award of $1,000 is awarded annually. Established in 1983. Reorganized in 1989.

★5766★ AIN Predoctoral Fellowships
American Institute of Nutrition (AIN)
9650 Rockville Pike
Bethesda, MD 20814
Ph: (301)530-7050   Fax: (301)571-1892

Qualifications: Applicants must be enrolled in a graduate program of nutrition that is listed in the AIN Directory of Graduate Programs in Nutritional Sciences. Selection criteria: Selection is made by the AIN Graduate Nutrition Education Committee. The Committee will evaluate significance, feasibility, communication and clarity, as well as the overall scientific technical quality of the proposal. Funds available: $5,000. Fellowships are non-renewable. Application details: Application forms are available from the AIN office. Forms must be accompanied by a summary of the research proposal not to exceed four single-spaced typewritten pages including objective, experimental approach, and selected references. Deadline: December 1.

★5767★ Conrad A. Elvehjem Award for Public Service in Nutrition
American Institute of Nutrition
9650 Rockville Pike
Bethesda, MD 20814-3990
Ph: (301)530-7050   Fax: (301)571-1892

For recognition of specific and distinguished service to the public through the science of nutrition. Such service would be rendered primarily through distinctive activities in the public interest in governmental, industrial, private, or international institutions, but contributions of an investigative character would not be excluded. A monetary award of $1,500 and a plaque are awarded annually. Established in 1966. Sponsored by Nabisco Brands.

★5768★ Robert H. Herman Award
American Society for Clinical Nutrition
9650 Rockville Pike
Bethesda, MD 20814-3998
Ph: (301)530-7110   Fax: (301)571-1892

To recognize outstanding research in clinical nutrition. Nominations must be submitted by November 15. A monetary award of $1,000 and a scroll are awarded annually. Established in 1982.

★5769★ E. V. McCollum Award
American Society for Clinical Nutrition
9650 Rockville Pike
Bethesda, MD 20814-3998
Ph: (301)530-7110   Fax: (301)571-1892

To recognize outstanding research in the field of clinical nutrition. Nominations must be submitted by November 15. A monetary award of $1,000 and a scroll are awarded annually. Established in 1965 by the National Dairy Counciland the Society. Sponsored by the National Dairy Council.

★5770★ Mead Johnson Award
American Institute of Nutrition
9650 Rockville Pike
Bethesda, MD 20814-3990
Ph: (301)530-7050   Fax: (301)571-1892

For recognition of a single, outstanding piece of recent research in nutrition or a series of recent papers on the same subject. Investigators who are under 40 years of age at the time of selection are eligible. The deadline for nominations is October 1. A monetary award of $1,500 and an inscribed scroll are awarded annually. Established in 1939. Sponsored by Mead Johnson and Company.

★5771★ Jonathan E. Rhoads Lecture
American Society for Parenteral and Enteral Nutrition
8630 Fenton St., Ste. 412
Silver Spring, MD 20910
Ph: (301)587-6315   Fax: (301)587-2365

For recognition of major contributions to the field of specialized nutrition support and a commitment to the provision of optimum nutrition to all patients. A $1,000 honorarium, and an invitation to deliver a lecture at the plenary session of the annual Clinical Congress are awarded annually. Established in 1978 in honor of Dr. Jonathan Rhoads, who had a pivotal role in the field of specialized nutrition support.

BASIC REFERENCE GUIDES AND HANDBOOKS

★5772★ The Biochemistry of Human Nutrition: A Desk Reference
West Publishing Co.
50 W. Kellogg Blvd.
PO Box 64526
St. Paul, MN 55164
Ph: (612)228-2778

Eva M. N. Hamilton and Sareen A. S. Gropper. 1987. Illustrated.

★5773★ Clinical Nutrition
Mosby-Year Book, Inc.
11830 Westline Industrial Dr.
St. Louis, MO 63146
Ph: (314)872-8370   Fax: (314)432-1380
Fr: 800-325-4177

David M. Paige, editor. Second edition, 1988. Includes bibliographies and an index.

★5774★ Handbook of Clinical Nutrition: Clinician's Manual for the Diagnosis and Management of Nutritional Problems
Mosby-Year Book, Inc.
11830 Westline Industrial Dr.
St. Louis, MO 63146
Ph: (314)872-8370   Fax: (314)432-1380
Fr: 800-325-4177

Roland L. Weinsier and C. E. Butterworth, Jr. 1988. Includes bibliographical references and an index. Illustrated.

★5775★ Handbook of Vitamins
Marcel Dekker, Inc.
270 Madison Ave.
New York, NY 10016
Ph: (212)696-9000   Fr: 800-228-1160

Lawrence J. Machlin, editor. Second revised and expanded edition, 1990.

★5776★ Manual of Nutritional Therapeutics
Little, Brown and Co., Inc.
34 Beacon St.
Boston, MA 02108
Ph: (617)227-0730

David H. Alpers, Ray E. Clouse, and William F. Stenson. Second edition, 1988. Includes bibliographies and an index. Illustrated.

★5777★ Modern Nutrition in Health and Disease
Lea and Febiger
200 Chesterfield Pkwy.
Malvern, PA 19355
Ph: (215)251-2230   Fr: 800-433-3850

Maurice E. Shils and Vernon R. Young, editors. Seventh edition, 1988.

★5778★ The Nutrition Desk Reference
Keats Publishing, Inc.
27 Pine St., Box 876
New Canaan, CT 06840
Ph: (203)966-8721

Robert H. Garrison and Elizabeth Somer. Second edition, 1990. Includes bibliographies and an index. Illustrated.

★5779★ Nutrition and Diagnosis-Related Care
Lea and Febiger
200 Chesterfield Pkwy.
Malvern, PA 19355
Ph: (215)251-2230

Sylvia Escott-Stump. Thrid edition, 1992. Includes a bibliography and an index.

★5780★ Nutrition for the Foodservice Professional
Van Nostrand Reinhold
115 5th Ave.
New York, NY 10013

Karen Eich Drummond. 1993.

★5781★ Nutritional Influences on Illness: A Sourcebook of Clinical Research
Third Line Press, Inc.
4751 Viviana Dr.
Tarzana, CA 91356
Ph: (818)996-0076

Melvyn R. Werbach. 1992. Discusses the effects of nutrients, toxins, and the environment on many common diseases.

★5782★ **Recommended Dietary Allowances**
National Academy Press
2101 Constitution Ave., NW
PO Box 285
Washington, DC 20055
Ph: (202)334-3318   Fr: 800-624-6242
Compiled by the National Research Council, Food and Nutrition Board. Tenth edition, 1989.

PROFESSIONAL AND TRADE PERIODICALS

★5783★ **American Journal of Clinical Nutrition**
American Society of Clinical Nutrition
9650 Rockville Pike
Bethesda, MD 20814-3998
Ph: (301)530-7038   Fax: (301)571-8303
Norman Kretchmer
Monthly. Journal of basic and clinical studies relevant to human nutrition.

★5784★ **Environmental Nutrition**
Environmental Nutrition, Inc.
52 Riverside Dr., 15A
New York, NY 10024
Ph: (212)362-0424   Fax: (212)362-2066
Denise Webb
Monthly. Keeps readers abreast of new findings and breakthroughs in nutrition and diet. Discusses nutrition in connection with food additives, food fads and diets, pharmaceuticals and vitamins, and disease prevention. Recurring features include weight manager, nutrition comparisons, letters to the editor, and resources.

★5785★ **Food Science and Nutrition Advisory Council—Newsletter**
Food Science and Nutrition Advisory Council
1334 Eckles Ave., Rm. 225
St. Paul, MN 55108
Ph: (612)624-2787
Vernal S. Packard
Informs the Council of Department programs, research, services, and staff news. Recurring features include columns titled Advisory Council News, Alumni News, and Grants & Awards.

★5786★ **Foodlines**
Food Research and Action Center
1875 Connecticut Ave. NW, Ste. 540
Washington, DC 20009
Ph: (202)986-2200   Fax: (202)986-2525
Christin M. Driscoll
Bimonthly. Informs readers of efforts to alleviate hunger and poverty in the U.S. Recurring features include strategies for local and state-wide anti-hunger activities, news of research, notices of publications available, and legislative updates.

★5787★ **HealthWatchers System**
Health Watchers System
13402 N. Scottsdale Rd., Ste. B. 150
Scottsdale, AZ 85254-4054
Fax: (602)948-8150   Fr: 800-654-3734
Gary A. Martin
Discusses the merits of various "natural health products" (mainly dietary supplements) available through Nutripathic Formulas, Inc. Also provides information on studies and research relating to health problems brought on by vitamin deficiencies. Recurring features include letters from students of the company's nutripathic program, an order form for available products, interviews, book reviews, and notices of publications available.

★5788★ **Journal of the American College of Nutrition**
John Wiley and Sons, Inc.
605 3rd Ave.
New York, NY 10158
Ph: (212)850-6000   Fax: (212)850-6799
Mildred S. Seelig
Bimonthly. Journal providing coverage of nutrition research applicable to patient care. Summarizes new developments and presents concepts affecting utilization and the requirements of nutrients. Topics include the use of calcium in hypertension, dietary management of diabetes mellitus, and the relation of nutrition to cancer metabolism.

★5789★ **Journal of Nutrition**
Willard J. Visek
Monthly. Journal on nutrition research in the U.S. and abroad.

★5790★ **NNFA Today**
National Nutritional Foods Association (NNFA)
150 Paularino Ave., Ste. 285
Costa Mesa, CA 92626-3302
Ph: (714)966-6632   Fax: (714)641-7005
Burton Kallman
Monthly. Supplies professionals in the health foods industry with analysis of business, legislative, social, technological, scientific, and economic developments affecting the industry. Provides information and suggestions on marketing, merchandising, public relations, and business management. Recurring features include interviews, reports of meetings, book reviews, news of nutrition research, a calendar of events, and columns titled Business Shorts, Science & Technology, and Legal/Legislation.

★5791★ **NOHA News**
Nutrition for Optimal Health Association (NOHA)
PO Box 380
Winnetka, IL 60093
Ph: (708)491-0429
Marjorie Fisher
Quarterly. Examines the links between good nutrition and health. Reports nutritional information and research findings culled from a wide range of scientific sources; includes a column written by the Professional Advisory Board.

★5792★ **Nutrition Action Healthletter**
Center for Science in the Public Interest
1875 Connecticut Ave. NW, No. 300
Washington, DC 20009-5728
Ph: (202)332-9110   Fax: (202)265-4954
Stephen Schmidt
Covers food and nutrition, the food industry, and relevant government regulations and legislation. Focuses on the connections among diet, lifestyle, and disease. Includes nutritional comparisons of food products, reader questions and answers, and health-promoting recipies.

★5793★ **Nutrition Health Review**
Vegetus Publications
27 Tunbridge Rd.
Haverford, PA 19041
Ph: (215)866-1857
Frank Ray Rifkin
Quarterly. Aims to educate the public about nutrition and health. Covers developments in areas including medical care, psychology, childraising, and geriatrics. Recurring features include news of research, editorials, letters to the editor, and book reviews.

★5794★ **Nutrition & the M.D.**
Raven Press
1185 Avenue of the Americas
New York, NY 10036
Fr: 800-365-2468
Mary K. Stein
Monthly. Covers such topics as foodborne illness, the effects of infection on nutrient metabolism, environmental contamination, food allergies, and amino acid therapy. Reports on specific food coloring dyes, preservatives, and other additives, and examines various health and nutrition studies conducted by major health institutions. Recurring features include news of research, reprints from national medical journals, book reviews, a bibliography, a question and answer section, and columns titled Diet-Obesity Update and Drug Spotlight.

★5795★ **Nutrition News**
Gurumantra S. Khalsa
4108 Watkins Dr.
Riverside, CA 92507
Ph: (909)784-7500
Siri Khalsa
Monthly. Disseminates current research on nutrition and wellness in non-technical, indepth articles. Focuses on one topic per issue.

★5796★ **Nutrition Research Newsletter**
Lyda Associates, Inc.
PO Box 700
Palisades, NY 10964
Ph: (914)359-8282   Fax: (914)359-1229
Lillian Langseth
Summarizes more than 400 biomedical journals to provide abstracts and citations to literature in nutrition research and clinical nutrition research. Recurring features include listing of reviews.

PROFESSIONAL MEETINGS AND CONVENTIONS

★5797★ American Dietetic Association Annual Meeting and Exhibition
American Dietetic Association
216 W. Jackson Blvd., Ste. 800
Chicago, IL 60606-6995
Ph: (312)899-0040   Fax: (312)899-1979
Fr: 800-877-1600
Annual. **Dates and Locations:** 1995 Oct 30-02; Chicago, IL.

★5798★ Society for Nutrition Education Annual Meeting
Society for Nutrition Education
2001 Killebrew Dr., Ste. 340
Minneapolis, MN 55425-1882
Ph: (612)854-0035   Fax: (612)854-7869
Annual.   ·5

OTHER SOURCES OF INFORMATION

★5799★ "Dietician" in *100 Best Jobs for the 1990s & Beyond*
Dearborn Financial Publishing, Inc.
520 N. Dearborn St.
Chicago, IL 60610-4354
Ph: (312)836-4400   Fax: (312)836-1021
Fr: 800-621-9621

Carol Kleiman. 1992. Describes 100 jobs ranging from accountants to veterinarians. Each job profile includes such information as education, experience, and certification needed, salaries, and job search suggestions.

★5800★ "Nutrition" in *Accounting to Zoology: Graduate Fields Defined* (pp. 277-279)
Petersons Guides, Inc.
PO Box 2123
Princeton, NJ 08543-2123
Ph: (609)243-9111   Fax: (609)243-9150
Fr: 800-338-3282

Amy J. Goldstein, editor. Revised and updated, 1987. Discusses types of graduate programs and degrees, graduate research, applied work, employment prospects and trends.

Occupational Therapists

Occupational therapists help mentally, physically, developmentally, or emotionally disabled individuals develop, recover, or maintain daily living and work skills. They help patients improve their basic motor functions and reasoning abilities, as well as help them learn to dress, bathe, cook, or operate machinery. Activities, ranging from cooking to using a computer, are used by occupational therapists. Computer programs have been designed to help patients improve problem solving, decision making, and perceptual skills, as well as memory and coordination. Occupational therapists also help permanently disabled patients cope with the physical and emotional effects of being disabled. With support and direction, patients learn (or relearn) many of the day-to-day skills necessary to establish an independent, productive, and satisfying lifestyle.

Salaries

Median salaries for occupational therapists are as follows:

Beginning occupational therapists, hospitals	$30,470/year
Experienced occupational therapists, hospital	$44,958/year

Employment Outlook

Growth rate until the year 2005: Much faster than the average.

Occupational Therapists

CAREER GUIDES

CAREER GUIDES

★5801★ Allied Health Professions
Simon & Schuster, Inc.
200 Old Tappan Rd.
Old Tappan, NJ 07675

1993. Includes information on available jobs, required training, a directory of training programs, and a full-sample Allied Health Professions Admission Test (AHPAT).

★5802★ Careers in Health and Fitness
Rosen Publishing Group
29 E. 21st St.
New York, NY 10010
Ph: (212)777-3017   Fax: (212)777-0277
Fr: 800-237-9932

Jackie Heron, R.N. 1990. Explores the opportunities and responsibilities of a career in health or fitness.

★5803★ Careers in Occupational Therapy
Rosen Publishing Group
29 E. 21st St.
New York, NY 10010
Ph: (212)777-3017   Fax: (212)777-0277
Fr: 800-237-9932

Margaret F. Brown. 1989.

★5804★ Careers in Occupational Therapy
American Occupational Therapy Association
1383 Piccard Dr., Ste. 301
PO Box 1725
Rockville, MD 20849-1725
Ph: (301)948-9626

1990. This sheet describes employment outlook for occupational therapists, as well as education, places of employment, and earnings.

★5805★ Careers in Social and Rehabilitation Services
National Textbook Co. (NTC)
VGM Career Books
4255 W. Touhy Ave.
Lincolnwood, IL 60646-1975
Ph: (708)679-5500   Fax: (708)679-2494
Fr: 800-323-4900

Geraldine O. Garner, Ph.D., editor. 1993. Describes dozens of careers in the field of social and rehabilitation services.

★5806★ The Certified Occupational Therapy Assistant: Roles and Responsibilities
Slack, Inc.
6900 Grove Rd.
Thorofare, NJ 08086
Ph: (609)848-1000   Fr: 800-257-8290

Sally E. Ryan, editor. 1992. Includes a bibliography. Illustrated.

★5807★ Certified Occupational Therapy Assistants: Opportunities and Challenges
Haworth Press, Inc.
10 Alice St.
Binghamton, NY 13904-1580
Ph: (607)722-2493   Fr: 800-342-9678

Jerry A. Johnson, editor. 1988. Includes bibliographical references. Illustrated.

★5808★ "Health Care" in Where the Jobs Are: The Hottest Careers for the 90s (pp. 143-166)
Career Press
180 5th Ave.
Hawthorne, NJ 07507
Ph: (201)427-0229   Fax: (201)427-2037
Fr: 800-CAREER-1

Joyce Hadley. 1995. Offers a job-hunting strategy for the 1990s as well as descriptions of growing careers of the decade. Each profile includes general information, forecasts, growth, education and training, licensing requirements, and salary information.

★5809★ The Health Care Worker: An Introduction to Health Occupations
Prentice-Hall, Inc.
200 Old Tappan Rd.
Old Tappan, NJ 07675
Ph: (201)767-5000

Shirley A. Badasch, and Doreen S. Chesebro. Second edition, 1988. Includes a bibliography and an index.

★5810★ Health Careers
Careers, Inc.
PO Box 135
Largo, FL 34649-0135
Ph: (813)584-7333

1994. Four-page brief describing duties, working conditions, personal qualifications, training, earnings and hours, employment outlook, places of employment, related careers, and where to write for more information.

★5811★ Occupational Therapist
Careers, Inc.
PO Box 135
Largo, FL 34649-0135
Ph: (813)584-7333

1992. Four-page brief offering the definition, history, duties, working conditions, personal qualifications, educational requirements, earnings, hours, employment outlook, advancement, and careers related to this position.

★5812★ Occupational Therapist
Vocational Biographies, Inc.
PO Box 31
Sauk Centre, MN 56378-0031
Ph: (612)352-6516   Fax: (612)352-5546
Fr: 800-255-0752

1992. Four-page pamphlet containing a personal narrative about a worker's job, work likes and dislikes, career path from high school to the present. Education and training, the rewards and frustrations, and the effects of the job on the rest of the worker's life. The data file portion of this pamphlet gives a concise occupational summary, including work descriptions, working conditions, places of employment, personal characteristics, education and training, job outlook, and salary range.

★5813★ "Occupational Therapist" in
150 Careers in the Health Care Field
Reed Reference Publishing
121 Chanlon Rd.
PO Box 31
New Providence, NJ 07974
Fax: (908)665-6688   Fr: 800-521-8110
Stanley Alperin. Third edition, 1993. Profiles health care occupations requiring a bachelor's degree or less. Describes the nature of the work, educational preparation, licensing requirements, and salary. Lists accredited educational programs.

★5814★ "Occupational Therapist" in
Allied Health Education Directory (pp. 160-164)
American Medical Association (AMA)
515 N. State St.
Chicago, IL 60610
Ph: (312)464-5000   Fr: 800-621-8335
William R. Burrow, editor. 1994. Describes allied health occupations and lists educational programs accredited by the Committee on Allied Health Education and Accreditation of the American Medical Association.

★5815★ "Occupational Therapist" in
Career Information Center (Vol.7)
Simon and Schuster
200 Old Tappan Rd.
Old Tappan, NJ 07675
Fax: 800-445-6991   Fr: 800-223-2348
Richard Lidz and Linda Perrin, editorial directors. Fifth edition, 1993. This 13-volume set profiles over 600 occupations. Each occupational profile describes job duties, entry-level requirements, educational requirements, advancement possibilities, employment outlook, working conditions, earnings and benefits, and where to write for more information.

★5816★ "Occupational Therapist" in
College Board Guide to Jobs and Career Planning (pp. 260)
The College Board
415 Columbus Ave.
New York, NY 10023-6992
Ph: (212)713-8165   Fax: (212)713-8143
Fr: 800-323-7155
Joyce S. Mitchell. Second edition, 1994. Describes the job, salaries, related careers, education needed, and where to write for more information.

★5817★ "Occupational Therapist" in
Jobs Rated Almanac
World Almanac
1 International Blvd., Ste. 444
Mahwah, NJ 07495
Ph: (201)529-6900   Fax: (201)529-6901
Les Krantz. Second edition, 1992. Ranks 250 jobs by environment, salary, outlooks, physical demands, stress, security, travel opportunities, and extra perks. Includes jobs the editor feels are the most common, most interesting, and the most rapidly growing.

★5818★ "Occupational Therapist and Occupational Therapy Assistant" in
Careers in Health Care (pp. 176-181)
National Textbook Co. (NTC)
VGM Career Books
4255 W. Touhy Ave.
Lincolnwood, IL 60646-1975
Ph: (708)679-5500   Fax: (708)679-2494
Fr: 800-323-4900
Swanson, Barbara M. Third edition, 1995. Describes job duties, work settings, salaries, licensing and certification requirements, educational preparation, and future outlook.

★5819★ "Occupational Therapist" in
Profitable Careers in Non-Profit (pp. 95-96)
John Wiley and Sons, Inc.
605 3rd Ave.
New York, NY 10158-0012
Ph: (212)850-6000   Fax: (212)850-6088
Fr: 800-526-5368
William Lewis and Carol Milano. 1987. Examines nonprofit organizations and the career opportunities they offer. Offers tips on how to target and explore occupational opportunities in the nonprofit sector.

★5820★ "Occupational Therapist" in
VGM's Careers Encyclopedia
National Textbook Co. (NTC)
VGM Career Books
4255 W. Touhy Ave.
Lincolnwood, IL 60646-1975
Ph: (708)679-5500   Fax: (708)679-2494
Fr: 800-323-4900
Third edition, 1991. Describes job duties, places of employment, working conditions, qualifications, education, and training, advancement potential, and salary for each occupation.

★5821★ "Occupational Therapist" in
VGM's Handbook of Health Care Careers
National Textbook Co.
4255 W. Touhy Ave.
Lincolnwood, IL 60646-1975
Ph: (708)679-5500   Fax: (708)679-2494
Fr: 800-323-4900
Annette Selden. 1993. Contains 42 two-page occupational profiles describing job duties, places of employment, working conditions, qualifications, education, employment outlook, and income.

★5822★ *Occupational Therapists*
Chronicle Guidance Publications, Inc.
66 Aurora St.
PO Box 1190
Moravia, NY 13118-1190
Ph: (315)497-0330   Fax: (315)497-3359
Fr: 800-622-7284
1993. Career brief describing the nature of the job, working conditions, hours and earnings, education and training, licensure, certification, unions, personal qualifications, social and psychological factors, location, employment outlook, entry methods, advancement, and related occupations.

★5823★ "Occupational Therapists" in
101 Careers: A Guide to the Fastest-Growing Opportunities (pp. 231-234)
John Wiley & Sons, Inc.
605 3rd Ave.
New York, NY 10158-0012
Ph: (212)850-6645   Fax: (212)850-6088
Michael Harkavy. 1990. Describes the nature of the job, working conditions, employment growth, qualifications, personal skills, projected salaries, and where to write for more information.

★5824★ "Occupational Therapists" in
American Almanac of Jobs and Salaries (p. 469)
Avon Books
1350 Avenue of the Americas
New York, NY 10019
Ph: (212)261-6800   Fr: 800-238-0658
John Wright, editor. Revised and updated, 1994-95. This is comprehensive guide to the wages of hundreds of occupations in a wide variety of industries and organizations.

★5825★ "Occupational Therapists" in
America's 50 Fastest Growing Jobs (pp. 48)
JIST Works, Inc.
720 N. Park Ave.
Indianapolis, IN 46202-3431
Ph: (317)264-3720   Fax: (317)264-3709
Fr: 800-648-5478
Michael J. Farr, compiler. 1994. Describes the 50 fastest growing jobs within major career clusters such as technicians, and marketing and sales. Each job profile explains the nature of the work, skills and abilities required, employment outlook, average earnings, related occupations, education and training requirements, and employment opportunities. Also contains career planning information and job search tips.

★5826★ "Occupational Therapists and Assistants" in *Jobs! What They Are—Where They Are—What They Pay* (p. 173)
Simon & Schuster, Inc.
Simon & Schuster Bldg.
1230 Avenue of the Americas
New York, NY 10020
Ph: (212)698-7000   Fr: 800-223-2348
Robert O. Snelling and Anne M. Snelling. 3rd edition, 1992. Describes duties and responsibilities, earnings, employment opportunities, training, and qualifications.

★5827★ "Occupational Therapists" in
Career Discovery Encyclopedia (Vol.4, pp. 136-137)
J.G. Ferguson Publishing Co.
200 W. Madison St., Ste. 300
Chicago, IL 60606
Ph: (312)580-5480   Fax: (312)580-4948
Russell E. Primm, editor-in chief. 1993. This six volume set contains two-page articles for 504 occupations. Each article describes job duties, earnings, and educational and training requirements. The whole set is arranged alphabetically by job title. Designed for junior high and older students.

★5828★ "Occupational Therapists" in
Encyclopedia of Careers and
Vocational Guidance (Vol.3, pp. 604-
606)
J.G. Ferguson Publishing Co.
200 W. Madison St., Ste. 300
Chicago, IL 60606
Ph: (312)580-5480   Fax: (312)580-4948

William E. Hopke, editor-in-chief. Ninth edition, 1993. Four-volume set that profiles 900 occupations and describes job trends in 74 industries. Includes career description, educational requirements, history of the job, methods of entry, advancement, employment outlook, earnings, conditions of work, social and psychological factors, and sources of further information.

★5829★ "Occupational Therapists" in
Guide to Federal Jobs (p. 132)
Resource Directories
3361 Executive Pkwy., Ste. 302
Toledo, OH 43606
Ph: (419)536-5353   Fax: (419)536-7056
Fr: 800-274-8515

Rod W. Durgin, editor. Third edition, 1992. Contains information on finding and applying for federal jobs. Describes more than 200 professional and technical jobs for college graduates. Covers the nature of the work, salary, and geographic location. Lists college majors preferred for that occupation. Section one describes the function and work of government agencies that hire the most significant number of college graduates.

★5830★ "Occupational Therapists" in
Health Care Job Explosion! (pp. 159-
167)
D-Amp Publications
401 Amherst Ave.
Coraopolis, PA 15108
Ph: (412)262-5578

Dennis V. Damp. 1993. Provides information on the nature of work for the major health care occupational groups. Descriptions include working conditions, training, job outlook, qualifications, and related occupations.

★5831★ "Occupational Therapists" in
Occupational Outlook Handbook
U.S. Government Printing Office
Superintendent of Documents
Washington, DC 20402
Ph: (202)512-1800   Fax: (202)512-2250

Biennial; latest edition, 1994-95. Encyclopedia of careers describing about 250 occupations and comprising about 85 percent of all jobs in the economy. Occupations that require lengthy education or training are given the most attention. Each occupation's profile describes what the worker does on the job, working conditions, education and training requirements, advancement possibilities, job outlook, earnings, and sources of additional information.

★5832★ Occupational Therapy:
Principles & Practice
Williams and Wilkins
428 E. Preston St.
Baltimore, MD 21202
Ph: (410)528-4000   Fr: 800-638-0672

Alice J. Punwar. Second edition, 1994. Includes bibliographies and an index. Illustrated.

★5833★ Opportunities in Fitness
Careers
National Textbook Co. (NTC)
VGM Career Books
4255 W. Touhy Ave.
Lincolnwood, IL 60646-1975
Ph: (708)679-5500   Fax: (708)679-2494
Fr: 800-323-4900

Jean Rosenbaum and Mary Prine. 1991. Surveys fitness related careers, including the physical therapy profession. Describes career opportunities, education and experience needed, how to get into entry-level jobs and what income to expect. Schools are listed in the appendix.

★5834★ Opportunities in Health and
Medical Careers
National Textbook Co. (NTC)
VGM Career Books
4255 W. Touhy Ave.
Lincolnwood, IL 60646-1975
Ph: (708)679-5500   Fax: (708)679-2494
Fr: 800-323-4900

I. Donald Snook Jr., Leo D'Orazio. Describes the working conditions of physicians, physician assistants, therapists, nurses, technicians, administrators, and hospital staff. Also includes information on educational requirements and salaries.

★5835★ Opportunities in Occupational
Therapy Careers
National Textbook Co. (NTC)
VGM Career Books
4255 W. Touhy Ave.
Lincolnwood, IL 60646-1975
Ph: (708)679-5500   Fax: (708)679-2494
Fr: 800-323-4900

Zona R. Weeks. 1994. Discusses history, educational and licensure requirements, and the working conditions. Describes the occupational therapist in clinical work, in administration, and in education. Covers salaries, educational programs, and where to write for more information.

PROFESSIONAL ASSOCIATIONS

★5836★ American Occupational
Therapy Association (AOTA)
4720 Montgomery Ln.
PO Box 31220
Bethesda, MD 20824-1220
Ph: (301)652-2682   Fax: (301)652-7711

Members: Registered occupational therapists and certified occupational therapy assistants who provide services to people whose lives have been disrupted by physical injury or illness, developmental problems, the aging process, or social or psychological difficulties. Occupational therapy focuses on the active involvement of the patient in specially designed therapeutic tasks and activities to improve function, performance capacity, and the ability to cope with demands of daily living. Conducts research and educational programs and compiles statistics. Supports the American Occupational Therapy Foundation, which administers a program of professional training and development in research and provides research information related to occupational therapy. **Publications:** *American Journal of Occupational Therapy*, monthly. • *Occupational Therapy Week*, weekly. • *Publications Catalog.*

STANDARDS/CERTIFICATION AGENCIES

★5837★ American Occupational
Therapy Association (AOTA)
4720 Montgomery Ln.
PO Box 31220
Bethesda, MD 20824-1220
Ph: (301)652-2682   Fax: (301)652-7711

Registered occupational therapists and certified occupational therapy assistants who provide services to people whose lives have been disrupted by physical injury or illness, developmental problems, the aging process, or social or psychological difficulties.

★5838★ American Occupational
Therapy Certification Board (AOTCB)
4 Research Pl., Ste. 160
Rockville, MD 20850-3226
Ph: (301)990-7979   Fax: (301)869-8492

Administers certification program and maintains certification records of certificants; operates disciplinary mechanisms.

TEST GUIDES

★5839★ Career Examination Series:
Chief Occupational Therapist
National Learning Corp.
212 Michael Dr.
Syosset, NY 11791
Ph: (516)921-8888   Fax: (516)921-8743
Fr: 800-645-6337

Jack Rudman. Test guide including questions and answers for students or professionals in the field who seek advancement through examination.

★5840★ Career Examination Series:
Occupational Therapist
National Learning Corp.
212 Michael Dr.
Syosset, NY 11791
Ph: (516)921-8888   Fax: (516)921-8743
Fr: 800-645-6337

Jack Rudman. A study guide for professionals and trainees in the field of occupational therapy. Includes a multiple-choice examination section; provides answers.

★5841★ Career Examination Series: Senior Occupational Therapist
National Learning Corp.
212 Michael Dr.
Syosset, NY 11791
Ph: (516)921-8888   Fax: (516)921-8743
Fr: 800-645-6337
Jack Rudman. A study guide for professionals and trainees in the field of occupational therapy. Includes a multiple-choice examination section; provides answers.

★5842★ Career Examination Series: Supervising Therapist
National Learning Corp.
212 Michael Dr.
Syosset, NY 11791
Ph: (516)921-8888   Fax: (516)921-8743
Fr: 800-645-6337
Jack Rudman. 1993. Test guide including questions and answers for students or professionals in the field who seek advancement through examination.

★5843★ Certification Examination for Occupational Therapy Assistant (OTA)
National Learning Corp.
212 Michael Dr.
Syosset, NY 11791
Ph: (516)921-8888   Fax: (516)921-8743
Fr: 800-645-6337
Jack Rudman. Part of the Admission Test series. A sample test for prospective occupational therapy assistants who are seeking admission to graduate and professional schools or seeking entrance or advancement in institutional and public career service.

EDUCATIONAL DIRECTORIES AND PROGRAMS

★5844★ Educational Programs in Occupational Therapy
American Occupational Therapy
  Association, Inc.
4720 Montgomery Ln.
PO Box 31220
Bethesda, MD 20824-1220
Ph: (301)652-2682   Fax: (301)652-7711
Martha S. O'Connor, Director, Accreditation
Annual, December. Covers over 108 accredited and developing programs in occupational therapy and over 114 accredited and developing occupational therapy assistant programs. Entries include: Institution name, address, level of program. Telecommunications Device for the Deaf, 800-377-8555. Arrangement: Geographical, then classified by educational institution. Separate listings for developing programs and assistant programs.

★5845★ Encyclopedia of Medical Organizations and Agencies
Gale Research Inc.
835 Penobscot Bldg.
Detroit, MI 48226-4094
Ph: (313)961-2242   Fax: (313)961-6741
Fr: 800-877-GALE
Karen Boyden, Contact
Biennial, November of odd years. Covers over 13,400 state, national, and international medical associations, foundations, research institutes, federal and state agencies, and medical and allied health schools. Entries include: Organization name, address, phone; many listings include names and titles of key personnel, descriptive annotations. Arrangement: Classified by subject, then by type of organization.

★5846★ Health & Medical Industry Directory
American Business Directories, Inc.
5711 S. 86th Circle
Omaha, NE 68127
Ph: (402)593-4600   Fax: (402)331-1505
Released 1993. Lists over 1.1 million physicians and surgeons, dentists, clinics, health clubs, and other health-related businesses in the U.S. and Canada. Entries include: Name, address, phone.

★5847★ Medical and Health Information Directory
Gale Research Inc.
835 Penobscot Bldg.
Detroit, MI 48226-4094
Ph: (313)961-2242   Fax: (313)961-6741
Fr: 800-877-GALE
Karen Boyden, Contact
Approximately biennial; latest edition 1994. Covers in Volume 1, almost 18,600 medical and health oriented associations, organizations, institutions, and government agencies, including health maintenance organizations (HMOs), preferred provider organizations (PPOs), insurance companies, pharmaceutical companies, research centers, and medical and allied health schools. In Volume 2, nearly 11,800 medical book publishers; medical periodicals, directories, audiovisual producers and services, medical libraries and information centers, and electronic resources. In Volume 3, nearly 26,000 clinics, treatment centers, care programs, and counseling/diagnostic services for 30 subject areas. Entries include: Institution, service, or firm name, address, phone; many include names of key personnel Arrangement: Classified by organization activity, service, etc..

★5848★ Therapists and Allied Health Professionals Career Directory
Gale Research Inc.
835 Penobscot Bldg.
Detroit, MI 48226-4094
Ph: (313)961-2242   Fax: (313)961-6083
Fr: 800-877-GALE
Bradley J. Morgan and Joseph M. Palmisano. 1993. A directory in the Career Advisor Series that provides essays written by industry professionals; job search information on resume and cover letter preparation, networking, and the interviewing process; approximately 300 companies and organizations offering job opportunities and internships, and additional job-hunting resources.

AWARDS, SCHOLARSHIPS, GRANTS, AND FELLOWSHIPS

★5849★ Department of Veterans Affairs Health Professional Scholarship Award
Department of Veterans Affairs
810 Vermont Ave, NW
Washington, DC 20420
Qualifications: Applicants must be accepted for enrollment as full-time students in an education program that is nationally accredited by either the National League for Nursing, American Physical Therapy Association, American Occupational Therapy Association, or the American Association of Nurse Anesthetists. Applicants must be citizens of the United States. Associate degree nursing students in their last year of study, and third-and-fourth year nursing students in baccalaureate degree nursing, physical therapym, and occupational therapy may apply. Students in masters degree programs in physical therapy, nurse anasthesia, and certain speciallty areas for nursing, physical therapy, and occupational therapy may also apply. Registered nurses may apply if they enrolled full-time or accepted for enrollment in an accredited baccalaureate nursing program or specialized masters program. These specialty programs vary, and a list of the programs can be obtained from the Department of Veterans Affairs (VA) at the above address. Selection criteria: Selections are based on academic performance; recommendation from the applicant's college/university Dean or Program Director of nursing, physical therapy, or occupational therapy; career goals; and work and/or volunteer recommendation and experiences. Funds available: The award provides direct payment for up to two years for tuition and fees to the participant's college/university, and provides an annual payment for books and other costs, and a tax-free stipend of $621 per month to the participant for the length of the award. The award is repaid through service obligation, where the participant works full-time as a registered nurse, nurse anesthetist, physical therapist, or occupational therapist at one of the VA medical centers in the United States. Service will not be in any branch of the armed forces or any other Federal agency. The minimum obligated service is two years upon completion of degree requirements and attainment of licensure or certification. Application details: Applicants can obtain application materials and application Information Bulletins by sending their name, address, and identifying the award for which they wish information, to Health Professional Scholarship Program (143 B) at the above address. Applications are available each March. Deadline: Applications must be postmarked no later than the last Tuesday in May.

★5850★ Department of Veterans Affairs Reserve Member Stipend Program Award
Department of Veterans Affairs
810 Vermont Ave., NW
Washington, DC 20420
Qualifications: Applicants must be accepted for enrollment as full-time students in an edu-

cation program that is nationally accredited by either the National League for Nursing, American Physical Therapy Association, American Occupational Therapy Association, or the American Association of Nurse Anesthetists. Applicants must be citizens of the United States. Associate degree nursing students in their last year of study, and third-and-fourth year nursing students in baccalaureate degree nursing may apply. Entry-level masters students in nursing, physical therapy, and occupational therapy may also apply. Also eligible are reservists who are members of the Selected Ready Reserves, eligible for the Reserve GI Bill, and have a score above the 50th percentile on the Armed Forces Qualification Test. Rregistered nurses may apply if enrolled full-time or accepted for enrollment in an accredited nursing program. Selection criteria: Selections are based on academic performance; recommendation from the applicant's college/university Dean or Program Director of nursing, physical therapy, or occupational therapy; career goals; work and/or volunteer recommendation and experiences; and commander's recommendation. Funds available: Awards have a maximum length of 24 months of funding support and pay $400 per month while the reservist is enrolled in full-time course work. Reservists may also receive the Reserve GI Bill. The award is repaid through service obligation, where the participant works full-time as a registered nurse, nurse anesthetist, physical therapist, or occupational therapist at one of the VA medical centers in the United States. Service will not be in any branch of the armed forces or any other Federal agency. The minimum obligated service is two years upon completion of degree requirements and attainment of licensure or certification. Application details: Applicants can obtain application materials and Application Information Bulletins by sending their name, address, and identifying the award for which they wish information, to Health Professional Scholarship Program (143 B) at the above address. Applications are available each March. Deadline: Applications must be submitted and postmarked no later than the last Tuesday in May.

★5851★ Golden Pen Award
American Physical Therapy Association
APTA Awards Program
1111 N. Fairfax St.
Alexandria, VA 22314
Ph: (703)684-2782   Fax: (703)684-7343

To recognize individuals who have made significant contributions to the advancement of *Physical Therapy*. Individuals who have demonstrated superior writing skill in one or more articles published in *Physical Therapy* or who have collaborated with or encouraged others to make similar contributions or contributed outstanding leadership and effort in initiating activities to improve *Physical Therapy* are eligible. Established in 1964.

★5852★ Health Advocate Award
American Occupational Therapy
    Association
c/o Strahan
1383 Piccard Dr., Ste. 301
PO Box 1725
Rockville, MD 20849-1725
Ph: (301)948-9626   Fax: (301)948-5512

For recognition of extraordinary contributions of national significance that led to the advancement of health and health care. Nominees may be members in good standing at the time of nomination or nonmembers who have made significant contributions towards the advancement of health and health care. These contributions may include, but are not limited to: legislation, political support of health care, financial contributions, and leadership in improving health care. A certificate is awarded annually at the AOTA Conference. Established in 1983.

★5853★ Veterans Affairs Health Professional Scholarship Awards
U.S. Department of Veterans Affairs
Central Office
810 Vermont Ave., NW
Washington, DC 20420
Ph: (202)535-7527

Purpose: To provide an adequate supply of nurses, occupational therapists, and physical therapists for the Department of Veterans Affairs and the nation. Qualifications: Applicants must be U.S. citizens, and accepted for enrollment or enrolled full-time in a nursing program accredited by the National League of Nursing, an occupational therapy program accredited by the American Occupational Therapy Association, or a physical therapy program accredited by the American Physical Therapy Association. Applicants may not be obligated for service under any other scholarship program. VA employees who meet eligibility may apply. Selection criteria: Selection is based upon academic performance, career goals, recommendations, and work/volunteer experience. Funds available: Tuition/fees, reasonable educational expenses, and a monthly stipend of $621, all exempt from Federal taxation. Application details: Applications are available from college/university financial aid offices, deans of Nursing, program directors of Occupational Therapy or Physical Therapy, all VA medical centers, and the VA Central Office. Deadline: May.

★5854★ Jack Walker Award
American Physical Therapy Association
APTA Awards Program
1111 N. Fairfax St.
Alexandria, VA 22314
Ph: (703)684-2782   Fax: (703)684-7343

For recognition of the best article on clinical practice published in *Physical Therapy*. The article should be a noteworthy contribution to the improvement of patient care (e.g., therapeutic procedures, patient/family education, or delivery of health care) and should have been published in *Physical Therapy* during the preceding year. A monetary prize of $1,000 and a certificate are awarded. Established in 1978.

★5855★ E.K. Wise Loan
American Occupational Therapy
    Foundation, Inc.
4720 Montgomery Ln.
PO Box 31220
Bethesda, MD 20824-1220
Ph: (301)948-9626   Fax: (301)948-5512

Purpose: To assist eligible students with the expenses of their occupational therapy education. Qualifications: Applicants must be female citizens or permanent residents of the United States, members of the American Occupational Therapy Association, have a bachelor's degree, be enrolled in an occupational therapy curriculum leading to a certificate or graduate degree in occupational therapy, and plan to seek future employment in the field of occupational therapy. Funds available: Loans of up to $2,000, which must be repaid within three years after graduation or earlier should the recipient withdraw from the approved course of study before graduation. Application details: Formal application required. Deadline: Application for a loan may be made at any time.

BASIC REFERENCE GUIDES AND HANDBOOKS

★5856★ Physical and Occupational Therapy: Drug Implications for Practice
J. B. Lippincott Co.
227 E. Washington Sq.
Philadelphia, PA 19106
Ph: (215)238-4436   Fr: 800-441-4526

Terry Malone, editor. 1989. Includes bibliographies and an index.

★5857★ Play in Occupational Therapy
Mosby-Year Book, Inc..
11830 Westline Industrial Dr.
St. Louis, MO 63146
Ph: (314)872-8370   Fax: (314)432-1380
Fr: 800-325-4177

Diane Parham. 1995.

★5858★ Spinal Cord Injury: A Guide to Functional Outcomes in Occupational Therapy
Aspen Publishers, Inc.
200 Orchard Ridge Dr., Ste. 200
Gaithersburg, MD 20878
Ph: (301)417-7500

Judy P. Hill. 1987. Includes a bibliography and an index. Illustrated.

PROFESSIONAL AND TRADE PERIODICALS

★5859★ *Administration/Management Special Interest Section—Newsletter*
Administration/Management Special Interest Section
1383 Piccard Dr.
PO Box 1725
Rockville, MD 20850
Ph: (202)948-9626   Fax: (301)948-5512
Gayle Green Smith

Quarterly. Focuses on the administration and management issues of occupational therapy practice.

★5860★ *The American Journal of Occupational Therapy*
American Occupational Therapy Assn. Inc.
1383 Piccard Drive
PO Box 1725
Rockville, MD 20850-4375
Ph: (301)948-9626   Fax: (301)948-5512
Fr: 800-491-1760
Elaine Viseltear

Monthly. Journal providing a forum for occupational therapy personnel to share research, case studies, and new theory.

★5861★ *American Occupational Therapy Association—Federal Report*
American Occupational Therapy Association (AOTA)
4720 Montgomery Ln.
Bethesda, MD 20824
Ph: (301)652-2682
Frederick P. Somers

Bimonthly. Analyzes legislative and regulatory issues related to occupational therapy, primarily Medicare and Medicaid. Carries information on health care inflation, cost reimbursement for hospitals, the prospective payment system, taxes, physician competition, rehabilitation services, hospitals, home health agencies, skilled nursing facilities, and health planning.

★5862★ *Gerontology Special Interest Section—Newsletter*
Gerontology Special Interest Section
1383 Piccard Dr.
PO Box 1725
Rockville, MD 20850
Ph: (301)948-9626   Fax: (301)948-5512
Jennifer Jones

Quarterly. Focuses on the clinical management of the elderly. Publishes articles relevant to occupational therapy practice, including such topics as assessment protocols, treatment approaches, and program administration. Recurring features include editorials, news of research, case reports, bibliographies, and notices of new equipment.

★5863★ *National Rehabilitation Information Center—Quarterly*
National Rehabilitation Information Center
Catholic University of America
8455 Colesville Rd., Ste. 935
Silver Spring, MD 20910
Fr: 800-346-2742
Adele Kirk

Quarterly. Carries information for those involved in all aspects of rehabilitation and disability. Recurring features include a calendar of events.

★5864★ *Physical Disabilities Special Interest Section—Newsletter*
Physical Disabilities Special Interest Section
1383 Piccard Dr.
Rockville, MD 20850
Ph: (301)948-9626   Fax: (301)948-5512

Quarterly. Focuses on the clinical management of people with physical disabilities. Publishes articles relevant to occupational therapy practice, including such topics as assessment protocols, treatment approaches, and program administration. Recurring features include editorials, news of research, case reports, bibliographies, and notices of new equipment.

★5865★ *Physical & Occupational Therapy in Geriatrics*
The Haworth Press, Inc.
10 Alice St.
Binghamton, NY 13904-1580
Ph: (607)722-5857   Fax: (607)722-1424
Fr: 800-342-9678
Ellen D. Taira

Quarterly. Journal for allied health professionals focusing on current practice and emerging issues in the health care of the older client.

PROFESSIONAL MEETINGS AND CONVENTIONS

★5866★ **American Occupational Health Conference**
Slack, Inc.
6900 Grove Rd.
Thorofare, NJ 08086
Ph: (609)848-1000   Fax: (609)853-5991
Fr: 800-257-8290

Annual. **Dates and Locations:** 1996 Apr 27-03; San Antonio, TX.

★5867★ **American Society of Hand Therapists Convention**
American Society of Hand Therapists
401 N. Michigan Ave.
Chicago, IL 60611-4212
Ph: (919)779-2748   Fax: (919)779-5642

Annual. **Dates and Locations:** 1996 Oct 09-13; Nashville, TN.

★5868★ **National Rehabilitation Association National Conference and Exhibit Show**
National Rehabilitation Association
633 S. Washington St.
Alexandria, VA 22314-4109
Ph: (703)836-0850   Fax: (703)836-0848
Annual.

OTHER SOURCES OF INFORMATION

★5869★ *American Occupational Therapy Certification Board Requirements*
American Occupational Therapy Association (AOTA)
1383 Piccard Dr.
Rockville, MD 20850-1725
Ph: (301)948-9626

This sheet describes the requirements to become a registered occupational therapist.

★5870★ *"Occupational Therapist" in 100 Best Jobs for the 1990s & Beyond*
Dearborn Financial Publishing, Inc.
520 N. Dearborn St.
Chicago, IL 60610-4354
Ph: (312)836-4400   Fax: (312)836-1021
Fr: 800-621-9621

Carol Kleiman. 1992. Describes 100 jobs ranging from accountants to veterinarians. Each job profile includes such information as education, experience, and certification needed, salaries, and job search suggestions.

★5871★ *"Occupational Therapist" in Career Selector 2001*
Barron's Educational Series, Inc.
250 Wireless Blvd.
Hauppauge, NY 11788
Ph: (516)434-3311   Fax: (516)434-3723
Fr: 800-645-3476

James C. Gonyea. 1993.

★5872★ *"Occupational Therapy" in Accounting to Zoology: Graduate Fields Defined (pp. 248-249)*
Petersons Guides, Inc.
PO Box 2123
Princeton, NJ 08543-2123
Ph: (609)243-9111   Fax: (609)243-9150
Fr: 800-338-3282

Amy J. Goldstein, editor. Revised and updated, 1987. Discusses types of graduate programs and degrees, graduate research, applied work, employment prospects and trends.

★5873★ *Occupational Therapy Scholarships, Fellowships, Grants, and Loans*
American Occupational Therapy Foundation (AOTF)
1383 Piccard Dr.
Rockville, MD 20850-1725
Ph: (301)948-9626

This eight-panel brochure describes financial aid for occupational therapy study at both the undergraduate and graduate level.

Pharmacists

Pharmacists advise the public, physicians, and other health professionals on the proper selection and use of medicines. The special knowledge of the pharmacist is needed because of the complexity and potential side effects of the large and growing number of pharmaceutical products on the market. In addition to providing information, pharmacists dispense drugs and medicines prescribed by health practitioners, such as physicians, podiatrists, and dentists. Pharmacists must understand the use, composition, and effects of drugs and how they are tested for purity and strength. Compounding, the actual mixing of ingredients to form powders, tablets, capsules, ointments, and solutions, is now only a small part of a pharmacist's practice since most medicines are produced by pharmaceutical companies in the dosage and form used by the patient.

Salaries

Salaries of pharmacists are influenced by the location, size, and type of employer; the education and professional attributes of the pharmacist; and the duties and responsibilities of their positions.

Lowest 10 percent	Less than $26,100/year
Median	$45,000/year
Top 10 percent	More than $59,500/year

Employment Outlook

Growth rate until the year 2005: Faster than the average.

Pharmacists

CAREER GUIDES

★5874★ Allied Health Professions
Simon & Schuster, Inc.
200 Old Tappan Rd.
Old Tappan, NJ 07675
1993. Includes information on available jobs, required training, a directory of training programs, and a full-sample Allied Health Professions Admission Test (AHPAT).

★5875★ A Career in Pharmacy
National Association of Retail Druggists
205 Daingerfield Rd.
Alexandria, VA 22314
Ph: (703)683-8200
1992. This one-page information sheet outlines high school courses, pre-pharmacy courses, and pharmacy school courses. Briefly describes professional opportunities in different work settings, working hours per week, salary, and employment outlook.

★5876★ Careers in Medicine: Traditional and Alternative Opportunities
Garrett Park Press
PO Box 1907
Garrett Park, MD 20896-0190
Ph: (301)946-2553
T. Donald Rucker and Martin D. Keller. Revised edition, 1990. Written for college students who are considering applying to medical school, medical students attempting to select a specialty, and physicians who want to explore nonclinical work. Provides descriptions and employment outlook for 900 medical-oriented occupations.

★5877★ Clinical Pharmacist
Vocational Biographies, Inc.
PO Box 31
Sauk Centre, MN 56378-0031
Ph: (612)352-6516   Fax: (612)352-5546
Fr: 800-255-0752
1992. Four-page pamphlet containing a personal narrative about a worker's job, work likes and dislikes, career path from high school to the present. Education and training, the rewards and frustrations, and the effects of the job on the rest of the worker's life. The data file portion of this pamphlet gives a concise occupational summary, including

work descriptions, working conditions, places of employment, personal characteristics, education and training, job outlook, and salary range.

★5878★ A Graduate Degree in the Pharmaceutical Sciences: An Option for You?
American Association of Colleges of Pharmacy
1426 Prince St.
Alexandria, VA 22314-2841
Ph: (703)739-2330
1991. Encourages students to consider earning a Ph.D. in pharmaceutical science. Provides practical information about selecting a graduate program and identifying a potential career path.

★5879★ The Health Care Worker: An Introduction to Health Occupations
Prentice-Hall, Inc.
200 Old Tappan Rd.
Old Tappan, NJ 07675
Ph: (201)767-5000
Shirley A. Badasch, and Doreen S. Chesebro. Second edition, 1988. Includes a bibliography and an index.

★5880★ Health Careers
Careers, Inc.
PO Box 135
Largo, FL 34649-0135
Ph: (813)584-7333
1994. Four-page brief describing duties, working conditions, personal qualifications, training, earnings and hours, employment outlook, places of employment, related careers, and where to write for more information.

★5881★ The Internship Experience—A Manual for Pharmacy Preceptors and Interns
National Association of Boards of Pharmacy (NABP)
700 Bussey Hwy.
Park Ridge, IL 60068
Ph: (708)698-6227
Paul Grussing, editor. 1991.

★5882★ Opportunities in Pharmacy Careers
National Textbook Co. (NTC)
VGM Career Books
4255 W. Touhy Ave.
Lincolnwood, IL 60646-1975
Ph: (708)679-5500   Fax: (708)679-2494
Fr: 800-323-4900
Fred B. Cable. 1990.

★5883★ Pharmacist
Careers, Inc.
PO Box 135
Largo, FL 34649-0135
Ph: (813)584-7333
1992. Four-page brief offering the definition, history, duties, working conditions, personal qualifications, educational requirements, earnings, hours, employment outlook, advancement, and careers related to this position.

★5884★ Pharmacist
Vocational Biographies, Inc.
PO Box 31
Sauk Centre, MN 56378-0031
Ph: (612)352-6516   Fax: (612)352-5546
Fr: 800-255-0752
1993. Four-page pamphlet containing a personal narrative about a worker's job, work likes and dislikes, career path from high school to the present. Education and training, the rewards and frustrations, and the effects of the job on the rest of the worker's life. The data file portion of this pamphlet gives a concise occupational summary, including work descriptions, working conditions, places of employment, personal characteristics, education and training, job outlook, and salary range.

★5885★ "Pharmacist" in 100 Best Careers for the Year 2000 (pp. 62-65)
Arco Pub.
201 W. 103rd St.
Indianapolis, IN 46290
Ph: 800-428-5331   Fax: 800-835-3202
Shelly Field. 1992. Describes 100 job opportunities expected to grow fast throughout the next decade. Provides information on job duties and responsibilities, training requirements, education, advancement opportunities, experience and qualifications, and typical salaries.

★5886★ "Pharmacist" in *Career Information Center* **(Vol.7)**
Simon and Schuster
200 Old Tappan Rd.
Old Tappan, NJ 07675
Fax: 800-445-6991   Fr: 800-223-2348
Richard Lidz and Linda Perrin, editorial directors. Fifth edition, 1993. This 13-volume set profiles over 600 occupations. Each occupational profile describes job duties, entry-level requirements, educational requirements, advancement possibilities, employment outlook, working conditions, earnings and benefits, and where to write for more information.

★5887★ "Pharmacist" in *Careers in Health Care* **(pp. 214-217)**
National Textbook Co. (NTC)
VGM Career Books
4255 W. Touhy Ave.
Lincolnwood, IL 60646-1975
Ph: (708)679-5500   Fax: (708)679-2494
Fr: 800-323-4900
Swanson, Barbara M. Third edition, 1995. Describes job duties, work settings, salaries, licensing and certification requirements, educational preparation, and future outlook.

★5888★ "Pharmacist" in *College Board Guide to Jobs and Career Planning* **(pp. 253)**
The College Board
415 Columbus Ave.
New York, NY 10023-6992
Ph: (212)713-8165   Fax: (212)713-8143
Fr: 800-323-7155
Joyce S. Mitchell. Second edition, 1994. Describes the job, salaries, related careers, education needed, and where to write for more information.

★5889★ "Pharmacist" in *Guide to Federal Jobs* **(p. 139)**
Resource Directories
3361 Executive Pkwy., Ste. 302
Toledo, OH 43606
Ph: (419)536-5353   Fax: (419)536-7056
Fr: 800-274-8515
Rod W. Durgin, editor. Third edition, 1992. Contains information on finding and applying for federal jobs. Describes more than 200 professional and technical jobs for college graduates. Covers the nature of the work, salary, and geographic location. Lists college majors preferred for that occupation. Section one describes the function and work of government agencies that hire the most significant number of college graduates.

★5890★ "Pharmacist" in *Jobs Rated Almanac*
World Almanac
1 International Blvd., Ste. 444
Mahwah, NJ 07495
Ph: (201)529-6900   Fax: (201)529-6901
Les Krantz. Second edition, 1992. Ranks 250 jobs by environment, salary, outlooks, physical demands, stress, security, travel opportunities, and extra perks. Includes jobs the editor feels are the most common, most interesting, and the most rapidly growing.

★5891★ "Pharmacist" in *VGM's Careers Encyclopedia* **(pp. 341-344)**
National Textbook Co. (NTC)
VGM Career Books
4255 W. Touhy Ave.
Lincolnwood, IL 60646-1975
Ph: (708)679-5500   Fax: (708)679-2494
Fr: 800-323-4900
Third edition, 1991. Describes job duties, places of employment, working conditions, qualifications, education, and training, advancement potential, and salary for each occupation.

★5892★ "Pharmacist" in *VGM's Handbook of Health Care Careers*
National Textbook Co.
4255 W. Touhy Ave.
Lincolnwood, IL 60646-1975
Ph: (708)679-5500   Fax: (708)679-2494
Fr: 800-323-4900
Annette Selden. 1993. Contains 42 two-page occupational profiles describing job duties, places of employment, working conditions, qualifications, education, employment outlook, and income.

★5893★ *Pharmacists*
Chronicle Guidance Publications, Inc.
66 Aurora St.
PO Box 1190
Moravia, NY 13118-1190
Ph: (315)497-0330   Fax: (315)497-3359
Fr: 800-622-7284
1994. Career brief describing the nature of the job, working conditions, hours and earnings, education and training, licensure, certification, unions, personal qualifications, social and psychological factors, location, employment outlook, entry methods, advancement, and related occupations.

★5894★ "Pharmacists" in *American Almanac of Jobs and Salaries* **(p. 474)**
Avon Books
1350 Avenue of the Americas
New York, NY 10019
Ph: (212)261-6800   Fr: 800-238-0658
John Wright, editor. Revised and updated, 1994-95. This is comprehensive guide to the wages of hundreds of occupations in a wide variety of industries and organizations.

★5895★ "Pharmacists" in *Best Jobs for the 1990s and Into the 21st Century*
Impact Publications
9104-N Manassas Dr.
Manassas Park, VA 22111
Ph: (703)361-7300   Fax: (703)335-9486
Ronald L. Krannich and Caryl Rae Krannich. 1993.

★5896★ "Pharmacists" in *Black Woman's Career Guide* **(p. 112)**
Bantam Doubleday Dell
1540 Broadway
New York, NY 10036
Fax: 800-233-3294   Fr: 800-223-5780
Beatryce Nivens. Revised edition, 1987. Part 1 describes career planning, resume writing, job hunting, and interviewing. Part 2 profiles 60 black women pioneers in 20 different career areas.

★5897★ "Pharmacists" in *Career Discovery Encyclopedia* **(Vol.5, pp. 28-29)**
J.G. Ferguson Publishing Co.
200 W. Madison St., Ste. 300
Chicago, IL 60606
Ph: (312)580-5480   Fax: (312)580-4948
Russell E. Primm, editor-in-chief. 1993. This six volume set contains two-page articles for 504 occupations. Each article describes job duties, earnings, and educational and training requirements. The whole set is arranged alphabetically by job title. Designed for junior high and older students.

★5898★ "Pharmacists" in *Encyclopedia of Careers and Vocational Guidance* **(Vol.4, pp. 57-60)**
J.G. Ferguson Publishing Co.
200 W. Madison St., Ste. 300
Chicago, IL 60606
Ph: (312)580-5480   Fax: (312)580-4948
William E. Hopke, editor-in-chief. Ninth edition, 1993. Four-volume set that profiles 900 occupations and describes job trends in 74 industries. Includes career description, educational requirements, history of the job, methods of entry, advancement, employment outlook, earnings, conditions of work, social and psychological factors, and sources of further information.

★5899★ "Pharmacists" in *Health Care Job Explosion!* **(pp. 168-177)**
D-Amp Publications
401 Amherst Ave.
Coraopolis, PA 15108
Ph: (412)262-5578
Dennis V. Damp. 1993. Provides information on the nature of work for the major health care occupational groups. Descriptions include working conditions, training, job outlook, qualifications, and related occupations.

★5900★ "Pharmacists" in *Jobs! What They Are—Where They Are—What They Pay* **(p. 288)**
Simon & Schuster, Inc.
Simon & Schuster Bldg.
1230 Avenue of the Americas
New York, NY 10020
Ph: (212)698-7000   Fr: 800-223-2348
Robert O. Snelling and Anne M. Snelling. 3rd edition, 1992. Describes duties and responsibilities, earnings, employment opportunities, training, and qualifications.

★5901★ "Pharmacists" in *Occupational Outlook Handbook*
U.S. Government Printing Office
Superintendent of Documents
Washington, DC 20402
Ph: (202)512-1800   Fax: (202)512-2250
Biennial; latest edition, 1994-95. Encyclopedia of careers describing about 250 occupations and comprising about 85 percent of all jobs in the economy. Occupations that require lengthy education or training are given the most attention. Each occupation's profile describes what the worker does on the job, working conditions, education and training requirements, advancement possibilities, job outlook, earnings, and sources of additional information.

★5902★ *Pharmacy: A Caring Profession*
American Association of Colleges of
  Pharmacy
1426 Prince St.
Alexandria, VA 22314-2841
Ph: (703)739-2330   Fax: (703)836-8982
1992. This six-panel brochure describes the
profession and educational preparation required and lists schools of pharmacy.

★5903★ *Pharmacy Education and Careers: The APhA Resource Book*
American Pharmaceutical Association
  (APhA)
2215 Constitution Ave., NW
Washington, DC 20037
Ph: (202)628-4410
Vicki L. Meade, editor. Biennial.

★5904★ *Shall I Study Pharmacy?*
American Association of Colleges of
  Pharmacy
1426 Prince St.
Alexandria, VA 22314-2841
Ph: (703)739-2330
Tenth edition, 1992. This 31-page booklet explains career opportunities in community and hospital pharmacy and the pharmaceutical industry; describes personal qualifications, educational preparation, professional courses, working conditions, and financial aid. Lists colleges and schools of pharmacy in the United States.

PROFESSIONAL ASSOCIATIONS

★5905★ American Association of Colleges of Pharmacy (AACP)
1426 Prince St.
Alexandria, VA 22314
Ph: (703)739-2330   Fax: (703)836-8982
Members: College of pharmacy programs accredited by American Council on Pharmaceutical Education corporations and individuals. Compiles statistics. **Publications:** *AACP News*, monthly. • *American Association of Colleges of Pharmacy—Graduate Programs in the Pharmaceutical Sciences*, annual. • *American Journal of Pharmaceutical Education*, quarterly. • *Pharmacy School Admission Requirements*, annual. • *Roster of Teaching Personnel in Colleges of Pharmacy*, annual.

★5906★ American Council on Pharmaceutical Education (ACPE)
311 W. Superior St., Ste. 512
Chicago, IL 60610
Ph: (312)664-3575   Fax: (312)664-4652
Members: Accrediting agency for the professional programs of colleges and schools of pharmacy and approval of providers of continuing pharmaceutical education. **Publications:** *Accredited Professional Programs of Colleges of Schools of Pharmacy*, annual. • *Approved Providers of Continuing Pharmaceutical Education*.

★5907★ American Managed Care Pharmacy Association (AMCPA)
2300 9th St. S., Ste. 210
Arlington, VA 22204
Ph: (703)920-8480   Fax: (703)920-8491
Members: Preferred provider organizations that specialize in maintainence drug therapy in managed care environments and make available home-delivery pharmacy services. **Purpose:** Promotes managed care prescription services as suppliers of medication to home-delivery pharmacy services. Seeks to assist health plan officers and consumers in obtaining maximum value from prescription services; inform consumers and health care organizations about members' efforts to improve prescription services through cost containment measures. Compiles statistics.

★5908★ American Society of Hospital Pharmacists (ASHP)
7272 Wisconsin Ave.
Bethesda, MD 20814
Ph: (301)657-3000   Fax: (301)652-8278
Members: Professional society of pharmacists employed by hospitals, HMOs, clinics, and other health systems. **Purpose:** Provides personnel placement service for members; sponsors professional and personal liability program. Conducts educational and exhibit programs. Has 30 practice interest areas, special sections for home care practitioners and clinical specialists, and research and education foundation. **Publications:** *AHFS Drug Information*, annual. • *American Journal of Hospital Pharmacy*, semimonthly. • *ASHP Newsletter*, monthly. • *Drug Products Information File*. • *Handbook on Injectable Drugs*, biennial. • *International Pharmaceutical Abstracts*, semimonthly.

★5909★ National Association of Boards of Pharmacy (NABP)
700 Busse Hwy.
Park Ridge, IL 60068
Ph: (708)698-6227   Fax: (708)698-0124
Members: Pharmacy boards of several states, District of Columbia, Puerto Rico, Virgin Islands, several Canadian provinces, and the states of Victoria, Australia, and New South Wales. **Purpose:** Provides for inter-state reciprocity in pharmaceutic licensure based upon a uniform minimum standard of pharmaceutic education and uniform legislation; improves the standards of pharmaceutical education licensure and practice. Provides legislative information; sponsors uniform licensure examination; also provides information on accredited school and college requirements. Maintains pharmacy and drug law statistics. **Publications:** *NABP Newsletter*, 10/year. • *The NABPLEX Candidate's Review Guide*, annual. • *State Board Newsletter*, quarterly. • *Survey of Pharmacy Law*, annual.

★5910★ National Association of Chain Drug Stores (NACDS)
413 N. Lee St.
PO Box 1417-D49
Alexandria, VA 22313
Ph: (703)549-3001   Fax: (703)836-4869
Members: Chain drug members (155); associate members (1100) include manufacturers, suppliers, manufacturer's representatives, publishers, and advertising agencies.

Purpose: Interprets actions by government agencies in such areas as drugs, public health, federal trade, labor, and excise taxes. Sponsors meetings and pharmacy student recruitment program. Maintains library. Offers insurance and discount services to members. **Publications:** *Chain Pharmacists Newsletter*, periodic. • *Environmental Affairs Newsletter*, periodic. • *Federal Report*. • *NACDS Health Events Resource Guide*, annual. • *NACDS Industry Calendar*, annual. • *NACDS Membership Directory*, annual. • *NACDS Sourcebook*, annual. • *National Association of Chain Drug Stores—Executive Newsletter*, biweekly.

★5911★ National Wholesale Druggists' Association (NWDA)
1821 Michael Faraday Dr., Ste. 400
Reston, VA 22090-5348
Ph: (703)787-0000   Fax: (703)787-6930
Members: Wholesalers and manufacturers of drug, toiletry, and sundry products; advertising agencies; others interested in improving the flow of merchandise from manufacturer to consumer. **Purpose:** Compiles statistics; sponsors research and specialized education programs; maintains video network. Offers speakers' bureau. **Publications:** *Fact Book*, annual. • *Government Update*, monthly. • *NWDA Executive Newsletter*, monthly. • *Operating Survey*, annual.

STANDARDS/CERTIFICATION AGENCIES

★5912★ American Council on Pharmaceutical Education (ACPE)
311 W. Superior St., Ste. 512
Chicago, IL 60610
Ph: (312)664-3575   Fax: (312)664-4652
Accrediting agency for the professional programs of colleges and schools of pharmacy and approval of providers of continuing pharmaceutical education.

★5913★ National Association of Boards of Pharmacy (NABP)
700 Busse Hwy.
Park Ridge, IL 60068
Ph: (708)698-6227   Fax: (708)698-0124
Pharmacy boards of several states, District of Columbia, Puerto Rico, Virgin Islands, several Canadian provinces, and the states of Victoria, Australia, and New South Wales. Provides for inter-state reciprocity in pharmaceutic licensure based upon a uniform minimum standard of pharmaceutic education and uniform legislation; improves the standards of pharmaceutical education licensure and practice. Sponsors uniform licensure examination; also provides information on accredited school and college requirements.

TEST GUIDES

★5914★ Career Examination Series: Pharmacist
National Learning Corp.
212 Michael Dr.
Syosset, NY 11791
Ph: (516)921-8888   Fax: (516)921-8743
Fr: 800-645-6337

Jack Rudman. A series of study guides with multiple-choice examination questions and solutions for trainees and professional pharmacists. Titles in the series include *Pharmacist I; Pharmacist II; Pharmacist III; Pharmacist Trainee; Pharmacologist; Senior Pharmacist.*

★5915★ Foreign Pharmacy Graduates Equivalency Examination
National Learning Corp.
212 Michael Dr.
Syosset, NY 11791
Ph: (516)921-8888   Fax: (516)921-8743
Fr: 800-645-6337

Jack Rudman. Part of the Admission Test series. A sample test for prospective pharmacists who are seeking admission to graduate and professional schools or seeking entrance or advancement in institutional and public career service.

★5916★ National Pharmacy Boards
National Learning Corp.
212 Michael Dr.
Syosset, NY 11791
Ph: (516)921-8888   Fax: (516)921-8743
Fr: 800-645-6337

Jack Rudman. Part of the Admission Test series. A sample test for prospective pharmacists who are seeking admission to graduate and professional schools or seeking entrance or advancement in institutional and public career service.

★5917★ PCAT: Pharmacy College Admission Test
Arco Pub.
201 W. 103rd St.
Indianapolis, IN 46290
Ph: 800-428-5331   Fax: 800-835-3202

D.R. Gourley. 1991, second edition. Contains hundreds of sample questions.

★5918★ Pharmacy College Admission Test (PCAT)
National Learning Corp.
212 Michael Dr.
Syosset, NY 11791
Ph: (516)921-8888   Fax: (516)921-8743
Fr: 800-645-6337

Jack Rudman. Part of the Admission Test series. A sample test for prospective pharmacists who are seeking admission to graduate and professional schools or seeking entrance or advancement in institutional and public career service.

★5919★ Student Guide to the PCAT, (Pharmacy College Admission Test): Comprehensive Manual for Self-Study and Review
Datar Publishing Co.
PO Box 16464
St. Louis, MO 63125
Ph: (314)843-5343

David M. Tarlow. 1991. Part of the Practice Examination Series.

EDUCATIONAL DIRECTORIES AND PROGRAMS

★5920★ Accredited Professional Programs of Colleges and Schools of Pharmacy
American Council on Pharmaceutical Education
311 W. Superior St., Ste. 512
Chicago, IL 60610
Ph: (312)664-3575   Fax: (312)664-4652
Lynn Moen, Contact

Annual, July. Covers accredited pharmacy colleges with professional degree programs in the United States and Puerto Rico. Entries include: College name, address, phone, dean's name, date of most recent and of next accreditation evaluation. Arrangement: Geographical.

★5921★ Approved Providers of Continuing Pharmaceutical Education
American Council on Pharmaceutical Education
311 W. Superior St., Ste. 512
Chicago, IL 60610
Ph: (312)664-3575   Fax: (312)664-4652
Lynn Moen, Executive Assistant

Annual, September. Covers about 335 universities, colleges, associations, publishers, and corporations that provide continuing pharmaceutical education seminars, workshops, demonstrations, publications, audiovisual materials, and correspondence courses. Entries include: Organization name, type of organization, address, phone, name and title of contact. Arrangement: Alphabetical.

★5922★ Encyclopedia of Medical Organizations and Agencies
Gale Research Inc.
835 Penobscot Bldg.
Detroit, MI 48226-4094
Ph: (313)961-2242   Fax: (313)961-6741
Fr: 800-877-GALE
Karen Boyden, Contact

Biennial, November of odd years. Covers over 13,400 state, national, and international medical associations, foundations, research institutes, federal and state agencies, and medical and allied health schools. Entries include: Organization name, address, phone; many listings include names and titles of key personnel, descriptive annotations. Arrangement: Classified by subject, then by type of organization.

★5923★ Gourman Report: A Rating of Graduate and Professional Programs in American and International Universities
National Education Standards
624 S. Grand Ave., Ste. 1210
Los Angeles, CA 90017
Ph: (213)623-9135
Jack Gourman

Irregular, previous edition 1989; latest edition January, 1993. Covers colleges and universities offering graduate programs in a variety of disciplines; medical schools; law schools; schools of dentistry; optometry; pharmacy. Entries include: Institution name, address, author's description and evaluation. Arrangement: Law, medical, dental, and pharmacy schools are listed by country; others (primarily in United States) are by discipline.

★5924★ Health & Medical Industry Directory
American Business Directories, Inc.
5711 S. 86th Circle
Omaha, NE 68127
Ph: (402)593-4600   Fax: (402)331-1505

Released 1993. Lists over 1.1 million physicians and surgeons, dentists, clinics, health clubs, and other health-related businesses in the U.S. and Canada. Entries include: Name, address, phone.

★5925★ Medical and Health Information Directory
Gale Research Inc.
835 Penobscot Bldg.
Detroit, MI 48226-4094
Ph: (313)961-2242   Fax: (313)961-6741
Fr: 800-877-GALE
Karen Boyden, Contact

Approximately biennial; latest edition 1994. Covers in Volume 1, almost 18,600 medical and health oriented associations, organizations, institutions, and government agencies, including health maintenance organizations (HMOs), preferred provider organizations (PPOs), insurance companies, pharmaceutical companies, research centers, and medical and allied health schools. In Volume 2, nearly 11,800 medical book publishers; medical periodicals, directories, audiovisual producers and services, medical libraries and information centers, and electronic resources. In Volume 3, nearly 26,000 clinics, treatment centers, care programs, and counseling/diagnostic services for 30 subject areas. Entries include: Institution, service, or firm name, address, phone; many include names of key personnel Arrangement: Classified by organization activity, service, etc..

★5926★ Pharmacy School Admission Requirements
American Association of Colleges of Pharmacy (AACP)
1426 Prince St.
Alexandria, VA 22314-2841
Ph: (703)739-2330   Fax: (703)836-8982
Susan M. Meyer, Contact

Annual, September. Covers 75 colleges and schools with pharmacy programs accredited by the American Council on Pharmaceutical Education. Entries include: School name, address, admission requirements, tuition, contact name, timetables for application and admission for one-year period in advance.

Descriptions of student life and housing, facilities, curriculum, and advanced placement are provided. Arrangement: Geographical, then alphabetical by school name.

★5927★ Therapists and Allied Health Professionals Career Directory
Gale Research Inc.
835 Penobscot Bldg.
Detroit, MI 48226-4094
Ph: (313)961-2242   Fax: (313)961-6083
Fr: 800-877-GALE

Bradley J. Morgan and Joseph M. Palmisano. 1993. A directory in the Career Advisor Series that provides essays written by industry professionals; job search information on resume and cover letter preparation, networking, and the interviewing process; approximately 300 companies and organizations offering job opportunities and internships, and additional job-hunting resources.

★5928★ United States and Canadian Programs for Graduate Training in Pharmacology
American Society for Pharmacology and Experimental Therapeutics
9650 Rockville Pike
Bethesda, MD 20814-3995
Ph: (301)530-7060
Kay A. Croker

Triennial, latest edition January 1992. Covers more than 200 institutions; limited Canadian coverage. Entries include: Institution name, department name, address, name of department chairperson, phone, pharmacological specialties offered, highest degree offered. Arrangement: Separate geographical sections for medicine, pharmacy, and veterinary medicine schools.

AWARDS, SCHOLARSHIPS, GRANTS, AND FELLOWSHIPS

★5929★ Award for Achievement in the Professional Practice of Hospital Pharmacy
American Society of Hospital Pharmacists Research and Education Foundation
7272 Wisconsin Ave.
Bethesda, MD 20814
Ph: (301)657-3000   Fax: (301)652-8278

For recognition of the most significant contribution to the literature in the professional practice of hospital pharmacy in the calendar year preceding the year in which the award is granted. Professional practice of hospital pharmacy refers to all aspects of professional practice, including management, drug use control, technological services, clinical services, and information processing. The deadline is May 15. A monetary award of $1,000, a $500 travel allowance to attend the ASHP Midyear Clinical Meeting, and a plaque are awarded annually. Established in 1971.

★5930★ Donald E. Francke Medal
American Society of Hospital Pharmacists
7272 Wisconsin Ave.
Bethesda, MD 20814
Ph: (301)657-3000   Fax: (301)652-8278

To honor a hospital pharmacist who has made significant contributions to the profession at the international level. A sterling silver medallion is awarded irregularly. Established in 1972.

★5931★ Takeru Higuchi Research Prize
American Pharmaceutical Association
2215 Constitution Ave. NW
Washington, DC 20037
Ph: (202)628-4410   Fax: (202)783-2351

To recognize a scientist who has demonstrated effective and persistent efforts in pioneering a new concept applicable to the pharmaceutical sciences. The prize consists of a bronze medal and an honorarium, and is bestowed no more frequently than every other year. Established in 1981 in honor of Takeru Higuchi, the first scientific academy President.

★5932★ HRSA-BHP Health Professions Student Loans
U.S. Public Health Service
Health Resources and Services Administration
Parklawn Bldg., Rm. 8-38
5600 Fishers Ln.
Rockville, MD 20857

Purpose: To assist students with need for financial assistance to undertake the course of study required to become physicians, dentists, osteopathic physicians, optometrists, pharmacists, podiatrists, or veterinarians. Qualifications: Applicants must be enrolled or accepted for enrollment as full-time students in a program leading to a doctoral degree in medicine, dental surgery or equivalent degree, pharmacy, osteopathic medicine, optometry or equivalent degree, podiatric medicine or equivalent degree, or veterinary medicine or equivalent degree; or a bachelor of science in pharmacy or equivalent degree. Applicants must also be citizens, nationals, or permanent residents of the United States or the District of Columbia, the Commonwealths of Puerto Rico or the Marianna Islands, the Virgin Islands, Guam, The American Samoa, the Trust Territory of the Pacific Islands, the Republic of Palau, the Republic of the Marshall Islands, and the Federated State of Micronesia. Applicants must also demonstrate financial need. Professional students, interns, residents, and students seeking advanced training are not eligible. Funds available: Up to the cost of tuition plus $2,500 or the amount of financial need, whichever is less. The interest rate is five percent and accrues during the repayment period. Loans are repayable over a ten year period and beginning one year after the student graduates or ceases to enroll full-time in a health program.

★5933★ HRSA-BHP Loans for Disadvantaged Students
U.S. Public Health Service
Health Resources and Services Administration
Parklawn Bldg., Rm. 8-38
5600 Fishers Ln.
Rockville, MD 20857

Purpose: To assist students who need financial assistance to pursue careers in medicine, osteopathic medicine, dentistry, optometry, podiatric medicine, pharmacy, or veterinary medicine. Qualifications: Applicants must be citizens, nationals, or lawful permanent residents of the United States or the District of Columbia, the Commonwealths of Puerto Rico or the Marianna Islands, the Virgin Islands, Guam, American Samoa, the Trust Territory of the Pacific Islands, the Republic of Palau, the Republic of the Marshall Islands, or the Federated State of Micronesia. They must also be enrolled or accepted for enrollment at a participating health professionals school full-time. Students must be determined by their school's financial aid director to meet financial need and "disadvantaged background" criteria. Those enrolled in schools of medicine or osteopathic medicine must demonstrate exceptional financial need. Preprofessional students, interns, residents, and students seeking advanced training are not eligible. Selection criteria: Schools are responsible for selecting recipients and for determining the amount of assistance. Funds available: The maximum loan amount allowed for each school year is the cost of tuition plus $2,500, or the amount of financial need, whichever is lesser. The repayment interest rate is five percent over a ten-year period, which begins one year after completion of cessation of full-time study. Interest begins accruing at the time the loan becomes repayable. Repayment may be deferred under special circumstances, and interest does not accrue during periods of deferment.

★5934★ Daniel B. Smith Award
American Pharmaceutical Association
2215 Constitution Ave. NW
Washington, DC 20037
Ph: (202)628-4410   Fax: (202)783-2351

To recognize the achievements of a community pharmacy practitioner who has distinguished himself/herself and the profession of pharmacy by outstanding professional performance, both in the recipient's practice setting and in the community in which it is located. A mounted bronze medallion is awarded annually. Established in 1964 in honor of Daniel B. Smith, the first president of APhA who was a community pharmacist and president of the Philadelphia College of Pharmacy and Science. Sponsored by Marion Merrell Dow, Inc.

★5935★ Harvey A. K. Whitney Award
American Society of Hospital Pharmacists
7272 Wisconsin Ave.
Bethesda, MD 20814
Ph: (301)657-3000   Fax: (301)652-8278

This, hospital pharmacy's highest honor, is given to honor outstanding contributions to the practice of hospital pharmacy. The awardee presents a lecture and receives a plaque. Awarded annually. Established in

1950 by the Michigan Society of Hospital Pharmacists (now the Southeastern Michigan Society of Hospital Pharmacists) to honor Harvey A.K. Whitney (1894-1957), editor, author, educator, practitioner, hospital pharmacy leader, and first chairman of the American Society of Hospital Pharmacists.

BASIC REFERENCE GUIDES AND HANDBOOKS

★5936★ AHFS Drug Information '95
American Society of Hospital Pharmacists (ASHP)
7272 Wisconsin Ave.
Bethesda, MD 20814
Ph: (301)657-3000

Annual with quarterly supplements. Contains two-or-three page articles describing the properties, uses, and effects of individual drugs.

★5937★ Fact Sheet: Health Education Assistance Loan Program (HEAL)
U.S. Department of Health and Human Services
Public Health Service
Health Resources and Services Administration
Bureau of Health Professions, Division of Student Assistance
Rockville, MD 20857
Ph: (301)443-2086

Fact sheet describing the HEAL Program; covers eligible schools, borrowers, and lenders, as well as loan limitations, interest, and repayment.

★5938★ PDR: Physicians' Desk Reference
Medical Economics Books
680 Kinderkamack Rd.
Oradell, NJ 07649
Ph: (201)358-7200   Fr: 800-223-0581
Barbara B. Huff, et al., editors. Annual. 1995. Contains descriptions of drugs including medical indications, pharmacological actions, and adverse reactions.

★5939★ Pharmaceutical Dosage Forms, Parenteral Medications
Marcel Dekker, Inc.
270 Madison Ave.
New York, NY 10016
Ph: (212)696-9000
Kenneth E. Avis, Leon Lachman, and Herbert A. Lieberman, editors. Volume 1 and 2, 1992; Volume 3, 1993. Includes bibliographies and an index.

★5940★ Remington's Pharmaceutical Sciences
Mack Publishing Co.
1991 Northhampton St.
Easton, PA 18042
Ph: (215)250-7241
Alfonso R. Gennaro, editor. Eighteenth edition, 1990. Textbook and reference work for pharmacists.

★5941★ The United States Pharmacopeia: The National Formulary
United States Pharmacopeial Convention, Inc.
12601 Twinbrook Pkwy.
Rockville, MD 20852
Ph: (301)881-0666   Fr: 800-227-8772
Twenty-third revision of The Pharmacopeia of the U.S.

PROFESSIONAL AND TRADE PERIODICALS

★5942★ American College of Apothecaries—Newsletter
American College of Apothecaries
205 Daingerfield Rd.
Alexandria, VA 22314
Ph: (703)684-8603
D.C. Huffman

Monthly. Presents national pharmacy news designed to assist Association members in their professional practices. Covers Association news, including items on membership, chapters, committees, elections, and conferences. Recurring features include book reviews and a necrology.

★5943★ American Druggist
Hearst Business Publishing
60 E. 42nd St.
New York, NY 10165
Ph: (212)297-9680   Fax: (212)286-9886
Scott E. PiercePublisher

Monthly. Magazine for pharmacists who practice in independent drug stores, chain drug stores, and hospitals. Also covers wholesale drug field.

★5944★ American Journal of Hospital Pharmacy
American Society of Hospital Pharmacists
7272 Wisconsin Ave.
Bethesda, MD 20814
Ph: (301)657-3000   Fax: (301)657-1258
C. Richard Talley

Monthly. Journal for directors and staffs of pharmaceutical departments in hospitals and health-care institutions.

★5945★ American Pharmacy
American Pharmaceutical Assn.
2215 Constitution Ave. NW
Washington, DC 20037
Ph: (202)628-4410   Fax: (202)783-2351
Marlene Bloom

Monthly. Journal for pharmacy professionals.

★5946★ Biopharmaceutics and Drug Disposition
John Wiley and Sons, Inc.
Subscription Dept.
605 3rd Ave.
New York, NY 10158
Ph: (212)850-6000   Fax: (212)850-6799
G.L. Mattok

Monthly. Journal covering biopharmaceutics, drug disposition, pharmacokinetics and related research.

★5947★ CNS Drugs
Adis International
Oxford Ct., Business Ctr., Ste. B-30
582 Middletown Blvd.
Langhorne, PA 19047
Ph: (215)752-4500

Monthly. Journal covering issues in the pharmacological treatment of neurological and psychiatric disorders.

★5948★ Diabetic Medicine
John Wiley and Sons, Inc.
Subscription Dept.
605 3rd Ave.
New York, NY 10158
Ph: (212)850-6000   Fax: (212)850-6799
Andrew Boulton

Monthly. Journal informing diabetic patients of research and better health care.

★5949★ InterPharmacy Forum
Michele Ryan, Contact
Monthly. Discusses timely questions and answers in an easy to read format. Topics apply to a variety of real world problems and solutions. Recurring features include "Notes and News" column which provides the latest information on all aspects of drugs.

★5950★ NARD Newsletter
National Association of Retail Druggists (NARD)
205 Daingerfield Rd.
Alexandria, VA 22314
Ph: (703)683-8200   Fax: (703)683-3619
Fr: 800-544-7447
Robert D. Appel

Semimonthly. Reports on topics affecting independents, including developments within the pharmaceutical industry, regulatory and legislative activity, and pricing and import information. Recurring features include reports of meetings, news of educational opportunities, notices of publications available, and news of NARD activities and events.

★5951★ Pharmacoepidemiology and Drug Safety
John Wiley and Sons, Inc.
605 3rd Ave.
New York, NY 10158
Ph: (212)850-6000   Fax: (212)850-6799
Ronald Mann

Bimonthly. Journal publishing data and opinions in the field of pharmacoepidemiology.

★5952★ Voice of the Pharmacist— Newsletter
American College of Apothecaries
205 Daingerfield Rd.
Alexandria, VA 22314
Ph: (703)684-8603   Fax: (703)683-3619
D.C. Huffman

Quarterly. Examines current issues and opportunities affecting the retail, hospital, and consultant practices of pharmacy. Discusses controversial issues, often with commentary by pharmacists. Recurring features include editorials, news of research, and letters to the editor.

PROFESSIONAL MEETINGS AND CONVENTIONS

★5953★ American College of Clinical Pharmacy Annual Meeting
American College of Clinical Pharmacy
3101 Broadway, Ste. 380
Kansas City, MO 64111
Ph: (816)531-2177   Fax: (816)531-4990
Annual.

★5954★ American Society of Consultant Pharmacists Annual Meeting
American Society of Consultant Pharmacists
1321 Duke St.
Alexandria, VA 22314-3563
Ph: (703)739-1300   Fax: (703)739-1321
Annual. **Dates and Locations:** 1995 Nov 15-19; San Francisco, CA.

★5955★ American Society of Hospital Pharmacists Annual Meeting
American Society of Hospital Pharmacists
4630 Montgomery Ave.
Bethesda, MD 20814
Ph: (301)657-3000   Fax: (301)652-8278
Annual.

★5956★ Pharmaceutical Society of the State of New York Annual Meeting
Pharmaceutical Society of the State of New York
Pine West Plaza IV
Washington Ave.
Albany, NY 12205
Ph: (518)869-6595   Fax: (518)464-0618
Annual. Always held during the last week of June.

★5957★ RX Expo - An Educational Forum and Buying Show
National Association of Retail Druggists
205 Daingerfield Rd.
Alexandria, VA 22314
Ph: (703)683-8200   Fax: (703)683-3619
Fr: 800-547-7447
Annual. Always held during May. **Dates and Locations:** 1996 May.

★5958★ Western Pharmacy Education Fair
California Pharmacists Association
1112 I St., Ste. 300
Sacramento, CA 95814
Ph: (916)444-7811   Fax: (916)444-7929
Annual. **Dates and Locations:** 1996 Oct 04-06; Reno, NV.

OTHER SOURCES OF INFORMATION

★5959★ Financial Aid Information for Pharmacy Students
American Association of Colleges of Pharmacy (AACP)
1426 Prince St.
Alexandria, VA 22314-2841
Ph: (703)739-2330
One-page sheet briefly describing federal scholarships and loans, state scholarships and loans, college scholarships and loans, and other sources of aid.

★5960★ NACDS and Pharmacy Education: Programs for Progress
National Assocation of Chain Drug Stores (NACDS)
PO Box 1417-D49
Alexandria, VA 22313
Ph: (703)549-3001
This pamphlet describes scholarship, internship, and fellowship programs offered by the National Association of Chain Drug Stores.

★5961★ "Pharmacist" in 100 Best Jobs for the 1990s & Beyond
Dearborn Financial Publishing, Inc.
520 N. Dearborn St.
Chicago, IL 60610-4354
Ph: (312)836-4400   Fax: (312)836-1021
Fr: 800-621-9621
Carol Kleiman. 1992. Describes 100 jobs ranging from accountants to veterinarians. Each job profile includes such information as education, experience, and certification needed, salaries, and job search suggestions.

★5962★ Pharmacy, Drugs, and Medical Care
Williams and Wilkins
428 E. Preston St.
Baltimore, MD 21202
Ph: (301)528-4000
Smith, Mickey C., and David A. Knapp. Fourth edition, 1987. Includes bibliographies and an index.

★5963★ "Pharmacy and Pharmaceutical Science" in Accounting to Zoology: Graduate Fields Defined (pp. 281-284)
Petersons Guides, Inc.
PO Box 2123
Princeton, NJ 08543-2123
Ph: (609)243-9111   Fax: (609)243-9150
Fr: 800-338-3282
Amy J. Goldstein, editor. Revised and updated, 1987. Discusses types of graduate programs and degrees, graduate research, applied work, employment prospects and trends.

★5964★ Survey of Pharmacy Law
National Association of Boards of Pharmacy (NABP)
1300 Higgins Rd., Ste. 103
700 Busse Hwy.
Park Ridge, IL 60068
Ph: (708)698-6227
Annual. Guide to state pharmacy laws including the organization of state boards, licensing of pharmacists, internship requirements, and drug laws. Includes data on issuance and renewal of licenses, prescribing authority, and state drug associations.

Physical Therapists

Physical therapists work to improve the mobility, relieve the pain, and prevent or limit the permanent disability of patients suffering from injuries or disease. Their patients include accident victims or handicapped individuals with such conditions as multiple sclerosis, cerebral palsy, nerve injuries, burns, amputations, head injuries, fractures, low back pain, arthritis, and heart disease. Patients range in age from the newborn to the elderly. Some physical therapists treat a wide variety of problems; others specialize in areas such as pediatrics, orthopedics, geriatrics, sports physical therapy, neurology, and cardiopulmonary physical therapy.

Salaries

Average earnings of physical therapists are as follows:

Lowest 10 percent	Less than $17,784/year
Median	$35,464/year
Top 10 percent	More than $52,468/year

Employment Outlook

Growth rate until the year 2005: Much faster than the average.

Physical Therapists

CAREER GUIDES

★5965★ Allied Health Professions
Simon & Schuster, Inc.
200 Old Tappan Rd.
Old Tappan, NJ 07675

1993. Includes information on available jobs, required training, a directory of training programs, and a full-sample Allied Health Professions Admission Test (AHPAT).

★5966★ Careers in Health and Fitness
Rosen Publishing Group
29 E. 21st St.
New York, NY 10010
Ph: (212)777-3017   Fax: (212)777-0277
Fr: 800-237-9932

Jackie Heron, R.N. 1990. Explores the opportunities and responsibilities of a career in health or fitness.

★5967★ Careers in Social and Rehabilitation Services
National Textbook Co. (NTC)
VGM Career Books
4255 W. Touhy Ave.
Lincolnwood, IL 60646-1975
Ph: (708)679-5500   Fax: (708)679-2494
Fr: 800-323-4900

Geraldine O. Garner, Ph.D., editor. 1993. Describes dozens of careers in the field of social and rehabilitation services.

★5968★ A Future in Physical Therapy
American Physical Therapy Association
1111 N. Fairfax St.
Alexandria, VA 22314
Ph: (703)684-2782

Annual. Sixteen-page booklet including a description of the field, what physical therapists do, education, licensure, and salaries. Gives a state-by-state listing of accredited programs. List sources of financial aid.

★5969★ The Health Care Worker: An Introduction to Health Occupations
Prentice-Hall, Inc.
200 Old Tappan Rd.
Old Tappan, NJ 07675
Ph: (201)767-5000

Shirley A. Badasch, and Doreen S. Chesebro. Second edition, 1988. Includes a bibliography and an index.

★5970★ Health Careers
Careers, Inc.
PO Box 135
Largo, FL 34649-0135
Ph: (813)584-7333

1994. Four-page brief describing duties, working conditions, personal qualifications, training, earnings and hours, employment outlook, places of employment, related careers, and where to write for more information.

★5971★ Opportunities in Fitness Careers
National Textbook Co. (NTC)
VGM Career Books
4255 W. Touhy Ave.
Lincolnwood, IL 60646-1975
Ph: (708)679-5500   Fax: (708)679-2494
Fr: 800-323-4900

Jean Rosenbaum and Mary Prine. 1991. Surveys fitness related careers, including the physical therapy profession. Describes career opportunities, education and experience needed, how to get into entry-level jobs and what income to expect. Schools are listed in the appendix.

★5972★ Opportunities in Health and Medical Careers
National Textbook Co. (NTC)
VGM Career Books
4255 W. Touhy Ave.
Lincolnwood, IL 60646-1975
Ph: (708)679-5500   Fax: (708)679-2494
Fr: 800-323-4900

I. Donald Snook Jr., Leo D'Orazio. Describes the working conditions of physicians, physician assistants, therapists, nurses, technicians, administrators, and hospital staff. Also includes information on educational requirements and salaries.

★5973★ Opportunities in Physical Therapy
National Textbook Co. (NTC)
VGM Career Books
4255 W. Touhy Ave.
Lincolnwood, IL 60646-1975
Ph: (708)679-5500   Fax: (708)679-2494
Fr: 800-323-4900

Bernice Krumhansl. Profiles the work of a physical therapist in various settings including hospital and schools, industrial clinics, and home health care institutions. Includes information on legal and professional requirements, licensing and insurance issues, salaries and wages, and opportunities for advancement.

★5974★ Opportunities in Physical Therapy Careers
National Textbook Co. (NTC)
VGM Career Books
4255 W. Touhy Ave.
Lincolnwood, IL 60646-1975
Ph: (708)679-5500   Fax: (708)679-2494
Fr: 800-323-4900

Bernice Krumhansl. 1987. Gives the history and an overview of physical therapy as a career. Discusses the many different settings where physical therapists work. Describes training requirements and lists colleges and universities offering programs in physical therapy.

★5975★ Passbooks for Career Opportunities: Physical Therapist
National Learning Corp.
212 Michael Dr.
Syosset, NY 11791
Ph: (516)921-8888   Fax: (516)921-8743
Fr: 800-645-6337

1992.

★5976★ Physical Therapist
Vocational Biographies, Inc.
PO Box 31
Sauk Centre, MN 56378-0031
Ph: (612)352-6516   Fax: (612)352-5546
Fr: 800-255-0752

1994. Four-page pamphlet containing a personal narrative about a worker's job, work likes and dislikes, career path from high school to the present. Education and training, the rewards and frustrations, and the effects of the job on the rest of the worker's life. The data file portion of this pamphlet gives a concise occupational summary, including work descriptions, working conditions, places of employment, personal characteristics, education and training, job outlook, and salary range.

★5977★ Physical Therapist
Careers, Inc.
PO Box 135
Largo, FL 34649-0135
Ph: (813)584-7333
1995. Four-page brief offering the definition, history, duties, working conditions, personal qualifications, educational requirements, earnings, hours, employment outlook, advancement, and careers related to this position.

★5978★ "Physical Therapist" in _100 Best Careers for the Year 2000_ (pp. 69-71)
Arco Pub.
201 W. 103rd St.
Indianapolis, IN 46290
Ph: 800-428-5331   Fax: 800-835-3202
Shelly Field. 1992. Describes 100 job opportunities expected to grow fast throughout the next decade. Provides information on job duties and responsibilities, training requirements, education, advancement opportunities, experience and qualifications, and typical salaries.

★5979★ "Physical Therapist" in _150 Careers in the Health Care Field_
Reed Reference Publishing
121 Chanlon Rd.
PO Box 31
New Providence, NJ 07974
Fax: (908)665-6688   Fr: 800-521-8110
Stanley Alperin. Third edition, 1993. Profiles health care occupations requiring a bachelor's degree or less. Describes the nature of the work, educational preparation, licensing requirements, and salary. Lists accredited educational programs.

★5980★ "Physical Therapist Assistants" in _Encyclopedia of Careers and Vocational Guidance_ (Vol.4, pp. 81-85)
J.G. Ferguson Publishing Co.
200 W. Madison St., Ste. 300
Chicago, IL 60606
Ph: (312)580-5480   Fax: (312)580-4948
William E. Hopke, editor-in-chief. Ninth edition, 1993. Four-volume set that profiles 900 occupations and describes job trends in 74 industries. Includes career description, educational requirements, history of the job, methods of entry, advancement, employment outlook, earnings, conditions of work, social and psychological factors, and sources of further information.

★5981★ "Physical Therapist" in _Career Information Center_ (Vol.7)
Simon and Schuster
200 Old Tappan Rd.
Old Tappan, NJ 07675
Fax: 800-445-6991   Fr: 800-223-2348
Richard Lidz and Linda Perrin, editorial directors. Fifth edition, 1993. This 13-volume set profiles over 600 occupations. Each occupational profile describes job duties, entry-level requirements, educational requirements, advancement possibilities, employment outlook, working conditions, earnings and

benefits, and where to write for more information.

★5982★ "Physical Therapist" in _Careers in Health and Fitness_
Rosen Publishing Group
29 E. 21st St.
New York, NY 10010
Ph: (212)777-3017   Fax: (212)777-0277
Fr: 800-237-9932
Jackie Heron. 1990. Occupational profiles contain information on job duties, skills, advantages, basic equipment used, employment possibilities, certification, and salary.

★5983★ "Physical Therapist" in _College Board Guide to Jobs and Career Planning_ (pp. 262)
The College Board
415 Columbus Ave.
New York, NY 10023-6992
Ph: (212)713-8165   Fax: (212)713-8143
Fr: 800-323-7155
Joyce S. Mitchell. Second edition, 1994. Describes job duties, salaries, related careers, education needed, and where to write for more information.

★5984★ "Physical Therapist" in _Guide to Federal Jobs_ (p. 133)
Resource Directories
3361 Executive Pkwy., Ste. 302
Toledo, OH 43606
Ph: (419)536-5353   Fax: (419)536-7056
Fr: 800-274-8515
Rod W. Durgin, editor. Third edition, 1992. Contains information on finding and applying for federal jobs. Describes more than 200 professional and technical jobs for college graduates. Covers the nature of the work, salary, and geographic location. Lists college majors preferred for that occupation. Section one describes the function and work of government agencies that hire the most significant number of college graduates.

★5985★ "Physical Therapist" in _Jobs Rated Almanac_
World Almanac
1 International Blvd., Ste. 444
Mahwah, NJ 07495
Ph: (201)529-6900   Fax: (201)529-6901
Les Krantz. Second edition, 1992. Ranks 250 jobs by environment, salary, outlooks, physical demands, stress, security, travel opportunities, and extra perks. Includes jobs the editor feels are the most common, most interesting, and the most rapidly growing.

★5986★ "Physical Therapist" and "Physical Therapist Assistant" in _Careers in Health Care_ (pp. 218-223)
National Textbook Co. (NTC)
VGM Career Books
4255 W. Touhy Ave.
Lincolnwood, IL 60646-1975
Ph: (708)679-5500   Fax: (708)679-2494
Fr: 800-323-4900
Swanson, Barbara M. Third edition, 1995. Describes job duties, work settings, salaries, licensing and certification requirements, educational preparation, and future outlook.

★5987★ "Physical Therapist" in _Profitable Careers in Non-Profit_ (pp. 98-100)
John Wiley and Sons, Inc.
605 3rd Ave.
New York, NY 10158-0012
Ph: (212)850-6000   Fax: (212)850-6088
Fr: 800-526-5368
William Lewis and Carol Milano. 1987. Examines nonprofit organizations and the career opportunities they offer. Offers tips on how to target and explore occupational opportunities in the nonprofit sector.

★5988★ "Physical Therapist" in _VGM's Careers Encyclopedia_ (pp. 348-350)
National Textbook Co. (NTC)
VGM Career Books
4255 W. Touhy Ave.
Lincolnwood, IL 60646-1975
Ph: (708)679-5500   Fax: (708)679-2494
Fr: 800-323-4900
Third edition, 1991. Describes job duties, places of employment, working conditions, qualifications, education, and training, advancement potential, and salary for each occupation.

★5989★ "Physical Therapist" in _VGM's Handbook of Health Care Careers_
National Textbook Co.
4255 W. Touhy Ave.
Lincolnwood, IL 60646-1975
Ph: (708)679-5500   Fax: (708)679-2494
Fr: 800-323-4900
Annette Selden. 1993. Contains 42 two-page occupational profiles describing job duties, places of employment, working conditions, qualifications, education, employment outlook, and income.

★5990★ Physical Therapists
Chronicle Guidance Publications, Inc.
66 Aurora St.
PO Box 1190
Moravia, NY 13118-1190
Ph: (315)497-0330   Fax: (315)497-3359
Fr: 800-622-7284
1993. Career brief describing the nature of the job, working conditions, hours and earnings, education and training, licensure, certification, unions, personal qualifications, social and psychological factors, location, employment outlook, entry methods, advancement, and related occupations.

★5991★ "Physical Therapists" in _101 Careers: A Guide to the Fastest-Growing Opportunities_ (pp. 246-249)
John Wiley & Sons, Inc.
605 3rd Ave.
New York, NY 10158-0012
Ph: (212)850-6645   Fax: (212)850-6088
Michael Harkavy. 1990. Describes the nature of the job, working conditions, employment growth, qualifications, personal skills, projected salaries, and where to write for more information.

★5992★ "Physical Therapists" in *American Almanac of Jobs and Salaries* (p. 468)
Avon Books
1350 Avenue of the Americas
New York, NY 10019
Ph: (212)261-6800   Fr: 800-238-0658
John Wright, editor. Revised and updated, 1994-95. This is comprehensive guide to the wages of hundreds of occupations in a wide variety of industries and organizations.

★5993★ "Physical Therapists" in *America's 50 Fastest Growing Jobs* (pp. 52)
JIST Works, Inc.
720 N. Park Ave.
Indianapolis, IN 46202-3431
Ph: (317)264-3720   Fax: (317)264-3709
Fr: 800-648-5478
Michael J. Farr, compiler. 1994. Describes the 50 fastest growing jobs within major career clusters such as technicians, and marketing and sales. Each job profile explains the nature of the work, skills and abilities required, employment outlook, average earnings, related occupations, education and training requirements, and employment opportunities. Also contains career planning information and job search tips.

★5994★ "Physical Therapists and Assistants" in *Jobs! What They Are— Where They Are—What They Pay* (p. 174)
Simon & Schuster, Inc.
Simon & Schuster Bldg.
1230 Avenue of the Americas
New York, NY 10020
Ph: (212)698-7000   Fr: 800-223-2348
Robert O. Snelling and Anne M. Snelling. 3rd edition, 1992. Describes duties and responsibilities, earnings, employment opportunities, training, and qualifications.

★5995★ "Physical Therapists" in *Best Jobs for the 1990s and Into the 21st Century*
Impact Publications
9104-N Manassas Dr.
Manassas Park, VA 22111
Ph: (703)361-7300   Fax: (703)335-9486
Ronald L. Krannich and Caryl Rae Krannich. 1993.

★5996★ "Physical Therapists" in *Desk Guide to Training and Work Advertisement* (p. 49)
Charles C. Thomas, Publisher
2600 S. 1st St.
Springfield, IL 62794-9265
Ph: (217)789-8980   Fax: (217)789-9130
Fr: 800-258-8980
Gail Baugher Kuenstler. 1988. Describes alternative methods of gaining entry into an occupation through different types of educational programs, internships, and apprenticeships.

★5997★ "Physical Therapists" in *Encyclopedia of Careers and Vocational Guidance* (Vol.4, pp. 86-88)
J.G. Ferguson Publishing Co.
200 W. Madison St., Ste. 300
Chicago, IL 60606
Ph: (312)580-5480   Fax: (312)580-4948
William E. Hopke, editor-in-chief. Ninth edition, 1993. Four-volume set that profiles 900 occupations and describes job trends in 74 industries. Includes career description, educational requirements, history of the job, methods of entry, advancement, employment outlook, earnings, conditions of work, social and psychological factors, and sources of further information.

★5998★ "Physical Therapists" in *Health Care Job Explosion!* (pp. 178-186)
D-Amp Publications
401 Amherst Ave.
Coraopolis, PA 15108
Ph: (412)262-5578
Dennis V. Damp. 1993. Provides information on the nature of work for the major health care occupational groups. Descriptions include working conditions, training, job outlook, qualifications, and related occupations.

★5999★ "Physical Therapists" in *Occupational Outlook Handbook*
U.S. Government Printing Office
Superintendent of Documents
Washington, DC 20402
Ph: (202)512-1800   Fax: (202)512-2250
Biennial; latest edition, 1994-95. Encyclopedia of careers describing about 225 occupations and comprising about 85 percent of all jobs in the economy. Occupations that require lengthy education or training are given the most attention. Each occupation's profile describes what the worker does on the job, working conditions, education and training requirements, advancement possibilities, job outlook, earnings, and sources of additional information.

PROFESSIONAL ASSOCIATIONS

★6000★ American Physical Therapy Association (APTA)
1111 N. Fairfax St.
Alexandria, VA 22314
Ph: (703)684-2782
Members: Professional organization of physical therapists and physical therapist assistants and students. **Purpose:** Fosters the development and improvement of physical therapy service, education, and research; evaluates the organization and administration of curricula; directs the maintenance of standards and promotes scientific research. Acts as an accrediting body for educational programs in physical therapy and is responsible for establishing standards. Offers advisory and consultation services to schools of physical therapy and facilities offering physical therapy services; provides placement services at conference. **Publications:** *Physical Therapy*, monthly. • *PT Bulletin*, weekly. • *PT Magazine*, monthly.

★6001★ Private Practice Section/ American Physical Therapy Association (PPS)
1101 17th St. NW, Ste. 1000
Washington, DC 20036
Ph: (202)457-1115   Fax: (202)457-9191
Members: Physical therapists who are members of the American Physical Therapy Association and who are in private practice. **Purpose:** Purposes are: to provide physical therapists with information on establishing and managing a private practice; to promote high standards of private practice physical therapy; to represent private practitioners before governmental and professional agencies; to disseminate information relating to private practice. Monitors federal and state legislation. Holds forums and seminars. Bestows Robert G. Dicus Award to recognize individuals for achievement in and commitment to the private practice of physical therapy. **Publications:** *An Employers Guide to Obtaining Physical Therapy Services.* • *An Employers Guide to Obtaining PT Services.* • *How to Start a PT Private Practice.* • *Physical Therapy Today*, quarterly. • *Private Practice Section Membership Directory*, annual. • *Private Practice Valuation Primer - How to Value a Practice for Sale or Purchase.* • *Twenty Questions About Private Practice.*

★6002★ U.S. Physical Therapy Association (USPTA)
1803 Avon Ln.
Arlington Heights, IL 60004
Members: Professional physical therapists and assistants. **Purpose:** Maintains U.S. Physical Therapy Academy which: conducts continuing education programs for members; sponsors workshops to acquaint personnel from other medical fields with physical therapy; accredits hospital and nursing home physical therapy departments, universities, and colleges of physical therapy; certifies physical therapists through board examinations. Promotes ethical standards; maintains placement service and charitable program; compiles statistics; conducts children's services.

STANDARDS/CERTIFICATION AGENCIES

★6003★ American Physical Therapy Association (APTA)
1111 N. Fairfax St.
Alexandria, VA 22314
Ph: (703)684-2782
Fosters the development and improvement of physical therapy service, education, and research; directs the maintenance of standards and promotes scientific research. Acts as an accrediting body for educational programs in physical therapy and is responsible for establishing standards. Offers advisory and consultation services to schools of physical therapy and facilities offering physical therapy services; provides placement services at conference.

TEST GUIDES

★6004★ Career Examination Series: Chief Physical Therapist
National Learning Corp.
212 Michael Dr.
Syosset, NY 11791
Ph: (516)921-8888   Fax: (516)921-8743
Fr: 800-645-6337

Jack Rudman. A study guide for professionals and trainees in the field of physical therapy. Includes a multiple-choice examination section; provides answers.

★6005★ Career Examination Series: Physical Therapist
National Learning Corp.
212 Michael Dr.
Syosset, NY 11791
Ph: (516)921-8888   Fax: (516)921-8743
Fr: 800-645-6337

Jack Rudman. A study guide for professionals and trainees in the field of physical therapy. Includes a multiple-choice examination section; provides answers.

★6006★ Career Examination Series: Senior Physical Therapist
National Learning Corp.
212 Michael Dr.
Syosset, NY 11791
Ph: (516)921-8888   Fax: (516)921-8743
Fr: 800-645-6337

Jack Rudman. A study guide for professionals and trainees in the field of physical therapy. Includes a multiple-choice examination section; provides answers.

★6007★ Career Examination Series: Supervising Physical Therapist
National Learning Corp.
212 Michael Dr.
Syosset, NY 11791
Ph: (516)921-8888   Fax: (516)921-8743
Fr: 800-645-6337

Jack Rudman. A study guide for professionals and trainees in the field of physical therapy. Includes a multiple-choice examination section; provides answers.

★6008★ Career Examination Series: Supervising Therapist
National Learning Corp.
212 Michael Dr.
Syosset, NY 11791
Ph: (516)921-8888   Fax: (516)921-8743
Fr: 800-645-6337

Jack Rudman. 1993. Test guide including questions and answers for students or professionals in the field who seek advancement through examination.

EDUCATIONAL DIRECTORIES AND PROGRAMS

★6009★ Encyclopedia of Medical Organizations and Agencies
Gale Research Inc.
835 Penobscot Bldg.
Detroit, MI 48226-4094
Ph: (313)961-2242   Fax: (313)961-6741
Fr: 800-877-GALE
Karen Boyden, Contact

Biennial, November of odd years. Covers over 13,400 state, national, and international medical associations, foundations, research institutes, federal and state agencies, and medical and allied health schools. Entries include: Organization name, address, phone; many listings include names and titles of key personnel, descriptive annotations. Arrangement: Classified by subject, then by type of organization.

★6010★ Health & Medical Industry Directory
American Business Directories, Inc.
5711 S. 86th Circle
Omaha, NE 68127
Ph: (402)593-4600   Fax: (402)331-1505
Released 1993. Lists over 1.1 million physicians and surgeons, dentists, clinics, health clubs, and other health-related businesses in the U.S. and Canada. Entries include: Name, address, phone.

★6011★ Medical and Health Information Directory
Gale Research Inc.
835 Penobscot Bldg.
Detroit, MI 48226-4094
Ph: (313)961-2242   Fax: (313)961-6741
Fr: 800-877-GALE
Karen Boyden, Contact

Approximately biennial; latest edition 1994. Covers in Volume 1, almost 18,600 medical and health oriented associations, organizations, institutions, and government agencies, including health maintenance organizations (HMOs), preferred provider organizations (PPOs), insurance companies, pharmaceutical companies, research centers, and medical and allied health schools. In Volume 2, nearly 11,800 medical book publishers; medical periodicals, directories, audiovisual producers and services, medical libraries and information centers, and electronic resources. In Volume 3, nearly 26,000 clinics, treatment centers, care programs, and counseling/diagnostic services for 30 subject areas. Entries include: Institution, service, or firm name, address, phone; many include names of key personnel Arrangement: Classified by organization activity, service, etc..

★6012★ Therapists and Allied Health Professionals Career Directory
Gale Research Inc.
835 Penobscot Bldg.
Detroit, MI 48226-4094
Ph: (313)961-2242   Fax: (313)961-6083
Fr: 800-877-GALE
Bradley J. Morgan and Joseph M. Palmisano. 1993. A directory in the Career Advisor Series that provides essays written by industry professionals; job search information on resume and cover letter preparation, networking, and the interviewing process; approximately 300 companies and organizations offering job opportunities and internships, and additional job-hunting resources.

AWARDS, SCHOLARSHIPS, GRANTS, AND FELLOWSHIPS

★6013★ Bernard M. Baruch Essay Award
American Congress of Rehabilitation Medicine
5700 Old Orchard Rd., 1st Fl.
Skokie, IL 60077
Ph: (708)966-0095   Fax: (708)966-9418

For recognition of an outstanding essay by a medical student pertaining to the field of physical medicine and rehabilitation. Topics must reflect the interdisciplinary character of rehabilitation. Essays may not exceed 3,000 words. The deadline for submissions is March 1. The following prizes are awarded: first prize - $200 and the Baruch Medal; second prize - $100; and third prize - $50. Awarded annually.

★6014★ Dorothy Briggs Memorial Scientific Inquiry Award
American Physical Therapy Association
APTA Awards Program
1111 N. Fairfax St.
Alexandria, VA 22314
Ph: (703)684-2782   Fax: (703)684-7343

To recognize a physical therapist member of the Association who as a student developed an experimental investigation that subsequently was published in *Physical Therapy*. One award may be granted for a study undertaken at each of three academic levels: (1) doctoral degree programs; (2) master's degree programs beyond entry level; (3) certificate, baccalaureate, and entry level master's degree programs. Established in 1969 in honor of Dorothy I. Briggs, Ph.D., former Chairman of the editorial board of *Physical Therapy*.

★6015★ Chattanooga Research Award
American Physical Therapy Association
APTA Awards Program
1111 N. Fairfax St.
Alexandria, VA 22314
Ph: (703)684-2782   Fax: (703)684-7343

To encourage the publication of outstanding physical therapy clinical research reports and for recognition of the best article on clinical research in *Physical Therapy* during the preceding year. Members are eligible. A monetary prize of $1,000 is awarded annually. Established in 1980. Sponsored by the Chattanooga Corporation.

★6016★ Milton Cohen Distinguished Career Award
American Rehabilitation Association
1910 Association Dr.
Reston, VA 22091
Ph: (703)648-9300   Fax: (703)648-0346
To recognize an individual with at least ten years of service to the rehabilitation field who has demonstrated a commitment to rehabilitation, and has accomplished a major project(s) that significantly advanced the status and lives of people with disabilities. A crystal carved egg is awarded annually. For further information, contact Chris Mason at (703)716-4020.

★6017★ Department of Veterans Affairs Health Professional Scholarship Award
Department of Veterans Affairs
810 Vermont Ave, NW
Washington, DC 20420
Qualifications: Applicants must be accepted for enrollment as full-time students in an education program that is nationally accredited by either the National League for Nursing, American Physical Therapy Association, American Occupational Therapy Association, or the American Association of Nurse Anesthetists. Applicants must be citizens of the United States. Associate degree nursing students in their last year of study, and third-and-fourth year nursing students in baccalaureate degree nursing, physical therapym, and occupational therapy may apply. Students in masters degree programs in physical therapy, nurse anasthesia, and certain speciallty areas for nursing, physical therapy, and occupational therapy may also apply. Registered nurses may apply if they enrolled full-time or accepted for enrollment in an accredited baccalaureate nursing program or specialized masters program. These specialty programs vary, and a list of the programs can be obtained from the Department of Veterans Affairs (VA) at the above address. Selection criteria: Selections are based on academic performance; recommendation from the applicant's college/university Dean or Program Director of nursing, physical therapy, or occupational therapy; career goals; and work and/or volunteer recommendation and experiences. Funds available: The award provides direct payment for up to two years for tuition and fees to the participant's college/university, and provides an annual payment for books and other costs, and a tax-free stipend of $621 per month to the participant for the length of the award. The award is repaid through service obligation, where the participant works full-time as a registered nurse, nurse anesthetist, physical therapist, or occupational therapist at one of the VA medical centers in the United States. Service will not be in any branch of the armed forces or any other Federal agency. The minimum obligated service is two years upon completion of degree requirements and attainment of licensure or certification. Application details: Applicants can obtain application materials and application Information Bulletins by sending their name, address, and identifying the award for which they wish information, to Health Professional Scholarship Program (143 B) at the above address. Applications are available each

March. Deadline: Applications must be postmarked no later than the last Tuesday in May.

★6018★ Department of Veterans Affairs Reserve Member Stipend Program Award
Department of Veterans Affairs
810 Vermont Ave., NW
Washington, DC 20420
Qualifications: Applicants must be accepted for enrollment as full-time students in an education program that is nationally accredited by either the National League for Nursing, American Physical Therapy Association, American Occupational Therapy Association, or the American Association of Nurse Anesthetists. Applicants must be citizens of the United States. Associate degree nursing students in their last year of study, and third-and-fourth year nursing students in baccalaureate degree nursing may apply. Entry-level masters students in nursing, physical therapy, and occupational therapy may also apply. Also eligible are reservists who are members of the Selected Ready Reserves, eligible for the Reserve GI Bill, and have a score above the 50th percentile on the Armed Forces Qualification Test. Rregistered nurses may apply if enrolled full-time or accepted for enrollment in an accredited nursing program. Selection criteria: Selections are based on academic performance; recommendation from the applicant's college/university Dean or Program Director of nursing, physical therapy, or occupational therapy; career goals; work and/or volunteer recommendation and experiences; and commander's recommendation. Funds available: Awards have a maximum length of 24 months of funding support and pay $400 per month while the reservist is enrolled in full-time course work. Reservists may also receive the Reserve GI Bill. The award is repaid through service obligation, where the participant works full-time as a registered nurse, nurse anesthetist, physical therapist, or occupational therapist at one of the VA medical centers in the United States. Service will not be in any branch of the armed forces or any other Federal agency. The minimum obligated service is two years upon completion of degree requirements and attainment of licensure or certification. Application details: Applicants can obtain application materials and Application Information Bulletins by sending their name, address, and identifying the award for which they wish information, to Health Professional Scholarship Program (143 B) at the above address. Applications are available each March. Deadline: Applications must be submitted and postmarked no later than the last Tuesday in May.

★6019★ Robert G. Dicus Award
American Physical Therapy Association
Private Practice Sector
1101 17th St. NW, Ste. 1000
Washington, DC 20036
Ph: (202)457-1115   Fax: (202)457-9191
To recognize significant and persistent achievement in the private practice of physical therapy in the following areas: clinical practice; education; delivery of new services; participation in the American Physical Therapy Association and the Private Practice Section; and commitment to private practice, public relations and community service. Members of the Association and the Section

may be nominated. A plaque is awarded annually. Established in 1981 to honor Robert G. Dicus.

★6020★ W. F. Faulkes Award
National Rehabilitation Association
633 S. Washington St.
Alexandria, VA 22314
Ph: (703)715-9090
To recognize technical and/or professional achievement in the field of rehabilitation. Individuals or organizations that have in the preceding years made major contributions of national importance to the increase of knowledge in the field of rehabilitation or to the development of techniques or methods in the application of such knowledge or to the prevention of disability are eligible. Eligibility for this award would be: (1) the author of a notable technical treatise on rehabilitation; (2) a physician or medical school that has discovered a new technique useful in rehabilitating certain groups of persons with disabilities; (3) a research scientist or laboratory whose work has led to the discovery of a preventive or cure for a handicapping condition; and (4) a rehabilitation worker who has put into practice a new rehabilitation technique or method which has had, nationally, an important effect on rehabilitation practice. The deadline for nominations is August 1. Established in 1954 to honor W.F. Faulkes, the Association's founder and first president.

★6021★ Gold Key Award
American Congress of Rehabilitation Medicine
5700 Old Orchard Rd., 1st Fl.
Skokie, IL 60077
Ph: (708)966-0095   Fax: (708)966-9418
To recognize and honor those members of the medical and allied professions who have rendered extraordinary service to the cause of rehabilitation medicine. Nominations must be postmarked by February 1. An inscribed gold medal with the seal of the Congress is awarded annually. Established in 1932.

★6022★ Honorary Member
American Physical Therapy Association
APTA Awards Program
1111 N. Fairfax St.
Alexandria, VA 22314
Ph: (703)684-2782   Fax: (703)684-7343
For recognition of individuals who have made contributions which are: (1) significant to the field of physical therapy; (2) national in recognition and scope; (3) beyond the scope of work done as part of paid employment; and (4) of a unique quality. The deadline for chapters to submit recommendations is December 1. At an appropriate occasion, chapter officers make the presentation to the recipient. Established in 1936.

★6023★ Henry O. Kendall and Florence P. Kendall Award for Outstanding Achievement in Clinical Practice
American Physical Therapy Association
APTA Awards Program
1111 N. Fairfax St.
Alexandria, VA 22314
Ph: (703)684-2782   Fax: (703)684-7343
To give public recognition to members of the Association who are outstanding clinicians as demonstrated by their dedication to their patients, their profession, and by their sharing of

knowledge with others. Members may be nominated by individual members, chapters, districts, or sections of the APTA by December 1. A plaque and a monetary donation made to the charity of the honoree's choice are awarded. Presented annually in honor of Henry O. Kendall (deceased 1978) and Florence P. Kendall, who have been outstanding physical therapist clinicians in Maryland for over 50 years.

★6024★ Mary McMillan Lecture Award
American Physical Therapy Association
APTA Awards Program
1111 N. Fairfax St.
Alexandria, VA 22314
Ph: (703)684-2782   Fax: (703)684-7343
For recognition of distinguished contribution to the profession of physical therapy in one or more of the following categories: administration; education; patient care; or research. The deadline for nominations is December 1. The honoree presents a lecture and receives an honorarium of $250, a plaque and a medallion. Awarded as merited. Established in 1963 in honor of Mary McMillan, a pioneer in physical therapy and founding President of the Association.

★6025★ Mary McMillan Scholarship
American Physical Therapy Association
APTA Awards Program
1111 N. Fairfax St.
Alexandria, VA 22314
Ph: (703)684-2782   Fax: (703)684-7343
To honor outstanding physical therapy students and to contribute to the growth of physical therapy as a profession by recognizing individuals with superior capabilities. Awards are made on a competitive basis. Recipients are selected on the basis of the following criteria: (1) Superior scholastic performance; (2) Evidence of potential contribution to physical therapy; and (3) Past productivity. Students who are members of the Association may be nominated in the following four levels of physical therapy education programs: (1) Entry level physical therapist educational programs accredited by the APTA; (2) Entry level physical therapist assistant educational programs accredited by APTA; (3) Educational programs that provide advanced educational opportunities for physical therapists leading to postgraduate master's degrees; and (4) Educational programs that provide advanced educational opportunities for physical therapists leading to postgraduate doctoral degrees. An award of $1,000 is granted to each physical therapist, entry-level physical therapist, and post-professional master's degree student recipient selected. An award of $5,000 is granted to each physical therapist in doctoral-level education programs. Established in 1963.

★6026★ Eugene Michels New Investigator Award
American Physical Therapy Association
APTA Awards Program
1111 N. Fairfax St.
Alexandria, VA 22314
Ph: (703)684-2782   Fax: (703)684-7343
To recognize an outstanding new investigator who has demonstrated a commitment to a defined, research theme. The nominee must be a physical therapist who is a member of the APTA and has been engaged in independent research activities for not more than five years after completion of formal education. There must be a demonstrated relationship between the research theme and the field of physical therapy. Any member of the Association may nominate candidates for this award by December 1. A monetary prize of $1,000 is awarded when merited. Established in 1989 in honor of Eugene Michels who has been instrumental in developing a plan to foster research among physical therapists.

★6027★ Veterans Affairs Health Professional Scholarship Awards
U.S. Department of Veterans Affairs
Central Office
810 Vermont Ave., NW
Washington, DC 20420
Ph: (202)535-7527

Purpose: To provide an adequate supply of nurses, occupational therapists, and physical therapists for the Department of Veterans Affairs and the nation. Qualifications: Applicants must be U.S. citizens, and accepted for enrollment or enrolled full-time in a nursing program accredited by the National League of Nursing, an occupational therapy program accredited by the American Occupational Therapy Association, or a physical therapy program accredited by the American Physical Therapy Association. Applicants may not be obligated for service under any other scholarship program. VA employees who meet eligibility may apply. Selection criteria: Selection is based upon academic performance, career goals, recommendations, and work/volunteer experience. Funds available: Tuition/fees, reasonable educational expenses, and a monthly stipend of $621, all exempt from Federal taxation. Application details: Applications are available from college/university financial aid offices, deans of Nursing, program directors of Occupational Therapy or Physical Therapy, all VA medical centers, and the VA Central Office. Deadline: May.

★6028★ Marian Williams Award for Research in Physical Therapy
American Physical Therapy Association
APTA Awards Program
1111 N. Fairfax St.
Alexandria, VA 22314
Ph: (703)684-2782   Fax: (703)684-7343
For recognition of research which has been conducted by a physical therapist in basic or clinical science or education. Criteria for nomination include evidence that research has been sustained and outstanding, that research results have been disseminated widely, and that the nominee has shown continuity of commitment to the profession. The Committee on Research recommends candidates by December 1. Established in 1963 to commemorate Marian Williams, Ph.D., whose professional life was dedicated to the promotion of physical therapy through teaching, writing, and research. A bronze medal is awarded as merited. Established in 1963.

★6029★ Catherine Worthingham Fellows of APTA
American Physical Therapy Association
APTA Awards Program
1111 N. Fairfax St.
Alexandria, VA 22314
Ph: (703)684-2782   Fax: (703)684-7343
To recognize those persons whose work has resulted in lasting and significant advances in the science, education, and practice of physical therapy. Criteria for nomination are that the individual should be an active member who has held active membership status for a minimum of 15 years; has demonstrated nationally prominent leadership in advancing at least one of the three areas of the science, education, or practice of physical therapy; has documented achievements in at least two of the three areas of the profession, or is known nationwide. The deadline for nominations is December 1. A pin and recognition as a fellow are awarded as merited. Established in 1980 in honor of Catherine Worthingham, a leader in physical therapy education, science, and practice for more than fifty years.

BASIC REFERENCE GUIDES AND HANDBOOKS

★6030★ Clinical Kinesiology for Physical Therapist Assistants
F.A. Davis Co.
1915 Arch St.
Philadelphia, PA 19103
Ph: (215)568-5065   Fax: (215)568-5065
Lynn Lippert, editor. 1993.

★6031★ Clinical Medicine for Physical Therapists
Mosby-Year Book, Inc.
11830 Westline Industrial Dr.
St. Louis, MO 63146
Ph: (314)872-8370   Fax: (314)432-1380
Fr: 800-325-4177
Catherine Certo. 1995.

★6032★ Fundamentals of Private Practice in Physical Therapy
Charles C Thomas, Publisher
2600 S. 1st St.
Springfield, IL 62794-9265
Ph: (217)789-8980
Mark A. Brimer. 1988. Covers starting a private practice, insurance, hiring personnel, managing the office, and marketing.

★6033★ Job's Body: A Handbook for Bodywork
Station Hill Press
Station Hill Rd.
Barrytown, NY 12507
Ph: (914)758-5840
Dean Jahan. 1991.

★6034★ Manual of Physical Therapy
Churchill Livingstone, Inc.
650 Avenue of the Americas
New York, NY 10011
Ph: (212)206-5000
Otto D. Payton, et al., editors. 1989. Includes bibliographies and an index. Illustrated.

★6035★ *Physical Therapy Procedures: Selected Techniques*
Charles C Thomas, Publisher
2600 S. 1st St.
Springfield, IL 62794-9265
Ph: (217)789-8980

Ann H. Downer. Fourth edition, 1988.

PROFESSIONAL AND TRADE PERIODICALS

★6036★ *AAPSM Newsletter*
American Academy of Podiatric Sports Medicine (AAPSM)
1729 Glastonberry Rd.
Potomac, MD 20854
Ph: (301)424-7440
Larry I. Shane

Quarterly. Features articles discussing injuries and treatments in the field of podiatry. Reports on Academy activities and meetings. Recurring features include news of research, editorials, and a calendar of events.

★6037★ *American Society of Hand Therapists—Newsletter*
American Society of Hand Therapists
401 N. Michigan Ave.
Chicago, IL 60611
Ph: (312)321-6866   Fax: (312)527-6636
Jennifer Bullock

Bimonthly. Promotes understanding of and builds membership/professional support for hand therapy. Provides information about improving health care to consumers, raising standards of practice in hand therapy, and encourages ongoing research. Recurring features include news of research and news of members.

★6038★ *National Rehabilitation Information Center—Quarterly*
National Rehabilitation Information Center
Catholic University of America
8455 Colesville Rd., Ste. 935
Silver Spring, MD 20910
Fr: 800-346-2742
Adele Kirk

Quarterly. Carries information for those involved in all aspects of rehabilitation and disability. Recurring features include a calendar of events.

★6039★ *Pacific Basin Rehabilitation Research & Training Center—Newsletter*
Pacific Basin Rehabilitation Research & Training Center
226 N. Kuakini St., Rm. 233
Honolulu, HI 96817
Ph: (808)537-5986   Fax: (808)531-8691
Joanne Y. Yamada

Semiannual. Focuses on the Center's research, training activities, and rehabilitation services. Recurring features include news of research, a calendar of events, and reports of meetings.

★6040★ *Physical Therapy*
American Physical Therapy Assn.
1111 N. Fairfax St.
Alexandria, VA 22314
Ph: (703)684-2782   Fax: (703)684-7343
Fr: 800-999-2782
Jules M. Rothstein

Monthly. Journal of the American Physical Therapy Association.

PROFESSIONAL MEETINGS AND CONVENTIONS

★6041★ **American Association for Respiratory Care Annual Meeting and Exhibition**
American Association for Respiratory Care
11030 Ables Ln.
Dallas, TX 75229
Ph: (214)243-2272   Fax: (214)484-2720

Annual. Usually held during December. **Dates and Locations:** 1995 Dec 02-05; Orlando, FL. • 1996 Nov 03-06; San Diego, CA. • 1997 Dec 06-09; New Orleans, LA. • 1998 Nov 07-10; Atlanta, GA.

★6042★ **American Physical Therapy Association Annual Conference**
American Physical Therapy Association
1111 N. Fairfax St.
Alexandria, VA 22314
Ph: (703)684-2782   Fax: (703)684-7343

Annual. Always held during June. **Dates and Locations:** 1996 Jun 15-18; Minneapolis, MN. • 1997 May 31-03; San Diego, CA.

★6043★ **American Physical Therapy Association Private Practice Section Convention**
American Physical Therapy Association, Private Practice Section
1101 17th St., NW, Ste. 1000
Washington, DC 20036
Ph: (202)457-1115   Fax: (202)457-9191

Annual. Always held during the second week of November.

★6044★ **American Society of Hand Therapists Convention**
American Society of Hand Therapists
401 N. Michigan Ave.
Chicago, IL 60611-4212
Ph: (919)779-2748   Fax: (919)779-5642

Annual. **Dates and Locations:** 1996 Oct 09-13; Nashville, TN.

OTHER SOURCES OF INFORMATION

★6045★ **"Physical Therapist" in** *100 Best Jobs for the 1990s & Beyond*
Dearborn Financial Publishing, Inc.
520 N. Dearborn St.
Chicago, IL 60610-4354
Ph: (312)836-4400   Fax: (312)836-1021
Fr: 800-621-9621

Carol Kleiman. 1992. Describes 100 jobs ranging from accountants to veterinarians. Each job profile includes such information as education, experience, and certification needed, salaries, and job search suggestions.

★6046★ **"Physical Therapist" in** *Career Selector 2001*
Barron's Educational Series, Inc.
250 Wireless Blvd.
Hauppauge, NY 11788
Ph: (516)434-3311   Fax: (516)434-3723
Fr: 800-645-3476

James C. Gonyea. 1993.

★6047★ **"Physical Therapy" in** *Accounting to Zoology: Graduate Fields Defined* (pp. 249-250)
Petersons Guides, Inc.
PO Box 2123
Princeton, NJ 08543-2123
Ph: (609)243-9111   Fax: (609)243-9150
Fr: 800-338-3282

Amy J. Goldstein, editor. Revised and updated, 1987. Discusses types of graduate programs and degrees, graduate research, applied work, employment prospects and trends.

Physician Assistants

Physician assistants are formally trained to perform many of the essential but time-consuming tasks involved in patient care. They take medical histories, perform physical examinations, order and interpret laboratory tests and X-rays, make preliminary diagnoses, prescribe appropriate treatments, and recommend medications and drug therapies. In a growing number of States, physician assistants may prescribe medication. They also treat minor problems such as lacerations, abrasions, and burns. Some physician assistants specializing in surgery, provide pre- and post-operative care and work as first or second assistants during major surgery. Physician assistants always work under the supervision of a licensed physician.

Salaries

Average earnings of physician assistants are as follows:

Physician assistant, median salary	$41,038/year
Average for all physician assistants	$32,466-$49,782/year

Employment Outlook

Growth rate until the year 2005: Faster than the average.

Physician Assistants

CAREER GUIDES

★6048★ Allied Health Professions
Simon & Schuster, Inc.
200 Old Tappan Rd.
Old Tappan, NJ 07675
1993. Includes information on available jobs, required training, a directory of training programs, and a full-sample Allied Health Professions Admission Test (AHPAT).

★6049★ Careers in Medicine: Traditional and Alternative Opportunities
Garrett Park Press
PO Box 1907
Garrett Park, MD 20896-0190
Ph: (301)946-2553
T. Donald Rucker and Martin D. Keller. Revised edition, 1990. Written for college students who are considering applying to medical school, medical students attempting to select a specialty, and physicians who want to explore nonclinical work. Provides descriptions and employment outlook for 900 medical-oriented occupations.

★6050★ "Health Care" in Where the Jobs Are: The Hottest Careers for the 90s (pp. 143-166)
Career Press
180 5th Ave.
Hawthorne, NJ 07507
Ph: (201)427-0229   Fax: (201)427-2037
Fr: 800-CAREER-1
Joyce Hadley. 1995. Offers a job-hunting strategy for the 1990s as well as descriptions of growing careers of the decade. Each profile includes general information, forecasts, growth, education and training, licensing requirements, and salary information.

★6051★ The Health Care Worker: An Introduction to Health Occupations
Prentice-Hall, Inc.
200 Old Tappan Rd.
Old Tappan, NJ 07675
Ph: (201)767-5000
Shirley A. Badasch, and Doreen S. Chesebro. Second edition, 1988. Includes a bibliography and an index.

★6052★ Health Careers
Careers, Inc.
PO Box 135
Largo, FL 34649-0135
Ph: (813)584-7333
1994. Four-page brief describing duties, working conditions, personal qualifications, training, earnings and hours, employment outlook, places of employment, related careers, and where to write for more information.

★6053★ Opportunities in Health and Medical Careers
National Textbook Co. (NTC)
VGM Career Books
4255 W. Touhy Ave.
Lincolnwood, IL 60646-1975
Ph: (708)679-5500   Fax: (708)679-2494
Fr: 800-323-4900
I. Donald Snook Jr., Leo D'Orazio. Describes the working conditions of physicians, physician assistants, therapists, nurses, technicians, administrators, and hospital staff. Also includes information on educational requirements and salaries.

★6054★ Opportunities in Physician Assistant Careers
National Textbook Co. (NTC)
VGM Career Books
4255 W. Toughy Ave.
Lincolnwood, IL 60646-1975
Ph: (708)679-5500   Fax: (708)679-2494
Fr: 800-323-4900
Terry Sacks. 1994.

★6055★ PA Fact Sheet
American Academy of Physician Assistants
950 N. Washington St.
Alexandria, VA 22314-1534
Ph: (703)836-2272   Fax: (703)684-1924
1991. This sheet describes what a physician assistant does, training and education required, prerequisites for entering a training program, certification, specialties, salaries, and the future of the profession.

★6056★ Physician Assistant
Careers, Inc.
PO Box 135
Largo, FL 34649-0135
Ph: (813)584-7333
1992. Two-page occupational summary card describing duties, working conditions, personal qualifications, training, earnings and hours, employment outlook, places of employment, related careers, and where to write for more information.

★6057★ "Physician Assistant" in 100 Best Careers for the Year 2000 (pp. 50-52)
Arco Pub.
201 W. 103rd St.
Indianapolis, IN 46290
Ph: 800-428-5331   Fax: 800-835-3202
Shelly Field. 1992. Describes 100 job opportunities expected to grow fast throughout the next decade. Provides information on job duties and responsibilities, training requirements, education, advancement opportunities, experience and qualifications, and typical salaries.

★6058★ "Physician Assistant" in 150 Careers in the Health Care Field
Reed Reference Publishing
121 Chanlon Rd.
PO Box 31
New Providence, NJ 07974
Fax: (908)665-6688   Fr: 800-521-8110
Stanley Alperin. Third edition, 1993. Profiles health care occupations requiring a bachelor's degree or less. Describes the nature of the work, educational preparation, licensing requirements, and salary. Lists accredited educational programs.

★6059★ "Physician Assistant" in Career Information Center (Vol.7)
Simon and Schuster
200 Old Tappan Rd.
Old Tappan, NJ 07675
Fax: 800-445-6991   Fr: 800-223-2348
Richard Lidz and Linda Perrin, editorial directors. Fifth edition, 1993. This 13-volume set profiles over 600 occupations. Each occupational profile describes job duties, entry-level requirements, educational requirements, advancement possibilities, employment outlook, working conditions, earnings and benefits, and where to write for more information.

★6060★ "Physician Assistant" in Careers in Health Care (pp. 224-232)
National Textbook Co. (NTC)
VGM Career Books
4255 W. Touhy Ave.
Lincolnwood, IL 60646-1975
Ph: (708)679-5500   Fax: (708)679-2494
Fr: 800-323-4900

Swanson, Barbara M. Third edition, 1995. Describes job duties, work settings, salaries, licensing and certification requirements, educational preparation, and future outlook.

★6061★ The Physician Assistant in a Changing Health Care Environment
Aspen Publishers, Inc.
1600 Research Blvd.
Rockville, MD 20850
Ph: (301)251-5554   Fr: 800-638-8437

Gretchen Engle Schafft, and James F. Cawley. 1987. Covers the development of the physician assistant profession and the profession's place in the current health care environment.

★6062★ "Physician Assistant" in Guide to Federal Jobs (p. 129)
Resource Directories
3361 Executive Pkwy., Ste. 302
Toledo, OH 43606
Ph: (419)536-5353   Fax: (419)536-7056
Fr: 800-274-8515

Rod W. Durgin, editor. Third edition, 1992. Contains information on finding and applying for federal jobs. Describes more than 200 professional and technical jobs for college graduates. Covers the nature of the work, salary, and geographic location. Lists college majors preferred for that occupation. Section one describes the function and work of government agencies that hire the most significant number of college graduates.

★6063★ "Physician Assistant" in Jobs Rated Almanac
World Almanac
1 International Blvd., Ste. 444
Mahwah, NJ 07495
Ph: (201)529-6900   Fax: (201)529-6901

Les Krantz. Second edition, 1992. Ranks 250 jobs by environment, salary, outlooks, physical demands, stress, security, travel opportunities, and extra perks. Includes jobs the editor feels are the most common, most interesting, and the most rapidly growing.

★6064★ "Physician Assistant" in Opportunities in Paramedical Careers (pp. 13-24)
National Textbook Co. (NTC)
VGM Career Books
4255 W. Touhy Ave.
Lincolnwood, IL 60646-1975
Ph: (708)679-5500   Fax: (708)679-2494
Fr: 800-323-4900

Alex Kacen. 1994. Describes paraprofessional careers in the health professions such as physician assistant, medical assistant, and emergency medical technician. Describes job duties, educational preparation, certification, earnings, and job outlook. Lists educational programs.

★6065★ "Physician Assistant" in Opportunities in Vocational and Technical Careers (p. 94)
National Textbook Co. (NTC)
VGM Career Books
4255 W. Touhy Ave.
Lincolnwood, IL 60646-1975
Ph: (708)679-5500   Fax: (708)679-2494
Fr: 800-323-4900

Adrian A. Paradis. 1992. This book describes careers which can be prepared for by attending vocational-technical schools. Gives the employment outlook and salary information.

★6066★ "Physician Assistant" in Profitable Careers in Non-Profit (pp. 93-95)
John Wiley and Sons, Inc.
605 3rd Ave.
New York, NY 10158-0012
Ph: (212)850-6000   Fax: (212)850-6088
Fr: 800-526-5368

William Lewis and Carol Milano. 1987. Examines nonprofit organizations and the career opportunities they offer. Offers tips on how to target and explore occupational opportunities in the nonprofit sector.

★6067★ Physician Assistant Programs Directory
American Academy of Physician Assistants
950 N. Washington St.
Alexandria, VA 22314-1552
Ph: (703)836-2272   Fr: (703)684-1924

1988. This information packet describes accreditation of physician assistant programs, curriculum, and degrees awarded to physician assistants.

★6068★ The Physician Assistant Up Close
Pennsylvania Society of Physician Assistants
PO Box 8988
Pittsburgh, PA 15221-8988
Ph: (412)836-6411

1989. Eight-panel brochure explaining education, credentials, and roles of physician assistants.

★6069★ "Physician Assistant" in VGM's Handbook of Health Care Careers
National Textbook Co.
4255 W. Touhy Ave.
Lincolnwood, IL 60646-1975
Ph: (708)679-5500   Fax: (708)679-2494
Fr: 800-323-4900

Annette Selden. 1993. Contains 42 two-page occupational profiles describing job duties, places of employment, working conditions, qualifications, education, employment outlook, and income.

★6070★ Physician Assistants
Chronicle Guidance Publications, Inc.
66 Aurora St.
PO Box 1190
Moravia, NY 13118-1190
Ph: (315)497-0330   Fax: (315)497-3359
Fr: 800-622-7284

Paul Downes, editor. 1993. Career brief describing the nature of the job, working conditions, hours and earnings, education and training, licensure, certification, unions, personal qualifications, social and psychological factors, location, employment outlook, entry

methods, advancement, and related occupations.

★6071★ "Physician Assistants" in American Almanac of Jobs and Salaries (p. 463)
Avon Books
1350 Avenue of the Americas
New York, NY 10019
Ph: (212)261-6800   Fr: 800-238-0658

John Wright, editor. Revised and updated, 1994-95. This is comprehensive guide to the wages of hundreds of occupations in a wide variety of industries and organizations.

★6072★ "Physician Assistants" in America's 50 Fastest Growing Jobs (pp. 53)
JIST Works, Inc.
720 N. Park Ave.
Indianapolis, IN 46202-3431
Ph: (317)264-3720   Fax: (317)264-3709
Fr: 800-648-5478

Michael J. Farr, compiler. 1994. Describes the 50 fastest growing jobs within major career clusters such as technicians, and marketing and sales. Each job profile explains the nature of the work, skills and abilities required, employment outlook, average earnings, related occupations, education and training requirements, and employment opportunities. Also contains career planning information and job search tips.

★6073★ "Physician Assistants" in Career Discovery Encyclopedia (Vol.5, pp. 40-41)
J.G. Ferguson Publishing Co.
200 W. Madison St., Ste. 300
Chicago, IL 60606
Ph: (312)580-5480   Fax: (312)580-4948

Russell E. Primm, editor-in chief. 1993. This six volume set contains two-page articles for 504 occupations. Each article describes job duties, earnings, and educational and training requirements. The whole set is arranged alphabetically by job title. Designed for junior high and older students.

★6074★ "Physician Assistants" in Career Paths in the Field of Aging: Professional Gerontology (p. 27)
Simon and Schuster
200 Old Tappan Rd.
Old Tappan, NJ 07675
Fax: 800-445-6991   Fr: 800-223-2348

David A. Peterson. 1987. Provides a history of the gerontology profession, and describes jobs, education and skills required, employment outlook and trends in the field.

★6075★ "Physician Assistants" in Encyclopedia of Careers and Vocational Guidance (Vol.4, pp. 89-91)
J.G. Ferguson Publishing Co.
200 W. Madison St., Ste. 300
Chicago, IL 60606
Ph: (312)580-5480   Fax: (312)580-4948

William E. Hopke, editor in chief. Ninth edition, 1993. Four-volume set that profiles 900 occupations and describes job trends in 74 industries. Includes a career description, educational requirements, history of the job, methods of entry, advancement, employment outlook, earnings, conditions of work, social and psychological factors, and sources of further information.

★6076★ "Physician Assistants" in
Health Care Job Explosion! **(pp. 317-323)**
D-Amp Publications
401 Amherst Ave.
Coraopolis, PA 15108
Ph: (412)262-5578
Dennis V. Damp. 1993. Provides information on the nature of work for the major health care occupational groups. Descriptions include working conditions, training, job outlook, qualifications, and related occupations.

★6077★ "Physician Assistants" in
Occupational Outlook Handbook
U.S. Government Printing Office
Superintendent of Documents
Washington, DC 20402
Ph: (202)512-1800   Fax: (202)512-2250
Biennial; latest edition, 1994-95. Encyclopedia of careers describing about 250 occupations and comprising about 85 percent of all jobs in the economy. Occupations that require lengthy education or training are given the most attention. Each occupation's profile describes what the worker does on the job, working conditions, education and training requirements, advancement possibilities, job outlook, earnings, and sources of additional information.

★6078★ *Physician Assistants: The Facts*
American Academy of Physician Assistants
950 N. Washington St.
Alexandria, VA 22314-1534
Ph: (703)836-2272   Fax: (703)684-1924
1993. Eighteen-page booklet describing roles, work settings, education, credentials, cost effectiveness, history, and organizations related to physician assistants.

★6079★ "Physician's Assistant" in
Allied Health Education Directory **(pp. 175-177)**
American Medical Association (AMA)
515 N. State St.
Chicago, IL 60610
Ph: (312)464-5000   Fr: 800-621-8335
William R. Burrow, editor. 1994. Describes allied health occupations and lists educational programs accredited by the Committee on Allied Health Education and Accreditation of the American Medical Association.

★6080★ "Physicians Assistants" in
Jobs! What They Are—Where They Are—What They Pay **(p. 91)**
Simon & Schuster, Inc.
Simon & Schuster Bldg.
1230 Avenue of the Americas
New York, NY 10020
Ph: (212)698-7000   Fr: 800-223-2348
Robert O. Snelling and Anne M. Snelling. 3rd edition, 1992. Describes duties and responsibilities, earnings, employment opportunities, training, and qualifications.

PROFESSIONAL ASSOCIATIONS

★6081★ Accreditation Review Committee on Education for Physician Assistants (ARC-PA)
1000 N. Oak Ave.
Marshfield, WI 54449-5788
Ph: (715)389-3785   Fax: (715)389-3131
Members: Serves as an accrediting review body for physician assistant education nationwide. **Purpose:** Makes recommendations to Commission on Accreditation of Allied Health Education Programs **

★6082★ American Academy of Physician Assistants (AAPA)
950 N. Washington St.
Alexandria, VA 22314
Ph: (703)836-2272   Fax: (703)684-1924
Members: Physician assistants who have graduated from an American Medical Association accredited program and/or are certified by the National Commission on Certification of Physician Assistants; individuals who are enrolled in an accredited PA educational program. **Purpose:** Purposes are to: educate the public about the physician assistant profession; represent physician assistants' interests before Congress, government agencies, and health-related organizations; assure the competence of physician assistants through development of educational curricula and accreditation programs; provide services for members. Organizes annual National PA Day. Develops research and education programs; compiles statistics. **Publications:** *AAPA Bulletin*, monthly. • *AAPA News*, monthly. • *Career Magazine*, monthly. • *Journal of the American Academy of Physician Assistants*, 11/year. • *Legislative Watch*, monthly.

★6083★ American Association of Managed Care Nurses (AAMCN)
PO Box 4975
Glen Allen, VA 23058-4975
Ph: (804)747-9698   Fax: (804)747-5316

★6084★ Association of Physician Assistant Programs (APAP)
950 N. Washington St.
Alexandria, VA 22314
Ph: (703)548-5538
Members: Educational institutions with training programs for assistants to primary care and surgical physicians. **Purpose:** Assists in the development and organization of educational curricula for physician assistant (PA) programs to assure the public of competent PAs; contributes to defining the roles of PAs in the field of medicine to maximize their benefit to the public; serves as a public information center on the profession; coordinates program logistics such as admissions and career placements. Sponsors Annual Survey of Physician Assistant Educational Programs in the United States. Conducts research projects; compiles statistics. **Publications:** *Annual Report on Physician Assistant Education in the U.S.*, annual. • *APAP Update*, monthly. • *National Directory of Physician Assistant Programs*, annual.

★6085★ Commission on Accreditation of Allied Health Education Programs (CAAHEP)
515 N. State St., Ste. 7530
Chicago, IL 60610
Ph: (312)464-4636   Fax: (312)464-5830
Members: Serves as an accrediting agency for allied health programs in 19 occupational areas.

★6086★ Council on Medical Education - of the American Medical Association (CME-AMA)
515 N. State St.
Chicago, IL 60610
Ph: (312)464-4804   Fax: (312)464-5830
Members: A council of the American Medical Association. **Purpose:** Participates in the accreditation of and provides consultation to medical school programs, graduate medical educational programs, and educational programs for several allied health occupations. Provides information on medical and allied health education at all levels. **Publications:** *Allied Health Education Directory*, annual. • *Annual Report of Medical Education in the Journal of the AMA*. • *Continuing Education Courses for Physicians Supplement to the Journal of the AMA*, semiannual. • *Directory of Graduate Medical Education Programs*, annual.

★6087★ National Commission on Certification of Physician Assistants (NCCPA)
2845 Henderson Mill Rd. NE
Atlanta, GA 30341
Ph: (404)493-9100   Fax: (404)493-7316
Members: Certifies physician assistants at the entry level and for continued competence. Has certified 22,750 physician assistants. **Publications:** *Directory of Physician Assistants - Certified*, annual.

STANDARDS/CERTIFICATION AGENCIES

★6088★ American Academy of Physician Assistants (AAPA)
950 N. Washington St.
Alexandria, VA 22314
Ph: (703)836-2272   Fax: (703)684-1924
Physician assistants who have graduated from an American Medical Association credited program and/or are certified by the National Commission on Certification of Physician Assistants; individuals who are enrolled in an accredited PA educational program.

★6089★ Commission on Accreditation of Allied Health Education Programs (CAAHEP)
515 N. State St., Ste. 7530
Chicago, IL 60610
Ph: (312)464-4636   Fax: (312)464-5830
Serves as an accrediting agency for allied health programs in 18 occupational areas.

★6090★ National Commission on Certification of Physician Assistants (NCCPA)
2845 Henderson Mill Rd. NE
Atlanta, GA 30341
Ph: (404)493-9100   Fax: (404)493-7316
Certifies physician assistants at the entry level and for continued competence. Has certified 22,750 physician assistants.

TEST GUIDES

★6091★ Career Examination Series: Physician's Assistant
National Learning Corp.
212 Michael Dr.
Syosset, NY 11791
Ph: (516)921-8888   Fax: (516)921-8743
Fr: 800-645-6337
Jack Rudman. A study guide for professional and trainee physician assistants. Includes a multiple-choice examination section; provides answers.

★6092★ National Certifying Examination for Physician's Assistants
National Learning Corp.
212 Michael Dr.
Syosset, NY 11791
Ph: (516)921-8888   Fax: (516)921-8743
Fr: 800-645-6337
Jack Rudman. Part of the Admission Test series. A sample test for prospective physician assistants who are seeking admission to graduate and professional schools or seeking entrance or advancement in institutional and public career service.

★6093★ Physician's Assistant Examination Review: 850 Multiple-Choice Questions With Explanatory Answers
Appleton & Lange
25 Van Zant St.
Norwalk, CT 06855
Ph: (203)838-4400
Richard R. Rahl and Bruce R. Niebuhr. Second edition, 1991. Revised edition of Physician's Assistant Examination Review and Patient Management Problems.

EDUCATIONAL DIRECTORIES AND PROGRAMS

★6094★ Encyclopedia of Medical Organizations and Agencies
Gale Research Inc.
835 Penobscot Bldg.
Detroit, MI 48226-4094
Ph: (313)961-2242   Fax: (313)961-6741
Fr: 800-877-GALE
Karen Boyden, Contact
Biennial, November of odd years. Covers over 13,400 state, national, and international medical associations, foundations, research institutes, federal and state agencies, and medical and allied health schools. Entries in-

clude: Organization name, address, phone; many listings include names and titles of key personnel, descriptive annotations. Arrangement: Classified by subject, then by type of organization.

★6095★ Health & Medical Industry Directory
American Business Directories, Inc.
5711 S. 86th Circle
Omaha, NE 68127
Ph: (402)593-4600   Fax: (402)331-1505
Released 1993. Lists over 1.1 million physicians and surgeons, dentists, clinics, health clubs, and other health-related businesses in the U.S. and Canada. Entries include: Name, address, phone.

★6096★ Medical and Health Information Directory
Gale Research Inc.
835 Penobscot Bldg.
Detroit, MI 48226-4094
Ph: (313)961-2242   Fax: (313)961-6741
Fr: 800-877-GALE
Karen Boyden, Contact
Approximately biennial; latest edition 1994. Covers in Volume 1, almost 18,600 medical and health oriented associations, organizations, institutions, and government agencies, including health maintenance organizations (HMOs), preferred provider organizations (PPOs), insurance companies, pharmaceutical companies, research centers, and medical and allied health schools. In Volume 2, nearly 11,800 medical book publishers; medical periodicals, directories, audiovisual producers and services, medical libraries and information centers, and electronic resources. In Volume 3, nearly 26,000 clinics, treatment centers, care programs, and counseling/diagnostic services for 30 subject areas. Entries include: Institution, service, or firm name, address, phone; many include names of key personnel Arrangement: Classified by organization activity, service, etc..

★6097★ National Directory of Physician Assistant Programs
Association of Physician Assistant Programs
950 N. Washington St.
Alexandria, VA 22314
Ph: (703)836-2272   Fax: (703)684-1924
Kevin Bayes, Contact
Annual. Covers over 55 accredited programs that educate physician assistants. Entries include: Program name, institution name, address, phone; description of program, including curriculum, selection criteria, degrees of certificates offered. Arrangement: Geographical.

★6098★ Therapists and Allied Health Professionals Career Directory
Gale Research Inc.
835 Penobscot Bldg.
Detroit, MI 48226-4094
Ph: (313)961-2242   Fax: (313)961-6083
Fr: 800-877-GALE
Bradley J. Morgan and Joseph M. Palmisano. 1993. A directory in the Career Advisor Series that provides essays written by industry professionals; job search information on resume and cover letter preparation, networking, and the interviewing process; approximately 300 companies and

organizations offering job opportunities and internships, and additional job-hunting resources.

BASIC REFERENCE GUIDES AND HANDBOOKS

★6099★ Mosby's Fundamentals of Medical Assisting
Mosby-Year Book, Inc.
11830 Westline Industrial Dr.
St. Louis, MO 63146
Ph: (314)872-8370   Fax: (314)432-1380
Fr: 800-325-4177
Margaret A. Shea and Sharron M. Zakus. 1990. Includes a bibliography and an index.

★6100★ Procedural Manual for the Utilization of Physician Extenders
Geisinger Medical Center
Kenneth Harbert, Physician Extender Services
Danville, PA 17822
Ph: (717)271-6094
1985. Manual providing general guidelines, job descriptions, and clinical privileges for physician assistants.

PROFESSIONAL AND TRADE PERIODICALS

★6101★ Association of Schools of Allied Health Professions—Trends
Associations of Schools of Allied Health Professions
1101 Connecticut Ave. NW, Ste. 700
Washington, DC 20036
Ph: (202)857-1150   Fax: (202)429-5108
Thomas W. Elwood
Monthly. Discusses the educational programs, grants and funding, and employment opportunities available to those employed in allied health professions. Recurring features include Association news and legislative, organizational, and institutional updates.

★6102★ Health Labor Relations Reports
Interwood Publications
PO Box 20241
Cincinnati, OH 45220
Ph: (513)221-3715
Frank J. Bardack
Biweekly. Focuses on employee and labor relations in the health care field. Reports on court and National Labor Relations Board (NLRB) decisions in the areas of wrongful discharge, employment-at-will, discrimination, and union organizing. Also notifies readers of arbitration awards and contract settlements.

★6103★ *Health Professions Report*
Whitaker Newsletters, Inc.
313 South Ave.
Fanwood, NJ 07023-0340
Ph: (908)889-6336   Fax: (908)889-6339
Anne C. Bittner

Reports on the education and training of doctors, nurses, and allied health professionals. Includes pending legislation, information on public and private funding sources, cost-cutting measures, curriculum ideas, recruiting efforts and admission policies, new medical breakthroughs, scientific research and advanced programs from America's leading medical training facilities.

★6104★ *Medical Staff Leader*
American Hospital Publishing, Inc.
737 N. Michigan Ave., Ste. 700
Chicago, IL 60611
Ph: (312)440-6800   Fr: 800-621-6902
Jim Montague

Monthly. Devoted to specific and common concerns of medical staff and hospital administration. Recurring features include articles on joint ventures, ethics, legislation, malpractice, and medical by-laws.

PROFESSIONAL MEETINGS AND CONVENTIONS

★6105★ **California Academy of Physician Assistants Convention**
California Academy of Physician Assistants
9778 Katella Ave., Ste. 115
Anaheim, CA 92804
Ph: (714)539-1430   Fax: (714)534-7223
Annual.

★6106★ **Physician Assistants Annual Conference**
American Academy of Physician Assistants
950 N. Washington St.
Alexandria, VA 22314
Ph: (703)836-2272   Fax: (703)684-1924

Annual. **Dates and Locations:** 1996 May 25-30; New York, NY.

★6107★ **Washington State Academy of Physician Assistants Convention**
Washington State Academy of Physician Assistants
2033 6th Ave., Ste. 1100
Seattle, WA 98121
Ph: (206)441-9762   Fax: (206)441-5863

Semiannual. Always held during Presidents' Day Weekend in Februrary at the Sea-Tac Marrriott in Seattle, Washington.

OTHER SOURCES OF INFORMATION

★6108★ *Certification and Recertification Fact Sheet*
American Academy of Physician Assistants (AAPA)
950 N. Washington St.
Alexandria, VA 22314-1534
Ph: (703)836-2272

This two-page fact sheet describes the certification/recertification process and explains how to prepare for the exam.

★6109★ *"Physician Assistant"* in *100 Best Jobs for the 1990s & Beyond*
Dearborn Financial Publishing, Inc.
520 N. Dearborn St.
Chicago, IL 60610-4354
Ph: (312)836-4400   Fax: (312)836-1021
Fr: 800-621-9621

Carol Kleiman. 1992. Describes 100 jobs ranging from accountants to veterinarians. Each job profile includes such information as education, experience, and certification needed, salaries, and job search suggestions.

Recreational Therapists

Recreational therapists employ activities to treat or maintain the mental, physical, and emotional well-being of patients. Activities include sports, games, dance, drama, arts and crafts, music, and field trips. Recreational therapists carefully observe and record patients' participation, reactions, and progress to the activities in which they are involved.

Salaries

Salaries of recreational therapists vary according to employment setting, educational background, work experience, and geographic region.

Recreation therapists	$25,557/year
Activities directors in nursing homes	$15,000-$25,000/year
Recreational therapists, federal government	$33,499/year

Employment Outlook

Growth rate until the year 2005: Faster than the average.

Recreational Therapists

CAREER GUIDES

★6110★ About Therapeutic Recreation
National Therapeutic Recreation Society
2775 S. Quincy St., Ste. 300
Arlington, VA 22206
Ph: (703)820-4940

1989. This 15-page booklet discusses the importance of therapeutic recreation and its role as part of the client treatment team; describes educational preparation, certification, and licensure.

★6111★ Allied Health Professions
Simon & Schuster, Inc.
200 Old Tappan Rd.
Old Tappan, NJ 07675

1993. Includes information on available jobs, required training, a directory of training programs, and a full-sample Allied Health Professions Admission Test (AHPAT).

★6112★ Careers in Health and Fitness
Rosen Publishing Group
29 E. 21st St.
New York, NY 10010
Ph: (212)777-3017   Fax: (212)777-0277
Fr: 800-237-9932

Jackie Heron, R.N. 1990. Explores the opportunities and responsibilities of a career in health or fitness.

★6113★ Careers in Social and Rehabilitation Services
National Textbook Co. (NTC)
VGM Career Books
4255 W. Touhy Ave.
Lincolnwood, IL 60646-1975
Ph: (708)679-5500   Fax: (708)679-2494
Fr: 800-323-4900

Geraldine O. Garner, Ph.D., editor. 1993. Describes dozens of careers in the field of social and rehabilitation services.

★6114★ The Health Care Worker: An Introduction to Health Occupations
Prentice-Hall, Inc.
200 Old Tappan Rd.
Old Tappan, NJ 07675
Ph: (201)767-5000

Shirley A. Badasch, and Doreen S. Chesebro. Second edition, 1988. Includes a bibliography and an index.

★6115★ Health Careers
Careers, Inc.
PO Box 135
Largo, FL 34649-0135
Ph: (813)584-7333

1994. Four-page brief describing duties, working conditions, personal qualifications, training, earnings and hours, employment outlook, places of employment, related careers, and where to write for more information.

★6116★ "Nursing" in Accounting to Zoology: Graduate Fields Defined (pp. 260-277)
Petersons Guides, Inc.
PO Box 2123
Princeton, NJ 08543-2123
Ph: (609)243-9111   Fax: (609)243-9150
Fr: 800-338-3282

Amy J. Goldstein, editor. Revised and updated, 1987. Discusses types of graduate programs and degrees, graduate research, applied work, employment prospects and trends.

★6117★ "Recreation/Creative Arts Therapists" in Guide to Federal Jobs (p. 136)
Resource Directories
3361 Executive Pkwy., Ste. 302
Toledo, OH 43606
Ph: (419)536-5353   Fax: (419)536-7056
Fr: 800-274-8515

Rod W. Durgin, editor. Third edition, 1992. Contains information on finding and applying for federal jobs. Describes more than 200 professional and technical jobs for college graduates. Covers the nature of the work, salary, and geographic location. Lists college majors preferred for that occupation. Section one describes the function and work of government agencies that hire the most significant number of college graduates.

★6118★ Recreation Therapist
Careers, Inc.
PO Box 135
Largo, FL 34649-0135
Ph: (813)584-7333

1992. Two-page occupational summary card describing duties, working conditions, personal qualifications, training, earnings and hours, employment outlook, places of employment, related careers, and where to write for more information.

★6119★ "Recreation Therapist" in College Board Guide to Jobs and Career Planning (pp. 264-265)
The College Board
45 Columbus Ave.
New York, NY 10023-6992
Ph: (212)713-8165   Fax: (212)713-8143
Fr: 800-323-7155

Second edition, 1994. Describes the job, salaries, related careers, education needed, and where to write for more information.

★6120★ "Recreational Therapist" in 100 Best Careers for the Year 2000 (pp. 97-99)
Arco Pub.
201 W. 103rd St.
Indianapolis, IN 46290
Ph: 800-428-5331   Fax: 800-835-3202

Shelly Field. 1992. Describes 100 job opportunities expected to grow fast throughout the next decade. Provides information on job duties and responsibilities, training requirements, education, advancement opportunities, experience and qualifications, and typical salaries.

★6121★ "Recreational Therapist" in Career Information Center (Vol.7)
Simon and Schuster
200 Old Tappan Rd.
Old Tappan, NJ 07675
Fax: 800-445-6991   Fr: 800-223-2348

Richard Lidz and Linda Perrin, editorial directors. Fifth edition, 1993. This 13-volume set profiles over 600 occupations. Each occupational profile describes job duties, entry-level requirements, educational requirements, advancement possibilities, employment outlook, working conditions, earnings and benefits, and where to write for more information.

★6122★ "Recreational Therapist" in
VGM's Handbook of Health Care
Careers
National Textbook Co.
4255 W. Touhy Ave.
Lincolnwood, IL 60646-1975
Ph: (708)679-5500   Fax: (708)679-2494
Fr: 800-323-4900
Annette Selden. 1993. Contains 42 two-page occupational profiles describing job duties, places of employment, working conditions, qualifications, education, employment outlook, and income.

★6123★ *Recreational Therapists*
Chronicle Guidance Publications, Inc.
66 Aurora St.
PO Box 1190
Moravia, NY 13118-1190
Ph: (315)497-0330   Fax: (315)497-3359
Fr: 800-622-7284
1992. Career brief describing the nature of the job, working conditions, hours and earnings, education and training, licensure, certification, unions, personal qualifications, social and psychological factors, location, employment outlook, entry methods, advancement, and related occupations.

★6124★ "Recreational Therapists" in
America's 50 Fastest Growing Jobs
(pp. 62)
JIST Works, Inc.
720 N. Park Ave.
Indianapolis, IN 46202-3431
Ph: (317)264-3720   Fax: (317)264-3709
Fr: 800-648-5478
Michael J. Farr, compiler. 1994. Describes the 50 fastest growing jobs within major career clusters such as technicians, and marketing and sales. Each job profile explains the nature of the work, skills and abilities required, employment outlook, average earnings, related occupations, education and training requirements, and employment opportunities. Also contains career planning information and job search tips.

★6125★ "Recreational Therapists" in
Encyclopedia of Careers and
Vocational Guidance **(Vol.4, pp. 258-**
261)
J.G. Ferguson Publishing Co.
200 W. Madison St., Ste. 300
Chicago, IL 60606
Ph: (312)580-5480   Fax: (312)580-4948
William E. Hopke, editor-in-chief. Ninth edition, 1993. Four-volume set that profiles 900 occupations and describes job trends in 74 industries. Includes career description, educational requirements, history of the job, methods of entry, advancement, employment outlook, earnings, conditions of work, social and psychological factors, and sources of further information.

★6126★ "Recreational Therapists" in
Health Care Job Explosion! **(pp. 187-**
194)
D-Amp Publications
401 Amherst Ave.
Coraopolis, PA 15108
Ph: (412)262-5578
Dennis V. Damp. 1993. Provides information on the nature of work for the major health care occupational groups. Descriptions in-

clude working conditions, training, job outlook, qualifications, and related occupations.

★6127★ "Recreational Therapists" in
Jobs! What They Are—Where They
Are—What They Pay **(pp. 175)**
Fireside
Simon & Schuster Bldg.
1230 Avenue of the Americas
New York, NY 10020
Ph: (212)698-7000   Fr: 800-223-2348
Robert O. Snelling and Anne M. Snelling. Revised and updated, 1992. Describes duties and responsibilities, earnings, employment opportunities, training, and qualifications.

★6128★ "Recreational Therapists" in
Occupational Outlook Handbook
U.S. Government Printing Office
Superintendent of Documents
Washington, DC 20402
Ph: (202)512-1800   Fax: (202)512-2250
Biennial; latest edition, 1994-95. Encyclopedia of careers describing about 250 occupations and comprising about 85 percent of all jobs in the economy. Occupations that require lengthy education or training are given the most attention. Each occupation's profile describes what the worker does on the job, working conditions, education and training requirements, advancement possibilities, job outlook, earnings, and sources of additional information.

★6129★ "Therapeutic Recreation" in
150 Careers in the Health Care Field
Reed Reference Publishing
121 Chanlon Rd.
PO Box 31
New Providence, NJ 07974
Fax: (908)665-6688   Fr: 800-521-8110
Stanley Alperin. Third edition, 1993. Profiles health care occupations requiring a bachelor's degree or less. Describes the nature of the work, educational preparation, licensing requirements, and salary.

★6130★ *Therapeutic Recreation:*
Comprehensive Approach to a
Continuum of Care
National Therapeutic Recreation Society
3101 Park Center Dr.
Alexandria, VA 22302
Ph: (703)820-4940
Pamphlet describing the role of recreation therapy and the recreation therapist in health care.

★6131★ *Therapeutic Recreation*
Specialists
Chronicle Guidance Publications, Inc.
66 Aurora St.
PO Box 1190
Moravia, NY 13118-1190
Ph: (315)497-0330   Fax: (315)497-3359
Fr: 800-622-7284
1993. Career brief describing the nature of the job, working conditions, hours and earnings, education and training, licensure, certification, unions, personal qualifications, social and psychological factors, location, employment outlook, entry methods, advancement, and related occupations.

PROFESSIONAL ASSOCIATIONS

★6132★ American Association for
Leisure and Recreation (AALR)
1900 Association Dr.
Reston, VA 22091
Ph: (703)476-3472   Fax: (703)476-9527
Members: Established by the American Alliance for Health, Physical Education, Recreation and Dance. Teachers of recreation and park administration, leisure studies, and recreation programming in colleges and universities; professional recreation and park practitioners; people involved in other areas of health, physical education, and recreation with an interest in recreation. **Purpose:** Goals are to: encourage professional involvement and exchange; monitor recreation legislation and render consultation at the request of legislators; disseminate information on topics of current interest in leisure and recreation; maintain liaison with organizations having allied interests in leisure and recreation; support, encourage, and provide guidance to members in the development of programs of leisure services; aid in the development of quality educational/recreational programs in the schools; facilitate communication between professionals and lay people and between the schools and the community; create opportunity for professional growth and development; sponsor programs at district and national conventions, workshops, and conferences; nurture the conceptualization of a philosophy of leisure through curriculum development and professional preparation. Maintains placement service. **Publications:** *AALReporter*, quarterly. • *Journal of Physical Education, Recreation and Dance.* • *Leisure Today*, semiannual.

★6133★ American Health Care
Association (AHCA)
1201 L St. NW
Washington, DC 20005
Ph: (202)842-4444   Fax: (202)842-3860
Members: Federation of state associations of long-term health care facilities. **Purpose:** Promotes standards for professionals in long-term health care delivery and quality care for patients and residents in a safe environment. Focuses on issues of availability, quality, affordability, and fair payment. Operates as liaison with governmental agencies, Congress, and professional associations. Compiles statistics. **Publications:** *AHCA Notes*, monthly. • *Provider: For Long Term Care Professionals*, monthly. • *Thinking About a Nursing Home?.* • *Welcome to Our Nursing Home.*

★6134★ American Therapeutic
Recreation Association (ATRA)
PO Box 15215
Hattiesburg, MS 39404-5215
Ph: (601)264-3413   Fax: (601)264-3337
Fr: 800-553-0304
Members: Therapeutic recreation professionals and students; interested others. (Therapeutic recreation involves the use of sports, handicrafts, and other recreational activities to improve the physical, mental, and emotional functions of persons with illnesses or disabling conditions.) **Purpose:** Promotes

the use of therapeutic recreation in hospitals, mental rehabilitation centers, physical rehabilitation centers, senior citizen treatment centers, and other public health facilities. Conducts discussions on certification and legislative and regulatory concerns that affect the industry. Sponsors seminars and workshops; conducts research. **Publications:** *Employment Update*, monthly. • *Evaluation of Therapeutic Recreation Through Quality Assurance.* • *Risk Management in Therapeutic Recreation.* • *The Therapeutic Recreation Journal*, annual. • *Third Party Reimbursements.*

★6135★ National Council for Therapeutic Recreation Certification (NCTRC)
479 Theills
Spring Valley, NY 10977
Ph: (914)947-4346

Members: Objectives are to: establish national evaluative standards for certification and recertification of individuals who work in the therapeutic recreation field; grant recognition to individuals who voluntarily apply and meet established standards; monitor adherence to standards by certified personnel. **Publications:** *NCTRC Newsletter*, semi-annual.

★6136★ National Therapeutic Recreation Society (NTRS)
2775 S. Quincy St., Ste. 300
Arlington, VA 22206
Ph: (703)578-5548   Fax: (703)671-6772
Fr: 800-626-6772

Members: Professionals, educators, and students involved in the provision of therapeutic recreation services for persons with disabilities in clinical facilities and in the community. **Purpose:** Offers technical assistance services to agencies, institutions, and individuals on matters related to the field. Encourages professional growth through research, training, and workshops. A branch of the National Recreation and Park Association. **Publications:** *Guidelines for the Administration of Therapeutic Recreation Services.* • *Management of Therapeutic Recreation Services.* • *NTRS Report*, quarterly. • *Parks and Recreation*, monthly. • *Philosophy of Therapeutic Recreation: Ideas and Issues.* • *Preparing for a Career in Therapeutic Recreation.* • *Protocols in Therapeutic Recreation.* • *Standards of Practice for Therapeutic Recreation Service.* • *Therapeutic Recreation Journal*, quarterly.

STANDARDS/CERTIFICATION AGENCIES

★6137★ American Health Care Association (AHCA)
1201 L St. NW
Washington, DC 20005
Ph: (202)842-4444   Fax: (202)842-3860
Promotes standards for professionals in long-term health care delivery and quality care for patients and residents in a safe environment.

Focuses on issues of availability, quality, affordability, and fair payment.

★6138★ National Council for Therapeutic Recreation Certification (NCTRC)
479 Theills
Spring Valley, NY 10977
Ph: (914)947-4346

Objectives are to: establish national evaluative standards for certification and recertification of individuals who work in the therapeutic recreation field; grant recognition to individuals who voluntarily apply and meet established standards; monitor adherence to standards by certified personnel.

★6139★ World Sports Medicine Association of Registered Therapists
206 Marine Ave.
PO Box 5642
Newport Beach, CA 92662
Ph: (818)574-1999

Athletic trainers, fitness trainers, and individuals involved in sports medicine and certified by any nationally recognized athletic trainers association. Establishes standards of competency for trainers, therapists, and sports care providers that are recognized worldwide.

TEST GUIDES

★6140★ *Basic Terminology for Therapeutic Recreation & Other Action Therapies*
Stipes Publishing Co.
10-12 Chester St.
Champaign, IL 61820
Ph: (217)356-8391
Scout Lee. 1990.

★6141★ *Career Examination Series: Chief Recreation Therapist*
National Learning Corp.
212 Michael Dr.
Syosset, NY 11791
Ph: (516)921-8888   Fax: (516)921-8743
Fr: 800-645-6337

Jack Rudman. A study guide for professionals and trainees in the field of recreational therapy. Includes a multiple-choice examination section; provides answers.

★6142★ *Career Examination Series: Developmental Disabilities Program Specialist*
National Learning Corp.
212 Michael Dr.
Syosset, NY 11791
Ph: (516)921-8888   Fax: (516)921-8743
Fr: 800-645-6337

Jack Rudman. 1993. Test guide including questions and answers for students or professionals in the field who seek advancement through examination.

★6143★ *Career Examination Series: Recreation Therapist*
National Learning Corp.
212 Michael Dr.
Syosset, NY 11791
Ph: (516)921-8888   Fax: (516)921-8743
Fr: 800-645-6337

Jack Rudman. A study guide for professionals and trainees in the field of recreational therapy. Includes a multiple-choice examination section; provides answers.

★6144★ *Career Examination Series: Senior Recreation Therapist*
National Learning Corp.
212 Michael Dr.
Syosset, NY 11791
Ph: (516)921-8888   Fax: (516)921-8743
Fr: 800-645-6337

Jack Rudman. 1993. Test guide including questions and answers for students or professionals in the field who seek advancement through examination.

★6145★ *Career Examination Series: Supervising Therapist*
National Learning Corp.
212 Michael Dr.
Syosset, NY 11791
Ph: (516)921-8888   Fax: (516)921-8743
Fr: 800-645-6337

Jack Rudman. 1993. Test guide including questions and answers for students or professionals in the field who seek advancement through examination.

EDUCATIONAL DIRECTORIES AND PROGRAMS

★6146★ *Encyclopedia of Medical Organizations and Agencies*
Gale Research Inc.
835 Penobscot Bldg.
Detroit, MI 48226-4094
Ph: (313)961-2242   Fax: (313)961-6741
Fr: 800-877-GALE
Karen Boyden, Contact

Biennial, November of odd years. Covers over 13,400 state, national, and international medical associations, foundations, research institutes, federal and state agencies, and medical and allied health schools. Entries include: Organization name, address, phone; many listings include names and titles of key personnel, descriptive annotations. Arrangement: Classified by subject, then by type of organization.

★6147★ *Medical and Health Information Directory*
Gale Research Inc.
835 Penobscot Bldg.
Detroit, MI 48226-4094
Ph: (313)961-2242   Fax: (313)961-6741
Fr: 800-877-GALE
Karen Boyden, Contact

Approximately biennial; latest edition 1994. Covers in Volume 1, almost 18,600 medical and health oriented associations, organizations, institutions, and government agencies, including health maintenance organizations

(HMOs), preferred provider organizations (PPOs), insurance companies, pharmaceutical companies, research centers, and medical and allied health schools. In Volume 2, nearly 11,800 medical book publishers; medical periodicals, directories, audiovisual producers and services, medical libraries and information centers, and electronic resources. In Volume 3, nearly 26,000 clinics, treatment centers, care programs, and counseling/diagnostic services for 30 subject areas. Entries include: Institution, service, or firm name, address, phone; many include names of key personnel Arrangement: Classified by organization activity, service, etc..

★6148★ Therapists and Allied Health Professionals Career Directory
Gale Research Inc.
835 Penobscot Bldg.
Detroit, MI 48226-4094
Ph: (313)961-2242   Fax: (313)961-6083
Fr: 800-877-GALE

Bradley J. Morgan and Joseph M. Palmisano. 1993. A directory in the Career Advisor Series that provides essays written by industry professionals; job search information on resume and cover letter preparation, networking, and the interviewing process; approximately 300 companies and organizations offering job opportunities and internships, and additional job-hunting resources.

BASIC REFERENCE GUIDES AND HANDBOOKS

★6149★ Behavior Modification in Therapeutic Recreation: An Introductory Learning Manual
Venture Publishing, Inc.
1999 Capo Ave.
State College, PA 16801
Ph: (814)234-4561

John Dattilo and William D. Murphy. 1987. Includes a bibliography.

★6150★ Therapeutic Recreation Intervention: An Ecological Perspective
Prentice-Hall, Inc.
Rte. 9W
Englewood Cliffs, NJ 07632
Ph: (201)592-2000

Roxanne Howe-Murphy and Becky G. Charboneau. 1987. Includes bibliographies and an index.

★6151★ Therapeutic Recreation for Long-Term Care Facilities
Human Sciences Press
233 Spring St.
New York, NY 10013
Ph: (212)620-8000

Fred S. Greenblatt. 1988. Includes a bibliography and an index.

PROFESSIONAL AND TRADE PERIODICALS

★6152★ Pacific Basin Rehabilitation Research & Training Center—Newsletter
Pacific Basin Rehabilitation Research & Training Center
226 N. Kuakini St., Rm. 233
Honolulu, HI 96817
Ph: (808)537-5986   Fax: (808)531-8691
Joanne Y. Yamada

Semiannual. Focuses on the Center's research, training activities, and rehabilitation services. Recurring features include news of research, a calendar of events, and reports of meetings.

★6153★ Physical Disabilities Special Interest Section—Newsletter
Physical Disabilities Special Interest Section
1383 Piccard Dr.
Rockville, MD 20850
Ph: (301)948-9626   Fax: (301)948-5512

Quarterly. Focuses on the clinical management of people with physical disabilities. Publishes articles relevant to occupational therapy practice, including such topics as assessment protocols, treatment approaches, and program administration. Re-

curring features include editorials, news of research, case reports, bibliographies, and notices of new equipment.

★6154★ Therapeutic Recreation Journal
National Recreation and Park Assn.
2775 S. Quincy St., Ste. 300
Arlington, VA 22206-2204
Ph: (703)820-4940   Fax: (703)671-6772
Rikki S. Epstein

Quarterly. Journal providing forum for research and discussion of therapeutic recreation for persons with disabilities.

★6155★ Work Programs Special Interest Section Newsletter
Work Programs Special Interest Section
1383 Piccard Dr.
PO Box 1725
Rockville, MD 20850
Ph: (301)948-9626   Fax: (301)948-5512
Jennifer Jones

Quarterly. Focuses on habilitation and rehabilitation of the worker in areas of physical disabilities, developmental disabilities, and mental health.

PROFESSIONAL MEETINGS AND CONVENTIONS

★6156★ American Alliance for Health, Physical Education, Recreation, and Dance - Midwest District Convention
American Alliance for Health, Physical Education, Recreation, and Dance
1900 Association Dr.
Reston, VA 22091
Ph: (703)476-3400

Registered Nurses

Registered nurses (R.N.'s) care for the sick and injured and help people stay well. Typically concerned with the "whole person," registered nurses provide for the physical, mental, and emotional needs of their patients. They observe, assess, and record symptoms, reactions, and progress; administer medications; assist in convalescence and rehabilitation; instruct patients and their families in proper care; and help individuals and groups take steps to improve or maintain their health. **Hospital nurses** constitute the largest group of nurses. Most are staff nurses, who provide skilled bedside nursing care and carry out the medical regimen prescribed by physicians. **Nursing home nurses** manage nursing care for residents with conditions ranging from a fracture to Alzheimer's disease. **Public health nurses** care for patients in clinics, schools, retirement and life care communities, and other community settings. **Private duty nurses** provide services to patients needing constant attention. **Office nurses** assist physicians in private practice, clinics, and health maintenance organizations. **Occupational health nurses** or **industrial nurses** provide nursing care to employees in industry and government. **Head nurses** or **nurse supervisors** direct nursing activities. They plan work schedules and assign duties to nurses and aides.

Salaries

In general, Veterans Administration and nursing home nurses have lower average yearly salaries. Salaries of full-time nurses are as follows:

Staff nurse	$33,278/year
Experienced head nurse	$47,335/year
R.N. staff nurses in nursing homes	$27,200-$33,400/year

Employment Outlook

Growth rate until the year 2005: Much faster than the average.

Registered Nurses

CAREER GUIDES

★6157★ The AJN Career Guide for 1995
American Journal of Nursing Co.
555 W. 57th St.
New York, NY 10019
Ph: (212)582-8820
Annual. Previously published under title, *AJN Guide to Nursing Career Oportunities.* Gives career planning, self-assessment, and job hunting advice. This is primarily a listing of hospitals and health centers. Profiles on each hospital describe the facilities, professional climate, and benefits.

★6158★ Allied Health Professions
Simon & Schuster, Inc.
200 Old Tappan Rd.
Old Tappan, NJ 07675
1993. Includes information on available jobs, required training, a directory of training programs, and a full-sample Allied Health Professions Admission Test (AHPAT).

★6159★ Become a Nurse . . . Touch Your World
American Nurses' Association
600 Maryland Ave., SW, Ste. 100-W
Washington, DC 20024
Ph: (202)554-4444
This eight-panel brochure explains opportunities in nursing and includes an education checklist.

★6160★ Career Guide for Nurse Educators
Appleton and Lange
25 Van Zant St.
E. Norwalk, CT 06855
Ph: (203)838-4400
Margaret Denise Zanecchia. 1988. Intended to serve as a resource guide for nurses considering a teaching career.

★6161★ Career Planning: A Nurse's Guide to Career Advancement
National League for Nursing (NLN)
350 Hudson St.
New York, NY 10014
Ph: (212)989-9393   Fr: 800-NOW-1NLN
Patricia Winstead-Fry. 1990. This is a guide to career planning and self assessment. De-

scribes opportunities in nurse-midwifery, independent practice, community health, administration, research and education. Gives advice on getting into the field and acquiring the education needed.

★6162★ Careers in Medicine: Traditional and Alternative Opportunities
Garrett Park Press
PO Box 1907
Garrett Park, MD 20896-0190
Ph: (301)946-2553
T. Donald Rucker and Martin D. Keller. Revised edition, 1990. Written for college students who are considering applying to medical school, medical students attempting to select a specialty, and physicians who want to explore nonclinical work. Provides descriptions and employment outlook for 900 medical-oriented occupations.

★6163★ Competencies of the Associate Degree Nurse: Valid Definers of Entry-Level Nursing Practice
National League for Nursing (NLN)
350 Hudson St.
New York, NY 10014
Ph: (212)989-9393   Fr: 800-NOW-1NLN
Verle H. Waters and Sharlene Limon. 1987. This book is an outcome of a study that clarifies the working skills or competencies of AD graduates.

★6164★ Developing Your Career in Nursing
Routledge, Chapman & Hall
29 W. 35th St.
New York, NY 10001
Ph: (212)244-3336   Fax: (212)563-2269
Desmond F.S. Cormack, editor. 1990.

★6165★ The Discipline of Nursing
Appleton and Lange
25 Van Zant St.
East Norwalk, CT 06855
Ph: (203)838-4400   Fr: 800-423-1359
Margaret O'Bryan Doheny, Christina B. Cook, and Mary C. Stopper. Third edition, 1992. Includes bibliographies and an index.

★6166★ Educational Outcomes of Associate Degree Nursing Programs: Roles and Competencies
Council of Associate Degree Programs, National League for Nursing (NLN)
350 Hudson St.
New York, NY 10014
Ph: (212)989-9393   Fr: 800-NOW-1NLN
Prepared by the NLN Council of AD Programs. 1990. Pamphlet describes the scope and roles of practice and competencies of nurse graduating from an associate degree program.

★6167★ Entering and Moving in the Professional Job Market: A Nurse's Resource Kit
American Nurses' Association (ANA)
2420 Pershing Rd.
Kansas City, MO 64108
Ph: (816)474-5720
Lyndia Flanagan. 1988. Contains one booklet and five brochures.

★6168★ "Environmental Nurse" in Opportunities in Environmental Careers
National Textbook Co. (NTC)
VGM Career Books
4255 W. Touhy Ave.
Lincolnwood, IL 60646-1975
Ph: (708)679-5500   Fax: (708)679-2494
Fr: 800-323-4900
Odom Fanning. 1991. Describes a broad range of opportunities in fields such as environmental health, recreation, physics, and hygiene.

★6169★ "Health Care" in Where the Jobs Are: The Hottest Careers for the 90s (pp. 143-166)
Career Press
180 5th Ave.
Hawthorne, NJ 07507
Ph: (201)427-0229   Fax: (201)427-2037
Fr: 800-CAREER-1
Joyce Hadley. 1995. Offers a job-hunting strategy for the 1990s as well as descriptions of growing careers of the decade. Each profile includes general information, forecasts, growth, education and training, licensing requirements, and salary information.

★6170★ *The Health Care Worker: An Introduction to Health Occupations*
Prentice-Hall, Inc.
200 Old Tappan Rd.
Old Tappan, NJ 07675
Ph: (201)767-5000

Shirley A. Badasch, and Doreen S. Chesebro. Second edition, 1988. Includes a bibliography and an index.

★6171★ *Health Careers*
Careers, Inc.
PO Box 135
Largo, FL 34649-0135
Ph: (813)584-7333

1994. Four-page brief describing duties, working conditions, personal qualifications, training, earnings and hours, employment outlook, places of employment, related careers, and where to write for more information.

★6172★ *"Health Technicians and Paraprofessionals" in Opportunities in Vocational Technical Careers (pp. 91-108)*
National Textbook Co. (NTC)
VGM Career Books
4255 W. Touhy Ave.
Lincolnwood, IL 60646-1975
Ph: (708)679-5500   Fax: (708)679-2494
Fr: 800-323-4900

Adrian A. Paradis. 1992. This book describes careers which can be prepared for by attending vocational-technical schools. Gives the employment outlook and salary information.

★6173★ *"Imprints" in Directory of Nursing Clinical and Occupational Specialties*
American Nurses' Association
600 W. Maryland Ave., SW, Ste. 100-W
Washington, DC 20024
Ph: (202)554-4444

B. J. Nerone, compiler and managing editor. Profiles 23 nursing career specialties. For each career specialty, the primary professional association, salary range, educational requirements, work settings, rewards, potential frustrations, and printed resources are given.

★6174★ *Issues in Graduate Nursing Education*
National League for Nursing (NLN)
350 Hudson St.
New York, NY 10014
Ph: (212)989-9393   Fr: 800-NOW-1NLN

Sylvia E. Hart, editor. 1987. Discusses the growing number of graduates of master and doctoral degrees in nursing, and how they should be utilized.

★6175★ *"Laser Nurse Coordinator" in Opportunities in Laser Technology Careers (pp. 32-35)*
National Textbook Co. (NTC)
VGM Career Books
4255 W. Touhy Ave.
Lincolnwood, IL 60646-1975
Ph: (708)679-5500   Fax: (708)679-2494
Fr: 800-323-4900

Jan Bone. 1989. Describes career opportunities using lasers in health care, manufacturing, the military, space communications, and research. Explains the education needed and gives job hunting tips.

★6176★ *Mosby's Tour Guide to Nursing School: A Student's Road Survival Kit*
Mosby-Year Book, Inc.
11830 Westline Industrial Dr.
St. Louis, MO 63146
Ph: (314)872-8370   Fax: (314)432-1380
Fr: 800-325-4177

Melodie Chenevert. 3rd edition, 1994. Provides students with a realistic look at nursing.

★6177★ *National Commission on Nursing Implementation Project: Models for the Future of Nursing*
National League for Nursing (NLN)
350 Hudson St.
New York, NY 10014
Ph: (212)989-9393   Fr: 800-NOW-1NLN
1988.

★6178★ *Nurse Anesthetist*
Careers, Inc.
PO Box 135
Largo, FL 34649-0135
Ph: (813)584-7333

1994. Two-page summary describing duties, working conditions, personal qualifications, training, earnings and hours, employment outlook, places of employment, related careers, and where to write for more information.

★6179★ *"Nurse" in Careers in Health Care (pp. 153-167)*
National Textbook Co. (NTC)
VGM Career Books
4255 W. Touhy Ave.
Lincolnwood, IL 60646-1975
Ph: (708)679-5500   Fax: (708)679-2494
Fr: 800-323-4900

Barbara M. Swanson. Third edition, 1995. Describes job duties, work settings, salaries, licensing and certification requirements, educational preparation, and future outlook.

★6180★ *"Nurse" in College Board Guide to Jobs and Career Planning (pp. 248)*
The College Board
415 Columbus Ave.
New York, NY 10023-6992
Ph: (212)713-8165   Fax: (212)713-8143
Fr: 800-323-7155

Joyce S. Mitchell. Second edition, 1994. Describes the job, salaries, related careers, education needed, and where to write for more information.

★6181★ *"Nurse" in Guide to Careers Without College (pp. 40-43)*
Franklin Watts, Inc.
PO Box 1741
Danbury, CT 06816
Ph: (212)686-7070   Fr: 800-672-6672

Kathleen S. Abrams. 1988. Discusses rewarding careers that do not require a college degree.

★6182★ *"Nurse" in Guide to Federal Jobs (p. 130)*
Resource Directories
3361 Executive Pkwy., Ste. 302
Toledo, OH 43606
Ph: (419)536-5353   Fax: (419)536-7056
Fr: 800-274-8515

Rod W. Durgin, editor. Third edition, 1992. Contains information on finding and applying for federal jobs. Describes more than 200 professional and technical jobs for college graduates. Covers the nature of the work, salary, and geographic location. Lists college majors preferred for that occupation. Section one describes the function and work of government agencies that hire the most significant number of college graduates.

★6183★ *Nurse, Licensed Practical*
Careers, Inc.
PO Box 135
Largo, FL 34649-0135
Ph: (813)584-7333

1991. Four-page brief describing duties, working conditions, personal qualifications, training, earnings and hours, employment outlook, places of employment, related careers, and where to write for more information.

★6184★ *Nurse-Midwife*
Vocational Biographies, Inc.
PO Box 31
Sauk Centre, MN 56378-0031
Ph: (612)352-6516   Fax: (612)352-5546
Fr: 800-255-0752

1994. Four-page pamphlet containing a personal narrative about a worker's job, work likes and dislikes, career path from high school to the present, education and training, the rewards and frustrations, and the effects of the job on the rest of the worker's life. The data file portion of this pamphlet gives a concise occupational summary, including work description, working conditions, places of employment, personal characteristics, education and training, job outlook, and salary range.

★6185★ *"Nurse Midwife" in Careers in Health Care (pp. 168-172)*
National Textbook Co. (NTC)
VGM Career Books
4255 W. Touhy Ave.
Lincolnwood, IL 60646-1975
Ph: (708)679-5500   Fax: (708)679-2494
Fr: 800-323-4900

Barbara M. Swanson. Third edition, 1995. Describes job duties, work settings, salaries, licensing and certification requirements, educational preparation, and future outlook.

★6186★ *Nurse, Occupational Health*
Careers, Inc.
PO Box 135
Largo, FL 34649-0135
Ph: (813)584-7333

1995. Two-page summary describing duties, working conditions, personal qualifications, training, earnings and hours, employment outlook, places of employment, related careers, and where to write for more information.

★6187★ Nurse Oncologist
Vocational Biographies, Inc.
PO Box 31
Sauk Centre, MN 56378-0031
Ph: (612)352-6516   Fax: (612)352-5546
Fr: 800-255-0752
1988. Four-page pamphlet containing a personal narrative about a worker's job, work likes and dislikes, career path from high school to the present, education and training, the rewards and frustrations, and the effects of the job on the rest of the worker's life. The data file portion of this pamphlet gives a concise occupational summary, including work description, working conditions, places of employment, personal characteristics, education and training, job outlook, and salary range.

★6188★ "Nurse Practitioner" in
Opportunities in Paramedical Careers
(pp. 13-24)
National Textbook Co. (NTC)
VGM Career Books
4255 W. Touhy Ave.
Lincolnwood, IL 60646-1975
Ph: (708)679-5500   Fax: (708)679-2494
Fr: 800-323-4900
Alex Kacen. 1994. Describes paraprofessional careers in the health professions such as physician assistant, medical assistant, and emergency medical techician. Describes job duties, educational preparation, certification, earnings, and job outlook. Lists educational programs.

★6189★ Nurse, Psychiatric
Careers, Inc.
PO Box 135
Largo, FL 34649-0135
Ph: (813)584-7333
1993. Two-page summary describing duties, working conditions, personal qualifications, training, earnings and hours, employment outlook, places of employment, related careers, and where to write for more information.

★6190★ Nurse, Registered
Careers, Inc.
PO Box 135
Largo, FL 34649-0135
Ph: (813)584-7333
1995. Four-page brief offering the definition, history, duties, working con ditions, personal qualifications, educational requirements, earnings, hours, employment outlook, advancement, and careers related to this position.

★6191★ "Nurse (Registered)" in Jobs
Rated Almanac
World Almanac
1 International Blvd., Ste. 444
Mahwah, NJ 07495
Ph: (201)529-6900   Fax: (201)529-6901
Les Krantz. Second edition, 1992. Ranks 250 jobs by environment, salary, outlooks, physical demands, stress, security, travel opportunities, and extra perks. Includes jobs the editor feels are the most common, most interesting, and the most rapidly growing.

★6192★ "Nurse, Registered" in VGM's
Handbook of Health Care Careers
National Textbook Co.
4255 W. Touhy Ave.
Lincolnwood, IL 60646-1975
Ph: (708)679-5500   Fax: (708)679-2494
Fr: 800-323-4900
Annette Selden. 1993. Contains 42 two-page occupational profiles describing job duties, places of employment, working conditions, qualifications, education, employment outlook, and income.

★6193★ "Nurses" in American Almanac
of Jobs and Salaries (pp. 453)
Avon Books
1350 Avenue of the Americas
New York, NY 10019
Ph: (212)261-6800   Fr: 800-238-0658
John Wright, editor. Revised and updated, 1994-95. This is comprehensive guide to the wages of hundreds of occupations in a wide variety of industries and organizations.

★6194★ "Nurses" in Career Paths in the
Field of Aging: Professional
Gerontology (pp. 25-26)
Simon and Schuster
200 Old Tappan Rd.
Old Tappan, NJ 07675
Fax: 800-445-6991   Fr: 800-223-2348
David A. Peterson. 1987. Provides a history of the gerontology profession, and describes jobs education and skills required, employment outlook and trends in the field.

★6195★ "Nurses" in Encyclopedia of
Careers and Vocational Guidance
J.G. Ferguson Publishing Co.
200 W. Madison St., Ste. 300
Chicago, IL 60606
Ph: (312)580-5480   Fax: (312)580-4948
William E. Hopke, editor-in-chief. Ninth edition, 1993. Four-volume set that profiles 900 occupations and describes job trends in 74 industries. Includes career description, educational requirements, history of the jobs, methods of entry, advancement, employment outlook, earnings, conditions of work, social and psychological factors, and sources of further information.

★6196★ "Nurses" in Jobs! What They
Are—Where They Are—What They Pay
(p. 170)
Simon & Schuster, Inc.
Simon & Schuster Bldg.
1230 Avenue of the Americas
New York, NY 10020
Ph: (212)698-7000   Fr: 800-223-2348
Robert O. Snelling and Anne M. Snelling. 3rd edition, 1992. Describes duties and responsibilities, earnings, employment opportunities, training, and qualifications.

★6197★ Nurses, Registered
Professional
Chronicle Guidance Publications, Inc.
66 Aurora St.
PO Box 1190
Moravia, NY 13118-1190
Ph: (315)497-0330   Fax: (315)497-3359
Fr: 800-622-7284
1991. Career brief describing the nature of the job, working conditions, hours and earnings, education and training, licensure, certifi-

cation, unions, personal qualifications, social and psychological factors, location, employment outlook, entry methods, advancement, and related occupations.

★6198★ "Nursing" in 150 Careers in the
Health Care Field
Reed Reference Publishing
121 Chanlon Rd.
PO Box 31
New Providence, NJ 07974
Fax: (908)665-6688   Fr: 800-521-8110
Stanley Alperin. Third edition, 1993. Profiles health care occupations requiring a bachelor's degree or less. Describes the nature of the work, educational preparation, licensing requirements, and salary. Lists accredited educational programs.

★6199★ "Nursing" in Accounting to
Zoology: Graduate Fields Defined (pp.
260-277)
Petersons Guides, Inc.
PO Box 2123
Princeton, NJ 08543-2123
Ph: (609)243-9111   Fax: (609)243-9150
Fr: 800-338-3282
Amy J. Goldstein, editor. Revised and updated, 1987. Discusses types of graduate programs and degrees, graduate research, applied work, employment prospects and trends.

★6200★ "Nursing" in Black Woman's
Career Guide (pp. 110-111)
Bantam Doubleday Dell
1540 Broadway
New York, NY 10036
Fax: 800-233-3294   Fr: 800-223-5780
Beatryce Nivens. Revised edition, 1987. Part 1 describes career planning, resume writing, job hunting, and interviewing. Part 2 profiles 60 black women pioneers in 20 different career areas.

★6201★ Nursing: From Education to
Practice
Appleton and Lange
PO Box 5630
Norwalk, CT 06856
Ph: (203)838-4400   Fr: 800-423-1359
Helen Frishe Hodges. 1988. Practical guide designed to help nursing students and registered nurses reentering the workforce make the transition to a clinical setting. Covers diagnostic related groups, ethics, and professional liability. Gives tips on time management, conflict management, and evaluating employers.

★6202★ Nursing Home Salary and
Benefits Report
Hospital Compensation Service
John R. Zabka Associates, Inc.
69 Minnehaha Blvd.
PO Box 376
Oakland, NJ 07436
Ph: (201)405-0075
Annual. Gives salaries and fringe benefits for registered and licensed practical nurses. Lists salaries by the annual gross revenue of the nursing home, bed size, and profit and nonprofit status.

★6203★ "Nursing and Related Services" in *College Majors and Careers: A Resource Guide to Effective Life Planning* (pp. 101-102)
Garrett Park Press
PO Box 1907
Garrett Park, MD 20896
Ph: (301)946-2553

Paul Phifer. Revised, 1993. Lists 60 college majors, with definitions; related occupations and leisure activities; skills, values, and personal attributesneeded; suggested readings; and a list of associations.

★6204★ *Nursing's New Directions*
American Nurses' Association
600 W. Maryland Ave., SW, Ste. 100-W
Washington, DC 20024
Ph: (202)554-4444

This brochure describes new specializations on nursing involving responsibilities and work settings.

★6205★ *Opportunities in Health and Medical Careers*
National Textbook Co. (NTC)
VGM Career Books
4255 W. Touhy Ave.
Lincolnwood, IL 60646-1975
Ph: (708)679-5500   Fax: (708)679-2494
Fr: 800-323-4900

I. Donald Snook Jr., Leo D'Orazio. Describes the working conditions of physicians, physician assistants, therapists, nurses, technicians, administrators, and hospital staff. Also includes information on educational requirements and salaries.

★6206★ *Opportunities in Nursing Careers*
National Textbook Co. (NTC)
VGM Career Books
4255 W. Touhy Ave.
Lincolnwood, IL 60646-1975
Ph: (708)679-5500   Fax: (708)679-2494
Fr: 800-323-4900

Keville Frederickson. 1989. Describes working conditions, job responsibilities, salary, and educational requirements.

★6207★ *Profiles of the Newly Licensed Nurse*
National League for Nursing (NLN)
350 Hudson St.
New York, NY 10014
Ph: (212)989-9393   Fr: 800-NOW-1NLN

Peri Rosenfeld. 1989. This book is based on a survey of over 38,000 recently licensed registered nurses, describing their background, professional activities, compensation, and likes and dislikes. Also gives data such as age, region, program type, length of time it took to find a job, and salaries.

★6208★ "Registered Nurse" in *150 Careers in the Health Care Field*
Reed Reference Publishing
121 Chanlon Rd.
PO Box 31
New Providence, NJ 07974
Fax: (908)665-6688   Fr: 800-521-8110

Stanley Alperin. Third edition, 1993. Profiles health care occupations requiring a bachelor's degree or less. Describes the nature of the work, educational preparation, licensing requirements, and salary. Lists accredited educational programs.

★6209★ "Registered Nurse" in *BLR Encyclopedia of Prewritten Job Descriptions*
Business and Legal Reports, Inc.
39 Academy St.
Madison, CT 06443-1513
Ph: (203)245-7448

Stephen D. Bruce, editor-in-chief. 1994. This book contains hundreds of sample job descriptions arranged by functional job category. The 1-3 page job descriptions cover what the worker normally does in the position, who they report to, and how that position fits in the organizational structure.

★6210★ "Registered Nurse" in *Career Information Center* (Vol.7)
Simon and Schuster
200 Old Tappan Rd.
Old Tappan, NJ 07675
Fax: 800-445-6991   Fr: 800-223-2348

Richard Lidz and Linda Perrin, editorial directors. Fifth edition, 1993. This 13-volume set profiles over 600 occupations. Each occupational profile describes job duties, entry-level requirements, educational requirements, advancement possibilities, employment outlook, working conditions, earnings and benefits, and where to write for more information.

★6211★ "Registered Nurse (R.N.)" in *100 Best Careers for the Year 2000* (pp. 12-14)
Arco Pub.
201 W. 103rd St.
Indianapolis, IN 46290
Ph: 800-428-5331   Fax: 800-835-3202

Shelly Field. 1992. Describes 100 job opportunities expected to grow fast throughout the next decade. Provides information on job duties and responsibilities, training requirements, education, advancement opportunities, experience and qualifications, and typical salaries.

★6212★ "Registered Nurse" in *VGM's Careers Encyclopedia* (pp. 301-304)
National Textbook Co. (NTC)
VGM Career Books
4255 W. Touhy Ave.
Lincolnwood, IL 60646-1975
Ph: (708)679-5500   Fax: (708)679-2494
Fr: 800-323-4900

Third edition, 1991. Describes job duties, places of employment, working conditions, qualifications, education, and training, advancement potential, and salary for each occupation.

★6213★ "Registered Nurses" in *101 Careers: A Guide to the Fastest-Growing Opportunities* (pp. 259-262)
John Wiley & Sons, Inc.
605 3rd Ave.
New York, NY 10158-0012
Ph: (212)850-6645   Fax: (212)850-6088

Michael Harkavy. 1990. Describes the nature of the job, working conditions, employment growth, qualifications, personal skills, projected salaries, and where to write for more information.

★6214★ "Registered Nurses" in *America's 50 Fastest Growing Jobs* (pp. 63)
JIST Works, Inc.
720 N. Park Ave.
Indianapolis, IN 46202-3431
Ph: (317)264-3720   Fax: (317)264-3709
Fr: 800-648-5478

Michael J. Farr, compiler. 1994. Describes the 50 fastest growing jobs within major career clusters such as technicians, and marketing and sales. Each job profile explains the nature of the work, skills and abilities required, employment outlook, average earnings, related occupations, education and training requirements, and employment opportunities. Also contains career planning information and job search tips.

★6215★ "Registered Nurses" in *Health Care Job Explosion!* (pp. 235-250)
D-Amp Publications
401 Amherst Ave.
Coraopolis, PA 15108
Ph: (412)262-5578

Dennis V. Damp. 1993. Provides information on the nature of work for the major health care occupational groups. Descriptions include working conditions, training, job outlook, qualifications, and related occupations.

★6216★ "Registered Nurses" in *Occupational Outlook Handbook*
U.S. Government Printing Office
Superintendent of Documents
Washington, DC 20402
Ph: (202)512-1800   Fax: (202)512-2250

Biennial; latest edition, 1994-95. Encyclopedia of careers describing about 250 occupations and comprising about 85 percent of all jobs in the economy. Occupations that require lengthy education or training are given the most attention. Each occupation's profile describes what the worker does on the job, working conditions, education and training requirements, advancement possibilities, job outlook, earnings, and sources of additional information.

★6217★ "Registered Nurses (R.N.)" in *Best Jobs for the 1990s and Into the 21st Century*
Impact Publications
9104-N Manassas Dr.
Manassas Park, VA 22111
Ph: (703)361-7300   Fax: (703)335-9486

Ronald L. Krannich and Caryl Rae Krannich. 1993.

★6218★ *Resume Writing for the Professional Nurse*
Continuing Education Systems, Inc.
112 S. Grant St.
Hinsdale, IL 60521
Ph: (312)654-2596

Nancy Kuzmich. 1988. Self-study guide written for the professional nurse on how to set career goals, interview for a job, and select the best job offer. Includes sample resumes and cover letters.

★6219★ "Speech-Language Pathologists" in *Career Discovery Encyclopedia* (Vol.6, pp. 48-49)
J.G. Ferguson Publishing Co.
200 W. Madison St., Ste. 300
Chicago, IL 60606
Ph: (312)580-5480   Fax: (312)580-4948
Russell E. Primm, editor-in chief. 1993. This six volume set contains two-page articles for 504 occupations. Each article describes job duties, earnings, and educational and training requirements. The whole set is arranged alphabetically by job title. Designed for junior high and older students.

★6220★ *Your Career in Nursing*
National League for Nursing (NLN)
350 Hudson St.
New York, NY 10014
Ph: (212)989-9393   Fr: 800-NOW-1NLN
Lila Anastas. Second edition, 1988. Describes types of nursing schools, salaries, specialties, opportunities, issues, and trends. Includes statistical information on nursing practice and education, graduate nursing, continuing education, and career mobility.

PROFESSIONAL ASSOCIATIONS

★6221★ American Association of Managed Care Nurses (AAMCN)
PO Box 4975
Glen Allen, VA 23058-4975
Ph: (804)747-9698   Fax: (804)747-5316

★6222★ American Association of Mental Health Professionals in Corrections (AAMHPC)
c/o John S. Zil, M.D., J.D.
PO Box 163359
Sacramento, CA 95816-9359
Ph: (707)864-0910   Fax: (707)864-0910
Members: Psychiatrists, psychologists, social workers, nurses, and other mental health professionals; individuals working in correctional settings. **Purpose:** Fosters the progress of behavioral sciences related to corrections. Goals are: to improve the treatment, rehabilitation, and care of the mentally ill, mentally retarded, and emotionally disturbed; to promote research and professional education in psychiatry and allied fields in corrections; to advance standards of correctional services and facilities; to foster cooperation between individuals concerned with the medical, psychological, social, and legal aspects of corrections; to share knowledge with other medical practitioners, scientists, and the public. Conducts scientific meetings to contribute to the advancement of the therapeutic community in all its institutional settings, including correctional institutions, hospitals, churches, schools, industry, and the family. **Publications:** *Corrective and Social Psychiatry*, quarterly.

★6223★ American Health Care Association (AHCA)
1201 L St. NW
Washington, DC 20005
Ph: (202)842-4444   Fax: (202)842-3860
Members: Federation of state associations of long-term health care facilities. **Purpose:** Promotes standards for professionals in long-term health care delivery and quality care for patients and residents in a safe environment. Focuses on issues of availability, quality, affordability, and fair payment. Operates as liaison with governmental agencies, Congress, and professional associations. Compiles statistics. **Publications:** *AHCA Notes*, monthly. • *Provider: For Long Term Care Professionals*, monthly. • *Thinking About a Nursing Home?*. • *Welcome to Our Nursing Home.*

★6224★ American Hospital Association (AHA)
1 N. Franklin, Ste. 27
Chicago, IL 60606
Ph: (312)422-3000   Fax: (312)422-4796
Members: Individuals and health care institutions including hospitals, health care systems, and pre- and postacute health care delivery organizations. **Purpose:** Is dedicated to promoting the welfare of the public through its leadership and assistance to its members in the provision of better health services for all people. Carries out research and education projects in such areas as health care administration, hospital economics, and community relations; represents hospitals in national legislation; offers programs for institutional effectiveness review, technology assessment, and hospital administrative services to hospitals; conducts educational programs furthering the in-service education of hospital personnel; collects and analyzes data; furnishes multimedia educational materials; maintains 44,000 volume health care administration library, and biographical archive. **Publications:** *AHANews*, weekly. • *Guide to the Health Care Field*, annual. • *Hospital Statistics*, annual. • *Hospitals and Health Networks*, biweekly.

★6225★ American Nurses Association (ANA)
600 Maryland Ave. SW, Ste. 100 W.
Washington, DC 20024-2571
Ph: (202)651-7000   Fax: (202)651-7001
Members: Member associations representing registered nurses. Sponsors American Nurses Foundation (for research), American Academy of Nursing , Center for Ethics and Human Rights, International Nursing Center, Ethnic/Racial Minority Fellowship Programs, and American Nurses Credentialing Center. Maintains hall of fame. **Publications:** *The American Nurse*, monthly. • *Facts About Nursing*, semiannual. • *Proceedings of the House of Delegates*, periodic.

★6226★ Association of Child and Adolescent Psychiatric Nurses (ACAPN)
1211 Locust St.
Philadelphia, PA 19107
Ph: (215)545-2843   Fax: (215)545-8107
Fr: 800-826-2950
Members: Nurses and others interested in child and adolescent psychiatry. **Purpose:** Works to promote mental health of infants, children, adolescents, and their families through clinical practice, public policy, and research. **Publications:** *ACAPN News*, 3/year. • *Journal of Child and Adolescent Psychiatric Nursing*, quarterly.

★6227★ National Association of Nurse Massage Therapists (NANMT)
PO Box 1268
Osprey, FL 34229
Ph: (813)966-6288   Fax: (813)918-0522
Members: Nurses and other healthcare professionals who practice massage therapy. **Purpose:** Promotes the integration of massage and other therapeutic forms of bodywork into existing healthcare practice. Promotes Nurse Massage Therapists as specialists within the nursing profession. Seeks to establish standards of professional practice and criteria for national certification of Nurse Massage Therapists. Educates the medical community and the general public about bodywork therapies. Monitors legislation. **Publications:** *NANMT Membership Directory*, annual. • *Nurse's Touch*, quarterly.

★6228★ National Student Nurses' Association (NSNA)
555 W. 57th St., Ste. 1327
New York, NY 10019
Ph: (212)581-2211   Fax: (212)581-2368
Members: Students enrolled in state-approved schools for the preparation of registered nurses. **Purpose:** Seeks to aid in the development of the individual nursing student and to urge students of nursing, as future health professionals, to be aware of and to contribute to improving the health care of all people. Encourages programs and activities in state groups concerning nursing, health, and the community. Provides assistance for state board review, as well as materials for preparation for state RN licensing examination. Cooperates with nursing organizations in recruitment of nurses and in professional, community, and civic programs. Sponsors essay writing contest for members. Sponsors Foundation of the National Student Nurses' Association in Honor of Frances Tompkins to award scholarships to student nurses. **Publications:** *Career Planning Guide*, annual. • *Convention News*. • *Dean's Notes*, 5/year. • *Imprint*, 5/year. • *NSNA News*, 5/year.

★6229★ Society of Trauma Nurses (STN)
1211 Locust St.
Philadelphia, PA 19107
Ph: (215)545-5687   Fax: (215)545-8107
Fr: 800-237-6966
Members: Nurses involved in all facets of trauma care. **Purpose:** Seeks to communicate trauma nursing information and recognize excellence and innovation in trauma nursing. Addresses legislative issues; assists in the development of standards. Facilitates research. **Publications:** *Journal of Trauma Nursing*, quarterly.

STANDARDS/CERTIFICATION AGENCIES

★6230★ American Health Care Association (AHCA)
1201 L St. NW
Washington, DC 20005
Ph: (202)842-4444   Fax: (202)842-3860
Promotes standards for professionals in long-term health care delivery and quality care for patients and residents in a safe environment. Focuses on issues of availability, quality, affordability, and fair payment.

★6231★ National Association of Nurse Massage Therapists (NANMT)
PO Box 1268
Osprey, FL 34229
Ph: (813)966-6288   Fax: (813)918-0522
Seeks to establish standards of professional practice and criteria for national certification of Nurse Massage Therapists. Educates the medical community and the general public about bodywork therapies.

★6232★ National League for Nursing (NLN)
350 Hudson St.
New York, NY 10014
Ph: (212)989-9393   Fax: (212)989-9256
Fr: 800-669-1656
Prepares tests for evaluating nursing student progress and nursing service tests. Nationally accredits nursing education programs and community health agencies.

TEST GUIDES

★6233★ ACT Proficiency Examination Program: Nursing
National Learning Corp.
212 Michael Dr.
Syosset, NY 11791
Ph: (516)921-8888   Fax: (516)921-8743
Fr: 800-645-6337
Jack Rudman. A series of practice test guides containing multiple-choice examinations designed to demonstrate proficiency in the subject of nursing. Titles in the series include *Adult Nursing; Commonalities in Nursing Care, Area I; Commonalities in Nursing Care, Area II; Differences in Nursing Care, Area I; Differences in Nursing Care, Area II; Differences in Nursing Care, Area III; Fundamentals of Nursing; Maternal and Child Nursing, Associate Degree; Maternal and Child Nursing, Baccalaureate Degree; Occupational Strategy, Nursing; Nursing Health Care; Professional Strategies, Nursing; Psychiatric/Mental Health Nursing; Maternity Nursing.*

★6234★ Addison-Wesley's Nursing Examination Review
Addison-Wesley Publishing Co.
1 Jacob Way
Reading, MA 01867
Ph: (617)944-3700   Fr: 800-358-4566
Sally L. Lagerquist and Geraldine C. Colombraro. Fourth edition, 1991, (paper). Includes a bibliography and an index.

★6235★ Admission Test Series: Nursing
National Learning Corp.
212 Michael Dr.
Syosset, NY 11791
Ph: (516)921-8888   Fax: (516)921-8743
Fr: 800-645-6337
Jack Rudman. A collection of sample examinations designed to prepare potential nurses for graduate and professional school entrance tests and for tests administered by private and public institutions for entrance and career advancement. Provides multiple-choice questions; includes correct answers. Titles in the series include *Nursing School Entrance Examinations for Registered and Graduate Nurses; State Nursing Boards for Registered Nurse; National Council Licensure Examination for Registered Nurses; Commission on Graduates of Foreign Nursing Schools Qualifying Examination.*

★6236★ Appleton and Lange's Review of Nursing for the New State Board Examination
Appleton and Lange
25 Van Zant St.
East Norwalk, CT 06855
Ph: (203)838-4400   Fr: 800-423-1359
Anna M. Desharnais, et al. Third edition, 1990. Preparation guide for medical-surgical nursing, maternal-child nursing, and psychiatric-mental health nursing. Contains Nursing Process Care Plans and multiple-choice questions.

★6237★ Career Examination Series: Registered Professional Nurse
National Learning Corp.
212 Michael Dr.
Syosset, NY 11791
Ph: (516)921-8888   Fax: (516)921-8743
Fr: 800-645-6337
Jack Rudman. A series of study guides with multiple-choice examination questions and solutions for trainees and professional nurses. Titles in the series include *Clinical Nurse; Community Mental Health Nurse; Head Nurse; Health Service Nurse; Infection Control Nurse; Mental Hygiene Nursing Program Coordinator; Nurse; Professional Nurse; Psychiatric Nurse; Public Health Nurse; Staff Nurse; Supervising Nurse; Supervising Public Health Nurse.*

★6238★ Certified Nurse Examination Series
National Learning Corp.
212 Michael Dr.
Syosset, NY 11791
Ph: (516)921-8888   Fax: (516)921-8743
Fr: 800-645-6337
Jack Rudman. Practice multiple-choice examinations for national certification of registered nurses. Includes solutions. Titles in the series include *Adult Nurse Practitioner; Child and Adolescent Nurse; Clinical Specialist in Adult Psychiatric and Mental Health Nursing; Clinical Specialist in Child and Adolescent Psychiatric and Mental Health Nursing; Clinical Specialist in Medical-Surgical Nursing; Community Health Nurse; Critical Care Nurse; Family Nurse Practitioner; Gerontological Nurse Practitioner; High Risk Perinatal Nurse; Maternal and Child Health Nurse; Medical-Surgical Nurse; Nursing Administration; Nursing Administration, Advanced; OB/GYN Nurse Practitioner; Pediatric Nurse Practitioner; Psychiatric and Mental Health Nurse; School Nurse Practitioner.*

★6239★ Emergency Nursing Examination Review
Springhouse Corp.
1111 Bethlehem Pk.
Spring House, PA 19477
Ph: (215)646-8700
Laura Gasparis Vonfrolio and Joanne Noone. Second edition, 1991. Includes bibliographies and an index. Illustrated.

★6240★ Lippincott's State Board Examination Review for NCLEX-PN
J. B. Lippincott Co.
227 E. Washington Sq.
Philadelphia, PA 19106
Ph: (215)238-4200
LuVerne Wolff Lewis. 1994. (paper). Includes a bibliography and an index.

★6241★ Mosby's AssessTest: A Practice Exam for RN Licensure
Mosby-Year Book, Inc.
11830 Westline Industrial Dr.
St. Louis, MO 63146
Ph: (314)872-8370   Fax: (314)432-1380
Fr: 800-325-4177
Delores F. Saxton. 1994.

★6242★ The National Council Licensure Examination for Registered Nurses
Chicago Review Press, Inc.
814 N. Franklin
Chicago, IL 60610
Ph: (312)337-0747
Eileen McQuaid and Carolyn J. Yocom. Fourth edition, 1988 (paper). Includes a bibliography.

★6243★ National Council Licensure Examination for Registered Nurses
Barron's Educational Series, Inc.
250 Wireless Blvd.
Hauppauge, NY 11788
Ph: (516)434-3311   Fax: (516)434-3723
Fr: 800-645-3476
Second edition. 1990.

★6244★ Nurse
Arco Publishing Co.
Macmillan General Reference
15 Columbus Cir.
New York, NY 10023
Fax: 800-835-3202   Fr: 800-858-7674
Carmen Sanchez. Seventh edition, 1987. A test guide for the registered, public health, or practical health nurse preparing for a civil service test.

★6245★ Nursing School Entrance Examinations
Arco Publishing Co.
Macmillan General Reference
15 Columbus Cir.
New York, NY 10023
Fax: 800-835-3202   Fr: 800-858-7674

Marion F. Gooding and Bernice Hughes. Twelfth edition, 1994. Contains sample questions for school entrance examinations for licensed practical and registered nurses with an explanation of the answers.

★6246★ Nursing School Entrance Examinations for Registered and Graduate Nurses
National Learning Corp.
212 Michael Dr.
Syosset, NY 11791
Ph: (516)921-8888   Fax: (516)921-8743
Fr: 800-645-6337

Jack Rudman. Part of the Admission Test series. A sample test for those seeking admission to graduate and professional schools or seeking entrance or advancement in institutional and public career service.

★6247★ Preparation for NCLEX-RN: Saunders Nursing Review and Practice Tests
W. B. Saunders Co.
W. Washington Sq.
Philadelphia, PA 19105
Ph: (215)238-7800

Dee Ann Gillies. Fourth edition, 1987. Includes bibliographies and an index.

★6248★ Regents College Proficiency Examination Series: Nursing
National Learning Corp.
212 Michael Dr.
Syosset, NY 11791
Ph: (516)921-8888   Fax: (516)921-8743
Fr: 800-645-6337

Jack Rudman. A series of sample tests for college credit-by-examination programs in the field of nursing. Multiple-choice style with answers included. Titles in the series includes *Adult Nursing; Fundamentals of Nursing; Maternal and Child Nursing—Associate; Maternal and Child Nursing—Baccalaureate; Medical-Surgical Nursing; Psychiatric-Mental Health Nursing.*

★6249★ Regents External Degree Series: Nursing
National Learning Corp.
212 Michael Dr.
Syosset, NY 11791
Ph: (516)921-8888   Fax: (516)921-8743
Fr: 800-645-6337

Jack Rudman. A multiple-choice examination for nursing professionals preparing to enter the Regents External Degree Program, an alternate route to a college degree. Test contains multiple-choice questions with answers provided. Titles in the series include *Commonalities in Nursing Care: Area A; Commonalities in Nursing Care: Area B; Differences in Nursing Care: Area A; Differences in Nursing Care: Area B; Differences in Nursing Care: Area C; Health Support: Area I; Health Support: Area II; Nursing Health Care; Occupational Strategy (Nursing); Professional Strategies (Nursing).*

★6250★ State Nursing Boards for Registered Nurse (SNB/RN)
National Learning Corp.
212 Michael Dr.
Syosset, NY 11791
Ph: (516)921-8888   Fax: (516)921-8743
Fr: 800-645-6337

Jack Rudman. Part of the Admission Test series. A sample test for those seeking admission to graduate and professional schools or seeking entrance or advancement in institutional and public career service.

EDUCATIONAL DIRECTORIES AND PROGRAMS

★6251★ Encyclopedia of Medical Organizations and Agencies
Gale Research Inc.
835 Penobscot Bldg.
Detroit, MI 48226-4094
Ph: (313)961-2242   Fax: (313)961-6741
Fr: 800-877-GALE
Karen Boyden, Contact

Biennial, November of odd years. Covers over 13,400 state, national, and international medical associations, foundations, research institutes, federal and state agencies, and medical and allied health schools. Entries include: Organization name, address, phone; many listings include names and titles of key personnel, descriptive annotations. Arrangement: Classified by subject, then by type of organization.

★6252★ Healthcare Career Directory—Nurses and Physicians
Gale Research Inc.
835 Penobscot Bldg.
Detroit, MI 48226-4094
Ph: (313)961-2242   Fax: (313)961-6083
Fr: 800-877-GALE

Bradley J. Morgan and Joseph M. Palmisano. Second edition, 1993. A directory in the Career Advisor Series that provides essays written by industry professionals; job search information on resume and cover letter preparation, networking, and the interviewing process; approximately 300 companies and organizations offering job opportunities and internships, and additional job-hunting resources.

★6253★ Medical and Health Information Directory
Gale Research Inc.
835 Penobscot Bldg.
Detroit, MI 48226-4094
Ph: (313)961-2242   Fax: (313)961-6741
Fr: 800-877-GALE
Karen Boyden, Contact

Approximately biennial; latest edition 1994. Covers in Volume 1, almost 18,600 medical and health oriented associations, organizations, institutions, and government agencies, including health maintenance organizations (HMOs), preferred provider organizations (PPOs), insurance companies, pharmaceutical companies, research centers, and medical and allied health schools. In Volume 2, nearly 11,800 medical book publishers; medi-

cal periodicals, directories, audiovisual producers and services, medical libraries and information centers, and electronic resources. In Volume 3, nearly 26,000 clinics, treatment centers, care programs, and counseling/diagnostic services for 30 subject areas. Entries include: Institution, service, or firm name, address, phone; many include names of key personnel Arrangement: Classified by organization activity, service, etc..

★6254★ National Directory of Nurse Practitioner Programs
Primary Health Care-FNP Program
Seattle, WA 98195
Phyllis Ann Zimmer, Contact

Covers about 140 certificate, bachelor's, and master's programs for nurse practitioners. Entries include: Institution name, address, phone, programs offered. Arrangement: Classified by program level, then geographical.

★6255★ School Guide
School Guide Publications
210 North Ave.
New Rochelle, NY 10801
Ph: (914)632-7771   Fax: (914)632-3412
Fr: 800-433-7771
Myles Ridder, Contact

Annual, March. Covers over 1,000 colleges, vocational schools, and nursing schools in the United States. Entries include: Institution name, address, phone, courses offered, degrees awarded. Arrangement: Classified by type of institution, then geographical.

★6256★ State-Approved Schools of Nursing: R.N.
National League for Nursing (NLN)
350 Hudson St.
New York, NY 10014
Ph: (212)989-9393   Fax: (212)989-3710
Fr: 800-669-1656
Nancy Jeffries

Annual, August. Covers associate degree, baccalaureate degree, and diploma programs offered in over 1,475 schools, leading to licensure as a registered nurse. Entries include: Name of school, address, names of deans and directors of programs, type of administrative control, sources of financial support, and information on National League for Nursing accreditation status. Arrangement: Geographical.

AWARDS, SCHOLARSHIPS, GRANTS, AND FELLOWSHIPS

★6257★ AACN Educational Advancement Scholarships for Graduates
American Association of Critical-Care Nurses (AACN)
101 Columbia
Aliso Viejo, CA 92656-1491
Ph: (714)362-2000

Qualifications: Candidates must be current AACN members, licensed as registered nurses, enrolled in a master's or doctorate level program, have a cumulative GPA of at least 3.0 on a 4.0 scale, and currently work in a critical unit or have worked in a critical care unit for at least one year in the last three years. Previous recipients are eligible to re-apply, but may receive no more than a total of $3,000. Members of the Board of Directors, Education Committee, and ACCN staff are not eligible. Funds available: 17 $1,500 scholarships. A minimum of 20 percent will be allocated to ethnic minorities. Recipients must also agree to participate in a follow-up study to discuss the impact of their degree on care of patients/families in critical care unit. Application details: Completed application forms (typed only) should include official tran-scripts of all coursework, verification of enroll-ment in a planned course of graduate study, verification of employment in a critical care unit for at least one year in the last three years, a curriculum vitae, a statement regard-ing how applicants see their nursing practice changing as a result of their graduate degree, and an exemplar (a situation where appli-cant's intervention made a difference in a pa-tient's outcome). Deadline: The 1993 dead-line was January 15.

★6258★ AACN Educational Advancement Scholarships for Undergraduates
American Association of Critical-Care Nurses (AACN)
101 Columbia
Aliso Viejo, CA 92656-1491
Ph: (714)362-2000

Qualifications: Candidates must be current AACN members, licensed as registered nurses, enrolled in an NLN-accredited bacca-laureate degree program in nursing with at least junior status, have a cumulative GPA of at least 3.0 on a 4.0 scale, and currently work in a critical unit or have worked in a critical care unit for at least one year in the last three years. Previous recipients are eligible to re-apply, but may receive no more than a total of $3,000. Members of the Board of Directors, Education Committee, and AACN staff are not eligible. Funds available: 37 $1,500 scholarships. A minimum of 20 percent will be allocated to ethnic minorities. Recipients must also agree to participate in a follow-up study to discuss impact of degree on care of patients/families in critical care units. Applica-tion details: Completed application forms (typed only) should include official transcripts of all coursework; verification of employment in a critical care unit for at least one year in the last three years; letter of enrollment from school of nursing director, faculty, or advisor that verifies junior or senior status; verifica-tion from Nursing Director of NLN accredita-tion status; and a statment regarding goals in returning to school and past and projected contributions to critical care nursing. Dead-line: The 1993 deadline was January 15.

★6259★ Luther Christman Award
American Assembly for Men in Nursing
PO Box 31753
Independence, OH 44131

To recognize a person who has demon-strated excellence, leadership, high stan-dards, principles, and contributions to the profession of nursing. A wood plaque with gold plate is awarded annually. Established in 1975 by Luther Christman, R.N., Ph.D.

★6260★ Hazel Corbin Assistance Fund Scholarships
Maternity Center Association
48 East 92nd St.
New York, NY 10128
Ph: (212)369-7300   Fax: (212)369-8747

Purpose: To support postgraduate studies in nurse-midwifery. Qualifications: Applicant may be of any nationality, but must be a regis-tered nurse who plans on practicing nurse-midwifery in the United States. Scholarships are intended to cover the daily living ex-penses of students enrolled in postgraduate courses in nurse-midwifery. Awards will not be given for other courses of study. Funds available: $50-1,000. Application details: Write to the Association for application guide-lines. Deadline: None.

★6261★ Department of Veterans Affairs Health Professional Scholarship Award
Department of Veterans Affairs
810 Vermont Ave, NW
Washington, DC 20420

Qualifications: Applicants must be accepted for enrollment as full-time students in an edu-cation program that is nationally accredited by either the National League for Nursing, American Physical Therapy Association, American Occupational Therapy Association, or the American Association of Nurse Anes-thetists. Applicants must be citizens of the United States. Associate degree nursing stu-dents in their last year of study, and third-and-fourth year nursing students in baccalaureate degree nursing, physical therapym, and oc-cupational therapy may apply. Students in masters degree programs in physical ther-apy, nurse anasthetesia, and certain spe-ciallty areas for nursing, physical therapy, and occupational therapy may also apply. Registered nurses may apply if they enrolled full-time or accepted for enrollment in an ac-credited baccalaureate nursing program or specialized masters program. These spe-cialty programs vary, and a list of the pro-grams can be obtained from the Department of Veterans Affairs (VA) at the above ad-dress. Selection criteria: Selections are based on academic performance; recom-mendation from the applicant's college/uni-versity Dean or Program Director of nursing, physical therapy, or occupational therapy; ca-reer goals; and work and/or volunteer recom-mendation and experiences. Funds avail-able: The award provides direct payment for up to two years for tuition and fees to the participant's college/university, and provides an annual payment for books and other costs, and a tax-free stipend of $621 per month to the participant for the length of the award. The award is repaid through service obli-gation, where the participant works full-time as a registered nurse, nurse anesthetist, physical therapist, or occupational therapist at one of the VA medical centers in the United States. Service will not be in any branch of the armed forces or any other Federal agency. The minimum obligated service is two years upon completion of degree require-ments and attainment of licensure or certifica-tion. Application details: Applicants can ob-tain application materials and application Information Bulletins by sending their name, address, and identifying the award for which they wish information, to Health Professional

Scholarship Program (143 B) at the above address. Applications are available each March. Deadline: Applications must be post-marked no later than the last Tuesday in May.

★6262★ Department of Veterans Affairs Reserve Member Stipend Program Award
Department of Veterans Affairs
810 Vermont Ave., NW
Washington, DC 20420

Qualifications: Applicants must be accepted for enrollment as full-time students in an edu-cation program that is nationally accredited by either the National League for Nursing, American Physical Therapy Association, American Occupational Therapy Association, or the American Association of Nurse Anes-thetists. Applicants must be citizens of the United States. Associate degree nursing stu-dents in their last year of study, and third-and-fourth year nursing students in baccalaureate degree nursing may apply. Entry-level mas-ters students in nursing, physical therapy, and occupational therapy may also apply. Also eligible are reservists who are members of the Selected Ready Reserves, eligible for the Reserve GI Bill, and have a score above the 50th percentile on the Armed Forces Qualification Test. Rregistered nurses may apply if enrolled full-time or accepted for en-rollment in an accredited nursing program. Selection criteria: Selections are based on academic performance; recommendation from the applicant's college/university Dean or Program Director of nursing, physical ther-apy, or occupational therapy; career goals; work and/or volunteer recommendation and experiences; and commander's recommen-dation. Funds available: Awards have a maxi-mum length of 24 months of funding support and pay $400 per month while the reservist is enrolled in full-time course work. Reservists may also receive the Reserve GI Bill. The award is repaid through service obligation, where the participant works full-time as a reg-istered nurse, nurse anesthetist, physical therapist, or occupational therapist at one of the VA medical centers in the United States. Service will not be in any branch of the armed forces or any other Federal agency. The mini-mum obligated service is two years upon completion of degree requirements and at-tainment of licensure or certification. Applica-tion details: Applicants can obtain application materials and Application Information Bulle-tins by sending their name, address, and identifying the award for which they wish in-formation, to Health Professional Scholarship Program (143 B) at the above address. Appli-cations are available each March. Deadline: Applications must be submitted and post-marked no later than the last Tuesday in May.

★6263★ Distinguished Scholar Program
American Nurses Foundation
600 Maryland Ave. SW, Ste. 100W
Washington, DC 20024-2571
Ph: (202)554-4444   Fax: (202)554-2262

To facilitate analysis of policy related to eco-nomics, delivery of nursing services, nursing practice, and nursing education. U.S. regis-tered nurses are named by the ANF Board of Trustees. A grant to conduct a project is awarded when determined by the ANF Board of Trustees. Established in 1984.

★6264★ Anna M. Fillmore Award
National League for Nursing
350 Hudson St.
New York, NY 10014
Ph: (212)989-9393   Fax: (212)989-3710

To recognize an individual nurse who demonstrates or has shown unusual leadership in developing and administering community health services on a local, state, or national level. A plaque is awarded biennially. Established in 1976.

★6265★ Caroline Holt Nursing Scholarships
National Society Daughters of The American Revolution
DAR Scholarship Committee
1776 D St., NW
Washington, DC 20006
Ph: (202)879-3292

Qualifications: Applicants must be United States citizens. The award is for any year of undergraduate study in an accredited school of nursing. No affiliation with the DAR is necessary. However, all applicants mut be sponsored by a local DAR Chapter. Selection criteria: Applicants are judged on the basis of academic excellence, commitment to field of study, and financial need. Funds available: $500. Application details: Write or call Office of Committees for application forms. A self-addressed, stamped envelope must accompany application requests. Applicants must submit a formal application, along with accompanying material, including: a statement of 1,000 words or less setting forth career goals and relevance of academic program to future profession; a financial need form; an official transcript of grades and test scores from high school; and a list of all extra-curricular activities, honors, and scholastic achievements. At least two and not more than four letters of recommendation from persons in authority at the student's high school who know the student's work, and a photocopy of the student's birth certificate or naturalization papers are also required. Proof of acceptance into a school of nursing program is required prior to payment of the scholarship. Deadline: Applications must be sent to the National Chairman by February 15 or August 15.

★6266★ Honorary Human Rights Award
American Nurses' Association
600 Maryland Ave. SW, Ste. 100W
Washington, DC 20024-2571
Ph: (202)554-4444   Fax: (202)554-2262

For recognition of an outstanding commitment to human rights and exemplifying the essence of nursing's philosophy about humanity. Current SNA members are eligible. The deadline for nominations is October. Awarded biennially. Established in 1986.

★6267★ HRSA-BHP Professional Nurse Traineeship
U.S. Public Health Service
Health Resources and Services Administration
Parklawn Bldg., Rm. 8-38
5600 Fishers Ln.
Rockville, MD 20857

Purpose: To meet the cost of traineeships for individuals in advanced degree nursing education programs, and to educate individuals to serve in and prepare for practice as nurse practitioners, nurse midwives, nurse educators, public health nurses, or in any other clinical nursing specialties. Qualifications: Candidates must be United States citizens, non-citizen nationals, or foreign nationals who possess a visa permitting permanent residence in the United States. They must be currently licensed as a registered nurse in a state, or have completed basic nursing preparations in a masters of nursing program (as determined by the school). They are also required to be enrolled full-time in eligible graduate programs and be pursuing a masters or doctoral degree. Preference will be given to individuals who are residents of health professional shortage areas designated under Section 332 of the Public Health Service Act. Selection criteria: Recipients are selected by the participating instututions in accordance with the institutions' admission policies and the purpose of the traineeship program. Funds available: Stipend up to $8,800 for tuition, books, fees and reasonable living expenses for a maximum of 36 months of study.

★6268★ Jean MacVicar Outstanding Nurse Executive Award
National League for Nursing
350 Hudson St.
New York, NY 10014
Ph: (212)989-9393   Fax: (212)989-3710

To recognize an individual for excellence in leadership, achievement, and creativity of national significance in the field of nursing service administration. A plaque is presented biennially at the convention. Established in 1983.

★6269★ NAPNAP-McNeil Scholarships
National Association of Pediatric Nurse Associates and Practitioners
1101 Kings Hwy. N., Ste. 206
Cherry Hill, NJ 08034
Ph: (609)667-1773   Fax: (609)667-7187

Qualifications: Applicants must be registered nurses with previous work experience in pediatrics, but have no formal nurse practitioner education. Candidates must demonstrate financial need and be accepted into a recognized pediatric nurse practitioner program either at continuing education or master's levels. Selection criteria: Applicants who make a formal committment to work in a geographic area of need or with an underserved population are given preference. Funds available: $2,000. Application details: A formal application is required. Candidates must present a philosophy and goals statement related to the use of PNP education, and employment plans after completion of the program. Description of how the employment plan fits the criterion of working in underserved population areas. A budget of expenses and income for the period for which the scholarship is requested must be presented. Deadline: Applications must be postmarked by September 30 for spring semester programs and May 30 for fall semester programs.

★6270★ NEF Scholarships
Nurses' Educational Funds, Inc. (NEF)
555 West 57th St.
New York, NY 10019
Ph: (212)582-8820

Purpose: To assist registered nurses with advanced study. Qualifications: Applicant must be a U.S. citizen or permanent resident with the intent to become a citizen. Applicant must be a registered nurse and a member of a national professional nursing association, and be enrolled in or applying to a master's or doctoral level program accredited by the National League for Nursing. Funds available: $2,500-10,000. Application details: Write to NEF for an application kit. Include U.S.$5.00 check. The kits are availabe between 1 August and 1 February. Deadline: 1 March. Successful applicants will be notified at the end of April or the beginning of May.

★6271★ Nurses' Educational Funds
Nurses' Educational Funds, Inc. (NEF)
555 West 57th St.
New York, NY 10019
Ph: (212)582-8820

Purpose: To fund registered nurses for higher education. Qualifications: Applicants must be registered nurses and members of a national, professional nursing association. They must be enrolled in or applying to a National League for Nursing accredited Master's program in nursing. If applicants are at the doctoral level, they must be in a nursing or nursing-related program and they must have their GRE/MAT scores. Selection criteria: Selection is based on academic excellence, current service to the profession, and potential for future service. Funds available: $2,500 to $10,000 is available for qualified nurses. Approximately 16 awards are given. Application details: Applicants must send $5.00 for an application kit. Applications will not be mailed after February 1. Deadline: March 1.

★6272★ Mary Adelaide Nutting Award
National League for Nursing
350 Hudson St.
New York, NY 10014
Ph: (212)989-9393   Fax: (212)989-3710

To recognize outstanding leadership and achievement in nursing education or service having more than local or regional significance. Individuals and groups of any country are eligible. A silver medal is awarded biennially. Established in 1943.

★6273★ Oncology Nursing Foundation Doctoral Scholarship
Oncology Nursing Foundation
501 Holiday Dr.
Pittsburgh, PA 15220-2749
Ph: (412)921-7373   Fax: (412)921-6565

Qualifications: Applicants must currently be licensed to practice as a registered nurse, and have an interest in and commitment to cancer nursing. They must currently be enrolled in or applying to a doctoral nursing degree or related program. Funds available: Five scholarships at $2,500 are awarded. Deadline: January 15.

★6274★ Oncology Nursing Foundation Graduate Scholarship
Oncology Nursing Foundation
501 Holiday Dr.
Pittsburgh, PA 15220-2749
Ph: (412)921-7373   Fax: (412)921-6565

Qualifications: Applicants must currently be licensed to practice as a registered nurse and have an interest in and commitment to cancer nursing. They must currently be enrolled in a graduate degree program in a NLN accredited school of Nursing. Funds available: Eight scholarships of $2,500 are awarded. Deadline: January 15.

★6275★ Oncology Nursing Foundation Undergraduate Scholarship
Oncology Nursing Foundation
501 Holiday Dr.
Pittsburgh, PA 15220-2749
Ph: (412)921-7373   Fax: (412)921-6565

Qualifications: Applicants must currently be licensed to practice as a registered nurse, and have an interest in and commitment to cancer nursing. They Must currently be enrolled in an undergraduate nursing degree program in a NLN accredited school of Nursing. Funds available: Ten scholarships of $1,000 each are awarded. Deadline: January 15.

★6276★ Recognition Award
National Association of School Nurses
PO Box 1300
Scarborough, ME 04070-1300
Ph: (207)883-2117   Fax: (207)883-2683

To recognize school nurses for their contributions to school nursing and NASN. Individuals, not necessarily school nurses, who have made outstanding achievements in the field are eligible. A special recognition plaque is awarded when merited. Established in 1976.

★6277★ Linda Richards Awards
National League for Nursing
350 Hudson St.
New York, NY 10014
Ph: (212)989-9393   Fax: (212)989-3710

To recognize a unique contribution of a pioneering nature to the field of nursing. Citizens of the United States who are active in nursing are eligible. An engraved pin bearing the likeness of Linda Richards centered on a maltese cross is awarded biennially. Established in 1962 by the Alumnae Association of the New England Hospital for Women and Children, Roxbury, MA.

★6278★ Martha E. Rogers Award
National League for Nursing
350 Hudson St.
New York, NY 10014
Ph: (212)989-9393   Fax: (212)989-3710

For recognition of a nurse scholar who has made significant contributions to nursing knowledge that advance the science of nursing. A plaque is awarded biennially. Established in 1985.

★6279★ School Nurse of the Year
National Association of School Nurses
PO Box 1300
Scarborough, ME 04070-1300
Ph: (207)883-2117   Fax: (207)883-2683

To recognize a school nurse who has done outstanding work. Each state school nurse association may nominate one candidate for this award. The person cannot be a nursing supervisor or an officer of the school nurse association. A plaque is awarded and expenses are paid to the NASN annual conference. Established in 1984.

★6280★ NSNA Frances Tompkins Breakthrough to Nursing Scholarships for Ethnic People of Color
The Foundation of the National Student Nurses' Association, Inc.
555 W. 57th St., Ste. 1325
New York, NY 10019
Ph: (212)581-2215

Qualifications: Applicants must be minority students who are currently enrolled in a state-approved school of nursing or pre-nursing in a program leading to an associate or baccalaureate degree, a diploma, or a generic doctorate or master's degree. Selection criteria: Awards are based on academic achievement, financial need, and involvement in nursing student organizations and community activities related to health care. All factors are weighed equally. Funds available: Scholarships range from $1,000 to $2,500 each. In 1992-93, more than $100,000 in scholarship funds were awarded. Application details: Students must submit a copy of their recent nursing school and college transcripts or grade reports and a $5 processing fee along with completed applications. NSNA members must submit proof of their membership. Application forms are available by sending a self-addressed, legal-size envelope with 52 cents postage. They are available from September through January. Deadline: February 1. Recipients are notified by March.

★6281★ NSNA Frances Tompkins Career Mobility Scholarships
The Foundation of the National Student Nurses' Association, Inc.
555 W. 57th St., Ste. 1325
New York, NY 10019
Ph: (212)581-2215

Qualifications: Applicants must be registered nurses who are enrolled in a state-approved school of nursing or pre-nursing in a program leading to a baccalaureate degree with a major in nursing. They may also be licensed practical/vocational nurses who are enrolled in a program that will lead to registered nurse licensure. Selection criteria: Awards are based on academic achievement, financial need, and involvement in nursing student organizations and community activities related to health care. All factors are equally weighed. Funds available: Scholarships range from $1,000 to $2,500 each. In 1992-93, more than $100,000 in scholarship funds were awarded. Application details: Students must submit copies of their recent nursing school and college transcripts or grade reports, nursing licenses, and a $5 processing fee along with completed applications. Members of NSNA must submit proof of their membership. Application forms are available by sending a self-addressed, legal-size envelope with 52 cents postage. They are available from September through January. Deadline: February 1. Recipients are notified by March.

★6282★ Frances Tompkins Speciality Scholarships
The Foundation of the National Student Nurses' Association, Inc.
555 W. 57th St., Ste. 1325
New York, NY 10019
Ph: (212)581-2215

Qualifications: Applicants must be currently enrolled in a state-approved school of nursing or pre-nursing in a program leading to an associate or baccalaureate degree, a diploma, or a generic doctorate or master's degree. Some area of specialty must also be acknowledged. Selection criteria: Awards are based on academic achievement, financial need, and involvement in nursing student organizations and community activities related to health care. All factors are weighed equally. Funds available: Scholarships range from $1,000 to $2,500 each. In 1992-93, more than $100,000 in scholarship funds were awarded. Application details: Students must submit a copy of their recent nursing school and college transcripts or grade reports and a $5 processing fee along with completed applications. Members of NSNA must submit proof of their membership. Application forms are available by sending a self-addressed, legal-size envelope with 52 cents postage. They are available from September through January. Deadline: February 1. Recipients are notified by March.

★6283★ Veterans Affairs Health Professional Scholarship Awards
U.S. Department of Veterans Affairs
Central Office
810 Vermont Ave., NW
Washington, DC 20420
Ph: (202)535-7527

Purpose: To provide an adequate supply of nurses, occupational therapists, and physical therapists for the Department of Veterans Affairs and the nation. Qualifications: Applicants must be U.S. citizens, and accepted for enrollment or enrolled full-time in a nursing program accredited by the National League of Nursing, an occupational therapy program accredited by the American Occupational Therapy Association, or a physical therapy program accredited by the American Physical Therapy Association. Applicants may not be obligated for service under any other scholarship program. VA employees who meet eligibility may apply. Selection criteria: Selection is based upon academic performance, career goals, recommendations, and work/volunteer experience. Funds available: Tuition/fees, reasonable educational expenses, and a monthly stipend of $621, all exempt from Federal taxation. Application details: Applications are available from college/university financial aid offices, deans of Nursing, program directors of Occupational Therapy or Physical Therapy, all VA medical centers, and the VA Central Office. Deadline: May.

BASIC REFERENCE GUIDES AND HANDBOOKS

★6284★ Definitions
Springhouse Corp.
1111 Bethlehem Pike
Spring House, PA 19477
Ph: (215)646-8700

1987. Contains nursing terms, drug names and interactions, and an anatomical atlas.

★6285★ Diseases
Springhouse Corp.
1111 Bethlehem Pike
Spring House, PA 19477
Ph: (215)646-8700

1992. Includes bibliographies and index.

★6286★ Duncan's Dictionary for Nurses
Springer Publishing Co.
536 Broadway, 11th Fl.
New York, NY 10012
Ph: (212)431-4370

Helen A. Duncan. Second edition, 1989.

★6287★ Mosby's Medical Dictionary
Mosby-Year Book, Inc.
11830 Westline Industrial Dr.
St. Louis, MO 63146
Ph: (314)872-8370   Fax: (314)432-1380
Fr: 800-325-4177

Walter D. Glanze, Kenneth N. Anderson, and Lois E. Anderson, editors. 1993. Illustrated.

★6288★ Mosby's Pharmacology in Nursing
Mosby-Year Book, Inc.
11830 Westline Industrial Dr.
St. Louis, MO 63146
Ph: (314)872-8370   Fax: (314)432-1380
Fr: 800-325-4177

nne Burgess Hahn, et al., editors. Eighteenth edition, 1991. This textbook contains information for nurses on drug therapy.

★6289★ Nursing
Springhouse Corp.
1111 Bethlehem Pike
Spring House, PA 19477
Ph: (215)646-8700

Maryanne Wagner, editor. Monthly. Practical nursing journal focusing on hospital nurses; includes articles for critical-care nurses and nurse managers.

★6290★ The Nursing Clinics of North America
W. B. Saunders Co.
Curtis Center
Independence Sq., W.
Philadelphia, PA 19106
Ph: (215)238-7800   Fr: 800-654-2452

Carol Wolfe, editor. Quarterly.

★6291★ The Nursing Process: Assessing, Planning, Implementing, Evaluating
Appleton and Lange
PO Box 56303
Norwalk, CT 06856
Ph: (203)838-4400   Fr: 800-423-1359

Helen Yura and Mary B. Walsh. Fifth edition, 1988. Covers nursing research, computers in nursing, and the future of nursing. Includes nursing diagnosis and case studies.

★6292★ Operating Room Nursing Handbook
Warren H. Green, Inc.
8356 Olive Blvd.
St. Louis, MO 63132
Ph: (324)991-1335

Nancy Girard. 1991.

PROFESSIONAL AND TRADE PERIODICALS

★6293★ American Journal of Nursing
American Journal of Nursing Co.
555 W. 57th St.
New York, NY 10019
Ph: (212)582-8820   Fax: (212)586-5462
Martin DiCarlantonio

Monthly. Journal for staff nurses, nurse managers, and clinical nurse specialists. Focuses on patient care in hospitals, hospital ICUs and homes. Provides news coverage of health care from the nursing perspective.

★6294★ The American Nurse
American Nurses Assn.
600 Maryland Ave. SW, Ste. 100
Washington, DC 20024-2571
Ph: (202)651-7000   Fax: (202)651-7001
Fr: 800-274-4262
Mandy Mikulencak

Newspaper (tabloid) for the nursing profession.

★6295★ American Society of Ophthalmic Registered Nurses— Insight
American Society of Ophthalmic Registered Nurses
PO Box 193030
San Francisco, CA 94119
Ph: (415)561-8513
Kay McCoy

Bimonthly. Designed to facilitate continuing education of registered nurses through the study, discussion, and exchange of knowledge, experience, and ideas in the field of ophthalmology. Features news of research and innovations in the field.

★6296★ AONE News
American Organization of Nurse Executives (AONE)
AHA Bldg.
840 N. Lake Shore Dr.
Chicago, IL 60611
Ph: (312)280-6409   Fax: (312)280-5995
Jacqueline M. Sapiente

Monthly. Discusses all aspects of improving the management and administration of nursing service in health care institutions. Disseminates information on administrative problems and profiles successful operations. Recurring features include let.

★6297★ Beginnings
American Holistic Nurses' Association
4101 Lake Boone Trail, Ste. 201
Raleigh, NC 27607
Ph: (919)787-5181   Fax: (919)787-4916
Noreen Frisch

Functions as the official newsletter of the Association, which seeks to "renew and enhance the art of nurturing and caring for the whole person." Offers educational information on holistic nursing and healing modalities, and provides news of the Association. Recurring features include editorials, news of research, letters to the editor, news of members, book reviews, a social and ethical column, and a calendar of events.

★6298★ Imprint
National Student Nurses Assn., Inc.
555 W. 57th St.
New York, NY 10019
Ph: (212)581-2211   Fax: (212)581-2368
Caroline Jaffe

Magazine for nursing students, focusing on issues and trends in nursing education.

★6299★ New York State Nursing Association—Report
Tammy Krutz, Contact

Contains news and features on nurses and nursing issues. Also provides information on the activities of the New York State Nurses Association. Recurring features include news of research, a calendar of events, and news of educational opportunities. Columns include Ask the Experts and Legislative Power.

★6300★ The Nightingale
National Association of Physician Nurses
900 S. Washington St., No. G13
Falls Church, VA 22046-4020
Ph: (703)237-8616
Sue Young

Monthly. Presents items on "medical and personal subjects pertaining to office nurses and other staff."

★6301★ The Nurse Practitioner
Vernon Publications Inc.
3000 Northup Way, Ste. 200
PO Box 96043
Bellevue, WA 98009-9643
Ph: (206)827-9900   Fax: (206)822-9372
Linda J. Pearson

Monthly. Magazine presenting clinical information to nurses in advanced primary care practice. Also covers legal, business, economic, ethical, research, pharmaceutical, and theoretical issues.

★6302★ Nursing Outlook
Mosby-Year Book, Inc.
11830 Westline Industrial Dr.
St. Louis, MO 63146
Ph: (314)872-8370   Fax: (314)432-1380
Fr: 800-325-4177
Jo Ann Anzalone

Bimonthly. Official magazine of the American Academy of Nursing, reporting on trends and issues in nursing.

★6303★ Nursing Research
American Journal of Nursing Co.
555 W. 57th St.
New York, NY 10019-2961
Ph: (212)582-8820   Fax: (212)315-3187
Florence Downs

Bimonthly. Magazine focusing on nursing research.

★6304★ RN Magazine
Medical Economics Publishing
5 Paragon Drive
Montvale, NJ 07645-1742
Ph: (201)358-7208   Fax: (201)573-1045
Marianne Dekker Mattera

Monthly. Clinical journal for registered nurses.

PROFESSIONAL MEETINGS AND CONVENTIONS

★6305★ The AJN Conference on Medical-Surgical and Geriatric Nursing
George Little Management, Inc.
10 Bank St., Ste. 1200
White Plains, NY 10606-1933
Ph: (914)421-3200   Fax: (914)948-6180
Annual. **Dates and Locations:** 1995 Oct.

★6306★ American Association of Critical-Care Nurses National Teaching Institute & Critical Care Exposition
American Association of Critical-Care
  Nurses
101 Columbia
Aliso Viejo, CA 92656
Ph: (714)362-2000   Fax: (714)362-2020
Annual. Always held during May. **Dates and Locations:** 1996 May 19-23; Anaheim, CA. • 1997 May 18-22; Orlando, FL. • 1998 May 30-04; Los Angeles, CA. • 1999 May 17-16; New Orleans, LA. • 2000 May 21-25; Orlando, FL.

★6307★ American Nephrology Nurses Association Symposium
Anthony J. Jannetti, Inc.
N. Woodbury Rd., Box 56
Pitman, NJ 08071
Ph: (609)589-2319   Fax: (609)589-7463
Annual.

★6308★ American Nurses Association Convention
American Nurses Association, Council of
  Community Health Nurses
600 Maryland Ave., SW, No. 100 W
Washington, DC 20024-2571
Ph: (202)554-4444   Fax: (202)554-2262
Biennial. **Dates and Locations:** 1996

★6309★ American Organization of Nurse Executives Meeting and Exposition
American Hospital Association
Convention and Meetings Division
840 N. Lake Shore Dr.
Chicago, IL 60611
Ph: (312)280-6000   Fax: (312)280-5995
Annual.

★6310★ Association of Operating Room Nurses Annual Congress
Association of Operating Room Nurses
  (AORN)
Highpoint Office Bldg.
2170 S. Parker Rd., Ste. 300
Denver, CO 80231-5711
Ph: (303)755-6300   Fax: (303)755-4511
Annual. **Dates and Locations:** 1996 Mar 03-08; Dallas, TX. • 1997 Apr 06-11; Anaheim, CA. • 1998 Mar 28-03; Orlando, FL.

★6311★ Association of Pediatric Oncology Nurses
The Phenix Corp.
11512 Allecingie Pkwy.
Richmond, VA 23235
Ph: (804)379-9150   Fax: (804)379-1386
Annual.

★6312★ National Association of Orthopedic Nurses Annual Congress
Anthony J. Jannetti, Inc.
N. Woodbury Rd., Box 56
Box 56
Pitman, NJ 08071
Ph: (609)589-2319   Fax: (609)589-7463
Annual. **Dates and Locations:** 1996 May 31-05; Dallas, TX. • 1997 May 18-22; Philadelphia, PA.

★6313★ National League for Nursing Convention
Slack, Inc.
6900 Grove Rd.
Thorofare, NJ 08086
Ph: (609)848-1000   Fax: (609)853-5991
Biennial.

★6314★ Nurses Care Fair
Texas Nurses Association
7600 Burnet Rd., Ste. 440
Austin, TX 78757
Ph: (512)452-0645   Fax: (512)452-0648

★6315★ Nursing Management Congress and Exposition
Conference Management Corp.
200 Connecticut Ave.
Norwalk, CT 06856
Ph: (203)852-0500   Fax: (203)838-3710
Fr: 800-243-3238
Annual. Always held during the Fall.

★6316★ World Conference of Operating Room Nurses
Association of Operating Room Nurses
  (AORN)
Highpoint Office Bldg
2170 S. Parker Rd., Ste. 300
Denver, CO 80231
Ph: (303)755-6300   Fax: (303)752-0299
Biennial. **Dates and Locations:** 1995.

OTHER SOURCES OF INFORMATION

★6317★ Creative Tuition Programs for Nursing Tuition
American Hospital Association (AHA)
840 N. Lake Shore Dr.
Chicago, IL 60611
Ph: (312)280-6000
1988. One-page sheet listing colleges offering creative tuition programs. Also lists colleges with special registered nursing degree programs for persons who already have a bachelor degree.

★6318★ Entrepreneuring: A Nurse's Guide to Starting a Business
National League for Nursing (NLN)
10 Columbus Circle
New York, NY 10019
Ph: (212)582-1022   Fr: 800-NOW-1NLN
Gerry Vogel and Nancy Doleysh. 1988. Includes an index.

★6319★ Exploring Careers in Nursing
Rosen Publishing Group
29 E. 21st St.
New York, NY 10010
Ph: 800-237-9932   Fax: (212)777-0277
Jackie Heron. Revised edition, 1990.

★6320★ The Nurses's Guide to Starting a Small Business
Pilot Books
103 Cooper St.
Babylon, NY 11702
Ph: (516)422-2225   Fax: (516)422-2227
1992.

★6321★ Nursing Today: Transition and Trends
W.B. Saunders Co.
Independence Sq. W.
Philadelphia, PA 19106
Ph: (215)238-7800
1994.

★6322★ "Registered Nurse" in 100 Best Jobs for the 1990s & Beyond
Dearborn Financial Publishing, Inc.
520 N. Dearborn St.
Chicago, IL 60610-4354
Ph: (312)836-4400   Fax: (312)836-1021
Fr: 800-621-9621
Carol Kleiman. 1992. Describes 100 jobs ranging from accountants to veterinarians.. Each job profile includes such information as education, experience, and certification needed, salaries, and job search suggestions.

★6323★ "Registered Nurse (RN)" in Allied Health Professions (pp. 9-11; 135)
Arco Publishing Co.
Simon & Schuster, Inc.
201 W. 103rd St.
Indianapolis, IN 46290
Ph: (516)428-5331   Fax: 800-835-3202
1993. Contains information on 28 representative careers in health care. Provides a sample of the Allied Health Professions Admission Test, lists professional societies and associa-

tions, and offers a directory of schools and programs for the careers listed.

★6324★ *Survival Skills in the Workplace: What Every Nurse Should Know*
American Nurses' Association
600 Maryland Ave., SW, Ste. 100W
Washington, DC 20024-2571
Ph: (202)554-4444
Lyndia Flanagan. 1990.

Respiratory Therapists

Respiratory therapists, also known as **respiratory care practitioners**, specialize in the evaluation, treatment, and care of patients with breathing disorders. They treat all sorts of patients, from premature infants whose lungs are not fully developed to elderly people with chronic asthma or emphysema and emergency care for heart failure, stroke, drowning, or shock victims.

Salaries

Salaries for respiratory therapists are as follows:

Lowest 10 percent	Less than $21,528/year
Respiratory therapists, hospitals	$32,084/year
Top 10 percent	More than $48,048/year

Employment Outlook

Growth rate until the year 2005: Much faster than the average.

Respiratory Therapists

CAREER GUIDES

★6325★ Allied Health Professions
Simon & Schuster, Inc.
200 Old Tappan Rd.
Old Tappan, NJ 07675
1993. Includes information on available jobs, required training, a directory of training programs, and a full-sample Allied Health Professions Admission Test (AHPAT).

★6326★ Careers in Social and Rehabilitation Services
National Textbook Co. (NTC)
VGM Career Books
4255 W. Touhy Ave.
Lincolnwood, IL 60646-1975
Ph: (708)679-5500   Fax: (708)679-2494
Fr: 800-323-4900
Geraldine O. Garner, Ph.D., editor. 1993. Describes dozens of careers in the field of social and rehabilitation services.

★6327★ The Health Care Worker: An Introduction to Health Occupations
Prentice-Hall, Inc.
200 Old Tappan Rd.
Old Tappan, NJ 07675
Ph: (201)767-5000
Shirley A. Badasch, and Doreen S. Chesebro. Second edition, 1988. Includes a bibliography and an index.

★6328★ Health Careers
Careers, Inc.
PO Box 135
Largo, FL 34649-0135
Ph: (813)584-7333
1994. Four-page brief describing duties, working conditions, personal qualifications, training, earnings and hours, employment outlook, places of employment, related careers, and where to write for more information.

★6329★ Life and Breath
American Association for Respiratory Care (AARC)
11030 Abies Ln.
Dallas, TX 75229
Ph: (214)243-2272
1987. Videocassette recording that discusses the career possibilities of a respiratory therapist.

★6330★ "Respiration Therapist" in Profitable Careers in Non-Profit (pp. 92-93)
John Wiley and Sons, Inc.
605 3rd Ave.
New York, NY 10158-0012
Ph: (212)850-6000   Fax: (212)850-6088
Fr: 800-526-5368
William Lewis and Carol Milano. 1987. Examines nonprofit organizations and the career opportunities they offer. Offers tips on how to target and explore occupational opportunities in the nonprofit sector.

★6331★ Respiratory Care: A Career for Now and the Future
American Association for Respiratory Care
11030 Abies Ln.
Dallas, TX 75229
Ph: (214)243-2272
This six-panel brochure describes the work of the respiratory therapist, educational preparation, and employment outlook.

★6332★ Respiratory Care Practitioners
Careers, Inc.
PO Box 135
Largo, FL 34649-0135
Ph: (813)584-7333
1991. Two-page occupational summary card describing duties, working conditions, personal qualifications, training, earnings and hours, employment outlook, places of employment, related careers, and where to write for more information.

★6333★ Respiratory Care Workers
Chronicle Guidance Publications, Inc.
66 Aurora St.
PO Box 1190
Moravia, NY 13118-1190
Ph: (315)497-0330   Fax: (315)497-3359
Fr: 800-622-7284
1994. Career brief describing the nature of the job, working conditions, hours and earn-ings, education and training, licensure, certification, unions, personal qualifications, social and psychological factors, location, employment outlook, entry methods, advancement, and related occupations.

★6334★ Respiratory Therapist
Vocational Biographies, Inc.
PO Box 31
Sauk Centre, MN 56378-0031
Ph: (612)352-6516   Fax: (612)352-5546
Fr: 800-255-0752
1990. Four-page pamphlet containing a personal narrative about a worker's job, work likes and dislikes, career path from high school to the present. Education and training, the rewards and frustrations, and the effects of the job on the rest of the worker's life. The data file portion of this pamphlet gives a concise occupational summary, including work descriptions, working conditions, places of employment, personal characteristics, education and training, job outlook, and salary range.

★6335★ "Respiratory Therapist" in Allied Health Education Directory (pp. 237-252)
American Medical Association (AMA)
515 N. State St.
Chicago, IL 60610
Ph: (312)464-5000   Fr: 800-621-8335
William R. Burrow, editor. 1994. Describes allied health occupations and lists educational programs accredited by the Committee on Allied Health Education and Accreditation of the American Medical Association.

★6336★ "Respiratory Therapist" in BLR Encyclopedia of Prewritten Job Descriptions
Business and Legal Reports, Inc.
39 Academy St.
Madison, CT 06443-1513
Ph: (203)245-7448
Stephen D. Bruce, editor-in-chief. 1994. This book contains hundreds of sample job descriptions arranged by functional job category. The 1-3 page job descriptions cover what the worker normally does in the position, who they report to, and how that position fits in the organizational structure.

★**6337**★ **"Respiratory Therapist" in** *Career Selector 2001*
Barron's Educational Series, Inc.
250 Wireless Blvd.
Hauppauge, NY 11788
Ph: (516)434-3311   Fax: (516)434-3723
Fr: 800-645-3476
James C. Gonyea. 1993.

★**6338**★ **"Respiratory Therapist" in** *College Board Guide to Jobs and Career Planning* **(pp. 265-266)**
The College Board
45 Columbus Ave.
New York, NY 10023-6992
Ph: (212)713-8165   Fax: (212)713-8143
Fr: 800-323-7155
Second edition, 1994. Describes the job, salaries, related careers, education needed, and where to write for more information.

★**6339**★ **"Respiratory Therapist" in** *Jobs Rated Almanac*
World Almanac
1 International Blvd., Ste. 444
Mahwah, NJ 07495
Ph: (201)529-6900   Fax: (201)529-6901
Les Krantz. Second edition, 1992. Ranks 250 jobs by environment, salary, outlooks, physical demands, stress, security, travel opportunities, and extra perks. Includes jobs the editor feels are the most common, most interesting, and the most rapidly growing.

★**6340**★ **"Respiratory Therapist, Respiratory Therapy Technician, and Respiratory Therapy Aide" in** *Careers in Health Care* **(pp. 251-255)**
National Textbook Co. (NTC)
VGM Career Books
4255 W. Touhy Ave.
Lincolnwood, IL 60646-1975
Ph: (708)679-5500   Fax: (708)679-2494
Fr: 800-323-4900
Barbara M. Swanson. Third edition, 1995. Describes job duties, work settings, salaries, licensing and certification requirements, educational preparation, and future outlook.

★**6341**★ **"Respiratory Therapist" in** *VGM's Careers Encyclopedia* **(pp. 404-407)**
National Textbook Co. (NTC)
VGM Career Books
4255 W. Touhy Ave.
Lincolnwood, IL 60646-1975
Ph: (708)679-5500   Fax: (708)679-2494
Fr: 800-323-4900
Third edition, 1991. Describes job duties, places of employment, working conditions, qualifications, education, and training, advancement potential, and salary for each occupation.

★**6342**★ **"Respiratory Therapist" in** *VGM's Handbook of Health Care Careers*
National Textbook Co.
4255 W. Touhy Ave.
Lincolnwood, IL 60646-1975
Ph: (708)679-5500   Fax: (708)679-2494
Fr: 800-323-4900
Annette Selden. 1993. Contains 42 two-page occupational profiles describing job duties, places of employment, working conditions, qualifications, education, employment outlook, and income.

★**6343**★ **"Respiratory Therapists" in** *101 Careers: A Guide to the Fastest-Growing Opportunities* **(pp. 263-265)**
John Wiley & Sons, Inc.
605 3rd Ave.
New York, NY 10158-0012
Ph: (212)850-6645   Fax: (212)850-6088
Michael Harkavy. 1990. Describes the nature of the job, working conditions, employment growth, qualifications, personal skills, projected salaries, and where to write for more information.

★**6344**★ **"Respiratory Therapists" in** *America's 50 Fastest Growing Jobs* **(pp. 65)**
JIST Works, Inc.
720 N. Park Ave.
Indianapolis, IN 46202-3431
Ph: (317)264-3720   Fax: (317)264-3709
Fr: 800-648-5478
Michael J. Farr, compiler. 1994. Describes the 50 fastest growing jobs within major career clusters such as technicians, and marketing and sales. Each job profile explains the nature of the work, skills and abilities required, employment outlook, average earnings, related occupations, education and training requirements, and employment opportunities. Also contains career planning information and job search tips.

★**6345**★ **"Respiratory Therapists" in** *Encyclopedia of Careers and Vocational Guidance* **(Vol.4, pp. 285-287)**
J.G. Ferguson Publishing Co.
200 W. Madison St., Ste. 300
Chicago, IL 60606
Ph: (312)580-5480   Fax: (312)580-4948
William E. Hopke, editor-in-chief. Ninth edition, 1993. Four-volume set that profiles 900 occupations and describes job trends in 74 industries. Includes career description, educational requirements, history of the job, methods of entry, advancement, employment outlook, earnings, conditions of work, social and psychological factors and sources of further information.

★**6346**★ **"Respiratory Therapists" in** *Health Care Job Explosion!* **(pp. 195-203)**
D-Amp Publications
401 Amherst Ave.
Coraopolis, PA 15108
Ph: (412)262-5578
Dennis V. Damp. 1993. Provides information on the nature of work for the major health care occupational groups. Descriptions include working conditions, training, job outlook, qualifications, and related occupations.

★**6347**★ **"Respiratory Therapists" in** *Occupational Outlook Handbook*
U.S. Government Printing Office
Superintendent of Documents
Washington, DC 20402
Ph: (202)512-1800   Fax: (202)512-2250
Biennial; latest edition, 1994-95. Encyclopedia of careers describing about 250 occupations and comprising about 85 percent of all jobs in the economy. Occupations that re-

quire lengthy education or training are given the most attention. Each occupation's profile describes what the worker does on the job, working conditions, education and training requirements, advancement possibilities, job outlook, earnings, and sources of additional information.

★**6348**★ **"Respiratory Therapy" in** *150 Careers in the Health Care Field*
Reed Reference Publishing
121 Chanlon Rd.
PO Box 31
New Providence, NJ 07974
Fax: (908)665-6688   Fr: 800-521-8110
Stanley Alperin. Third edition, 1993. Profiles health care occupations requiring a bachelor's degree or less. Describes the nature of the work, educational preparation, licensing requirements, and salary. Lists accredited educational programs.

PROFESSIONAL ASSOCIATIONS

★**6349**★ **American Association for Respiratory Care (AARC)**
11030 Ables Ln.
Dallas, TX 75229
Ph: (214)243-2272   Fax: (214)484-2720
Members: Allied health society of respiratory care technicians and therapists employed by hospitals, skilled nursing facilities, home care companies, group practices, educational institutions, and municipal organizations. **Purpose:** To encourage, develop, and provide educational programs for persons interested in the profession of respiratory care; and to advance the science of respiratory care. **Publications:** *AARC Times: The Magazine for the Respiratory Care Professional*, monthly. • *Respiratory Care*, monthly.

★**6350**★ **Joint Review Committee for Respiratory Therapy Education (JRCRTE)**
1701 W. Euless Blvd., Ste. 300
Euless, TX 76040
Ph: (817)283-2835   Fax: (817)354-8519
Fr: 800-874-5615
Members: Physicians (6); respiratory therapists (6); public representative (1). **Purpose:** Purposes are to develop standards and requirements for accredited educational programs of respiratory therapy for recommendation to the American Medical Association; to conduct evaluations of educational programs that have applied for accreditation of the AMA and to make recommendations to the AMA's Committee on Allied Health Education and Accreditation to maintain a working liaison with other organizations interested in respiratory therapy education and evaluation.

★**6351**★ **National Board for Respiratory Care (NBRC)**
8310 Nieman Rd.
Lenexa, KS 66214
Ph: (913)599-4200
Members: Offers credentialing examinations for respiratory therapists, respiratory therapy technicians, pulmonary technologists, and

perinatal/pediatric respiratory care specialists.

STANDARDS/CERTIFICATION AGENCIES

★6352★ Joint Review Committee for Respiratory Therapy Education (JRCRTE)
1701 W. Euless Blvd., Ste. 300
Euless, TX 76040
Ph: (817)283-2835   Fax: (817)354-8519
Fr: 800-874-5615

Purposes are to develop standards and requirements for accredited educational programs of respiratory therapy for recommendation to the American Medical Association; to conduct evaluations of educational programs that have applied for accreditation of the AMA and to make recommendations to the AMA's Committee on Allied Health Education and Accreditation.

★6353★ National Board for Respiratory Care (NBRC)
8310 Nieman Rd.
Lenexa, KS 66214
Ph: (913)599-4200

Offers credentialing examinations for respiratory therapists, respiratory therapy technicians, pulmonary technologists, and perinatal/pediatric respiratory care specialists.

TEST GUIDES

★6354★ Career Examination Series: Respiratory Therapy Technician
National Learning Corp.
212 Michael Dr.
Syosset, NY 11791
Ph: (516)921-8888   Fax: (516)921-8743
Fr: 800-645-6337

Jack Rudman. Test guide including questions and answers for students or professionals in the field who seek advancement through examination.

★6355★ Career Examination Series: Supervising Therapist
National Learning Corp.
212 Michael Dr.
Syosset, NY 11791
Ph: (516)921-8888   Fax: (516)921-8743
Fr: 800-645-6337

Jack Rudman. 1993. Test guide including questions and answers for students or professionals in the field who seek advancement through examination.

★6356★ A Comprehensive Review in Respiratory Care
Appleton and Lange
PO Box 56303
Norwalk, CT 06856
Ph: (203)838-4400

Vijay Deshpande, Susan P. Pilbeam, and Robin J. Dixon. 1988. Includes bibliographies and an index.

★6357★ Respiratory Care Certification Guide
Mosby-Year Book, Inc..
11830 Westline Industrial Dr.
St. Louis, MO 63146
Ph: (314)872-8370   Fax: (314)432-1380
Fr: 800-325-4177

James R. Sills. 2nd edition, 1994. Provides analysis of the content areas of the CRTT exam.

EDUCATIONAL DIRECTORIES AND PROGRAMS

★6358★ Encyclopedia of Medical Organizations and Agencies
Gale Research Inc.
835 Penobscot Bldg.
Detroit, MI 48226-4094
Ph: (313)961-2242   Fax: (313)961-6741
Fr: 800-877-GALE
Karen Boyden, Contact

Biennial, November of odd years. Covers over 13,400 state, national, and international medical associations, foundations, research institutes, federal and state agencies, and medical and allied health schools. Entries include: Organization name, address, phone; many listings include names and titles of key personnel, descriptive annotations. Arrangement: Classified by subject, then by type of organization.

★6359★ Health & Medical Industry Directory
American Business Directories, Inc.
5711 S. 86th Circle
Omaha, NE 68127
Ph: (402)593-4600   Fax: (402)331-1505

Released 1993. Lists over 1.1 million physicians and surgeons, dentists, clinics, health clubs, and other health-related businesses in the U.S. and Canada. Entries include: Name, address, phone.

★6360★ Medical and Health Information Directory
Gale Research Inc.
835 Penobscot Bldg.
Detroit, MI 48226-4094
Ph: (313)961-2242   Fax: (313)961-6741
Fr: 800-877-GALE
Karen Boyden, Contact

Approximately biennial; latest edition 1994. Covers in Volume 1, almost 18,600 medical and health oriented associations, organizations, institutions, and government agencies, including health maintenance organizations (HMOs), preferred provider organizations (PPOs), insurance companies, pharmaceutical companies, research centers, and medi-

cal and allied health schools. In Volume 2, nearly 11,800 medical book publishers; medical periodicals, directories, audiovisual producers and services, medical libraries and information centers, and electronic resources. In Volume 3, nearly 26,000 clinics, treatment centers, care programs, and counseling/diagnostic services for 30 subject areas. Entries include: Institution, service, or firm name, address, phone; many include names of key personnel Arrangement: Classified by organization activity, service, etc..

★6361★ Therapists and Allied Health Professionals Career Directory
Gale Research Inc.
835 Penobscot Bldg.
Detroit, MI 48226-4094
Ph: (313)961-2242   Fax: (313)961-6083
Fr: 800-877-GALE

Bradley J. Morgan and Joseph M. Palmisano. 1993. A directory in the Career Advisor Series that provides essays written by industry professionals; job search information on resume and cover letter preparation, networking, and the interviewing process; approximately 300 companies and organizations offering job opportunities and internships, and additional job-hunting resources.

AWARDS, SCHOLARSHIPS, GRANTS, AND FELLOWSHIPS

★6362★ Morton B. Duggan Jr. Memorial Scholarships
American Respiratory Care Foundation
11030 Ables Ln.
Dallas, TX 75229-4593
Ph: (214)243-2272   Fax: (214)484-2720

Qualifications: Candidates must be United States citizens or submit a copy of an immigration visa and be enrolled in an AMA-approved respiratory care training program. Selection criteria: Applications are accepted from all states with preference to Georgia and South Carolina candidates. Funds available: The scholarship award is $500. Application details: The application must be accompanied by an official grade transcript showing a 3.0 average at the minimum, on a 4.0 scale or the equivalent, and at least two letters of recommendation, one attesting to the candidate's worthiness and potential in the field of respiratory care. One letter must be from the program director or a senior faculty member and the other from the medical director or other physician instructor. Submission of six copies of an original referenced paper on some facet of respiratory care accompanied by letters of approval by knowledgeable persons is also required. Deadline: Deadline for receipt of application is June 30; the scholarship is awarded September 1.

★6363★ **Jimmy A. Young Memorial Scholarships**
American Respiratory Care Foundation
11030 Ables Ln.
Dallas, TX 75229-4593
Ph: (214)243-2272   Fax: (214)484-2720
Purpose: To assist minority students in respiratory therapy programs based on academic achievement. Qualifications: Applicants must be United States citizens or submit a copy of their immigrant visa. They must be members of minority groups, which include American Indians, Asian or Pacific Islanders, Black-Americans, Spanish-Americans, and Mexican-Americans. They must provide evidence of enrollment in an AMA-approved respiratory care program and have a minimum grade point average of 3.0 on a 4.0 scale. Funds available: $1,000. Application details: Candidates must submit official transcripts of grades, and two letters of recommendation from the program director and medical director that verifies the applicant is deserving and a member of a designated minority group. A budget must be submitted. An original essay on some facet of respiratory care is also required. Deadline: Applications are accepted between April 1 and June 1. Scholarships are awarded by September 1.

BASIC REFERENCE GUIDES AND HANDBOOKS

★6364★ **Comprehensive Respiratory Care**
Mosby-Year Book, Inc.
11830 Westline Industrial Dr.
St. Louis, MO 63146
Ph: (314)872-8370   Fax: (314)432-1380
Fr: 800-325-4177
1995.

★6365★ **A Comprehensive Review in Respiratory Care**
Appleton and Lange
PO Box 56303
Norwalk, CT 06856
Ph: (203)838-4400
Vijay Deshpande, Susan P. Pilbeam, and Robin J. Dixon. 1988. Includes bibliographies and an index.

★6366★ **Core Textbook of Respiratory Care Practice**
Mosby-Year Book, Inc..
11830 Westline Industrial Dr.
St. Louis, MO 63146
Ph: (314)872-8370   Fax: (314)432-1380
Fr: 800-325-4177
Thomas A. Barnes. 2nd edition, 1994.

★6367★ **Manual of Respiratory Care Procedures**
J. B. Lippincott Co.
227 E. Washington Sq.
Philadelphia, PA 19106
Ph: (215)238-4436
Diane Blodgett. Second edition, 1987. Includes bibliographies and an index.

★6368★ **Respiratory Facts**
F. A. Davis Co.
1915 Arch St.
Philadelphia, PA 19103
Ph: (215)568-2270
John H. Riggs. 1988. Includes bibliographies and an index.

PROFESSIONAL AND TRADE PERIODICALS

★6369★ **IVUN News**
International Ventilator Users Network (IVUN)
5100 Oakland Ave., No. 206
St. Louis, MO 63110
Ph: (314)534-0475   Fax: (314)534-5070
Judith Fischer
Semiannual. Disseminates information on breathing techniques and equipment to help persons who use mechanical ventilation to live at home rather than in an institution. Discusses related issues such as adaptation and psychological adjustment, attendant care, funding sources, travel with ventilators, and sleep-disordered breathing. Recurring features include a calendar of events and news of relevant legislation.

★6370★ **National Rehabilitation Information Center—Quarterly**
National Rehabilitation Information Center
Catholic University of America
8455 Colesville Rd., Ste. 935
Silver Spring, MD 20910
Fr: 800-346-2742
Adele Kirk
Quarterly. Carries information for those involved in all aspects of rehabilitation and dis-

ability. Recurring features include a calendar of events.

★6371★ **Respiratory Care**
Daedalus Enterprises, Inc.
11030 Ables Ln.
Dallas, TX 75229
Ph: (214)243-2272   Fax: (214)484-2720
Pat Brougher
Monthly. Science journal about cardiorespiratory care.

★6372★ **Technology for Health Care Series**
ECRI
5200 Butler Pike
Plymouth Meeting, PA 19462
Ph: (215)825-6000   Fax: (215)834-1275
Michele Moscariello
Monthly. Concerned with the safety, performance, reliability, and cost effectiveness of health care technology. Covers areas of anesthesia, cardiology, imaging and radiology, and respiratory therapy. Reviews device test results and warns of hazards and deficiencies. Recurring features include news of research, Institute reports, and news of members.

★6373★ **Technology for Respiratory Therapy**
ECRI
5200 Butler Pike
Plymouth Meeting, PA 19462
Ph: (215)825-6000   Fax: (215)834-1275
Michele Moscariello
Monthly. Reviews medical device technology and summarizes reported problems, hazards, and recalls. Recurring features include news of research and health care technology abstracts.

PROFESSIONAL MEETINGS AND CONVENTIONS

★6374★ **American Association for Respiratory Care Annual Meeting and Exhibition**
American Association for Respiratory Care
11030 Ables Ln.
Dallas, TX 75229
Ph: (214)243-2272   Fax: (214)484-2720
Annual. Usually held during December. **Dates and Locations:** 1995 Dec 02-05; Orlando, FL. • 1996 Nov 03-06; San Diego, CA. • 1997 Dec 06-09; New Orleans, LA. • 1998 Nov 07-10; Atlanta, GA.

Speech-Language Pathologists and Audiologists

Speech-language pathologists identify, assess, and treat persons with speech, language, voice, and fluency disorders while **audiologists** assess and treat hearing impaired individuals. Because both occupations are concerned with communication, individuals competent in one area must be familiar with the other. Speech-language pathologists identify and treat speech, language, and swallowing disorders resulting from conditions such as total or partial hearing loss, brain injury, cerebral palsy, cleft palate, voice pathology, mental retardation, faulty learning, emotional problems, or foreign dialect. They also counsel patients and families about communication disorders and how to cope with the stress and misunderstanding that often accompany a communication disorder. Audiologists identify, assess, treat, and work to prevent hearing problems. The duties of speech-language pathologists and audiologist vary. Most, however, provide direct clinical services to individuals with communication disorders.

Salaries

Salaries for speech-language pathologists and audiologists are as follows:

Beginning speech-language pathologists and audiologists, hospitals/medical centers	$29,050/year
Experienced speech-language pathologists	$41,300/year
Experienced audiologists	$45,000/year.

Employment Outlook

Growth rate until the year 2005: Much faster than the average.

Speech-Language Pathologists and Audiologists

CAREER GUIDES

★6375★ Allied Health Professions
Simon & Schuster, Inc.
200 Old Tappan Rd.
Old Tappan, NJ 07675

1993. Includes information on available jobs, required training, a directory of training programs, and a full-sample Allied Health Professions Admission Test (AHPAT).

★6376★ Audiologist
Vocational Biographies, Inc.
PO Box 31
Sauk Centre, MN 56378-0031
Ph: (612)352-6516   Fax: (612)352-5546
Fr: 800-255-0752

1991. Four-page pamphlet containing a personal narrative about a worker's job, work likes and dislikes, career path from high school to the present. Education and training, the rewards and frustrations, and the effects of the job on the rest of the worker's life. The data file portion of this pamphlet gives a concise occupational summary, including work descriptions, working conditions, places of employment, personal characteristics, education and training, job outlook, and salary range.

★6377★ Audiologist
Careers, Inc.
PO Box 135
Largo, FL 34649-0135
Ph: (813)584-7333

1992. Four-page brief offering the definition, history, duties, working conditions, personal qualifications, educational requirements, earnings, hours, employment outlook, advancement, and careers related to this position.

★6378★ "Audiologist" in BLR Encyclopedia of Prewritten Job Descriptions
Business and Legal Reports, Inc.
39 Academy St.
Madison, CT 06443-1513
Ph: (203)245-7448

Stephen D. Bruce, editor-in-chief. 1994. This book contains hundreds of sample job descriptions arranged by functional job category. The 1-3 page job descriptions cover what the worker normally does in the position, who they report to, and how that position fits in the organizational structure.

★6379★ "Audiologist" in Jobs Rated Almanac
World Almanac
1 International Blvd., Ste. 444
Mahwah, NJ 07495
Ph: (201)529-6900   Fax: (201)529-6901

Les Krantz. Second edition, 1992. Ranks 250 jobs by environment, salary, outlooks, physical demands, stress, security, travel opportunities, and extra perks. Includes jobs the editor feels are the most common, most interesting, and the most rapidly growing.

★6380★ Audiologists
Chronicle Guidance Publications, Inc.
66 Aurora St.
PO Box 1190
Moravia, NY 13118-1190
Ph: (315)497-0330   Fax: (315)497-3359
Fr: 800-622-7284

1991. Career brief describing the nature of the job, working conditions, hours and earnings, education and training, licensure, certification, unions, personal qualifications, social and psychological factors, location, employment outlook, entry methods, advancement, and related occupations.

★6381★ "Audiologists" in Career Discovery Encyclopedia (Vol.1, pp. 80-81)
J.G. Ferguson Publishing Co.
200 W. Madison St., Ste. 300
Chicago, IL 60606
Ph: (312)580-5480   Fax: (312)580-4948

Russell E. Primm, editor-in chief. 1993. This six volume set contains two-page articles for 504 occupations. Each article describes job duties, earnings, and educational and training requirements. The whole set is arranged alphabetically by job title. Designed for junior high and older students.

★6382★ "Audiology/Speech Pathology" in Liberal Arts Jobs
Petersons Guides, Inc.
PO Box 2123
Princeton, NJ 08543-2123
Ph: (609)243-9111   Fax: (609)243-9150
Fr: 800-338-3282

Burton Jay Nadler. Second edition, 1989. Strives to help the liberal arts graduate identify skills for entry-level positions. Gives goal setting and job search advice.

★6383★ Careers in Speech-Language Pathology and Audiology
American Speech-Language-Hearing Association (ASHA)
10801 Rockville Pike
Rockville, MD 20852
Ph: (301)897-5700

1994. Packet containing four information sheets describing what speech-language pathologists and audiologists do, as well as certification, educational preparation, and financial aid.

★6384★ Exciting Opportunities Ahead for Speech, Language and Hearing Scientists
American Speech-Language-Hearing Association
10801 Rockville Pike
Rockville, MD 20852
Ph: (301)897-5700

1990. Eight-panel brochure describing research careers in communication sciences and disorders; also explains educational preparation required.

★6385★ The Health Care Worker: An Introduction to Health Occupations
Prentice-Hall, Inc.
200 Old Tappan Rd.
Old Tappan, NJ 07675
Ph: (201)767-5000
Shirley A. Badasch, and Doreen S. Chesebro. Second edition, 1988. Includes a bibliography and an index.

★6386★ Health Careers
Careers, Inc.
PO Box 135
Largo, FL 34649-0135
Ph: (813)584-7333
1994. Four-page brief describing duties, working conditions, personal qualifications, training, earnings and hours, employment outlook, places of employment, related careers, and where to write for more information.

★6387★ Opportunities in Speech-Language Pathology Careers
National Textbook Co. (NTC)
VGM Career Books
4255 W. Touhy Ave.
Lincolnwood, IL 60646-1975
Ph: (708)679-5500   Fax: (708)679-2494
Fr: 800-323-4900
Patricia G. Larkins. 1988. Describes the job responsibilities, educational prepartation, work settings, and related careers.

★6388★ Speech-Language Pathologist
Careers, Inc.
PO Box 135
Largo, FL 34649-0135
Ph: (813)584-7333
1995. Four-page brief offering the definition, history, duties, working conditions, personal qualifications, educational requirements, earnings, hours, employment outlook, advancement, and careers related to this position.

★6389★ Speech-Language Pathologist
Vocational Biographies, Inc.
PO Box 31
Sauk Centre, MN 56378-0031
Ph: (612)352-6516   Fax: (612)352-5546
Fr: 800-255-0752
1990. Four-page pamphlet containing a personal narrative about a worker's job, work likes and dislikes, career path from high school to the present, education and training, the rewards and frustrations, and the effects of the job on the rest of the worker's life. The data file portion of this pamphlet gives a concise occupational summary, including work description, working conditions, places of employment, personal characteristics, education and training, job outlook, and salary range.

★6390★ "Speech Language Pathologist and Audiologist" in Careers in Health Care (pp. 261-264)
National Textbook Co. (NTC)
VGM Career Books
4255 W. Touhy Ave.
Lincolnwood, IL 60646-1975
Ph: (708)679-5500   Fax: (708)679-2494
Fr: 800-323-4900
Barbara M. Swanson. Third edition, 1995. Describes job duties, work settings, salaries,

licensing and certification requirements, educational preparation, and future outlook.

★6391★ Speech-Language Pathologists
Chronicle Guidance Publications, Inc.
66 Aurora St.
PO Box 1190
Moravia, NY 13118-1190
Ph: (315)497-0330   Fax: (315)497-3359
Fr: 800-622-7284
1991. Career brief describing the nature of the job, working conditions, hours and earnings, education and training, licensure, certification, unions, personal qualifications, social and psychological factors, location, employment outlook, entry methods, advancement, and related occupations.

★6392★ Speech Language Pathologists and Audiologists
Chronicle Guidance Publications, Inc.
66 Aurora St.
PO Box 1190
Moravia, NY 13118-1190
Ph: (315)497-0330   Fax: (315)497-3359
Fr: 800-622-7284
1992. Career brief describing the nature of the job, working conditions, hours and earnings, education and training, licensure, certification, unions, personal qualifications, social and psychological factors, location, employment outlook, entry methods, advancement, and related occupations.

★6393★ "Speech-Language Pathologists and Audiologists" in 101 Careers: A Guide to the Fastest-Growing Opportunities (pp. 266-268)
John Wiley & Sons, Inc.
605 3rd Ave.
New York, NY 10158-0012
Ph: (212)850-6645   Fax: (212)850-6088
Michael Harkavy. 1990. Describes the nature of the job, working conditions, employment growth, qualifications, personal skills, projected salaries, and where to write for more information.

★6394★ "Speech-Language Pathologists and Audiologists" in America's 50 Fastest Growing Jobs (pp. 71)
JIST Works, Inc.
720 N. Park Ave.
Indianapolis, IN 46202-3431
Ph: (317)264-3720   Fax: (317)264-3709
Fr: 800-648-5478
Michael J. Farr, compiler. 1994. Describes the 50 fastest growing jobs within major career clusters such as technicians, and marketing and sales. Each job profile explains the nature of the work, skills and abilities required, employment outlook, average earnings, related occupations, education and training requirements, and employment opportunities. Also contains career planning information and job search tips.

★6395★ "Speech-Language Pathologists/Audiologists" in Best Jobs for the 1990s and Into the 21st Century
Impact Publications
9104-N Manassas Dr.
Manassas Park, VA 22111
Ph: (703)361-7300   Fax: (703)335-9486
Ronald L. Krannich and Caryl Rae Krannich. 1993.

★6396★ "Speech-language Pathologists and Audiologists" in Encyclopedia of Careers and Vocational Guidance (Vol.4, pp. 403-405)
J.G. Ferguson Publishing Co.
200 W. Madison St., Ste. 300
Chicago, IL 60606
Ph: (312)580-5480   Fax: (312)580-4948
William E. Hopke, editor-in-chief. Ninth edition, 1993. Four-volume that profiles 900 occupations and describes job trends in 74 industries. Includes career description, educational requirements, history of the job, methods of entry, advancement, employment outlook, earnings, conditions of work, social and psychological factors, and sources of further information.

★6397★ "Speech-Language Pathologists and Audiologists" in Health Care Job Explosion! (pp. 204-212)
D-Amp Publications
401 Amherst Ave.
Coraopolis, PA 15108
Ph: (412)262-5578
Dennis V. Damp. 1993. Provides information on the nature of work for the major health care occupational groups. Descriptions include working conditions, training, job outlook, qualifications, and related occupations.

★6398★ "Speech-Language Pathologists and Audiologists" in Occupational Outlook Handbook
U.S. Government Printing Office
Superintendent of Documents
Washington, DC 20402
Ph: (202)512-1800   Fax: (202)512-2250
Biennial; latest edition, 1994-95. Encyclopedia of careers describing about 250 occupations and comprising about 85 percent of all jobs in the economy. Occupations that require lengthy education or training are given the most attention. Each occupation's profile describes what the worker does on the job, working conditions, education and training requirements, advancement possibilities, job outlook, earnings, and sources of additional information.

★6399★ "Speech Pathologist/Audiologist" in Guide to Federal Jobs (p. 141)
Resource Directories
3361 Executive Pkwy., Ste. 302
Toledo, OH 43606
Ph: (419)536-5353   Fax: (419)536-7056
Fr: 800-274-8515
Rod W. Durgin, editor. Third edition, 1992. Contains information on finding and applying for federal jobs. Describes more than 200 professional and technical jobs for college graduates. Covers the nature of the work,

salary, and geographic location. Lists college majors preferred for that occupation. Section one describes the function and work of government agencies that hire the most significant number of college graduates.

★6400★ "Speech Pathologist and Audiologist" in VGM's Careers Encyclopedia (pp. 439-440)
National Textbook Co. (NTC)
VGM Career Books
4255 W. Touhy Ave.
Lincolnwood, IL 60646-1975
Ph: (708)679-5500   Fax: (708)679-2494
Fr: 800-323-4900

Third edition, 1991. Describes job duties, places of employment, working conditions, qualifications, education, and training, advancement potential, and salary for each occupation.

★6401★ "Speech Pathologist and Audiologist" in VGM's Handbook of Health Care Careers
National Textbook Co.
4255 W. Touhy Ave.
Lincolnwood, IL 60646-1975
Ph: (708)679-5500   Fax: (708)679-2494
Fr: 800-323-4900

Annette Selden. 1993. Contains 42 two-page occupational profiles describing job duties, places of employment, working conditions, qualifications, education, employment outlook, and income.

★6402★ "Speech Pathologist" in Jobs Rated Almanac
World Almanac
1 International Blvd., Ste. 444
Mahwah, NJ 07495
Ph: (201)529-6900   Fax: (201)529-6901

Les Krantz. Second edition, 1992. Ranks 250 jobs by environment, salary, outlooks, physical demands, stress, security, travel opportunities, and extra perks. Includes jobs the editor feels are the most common, most interesting, and the most rapidly growing.

★6403★ "Speech Pathologists and Audiologists" in Jobs! What They Are—Where They Are—What They Pay (p. 176)
Simon & Schuster, Inc.
Simon & Schuster Bldg.
1230 Avenue of the Americas
New York, NY 10020
Ph: (212)698-7000   Fr: 800-223-2348

Robert O. Snelling and Anne M. Snelling. 3rd edition, 1992. Describes duties and responsibilities, earnings, employment opportunities, training, and qualifications.

★6404★ "Speech Therapist, Hearing Therapist" in College Board Guide to Jobs and Career Planning (pp. 267)
The College Board
415 Columbus Ave.
New York, NY 10023-6992
Ph: (212)713-8165   Fax: (212)713-8143
Fr: 800-323-7155

Joyce S. Mitchell. Second edition, 1994. Describes the job, salaries, related careers, education needed, and where to write for more information.

★6405★ "Speech Therapists and Audiologists" in American Almanac of Jobs and Salaries (p. 473)
Avon Books
1350 Avenue of the Americas
New York, NY 10019
Ph: (212)261-6800   Fr: 800-238-0658

John Wright, editor. Revised and updated, 1994-95. This is comprehensive guide to the wages of hundreds of occupations in a wide variety of industries and organizations.

PROFESSIONAL ASSOCIATIONS

★6406★ American Auditory Society (AAS)
512 E. Canterbury Ln.
Phoenix, AZ 85022
Ph: (602)789-0755   Fax: (602)942-1486

Members: Audiologists, otolaryngologists, scientists, hearing aid industry professionals, and educators of hearing impaired people; individuals involved in industries serving hearing impaired people, including the amplification systems industry. Purpose: Works to increase knowledge and understanding of: the ear, hearing, and balance; disorders of the ear, hearing, and balance; prevention of these disorders; habilitation and rehabilitation of individuals with hearing and balance dysfunction. Publications: The Bulletin of the AAS. • Ear and Hearing, bimonthly.

★6407★ American Speech-Language-Hearing Association (ASHA)
10801 Rockville Pke.
Rockville, MD 20852
Ph: (301)897-5700   Fax: (301)571-0457
Fr: 800-638-8255

Members: Professional association for speech-language pathologists and audiologists. Acts as an accrediting agency for college and university graduate school programs and clinic and hospital programs and as a certifying body for professionals providing speech, language, and hearing therapy to the public. Purpose: Offers career information, listing of university training programs, and certification requirements. Conducts research on communication disorders and community needs. Publications: American Journal of Audiology: A Journal of Clinical Practice. • American Journal of Speech Language Pathology: A Journal of Clinical Practice, periodic. • Asha, monthly. • ASHA Monographs, periodic. • ASHA Reports, periodic. • Guide to Graduate Education in Speech-Language Pathology and Audiology, biennial. • Journal of Speech and Hearing Research, bimonthly. • Language, Speech, and Hearing Services in Schools, quarterly.

★6408★ Council on Professional Standards in Speech-Language Pathology and Audiology
American Speech-Language-Hearing Association
10801 Rockville Pike
Rockville, MD 20852
Ph: (301)897-5700

Members: Defines standards for clinical certification and for the accreditation of graduate education programs, as well as for professional service programs. Purpose: Monitors the interpretation and application of these standards to individuals, institutions, and organizations. Hears appeals regarding certification and accreditation.

STANDARDS/CERTIFICATION AGENCIES

★6409★ American Speech-Language-Hearing Association (ASHA)
10801 Rockville Pke.
Rockville, MD 20852
Ph: (301)897-5700   Fax: (301)571-0457
Fr: 800-638-8255

Acts as an accrediting agency for college and university graduate school programs and clinic and hospital programs and as a certifying body for professionals providing speech, language, and hearing therapy to the public. Offers career information, listing of university training programs, and certification requirements.

★6410★ Council on Professional Standards in Speech-Language Pathology and Audiology
American Speech-Language-Hearing Association
10801 Rockville Pike
Rockville, MD 20852
Ph: (301)897-5700

Defines standards for clinical certification and for the accreditation of graduate education programs, as well as for professional service programs. Monitors the interpretation and application of these standards to individuals, institutions, and organizations. Hears appeals regarding certification and accreditation.

TEST GUIDES

★6411★ Career Examination Series: Audiologist
National Learning Corp.
212 Michael Dr.
Syosset, NY 11791
Ph: (516)921-8888   Fax: (516)921-8743
Fr: 800-645-6337

Jack Rudman. A series of study guides with multiple-choice examination questions and solutions for trainees and professional speech/language pathologists and audiologists. Titles in the series include Audiologist-Speech Pathologist; Consultant in

Audiology; Senior Speech and Hearing Therapist; Speech Audiologist; Speech and Hearing Therapist; Speech Pathologist.

★6412★ Career Examination Series: Speech Audiologist/Pathologist

National Learning Corp.
212 Michael Dr.
Syosset, NY 11791
Ph: (516)921-8888   Fax: (516)921-8743
Fr: 800-645-6337

Jack Rudman. Test guide including questions and answers for students or professionals in the field who seek advancement through examination.

★6413★ Career Examination Series: Supervising Audiologist

National Learning Corp.
212 Michael Dr.
Syosset, NY 11791
Ph: (516)921-8888   Fax: (516)921-8743
Fr: 800-645-6337

Jack Rudman. 1993. Test guide including questions and answers for students or professionals in the field who seek advancement through examination.

★6414★ Speech Pathology and Audiology

National Learning Corp.
212 Michael Dr.
Syosset, NY 11791
Ph: (516)921-8888   Fax: (516)921-8743
Fr: 800-645-6337

Jack Rudman. Part of the Undergraduate Program Field Test series. A practice examination fashioned after tests given in the Regents External Degree Program. Designed to measure knowledge received outside the college classroom in the subject of speech pathology and audiology. Contains multiple-choice questions; provides solutions.

EDUCATIONAL DIRECTORIES AND PROGRAMS

★6415★ Encyclopedia of Medical Organizations and Agencies

Gale Research Inc.
835 Penobscot Bldg.
Detroit, MI 48226-4094
Ph: (313)961-2242   Fax: (313)961-6741
Fr: 800-877-GALE
Karen Boyden, Contact

Biennial, November of odd years. Covers over 13,400 state, national, and international medical associations, foundations, research institutes, federal and state agencies, and medical and allied health schools. Entries include: Organization name, address, phone; many listings include names and titles of key personnel, descriptive annotations. Arrangement: Classified by subject, then by type of organization.

★6416★ Guide to Graduate Education in Speech-Language Pathology and Audiology

American Speech-Language-Hearing Association
10801 Rockville Pike
Rockville, MD 20852
Ph: (301)897-5700   Fax: (301)571-0457
Fr: 800-638-8255
Joanne Jessen, Contact

Irregular, previous edition 1991; latest edition 1995. Covers more than 240 colleges and universities offering graduate training in speech-language pathology and audiology. Entries include: Institution name, location, size, faculty, student characteristics, admission requirements, tuition, degrees granted, program description, costs, availability of financial aid. Arrangement: Separate geographical sections for accredited and unaccredited schools.

★6417★ Medical and Health Information Directory

Gale Research Inc.
835 Penobscot Bldg.
Detroit, MI 48226-4094
Ph: (313)961-2242   Fax: (313)961-6741
Fr: 800-877-GALE
Karen Boyden, Contact

Approximately biennial; latest edition 1994. Covers in Volume 1, almost 18,600 medical and health oriented associations, organizations, institutions, and government agencies, including health maintenance organizations (HMOs), preferred provider organizations (PPOs), insurance companies, pharmaceutical companies, research centers, and medical and allied health schools. In Volume 2, nearly 11,800 medical book publishers; medical periodicals, directories, audiovisual producers and services, medical libraries and information centers, and electronic resources. In Volume 3, nearly 26,000 clinics, treatment centers, care programs, and counseling/diagnostic services for 30 subject areas. Entries include: Institution, service, or firm name, address, phone; many include names of key personnel Arrangement: Classified by organization activity, service, etc..

★6418★ Therapists and Allied Health Professionals Career Directory

Gale Research Inc.
835 Penobscot Bldg.
Detroit, MI 48226-4094
Ph: (313)961-2242   Fax: (313)961-6083
Fr: 800-877-GALE

Bradley J. Morgan and Joseph M. Palmisano. 1993. A directory in the Career Advisor Series that provides essays written by industry professionals; job search information on resume and cover letter preparation, networking, and the interviewing process; approximately 300 companies and organizations offering job opportunities and internships, and additional job-hunting resources.

AWARDS, SCHOLARSHIPS, GRANTS, AND FELLOWSHIPS

★6419★ American Speech-Language-Hearing Foundation Graduate Student Scholarships

American Speech-Language-Hearing Foundation
10801 Rockville Pike
Rockville, MD 20852
Ph: (301)897-5700   Fax: (301)571-0457

Purpose: To support graduate studies in fields of interest to the Foundation. Qualifications: Candidate may be of any nationality. Applicant must be accepted for full-time graduate study in an ASHA Educational Standards Board accredited communication sciences and disorders program at a U.S. institution; this requirement is not mandatory for doctoral degree candidates. The student must be enrolled full-time. Applicants must submit official University transcripts of coursework, credits, and grades, plus recommendations of a committee of two or more persons who are: faculty at the student's current college or university program; or faculty at the student's past college or university program if the student is a recent undergraduate; and colleagues at the student's current place of employment. Candidate may not have previously received a scholarship from the Foundation. In addition to general graduate scholarships, the Foundation administers two scholarships with additional stipulations. The Kala Singh Memorial Scholarship gives priority to a non-U.S. citizen or a U.S. minority student applicant must be studying in the continental United States. The Leslie Isenberg Fund Scholarship gives priority to a disabled student. Separate applications are not necessary for these awards; students will be automatically considered for all awards for which they are eligible. Funds available: General scholarships: $4,000; Isenberg and Singh Scholarships: $2,000. Application details: Write to the Foundation for application materials and guidelines. Deadline: 15 June. Scholarship recipients will be announced in November.

★6420★ Fellows of the Association

American Speech-Language-Hearing Association
10801 Rockville Pike
Rockville, MD 20852
Ph: (301)897-5700   Fax: (301)571-0457
Fr: 800-638-8255

To recognize a member for achievement. A fellow must have been active in the Association as evidenced by publications, appearance on the convention programs, or service on committees and must have a record of achievement, unquestionable and sustained, of one or more of the following types: original contributions to the advancement of knowledge; distinguished educational, professional, or administrative activity; and outstanding service to the Association. Awarded annually at the convention. Established in 1951.

★6421★ Honors of the Association
American Speech-Language-Hearing
  Association
10801 Rockville Pike
Rockville, MD 20852
Ph: (301)897-5700   Fax: (301)571-0457
Fr: 800-638-8255

For recognition of distinguished service to the profession. Individuals are recommended by the Committee on Honors with the approval of the Council. Awarded annually at the convention. Established in 1944.

BASIC REFERENCE GUIDES AND HANDBOOKS

★6422★ A Comprehensive Dictionary of Audiology
Hearing Aid Journal
63 Great Rd.
Maynard, MA 01754-2025
Ph: (508)897-5552

James H. Delk. Fourth edition, 1991.

★6423★ A Dictionary of Communication Disorders
Singular Publishing Group
4284 41st St.
San Diego, CA 92105
Ph: 800-521-8545   Fax: (619)563-9008

David W. H. Morris. Second edition, 1992. Terms are grouped under such subjects as speech pathology, linguistics, phonetics/phonology, psychology/psychiatry, medicine, hearing, electronic devices, and microcomputers. Includes a bibliography and appendixes.

PROFESSIONAL AND TRADE PERIODICALS

★6424★ Communication Outlook
Artificial Language Laboratory
405 Computer Center
East Lansing, MI 48824-1042
Ph: (517)353-0870
Annette Vasquez

Quarterly. Provides information on modern techniques and aids for persons who experi-

ence communication handicaps due to neurological or neuromuscular conditions. Reports on current research, centers, programs, and projects in the field. Recurring features include listings of new publications, questions and letters from readers, and a calendar of events.

★6425★ Division for Children With Communication Disorders—Newsletter
Division for Children With Communication
  Disorders
1920 Association Dr.
Reston, VA 22091-1589
Ph: (703)620-3660
Chris DeSouza

Semiannual. Serves to inform members of the Division activities in the field of communication disorders. Recurring features include reports from the Division's committees and executive board members, convention news, information on similar organizations, a calendar of events, and a column titled A Message From the President.

★6426★ Ear and Hearing
Williams & Wilkins
428 E. Preston St.
Baltimore, MD 21202-3993
Ph: (410)528-4176   Fax: (410)428-4452
Susan Jerger

Bimonthly. Original aricles on auditory disorders.

PROFESSIONAL MEETINGS AND CONVENTIONS

★6427★ American Speech-Language-Hearing Association Annual Convention
American Speech-Language-Hearing
  Association
10801 Rockville Pke.
Rockville, MD 20852
Ph: (301)897-5700   Fax: (301)571-0457

Annual. **Dates and Locations:** 1995 Nov 17-20; Cincinnati, OH. • 1996 Nov 22-25; Seattle, WA.

OTHER SOURCES OF INFORMATION

★6428★ "Speech Language Pathology and Audiology" in Accounting to Zoology: Graduate Fields Defined (pp. 250-251)
Petersons Guides, Inc.
PO Box 2123
Princeton, NJ 08543-2123
Ph: (609)243-9111   Fax: (609)243-9150
Fr: 800-338-3282

Amy J. Goldstein, editor. Revised and updated, 1987. Discusses types of graduate programs and degrees, graduate research, applied work, employment prospects and trends.

★6429★ "Speech Pathologist/ Audiologist" in 100 Best Jobs for the 1990s & Beyond
Dearborn Financial Publishing, Inc.
520 N. Dearborn St.
Chicago, IL 60610-4354
Ph: (312)836-4400   Fax: (312)836-1021
Fr: 800-621-9621

Carol Kleiman. 1992. Describes 100 jobs ranging from accountants to veterinarians. Each job profile includes such information as education, experience, and certification needed, salaries, and job search suggestions.

★6430★ "Speech Pathologist" in Career Selector 2001
Barron's Educational Series, Inc.
250 Wireless Blvd.
Hauppauge, NY 11788
Ph: (516)434-3311   Fax: (516)434-3723
Fr: 800-645-3476

James C. Gonyea. 1993.

Public Relations Specialist

Public relations specialists help businesses, governments, universities, hospitals, schools, and other organizations build and maintain positive relationships with the public. Public relations specialists handle such functions as media, community, consumer, and governmental relations; political campaigns; interest-group representation; fundraising; or employee relations. Understanding the attitudes and concerns of customers, employees, and various other "publics" and communicating this information to management to help to formulate sound policy is also an important part of the job. To improve communications, public relations workers establish and maintain cooperative relationships with representatives of community, consumer, and public interest groups and those in print and broadcast journalism.

Salaries

Salaries for public relations specialists vary by employer. Persons working in large organizations with extensive public relation programs generally earn the most. Median annual earnings for public relations specialists who are not self-employed are as follows:

Lowest 10 percent	Less than $17,000/year
Middle 50 percent	$24,000-$51,000/year
Top 10 percent	More than $62,000/year
Public affairs in federal government	$45,400/year

Employment Outlook

Growth rate until the year 2005: Average.

Public Relations Specialists

★6431★ "Advertising/Public Relations"
in *Internships: 1995* (pp. 38-49)
Petersons Guides, Inc.
PO Box 2123
Princeton, NJ 08543-2123
Ph: (609)243-9111   Fax: (609)243-9150
Fr: 800-338-3282

Fifteenth edition, 1995. Lists internship opportunities under six broad categories: communications, creative, performing, and fine, performing, and fine arts, human services, international relations, business and technology, and public relations. Includes a special section on internships in Washington, DC. For each internship program, gives the name, phone number, contact person, description, eligibility requirements, and benefits.

★6432★ *Career Opportunities in*
**   *Advertising and Public Relations***
Facts on File
460 Park Ave. S.
New York, NY 10016-7382
Ph: (212)683-2244   Fax: 800-678-3633
Fr: 800-322-8755

Shelly Field. 1993. Guidebook offering complete career information for those entering advertising or public relations. Describes 85 jobs and includes salary information, employment prospects, and education and skills needed for the jobs.

★6433★ *Career Opportunities in the*
**   *Sports Industry***
Facts on File
460 Park Ave. S.
New York, NY 10016-7382
Ph: (212)683-2244   Fax: 800-678-3633
Fr: 800-322-8755

Shelly Field. 1993. Sourcebook combining a variety of information including sports-related academic programs, league lists, professional associations, and more of interest to those considering employment in organized amateur or professional sports.

★6434★ *Career Opportunities in*
**   *Television, Cable and Video***
Facts on File
460 Park Ave. S.
New York, NY 10016-7382
Ph: (212)683-2244   Fax: 800-678-3633
Fr: 800-322-8755

Maxine K. Reed and Robert M. Reed. Third edition, 1993. Includes information on employment and advancement prospects, education, experience and skills requiresn salary range, and tips for entry into the field.

★6435★ *Career Opportunities for*
**   *Writers***
Facts on File
460 Park Ave. S.
New York, NY 10016-7382
Ph: (212)683-2244   Fax: 800-678-3633
Fr: 800-322-8755

Rosemary Ellen Guiley. 1993. Sourcebook on over 100 careers for writers from various fields.

★6436★ *Careers in Communications*
National Textbook Co. (NTC)
VGM Career Books
4255 W. Touhy Ave.
Lincolnwood, IL 60646-1975
Ph: (708)679-5500   Fax: (708)679-2494
Fr: 800-323-4900

Shonan F. Noronha. 1987. Provides facts about careers in communications, including journalism, publishing, photography and film, advertising, public relations, and telecommunication.

★6437★ *Careers in Public Relations*
Public Relations Society of America (PRSA)
33 Irving Pl., 3rd Fl.
15th & 16th Sts.
New York, NY 10003
Ph: (212)995-2230

Describes the field of public relations, salaries, nature of the work, personal qualifications, educational preparation, work experience, fields of public relations, and finding a job.

★6438★ *Celebrity Publicist*
Vocational Biographies, Inc.
PO Box 31
Sauk Centre, MN 56378-0031
Ph: (612)352-6516   Fax: (612)352-5546
Fr: 800-255-0752

1992. Four-page pamphlet containing a personal narrative about a worker's job, work likes and dislikes, career path from high school to the present. Education and training, the rewards and frustrations, and the effects of the job on the rest of the worker's life. The data file portion of this pamphlet gives a concise occupational summary, including work descriptions, working conditions, places of employment, personal characteristics, education and training, job outlook, and salary range.

★6439★ *Hospital Public Relations*
**   *Director***
Vocational Biographies, Inc.
PO Box 31
Sauk Centre, MN 56378-0031
Ph: (612)352-6516   Fax: (612)352-5546
Fr: 800-255-0752

1992. Four-page pamphlet containing a personal narrative about a worker's job, work likes and dislikes, career path from high school to the present. Education and training, the rewards and frustrations, and the effects of the job on the rest of the worker's life. The data file portion of this pamphlet gives a concise occupational summary, including work descriptions, working conditions, places of employment, personal characteristics, education and training, job outlook, and salary range.

★6440★ *Making It in Public Relations:*
**   *An Insider's Guide to Career***
**   *Opportunities***
Macmillan Publishing Co.
866 3rd Ave.
New York, NY 10022
Ph: (212)702-2000

Leonard Mogel. 1993.

★6441★ *Opportunities in Public Relations Careers*
National Textbook Co. (NTC)
VGM Career Books
4255 W. Touhy Ave.
Lincolnwood, IL 60646-1975
Ph: (708)679-5500   Fax: (708)679-2494
Fr: 800-323-4900

Morris B. Rotman. 1988. Describes the history and future of public relations; what public relations people do; and the market for public relations. Lists colleges offering public relations courses and the largest public relations firms. Charts public relations salaries.

★6442★ "Press Relations Coordinator" in *Opportunities in Laser Technology Careers* (pp. 76-78)
National Textbook Co. (NTC)
VGM Career Books
4255 W. Touhy Ave.
Lincolnwood, IL 60646-1975
Ph: (708)679-5500   Fax: (708)679-2494
Fr: 800-323-4900

Jan Bone. 1989. Describes career opportunities using lasers in health care, manufacturing, the military, space communications, and research. Explains the education needed and provides job hunting tips.

★6443★ *"Press Secretary" in How to Land a Job in Journalism* (pp. 170-171)
Betterway Publications
PO Box 219
Crozet, VA 22932
Ph: (804)823-5661

Phil Swann and Ed Achorn. 1988. Offers advice on college preparation, financial aid, internships, and job hunting for those interested in a career in journalism. Contains tips from journalists.

★6444★ "Public Affairs Specialist" in *Guide to Federal Jobs* (p. 187)
Resource Directories
3361 Executive Pkwy., Ste. 302
Toledo, OH 43606
Ph: (419)536-5353   Fax: (419)536-7056
Fr: 800-274-8515

Rod W. Durgin, editor. Third edition, 1992. Contains information on finding and applying for federal jobs. Describes more than 200 professional and technical jobs for college graduates. Covers the nature of the work, salary, and geographic location. Lists college majors preferred for that occupation. Section one describes the function and work of government agencies that hire the most significant number of college graduates.

★6445★ "Public Relations" in *American Almanac of Jobs and Salaries* (pp. 350)
Avon Books
1350 Avenue of the Americas
New York, NY 10019
Ph: (212)261-6800   Fr: 800-238-0658

John Wright, editor. Revised and updated, 1994-95. A comprehensive guide to the wages of hundreds of occupations in a wide variety of industries and organizations.

★6446★ "Public Relations Assistant" in *Career Opportunities in Art*
Facts on File
460 Park Ave. S.
New York, NY 10016-7382
Ph: (212)683-2244   Fax: 800-678-3633
Fr: 800-322-8755

Susan H. Haubenstock. 1988. This book profiles seventy-five art-related jobs. Each profile includes a career description, career ladder, employment and advancement prospects, education, experience and skills required, salary range, and tips for entry into the field. Chapters include "Information Coordinator" "Public Relations Assistant," and "Publicist."

★6447★ "Public Relations" in *Black Woman's Career Guide* (p. 182)
Bantam Doubleday Dell
1540 Broadway
New York, NY 10036
Fax: 800-233-3294   Fr: 800-223-5780

Beatryce Nivens. Revised edition, 1987. Describes career planning, resume writing, job hunting, and interviewing. Profiles 60 black women pioneers in 20 different careers.

★6448★ "Public Relations" in *Career Choices for the 90's for Students of Psychology* (pp. 165-183)
Walker and Co.
435 Hudson St.
New York, NY 10014
Ph: (212)727-8300   Fax: (212)727-0984
Fr: 800-289-2553

1990. Offers alternatives for students of psychology. Gives information about the outlook and competition for entry-level candidates. Provides job-hunting tips.

★6449★ "Public Relations" in *Careers in Business*
National Textbook Co. (NTC)
VGM Career Books
4255 W. Touhy Ave.
Lincolnwood, IL 60646-1975
Ph: (708)679-5500   Fax: (708)679-2494
Fr: 800-323-4900

Lila B. Stair and Dorothy Domkowski, editors. 1992. Provides facts about business areas such as marketing, accounting, production, human resources, management, public relations, and finance. Focuses on job duties, salaries, career paths, employment outlook, trends, educational preparation, and skills needed.

★6450★ "Public Relations" in *Careers in Communications*
National Textbook Co. (NTC)
VGM Career Books
4255 W. Touhy Ave.
Lincolnwood, IL 60646-1975
Ph: (708)679-5500   Fax: (708)679-2494
Fr: 800-323-4900

Shonan F. Noronha. 1987. Examines the fields of journalism, photography, radio, television, film, public relations, and advertising. Gives concrete details on job locations and how to secure a job. Suggests many resources for job hunting.

★6451★ "Public Relations" in *Careers in Health and Fitness*
Rosen Publishing Group
29 E. 21st St.
New York, NY 10010
Ph: (212)777-3017   Fax: (212)777-0277
Fr: 800-237-9932

Jackie Heron. 1990. Occupational profiles contain information on job duties, skills, advantages, basic equipment used, employment possibilities, certification, and salary.

★6452★ "Public Relations" in *Careers for Women Without College Degrees* (pp. 53-55)
McGraw-Hill, Inc.
1221 Avenue of the Americas
New York, NY 10020-3825
Ph: (212)512-2000   Fr: 800-722-4726

Beatryce Nivens. 1988. Contains exercises in goal setting, decision making and skills assessment. Explores 19 careers with the best occupational outlook; describes nontraditional college degree programs.

★6453★ *Public Relations Consultant*
Vocational Biographies, Inc.
PO Box 31
Sauk Centre, MN 56378-0031
Ph: (612)352-6516   Fax: (612)352-5546
Fr: 800-255-0752

1991. Four-page pamphlet containing a personal narrative about a worker's job, work likes and dislikes, career path from high school to the present. Education and training, the rewards and frustrations, and the effects of the job on the rest of the worker's life. The data file portion of this pamphlet gives a concise occupational summary, including work descriptions, working conditions, places of employment, personal characteristics, education and training, job outlook, and salary range.

★6454★ "Public Relations Counselor" in *Career Opportunities in the Music Industry* (pp. 135-138)
Facts on File
460 Park Ave. S.
New York, NY 10016-7382
Ph: (212)683-2244   Fax: 800-678-3633
Fr: 800-322-8755

Shelly Field. 1990. Discusses approximately 80 jobs in music including the performing arts, business, and education. Each job description provides basic career information, salary, employment prospects, advancement opportunities, education, training, and experience required.

★6455★ *Public Relations Director*
Vocational Biographies, Inc.
PO Box 31
Sauk Centre, MN 56378-0031
Ph: (612)352-6516   Fax: (612)352-5546
Fr: 800-255-0752

1994. Four-page pamphlet containing a personal narrative about a worker's job, work likes and dislikes, career path from high school to the present. Education and training, the rewards and frustrations, and the effects of the job on the rest of the worker's life. The data file portion of this pamphlet gives a concise occupational summary, including work descriptions, working conditions, places of employment, personal characteristics, education and training, job outlook, and salary range.

★6456★ "Public Relations" in *Encyclopedia of Career Choices for the 1990s: A Guide to Entry Level Jobs* (pp. 700-718)
Berkley Pub.
PO Box 506
East Rutherford, NJ 07073
Fax: (201)933-2316   Fr: 800-788-6262
1992. Describes entry-level careers in a variety of industries. Presents qualifications required, working conditions, salary, internships, and professional associations.

★6457★ "Public Relations" in *Encyclopedia of Careers and Vocational Guidance* (Vol.1, pp. 387-392)
J.G. Ferguson Publishing Co.
200 W. Madison St., Ste. 300
Chicago, IL 60606
Ph: (312)580-5480   Fax: (312)580-4948
William E. Hopke, editor-in-chief. Ninth edition, 1993. Four-volume set that profiles 900 occupations and describes job trends in 74 industries. Includes career description, educational requirements, history of the job, methods of entry, advancement, employment outlook, earnings, conditions of work, social and psychological factors, and sources of further information.

★6458★ "Public Relations" in *Fast Track Careers: A Guide to the Highest Paying Jobs* (pp. 90-93)
John Wiley and Sons, Inc.
605 3rd Ave.
New York, NY 10158-0012
Ph: (212)850-6000   Fax: (212)850-6088
Fr: 800-526-5368
William Lewis and Nancy Schuman. 1987. Describes eight fast-track careers, the public relations industry, entry-level opportunities, leading companies, expected earnings; includes a glossary of industry jargon.

★6459★ "Public Relations" in *Liberal Arts Jobs*
Petersons Guides, Inc.
PO Box 2123
Princeton, NJ 08543-2123
Ph: (609)243-9111   Fax: (609)243-9150
Fr: 800-338-3282
Burton Jay Nadler. Second edition, 1989. Strives to help the liberal arts graduate identify skills for entry-level positions. Also includes a chapter on public affairs. Gives goal setting and job search advice.

★6460★ "Public Relations Manager" in *College Board Guide to Jobs and Career Planning* (pp. 115)
The College Board
415 Columbus Ave.
New York, NY 10023-6992
Ph: (212)713-8165   Fax: (212)713-8143
Fr: 800-323-7155
Joyce S. Mitchell. Second edition, 1994. Describes a variety of careers. Includes information on salaries, related careers, education needed, and sources of additional information.

★6461★ "Public Relations" in *New Careers in Hospitals*
Rosen Publishing Group
29 E. 21st St.
New York, NY 10010
Ph: (212)777-3017   Fax: (212)777-0277
Fr: 800-237-9932
Lois S. Siegel. Revised edition, 1990. Describes a variety of hospital careers and covers background, professional preparation, functions, salary, and job outlook.

★6462★ "Public Relations" in *Opportunities in Marketing Careers* (pp. 20-21)
National Textbook Co. (NTC)
VGM Career Books
4255 W. Touhy Ave.
Lincolnwood, IL 60646-1975
Ph: (708)679-5500   Fax: (708)679-2494
Fr: 800-323-4900
Margery S. Steinberg. 1988. Defines marketing and surveys marketing fields, such as research and retailing. Gives the employment outlook; describes the rewards of a career in marketing. Includes information on the education needed, and how to find a job. Lists colleges with majors in marketing.

★6463★ "Public Relations Practitioner" in *Opportunities in Insurance Careers*
National Textbook Co. (NTC)
VGM Career Books
4255 W. Touhy Ave.
Lincolnwood, IL 60646-1975
Ph: (708)679-5500   Fax: (708)679-2494
Fr: 800-323-4900
Robert M. Schrayer. 1993. Provides an introduction to the world of insurance careers through an exploration of the industry's history; academic requirements; certification, licensing, and education requirements; positions available; as well as some careers associated with the insurance industry, such as data processing, human resources, and public relations.

★6464★ "Public Relations" in *Profitable Careers in Non-Profit* (pp. 136-147)
John Wiley and Sons, Inc.
605 3rd Ave.
New York, NY 10158-0012
Ph: (212)850-6000   Fax: (212)850-6088
Fr: 800-526-5368
William Lewis and Carol Milano. 1987. Examines nonprofit organizations and the career opportunities they offer. Offers tips on how to target and explore occupational opportunities in the nonprofit sector.

★6465★ "Public Relations and Publicity" in *Advertising: A VGM Career Planner* (pp. 93-98)
National Textbook Co. (NTC)
VGM Career Books
4255 W. Touhy Ave.
Lincolnwood, IL 60646-1975
Ph: (708)679-5500   Fax: (708)679-2494
Fr: 800-323-4900
Pattis, S. William. 1989. Describes the development of advertising. Explains the role of the media in advertising, personal characteristics needed to succeed in this field, educational requirements, and related jobs. Gives job hunting tips.

★6466★ *Public Relations Specialist*
Careers, Inc.
PO Box 135
Largo, FL 34649-0135
Ph: (813)584-7333
1992. Four-page brief offering the definition, history, duties, working conditions, personal qualifications, educational requirements, earnings, hours, employment outlook, advancement, and careers related to this position.

★6467★ *Public Relations Specialists*
Chronicle Guidance Publications, Inc.
66 Aurora St.
PO Box 1190
Moravia, NY 13118-1190
Ph: (315)497-0330   Fax: (315)497-3359
Fr: 800-622-7284
1992. Career brief describing the nature of the job, working conditions, hours and earnings, education and training, licensure, certification, unions, personal qualifications, social and psychological factors, location, employment outlook, entry methods, advancement, and related occupations.

★6468★ "Public Relations Specialists" in *101 Careers: A Guide to the Fastest-Growing Opportunities* (pp. 42-44)
John Wiley & Sons, Inc.
605 3rd Ave.
New York, NY 10158-0012
Ph: (212)850-6645   Fax: (212)850-6088
Michael Harkavy. 1990. Describes the nature of the job, working conditions, employment growth, qualifications, personal skills, projected salaries, and where to write for more information.

★6469★ "Public Relations Specialists" in *Career Opportunities for Writers* (pp. 40-41)
Facts on File
460 Park Ave. S.
New York, NY 10016-7382
Ph: (212)683-2244   Fax: 800-678-3633
Fr: 800-322-8755
Rosemary Guiley. 1992. Describes approximately 90 careers in eight major fields, offering such details as duties, salaries, prerequisites, employment and advancement opportunities, organizations to join, and opportunities for women and minorities.

★6470★ "Public Relations Specialists" in *Encyclopedia of Careers and Vocational Guidance* (Vol.4, pp. 201-204)
J.G. Ferguson Publishing Co.
200 W. Madison St., Ste. 300
Chicago, IL 60606
Ph: (312)580-5480   Fax: (312)580-4948
William E. Hopke, editor-in-chief. Ninth edition, 1993. Four-volume set that profiles 900 occupations and describes job trends in 74 industries. Volume 2—*Professional Careers*—contains a chapter titled "Public Relations Specialists" (p. 548). Includes career description, educational requirements, history of the job, methods of entry, advancement, employment outlook, earnings, conditions of work, social and psychological factors, and sources of further information.

★6471★ "Public Relations Specialists" in *Jobs! What They Are—Where They Are—What They Pay* (p. 271)
Simon & Schuster, Inc.
Simon & Schuster Bldg.
1230 Avenue of the Americas
New York, NY 10020
Ph: (212)698-7000   Fr: 800-223-2348
Robert O. Snelling and Anne M. Snelling. 3rd edition, 1992. Describes duties and responsibilities, earnings, employment opportunities, training, and qualifications.

★6472★ "Public Relations Specialists" in *Occupational Outlook Handbook*
U.S. Government Printing Office
Superintendent of Documents
Washington, DC 20402
Ph: (202)512-1800   Fax: (202)512-2250
Biennial; latest edition, 1994-95. Encyclopedia of careers describing about 250 occupations and comprising about 85 percent of all jobs in the economy. Occupations that require lengthy education or training are given the most attention. Each occupation's profile describes what the worker does on the job, working conditions, education and training requirements, advancement possibilities, job outlook, earnings, and sources of additional information.

★6473★ "Public Relations" in *Wanted: Liberal Arts Graduates* (pp. 44-45)
Doubleday and Co.
666 5th Ave.
New York, NY 10103
Ph: (212)765-6500   Fr: 800-223-6834
Maran L. Salzman. 1987. Recommends that liberal arts graduates analyze their skills and research the job market. Describes companies that hire liberal arts graduates. Gives tips on how to find work.

★6474★ "Public Relations" in *Where the Jobs Are: The Hottest Careers for the 90s* (pp. 211-220)
Career Press
180 5th Ave.
Hawthorne, NJ 07507
Ph: (201)427-0229   Fax: (201)427-2037
Fr: 800-CAREER-1
Joyce Hadley. 1995. Offers a job-hunting strategy for the 1990s as well as descriptions of growing careers of the decade. Each profile includes general information, forecasts, growth, education and training, licensing requirements, and salary information.

★6475★ "Public Relations Worker" in *VGM's Careers Encyclopedia* (pp. 381-384)
National Textbook Co. (NTC)
VGM Career Books
4255 W. Touhy Ave.
Lincolnwood, IL 60646-1975
Ph: (708)679-5500   Fax: (708)679-2494
Fr: 800-323-4900
Third edition, 1991. Profiles 200 occupations. Describes job duties, places of employment, working conditions, qualifications, education and training, advancement potential, and salary for each occupation.

★6476★ "Public Relations Worker" in *VGM's Handbook of Business and Management Careers*
National Textbook Co.
4255 W. Touhy Ave.
Lincolnwood, IL 60646-1975
Ph: (708)679-5500   Fax: (708)679-2494
Fr: 800-323-4900
Annette Selden. Second edition, 1993. Contains 42 two-page occupational profiles describing job duties, places of employment, working conditions, qualifications, education, employment outlook, and income.

★6477★ "Public Relations Workers" in *Career Information Center* (Vol.3)
Simon and Schuster
200 Old Tappan Rd.
Old Tappan, NJ 07675
Fax: 800-445-6991   Fr: 800-223-2348
Richard Lidz and Linda Perrin, editorial directors. Fifth edition, 1993. A multi-volume set that profiles more than 600 occupations. Each occupational profile describes job duties, educational requirements, getting a job, advancement possibilities, employment outlook, working conditions, earnings and benefits, and sources of additional information.

★6478★ "Publicity" in *Career Choices for the 90's for Students of Communications and Journalism* (pp. 33-35)
Walker and Co.
435 Hudson St.
New York, NY 10014
Ph: (212)727-8300   Fax: (212)727-0984
Fr: 800-289-2553
1990. Offers alternatives for students of communications and journalism. Gives information about the job outlook and competition for entry-level candidates. Provides job-hunting tips.

★6479★ *School Public Relations Specialist*
Vocational Biographies, Inc.
PO Box 31
Sauk Centre, MN 56378-0031
Ph: (612)352-6516   Fax: (612)352-5546
Fr: 800-255-0752
1991. Four-page pamphlet containing a personal narrative about a worker's job, work likes and dislikes, career path from high school to the present. Education and training, the rewards and frustrations, and the effects of the job on the rest of the worker's life. The data file portion of this pamphlet gives a concise occupational summary, including work descriptions, working conditions, places of employment, personal characteristics, education and training, job outlook, and salary range.

PROFESSIONAL ASSOCIATIONS

★6480★ American Society for Health Care Marketing and Public Relations (ASHCMPR)
c/o American Hospital Association
840 N. Lake Shore Dr.
Chicago, IL 60611
Ph: (312)422-3737   Fax: (312)422-4579
Persons in hospitals, hospital councils or associations, hospital-related schools, and health care organizations responsible for marketing and public relations. **Publications:** *Directory of Health Care Strategic Management and Communications Consultants*, annual. • *Membership Directory of the American Society for Health Care Marketing and Public Relations*, annual. • *MPR Exchange*, bimonthly.

★6481★ Public Relations Society of America (PRSA)
33 Irving Pl., 3rd Fl.
New York, NY 10003
Ph: (212)995-2230   Fax: (212)995-0757
Members: Professional society of public relations practitioners in business and industry, counseling firms, government, associations, hospitals, schools, and nonprofit organizations. **Purpose:** Conducts professional development programs. Maintains job referral service, speakers' bureau, and research information center. Offers accreditation program. **Publications:** *Public Relations Journal*, semiannual. • *Public Relations Tactics*, monthly.

STANDARDS/CERTIFICATION AGENCIES

★6482★ Public Relations Society of America (PRSA)
33 Irving Pl., 3rd Fl.
New York, NY 10003
Ph: (212)995-2230   Fax: (212)995-0757
Conducts professional development programs. Maintains job referral service, speakers' bureau, and research information center. Offers accreditation program.

TEST GUIDES

★6483★ *Career Examination Series: Public Relations Specialist*
National Learning Corp.
212 Michael Dr.
Syosset, NY 11791
Ph: (516)921-8888   Fax: (516)921-8743
Fr: 800-645-6337
Jack Rudman. 1993. Test guide including questions and answers for students or professionals in the field who seek advancement through examination.

EDUCATIONAL DIRECTORIES AND PROGRAMS

★6484★ Public Administration Career Directory
Gale Research Inc.
835 Penobscot Bldg.
Detroit, MI 48226
Ph: (313)961-2242   Fr: 800-877-GALE
1994. For job seekers contemplating careers in public service.

★6485★ Public Relations Career Directory
Gale Research Inc.
835 Penobscot Bldg.
Detroit, MI 48226-4094
Ph: (313)961-2242   Fax: (313)961-6083
Fr: 800-877-GALE
Bradley J. Morgan, Contact
Latest edition 1993. Covers Approximately 125 companies offering job opportunities, internships, and training possibilities for those seeking a career in public relations; sources of help-wanted ads, professional associations, videos, databases, career guides, and professional guides and handbooks. Entries include: For companies—Name, address, phone, fax, business description, names and titles of key personnel, number of employees, average number of entry-level positions available, human resources contact, description of internships including contact, type and number available, application procedures, qualifications, and duties. For others—Name or title, address, phone, description. Paperback edition is available from Visible Ink Press. Arrangement: Companies are alphabetical; others are classified by type of resource.

AWARDS, SCHOLARSHIPS, GRANTS, AND FELLOWSHIPS

★6486★ National Public Relations Achievement Award
Ball State University
Department of Journalism
Muncie, IN 47306-0485
Ph: (317)285-8200   Fax: (317)285-7997
To recognize an outstanding individual in the field of public relations. Honorees are selected by the faculty. Established in 1977.

BASIC REFERENCE GUIDES AND HANDBOOKS

★6487★ The Business of Public Relations
Praeger Publishers
1 Madison Ave., 11th Fl.
New York, NY 10010
Ph: (212)685-5300
E. W. Brody. 1987. Includes a bibliography and an index.

★6488★ The Complete Book of Product Publicity
AMACOM
135 W. 50th St.
New York, NY 10020-1201
Ph: (212)903-8089   Fr: 800-262-9699
James D. Barhydt. 1987. Includes an index.

★6489★ The Dartnell Public Relations Handbook
Dartnell Corp.
4660 Ravenswood Ave.
Chicago, IL 60640
Ph: (312)561-4000
Robert L. Dilenschneider and Dan J. Forrestal. Third revised edition, 1987. Includes a bibliograpy and an index.

★6490★ Effective Corporate Relations: Applying Public Relations in Business and Industry
McGraw-Hill, Inc.
1221 Avenue of the Americas
New York, NY 10020
Ph: (212)512-2000   Fr: 800-722-4726
Norman A. Hart, editor. 1987. Includes bibliographies and an index.

★6491★ Lesly's Handbook of PR & Communications
AMACOM
135 W. 50th St.
New York, NY 10020-1201
Ph: (212)903-8089   Fr: 800-262-9699
Philip Lesly, editor. Fourth edition, 1991.

★6492★ The Marketer's Guide to Public Relations: How Today's Top Companies Are Using the New PR to Gain a Competitive Edge
John Wiley and Sons, Inc.
605 3rd Ave.
New York, NY 10158-0012
Ph: (212)850-6000   Fax: (212)850-6088
Fr: 800-526-5368
Thomas L. Harris. 1991. Simplifies public relations into a tool that can be used by marketing departments of companies for increased business success.

★6493★ Professional's Guide to Public Relations Services
Gale Research Inc.
835 Penobscot Bldg.
Detroit, MI 48226
Ph: (313)961-2242   Fax: (313)961-6083
Fr: 800-347-GALE
Richard Weiner. Sixth edition, 1988. Published by the American Management Association. Includes index.

★6494★ Promoting Issues and Ideas: A Guide to Public Relations for Nonprofit Organizations
Foundation Center (FC)
79 5th Ave.
New York, NY 10003-3076
Ph: (212)620-4230   Fr: 800-424-9836
1995. Includes a bibliography and an index.

★6495★ Public Relations in Action
TAB/McGraw-Hill, Inc.
PO Box 182607
Columbus, OH 43218-2607
Fax: (614)759-3644   Fr: 800-822-8158
Robert T. Reilly. Second edition, 1987. Includes bibliographies and an index.

★6496★ Public Relations Handbook
Dartnell Corp.
4660 Ravenswood Ave.
Chicago, IL 60640
Ph: (312)561-4000   Fr: 800-621-5463
Robert L. Dilenschneider and Dan J. Forrestal. Third revised edition, 1987. Covers planning, policy making, budgeting, staffing, and creative writing.

★6497★ Public Relations Programming and Production
Praeger Publishers
1 Madison Ave., 11th Fl.
New York, NY 10010
Ph: (212)685-5300
E. W. Brody. 1988. Includes a bibliography and an index.

★6498★ Strategic Public Relations Counseling: Models From the Counselor's Academy
University Press of America
4720 Boston Way
Lanham, MD 20706
Ph: (301)459-3366
Norman R. Nager and Richard H. Truitt. 1991. Includes a bibliography and an index.

PROFESSIONAL AND TRADE PERIODICALS

★6499★ Bulldog Reporter: West
Infocom Group
2115 4th St., Ste. B
Berkeley, CA 94710
Ph: (510)549-4338
Mike Moran
Semimonthly. Covers public relations and Western U.S. news media. Recurring features include interviews, job listings, book reviews, and agency news.

★6500★ Communication Briefings
Encoders, Inc.
700 Black Horse Pike, Ste. 110
Blackwood, NJ 08012
Ph: (609)232-6380   Fax: (609)232-8229
Frank Grazian
Monthly. Provides communication ideas and techniques for a wide variety of areas, including public relations, advertising, fund raising, speeches, media relations, human resources, and employee/manager relations.

Carries interviews with top communicators, business leaders, university experts, and research specialists. Recurring features include news of research, book reviews, and abstracts of articles from national publications.

★6501★ The Community Relations Report
Joe Williams Communications
PO Box 924
Bartlesville, OK 74005
Ph: (918)336-2267   Fax: (918)336-2733
Joe Williams

Monthly. Reports on innovative and creative corporate community relations activities throughout the country. Covers different techniques of improving community relations such as programs, activities, cultural events, and philanthropy grants. Recurring features include profiles of community relations practitioners and announcements of useful programs and books.

★6502★ Corporate Public Issues and Their Management
Issue Action Publications, Inc.
207 Loudoun St. SE
Leesburg, VA 22075-3115
Ph: (703)777-8450
Teresa Yancey Crane

Semimonthly. Concerned with sound public relations and strategic planning for effective public affairs and public policy management. Covers topics such as pertinent legislation, regulations, media interpretation, and community confrontation. Recurring features include profiles of corporate and association issue management programs, case histories, reports on seminars, and references for further reading.

★6503★ The National Business Wire Newsletter
Business Wire
44 Montgomery St., No. 3900
San Francisco, CA 94104
Ph: (415)986-4422   Fax: (415)788-5335
Lorry I. Lokey

Monthly. Published for those who use the Business Wire service to transmit news releases nationally and internationally via high speed (9600 baud) satellite. Carries updates on personnel changes in the media and public relations world as well as news items concerning print and electronic journalism and all aspects of public relations. Recurring features include job listings and obituaries.

★6504★ Public Relations Review
JAI Press, Inc.
55 Old Post Rd., No. 2
PO Box 1678
Greenwich, CT 06836-1678
Ph: (203)661-7602   Fax: (203)661-0792
Ray E. Hiebert

Quarterly. Communications journal covering public relations education, government, survey research, public policy, history, and bibliographies.

PROFESSIONAL MEETINGS AND CONVENTIONS

★6505★ Public Relations Society of America Annual Conference
Public Relations Society of America
33 Irving Pl.
New York, NY 10003
Ph: (212)995-2230   Fax: (212)995-0757
Annual. **Dates and Locations:** 1995 Nov 05-08; Seattle, WA.

OTHER SOURCES OF INFORMATION

★6506★ "Advertising and Public Relations" in Accounting to Zoology: Graduate Fields Defined (pp. 33-36)
Petersons Guides, Inc.
PO Box 2123
Princeton, NJ 08543-2123
Ph: (609)243-9111   Fax: (609)243-9150
Fr: 800-338-3282

Amy J. Goldstein, editor. Revised and updated, 1987. Discusses types of graduate programs and degrees, graduate research, applied work, employment prospects and trends.

★6507★ Effective Public Relations
Prentice-Hall, Inc.
Rte. 9W
Englewood Cliffs, NJ 07632
Ph: (201)592-2000   Fr: 800-947-7700

Scott M. Cutlip, Allen H. Center, and Glen M. Broom. Sixth edition, 1993. Includes bibiographies and an index.

★6508★ "Public Relations Specialist" in 100 Best Jobs for the 1990s & Beyond
Dearborn Financial Publishing, Inc.
520 N. Dearborn St.
Chicago, IL 60610-4354
Ph: (312)836-4400   Fax: (312)836-1021
Fr: 800-621-9621

Carol Kleiman. 1992. Describes 100 jobs ranging from accountants to veterinarians.. Each job profile includes such information as education, experience, and certification needed, salaries, and job search suggestions.

Radio and Television Announcers and Newscasters

Announcers and newscasters are well-known personalities to radio and television audiences. **Radio announcers**, often called **disc jockeys**, select and introduce recorded music; present news, sports, weather, and commercials; interview guests; and report on community activities and other matters of interest to the audience. If a written script is required, they may do the research and writing. Announcers at large stations usually specialize in sports or weather, or in general news, and may be called newscasters or **anchors**. Some are **news analysts**. In small stations, one announcer may do everything. News anchors, or a pair of co-anchors, present news stories and introduce in-depth videotaped news or live transmissions from on-the-scene reporters. **Weathercasters**, also called **weather reporters or meteorologists**, report and forecast-weather conditions. Sportscasters select, write, and deliver sports news. This may include interviews with sports personalities and live coverage of games. **Broadcast news analysts**, called **commentators** present news stories and interpret them or discuss how they may affect the nation or listeners personally.

Salaries

Salaries in broadcasting vary widely. They are higher in television than in radio, higher in larger markets than in small ones, and higher in commercial than in public broadcasting.

Experienced radio announcers	$13,000-$45,000/year
Experienced radio announcers (average)	$17,000/year
Television news anchors	$28,000-$163,000/year
Television news anchors (average)	$41,000/year
Weathercasters	$25,200-$103,321/year
Sportscasters	$23,000-$109,000/year
Radio sportscasters	$12,500-30,600/year

Employment Outlook

Growth rate until the year 2005: Average.

Radio and Television Announcers and Newscasters

CAREER GUIDES

★6509★ Announcer, Radio-TV
Careers, Inc.
PO Box 135
Largo, FL 34649-0135
Ph: (813)584-7333

1992. Four-page brief offering the definition, history, duties, working conditions, personal qualifications, educational requirements, earnings, hours, employment outlook, advancement, and careers related to this position.

★6510★ "Announcers" in Career Information Center (Vol.3)
Simon and Schuster
200 Old Tappan Rd.
Old Tappan, NJ 07675
Fax: 800-445-6991   Fr: 800-223-2348

Richard Lidz and Linda Perrin, editorial directors. Fifth edition, 1993. A multi-volume set that profiles more than 600 occupations. Each occupational profile describes job duties, educational requirements, getting a job, advancement possibilities, employment outlook, working conditions, earnings and benefits, and sources of additional information.

★6511★ Announcers and Disc Jockeys
Chronicle Guidance Publications, Inc.
66 Aurora St.
PO Box 1190
Moravia, NY 13118-1190
Ph: (315)497-0330   Fax: (315)497-3359
Fr: 800-622-7284

1994. Career brief describing the nature of the job, working conditions, hours and earnings, education and training, licensure, certification, unions, personal qualifications, social and psychological factors, location, employment outlook, entry methods, advancement, and related occupations.

★6512★ "Art, Entertainment, and Media Careers" in Best Jobs for the 1990s and Into the 21st Century
Impact Publications
9104-N Manassas Dr.
Manassas Park, VA 22111
Ph: (703)361-7300   Fax: (703)335-9486

Ronald L. Krannich and Caryl Rae Krannich. 1993. Includes information on designers, photographers and camera operators, and radio and TV news announcers and newscasters.

★6513★ Break into Broadcasting
Carlton Press, Inc.
11 W. 32nd St.
New York, NY 10001
Ph: (212)714-0300

Robert L. Shannon. 1991.

★6514★ "Broadcaster (Sports)" in Careers in Health and Fitness
Rosen Publishing Group
29 E. 21st St.
New York, NY 10010
Ph: (212)777-3017   Fax: (212)777-0277
Fr: 800-237-9932

Jackie Heron. 1990. Occupational profiles contain information on job duties, skills, advantages, basic equipment used, employment possibilities, certification, and salary.

★6515★ "Broadcasting" in Black Woman's Career Guide (pp. 173-177)
Bantam Doubleday Dell
1540 Broadway
New York, NY 10036
Fax: 800-233-3294   Fr: 800-223-5780

Beatryce Nivens. Revised edition, 1987. Describes career planning, resume writing, job hunting, and interviewing. Profiles 60 black women pioneers in 20 different careers.

★6516★ "Broadcasting" in Career Choices for the 90's for Students of Political Science and Government
Walker and Co.
435 Hudson St.
New York, NY 10014
Ph: (212)727-8300   Fax: (212)727-0984
Fr: 800-289-2553

1990. Offers alternatives for students of political science. Gives information about job outlook and competition for entry-level candidates. Provides job-hunting tips.

★6517★ Career Opportunities in the Sports Industry
Facts on File
460 Park Ave. S.
New York, NY 10016-7382
Ph: (212)683-2244   Fax: 800-678-3633
Fr: 800-322-8755

Shelly Field. 1993. Sourcebook combining a variety of information including sports-related academic programs, league lists, professional associations, and more of interest to those considering employment in organized amateur or professional sports.

★6518★ Career Opportunities in Television, Cable and Video
Facts on File
460 Park Ave. S.
New York, NY 10016-7382
Ph: (212)683-2244   Fax: 800-678-3633
Fr: 800-322-8755

Maxine K. Reed and Robert M. Reed. Third edition, 1993. Includes information on employment and advancement prospects, education, experience and skills requiresn salary range, and tips for entry into the field.

★6519★ Career Opportunities for Writers
Facts on File
460 Park Ave. S.
New York, NY 10016-7382
Ph: (212)683-2244   Fax: 800-678-3633
Fr: 800-322-8755

Rosemary Ellen Guiley. 1993. Sourcebook on over 100 careers for writers from various fields.

★6520★ Careers in Communications
National Textbook Co. (NTC)
VGM Career Books
4255 W. Touhy Ave.
Lincolnwood, IL 60646-1975
Ph: (708)679-5500   Fax: (708)679-2494
Fr: 800-323-4900

Shonan F. Noronha. 1987. Provides facts about careers in communications, including journalism, publishing, photography and film, advertising, public relations, and telecommunication.

★6521★ Careers in Radio and Television News
Radio-Television News Directors Association
1000 Connecticut Ave., NW, Ste. 615
Washington, DC 20036
Ph: (202)659-6510

Vernon A. Stone. Seventh edition, 1993. Describes careers in radio and television, job locations, salaries, opportunities for women and minorities, and how to get started in the field.

★6522★ Careers in Television
National Association of Broadcasters
1771 N St., NW
Washington, DC 20036-2898
Ph: (202)429-5376

Rich Adams and Dwight Ellis. 1991. Describes various jobs in television broadcasting, including educational requirements and job-related experience needed.

★6523★ "Disc Jockeys" in Opportunities in Broadcasting Careers (pp. 67-86)
National Textbook Co. (NTC)
VGM Career Books
4255 W. Touhy Ave.
Lincolnwood, IL 60646-1975
Ph: (708)679-5500   Fax: (708)679-2494
Fr: 800-323-4900

Elmo Israel Ellis. 1992. Describes the history and future of radio, television, and cable TV broadcasting. Includes information on working conditions and education requirements.

★6524★ Exploring Careers in Video
Rosen Publishing Group
29 E. 21st St.
New York, NY 10010
Ph: (212)777-3017   Fax: (212)777-0277
Fr: 800-237-9932

Paul Allman. Revised edition, 1989. Describes various careers available in television and tells how to acquire necessary training and preparation. Covers work in network and cable TV, industrial television, and commercial production.

★6525★ Into the Newsroom: An Introduction to Journalism
Globe Pequot Press
1001 N. Calvert St.
Chester, CT 06412
Ph: (203)526-9571   Fr: 800-243-0495

Leonard R. Teel and Ron Taylor. Second edition, 1988. Includes an index.

★6526★ Making It in the Media Professions: A Realistic Guide to Career Opportunities in Newspapers, Magazines, Books, Television, Radio, the Movies
Globe Pequot
1001 N. Calvert St.
Chester, CT 06412
Ph: (203)526-9571

Leonard Mogel. 1988. Describes the history and scope of the field, education, and training needed. Profiles people working in media professions. Lists the ten best companies in each field. Lists college degree programs and workshops.

★6527★ "Music Director" in Career Opportunities in the Music Industry (p. 65-66)
Facts on File
460 Park Ave. S.
New York, NY 10016-7382
Ph: (212)683-2244   Fax: 800-678-3633
Fr: 800-322-8755

Shelly Field. 1990. Discusses approximately 80 jobs in music including the performing arts, business, and education. Each job description provides basic career information, salary, employment prospects, advancement opportunities, education, training, and experience required.

★6528★ "News (Broadcasting)" in Career Choices for the 90's for Students of History (pp. 30-33)
Walker and Co.
435 Hudson St.
New York, NY 10014
Ph: (212)727-8300   Fax: (212)727-0984
Fr: 800-289-2553

1990. Offers alternatives for students of history. Gives information about the outlook and competition for entry-level candidates. Provides job-hunting tips.

★6529★ "News" in Career Choices for the 90's for Students of Communications and Journalism (pp. 146-148)
Walker and Co.
435 Hudson St.
New York, NY 10014
Ph: (212)727-8300   Fax: (212)727-0984
Fr: 800-289-2553

1990. Offers alternatives for students of communications and journalism. Gives information about the job outlook and competition for entry-level candidates. Provides job-hunting tips.

★6530★ Opportunities in Broadcasting
National Textbook Co. (NTC)
VGM Career Books
4255 W. Touhy Ave.
Lincolnwood, IL 60646-1975
Ph: (708)679-5500   Fax: (708)679-2494
Fr: 800-323-4900

Elmo Israel Ellis. 1992. Describes the history and future of radio, television, and cable TV broadcasting. Includes information on working conditions and educational requirements.

★6531★ Opportunities in Television and Video Careers
National Textbook Co. (NTC)
VGM Career Books
4255 W. Touhy Ave.
Lincolnwood, IL 60646-1975
Ph: (708)679-5500   Fax: (708)679-2494
Fr: 800-323-4900

Shonan F.R. Noronha. 1988.

★6532★ Radio Disc Jockey
Vocational Biographies, Inc.
PO Box 31
Sauk Centre, MN 56378-0031
Ph: (612)352-6516   Fax: (612)352-5546
Fr: 800-255-0752

1991. Four-page pamphlet containing a personal narrative about a worker's job, work likes and dislikes, career path from high school to the present. Education and training, the rewards and frustrations, and the effects of the job on the rest of the worker's life. The data file portion of this pamphlet gives a concise occupational summary, including work descriptions, working conditions, places of employment, personal characteristics, education and training, job outlook, and salary range.

★6533★ "Radio" in Internships: 1995 (pp. 87-92)
Petersons Guides, Inc.
PO Box 2123
Princeton, NJ 08543-2123
Ph: (609)243-9111   Fax: (609)243-9150
Fr: 800-338-3282

Fifteenth edition, 1995. Lists internship opportunities under six broad categories: communications, creative, performing, and fine arts, human services, international relations, business and technology, and public relations. Includes a special section on internships in Washington, D.C. For each internship program, gives the name, phone number, contact person, description, eligibility requirements, and benefits.

★6534★ "Radio/Television Announcer" in VGM's Careers Encyclopedia (pp. 389-391)
National Textbook Co. (NTC)
VGM Career Books
4255 W. Touhy Ave.
Lincolnwood, IL 60646-1975
Ph: (708)679-5500   Fax: (708)679-2494
Fr: 800-323-4900

Third edition, 1991. Profiles 200 occupations. Describes job duties, places of employment, working conditions, qualifications, education and training, advancement potential, and salary for each occupation.

★6535★ "Radio and Television Announcers and Newscasters" in Occupational Outlook Handbook
U.S. Government Printing Office
Superintendent of Documents
Washington, DC 20402
Ph: (202)512-1800   Fax: (202)512-2250

Biennial; latest edition, 1994-95. Encyclopedia of careers describing about 250 occupations and comprising about 85 percent of all jobs in the economy. Occupations that require lengthy education or training are given the most attention. Each occupation's profile describes what the worker does on the job, working conditions, education and training requirements, advancement possibilities, job outlook, earnings, and sources of additional information.

★6536★ "Radio and Television Newscasters and Announcers" in *Encyclopedia of Careers and Vocational Guidance* **(Vol.4, pp. 223-227)**
J.G. Ferguson Publishing Co.
200 W. Madison St., Ste. 300
Chicago, IL 60606
Ph: (312)580-5480   Fax: (312)580-4948
William E. Hopke, editor-in-chief. Ninth edition, 1993. Four-volume set that profiles 900 occupations and describes job trends in 74 industries. Includes career description, educational requirements, history of the job, methods of entry, advancement, employment outlook, earnings, conditions of work, social and psychological factors, and sources of further information.

★6537★ "Radio and TV Announcers and Broadcasters" in *101 Careers: A Guide to the Fastest-Growing Opportunities* **(pp. 297-300)**
John Wiley & Sons, Inc.
605 3rd Ave.
New York, NY 10158-0012
Ph: (212)850-6645   Fax: (212)850-6088
Michael Harkavy. 1990. Describes the nature of the job, working conditions, employment growth, qualifications, personal skills, projected salaries, and where to write for more information.

★6538★ "Television" in *Internships: 1995* **(pp. 93-112)**
Petersons Guides, Inc.
PO Box 2123
Princeton, NJ 08543-2123
Ph: (609)243-9111   Fax: (609)243-9150
Fr: 800-338-3282
Fifteenth edition, 1995. Lists internship opportunities under six broad categories: communications, creative, performing, and fine arts, human services, international relations, business and technology, and public relations. Includes a special section on internships in Washington, D.C. For each internship program, gives the name, phone number, contact person, description, eligibility requirements, and benefits.

★6539★ "Television and Radio Announcers, Reporters, and Newscasters" in *Jobs! What They Are—Where They Are—What They Pay* **(p. 278)**
Simon & Schuster, Inc.
Simon & Schuster Bldg.
1230 Avenue of the Americas
New York, NY 10020
Ph: (212)698-7000   Fr: 800-223-2348
Robert O. Snelling and Anne M. Snelling. 3rd edition, 1992. Describes duties and responsibilities, earnings, employment opportunities, training, and qualifications.

★6540★ *TV News: Building a Career in Broadcast Journalism*
Butterworth Publishers
80 Montvale Ave.
Stoneham, MA 02180
Ph: (617)438-8464
Ray White, 1990.

PROFESSIONAL ASSOCIATIONS

★6541★ Broadcast Education Association (BEA)
1771 N St. NW
Washington, DC 20036-2891
Ph: (202)429-5355
Members: Universities and colleges; faculty and students; radio and television stations that belong to the National Association of Broadcasters. **Purpose:** Promotes improvement of curriculum and teaching methods, broadcasting research, television and radio production, and programming teaching. Offers placement services. **Publications:** *Feedback*, quarterly. • *Journal of Broadcasting and Electronic Media*, quarterly.

★6542★ National Association of Broadcasters (NAB)
1771 N St. NW
Washington, DC 20036
Ph: (202)429-5300   Fax: (202)429-5343
Members: Representatives of radio and television stations and networks; associate members include producers of equipment and programs. **Purpose:** Seeks to ensure the viability, strength, and success of free, over-the-air broadcasters; serves as an information resource to the industry. Monitors and reports on events regarding radio and television broadcasting. Maintains Broadcasting Hall of Fame. Offers minority placement service and employment clearinghouse. **Publications:** *Broadcast Engineering Conference Proceedings*, annual. • *Member Services Catalog*, annual. • *RadioWeek*, weekly. • *TV Today*, weekly.

★6543★ National Association of Radio Talk Show Hosts
134 Saint Botolph
Boston, MA 02115-4819
Ph: (617)437-9757   Fax: (617)437-0797
Members: Talk show hosts, producers, and others interested in the industry. **Purpose:** Seeks to encourage interest and promote excellence in all aspects of national, international, and community broadcast, and to promote freedom of speech. Goals are to protect the first amendment; to advance the status of talk programming; to promote and encourage the exchange of ideas, information, and experiences among professionals in the field; and to encourage and assist qualified and dedicated people to advance in talk broadcasting. Offers educational and charitable programs; maintains a speakers' bureau and hall of fame. **Publications:** *Open Line*, monthly.

★6544★ Radio-Television News Directors Association (RTNDA)
1000 Connecticut Ave. NW, Ste. 615
Washington, DC 20036
Ph: (202)659-6510   Fax: (202)223-4007
Fr: 800-80-RTNDA
Members: Professional society of heads of news departments for broadcast and cable stations and networks; associate members are journalists engaged in the preparation and presentation of broadcast news and teachers of electronic journalism; other members represent industry services, public relations departments of business firms, public relations firms, and networks. **Purpose:** Works to improve standards of electronic journalism; defends rights of journalists to access news; promotes journalism training to meet specific needs of the industry. Operates placement service and speakers' bureau. **Publications:** *Careers in Radio and Television*. • *Job Bulletin*, monthly. • *Radio-Television News Directors Association—Communicator*, monthly. • *Radio-Television News Directors Association—Membership Directory*, semiannual.

STANDARDS/CERTIFICATION AGENCIES

★6545★ Radio-Television News Directors Association (RTNDA)
1000 Connecticut Ave. NW, Ste. 615
Washington, DC 20036
Ph: (202)659-6510   Fax: (202)223-4007
Fr: 800-80-RTNDA
Works to improve standards of electronic journalism; defends rights of journalists to access news; promotes journalism training to meet specific needs of the industry. Operates placement service and speakers' bureau.

TEST GUIDES

★6546★ *Career Examination Series: Announcer*
National Learning Corp.
212 Michael Dr.
Syosset, NY 11791
Ph: (516)921-8888   Fax: (516)921-8743
Fr: 800-645-6337
Jack Rudman. A study guide for professional and trainees in the field of radio and television announcing. Includes a multiple-choice examination section; provides answers.

EDUCATIONAL DIRECTORIES AND PROGRAMS

★6547★ *Radio and Television Career Directory*
Gale Research Inc.
835 Penobscot Bldg.
Detroit, MI 48226-4094
Ph: (313)961-2242   Fax: (313)961-6083
Fr: 800-877-GALE

Bradley J. Morgan and Joseph M. Palmisano. Second edition, 1993. A directory in the Career Advisor Series that provides essays written by industry professionals; job search information on resume and cover letter preparation, networking, and the interviewing process; approximately 300 companies and organizations offering job opportunities and internships, and additional job-hunting resources.

AWARDS, SCHOLARSHIPS, GRANTS, AND FELLOWSHIPS

★6548★ **Award for Outstanding Service by a Broadcast Meteorologist**
American Meteorological Society
45 Beacon St.
Boston, MA 02108-3693
Ph: (617)227-2425   Fax: (617)742-8718

To recognize outstanding service to the community by a weathercaster. Nominations may be made by an individual or a group. A certificate is awarded annually. Established in 1975.

★6549★ **Broadcast/Cable Journalism Awards - Jack R. Howard Awards**
Scripps Howard Foundation
312 Walnut St.
PO Box 5380
Cincinnati, OH 45201
Ph: (513)977-3035   Fax: (513)977-3810

To recognize journalistic excellence in electronic media and to honor the best investigative or in-depth reporting of events. Any length program or series of programs broadcast during the preceding calendar year is considered. Any television or radio station or cable system originating local programs in the United States is eligible. No network syndicated programs, or production companies may compete. Judges look for importance, relevance, courage and localism. The deadline for entries is January 31. (Fact sheets and entry blanks are available in the fall of the year for all awards.) A monetary award of $2,000 and a bronze plaque are awarded to each winner in four categories. Established in 1972.

★6550★ **Broadcaster of the Year Award**
International Radio and Television Society
420 Lexington Ave.
New York, NY 10170
Ph: (212)867-6650   Fax: (212)867-6653

To recognize an outstanding individual, usually a performer. Awarded at the IRTS Annual Meeting in June. Established in 1964.

★6551★ **Grover C. Cobb Memorial Award**
National Association of Broadcasters
1771 N St. NW
Washington, DC 20036
Ph: (202)429-5300   Fax: (202)775-3520

To recognize a broadcaster or public servant who demonstrates unusual dedication to improving broadcasting's relationship with the federal government. A plaque and a grant are awarded annually at the Association's spring convention. Established in 1976 by TARPAC in memory of Grover C. Cobb, NAB senior vice president, government relations.

★6552★ **Distinguished Service Award**
National Association of Broadcasters
1771 N St. NW
Washington, DC 20036
Ph: (202)429-5300   Fax: (202)775-3520

For recognition of outstanding contributions to the field of broadcasting. Individuals in the American broadcasting industry are eligible. A plaque is awarded annually at the Association's spring convention. Established in 1953.

★6553★ **Douglas Edwards Award**
St. Bonaventure University
Department of Mass Communication
Drawer J
St. Bonaventure, NY 14778
Ph: (716)375-2520   Fax: (716)375-2389

To honor a renowned broadcaster who has displayed high moral and ethical conduct in his or her profession. A person of national renown in any phase of the broadcasting profession is eligible. A certificate is awarded annually at the Mark Hellinger Awards Luncheon in New York City. Established in 1986 by Russell J. Jandoli to honor Douglas Edwards, formerly of CBS News.

BASIC REFERENCE GUIDES AND HANDBOOKS

★6554★ *Les Brown's Encyclopedia of Television*
New York Zoetrope
838 Broadway
New York, NY 10003
Ph: (212)420-0590

Les Brown. Third edition, 1992. Includes a bibliography.

★6555★ *NBC Handbook of Pronunciation*
Harper Collins Publishers, Inc.
10 E. 53rd St.
New York, NY 10022
Ph: (212)207-7000

Eugene H. Ehrlich and Raymond Hand, Jr. Fourth edition, 1991.

★6556★ *The Practice of Journalism: A Guide to Reporting and Writing the News*
Prentice-Hall, Inc.
Rte. 9W
Englewood Cliffs, NJ 07632
Ph: (201)592-2000

Bruce Porter and Timothy Ferris. 1988. Includes a bibliography and an index .

★6557★ *The Radio Documentary Handbook: Creating, Producing, and Selling for Broadcast*
International Self-Counsel Press Ltd.
1704 N. State St.
Bellingham, WA 98225
Ph: (206)676-4530   Fr: 800-663-3007

Jurgen Hesse. 1987.

★6558★ *Skills for Radio Broadcasters*
Tab Books, Inc.
PO Box 40
Blue Ridge Summit, PA 17294-0850
Ph: (717)794-2191   Fr: 800-233-1128

Curtis Holsoppe. Third edition, 1988.

★6559★ *The Television News Interview*
Sage Publications, Inc.
2455 Teller Rd.
Newbury Park, CA 91320
Ph: (805)499-0721

Akiba A. Cohen. 1987. Includes a bibliography and an index.

★6560★ *Television and Radio Announcing*
Houghton Mifflin Co.
222 Berkeley St.
Boston, MA 02116
Ph: (617)351-5000

Stuart W. Hyde. Sixth edition, 1991. Includes an index.

PROFESSIONAL AND TRADE PERIODICALS

★6561★ *Broadcasting and Cable*
Cahners Publishing Co.
249 W. 17th St.
New York, NY 10011
Ph: (212)463-6759   Fax: (212)463-6734
Donald V. West

Weekly. News magazine covering The Fifth Estate (radio, TV, cable, and satellite), and the regulatory commissions involved.

★6562★ *Community Radio News*
National Federation of Community Broadcasters (NFCB)
666 11th St. NW, No. 805
Washington, DC 20001
Ph: (202)393-2355
Charmaine Peters

Monthly. Serves as a medium of communication for independent, community-licensed radio stations. Contains brief articles and news items on such topics as public broadcasting and programming, legislative developments, activities of the Federal Communications Commission, and local stations. Recurring features include notices of grants and awards received and a calendar for noncommercial broadcasters.

★6563★ The M Street Journal
M Street Corporation
304 Park Ave. S., 7th Fl.
New York, NY 10010
Ph: (212)473-4668   Fax: (212)473-4626
Fr: 800-248-4242
Robert Unmacht

Weekly. Reports on "radio station regulatory applications, actions, and filings; construction permit activity; format changes; and other U.S. and Canadian radio news of interest to the broadcast industry." Covers all radio markets, large and small.

★6564★ The Media Messenger
Western Press Clipping Services
8401 73rd Ave. N., Ste. 82
Brooklyn Park, MN 55428
Ph: (612)537-7730   Fr: 800-328-4827
Mary Sis

Monthly. Reports news summaries within the publishing, advertising, public relations, radio, and television industries.

★6565★ NAB RadioWeek
National Association of Broadcasters (NAB)
Public Affairs & Communications
1771 N St. NW
Washington, DC 20036-2891
Ph: (202)429-5416   Fax: (202)429-5406
Kirk Rafdal

Weekly. Covers radio broadcasting from legislative, regulatory, political, technical, management, and sales/marketing perspectives. Contains pertinent industry news, promotions of NAB conferences, product announcements, and coverage of awards competitions.

★6566★ One to One
CreeYadio Services
PO Box 9787
Fresno, CA 93794
Ph: (209)226-0558   Fax: (209)226-7481
Jay Trachman

Contains talent tips, topical humor, jokes, and one-liners. Offers no exclusivity. Recurring features include day-to-day calendar information, artist profiles and information, promotions, record introductions, editorials, letters to the editor, a calendar of events, and columns titled Promotions, Production Tips, Today in History, and Female Perspective.

★6567★ Television Digest
Warren Publishing, Inc.
2115 Ward Ct. NW
Washington, DC 20037
Ph: (202)872-9200   Fax: (202)393-3435
Albert Warren

Weekly. Monitors trends in the television broadcasting and cable industries and in consumer electronics equipment manufacturing and distribution. Reports on networks, stations, ratings, advertising, federal agencies, programming, technology, foreign developments, finance, and related subjects. Recurring features include a column on people in the industry. Consumer Electronics appears as a part of this newsletter.

★6568★ Variety
Cahners Publishing Co.
475 Park Ave. S.
New York, NY 10016-6999
Ph: (212)689-3600   Fax: (212)545-5400
Peter Bart

Weekly. Newspaper (tabloid) reporting on theatre, television, radio, music, records, and movies.

PROFESSIONAL MEETINGS AND CONVENTIONS

★6569★ National Association of Broadcasters International Convention and Exposition
National Association of Broadcasters
1771 N St., NW
Washington, DC 20036
Ph: (202)429-5335   Fax: (202)429-5343
Annual. Always held during April at the Convention Center in Las Vegas, Nevada. **Dates and Locations:** 1996 Apr 15-18; Las Vegas, NV. • 1997 Apr 07-10; Las Vegas, NV.

OTHER SOURCES OF INFORMATION

★6570★ "Radio/TV News Reporter" in 100 Best Jobs for the 1990s & Beyond
Dearborn Financial Publishing, Inc.
520 N. Dearborn St.
Chicago, IL 60610-4354
Ph: (312)836-4400   Fax: (312)836-1021
Fr: 800-621-9621
Carol Kleiman. 1992. Describes 100 jobs ranging from accountants to veterinarians. Each job profile includes such information as education, experience, and certification needed, salaries, and job search suggestions.

★6571★ Working in TV News: An Insiders Guide
Mustang Publishing Co.
PO Box 3004
Memphis, TN 38173
Ph: (901)521-1406   Fax: (901)521-1412
1993.

Reporters and Correspondents

Reporters and correspondents gather information and prepare stories on local, state, national, and international events; present points of view on current issues; and monitor the actions of public officials, corporate executives, special interest groups, and others who exercise power. In covering a story, they investigate leads and news tips, look at documents, observe on the scene, and interview people. Reporters in radio and television broadcasting often compose their story and report "live" from the scene of a newsworthy event. Later, they may do commentary for a taped report in the studio and appear on camera to introduce it. **General assignment reporters** write up local news as assigned, such as a political rally or a local company going out of business. **Investigative reporters** cover stories that take many days or weeks of information gathering. Reporters on small newspapers cover all aspects of local news, and also may take photographs, write headlines, edit wire service copy, and write editorials.

Salaries

Salaries for reporters and correspondents are as follows:

Radio reporters	$12,000-$33,388/year
Radio reporters (average)	$16,000/year
Television reporters	$16,052-$69,500/year
Television reporters (average)	$21,825/year
Beginning newspaper reporters	$300/week or less-$567/week or more
Experienced newspaper reporters	$479/week or less -$856/week or more

Employment Outlook

Growth rate until the year 2005: Average.

Reporters and Correspondents

CAREER GUIDES

★6572★ Career Choices for the 90's for Students of Communications and Journalism
Walker and Co.
435 Hudson St.
New York, NY 10014
Ph: (212)727-8300   Fax: (212)727-0984
Fr: 800-289-2553

1990. Offers alternatives for students of communications and journalism. Gives information about the job outlook and competition for entry-level candidates. Provides job-hunting tips.

★6573★ Career Opportunities in the Sports Industry
Facts on File
460 Park Ave. S.
New York, NY 10016-7382
Ph: (212)683-2244   Fax: 800-678-3633
Fr: 800-322-8755

Shelly Field. 1993. Sourcebook combining a variety of information including sports-related academic programs, league lists, professional associations, and more of interest to those considering employment in organized amateur or professional sports.

★6574★ Career Opportunities in Television, Cable and Video
Facts on File
460 Park Ave. S.
New York, NY 10016-7382
Ph: (212)683-2244   Fax: 800-678-3633
Fr: 800-322-8755

Maxine K. Reed and Robert M. Reed. Third edition, 1993. Includes information on employment and advancement prospects, education, experience and skills requiresn salary range, and tips for entry into the field.

★6575★ Career Opportunities for Writers
Facts on File
460 Park Ave. S.
New York, NY 10016-7382
Ph: (212)683-2244   Fax: 800-678-3633
Fr: 800-322-8755

Rosemary Ellen Guiley. 1993. Sourcebook on over 100 careers for writers from various fields.

★6576★ Careers in Communications
National Textbook Co. (NTC)
VGM Career Books
4255 W. Touhy Ave.
Lincolnwood, IL 60646-1975
Ph: (708)679-5500   Fax: (708)679-2494
Fr: 800-323-4900

Shonan F. Noronha. 1987. Provides facts about careers in communications, including journalism, publishing, photography and film, advertising, public relations, and telecommunication.

★6577★ Careers in Journalism
National Textbook Co. (NTC)
VGM Career Books
4255 W. Toughy Ave.
Lincolnwood, IL 60646-1975
Ph: (708)679-5500   Fax: (708)679-2494
Fr: 800-323-4900

Jan Goldberg. 1994. Looks at educational requirements, salary ranges, working conditions, and employment outlook for different careers in journalism.

★6578★ "Critic" in Career Opportunities in Art
Facts on File
460 Park Ave. S.
New York, NY 10016-7382
Ph: (212)683-2244   Fax: 800-678-3633
Fr: 800-322-8755

Susan H. Haubenstock. 1994. This book profiles 75 art-related jobs. Each profile includes a career description, career ladder, employment and advancement prospects, education, experience and skills required, salary range, and tips for entry into the field.

★6579★ How to Land a Job in Journalism
Betterway Publications
PO Box 219
Crozet, VA 22932
Ph: (804)823-5661

Phil Swann and Ed Achorn. 1988. Offers advice on college preparation, financial aid, internships, and job hunting for those interested in a career in journalism. Contains tips from journalists. Includes chapters on copy editing and newsletter editing.

★6580★ "International Journalism" in Guide to Careers in World Affairs
Impact Publications
10655 Big Oak Circle
Manassas Park, VA 22111
Ph: (703)361-7300

Third ed., 1993. Describes jobs in business, government, and nonprofit organizations. Explains the methods and credentials required to secure a job. Contains sections on internships and graduate programs.

★6581★ "Journalism" in Black Woman's Career Guide (pp. 171-173)
Bantam Doubleday Dell
1540 Broadway
New York, NY 10036
Fax: 800-233-3294   Fr: 800-223-5780

Beatryce Nivens. Revised edition, 1987. Describes career planning, resume writing, job hunting, and interviewing. Profiles 60 black women pioneers in 20 different careers.

★6582★ "Journalism" in Career Connection for Technical Education (pp. 98-99)
JIST Works, Inc.
720 N. Park Ave.
Indianapolis, IN 46202-3431
Ph: (317)264-3720   Fax: (317)264-3709

Fred A. Rowe. 1994, second edition. Describes in detail technical occupations. Includes information on recommended high school courses, course requirements, related careers, and a self-assessment guide.

★6583★ Journalism Career and Scholarship Guide
Dow Jones Newspaper Fund
PO Box 300
Princeton, NJ 08543-0300
Ph: (609)452-2820

Annual. Provides information on newspaper careers and salaries, and how to apply for a newspaper job. Explains how to choose a journalism school and lists colleges and universities offering journalism majors; descibes undergraduate and graduate financial aid programs. Lists scholarships, fellowships, internships, and continuing education opportunities.

★6584★ "Journalism" in Careers in Communications (pp. 6-22)
National Textbook Co. (NTC)
VGM Career Books
4255 W. Touhy Ave.
Lincolnwood, IL 60646-1975
Ph: (708)679-5500   Fax: (708)679-2494
Fr: 800-323-4900

Shonan F. Noronha. 1987. Examines the fields of journalism, photography, radio, television, film, public relations, and advertising. Gives concrete details on job locations and how to secure a job. Suggests many resources for job hunting.

★6585★ "Journalism/Reporting" in Straight Talk on Careers: Eighty Pros Take You Into Their Professions (pp. 145-159)
Garrett Park Press
PO Box 1907
Garrett Park, MD 20896
Ph: (301)946-2553

Mary Barbera-Hogan. 1987. Contains candid interviews from people who give an inside view of their work in 80 different careers. These professionals describe a day's work and the stresses and rewards accompanying their work.

★6586★ Journalism: Your Newspaper Career and How to Prepare for It
National Newspaper Foundation
1627 K St., NW, Ste. 400
Washington, DC 20006-1790
Ph: (202)466-7200

1987. Gives an overview of jobs with newspapers, preparation, and where to write for more information.

★6587★ Journalist News
Careers, Inc.
PO Box 135
Largo, FL 34649-0135
Ph: (813)584-7333

1992. Four-page brief offering the definition, history, duties, working conditions, personal qualifications, educational requirements, earnings, hours, employment outlook, advancement, and careers related to this position.

★6588★ "Journalists" in Career Information Center (Vol.3)
Simon and Schuster
200 Old Tappan Rd.
Old Tappan, NJ 07675
Fax: 800-445-6991   Fr: 800-223-2348

Richard Lidz and Linda Perrin, editorial directors. Fifth edition, 1993. A multi-volume set

that profiles more than 600 occupations. Each occupational profile describes job duties, educational requirements, getting a job, advancement possibilities, employment outlook, working conditions, earnings and benefits, and sources of additional information.

★6589★ News Reporters (Radio and Television)
Chronicle Guidance Publications, Inc.
66 Aurora St.
PO Box 1190
Moravia, NY 13118-1190
Ph: (315)497-0330   Fax: (315)497-3359
Fr: 800-622-7284

1994. Career brief describing the nature of the job, working conditions, hours and earnings, education and training, licensure, certification, unions, personal qualifications, social and psychological factors, location, employment outlook, entry methods, advancement, and related occupations.

★6590★ "News Reporting" in Career Choices for the 90's for Students of Political Science and Government
Walker and Co.
435 Hudson St.
New York, NY 10014
Ph: (212)727-8300   Fax: (212)727-0984
Fr: 800-289-2553

1990. Offers alternatives for students of political science. Gives information about job outlook and competition for entry-level candidates. Provides job-hunting tips.

★6591★ "Newspaper Publishing" in Encyclopedia of Career Choices for the 1990s: Guide to Entry Level Jobs (pp. 602-624)
Berkley Pub.
PO Box 506
East Rutherford, NJ 07073
Fax: (201)933-2316   Fr: 800-788-6262

1992. Describes entry-level careers in a variety of industries. Presents qualifications required, working conditions, salary, internships, and professional associations.

★6592★ "Newspaper Reporter" in VGM's Careers Encyclopedia (pp. 297-299)
National Textbook Co. (NTC)
VGM Career Books
4255 W. Touhy Ave.
Lincolnwood, IL 60646-1975
Ph: (708)679-5500   Fax: (708)679-2494
Fr: 800-323-4900

Third edition, 1991. Profiles 200 occupations. Describes job duties, places of employment, working conditions, qualifications, education and training, advancement potential, and salary for each occupation.

★6593★ Newspaper Reporters
Chronicle Guidance Publications, Inc.
66 Aurora St.
PO Box 1190
Moravia, NY 13118-1190
Ph: (315)497-0330   Fax: (315)497-3359
Fr: 800-622-7284

1992. Career brief describing the nature of the job, working conditions, hours and earnings, education and training, licensure, certification, unions, personal qualifications, social and psychological factors, location, employ-

ment outlook, entry methods, advancement, and related occupations.

★6594★ "Newspapers/Journalism" in Internships: 1995 (pp. 72-86)
Petersons Guides, Inc.
PO Box 2123
Princeton, NJ 08543-2123
Ph: (609)243-9111   Fax: (609)243-9150
Fr: 800-338-3282

1995. Lists internship opportunities under six broad categories: communications, creative, performing, and fine arts, human services, international relations, business and technology, and public relations. Includes a special section on internships in Washington, DC. For each internship program, gives the name, phone number, contact person, description, eligibility requirements, and benefits.

★6595★ "Newspapers and News Services" in Career Opportunities for Writers
Facts on File
460 Park Ave. S.
New York, NY 10016-7382
Ph: (212)683-2244   Fax: 800-678-3633
Fr: 800-322-8755

Rosemary Guiley. 1992. Describes approximately 90 careers in eight major fields, offering such details as duties, salaries, prerequisites, employment and advancement oportunities, organizations to join, and opportunities for women and minorities.

★6596★ Opportunities in Journalism Careers
National Textbook Co. (NTC)
VGM Career Books
4255 W. Touhy Ave.
Lincolnwood, IL 60646-1975
Ph: (708)679-5500   Fax: (708)679-2494
Fr: 800-323-4900

Donald L. Ferguson. Describes job responsibilities, working conditions, salary, and educational requirements.

★6597★ Opportunities in Newspaper Publishing Careers
National Textbook Co. (NTC)
VGM Career Books
4255 W. Touhy Ave.
Lincolnwood, IL 60646-1975
Ph: (708)679-5500   Fax: (708)679-2494
Fr: 800-323-4900

John Tebbel. 1989. Describes working for big and small newspapers and addresses the changing technology in the publishing field.

★6598★ Opportunities in Writing Careers
National Textbook Co. (NTC)
VGM Career Books
4255 W. Touhy Ave.
Lincolnwood, IL 60646-1975
Ph: (708)679-5500   Fax: (708)679-2494
Fr: 800-323-4900

Elizabeth Foote-Smith. 1989. Describes writing career opportunities. Covers articles, novels, short stories, nonfiction books, reviews, and interviews. Also includes information on playwrights, poets, journalists, and broadcasters. Discusses educational preparation. Includes a bibliography.

★6599★ "Reporter" in *College Board Guide to Jobs and Career Planning* **(pp. 162-163)**
The College Board
45 Columbus Ave.
New York, NY 10023-6992
Ph: (212)713-8165   Fax: (212)713-8143
Fr: 800-323-7155
Second edition, 1994. Describes the job, salaries, related careers, education needed, and where to write for more information.

★6600★ "Reporter" in *Jobs Rated Almanac*
World Almanac
1 International Blvd., Ste. 444
Mahwah, NJ 07495
Ph: (201)529-6900   Fax: (201)529-6901
Les Krantz. Second edition, 1992. Ranks 250 jobs by environment, salary, outlooks, physical demands, stress, security, travel opportunities, and extra perks. Includes jobs the editor feels are the most common, most interesting, and the most rapidly growing.

★6601★ *Reporter, Newspaper*
Careers, Inc.
PO Box 135
Largo, FL 34649-0135
Ph: (813)584-7333
1991. Two-page occupational summary card describing duties, working conditions, personal qualifications, training, earnings and hours, employment outlook, places of employment, related careers, and where to write for more information.

★6602★ "Reporter (print)" in *100 Best Careers for the Year 2000* **(pp. 149-150)**
Arco Pub.
201 W. 103rd St.
Indianapolis, IN 46290
Ph: 800-428-5331   Fax: 800-835-3202
Shelly Field. 1992. Describes 100 job opportunities expected to grow fast throughout the next decade. Provides information on job duties and responsibilities, training requirements, education, advancement opportunities, experience and qualifications, and typical salaries.

★6603★ "Reporters and Correspondents" in *101 Careers: A Guide to the Fastest-Growing Opportunities* **(pp. 301-302)**
John Wiley & Sons, Inc.
605 3rd Ave.
New York, NY 10158-0012
Ph: (212)850-6645   Fax: (212)850-6088
Michael Harkavy. 1990. Describes the nature of the job, working conditions, employment growth, qualifications, personal skills, projected salaries, and where to write for more information.

★6604★ "Reporters and Correspondents" in *Encyclopedia of Careers and Vocational Guidance* **(Vol.4, pp. 272-276)**
J.G. Ferguson Publishing Co.
200 W. Madison St., Ste. 300
Chicago, IL 60606
Ph: (312)580-5480   Fax: (312)580-4948
William E. Hopke, editor-in-chief. Ninth edition, 1993. Four-volume set that profiles 900 occupations and describes job trends in 74 industries. Includes career description, educational requirements, history of the job, methods of entry, advancement, employment outlook, earnings, conditions of work, social and psychological factors, and sources of further information.

★6605★ "Reporters and Correspondents" in *Occupational Outlook Handbook*
U.S. Government Printing Office
Superintendent of Documents
Washington, DC 20402
Ph: (202)512-1800   Fax: (202)512-2250
Biennial, 1994-95. Encyclopedia of careers describing about 250 occupations and comprising about 85 percent of all jobs in the economy. Occupations that require lengthy education or training are given the most attention. Each occupation's profile describes what the worker does on the job, working conditions, education and training requirements, advancement possibilities, job outlook, earnings, and sources of additional information.

★6606★ "Reporters and Correspondents (Print)" in *Jobs! What They Are— Where They Are—What They Pay* **(p. 273)**
Simon & Schuster, Inc.
Simon & Schuster Bldg.
1230 Avenue of the Americas
New York, NY 10020
Ph: (212)698-7000   Fr: 800-223-2348
Robert O. Snelling and Anne M. Snelling. 3rd edition, 1992. Describes duties and responsibilities, earnings, employment opportunities, training, and qualifications.

PROFESSIONAL ASSOCIATIONS

★6607★ Accrediting Council on Education in Journalism and Mass Communications (ACEJMC)
University of Kansas
School of Journalism
Stauffer-Flint Hall
Lawrence, KS 66045
Ph: (913)864-3973
Members: Journalism education associations; related industry groups. **Purpose:** Encourages cooperation between the mass media and colleges and universities in education for journalism and accredits professional programs in schools and departments of journalism. Approved list currently includes 215 sequences (such as Advertising, Community Journalism, Magazine, Management, News-Editorial, Photojournalism, Public Relations, Publishing, Radio-Television, and Technical Journalism) in 95 colleges and universities. **Publications:** *Accredited Journalism and Mass Communications Education*, annual.

★6608★ Association for Education in Journalism and Mass Communication (AEJMC)
1621 College St.
University of South Carolina
Columbia, SC 29208
Ph: (803)777-2005   Fax: (803)777-4728
Members: Professional organization of college and university journalism teachers. **Purpose:** Works to improve methods and standards of teaching and stimulate research. Compiles statistics on enrollments and current developments in journalism education. Maintains a listing of journalism teaching positions available and teaching positions wanted, revised bimonthly. **Publications:** *Journalism and Mass Communication Educator*, quarterly. • *Journalism and Mass Communication Monographs*, quarterly. • *Journalism and Mass Communication Quarterly*, quarterly. • *Journalism and Mass Communicator Abstracts*, annual.

★6609★ Dow Jones Newspaper Fund (DJNF)
PO Box 300
Princeton, NJ 08543
Ph: (609)452-2820   Fax: (609)520-5804
Members: Established by Dow Jones and Company, publishers of *The Wall Street Journal*, to encourage careers in journalism among young people. **Purpose:** Operates Editing Internship Program for all junior, senior, and graduate level college students interested in journalism. Students work as copy editors during the summer for a daily newspaper or wire service and receive monetary scholarships to return to school in the fall. Offers information on careers in print journalism. **Publications:** *Advisor Update*, quarterly. • *The Journalists' Road to Success*, annual. • *Newspapers, Diversity, and You*.

★6610★ National Newspaper Association (NNA)
1525 Wilson Blvd., Ste. 550
Arlington, VA 22209
Ph: (703)907-7900   Fax: (703)907-7901
Members: Representatives of weekly, semiweekly, and daily newspapers. **Purpose:** Operates American Newspaper Representatives, Inc. Compiles statistics. **Publications:** *National Directory of Weekly Newspapers*, annual. • *Publishers' Auxiliary: The Newspaper Industry's Oldest Newspaper*, biweekly.

★6611★ The Newspaper Guild (TNG)
8611 2nd Ave.
Silver Spring, MD 20910
Ph: (301)585-2990
Members: AFL-CIO; Canadian Labour Congress. Sponsors Newspaper Guild International Pension Fund which provides retirement benefits to persons employed in the news industry. **Publications:** *Constitution*, annual. • *Guild Reporter*, monthly. • *Newspaper Guild—Proceedings*, annual.

★6612★ Women in Communications, Inc. (WICI)
3717 Columbia Pike, No. 310
Arlington, VA 22204-4255
Ph: (703)528-4200
Members: Professional society - journalism and communications. **Purpose:** Offers place-

ment service; compiles statistics. **Publications:** *Careers in Communications.* • *Leading Change*, periodic. • *Membership and Resource Directory*, biennial. • *The Professional Communicator.*

STANDARDS/CERTIFICATION AGENCIES

★6613★ **Accrediting Council on Education in Journalism and Mass Communications (ACEJMC)**
University of Kansas
School of Journalism
Stauffer-Flint Hall
Lawrence, KS 66045
Ph: (913)864-3973

Encourages cooperation between the mass media and colleges and universities in education for journalism and accredits professional programs in schools and departments of journalism. Approved list currently includes 215 sequences (such as Advertising, Community Journalism, Magazine, Management, News-Editorial, Photojournalism, Public Relations, Publishing, Radio-Television, and Technical Journalism) in 95 colleges and universities.

★6614★ **Association for Education in Journalism and Mass Communication (AEJMC)**
1621 College St.
University of South Carolina
Columbia, SC 29208
Ph: (803)777-2005   Fax: (803)777-4728
Works to improve methods and standards of teaching and stimulate research.

EDUCATIONAL DIRECTORIES AND PROGRAMS

★6615★ *Accredited Journalism and Mass Communications Education*
Accrediting Council on Education in Journalism and Mass Communications
School of Journalism
Stauffer-Flint Hall
University of Kansas
Lawrence, KS 66045
Ph: (913)864-3973   Fax: (913)864-5225
Susanne Shaw, Contact

Annual, September. Publication includes: about 95 institutions with accredited programs in journalism, journalism associations, accrediting committee and council members. Principal content of publication is purpose/benefits of accreditation, accredition guidelines and standards. Entries include: For institutions—Name, address; name and phone of department chairman or contact; degree(s) offered; scope and date of accreditation. For associations—Name, address, phone, name and title of executive. For accrediting council members—Name, title, co. name, address, phone, year term expires. Arrangement: Classified by type of organization.

★6616★ *Magazine Career Directory*
Gale Research Inc.
835 Penobscot Bldg.
Detroit, MI 48226-4094
Ph: (313)961-2242   Fax: (313)961-6083
Fr: 800-877-GALE

Bradley J. Morgan and Joseph M. Palmisano. Fifth edition, 1993. A directory in the Career Advisor Series that provides essays written by industry professionals; job search information on resume and cover letter preparation, networking, and the interviewing process; approximately 300 companies and organizations offering job opportunities and internships, and additional job-hunting resources.

★6617★ *Newspapers Career Directory*
Gale Research Inc.
835 Penobscot Bldg.
Detroit, MI 48226-4094
Ph: (313)961-2242   Fax: (313)961-6083
Fr: 800-877-GALE

Bradley J. Morgan and Joseph M. Palmisano. 1993. A directory in the Career Advisor Series that provides essays written by industry professionals; job search information on resume and cover letter preparation, networking, and the interviewing process; approximately 300 companies and organizations offering job opportunities and internships, and additional job-hunting resources.

★6618★ *Radio and Television Career Directory*
Gale Research Inc.
835 Penobscot Bldg.
Detroit, MI 48226-4094
Ph: (313)961-2242   Fax: (313)961-6083
Fr: 800-877-GALE

Bradley J. Morgan and Joseph M. Palmisano. Second edition, 1993. A directory in the Career Advisor Series that provides essays written by industry professionals; job search information on resume and cover letter preparation, networking, and the interviewing process; approximately 300 companies and organizations offering job opportunities and internships, and additional job-hunting resources.

AWARDS, SCHOLARSHIPS, GRANTS, AND FELLOWSHIPS

★6619★ **Worth Bingham Prize**
Worth Bingham Memorial Fund
1155 Connecticut Ave. NW, Ste. 601
Washington, DC 20036-2001
Ph: (202)466-8217   Fax: (202)862-3956

To honor newspaper or magazine reporting that investigates and analyzes situations of national significance where the public interest is being ill-served. There may be actual violations of the law, rule or code; lax or ineffective administration or enforcement; or activites which, while not specific violations of anything on the statute books, create conflicts of interest, entail excessive secrecy or otherwise raise questions of propriety. Judges are guided by such factors as the reporting enter-

prise, obstacles overcome in getting information, accuracy, clarity of analysis and writing style, magnitude of the situation, and impact on the public, including any reforms that may have resulted. Entries may include a single story, a related series of stories, or up to three unrelated stories. Columns and editorials are eligible. The entry deadline is February 15. A monetary award of $10,000 is presented at the White House Correspondents' Dinner in the spring. Awarded annually. Established in 1966 in memory of Robert Worth Bingham, a young journalist-editor who was killed in an accident at the age of 34.

★6620★ **Arthur F. Burns Fellowships**
Center for Foreign Journalists
11690 A Sunrise Valley Dr.
Reston, VA 22091
Ph: (703)620-5984

Purpose: To enable U.S. and German journalists to work with the press in the United States or Germany. Qualifications: Applicant must be a U.S. or German citizen or permanent resident. Candidate should be between the ages of 21 and 31 years. Applicant must be a working journalist in any news medium. U.S. citizens are placed with news organizations in Germany; Germany citizens are placed with U.S. news organizations. Funds available: $5,000. Application details: Write to the office manager for application guidelines. Deadline: 15 March. Notification by 15 Apirl.

★6621★ **Raymond Clapper Memorial Awards**
Standing Committee of Correspondents
U.S. Senate Press Gallery
Capitol Bldg., S 316
Washington, DC 20510-9042
Ph: (202)224-0241

To recognize meritorious local, national, or international news coverage. Washington-based daily newspaper writers, or a writing team of not more than two individuals, whose work during the previous year approximates the ideals of fair and painstaking reporting and good craftsmanship characteristic of Raymond Clapper are considered for the award. Subjects can be local, national, or international. The deadline is April 7. A monetary award of $1,500 for First Prize and $500 for Second Prize are awarded annually at the White House Correspondents' Association Dinner in April. Established in 1944.

★6622★ **Columbia Journalism Award**
Columbia University
Office of the Pres.
202 Low Memorial Library
New York, NY 10027
Ph: (212)854-5017

To honor individuals not usually recognized in other major journalistic prizes for distinguished service in the public interest. A silver plaque is awarded as deemed appropriate by the faculty of journalism. Established in 1958.

★6623★ Walter Cronkite Award for Excellence in Journalism and Telecommunication
Walter Cronkite Endowment for Journalism and Telecommunication
Walter Cronkite School of Journalism & Telecommunication
Arizona State Univ.
Tempe, AZ 85287-1305
Ph: (602)965-5011　　Fax: (602)965-7041
For recognition of outstanding contributions to the media fields. Individuals who have evidenced excellence during the years that they have been associated with the media may be nominated. The endowment selection committee reviews the nominations and makes the selection. A plaque is awarded annually in the fall. Established in 1984.

★6624★ Freedom of Information Award
Associated Press
Managing Editors Association
50 Rockefeller Plaza
New York, NY 10020-1668
Ph: (212)621-1552　　Fax: (212)621-7529
To recognize outstanding contributions in maintaining freedom of information standards or for widening the scope of information available to the public. Journalists and newspapers are eligible. An engraved plaque is awarded annually. Established in 1971.

★6625★ Hearst Foundation Journalism Writing Competition
William Randolph Hearst Foundation
90 New Montgomery St., Ste. 1212
San Francisco, CA 94105
Ph: (415)543-4057
Purpose: To provide support, encouragement, and assistance to undergraduate journalism students. Qualifications: Only undergraduate students enrolled in member colleges and universities of the Association of Schools of Journalism and Mass Communication are eligible. Entrants must be full-time undergraduate journalism majors at the time the entries are produced and submitted. Students who have had full-time professional newspaper or broadcast news experience, or its equivalent, for three years or more, are not eligible. Selection criteria: Knowledge of subject, understandability, clarity, color, reporting in depth, and construction. Funds available: $300 to $2,000. Application details: A contest entry must be a single article originating with and produced by the undergraduate student. The entry must have been printed in either a campus or professional publication. If the entry is from a professional publication, it must be verified in accompanying letters by the editor of the publication and Journalism Unit Administrator that the entry is student work with minimal editing and no editor rewriting. Articles must not have multiple bylines unless accompanied by a letter from the Journalism Unit Administrator verifying that, while others may have participated in the research, the article was written by the entrant. Side bars, subordinate in length and content to the article submitted, written by the same student on the same topic the same day, will be considered as part of a single entry. Four tear sheets of each published article showing date of publication and full name of publication must be submitted with each entry. An official entry blank must be completed and

signed by the entrant, Journalism Unit Administrator, and Chief Journalism Administrator.

★6626★ Inter-American Press Association Scholarships
Inter-American Press Association Scholarship Fund, Inc.
2911 N.W. 39th St.
Miami, FL 33142
Ph: (305)634-2465　　Fax: (305)635-2272
Purpose: To support the exchange of journalists between the United States, Canada, Latin America, and the Caribbean. Qualifications: Applicant must be a citizen of the United States, Canada, Latin America, or the Caribbean. Applicant must be a journalist or journalism school graduate, and be between the ages of 21 and 35 years. Students must have finished their degree before beginning the scholarship term. U.S. and Canadian scholars spend the award tenure studying and reporting in Latin America and the Caribbean. Journalists from the Caribbean and Latin America use the awards to study at Canadian and U.S. journalism schools. Candidates must be fluent in the language of the host country. U.S. and Canadian candidates must have their language ability attested to by a recognized authority. Latin American candidates must take the Test of English as a Foreign Language. Funds available: $10,000. Application details: Write for an application form and guidelines. Submit form with a study and work plan. Deadline: 1 August. Notification by November.

★6627★ IRE Awards
Investigative Reporters and Editors
PO Box 838
Columbia, MO 65205
Ph: (314)882-2042　　Fax: (314)882-5431
To honor the best examples of investigative reporting in the United States each year and to promote high standards within the profession. Awards are given in the following categories: newspapers over 75,000 circulation, newspapers under 75,000 circulation, network and syndicated programs, television in the top 20 markets, television below the top 20 markets, radio, books, magazines, and specialty publications. There are up to three winners in each of the seven categories. The entry deadline is January 15 for the previous year's work. The first round winners receive scrolls and the second round winners receive plaques. Winners also appear as panelists at the national conference. Awarded annually. Established in 1979.

★6628★ Knight-Bagehot Fellowships in Economics and Business Journalism
Columbia University
Graduate School of Journalism
Knight-Bagehot Fellowship Program
New York, NY 10027
Ph: (212)854-2711　　Fax: (212)854-7837
Purpose: To improve the coverage of business, economics, and finance. Qualifications: Applicant may be of any nationality, but must be either a freelance journalist or a full-time editorial employee of a newspaper, magazine, wire service, or broadcast news program. Applicant must have at least four years of experience. The fellowship is open only to journalists whose work regularly appears in the United States or Canada. There are no age requirements, but those selected are typ-

ically between the ages of 27 and 40 years. There are no educational prerequisites. Fellowships are tenable only at the Graduate School of Journalism, Columbia University. Funds available: $16,000/year, plus tuition. Application details: Write or phone the fellowship director for application form and guidelines. Submit with four references, an essay on economics, a personal essay, and samples of work. Deadline: March 1. Fellowships are announced by May 1.

★6629★ Edward R. Murrow Fellowship for American Foreign Correspondents
Council on Foreign Relations
58 E. 68th St.
New York, NY 10021
Ph: (212)734-0400　　Fax: (212)861-2504
Purpose: To help journalists to increase their competence to report and interpret events abroad, and to allow them a period for sustained analysis and writing free from the daily pressures of journalism. Qualifications: Applicant must be a U.S. citizen and a correspondent, editor, or producer of an American newspaper, magazine, radio, or television station. Applicant either must be serving abroad now or, having recently served abroad, must plan to return to a foreign post. There are no set work requirements for the term of the fellowship, but preference will be given to those candidates who have a thorough plan of study and writing relating to foreign affairs. Fellows are expected to be in residence in New York City and to participate fully in the activities of the Council. The stipend granted the fellow will not normally exceed the amount of salary relinquished during the fellowship term. Funds available: $60,000 maximum. Application details: Forward a brief outline of proposal with curriculum vitae to Kempton Dunn at the Council. After internal review, an invitation to apply and application form may be forwarded. With application, include research proposal, photograph, and five samples of journalistic work from abroad. A letter from employer granting leave of absence in the event of selection should be sent directly from the employer to the fellowship director. Deadline: Nov. 15 for preliminary letters; Feb. 1 for completed applications.

★6630★ NAA Foundation—National Scholastic Press Association Pacemaker Awards
Newspaper Association of America Foundation
The Newspaper Center
11600 Sunrise Valley Dr.
Reston, VA 22091
Ph: (703)648-1047　　Fax: (703)620-1265
To encourage vital high school journalism by honoring outstanding high school newspapers. Plaques are awarded annually to six high school newspapers. Administered by the National Scholastic Press Association, 620 Rarig Center, 330 South 21st Avenue, Minneapolis, MN 55455-0478.

★6631★ National Association of Black Journalists Salute to Excellence Awards

National Association of Black Journalists
11600 Sunrise Valley Dr.
Reston, VA 22091-1412
Ph: (703)648-1270   Fax: (703)476-6245

To recognize outstanding stories and photographs that highlight Black people or programs and issues of special concern to the Black community. Entries are judged for impact, sensitivity, quality, and significance. An entry can be a single news story, photo, or TV or radio program or a series of stories, photos, or TV or radio programs on a related subject. Newspaper entries for each category are grouped and judged according to circulation, entries from papers with a circulation of less than 75,000, and entries from papers of a circulation of 75,000 or more. Television entries for each category are judged based on market ranking. Monetary awards of $100 are given in the following categories: in radio categories for Spot News Reporting and Public Affairs-Documentary; in print categories for international reporting, general news, feature, sports, commentary, and photojournalism; and in television categories for international reporting, general news, features, sports, documentary, and photojournalism. The following special awards are also presented: Journalist of the Year Award, Lifetime Achievement Award, and Percy Qoboza Award for Foreign Journalists. Established in 1975. Additional information is available from Carl E. Morris, Sr., Executive Director, PO Box 17212, Washington, DC 20041, phone: (703) 648-1270 or Jackie Greene, *USA Today*, 1000 Wilson Boulevard, Arlington, VA 22209.

★6632★ NFPW Member Graduate Scholarships

National Federation of Press Women, Inc.
PO Box 99
Blue Springs, MO 64013
Ph: (816)229-1666

Qualifications: Applicants must be college students who are seeking a graduate degree in journalism. Applicants may be men or women who possess two years active professional membership in the National Federation of Press Women. Selection criteria: Recipient is selected on the basis of career potential, scholarship, and financial need. Funds available: One $1,000 scholarship is awarded annually. Application details: Applications must include a transcript of college credit, work samples, and letters of recommendation in sealed envelopes from at least two persons acquainted with the applicant's work and/or schooling achievements. A photograph, a description of the study plan, a timetable for completion, a budget for use of the scholarship, and how the scholarship will be augmented to achieve study goals are also required. Deadline: Applications must be received by May 1.

★6633★ Nixon National Journalism Writing Award

Ball State University
Department of Journalism
Muncie, IN 47306-0485
Ph: (317)285-8200   Fax: (317)285-7997

To recognize an American print writer. The writing is judged by a panel. Established in 1960. Renamed in 1985. Sponsored by Nixon Newspapers, Inc.

★6634★ Outdoor Writers Association of America Scholarship Awards

Outdoor Writers Association of America (OWAA)
2017 Cato Ave., Ste. 101
State College, PA 16801-2768
Ph: (814)234-1011   Fax: (814)234-9692

Purpose: To reward outstanding students who are working toward careers in outdoor writing, broadcasting, photography, or art. Qualifications: Applicants should be in their last two years of college or master's degree students in any accredited school of journalism or mass communication listed by the Association for Education in Journalism and Mass Communication, or those schools accepted on application to the Outdoor Writers Association of America. There shall be no more than one applicant from each school per school year. Each school will be responsible for selecting its candidate. Selection criteria: Judges look for applicants with talent, promise, and first-hand outdoor knowledge. Applications are rated on clarity, organization, and originality. Grade point average is considered. Funds available: The amount of the scholarship varies, but is usually at least $3,000. Application details: An applicant must submit an OWAA application form, school recommendation, grade transcript, examples of outdoor communication work (including published samples), a one- to two-page statement by the nominee detailing career goals, and optional letters of recommendation from outdoor communicators or employers familiar with the applicant's work. The application package must be submitted to the Executive Director, Outdoor Writers Association of America. Deadline: March 1.

★6635★ Patterson Fellowships

Alicia Patterson Foundation (APF)
1001 Pennsylvania Ave., N.W., Ste. 1250
Washington, DC 20004
Ph: (202)393-5995

Purpose: To enable working journalists to pursue independent projects. Qualifications: Applicant must be a U.S. citizen. Candidate must currently be a newspaper, magazine, freelance, or wire-service journalist with at least five years of professional experience. Applicant must be able to take a leave of absence from work for the fellowship period. Fellows are expected to write four magazine-length articles based on investigations in topics of their own choosing. Grants are not offered for academic study. Funds available: $30,000. Application details: Write or phone the executive director for application form and guidelines. Submit form, two-page autobiographical essay, three-page research proposal, three samples of journalistic work, and four letters of reference. Deadline: October 1.

★6636★ George Foster Peabody Broadcasting Awards

University of Georgia
College of Journalism and Mass Communication
Athens, GA 30602
Ph: (706)542-5798   Fax: (706)542-4785

For recognition of distinguished achievement and the most meritorious public service rendered by electronically-delivered programming (radio, television and cable). Programs, stations, networks, and individuals are considered for the award. Entries may be submitted by radio and television networks worldwide. Medals and certificates are awarded annually in May. Established in 1940 to honor George Foster Peabody, a Columbus, Georgia, native who was a successful New York banker and philanthropist.

★6637★ Pulitzer Prizes

Columbia University
Office of Public Information
116th & Broadway
New York, NY 10027
Ph: (212)854-3841

To recognize outstanding accomplishments in journalism, letters, music, and drama. Awards are given in the following categories: Journalism - Public Service, for meritorious public service by a newspaper through the use of its journalistic resources, which may include editorials, cartoons, photographs and reporting; Spot News Reporting, for local reporting of sport news; Investigative Reporting, for investigative reporting within a newspaper's area of circulation by an individual or team, presented as a single article or series; Explanatory Journalism, for explanatory journalism that illuminates significant and complex issues; Beat Reporting; National Reporting; International Reporting (two prizes); Feature Writing, for feature writing giving prime consideration to high quality and originality; Commentary; Criticism; Editorial Writing, the test of excellence being clearness of style, moral purpose, sound reasoning, and power to influence public opinion in what the writer conceives to be the right direction, due account being taken of the whole volume of the editorial writer's work during the year; Editorial Cartooning, for a cartoon that embodies an idea made clearly apparent, shows good drawing and striking pictorial effect, and intended to be helpful to some commendable cause, due account being taken of the whole volume of the artist's work during the year; Spot News Photography, for spot news photography in black and white or color, which may consist of a photograph or photographs, a sequence, or album; and Feature Photography, for feature photography in black or white or color, which may consist of a photograph or photographs, a sequence or an album. Letters and Drama - Fiction, by an American author, preferably dealing with American life; History, for a book about the United States; Biography by an American author; Poetry, by an American poet; General Non-Fiction, by an American author that is not eligible for consideration in any other category; Drama, by an American author, preferably dealing with American life. Music - for a composition by an American in any of the larger forms including chamber, orchestral, choral, opera, song, dance, or other forms of musical theater, which has had its first performance in the United States during the year. The nominees are screened by juries appointed in each category and recommended to the Pulitzer Prize Board. The awardee for Public Service in Journalism receives a gold medal. All other awardees receive a monetary award of $3,000. Awarded annually. Established in 1917 and endowed by Joseph Pulitzer, the noted Hungarian-born American journalist who founded the Columbia University School of Journalism.

★6638★ Pulliam Journalism Fellowships
Central Newspapers, Inc.
c/o The Indianapolis News
PO Box 145
Indianapolis, IN 46206-0145
Ph: (317)633-9121

Purpose: To provide specialized training in journalism to recent college graduates. Qualifications: Applicant must be a U.S. citizen or permanent resident who will earn a bachelor's degree during the eleven months directly prior to the start of the fellowship in June. Candidate may be a newspaper journalism major or a liberal arts major with part-time or full-time newspaper experience. Applicant must have a proven potential in reporting, writing and editing and have high scholastic attainment, especially in the liberal arts. Fellows are granted work-study internships at the Indianapolis Star, the Indianapolis News, the Arizona Republic or the Phoenix Gazette. In addition to working as reporters, editorial writers or copy editors, fellows meet with guest speakers and participate in group and individual sessions conducted by a writing coach. Selection criteria: Based on scholastic achievement, writing ability, newspaper internships and references. Funds available: $4,200. Application details: Write to Mr. Pulliam for application form and guidelines. Submit form with samples of published writing, transcripts, a recent photograph, three letters of recommendation and a 400- to 600-word editorial written expressly for the application. Deadline: March 1.

★6639★ Garth Reeves Jr. Memorial Scholarships
Society of Professional Journalists
Greater Miami Chapter
c/o Miami Herald
1 Herald Plaza
Miami, FL 33132-1693

Purpose: To assist undergraduate and graduate-level minority students majoring in journalism. Qualifications: Applicants must be South Florida residents. Selection criteria: Applicants are choosen based on need, scholastic achievement, and extracurricular journalism activity. Funds available: Minimum grant $500; amount of each scholarship is determined by need. Application details: Applications available in January. Deadline: March 1.

★6640★ Scripps Howard Foundation Scholarships
Scripps Howard Foundation
PO Box 5380
Cincinnati, OH 45201
Ph: (513)977-3036   Fax: (513)977-3810

Purpose: To encourage deserving students to prepare for careers in Print and Broadcast Journalism. Qualifications: Applicant must be

a U.S. citizen or resident alien, or have a U.S. visa. Applicant must be a full-time student in good scholastic standing with a proven interest in the field of journalism. Candidate must demonstrate financial need. Non-U.S. citizens must use the scholarship at a U.S. institution. U.S. citizens may use the scholarship worldwide. Funds available: $500-3,000. Application details: Send a letter stating college major and career goal to request an application before 20 December. Submit application with letters of recommendation and samples of journalistic work. Graduate Record Examination scores are also required. Deadline: 25 February. Written notification sent on 15 May.

★6641★ Service to the First Amendment - Edward Willis Scripps Award
Scripps Howard Foundation
312 Walnut St.
PO Box 5380
Cincinnati, OH 45201
Ph: (513)977-3035   Fax: (513)977-3810

To recognize a daily newspaper or wire service that contributes significantly to the cause of the First Amendment guarantee of a free press. The award reflects service to the First Amendment in one or more of a variety of ways: fighting the growing threat of censorship in America, overcoming public uneasiness with regard to press credibility, combating government secrecy at all levels, and instilling in the public an appreciation of its need as well as its right to know, as guaranteed by the First Amendment. Submitted material must have been published in a daily newspaper during the preceding calendar year. The deadline is February 9. A monetary award of $2,500 and a bronze plaque are awarded annually. Established in 1976.

★6642★ SPA Journalism Recognition Awards
Software Publishers Association
1730 M St. NW, Ste. 700
Washington, DC 20036-4510
Ph: (202)452-1600   Fax: (202)223-8756

To honor those individuals who cover the software industry in an accurate and insightful manner. The association presents the following four awards: Best Software Reviewer, Best Industry/Editorial, Best Trade or General Press News Reporting, and Best Financial Reporting and Analysis. Awards are presented at the annual special luncheon in early spring. Established in 1988.

★6643★ United Press International National Broadcast Awards
United Press International
1400 I St. NW, 9th Fl.
Washington, DC 20005
Ph: (202)898-8254   Fax: (202)842-3625

To recognize excellence in broadcast journalism. Awards are given to both small and large television and radio stations in the following categories: (1) Outstanding Spot News; (2) Outstanding Newscast; (3) Outstanding Sports Coverage; (4) Outstanding Feature; (5) Outstanding Documentary; (6) Outstanding Videography; and (7) Outstanding Reporting/Individual Achievement. UPI clients are eligible. Judging is carried out by broadcasters from different regions of the country. Engraved UPI statues are awarded annually. Established in 1980.

★6644★ Edward Weintal Prize for Diplomatic Reporting
Georgetown University
Institute for the Study of Diplomacy
School of Foreign Service
514 ICC
Washington, DC 20057
Ph: (202)687-6279   Fax: (202)687-8312

To honor journalists for distinguished reporting on American foreign policy and diplomacy. One award is given to a member of the print media, and one to a member of the television and radio industries. The 1994 deadline for submissions was January 14. Nominations may be made on the basis of a specific story or series or on the basis of a journalist's overall news coverage. Monetary prizes totaling $8,000 and certificates are awarded annually. Established in 1974 in memory of Edward Weintal (1901-1973), a diplomatic correspondent for *Newsweek* magazine.

BASIC REFERENCE GUIDES AND HANDBOOKS

★6645★ *The Associated Press Stylebook and Libel Manual*
Addison-Wesley Publishing Co.
1 Jacob Way
Reading, MA 01867
Ph: (617)944-3700   Fr: 800-447-2226

Norm Goldstein, editor. 1994. Includes a guide to capitalization, abbreviations, spelling, numerals, and usage. Also covers libel rules, photo captions, and wire service material.

★6646★ *The Complete Reporter: Fundamentals of News Gathering, Writing, and Editing, Complete With Exercises*
Macmillan Publishing Co.
866 3rd Ave.
New York, NY 10022
Ph: (212)702-2000   Fr: 800-257-5755

Julian Harriss, Kelly Leiter, and Stanley Johnson. Sixth edition, 1991. Includes a bibliography and an index.

★6647★ *A Guide for Newspaper Stringers*
Lawrence Erlbaum Associates, Inc.
365 Broadway
Hillsdale, NJ 07642
Ph: (201)666-4110   Fax: (201)666-2394

Margaret G. Davidson. 1990.

★6648★ *The Reporter & the Law: Techniques of Covering the Courts*
Columbia University Press
562 W. 113th St.
New York, NY 10025
Ph: (212)316-7100

Lyle W. Denniston, editor. 1992.

★6649★ *Writing and Reporting the News*
Holt, Rinehart and Winston, Inc.
Orlando, FL 32887
Ph: (407)345-2000

Mitchell Stephens. Second edition, 1993. Includes an index.

PROFESSIONAL AND TRADE PERIODICALS

★6650★ *Columbia Journalism Review*
Columbia Journalism Review
700 Journalism Bldg.
Columbia University
New York, NY 10027
Ph: (212)854-1881   Fax: (212)854-8580
Suzanne Braun Levine

Bimonthly. Magazine focusing on journalism.

★6651★ *Editor & Publisher*
Editor & Publisher Co.
11 W. 19th St.
New York, NY 10011
Ph: (212)675-4380   Fax: (212)929-1259
John P. Consoli

Weekly. Magazine focusing on journalism, advertising, and printing equipment.

★6652★ *National Press Club—Record*
National Press Club
National Press Bldg.
Washington, DC 20045
Ph: (202)662-7500
Dennis S. Feldman

Covers only Club activities and programs. Recurring features include a calendar of events and a column titled Job Opportunities.

★6653★ *National Press Foundation—Update*
National Press Foundation (NPF)
National Press Bldg.
Washington, DC 20045
Ph: (202)662-7350
Frank Holeman

Quarterly. Publishes news of the National Press Foundation, a professional organization working toward "excellence in journalism." Reports on NPF meetings, conferences, and member activities and accomplishments.

★6654★ *Quill & Scroll*
Quill and Scroll Society
University of Iowa
School of Journalsm and Mass
  Communication
Iowa City, IA 52242
Ph: (319)335-5795   Fax: (319)335-5386
Richard P. Johns

Quarterly. High school honorary journalism magazine.

OTHER SOURCES OF INFORMATION

★6655★ "Journalism" in *Accounting to Zoology: Graduate Fields Defined* (pp. 50-51)
Petersons Guides, Inc.
PO Box 2123
Princeton, NJ 08543-2123
Ph: (609)243-9111   Fax: (609)243-9150
Fr: 800-338-3282

Amy J. Goldstein, editor. Revised and updated, 1987. Defines 298 graduate and professional fields. Discusses types of graduate programs and degrees, graduate research, applied work, employment prospects, and trends.

★6656★ "Journalist" in *Encyclopedia of Danger: Dangerous Professions* (pp. 54-57)
Chelsea House Publishers
1974 Sproul Rd., Ste. 400
Broomall, PA 19008
Ph: (215)353-5166   Fax: (215)359-1439

Missy Allen and Michel Peissel. 1993. Provides descriptions of 24 dangerous occupations, their risky characteristics, and safety precautions.

★6657★ "Reporter" in *Career Selector 2001*
Barron's Educational Series, Inc.
250 Wireless Blvd.
Hauppauge, NY 11788
Ph: (516)434-3311   Fax: (516)434-3723
Fr: 800-645-3476

James C. Gonyea. 1993.

★6658★ "Reporter/Correspondent" in *100 Best Jobs for the 1990s & Beyond*
Dearborn Financial Publishing, Inc.
520 N. Dearborn St.
Chicago, IL 60610-4354
Ph: (312)836-4400   Fax: (312)836-1021
Fr: 800-621-9621

Carol Kleiman. 1992. Describes 100 jobs ranging from accountants to veterinarians. Each job profile includes such information as education, experience, and certification needed, salaries, and job search suggestions.

★6659★ *Speaking of Journalism*
HarperCollins
10 E. 53rd St.
New York, NY 10022
Fr: 800-2-HARPER

1994. Twelve writers and editors discuss their work.

★6660★ *Truth Needs No Ally: Inside Photojournalism*
Crestwood House
866 3rd Ave.
New York, NY 10022
Ph: (212)702-9632
1994.

Writers and Editors

Writers and editors communicate through the written word. Writers develop original fiction and nonfiction for books, magazines, trade journals, newspapers, technical studies and reports, company newsletters, radio and television broadcasts, and advertisements. Editors supervise writers and select and prepare material for publication or broadcasting. From the information they gather, writers select and organize the material and put it into words that will convey it to the reader with the desired effect. Writers often revise or rewrite sections, searching for the best organization of the material or just the right phrasing. **Newswriters** write news items for inclusion in newspapers or news broadcasts based on information supplied by reporters or wire services. **Columnists** analyze news and write columns or commentaries, based on personal knowledge and experience. **Editorial writers** write comments to stimulate or mold public opinion, in accordance with their publication's viewpoint. Reporters and correspondents may also write copies for broadcast. **Technical writers** put scientific and technical information into readily understandable language. **Copy writers** write advertising copy for use by publication or broadcast media to promote the sale of goods and services. Editors frequently do some writing and almost always do much rewriting and editing, but their primary duties are to plan the contents of books, magazines, or newspapers and to supervise their preparation. In broadcasting companies, **program directors** have responsibilities comparable to those of editors. Most writers and editors use personal computers or word processors; many use desktop or electronic publishing systems.

Salaries

Salaries for writers and editors are as follows:

Beginning writers and editorial assistants	$20,000/year
Experienced writers and researchers	$30,000/year
Technical writers, federal government	$40,669/year
Technical writers, entry-level	$26,700/year
Technical writers, mid-level	$35,000/year
Technical writers, mid-level management	$40,000/year
Technical writers, senior management	$45,400/year
Senior editors, large circulation newspapers and magazines	More than $60,000/year
Writers and editors, federal government	$39,077/year

Employment Outlook

Growth rate until the year 2005: Average.

Writers and Editors

CAREER GUIDES

★6661★ "Advertising Copywriter" in
Liberal Arts Jobs
Petersons Guides, Inc.
PO Box 2123
Princeton, NJ 08543-2123
Ph: (609)243-9111   Fax: (609)243-9150
Fr: 800-338-3282
Burton Jay Nadler. Second edition, 1989. Strives to help the liberal arts graduate identify skills for entry-level positions. Gives goal setting and job search advice.

★6662★ "Advertising Copywriters",
"Copy Editors", "Magazine Editors",
and "Fiction Writers" in *Career*
Information Center (vol.3)
Simon and Schuster
200 Old Tappan Rd.
Old Tappan, NJ 07675
Fax: 800-445-6991   Fr: 800-223-2348
Richard Lidz and Linda Perrin, editorial directors. Fifth edition, 1993. A multi-volume set that profiles more than 600 occupations. Each occupational profile describes job duties, educational requirements, getting a job, advancement possibilities, employment outlook, working conditions, earnings and benefits, and sources of additional information.

★6663★ "Advertising Copywriters" in
Jobs! What They Are—Where They
Are—What They Pay (pp. 35)
Simon & Schuster, Inc.
Simon & Schuster Bldg.
1230 Avenue of the Americas
New York, NY 10020
Ph: (212)698-7000   Fr: 800-223-2348
Robert O. Snelling and Anne M. Snelling. Third revised edition, 1992. Includes chapters titled "Writers, Fiction and Nonfiction," "Copy Editors and Proofreaders" , and "Technical Writers". Describes duties and responsibilities, earnings, employment opportunities, training, and qualifications.

★6664★ *Book Editor*
Vocational Biographies, Inc.
PO Box 31
Sauk Centre, MN 56378-0031
Ph: (612)352-6516   Fax: (612)352-5546
Fr: 800-255-0752
1991. Four-page pamphlet containing a personal narrative about a worker's job, work likes and dislikes, career path from high school to the present, education and training, the rewards and frustrations, and the effects of the job on the rest of the worker's life. The data file portion of this pamphlet gives a concise occupational summary, including work description, working conditions, places of employment, personal characteristics, education and training, job outlook, and salary range.

★6665★ "Book Editors" in *Career*
Discovery Encyclopedia (Vol.1, pp.
120-121)
J.G. Ferguson Publishing Co.
200 W. Madison St., Ste. 300
Chicago, IL 60606
Ph: (312)580-5480   Fax: (312)580-4948
Russell E. Primm, editor-in chief. 1993. This six volume set contains two-page articles for 504 occupations. Each article describes job duties, earnings, and educational and training requirements. The whole set is arranged alphabetically by job title. Designed for junior high and older students.

★6666★ "Book Editors" in *Encyclopedia*
of Careers and Vocational Guidance
(Vol.2, pp. 204-208)
J.G. Ferguson Publishing Co.
200 W. Madison St., Ste. 300
Chicago, IL 60606
Ph: (312)580-5480   Fax: (312)580-4948
William E. Hopke, editor-in-chief. Ninth edition, 1993. Four-volume set that profiles 900 occupations and describes job trends in 74 industries. Includes career description, educational requirements, history of the job, methods of entry, advancement, employment outlook, earnings, conditions of work, social and psychological factors, and sources of further information.

★6667★ "Book Editors", "Newspaper
Editors", and "Technical Writers" in
Career Information Center (Vol.3)
Simon and Schuster
200 Old Tappan Rd.
Old Tappan, NJ 07675
Fax: 800-445-6991   Fr: 800-223-2348
Richard Lidz and Linda Perrin, editorial directors. Fifth edition, 1993. A multi-volume set that profiles more than 600 occupations. Each occupational profile describes job duties, educational requirements, getting a job, advancement possibilities, employment outlook, working conditions, earnings and benefits, and sources of additional information.

★6668★ *Career Choices for the 90's for*
Students of Communications and
Journalism
Walker and Co.
435 Hudson St.
New York, NY 10014
Ph: (212)727-8300   Fax: (212)727-0984
Fr: 800-289-2553
1990. Offers alternatives for students of communications and journalism. Gives information about the job outlook and competition for entry-level candidates. Provides job-hunting tips.

★6669★ *Career Opportunities in the*
Sports Industry
Facts on File
460 Park Ave. S.
New York, NY 10016-7382
Ph: (212)683-2244   Fax: 800-678-3633
Fr: 800-322-8755
Shelly Field. 1993. Sourcebook combining a variety of information including sports-related academic programs, league lists, professional associations, and more of interest to those considering employment in organized amateur or professional sports.

★6670★ *Career Opportunities in*
Television, Cable and Video
Facts on File
460 Park Ave. S.
New York, NY 10016-7382
Ph: (212)683-2244   Fax: 800-678-3633
Fr: 800-322-8755
Maxine K. Reed and Robert M. Reed. Third edition, 1993. Includes information on employment and advancement prospects, edu-

cation, experience and skills requiresn salary range, and tips for entry into the field.

★6671★ **Career Opportunities for Writers**
Facts on File
460 Park Ave. S.
New York, NY 10016-7382
Ph: (212)683-2244   Fax: 800-678-3633
Fr: 800-322-8755
Rosemary Ellen Guiley. 1993. Sourcebook on over 100 careers for writers from various fields.

★6672★ **Careers for Bookworms & Other Literary Types**
National Textbook Co. (NTC)
VGM Career Books
4255 W. Touhy Ave.
Lincolnwood, IL 60646-1975
Ph: (708)679-5500   Fax: (708)679-2494
Fr: 800-323-4900
Marjorie Eberts and Margaret Gisler. 1991. Describes employment opportunities for jobs in education, publishing, libraries, museums, and more.

★6673★ **Careers in Communications**
National Textbook Co. (NTC)
VGM Career Books
4255 W. Touhy Ave.
Lincolnwood, IL 60646-1975
Ph: (708)679-5500   Fax: (708)679-2494
Fr: 800-323-4900
Shonan F. Noronha. 1987. Provides facts about careers in communications, including journalism, publishing, photography and film, advertising, public relations, and telecommunication.

★6674★ **Careers in Journalism**
National Textbook Co. (NTC)
VGM Career Books
4255 W. Toughy Ave.
Lincolnwood, IL 60646-1975
Ph: (708)679-5500   Fax: (708)679-2494
Fr: 800-323-4900
Jan Goldberg. 1994. Looks at educational requirements, salary ranges, working conditions, and employment outlook for different careers in journalism.

★6675★ **Careers in Word Processing and Desktop Publishing**
Rosen Publishing Group
29 E. 21st St.
New York, NY 10010
Ph: (212)777-3017   Fax: (212)777-0277
Fr: 800-237-9932
Jean Spencer. 1990. Overviews the exciting job possibilities available in this field as desktop publishers continue to grow.

★6676★ **Children's Book Writer**
Vocational Biographies, Inc.
PO Box 31
Sauk Centre, MN 56378-0031
Ph: (612)352-6516   Fax: (612)352-5546
Fr: 800-255-0752
1992. Four-page pamphlet containing a personal narrative about a worker's job, work likes and dislikes, career path from high school to the present, education and training, the rewards and frustrations, and the effects of the job on the rest of the worker's life. The data file portion of this pamphlet gives a concise occupational summary, including

work description, working conditions, places of employment, personal characteristics, education and training, job outlook, and salary range.

★6677★ **Comedy/Gag Writer**
Vocational Biographies, Inc.
PO Box 31
Sauk Centre, MN 56378-0031
Ph: (612)352-6516   Fax: (612)352-5546
Fr: 800-255-0752
1991. Four-page pamphlet containing a personal narrative about a worker's job, work likes and dislikes, career path from high school to the present. Education and training, the rewards and frustrations, and the effects of the job on the rest of the worker's life. The data file portion of this pamphlet gives a concise occupational summary, including work descriptions, working conditions, places of employment, personal characteristics, education and training, job outlook, and salary range.

★6678★ **Copy/Assignment Editor**
Vocational Biographies, Inc.
PO Box 31
Sauk Centre, MN 56378-0031
Ph: (612)352-6516   Fax: (612)352-5546
Fr: 800-255-0752
1994. Four-page pamphlet containing a personal narrative about a worker's job, work likes and dislikes, career path from high school to the present. Education and training, the rewards and frustrations, and the effects of the job on the rest of the worker's life. The data file portion of this pamphlet gives a concise occupational summary, including work descriptions, working conditions, places of employment, personal characteristics, education and training, job outlook, and salary range.

★6679★ **Copy Editor**
Vocational Biographies, Inc.
PO Box 31
Sauk Centre, MN 56378-0031
Ph: (612)352-6516   Fax: (612)352-5546
Fr: 800-255-0752
1993. Four-page pamphlet containing a personal narrative about a worker's job, work likes and dislikes, career path from high school to the present, education and training, the rewards and frustrations, and the effects of the job on the rest of the worker's life. The data file portion of this pamphlet gives a concise occupational summary, including work description, working conditions, places of employment, personal characteristics, education and training, job outlook, and salary range.

★6680★ **Copywriter**
Careers, Inc.
PO Box 135
Largo, FL 34649-0135
Ph: (813)584-7333
1994. Two-page occupational summary card describing duties, working conditions, personal qualifications, training, earnings and hours, employment outlook, places of employment, related careers, and where to write for more information.

★6681★ **Copywriter**
Vocational Biographies, Inc.
PO Box 31
Sauk Centre, MN 56378-0031
Ph: (612)352-6516   Fax: (612)352-5546
Fr: 800-255-0752
1990. Four-page pamphlet containing a personal narrative about a worker's job, work likes and dislikes, career path from high school to the present. Education and training, the rewards and frustrations, and the effects of the job on the rest of the worker's life. The data file portion of this pamphlet gives a concise occupational summary, including work descriptions, working conditions, places of employment, personal characteristics, education and training, job outlook, and salary range.

★6682★ **"Copywriter" in 100 Best Careers for the Year 2000 (pp. 143-145)**
Arco Pub.
201 W. 103rd St.
Indianapolis, IN 46290
Ph: 800-428-5331   Fax: 800-835-3202
Shelly Field. 1992. Describes 100 job opportunities expected to grow fast throughout the next decade. Provides information on job duties and responsibilities, training requirements, education, advancement opportunities, experience and qualifications, and typical salaries.

★6683★ **"Crafts Writer" in Opportunities in Crafts Careers (pp. 79-88)**
National Textbook Co. (NTC)
VGM Career Books
4255 W. Touhy Ave.
Lincolnwood, IL 60646-1975
Ph: (708)679-5500   Fax: (708)679-2494
Fr: 800-323-4900
Marianne Munday. 1994. Provides a general overview of crafts and some traditional and non-traditional jobs related to crafts. Gives information on how to start a crafts business.

★6684★ **"Editing" in Career Choices for the 90's for Students of Political Science and Government**
Walker and Co.
435 Hudson St.
New York, NY 10014
Ph: (212)727-8300   Fax: (212)727-0984
Fr: 800-289-2553
1990. Offers alternatives for students of political science. Gives information about job outlook and competition for entry-level candidates. Provides job-hunting tips.

★6685★ **"Editor" in 100 Best Careers for the Year 2000 (pp. 157-158)**
Arco Pub.
201 W. 103rd St.
Indianapolis, IN 46290
Ph: 800-428-5331   Fax: 800-835-3202
Shelly Field. 1992. Describes 100 job opportunities expected to grow fast throughout the next decade. Provides information on job duties and responsibilities, training requirements, education, advancement opportunities, experience and qualifications, and typical salaries.

★6686★ "Editor, Book Publishing",
"Editor, Newspaper and Magazine",
and "Technical Writer" in *VGM's
Careers Encyclopedia*
National Textbook Co. (NTC)
VGM Career Books
4255 W. Touhy Ave.
Lincolnwood, IL 60646-1975
Ph: (708)679-5500   Fax: (708)679-2494
Fr: 800-323-4900

Third edition, 1991. Profiles 200 occupations.
Describes job duties, places of employment,
working conditions, qualifications, education,
and training, advancement potential, and salary for each occupation.

★6687★ *Editor, Newspaper*
Careers, Inc.
PO Box 135
Largo, FL 34649-0135
Ph: (813)584-7333

1992. Two-page occupational summary card
describing duties, working conditions, personal qualifications, training, earnings and
hours, employment outlook, places of employment, related careers, and where to write
for more information.

★6688★ "Editor" in *Opportunities in
Magazine Publishing* (pp. 42-43, 67-82)
National Textbook Co. (NTC)
VGM Career Books
4255 W. Touhy Ave.
Lincolnwood, IL 60646-1975
Ph: (708)679-5500   Fax: (708)679-2494
Fr: 800-323-4900

S. William Pattis. 1992. Describes history, organizations, and types of magazine publishing (including consumer, business, technical
and trade magazines). Covers career opportunities in different departments in a publishing company, future trends, and job hunting
techniques.

★6689★ "Editorial Assistant" in *Guide
to Federal Technical, Trades and Labor
Jobs* (p. 196)
Resource Directories
3361 Executive Pkwy., Ste. 302
Toledo, OH 43606
Ph: (419)536-5353   Fax: (419)536-7056
Fr: 800-274-8515

Rod W. Durgin, editor. Second edition, 1992.
Describes where and how to apply for a federal job. Profiles 300 federal jobs that do not
require a college degree. Gives a description,
salary, locations, and the agencies that hire
the most employees for each job.

★6690★ *Editorial Staff Members*
Chronicle Guidance Publications, Inc.
66 Aurora St.
PO Box 1190
Moravia, NY 13118-1190
Ph: (315)497-0330   Fax: (315)497-3359
Fr: 800-622-7284

1991. Career brief describing the nature of
the job, working conditions, hours and earnings, education and training, licensure, certification, unions, personal qualifications, social
and psychological factors, location, employment outlook, entry methods, advancement,
and related occupations.

★6691★ "Editors-Books and
Magazines" in *101 Careers: A Guide to
the Fastest-Growing Opportunities* (pp.
285-287)
John Wiley & Sons, Inc.
605 3rd Ave.
New York, NY 10158-0012
Ph: (212)850-6645   Fax: (212)850-6088

Michael Harkavy. 1990. Describes the nature
of the job, working conditions, employment
growth, qualifications, personal skills, projected salaries, and where to write for more
information.

★6692★ "Editors" in *Career
Opportunities in Art*
Facts on File
460 Park Ave. S.
New York, NY 10016-7382
Ph: (212)683-2244   Fax: 800-678-3633
Fr: 800-322-8755

Susan H. Haubenstock. 1988. This book profiles seventy-five art-related jobs. Each profile
includes a career description, career ladder,
employment and advancement prospects,
education, experience and skills required,
salary range, and tips for entry into the field.

★6693★ *Editors, General*
Careers, Inc.
PO Box 135
Largo, FL 34649-0135
Ph: (813)584-7333

1993. Four-page brief offering the definition,
history, duties, working conditions, personal
qualifications, educational requirements,
earnings, hours, employment outlook, advancement, and careers related to this position.

★6694★ "Editors" in *Opportunities in
Book Publishing Careers* (pp. 128-135)
National Textbook Co. (NTC)
VGM Career Books
4255 W. Touhy Ave.
Lincolnwood, IL 60646-1975
Ph: (708)679-5500   Fax: (708)679-2494
Fr: 800-323-4900

Robert A. Carter. 1987. Describes the history
of book publishing and jobs in different types
of publishing: trade, religious, textbook, technical, scientific, medical, university presses,
paperback, and mail order. Includes information on educational preparation, personal requirements, advancement possibilities, unions, and related fields.

★6695★ *Editors, Weekly Newspaper*
Chronicle Guidance Publications, Inc.
66 Aurora St.
PO Box 1190
Moravia, NY 13118-1190
Ph: (315)497-0330   Fax: (315)497-3359
Fr: 800-622-7284

1992. Career brief describing the nature of
the job, working conditions, hours and earnings, education and training, licensure, certification, unions, personal qualifications, social
and psychological factors, location, employment outlook, entry methods, advancement,
and related occupations.

★6696★ *The Encyclopedia of Career
Choices for the 1990s: A Guide to
Entry Level Jobs*
Berkley Pub.
PO Box 506
East Rutherford, NJ 07073
Fax: (201)933-2316   Fr: 800-788-6262

1992. Describes entry-level careers in a variety of industries. Chapters of particular interest to writers and editors include "Editing"
(pp. 501-520, 602-624, 700-718) and "Technical Writing" (pp. 805-817). Presents qualifications required, working conditions, salary,
internships, and professional associations.

★6697★ *Executive Editor*
Vocational Biographies, Inc.
PO Box 31
Sauk Centre, MN 56378-0031
Ph: (612)352-6516   Fax: (612)352-5546
Fr: 800-255-0752

1995. Four-page pamphlet containing a personal narrative about a worker's job, work
likes and dislikes, career path from high
school to the present. Education and training,
the rewards and frustrations, and the effects
of the job on the rest of the worker's life. The
data file portion of this pamphlet gives a
concise occupational summary, including
work descriptions, working conditions, places
of employment, personal characteristics, education and training, job outlook, and salary
range.

★6698★ *Exploring Careers in Video*
Rosen Publishing Group
29 E. 21st St.
New York, NY 10010
Ph: (212)777-3017   Fax: (212)777-0277
Fr: 800-237-9932

Paul Allman. Revised edition, 1989. Describes various careers available in television
and tells how to acquire necessary training
and preparation. Covers work in network and
cable TV, industrial television, and commercial production.

★6699★ *Farm News Editor*
Vocational Biographies, Inc.
PO Box 31
Sauk Centre, MN 56378-0031
Ph: (612)352-6516   Fax: (612)352-5546
Fr: 800-255-0752

1994. Four-page pamphlet containing a personal narrative about a worker's job, work
likes and dislikes, career path from high
school to the present. Education and training,
the rewards and frustrations, and the effects
of the job on the rest of the worker's life. The
data file portion of this pamphlet gives a
concise occupational summary, including
work descriptions, working conditions, places
of employment, personal characteristics, education and training, job outlook, and salary
range.

★6700★ "Film Editors" in *Encyclopedia
of Careers and Vocational Guidance*
(Vol.2, pp.649-652)
J.G. Ferguson Publishing Co.
200 W. Madison St., Ste. 300
Chicago, IL 60606
Ph: (312)580-5480   Fax: (312)580-4948

William E. Hopke, editor-in-chief. Ninth edition, 1993. Four-volume set that profiles 900
occupations and describes job trends in 74

industries. Includes career description, educational requirements, history of the job, methods of entry, advancement, employment outlook, earnings, conditions of work, social and psychological factors, and sources of further information.

★6701★ Film and Video Career Directory
Gale Research Inc.
835 Penobscot Bldg.
Detroit, MI 48226
Ph: (313)961-2242   Fr: 800-877-GALE
1994. Profiles careers in the film and video industry.

★6702★ Guide to Careers in Abstracting and Indexing
National Federation of Abstracting and Information Services (NFAIS)
1429 Walnut St.
Philadelphia, PA 19102
Ph: (215)563-2406
Ann Marie Cunningham and Wendey Wicks. 1992.

★6703★ How to Get Your First Copywriting Job in Advertising
E. P. Dutton
2 Park Ave.
New York, NY 10016
Ph: (212)366-2000
Dick Wasserman. 1987. Gives advice on putting a portfolio together, becoming a first-rate copywriter, and job hunting in the advertising field.

★6704★ How to Land a Job in Journalism
Betterway Publications
PO Box 219
Crozet, VA 22932
Ph: (804)823-5661
Phil Swann and Ed Achorn. 1988. Offers advice on college preparation, financial aid, internships, and job hunting for those interested in a career in journalism. Contains tips from journalists. Includes chapters on copy editing and newsletter editing.

★6705★ How to Start and Run a Writing and Editing Business
John Wiley and Sons, Inc.
605 3rd Ave.
New York, NY 10158-0012
Ph: (212)850-6000   Fax: (212)850-6088
Fr: 800-526-5368
Herman Holtz. 1992. Provides information on how to market newsletters, manuals, catalogs, brochures and proposals. Also discusses methods of composition and production using desktop publishing.

★6706★ In Their Own Words: Contemporary American Playwrights
Theatre Communications Group TCG
355 Lexington Ave.
New York, NY 10017
Ph: (212)697-5230
David Savran. 1988. Playwrights describe their early experiences in the theatre, their working methods, and their plays in various interviews.

★6707★ "Magazine/Book Publishing" in Internships: 1995 (pp. 57-71)
Petersons Guides, Inc.
PO Box 2123
Princeton, NJ 08543-2123
Ph: (609)243-9111   Fax: (609)243-9150
Fr: 800-338-3282
Fifteenth edition, 1995. Lists internship opportunities under six broad categories: communications, creative, performing, and fine arts, human services, international relations, business and technology, and public relations. Includes a special section on internships in Washington, DC. For each internship program, gives the name, phone number, contact person, description, eligibility requirements, and benefits.

★6708★ "Marketing and Advertising" in Where the Jobs Are: The Hottest Careers for the 90s (pp. 195-210)
Career Press
180 5th Ave.
Hawthorne, NJ 07507
Ph: (201)427-0229   Fax: (201)427-2037
Fr: 800-CAREER-1
Joyce Hadley. 1995. Offers a job-hunting strategy for the 1990s as well as descriptions of growing careers of the decade. Each profile includes general information, forecasts, growth, education and training, licensing requirements, and salary information.

★6709★ "Medical Writer and Editor" in 150 Careers in the Health Care Field
Reed Reference Publishing
121 Chanlon Rd.
PO Box 31
New Providence, NJ 07974
Fax: (908)665-6688   Fr: 800-521-8110
Stanley Alperin. Third edition, 1993. Profiles 150 health care occupations requiring a bachelor's degree or less. Describes the nature of the work, educational preparation, licensing requirements, and salary. Lists accredited educational programs.

★6710★ "Newspaper Editors" in Encyclopedia of Careers and Vocational Guidance (Vol.3, pp. 547-552)
J.G. Ferguson Publishing Co.
200 W. Madison St., Ste. 300
Chicago, IL 60606
Ph: (312)580-5480   Fax: (312)580-4948
William E. Hopke, editor-in-chief. Ninth edition, 1993. Four-volume set that profiles 900 occupations and describes job trends in 74 industries. Includes career description, educational requirements, history of the job, methods of entry, advancement, employment outlook, earnings, conditions of work, social and psychological factors, and sources of further information.

★6711★ Newspaper Features Editor
Vocational Biographies, Inc.
PO Box 31
Sauk Centre, MN 56378-0031
Ph: (612)352-6516   Fax: (612)352-5546
Fr: 800-255-0752
1995. Four-page pamphlet containing a personal narrative about a worker's job, work likes and dislikes, career path from high school to the present. Education and training, the rewards and frustrations, and the effects

of the job on the rest of the worker's life. The data file portion of this pamphlet gives a concise occupational summary, including work descriptions, working conditions, places of employment, personal characteristics, education and training, job outlook, and salary range.

★6712★ Newspaper Managing Editor
Vocational Biographies, Inc.
PO Box 31
Sauk Centre, MN 56378-0031
Ph: (612)352-6516   Fax: (612)352-5546
Fr: 800-255-0752
1995. Four-page pamphlet containing a personal narrative about a worker's job, work likes and dislikes, career path from high school to the present, education and training, the rewards and frustrations, and the effects of the job on the rest of the worker's life. The data file portion of this pamphlet gives a concise occupational summary, including work description, working conditions, places of employment, personal characteristics, education and training, job outlook, and salary range.

★6713★ Opportunities in Newspaper Publishing Careers
National Textbook Co. (NTC)
VGM Career Books
4255 W. Touhy Ave.
Lincolnwood, IL 60646-1975
Ph: (708)679-5500   Fax: (708)679-2494
Fr: 800-323-4900
John Tebbel. 1989. Describes working for big and small newspapers and addresses the changing technology in the publishing field.

★6714★ Opportunities in Technical Writing and Communications Careers
National Textbook Co. (NTC)
VGM Career Books
4255 W. Toughy Ave.
Lincolnwood, IL 60646-1975
Ph: (708)679-5500   Fax: (708)679-2494
Fr: 800-323-4900
Joy Gould.

★6715★ Opportunities in Writing Careers
National Textbook Co. (NTC)
VGM Career Books
4255 W. Touhy Ave.
Lincolnwood, IL 60646-1975
Ph: (708)679-5500   Fax: (708)679-2494
Fr: 800-323-4900
Elizabeth Foote-Smith. 1989. Describes writing career opportunities. Covers articles, novels, short stories, nonfiction books, reviews, and interviews. Also includes information on playwrights, poets, journalists, and broadcasters. Discusses educational preparation. Includes a bibliography.

★6716★ Playwright and Screen Writer
Careers, Inc.
PO Box 135
Largo, FL 34649-0135
Ph: (813)584-7333
1993. Two-page occupational summary card describing duties, working conditions, personal qualifications, training, earnings and hours, employment outlook, places of employment, related careers, and where to write for more information.

★6717★ *Proofreader*
Vocational Biographies, Inc.
PO Box 31
Sauk Centre, MN 56378-0031
Ph: (612)352-6516   Fax: (612)352-5546
Fr: 800-255-0752

1990. Four-page pamphlet containing a personal narrative about a worker's job, work likes and dislikes, career path from high school to the present, education and training, the rewards and frustrations, and the effects of the job on the rest of the worker's life. The data file portion of this pamphlet gives a concise occupational summary, including work description, working conditions, places of employment, personal characteristics, education and training, job outlook, and salary range.

★6718★ "Publication Editor",
"Technical Writer", and "Author
(Books)" in *Jobs Rated Almanac*
World Almanac
1 International Blvd., Ste. 444
Mahwah, NJ 07495
Ph: (201)529-6900   Fax: (201)529-6901

Les Krantz. Second edition, 1992. Ranks 250 jobs by environment, salary, outlooks, physical demands, stress, security, travel opportunities, and extra perks. Includes jobs the editor feels are the most common, most interesting, and the most rapidly growing.

★6719★ "Publications (Art Museums)"
in *Career Choices for the 90's for
Students of History* (p. 13)
Walker and Co.
435 Hudson St.
New York, NY 10014
Ph: (212)727-8300   Fax: (212)727-0984
Fr: 800-289-2553

1990. Offers alternatives for students of history. Gives information about the outlook and competition for entry-level candidates. Provides job-hunting tips.

★6720★ "Screenwriters" in *Career
Discovery Encyclopedia* (Vol.5, pp.
176-177)
J.G. Ferguson Publishing Co.
200 W. Madison St., Ste. 300
Chicago, IL 60606
Ph: (312)580-5480   Fax: (312)580-4948

Russell E. Primm, editor-in-chief. 1993. This six volume set contains two-page articles for 504 occupations. Each article describes job duties, earnings, and educational and training requirements. The whole set is arranged alphabetically by job title. Designed for junior high and older students.

★6721★ "Screenwriters" in
*Encyclopedia of Careers and
Vocational Guidance* (Vol.4, pp. 329-
331)
J.G. Ferguson Publishing Co.
200 W. Madison St., Ste. 300
Chicago, IL 60606
Ph: (312)580-5480   Fax: (312)580-4948

William E. Hopke, editor-in-chief. Ninth edition, 1993. Four-volume set that profiles 900 occupations and describes job trends in 74 industries. Includes career description, educational requirements, history of the job, methods of entry, advancement, employment outlook, earnings, conditions of work, social and psychological factors, and sources of further information.

★6722★ *Scriptwriter*
Vocational Biographies, Inc.
PO Box 31
Sauk Centre, MN 56378-0031
Ph: (612)352-6516   Fax: (612)352-5546
Fr: 800-255-0752

1993. Four-page pamphlet containing a personal narrative about a worker's job, work likes and dislikes, career path from high school to the present. Education and training, the rewards and frustrations, and the effects of the job on the rest of the worker's life. The data file portion of this pamphlet gives a concise occupational summary, including work descriptions, working conditions, places of employment, personal characteristics, education and training, job outlook, and salary range.

★6723★ *The Tech Writing Game*
Facts on File
460 Park Ave. S.
New York, NY 10016-7382
Ph: (212)683-2244   Fax: 800-678-3633
Fr: 800-322-8755

Janet Van Wicklen. 1993. Includes the how and where to training, landing, and holding a job. Also includes appendices, bibliography, and tables.

★6724★ *Technical Writer*
Vocational Biographies, Inc.
PO Box 31
Sauk Centre, MN 56378-0031
Ph: (612)352-6516   Fax: (612)352-5546
Fr: 800-255-0752

1990. Four-page pamphlet containing a personal narrative about a worker's job, work likes and dislikes, career path from high school to the present. Education and training, the rewards and frustrations, and the effects of the job on the rest of the worker's life. The data file portion of this pamphlet gives a concise occupational summary, including work descriptions, working conditions, places of employment, personal characteristics, education and training, job outlook, and salary range.

★6725★ "Technical Writer" in *BLR
Encyclopedia of Prewritten Job
Descriptions*
Business and Legal Reports, Inc.
39 Academy St.
Madison, CT 06443-1513
Ph: (203)245-7448

Stephen D. Bruce, editor-in-chief. 1994. This book contains hundreds of sample job descriptions arranged by functional job category. The 1-3 page job descriptions cover what the worker normally does in the position, who they report to, and how that position fits in the organizational structure.

★6726★ "Technical Writer" in
Opportunities in High-Tech Careers
(pp. 97-98)
National Textbook Co. (NTC)
VGM Career Books
4255 W. Touhy Ave.
Lincolnwood, IL 60646-1975
Ph: (708)679-5500   Fax: (708)679-2494
Fr: 800-323-4900

Gary D. Colter and Deborah Yanuck. 1987. Explores high-technology careers. Written for the student and displaced worker. Describes job opportunities, how to make a career decision, how to prepare for high technology jobs, job hunting techniques, and future trends.

★6727★ "Technical Writing" in *Career
Choices for the 90's for Students of
English*
Walker and Co.
435 Hudson St.
New York, NY 10014
Ph: (212)727-8300   Fax: (212)727-0984
Fr: 800-289-2553

1990. Offers career alternatives for students of English. Gives the job outlook and competition for entry-level candidates. Provides job-hunting tips.

★6728★ "Technical Writing" in *Careers
in High-Tech*
Arco Publishing Co.
Macmillan General Reference
15 Columbus Cir.
New York, NY 10023
Fax: 800-835-3202   Fr: 800-858-7674

Connie Winkler. 1987. Surveys occupations in data processing, personal computers, telecommunications, manufacturing technology, artificial intelligence, computer graphics, medicine, biotechnology, lasers, technical writing, and publishing. Separate chapters cover education and training.

★6729★ "Technical Writing" in
Exploring High-Tech Careers
Rosen Publishing Group
29 E. 21st St.
New York, NY 10010
Ph: (212)777-3017   Fax: (212)777-0277
Fr: 800-237-9932

Scott Southworth. Revised edition, 1993. Gives an orientation to the field of high technology and high-tech jobs. Describes educational preparation and job hunting. Includes a glossary and bibliography.

★6730★ "Television Writer" in *Profiles
in Achievement* (pp. 41-58)
The College Board
45 Columbus Ave.
New York, NY 10023-6992
Ph: (212)713-8165   Fax: (212)713-8143
Fr: 800-323-7155

Charles M. Holloway. 1987. Profiles eight men and women who have overcome the the barriers of race, gender, tradition, and economic circumstances in their quest to become successful professionals.

★6731★ Travel Writer
Vocational Biographies, Inc.
PO Box 31
Sauk Centre, MN 56378-0031
Ph: (612)352-6516   Fax: (612)352-5546
Fr: 800-255-0752
1993. Four-page pamphlet containing a personal narrative about a worker's job, work likes and dislikes, career path from high school to the present. Education and training, the rewards and frustrations, and the effects of the job on the rest of the worker's life. The data file portion of this pamphlet gives a concise occupational summary, including work descriptions, working conditions, places of employment, personal characteristics, education and training, job outlook, and salary range.

★6732★ Writer
Careers, Inc.
PO Box 135
Largo, FL 34649-0135
Ph: (813)584-7333
1992. Four-page brief offering the definition, history, duties, working conditions, personal qualifications, educational requirements, earnings, hours, employment outlook, advancement, and careers related to this position.

★6733★ "Writer and Editor" in Career Opportunities for Writers (pp. 148-149)
Facts on File
460 Park Ave. S.
New York, NY 10016-7382
Ph: (212)683-2244   Fax: 800-678-3633
Fr: 800-322-8755
Rosemary Guiley. 1992. Describes approximately 90 careers in eight major fields, offering such details as duties, salaries, prerequisites, employment and advancement opportunities, organizations to join, and opportunities for women and minorities.

★6734★ "Writer, Editor" in College Board Guide to Jobs and Career Planning (pp. 164)
The College Board
415 Columbus Ave.
New York, NY 10023-6992
Ph: (212)713-8165   Fax: (212)713-8143
Fr: 800-323-7155
Joyce S. Mitchell. Second edition, 1994. Describes a variety of careers. Includes information on salaries, related careers, education needed, and sources of additional information.

★6735★ "Writer/Editor" in Guide to Federal Jobs
Resource Directories
3361 Executive Pkwy., Ste. 302
Toledo, OH 43606
Ph: (419)536-5353   Fax: (419)536-7056
Fr: 800-274-8515
Rod W. Durgin, editor. Third edition, 1992. Contains information on finding and applying for federal jobs. Describes more than 200 professional and technical jobs for college graduates. Covers the nature of the work, salary, and geographic location. Lists college majors preferred for that occupation. Section one describes the function and work of government agencies that hire the most significant number of college graduates.

★6736★ Writer, Technical
Careers, Inc.
PO Box 135
Largo, FL 34649-0135
Ph: (813)584-7333
1994. Four-page brief offering the definition, history, duties, working conditions, personal qualifications, educational requirements, earnings, hours, employment outlook, advancement, and careers related to this position.

★6737★ "Writers" in Advertising: A VGM Career Planner (pp. 49-50)
National Textbook Co. (NTC)
VGM Career Books
4255 W. Touhy Ave.
Lincolnwood, IL 60646-1975
Ph: (708)679-5500   Fax: (708)679-2494
Fr: 800-323-4900
S. William Pattis. 1989. Describes the development of advertising. Explains the role of the media in advertising, personal characteristics needed to succeed in this field, educational requirements, and related jobs. Gives job hunting tips.

★6738★ "Writers" in American Almanac of Jobs and Salaries (pp. 194, 551)
Avon Books
1350 Avenue of the Americas
New York, NY 10019
Ph: (212)261-6800   Fr: 800-238-0658
John Wright, editor. Revised and updated, 1994-95. A comprehensive guide to the wages of hundreds of occupations in a wide variety of industries and organizations.

★6739★ Writers, Artistic and Dramatic
Chronicle Guidance Publications, Inc.
66 Aurora St.
PO Box 1190
Moravia, NY 13118-1190
Ph: (315)497-0330   Fax: (315)497-3359
Fr: 800-622-7284
1993. Occupational brief describing the nature of the job, working conditions, hours and earnings, education and training, licensure, certification, unions, personal qualifications, social and psychological factors, location, employment outlook, entry methods, advancement, and related occupations.

★6740★ "Writers and Authors" in Career Discovery Encyclopedia (Vol.6, pp. 160-161)
J.G. Ferguson Publishing Co.
200 W. Madison St., Ste. 300
Chicago, IL 60606
Ph: (312)580-5480   Fax: (312)580-4948
Russell E. Primm, editor-in chief. 1993. This six volume set contains two-page articles for 504 occupations. Each article describes job duties, earnings, and educational and training requirements. The whole set is arranged alphabetically by job title. Designed for junior high and older students.

★6741★ "Writers and Editors" in Occupational Outlook Handbook
U.S. Government Printing Office
Superintendent of Documents
Washington, DC 20402
Ph: (202)512-1800   Fax: (202)512-2250
Biennial, 1994-95. Encyclopedia of careers describing about 250 occupations and comprising about 85 percent of all jobs in the economy. Occupations that require lengthy education or training are given the most attention. Each occupation's profile describes what the worker does on the job, working conditions, education and training requirements, advancement possibilities, job outlook, earnings, and sources of additional information.

★6742★ "Writers" in Encyclopedia of Careers and Vocational Guidance (Vol.4, pp. 619-623)
J.G. Ferguson Publishing Co.
200 W. Madison St., Ste. 300
Chicago, IL 60606
Ph: (312)580-5480   Fax: (312)580-4948
William E. Hopke, editor-in-chief. Ninth edition, 1993. Four-volume set that profiles 900 occupations and describes job trends in 74 industries. Includes career description, educational requirements, history of the job, methods of entry, advancement, employment outlook, earnings, conditions of work, social and psychological factors, and sources of further information.

★6743★ Writers, Free-lance
Chronicle Guidance Publications, Inc.
66 Aurora St.
PO Box 1190
Moravia, NY 13118-1190
Ph: (315)497-0330   Fax: (315)497-3359
Fr: 800-622-7284
1992. Career brief describing the nature of the job, working conditions, hours and earnings, education and training, licensure, certification, unions, personal qualifications, social and psychological factors, location, employment outlook, entry methods, advancement, and related occupations.

★6744★ Writers, Technical
Chronicle Guidance Publications, Inc.
66 Aurora St.
PO Box 1190
Moravia, NY 13118-1190
Ph: (315)497-0330   Fax: (315)497-3359
Fr: 800-622-7284
1992. Career brief describing the nature of the job, working conditions, hours and earnings, education and training, licensure, certification, unions, personal qualifications, social and psychological factors, location, employment outlook, entry methods, advancement, and related occupations.

★6745★ "Writing" in Straight Talk on Careers: Eighty Pros Take You Into Their Professions (pp. 74-96)
Garrett Park Press
PO Box 1907
Garrett Park, MD 20896
Ph: (301)946-2553
Mary Barbera-Hogan. 1987. Contains candid interviews from people who give an inside view of their work in 80 different careers. These professionals describe a day's work and the stresses and rewards accompanying their work.

PROFESSIONAL ASSOCIATIONS

★6746★ American Society of Magazine Editors (ASME)
919 3rd Ave.
New York, NY 10022
Ph: (212)872-3700   Fax: (212)888-4217
Members: Purpose: Professional organization of senior magazine editors. Sponsors annual editorial internship program for college juniors.

★6747★ Association for Business Communication (ABC)
University of North Texas
College of Business
Department of Management
Denton, TX 76203
Ph: (817)565-4423   Fax: (817)565-4930
Members: College teachers of business communication; management consultants in business communications; training directors and correspondence supervisors of business firms, direct mail copywriters, public relations writers, and others interested in communication for business. Sponsors research programs. **Publications:** *Bulletin of the Association for Business Communication*, quarterly. • *Journal of Business Communication*, quarterly.

★6748★ Dow Jones Newspaper Fund (DJNF)
PO Box 300
Princeton, NJ 08543
Ph: (609)452-2820   Fax: (609)520-5804
Established by Dow Jones and Company, publishers of *The Wall Street Journal*, to encourage careers in journalism among young people. Operates Editing Internship Program for all junior, senior, and graduate level college students interested in journalism. Students work as copy editors during the summer for a daily newspaper or wire service and receive monetary scholarships to return to school in the fall. Offers information on careers in print journalism. **Publications:** *Advisor Update*, quarterly. • *The Journalists' Road to Success*, annual. • *Newspapers, Diversity, and You*.

★6749★ Society for Technical Communication (STC)
901 N. Stuart St., Ste. 904
Arlington, VA 22203
Ph: (703)522-4114   Fax: (703)522-2075
Members: Writers, editors, educators, scientists, engineers, artists, publishers, and others professionally engaged in or interested in some phase of the field of technical communications; companies, corporations, organizations, and agencies interested in the aims of the society. **Purpose:** Seeks to advance the theory and practice of technical communication in all media. Sponsors high school writing contests. **Publications:** *Annual Conference Proceedings*, annual. • *Intercom Newsletter*, monthly. • *Technical Communication*, quarterly.

★6750★ Women in Communications, Inc. (WICI)
3717 Columbia Pike, No. 310
Arlington, VA 22204-4255
Ph: (703)528-4200
Members: Professional society - journalism and communications. **Purpose:** Offers placement service; compiles statistics. **Publications:** *Careers in Communications*. • *Leading Change*, periodic. • *Membership and Resource Directory*, biennial. • *The Professional Communicator*.

TEST GUIDES

★6751★ *Career Examination Series: Publications Editor*
National Learning Corp.
212 Michael Dr.
Syosset, NY 11791
Ph: (516)921-8888   Fax: (516)921-8743
Fr: 800-645-6337
Jack Rudman. A series of study guides with multiple-choice examination questions and solutions for trainees and professional writers and editors. Titles in the series include *Editorial Assistant; Editorial Clerk*.

EDUCATIONAL DIRECTORIES AND PROGRAMS

★6752★ *Advertising Career Directory*
Gale Research Inc.
835 Penobscot Bldg.
Detroit, MI 48226-4094
Ph: (313)961-2242   Fax: (313)961-6083
Fr: 800-877-GALE
Bradley J. Morgan and Joseph M. Palmisano. Fifth edition, 1992. A directory in the Career Advisor Series that provides essays written by industry professionals; job search information on resume and cover letter preparation, networking, and the interviewing process; approximately 300 companies and organizations offering job opportunities and internships, and additional job-hunting resources.

★6753★ *The AWP Official Guide to Writing Programs*
Associated Writing Programs (AWP)
Tallwood House, Mail Stop 1E3
George Mason Universtiy
Fairfax, VA 22030
Ph: (804)683-3839   Fax: (703)993-4302
D.W. Fenza, Publications Editor
Biennial, February of even years. Covers about 300 colleges and universities offering workshops and degree programs (undergraduate and graduate) in creative writing; approximately 100 writers' conferences, colonies, and centers; coverage includes Canada. Entries include: Institution name, department name, contact name and address; description of program, including degree or other credit offered; description of faculty, in-

cluding titles of their publications. Arrangement: Alphabetical.

★6754★ *Book Publishing Career Directory*
Gale Research Inc.
835 Penobscot Bldg.
Detroit, MI 48226-4094
Ph: (313)961-2242   Fax: (313)961-6083
Fr: 800-877-GALE
Bradley J. Morgan and Joseph M. Palmisano. Fifth edition, 1992. A directory in the Career Advisor Series that provides essays written by industry professionals; job search information on resume and cover letter preparation, networking, and the interviewing process; approximately 300 companies and organizations offering job opportunities and internships, and additional job-hunting resources.

★6755★ *CRTentertainment*
Sofprotex
PO Box 271
Belmont, CA 94002
Current. Diskette; requires a FileMaker compatible database. Covers over 500 theatrical agencies and entertainment industry organizations and 1,000 movie stars, musicians, producers, directors, and writers in the U.S. Database includes: Name, home address, business address and phone.

★6756★ *Directory of Publications Resources*
Editorial Experts, Inc. (EEI)
66 Canal Center Plaza, Ste. 200
Alexandria, VA 22314-5507
Ph: (703)683-0683   Fax: (703)683-4915
Eleanor A. Johnson, Contact
Biennial, January of odd years. Covers over 100 books and periodicals for the professional editor and writer; 90 professional organizations; 55 colleges and universities that sponsor training programs for writers and editors. Entries include: For publishers—Name, address, phone, publication title, price. For organizations—Organization name, address, phone, description of activities, number of members, services, publications, dues. For colleges and universities—Name, address, phone, types of courses offered, credit earned, schedule. Arrangement: Separate sections for periodicals, books, professional organizations, software packages, and training opportunities.

★6757★ *FYI Directory of News Sources and Information*
JSC Group Ltd.
2 Evergreen Rd., Ste. 2A
Severna Park, MD 21146
Ph: (410)647-1013   Fax: (410)647-9557
Julia Stocks Corneal
Annual, June. Covers about 400 associations, corporations, individuals, and sources for background story gathering for journalists. Entries include: Co. or organization name, address, phone, name and title of contact, description. Arrangement: Classified by subject.

★6758★ Magazine Career Directory
Gale Research Inc.
835 Penobscot Bldg.
Detroit, MI 48226-4094
Ph: (313)961-2242   Fax: (313)961-6083
Fr: 800-877-GALE

Bradley J. Morgan and Joseph M. Palmisano. Fifth edition, 1993. A directory in the Career Advisor Series that provides essays written by industry professionals; job search information on resume and cover letter preparation, networking, and interviewing process; approximately 300 companies and organizations offering job opportunities and internships, and additional job-hunting resources.

★6759★ Newspapers Career Directory
Gale Research Inc.
835 Penobscot Bldg.
Detroit, MI 48226-4094
Ph: (313)961-2242   Fax: (313)961-6083
Fr: 800-877-GALE

Bradley J. Morgan and Joseph M. Palmisano. 1993. A directory in the Career Advisor Series that provides essays written by industry professionals; job search information on resume and cover letter preparation, networking, and the interviewing process; approximately 300 companies and organizations offering job opportunities and internships, and additional job-hunting resources.

★6760★ Radio and Television Career Directory
Gale Research Inc.
835 Penobscot Bldg.
Detroit, MI 48226-4094
Ph: (313)961-2242   Fax: (313)961-6083
Fr: 800-877-GALE

Bradley J. Morgan and Joseph M. Palmisano. Second edition, 1993. A directory in the Career Advisor Series that provides essays written by industry professionals; job search information on resume and cover letter preparation, networking, and the interviewing process; approximately 300 companies and organizations offering job opportunities and internships, and additional job-hunting resources.

AWARDS, SCHOLARSHIPS, GRANTS, AND FELLOWSHIPS

★6761★ Aga Khan Prize for Fiction
The Paris Review
541 E. 72 St.
New York, NY 10021
Ph: (212)861-0016   Fax: (212)861-4504

To recognize the author of an unpublished short work of contemporary fiction written in English. Manuscripts between 1,000 and 10,000 words may be submitted between May 1 and June 1. SASE is required. A monetary prize of $1,000 is awarded annually. The winning short story is announced in the fall issue. Established in 1955 by Prince Aga Khan.

★6762★ American Poetry Association Annual Poetry Contest
American Poetry Association
250 - A Potrero St.
PO Box 1803
Santa Cruz, CA 95061

To reward fine poetry and to give recognition to new talent. All poets may submit up to six original poems, no more than 20 lines in each poem. The deadline for entry is June 30 and December 31. A monetary award of $1,000, publication, and a certificate are awarded for the best poem every six months to the Grand Prize winner; there are also 150 more prizes of cash, certificate, or publication. Winners are announced in August and February. Established in 1981.

★6763★ American Society of Magazine Editors Magazine Internship Program
American Society of Magazine Editors (ASME)
575 Lexington Ave.
New York, NY 10022
Ph: (212)752-0055   Fax: (212)888-4217

Purpose: Designed to integrate the interests of magazine editors and their staffs, college students working toward careers in magazine journalism and schools of journalism. Qualifications: Applicants must have completed their junior year of college by June and be entering a full senior year in the fall after the internship program. Their interest in journalism must be evident from such activities as: academic courses in journalism, especially reporting, writing and editing; participation in campus journalism, especially as editor or senior staff member; previous summer internships or jobs at magazines or newspapers; and published articles in magazines or newspapers. Selection criteria: Strong consideration is given to heavy involvement in journalism and interest in magazine work. Funds available: Interns become employees of the magazines to which they are assigned at a minimum weekly stipend of $275 before deductions. The program runs ten weeks from June to August. Interns are responsible for their own travel expenses between assignment and home or school. They are also responsible for their own housing and maintenance. Arrangements are made with New York University or elsewhere for dormitory accommodations. Students who live in the area may live at home. Application details: Invitations to participate are sent to deans of journalism schools and heads of journalism departments; deans or department heads of liberal arts universities and colleges which have previously participated; university and college offices handling summer internships for students that have requested information; and individual students who have requested information. Each dean or department head may nominate one candidate, except those having a magazine sequence accredited by the American Council on Education for Journalism, which may submit two nominations. Submission of a formal application is required. Each application must include an application form signed by the nominee and by a dean or department head; a letter from the nominee expanding on the application, such as relevant experience, why the nominee wants to be an intern, what is expected from the experience and what the nominee hopes to contribute to the assigned magazine, the attitude of candidates towards magazines, and their willingness to dig-in as full-time employees; a supporting letter from a dean, department head, or professor who personally knows the nominees journalistic excellence; writing samples; a letter from a former intern (if possible); a recent black and white photograph (passport photo size); and a self-addressed stamped postcard for notification of receipt of application material. Deadline: December 15. Recipients will be notified no later than March 1.

★6764★ Artists' Fellowship Program
New York Foundation for the Arts
155 6th Ave., No. 14FL
New York, NY 10013-1507
Ph: (212)233-3900   Fax: (212)791-1813

To encourage professional development and to provide fellowships to individual New York State creative artists in the following categories: Architecture, Choreography, Crafts, Fiction, Film, Music Composition, Nonfiction Literature, Painting, Performance Art/Emergent Forms, Photography, Playwriting/Screenwriting, Poetry, Printmaking/Drawing/Artists' Books, Sculpture, and Video. The Program assists eligible New York State artists in their work through direct grants awarded solely on the basis of creative excellence. These awards are not to be considered project support. All applicants to the Artists' Fellowship Program are required to submit a representative body of work to demonstrate professional accomplishment and commitment to a professional career. They must be at least 18 years of age, and must have resided in New York State for the two years immediately prior to application. Graduate or undergraduate matriculated students enrolled in a degree program at the time of application may not apply. No faxed applications are accepted. Fellowships of $7,000 are awarded in some of the categories annually. In 1992, an average of 11 Fellowships were awarded in each of the following categories: Crafts, Film, Nonfiction, Literature, Performance Art/Emergent Forms, Poetry, Printmaking/Drawing/Artists' Books and Sculpture. Established in 1984. The New York Foundation for the Arts also administers four other major statewide programs: (1) The Artists-in-Residence Program, a re-grant program to create artists-in-residence opportunities in educational, cultural, and community organizations; (2) The Artists' New Works Program, a sponsorship program that provides advisory and fiscal services to professional artists who are developing individual projects; and (3) The Revolving Loan Program, a short-term, loan service for nonprofit cultural organizations.

★6765★ Oscar Blumenthal Prize
Poetry
Modern Poetry Association
60 W. Walton St.
Chicago, IL 60610
Ph: (312)280-4870

To recognize an outstanding poem or group of poems published in *Poetry* magazine. A monetary prize of $250 is awarded annually. Established in 1936.

★6766★ Bollingen Prize in Poetry
Yale University
Beinecke Library
208240 Box
New Haven, CT 06520-8240
Ph: (203)432-2962   Fax: (203)432-4047

To recognize an American poet for the best collection published in a two year period, or for a body of poetry written over several years. A monetary prize of $10,000 is awarded biennially in odd-numbered years. Established in 1948 by the Bollingen Foundation, financed by Paul Mellon for support of learning in the humanities, and named for the Swiss home of Carl Yung. In 1973, the prize received a permanent endowment from the Andrew F. Mellon Foundation.

★6767★ Arthur F. Burns Fellowships
Center for Foreign Journalists
11690 A Sunrise Valley Dr.
Reston, VA 22091
Ph: (703)620-5984

Purpose: To enable U.S. and German journalists to work with the press in the United States or Germany. Qualifications: Applicant must be a U.S. or German citizen or permanent resident. Candidate should be between the ages of 21 and 31 years. Applicant must be a working journalist in any news medium. U.S. citizens are placed with news organizations in Germany; Germany citizens are placed with U.S. news organizations. Funds available: $5,000. Application details: Write to the office manager for application guidelines. Deadline: 15 March. Notification by 15 Aiprl.

★6768★ Raymond Clapper Memorial Awards
Standing Committee of Correspondents
U.S. Senate Press Gallery
Capitol Bldg., S 316
Washington, DC 20510-9042
Ph: (202)224-0241

To recognize meritorious local, national, or international news coverage. Washington-based daily newspaper writers, or a writing team of not more than two individuals, whose work during the previous year approximates the ideals of fair and painstaking reporting and good craftsmanship characteristic of Raymond Clapper are considered for the award. Subjects can be local, national, or international. The deadline is April 7. A monetary award of $1,500 for First Prize and $500 for Second Prize are awarded annually at the White House Correspondents' Association Dinner in April. Established in 1944.

★6769★ Dobie-Paisano Fellowships
The Dobie-Paisano Project
The Graduate School
The University of Texas at Austin
Austin, TX 78712-1191
Ph: (512)471-7213   Fax: (512)471-7620

Purpose: The fellowship is primarily for creative writing. It is not suitable for those who are looking for academic and research opportunities. Qualifications: This fellowship is open to native Texans, those living in Texas now, or individuals whose work focuses on Texas and the Southwest. Funds available: Awards include residence at the ranch and a stipend of approximately $7,200 for six months. The house is furnished and utilities and maintenance are provided by the University of Texas at Austin. Two fellowships are awarded annually, the Jesse Jones Writing Fellowship and the Ralph A. Johnston Memorial Fellowship. Application details: A formal application must be filed. Visual artists with a publication in mind may request a special application. Both visual material and written text must be submitted. Deadline: An application and a sample of the author's work must be submitted by the fourth Friday in January. Announcement of the award is made by May 1. Recipients take up residence August 1.

★6770★ Editing Internships
The Dow Jones Newspaper Fund
PO Box 300
Princeton, NJ 08543-0300
Ph: (609)452-2820

Purpose: To provide students with the opportunity to work as copy editors for daily newspapers. Qualifications: Applicant must be a U.S. citizen. Candidate should be a graduate student or a junior or senior undergraduate. Internship is tenable in the summer at a U.S. daily newspaper. In addition to regular wages paid by the newspaper the Fund awards interns with a scholarship to interns returning to school full-time following the internship. Funds available: $1,000 scholarship. Application details: Write for application form and guidelines, available between 1 September to 1 November. Deadline: November 15.

★6771★ Editor of the Year Award
National Press Photographers Association
3200 Croasdaile Dr., Ste. 306
Durham, NC 27705
Ph: (919)383-7246   Fax: (919)383-7261

For recognition of outstanding service by a newspaper or magazine editor to the profession of photojournalism and to the progress and ideals of NPPA. A citation is awarded annually. Established in 1958.

★6772★ Emmy Awards for Primetime Programming
Academy of Television Arts and Sciences
5220 Lankershim Blvd.
North Hollywood, CA 91601
Ph: (818)754-2800   Fax: (818)761-2927

To recognize the advancement of the arts and sciences of television and achievements broadcast nationally during primetime. Awards are given in the following categories: (1) Program Category Awards - (a) Outstanding Comedy Series; (b) Outstanding Drama Series; (c) Outstanding Miniseries; (d) Outstanding Variety, Music, or Comedy Series; (e) Outstanding Made for T.V. Movie; (f) Outstanding Classical Program in the Performing Arts; (g) Outstanding Informational Special; (h) Outstanding Informational Series; (i) Outstanding Animated Program; and (j) Outstanding Children's Program; (2) Individual Awards - (a) Lead, Supporting, and Guest Acting in Comedy Series, Drama Series, Miniseries, or Special; (b) Performance in Variety or Music Program, Informational Programming, and Classical Music/Dance Programming; (c) Directing in Comedy Series, Drama Series, Variety or Music Program, Miniseries or Special, Classical Music/Dance Programming, and Informational Programming; (d) Casting for a Miniseries or Special; (e) Writing in Comedy Series, Drama Series, Variety or Music Program, Miniseries or Special, Informational Programming, and Classi-

cal Music/Dance Programming; and (3) Technical Awards - (a) Choreography; (b) Cinematography; (c) Art Direction; (d) Music Composition; (e) Main Title Theme Music; (f) Music Direction; (g) Music and Lyrics; (h) Costume Design; (i) Costuming; (j) Makeup; (k) Hairstyling; (l) Editing; (m) Sound Editing; (n) Sound Mixing; (o) Technical Direction/Camera/Video; (p) Special Visual Effects; (q) Graphic Design and Title Sequences; (r) Lighting Direction; (s) Engineering Development; and (4) ATAS Governors Award. Nominees are voted upon by a jury. An Emmy statuette is presented annually at the Emmy Awards Ceremony. Established in 1948 and administered by the Academy of Television Arts and Sciences until 1977.

★6773★ Fellowship for Poets of Proven Merit
Academy of American Poets
584 Broadway, Ste. 1208
New York, NY 10012
Ph: (212)274-0343

To recognize a poet of proven merit and distinguished poetic achievement. U.S. citizens are eligible. Nomination and election are made by the Academy's Board of Chancellors. A monetary award of $20,000 is awarded annually. Established in 1937.

★6774★ Fine Arts Work Center Fellowships
Fine Arts Work Center in Provincetown
24 Pearl St.
Provincetown, MA 02657
Ph: (508)487-9960   Fax: (508)487-8873

Purpose: To encourage and support emerging artists and writers by giving them the freedom to work without distraction in a community of peers. Qualifications: Applicant may be any age, but the Center aims to help emerging talents who have completed their formal training and are already working on their own. Fellowships are based on the quality of the applicant's work. No other restrictions apply. Fellowships include a residency at the Center. Funds available: Small monthly stipend, plus living and studio space. Application details: Send a self-addressed stamped envelope with request for application form and guidelines; specify interest in writing or visual arts. Information on submission of creative works is included in the application forms. Deadline: February 1. Notification around May 1.

★6775★ Golden Quill Award
North American Ski Journalists Association
PO Box 5334
Takoma Park, MD 20912
Ph: (301)864-8428   Fax: (301)864-8428

To recognize an individual who has made great contributions to winter sports. A plaque or trophy is awarded annually if merited. Established in 1965.

★6776★ Nate Haseltine Memorial Fellowship in Science Writing
Council for the Advancement of Science Writing
PO Box 404
Greenlawn, NY 11740
Ph: (516)757-5664   Fax: (516)757-0069

Purpose: To improve the quality of science writing through graduate study. Qualifications: Applicant must be a U.S. citizen and a journalist who has a minimum of two years experience at a daily newspaper, wire service, news magazine, radio or television station or network. Applicant must also hold an undergraduate degree in journalism or science and demonstrate a desire to pursue science journalism. Funds available: $2,000. Application details: Write to the Executive Director for application form and guidelines. Application must contain a resume, undergraduate transcripts, three letters of recommendation, three writing samples, and a state of career goals. Deadline: June 15.

★6777★ Hearst Foundation Journalism Writing Competition

William Randolph Hearst Foundation
90 New Montgomery St., Ste. 1212
San Francisco, CA 94105
Ph: (415)543-4057

Purpose: To provide support, encouragement, and assistance to undergraduate journalism students. Qualifications: Only undergraduate students enrolled in member colleges and universities of the Association of Schools of Journalism and Mass Communication are eligible. Entrants must be full-time undergraduate journalism majors at the time the entries are produced and submitted. Students who have had full-time professional newspaper or broadcast news experience, or its equivalent, for three years or more, are not eligible. Selection criteria: Knowledge of subject, understandability, clarity, color, reporting in depth, and construction. Funds available: $300 to $2,000. Application details: A contest entry must be a single article originating with and produced by the undergraduate student. The entry must have been printed in either a campus or professional publication. If the entry is from a professional publication, it must be verified in accompanying letters by the editor of the publication and Journalism Unit Administrator that the entry is student work with minimal editing and no editor rewriting. Articles must not have multiple bylines unless accompanied by a letter from the Journalism Unit Administrator verifying that, while others may have participated in the research, the article was written by the entrant. Side bars, subordinate in length and content to the article submitted, written by the same student on the same topic the same day, will be considered as part of a single entry. Four tear sheets of each published article showing date of publication and full name of publication must be submitted with each entry. An official entry blank must be completed and signed by the entrant, Journalism Unit Administrator, and Chief Journalism Administrator.

★6778★ Ernest Hemingway Foundation Award

PEN American Center
568 Broadway
New York, NY 10012
Ph: (212)334-1660   Fax: (212)334-2181

To encourage the publication of first fiction by young and developing American writers. Authors of novels or collections of short stories in English, excluding children's books, are eligible. The deadline is December 31. A monetary prize of $7,500 is awarded annually. Established in 1975 by Mary Hemingway in memory of her husband.

★6779★ Inter-American Press Association Scholarships

Inter-American Press Association
 Scholarship Fund, Inc.
2911 N.W. 39th St.
Miami, FL 33142
Ph: (305)634-2465   Fax: (305)635-2272

Purpose: To support the exchange of journalists between the United States, Canada, Latin America, and the Caribbean. Qualifications: Applicant must be a citizen of the United States, Canada, Latin America, or the Caribbean. Applicant must be a journalist or journalism school graduate, and be between the ages of 21 and 35 years. Students must have finished their degree before beginning the scholarship term. U.S. and Canadian scholars spend the award tenure studying and reporting in Latin America and the Caribbean. Journalists from the Caribbean and Latin America use the awards to study at Canadian and U.S. journalism schools. Candidates must be fluent in the language of the host country. U.S. and Canadian candidates must have their language ability attested to by a recognized authority. Latin American candidates must take the Test of English as a Foreign Language. Funds available: $10,000. Application details: Write for an application form and guidelines. Submit form with a study and work plan. Deadline: 1 August. Notification by November.

★6780★ Knight-Bagehot Fellowships in Economics and Business Journalism

Columbia University
Graduate School of Journalism
Knight-Bagehot Fellowship Program
New York, NY 10027
Ph: (212)854-2711   Fax: (212)854-7837

Purpose: To improve the coverage of business, economics, and finance. Qualifications: Applicant may be of any nationality, but must be either a freelance journalist or a full-time editorial employee of a newspaper, magazine, wire service, or broadcast news program. Applicant must have at least four years of experience. The fellowship is open only to journalists whose work regularly appears in the United States or Canada. There are no age requirements, but those selected are typically between the ages of 27 and 40 years. There are no educational prerequisites. Fellowships are tenable only at the Graduate School of Journalism, Columbia University. Funds available: $16,000/year, plus tuition. Application details: Write or phone the fellowship director for application form and guidelines. Submit with four references, an essay on economics, a personal essay, and samples of work. Deadline: March 1. Fellowships are announced by May 1.

★6781★ Lamont Poetry Selection

Academy of American Poets
584 Broadway, Ste. 1208
New York, NY 10012
Ph: (212)274-0343

To recognize and encourage poetic genius by supporting the publication of an American poet's second book. The honoree must have published one book of poems in a standard edition. The Academy contracts to purchase 2,000 copies of the winning book from the publisher, and the poet receives a monetary award of $1,000. Awarded annually. Estab-

lished in 1954 by a bequest by Mrs. Thomas W. Lamont.

★6782★ Loft-McKnight Award

The Loft, a place for writing and literature
66 Malcolm Ave. SE
Minneapolis, MN 55406
Ph: (612)379-8999   Fax: (612)627-2281

To recognize Minnesota writers and to give Minnesota writers of demonstrated ability an opportunity to work for a concentrated period of time on their writing. Writers who are residents of Minnesota (as determined by income tax return or driver's license) may apply. Eight monetary awards of $7,500 each are awarded annually. Winners are designated Loft-McKnight Fellows. Established in 1981.

★6783★ Edward R. Murrow Fellowship for American Foreign Correspondents

Council on Foreign Relations
58 E. 68th St.
New York, NY 10021
Ph: (212)734-0400   Fax: (212)861-2504

Purpose: To help journalists to increase their competence to report and interpret events abroad, and to allow them a period for sustained analysis and writing free from the daily pressures of journalism. Qualifications: Applicant must be a U.S. citizen and a correspondent, editor, or producer of an American newspaper, magazine, radio, or television station. Applicant either must be serving abroad now or, having recently served abroad, must plan to return to a foreign post. There are no set work requirements for the term of the fellowship, but preference will be given to those candidates who have a thorough plan of study and writing relating to foreign affairs. Fellows are expected to be in residence in New York City and to participate fully in the activities of the Council. The stipend granted the fellow will not normally exceed the amount of salary relinquished during the fellowship term. Funds available: $60,000 maximum. Application details: Forward a brief outline of proposal with curriculum vitae to Kempton Dunn at the Council. After internal review, an invitation to apply and application form may be forwarded. With application, include research proposal, photograph, and five samples of journalistic work from abroad. A letter from employer granting leave of absence in the event of selection should be sent directly from the employer to the fellowship director. Deadline: Nov. 15 for preliminary letters; Feb. 1 for completed applications.

★6784★ NAA Foundation—National Scholastic Press Association Pacemaker Awards

Newspaper Association of America
 Foundation
The Newspaper Center
11600 Sunrise Valley Dr.
Reston, VA 22091
Ph: (703)648-1047   Fax: (703)620-1265

To encourage vital high school journalism by honoring outstanding high school newspapers. Plaques are awarded annually to six high school newspapers. Administered by the National Scholastic Press Association, 620 Rarig Center, 330 South 21st Avenue, Minneapolis, MN 55455-0478.

★6785★ National Book Awards
National Book Foundation
National Book Awards
260 5th Ave., 9th Fl.
New York, NY 10001
Ph: (212)685-0261   Fax: (212)213-6570

To honor American books of the highest literary merit. For four decades, these award-winning books have earned a permanent place in world literature, a distinction made possible by the participation of discerning and dedicated judges and the faithful support of the American publishing industry. Awards are given in three categories: fiction, poetry, and nonfiction. There are separate judging panels for each category. The chairmen of the judging panels announce a short list of five finalists in each category on or about October 15. Six weeks later, the winners are announced at a ceremony and reception in New York. Full-length books, collections of short stories and essays, and collected and selected poems written by American authors and published by American publishers between December 1 and November 30 are eligible to be submitted by a publisher for a $100 entry fee per title. Authors may not submit their own work. Reprints and translations are not accepted. A monetary award of $10,000 is awarded to the winner in each category and $1,000 to each runner-up. Awarded annually. Established in 1950 as the National Book Awards. Re-named the American Book Awards (TABA) from 1980 to 1986. Currently administered by the nonprofit National Book Foundation, co-sponsor of National Book Weekin January with the Center for the Book at the Library of Congress.

★6786★ NFPW Member Graduate Scholarships
National Federation of Press Women, Inc.
PO Box 99
Blue Springs, MO 64013
Ph: (816)229-1666

Qualifications: Applicants must be college students who are seeking a graduate degree in journalism. Applicants may be men or women who possess two years active professional membership in the National Federation of Press Women. Selection criteria: Recipient is selected on the basis of career potential, scholarship, and financial need. Funds available: One $1,000 scholarship is awarded annually. Application details: Applications must include a transcript of college credit, work samples, and letters of recommendation in sealed envelopes from at least two persons acquainted with the applicant's work and/or schooling achievements. A photograph, a description of the study plan, a timetable for completion, a budget for use of the scholarship, and how the scholarship will be augmented to achieve study goals are also required. Deadline: Applications must be received by May 1.

★6787★ NWC Poetry Award
National Writers Club
1450 S. Havana, Ste. 620
Aurora, CO 80012
Ph: (303)751-7844   Fax: (303)751-8593

To encourage the writing of poetry and to recognize outstanding poets. Poems written in English that do not exceed 40 lines may be submitted. A monetary prize and certificate

are awarded annually in September. Established in 1942.

★6788★ NWC Short Story Award
National Writers Club
1450 S. Havana, Ste. 620
Aurora, CO 80012
Ph: (303)751-7844   Fax: (303)751-8593

To encourage writers of short stories, and to recognize outstanding creative fiction writing. Unpublished fiction or nonfiction written in English that does not exceed 5,000 words may be submitted. Monetary prizes and certificates are awarded annually in June. Established in 1942.

★6789★ Outdoor Writers Association of America Scholarship Awards
Outdoor Writers Association of America (OWAA)
2017 Cato Ave., Ste. 101
State College, PA 16801-2768
Ph: (814)234-1011   Fax: (814)234-9692

Purpose: To reward outstanding students who are working toward careers in outdoor writing, broadcasting, photography, or art. Qualifications: Applicants should be in their last two years of college or master's degree students in any accredited school of journalism or mass communication listed by the Association for Education in Journalism and Mass Communication, or those schools accepted on application to the Outdoor Writers Association of America. There shall be no more than one applicant from each school per school year. Each school will be responsible for selecting its candidate. Selection criteria: Judges look for applicants with talent, promise, and first-hand outdoor knowledge. Applications are rated on clarity, organization, and originality. Grade point average is considered. Funds available: The amount of the scholarship varies, but is usually at least $3,000. Application details: An applicant must submit an OWAA application form, school recommendation, grade transcript, examples of outdoor communication work (including published samples), a one- to two-page statement by the nominee detailing career goals, and optional letters of recommendation from outdoor communicators or employers familiar with the applicant's work. The application package must be submitted to the Executive Director, Outdoor Writers Association of America. Deadline: March 1.

★6790★ Robert Troup Paine Prize
Harvard University Press
79 Garden St.
Cambridge, MA 02138
Ph: (617)495-2600

To recognize the author of an unpublished manuscript of book length that is judged to be the best work on a specified subject accepted by the Harvard University Press during the preceding four years. In 1993, the subject is human physiology. A monetary prize of $3,000 over and above the usual publication royalties is awarded every four years. Not open to the public. Established in 1962.

★6791★ Patterson Fellowships
Alicia Patterson Foundation (APF)
1001 Pennsylvania Ave., N.W., Ste. 1250
Washington, DC 20004
Ph: (202)393-5995

Purpose: To enable working journalists to pursue independent projects. Qualifications: Applicant must be a U.S. citizen. Candidate must currently be a newspaper, magazine, freelance, or wire-service journalist with at least five years of professional experience. Applicant must be able to take a leave of absence from work for the fellowship period. Fellows are expected to write four magazine-length articles based on investigations in topics of their own choosing. Grants are not offered for academic study. Funds available: $30,000. Application details: Write or phone the executive director for application form and guidelines. Submit form, two-page autobiographical essay, three-page research proposal, three samples of journalistic work, and four letters of reference. Deadline: October 1.

★6792★ PEN/Faulkner Award for Fiction
PEN/Faulkner Foundation
FolgerShakespeare Library
201 E. Capitol St. SE
Washington, DC 20003
Ph: (202)544-7077

To honor the best work of fiction published by an American writer in a calendar year. American citizens are eligible. The deadline for submitting four copies of the published book is December 31. A monetary prize of $15,000 is awarded to the winner, and $5,000 to each of four other nominees. Awarded annually. Established in 1980.

★6793★ Art Peters Minority Internships
Philadelphia Inquirer
PO Box 8263
Philadelphia, PA 19101
Ph: (215)854-2419   Fax: (215)854-4794
Fr: 800-444-1133

Purpose: To provide minority college students with the opportunity to participate in a 10-week course of instruction and practical work in copyediting at the Philadelphia Inquirer. After a week of intensive instruction, students are assigned to copy desks. Qualifications: Minority students from all college classes are eligible for these internships. Funds available: Interns' wages are based on Newspaper Guild scale for student interns. Application details: Applicants should send a letter and resume. Deadline: December 31.

★6794★ The Poetry Center Book Award
The Poetry Center
San Francisco State Univ.
1600 Holloway Ave.
San Francisco, CA 94132
Ph: (415)338-2227

For recognition of the year's outstanding poetry publication. The book must have been copyrighted in the year of the current award, be the work of a living author, and be published in the year of the award. Books may be submitted for consideration by December 31. A monetary prize of $500 and an invitation to read in The Poetry Center's reading series of the following year are awarded annually. Established in 1980.

★6795★ Pulitzer Prizes

Columbia University
Office of Public Information
116th & Broadway
New York, NY 10027
Ph: (212)854-3841

To recognize outstanding accomplishments in journalism, letters, music, and drama. Awards are given in the following categories: Journalism - Public Service, for meritorious public service by a newspaper through the use of its journalistic resources, which may include editorials, cartoons, photographs and reporting; Spot News Reporting, for local reporting of sport news; Investigative Reporting, for investigative reporting within a newspaper's area of circulation by an individual or team, presented as a single article or series; Explanatory Journalism, for explanatory journalism that illuminates significant and complex issues; Beat Reporting; National Reporting; International Reporting (two prizes); Feature Writing, for feature writing giving prime consideration to high quality and originality; Commentary; Criticism; Editorial Writing, the test of excellence being clearness of style, moral purpose, sound reasoning, and power to influence plublic opinion in what the writer conceives to be the right direction, due account being taken of the whole volume of the editorial writer's work during the year; Editorial Cartooning, for a cartoon that embodies an idea made clearly apparent, shows good drawing and striking pictorial effect, and intended to be helpful to some commendable cause, due account being taken of the whole volume of the artist's work during the year; Spot News Photography, for spot news photography in black and white or color, which may consist of a photograph or photographs, a sequence, or album; and Feature Photography, for feature photography in black or white or color, which may consist of a photograph or photographs, a sequence or an album. Letters and Drama - Fiction, by an American author, preferably dealing with American life; History, for a book about the United States; Biography by an American author; Poetry, by an American poet; General Non-Fiction, by an American author that is not eligible for consideration in any other category; Drama, by an American author, preferably dealing with American life. Music - for a composition by an American in any of the larger forms including chamber, orchestral, choral, opera, song, dance, or other forms of musical theater, which has had its first performance in the United States during the year. The nominees are screened by juries appointed in each category and recommended to the Pulitzer Prize Board. The awardee for Public Service in Journalism receives a gold medal. All other awardees receive a monetary award of $3,000. Awarded annually. Established in 1917 and endowed by Joseph Pulitzer, the noted Hungarian-born American journalist who founded the Columbia University School of Journalism.

★6796★ Pulliam Journalism Fellowships

Central Newspapers, Inc.
c/o The Indianapolis News
PO Box 145
Indianapolis, IN 46206-0145
Ph: (317)633-9121

Purpose: To provide specialized training in journalism to recent college graduates. Qualifications: Applicant must be a U.S. citizen or permanent resident who will earn a bachelor's degree during the eleven months directly prior to the start of the fellowship in June. Candidate may be a newspaper journalism major or a liberal arts major with part-time or full-time newspaper experience. Applicant must have a proven potential in reporting, writing and editing and have high scholastic attainment, especially in the liberal arts. Fellows are granted work-study internships at the Indianapolis Star, the Indianapolis News, the Arizona Republic or the Phoenix Gazette. In addition to working as reporters, editorial writers or copy editors, fellows meet with guest speakers and participate in group and individual sessions conducted by a writing coach. Selection criteria: Based on scholastic achievement, writing ability, newspaper internships and references. Funds available: $4,200. Application details: Write to Mr. Pulliam for application form and guidelines. Submit form with samples of published writing, transcripts, a recent photograph, three letters of recommendation and a 400- to 600-word editorial written expressly for the application. Deadline: March 1.

★6797★ Quill and Scroll National Writing/Photo Contest

Quill and Scroll
School of Journalism and Mass
  Communication
University of Iowa
Iowa City, IA 52242-1528
Ph: (319)335-5795

Qualifications: Competition is open to all high school students; Quill and Scroll membership is not required. Each school may submit two entries in each of 10 categories: Editorial, Editorial Cartoon, In-Depth Reporting (Individual and Team), News Story, Feature Story, Sports Story, Advertisement, and Photography (News/Feature and Sports). Application details: Contest rules are sent in late December to all schools on the Society's mailing list. Guidelines and entry forms also appear in the Dec/Jan issue of Quill & Scroll magazine. A $2.00 fee must accompany each entry. Deadline: February 5.

★6798★ Garth Reeves Jr. Memorial Scholarships

Society of Professional Journalists
Greater Miami Chapter
c/o Miami Herald
1 Herald Plaza
Miami, FL 33132-1693

Purpose: To assist undergraduate and graduate-level minority students majoring in journalism. Qualifications: Applicants must be South Florida residents. Selection criteria: Applicants are choosen based on need, scholastic achievement, and extracurricular journalism activity. Funds available: Minimum grant $500; amount of each scholarship is determined by need. Application details: Appli-

cations available in January. Deadline: March 1.

★6799★ Scripps Howard Foundation Scholarships

Scripps Howard Foundation
PO Box 5380
Cincinnati, OH 45201
Ph: (513)977-3036   Fax: (513)977-3810

Purpose: To encourage deserving students to prepare for careers in Print and Broadcast Journalism. Qualifications: Applicant must be a U.S. citizen or resident alien, or have a U.S. visa. Applicant must be a full-time student in good scholastic standing with a proven interest in the field of journalism. Candidate must demonstrate financial need. Non-U.S. citizens must use the scholarship at a U.S. institution. U.S. citizens may use the scholarship worldwide. Funds available: $500-3,000. Application details: Send a letter stating college major and career goal to request an application before 20 December. Submit application with letters of recommendation and samples of journalistic work. Graduate Record Examination scores are also required. Deadline: 25 February. Written notification sent on 15 May.

★6800★ Mildred and Harold Strauss Livings

American Academy of Arts and Letters
633 W. 155 St.
New York, NY 10032
Ph: (212)368-5900   Fax: (212)491-4615

To provide writers of English prose literature with an annual stipend to cover their living expenses so that they can devote their time exclusively to writing. Recipients must resign positions of paid employment before receiving the Livings. Applications are not accepted. Nominations are made by members of the Academy. Two writers are selected every five years to receive a stipend of $50,000 for a five-year period. Established in 1981 by Mildred and Harold Strauss.

★6801★ Thurber House Residencies

Thurber House
77 Jefferson Ave.
Columbus, OH 43215
Ph: (614)464-1032   Fax: (614)228-7445

Purpose: To support and encourage novelists, poets, playwrights, and journalists. Qualifications: Residencies are offered to candidates in three categories: journalism, playwriting, and writing. Candidate may be of any nationality. Journalist-in-Residence award recipients must have experience in reporting, feature writing, reviewing, or other areas of journalism, as well as significant publications. Awardee will teach once a week at the Ohio State University School of Journalism and act as a staff writing coach for reporters at the Columbus Dispatch for approximately eight hours per week. The remaining time should be spent on the awardee's work-in-progress. Applicant for the Playwright-in-Residence award must have had at least one play published and/or produced by a significant company. Awardee will teach a class in playwriting once a week at the Ohio State University Department of Theatre. The majority of the awardee's time will be reserved for current writing projects. One play by the candidate may be considered for mounting, public reading, or production by the Department of Theatre. Candidate for the

Writer-in-Residence award must have published at least one book with a major publisher, in any area of fiction, nonfiction, or poetry. Applicant should have some teaching experience. Awardee will teach one class in the Creative Writing Program at Ohio State University, and will offer one public reading and a short workshop for writers in the community. Significant time outside of teaching is reserved for the writer's own work-in-progress. All residencies are tenable at the Thurber House. Awardees are responsible for the cost of travel to and from Thurber House. Funds available: $5,000 stipend, plus housing. Application details: Send a letter of interest and curriculum vitae to the Literary Director by December 15. Deadline: January 1. Awards are announced by March 15.

★6802★ Whiting Writers' Award
Mrs. Giles Whiting Foundation
30 Rockefeller Plaza, Rm. 3500
New York, NY 10112
Ph: (212)698-2138
To identify and support deserving writers of exceptional promise. The program places special emphasis on exceptionally promising emerging talent. To qualify, writers need not be "young," given that new talent may emerge at any age. Occasionally, the program also considers proven authors for whom a Whiting Award would provide further recognition and encouragement at a critical stage of their careers. Recipients of the award are selected by a selection committee from nominations made by writers, educators, and editors from communities across the country whose experience and vocations bring them in contact with individuals of unusual talent. The nominators and selectors are appointed by the foundation and serve anonymously. Direct applications and informal nominations are not accepted by the foundation. Nominated candidates may be writers of fiction, poetry, or nonfiction; they may be essayists, literary scholars, playwrights, novelists, poets, or critics. Selections are based on the quality of writing and the likelihood of outstanding future work. Monetary awards of $30,000 each are awarded annually to ten candidates. Established in 1985.

BASIC REFERENCE GUIDES AND HANDBOOKS

★6803★ Basic Technical Writing
Society for Technical Communication (STC)
901 N. Stuart St., Ste. 304
Arlington, VA 22203
Ph: (703)522-4114
Frances J. Sullivan, editor. 1991.

★6804★ The Business Writer's Handbook
St. Martin's Press, Inc.
175 5th Ave. Rm. 1715
New York, NY 10010
Ph: (212)674-5151   Fr: 800-221-7945
Charles T. Brusaw, Gerald J. Alred, and Walter E. Oliu. Fourth revised edition, 1993. Contains entries on style, usage, and documentation. Arranged alphabetically.

★6805★ Chicago Guide to Preparing Electronic Manuscripts: For Authors and Publishers
University of Chicago Press
5801 S. Ellis Ave., 4th Fl.
Chicago, IL 60637
Ph: (312)702-7700   Fr: 800-621-2736
1987. A guide to using electronic media to produce books.

★6806★ The Chicago Manual of Style: The Essential Guide for Authors, Editors, & Publishers
University of Chicago Press
5801 S. Ellis Ave., 4th Fl.
Chicago, IL 60637
Ph: (312)702-7700
Fourteenth edition, 1993. Contains guidelines on bookmaking, editorial style, and production and printing. Includes a bibliography and an index.

★6807★ Copyediting: A Practical Guide
Crisp Publications, Inc.
1200 Hamilton CT
Menlo Park, CA 94025
Ph: (415)323-6100
Karen Judd. Second edition. 1991. Covers word transposition, handling artwork, rights and permissions, and diction and style.

★6808★ Creative Editing for Print Media
Wadsworth Publishing Co.
10 Davis Dr.
Belmont, CA 94002
Ph: (415)595-2350   Fax: (415)637-9955
Dorothy A. Bowles, editor. 1993.

★6809★ Dramatist Sourcebook 1993-1994
Theatre Communications Group
355 Lexington Ave.
New York, NY 10017
Ph: (212)697-5230
Gillian Richards and Linda MacColl, editors. 1993. Written for playwrights. Filled with more than 700 entries describing script submission policies of more than 225 theatres, playwriting contests, publishing outlets, developmental workshops, conferences, and service organizations that aid playwrights.

★6810★ Editing in the Electronic Era
Iowa State University Press
2121 S. State Ave.
Ames, IA 50010
Ph: (515)292-0140   Fax: (515)292-3348
Martin L. Gibson, editor. Third edition, 1991.

★6811★ Editing for Print
Writer's Digest Books
1507 Dana Ave.
Cincinnati, OH 45207
Ph: (513)531-2222
Barbara Horn. 1985. Includes a bibliography and an index.

★6812★ The Fine Art of Copyediting
Columbia University Press
562 W. 113th St.
New York, NY 10025
Ph: (212)316-7100
Elsie M. Stainton, editor. 1992.

★6813★ Get Published: Editors From the Nation's Top Magazines Tell You What They Want
Henry Holt and Co.
115 W. 18th St.
New York, NY 10011
Ph: (212)886-9200
Diane Gage and Marcia H. Coppess. 1993. Includes an index.

★6814★ Great Print Advertising: Creative Approaches, Strategies, and Tactics
John Wiley and Sons, Inc.
605 3rd Ave.
New York, NY 10158-0012
Ph: (212)850-6000   Fax: (212)850-6088
Fr: 800-526-5368
Tony Antin. 1993. Gives detailed instructions for developing print ads. Provides examples of ads that work and those that don't, plus explains the differences between them.

★6815★ The Gregg Reference Manual
McGraw-Hill, Inc.
1221 Avenue of the Americas
New York, NY 10020
Ph: (212)512-2000   Fr: 800-722-4726
William A. Sabin. Seventh edition, 1992. Includes an index.

★6816★ Guide for Authors: Manuscript, Proof and Illustration
Charles C. Thomas, Publisher
2600 S. 1st St.
Springfield, IL 62794-9265
Ph: (217)789-8980   Fax: (217)789-9130
Fr: 800-258-8980
Payne E. Thomas. 1993.

★6817★ A Guide to Documentary Editing
Johns Hopkins University Press
701 W. 40th St., Ste. 275
Baltimore, MD 21211
Ph: (410)516-6900
Mary-Jo Kline. 1987. Includes bibliographies and an index.

★6818★ A Guide to Information Sources for the Preparation, Editing, and Production of Documents
Gower Publishing Co.
Old Post Rd.
Brookfield, VT 05036
Ph: (802)276-3162
Dorothy Anderson. 1989.

★6819★ Handbook for Academic Authors
Cambridge University Press
110 Midland Ave.
Port Chester, NY 10573
Ph: (212)924-3900   Fr: 800-227-0247
Beth Luey. 1990. Describes how to prepare a manuscript for publication and work with a publisher on contract negotiation and editing.

★6820★ Honk If You're a Writer: Unabashed Advice, Undiluted Experience, & Unadulterated Inspiration for Writers & Writers-to-Be
Simon & Schuster Trade
Simon & Schuster Bldg.
1230 Avenue of the Americas
New York, NY 10020
Ph: (212)698-7000
Arthur Plotnik, editor. 1992.

★6821★ How to Copyedit Scientific Books and Journals
William & Wilkins
351 W. Camden St.
Baltimore, MD 21201
Fr: 800-638-0672
Maeve O'Connor. 1989. This is a how-to-do-it book which describes technical editing, coding manuscripts, and proofreading.

★6822★ Magazine Writers Nonfiction Guidelines: Over 200 Periodical Editors' Instructions Reproduced
McFarland and Co., Inc.
Hwy. 88
PO Box 611
Jefferson, NC 28640
Ph: (919)246-4460
Judy Mandell, editor. 1987. Includes an index.

★6823★ MLA Handbook for Writers of Research Papers
Modern Language Association of America (MLA)
10 Astor Pl.
New York, NY 10003
Ph: (212)475-9500
Joseph Gibaldi and Walter S. Achtert. Third edition, 1988. This guide describes the MLA format for writers. Explains rules and includes samples.

★6824★ Technical Editing: The Practical Guide for Editors & Writers
Addison-Wesley Publishing Co.
1 Jacov Way
Reading, MA 01867
Ph: (617)944-3700   Fr: 800-358-4566
Judith Tarutz, editor. 1993.

★6825★ The Theory & Practice of Text-Editing: Essays in Honour of James T. Boulton
Cambridge University Press
40 W. 20th St.
New York, NY 10011
Ph: (212)924-3900   Fax: (212)691-3239
Ian Small, editor. 1992.

★6826★ UPI Stylebook: The Authoritative Handbook for Writers, Editors, & News Directors
NTC Publishing Group
4255 W. Touhy Ave.
Lincolnwood, IL 60646
Ph: (708)679-5500   Fax: (708)679-2494
United Press International Staff. 1993.

★6827★ Writer's A-Z
Writer's Digest Books
1507 Dana Ave.
Cincinnati, OH 45207
Ph: (513)531-2222
Kirk Polking, Joan Bloss, and Colleen Cannon, editors. 1990. Includes a bibliography.

★6828★ The Writer's Handbook
The Writer's Magazine
120 Boylston St.
Boston, MA 02116
Ph: (617)423-3157
Sylvia K. Burack, editor. Revised edition, 1993. Annual. Contains information on getting published, writing techniques, and working with agents and editors. Describes specialized writing markets and lists publishers, writers' organizations, and literary agents.

★6829★ Writing Effectively with Your PC: Computer Tools, Tips, and Tricks for Modern Writers
Random House, Inc.
201 E. 50th St.
New York, NY 10022
Ph: (212)751-2600
Larry Magid, editor. 1993.

★6830★ Writing: From Topic to Evaluation
Allyn and Bacon, Inc.
PO Box 11071
Des Moines, IA 50336
Fr: 800-278-3525
Iris M. Tiedt. 1989. Includes bibliographies and an index.

PROFESSIONAL AND TRADE PERIODICALS

★6831★ Columbia Journalism Review
Columbia Journalism Review
700 Journalism Bldg.
Columbia University
New York, NY 10027
Ph: (212)854-1881   Fax: (212)854-8580
Suzanne Braun Levine
Bimonthly. Magazine focusing on journalism.

★6832★ Computeriter
Creative Business Communications, Inc.
PO Box 476
Columbia, MD 21045
Ph: (301)596-5591   Fax: (301)997-7946
Linda J. Elengold
Monthly. Supplies announcements of new products, product evaluations, and suggestions on computer usage for writers and editors. Reviews hardware, software, online databases, and peripherals. Recurring features include editorials, news of research, and book reviews.

★6833★ Contents
Contents
PO Box 8879
Savannah, GA 31412
Joseph Alfieris
Magazine covering art, design, literature and music.

★6834★ Dramatists Guild Newsletter
Authors Guild/Dramatists Guild, Inc.
234 W. 44th St.
New York, NY 10036-3988
Ph: (212)398-9366
Scott Segal, Contact
Provides members with information on the artistic and business aspects of professional theatre writing. Also lists symposiums, marketing guides, and script opportunities. Recurring features include a calendar of events, reports of meetings, news of educational opportunities, and notices of publications available. Columns titled Business Affairs, Taxes, and Theatre Updates.

★6835★ Harmony International Screenwriters Group
Harmony International, Inc.
901 S. Ashland Ave., No. 218A
Chicago, IL 60607
Ph: (312)733-0662
Provides tips on screenwriting and discusses strategies to promote the sales of literary works of screenwriters and novelists. Also focuses on social functions of the Group. Recurring features include news of research, a calendar of events, reports of meetings, and job listings.

★6836★ Ideas Unlimited for Editors
Newsletter Services, Inc.
9700 Philadelphia Ct.
Lanham, MD 20706-4405
Ph: (301)731-5202   Fax: (301)731-5203
Jerry Boin, Contact
Monthly. Contains pre-formatted editorial fillers and camera-ready art for editors of company publications.

★6837★ Poets & Writers Magazine
Poets & Writers, Inc.
72 Spring St.
New York, NY 10012
Ph: (212)226-3586   Fax: (212)226-3963
Daryln Brewer
Bimonthly. Magazine containing essays, interviews with writers, news and comment on publishing, political issues, and practical topics of interest to writers. Includes coverage of grants and awards, deadlines for applications, and calls for manuscript submissions.

★6838★ Publishers Weekly
Publisher's Weekly
249 W. 17th St.
New York, NY 10011
Ph: (212)463-6758   Fax: (212)463-6631
Nora Rawlinson
Weekly.

★6839★ Quill & Scroll
Quill and Scroll Society
University of Iowa
School of Journalsm and Mass Communication
Iowa City, IA 52242
Ph: (319)335-5795   Fax: (319)335-5386
Richard P. Johns
Quarterly. High school honorary journalism magazine.

★6840★ Technical Communication
Society for Technical Communication
901 N. Stuart St., Ste. 304
Arlington, VA 22203-1822
Ph: (703)522-4114   Fax: (703)522-2075
Frank R. Smith

Quarterly. Journal for those engaged in technical communication.

★6841★ The Writer
Plays, Inc.
120 Boylston St.
Boston, MA 02116-4615
Ph: (617)423-3157
Sylvia K. Burack

Monthly. Magazine for free-lance writers. Publishing practical information and advice on how to write publishable material and where to sell it.

★6842★ Writers Club Newsletter
Jacklyn Barlow
67 Aberdeen Circle
Leesburg, FL 34788
Ph: (904)742-1224
Jacklyn Barlow

Quarterly. Serves as a forum for writers wishing to share experiences, resources, writing problems, and successes.

★6843★ Writer's Digest
F&W Publications, Inc.
1507 Dana Ave.
Cincinnati, OH 45207
Ph: (513)531-2222   Fax: (513)531-1843
Bruce Woods

Monthly. Professional magazine for writers.

PROFESSIONAL MEETINGS AND CONVENTIONS

★6844★ International Black Writers and Artists Convention
International Black Writers and Artists
PO Box 43576
Los Angeles, CA 90043
Ph: (415)532-6179

Annual. **Dates and Locations:** 1995.

OTHER SOURCES OF INFORMATION

★6845★ "Copy Writer" in Career Selector 2001
Barron's Educational Series, Inc.
250 Wireless Blvd.
Hauppauge, NY 11788
Ph: (516)434-3311   Fax: (516)434-3723
Fr: 800-645-3476

James C. Gonyea. 1993.

★6846★ "Editor/Writer" in 100 Best Jobs for the 1990s & Beyond
Dearborn Financial Publishing, Inc.
520 N. Dearborn St.
Chicago, IL 60610-4354
Ph: (312)836-4400   Fax: (312)836-1021
Fr: 800-621-9621

Carol Kleiman. 1992. Describes 100 jobs ranging from accountants to veterinarians. Each job profile includes such information as education, experience, and certification needed, salaries, and job search suggestions.

★6847★ Speaking of Journalism
HarperCollins
10 E. 53rd St.
New York, NY 10022
Fr: 800-2-HARPER

1994. Twelve writers and editors discuss their work.

★6848★ "Writing" in Accounting to Zoology: Graduate Fields Defined (pp. 153-154)
Petersons Guides, Inc.
PO Box 2123
Princeton, NJ 08543-2123
Ph: (609)243-9111   Fax: (609)243-9150
Fr: 800-338-3282

Amy J. Goldstein, editor. Revised and updated, 1987. Defines 298 graduate and professional fields. Discusses types fo graduate programs and degrees, graduate research, applied work, employment prospects, and trends.

Designers

Designers organize and design articles, products, and materials in such a way that they not only serve the purpose for which they were intended but are visually pleasing as well. Designers usually specialize in one particular area of design, for example, automobiles, clothing, furniture, home appliances, industrial equipment, movie and theater sets, packaging, or floral arrangements. Designers in some specialties are increasingly using computer-aided design (CAD) to create and better visualize a final product. **Industrial designers** develop and design countless manufactured products like cars, home appliances, computers, stethoscopes, filing cabinets, fishing rods, pens, and children's toys. **Interior designers** plan and furnish the interiors of private homes, public buildings, and commercial establishments. **Set designers** design movie, television, and theater sets. **Fashion designers** design coats, suits, dresses, hats, handbags, shoes, gloves, jewelry, underwear, and other apparel. **Textile designers** design fabrics for garments, upholstery, rugs, and other products, using their knowledge of textile materials and fashion trends. **Furniture designers** design furniture for manufacturers. **Floral designers** cut and arrange fresh, dried, or artificial flowers and foliage into a design to express the sentiments of the sender.

Salaries

Earnings of self-employed designers vary greatly, depending on their talents and business abilities, but generally are higher than those of salaried designers. Median annual salaries for full-time designers are as follows:

Lowest 10 percent	Less than $260/week
Median	$585/week
Top 10 percent	More than $1,120/week
Beginning floral designers	$5.40/hour
Experienced floral designers	$7.60/hour

Employment Outlook

Growth rate until the year 2005: Average.

Designers

Career Guides

★6849★ "Apparel Design" in Opportunities in Fashion Careers (pp. 1-18)
National Textbook Co. (NTC)
VGM Career Books
4255 W. Touhy Ave.
Lincolnwood, IL 60646-1975
Ph: (708)679-5500   Fax: (708)679-2494
Fr: 800-323-4900
Roslyn Dolber. 1993. Describes career opportunities in apparel design and fashion merchandising. Gives job hunting advice. Lists schools which offer fashion-related majors.

★6850★ "Art Directors" and "Interior Designers" in Career Information Center (Vol.3)
Simon and Schuster
200 Old Tappan Rd.
Old Tappan, NJ 07675
Fax: 800-445-6991   Fr: 800-223-2348
Richard Lidz and Linda Perrin, editorial directors. Fifth edition, 1993. A multi-volume set that profiles more than 600 occupations. Each occupational profile describes job duties, educational requirements, getting a job, advancement possibilities, employment outlook, working conditions, earnings and benefits, and sources of additional information.

★6851★ "Art, Entertainment, and Media Careers" in Best Jobs for the 1990s and Into the 21st Century
Impact Publications
9104-N Manassas Dr.
Manassas Park, VA 22111
Ph: (703)361-7300   Fax: (703)335-9486
Ronald L. Krannich and Caryl Rae Krannich. 1993. Includes information on designers, photographers and camera operators, and radio and TV news announcers and newscasters.

★6852★ "Book Design, Exhibition Design, and Industrial Design" in School of Visual Arts Guide to Careers (pp. 156-157, 168-169, 258-270)
McGraw-Hill, Inc.
1221 Avenue of the Americas
New York, NY 10020
Ph: (212)512-2000   Fr: 800-722-4726
Dee Ito. 1987. Gives a broad overview of each field included, with educational requirements and employment opportunities.

★6853★ Career Opportunities in Advertising and Public Relations
Facts on File
460 Park Ave. S.
New York, NY 10016-7382
Ph: (212)683-2244   Fax: 800-678-3633
Fr: 800-322-8755
Shelly Field. 1993. Guidebook offering complete career information for those entering advertising or public relations. Describes 85 jobs and includes salary information, employment prospects, and education and skills needed for the jobs.

★6854★ Career Opportunities in Art
Facts on File
460 Park Ave. S.
New York, NY 10016-7382
Ph: (212)683-2244   Fax: 800-678-3633
Fr: 800-322-8755
Susan H. Haubenstock and David Joselit. 1993. Guidebook containing valuable information on obtaining practical employment in 83 art-related fields. Includes contact information for degree programs as well as professional associations. Includes information on jobs in advertising, graphic desing, printmaking, photography, architecture, interior design, textile design, and others.

★6855★ Career Opportunities in Television, Cable and Video
Facts on File
460 Park Ave. S.
New York, NY 10016-7382
Ph: (212)683-2244   Fax: 800-678-3633
Fr: 800-322-8755
Maxine K. Reed and Robert M. Reed. Third edition, 1993. Includes information on employment and advancement prospects, education, experience and skills requiresn salary range, and tips for entry into the field.

★6856★ Careers in Clothing and Textiles
Glencoe Publishing Co.
866 3rd Ave.
New York, NY 10022-6299
Ph: (212)702-3276
Videotape that explores career possibilities in the manufacturing, designing, merchandising, and selling of clothes.

★6857★ "Costume Designers" in Encyclopedia of Careers and Vocational Guidance (Vol.2, pp. 402-404)
J.G. Ferguson Publishing Co.
200 W. Madison St., Ste. 300
Chicago, IL 60606
Ph: (312)580-5480   Fax: (312)580-4948
William E. Hopke, editor-in-chief. Ninth edition, 1993. Four-volume set that profiles 900 occupations and describes job trends in 74 industries. Includes career description, educational requirements, history of the job, methods of entry, advancement, employment outlook, earnings, conditions of work, social and psychological factors, and sources of further information.

★6858★ "Design" in Encyclopedia of Careers and Vocational Guidance (Vol.1, pp. 135-141)
J.G. Ferguson Publishing Co.
200 W. Madison St., Ste. 300
Chicago, IL 60606
Ph: (312)580-5480   Fax: (312)580-4948
William E. Hopke, editor-in-chief. Ninth edition, 1993. Four-volume set that profiles 900 occupations and describes job trends in 74 industries. Includes career description, educational requirements, history of the job, methods of entry, advancement, employment outlook, earnings, conditions of work, social and psychological factors, and sources of further information.

★6859★ "Design" in Liberal Arts Jobs
Petersons Guides, Inc.
PO Box 2123
Princeton, NJ 08543-2123
Ph: (609)243-9111   Fax: (609)243-9150
Fr: 800-338-3282
Burton Jay Nadler. Second edition, 1989. Strives to help the liberal arts graduate identify skills for entry-level positions. Gives goal setting and job search advice.

★6860★ "Designer" in *Career Opportunities in Art*

Facts on File
460 Park Ave. S.
New York, NY 10016-7382
Ph: (212)683-2244   Fax: 800-678-3633
Fr: 800-322-8755

Susan H. Haubenstock. 1988. Profiles seventy-five art-related jobs. Each profile includes a career description, career ladder, employment and advancement prospects, education, experience and skills required, salary range, and tips for entry into the field.

★6861★ *Designer, Clothing*

Careers, Inc.
PO Box 135
Largo, FL 34649-0135
Ph: (813)584-7333

1995. Two-page occupational summary card describing duties, working conditions, personal qualifications, training, earnings and hours, employment outlook, places of employment, related careers, and where to write for more information.

★6862★ "Designer" and "Interior Designer" in *College Board Guide to Jobs and Career Planning* **(pp. 69-71)**

The College Board
415 Columbus Ave.
New York, NY 10023-6992
Ph: (212)713-8165   Fax: (212)713-8143
Fr: 800-323-7155

Joyce S. Mitchell. Second edition, 1994. Covers a variety of careers. Each career profile contains information on salaries, related careers, education needed, and sources of additional information. Chapters include "Industrial Designer" (pp. 76, 190, 197), "Interior Designer" (pp. 70-71), and "Set Designer" (pp. 20-21).

★6863★ "Designer" in *Opportunities in Book Publishing Careers* **(pp. 135-137)**

National Textbook Co. (NTC)
VGM Career Books
4255 W. Touhy Ave.
Lincolnwood, IL 60646-1975
Ph: (708)679-5500   Fax: (708)679-2494
Fr: 800-323-4900

Robert A. Carter. 1987. Describes the history of book publishing and jobs in different types of publishing: trade, religious, textbook, technical, scientific, medical, university presses, paperback, and mail order. Includes information on educational preparation, personal requirements, advancement possibilities, unions, and related fields.

★6864★ "Designers" in *Advertising: A VGM Career Planner* **(pp. 50-52)**

National Textbook Co. (NTC)
VGM Career Books
4255 W. Touhy Ave.
Lincolnwood, IL 60646-1975
Ph: (708)679-5500   Fax: (708)679-2494
Fr: 800-323-4900

Pattis, S. William. 1989. Describes the development of advertising. Explains the role of the media in advertising, personal characteristics needed to succeed in this field, educational requirements, and related jobs. Gives job hunting tips.

★6865★ "Designers" in *American Almanac of Jobs and Salaries* **(pp. 201)**

Avon Books
1350 Avenue of the Americas
New York, NY 10019
Ph: (212)261-6800   Fr: 800-238-0658

John Wright, editor. Revised and updated, 1994-95. A comprehensive guide to the wages of hundreds of occupations in a wide variety of industries and organizations.

★6866★ "Designers" in *Career Discovery Encyclopedia* **(Vol.2, pp. 94-95)**

J.G. Ferguson Publishing Co.
200 W. Madison St., Ste. 300
Chicago, IL 60606
Ph: (312)580-5480   Fax: (312)580-4948

Russell E. Primm, editor-in chief. 1993. This six volume set contains two-page articles for 504 occupations. Each article describes job duties, earnings, and educational and training requirements. The whole set is arranged alphabetically by job title. Designed for junior high and older students.

★6867★ "Designers" in *Occupational Outlook Handbook*

U.S. Government Printing Office
Superintendent of Documents
Washington, DC 20402
Ph: (202)512-1800   Fax: (202)512-2250

Biennial; latest edition, 1994-95. Encyclopedia of careers describing about 250 occupations and comprising about 85 percent of all jobs in the economy. Occupations that require lengthy education or training are given the most attention. Each occupation's profile describes what the worker does on the job, working conditions, education and training requirements, advancement possibilities, job outlook, earnings, and sources of additional information.

★6868★ "Exhibit Designer" in *Career Opportunities in Art*

Facts on File
460 Park Ave. S.
New York, NY 10016-7382
Ph: (212)683-2244   Fax: 800-678-3633
Fr: 800-322-8755

Susan H. Haubenstock. 1988. This book profiles seventy-five art-related jobs. Each profile includes a career description, career ladder, employment and advancement prospects, education, experience and skills required, salary range, and tips for entry into the field.

★6869★ *Fashion Coordinator*

Vocational Biographies, Inc.
PO Box 31
Sauk Centre, MN 56378-0031
Ph: (612)352-6516   Fax: (612)352-5546
Fr: 800-255-0752

1992. Four-page pamphlet containing a personal narrative about a worker's job, work likes and dislikes, career path from high school to the present, education and training, the rewards and frustrations, and the effects of the job on the rest of the worker's life. The data file portion of this pamphlet gives a concise occupational summary, including work description, working conditions, places of employment, personal characteristics, education and training, job outlook, and salary range.

★6870★ "Fashion Design and Merchandising" in *Opportunities in Home Economics Careers* **(pp. 103-115)**

National Textbook Co. (NTC)
VGM Career Books
4255 W. Touhy Ave.
Lincolnwood, IL 60646-1975
Ph: (708)679-5500   Fax: (708)679-2494
Fr: 800-323-4900

Rhea Shields. 1988. Gives the history and trends of home economics. Separate chapters cover home economics-related careers such as art, interior design, and hospitality. Lists colleges and universities offering programs in home economics.

★6871★ "Fashion Designer" in *Jobs Rated Almanac*

World Almanac
1 International Blvd., Ste. 444
Mahwah, NJ 07495
Ph: (201)529-6900   Fax: (201)529-6901

Les Krantz. Second edition, 1992. Ranks 250 jobs by environment, salary, outlooks, physical demands, stress, security, travel opportunities, and extra perks. Includes jobs the editor feels are the most common, most interesting, and the most rapidly growing.

★6872★ "Fashion Designers" in *Encyclopedia of Careers and Vocational Guidance* **(Vol.2, pp. 633-635)**

J.G. Ferguson Publishing Co.
200 W. Madison St., Ste. 300
Chicago, IL 60606
Ph: (312)580-5480   Fax: (312)580-4948

William E. Hopke, editor in chief. Ninth edition, 1993. Four-volume set that profiles 900 occupations and describes job trends in 74 industries. Chapters on designers include "Designers", "Industrial Designers", and "Interior Designers and Decorators". Includes career description, educational requirements, history of the job, methods of entry, advancement, employment outlook, earnings, conditions of work, social and psychological factors, and sources of further information.

★6873★ "Fashion Designers" in *Jobs! What They Are—Where They Are—What They Pay!* **(p. 318)**

Simon & Schuster, Inc.
Simon & Schuster Bldg.
1230 Avenue of the Americas
New York, NY 10020
Ph: (212)698-7000   Fr: 800-223-2348

Robert O. Snelling and Anne M. Snelling. Third revised edition, 1992. Includes chapters titled "Floral Designers", "Industrial Designers", and "Interior Designers". Describes duties and responsibilities, earnings, employment opportunities, training, and qualifications.

★6874★ "Fashion, Textile, and Interior Design" in *Career Choices for the 90's for Students of Art* **(pp. 66-91)**

Walker and Co.
435 Hudson St.
New York, NY 10014
Ph: (212)727-8300   Fax: (212)727-0984
Fr: 800-289-2553

1990. Offers alternatives for students of art. Gives information about the outlook and competition for entry-level candidates. Provides job-hunting tips.

★6875★ "Fashion, Textile Interior, and Design" in *Encyclopedia of Career Choices for the 1990s: A Guide to Entry Level Jobs*
Berkley Pub.
PO Box 506
East Rutherford, NJ 07073
Fax: (201)933-2316   Fr: 800-788-6262
1992. Describes entry-level careers in a variety of industries. Presents qualifications required, working conditions, salary, internships, and professional associations.

★6876★ *Floral Designer*
Careers, Inc.
PO Box 135
Largo, FL 34649-0135
Ph: (813)584-7333
1995. Four-page brief offering the definition, history, duties, working conditions, personal qualifications, educational requirements, earnings, hours, employment outlook, advancement, and careers related to this position.

★6877★ "Floral Designer", "Fashion Designer", "Industrial Designer", and "Interior Designer" in *VGM's Careers Encyclopedia*
National Textbook Co. (NTC)
VGM Career Books
4255 W. Touhy Ave.
Lincolnwood, IL 60646-1975
Ph: (708)679-5500   Fax: (708)679-2494
Fr: 800-323-4900
Third edition, 1991. Profiles 200 occupations. Describes job duties, places of employment, working conditions, qualifications, education and training, advancement potential, and salary for each occupation.

★6878★ *Floral Designers (Florists)*
Chronicle Guidance Publications, Inc.
66 Aurora St.
PO Box 1190
Moravia, NY 13118-1190
Ph: (315)497-0330   Fax: (315)497-3359
Fr: 800-622-7284
1993. Career brief describing the nature of the job, working conditions, hours and earnings, education and training, licensure, certification, unions, personal qualifications, social and psychological factors, location, employment outlook, entry methods, advancement, and related occupations.

★6879★ *Getting Started as a Freelance Illustrator or Designer*
North Light Books
1507 Dana Ave.
Cincinnati, OH 45207
Ph: (513)531-2222   Fax: (513)531-4744
Michael Fleishman, editor. 1990.

★6880★ *Industrial Designer*
Careers, Inc.
PO Box 135
Largo, FL 34649-0135
Ph: (813)584-7333
1991. Four-page brief offering the definition, history, duties, working conditions, personal qualifications, educational requirements, earnings, hours, employment outlook, ad-

vancement, and careers related to this position.

★6881★ *Industrial Designers*
Chronicle Guidance Publications, Inc.
66 Aurora St.
PO Box 1190
Moravia, NY 13118-1190
Ph: (315)497-0330   Fax: (315)497-3359
Fr: 800-622-7284
1993. Career brief describing the nature of the job, working conditions, hours and earnings, education and training, licensure, certification, unions, personal qualifications, social and psychological factors, location, employment outlook, entry methods, advancement, and related occupations.

★6882★ "Industrial Designers" in *Career Information Center* (Vol.9)
Simon and Schuster
200 Old Tappan Rd.
Old Tappan, NJ 07675
Fax: 800-445-6991   Fr: 800-223-2348
Richard Lidz and Linda Perrin, editorial directors. Fifth edition, 1993. This 13-volume set profiles over 600 occupations. Each occupational profile describes job duties, educational requirements, advancement possibilities, employment outlook, working conditions, earnings and benefits, and where to write for more information.

★6883★ "Interior Design" in *Career Connection for Technical Education* (pp. 94-95)
JIST Works, Inc.
720 N. Park Ave.
Indianapolis, IN 46202-3431
Ph: (317)264-3720   Fax: (317)264-3709
Fred A. Rowe. 1994, second edition. Describes in detail technical occupations. Includes information on recommended high school courses, course requirements, related careers, and a self-assessment guide.

★6884★ *Interior Design Career Guide*
American Society of Interior Designers (ASID)
1430 Broadway
New York, NY 10018
Ph: (202)546-3480
Annual. Free (first copy). Booklet of basic information on the profession, including overview, educational requirements, employment prospects, and compensation. Lists three-, four-, and five-year design programs, with ASID student chapters and Foundation for Interior Design Education Research accreditation.

★6885★ "Interior Design" in *Opportunities in Home Economics Careers* (pp. 9-17)
National Textbook Co. (NTC)
VGM Career Books
4255 W. Touhy Ave.
Lincolnwood, IL 60646-1975
Ph: (708)679-5500   Fax: (708)679-2494
Fr: 800-323-4900
Rhea Shields. 1988. Gives the history and trends of home economics. Separate chapters cover home economics-related careers such as art, interior design, and hospitality. Lists colleges and universities offering programs in home economics.

★6886★ *Interior Designer*
Chronicle Guidance Publications, Inc.
66 Aurora St.
PO Box 1190
Moravia, NY 13118-1190
Ph: (315)497-0330   Fax: (315)497-3359
Fr: 800-622-7284
1993. Career brief describing the nature of the job, working conditions, hours and earnings, education and training, licensure, certification, unions, personal qualifications, social and psychological factors, location, employment outlook, entry methods, advancement, and related occupations.

★6887★ *Interior Designer*
Careers, Inc.
PO Box 135
Largo, FL 34649-0135
Ph: (813)584-7333
1994. Four-page brief offering the definition, history, duties, working conditions, personal qualifications, educational requirements, earnings, hours, employment outlook, advancement, and careers related to this position.

★6888★ "Marketing and Advertising" in *Where the Jobs Are: The Hottest Careers for the 90s* (pp. 195-210)
Career Press
180 5th Ave.
Hawthorne, NJ 07507
Ph: (201)427-0229   Fax: (201)427-2037
Fr: 800-CAREER-1
Joyce Hadley. 1995. Offers a job-hunting strategy for the 1990s as well as descriptions of growing careers of the decade. Each profile includes general information, forecasts, growth, education and training, licensing requirements, and salary information.

★6889★ *Opportunities in Interior Design Careers*
National Textbook Co. (NTC)
VGM Career Books
4255 W. Touhy Ave.
Lincolnwood, IL 60646-1975
Ph: (708)679-5500   Fax: (708)679-2494
Fr: 800-323-4900
Victoria Kloss Ball. 1988. Describes careers in interior design. Includes job descriptions, training and education requirements, future of the profession, professional organizations, and specialties within the field.

★6890★ "Set/Scenic Designers" in *TV Careers Behind the Screen* (pp. 43, 65-67, 78-79)
John Wiley and Sons, Inc.
605 3rd Ave.
New York, NY 10158-0012
Ph: (212)850-6000   Fax: (212)850-6088
Fr: 800-526-5368
Jane Blanksteen and Ovi Odeni. 1987. Describes the organization of the television broadcasting industry. Explains the role each job plays in television production, career paths, education, and training. Includes job-hunting tips and information on trends in the industry.

★6891★ "Textile Design" in
Opportunities in Fashion Careers **(pp. 41- 42, 44)**
National Textbook Co. (NTC)
VGM Career Books
4255 W. Touhy Ave.
Lincolnwood, IL 60646-1975
Ph: (708)679-5500   Fax: (708)679-2494
Fr: 800-323-4900

Roslyn Dolber. 1993. Describes career opportunities in apparel design and fashion merchandising. Gives job hunting advice. Lists schools which offer fashion-related majors.

★6892★ "Zabelle Bedrosin—Interior Designer" in *Straight Talk on Careers: Eighty Pros Take You Into Their Professions* **(pp. 15-17)**
Garrett Park Press
PO Box 1907
Garrett Park, MD 20896
Ph: (301)946-2553

Mary Barbera-Hogan. 1987. Contains candid interviews from people who give an inside view of their work in 80 different careers. These professionals describe a day's work and the stresses and rewards accompanying their work.

Professional Associations

★6893★ American Design Drafting Association (ADDA)
PO Box 799
Rockville, MD 20848-0799
Ph: (301)460-6875   Fax: (301)460-8591
Members: Designers, drafters, drafting managers, chief drafters, supervisors, administrators, instructors, and students of design and drafting. **Purpose:** Encourages a continued program of education for self-improvement and professionalism in design and drafting and computer-aided design/drafting. Informs members of effective techniques and materials used in drawings and other graphic presentations. Evaluates curriculum of educational institutions through certification program; sponsors drafter certification program. **Publications:** *Compensation Survey*, biennial. • *Design and Drafting News*, monthly. • *Guide to Writing Design/Drafting Job Descriptions*.

★6894★ American Institute of Graphic Arts (AIGA)
164 5th Ave.
New York, NY 10010
Ph: (212)807-1990   Fax: (212)807-1799
Fr: 800-548-1634
Members: Graphic designers, art directors, art directors, illustrators, packaging designers, and craftsmen involved in printing and allied graphic fields. **Purpose:** Sponsors exhibits and projects in the public interest. Sponsors traveling exhibitions. Operates gallery. Maintains library of design books and periodicals; offers slide archives. **Publications:** *AIGA Journal of Graphic Design*, quarterly. • *AIGA Membership Directory*, biennial. • *AIGA News*, bimonthly. • *Graphic Design USA*, annual.

★6895★ American Society of Interior Designers (ASID)
608 Massachusetts Ave. NE
Washington, DC 20002
Ph: (202)546-3480   Fax: (202)546-3480
Members: Practicing professional interior designers and affiliate members in allied design fields. **Purpose:** ASID Educational Foundation sponsors scholarship competitions, finances educational research, and awards special grants. Operates speakers' bureau; maintains placement service. **Publications:** *ASID Report*, bimonthly. • *Interior Design Career Guide*, annual.

★6896★ Florists' Transworld Delivery Association (FTDA)
29200 Northwestern Hwy.
Southfield, MI 48034
Ph: (810)355-9300
Members: Retail florist shops in North America selling flowers, gifts, candy, and fruit by wire. **Purpose:** Conducts specialized advertising, education, and research programs; compiles statistics. Conducts ZIP code marketing service. **Publications:** *Florist Magazine*, monthly. • *FTD Family*, monthly.

★6897★ Foundation for Interior Design Education Research (FIDER)
60 Monroe Center NW, Ste. 300
Grand Rapids, MI 49503-2920
Ph: (616)458-0400   Fax: (616)458-0460
Members: Formed by Interior Design Educators Council and American Society of Interior Designers. **Purpose:** Administers voluntary plan for the special accreditation of interior design education programs offered at institutions of higher learning throughout the U.S. and its possessions and Canada; emphasizes the use of accreditation procedures to assure that the purposes and accomplishments of programs of interior design education meet the needs of society, students, and the interior design profession. Recognized by the United States Department of Education as a national accrediting agency for programs in interior design in schools throughout the country. **Publications:** *Directory of Interior Design Programs Accredited by FIDER*, semiannual. • *Foundation for Interior Design Education Research—Newsletter*, semi-annual. • *Guide to FIDER Accredited Interior Design Programs in North America*, annual.

★6898★ Industrial Designers Society of America (IDSA)
1142-E Walker Rd.
Great Falls, VA 22066
Ph: (703)759-0100   Fax: (703)759-7679
Members: Professional society of industrial designers. **Purpose:** Maintains the standards of the profession in its relations with business, industry, government, and international designers; promotes the industrial design profession. Operates the WORLDESIGN Foundation, the research branch of IDSA. Maintains referral service and speakers' bureau. Sponsors children's services; conducts research, educational, and charitable programs. Compiles statistics. **Publications:** *Compensation Studies*, biennial. • *Consultant Operating Studies*. • *Design Perspectives*, monthly. • *Innovation*.

★6899★ National Association of Schools of Art and Design (NASAD)
11250 Roger Bacon Dr., Ste. 21
Reston, VA 22090
Ph: (703)437-0700   Fax: (703)437-6312
Members: Serves as the accrediting agency for educational programs in the visual arts and design. **Purpose:** Aims are to: establish a national forum to stimulate the understanding and acceptance of the educational disciplines inherent in the creative arts in higher education in the U.S.; develop reasonable standards in areas of budget, faculty qualifications, faculty-student ratios, class time requirements, and library and physical facilities; evaluate, through the process of accreditation, schools of art and design and programs of studio art instruction in terms of the quality and results they achieve; assure students and parents that accredited art and design programs provide competent teachers, adequate equipment, and sound curricula; assist schools in developing their programs and encourage self-evaluation and continuing self-improvement.

★6900★ Society of American Florists (SAF)
1601 Duke St.
Alexandria, VA 22314-3406
Ph: (703)836-8700   Fax: (703)836-8705
Fr: 800-336-4743
Members: Growers, wholesalers, retailers, and allied tradesmen in the floral industry. **Purpose:** Lobbies Congress on behalf of the industry; sponsors educational programs; promotes the floral industry; prepares materials for consumers and for high school and college students; provides business resources. Sponsors Floricultural Hall of Fame, American Academy of Floriculture, American Floral Marketing Council and Professional Floral Commentators - International. Compiles statistics; sponsors competitions. **Publications:** *Dateline: Washington*. • *Floral Management*, monthly.

Standards/Certification Agencies

★6901★ American Design Drafting Association (ADDA)
PO Box 799
Rockville, MD 20848-0799
Ph: (301)460-6875   Fax: (301)460-8591
Evaluates curriculum of educational institutions through certification program; sponsors drafter certification program.

★6902★ Industrial Designers Society of America (IDSA)
1142-E Walker Rd.
Great Falls, VA 22066
Ph: (703)759-0100   Fax: (703)759-7679
Maintains the standards of the profession in its relations with business, industry, government, and international designers; promotes the industrial design profession.

★6903★ National Association of Schools of Art and Design (NASAD)
11250 Roger Bacon Dr., Ste. 21
Reston, VA 22090
Ph: (703)437-0700   Fax: (703)437-6312
Serves as the accrediting agency for educational programs in the visual arts and design. Aims are to: develop reasonable standards in areas of budget, faculty qualifications, faculty-student ratios, class time requirements, and library and physical facilities; evaluate, through the process of accreditation, schools of art and design and programs of studio art instruction in terms of the quality and results they achieve; assure students and parents that accredited art and design programs provide competent teachers, adequate equipment, and sound curricula.

EDUCATIONAL DIRECTORIES AND PROGRAMS

★6904★ Advertising Career Directory
Gale Research Inc.
835 Penobscot Bldg.
Detroit, MI 48226-4094
Ph: (313)961-2242   Fax: (313)961-6083
Fr: 800-877-GALE
Bradley J. Morgan and Joseph M. Palmisano. Fifth edition, 1992. A directory in the Career Advisor Series that provides essays written by industry professionals; job search information on resume and cover letter preparation, networking, and the interviewing process; approximately 300 companies and organizations offering job opportunities and internships, and additional job-hunting resources.

★6905★ Book Publishing Career Directory
Gale Research Inc.
835 Penobscot Bldg.
Detroit, MI 48226-4094
Ph: (313)961-2242   Fax: (313)961-6083
Fr: 800-877-GALE
Bradley J. Morgan and Joseph M. Palmisano. Fifth edition, 1992. A directory in the Career Advisor Series that provides essays written by industry professionals; job search information on resume and cover letter preparation, networking, and the interviewing process; approximately 300 companies and organizations offering job opportunities and internships, and additional job-hunting resources.

★6906★ Directory of Interior Design Programs Accredited by FIDER
Foundation for Interior Design Education Research (FIDER)
60 Monroe Center NW, Ste. 300
Grand Rapids, MI 49503-2920
Ph: (616)458-0400   Fax: (616)458-0460
Pam Jennings, Contact
Semiannual, April and August. Covers 108 interior design programs in the United States and Canada in conformance with the accreditation standards of the foundation. Entries include: Type of program, name of institution, address, name of department chair or pro-

gram head, phone, dates of last and next accreditation review, degrees offered. Arrangement: Geographical, degree level offered, then alphabetical by institution name.

★6907★ National Association of Schools of Art and Design—Directory
National Association of Schools of Art and Design
11250 Roger Bacon Dr., No. 21
Reston, VA 22090
Ph: (703)437-0700   Fax: (703)437-6312
Annual, March. Covers approximately 180 independent and university-affiliated schools of art and design accredited by the association. Entries include: Institution name, address, phone, names of executives, major programs (drawing, graphic design, etc.) and duration, summer programs, degrees. Arrangement: Alphabetical.

★6908★ Performing Arts Career Directory
Gale Research Inc.
835 Penobscot Bldg.
Detroit, MI 48226
Ph: (313)961-2242   Fr: 800-877-GALE
1994. Profiles careers in the performing arts industry.

★6909★ Radio and Television Career Directory
Gale Research Inc.
835 Penobscot Bldg.
Detroit, MI 48226-4094
Ph: (313)961-2242   Fax: (313)961-6083
Fr: 800-877-GALE
Bradley J. Morgan and Joseph M. Palmisano. Second edition, 1993. A directory in the Career Advisor Series that provides essays written by industry professionals; job search information on resume and cover letter preparation, networking, and the interviewing process; approximately 300 companies and organizations offering job opportunities and internships, and additional job-hunting resources.

AWARDS, SCHOLARSHIPS, GRANTS, AND FELLOWSHIPS

★6910★ ACTF Awards for Theatrical Design Excellence
American College Theatre Festival
John F. Kennedy Center for the Performing Arts
Education Division
Washington, DC 20566
Ph: (202)416-8800   Fax: (202)416-8802
To recognize outstanding student designers by exhibiting their work at the Kennedy Center. Any full-length production entered in the American College Theatre Festival that has one or more of the visual elements designed by a student is eligible. National winners in set design and costume design receive an honorarium of $100 and an all-expenses-paid trip to New York City for seven days to visit the studios of distinguished designers. *Theatre Crafts* magazine and *USITT Journal of Theatre and Technology* publish information

on the national set and costume design winners.

★6911★ American Theatre Wing Design Awards
American Theatre Wing
250 W. 57th St.
New York, NY 10107
Ph: (212)765-0609   Fax: (212)765-0606
To recognize outstanding theatrical designers of Broadway, off-Broadway, and off-off Broadway plays and musicals for designs originating in the United States. American stage and costume designers are eligible. Four awards of $250 are presented in the following categories: scenic design, costume design, lighting, and unusual effects. Honoraria and citations are awarded annually at the American Theatre Wing's Design Seminar at the Graduate Center of the City University of New York, 33 West 42nd Street, New York City. Established in 1965.

★6912★ CFDA Fashion Awards
Council of Fashion Designers of America
1412 Broadway, Ste. 933
New York, NY 10018
Ph: (212)302-1821
To recognize outstanding contributions made to American fashion by individuals from all areas of the arts and industry. Awards are given in such varied fields as publishing, retailing, photography, jewelry, and television. The Eugenia Sheppard Award is presented for fashion journalism. The Perry Ellis Award recognizes new talent. Awards are presented annually. Established in 1982.

★6913★ Creativity Show
Art Direction Book Company
10 E. 39th St., 6th Fl.
New York, NY 10016
Ph: (212)889-6500   Fax: (212)889-6504
To recognize outstanding visual professionals internationally and to commend the best work in advertising art, design, photography, or illustration during the preceding 12 months. The recipient must be an art director, advertising designer, photographer, or illustrator. Each year, the entire show is displayed in major cities. All material in print or on the air from May to May each year is eligible. The deadline for entry is May 4. Art directors are judged for concept and design. Artists, illustrators, photographers, and production houses are judged for art, photography, etc. All accepted entries are reproduced in the annual Creativity book, a worldwide volume. The Creativity Show is the annual showcase for the year's best work. Certificates of Distinction are awarded annually. Established in 1970.

★6914★ Industrial Design Excellence Awards (IDEA)
Industrial Designers Society of America
1142 Walker Rd., Ste. E
Great Falls, VA 22066-1836
Ph: (703)759-0100   Fax: (703)759-7679
To foster and promote industrial design excellence and recognize the role industrial design plays in stimulating economic competitiveness and meet the changing needs of consumers. Awards are given in the following categories: products, instruments, equipment, furniture and fixtures, transportation, packaging, signage, toys and games, ex-

hibits, environments, design exploration, student design projects, and machinery. A design must be primarily the work of a U.S. based design group placed on the market within two years of the February deadline for entry. Three levels of awards are given: Gold, Silver, and Bronze. Trophies are presented at the annual conference. Established in 1980. Sponsored by *Business Week.*

★6915★ National Endowment for the Arts - Design Arts Program USA Fellowships
National Endowment for the Arts
Visual Arts Program/Fellowships, Rm. 729
Nancy Hanks Center
1100 Pennsylvania Ave., NW
Washington, DC 20506-0001
Ph: (202)682-5422   Fax: (202)682-5699
Purpose: To enable designers and those in design-related professions who have made significant contributions to the design field to travel and study independently within the United States. The grants provide desingers the time and flexibility to explore new concepts, generate fresh ideas, or compile information for a book or study. Qualifications: Fellowships are awarded to professional designers and other qualified individuals working on innovative design projects. They are intended for those for whom a more extensive first-hand knowledge of the American design environment is critical to their work. Eligible fields include architecture, landscape architecture, urban design and planning, historic preservation, interior design, industrial and product design, and graphic design. Applicants must be United States citizens or permanent residents. Selection criteria: The Endowment places a strong emphasis on quality as the first criterion in evaluating applications. Funds available: Fellowships include awards of up to $20,000.

★6916★ OBIE Awards
The Village Voice
Promotion Dept.
842 Broadway
New York, NY 10003
Ph: (212)475-3300   Fax: (212)475-8947
To recognize achievement in Off and Off-Off Broadway theatre. Awards are given in the following categories: Best New American Play, Sustained Achievement, Sustained Excellence of Performance, Performance, Direction, Sustained Excellence of Lighting Design, Lighting Design, and Set and Costume Design. All Off and Off-Off Broadway theatres are eligible. Monetary prizes, certificates, and cash grants are presented annually at the OBIE awards ceremony. Established in 1955 by the Plumsock Fund and *The Village Voice.*

★6917★ Presidential Awards for Design Excellence
National Endowment for the Arts
Nancy Hanks Center
1100 Pennsylvania Ave. NW
Washington, DC 20506
Ph: (202)682-5400
To honor exemplary achievements in federal design in the fields of architecture, engineering design, graphic design, historic preservation, interior design landscape architecture, product/industrial design, and urban design and planning. Works that have been authorized, commissioned, produced, supported or

promulgated by the federal government are eligible. Current and former federal employees having professional responsibility for design work; and federal contractors, state and local governments, and non-profit organizations that have completed design work for the federal government are eligible for work completed or implemented and in use during the 10 year period preceding the award year. Award-winning projects must: improve the federal government's ability to fulfill its mission; establish exemplary design practices, standards, or guidelines that can serve as models for federal design activities; demonstrate cost-effectiveness on a life-cycle basis, and demonstrate careful design and planning without sacrificing performance or quality; exemplify aesthetic merit; and show a high level of technical and functional proficiency in all aspects of performance. Entries are judged in a two-stage jury process. In the first stage, winners receive Federal Design Achievement Awardsfrom the National Endowment for the Arts. From among the Achievement Awards recipients, a second jury of design experts select and recommend to the President recipients for the Presidential Design Awards. Certificates are awarded quadrennially. Established in 1983 by President Reagan. Administered by the Design Arts Program of the National Endowment for the Arts, as a part of the Federal Design Improvement Program. Sponsored by the United States Executive Office of the President.

BASIC REFERENCE GUIDES AND HANDBOOKS

★6918★ *The Business of Design*
Van Nostrand Reinhold Co., Inc.
115 5th Ave.
New York, NY 10003
Ph: (212)254-3232   Fr: 800-842-3636
Ian Linton. 1988. Includes an index.

★6919★ *Concise Encyclopedia of Interior Design*
Van Nostrand Reinhold Co., Inc.
115 5th Ave.
New York, NY 10003
Ph: (212)254-3232
Allen A. Dizik. Second edition, 1988. Contains short articles and definitions on furniture periods, fabrics, wall and floor coverings, and room arrangements.

★6920★ *Graphics Master 5*
Dean Lem Associates, Inc.
PO Box 959
Kihei, HI 96753-0959
Ph: (808)874-5461   Fax: (808)875-1404
Fr: 800-562-2562

★6921★ *The Image*
Watson-Guptill Publications
1515 Broadway
New York, NY 10036
Ph: (212)764-7300
Michael Freeman. 1987. Includes a bibliography and an index.

PROFESSIONAL AND TRADE PERIODICALS

★6922★ *Architecture*
Billboard Magazine
33 Commercial St.
Gloucester, MA 01930
Ph: (508)281-3110   Fax: (508)281-0136
Monthly. Official publication of the American Institute of Architects. For architects, interior designers, engineers, and architectural students.

★6923★ *Board Report's Creative Training*
American Professional Graphic Artists
PO Box 300789
Denver, CO 80203
Ph: (303)839-9058
Drew Allen Miller
Monthly. Serves graphic artists, designers, printers, and advertising agencies. Consists of three publications: The Graphic Artists Newsletter, the Designer's Compendium, and Trademark Trends. Provides creative ideas and current trade information on a wide range of subjects: new postal regulations, advertising claims and liability, tax tips for freelancers, current pay scales, how to run a graphic communication business, and modern printing and bindery equipment. Recurring features include results of surveys, news of research, statistics, reviews of fresh designs and trends, and indexed subsections for rapid research.

★6924★ *The CAUS Newsletter*
Color Association of the United States (CAUS)
409 W. 44th St.
New York, NY 10036
Ph: (212)582-6884   Fax: (212)757-4557
Margaret Walch
Explores aspects of color design, discussing applications to a wide variety of fields, including fashion, textiles, interior decorating, environmental construction, marketing, and advertising. Contains news of research, book reviews, and editorials. Recurring features include letters to the editor, news of members, and a calendar of events.

★6925★ *Contents*
Contents
PO Box 8879
Savannah, GA 31412
Joseph Alfieris
Magazine covering art, design, literature and music.

★6926★ *Design Perspectives*
Industrial Designers Society of America (IDSA)
1142 Walker Rd., Ste. E
Great Falls, VA 22066-1836
Ph: (703)759-0100   Fax: (703)759-7679
Karen Berube
Discusses issues relevant to the profession. Recurring features include reports of chapter and national activities of IDSA, a section on employment opportunities in the field, resource section, and a calendar of events.

★6927★ *Design Quarterly*
MIT Press Journals
55 Hayward St.
Cambridge, MA 02142
Ph: (617)253-2889   Fax: (617)258-6779
Martin Filler
Quarterly. Journal covering architecture, design, and contemporary graphics.

★6928★ *Designer*
University and College Designers
   Association
615 1/2 Roosevelt Rd., Ste. 2
Walkerton, IN 46574
Ph: (219)586-2988
Bill Noblitt
Quarterly. Focuses on different areas of visual communication design, including graphics, photography, signage, films, and other related fields. Reviews communication and design technologies and techniques. Recurring features include information on the Association's educational programs and other activities.

★6929★ *Interior Design*
Cahners Publishing Co.
249 W. 17th St.
New York, NY 10011
Ph: (212)463-6759   Fax: (212)463-6734
Stan Abercrombie
Monthly. Interior designing and furnishings magazine.

★6930★ *Print*
R.C. Publications, Inc.
104 5th Ave., 9th Fl.
New York, NY 10011
Ph: (212)463-0600   Fax: (212)989-9891
Martin Fox
Bimonthly. Covers all aspects of graphic design for visual communication.

★6931★ *Progressive Architecture*
P/A 600 Summer St.
Stamford, CT 06904 ,
Ph: (203)348-7531   Fax: (203)348-4023
Monthly. National magazine on architecture, interior designs, and planning.

★6932★ *Women's Wear Daily*
Fairchild Publications
7 W. 34th St.
New York, NY 10001
Ph: (212)630-4880   Fax: (212)630-4879
Ed NardozaVice President
Daily. Newspaper (tabloid) on women's and children's apparel, textiles, and technology.

PROFESSIONAL MEETINGS AND CONVENTIONS

★6933★ **American Society of Interior Designers National Conference and International Exposition of Designer Sources**
American Society of Interior Designers
608 Massachusetts Ave., NE
Washington, DC 20002-6006
Ph: (202)546-3480   Fax: (202)546-3240
Annual.

★6934★ **Design Professionals Annual Convention and Products Show/ Louisiana Architects Association/ American Society of Interior Design**
Louisiana Architects Association
521 America St.
Baton Rouge, LA 70802
Ph: (504)387-5579   Fax: (504)387-2743
Annual. **Dates and Locations:** 1995 Oct 19-21; Kenner, LA.

OTHER SOURCES OF INFORMATION

★6935★ *Color Drawing*
Van Nostrand Reinhold
115 5th Ave.
New York, NY 10013
Michael E. Doyle. 1993.

★6936★ *The Complete Illustration Guide For Architects, Designers, Artists, and Students*
Van Nostrand Reinhold
115 5th Ave.
New York, NY 10013
Larry Evans. 1993.

★6937★ "Floral Designer" in *Career Selector 2001*
Barron's Educational Series, Inc.
250 Wireless Blvd.
Hauppauge, NY 11788
Ph: (516)434-3311   Fax: (516)434-3723
Fr: 800-645-3476
James C. Gonyea. 1993.

★6938★ *Guide to the National Endowment for the Arts, 1993-94*
National Endowment of the Arts
Nancy Hanks Center, Rm. 803
1100 Pennsylvania Ave., NW
Washington, DC 20506
Ph: (202)682-5400

1993. Describes the overall purpose of each of the endowment's programs and outlines the types of support available in each funding category.

★6939★ "Interior Design" in *Accounting to Zoology: Graduate Fields Defined*
Petersons Guides, Inc.
PO Box 2123
Princeton, NJ 08543-2123
Ph: (609)243-9111   Fax: (609)243-9150
Fr: 800-338-3282

Amy J. Goldstein, editor. Revised and updated, 1987. Defines 298 graduate and professional fields. Discusses types of graduate programs and degrees, graduate research, applied work, employment prospects, and trends. Contains chapters titled "Applied Arts and Design" (pp. 3-4), "Industrial Design" (pp. 8-9), and "Textile Designs" (pp. 11-12).

★6940★ "Interior Designer" in *100 Best Jobs for the 1990s & Beyond*
Dearborn Financial Publishing, Inc.
520 N. Dearborn St.
Chicago, IL 60610-4354
Ph: (312)836-4400   Fax: (312)836-1021
Fr: 800-621-9621

Carol Kleiman. 1992. Describes 100 jobs ranging from accountants to veterinarians. Each job profile includes such information as education, experience, and certification needed, salaries, and job search suggestions.

Photographers and Camera Operators

Photographers or camera operators accurately or artistically portray people, places, and events. Skillful photographers can capture the special feeling, mood, or personality that sells products, spurs interest in news stories, or brings back happy memories such as weddings. Because the skills required of photographers are quite different from those needed by camera operators, workers generally specialize in one area or the other. Photographers may specialize in a particular type of photography, such as portrait, fashion, or advertising. **Portrait photographers** take pictures of individuals or groups of persons and often work in their own studios. **Commercial, editorial, or industrial photographers** take pictures of a wide range of subjects, including manufactured articles, buildings, livestock, and groups of people. They frequently do work for catalogs and magazines. **Scientific photographers and biological photographers** provide illustrations and documentation for scientific publications and research reports. **Photojournalists** photograph newsworthy events, places, people, and things for publications such as newspapers and magazines. Some camera operators work for television networks and individual stations, covering news events as part of a team that includes a reporter and other technicians. Camera operators also are employed in the entertainment field to film movies, television programs, and commercials. **Animation camera operators** film cartoons; **optical-effects camera operators** create illusions for television and movies.

Salaries

Some self-employed and free-lance photographers earn more than salaried workers, but many do not.

Salaried photographers and camera operators	$24,814-$37,273/year
Beginning photographers, newspaper	$426/week
Experienced photographers, newspaper	$659/week
Photographers, federal government	$33,000/year

Employment Outlook

Growth rate until the year 2005: Average.

Photographers and Camera Operators

★6941★ *Aerial Photographers*
Chronicle Guidance Publications, Inc.
66 Aurora St.
PO Box 1190
Moravia, NY 13118-1190
Ph: (315)497-0330   Fax: (315)497-3359
Fr: 800-622-7284

1994. Career brief describing the nature of the job, working conditions, hours and earnings, education and training, licensure, certification, unions, personal qualifications, social and psychological factors, location, employment outlook, entry methods, advancement, and related occupations.

★6942★ "Art, Entertainment, and Media Careers" in *Best Jobs for the 1990s and Into the 21st Century*
Impact Publications
9104-N Manassas Dr.
Manassas Park, VA 22111
Ph: (703)361-7300   Fax: (703)335-9486

Ronald L. Krannich and Caryl Rae Krannich. 1993. Includes information on designers, photographers and camera operators, and radio and TV news announcers and newscasters.

★6943★ "Biological Photographer" in *Careers in Health Care* (pp. 8-11)
National Textbook Co. (NTC)
VGM Career Books
4255 W. Touhy Ave.
Lincolnwood, IL 60646-1975
Ph: (708)679-5500   Fax: (708)679-2494
Fr: 800-323-4900

Barbara M. Swanson. Third edition, 1995. Profiles 58 health careers. Describes job duties, work settings, salaries, licensing and certification requirements, educational preparation, and future outlook.

★6944★ "Camera Operator" in *TV Careers Behind the Screen* (pp. 42, 57-59, 79-81)
John Wiley and Sons, Inc.
605 3rd Ave.
New York, NY 10158-0012
Ph: (212)850-6000   Fax: (212)850-6088
Fr: 800-526-5368

Jane Blanksteen and Ovi Odeni. 1987. Describes the organization of the television broadcasting industry. Explains the role each job plays in television production, career paths, education, and training. Includes job-hunting tips and information on trends in the industry.

★6945★ "Camera Operators" and "Photographers" in *Career Information Center* (Vol.3)
Simon and Schuster
200 Old Tappan Rd.
Old Tappan, NJ 07675
Fax: 800-445-6991   Fr: 800-223-2348

Richard Lidz and Linda Perrin, editorial directors. Fifth edition, 1993. A multi-volume set that profiles more than 600 occupations. Each occupational profile describes job duties, educational requirements, getting a job, advancement possibilities, employment outlook, working conditions, earnings and benefits, and sources of additional information.

★6946★ *Career Opportunities in Art*
Facts on File
460 Park Ave. S.
New York, NY 10016-7382
Ph: (212)683-2244   Fax: 800-678-3633
Fr: 800-322-8755

Susan H. Haubenstock and David Joselit. 1993. Guidebook containing valuable information on obtaining practical employment in 83 art-related fields. Includes contact information for degree programs as well as professional associations. Includes information on jobs in advertising, graphic desing, printmaking, photography, architecture, interior design, textile design, and others.

★6947★ *Career Opportunities in the Sports Industry*
Facts on File
460 Park Ave. S.
New York, NY 10016-7382
Ph: (212)683-2244   Fax: 800-678-3633
Fr: 800-322-8755

Shelly Field. 1993. Sourcebook combining a variety of information including sports-related academic programs, league lists, professional associations, and more of interest to those considering employment in organized amateur or professional sports.

★6948★ *Career Opportunities in Television, Cable and Video*
Facts on File
460 Park Ave. S.
New York, NY 10016-7382
Ph: (212)683-2244   Fax: 800-678-3633
Fr: 800-322-8755

Maxine K. Reed and Robert M. Reed. Third edition, 1993. Includes information on employment and advancement prospects, education, experience and skills requiresn salary range, and tips for entry into the field.

★6949★ *Careers for Shutterbugs & Other Candid Types*
National Textbook Co. (NTC)
VGM Career Books
4255 W. Toughy Ave.
Lincolnwood, IL 60646-1975
Ph: (708)679-5500   Fax: (708)679-2494
Fr: 800-323-4900

1994. Describes different career opportunities for photographers.

★6950★ "Cinematographers" in *Jobs! What They Are—Where They Are—What They Pay* (p. 263)
Simon & Schuster, Inc.
Simon & Schuster Bldg.
1230 Avenue of the Americas
New York, NY 10020
Ph: (212)698-7000   Fr: 800-223-2348

Robert O. Snelling and Anne M. Snelling. 3rd edition, 1992. Describes duties and responsibilities, earnings, employment opportunities, training, and qualifications.

★6951★ "Crafts Photography" in
Opportunities in Crafts Careers **(pp. 79-88)**
National Textbook Co. (NTC)
VGM Career Books
4255 W. Touhy Ave.
Lincolnwood, IL 60646-1975
Ph: (708)679-5500   Fax: (708)679-2494
Fr: 800-323-4900

Marianne Munday. 1994. Provides a general overview of crafts and some traditional and non-traditional jobs related to crafts. Gives information on how to start a crafts business.

★6952★ *Exploring Nontraditional Jobs*
for Women
Rosen Publishing Group
29 E. 21st St.
New York, NY 10010
Ph: (212)777-3017   Fax: (212)777-0277
Fr: 800-237-9932

Rose Neufeld. Revised edition, 1989. Describes occupations where few women are found, including the job of camera operator. Covers job duties, training routes, where to apply for jobs, tools used, salary, and advantages and disadvantages of the job.

★6953★ "Motion Picture Camera
Operators" in *Encyclopedia of Careers*
and Vocational Guidance **(Vol.3, pp. 476-479)**
J.G. Ferguson Publishing Co.
200 W. Madison St., Ste. 300
Chicago, IL 60606
Ph: (312)580-5480   Fax: (312)580-4948

William E. Hopke, editor-in-chief. Ninth edition, 1993. Four-volume set that profiles 900 occupations and describes job trends in 74 industries. Includes career description, educational requirements, history of the job, methods of entry, advancement, employment outlook, earnings, conditions of work, social and psychological factors, and sources of further information.

★6954★ *Opportunities in Photography*
Careers
National Textbook Co. (NTC)
VGM Career Books
4255 W. Touhy Ave.
Lincolnwood, IL 60646-1975
Ph: (708)679-5500   Fax: (708)679-2494
Fr: 800-323-4900

Bervin M. Johnson, Robert E. Mayer, and Fred Schmidt. 1991. Describes the history of photography and employment outlook; covers educational preparation required; gives advice on how to find a job. Describes different types of photography including portrait, commercial, industrial, scientific and technical, and photojournalism. Includes a bibliography.

★6955★ *Opportunities in Television and*
Video Careers
National Textbook Co. (NTC)
VGM Career Books
4255 W. Touhy Ave.
Lincolnwood, IL 60646-1975
Ph: (708)679-5500   Fax: (708)679-2494
Fr: 800-323-4900

Shonan F.R. Noronha. 1988.

★6956★ *Photographer*
Careers, Inc.
PO Box 135
Largo, FL 34649-0135
Ph: (813)584-7333

1993. Four-page brief offering the definition, history, duties, working conditions, personal qualifications, educational requirements, earnings, hours, employment outlook, advancement, and careers related to this position.

★6957★ "Photographer, Camera
Operator" in *College Board Guide to*
Jobs and Career Planning **(pp. 73)**
The College Board
415 Columbus Ave.
New York, NY 10023-6992
Ph: (212)713-8165   Fax: (212)713-8143
Fr: 800-323-7155

Joyce S. Mitchell. Second edition, 1994. Describes a variety of careers. Each profile includes information on salaries, related careers, education needed, and sources of additional information.

★6958★ "Photographer" in *Career*
Opportunities in Art
Facts on File
460 Park Ave. S.
New York, NY 10016-7382
Ph: (212)683-2244   Fax: 800-678-3633
Fr: 800-322-8755

Susan H. Haubenstock. 1988. This book profiles seventy-five art-related jobs. Each profile includes a career description, career ladder, employment and advancement prospects, education, experience and skills required, salary range, and tips for entry into the field.

★6959★ *Photographer, Commercial*
Careers, Inc.
PO Box 135
Largo, FL 34649-0135
Ph: (813)584-7333

1995. Two-page occupational summary card describing duties, working conditions, personal qualifications, training, earnings and hours, employment outlook, places of employment, related careers, and where to write for more information.

★6960★ "Photographer" in *Jobs Rated*
Almanac
World Almanac
1 International Blvd., Ste. 444
Mahwah, NJ 07495
Ph: (201)529-6900   Fax: (201)529-6901

Les Krantz. Second edition, 1992. Ranks 250 jobs by environment, salary, outlooks, physical demands, stress, security, travel opportunities, and extra perks. Includes jobs the editor feels are the most common, most interesting, and the most rapidly growing.

★6961★ "Photographer" in *VGM's*
Careers Encyclopedia **(pp. 344-346)**
National Textbook Co. (NTC)
VGM Career Books
4255 W. Touhy Ave.
Lincolnwood, IL 60646-1975
Ph: (708)679-5500   Fax: (708)679-2494
Fr: 800-323-4900

Third edition, 1991. Describes job duties, places of employment, working conditions, qualifications, education, and training, ad-

vancement potential, and salary for each occupation.

★6962★ *Photographers*
Chronicle Guidance Publications, Inc.
66 Aurora St.
PO Box 1190
Moravia, NY 13118-1190
Ph: (315)497-0330   Fax: (315)497-3359
Fr: 800-622-7284

1993. Career brief describing the nature of the job, working conditions, hours and earnings, education and training, licensure, certification, unions, personal qualifications, social and psychological factors, location, employment outlook, entry methods, advancement, and related occupations.

★6963★ "Photographers" in *101*
Careers: A Guide to the Fastest-
Growing Opportunities **(pp. 294-296)**
John Wiley & Sons, Inc.
605 3rd Ave.
New York, NY 10158-0012
Ph: (212)850-6645   Fax: (212)850-6088

Michael Harkavy. 1990. Describes the nature of the job, working conditions, employment growth, qualifications, personal skills, projected salaries, and where to write for more information.

★6964★ "Photographers" in *American*
Almanac of Jobs and Salaries **(pp. 209)**
Avon Books
1350 Avenue of the Americas
New York, NY 10019
Ph: (212)261-6800   Fr: 800-238-0658

John Wright, editor. Revised and updated, 1994-95. A comprehensive guide to the wages of hundreds of occupations in a wide variety of industries and organizations.

★6965★ "Photographers and Camera
Operators" in *Encyclopedia of Careers*
and Vocational Guidance **(Vol.4, pp. 71-74)**
J.G. Ferguson Publishing Co.
200 W. Madison St., Ste. 300
Chicago, IL 60606
Ph: (312)580-5480   Fax: (312)580-4948

William E. Hopke, editor-in-chief. Ninth edition, 1993. Four-volume set that profiles 900 occupations and describes job trends in 74 industries. Includes career description, educational requirements, history of the job, methods of entry, advancement, employment outlook, earnings, conditions of work, social and psychological factors, and sources of further information.

★6966★ "Photographers and Camera
Operators" in *Occupational Outlook*
Handbook
U.S. Government Printing Office
Superintendent of Documents
Washington, DC 20402
Ph: (202)512-1800   Fax: (202)512-2250

Biennial; latest edition, 1994-95. Encyclopedia of careers describing about 250 occupations and comprising about 85 percent of all jobs in the economy. Occupations that require lengthy education or training are given the most attention. Each occupation's profile describes what the worker does on the job, working conditions, education and training requirements, advancement possibilities, job

outlook, earnings, and sources of additional information.

★6967★ "Photographers" in *Career Discovery Encyclopedia* (Vol.5, pp. 36-37)
J.G. Ferguson Publishing Co.
200 W. Madison St., Ste. 300
Chicago, IL 60606
Ph: (312)580-5480   Fax: (312)580-4948
Russell E. Primm, editor-in chief. 1993. This six volume set contains two-page articles for 504 occupations. Each article describes job duties, earnings, and educational and training requirements. The whole set is arranged alphabetically by job title. Designed for junior high and older students.

★6968★ "Photographers" in *Jobs! What They Are—Where They Are—What They Pay* (pp. 270)
Fireside
Simon & Schuster Bldg.
1230 Avenue of the Americas
New York, NY 10020
Ph: (212)698-7000   Fr: 800-223-2348
Robert O. Snelling and Anne M. Snelling. Revised and updated, 1992. Describes duties and responsibilities, earnings, employment opportunities, training, and qualifications.

★6969★ "Photography" in *Career Choices for the 90's for Students of Art* (pp. 181-202)
Walker and Co.
435 Hudson St.
New York, NY 10014
Ph: (212)727-8300   Fax: (212)727-0984
Fr: 800-289-2553
1990. Offers alternatives for students of art. Gives information about the job outlook and competition for entry-level candidates. Provides job-hunting tips.

★6970★ "Photography" in *Career Connection for Technical Education* (pp. 122-123)
JIST Works, Inc.
720 N. Park Ave.
Indianapolis, IN 46202-3431
Ph: (317)264-3720   Fax: (317)264-3709
Fred A. Rowe. 1994, second edition. Describes in detail technical occupations. Includes information on recommended high school courses, course requirements, related careers, and a self-assessment guide.

★6971★ "Photography" in *Careers in Communications* (pp. 23-42)
National Textbook Co. (NTC)
VGM Career Books
4255 W. Touhy Ave.
Lincolnwood, IL 60646-1975
Ph: (708)679-5500   Fax: (708)679-2494
Fr: 800-323-4900
Shonan F. Noronha. 1994. This book examines the fields of journalism, photography, radio, television, film, public relations, and advertising. Gives concrete details on job locations and how to secure a job. Suggests many resources for job hunting.

★6972★ "Photography" in *Desk Guide to Training and Work Advertisement* (pp. 109-110)
Charles C. Thomas, Publisher
2600 S. 1st St.
Springfield, IL 62794-9265
Ph: (217)789-8980   Fax: (217)789-9130
Fr: 800-258-8980
Gail Baugher Keunstler. 1988. Describes alternative methods of gaining entry into an occupation through different types of educational programs, internships, and apprenticeships.

★6973★ "Photography" in *Encyclopedia of Career Choices for the 1990s: A Guide to Entry Level Jobs* (pp. 658-679)
Berkley Pub.
PO Box 506
East Rutherford, NJ 07073
Fax: (201)933-2316   Fr: 800-788-6262
1992. Describes entry-level careers in a variety of industries. Presents qualifications required, working conditions, salary, internships, and professional associations.

★6974★ *Photojournals (News Photographer)*
Careers, Inc.
PO Box 135
Largo, FL 34649-0135
Ph: (813)584-7333
1992. Two-page occupational summary card describing duties, working conditions, personal qualifications, training, earnings and hours, employment outlook, places of employment, related careers, and where to write for more information.

★6975★ *Portrait Photographer*
Vocational Biographies, Inc.
PO Box 31
Sauk Centre, MN 56378-0031
Ph: (612)352-6516   Fax: (612)352-5546
Fr: 800-255-0752
1989. Four-page pamphlet containing a personal narrative about a worker's job, work likes and dislikes, career path from high school to the present, education and training, the rewards and frustrations, and the effects of the job on the rest of the worker's life. The data file portion of this pamphlet gives a concise occupational summary, including work description, working conditions, places of employment, personal characteristics, education and training, job outlook, and salary range.

★6976★ "Sports Photographer" in *Careers in Health and Fitness*
Rosen Publishing Group
29 E. 21st St.
New York, NY 10010
Ph: (212)777-3017   Fax: (212)777-0277
Fr: 800-237-9932
Jackie Heron. 1990. Occupational profiles contain information on job duties, skills, advantages, basic equipment used, employment possibilities, certification, and salary.

★6977★ "Staff Photographer" in *How to Land a Job in Journalism* (pp. 140-141)
Betterway Publications
PO Box 219
Crozet, VA 22932
Ph: (804)823-5661
Phil Swann and Ed Achorn. 1988. Offers advice on college preparation, financial aid, internships, and job hunting for those interested in a career in journalism. Contains tips from journalists.

PROFESSIONAL ASSOCIATIONS

★6978★ **American Society of Media Photographers (ASMP)**
14 Washington Rd., Ste. 502
Princeton Junction, NJ 08550-1033
Ph: (609)799-8300   Fax: (609)799-2233
Members: Professional society of freelance photographers. **Purpose:** Works to evolve trade practices for photographers in communications fields. Provides business information to photographers and their potential clients; promotes ethics and rights of members. Holds educational programs and seminars. Compiles statistics. **Publications:** *ASMP Bulletin*, monthly. • *The ASMP Business Bible*. • *ASMP Members Only*, monthly. • *Assignment Photography Monograph*. • *Copyright Guide for Photographers*. • *Forms*. • *Magazine Photography*. • *Photographers' Guide to Negotiating*. • *Stock Photography Handbook*, quadrennial. • *10,000 Eyes*. • *Valuation of Lost or Damaged Transparencies*.

★6979★ **Professional Photographers of America**
57 Forsyth St. NW, Ste. 1600
Atlanta, GA 30303
Ph: (404)522-8600   Fr: 800-742-7468
Members: Professional society of portrait, wedding, commercial, and industrial, and specialized photographers. Sponsors Winona International School of Professional Photography, Mt. Prospect, IL. Maintains speakers' bureau. **Publications:** *Directory of Professional Photography*, annual. • *Photo Electronic Imaging*, monthly. • *PP of A Today*, monthly. • *Professional Photographer*, monthly. • *Who's Who in Professional Photography*, annual.

★6980★ **The Zebras**
163 Amsterdam Ave., No. 201
New York, NY 10023
Ph: (212)362-6637   Fax: (212)873-7065
Members: Photographers. **Purpose:** Promotes the practice of silver-based writing with light, known as black and white photography. Maintains speakers' bureau; conducts educational programs.

STANDARDS/CERTIFICATION AGENCIES

★6981★ Evidence Photographers International Council (EPIC)
600 Main St.
Honesdale, PA 18431
Ph: (717)253-5450   Fax: (717)253-5011
Fr: 800-356-3742

Offers certification upon satisfactory completion of an oral or written examination by a three-member panel, receipt of a minimum of 30 prints for review, and a $150 application fee.

★6982★ Ophthalmic Photographers' Society (OPS)
Davis Dueher Eye Associates
1025 Regent St.
462 Grider St.
Madison, WI 53715

Provides testing, and subsequent certification as Certified Retinal Angiographer and Certified Ophthalmic Photographer Retinal Angiographer, in performance of ophthalmic photography.

TEST GUIDES

★6983★ Career Examination Series: Medical Photographer
National Learning Corp.
212 Michael Dr.
Syosset, NY 11791
Ph: (516)921-8888   Fax: (516)921-8743
Fr: 800-645-6337

Jack Rudman. 1993. Test guide including questions and answers for students or professionals in the field who seek advancement through examination.

★6984★ Career Examination Series: Photographer
National Learning Corp.
212 Michael Dr.
Syosset, NY 11791
Ph: (516)921-8888   Fax: (516)921-8743
Fr: 800-645-6337

Jack Rudman. A series of study guides with multiple-choice examination questions and solutions for trainees and professional photographers.

★6985★ Commercial Photography
National Learning Corp.
212 Michael Dr.
Syosset, NY 11791
Ph: (516)921-8888   Fax: (516)921-8743
Fr: 800-645-6337

Jack Rudman. Occupational Competency Examination series. A test for professional photographers seeking to provide evidence of proficiency in their field to become vocational teachers. Multiple choice with solutions.

EDUCATIONAL DIRECTORIES AND PROGRAMS

★6986★ Green Book: Directory of Natural History and General Stock Photography
A G Editions, Inc.
142 Bank St., Ste. GA
New York, NY 10014
Ph: (212)929-0959   Fax: (212)924-4796
Ann Guilfoyle, Contact

Biennial, January of odd years. Covers over 400 photographers and photo agencies that provide stock photography; most specialize in natural history subjects; international coverage. Entries include: Name, address, phone, file size, general stock coverage, specialties, geographic areas, most recent coverage, photographic plans, selected credits, related credentials, stock agents, comments, noneditorial services. Arrangement: Alphabetical.

★6987★ Guide to Photography Workshops
ShawGuides, Inc.
10 W. 66th St. 30H
New York, NY 10023
Ph: (212)799-6464   Fax: (212)724-9287
D. KaplanPresident

Biennial, even years. Covers more than 300 photography workshops worldwide for amateurs and professionals, including photo tours, studio intensives, and specialized instruction; 37 residencies and retreats; 20 photography organizations. Entries include: For workshops and organizations—Name, address, phone, fax, admission requirements and dues, member services. For residences and retreats—Name, address, phone, description of facilities, admission and application requirements, costs. Arrangement: Alphabetical.

★6988★ Magazine Career Directory
Gale Research Inc.
835 Penobscot Bldg.
Detroit, MI 48226-4094
Ph: (313)961-2242   Fax: (313)961-6083
Fr: 800-877-GALE

Bradley J. Morgan and Joseph M. Palmisano. Fifth edition, 1993. A directory in the Career Advisor Series that provides essays written by industry professionals; job search information on resume and cover letter preparation, networking, and the interviewing process; approximately 300 companies and organizations offering job opportunities and internships, and additional job-hunting resources.

★6989★ Newspapers Career Directory
Gale Research Inc.
835 Penobscot Bldg.
Detroit, MI 48226-4094
Ph: (313)961-2242   Fax: (313)961-6083
Fr: 800-877-GALE

Bradley J. Morgan and Joseph M. Palmisano. 1993. A directory in the Career Advisor Series that provides essays written by industry professionals; job search information on resume and cover letter preparation, networking, and the interviewing process; ap-

proximately 300 companies and organizations offering job opportunities and internships, and additional job-hunting resources.

★6990★ Photographer's Complete Guide to Exhibition & Sales Spaces
The Consultant Press, Ltd.
163 Amsterdam Ave., No. 201
New York, NY 10023
Ph: (212)838-8640   Fax: (212)873-7065
Robert S. Persky, Contact

Irregular, previous edition 1989; latest edition January 1995. Covers over 1,800 places where photographers can exhibit and sell their work; 150 colleges and universities that offer courses and degrees in photography; restorers, conservators, and suppliers of conservation products; associations, information centers, and publishers of photography books, magazines, and newsletters; international coverage. Entries include: Name of space, workshop, or university, name of contact, address, phone, specialty. Arrangement: Geographical.

★6991★ Radio and Television Career Directory
Gale Research Inc.
835 Penobscot Bldg.
Detroit, MI 48226-4094
Ph: (313)961-2242   Fax: (313)961-6083
Fr: 800-877-GALE

Bradley J. Morgan and Joseph M. Palmisano. Second edition, 1993. A directory in the Career Advisor Series that provides essays written by industry professionals; job search information on resume and cover letter preparation, networking, and the interviewing process; approximately 300 companies and organizations offering job opportunities and internships, and additional job-hunting resources.

★6992★ Registry of Freelance Photographers
Publishers Network, Inc.
PO Box 3190
Vista, CA 92085
Ph: (619)941-4100   Fax: (619)941-0773
Richard M. Kutner, Contact

Semiannual, January and June. Covers Approximately 1,000 photographers available for assignment in the cities in which they reside; coverage is mostly U.S. and Canada, with a few in Europe and Asia. Entries include: Name, geographical area served, phone, biographical data, qualifications, interests and experience. Arrangement: Geographical by ZIP code.

★6993★ TIPS: The International Photographic Sourcebook
L.A. Photogram
Box 2015
San Gabriel, CA 91778
Ph: (818)286-7510
Bill Whitmore, Contact

Irregular, latest edition fall 1991; updated through "Photographic Digest". Covers over 2,000 manufacturers and distributors of photographic and audiovisual equipment, including speciality bookstores, retail stores, photographic laboratories, photochemical companies, photography organizations; traveling, outdoor, and underwater photographers; colleges and universities offering photography programs, institutions housing largest photo collections; publishers of photography magazines, reference books, and supply catalogs; photo agencies that purchase photographs; limited international coverage. Entries include: Name, address, phone; entries for manufacturers and distributors also include description of products. Arrangement: Classified by line of business.

AWARDS, SCHOLARSHIPS, GRANTS, AND FELLOWSHIPS

★6994★ Reid Blackburn Scholarship
National Press Photographers Foundation
3200 Croasdaile Dr., Ste. 306
Durham, NC 27705
Ph: (919)383-7246   Fax: (919)383-7261
Purpose: To encourage those who have talent and dedication to photojournalism, and who need financial help to continue their studies. Qualifications: Applicants must be high school graduates and may already be in college or in the working world. Selection criteria: Those selected are most deserving of financial need and can demonstrate potential in photojournalism. The philosophy and goals statement (see below) is particularly important in the selection process. Funds available: $1,000. Application details: Applicants must provide evidence of financial need, send a letter of recommendation from a college instructor, and submit a philosophy and goals statement along with a portfolio, which gives evidence of the applicant's academic ability and photo aptitude. For photographers, the portfolio should contain a minimum of six pictures (a picture story counts as one) with the applicant's name printed clearly on the back of each print or on the slide margins (keep caption information concise); for picture editors, three tear sheets; and for video journalists, a sample tape. Applicants' choice of school must be in the United States or Canada and the scholarship award must be used at the beginning of the next semester. Images will not be returned and should be 8x10 unmounted prints or 35mm duplicate slides. Persons may apply for as many different scholarships as they choose but will only be awarded one in any given year. Deadline: March 1.

★6995★ CFDA Fashion Awards
Council of Fashion Designers of America
1412 Broadway, Ste. 933
New York, NY 10018
Ph: (212)302-1821

To recognize outstanding contributions made to American fashion by individuals from all areas of the arts and industry. Awards are given in such varied fields as publishing, retailing, photography, jewelry, and television. The Eugenia Sheppard Award is presented for fashion journalism. The Perry Ellis Award recognizes new talent. Awards are presented annually. Established in 1982.

★6996★ Creativity Show
Art Direction Book Company
10 E. 39th St., 6th Fl.
New York, NY 10016
Ph: (212)889-6500   Fax: (212)889-6504
To recognize outstanding visual professionals internationally and to commend the best work in advertising art, design, photography, or illustration during the preceding 12 months. The recipient must be an art director, advertising designer, photographer, or illustrator. Each year, the entire show is displayed in major cities. All material in print or on the air from May to May each year is eligible. The deadline for entry is May 4. Art directors are judged for concept and design. Artists, illustrators, photographers, and production houses are judged for art, photography, etc. All accepted entries are reproduced in the annual Creativity book, a worldwide volume. The Creativity Show is the annual showcase for the year's best work. Certificates of Distinction are awarded annually. Established in 1970.

★6997★ Bob East Scholarship
National Press Photographers Foundation
3200 Croasdaile Dr., Ste. 306
Durham, NC 27705
Ph: (919)383-7246   Fax: (919)383-7261
Purpose: To encourage those who have talent and dedication to photojournalism, and who need financial help to continue their studies. Qualifications: Applicants must be either undergraduates in their first three and one-half years in college or offer some indication of acceptance to post-graduate work. Selection criteria: Those selected are most deserving of financial need and can demonstrate potential in photojournalism. Funds available: $1,000. Application details: Applicants must provide evidence of financial need, send a letter of recommendation from a college instructor, and submit a portfolio that includes at least five single images in addition to a picture story. Caption information for the prints or slides is useful but should be concise. Applicant's choice of school must be in the United States or Canada and the scholarship award must be used at the beginning of the next semester. Images will not be returned and should be 8x10 unmounted prints or 35mm duplicate slides. Persons may apply for as many different scholarships as they choose but will only be awarded one in any given year. Deadline: March 1.

★6998★ Joseph Ehrenreich Scholarships
National Press Photographers Foundation
3200 Croasdaile Dr., Ste. 306
Durham, NC 27705
Ph: (919)383-7246   Fax: (919)383-7261
Purpose: To encourage those who have talent and dedication to photojournalism, and who need financial help to continue their studies. Qualifications: Students must be enrolled in a recognized four-year college or university having courses in photojournalism and must be continuing in a program leading to a bachelor's degree. They must have at least one-half year of undergraduate schooling remaining at the time of the award. The awards are intended for those with journalism potential, but with little opportunity and great need. Selection criteria: Those selected are

most deserving of financial need and can demonstrate potential in photojournalism. Funds available: Five $1,000. Application details: Applicants must submit an application, portfolio, and a letter of recommendation from a college instructor. The portfolio should demonstrate evidence of photo aptitude. For photographers, the portfolio should contain a minimum of six pictures (a picture story counts as one) with the applicant's name printed clearly on the back of each or on slide margins (keep caption information concise); for picture editors, three tear sheets; for video journalists, a sample tape. Images will not be returned and should be 8x10 unmounted prints or 35mm duplicate slides. Applicant's choice of school must be in the United States or Canada and the scholarship award must be used at the beginning of the next semester. Deadline: March 1.

★6999★ Ferguson Award
The Friends of Photography
Ansel Adams Center
250 Fourth St.
San Francisco, CA 94103
Ph: (415)495-7000   Fax: (415)495-8517
Purpose: To recognize emerging artists accomplishments in the field of creative photography and to support their continued creative growth. Qualifications: All photographers are eligible to apply for the award. Selection criteria: Preference is given to emerging artists who have begun to establish a record of contributions to the field and who show promise of continuing that record. Funds available: $2,000 award. Application details: Applicants must submit twenty slides in a clear plastic slide page. They should not send glass-mounted slides. Applications with slide guidelines are available from Friends of Photography, and must be submitted with a resume or one-page biographical statement and a self-addressed, stamped envelope. A brief statement about the work is optional. Deadline: Applications and slides for the award will be accepted between September 15 and September 26. In late October, a selected group of finalists will be invited to submit portfolios of prints for a final selection process. These will be due in late November, with the award being made shortly thereafter.

★7000★ Grant in Humanistic Photography
W. Eugene Smith Memorial Fund
c/o International Center of Photography
1130 5th Ave.
New York, NY 10128
Ph: (212)860-1770   Fax: (212)360-6490
Purpose: To identify, encourage, and support works-in-progress of photojournalists engaged in humanistic documentary photography. Qualifications: Candidate may be of any nationality. Applicant must be a highly qualified photojournalist interested in recording aspects of human life. The project proposal must be cogent, concise, journalistically realizable, visually translatable, and justifiable in humanistic terms. Selection criteria: A candidate must prove worthiness of project and demonstrated ability. Funds available: $20,000. Application details: Write for application form and guidelines. Submit completed form with photographic prints or duplicate transparencies and project proposals. Finalists will be asked to submit a compre-

hensive portfolio. Deadline: July 15. Notification by October 15.

★7001★ International Exhibition of Photography

Del Mar Fair
Southern California Exposition
2260 Jimmy Durante Blvd.
Del Mar, CA 92014-2216
Ph: (619)755-1161

To recognize outstanding photographic endeavors by professional and amateur still photographers in the black and white (monochrome) print, color print, and creative categories. The pre-registration deadline is April 29. A monetary award of $300 and a rosette are awarded annually for the Best of Show in each of the three categories. A total of $3,505 is awarded. Established in 1948. For more information, send a No. 10 SASE.

★7002★ International Exhibition of Professional Photography

Professional Photographers of America
1090 Exec. Way
Des Plaines, IL 60018

To recognize outstanding professional photography in the following categories: (1) commercial/industrial; (2) portrait; (3) scientific/technical; (4) unclassified; (5) illustrtive; (6) wedding; (7) wedding album; (8) electronic imaging; and (9) specialist (negative retoucher/color artist). Established in 1891.

★7003★ Kit C. King Graduate Scholarship

National Press Photographers Foundation
3200 Croasdaile Dr., Ste. 306
Durham, NC 27705
Ph: (919)383-7246   Fax: (919)383-7261

Purpose: To encourage those who have talent and dedication to photojournalism, and who need financial help to continue their studies. Qualifications: The scholarship is open to anyone pursuing an advanced degree in photojournalism and who can provide some indication of acceptance to an accredited graduate program in photojournalism. Selection criteria: Those selected are most deserving of financial need and can demonstrate potential in photojournalism. Funds available: $500. Application details: Applicants must provide evidence of financial need and send a letter of recommendation from a college instructor. They are also required to submit a philosophy and goals statement and a portfolio, both of which should demonstrate talent and initiative in documentary photojournalism. For photographers, the portfolio should contain a minimum of six pictures (a picture story counts as one) with the applicant's name printed clearly on the back of each print or on slide margins (keep caption information concise); for picture editors, three tear sheets; for video journalists, a sample tape. Images will not be returned and should be 8x10 mounted prints or 35mm duplicate slides. Applicant's choice of school must be in the United States or Canada and the scholarship award must be used at the beginning of the next semester. Deadline: March 1.

★7004★ Man of the Year

International Fire Photographers
  Association
3914 77th Pl. E
Sarasota, FL 34243
Ph: (813)355-3421

To provide recognition for service of outstanding quality to the Association. Current active members of the Association are eligible. A wall plaque is awarded when merited. Established in 1974 in memory of Ralph E. Fox.

★7005★ Rae Mitsuoka Photography Scholarships

Washington Press Association
14243 156th Ave., SE
Renton, WA 98059
Ph: (206)654-5100   Fax: (206)277-8584

Purpose: To further knowledge of photography. Qualifications: Applicants must be high school seniors entered in WPA's High School Photography Contest. Selection criteria: Scholarship award is based on talent, financial need, and academic performance and must be used for a photography workshop or tuition at a college or university in the state. Preference is given to Washington students. Funds available: $250. Application details: Applicants must submit a completed application form, a letter including education and career goals and how the funds would be used, two samples of work, a high school transcript, and a self-addressed, stamped envelope. Deadline: April 1.

★7006★ National Endowment for the Arts - Visual Artists Fellowships

National Endowment for the Arts
Visual Arts Program/Fellowships, Rm. 729
Nancy Hanks Center
1100 Pennsylvania Ave., NW
Washington, DC 20506-0001
Ph: (202)682-5422   Fax: (202)682-5699

Purpose: To encourage the creative development of professional artists by enabling them to set aside time to pursue their work. Qualifications: Fellowships are available to practicing professional artists of exceptional talent with demonstrated ability working in a wide variety of visual media, including painting, sculpture, photography, crafts, printmaking, drawing, artists books, video, performance art, conceptual art, and new genres. Applicants must be United States citizens or permanent residents. Funds available: Fellowships include awards from $15,000 to $20,000. Deadline: Application deadlines vary.

★7007★ Nature Division Awards

Photographic Society of America
3000 United Founders Blvd., Ste. 103
Oklahoma City, OK 73112
Ph: (405)843-1437   Fax: (405)843-1438

For recognition of the most outstanding nature slides and prints at the PSA International Exhibition. The following prizes are awarded: (1) Charles A. Kinsley Memorial Trophy for the best three accepted entries showing diversification; (2) PSA-ND Gold Medal for Best of Show; (3) PSA-ND Silver Medal for Second Best of Show; (4) PSA-ND Bronze Medal for Third Best of Show; (5) PSA-ND Gold Medal for Best Wildlife; (6) PSA-ND Silver Medal for Second Best Wildlife; (7) PSA-ND

Bronze Medal for Third Best Wildlife; (8) PSA-ND Best Botany Award in memory of Leslie B. Henney; (9) Lorena Medbery Nature Landscape/Seascape Award; (10) PSA-ND Geological Award in memory of Lloyd L. Reise, FPSA; (11) PSA-ND Ornithological Wildlife Award in memory of Alice B. Kessler, FPSA; and (12) PSA-ND Nature Division Best Insect Award. Awarded annually.

★7008★ NPPA Association Fellowship Award

National Press Photographers Association
3200 Croasdaile Dr., Ste. 306
Durham, NC 27705
Ph: (919)383-7246   Fax: (919)383-7261

To recognize an individual for continuous outstanding service in the interests of press photography and for outstanding technical achievement in photography. Awarded annually. Established in 1948.

★7009★ NPPF Still Scholarship

National Press Photographers Foundation
3200 Croasdaile Dr., Ste. 306
Durham, NC 27705
Ph: (919)383-7246   Fax: (919)383-7261

Purpose: To encourage those who have talent and dedication to photojournalism, and who need financial help to continue their studies. Qualifications: Students must be enrolled in a recognized four-year college or university having courses in photojournalism and must be continuing in a program leading to a bachelor's degree. They must have at least one-half year of undergraduate schooling remaining at the time of the award. The awards are intended for those with journalism potential, but with little opportunity and great need. Selection criteria: Those selected are most deserving of financial need and can demonstrate potential in photojournalism. Funds available: $1,000. Application details: Applicants must submit an application, portfolio, and a letter of recommendation from a college instructor. The portfolio should demonstrate evidence of photo aptitude, and contain the following: for photographers, a minimum of six pictures (a picture story counts as one) with the applicant's name printed clearly on each print or on the slide margins (keep captions concise); for picture editors, three tear sheets; for video journalists, a sample tape. Applicant's choice of school must be in the United States or Canada and the scholarship award must be used at the beginning of the next semester. Images will not be returned and should be 8x10 unmounted prints or 35mm duplicate slides. Deadline: March 1.

★7010★ Outdoor Writers Association of America Scholarship Awards

Outdoor Writers Association of America
  (OWAA)
2017 Cato Ave., Ste. 101
State College, PA 16801-2768
Ph: (814)234-1011   Fax: (814)234-9692

Purpose: To reward outstanding students who are working toward careers in outdoor writing, broadcasting, photography, or art. Qualifications: Applicants should be in their last two years of college or master's degree students in any accredited school of journalism or mass communication listed by the Association for Education in Journalism and Mass Communication, or those schools accepted on application to the Outdoor Writers

Association of America. There shall be no more than one applicant from each school per school year. Each school will be responsible for selecting its candidate. Selection criteria: Judges look for applicants with talent, promise, and first-hand outdoor knowledge. Applications are rated on clarity, organization, and originality. Grade point average is considered. Funds available: The amount of the scholarship varies, but is usually at least $3,000. Application details: An applicant must submit an OWAA application form, school recommendation, grade transcript, examples of outdoor communication work (including published samples), a one- to two-page statement by the nominee detailing career goals, and optional letters of recommendation from outdoor communicators or employers familiar with the applicant's work. The application package must be submitted to the Executive Director, Outdoor Writers Association of America. Deadline: March 1.

★7011★ **Photo-Journalism Division Awards**
Photographic Society of America
3000 United Founders Blvd., Ste. 103
Oklahoma City, OK 73112
Ph: (405)843-1437   Fax: (405)843-1438
For recognition of outstanding work in photojournalism. Awards are given in the following categories: (1) Class "A" Large Prints; (2) Class "B" Small Prints; and (3) Color "C" Slides. The following prizes are awarded: (1) PSA PJD Gold Medal Award for Best of Show; (2) PSA PJD Silver Medal for Best Man in Action; and (3) Charles A. Kinsley Memorial Trophy - one for a print, large or small; and one for a slide. Awarded annually.

★7012★ **Photo-Travel Division Awards**
Photographic Society of America
3000 United Founders Blvd., Ste. 103
Oklahoma City, OK 73112
Ph: (405)843-1437   Fax: (405)843-1438
For recognition of the most outstanding photo travel slides at the PSA International Exhibition. The following prizes are awarded: (1) Charles A. Kinsley Memorial Trophy for the best three accepted entries showing diversification; (2) Joseph Van Gelder award for Best of Show; (3) PSA PTD Gold Medal for runner-up; (4) PSA PTD Gold Medal for runner-up; and (5) People at Work Award in memory of Joe Seckendorf, FPSA.

★7013★ **Regional Television Photographers of the Year**
National Press Photographers Association
3200 Croasdaile Dr., Ste. 306
Durham, NC 27705
Ph: (919)383-7246   Fax: (919)383-7261
To recognize television photographers from 11 regions. Awarded annually. Established in 1980.

★7014★ **Ruttenberg Foundation Award**
The Friends of Photography
Ansel Adams Center
250 Fourth St.
San Francisco, CA 94103
Ph: (415)495-7000   Fax: (415)495-8517
Purpose: To support the work of an emerging artist and to encourage that artist's continued creative growth. Qualifications: All photographers are eligible to apply for the award. Applicants must demonstrate excellence in and

commitment to the medium and concentrate their efforts on portraiture in the context of fine art photography. Selection criteria: Preference is given to emerging artists who have begun to establish a record of contributions to the field and who show promise of continuing that record. Funds available: $2,000. Application details: Applicants must submit twenty slides in a clear plastic slide page. They should not send glass-mounted slides. Applications with slide guidelines are available from the Friends of Photography, and must be accompanied by a resume or one-page biographical statement and a self-addressed, stamped envelope. A brief statement about the work is optional. Deadline: Applications and slides for the award will be accepted between September 22 and October 3. In early October, a selected group of finalists will be invited to submit portfolios of prints for a final selection process. These will be due in late November, with the award being made shortly thereafter.

★7015★ **Joseph A. Sprague Memorial Award**
National Press Photographers Association
3200 Croasdaile Dr., Ste. 306
Durham, NC 27705
Ph: (919)383-7246   Fax: (919)383-7261
This is the highest honor in the field of photojournalism. Two awards are given each year: to a working photojournalist who advances, elevates, or attains unusual recognition for the profession of photojournalism by conduct, initiative leadership, skill and devotion to duty; and to an individual, not a working photojournalist, for unusual service or achievement beneficial to photojournalism or for an outstanding technology advance in equipment or processes of photojournalism. Plaques, rings, and citations are awarded annually in both categories. Established in 1947 in memory of Joseph A. Sprague, a press technical representative for Graflex Corporation, Rochester, NY.

★7016★ **Lila Wallace-Reader's Digest International Artists**
Arts International Program of the Institute of International Education
c/o Institute of International Education
809 University Plaza
New York, NY 10017
Ph: (212)984-5370
Purpose: To provide visual artists (painters, sculptors, photographers, video artists, and craft artists) with three- to six-month international residencies, followed by an active partnership with an arts organization in the U.S. to present community programs based on the artists' experiences abroad. Qualifications: Applicants must be visual artists. The artist must apply jointly with a sponsoring organization and work together to define their interests and develop innovative, interactive, or collaborative approaches to the community activity stage of the program. Funds available: Financial support to live, work and travel three- to six-months. Application details: Guidelines and application forms are available from Arts International. Deadline: The 1992 deadline was December 11.

★7017★ **White House News Photographers' Association Awards**
White House News Photographers' Association
7119 Ben Franklin Sta.
Washington, DC 20044-7119
Ph: (202)785-5230   Fax: (301)428-4904
To recognize outstanding photojournalists who daily cover the Office of the President of the United States and major events in Washington, DC, as well as other parts of the world. Awards are presented in categories in the following classes: Still Division: Presidential; Insiders' Washington; News; Sports/Action; Sports/Feature; Personalities/Color; Personalities/Black & White; Feature/Color; Feature Black & White; Pictorial; Picture Story/News; Picture Story/Feature; and Campaign '88; and Tape/Film Division: News Feature; Presidential; Spot News; General News; Day Feature; Feature; Series; Sports; Editing; Sound; Magazine Feature; and Lighting. First, second, third place, and often honorable mention winners are selected in each class. Prizes vary from year to year depending on sponsors, and are often camera equipment and monetary prizes. In addition, the Eastman Kodak Companypresents the Kodak/WHNPA Achievement Award. The 3M Companypresents the Winner Takes All Awardto the Cameraman of the Year. The Still Photographer of the Year Award is presented. Awarded annually. Established in 1921. All winning photographs are displayed at photo exhibitions that travel around the United States and abroad.

BASIC REFERENCE GUIDES AND HANDBOOKS

★7018★ **ASMP Stock Photography Handbook**
American Society of Media Photographers (ASMP)
419 Park Ave. S., Ste. 1407
New York, NY 10016
Ph: (609)799-8300
1990. Michael Heron, editor. Gives an overview of stock photography, selling stock photography, and using a stock agency.

★7019★ **The Glamour Photographer Sourcebook**
Jax Photo Books & Videos
5491 Mantva Ct.
San Diego, CA 92124
Ph: (619)268-1727
Jack Qualman, editor. 1992.

★7020★ **The Photographer's Sourcebook of Creative Ideas**
Alfred A. Knopf, Inc.
201 E. 50th St.
New York, NY 10022
Ph: (212)751-2600
John Hedgecoe. First edition, 1987. Includes an index.

★7021★ The Ultimate Photo Data Guide
Simon & Schuster, Inc.
Simon & Schuster Bldg.
1230 Avenue of the Americas
New York, NY 10020
Ph: (212)698-7000   Fr: 800-722-4726
Richard Platt. 1989. A guide to taking pictures anytime, anywhere in the world. Contains rules of thumb and step-by-step formulas, and tables to determine lighting and image calculations, conversion factors, lenses, film, and repairs. Also are included are a filter-selection guide, a five-language phrase book, and a country-by-country chart for special requirements and restrictions on photography.

PROFESSIONAL AND TRADE PERIODICALS

★7022★ American Cinematographer
ASC Holding Corp.
PO Box 2230
Los Angeles, CA 90078
Ph: (213)969-4333   Fax: (213)876-4973
David Heuring
Monthly. Magazine of the American Society of Cinematographers; covering film and video production.

★7023★ Aperture
Aperture Foundation, Inc.
20 E. 23rd St.
New York, NY 10010
Ph: (212)505-5555   Fax: (212)979-7759
Michael E. Hoffman
Quarterly. Photography magazine.

★7024★ Industrial Photography
PTN Publishing Co.
445 Broad Hollow Rd., Ste. 21
Melville, NY 11747
Ph: (516)845-2700   Fax: (516)845-7109
Steve Shaw
Monthly. Magazine on industrial photography.

★7025★ News Photographer Magazine
National Press Photographers Association
3200 Croasdaile Dr., Ste. 306
Durham, NC 27705
Ph: (919)383-7246   Fax: (919)383-7261
Fr: 800-289-6772
Jim Gordon
Monthly. Carries items of professional interest to members—news photographers and others whose occupation has a direct professional relationship with photojournalism. Discusses legal and ethical aspects of photojournalism and publishes results of the Association's monthly contests for still clipping and television-newsfilm. Recurring features include member and Association news, news of educational opportunities, and a calendar of events.

★7026★ PHOTO Electronic Imaging
PPA Publications & Events, Inc.
57 Forsyth Street, NW
Atlanta, GA 30303
Ph: (404)522-8600   Fax: (404)614-6405
Kim Brady
Monthly. Technical business magazine.

★7027★ PhotoBulletin
PhotoSource International
Pine Lake Farm
Osceola, WI 54020
Ph: (715)248-3800   Fax: (715)248-7394
Fr: 800-223-3860
Lori Johnson
Weekly. Announces current photograph needs of book and magazine publishers, corporations, government, and advertising agencies. Includes specific information on deadlines and prices.

★7028★ Photograph America Newsletter
Photograph America
1333 Monte Maria Ave.
Novato, CA 94947
Ph: (415)898-3736   Fr: 800-GET-FOTO
Robert Hitchman
Bimonthly. Provides details, maps, and directions to spots to produce photographs of professional quality. Features one specific location, such as Death Valley, the Florida Everglades, Yellowstone, or Hawaiian rainforests, in each issue.

★7029★ The PhotoLetter
PhotoSource International
Pine Lake Farm
Osceola, WI 54020
Ph: (715)248-3800   Fax: (715)248-7394
Fr: 800-223-3860
Lynette Layer
Monthly. Informs photographers of a large network of publishers, art directors, and photo editors who currently need material for textbooks, magazines, and encyclopedias.

★7030★ PhotoMarket
PhotoSource International
Pine Lake Farm
Osceola, WI 54020
Ph: (715)248-3800   Fax: (715)248-7394
Fr: 800-223-3860
Lori Johnson
Semimonthly. Lists current photography needs of editors, publications, and advertising agencies. Includes type of photographs needed, subject matter, rate, contact person, address, phone number, and deadline.

★7031★ Professional Photographer
Professional Photographers of America, Inc.
57 Forsyth St. N.W. #1600
Atlanta, GA 30303
Ph: (404)522-8600   Fax: (404)614-6405
Kimberly Brady
Monthly.

★7032★ Shots
PO Box 109
Joseph, OR 97846
Informal photography magazine.

PROFESSIONAL MEETINGS AND CONVENTIONS

★7033★ Annual International Fire Photographers Association Training Conference
International Fire Photographers Association
PO Box 8337
Rolling Meadows, IL 60008
Ph: (708)747-2080
Annual. Always held during June/July. **Dates and Locations:** 1996.

★7034★ International Exposition of Professional Photography
Professional Photographers of America
57 Forsyth St. NW, Ste. 1600
Atlanta, GA 30303-2206
Ph: (404)522-8600   Fax: (404)614-6400
Annual. **Dates and Locations:** 1996 Jul 12-17; Orlando, FL.

★7035★ Professional Photographers of America Marketing and Management Conference
Professional Photographers of America
1090 Executive Way
Des Plaines, IL 60018
Ph: (708)299-8161   Fax: (708)299-1975
Annual. Always held during January.

★7036★ Professional Photography Annual Exposition
Professional Photographers of America
1090 Executive Way
Des Plaines, IL 60018
Ph: (708)299-8161
Annual.

OTHER SOURCES OF INFORMATION

★7037★ "Photographer/Camera Operator" in 100 Best Jobs for the 1990s & Beyond
Dearborn Financial Publishing, Inc.
520 N. Dearborn St.
Chicago, IL 60610-4354
Ph: (312)836-4400   Fax: (312)836-1021
Fr: 800-621-9621
Carol Kleiman. 1992. Describes 100 jobs ranging from accountants to veterinarians. Each job profile includes such information as education, experience, and certification needed, salaries, and job search suggestions.

★7038★ "Photographer" in Career Selector 2001
Barron's Educational Series, Inc.
250 Wireless Blvd.
Hauppauge, NY 11788
Ph: (516)434-3311   Fax: (516)434-3723
Fr: 800-645-3476
James C. Gonyea. 1993.

★7039★ *The Photographer's Assistant*
Allworth Press
10 E. 23rd St., Ste. 400
New York, NY 10010
Ph: (212)777-8395   Fax: (212)777-8261
Fr: 800-247-6553

1992.

★7040★ *The Photographer's Guide to Marketing and Self-Promotion*
Writer's Digest Books
1507 Dana Ave.
Cincinnati, OH 45207
Ph: (513)531-2222   Fr: 800-543-4644

Maria Piscopo. 1987.

★7041★ *Photographs: The International Annual of Advertising and Editorial Photography*
Watson-Guptill Publications
1515 Broadway
New York, NY 10036
Ph: (908)363-5679   Fr: 800-526-3641
Walter Herleg, editor. Annual.

★7042★ "Photography" in *Accounting to Zoology: Graduate Fields Defined* (pp. 10-11)
Petersons Guides, Inc.
PO Box 2123
Princeton, NJ 08543-2123
Ph: (609)243-9111   Fax: (609)243-9150
Fr: 800-338-3282

Amy J. Goldstein, editor. Revised and updated, 1987. Defines 298 graduate and professional fields. Discusses types of graduate programs and degrees, graduate research, applied work, employment prospects, and trends.

★7043★ *Truth Needs No Ally: Inside Photojournalism*
Crestwood House
866 3rd Ave.
New York, NY 10022
Ph: (212)702-9632

1994.

Visual Artists

Visual artists use an almost limitless variety of methods and materials to communicate ideas, thoughts, and feelings. They may use oils, watercolors, acrylics, pastels, magic markers, pencils, pen and ink, silkscreen, plaster, clay, or any of a number of other media, including computers, to create realistic and abstract works or images of objects, people, nature, topography, or events. Visual artists generally fall into one of two categories, graphic artists and fine artists, depending not so much on the medium, but on the artist's purpose in creating a work of art. **Fine artists**, on the other hand, often create art to satisfy their own need for self-expression, and may display their work in museums, art galleries, and homes. Fine artists usually work independently, choosing the subject matter and medium they deem fit. **Painters** generally work with two-dimensional art forms. **Sculptors** design three-dimensional art works either molding and joining materials such as clay, stone. **Printmakers** create printed images from designs cut into wood, stone, or metal, or from computer-driven data. **Painting restorers** preserve and restore damage and faded paintings. Graphic artists, whether freelancers or employees of a firm, use a variety of print and film media to create and execute art that meets a client's needs. **Graphic artists** put their artistic skills and vision at the service of commercial clients such as major corporations, retail stores, advertising firms, and production companies. Graphic artists perform different jobs depending on their area of expertise. **Graphic designers** may design packaging and promotional displays for a new product, an annual report, or a distinctive logo for a store chain, company stationery, and products. **Illustrators** paint or draw pictures for books, magazines, and films. **Editorial artists** do illustrations for magazines, album and compact disk covers, films, theater posters, and other publications. **Medical and scientific illustrators** combine artist's skills with knowledge of the biological sciences. **Fashion artists** draw illustrations of women's and men's and children's clothing and accessories for newspapers, magazines, and other media. **Cartoonists** draw political, advertising, social, and sports cartoons. **Animators** work in the motion picture and television industry. **Art directors**, also called **visual journalists**, read the material to be printed in periodicals, newspapers, and other printed media, and determine how to visually present the information.

Salaries

Earnings for self-employed visual artists vary widely.

Lowest 10 percent	Less than $14,600/year
Median	$23,000/year
Top 10 percent	More than $43,500/year

Employment Outlook

Growth rate until the year 2005: Average.

Visual Artists

★7044★ AAA in *Exploring Careers in Computer Graphics*
Rosen Publishing Group
29 E. 21st St.
New York, NY 10010
Ph: (212)777-3017   Fax: (212)777-0277
Fr: 800-237-9932

Richard Masterson. Revised edition, 1990. Explores careers in computer graphics describing educational preparation and job-hunting strategies. Includes information on applications such as CAD/CAM and business. Appendices include a glossary, trade journals, associations, colleges, and a bibliography.

★7045★ "Art" in *College Majors and Careers: A Resource Guide to Effective Life Planning* (pp. 21-22)
Garrett Park Press
PO Box 1907
Garrett Park, MD 20896
Ph: (301)946-2553

Paul Phifer. Revised, 1993. Lists 60 college majors, with definitions; related occupations and leisure activities; skills, values, and personal attributesneeded; suggested readings; and a list of associations.

★7046★ "Art" in *Internships: 1995* (pp. 113-121)
Petersons Guides, Inc.
PO Box 2123
Princeton, NJ 08543-2123
Ph: (609)243-9111   Fax: (609)243-9150
Fr: 800-338-3282

1991. Lists internship opportunities under six broad categories: communications, creative, performing, and fine arts, human services, international relations, business and technology, and public relations. Includes a special section on internships in Washington, DC. For each internship program, gives the name, phone number, contact person, description, eligibility requirements, and benefits.

★7047★ "Art Specialist" and "Illustrator" in *Guide to Federal Jobs* (pp. 191, 186)
Resource Directories
3361 Executive Pkwy., Ste. 302
Toledo, OH 43606
Ph: (419)536-5353   Fax: (419)536-7056
Fr: 800-274-8515

Rod W. Durgin, editor. Third edition, 1992. Contains information on finding and applying for federal jobs. Describes more than 200 professional and technical jobs for college graduates. Covers the nature of the work, salary, and geographic location. Lists college majors preferred for that occupation. Section one describes the function and work of government agencies that hire the most significant number of college graduates.

★7048★ "Artist (Fine Art)" in *Jobs Rated Almanac*
World Almanac
1 International Blvd., Ste. 444
Mahwah, NJ 07495
Ph: (201)529-6900   Fax: (201)529-6901

Les Krantz. Second edition, 1992. Ranks 250 jobs by environment, salary, outlooks, physical demands, stress, security, travel opportunities, and extra perks. Includes jobs the editor feels are the most common, most interesting, and the most rapidly growing.

★7049★ *Artist, Graphic*
Careers, Inc.
PO Box 135
Largo, FL 34649-0135
Ph: (813)584-7333

1994. Two-page occupational summary card describing duties, working conditions, personal qualifications, training, earnings and hours, employment outlook, places of employment, related careers, and where to write for more information.

★7050★ *Artists*
Careers, Inc.
PO Box 135
Largo, FL 34649-0135
Ph: (813)584-7333

1992. Four-page brief offering the definition, history, duties, working conditions, personal qualifications, educational requirements, earnings, hours, employment outlook, advancement, and careers related to this position.

★7051★ "Artists and Painters" in *Career Discovery Encyclopedia* (Vol.1, pp. 64-65)
J.G. Ferguson Publishing Co.
200 W. Madison St., Ste. 300
Chicago, IL 60606
Ph: (312)580-5480   Fax: (312)580-4948

Russell E. Primm, editor-in chief. 1993. This six volume set contains two-page articles for 504 occupations. Each article describes job duties, earnings, and educational and training requirements. The whole set is arranged alphabetically by job title. Designed for junior high and older students.

★7052★ *A Brief Guide to Art and Design Studies*
National Association of Schools of Art and Design (NASAD)
11250 Roger Bacon Dr., Ste. 21
Reston, VA 22090
Ph: (703)437-0700

Describes major options in the field of art, including fine arts, crafts, visual communication, and industrial and environmental design. Also generally comments on related fields, institutions for vocational training in art and design, college and university departments of art and design, art teacher education, and professional schools of art and design.

★7053★ *The Business of Art*
Prentice-Hall, Inc.
200 Old Tappan Rd.
Old Tappan, NJ 07675
Ph: (201)767-5000

Art Caplin. Second edition, 1989. Covers financial planning; working with galleries, dealers, and museums; packaging and promoting art. Describes how to choose the most profitable crafts fairs, and how to secure endowments and grants.

★7054★ *Career Choices for the 90's for Students of Art*
Walker and Co.
435 Hudson St.
New York, NY 10014
Ph: (212)727-8300   Fax: (212)727-0984
Fr: 800-289-2553

1990. Describes alternative careers for students of art. Offers information about job outlook and competition for entry-level candidates. Includes a bibliography and an index.

★7055★ Career Opportunities in Advertising
American Advertising Federation (AAF)
1101 Vermont Ave., NW, Ste. 500
Washington, DC 20005
Ph: (202)898-0089   Fax: (202)898-0159
Describes advertising job opportunities and educational preparation. Gives job-hunting tips.

★7056★ Career Opportunities in Advertising and Public Relations
Facts on File
460 Park Ave. S.
New York, NY 10016-7382
Ph: (212)683-2244   Fax: 800-678-3633
Fr: 800-322-8755
Shelly Field. 1993. Guidebook offering complete career information for those entering advertising or public relations. Describes 85 jobs and includes salary information, employment prospects, and education and skills needed for the jobs.

★7057★ Career Opportunities in Art
Facts on File
460 Park Ave. S.
New York, NY 10016-7382
Ph: (212)683-2244   Fax: 800-678-3633
Fr: 800-322-8755
Susan H. Haubenstock and David Joselit. 1993. Guidebook containing valuable information on obtaining practical employment in 83 art-related fields. Includes contact information for degree programs as well as professional associations. Includes information on jobs in advertising, graphic desing, printmaking, photography, architecture, interior design, textile design, and others.

★7058★ Career Opportunities in Television, Cable and Video
Facts on File
460 Park Ave. S.
New York, NY 10016-7382
Ph: (212)683-2244   Fax: 800-678-3633
Fr: 800-322-8755
Maxine K. Reed and Robert M. Reed. Third edition, 1993. Includes information on employment and advancement prospects, education, experience and skills requiresn salary range, and tips for entry into the field.

★7059★ Careers in the Graphic Arts
Rosen Publishing Group
29 E. 21st St.
New York, NY 10010
Ph: (212)777-3017   Fax: (212)777-0277
Fr: 800-237-9932
Virginia Lee Robertson. Revised edition, 1993. Discusses a career in graphic arts; outlines educational requirements, training, and skills needed to become an illustrator, layout artist, designer, and paste-up artist. Gives job hunting advice describes how to write a resume, prepare the portfolio, and interview preparation. Gives a state-by-state listing of schools offering graphic arts.

★7060★ Cartoonist
Careers, Inc.
PO Box 135
Largo, FL 34649-0135
Ph: (813)584-7333
1995. Four-page brief offering the definition, history, duties, working conditions, personal qualifications, educational requirements, earnings, hours, employment outlook, advancement, and careers related to this position.

★7061★ "Cartoonist" in VGM's Careers Encyclopedia (pp. 78-81)
National Textbook Co. (NTC)
VGM Career Books
4255 W. Touhy Ave.
Lincolnwood, IL 60646-1975
Ph: (708)679-5500   Fax: (708)679-2494
Fr: 800-323-4900
Third edition, 1991. Profiles 200 occupations. Describes job duties, places of employment, working conditions, qualifications, education and training, advancement potential, and salary for each occupation.

★7062★ Cartoonists
Chronicle Guidance Publications, Inc.
66 Aurora St.
PO Box 1190
Moravia, NY 13118-1190
Ph: (315)497-0330   Fax: (315)497-3359
Fr: 800-622-7284
1992. Career brief describing the nature of the job, working conditions, hours and earnings, education and training, licensure, certification, unions, personal qualifications, social and psychological factors, location, employment outlook, entry methods, advancement, and related occupations.

★7063★ "Cartoonists", "Commercial Artists", and "Artists" in Career Information Center (Vol.3)
Simon and Schuster
200 Old Tappan Rd.
Old Tappan, NJ 07675
Fax: 800-445-6991   Fr: 800-223-2348
Richard Lidz and Linda Perrin, editorial directors. Fifth edition, 1993. A multi-volume set that profiles more than 600 occupations. Each occupational profile describes job duties, educational requirements, getting a job, advancement possibilities, employment outlook, working conditions, earnings and benefits, and sources of additional information.

★7064★ For the Working Artist: A Survival Guide for Artists
California Institute of the Arts
Placement Office
24700 McBean Pkwy.
Valencia, CA 91355
Ph: (805)253-7871
Judith Luther and Eric Vollmer. Second edition, 1991.

★7065★ "Graphic Artist" in 100 Best Careers for the Year 2000 (pp. 149-150)
Arco Pub.
201 W. 103rd St.
Indianapolis, IN 46290
Ph: 800-428-5331   Fax: 800-835-3202
Shelly Field. 1992. Describes 100 job opportunities expected to grow fast throughout the next decade. Provides information on job duties and responsibilities, training requirements, education, advancement opportunities, experience and qualifications, and typical salaries.

★7066★ "Graphic Arts" in Career Connection for Technical Education (pp. 84-85)
JIST Works, Inc.
720 N. Park Ave.
Indianapolis, IN 46202-3431
Ph: (317)264-3720   Fax: (317)264-3709
Fred A. Rowe. 1994, second edition. Describes in detail technical occupations. Includes information on recommended high school courses, course requirements, related careers, and a self-assessment guide.

★7067★ "Graphic Arts" in Liberal Arts Jobs
Petersons Guides, Inc.
PO Box 2123
Princeton, NJ 08543-2123
Ph: (609)243-9111   Fax: (609)243-9150
Fr: 800-338-3282
Burton Jay Nadler. Second edition, 1989. Strives to help the liberal arts graduate identify skills for entry-level positions. Gives goal setting and job search advice.

★7068★ "Graphic Design" in Encyclopedia of Career Choices for the 1990s: A Guide to Entry Level Jobs (pp. 377-396)
Berkley Pub.
PO Box 506
East Rutherford, NJ 07073
Fax: (201)933-2316   Fr: 800-788-6262
1992. Describes entry-level careers in a variety of industries. Presents qualifications required, working conditions, salary, internships, and professional associations.

★7069★ "Graphic Designer" in VGM's Careers Encyclopedia (pp. 198-200)
National Textbook Co. (NTC)
VGM Career Books
4255 W. Touhy Ave.
Lincolnwood, IL 60646-1975
Ph: (708)679-5500   Fax: (708)679-2494
Fr: 800-323-4900
Third edition, 1991. Profiles 200 occupations. Describes job duties, places of employment, working conditions, qualifications, education and training, advancement potential, and salary for each occupation.

★7070★ "Graphic Designers" in Encyclopedia of Careers and Vocational Guidance (Vol.3, pp. 104-107)
J.G. Ferguson Publishing Co.
200 W. Madison St., Ste. 300
Chicago, IL 60606
Ph: (312)580-5480   Fax: (312)580-4948
William E. Hopke, editor-in-chief. Ninth edition, 1993. Four-volume set that profiles 900 occupations and describes job trends in 74 industries. Each chapter offers a career description, educational requirements, history of the job, methods of entry, advancement, employment outlook, earnings, conditions of work, social and psychological factors, and sources of further information.

★7071★ "Graphic Designers" in *Jobs! What They Are—Where They Are— What They Pay* (p. 31)
Simon & Schuster, Inc.
Simon & Schuster Bldg.
1230 Avenue of the Americas
New York, NY 10020
Ph: (212)698-7000   Fr: 800-223-2348
Robert O. Snelling and Anne M. Snelling. 3rd edition, 1992. Describes duties and responsibilities, earnings, employment opportunities, training, and qualifications.

★7072★ "Graphics" in *Desk Guide to Training and Work Advertisement* (pp. 115-118)
Charles C. Thomas, Publisher
2600 S. 1st St.
Springfield, IL 62794-9265
Ph: (217)789-8980   Fax: (217)789-9130
Fr: 800-258-8980
Gail Baugher Keunstler. 1988. Describes alternative methods of gaining entry into an occupation through different types of educational programs, internships, and apprenticeships.

★7073★ *Illustrator, Fashion*
Careers, Inc.
PO Box 135
Largo, FL 34649-0135
Ph: (813)584-7333
1992. Two-page occupational summary card describing duties, working conditions, personal qualifications, training, earnings and hours, employment outlook, places of employment, related careers, and where to write for more information.

★7074★ *Illustrator, Medical*
Careers, Inc.
PO Box 135
Largo, FL 34649-0135
Ph: (813)584-7333
1993. Two-page occupational summary card describing duties, working conditions, personal qualifications, training, earnings and hours, employment outlook, places of employment, related careers, and where to write for more information.

★7075★ *Illustrator, Technical*
Careers, Inc.
PO Box 135
Largo, FL 34649-0135
Ph: (813)584-7333
1993. Two-page occupational summary card describing duties, working conditions, personal qualifications, training, earnings and hours, employment outlook, places of employment, related careers, and where to write for more information.

★7076★ *Illustrators, Technical*
Chronicle Guidance Publications, Inc.
66 Aurora St.
PO Box 1190
Moravia, NY 13118-1190
Ph: (315)497-0330   Fax: (315)497-3359
Fr: 800-622-7284
1994. Career brief describing the nature of the job, working conditions, hours and earnings, education and training, licensure, certification, unions, personal qualifications, social and psychological factors, location, employ-

ment outlook, entry methods, advancement, and related occupations.

★7077★ *Medical Illustration*
Association of Medical Illustrators (AMI)
2692 Huguenot Springs Rd.
Midlothian, VA 23113
Ph: (804)794-2908
This ten-panel brochure describes the nature of the work, educational requirements, advancement opportunities, and salaries. Lists schools of medical illustration.

★7078★ "Medical Illustrator" in *150 Careers in the Health Care Field*
Reed Reference Publishing
121 Chanlon Rd.
PO Box 31
New Providence, NJ 07974
Fax: (908)665-6688   Fr: 800-521-8110
Stanley Alperin. Third edition, 1993. Profiles 150 health care occupations requiring a bachelor's degree or less. Describes the nature of the work, educational preparation, licensing requirements, and salary. Lists accredited educational programs.

★7079★ "Medical Illustrator" in *Careers in Health Care* (pp. 125-128)
National Textbook Co. (NTC)
VGM Career Books
4255 W. Touhy Ave.
Lincolnwood, IL 60646-1975
Ph: (708)679-5500   Fax: (708)679-2494
Fr: 800-323-4900
Barbara M. Swanson. Third edition, 1995. Profiles 58 health careers. Describes job duties, work settings, salaries, licensing and certification requirements, educational preparation, and future outlook.

★7080★ *Medical Illustrators*
Chronicle Guidance Publications, Inc.
66 Aurora St.
PO Box 1190
Moravia, NY 13118-1190
Ph: (315)497-0330   Fax: (315)497-3359
Fr: 800-622-7284
1992. Career brief describing the nature of the job, working conditions, hours and earnings, education and training, licensure, certification, unions, personal qualifications, social and psychological factors, location, employment outlook, entry methods, advancement, and related occupations.

★7081★ *Opportunities in Commercial Art and Graphic Design*
National Textbook Co. (NTC)
VGM Career Books
4255 W. Touhy Ave.
Lincolnwood, IL 60646-1975
Ph: (708)679-5500   Fax: (708)679-2494
Fr: 800-323-4900
Barbara Gordon. 1992. This volume offers an overview of the many possibilities for employment in advertising, public relations, and publishing.

★7082★ *Opportunities in Printing Careers*
National Textbook Co. (NTC)
VGM Career Books
4255 W. Touhy Ave.
Lincolnwood, IL 60646-1975
Ph: (708)679-5500   Fax: (708)679-2494
Fr: 800-323-4900
Irvin J. Borowsky. 1992. Describes various jobs for commercial artists in the printing industry including layout artist, package designer, and paste-up artist. Includes information on places of employment, job duties, and salaries.

★7083★ *Opportunities in Visual Arts Careers*
National Textbook Co. (NTC)
VGM Career Books
4255 W. Touhy Ave.
Lincolnwood, IL 60646-1975
Ph: (708)679-5500   Fax: (708)679-2494
Fr: 800-323-4900
Mark Salmon. 1993. Reviews the education, training and talent required for success in the visual arts fields. Overviews opportunities in design, painting, sculpting, illustration, animation, photography, art therapy, education, and more.

★7084★ *The School of Visual Arts Guide to Careers*
McGraw-Hill, Inc.
1221 Avenue of the Americas
New York, NY 10020
Ph: (212)512-3825   Fr: 800-722-4726
Dee Ito. 1987. Out of print; check local libraries. Provides a broad overview of careers, with educational requirements and employment opportunities.

★7085★ *Supporting Yourself as an Artist*
Oxford University Press
200 Madison Ave.
New York, NY 10016
Ph: (212)679-7300
Deborah A. Hoover. Second edition, 1989. Assists artists in identifying organizations and individuals that can provide the financial and nonfinancial support needed to survive.

★7086★ "Technical Illustrating" in *Exploring High-Tech Careers*
Rosen Publishing Group
29 E. 21st St.
New York, NY 10010
Ph: (212)777-3017   Fax: (212)777-0277
Fr: 800-237-9932
Scott Southworth. Revised edition, 1993. Gives an orientation to the field of high technology and high-tech jobs. Describes educational preparation and job hunting. Includes a glossary and bibliography.

★7087★ "Visual Artist" in *College Board Guide to Jobs and Career Planning* (pp. 75-78)
The College Board
45 Columbus Ave.
New York, NY 10023-6992
Ph: (212)713-8165   Fax: (212)713-8143
Fr: 800-323-7155
Second edition, 1994. Describes the job, salaries, related careers, education needed, and where to write for more information.

★7088★ "Visual Artists" in
Occupational Outlook Handbook
U.S. Government Printing Office
Superintendent of Documents
Washington, DC 20402
Ph: (202)512-1800   Fax: (202)512-2250
Biennial, 1994-95. Encyclopedia of careers describing about 250 occupations and comprising about 85 percent of all jobs in the economy. Occupations that require lengthy education or training are given the most attention. Each occupation's profile describes what the worker does on the job, working conditions, education and training requirements, advancement possibilities, job outlook, earnings, and sources of additional information.

PROFESSIONAL ASSOCIATIONS

★7089★ American Institute of Graphic
Arts (AIGA)
164 5th Ave.
New York, NY 10010
Ph: (212)807-1990   Fax: (212)807-1799
Fr: 800-548-1634
Members: Graphic designers, art directors, art directors, illustrators, packaging designers, and craftsmen involved in printing and allied graphic fields. **Purpose:** Sponsors exhibits and projects in the public interest. Sponsors traveling exhibitions. Operates gallery. Maintains library of design books and periodicals; offers slide archives. **Publications:** *AIGA Journal of Graphic Design*, quarterly. • *AIGA Membership Directory*, biennial. • *AIGA News*, bimonthly. • *Graphic Design USA*, annual.

★7090★ American Society of Furniture
Designers (ASFD)
PO Box 2688
High Point, NC 27261
Ph: (910)884-4074
Members: Professional furniture designers, teachers, students, corporate suppliers of products and services; others who supply products and services related to furniture design. Seeks to promote the profession of furniture design. Conducts and cooperates in educational courses and seminars for furniture designers and persons planning to enter the field. Maintains placement service. **Publications:** *ASFD Official Directory*, annual. • *Designer Forum*, quarterly.

★7091★ Black Gold Group
223 Parker St. NE
Washington, DC 20002
Ph: (202)667-0355
Members: African-American artists. **Purpose:** Provides support and technical assistance to artists. **Publications:** *Black Gold National Shoppers' Guide*, biennial.

★7092★ Enabled Artists United (EAU)
Box 178
Dobbins, CA 95935
Ph: (916)692-1581
Purpose: Advocates the right of all persons to the means for creative expression. Promotes partnerships between artists with and

without disabilities and assists the implementation of the Americans with Disabilities Act. Provides consultation on accessibility of art events and programs. **Publications:** *Enabled Courier*, quarterly.

★7093★ Graphic Artists Guild (GAG)
11 W. 20th St., 8th Fl.
New York, NY 10011
Ph: (212)463-7730   Fax: (212)463-8779
Members: Graphic, textile, and needleart designers; cartoonists, computer artists, production artists, and illustrators. **Purpose:** Promotes professional and economic interests of graphic artists. Seeks to establish standards for ownership rights, reproduction rights, business pratices, and copyrights. Has grievance procedure for members in disputes. Maintains artist-to-artist hot line, placement service, and speakers' bureau. Provides legal and accounting referrals and discount program for products and services. Offers specialized education in business school courses and seminars. **Publications:** *Directory of Illustration*, annual. • *Graphic Artists Guild Handbook: Pricing and Ethical Guidelines*, biennial. • *Graphic Artists Guild—National Newsletter*, quarterly. • *Graphic Artists Guild—The Update*, periodic.

★7094★ Graphic Artists Guild
Foundation (GAGF)
11 W. 20th St., 8th Fl.
New York, NY 10011
Ph: (212)463-7730   Fax: (212)463-8779
Members: Purpose: Goals are to stimulate public interest in graphic arts and to offer the public an opportunity to view and create graphic arts. Formulated ethical guidelines in the sponsorship of art competitions and contests. Sponsors training sessions, and lectures. Maintains graphic arts research center. Completed library of 12 Disability Access Symbols, available in print and digital formats.

★7095★ Grupo de Artistas Latino
Americanos (GALA)
21 W. 112th St., Apt 9J
New York, NY 10026
Members: Professional Latin American painters and sculptors. **Purpose:** Promotes appreciation, suppport, and recognition of Latin American art and artists. Organizes exhibitions of members' work. Conducts educational and research programs; maintains museum. **Publications:** *GALA in Action Newsletter*, 3/year.

★7096★ National Association of
Schools of Art and Design (NASAD)
11250 Roger Bacon Dr., Ste. 21
Reston, VA 22090
Ph: (703)437-0700 ·   Fax: (703)437-6312
Members: Serves as the accrediting agency for educational programs in the visual arts and design. **Purpose:** Aims are to: establish a national forum to stimulate the understanding and acceptance of the educational disciplines inherent in the creative arts in higher education in the U.S.; develop reasonable standards in areas of budget, faculty qualifications, faculty-student ratios, class time requirements, and library and physical facilities; evaluate, through the process of accreditation, schools of art and design and programs of studio art instruction in terms of the quality

and results they achieve; assure students and parents that accredited art and design programs provide competent teachers, adequate equipment, and sound curricula; assist schools in developing their programs and encourage self-evaluation and continuing self-improvement.

★7097★ Society of Illustrators (SI)
128 E. 63rd St.
New York, NY 10021
Ph: (212)838-2560   Fax: (212)838-2561
Members: Professional society of illustrators and art directors. Maintains Museum of American Illustration which sponsors continuous exhibits; holds annual exhibit (February-April) of best illustrations of the year; conducts benefit and sale in gallery in December. Awards annual scholarships to students of accredited college-level art schools. Participates in annual U.S. Air Force and U.S. Coast Guard exhibits. Maintains hall of fame. **Publications:** *Annual of American Illustration*, annual.

STANDARDS/CERTIFICATION AGENCIES

★7098★ Graphic Artists Guild (GAG)
11 W. 20th St., 8th Fl.
New York, NY 10011
Ph: (212)463-7730   Fax: (212)463-8779
Seeks to establish standards for ownership rights, reproduction rights, business pratices, and copyrights. Has grievance procedure for members in disputes.

TEST GUIDES

★7099★ Career Examination Series:
Illustrator
National Learning Corp.
212 Michael Dr.
Syosset, NY 11791
Ph: (516)921-8888   Fax: (516)921-8743
Fr: 800-645-6337
Jack Rudman. A series of study guides with multiple-choice examination questions and solutions for trainees and professional visual artists. Titles in the series include *Associate Graphic Artist; Graphic Arts Specialist; Principal Illustrator; Senior Illustrator.*

EDUCATIONAL DIRECTORIES AND PROGRAMS

★7100★ Advertising Career Directory
Gale Research Inc.
835 Penobscot Bldg.
Detroit, MI 48226-4094
Ph: (313)961-2242   Fax: (313)961-6083
Fr: 800-877-GALE

Bradley J. Morgan and Joseph M. Palmisano. Fifth edition, 1992. A directory in the Career Advisor Series that provides essays written by industry professionals; job search information on resume and cover letter preparation, networking, and the interviewing process; approximately 300 companies and organizations offering job opportunities and internships, and additional job-hunting resources.

★7101★ American Art Directory
R. R. Bowker Co.
121 Chanlon Rd.
New Providence, NJ 07974
Ph: (908)464-6800   Fax: (908)771-7704
Van Hudes, Marketing Director

Approximately biennial; latest edition March 1993; new edition expected December 1994. Covers over 7,000 museums, art libraries, and art organizations, and 1,700 art schools; also includes lists of state directors and supervisors of art education in schools, traveling exhibition booking agencies, corporations having art holdings for public viewing, newspapers that carry art notes, art scholarships and fellowships; and 190 national, regional, and state open art exhibitions. Entries include: For museums—Name, address, phone, fax, electronic mail address, name of curator; days and hours of operation, collection, budget, publications. For exhibits—Name, address, phone, fax, electronic mail address, name of contact; date, deadline. For schools—Name, address, phone, name of director, names of faculty members, majors or degrees offered, tuition Arrangement: Geographical.

★7102★ American Artist—Directory of Arts Schools and Workshops Issue
BPI Communications
1515 Broadway, 39th Fl.
New York, NY 10036
Ph: (212)536-5161   Fax: (212)536-5351
M. Stephen Doherty, Contact

Annual, March. Publication includes: Directory of arts schools, summer schools, private art teachers, and travel art workshops; limited international coverage. Entries include: For schools and workshops—Name, address, phone; workshops also give student-to-teacher ratio, courses available, whether scholarships are available, academic year, enrollment, number of faculty, memberships and accreditation; educational degrees available, number of students having received them during the previous year, additional information on itineraries, etc. Arrangement: Schools are geographical; teachers and workshops are alphabetical.

★7103★ Art in America—Guide to Galleries, Museums, and Artists
Brant Publications, Inc.
575 Broadway
New York, NY 10012
Ph: (212)941-2800
Janet Podell

Annual, August. Publication includes: List of over 3,700 museums, galleries, and other display areas. Entries include: Generally, name of exhibit area, address, phone, fax; name of director, artists exhibited, type of art exhibited, hours of operation, category code (gallery, private dealer, corporate consultant, museum, university museum/gallery, non-profit space); some include catalogs published and upcoming one-person shows. Arrangement: Geographical.

★7104★ Book Publishing Career Directory
Gale Research Inc.
835 Penobscot Bldg.
Detroit, MI 48226-4094
Ph: (313)961-2242   Fax: (313)961-6083
Fr: 800-877-GALE

Bradley J. Morgan and Joseph M. Palmisano. Fifth edition, 1992. A directory in the Career Advisor Series that provides essays written by industry professionals; job search information on resume and cover letter preparation, networking, and the interviewing process; approximately 300 companies and organizations offering job opportunities and internships, and additional job-hunting resources.

★7105★ Directory of MFA Programs in the Visual Arts
College Art Association
275 7th Ave.
New York, NY 10001
Ph: (212)691-1051   Fax: (212)627-2381
Virginia Wageman, Contact

Irregular, previous edition 1991; latest edition 1992. Covers master of Fine Arts degree programs offered at over 180 institutions. Entries include: Institution name, name of department, address; admission requirements, application deadline, areas of concentration, tuition, financial aid, degree requirements, faculty, curriculum, campus resources, studio space. Arrangement: Alphabetical.

★7106★ International Guide to Afrocentric Talent
Osborne Communications
18565 NE 1 Ct.
Miami, FL 33179
Ph: (305)654-8298
Eddie Osborne, Contact

Annual, winter. Covers Approximately 500 vocalists, musicians, dance and theatre troupes, speakers, storytellers, and other talent of African descent, theme, or focus; coverage includes the U.S., Canada, the Caribbean, Africa, Europe, and regions of the Pacific. Entries include: Organization or individual name, address, phone, name and title of contact, number of members (for groups), geographical area served, description. Arrangement: Classified by type of talent.

★7107★ Magazine Career Directory
Gale Research Inc.
835 Penobscot Bldg.
Detroit, MI 48226-4094
Ph: (313)961-2242   Fax: (313)961-6083
Fr: 800-877-GALE

Bradley J. Morgan and Joseph M. Palmisano. Fifth edition, 1993. A directory in the Career Advisor Series that provides essays written by industry professionals; job search information on resume and cover letter preparation, networking, and the interviewing process; approximately 300 companies and organizations offering job opportunities and internships, and additional job-hunting resources.

★7108★ National Association of Schools of Art and Design—Directory
National Association of Schools of Art and Design
11250 Roger Bacon Dr., No. 21
Reston, VA 22090
Ph: (703)437-0700   Fax: (703)437-6312

Annual, March. Covers approximately 180 independent and university-affiliated schools of art and design accredited by the association. Entries include: Institution name, address, phone, names of executives, major programs (drawing, graphic design, etc.) and duration, summer programs, degrees. Arrangement: Alphabetical.

★7109★ National Directory of Arts Internships
National Network for Artist Placement
935 W. Ave. 37
Los Angeles, CA 90065
Ph: (213)222-4035   Fax: (213)222-4035
Warren Christensen, Contact

Biennial, odd years. Covers Approximately 2,000 internship opportunities in dance, music, theater, art, design, film, and video. Entries include: Name of sponsoring organization, address, name of contact; description of positions available, eligibility requirements, stipend or salary (if any), application procedures. Arrangement: Classified by discipline, then geographical.

★7110★ National Guild of Community Schools of the Arts—Membership Directory
National Guild of Community Schools of the Arts
40 N. Van Brunt St., Rm. 32
PO Box 8018
Englewood, NJ 07631
Ph: (201)871-3337   Fax: (201)871-7639
Lolita Mayadas

Annual, July. Covers over 220 member schools, including community schools, social service centers, and collegiate divisions with programs in music, dance, drama, and visual arts; about 150 individual members, trustees, and board members; coverage includes Canada. Entries include: For schools—School name, address, phone, name and title of director, year established, year and status of NGCSA membership, number of branches (affiliate programs), areas of instruction, organizational affiliations, profile of school guild membership, special programs and classes, number of students. For individuals—Name, title, affiliation, address. Arrangement: Institutions are geographical; individuals are alphabetical.

★7111★ Newspapers Career Directory
Gale Research Inc.
835 Penobscot Bldg.
Detroit, MI 48226-4094
Ph: (313)961-2242   Fax: (313)961-6083
Fr: 800-877-GALE
Bradley J. Morgan and Joseph M. Palmisano. 1993. A directory in the Career Advisor Series that provides essays written by industry professionals; job search information on resume and cover letter preparation, networking, and the interviewing process; approximately 300 companies and organizations offering job opportunities and internships, and additional job-hunting resources.

★7112★ Radio and Television Career Directory
Gale Research Inc.
835 Penobscot Bldg.
Detroit, MI 48226-4094
Ph: (313)961-2242   Fax: (313)961-6083
Fr: 800-877-GALE
Bradley J. Morgan and Joseph M. Palmisano. Second edition, 1993. A directory in the Career Advisor Series that provides essays written by industry professionals; job search information on resume and cover letter preparation, networking, and the interviewing process; approximately 300 companies and organizations offering job opportunities and internships, and additional job-hunting resources.

★7113★ Technical Schools, Colleges and Universities Offering Courses in Graphic Communications
National Scholarship Trust Fund of the Graphic Arts
4615 Forbes Ave.
Pittsburgh, PA 15213-3796
Ph: (412)621-6941   Fax: (412)621-3049
M. Margaret Dimperio, Business Manager
Biennial, Odd years. Covers about 320 accredited technical schools, colleges, and universities in the U.S., Canada, and Puerto Rico. Entries include: School name, address, phone, name of contact; types of programs offered, degrees or certificates awarded. Arrangement: Geographical.

AWARDS, SCHOLARSHIPS, GRANTS, AND FELLOWSHIPS

★7114★ Benjamin Altman (Figure) Prize
National Academy of Design
1083 5th Ave.
New York, NY 10128
Ph: (212)369-4880   Fax: (212)360-6795
For recognition of achievement in figure paintings in oil by native born Americans. Monetary prizes of $3,000 and $1,500 are awarded annually at the Academy's Exhibition. Established in 1915.

★7115★ Benjamin Altman (Landscape) Prize
National Academy of Design
1083 5th Ave.
New York, NY 10128
Ph: (212)369-4880   Fax: (212)360-6795
For recognition of achievement in landscape paintings in oil by American born citizens. Monetary prizes of $3,000 and $1,500 are awarded annually at the Academy's Exhibition. Established in 1916.

★7116★ Annual Exhibition
Audubon Artists, Inc.
32 Union Sq. E., Studio 1214
New York, NY 10003
Ph: (212)260-5706
To recognize outstanding art displayed at the annual exhibition. Selection is based on works in oil, aquamedia, sculpture, and graphics. The following prizes are awarded annually: Medals of Honor and monetary awards; and silver medals. Established in 1942.

★7117★ Annual Open Exhibition
Catharine Lorillard Wolfe Art Club
c/o Karin Strong
PO Box 2734
Sag Harbor, NY 11963
Ph: (516)725-3103
To recognize outstanding women artists whose works exemplify the finest representations of contemporary traditional art. The entry deadline for slides is usually in July. Awards are given in some of the following categories: oil, watercolor, pastel, graphics, acrylics, and sculpture. Monetary awards totaling $5,000 are presented. Some of the awards presented are: the Catharine Lorillard Wolfe Medal of Honor - a $250 award in each of the four categories; the Anna Hyatt Huntington Bronze Medals - awarded in each of the four categories; the M. Grumbacher Silver Medallion - $200 for an oil or watercolor painting; and the Harriet W. Frishmuth Memorial Award - $200 for an oil or watercolor painting. Awarded annually. Established in 1896 by a group of women at Grace Church in New York to help the struggling, young, women art students.

★7118★ Randolph Caldecott Medal
American Library Association
Association for Library Service to Children
50 E. Huron St.
Chicago, IL 60611
Ph: (312)944-6780   Fax: (312)440-9374
For recognition of the most distinguished American picture book for children. Illustrators who are United States citizens or residents are eligible for books published in the United States during the preceding year. A bronze medal and possibly Caldecott Honor Books are awarded annually at the Newbery/Caldecott Awards celebration during ALA's annual conference. Established in 1937 by Frederic C. Melcher, the distinguished publisher who originated and first donated the bronze medals. The award is named in honor of Randolph Caldecott, the noted nineteenth century English illustrator.

★7119★ Cannon Prize
National Academy of Design
1083 5th Ave.
New York, NY 10128
Ph: (212)369-4880   Fax: (212)360-6795
For recognition of outstanding painting in watercolor by an American artist. A monetary prize of $400 is awarded annually at the Academy's Exhibition. Established in 1951.

★7120★ Andrew Carnegie Medal
American Library Association
Association for Library Service to Children
50 E. Huron St.
Chicago, IL 60611
Ph: (312)944-6780   Fax: (312)440-9374
To recognize a U.S. producer of the most distinguished video for children in the previous year. Established in 1991. Sponsored by Carnegie Corporation of New York.

★7121★ Creativity Show
Art Direction Book Company
10 E. 39th St., 6th Fl.
New York, NY 10016
Ph: (212)889-6500   Fax: (212)889-6504
To recognize outstanding visual professionals internationally and to commend the best work in advertising art, design, photography, or illustration during the preceding 12 months. The recipient must be an art director, advertising designer, photographer, or illustrator. Each year, the entire show is displayed in major cities. All material in print or on the air from May to May each year is eligible. The deadline for entry is May 4. Art directors are judged for concept and design. Artists, illustrators, photographers, and production houses are judged for art, photography, etc. All accepted entries are reproduced in the annual Creativity book, a worldwide volume. The Creativity Show is the annual showcase for the year's best work. Certificates of Distinction are awarded annually. Established in 1970.

★7122★ Emmy Awards for Primetime Programming
Academy of Television Arts and Sciences
5220 Lankershim Blvd.
North Hollywood, CA 91601
Ph: (818)754-2800   Fax: (818)761-2927
To recognize the advancement of the arts and sciences of television and achievements broadcast nationally during primetime. Awards are given in the following categories: (1) Program Category Awards - (a) Outstanding Comedy Series; (b) Outstanding Drama Series; (c) Outstanding Miniseries; (d) Outstanding Variety, Music, or Comedy Series; (e) Outstanding Made for T.V. Movie; (f) Outstanding Classical Program in the Performing Arts; (g) Outstanding Informational Special; (h) Outstanding Informational Series; (i) Outstanding Animated Program; and (j) Outstanding Children's Program; (2) Individual Awards - (a) Lead, Supporting, and Guest Acting in Comedy Series, Drama Series, Miniseries, or Special; (b) Performance in Variety or Music Program, Informational Programming, and Classical Music/Dance Programming; (c) Directing in Comedy Series, Drama Series, Variety or Music Program, Miniseries or Special, Classical Music/Dance Programming, and Informational Programming; (d) Casting for a Miniseries or Special;

(e) Writing in Comedy Series, Drama Series, Variety or Music Program, Miniseries or Special, Informational Programming, and Classical Music/Dance Programming; and (3) Technical Awards - (a) Choreography; (b) Cinematography; (c) Art Direction; (d) Music Composition; (e) Main Title Theme Music; (f) Music Direction; (g) Music and Lyrics; (h) Costume Design; (i) Costuming; (j) Makeup; (k) Hairstyling; (l) Editing; (m) Sound Editing; (n) Sound Mixing; (o) Technical Direction/Camera/Video; (p) Special Visual Effects; (q) Graphic Design and Title Sequences; (r) Lighting Direction; (s) Engineering Development; and (4) ATAS Governors Award. Nominees are voted upon by a jury. An Emmy statuette is presented annually at the Emmy Awards Ceremony. Established in 1948 and administered by the Academy of Television Arts and Sciences until 1977.

★7123★ Fine Arts Work Center Fellowships
Fine Arts Work Center in Provincetown
24 Pearl St.
Provincetown, MA 02657
Ph: (508)487-9960   Fax: (508)487-8873
Purpose: To encourage and support emerging artists and writers by giving them the freedom to work without distraction in a community of peers. Qualifications: Applicant may be any age, but the Center aims to help emerging talents who have completed their formal training and are already working on their own. Fellowships are based on the quality of the applicant's work. No other restrictions apply. Fellowships include a residency at the Center. Funds available: Small monthly stipend, plus living and studio space. Application details: Send a self-addressed stamped envelope with request for application form and guidelines; specify interest in writing or visual arts. Information on submission of creative works is included in the application forms. Deadline: February 1. Notification around May 1.

★7124★ Reuben Award: Rube Goldberg Award
National Cartoonists Society
PO Box 20267, Columbus Circle Sta.
New York, NY 10023
Ph: (212)627-1550
To honor the outstanding cartoonist of the year. Professional cartoonists are eligible. Submissions are not accepted. The Reuben, a bronze statuette designed by the late Rube Goldberg, is awarded annually in April. Established in 1946 in memory of Rube Goldberg, the first NCS President.

★7125★ Hoyt National Art Show
Hoyt Institute of Fine Arts
124 E. Leasure Ave.
New Castle, PA 16101
Ph: (412)652-2882
For recognition of art work of the highest quality and greatest diversity. Open to residents of the United States, 18 years of age or older, working in any fine arts medium, including fine arts, crafts, sculpture, and photography. Two and three-dimensional size limits must not exceed 48 inches in any direction. Up to three works may be entered. Juror selection is by 35mm slides. The deadline for entry is July 25. Monetary prizes are awarded in the following categories: First Prize - $500; Sec-

ond Prize \$300; Third Prize - \$100; The Grumbacher Corporation Award- a medal and a gift certificate; and Purchase Awards - usually exceeding \$3,000. Established in 1982.

★7126★ Joseph S. Isidor Memorial Medal
National Academy of Design
1083 5th Ave.
New York, NY 10128
Ph: (212)369-4880   Fax: (212)360-6795
For recognition of an outstanding figure composition painted in oil. American artists are eligible. A gold medal is awarded annually when merited at the Academy's Exhibition. Established in 1907.

★7127★ National Academy of Design Gold Medal
National Academy of Design
1083 5th Ave.
New York, NY 10128
Ph: (212)369-4880   Fax: (212)360-6795
For recognition of an outstanding work of sculpture or painting. Presented annually when merited at the Academy's Exhibition. Established in 1945.

★7128★ National Cartoonists Society Category Awards
National Cartoonists Society
PO Box 20267, Columbus Circle Sta.
New York, NY 10023
Ph: (212)627-1550
For recognition of distinguished attainment by professional cartoonists for published works in the following categories: advertising, animation, comic books, editorial cartoons, humor strips, illustration, magazines, special features, sports cartoons, story strips and syndicated panels. Submissions are not accepted. The best in each category is awarded a silver plaque. Awarded annually. Established in 1956.

★7129★ National Endowment for the Arts - Visual Artists Fellowships
National Endowment for the Arts
Visual Arts Program/Fellowships, Rm. 729
Nancy Hanks Center
1100 Pennsylvania Ave., NW
Washington, DC 20506-0001
Ph: (202)682-5422   Fax: (202)682-5699
Purpose: To encourage the creative development of professional artists by enabling them to set aside time to pursue their work. Qualifications: Fellowships are available to practicing professional artists of exceptional talent with demonstrated ability working in a wide variety of visual media, including painting, sculpture, photography, crafts, printmaking, drawing, artists books, video, performance art, conceptual art, and new genres. Applicants must be United States citizens or permanent residents. Funds available: Fellowships include awards from \$15,000 to \$20,000. Deadline: Application deadlines vary.

★7130★ National Society of Painters in Casein and Acrylic Awards
National Society of Painters in Casein and Acrylic
969 Catasauqua Rd.
Whitehall, PA 18052
To recognize outstanding works of art at the Society's annual exhibition. Monetary awards and medals are awarded annually. Established in 1954.

★7131★ Outdoor Writers Association of America Scholarship Awards
Outdoor Writers Association of America (OWAA)
2017 Cato Ave., Ste. 101
State College, PA 16801-2768
Ph: (814)234-1011   Fax: (814)234-9692
Purpose: To reward outstanding students who are working toward careers in outdoor writing, broadcasting, photography, or art. Qualifications: Applicants should be in their last two years of college or master's degree students in any accredited school of journalism or mass communication listed by the Association for Education in Journalism and Mass Communication, or those schools accepted on application to the Outdoor Writers Association of America. There shall be no more than one applicant from each school per school year. Each school will be responsible for selecting its candidate. Selection criteria: Judges look for applicants with talent, promise, and first-hand outdoor knowledge. Applications are rated on clarity, organization, and originality. Grade point average is considered. Funds available: The amount of the scholarship varies, but is usually at least \$3,000. Application details: An applicant must submit an OWAA application form, school recommendation, grade transcript, examples of outdoor communication work (including published samples), a one- to two-page statement by the nominee detailing career goals, and optional letters of recommendation from outdoor communicators or employers familiar with the applicant's work. The application package must be submitted to the Executive Director, Outdoor Writers Association of America. Deadline: March 1.

★7132★ Arthur Ross Awards
Classical America
227 E. 50th St.
New York, NY 10022
Ph: (212)753-4376
For recognition of contemporary contributions to the classical tradition in the arts. Painters, sculptors, architects, craftsmen, landscape architects, architectural renderers, gardeners, and patrons who are citizens of the United States are eligible. Mature work that exhibits a continued excellence and integrity in its application of classical ideals and canons is considered. Certificates are awarded annually at the National Academy of Design. Established in 1982 in honor of Arthur Ross.

★7133★ Augustus St. Gaudens Medal
Cooper Union for the Advancement of
  Science and Art
30 Cooper Sq.
New York, NY 10003-7120
Ph: (212)353-4164

To recognize professional achievement in art
and architecture. A committee evaluates past
achievements of the candidates for the
award. A medal is presented annually. Established in 1955 and named after one of America's leading sculptors, Augustus St.
Gaudens.

**★7134★ Lila Wallace-Reader's Digest
International Artists**
Arts International Program of the Institute of
  International Education
c/o Institute of International Education
809 University Plaza
New York, NY 10017
Ph: (212)984-5370

Purpose: To provide visual artists (painters,
sculptors, photographers, video artists, and
craft artists) with three- to six-month international residencies, followed by an active partnership with an arts organization in the U.S.
to present community programs based on the
artists' experiences abroad. Qualifications:
Applicants must be visual artists. The artist
must apply jointly with a sponsoring organization and work together to define their interests
and develop innovative, interactive, or collaborative approaches to the community activity
stage of the program. Funds available: Financial support to live, work and travel three- to
six-months. Application details: Guidelines
and application forms are available from Arts
International. Deadline: The 1992 deadline
was December 11.

BASIC REFERENCE GUIDES AND HANDBOOKS

**★7135★ Art in America—Guide to
Galleries, Museums, and Artists**
Brant Publications, Inc.
575 Broadway
New York, NY 10012
Ph: (212)941-2800

Steven Anzovin and Janet Podell, editors.
Annual, August. List of over 3,900 museums,
galleries, and other display areas. Entries include: Generally, name of exhibit area, address, phone, fax; name of director, artists
exhibited, up-coming one-person shows,
type of art exhibited, hours of operation; profit
or nonprofit status; and catalogs published.
Arrangement: Geographical. Indexes: Gallery/museum name, artist, catalog title (with
author, number of pages, and price). **Other
Information:**

**★7136★ Great Print Advertising:
Creative Approaches, Strategies, and
Tactics**
John Wiley and Sons, Inc.
605 3rd Ave.
New York, NY 10158-0012
Ph: (212)850-6000   Fax: (212)850-6088
Fr: 800-526-5368

Tony Antin. 1993. Gives detailed instructions
for developing print ads. Provides examples
of ads that work and those that don't, plus
explains the differences between them.

★7137★ The Oxford Dictionary of Art
Oxford University Press, Inc.
200 Madison Ave.
New York, NY 10016
Ph: (212)679-7300   Fr: 800-451-7556

Ian Chilvers, editor. 1994. Contains entries
on individual artists and definitions of art
terms.

**★7138★ The Thames and Hudson
Dictionary of Art and Artists**
Thames and Hudson, Inc.
500 5th Ave.
New York, NY 10110
Ph: (212)354-3763

Herbert Read. Revised edition, 1988.

PROFESSIONAL AND TRADE PERIODICALS

★7139★ American Artist
BPI Communications, Inc.
1515 Broadway, 14th Fl.
New York, NY 10036
Ph: (212)536-5336   Fax: (212)536-5336
Fr: 800-274-4100
M. Stephen Doherty

Monthly. Art and educational journal.

★7140★ Art in America
Brant Publications Inc.
575 Broadway
New York, NY 10012
Ph: (212)941-2800   Fax: (212)941-2885
Fr: 800-925-8055
Elizabeth C. Baker

Art magazine.

★7141★ Art Direction
Advertising Trade Publications, Inc.
10 E. 39th St., 6th Fl.
New York, NY 10016-0199
Ph: (212)889-6500   Fax: (212)889-6504
Dan Barron

Monthly. Magazine on advertising art and
photography.

★7142★ ARTnews Magazine
Art News Associates
48 W. 38th St.
New York, NY 10018
Ph: (212)398-1690   Fax: (212)768-4002
Milton Esterow

Monthly. News magazine reporting on art,
personalities, issues, trends, and events that
shape the international art world.

★7143★ ARTWEEK
12 S. 1st St., Ste. 520
San Jose, CA 95113-2404
Ph: (408)279-2293   Fax: (408)279-2432
Fr: 800-733-2916
Kitty SpauldingPublisher

Semiweekly. Magazine containing contemporary West Coast art, photography reviews,
commentary features, and interviews.

**★7144★ Board Report's Creative
Training**
American Professional Graphic Artists
PO Box 300789
Denver, CO 80203
Ph: (303)839-9058
Drew Allen Miller

Monthly. Serves graphic artists, designers,
printers, and advertising agencies. Consists
of three publications: The Graphic Artists
Newsletter, the Designer's Compendium,
and Trademark Trends. Provides creative
ideas and current trade information on a wide
range of subjects: new postal regulations, advertising claims and liability, tax tips for freelancers, current pay scales, how to run a
graphic communication business, and modern printing and bindery equipment. Recurring features include results of surveys, news
of research, statistics, reviews of fresh designs and trends, and indexed subsections
for rapid research.

★7145★ Contents
Contents
PO Box 8879
Savannah, GA 31412
Joseph Alfieris

Magazine covering art, design, literature and
music.

★7146★ Graphic Artists Guild—Interim
Mary M. Bono
Provides information of interest to Guild
members and others involved in the graphic
arts industry, especially in New York. Recurring features include a calendar of events.

**★7147★ Graphic Artists Guild Jobline
News**
Graphic Artists Guild
11 W. 20th St., 8th Fl.
New York, NY 10011-3704
Ph: (212)463-7759
Pamela Fehl

Weekly. Lists jobs for freelance artists in
areas such as graphic design, illustration,
and art education. Most jobs listed are in the
New York area.

★7148★ Graphic Arts Monthly
Cahners Publishing Co.
249 W. 17th St.
New York, NY 10011
Ph: (212)463-6759   Fax: (212)463-6734
Roger Ynostroza

Monthly. Magazine featuring commercial
printing and graphic arts.

★7149★ Graphic Design: USA
Kaye Publishing
1556 3rd Ave., Ste. 405
New York, NY 10128
Ph: (212)534-5500   Fax: (212)534-4415
Susan Benson

Monthly. Magazine reporting on creating and
producing advertising art.

PROFESSIONAL MEETINGS AND CONVENTIONS

★7150★ Arts and Crafts Annual Spring Easter Show and Sale
Finger Lakes Craftsmen Shows
1 Freshour Dr.
Shortsville, NY 14548
Ph: (716)289-9439   Fax: (716)289-9440
Annual. Always held Palm Sunday weekend at the Dome Center in Rochester, New York. **Dates and Locations:** 1996 Mar 30-31; Rochester, NY.

★7151★ Arts and Crafts Annual Summer Show and Sale
Finger Lakes Craftsmen Shows
1 Freshour Dr.
Shortsville, NY 14548
Ph: (716)289-9439   Fax: (716)289-9440
Annual. Always held during July at the Dome Center in Rochester, New York. **Dates and Locations:** 1996 Jul 27-28; Rochester, NY.

★7152★ Grafix
Conference Management Corp.
200 Connecticut Ave.
Norwalk, CT 06856-4990
Ph: (203)852-0500   Fax: (203)838-3710
Fr: 800-342-3238
Annual. Always held in New York, New York, during the fall at the Jacob K. Javits Convention Center.

★7153★ International Black Writers and Artists Convention
International Black Writers and Artists
PO Box 43576
Los Angeles, CA 90043
Ph: (415)532-6179
Annual.

OTHER SOURCES OF INFORMATION

★7154★ "Art/Fine Arts" in *Accounting to Zoology: Graduate Fields Defined*
Petersons Guides, Inc.
PO Box 2123
Princeton, NJ 08543-2123
Ph: (609)243-9111   Fax: (609)243-9150
Fr: 800-338-3282
Amy J. Goldstein, editor. Revised and updated, 1987. Defines 298 graduate and professional fields. Discusses types of graduate programs and degrees, graduate research, applied work, employment prospects, and

trends. Chapters include "Graphic Design" (p. 6) and "Illustration" (pp. 6-8).

★7155★ "Artist" in *Encyclopedia of Danger: Dangerous Professions* **(pp. 10-13)**
Chelsea House Publishers
1974 Sproul Rd., Ste. 400
Broomall, PA 19008
Ph: (215)353-5166   Fax: (215)359-1439
Missy Allen and Michel Peissel. 1993. Provides descriptions of 24 dangerous occupations, their risky characteristics, and safety precautions.

★7156★ The Artist's Resource Handbook
Allworth Press
10 E. 23rd St., Ste. 400
New York, NY 10010
Ph: (212)777-8395   Fax: (212)777-8261
Fr: 800-247-6553
1994.

★7157★ Careers by Design: A Headhunter's Secrets for Success and Survival in Graphic Design
Allworth Press
10 E. 23rd St., Ste. 400
New York, NY 10010
Ph: (212)777-8395   Fax: (212)777-8261
Fr: 800-247-6553
1993.

★7158★ Careers in the Visual Arts
Watson-Guptill Publications
1515 Broadway
New York, NY 10036
Ph: (212)764-7300   Fax: (212)536-5359
Fr: 800-451-1741
1993. A Guide to jobs, money, opportunities, and an artistic life.

★7159★ Color Drawing
Van Nostrand Reinhold
115 5th Ave.
New York, NY 10013
Michael E. Doyle. 1993.

★7160★ "Commercial and Graphic Artists" in *100 Best Jobs for the 1990s & Beyond*
Dearborn Financial Publishing, Inc.
520 N. Dearborn St.
Chicago, IL 60610-4354
Ph: (312)836-4400   Fax: (312)836-1021
Fr: 800-621-9621
Carol Kleiman. 1992. Describes 100 jobs ranging from accountants to veterinarians.. Each job profile includes such information as education, experience, and certification needed, salaries, and job search suggestions.

★7161★ The Complete Illustration Guide For Architects, Designers, Artists, and Students
Van Nostrand Reinhold
115 5th Ave.
New York, NY 10013
Larry Evans. 1993.

★7162★ The Graphic Artists Guild Handbook: Pricing and Ethical Guidelines
Graphic Artists Guild (GAG)
11 W. 20th St., 8th Fl.
New York, NY 10011
Ph: (212)463-7730
Sixth edition, 1994. Contains material on buying and selling art, pricing surveys, standard contract forms, and information on the laws that pertain to the graphic arts industry.

★7163★ Graphic Design
Watson-Guptill Publications
1515 Broadway
New York, NY 10036
Ph: (908)363-5679   Fr: 800-451-1741
B. Martin, editor. 1988. Annual.

★7164★ Guide to the National Endowment for the Arts, 1993-94
National Endowment of the Arts
Nancy Hanks Center, Rm. 803
1100 Pennsylvania Ave., NW
Washington, DC 20506
Ph: (202)682-5400
1993. Describes the overall purpose of each of the endowment's programs and outlines the types of support available in each funding category.

★7165★ How to Survive and Prosper as an Artist
Henry Holt and Co.
115 W. 18th St., 6th Fl.
New York, NY 10011
Ph: (212)886-9200
Third edition, 1992.

★7166★ The Painter Speaks
Greenwood Press Inc.
88 Post Rd., W
PO Box 5007
Westport, CT 06881
Ph: (203)226-3571   Fax: (203)222-1502
1993.

Actors, Directors, and Producers

Actors entertain and communicate with people through their interpretation of dramatic roles. They rely on facial and verbal expression as well as body motion for creative effect. **Directors** interpret plays or scripts. In addition, they usually conduct rehearsals and auditions and select cast members as well as direct the work of the cast and crew. Directors use their knowledge of acting, voice, and movement to achieve the best possible performance and usually approve the scenery, costumes, choreography, and music. **Producers** select plays or scripts and hire directors, principal members of the cast, and key production staff members. They negotiate contracts with artistic personnel, often dealing with collective bargaining agreements with labor unions. Producers also coordinate the activities of writers, directors, managers, and other personnel, arrange financing, and decide on the size of the production and its budget.

Salaries

Earnings of most actors from acting jobs are low because of irregular employment. Many actors supplement their incomes with other jobs. Similarly, salaries for directors vary widely depending on experience and genre. Producers, on the other hand, usually receive percentages of productions' earnings instead of salaries.

Actors, Broadway	$950/week minimum
Actors, off-Broadway	$340-$579/week minimum
Actors, motion picture and television	$485/day minimum
Directors, Broadway	$36,750/rehearsal period (5 weeks)
Directors, small dinner theaters and summer stock	$685-$1,311/week

Employment Outlook

Growth rate until the year 2005: Much faster than the average.

Actors, Directors, and Producers

★7177★ "Actors, Directors, and Producers" in *101 Careers: A Guide to the Fastest-Growing Opportunities* (pp.273-277)
John Wiley & Sons, Inc.
605 3rd Ave.
New York, NY 10158-0012
Ph: (212)850-6645   Fax: (212)850-6088
Michael Harkavy. 1990. Describes the nature of the job, working conditions, employment growth, qualifications, personal skills, projected salaries, and where to write for more information.

★7178★ "Actors, Directors, and Producers" in *America's 50 Fastest Growing Jobs* (pp. 29)
JIST Works, Inc.
720 N. Park Ave.
Indianapolis, IN 46202-3431
Ph: (317)264-3720   Fax: (317)264-3709
Fr: 800-648-5478
Michael J. Farr, compiler. 1994. Describes the 50 fastest growing jobs within major career clusters such as technicians, and marketing and sales. Each job profile explains the nature of the work, skills and abilities required, employment outlook, average earnings, related occupations, education and training requirements, and employment opportunities. Also contains career planning information and job search tips.

★7179★ "Actors", "Directors", and "Producers" in *Career Information Center* (Vol.3)
Simon and Schuster
200 Old Tappan Rd.
Old Tappan, NJ 07675
Fax: 800-445-6991   Fr: 800-223-2348
Richard Lidz and Linda Perrin, editorial directors. Fifth edition, 1993. A multi-volume set that profiles more than 600 occupations. Each occupational profile describes job duties, educational requirements, getting a job, advancement possibilities, employment outlook, working conditions, earnings and benefits, and sources of additional information.

★7180★ "Actors, Directors, and Producers" in *Occupational Outlook Handbook*
U.S. Government Printing Office
Superintendent of Documents
Washington, DC 20402
Ph: (202)512-1800   Fax: (202)512-2250
Biennial, 1994-95. Encyclopedia of careers describing about 250 occupations and comprising about 85 percent of all jobs in the economy. Occupations that require lengthy education or training are given the most attention. Each occupation's profile describes what the worker does on the job, working conditions, education and training requirements, advancement possibilities, job outlook, earnings, and sources of additional information.

★7181★ "Actors" in *Encyclopedia of Careers and Vocational Guidance* (Vol.2, pp. 5-8)
J.G. Ferguson Publishing Co.
200 W. Madison St., Ste. 300
Chicago, IL 60606
Ph: (312)580-5480   Fax: (312)580-4948
William E. Hopke, editor-in-chief. Ninth edition, 1993. Four-volume set that profiles 900 occupations and describes job trends in 74 industries. Includes career description, educational requirements, history of the job, methods of entry, advancement, employment outlook, earnings, conditions of work, social and psychological factors, and sources of further information.

★7182★ "Actors" and "Television Directors and Producers" in *American Almanac of Jobs and Salaries* (pp. 126, 192, 186)
Avon Books
1350 Avenue of the Americas
New York, NY 10019
Ph: (212)261-6800   Fr: 800-238-0658
John Wright, editor. Revised and updated, 1994-95. A comprehensive guide to the wages of hundreds of occupations in a wide variety of industries and organizations.

★7183★ *Career Opportunities in Television, Cable and Video*
Facts on File
460 Park Ave. S.
New York, NY 10016-7382
Ph: (212)683-2244   Fax: 800-678-3633
Fr: 800-322-8755
Maxine K. Reed and Robert M. Reed. Third edition, 1993. Includes information on employment and advancement prospects, education, experience and skills requiresn salary range, and tips for entry into the field.

★7184★ *Career Opportunities in Theater and the Performing Arts*
Facts on File
460 Park Ave. S.
New York, NY 10016-7382
Ph: (212)683-2244   Fax: 800-678-3633
Fr: 800-322-8755
Shelly Field. 1993. Guidebook offering complete career information for those entering the theater or any of the performing arts. Includes an index, appendices, bibliography, and glossary.

★7185★ "Directors, Film and Television" in *Career Discovery Encyclopedia* (Vol.2, pp. 106-107)
J.G. Ferguson Publishing Co.
200 W. Madison St., Ste. 300
Chicago, IL 60606
Ph: (312)580-5480   Fax: (312)580-4948
Russell E. Primm, editor-in chief. 1993. This six volume set contains two-page articles for 504 occupations. Each article describes job duties, earnings, and educational and training requirements. The whole set is arranged alphabetically by job title. Designed for junior high and older students.

★7186★ *The Director's Voice*
Theatre Communications Group
355 Lexington Ave.
New York, NY 10017
Ph: (212)697-5230
Arthur Bartow. 1988. Includes interviews with 21 directors who reveal their methods for collaborating with actors, designers, musicians, and playwrights. They also discuss how their training and early influences, as well as imagination and command of craft, impact their productions.

★7187★ "Entertainment and Leisure" in *Where the Jobs Are: The Hottest Careers for the 90s* (pp. 125-142)
Career Press
180 5th Ave.
Hawthorne, NJ 07507
Ph: (201)427-0229   Fax: (201)427-2037
Fr: 800-CAREER-1
Joyce Hadley. 1995. Offers a job-hunting strategy for the 1990s as well as descriptions of growing careers of the decade. Each profile includes general information, forecasts, growth, education and training, licensing requirements, and salary information.

★7188★ "Film/Audio/Video" in *Internships: 1995* (pp. 50-56)
Petersons Guides, Inc.
PO Box 2123
Princeton, NJ 08543-2123
Ph: (609)243-9111   Fax: (609)243-9150
Fr: 800-338-3282
Fifteen edition, 1995. Lists internship opportunities under six broad categories: communications, creative, performing, and fine arts, human services, international relations, business and technology, and public relations. Includes a special section on internships in Washington, DC. For each internship program, gives the name, phone number, contact person, description, eligibility requirements, and benefits.

★7189★ "Film Extra" in *Offbeat Careers: Directory of Unusual Work*
Ten Speed Press
PO Box 7123
Berkeley, CA 94707
Fax: (510)559-1629   Fr: 800-841-2665
Al Sacharov. 1991. Contains an occupational profile on acting. Describes places of employment, employment outlook, advantages and disadvantages of the work, and personal characteristics needed.

★7190★ "Film Production" in *Desk Guide to Training and Work Advertisement* (pp. 111-112)
Charles C. Thomas, Publisher
2600 S. 1st St.
Springfield, IL 62794-9265
Ph: (217)789-8980   Fax: (217)789-9130
Fr: 800-258-8980
Gail Baugher Kenstler. 1988. Describes alternative methods of gaining entry into an occupation through different types of educational programs, internships, and apprenticeships.

★7191★ *Film and Video Career Directory*
Gale Research Inc.
835 Penobscot Bldg.
Detroit, MI 48226
Ph: (313)961-2242   Fr: 800-877-GALE
1994. Profiles careers in the film and video industry.

★7192★ *For the Working Artists: A Survival Guide*
Warren Christianson
935 W. Ave. 37
Los Angeles, CA 90065
Ph: (213)222-4035
Judith Luther and Eric Vollmer. Second edition, 1991.

★7193★ *The Hand That Holds the Camera: Interviews With Women Film and Video Directors*
Garland Publishing Co., Inc.
717 5th Ave., Ste. 2500
New York, NY 10022
Ph: (212)751-7447   Fr: 800-627-6273
Lynn Fieldman Miller. 1988. Contains interviews with women directors who describe their own work and experiences in a traditionally male occupation.

★7194★ *How to Be a Working Actor: An Insider's Guide to Finding Jobs in Theatre, Film, and Television*
M. Evans and Co.
216 E. 49th St.
New York, NY 10017
Ph: (212)688-2810
Mari Lyn Henry and Lynne Rogers. Third edition, 1994. Gives advice on putting together a portfolio, finding leads, and dealing with agents and managers. Covers unions, interviewing, auditions, and screen tests.

★7195★ *How to Sell Yourself As an Actor*
Sweden Press
Box 1612
Studio City, CA 91614
Ph: (818)995-4250
K. Callan. Second edition, completely revised, 1990.

★7196★ *"Media Production" in Career Choices for the 90's for Students of Art* (pp. 132-158)
Walker and Co.
435 Hudson St.
New York, NY 10014
Ph: (212)727-8300   Fax: (212)727-0984
Fr: 800-289-2553
1990. Offers alternatives for students of art. Gives information about the job outlook and competition for entry-level candidates. Provides job-hunting tips.

★7197★ *"Media Production" in Encyclopedia of Career Choices for the 1990s: A Guide to Entry Level Jobs* (pp. 575-601)
Berkley Pub.
PO Box 506
East Rutherford, NJ 07073
Fax: (201)933-2316   Fr: 800-788-6262
1992. Describes entry-level careers in a variety of industries. Presents qualifications required, working conditions, salary, internships, and professional associations.

★7198★ *"Motion Picture Directors" in Encyclopedia of Careers and Vocational Guidance* (Vol.3, pp. 480-484)
J.G. Ferguson Publishing Co.
200 W. Madison St., Ste. 300
Chicago, IL 60606
Ph: (312)580-5480   Fax: (312)580-4948
William E. Hopke, editor-in-chief. Ninth edition, 1993. Four-volume set that profiles 900 occupations and describes job trends in 74 industries. Includes career description, educational requirements, history of the job, methods of entry, advancement, employment outlook, earnings, conditions of work, social and psychological factors, and sources of further information.

★7199★ *"Motion Picture Producers" in Encyclopedia of Careers and Vocational Guidance* (Vol.3, pp. 485-487)
J.G. Ferguson Publishing Co.
200 W. Madison St., Ste. 300
Chicago, IL 60606
Ph: (312)580-5480   Fax: (312)580-4948
William E. Hopke, editor-in-chief. Ninth edition, 1993. Four-volume set that profiles 900 occupations and describes job trends in 74 industries. Includes career description, educational requirements, history of the job, methods of entry, advancement, employment outlook, earnings, conditions of work, social and psychological factors, and sources of further information.

★7200★ *Opportunities in Acting Careers*
National Textbook Co. (NTC)
VGM Career Books
4255 W. Touhy Ave.
Lincolnwood, IL 60646-1975
Ph: (708)679-5500   Fax: (708)679-2494
Fr: 800-323-4900
Dick Moore. Revised edition, 1993. Describes acting positions in show business; discusses how much actors earn, unions, working with agents, and schools. Gives advice on how to get started. Includes a bibliography.

★7201★ *Opportunities in Performing Arts Careers*
National Textbook Co. (NTC)
VGM Career Books
4255 W. Touhy Ave.
Lincolnwood, IL 60646-1975
Ph: (708)679-5500   Fax: (708)679-2494
Fr: 800-323-4900
Bonnie Bjorguine Bekken. 1991. Overviews the exciting world of performing arts, including opportunities in classical and popular music; theater, television, and movie acting; dance; performance art; and teaching and therapy. Also offers information on developing a portfolio and preparing for auditions.

★7202★ *"Producer/Director of Radio, Television, Movies, and Theater" in VGM's Careers Encyclopedia* (pp. 370-373)
National Textbook Co. (NTC)
VGM Career Books
4255 W. Touhy Ave.
Lincolnwood, IL 60646-1975
Ph: (708)679-5500   Fax: (708)679-2494
Fr: 800-323-4900
Third edition, 1991. Profiles 200 occupations. Describes job duties, places of employment, working conditions, qualifications, education and training, advancement potential, and salary for each occupation.

★7203★ *"Producers, Film and Television" in Career Discovery Encyclopedia* (Vol.5, pp. 88-89)
J.G. Ferguson Publishing Co.
200 W. Madison St., Ste. 300
Chicago, IL 60606
Ph: (312)580-5480   Fax: (312)580-4948
Russell E. Primm, editor-in chief. 1993. This six volume set contains two-page articles for 504 occupations. Each article describes job duties, earnings, and educational and training requirements. The whole set is arranged alphabetically by job title. Designed for junior high and older students.

★7204★ *Program Directors, Radio and Television*
Chronicle Guidance Publications, Inc.
66 Aurora St.
PO Box 1190
Moravia, NY 13118-1190
Ph: (315)497-0330   Fax: (315)497-3359
Fr: 800-622-7284
1991. Career brief describing the nature of the job, working conditions, hours and earnings, education and training, licensure, certification, unions, personal qualifications, social and psychological factors, location, employment outlook, entry methods, advancement, and related occupations.

★7205★ *Television Directors*
Careers, Inc.
PO Box 135
Largo, FL 34649-0135
Ph: (813)584-7333
1992. Four-page brief describing duties, working conditions, personal qualifications, training, earnings and hours, employment outlook, places of employment, related careers, and where to write for more information.

★7206★ *"Television Programming and Production" in Television and Video: A VGM Career Planner* (pp. 32-43)
National Textbook Co. (NTC)
VGM Career Books
4255 W. Touhy Ave.
Lincolnwood, IL 60646-1975
Ph: (708)679-5500   Fax: (708)679-2494
Fr: 800-323-4900
Shonan Noronha. 1989. Describes career opportunities in broadcasting organizations. Discusses working conditions, compensation, education, professional development and job-search strategies.

★7207★ "Theatre" in *Internships: 1995* (pp. 166-196)
Petersons Guides, Inc.
PO Box 2123
Princeton, NJ 08543-2123
Ph: (609)243-9111   Fax: (609)243-9150
Fr: 800-338-3282
Fifteenth edition, 1995. Lists internship opportunities under six broad categories: communications, creative, performing, and fine arts, human services, international relations, business and technology, and public relations. Includes a special section on internships in Washington, DC. For each internship program, gives the name phone number, contact person, description, eligibility requirements, and benefits.

★7208★ *The Working Actor: A Guide to the Profession*
Viking Penguin
375 Hudson St.
New York, NY 10014
Ph: (212)366-2000
Katinka Matson, editor. Revised edition, 1993. Includes information on education, training, where to find work, auditioning, screen testing, and factys about unions, agents, and managers.

PROFESSIONAL ASSOCIATIONS

★7209★ Actors' Equity Association (AEA)
165 W. 46th St.
New York, NY 10036
Ph: (212)869-8530   Fax: (212)719-9815
Members: AFL-CIO. **Purpose:** Represents professional actors and stage managers. Maintains Actors' Equity Foundation that makes awards and grants to organizations or charities that work in the best interests of theatre. **Publications:** *Equity News*, 10/year.

★7210★ Aspiring Actors Club
PO Box 2203
Carmichael, CA 95609
Ph: (916)488-3011
Members: Aspiring actors. **Purpose:** Offers the opportunity for aspiring actors to meet each other. Displays photographs and information on aspiring actors. **Publications:** *Aspiring Actors Newsletter*, quarterly.

★7211★ Directors Guild of America (DGA)
7920 Sunset Blvd.
Hollywood, CA 90046
Ph: (310)289-2000   Fax: (310)289-2029
Members: Purpose: Independent. Negotiates agreements for members. **Publications:** *Directory of Members*, annual.

★7212★ National Association of Schools of Theatre (NAST)
11250 Roger Bacon Dr., Ste. 21
Reston, VA 22090
Ph: (703)437-0700   Fax: (703)437-6312
Purpose: Accrediting agency for postsecondary educational programs in theatre. Seeks to improve educational practices and maintain high professional standards in theatre education. Counsels and assists institutions in developing their programs, and encourages the cooperation of professional theatre groups and individuals in the formulation of appropriate curricula and standards. Compiles statistics.

★7213★ Theatre Communications Group (TCG)
355 Lexington Ave.
New York, NY 10017
Ph: (212)697-5230   Fax: (212)983-4847
Members: Service organization for nonprofit professional theatres and theatre artists, administrators, and technicians; associate members include smaller, emerging and educational theatres. **Purpose:** Objectives are to: foster cooperation, information sharing, and interaction among members; expand the artistic and administrative capabilities of the professional theatre; develop public awareness and appreciation of the theatre's role in society; act as a resource for the press, funding sources, and government agencies. Operates the National Theatre Artist Residency Program which bestows up to 10 grants of $100,000 annually to nonprofit professional theatres to enable one or more artists to spend substantial time in residence at each grantee institution, as well as other grants and fellowships. Conducts research; assists theatres in the areas of budgeting, long-range planning, fundraising, and advocacy. Operates play distribution service; offers advisory and consultation services; sponsors symposia, workshops, conferences, and seminars. Maintains artist and theatre resource files. **Publications:** *American Theatre Magazine*, monthly. • *Art SEARCH*, biweekly. • *Dramatists Sourcebook*, annual. • *Plays in Process*, bimonthly. • *Survey*, annual. • *Theatre Directory*, annual. • *Theatre Profiles*, biennial.

TEST GUIDES

★7214★ *Drama and Theatre*
National Learning Corp.
212 Michael Dr.
Syosset, NY 11791
Ph: (516)921-8888   Fax: (516)921-8743
Fr: 800-645-6337
Jack Rudman. Undergraduate Program Field Test series. A practice examination fashioned after tests given in the Regents External Degree Program. Designed to measure knowledge received outside the college classroom in the subject of drama and theatre. Contains multiple-choice questions; provides solutions.

EDUCATIONAL DIRECTORIES AND PROGRAMS

★7215★ *Advertising Career Directory*
Gale Research Inc.
835 Penobscot Bldg.
Detroit, MI 48226-4094
Ph: (313)961-2242   Fax: (313)961-6083
Fr: 800-877-GALE
Bradley J. Morgan and Joseph M. Palmisano. Fifth edition, 1992. A directory in the Career Advisor Series that provides essays written by industry professionals; job search information on resume and cover letter preparation, networking, and the interviewing process; approximately 300 companies and organizations offering job opportunities and internships, and additional job-hunting resources.

★7216★ *CRTentertainment*
Sofprotex
PO Box 271
Belmont, CA 94002
Current. Diskette; requires a FileMaker compatible database. Covers over 500 theatrical agencies and entertainment industry organizations and 1,000 movie stars, musicians, producers, directors, and writers in the U.S. Database includes: Name, home address, business address and phone.

★7217★ *Directory of Theatre Programs*
Association for Communication
   Administration
5105 Backlick Rd., No. 6
Annandale, VA 22003
Ph: (703)750-0533   Fax: (703)914-9471
Jim Gaudino, Contact
Biennial, fall of odd years. Covers about 775 university and college programs in theater in the United States and Canada. Entries include: Name of institution, address, phone, name of theater program administrator, graduate and undergraduate areas of study in theater (coded), degrees offered, number of students per degree program, number of full-time and part-time faculty. Arrangement: Geographical.

★7218★ *Directory of Theatre Training Programs*
American Theatre Works, Inc.
PO Box 519
Dorset, VT 05251
Ph: (802)867-2223   Fax: (802)867-0144
Jill Charles, Contact
Biennial, fall of odd years. Covers 381 colleges, universities, and conservatories offering theater study programs at undergraduate and graduate levels. Entries include: Institute name, address, phone, contact person, degree offered, description of faculty and curriculum, Tuition fees, available scholarships, type of productions presented, theatrical facilities, methods and aim of training. Arrangement: Geographical.

★7219★ Dramatics Magazine—Summer Theatre Directory Issue
International Thespian Society
3368 Central Pkwy.
Cincinnati, OH 45225
Ph: (513)559-1996
Don Corathers, Contact

Annual, February. Publication includes: List of over 150 study and performance opportunities in summer schools and summer theater education programs. Entries include: Organization, school or group name, address, phone, name of contact; description of program, dates, requirements, cost, financial aid availability, etc. Arrangement: Geographical.

★7220★ Hollywood Who's Who: The Actors and Directors in Today's Hollywood
Continuum Publishing Corp.
370 Lexington Ave.
New York, NY 10017
Ph: (212)953-5858   Fax: (615)793-3915
Fr: 800-937-5557
Robyn Karney

Published 1993. Covers over 600 actors and directors, including legends and recent stars, most still active in Hollywood. Entries include: Name, biographical data, career description, film credits. No addresses are given. Arrangement: Alphabetical..

★7221★ Performing Arts Career Directory
Gale Research Inc.
835 Penobscot Bldg.
Detroit, MI 48226
Ph: (313)961-2242   Fr: 800-877-GALE
1994. Profiles careers in the performing arts industry.

★7222★ Regional Theatre Directory 1994-1995: A National Guide to Employment in Regional Theatres
Theatre Directories
PO Box 519
Dorset, VT 05251
Ph: (802)867-2223
Jill Charles, C. Barrack Evans, and Gene Sirotof, editors. 1994. Gives job-hunting tips and information on unions, contracts, and auditions.

★7223★ Summer Theater Directory
American Theatre Works, Inc.
PO Box 519
Dorset, VT 05251
Ph: (802)867-2223   Fax: (802)867-0144
Jill Charles, Contact

Annual, December. Covers summer theater companies that offer employment opportunities in acting, design, production, and management; summer theater training programs. Entries include: Co. name, address, phone, name and title of contact; type of company, activities and size of house; whether union affiliated, whether nonprofit or commercial; year established; hiring procedure and number of positions hired annually, season; description of stage; internships; description of company's artistic goals and audience. Arrangement: Geographical.

★7224★ University Resident Theatre Association—Directory
University Resident Theatre Association
1560 Broadway, Ste. 903
New York, NY 10036
Ph: (212)221-1130   Fax: (212)869-2752
Gina Cesari, Director of Operations

Annual. Covers over 32 member colleges, universities, and resident theaters organized to promote professionalism among graduate training programs in theatre. Entries include: Institution name, address; name and phone of contact; description of program, positions available, tuitions, stipends, terms. Arrangement: Alphabetical.

AWARDS, SCHOLARSHIPS, GRANTS, AND FELLOWSHIPS

★7225★ Academy Awards of Merit (Oscar)
Academy of Motion Picture Arts and Sciences
8949 Wilshire Blvd.
Beverly Hills, CA 90211
Ph: (310)247-3000   Fax: (310)859-9351

To recognize outstanding achievements in connection with motion pictures. Awards are presented in the following categories: Acting - best performance by an actor and actress in a leading role; best performance by an actor and actress in a supporting role; Art Direction; Cinematography; Costume Design; Directing; Documentary - feature and short subject; Film Editing; Foreign Language Film; Makeup; Music - best original score, original song score, and best original song; Best Picture; Short Films - animated and live action; Sound; Sound Effects Editing; Visual Effects; and Writing - best screenplay written directly for the screen; and best screenplay based on material previously produced or published. An Award of Merit in the form of a gold statuette, known as the "Oscar", is presented in each category. Awarded annually at a gala event. Established in 1927.

★7226★ American Film and Video Festival Awards
American Film and Video Association
8050 Millawake
PO Box 48659
Niles, IL 60714
Ph: (708)698-6440

To recognize outstanding films and tapes produced within the preceding two calendar years and presented at the American Film Festival. Awards are given in several dozen categories such as fine arts, literature, social studies, religion and society, etc. The following prizes are awarded annually in each category: Blue Ribbon Awards for first place; and Red Ribbon Awards for second place. Established in 1959.

★7227★ Award of Excellence
Film Advisory Board
1727 1/2 N. Sycamore
Hollywood, CA 90028
Ph: (213)874-3644   Fax: (213)969-0635

Three awards are presented in the following catagories: to recognize motion pictures, television programs, and videos as excellent family entertainment; to recognize the "Most Promising Young Newcomer" in the areas of film and television, and audio tapes, books, and inventions pertaining to the entertainment industry; and to recognize celebrities for their contributions to entertainment. Tapes may be submitted at any time. A plaque is awarded monthly. Established in 1975.

★7228★ Frank Capra Achievement Award
Directors Guild of America
7920 Sunset Blvd.
Los Angeles, CA 90046-0907
Ph: (310)289-2038   Fax: (310)289-2024

For recognition of a unit production manager or assistant director for a history of service to the guild and to the industry. A plaque is awarded when merited. Established in 1980.

★7229★ Clarence Derwent Award
Actors' Equity Foundation
165 W. 46th St.
New York, NY 10036
Ph: (212)869-8530   Fax: (212)921-8454

To recognize the most promising female and male actors on the New York Metropolitan scene. A monetary award of $1,000 and an engraved crystal memento are awarded to each person annually. Established in 1944 by Clarence Derwent, distinguished actor and former president of Actors' Equity Association.

★7230★ Emmy Awards for Daytime Programming
National Academy of Television Arts and Sciences
111 W. 57th St., Ste. 1020
New York, NY 10019
Ph: (212)586-8424

For recognition of outstanding daytime program and individual achievements that advance the arts and sciences of television. A gold Emmy statuette is awarded annually. Established in 1974.

★7231★ Emmy Awards for Primetime Programming
Academy of Television Arts and Sciences
5220 Lankershim Blvd.
North Hollywood, CA 91601
Ph: (818)754-2800   Fax: (818)761-2927

To recognize the advancement of the arts and sciences of television and achievements broadcast nationally during primetime. Awards are given in the following categories: (1) Program Category Awards - (a) Outstanding Comedy Series; (b) Outstanding Drama Series; (c) Outstanding Miniseries; (d) Outstanding Variety, Music, or Comedy Series; (e) Outstanding Made for T.V. Movie; (f) Outstanding Classical Program in the Performing Arts; (g) Outstanding Informational Special; (h) Outstanding Informational Series; (i) Outstanding Animated Program; and (j) Outstanding Children's Program; (2) Individual Awards - (a) Lead, Supporting, and Guest

Acting in Comedy Series, Drama Series, Miniseries, or Special; (b) Performance in Variety or Music Program, Informational Programming, and Classical Music/Dance Programming; (c) Directing in Comedy Series, Drama Series, Variety or Music Program, Miniseries or Special, Classical Music/Dance Programming, and Informational Programming; (d) Casting for a Miniseries or Special; (e) Writing in Comedy Series, Drama Series, Variety or Music Program, Miniseries or Special, Informational Programming, and Classical Music/Dance Programming; and (3) Technical Awards - (a) Choreography; (b) Cinematography; (c) Art Direction; (d) Music Composition; (e) Main Title Theme Music; (f) Music Direction; (g) Music and Lyrics; (h) Costume Design; (i) Costuming; (j) Makeup; (k) Hairstyling; (l) Editing; (m) Sound Editing; (n) Sound Mixing; (o) Technical Direction/Camera/Video; (p) Special Visual Effects; (q) Graphic Design and Title Sequences; (r) Lighting Direction; (s) Engineering Development; and (4) ATAS Governors Award. Nominees are voted upon by a jury. An Emmy statuette is presented annually at the Emmy Awards Ceremony. Established in 1948 and administered by the Academy of Television Arts and Sciences until 1977.

★7232★ Golden Globe Awards
Hollywood Foreign Press Association
292 S. LaCienega Blvd., Ste. 316
Beverly Hills, CA 90211
Ph: (310)657-1731   Fax: (310)657-5576

This, the highest award of the organization, is given for recognition of outstanding efforts in the entertainment field. Awards are given for motion pictures and television in the following categories: best motion picture - drama; best motion picture - musical/comedy; best foreign language film; best performance by an actress in a motion picture - drama; best performance by an actor in a motion picture - drama; best performance by an actress in a motion picture - comedy/musical; best performance by an actor in a motion picture - comedy/musical; best performance by an actress in a supporting role in a motion picture; best performance by an actor in a supporting role in a motion picture; best director - motion picture; best screenplay - motion picture; best original score - motion picture; best original song - motion picture; best television series - drama; best television series - comedy/musical; best mini-series or motion picture made for television; best performance by an actress in a television series - drama; best performance by an actor in a television series - drama; best performance by an actress in a television series musical/comedy; best performance by an actor in a television series - musical/comedy; best performance by an actress in a mini-series. or motion picture made for television; best performance by an actor in a mini-series, or motion picture made for television; best performance by an actress in a supporting role in a series, mini-series, or motion picture made for television; and best performance by an actor in a supporting role in a series, mini-series, or motion picture made for television. Golden Globe statuettes are awarded annually. Established in 1944.

★7233★ David Wark Griffith Awards
National Board of Review of Motion
  Pictures
PO Box 589
New York, NY 10021
Ph: (212)628-1594

To recognize outstanding accomplishment in motion pictures. The following awards are presented: (1) Best Picture Award - to increase public awareness of the meritorious aspects of movies. Awarded annually. Established in 1917; (2) Best Actor Award. Awarded annually. Established in 1945; (3) Best Actress Award. Awarded annually. Established in 1945; (4) Best Director Award. Awarded annually. Established in 1945; (5) Best Foreign Film Award. Awarded annually. Established in 1930; (6) Best Supporting Actor Award. Awarded annually. Established in 1954; (7) Best Supporting Actress award. Awarded annually. Established in 1954; (8) Best Television Film Award. Established in 1980; (9) Career Achievement Award. Established in 1980; (10) Ten Best Awards - for the ten most outstanding American motion pictures of the year. Awarded annually. Established in 1930. The awards consist of shield-shaped brass and walnut plaques. The awards program was renamed in 1980 to honor David Wark Griffith, the noted pioneer director.

★7234★ Kennedy Center Honors
John F. Kennedy Center for the Performing
  Arts
Washington, DC 20566
Ph: (202)416-8000   Fax: (202)416-8205

To recognize individuals for their distinguished artistic achievements and career contributions to American culture. The primary criterion in the selection of the recipients is artistic achievement as a performer, composer, choreographer, playwright, director or conductor. Honorees are nominated by the Artists Committee in the areas of dance, music, theater, opera, motion pictures and television. Final selection is made by the Kennedy Center Board of Trustees. A unique beribboned medal, created for the Kennedy Center Honors, is awarded each year at an annual celebration consisting of a traditional Board of Trustees dinner and an Honors Gala performance, preceeded by a reception hosted by the President of the United States. Established in 1978. Additional information is available from Laura Langley, phone: (202) 416-8430.

★7235★ OBIE Awards
The Village Voice
Promotion Dept.
842 Broadway
New York, NY 10003
Ph: (212)475-3300   Fax: (212)475-8947

To recognize achievement in Off and Off-Off Broadway theatre. Awards are given in the following categories: Best New American Play, Sustained Achievement, Sustained Excellence of Performance, Performance, Direction, Sustained Excellence of Lighting Design, Lighting Design, and Set and Costume Design. All Off and Off-Off Broadway theatres are eligible. Monetary prizes, certificates, and cash grants are presented annually at the OBIE awards ceremony. Established in 1955 by the Plumsock Fundand *The Village Voice*.

★7236★ Outstanding Directorial Achievement Award for Feature Films
Directors Guild of America
7920 Sunset Blvd.
Los Angeles, CA 90046-0907
Ph: (310)289-2038   Fax: (310)289-2024

For recognition of outstanding directorial achievement in a feature film. Directors of feature films released in the New York and Los Angeles areas during the year are eligible. A gold medallion is awarded annually. Established in 1948.

★7237★ Outstanding Directorial Achievement Award for Television
Directors Guild of America
7920 Sunset Blvd.
Los Angeles, CA 90046-0907
Ph: (310)289-2038   Fax: (310)289-2024

For recognition of outstanding directorial achievement in the following categories in television: Comedy Series, Dramatic Series - Night, Musical/Variety, Documentary/Actuality, and Dramatic Specials. Directors of television programs presented during the year are eligible. A gold medallion is awarded annually. Established in 1953.

★7238★ Student Academy Awards
Academy of Motion Picture Arts and
  Sciences
8949 Wilshire Blvd.
Beverly Hills, CA 90211
Ph: (310)247-3000   Fax: (310)859-9351

To recognize a student for an outstanding achievement in student filmmaking in the animation, documentary, dramatic, or experimental categories. Films of any length in 16mm or larger completed in a student-teacher relationship in a curricular structure of institutions of higher learning are eligible. Gold, silver, and bronze trophies are awarded annually. Established in 1973.

BASIC REFERENCE GUIDES AND HANDBOOKS

★7239★ *Acting From the Ultimate Consciousness*
Putnam Publishing Group, Inc.
200 Madison Ave.
New York, NY 10016
Ph: (212)951-8400
Eric Morris. 1992.

★7240★ *Acting Step by Step*
Resource Publications, Inc.
160 E. Virginia St., Ste. 290
San Jose, CA 95112
Ph: (408)286-8505
Marshall Cassady. 1988. Includes bibliographical references.

★7241★ *Actor*
Warner Books, Inc.
Time & Life Bldg.
1271 Avenue of the Americas
New York, NY 10020
Ph: (212)522-7200
Parnell Hall, editor. 1994.

★7242★ The Actor: A Practical Guide to a Professional Career
Donald I. Fine, Inc.
19 W. 21st St.
New York, NY 10010
Ph: (212)727-3270   Fr: 800-331-4624
Eve Brandstein and Joanna Lipari. 1987.

★7243★ The Actor and The Text
Applause Theatre Book Publishers
211 W. 71st St.
New York, NY 10023
Ph: (212)595-4735
Cicely Berry. Revised edition, 1992.

★7244★ The Actor's Book of Classical Monologues
Penguin Books
375 Hudson St.
New York, NY 10014
Ph: (212)366-2000
Stefan Rudnicki, editor. 1988.

★7245★ The Back Stage Handbook for Performing Artists
Waton-Guptill Publications, Inc.
1515 Broadway
New York, NY 10036
Ph: (212)764-7300
Sherry Eaker, editor. 1991.

★7246★ Directing Television and Film
Wadsworth Publishing Co.
10 Davis Dr.
Belmont, CA 94002
Ph: (415)595-2350
Alan A. Armer. Second edition, 1990. Includes a bibliography and an index.

★7247★ Feature Filmmaking at Used-Car Prices
Viking Penguin, Inc.
375 Hudson St.
New York, NY 10014
Ph: (212)366-2000
Rick Schmidt. 1988.

★7248★ The Film Producer
Saint Martin's Press, Inc.
175 5th Ave.
New York, NY 10010
Ph: (212)674-5151
Paul N. Lazarus, III, editor. 1992.

★7249★ Film Producers, Studios, Agents & Casting Directors Guide
Lone Eagle Publishing Co.
9903 Santa Monica Blvd., Ste. 204
Beverly Hills, CA 90212
Ph: (310)471-8066
Susan Avallone, editor. Fourth edition, 1994.

★7250★ Film Producers, Studios & Agents Guide
Lone Eagle Publishing Co.
9903 Santa Monica Blvd., Ste. 204
Beverly Hills, CA 90212
Ph: (213)471-8066
Second edition, 1994.

★7251★ Making Movies
Dell Publishing Co.
1540 Broadway
New York, NY 10036
Ph: (212)354-6500
John Russo. 1989. Includes bibliography and an index.

★7252★ New York Casting and Survival Guide
Peter Glenn Publications Ltd.
17 E. 48th St.
New York, NY 10017
Ph: (212)688-7940   Fr: 800-223-1254
Peter Glenn and Chip Brill, editors. Annual. 1993.

★7253★ On Performing: A Handbook for Actors, Dancers, Singers on the Musical Stage
McGraw-Hill, Inc.
1221 Avenue of the Americas
New York, NY 10020
Ph: (212)512-2000   Fr: 800-722-4726
David Craig. 1987.

★7254★ The Practical Director
Focal Press
80 Montvale Ave.
Stoneham, MA 02180
Ph: (617)438-8464   Fax: (617)438-1979
Mike Crisp, editor. 1993.

★7255★ The Producer's Masterguide 1995: The International Production Manual for Motion Pictures, Broadcast Television, Commercials . . .
New York Production Manual, Inc.
611 Broadway, Ste. 807
New York, NY 10012-2608
Ph: (212)777-4002
Shmuel Bension, editor. Fifteenth edition, 1995. Contains information about laws and unions in the film industry.

★7256★ The Shifting Point, 1946-1987
Harper & Row Publishers, Inc.
10 E. 53rd St.
New York, NY 10022
Ph: (212)207-7000
Peter Brook. 1989. Includes an index.

★7257★ The Technique of Acting
Bantam Books
666 5th Ave.
New York, NY 10103
Ph: (212)765-6500
Stella Adler. 1990.

★7258★ Television Production
McGraw-Hill, Inc.
1221 Avenue of the Americas
New York, NY 10020
Ph: (212)512-2000   Fr: 800-722-4726
Alan Wurtzel and Stephen R. Acker. Third revised edition, 1989. Covers the equipment, processes, and techniques of television production.

★7259★ Working Actors: The Craft of Televison, Film, & Stage Performance
Focal Press
Butterworth Publishers
80 Montvale Ave.
Stoneham, MA 02180
Ph: (617)438-8464   Fax: (617)438-1479
Richard A. Blum. 1989.

PROFESSIONAL AND TRADE PERIODICALS

★7260★ American Theatre
Theatre Communications Group
355 Lexington Ave.
New York, NY 10017
Ph: (212)697-5230   Fax: (212)983-4847
Jim O'Quinn
Monthly. Magazine containing news, features, and opinion on American and international theatre. Full length play published seven times a year.

★7261★ Dramatists Guild—Newsletter
Dramatists Guild
234 W. 44th St.
New York, NY 10036
Ph: (212)398-9366   Fax: (212)944-0420
Jason Milligan
Contains news of Guild activities, including symposia, seminars, regional theater activity, playwriting contests and workshops, and playreading units. Offers information on organizations which are looking for new plays. Features business advice columns, articles on taxes for the writer, and other related pieces.

★7262★ Dramatists Guild Newsletter
Authors Guild/Dramatists Guild, Inc.
234 W. 44th St.
New York, NY 10036-3988
Ph: (212)398-9366
Scott Segal, Contact
Provides members with information on the artistic and business aspects of professional theatre writing. Also lists symposiums, marketing guides, and script opportunities. Recurring features include a calendar of events, reports of meetings, news of educational opportunities, and notices of publications available. Columns titled Business Affairs, Taxes, and Theatre Updates.

★7263★ International Theatre Institute of the United States, Inc.—Newsletter
International Theatre Institute of the United States, Inc.
220 W. 42nd St.
New York, NY 10036
Ph: (212)254-4141   Fax: (212)944-1506
Louis A. Rachow
Quarterly. Reports on the activities of ITI/Worldwide, ITI/US, and the theatre professionals who are served by ITI's international programs. Recurring features include news of educational opportunities, book reviews, notices of publications available, and columns titled World Notes and Book Notes.

★7264★ Performing Arts
Performing Arts Network
3539 Motor Ave.
Los Angeles, CA 90034
Ph: (310)839-8000   Fax: (310)839-5651
Jeffrey Hirsch

Monthly. In-theatre magazine for all major theatres in California and Texas.

★7265★ Theatre Crafts
Theatre Crafts
32 W. 18th St.
New York, NY 10011-4612
Ph: (212)229-2965   Fax: (212)229-2084
Patricia MackayPublisher

The business of entertainment technology and design.

PROFESSIONAL MEETINGS AND CONVENTIONS

★7266★ International Society of Performing Arts Administrators Annual Conference
International Society of Performing Arts
  Administrators
4920 Plainfield NE, Ste. 3
Grand Rapids, MI 49505
Ph: (616)364-3000   Fax: (616)364-9010

Semiannual. Always held during the second week in December in New York City and abroad each June.

★7267★ Radio-Television News Directors Association International Conference and Exhibit
Radio-Television News Directors
  Association
1000 Connecticut Ave., NW, Ste. 615
Washington, DC 20036
Ph: (202)659-6510

Annual.

OTHER SOURCES OF INFORMATION

★7268★ Acting Like a Pro: Who's Who, What's What, and the Way Things Really Work in the Theatre
Betterway Publications, Inc.
Box 219
Crozet, VA 22932
Ph: (804)823-5661
1992.

★7269★ "Actor" in Career Selector 2001
Barron's Educational Series, Inc.
250 Wireless Blvd.
Hauppauge, NY 11788
Ph: (516)434-3311   Fax: (516)434-3723
Fr: 800-645-3476
James C. Gonyea. 1993.

★7270★ "Actor/Director/Producer" in 100 Best Jobs for the 1990s & Beyond
Dearborn Financial Publishing, Inc.
520 N. Dearborn St.
Chicago, IL 60610-4354
Ph: (312)836-4400   Fax: (312)836-1021
Fr: 800-621-9621

Carol Kleiman. 1992. Describes 100 jobs ranging from accountants to veterinarians.. Each job profile includes such information as education, experience, and certification needed, salaries, and job search suggestions.

★7271★ "Drama/Theater Arts" and "Radio, Television, and Film" in Accounting to Zoology: Graduate Fields Defined
Petersons Guides, Inc.
PO Box 2123
Princeton, NJ 08543-2123
Ph: (609)243-9111   Fax: (609)243-9150
Fr: 800-338-3282

Amy J. Goldstein, editor. Revised and updated, 1987. Defines 298 graduate and professional fields. Discusses types of graduate programs and degrees, graduate research, applied work, employment prospects, and trends.

★7272★ Film
Crestwood House
866 3rd Ave.
New York, NY 10022
Ph: (212)702-9632
1994.

★7273★ Guide to the National Endowment for the Arts, 1993-94
National Endowment of the Arts
Nancy Hanks Center, Rm. 803
1100 Pennsylvania Ave., NW
Washington, DC 20506
Ph: (202)682-5400

1993. Describes the overall purpose of each of the endowment's programs and outlines the types of support available in each funding category.

★7274★ The Hollywood Job Hunter's Survival Guide
Lone Eagle
2337 Roscomare Rd., No. 9
Los Angeles, CA 90077
Ph: (310)471-8066   Fax: (310)471-4969
Fr: 800-345-6257
1993.

★7275★ International Motion Picture Almanac, 1994
Quigley Publishing Co.
159 W. 53rd St.
New York, NY 10019
Ph: (212)247-3100

Jane Klain and William Pay, editors. Annual. Lists studios, producers, and related services and suppliers. Reviews events in the motion picture industry for the past year. Provides statistics and information on the world market.

★7276★ International Television and Video Almanac, 1994
Quigley Publishing Co., Inc.
159 W. 53rd St.
New York, NY 10019
Ph: (212)247-3100

Jane Klain, William Pay, and Patricia Thompson, editors. Annual. Provides statistics and an overview of the televison and video industry. Reports on the world market. Lists television companies and producers.

★7277★ The Movie Business Book
Simon & Schuster, Inc.
Simon & Schuster Bldg.
1230 Avenue of the Americas
New York, NY 10020
Ph: (212)698-7000

Jason E. Squire, editor. 1992. Forty-one producers, distributors, and agents reveal the workings of the motion picture business.

★7278★ Television
Crestwood House
866 3rd Ave.
New York, NY 10022
Ph: (212)702-9632
1994.

Dancers and Choreographers

Dancers express ideas, stories, rhythm, and sound with their bodies. They may perform in classical ballet, modern dance, dance adaptation for musical shows, folk, ethnic, and jazz dances, and other popular kinds of dancing. Many dancers combine stage work with teaching. **Choreographers** often create original dances, teach them to performers, and sometimes direct and stage the presentations of their work.

Salaries

Earnings of most dancers from dancing are generally low because of irregular employment. Dancers often must supplement their incomes with other jobs. In addition, earnings of most professional dancers are governed by union contracts.

Dancers, ballet and modern productions	$587/week minimum
Dancers, television	$569/one-hour show
Beginning choreographers	$970/week

Employment Outlook

Growth rate until the year 2005: Average.

Dancers and Choreographers

CAREER GUIDES

★7279★ Career Opportunities in Television, Cable and Video
Facts on File
460 Park Ave. S.
New York, NY 10016-7382
Ph: (212)683-2244   Fax: 800-678-3633
Fr: 800-322-8755

Maxine K. Reed and Robert M. Reed. Third edition, 1993. Includes information on employment and advancement prospects, education, experience and skills requiresn salary range, and tips for entry into the field.

★7280★ Career Opportunities in Theater and the Performing Arts
Facts on File
460 Park Ave. S.
New York, NY 10016-7382
Ph: (212)683-2244   Fax: 800-678-3633
Fr: 800-322-8755

Shelly Field. 1993. Guidebook offering complete career information for those entering the theater or any of the performing arts. Includes an index, appendices, bibliography, and glossary.

★7281★ Choreographer
Vocational Biographies, Inc.
PO Box 31
Sauk Centre, MN 56378-0031
Ph: (612)352-6516   Fax: (612)352-5546
Fr: 800-255-0752

1992. Four-page pamphlet containing a personal narrative about a worker's job, work likes and dislikes, career path from high school to the present. Education and training, the rewards and frustrations, and the effects of the job on the rest of the worker's life. The data file portion of this pamphlet gives a concise occupational summary, including work descriptions, working conditions, places of employment, personal characteristics, education and training, job outlook, and salary range.

★7282★ "Choreographer" and "Dancer" in Jobs Rated Almanac
World Almanac
1 International Blvd., Ste. 444
Mahwah, NJ 07495
Ph: (201)529-6900   Fax: (201)529-6901

Les Krantz. Second edition, 1992. Ranks 250 jobs by environment, salary, outlooks, physical demands, stress, security, travel opportunities, and extra perks. Includes jobs the editor feels are the most common, most interesting, and the most rapidly growing.

★7283★ "Choreographers" in Career Discovery Encyclopedia (Vol.1, pp. 172-173)
J.G. Ferguson Publishing Co.
200 W. Madison St., Ste. 300
Chicago, IL 60606
Ph: (312)580-5480   Fax: (312)580-4948

Russell E. Primm, editor-in chief. 1993. This six volume set contains two-page articles for 504 occupations. Each article describes job duties, earnings, and educational and training requirements. The whole set is arranged alphabetically by job title. Designed for junior high and older students.

★7284★ Chorus Dancer
Vocational Biographies, Inc.
PO Box 31
Sauk Centre, MN 56378-0031
Ph: (612)352-6516   Fax: (612)352-5546
Fr: 800-255-0752

1990. Four-page pamphlet containing a personal narrative about a worker's job, work likes and dislikes, career path from high school to the present. Education and training, the rewards and frustrations, and the effects of the job on the rest of the worker's life. The data file portion of this pamphlet gives a concise occupational summary, including work descriptions, working conditions, places of employment, personal characteristics, education and training, job outlook, and salary range.

★7285★ Dance: A Career for You
National Dance Association (NDA)
1900 Association Dr.
Reston, VA 22091
Ph: (703)476-3436

Suggests career opportunities as a teacher, therapist, performer, recreation leader, and choreographer. Describes employment op-

portunities, personal qualifications, training, knowledge, and skills required for a career in dance.

★7286★ "Dance Instruction" in Career Connection for Technical Education (pp. 50-51)
JIST Works, Inc.
720 N. Park Ave.
Indianapolis, IN 46202-3431
Ph: (317)264-3720   Fax: (317)264-3709

Fred A. Rowe. 1994, second edition. Describes in detail technical occupations. Includes information on recommended high school courses, course requirements, related careers, and a self-assessment guide.

★7287★ "Dancer, Choreographer" in College Board Guide to Jobs and Career Planning (pp. 61)
The College Board
415 Columbus Ave.
New York, NY 10023-6992
Ph: (212)713-8165   Fax: (212)713-8143
Fr: 800-323-7155

Joyce S. Mitchell. Second edition, 1994. Covers a variety of careers. Each profile contains information on salaries, related careers, education needed, and sources of additional information.

★7288★ The Dancer Prepares: Modern Dance for Beginners
Mayfield Publishing Co.
1240 Villa St.
Mountain View, CA 94041
Ph: (415)960-3222   Fax: (415)960-0328

James Penrod, editor. Third edition, 1990.

★7289★ "Dancer" in VGM's Careers Encyclopedia (pp. 129-132)
National Textbook Co. (NTC)
VGM Career Books
4255 W. Touhy Ave.
Lincolnwood, IL 60646-1975
Ph: (708)679-5500   Fax: (708)679-2494
Fr: 800-323-4900

Third edition, 1991. Profiles 200 occupations. Describes job duties, places of employment, working conditions, qualifications, education and training, advancement potential, and salary for each occupation.

★7290★ Dancers
Careers, Inc.
PO Box 135
Largo, FL 34649-0135
Ph: (813)584-7333

1992. Two-page occupational summary card describing duties, working conditions, personal qualifications, training, earnings and hours, employment outlook, places of employment, related careers, and where to write for more information.

★7291★ Dancers
Chronicle Guidance Publications, Inc.
66 Aurora St.
PO Box 1190
Moravia, NY 13118-1190
Ph: (315)497-0330   Fax: (315)497-3359
Fr: 800-622-7284

1992. Career brief describing the nature of the job, working conditions, hours and earnings, education and training, licensure, certification, unions, personal qualifications, social and psychological factors, location, employment outlook, entry methods, advancement, and related occupations.

★7292★ "Dancers" in American Almanac of Jobs and Salaries (pp. 140)
Avon Books
1350 Avenue of the Americas
New York, NY 10019
Ph: (212)261-6800   Fr: 800-238-0658

John Wright, editor. Revised and updated, 1994-95. A comprehensive guide to the wages of hundreds of occupations in a wide variety of industries and organizations.

★7293★ "Dancers" in Career Discovery Encyclopedia (Vol.2, pp. 76-77)
J.G. Ferguson Publishing Co.
200 W. Madison St., Ste. 300
Chicago, IL 60606
Ph: (312)580-5480   Fax: (312)580-4948

Russell E. Primm, editor-in chief. 1993. This six volume set contains two-page articles for 504 occupations. Each article describes job duties, earnings, and educational and training requirements. The whole set is arranged alphabetically by job title. Designed for junior high and older students.

★7294★ "Dancers" in Career Information Center (Vol.3)
Simon and Schuster
200 Old Tappan Rd.
Old Tappan, NJ 07675
Fax: 800-445-6991   Fr: 800-223-2348

Richard Lidz and Linda Perrin, editorial directors. Fifth edition, 1993. A multi-volume set that profiles more than 600 occupations. Each occupational profile describes job duties, educational requirements, getting a job, advancement possibilities, employment outlook, working conditions, earnings and benefits, and sources of additional information.

★7295★ "Dancers and Choreographers" in 101 Careers: A Guide to the Fastest-Growing Opportunities (pp. 281 = 284)
John Wiley & Sons, Inc.
605 3rd Ave.
New York, NY 10158-0012
Ph: (212)850-6645   Fax: (212)850-6088

Michael Harkavy. 1990. Describes the nature of the job, working conditions, employment growth, qualifications, personal skills, projected salaries, and where to write for more information.

★7296★ "Dancers and Choreographers" in America's 50 Fastest Growing Jobs (pp. 38)
JIST Works, Inc.
720 N. Park Ave.
Indianapolis, IN 46202-3431
Ph: (317)264-3720   Fax: (317)264-3709
Fr: 800-648-5478

Michael J. Farr, compiler. 1994. Describes the 50 fastest growing jobs within major career clusters such as technicians, and marketing and sales. Each job profile explains the nature of the work, skills and abilities required, employment outlook, average earnings, related occupations, education and training requirements, and employment opportunities. Also contains career planning information and job search tips.

★7297★ "Dancers and Choreographers" in Occupational Outlook Handbook
U.S. Government Printing Office
Superintendent of Documents
Washington, DC 20402
Ph: (202)512-1800   Fax: (202)512-2250

Biennial; latest edition, 1994-95. Encyclopedia of careers describing about 250 occupations and comprising about 85 percent of all jobs in the economy. Occupations that require lengthy education or training are given the most attention. Each occupation's profile describes what the worker does on the job, working conditions, education and training requirements, advancement possibilities, job outlook, earnings, and sources of additional information.

★7298★ "Dancers and Chorepographers" in Encyclopedia of Careers and Vocational Guidance (Vol.2, pp. 424-426)
J.G. Ferguson Publishing Co.
200 W. Madison St., Ste. 300
Chicago, IL 60606
Ph: (312)580-5480   Fax: (312)580-4948

William E. Hopke, editor-in-chief. Ninth edition, 1993. Four-volume set that profiles 900 occupations and describes job trends in 74 industries. Includes career description, educational requirements, history of the job, methods of entry, advancement, employment outlook, earnings, conditions of work, social and psychological factors, and sources of further information.

★7299★ The Dancer's Complete Guide to Healthcare and a Long Career
Bonus Books
160 E. Illinois St.
Chicago, IL 60611
Ph: (312)467-0580

Allan J. Ryan and Robert E. Stephens. 1988. Contains advice on starting, maintaining, and extending a career in dance. Includes information on training, diet, nutrition, and preventing and treating injuries.

★7300★ Dancer's Survival Manual: Everything You Need to Know About Being a Dancer... Except How to Dance
Harper and Row, Publishers
10 E. 53rd St.
New York, NY 10022
Ph: (212)207-7000   Fr: 800-242-7737

Marian Horosko and Judith F. Kupersmith. 1987. Out of print; check local libraries.

★7301★ Exchanges: Life After Dance
AAHPERD Publications
PO Box 704
Waldorf, MD 20604
Ph: (703)476-3481

Joysanne Sidimus. 1987. Discusses career transitions for dancers.

★7302★ For the Working Artists: A Survival Guide
Warren Christianson
935 W. Ave. 37
Los Angeles, CA 90065
Ph: (213)222-4035

Judith Luther and Eric Vollmer. Second edition, 1991.

★7303★ "Music/Dance" in Internships: 1995 (pp. 154-165)
Petersons Guides, Inc.
PO Box 2123
Princeton, NJ 08543-2123
Ph: (609)243-9111   Fax: (609)243-9150
Fr: 800-338-3282

Fifteenth edition, 1995. Lists internship opportunities under six broad categories: communications, creative, performing, and fine arts, human services, international relations, business and technology, and public relations. Includes a special section on internships in Washington, DC. For each internship program, gives the name, phone number, contact person, description, eligibility requirements, and benefits.

★7304★ Opportunities in Dance Careers
National Textbook Co. (NTC)
VGM Career Books
4255 W. Toughy Ave.
Lincolnwood, IL 60646-1975
Ph: (708)679-5500   Fax: (708)679-2494
Fr: 800-323-4900

Paul Denis.

★7305★ Opportunities in Performing Arts Careers
National Textbook Co. (NTC)
VGM Career Books
4255 W. Touhy Ave.
Lincolnwood, IL 60646-1975
Ph: (708)679-5500   Fax: (708)679-2494
Fr: 800-323-4900

Bonnie Bjorguine Bekken. 1991. Overviews the exciting world of performing arts, including opportunities in classical and popular music; theater, television, and movie acting; dance; performance art; and teaching and therapy. Also offers information on developing a portfolio and preparing for auditions.

PROFESSIONAL ASSOCIATIONS

★7306★ American Dance Guild (ADG)
31 W. 21st St., 3rd Fl.
New York, NY 10010
Ph: (212)627-3790   Fax: (212)675-9657
Members: Teachers, performers, historians, critics, writers, and students in the field of dance, including ballet, modern dance, modern jazz dance, tap dance, and ethnological dance forms. **Purpose:** Initiates programs of national significance in the field. Maintains speakers' bureau; operates career counseling service and Job Express Registry, a monthly job listing for people looking for work in the dance field. **Publications:** *American Dance*, quarterly. • *American Dance Guild—Job Express Registry*. • *Souvenir Journal*, annual.

★7307★ American Dance Therapy Association (ADTA)
2000 Century Plz., Ste. 108
Columbia, MD 21044
Ph: (410)997-4040   Fax: (410)997-4048
Members: Individuals professionally practicing dance therapy, students interested in becoming dance therapists, university departments with dance therapy programs, and individuals in related therapeutic fields. **Purpose:** Purpose is to establish and maintain high standards of professional education and competence in dance therapy. Acts as information center; develops guidelines for educational programs and for approval of programs; maintains registry of qualified dance therapists. Maintains Marian Chace Memorial Fund to be used for educational, literary, or scientific projects related to dance in the field of mental health. **Publications:** *American Journal of Dance Therapy*, semi-annual. • *Conference Proceedings*. • *Dance Therapy Bibliography*.

★7308★ American Guild of Musical Artists (AGMA)
1727 Broadway
New York, NY 10019
Ph: (212)265-3687
Members: AFL-CIO. Opera and classical concert singers, classical ballet and modern dance performers, and affiliated stage directors and stage managers. **Publications:** *AGMAzine*.

★7309★ Dance/U.S.A.
1156 15th St., NW, Ste. 820
Washington, DC 20005
Ph: (202)833-1717   Fax: (202)833-2686
Members: Dancers, dance companies, artists, and others involved in nonprofit professional dance. **Purpose:** Seeks to advance dance as an art form by encouraging higher standards; works to further knowledge, appreciation, and support of dance. Provides a forum for the discussion of issues of concern to members; supports network for exchange of information; compiles statistics. Assists dance professionals in improving their capabilities. Administers two regranting programs and other special projects. **Publications:** *AIDS in the Dance/Arts Workplace*. • *Dance/USA Journal*, quarterly. • *Dance/USA Mem-* *bership Directory*, biennial. • *Dance/USA Touring Task Force Report*. • *Update*, monthly.

★7310★ National Association of Schools of Dance (NASD)
11250 Roger Bacon Dr., Ste. 21
Reston, VA 22090
Ph: (703)437-0700   Fax: (703)437-6312
Purpose: Serves as accrediting agency for educational programs in dance. Provides prospective students with current, accurate information about schools offering instruction in dance. Seeks to establish standards in the field regarding budget, class time requirements, faculty qualifications, faculty-student ratios, and library and physical facilities. Fosters public understanding and acceptance of the educational disciplines inherent in the creative arts in the nation's system of higher education. Encourages high-quality teaching, as well as varied and experimental methods and theories of dance instruction. Provides national representation in matters pertaining to dance and affecting member institutions and their goals. Encourages the collaboration of individuals and professional dance groups in formulating curricula and standards. Offers members general assistance and counseling in program development and encourages self-evaluation and continuing efforts toward improvement. Evaluates dance schools and dance instruction programs through voluntary accreditation processes; assures students and parents that accredited programs offer competent instructors and adequate curricula and facilities.

★7311★ National Dance Association (NDA)
1900 Association Dr.
Reston, VA 22091
Ph: (703)476-3436   Fax: (703)476-9527
Fr: 800-321-0789
Members: Public and private schools; college teachers of dance. **Purpose:** Promotes the development of sound philosophies and policies for dance as education through conferences, convention programs, special projects, and publications. Acts as advocate for better dance education programs through liaison activities with government, foundations, and special agencies. Provides reports and publications on dance research, career opportunities, current information on dance education, professional preparation, and certification. Maintains oral history archives of leaders in dance. Offers placement service and speakers' bureau; makes consultant referrals. **Publications:** *Dance Directory*, biennial. • *Focus on Dance*, biennial. • *Journal of Physical Education, Recreation, and Dance*. • *Spotlight on Dance*, 3/year. • *Update*, 9/year.

STANDARDS/CERTIFICATION AGENCIES

★7312★ Laban/Bartenieff Institute of Movement Studies (LIMS)
11 E. 4th St., 3rd Fl.
New York, NY 10003
Ph: (212)477-4299   Fax: (212)477-3702
Offers certificate program in Laban movement studies, workshops, and seminars. Supports research and development projects of practicing movement analysts.

★7313★ National Dance Association (NDA)
1900 Association Dr.
Reston, VA 22091
Ph: (703)476-3436   Fax: (703)476-9527
Fr: 800-321-0789
Promotes the development of sound philosophies and policies for dance as education through conferences, convention programs, special projects, and publications. Provides reports and publications on dance research, professional preparation, and certification.

★7314★ World Congress of Teachers of Dancing (WCTD)
38 S. Arlington Ave.
PO Box 245
East Orange, NJ 07019
Ph: (201)673-9225
Seeks to maintain global standards of excellence in dance. Conducts educational programs and examinations; certifies teachers of dancing. Researches and disseminates information on the history and status of dance from local to international levels.

EDUCATIONAL DIRECTORIES AND PROGRAMS

★7315★ *Dance Directory—Programs of Professional Preparation in American Colleges and Universities*
American Alliance for Health, Physical Education, Recreation, and Dance
PO Box 385
Oxon Hill, MD 20750-0385
Fax: (301)567-9553   Fr: 800-321-0789
Biennial, even years. Covers over 230 institutions with dance curriculums at undergraduate or graduate levels; coverage includes Canada. Entries include: Institution name, address, phone, course offerings, teaching personnel, performing groups, degrees offered. Arrangement: Geographical.

★7316★ Dance Magazine College Guide: A Directory of Dance in North American Colleges and Universities
Dance Magazine, Inc.
33 W. 60th St., 10th Fl.
New York, NY 10023
Ph: (212)245-9050   Fax: (212)956-6487
Fr: 800-458-2845
Allen E. McCormack, Contact

Biennial. Covers Approximately 500 college-level dance programs. Entries include: College name, address, phone, and name of contact for dance department; degrees offered; degree requirements; facilities; special programs; admission requirements; tuition and fees; financial aid available. Arrangement: Alphabetical..

★7317★ Dancing Studios/Instruction Directory
American Business Directories, Inc.
5711 S. 86th Circle
Omaha, NE 68127
Ph: (402)593-4600   Fax: (402)331-1505

Annual. Number of listings: 12,621 (U.S. edition); 1,058 (Canadian edition). Entries include: Name, address, phone (including area code), size of advertisement, year first in "Yellow Pages," name of owner or manager, number of employees. Compiled from telephone company "Yellow Pages," nationwide. Arrangement: Geographical.

★7318★ International Guide to Afrocentric Talent
Osborne Communications
18565 NE 1 Ct.
Miami, FL 33179
Ph: (305)654-8298
Eddie Osborne, Contact

Annual, winter. Covers Approximately 500 vocalists, musicians, dance and theatre troupes, speakers, storytellers, and other talent of African descent, theme, or focus; coverage includes the U.S., Canada, the Caribbean, Africa, Europe, and regions of the Pacific. Entries include: Organization or individual name, address, phone, name and title of contact, number of members (for groups), geographical area served, description. Arrangement: Classified by type of talent.

★7319★ National Directory of Arts Internships
National Network for Artist Placement
935 W. Ave. 37
Los Angeles, CA 90065
Ph: (213)222-4035   Fax: (213)222-4035
Warren Christensen, Contact

Biennial, odd years. Covers Approximately 2,000 internship opportunities in dance, music, theater, art, design, film, and video. Entries include: Name of sponsoring organization, address, name of contact; description of positions available, eligibility requirements, stipend or salary (if any), application procedures. Arrangement: Classified by discipline, then geographical.

★7320★ Performing Arts Career Directory
Gale Research Inc.
835 Penobscot Bldg.
Detroit, MI 48226
Ph: (313)961-2242   Fr: 800-877-GALE
1994. Profiles careers in the performing arts industry.

AWARDS, SCHOLARSHIPS, GRANTS, AND FELLOWSHIPS

★7321★ American Ballet Competition
American Ballet Competition
PO Box 328
Philadelphia, PA 19105
Ph: (215)829-9800   Fax: (215)829-0508
To select and financially support American dancers participating in international ballet competitions. The primary goals of the program are: to ensure that the best dancers, partners, and coaches represent the United States in international competitions; to discover and publicize these promising dancers through regional and national competitions; to provide artistic guidance and administrative support to the American team; to award financial grants-in-aid to competitors for travel, lodging expenses, coaches, partners, music, rehearsal space, costumes, and shoes; to develop skills necessary for success in international competitions through workshops and seminars involving world-class coaches, choreographers, and dancers; to solidify the cultural and educational exchange process by providing opportunities for United States artists to meet and share ideas with their foreign peers; and to provide grants to schools and companies who developed and fostered those talented dancers selected for competition. The American team of dancers is selected following regional and national auditions. An excess of $200,000 in stipends has been awarded to more than 30 dancers participating in 11 international competitions. Established in 1979.

★7322★ American Dance Guild Award for Outstanding Achievement in Dance
American Dance Guild
31 W. 21st St., 3rd Fl.
New York, NY 10010
Ph: (212)627-3790   Fax: (212)675-9657
To recognize meritorious and unique contributions to the field of dance. Individuals outstanding in the field of dance are eligible. A statuette is awarded annually. Established in 1970.

★7323★ Artists' Fellowship Program
New York Foundation for the Arts
155 6th Ave., No. 14FL
New York, NY 10013-1507
Ph: (212)233-3900   Fax: (212)791-1813
To encourage professional development and to provide fellowships to individual New York State creative artists in the following categories: Architecture, Choreography, Crafts, Fiction, Film, Music Composition, Nonfiction Literature, Painting, Performance Art/Emergent

Forms, Photography, Playwriting/Screenwriting, Poetry, Printmaking/Drawing/Artists' Books, Sculpture, and Video. The Program assists eligible New York State artists in their work through direct grants awarded solely on the basis of creative excellence. These awards are not to be considered project support. All applicants to the Artists' Fellowship Program are required to submit a representative body of work to demonstrate professional accomplishment and commitment to a professional career. They must be at least 18 years of age, and must have resided in New York State for the two years immediately prior to application. Graduate or undergraduate matriculated students enrolled in a degree program at the time of application may not apply. No faxed applications are accepted. Fellowships of $7,000 are awarded in some of the categories annually. In 1992, an average of 11 Fellowships were awarded in each of the following categories: Crafts, Film, Nonfiction, Literature, Performance Art/Emergent Forms, Poetry, Printmaking/Drawing/Artists' Books and Sculpture. Established in 1984. The New York Foundation for the Arts also administers four other major statewide programs: (1) The Artists-in-Residence Program, a re-grant program to create artists-in-residence opportunities in educational, cultural, and community organizations; (2) The Artists' New Works Program, a sponsorship program that provides advisory and fiscal services to professional artists who are developing individual projects; and (3) The Revolving Loan Program, a short-term, loan service for nonprofit cultural organizations.

★7324★ Dance Magazine Annual Awards
Dance Magazine
33 W. 60th St.
New York, NY 10023
Ph: (212)245-9050   Fax: (212)956-6487
For recognition of outstanding contributions to the field of dance. Performers, choreographers, designers, musicians, administrators, and teachers are eligible. Sterling silver bowls are awarded annually. Established in 1954.

★7325★ Dance/USA National Honors
Dance/USA
777 14th St. NW, Ste. 540
Washington, DC 20005-3270
Ph: (202)628-0144   Fax: (202)628-0375
To recognize individuals and/or organizations that have made important contributions to the dance art form and field. The Board of Trustees makes the selection. A framed citation, and a piece of artwork are awarded biennially. Established in 1986.

★7326★ DMA Annual Award
Dance Masters of America
1430 Futura
Beaumont, TX 77706
Ph: (409)892-7093
To recognize an individual for significant contributions to the dance profession. Individuals are nominated by the Board of Directors. Plaques are presented annually in August. Established in 1963.

★7327★ Emmy Awards for Primetime Programming
Academy of Television Arts and Sciences
5220 Lankershim Blvd.
North Hollywood, CA 91601
Ph: (818)754-2800   Fax: (818)761-2927

To recognize the advancement of the arts and sciences of television and achievements broadcast nationally during primetime. Awards are given in the following categories: (1) Program Category Awards - (a) Outstanding Comedy Series; (b) Outstanding Drama Series; (c) Outstanding Miniseries; (d) Outstanding Variety, Music, or Comedy Series; (e) Outstanding Made for T.V. Movie; (f) Outstanding Classical Program in the Performing Arts; (g) Outstanding Informational Special; (h) Outstanding Informational Series; (i) Outstanding Animated Program; and (j) Outstanding Children's Program; (2) Individual Awards - (a) Lead, Supporting, and Guest Acting in Comedy Series, Drama Series, Miniseries, or Special; (b) Performance in Variety or Music Program, Informational Programming, and Classical Music/Dance Programming; (c) Directing in Comedy Series, Drama Series, Variety or Music Program, Miniseries or Special, Classical Music/Dance Programming, and Informational Programming; (d) Casting for a Miniseries or Special; (e) Writing in Comedy Series, Drama Series, Variety or Music Program, Miniseries or Special, Informational Programming, and Classical Music/Dance Programming; and (3) Technical Awards - (a) Choreography; (b) Cinematography; (c) Art Direction; (d) Music Composition; (e) Main Title Theme Music; (f) Music Direction; (g) Music and Lyrics; (h) Costume Design; (i) Costuming; (j) Makeup; (k) Hairstyling; (l) Editing; (m) Sound Editing; (n) Sound Mixing; (o) Technical Direction/Camera/Video; (p) Special Visual Effects; (q) Graphic Design and Title Sequences; (r) Lighting Direction; (s) Engineering Development; and (4) ATAS Governors Award. Nominees are voted upon by a jury. An Emmy statuette is presented annually at the Emmy Awards Ceremony. Established in 1948 and administered by the Academy of Television Arts and Sciences until 1977.

★7328★ Heritage Award
National Dance Association
Assn. of Amer. Alliance for Hlth., Phys. Ed., Rec., & Dance
1900 Association Dr.
Reston, VA 22090
Ph: (703)476-3436   Fax: (703)476-9527

To honor an individual for comprehensive contributions of national or international significance over a long period of years, to dance in one or more of the following categories: teaching excellence; establishment or administration of a functioning dance department, center, or program; service, research, or publication; consulting; choregraphy; performance; notation; and education and related arts. Nominations are accepted at any time. A plaque is awarded annually when merited at the Dance Heritage Luncheon. Established in 1963.

★7329★ Kennedy Center Honors
John F. Kennedy Center for the Performing Arts
Washington, DC 20566
Ph: (202)416-8000   Fax: (202)416-8205

To recognize individuals for their distinguished artistic achievements and career contributions to American culture. The primary criterion in the selection of the recipients is artistic achievement as a performer, composer, choreographer, playwright, director or conductor. Honorees are nominated by the Artists Committee in the areas of dance, music, theater, opera, motion pictures and television. Final selection is made by the Kennedy Center Board of Trustees. A unique beribboned medal, created for the Kennedy Center Honors, is awarded each year at an annual celebration consisting of a traditional Board of Trustees dinner and an Honors Gala performance, preceeded by a reception hosted by the President of the United States. Established in 1978. Additional information is available from Laura Langley, phone: (202) 416-8430.

★7330★ New York Dance and Performance Awards (Bessie Awards)
Dance Theater Workshop
219 West 19th St.
New York, NY 10011
Ph: (212)691-6500   Fax: (212)633-1974

To honor outstanding creative achievements by innovative artists working in the fields of contemporary dance and related performance. Any performing artist presenting new work in New York City during the course of a particular performance season is eligible. Nomination is by a committee of producers and reviewers. Monetary awards and framed certificates are presented to choreographers, performance-art creators, and persons in other categories. Awarded annually in September. Established in 1984 by the Dance Theater Workshop with special funding from Morgan Guaranty Trust Companyin honor of Bessie Schonberg, a renowned teacher of dance composition and mentor to many choreographers.

★7331★ New York International Ballet Competition
New York International Ballet Competition
111 W. 57th St., Ste. 1400
New York, NY 10019
Ph: (212)956-1520   Fax: (212)397-1580

For recognition of the best ballet dancers chosen to participate in NYIBC. The triennial competition is open to female ballet dancers 17 to 23 years of age and male ballet dancers 18 to 24 years of age from all countries. During the first two weeks, three pas de deux and classes are taught by world renowned teachers and coaches. During the third week, four competition rounds (six performances), an awards ceremony, and Gala Performance are held at Lincoln Center for the Performing Arts. All performances are open to the public. Gussie and Samuel Arbuse Gold Medals, Silver Medals, and Bronze Medals are awarded to the best dancers. The next competition is scheduled for June, 1996. Also awarded is the Lefkowitz Awardfor excellence in partnering. All awards include cash prizes and all participants receive diplomas. Established in

1983 by Ilona Copen. The first competition was held in June 1984.

★7332★ Antoinette Perry Awards (Tony Awards)
League of American Theatres and Producers
226 W. 47 St.
New York, NY 10036
Ph: (212)764-2929   Fax: (212)719-4389

To recognize outstanding theatrical achievement in the Broadway theatre. Legitimate theatrical productions opening in an eligible Broadway house with 499 or more seats during the Tony season (May to May) are eligible for nomination. Awards are presented in the following creative categories: Best Play - awards to the author and producer; Best Musical - award to the producer; Best Book of a Musical; Best Original Score of a Musical written for the theater; Best Revival of a Play or a Musical - award to the producer; Best Actor in a Play; Best Actress in a Play; Best Featured Actor in a Play; Best Featured Actress in a Play; Best Actor in a Musical; Best Actress in a Musical; Best Featured Actor in a Musical; Best Featured Actress in a Musical; Best Direction of a Play; Best Direction of a Musical; Best Scenic Design; Best Costume Design; Best Lighting Design; and Best Choreography. Tony Awards- a silver medallion embossed with masks of comedy and tragedy mounted on black lucite-base, are awarded annually in each category. Established in 1947 in honor of Antoinette Perry of the American Theatre Wing.

★7333★ Presidential Recognition Awards
American Alliance for Health, Physical Education, Recreation, and Dance
1900 Association Dr.
Reston, VA 22091
Ph: (703)476-3405

To recognize outstanding achievement. One award is presented annually.

★7334★ Residency Fellowships for Artists and Ensembles Developing New Works
Yellow Springs Institute
1645 Art School Rd.
Chester Springs, PA 19425
Ph: (215)827-9111   Fax: (215)827-7093

To provide artists with an opportunity to develop, rehearse, and present untried new works, particularly in music, dance, performance art, and inter-disciplinary projects. Applicants must have a minimum of three years professional experience in the field. Only works previously unproduced and unperformed are considered. Students are ineligible. Applications must be submitted by October 15. Call for application forms. Residencies are for two to three weeks, including room, board, professionally staffed rehearsal and performance space, documentation, and transportation assistance. Established in 1979 by John A. Clauser, AIA.

BASIC REFERENCE GUIDES AND HANDBOOKS

★7335★ The Art of Making Dances
Princeton Book Co., Publishers
12 W. Deleware Ave.
PO Box 57
Pennington, NJ 08534
Ph: (609)737-8177　　　Fr: 800-326-7149
Doris Humphrey, author; Barbara Pollack, editor. 1991.

★7336★ Choreographing the Stage Musical
Routledge, Chapman & Hall, Inc.
29 W. 35th St.
New York, NY 10001-2291
Ph: (212)244-3336
Margot Sunderland, editor. 1990.

★7337★ The Dance Handbook
Macmillan Publishing Co.
866 3rd Ave, 7th Fl.
New York, NY 10022
Ph: (617)423-3990　　　Fr: 800-257-5755
Allen Robertson, editor. 1990.

★7338★ Modern Dance in Germany and the United States: Cross Currents & Influences
Gordon & Breach Science Publishers, Inc.
270 8th Ave.
New York, NY 10011
Ph: (212)206-8900
Isa Partsch-Bergsohn, editor. 1994.

★7339★ Musical Theater Choreography
Watson-Guptill Publications
1515 Broadway
New York, NY 10036
Ph: (212)764-7300　　　Fax: (212)536-5359
Fr: 800-451-1741
Robert Berkson, editor. 1990.

★7340★ A Primer for Choreographers
Waveland Press, Inc.
PO Box 400
Prospect Heights, IL 60070
Ph: (708)634-0081
Lois Ellfeldt. 1988. An introductory text for choreographers. Covers spacial relationships, visual images, settings, and accompaniment.

★7341★ Relationships Between Score & Choreography in Twentieth-Century Dance: Music, Movement, Metaphor
The Edwin Mellen Press
415 Ridge St.
PO Box 450
Lewiston, NY 14092
Ph: (716)754-2266
Paul Hodgins, editor. 1992.

PROFESSIONAL AND TRADE PERIODICALS

★7342★ American Dance
American Dance Guild
31 W. 21st St., 3rd Fl.
New York, NY 10010-6807
Ph: (212)627-3790
Ann Vachon

Quarterly. Presents information for those interested in dance. Contains news about the activities of schools, companies, and individuals; governmental and foundation grants; the activities of arts councils; dance reviews; and association news.

★7343★ Dance Magazine
Dance Magazine
33 W. 60th St.
New York, NY 10023-7990
Ph: (212)245-9050　　　Fax: (212)956-6487
Richard Philp

Monthly. Performing arts magazine featuring all forms of dance with profiles, news, photos, reviews of performances, and information on books, videos, films, schools, health, and technique.

PROFESSIONAL MEETINGS AND CONVENTIONS

★7344★ International Society of Performing Arts Administrators Annual Conference
International Society of Performing Arts Administrators
4920 Plainfield NE, Ste. 3
Grand Rapids, MI 49505
Ph: (616)364-3000　　　Fax: (616)364-9010

Semiannual. Always held during the second week in December in New York City and abroad each June.

★7345★ Texas Association for Health, Physical Education, Recreation, and Dance Annual State Convention
Texas Association for Health, Physical Education, Recreation, and Dance
6300 La Calma Dr., No. 100
Austin, TX 78752-3890
Ph: (512)459-1299　　　Fax: (512)459-1290

Annual. **Dates and Locations:** 1995 Nov 29-02; Dallas, TX. • 1996 Dec 04-07; Corpus Christi, TX.

OTHER SOURCES OF INFORMATION

★7346★ "Choreographer" in Career Selector 2001
Barron's Educational Series, Inc.
250 Wireless Blvd.
Hauppauge, NY 11788
Ph: (516)434-3311　　　Fax: (516)434-3723
Fr: 800-645-3476
James C. Gonyea. 1993.

★7347★ "Dance" in Accounting to Zoology: Graduate Fields Defined (pp. 160-162)
Petersons Guides, Inc.
PO Box 2123
Princeton, NJ 08543-2123
Ph: (609)243-9111　　　Fax: (609)243-9150
Fr: 800-338-3282

Amy J. Goldstein, editor. Revised and updated, 1987. Defines 298 graduate and professional fields. Discusses types of graduate programs and degrees, graduate research, applied work, employment prospects, and trends.

★7348★ "Dancer" in Career Selector 2001
Barron's Educational Series, Inc.
250 Wireless Blvd.
Hauppauge, NY 11788
Ph: (516)434-3311　　　Fax: (516)434-3723
Fr: 800-645-3476
James C. Gonyea. 1993.

★7349★ Guide to the National Endowment for the Arts, 1993-94
National Endowment for the Arts
Nancy Hanks Center, Rm. 803
1100 Pennsylvania Ave., NW
Washington, DC 20506
Ph: (202)682-5400

1993. Describes the overall purpose of each of the endowment's programs and outlines the types of support available in each funding category.

★7350★ Poor Dancer's Almanac: Managing a Life and Work in the Performing Arts
Duke University Press
PO Box 90660
Durham, NC 27708
Ph: (919)687-3600　　　Fax: (919)688-4574
1993.

Musicians

Professional **musicians** may specialize in several areas of music such as rock, gospel, classical, blues, or jazz. They may sing, write musical compositions, or conduct instrumental or vocal performances. Musicians may perform alone or as part of a group on stage, radio, or in TV or movie productions. **Instrumental musicians** play a musical instrument in an orchestra, band, rock group, or jazz "combo." Musicians play string, brass, woodwind, or percussion instruments. **Singers** interpret music using their knowledge of voice production, melody, and harmony. **Composers** create original music such as symphonies operas, sonatas, or popular songs. They transcribe ideas into musical notation using harmony, rhythm, melody, and tonal structure. Many songwriters now compose and edit music using computers. **Orchestra conductors** lead orchestras and bands. They audition and select musicians and direct rehearsals and performances. They apply conducting techniques, music theory, and harmony to achieve desired musical effects. **Choral directors** conduct choirs and glee clubs. They audition and select singers and direct them at rehearsals and performances to achieve harmony, rhythm, tempo, shading, and other desired musical effects.

Salaries

Earnings often depend on a performer's professional reputation as well as on geographic location and on the number of hours worked. Minimum salaries for musicians are as follows:

Musicians, symphony orchestras with largest budgets	$473-$1,140/week
Musicians, motion picture or television recording	$185-$234/three-hour session minimum
Principal singers, television	$448/day

Employment Outlook

Growth rate until the year 2005: Average.

Musicians

CAREER GUIDES

★7351★ **Breaking into the Music Business**
Simon & Schuster, Inc
Simon & Schuster Bldg.
1230 Avenue of the Americas
New York, NY 10020
Ph: (212)698-7000   Fr: 800-354-4004
Alan H. Siegel. Revised edition, 1990. Describes the record deal; the artist-manager relationship; working with copyrights, demos, and the terminology used in the industry.

★7352★ **Career Opportunities in the Music Industry**
Facts on File
460 Park Ave. S.
New York, NY 10016-7382
Ph: (212)683-2244   Fax: 800-678-3633
Fr: 800-322-8755
Shelly Field. 1990. Discusses approximately 80 jobs in music, including the performing arts, business, and education. Each job description provides basic career information, salary, employment prospects, advancement opportunities, education, training, and experience required.

★7353★ **Career Opportunities in Television, Cable and Video**
Facts on File
460 Park Ave. S.
New York, NY 10016-7382
Ph: (212)683-2244   Fax: 800-678-3633
Fr: 800-322-8755
Maxine K. Reed and Robert M. Reed. Third edition, 1993. Includes information on employment and advancement prospects, education, experience and skills requiresn salary range, and tips for entry into the field.

★7354★ **Career Opportunities in Theater and the Performing Arts**
Facts on File
460 Park Ave. S.
New York, NY 10016-7382
Ph: (212)683-2244   Fax: 800-678-3633
Fr: 800-322-8755
Shelly Field. 1993. Guidebook offering complete career information for those entering the theater or any of the performing arts. Includes an index, appendices, bibliography, and glossary.

★7355★ **Creating Careers in Music Theatre**
Peter Lang Publishing, Inc.
62 W. 45th St.
New York, NY 10036
Ph: (212)302-6740
Glenn Loney and Meredith and William Boswell. 1988.

★7356★ **For the Working Artists: A Survival Guide**
Warren Christianson
935 W. Ave. 37
Los Angeles, CA 90065
Ph: (213)222-4035
Judith Luther and Eric Vollmer. Second edition, 1991.

★7357★ **Making It in the New Music Business**
Writer's Digest Books
1507 Dana Ave.
Cincinnati, OH 45207
Ph: (513)531-2222   Fr: 800-289-0963
James Riordan. Revised and updated, 1991. Covers how to make records and establish an audience.

★7358★ **The Music Business: Career Opportunities and Self-Defense**
Crown Publishers, Inc.
225 Park Ave. S.
New York, NY 10003
Ph: (212)254-1600
Dick Weissman. New, revised, updated edition, 1990.

★7359★ **Music Careers**
Careers, Inc.
PO Box 135
Largo, FL 34649-0135
Ph: (813)584-7333
1992. Four-page brief offering the definition, history, duties, working conditions, personal qualifications, educational requirements, earnings, hours, employment outlook, advancement, and careers related to this position.

★7360★ **"Music/Dance" in** *Internships: 1995* **(pp. 154-165)**
Petersons Guides, Inc.
PO Box 2123
Princeton, NJ 08543-2123
Ph: (609)243-9111   Fax: (609)243-9150
Fr: 800-338-3282
Fifteenth edition, 1995. Lists internship opportunities under six broad categories: communications, creative, performing, and fine arts, human services, international relations, business and technology, and public relations. Includes a special section on internships in Washington, DC. For each internship program, gives the name, phone number, contact person, description, eligibility requirements, and benefits.

★7361★ **"Music" in** *Desk Guide to Training and Work Advisement* **(pp. 125-126)**
Charles C. Thomas, Publisher
2600 S. 1st St.
Springfield, IL 62794-9265
Ph: (217)789-8980   Fax: (217)789-9130
Fr: 800-258-8980
Gail Baugher Keunstler. 1988. Describes alternative methods of gaining entry into an occupation through different types of educational programs, internships, and apprenticeships.

★7362★ **"Music Specialist" in** *Guide to Federal Jobs* **(p. 189)**
Resource Directories
3361 Executive Pkwy., Ste. 302
Toledo, OH 43606
Ph: (419)536-5353   Fax: (419)536-7056
Fr: 800-274-8515
Rod W. Durgin, editor. Third edition, 1992. Contains information on finding and applying for federal jobs. Describes more than 200 professional and technical jobs for college graduates. Covers the nature of the work, salary, and geographic location. Lists college majors preferred for that occupation. Section one describes the function and work of government agencies that hire the most significant number of college graduates.

★7363★ "Music" in *Straight Talk on Careers: Eighty Pros Take You Into Their Professions* **(pp. 113-130)**
Garrett Park Press
PO Box 1907
Garrett Park, MD 20896
Ph: (301)946-2553

Mary Barbera-Hogan. 1987. Contains candid interviews from people who give an inside view of their work in 80 different careers. These professionals describe a day's work and the stresses and rewards accompanying their work.

★7364★ "Musician" in *College Board Guide to Jobs and Career Planning* **(pp. 61-63)**
The College Board
45 Columbus Ave.
New York, NY 10023-6992
Ph: (212)713-8165   Fax: (212)713-8143
Fr: 800-323-7155

Second edition, 1994. Describes the job, salaries, related careers, education needed, and where to write for more information.

★7365★ *Musician/Entertainer*
Vocational Biographies, Inc.
PO Box 31
Sauk Centre, MN 56378-0031
Ph: (612)352-6516   Fax: (612)352-5546
Fr: 800-255-0752

1993. Four-page pamphlet containing a personal narrative about a worker's job, work likes and dislikes, career path from high school to the present. Education and training, the rewards and frustrations, and the effects of the job on the rest of the worker's life. The data file portion of this pamphlet gives a concise occupational summary, including work descriptions, working conditions, places of employment, personal characteristics, education and training, job outlook, and salary range.

★7366★ *Musician, Instrumental*
Careers, Inc.
PO Box 135
Largo, FL 34649-0135
Ph: (813)584-7333

1991. Two-page occupational summary card describing duties, working conditions, personal qualifications, training, earnings and hours, employment outlook, places of employment, related careers, and where to write for more information.

★7367★ "Musician" in *Jobs Rated Almanac*
World Almanac
1 International Blvd., Ste. 444
Mahwah, NJ 07495
Ph: (201)529-6900   Fax: (201)529-6901

Les Krantz. Second edition, 1992. Ranks 250 jobs by environment, salary, outlooks, physical demands, stress, security, travel opportunities, and extra perks. Includes jobs the editor feels are the most common, most interesting, and the most rapidly growing.

★7368★ "Musician" in *VGM's Careers Encyclopedia* **(pp. 294-296)**
National Textbook Co. (NTC)
VGM Career Books
4255 W. Touhy Ave.
Lincolnwood, IL 60646-1975
Ph: (708)679-5500   Fax: (708)679-2494
Fr: 800-323-4900

Third edition, 1991. Profiles 200 occupations. Describes job duties, places of employment, working conditions, qualifications, education and training, advancement potential, and salary for each occupation.

★7369★ "Musicians" in *101 Careers: A Guide to the Fastest-Growing Opportunities* **(pp. 291-293)**
John Wiley & Sons, Inc.
605 3rd Ave.
New York, NY 10158-0012
Ph: (212)850-6645   Fax: (212)850-6088

Michael Harkavy. 1990. Describes the nature of the job, working conditions, employment growth, qualifications, personal skills, projected salaries, and where to write for more information.

★7370★ "Musicians" in *American Almanac of Jobs and Salaries* **(pp. 147)**
Avon Books
1350 Avenue of the Americas
New York, NY 10019
Ph: (212)261-6800   Fr: 800-238-0658

John Wright, editor. Revised and updated, 1994-95. A comprehensive guide to the wages of hundreds of occupations in a wide variety of industries and organizations.

★7371★ "Musicians" in *Career Discovery Encyclopedia* **(Vol.4, pp. 116-117)**
J.G. Ferguson Publishing Co.
200 W. Madison St., Ste. 300
Chicago, IL 60606
Ph: (312)580-5480   Fax: (312)580-4948

Russell E. Primm, editor-in chief. 1993. This six volume set contains two-page articles for 504 occupations. Each article describes job duties, earnings, and educational and training requirements. The whole set is arranged alphabetically by job title. Designed for junior high and older students.

★7372★ "Musicians", "Composers", and "Singers" in *Career Information Center* **(Vol.3)**
Simon and Schuster
200 Old Tappan Rd.
Old Tappan, NJ 07675
Fax: 800-445-6991   Fr: 800-223-2348

Ricard Lidz and Linda Perrin, editorial directors. Fifth edition, 1993. A multi-volume set that profiles more than 600 occupations. Each occupational profile describes job duties, educational requirements, getting a job, advancement possibilities, employment outlook, working conditions, earnings and benefits, and sources of additional information.

★7373★ "Musicians" in *Encyclopedia of Careers and Vocational Guidance* **(Vol.3, pp. 533-539)**
J.G. Ferguson Publishing Co.
200 W. Madison St., Ste. 300
Chicago, IL 60606
Ph: (312)580-5480   Fax: (312)580-4948

William E. Hopke, editor-in-chief. Ninth edition, 1993. Four-volume set that profiles 900 occupations and describes job trends in 74 industries. Includes career description, educational requirements, history of the job, methods of entry, advancement, employment outlook, earnings, conditions of work, social and psychological factors, and sources of further information.

★7374★ *Musicians, Instrumental*
Chronicle Guidance Publications, Inc.
66 Aurora St.
PO Box 1190
Moravia, NY 13118-1190
Ph: (315)497-0330   Fax: (315)497-3359
Fr: 800-622-7284

1993. Career brief describing the nature of the job, working conditions, hours and earnings, education and training, licensure, certification, unions, personal qualifications, social and psychological factors, location, employment outlook, entry methods, advancement, and related occupations.

★7375★ "Musicians" in *Jobs! What They Are—Where They Are—What They Pay* **(pp. 301)**
Fireside
Simon & Schuster Bldg.
1230 Avenue of the Americas
New York, NY 10020
Ph: (212)698-7000   Fr: 800-223-2348

Robert O. Snelling and Anne M. Snelling. Revised and updated, 1992. Describes duties and responsibilities, earnings, employment opportunities, training, and qualifications.

★7376★ "Musicians" in *Occupational Outlook Handbook*
U.S. Government Printing Office
Superintendent of Documents
Washington, DC 20402
Ph: (202)512-1800   Fax: (202)512-2250

Biennial; latest edition, 1994-95. Encyclopedia of careers describing about 250 occupations and comprising about 85 percent of all jobs in the economy. Occupations that require lengthy education or training are given the most attention. Each occupation's profile describes what the worker does on the job, working conditions, education and training requirements, advancement possibilities, job outlook, earnings, and sources of additional information.

★7377★ *Opportunities in Music Careers*
National Textbook Co. (NTC)
VGM Career Books
4255 W. Touhy Ave.
Lincolnwood, IL 60646-1975
Ph: (708)679-5500   Fax: (708)679-2494
Fr: 800-323-4900

Robert Gerardi. 1991. Includes a bibliography.

★7378★ Opportunities in Performing Arts Careers
National Textbook Co. (NTC)
VGM Career Books
4255 W. Touhy Ave.
Lincolnwood, IL 60646-1975
Ph: (708)679-5500   Fax: (708)679-2494
Fr: 800-323-4900

Bonnie Bjorguine Bekken. 1991. Overviews the exciting world of performing arts, including opportunities in classical and popular music; theater, television, and movie acting; dance; performance art; and teaching and therapy. Also offers information on developing a portfolio and preparing for auditions.

★7379★ "Singer" in College Board Guide to Jobs and Career Planning (pp. 67)
The College Board
415 Columbus Ave.
New York, NY 10023-6992
Ph: (212)713-8165   Fax: (212)713-8143
Fr: 800-323-7155

Joyce S. Mitchell. Second edition, 1994. Describes a variety of careers. Each profile contains information on salaries, related careers, education needed, and sources of additional information.

★7380★ Singers
Chronicle Guidance Publications, Inc.
66 Aurora St.
PO Box 1190
Moravia, NY 13118-1190
Ph: (315)497-0330   Fax: (315)497-3359
Fr: 800-622-7284

1994. Career brief describing the nature of the job, working conditions, hours and earnings, education and training, licensure, certification, unions, personal qualifications, social and psychological factors, location, employment outlook, entry methods, advancement, and related occupations.

★7381★ "Singers" in American Almanac of Jobs and Salaries (pp. 150)
Avon Books
1350 Avenue of the Americas
New York, NY 10019
Ph: (212)261-6800   Fr: 800-238-0658

John Wright, editor. Revised and updated, 1994-95. A comprehensive guide to the wages of hundreds of occupations in a wide variety of industries and organizations.

★7382★ "Symphony Conductor" in Offbeat Careers: Directory of Unusual Work
Ten Speed Press
PO Box 7123
Berkeley, CA 94707
Fax: (510)559-1629   Fr: 800-841-2665

Al Sacharov. 1991. Each occupational profile describes places of employment, employment outlook, advantages and disadvantages of the work, and personal characteristics needed.

★7383★ Violinist
Vocational Biographies, Inc.
PO Box 31
Sauk Centre, MN 56378-0031
Ph: (612)352-6516   Fax: (612)352-5546
Fr: 800-255-0752

1993. Four-page pamphlet containing a personal narrative about a worker's job, work likes and dislikes, career path from high school to the present. Education and training, the rewards and frustrations, and the effects of the job on the rest of the worker's life. The data file portion of this pamphlet gives a concise occupational summary, including work descriptions, working conditions, places of employment, personal characteristics, education and training, job outlook, and salary range.

★7384★ Your Own Way in Music: A Career and Resource Guide
St. Martin's Press, Inc.
175 5th Ave.
New York, NY 10010
Ph: (212)674-5151

Nancy Uscher. 1990.

PROFESSIONAL ASSOCIATIONS

★7385★ American Federation of Musicians of the United States and Canada (AFM)
Paramount Bldg.
1501 Broadway, Ste. 600
New York, NY 10036
Ph: (212)869-1330   Fax: (212)764-6134
Fr: 800-762-3444

Members: AFL-CIO. Musicians interested in advancing the music industry. **Purpose:** Offers legal representation on issues dealing with breach of contract, job protection, and wage scale negotiations. **Publications:** International Musician, monthly.

★7386★ American Guild of Musical Artists (AGMA)
1727 Broadway
New York, NY 10019
Ph: (212)265-3687

Members: AFL-CIO. Opera and classical concert singers, classical ballet and modern dance performers, and affiliated stage directors and stage managers. **Publications:** AGMAzine.

★7387★ American Guild of Organists (AGO)
475 Riverside Dr., Ste. 1260
New York, NY 10115
Ph: (212)870-2310   Fax: (212)870-2163

Members: Purpose: Educational and service organization organized to advance the cause of organ and choral music and to maintain standards of artistic excellence of organists and choral conductors. Offers professional certification in organ playing, choral and instrumental training, and theory and general knowledge of music. **Publications:** The American Organist, monthly.

★7388★ American Symphony Orchestra League
777 14th St. NW, Ste. 500
Washington, DC 20005
Ph: (202)628-0099   Fax: (202)783-7228

Members: Symphony orchestras; associate members include educational institutions, arts councils, public libraries, business firms, orchestra professionals, and individuals interested in symphony orchestras. **Purpose:** Engages in extensive research on diverse facets of symphony orchestra operations and development. Provides consulting services for orchestras, their boards, and volunteer organizations. Sponsors management seminars and workshops for professional symphony orchestra administrative and artistic staff, volunteers, and prospective management personnel. Maintains employment services; collects and distributes resource materials, financial data, and statistical reports on many aspects of orchestra operations. Compiles statistics; sponsors educational programs; maintains resource center. **Publications:** Education Programs. • The Gold Book: Director of Successful Projects for Volunteers. • Orchestra/Business Directory, annual. • SYMPHONY, bimonthly.

★7389★ Music Educators National Conference (MENC)
1806 Robert Fulton Dr.
Reston, VA 22091
Ph: (703)860-4000   Fax: (703)860-1531
Fr: 800-336-3768

Members: Professional organization of music educators, administrators, supervisors, consultants, and music education majors in colleges. Compiles statistics. **Publications:** General Music Today, quarterly. • Journal of Research in Music Education, quarterly. • Music Educators Journal, bimonthly. • Teaching Music, bimonthly.

★7390★ Music Teachers National Association (MTNA)
441 Vine St., Ste. 505
Cincinnati, OH 45202-2814
Ph: (513)421-1420   Fax: (513)421-2503

Members: Professional society of independent and collegiate music teachers committed to furthering the art of music through programs that encourage and support teaching, performance, composition, and scholarly research. **Publications:** American Music Teacher Journal, bimonthly. • MTNA Newsletter, 3/year. • Music Teachers National Association—Directory of Nationally Certified Teachers of Music, annual.

★7391★ National Association of Schools of Music (NASM)
11250 Roger Bacon Dr., Ste. 21
Reston, VA 22090
Ph: (703)437-0700   Fax: (703)437-6312

Members: Purpose: Accrediting agency for music educational programs. Compiles statistics. **Publications:** National Association of Schools of Music—Directory, annual. • National Association of Schools of Music—Handbook, biennial. • National Association of Schools of Music—Proceedings, annual.

STANDARDS/CERTIFICATION AGENCIES

★7392★ American Guild of Organists (AGO)
475 Riverside Dr., Ste. 1260
New York, NY 10115
Ph: (212)870-2310   Fax: (212)870-2163
Educational and service organization organized to advance the cause of organ and choral music and to maintain standards of artistic excellence of organists and choral conductors. Offers professional certification in organ playing, choral and instrumental training, and theory and general knowledge of music.

TEST GUIDES

★7393★ Music
National Learning Corp.
212 Michael Dr.
Syosset, NY 11791
Ph: (516)921-8888   Fax: (516)921-8743
Fr: 800-645-6337
Jack Rudman. Undergraduate Program Field Test series. A practice examination fashioned after tests given in the Regents External Degree Program. Designed to measure knowledge received outside the college classroom in the subject of music. Contains multiple-choice questions; provides solutions.

★7394★ Music
National Learning Corp.
212 Michael Dr.
Syosset, NY 11791
Ph: (516)921-8888   Fax: (516)921-8743
Fr: 800-645-6337
Jack Rudman. A test from the Graduate Record Examination series. Multiple-choice test for those seeking admission to graduate school for study in the field of music. Includes solutions to examination questions.

★7395★ Practicing to Take the GRE Revised Music Test
Educational Testing Service
Rosedale Rd.
Princeton, NJ 08541
Ph: (609)921-9000
1990. One booklet and one cassette. Published by the Educational Testing Service for the Graduate Record Examination Board.

EDUCATIONAL DIRECTORIES AND PROGRAMS

★7396★ Chamber Music America— Membership Directory
Chamber Music America
545 8th Ave.
New York, NY 10018
Ph: (212)244-2772   Fax: (212)244-2776
Daniel J. Myers, Contact
Annual, fall. Covers over 800 member ensembles, presenters, festivals, and training programs; over 4,000 associate members, including managers, publishers, arts organizations, instrument manufacturers, libraries and individuals. Entries include: For members— Name, address, phone, name of contact, activities, awards. For associates—Name, address, phone. Arrangement: Separate geographical sections for ensembles, presenters, festivals and training programs; associate members are classified by type of organization, then alphabetical.

★7397★ CRTentertainment
Sofprotex
PO Box 271
Belmont, CA 94002
Current. Diskette; requires a FileMaker compatible database. Covers over 500 theatrical agencies and entertainment industry organizations and 1,000 movie stars, musicians, producers, directors, and writers in the U.S. Database includes: Name, home address, business address and phone.

★7398★ Directory of Music Faculties in Colleges and Universities, U.S. and Canada
CMS Publications, Inc.
PO Box 8208
Missoula, MT 59807-8208
Ph: (406)728-2002   Fax: (406)721-9419
Fr: 800-729-0235
Robby D. Gunstream
Annual. Covers Over 1,800 postsecondary institutions and over 31,000 faculty members throughout the United States and Canada. Entries include: For institutions—Name, address, phone, fax, e-mail, and degree programs offered. For faculty members—Name, academic rank, highest degree earned, teaching areas in field of music. Arrangement: Geographical.

★7399★ Instrumentalist—Directory of Music Schools Issue
The Instrumentalist Co.
200 Northfield Rd.
Northfield, IL 60093
Ph: (708)446-5000
Katherine Olsen, Contact
Annual, October; November addendum. Publication includes: List of nearly 220 college and university music departments; coverage includes Canada. Entries include: School name, address, phone, name of contact; fees, financial aid available, deadlines. Arrangement: Geographical.

★7400★ International Guide to Afrocentric Talent
Osborne Communications
18565 NE 1 Ct.
Miami, FL 33179
Ph: (305)654-8298
Eddie Osborne, Contact
Annual, winter. Covers Approximately 500 vocalists, musicians, dance and theatre troupes, speakers, storytellers, and other talent of African descent, theme, or focus; coverage includes the U.S., Canada, the Caribbean, Africa, Europe, and regions of the Pacific. Entries include: Organization or individual name, address, phone, name and title of contact, number of members (for groups), geographical area served, description. Arrangement: Classified by type of talent.

★7401★ The Kerrville Directory
Kerrville Music Foundation, Inc.
PO Box 1466
Kerrville, TX 78029
Ph: (210)257-3600   Fax: (210)257-8680
Steve Gillette
Annual, March. Covers International information for singers, songwriters, and acoustic musicians, including performance venues, radio stations/shows/producers, commercial press, entertainment editors, folk press/organizations, songwriter organizations/services, performers, writers, agents, managers, publicists, and retail sales of instruments and musical supplies. Entries include: For performance venues—Name, address, phone, name and title of contact, description/performance opportunities. For radio stations—Call letters, address, name and title of contact, phone; wattage; name of radio program, host. All other entries—Name, address, phone, name and title of contact; some listings give descriptions.

★7402★ Musical America's International Directory of the Performing Arts
K-III Directory Corp.
424 W. 33rd St., 11th Fl.
New York, NY 10001
Ph: (212)714-3100   Fax: (212)714-3157
Fr: 800-221-5488
Robert Rund, Contact
Annual, December. Covers U.S., Canadian, and international orchestras, musicians, singers, performing arts series, dance and opera companies, festivals, contests, foundations and awards, publishers of music, artist managers, booking agents, music magazines, and service and professional music organizations. Section for U.S. and Canada also includes listings of choral groups, music schools and departments, and newspaper music critics; international directory section also lists concert managers. Entries include: Name of organization, institution, address, phone, fax, telex, key personnel; most entries include name of contact, manager, conductor, etc. For schools—Number of students and faculty. For Arrangement: Geographical.

★7403★ **National Association of Schools of Music—Directory**
National Association of Schools of Music
11250 Roger Bacon Dr., No. 21
Reston, VA 22090
Ph: (703)437-0700   Fax: (703)437-6312
Betty Weir, Contact
Annual, March. Covers approximately 550 college and university departments of music and music conservatories accredited by the association. Entries include: School name, address, type of membership, description of music program, name of chief administrator, phone, degree or other study programs offered in music. Arrangement: Alphabetical.

★7404★ **National Directory of Arts Internships**
National Network for Artist Placement
935 W. Ave. 37
Los Angeles, CA 90065
Ph: (213)222-4035   Fax: (213)222-4035
Warren Christensen, Contact
Biennial, odd years. Covers Approximately 2,000 internship opportunities in dance, music, theater, art, design, film, and video. Entries include: Name of sponsoring organization, address, name of contact; description of positions available, eligibility requirements, stipend or salary (if any), application procedures. Arrangement: Classified by discipline, then geographical.

★7405★ **National Opera Association— Membership Directory**
National Opera Association, Inc.
School of Music
Northwestern University
711 Elgin Rd.
Evanston, IL 60208
Ph: (708)467-2422   Fax: (708)491-5260
Jeffery Wright, Executive Administrator
Annual, October. Covers About 675 music and singing teachers, singers, directors, and about 300 schools, colleges, and organizations interested in opera; international coverage. Entries include: Name, address, phone, activity or occupation. Arrangement: Alphabetical within membership divisions..

★7406★ **Performing Arts Career Directory**
Gale Research Inc.
835 Penobscot Bldg.
Detroit, MI 48226
Ph: (313)961-2242   Fr: 800-877-GALE
1994. Profiles careers in the performing arts industry.

★7407★ **Schirmer Guide to Schools of Music and Conservatories throughout the World**
Schirmer Books
866 3rd Ave.
New York, NY 10022
Ph: (212)702-3445   Fax: (212)605-9368
Fr: 800-257-5755
Soo Mee Kwon, Contact
Reported as every four-five years; latest edition 1988. Covers more than 750 conservatories and university departments and schools of music. Entries include: Institution name, address, phone, name of chief administrative officer, programs and degrees of certificates offered, instruments taught; practice, concert, and recording facilities; library facilities and special collections, performance groups and featured programs, exchange programs, tuition and financial aid, accreditations, description of community life. Arrangement: Geographical.

AWARDS, SCHOLARSHIPS, GRANTS, AND FELLOWSHIPS

★7408★ **Artists' Fellowship Program**
New York Foundation for the Arts
155 6th Ave., No. 14FL
New York, NY 10013-1507
Ph: (212)233-3900   Fax: (212)791-1813
To encourage professional development and to provide fellowships to individual New York State creative artists in the following categories: Architecture, Choreography, Crafts, Fiction, Film, Music Composition, Nonfiction Literature, Painting, Performance Art/Emergent Forms, Photography, Playwriting/Screenwriting, Poetry, Printmaking/Drawing/Artists' Books, Sculpture, and Video. The Program assists eligible New York State artists in their work through direct grants awarded solely on the basis of creative excellence. These awards are not to be considered project support. All applicants to the Artists' Fellowship Program are required to submit a representative body of work to demonstrate professional accomplishment and commitment to a professional career. They must be at least 18 years of age, and must have resided in New York State for the two years immediately prior to application. Graduate or undergraduate matriculated students enrolled in a degree program at the time of application may not apply. No faxed applications are accepted. Fellowships of $7,000 are awarded in some of the categories annually. In 1992, an average of 11 Fellowships were awarded in each of the following categories: Crafts, Film, Nonfiction, Literature, Performance Art/Emergent Forms, Poetry, Printmaking/Drawing/Artists' Books and Sculpture. Established in 1984. The New York Foundation for the Arts also administers four other major statewide programs: (1) The Artists-in-Residence Program, a re-grant program to create artists-in-residence opportunities in educational, cultural, and community organizations; (2) The Artists' New Works Program, a sponsorship program that provides advisory and fiscal services to professional artists who are developing individual projects; and (3) The Revolving Loan Program, a short-term, loan service for nonprofit cultural organizations.

★7409★ **BMI Awards to Student Composers**
Broadcast Music, Inc.
320 W. 57th St.
New York, NY 10019
Ph: (212)586-2000   Fax: (212)262-2824
To honor the best original vocal or instrumental composition and to encourage the creation of concert music by student composers. Students actively engaged in the study of music who are under 26 years of age and are citizens or permanent residents of countries within the Western Hemisphere are eligible. Monetary prizes totalling $16,000 and ranging from $500 to $3,000 are awarded annually at the discretion of the judges, permanently chaired by the American composer, Milton Babbitt. Established in 1951.

★7410★ **Concert Artists Guild New York Competition**
Concert Artists Guild
850 7th Ave., Ste. 1003
New York, NY 10019
Ph: (212)333-5200   Fax: (212)977-7149
To assist the career development of young classical music artists. Instrumentalists (except organists), vocalists, and chamber ensembles are eligible. Applicants under professional United States management, are not eligible. Artists of all nationalities without regard to age may submit applications by January 17. Award winners are chosen through the CAG Annual New York Competition. The first prize award consists of a fully sponsored New York recital, a commissioned work from a composer of the winner's choice, free professional management leading to recitals and solo appearances with orchestras and more. A maximum of three first prize CAG Awards are available annually. One of the first prize winners is selected to receive a recording contract with Amsterdam's Channel Classics Records. Nathan Wedeen Awards are given to extraordinary competitors ath the descretion of staff and judges. The awards provide the winners with free professional U.S. management by Concert Artists Guild. Established in 1951.

★7411★ **Emmy Awards for Primetime Programming**
Academy of Television Arts and Sciences
5220 Lankershim Blvd.
North Hollywood, CA 91601
Ph: (818)754-2800   Fax: (818)761-2927
To recognize the advancement of the arts and sciences of television and achievements broadcast nationally during primetime. Awards are given in the following categories: (1) Program Category Awards - (a) Outstanding Comedy Series; (b) Outstanding Drama Series; (c) Outstanding Miniseries; (d) Outstanding Variety, Music, or Comedy Series; (e) Outstanding Made for T.V. Movie; (f) Outstanding Classical Program in the Performing Arts; (g) Outstanding Informational Special; (h) Outstanding Informational Series; (i) Outstanding Animated Program; and (j) Outstanding Children's Program; (2) Individual Awards - (a) Lead, Supporting, and Guest Acting in Comedy Series, Drama Series, Miniseries, or Special; (b) Performance in Variety or Music Program, Informational Programming, and Classical Music/Dance Programming; (c) Directing in Comedy Series, Drama Series, Variety or Music Program, Miniseries or Special, Classical Music/Dance Programming, and Informational Programming; (d) Casting for a Miniseries or Special; (e) Writing in Comedy Series, Drama Series, Variety or Music Program, Miniseries or Special, Informational Programming, and Classical Music/Dance Programming; and (3) Technical Awards - (a) Choreography; (b) Cinematography; (c) Art Direction; (d) Music Composition; (e) Main Title Theme Music; (f) Music Direction; (g) Music and Lyrics; (h) Costume Design; (i) Costuming; (j) Makeup;

(k) Hairstyling; (l) Editing; (m) Sound Editing; (n) Sound Mixing; (o) Technical Direction/Camera/Video; (p) Special Visual Effects; (q) Graphic Design and Title Sequences; (r) Lighting Direction; (s) Engineering Development; and (4) ATAS Governors Award. Nominees are voted upon by a jury. An Emmy statuette is presented annually at the Emmy Awards Ceremony. Established in 1948 and administered by the Academy of Television Arts and Sciences until 1977.

★7412★ Avery Fisher Artist Program
Avery Fisher Artist Program
Lincoln Center for the Performing Arts
70 Lincoln Center Plaza
New York, NY 10023
Ph: (212)875-5540   Fax: (212)875-5414

To recognize artists for outstanding achievement and excellence in music. Awards are made to solo instrumentalists who are United States citizens. Nominations are made by the recommendation board; recipients are chosen by the executive committee. The following awards are given: Avery Fisher Prize - a monetary award of $25,000 and the recipient's name engraved on a plaque in the Avery Fisher Hall; and Avery Fisher Career Grant - three to five grants of $10,000 each to be used by the recipients for specific needs to further careers. Established in 1974. Additional information is available from M.L. Falcone, Public Relations, 155 W. 68th St., New York, NY 10023.

★7413★ Gold Medal
American Academy of Arts and Letters
633 W. 155 St.
New York, NY 10032
Ph: (212)368-5900   Fax: (212)491-4615

For distinguished achievement in the following categories of the arts: architecture (including landscape architecture) and history, drama and graphic arts, belles letters, criticism, painting, poetry and music, fiction and sculpture, and biography and music. Criteria for selection is based on the entire work of the recipient, who must be a United States citizen. Applications are not accepted. Nominations are made by members of the Academy. Awarded annually in rotation in the above categories.

★7414★ Golden Score Award
American Society of Music Arrangers
PO Box 11
Hollywood, CA 90078
Ph: (213)658-5997   Fax: (213)658-6521

For recognition of continued excellence and achievement in the arts of music composing, arranging, and orchestrating. Nominations may be made by the Board of Directors based on the length of professional career and maintenance of high standards. A plaque is awarded annually. Established in 1982.

★7415★ John Simon Guggenheim Memorial Foundation Fellowships
John Simon Guggenheim Memorial Foundation
90 Park Ave.
New York, NY 10016
Ph: (212)687-4470

To recognize men and women who have demonstrated an exceptional capacity for productive scholarship or exceptional creative ability in the arts. Fellowships are awarded through two annual competitions: one open to citizens and permanent residents of the United States and Canada, and the other open to citizens and permanent residents of Latin America and the Caribbean. The Fellowships are awarded by the Trustees upon nominations made by a Committee of Selection. The Foundation consults with distinguished scholars and artists regarding the accomplishments and promise of the applicants in relation to the plans that they propose. Appointments are ordinarily made for one year, but in no instance for less than six consecutive months. The amount of each grant is adjusted to the needs of the Fellows, considering their other resources and the purpose and scope of their plans. Established by U. S. Senator Simon Guggenheim and Mrs. Guggenheim as a memorial to their son who died April 26, 1922.

★7416★ Jazz Hall of Fame
Institute of Jazz Studies
135 Bradley Hall
Rutgers Univ.
Newark, NJ 07102
Ph: (201)648-5595   Fax: (201)648-5944

For recognition of outstanding contributions to jazz, past and present. The award is intended primarily for instrumentalists and singers, but non-performers (critics, scholars, producers) are also eligible. A plaque and permanent representation in the Hall of Fame are awarded posthumously as well as to the living. Awarded annually. Established in 1983 by Rutgers University and the New Jersey Jazz Society.

★7417★ Kennedy Center Honors
John F. Kennedy Center for the Performing Arts
Washington, DC 20566
Ph: (202)416-8000   Fax: (202)416-8205

To recognize individuals for their distinguished artistic achievements and career contributions to American culture. The primary criterion in the selection of the recipients is artistic achievement as a performer, composer, choreographer, playwright, director or conductor. Honorees are nominated by the Artists Committee in the areas of dance, music, theater, opera, motion pictures and television. Final selection is made by the Kennedy Center Board of Trustees. A unique beribboned medal, created for the Kennedy Center Honors, is awarded each year at an annual celebration consisting of a traditional Board of Trustees dinner and an Honors Gala performance, preceeded by a reception hosted by the President of the United States. Established in 1978. Additional information is available from Laura Langley, phone: (202) 416-8430.

★7418★ Musician of the Year
Musical America Publishing
424 W. 33rd St., No. 11FL
New York, NY 10001-2604
Ph: (212)714-3103   Fax: (212)695-5025

To honor an outstanding classical singer, instrumentalist, conductor, composer, or choreographer for artistic achievement over the years. A plaque and a full-color photograph on the cover of *Musical America International Directory of the Performing Arts* are awarded annually in December. Established in 1960. In addition, in 1992, awards for Composer of the Year, Conductor of the Year, Instrumentalist of the Year, and Vocalist of the Yearwere established.

★7419★ National Endowment for the Arts Programs
National Endowment for the Arts
Nancy Hanks Center
1100 Pennsylvania Ave. NW
Washington, DC 20506
Ph: (202)682-5400

To encourage and support American arts and artists. The Endowment serves as a catalyst to promote the continuing vitality and excellence of the arts in America and to provide access to, and appreciation of, such excellence and vitality. The National Council on the Arts advises the Endowment on policies, programs, and procedures and reviews and makes recommendations on applications for grants. The Endowment provides three major types of financial assistance: non-matching fellowships to artists of exceptional talent (fellowships are given only to citizens or permanent residents of the United States); matching grants to non-profit, tax-exempt organizations and projects of the highest artistic level and of national or regional significance; and matching grants to state and local arts agencies and regional arts groups. Awards are presented in the following areas: dance, design arts, expansion arts, folk arts, literature, media arts, film/radio/television, museums, music, opera-musical theater, presenting and commissioning, inter-arts, theater, visual arts, and international. Established in 1965.

★7420★ George Peabody Medal
Peabody Institute of The Johns Hopkins University
1 E. Mt. Vernon Pl.
Baltimore, MD 21202-2397
Ph: (410)659-8160   Fax: (410)659-8168

For recognition of outstanding contributions to music in America. Contributions to music may be considered in one of the following areas: performance, composition, philanthropy, and musicology. A pewter medal is awarded annually at the Peabody Conservatory May Graduation Exercises. Established in 1980. Sponsored by the Peabody Conservatory of Music.

★7421★ Antoinette Perry Awards (Tony Awards)
League of American Theatres and Producers
226 W. 47 St.
New York, NY 10036
Ph: (212)764-2929   Fax: (212)719-4389

To recognize outstanding theatrical achievement in the Broadway theatre. Legitimate theatrical productions opening in an eligible Broadway house with 499 or more seats during the Tony season (May to May) are eligible for nomination. Awards are presented in the following creative categories: Best Play - awards to the author and producer; Best Musical - award to the producer; Best Book of a Musical; Best Original Score of a Musical written for the theater; Best Revival of a Play or a Musical - award to the producer; Best Actor in a Play; Best Actress in a Play; Best Featured Actor in a Play; Best Featured Actress in a Play; Best Actor in a Musical; Best Actress in a Musical; Best Featured Actor in a

Musical; Best Featured Actress in a Musical; Best Direction of a Play; Best Direction of a Musical; Best Scenic Design; Best Costume Design; Best Lighting Design; and Best Choreography. Tony Awards- a silver medallion embossed with masks of comedy and tragedy mounted on black lucite-base, are awarded annually in each category. Established in 1947 in honor of Antoinette Perry of the American Theatre Wing.

★7422★ **Residency Fellowships for Artists and Ensembles Developing New Works**
Yellow Springs Institute
1645 Art School Rd.
Chester Springs, PA 19425
Ph: (215)827-9111   Fax: (215)827-7093
To provide artists with an opportunity to develop, rehearse, and present untried new works, particularly in music, dance, performance art, and inter-disciplinary projects. Applicants must have a minimum of three years professional experience in the field. Only works previously unproduced and unperformed are considered. Students are ineligible. Applications must be submitted by October 15. Call for application forms. Residencies are for two to three weeks, including room, board, professionally staffed rehearsal and performance space, documentation, and transportation assistance. Established in 1979 by John A. Clauser, AIA.

★7423★ **Rock and Roll Hall of Fame**
Rock and Roll Hall of Fame and Museum
50 Public Sq., Ste. 545
Cleveland, OH 44113
Ph: (216)781-ROCK   Fax: (216)781-1832
For recognition of outstanding rock and roll performers. To be eligible, a performer must have recorded an album or single at least 25 years ago. In addition, non- performers and musicians who had an early influence on rock and roll are also considered. Established in 1986. Additional information is available from the Rock and Roll Hall of Fame Foundation, Suzan Evans, phone: (212) 484-6427.

★7424★ **Rome Prize Fellowships**
American Academy in Rome
7 East 60th St.
New York, NY 10022-1001
Ph: (212)751-7200   Fax: (212)751-7220
To provide artists and scholars with a year in Rome at the Academy for independent work or research in the following fields: architecture; landscape architecture; musical composition; design arts; painting, sculpture and visual arts; literature; classical studies; history of art; medieval/renaissance studies; post-classical humanistic studies; and modern Italian studies. U.S. citizens (or permanent residents if applying for the Andrew W. Mellon Fellowship(post-doctoral) in the humanities) with a B.A. or equivalent degree in a field of fine arts, or a pre-doctoral or post-doctoral candidate in a field of the humanities, may apply by November 15 each year. Fellowships that provide travel, room, board, studio/study, and a stipend are awarded annually to approximately 30 artists and scholars. Established in 1894 by Charles Follen McKim. The Italian address for the American Academy in Rome is Via Angelo Masina 5, 00153 Rome, Italy.

★7425★ **William Schuman Award**
Columbia University
School of the Arts
305 Dodge Hall
New York, NY 10027
Ph: (212)854-2875   Fax: (212)854-1309
To recognize the lifetime achievement of an American composer whose works have been widely performed and generally acknowledged to be of lasting significance. The Dean of the School of the Arts and composers choose the winner of the prize. A monetary prize of $50,000 is awarded biennially or when $50,000 has accumulated. Established in 1981 by the James Warburg family in honor of the American composer, William Schuman. The Bydale Foundation(a Warburg family foundation) established the award through a grant of $250,000 to the School of the Arts.

★7426★ **Young Composers Awards**
National Guild of Community Schools of the Arts
PO Box 8018
Englewood, NJ 07631
Ph: (201)871-3337   Fax: (201)871-7639
To encourage the composition of serious music by young people. Students between 13 and 19 years of age who are residents of the United States or Canada may submit scores by April 1. The following monetary prizes are awarded: first prize - $1,000; second prize - $750; and third prize - $500. Awarded annually. Established in 1984 by Dr. Herbert Zipper with support from the Rockefeller Foundation.

BASIC REFERENCE GUIDES AND HANDBOOKS

★7427★ *The Anchor Companion to the Orchestra*
Doubleday and Co., Inc.
1540 Broadway
New York, NY 10036-4094
Ph: (212)354-6500   Fr: 800-223-6834
Norman Del Mar. 1987. Contains entries on musical instruments, orchestral performance, and musical arrangement.

★7428★ *Benet's Reader's Encyclopedia*
Harper and Row Publishers, Inc.
10 E. 53rd St.
New York, NY 10022
Ph: (212)207-7000
William Benet. Third edition, 1987.

★7429★ *Fundamentals of Music*
Prentice-Hall, Inc.
Rte. 9W
Englewood Cliffs, NJ 07632
Ph: (201)592-2000   Fr: 800-634-2863
Raymond Elliott. Fourth edition, 1989. Covers the basic elements of music: rhythm, melody, and harmony.

★7430★ *The Jazz Musician*
Saint Martin's Press Inc.
175 5th Ave.
New York, NY 10010
Ph: (212)674-5151
Tony Scherman, editor. 1994.

★7431★ *The Master Musician*
Zondervan Publishing Corp.
5300 Patterson Ave. SE
Grand Rapids, MI 49530
Ph: (616)698-6900   Fax: (616)698-3235
Fr: 800-272-3480
John M. Talbot, editor. 1992.

★7432★ *Music Business Handbook & Career Guide*
Sherwood Co.
PO Box 4198
Thousand Oaks, CA 91359
Ph: (805)379-6820
David Baskerville. Fifth edition, 1990.

★7433★ *Playing for Pay: How to be a Working Musician*
Writer's Digest Books
1507 Dana Ave.
Cincinnati, OH 45207
Ph: (513)531-2222   Fax: (513)531-4744
Fr: 800-289-0963
James Gibson, editor. 1990.

★7434★ *The Rock Musician*
Saint Martin's Press
175 5th Ave.
New York, NY 10010
Ph: (212)674-5151
Tony Scherman, editor. 1993.

★7435★ *The Songwriter's and Musician's Guide to Making Great Demos*
Writer's Digest Books
1507 Dana Ave.
Cincinnati, OH 45207
Ph: (513)531-2222
Harvey Rachlin. 1990. Includes an index.

PROFESSIONAL AND TRADE PERIODICALS

★7436★ *American Recorder*
American Recorder Society
PO Box 631
Littleton, CO 80160
Ph: (303)347-1120
Benjamin Dunham
Magazine containing articles, reports, and reviews for the vocational and professional recorder player. Music for recorder in most issues.

★7437★ *British Journal of Music Education*
Cambridge University Press
40 W. 20th St.
New York, NY 10011
Ph: (212)924-3900   Fax: (212)691-3239
John Paynter
Journal focusing on current issues in music education.

★7438★ Cambridge Opera Journal
Cambridge University Press
40 W. 20th St.
New York, NY 10011
Ph: (212)924-3900   Fax: (212)691-3239
Roger Parker

Journal focusing on opera and related disciplines.

★7439★ Contents
Contents
PO Box 8879
Savannah, GA 31412
Joseph Alfieris

Magazine covering art, design, literature and music.

★7440★ Down Beat
Maher Publications, Inc.
180 W. Park Ave.
Elmhurst, IL 60126
Ph: (708)941-2030   Fax: (708)941-3210
Fr: 800-535-7496
John Ephland

Monthly. Magazine edited for the learning musician.

★7441★ Hot Line News
Musicians National Hot Line Association
277 East 6100 South
Salt Lake City, UT 84107
Ph: (801)268-2000
Nancy W. Zitting

Carries news of individual musicians and groups, and addresses ways to stay employed in music. Carries brief autobiographical sketches and lists of employment needs and opportunities. Recurring features include a column titled Spotlight.

★7442★ International Musician
American Federation of Musicians
1501 Broadway, Ste. 600
New York, NY 10036
Ph: (212)869-1330   Fax: (212)302-4374
Stephen R. Sprague

Monthly. Tabloid for labor union musicians.

★7443★ Jersey Jazz
New Jersey Jazz Society
PO Box 173
Brookside, NJ 07926
Ph: (201)543-2039
Don Robertson

Dedicated to the performance, promotion, and preservation of jazz.

★7444★ Music Notation News
Music Notation Modernization Association
PO Box 241
Kirksville, MO 63501
Ph: (816)665-8098   Fax: (816)665-8098
Mark Gaare

Quarterly. Serves as the official organ of the Association, which is devoted to "finding ways to improve the basic system of musical notation for greater simplicity and efficiency in reading, writing, and printing music."

★7445★ SYMPHONY
American Symphony Orchestra League
777 14th St. NW, Ste. 500
Washington, DC 20005-3201
Ph: (202)628-0099   Fax: (202)783-7228
Sandra Hyslop

Bimonthly. Magazine with news and articles for symphonic orchestra managers, trustees, volunteers, and musicians.

PROFESSIONAL MEETINGS AND CONVENTIONS

★7446★ American Harp Society National Conference
American Harp Society
6331 Quebec Dr.
Hollywood, CA 90068-2831
Ph: (213)463-0716   Fax: (213)464-2950

Annual. Always held during June. **Dates and Locations:** 1996 Jun.

★7447★ American Musicological Society Convention
American Musicological Society
201 S. 34th St.
Philadelphia, PA 19104
Ph: (215)898-8698

Annual. **Dates and Locations:** 1995 Oct 26-29; New York, NY. • 1996; Cincinnati, OH.

★7448★ International Blues Conference
Blues Foundation
174 Beale St.
Memphis, TN 38103-3714
Ph: (901)527-BLUE

Annual. Always held during November in Memphis, Tennessee. **Dates and Locations:** 1995 Nov; Memphis, TN.

★7449★ Midwest International Band and Orchestra Clinic
Midwest International Band and Orchestra Clinic
1503 Huntington Dr.
Glenview, IL 60025
Ph: (708)729-4629   Fax: (708)729-4635

Annual. Always held during December at the Hilton in Chicago, Illinois. **Dates and Locations:** 1995 Dec 19-23; Chicago, IL. • 1996 Dec 17-21; Chicago, IL.

★7450★ Violin Society of America Convention
Violin Society of America
85-07 Abingdon Rd.
Kew Gardens, NY 11415
Ph: (718)849-1373   Fax: (718)849-1374
Annual.

OTHER SOURCES OF INFORMATION

★7451★ Careers as a Rock Musician
Rosen Publishing Group
29 E. 21st St.
New York, NY 10010
Ph: 800-237-9932   Fax: (212)777-0277
Del and Margaret Hopkins. 1993.

★7452★ Guide to the National Endowment for the Arts, 1993-94
National Endowment of the Arts
Nancy Hanks Center, Rm. 803
1100 Pennsylvania Ave., NW
Washington, DC 20506
Ph: (202)682-5400

1993. Describes the overall purpose of each of the endowment's programs and outlines the types of support available in each funding category.

★7453★ Music
Crestwood House
866 3rd Ave.
New York, NY 10022
Ph: (212)702-9632
1994.

★7454★ "Music" in Accounting to Zoology: Graduate Fields Defined (pp. 164)
Petersons Guides, Inc.
PO Box 2123
Princeton, NJ 08543-2123
Ph: (609)243-9111   Fax: (609)243-9150
Fr: 800-338-3282
Amy J. Goldstein, editor. Revised and updated, 1987. Defines 298 graduate and professional fields. Discusses types of graduate programs and degrees, graduate research, applied work, employment prospects, and trends.

★7455★ "Musician" in Career Selector 2001
Barron's Educational Series, Inc.
250 Wireless Blvd.
Hauppauge, NY 11788
Ph: (516)434-3311   Fax: (516)434-3723
Fr: 800-645-3476
James C. Gonyea. 1993.

★7456★ "Musician" in Encyclopedia of Danger: Dangerous Professions (pp. 70-73)
Chelsea House Publishers
1974 Sproul Rd., Ste. 400
Broomall, PA 19008
Ph: (215)353-5166   Fax: (215)359-1439
Missy Allen and Michel Peissel. 1993. Provides descriptions of 24 dangerous occupations, their risky characteristics, and safety precautions.

★7457★ Orchestra Management Fellowship Program
American Symphony Orchestra League
777 14th St., NW, Ste. 500
Washington, DC 20005
Ph: (202)628-0099
Describes the fellowship program to train general managers in concert production,

fundraising, financial management, marketing, public relations, and contract negotiation.

★7458★ *Radio*
Crestwood House
866 3rd Ave.
New York, NY 10022
Ph: (212)702-9632

1994.

★7459★ *Rock, Rap, and Rad: How to Be a Rock or Rap Star*
Avon Books
1350 Avenue of the Americas
New York, NY 10019
Ph: (212)261-6800   Fr: 800-238-0658
1992.

Clinical Laboratory Technologists and Technicians

Clinical laboratory workers run routine tests while others perform complex analyses. The types of tests performed and the amount of responsibility these workers assume depend largely on the educational preparation and experience they have. **Medical technologists** generally have a bachelor's degree in medical technology or in one of the life sciences, or have a combination of formal training and work experience. They perform complicated chemical, biological, hematological, immunologic, microscopic, and bacteriological tests. These may include chemical tests to determine blood glucose or cholesterol levels, for example, or examinations of tissue to detect the presence of infections or diseases. Technologists who prepare specimens and analyze the chemical and hormonal contents of body fluids are **clinical chemistry technologists**. Those who examine and identify bacteria and other micro-organisms are **microbiology technologists**. Other specialty groups include **histology technicians**, who cut and stain tissue specimens for microscopic examination by pathologists; **phlebotomists and blood bank technologists**, who collect, type, and prepare blood and its components for transfusions; and **immunology technologists**, who examine elements and responses of the human immune system to foreign bodies. **Cytotechnologists**, who receive their training in specialized programs, prepare slides of body cells and microscopically examine these cells for abnormalities. **Medical laboratory technicians** generally have an associate degree from a community or junior college, or a diploma or certificate from a vocational or technical school. They are midlevel laboratory workers or laboratory supervisor. They perform a wide range of routine tests and laboratory procedures.

Salaries

Salaries of clinical laboratory personnel vary depending on the employer and geographic location. In general, those in large cities receive the highest salaries.

Medical technologist	$14.71/hour
Medical laboratory technician	$11.33/hour
Medical technologists, federal government	$32,023/year

Employment Outlook

Growth rate until the year 2005: More slowly than the average.

Clinical Laboratory
Technologists and Technicians

★7460★ Answers to Your Questions About an Exciting Career in Medical Technology
American Medical Technologists
710 Higgins Rd.
Park Ridge, IL 60068
Ph: (708)823-5169
1990. This six-panel brochure defines medical technology and describes the difference between a medical technologist and a medical laboratory technician. Outlines places of employment, employment outlook working conditions, and educational preparation.

★7461★ The Art and Science of Histotechnology: A Career to Consider
National Society For Histotechnology
5900 Princess Garden Pkwy., Ste. 805
Lanham, MD 20706
Ph: (301)577-4907
1987. Describes job duties, where the work is done, and gives a state-by-state history of accredited training programs in histotechnology.

★7462★ Blood Bank Specialists
Chronicle Guidance Publications, Inc.
66 Aurora St.
PO Box 1190
Moravia, NY 13118-1190
Ph: (315)497-0330   Fax: (315)497-3359
Fr: 800-622-7284
1994. Career brief describing the nature of the job, working conditions, hours and earnings, education and training, licensure, certification, unions, personal qualifications, social and psychological factors, location, employment outlook, entry methods, advancement, and related occupations.

★7463★ Blood Bank Technology
American Association of Blood Banks
8101 Glenbrook Rd.
Bethesda, MD 20814
Ph: (301)907-6977   Fax: (301)907-6895
This 17-page booklet includes a description of careers in blood banks, a list of accredited

educational programs, and information on scholarships and the certification examination.

★7464★ Body of Knowledge and Task Delineations and Addendum to Body of Knowledge
American Society for Medical Technology (ASMT)
7910 Woodmont Ave., Ste. 1301
Bethesda, MD 20814-3015
Ph: (301)657-2768
Revised edition, 1987. Includes content outlines for all clinical laboratory science disciplines; delineates tasks for present and potential areas of practice; and defines knowledge, skills, and attitudes for competent performance of each clinical laboratory test.

★7465★ A Career in Cytotechnology
American Society of Cytology
1015 Chesnut St., Ste. 1518
Philadelphia, PA 19107
Ph: (215)922-3880
1991. This six-panel pamphlet explains what a cytotechnologist is, and describes the duties, educational requirements, and personal characteristics necessary for the job. Also provides the salary range.

★7466★ Clinical Laboratory Sciences: Levels of Practice
American Society for Medical Technology (ASMT)
7910 Woodmont Ave., Ste. 1301
Bethesda, MD 20814-3015
Ph: (301)657-2768
1987. Revised, 1989. Details performance expectations for current and potential clinical laboratory positions.

★7467★ "Clinical Laboratory Technologist" in 100 Best Careers for the Year 2000 (pp. 53-55)
Arco Pub.
201 W. 103rd St.
Indianapolis, IN 46290
Ph: 800-428-5331   Fax: 800-835-3202
Shelly Field. 1992. Describes 100 job opportunities expected to grow fast throughout the next decade. Provides information on job

duties and responsibilities, training requirements, education, advancement opportunities, experience and qualifications, and typical salaries.

★7468★ "Clinical Laboratory Technologists and Technicians" in 101 Careers: A Guide to the Fastest-Growing Opportunities (pp. 188-190)
John Wiley & Sons, Inc.
605 3rd Ave.
New York, NY 10158-0012
Ph: (212)850-6645   Fax: (212)850-6088
Michael Harkavy. 1990. Describes the nature of the job, working conditions, employment growth, qualifications, personal skills, projected salaries, and where to write for more information.

★7469★ "Clinical Laboratory Technologists and Technicians" in Best Jobs for the 1990s and Into the 21st Century (pp. 103)
Impact Publications
9104-N Manassas Dr.
Manassas Park, VA 22111
Ph: (703)361-7300   Fax: (703)335-9486
Ronald L. Krannich and Caryl Rae Krannich. 1993.

★7470★ "Clinical Laboratory Technologists and Technicians" in Health Care Job Explosion! (pp. 53-66)
D-Amp Publications
401 Amherst Ave.
Coraopolis, PA 15108
Ph: (412)262-5578
Dennis V. Damp. 1993. Provides information on the nature of work for the major health care occupational groups. Descriptions include working conditions, training, job outlook, qualifications, and related occupations.

★7471★ "Clinical Laboratory Technologists and Technicians" in *Occupational Outlook Handbook*
U.S. Government Printing Office
Superintendent of Documents
Washington, DC 20402
Ph: (202)512-1800   Fax: (202)512-2250
Biennial; latest edition, 1994-95. Encyclopedia of careers describing about 250 occupations and comprising about 85 percent of all jobs in the economy. Occupations that require lengthy education or training are given the most attention. Each occupation's profile describes what the worker does on the job, working conditions, education and training requirements, advancement possibilities, job outlook, earnings, and sources of additional information.

★7472★ "Cytotechnologist" in *VGM's Handbook of Health Care Careers*
National Textbook Co.
4255 W. Touhy Ave.
Lincolnwood, IL 60646-1975
Ph: (708)679-5500   Fax: (708)679-2494
Fr: 800-323-4900
Annette Selden. 1993. Contains 42 two-page occupational profiles describing job duties, places of employment, working conditions, qualifications, education, employment outlook, and income.

★7473★ *Health Careers*
Careers, Inc.
PO Box 135
Largo, FL 34649-0135
Ph: (813)584-7333
1994. Four-page brief describing duties, working conditions, personal qualifications, training, earnings and hours, employment outlook, places of employment, related careers, and where to write for more information.

★7474★ "Medical Laboratory" in *150 Careers in the Health Care Field*
Reed Reference Publishing
121 Chanlon Rd.
PO Box 31
New Providence, NJ 07974
Fax: (908)665-6688   Fr: 800-521-8110
Stanley Alerin. Third edition, 1993. Profiles health care occupations requiring a bachelor's degree or less. Describes the nature of the work, educational preparation, licensing requirements, and salary. Lists accredited educational programs.

★7475★ "Medical Laboratory Technologist" in *VGM's Careers Encyclopedia* (pp. 274-277)
National Textbook Co. (NTC)
VGM Career Books
4255 W. Touhy Ave.
Lincolnwood, IL 60646-1975
Ph: (708)679-5500   Fax: (708)679-2494
Fr: 800-323-4900
Third edition, 1991. Describes job duties, places of employment, working conditions, qualifications, education and training, advancement potential, and salary for each occupation.

★7476★ "Medical Laboratory Technologist" in *VGM's Handbook of Health Care Careers*
National Textbook Co.
4255 W. Touhy Ave.
Lincolnwood, IL 60646-1975
Ph: (708)679-5500   Fax: (708)679-2494
Fr: 800-323-4900
Annette Selden. 1993. Contains 42 two-page occupational profiles describing job duties, places of employment, working conditions, qualifications, education, employment outlook, and income.

★7477★ "Medical-Laboratory Workers" in *Jobs! What They Are—Where They Are—What They Pay* (p. 186)
Simon & Schuster, Inc.
Simon & Schuster Bldg.
1230 Avenue of the Americas
New York, NY 10020
Ph: (212)698-7000   Fr: 800-223-2348
Robert O. Snelling and Anne M. Snelling. 3rd edition, 1992. Describes duties and responsibilities, earnings, employment opportunities, training, and qualifications.

★7478★ *Medical Technologist*
Careers, Inc.
PO Box 135
Largo, FL 34649-0135
Ph: (813)584-7333
1993. Four-page brief offering the definition, history, duties, working conditions, personal qualifications, educational requirements, earnings, hours, employment outlook, advancement, and careers related to this position.

★7479★ "Medical Technologist" in *College Board Guide to Jobs and Career Planning* (pp. 270)
The College Board
415 Columbus Ave.
New York, NY 10023-6992
Ph: (212)713-8165   Fax: (212)713-8143
Fr: 800-323-7155
Joyce S. Mitchell. Second edition, 1994. Describes the job, salaries, related careers, education needed, and where to write for more information.

★7480★ "Medical Technologist" in *Guide to Federal Jobs* (p. 138)
Resource Directories
3361 Executive Pkwy., Ste. 302
Toledo, OH 43606
Ph: (419)536-5353   Fax: (419)536-7056
Fr: 800-274-8515
Rod W. Durgin, editor. Third edition, 1992. Contains information on finding and applying for federal jobs. Describes more than 200 professional and technical jobs for college graduates. Covers the nature of the work, salary, and geographic location. Lists college majors preferred for that occupation. Section one describes the function and work of government agencies that hire the most significant number of college graduates.

★7481★ "Medical Technologist and Medical Laboratory Technician" in *Careers in Health Care* (pp. 134-139)
National Textbook Co. (NTC)
VGM Career Books
4255 W. Touhy Ave.
Lincolnwood, IL 60646-1975
Ph: (708)679-5500   Fax: (708)679-2494
Fr: 800-323-4900
Barbara M. Swanson. Third edition, 1995. Describes job duties, work settings, salaries, licensing and certification requirements, educational preparation, and future outlook.

★7482★ *Medical Technologists*
Chronicle Guidance Publications, Inc.
66 Aurora St.
PO Box 1190
Moravia, NY 13118-1190
Ph: (315)497-0330   Fax: (315)497-3359
Fr: 800-622-7284
1991. Career brief describing the nature of the job, working conditions, hours and earnings, education and training, licensure, certification, unions, personal qualifications, social and psychological factors, location, employment outlook, entry methods, advancement, and related occupations.

★7483★ "Medical Technologists" in *Encyclopedia of Careers and Vocational Guidance* (Vol.3, 421-424)
J.G. Ferguson Publishing Co.
200 W. Madison St., Ste. 300
Chicago, IL 60606
Ph: (312)580-5480   Fax: (312)580-4948
William E. Hopke, editor-in-chief. Eighth 1990. Four-volume set that profiles 900 occupations and describes job trends in 76 industries. Chapters include "Laboratory Technicians" (p. 263) and "Medical Laboratory Technicians" (p. 307). Includes career description, educational requirements, history of the job, methods of entry, advancement, employment outlook, earnings, conditions of work, social and psychological factors, and sources of further information.

★7484★ "Medical Technology" in *Accounting to Zoology: Graduate Fields Defined* (pp. 247-248)
Petersons Guides, Inc.
PO Box 2123
Princeton, NJ 08543-2123
Ph: (609)243-9111   Fax: (609)243-9150
Fr: 800-338-3282
Amy J. Goldstein, editor. Revised and updated, 1987. Discusses types of graduate programs and degrees, graduate research, applied work, employment prospects and trends.

★7485★ "Medical Technology" in *Careers in High-Tech*
Arco Publishing Co.
Macmillan General Reference
15 Columbus Cir.
New York, NY 10023
Fax: 800-835-3202   Fr: 800-858-7674
Connie Winkler. 1987. Surveys occupations in data processing, personal computers, telecommunications, manufacturing technology, artificial intelligence, computer graphics, medicine, biotechnology, lasers, technical writing, and publishing. Separate chapters cover education and training.

★7486★ Opportunities in Medical Technology
National Textbook Co. (NTC)
VGM Career Books
4255 W. Touhy Ave.
Lincolnwood, IL 60646-1975
Ph: (708)679-5500   Fax: (708)679-2494
Fr: 800-323-4900
Karen R. Karni, Jane Sidney Oliver. Overviews opportunities for laboratory technicians, nuclear medicine and radiologic technologists, and others. Includesinformation on training, salaries, and the employment outlook.

★7487★ Preparing for a Career in the Medical Laboratory
American Society of Clinical Pathologists
2100 W. Harrison
Chicago, IL 60612
Ph: (312)738-1336
1988. Eight-panel brochure describing certification, education, and training requirements for eight different clinical laboratory specialities.

★7488★ "Specialist in Blood Bank Technology" in Careers in Health Care (pp. 256-260)
National Textbook Co. (NTC)
VGM Career Books
4255 W. Touhy Ave.
Lincolnwood, IL 60646-1975
Ph: (708)679-5500   Fax: (708)679-2494
Fr: 800-323-4900
Barbara M. Swanson. Third edition, 1995. Describes job duties, work settings, salaries, licensing and certification requirements, educational preparation, and future outlook.

★7489★ Would You Like to Solve a Mystery and Help Save a Life? Consider a Career in Cytotechnology
American Society of Cytology
1015 Chestnut St., Ste. 1518
Philadelphia, PA 19107
Ph: (215)922-3880
This six-panel pamphlet describes responsibilities, opportunities, education, certification, and employment for cytotechnologists.

PROFESSIONAL ASSOCIATIONS

★7490★ Accrediting Bureau of Health Education Schools (ABHES)
Oak Manor Office
29089 U.S. 20 W.
Elkhart, IN 46514
Ph: (219)293-0124   Fax: (219)295-8564
Members: Serves as a nationally recognized accrediting agency of health education institutions and schools conducting medical laboratory technician and medical assistant education programs. **Purpose:** Establishes criteria and standards for the administration and operation of health education institutions. Seeks to enhance the profession through the improvement of schools, courses, and the competence of graduates. Schools must apply voluntarily for accreditation; once accredited, they must report to the bureau annually and be reexamined at least every 6 years.

Has accredited 15 programs for medical laboratory technicians, 124 medical assistants, and 80 institutions of allied health. **Publications:** ABHES News, periodic. • Accrediting Bureau of Health Education Schools— Directory of Accredited Schools and Programs, periodic.

★7491★ American Association of Blood Banks (AABB)
8101 Glenbrook Rd.
Bethesda, MD 20814
Ph: (301)907-6977   Fax: (301)907-6895
Members: Community and hospital blood centers and transfusion and transplantation services, physicians, nurses, technologists, administrators, blood donor recruiters, scientists, and individuals involved in related activities. **Purpose:** Encourages the voluntary donation of blood and other tissues and organs through education, public information, and research. Operates the National Blood Exchange; inspects and accredits blood banks and parentage testing laboratories; sponsors the National Blood Foundation; maintains a rare donor file and reference laboratory system. Maintains over 40 scientific, technical, and administrative committees and three councils. **Publications:** AABB News Briefs, 11/year. • American Association of Blood Banks—Membership Directory, biennial. • Blood Bank Week. • Directory of Community Blood Centers, biennial. • Standards for Blood Banks and Transfusion Services. • Technical Manual, triennial. • Transfusion, monthly.

★7492★ American Association for Clinical Chemistry (AACC)
2101 L St. NW, Ste. 202
Washington, DC 20037-1526
Ph: (202)857-0717   Fax: (202)887-5093
Fr: 800-892-1400
Members: Clinical laboratory scientists and others engaged in the practice of clinical chemistry in independent laboratories, hospitals, and allied institutions. **Purpose:** Maintains Endowment Fund for Research in Clinical Chemistry. Maintains employment service. Sponsors: therapeutic drug monitoring and endocrinology programs; continuing education programs; quality control programs. Compiles statistics; sponsors speakers' bureau. **Publications:** Clinical Chemistry Journal, monthly. • Clinical Chemistry News, monthly. • Clinical Chemistry Reference Edition, monthly.

★7493★ American Medical Technologists (AMT)
710 Higgins Rd.
Park Ridge, IL 60068
Ph: (708)823-5169   Fax: (708)823-0458
Fr: 800-275-1268
Members: National professional registry of medical laboratory technologists, technicians, medical assistants, dental assistants, and phlebotomists. **Purpose:** Maintains job information service. Sponsors AMT Institute for Education, which has developed continuing education programs. **Publications:** AMT Events and Continuing Education Supplement, 8/year.

★7494★ American Society for Clinical Laboratory Science (ASMT)
7910 Woodmont Ave., Ste. 1301
Bethesda, MD 20814
Ph: (301)657-2768   Fax: (301)657-2909
Members: Primarily clinical laboratory personnel who have an associate or baccalaureate degree and clinical training and specialists who hold at least a master's degree in one of the major fields of clinical laboratory science such as bacteriology, mycology, or biochemistry; also includes technicians, specialists, and educators with limited certificates and students enrolled in approved programs of clinical laboratory studies and military medical technology schools. **Purpose:** Promotes and maintains high standards in clinical laboratory methods and research and advances standards of education and training of personnel. Conducts educational program of seminars and workshops. Sponsors award competition to encourage the writing of scientific papers. Approves programs of continuing education and maintains records on participation in continuing education programs for members. Maintains speakers' bureau. **Publications:** ASCLS Today, monthly. • Clinical Laboratory Science, bimonthly.

★7495★ American Society of Clinical Pathologists (ASCP)
2100 W. Harrison
Chicago, IL 60612
Ph: (312)738-1336   Fax: (312)738-1619
Fr: 800-621-4142
Members: Purpose: Works to promote public health and safety by the appropriate application of pathology and laboratory medicine. Provides educational, scientific, and charitable services. **Publications:** American Journal of Clinical Pathology, monthly. • ASCP News, monthly. • Laboratory Medicine, monthly. • Pathology Patterns, semiannual.

★7496★ American Society of Cytology (ASC)
400 W. 9th St., Ste. 201
Wilmington, DE 19801
Ph: (302)429-8802   Fax: (302)429-8807
Members: Cytologists, pathologists, and clinicians with M.D.s; nonmedical professional personnel (Ph.D.s); associate members are cytotechnologists. (Cytology is the biological study of the formation, structure, and function of cells.) **Purpose:** Seeks to make the cytological method of early cancer detection universally available to potential victims. Promotes establishment of additional educational and training facilities; encourages implementaion of research programs; inspects and accredits cytology laboratories; assists in preparation of national registry examination for cytotechnologists. Reviews cytotechnology training programs for accreditation. **Publications:** Acta Cytologica, bimonthly. • The ASC Bulletin, bimonthly. • Consider a Career in Cytotechnology. • Cytopathology Review Course Syllabus.

★7497★ Association for Practitioners in Infection Control (APIC)
1016 16th St. NW, 6th Fl.
Washington, DC 20036
Ph: (202)296-2742   Fax: (202)296-5645
Members: Physicians, microbiologists, nurses, epidemiologists, medical technicians,

sanitarians, and pharmacists. **Purpose:** Purpose is to improve patient care by improving the profession of infection control through the development of educational programs and standards. Promotes quality research and standardization of practices and procedures. Develops communications among members, and assesses and influences legislation related to the field. Conducts seminars at local level. **Publications:** *American Journal of Infection Control*, bimonthly.

★7498★ Commission on Accreditation of Allied Health Education Programs (CAAHEP)
515 N. State St., Ste. 7530
Chicago, IL 60610
Ph: (312)464-4636   Fax: (312)464-5830
Members: Serves as an accrediting agency for allied health programs in 19 occupational areas.

★7499★ International Society for Clinical Laboratory Technology (ISCLT)
818 Olive St., Ste. 918
St. Louis, MO 63101-1598
Ph: (314)241-1445   Fax: (314)241-1449
Members: Clinical laboratory supervisors, technologists and technicians; physician's office laboratory technicians. Conducts educational programs; maintains placement service; offers specialized education. **Publications:** *ISCLT Alert*, periodic. • *ISCLT Newsletter*, bimonthly.

STANDARDS/CERTIFICATION AGENCIES

★7500★ Accrediting Bureau of Health Education Schools (ABHES)
Oak Manor Office
29089 U.S. 20 W.
Elkhart, IN 46514
Ph: (219)293-0124   Fax: (219)295-8564
Serves as a nationally recognized accrediting agency of health education institutions and schools conducting medical laboratory technician and medical assistant education programs. Establishes criteria and standards for the administration and operation of health education institutions. Seeks to enhance the profession through the improvement of schools, courses, and the competence of graduates. Schools must apply voluntarily for accreditation; once accredited, they must report to the bureau annually and be reexamined at least every 6 years. Has accredited 15 programs for medical laboratory technicians, 124 medical assistants, and 80 institutions of allied health.

★7501★ American Association of Blood Banks (AABB)
8101 Glenbrook Rd.
Bethesda, MD 20814
Ph: (301)907-6977   Fax: (301)907-6895
Trains and certifies blood bank technologists.

★7502★ American Medical Technologists (AMT)
710 Higgins Rd.
Park Ridge, IL 60068
Ph: (708)823-5169   Fax: (708)823-0458
Fr: 800-275-1268
National professional registry of medical laboratory technologists, technicians, medical assistants, dental assistants, and phlebotomists. Maintains job information service. Sponsors AMT Institute for Education, which has developed continuing education programs.

★7503★ American Society for Clinical Laboratory Science (ASMT)
7910 Woodmont Ave., Ste. 1301
Bethesda, MD 20814
Ph: (301)657-2768   Fax: (301)657-2909
Promotes and maintains high standards in clinical laboratory methods and research and advances standards of education and training of personnel. Conducts educational program of seminars and workshops. Approves programs of continuing education and maintains records on participation in continuing education programs for members.

★7504★ American Society of Clinical Pathologists (ASCP)
2100 W. Harrison
Chicago, IL 60612
Ph: (312)738-1336   Fax: (312)738-1619
Fr: 800-621-4142
Works to promote public health and safety by the appropriate application of pathology and laboratory medicine. Provides educational, scientific, and charitable services.

★7505★ American Society of Cytology (ASC)
400 W. 9th St., Ste. 201
Wilmington, DE 19801
Ph: (302)429-8802   Fax: (302)429-8807
Promotes establishment of additional educational and training facilities; encourages implementaion of research programs; inspects and accredits cytology laboratories; assists in preparation of national registry examination for cytotechnologists. Reviews cytotechnology training programs for accreditation.

★7506★ American Society for Medical Technology (ASMT)
2021 L St. NW, Ste. 400
Washington, DC 20036
Ph: (202)785-3311   Fax: (202)466-2254
Promotes and maintains high standards in clinical laboratory methods and research and advances standards of education and training of personnel.

★7507★ Commission on Accreditation of Allied Health Education Programs (CAAHEP)
515 N. State St., Ste. 7530
Chicago, IL 60610
Ph: (312)464-4636   Fax: (312)464-5830
Serves as an accrediting agency for allied health programs in 18 occupational areas.

★7508★ Credentialing Commission (CC)
818 Olive St., Ste. 918
St. Louis, MO 63101-1598
Ph: (314)241-1445   Fax: (314)241-1449
Autonomous certifying agency for general supervison, medical technologists, laboratory technicians, and physician office laboratory technicians. Maintains Continuing Education for Professional Advancement (CEPA) program to approve and record continuing education unit credits.

★7509★ National Certification Agency for Medical Lab Personnel (NCA)
7910 Woodmont Ave., Ste. 1301
Bethesda, MD 20814
Ph: (301)654-1622   Fax: (301)657-2909
Persons who direct, educate, supervise, or practice in clinical laboratory science. To assure the public and employers of the competence of clinical laboratory personnel; to provide a mechanism for individuals demonstrating competency in the field to achieve career mobility. Develops and administers competency-based examinations for certification of clinical laboratory personnel; provides for periodic recertification by examination or through documentation of continuing education.

TEST GUIDES

★7510★ *Career Examination Series: Medical Research Technician*
National Learning Corp.
212 Michael Dr.
Syosset, NY 11791
Ph: (516)921-8888   Fax: (516)921-8743
Fr: 800-645-6337
Jack Rudman. 1993. Test guide including questions and answers for students or professionals in the field who seek advancement through examination.

★7511★ *Career Examination Series: Medical Technologist*
National Learning Corp.
212 Michael Dr.
Syosset, NY 11791
Ph: (516)921-8888   Fax: (516)921-8743
Fr: 800-645-6337
Jack Rudman. A series of study guides with multiple-choice examination questions and solutions for trainees and professional laboratory technicians. Titles in the series include *Certified Laboratory Assistant; Laboratory Assistant; Medical Laboratory Technician; Medical Laboratory Technician (Substance Abuse); Medical Technical Assistant; Medical Technician; Medical Technician Trainee; Principal Laboratory Technician; Registered Technologist, R.T.; Senior Laboratory Technician; Senior Laboratory Technician (Biochemistery); Senior Laboratory Technician (Chemistry); Senior Laboratory Technician (Food Chemistry); Senior Laboratory Techni nici an (Microbiology); Senior Medical Laboratory Technician.*

★7512★ **Medical Technology: Examination Review and Study Guide**
Appleton and Lange
25 Van Zant St.
East Norwalk, CT 06855
Ph: (203)838-4400   Fr: 800-423-1359

Anna P. Ciulla and Georganne K. Buescher. Second edition, 1992. A guide for certification and licensure examinations in medical technology. Includes 2000 questions with answers and explanations.

EDUCATIONAL DIRECTORIES AND PROGRAMS

★7513★ **Medical Technologists and Technicians Career Directory**
Gale Research Inc.
835 Penobscot Bldg.
Detroit, MI 48226-4094
Ph: (313)961-2242   Fax: (313)961-6083
Fr: 800-877-GALE

Bradley J. Morgan and Joseph M. Palmisano. 1993. A directory in the Career Advisor Series that provides essays written by industry professionals; job search information on resume and cover letter preparation, networking, and the interviewing process; approximately 300 companies and organizations offering job opportunities and internships, and additional job-hunting resources.

★7514★ **Specialized Programs for Medical Laboratory Technicians and Medical Assistants and Institutions of Allied Health**
Accrediting Bureau of Health Education Schools/Programs
29089 U.S. 20 W.
Elkhart, IN 46514
Ph: (219)293-0124   Fax: (219)295-8564
Mary Lou Reed, Contact

Annual, March. Covers 164 institutions offering programs accredited by the Accrediting Bureau of Health Education Schools; includes programs of preparation for medical laboratory technician, medical assistant, and allied health education careers. Entries include: Institution name, address, phone, name and title of director, programs accredited, year of initial accreditation, year of next accreditation review. Arrangement: Separate geographical lists for laboratory technician/medical assistant and the allied careers.

AWARDS, SCHOLARSHIPS, GRANTS, AND FELLOWSHIPS

★7515★ **American Society for Clinical Laboratory Science Scholarships**
American Society for Clinical Laboratory Science (ASMT)
Education and Research Fund, Inc.
7910 Woodmont Ave., No. 1301
Bethesda, MD 20814
Ph: (301)657-2768

Purpose: To assist experienced professionals who wish to pursue graduate, continuing, or advanced studies relevant to the interests of the Society. Qualifications: Applicant for most ASMT scholarships must be a U.S. citizen or permanent resident, and be a clinical laboratory practitioner or educator, who has performed clinical laboratory functions for at least one year. For the Baxter Healthcare Scientific Products Division Graduate Scholarship candidate must be pursuing master's or doctoral study in the clinical laboratory or related sciences. Funds available: $250-$3,000. Application details: Write to the executive secretary for application form and guidelines. Deadline: 1 February.

BASIC REFERENCE GUIDES AND HANDBOOKS

★7516★ **Basic Techniques in Clinical Laboratory Science**
Mosby-Year Book, Inc.
11830 Westline Industrial Dr.
St. Louis, MO 63146
Ph: (314)872-8370   Fax: (314)432-1380
Fr: 800-325-4177

Linne, editor. Third edition, 1991.

★7517★ **Clinical Chemistry: Theory, Analysis, and Correlation**
Mosby-Year Book, Inc.
11830 Westline Industrial Dr.
St. Louis, MO 63146
Ph: (314)872-8370   Fax: (314)432-1380
Fr: 800-325-4177

Lawrence Kaplan and Amadeo J. Pesce, et al. Second edition, 1989. Emphasizes the core concepts of clinical chemistry. Includes case studies requiring knowledge of pathophysiology, biochemistry, and principles of laboratory practice. Also contains laboratory experiments and review questions and answers.

★7518★ **Introduction to Lab Science & Basic Technique Clinical Laboratory**
Mosby-Year Book, Inc.
11830 Westline Industrial Dr.
St. Louis, MO 63146
Ph: (314)872-8370   Fax: (314)432-1380
Fr: 800-325-4177

Clerc, editor. 1992.

★7519★ **Principles & Practice of Clinical Anaerobic Bacteriology**
Star Publishing Co.
940 Emmett Ave.
Belmont, CA 94002
Ph: (415)591-3505   Fax: (415)591-3898

Paul Engelkirk, editor. 1992.

PROFESSIONAL AND TRADE PERIODICALS

★7520★ **Clinical Lab Letter**
Quest Publishing Company
1351 Titan Way
Brea, CA 92621
Ph: (714)738-6400   Fax: (714)525-6258
Gregory F. Nighswonger

Semimonthly. Covers the latest advances in clinical laboratory technology, with special attention to safety and management in laboratories. Includes regular sections on government activities, safety hazards and product recalls, new diagnostic technology, professional activities of clinical lab personnel, information sources, business news, meetings and conventions, and educational opportunities.

★7521★ **Lab Report**
Raymond Gambino, M.D.
155 Federal St., 16th Fl.
Boston, MA 02110
Ph: (617)338-8860   Fax: (617)723-4785
Raymond Gambino

Monthly. Presents information on developments in laboratory medicine. Discusses which tests are best, and why. Identifies outdated and ineffective tests, and identifies important new tests. Includes the latest, most practical information relevant to laboratory medicine. Recurring features include a column titled Diagnostic Bulletins.

★7522★ **NAACLS News**
National Accrediting Agency for Clinical Laboratory Sciences (NAACLS)
8410 W. Bryn Mawr, Ste. 670
Chicago, IL 60631
Ph: (312)714-8880   Fax: (312)714-8886
Megan Hennessy Eggert

Provides news of the activities of the Agency as well as issues related to laboratory scientists.

★7523★ **National Committee for Clinical Laboratory Standards—Update**
National Committee for Clinical Laboratory Standards
771 E. Lancaster Ave.
Villanova, PA 19085
Ph: (215)525-2435
Mary Barr Martin

Bimonthly. Reports on Committee projects, activities, and publications and carries items of interest to professionals in the clinical laboratory testing community. Recurring features include a calendar of events and meetings reports.

★7524★ Technology for Health Care Series
ECRI
5200 Butler Pike
Plymouth Meeting, PA 19462
Ph: (215)825-6000   Fax: (215)834-1275
Michele Moscariello

Monthly. Concerned with the safety, performance, reliability, and cost effectiveness of health care technology. Covers areas of anesthesia, cardiology, imaging and radiology, and respiratory therapy. Reviews device test results and warns of hazards and deficiencies. Recurring features include news of research, Institute reports, and news of members.

PROFESSIONAL MEETINGS AND CONVENTIONS

★7525★ American Association of Blood Banks Annual Meeting
American Association of Blood Banks
8101 Glenbrock Rd.
Bethesda, MD 20814-2749
Ph: (301)907-6977   Fax: (301)907-6895
Annual. **Dates and Locations:** 1995 Nov 11-16; New Orleans, LA. • 1996 Oct 12-17; Or-lando, FL. • 1997 Oct 25-30; Dallas, TX. • 1998 Oct 31-05; Philadelphia, PA.

★7526★ Association for Practitioners in Infection Control Annual Educational Conference
Association for Practitioners in Infection Control
505 E. Hawley St.
Mundelein, IL 60060
Ph: (708)949-6052

Annual. **Dates and Locations:** 1995; Las Vegas, NV. • 1996; Atlanta, GA.

★7527★ College of American Pathologists and American Society of Clinical Pathologists Fall Meeting
American Society of Clinical Pathologists
2100 W. Harrison
Chicago, IL 60612
Ph: (312)738-1336   Fax: (312)738-1619

Annual. **Dates and Locations:** 1996 Sep 30-02; San Diego, CA. • 1997 Sep 22-24; Philadelphia, PA. • 1998 Oct 19-21; Washington, DC.

OTHER SOURCES OF INFORMATION

★7528★ Standards for Blood Banks and Transfusion Services
American Association of Blood Banks (AABB)
8101 Glenbrook Rd.
Bethesda, MD 20814-2749
Ph: (301)907-6977

Paul Holland, editor. 1993. This handbook sets standards for practice and provides the basis for accreditation and licensing.

★7529★ Statements of Competence
American Society for Medical Technology (ASMT)
2021 L St., NW, Ste. 400
Washington, DC 20036
Ph: (202)785-3311

Revised edition, 1987. This six-page statement describes abilities essential for competent clinical laboratory practice.

Dental Hygienists

Dental hygienists provide preventive dental care and encourage patients to develop good oral hygiene skills. In addition to carrying out clinical responsibilities such as cleaning and scaling teeth, hygienists help patients develop and maintain good oral health by explaining the relationship between diet or smoking and oral health, for example, and showing patients how to select toothbrushes and use dental floss. Although most hygienists work with individual patients, some develop and promote community dental health programs.

Salaries

Earnings of dental hygienists are affected by geographic location, employment setting, and education and experience of individual.

Dental hygienists $38,480/year

Employment Outlook

Growth rate until the year 2005: Much faster than the average.

Dental Hygienists

CAREER GUIDES

★7530★ "Dental Assistants and Dental Hygienists" in *American Almanac of Jobs and Salaries* **(p. 480)**
Avon Books
1350 Avenue of the Americas
New York, NY 10019
Ph: (212)261-6800   Fr: 800-238-0658
John Wright, editor. Revised and updated, 1994-95. This is comprehensive guide to the wages of hundreds of occupations in a wide variety of industries and organizations.

★7531★ "Dental Assistants and Hygienists" in *Jobs! What They Are— Where They Are—What They Pay* **(p. 180)**
Simon & Schuster, Inc.
Simon & Schuster Bldg.
1230 Avenue of the Americas
New York, NY 10020
Ph: (212)698-7000   Fr: 800-223-2348
Robert O. Snelling and Anne M. Snelling. 3rd edition, 1992. Describes duties and responsibilities, earnings, employment opportunities, training, and qualifications.

★7532★ "Dental Hygiene" in *Accounting to Zoology: Graduate Fields Defined* **(pp. 245)**
Petersons Guides, Inc.
PO Box 2123
Princeton, NJ 08543-2123
Ph: (609)243-9111   Fax: (609)243-9150
Fr: 800-338-3282
Amy J. Goldstein, editor. Revised and updated, 1987. Discusses types of graduate programs and degrees, graduate research, applied work, employment prospects and trends.

★7533★ *Dental Hygienist*
Careers, Inc.
PO Box 135
Largo, FL 34649-0135
Ph: (813)584-7333
1994. Two-page occupational summary card describing duties, working conditions, personal qualifications, training, earnings and hours, employment outlook, places of em-

ployment, related careers, and where to write for more information.

★7534★ *Dental Hygienist*
Vocational Biographies, Inc.
PO Box 31
Sauk Centre, MN 56378-0031
Ph: (612)352-6516   Fax: (612)352-5546
Fr: 800-255-0752
1993. Four-page pamphlet containing a personal narrative about a worker's job, work likes and dislikes, career path from high school to the present. Education and training, the rewards and frustrations, and the effects of the job on the rest of the worker's life. The data file portion of this pamphlet gives a concise occupational summary, including work descriptions, working conditions, places of employment, personal characteristics, education and training, job outlook, and salary range.

★7535★ "Dental Hygienist" in *100 Best Careers for the Year 2000* **(pp. 26-28)**
Arco Pub.
201 W. 103rd St.
Indianapolis, IN 46290
Ph: 800-428-5331   Fax: 800-835-3202
Shelly Field. 1992. Describes 100 job opportunities expected to grow fast throughout the next decade. Provides information on job duties and responsibilities, training requirements, education, advancement opportunities, experience and qualifications, and typical salaries.

★7536★ "Dental Hygienist" in *150 Careers in the Health Care Field*
Reed Reference Publishing
121 Chanlon Rd.
PO Box 31
New Providence, NJ 07974
Fax: (908)665-6688   Fr: 800-521-8110
Stanley Alperin. Third edition, 1993. Profiles health care occupations requiring a bachelor's degree or less. Describes the nature of the work, educational preparation, licensing requirements, and salary. Lists accredited educational programs.

★7537★ "Dental Hygienist" in *Career Information Center* **(Vol.7)**
Simon and Schuster
200 Old Tappan Rd.
Old Tappan, NJ 07675
Fax: 800-445-6991   Fr: 800-223-2348
Richard Lidz and Linda Perrin, editorial directors. Fifth edition, 1993. This 13-volume set profiles over 600 occupations. Each occupational profile describes job duties, entry-level requirements, educational requirements, advancement possibilities, employment outlook, working conditions, earnings and benefits, and where to write for more information.

★7538★ "Dental Hygienist" in *Careers in Health Care* **(pp. 55-58)**
National Textbook Co. (NTC)
VGM Career Books
4255 W. Touhy Ave.
Lincolnwood, IL 60646-1975
Ph: (708)679-5500   Fax: (708)679-2494
Fr: 800-323-4900
Barbara M. Swanson. Third edition, 1995. Describes job duties, work settings, salaries, licensing and certification requirements, educational preparation, and future outlook.

★7539★ "Dental Hygienist" in *College Board Guide to Jobs and Career Planning* **(pp. 241)**
The College Board
415 Columbus Ave.
New York, NY 10023-6992
Ph: (212)713-8165   Fax: (212)713-8143
Fr: 800-323-7155
Joyce S. Mitchell. Second edition, 1994. Describes the job, salaries, related careers, education needed, and where to write for more information.

★7540★ "Dental Hygienist" in *Jobs Rated Almanac*
World Almanac
1 International Blvd., Ste. 444
Mahwah, NJ 07495
Ph: (201)529-6900   Fax: (201)529-6901
Les Krantz. Second edition, 1992. Ranks 250 jobs by environment, salary, outlooks, physical demands, stress, security, travel opportunities, and extra perks. Includes jobs the editor feels are the most common, most interesting, and the most rapidly growing.

★7541★ "Dental Hygienist" in
Opportunities in Paramedical Careers
(pp. 41-44)
National Textbook Co. (NTC)
VGM Career Books
4255 W. Touhy Ave.
Lincolnwood, IL 60646-1975
Ph: (708)679-5500   Fax: (708)679-2494
Fr: 800-323-4900

Alex Kacen. 1994. Describes paraprofessional careers in the health professions such as physician assistant, medical assistant, and emergency medical technician. Describes job duties, educational preparation, certification, earnings, and job outlook. Lists educational programs.

★7542★ "Dental Hygienist" in *VGM's
Careers Encyclopedia **(pp. 134-136)**
National Textbook Co. (NTC)
VGM Career Books
4255 W. Touhy Ave.
Lincolnwood, IL 60646-1975
Ph: (708)679-5500   Fax: (708)679-2494
Fr: 800-323-4900

Third edition, 1991. Describes job duties, places of employment, working conditions, qualifications, education and training, advancement potential, and salary for each occupation.

★7543★ "Dental Hygienist" in *VGM's
Handbook of Health Care Careers
National Textbook Co.
4255 W. Touhy Ave.
Lincolnwood, IL 60646-1975
Ph: (708)679-5500   Fax: (708)679-2494
Fr: 800-323-4900

Annette Selden. 1993. Contains 42 two-page occupational profiles describing job duties, places of employment, working conditions, qualifications, education, employment outlook, and income.

★7544★ *Dental Hygienists*
Chronicle Guidance Publications, Inc.
66 Aurora St.
PO Box 1190
Moravia, NY 13118-1190
Ph: (315)497-0330   Fax: (315)497-3359
Fr: 800-622-7284

1992. Career brief describing the nature of the job, working conditions, hours and earnings, education and training, licensure, certification, unions, personal qualifications, social and psychological factors, location, employment outlook, entry methods, advancement, and related occupations.

★7545★ "Dental Hygienists" in *101
*Careers: A Guide to the Fastest-
Growing Opportunities* **(pp. 191-194)**
John Wiley & Sons, Inc.
605 3rd Ave.
New York, NY 10158-0012
Ph: (212)850-6645   Fax: (212)850-6088

Michael Harkavy. 1990. Describes the nature of the job, working conditions, employment growth, qualifications, personal skills, projected salaries, and where to write for more information.

★7546★ "Dental Hygienists" in
America's 50 Fastest Growing Jobs
(p. 78)
JIST Works, Inc.
720 N. Park Ave.
Indianapolis, IN 46202-3431
Ph: (317)264-3720   Fax: (317)264-3709
Fr: 800-648-5478

Michael J. Farr, compiler. 1994. Describes the 50 fastest growing jobs within major career clusters such as technicians, and marketing and sales. Each job profile explains the nature of the work, skills and abilities required, employment outlook, average earnings, related occupations, education and training requirements, and employment opportunities. Also contains career planning information and job search tips.

★7547★ "Dental Hygienists" in *Best
*Jobs for the 1990s and Into the 21st
Century*
Impact Publications
9104-N Manassas Dr.
Manassas Park, VA 22111
Ph: (703)361-7300   Fax: (703)335-9486

Ronald L. Krannich and Caryl Rae Krannich. 1993.

★7548★ "Dental Hygienists" in *Career
Discovery Encyclopedia **(Vol.2, pp. 86-
87)**
J.G. Ferguson Publishing Co.
200 W. Madison St., Ste. 300
Chicago, IL 60606
Ph: (312)580-5480   Fax: (312)580-4948

Russell E. Primm, editor-in chief. 1993. This six volume set contains two-page articles for 504 occupations. Each article describes job duties, earnings, and educational and training requirements. The whole set is arranged alphabetically by job title. Designed for junior high and older students.

★7549★ "Dental Hygienists" in
*Encyclopedia of Careers and
Vocational Guidance* **(Vol.2, pp. 447-
449)**
J.G. Ferguson Publishing Co.
200 W. Madison St., Ste. 300
Chicago, IL 60606
Ph: (312)580-5480   Fax: (312)580-4948

William E. Hopke, editor. Ninth edition, 1993. Four-volume set that profiles 900 occupations and describes job trends in 76 industries. Includes career description, educational requirements, history of the job, methods of entry advancement, employment outlook, earnings, conditions of work, social and psychological factors, and sources of further information.

★7550★ "Dental Hygienists" in *Guide to
Careers Without College **(pp. 36-38)**
Franklin Watts, Inc.
387 Park Ave., S.
New York, NY 10016
Ph: (212)686-7070   Fr: 800-672-6672

Kathleen S. Abrams. 1988. Discusses rewarding careers that do not require a college degree.

★7551★ "Dental Hygienists" in *Health
Care Job Explosion! **(pp. 104-112)**
D-Amp Publications
401 Amherst Ave.
Coraopolis, PA 15108
Ph: (412)262-5578

Dennis V. Damp. 1993. Provides information on the nature of work for the major health care occupational groups. Descriptions include working conditions, training, job outlook, qualifications, and related occupations.

★7552★ "Dental Hygienists" in
Occupational Outlook Handbook
U.S. Government Printing Office
Superintendent of Documents
Washington, DC 20402
Ph: (202)512-1800   Fax: (202)512-2250

Biennial; latest edition, 1994-95. Encyclopedia of careers describing about 250 occupations and comprising about 85 percent of all jobs in the economy. Occupations that require lengthy education or training are given the most attention. Each occupation's profile describes what the worker does on the job, working conditions, education and training requirements, advancement possibilities, job outlook, earnings, and sources of additional information.

★7553★ "Dental Hygienists" in
Opportunities in Public Health Careers
(pp. 63-64)
National Textbook Co. (NTC)
VGM Career Books
4255 W. Touhy Ave.
Lincolnwood, IL 60646-1975
Ph: (708)679-5500   Fax: (708)679-2494
Fr: 800-323-4900

George E. Pickett. 1988. Defines the public health field and describes career opportunities as well as educational preparation and the future of the public health field. The appendixes list public health organizations, state and federal public health agencies, and graduate schools offering public health programs.

★7554★ *Have You Considered Dental
Hygiene?
American Dental Association (ADA)
211 E. Chicago Ave.
Chicago, IL 60611
Ph: (312)440-2500   Fr: 800-947-4746

1988. This nine-page booklet describes what dental hygienists do and where they work, earnings, accreditation, licensure, and education.

★7555★ *Health Careers*
Careers, Inc.
PO Box 135
Largo, FL 34649-0135
Ph: (813)584-7333

1994. Four-page brief describing duties, working conditions, personal qualifications, training, earnings and hours, employment outlook, places of employment, related careers, and where to write for more information.

PROFESSIONAL ASSOCIATIONS

★7556★ Academy of Laser Dentistry
401 N. Michigan Ave.
Chicago, IL 60611
Ph: (312)644-6610   Fax: (312)321-6869
Members: Dentists, hygienists, dental teachers, and corporate laser dental vendors. **Purpose:** Promotes clinical education, research, and development of standards and guidelines for the safe and ethical use of dental laser technology. Conducts educational programs. Provides certification. **Publications:** *Journal of Clinical, Laser, Medical, and Surgery*, bimonthly. • *Wavelengths*, quarterly.

★7557★ American Association of Dental Examiners (AADE)
211 E. Chicago Ave., Ste. 844
Chicago, IL 60611
Ph: (312)440-7464   Fax: (312)440-7494
Members: Present and past members of state dental examining boards and board administrators. To assist member agencies with problems related to state dental board examinations and licensure, and enforcement of the state dental practice act. Conducts research; compiles statistics. **Publications:** *American Association of Dental Examiners Bulletin*, quarterly.

★7558★ American Board of Endodontics (ABE)
211 E. Chicago Ave.
Chicago, IL 60611
Ph: (312)266-7310
Members: Dentists who have successfully completed study and training in an advanced endodontics education program which is accredited by the Commission on Dental Accreditation of the American Dental Association. **Purpose:** Administers examinations and certifies dentists who successfully complete the examinations. Primary objective is to protect the public by raising the standards of endodontic practice and requiring candidates for diplomate status to show strong evidence of specialized skills and knowledge in endodontics. **Publications:** *Membership Roster*, annual.

★7559★ American Dental Assistants Association (ADAA)
203 N. LaSalle St., Ste. 1320
Chicago, IL 60601-1225
Ph: (312)541-1550   Fax: (312)541-1496
Members: Individuals employed as dental assistants in dental offices, clinics, hospitals, or institutions; instructors of dental assistants; dental students. Sponsors workshops and seminars; maintains governmental liaison. **Purpose:** Offers group insurance; maintains scholarship trust fund. Dental Assisting National Board examines members who are candidates for title of Certified Dental Assistant. **Publications:** *The Dental Assistant*, 5/year. • *The Dental Assistant Update*, semiannual.

★7560★ American Dental Hygienists' Association (ADHA)
444 N. Michigan Ave., Ste. 3400
Chicago, IL 60611
Ph: (312)440-8929   Fax: (312)440-8929
Fr: 800-243-ADHA
Members: Professional organization of licensed dental hygienists possessing a degree or certificate in dental hygiene granted by an accredited school of dental hygiene. **Purpose:** Administers Dental Hygiene Candidate Aptitude Testing Program and makes available scholarships, research grants, and continuing education programs. Maintains accrediting service through the American Dental Association's Commission on Dental Accreditation. Compiles statistics. **Publications:** *American Dental Hygienists' Association Access*. • *Dental Hygiene*.

STANDARDS/CERTIFICATION AGENCIES

★7561★ Academy of Laser Dentistry
401 N. Michigan Ave.
Chicago, IL 60611
Ph: (312)644-6610   Fax: (312)321-6869
Promotes clinical education, research, and development of standards and guidelines for the safe and ethical use of dental laser technology. Provides certification.

★7562★ American Board of Endodontics (ABE)
211 E. Chicago Ave.
Chicago, IL 60611
Ph: (312)266-7310
Administers examinations and certifies dentists who successfully complete the examinations. Primary objective is to protect the public by raising the standards of endodontic practice and requiring candidates for diplomate status to show strong evidence of specialized skills and knowledge in endodontics.

★7563★ American Dental Association (ADA)
211 E. Chicago Ave.
Chicago, IL 60611
Ph: (312)440-2500   Fax: (312)440-7494
Inspects and accredits dental schools and schools for dental hygienists, assistants, and laboratory technicians.

★7564★ American Dental Hygienists' Association (ADHA)
444 N. Michigan Ave., Ste. 3400
Chicago, IL 60611
Ph: (312)440-8929   Fax: (312)440-8929
Fr: 800-243-ADHA
Professional organization of licensed dental hygienists possessing a degree or certificate in dental hygiene granted by an accredited school of dental hygiene. Administers Dental Hygiene Candidate Aptitude Testing Program and makes available scholarships, research grants, and continuing education programs. Maintains accrediting service through the American Dental Association's Commission on Dental Accreditation.

TEST GUIDES

★7565★ Admission Test Series: Dental Hygiene Aptitide Test
National Learning Corp.
212 Michael Dr.
Syosset, NY 11791
Ph: (516)921-8888   Fax: (516)921-8743
Fr: 800-645-6337
Jack Rudman. A collection of sample examinations designed to prepare potential dental hygienists for professional school entrance tests and for tests administered by private and public institutions for entrance and career advancement. Provides multiple-choice questions; includes correct answers. Titles in the series include *National Dental Hygiene Boards; National Dental Assistant Boards*.

★7566★ Appleton and Lange's Review for the Dental Hygiene Examination
Appleton and Lange
25 Van Zant St.
East Norwalk, CT 06855
Ph: (203)838-4400   Fr: 800-423-1359
Caren M. Barnes. Fourth edition, 1994. This is a guide to help dental hygiene students prepare for the National Board Dental Hygiene Examination and the comprehensive written examination for state boards. Includes sample questions with answers and explanations.

★7567★ Career Examination Series: Dental Hygienist
National Learning Corp.
212 Michael Dr.
Syosset, NY 11791
Ph: (516)921-8888   Fax: (516)921-8743
Fr: 800-645-6337
Jack Rudman. A study guide for professionals and trainees in the field of dental hygiene. Includes a multiple-choice examination section; provides answers.

★7568★ Career Examination Series: Senior Dental Hygienist
National Learning Corp.
212 Michael Dr.
Syosset, NY 11791
Ph: (516)921-8888   Fax: (516)921-8743
Fr: 800-645-6337
Jack Rudman. A study guide for professionals and trainees in the field of dental hygiene. Includes a multiple-choice examination section; provides answers.

★7569★ Dental Hygiene Aptitude Test (DHAT)
National Learning Corp.
212 Michael Dr.
Syosset, NY 11791
Ph: (516)921-8888   Fax: (516)921-8743
Fr: 800-645-6337
Jack Rudman. Part of the Admission Test series. A sample test for those seeking admission to graduate and professional schools or seeking entrance or advancement in institutional and public career service.

EDUCATIONAL DIRECTORIES AND PROGRAMS

★7570★ Annual Report on Allied Dental Education
Survey Center
211 E. Chicago Ave.
Chicago, IL 60611
Ph: (312)440-2568   Fax: (312)440-7461
Annual, April. Covers about 550 institutions conducting dental assisting, dental hygiene, and dental laboratory technology programs. Entries include: Institution name, address, name of program director. Arrangement: Separate geographical sections for dental hygiene, dental assisting, and laboratory technology programs.

★7571★ Health & Medical Industry Directory
American Business Directories, Inc.
5711 S. 86th Circle
Omaha, NE 68127
Ph: (402)593-4600   Fax: (402)331-1505
Released 1993. Lists over 1.1 million physicians and surgeons, dentists, clinics, health clubs, and other health-related businesses in the U.S. and Canada. Entries include: Name, address, phone.

★7572★ Therapists and Allied Health Professionals Career Directory
Gale Research Inc.
835 Penobscot Bldg.
Detroit, MI 48226-4094
Ph: (313)961-2242   Fax: (313)961-6083
Fr: 800-877-GALE
Bradley J. Morgan and Joseph M. Palmisano. 1993. A directory in the Career Advisor Series that provides essays written by industry professionals; job search information on resume and cover letter preparation, networking, and the interviewing process; approximately 300 companies and organizations offering job opportunities and internships, and additional job-hunting resources.

AWARDS, SCHOLARSHIPS, GRANTS, AND FELLOWSHIPS

★7573★ Dental Hygiene Scholarship Program
ADA Endowment Fund and Assistance Fund Inc
211 East Chicago Ave., 17th Fl.
Chicago, IL 60611
Ph: (312)440-2567   Fax: (312)440-2822
Purpose: To assist students in need of financial assistance in the field of dental hygiene. Qualifications: Applicants must be a U.S. citizen entering or in the first year at an accredited dental hygiene program. Selection criteria: 2.8 GPA; demonstrate financial need; 21 letters of reference; typed summary of personal/professional goals. Funds available: $1,000. Application details: Contact the Fund

for guidelines and application forms. Deadline: August 15.

★7574★ Senior Dental and Dental Hygiene Student Awards
Academy of Dentistry for the Handicapped
211 E. Chicago, 17th Fl.
Chicago, IL 60611
Ph: (312)440-2660
To encourage the sensitivity and sensibility of the dental profession and allied health professionals toward the needs of the handicapped and special patient populations. Graduating senior dental and dental hygiene students may qualify for the award by demonstrating a sincere interest and concern for the dental needs of the handicapped and special patients while an undergraduate dental or dental hygiene student. Certificates are awarded annually.

★7575★ Student Merit Award for Outstanding Achievement in Community Dentistry
American Association of Public Health Dentistry
National Office
10619 Jousting Ln.
Richmond, VA 23235
Ph: (804)272-8344   Fax: (804)272-0802
To recognize outstanding achievement by dental students and dental hygiene students in the field of community dentistry. Full-time dental hygiene students or predoctoral dental students in an accredited dental or dental hygiene school in the United States are eligible. First prize includes a monetary award, a one-year subscription to the *Journal of Public Health Dentistry*, and partial expenses to the association's annual meeting; second and third prizes consist of plaques and *Journal* subscriptions. Awarded annually. Established in 1970.

BASIC REFERENCE GUIDES AND HANDBOOKS

★7576★ Clinical Practice of the Dental Hygienist
Lea and Febiger
200 Chesterfield Pkwy.
Malvern, PA 19355
Ph: (215)251-2230   Fr: 800-638-0672
Esther M. Wilkins. 1994. Includes bibliographies and an index.

★7577★ Dental Hygienist
R & E Publishers, Inc.
PO Box 2008
Saratoga, CA 95070
Ph: (408)866-6303   Fax: (408)866-0825
Ronald R. Smith, editor. 1993. Part of the Smith's Career Notes Series.

★7578★ Essentials of Clinical Dental Assisting
Mosby-Year Book, Inc.
11830 Westline Industrial Dr.
St. Louis, MO 63146
Ph: (314)872-8370   Fax: (314)432-1380
Fr: 800-325-4177
Joseph E. Chasteen. Fourth edition, 1989. Includes bibliographies and an index. Illustrated.

★7579★ General & Oral Pathology for the Dental Hygienist
Mosby-Year Book, Inc.
11830 Westline Industrial Dr.
St. Louis, MO 63146
Ph: (314)872-8370   Fax: (314)432-1380
Fr: 800-325-4177
Miller, editor. 1993.

★7580★ Oral Pathology for the Dental Hygienist
W. B. Saunders Co.
Curtis Center
Independence Sq. W.
Philadelphia, PA 19106
Ph: (215)238-7800
Olga A. C. Ibsen, editor. 1991.

★7581★ Radiographic Interpretation for the Dental Hygienist
W. B. Saunders Co.
Curtis Center
Independence Sq. W.
Philadelphia, PA 19106
Ph: (215)237-7800
Joen I. Haring, editor. 1993.

PROFESSIONAL AND TRADE PERIODICALS

★7582★ Current Opinion in Dentistry
Current Science
20 N. 3rd St.
Philadelphia, PA 19106-2113
Ph: (215)574-2266   Fax: (215)574-2270
Fr: 800-552-5866
S.T. Sonis
Quarterly. Journal for dental professionals.

★7583★ The Explorer
National Association of Dental Assistants
900 S. Washington St., No. G13
Falls Church, VA 22046-4020
Ph: (703)237-8616
Sue Young
Monthly. Reflects the Association's goal of improving the professional and personal lives of dental assistants and other staff. Provides information relating to the field of dentistry.

★7584★ Journal of Dental Hygiene
American Dental Hygienists' Assn.
444 N. Michigan Ave., Ste. 3400
Chicago, IL 60611
Ph: (312)440-8900   Fax: (312)440-8929
Rosetta Gervasi
Professional journal on dental hygiene.

★7585★ *Journal of the Michigan Dental Association*
Michigan Dental Assn.
230 N. Washington Ave., Ste. 208
Lansing, MI 48933
Ph: (517)372-9070   Fax: (517)372-0008
David Foe

Journal focusing on the Michigan Dental Association and dentistry.

★7586★ *Pediatric Dentistry Today*
American Academy of Pediatric Dentistry
211 E. Chicago Ave., Ste. 1036
Chicago, IL 60611
Ph: (312)351-8387   Fax: (312)337-6329
Amy Fox

Reports on the activities of the Academy, which seeks to advance the specialty of pediatric dentistry through practice, education, and research. Recurring features include news of research, profiles of members, and legislative updates.

★7587★ *Westviews*
Western Dental Society (WDS)
6242 Westchester Pkwy., Ste. 220
Los Angeles, CA 90045
Ph: (213)641-5561   Fax: (213)641-3258
James Mead

Carries items relating to organized dentistry and the clinical aspects of dentistry. Covers local community events involving the organization or the profession; provides updates of states agency actions affecting dentistry.

PROFESSIONAL MEETINGS AND CONVENTIONS

★7588★ *American Dental Hygienists' Association Convention*
American Dental Hygienists' Association
444 N. Michigan Ave., Ste. 3400
Chicago, IL 60611
Ph: (312)440-8900   Fax: (312)440-8929
Annual. **Dates and Locations:** 1996 Jun 21-22.

★7589★ *Liberty Dental Conference*
Philadelphia County Dental Society
225 Washington E.
Philadelphia, PA 19106
Ph: (215)925-6050   Fax: (215)925-6998
Annual. **Dates and Locations:** 1996 Mar 08-10; Philadelphia, PA.

★7590★ *National Dental Association Annual Convention*
National Dental Association, Inc.
5506 Connecticut Ave., NW, Ste. 24-25
Washington, DC 20015
Ph: (202)244-7555   Fax: (202)244-5992
Annual. **Dates and Locations:** 1995; Philadelphia, PA.

★7591★ *Yankee Dental Congress*
Massachusetts Dental Society
83 Speen St.
Natick, MA 01760-4125
Ph: (508)651-7511   Fax: (508)653-7115

OTHER SOURCES OF INFORMATION

★7592★ *"Dental Hygienist" in 100 Best Jobs for the 1990s & Beyond*
Dearborn Financial Publishing, Inc.
520 N. Dearborn St.
Chicago, IL 60610-4354
Ph: (312)836-4400   Fax: (312)836-1021
Fr: 800-621-9621
Carol Kleiman. 1992. Describes 100 jobs ranging from accountants to veterinarians. Each job profile includes such information as education, experience, and certification needed, salaries, and job search suggestions.

★7593★ *"Dental Hygienist" in Allied Health Professions (pp. 14-15; 138)*
Arco Publishing Co.
Simon & Schuster, Inc.
201 W. 103rd St.
Indianapolis, IN 46290
Ph: 800-428-5331   Fax: 800-835-3202
1993. Contains information on 28 representative careers in health care. Provides a sample of the Allied Health Professions Admission Test, lists professional societies and associations, and offers a directory of schools and programs for the careers listed.

★7594★ *"Dental Hygienist" in Career Selector 2001*
Barron's Educational Series, Inc.
250 Wireless Blvd.
Hauppauge, NY 11788
Ph: (516)434-3311   Fax: (516)434-3723
Fr: 800-645-3476
James C. Gonyea. 1993.

Dispensing Opticians

Dispensing opticians fit eyeglasses and contact lenses. Dispensing opticians order the necessary ophthalmic laboratory work, help the customer select appropriate frames, and adjust the finished eyeglasses. They fit contact lenses under the supervision of an optometrist or ophthalmologist. The majority of dispensing opticians fit eyeglasses. A small number specialize in fitting contacts, artificial eyes, or cosmetic shells to cover blemished eyes.

Salaries

Earnings of dispensing opticians vary considerably; those who work in states that require licensure often earn the most.

Dispensing opticians $20,971-$30,000/year

Employment Outlook

Growth rate until the year 2005: Faster than the average.

Dispensing Opticians

★7595★ *Description of the Profession*
Commission on Opticianry Accreditation
10111 Martin Luther King, Jr., Hwy., Ste. 112
Bowie, MD 20720
Ph: (301)577-4829
This one-page sheet details the job duties of dispensing opticians. Lists accredited programs across the United States.

★7596★ *"Dispensing Optician" in 100 Best Careers for the Year 2000 (pp. 59-61)*
Arco Pub.
201 W. 103rd St.
Indianapolis, IN 46290
Ph: 800-428-5331   Fax: 800-835-3202
Shelly Field. 1992. Describes 100 job opportunities expected to grow fast throughout the next decade. Provides information on job duties and responsibilities, training requirements, education, advancement opportunities, experience and qualifications, and typical salaries.

★7597★ *"Dispensing Optician" in 150 Careers in the Health Care Field*
Reed Reference Publishing
121 Chanlon Rd.
PO Box 31
New Providence, NJ 07974
Fax: (908)665-6688   Fr: 800-521-8110
Stanley Alperin. Third edition, 1993. Profiles health care occupations requiring a bachelor's degree or less. Describes the nature of the work, educational preparation, licensing requirements, and salary. Lists accredited educational programs.

★7598★ *"Dispensing Optician" in VGM's Careers Encyclopedia (pp. 324-326)*
National Textbook Co. (NTC)
VGM Career Books
4255 W. Touhy Ave.
Lincolnwood, IL 60646-1975
Ph: (708)679-5500   Fax: (708)679-2494
Fr: 800-323-4900
Third edition, 1991. Describes job duties, places of employment, working conditions,
qualifications, education, and training, advancement potential, and salary for each occupation.

★7599★ *"Dispensing Opticians" in 101 Careers: A Guide to the Fastest-Growing Opportunities (pp. 201-203)*
John Wiley & Sons, Inc.
605 3rd Ave.
New York, NY 10158-0012
Ph: (212)850-6645   Fax: (212)850-6088
Michael Harkavy. 1990. Describes the nature of the job, working conditions, employment growth, qualifications, personal skills, projected salaries, and where to write for more information.

★7600★ *"Dispensing Opticians" in America's 50 Fastest Growing Jobs (pp. 79)*
JIST Works, Inc.
720 N. Park Ave.
Indianapolis, IN 46202-3431
Ph: (317)264-3720   Fax: (317)264-3709
Fr: 800-648-5478
Michael J. Farr, compiler. 1994. Describes the 50 fastest growing jobs within major career clusters such as technicians, and marketing and sales. Each job profile explains the nature of the work, skills and abilities required, employment outlook, average earnings, related occupations, education and training requirements, and employment opportunities. Also contains career planning information and job search tips.

★7601★ *"Dispensing Opticians" in Career Discovery Encyclopedia (Vol.2, pp. 112-113)*
J.G. Ferguson Publishing Co.
200 W. Madison St., Ste. 300
Chicago, IL 60606
Ph: (312)580-5480   Fax: (312)580-4948
Russell E. Primm, editor-in chief. 1993. This six volume set contains two-page articles for 504 occupations. Each article describes job duties, earnings, and educational and training requirements. The whole set is arranged alphabetically by job title. Designed for junior high and older students.

★7602★ *"Dispensing Opticians" in Encyclopedia of Careers and Vocational Guidance (Vol.2, pp. 485-487)*
J.G. Ferguson Publishing Co.
200 W. Madison St., Ste. 300
Chicago, IL 60606
Ph: (312)580-5480   Fax: (312)580-4948
William E. Hopke, editor-in-chief. Ninth edition, 1993. Four-volume set that profiles 900 occupations and describes job trends in 74 industries. Includes career description, educational requirements, history of the job, methods of entry, advancement, employment outlook, earnings, conditions of work, social and psychological factors, and sources of further information.

★7603★ *"Dispensing Opticians" in Health Care Job Explosion! (pp. 120-127)*
D-Amp Publications
401 Amherst Ave.
Coraopolis, PA 15108
Ph: (412)262-5578
Dennis V. Damp. 1993. Provides information on the nature of work for the major health care occupational groups. Descriptions include working conditions, training, job outlook, qualifications, and related occupations.

★7604★ *"Dispensing Opticians" in Jobs! What They Are—Where They Are—What They Pay (p. 183)*
Simon & Schuster, Inc.
Simon & Schuster Bldg.
1230 Avenue of the Americas
New York, NY 10020
Ph: (212)698-7000   Fr: 800-223-2348
Robert O. Snelling and Anne M. Snelling. 3rd edition, 1992. Describes duties and responsibilities, earnings, employment opportunities, training, and qualifications.

★7605★ *"Dispensing Opticians: Lens Workers" in Careers for Women Without College Degrees (pp. 212-215)*
McGraw-Hill, Inc.
Blue Ridge Summit
Philadelphia, PA 17294
Ph: (212)512-2000   Fr: 800-722-4726
Beatryce Nivens. 1988. Part 1 contains exercises in goal setting, decision making, and skills assessment. Part 2 explores 19 careers

with the best occupational outlook. Part 3 describes nontraditional college degree programs.

★7606★ "Dispensing Opticians" in *Occupational Outlook Handbook*
U.S. Government Printing Office
Superintendent of Documents
Washington, DC 20402
Ph: (202)512-1800   Fax: (202)512-2250

Biennial; latest edition, 1994-95. Encyclopedia of careers describing about 250 occupations and comprising about 85 percent of all jobs in the economy. Occupations that require lengthy education or training are given the most attention. Each occupation's profile describes what the worker does on the job, working conditions, education and training requirements, advancement possibilities, job outlook, earnings, and sources of additional information.

★7607★ *Health Careers*
Careers, Inc.
PO Box 135
Largo, FL 34649-0135
Ph: (813)584-7333

1994. Four-page brief describing duties, working conditions, personal qualifications, training, earnings and hours, employment outlook, places of employment, related careers, and where to write for more information.

★7608★ "Ophthalmic Dispensing Optician" in *Desk Guide to Training and Work Advertisement* (p. 60)
Charles C. Thomas, Publisher
2600 S. 1st St.
Springfield, IL 62794-9265
Ph: (217)789-8980   Fax: (217)789-9130
Fr: 800-258-8980

Gail Baugher Kuenstler. 1988. Describes alternative methods of gaining entry into an occupation through different types of educational programs, internships, and apprenticeships.

★7609★ *Opportunities in Eye Care Careers*
National Textbook Co. (NTC)
VGM Career Books
4255 W. Touhy Ave.
Lincolnwood, IL 60646-1975
Ph: (708)679-5500   Fax: (708)679-2494
Fr: 800-323-4900

Kathleen M. Ahrens. 1991. Describes job responsibilities, working conditions, salaries, and educational requirements.

★7610★ *Optician*
Careers, Inc.
PO Box 135
Largo, FL 34649-0135
Ph: (813)584-7333

1993. Four-page brief offering the definition, history, duties, working conditions, personal qualifications, educational requirements, earnings, hours, employment outlook, advancement, and careers related to this position.

★7611★ "Optician" in *Careers in Health Care* (pp. 188-190)
National Textbook Co. (NTC)
VGM Career Books
4255 W. Touhy Ave.
Lincolnwood, IL 60646-1975
Ph: (708)679-5500   Fax: (708)679-2494
Fr: 800-323-4900

Barbara M. Swanson. Third edition, 1995. Describes job duties, work settings, salaries, licensing and certification requirements, educational preparation, and future outlook.

★7612★ "Optician, Dispensing" in *VGM's Handbook of Health Care Careers*
National Textbook Co.
4255 W. Touhy Ave.
Lincolnwood, IL 60646-1975
Ph: (708)679-5500   Fax: (708)679-2494
Fr: 800-323-4900

Annette Selden. 1993. Contains 42 two-page occupational profiles describing job duties, places of employment, working conditions, qualifications, education, employment outlook, and income.

★7613★ *Opticians, Dispensing*
Chronicle Guidance Publications, Inc.
66 Aurora St.
PO Box 1190
Moravia, NY 13118-1190
Ph: (315)497-0330   Fax: (315)497-3359
Fr: 800-622-7284

1991. Occupational brief describing the nature of the job, working conditions, hours and earnings, education and training, licensure, certification, unions, personal qualifications, social and psychological factors, location, employment outlook, entry methods, advancement, and related occupations.

PROFESSIONAL ASSOCIATIONS

★7614★ Commission on Opticianry Accreditation (COA)
10111 Martin Luther King, Jr. Hwy., No. 100
Bowie, MD 20720
Ph: (301)459-8075   Fax: (301)577-3880

Members: Purpose: Accrediting agency for ophthalmic dispensing and ophthalmic laboratory technology programs in postsecondary institutions. Conducts an evaluator's workshop to train on-site evaluators. **Publications:** *Accreditation Guide for Ophthalmic Dispensing Programs.* • *COA News,* semiannual. • *Evaluator's Checklist for Ophthalmic Laboratory Technology Programs.* • *Evaluator's Handbook for Ophthalmic Dispensing Programs.* • *Evaluator's Handbook for Ophthalmic Laboratory Technology Programs.* • *Self-Study Report Format for Ophthalmic Dispensing Programs.*

★7615★ National Academy of Opticianry (NAO)
10111 Martin Luther King, Jr. Hwy., Ste. 112
Bowie, MD 20720
Ph: (301)577-4828   Fax: (301)577-3880

Members: Offers review courses for national certification and state licensure examinations to members. Maintains speakers' bureau and Career Progression Program. **Publications:** *Academy Newsletter,* quarterly. • *Exam Review for Ophthalmic Dispensing.* • *Ophthalmic Dispensing Review Book.* • *Optical Math Review.*

★7616★ Opticians Association of America (OAA)
10341 Democracy Ln.
Fairfax, VA 22030
Ph: (703)691-8355   Fax: (703)691-3929

Members: Retail dispensing opticians who fill prescriptions for glasses or contact lenses written by a vision care specialist. **Purpose:** Works to advance the science of ophthalmic optics. Conducts research and educational programs. Maintains museum and speakers' bureau. Compiles statistics. **Publications:** *American Optician,* bimonthly.

STANDARDS/CERTIFICATION AGENCIES

★7617★ American Board of Opticianry (ABO)
10341 Democracy Ln.
Fairfax, VA 22030
Ph: (703)691-8356   Fax: (703)691-3929

Provides uniform standards for dispensing opticians by administering the National Opticianry Competency Examination and by issuing the Certified Optician Certificate to those passing the exam. Also administers the Master in Ophthalmic Optics Examination and issues certificates to opticians at the advanced level passing the exam. Maintains records of persons certified for competency in eyeglass dispensing. Adopts and enforces continuing education requirements; assists and encourages state licensing boards in the use of the National Opticianry Competency Examination for licensure purposes.

★7618★ National Academy of Opticianry (NAO)
10111 Martin Luther King, Jr. Hwy., Ste. 112
Bowie, MD 20720
Ph: (301)577-4828   Fax: (301)577-3880

Offers review courses for national certification and state licensure examinations to members. Maintains speakers' bureau and Career Progression Program.

★7619★ National Contact Lens Examiners (NCLE)
10341 Democracy Ln.
Fairfax, VA 22030
Ph: (703)691-1061   Fax: (703)691-3929

National certifying agency promoting continued development of opticians and technicians as contact lens fitters by formulating standards and procedures for determination of entry-level competency. Assists in the continuation, development, administration, and monitoring of a national Contact Lens Registry Examination (CLRE), which verifies entry-level competency of contact lens fitters. Issues certificates.

EDUCATIONAL DIRECTORIES AND PROGRAMS

★7620★ Health & Medical Industry Directory
American Business Directories, Inc.
5711 S. 86th Circle
Omaha, NE 68127
Ph: (402)593-4600   Fax: (402)331-1505
Released 1993. Lists over 1.1 million physicians and surgeons, dentists, clinics, health clubs, and other health-related businesses in the U.S. and Canada. Entries include: Name, address, phone.

★7621★ Therapists and Allied Health Professionals Career Directory
Gale Research Inc.
835 Penobscot Bldg.
Detroit, MI 48226-4094
Ph: (313)961-2242   Fax: (313)961-6083
Fr: 800-877-GALE
Bradley J. Morgan and Joseph M. Palmisano. 1993. A directory in the Career Advisor Series that provides essays written by industry professionals; job search information on resume and cover letter preparation, networking, and the interviewing process; approximately 300 companies and organizations offering job opportunities and internships, and additional job-hunting resources.

BASIC REFERENCE GUIDES AND HANDBOOKS

★7622★ Dispensing Optician
R & E Publishers, Inc.
PO Box 2008
Saratoga, CA 95070
Ph: (408)866-6303   Fax: (408)866-0825
Ronald R. Smith, editor. 1993.

PROFESSIONAL AND TRADE PERIODICALS

★7623★ Eyewitness
Contact Lens Society of America
11735 Bowman Green Dr.
Reston, VA 22090
Ph: (703)437-5100   Fax: (703)437-0727
Thomas V. Appler

Quarterly. Informs members of developments in the contact lens industry. Also reports on related educational information and technical papers. Recurring features include news of research, calendar of events, reports of meetings, and associate member listing.

PROFESSIONAL MEETINGS AND CONVENTIONS

★7624★ International Vision Expo and Conference East
Association Expositions & Services
1100 Summer St.
Stamford, CT 06905
Ph: (203)325-5099   Fax: (203)325-5001
Annual. Always held during March at the Jacob Javits Convention Center in New York, New York. **Dates and Locations:** 1996 Mar 29-31; New York, NY. • 1997 Mar 21-23; New York, NY.

★7625★ National Academy of Opticianry Convention
National Academy of Opticianry
10111 Martin Luther King, Jr. Hwy., Ste. 112
Bowie, MD 20720
Ph: (301)577-4828   Fax: (301)577-3880
Annual.

OTHER SOURCES OF INFORMATION

★7626★ Opticianry Licensing and Certification Boards
Opticians Associaton of America (OAA)
10341 Democracy Ln.
Fairfax, VA 22030
Ph: (703)691-8355
1993. Four-page list of state optician licensing boards. Includes name, address, phone number, and contact person.

EEG Technologists

Electroencephalography is a procedure that measures the electrical activity of the brain. An instrument called an electroencephalograph records this activity and produces a written tracing of the brain's electrical impulses. The people who operate electroencephalographs are called **EEG technologists**. The tests performed help neurologists diagnose brain tumors, strokes, toxic/metabolic disorders, and epilepsy. They also measure the effects of diseases on the brain and determine whether individuals with mental disorders have an organic impairment.

Salaries

Salaries for EEG technologists is as follows:

EEG technologists, average	$23,369/year

Employment Outlook

Growth rate until the year 2005: Much faster than the average.

EEG Technologists

CAREER GUIDES

★7627★ "EEG and EKG Technician" in Career Information Center (Vol.7)
Simon and Schuster
200 Old Tappan Rd.
Old Tappan, NJ 07675
Fax: 800-445-6991   Fr: 800-223-2348
Richard Lidz and Linda Perrin, editorial directors. Fifth edition, 1993. This 13-volume set profiles over 600 occupations. Each occupational profile describes job duties, entry-level requirements, educational requirements, advancement possibilities, employment outlook, working conditions, earnings and benefits, and where to write for more information.

★7628★ "EEG Technologist/Technician" in 100 Best Careers for the Year 2000 (pp. 38-40)
Arco Pub.
201 W. 103rd St.
Indianapolis, IN 46290
Ph: 800-428-5331   Fax: 800-835-3202
Shelly Field. 1992. Describes 100 job opportunities expected to grow fast throughout the next decade. Provides information on job duties and responsibilities, training requirements, education, advancement opportunities, experience and qualifications, and typical salaries.

★7629★ "EEG Technologists" in America's 50 Fastest Growing Jobs (pp. 81)
JIST Works, Inc.
720 N. Park Ave.
Indianapolis, IN 46202-3431
Ph: (317)264-3720   Fax: (317)264-3709
Fr: 800-648-5478
Michael J. Farr, compiler. 1994. Describes the 50 fastest growing jobs within major career clusters such as technicians, and marketing and sales. Each job profile explains the nature of the work, skills and abilities required, employment outlook, average earnings, related occupations, education and training requirements, and employment opportunities. Also contains career planning information and job search tips.

★7630★ "EEG Technologists" in Health Care Job Explosion! (pp. 67-72)
D-Amp Publications
401 Amherst Ave.
Coraopolis, PA 15108
Ph: (412)262-5578
Dennis V. Damp. 1993. Provides information on the nature of work for the major health care occupational groups. Descriptions include working conditions, training, job outlook, qualifications, and related occupations.

★7631★ "EEG Technologists" in Occupational Outlook Handbook
U.S. Government Printing Office
Superintendent of Documents
Washington, DC 20402
Ph: (202)512-1800   Fax: (202)512-2250
Biennial; latest edition, 1994-95. Encyclopedia of careers describing about 250 occupations and comprising about 85 percent of all jobs in the economy. Occupations that require lengthy education or training are given the most attention. Each occupation's profile describes what the worker does on the job, working conditions, education and training requirements, advancement possibilities, job outlook, earnings, and sources of additional information.

★7632★ "EEG Technologists and Technicians" in 101 Careers: A Guide to the Fastest-Growing Opportunities (pp. 204-206)
John Wiley & Sons, Inc.
605 3rd Ave.
New York, NY 10158-0012
Ph: (212)850-6645   Fax: (212)850-6088
Michael Harkavy. 1990. Describes the nature of the job, working conditions, employment growth, qualifications, personal skills, projected salaries, and where to write for more information.

★7633★ "EEG Technologists and Technicians" in Best Jobs for the 1990s and Into the 21st Century
Impact Publications
9104-N Manassas Dr.
Manassas Park, VA 22111
Ph: (703)361-7300   Fax: (703)335-9486
Ronald L. Krannich and Caryl Rae Krannich. 1993.

★7634★ "Electroencephalograph (EEG) Technician" in VGM's Handbook of Health Care Careers
National Textbook Co.
4255 W. Touhy Ave.
Lincolnwood, IL 60646-1975
Ph: (708)679-5500   Fax: (708)679-2494
Fr: 800-323-4900
Annette Selden. 1993. Contains 42 two-page occupational profiles describing job duties, places of employment, working conditions, qualifications, education, employment outlook, and income.

★7635★ "Electroencephalographic Technicians" in Encyclopedia of Careers and Vocational Guidance (Vol.2, pp. 554-558)
J.G. Ferguson Publishing Co.
200 W. Madison St., Ste. 300
Chicago, IL 60606
Ph: (312)580-5480   Fax: (312)580-4948
William E. Hopke, editor-in-chief. Ninth edition, 1993. Four-volume set that profiles 900 occupations and describes job trends in 74 industries. Includes career description, educational requirements, history of the job, methods of entry, advancement, employment outlook, earnings, conditions of work, social and psychological factors, and sources of further information.

★7636★ "Electroencephalographic Technologist" in 150 Careers in the Health Care Field
Reed Reference Publishing
121 Chanlon Rd.
PO Box 31
New Providence, NJ 07974
Fax: (908)665-6688   Fr: 800-521-8110
Stanley Alperin. Third edition, 1993. Profiles health care occupations requiring a bachelor's degree or less. Describes the nature of the work, educational preparation, licensing requirements, and salary. Lists accredited educational programs.

★7637★ "Electroencephalographic Technologist and Electroencephalographic Technician" in *Careers in Health Care* (pp. 74-78)
National Textbook Co. (NTC)
VGM Career Books
4255 W. Touhy Ave.
Lincolnwood, IL 60646-1975
Ph: (708)679-5500   Fax: (708)679-2494
Fr: 800-323-4900

Barbara M. Swanson. Third edition, 1995. Describes job duties, work settings, salaries, licensing and certification requirements, educational preparation, and future outlook.

★7638★ *Electroencephalographic Technologists*
Chronicle Guidance Publications, Inc.
66 Aurora St.
PO Box 1190
Moravia, NY 13118-1190
Ph: (315)497-0330   Fax: (315)497-3359
Fr: 800-622-7284

1992. Career brief describing the nature of the job, working conditions, hours and earnings, education and training, licensure, certification, unions, personal qualifications, social and psychological factors, location, employment outlook, entry methods, advancement, and related occupations.

★7639★ *Electroencephalographic Technologists*
American Society of Electroneurodiagnostic Technologists (ASET)
204 W. 7th St.
Carroll, IA 51401
Ph: (712)792-2978

This two-page pamphlet explains what an electroencephalogram (EEG) is, how it is used, what EEG technologists do, earnings, basic qualifications needed, advancement, possibilities, training, and the cost of training.

★7640★ "Electroencephalographic Technology" in *Allied Health Education Directory* (pp. 30-31)
American Medical Association (AMA)
515 N. State St.
Chicago, IL 60610
Ph: (312)464-5000   Fr: 800-621-8335

William R. Burrow, editor. Sixteenth edition, 1988. Describes 26 allied health occupations and lists educational programs accredited by the Committee on Allied Health Education and Accreditation of the American Medical Association.

★7641★ *Health Careers*
Careers, Inc.
PO Box 135
Largo, FL 34649-0135
Ph: (813)584-7333

1994. Four-page brief describing duties, working conditions, personal qualifications, training, earnings and hours, employment outlook, places of employment, related careers, and where to write for more information.

PROFESSIONAL ASSOCIATIONS

★7642★ American Board of Registration of EEG and EP Technologists (ABRET)
PO Box 11434
Norfolk, VA 23517
Ph: (804)627-5503

Members: Purpose: Determines the competency of electroencephalography technologists through administration of written and oral examinations.

★7643★ American Society of Electroneurodiagnostic Technologists (ASET)
204 W. 7th St.
Carroll, IA 51401-2317
Ph: (712)792-2978   Fax: (712)792-6962

Members: Persons engaged mainly in clinical electroencephalographic technology, with some doing both clinical and research EEG and related neurodiagnostic procedures, such as Evoked Potential Responses and polysomnography. **Purpose:** Objective is the advancement of electroneurodiagnostic technology and the development and maintenance of high standards of training and practice in this field. Conducts a scientific program and structured, short courses in various aspects of EEG technology and electroneurodiagnostics. Joint projects with the American Electroencephalographic Society Works for complete equality and integration of the blind in society. Provides support and information services. include the drawing up of job descriptions in EEG technology as guidelines for classification of personnel and working toward approved programs for training EEG technologists. Collaborates in videocassette/television productions. Provides employment exchange service. Is developing a library. **Publications:** *American Journal of EEG Technology*, quarterly. • *ASET Newsletter*, quarterly. • *Who's Who in Electroneurodiagnostics—Membership Directory*, annual.

STANDARDS/CERTIFICATION AGENCIES

★7644★ American Board of Registration of EEG and EP Technologists (ABRET)
PO Box 11434
Norfolk, VA 23517
Ph: (804)627-5503

Determines the competency of electroencephalography technologists through administration of written and oral examinations.

TEST GUIDES

★7645★ *Career Examination Series: EEG Technician*
National Learning Corp.
212 Michael Dr.
Syosset, NY 11791
Ph: (516)921-8888   Fax: (516)921-8743
Fr: 800-645-6337

Jack Rudman. A study guide for professional and trainee EEG technicians. Includes a multiple-choice examination section; provides answers.

★7646★ *Registration Examination for Electroencephalographic Technologists Handbook for Candidates*
ABRET Examination
The Psychological Corporation Project 617/ABRET
555 Academic Ct.
San Antonio, TX 78204
Ph: (512)299-1061

This booklet describes the test for registration, gives an outline of the test, sample questions, eligibility requirements, application procedures; also lists testing centers. Includes an application schedule of testing dates and deadlines.

EDUCATIONAL DIRECTORIES AND PROGRAMS

★7647★ *Health & Medical Industry Directory*
American Business Directories, Inc.
5711 S. 86th Circle
Omaha, NE 68127
Ph: (402)593-4600   Fax: (402)331-1505

Released 1993. Lists over 1.1 million physicians and surgeons, dentists, clinics, health clubs, and other health-related businesses in the U.S. and Canada. Entries include: Name, address, phone.

★7648★ *Medical Technologists and Technicians Career Directory*
Gale Research Inc.
835 Penobscot Bldg.
Detroit, MI 48226-4094
Ph: (313)961-2242   Fax: (313)961-6083
Fr: 800-877-GALE

Bradley J. Morgan and Joseph M. Palmisano. 1993. A directory in the Career Advisor Series that provides essays written by industry professionals; job search information on resume and cover letter preparation, networking, and the interviewing process; approximately 300 companies and organizations offering job opportunities and internships, and additional job-hunting resources.

BASIC REFERENCE GUIDES AND HANDBOOKS

★7649★ Basic Mechanisms of the EEG
Birkhauser Boston
675 Massachusettes Ave.
Cambridge, MA 02139
Ph: (617)876-2333
Stephan Zschocke, editor. 1993. Part of the Brain Dynamics Series.

★7650★ Clinical Electroencephalography and Topographic Brain Mapping: Technology and Practice
Springer-Verlag New York, Inc.
175 5th Ave.
New York, NY 10010
Ph: (212)460-1500
Frank H. Duffy, V. G. Iyer, and W. W. Surwillo. 1989. Includes bibliographies and an index. Illustrated.

★7651★ Current Practice of Clinical Electroencephalography
Raven Press
1185 Avenue of the Americas
New York, NY 10036
Ph: (212)930-9500
D. D. Daly and T. A. Pedley, editors. Second edition, 1990.

★7652★ Electroencephalography: Basic Principles, Clinical Applications, and Related Fields
Williams & Wilkins
428 E. Preston St.
Baltimore, MD 21202
Ph: (410)528-4000
Ernst Niedermeyer and Fernando Lopes da Silva. Third edition, 1993. Includes bibliographies and an index.

★7653★ Spehlmann's EEG Primer
Elsevier Science Publishing Co., Inc.
655 Avenue of the Americas
New York, NY 10010
Ph: (212)989-5800
B. J. Fisch, editor. Second edition, 1990.

PROFESSIONAL AND TRADE PERIODICALS

★7654★ Biomedical Technology Information Service
Quest Publishing Company
1351 Titan Way
Brea, CA 92621
Ph: (714)738-6400   Fax: (714)525-6258
Gregory F. Nighswonger
Semimonthly. Monitors latest advances in medical technology, including developments in medical devices and electronics. Recurring features include new technology, computer applications, legislation and regulations, new inventions, and professional activities. Also includes book reviews, letters to the editor, and a calendar of events.

★7655★ Brain Topography
Human Sciences Press
233 Spring St.
New York, NY 10013
Ph: (212)620-8000   Fax: (212)463-0742
R. Eugene Ramsay
Quarterly.

★7656★ Neurology
Advanstar Communications, Inc.
270 Madison Ave.
New York, NY 10016-0601
Ph: (212)951-6600   Fax: (212)481-6561
Robert B. Daroff
Monthly. Official journal of the American Academy of Neurology.

★7657★ Technology for Health Care Series
ECRI
5200 Butler Pike
Plymouth Meeting, PA 19462
Ph: (215)825-6000   Fax: (215)834-1275
Michele Moscariello
Monthly. Concerned with the safety, performance, reliability, and cost effectiveness of health care technology. Covers areas of anesthesia, cardiology, imaging and radiology, and respiratory therapy. Reviews device test results and warns of hazards and deficiencies. Recurring features include news of research, Institute reports, and news of members.

PROFESSIONAL MEETINGS AND CONVENTIONS

★7658★ American Association of Electrodiagnostic Medicine Meeting
American Association of Electrodiagnostic Medicine
21 2nd St. SW, Ste. 103
Rochester, MN 55902-3018
Ph: (507)288-0100   Fax: (507)288-1225
Annual. **Dates and Locations:** 1996 Oct 02-06; Minneapolis, MN. • 1997 Sep 17-21; San Diego, CA. • 1998 Oct 14-18; Lake Buena Vista, FL.

★7659★ American Society of Electroneurodiagnostic Technologists Convention
American Society of Electroneurodiagnostic Technologists
c/o M. Fran Pedelty
204 West 7th St.
Carroll, IA 51401
Ph: (712)792-2978   Fax: (712)792-6962
Annual. **Dates and Locations:** 1996 Aug.

OTHER SOURCES OF INFORMATION

★7660★ "EEG Technologist/Technician" in Allied Health Professions (pp. 23-24; 141)
Arco Publishing Co.
Simon & Schuster, Inc.
201 W. 103rd St.
Indianapolis, IN 46290
Ph: 800-428-5331   Fax: 800-835-3202
1993. Contains information on 28 representative careers in health care. Provides a sample of the Allied Health Professions Admission Test, lists professional societies and associations, and offers a directory of schools and programs for the careers listed.

EKG Technicians

Electrocardiograph technicians (EKG's, also called ECG's), operate a machine called an electrocardiograph, which records graphic tracings of heartbeats known as electrocardiograms. These tracings indicate the electrical impulses transmitted by the heart muscle during and between heart beats. EKG's help physicians diagnose heart disease, monitor the effect of drug therapy, and analyze changes in a patient's heart. More skilled EKG technicians perform ambulatory monitoring and stress testing.

Salaries

Salaries for EKG technicians are as follows:

EKG technicians $8.66/hour

Employment Outlook

Growth rate until the year 2005: More slowly than the average.

EKG Technicians

CAREER GUIDES

★7661★ "Cardiographic Technician (EKG Technician)" in 150 Careers in the Health Care Field
Reed Reference Publishing
121 Chanlon Rd.
PO Box 31
New Providence, NJ 07974
Fax: (908)665-6688   Fr: 800-521-8110

Stanley Alperin. Third edition, 1993. Profiles health care occupations requiring a bachelor's degree or less. Describes the nature of the work, educational preparation, licensing requirements, and salary. Lists accredited educational programs.

★7662★ "Cardiology and Cardiopulmonary Technologists" in Careers in High-Tech
Arco Publishing Co.
Macmillan General Reference
15 Columbus Cir.
New York, NY 10023
Fax: 800-835-3202   Fr: 800-858-7674

Winkler, Connie. 1987. Surveys occupations in data processing, personal computers, telecommunications, manufacturing technology, artificial intelligence, computer graphics, medicine, biotechnology, lasers, technical writing, and publishing. Separate chapters cover education and training.

★7663★ "Cardiovascular Technology Personnel" in Careers in Health Care (pp. 27-31)
National Textbook Co. (NTC)
VGM Career Books
4255 W. Touhy Ave.
Lincolnwood, IL 60646-1975
Ph: (708)679-5500   Fax: (708)679-2494
Fr: 800-323-4900

Barbara M. Swanson. Third edition, 1995. Describes job duties, work settings, salaries, licensing and certification requirements, educational preparation, and future outlook.

★7664★ "EEG and EKG Technician" in Career Information Center (Vol.7)
Simon and Schuster
200 Old Tappan Rd.
Old Tappan, NJ 07675
Fax: 800-445-6991   Fr: 800-223-2348

Richard Lidz and Linda Perrin, editorial directors. Fifth edition, 1993. This 13-volume set profiles over 600 occupations. Each occupational profile describes job duties, entry-level requirements, educational requirements, advancement possibilities, employment outlook, working conditions, earnings and benefits, and where to write for more information.

★7665★ EKG Technician
Vocational Biographies, Inc.
PO Box 31
Sauk Centre, MN 56378-0031
Ph: (612)352-6516   Fax: (612)352-5546
Fr: 800-255-0752

1990. Four-page pamphlet containing a personal narrative about a worker's job, work likes and dislikes, career path from high school to the present. Education and training, the rewards and frustrations, and the effects of the job on the rest of the worker's life. The data file portion of this pamphlet gives a concise occupational summary, including work descriptions, working conditions, places of employment, personal characteristics, education and training, job outlook, and salary range.

★7666★ "EKG Technician" in 100 Best Careers for the Year 2000 (pp. 41-43)
Arco Pub.
201 W. 103rd St.
Indianapolis, IN 46290
Ph: 800-428-5331   Fax: 800-835-3202

Shelly Field. 1992. Describes 100 job opportunities expected to grow fast throughout the next decade. Provides information on job duties and responsibilities, training requirements, education, advancement opportunities, experience and qualifications, and typical salaries.

★7667★ "EKG Technicians" in 101 Careers: A Guide to the Fastest-Growing Opportunities (pp. 207-209)
John Wiley & Sons, Inc.
605 3rd Ave.
New York, NY 10158-0012
Ph: (212)850-6645   Fax: (212)850-6088

Michael Harkavy. 1990. Describes the nature of the job, working conditions, employment growth, qualifications, personal skills, projected salaries, and where to write for more information.

★7668★ "EKG Technologists" in Health Care Job Explosion! (pp. 73-78)
D-Amp Publications
401 Amherst Ave.
Coraopolis, PA 15108
Ph: (412)262-5578

Dennis V. Damp. 1993. Provides information on the nature of work for the major health care occupational groups. Descriptions include working conditions, training, job outlook, qualifications, and related occupations.

★7669★ "Electrocardiograph (EKG) Technician" in VGM's Handbook of Health Care Careers
National Textbook Co.
4255 W. Touhy Ave.
Lincolnwood, IL 60646-1975
Ph: (708)679-5500   Fax: (708)679-2494
Fr: 800-323-4900

Annette Selden. 1993. Contains 42 two-page occupational profiles describing job duties, places of employment, working conditions, qualifications, education, employment outlook, and income.

★7670★ Electrocardiograph Technician
Careers, Inc.
PO Box 135
Largo, FL 34649-0135
Ph: (813)584-7333

1992. Two-page summary describing duties, working conditions, personal qualifications, training, earnings and hours, employment outlook, places of employment, related careers, and where to write for more information.

★7671★ *Electrocardiograph Technicians*
Chronicle Guidance Publications, Inc.
66 Aurora St.
PO Box 1190
Moravia, NY 13118-1190
Ph: (315)497-0330   Fax: (315)497-3359
Fr: 800-622-7284
1993. Career brief describing the nature of the job, working conditions, hours and earnings, education and training, licensure, certification, unions, personal qualifications, social and psychological factors, location, employment outlook, entry methods, advancement, and related occupations.

★7672★ "Electrocardiograph Technicians" in *Encyclopedia of Careers and Vocational Guidance* (Vol.2, pp. 550-553)
J.G. Ferguson Publishing Co.
200 W. Madison St., Ste. 300
Chicago, IL 60606
Ph: (312)580-5480   Fax: (312)580-4948
William E. Hopke, editor in chief. Ninth edition, 1993. Four-volume set that profiles 900 occupations and describes job trends in 74 industries. Includes career description, educational requirements, history of the job, methods of entry, advancement, employment outlook, earnings, conditions of work, social and psychological factors, and sources of further information.

★7673★ "Electrocardiograph Technicians" in *Jobs! What They Are—Where They Are—What They Pay* (p. 184)
Simon & Schuster, Inc.
Simon & Schuster Bldg.
1230 Avenue of the Americas
New York, NY 10020
Ph: (212)698-7000   Fr: 800-223-2348
Robert O. Snelling and Anne M. Snelling. 3rd edition, 1992. Describes duties and responsibilities, earnings, employment opportunities, training, and qualifications.

★7674★ *Health Careers*
Careers, Inc.
PO Box 135
Largo, FL 34649-0135
Ph: (813)584-7333
1994. Four-page brief describing duties, working conditions, personal qualifications, training, earnings and hours, employment outlook, places of employment, related careers, and where to write for more information.

Professional Associations

★7675★ American College of International Physicians (ACIP)
711 2nd St. NE, Ste. 200
Washington, DC 20002
Ph: (202)544-7498   Fax: (202)546-7105
Members: Physicians and surgeons interested in initiatives to promote national efforts in international health, education, research, training, and welfare. **Purpose:** Promotes the betterment of the health of all peoples and seeks to advance the art and science of medi-

cine. Emphasizes the international character of medicine and the education of international physicians. Seeks parity for foreign medical graduates. Supports relief programs to areas struck by natural calamities or epidemic diseases. **Publications:** *International Medical Journal*, semiannual. • *The International Physician*, quarterly.

★7676★ American Society of Cardiovascular Professionals (ASCP)
120 Falcon Dr.
Fredericksburg, VA 22408
Ph: (703)891-0079   Fax: (703)898-2393
Fr: 800-683-NSCT
Members: Dedicated to determining educational needs, developing programs to meet those needs, and providing a structure to offer the cardiovascular and pulmonary technology professional a key to the future as a valuable member of the medical team. Seeks advancement for members through communication and education. **Purpose:** Provides coordinated programs to orient the newer professional to his field and continuing educational opportunities for technologist personnel. Has established guidelines for educational programs in the hospital and university setting. Works with educators and physicians to provide basic, advanced, and in-service programs for technologists. Sponsors registration and certification programs which provide technology professionals with further opportunity to clarify their level of expertise. Compiles statistics. **Publications:** *ASCP Membership Directory*, annual. • *CP Digest*, bimonthly. • *Journal of Cardiovascular Technology*, semiannual. • *Pulmonary News*, quarterly.

★7677★ Cardiovascular Credentialing International (CCI)
4456 Corporation Ln., Ste. 120
Virginia Beach, VA 23462
Ph: (804)497-3380   Fax: (804)497-3491
Fr: 800-326-0268
Members: Cardiovascular technologists involved in the allied health professions. **Purpose:** Conducts testing of allied health professionals throughout the U.S. and Canada. Provides study guides and reliability and validity testing. Compiles statistics. **Publications:** *Pulse*, quarterly.

Standards/Certification Agencies

★7678★ American Society of Cardiovascular Professionals (ASCP)
120 Falcon Dr.
Fredericksburg, VA 22408
Ph: (703)891-0079   Fax: (703)898-2393
Fr: 800-683-NSCT
Dedicated to determining educational needs, developing programs to meet those needs, and providing a structure to offer the cardiovascular and pulmonary technology professional a key to the future as a valuable member of the medical team. Sponsors registration and certification programs which

provide technology professionals with further opportunity to clarify their level of expertise.

★7679★ National Society for Cardiovascular and Pulmonary Technology (NSCPT)
1101 14th St. Nw, Ste. 1100
Washington, DC 20005
Ph: (202)371-1267
Promotes efficiency and advancements in the field of cardiology technology by encouraging the application of scientific methods and standardization of procedures.

Test Guides

★7680★ *Career Examination Series: EKG Technician*
National Learning Corp.
212 Michael Dr.
Syosset, NY 11791
Ph: (516)921-8888   Fax: (516)921-8743
Fr: 800-645-6337
Jack Rudman. A study guide for professional and trainee EKG technicians. Includes a multiple-choice examination section; provides answers.

★7681★ *Career Examination Series: Electrocardiograph Technician*
National Learning Corp.
212 Michael Dr.
Syosset, NY 11791
Ph: (516)921-8888   Fax: (516)921-8743
Fr: 800-645-6337
Jack Rudman. A study guide for professional and trainee EKG technicians. Includes a multiple-choice examination section; provides answers.

Educational Directories and Programs

★7682★ *Health & Medical Industry Directory*
American Business Directories, Inc.
5711 S. 86th Circle
Omaha, NE 68127
Ph: (402)593-4600   Fax: (402)331-1505
Released 1993. Lists over 1.1 million physicians and surgeons, dentists, clinics, health clubs, and other health-related businesses in the U.S. and Canada. Entries include: Name, address, phone.

★7683★ *Medical Technologists and Technicians Career Directory*
Gale Research Inc.
835 Penobscot Bldg.
Detroit, MI 48226-4094
Ph: (313)961-2242   Fax: (313)961-6083
Fr: 800-877-GALE
Bradley J. Morgan and Joseph M. Palmisano. 1993. A directory in the Career Advisor Series that provides essays written by industry professionals; job search information on resume and cover letter preparation, net-

working, and the interviewing process; approximately 300 companies and organizations offering job opportunities and internships, and additional job-hunting resources.

BASIC REFERENCE GUIDES AND HANDBOOKS

★7684★ Comprehensive Electrocardiology: Theory and Practice in Health and Disease
Pergamon Press, Inc.
Fairview Park
Elmsford, NY 10523
Ph: (914)524-9200

Peter W. McFarlane and T. D. Veitch Lawrie, editors. 1988. Includes bibliographical references and an index.

★7685★ The Electrocardiogram: An Illustrated Manual
Thieme Medical Publishers
381 Park Ave., S., 15th Fl.
New York, NY 10016
Ph: (212)683-5088

Rainer Klinge. 1988. Includes bibliographies and an index.

★7686★ Electrocardiography and Cardiac Drug Therapy
Kluwer Academic Publishers
101 Philip Dr.
Norwell, MA 02061
Ph: (617)871-6300

V. Hombach, H. H. Hilger, and H. L. Kennedy, editors. 1989. Includes bibliographies and an index.

★7687★ How to Quickly and Accurately Master Arrhythmia Interpretation
J. B. Lippincott Co.
227 E. Washington Sq.
Philadelphia, PA 19106
Ph: (215)238-4436

Dale Davis. 1989. Includes an index. Illustrated.

★7688★ Learning Electrocardiography: A Complete Course
Little, Brown and Co., Inc.
34 Beacon St.
Boston, MA 02108
Ph: (617)227-0730

Jules Constant. Third edition, 1987. Includes bibliographies and an index.

★7689★ Lessons in EKG Interpretation: A Basic Self-Instructional Guide
Churchill Livingstone, Inc.
650 Avenue of the Americas
New York, NY 10011
Ph: (212)206-5000

Charles P. Summerall, III, editor. Second edition, 1991.

★7690★ The Only EKG Book You'll Ever Need
J. B. Lippincott Co.
227 E. Washington Sq.
Philadelphia, PA 19106
Ph: (215)238-4436   Fr: 800-441-4526

Malcolm S. Thaler. 1994. Includes an index.

★7691★ Practical Electrocardiography
Williams and Wilkins
428 E. Preston St.
Baltimore, MD 21202
Ph: (410)528-4000

Henry J. L. Henry. Eighth edition, 1988. Includes bibliographies and an index.

★7692★ Principles of Clinical Electrocardiography
Appleton and Lange
PO Box 56303
Norwalk, CT 06856
Ph: (203)838-4400   Fr: 800-423-1359

Nora Goldschlager and Mervin J. Goldman. Thirteenth edition, 1989. Covers basic concepts of electrocardiography and its clinical diagnostic value.

★7693★ Simplified EKG Analysis: A Sequential Guide to Interpretation
Hanley & Belfus, Inc.
210 S. 13th St.
Philadelphia, PA 19107
Ph: (215)546-4995

Charles B. Seelig, editor. 1992.

PROFESSIONAL AND TRADE PERIODICALS

★7694★ Biomedical Technology Information Service
Quest Publishing Company
1351 Titan Way
Brea, CA 92621
Ph: (714)738-6400   Fax: (714)525-6258
Gregory F. Nighswonger

Semimonthly. Monitors latest advances in medical technology, including developments in medical devices and electronics. Recurring features include new technology, computer applications, legislation and regulations, new inventions, and professional activities. Also includes book reviews, letters to the editor, and a calendar of events.

★7695★ Journal of Electrocardiology
Churchill Livingstone, Inc.
650 Avenue of the Americas
New York, NY 10011
Ph: (212)206-5040   Fax: (212)727-7808
Fr: 800-553-5426
Ronald H. Selvester

Quarterly. Journal covering clinical and experimental studies of the electrical activities of the heart.

★7696★ Society of Cardiovascular Anesthesiologists—Newsletter
Society of Cardiovascular Anesthesiologists
PO Box 11086
Richmond, VA 23230-1086
Ph: (804)282-0084   Fax: (804)282-0090
Salwa Shenaq

Includes pro and con discussions of major issues within the cardiovascular anesthesiology field and reviews of related literature being published. Covers Society news, chapter reports, meeting programs and information, and lists new members.

★7697★ Technology for Health Care Series
ECRI
5200 Butler Pike
Plymouth Meeting, PA 19462
Ph: (215)825-6000   Fax: (215)834-1275
Michele Moscariello

Monthly. Concerned with the safety, performance, reliability, and cost effectiveness of health care technology. Covers areas of anesthesia, cardiology, imaging and radiology, and respiratory therapy. Reviews device test results and warns of hazards and deficiencies. Recurring features include news of research, Institute reports, and news of members.

PROFESSIONAL MEETINGS AND CONVENTIONS

★7698★ Annual Scientific Session of the American College of Cardiology
American College of Cardiology
9111 Old Georgetown Rd.
Bethesda, MD 20814-1699
Ph: (301)897-2693   Fax: (301)897-9745

Annual. **Dates and Locations:** 1996 Mar 24-27; Orlando, FL. • 1997 Mar 16-20; Anaheim, CA. • 1998 Mar 29-02; Atlanta, GA. • 1999 Mar 07-11; New Orleans, LA. • 2000 Mar 12-16; Anaheim, CA.

OTHER SOURCES OF INFORMATION

★7699★ "EKG Technician" in Allied Health Professions (pp. 25-26; 143)
Arco Publishing Co.
Simon & Schuster, Inc.
201 W. 103rd St.
Indianapolis, IN 46290
Ph: 800-428-5331   Fax: 800-835-3202

1993. Contains information on 28 representative careers in health care. Provides a sample of the Allied Health Professions Admission Test, lists professional societies and associations, and offers a directory of schools and programs for the careers listed.

Emergency Medical Technicians

Emergency medical technicians (EMT's) give immediate emergency care. This may include opening airways, restoring breathing, controlling bleeding, treating for shock, administering oxygen, immobilizing fractures, bandaging, assisting in childbirth, managing emotionally disturbed patients, treating and resuscitating heart attack victims, and giving initial care to poison and burn victims. Some procedures are carried out under the step-by-step direction of medical staff with whom the EMT's are in radio contact. The entry-level worker is an **EMT-Ambulance (EMT-A) or basic EMT**. There are two other levels of EMT's: **EMT-Intermediates and EMT-Paramedics**. These workers have more training than EMT-A's and can perform additional procedures, as specified by state law. In most states, EMT-Intermediates may treat trauma patients with intravenous fluid, and with antishock garments and airways management techniques. EMT-Intermediates are widely used in rural areas, where the number and type of services called for require an individual with more training than an EMT-A but less than an EMT-Paramedic. EMT-Paramedics are trained in advanced life support skills. EMT-Paramedics in most states may administer drugs both orally and intravenously, interpret EKG's, perform endotracheal intubation, and use complex equipment such as a monitor or defibrillator.

Salaries

Earnings tend to vary by employment setting, geographic location, and individual training and experience. EMT's working in the public sector or areas where there is a heavy volume of calls typically earn the highest salaries. Average starting salaries for emergency medical technicians (EMT's) are as follows:

Average, EMT-Ambulance	$20,092/year
Average, EMT-Intermediate	$19,530/year
Average, EMT-Paramedic	$24,390/year

Employment Outlook

Growth rate until the year 2005: Faster than the average.

Emergency Medical Technicians

★7700★ *Board Certification Registered EMT-Paramedic*
National Registry of Emergency Medical Technicians (NREMT)
PO Box 29233
Columbus, OH 43229
Ph: (614)888-4484
1991. This ten-panel brochure describes the certification procedure, professional registration, examination process, and continuing education requirements in becoming an emergency medical technician.

★7701★ **"Emergency Medical Services Paramedic" in** *Allied Health Education Directory* **(pp. 49-57)**
American Medical Association (AMA)
515 N. State St.
Chicago, IL 60610
Ph: (312)464-5000   Fr: 800-621-8335
Willaim R. Burrow, editor. 1994. Describes allied health occupations and lists educational programs accredited by the Committee on Allied Health Education and Accreditation of the American Medical Association.

★7702★ *Emergency Medical Technician*
Careers, Inc.
PO Box 135
Largo, FL 34649-0135
Ph: (813)584-7333
1994. Two-page occupational summary card describing duties, working conditions, personal qualifications, training, earnings and hours, employment outlook, places of employment, related careers, and where to write for more information.

★7703★ **"Emergency Medical Technician" in** *100 Best Careers for the Year 2000* **(pp. 44-47)**
Arco Pub.
201 W. 103rd St.
Indianapolis, IN 46290
Ph: 800-428-5331   Fax: 800-835-3202
Shelly Field. 1992. Describes 100 job opportunities expected to grow fast throughout the next decade. Provides information on job duties and responsibilities, training requirements, education, advancement opportunities, experience and qualifications, and typical salaries.

★7704★ **"Emergency Medical Technician" in** *Career Information Center* **(Vol.7)**
Simon and Schuster
200 Old Tappan Rd.
Old Tappan, NJ 07675
Fax: 800-445-6991   Fr: 800-223-2348
Richard Lidz and Linda Perrin, editorial directors. Fifth edition, 1993. This 13-volume set profiles over 600 occupations. Each occupational profile describes job duties, entry-level requirements, educational requirements, advancement possibilities, employment outlook, working conditions, earnings and benefits, and where to write for more information.

★7705★ **"Emergency Medical Technician" in** *Careers in Health Care* **(pp. 79-83)**
National Textbook Co. (NTC)
VGM Career Books
4255 W. Touhy Ave.
Lincolnwood, IL 60646-1975
Ph: (708)679-5500   Fax: (708)679-2494
Fr: 800-323-4900
Barbara M. Swanson. Third edition, 1995. Describes job duties, work settings, salaries, licensing and certification requirements, educational preparation, and future outlook.

★7706★ **"Emergency Medical Technician (EMT)" in** *150 Careers in the Health Care Field*
Reed Reference Publishing
121 Chanlon Rd.
PO Box 31
New Providence, NJ 07974
Fax: (908)665-6688   Fr: 800-521-8110
Stanley Alperin. Third edition, 1993. Profiles health care occupations requiring a bachelor's degree or less. Describes the nature of the work, educational preparation, licensing requirements, and salary. Lists accredited educational programs.

★7707★ **"Emergency Medical Technician" in** *Jobs Rated Almanac*
World Almanac
1 International Blvd., Ste. 444
Mahwah, NJ 07495
Ph: (201)529-6900   Fax: (201)529-6901
Les Krantz. Second edition, 1992. Ranks 250 jobs by environment, salary, outlooks, physical demands, stress, security, travel opportunities, and extra perks. Includes jobs the editor feels are the most common, most interesting, and the most rapidly growing.

★7708★ **"Emergency Medical Technician" in** *VGM's Handbook of Health Care Careers*
National Textbook Co.
4255 W. Touhy Ave.
Lincolnwood, IL 60646-1975
Ph: (708)679-5500   Fax: (708)679-2494
Fr: 800-323-4900
Annette Selden. 1993. Contains 42 two-page occupational profiles describing job duties, places of employment, working conditions, qualifications, education, employment outlook, and income.

★7709★ *Emergency Medical Technicians*
Chronicle Guidance Publications, Inc.
66 Aurora St.
PO Box 1190
Moravia, NY 13118-1190
Ph: (315)497-0330   Fax: (315)497-3359
Fr: 800-622-7284
1994. Career brief describing the nature of the job, working conditions, hours and earnings, education and training, licensure, certification, unions, personal qualifications, social and psychological factors, location, employment outlook, entry methods, advancement, and related occupations.

★7710★ "Emergency Medical Technicians" in *101 Careers: A Guide to the Fastest-Growing Opportunities* (pp. 210-213)
John Wiley & Sons, Inc.
605 3rd Ave.
New York, NY 10158-0012
Ph: (212)850-6645   Fax: (212)850-6088
Michael Harkavy. 1990. Describes the nature of the job, working conditions, employment growth, qualifications, personal skills, projected salaries, and where to write for more information.

★7711★ "Emergency Medical Technicians" in *American Almanac of Jobs and Salaries* (p. 467)
Avon Books
1350 Avenue of the Americas
New York, NY 10019
Ph: (212)261-6800   Fr: 800-238-0658
John Wright, editor. Revised and updated, 1994-95. This is a comprehensive guide to the wages of hundreds of occupations in a wide variety of industries and organizations.

★7712★ "Emergency Medical Technicians" in *Best Jobs for the 1990s and Into the 21st Century*
Impact Publications
9104-N Manassas Dr.
Manassas Park, VA 22111
Ph: (703)361-7300   Fax: (703)335-9486
Ronald L. Krannich and Caryl Rae Krannich. 1993.

★7713★ "Emergency Medical Technicians" in *Career Discovery Encyclopedia* (Vol.2, pp. 158-159)
J.G. Ferguson Publishing Co.
200 W. Madison St., Ste. 300
Chicago, IL 60606
Ph: (312)580-5480   Fax: (312)580-4948
Russell E. Primm, editor-in chief. 1993. This six volume set contains two-page articles for 504 occupations. Each article describes job duties, earnings, and educational and training requirements. The whole set is arranged alphabetically by job title. Designed for junior high and older students.

★7714★ "Emergency Medical Technicians: Dealing With Emergencies" in *Careers for Women Without College Degrees* (pp. 215-218)
McGraw-Hill, Inc.
1221 Avenue of the Americas
New York, NY 10020
Ph: (212)512-3825   Fr: 800-722-4726
Beatryce Nivens. 1988. Part 1 contains exercises in goal setting, decision making, and skills assessment. Part 2 explores 19 careers with the best occupational outlook. Part 3 describes nontraditional college degree programs.

★7715★ "Emergency Medical Technicians" in *Encyclopedia of Careers and Vocational Guidance* (Vol.2, pp. 585-590)
J.G. Ferguson Publishing Co.
200 W. Madison St., Ste. 300
Chicago, IL 60606
Ph: (312)580-5480   Fax: (312)580-4948
William E. Hopke, editor-in-chief. Ninth edition, 1993. Four-volume set that profiles 900 occupations and describes job trends in 74 industries. Includes career description, educational requirements, history of the job, methods of entry, advancement, employment outlook, earnings, conditions of work, social and psychological factors, and sources of further information.

★7716★ "Emergency Medical Technicians" in *Guide to Careers Without College* (pp. 34-36)
Franklin Watts, Inc.
387 Park Ave., S. 4th Fl.
New York, NY 10016
Ph: (212)686-7070   Fr: 800-672-6672
Kathleen S. Abrams. 1988. Discusses rewarding careers that do not require a college degree.

★7717★ "Emergency Medical Technicians" in *Health Care Job Explosion!* (pp. 128-135)
D-Amp Publications
401 Amherst Ave.
Coraopolis, PA 15108
Ph: (412)262-5578
Dennis V. Damp. 1993. Provides information on the nature of work for the major health care occupational groups. Descriptions include working conditions, training, job outlook, qualifications, and related occupations.

★7718★ "Emergency Medical Technicians" in *Jobs! What They Are—Where They Are—What They Pay* (p.185)
Simon & Schuster, Inc.
Simon & Schuster Bldg.
1230 Avenue of the Americas
New York, NY 10020
Ph: (212)698-7000   Fr: 800-223-2348
Robert O. Snelling and Anne M. Snelling. 3rd edition, 1992. Describes duties and responsibilities, earnings, employment opportunities, training, and qualifications.

★7719★ "Emergency Medical Technicians" in *Occupational Outlook Handbook*
U.S. Government Printing Office
Superintendent of Documents
Washington, DC 20402
Ph: (202)512-1800   Fax: (202)512-2250
Biennial; latest edition, 1994-95. Encyclopedia of careers describing about 250 occupations and comprising about 85 percent of all jobs in the economy. Occupations that require lengthy education or training are given the most attention. Each occupation's profile describes what the worker does on the job, working conditions, education and training requirements, advancement possibilities, job outlook, earnings, and sources of additional information.

★7720★ "Emergency Medical Technicians" in *Opportunities in Paramedical Careers* (pp. 35-39)
National Textbook Co. (NTC)
VGM Career Books
4255 W. Touhy Ave.
Lincolnwood, IL 60646-1975
Ph: (708)679-5500   Fax: (708)679-2494
Fr: 800-323-4900
Alex Kacen. 1994. Describes paraprofessional careers in the health professions such as physician assistant, medical assistant, and emergency medical technician. Describes job duties, educational preparation, certification, earnings, and job outlook. Lists educational programs.

★7721★ "Emergency Medical Technology" in *Career Connection for Technical Education* (pp. 68-69)
JIST Works, Inc.
720 N. Park Ave.
Indianapolis, IN 46202-3431
Ph: (317)264-3720   Fax: (317)264-3709
Fred A. Rowe. 1994, second edition. Describes in detail technical occupations. Includes information on recommended high school courses, course requirements, related careers, and a self-assessment guide.

★7722★ "EMT-Ambulance, EMT-Intermediate, EMT Paramedic" in *150 Careers in the Health Care Field*
Reed Reference Publishing
121 Chanlon Rd.
PO Box 31
New Providence, NJ 07974
Fax: (908)665-6688   Fr: 800-521-8110
Stanley Alperin. Third edition, 1993. Profiles health care occupations requiring a bachelor's degree or less. Describes the nature of the work, educational preparation, licensing requirements, and salary. Lists accredited educational programs.

★7723★ *Health Careers*
Careers, Inc.
PO Box 135
Largo, FL 34649-0135
Ph: (813)584-7333
1994. Four-page brief describing duties, working conditions, personal qualifications, training, earnings and hours, employment outlook, places of employment, related careers, and where to write for more information.

★7724★ "Health Technicians and Paraprofessionals" in *Opportunities in Vocational Technical Careers* (pp. 91-108)
National Textbook Co. (NTC)
VGM Career Books
4255 W. Touhy Ave.
Lincolnwood, IL 60646-1975
Ph: (708)679-5500   Fax: (708)679-2494
Fr: 800-323-4900
Adrian A. Paradis. 1992. This book describes careers which can be prepared for by attending vocational-technical schools. Gives the employment outlook and salary information.

★7725★ *Opportunities in Medical Technology*
National Textbook Co. (NTC)
VGM Career Books
4255 W. Touhy Ave.
Lincolnwood, IL 60646-1975
Ph: (708)679-5500   Fax: (708)679-2494
Fr: 800-323-4900
Karen R. Karni, Jane Sidney Oliver. Overviews opportunities for laboratory technicians, nuclear medicine and radiologic technologists, and others. Includesinformation on training, salaries, and the employment outlook.

PROFESSIONAL ASSOCIATIONS

★7726★ National Association of Emergency Medical Technicians (NAEMT)
102 W. Leake St.
Clinton, MS 39056
Ph: (601)924-7744   Fax: (601)924-7325
Fr: 800-34-NAEMT
Members: Nationally registered or state certified emergency medical technicians (EMTs) and EMT-paramedics. **Purpose:** Promotes the professional status of EMTs and national acceptance of a uniform standard of recognition for their skills; encourages constant upgrading of these skills and EMT qualifications and educational requirements; engages in scientific research related to the care and transportation of the sick and injured; supports the establishment of emergency medical services systems. Sponsors insurance, credit card and member loan programs. Maintains placement services. **Publications:** *NAEMT News*, monthly.

★7727★ National Registry of Emergency Medical Technicians (NREMT)
PO Box 29233
Columbus, OH 43229
Ph: (614)888-4484
Members: Purpose: Promotes the improved delivery of emergency medical services by: assisting in the development and evaluation of educational programs to train emergency medical technicians; establishing qualifications for eligibility to apply for registration; preparing and conducting examinations designed to assure the competency of emergency medical technicians and paramedics; establishing a system for biennial registration; establishing procedures for revocation of certificates of registration for cause; maintaining a directory of registered emergency medical technicians.

STANDARDS/CERTIFICATION AGENCIES

★7728★ Commission on Accreditation of Allied Health Education Programs (CAAHEP)
515 N. State St., Ste. 7530
Chicago, IL 60610
Ph: (312)464-4636   Fax: (312)464-5830
Serves as an accrediting agency for allied health programs in 18 occupational areas.

★7729★ Committee on Allied Health Education and Accreditation (CAHEA)
515 N. Dearborn St.
Chicago, IL 60610
Ph: (312)464-4660   Fax: (312)464-4184
Serves as an accrediting agency for 2885 allied health programs, in 28 occupational areas. Sponsored by the American Medical Association.

★7730★ National Association of Emergency Medical Technicians (NAEMT)
102 W. Leake St.
Clinton, MS 39056
Ph: (601)924-7744   Fax: (601)924-7325
Fr: 800-34-NAEMT
Nationally registered or state certified emergency medical technicians (EMTs) and EMT-paramedics. Promotes the professional status of EMTs and national acceptance of a uniform standard of recognition for their skills; encourages constant upgrading of these skills and EMT qualifications and educational requirements; engages in scientific research related to the care and transportation of the sick and injured; supports the establishment of emergency medical services systems.

★7731★ National Registry of Emergency Medical Technicians (NREMT)
PO Box 29233
Columbus, OH 43229
Ph: (614)888-4484
Promotes the improved delivery of emergency medical services by: assisting in the development and evaluation of educational programs to train emergency medical technicians; establishing qualifications for eligibility to apply for registration; preparing and conducting examinations designed to assure the competency of emergency medical technicians and paramedics; establishing procedures for revocation of certificates of registration for cause.

TEST GUIDES

★7732★ Career Examination Series: Ambulance Attendant
National Learning Corp.
212 Michael Dr.
Syosset, NY 11791
Ph: (516)921-8888   Fax: (516)921-8743
Fr: 800-645-6337
Jack Rudman. A study guide for professional and trainee emergency medical technicians. Includes a multiple-choice examination section; provides answers.

★7733★ Career Examination Series: Ambulance Corpsman
National Learning Corp.
212 Michael Dr.
Syosset, NY 11791
Ph: (516)921-8888   Fax: (516)921-8743
Fr: 800-645-6337
Jack Rudman. A study guide for professional and trainee emergency medical technicians. Includes a multiple-choice examination section; provides answers.

★7734★ Career Examination Series: Ambulance Driver
National Learning Corp.
212 Michael Dr.
Syosset, NY 11791
Ph: (516)921-8888   Fax: (516)921-8743
Fr: 800-645-6337
Jack Rudman. A study guide for professional and trainee emergency medical technicians.

Includes a multiple-choice examination section; provides answers.

★7735★ Career Examination Series: Supervising Emergency Medical Service Specialist
National Learning Corp.
212 Michael Dr.
Syosset, NY 11791
Ph: (516)921-8888   Fax: (516)921-8743
Fr: 800-645-6337
Jack Rudman. A study guide for professional and trainee emergency medical technicians. Includes a multiple-choice examination section; provides answers.

★7736★ Emergency Medical Technicians—Paramedic Examination (EMT)
National Learning Corp.
212 Michael Dr.
Syosset, NY 11791
Ph: (516)921-8888   Fax: (516)921-8743
Fr: 800-645-6337
Jack Rudman. Part of the Admission Test series. A sample test for emergency medical technicians who are seeking admission to graduate and professional schools or seeking entrance or advancement in institutional and public career service.

★7737★ EMT Review: Examination Preparation
Prentice-Hall, Inc.
200 Old Tappan Rd.
Old Tappan, NJ 07675
Ph: (201)767-5000
Carolyn C. Hanes. Third edition, 1991.

★7738★ EMT Review Manual: Self-Assessment Practice Tests for Basic Life Support Skills
W.B. Saunders Co.
Curtis Center
Independence Sq. W
Philadelphia, PA 19106
Ph: (215)238-7800
Donald J. Ptacnik. Fourth edition, 1993. Includes a bibliography.

EDUCATIONAL DIRECTORIES AND PROGRAMS

★7739★ Medical Technologists and Technicians Career Directory
Gale Research Inc.
835 Penobscot Bldg.
Detroit, MI 48226-4094
Ph: (313)961-2242   Fax: (313)961-6083
Fr: 800-877-GALE
Bradley J. Morgan and Joseph M. Palmisano. 1993. A directory in the Career Advisor Series that provides essays written by industry professionals; job search information on resume and cover letter preparation, networking, and the interviewing process; approximately 300 companies and organizations offering job opportunities and internships, and additional job-hunting resources.

AWARDS, SCHOLARSHIPS, GRANTS, AND FELLOWSHIPS

★7740★ Asmund S. Laerdal Award for Excellence (EMT-Paramedic of the Year)
National Association of Emergency Medical Technicians
9140 Ward Pkwy., Ste. 200
Kansas City, MO 64114
Ph: (816)444-3500   Fax: (816)444-0330
Fr: 800-34-NAEMT

To recognize an EMT-Paramedic who has contributed significantly to EMS at the community, state, or national level. Nationally registered EMT-Paramedics are eligible. A stipend of $1,000 and a carved Norwegian crystal are awarded annually. Established in 1984. Sponsored by Laerdal Medical Corporation.

★7741★ Rocco V. Morando Lifetime Achievement Award
National Association of Emergency Medical Technicians
9140 Ward Pkwy., Ste. 200
Kansas City, MO 64114
Ph: (816)444-3500   Fax: (816)444-0330
Fr: 800-34-NAEMT

To recognize an individual whose contributions to emergency medical services have been consistent and longlasting, representing in effect a lifetime of outstanding service to the profession and the public. A plaque is awarded when merited at the annual awards banquet. Established in 1984.

★7742★ Robert E. Motley EMT (Emergency Medical Technician) of the Year Award
National Association of Emergency Medical Technicians
9140 Ward Pkwy., Ste. 200
Kansas City, MO 64114
Ph: (816)444-3500   Fax: (816)444-0330
Fr: 800-34-NAEMT

To recognize excellence in various aspects of emergency medical services at the community, state, or national level. Criteria considered are: community support and involvement; EMS involvement; contribution to local, state, and national EMS; personal press coverage; letters of recommendation; and level of training and education. An educational stipend of $1,000 and a plaque are presented annually at the awards banquet. Established in 1978. Sponsored by Mosby Lifelines.

BASIC REFERENCE GUIDES AND HANDBOOKS

★7743★ Emergency Medical Technician
R & E Publishers, Inc.
PO Box 2008
Saratoga, CA 95070
Ph: (408)866-6303   Fax: (408)866-0825
Ronald R. Smith, editor. 1993. Part of the Smith's Career Notes Series.

★7744★ Emergency Medical Technician: Ambulance
Gordon Press Publishers, Inc.
PO Box 459
Bowling Green Sta.
New York, NY 10004
1992.

★7745★ Emergency Medical Technician: Intermediate
Gordon Press Publishers
PO Box 459
Bowling Green Sta.
New York, NY 10004
1992.

★7746★ Emergency Medical Technician: Paramedic
Gordon Press Publishers
PO Box 459
Bowling Green Sta.
New York, NY 10004
1992.

★7747★ Prehospital Pediatric Life Support
Mosby-Year Book, Inc.
11830 Westline Industrial Dr.
St. Louis, MO 63146
Ph: (314)872-8370   Fax: (314)432-1380
Fr: 800-325-4177
Joseph E. Simon and Aron T. Goldberg. 1989. Includes a bibliography and an index.

★7748★ The Sixty Second EMT
Mosby-Year Book, Inc.
11830 Westline Industrial Dr.
St. Louis, MO 63146
Ph: (314)872-8370   Fax: (314)432-1380
Fr: 800-325-4177
Gideon Bosker. Second edition, 1994. Includes an index.

PROFESSIONAL AND TRADE PERIODICALS

★7749★ ACEP News
American College of Emergency Physicians (ACEP)
PO Box 619911
Dallas, TX 75261-9911
Ph: (214)550-0911   Fax: (214)580-2816
Fr: 800-798-1822
Earl Schwartz
Monthly. Informs emergency physicians of socioeconomic issues affecting the specialty of emergency medicine. Contains information on medical practice management, pertinent federal and state legislation, and college activities and services.

★7750★ JEMS
Jems Communications
PO Box 2789
Carlsbad, CA 92018-2789
Ph: (619)431-9797   Fax: (619)431-8176
Keith Griffiths
Monthly.

★7751★ NAFAC News
National Association for Ambulatory Care (NAFAC)
29 W. Susquehanna Ave.
Baltimore, MD 21204
Ph: (410)296-4600   Fax: (410)828-6084
Fr: 800-999-9722
William Wenmark

Quarterly. Reports on issues current to the ambulatory care industry, including government activity, national developments, and trends in health care. Recurring features include editorials, news of research, letters to the editor, Association news, and stock watch column.

PROFESSIONAL MEETINGS AND CONVENTIONS

★7752★ EMS - Emergency Medical Services Expo
Conference Management Corp.
200 Connecticut Ave.
Norwalk, CT 06856-4990
Ph: (203)852-0500   Fax: (203)838-3710
Fr: 800-243-3238
Annual.

★7753★ National Association of Emergency Medical Technicians Annual National Educational Conference
National Association of Emergency Medical Technicians
9140 Ward Pkwy.
Kansas City, MO 64114
Ph: (816)444-3500   Fax: (816)444-0330
Annual.

OTHER SOURCES OF INFORMATION

★7754★ "Emergency Medical Technician" in Career Selector 2001
Barron's Educational Series, Inc.
250 Wireless Blvd.
Hauppauge, NY 11788
Ph: (516)434-3311   Fax: (516)434-3723
Fr: 800-645-3476
James C. Gonyea. 1993.

Licensed Practical Nurses

Licensed practical nurses (LPN's) or **licensed vocational nurses (LVN's)** as they are called in Texas and California, help care for the sick under the direction of physicians and registered nurses. Most LPN's provide basic bedside care. LPN's in nursing homes, in addition to providing routine bedside care, may also help evaluate residents' needs, develop care treatment plans, and supervise nursing aides. In doctors' offices, walk-in clinics, health maintenance organizations, they also perform clerical duties such as making appointments and keeping records. LPN's who work in private homes may also prepare meals and teach family members simple nursing tasks.

Salaries

Median annual earnings for full-time licensed practical nurses are as follows:

Lowest 10 percent	$15,392/year
Middle 50 percent	$21,476/year
Top 10 percent	$31,668/year
Median, LPN's in hospitals	$22,360/year
Median, LPN's in nursing homes	$21,900/year

Employment Outlook

Growth rate until the year 2005: Faster than the average.

Licensed Practical Nurses

CAREER GUIDES

★7755★ Addison-Wesley's Nursing Examination Review
Addison-Wesley Publishing Co.
1 Jacob Way
Reading, MA 01867
Ph: (617)944-3700   Fr: 800-358-4566
Sally L. Lagerquist and Geraldine C. Colombraro. Fourth edition, 1991, (paper). Includes a bibliography and an index.

★7756★ The Discipline of Nursing
Appleton and Lange
25 Van Zant St.
East Norwalk, CT 06855
Ph: (203)838-4400   Fr: 800-423-1359
Margaret O'Bryan Doheny, Christina B. Cook, and Mary C. Stopper. Third edition, 1992. Includes bibliographies and an index.

★7757★ Entering and Moving in the Professional Job Market: A Nurse's Guide
American Nurses' Association (ANA)
2420 Pershing Rd.
Kansas City, MO 64108
Ph: (816)474-5720   Fr: 800-274-4262
1988. Contains one booklet, by Lyndia Flanagan, and five brochures.

★7758★ Health Careers
Careers, Inc.
PO Box 135
Largo, FL 34649-0135
Ph: (813)584-7333
1994. Four-page brief describing duties, working conditions, personal qualifications, training, earnings and hours, employment outlook, places of employment, related careers, and where to write for more information.

★7759★ Licensed Practical Nurse
Vocational Biographies, Inc.
PO Box 31
Sauk Centre, MN 56378-0031
Ph: (612)352-6516   Fax: (612)352-5546
Fr: 800-255-0752
1994. Four-page pamphlet containing a personal narrative about a worker's job, work likes and dislikes, career path from high

school to the present. Education and training, the rewards and frustrations, and the effects of the job on the rest of the worker's life. The data file portion of this pamphlet gives a concise occupational summary, including work descriptions, working conditions, places of employment, personal characteristics, education and training, job outlook, and salary range.

★7760★ "Licensed Practical Nurse" in BLR Encyclopedia of Prewritten Job Descriptions
Business and Legal Reports, Inc.
39 Academy St.
Madison, CT 06443-1513
Ph: (203)245-7448
Stephen D. Bruce, editor-in-chief. 1994. This book contains hundreds of sample job descriptions arranged by functional job category. The 1-3 page job descriptions cover what the worker normally does in the position, who they report to, and how that position fits in the organizational structure.

★7761★ "Licensed Practical Nurse" in Career Information Center (Vol.7)
Simon and Schuster
200 Old Tappan Rd.
Old Tappan, NJ 07675
Fax: 800-445-6991   Fr: 800-223-2348
Richard Lidz and Linda Perrin, editorial directors. Fifth edition, 1993. This 13-volume set profiles over 600 occupations. Each occupational profile describes job duties, entry-level requirements, educational requirements, advancement possibilities, employment outlook, working conditions, earnings and benefits, and where to write for more information.

★7762★ "Licensed Practical Nurse (L.P.N.)" in 100 Best Careers for the Year 2000 (pp. 15-16)
Arco Pub.
201 W. 103rd St.
Indianapolis, IN 46290
Ph: 800-428-5331   Fax: 800-835-3202
Shelly Field. 1992. Describes 100 job opportunities expected to grow fast throughout the next decade. Provides information on job duties and responsibilities, training requirements, education, advancement opportunities, experience and qualifications, and typical salaries.

★7763★ "Licensed Practical Nurse" in Opportunities in Child Care (pp. 64-66)
National Textbook Co. (NTC)
VGM Career Books
4255 W. Touhy Ave.
Lincolnwood, IL 60646-1975
Ph: (708)679-5500   Fax: (708)679-2494
Fr: 800-323-4900
Renne Wittenberg. 1987. This book offers a detailed survey of the career choices available in child care. Outlines the many job opportunities available in day care, child welfare, child development, and social services. Describes the challenges and rewards, and educational and training requirements.

★7764★ "Licensed Practical Nurse" in VGM's Careers Encyclopedia (pp. 299-301)
National Textbook Co. (NTC)
VGM Career Books
4255 W. Touhy Ave.
Lincolnwood, IL 60646-1975
Ph: (708)679-5500   Fax: (708)679-2494
Fr: 800-323-4900
Third edition, 1991. Describes job duties, places of employment, working conditions, qualifications, education and training, advancement potential, and salary for each occupation.

★7765★ Licensed Practical Nurses
Careers, Inc.
PO Box 135
Largo, FL 34649-0135
Ph: (813)584-7333
1991. Four-page brief offering the definition, history, duties, working conditions, personal qualifications, educational requirements, earnings, hours, employment outlook, advancement, and careers related to this position.

★7766★ Licensed Practical Nurses
Chronicle Guidance Publications, Inc.
66 Aurora St.
PO Box 1190
Moravia, NY 13118-1190
Ph: (315)497-0330   Fax: (315)497-3359
Fr: 800-622-7284
1987. Career brief describing the nature of the job, working conditions, hours and earnings, education and training, licensure, certification, unions, personal qualifications, social and psychological factors, location, employ-

ment outlook, entry methods, advancement, and related occupations.

★7767★ Licensed Practical Nurses
Chronicle Guidance Publications, Inc.
66 Aurora St.
PO Box 1190
Moravia, NY 13118-1190
Ph: (315)497-0330   Fax: (315)497-3359
Fr: 800-622-7284
1994. Career brief describing the nature of the job, working conditions, hours and earnings, education and training, licensure, certification, unions, personal qualifications, social and psychological factors, location, employment outlook, entry methods, advancement, and related occupations.

★7768★ "Licensed Practical Nurses" in 101 Careers: A Guide to the Fastest-Growing Opportunities (pp. 222-224)
John Wiley & Sons, Inc.
605 3rd Ave.
New York, NY 10158-0012
Ph: (212)850-6645   Fax: (212)850-6088
Michael Harkavy. 1990. Describes the nature of the job, working conditions, employment growth, qualifications, personal skills, projected salaries, and where to write for more information.

★7769★ "Licensed Practical Nurses" in 150 Careers in the Health Care Field
Reed Reference Publishing
121 Chanlon Rd.
PO Box 31
New Providence, NJ 07974
Fax: (908)665-6688   Fr: 800-521-8110
Stanley Alperin. Third edition, 1993. Profiles health care occupations requiring a bachelor's degree or less. Describes the nature of the work, educational preparation, licensing requirements, and salary. Lists accredited educational programs.

★7770★ "Licensed Practical Nurses" in America's 50 Fastest Growing Jobs (pp. 82)
JIST Works, Inc.
720 N. Park Ave.
Indianapolis, IN 46202-3431
Ph: (317)264-3720   Fax: (317)264-3709
Fr: 800-648-5478
Michael J. Farr, compiler. 1994. Describes the 50 fastest growing jobs within major career clusters such as technicians, and marketing and sales. Each job profile explains the nature of the work, skills and abilities required, employment outlook, average earnings, related occupations, education and training requirements, and employment opportunities. Also contains career planning information and job search tips.

★7771★ "Licensed Practical Nurses" in Career Discovery Encyclopedia (Vol.4, pp. 10-11)
J.G. Ferguson Publishing Co.
200 W. Madison St., Ste. 300
Chicago, IL 60606
Ph: (312)580-5480   Fax: (312)580-4948
Russell E. Primm, editor-in chief. 1993. This six volume set contains two-page articles for 504 occupations. Each article describes job duties, earnings, and educational and training requirements. The whole set is arranged al-

phabetically by job title. Designed for junior high and older students.

★7772★ "Licensed Practical Nurses" in Health Care Job Explosion! (pp. 215-225)
D-Amp Publications
401 Amherst Ave.
Coraopolis, PA 15108
Ph: (412)262-5578
Dennis V. Damp. 1993. Provides information on the nature of work for the major health care occupational groups. Descriptions include working conditions, training, job outlook, qualifications, and related occupations.

★7773★ "Licensed Practical Nurses (L.P.N.)" in Best Jobs for the 1990s and Into the 21st Century
Impact Publications
9104-N Manassas Dr.
Manassas Park, VA 22111
Ph: (703)361-7300   Fax: (703)335-9486
Ronald L. Krannich and Caryl Rae Krannich. 1993.

★7774★ "Licensed Practical Nurses" in Occupational Outlook Handbook
U.S. Government Printing Office
Superintendent of Documents
Washington, DC 20402
Ph: (202)512-1800   Fax: (202)512-2250
Biennial; latest edition, 1994-95. Encyclopedia of careers describing about 250 occupations and comprising about 85 percent of all jobs in the economy. Occupations that require lengthy education or training are given the most attention. Each occupation's profile describes what the worker does on the job, working conditions, education and training requirements, advancement possibilities, job outlook, earnings, and sources of additional information.

★7775★ Licensed Practical/Vocational Nurses in the Department of Veterans Affairs: Nationwide Opportunities
Department of Veterans Affairs
Veterans Health Services and Research Administration
810 Vermont Ave., NW
Washington, DC 20420
Ph: (202)535-7444
Revised, 1989. This six-page pamphlet describes job opportunities and employee benefits for practical nurses. Gives a state-by-state listing of U.S. Veterans Administration Medical Centers.

★7776★ Mosby's Tour Guide to Nursing School: A Student's Road Survival Kit
Mosby-Year Book, Inc.
11830 Westline Industrial Dr.
St. Louis, MO 63146
Ph: (314)872-8370   Fax: (314)432-1380
Fr: 800-325-4177
Melodie Chenevert. 3rd edition, 1994. Provides students with a realistic look at nursing.

★7777★ National Commission on Nursing Implementation Project: Models for the Future of Nursing
National League for Nursing (NLN)
350 Hudson St.
New York, NY 10014
Ph: (212)989-9393   Fr: 800-NOW-1NLN
1988.

★7778★ "Nurse" in Careers in Health Care (pp. 153-167)
National Textbook Co. (NTC)
VGM Career Books
4255 W. Touhy Ave.
Lincolnwood, IL 60646-1975
Ph: (708)679-5500   Fax: (708)679-2494
Fr: 800-323-4900
Barbara M. Swanson. Third edition, 1995. Describes job duties, work settings, salaries, licensing and certification requirements, educational preparation, and future outlook.

★7779★ "Nurse" in Guide to Federal Jobs (p. 130)
Resource Directories
3361 Executive Pkwy., Ste. 302
Toledo, OH 43606
Ph: (419)536-5353   Fax: (419)536-7056
Fr: 800-274-8515
Rod W. Durgin, editor. Third edition, 1992. Contains information on finding and applying for federal jobs. Describes more than 200 professional and technical jobs for college graduates. Covers the nature of the work, salary, and geographic location. Lists college majors preferred for that occupation. Section one describes the function and work of government agencies that hire the most significant number of college graduates.

★7780★ Nurse, Licensed Practical
Careers, Inc.
PO Box 135
Largo, FL 34649-0135
Ph: (813)584-7333
1991. Four-page brief describing duties, working conditions, personal qualifications, training, earnings and hours, employment outlook, places of employment, related careers, and where to write for more information.

★7781★ "Nurse (Licensed Practical)" in Jobs Rated Almanac
World Almanac
1 International Blvd., Ste. 444
Mahwah, NJ 07495
Ph: (201)529-6900   Fax: (201)529-6901
Les Krantz. Second edition, 1992. Ranks 250 jobs by environment, salary, outlooks, physical demands, stress, security, travel opportunities, and extra perks. Includes jobs the editor feels are the most common, most interesting, and the most rapidly growing.

★7782★ "Nurse, Licensed Practical" in VGM's Handbook of Health Care Careers
National Textbook Co.
4255 W. Touhy Ave.
Lincolnwood, IL 60646-1975
Ph: (708)679-5500   Fax: (708)679-2494
Fr: 800-323-4900
Annette Selden. 1993. Contains 42 two-page occupational profiles describing job duties, places of employment, working conditions,

qualifications, education, employment outlook, and income.

★7783★ Nurse, Practitioner
Careers, Inc.
PO Box 135
Largo, FL 34649-0135
Ph: (813)584-7333
1993. Two-page summary describing duties, working conditions, personal qualifications, training, earnings and hours, employment outlook, places of employment, related careers, and where to write for more information.

★7784★ "Nurses" in American Almanac of Jobs and Salaries (pp. 453)
Avon Books
1350 Avenue of the Americas
New York, NY 10019
Ph: (212)261-6800   Fr: 800-238-0658
John Wright, editor. Revised and updated, 1994-95. This is comprehensive guide to the wages of hundreds of occupations in a wide variety of industries and organizations.

★7785★ "Nursing, Licensed Practical" in Career Connection for Technical Education (pp. 118-119)
JIST Works, Inc.
720 N. Park Ave.
Indianapolis, IN 46202-3431
Ph: (317)264-3720   Fax: (317)264-3709
Fred A. Rowe. 1994, second edition. Describes in detail technical occupations. Includes information on recommended high school courses, course requirements, related careers, and a self-assessment guide.

★7786★ Opportunities in Nursing Careers
National Textbook Co. (NTC)
VGM Career Books
4255 W. Touhy Ave.
Lincolnwood, IL 60646-1975
Ph: (708)679-5500   Fax: (708)679-2494
Fr: 800-323-4900
Keville Frederickson. 1989. Describes working conditions, job responsibilities, salary, and educational requirements.

★7787★ "Practical Nurse" in Guide to Federal Technical, Trades and Labor Jobs (p. 177)
Resource Directories
3361 Executive Pkwy., Ste. 302
Toledo, OH 43606
Ph: (419)536-5353   Fax: (419)536-7056
Fr: 800-274-8515
Rod W. Durgin, editor in chief. Second edition, 1992. Describes where and how to apply for a federal job in practical nursing. For each job included, gives a description, salary, locations, and the agencies that hire the most employees for that job.

★7788★ Your Career in Nursing
National League for Nursing (NLN)
350 Hudson St.
New York, NY 10014
Ph: (212)989-9393   Fr: 800-NOW-1NLN
Lila Anastas. Second edition, 1988. Describes types of nursing schools, salaries, specialties, opportunities, issues, and trends. Includes statistical information on nursing practice and education, graduate nursing, continuing education, and career mobility.

PROFESSIONAL ASSOCIATIONS

★7789★ American Association of Managed Care Nurses (AAMCN)
PO Box 4975
Glen Allen, VA 23058-4975
Ph: (804)747-9698   Fax: (804)747-5316

★7790★ American Association of Mental Health Professionals in Corrections (AAMHPC)
c/o John S. Zil, M.D., J.D.
PO Box 163359
Sacramento, CA 95816-9359
Ph: (707)864-0910   Fax: (707)864-0910
Members: Psychiatrists, psychologists, social workers, nurses, and other mental health professionals; individuals working in correctional settings. **Purpose:** Fosters the progress of behavioral sciences related to corrections. Goals are: to improve the treatment, rehabilitation, and care of the mentally ill, mentally retarded, and emotionally disturbed; to promote research and professional education in psychiatry and allied fields in corrections; to advance standards of correctional services and facilities; to foster cooperation between individuals concerned with the medical, psychological, social, and legal aspects of corrections; to share knowledge with other medical practitioners, scientists, and the public. Conducts scientific meetings to contribute to the advancement of the therapeutic community in all its institutional settings, including correctional institutions, hospitals, churches, schools, industry, and the family. **Publications:** Corrective and Social Psychiatry, quarterly.

★7791★ American Health Care Association (AHCA)
1201 L St. NW
Washington, DC 20005
Ph: (202)842-4444   Fax: (202)842-3860
Members: Federation of state associations of long-term health care facilities. **Purpose:** Promotes standards for professionals in long-term health care delivery and quality care for patients and residents in a safe environment. Focuses on issues of availability, quality, affordability, and fair payment. Operates as liaison with governmental agencies, Congress, and professional associations. Compiles statistics. **Publications:** AHCA Notes, monthly. • Provider: For Long Term Care Professionals, monthly. • Thinking About a Nursing Home?. • Welcome to Our Nursing Home.

★7792★ American Hospital Association (AHA)
1 N. Franklin, Ste. 27
Chicago, IL 60606
Ph: (312)422-3000   Fax: (312)422-4796
Members: Individuals and health care institutions including hospitals, health care systems, and pre- and postacute health care delivery organizations. **Purpose:** Is dedicated to promoting the welfare of the public through its leadership and assistance to its members in the provision of better health services for all people. Carries out research and education projects in such areas as health care administration, hospital economics, and community relations; represents hospitals in national legislation; offers programs for institutional effectiveness review, technology assessment, and hospital administrative services to hospitals; conducts educational programs furthering the in-service education of hospital personnel; collects and analyzes data; furnishes multimedia educational materials; maintains 44,000 volume health care administration library, and biographical archive. **Publications:** AHANews, weekly. • Guide to the Health Care Field, annual. • Hospital Statistics, annual. • Hospitals and Health Networks, biweekly.

★7793★ Association of Child and Adolescent Psychiatric Nurses (ACAPN)
1211 Locust St.
Philadelphia, PA 19107
Ph: (215)545-2843   Fax: (215)545-8107
Fr: 800-826-2950
Members: Nurses and others interested in child and adolescent psychiatry. **Purpose:** Works to promote mental health of infants, children, adolescents, and their families through clinical practice, public policy, and research. **Publications:** ACAPN News, 3/year. • Journal of Child and Adolescent Psychiatric Nursing, quarterly.

★7794★ National Association of Nurse Massage Therapists (NANMT)
PO Box 1268
Osprey, FL 34229
Ph: (813)966-6288   Fax: (813)918-0522
Members: Nurses and other healthcare professionals who practice massage therapy. **Purpose:** Promotes the integration of massage and other therapeutic forms of bodywork into existing healthcare practice. Promotes Nurse Massage Therapists as specialists within the nursing profession. Seeks to establish standards of professional practice and criteria for national certification of Nurse Massage Therapists. Educates the medical community and the general public about bodywork therapies. Monitors legislation. **Publications:** NANMT Membership Directory, annual. • Nurse's Touch, quarterly.

★7795★ National Association for Practical Nurse Education and Service (NAPNES)
1400 Spring St., Ste. 310
Silver Spring, MD 20910
Ph: (301)588-2491   Fax: (301)588-2839
Members: Licensed practical/vocational nurses, registered nurses, physicians, hospital and nursing home administrators, and interested others. **Purpose:** Provides consultation service to advise schools wishing to develop a practical/vocational nursing program on facilities, equipment, policies, curriculum, and staffing. Promotes recruitment of students through preparation and distribution of recruitment materials. Sponsors seminars for directors and instructors in schools of practical/vocational nursing and continuing education programs for LPNs/LVNs; approves continuing education programs and awards contact hours; holds national certification courses in pharmacology and gerontics. Maintains library of nursing and health publications. Compiles statistics. **Publications:** Journal of Practical Nursing, quarterly. • NAPNES Forum.

★7796★ National Federation of Licensed Practical Nurses (NFLPN)
1418 Aversboro Rd.
Garner, NC 27529-4547
Ph: (919)779-0046   Fax: (919)779-5642
Members: Federation of state associations of licensed practical and vocational nurses. **Purpose:** Aims to: preserve and foster the ideal of comprehensive nursing care for the ill and aged; improve standards of practice; secure recognition and effective utilization of LPNs; further continued improvement in the education of LPNs. Acts as clearinghouse for information on practical nursing and cooperates with other groups concerned with better patient care. Maintains loan program. **Publications:** *Licensed Practical Nurse*, quarterly. • *LPN*, quarterly.

★7797★ National League for Nursing (NLN)
350 Hudson St.
New York, NY 10014
Ph: (212)989-9393   Fax: (212)989-9256
Fr: 800-669-1656
Members: Individuals and leaders in nursing and other health professions, and community members interested in solving health care problems (18,000); agencies, nursing educational institutions, departments of nursing in hospitals and related facilities, and home and community health agencies (1800). **Purpose:** Works to assess nursing needs, improve organized nursing services and nursing education, and foster collaboration between nursing and other health and community services. Provides tests used in selection of applicants to schools of nursing; also prepares tests for evaluating nursing student progress and nursing service tests. Nationally accredits nursing education programs and community health agencies. Collects and disseminates data on nursing services and nursing education. Conducts studies and demonstration projects on community planning for nursing and nursing service and education. **Publications:** *NLN Newsletter*, periodic. • *Nurse Faculty Census*, biennial. • *Nursing and Health Care*, 10/year. • *Nursing Data Review*, annual. • *Nursing Student Census*, annual. • *Public Policy Bulletin*, periodic. • *State Approved Schools of Nursing - LPN*, annual. • *State Approved Schools of Nursing - RN*, annual.

★7798★ Society of Trauma Nurses (STN)
1211 Locust St.
Philadelphia, PA 19107
Ph: (215)545-5687   Fax: (215)545-8107
Fr: 800-237-6966
Members: Nurses involved in all facets of trauma care. **Purpose:** Seeks to communicate trauma nursing information and recognize excellence and innovation in trauma nursing. Addresses legislative issues; assists in the development of standards. Facilitates research. **Publications:** *Journal of Trauma Nursing*, quarterly.

STANDARDS/CERTIFICATION AGENCIES

★7799★ National Association for Practical Nurse Education and Service (NAPNES)
1400 Spring St., Ste. 310
Silver Spring, MD 20910
Ph: (301)588-2491   Fax: (301)588-2839
Provides consultation service to advise schools wishing to develop a practical/vocational nursing program on facilities, equipment, policies, curriculum, and staffing. Sponsors seminars for directors and instructors in schools of practical/vocational nursing and continuing education programs for LPNs/LVNs; holds national certification courses in pharmacology and gerontics.

★7800★ National League for Nursing (NLN)
350 Hudson St.
New York, NY 10014
Ph: (212)989-9393   Fax: (212)989-9256
Fr: 800-669-1656
Prepares tests for evaluating nursing student progress and nursing service tests. Nationally accredits nursing education programs and community health agencies.

TEST GUIDES

★7801★ *Admission Test Series: Nursing*
National Learning Corp.
212 Michael Dr.
Syosset, NY 11791
Ph: (516)921-8888   Fax: (516)921-8743
Fr: 800-645-6337
Jack Rudman. A collection of sample examinations designed to prepare potential nurses for graduate and professional school entrance tests and for tests administered by private and public institutions for entrance and career advancement. Provides multiple-choice questions; includes correct answers. Titles in the series include *Nursing School Entrance Examinations for Registered and Graduate Nurses; State Nursing Boards for Registered Nurse; National Council Licensure Examination for Registered Nurses; Commission on Graduates of Foreign Nursing Schools Qualifying Examination*.

★7802★ *Appleton and Lange's Review of Nursing for the New State Board Examination*
Appleton and Lange
25 Van Zant St.
East Norwalk, CT 06855
Ph: (203)838-4400   Fr: 800-423-1359
Anna M. Desharnais, et al. Third edition, 1990. Preparation guide for medical-surgical nursing, maternal-child nursing, and psychiatric-mental health nursing. Contains Nursing Process Care Plans and multiple-choice questions.

★7803★ *Career Examination Series: Licensed Practical Nurse*
National Learning Corp.
212 Michael Dr.
Syosset, NY 11791
Ph: (516)921-8888   Fax: (516)921-8743
Fr: 800-645-6337
Jack Rudman. A series of study guides with multiple-choice examination questions and solutions for trainees and professional nurses. Titles in the series include *Clinical Nurse; Community Mental Health Nurse; Health Service Nurse; Infection Control Nurse; Nurse; Practical Nurse; Professional Nurse; Psychiatric Nurse; Public Health Nurse; Staff Nurse*.

★7804★ *Lippincott's State Board Examination Review for NCLEX-PN*
J. B. Lippincott Co.
227 E. Washington Sq.
Philadelphia, PA 19106
Ph: (215)238-4200
LuVerne Wolff Lewis. 1994. (paper). Includes a bibliography and an index.

★7805★ *National Council Licensure Examination for Practical Nurses*
Barron's Educational Series, Inc.
250 Wireless Blvd.
Hauppauge, NY 11788
Ph: (516)434-3311   Fax: (516)434-3723
Fr: 800-645-3476
Second edition. 1990.

★7806★ *Nurse*
Arco Publishing Co.
Macmillan General Reference
15 Columbus Cir.
New York, NY 10023
Fax: 800-835-3202   Fr: 800-858-7674
Carmen Sanchez. Seventh edition, 1987. A test guide for the registered, public health, or practical health nurse preparing for a civil service test.

★7807★ *Nursing School Entrance Examinations*
Arco Publishing Co.
Macmillan General Reference
15 Columbus Cir.
New York, NY 10023
Fax: 800-835-3202   Fr: 800-858-7674
Marion F. Gooding and Bernice Hughes. Twelfth edition, 1994. Contains sample questions for school entrance examinations for licensed practical and registered nurses with an explanation of the answers.

★7808★ *Regents College Proficiency Examination Series: Nursing*
National Learning Corp.
212 Michael Dr.
Syosset, NY 11791
Ph: (516)921-8888   Fax: (516)921-8743
Fr: 800-645-6337
Jack Rudman. A series of sample tests for college credit-by-examination programs in the field of nursing. Multiple-choice style with answers included. Titles in the series includes *Adult Nursing; Fundamentals of Nursing; Maternal and Child Nursing—Associate; Maternal and Child Nursing—Baccalaureate; Medical-Surgical Nursing; Psychiatric-Mental Health Nursing*.

★7809★ *Regents External Degree Series: Nursing*
National Learning Corp.
212 Michael Dr.
Syosset, NY 11791
Ph: (516)921-8888   Fax: (516)921-8743
Fr: 800-645-6337

Jack Rudman. A multiple-choice examination for nursing professionals preparing to enter the Regents External Degree Program, an alternate route to a college degree. Test contains multiple-choice questions with answers provided. Titles in the series include *Commonalities in Nursing Care: Area A; Commonalities in Nursing Care: Area B; Differences in Nursing Care: Area A; Differences in Nursing Care: Area B; Differences in Nursing Care: Area C; Health Support: Area I; Health Support: Area II; Nursing Health Care; Occupational Strategy (Nursing); Professional Strategies (Nursing).*

★7810★ *Saunders Review of Practical Nursing for NCLEX-PN*
W. B. Saunders Co.
W. Washington Sq.
Philadelphia, PA 19105
Ph: (215)238-7800

Esther Matassarin-Jacobs. Second edition, 1992 (paper). Includes bibliographical references and an index.

EDUCATIONAL DIRECTORIES AND PROGRAMS

★7811★ *Healthcare Career Directory— Nurses and Physicians*
Gale Research Inc.
835 Penobscot Bldg.
Detroit, MI 48226-4094
Ph: (313)961-2242   Fax: (313)961-6083
Fr: 800-877-GALE

Bradley J. Morgan and Joseph M. Palmisano. Second edition, 1993. A directory in the Career Advisor Series that provides essays written by industry professionals; job search information on resume and cover letter preparation, networking, and the interviewing process; approximately 300 companies and organizations offering job opportunities and internships, and additional job-hunting resources.

★7812★ *State-Approved Schools of Nursing: L.P.N./L.V.N.*
National League for Nursing (NLN)
350 Hudson St.
New York, NY 10014
Ph: (212)989-9393   Fax: (212)989-3710
Fr: 800-669-1656
Lisa Moss, V.P. Communications

Annual, July. Covers licensed practical nurse and licensed vocational nurse programs in about 1,320 schools. Entries include: Name of school, address, types of programs, admission policies, type of administrative control, sources of financial support, length of program, information on state board approval and National League for Nursing accreditation. Arrangement: Geographical.

AWARDS, SCHOLARSHIPS, GRANTS, AND FELLOWSHIPS

★7813★ **AACN Educational Advancement Scholarships for Graduates**
American Association of Critical-Care Nurses (AACN)
101 Columbia
Aliso Viejo, CA 92656-1491
Ph: (714)362-2000

Qualifications: Candidates must be current AACN members, licensed as registered nurses, enrolled in a master's or doctorate level program, have a cumulative GPA of at least 3.0 on a 4.0 scale, and currently work in a critical unit or have worked in a critical care unit for at least one year in the last three years. Previous recipients are eligible to reapply, but may receive no more than a total of $3,000. Members of the Board of Directors, Education Committee, and ACCN staff are not eligible. Funds available: 17 $1,500 scholarships. A minimum of 20 percent will be allocated to ethnic minorities. Recipients must also agree to participate in a follow-up study to discuss the impact of their degree on care of patients/families in critical care unit. Application details: Completed application forms (typed only) should include official transcripts of all coursework, verification of enrollment in a planned course of graduate study, verification of employment in a critical care unit for at least one year in the last three years, a curriculum vitae, a statement regarding how applicants see their nursing practice changing as a result of their graduate degree, and an exemplar (a situation where applicant's intervention made a difference in a patient's outcome). Deadline: The 1993 deadline was January 15.

★7814★ **AACN Educational Advancement Scholarships for Undergraduates**
American Association of Critical-Care Nurses (AACN)
101 Columbia
Aliso Viejo, CA 92656-1491
Ph: (714)362-2000

Qualifications: Candidates must be current AACN members, licensed as registered nurses, enrolled in an NLN-accredited baccalaureate degree program in nursing with at least junior status, have a cumulative GPA of at least 3.0 on a 4.0 scale, and currently work in a critical unit or have worked in a critical care unit for at least one year in the last three years. Previous recipients are eligible to reapply, but may receive no more than a total of $3,000. Members of the Board of Directors, Education Committee, and AACN staff are not eligible. Funds available: 37 $1,500 scholarships. A minimum of 20 percent will be allocated to ethnic minorities. Recipients must also agree to participate in a follow-up study to discuss impact of degree on care of patients/families in critical care units. Application details: Completed application forms (typed only) should include official transcripts of all coursework; verification of employment in a critical care unit for at least one year in the last three years; letter of enrollment from school of nursing director, faculty, or advisor that verifies junior or senior status; verification from Nursing Director of NLN accreditation status; and a statment regarding goals in returning to school and past and projected contributions to critical care nursing. Deadline: The 1993 deadline was January 15.

★7815★ **Luther Christman Award**
American Assembly for Men in Nursing
PO Box 31753
Independence, OH 44131

To recognize a person who has demonstrated excellence, leadership, high standards, principles, and contributions to the profession of nursing. A wood plaque with gold plate is awarded annually. Established in 1975 by Luther Christman, R.N., Ph.D.

★7816★ **Anna M. Fillmore Award**
National League for Nursing
350 Hudson St.
New York, NY 10014
Ph: (212)989-9393   Fax: (212)989-3710

To recognize an individual nurse who demonstrates or has shown unusual leadership in developing and administering community health services on a local, state, or national level. A plaque is awarded biennially. Established in 1976.

★7817★ **Caroline Holt Nursing Scholarships**
National Society Daughters of The American Revolution
DAR Scholarship Committee
1776 D St., NW
Washington, DC 20006
Ph: (202)879-3292

Qualifications: Applicants must be United States citizens. The award is for any year of undergraduate study in an accredited school of nursing. No affiliation with the DAR is necessary. However, all applicants mut be sponsored by a local DAR Chapter. Selection criteria: Applicants are judged on the basis of academic excellence, commitment to field of study, and financial need. Funds available: $500. Application details: Write or call Office of Committees for application forms. A self-addressed, stamped envelope must accompany application requests. Applicants must submit a formal application, along with accompanying material, including: a statement of 1,000 words or less setting forth career goals and relevance of academic program to future profession; a financial need form; an official transcript of grades and test scores from high school; and a list of all extra-curricular activities, honors, and scholastic achievements. At least two and not more than four letters of recommendation from persons in authority at the student's high school who know the student's work, and a photocopy of the student's birth certificate or naturalization papers are also required. Proof of acceptance into a school of nursing program is required prior to payment of the scholarship. Deadline: Applications must be sent to the National Chairman by February 15 or August 15.

★7818★ Honorary Human Rights Award
American Nurses' Association
600 Maryland Ave. SW, Ste. 100W
Washington, DC 20024-2571
Ph: (202)554-4444   Fax: (202)554-2262

For recognition of an outstanding commitment to human rights and exemplifying the essence of nursing's philosophy about humanity. Current SNA members are eligible. The deadline for nominations is October. Awarded biennially. Established in 1986.

★7819★ HRSA-BHP Professional Nurse
Traineeship
U.S. Public Health Service
Health Resources and Services
  Administration
Parklawn Bldg., Rm. 8-38
5600 Fishers Ln.
Rockville, MD 20857

Purpose: To meet the cost of traineeships for individuals in advanced degree nursing education programs, and to educate individuals to serve in and prepare for practice as nurse practitioners, nurse midwives, nurse educators, public health nurses, or in any other clinical nursing specialties. Qualifications: Candidates must be United States citizens, non-citizen nationals, or foreign nationals who possess a visa permitting permanent residence in the United States. They must be currently licensed as a registered nurse in a state, or have completed basic nursing preparations in a masters of nursing program (as determined by the school). They are also required to be enrolled full-time in eligible graduate programs and be pursuing a masters or doctoral degree. Preference will be given to individuals who are residents of health professional shortage areas designated under Section 332 of the Public Health Service Act. Selection criteria: Recipients are selected by the participating instututions in accordance with the institutions' admission policies and the purpose of the traineeship program. Funds available: Stipend up to $8,800 for tuition, books, fees and reasonable living expenses for a maximum of 36 months of study.

★7820★ Mary Adelaide Nutting Award
National League for Nursing
350 Hudson St.
New York, NY 10014
Ph: (212)989-9393   Fax: (212)989-3710

To recognize outstanding leadership and achievement in nursing education or service having more than local or regional significance. Individuals and groups of any country are eligible. A silver medal is awarded biennially. Established in 1943.

★7821★ Outstanding Service Award
American Assembly for Men in Nursing
PO Box 31753
Independence, OH 44131

To recognize a licensed professional nurse employed in the nursing profession who contributes outstanding service toward nursing. The AAMN is not part of the award committee. A plaque with gold plate is awarded annually. Established in 1972.

★7822★ Linda Richards Awards
National League for Nursing
350 Hudson St.
New York, NY 10014
Ph: (212)989-9393   Fax: (212)989-3710

To recognize a unique contribution of a pioneering nature to the field of nursing. Citizens of the United States who are active in nursing are eligible. An engraved pin bearing the likeness of Linda Richards centered on a maltese cross is awarded biennially. Established in 1962 by the Alumnae Association of the New England Hospital for Women and Children, Roxbury, MA.

★7823★ Martha E. Rogers Award
National League for Nursing
350 Hudson St.
New York, NY 10014
Ph: (212)989-9393   Fax: (212)989-3710

For recognition of a nurse scholar who has made significant contributions to nursing knowledge that advance the science of nursing. A plaque is awarded biennially. Established in 1985.

★7824★ NSNA Frances Tompkins
Career Mobility Scholarships
The Foundation of the National Student
  Nurses' Association, Inc.
555 W. 57th St., Ste. 1325
New York, NY 10019
Ph: (212)581-2215

Qualifications: Applicants must be registered nurses who are enrolled in a state-approved school of nursing or pre-nursing in a program leading to a baccalaureate degree with a major in nursing. They may also be licensed practical/vocational nurses who are enrolled in a program that will lead to registered nurse licensure. Selection criteria: Awards are based on academic achievement, financial need, and involvement in nursing student organizations and community activities related to health care. All factors are equally weighed. Funds available: Scholarships range from $1,000 to $2,500 each. In 1992-93, more than $100,000 in scholarship funds were awarded. Application details: Students must submit copies of their recent nursing school and college transcripts or grade reports, nursing licenses, and a $5 processing fee along with completed applications. Members of NSNA must submit proof of their membership. Application forms are available by sending a self-addressed, legal-size envelope with 52 cents postage. They are available from September through January. Deadline: February 1. Recipients are notified by March.

★7825★ Veterans Affairs Health
Professional Scholarship Awards
U.S. Department of Veterans Affairs
Central Office
810 Vermont Ave., NW
Washington, DC 20420
Ph: (202)535-7527

Purpose: To provide an adequate supply of nurses, occupational therapists, and physical therapists for the Department of Veterans Affairs and the nation. Qualifications: Applicants must be U.S. citizens, and accepted for enrollment or enrolled full-time in a nursing program accredited by the National League of Nursing, an occupational therapy program

accredited by the American Occupational Therapy Association, or a physical therapy program accredited by the American Physical Therapy Association. Applicants may not be obligated for service under any other scholarship program. VA employees who meet eligibility may apply. Selection criteria: Selection is based upon academic performance, career goals, recommendations, and work/volunteer experience. Funds available: Tuition/fees, reasonable educational expenses, and a monthly stipend of $621, all exempt from Federal taxation. Application details: Applications are available from college/university financial aid offices, deans of Nursing, program directors of Occupational Therapy or Physical Therapy, all VA medical centers, and the VA Central Office. Deadline: May.

BASIC REFERENCE GUIDES AND HANDBOOKS

★7826★ Definitions
Springhouse Corp.
1111 Bethlehem Pike
Spring House, PA 19477
Ph: (215)646-8700

1987. Contains nursing terms, drug names and interactions, and an anatomical atlas.

★7827★ Diseases
Springhouse Corp.
1111 Bethlehem Pike
Spring House, PA 19477
Ph: (215)646-8700

1992. Includes bibliographies and index.

★7828★ Duncan's Dictionary for Nurses
Springer Publishing Co.
536 Broadway, 11th Fl.
New York, NY 10012
Ph: (212)431-4370

Helen A. Duncan. Second edition, 1989.

★7829★ Licensed Practical Nurse
R & E Publishers, Inc.
PO Box 2008
Saratoga, CA 95070
Ph: (408)866-6303   Fax: (408)866-0825

Ronald R. Smith, editor. 1993. Part of the Smith's Career Notes Series.

★7830★ Mosby's Medical Dictionary
Mosby-Year Book, Inc.
11830 Westline Industrial Dr.
St. Louis, MO 63146
Ph: (314)872-8370   Fax: (314)432-1380
Fr: 800-325-4177

Walter D. Glanze, Kenneth N. Anderson, and Lois E. Anderson, editors. 1993. Illustrated.

PROFESSIONAL AND TRADE PERIODICALS

★7831★ *The American Nurse*
American Nurses Assn.
600 Maryland Ave. SW, Ste. 100
Washington, DC 20024-2571
Ph: (202)651-7000   Fax: (202)651-7001
Fr: 800-274-4262
Mandy Mikulencak
Newspaper (tabloid) for the nursing profession.

★7832★ *Journal of Nursing Administration*
J.B. Lippincott Co.
227 E. Washington Sq.
Philadelphia, PA 19106
Ph: (215)238-4492   Fax: (215)238-4461
Suzanne Smith Blancett
Journal covering developments and advances in nursing administration and management.

★7833★ *Journal of Practical Nursing*
National Assn. for Practical Nurse
   Education & Service
1400 Spring St., No. 310
Silver Spring, MD 20910
Ph: (301)588-2491   Fax: (301)588-2839
Kathy Jentz
Quarterly. Journal providing information on licensed practical nursing for LPNs, PN educators, and students.

★7834★ *New York State Nursing Association—Report*
Tammy Krutz, Contact
Contains news and features on nurses and nursing issues. Also provides information on the activities of the New York State Nurses Association. Recurring features include news of research, a calendar of events, and news of educational opportunities. Columns include Ask the Experts and Legislative Power.

★7835★ *The Nightingale*
National Association of Physician Nurses
900 S. Washington St., No. G13
Falls Church, VA 22046-4020
Ph: (703)237-8616
Sue Young
Monthly. Presents items on "medical and personal subjects pertaining to office nurses and other staff."

★7836★ *Technology for Health Care Series*
ECRI
5200 Butler Pike
Plymouth Meeting, PA 19462
Ph: (215)825-6000   Fax: (215)834-1275
Michele Moscariello
Monthly. Concerned with the safety, performance, reliability, and cost effectiveness of health care technology. Covers areas of anesthesia, cardiology, imaging and radiology, and respiratory therapy. Reviews device test results and warns of hazards and deficiencies. Recurring features include news of research, Institute reports, and news of members.

PROFESSIONAL MEETINGS AND CONVENTIONS

★7837★ The AJN Conference on Medical-Surgical and Geriatric Nursing
George Little Management, Inc.
10 Bank St., Ste. 1200
White Plains, NY 10606-1933
Ph: (914)421-3200   Fax: (914)948-6180
Annual. **Dates and Locations:** 1995 Oct.

★7838★ American Association of Critical-Care Nurses National Teaching Institute & Critical Care Exposition
American Association of Critical-Care
   Nurses
101 Columbia
Aliso Viejo, CA 92656
Ph: (714)362-2000   Fax: (714)362-2020
Annual. Always held during May. **Dates and Locations:** 1996 May 19-23; Anaheim, CA. • 1997 May 18-22; Orlando, FL. • 1998 May 30-04; Los Angeles, CA. • 1999 May 17-16; New Orleans, LA. • 2000 May 21-25; Orlando, FL.

★7839★ American Association of Neuroscience Nurses Convention
American Association of Neuroscience
   Nurses
224 N. Des Planes, No. 601
Chicago, IL 60661
Ph: (312)993-0043
Annual. **Dates and Locations:** 1996 Apr 28-02; Toronto, ON.

★7840★ American Organization of Nurse Executives Meeting and Exposition
American Hospital Association
Convention and Meetings Division
840 N. Lake Shore Dr.
Chicago, IL 60611
Ph: (312)280-6000   Fax: (312)280-5995
Annual.

★7841★ Association of Pediatric Oncology Nurses
The Phenix Corp.
11512 Allecingie Pkwy.
Richmond, VA 23235
Ph: (804)379-9150   Fax: (804)379-1386
Annual.

★7842★ National Association of Orthopedic Nurses Annual Congress
Anthony J. Jannetti, Inc.
N. Woodbury Rd., Box 56
Box 56
Pitman, NJ 08071
Ph: (609)589-2319   Fax: (609)589-7463
Annual. **Dates and Locations:** 1996 May 31-05; Dallas, TX. • 1997 May 18-22; Philadelphia, PA.

★7843★ National League for Nursing Convention
Slack, Inc.
6900 Grove Rd.
Thorofare, NJ 08086
Ph: (609)848-1000   Fax: (609)853-5991
Biennial.

★7844★ Nurses Care Fair
Texas Nurses Association
7600 Burnet Rd., Ste. 440
Austin, TX 78757
Ph: (512)452-0645   Fax: (512)452-0648

★7845★ Nursing Management Congress and Exposition
Conference Management Corp.
200 Connecticut Ave.
Norwalk, CT 06856
Ph: (203)852-0500   Fax: (203)838-3710
Fr: 800-243-3238
Annual. Always held during the Fall.

★7846★ World Conference of Operating Room Nurses
Association of Operating Room Nurses
   (AORN)
Highpoint Office Bldg
2170 S. Parker Rd., Ste. 300
Denver, CO 80231
Ph: (303)755-6300   Fax: (303)752-0299
Biennial. **Dates and Locations:** 1995.

OTHER SOURCES OF INFORMATION

★7847★ *Entrepreneuring: A Nurse's Guide to Starting a Business*
National League for Nursing (NLN)
10 Columbus Circle
New York, NY 10019
Ph: (212)582-1022   Fr: 800-NOW-1NLN
Gerry Vogel and Nancy Doleysh. 1988. Includes an index.

★7848★ *Exploring Careers in Nursing*
Rosen Publishing Group
29 E. 21st St.
New York, NY 10010
Ph: 800-237-9932   Fax: (212)777-0277
Jackie Heron. Revised edition, 1990.

★7849★ "Licensed Practical Nurse" in *100 Best Jobs for the 1990s & Beyond*
Dearborn Financial Publishing, Inc.
520 N. Dearborn St.
Chicago, IL 60610-4354
Ph: (312)836-4400   Fax: (312)836-1021
Fr: 800-621-9621
Carol Kleiman. 1992. Describes 100 jobs ranging from accountants to veterinarians. Each job profile includes such information as education, experience, and certification needed, salaries, and job search suggestions.

★7850★ "Licensed Practical Nurse (LPN)" in *Allied Health Professions* (pp. 12-13; 135)
Arco Publishing Co.
Simon & Schuster, Inc.
201 W. 103rd St.
Indianapolis, IN 46290
Ph: 800-428-5331   Fax: 800-835-3202
1993. Contains information on 28 representative careers in health care. Provides a sample of the Allied Health Professions Admission Test, lists professional societies and associa-

tions, and offers a directory of schools and programs for the careers listed.

★7851★ "Nurse (Licensed Practical)" in Career Selector 2001
Barron's Educational Series, Inc.
250 Wireless Blvd.
Hauppauge, NY 11788
Ph: (516)434-3311   Fax: (516)434-3723
Fr: 800-645-3476
James C. Gonyea. 1993.

★7852★ The Nurses's Guide to Starting a Small Business
Pilot Books
103 Cooper St.
Babylon, NY 11702
Ph: (516)422-2225   Fax: (516)422-2227

1992.

★7853★ Nursing Today: Transition and Trends
W.B. Saunders Co.
Independence Sq. W.
Philadelphia, PA 19106
Ph: (215)238-7800

1994.

Medical Record Technicians

Managing an information system that meets medical, administrative, ethical, and legal requirements involves the teamwork of medical record administrators, **medical record technicians**, medical record clerks, and medical transcriptionists, known collectively as medical record personnel. Directing the activities of the medical record department is the **medical record administrator**, whose job is to develop systems for documenting, storing, and retrieving medical information. **Medical record technicians** are the people who actually handle the records, organizing and evaluating them for completeness and accuracy.

Salaries

Earnings of medical record technicians vary according to locality.

Average, Medical record technicians	$9.77/hour
Medical record technicians, federal government	$22,008/year

Employment Outlook

Growth rate until the year 2005: Much faster than the average.

Medical Record Technicians

CAREER GUIDES

★7854★ *Health Careers*
Careers, Inc.
PO Box 135
Largo, FL 34649-0135
Ph: (813)584-7333

1994. Four-page brief describing duties, working conditions, personal qualifications, training, earnings and hours, employment outlook, places of employment, related careers, and where to write for more information.

★7855★ "Health Technicians and Paraprofessionals" in *Opportunities in Vocational Technical Careers* (pp. 91-108)
National Textbook Co. (NTC)
VGM Career Books
4255 W. Touhy Ave.
Lincolnwood, IL 60646-1975
Ph: (708)679-5500   Fax: (708)679-2494
Fr: 800-323-4900

Adrian A. Paradis. 1992. This book describes careers which can be prepared for by attending vocational-technical schools. Gives the employment outlook and salary information.

★7856★ "Medical Record Administrator" in *150 Careers in the Health Care Field*
Reed Reference Publishing
121 Chanlon Rd.
PO Box 31
New Providence, NJ 07974
Fax: (908)665-6688   Fr: 800-521-8110

Stanley Alperin. Third edition, 1993. Profiles health care occupations requiring a bachelor's degree or less. Describes the nature of the work, educational preparation, licensing requirements, and salary. Lists accredited educational programs.

★7857★ *Medical Record Administrators*
Chronicle Guidance Publications, Inc.
66 Aurora St.
PO Box 1190
Moravia, NY 13118-1190
Ph: (315)497-0330   Fax: (315)497-3359
Fr: 800-622-7284

1991. Occupational brief describing the nature of the job, working conditions, hours and earnings, education and training, licensure, certification, unions, personal qualifications, social and psychological factors, location, employment outlook, entry methods, advancement, and related occupations.

★7858★ "Medical Record Technician" in *150 Careers in the Health Care Field*
Reed Reference Publishing
121 Chanlon Rd.
PO Box 31
New Providence, NJ 07974
Fax: (908)665-6688   Fr: 800-521-8110

Stanley Alperin. Third edition, 1993. Profiles health care occupations requiring a bachelor's degree or less. Describes the nature of the work, educational preparation, licensing requirements, and salary. Lists accredited educational programs.

★7859★ "Medical Record Technician" in *Allied Health Education Directory* (pp. 135-141)
American Medical Association (AMA)
515 N. State St.
Chicago, IL 60610
Ph: (312)464-5000   Fr: 800-621-8335

William R. Burrow, editor. 1994. Describes allied health occupations and lists educational programs accredited by the Committee on Allied Health Education and Accreditation of the American Medical Association.

★7860★ "Medical Record Technician/ Clerk" in *Career Information Center* (Vol.7)
Simon and Schuster
200 Old Tappan Rd.
Old Tappan, NJ 07675
Fax: 800-445-6991   Fr: 800-223-2348

Richard Lidz and Linda Perrin, editorial directors. Fifth edition, 1993. This 13-volume set profiles over 600 occupations. Each occupational profile describes job duties, entry-level requirements, educational requirements, advancement possibilities, employment outlook, working conditions, earnings and benefits, and where to write for more information.

★7861★ "Medical Record Technician" in *Guide to Federal Technical, Trades and Labor Jobs* (p. 184)
Resource Directories
3361 Executive Pkwy., Ste. 302
Toledo, OH 43606
Ph: (419)536-5353   Fax: (419)536-7056
Fr: 800-274-8515

Rod W. Durgin, editor in chief. Second edition, 1992. Describes where and how to apply for a federal job as a medical record technician. For each job included, gives a description, salary, locations, and the agencies that hire the most employees for that job.

★7862★ "Medical Record Technician" in *VGM's Handbook of Health Care Careers*
National Textbook Co.
4255 W. Touhy Ave.
Lincolnwood, IL 60646-1975
Ph: (708)679-5500   Fax: (708)679-2494
Fr: 800-323-4900

Annette Selden. 1993. Contains 42 two-page occupational profiles describing job duties, places of employment, working conditions, qualifications, education, employment outlook, and income.

★7863★ "Medical Record Technicians" in *101 Careers: A Guide to the Fastest-Growing Opportunities* (pp. 225-227)
John Wiley & Sons, Inc.
605 3rd Ave.
New York, NY 10158-0012
Ph: (212)850-6645   Fax: (212)850-6088

Michael Harkavy. 1990. Describes the nature of the job, working conditions, employment growth, qualifications, personal skills, projected salaries, and where to write for more information.

★7864★ "Medical Record Technicians" in *America's 50 Fastest Growing Jobs* (pp. 83)
JIST Works, Inc.
720 N. Park Ave.
Indianapolis, IN 46202-3431
Ph: (317)264-3720   Fax: (317)264-3709
Fr: 800-648-5478
Michael J. Farr, compiler. 1994. Describes the 50 fastest growing jobs within major career clusters such as technicians, and marketing and sales. Each job profile explains the nature of the work, skills and abilities required, employment outlook, average earnings, related occupations, education and training requirements, and employment opportunities. Also contains career planning information and job search tips.

★7865★ "Medical Record Technicians" in *Best Jobs for the 1990s and Into the 21st Century*
Impact Publications
9104-N Manassas Dr.
Manassas Park, VA 22111
Ph: (703)361-7300   Fax: (703)335-9486
Ronald L. Krannich and Caryl Rae Krannich. 1993.

★7866★ "Medical Record Technicians" in *Encyclopedia of Careers and Vocational Guidance* (Vol.3, pp. 415-420)
J.G. Ferguson Publishing Co.
200 W. Madison St., Ste. 300
Chicago, IL 60606
Ph: (312)580-5480   Fax: (312)580-4948
William E. Hopke, editor in chief. Ninth edition, 1993. Four-volume set that profiles 900 occupations and describes job trends in 74 industries. Includes career description, educational requirements, history of the job, methods of entry, advancement, employment outlook, earnings, conditions of work, social and psychological factors, and sources of further information.

★7867★ "Medical Record Technicians" in *Health Care Job Explosion!* (pp. 136-141)
D-Amp Publications
401 Amherst Ave.
Coraopolis, PA 15108
Ph: (412)262-5578
Dennis V. Damp. 1993. Provides information on the nature of work for the major health care occupational groups. Descriptions include working conditions, training, job outlook, qualifications, and related occupations.

★7868★ "Medical Record Technicians" in *Occupational Outlook Handbook*
U.S. Government Printing Office
Superintendent of Documents
Washington, DC 20402
Ph: (202)512-1800   Fax: (202)512-2250
Biennial; latest edition, 1994-95. Encyclopedia of careers describing about 250 occupations and comprising about 85 percent of all jobs in the economy. Occupations that require lengthy education or training are given the most attention. Each occupation's profile describes what the worker does on the job, working conditions, education and training requirements, advancement possibilities, job

outlook, earnings, and sources of additional information.

★7869★ "Medical Records Administrators" in *Jobs! What They Are—Where They Are—What They Pay* (p. 165)
Simon & Schuster, Inc.
Simon & Schuster Bldg.
1230 Avenue of the Americas
New York, NY 10020
Ph: (212)698-7000   Fr: 800-223-2348
Robert O. Snelling and Anne M. Snelling. 3rd edition, 1992. Describes duties and responsibilities, earnings, employment opportunities, training, and qualifications.

★7870★ "Medical Records Manager" in *College Board Guide to Jobs and Career Planning* (pp. 237-238)
The College Board
45 Columbus Ave.
New York, NY 10023-6992
Ph: (212)713-8165   Fax: (212)713-8143
Fr: 800-323-7155
Second edition, 1994. Describes the job, salaries, related careers, education needed, and where to write for more information.

★7871★ "Medical Records Technician" in *100 Best Careers for the Year 2000* (pp. 48-49)
Arco Pub.
201 W. 103rd St.
Indianapolis, IN 46290
Ph: 800-428-5331   Fax: 800-835-3202
Shelly Field. 1992. Describes 100 job opportunities expected to grow fast throughout the next decade. Provides information on job duties and responsibilities, training requirements, education, advancement opportunities, experience and qualifications, and typical salaries.

★7872★ "Medical Records Technician" in *Jobs Rated Almanac*
World Almanac
1 International Blvd., Ste. 444
Mahwah, NJ 07495
Ph: (201)529-6900   Fax: (201)529-6901
Les Krantz. Second edition, 1992. Ranks 250 jobs by environment, salary, outlooks, physical demands, stress, security, travel opportunities, and extra perks. Includes jobs the editor feels are the most common, most interesting, and the most rapidly growing.

★7873★ *Medical Records Today, Your Career Tomorrow*
American Medical Record Association
919 N. Michigan Ave., Ste. 1400
Chicago, IL 60611
Ph: (312)787-2672
This eight-panel brochure describes what medical record technicians do, and how they become an Accredited Record Technician.

PROFESSIONAL ASSOCIATIONS

★7874★ American Association of Managed Care Nurses (AAMCN)
PO Box 4975
Glen Allen, VA 23058-4975
Ph: (804)747-9698   Fax: (804)747-5316

★7875★ American Health Information Management Association (AMRA)
919 N. Michigan Ave., Ste. 1400
Chicago, IL 60611-1683
Ph: (312)787-2672   Fax: (312)787-9793
Members: Registered record administrators; accredited record technicians with expertise in health information management, biostatistics, classification systems, and systems analysis. **Purpose:** Sponsors Independent Study Program in Medical Record Technology. Conducts annual qualification examinations to credential medical record personnel as Registered Record Administrators (RRA) and Accredited Record Technicians (ART). Maintains Foundation of Record Education Resource Center. Provides resume referral service; maintains speakers' bureau. **Publications:** *American Medical Record Association—Membership Roster*, semiannual. • *From the Couch: Official Newsletter of the Mental Health Record Section of the American Medical Record Association*, quarterly. • *The Gavel: AMRA State Presidents' Newsletter*, quarterly. • *Journal of AMRA: America's Health Information Leaders*, monthly. • *Medical Record Educator*, quarterly. • *QA Section Connection*, bimonthly. • *Spectrum*, quarterly.

★7876★ American Medical Association (AMA)
515 N. State St.
Chicago, IL 60610
Ph: (312)464-5000   Fax: (312)464-4184
Members: County medical societies and physicians. **Purpose:** Disseminates scientific information to members and the public. Informs members on significant medical and health legislation on state and national levels and represents the profession before Congress and governmental agencies. Cooperates in setting standards for medical schools, hospitals, residency programs, and continuing medical education courses. Offers physician placement service and counseling on practice management problems. Operates library which lends material and provides specific medical information to physicians. Adhoc committees are formed for such topics as health care planning and principles of medical ethics. **Publications:** *American Medical News*, weekly. • *Archives of Dermatology*, monthly. • *Archives of Family Medicine*, monthly. • *Archives of General Psychiatry*, monthly. • *Archives of Internal Medicine*, semimonthly. • *Archives of Neurology*, monthly. • *Archives of Ophthalmology*, monthly. • *Archives of Otolaryngology—Head and Neck Surgery*, monthly. • *Archives of Pediatrics & Adolescent Medicine*, monthly. • *Archives of Surgery*, monthly. • *Journal of the American Medical Association*, weekly.

★7877★ Society of Vascular Technology (SVT)
4601 Presidents Dr., Ste. 260
Lanham, MD 20706-4365
Ph: (301)459-7550   Fax: (301)459-5651
Fr: 800-SVT-VEIN
Medical technologists and others in the field of noninvasive vascular technology. (Noninvasive vascular technology is a highly technical and specialized method of monitoring the blood flow in arms and legs in order to better diagnose disease and blood clots.) Seeks to establish an information clearinghouse providing reference and assistance in matters relating to noninvasive vascular technology; facilitate cooperation among noninvasive vascular facilities and other health professions; provide continuing education for individuals in the field. **Publications:** *Glossary of Terms.* • *Journal of Vascular Technology.* • *Patient Education Pamphlets.* • *Referenced Study Outline.* • *Spectrum*, quarterly. • *Training Centers Directory.* • *Vascular Registry Review.*

STANDARDS/CERTIFICATION AGENCIES

★7878★ American Health Information Management Association (AMRA)
919 N. Michigan Ave., Ste. 1400
Chicago, IL 60611-1683
Ph: (312)787-2672   Fax: (312)787-9793
Conducts annual qualification examinations to credential medical record personnel as Registered Record Administrators (RRA) and Accredited Record Technicians (ART). Maintains Foundation of Record Education Resource Center.

★7879★ American Medical Record Association (AMRA)
919 N. Michigan Ave.
Chicago, IL 60611
Ph: (312)787-2672
Conducts annual qualification examinations to credential medical record personnel as Registered Record Administrators (RRA) and Accredited Record Technicians (ART).

TEST GUIDES

★7880★ AMRA Medical Record Technician National Registration Examination
National Learning Corp.
212 Michael Dr.
Syosset, NY 11791
Ph: (516)921-8888   Fax: (516)921-8743
Fr: 800-645-6337
Jack Rudman. Part of the Admission Test series. A sample test for those seeking admission to graduate and professional schools or seeking entrance or advancement in institutional and public career service.

★7881★ Career Examination Series: Medical Record Technician
National Learning Corp.
212 Michael Dr.
Syosset, NY 11791
Ph: (516)921-8888   Fax: (516)921-8743
Fr: 800-645-6337
Jack Rudman. A study guide for professional and trainee medical record technicians. Includes a multiple-choice examination section; provides answers.

EDUCATIONAL DIRECTORIES AND PROGRAMS

★7882★ Accredited Educational Programs in Health Information Technology and Health Information Administration
American Health Information Management Association
919 N. Michigan Ave., Ste. 1400
Chicago, IL 60611
Ph: (312)787-2672   Fax: (312)787-5926
Paula Johnson, Contact
Three issues per year. Covers over 50 schools that offer accredited baccalaureate programs or post-baccalaureate certificates in health information administration; over 130 associate degree programs in health information technology. Entries include: College or university name, location, name of school or department, name of program director, phone, key indicating type of degree or certificate awarded. Arrangement: Geographical.

★7883★ Health & Medical Industry Directory
American Business Directories, Inc.
5711 S. 86th Circle
Omaha, NE 68127
Ph: (402)593-4600   Fax: (402)331-1505
Released 1993. Lists over 1.1 million physicians and surgeons, dentists, clinics, health clubs, and other health-related businesses in the U.S. and Canada. Entries include: Name, address, phone.

★7884★ Medical Technologists and Technicians Career Directory
Gale Research Inc.
835 Penobscot Bldg.
Detroit, MI 48226-4094
Ph: (313)961-2242   Fax: (313)961-6083
Fr: 800-877-GALE
Bradley J. Morgan and Joseph M. Palmisano. 1993. A directory in the Career Advisor Series that provides essays written by industry professionals; job search information on resume and cover letter preparation, networking, and the interviewing process; approximately 300 companies and organizations offering job opportunities and internships, and additional job-hunting resources.

BASIC REFERENCE GUIDES AND HANDBOOKS

★7885★ Data Quality and DRGs
American Health Information Management Association
919 N. Michigan Ave., Ste. 1400
Chicago, IL 60611
Ph: (312)787-2672
Rita Finnegan. 1993. Includes a bibliography.

★7886★ Medical Records: Management in a Changing Environment
Aspen Publishers, Inc.
200 Orchard Ridge Dr., Ste. 200
Gaithersburg, MD 20878
Ph: (301)417-7500
Susan M. Murphy-Muth. 1987. Includes bibliographies and an index.

★7887★ Organization of Medical Record Departments in Hospitals
American Hospital Publishing, Inc.
737 N. Michigan Ave., Ste. 700
Chicago, IL 60611
Ph: (312)440-6800   Fr: 800-621-6902
Margaret F. Skurka. Second edition, 1988. Includes an index.

PROFESSIONAL AND TRADE PERIODICALS

★7888★ AOE Network
American Health Information Management Association
919 N. Michigan Ave., Ste. 1400
Chicago, IL 60611
Ph: (312)787-2672
Linda Bergen
Quarterly. Reviews developments in the field of education for those teaching medical record management and technology. Reports on Association educational programs. Recurring features include Association news, notes on members, news of research, and a calendar of events.

★7889★ From the Couch
Mental Health Record Section
919 Michigan Ave., Ste. 1400
Chicago, IL 60611
Ph: (312)787-2672   Fax: (312)787-9793
Quarterly. Covers aspects of the medical records industry that pertain to mental health records.

OTHER SOURCES OF INFORMATION

★7890★ "Medical Records
  Administrator" in *100 Best Jobs for the
  1990s & Beyond*
Dearborn Financial Publishing, Inc.
520 N. Dearborn St.
Chicago, IL 60610-4354
Ph: (312)836-4400   Fax: (312)836-1021
Fr: 800-621-9621
Carol Kleiman. 1992. Describes 100 jobs
ranging from accountants to veterinarians.

Each job profile includes such information as
education, experience, and certification
needed, salaries, and job search suggestions.

★7891★ "Medical Records Technician"
  in *Allied Health Professions* (pp. 29-30;
  145)
Arco Publishing Co.
Simon & Schuster, Inc.
201 W. 103rd St.
Indianapolis, IN 46290
Ph: 800-428-5331   Fax: 800-835-3202
1993. Contains information on 28 representative careers in health care. Provides a sample
of the Allied Health Professions Admission

Test, lists professional societies and associations, and offers a directory of schools and
programs for the careers listed.

Nuclear Medicine Technologists

Nuclear medicine technologists are trained to use radiopharmaceuticals in a variety of areas. They may conduct laboratory studies, do research, or develop and administer procedures for purchasing, using, and disposing of radioactive nuclides. Implementing safety procedures is another important role. Most of the time, however, technologists work directly with patients, performing nuclear medicine procedures that are used to diagnose or treat disease. Nuclear medicine technologists, like radiologic technologists, operate diagnostic imaging equipment. In nuclear medicine, the technologist prepares the radiopharmaceutical for the patient to take, administers it, and then operates a camera that detects and maps the radioactive drug in patient's body.

Salaries

Salaries for nuclear medical technologists are as follows:

Average minimum	$26,402/year
Median	$32,843/year
Average maximum	$38,840/year

Employment Outlook

Growth rate until the year 2005: Much faster than the average.

Nuclear Medicine Technologists

★7892★ Health Careers
Careers, Inc.
PO Box 135
Largo, FL 34649-0135
Ph: (813)584-7333
1994. Four-page brief describing duties, working conditions, personal qualifications, training, earnings and hours, employment outlook, places of employment, related careers, and where to write for more information.

★7893★ "Nuclear Medicine Technicians" in *101 Careers: A Guide to the Fastest-Growing Opportunities* (pp. 228-230)
John Wiley & Sons, Inc.
605 3rd Ave.
New York, NY 10158-0012
Ph: (212)850-6645   Fax: (212)850-6088
Michael Harkavy. 1990. Describes the nature of the job, working conditions, employment growth, qualifications, personal skills, projected salaries, and where to write for more information.

★7894★ *The Nuclear Medicine Technologist—A Career For You?*
American Society of Radiologic Technologists
15000 Central Ave., S.E.
Albuquerque, NM 87123-3917
Ph: (505)298-4500
1991. This six-panel brochure describes nuclear medicine technology, including job duties, educational preparation, and career opportunities.

★7895★ "Nuclear Medicine Technologist" in *Allied Health Education Directory* (pp. 144-152)
American Medical Association (AMA)
515 N. State St.
Chicago, IL 60610
Ph: (312)464-5000   Fr: 800-621-8335
William R. Burrow, editor. 1994. Describes allied health occupations and lists educational programs accredited by the Committee on Allied Health Education and Accreditation of the American Medical Association.

★7896★ "Nuclear Medicine Technologist" in *Careers in Health Care* (pp. 147-152)
National Textbook Co. (NTC)
VGM Career Books
4255 W. Touhy Ave.
Lincolnwood, IL 60646-1975
Ph: (708)679-5500   Fax: (708)679-2494
Fr: 800-323-4900
Barbara M. Swanson. Third edition, 1995. Describes job duties, work settings, salaries, licensing and certification requirements, educational preparation, and future outlook.

★7897★ "Nuclear Medicine Technologist" in *Careers in High-Tech*
Arco Publishing Co.
Macmillan General Reference
15 Columbus Cir.
New York, NY 10023
Fax: 800-835-3202   Fr: 800-858-7674
Connie Winkler. 1987. Surveys occupations in data processing, personal computers, telecommunications, manufacturing technology, artificial intelligence, computer graphics, medicine, biotechnology, lasers, technical writing, and publishing. Separate chapters cover education and training.

★7898★ "Nuclear Medicine Technologist" in *College Board Guide to Jobs and Career Planning* (pp. 272-273)
The College Board
45 Columbus Ave.
New York, NY 10023-6992
Ph: (212)713-8165   Fax: (212)713-8143
Fr: 800-323-7155
Second edition, 1994. Describes the job, salaries, related careers, education needed, and where to write for more information.

★7899★ "Nuclear Medicine Technologist" in *Jobs! What They Are—Where They Are—What They Pay* (pp. 188)
Fireside
Simon & Schuster Bldg.
1230 Avenue of the Americas
New York, NY 10020
Ph: (212)698-7000   Fr: 800-223-2348
Robert O. Snelling and Anne M. Snelling. Revised and updated, 1992. Describes duties and responsibilities, earnings, employment opportunities, training, and qualifications.

★7900★ "Nuclear Medicine Technologist" in *Opportunities in High-Tech Careers* (pp. 78-80)
National Textbook Co. (NTC)
VGM Career Books
4255 W. Touhy Ave.
Lincolnwood, IL 60646-1975
Ph: (708)679-5500   Fax: (708)679-2494
Fr: 800-323-4900
Gary D. Colter and Deborah Yanuck. 1987. Explores high-technology careers. Written for the student and displaced worker. Describes job opportunities, how to make a career decision, how to prepare for high-technology jobs, job hunting techniques, and future trends.

★7901★ "Nuclear Medicine Technologist" in *VGM's Handbook of Health Care Careers*
National Textbook Co.
4255 W. Touhy Ave.
Lincolnwood, IL 60646-1975
Ph: (708)679-5500   Fax: (708)679-2494
Fr: 800-323-4900
Annette Selden. 1993. Contains 42 two-page occupational profiles describing job duties, places of employment, working conditions, qualifications, education, employment outlook, and income.

★7902★ Nuclear Medicine Technologists
Chronicle Guidance Publications, Inc.
66 Aurora St.
PO Box 1190
Moravia, NY 13118-1190
Ph: (315)497-0330   Fax: (315)497-3359
Fr: 800-622-7284

1993. Career brief describing the nature of the job, working conditions, hours and earnings, education and training, licensure, certification, unions, personal qualifications, social and psychological factors, location, employment outlook, entry methods, advancement, and related occupations.

★7903★ "Nuclear Medicine Technologists" in America's 50 Fastest Growing Jobs (pp. 85)
JIST Works, Inc.
720 N. Park Ave.
Indianapolis, IN 46202-3431
Ph: (317)264-3720   Fax: (317)264-3709
Fr: 800-648-5478

Michael J. Farr, compiler. 1994. Describes the 50 fastest growing jobs within major career clusters such as technicians, and marketing and sales. Each job profile explains the nature of the work, skills and abilities required, employment outlook, average earnings, related occupations, education and training requirements, and employment opportunities. Also contains career planning information and job search tips.

★7904★ "Nuclear Medicine Technologists" in Health Care Job Explosion! (pp. 79-84)
D-Amp Publications
401 Amherst Ave.
Coraopolis, PA 15108
Ph: (412)262-5578

Dennis V. Damp. 1993. Provides information on the nature of work for the major health care occupational groups. Descriptions include working conditions, training, job outlook, qualifications, and related occupations.

★7905★ "Nuclear Medicine Technologists" in Occupational Outlook Handbook
U.S. Government Printing Office
Superintendent of Documents
Washington, DC 20402
Ph: (202)512-1800   Fax: (202)512-2250

Biennial; latest edition, 1994-95. Encyclopedia of careers describing about 250 occupations and comprising about 85 percent of all jobs in the economy. Occupations that require lengthy education or training are given the most attention. Each occupation's profile describes what the worker does on the job, working conditions, education and training requirements, advancement possibilities, job outlook, earnings, and sources of additional information.

★7906★ "Nuclear Medicine Technology/ Technician" in 150 Careers in the Health Care Field
Reed Reference Publishing
121 Chanlon Rd.
PO Box 31
New Providence, NJ 07974
Fax: (908)665-6688   Fr: 800-521-8110

Stanley Alperin. Third edition, 1993. Profiles health care occupations requiring a bachelor's degree or less. Describes the nature of the work, educational preparation, licensing requirements, and salary. Lists accredited educational programs.

★7907★ Opportunities in Medical Technology
National Textbook Co. (NTC)
VGM Career Books
4255 W. Touhy Ave.
Lincolnwood, IL 60646-1975
Ph: (708)679-5500   Fax: (708)679-2494
Fr: 800-323-4900

Karen R. Karni, Jane Sidney Oliver. Overviews opportunities for laboratory technicians, nuclear medicine and radiologic technologists, and others. Includesinformation on training, salaries, and the employment outlook.

PROFESSIONAL ASSOCIATIONS

★7908★ American Medical Association (AMA)
515 N. State St.
Chicago, IL 60610
Ph: (312)464-5000   Fax: (312)464-4184

Members: County medical societies and physicians. **Purpose:** Disseminates scientific information to members and the public. Informs members on significant medical and health legislation on state and national levels and represents the profession before Congress and governmental agencies. Cooperates in setting standards for medical schools, hospitals, residency programs, and continuing medical education courses. Offers physician placement service and counseling on practice management problems. Operates library which lends material and provides specific medical information to physicians. Ad-hoc committees are formed for such topics as health care planning and principles of medical ethics. **Publications:** American Medical News, weekly. • Archives of Dermatology, monthly. • Archives of Family Medicine, monthly. • Archives of General Psychiatry, monthly. • Archives of Internal Medicine, semimonthly. • Archives of Neurology, monthly. • Archives of Ophthalmology, monthly. • Archives of Otolaryngology— Head and Neck Surgery, monthly. • Archives of Pediatrics & Adolescent Medicine, monthly. • Archives of Surgery, monthly. • Journal of the American Medical Association, weekly.

★7909★ American Registry of Radiologic Technologists (ARRT)
1255 Northland Dr.
St. Paul, MN 55120
Ph: (612)687-0048

Members: Radiologic certification boards that administer examinations, issues certificates of registration to radiographers, nuclear medicine technologists, and radiation therapists, and investigates the qualifications of practicing radiologic technologists. Governed by trustees appointed from American College of Radiology and American Society of Radiologic Technologists. **Publications:** Directory of Registered Technologists, biennial.

★7910★ American Society of Radiologic Technologists (ASRT)
15000 Central Ave. SE
Albuquerque, NM 87123
Ph: (505)298-4500   Fax: (505)298-5063

Members: Professional society of diagnostic radiography, radiation therapy, ultrasound, and nuclear medicine technologists. **Purpose:** Advances the science of radiologic technology; establishes and maintains high standards of education; evaluates the quality of patient care; improves the welfare and socioeconomics of radiologic technologists. Operates ASRT Educational Foundation, which provides educational materials to radiologic technologist programs. **Publications:** ASRT Scanner, bimonthly. • Radiologic Technology, bimonthly.

★7911★ Nuclear Medicine Technology Certification Board (NMTCB)
2970 Clairmont Rd., Ste. 610
Atlanta, GA 30329
Ph: (404)315-1739   Fax: (404)315-6502

Members: Purpose: Purposes are to provide for the certification of nuclear medical technologists and to develop, assess, and administer an examination relevant to nuclear medicine technology. Compiles statistics. **Publications:** Certification Examination Validation Report, annual. • Examination Report, annual. • NMTCB News, semiannual.

★7912★ Society of Nuclear Medicine (SNM)
1850 Samuel Morse Dr.
Reston, VA 22090
Ph: (703)708-9000   Fax: (703)708-9015

Members: Professional society of physicians, physicists, chemists, radiopharmacists, nuclear medicine technologists, and others interested in nuclear medicine, nuclear magnetic resonance, and the use of radioactive isotopes in clinical practice, research, and teaching. **Purpose:** Disseminates information concerning the utilization of nuclear phenomena in the diagnosis and treatment of disease. Oversees the Technologist Section of the Society of Nuclear Medicine . **Publications:** The Journal of Nuclear Medicine, monthly. • Journal of Nuclear Medicine Technology, quarterly. • Society of Nuclear Medicine Membership Directory.

★7913★ **Technologist Section of the Society of Nuclear Medicine (TSSNM)**
136 Madison Ave.
New York, NY 10016
Ph: (703)708-9000   Fax: (703)708-9015

Members: Members of the Society of Nuclear Medicine who have received formal training in nuclear medicine technology. **Purpose:** Purposes are to: promote the continued development and improvement of nuclear medicine technology; enhance the development of nuclear medicine technologists; stimulate continuing education; develop a forum for the exchange of ideas and information. Serves as the central source of information for those interested and involved in the field of nuclear medicine technology. Represents the field in areas of licensure, accreditation, and certification. Sponsors training sessions. Conducts surveys; compiles statistics. **Publications:** *Journal of Nuclear Medicine Technology*, quarterly.

STANDARDS/CERTIFICATION AGENCIES

★7914★ **American Medical Association (AMA)**
515 N. State St.
Chicago, IL 60610
Ph: (312)464-5000   Fax: (312)464-4184

Cooperates in setting standards for medical schools, hospitals, residency programs, and continuing medical education courses.

★7915★ **American Registry of Radiologic Technologists (ARRT)**
1255 Northland Dr.
St. Paul, MN 55120
Ph: (612)687-0048

Radiologic certification boards that administer examinations, issues certificates of registration to radiographers, nuclear medicine technologists, and radiation therapists, and investigates the qualifications of practicing radiologic technologists.

★7916★ **Nuclear Medicine Technology Certification Board (NMTCB)**
2970 Clairmont Rd., Ste. 610
Atlanta, GA 30329
Ph: (404)315-1739   Fax: (404)315-6502

Purposes are to provide for the certification of nuclear medical technologists and to develop, assess, and administer an examination relevant to nuclear medicine technology.

EDUCATIONAL DIRECTORIES AND PROGRAMS

★7917★ *Medical Technologists and Technicians Career Directory*
Gale Research Inc.
835 Penobscot Bldg.
Detroit, MI 48226-4094
Ph: (313)961-2242   Fax: (313)961-6083
Fr: 800-877-GALE

Bradley J. Morgan and Joseph M. Palmisano. 1993. A directory in the Career Advisor Series that provides essays written by industry professionals; job search information on resume and cover letter preparation, networking, and the interviewing process; approximately 300 companies and organizations offering job opportunities and internships, and additional job-hunting resources.

AWARDS, SCHOLARSHIPS, GRANTS, AND FELLOWSHIPS

★7918★ **Berson-Yalow Award**
Society of Nuclear Medicine
136 Madison Ave., 8th Fl.
New York, NY 10016-6760
Ph: (212)889-0717   Fax: (212)545-0221

To recognize originality in, and contributions to, basic or clinical radioassay. Awarded annually when merited. Established in 1977.

★7919★ **SNM Honorary Member**
Society of Nuclear Medicine
136 Madison Ave., 8th Fl.
New York, NY 10016-6760
Ph: (212)889-0717   Fax: (212)545-0221

To recognize individuals for outstanding contributions to the field of nuclear medicine.

BASIC REFERENCE GUIDES AND HANDBOOKS

★7920★ *Essentials of Nuclear Medicine Science*
Williams and Wilkins
428 E. Preston St.
Baltimore, MD 21202
Ph: (410)528-4000

William B. Hladik III, Gopal B. Saha, and Kenneth T. Study, editors. 1987. Includes bibliographies and an index.

★7921★ *Examples of Monitoring and Evaluation in Diagnostic Radiology, Radiation Oncology, and Nuclear Medicine Services*
Joint Commission on Accreditation of Healthcare Organizations
1 Renaissance Blvd.
Oakbrook Terrace, IL 60181
Ph: (708)916-5600

1988. Includes bibliographies.

★7922★ *Fundamentals of Nuclear Medicine*
Society of Nuclear Medicine, Inc.
136 Madison Ave.
New York, NY 10016-6760
Ph: (212)889-0717

Naomi P. Alazraki and Fred S. Mishkin, editors. Second edition, 1991. Includes bibliographies and an index.

★7923★ *Introductory Physics of Nuclear Medicine*
Lea and Febiger
200 Chesterfield Pkwy.
Malvern, PA 19355
Ph: (215)251-2230

Ramesh Chandra. Fourth edition, 1992. Includes a bibliography and an index.

★7924★ *Nuclear Medicine Technologist*
R & E Publishers, Inc.
PO Box 2008
Saratoga, CA 95070
Ph: (408)866-6303   Fax: (408)866-0825

Ronald R. Smith, editor. 1993. Part of the Smith's Career Notes series.

★7925★ *Nuclear Medicine Technology and Techniques*
Mosby-Year Book, Inc.
11830 Westline Industrial Dr.
St. Louis, MO 63146
Ph: (314)872-8370   Fax: (314)432-1380
Fr: 800-325-4177

Donald R. Bernier, James K. Langan, and Paul E. Christian, editors. Third edition, 1993. Includes bibliographies and an index.

PROFESSIONAL AND TRADE PERIODICALS

★7926★ *The Journal of Nuclear Medicine*
Society of Nuclear Medicine
136 Madison Ave.
New York, NY 10016-6760
Ph: (212)889-0717   Fax: (212)545-0221
H. William Strauss

Monthly. Scientific peer-reviewed journal presenting original research and commentary on significant trends and discoveries in nuclear medicine.

★7927★ *Journal of Nuclear Medicine Technology*
Society of Nuclear Medicine
136 Madison Ave.
New York, NY 10016-6760
Ph: (212)889-0717   Fax: (212)545-0221
Susan Weiss
Quarterly. Peer-reviewed scientific journal for technologists presenting original research, clinical reports, continuing education articles, and commentary on scientific trends and discoveries in nuclear medicine.

★7928★ *Radiology & Imaging Letter*
Quest Publishing Company
1351 Titan Way
Brea, CA 92621
Ph: (714)738-6400   Fax: (714)525-6258
Gregory F. Nighswonger
Semimonthly. Covers the latest advances in medical imaging technology, spanning the fields of radiation therapy, ultrasonics, nuclear medicine, and diagnostic procedures. Recurring features include sections on new technology and procedures, recalls and safety hazards, legislation and regulations, professional activities, business briefs, meetings and events, and resources available.

★7929★ *Society of Nuclear Medicine— Newsline*
Society of Nuclear Medicine
136 Madison Ave.
New York, NY 10016-6760
Ph: (212)889-0717   Fax: (212)545-0221
Lantz Miller
Monthly. Provides socio-economic and regulatory news affecting the climate of nuclear medicine.

PROFESSIONAL MEETINGS AND CONVENTIONS

★7930★ American Association of Physicists in Medicine Annual Meeting
American Association of Physicists in Medicine
335 E. 45th St.
New York, NY 10017
Ph: (212)661-9404   Fax: (212)661-7026
Annual.

★7931★ Society of Nuclear Medicine Annual Meeting, Southeastern Chapter
Society of Nuclear Medicine
5987 Turpin Hills Dr.
Cincinnati, OH 45244
Ph: (513)231-6955
Annual.

★7932★ Society of Nuclear Medicine Convention
Society of Nuclear Medicine
136 Madison Ave.
New York, NY 10016
Ph: (212)889-0717   Fax: (212)545-0221
Annual. **Dates and Locations:** 1996 Jun 03-06; Denver, CO. • 1997 Jun 02-05; San Antonio, TX. • 1998 Jun 01-04; New Orleans, LA.

★7933★ Southwestern Chapter, Society of Nuclear Medicine
Society of Nuclear Medicine
PO Box 31096
San Francisco, CA 94131
Ph: (415)333-6472   Fax: (415)469-9887
Annual. **Dates and Locations:** 1996 Mar 28-31; Austin, TX.

Radiologic Technologists

Radiologic personnel may be called **radiologic technologists** in one hospital, radiographers in another, and X-ray technicians in yet a third. The size of the facility, amount of specialization, and organizational policy are among the factors that determine which job titles are used. Another reason for inconsistency in job titles is the rapidity with which new medical technologies have emerged and practice patterns have changed. When new equipment is introduced, existing staff are taught to operate it, and it may be some time before job titles are changed. **Radiographers** take X-ray films (radiographs) of all parts of the human body for use in diagnosing medical problems. **Radiation therapy technologists** prepare cancer patients for treatment and administer prescribed doses of ionizing radiation to specific body parts. **Sonographers**, also known as **ultrasound technologists**, use non-ionizing equipment to transmit sound waves at high frequencies into the patients body, then collect reflected echoes to form an image.

Salaries

Radiologic technologists	$12.75/hour
Diagnostic medical sonographers	$14.47/hour
Radiation therapy technologists	$29,162/year

Employment Outlook

Growth rate until the year 2005: Much faster than the average.

Radiologic Technologists

CAREER GUIDES

★7934★ "Diagnostic Medical
Sonographer" in *Careers in Health
Care* (pp. 62-66)
National Textbook Co. (NTC)
VGM Career Books
4255 W. Touhy Ave.
Lincolnwood, IL 60646-1975
Ph: (708)679-5500   Fax: (708)679-2494
Fr: 800-323-4900

Barbara M. Swanson. Third edition, 1995.
Describes job duties, work settings, salaries,
licensing and certification requirements, educational preparation, and future outlook.

★7935★ "Diagnostic Medical
Sonographer" in *Jobs! What They
Are—Where They Are—What They
Pay!* (p. 182)
Simon & Schuster, Inc.
Simon & Schuster Bldg.
1230 Avenue of the Americas
New York, NY 10020
Ph: (212)698-7000   Fr: 800-223-2348

Robert O. Snelling and Anne M. Snelling.
Third revised edition, 1992. Includes a chapter titled "Radiologic (X-Ray) Technologists"
(p. 192). Describes duties and responsibilities, earnings, employment opportunities,
training, and qualifications.

★7936★ *Diagnostic Medical
Sonographers*
Chronicle Guidance Publications, Inc.
66 Aurora St.
PO Box 1190
Moravia, NY 13118-1190
Ph: (315)497-0330   Fax: (315)497-3359
Fr: 800-622-7284

1992. Career brief describing the nature of
the job, working conditions, hours and earnings, education and training, licensure, certification, unions, personal qualifications, social
and psychological factors, location, employment outlook, entry methods, advancement,
and related occupations.

★7937★ "Diagnostic Medical
Sonographers or Ultrasound
Technologists" in *Careers in High-
Tech*
Arco Publishing Co.
Macmillan General Reference
15 Columbus Cir.
New York, NY 10023
Fax: 800-835-3202   Fr: 800-858-7674

Connie Winkler. 1987. Surveys occupations
in data processing, personal computers, telecommunications, manufacturing technology,
artificial intelligence, computer graphics,
medicine, biotechnology, lasers, technical
writing, and publishing. Separate chapters
cover education and training.

★7938★ *Health Careers*
Careers, Inc.
PO Box 135
Largo, FL 34649-0135
Ph: (813)584-7333

1994. Four-page brief describing duties,
working conditions, personal qualifications,
training, earnings and hours, employment
outlook, places of employment, related careers, and where to write for more information.

★7939★ *Introduction to Radiologic
Technology*
Mosby-Year Book, Inc.
11830 Westline Industrial Dr.
St. Louis, MO 63146
Ph: (314)872-8370   Fax: (314)432-1380
Fr: 800-325-4177

LaVerne Tolley Gurley and William J.
Callaway, editors. Third edition, 1992.

★7940★ *Opportunities in Medical
Technology*
National Textbook Co. (NTC)
VGM Career Books
4255 W. Touhy Ave.
Lincolnwood, IL 60646-1975
Ph: (708)679-5500   Fax: (708)679-2494
Fr: 800-323-4900

Karen R. Karni, Jane Sidney Oliver. Overviews opportunities for laboratory technicians, nuclear medicine and radiologic technologists, and others. Includes information on
training, salaries, and the employment
outlook.

★7941★ "Radiation Therapist" in
Careers in Health Care (pp. 236-240)
National Textbook Co. (NTC)
VGM Career Books
4255 W. Touhy Ave.
Lincolnwood, IL 60646-1975
Ph: (708)679-5500   Fax: (708)679-2494
Fr: 800-323-4900

Barbara M. Swanson. Third edition, 1995.
Describes job duties, work settings, salaries,
licensing and certification requirements, educational preparation, and future outlook.

★7942★ *The Radiation Therapy
Technologist: A Career in Cancer
Management*
American Society of Radiologic
Technologists
15000 Central Ave., S.E.
Albuquerque, NM 87123-3917
Ph: (505)298-4500

1993. This six-panel brochure describes radiation therapy and explains what radiation
therapists do. Covers educational preparation required.

★7943★ "Radiation Therapy
Technologists" in *Careers in High-
Tech*
Arco Publishing Co.
Macmillan General Reference
15 Columbus Cir.
New York, NY 10023
Fax: 800-835-3202   Fr: 800-858-7674

Connie Winkler. 1987. Surveys occupations
in data processing, personal computers, telecommunications, manufacturing technology,
artificial intelligence, computer graphics,
medicine, biotechnology, lasers, technical
writing, and publishing. Separate chapters
cover education and training. TO 800-223-
2336.

★7944★ *Radiographer*
Careers, Inc.
PO Box 135
Largo, FL 34649-0135
Ph: (813)584-7333

1993. Two-page occupational summary card
describing duties, working conditions, personal qualifications, training, earnings and
hours, employment outlook, places of employment, related careers, and where to write
for more information.

★7945★ *The Radiographer—A Career for You?*
American Society of Radiologic Technologists
15000 Central Ave., S.E.
Albuquerque, NM 87123-3917
Ph: (505)298-4500

1993. Six-panel brochure describing the job of a radiographer and the educational preparation necessary for this career.

★7946★ "Radiographer" in *Careers in Health Care* (pp. 241-244)
National Textbook Co. (NTC)
VGM Career Books
4255 W. Touhy Ave.
Lincolnwood, IL 60646-1975
Ph: (708)679-5500   Fax: (708)679-2494
Fr: 800-323-4900

Barbara M. Swanson. Third edition, 1995. Describes job duties, work settings, salaries, licensing and certification requirements, educational preparation, and future outlook.

★7947★ *Radiologic Technologist*
Careers, Inc.
PO Box 135
Largo, FL 34649-0135
Ph: (813)584-7333

1994. Four-page brief offering the definition, history, duties, working conditions, personal qualifications, educational requirements, earnings, hours, employment outlook, advancement, and careers related to this position.

★7948★ *Radiologic Technologist*
Vocational Biographies, Inc.
PO Box 31
Sauk Centre, MN 56378-0031
Ph: (612)352-6516   Fax: (612)352-5546
Fr: 800-255-0752

1991. Four-page pamphlet containing a personal narrative about a worker's job, work likes and dislikes, career path from high school to the present. Education and training, the rewards and frustrations, and the effects of the job on the rest of the worker's life. The data file portion of this pamphlet gives a concise occupational summary, including work descriptions, working conditions, places of employment, personal characteristics, education and training, job outlook, and salary range.

★7949★ "Radiologic Technologist" in *100 Best Careers for the Year 2000* (pp. 66-68)
Arco Pub.
201 W. 103rd St.
Indianapolis, IN 46290
Ph: 800-428-5331   Fax: 800-835-3202

Shelly Field. 1992. Describes 100 job opportunities expected to grow fast throughout the next decade. Provides information on job duties and responsibilities, training requirements, education, advancement opportunities, experience and qualifications, and typical salaries.

★7950★ "Radiologic Technologist" in *Career Information Center* (Vol.7)
Simon and Schuster
200 Old Tappan Rd.
Old Tappan, NJ 07675
Fax: 800-445-6991   Fr: 800-223-2348

Richard Lidz and Linda Perrin, editorial directors. Fifth edition, 1993. This 13-volume set profiles over 600 occupations. Each occupational profile describes job duties, entry-level requirements, educational requirements, advancement possibilities, employment outlook, working conditions, earnings and benefits, and where to write for more information.

★7951★ "Radiologic Technologist" in *Guide to Careers Without College* (pp. 39-40)
Franklin Watts, Inc.
387 Park Ave., S.
New York, NY 10016
Ph: (212)686-7070   Fr: 800-672-6672

Kathleen S. Abrams. 1988. Discusses rewarding careers that do not require a college degree.

★7952★ "Radiologic Technologists" in *101 Careers: A Guide to the Fastest-Growing Opportunities* (pp. 256-258)
John Wiley & Sons, Inc.
605 3rd Ave.
New York, NY 10158-0012
Ph: (212)850-6645   Fax: (212)850-6088

Michael Harkavy. 1990. Describes the nature of the job, working conditions, employment growth, qualifications, personal skills, projected salaries, and where to write for more information.

★7953★ "Radiologic Technologists" in *America's 50 Fastest Growing Jobs* (pp. 89)
JIST Works, Inc.
720 N. Park Ave.
Indianapolis, IN 46202-3431
Ph: (317)264-3720   Fax: (317)264-3709
Fr: 800-648-5478

Michael J. Farr, compiler. 1994. Describes the 50 fastest growing jobs within major career clusters such as technicians, and marketing and sales. Each job profile explains the nature of the work, skills and abilities required, employment outlook, average earnings, related occupations, education and training requirements, and employment opportunities. Also contains career planning information and job search tips.

★7954★ "Radiologic Technologists" in *Best Jobs for the 1990s and Into the 21st Century*
Impact Publications
9104-N Manassas Dr.
Manassas Park, VA 22111
Ph: (703)361-7300   Fax: (703)335-9486

Ronald L. Krannich and Caryl Rae Krannich. 1993.

★7955★ "Radiologic Technologists" in *Health Care Job Explosion!* (pp. 85-94)
D-Amp Publications
401 Amherst Ave.
Coraopolis, PA 15108
Ph: (412)262-5578

Dennis V. Damp. 1993. Provides information on the nature of work for the major health care occupational groups. Descriptions include working conditions, training, job outlook, qualifications, and related occupations.

★7956★ "Radiologic Technologists" in *Occupational Outlook Handbook*
U.S. Government Printing Office
Superintendent of Documents
Washington, DC 20402
Ph: (202)512-1800   Fax: (202)512-2250

Biennial; latest edition, 1994-95. Encyclopedia of careers describing about 250 occupations and comprising about 85 percent of all jobs in the economy. Occupations that require lengthy education or training are given the most attention. Each occupation's profile describes what the worker does on the job, working conditions, education and training requirements, advancement possibilities, job outlook, earnings, and sources of additional information.

★7957★ "Radiologic Technology" in *150 Careers in the Health Care Field*
Reed Reference Publishing
121 Chanlon Rd.
PO Box 31
New Providence, NJ 07974
Fax: (908)665-6688   Fr: 800-521-8110

Stanley Alperin. Third edition, 1993. Profiles health care occupations requiring a bachelor's degree or less. Describes the nature of the work, educational preparation, licensing requirements, and salary. Lists accredited educational programs.

★7958★ "Radiologic Technology" in *Allied Health Education Directory* (pp. 179-180)
American Medical Association (AMA)
515 N. State St.
Chicago, IL 60610
Ph: (312)464-5000   Fr: 800-621-8335

William R. Burrow, editor. 1994. Describes allied health occupations and lists educational programs accredited by the Committee on Allied Health Education and Accreditation of the American Medical Association.

★7959★ "Radiologic (X-Ray) Technician" in *VGM's Handbook of Health Care Careers*
National Textbook Co.
4255 W. Touhy Ave.
Lincolnwood, IL 60646-1975
Ph: (708)679-5500   Fax: (708)679-2494
Fr: 800-323-4900

Annette Selden. 1993. Contains 42 two-page occupational profiles describing job duties, places of employment, working conditions, qualifications, education, employment outlook, and income.

★7960★ "Radiologic (X-Ray) Technologist" in VGM's Careers Encyclopedia (pp. 391-393)
National Textbook Co. (NTC)
VGM Career Books
4255 W. Touhy Ave.
Lincolnwood, IL 60646-1975
Ph: (708)679-5500   Fax: (708)679-2494
Fr: 800-323-4900
Third edition, 1991. Describes job duties, places of employment, working conditions, qualifications, education and training, advancement potential, and salary for each occupation.

★7961★ "Radiological Technology" in Career Connection for Technical Education (pp. 130-131)
JIST Works, Inc.
720 N. Park Ave.
Indianapolis, IN 46202-3431
Ph: (317)264-3720   Fax: (317)264-3709
Fred A. Rowe. 1994, second edition. Describes in detail technical occupations. Includes information on recommended high school courses, course requirements, related careers, and a self-assessment guide.

★7962★ "Radiological (X-Ray) Technologists" in Encyclopedia of Careers and Vocational Guidance (Vol.4, pp. 231-235)
J.G. Ferguson Publishing Co.
200 W. Madison St., Ste. 300
Chicago, IL 60606
Ph: (312)580-5480   Fax: (312)580-4948
William E. Hopke, editor in chief. Ninth edition, 1993. Four-volume set that profiles 900 occupations and describes job trends in 74 industries. Includes career description, educational requirements, history of the job, methods of entry, advancement, employment outlook, earnings, conditions of work, social and psychological factors, and sources of further information.

★7963★ Radiologists
Chronicle Guidance Publications, Inc.
66 Aurora St.
PO Box 1190
Moravia, NY 13118-1190
Ph: (315)497-0330   Fax: (315)497-3359
Fr: 800-622-7284
1991. Career brief describing the nature of the job, working conditions, hours and earnings, education and training, licensure, certification, unions, personal qualifications, social and psychological factors, location, employment outlook, entry methods, advancement, and related occupations.

Professional Associations

★7964★ American Cancer Society (ACS)
1599 Clifton Rd. NE
Atlanta, GA 30329
Ph: (404)320-3333   Fax: (404)325-0230
Fr: 800-ACS-2345
Members: Volunteers (2,500,000) supporting education and research in cancer prevention, diagnosis, detection, and treatment. Provides special services to cancer patients.

Sponsors Reach to Recovery and I Can Cope. Conducts medical and educational programs. **Publications:** *American Cancer Society.* • *CA-A Cancer Journal for Clinicians*, bimonthly. • *Cancer*, semimonthly. • *Cancer Facts and Figures*, annual. • *Cancer News*, 3/year. • *Cancer Nursing News*, quarterly. • *World Smoking and Health*, 3/year.

★7965★ American Medical Association (AMA)
515 N. State St.
Chicago, IL 60610
Ph: (312)464-5000   Fax: (312)464-4184
Members: County medical societies and physicians. **Purpose:** Disseminates scientific information to members and the public. Informs members on significant medical and health legislation on state and national levels and represents the profession before Congress and governmental agencies. Cooperates in setting standards for medical schools, hospitals, residency programs, and continuing medical education courses. Offers physician placement service and counseling on practice management problems. Operates library which lends material and provides specific medical information to physicians. Adhoc committees are formed for such topics as health care planning and principles of medical ethics. **Publications:** *American Medical News*, weekly. • *Archives of Dermatology*, monthly. • *Archives of Family Medicine*, monthly. • *Archives of General Psychiatry*, monthly. • *Archives of Internal Medicine*, semimonthly. • *Archives of Neurology*, monthly. • *Archives of Ophthalmology*, monthly. • *Archives of Otolaryngology—Head and Neck Surgery*, monthly. • *Archives of Pediatrics & Adolescent Medicine*, monthly. • *Archives of Surgery*, monthly. • *Journal of the American Medical Association*, weekly.

★7966★ American Registry of Diagnostic Medical Sonographers (ARDMS)
2368 Victory Pky., Ste. 510
Cincinnati, OH 45206-2810
Ph: (513)281-7111   Fax: (513)281-7524
Fr: 800-541-9754
Members: Administers examinations in the field of diagnostic medical sonography and vascular technology throughout the U.S. and Canada and registers candidates passing those exams in the specialties of their expertise. **Purpose:** Maintains central office for administering examination plans and schedules and assisting registered candidates and those interested in becoming registered. **Publications:** *American Registry of Diagnostic Medical Sonographers Directory*, annual. • *Annual Examination Information and Application Booklet*. • *Continuing Competency Requirements*. • *Informational Brochure*, annual. • *Mailing List Brochure*.

★7967★ American Society of Radiologic Technologists (ASRT)
15000 Central Ave. SE
Albuquerque, NM 87123
Ph: (505)298-4500   Fax: (505)298-5063
Members: Professional society of diagnostic radiography, radiation therapy, ultrasound, and nuclear medicine technologists. **Purpose:** Advances the science of radiologic technology; establishes and maintains high

standards of education; evaluates the quality of patient care; improves the welfare and socioeconomics of radiologic technologists. Operates ASRT Educational Foundation, which provides educational materials to radiologic technologist programs. **Publications:** *ASRT Scanner*, bimonthly. • *Radiologic Technology*, bimonthly.

★7968★ Society of Diagnostic Medical Sonographers (SDMS)
12770 Coit Rd., Ste. 508
Dallas, TX 75251
Ph: (214)239-7367   Fax: (214)239-7378
Members: Sonographers, physician sonologists, and those in medical specialties utilizing high frequency sound for diagnostic purposes. **Purpose:** Works to advance the science of diagnostic medical sonography to establish and maintain high standards of education, to provide an identity and sense of direction for members. Collects information concerning educational programs and informs schools of minimum standards currently being proposed. Has developed American Registry of Diagnostic Medical Sonographers, the first registering body for the field of diagnostic ultrasound. Maintains list of job openings. **Publications:** *Directory of Education*. • *Guidelines for Student Review*. • *Journal of Diagnostic Medical Sonography*, biennial. • *News Wave*, biennial. • *1995 Compensation Survey*.

Standards/Certification Agencies

★7969★ American Medical Association (AMA)
515 N. State St.
Chicago, IL 60610
Ph: (312)464-5000   Fax: (312)464-4184
Cooperates in setting standards for medical schools, hospitals, residency programs, and continuing medical education courses.

★7970★ American Registry of Clinical Radiography Technologists (ARCRT)
710 Higgins Rd.
Park Ridge, IL 60068
Ph: (708)318-9050
Registers X-ray technologists who meet ARCRT educational and training standards. Sponsors a Registry Examination for Clinical Radiography Technologists program, which provides an alternate means of certification for technologists who do not have the prerequisite formal educational program.

★7971★ American Registry of Diagnostic Medical Sonographers (ARDMS)
2368 Victory Pky., Ste. 510
Cincinnati, OH 45206-2810
Ph: (513)281-7111   Fax: (513)281-7524
Fr: 800-541-9754
Administers examinations in the field of diagnostic medical sonography and vascular technology throughout the U.S. and Canada and registers candidates passing those exams in the specialties of their expertise.

Maintains central office for administering examination plans and schedules and assisting registered candidates and those interested in becoming registered.

★7972★ **American Registry of Radiologic Technologists (ARRT)**
1255 Northland Dr.
St. Paul, MN 55120
Ph: (612)687-0048

Radiologic certification boards that administer examinations, issues certificates of registration to radiographers, nuclear medicine technologists, and radiation therapists, and investigates the qualifications of practicing radiologic technologists.

TEST GUIDES

★7973★ *The American Registry of Diagnostic Medical Sonographers Information Booklet*
American Registry of Diagnostic Medical Sonographers (ARDMS)
2368 Victor Pkwy., Ste. 510
Cincinnati, OH 45206
Ph: (513)281-7111

1988. This 24-page pamphlet explains the examination to become a registered diagnostic medical sonographer. Includes test registration requirements, fees, and an outline of the subject matter. Lists testing centers; provides sample test questions.

★7974★ *Career Examination Series: Assistant Radiologist*
National Learning Corp.
212 Michael Dr.
Syosset, NY 11791
Ph: (516)921-8888   Fax: (516)921-8743
Fr: 800-645-6337

Jack Rudman. 1993. Test guide including questions and answers for students or professionals in the field who seek advancement through examination.

★7975★ *Career Examination Series: Radiologic Technologist*
National Learning Corp.
212 Michael Dr.
Syosset, NY 11791
Ph: (516)921-8888   Fax: (516)921-8743
Fr: 800-645-6337

Jack Rudman. Test guide including questions and answers for students or professionals in the field who seek advancement through examination.

★7976★ *Career Examination Series: X-Ray Coordinator*
National Learning Corp.
212 Michael Dr.
Syosset, NY 11791
Ph: (516)921-8888   Fax: (516)921-8743
Fr: 800-645-6337

Jack Rudman. A series of study guides with multiple-choice examination questions and solutions for trainees and professional radiologic technologists. Titles in the series include *Medical Radiology Technologist; Principal X-Ray Technician; Radiologic Technologist; Senior Radiologic Technologist; Senior X-*

Ray Technician; X-Ray Coordinator; X-Ray Technician I; X-Ray Technician II; X-Ray Technician III.

★7977★ *Registry Examination for Radiography Technologist*
American Registry of Clinical Radiography Technologists (ARCRT)
710 Higgins Rd.
Park Ridge, IL 60068
Ph: (708)318-9050

This pamphlet explains the registration examination for radiography technologist, including eligibility qualifications, fees and dates, and the subjects the test examines.

EDUCATIONAL DIRECTORIES AND PROGRAMS

★7978★ *Medical Technologists and Technicians Career Directory*
Gale Research Inc.
835 Penobscot Bldg.
Detroit, MI 48226-4094
Ph: (313)961-2242   Fax: (313)961-6083
Fr: 800-877-GALE

Bradley J. Morgan and Joseph M. Palmisano. 1993. A directory in the Career Advisor Series that provides essays written by industry professionals; job search information on resume and cover letter preparation, networking, and the interviewing process; approximately 300 companies and organizations offering job opportunities and internships, and additional job-hunting resources.

AWARDS, SCHOLARSHIPS, GRANTS, AND FELLOWSHIPS

★7979★ **Certificates of Honor and Appreciation**
American College of Radiology
Attn. Executive Office
1891 Preston White Dr.
Reston, VA 22091
Ph: (703)648-8900   Fax: (703)648-9176

To recognize assistance to the American College of Radiology, usually in its educational programs. Certificates are awarded intermittently.

★7980★ **George W. Holmes Lectureship**
New England Roentgen Ray Society
Radiology Dept.
New England Deaconess Hospital
185 Pilgrim Rd.
Boston, MA 02215
Ph: (617)732-8460   Fax: (617)632-0762

To recognize outstanding achievements in the field of radiology. A silver pitcher is awarded annually. Established in 1945. Additional information is available from Robert Cleveland, M.D., Secretary, NERRS; c/o Dept. of Radiology, Children's Hospital Medi-

cal Ctr., 300 Longwood Ave., Boston, MA 02115, phone (617) 735-6298.

BASIC REFERENCE GUIDES AND HANDBOOKS

★7981★ *Basic Medical Techniques and Patient Care for Radiologic Technologists*
J. B. Lippincott Co.
227 E. Washington Sq.
Philadelphia, PA 19106-3780
Ph: (215)238-4436

Lillian S. Torres. Fourth edition, 1993. Includes a bibliography and an index.

★7982★ *Examples of Monitoring and Evaluation in Diagnostic Radiology, Radiation Oncology, and Nuclear Medicine Services*
Joint Commission on Accreditation of Healthcare Organizations
1 Renaissance Blvd.
Oakbrook Terrace, IL 60181
Ph: (708)916-5600

1988. Includes bibliographies.

★7983★ *Radiology*
McGraw-Hill Inc.
11 W. 19 St.
New York, NY 10011
Ph: 800-722-4726

David Hovsepian, M.D. 1993.

★7984★ *Textbook of Radiographic Positioning and Related Anatomy*
Mosby-Year Book, Inc.
11830 Westline Industrial Dr.
St. Louis, MO 63146
Ph: (314)872-8370   Fax: (314)432-1380
Fr: 800-325-4177

Kenneth L. Bontrager and Barry T. Anthony. Third edition, 1992. Includes a bibliography and an index. Illustrated.

★7985★ *A Word Book in Radiology: With Anatomic Plates and Tables*
W. B. Saunders Co.
Independence Sq., W.
Philadelphia, PA 19106
Ph: (215)238-7800   Fr: 800-545-2522

Sheila B. Sloane. 1988. Illustrated.

PROFESSIONAL AND TRADE PERIODICALS

★7986★ *American Journal of Roentgenology*
Williams & Wilkins
428 E. Preston St.
Baltimore, MD 21202
Ph: (410)528-8553   Fax: (410)528-4452
Robert N. Berk

Monthly. Journal publishing orginal articles on general and diagnostic radiology.

★7987★ Investigative Radiology
J.B. Lippincott Co.
227 E. Washington Sq.
Philadelphia, PA 19106
Ph: (215)238-4492   Fax: (215)238-4461
Bruce J. Hillman

Monthly. Journal covering clinical and laboratory investigations in diagnostic imaging.

★7988★ Journal of Clinical Ultrasound
John Wiley and Sons, Inc.
605 3rd Ave.
New York, NY 10158
Ph: (212)850-6000   Fax: (212)850-6799
Russell L. Deter

International journal devoted to the clinical applications of ultrasound in medicine. Features include scholarly, peer-reviewed articles on research procedures and techniques encompassing all phases of diagnostic ultrasound.

★7989★ Radiologic Technology
American Society of Radiologic
    Technologists
15000 Central Ave. SE
Albuquerque, NM 87123-3909
Ph: (505)298-4500   Fax: (505)298-5063
Ceela McElveny

Bimonthly. Medical imaging technology magazine. Includes annual index.

★7990★ Radiology
Radiological Society of North America
2021 Spring Rd., Ste. 600
Oak Brook, IL 60521
Ph: (708)571-2670   Fax: (708)571-7837
Stanley S. Siegelman

Monthly. Journal focusing on radiology.

★7991★ Radiology & Imaging Letter
Quest Publishing Company
1351 Titan Way
Brea, CA 92621
Ph: (714)738-6400   Fax: (714)525-6258
Gregory F. Nighswonger

Semimonthly. Covers the latest advances in medical imaging technology, spanning the fields of radiation therapy, ultrasonics, nuclear medicine, and diagnostic procedures. Recurring features include sections on new technology and procedures, recalls and safety hazards, legislation and regulations, professional activities, business briefs, meetings and events, and resources available.

★7992★ Scanner
American Society of Radiologic
    Technologists
15000 Central Ave. SE
Albuquerque, NM 87123-4605
Ph: (505)298-4500   Fax: (505)298-5063
Anna Stecher

Bimonthly. Reflects the aims of the Society, which seeks to "advance the science of radiologic technology, to establish and maintain high standards of education and training, to elevate the quality of patient care, and to improve the welfare and socioeconomics of radiologic technologists." Recurring features include news of research and news of members.

★7993★ Technology for Health Care Series
ECRI
5200 Butler Pike
Plymouth Meeting, PA 19462
Ph: (215)825-6000   Fax: (215)834-1275
Michele Moscariello

Monthly. Concerned with the safety, performance, reliability, and cost effectiveness of health care technology. Covers areas of anesthesia, cardiology, imaging and radiology, and respiratory therapy. Reviews device test results and warns of hazards and deficiencies. Recurring features include news of research, Institute reports, and news of members.

PROFESSIONAL MEETINGS AND CONVENTIONS

★7994★ Harvard Medical School, Brigham and Women's Hospital Department of Radiology Ultrasound Convention
Harvard Medical School, Brigham and
    Women's Hospital
Department of Radiology
75 Francis St.
Boston, MA 02115
Ph: (617)732-6265   Fax: (617)732-6509
Annual. Always held during March or April in Boston, Massachusetts.

★7995★ Radiological Society of North America Scientific Assembly and Annual Meeting
Radiological Society of North America
2021 Spring Rd., Ste. 600
Oak Brook, IL 60521-1860
Ph: (708)571-2670   Fax: (708)571-7837
Annual. Always held during November or December at the McCormick Place in Chicago,

Illinois. **Dates and Locations:** 1995 Nov 26-01; Chicago, IL. • 1996 Nov 26-01; Chicago, IL. • 1997 Dec 30-05; Chicago, IL.

★7996★ Rocky Mountain Radiological Society Annual Midsummer Conference
Rocky Mountain Radiological Society
PO Box 200532
Denver, CO 80220-2511
Ph: (303)753-1191
Annual.

OTHER SOURCES OF INFORMATION

★7997★ "Radiologic Technologist" in 100 Best Jobs for the 1990s & Beyond
Dearborn Financial Publishing, Inc.
520 N. Dearborn St.
Chicago, IL 60610-4354
Ph: (312)836-4400   Fax: (312)836-1021
Fr: 800-621-9621

Carol Kleiman. 1992. Describes 100 jobs ranging from accountants to veterinarians.. Each job profile includes such information as education, experience, and certification needed, salaries, and job search suggestions.

★7998★ "Radiologic Technologist" in Allied Health Professions (pp. 42-44; 160)
Arco Publishing Co.
Simon & Schuster, Inc.
201 W. 103rd St.
Indianapolis, IN 46290
Ph: 800-428-5331   Fax: 800-835-3202

1993. Contains information on 28 representative careers in health care. Provides a sample of the Allied Health Professions Admission Test, lists professional societies and associations, and offers a directory of schools and programs for the careers listed.

★7999★ "Radiologic Technologist" in Career Selector 2001
Barron's Educational Series, Inc.
250 Wireless Blvd.
Hauppauge, NY 11788
Ph: (516)434-3311   Fax: (516)434-3723
Fr: 800-645-3476

James C. Gonyea. 1993.

Surgical Technicians

Surgical technologists, also called **operating room technicians**, work with, and under the supervision of, surgeons or registered nurses. They help set up the operating room with surgical instruments, equipment, sterile linens, and fluids such as saline (a salt solution) or glucose (a sugar solution). Surgical technologists also may prepare patients for surgery by washing, shaving, and disinfecting body areas where the surgeon will operate. They may transport patients to the operating room and help drape them and position them on the operating table. During surgery, they pass instruments and other sterile supplies to the surgeons and the surgeons' assistants. They may hold retractors, cut sutures, and help count the sponges, needles, supplies, and instruments used during the operation. Surgical technologists help prepare, care for, and dispose of specimens taken for laboratory analysis during the operation and may help apply dressings. At times, surgical technologists may operate sterilizers, lights, or suction machines, and help operate diagnostic equipment. After the operation, **surgical technicians** may help transfer patients to the recovery room and assist nurses in cleaning and stocking the operating room for the next operation.

Salaries

Salaries vary widely by geographic location, those on the east and west coasts generally being higher. Surgical technicians employed by a surgeon tend to earn more than those employed by hospitals and similar institutions.

Surgical technicians	$9.46-$13.03/hour

Employment Outlook

Growth rate until the year 2005: Much faster than the average.

Surgical Technicians

★8000★ Health Careers
Careers, Inc.
PO Box 135
Largo, FL 34649-0135
Ph: (813)584-7333
1994. Four-page brief describing duties, working conditions, personal qualifications, training, earnings and hours, employment outlook, places of employment, related careers, and where to write for more information.

★8001★ Job Description: Certified Surgical Technologist in the O.R.
Association of Surgical Technologists
7108-C S. Alton Way
Englewood, CO 80112
Ph: (303)694-9130   Fax: (303)694-9169
Fr: 800-637-7433
1990. This six-panel brochure defines surgical technology and describes education, credentials, job and surgery knowledge, and equipment used in surgery.

★8002★ Opportunities in Medical Technology
National Textbook Co. (NTC)
VGM Career Books
4255 W. Touhy Ave.
Lincolnwood, IL 60646-1975
Ph: (708)679-5500   Fax: (708)679-2494
Fr: 800-323-4900
Karen R. Karni, Jane Sidney Oliver. Overviews opportunities for laboratory technicians, nuclear medicine and radiologic technologists, and others. Includesinformation on training, salaries, and the employment outlook.

★8003★ A Profile of the Surgical Technologist
Association of Surgical Technologists
7108-C S. Alton Way
Englewood, CO 80112
Ph: (303)694-9130   Fax: (303)694-9169
Fr: 800-637-7433
1990. This eight-panel pamphlet describes the role of surgical technologists, including educational preparation, personal characteristics, working conditions, and employment.

★8004★ "Surgeon's Assistant" in 150 Careers in the Health Care Field
Reed Reference Publishing
121 Chanlon Rd.
PO Box 31
New Providence, NJ 07974
Fax: (908)665-6688   Fr: 800-521-8110
Stanley Alperin. Third edition, 1993. Profiles health care occupations requiring a bachelor's degree or less. Describes the nature of the work, educational preparation, licensing requirements, and salary. Lists accredited educational programs.

★8005★ Surgical Technician
Careers, Inc.
PO Box 135
Largo, FL 34649-0135
Ph: (813)584-7333
1994. Two-page occupational summary card describing duties, working conditions, personal qualifications, training, earnings and hours, employment outlook, places of employment, related careers, and where to write for more information.

★8006★ "Surgical Technicians" in Encyclopedia of Careers and Vocational Guidance (Vol.4, pp. 456-559)
J.G. Ferguson Publishing Co.
200 W. Madison St., Ste. 300
Chicago, IL 60606
Ph: (312)580-5480   Fax: (312)580-4948
William E. Hopke, editor-in-chief. Ninth edition, 1993. Four-volume set that profiles 900 occupations and describes job trends in 74 industries. Includes career description, educational requirements, history of the job, methods of entry, advancement, employment outlook, earnings, conditions of work, social and psychological factors, and sources of further information.

★8007★ "Surgical Technicians" in Occupational Outlook Handbook
U.S. Government Printing Office
Superintendent of Documents
Washington, DC 20402
Ph: (202)512-1800   Fax: (202)512-2250
Biennial; latest edition, 1994-95. Encyclopedia of careers describing about 250 occupations and comprising about 85 percent of all jobs in the economy. Occupations that require lengthy education or training are given

the most attention. Each occupation's profile describes what the worker does on the job, working conditions, education and training requirements, advancement possibilities, job outlook, earnings, and sources of additional information.

★8008★ "Surgical Technologist" in 150 Careers in the Health Care Field
Reed Reference Publishing
121 Chanlon Rd.
PO Box 31
New Providence, NJ 07974
Fax: (908)665-6688   Fr: 800-521-8110
Stanley Alperin. Third edition, 1993. Profiles health care occupations requiring a bachelor's degree or less. Describes the nature of the work, educational preparation, licensing requirements, and salary. Lists accredited educational programs.

★8009★ "Surgical Technologist" in Careers in Health Care (pp. 265-268)
National Textbook Co. (NTC)
VGM Career Books
4255 W. Touhy Ave.
Lincolnwood, IL 60646-1975
Ph: (708)679-5500   Fax: (708)679-2494
Fr: 800-323-4900
Barbara M. Swanson. Third edition, 1995. Describes job duties, work settings, salaries, licensing and certification requirements, educational preparation, and future outlook.

★8010★ "Surgical Technologist" in Health Care Job Explosion! (pp. 95-100)
D-Amp Publications
401 Amherst Ave.
Coraopolis, PA 15108
Ph: (412)262-5578
Dennis V. Damp. 1993. Provides information on the nature of work for the major health care occupational groups. Descriptions include working conditions, training, job outlook, qualifications, and related occupations.

★8011★ "Surgical Technologist" in VGM's Handbook of Health Care Careers
National Textbook Co.
4255 W. Touhy Ave.
Lincolnwood, IL 60646-1975
Ph: (708)679-5500   Fax: (708)679-2494
Fr: 800-323-4900
Annette Selden. 1993. Contains 42 two-page occupational profiles describing job duties, places of employment, working conditions, qualifications, education, employment outlook, and income.

★8012★ Surgical Technologists
Chronicle Guidance Publications, Inc.
66 Aurora St.
PO Box 1190
Moravia, NY 13118-1190
Ph: (315)497-0330   Fax: (315)497-3359
Fr: 800-622-7284
1992. Career brief describing the nature of the job, working conditions, hours and earnings, education and training, licensure, certification, unions, personal qualifications, social and psychological factors, location, employment outlook, entry methods, advancement, and related occupations.

★8013★ "Surgical Technologists" in America's 50 Fastest Growing Jobs (pp. 91)
JIST Works, Inc.
720 N. Park Ave.
Indianapolis, IN 46202-3431
Ph: (317)264-3720   Fax: (317)264-3709
Fr: 800-648-5478
Michael J. Farr, compiler. 1994. Describes the 50 fastest growing jobs within major career clusters such as technicians, and marketing and sales. Each job profile explains the nature of the work, skills and abilities required, employment outlook, average earnings, related occupations, education and training requirements, and employment opportunities. Also contains career planning information and job search tips.

★8014★ "Surgical Technologists" in Jobs! What They Are—Where They Are—What They Pay (p. 193)
Simon & Schuster, Inc.
Simon & Schuster Bldg.
1230 Avenue of the Americas
New York, NY 10020
Ph: (212)698-7000   Fr: 800-223-2348
Robert O. Snelling and Anne M. Snelling. 3rd edition, 1992. Describes duties and responsibilities, earnings, employment opportunities, training, and qualifications.

★8015★ "Surgical Technology" in Allied Health Education Directory (pp. 264-265)
American Medical Association (AMA)
515 N. State St.
Chicago, IL 60610
Ph: (312)464-5000   Fr: 800-621-8335
William R. Burrow, editor. 1994. Describes allied health occupations and lists educational programs accredited by the Committee on Allied Health Education and Accreditation of the American Medical Association.

★8016★ "Surgical Technology" in Career Connection for Technical Education (pp. 138-139)
JIST Works, Inc.
720 N. Park Ave.
Indianapolis, IN 46202-3431
Ph: (317)264-3720   Fax: (317)264-3709
Fred A. Rowe. 1994, second edition. Describes in detail technical occupations. Includes information on recommended high school courses, course requirements, related careers, and a self-assessment guide.

PROFESSIONAL ASSOCIATIONS

★8017★ Association of Surgical Technologists (AST)
7108-C S. Alton Way
Englewood, CO 80112
Ph: (303)694-9130   Fax: (303)694-9169
Members: Individuals who have received specific education and training to deliver surgical patient care in the operating room. Membership categories are available for both certified and uncertified technologists. **Purpose:** Emphasis is placed on encouraging members to participate actively in a continuing education program. Aims are: to study, discuss, and exchange knowledge, experience, and ideas in the field of surgical technology; to promote a high standard of surgical technology performance in the community for quality patient care; to stimulate interest in continuing education. Local groups sponsor workshops and institutes. Conducts research. **Publications:** AST Core Curriculum for Surgical First Assisting. • AST Core Curriculum for Surgical Technology. • AST News, bimonthly. • Study and Test Skills for Health Professionals. • The Surgical Technologist, monthly.

STANDARDS/CERTIFICATION AGENCIES

★8018★ Association of Surgical Technologists (AST)
7108-C S. Alton Way
Englewood, CO 80112
Ph: (303)694-9130   Fax: (303)694-9169
Membership categories are available for both certified and uncertified technologists. Emphasis is placed on encouraging members to participate actively in a continuing education program. Aims are: to study, discuss, and exchange knowledge, experience, and ideas in the field of surgical technology; to promote a high standard of surgical technology performance in the community for quality patient care; to stimulate interest in continuing education.

TEST GUIDES

★8019★ Appleton and Lange's Review for the Surgical Technology Examination
Appleton and Lange
25 Van Zant St.
East Norwalk, CT 06855
Ph: (203)838-4400   Fr: 800-423-1359
Nancy M. Allmers and Joan Ann Verderame. Third edition, 1993. This is a preparation guide for the certification exam for surgical technologists. Includes sample questions with answers and explanations.

EDUCATIONAL DIRECTORIES AND PROGRAMS

★8020★ Medical Technologists and Technicians Career Directory
Gale Research Inc.
835 Penobscot Bldg.
Detroit, MI 48226-4094
Ph: (313)961-2242   Fax: (313)961-6083
Fr: 800-877-GALE
Bradley J. Morgan and Joseph M. Palmisano. 1993. A directory in the Career Advisor Series that provides essays written by industry professionals; job search information on resume and cover letter preparation, networking, and the interviewing process; approximately 300 companies and organizations offering job opportunities and internships, and additional job-hunting resources.

BASIC REFERENCE GUIDES AND HANDBOOKS

★8021★ Surgical Technologist
R & E Publishers, Inc.
PO Box 2008
Saratoga, CA 95070
Ph: (408)866-6303   Fax: (408)866-0825
Ronald R. Smith, editor. 1993. Part of the Smith's Career Notes Series.

★8022★ Surgical Technology: Principles & Practice
W. B. Saunders Co.
Curtis Center
Independence Sq. W.
Philadelphia, PA 19106
Ph: (215)238-7800
Joanna R. Fuller, editor. Third edition, 1993.

PROFESSIONAL AND TRADE PERIODICALS

★8023★ Biomedical Technology Information Service
Quest Publishing Company
1351 Titan Way
Brea, CA 92621
Ph: (714)738-6400   Fax: (714)525-6258
Gregory F. Nighswonger
Semimonthly. Monitors latest advances in medical technology, including developments in medical devices and electronics. Recurring features include new technology, computer applications, legislation and regulations, new inventions, and professional activities. Also includes book reviews, letters to the editor, and a calendar of events.

★8024★ Technology for Health Care Series
ECRI
5200 Butler Pike
Plymouth Meeting, PA 19462
Ph: (215)825-6000   Fax: (215)834-1275
Michele Moscariello
Monthly. Concerned with the safety, performance, reliability, and cost effectiveness of health care technology. Covers areas of anesthesia, cardiology, imaging and radiology, and respiratory therapy. Reviews device test results and warns of hazards and deficiencies. Recurring features include news of research, Institute reports, and news of members.

Aircraft Pilots

Pilots are highly trained, skilled professionals who fly numerous kinds of airplanes and helicopters to carry out a wide variety of tasks. Some pilots transport passengers, cargo, and mail, while others dust crops, spread seed for reforestation, test aircraft, and take aerial photographs. **Helicopter pilots** are involved in firefighting, police work, offshore exploration for natural resources, evacuation and rescue efforts, logging operations, construction work, and weather station operations; some also transport passengers.

Salaries

Airline pilots command the best salaries; pilots who fly jet aircraft earn higher salaries than non-jet pilots. Average salaries for pilots are as follows:

Airline pilots	$80,000/year
Copilots, airline	$65,000/year
Chief pilots, non-airline	$45,000-$62,000/year
Copilots, non-airline	$42,000/year
Flight engineers	$42,000/year
Captains	$107,000/year

Employment Outlook

Growth rate until the year 2005: Faster than the average.

Aircraft Pilots

CAREER GUIDES

★8025★ *Agricultural Aircraft Pilots*
Chronicle Guidance Publications, Inc.
66 Aurora St.
PO Box 1190
Moravia, NY 13118-1190
Ph: (315)497-0330   Fax: (315)497-3359
Fr: 800-622-7284

1993. This career brief describes the nature of the job, working conditions, hours and earnings, education and training, licensure, certification, unions, personal qualifications, social and psychological factors, location, employment outlook, entry methods, advancement, and related occupations.

★8026★ "Aircraft Pilot" in *Jobs! What They Are—Where They Are—What They Pay* (p. 96)
Fireside/Simon & Schuster, Inc.
Simon & Schuster Bldg.
1230 Avenue of the Americas
New York, NY 10020
Ph: (212)698-7000

Robert O. Snelling, author. 1992. This book profiles 241 occupations, describing duties and responsiblities, educational preparation, earnings, opportunities, qualifications, and where to write for more information. Occupations are arranged under 29 broad career fields.

★8027★ "Aircraft Pilots" in *101 Careers: A Guide to the Fastest-Growing Opportunities* (pp. 310-312)
John Wiley & Sons, Inc.
605 3rd Ave.
New York, NY 10158-0012
Ph: (212)850-6645   Fax: (212)850-6088

Michael Harkavy. 1990. Describes the nature of the job, working conditions, employment growth, qualifications, personal skills, projected salaries, and where to write for more information.

★8028★ "Aircraft Pilots" in *America's 50 Fastest Growing Jobs* (pp. 73)
JIST Works, Inc.
720 N. Park Ave.
Indianapolis, IN 46202-3431
Ph: (317)264-3720   Fax: (317)264-3709
Fr: 800-648-5478

Michael J. Farr, compiler. 1994. Describes the 50 fastest growing jobs within major career clusters such as technicians, and marketing and sales. Each job profile explains the nature of the work, skills and abilities required, employment outlook, average earnings, related occupations, education and training requirements, and employment opportunities. Also contains career planning information and job search tips.

★8029★ "Aircraft Pilots" in *Occupational Outlook Handbook*
U.S. Government Printing Office
Superintendent of Documents
Washington, DC 20402
Ph: (202)512-1800   Fax: (202)512-2250

Biennial, 1992-1993. This encyclopedia of careers describes in detail 250 occupations—comprising about 85 percent of all jobs in the economy. Occupations that require lengthy education or training are given the most attention. For each occupation, the handbook covers job duties, working conditions, training, educational preparation, personal qualities, advancement possibilities, job outlook, earnings, and sources of additional information.

★8030★ *Airline Pilot*
Arco Publishing Co.
Macmillan General Reference
15 Columbus Cir.
New York, NY 10023
Fax: 800-835-3202   Fr: 800-858-7674

Edited by the Future Aviation Professionals of America (FAPA). 1990. Professional guide for aspiring pilots. Covers job qualifications, requirements, application procedures, and training programs.

★8031★ *Airline Pilot Career Information*
Air Line Pilots Association
1625 Massachusetts Ave., NW
Washington, DC 20036
Ph: (703)689-2270   Fax: (202)797-4052

This 19 page booklet describes the career path of a pilot, and explains personal, educa-

tional and training qualifications. Surveys four types of licensure including age, and physical and training requirements.

★8032★ "Airline Pilot" in *Opportunities in Aerospace Careers* (pp. 10-15)
National Textbook Co. (NTC)
VGM Career Books
4255 W. Touhy Ave.
Lincolnwood, IL 60646-1975
Ph: (708)679-5500   Fax: (708)679-2494
Fr: 800-323-4900

Maples R. Wallace, author. 1991. Surveys jobs with the airlines, airports, the government, the military, in manufacturing, and in research and development. Describes educational requirements, working conditions, salaries, employment outlook, and licensure.

★8033★ "Airline Pilot" in *Top Professions: The 100 Most Popular, Dynamic, and Profitable Careers in America Today* (pp. 61-63)
Petersons Guides, Inc.
PO Box 2123
Princeton, NJ 08543-2123
Ph: (609)243-9111   Fax: (609)243-9150
Fr: 800-338-3282

1989. Includes occupations requiring a college or advanced degree. Describes job duties, earnings, typical job titles, career opportunities at different degree levels, and lists associations to write to for more information.

★8034★ *Airline Pilots, Commercial*
Chronicle Guidance Publications, Inc.
66 Aurora St.
PO Box 1190
Moravia, NY 13118-1190
Ph: (315)497-0330   Fax: (315)497-3359
Fr: 800-622-7284

1992. This career brief describes the nature of the job, working conditions, hours and earnings, education and training, licensure, certification, unions, personal qualifications, social and psychological factors, location, employment outlook, entry methods, advancement, and related occupations.

★8035★ "Airplane Pilot" in *Career Information Center* (Vol.12)
Simon and Schuster
200 Old Tappan Rd.
Old Tappan, NJ 07675
Fax: 800-445-6991   Fr: 800-223-2348
Richard Lidz and Dale Anderson, editorial directors. Fifth edition, 1993. For 600 occupations, this 13 volume set describes job duties, entry-level requirements, education and training needed, advancement possibilities, employment outlook, earnings, and benefits. Each of the first 12 volumes includes jobs related under a broad career field. Volume 13 is the index.

★8036★ "Airplane Pilot" in *Jobs Rated Almanac*
World Almanac
1 International Blvd., Ste. 444
Mahwah, NJ 07495
Ph: (201)529-6900   Fax: (201)529-6901
Les Krantz. Second edition, 1992. Ranks 250 jobs by environment, salary, outlooks, physical demands, stress, security, travel opportunities, and extra perks. Includes jobs the editor feels are the most common, most interesting, and the most rapidly growing.

★8037★ "Airplane Pilots" in *VGM's Careers Encyclopedia* (pp. 34-38)
National Textbook Co. (NTC)
VGM Career Books
4255 W. Touhy Ave.
Lincolnwood, IL 60646-1975
Ph: (708)679-5500   Fax: (708)679-2494
Fr: 800-323-4900
Third edition, 1991. Arranged alphabetically A-Z, this book contains 2-5 page descriptions of 200 managerial, professional, technical, trade, and service occupations. Each profile describes job duties, places of employment, qualifications, educational preparation, training, employment potential, advancement, income, and additional sources of information.

★8038★ *Becoming an Airline Pilot*
TAB/McGraw-Hill
Blue Ridge Summit, PA 17294-0850
Ph: (717)794-2191   Fr: 800-822-8138
Jeff Griffin. 1990.

★8039★ *Careers in Aviation*
Rosen Publishing Group
29 E. 21st St.
New York, NY 10010
Ph: (212)777-3017   Fax: (212)777-0277
Fr: 800-237-9932
Sharon Carter. 1990. Covers careers with the commercial airliners, as a crop duster, helicopter pilot, flight attendant, and air traffic controller.

★8040★ *Commercial Pilot*
Careers, Inc.
PO Box 135
Largo, FL 34649-0135
Ph: (813)584-7333
1995. Four-page brief offering the definition, history, duties, working conditions, personal qualifications, educational requirements, earnings, hours, employment outlook, advancement, and careers related to this position.

★8041★ *Corporate Pilot*
Vocational Biographies, Inc.
PO Box 31
Sauk Centre, MN 56378-0031
Ph: (612)352-6516   Fax: (612)352-5546
Fr: 800-255-0752
1992. Four-page pamphlet containing a personal narrative about a worker's job, work likes and dislikes, career path from high school to the present. Education and training, the rewards and frustrations, and the effects of the job on the rest of the worker's life. The data file portion of this pamphlet gives a concise occupational summary, including work descriptions, working conditions, places of employment, personal characteristics, education and training, job outlook, and salary range.

★8042★ *Express Freight Pilot*
Vocational Biographies, Inc.
PO Box 31
Sauk Centre, MN 56378-0031
Ph: (612)352-6516   Fax: (612)352-5546
Fr: 800-255-0752
1994. Four-page pamphlet containing a personal narrative about a worker's job, work likes and dislikes, career path from high school to the present. Education and training, the rewards and frustrations, and the effects of the job on the rest of the worker's life. The data file portion of this pamphlet gives a concise occupational summary, including work descriptions, working conditions, places of employment, personal characteristics, education and training, job outlook, and salary range.

★8043★ "Flight Instructor" in *Career Information Center* (Vol.12)
Simon and Schuster
200 Old Tappan Rd.
Old Tappan, NJ 07675
Fax: 800-445-6991   Fr: 800-223-2348
Richard Lidz and Dale Anderson, editorial directors. Fifth edition, 1993. For 600 occupations, this 13 volume set describes job duties, entry-level requirements, education and training needed, advancement possibilities, employment outlook, earnings, and benefits. Each of the first 12 volumes includes jobs related under a broad career field. Volume 13 is the index.

★8044★ "Flight Instructor" in *Complete Aviation/Aerospace Career Guide* (p. 149)
Aero Publishers, Inc.
13311 Monterey Ave.
Blue Ridge Summit, PA 17294
Ph: (717)794-2191
1989. This is a comprehensive guide to hundreds of aviation related jobs. Surveys many different types of piloting jobs including airline, helicopter, and test piloting. Provides job descriptons, training requirements, advancement opportunities and outlook. Lists FAA (Federal Aviation Administration) certified pilot shcools, four-year colleges offering aviation degrees, and aviation organizations and publications.

★8045★ "Flight Instructor" in *Opportunities in Airline Careers* (pp. 97-98)
National Textbook Co. (NTC)
VGM Career Books
4255 W. Touhy Ave.
Lincolnwood, IL 60646-1975
Ph: (708)679-5500   Fax: (708)679-2494
Fr: 800-323-4900
Adrian A. Paradis. 1987. Surveys trends in the industry and career opportunities with the airlines including management, sales, customer service, flying, and maintenance. Describes pilots' job duties, working conditions, and basic educational and training requirements.

★8046★ *Flight Instructors*
Chronicle Guidance Publications, Inc.
66 Aurora St.
PO Box 1190
Moravia, NY 13118-1190
Ph: (315)497-0330   Fax: (315)497-3359
Fr: 800-622-7284
1991. This career brief describes the nature of the job, working conditions, hours and earnings, education and training, licensure, certification, unions, personal qualifications, social and psychological factors, location, employment outlook, entry methods, advancement, and related occupations.

★8047★ *Helicopter Pilot*
Careers, Inc.
PO Box 135
Largo, FL 34649-0135
Ph: (813)584-7333
1993. Two-page occupational summary card describing duties, working conditions, personal qualifications, training, earnings and hours, employment outlook, places of employment, related careers, and where to write for more information.

★8048★ *Helicoptor Pilots*
Chronicle Guidance Publications, Inc.
66 Aurora St.
PO Box 1190
Moravia, NY 13118-1190
Ph: (315)497-0330   Fax: (315)497-3359
Fr: 800-622-7284
1994. This career brief describes the nature of the job, working conditions, hours and earnings, education and training, licensure, certification, unions, personal qualifications, social and psychological factors, location, employment outlook, entry methods, advancement, and related occupations.

★8049★ "In the Air" in *Careers in Aviation* (pp. 43-122)
Rosen Publishing Group
29 E. 21st St.
New York, NY 10010
Ph: (212)777-3017   Fax: (212)777-0277
Fr: 800-237-9932
Sharon Carter. 1990. Explores a wide variety of piloting jobs including aerial patrolling, corporate flying, flying for the media, law enforcement, and the airlines, helicopter ambulance flying, and stunt flying. Discusses being licensed, and opportunities for women. Most of the book is based on interviews with people who describe what they do on the job.

★8050★ "Instructional Flying" in
Opportunities in Aerospace Careers
(pp. 69-70)
National Textbook Co. (NTC)
VGM Career Books
4255 W. Touhy Ave.
Lincolnwood, IL 60646-1975
Ph: (708)679-5500   Fax: (708)679-2494
Fr: 800-323-4900
Wallace R. Maples, author. 1991. Surveys jobs with the airlines, airports, the government, the military, in manufacturing, and in research and development. Describes educational requirements, working conditions, salaries, employment outlook and certification.

★8051★ *Opportunities in Aerospace*
Careers
National Textbook Co. (NTC)
VGM Career Books
4255 W. Touhy Ave.
Lincolnwood, IL 60646-1975
Ph: (708)679-5500   Fax: (708)679-2494
Fr: 800-323-4900
Wallace R. Maples, author. 1991. Surveys jobs with the airlines, airports, the government, the military, in manufacturing, and in research and development. Describes educational requirements, working conditions, salaries, employment outlook, and certification.

★8052★ *Opportunities in Airline Careers*
National Textbook Co. (NTC)
VGM Career Books
4255 W. Touhy Ave.
Lincolnwood, IL 60646-1975
Ph: (708)679-5500   Fax: (708)679-2494
Fr: 800-323-4900
Adrian A. Paradis, author. 1987. Surveys trends in the industry and career opportunities with the airlines including management, customer service, flying, and maintenance. Describes pilots job duties, working conditions, and basic educational and training requirements.

★8053★ "Pilot" in *100 Best Careers for*
the Year 2000 **(pp. 239-241)**
Arco Pub.
201 W. 103rd St.
Indianapolis, IN 46290
Ph: 800-428-5331   Fax: 800-835-3202
Shelly Field. 1992. Describes 100 job opportunities expected to grow fast throughout the next decade. Provides information on job duties and responsibilities, training requirements, education, advancement opportunities, experience and qualifications, and typical salaries.

★8054★ "Pilot" in *College Board Guide*
to Jobs and Career Planning **(pp. 85)**
The College Board
415 Columbus Ave.
New York, NY 10023-6992
Ph: (212)713-8165   Fax: (212)713-8143
Fr: 800-323-7155
Joyce Slayton Mitchell, author. Second edition, 1994. Written for high school and college students, this guide includes career planning tips and information about the 90's labor market. Profiles over 100 careers in 15 fields. Each profile describes occupational experience, educational preparation needed, sala-

ries, job opportunities, related careers, and additional information sources.

★8055★ "Pilot, Commercial" in *Occu-*
Facts: Information on 580 Careers in
Outline Form
Careers, Inc.
PO Box 135
Largo, FL 34649-0135
Ph: (813)584-7333
Biennial, 1995-96 edition. Each four-page occupational profile describes duties, working conditions, physical surroundings and demands, aptitudes, temperament, educational requirements, employment outlook, earnings, and places of employment.

★8056★ "Pilot" in *Desk Guide to*
Training and Work Advisement **(p. 90)**
Charles C. Thomas, Publisher
2600 S. 1st St.
Springfield, IL 62794-9265
Ph: (217)789-8980   Fax: (217)789-9130
Fr: 800-258-8980
Gail Kuenstler. 1988. Describes alternative methods of entry into an occupation through different types of educational programs, internships, and apprenticeships.

★8057★ "Pilot, Helicopter" in *Occu-*
Facts: Information on 580 Careers in
Outline Form
Careers, Inc.
PO Box 135
Largo, FL 34649-0135
Ph: (813)584-7333
Biennial, 1995-96. Contains two-page occupational profiles describing duties, working conditions, physical surroundings and demands, aptitudes, temperament, educational requirements, employment outlook, earnings, and places of employment.

★8058★ "Pilots" in *American Almanac*
of Jobs and Salaries **(pp.391)**
Avon Books
1350 Avenue of the Americas
New York, NY 10019
Ph: (212)261-6800   Fr: 800-238-0658
John W. Wright, editor. Revised edition, 1994-95. This is a comprehensive guide to the wages of hundreds of occupations in a wide variety of industries and organizations.

★8059★ "Pilots" in *Career Discovery*
Encyclopedia **(Vol.5, pp. 48-49)**
J.G. Ferguson Publishing Co.
200 W. Madison St., Ste. 300
Chicago, IL 60606
Ph: (312)580-5480   Fax: (312)580-4948
Russell E. Primm, editor-in-chief. 1993. This six volume set contain two-page articles for 504 occupations. Each article describes job duties, earnings, and educational and training requirements. The set is arranged alphabetically by job title.

★8060★ "Pilots" in *Encyclopedia of*
Careers and Vocational Guidance
(Vol.4, pp. 109-113)
J.G. Ferguson Publishing Co.
200 W. Madison St., Ste. 300
Chicago, IL 60606
Ph: (312)580-5480   Fax: (312)580-4948
William E. Hopke, editor-in-chief. Ninth edition, 1993. This four volume set describes 74 industries and 900 occupations. The occupa-

tional profiles cover the nature of the work, educational requirements, history methods of entry, advancement, employment outlook, earnings, working conditions, social and psychological factors, and sources of further information. Volume 2 covers professional careers.

PROFESSIONAL ASSOCIATIONS

★8061★ Air Line Pilots Association
(ALPA)
1625 Massachusetts Ave. NW
Washington, DC 20036
Ph: (202)797-4600   Fax: (202)797-4052
Members: Collective bargaining agent for air line pilots. **Publications:** *Air Line Pilot: The Magazine of Professional Flight Crews*, monthly.

★8062★ Air Transport Association of
America (ATA)
1301 Pennsylvania Ave., Ste. 1100
Washington, DC 20004-7017
Ph: (202)626-4000   Fax: (202)626-4166
Members: Airlines engaged in transporting persons, goods, and mail by aircraft between fixed terminals on regular schedules. **Publications:** *Air Transport*, annual.

★8063★ American Pilots' Association
(APA)
499 S. Capital St. SW, Ste. 409
Washington, DC 20003
Ph: (202)484-0700   Fax: (202)484-9320
Members: State associations of licensed state marine pilots representing 950 members. **Purpose:** Seeks to improve pilotage services. **Publications:** *On Station*, quarterly.

★8064★ Helicopter Association
International (HAI)
1635 Prince St.
Alexandria, VA 22314-2818
Ph: (703)683-4646   Fax: (703)683-4745
Fr: 800-435-4976
Owners, operators, helicopter enthusiasts, and affiliated companies in the civil helicopter industry. Receives and disseminates information concerning the use, operation, hiring, contracting, and leasing of helicopters. Offers Helicopter Operators Management Course and continuing education courses. Provides speakers for Fly Neighborly program; compiles statistics. Maintains a collection of current helicopter service bulletins and technical data; organizes safety seminars. **Publications:** *Fly Neighborly Guide*. • *Helicopter Annual*. • *Heliport Development Guide*, biennial. • *Heliport Directory*, periodic. • *Operations and Management Guide*. • *Operations Update*, monthly. • *Preliminary Accident Reports and Technical Notes*, monthly. • *Rotor: By the Industry - For the Industry*, quarterly. • *Safety Management Reference Guide*. • *Safety Manual*. • *Visibility Unlimited*.

Standards/Certification Agencies

★8065★ Aviation Safety Institute
6797 N. High St., Ste. 316
Worthington, OH 43085
Ph: (614)885-4242
Works to promote and improve aviation safety.

★8066★ Federal Aviation Administration
800 Independence Ave., S.W.
Washington, DC 20591
Ph: (202)267-3484
Issues and enforces rules, regulations, and standards relating to the rating and certification of pilots.

★8067★ National EMS Pilots Association (NEMSPA)
5810 Hornwood
Houston, TX 77081
Ph: (713)668-6144   Fr: 800-848-7386
Developed EMS guidelines to address pilot, aircraft, and operating standards for EMS helicopter operations. Plans to offer training and professionalism certification.

Test Guides

★8068★ Commercial Pilot FAA Written Exam
Gleim Publiccations, Inc.
PO Box 12848
University Sta.
Gainesville, FL 32604
Ph: 800-874-5346
Irvin N. Gleim and Patrick R. Delaney. Fourth edition, 1992-1994.

★8069★ Commercial Pilot Test Guide: Questions, Answers & Explanations
Gleim Publications, Inc.
PO Box 12848
University Sta.
Gainesville, FL 32604
Ph: 800-874-5346
Edited by Aviation Supplies & Academics staff. 1992.

★8070★ Military Flight Aptitude Tests
Arco Publishing Co.
Macmillan General Reference
15 Columbus Cir.
New York, NY 10023
Fax: 800-835-3202   Fr: 800-858-7674
Solomon Wiener, editor. 1989. Prepares officer candidates who seek flight training as pilots, navigators, or flight officers in the Army, Navy, Air Force, Marine Corps, or Coast Guard. Covers: Army Flight Aptitude Selection Test (FAST), the Air Force Officer Qualifying Test (AFOQT), and the Navy and Marine Corps Aviation Selection Battery.

Educational Directories and Programs

★8071★ Aircraft Schools Directory
American Business Directories, Inc.
5711 S. 86th Circle
Omaha, NE 68127
Ph: (402)593-4600   Fax: (402)331-1505
Annual. Number of listings: 2,458. Entries include: Name, address, phone (including area code), size of advertisement, year first in "Yellow Pages," name of owner or manager, number of employees. Compiled from telephone company "Yellow Pages," nationwide. Arrangement: Geographical.

★8072★ Travel and Hospitality Career Directory
Gale Research Inc.
835 Penobscot Bldg.
Detroit, MI 48226-4094
Ph: (313)961-2242   Fax: (313)961-6083
Fr: 800-877-GALE
Bradley J. Morgan and Joseph M. Palmisano. Second edition, 1992. A directory in the Career Advisor Series that provides essays written by industry professionals; job search information on resume and cover letter preparation, networking, and the interviewing process; approximately 300 companies and organizations offering job opportunities and internships, and additional job-hunting resources.

Awards, Scholarships, Grants, and Fellowships

★8073★ Agrinaut Award
National Agricultural Aviation Association
1005 E St. SE
Washington, DC 20003
Ph: (202)546-5722   Fax: (202)546-5726
To recognize the agricultural aircraft operator or operating organization that has made public an outstanding contribution in the field of agricultural aircraft operations. The recipient of the award must have been actively engaged in commercial agricultural applications with an agricultural aircraft and the achievement cited must have contributed to the state-of-the-art for the benefit of the agricultural aircraft industry as a whole. A freestanding cup inscribed with the award winner's achievements is awarded annually. Established in 1967 by Agrinautics of Las Vegas, Nevada, and by the NAAA under procedures established for noting new operating techniques, new and novel equipment, new successful crop applications, or other contributions.

★8074★ Frederick L. Feinberg Award
American Helicopter Society
217 N. Washington St.
Alexandria, VA 22314-2538
Ph: (703)684-6777   Fax: (703)739-9279
To recognize the helicopter pilot who accomplished the most outstanding achievement during the preceding year. Military or civilian pilots are eligible. A monetary award of $200 and a certificate are awarded annually. Established in 1959 by the Kaman Aerospace Corporation in memory of Frederick L. Feinberg, an outstanding helicopter test pilot.

★8075★ John Robert Horne Memorial Award
National Agricultural Aviation Association
1005 E St. SE
Washington, DC 20003
Ph: (202)546-5722   Fax: (202)546-5726
To recognize a pilot with five years or less experience in the agricultural aviation industry who has an exemplary safety record and/or has contributed to safety in agricultural aviation. A wall plaque inscribed with the recipient's name and year is awarded annually. Established in 1980 by John and Jewell Horne in memory of their son, John Robert Horne.

★8076★ Iven C. Kincheloe Award
Society of Experimental Test Pilots
PO Box 986
Lancaster, CA 93534
Ph: (805)942-9574   Fax: (805)940-0398
To recognize outstanding professional accomplishment in the conduct of flight testing. Members of the Society are eligible. A trophy is awarded annually. Established in 1958.

★8077★ MBB Golden Hour Award
Helicopter Association International
1619 Duke St.
Alexandria, VA 22314-3406
Ph: (703)683-4646   Fax: (703)683-4745
To recognize an emergency medical services (EMS) helicopter pilot who has most distinguished himself by performing above and beyond the already high EMS standards, and who has made an outstanding contribution to a specific emergency, thereby advancing the helicopter in lifesaving operations. Awarded annually. Established in 1982.

★8078★ Doris Muellen Whirly-Girls Scholarship
Whirly-Girls
c/o Charollete Kelley
Executive Towers 10-D
207 W. Clarendon
Phoenix, AZ 85013
Ph: (602)263-0190
To assist a financially deserving woman to further her career in the helicopter industry through add-on ratings to her helicopter license. Members of the Whirly-Girls who show financial need and commitment to aviation are eligible. A scholarship of $4,500 is awarded annually. Established in 1967 in memory of Doris Muellen, No. 84, who was fatally injured in an airplane accident in 1967. Doris personified the high standards and ideals of women in aviation.

★8079★ National Aviation Hall of Fame Award
National Aviation Hall of Fame
One Chamber Plaza
Dayton, OH 45402
Ph: (513)226-0800   Fax: (513)226-8294
To honor aviation leaders, pilots, teachers, scientists, engineers, inventors, governmental leaders, and other individuals who have helped to make the United States great by their outstanding contributions to aviation.

Nominees must be United States citizens or residents. No persons shall be honored for achievement attained less than five years prior to election to the National Aviation Hall of Fame enshrinement. A plaque with a statement of the recipient's accomplishments is hung in the National Aviation Hall of Fame. Four to eight individuals are inducted annually. Established in 1962.

★8080★ Ninety-Nines NIFA Achievement Award
Ninety-Nines
International Women Pilots Association
PO Box 59965
Will Rogers World Airport
Oklahoma City, OK 73159
Ph: (405)685-7969   Fax: (405)685-7985

To encourage active participation by women in aviation. Female university students in good standing who have Private Pilot Certificates are eligible. The following prizes are awarded: first place - a monetary prize of $200 and the Gold Amelia Earhart Medal; second place - $150 and the Silver Amelia Earhart Medal; and third place - $100 and the Bronze Amelia Earhart Medal. In addition, the Top Female Pilot award is presented. Awarded annually. Established in the late 1940s.

★8081★ Pilot of the Year
Seaplane Pilots Association
421 Aviation Way
Frederick, MD 21701
Ph: (301)695-2083

To recognize an individual whose promotion and support of seaplane flying has been outstanding. Nominations may be submitted by July. A plaque is awarded annually. Established in 1983.

★8082★ Pilot of the Year Award
Helicopter Association International
1619 Duke St.
Alexandria, VA 22314-3406
Ph: (703)683-4646   Fax: (703)683-4745

To recognize an outstanding single feat performed by a helicopter pilot during the year, or extraordinary professionalism over a period of time. Nominees must be active civilian pilots. An engraved plaque is awarded annually. Established in 1960 by Stanley Hiller, Junior, then president of Hiller Aircraft Corporation.

★8083★ Igor I. Sikorsky Award for Humanitarian Service
Helicopter Association International
1619 Duke St.
Alexandria, VA 22314-3406
Ph: (703)683-4646   Fax: (703)683-4745

To recognize the individual(s) who best demonstrates the value of civil rotorcraft to society and their operators through the saving of life, protection of property, and amelioration of distress. Established in 1989 to honor Igor I. Sikorsky, founder of Sikorsky Aircraft.

BASIC REFERENCE GUIDES AND HANDBOOKS

★8084★ Aviator's Guide to Flight Planning
TAB Books
PO Box 40
Blue Ridge Summit, PA 17294-0850
Ph: (717)794-2191   Fr: 800-822-8138
Donald J. Clausing. 1995. Includes illustrations.

★8085★ OAG Desktop Guide
Official Airline Guides
2000 Clearwater Dr.
Oak Brook, IL 60521
Ph: (708)574-6000   Fax: (708)574-6565
North American edition. Two issues/month. Guide containing schedules of airlines operating within North America and the Caribbean areas. Published as a service for airlines, travel agents, and volume users of air transportation.

★8086★ The Official Airline Career Handbook
Market Plus Inc.
PO Box 2255
Silverthorne, CO 80498
Ron Hooson. 25th edition, 1995. Offers job descriptions and requirements, salaries information, and application and interview procedures. Also provides a list of national, regional, and charter airlines.

★8087★ Pilot's Handbook of Aeronautical Knowledge
TAB Books
PO Box 40
Blue Ridge Summit, PA 17294-0850
Ph: (717)794-2191   Fr: 800-822-8138
Paul E. Illman. Revised edition, 1990. Includes illustrations.

★8088★ The Student Pilot's Flight Manual
Iowa State University Press
2121 S. State Ave.
Ames, IA 50010
Ph: (515)292-0140   Fax: (515)292-3348
William K. Kershner. Seventh edition, 1993. Includes illustrations.

PROFESSIONAL AND TRADE PERIODICALS

★8089★ Air Line Pilot
Air Line Pilots Assn.
535 Herndon Pkwy.
PO Box 1169
Herndon, VA 22070
Ph: (703)689-4176   Fax: (703)689-4370
Esperison Martinez
Monthly. Magazine covering industry trends and developments, flight technology, and air safety.

★8090★ General Aviation News & Flyer
PO Box 39099
Tacoma, WA 98439-0099
Ph: (206)471-9888   Fax: (206)471-9911
Dave SclairPublisher
Biweekly. General aviation newspaper (tabloid) for aircraft pilots and owners.

★8091★ Journal of the American Helicopter Society
American Helicopter Society
217 N. Washington St.
Alexandria, VA 22314
Ph: (703)684-6777   Fax: (703)739-9279
Robert J. Huston
Quarterly. Technical journal on vertical flight research and developments.

★8092★ OAG Desktop Flight Guide-North American Edition
Official Airline Guides
2000 Clearwater Drive
Oak Brook, IL 60521
Ph: (708)574-6000   Fax: (708)474-6667
Richard A. NelsonPublisher
SWY. Guide containing schedules of airlines operating within North America and the Caribbean areas. Published as a service for business travelers, travel agents, and airlines.

★8093★ Private Pilot Magazine
Fancy Publications, Inc.
PO Box 6050
Mission Viejo, CA 92690
Ph: (714)855-8822   Fax: (714)855-3045
Dennis Shattuck
Monthly. Magazine covering general aviation interests.

★8094★ Professional Pilot
Queensmith Communications Corp.
3014 Colvin St.
Alexandria, VA 22314
Ph: (703)370-0606   Fax: (703)370-7082
Murray Q. SmithPublisher
Monthly. Magazine serving pilots of corporate, charter, commuter, and major airlines.

PROFESSIONAL MEETINGS AND CONVENTIONS

★8095★ AIR - Aircraft Owners and Pilots Association Aircraft Sales, Seminars, and Trade Show
Aircraft Owners and Pilots Association
421 Aviation Way
Frederick, MD 21701
Ph: (301)695-2000
Annual.

★8096★ National Business Aircraft Association Annual Meeting and Convention
National Business Aircraft Association
1200 18th St. NW, Ste. 200
Washington, DC 20036
Ph: (202)783-9000   Fax: (202)862-5552
Annual.

OTHER SOURCES OF INFORMATION

★8097★ *Choosing an Airline Career: In-Depth Descriptions of Entry-Level Positions, Travel Benefits, How to Apply and Interview*
Capri Publishing Co.
PO Box 625 FDR Station
New York, NY 10150-0625
Ph: (212)421-3709   Fax: (212)223-2878
Fr: 800-247-6553
1992.

★8098★ "Commercial Airplane Pilot" in *Career Selector 2001*
Barron's Educational Series, Inc.
250 Wireless Blvd.
Hauppauge, NY 11788
Ph: (516)434-3311   Fax: (516)434-3723
Fr: 800-645-3476
James C. Gonyea. 1993.

★8099★ "Pilot" in *100 Best Jobs for the 1990s & Beyond*
Dearborn Financial Publishing, Inc.
520 N. Dearborn St.
Chicago, IL 60610-4354
Ph: (312)836-4400   Fax: (312)836-1021
Fr: 800-621-9621
Carol Kleiman. 1992. Describes 100 jobs ranging from accountants to veterinarians.

Each job profile includes such information as education, experience, and certification needed, salaries, and job search suggestions.

★8100★ *Pilots*
Lodestar Books
375 Hudson St.
New York, NY 10014
Ph: (212)366-2627   Fax: (212)366-2011
1992.

Air Traffic Controllers

Air traffic controllers are the guardians of the airways. They keep track of planes flying within their assigned area and make certain that they are safe distances apart. Their immediate concern is safety, but controllers also must direct planes efficiently to minimize delays. Some regulate airport traffic; others regulate flights between airports. Although airport tower or terminal controllers watch over all planes traveling through the airport's airspace, their main responsibility is to organize the flow of aircraft in and out of the airport. The **ground controller** directs the plane to the proper runway. The **local controller** then informs the pilot about conditions at the airport, such as the weather, speed and direction of wind, and visibility. **En route controllers** work in teams of up to three members, depending on how heavy traffic is; each team is responsible for a section of the center's airspace. To prepare for planes about to enter the team's airspace, the **radar associate controller** organizes flight plans coming from printing machines. The **radar controller**, who is the senior team member, observes the planes in the team's airspace on radar and communicates with the pilots when necessary. In addition to airport towers and En route centers, air traffic controllers also work in flight service stations operated at 100 locations. These controllers provide pilots with information on the station's particular area, including terrain, preflight and in-flight weather information, suggested routes, and other information important to the safety of a flight.

Salaries

A controller's pay is determined by the worker's job responsibilities and by the complexity of the facility. Earnings are higher at facilities where traffic patterns are more complex.

Beginning air traffic controllers with the FAA	$21,000/year
Average for all controllers	$47,200/year

Employment Outlook

Growth rate until the year 2005: Slower than the average.

Air Traffic Controllers

CAREER GUIDES

★8101★ Air Traffic Control: How to Become an FAA Air Traffic Controller
Random House
201 E. 50th St.
New York, NY 10022
Ph: (212)751-2600   Fr: 800-726-0600
Walter S. Luffsey. 1990.

★8102★ "Air Traffic Control" in Liberal Arts Jobs
Petersons Guides, Inc.
PO Box 2123
Princeton, NJ 08543-2123
Ph: (609)243-9111   Fax: (609)243-9150
Fr: 800-338-3282
Burton Jay Nadler. Second edition, 1989. Strives to help the liberal arts graduate identify skills for entry-level positions. Gives goal setting and job search advice.

★8103★ "Air Traffic Control" in Opportunities in Airline Careers (pp. 125-137)
National Textbook Co. (NTC)
VGM Career Books
4255 W. Touhy Ave.
Lincolnwood, IL 60646-1975
Ph: (708)679-5500   Fax: (708)679-2494
Fr: 800-323-4900
Adrian A. Paradis. 1987. Gives an overview of the airline industry including job opportunities and salaries. Describes careers in management, finance, sales, customer service and safety.

★8104★ "Air Traffic Control Specialist" in Guide to Federal Technical, Trades and Labor Jobs (p. 216)
Resource Directories
3361 Executive Pkwy., Ste. 302
Toledo, OH 43606
Ph: (419)536-5353   Fax: (419)536-7056
Fr: 800-274-8515
Rod W. Durgin, editor. Second edition, 1992. Describes where and how to apply for a federal job in air traffic control. For each job included, gives a description, salary, locations, and the agencies that hire the most employees for that job.

★8105★ Air Traffic Control Specialists
Chronicle Guidance Publications, Inc.
66 Aurora St.
PO Box 1190
Moravia, NY 13118-1190
Ph: (315)497-0330   Fax: (315)497-3359
Fr: 800-622-7284
1993. Career brief describing the nature of the job, working conditions, hours and earnings, education and training, licensure, certification, unions, personal qualifications, social and psychological factors, location, employment outlook, entry methods, advancement, and related occupations.

★8106★ Air Traffic Controller
Careers, Inc.
PO Box 135
Largo, FL 34649-0135
Ph: (813)584-7333
1992. Four-page brief offering the definition, history, duties, working conditions, personal qualifications, educational requirements, earnings, hours, employment outlook, advancement, and careers related to this position.

★8107★ "Air Traffic Controller" in Career Information Center (Vol.12)
Simon and Schuster
200 Old Tappan Rd.
Old Tappan, NJ 07675
Fax: 800-445-6991   Fr: 800-223-2348
Richard Lidz and Linda Perrin, editorial directors. Fifth edition, 1993. This 13-volume set profiles over 600 occupations. Each occupational profile describes job duties, educational requirements, how to get the job, advancement possibilities, employment outlook, working conditions, earnings and benefits, and where to write for more information.

★8108★ "Air Traffic Controller" in College Board Guide to Jobs and Career Planning (pp. 80)
The College Board
415 Columbus Ave.
New York, NY 10023-6992
Ph: (212)713-8165   Fax: (212)713-8143
Fr: 800-323-7155
Joyce S. Mitchell. Second edition, 1994. Describes the job, salaries, related careers, education needed, and where to write for more information.

★8109★ "Air Traffic Controller" in Jobs Rated Almanac
World Almanac
1 International Blvd., Ste. 444
Mahwah, NJ 07495
Ph: (201)529-6900   Fax: (201)529-6901
Les Krantz. Second edition, 1992. Ranks 250 jobs by environment, salary, outlooks, physical demands, stress, security, travel opportunities, and extra perks. Includes jobs the editor feels are the most common, most interesting, and the most rapidly growing.

★8110★ "Air Traffic Controller" in VGM's Careers Encyclopedia (pp. 41-43)
National Textbook Co. (NTC)
VGM Career Books
4255 W. Touhy Ave.
Lincolnwood, IL 60646-1975
Ph: (708)679-5500   Fax: (708)679-2494
Fr: 800-323-4900
Third edition, 1991. Describes job duties, places of employment, working conditions, qualifications, education, and training, advancement potential, and salary for each occupation.

★8111★ "Air Traffic Controllers" in 101 Careers: A Guide to the Fastest-Growing Opportunities (pp. 313-315)
John Wiley & Sons, Inc.
605 3rd Ave.
New York, NY 10158-0012
Ph: (212)850-6645   Fax: (212)850-6088
Michael Harkavy. 1990. Describes the nature of the job, working conditions, employment growth, qualifications, personal skills, projected salaries, and where to write for more information.

★8112★ "Air Traffic Controllers" in Encyclopedia of Careers and Vocational Guidance (Vol.2, pp. 57-59)
J.G. Ferguson Publishing Co.
200 W. Madison St., Ste. 300
Chicago, IL 60606
Ph: (312)580-5480   Fax: (312)580-4948
William E. Hopke, editor-in-chief. Ninth edition, 1993. Four-volume set that profiles 900 occupations and describes job trends in 74 industries. Includes career description, educational requirements, history of the job, methods of entry, advancement, employment outlook, earnings, conditions of work, social

and psychological factors, and sources of further information.

★8113★ "Air Traffic Controllers" in
Jobs! What They Are—Where They
Are—What They Pay (p. 131)
Simon & Schuster, Inc.
Simon & Schuster Bldg.
1230 Avenue of the Americas
New York, NY 10020
Ph: (212)698-7000   Fr: 800-223-2348
Robert O. Snelling and Anne M. Snelling. 3rd edition, 1992. Describes duties and responsibilities, earnings, employment opportunities, training, and qualifications.

★8114★ "Air Traffic Controllers" in
Occupational Outlook Handbook
U.S. Government Printing Office
Superintendent of Documents
Washington, DC 20402
Ph: (202)512-1800   Fax: (202)512-2250
Biennial; latest edition, 1994-95. Encyclopedia of careers describing about 250 occupations and comprising about 85 percent of all jobs in the economy. Occupations that require lengthy education or training are given the most attention. Each occupation's profile describes what the worker does on the job, working conditions, education and training requirements, advancement possibilities, job outlook, earnings, and sources of additional information.

★8115★ *Careers in Aviation*
Rosen Publishing Group
29 E. 21st St.
New York, NY 10010
Ph: (212)777-3017   Fax: (212)777-0277
Fr: 800-237-9932
Sharon Carter. 1990. Covers careers with the commercial airliners, as a crop duster, helicopter pilot, flight attendant, and air traffic controller.

PROFESSIONAL ASSOCIATIONS

★8116★ Air Traffic Control Association
(ATCA)
2300 Clarendon Blvd., Ste. 711
Arlington, VA 22201
Ph: (703)522-5717   Fax: (703)527-7251
Members: Air traffic controllers; private, commercial, and military pilots; private and business aircraft owners and operators; aircraft and electronics engineers; airlines, aircraft manufacturers, and electronic and human engineering firms interested in the establishment and maintenance of a safe and efficient air traffic control system. **Purpose:** Conducts special surveys and studies on air traffic control problems. Participates in aviation community conferences. **Publications:** *Fall Conference Proceedings*, annual. • *Journal of Air Traffic Control*, quarterly.

★8117★ National Air Traffic Controllers
Association (NATCA)
1150 17th St. NW, Ste. 201
Washington, DC 20036
Ph: (202)347-4572
Members: AFL-CIO. Represents U.S. air traffic controllers within the aviation industry and before the government. **Purpose:** Negotiates on members' behalf with the Federal Aviation Administration. Conducts educational programs; compiles statistics. Maintains speakers' bureau.

TEST GUIDES

★8118★ *Air Traffic Control Specialist*
Employment Study Guide
Aviation Book Co.
25133 Anza Dr., Unit E
Santa Clarita, CA 91355
Ph: (805)294-0101   Fax: (818)240-1196
Clark St. John. 1990.

★8119★ *Air Traffic Controller*
Arco Pub.
201 W. 103rd St.
Indianapolis, IN 46290
Ph: 800-428-5331   Fax: 800-835-3202
Dr. James E. Turner. 1994, third edition. Features a sample test with answers, information on application procedures, and job requirements.

★8120★ *Air Traffic Controller Test*
Random House, Inc.
201 E. 50th St.
New York, NY 10022
Ph: (212)751-2600
Air Traffic Control Association Staff. 1990.

★8121★ *Career Examination Series: Air*
Traffic Control Specialist
National Learning Corp.
212 Michael Dr.
Syosset, NY 11791
Ph: (516)921-8888   Fax: (516)921-8743
Fr: 800-645-6337
Jack Rudman. A study guide for professionals and trainees in the field of air traffic control. Includes a multiple-choice examination section; provides answers.

AWARDS, SCHOLARSHIPS, GRANTS, AND FELLOWSHIPS

★8122★ ATCA Industrial Award
Air Traffic Control Association
2300 Clarendon Blvd., Ste. 711
Arlington, VA 22201
Ph: (703)522-5717   Fax: (703)527-7251
To recognize an industry or group of industries for an outstanding achievement or contribution which has added to the quality, safety, or efficiency of the air traffic control system. A medallion is awarded.

★8123★ Glen A. Gilbert Memorial Award
Air Traffic Control Association
2300 Clarendon Blvd., Ste. 711
Arlington, VA 22201
Ph: (703)522-5717   Fax: (703)527-7251
To honor the outstanding long-term achievements of an individual in the field of aviation. Anyone who has demonstrated a long-term commitment to excellence in aviation from government, industry, education, or the private sector is eligible. The award is open to foreign nationals, as well as citizens of the United States. A trophy is awarded annually when merited. Established in 1986 in honor of Glen A. Gilbert, known as one of the "Fathers of Air Traffic Control," whose life personified commitment to achievement, professionalism, and excellence.

★8124★ George W. Kriskie Memorial
Award
Air Traffic Control Association
2300 Clarendon Blvd., Ste. 711
Arlington, VA 22201
Ph: (703)522-5717   Fax: (703)527-7251
To recognize an individual for an outstanding career which has added to the quality, safety, or efficiency of the air traffic control system. A medallion is awarded.

★8125★ William A. Parenteau Memorial
Award
Air Traffic Control Association
2300 Clarendon Blvd., Ste. 711
Arlington, VA 22201
Ph: (703)522-5717   Fax: (703)527-7251
To recognize an individual for an outstanding achievement or contribution during the previous year which has added to the quality, safety, or efficiency of the air traffic control system. A medallion is awarded.

★8126★ General E. R. Quesada Award
Air Traffic Control Association
2300 Clarendon Blvd., Ste. 711
Arlington, VA 22201
Ph: (703)522-5717   Fax: (703)527-7251
To recognize an individual for an outstanding achievement and contribution during the previous year as a manager in the air traffic control system. A medallion is awarded.

BASIC REFERENCE GUIDES AND HANDBOOKS

★8127★ *The Air Traffic System: A*
Commonsense Guide
Iowa State University Press
2121 S. State Ave.
Ames, IA 50010
Ph: (515)292-0140
Milovan S. Brenlove. First edition, 1987. Includes an index.

★8128★ *The Official Airline Career*
Handbook
Market Plus Inc.
PO Box 2255
Silverthorne, CO 80498
Ron Hooson. 25th edition, 1995. Offers job descriptions and requirements, salaries infor-

mation, and application and interview procedures. Also provides a list of national, regional, and charter airlines.

PROFESSIONAL AND TRADE PERIODICALS

★8129★ *ATCA Bulletin*
Air Traffic Control Association (ATCA)
2300 Clarendon Blvd., Ste. 711
Arlington, VA 22201
Ph: (703)522-5717   Fax: (703)527-7251
Carol Newmaster

Monthly. Features news of the Association, which is interested in the establishment and maintenance of a safe and efficient air traffic control system.

★8130★ *Aviation Safety Institute— Monitor*
Aviation Safety Institute
6797 N. High St., No. 316
Worthington, OH 43085-2533
Ph: (614)885-4242   Fax: (614)885-5891
Mike Overly

Monthly. Concerned with all aspects of aviation safety, civil and military: air traffic control, airframe and powerplants, avionics, human factors, weather, accident prevention and investigation, and hazard reports. Recurring features include summaries of recent hazards reported and a listing of a toll-free hazard number.

PROFESSIONAL MEETINGS AND CONVENTIONS

★8131★ **Air Traffic Control Association Convention**
Air Traffic Control Association
2300 Clarendon Blvd., Ste. 711
Arlington, VA 22201
Ph: (703)522-5717   Fax: (703)527-7251
Annual.

OTHER SOURCES OF INFORMATION

★8132★ **"Air-Traffic Control Specialist"** in *Career Selector 2001*
Barron's Educational Series, Inc.
250 Wireless Blvd.
Hauppauge, NY 11788
Ph: (516)434-3311   Fax: (516)434-3723
Fr: 800-645-3476

James C. Gonyea. 1993.

★8133★ *Vectors to Spare: The Life of an Air Traffic Controller*
Iowa State University Press
2121 S. State Ave.
Ames, IA 50010
Ph: (515)292-0140   Fax: (515)292-3348

1993.

Broadcast Technicians

Broadcast technicians install, test, repair, set up, and operate the electronic equipment used to record and transmit radio and television programs. They work with television cameras, microphones, tape recorders, light and sound effects, transmitters, antennas, and other equipment. The terms "operator," "engineer," and "technician" often are used interchangeably to describe these jobs. **Transmitter operators** monitor and log outgoing signals and operate transmitters. **Maintenance technicians** set up, adjust, service, and repair electronic broadcasting equipment. **Audio control engineers** regulate sound pickup, transmission, and switching, and **video control engineers** regulate the quality, brightness, and contrast of television pictures. **Recording engineers** operate and maintain video and sound recording equipment. Technicians operate equipment designed to produce special effects, such as the illusions of a bolt of lightning or a police siren. **Field technicians** set up and operate broadcasting equipment outside the studio. **Chief engineers**, **transmission engineers**, and **broadcast field supervisors** supervise the technicians who operate and maintain broadcasting equipment. Technicians in the motion picture industry are called **sound mixers** or rerecording mixers.

Salaries

Television stations usually pay higher salaries than radio stations; commercial broadcasting usually pays more than educational broadcasting; and stations in large markets pay more than those in small ones.

Broadcast technicians, radio	$22,725/year
Chief broadcast technicians, radio	$26,140/year
Operator technician, television	$22,136/year
Technical director, television	$24,705/year
Maintenance technician	$28,280/year
Chief engineer, television	$47,741/year

Employment Outlook

Growth rate until the year 2005: More slowly than the average.

Broadcast Technicians

★8134★ "Audio Engineering" in *TV Careers Behind the Screen* (pp. 43, 44-45, 54-55)
John Wiley and Sons, Inc.
605 3rd Ave.
New York, NY 10158-0012
Ph: (212)850-6000   Fax: (212)850-6088
Fr: 800-526-5368

Jane Blanksteen and Ovi Odeni. 1987. Describes the organization of the television broadcasting industry. Explains the role each job plays in television production, career paths, education, and training. Includes job-hunting tips and information on trends in the industry.

★8135★ "Broadcast Engineering" in *Desk Guide to Training and Work Advisement* (pp. 87-88)
Charles C. Thomas, Publisher
2600 S. 1st St.
Springfield, IL 62794-9265
Ph: (217)789-8980   Fax: (217)789-9130
Fr: 800-258-8980

Gail Baugher Keunstler. 1988. Describes alternative methods of gaining entry into an occupation through different types of educational programs, internships, and apprenticeships.

★8136★ *Broadcast Technician*
Careers, Inc.
PO Box 135
Largo, FL 34649-0135
Ph: (813)584-7333

1991. Two-page occupational summary card describing duties, working conditions, personal qualifications, training, earnings and hours, employment outlook, places of employment, related careers, and where to write for more information.

★8137★ "Broadcast Technician" in *Exploring Nontraditional Jobs for Women*
Rosen Publishing Group
29 E. 21st St.
New York, NY 10010
Ph: (212)777-3017   Fax: (212)777-0277
Fr: 800-237-9932

Rose Neufeld. 1989. Describes occupations where few women are found. Covers job duties, training routes, where to apply for jobs, tools used, salary, and advantages and disadvantages of the job.

★8138★ "Broadcast Technician" in *Jobs Rated Almanac*
World Almanac
1 International Blvd., Ste. 444
Mahwah, NJ 07495
Ph: (201)529-6900   Fax: (201)529-6901

Les Krantz. Second edition, 1992. Ranks 250 jobs by environment, salary, outlooks, physical demands, stress, security, travel opportunities, and extra perks. Includes jobs the editor feels are the most common, most interesting, and the most rapidly growing.

★8139★ "Broadcast Technician" in *VGM's Careers Encyclopedia* (pp. 66-68)
National Textbook Co. (NTC)
VGM Career Books
4255 W. Touhy Ave.
Lincolnwood, IL 60646-1975
Ph: (708)679-5500   Fax: (708)679-2494
Fr: 800-323-4900

Third edition, 1991. Profiles 200 occupations. Describes job duties, places of employment, working conditions, qualifications, education and training, advancement potential, and salary for each occupation.

★8140★ "Broadcast Technicians" in *101 Careers: A Guide to the Fastest-Growing Opportunities* (pp. 278-280)
John Wiley & Sons, Inc.
605 3rd Ave.
New York, NY 10158-0012
Ph: (212)850-6645   Fax: (212)850-6088

Michael Harkavy. 1990. Describes the nature of the job, working conditions, employment growth, qualifications, personal skills, projected salaries, and where to write for more information.

★8141★ "Broadcast Technicians" in *Career Information Center* (Vol.3)
Simon and Schuster
200 Old Tappan Rd.
Old Tappan, NJ 07675
Fax: 800-445-6991   Fr: 800-223-2348

Richard Lidz and Linda Perrin, editorial directors. Fifth edition, 1993. A multi-volume set that profiles more than 600 occupations. Each occupational profile describes job duties, educational requirements, getting a job, advancement possibilities, employment outlook, working conditions, earnings and benefits, and sources of additional information.

★8142★ "Broadcast Technicians" in *Jobs! What They Are—Where They Are—What They Pay* (pp. 36)
Fireside
Simon & Schuster Bldg.
1230 Avenue of the Americas
New York, NY 10020
Ph: (212)698-7000   Fr: 800-223-2348

Robert O. Snelling and Anne M. Snelling. Revised and updated, 1992. Describes duties and responsibilities, earnings, employment opportunities, training, and qualifications.

★8143★ "Broadcast Technicians" in *Occupational Outlook Handbook*
U.S. Government Printing Office
Superintendent of Documents
Washington, DC 20402
Ph: (202)512-1800   Fax: (202)512-2250

Biennial; latest edition, 1994-95. Encyclopedia of careers describing about 250 occupations and comprising about 85 percent of all jobs in the economy. Occupations that require lengthy education or training are given the most attention. Each occupation's profile describes what the worker does on the job, working conditions, education and training requirements, advancement possibilities, job outlook, earnings, and sources of additional information.

★8144★ "Broadcasting Technology" in Career Connection for Technical Education (pp. 32-33)
JIST Works, Inc.
720 N. Park Ave.
Indianapolis, IN 46202-3431
Ph: (317)264-3720   Fax: (317)264-3709
Fred A. Rowe. 1994, second edition. Describes in detail technical occupations. Includes information on recommended high school courses, course requirements, related careers, and a self-assessment guide.

★8145★ Career Opportunities in the Music Industry
Facts on File
460 Park Ave. S.
New York, NY 10016-7382
Ph: (212)683-2244   Fax: 800-678-3633
Fr: 800-322-8755
Shelly Field. 1990. Discusses approximately 80 jobs in music, including the performing arts, business, and education. Each job description provides basic career information, salary, employment prospects, advancement opportunities, education, training, and experience required.

★8146★ Career Opportunities in Television, Cable and Video
Facts on File
460 Park Ave. S.
New York, NY 10016-7382
Ph: (212)683-2244   Fax: 800-678-3633
Fr: 800-322-8755
Maxine K. Reed and Robert M. Reed. Third edition, 1993. Includes information on employment and advancement prospects, education, experience and skills requiresn salary range, and tips for entry into the field.

★8147★ Careers in Radio
National Association of Broadcasters
1771 N St., NW
Washington, DC 20036
Ph: (202)429-5376   Fr: 800-368-5644
Revised by Kathy Checkley and produced in cooperation with member radio stations of the National Association of Broadcasters. 1991. Describes various careers in radio broadcasting including educational requirements and job-related experience needed.

★8148★ Opportunities in Broadcasting
National Textbook Co. (NTC)
VGM Career Books
4255 W. Touhy Ave.
Lincolnwood, IL 60646-1975
Ph: (708)679-5500   Fax: (708)679-2494
Fr: 800-323-4900
Elmo Israel Ellis. 1992. Describes the history and future of radio, television, and cable TV broadcasting. Includes information on working conditions and educational requirements.

★8149★ "Radio Engineering" in Opportunities in Broadcasting (pp. 67-86)
National Textbook Co. (NTC)
VGM Career Books
4255 W. Touhy Ave.
Lincolnwood, IL 60646-1975
Ph: (708)679-5500   Fax: (708)679-2494
Fr: 800-323-4900
Elmo Israel Ellis. 1992. Describes the history and future of radio, television, and cable TV

broadcasting. Includes information on working conditions and education requirements.

★8150★ Radio and Television Broadcasting Workers
Chronicle Guidance Publications, Inc.
66 Aurora St.
PO Box 1190
Moravia, NY 13118-1190
Ph: (315)497-0330   Fax: (315)497-3359
Fr: 800-622-7284
1992. Occupational brief describing the nature of the job, working conditions, hours and earnings, education and training, licensure, certification, unions, personal qualifications, social and psychological factors, location, employment outlook, entry methods, advancement, and related occupations.

★8151★ "Recording Engineer" in Career Opportunities in the Music Industry (pp. 51-54)
Facts on File
460 Park Ave. S.
New York, NY 10016-7382
Ph: (212)683-2244   Fax: 800-678-3633
Fr: 800-322-8755
Shelly Field. 1990. Discusses approximately 80 jobs in music including the performing arts, business, and education. Each job description provides basic career information, salary, employment prospects, advancement opportunities, education, training, and experience required.

★8152★ "Recording Engineer" in Jobs! What They Are—Where They Are—What They Pay! (p. 272)
Simon & Schuster, Inc.
Simon & Schuster Bldg.
1230 Avenue of the Americas
New York, NY 10020
Ph: (212)698-7000   Fr: 800-223-2348
Robert O. Snelling and Anne M. Snelling. Third revised edition, 1992. Includes a chapter titled "Broadcast Technicians". Describes duties and responsibilities, earnings, employment opportunities, training, and qualifications.

★8153★ "Sound Technician" and "Resident Sound Technician" in Career Opportunities in the Music Industry (pp. 81-82, 183-184)
Facts on File
460 Park Ave. S.
New York, NY 10016-7382
Ph: (212)683-2244   Fax: 800-678-3633
Fr: 800-322-8755
Shelly Field. 1990. Discusses approximately 80 jobs in music including the performing arts, business, and education. Each job description provides basic career information, salary, employment prospects, advancement opportunities, education, training, and experience required.

PROFESSIONAL ASSOCIATIONS

★8154★ American-Hispanic Owned Radio Association
1400 Central SE Ste. 2300
Albuquerque, NM 87106
Ph: (505)243-1744   Fax: (505)842-1990
Members: Hispanic broadcasters. **Purpose:** Promotes American-Hispanic owned radio stations. Conducts research and educational programs. Lobbies issues concerning the broadcasting industry. **Publications:** Hispanic Broadcasters, periodic.

★8155★ Broadcast Education Association (BEA)
1771 N St. NW
Washington, DC 20036-2891
Ph: (202)429-5355
Members: Universities and colleges; faculty and students; radio and television stations that belong to the National Association of Broadcasters. **Purpose:** Promotes improvement of curriculum and teaching methods, broadcasting research, television and radio production, and programming teaching. Offers placement services. **Publications:** Feedback, quarterly. • Journal of Broadcasting and Electronic Media, quarterly.

★8156★ Indigenous Communications Association (ICA)
948 Sage St.
Grants, NM 87020
Ph: (505)775-3215
Members: Radio stations in the continental U.S. and Canada, mainly located on Indian reservations. **Purpose:** Provides development, advocacy, and technical support to member stations, including: financial resource development and management; advocacy and communications that promote station stability and growth; station staff development and training; international, national, and regional program production and dissemination; cross-cultural programming. Conducts fundraising.

★8157★ National Association Broadcast Employees and Technicians (NABET)
501 3rd St. NW, 8th Fl.
Washington, DC 20001
Ph: (202)434-1254   Fax: (202)434-1426
Members: AFL-CIO. **Publications:** NABET News, bimonthly.

★8158★ National Association of Broadcasters (NAB)
1771 N St. NW
Washington, DC 20036
Ph: (202)429-5300   Fax: (202)429-5343
Members: Representatives of radio and television stations and networks; associate members include producers of equipment and programs. **Purpose:** Seeks to ensure the viability, strength, and success of free, over-the-air broadcasters; serves as an information resource to the industry. Monitors and reports on events regarding radio and television broadcasting. Maintains Broadcasting Hall of Fame. Offers minority placement service and employment clearinghouse. **Publications:** Broadcast Engineering Con-

ference Proceedings, annual. • *Member Services Catalog*, annual. • *RadioWeek*, weekly. • *TV Today*, weekly.

★8159★ **National Broadcast Association for Community Affairs**
1200 19th St. NW, Ste. 300
Washington, DC 20036
Ph: (202)857-1155
Professionals from radio and television industries seeking to promote public affairs programming and improve community relations. Offers educational programs. **Publications:** *NBACA News*, quarterly.

★8160★ **National Cable Television Association (NCTA)**
1724 Massachusetts Ave. NW
Washington, DC 20036
Ph: (202)775-3550   Fax: (202)775-3695
Members: Franchised cable operators, programmers, and cable networks; associate members are cable hardware suppliers and distributors; affiliate members are brokerage and law firms and financial institutions; state and regional cable television associations cooperate, but are not affiliated, with NCTA. **Purpose:** Serves as national medium for exchange of experiences and opinions through research, study, discussion, and publications. Represents the cable industry before Congress, the Federal Communications Commission, and various courts on issues of primary importance. Conducts research program in conjunction with National Academy of Cable Programming. Sponsors, in conjunction with Motion Picture Association of America, the Coalition Opposing Signal Theft, an organization designed to deter cable signal theft and to develop antipiracy materials. Provides promotional aids and information on legal, legislative, and regulatory matters. Compiles statistics. **Publications:** *Cable Primer.* • *Careers in Cable.* • *FCC Cable Rules.* • *Linking Up*, quarterly. • *National Cable Television Association—Producer's Sourcebook: A Guide to Cable TV Program Buyers*, annual. • *TechLine.*

★8161★ **Society of Broadcast Engineers (SBE)**
8445 Keystone Crossing, Ste. 140
Indianapolis, IN 46240
Ph: (317)253-1640   Fax: (317)253-0418
Members: Broadcast engineers, students, and broadcast professionals in closely allied fields. **Purpose:** Promotes professional abilities of members and provides information exchange. Provides support to local chapters. Maintains certification program; represents members' interests before the Federal Communications Commission and other governmental and industrial groups. **Publications:** *SBE Signal*, quarterly. • *Short Circuits.*

★8162★ **Television Operators Caucus (TOC)**
c/o Mary Jo Manning
901 31st St. NW
Washington, DC 20007-4423
Ph: (202)944-5109   Fax: (202)333-1638
Members: Participants are executive officers in charge of operating full-service television stations in the U.S. that are not owned by the national networks. **Purpose:** Provides forum for the definition and discussion of public policy regulatory and other issues faced by

members. Conducts activities on behalf of members.

STANDARDS/CERTIFICATION AGENCIES

★8163★ **Society of Broadcast Engineers (SBE)**
8445 Keystone Crossing, Ste. 140
Indianapolis, IN 46240
Ph: (317)253-1640   Fax: (317)253-0418
Maintains certification program; represents members' interests before the Federal Communications Commission and other governmental and industrial groups.

TEST GUIDES

★8164★ *Career Examination Series: Radio Broadcast Technician*
National Learning Corp.
212 Michael Dr.
Syosset, NY 11791
Ph: (516)921-8888   Fax: (516)921-8743
Fr: 800-645-6337
Jack Rudman. 1993. Test guide including questions and answers for students or professionals in the field who seek advancement through examination.

★8165★ *Career Examination Series: Radio Technologist*
National Learning Corp.
212 Michael Dr.
Syosset, NY 11791
Ph: (516)921-8888   Fax: (516)921-8743
Fr: 800-645-6337
Jack Rudman. A series of study guides with multiple-choice examination questions and solutions for trainees and professional broadcast technicians. Titles in the series include *Audio-Visual Technician; Radio Broadcast Technician; Radio and Television Engineer; Radio and Television Technician; Senior Audio-Visual Aid Technician.*

AWARDS, SCHOLARSHIPS, GRANTS, AND FELLOWSHIPS

★8166★ **Gold Medal Award**
Audio Engineering Society
60 E. 42nd St., Rm. 2520
New York, NY 10165
Ph: (212)661-8528
For recognition of outstanding achievements, sustained over a period of years, in the field of audio engineering. Awarded annually. Established in memory of John H. Potts by his widow in 1949.

★8167★ **RTNDF Undergraduate Scholarships**
Radio and Television News Directors Foundation (RTNDF)
1000 Connecticut Ave., NW, Ste. 615
Washington, DC 20036
Ph: (202)659-6910   Fax: (202)223-4007
Qualifications: Any sophomore or more advanced undergraduate or graduate student whose career objective is broadcast or cable news and who has declared a major in electronic journalism may apply. All recipients must have at least one full year of school remaining. Previous winners are not eligible. Funds available: One $2,000 and 11 $1,000 scholarships are awarded. Application details: Applications may be obtained from the applicant's faculty advisor, dean's office, or from the Foundation. Entries must include a completed application form, three to five examples of reporting or producing skills, a statement explaining why the applicant seeks a career in broadcast or cable journalism, and a letter of endorsement from applicant's faculty sponsor that includes a description of available facilities for electronic news production. Deadline: March 15.

★8168★ **Abe Schechter Graduate Scholarship**
Radio and Television News Directors Foundation (RTNDF)
1000 Connecticut Ave., NW, Ste. 615
Washington, DC 20036
Ph: (202)659-6910   Fax: (202)223-4007
Qualifications: Any continuing or incoming graduate student whose career objective is broadcast or cable news or electronic journalism research or teaching may apply. Applicants must have at least one full year of school remaining. Funds available: $1,000 for one year of study. Application details: Applications may be obtained from faculty advisors, dean's offices, or from the RTNDF. Deadline: March 15.

★8169★ **Silver Medal Award**
Audio Engineering Society
60 E. 42nd St., Rm. 2520
New York, NY 10165
Ph: (212)661-8528
For recognition of a single outstanding development or achievement in the field of audio engineering. Awarded annually. Established by the Berliner family in 1953. The award now honors the audio pioneers Alexander Graham Bell, Emile Berliner, and Thomas A. Edison.

★8170★ **Carole Simpson Scholarship**
Radio and Television News Directors Foundation (RTNDF)
1000 Connecticut Ave., NW, Ste. 615
Washington, DC 20036
Ph: (202)659-6910   Fax: (202)223-4007
Qualifications: Applicants may be any sophomore or more advance undergraduate or graduate minority student whose career objectives are broadcast or cable news, and who have declared a major in electronic journalism at an accredited or nationally recognized college or university. Applicants must have at least one full year of school remaining. Funds available: $2,000 for one year of study. Application details: Applications may be obtained from faculty advisors, dean's of-

fices, or from the Foundation. Deadline: March 15.

BASIC REFERENCE GUIDES AND HANDBOOKS

★8171★ Careers in Television
National Association of Broadcasters
1771 N St., NW
Washington, DC 20036-2898
Ph: (202)429-5376
Rich Adams and Dwight Ellis. 1991. Describes various jobs in television broadcasting, including educational requirements and job-related experience needed.

PROFESSIONAL AND TRADE PERIODICALS

★8172★ Broadcast Engineering
Intertec Publishing Corp.
9800 Metcalf
Overland Park, KS 66212-2215
Ph: (913)341-1300   Fax: (913)967-1898
Brad Dick
Magazine on radio and television broadcast equipment, products & technology.

★8173★ SMPTE Journal
Society of Motion Picture and Television
  Engineers
595 W. Hartsdale Ave.
White Plains, NY 10607
Ph: (914)761-1100   Fax: (914)761-3115
Jeffrey B. Friedman

Monthly. Journal containing articles pertaining to new developments in motion-picture and television technology; standards and recommended practices; general news of the industry.

★8174★ Television Digest
Warren Publishing, Inc.
2115 Ward Ct. NW
Washington, DC 20037
Ph: (202)872-9200   Fax: (202)393-3435
Albert Warren

Weekly. Monitors trends in the television broadcasting and cable industries and in consumer electronics equipment manufacturing and distribution. Reports on networks, stations, ratings, advertising, federal agencies, programming, technology, foreign developments, finance, and related subjects. Recurring features include a column on people in the industry. Consumer Electronics appears as a part of this newsletter.

PROFESSIONAL MEETINGS AND CONVENTIONS

★8175★ Society of Motion Picture and Television Engineers Convention
Society of Motion Picture and Television
  Engineers
595 W. Hartsdale Ave.
White Plains, NY 10607
Ph: (914)761-1100   Fax: (914)761-3115
Annual. **Dates and Locations:** 1995 Oct.

OTHER SOURCES OF INFORMATION

★8176★ Making it in Broadcasting: An Insider's Guide to Career Opportunities
Macmillian Publishing Co., Inc.
866 3rd Ave.
New York, NY 10022
Ph: (202)702-2000   Fr: 800-257-5755
1994.

Computer Programmers

Computer programmers write, update, and maintain the detailed instructions (called programs or software) that list in a logical order the steps the machine must follow. Programmers write specific programs by breaking down each step into a logical series of instructions the computer can follow. Programmers often are grouped into two broad types: Applications programmers and systems programmers. **Applications programmers** usually are oriented toward business, engineering, or science. They write software to handle specific jobs, such as a program used in an inventory control system or one to guide a missile after it has been fired. **Systems programmers**, on the other hand, maintain the software that controls the operation of the entire computer system.

Salaries

On the average systems programmers earn more than applications programmers. Earnings for programmers are as follows:

Lowest 10 percent	Less than $19,700/year
Median	$35,600/year
Top 10 percent	More than $58,000/year
Starting salary, programmers, Federal government	$18,300/year

Employment Outlook

Growth rate until the year 2005: Faster than the average.

Computer Programmers

CAREER GUIDES

★8177★ Applications and Systems Programmers
Chronicle Guidance Publications, Inc.
66 Aurora St.
PO Box 1190
Moravia, NY 13118-1190
Ph: (315)497-0330   Fax: (315)497-3359
Fr: 800-622-7284
1992. Career brief describing the nature of the job, working conditions, hours and earnings, education and training, licensure, certification, unions, personal qualifications, social and psychological factors, location, employment outlook, entry methods, advancement, and related occupations.

★8178★ Career Choices for the 90's for Students of Computer Science
Walker and Co.
435 Hudson St.
New York, NY 10014
Ph: (212)727-8300   Fax: (212)727-0984
Fr: 800-289-2553
1990. Offers alternatives for students of computer science. Gives information about the job outlook and competition for entry-level candidates. Provides job-hunting tips.

★8179★ Careers for Computer Buffs and Other Technological Types
National Textbook Co. (NTC)
VGM Career Books
4255 W. Touhy Ave.
Lincolnwood, IL 60646-1975
Ph: (708)679-5500   Fax: (708)679-2494
Fr: 800-323-4900
Marjorie Eberts and Margaret Gisler, editors. 1993. Career manual for those interested in computers and other technological fields.

★8180★ "Computer Careers" in Best Jobs for the 1990s and Into the 21st Century
Impact Publications
9104-N Manassas Dr.
Manassas Park, VA 22111
Ph: (703)361-7300   Fax: (703)335-9486
Ronald L. Krannich and Caryl Rae Krannich. 1993. Includes information on computer pro-

grammers, systems analysts, and operations research analysts.

★8181★ "The Computer Industry" in Encyclopedia of Career Choices for the 1990s: A Guide to Entry Level Jobs (pp. 152-173)
Berkley Pub.
PO Box 506
East Rutherford, NJ 07073
Fax: (201)933-2316   Fr: 800-788-6262
1992. Describes entry-level careers in a variety of industries. Presents qualifications required, working conditions, salary, internships, and professional associations.

★8182★ "Computer and Information Services" in Where the Jobs Are: The Hottest Careers for the 90s (pp. 77-96)
Career Press
180 5th Ave.
Hawthorne, NJ 07507
Ph: (201)427-0229   Fax: (201)427-2037
Fr: 800-CAREER-1
Joyce Hadley. 1995. Offers a job-hunting strategy for the 1990s as well as descriptions of growing careers of the decade. Each profile includes general information, forecasts, growth, education and training, licensing requirements, and salary information.

★8183★ "Computer Programers" in Encyclopedia of Careers and Vocational Guidance (Vol.2, pp. 360-362)
J.G. Ferguson Publishing Co.
200 W. Madison St., Ste. 300
Chicago, IL 60606
Ph: (312)580-5480   Fax: (312)580-4948
William E. Hopke, editor in chief. Ninth edition, 1993. Four-volume set that profiles 900 occupations and describes job trends in 74 industries. Includes career description, educational requirements, history of the job, methods of entry, advancement, employment outlook, earnings, conditions of work, social and psychological factors, and sources of further information.

★8184★ "Computer Programmer" in 100 Best Careers for the Year 2000 (pp. 115-117)
Arco Pub.
201 W. 103rd St.
Indianapolis, IN 46290
Ph: 800-428-5331   Fax: 800-835-3202
Shelly Field. 1992. Describes 100 job opportunities expected to grow fast throughout the next decade. Provides information on job duties and responsibilities, training requirements, education, advancement opportunities, experience and qualifications, and typical salaries.

★8185★ "Computer Programmer" in Jobs Rated Almanac
World Almanac
1 International Blvd., Ste. 444
Mahwah, NJ 07495
Ph: (201)529-6900   Fax: (201)529-6901
Les Krantz. Second edition, 1992. Ranks 250 jobs by environment, salary, outlooks, physical demands, stress, security, travel opportunities, and extra perks. Includes jobs the editor feels are the most common, most interesting, and the most rapidly growing.

★8186★ "Computer Programmer" in VGM's Careers Encyclopedia (pp. 114-116)
National Textbook Co. (NTC)
VGM Career Books
4255 W. Touhy Ave.
Lincolnwood, IL 60646-1975
Ph: (708)679-5500   Fax: (708)679-2494
Fr: 800-323-4900
Third edition, 1991. Profiles 200 occupations. Describes job duties, places of employment, working conditions, qualifications, education and training, advancement potential, and salary for each occupation.

★8187★ "Computer Programmer" in VGM's Handbook of Business and Management Careers
National Textbook Co.
4255 W. Touhy Ave.
Lincolnwood, IL 60646-1975
Ph: (708)679-5500   Fax: (708)679-2494
Fr: 800-323-4900
Annette Selden. Second edition, 1993. Contains 42 two-page occupational profiles describing job duties, places of employment,

working conditions, qualifications, education, employment outlook, and income.

★8188★ Computer Programmers
Chronicle Guidance Publications, Inc.
66 Aurora St.
PO Box 1190
Moravia, NY 13118-1190
Ph: (315)497-0330   Fax: (315)497-3359
Fr: 800-622-7284

1993. Career brief describing the nature of the job, working conditions, hours and earnings, education and training, licensure, certification, unions, personal qualifications, social and psychological factors, location, employment outlook, entry methods, advancement, and related occupations.

★8189★ "Computer Programmers" in 101 Careers: A Guide to the Fastest-Growing Opportunities (pp. 73-75)
John Wiley & Sons, Inc.
605 3rd Ave.
New York, NY 10158-0012
Ph: (212)850-6645   Fax: (212)850-6088

Michael Harkavy. 1990. Describes the nature of the job, working conditions, employment growth, qualifications, personal skills, projected salaries, and where to write for more information.

★8190★ "Computer Programmers" in America's 50 Fastest Growing Jobs (pp. 75)
JIST Works, Inc.
720 N. Park Ave.
Indianapolis, IN 46202-3431
Ph: (317)264-3720   Fax: (317)264-3709
Fr: 800-648-5478

Michael J. Farr, compiler. 1994. Describes the 50 fastest growing jobs within major career clusters such as technicians, and marketing and sales. Each job profile explains the nature of the work, skills and abilities required, employment outlook, average earnings, related occupations, education and training requirements, and employment opportunities. Also contains career planning information and job search tips.

★8191★ "Computer Programmers" in Career Information Center (Vol.1)
Simon and Schuster
200 Old Tappan Rd.
Old Tappan, NJ 07675
Fax: 800-445-6991   Fr: 800-223-2348

Richard Lidz and Linda Perrin, editorial directors. Fifth edition, 1993. A multi-volume set that profiles over 600 occupations. Each occupational profile describes job duties, educational requirements, advancement possibilities, employment outlook, working conditions, earnings and benefits, and where to write for more information.

★8192★ "Computer Programmers" in Careers in High-Tech
Arco Publishing Co.
Macmillan General Reference
15 Columbus Cir.
New York, NY 10023
Fax: 800-835-3202   Fr: 800-858-7674

Connie Winkler. 1987. Surveys occupations in data processing, personal computers, telecommunications, manufacturing technology, artificial intelligence, computer graphics, medicine, biotechnology, lasers, technical

writing and publishing. Separate chapters cover education and training.

★8193★ "Computer Programmers" in Occupational Outlook Handbook
U.S. Government Printing Office
Superintendent of Documents
Washington, DC 20402
Ph: (202)512-1800   Fax: (202)512-2250

Biennial, 1994-95. Encyclopedia of careers describing about 250 occupations and comprising about 85 percent of all jobs in the economy. Occupations that require lengthy education or training are given the most attention. Each occupation's profile describes what the worker does on the job, working conditions, education and training requirements, advancement possibilities, job outlook, earnings, and sources of additional information.

★8194★ "Computer Programming" in Opportunities in High-Tech Careers (pp. 37-38, 70-71, 103-104)
National Textbook Co. (NTC)
VGM Career Books
4255 W. Touhy Ave.
Lincolnwood, IL 60646-1975
Ph: (708)679-5500   Fax: (708)679-2494
Fr: 800-323-4900

Gary D. Golter and Deborah Yanuck. 1987. Explores high-technology careers. Written for the student and displaced worker. Describes job opportunities, how to make a career decision, how to prepare for high-technology jobs, job hunting techniques, and future trends.

★8195★ "Computer Programming" in Opportunities in Word Processing
National Textbook Co. (NTC)
VGM Career Books
4255 W. Touhy Ave.
Lincolnwood, IL 60646-1975
Ph: (708)679-5500   Fax: (708)679-2494
Fr: 800-323-4900

Marianne Forrester Munday. 1991. Explains the development of word processing and how it works. Discusses the training needed, major employers of word processing personnel, and related careers.

★8196★ Computer, Salary Survey and Career Planning Guide
Source EDP
120 Broadway, Ste. 1010
New York, NY 10271
Ph: (212)557-8611

Annual. Describes career paths in the computer field and trends in the computer field. Lists job titles. Charts salaries by job titles, years of experience, and industry.

★8197★ "Computer Technologists and Professionals" in American Almanac of Jobs and Salaries (pp. 284-295)
Avon Books
1350 Avenue of the Americas
New York, NY 10019
Ph: (212)261-6800   Fr: 800-238-0658

John Wright, editor. Revised and updated, 1994-95. A comprehensive guide to the wages of hundreds of occupations in a wide variety of industries and organizations.

★8198★ "Computers" in College Majors and Careers: A Resource Guide to Effective Life Planning (pp. 41-42)
Garrett Park Press
PO Box 1907
Garrett Park, MD 20896
Ph: (301)946-2553

Paul Phifer. 1993. Lists 60 college majors, with definitions; related occupations and leisure activities; skills, values, and personal needed attributes; suggested readings; and a list of associations.

★8199★ "Computers" in Internships 1995
Petersons Guides, Inc.
PO Box 2123
Princeton, NJ 08543-2123
Ph: (609)243-9111   Fr: 800-338-3282

Fifteenth edition, 1995. Lists internship opportunities under six broad categories: communications, creative, performing, and fine arts, human services, international relations, business and technology, and public affairs. For each internship program, gives the names, phone number, contact person, description, eligibility requirements, and benefits.

★8200★ Exploring Careers in the Computer Field
Rosen Publishing Group
29 E. 21st St.
New York, NY 10010
Ph: (212)777-3017   Fax: (212)777-0277
Fr: 800-237-9932

Joseph Weintraub. Revised edition, 1993. Describes future trends in computers including opportunities in hardware and software. Includes interviews with people in different computer careers including programming, consulting, and systems management. Provides state-by-state listing of universities and colleges offering two- and four-year degree programs in data processing and computer science.

★8201★ Exploring High-Tech Careers
Rosen Publishing Group
29 E. 21st St.
New York, NY 10010
Ph: (212)777-3017   Fax: (212)777-0277
Fr: 800-237-9932

Scott Southworth. Revised edition, 1993. Gives an orientation to the field of high technology and high-tech jobs. Describes educational preparation and job hunting. Includes a glossary and a bibliography.

★8202★ Graphic Programmers
Chronicle Guidance Publications, Inc.
66 Aurora St.
PO Box 1190
Moravia, NY 13118-1190
Ph: (315)497-0330   Fax: (315)497-3359
Fr: 800-622-7284

1991. Occupational brief describing the nature of the job, working conditions, hours and earnings, education and training, licensure, certification, unions, personal qualifications, social and psychological factors, location, employment outlook, entry methods, advancement, and related occupations.

★8203★ Opportunities in Computer Science Careers
National Textbook Co. (NTC)
VGM Career Books
4255 W. Touhy Ave.
Lincolnwood, IL 60646-1975
Ph: (708)679-5500   Fax: (708)679-2494
Fr: 800-323-4900
Julie L. Kling. 1991. Includes a bibliography. Describes job duties, educaitonal requirements, salary, working conditions, employment outlook, and advancement opportunities.

★8204★ Peterson's Job Opportunities for Engineering and Technology
Petersons Guides, Inc.
PO Box 2123
Princeton, NJ 08543-2123
Ph: (609)243-9111   Fax: (609)243-9150
Fr: 800-338-3282
1994. Gives job hunting advice including information on resume writing, interviewing, and handling salary negotiations. Lists companies that hire college graduates in science and engineering at the bachelor and master's level. Companies are indexed by industry, starting location, and major. Company profiles include contact information and types of hires.

★8205★ Programmer
Careers, Inc.
PO Box 135
Largo, FL 34649-0135
Ph: (813)584-7333
1993. Four-page brief offering the definition, history, duties, working conditions, personal qualifications, educational requirements, earnings, hours, employment outlook, advancement, and careers related to this position.

★8206★ "Programmers" in Jobs! What They Are—Where They Are—What They Pay (p. 80)
Simon & Schuster, Inc.
Simon & Schuster Bldg.
1230 Avenue of the Americas
New York, NY 10020
Ph: (212)698-7000   Fr: 800-223-2348
Robert O. Snelling and Anne M. Snelling. 3rd edition, 1992. Describes duties and responsibilities, earnings, employment opportunities, training, and qualifications.

★8207★ The Programmer's Survival Guide: Career Strategies for Computer Professionals
Prentice-Hall, Inc.
200 Old Tappan Rd.
Old Tappan, NJ 07675
Ph: (201)767-5000   Fr: 800-223-2348
Janet Lehrman Ruhl. 1988. Contains information on career planning, job hunting, and job changing. Gives advice on the software packages needed in corporate America, how to interview, and when to change jobs.

★8208★ "Programming" in Career Choices for the 90's for Students of Mathematics (pp. 48-52)
Walker and Co.
435 Hudson St.
New York, NY 10014
Ph: (212)727-8300   Fax: (212)727-0984
Fr: 800-289-2553
1990. Offers alternatives for students of mathematics. Gives information about the outlook and competition for entry-level candidates. Provides job-hunting tips.

★8209★ "Waverly Hagey—Espie, Programmer" in Straight Talk on Careers: Eighty Pros Take You Into Their Professions (pp. 5-6)
Garrett Park Press
PO Box 1907
Garrett Park, MD 20896
Ph: (301)946-2553
Mary Barbera-Hogan. 1987. Contains candid interviews from people who give an inside view of their work in 80 different careers. These professionals describe a day's work and the stresses and rewards accompanying their work.

PROFESSIONAL ASSOCIATIONS

★8210★ Back Bay Lisa
49 Searle St.
Georgetown, MA 01833
Members: Computer programmers and system administrators interested in professional development. Conducts monthly meetings with featured speakers on a wide variety of computer-related topics.

★8211★ Institute for Certification of Computer Professionals (ICCP)
2200 E. Devon Ave., Ste. 268
Des Plaines, IL 60018
Ph: (708)299-4227   Fax: (708)299-4280
Members: Professional societies united to **Purpose:** promote the development of computer examinations which are of high quality, directed toward information technology professionals, and designed to encourage competence and professionalism. Individuals passing the exams automatically become members of the Association of the Institute for Certification of Computer Professionals. Has developed code of ethics and good practice to which those taking the exams promise to adhere. Maintains speakers' bureau; compiles statistics.

★8212★ Office Automation Society International (OASI)
5170 Meadow Wood Blvd.
Lyndhurst, OH 44124
Ph: (216)461-4803   Fax: (216)461-4803
Members: Office professionals and vendor employees united to discuss problems concerning automation in the office and evaluate and disseminate information on potential solutions. **Purpose:** Provides training on automated devices. Confers professional certification. **Publications:** Conference Proceedings, annual. • OASI Newsletter, bimonthly. • Office Automation Glossary.

STANDARDS/CERTIFICATION AGENCIES

★8213★ Institute for Certification of Computer Professionals (ICCP)
2200 E. Devon Ave., Ste. 268
Des Plaines, IL 60018
Ph: (708)299-4227   Fax: (708)299-4280
Individuals passing the exams automatically become members of the Association of the Institute for Certification of Computer Professionals. Has developed code of ethics and good practice to which those taking the exams promise to adhere.

★8214★ Office Automation Society International (OASI)
5170 Meadow Wood Blvd.
Lyndhurst, OH 44124
Ph: (216)461-4803   Fax: (216)461-4803
Provides training on automated devices. Confers professional certification.

TEST GUIDES

★8215★ Advanced Placement Examination in Computer Science
Arco Publishing Co.
Macmillan General Reference
15 Columbus Cir.
New York, NY 10023
Fax: 800-835-3202   Fr: 800-858-7674
Elayne Schulman. Second edition, 1988. Includes two full-length model examinations in computer science, plus review and drill.

★8216★ Career Examination Series: Computer Programmer
National Learning Corp.
212 Michael Dr.
Syosset, NY 11791
Ph: (516)921-8888   Fax: (516)921-8743
Fr: 800-645-6337
Jack Rudman. A series of study guides with multiple-choice examination questions and solutions for trainees and professional computer programmers. Titles in the series include Associate Computer Programmer; Computer Associate (Applications Programming); Computer Programmer Analyst; Computer Programmer Analyst Trainee; Computer Programming Supervisor; Computer Specialist (Applications Programming); Digital Computer Programmer; Programmer; Programmer/Programmer Analyst; Programmer Aptitude Test (PAT); Programmer Trainee; Senior Computer Programmer; Senior Computer Programmer/Analyst; Senior Programmer.

★8217★ Career Examination Series: Digital Computer Systems Programmer
National Learning Corp.
212 Michael Dr.
Syosset, NY 11791
Ph: (516)921-8888 Fax: (516)921-8743
Fr: 800-645-6337

Jack Rudman. 1993. Test guide including questions and answers for students or professionals in the field who seek advancement through examination.

★8218★ Career Examination Series: Principal Computer Programmer
National Learning Corp.
212 Michael Dr.
Syosset, NY 11791
Ph: (516)921-8888 Fax: (516)921-8743
Fr: 800-645-6337

Jack Rudman. 1993. Test guide including questions and answers for students or professionals in the field who seek advancement through examination.

★8219★ Career Examination Series: Systems Programmer
National Learning Corp.
212 Michael Dr.
Syosset, NY 11791
Ph: (516)921-8888 Fax: (516)921-8743
Fr: 800-645-6337

Jack Rudman. 1993. Test guide including questions and answers for students or professionals in the field who seek advancement through examination.

★8220★ College-Level Examination Series: Computer Programming
National Learning Corp.
212 Michael Dr.
Syosset, NY 11791
Ph: (516)921-8888 Fax: (516)921-8743
Fr: 800-645-6337

Jack Rudman. Multiple-choice preparatory examinations for professional computer programmers considering the College-Level Examination Program (CLEP) as an alternative to college course matriculation. Includes solutions to sample test questions.

★8221★ Computer Programming
National Learning Corp.
212 Michael Dr.
Syosset, NY 11791
Ph: (516)921-8888 Fax: (516)921-8743
Fr: 800-645-6337

Jack Rudman. Part of the Test Your Knowledge Series. Contains multiple choice questions with answers.

★8222★ EZ 101 Study Keys: Computer Science
Barron's Educational Series, Inc.
250 Wireless Blvd.
Hauppauge, NY 11788
Ph: (516)434-3311 Fax: (516)434-3723
Fr: 800-645-3476

1991. Provides themes and a glossary of terms.

★8223★ Graduate Record Examination: Computers
Arco Publishing Co.
Macmillan General Reference
15 Columbus Cir.
New York, NY 10023
Fax: 800-835-3202 Fr: 800-858-7674
Thomas H. Martinson. Fifth edition, 1994. Includes six practice exams.

EDUCATIONAL DIRECTORIES AND PROGRAMS

★8224★ Computing and Software Design Career Directory
Gale Research Inc.
835 Penobscot Bldg.
Detroit, MI 48226-4094
Ph: (313)961-2242 Fax: (313)961-6083
Fr: 800-877-GALE

Bradley J. Morgan and Joseph M. Palmisano. 1993. A directory in the Career Advisor Series that provides essays written by industry professionals; job search information on resume and cover letter preparation, networking, and the interviewing process; approximately 300 companies and organizations offering job opportunities and internships, and additional job-hunting resources.

★8225★ Graduate Assistantship Directory in Computing
Association for Computing Machinery
1515 Broadway, 17th Fl.
New York, NY 10036
Ph: (212)869-7440 Fax: (212)869-0481
Fr: 800-342-6626

Annual, fall. Covers fellowships and assistantships in the computer sciences offered at U.S. and Canadian educational institutions. Entries include: Institution name, address, name and title of contact, degrees offered, area of expertise, financial aid offered, stipend amount, department facilities (hardware and software), school enrollment, required exams, admission deadlines. Arrangement: Geographical.

AWARDS, SCHOLARSHIPS, GRANTS, AND FELLOWSHIPS

★8226★ Computer Pioneer Award
Institute of Electrical and Electronics Engineers
Computer Society
Technical & Area Activities
1730 Massachusetts Ave. NW
Washington, DC 20036-1903
Ph: (202)371-0101 Fax: (202)728-9614

To recognize and honor the vision of those people whose efforts resulted in the creation and continued vitality of the electronic computer industry. Individuals whose main contribution to the concepts and development of the computer field was made at least 15 years earlier are considered. A medal is awarded annually. Established in 1981.

★8227★ FIGGIE
FORTH Dimensions Interest Group
PO Box 2154
Oakland, CA 94621-0054
Ph: (408)277-0668 Fax: (408)286-8988

For recognition of contributions to the promotions of the FORTH (an interpretive computer language) Interest Group. Nominations are accepted from previous winners prior to the annual convention in October. A plaque is presented annually. Established in 1978 by William Ragsdale.

★8228★ Andrew Fluegelman Award
PCW Communications
501 2nd St.
San Francisco, CA 94107
Ph: (415)243-0500

To encourage personal computer software excellence and to recognize a software programmer or team of programmers. Innovative contributions by individuals to the personal computer community in commercial, shareware, or public-domain software including utilities, applications, and languages, are considered. Only individuals, not companies, may be nominated. A monetary award of $5,000 and a marble plaque are awarded at the annual Software Publishers AssociationAwards Dinner. Established in 1986 to honor Andrew Fluegelman. Sponsored by the Software Publishers Association.

★8229★ Richard W. Hamming Medal
Institute of Electrical and Electronics Engineers
345 E. 47th St.
New York, NY 10017-2394
Ph: (212)705-7882 Fax: (212)223-2911

To recognize exceptional contributions to information sciences and systems. Preference is given to an individual, but may be conferred on a team of not more than three. A monetary award of $10,000, a gold medal, a bronze replica, and a certificate are awarded annually. Established in 1986. Sponsored by AT&T +Bell Laboratories.

★8230★ Augusta Ada Lovelace Award
Association for Women in Computing
41 Sutter St., Ste. 1006
San Francisco, CA 94104

To recognize individuals who have excelled in either, or both outstanding scientific and technical achievement and extraordinary service to the computing community through their accomplishments and contributions on behalf of women in computing. Any person who has rendered extraordinary service to the computing industry through contributions on behalf of women in computing, or whose technical and scientific accomplishments are outstanding, is eligible for nomination. A certificate is awarded annually when merited. Established in 1981 in memory of Augusta Ada, Countess of Lovelace, considered to be the first woman in computing for her work with Charles Babbage, inventor of the "analytical engine," the first computer. She programmed the machine and understood its implications for the future.

★8231★ W. Wallace McDowell Award
Institute of Electrical and Electronics
  Engineers
Computer Society
Technical & Area Activities
1730 Massachusetts Ave. NW
Washington, DC 20036-1903
Ph: (202)371-0101   Fax: (202)728-9614

To recognize an individual whose professional work has been outstanding in concepts, technology, programming, education, or management in the computer field. A monetary prize of $2,000 is presented annually. Established in 1966 by the International Business Machines Corporation. The award honors W. Wallace McDowell, a retired Vice President of International Business Machines Corporation.

★8232★ Emanuel R. Piore Award
Institute of Electrical and Electronics
  Engineers
345 E. 47th St.
New York, NY 10017-2394
Ph: (212)705-7882   Fax: (212)223-2911

To recognize outstanding achievement in the field of information processing, in relation to computer science, deemed to have contributed significantly to the advancement of science and to the betterment of society. Preference is given for achievement by a single individual, but may be conferred on a team of two individuals. The deadline for nominations is January 31. A monetary prize of $5,000, a gold- plated bronze medal, and a certificate are awarded annually. Established in 1976. Sponsored by IBM Corporation.

★8233★ Software System Award
Association for Computing Machinery
1515 Broadway
New York, NY 10036-1998
Ph: (212)869-7440   Fax: (212)944-1318

To recognize a software system that has had a lasting influence, as reflected in contributions to concepts or in commercial practice or in both. Either institutions or individuals responsible for developing and introducing the software system are eligible. A monetary award of $10,000, engraved plaque, and a certificate are awarded. Established in 1969. Renamed in 1983. Financial support is provided by IBM.

Basic Reference Guides and Handbooks

★8234★ Computer Science Source Book
McGraw-Hill, Inc.
1221 Avenue of the Americas
New York, NY 10020
Ph: (212)512-2000   Fr: 800-722-4726

1989. Sixty articles cover topics such as computer science, data processing, artificial intelligence, operating systems, programming languages, electronic mail, and super computers.

★8235★ Computers Today with BASIC
McGraw-Hill, Inc.
1221 Avenue of the Americas
New York, NY 10020
Ph: (212)512-2000   Fr: 800-722-4726

D.H. Sanders. Third edition, 1989. Covers computer capabilities and limitations, software applications, information systems, and the computer's impact on society.

★8236★ McGraw-Hill Encyclopedia of Electronics and Computers
McGraw-Hill, Inc.
1221 Avenue of the Americas
New York, NY 10020
Ph: (212)512-2000   Fr: 800-722-4726

Sybil P. Parker, editor. Second edition, 1988. Contains articles on electronics and computers.

★8237★ McGraw-Hill Microcomputing
McGraw-Hill, Inc.
1221 Avenue of the Americas
New York, NY 10020
Ph: (212)512-2000   Fr: 800-722-4726

Timothy J. O'Leary and Bryan K. Williams. Annual, third edition 1991-92. Describes computer concepts in general and specific software such as Wordperfect, dBase, and Lotus.

★8238★ McGraw-Hill Personal Computer Programming Encyclopedia: Languages and Operating Systems
McGraw-Hill, Inc.
1221 Avenue of the Americas
New York, NY 10020
Ph: (212)512-2000   Fr: 800-722-4726

William J. Birnes, editor. Second edition, 1989. Provides functional and operating definitions for all statement commands, and source codes in all high-level programming languages. Includes articles on CAD/CAM, desktop publishing, and artificial intelligence.

Professional and Trade Periodicals

★8239★ Ada Letters
Special Interest Group on Ada
1515 Broadway
New York, NY 10036
Ph: (212)869-7440
Cammie Donaldson

Bimonthly. Disseminates information about Ada computer language, including its usage, environment, standardization, and implementation. Updates members on the activities of the association, which functions as a special interest group of the Association for Computing Machinery. Recurring features include data on technological developments and announcements of technical conferences.

★8240★ Computer Wave
PO Box 19491
Seattle, WA 98109
Ph: (206)284-5476   Fax: (206)283-1020
Robert L. Crowther

★8241★ Concurrency
John Wiley and Sons, Inc.
Subscription Dept.
605 3rd Ave.
New York, NY 10158
Ph: (212)850-6000   Fax: (212)850-6799
G.C. Fox

Scientific journal focussing on concurrent computers and solutions to problems specific to concurrent computer designers.

★8242★ Expert Systems
Learned Information, Inc.
143 Old Marlton Pike
Medford, NJ 08055
Ph: (609)654-6500   Fax: (609)654-4309
Ian F. Croall

Quarterly. Journal for business professionals. Deals with expert computer systems and their applications to government, business, and industry.

★8243★ Journal of Programming Languages
Chapman & Hall
29 W. 35th St.
New York, NY 10001-2291
Ph: (212)244-3336

Quarterly. Journal providing research in high level language design and implementation.

★8244★ SIGDOC Newsletter
Special Interest Group for Systems
  Documentation (SIGDOC)
1515 Broadway, 17th Fl.
New York, NY 10036
Ph: (212)869-7440   Fr: 800-932-0878
Russel Boiland

Quarterly. Contains announcements and reports about international conferences on systems documentation. Examines documents produced by systems analysts, programmers, and project managers in their work to investigate, design, and develop new systems. Reviews techniques applied by technical writers and others in preparing user documents and reference material. Reports on hardware and software used to aid the documentation process.

★8245★ SIGPLAN Notices
Special Interest Group on Programming
  Languages (SIGPLAN)
1515 Broadway, 17th Fl.
New York, NY 10036
Ph: (212)869-7440   Fr: 800-526-0359
Richard L. Wexelblat

Monthly. Examines all aspects of programming languages and programming languages processors. Utilizes practical and theoretical approaches to such areas as programming methodology; language definition and design; principles and techniques of computer implementation; general purpose and application-oriented languages; and teaching of programming languages. Recurring features include standards information and proceedings of SIGPLAN symposia.

★8246★ SIGSOFT Software Engineering Notes
Special Interest Group on Software Engineering (SIGSOFT)
1515 Broadway, 17th Fl.
New York, NY 10036
Ph: (212)869-7440   Fr: 800-932-0878
Will Tracz
Quarterly. Tracks developments in programming and software maintenance processes, as well as the use of computers to provide and maintain timely, higher quality, cost-effective, and durable software. Contains proceedings of software engineering workshops and symposia.

★8247★ West Coast Online
West Coast Online
PO Box 360588
Milpitas, CA 95036-0588
Ph: (408)946-3823   Fax: (408)946-5331
Mark ShapiroPublisher
Monthly. Magazine covering Internet and on-line information.

PROFESSIONAL MEETINGS AND CONVENTIONS

★8248★ Association for Computing Machinery Computer Science Conference
Association for Computing Machinery (ACM)
1515 Broadway
New York, NY 10017
Ph: (212)869-7440   Fax: (212)944-1318
Annual. Always held during the winter.

★8249★ Society for Computer Simulation International Western Multi-conference
Society for Computer Simulation International
PO Box 17900
San Diego, CA 92117
Ph: (619)277-3888   Fax: (619)277-3930
Annual. **Dates and Locations:** 1995

★8250★ Summer Computer Simulation Conference
Society for Computer Simulation International
PO Box 17900
San Diego, CA 92117
Ph: (619)277-3888   Fax: (619)277-3930
Annual. Always held during July. **Dates and Locations:** 1996 Jul 21-24; Portland, OR.

OTHER SOURCES OF INFORMATION

★8251★ The Computer Industry Almanac, 1989: The Insider's Guide to People, companies, Products, & Trends in the Fascinating Fast-Paced Computer . . .
Simon & Schuster, Inc.
Simon & Schuster Bldg.
1230 Avenue of the Americas
New York, NY 10020
Ph: (212)698-7000   Fr: 800-223-2348
Juliussen, Egil, and Kawren Juliussen, editors. 1989. A compendium of a variety of information on the computer industry compiled from newsletters, reports and magazines.

★8252★ "Computer Programmer" in 100 Best Jobs for the 1990s & Beyond
Dearborn Financial Publishing, Inc.
520 N. Dearborn St.
Chicago, IL 60610-4354
Ph: (312)836-4400   Fax: (312)836-1021
Fr: 800-621-9621

Carol Kleiman. 1992. Describes 100 jobs ranging from accountants to veterinarians. Each job profile includes such information as education, experience, and certification needed, salaries, and job search suggestions.

★8253★ Introduction to Information Processing
McGraw-Hill, Inc.
1221 Avenue of the Americas
New York, NY 10020
Ph: (212)512-2000   Fr: 800-722-4726

Beryl Robichaud and Eugene J. Muscat. Fourth edition, 1989. Covers networks, telecommunications, computer conferencing, and artificial intelligence. Describes job opportunities in information processing in the public and private sectors.

Drafters

Drafters prepare technical drawings used by workers who build spacecraft, industrial machinery and other manufactured products, and office buildings, bridges, and other structures. Their drawings show the technical details of the products and structures and specify materials to be used, procedures to be followed, and other information needed to carry out the job. Drafters prepare and fill in technical details, using drawings, rough sketches, specifications, and calculations made by engineers, surveyors, architects, and scientists. There are two methods by which drawings are prepared. In the traditional method, drafters sit at drawing boards and use compasses, dividers, protractors, triangles, and other drafting devices to prepare the drawing manually. Today, drafters also use computer-aided drafting (CAD) systems. They sit at computer work stations and draw on a video screen. They may put the drawing on paper or just store it electronically. Many drafters specialize. **Architectural drafters** draw architectural and structural features of buildings and other structures, such as schools or office buildings. **Aeronautical drafters** prepare engineering drawings used for the manufacture of aircraft and missiles. **Electrical drafters** draw wiring and layout diagrams used by workers who erect, install, and repair electrical equipment and wiring in powerplants, electrical distribution systems, and buildings. **Electronic drafters** draw wiring diagrams, schematics, and layout drawings used in the manufacture , installation, and repair of electronic equipment. **Civil drafters** prepare drawings and topographical and relief maps used in civil engineering projects such as highways, bridges, flood control projects, and water and sewage systems. **Mechanical drafters** draw detailed working diagrams of machinery and mechanical devices, including dimensions, fastening methods, and other engineering information.

Salaries

Earnings for drafters are as follows:

Median	$25,900/year
Experienced drafters in manufacturing, transportation, and utilities	$18,600-$31,500/year
Senior drafter	$36,200/year

Drafters

CAREER GUIDES

★8254★ "Architectural Drafter" in *Guide to Careers Without College* **(pp. 76-77)**
Franklin Watts, Inc.
387 Park Ave., S., 4th Fl.
New York, NY 10016
Ph: (212)686-7070   Fr: 800-672-6672
Kathleen S. Abrams. 1988. Discusses rewarding careers that do not require a college degree.

★8255★ "Architectural Drafter" in *Jobs Rated Almanac*
World Almanac
1 International Blvd., Ste. 444
Mahwah, NJ 07495
Ph: (201)529-6900   Fax: (201)529-6901
Les Krantz. Second edition, 1992. Ranks 250 jobs by environment, salary, outlooks, physical demands, stress, security, travel opportunities, and extra perks. Includes jobs the editor feels are the most common, most interesting, and the most rapidly growing.

★8256★ "Architectural Drafters" in *Career Information Center* **(Vol.4)**
Simon and Schuster
200 Old Tappan Rd.
Old Tappan, NJ 07675
Fax: 800-445-6991   Fr: 800-223-2348
Richard Lidz and Linda Perrin, editorial directors. Fifth edition, 1993. A multi-volume set that profiles more than 600 occupations. Each occupational profile describes job duties, educational requirements, getting a job, advancement possibilities, employment outlook, working conditions, earnings and benefits, and sources of additional information.

★8257★ "Architecture Drafter" in *Liberal Arts Jobs*
Petersons Guides, Inc.
PO Box 2123
Princeton, NJ 08543-2123
Ph: (609)243-9111   Fax: (609)243-9150
Fr: 800-338-3282
Burton Jay Nadler. Second edition, 1989. Strives to help the liberal arts graduate identify skills for entry-level positions. Gives goal setting and job search advice.

★8258★ "CAD/CAM" in *Exploring Careers in Computer Graphics*
Rosen Publishing Group
29 E. 21st St.
New York, NY 10010
Ph: (212)777-3017   Fax: (212)777-0277
Fr: 800-237-9932
Richard Masterson. 1990. Explores careers in computer graphics describing educational preparation and job-hunting strategies. Includes information on applications such as CAD/CAM and business. Appendices include a glossary, trade journals, associations, colleges, and a bibliography.

★8259★ "CAD" in *Complete Computer Career Guide (pp. 79-83)*
Tab/McGraw-Hill
Blue Ridge Summit, PA 17214-8050
Ph: (717)794-2191   Fr: 800-822-8138
Judith Norback. 1987. Describes how to enter a career in computers. Explains education needed, the most promising opportunities, and industry trends. Offers job hunting tips.

★8260★ "CAD: Computer-Aided Design" in *Careers in High-Tech*
Arco Publishing Co.
Macmillan General Reference
15 Columbus Cir.
New York, NY 10023
Fax: 800-835-3202   Fr: 800-858-7674
Connie Winkler. 1987. Surveys occupations in data processing, personal computers, telecommunications, manufacturing technology, artificial intelligence, computer graphics, medicine, biotechnology, lasers, technical writing, and publishing. Separate chapters cover education and training.

★8261★ *Drafter, Aeronautical*
Careers, Inc.
PO Box 135
Largo, FL 34649-0135
Ph: (813)584-7333
1994. Two-page occupational summary card describing duties, working conditions, personal qualifications, training, earnings and hours, employment outlook, places of employment, related careers, and where to write for more information.

★8262★ *Drafter, Architectural*
Careers, Inc.
PO Box 135
Largo, FL 34649-0135
Ph: (813)584-7333
1993. Two-page occupational summary card describing duties, working conditions, personal qualifications, training, earnings and hours, employment outlook, places of employment, related careers, and where to write for more information.

★8263★ "Drafter and Design Technician" in *Career Information Center* **(Vol.6)**
Simon and Schuster
200 Old Tappan Rd.
Old Tappan, NJ 07675
Fax: 800-445-6991   Fr: 800-223-2348
Richard Lidz and Linda Perrin, editorial directors. Fifth edition, 1993. This 13-volume set profiles over 600 occupations. Each occupational profile describes job duties, entry-level requirements, educational requirements, advancement possibilities, employment outlook, working conditions, earnings and benefits, and where to write for more information.

★8264★ *Drafter, Mechanical*
Careers, Inc.
PO Box 135
Largo, FL 34649-0135
Ph: (813)584-7333
1992. Two-page occupational summary card describing duties, working conditions, personal qualifications, training, earnings and hours, employment outlook, places of employment, related careers, and where to write for more information.

★8265★ "Drafter Technician" in *Opportunities in High-Tech Careers* **(pp. 133-134)**
National Textbook Co. (NTC)
VGM Career Books
4255 W. Touhy Ave.
Lincolnwood, IL 60646-1975
Ph: (708)679-5500   Fax: (708)679-2494
Fr: 800-323-4900
Gary D. Golter and Deborah Yanuck. 1987. Explores high-technology careers. Written for the student and displaced worker. Describes job opportunities, how to make a career deci-

sion, how to prepare for high-technology jobs, job hunting techniques, and future trends.

★8266★ "Drafter" in *VGM's Careers Encyclopedia* (pp. 141-143)
National Textbook Co. (NTC)
VGM Career Books
4255 W. Touhy Ave.
Lincolnwood, IL 60646-1975
Ph: (708)679-5500   Fax: (708)679-2494
Fr: 800-323-4900

Third edition, 1991. Profiles 200 occupations. Describes job duties, places of employment, working conditions, qualifications, education and training, advancement potential, and salary for each occupation.

★8267★ *Drafters*
Careers, Inc.
PO Box 135
Largo, FL 34649-0135
Ph: (813)584-7333

1993. Four-page brief offering the definition, history, duties, working conditions, personal qualifications, educational requirements, earnings, hours, employment outlook, advancement, and careers related to this position.

★8268★ *Drafters*
Chronicle Guidance Publications, Inc.
66 Aurora St.
PO Box 1190
Moravia, NY 13118-1190
Ph: (315)497-0330   Fax: (315)497-3359
Fr: 800-622-7284

1993. Career brief describing the nature of the job, working conditions, hours and earnings, education and training, licensure, certification, unions, personal qualifications, social and psychological factors, location, employment outlook, entry methods, advancement, and related occupations.

★8269★ "Drafters" in *Career Discovery Encyclopedia* (Vol.2, pp. 122-123)
J.G. Ferguson Publishing Co.
200 W. Madison St., Ste. 300
Chicago, IL 60606
Ph: (312)580-5480   Fax: (312)580-4948
Russell E. Primm, editor-in chief. 1993. This six volume set contains two-page articles for 504 occupations. Each article describes job duties, earnings, and educational and training requirements. The whole set is arranged alphabetically by job title. Designed for junior high and older students.

★8270★ "Drafters" in *Encyclopedia of Careers and Vocational Guidance* (Vol.2, pp. 506-508)
J.G. Ferguson Publishing Co.
200 W. Madison St., Ste. 300
Chicago, IL 60606
Ph: (312)580-5480   Fax: (312)580-4948
William E. Hopke, editor-in-chief. Ninth edition, 1993. Four-volume set that profiles 900 occupations and describes job trends in 74 industries. Includes career description, educational requirements, history of the job, methods of entry, advancement, employment outlook, earnings, conditions of work, social and psychological factors, and sources of further information.

★8271★ "Drafters" in *Jobs! What They Are—Where They Are—What They Pay* (p. 60)
Simon & Schuster, Inc.
Simon & Schuster Bldg.
1230 Avenue of the Americas
New York, NY 10020
Ph: (212)698-7000   Fr: 800-223-2348
Robert O. Snelling and Anne M. Snelling. 3rd edition, 1992. Describes duties and responsibilities, earnings, employment opportunities, training, and qualifications.

★8272★ "Drafters" in *Occupational Outlook Handbook*
U.S. Government Printing Office
Superintendent of Documents
Washington, DC 20402
Ph: (202)512-1800   Fax: (202)512-2250
Biennial; latest edition, 1994-95. Encyclopedia of careers describing about 250 occupations and comprising about 85 percent of all jobs in the economy. Occupations that require lengthy education or training are given the most attention. Each occupation's profile describes what the worker does on the job, working conditions, education and training requirements, advancement possibilities, job outlook, earnings, and sources of additional information.

★8273★ "Drafting and Design Technicians" in *Encyclopedia of Careers and Vocational Guidance* (Vol.2, pp. 509-513)
J.G. Ferguson Publishing Co.
200 W. Madison St., Ste. 300
Chicago, IL 60606
Ph: (312)580-5480   Fax: (312)580-4948
William E. Hopke, editor in chief. Ninth edition, 1993. Four-volume set that profiles 900 occupations and describes job trends in 74 industries. Includes career description, educational requirements, history of the job, methods of entry, advancement, employment outlook, earnings, conditions of work, social and psychological factors, and sources of further information.

★8274★ "Drafting and Layout Design" in *Exploring High-Tech Careers*
Rosen Publishing Group
29 E. 21st St.
New York, NY 10010
Ph: (212)777-3017   Fax: (212)777-0277
Fr: 800-237-9932
Scott Southworth. Revised edition, 1993. Gives an orientation to the field of high technology and high-tech jobs. Describes educational preparation and job hunting. Includes a glossary and bibliography.

★8275★ "Drafting Technology" in *Career Connection for Technical Education* (pp. 60-61)
JIST Works, Inc.
720 N. Park Ave.
Indianapolis, IN 46202-3431
Ph: (317)264-3720   Fax: (317)264-3709
Fred A. Rowe. 1994, second edition. Describes in detail technical occupations. Includes information on recommended high school courses, course requirements, related careers, and a self-assessment guide.

★8276★ "Engineering Draftsman" in *Guide to Federal Technical, Trades and Labor Jobs* (p. 190)
Resource Directories
3361 Executive Pkwy., Ste. 302
Toledo, OH 43606
Ph: (419)536-5353   Fax: (419)536-7056
Fr: 800-274-8515
Rod W. Durgin, editor. Second edition. 1992. Describes where and how to apply for a federal job. Profiles 300 federal jobs that do not require a college degree. Gives a description, salary, locations, and the agencies that hire the most employees for each job.

★8277★ *Opportunities in Drafting Careers*
National Textbook Co. (NTC)
VGM Career Books
4255 W. Toughy Ave.
Lincolnwood, IL 60646-1975
Ph: (708)679-5500   Fax: (708)679-2494
Fr: 800-323-4900
Mark Rowh

PROFESSIONAL ASSOCIATIONS

★8278★ American Design Drafting Association (ADDA)
PO Box 799
Rockville, MD 20848-0799
Ph: (301)460-6875   Fax: (301)460-8591
Members: Designers, drafters, drafting managers, chief drafters, supervisors, administrators, instructors, and students of design and drafting. **Purpose:** Encourages a continued program of education for self-improvement and professionalism in design and drafting and computer-aided design/drafting. Informs members of effective techniques and materials used in drawings and other graphic presentations. Evaluates curriculum of educational institutions through certification program; sponsors drafter certification program. **Publications:** *Compensation Survey*, biennial. • *Design and Drafting News*, monthly. • *Guide to Writing Design/Drafting Job Descriptions*.

★8279★ Career College Association (CCA)
750 1st St. NE, Ste. 900
Washington, DC 20002
Ph: (202)336-6700   Fax: (202)336-6828
Members: Private postsecondary schools providing career education. **Purpose:** Seeks to inform members of the accreditation process and regulations affecting vocational education. Conducts workshops and institutes for staffs of member schools; provides legislative, administrative, and public relations assistance. Has established Career Training Foundation to support research into private vocational education. Sponsors research programs. Maintains hall of fame; compiles statistics. **Publications:** *Career College Times*, monthly. • *Career Education.* • *Career News Digest.* • *Classroom Companion*, quarterly. • *Directory of Private Accredited Career Colleges and Schools*, annual.

STANDARDS/CERTIFICATION AGENCIES

★8280★ American Design Drafting Association (ADDA)
PO Box 799
Rockville, MD 20848-0799
Ph: (301)460-6875   Fax: (301)460-8591
Evaluates curriculum of educational institutions through certification program; sponsors drafter certification program.

TEST GUIDES

★8281★ Career Examination Series: Civil Engineering Draftsman
National Learning Corp.
212 Michael Dr.
Syosset, NY 11791
Ph: (516)921-8888   Fax: (516)921-8743
Fr: 800-645-6337
Jack Rudman. 1993. Test guide including questions and answers for students or professionals in the field who seek advancement through examination.

★8282★ Career Examination Series: Draftsman
National Learning Corp.
212 Michael Dr.
Syosset, NY 11791
Ph: (516)921-8888   Fax: (516)921-8743
Fr: 800-645-6337
Jack Rudman. A series of study guides with multiple-choice examination questions and solutions for trainees and professional drafters. Titles in the series include *Cartographer-Draftsman; Chief Cartographer-Draftsman; Drafting Aide; Drafting Technician; Draftsman; Junior Draftsman; Mechanical Engineering Draftsman; Principal Draftsman; Principal Engineering Technician (Drafting); Senior Architectural Draftsman; Senior Drafting Technician; Senior Draftsman; Senior Engineering Technician (Drafting).*

★8283★ Career Examination Series: Electrical Engineering Draftsman
National Learning Corp.
212 Michael Dr.
Syosset, NY 11791
Ph: (516)921-8888   Fax: (516)921-8743
Fr: 800-645-6337
Jack Rudman. 1993. Test guide including questions and answers for students or professionals in the field who seek advancement through examination.

★8284★ Career Examination Series: Engineering Draftsman
National Learning Corp.
212 Michael Dr.
Syosset, NY 11791
Ph: (516)921-8888   Fax: (516)921-8743
Fr: 800-645-6337
Jack Rudman. 1993. Test guide including questions and answers for students or professionals in the field who seek advancement through examination.

★8285★ Drafting
National Learning Corp.
212 Michael Dr.
Syosset, NY 11791
Ph: (516)921-8888   Fax: (516)921-8743
Fr: 800-645-6337
Jack Rudman. Part of the Test Your Knowledge Series. Contains multiple choice questions with answers.

★8286★ Technical Drawing and Graphics
National Learning Corp.
212 Michael Dr.
Syosset, NY 11791
Ph: (516)921-8888   Fax: (516)921-8743
Fr: 800-645-6337
Jack Rudman. Dantes Subject Standardized Test series. A standardized graduate and college level examination given by graduate schools, colleges, and the Armed Forces as a final examination for course evaluation in the field of drafting. Multiple-choice format with correct answers.

BASIC REFERENCE GUIDES AND HANDBOOKS

★8287★ Architectural Programming
Van Nostrand Reinhold
115 5th Ave.
New York, NY 10013
Donna Duerk. 1993.

★8288★ Machinery's Handbook: A Reference Book for the Mechanical Engineer, Designer, Manufacturing Engineer, Draftsman, Toolmaker, and Machinist
Industrial Press, Inc.
200 Madison Ave.
New York, NY 10016
Ph: (212)889-6330
Erik Oberg, Franklin D. Jones, and Holbrook L. Horton, editors. Twenty-fourth edition, 1992. Covers all aspects of machine shop practice.

PROFESSIONAL AND TRADE PERIODICALS

★8289★ Design & Drafting News
American Design Drafting Association
PO Box 799
Rockville, MD 20848-0799
Ph: (301)460-6875
Rachel Howard
Bimonthly. Monitors new developments, techniques, and products related to design and drafting. Carries information about metrication and standards. Recurring features include news of the Association and its members, book reviews, and a calendar of events.

★8290★ Design Perspectives
Industrial Designers Society of America (IDSA)
1142 Walker Rd., Ste. E
Great Falls, VA 22066-1836
Ph: (703)759-0100   Fax: (703)759-7679
Karen Berube
Discusses issues relevant to the profession. Recurring features include reports of chapter and national activities of IDSA, a section on employment opportunities in the field, resource section, and a calendar of events.

OTHER SOURCES OF INFORMATION

★8291★ "Drafter" in *100 Best Jobs for the 1990s & Beyond*
Dearborn Financial Publishing, Inc.
520 N. Dearborn St.
Chicago, IL 60610-4354
Ph: (312)836-4400   Fax: (312)836-1021
Fr: 800-621-9621
Carol Kleiman. 1992. Describes 100 jobs ranging from accountants to veterinarians. Each job profile includes such information as education, experience, and certification needed, salaries, and job search suggestions.

Engineering Technicians

Engineering technicians use the principles and theories of science, engineering, and mathematics to solve problems in research and development, manufacturing, sales, construction, and customer service. Their jobs are more limited in scope and more practically oriented than those of scientists and engineers. Many engineering technicians assist engineers and scientists, especially in research and development. Some technicians work on their own, servicing equipment at customers' work sites. Others work in production or inspection jobs. **Civil engineering technicians** help civil engineers plan and build highways, buildings, bridges, dams, wastewater treatment systems, and other structures, and do related surveys and studies. **Electronics engineering technicians** develop, manufacture, and service electronic equipment such as radios, radar, sonar, television, industrial and medical measuring or control devices, navigational equipment, and computers, often using measuring and diagnostic devices to test, adjust, and repair equipment. **Industrial engineering technicians** study the efficient use of personnel, materials, and machines in factories, stores, repair shops, and offices. **Mechanical engineering technicians** help engineers design and develop machinery and other equipment by making sketches and rough layouts. **Chemical engineering technicians** help design, install, and test or maintain process equipment of computer control instrumentation, monitor quality control in processing plants, and make needed adjustments.

Salaries

Annual earnings of full-time engineering technicians are as follows:

Beginning technicians	$20,90/year
Experienced technicians	$28,800/year
Supervisory technicians	$41,400/year
Federal government technicians	$37,337/year

Employment Outlook

Growth rate until the year 2005: Average.

Engineering Technicians

CAREER GUIDES

★8292★ *Aerospace Engineering Technician*
Careers, Inc.
PO Box 135
Largo, FL 34649-0135
Ph: (813)584-7333
1991. Two-page occupational summary card describing duties, working conditions, personal qualifications, training, earnings and hours, employment outlook, places of employment, related careers, and where to write for more information.

★8293★ *"Biomedical Equipment Technician"* in *150 Careers in the Health Care Field*
Reed Reference Publishing
121 Chanlon Rd.
PO Box 31
New Providence, NJ 07974
Fax: (908)665-6688   Fr: 800-521-8110
Stanley Alperin. Third edition, 1993. Profiles health care occupations requiring a bachelor's degree or less. Describes the nature of the work, educational preparation, licensing requirements, and salary. Lists accredited educational programs.

★8294★ *Careers in the Electronics Industry*
International Society of Certified Electronics
  Technicians (ISCET)
2708 W. Berry St.
Fort Worth, TX 76109
Ph: (817)921-9101
Describes the work of electronic technicians and consumer electronic technicians. Covers training and qualifications, employment outlook, earnings, and working conditions. Lists schools which offer CET (Certified Electronic Technician) Associates Certification programs.

★8295★ *Civil Engineering Technician*
Careers, Inc.
PO Box 135
Largo, FL 34649-0135
Ph: (813)584-7333
1995. Two-page occupational summary card describing duties, working conditions, per-

sonal qualifications, training, earnings and hours, employment outlook, places of employment, related careers, and where to write for more information.

★8296★ *"Civil Engineering Technicians"* in *Career Information Center* (Vol.4)
Simon and Schuster
200 Old Tappan Rd.
Old Tappan, NJ 07675
Fax: 800-445-6991   Fr: 800-223-2348
Richard Lidz and Linda Perrin, editorial directors. Fifth edition, 1993. A multi-volume set that profiles more than 600 occupations. Each occupational profile describes job duties, educational requirements, getting a job, advancement possibilities, employment outlook, working conditions, earnings and benefits, and sources of additional information.

★8297★ *Electrical Engineering Technician*
Careers, Inc.
PO Box 135
Largo, FL 34649-0135
Ph: (813)584-7333
1992. Two-page summary describing duties, working conditions, personal qualifications, training, earnings and hours, employment outlook, places of employment, related careers, and where to write for more information.

★8298★ *Electrical Engineers and Technicians*
Chronicle Guidance Publications, Inc.
66 Aurora St.
PO Box 1190
Moravia, NY 13118-1190
Ph: (315)497-0330   Fax: (315)497-3359
Fr: 800-622-7284
1992. Career brief describing the nature of the job, working conditions, hours and earnings, education and training, licensure, certification, unions, personal qualifications, social and psychological factors, location, employment outlook, entry methods, advancement, and related occupations.

★8299★ *"Electrical Technicians"* in *Encyclopedia of Careers and Vocational Guidance* (Vol.2, pp. 542-545)
J.G. Ferguson Publishing Co.
200 W. Madison St., Ste. 300
Chicago, IL 60606
Ph: (312)580-5480   Fax: (312)580-4948
William E. Hopke, editor in chief. Ninth edition, 1993. Four-volume set that profiles 900 occupations and describes job trends in 74 industries. Chapters include "Civil Engineering Technicians" and "Industrial Engineering Techinicians". Includes career description, educational requirements, history of the job, methods of entry, advancement, employment outlook, earnings, conditions of work, social and psychological factors, and sources of further information.

★8300★ *Electronics Technician*
Careers, Inc.
PO Box 135
Largo, FL 34649-0135
Ph: (813)584-7333

1991. Two-page occupational summary card describing duties, working conditions, personal qualifications, training, earnings and hours, employment outlook, places of employment, related careers, and where to write for more information.

★8301★ *"Electronics Technician"* in *Guide to Federal Technical, Trades and Labor Jobs* (p. 191)
Resource Directories
3361 Executive Pkwy., Ste. 302
Toledo, OH 43606
Ph: (419)536-5353   Fax: (419)536-7056
Fr: 800-274-8515

Rod W. Durgin, editor. Second edition, 1992. Describes where and how to apply for a federal job. Profiles 300 federal jobs that do not require a college degree. Gives a description, salary, locations, and the agencies that hire the most employees for each job.

★8302★ Electronics Technicians
Chronicle Guidance Publications, Inc.
66 Aurora St.
PO Box 1190
Moravia, NY 13118-1190
Ph: (315)497-0330   Fax: (315)497-3359
Fr: 800-622-7284
1994. Career brief describing the nature of the job, working conditions, hours and earnings, education and training, licensure, certification, unions, personal qualifications, social and psychological factors, location, employment outlook, entry methods, advancement, and related occupations.

★8303★ "Engineering and Science Technicians" in *Jobs! What They Are—Where They Are—What They Pay!* **(pp. 122)**
Simon & Schuster, Inc.
Simon & Schuster Bldg.
1230 Avenue of the Americas
New York, NY 10020
Ph: (212)698-7000   Fr: 800-223-2348
Robert O. Snelling and Anne M. Snelling. Third revised edition, 1992. Includes a chapter titled "Electronics and Mathematical Technicians". Describes duties and responsibilities, earnings, employment opportunities, training, and qualifications.

★8304★ "Engineering Technician" in *Jobs Rated Almanac*
World Almanac
1 International Blvd., Ste. 444
Mahwah, NJ 07495
Ph: (201)529-6900   Fax: (201)529-6901
Les Krantz. Second edition, 1992. Ranks 250 jobs by environment, salary, outlooks, physical demands, stress, security, travel opportunities, and extra perks. Includes jobs the editor feels are the most common, most interesting, and the most rapidly growing.

★8305★ "Engineering Technician" in *Opportunities in Public Health Careers* **(pp. 71-72)**
National Textbook Co. (NTC)
VGM Career Books
4255 W. Touhy Ave.
Lincolnwood, IL 60646-1975
Ph: (708)679-5500   Fax: (708)679-2494
Fr: 800-323-4900
George E. Pickett. 1988. Defines the public health field and describes career opportunities as well as educational preparation and the future of the public health field. The appendices list public health organizations, state and federal public health agencies, and graduate schools offering public health programs.

★8306★ "Engineering Technicians" in *Occupational Outlook Handbook*
U.S. Government Printing Office
Superintendent of Documents
Washington, DC 20402
Ph: (202)512-1800   Fax: (202)512-2250
Biennial; latest edition, 1994-95. Encyclopedia of careers describing about 250 occupations and comprising about 85 percent of all jobs in the economy. Occupations that require lengthy education or training are given the most attention. Each occupation's profile describes what the worker does on the job, working conditions, education and training re-

quirements, advancement possibilities, job outlook, earnings, and sources of additional information.

★8307★ "Engineering Technology" in *Career Connection for Technical Education* **(pp. 70-71)**
JIST Works, Inc.
720 N. Park Ave.
Indianapolis, IN 46202-3431
Ph: (317)264-3720   Fax: (317)264-3709
Fred A. Rowe. 1994, second edition. Describes in detail technical occupations. Includes information on recommended high school courses, course requirements, related careers, and a self-assessment guide.

★8308★ Industrial Engineering Technicians
Chronicle Guidance Publications, Inc.
66 Aurora St.
PO Box 1190
Moravia, NY 13118-1190
Ph: (315)497-0330   Fax: (315)497-3359
Fr: 800-622-7284
1994. Career brief describing the nature of the job, working conditions, hours and earnings, education and training, licensure, certification, unions, personal qualifications, social and psychological factors, location, employment outlook, entry methods, advancement, and related occupations.

★8309★ Mechanical Engineer Technician
Careers, Inc.
PO Box 135
Largo, FL 34649-0135
Ph: (813)584-7333
1992. Two-page occupational summary card describing duties, working conditions, personal qualifications, training, earnings and hours, employment outlook, places of employment, related careers, and where to write for more information.

★8310★ Mechanical Engineering Technicians
Chronicle Guidance Publications, Inc.
66 Aurora St.
PO Box 1190
Moravia, NY 13118-1190
Ph: (315)497-0330   Fax: (315)497-3359
Fr: 800-622-7284
1991. Career brief describing the nature of the job, working conditions, hours and earnings, education and training, licensure, certification, unions, personal qualifications, social and psychological factors, location, employment outlook, entry methods, advancement, and related occupations.

★8311★ Mechanical Engineering Technology
American Society of Mechanical Engineers (ASME)
345 E. 47th St.
New York, NY 10017
Ph: (212)705-7722   Fr: 800-321-2633
1987. Covers high school and college preparation, associate and bachelor degree programs, and career opportunities for mechanical engineer technologists.

★8312★ Nuclear Power Plant Engineers & Technicians
Chronicle Guidance Publications, Inc.
66 Aurora St.
PO Box 1190
Moravia, NY 13118-1190
Ph: (315)497-0330   Fax: (315)497-3359
Fr: 800-622-7284
1993. Career brief describing the nature of the job, working conditions, hours and earnings, education and training, licensure, certification, unions, personal qualifications, social and psychological factors, location, employment outlook, entry methods, advancement, and related occupations.

★8313★ Opportunities in Engineering Technology Careers
National Textbook Co. (NTC)
VGM Career Books
4255 W. Touhy Ave.
Lincolnwood, IL 60646-1975
Ph: (708)679-5500   Fax: (708)679-2494
Fr: 800-323-4900
John E. Heer and D. Joseph Hagerty. 1987. Describes the many opportunities available for engineering technicians. Explains job duties, educational requirements, salary, working conditions, employment outlook, and advancement opportunities. Lists accredited engineering technology programs.

★8314★ The Power of the Profession: Your Career as an Electronics Technician
Electronic Industries Association (EIA)
2001 Pennsylvania Ave., NW, Ste. 110
Washington, DC 20006-1813
Ph: (202)457-4900
1992. This 12 page pamphlet includes information on employment outlook, earnings, education, continuing education, and advancement opportunities for electronics technicians.

★8315★ Technicians, Science and Engineering
Careers, Inc.
PO Box 135
Largo, FL 34649-0135
Ph: (813)584-7333
1992. Four-page brief offering the definition, history, duties, working conditions, personal qualifications, educational requirements, earnings, hours, employment outlook, advancement, and careers related to this position.

Professional Associations

★8316★ Electronics Technicians Association, International (ETA-I)
602 N. Jackson
Greencastle, IN 46135
Ph: (317)653-8262   Fax: (317)653-8262
Members: Skilled electronics technicians. **Purpose:** Provides placement service; offers certification examinations for electronics technicians and satellite installers. Compiles wage and manpower statistics. **Publications:** *Directory of Professional Electronics Technicians*, annual. • *EEA Training Pro-*

gram, monthly. • *Management Update*, monthly. • *Technician Association News*, monthly.

★8317★ International Society of Certified Electronics Technicians (ISCET)
2708 W. Berry, Ste. 3
Fort Worth, TX 76109
Ph: (817)921-9101   Fax: (817)921-3741
Members: Technicians in 37 countries who have been certified by the society. **Purpose:** Seeks to provide a fraternal bond among certified electronics technicians, raise their public image, and improve the effectiveness of industry education programs for technicians. Offers training programs in new electronics information. Maintains library of service literature for consumer electronic equipment, including manuals and schematics for out-of-date equipment. Offers general radiotelephone license. Sponsors testing program for certification of electronics technicians in the fields of audio, communications, computer, consumer, industrial, medical electronics, radar, radio-television, and video. Operates Hall of Fame. **Publications:** *ISCET Update*, quarterly. • *Professional Electronics Magazine*, bimonthly. • *Technical Log*, quarterly.

STANDARDS/CERTIFICATION AGENCIES

★8318★ Electronics Technicians Association, International (ETA-I)
602 N. Jackson
Greencastle, IN 46135
Ph: (317)653-8262   Fax: (317)653-8262
Provides placement service; offers certification examinations for electronics technicians and satellite installers. Compiles wage and manpower statistics.

★8319★ International Society of Certified Electronics Technicians (ISCET)
2708 W. Berry, Ste. 3
Fort Worth, TX 76109
Ph: (817)921-9101   Fax: (817)921-3741
Technicians in 37 countries who have been certified by the society. Seeks to provide a fraternal bond among certified electronics technicians, raise their public image, and improve the effectiveness of industry education programs for technicians. Offers general radiotelephone license. Sponsors testing program for certification of electronics technicians in the fields of audio, communications, computer, consumer, industrial, medical electronics, radar, radio-television, and video.

TEST GUIDES

★8320★ *Career Examination Series: Assistant Air Pollution Control Engineer*
National Learning Corp.
212 Michael Dr.
Syosset, NY 11791
Ph: (516)921-8888   Fax: (516)921-8743
Fr: 800-645-6337
Jack Rudman. 1993. Test guide including questions and answers for students or professionals in the field who seek advancement through examination.

★8321★ *Career Examination Series: Assistant Engineering Technician*
National Learning Corp.
212 Michael Dr.
Syosset, NY 11791
Ph: (516)921-8888   Fax: (516)921-8743
Fr: 800-645-6337
Jack Rudman. 1993. Test guide including questions and answers for students or professionals in the field who seek advancement through examination.

★8322★ *Career Examination Series: Associate Engineering Technician*
National Learning Corp.
212 Michael Dr.
Syosset, NY 11791
Ph: (516)921-8888   Fax: (516)921-8743
Fr: 800-645-6337
Jack Rudman. 1993. Test guide including questions and answers for students or professionals in the field who seek advancement through examination.

★8323★ *Career Examination Series: Engineering Materials Technician*
National Learning Corp.
212 Michael Dr.
Syosset, NY 11791
Ph: (516)921-8888   Fax: (516)921-8743
Fr: 800-645-6337
Jack Rudman. 1993. Test guide including questions and answers for students or professionals in the field who seek advancement through examination.

★8324★ *Career Examination Series: Engineering Technician*
National Learning Corp.
212 Michael Dr.
Syosset, NY 11791
Ph: (516)921-8888   Fax: (516)921-8743
Fr: 800-645-6337
Jack Rudman. Test guide including questions and answers for students or professionals in the field who seek advancement through examination.

★8325★ *The CET Exam Book (Engineering Technicians)*
TAB/McGraw-Hill
Blue Ridge Summit, PA 17294-0850
Ph: (717)794-2191   Fr: 800-233-1128
Dick Glass and Ron Crow. Third edition, 1992. Helps prepare individuals for the associate-level CET (Certified Electronic Technician) examination.

EDUCATIONAL DIRECTORIES AND PROGRAMS

★8326★ *CED Directory of Engineering and Engineering Technology Co-Op Programs*
Cooperative Education Division (CED)
c/o Cooperative Education Program
Mississippi State University
Box 6046
Mississippi State, MS 39762
Ph: (601)325-3823   Fax: (601)325-8733
Mike Mathews, Contact
Biennial, January of odd years. Covers about 180 colleges and universities with cooperative education programs in engineering and engineering technology; coverage includes the United States and Canada. Entries include: School name, address, phone, fax, electronic mail address, names and titles of key personnel, description of program, accreditation, enrollment, number of staff. Arrangement: Alphabetical.

★8327★ *Directory of Manufacturing Education Programs in Colleges, Universities, and Technical Institutes*
Society of Manufacturing Engineers
1 SME Dr.
PO Box 930
Dearborn, MI 48121-0930
Ph: (313)271-1500   Fax: (313)271-2861
Fr: 800-733-4763
Nancy Nowitzke, Contact
Biennial, even years. Covers over 500 educational institutions offering graduate and undergraduate programs and course work in manufacturing engineering and manufacturing engineering technology; coverage includes Canada. Entries include: Institution name, address; names and phone numbers of dean and department chairman; degree programs offered, whether night courses or a cooperative program are offered. Arrangement: Alphabetical by school name.

AWARDS, SCHOLARSHIPS, GRANTS, AND FELLOWSHIPS

★8328★ Technician of the Month Award
American Society of Certified Engineering Technicians
PO Box 371474
El Paso, TX 79937
Ph: (915)591-5115
To recognize a certified engineering technician for outstanding achievement. Members are eligible. A picture and an article in *Certified Engineering Technician* magazine are awarded monthly. Established in 1966.

★8329★ Technician of the Year Award
American Society of Certified Engineering
  Technicians
PO Box 371474
El Paso, TX 79937
Ph: (915)591-5115

To recognize engineering technicians for extraordinary technical achievements. Honorees receive a plaque at the annual meeting and a picture and article in the annual meeting program and *Certified Engineering Technician* magazine. Established in 1965.

BASIC REFERENCE GUIDES AND HANDBOOKS

★8330★ Complete Construction Handbook
McGraw-Hill Inc.
11 W. 19 St.
New York, NY 10011
Ph: 800-722-4726

Joseph J. Waddell and Joseph A. Dobrowlski. 1993.

★8331★ Standard Handbook for Electrical Engineers
McGraw-Hill, Inc.
1221 Avenue of the Americas
New York, NY 10020
Ph: (212)512-2000   Fr: 800-722-4726

Donald G. Fink and H. Wayne Beaty, editors. Thirteenth edition, 1993. Covers new developments, and the generation, transmission, distribution, control, conservation, and application of electrical power. Lists current standards governing the electrical engineering field.

★8332★ The VNR Dictionary of Civil Engineering
Van Nostrand Reinhold
115 5th Ave.
New York, NY 10013
John S. Scott. 1993.

PROFESSIONAL AND TRADE PERIODICALS

★8333★ ETA Technician Association News
Electronic Technicians Association (ETA)
602 N. Jackson St.
Greencastle, IN 46135
Ph: (317)653-5541   Fax: (317)653-8262
Fr: 800-359-6706
Dick Glass

Monthly. Serves member technicians with news of the Association and the electronics industry, including items on service, education, employment, management, and events. Contains information on membership, management, telecommunications, and business and technical training programs. Recurring features include editorials, news of research, letters to the editor, book reviews, and a calendar of events.

★8334★ International Society of Certified Electronics Technicians— Update
International Society of Certified Electronics
  Technicians
2708 W. Berry St.
Ft. Worth, TX 76109
Ph: (817)921-9101   Fax: (817)921-3741
Barbara Rubin

Quarterly. Reflects the aims of the Society, which are to raise the public image of certified electronics technicians and to improve the effectiveness of industry education programs for technicians. Recurring features include news of research, a calendar of events, reports of meetings, news of educational opportunities, and job listings.

Library Technicians

Library technicians help librarians acquire, prepare, and organize material, and help users find materials and information. Technicians in small libraries handle a wide range of duties; those in large libraries usually specialize. Library technicians are also known as **library technical assistants**. Technicians assist in the use of public catalogs, direct library users to references, organize and maintain periodicals, and perform routine cataloging and coding of library materials.

Salaries

Salaries for library technicians vary widely depending on the type of the library and geographic location.

Library technicians, federal government $23,900/year

Employment Outlook

Growth rate until the year 2005: Average.

Library Technicians

CAREER GUIDES

★8335★ Careers for Bookworms & Other Literary Types
National Textbook Co. (NTC)
VGM Career Books
4255 W. Touhy Ave.
Lincolnwood, IL 60646-1975
Ph: (708)679-5500   Fax: (708)679-2494
Fr: 800-323-4900
Marjorie Eberts and Margaret Gisler. 1991.
Describes employment opportunities for jobs in education, publishing, libraries, museums, and more.

★8336★ "Health Sciences Library Assistant" in 150 Careers in the Health Care Field
Reed Reference Publishing
121 Chanlon Rd.
PO Box 31
New Providence, NJ 07974
Fax: (908)665-6688   Fr: 800-521-8110
Stanley Alperin. Third edition, 1993. Profiles health care occupations requiring a bachelor's degree or less. Describes the nature of the work, educational preparation, licensing requirements, and salary. Lists accredited educational programs.

★8337★ "Library Aide and Technician" in Guide to Federal Technical, Trades and Labor Jobs (p. 204)
Resource Directories
3361 Executive Pkwy., Ste. 302
Toledo, OH 43606
Ph: (419)536-5353   Fax: (419)536-7056
Fr: 800-274-8515
Rod W. Durgin, editor. Second edition, 1992. Describes where and how to apply for a federal job as a library aide or technician. Provides description, salary, locations, and the agencies that hire the most employees for that job.

★8338★ Library Technical Assistant
Careers, Inc.
PO Box 135
Largo, FL 34649-0135
Ph: (813)584-7333
1994. Two-page occupational summary card describing duties, working conditions, per-

sonal qualifications, training, earnings and hours, employment outlook, places of employment, related careers, and where to write for more information.

★8339★ Library Technicians and Assistants
Chronicle Guidance Publications, Inc.
66 Aurora St.
PO Box 1190
Moravia, NY 13118-1190
Ph: (315)497-0330   Fax: (315)497-3359
Fr: 800-622-7284
1993. Career brief describing the nature of the job, working conditions, hours and earnings, education and training, licensure, certification, unions, personal qualifications, social and psychological factors, location, employment outlook, entry methods, advancement, and related occupations.

★8340★ "Library Technicians and Assistants" in Jobs! What They Are— Where They Are—What They Pay (p. 113)
Simon & Schuster, Inc.
Simon & Schuster Bldg.
1230 Avenue of the Americas
New York, NY 10020
Ph: (212)698-7000   Fr: 800-223-2348
Robert O. Snelling and Anne M. Snelling. 3rd edition, 1992. Describes duties and responsibilities, earnings, employment opportunities, training, and qualifications.

★8341★ "Library Technicians" in Encyclopedia of Careers and Vocational Guidance (Vol.3, pp. 297-298)
J.G. Ferguson Publishing Co.
200 W. Madison St., Ste. 300
Chicago, IL 60606
Ph: (312)580-5480   Fax: (312)580-4948
William E. Hopke, editor in chief. Ninth edition, 1993. Four-volume set that profiles 900 occupations and describes job trends in 74 industries. Includes career description, educational requirements, history of the job, methods of entry, advancement, employment outlook, earnings, conditions of work, social and psychological factors, and sources of further information.

★8342★ "Library Technicians" in Occupational Outlook Handbook
U.S. Government Printing Office
Superintendent of Documents
Washington, DC 20402
Ph: (202)512-1800   Fax: (202)512-2250
Biennial; latest edition, 1994-95. Encyclopedia of careers describing about 250 occupations and comprising about 85 percent of all jobs in the economy. Occupations that require lengthy education or training are given the most attention. Each occupation's profile describes what the worker does on the job, working conditions, education and training requirements, advancement possibilities, job outlook, earnings, and sources of additional information.

★8343★ "Service Occupations" in Opportunities in Vocational and Technical Career (pp. 76-90)
National Textbook Co. (NTC)
VGM Career Books
4255 W. Touhy Ave.
Lincolnwood, IL 60646-1975
Ph: (708)679-5500   Fax: (708)679-2494
Fr: 800-323-4900
Adrian A. Paradis. 1992. This book describes careers which can be prepared for by attending vocational or technical schools. Gives the employment outlook and salary information.

PROFESSIONAL ASSOCIATIONS

★8344★ American Library Association (ALA)
50 E. Huron St.
Chicago, IL 60611
Ph: (312)944-6780   Fax: (312)280-3255
Fr: 800-545-2433
Members: Librarians, libraries, trustees, friends of libraries, and others interested in the responsibilities of libraries in the educational, social, and cultural needs of society.
Purpose: Promotes and improves library service and librarianship. Establishes standards of service, support, education, and welfare for libraries and library personnel; promotes the adoption of such standards in libraries of all kinds; safeguards the professional status of

librarians; encourages the recruiting of competent personnel for professional careers in librarianship; promotes popular understanding and public acceptance of the value of library service and librarianship. Works in liaison with federal agencies to initiate the enactment and administration of legislation that will extend library services. Offers placement services. **Publications:** *ALA Handbook of Organization and Membership Directory*, annual. • *ALA Washington Newsletter*, periodic. • *American Libraries*, 11/year. • *Book Links*, bimonthly. • *Booklist*, biweekly. • *Library Systems Newsletter*, monthly. • *Library Technology Reports*, bimonthly.

★8345★ Council on Library-Media Technical-Assistants (COLT)
c/o Margaret Barron
Cuyahoga Community College
Library/Media Technology Dept., SC 201
2900 Community College Ave.
Cleveland, OH 44115
Ph: (216)987-4296   Fax: (216)987-4404
Members: Persons involved in two-year associate degree programs for the training of library technical assistants (professional-support workers) and graduates of programs employed as library/media technical assistants (B.A. degree holders without M.L.S. degree). Membership includes junior college deans, librarians, curriculum directors, professors, employers, special libraries, university libraries, library schools, publishers, and library technical assistants. Provides a channel of communication among the institutions and personnel that have developed such training programs; attempts to standardize curriculum offerings; develops educational standards; conducts research on graduates of the programs; represents the interests of library technical assistants and support staff . The council's concerns also include development of clear job descriptions and criteria for employment of technicians and dissemination of information to the public and to prospective students. Sponsors workshops for support staff in areas such as management, supervisory skills, interpersonal communication, business writing, and media center management. Maintains speakers' bureau. Is developing a program for certification of library media technicians and a continuing education program for library support staff. **Publications:** *Membership Directory and Data Book*, biennial. • *Mosaic*, monthly.

STANDARDS/CERTIFICATION AGENCIES

★8346★ American Library Association (ALA)
50 E. Huron St.
Chicago, IL 60611
Ph: (312)944-6780   Fax: (312)280-3255
Fr: 800-545-2433
Establishes standards of service, support, education, and welfare for libraries and library personnel; promotes the adoption of such standards in libraries of all kinds.

★8347★ Council on Library-Media Technical-Assistants (COLT)
c/o Margaret Barron
Cuyahoga Community College
Library/Media Technology Dept., SC 201
2900 Community College Ave.
Cleveland, OH 44115
Ph: (216)987-4296   Fax: (216)987-4404
Provides a channel of communication among the institutions and personnel that have developed such training programs; attempts to standardize curriculum offerings; develops educational standards; conducts research on graduates of the programs; represents the interests of library technical assistants and support staff. Is developing a program for certification of library media technicians.

TEST GUIDES

★8348★ Career Examination Series: Audio—Visual Aid Technician
National Learning Corp.
212 Michael Dr.
Syosset, NY 11791
Ph: (516)921-8888   Fax: (516)921-8743
Fr: 800-645-6337
Jack Rudman. 1993. Test guide including questions and answers for students or professionals in the field who seek advancement through examination.

★8349★ Career Examination Series: Library Technician
National Learning Corp.
212 Michael Dr.
Syosset, NY 11791
Ph: (516)921-8888   Fax: (516)921-8743
Fr: 800-645-6337
Jack Rudman. A study guide for professional and trainee library technicians. Includes a multiple-choice examination section; provides answers.

EDUCATIONAL DIRECTORIES AND PROGRAMS

★8350★ Undergraduate Programs in Library Education
Standing Committee on Library Education
50 E. Huron St.
Chicago, IL 60611
Ph: (312)280-4277   Fax: (312)280-3256
Fr: 800-545-2433
Margaret Myers, Contact
Irregular, latest edition April 1991. Covers four-year schools that offer undergraduate programs in library science. Entries include: Institution name, address, phone, degree offered. Arrangement: Geographical.

PROFESSIONAL AND TRADE PERIODICALS

★8351★ ALCTS Newsletter
Association for Library Collections and Technical Services (ALCTS)
50 E. Huron St.
Chicago, IL 60611
Ph: (708)892-7465   Fax: (708)892-7466
Ann Swartzell
Concerned with collection development, cataloging, acquisitions, microform management, serials management, and preservation of materials in libraries. Contains news of activities of the Division and news items contributed by press releases from agencies and publishers. Recurring features include a calendar of events, notices of new publications, and a column titled Council of Regional Groups Update.

★8352★ B/ITE
Information Technology Division
c/o Karol Feltes Battelle
505 King Ave.
Columbus, OH 43201
Ph: (614)424-6307   Fax: (614)424-4738
Karol Feltes
Quarterly. Presents information technology and its applications to libraries. Provides a forum and means of communication for Division members. Recurring features include a calendar of events, reports of meetings, news of educational opportunities, and notices of publications available.

★8353★ Friends of Libraries U.S.A. News Update
American Library Association, Reference and Adult Services Division
E Huron St.
Chicago, IL 60611-2795
Ph: (312)944-6780   Fax: (312)440-9374
Sandy Dolnick, Contact
Quarterly. Informs members on activities of benefit to them, including organizing, fundraising, literacy programs, and book and author events. Recurring features include book reviews. columns titled Friends in Action and New Books: Eclectic Selections for Reading Groups, Programs and Reading Enjoyment.

★8354★ The Primary Source
Soc. of Mississippi Archivists
PO Box 1151
Jackson, MS 39215-1151
Ph: (601)359-6868
Mattie Sink
Quarterly. Focuses on activities and trends in the archival and library community both regionally and nationally. Includes information on conservation and articles on state repositories and their holdings. Recurring features include news of research, book reviews, and a calendar of events.

★8355★ *Technicalities*
Media Periodicals
4050 Pennsylvania Ave., Ste. 310
Kansas City, MO 64111-3051
Ph: (816)756-1490   Fax: (816)756-0159
Fr: 800-347-2665
Brian Alley
Monthly. Presents discussion, opinions, and reviews on library management topics, in-cluding computer applications, online public access catalogs, library budgets, collection building, automation, software, library marketplace trends, and the Library of Congress.

Paralegals

Lawyers are often assisted in their work by **paralegals**, also called **legal assistants**, who perform many of the same tasks as lawyers, except for those tasks considered as being the practice of law. Paralegals work directly under the supervision of a lawyer. While the lawyer assumes responsibility for the paralegal's work, a paralegal is often allowed to perform all the functions of a lawyer other than accepting clients, setting legal fees, giving legal advice, or presenting a case in court. Paralegals generally do background work for lawyers. They may conduct research to identify appropriate laws, judicial decisions, legal articles, and other material that will be used to determine whether or not the client has a good case.

Salaries

Earnings of legal assistants vary greatly depending on education, training, experience type of employer, and geographic location. Average annual salaries of paralegals are as follows:

Beginning paralegals	$23,400/year
Paralegals, 6-10 years experience	$28,200/year
Paralegals, over 10 years experience	$29,800/year
Paralegals, federal government	$37,600/year

Employment Outlook

Growth rate until the year 2005: Much faster than the average.

Paralegals

CAREER GUIDES

★8356★ "Corporate Legal Assistants" in
Career Information Center **(Vol.11)**
Simon and Schuster
200 Old Tappan Rd.
Old Tappan, NJ 07675
Fax: 800-445-6991   Fr: 800-223-2348
Richard Lidz and Linda Perrin, editorial directors. Fifth edition, 1993. A multi-volume set that profiles over 600 occupations. Each occupational profile describes job duties, educational requirements, advancement possibilities, employment outlook, working conditions, earnings and benefits, and where to write for more information.

★8357★ How to Find a Job As a
Paralegal: A Step-by-Step Job Search
Guide
West Publishing Co.
610 Opperman Dr.
Eagan, MN 55123
Ph: (612)687-7000
Marie Kisiel, editor. Second edition, 1992.

★8358★ "Law and Legal Services" in
Where the Jobs Are: The Hottest
Careers for the 90s (pp. 183-194)
Career Press
180 5th Ave.
Hawthorne, NJ 07507
Ph: (201)427-0229   Fax: (201)427-2037
Fr: 800-CAREER-1
Joyce Hadley. 1995. Offers a job-hunting strategy for the 1990s as well as descriptions of growing careers of the decade. Each profile includes general information, forecasts, growth, education and training, licensing requirements, and salary information.

★8359★ "Legal Assistants" in American
Almanac of Jobs and Salaries (pp. 246)
Avon Books
1350 Avenue of the Americas
New York, NY 10019
Ph: (212)261-6800   Fr: 800-238-0658
John Wright, editor. Revised and updated, 1994-95. A comprehensive guide to the wages of hundreds of occupations in a wide variety of industries and organizations.

★8360★ "Legal Assistants" in *Career*
Discovery Encyclopedia **(Vol.3, pp.**
172-173)
J.G. Ferguson Publishing Co.
200 W. Madison St., Ste. 300
Chicago, IL 60606
Ph: (312)580-5480   Fax: (312)580-4948
Russell E. Primm, editor-in chief. 1993. This six volume set contains two-page articles for 504 occupations. Each article describes job duties, earnings, and educational and training requirements. The whole set is arranged alphabetically by job title. Designed for junior high and older students.

★8361★ "Legal Assistants" in *Career*
Opportunities for Writers **(pp. 219-220)**
Facts on File
460 Park Ave. S.
New York, NY 10016-7382
Ph: (212)683-2244   Fax: 800-678-3633
Fr: 800-322-8755
Rosemary Guiley. 1992. Describes approximately 90 careers in eight major fields, offering such details as prerequisites, employment and advancement oportunities, organizations to join, and opportunities for women and minorities.

★8362★ "Legal Assistants" in *Guide to*
Careers Without College **(pp. 49-51)**
Franklin Watts, Inc.
387 Park Ave. S., 4th Fl.
New York, NY 10016
Ph: (212)686-7070   Fr: 800-672-6672
Kathleen S. Abrams. 1988. Discusses rewarding careers that do not require a college degree.

★8363★ "Legal Assistants" in *Jobs!*
What They Are—Where They Are—
What They Pay **(p. 223)**
Simon & Schuster, Inc.
Simon & Schuster Bldg.
1230 Avenue of the Americas
New York, NY 10020
Ph: (212)698-7000   Fr: 800-223-2348
Robert O. Snelling and Anne M. Snelling. 3rd edition, 1992. Describes duties and responsibilities, earnings, employment opportunities, training, and qualifications.

★8364★ "Legal Assistants: Lawyer's
Helpers" in Careers for Women
Without College Degrees **(pp. 227-230)**
McGraw-Hill, Inc.
1221 Avenue of the Americas
New York, NY 10020
Ph: (212)512-2000   Fr: 800-722-4726
Beatryce Nivens. 1988. Contains exercises in goal setting, decision making, and skills assessment. Explores 19 careers with the best occupational outlook; Describes nontraditional college-degree programs.

★8365★ Legal Assistants (Paralegals)
Chronicle Guidance Publications, Inc.
66 Aurora St.
PO Box 1190
Moravia, NY 13118-1190
Ph: (315)497-0330   Fax: (315)497-3359
Fr: 800-622-7284
1991. Career brief describing the nature of the job, working conditions, hours and earnings, education and training, licensure, certification, unions, personal qualifications, social and psychological factors, location, employment outlook, entry methods, advancement, and related occupations.

★8366★ NFPA Affirmation of
Professional Responsibility
National Federation of Paralegal
   Associations (NFPA)
5700 Old Orchard Rd.
Skokie, IL 60077-1057
Ph: (708)966-6066
1990. Describes the professional responsibility and conduct of the paralegal.

★8367★ "Office Employees" in
Opportunities in Vocational and
Technical Careers (pp. 47-58)
National Textbook Co. (NTC)
VGM Career Books
4255 W. Touhy Ave.
Lincolnwood, IL 60646-1975
Ph: (708)679-5500   Fax: (708)679-2494
Fr: 800-323-4900
Adrian A. Paradis. 1992. Describes careers which can be prepared for by attending vocational-technical schools. Gives the employment outlook and salary information.

★8368★ *Opportunities in Paralegal Careers*
National Textbook Co. (NTC)
VGM Career Books
4255 W. Touhy Ave.
Lincolnwood, IL 60646-1975
Ph: (708)679-5500   Fax: (708)679-2494
Fr: 800-323-4900

Alice Fins. 1990. Describes paralegal work. Includes information on working conditions, salary, educational preparation, and related careers.

★8369★ "Paralegal" in *100 Best Careers for the Year 2000* (pp. 182-184)
Arco Pub.
201 W. 103rd St.
Indianapolis, IN 46290
Ph: 800-428-5331   Fax: 800-835-3202

Shelly Field. 1992. Describes 100 job opportunities expected to grow fast throughout the next decade. Provides information on job duties and responsibilities, training requirements, education, advancement opportunities, experience and qualifications, and typical salaries.

★8370★ "Paralegal Aides" in *Career Information Center* (Vol.11)
Simon and Schuster
200 Old Tappan Rd.
Old Tappan, NJ 07675
Fax: 800-445-6991   Fr: 800-223-2348

Richard Lidz and Linda Perrin, editorial directors. Fifth edition, 1993. This 13-volume set profiles over 600 occupations. Each occupational profile describes job duties, educational requirements, advancement possibilities, employment outlook, working conditions, earnings and benefits, and where to write for more information.

★8371★ *Paralegal: An Insider's Guide to One of the Fastest-Growing Occupations of the 1990s*
Petersons Guides, Inc.
PO Box 2123
Princeton, NJ 08543-2123
Ph: (609)243-9111   Fax: (609)243-9150
Fr: 800-338-3282

Barbara Bernardo, editor. Second edition. Offers career tips, nationwide salary survey results, information on pararalegal training programs, and additional information on the legal industry.

★8372★ "Paralegal Assistant" in *Jobs Rated Almanac*
World Almanac
1 International Blvd., Ste. 444
Mahwah, NJ 07495
Ph: (201)529-6900   Fax: (201)529-6901

Les Krantz. Second edition, 1992. Ranks 250 jobs by environment, salary, outlooks, physical demands, stress, security, travel opportunities, and extra perks. Includes jobs the editor feels are the most common, most interesting, and the most rapidly growing.

★8373★ "Paralegal" in *Career Choices for the 90's for Students of English*
Walker and Co.
435 Hudson St.
New York, NY 10014
Ph: (212)727-8300   Fax: (212)727-0984
Fr: 800-289-2553

1990. Offers career alternatives for students of English. Gives the outlook and competition for entry-level candidates. Provides job-hunting tips.

★8374★ *Paralegal Employment: Facts and Strategies for the 1990's*
West Publishing Co.
50 W. Kellogg Blvd.
PO Box 64526
St. Paul, MN 55164
Ph: (612)228-2778

William P. Statsky. Second edition, 1993. Includes an index.

★8375★ "Paralegal Profession" in *Career Choices for the 90's for Students of History* (pp. 139-152)
Walker and Co.
435 Hudson St.
New York, NY 10014
Ph: (212)727-8300   Fax: (212)727-0984
Fr: 800-289-2553

1990. Offers alternatives for students of history. Gives information about the outlook and competition for entry-level candidates. Provides job-hunting tips.

★8376★ "Paralegal Profession" in *Encyclopedia of Career Choices for the 1990s: A Guide to Entry Level Jobs* (pp. 625-638)
Berkley Pub.
PO Box 506
East Rutherford, NJ 07073
Fax: (201)933-2316   Fr: 800-788-6262

1992. Describes entry-level careers in a variety of industries. Presents qualifications required, working conditions, salary, internships, and professional associations.

★8377★ *Paralegal Responsibilites*
National Federation of Paralegal Associations (NFPA)
5700 Old Orchard Rd.
Skokie, IL 60077-1057
Ph: (708)966-6066

Typical duties of paralegals are itemized.

★8378★ "Paralegal Services" in *Career Connection for Technical Education* (pp. 120-121)
JIST Works, Inc.
720 N. Park Ave.
Indianapolis, IN 46202-3431
Ph: (317)264-3720   Fax: (317)264-3709

Fred A. Rowe. 1994, second edition. Describes in detail technical occupations. Includes information on recommended high school courses, course requirements, related careers, and a self-assessment guide.

★8379★ "Paralegals" in *America's 50 Fastest Growing Jobs* (pp. 86)
JIST Works, Inc.
720 N. Park Ave.
Indianapolis, IN 46202-3431
Ph: (317)264-3720   Fax: (317)264-3709
Fr: 800-648-5478

Michael J. Farr, compiler. 1994. Describes the 50 fastest growing jobs within major career clusters such as technicians, and marketing and sales. Each job profile explains the nature of the work, skills and abilities required, employment outlook, average earnings, related occupations, education and training requirements, and employment opportunities. Also contains career planning information and job search tips.

★8380★ "Paralegals" in *Career Discovery Encyclopedia* (Vol.4, pp. 168-169)
J.G. Ferguson Publishing Co.
200 W. Madison St., Ste. 300
Chicago, IL 60606
Ph: (312)580-5480   Fax: (312)580-4948

Russell E. Primm, editor-in chief. 1993. This six volume set contains two-page articles for 504 occupations. Each article describes job duties, earnings, and educational and training requirements. The whole set is arranged alphabetically by job title. Designed for junior high and older students.

★8381★ "Paralegals" in *Encyclopedia of Careers and Vocational Guidance* (Vol.3, pp. 676-679)
J.G. Ferguson Publishing Co.
200 W. Madison St., Ste. 300
Chicago, IL 60606
Ph: (312)580-5480   Fax: (312)580-4948

William E. Hopke, editor-in-chief. Ninth edition, 1993. Four-volume set that profiles 900 occupations and describes job trends in 74 industries. Includes career description, educational requirements, history of the job, methods of entry, advancement, employment outlook, earnings, conditions of work, social and psychological factors, and sources of further information.

★8382★ "Paralegals, or Legal Assistants" in *101 Careers: A Guide to the Fastest-Growing Opportunities* (pp. 136-139)
John Wiley & Sons, Inc.
605 3rd Ave.
New York, NY 10158-0012
Ph: (212)850-6645   Fax: (212)850-6088

Michael Harkavy. 1990. Describes the nature of the job, working conditions, employment growth, qualifications, personal skills, projected salaries, and where to write for more information.

★8383★ "Paralegals" in *Occupational Outlook Handbook*
U.S. Government Printing Office
Superintendent of Documents
Washington, DC 20402
Ph: (202)512-1800   Fax: (202)512-2250

Biennial; latest edition, 1994-95. Encyclopedia of careers describing about 250 occupations and comprising about 85 percent of all jobs in the economy. Occupations that require lengthy education or training are given the most attention. Each occupation's profile describes what the worker does on the job, working conditions, education and training requirements, advancement possibilities, job outlook, earnings, and sources of additional information.

★8384★ What Is a Paralegal? Often Asked Questions About the Paralegal Profession
National Federation of Paralegal
Associations (NFPA)
5700 Old Orchard Rd.
Skokie, IL 60077-1057
Ph: (708)966-6066
Describes where paralegals work, what they do, and how to become a paralegal.

PROFESSIONAL ASSOCIATIONS

★8385★ American Association for Paralegal Education (AAFPE)
PO Box 40244
Overland Park, KS 66204
Ph: (913)381-4458   Fax: (913)381-9308
Members: Paralegal educators and institutions of higher learning offering paralegal programs. **Purpose:** Aims to promote and maintain high standards for paralegal education. Serves as a forum and clearinghouse for information on the professional improvement of paralegal educators and education. Develops guidelines for paralegal education programs in cooperation with the American Bar Association and other institutional and professional associations. Promotes research and offers consultation services to institutions; maintains speakers' bureau. **Publications:** Journal of Paralegal Education and Practice, annual. • The Paralegal Educator, quarterly.

★8386★ Legal Assistant Management Association (LAMA)
638 Prospect Ave.
Hartford, CT 06105-4298
Ph: (203)586-7507   Fax: (203)586-7550
Members: Individuals who manage legal assistants. **Purpose:** Promotes the field of legal assistant management; conducts continuing education program for members; provides for information exchange among members and those planning to enter the field. Maintains 15 chapters and speakers' bureau. **Publications:** The LAMA Manager, quarterly. • Legal Assistant Management Association—Directory, annual.

★8387★ National Association of Legal Assistants (NALA)
1516 S. Boston, Ste. 200
Tulsa, OK 74119
Ph: (918)587-6828   Fax: (918)582-6772
Members: Professional paralegals employed for over six months; graduates or students of legal assistant training programs; attorneys. Members subscribe to and are bound by the NALA Code of Ethics and Professional Responsibility. **Purpose:** Cooperates with local, state, and national bar associations in setting standards and guidelines for legal assistants. Promotes the profession and attempts to broaden public understanding of the function of the legal assistant. Offers continuing edu-

cation for legal assistants both nationwide and statewide, and professional certification on a national basis to members and nonmembers who meet certain criteria. Conducts regional seminars; makes available courses on audio- and videotapes. **Publications:** National Association of Legal Assistants - Career Chronicle, annual. • National Association of Legal Assistants—Facts and Findings, quarterly. • Occupational Survey Report, biennial.

★8388★ National Federation of Paralegal Associations (NFPA)
PO Box 33108
Kansas City, MO 64114-0108
Ph: (816)941-4000   Fax: (816)941-2725
Members: State and local paralegal associations and other organizations supporting the goals of the federation (62); individual paralegals (17,000). **Purpose:** To serve as a national voice of the paralegal profession; to advance, foster, and promote the paralegal concept; to monitor and participate in developments in the paralegal profession; to maintain a nationwide communications network among paralegal associations and other members of the legal community. Provides a resource center of books, publications, and literature of the field. Monitors activities of local, state, and national bar associations and legislative bodies; presents testimony on matters affecting the profession. Has established a 15-member advisory council of attorneys, paralegals, educators, paralegal administrators, and members of the public to advise on policy and issues of concern to the paralegal and legal professions. **Publications:** Alert, quarterly. • Bankruptcy and Collections: The Paralegal Perspective. • Computers and the Law. • Directory of Paralegal Associations, periodic. • Directory of Paralegal Training Programs. • Ethical Wall. • Fee Recoverability. • How to Choose a Paralegal Education Program. • National Paralegal Reporter, quarterly.

★8389★ National Foundation for Professional Legal Assistants (NFPLA)
120 Penmarc Dr., Ste. 118
Raleigh, NC 27603
Ph: (919)821-7762   Fax: (919)832-6378

★8390★ National Paralegal Association (NPA)
Box 406
Solebury, PA 18963
Ph: (215)297-8333   Fax: (215)297-8358
Members: Paralegals, paralegal students, educators, supervisors, paralegal schools, administrators, law librarians, law clinics, and attorneys. **Purpose:** Objective is to advance the paralegal profession by promoting recognition, economic benefits, and high standards. Registers paralegals; maintains speakers' bureau, job bank, and placement service; offers resume preparation assistance. Sponsors commercial exhibits. Operates mail order bookstore and gift shop. Compiles statistics. Is developing promotion and public relations, insurance, certification, and computer bank programs. **Publications:** Directory of Corporate Legal Departments. • Directory of Local Paralegal Clubs, annual. • Legal Book Publishers Directory. • Local Paralegal Club Directory. • National Paralegal Employment and Salary Survey,

annual. • The Paralegal Bookstore, annual. • Paralegal Career Booklet, periodic. • The Paralegal Journal, periodic. • Paralegal School Directory, semiannual. • Paralegal Schools-State Listings.

★8391★ Professional Legal Assistants (PLA)
120 Penmarc Dr., Ste. 118
Raleigh, NC 27603
Ph: (919)821-7762   Fax: (919)832-6378
Members: Individuals who have completed or are engaged in a course of study designed to train paraprofessionals in the law as legal assistants; members of the bar, judiciary, and court system, legal assistant educators, and others interested in promoting the legal assistant profession; law firms, corporations, governmental agencies, and educational institutions. **Purpose:** Promotes development and advancement of certified legal assistants; works with bar associations and educators to develop guidelines and curricula for training programs; provides a forum for the exchange of ideas, opinions, and experiences among members and other organizations; advances understanding of the services provided by legal assistants. Sponsors training programs. **Publications:** Legal Assistant Today, bimonthly. • PLA News, quarterly.

STANDARDS/CERTIFICATION AGENCIES

★8392★ National Association of Legal Assistants (NALA)
1516 S. Boston, Ste. 200
Tulsa, OK 74119
Ph: (918)587-6828   Fax: (918)582-6772
Offers continuing education for legal assistants both nationwide and statewide, and professional certification on a national basis to members and nonmembers who meet certain criteria.

★8393★ National Federation of Paralegal Associations (NFPA)
PO Box 33108
Kansas City, MO 64114-0108
Ph: (816)941-4000   Fax: (816)941-2725
Has established a 15-member advisory council of attorneys, paralegals, educators, paralegal administrators, and members of the public to advise on policy and issues of concern to the paralegal and legal professions.

★8394★ National Paralegal Association (NPA)
Box 406
Solebury, PA 18963
Ph: (215)297-8333   Fax: (215)297-8358
Objective is to advance the paralegal profession by promoting recognition, economic benefits, and high standards. Is developing promotion and public relations, insurance, certification, and computer bank programs.

TEST GUIDES

★8395★ Career Examination Series: Legal Assistant
National Learning Corp.
212 Michael Dr.
Syosset, NY 11791
Ph: (516)921-8888   Fax: (516)921-8743
Fr: 800-645-6337

Jack Rudman. A series of study guides with multiple-choice examination questions and solutions for trainees and professional legal assistants. Titles in the series include *Legal Assistant I; Legal Assistant II; Legal Assistant Trainee; Paralegal Aide.*

★8396★ Career Examination Series: Legal Careers
National Learning Corp.
212 Michael Dr.
Syosset, NY 11791
Ph: (516)921-8888   Fax: (516)921-8743
Fr: 800-645-6337

Jack Rudman. 1993. Test guide including questions and answers for students or professionals in the field who seek advancement through examination.

★8397★ Career Examination Series: Paralegal Aide
National Learning Corp.
212 Michael Dr.
Syosset, NY 11791
Ph: (516)921-8888   Fax: (516)921-8743
Fr: 800-645-6337

Jack Rudman. Test guide including questions and answers for students or professionals in the field who seek advancement through examination.

BASIC REFERENCE GUIDES AND HANDBOOKS

★8398★ Independent Paralegal's Handbook: How to Provide Legal Services Without Becoming a Lawyer
Nolo Press
950 Parker St.
Berkeley, CA 94710
Ph: (415)549-1976

Ralph E. Warner. Second edition, 1991. Illustrated.

★8399★ An Introduction to Paralegal Studies
South-Western Publishing Co.
5101 Madison Rd.
Cincinnati, OH 45227
Ph: (513)271-8811   Fax: (513)527-6056
Fr: 800-543-0487

David G. Cooper, editor. 1993.

★8400★ Legal Assistants Handbook
BNA Books
1250 23rd St., NW
Washington, DC 20037
Ph: (202)452-4276

Thomas W. Brunner, and Julie P. Hamre. Second edition, 1988.

★8401★ Legal Assistants: Update
American Bar Association (ABA)
750 N. Lake Shore Dr.
Chicago, IL 60611
Ph: (312)988-5000
Annual.

★8402★ Legal Research
Prentice-Hall, Inc.
Rte. 9W
Englewood Cliffs, NJ 07632
Ph: (201)592-2000   Fr: 800-634-2863
Charles P. Nemeth. 1987.

★8403★ Legal Research Manual: A Game Plan for Legal Research and Analysis
Adams and Ambrose Publishing
PO Box 9684
Madison, WI 53715-0684
Ph: (608)257-5700

Christopher G. Wren and Jill R. Wren. Second edition, 1989. Includes checklist flow charts, glossaries, and index.

★8404★ Legal Research, Writing and Advocacy
Anderson Publishing Co.
2035 Reading Rd.
Cincinnati, OH 45202-1576
Ph: (513)421-4142   Fr: 800-543-0883
Wesley Gilmer. 1993. Answers the most frequently asked questions received by legal researchers.

★8405★ Manual for Legal Assistants
West Publishing Co.
50 W. Kellogg Blvd.
PO Box 64526
St. Paul, MN 55164
Ph: (612)228-2778

William R. Park, editor. Second edition, 1991. Includes an index.

★8406★ The Paralegal's Desk Reference
Arco Pub.
201 W. 103rd St.
Indianapolis, IN 46290
Ph: 800-428-5331   Fax: 800-835-3202
Steve Albrecht. 1993. Features information on interviewing clients, reading police reports working with experts, and drafting legal documents.

★8407★ Working With Legal Assistants: A Team Approach for Lawyers and Legal Assistants
American Bar Association (ABA)
750 N. Lake Shore Dr.
Chicago, IL 60611
Ph: (312)988-5000

Paul G. Ulrich and Robert S. Mucklestone, editors. Includes a bibliography and an index.

PROFESSIONAL AND TRADE PERIODICALS

★8408★ Legal Assistant Today
James Publishing, Inc.
3520 Cadillac Ave., Ste. E
Costa Mesa, CA 92626-1419
Ph: (714)755-5450   Fax: (714)751-5508
Leanne Cazares

Bimonthly. Magazine for Paralegals. Covers career development and ethics; products, services, and technology.

★8409★ Legal Management
Assn. of Legal Administrators
175 E. Hawthorn Pkwy., Ste. 325
Vernon Hills, IL 60061-1428
Ph: (708)816-1212   Fax: (708)816-1213
Nancy Blodgett

Bimonthly. Magazine covering aspects of law office management, including systems and technology, human resource management, finance, planning, and marketing.

★8410★ National Paralegal Reporter
National Federation of Paralegal Associations (NFPA)
PO Box 33108
Kansas City, MO 64114
Ph: (816)941-4000

Quarterly. Focuses on issues of concern to the paralegal profession such as responsibility and ethics, new developments in the field, and educational opportunities. Promotes the recognition and advancement of paralegals and provides information on programs and help offered by paralegal associations. Reports regional NFPA news and news of paralegal associations throughout the U.S. Recurring features include book reviews, news of research, and President's Column.

PROFESSIONAL MEETINGS AND CONVENTIONS

★8411★ American Association for Paralegal Education Convention
American Association for Paralegal Education
PO Box 40244
Overland Park, KS 66204
Ph: (913)381-4458   Fax: (913)381-9308
Annual.

OTHER SOURCES OF INFORMATION

★8412★ How to Land Your First Paralegal Job
Estrin Publishing
1900 Avenue of the Stars, No. 670
Los Angeles, CA 90067-4307
Ph: (310)552-9988   Fr: 800-358-5897
1992.

★8413★ "Paralegal" in 100 Best Jobs for the 1990s & Beyond
Dearborn Financial Publishing, Inc.
520 N. Dearborn St.
Chicago, IL 60610-4354
Ph: (312)836-4400   Fax: (312)836-1021
Fr: 800-621-9621
Carol Kleiman. 1992. Describes 100 jobs ranging from accountants to veterinarians. Each job profile includes such information as education, experience, and certification needed, salaries, and job search suggestions.

★8414★ "Paralegal Assistant" in Career Selector 2001
Barron's Educational Series, Inc.
250 Wireless Blvd.
Hauppauge, NY 11788
Ph: (516)434-3311   Fax: (516)434-3723
Fr: 800-645-3476
James C. Gonyea. 1993.

★8415★ Paralegal Career Guide
John Wiley and Sons, Inc.
605 3rd Ave.
New York, NY 10158-0012
Ph: (212)850-6000   Fax: (212)850-6088
Fr: 800-526-5368
1992.

★8416★ The Paralegal's Guide to U.S. Government Jobs: How to Land a Job in 70 Law-Related Career Fields
Federal Reports, Inc.
1010 Vermont Ave., NW, Ste. 408
Washington, DC 20005
Ph: (202)393-3311
Sixth edition, 1993. Explains U.S. Government hiring procedures and describes 70 law-related federal careers for which paralegals may qualify. Includes a directory of several hundred federal agency personnel offices that hire the most paralegal and law-related talents.

Science Technicians

Science technicians use the principles and theories of science and mathematics to solve problems in research and development, production, and oil and gas exploration. Their jobs are more practically oriented than those of scientists. In recent years, the increasing use of robotics to perform many routine tasks has freed technicians to operate more sophisticated equipment. They use such equipment as computers, computer-interfaced equipment, and high-technology industrial applications. Most science technicians specialize in agriculture, biology, chemistry, the nuclear field, or a particular industry such as petroleum. **Agricultural technicians** work with agricultural scientists in food and fiber research, production, and processing. **Biological technicians** work with biologists, studying living organisms. **Chemical technicians** work with chemists and chemical engineers, developing and using chemicals and related products and equipment. **Nuclear technicians** operate nuclear test and research equipment, monitor radiation, and assist nuclear engineers and physicists in research. **Petroleum technicians** measure and record physical and geologic conditions in oil or gas wells using instruments lowered into wells or by analysis of the mud from wells. Other science technicians collect weather information or assist oceanographers.

Salaries

Annual earnings of science technicians are as follows:

Lowest 10 percent	Less than $14,400/year
Median	$25,300/year
Top 10 percent	More than $42,400/year
Starting, federal government	$14,600-$18340/year

Employment Outlook

Growth rate until the year 2005: Average.

Science Technicians

CAREER GUIDES

★8417★ "Agricultural and Biological Technicians" in Jobs! What They Are—Where They Are—What They Pay (p. 406)
Simon & Schuster, Inc.
Simon & Schuster Bldg.
1230 Avenue of the Americas
New York, NY 10020
Ph: (212)698-7000   Fr: 800-223-2348
Robert O. Snelling and Anne M. Snelling. 3rd edition, 1992. Describes duties and responsibilities, earnings, employment opportunities, training, and qualifications.

★8418★ "Biological Laboratory Technician" in Desk Guide to Training and Work Advisement (p. 65)
Charles C. Thomas, Publisher
2600 S. 1st St.
Springfield, IL 62794-9265
Ph: (217)789-8980   Fax: (217)789-9130
Fr: 800-258-8980
Keunstler, Gail Baugher. 1988. Describes alternative methods of gaining entry into an occupation through different types of educational programs, internships, and apprenticeships.

★8419★ A Career as a Chemical Technician
American Chemical Society (ACS)
1155 16th St., NW
Washington, DC 20036
Ph: (202)872-4600
1993. Describes what chemical technicians do on the job, where they work, qualifications and skills needed, educational preparation, financial aid, salaries, and employment outlook.

★8420★ Chemical Laboratory Technician
Careers, Inc.
PO Box 135
Largo, FL 34649-0135
Ph: (813)584-7333
1994. Two-page summary describing duties, working conditions, personal qualifications, training, earnings and hours, employment outlook, places of employment, related careers, and where to write for more information.

★8421★ Chemical Laboratory Technicians
Chronicle Guidance Publications, Inc.
66 Aurora St.
PO Box 1190
Moravia, NY 13118-1190
Ph: (315)497-0330   Fax: (315)497-3359
Fr: 800-622-7284
1993. Career brief describing the nature of the job, working conditions, hours and earnings, education and training, licensure, certification, unions, personal qualifications, social and psychological factors, location, employment outlook, entry methods, advancement, and related occupations.

★8422★ "Chemical Technician" in Opportunities in High-Tech Careers (p. 141)
National Textbook Co. (NTC)
VGM Career Books
4255 W. Touhy Ave.
Lincolnwood, IL 60646-1975
Ph: (708)679-5500   Fax: (708)679-2494
Fr: 800-323-4900
Gary D. Golter and Deborah Yanuck. 1987. Explores high-technology careers. Written for the student and displaced worker. Describes job opportunities, how to make a career decision, how to prepare for high-technology jobs, job hunting techniques, and future trends.

★8423★ "Chemical Technicians" in Encyclopedia of Careers and Vocational Guidance (Vol.2, pp. 279-284)
J.G. Ferguson Publishing Co.
200 W. Madison St., Ste. 300
Chicago, IL 60606
Ph: (312)580-5480   Fax: (312)580-4948
William E. Hopke, editor in chief. Ninth edition, 1993. Four-volume set that profiles 900 occupations and describes job trends in 74 industries. Chapters include "Biological Technicians", "Nuclear Power Plant Radiation Control Technicians", "Nuclear Power Plant Quality Control Technicians", "Nuclear Materials Handling Technicians", "Petroleum Technicians", and "Nuclear Reactor Operator Technicians". Includes career description, educational requirements, history of the job, methods of entry, advancement, employ-

ment outlook, earnings, conditions of work, social and psychological factors, and sources of further information.

★8424★ "Chemical Technicians" in Opportunities in Chemistry Careers (pp. 86-89)
National Textbook Co. (NTC)
VGM Career Books
4255 W. Touhy Ave.
Lincolnwood, IL 60646-1975
Ph: (708)679-5500   Fax: (708)679-2494
Fr: 800-323-4900
John H. Woodburn. 1987. Defines chemistry and describes history, entry-level jobs, future trends, personal qualities needed, educational requirements, earnings, and career specializations. Includes a list of professional associations and a bibliograpy of further readings.

★8425★ "Engineering and Science Technicians" in Jobs! What They Are—Where They Are—What They Pay! (pp. 122)
Simon & Schuster, Inc.
Simon & Schuster Bldg.
1230 Avenue of the Americas
New York, NY 10020
Ph: (212)698-7000   Fr: 800-223-2348
Robert O. Snelling and Anne M. Snelling. Third revised edition, 1992. Includes a chapter titled "Electronics and Mathematical Technicians". Describes duties and responsibilities, earnings, employment opportunities, training, and qualifications.

★8426★ "Nuclear Chemical Technicians" in Opportunities in High-Tech Careers (pp. 138-139)
National Textbook Co. (NTC)
VGM Career Books
4255 W. Touhy Ave.
Lincolnwood, IL 60646-1975
Ph: (708)679-5500   Fax: (708)679-2494
Fr: 800-323-4900
Gary D. Colter and Deborah Yanuck. 1987. Explores high-technology careers. Written for the student and displaced worker. Describes job opportunities, how to make a career decision, how to prepare for high-technology jobs, job hunting techniques, and future trends.

★8427★ Nuclear Technician
Careers, Inc.
PO Box 135
Largo, FL 34649-0135
Ph: (813)584-7333
1991. Two-page occupational summary card describing duties, working conditions, personal qualifications, training, earnings and hours, employment outlook, places of employment, related careers, and where to write for more information.

★8428★ Physicist Technician
Careers, Inc.
PO Box 135
Largo, FL 34649-0135
Ph: (813)584-7333
1993. Two-page summary describing duties, working conditions, personal qualifications, training, earnings and hours, employment outlook, places of employment, related careers, and where to write for more information.

★8429★ "Science Technicians" in Occupational Outlook Handbook
U.S. Government Printing Office
Superintendent of Documents
Washington, DC 20402
Ph: (202)512-1800   Fax: (202)512-2250
Biennial; latest edition, 1994-95. Encyclopedia of careers describing about 250 occupations and comprising about 85 percent of all jobs in the economy. Occupations that require lengthy education or training are given the most attention. Each occupation's profile describes what the worker does on the job, working conditions, education and training requirements, advancement possibilities, job outlook, earnings, and sources of additional information.

★8430★ Technicians, Science and Engineering
Careers, Inc.
PO Box 135
Largo, FL 34649-0135
Ph: (813)584-7333
1992. Four-page brief offering the definition, history, duties, working conditions, personal qualifications, educational requirements, earnings, hours, employment outlook, advancement, and careers related to this position.

PROFESSIONAL ASSOCIATIONS

★8431★ American Astronomical Society (AAS)
2000 Florida Ave. NW, Ste. 400
Washington, DC 20009
Ph: (202)328-2010   Fax: (202)234-2560
Members: Astronomers, physicists, and scientists in related fields. **Purpose:** Conducts Visiting Professor in Astronomy Program. Maintains placement service. **Publications:** AAS Job Register, monthly. • AAS Newsletter, 5/year. • American Astronomical Society—Membership Directory, annual. • Astronomical Journal, monthly. • Astrophysical Journal. • Bulletin of the American Astronomical Society, quarterly.

★8432★ American Chemical Society (ACS)
1155 16th St. NW
Washington, DC 20036
Ph: (202)872-4600   Fr: 800-227-5558
Members: Scientific and educational society of chemists and chemical engineers. Conducts: studies and surveys; special programs for disadvantaged persons; legislation monitoring, analysis, and reporting; courses for graduate chemists and chemical engineers; radio and television programming. Offers career guidance counseling; administers the Petroleum Research Fund and other grants and fellowship programs. Operates Employment Clearing Houses. Compiles statistics. Maintains speakers' bureau. Maintains 33 divisions. **Publications:** Accounts of Chemical Research, monthly. • Analytical Chemistry, semimonthly. • Biochemistry, weekly. • Bioconjugate Chemistry, bimonthly. • Biotechnology Progress, bimonthly. • Chemical Abstracts, weekly. • Chemical and Engineering News, weekly. • Chemical Health & Safety, bimonthly. • Chemical Research in Toxicology, bimonthly. • Chemical Reviews, 8/year. • Chemical Titles. • Chemistry of Materials, monthly. • Chemtech, monthly. • Energy and Fuels, bimonthly. • Environmental Science and Technology, monthly. • Industrial and Engineering Chemistry Research, monthly. • Inorganic Chemistry, biweekly. • Journal of Agricultural and Food Chemistry, monthly. • Journal of Chemical and Engineering Data, quarterly. • Journal of Chemical Information and Computer Sciences, bimonthly. • Journal of Medicinal Chemistry, biweekly. • Journal of Organic Chemistry, biweekly. • Journal of Pharmaceutical Sciences, monthly. • Journal of Physical and Chemical Reference Data, bimonthly. • Journal of Physical Chemistry, weekly. • Journal of the American Chemical Society, biweekly. • Langmuir, monthly. • Macromolecules, biweekly. • Organometallics, monthly.

★8433★ American Institute of Biological Sciences (AIBS)
730 11th St. NW
Washington, DC 20001-4521
Ph: (202)628-1500   Fax: (202)628-1509
Fr: 800-992-AIBS
Members: Professional biological associations and laboratories whose members have an interest in the life sciences. **Purpose:** Promotes unity and effectiveness of effort among persons engaged in biological research, education, and application of biological sciences, including agriculture, environment, and medicine. Seeks to further the relationships of biological sciences to other sciences, the arts, and industries. Conducts symposium series; provides names of prominent biologists who are willing to serve as speakers and curriculum consultants; provides advisory committees and other services to the Department of Energy, Environmental Protection Agency, National Science Foundation, Department of Defense, and National Aeronautics and Space Administration. Maintains educational consultant panel. **Publications:** American Institute of Biological Sciences—Forum: Public Issues, the Life Sciences, and You, bimonthly. • Annual Meeting Program, annual. • BioScience, 11/year.

TEST GUIDES

★8434★ Career Examination Series: Environmental Technician
National Learning Corp.
212 Michael Dr.
Syosset, NY 11791
Ph: (516)921-8888   Fax: (516)921-8743
Fr: 800-645-6337

Jack Rudman. 1993. Test guide including questions and answers for students or professionals in the field who seek advancement through examination.

★8435★ Career Examination Series: Horticulturist
National Learning Corp.
212 Michael Dr.
Syosset, NY 11791
Ph: (516)921-8888   Fax: (516)921-8743
Fr: 800-645-6337

Jack Rudman. A study guide for professionals and prospective science technicians. Includes a multiple-choice examination section; provides answers.

★8436★ Career Examination Series: Laboratory Technician
National Learning Corp.
212 Michael Dr.
Syosset, NY 11791
Ph: (516)921-8888   Fax: (516)921-8743
Fr: 800-645-6337

Jack Rudman. 1993. Test guide including questions and answers for students or professionals in the field who seek advancement through examination.

★8437★ Career Examination Series: Medical Research Technician
National Learning Corp.
212 Michael Dr.
Syosset, NY 11791
Ph: (516)921-8888   Fax: (516)921-8743
Fr: 800-645-6337

Jack Rudman. 1993. Test guide including questions and answers for students or professionals in the field who seek advancement through examination.

★8438★ Career Examination Series: Physical Science Technician
National Learning Corp.
212 Michael Dr.
Syosset, NY 11791
Ph: (516)921-8888   Fax: (516)921-8743
Fr: 800-645-6337

Jack Rudman. 1993. Test guide including questions and answers for students or professionals in the field who seek advancement through examination.

PROFESSIONAL AND TRADE PERIODICALS

★8439★ *Biomedical Safety & Standards*
Quest Publishing Company
1351 Titan Way
Brea, CA 92621
Ph: (714)738-6400   Fax: (714)525-6258
Gregory F. Nighswonger

Semimonthly. Reports on biomedical safety and standards. Provides information on safety hazards, product recalls, product and facilities standards, legal actions, legislation and regulations, hospital safety, and biomedical equipment technician activities. Recurring features include news of research, employment opportunities, book reviews, and a calendar of events.

★8440★ *BIOSIS Evolution*
BioSciences Information Service (BIOSIS)
2100 Arch St.
Philadelphia, PA 19103-1399
Ph: (215)587-4800   Fax: (215)587-2016
Fr: 800-523-4806
Denise Civa

Bimonthly. Serves subscribers to BIOSIS, "the world's largest English language ab-stracting and indexing service for biological and biomedical research." Reports on new BIOSIS product developments, pricing and distribution of current products and services, and educational programs. Provides descriptions on training courses for BIOSIS online services, vendor news affecting BIOSIS databases, information on the availability of the databases, and tips on searching the databases. Recurring features include news of employees, a BIOSIS training schedule, news of research, columns titled title CD-ROM Corner, Vendor News, International Notes, and In Search of . . . (sample searches on various life science topics).

★8441★ *National Research Council News Report*
National Academy of Sciences
2101 Constitution Ave. NW
Washington, DC 20418
Ph: (202)334-2138
Patricia Worns

Quarterly. Covers the activities of the National Academy of Sciences, National Academy of Engineering, Institute of Medicine, and the National Research Council and studies by their units. Includes feature articles on significant reports and activities and lists new project.

PROFESSIONAL MEETINGS AND CONVENTIONS

★8442★ O-E/LASE - Optoelectronics and Laser Applications in Science and Engineering Exhibit
SPIE - International Society for Optical Engineering
PO Box 10
Bellingham, WA 98227
Ph: (206)676-3290   Fax: (206)647-1445

Annual. Four symposia per year.

Tool Programmers, Numerical Control

Tool programmers write coded instructions used by machines to perform a specific job. They must have a broad knowledge of machining operations, mathematics, and blueprint reading. They must know how various machine tools operate and the working properties of the metals and plastics used to make parts. Although machinery manufacturers are trying to standardize programming languages, currently there are numerous languages in use. Because of this, tool programmers must know the languages for each of the machines with which they work.

Salaries

Earnings for tool programmers are as follows:

Tool programmers	$13-$18/hour

Employment Outlook

Growth rate until the year 2005: Slower than the average.

Tool Programmers, Numerical Control

CAREER GUIDES

★8443★ "Numerical Control Tool Programmers" in *Encyclopedia of Careers and Vocational Guidance* (Vol.3, pp. 589-591)
J.G. Ferguson Publishing Co.
200 W. Madison St., Ste. 300
Chicago, IL 60606
Ph: (312)580-5480   Fax: (312)580-4948

William E. Hopke, editor in chief. Ninth edition, 1993. Four-volume set that profiles 900 occupations and describes job trends in 74 industries. Includes career description, educational requirements, history of the job, methods of entry, advancement, employment outlook, earnings, conditions of work, social and psychological factors, and sources of further information.

★8444★ "Tool Programmers, Numerical Control" in *Occupational Outlook Handbook*
U.S. Government Printing Office
Superintendent of Documents
Washington, DC 20402
Ph: (202)512-1800   Fax: (202)512-2250

Biennial; latest edition, 1994-95. Encyclopedia of careers describing about 250 occupations and comprising about 85 percent of all jobs in the economy. Occupations that require lengthy education or training are given the most attention.Each occupation's profile describes what the worker does on the job, working conditions, education and training requirements, advancement possibilities, job outlook, earnings, and sources of additional information.

PROFESSIONAL ASSOCIATIONS

★8445★ AMT - Association for Manufacturing Technology
7901 Westpark Dr.
Mc Lean, VA 22102
Ph: (703)893-2900   Fax: (703)893-1151
Fr: 800-544-3597
Members: Makers of power driven machines used in the process of transforming man-made materials into durable goods, including machine tools, assembly machines, inspection and testing machinery, robots, parts loaders, and plastics molding machines; associate members are producers of tools and tooling parts and components, attachments and accessories, controls and software, and engineering and systems design services. **Purpose:** Seeks to improve methods of producing and marketing machine tools; promotes research and development in the industry. Sponsors: seminars for training production supervisors, accident prevention and safety, and advertising management; industry standards and technical aspects of the industry. Serves as a clearinghouse for technical aspects of the industry. Promotes orderly disposal of government-owned surplus machine tools. **Publications:** *Directories of Machine Tools*, annual. • *Economic Handbook of the Machine Tool Industry*, annual.

★8446★ National Tooling and Machining Association (NTMA)
9300 Livingston Rd.
Fort Washington, MD 20744
Ph: (301)248-6200   Fax: (301)248-7104
Fr: 800-248-NTMA
Members: Manufacturers of tools, dies, jigs, fixtures, molds, gages, or special machinery; companies that do precision machining on a contract basis; past service and associate members. **Purpose:** Provides management services; represents members in legislative matters. Promotes apprenticeship programs. Compiles management surveys; conducts management training workshops; maintains speakers' bureau. Has produced motion pictures and videocassettes on tool, die, and precision machining for educational showings. **Publications:** *Business Management Advisories*, periodic. • *Buyers Guide of Special Tooling and Precision Machining Services*, annual. • *Catalog of Publications and Training Materials*, periodic. • *Precision*, bimonthly. • *Record*, monthly.

STANDARDS/CERTIFICATION AGENCIES

★8447★ Association for Manufacturing Technology (AMT)
7901 Westpark Dr.
Mc Lean, VA 22102
Ph: (703)893-2900   Fax: (703)893-1151
Fr: 800-544-3597

Sponsors: seminars for training production supervisors, accident prevention and safety, and advertising management; industry standards and technical aspects of the industry. Serves as a clearinghouse for technical aspects of the industry.

BASIC REFERENCE GUIDES AND HANDBOOKS

★8448★ *Discrete and Numerical Control Systems with Variable Structure*
C R C Press, Inc.
2000 Corporate Blvd. NW
Boca Raton, FL 33431
Ph: (407)994-0555   Fax: (407)241-7856
'Yanov Emel, editor. 1993.

★8449★ *Fundamentals of Numerical Control*
Delmar Publishers, Inc.
3 Columbia Circle
PO Box 15015
Albany, NY 12212-5015
Ph: (518)459-1150   Fr: 800-347-7707
William W. Luggen. Second edition, 1988.

★8450★ *Learning Computer Numerical Control*
Delmar Publishers, Inc.
2 Computer Dr. W.
Albany, NY 12212
Ph: (518)459-1150   Fax: (518)453-6472
Michael Janke, editor. 1992.

★8451★ *Learning Numerical Control*
Delmar Publishers, Inc.
2 Computer Dr., W.
Albany, NY 12212
Ph: (518)459-1150   Fax: (518)453-6472
Michael Janke, editor. 1992.

PROFESSIONAL AND TRADE PERIODICALS

★8452★ *NTMA Record*
National Tooling and Machining Association (NTMA)
9300 Livingston Rd.
Fort Washington, MD 20744
Ph: (301)248-6200   Fax: (301)248-7104
Fr: 800-248-6862
Sandra S. Bailey

Monthly. Focuses on business management techniques and government relations for the contract tool, die, and precision machining industry. Supplies information on Association activities. Recurring features include editorials, tax information, and technical notes.

OTHER SOURCES OF INFORMATION

★8453★ *Geometric Modelling for Numerically Controlled Machining*
Oxford University Press, Inc.
200 Madison Ave.
New York, NY 10016
Ph: (212)679-7300   Fax: (212)725-2972

State Occupational and Professional Licensing Agencies

This appendix covers state government agencies responsible for granting professional and occupational licenses. Entries are arranged alphabetically by state and include the state agency's or department's name, address, and phone number.

State Occupational and Professional Licensing Agencies

★8454★ Alaska State Division of Occupational Licensing
PO Box 110806
Juneau, AK 99811-0806
Ph: (907)465-2534   Fax: (907)465-2974

★8455★ Arizona State Department of Administration
State Boards Office
1400 W. Jefferson St., St. 230
Phoenix, AZ 85007
Ph: (602)542-3095

★8456★ California Department of Consumer Affairs
400 R St., Ste. 3000
Sacramento, CA 95814-6200
Ph: (916)445-1591

★8457★ Colorado State Department of Regulatory Agencies
1560 Broadway, Ste. 1300
Denver, CO 80202
Ph: (303)894-7711   Fax: (303)894-7692

★8458★ Connecticut State Department of Consumer Protection
Bureau of Licensing and Administration
165 Capitol Ave.
Hartford, CT 06106
Ph: (203)566-4999

★8459★ Delaware State Department of Administrative Services
Division of Professional Regulations
PO Box 1401
Dover, DE 19903
Ph: (302)739-4522

★8460★ District of Columbia Department of Consumer and Regulatory Affairs
Occupational and Professional Licensing Administration
614 H St. NW
Washington, DC 20001
Ph: (202)727-7480

★8461★ Florida State Department of Business and Professional Regulation
1940 N. Monroe St.
Tallahassee, FL 32399-0797
Ph: (904)488-7176   Fax: (904)922-3040

★8462★ Georgia Secretary of State
Professional Examining Boards
166 Pryor St. SW
Atlanta, GA 30303
Ph: (404)656-3900   Fax: (404)651-9532

★8463★ Hawaii State Department of Commerce and Consumer Affairs
PO Box 3469
Honolulu, HI 96801
Ph: (808)586-2850   Fax: (808)586-2856

★8464★ Idaho State Board of Occupational Licenses
1109 Main St.
Owyhee Plaza, Ste. 220
Boise, ID 83702-5642
Ph: (208)334-3233   Fax: (208)334-3945

★8465★ Illinois State Department of Professional Regulation
320 W. Washington St., 3rd Fl.
Springfield, IL 62786
Ph: (217)785-2145   Fax: (217)524-2470

★8466★ Indiana Professional Licensing Agency
1021 Government Center N.
100 N. Senate Ave.
Indianapolis, IN 46204
Ph: (317)232-2980   Fax: (317)232-2312

★8467★ Iowa State Department of Commerce
Professional Licensing and Regulation Division
1918 SE Hulsizer Ave.
Ankeny, IA 50021
Ph: (515)281-5602   Fax: (515)281-7372

★8468★ Kentucky Division of Occupations and Professions
PO Box 456
Frankfort, KY 40602-0456
Ph: (502)564-3296   Fax: (502)564-4818

★8469★ Louisiana State Department of Health and Human Resources
Office of Licensing Regulation
PO Box 3767
Baton Rouge, LA 70821-3767
Ph: (504)342-0138

★8470★ Maine State Division of Licensing and Enforcement
State House Station 35
Augusta, ME 04333
Ph: (207)582-8723

★8471★ Maryland State Department of Licensing and Regulation
Division of Occupational and Professional Licensing
501 St. Paul Pl., 15th Fl.
Baltimore, MD 21202-2272
Ph: (410)333-6209   Fax: (410)333-1229

★8472★ Massachusetts State Executive Office of Consumer Affairs
100 Cambridge St., Rm. 1520
Boston, MA 02202
Ph: (617)727-3074   Fax: (617)727-7378

★8473★ Michigan State Department of Commerce
Bureau of Occupational and Professional Regulation
PO Box 30018
Lansing, MI 48909
Ph: (517)373-1870   Fax: (517)335-6696

★8474★ Minnesota State Department of Commerce
133 E. 7th St.
St. Paul, MN 55101
Ph: (612)296-3528

★8475★ Mississippi Secretary of State
401 Mississippi St.
Jackson, MS 39215
Ph: (601)359-1350

★8476★ Missouri State Department of Professional Registration
PO Box 135
Jefferson City, MO 65102-0293
Ph: (314)751-1081   Fax: (314)751-4176

★8477★ **Montana State Department of Commerce**
Bureau of Professional and Occupational Licensing
111 N. Jackson
PO Box 200513
Helena, MT 59620-0513
Ph: (406)444-1488

★8478★ **Nebraska State Bureau of Examining Boards**
Department of Health
301 Centennial Mall S.
Box 95007
Lincoln, NE 68509
Ph: (402)471-2115

★8479★ **New Jersey State Department of Law and Public Safety**
Division of Consumer Affairs
124 Halsey St.
PO Box 45027
Newark, NJ 07102
Fax: (201)648-3538

★8480★ **New Mexico State Department of Regulation and Licensing**
725 St. Michaels Dr.
PO Box 25101
Santa Fe, NM 87504
Ph: (505)827-7000   Fax: (505)827-7095

★8481★ **New York Education Department**
Division of Professional Licensing Services
Cultural Education Center, Rm. 3029
Albany, NY 12230
Ph: (518)486-1765

★8482★ **North Dakota Secretary of State**
600 E. Blvd. Ave.
State Capitol, 1st Fl.
Bismarck, ND 58505-0500
Ph: (701)224-2905   Fax: (701)224-2992

★8483★ **Ohio State Department of Commerce**
Division of Licensing
77 S. High St., 23rd Fl.
Columbus, OH 43266-0546
Ph: (614)466-4130

★8484★ **Oregon State Department of Insurance and Finance**
350 Winter St., NW
Salem, OR 97310
Ph: (503)378-4100

★8485★ **Pennsylvania State Department**
Bureau of Professional and Occupational Affairs
618 Transportation and Safety Bldg.
Harrisburg, PA 17120
Ph: (717)787-8503   Fax: (717)787-7769

★8486★ **Rhode Island State Department of Health**
Division of Professional Regulation
3 Capitol Hill, Cannon Bldg.
Providence, RI 02908-5097
Ph: (401)277-2827   Fax: (401)277-1272

★8487★ **South Carolina Department of Labor**
Division of Licensing and Regulations
PO Box 11329
Columbia, SC 29211
Ph: (803)734-9600

★8488★ **South Dakota State Department of Commerce**
Professional and Occupational Licensing Department
910 E. Sioux Ave.
Pierre, SD 57501
Ph: (605)773-3178   Fax: (605)773-5369

★8489★ **Tennessee State Department of Commerce and Insurance**
Division of Regulatory Boards
500 James Roberston Pkwy., 2nd Fl.
Nashville, TN 37243-0572
Ph: (615)741-3449   Fax: (615)741-6470

★8490★ **Texas State Department of Licensing and Regulation**
PO Box 12157
Austin, TX 78711
Ph: (512)463-5520

★8491★ **Utah State Division of Occupational and Professional Licensing**
PO Box 45805
Salt Lake City, UT 84145-0805
Ph: (801)530-6628   Fax: (801)530-6511

★8492★ **Vermont Secretary of State**
Office od Professional Regulation
109 State St.
Montpelier, VT 05609-1106
Ph: (802)828-2458

★8493★ **Virginia Department of Health Professions**
6606 W. Broad St., 4th Fl.
Richmond, VA 23230-1717
Ph: (804)662-9904

★8494★ **Washington State Department of Licensing**
Highway-Licenses Bldg.
PO Box 01
Olympia, WA 98504-8001
Ph: (206)753-6918

★8495★ **Wisconsin State Department of Regulation and Licensing**
PO Box 8935
Madison, WI 53708
Ph: (608)266-2811

Appendix II: Employment Growth Rankings and Statistics

This section provides U.S. Bureau of Labor Statistics figures indicating expected employment growth for the occupations covered in this edition of *PCS*.

Bureau of Labor Statistics Occupational Data

Below is an extract of the Bureau of Labor Statistics' Industry-Occupation Matrix (1994). Occupations listed in *Professional Careers Sourcebook* are ranked alphabetically and in order of growth. Annual figures are presented in thousands. Page numbers to the occupation profile are in parentheses.

Occupational Growth from 1992 to 2005
(Occupations in Alphabetical Order)

	1992	2005	% Change		1992	2005	% Change
Accountants and auditors (1)	939	1243	32.3	Dentists (503)	183	192	5.2
				Designers (650)	302	359	18.7
Actors, directors, and producers (678)	129	198	53.5	Dietitians and nutritionists (545)	50	63	26.3
				Dispensing opticians (512)	63	86	35.7
Actuaries (270)	15	19	29.4	Drafters (786)	314	350	11.3
Administrative services managers (12)	226	256	13.1	Economists and market research analysts (104)	51	64	25.3
Adult and vocational education teachers (441)	540	712	31.8	Education administrators (34)	351	432	23.2
				EEG technologists (721)	6	10	53.8
Aerospace engineers (161)	66	75	14.1	EKG technicians (725)	16	14	-14.4
Agricultural scientists (288)	29	33	14.4	Electrical and electronics engineers (185)	370	459	24.2
Air traffic controllers (770)	23	25	9.9	Emergency medical technicians (729)	114	155	35.9
Aircraft pilots (760)	85	115	35.2	Employment interviewers (42)	79	96	21.8
Anthropologists (357)	35	42	20.3	Engineering, science, and data processing managers (45)	337	444	31.5
Archaeologists (363)	35	42	20.3	Engineering technicians (790)	695	827	19.0
Architects (238)	96	121	26.3	Financial Managers (51)	701	875	24.8
Archivists and curators (447)	19	23	18.2	Foresters and conservation scientists (303)	35	40	12.2
Biological scientists (388)	78	97	25.0	Funeral directors and morticians (61)	27	32	17.6
Broadcast technicians (774)	35	37	4.0				
Budget analysts (16)	67	81	20.1	General managers and top executives (67)	2871	3251	13.2
Chemical engineers (168)	52	62	19.4	Geographers (376)	35	42	20.3
Chemists (310)	92	112	21.2	Geologists and geophysicists (320)	48	59	22.2
Chiropractors (498)	46	62	35.8	Government chief executives and legislators (73)	73	76	3.1
Civil engineers (177)	173	214	23.6	Health services managers (412)	413	595	43.9
Clinical laboratory technologists and technicians (704)	268	339	26.5	Historians (380)	35	42	20.3
College and university faculty (454)	812	1026	26.4	Hotel managers and assistants (86)	532	764	43.5
Computer programmers (779)	555	723	30.4	Human services workers (412)	189	445	135.9
Computer scientist and systems analysts (265)	455	956	110.1	Industrial engineers (193)	119	138	16.8
Construction and building inspectors (20)	66	86	29.8	Industrial production managers (92)	203	208	2.4
Construction contractors and managers (25)	180	265	47.0	Inspectors and compliance officers, except construction (96)	155	196	27.0
Cost estimators (31)	163	211	29.8				
Counselors (461)	154	204	32.2				
Dancers and choreographers (687)	18	23	24.8				
Dental hygienists (711)	108	154	42.7				

Rankings and Statistics

	1990	2005	% Change		1990	2005	% Change
Kindergarten and elementary school teachers (470)	1456	1767	21.3	Property and real estate managers (132)	243	328	35.0
Landscape architects (248)	19	24	26.3	Protestant ministers (429)	189	245	29.8
Lawyers and judges (345)	716	913	27.5	Psychologists (392)	143	212	48.0
Librarians (478)	141	158	12.3	Public relations specialists (109)	98	123	26.3
Library Technicians (795)	71	89	25.0	Purchasers and buyers (138)	221	252	13.9
Licensed practical nurses (734)	659	920	39.7	Rabbis (433)	189	245	29.8
Loan officers and counselors (100)	171	239	40.0	Radio and television announcers and newscasters (619)	56	70	25.1
Management analysts and consultants (104)	208	297	42.7	Radiologic technologists (753)	162	264	62.7
Marketing, advertising, and public relations managers (109)	432	588	36.1	Recreation workers (416)	204	282	38.1
Mathematicians (272)	16	18	7.6	Recreational therapists (582)	30	42	39.8
Mechanical engineers (218)	227	273	20.3	Registered nurses (587)	1835	2601	41.7
Medical record technicians (743)	76	123	61.5	Reporters and correspondents (634)	58	73	26.1
Metallurgical, ceramic, and materials engineers (208)	19	24	28.3	Respiratory therapists (601)	74	109	48.3
Meteorologists (320)	6	8	24.4	Restaurant and food service managers (142)	532	764	43.5
Mining engineers (218)	4	4	3.1	Retail managers (148)	1676	2258	34.7
Musicians (694)	236	294	24.9	Roman Catholic priests (437)	189	245	29.8
Nuclear engineers (225)	17	17	.5	Science technicians (805)	244	305	25.0
Nuclear medicine technologists (748)	12	18	50.1	Secondary school teachers (490)	1263	1724	36.6
Occupational therapists (553)	40	64	59.6	Social workers (421)	484	676	39.5
Operations research analysts (279)	45	72	61.4	Sociologists (402)	35	42	20.3
Optometrists (512)	31	36	15.7	Speech-language pathologists and audiologists (606)	73	110	51.3
Paralegals (320)	95	176	86.1	Statisticians (283)	16	18	9.3
Personnel, training, and labor relations specialists and managers (121)	281	383	36.1	Surgical technicians (759)	44	62	42.4
Petroleum engineers (282)	14	14	-2.4	Surveyors (259)	99	112	13.2
Pharmacists (560)	163	211	29.0	Tool programmers, numerical control (809)	7	8	8.1
Photographers and camera operators (658)	118	147	24.7	Underwriters (151)	100	124	24.1
Physical therapists (568)	90	170	88.0	Urban and regional planners (408)	28	34	23.2
Physician assistants (576)	58	78	33.8	Veterinarians (537)	44	58	32.7
Physicians (518)	556	751	35.0	Visual artists (774)	1606	2012	25.3
Physicists and astronomers (335)	21	20	-3.2	Wholesale and retail buyers and merchandise managers (157)	180	204	13.3
Podiatrists (531)	15	20	37.4	Writers and editors (625)	283	348	23.2
Political scientists (386)	35	42	20.3				

Occupational Growth from 1992 to 2005
(Occupations by Percentage of Change)

	1990	2005	% Change		1990	2005	% Change
Human services workers (412)	189	445	135.9	Medical record technicians (743)	76	123	61.5
Computer scientist and systems analysts (265)	455	956	110.1	Operations research analysts (279)	45	72	61.4
Physical therapists (568)	90	170	88.0	Occupational therapists (553)	40	64	59.6
Paralegals (799)	95	176	86.1	EEG technologists (721)	6	10	53.8
Radiologic technologists (753)	162	264	62.7				

	1992	2005	% Change
Actors, directors, and producers (678)	129	198	53.5
Speech-language pathologists and audiologists (606)	73	110	51.3
Nuclear medicine technologists (748)	12	18	50.1
Respiratory therapists (601)	74	109	48.3
Psychologists (392)	143	212	48.0
Construction contractors and managers (25)	180	265	47.0
Health services managers (79)	413	595	43.9
Hotel managers and assistants (86)	532	764	43.5
Restaurant and food service managers (142)	532	764	43.5
Dental hygienists (711)	108	154	42.7
Management analysts and consultants (104)	208	297	42.7
Surgical technicians (759)	44	62	42.4
Registered nurses (587)	1835	2601	41.7
Loan officers and counselors (100)	171	239	40.0
Recreational therapists (582)	30	42	39.8
Licensed practical nurses (734)	659	920	39.7
Social workers (421)	484	676	39.5
Recreation workers (416)	204	282	38.1
Podiatrists (531)	15	20	37.4
Secondary school teachers (490)1	1263	1724	36.6
Marketing, advertising, and public relations managers (109)	432	588	36.1
Personnel, training, and labor relations specialists and managers (121)	281	383	36.1
Emergency medical technicians (729)	114	155	35.9
Chiropractors (498)	46	62	35.8
Dispensing opticians (717)	63	86	35.7
Aircraft pilots (763)	85	115	35.2
Physicians (518)	556	751	35.0
Property and real estate managers (132)	243	328	35.0
Retail managers (148)	1676	2258	34.7
Physician assistants (576)	58	78	33.8
Veterinarians (537)	44	58	32.7
Accountants and auditors (1)	939	1243	32.3
Adult and vocational education teachers (441)	540	712	31.8
Engineering, science, and data processing managers (45)	337	444	31.5
Counselors (461)	154	204	32.2
Computer programmers (779)	555	723	30.4
Construction and building inspectors (20)	66	86	29.8
Cost estimators (31)	163	211	29.8
Protestant ministers (429)	189	245	29.8

	1990	2005	% Change
Rabbis (433)	189	245	29.8
Roman Catholic priests (437)	189	245	29.8
Actuaries (260)	15	19	29.4
Pharmacists (560)	163	211	29.0
Metallurgical, ceramic, and materials engineers (208)	19	24	28.3
Lawyers and judges (345)	716	913	27.5
Inspectors and compliance officers, except construction (96)	155	196	27.0
Clinical laboratory technologists and technicians (704)	268	339	26.5
College and university faculty (454)	812	1026	26.4
Architects (239)	96	121	26.3
Dietitians and nutritionists (545)	50	63	26.3
Landscape architects (248)	19	24	26.3
Public relations specialists (612)	98	123	26.3
Reporters and correspondents (625)	58	73	26.1
Economists and market research analysts (369)	51	64	25.3
Visual artists (668)	1606	2012	25.3
Radio and television announcers and newscasters (619)	56	70	25.1
Biological scientists (294)	78	97	25.0
Library Technicians (795)	71	89	25.0
Science technicians (805)	244	305	25.0
Musicians (694)	236	294	24.9
Dancers and choreographers (687)	18	23	24.8
Financial Managers (51)	701	875	24.8
Photographers and camera operators (658)	118	147	24.7
Meteorologists (329)	6	8	24.4
Electrical and electronics engineers (185)	370	459	24.2
Underwriters (151)	100	124	24.1
Civil engineers (177)	173	214	23.6
Education administrators (34)	351	432	23.2
Urban and regional planners (408)	28	34	23.2
Writers and editors (634)	283	348	23.2
Geologists and geophysicists (320)	48	59	22.2
Employment interviewers (42)	79	96	21.8
Kindergarten and elementary school teachers (470)	1456	1767	21.3
Chemists (310)	92	112	21.2
Anthropologists (357)	35	42	20.3
Archaeologists (363)	35	42	20.3
Geographers (376)	35	42	20.3
Historians (380)	35	42	20.3
Mechanical engineers (200)	227	273	20.3
Political scientists (386)	35	42	20.3
Sociologists (402)	35	42	20.3
Budget analysts (16)	67	81	20.1
Chemical engineers (168)	52	62	19.4
Engineering technicians (790)	695	827	19.0

Rankings and Statistics

	1990	2005	% Change		1990	2005	% Change
Designers (650)	302	359	18.7	Foresters and conservation scientists (303)	35	40	12.2
Archivists and curators (447)	19	23	18.2	Drafters (786)	314	350	11.3
Funeral directors and morticians (61)	27	32	17.6	Air traffic controllers (770)	23	25	9.9
Industrial engineers (193)	119	138	16.8	Statisticians (283)	16	18	9.3
Optometrists (512)	31	36	15.7	Tool programmers, numerical control (809)	7	8	8.1
Agricultural scientists (288)	29	33	14.4	Mathematicians (272)	16	18	7.6
Aerospace engineers (161)	66	75	14.1	Dentists (503)	183	192	5.2
Purchasers and buyers (138)	221	252	13.9	Broadcast technicians (774)	35	37	4.0
Wholesale and retail buyers and merchandise managers (157)	180	204	13.3	Government chief executives and legislators (73)	73	76	3.1
General managers and top executives (67)	2871	3251	13.2	Mining engineers (218)	4	4	3.1
Surveyors (254)	99	112	13.2	Industrial production managers (92)	203	208	2.4
Administrative services managers (12)	226	256	13.1	Nuclear engineers (225)	17	17	.5
Librarians (478)	141	158	12.3	Petroleum engineers (232)	14	14	-2.4
				Physicists and astronomers (335)	21	20	-3.2
				EKG technicians (725)	16	14	-14.4

Index to Information Sources

This Index is an alphabetical listing of all organizations, agencies, and publications included in *PCS*. Index references are to **entry numbers** rather than to page numbers. Publication and film titles are rendered in italics. Consult the "User's Guide" for more detailed information about the index.

A

A & D Digest **1705**
A/E/C Systems and CMC Fall **296, 502**
A/E/C SYSTEMS - International Computer and Management Show for the Design and Construction Industries **236**
A. M. Skeffington Award **5381**
AAA in *Exploring Careers in Computer Graphics* **7044**
AABP Amstutz - Williams Award **5668**
AACE International **307**
AACN Educational Advancement Scholarships for Graduates **6257, 7813**
AACN Educational Advancement Scholarships for Undergraduates **6258, 7814**
AAFP President's Award **5482**
AAHA Award **5669**
AAHCPA Scholarship **92**
AAHE Bulletin **381, 4713**
AAIS Viewpoint **2717**
AAMD Salary **4604**
AAOMS Surgical Update **5298**
AAPSM Newsletter **5610, 6036**
AASA and Convention Exhibitors Scholarships **363**
AASL Distinguished School Administrators Award **364**
ABA Banking Journal **585**
ABA/BNA Lawyers' Manual on Professional Conduct **3685**
ABA Journal **3686**
Abbe Award for Distinguished Service to Atmospheric Sciences by an Individual; Cleveland **3419**
The Abbey Newsletter **4658**
ABC-CLIO America: History and Life Award **3975**
ABC Today **234**
Abe Schechter Graduate Scholarship **8168**
ABET Accreditation Yearbook **1689, 1778, 1878, 1964, 2049, 2128, 2222, 2312, 2377, 2453**
About Therapeutic Recreation **6110**
ACA Outstanding Achievement Award **2649**
Academic Deans **322**
Academic Leader **382, 4714**
Academic and Public Librarians: Data by Race, Ethnicity and Sex **4933**
Academy Awards of Merit (Oscar) **7225**
Academy of General Dentistry Annual Meeting **5316**
Academy of Laser Dentistry **5252, 5258, 7556, 7561**
Academy of Political Science **4016**
Accountant **1, 121**
"Accountant" in *100 Best Careers for the Year 2000* (pp. 167-169) **2**
"Accountant" and "Accountant Student Trainee" in *Guide to Federal Jobs* (pp. 124, 127) **3**

"Accountant/Auditor" in *100 Best Jobs for the 1990s & Beyond* **135**
"Accountant/Auditor" in *BLR Encyclopedia of Prewritten Job Descriptions* **4**
"Accountant" in *Career Selector 2001* **136**
"Accountant" in *College Board Guide to Jobs and Career Planning* (pp. 127-128) **5**
Accountant, Cost **6**
"Accountant" in *Jobs Rated Almanac* **7**
"Accountant" in *Opportunities in Office Occupations* (pp. 131-145) **8**
"Accountant" in *VGM's Careers Encyclopedia* (pp. 1-4) **9**
"Accountant" in *VGM's Handbook of Business and Management Careers* **10**
Accountants **11**
"Accountants" in *American Almanac of Jobs and Salaries* (pp. 262-272) **12**
"Accountants and Auditors" in *101 Careers: A Guide to the Fastest-Growing Opportunities* (pp. 1-3) **13**
"Accountants and Auditors" in *America's 50 Fastest Growing Jobs* (pp. 12) **14**
"Accountants, Auditors, Budget Analysts, and Credit Specialists" in *Jobs '95* **162**
"Accountants and Auditors" in *Encyclopedia of Careers and Vocational Guidance* (Vol.2, pp. 1-4) **15**
"Accountants and Auditors" in *Jobs! What They Are—Where They Are—What They Pay* (p. 156) **16**
"Accountants and Auditors" in *Occupational Outlook Handbook* **17**
The Accountant's Business Manual **105**
"Accountants" in *Career Discovery Encyclopedia* (Vol.1, pp. 7-9) **18**
Accountant's Desk Handbook **106**
"Accountants" in *Opportunities in Insurance Careers* (pp. 129-132) **19**
"Accountants", "Public Accountants", and "Auditor" in *Career Information Center* (Vol.1) **20**
Accounting **66**
Accounting and Auditing in a New Environment **107**
"Accounting" in *Black Woman's Career Guide* (pp. 244-248) **21**
"Accounting" in *Career Choices for the 90's for Students of Business* (pp. 1-23) **22**
"Accounting" in *Career Choices for the 90's for Students of Economics* (pp. 1-23) **23**
"Accounting" in *Career Choices for the 90's for Students of MBA* (pp. 1-22) **24**
"Accounting" in *College Majors and Careers: A Resource Guide to Effective Life Planning* (pp. 7-8) **25**
Accounting Desk Book: The Accountant's Everyday Instant Answerbook **108**
"Accounting" in *Encyclopedia of Career Choices for the 1990s: A Guide to Entry Level Jobs* (pp. 1-23) **26**

"Accounting" in *Encyclopedia of Careers and Vocational Guidance* (Vol.1, pp. 1-6) **27**
Accounting and Finance Salary Survey **28**
"Accounting" in *Internships 1995* **29**
"Accounting" in *Liberal Arts Jobs* **30**
"Accounting" in *Opportunities in Financial Careers* (pp. 77-94) **31**
"Accounting" in *Opportunities in Hotel and Motel Careers* (pp. 37-86) **32**
Accounting Review **122**
Accounting: Systems and Procedures **109**
"Accounting" in *Where the Jobs Are: The Hottest Careers for the 90s* (pp. 43-51) **33**
Accreditation Board for Engineering and Technology **1753, 1763, 1852, 1859, 1941, 1950, 2030, 2037, 2101, 2108, 2197, 2209, 2295, 2302, 2360, 2367, 2434, 2443**
Accreditation Council for Accountancy and Taxation **56**
Accreditation Review Committee on Education for Physician Assistants **6081**
Accredited Advanced Dental Educational Programs **5265**
Accredited Educational Programs in Health Information Technology and Health Information Administration **7882**
Accredited Journalism and Mass Communications Education **6615**
Accredited Professional Programs of Colleges and Schools of Pharmacy **5920**
Accredited University Planning Programs **4254**
Accrediting Association of Bible Colleges— Directory **4460**
Accrediting Bureau of Health Education Schools **7490, 7500**
Accrediting Commission on Education for Health Services Administration **822**
Accrediting Council on Education in Journalism and Mass Communications **6607, 6613**
ACE Fellows Program **365, 4705**
ACEP News **5512, 7749**
Achievement Award **3656**
Achieving Results From Training: How to Evaluate Human Resource Development to Strengthen Programs and Increase Impact **1303**
Acme—Directory of Members, 1994-95 **1068**
ACME - The Association of Management Consulting Firms **1058**
ACRL Doctoral Dissertation Fellowship **5007**
ACS Award in Analytical Chemistry **3238**
ACS Award in the Chemistry of Materials **3239**
ACS Award for Creative Invention **1787, 3240**
ACS Award in Inorganic Chemistry **3241**
ACS Award in Pure Chemistry **3242**
ACS Directory of Graduate Research **1779, 3233**
ACS Washington Alert **1804, 3275**
ACSM Map Design Competition Awards **2650**

Architectural Record 2551
Architectural Woodwork Institute Annual Trade Show and Convention 2558
Architecture 2552, 6922
"Architecture" in *Accounting to Zoology: Graduate Fields Defined* (pp. 12-13) 2563
"Architecture" in *College Majors and Careers: A Resource Guide to Effective Life Planning* (pp. 19-20) 2496
"Architecture Drafter" in *Liberal Arts Jobs* 8257
"Architecture" in *Exploring Careers in Computer Graphics* (pp. 62-66) 2497
"Architecture" in *Liberal Arts Jobs* 2498
"Architecture" in *Opportunities in Environmental Careers* 2499
Architecture Schools: Special Programs 2517
Archival Outlook 4661
Archivist 4605, 4606
"Archivist" in *Career Opportunities in Art* (pp. 76) 4607
"Archivist" and "Curator" in *Museum Jobs form A-Z: What They Are, How to Prepare, and Where to Find Them* 4608
"Archivist" in *Guide to Federal Jobs* (pp. 234) 4609
Archivists 4610
"Archivists" in *Career Discovery Encyclopedia* (Vol.1, pp. 60-61) 4611
"Archivists and Curators" in *101 Careers: A Guide to the Fastest-Growing Opportunities* (pp. 157-160) 4612
"Archivists and Curators" in *Occupational Outlook Handbook* 4613
Arctowski Medal 3501
Are You Interested in: Helping Others? . . . Have You Considered . . . Funeral Service? 619
ARI Newsletter 2999
Arizona State Department of Administration - State Boards Office 8455
Arnold Guyot Memorial Award 3357
Arnold W. Brunner Memorial Prize in Architecture 2529
Art in America 7140
Art in America—Guide to Galleries, Museums, and Artists 7103, 7135
"Art" in *College Majors and Careers: A Resource Guide to Effective Life Planning* (pp. 21-22) 7045
Art Direction 7141
"Art Directors" and "Interior Designers" in *Career Information Center* (Vol.3) 6850
"Art, Entertainment, and Media Careers" in *Best Jobs for the 1990s and Into the 21st Century* 6512, 6851, 6942
"Art/Fine Arts" in *Accounting to Zoology: Graduate Fields Defined* 7154
"Art" in *Internships: 1995* (pp. 113-121) 7046
Art Libraries Society of North America Annual Conference 5067
The Art of Making Dances 7335
Art Peters Minority Internships 6793
The Art and Science of Histotechnology: A Career to Consider 7461
The Art and Science of Hospitality Management 925, 1488
"Art Specialist" and "Illustrator" in *Guide to Federal Jobs* (pp. 191, 186) 7047
Arthur C. Cope Award 3247
Arthur C. Cope Scholar Award 3248
Arthur F. Burns Fellowships 6620, 6767
Arthur H. Carter Scholarship 97
Arthur J. Boase Award of the Reinforced Concrete Research Council 1882
Arthur L. Day Medal 3355
Arthur Ross Awards 7132
Arthur von Briesen Award 3678
"Artist" in *Encyclopedia of Danger: Dangerous Professions* (pp. 10-13) 7155
"Artist (Fine Art)" in *Jobs Rated Almanac* 7048
Artist, Graphic 7049
Artists 7050
Artists' Fellowship Program 2525, 6764, 7323, 7408

"Artists and Painters" in *Career Discovery Encyclopedia* (Vol.1, pp. 64-65) 7051
The Artist's Resource Handbook 7156
ARTnews Magazine 7142
Arts and Crafts Annual Spring Easter Show and Sale 7150
Arts and Crafts Annual Summer Show and Sale 7151
Arts Management Award for Arts Administrator of the Year 713
Arts Management Award for Career Service 714
ARTWEEK 7143
ASCE Guide to Employment Conditions for Civil Engineers 1820
ASCE President's Medal 1880
ASCE Salary Survey 1821
ASCUS Annual: A Job Search Handbook for Educators 4542, 4670, 4842, 5083
ASDA Handbook 5329
ASECS News Circular 3991
ASGD-InterFace 5305
Ashworth Fellowship 2526, 2591, 3976, 4258
Asian American Architects and Engineers 2508
ASLA Medal 2592
ASM International 2201
ASM International and The Minerals, Metals and Materials Society Distinguished Lectureship in Materials and Society 2227
ASME Medal 2129
ASMP Stock Photography Handbook 7018
Asmund S. Laerdal Award for Excellence (EMT-Paramedic of the Year) 7740
Aspiring Actors Club 7210
The ASPRS Newsletter 2668
AssemblyLine 4306, 4439
"Assistant Buyers and Buyers" and "Resident Buying Offices and Central Buying Offices" in *Opportunities in Retailing Careers* (chaps. 4 and 6) 1606
"Assistant Professor" in *Career Opportunities for Writers* (pp. 164-165) 4671
Associated Builders and Contractors 257
Associated Funeral Directors International 632
Associated Funeral Directors International— Membership Directory 644
Associated General Contractors of America 258
Associated General Contractors National Convention and Constructor Exposition 297
The Associated Press Stylebook and Libel Manual 6645
Associated Schools of Construction 259
Association for Advancement of Behavior Therapy Convention 4166
Association of American Geographers 3915
Association of American Geographers Annual Meeting 3942
Association of American Law Schools 3619
Association of American Law Schools Annual Meeting 3711
Association of American Medical Colleges 5443
Association of American Medical Colleges— Curriculum Directory 5465
Association of American Medical Colleges— Directory of American Medical Education 5466
Association of American State Geologists 3330
Association of American Veterinary Medical Colleges 5655
Association of Analytical Chemists 3210
Association of Astronomy Educators 3484, 4696, 4871, 5113
Association of Black Psychologists 4094
Association for Business Communication 4697, 6747
Association of Child and Adolescent Psychiatric Nurses 6226, 7793
Association for Childhood Education International Annual Study Conference 4918
Association of College and Research Libraries National Conference 5068

Association of Collegiate Schools of Architecture 2509
Association of Collegiate Schools of Planning 4249
Association for Computing Machinery 2763
Association for Computing Machinery Computer Science Conference 8248
Association of Consulting Chemists and Chemical Engineers 1759, 3211
Association for Continuing Higher Education— Directory 4570
Association for Education in Journalism and Mass Communication 6608, 6614
Association for Education in Journalism and Mass Communication Annual Convention 4727
Association of Engineering Geologists 3331
Association for Gerontology in Higher Education Annual Meeting 4728
Association for the History of Chiropractic— Bulletin 5215
Association of International Education Administrators 350
Association for Investment Management and Research 169
Association of Iron and Steel Engineers 2202
Association for Jewish Studies— Newsletter 4499
Association of Legal Administrators Meeting 161
Association for Library and Information Science Education 4988
Association for Library and Information Science Education—Annual Directory 4999
Association for Manufacturing Technology 8447
Association of Operating Room Nurses Annual Congress 6310
Association of Pediatric Oncology Nurses 6311, 7841
Association of Physician Assistant Programs 6084
Association for Practitioners in Infection Control 7497
Association for Practitioners in Infection Control Annual Educational Conference 7526
Association of School Business Officials Annual Meeting and Exhibits 4595
Association of Schools of Allied Health Professions—Trends 6101
Association of Schools and Colleges of Optometry 5360
Association for Social Anthropology in Oceania—Newsletter 3765
Association for the Study of Higher Education 351
Association of Surgical Technologists 8017, 8018
Association for Systems Management 2764
Association of Teacher Educators Annual Conference 405, 4729, 4919, 5161
Association of Trial Lawyers of America Convention/Exposition 3712
Association of University Programs in Health Administration 827
Association for Women in Psychology 4095
Association for Women Veterinarians 5656
Astronomer 3448
"Astronomer" in *Career Information Center* (Vol.6) 3449
"Astronomer" in *Career Selector 2001* 3556
"Astronomer" in *Jobs Rated Almanac* 3450
Astronomers 3451, 3452, 3557
"Astronomers" in *Career Discovery Encyclopedia* (Vol.1, pp. 72-73) 3453
"Astronomers" in *Encyclopedia of Careers and Vocational Guidance* (Vol.2, pp. 120-123) 3454
"Astronomers" in *Jobs! What They Are— Where They Are—What They Pay!* (p. 307) 3455
Astronomical Almanac 3558
Astronomical League 3485
ATCA Bulletin 8129
ATCA Industrial Award 8122

"Biologists" in *Encyclopedia of Careers and Vocational Guidance* **3021**

"Biology" in *Accounting to Zoology: Graduate Fields Defined* (pp. 199-200) **3099**

"Biology", "Botony", and "Physiology" in *College Majors and Careers: A Resource Guide to Effective Life Planning* **3022**

"Biology" in *Opportunities in Environmental Careers* **3023**

"Biomedical Equipment Technician" in *150 Careers in the Health Care Field* **8293**

Biomedical Safety & Standards **8439**

Biomedical Technology Information Service **7654, 7694, 8023**

Biometric Bulletin **2932**

Biopharmaceutics and Drug Disposition **5946**

Biophysical Society Annual Meeting **3095**

Biophysicist **3456**

BioScience **3089**

BIOSIS Evolution **3090, 8440**

Biotechnology & Bioengineering **1806**

Birdsall Prize in European Military and Strategic History; Paul **3977**

Bishop's Committee on Vocations **4513**

Black Gold Group **7091**

Blackburn Scholarship; Reid **6994**

Black's Law Dictionary; Definitions of the Terms and Phrases of American and English Jurisprodence . . . **3679**

Black's Veterinary Dictionary **5685**

Blackwell Medal; Elizabeth **5484**

Blood Bank Specialists **7462**

Blood Bank Technology **7463**

Blue Book of Optometrists **5364**

Blumenthal Prize; Oscar **6765**

BMI Awards to Student Composers **7409**

Board Certification Registered EMT-Paramedic **7700**

Board Report's Creative Training **6923, 7144**

Boase Award of the Reinforced Concrete Research Council; Arthur J. **1882**

Bob East Scholarship **6997**

Body of Knowledge and Task Delineations and Addendum to Body of Knowledge **7464**

Boggs Award; Lindy **773**

Bollingen Prize in Poetry **6766**

BOMA International Awards Program **1398**

Bonner Prize in Nuclear Physics; Tom W. **3504**

"Book Design, Exhibition Design, and Industrial Design" in School of Visual Arts Guide to Careers (pp. 156-157, 168-169, 258-270) **6852**

Book Editor **6664**

"Book Editors" in *Career Discovery Encyclopedia* (Vol.1, pp. 120-121) **6665**

"Book Editors" in *Encyclopedia of Careers and Vocational Guidance* (Vol.2, pp. 204-208) **6666**

"Book Editors", "Newspaper Editors", and "Technical Writers" in *Career Information Center* (Vol.3) **6667**

Book Publishing Career Directory **6754, 6905, 7104**

Botanical Society of America **3050**

Botanist **3024**

The Bottom Line: Inside Accounting Today **36**

Boucher's Clinical Dental Terminology: Glossary of Accepted Terms in All Disciplines of Dentistry **5295**

Bound to Stay Bound Books Scholarships **5008**

Bouwhuis Memorial Scholarships; Reverend Andrew L. **5009**

Bowie Medal; William **3352**

Bowker Annual: Library and Book Trade Almanac **5000**

Bowker/Ulrich's Serials Librarianship Award **5010**

Bradford Cadmus Memorial Award **96**

Brain Topography **7655**

Branch Management: What You Need to Know to Succeed **575**

Brandweek **3884**

Break into Broadcasting **6513**

Breaking into the Music Business **7351**

Bricker's International Directory: Long-Term University—Based Executive Programs **711**

The Bridge **479**

A Brief Guide to Art and Design Studies **7052**

Briggs Memorial Scientific Inquiry Award; Dorothy **6014**

British Journal of Music Education **7437**

Broadcast/Cable Journalism Awards - Jack R. Howard Awards **6549**

Broadcast Education Association **6541, 8155**

Broadcast Engineering **8172**

"Broadcast Engineering" in *Desk Guide to Training and Work Advisement* (pp. 87-88) **8135**

Broadcast Meteorologist **3394**

Broadcast Technician **8136**

"Broadcast Technician" in *Exploring Nontraditional Jobs for Women* **8137**

"Broadcast Technician" in *Jobs Rated Almanac* **8138**

"Broadcast Technician" in *VGM's Careers Encyclopedia* (pp. 66-68) **8139**

"Broadcast Technicians" in *101 Careers: A Guide to the Fastest-Growing Opportunities* (pp. 278-280) **8140**

"Broadcast Technicians" in *Career Information Center* (Vol.3) **8141**

"Broadcast Technicians" in *Jobs! What They Are—Where They Are—What They Pay* (p. 36) **8142**

"Broadcast Technicians" in *Occupational Outlook Handbook* **8143**

"Broadcaster (Sports)" in Careers in *Health and Fitness* **6514**

Broadcaster of the Year Award **6550**

"Broadcasting" in *Black Woman's Career Guide* (pp. 173-177) **6515**

Broadcasting and Cable **6561**

"Broadcasting" in *Career Choices for the 90's for Students of Political Science and Government* **6516**

"Broadcasting Technology" in *Career Connection for Technical Education* (pp. 32-33) **8144**

Broida Prize in Atomic, Molecular, or Chemical Physics; Herbert P. **3505**

The Brookings Review **3885**

Brouwer Award; Dirk **1697, 3506**

Bruce Medal; Catherine Wolfe **3507**

Brudney Award; Ruth P. **4430**

Bruel Noise Control and Acoustics Medal; Per **2130**

Brunner Memorial Prize in Architecture; Arnold W. **2529**

Bruno Rossi Prize **3530**

Bryant Gold Medal; Henry Grier **3923**

Bucher Medal; Walter H. **3353**

Buckley Condensed-Matter Physics Prize; Oliver E. **3508**

"Budget Analyst" in *Career Selector 2001* **194**

"Budget Analysts" in *101 Careers: A Guide to the Fastest-Growing Opportunities* (pp. 10-13) **163**

"Budget Analysts" in *Occupational Outlook Handbook* **164**

Budget and Management Analyst **165**

"Building Contractor" in *VGM's Careers Encyclopedia* (pp. 68-69) **239**

Building Design & Construction **277**

Building Industry Technology: An Abstract Newsletter **2553**

Building Inspection as a Career **195**

Building Inspector **196**

"Building Inspector" in *Career Information Center* (Vol.4) **197**

"Building Inspector" in *Career Selector 2001* **237**

Building Managers **1359**

Building Officials and Code Administrators International **206, 210**

Building Owners and Managers Association International **1383, 1389**

Building Owners and Managers Association International Annual Convention and the Office Building Show **1416**

"Building or Property Manager" in *VGM's Careers Encyclopedia* (pp. 69-71) **1360**

"Building or Property Manager" in *VGM's Handbook of Business and Management Careers* **1361**

Buildings **1410**

Bulldog Reporter: West **6499**

Bulletin to Management **1333**

Bulletin of the Society for American Archaeology **3817**

Bunche Award; Ralph J. **4028**

Burdette Pi Sigma Alpha Award; Franklin L. **4029**

Burns Fellowships; Arthur F. **6620, 6767**

Burr Award; Franklin L. **3924**

"Business Administration and Management" in *Accounting to Zoology: Graduate Fields Defined* (pp. 31-33) **741**

"Business Administration and Management" in *College Majors and Careers: A Resource Guide to Effective Life Planning* (pp. 31-32) **678**

The Business of Art **7053**

The Business of Construction **240**

The Business of Design **6918**

Business Economics **3886**

The Business-Education Partnership **377**

"Business Executive" in *College Board Guide to Jobs and Career Planning* (pp. 90) **679**

Business and Finance Career Directory **91, 173, 562, 1069, 1587**

Business Ideas Newsletter **1197**

Business & Industry **964**

Business Law **3630**

Business and Management Jobs **680**

Business Marketing **3887**

The Business of Public Relations **6487**

Business Trends **3888**

Business Week **733**

The Business Writer's Handbook **6804**

Buyers **1607**

"Buyers" in *Jobs! What They Are—Where They Are—What They Pay* (p. 316) **1608**

"Buyers" in *Liberal Arts Jobs* **1609**

"Buyers, Wholesale and Retail" in *Encyclopedia of Careers and Vocational Guidance* (Vol.2, pp. 229-232) **1610**

"Buying" in *Career Choices for the 90's for Students of Art* (pp. 52-54) **1611**

"Buying" in *Career Choices for the 90's for Students of Business* (pp. 75-77) **1612**

"Buying" in *Career Choices for the 90's for Students of English* **1613**

"Buying" in *Career Choices for the 90's for Students of Political Science and Government* **1614**

"Buying" in *Career Choices for the 90's for Students of Psychology* (pp. 30-32) **1615**

Buying Strategy Forecast **1450**

C

C. Albert Koob Award **4523**

"CAD/CAM" in *Exploring Careers in Computer Graphics* **8258**

"CAD" in *Complete Computer Career Guide* (pp. 79-83) **8259**

"CAD: Computer-Aided Design" in *Careers in High-Tech* **8260**

Cadbury Award; William and Charlotte **5485**

Cadmus Memorial Award; Bradford **96**

Cady Award; Gilbert H. **3354**

Cafeteria Manager Industrial **1456**

Caldecott Medal; Randolph **7118**

California Academy of Physician Assistants Convention **6105**

California Department of Consumer Affairs **8456**

California Land Surveyors Association Conference **2674**

Cambridge Archaeological Journal **3818**

The Cambridge Law Journal **3690**

Cambridge Opera Journal **7438**

"Camera Operator" in *TV Careers Behind the Screen* (pp. 42, 57-59, 79-81) **6944**

"Camera Operators" and "Photographers" in *Career Information Center* (Vol.3) **6945**

Campbell Memorial Lecture; Edward DeMille **2228**

Camping Magazine **4354**

Can-AM Civil Engineering Amity Award **1883**

Cannon Award in Astronomy; Annie Jump **3509**

Cannon Prize **7119**

Capra Achievement Award; Frank **7228**

CARA Seminary Directory **4519**

"Cardiographic Technician (EKG Technician)" in *150 Careers in the Health Care Field* **7661**

"Cardiology and Cardiopulmonary Technologists" in *Careers in High-Tech* **7662**

Cardiovascular Credentialing International **7677**

"Cardiovascular Technology Personnel" in *Careers in Health Care* (pp. 27-31) **7663**

A Career as a Chemical Technician **8419**

Career Choices for the 90's for Students of Art **7054**

Career Choices for the 90's for Students of Business **681, 1362, 1551**

Career Choices for the 90's for Students of Communications and Journalism **1100, 6572, 6668**

Career Choices for the 90's for Students of Computer Science **2732, 8178**

Career Choices for the 90's for Students of Economics **3829**

Career Choices for the 90's for Students of English **1101**

Career Choices for the 90's for Students of History **3944**

Career Choices for the 90's for Students of Law **3569**

Career Choices for the 90's for Students of Mathematics **1552, 2807**

Career Choices for the 90's for Students of MBA **682**

Career Choices for the 90's for Students of Political Science and Government **4005**

Career Choices for the 90's for Students of Psychology **1102, 1232, 1363, 4057**

Career College Association **907, 1476, 4561, 4698, 8279**

Career Counselor **4746**

Career Counselors **4747**

A Career in Cytotechnology **7465**

Career Development for Engineers and Scientists: Organizational Programs and Individual Choices **1658, 1723, 1822, 1912, 2003, 2071, 2163, 2274, 2339, 2408**

Career Development Quarterly **4821**

Career of Distinguished Scholarship Award **4216**

Career Examination Series: Accountant **70**

Career Examination Series: Accountant/ Auditor **71**

Career Examination Series: Accounting Assistant **72**

Career Examination Series: Activities Director **4337**

Career Examination Series: Actuary **2705**

Career Examination Series: Addiction Specialist **4410, 4799**

Career Examination Series: Administrative Associate **144**

Career Examination Series: Administrative Careers with America **145**

Career Examination Series: Administrative Careers Examination **146**

Career Examination Series: Administrative Claim Examiner **73**

Career Examination Series: Administrative Consultant **1060**

Career Examination Series: Administrative Education Analyst **1061**

Career Examination Series: Administrative Management Auditor **74**

Career Examination Series: Administrative Manager **147**

Career Examination Series: Administrative Service Officer **148**

Career Examination Series: Administrative Services Manager **149**

Career Examination Series: Administrator **707**

Career Examination Series: Aerospace Engineer **1679**

Career Examination Series: Aging Services Representative **4289, 4338**

Career Examination Series: Air Traffic Control Specialist **8121**

Career Examination Series: Alcoholism Counselor **4290**

Career Examination Series: Alcoholism Educator **4291, 4563**

Career Examination Series: Alcoholism Rehabilitation Consultant **4292, 4411**

Career Examination Series: Ambulance Attendant **7732**

Career Examination Series: Ambulance Corpsman **7733**

Career Examination Series: Ambulance Driver **7734**

Career Examination Series: Announcer **6546**

Career Examination Series: Architect **2514**

Career Examination Series: Archivist **4638**

Career Examination Series: Assistant Accountant **75**

Career Examination Series: Assistant Air Pollution Control Engineer **8320**

Career Examination Series: Assistant Chemical Engineer **1767**

Career Examination Series: Assistant Chemist **3221**

Career Examination Series: Assistant Engineering Technician **8321**

Career Examination Series: Assistant Heating & Ventilating Engineer **2039**

Career Examination Series: Assistant Physicist **3492**

Career Examination Series: Assistant Radiologist **7974**

Career Examination Series: Assistant Teacher **4879, 5119**

Career Examination Series: Associate Chemist **3222**

Career Examination Series: Associate Engineering Technician **8322**

Career Examination Series: Associate Transit Management Analyst **1062**

Career Examination Series: Associate Urban Park Ranger **4339**

Career Examination Series: Associate Water Use Inspector **991**

Career Examination Series: Astronomer **3493**

Career Examination Series: Attorney **3631**

Career Examination Series: Audio—Visual Aid Technician **8348**

Career Examination Series: Audiologist **6411**

Career Examination Series: Auto Equipment Inspector **992**

Career Examination Series: Automotive Facilities Inspector **993**

Career Examination Series: Bacteriologist **3053**

Career Examination Series: Beach Supervisor **4340**

Career Examination Series: Beverage Control Inspector **994**

Career Examination Series: Beverage Control Investigator **995**

Career Examination Series: Biologist **3054**

Career Examination Series: Budget Analyst **170**

Career Examination Series: Building Construction Inspector **214**

Career Examination Series: Building Construction Program Manager **263**

Career Examination Series: Building Mechanical Engineer **2111**

Career Examination Series: Building Structural Engineer **1861**

Career Examination Series: Buyer **1635**

Career Examination Series: Certified Mental Health Counselor **4800**

Career Examination Series: Certified Social Worker (CSW) **4412**

Career Examination Series: Chemical Engineer **1768**

Career Examination Series: Chemist **3223**

Career Examination Series: Chief Beverage Control Investigator **996**

Career Examination Series: Chief Compensation Investigator **171**

Career Examination Series: Chief Compliance Investigator **997**

Career Examination Series: Chief Consumer Affairs Investigator **998**

Career Examination Series: Chief Marketing Representative **1148**

Career Examination Series: Chief Meat Inspector **999**

Career Examination Series: Chief Multiple Residence Inspector **1000**

Career Examination Series: Chief Occupational Therapist **5839**

Career Examination Series: Chief Physical Therapist **6004**

Career Examination Series: Chief Recreation Therapist **6141**

Career Examination Series: Chief Water Pollution Control Inspector **1001**

Career Examination Series: Civil Engineer **1862**

Career Examination Series: Civil Engineering Draftsman **8281**

Career Examination Series: Community Relations Specialist **4293**

Career Examination Series: Compensation Claims Auditor **76**

Career Examination Series: Computer Programmer **8216**

Career Examination Series: Computer Systems Analyst **2767**

Career Examination Series: Conservation Biologist **3055**

Career Examination Series: Construction Analyst **264**

Career Examination Series: Construction Cost Specialist **313**

Career Examination Series: Construction Inspector **215**

Career Examination Series: Consultant **1063**

Career Examination Series: Coordinator of Drug Abuse Educational Programs **358**

Career Examination Series: Coordinator, Senior Citizen Planning and Research **4294, 4341**

Career Examination Series: Coordinator of Surveying Services **2645**

Career Examination Series: Cost and Statistical Analyst **172, 314, 2918**

Career Examination Series: Counselor **4801**

Career Examination Series: Dairy Products Specialist **2983**

Career Examination Series: Data Processing Operations Supervisor **468**

Career Examination Series: Database Programmer Analyst **2768**

Career Examination Series: Dental Hygienist **7567**

Career Examination Series: Dentist **5261**

Career Examination Series: Deputy Commissioner of Recreation and Community Services **4342**

Career Examination Series: Deputy Director of Planning **4251**

Career Examination Series: Developmental Disabilities Program Specialist **6142**

Career Examination Series: Dietitian **5754**

Career Examination Series: Digital Computer Specialist **2769**

Career Examination Series: Digital Computer Systems Analyst **2770**

Career Examination Series: Digital Computer Systems Programmer **8217**

Career Examination Series: Digital Computer Systems Specialist **2771**

Munson Memorial Student Award; Emily **2535**
Murphree Award in Industrial and Engineering Chemistry; E. V. **1794**
Murray Prize Competition; Roger F. **570**
Murrow Fellowship for American Foreign Correspondents; Edward R. **6629, 6783**
Museum Anthropology **3769**
"Museum Careers: Curator, Archivist" in *College Board Guide to Jobs and Career Planning* (pp. 184-185) **4620**
Museum Careers and Training: A Professional Guide **4668**
Museum Curator **4621**
"Museum Curator" in *Career Information Center* (Vol.8) **4622**
"Museum Curator" in *Career Selector 2001* **4669**
"Museum Curator" in *Jobs Rated Almanac* **4623**
"Museum Curator" in *Opportunities in Crafts* (pp. 55-64) **4624**
"Museum Curator" in *VGM's Careers Encyclopedia* (pp. 292-294) **4625**
Museum Curators **4626**
"Museum Curators" in *Career Discovery Encyclopedia* (Vol.4, pp. 108-109) **4627**
"Museum Curators" in *Encyclopedia of Careers and Vocational Guidance* (Vol.3, pp. 493-497) **4628**
Museum Monthly **3823**
Museum News **4664**
"Museums/Cultural Organizations" in *Internships: 1995* (pp. 122-153) **4629**
Music **7393, 7394, 7453**
"Music" in *Accounting to Zoology: Graduate Fields Defined* (pp. 164) **7454**
The Music Business: Career Opportunities and Self-Defense **7358**
Music Business Handbook & Career Guide **7432**
Music Careers **7359**
"Music/Dance" in *Internships: 1995* (pp. 154-165) **7303, 7360**
"Music" in *Desk Guide to Training and Work Advisement* (pp. 125-126) **7361**
"Music Director" in *Career Opportunities in the Music Industry* (p. 65-66) **6527**
Music Educators National Conference **7389**
"Music Librarian" in *Career Opportunities in the Music Industry* (pp. 201-204) **4975**
Music Notation News **7444**
"Music Specialist" in *Guide to Federal Jobs* (p. 189) **7362**
"Music" in *Straight Talk on Careers: Eighty Pros Take You Into Their Professions* (pp. 113-130) **7363**
Music Teachers National Association **7390**
Musical America's International Directory of the Performing Arts **7402**
Musical Theater Choreography **7339**
"Musician" in *Career Selector 2001* **7455**
"Musician" in *College Board Guide to Jobs and Career Planning* (pp. 61-63) **7364**
"Musician" in *Encyclopedia of Danger: Dangerous Professions* (pp. 70-73) **7456**
Musician/Entertainer **7365**
Musician, Instrumental **7366**
"Musician" in *Jobs Rated Almanac* **7367**
"Musician" in *VGM's Careers Encyclopedia* (pp. 294-296) **7368**
Musician of the Year **7418**
"Musicians" in *101 Careers: A Guide to the Fastest-Growing Opportunities* (pp. 291-293) **7369**
"Musicians" in *American Almanac of Jobs and Salaries* (pp. 147) **7370**
"Musicians" in *Career Discovery Encyclopedia* (Vol.4, pp. 116-117) **7371**
"Musicians", "Composers", and "Singers" in *Career Information Center* (Vol.3) **7372**
"Musicians" in *Encyclopedia of Careers and Vocational Guidance* (Vol.3, pp. 533-539) **7373**
Musicians, Instrumental **7374**
"Musicians" in *Jobs! What They Are—Where They Are—What They Pay* (pp. 301) **7375**

"Musicians" in *Occupational Outlook Handbook* **7376**
Myles Standish Award **1178**

N

NAA Foundation—National Scholastic Press Association Pacemaker Awards **6630, 6784**
NAACLS News **7522**
NAACP Willems Scholarship **2783, 2847, 3256, 3524**
NAB RadioWeek **6565**
NABE Executive Officer of the Year **4526**
NACDS and Pharmacy Education: Programs for Progress **5960**
Nacore International **1386**
Nacore International Symposium and Exposition **1417**
NAFAC News **7751**
NAFSA - Association of International Educators Annual Conference **406, 4730, 4920, 5162**
NAIEC Newsletter **4589**
The Naked Anthropologist: Tales from Around the World **3773**
NAMP Scholarships **916, 1487**
NAMS News **1600**
NAPNAP-McNeil Scholarships **6269**
NARD Newsletter **5950**
Nashreeye B'nei Torah **4500**
NASPA Forum **393, 4721**
Nate Haseltine Memorial Fellowship in Science Writing **6776**
National Academy of Design Gold Medal **7127**
National Academy of Opticianry **7615, 7618**
National Academy of Opticianry Convention **7625**
National Academy for School Executives Internships **373**
National Academy of Sciences Award in Applied Mathematics and Numerical Analysis **2848**
National Academy of Sciences Award in Chemical Sciences **3257**
National Academy of Sciences Award in Mathematics **2849**
National Academy of Sciences Award in Molecular Biology **3075**
National Action Council for Minorities in Engineering **1856, 1947, 2034, 2105, 2204, 2298, 2364, 2438**
National Air Traffic Controllers Association **8117**
National Apartment Association **1387, 1392**
National Art Education Association Convention **4921, 5163**
National Association of Affordable Housing Lenders **1020**
National Association of Biology Teachers National Convention **4731, 5164**
National Association of Black Geologists and Geophysicists **3335**
National Association of Black Journalists Salute to Excellence Awards **6631**
National Association of Black Social Workers Convention **4445**
National Association of Boards of Pharmacy **5909, 5913**
National Association Broadcast Employees and Technicians **8157**
National Association of Broadcasters **6542, 8158**
National Association of Broadcasters International Convention and Exposition **6569**
National Association of Business Economists **3859**
National Association of Chain Drug Stores **5910**
National Association of College and University Business Officers **4702**
National Association of Conservation Districts **3131**

National Association of Convenience Stores **1479**
National Association of Counties **769**
National Association of Credit Management **551**
National Association for the Education of Young Children **4872**
National Association for the Education of Young Children Annual Conference **407, 4922**
National Association of Elementary School Principals **352**
National Association of Elementary School Principals Convention and Exhibition **408**
National Association of Emergency Medical Technicians **7726, 7730**
National Association of Emergency Medical Technicians Annual National Educational Conference **7753**
National Association of Federal Veterinarians **5657**
National Association of Food Equipment Manufacturers Convention **1516**
National Association of Government Inspectors and Quality Assurance Personnel **984**
National Association of Governmental Labor Officials **985**
National Association of Health Underwriters **1585**
National Association of Home Builders of the U.S. **1388**
National Association for Law Placement **3621, 3627**
National Association of Legal Assistants **8387, 8392**
National Association of Media Brokers **3860**
National Association of Men's Sportswear Buyers **1632**
National Association of Men's Sportswear Buyers (NAMSB) Show **1641**
National Association of Nurse Massage Therapists **6227, 6231, 7794**
National Association of Orthopedic Nurses Annual Congress **6312, 7842**
National Association of Personnel Consultants **420**
National Association of Personnel Services **418, 421**
National Association for Practical Nurse Education and Service **7795, 7799**
National Association for the Practice of Anthropology **3742**
National Association of Professional Mortgage Women **1021, 1023**
National Association of Property Inspectors **986, 989**
National Association of Purchasing Management **1441, 1444**
National Association of Radio Talk Show Hosts **6543**
National Association of Retail Dealers of America **1539**
National Association of Review Appraisers and Mortgage Underwriters **1579**
National Association of Review Appraisers and Mortgage Underwriters Convention **1603**
National Association of School Psychologists **4097, 4099**
National Association of Schools of Art and Design **6899, 6903, 7096**
National Association of Schools of Art and Design—Directory **6907, 7108**
National Association of Schools of Dance **7310**
National Association of Schools of Music **7391**
National Association of Schools of Music—Directory **7403**
National Association of Schools of Public Affairs and Administration **4020**
National Association of Schools of Theatre **7212**
National Association of Secondary School Principals **353**
National Association of Secondary School Principals Annual Convention **409**